NATIONAL ACCOUNTS STATISTICS: MAIN AGGREGATES AND DETAILED TABLES, 1986

PART II

UNITED NATIONS
NEW YORK, 1989

NOTE

Symbols of United Nations documents are composed of capital letters combined with figures. Mention of such a symbol indicates a reference to a United Nations document.

The first 14 editions of the *Yearbook* were issued without series symbols.

ST/ESA/STAT/SER.X/11

UNITED NATIONS PUBLICATION

Sales No. E.89.XVII.7,Part II

10000
(not to be sold separately)

ISBN 92-1-161305-1

Inquiries should be directed to:

PUBLISHING DIVISION
UNITED NATIONS
NEW YORK, N.Y. 10017

Copyright © United Nations, 1989
All rights reserved
Manufactured in the United States of America

CONTENTS (continued)

	Page
Introduction	v
I. System of National Accounts (SNA)	ix
II. System of Material Product Balances (MPS)	xxi
III. Country tables	1

	Page		Page
Kenya	842	Romania	1258
Kiribati	853	Rwanda	1261
Korea, Republic of	854	Saint Christopher and Nevis	1270
Kuwait	872	Saint Lucia	1273
Lebanon	881	Saint Vincent and the Grenadines	1275
Lesotho	883	Samoa	1277
Liberia	888	Saudi Arabia	1278
Libyan Arab Jamahiriya	892	Senegal	1282
Luxembourg	906	Seychelles	1285
Madagascar	917	Sierra Leone	1293
Malawi	921	Singapore	1301
Malaysia	926	Solomon Islands	1305
Maldives	932	Somalia	1306
Mali	935	South Africa	1309
Malta	938	Spain	1320
Martinique	959	Sri Lanka	1343
Mauritania	961	Sudan	1359
Mauritius	964	Suriname	1373
Mexico	977	Swaziland	1376
Mongolia	987	Sweden	1385
Montserrat	988	Switzerland	1435
Morocco	992	Syrian Arab Republic	1440
Mozambique	995	Thailand	1446
Nepal	996	Togo	1464
Netherlands	999	Tonga	1469
Netherlands Antilles	1037	Trinidad and Tobago	1475
New Caledonia	1043	Tunisia	1483
New Zealand	1047	Turkey	1488
Nicaragua	1061	Uganda	1496
Niger	1065	Ukrainian SSR	1499
Nigeria	1069	United Arab Emirates	1500
Norway	1075	United Kingdom	1504
Oman	1122	United Republic of Tanzania	1549
Pakistan	1127	United States	1555
Panama	1134	Uruguay	1609
Papua New Guinea	1147	U.S.S.R.	1614
Paraguay	1157	Venezuela	1616
Peru	1165	Viet Nam	1633
Philippines	1195	Yemen	1634
Poland	1208	Yugoslavia	1641
Portugal	1220	Zaire	1643
Puerto Rico	1249	Zambia	1646
Qatar	1255	Zimbabwe	1656
Reunion	1256		

INTRODUCTION

This is the thirtieth issue of *National Accounts Statistics: Main Aggregates and Detailed Tables*,[1] showing detailed national accounts estimates for 165 countries and areas. Like the first 29 issues, it has been prepared by the Statistical Office of the Department of International Economic and Social Affairs of the United Nations Secretariat with the generous co-operation of national statistical services. It is issued in accordance with the request of the Statistical Commission [2] that the most recent available data on national accounts for as many countries and areas as possible be published regularly.

The present publication (Parts I and II) forms part of a *National Accounts Statistics* series. Another publication in the same series, issued separately is *National Accounts Statistics: Analysis of Main Aggregates*,[3] presenting in the form of analytical tables a summary of main national accounts aggregates extracted from this publication and supplemented by estimates made by the Statistical Office where official data are not available.

SCOPE OF PUBLICATION

National accounts estimates for countries or areas with market economies are shown, where available, for each of the subjects below. Estimates for the matrix tables are shown for some or all of the years 1980 through 1986. For other tables, estimates are shown for some or all of the years 1970, 1975, 1977 through 1986.

Part 1. Summary information

  1.1 Expenditures on the gross domestic product (current prices)
  1.2 Expenditures on the gross domestic product (constant prices)
  1.3 Cost components of the gross domestic product
  1.4 General government current receipts and expenditures, summary
  1.5 Current income and outlay of corporate and quasi-corporate enterprises, summary
  1.6 Current income and outlay of households and non-profit institutions, summary
  1.7 External transactions on current account, summary
  1.8 Capital transactions of the nation, summary
  1.9 Gross domestic product by institutional sector of origin
  1.10 Gross domestic product by kind of activity (current prices)
  1.11 Gross domestic product by kind of activity (constant prices)
  1.12 Relations among national accounting aggregates

Part 2. Final expenditures on gross domestic product: detailed breakdowns and supporting tables

  2.1 General government final consumption expenditure by function (current prices)
  2.2 General government final consumption expenditure by function (constant prices)
  2.3 Total government outlays by function and type (current prices)
  2.4 Composition of general government social security benefits and social assistance grants to households
  2.5 Private final consumption expenditure by type (current prices)
  2.6 Private final consumption expenditure by type (constant prices)
  2.7 Gross capital formation by type of good and owner (current prices)
  2.8 Gross capital formation by type of good and owner (constant prices)
  2.9 Gross capital formation by kind of activity of owner, ISIC major divisions (current prices)
  2.10 Gross capital formation by kind of activity of owner, ISIC major divisions (constant prices)
  2.11 Gross fixed capital formation by kind of activity of owner, ISIC divisions (current prices)
  2.12 Gross fixed capital formation by kind of activity of owner, ISIC divisions (constant prices)
  2.13 Stocks of reproducible fixed assets, by type of good and owner (current prices)
  2.14 Stocks of reproducible fixed assets, by type of good and owner (constant prices)
  2.15 Stocks of reproducible fixed assets by kind of activity (current prices)
  2.16 Stocks of reproducible fixed assets by kind of activity (constant prices)
  2.17 Exports and imports of goods and services, detail

Part 3. Institutional sector accounts: detailed flow accounts [4]

  1. General government

     3.11 Production account
     3.12 Income and outlay account
     3.13 Capital accumulation account
     3.14 Capital finance account

2. Corporate and quasi-corporate enterprises

   3.21 Production account: total and subsectors
   3.22 Income and outlay account: total and subsectors
   3.23 Capital accumulation account: total and subsectors
   3.24 Capital finance account: total and subsectors

3. Households and private unincorporated enterprises

   3.31 Production account: total and subsectors
   3.32 Income and outlay account: total and subsectors
   3.33 Capital accumulation account: total and subsectors
   3.34 Capital finance account: total and subsectors

4. Private non-profit institutions serving households

   3.41 Production account
   3.42 Income and outlay account
   3.43 Capital accumulation account
   3.44 Capital finance account

5. External transactions

   3.51 Current account, detail
   3.52 Capital accumulation account
   3.53 Capital finance account

Part 4. Production by kind of activity: detailed breakdowns and supporting tables

   4.1 Derivation of value added by kind of activity (current prices)
   4.2 Derivation of value added by kind of activity (constant prices)
   4.3 Cost components of value added

For the countries with centrally planned economies, estimates are shown, where available, in terms of the System of Material Product Balances (MPS), for each of the following subjects, as a rule, for some or all of the years 1970, 1975, 1977 through 1986.

1. Net material product by use
2. Net material product by kind of activity of the material sphere
3. Primary incomes by kinds of activity of the material sphere
4. Primary incomes from net material product
5. Supply and disposition of goods and material services
6. Capital formation by kind of activity of the material and non-material spheres
7. Final consumption
8. Personal consumption according to source of supply of goods and material services
9. Total consumption of the population by object, commodity and service, and mode of acquisition.

CONCEPTUAL REFERENCES

The form and concepts of the statistical tables in the present publication generally conform, for the countries or areas with market economies, to the recommendations in *A System of National Accounts*, Studies in Methods, Series F, No. 2, Rev. 3. [5] For the countries with centrally planned economies, the form and concepts generally conform to the recommendations in *Basic Principles of the System of Balances of the National Economy*, Studies in Methods, Series F, No.17. [6] A summary of the conceptual framework of both systems, their classifications and definitions of transactions items, is provided in chapters I and II of the present publication.

COMPILATION OF DATA

To compile the large volume of national accounts data, the Statistical Office each year sends to countries or areas with market economies a national accounts questionnaire; those with centrally planned economies receive a material balances questionnaire. The recipients of the questionnaires are also requested to indicate where the scope and coverage of the country estimates differ for conceptual or statistical reasons from the definitions and classifications recommended in the System of National Accounts (SNA) or in MPS. Data obtained from these replies are supplemented by information gathered from correspondence with the national statistical services and from national and international source publications.

In the present publication, the data for each country or area are presented in separate chapters, as far as possible, under uniform table headings and classifications of SNA or the material balances questionnaire, as the case may be. Each country chapter contains a brief introductory text (source and general note). The general note describes the extent to which the estimates conform conceptually to the recommendations of SNA or the material balances questionnaire. Important deviations from the two systems, where known, are described in the general note, while differences in definition and coverage of specific items are indicated in footnotes to the relevant tables.

Country data in chapter III are presented in alphabetical order. Unless otherwise stated, the data in the country tables relate to the calendar year against which they are shown.

COMPARABILITY OF THE NATIONAL ESTIMATES

Every effort has been made to present the estimates of the various countries or areas in a form designed to facilitate international comparability. To this end, important differences in concept, scope, coverage and classification have been described in the notes which precede and accompany the country tables. Such differences should be taken into account if misleading comparisons among countries or areas are to be avoided.

REVISIONS

The figures shown are the most recent estimates and revisions available at the time of compilation. In general, figures for the most recent year are to be regarded as provisional. For more up to date information, reference is made to the December issue of the *United Nations Monthly Bulletin of Statistics*. 7/

EXPLANATION OF SYMBOLS

The following symbols have been employed:
Data not available ....
Category not applicable ....
Magnitude nil or less than half of the unit employed .... -
Decimal figures are always preceded by a point (.)

When a series is not homogeneous, this is indicated by presenting the figures in separate rows.

Details and percentages in tables do not necessarily add to totals shown because of rounding.

GENERAL DISCLAIMER

The designations employed and the presentation of material in this publication do not imply the expression of any opinion whatsoever on the part of the Secretariat of the United Nations concerning the legal status of any country, territory, city or area or of its authorities, or concerning the delimitation of its frontiers or boundaries.

Where the designation "country or area" appears in the headings of tables, it covers countries, territories, cities or areas. In prior issues of this publication, where the designation "country" appears in the headings of tables, it covers countries, territories, cities or areas.

In some tables, the designations "developed" and "developing" economies are intended for statistical convenience and do not, necessarily, express a judgement about the stage reached by a particular country or area in the development process.

1/ United Nations publication. The first 25 editions of this publication were issued under the title *Yearbook of National Accounts Statistics* and under the following sales number: *1957*, 58.XVII.3; *1958*, 59.XVII.3; *1959*, 60.XVII.3; *1960*, 61.XVII.4; *1961*, 62.XVII.2; *1962*, 63.XVII.2;. *1963*, 64.XVII.4; *1964*, 65.XVII.2; *1965*, 66.XVII.2; *1966*, 67.XVII.14; *1967*, 69.XVII.6; *1968*, vol. I, 70.XVII.2, vol. II. 70.XVII.3; *1969*, vol. I, 71.XVII.2, vol. II. 71.XVII.3; *1970*, 72.XVII.3, vol. I, 72.XVII.3, vol. II; *1971*, (3 volumes), E.73.XVII.3; *1972*, (3 volumes), E.74.XVII.3; *1973*, (3 volumes), E.75.XVII.2; *1974*, (3 volumes), E.75.XVII.5; *1975*, (3 volumes), E.76.XVII.2; *1976* (2 volumes), E.77.XVII.2; *1977*, (2 volumes), E.78.XVII.2; *1978*, (2 volumes) E.79.XVII.8; *1979*, (2 volumes), E.80.XVII.11; *1980*, (2 volumes) E.82.XVII.6; *1981*, (2 volumes), E.83.XVII.3. Beginning with the twenty-sixth edition, this publication replaced Volume I *Individual country data*, of the Yearbook and it was issued under the following sales number: *1982*, E.85.XVII.4; *1983*, E.86.XVII.3; *1984*, E.86.XVII.26; *1985*,E.87.XVII.10.

2/ See *Official Records of the Economic and Social Council, First Year, Second Session*, (E/39), annex III, chap. IV.

3/ United Nations publication. Sales No. E.87.XVII.11.

4/ Institutional sector accounts are shown only for those countries which have tables for all the institutional sectors.

5/ United Nations publication, Sales No. E.69.XVII.3. The first edition of the report, published in 1953, was prepared by an expert committee appointed by the Secretary-General of the United Nations.

6 United Nations publication. Sales. No. E.71.XVII.10.

7/ United Nations publication, ST/ESA/STAT/SER.Q.

I. SYSTEM OF NATIONAL ACCOUNTS (SNA)

The revised System of National Accounts (SNA) was adopted by the Statistical Commission at its fifteenth session [1] for the use of national statistical authorities and in the international reporting of comparable national accounting data. The present System [2] is a revision and extension of the former SNA which was first formulated in 1952.

A. STRUCTURE OF SNA

SNA provides a comprehensive and detailed framework for the systematic and integrated recording of transaction flows in an economy. It brings together into an articulated and coherent system data ranging in degree of aggregation from consolidated accounts of the nation to detailed input-output and flow-of-funds tables. It includes production and goods and services and outlay and capital finance accounts for institutional sectors and subsectors.

The country tables are divided into four parts. These are listed in the above introduction. Part 1 contains summary but comprehensive information, at current and, where appropriate, constant prices. This part includes not only the basic gross domestic product (final expenditures and cost composition) but also summary information on government receipts and disbursements, enterprise and household income and outlay, and external transactions, a summary capital transactions account, information on gross product by institutional sector of origin and kind of activity and, finally, a table showing the relations among the aggregate concepts used in the revised SNA and also commonly in national statistical systems. Tables 1.1, 1.3, 1.4, 1.5, 1.6, 1.7 and 1.8 form a simple, closed and balancing set of flow accounts, drawn from the much more complex and elaborate standard accounts of SNA; these tables can therefore be used not only to provide an overview of the operation of the economic system but also as a guide to the more detailed data that follow and as a framework to enforce conceptual and statistical consistency.

Part 2 shows detailed breakdowns of the final expenditure components on gross domestic product (consumption, capital formation, imports and exports), in current and constant prices, together with supporting tables giving additional information on government outlays and capital stock. This part also shows tables relating to stocks of reproducible tangible assets at current and constant prices.

Part 3 shows detailed institutional sector accounts. For each sector and subsector, five accounts are given: a production account, an income and outlay account, a capital formation account, a capital finance account, and a balance sheet. The latter four are standard SNA accounts, as shown in annex 8.3 to *A System of National Accounts* [2] and in annex 8.2 to *Provisional Guidelines on National and Sector Balance Sheets and Reconciliation Accounts of the System of National Accounts.* [4]

The SNA standard accounts do not include institutional sector production accounts, but provision is made for this information in the supporting tables.

The sectors and subsectors distinguished in part 3 are: general government (central, state or provincial, local, social security funds), corporate and quasi-corporate enterprises (non-financial, financial), households and private unincorporated enterprises (farm entrepreneurial, other farm, non-farm entrepreneurial, non-farm wage earner, other) and non-profit institutions serving households.

Part 4 contains kind-of-activity breakdowns. Two levels of detail are employed. All of the information is asked for at the major division (1-digit) level of the *International Standard Industrial Classification of All Economic Activities* [5] (ISIC). In some cases, data are also asked for at the ISIC division (2-digit) level, with a very small amount of further breakdown to the 3-digit level. Where appropriate, both current and constant prices are specified. The tables show the derivation of value added (gross output less intermediate consumption), the cost components of value added, and employment.

B. STANDARD CLASSIFICATIONS OF THE SNA

Detailed discussions of definitions and classifications are to be found in *A System of National Accounts,* [2] and in the other publications on SNA cited above. SNA distinguishes between transactor and transaction classifications. Below is a short summary of the main characteristics of each of the classifications used by the system.

I. *Classifications of transactors*

1. *Kind of activity*

The kind-of-activity classification employed is the major division (1-digit) level or, in some tables the division (2-digit) level of ISIC.

In SNA, this classification is intended to be applied to establishment-type units, defined as the smallest units for which separate production accounts can be compiled. SNA also employs a much broader kind of activity classification which divides producers into "industries" and three categories of "other producers". Industries are, broadly, establishments whose activities are intended to be self-sustaining, whether through production for the market or for own use, and it is to this category that the ISIC breakdown is generally applied.

All establishments falling into ISIC major divisions 1-8 should be classed as industries. Producers of government services, private non-profit services to households, and

ix

domestic services are classed as "other producers"; all of these should fall into ISIC category 9 "Community, social and personal services". ISIC category 9 also may, of course, include some establishments classed as industries. Where countries consider, however, that some establishments classed as other producers should appear in ISIC categories other than 9, the nature of the exceptions would be specified in footnotes to tables 1.10 and 1.11.

2. *Institutional sectors*

The basic SNA institutional sectoring is given in *A System of National Accounts,* [3/] table 5.1.

Institutional sectoring, in SNA, is intended to be applied to enterprise-type units, that is, units for which complete accounts can be compiled, as opposed to the establishment-type units employed in the kind-of-activity classification. This distinction is applicable mainly to the corporate and quasi-corporate enterprise sector.

The sectoring and subsectoring employed in the institutional sector accounts in part 3 is as follows:

General government

    Central
    State or provincial
    Local
    Social security funds

Corporate and quasi-corporate enterprises

    Non-financial
    Financial

Households and private unincorporated enterprises

    Farm entrepreneurial
    Other farm
    Non-farm entrepreneurial
    Non-farm wage earner
    Other

Non-profit institutions serving households

Rest of the world

(a) *General government.* This sector includes (1) *producers of government services,* all bodies, departments and establishments of any level of government that engage in administration, defence, regulation of the public order and health, cultural, recreational and other social services and social security arrangements that are furnished but not normally sold to the public; and (2) *industries of government,* ancillary departments and establishments mainly engaged in supplying goods and services to other units of government, such as printing plants, central transport pools and arsenals, and agencies mainly selling goods and services to the public but operating on a small scale and financially integrated with general government, such as government restaurant facilities in public buildings.

Non-profit institutions which, while not an official part of any organ of government, are wholly or mainly financed and controlled by it should be included in producers of government services. Ancillary agencies may occur in any kind of activity. Producers of government services normally occur only in major division 9 (which of course may also include ancillary agencies).

Provision is made for four subsectors of general government, all of which may include the two components noted above. However, it is not intended that artificial distinctions should be introduced where they do not exist in the institutions of a particular country. It will, for instance, usually be desirable to separate state or provincial government from local government only in countries in which state or provincial governments exercise a considerable degree of autonomy. Similarly, social security funds should in general be distinguished separately only where they are organized separately from the other activities of general government and exercise substantial autonomy in their operations.

(b) *Corporate and quasi-corporate enterprises.* SNA defines this sector to include enterprises which meet any one of the following criteria: (1) they are incorporated; (2) they are owned by a non-resident; (3) they are relatively large partnerships or proprietorships with complete income statements and balance sheets; (4) they are non-profit institutions mainly serving business and financed and controlled by business; or (5) they are engaged in financial activities. Because of the difficulty that may be encountered in compiling separate production account data for incorporated and unincorporated units, a combined production account for these two sectors has also been provided for.

(c) *Households and private unincorporated enterprises.* This sector includes all private unincorporated enterprises not classed as quasi-corporations. SNA also includes in this sector private non-profit institutions serving households that employ less than the equivalent of two full-time persons.

The criterion for classifying the subsectors of the household sector in these tables differs slightly from that tentatively proposed in SNA. There, the subsectoring is based on the occupational status of the person designated "head of household". Here, the classification is based on the most important source of household income, taking all household members into account. It is considered that this criterion more accurately reflects both changing social views and changing labour force participation practices; it also responds to recent directives relating to the elimination of sex-based stereotypes.

(d) *Private non-profit institutions serving households.* This sector includes institutions, not mainly financed and controlled by general governments and employing the equivalent of two or more persons, that furnish educational, health, cultural, recreational and other social and community services to households free of charge or at prices that do not fully cover their costs of production.

As in the case of general government, SNA includes two components in this sector: (1) *producers of private non-profit services to households,* which engage in the activities enumerated above, and (2) *commercial activities* of these institutions, such as owning and letting dwellings, operating eating and lodging facilities, and publishing and selling books, for which it is possible to compile separate production accounts but not complete separate financial accounts. (Where separate financial accounts can be compiled, such activities would be classed as ordinary quasi-corporations.) In SNA, these commercial activities are considered to be "industries" and should be classed in the appropriate ISIC categories, whereas the non-profit services proper will all fall into ISIC category 9.

II. *Classifications of transactions*

1. *Classification of the functions of government*

Table 5.3 of *A System of National Accounts* [3] contains a classification of the purposes of government, the 1-digit level of which was used in previous publications for classifying general government outlays. This classification has now been superseded by the *Classification of the Functions of Government.* [6]

2. *Household consumption expenditure*

Table 6.1 of SNA provides a classification of household goods and services. The classification used in the present publication is a slightly condensed version of the second level of this classification, in which some second-level categories have been combined.

3. *Purposes of private non-profit bodies serving households*

This classification appears in table 5.4 of SNA. It is used for classifying the final consumption expenditures of private non-profit institutions serving households.

4. *Gross capital formation*

Table 6.2 of SNA classifies stocks according to type, and table 6.3 classifies gross fixed capital formation according to type. These classifications are used in the present publication in slightly modified form, calling for less detail in some areas and slightly more detail in others (specifically, transport equipment).

5. *Exports and imports of goods and services*

This classification is given in table 6.4 of SNA.

6. *Transfers*

Table 7.1 of SNA contains a classification of unrequited current transfers, including direct taxes. This classification is not employed directly in the present publication but it is the source of the definitions of a number of flows, and will be referred to in that connection.

7. *Financial assets and liabilities*

Table 7.2 of SNA gives a classification of items appearing in the capital finance account.

8. *Balance sheet categories*

Classifications of the various types of assets not included in the previous classification are given in tables 5.1 and 5.2 of *Provisional Guidelines on National and Sector Balance Sheets and Reconciliation Accounts of the System of National Accounts,* [4], which deal respectively, with stocks and fixed assets, and non-reproducible tangible assets. These classifications are used in the capital stock tables in part 2 and the balance sheet tables in part 3 of the present publication.

C. DEFINITIONS OF FLOWS

The following section briefly defines the content of the flows appearing in the SNA tables of chapter III of the present publication.

I. *Total supply of goods and services*

1. *Gross output of goods and services*

Gross output of goods and services covers both the value of goods and services produced for sale and the value of goods and services produced for own use. It includes (a) the domestic production of goods and services which are either for sale or for transfer to others, (b) net additions to work in progress valued at cost and to stocks of finished goods valued in producers' prices; (c) products made on own account for government or private consumption or for gross fixed capital formation; and (d) rents received on structures, machinery and equipment (but not on land) and imputed rent for owner-occupied dwellings.

Production for own consumption of households includes all own-account production of primary products (agricultural, fishing, forestry, mining and quarrying), own-account production of such items as butter, flour, wine, cloth or furniture made from primary products, and other goods and services that are also commonly sold. Gross output of the distributive trades is defined as the difference between sales and purchase values of goods sold. Gross output of banks and similar financial institutions is defined as the sum of actual service charges and imputed service charges; the latter is equal to the excess of property income received over interest paid out on deposits. For casualty insurance companies, gross output is defined as the excess of premiums received over claims paid, and for life insurance schemes it is the excess of premiums received over the sum of claims paid and net additions to actuarial reserves, excluding the accrued interest of the policy-holders in these reserves. Gross output of general government includes the market value of sales and goods and services produced for own use. The latter should be valued at cost, that is, the sum of net purchases of goods and services for intermediate consumption (at purchasers' prices), consumption of fixed capital, compensation of employees and any indirect taxes paid.

The concept of gross output appears in the tables in both part 3 and part 4. In part 3, each sector production account aggregates to its gross output. In part 4, gross output of various kind-of-activity sectors appears in tables 4.1 - 4.2 and 4.5 - 4.10. In the sector production accounts (tables 3.11, 3.21, 3.31 and 3.41) and the supply tables (4.5, 4.6, 4.9 and 4.10), gross output is divided into marketed and non-marketed components. The marketed component includes all output offered for sale (whether or not a buyer is actually found) or valued on the basis of a market transaction, even if it reaches the ultimate recipient through a transfer.

2. *Imports of goods and services*

Imports of goods and services include broadly the equivalent of general imports of merchandise as defined in external trade statistics, plus imports of services and direct purchases abroad made by resident households and by the government on current account. Transfer of migrants' household and personal effects and gifts between households are also included. The following additions and deductions are required, however, to move from the general trade concept to the national accounting concept. Additions required include (1) the value of purchases of bankers, stores and ballast for ships, aircraft, etc., (2) fish and salvage purchased from foreign vessels, and (3) purchases from abroad of gold ore and gold for industrial uses Deductions required include (4) goods imported solely for improvement or repair and subsequently re-exported; and (5) leased or rented machinery, equipment and other goods; the value of the repairs or leasing and rental services is included, however. The valuation of imports is c.i.f. In principle, transactions should be recorded at the moment the transfer of ownership takes place and not when goods physically enter the domestic territory, but in practice the time of recording used in the national accounts usually must follow that used in the external trade statistics.

Total imports of goods and services appear in tables 1.1, 1.2, 1.7 and 3.51. A detailed breakdown is given in table 2.17.

II. *Disposition of total supply: intermediate and final uses*

1. *Intermediate consumption*

Intermediate consumption covers non-durable goods and services used up in production, including repair and maintenance, research and development and exploration costs. It also includes indirect outlays on financing capital formation, such as flotation costs for loans and transfer costs involved in the purchase and sale of intangible assets and financial claims. Intermediate consumption is, as far as possible, valued in purchasers' prices at the moment of use.

For producers of government services and private non-profit services to households, intermediate consumption includes (1) purchases of goods and services on current account *less* sales of similar second-hand goods and scraps and wastes, (2) value of goods in kind received as transfers or gifts from foreign governments, except those received for distribution to households without renovation or alteration, (3) durable goods acquired primarily for military purposes, and (4) goods and services paid for by government but furnished by private suppliers to individuals (e.g., medical services), provided that the individuals have no choice of supplier. However, intermediate consumption of these producers does not include (1) goods and services acquired for use in constructing capital assets, such as roads or buildings, (2) goods and services paid for by government but furnished by private suppliers to individuals, when the individuals can choose the supplier and (3) purchases of strategic materials for government stockpiles.

Intermediate consumption appears in each institutional sector production account in part 3, and in tables 4.1-4.2 by kind of activity. In addition to the flow numbers assigned in SNA, flow numbers have been introduced for two categories of intermediate consumption not separately numbered in *A System of National Accounts.* [3/] The first is imputed bank service charges. The imputed bank service charge is defined as the excess of property income accruing to banks and similar financial institutions from the investment of deposits over the interest accruing to their depositors. This imputation is made because of the view that banks perform services for depositors for which no explicit payment is made, in return for the use of the deposits as earning assets. It is not possible to allocate the imputation to specific recipients of the services, however, so that it cannot be included, as would be desirable, as part of the intermediate consumption of each reception. It is therefore deducted as a lump-sum adjustment. The adjustment appears in the tables showing kind-of-activity breakdowns of value added or intermediate consumption, including tables 1.10, 1.11 and 4.1-4.2. The second addition is intermediate consumption of industries of government, required for constructing a production account for general government (table 3.11).

2. *Government final consumption expenditure*

Government final consumption expenditure is equal to the service produced by general government for its own use. Since these services are not sold, they are valued in the gross domestic product at their cost to the government. This cost is defined as the sum of (1) intermediate consumption, (2) compensation of employees, (3) consumption of fixed capital and (4) payments of indirect taxes, *less* (5) the value of own-account production of fixed assets, and *less* (6) sales of goods and services.

The latter item, government sales, includes all payments made by individuals for services received (whether nominal or full cost) and it also includes the provision of second-hand goods from government stores as transfers in kind to foreign governments. Sales of such items as timber from forest preserves, seeds from agricultural experiment stations and government publications would also appear here. Compensation of employees, consumption of fixed capital and indirect taxes paid (if any) should preferably relate to all general government activity, with intra-governmental purchases and sales of goods and services eliminated in order to avoid double counting. With this treatment, there will be no operating surplus for any general government unit. Where countries consider that ancillary agencies and/or unincorporated government enterprises selling to the general public are operated on commercial principles and that the prices charged reflect market values, treatment of these entities on a net basis is an acceptable alternative. In this treatment, their sales to other government agencies will appear as intermediate consumption of the latter, and their operating surplus will appear as an item of general government income. This treatment has a number of disadvantages: the boundary between ancillary agencies and other government agencies is very difficult to specify precisely, and variations in treatment are likely to lead to incomparability among countries. Also, the net treatment makes it impossible to obtain figures for such flows as total compensation of general government employees. Finally, the level of gross domestic product will vary when the government's internal transfer prices are altered, a result that is somewhat incongruous.

Total government consumption expenditures appear in tables 1.1, 1.2, 4.7 and 4.8. A breakdown by government subsectors appears in table 3.12. Tables 2.1-2.2 show detailed breakdowns by function.

3. *Private final consumption expenditure*

Private consumption expenditure measures the final consumption expenditure of all resident non-governmental units. Thus, it is the sum of final consumption expenditure of households and that of private non-profit institutions serving households.

(a) *Private non profit institutions serving households.* Final consumption expenditure of these units, as in the case of government, is equal to services they produce for their own use and is valued at cost. Cost includes purchases and the value (in purchasers' prices) of transfers of goods and services received in kind, compensation of employees, consumption of fixed capital, and indirect taxes paid by these institutions, *less* their sales of goods and services. The definitions of purchases and sales on current account are much the same as those for general government. Private non-profit institutions serving households are defined to include units employing the equivalent of two or more full-time persons and providing educational, health, cultural, recreational, and other social and community services to households free of charge or at prices that are not intended to cover the full costs of their production. Units mainly financed and controlled by general government, however, are included in general government rather than here. Units primarily serving business, such as trade associations, are included with corporate and quasi-corporate enterprises. In applying these definitions, some judgement is required, and it will often be necessary to examine intent, as well as outcome. A normally profit-making unit that sustains a loss does not thereby become a non-profit institution.

Final expenditures of private non-profit institutions serving households appear in tables 1.1, 1.2 and 3.42, and a breakdown by purpose appears in tables 2.5 and 2.6. Definitions of the purpose categories are given in SNA classification 5.4

(b) *Resident households.* What is wanted as a component of the final uses of gross domestic product is the final consumption expenditure of resident households. What is most commonly available in the statistics, however, is not expenditure of resident units but expenditure in the domestic market. To adjust expenditure in the domestic market to expenditure of resident units, purchases abroad and net gifts in kind received from abroad have been added, and subtracted are purchases in the domestic market of non-resident units. Corresponding adjustments are made to exports (to ensure that they include purchases of non-residents in the domestic market) and to imports (to ensure that they include purchases of residents abroad). These adjustments include expenditures by tourists, ships' crews, border and seasonal workers and diplomatic and military personnel on goods and services, including local transportation, but they exclude expenditures reimbursible as travel expenses (which are counted as intermediate consumption). These adjustments are shown in tables 2.5 and 2.6.

Household final consumption expenditure includes outlays on non-durable and durable goods and services, *less* sales of second-hand goods and of scraps and wastes. In addition to market purchases, household final consumption expenditure includes the imputed gross rent of owner-occupied dwellings, food and other items produced on own account and consumed, and items provided as wages and salaries in kind by an employer, such as food, shelter or clothing, and other fringe benefits included in compensation of employees, except those considered to add to household saving. The imputed gross rent of owner-occupied dwellings should, in principle, be valued at the rent of similar facilities on the market but has been approximated by costs, including operating maintenance and repair charges, depreciation, mortgage interest, and interest on the owner's equity. Other non-marketed output included in final consumption is valued at producers' prices.

Total resident final consumption expenditure appears in tables 1.1, 1.2, 1.6 and 1.12. It is broken down by institutional subsectors in tables 3.32, and in tables 4.7 and 4.8 it is broken down by industrial origin. A detailed breakdown by type of good is shown in tables 2.5 and 2.6. The type-of-good categories are defined in SNA classification 6.1.

4. *Gross capital formation*

Gross capital formation is the sum of the increase in stocks and gross fixed capital formation, defined below. It appears in tables 1.1, 1.2 and 1.8. Breakdowns of gross capital formation appear in tables 2.7-2.12, 4.7 and 4.8. Gross capital formation of individual institutional sectors appears in tables 3.13, 3.23, 3.33. and 3.43.

(a) *Increase in stocks*. This flow includes the value of the physical change in (a) stocks of raw materials, work in progress and finished goods held by private producers, and (b) stocks of strategic materials held by the government. Work put in place on buildings and other structures, roads and other construction projects is treated as gross fixed capital formation rather than increase in stocks but is distinguished separately there to facilitate analysis. Increases in livestock raised for slaughter should be included in the increase in stocks, but breeding and draft animals, dairy cattle, and animals raised for wool clips are treated as fixed capital. The physical change in stocks during a period of account should be valued at average purchasers' prices during the period. In some cases, the available data relate to the change in the value of stocks held rather than the value of the physical change.

A classification of the increase in stocks by type is given in tables 2.7 and 2.8, and defined in SNA classification 6.2. The increase in stocks by kind of activity of owner is shown in tables 2.9 and 2.10.

(b) *Gross capital formation*. This flow is defined to include purchases and own-account production of new producers' durable goods, reduced by net sales to the rest of the world of similar second-hand or scrapped goods. Outlays of producers of government services for military purposes (except on land and certain civilian-type items, such as schools, hospitals, family-type housing and, in some cases, roads when for civilian use) are, however, considered to be current expenditures. "Military purposes" are here construed in terms of final expenditures: they include the military airport, but not the bulldozer used in constructing the airport. Gross fixed capital formation includes outlays on reclamation and improvement of land and development and extension of timber tracts, mines, plantations, orchards, vineyards etc., and on breeding and dairy cattle, draft animals, and animals raised for wool. Outlays on alteration or extension of fixed assets, which significantly extend their life or increase their productivity, are included, but outlays on repair and maintenance to keep fixed assets in good working order are not. All costs are included that are directly connected with the acquisition and installation of the fixed assets, such as customs duties and other indirect taxes, transport, delivery and installation charges, site clearing, planning and designing costs, legal fees and other transfer costs with respect to transactions in land, mineral deposits, timber tracts etc. However, the costs of financing, such as flotation costs, underwriters' commissions and the cost of advertising bond issues, are excluded; these items are included in intermediate consumption. The acquisition of fixed assets is to be recorded at the moment that the ownership of the goods passes to the buyer. In the case of construction projects, this is taken to be the time that the work is put in place but, as noted above, uncompleted construction projects are shown separately from completed ones.

A classification of fixed assets by type is given in tables 2.7 and 2.8, and the categories are defined in SNA classification 6.3. A classification by kind of activity of purchaser is given in tables 2.9, 2.10, 2.11 and 2.12, and a classification by producing industry is given in tables 4.7 and 4.8. Breakdowns by institutional sector are given in tables 3.13, 3.23, 3.33 and 3.43.

5. *Exports of goods and services*

Exports of goods and services are defined to be parallel to the definition of imports given above, and they are shown in the same tables and classifications. Exports are, however, valued f.o.b., whereas imports are valued c.i.f.

III. *Cost components and income shares*

1. *Value added and gross domestic product*

The value added of industries at producers' prices is equal to the gross output of the industries at producers' prices *less* the value of their intermediate consumption at purchasers' prices. Value added for the total of all domestic producers (*plus* import duties and value added tax which are not included in the value added of any domestic producer, and *less* imputed bank service charges which are deducted in a single line) is equal to the gross domestic product is shown in tables 1.9-1.11, and 4.1 - 4.2. Gross domestic product may be defined alternatively as the sum of final expenditures in the domestic economy (tables 1.1 and 1.2) or as the sum of incomes received in the domestic economy (tables 1.3, 1.9 and 4.3). In principle, all three methods should yield the same result but in statistical practice there are likely to be small discrepancies. Such statistical discrepancies are shown where they exist.

2. Compensation of employees

Compensation of employees appears in SNA as a domestic concept and as a national concept. Table 1.3 employs the domestic concept, that is, compensation of employees paid by resident producers. This includes payments to non-resident employees working in the country but excludes payments to resident employees temporarily working abroad. In order to show the relation of this concept to compensation received by resident households (shown in tables 1.6 and 3.32) and compensation paid to the rest of the world (shown in tables 1.7 and 3.51), the two components are shown separately in table 1.3. Each component includes (a) wages and salaries, (b) employers' contributions to social security schemes and (c) employers' contributions to private pension, insurance and similar schemes. The national concept of compensation of employees is shown in the household sector income and outlay account (tables 1.6 and 3.31), where compensation received by resident households from domestic producers and that received from the rest of the world are gathered together. The portion paid by resident producers appears in table 1.3; that paid by the rest of the world appears in table 1.7.

Wages and salaries include all payments to employees for their labour, whether in cash or in kind, before deduction of employee contributions to social security schemes, withholding taxes and the like. They include commissions, bonuses and tips, and cost of living, vacation and sick leave allowances paid directly by the employers to the employee but exclude reimbursement for travel and other expenses incurred by employees for business purposes, which is included in intermediate consumption. The pay and allowances of members of the armed forces, the fees, salaries and bonuses of members of boards of directors, managing directors, executives and other employees of incorporated enterprises and the fees of ministers of religion are included. Wages and salaries in kind are valued at their cost to the employer, and include goods and services furnished to employees free of charge or at markedly reduced cost that are clearly and primarily of benefit to the employees as consumers.

Employers' contributions to social security schemes include all social security contributions that employers make on behalf of their employees, but not the employees' own share of such contributions. Social security contributions may be broader than payments to social security funds, since not all social security arrangements are funded.

Employers' contributions to pension, insurance and similar schemes include paid and imputed contributions by employers on behalf of their employees to private funds, reserves or other schemes for providing pensions, family allowances, lay-off and severance pay, maternity leave, workmen's compensation, health and other casualty insurance life insurance and the like. Where employers make payments to employees for such benefits without the establishment a formal fund for this purpose, the contributions that would be required to support such a fund are imputed both here and subsequently as an imputed transfer from households to their employers, since of course the employees do not control the use of the fund.

3. Operating surplus

Operating surplus is the balancing item in the SNA production account. For an individual establishment, it is defined as the excess of value added over the sum of compensation of employees, consumption of fixed capital, and net indirect taxes. The operating surplus of all types of establishments -- corporate, quasi-corporate, and unincorporated, public and private -- is included in the figure shown in table 1.3. Operating surplus for each of the institutional sectors individually is shown in tables 3.11, 3.21 and 3.31; its breakdown by kind of activity is shown in table 4.3 . It is also included in the totals for property and entrepreneurial income shown in tables 1.4, 1.5 and 1.6.

4. Consumption of fixed capital

Consumption of fixed capital includes allowances for normal wear and tear, foreseen obsolescence and probable (normally expected) accidental damage to fixed capital not made good by repair, all valued at current replacement cost. Unforeseen obsolescence, damages due to calamities, and depletion of natural resources are not included, since these are capital losses and should appear as changes in the balance sheet. Also not included is the revaluation of past allowances for consumption of fixed capital due to changes in the current replacement cost of fixed assets; this also will appear as part of the change in accumulated allowances shown in the balance sheet. Total consumption of fixed capital appears in tables 1.3, 1.8 and 1.12, consumption of fixed capital of individual institutional sectors in tables 3.11, 3.21, 3.31 and 3.41, and consumption of fixed capital by kind of activity in table 4.3. The accumulated consumption of fixed capital for specific types of assets and kind-of-activity sectors appears as the difference between the gross and net capital stock in tables 2.13-2.16, and for individual institutional sectors it appears in tables 3.15, 3.25, 3.35 and 3.45.

5. Indirect taxes

Indirect taxes are defined as taxes chargeable to the cost of production or sale of goods and services. They include (a) import and export duties, (b) excise, sales, entertainment and turnover taxes, (c) real estate and land taxes, unless they are merely an administrative device for collecting income tax, (d) levies on value added and the employment of labour (but not social security contributions), (e) motor-vehicle, driving-test, licence, airport and passport fees, when paid by producers, and (f) the operating surplus of government fiscal monopolies on such items as alcoholic beverages and tobacco (in principle reduced by the normal profit margin of similar business units). In the present publication, indirect taxes paid and subsidies received from supranational organizations (e.g., the European Economic Community) are shown separately. Also, the net treatment of value added taxes recommended by the European Economic Community has been employed.

Unlike all other indirect taxes, SNA does not allocate import duties among producers in tables by kind of activity. Indirect taxes are only allocated to a particular kind of activity where they are levied directly on the output of that activity (e.g., excise duties) or on the process of producing that output (e.g., employment taxes). Import duties, however, are levied on the output of foreign rather than domestic producers, and are therefore shown separately in tables by kind of activity, including tables 1.10, 1.11, 4.1, 4.2, 4.3, 4.5 and 4.6.

Total indirect taxes appear in table 1.3. Indirect taxes paid by individual institutional sectors appear in tables 3.11, 3.21, 3.31, and 3.41. Indirect taxes paid to supranational organizations appear in tables 1.7 and 1.12. Indirect taxes retained by government are shown in table 3.12.

6. Subsidies

Subsidies are grants on current account by the government to (a) private enterprises and public corporations, or (b) unincorporated public enterprises when clearly intended to compensate for losses resulting from the price policies of government. Total subsidies, including those paid by supranational organizations, as well as by government, appear in table 1.3; subsidies paid by supranational organizations in tables 1.7 and 1.12; and those paid by government in tables 1.4 and 3.12. Subsidies received by individual institutional sectors appear in tables 3.21, 3.31 and 3.41.

7. *Withdrawals from quasi-corporations*

Withdrawals from the entrepreneurial income of quasi-corporations consist of the actual payments made to the proprietors of quasi-corporations from the entrepreneurial income of these units. Entrepreneurial income of quasi-corporations is equal to their income from production (net operating surplus) *plus* their net income (receipts *less* payments) from property. In some cases, the whole of the entrepreneurial income will be treated as if paid out to the proprietors; in other cases, some of it is retained as net saving within the quasi-corporation. Withdrawals from quasi-corporations also include withdrawals from foreign branches of domestic companies or from domestic branches of foreign companies, since both of these categories are treated as quasi-corporations. The withdrawals may be negative, since proprietors may provide funds to the enterprises to compensate for losses.

SNA assigns separate flow numbers to withdrawals as they appear in the paying sectors (flow 4.4) and in the receiving sectors (flow 4.5). As disbursements, they appear in table 3.22 and as part of a larger total in table 1.5. As receipts, they appear in tables 3.12, 3.22, 3.32 and 3.42, and as parts of the larger total in tables 1.4, 1.5 and 1.6

8. *Property income*

Property income consists of payments of interest, dividends and land rents and royalties, all of which are assigned separate SNA flow numbers, both as payments and as receipts. Interest is defined as income payable and receivable on financial claims, such as bank and other deposits, bills and bonds, including public debt, and the equity of households in life insurance actuarial reserves and pension funds. Dividends consist of income payable and receivable on corporate equity securities and other forms of participation in the equity of private incorporated enterprises, public corporations and co-operatives. Rent payments include, in addition to net land rent, royalty payments for concessions to exploit mineral deposits or for the use of patents, copyrights, trademarks and the like. They exclude rent payments on machinery and equipment or buildings, which are treated as the purchase of a service rather than property income and appear in gross output of the seller and intermediate consumption of the purchaser. Payments of land rent are always treated as a domestic flow since the foreign owners are, for national accounting purposes, dealt with as residents of the country in which the land is located. When it is not possible to separate rent of buildings and rent of the land on which the buildings stand, the whole flow is attributed to the buildings, that is, excluded from property income and included in intermediate consumption.

Property income paid and received by individual institutional sectors is shown in tables 3.12, 3.22, 3.32 and 3.42. As part of a larger total it appears in the summary tables 1.4, 1.5 and 1.6.

IV. *Taxes and unrequited transfers*

The categories of taxes and unrequited transfers are classified and defined in SNA classification 7.1. SNA does not provide the full articulation of the to-whom from-whom relationships of these flows, but assigns flow numbers to the various combinations of them used in specific standard tables and accounts. In order to define less ambiguosly the flows used in the present publication, a somewhat fuller listing of individual flow components is used.

1. *Casualty insurance transactions*

Casualty insurance transactions refer to health, accident fire, theft, unemployment and similar insurance schemes. The total of net premiums for the economy as a whole is equal to the total premiums payable *less* an imputed service charge which in turn is defined to be equal to the difference between premiums and claims. As a consequence, for the economy as a whole, net premiums and claims are equal. However, the total service charge is distributed to sectors of receipt and disbursement in proportion to the total (not net) premiums paid, so that net premiums and claims are not necessarily equal for each sector. In the former SNA, these insurance transactions were considered to be in part capital items, and this practice continues in the accounts of a number of countries. In the revised SNA, however, all casualty insurance transactions, including compensation for capital losses, are considered to be current flows. They are shown in detail in tables 3.12, 3.22, 3.32 and 3.42.

2. *Taxes and other government receipts*

Taxes and other government receipts include direct taxes, compulsory fees, fines and penalties, social security contributions, and other current transfers received by general government.

Direct taxes include two components. Direct taxes on income cover levies by public authorities at regular intervals (except social security contributions) on income from employment, property, capital gains or any other source. Real estate and land taxes are included only if they are merely administrative procedures for the assessment and collection of income tax. Other direct taxes cover levies by public authorities at regular intervals on the financial assets and the net of total worth of enterprises, private non-profit institutions and households, and on the possession or use of goods by households. Direct taxes received are shown in tables 1.4 and 3.2; payments of other sectors are shown in tables 3.22, 3.32 and 3.42.

Compulsory fees are payments to public authorities by households for services that are obligatory and unavoidable in the only circumstances in which they are useful. Examples of such fees are payments by households for driving tests and licenses, airport and court fees and the like. Similar payments by business units are treated as indirect taxes. Fines and penalties, however, include not only those paid by households but also those paid by corporate and quasi-corporate enterprises and private non-profit institutions serving households. They appear in the same tables as direct taxes.

Social security contributions consist of contributions for the account of employees, whether made by employees or by employers on their behalf, to the social security arrangements that are imposed, controlled or financed by the government for the purpose of providing social security benefits for the community or large sections of the community. They appear as receipts in tables 1.4 and 3.12, and as payments in tables 1.6 and 3.32.

Current transfers n.e.c. received by general government consist primarily of transfers received from the rest of the world and imputed employee welfare contributions. Transfers from the rest of the world include grants between governments to finance military outlays, outlays for health and educational purposes, and similar transfers in kind of military equipment, food, clothing etc. Payments and assessments and other periodic contributions to international organizations are also included. In addition to actual transfers, this item also includes imputed transfers arising from the obligation of the government as an employer to pay directly to its employees pensions, family allowances, severance and lay-off pay and other welfare benefits when there is no special fund, reserve or insurance for these purposes. In these circumstances, SNA provides for the establishment of an imputed fund to which imputed contributions are made, of a magnitude sufficient to support the unfunded benefit payments. The imputed contributions are included in compensation of employees, as an addition to actual payments, and are then shown as an imputed payment by the employees back to the government as an employer. These transfers appear in table 1.4 as an aggregate, and in table 3.12 in more detail.

3. *Household transfer receipts*

Household transfer receipts include social security benefits, social assistance grants, and unfunded employee welfare benefits. These flows, in varying detail, are shown in tables 1.6, 2.4 and 3.32.

Social security benefits are payments to individuals under the social security arrangements described above. The payments are often made out of a special fund and may be related to the income of individuals from employment or to contributions to social security arrangements made on their behalf. Examples are unemployment insurance benefits, old-age, disability and survivors' pensions, family allowances and reimbursements for medical and hospital expenses. It may be difficult to distinguish social security benefits from social assistance grants, on the one hand, and insurance benefits, on the other. The main criterion is method of finance; the actual content will vary from country to country. Medical services, for instance, may be supplied as social assistance, as a part of social security, as a casualty insurance benefit, or as a free government service.

Social assistance grants are cash grants to individuals and households, except social security benefits and unfunded employee welfare benefits. They may be made by public authorities, private non-profit institutions, or corporate and quasi-corporate enterprises. Examples are relief payments;

widows', guardians' and family allowances and payments of medical and dental expenses which are not part of social insurance schemes; war bonuses, pensions and service grants; and scholarships, fellowships and maintenance allowances for educational, training and similar purposes. They include payments made by public authorities for services provided by business enterprises and private non-profit institutions directly and individually to persons, whether these payments are made to the individuals or directly to the providers of the services that the persons are considered to have purchased. They exclude, however, transfers to persons or households as indemnities for property losses during floods, wars and similar calamities; these are considered to be capital items.

Unfunded employee welfare benefits are pensions, family allowances, severance and lay-off pay, maternity leave pay, workmen's and disability compensation and reimbursements for medical expenses and other casualties which employers pay directly to their former or present employees when there is no special fund, reserve or insurance for these purposes.

4. *Transfers received by private non-profit institutions*

Transfers received by private non-profit institutions serving households include grants and gifts, in cash and in kind, to non-profit institutions serving households which are intended to cover partially the cost of the provision of services by these institutions. They also include membership dues paid to political organizations, fraternal bodies and the like. They appear as a receipt in table 3.42, and as payments sometimes as part of a larger total, in tables 3.12, 3.22 and 3.32.

5. *Other current transfers n.e.c.*

Other current transfers n.e.c. include transfers to and from resident sectors that are not specifically included in any other flows. They may include migrants' remittances, transfers of immigrants' personal and household goods, and transfers between resident and non-resident households, in cash and in kind. They include allowances for bad debts.

V. *Finance of gross accumulation*

1. *Net saving*

Net saving is the balancing item in the SNA income and outlay account. It is defined as the difference between current receipts and current disbursements. Net saving for the nation as a whole appears in tables 1.8 and 1.12. Net saving for individual institutional sectors appears in tables 3.12, 3.13, 3.22, 3.23, 3.32, 3.33, 3.42 and 3.43.

2. *Surplus of the nation on current transactions*

The surplus of the nation on current transactions is the balancing item in the external transactions current accounts (tables 1.7 and 3.51). It also appears in table 1.8, the capital transactions account, in table 1.12, the table showing relationships among the national accounting aggregates, and table 3.52, the external transactions capital accumulation account.

3. *Purchases of land, net*

Purchases of land, net, include purchases *less* sales of land, subsoil deposits, forests and inland waters, including any improvements that are an integral part of these assets except buildings and other structures. The purchases and sales are valued at the transaction (sales) price of the land, forests etc., not including the transfer costs involved; such transfer costs are included in gross capital formation. Purchases and sales are assumed to take place when the legal title to the land is passed. They are considered to take place between resident institutions only. Where the land is purchased by a non-resident, a nominal resident institution is considered to be the owner of the land. The foreign owner is assigned equity in the resident institution equivalent to the purchase price of the land. The value recorded in the flow is the same for both the buyer and the seller. For the country as a whole, therefore, purchases and sales will cancel out. If the sales value of the structures situated on the land cannot be separated from the sales value of the land itself, the entire transaction should be recorded as a purchase and sale of structures (i.e., of second-hand assets), unless the structures are intended for immediate demolition. Purchases of land appear in the capital accumulation accounts of the individual institutional sectors, (tables 3.13, 3.23, 3.33 and 3.43.

4. *Purchases of intangible assets, net*

Purchases of intangible assets, net, are defined as purchases, *less* sales, of exclusive rights to mineral, fishing and other concessions and of patents, copyrights etc. These transactions involve the once-and-for-all relinquishment and acquisition of the exclusive rights, although they may be paid for over a period of years; they do not include concessions, leases, licences to use patents and permission to publish copyrighted materials which involve the periodic payment of royalties or rents, with eventual reversion of the rights to the seller. The purchases and sales are valued at the transaction (sales) value of the mineral concession, lease, patent, etc., not including any transfer costs involved. (The transfer costs are included in gross capital formation.) Purchases of intangible assets appear in the individual institutional sector capital accumulation accounts (tables 3.13, 3.23, 3.33, and 3.43) as a part of gross accumulation. Purchases from the rest of the world appear in table 3.52.

5. *Capital transfers*

Capital transfers are defined as unrequited transfers, in cash or in kind, which are used for purposes of capital formation or other forms of capital accumulation, are made out of wealth, or are non-recurrent. Examples of capital transfers are grants from one government to another to finance deficits in external trade, investment grants, unilateral transfers of capital goods, legacies, death duties and inheritance taxes, migrants' transfers of financial assets and indemnities in respect of calamities. Mixed transfers, considered by one party to the transaction as capital and the other as current, are treated as capital. Capital transfers appear in tables 3.13, 3.23, 3.33, 3.43 and 3.52.

6. *Net lending*

Net lending is defined as the excess of the sources of finance of accumulation (i.e., net saving, consumption of fixed capital and capital transfers received) over the uses of these funds for gross capital formation, net purchases of land and intangibles, and capital transfers paid. It appears in the capital accumulation accounts of the individual institutional sectors (tables 3.13, 3.23, 3.33 and 3.43), and in the external transactions capital accumulation account (table 3.52). Net lending is also equal to the difference between a sector's net acquisition of financial assets and its net incurrence of financial liabilities. It thus also appears in the institutional sector capital finance accounts (tables 3.14, 3.24, 3.34, 3.44 and 3.53). Although not for all countries, net lending derived in these two different ways are statistically identical.

VI. *Financial assets and liabilities*

Net acquisition of financial assets is defined as the difference between, on the one hand, acquisitions or purchases and, on the other, relinquishment or sales by given transactors of financial claims on second parties. Net incurrence of liabilities is equal to the issue or sale *less* redemption or payment of financial claims of second parties. A classification and definitions of financial assets and liabilities is given in SNA classification 7.2. Changes in financial assets and liabilities for individual institutional sectors appear in the capital finance accounts (tables 3.14, 3.24, 3.34, 3.44 and 3.53). Their total amount is shown in the sector balance sheets (tables 3.15, 3.25, 3.35 and 3.45).

VII. *Other assets*

1. *Reproducible tangible assets*

Reproducible tangible assets are classified and defined in table 5.1 of the *Provisional Guidelines on National and Sector Balance Sheets and Reconciliation Accounts of the System of National Accounts.* [4] They appear, classified by type of asset and broad sector, in tables 2.13 and 2.14, by kind of activity in tables 2.15 and 2.16 and for individual institutional sectors, in the sector balance sheets in tables 3.15, 3.25, 3.35 and 3.45

2. *Non-reproducible tangible assets*

Non-reproducible tangible assets are classified and defined in table 5.2 of the *Provisional Guidelines* (see above). Only the total appears in the tables, in the sector balance sheets (tables 3.15, 3.25, and 3.45).

3. *Non-financial intangible assets*

Non-financial intangible assets include the mineral, fishing and other concessions, leases, patents, copyrights etc., the purchase and sale of which is recorded in the capital accumulation account. These intangible assets are created at the time of the purchase or sale, that is, when a once-and-for-all lump-sum payment has been made for the lease, concession, patent or copyright. They appear in the sector balance sheets (tables 3.15, 3.25, 3.35 and 3.45).

---

[1] *Official records of the Economic and Social Council, Forty-fourth Session, Supplement No. 10,* (E/4471), paras. 8-24.

[2] The present system is published in *A System of National Accounts,* Studies in Methods, Series F, No. 2, Rev. 3 (United Nations publication, Sales No. E.69.XVII.3).

[3] *Ibid*

[4] Statistical Papers, Series M, No. 60 United Nations publication, Sales No. 77.XVII.10.

[5] Statistical Papers, Series M, No. 4, Rev. 2, Add. 1 (United Nations publication, Sales No. E.71.XVII.8).

[6] Statistical Papers, Series M, No. 70 (United Nations publication, Sales No. 80.XVII.17).

II. SYSTEM OF MATERIAL PRODUCT BALANCES (MPS)

The System of Material Product Balances (MPS) furnishes the means for standardizing the national accounting data which the Statistical Office of the the Department of International Economic and Social Affairs of the United Nations Secretariat receives from countries with centrally planned economies. Data collection follows the principles found in the *Basic Methodological Rules for the Compilation of the Statistical Balance of the National Economy.* [1] This system is also described in the *Basic Principles of the System of Balances of the National Economy.* [2]

A. STRUCTURE OF MPS

MPS is based on a system of balances. It includes material and financial balances, the balance of manpower resources and the balance of fixed capital and indicators of national wealth. The material balance is a presentation of the volume of the supply of goods and material services originating in domestically produced global product and imports and their disposition to consumption, capital formation and exports, classified by different production activity categories. The financial balance is a presentation of income flows generated in production in the material sphere, their redistribution through transactions in the non-material sphere and through other transfers flows and, finally, their disbursement to consumption and capital formation. The income flows of the financial balance are classified by institutional (social) sectors. The presentation is therefore comparable to that of production, income and outlay and capital finance accounts by institutional sectors in the System of National Accounts (SNA). The third type of balance, that is, the manpower balance, presents the allocation of available manpower to production activities and institutional or social sectors. This balance is expressed in the number of persons employed. The last balance is the one of national wealth and capital assets. It is a presentation of the volume of the stocks of tangible fixed and other assets available at the beginning and the end of the year and the increase that has taken place during the year. The tangible assets are classified by type of asset and by form of ownership and production activities of the national economy.

The MPS tables that are presented in chapter III and are listed in the introduction provide further detail on the material balances. Table 1 on net material product by use is similar to the SNA table on gross domestic product by kind of economic activity. Data regarding the production and goods and services transactions are included in tables 2, 3, 4 and 5 which present, respectively, activity breakdowns of net material product and of primary incomes, of the population and of enterprises, a breakdown by socio-economic sectors of these two types of primary incomes, and a breakdown of supply and disposition of goods and material services by kind of activity of the producers. Tables 6, 7, 8 and 9 present further details on the expenditure categories, such as a breakdown of fixed capital formation by kind of economic activity and by socio-economic sector and of increases in material circulating assets and of stocks by kind of activity, and a classification of final consumption, personal consumption and of total consumption of the population by type of expenditure.

B. DIFFERENCES BETWEEN MPS AND SNA

Apart from the differences in structure of the two systems, there are considerable differences between the coverage of the concepts used in MPS and in SNA. Since these differences limit the use of MPS and SNA data in cross-country types of analyses, a summary of those that are relevant to the MPS data published in chapter III of the present publication is reproduced below. [3]

1. *The treatment of material and non-material services*

In MPS there is a distinction different to that made in SNA, between the production of material and non-material services. Only the production of material services, together with that of goods, is covered by the gross output (global product) concept of MPS. The production of non-material services is excluded. Material goods and services used as input in the production of non-material services are considered to be a part of final consumption expenditure, while income flows resulting from this type of production are treated as income transfers. The material services are those that are directly linked to the production of goods and cover the services related to the repair, transportation and distribution of goods. All other services are treated as non-material services. This important difference between MPS and the present SNA results in the following concrete differences between the two systems:

(a) Expenditures by enterprises on cultural, sports and similar facilities for their employees are excluded in MPS from intermediate consumption. Instead, a transfer between enterprises and households is included, while the material goods and services involved in the above expenditures are allocated to final consumption of the population. SNA treats these expenditures as intermediate consumption;

(b) Depreciation of dwellings and other material goods and services involved in the provision of housing are allocated in MPS to final consumption expenditure. Since these are non-material services, no value-added contribution is included in net material product. In SNA, this contribution is included in gross domestic product;

xxi

(c) Travel expenses in connection with business are not included in intermediate consumption in MPS as they are in the present SNA. Instead, they are treated as a part of compensation of employees and the material goods and services involved are allocated to private final consumption expenditure;

(d) In SNA and MPS a different distinction is drawn between uniforms to be treated as intermediate consumption and those to be included in compensation of employees and final consumption expenditure of households. In SNA, the distinction is drawn between civilian (intermediate consumption) and military uniforms and in MPS, between dress and working uniforms;

(e) Tips are treated in SNA as a part of compensation of employees, while in MPS they are treated as income transfers, when they exceed the normal service charge.

2. *Capital formation*

The MPS and SNA guidelines differ, on the one hand, with regard to the treatment of capital gains and losses and the coverage of depreciation and, on the other, in the coverage of fixed capital formation and increases in stocks. The main differences are the following:

(a) In MPS, depreciation, as well as the replacement for losses due to certain foreseeable and non-forseeable damages to fixed assets and stocks, including those caused by accidents and calamities, are deducted in order to arrive at net fixed capital formation. In SNA, generally uses the concept of gross fixed capital formation only is generally used. However, if net capital formation were to be estimated, only depreciation on fixed assets would have to be deducted in that system. Losses in stocks or fixed assets would never be considered for deduction. Losses on fixed assets would be treated as capital losses and dealt with outside the national accounts flows, while losses in stocks would be treated as a part of intermediate consumption or as capital losses, depending on whether they are due to normal events in production or to calamities. The dividing line between losses and depreciation of fixed assets also differs in the two systems. In SNA, depreciation is assumed to cover, among other things, the average amount of accidental damage to fixed assets that is not made good by repair or replacement of parts--for example, damage arising from fire and accidents. In MPS, such damages are not reflected in depreciation but covered under losses;

(b) Depreciation in MPS is based on the original cost of the assets. However, every eight to ten years, adjustments to replacement cost are made to this asset value and these adjustments are also reflected in a corrected value of depreciation. Furthermore, differences that arise between the actual value and the written-off book value at the moment the assets are scrapped or sold are included in the value of depreciation for the year in which the sale or scrapping occurs. In SNA, instead, the replacement value of the assets is used as a basis for depreciation. Any change in this value, whether it happens at the moment the asset is sold or during the time it is used, is considered to be a capital gain or loss and is not accounted for in the national accounting flows;

(c) In addition, in MPS, depreciation includes capital consumption allowances with respect to afforestation, land improvements, roads, bridges and similar structures. In SNA, no imputations for depreciation of this type of asset are included;

(d) Expenditures on fixed assets for military purposes are treated in MPS as a part of net fixed capital formation. In SNA, these outlays are allocated to government final consumption expenditure, except for outlays by government on the construction and alteration of family dwellings for personnel of the armed forces, which are included in gross fixed capital formation;

(e) Transfer cost with regard to purchases and sales of existing fixed assets are treated in MPS as transfers since these are non-material services. In SNA, these costs are included in gross fixed capital formation;

(f) Work put in place on structures, roads, dams, ports and other forms of construction is allocated in MPS to increases in material circulating assets and stocks. Only when the construction is finished is its total value transferrred to net fixed capital formation. In SNA, these outlays are immediately allocated to gross fixed capital formation.

3. *External transactions*

The third area in which MPS and SNA differ is in the coverage of exports and imports of goods and services, in the distinction between residents and non-residents and in the treatment of monetary, as opposed to non-monetary gold. The differences are the following:

(a) In MPS, embassies, consulates and international bodies are treated as residents of the country in which they are located, while in SNA they are treated as residents of the country they represent. This difference in the residence concept has consequences for the allocation between countries of capital formation and government final consumption expenditure and also for the allocation of the income flows. Wages and salaries paid to local employees of these extraterritorial bodies are not included in SNA concept of gross domestic product. They are dealt with, however, as factor income from abroad and therefore accounted for in the national income concept in SNA. In MPS, such wages and salaries, if earned in the sphere of material production, are included in primary incomes of the population, as well as in net material product;

(b) In MPS, the territorial concept of final consumption expenditure, which includes purchases by non-residents in the domestic market and excludes purchases abroad by residents, is used. As a result, such flows are not accounted for in exports or imports. On the other hand, it does include, in exports and imports, transactions that, though they take place in the domestic market, are conducted in foreign currency. These transactions are treated as if they were transactions with non-residents. In SNA, the national concept of final consumption expenditure is used; taken into account in exports and imports, respectively, are the direct purchases in the domestic market by non-residents and the direct purchases abroad by non-residents. Furthermore, no distinction is made in SNA between transactions that are conducted in local or in foreign currency;

(c) Purchases and sales by external trade organizations of goods that do not cross the border of the country in question and also imported goods that are re-exported without being processed are treated in MPS as part of respectively, imports and exports. In SNA, they are not accounted for in the export and import flows, except for the margins received by resident units as payments for services rendered;

(d) Gifts in kind by households to and from abroad are included in exports and imports in SNA. In MPS, they are excluded from these flows;

(e) Transactions in intangible assets (patents, copyrights, trade-marks, exclusive rights to exploit mineral deposits etc.) with the rest of the world are included in MPS in exports and imports. In SNA, they are treated as property income or as sales or purchases of intangible assets to or from abroad, depending on whether the payment is for the use of the rights or for the outright transfer of those rights;

(f) Transactions with the rest of the world in monetary and non-monetary gold are included in MPS in exports and imports. In SNA, included in exports and imports are actual transactions in non-monetary gold only. Exports in addition include newly mined gold (whether actually exported or not) in order to transform gold as a commodity into a financial asset.

C. STANDARD CLASSIFICATIONS OF MPS

Two classifications are used in the MPS standard tables presented, that is, the kind-of-activity classification and the classification by socio-economic group. Contrary to SNA usage with respect to the activity and institutional classifications for different groups of transactions, the two MPS classifications are parallel ones that are applied to the same transaction categories: net material product and its component primary incomes and capital formation. Each of these classifications is described briefly below

1. Kind of activity

All forms of activity in production are classified according to groups or branches, depending on the nature and results of the application of labour. The two major categories constitute branches of the material sphere and branches of the non-material sphere. The first category covers the production of goods, and services that are related to the production of goods, such as repair services, transportation services and goods distribution services. The second category includes the remaining services-producing activities. Each of the two categories is further broken down by branches which are similar in character to the ISIC categories used in SNA. The unit of classification is not the organizational unit (i.e., enterprise) but a smaller unit that performs one type of activity (i.e., establishment). If an enterprise or institution or other organizational unit carries on more than one type of economic activity, it is considered to consist of two or more establishments that perform different activities.

For the subclassification of net material product by kind of activity, only the activity breakdown of the material sphere is used since net material product originates in this sphere only. For capital formation, however, the activity categories of the non-material sphere are also used, since capital formation relates not only to the material sphere but also to non-material branches.

A rough correspondence based on the names of the activity categories can be established between the activity categories presented in SNA and in the MPS branches. The user should be aware, however, of the limitations that such a linkage may entail, as indicated in the following points:

(a) Mining and quarrying, manufacturing, and electricity, gas and water are shown as three separate categories in the SNA presentation and as one category (industrial production), in the MPS presentation;

(b) Hunting and the collection of forestry products is treated as a part of agriculture in the SNA presentation and as a part of forestry and logging in MPS;

(c) The distribution of gas, electricity and water to households is treated in MPS as a non-material service (including in housing). This activity is therefore not reflected in net material product, while its capital formation is dealt with as capital formation of the non-material sphere. In SNA, these distribution activities are an integral part of the activity category for electricity, gas and water;

(d) Printing and publishing, which is treated as a material activity in MPS, is allocated to the MPS category known as "other activities of the material sphere". In SNA, this activity is included with manufacturing;

(e) Cleaning, dyeing and repair services are included with industrial activity (manufacturing) in the MPS presentation and with community, social and personal services in SNA;

(f) In comparing the activity breakdown of net material product and gross domestic product, the user should be aware that the coverage of the MPS category known as "other activities of the material sphere" falls far short of the combined coverage of the two SNA categories for finance, insurance, real estate and business services and for community, social and personal services. The SNA categories include all non-material activities that are excluded from the MPS coverage of net material product. In addition, the shifts between activity categories that were outlined in the previous points affect this group. Other activities in the presentation of net material product include telegraph, news-gathering and editorial agencies, industrial services other than architectural design services, printing and publishing services, the production of motion pictures, phonograph records and prerecorded tapes, data-processing and tabulating services, waterway-maintenance services and the operation of flood-control systems, and services related to the conservation of natural resources and the protection of the environment.

2. *Socio-economic sectors*

The rates of development of the national economy and the basic features of production that support this development are largely determined by the social structure of the community. In order to study the process, the various activities involved in the production of material goods and services are classified in MPS by socio-economic sector. This classification is based on the form of ownership of the fixed and circulating capital. The form of ownership of the means of production determines the forms of ownership of the product and of the incomes generated by its disposal.

The basic socio-economic sectors are the socialist sector and the private sector.

The socialist sector embraces the enterprises and institutions in public, socialist ownership. The fixed and circulating assets of these enterprises are public property. The socialist sector also includes the personal plots of employees and members of co-operatives.

Within the socialist sector, the following socio-economic subsectors are distinguished: the state subsector; the co-operative subsector, which includes agricultural producers' co-operatives; associations; personal plots of employees; personal plots of members of co-operatives.

The state subsector includes the enterprises and institutions in state ownership. The State furnishes them with the fixed and circulating assets required for their operation. These economic units are administratively subordinated to central or local organs of state authority. The production of the state subsector and the income generated in it belong to the people as a country.

The co-operative subsector embraces the enterprises and institutions in collective or group onwership. The fixed and circulating assets of these economic bodies are originally built up from the entrance fees (initiation fees) of their members and the proceeds of sales of shares to them; and are later supplemented from part of their operating surplus. The output and income of the enterprises and institutions of the co-operative subsector are the property of their members.

The association subsector includes the enterprises and institutions owned by voluntary or semi-voluntary associations. The fixed and circulating assets of the economic bodies of this subsector are built up from the voluntary contributions of their members and from part of the operating surplus of such bodies. The output and income of this subsector belong to the associations.

The personal plots of employees and members of co-operatives embrace agricultural output, construction and other forms of activity (gathering of wild fruits and berries, scrap collection etc.).

The private sector includes the enterprises and institutions, the fixed and circulating assets of which are privately owned. The classification of enterprises and institutions of the private sector is based on the specific economic conditions in the country concerned. Within this sector, the subsector of craftsmen, artisans and peasants who are not members of co-operatives may be distinguished.

Peasants, craftsmen and artisans who do not belong to co-operatives operate small private ventures in which the productive process is carried out by their owners in person, as a rule without recourse to hired labour. This group also includes the subsidiary activities of the population occupied in the private sector of the national economy.

D. DEFINITIONS OF FLOWS

Given below are the definitions of the flows that appear in the MPS standard tables of chapter III. To make possible a comparison between SNA and MPS data, a description of the differences between the MPS and the SNA coverage is added to each of the sections. The items needed in order to convert the MPS coverage into a coverage that conforms to the SNA definition are only summarily indicated. For more information on these items, the user is therefore referred to the description of the differences between the two systems in section B above. The items described below have been grouped together into categories similar to those used for the SNA flows (see chap. I above, sect. C).

I. *Total supply and disposition of goods and material services*

1. *Gross output*

Global product covers the value of goods and material services produced. Deliveries of goods and material services within the same enterprise are generally excluded. Included are, among other things, the value of own-account constructed capital goods and capital repairs to fixed assets, the value of work-in-progress and the value of finished goods added to stocks. Covered is, furthermore, the value of goods and material services provided free to employees (the material services are valued at the material cost involved). Included in the contribution to global product by agriculture are seeds and feed produced and consumed at the same farm and agricultural and other goods produced on personal plots for own consumption or for sale, including the cost of their processing. This concept of gross output appears in MPS table 5.

To derive gross output in producers' prices as defined in SNA, global product as described above needs to be increased by:

plus: the gross output value of non-material services (including those of government), including the transfer cost on purchases and sales of existing second-hand fixed assets and land.

2. *Trade margins and transport charges*

The gross output of material goods and services is valued at both producers' and purchasers' values. The difference between the two sets of values gives the distributive trade margins (including restaurants, cafés and other catering) and the transportation margins. The gross output of the distributive-trade units is equal to the value of their gross margins on internal and external trade.

The gross margins on external trade are equivalent to the sum in domestic currency of (a) the value of imports of goods and material services in the domestic market *less* the actual value at which these imports are purchased from abroad and (b) the actual value at which exports of goods and material services are sold to abroad *less* the value of these exports in the domestic market. Trade margins and transport charges appear in MPS table 5.

3. *Intermediate material consumption, including depreciation*

Intermediate material consumption consists of the value of the goods and material services used up in the process of production during a period of account by units of the material sphere, including the consumption of fixed assets during the period. Consistent with the scope of the gross output of goods and material services included in intermediate consumption are certain items, for example, seeds and animal feed, which are produced and used by the same unit. The intermediate output of raw materials etc., is valued net of the value of scraps and wastes originating in the process of production. Purchased items are valued at purchasers' values; items produced on own account are valued at cost in the case of state and co-operative enterprises and at average purchasers' prices in the case of personal plots of households. This concept of intermediate material consumption appears in MPS table 5.

Depreciation or consumption of fixed assets includes an allowance for normal wear and tear and foreseen obsolescence of fixed assets based on standard rates of depreciation and, furthermore, the difference between the book value of scrapped fixed assets and their scrap value. The allowances for depreciation are often based on the original cost of the assets which may be periodically adjusted to replacement cost.

To arrive from intermediate material consumption, including depreciation as defined above, at the SNA concept of intermediate consumption, the MPS coverage needs to be increased and decreased by the following items:

plus: (i) material cost of non-material services;

plus: (ii) material expenditures by enterprises on cultural, sports and similar facilities for their employees;

plus: (iii) reimbursable expenditures for material goods and services purchased during business trips;

minus: (iv) consumption of fixed capital in the material sphere.

4. *Personal consumption*

This consists of all consumer goods, irrespective of durability, and material services (repair, transport, communication and similar services) which are purchased by households, received in kind as payment for work in state and collective enterprises and in private plots, or produced on own account on personal plots. Excluded is the purchase by households of dwellings (which is dealt with as capital formation) but included is the maintenance and depreciation of dwellings. Also included are reimbursable expenditures for material goods and services purchased during business trips. This concept of personal consumption appears in MPS tables 1 and 7. It appears according to source of supply of goods and material services in MPS table 8. In MPS, the domestic concept of consumption is used, so that direct purchases by foreign tourists, diplomatic personnel and other non-residents in the domestic market are included, while similar purchases abroad by residents are excluded.

5. *Material consumption in the units of the non-material sphere serving individuals*

This flow covers expenditures on non-durable goods and material services by units of the non-material sphere serving individuals, reduced by the increases in their stocks of goods. Also included is consumption of fixed assets used by these units. It appears in MPS tables 1 and 7.

6. *Material consumption in the units of the non-material sphere serving the community as a whole*

This flow consists of non-durable goods and material services purchased during a period of account by units of the non-material sphere serving the community as a whole, reduced by the increases in their stocks of goods during the period of account. Also included is consumption of fixed assets of these units. It appears in MPS tables 1 and 7.

To arrive from this concept at government final consumption expenditure as defined in SNA, the following additions to and subtraction from the MPS concept have to be made:

plus: (i) the difference between the value of non-material services produced by government and their material cost and depreciation

plus: (ii) government expenditures on fixed assets that have military uses;

plus: (iii) the difference between consumption expenditures (i.e., material and non-material cost, depreciation and compensation of employees) of extraterritorial bodies that represent the country abroad *minus* consumption expenditures incurred by extraterritorial bodies of other countries and international organizations located in the country in question;

plus: (iv) material expenditures by government (units in the non-material sphere serving individuals) on education, health, culture and other services provided free to individuals.

7. *Final consumption*

This flow is equal to the sum of personal consumption and material consumption in the units of the non-material sphere serving individuals and of those serving the community as a whole. Each of these concepts has been defined above. They appear in MPS tables 5 and 7.

8. *Consumption of the population*

Consumption of the population is the sum of personal consumption and material consumption in the units of the non-material sphere serving individuals. This concept is comparable to private final consumption expenditure in SNA, which can be derived from this MPS concept by adding and subtracting the following items:

plus: (i) the difference between the value of non-material services purchased by households, including housing services and the material cost and depreciation included in the value of these services;

minus: (ii) material expenditures by government (units in the non-material sphere serving individuals) on education, health, culture and other services provided free to individuals;

plus: (iii) the difference between direct purchases abroad by resident households and direct purchases in the domestic market by non-resident households as well as the difference between gifts sent abroad by household *minus* gifts received from abroad;

minus: (iv) reimbursable expenditures for material goods and services purchased during business trips;

minus: (v) material expenditures by enterprises on cultural sports and similar facilities for their employees.

9. *Total consumption of the population*

Total consumption of the population covers the consumption by the population of goods and material services and of non-material services, whether purchased by households or furnished free of charge. It therefore exceeds the consumption of the population (i.e., the sume of personal consumption and material consumption in the units of the non-material sphere serving individuals) by the value of the services of the units of the non-material sphere serving individuals, reduced by the consumption of goods and material services by these units. The value of the services of the units is equivalent to their costs of production, including operating surplus in some instances. In the case of dwellings provided by these units, their depreciation is not included when evaluating costs of production, since charges in respect of depreciation of these dwellings are included in personal consumption. Total consumption of the population appears classified by object in MPS table 9.

10. *Net fixed capital formation*

Net fixed capital formation consists of the value of new fixed assets purchased or constructed on own account and of completed capital repairs to these assets reduced by consumption of fixed assets for renewal of assets and capital repairs, and capital losses due to fire, floods and other calamities and furthermore reduced by the remaining value of scrapped fixed assets. Thus, it measures the net increase in the value of fixed assets during a period of account. This flow appears in MPS tables 5 and 6.

Fixed assets include completed dwellings, buildings and other structures; machinery, equipment and other durable goods acquired by units of the material and non-material sphere; cattle, excluding young cattle and cattle raised for meat; perennial plants; and expenditures on the improvement of land, forests and other natural resources. New fixed assets put into use are generally valued inclusive of acquisition and installation cost.

Capital repairs cover outlays on repairs that make up at least in part for the physical depreciation of the fixed assets and/or significantly raise the capacity and productivity of the fixed assets.

In order to convert the MPS concept of net fixed capital formation into gross fixed capital formation as defined in SNA, the following additions to and substractions from the MPS concept have to be made:

plus: (i) consumption of fixed capital in the material and non-material sphere, including that on afforestation, roads, bridges and similar structures;

plus: (ii) losses due to foreseeable as well as non-foreseeable damages to fixed assets;

plus: (iii) transfer cost with regard to purchases and sales of existing second-hand fixed assets, including land;

plus: (iv) work in progress on the construction of structures, roads, dams and ports on other forms of construction;

plus: (v) the difference between outlays on fixed capital formation by extraterritorial bodies representing the country in question abroad, *less* similar outlays by extraterritorial bodies of other countries and international organizations located in the country in question;

minus: (vi) government expenditures on fixed assets that have military uses.

11. *Gross fixed capital formation*

Gross fixed capital formation is equal to net fixed capital formation as defined above *plus* depreciation. Depreciation is defined in section 3 above, together with intermediate material consumption. Gross fixed capital formation classified by kind of activity appears in MPS table 6.

12. *Increases in material circulating assets and stocks*

This item consists of increases during the period of account in the stocks of enterprises in the material sphere, including wholesale and retail trade units, reduced by losses. Also covered are increases in government stockpiles, including stocks of defense items and state reserves of precious metals and precious stones. The stocks in the material sphere consist of raw materials, fuels, supplies and other non-durable goods; young cattle and cattle raised for meat; work in progress, including uncompleted construction projects; and finished goods not yet sold. Increases in material circulating assets and stocks appear in MPS tables 1 and 6.

In order to convert the MPS concept of increases in material circulating assets and stocks into increases in stocks as defined in SNA, the following addition to and subtractions from the MPS concept are needed:

plus: (i) losses due to foreseeable and non-foreseeable damages to stocks;

minus: (ii) work in progress on the construction of structures, roads, dams and ports and on other forms of construction;

minus: (iii) net increases in the holdings of gold ingots and other monetary gold.

13. *Losses*

This item is the sum of the value of the losses in fixed assets and losses in material circulating assets and stocks.

Included are losses (a) due to fires, floods and other calamities, (b) in adult productive and working cattle, (c) due to abandoned or interrupted construction works and (d) in agricultural products in storage at state and co-operative agricultural enterprises and at farms. This flow appears in MPS tables 1 and 5.

In SNA, this final demand category is not identified separately from gross capital formation.

14. *Exports and imports of goods and material services*

Exports are defined to include: (a) outward-bound goods thast cross the border of the country, including imported goods which are exported without being processed; (b) goods which are purchased outside the country by an external trade organization of the country in question and shipped directly to a third country; (c) outward-bound monetary and non-monetary gold and other precious metals; (d) unilateral transfers of goods by the government and public organizations of the country (uncompensated foreign aid); (e) material services, such as transport, forwarding and communication services, rental, including rental payments for time-charter of ships and other transport equipment and, furthermore, export contract services rendered to other countries. The imports cover the same categories of goods and material services which are inward bound. Exports are valued f.o.b. while imports are valued c.i.f. They appear in MPS tables 1 and 5.

To arrive at the SNA coverage of exports of goods and services, the following additions to and subtractions from the MPS concept are needed:

plus: (i) the difference between the export value of non-material services and the material cost and depreciation included in these services;

plus: (ii) consumption expenditure (material and non-material cost, depreciation and compensation of employees) and outlays on fixed capital formation by extraterritorial bodies of foreign governments and international organizations located in the country in question;

plus: (iii) direct purchases in the domestic market by non-resident households and gifts sent abroad by households;

minus: (iv) sales abroad by an external trade organization of the country of goods that have not crossed the border of the country in question; as well as of goods that have crossed the border but that are re-exported without being processed;

minus: (v) the difference between exported monetary gold and the value of sales of newly produced gold ingots and bars.

MPS imports have to be adjusted in a similar manner. To be added are the import value of non-material services *minus* material cost and depreciation, consumption expenditure and fixed capital formation of extraterritorial bodies that represent the country abroad and direct purchases abroad by residents. To be deducted are re-exports and purchases abroad by external trade organizations of goods that do not cross the border of the country, and also the value of imported monetary gold and gifts received households from abroad.

III. Cost components and income shares

1. Net material product

Net material product is defined in MPS and is used in countries with centrally planned economies. It can be estimated from the production income and expenditure side in the same manner, as is indicated in chapter I above, section C.III, in which the SNA coverage of gross domestic product is described. Following the production approach, net material product is the difference between global product (i.e., gross output) of goods and material services and intermediate material consumption, including consumption of fixed assets. Net material product defined from the income side is the sum of primary incomes of the population (comparable to compensation of employees in SNA) and primary incomes of enterprises (comparable to operating surplus in SNA). The expenditure approach finally defines net material product as the sum of the final uses of goods and material services, that is, personal consumption, and material consumption of units in the non-material sphere serving individuals and that of similar units serving the community as a whole, net capital formation (i.e., net of depreciation), replacement for losses and the balance between exports and imports of goods and material services. These three different methods for deriving net material product are shown in MPS tables 1, 2 and 4.

To arrive at the SNA concept of gross domestic product, net material product needs to be increased and reduced as follows:

plus: (i) the excess value of non-material services (i.e., the gross output value *minus* material cost and depreciation) consumed by households and by government *plus* the difference between these excess values of exported and imported non-material services;

minus: (ii) material expenditures by enterprises on cultural, sports and similar facilities for their employees;

minus: (iii) reimbursable expenditures for material goods and services purchased during business trips;

plus: (iv) consumption of fixed capital in the material and non-material sphere, including that on afforestation, roads, bridges and similar structures;

plus: (v) losses of fixed assets and stocks due to accidental damage, such as fire, accidents etc.;

plus: (vi) transfer cost with regard to purchases and sales of existing second-hand fixed assets, including land.

2. Primary income of the population

The primary income of the population consists of (a) wages and salaries, including receipts in kind, and related income, such as bonuses and reimbursements of expenses on business trips received from state, co-operative and private units of the material sphere; (b) the net material product (net value added) originating from the personal plots of households; and (c) the net material product of self-employed craftsmen, artisans and peasants. This flow appears in MPS tables 3 and 4.

Primary income of the population is roughly comparable to the SNA concept of compensation of employees. However, several differences remain and in order to arrive from the MPS concept at compensation of employees as defined in SNA, the following additions and subtractions are needed:

plus: (i) compensation of employees, including employers' contributions to social security funds, paid out in connection with non-material activities, inclusive of those that are paid out in connection with the provision of cultural, sports and similar facilities by industries in the material sphere;

plus: (ii) employers' contributions to social security funds paid out in connection with material activities;

minus: (iii) income from private enterprises;

minus: (iv) reimbursable expenditures for material goods and services purchased during business trips.

3. Primary income of enterprises

Primary income of enterprises consists of the sum of the net material product of the units of the material sphere which have employees *less* the wages and salaries and related incomes which they pay out. The primary incomes of these units are the source of such items as their net income, turnover taxes, contributions to social insurance, payments of taxes, fines and other compulsory items, finance of purchases of non-material services, insurance premiums, interest on bank loans and other business costs. This flow appears in MPS tables 3 and 4.

Although the coverage of primary income of enterprises is similar to that of operating surplus in SNA, the following additions to and subtractions from the MPS concept are needed in order to arrive at operating surplus as defined in SNA:

plus: (i) the remaining value of non-material services (i.e., the gross output value *minus* material cost, depreciation and compensation of employees) consumed by households and government, *plus* the difference between the remaining values of exported and imported non-material services;

minus: (ii) material expenditures by enterprises on cultural, sports and similar facilities for their employees;

plus: (iii) consumption of fixed capital in the material and non-material sphere, including that on afforestation, roads, bridges and similar structures;

plus: (iv) losses of fixed assets and stocks due to accidental damage, such as fire, accidents etc.;

plus: (v) transfer cost with regard to purchases and sales of existing fixed assets, including land;

minus: (vi) employers' contributions to social security funds, paid out in connection with material activities;

plus: (vii) income from private plots and private enterprises.

1/ Standing Statistical Commission, Council of Mutual Economic Assistance (Moscow, 1969).

2/ Studies in Methods, Series F, No. 17 (United Nations publication, Sales No. E.71.XVII.10).

3/ For a more exhaustive list of differences between MPS and SNA, the user should refer to *Comparisons of the System of National Accounts and the System of Balances of the National Economy*, part One, *Conceptual Relationships* (United Nations publication, Sales No. 77.XVII.6).

Although the coverage of primary income of enterprises is similar to that of operating surplus in SNA, the following additions to and subtractions from the MPS concept are needed in order to arrive at operating surplus as defined in SNA:

plus: (i) the remaining value of non-material services (i.e., the gross output value *minus* material cost, depreciation and compensation of employees) consumed by households and government, *plus* the difference between the remaining values of exported and imported non-material services;

minus: (ii) material expenditures by enterprises on cultural, sports and similar facilities for their employees;

plus: (iii) consumption of fixed capital in the material and non-material sphere, including that on afforestation, roads, bridges and similar structures;

plus: (iv) losses of fixed assets and stocks due to accidental damage, such as fire, accidents etc.;

plus: (v) transfer cost with regard to purchases and sales of existing fixed assets, including land;

minus: (vi) employers' contributions to social security funds, paid out in connection with material activities;

plus: (vii) income from private plots and private enterprises.

1/ Standing Statistical Commission, Council of Mutual Economic Assistance (Moscow, 1969).

2/ Studies in Methods, Series F, No. 17 (United Nations publication, Sales No. E.71.XVII.10).

3/ For a more exhaustive list of differences between MPS and SNA the user should refer to *Comparisons of the System of National Accounts and the System of Balances of the National Economy*, part One, *Conceptual Relationships* (United Nations publication, Sales No. 77.XVII.6).

III. COUNTRY TABLES

Kenya

General note. The preparation of national accounts statistics in Kenya is undertaken by the Central Bureau of Statistics, Nairobi. The official estimates are published annually in the 'Statistical Abstract'. The estimates are generally in accordance with the classifications and definitions recommended in the United Nations System of National Accounts (SNA). A full revision of previous estimastes for the years 1972-1975 were published in 1976, implementing improved methods and sources of estimation. Input-out tables for 1967 and 1971 were published in 1972 and 1976 respectively in 'Input-Output Tables for Kenya'. The following tables have been prepared from successive replies to the United Nations national accounts questionnaire. When the scope and coverage of the estimates differ for conceptual or statistical reasons from the definitions and classifications recommended in SNA, a footnote is indicated to the relevant tables.

Sources and methods:

(a) Gross domestic product. Gross domestic product is estimated mainly through the production approach.

(b) Expenditure on the gross domestic product. The expenditure approach is used to estimate government final consumption expenditure and exports and imports of goods and services. A combination of the commodity-flow and expenditure approaches is used to estimate gross capital formation. The estimates of government final consumption expenditure are derived from the accounts of the central and local government, the East African Community, the relevant statutory boards and the National Security Fund. All accounts are prepared on a cash basis. Private consumption expenditure is obtained as a residual. Changes in stocks are recorded for agriculture, industrial activity, building and construction and wholesale and retail trade sectors. The sources of information are the large-farm censuses, the integrated rural survey, annual surveys or reports from concerned sectors and the survey of Distribution. The estimate of capital formation in building and construction is derived from 'completions' reported by municipalities and from expenditure on other construction undertaken by government and industry. Included in gross fixed capital formation is the value of development of permanent crops. Expenditure estimates on machinery and equipment are derived by using the commodity-flow method. For import items, import duties are added to the c.i.f. values. For domestic production, the annual surveys of manufacturing are the source of information. The figures derived are converted to purchasers' values by adding transport and distribution margins. Exports and imports of goods and services are based on foreign trade reports and balance of payments estimates. For the constant price estimates, government expenditure on wages and salaries are extrapolated by an index of employment, while purchases of goods and services are deflated by various price indexes. Private consumption expenditure is obtained as a residual. For the remaining expenditure items, price deflation is used.

(c) Cost-structure of the gross domestic product. Wages and salaries paid in most industries are obtained from the annual surveys of employees and self-employed persons. Other sources include the integrated rural survey for small farms, logger licences and wage rate for forestry, reports and special surveys for transport, government accounts for the government sector and annual questionnaires for the private non-profit services. Information on indirect taxes and subsidies is obtained from concerned enterprises and from government records. Operating surplus, including consumption of fixed capital, is obtained as a residual.

(d) Gross domestic product by kind of economic activity. The table of gross domestic product by kind of economic activity is prepared in factor values. The production approach is used to estimate value added of most industries. The expenditure approach is used for construction and capital formation in residential and non-residential buildings while the income approach is used for insurance and real estate. For the agricultural sector, the main sources of information are the annual large-farm censuses, annual integrated rural surveys and purchases by boards, co-operatives and large factories. The Ministry of Agriculture provides supplementary information. The censuses and surveys provide information on quantity and value of sales and quantity consumed at the farms. The prices for agricultural products sold to boards and co-operatives are those paid by the boards while prices used for other products are those obtained from integrated rural survey, reflecting prices in the local markets. Estimates for forestry and fishing are obtained from concerned departments. Information on gross output and intermediate consumption of mining and quarrying and electricity is obtained from the companies concerned. A census of manufacturing industry was held in 1972 covering all establishments. Annual surveys are undertaken for all firms employing 50 or more persons and a sample is taken for firms employing between 20 and 49 persons. For firms with less than 20 employees, estimates are derived by inflating the value of gross output and intermediate consumption obtained in the 1972 census. The bench-mark estimate for construction contractors is based on the 1972 census of industry and the rural enterprise survey. Information from large contractors are available annually while those with less than 4 employees are covered by the labour force survey. Their estimates are obtained by applying an increasing factor to the census figures. The estimates of own-account construction are obtained from the large-farm censuses. Certain percentages are added for maintenance and labour costs. The East African Power and Lighting co., Ministry of Works, Forests Department and other local authorities provide information on their own-account construction activities. In the non-monetary sector, the value of output is the number of huts built multiplied by its current cost and 15 percent added for maintenance. For trade, the Survey of Distribution 1967 provided bench-mark information on the value of output and intermediate consumption. Value added by each sub-division is then extrapolated by using various indicators. The rural enterprise survey in 1972 provided bench-mark estimates for the rural areas. The sources of information for railway, shipping and air transports are the annual reports of the concerned companies and special questionnaires. For buses, data are obtained from the Kenya Bus Services Co. only and their ratios are applied to other bus firms. For the financial sector, the Central Bank of Kenya provides the information needed. Value added of real estate is calculated as net trade receipts of companies and individuals and 50 per cent of the rentals of companies. For ownership of dwellings, a stratified multi-stage sample is taken annually. The estimates of producers of government services are obtained from the accounts of the government, East-African Community and National Security Fund. For private services, bench-mark estimates are derived from a survey conducted in 1972. Domestic services are calculated from the estimated number of servants and their wage rates. For the constant price estimates, double deflation is used for agriculture, with current year's quantities revalued at base-year prices. Double deflation is also used for mining and quarrying, manufacturing and construction. For electricity, gas and water, trade, transport and community services, value added is extrapolated by various quantity indicators and indexes. Current values of financial institutions, insurance and real estate are deflated by price indexes.

1.1 Expenditure on the Gross Domestic Product, in Current Prices

Million Kenyan pounds

		1970	1975	1977	1978	1979	1980	1981	1982	1983	1984	1985	1986
1	Government final consumption expenditure	93.10	219.30	322.05	398.60	447.31	533.77	576.42	647.44	739.43	784.61	863.72	...
2	Private final consumption expenditure	344.69	813.75	1028.30	1240.48	1447.07	1605.93	1861.57	2157.03	2316.28	2646.71	3109.58	...
3	Gross capital formation	139.66	217.08	441.23	610.63	516.25	789.19	858.81	764.53	810.35	915.89	882.57	...
	A Increase in stocks	26.96	-24.81	51.22	96.62	-24.20	166.66	133.40	96.20	89.46	150.49	34.11	...
	B Gross fixed capital formation	112.70	241.89	390.01	514.01	540.45	622.53	725.41	668.33	720.89	765.40	848.46	...
	Residential buildings	18.66	42.47	49.41	70.36	93.08	105.86	119.55	125.46	112.63	132.81	141.37	...
	Non-residential buildings	14.09	31.42	41.43	45.75	69.35	89.34	101.81	88.00	87.04	85.85	131.56	...
	Other construction and land improvement etc.	22.80	62.96	83.98	93.98	93.51	124.76	148.33	157.84	142.80	147.22	161.59	...
	Other	57.15	105.04	215.19	303.92	284.49	302.88	355.72	297.03	378.42	399.52	413.94	...
4	Exports of goods and services	170.83	356.90	650.20	593.10	600.10	753.30	773.70	847.00	979.56	1143.70	1211.26	...
5	Less: Imports of goods and services	175.62	413.00	587.60	793.00	736.60	1052.70	1045.70	1005.23	1019.67	1244.81	1325.34	...
	Equals: Gross Domestic Product [a]	572.66	1194.03	1854.18	2049.81	2274.13	2629.49	3024.80	3410.77	3825.95	4246.10	4741.79	...

a) Data in this table have been revised, therefore they are not strictly comparable with the unrevised data in the other tables.

Kenya

1.2 Expenditure on the Gross Domestic Product, in Constant Prices

Million Kenyan pounds

	1970	1975	1977	1978	1979	1980	1981	1982	1983	1984	1985	1986
		1964			At constant prices of:			1982				
1 Government final consumption expenditure	84.58	472.79	579.91	670.77	679.32	694.74	657.26	647.44	662.04	634.53	648.08	...
2 Private final consumption expenditure	320.85	1732.20	1805.47	2132.29	2192.38	2177.93	2106.70	2157.03	2109.86	2345.98	2394.77	...
3 Gross capital formation	122.48	532.33	815.01	1007.37	766.22	1031.00	995.09	764.53	652.28	668.84	595.31	...
A Increase in stocks	26.96	-72.89	91.97	155.14	-21.29	223.72	151.12	96.20	73.90	103.88	16.00	...
B Gross fixed capital formation	95.52	605.22	723.04	852.23	787.51	807.28	843.97	668.33	578.38	564.96	579.31	...
Residential buildings	13.40	104.61	93.88	122.15	140.61	131.99	136.94	125.46	100.65	111.05	103.87	...
Non-residential buildings	10.11	71.41	74.99	75.61	99.64	106.49	113.88	88.00	79.71	72.26	99.97	...
Other construction and land improvement etc.	16.64	127.76	139.67	141.26	123.19	148.28	167.31	157.84	128.46	107.34	110.46	
Other	55.37	301.42	418.41	513.21	424.07	420.52	425.84	297.03	269.55	274.31	265.01	...
4 Exports of goods and services	159.65	822.47	868.87	883.53	842.02	887.72	850.55	847.00	846.04	851.54	883.11	...
5 Less: Imports of goods and services	164.13	1150.98	1333.74	1711.63	1385.69	1524.08	1203.47	1005.23	809.73	960.04	871.81	...
Equals: Gross Domestic Product [a]	523.43	2408.81	2735.52	2982.33	3094.25	3267.31	3389.82	3376.83	3467.46	3540.85	3649.43	...

a) Data in this table have been revised, therefore they are not strictly comparable with the unrevised data in the other tables.

1.3 Cost Components of the Gross Domestic Product

Million Kenyan pounds

	1970	1975	1977	1978	1979	1980	1981	1982	1983	1984	1985	1986
1 Indirect taxes, net	53.72	139.67	219.23	269.78	296.98	397.08	441.35	466.15	509.41	591.19	615.59	...
A Indirect taxes	54.88	140.48	219.78	270.25	297.58	397.78	442.57	467.73	510.99	593.37	617.55	...
B Less: Subsidies	1.16	0.81	0.55	0.47	0.60	0.70	1.22	1.58	1.58	2.18	1.96	...
2 Consumption of fixed capital	...	...	...	...	...	...	...	...	...	...	...	...
3 Compensation of employees paid by resident producers to:	236.86	445.27	592.59	689.90	800.29	931.65	1099.18	1243.11	1352.65	1537.78	1736.78	...
4 Operating surplus	282.08	609.09	1042.36	1090.13	1176.86	1300.76	1484.27	1701.51	1963.89	2117.13	2389.42	...
Equals: Gross Domestic Product [a]	572.66	1194.03	1854.18	2049.81	2274.13	2629.49	3024.80	3410.77	3825.95	4246.10	4741.79	...

a) Data in this table have been revised, therefore they are not strictly comparable with the unrevised data in the other tables.

1.7 External Transactions on Current Account, Summary

Million Kenyan pounds

	1970	1975	1977	1978	1979	1980	1981	1982	1983	1984	1985	1986
					Payments to the Rest of the World							
1 Imports of goods and services	...	413.00	587.60	793.00	736.60	1052.70	1045.70	1005.23	1019.67	1244.81	1325.34	...
A Imports of merchandise c.i.f.	...	314.50	529.30	724.90	684.90	994.60	971.80	939.93	929.05	1118.56	1219.38	...
B Other	...	98.50	58.30	68.10	51.70	58.10	73.90	65.30	90.62	126.25	105.96	...
2 Factor income to the rest of the world	...	67.70	98.70	108.50	106.50	104.00	132.20	174.93	157.36	185.35	220.36	...
A Compensation of employees	...	13.00	16.30	17.70	15.50	12.40	12.90	13.60	9.40	11.95	1.31	...
B Property and entrepreneurial income	...	54.70	82.40	90.80	91.00	91.60	119.30	161.33	147.96	173.40	207.26	...
3 Current transfers to the rest of the world	...	16.40	13.50	13.10	12.40	7.20	11.50	21.60	23.00	26.67	21.06	...
4 Surplus of the nation on current transactions	...	...	...	...	...	...	...	...	...	...	...	...
Payments to the Rest of the World and Surplus of the Nation on Current Transactions [a]	...	...	...	...	...	...	...	...	...	...	...	...
					Receipts From The Rest of the World							
1 Exports of goods and services	...	356.90	650.20	593.10	600.10	753.30	773.70	847.00	979.56	1143.70	1211.26	...

Kenya

1.7 External Transactions on Current Account, Summary
(Continued)

Million Kenyan pounds

		1970	1975	1977	1978	1979	1980	1981	1982	1983	1984	1985	1986
	A Exports of merchandise f.o.b.	...	232.40	468.00	369.40	385.50	468.00	474.80	509.90	615.80	745.14	774.02	...
	B Other	...	124.50	182.20	223.70	214.60	285.30	298.90	337.10	363.76	398.56	437.24	...
2	Factor income from rest of the world	...	21.40	20.00	17.90	22.60	20.00	25.10	35.58	28.10	33.69	42.54	...
	A Compensation of employees	...	2.10	3.10	1.50	3.60	...	...	...	...	...	...	...
	B Property and entrepreneurial income	...	19.30	16.90	16.40	19.00	...	...	...	...	...	...	...
3	Current transfers from rest of the world	...	23.20	29.00	35.10	31.10	40.00	33.70	33.10	39.70	54.36	58.53	...
	Receipts from the Rest of the World on Current Transactions [a]	...	...	...	...	...	...	...	...	...	...	...	...

a) Data in this table have been revised, therefore they are not strictly comparable with the unrevised data in the other tables.

1.10 Gross Domestic Product by Kind of Activity, in Current Prices

Million Kenyan pounds

		1970	1975	1977	1978	1979	1980	1981	1982	1983	1984	1985	1986
1	Agriculture, hunting, forestry and fishing	172.77	361.38	688.29	657.23	681.03	725.37	836.93	960.81	1092.53	1152.40	1273.36	...
2	Mining and quarrying	2.41	3.42	4.17	4.41	5.04	5.73	5.91	6.61	7.37	8.51	10.04	...
3	Manufacturing	62.16	127.00	179.94	219.32	249.84	295.14	328.16	372.32	408.26	460.96	518.40	...
4	Electricity, gas and water	11.96	19.98	31.07	35.71	44.27	47.73	58.30	66.27	68.92	76.80	89.11	...
5	Construction	26.39	63.65	79.93	97.88	119.45	146.74	168.60	169.54	202.69	218.93	226.28	...
6	Wholesale and retail trade, restaurants and hotels [a]	48.67	114.88	164.63	189.34	214.07	244.66	274.03	299.40	381.89	422.56	524.71	...
7	Transport, storage and communication	40.84	60.25	78.62	100.84	114.65	127.81	143.39	195.87	195.26	235.86	264.11	...
8	Finance, insurance, real estate and business services [b]	53.04	132.14	186.06	219.19	256.89	296.88	363.65	421.20	493.09	541.30	603.50	...
9	Community, social and personal services [ab]	20.08	23.33	30.80	35.46	39.59	49.41	56.15	62.68	70.17	81.93	96.50	...
	Total, Industries	438.32	906.03	1443.51	1559.38	1724.83	1939.47	2235.12	2554.70	2920.18	3199.25	3606.01	...
	Producers of Government Services	76.48	162.07	215.40	250.66	289.26	332.46	390.92	441.36	475.25	530.58	601.03	...
	Other Producers	4.14	8.86	13.44	17.06	19.16	23.34	28.62	32.75	35.71	44.89	52.80	...
	Subtotal [c]	518.94	1076.96	1672.35	1827.10	2033.25	2295.27	2654.66	3028.81	3431.14	3774.72	4259.84	...
	Less: Imputed bank service charge	...	22.60	37.40	47.07	56.10	62.86	71.21	84.19	114.51	120.18	133.64	...
	Plus: Import duties	28.58	47.37	81.84	106.42	90.30	141.82	149.41	158.57	151.10	188.09	167.37	...
	Plus: Value added tax	...	...	...	...	...	...	...	...	...	...	...	...
	Plus: Other adjustments [d]	25.14	92.30	137.39	163.36	206.68	255.26	291.94	307.58	358.22	403.47	448.22	...
	Equals: Gross Domestic Product [e]	572.66	1194.03	1854.18	2049.81	2274.13	2629.49	3024.80	3410.77	3825.95	4246.10	4741.79	...

a) For the first series, restaurants and hotels are included in item 'Community, social and personal services'.
b) For the first series, business services are included in item 'Community, social and personal services'.
c) Gross domestic product in factor values.
d) Item 'Other adjustments' refers to net indirect taxes other than import duties.
e) Data in this table have been revised, therefore they are not strictly comparable with the unrevised data in the other tables.

1.11 Gross Domestic Product by Kind of Activity, in Constant Prices

Million Kenyan pounds

		1970	1975	1977	1978	1979	1980	1981	1982	1983	1984	1985	1986
			1964			At constant prices of:			**1982**				
1	Agriculture, hunting, forestry and fishing	173.58	708.81	805.67	855.01	857.01	866.88	917.53	960.82	1004.11	970.69	1005.17	...
2	Mining and quarrying	2.60	7.08	6.62	7.63	7.95	8.75	5.45	6.61	7.28	8.16	9.43	...
3	Manufacturing	52.49	200.68	275.89	310.51	333.97	351.47	364.13	372.32	389.07	405.84	424.07	...
4	Electricity, gas and water	9.81	42.51	48.62	54.26	58.51	57.97	64.30	66.27	69.03	70.89	73.08	...
5	Construction	18.98	133.64	140.06	153.48	163.66	174.66	184.75	169.54	160.54	154.50	158.42	...

Kenya

1.11 Gross Domestic Product by Kind of Activity, in Constant Prices
(Continued)

Million Kenyan pounds

	1970	1975	1977	1978	1979	1980	1981	1982	1983	1984	1985	1986
	1964				At constant prices of:			**1982**				
6 Wholesale and retail trade, restaurants and hotels	43.81[a]	... 243.77	261.14	291.07	303.33	318.38	322.52	299.40	307.78	324.83	351.12	...
7 Transport, storage and communication	41.18	... 107.09	124.02	132.72	140.87	148.95	185.06	195.87	201.51	202.29	206.54	...
8 Finance, insurance, real estate and business services	45.00[b]	... 261.63	285.39	313.51	353.57	361.36	398.46	421.20	435.28	448.36	458.93	...
9 Community, social and personal services	20.33[ab]	... 41.18	45.27	44.64	51.85	56.09	59.32	62.68	68.46	72.02	77.23	...
Total, Industries	407.79	... 1746.39	1992.68	2162.83	2270.72	2344.51	2501.52	2554.71	2643.06	2657.58	2763.99	...
Producers of Government Services	73.75	... 303.83	335.60	357.05	382.39	403.84	425.20	441.36	459.89	473.13	494.31	...
Other Producers	3.55	... 13.99	17.68	20.42	24.06	20.33	30.67	32.75	34.88	37.16	39.74	...
Subtotal [c]	485.09	... 2064.21	2345.96	2540.30	2677.17	2776.68	2957.39	3028.82	3137.83	3167.87	3298.04	...
Less: Imputed bank service charge	...	... 43.93	53.19	67.14	81.14	78.41	80.94	84.19	102.88	104.50	108.21	...
Plus: Import duties	26.72	... 187.40	219.84	255.87	209.03	239.67	187.40	158.57	125.27	147.47	136.37	...
Plus: Value added tax	...	...	...	...	...	...	...	...	...	...	...	...
Plus: Other adjustments [d]	11.62	... 201.13	222.91	253.30	289.19	329.37	325.97	273.63	307.24	330.01	323.23	...
Equals: Gross Domestic Product [e]	523.43	... 2408.81	2735.52	2982.33	3094.25	3267.31	3389.82	3376.83	3467.46	3540.85	3649.43	...

a) Restaurants and hotels are included in item 'Community, social and personal services'.
b) Business services are included in item 'Community, social and personal services'.
c) Gross domestic product in factor values.
d) Item 'Other adjustments' refers to net indirect taxes other than import duties.
e) Data in this table have been revised, therefore they are not strictly comparable with the unrevised data in the other tables.

1.12 Relations Among National Accounting Aggregates

Million Kenyan pounds

	1970	1975	1977	1978	1979	1980	1981	1982	1983	1984	1985	1986
Gross Domestic Product	572.66	... 1194.03	1854.18	2049.81	2274.13	2629.49	3024.80	3410.77	3825.95	4246.10	4741.79	...
Plus: Net factor income from the rest of the world	-20.99	... -46.30	-78.70	-90.60	-83.90	-84.00	-107.10	-139.35	-129.26	-151.66	-177.82	...
Factor income from the rest of the world	...	... 21.40	20.00	17.90	22.60	20.00	25.10	35.58	28.10	33.69	42.54	...
Less: Factor income to the rest of the world	...	... 67.70	98.70	108.50	106.50	104.00	132.20	174.93	157.36	185.35	220.36	...
Equals: Gross National Product	551.67	... 1147.73	1775.48	1959.21	2190.23	2545.49	2921.70	3271.42	3696.69	4094.44	4563.97	...
Less: Consumption of fixed capital	...	...	...	...	...	...	...	...	...	...	...	...
Equals: National Income [a]	551.67	... 1147.73	1775.48	1959.21	2190.23	2545.49	2921.70	3271.42	3696.69	4094.44	4563.97	...
Plus: Net current transfers from the rest of the world	9.13	... 6.80	15.50	22.00	18.70	32.80	22.20	11.50	16.70	27.69	37.47	...
Current transfers from the rest of the world	...	... 23.20	29.00	35.10	31.10	40.00	33.70	33.10	39.70	54.36	58.53	...
Less: Current transfers to the rest of the world	...	... 16.40	13.50	13.10	12.40	7.20	11.50	21.00	23.00	26.67	21.06	...
Equals: National Disposable Income [b]	560.80	... 1154.53	1790.98	1981.21	2208.93	2578.29	2939.90	3282.92	3713.39	4122.13	4601.44	...
Less: Final consumption	437.79	... 1033.05	1350.35	1639.08	1894.38	2139.70	2437.99	2804.47	3055.71	3431.32	3973.30	...
Equals: Net Saving [c]	123.01	... 121.48	440.63	342.13	314.55	438.59	501.91	478.45	657.68	690.81	628.14	...
Less: Surplus of the nation on current transactions	...	...	...	...	...	...	...	...	...	...	...	...
Equals: Net Capital Formation	...	...	...	...	...	...	...	...	...	...	...	...

a) Item 'National income' includes consumption of fixed capital.
b) Item 'National disposable income' includes consumption of fixed capital.
c) Item 'Net saving' includes consumption of fixed capital.

Kenya

2.1 Government Final Consumption Expenditure by Function, in Current Prices

Million Kenyan pounds

	1970	1975	1977	1978	1979	1980	1981	1982	1983	1984	1985	1986
1 General public services	28.54	53.12	70.44	82.29	94.76	112.90	136.46	135.10	140.36	165.85	...	...
2 Defence	8.03	23.37	67.98	94.13	91.36	96.62	60.66	87.05	149.47	136.71	...	...
3 Public order and safety	...	...										
4 Education	25.81	77.68	100.37	114.82	132.29	175.74	201.98	226.07	239.83	278.83	...	...
5 Health	11.03	24.78	33.55	42.54	48.11	61.12	68.96	75.79	77.40	82.92	...	...
6 Social security and welfare											...	...
7 Housing and community amenities	19.69	40.35	49.71	64.82	80.79	87.39	108.36	123.43	132.37	144.73	...	...
8 Recreational, cultural and religious affairs											...	...
9 Economic services	...	...									...	...
10 Other functions	...	...										
Total Government Final Consumption Expenditure	93.10	219.30	322.05	398.60	447.31	533.77	576.42	647.44	739.43	809.04	...	...

2.5 Private Final Consumption Expenditure by Type and Porpose, in Current Prices

Million Kenyan pounds

	1970	1975	1977	1978	1979	1980	1981	1982	1983	1984	1985	1986

Final Consumption Expenditure of Resident Households

	1970	1975	1977	1978	1979	1980	1981	1982	1983	1984	1985	1986
1 Food, beverages and tobacco	...	400.35	...	...	...	791.54	...	...	...	...	...	...
A Food	...	336.42	...	...	...	665.15	...	...	...	...	...	...
B Non-alcoholic beverages	...	8.58	...	...	...	16.96	...	...	...	...	...	...
C Alcoholic beverages	...	33.72	...	...	...	66.67	...	...	...	...	...	...
D Tobacco	...	21.62	...	...	...	42.75	...	...	...	...	...	...
2 Clothing and footwear	...	62.69	...	...	...	123.94	...	...	...	...	...	...
3 Gross rent, fuel and power	...	102.42	...	...	...	202.50	...	...	...	...	...	...
A Fuel and power	...	21.10	...	...	...	41.72	...	...	...	...	...	...
B Other	...	81.31	...	...	...	160.78	...	...	...	...	...	...
4 Furniture, furnishings and household equipment and operation	...	76.55	...	...	...	151.35	...	...	...	...	...	...
5 Medical care and health expenses	...	17.90	...	...	...	35.39	...	...	...	...	...	...
6 Transport and communication	...	68.38	...	...	...	135.20	...	...	...	...	...	...
A Personal transport equipment	...	6.93	...	...	...	13.70	...	...	...	...	...	...
B Other	...	61.45	...	...	...	121.49	...	...	...	...	...	...
7 Recreational, entertainment, education and cultural services	...	33.41	...	...	...	66.06	...	...	...	...	...	...
A Education	...	8.38	...	...	...	16.57	...	...	...	...	...	...
B Other	...	25.03	...	...	...	49.49	...	...	...	...	...	...
8 Miscellaneous goods and services	...	52.04	...	...	...	102.89	...	...	...	...	...	...
A Personal care	...	15.52	...	...	...	30.69	...	...	...	...	...	...
B Expenditures in restaurants, cafes and hotels	...	31.24	...	...	...	61.76	...	...	...	...	...	...
C Other	...	5.28	...	...	...	10.44	...	...	...	...	...	...

Kenya

2.5 Private Final Consumption Expenditure by Type and Porpose, in Current Prices
(Continued)

Million Kenyan pounds

	1970	1975	1977	1978	1979	1980	1981	1982	1983	1984	1985	1986
Statistical discrepancy	...	...	...	...	...	-2.96	...	...	...	...	...	...
Total Final Consumption Expenditure in the Domestic Market by Households, of which	...	813.75	...	...	...	1605.93	...	...	...	...	...	...
Plus: Direct purchases abroad by resident households	...	...										
Less: Direct purchases in the domestic market by non-resident households	...	...										
Equals: Final Consumption Expenditure of Resident Households [a]	...	813.75	...	...	...	1605.93	...	...	...	...	...	...

Final Consumption Expenditure of Private Non-profit Institutions Serving Households

	1970	1975	1977	1978	1979	1980	1981	1982	1983	1984	1985	1986
Equals: Final Consumption Expenditure of Private Non-profit Organisations Serving Households	...	...	...	...	...	...	...	...	...	.		
Private Final Consumption Expenditure	344.69	813.75	1028.30	1240.48	1447.07	1605.93	1860.17	2123.09	2363.49	2638.87	...	...

a) Item 'Final consumption expenditure of resident households' includes consumption expenditure of private non-profit institutions serving households.

2.11 Gross Fixed Capital Formation by Kind of Activity of Owner, ISIC Divisions, in Current Prices

Million Kenyan pounds

	1970	1975	1977	1978	1979	1980	1981	1982	1983	1984	1985	1986
					All Producers							
1 Agriculture, hunting, forestry and fishing	12.58	22.69	43.61	51.86	42.74	48.19	55.43	52.30	54.84	58.92	...	...
2 Mining and quarrying	1.28	1.53	1.94	4.95	4.10	5.02	4.84	4.05	5.09	7.13	...	...
3 Manufacturing	12.95	31.23	63.27	83.71	88.52	76.91	88.45	66.05	111.49	99.48	...	...
4 Electricity, gas and water	3.68	17.19	33.72	40.20	31.99	41.26	65.47	75.22	57.19	46.75	...	...
5 Construction	6.96	7.81	15.50	32.25	25.68	33.41	32.90	28.86	59.35	65.69	...	...
6 Wholesale and retail trade, restaurants and hotels [a]	4.40	14.47	21.42	20.24	17.30	28.29	21.44	23.97	29.54	30.98	...	...
7 Transport, storage and communication	19.86	50.39	79.41	110.50	101.65	102.80	113.94	102.06	110.97	131.36	...	...
8 Finance, insurance, real estate and business services [b]	20.79	47.97	55.05	79.40	103.00	116.76	145.24	136.54	131.47	147.75	...	...
9 Community, social and personal services [a,b]	8.30	7.18	17.25	20.33	31.76	41.25	49.39	52.63	58.93	59.18	...	...
Total Industries	90.82	200.44	331.17	443.44	446.74	493.89	577.10	541.68	618.87	647.25	...	...
Producers of Government Services	21.89	41.45	58.84	70.56	93.70	128.64	148.31	126.65	102.03	188.87		
Private Non-Profit Institutions Serving Households	...	...	...	...	...	...	...	...	...	...		
Total	112.70	241.89	390.01	514.01	540.45	622.53	725.41	668.33	720.89	836.12	...	...

a) For the first series, restaurants and hotels are included in item 'Community, social and personal services'. b) For the first series, business services are included in item 'Community, social and personal services'.

2.12 Gross Fixed Capital Formation by Kind of Activity of Owner, ISIC Divisions, in Constant Prices

Million Kenyan pounds

	1970	1975	1977	1978	1979	1980	1981	1982	1983	1984	1985	1986
		1964			At constant prices of			1982				
					All Producers							
1 Agriculture, hunting, forestry and fishing	11.10	60.17	83.11	86.94	62.51	63.08	57.62	52.29	44.58	42.65	...	...
2 Mining and quarrying	1.24	4.80	3.84	8.92	6.57	7.55	6.02	4.05	3.58	4.89	...	...
3 Manufacturing	12.31	92.62	125.82	147.83	137.66	110.08	107.33	66.05	80.85	68.58	...	...
4 Electricity, gas and water	3.22	36.54	56.74	61.74	42.69	49.88	76.01	75.22	49.52	34.20	...	...

Kenya

2.12 Gross Fixed Capital Formation by Kind of Activity of Owner, ISIC Divisions, in Constant Prices
(Continued)

Million Kenyan pounds

	1970	1975	1977	1978	1979	1980	1981	1982	1983	1984	1985	1986
	1964				At constant prices of:			**1982**				
5 Construction	6.55	23.31	30.75	57.11	40.78	48.14	40.16	28.86	41.82	45.02	...	...
6 Wholesale and retail trade, restaurants and hotels	3.84[a]	43.13	41.74	35.22	26.88	39.51	25.62	23.97	23.61	23.00	...	...
7 Transport, storage and communication	18.47	115.05	139.05	170.31	134.43	127.84	130.30	102.06	83.86	91.53	...	...
8 Finance, insurance, real estate and business services	15.27[b]	119.16	105.08	138.13	155.95	145.74	166.21	136.53	116.48	122.00	...	...
9 Community, social and personal services	6.93[ab]	17.73	32.09	33.89	49.42	55.28	58.34	52.63	46.06	43.93	...	...
Total Industries	78.92	512.51	618.22	739.78	656.88	647.08	674.73	541.68	490.36	475.80	...	...
Producers of Government Services	16.60	92.71	104.82	112.44	130.63	160.19	169.24	126.66	88.02	141.23	...	...
Private Non-Profit Institutions Serving Households	...	...	...	...	...	...	...	...	...	...	...	...
Total	95.52	605.22	723.04	852.23	787.51	807.28	843.97	668.33	578.38	617.03	...	...

a) For the first series, restaurants and hotels are included in item 'Community, social and personal services'.
b) For the first series, business services are included in item 'Community, social and personal services'.

4.1 Derivation of Value Added by Kind of Activity, in Current Prices

Million Kenyan pounds

	1980			1981			1982			1983		
	Gross Output	Intermediate Consumption	Value Added	Gross Output	Intermediate Consumption	Value Added	Gross Output	Intermediate Consumption	Value Added	Gross Output	Intermediate Consumption	Value Added
					All Producers							
1 Agriculture, hunting, forestry and fishing	...	...	725.37	...	...	836.93	...	...	960.81	...	...	1092.54
A Agriculture and hunting	...	...	688.13	...	...	791.74	...	...	907.16	...	...	1030.61
B Forestry and logging	...	...	32.32	...	...	37.81	...	...	44.29	...	...	51.79
C Fishing	...	...	4.92	...	...	7.38	...	...	9.36	...	...	10.14
2 Mining and quarrying	...	...	5.73	...	...	5.91	...	...	6.61	...	...	7.37
3 Manufacturing	...	...	295.14	...	...	328.16	...	...	372.32	...	...	408.26
4 Electricity, gas and water	...	...	47.73	...	...	58.30	...	...	66.27	...	...	68.92
A Electricity, gas and steam	...	...	23.85	...	...	30.69	...	...	34.80	...	...	35.31
B Water works and supply	...	...	23.88	...	...	27.61	...	...	31.47	...	...	33.61
5 Construction	...	...	146.74	...	...	167.20	...	...	169.54	...	...	212.66
6 Wholesale and retail trade, restaurants and hotels	...	...	244.66	...	...	274.03	...	...	299.40	...	...	381.89
A Wholesale and retail trade	...	...	203.74	...	...	220.20	...	...	245.57	...	...	...
B Restaurants and hotels	...	...	40.92	...	...	53.83	...	...	53.83	...	...	...
7 Transport, storage and communication	...	...	127.81	...	...	143.39	...	...	161.93	...	...	195.26
8 Finance, insurance, real estate and business services	...	...	296.88	...	...	363.65	...	...	421.20	...	...	493.09
9 Community, social and personal services	...	...	49.41	...	...	56.15	...	...	62.68	...	...	70.17
Total, Industries	...	...	1939.47	...	...	2233.72	...	...	2520.76	...	...	2930.16
Producers of Government Services	...	...	332.46	...	...	390.92	...	...	441.36	...	...	475.25
Other Producers	...	...	23.34	...	...	28.62	...	...	32.75	...	...	35.71
Total [a]	...	...	2295.27	...	...	2653.26	...	...	2994.87	...	...	3441.12
Less: Imputed bank service charge	...	...	62.86	...	...	71.21	...	...	84.19	...	...	114.51
Import duties	...	...	141.82	...	...	149.41	...	...	158.57	...	...	151.10
Value added tax	...	...	...	...	...	...	...	...	...	...	...	...
Other adjustments [b]	...	...	255.26	...	...	291.94	...	...	307.58	...	...	395.57
Total	...	...	2629.49	...	...	3023.40	...	...	3376.83	...	...	3873.28

Kenya

4.1 Derivation of Value Added by Kind of Activity, in Current Prices

Million Kenyan pounds

	1984 Gross Output	1984 Intermediate Consumption	1984 Value Added
All Producers			
1 Agriculture, hunting, forestry and fishing	...	...	1148.06
A Agriculture and hunting	...	...	1083.89
B Forestry and logging	...	...	56.17
C Fishing	...	...	8.00
2 Mining and quarrying	...	...	8.51
3 Manufacturing	...	...	460.96
4 Electricity, gas and water	...	...	65.70
A Electricity, gas and steam	...	...	24.50
B Water works and supply	...	...	41.20
5 Construction	...	...	231.31
6 Wholesale and retail trade, restaurants and hotels	...	...	484.24
A Wholesale and retail trade	...	...	...
B Restaurants and hotels	...	...	...
7 Transport, storage and communication	...	...	218.94
8 Finance, insurance, real estate and business services	...	...	557.31
9 Community, social and personal services	...	...	81.93
Total, Industries	...	...	3256.96
Producers of Government Services	...	...	527.92
Other Producers	...	...	44.89
Total [a]	...	...	3829.77
Less: Imputed bank service charge	...	...	128.71
Import duties	...	...	188.10
Value added tax	...	...	...
Other adjustments [b]	...	...	404.90
Total	...	...	4294.06

a) Gross domestic product in factor values.
b) Item 'Other adjustments' refers to net indirect taxes other than import duties.

4.2 Derivation of Value Added by Kind of Activity, in Constant Prices

Million Kenyan pounds

At constant prices of: 1982

	1980 GO	1980 IC	1980 VA	1981 GO	1981 IC	1981 VA	1982 GO	1982 IC	1982 VA	1983 GO	1983 IC	1983 VA
All Producers												
1 Agriculture, hunting, forestry and fishing	...	...	866.26	...	...	917.53	...	...	960.81	...	...	1004.11
A Agriculture and hunting	...	...	817.66	...	...	867.33	...	...	907.16	...	...	945.65
B Forestry and logging	...	...	41.68	...	...	42.98	...	...	44.29	...	...	46.22
C Fishing	...	...	6.92	...	...	7.22	...	...	9.36	...	...	12.24
2 Mining and quarrying	...	...	8.75	...	...	5.45	...	...	6.61	...	...	7.21
3 Manufacturing	...	...	351.47	...	...	364.13	...	...	372.32	...	...	389.07
4 Electricity, gas and water	...	...	57.97	...	...	64.30	...	...	66.27	...	...	69.03
A Electricity, gas and steam	...	...	28.66	...	...	33.82	...	...	34.80	...	...	36.47
B Water works and supply	...	...	29.31	...	...	30.48	...	...	31.47	...	...	32.56
5 Construction	...	...	174.99	...	...	104.76	...	...	109.94	...	...	100.54
6 Wholesale and retail trade, restaurants and hotels	...	...	318.38	...	...	322.52	...	...	299.40	...	...	307.78
7 Transport, storage and communication	...	...	148.95	...	...	151.71	...	...	161.93	...	...	168.85
8 Finance, insurance, real estate and business services	...	...	361.36	...	...	427.92	...	...	421.20	...	...	453.29
9 Community, social and personal services	...	...	56.09	...	...	59.32	...	...	62.68	...	...	68.46
Total, Industries	...	...	2343.89	...	...	2497.63	...	...	2520.76	...	...	2628.34
Producers of Government Services	...	...	403.84	...	...	425.20	...	...	441.36	...	...	459.89

Kenya

4.2 Derivation of Value Added by Kind of Activity, in Constant Prices
(Continued)

Million Kenyan pounds

	1980			1981			1982			1983		
	Gross Output	Intermediate Consumption	Value Added	Gross Output	Intermediate Consumption	Value Added	Gross Output	Intermediate Consumption	Value Added	Gross Output	Intermediate Consumption	Value Added
	At constant prices of:1982										
Other Producers	...	...	28.33	...	...	30.67	...	...	32.75	...	...	34.88
Total a	...	...	2776.06	...	...	2953.50	...	...	2994.87	...	...	3123.11
Less: Imputed bank service charge	...	...	78.41	...	...	93.36	...	...	84.19	...	...	111.17
Import duties	...	...	239.67	...	...	187.40	...	...	158.57	...	...	125.27
Value added tax	...	...	...	...	...	...	...	...	...	...	...	...
Other adjustments b	...	...	329.99	...	...	342.28	...	...	307.58	...	...	330.25
Total	...	...	3267.31	...	...	3389.82	...	...	3376.83	...	...	3467.46

	1984		
	Gross Output	Intermediate Consumption	Value Added
	At constant prices of:1982		
	All Producers		
1 Agriculture, hunting, forestry and fishing	...	...	969.31
A Agriculture and hunting	...	...	910.77
B Forestry and logging	...	...	47.84
C Fishing	...	...	10.70
2 Mining and quarrying	...	...	8.16
3 Manufacturing	...	...	405.84
4 Electricity, gas and water	...	...	71.55
A Electricity, gas and steam	...	...	37.41
B Water works and supply	...	...	34.14
5 Construction	...	...	154.43
6 Wholesale and retail trade, restaurants and hotels	...	...	320.06
7 Transport, storage and communication	...	...	169.70
8 Finance, insurance, real estate and business services	...	...	474.26
9 Community, social and personal services	...	...	72.02
Total, Industries	...	...	2645.33
Producers of Government Services	...	...	473.13
Other Producers	...	...	37.16
Total a	...	...	3155.62
Less: Imputed bank service charge	...	...	116.42
Import duties	...	...	144.30
Value added tax	...	...	...
Other adjustments b	...	...	296.72
Total	...	...	3480.22

a) Gross domestic product in factor values.
b) Item 'Other adjustments' refers to net indirect taxes other than import duties.

4.3 Cost Components of Value Added

Million Kenyan pounds

	1980						1981					
	Compensation of Employees	Capital Consumption	Net Operating Surplus	Indirect Taxes	Less: Subsidies Received	Value Added	Compensation of Employees	Capital Consumption	Net Operating Surplus	Indirect Taxes	Less: Subsidies Received	Value Added
	All Producers											
1 Agriculture, hunting, forestry and fishing	91.10	...	634.27	...	...	725.37	102.60	...	734.33	...	...	836.93
A Agriculture and hunting	78.03	...	610.11	...	...	688.13	86.50	...	705.24	...	...	791.74
B Forestry and logging	11.98	...	20.34	...	...	32.32	14.46	...	23.35	...	...	37.81
C Fishing	1.09	...	3.83	...	...	4.92	1.64	...	5.74	...	...	7.38
2 Mining and quarrying	2.71	...	3.02	...	...	5.73	3.28	...	2.63	...	...	5.91
3 Manufacturing	116.11	...	179.03	...	...	295.14	146.08	...	182.08	...	...	328.16
4 Electricity, gas and water	9.39	...	38.34	...	...	47.73	14.29	...	44.01	...	...	58.30
A Electricity, gas and steam	3.18	...	20.67	...	...	23.85	3.82	...	26.87	...	...	30.69
B Water works and supply	6.21	...	17.67	...	...	23.88	10.47	...	17.14	...	...	27.61

Kenya

4.3 Cost Components of Value Added
(Continued)

Million Kenyan pounds

	1980						1981					
	Compensation of Employees	Capital Consumption	Net Operating Surplus	Indirect Taxes	Less: Subsidies Received	Value Added	Compensation of Employees	Capital Consumption	Net Operating Surplus	Indirect Taxes	Less: Subsidies Received	Value Added
5 Construction	84.53	...	62.21	...	...	146.74	95.87	...	71.33	...	...	167.20
6 Wholesale and retail trade, restaurants and hotels	107.86	...	136.80	...	...	244.66	118.89	...	155.14	...	...	274.03
A Wholesale and retail trade	87.42	...	116.32	...	...	203.74	91.24	...	128.96	...	...	220.20
B Restaurants and hotels	20.44	...	20.48	...	...	40.92	27.65	...	26.18	...	...	53.83
7 Transport, storage and communication	73.54	...	54.27	...	...	127.81	86.59	...	56.80	...	...	143.39
8 Finance, insurance, real estate and business services	62.76	...	234.12	...	...	296.88	74.10	...	289.55	...	...	363.65
9 Community, social and personal services	38.47	...	10.94	...	...	49.41	43.90	...	12.25	...	...	56.15
Total, Industries	586.47	...	1353.00	...	...	1939.47	685.60	...	1548.12	...	...	2233.72
Producers of Government Services	325.27	...	7.19	...	...	332.46	386.13	...	4.79	...	...	390.92
Other Producers	23.34	...	-	...	...	23.34	28.62	...	-	...	...	28.62
Total [a]	935.08	...	1360.19	...	...	2295.27	1100.35	...	1552.91	...	...	2653.26
Less: Imputed bank service charge	...	...	62.86	...	...	62.86	...	...	71.21	...	...	71.21
Import duties	...	...	...	141.82	...	141.82	...	...	...	149.41	...	149.41
Value added tax	...	...	...	...	...	...	...	...	...	...	...	...
Other adjustments [b]	...	...	...	255.26	...	255.26	...	...	...	291.94	...	291.94
Total [c]	935.08	...	1297.33	397.08	...	2629.49	1100.35	...	1481.70	441.35	...	3023.40

	1982						1983					
	Compensation of Employees	Capital Consumption	Net Operating Surplus	Indirect Taxes	Less: Subsidies Received	Value Added	Compensation of Employees	Capital Consumption	Net Operating Surplus	Indirect Taxes	Less: Subsidies Received	Value Added

All Producers

1 Agriculture, hunting, forestry and fishing	106.57	...	854.24	...	...	960.81	111.22	...	981.32	...	...	1092.54
A Agriculture and hunting	89.22	...	817.94	...	...	907.16	92.90	...	937.70	...	...	1030.61
B Forestry and logging	15.28	...	29.01	...	...	44.29	15.81	...	35.98	...	...	51.79
C Fishing	2.07	...	7.29	...	...	9.36	2.51	...	7.63	...	...	10.14
2 Mining and quarrying	3.68	...	2.93	...	...	6.61	4.32	...	3.06	...	...	7.37
3 Manufacturing	165.98	...	206.33	...	...	372.32	181.87	...	226.39	...	...	408.26
4 Electricity, gas and water	16.82	...	49.45	...	...	66.27	16.93	...	51.99	...	...	68.92
A Electricity, gas and steam	4.33	...	30.47	...	...	34.80	3.86	...	31.45	...	...	35.31
B Water works and supply	12.49	...	18.98	...	...	31.47	13.07	...	20.54	...	...	33.61
5 Construction	95.68	...	73.86	...	...	169.54	121.39	...	91.27	...	...	212.66
6 Wholesale and retail trade, restaurants and hotels	133.68	...	165.72	...	...	299.40	167.78	...	214.11	...	...	381.89
A Wholesale and retail trade	105.83	...	139.74	...	...	245.57	...	...	...	...	...	...
B Restaurants and hotels	27.85	...	25.98	...	...	53.83	...	...	...	...	...	...
7 Transport, storage and communication	90.41	...	71.52	...	...	161.93	101.95	...	93.31	...	...	195.26
8 Finance, insurance, real estate and business services	86.08	...	335.12	...	...	421.20	102.33	...	390.76	...	...	493.09
9 Community, social and personal services	49.12	...	13.56	...	...	62.68	55.69	...	14.48	...	...	70.17
Total, Industries	748.02	...	1772.73	...	...	2520.76	863.48	...	2066.68	...	...	2930.16
Producers of Government Services	440.00	...	1.36	...	...	441.36	474.25	...	1.00	...	...	475.25
Other Producers	32.75	...	-	...	...	32.75	35.71	...	-	...	...	35.71
Total [a]	1220.77	...	1774.09	...	...	2994.87	1373.44	...	2067.68	...	...	3441.12
Less: Imputed bank service charge	...	...	84.19	...	...	84.19	...	...	114.51	...	...	114.51
Import duties	...	...	...	158.57	...	158.57	...	...	...	151.10	...	151.10
Value added tax	...	...	...	...	...	...	...	...	...	...	...	...
Other adjustments [b]	...	...	...	307.58	...	307.58	...	...	...	395.57	...	395.57
Total [c]	1220.77	...	1689.90	466.15	...	3376.83	1373.44	...	1953.17	546.67	...	3873.28

	1984					
	Compensation of Employees	Capital Consumption	Net Operating Surplus	Indirect Taxes	Less: Subsidies Received	Value Added

All Producers

1 Agriculture, hunting, forestry and fishing	118.94	...	1029.12	...	...	1148.06
A Agriculture and hunting	99.51	...	984.38	...	...	1083.89
B Forestry and logging	17.41	...	38.76	...	...	56.17
C Fishing	2.02	...	5.98	...	...	8.00

Kenya

4.3 Cost Components of Value Added
(Continued)

Million Kenyan pounds

	Compensation of Employees	Capital Consumption	Net Operating Surplus	Indirect Taxes	Less: Subsidies Received	Value Added
	\multicolumn{6}{l}{1984}
2 Mining and quarrying	5.08	...	3.43	...	...	8.51
3 Manufacturing	205.54	...	255.42	...	...	460.96
4 Electricity, gas and water	11.87	...	53.83	...	...	65.70
A Electricity, gas and steam	3.41	...	21.09	...	...	24.50
B Water works and supply	8.46	...	32.74	...	...	41.20
5 Construction	129.13	...	102.18	...	...	231.31
6 Wholesale and retail trade, restaurants and hotels	220.06	...	264.18	...	...	484.24
A Wholesale and retail trade	...	...	...	...	...	...
B Restaurants and hotels	...	...	...	...	...	...
7 Transport, storage and communication	130.09	...	88.85	...	...	218.94
8 Finance, insurance, real estate and business services	119.10	...	438.21	...	...	557.31
9 Community, social and personal services	66.75	...	15.17	...	...	81.93
Total, Industries	1006.56	...	2250.40	...	...	3256.96
Producers of Government Services	526.10	...	1.82	...	...	527.92
Other Producers	44.89	...	-	...	...	44.89
Total [a]	1577.55	...	2252.22	...	...	3829.77
Less: Imputed bank service charge	...	...	128.71	...	...	128.71
Import duties	...	...	...	188.10	...	188.10
Value added tax	...	...	...	...	...	...
Other adjustments [b]	...	...	...	404.90	...	404.90
Total [c]	1577.55	...	2123.51	593.00	...	4294.06

a) Gross domestic product in factor values.
b) Item 'Other adjustments' refers to net indirect taxes other than import duties.
c) Column 4 refers to indirect taxes less subsidies received.

Kiribati

Source. Reply to the United Nations National Accounts Questionnaire from the Planning Office, Ministry of Finance, Tarawa.
General note. The estimates shown in the following tables have been prepared in accordance with the United Nations System of National Accounts so far as the existing data would permit. It should be noted that the estimates for 1972-1974 include data for Tuvalu (former Ellice Islands).

1.1 Expenditure on the Gross Domestic Product, in Current Prices

Thousand Australian dollars

	1970	1975	1977	1978	1979	1980	1981	1982	1983	1984	1985	1986
1 Government final consumption expenditure	...	...	...	7700	7900	7600	...	...	...	...	...	...
2 Private final consumption expenditure	...	...	...	20200	21000	19400	...	...	...	...	...	...
3 Gross capital formation	...	...	...	8200	8200	9200	...	...	...	...	...	...
A Increase in stocks	...	...	...	300	...	...	...	...	...	...	...	...
B Gross fixed capital formation	...	...	...	7900	...	...	...	...	...	...	...	...
4 Exports of goods and services	...	...	...	21600	22700	4700	...	...	...	...	...	...
5 Less: Imports of goods and services	...	...	...	18200	21300	20000	...	...	...	...	...	...
Statistical discrepancy	...	...	...	-100	...	...	...	...	...	...	...	...
Equals: Gross Domestic Product	...	42077	34943	39400	38500	20900	...	...	...	...	...	...

1.10 Gross Domestic Product by Kind of Activity, in Current Prices

Thousand Australian dollars

	1970	1975	1977	1978	1979	1980	1981	1982	1983	1984	1985	1986
1 Agriculture, hunting, forestry and fishing	...	...	...	7300	...	...	...	...	...	...	...	...
2 Mining and quarrying	...	...	...	16800	...	...	...	...	...	...	...	...
3 Manufacturing	...	...	...	700	...	...	...	...	...	...	...	...
4 Electricity, gas and water	...	...	...	600	...	...	...	...	...	...	...	...
5 Construction	...	...	...	3100	...	...	...	...	...	...	...	...
6 Wholesale and retail trade, restaurants and hotels	...	...	...	2400	...	...	...	...	...	...	...	...
7 Transport, storage and communication	...	...	...	1000	...	...	...	...	...	...	...	...
8 Finance, insurance, real estate and business services	...	...	...	600	...	...	...	...	...	...	...	...
9 Community, social and personal services [a]	...	...	...	4700	...	...	...	...	...	...	...	...
Total, Industries	...	...	...	37100	...	...	...	...	...	...	...	...
Producers of Government Services	...	...	...	...	...	...	...	...	...	...	...	...
Other Producers	...	...	...	...	...	...	...	...	...	...	...	...
Subtotal [b]	...	...	...	37100	...	...	...	...	...	...	...	...
Less: Imputed bank service charge	...	...	...	...	...	...	...	...	...	...	...	...
Plus: Import duties	...	...	...	...	...	...	...	...	...	...	...	...
Plus: Value added tax	...	...	...	...	...	...	...	...	...	...	...	...
Plus: Other adjustments [c]	...	...	...	2300	...	...	...	...	...	...	...	...
Equals: Gross Domestic Product	...	...	...	39400	...	...	...	...	...	...	...	...

a) Item 'Community, social and personal services' includes public services n.e.c. and 'Other producers'.
b) Gross domestic product in factor values.
c) Item 'Other adjustments' relates to compensation of employees received in kind in the first series and to indirect taxes net of subsidies in the second series.

Korea, Republic of

General note. The preparation of national accounts statistics in the Republic of Korea is undertaken by the Statistics Department of the Bank of Korea, Seoul. The official estimates and methodological notes on sources and methods are published annually by the Bank in 'National Income Statistics Yearbook'. The following presentation is based mainly on information contained in 'National Accounts in Developing Countries in Asia' issued by the Development Centre of the Organization for Economic Co-operation and Development in 1972. The estimates are generally in accordance with the classifications and definitions recommended in the United Nations System of National Accounts (SNA). Input-output tables have been compiled and published by the Bank. The following tables have been prepared from successive replies to the United Nations national accounts questionnaire. When the scope and coverage differ for conceptual or statistical reasons from the definitions and classifications recommended in SNA, a footnote is indicated to the relevant tables.

Sources and methods:

(a) Gross domestic product. Gross domestic product is estimated mainly through the production approach.

(b) Expenditure on the gross domestic product. All items of GDP by expenditure type are estimated through the expenditure approach except part of private final consumption expenditure and the purchases of producers' durable equipment which are estimated through the commodity-flow approach. The estimates of government consumption expenditure are derived from government fiscal data. Expenditure on all consumer goods, except food grain, is estimated by the commodity-flow method using industry's production data, export and import data, changes in stocks and input-output tables. Adjustment are made for net expenditure abroad by residents. For food grain, consumption per household or per head is multiplied by the total number of household or population. Changes in stocks of grain, livestock and imported raw materials are estimated by deducting total domestic demand from total domestic supply, valued at average prices. For mining and manufacturing products, estimates are based on the ratio of change in stocks to total production, this ratio is applied to the value of output by subgroups. Investment in the government sector is derived from government accounts. For the private sector, estimates of investment in construction are derived from output data adding incidental costs and excluding repair cost and construction for defence. Estimates for durable equipment are based on production data, import and exports and changes in stocks. Estimates for exports and imports of goods and services are based on balance-of-payments statements. For the constant price estimates, price deflation is used for government consumption expenditure, net expenditure abroad by resident and exports and imports of goods and services. Private expenditure on food grain is extrapolated by the index of consumption while other expenditure are based on constant value of production, imports and exports and increase in stocks. This latter source and method is also used for estimating producers' durable equipment. For increase in stocks of mineral and manufactured goods, the constant output value is multiplied by the rate of inventory change while for agricultural products and imported raw materials, the method is the same as the one used to estimate these items at current market prices.

(c) Cost-structure of the gross domestic product. The cost-structure estimates of GDP are compiled by aggregating the value added at factor cost of each industry, making adjustments for net indirect taxes which are obtained from taxation statistics.

(d) Gross domestic product by kind of economic activity. The table of GDP by kind of economic activity is prepared at market prices, i.e., producers' values. The production approach is used to estimate the value added of most industries. The income approach is used for electricity, gas and water, part of transport and communication and part of other services. The value of output of agriculture is obtained by multiplying the quantities produced by the corresponding prices, the data of which are supplied by the National Agricultural Co-operative Federation. The financial data contained in the 'Yearbook of Agriculture and Forestry Statistics' are used to obtain the value added of agricultural services. The value added of forestry is obtained by multiplying the value of production by the value-added ratio calculated from the input-output tables. For fisheries, the current value of output is obtained from fishing and marine statistics while the constant price value of intermediate inputs, extrapolated by the index of tonnage of fishing boats, is revalued at current prices by using the appropriate price indexes. Value added of the mining and manufacturing sectors is estimated by applying the value-added ratio to current value of output. Value-added ratio of subsectors are calculated from the input-output table and the Financial Statement Analysis of Enterprises. For mining, output is estimated by multiplying quantities produced by unit prices collected from wholesale price, export unit value and representative producers' prices while quantity data are obtained from the mineral production statistics. For manufacturing, output is obtained by inflating the constant-price of output by a weighted price index while quantity data are obtained from industrial production and shipment index statistics. Value added of electricity, gas and water is derived from the financial data of concerned enterprises. Value added of the construction sector is obtained by multiplying the construction value of each sector by a corresponding value-added ratio. The construction unit cost and value added ratio are specially calculated by using the base-year composition of input to total construction value. The construction value is estimated by multiplying total floor area by construction unit cost for the private sector and for the public sector, derived from fiscal data. Value added of the trade sector is estimated by multiplying total mark-up by the value-added ratio calculated from the input-output table. For restaurants and hotels, value-added in the base-year is extrapolated by volume indicators and re-valued at current prices. Value added of railway and air transportation and communication is derived directly from the respective financial data while for other transportation and storage, the gross earnings in the base-year are extrapolated by a quantity index and then revalued by appropriate price indexes. The value-added of financing and insurance and real-estate is obtained from financial data and taxation data, respectively. For business services, value added is estimated by extrapolating the base-year estimate. The government executed budget is used to estimate the contribution of public administration and defence to GDP. For the private services, estimates are calculated by multipluing the constant price estimate by appropriate price index, using such sources as Statistical Yearbook of Education and Yearbook of Public Health and Social Statistics. For the constant price estimates, double deflation is used for agriculture and fishing. Current estimates of agriculture services, government construction, financial institutions and insurance and government services are deflated by approriate price indexes. For the remaining sectors of the economic activity, value added in the base-year is extrapolated by quantity indicators.

1.1 Expenditure on the Gross Domestic Product, in Current Prices

Thousand Million Korean won

	1970	1975	1977	1978	1979	1980	1981	1982	1983	1984	1985	1986
1 Government final consumption expenditure	263.4	1121.1	1919.2	2501.2	3059.4	4268.0	5383.4	6110.3	6753.4	7079.1	7893.4	8884.6
2 Private final consumption expenditure	2063.9	7247.9	11306.1	14902.0	19532.0	24786.1	30497.6	34001.3	37281.9	40778.3	44125.8	47473.9
A Households	2044.0	7186.4	11202.0	14758.8	19345.5	24542.5	30224.7	33700.1	36893.3	40298.9	43568.7	46846.6
B Private non-profit institutions serving households	19.9	61.5	104.1	143.2	186.5	243.6	272.9	301.2	388.6	479.4	557.1	627.3
3 Gross capital formation	682.5	2767.1	4903.9	7624.0	11074.3	11788.9	13679.0	14509.6	17620.8	21207.3	22644.8	25281.1
A Increase in stocks	-4.1	217.0	64.2	136.2	883.0	-46.8	748.0	-976.9	-858.8	412.3	208.5	-964.6
B Gross fixed capital formation	686.6	2550.1	4839.7	7487.8	10191.3	11835.7	12931.0	15486.5	18479.6	20795.0	22436.3	26245.7
Residential buildings	146.3	527.0	863.5	1409.9	1709.3	2179.1	2007.4	2578.1	3452.0	3408.8	3494.1	4379.4
Non-residential buildings	153.8	379.7	668.9	1096.5	1605.7	2030.0	2098.0	2715.8	3456.2	4136.6	4138.1	4373.2
Other construction and land improvement etc.	173.2	518.4	1049.3	1382.3	2082.3	2731.1	3308.8	4117.5	4713.7	5368.5	6131.6	5953.0
Other	213.3	1125.0	2258.0	3599.1	4794.0	4895.5	5516.8	6075.1	6857.7	7881.1	8672.5	11540.1
4 Exports of goods and services	389.0	2854.8	5848.2	7335.7	8563.5	12765.4	17191.5	18802.3	22245.7	25829.6	27326.9	35340.6
5 Less: Imports of goods and services	657.6	3727.6	5811.0	8062.2	10828.7	15729.3	19712.3	20153.6	23027.9	26037.2	26922.8	30354.6
Statistical discrepancy	18.6	-39.4	-181.2	-58.2	-176.4	35.8	-15.5	-357.2	129.0	9.6	442.6	-115.7
Equals: Gross Domestic Product	2759.8	10223.9	17985.2	24242.5	31224.1	37914.9	47023.7	52912.7	61002.9	68866.7	75510.7	86509.9

Korea, Republic of

1.2 Expenditure on the Gross Domestic Product, in Constant Prices

Thousand Million Korean won

	1970	1975	1977	1978	1979	1980	1981	1982	1983	1984	1985	1986
					At constant prices of:1980							
1 Government final consumption expenditure	2152.1	3194.5	3554.3	3993.7	4009.2	4268.0	4531.9	4569.1	4810.9	4835.0	5145.2	5625.0
2 Private final consumption expenditure	12649.8	18019.2	20870.0	22896.6	24959.0	24786.1	25578.3	26798.0	28815.8	30538.3	32046.4	34064.5
A Households	12542.1	17864.9	20678.3	22673.6	24720.8	24542.5	25352.9	26575.7	28539.8	30213.6	31676.3	33657.8
B Private non-profit institutions serving households	107.7	154.3	191.7	223.0	238.2	243.6	225.4	222.3	276.0	324.7	370.1	406.7
3 Gross capital formation	4186.6	6818.2	9878.1	12820.8	14864.0	11788.9	12535.9	12553.2	14745.0	17492.1	17769.1	19639.3
A Increase in stocks	414.8	832.5	730.5	646.2	1645.7	-46.8	1176.4	-266.9	-271.9	874.6	413.4	-311.1
B Gross fixed capital formation	3771.8	5985.7	9147.6	12174.6	13218.3	11835.7	11359.5	12820.1	15016.9	16617.5	17355.7	19950.4
Residential buildings	855.8	1490.8	1881.9	2507.7	2260.7	2179.1	1758.7	2152.8	2853.9	2735.4	2742.3	3428.7
Non-residential buildings	914.6	1087.9	1452.5	1909.0	2065.0	2030.0	1841.1	2282.9	2871.0	3325.3	3237.9	3405.3
Other construction and land improvement etc.	1049.9	1493.8	2256.1	2434.4	2709.1	2731.1	2875.7	3410.1	3878.9	4280.5	4790.0	4661.1
Other	951.5	1913.2	3557.1	5323.5	6183.5	4895.5	4884.0	4974.3	5413.8	6276.3	6585.5	8455.3
4 Exports of goods and services	2006.4	5972.4	10413.3	11719.7	11586.6	12765.4	14684.5	15637.9	18054.0	19854.7	20279.5	25682.3
5 Less: Imports of goods and services	4002.0	7037.3	11700.2	14090.0	16617.7	15720.0	16432.1	16763.0	18503.4	20464.7	20124.1	23860.0
Statistical discrepancy	-106.8	-19.2	-174.0	-123.8	298.5	35.8	-175.2	240.8	-88.6	-382.9	-441.7	14.3
Equals: Gross Domestic Product	16885.3	26147.8	32833.5	36411.0	39099.6	37914.9	40723.3	43035.7	47743.7	51872.5	54674.4	61166.4

1.3 Cost Components of the Gross Domestic Product

Thousand Million Korean won

	1970	1975	1977	1978	1979	1980	1981	1982	1983	1984	1985	1986
1 Indirect taxes, net	254.9	985.5	1867.2	2620.3	3469.4	4538.6	5657.7	6619.0	8135.9	8719.6	9370.5	10533.8
A Indirect taxes	267.4	1150.3	2124.9	2948.9	3867.7	4919.7	6074.1	7041.8	8638.9	9329.9	9895.1	...
B Less: Subsidies	12.5	164.8	257.7	328.6	398.3	381.1	416.4	422.8	503.0	610.3	524.6	...
2 Consumption of fixed capital	175.1	759.2	1339.2	1710.4	2344.2	2896.2	3617.5	4390.2	5191.2	6070.2	6657.3	7758.7
3 Compensation of employees paid by resident producers to:	921.2	3358.4	6379.6	9113.5	12154.0	15266.2	18553.4	21274.6	25154.2	28171.0	30991.2	35552.6
A Resident households	919.3	3342.1	6345.9	9073.2	12091.7	15188.8	18486.2	21149.6	25014.6	27945.3	30696.2	35147.9
B Rest of the world	1.9	16.3	33.7	40.3	62.3	77.4	67.2	125.0	139.6	225.7	295.0	404.7
4 Operating surplus	1408.6	5120.8	8399.2	10798.3	13256.5	15213.9	19195.1	20628.9	22521.6	25905.9	28491.7	32664.8
A Corporate and quasi-corporate enterprises	...	743.1	1793.2	2528.0	3232.9	4603.5	6029.8	6092.5	7222.3	8241.3	9532.7	...
B Private unincorporated enterprises	...	4377.7	6606.0	8270.3	10023.6	10610.4	13165.3	14536.4	15299.3	17664.6	18959.0	...
C General government	...	...	...	...	...	...	...	...	...	...	...	...
Equals: Gross Domestic Product	2759.8	10223.9	17985.2	24242.5	31224.1	37914.9	47023.7	52912.7	61002.9	68866.7	75510.7	86509.9

1.4 General Government Current Receipts and Disbursements

Thousand Million Korean won

	1970	1975	1977	1978	1979	1980	1981	1982	1983	1984	1985	1986
					Receipts							
1 Operating surplus	...	...	...	...	...	...	...	...	...	...	...	...
2 Property and entrepreneurial income	...	46.2	92.5	102.2	142.6	242.4	343.7	402.0	468.5	502.2	590.3	...
3 Taxes, fees and contributions	...	1579.9	3085.1	4281.7	5768.0	7060.7	8859.1	10403.8	12436.5	13489.0	14692.4	...
A Indirect taxes	...	1150.3	2124.9	2948.9	3867.7	4919.7	6074.1	7041.8	8638.9	9329.9	9895.1	...
B Direct taxes	...	396.2	868.2	1175.6	1605.7	1786.6	2307.1	2755.4	3039.2	3308.0	3815.2	...
C Social security contributions	...	12.7	40.7	76.8	165.5	223.4	329.7	430.6	534.2	642.1	751.2	...
D Compulsory fees, fines and penalties	...	20.7	51.3	80.4	129.1	131.0	148.2	176.0	224.2	209.0	230.9	...
4 Other current transfers	...	33.8	28.3	38.0	55.3	64.0	64.2	68.2	62.1	73.5	82.9	...
Total Current Receipts of General Government	...	1659.9	3205.9	4421.9	5965.9	7367.1	9267.0	10874.0	12967.1	14064.7	15365.8	...
					Disbursements							
1 Government final consumption expenditure	...	1121.1	1919.2	2501.2	3059.4	4268.0	5383.4	6110.3	6753.4	7079.1	7893.4	...

Korea, Republic of

1.4 General Government Current Receipts and Disbursements
(Continued)

Thousand Million Korean won

	1970	1975	1977	1978	1979	1980	1981	1982	1983	1984	1985	1986
A Compensation of employees	...	620.3	1252.2	1595.2	2054.2	2735.7	3413.0	4093.9	4573.4	4914.4	5499.0	...
B Consumption of fixed capital	...	28.8	43.7	52.5	68.2	86.2	107.4	130.8	135.5	143.7	150.6	...
C Purchases of goods and services, net	...	471.4	622.7	852.6	935.6	1444.4	1861.2	1883.8	2042.3	2018.9	2242.1	...
D Less: Own account fixed capital formation	...	...	...	...	...	...	...	...	...	...	...	...
E Indirect taxes paid, net	...	0.6	0.6	0.9	1.4	1.7	1.8	1.8	2.2	2.1	1.7	...
2 Property income	...	45.0	84.1	117.9	143.5	226.6	295.4	397.9	507.7	577.4	595.6	...
A Interest	...	44.9	83.9	117.5	143.3	226.3	294.6	397.5	507.5	576.7	595.3	...
B Net land rent and royalties	...	0.1	0.2	0.2	0.2	0.3	0.8	0.4	0.2	0.7	0.3	...
3 Subsidies	...	164.8	257.7	328.6	398.3	381.1	416.4	422.8	503.0	610.3	524.6	...
4 Other current transfers	...	94.5	178.5	240.8	416.4	579.0	744.7	953.3	1071.0	1258.9	1451.2	...
A Social security benefits	...	10.9	29.0	51.3	135.9	211.4	289.4	436.8	556.4	675.5	803.5	...
B Social assistance grants	...	63.6	113.9	138.4	190.7	266.9	314.9	347.0	334.3	357.9	388.8	...
C Other	...	20.0	35.6	51.1	89.8	100.7	140.4	169.5	180.3	225.5	258.9	...
5 Net saving	...	234.5	766.4	1233.6	1948.3	1912.4	2427.1	2989.7	4132.0	4539.0	4901.0	...
Total Current Disbursements and Net Saving of General Government	...	1659.9	3205.9	4421.9	5965.9	7367.1	9267.0	10874.0	12967.1	14064.7	15365.8	...

1.6 Current Income and Outlay of Households and Non-Profit Institutions

Thousand Million Korean won

	1970	1975	1977	1978	1979	1980	1981	1982	1983	1984	1985	1986
					Receipts							
1 Compensation of employees	...	3394.5	6411.4	9167.6	12242.6	15319.3	18679.8	21417.4	25362.8	28347.1	31143.4	...
A From resident producers	...	3342.0	6345.9	9073.2	12091.7	15188.8	18486.2	21149.6	25014.6	27945.3	30696.2	...
B From rest of the world	...	52.5	65.5	94.4	150.9	130.5	193.6	267.8	348.2	401.8	447.2	...
2 Operating surplus of private unincorporated enterprises	...	4377.7	6606.0	8270.3	10023.6	10610.4	13165.3	14536.4	15299.3	17664.6	18959.0	...
3 Property and entrepreneurial income	...	252.0	628.9	911.2	1482.3	2518.1	3309.8	3687.3	3188.3	3700.6	4469.9	...
4 Current transfers	...	468.5	843.6	1469.9	2109.6	2777.9	3809.3	4480.8	5250.7	6221.4	7028.3	...
A Social security benefits	...	10.9	29.0	51.3	135.9	211.4	289.4	436.8	556.4	675.5	803.5	...
B Social assistance grants	...	63.6	113.9	138.4	190.7	266.9	314.9	347.0	334.3	357.9	388.8	...
C Other	...	394.0	700.7	1280.2	1783.0	2299.6	3205.0	3697.0	4360.0	5188.0	5836.0	...
Total Current Receipts	...	8492.8	14489.9	19819.0	25858.1	31225.7	38964.2	44121.9	49101.1	55933.7	61600.6	...
					Disbursements							
1 Private final consumption expenditure	...	7247.9	11306.1	14902.0	19532.0	24786.1	30497.6	34001.3	37281.9	40778.3	44125.8	...
2 Property income	...	136.8	231.4	342.4	680.3	1280.6	1650.6	1798.4	1827.6	2435.7	2641.1	...
3 Direct taxes and other current transfers n.e.c. to general government	...	262.3	559.6	752.4	1087.0	1253.5	1694.3	2094.3	2337.9	2629.3	2970.5	...
A Social security contributions	...	12.7	40.7	76.8	165.5	223.4	329.7	430.6	534.2	642.1	751.2	...
B Direct taxes	...	235.9	485.9	622.2	834.8	948.3	1265.2	1546.5	1661.1	1851.7	2071.4	...
C Fees, fines and penalties	...	13.7	33.0	53.4	86.7	81.8	99.4	117.2	142.6	135.5	147.9	...
4 Other current transfers	...	250.4	411.9	677.0	898.2	1071.6	1430.3	1635.8	2148.7	2853.4	3449.9	...
5 Net saving	...	595.4	1980.9	3145.2	3660.6	2833.9	3691.4	4592.1	5505.0	7237.0	8413.3	...
Total Current Disbursements and Net Saving	...	8492.8	14489.9	19819.0	25858.1	31225.7	38964.2	44121.9	49101.1	55933.7	61600.6	...

1.7 External Transactions on Current Account, Summary

Thousand Million Korean won

	1970	1975	1977	1978	1979	1980	1981	1982	1983	1984	1985	1986
				Payments to the Rest of the World								
1 Imports of goods and services	657.6	3727.6	5811.0	8062.2	10828.7	15729.3	19712.3	20153.6	23027.9	26037.2	26922.8	30354.6
A Imports of merchandise c.i.f.	612.5	3461.6	5347.8	7364.7	9915.8	14203.7	17462.5	17880.0	20611.9	23559.2	24508.3	27711.0
B Other	45.1	266.0	463.2	697.5	912.9	1525.6	2249.8	2273.6	2416.0	2478.0	2414.5	2643.6
2 Factor income to the rest of the world	25.6	235.5	390.4	538.8	795.2	1710.8	2579.4	2958.2	2821.7	3443.3	3800.8	3986.8

Korea, Republic of

1.7 External Transactions on Current Account, Summary
(Continued)

Thousand Million Korean won

	1970	1975	1977	1978	1979	1980	1981	1982	1983	1984	1985	1986
A Compensation of employees	1.9	16.3	33.7	40.3	62.3	77.4	67.2	125.0	139.6	225.7	295.0	404.7
B Property and entrepreneurial income	23.7	219.2	356.7	498.5	732.9	1633.4	2512.2	2833.2	2682.1	3217.6	3505.8	3582.1
3 Current transfers to the rest of the world	10.6	54.6	120.4	99.3	128.7	224.7	247.7	295.6	302.8	302.9	349.7	294.8
4 Surplus of the nation on current transactions	-194.2	-900.0	42.1	-504.9	-1996.6	-3210.1	-3062.1	-1954.5	-1263.7	-1096.3	-758.2	4048.0
Payments to the Rest of the World and Surplus of the Nation on Current Transactions	499.6	3117.7	6363.9	8195.4	9756.0	14454.7	19477.3	21452.9	24888.7	28687.1	30315.1	38684.2
Receipts From The Rest of the World												
1 Exports of goods and services	389.0	2854.8	5848.2	7335.7	8563.5	12765.4	17191.5	18802.3	22245.7	25829.6	27326.9	35340.6
A Exports of merchandise f.o.b.	272.3	2450.7	4792.0	6027.3	7055.9	10373.3	13881.1	14758.0	17980.0	21241.0	23044.9	29866.0
B Other	116.7	404.1	1056.2	1308.4	1507.6	2392.1	3310.4	4044.3	4265.7	4588.6	4282.0	5474.6
2 Factor income from rest of the world	42.7	76.2	133.8	233.1	312.2	468.2	681.9	770.1	804.6	984.8	1139.9	1309.9
A Compensation of employees	30.9	52.5	65.5	94.4	150.9	130.5	193.6	267.8	348.2	401.8	447.2	580.4
B Property and entrepreneurial income	11.8	23.7	68.3	138.7	161.3	337.7	488.3	502.3	456.4	583.0	692.7	729.5
3 Current transfers from rest of the world	67.9	186.7	381.9	626.6	880.3	1221.1	1603.9	1880.5	1838.4	1872.7	1848.3	2033.7
Receipts from the Rest of the World on Current Transactions	499.6	3117.7	6363.9	8195.4	9756.0	14454.7	19477.3	21452.9	24888.7	28687.1	30315.1	38684.2

1.8 Capital Transactions of The Nation, Summary

Thousand Million Korean won

	1970	1975	1977	1978	1979	1980	1981	1982	1983	1984	1985	1986
Finance of Gross Capital Formation												
Gross saving	506.9	1827.7	4764.8	7060.9	8901.3	8614.6	10601.4	12197.9	16486.1	20120.6	22329.2	29213.4
1 Consumption of fixed capital	175.1	759.2	1339.2	1710.4	2344.2	2896.2	3617.5	4390.2	5191.2	6070.2	6657.3	7758.7
A General government	...	28.8	43.7	52.5	68.2	86.2	107.4	130.8	135.5	143.7	150.6	...
B Corporate and quasi-corporate enterprises	...	522.4	929.1	1182.7	1764.2	2247.8	2848.4	3810.0	4513.0	5030.1	5730.0	...
C Other	...	208.0	366.4	475.2	511.8	562.2	661.7	449.4	542.7	896.4	776.7	...
2 Net saving	331.8	1068.5	3425.6	5350.5	6557.1	5718.4	6983.9	7807.7	11294.9	14050.4	15671.9	21454.7
A General government	...	234.5	766.4	1233.6	1948.3	1912.4	2427.1	2989.7	4132.0	4539.0	4901.0	...
B Corporate and quasi-corporate enterprises	...	238.6	678.3	971.7	948.2	972.1	865.4	225.9	1657.9	2274.4	2357.6	...
C Other	...	595.4	1980.9	3145.2	3660.6	2833.9	3691.4	4592.1	5505.0	7237.0	8413.3	...
Less: Surplus of the nation on current transactions	-194.2	-900.0	42.1	-504.9	-1996.6	-3210.1	-3062.1	-1954.5	-1263.7	-1096.3	-758.2	4048.0
Statistical discrepancy	-18.6	39.4	181.2	58.2	176.4	-35.8	15.5	357.2	-129.0	-9.6	-442.6	115.7
Finance of Gross Capital Formation	682.5	2767.1	4903.9	7624.0	11074.3	11788.9	13679.0	14509.6	17620.8	21207.3	22644.8	25281.1
Gross Capital Formation												
Increase in stocks	-4.1	217.0	64.2	136.2	883.0	-46.8	748.0	-976.9	868.8	412.0	208.5	-964.6
Gross fixed capital formation	686.6	2550.1	4839.7	7487.8	10191.3	11835.7	12931.0	15486.5	18479.6	20795.0	22436.3	26245.7
1 General government	...	338.2	623.0	921.3	1323.0	1660.5	1921.6	2329.6	2747.0	3179.8	3426.5	...
2 Corporate and quasi-corporate enterprises	...	1717.5	3227.6	4795.0	6650.1	7332.5	8552.7	10992.1	12056.0	13052.3	14295.4	...
3 Other	...	494.4	989.1	1771.5	2218.2	2842.7	2456.7	2164.8	3676.6	4562.9	4714.4	...
Gross Capital Formation	682.5	2767.1	4903.9	7624.0	11074.3	11788.9	13679.0	14509.6	17620.8	21207.3	22644.8	25281.1

1.10 Gross Domestic Product by Kind of Activity, in Current Prices

Thousand Million Korean won

	1970	1975	1977	1978	1979	1980	1981	1982	1983	1984	1985	1986
1 Agriculture, hunting, forestry and fishing	717.6	2503.8	3957.6	4890.4	5877.6	5524.7	7442.3	7731.5	8292.6	9181.2	10158.0	10648.5
2 Mining and quarrying	35.3	144.6	258.4	332.8	363.4	520.0	734.3	772.6	873.1	977.8	1098.2	1158.7
3 Manufacturing	583.9	2676.2	4943.4	6788.4	8949.3	11214.3	13713.8	14996.2	17301.7	20019.4	21285.1	25965.5
4 Electricity, gas and water	42.3	125.2	259.2	318.8	523.2	786.2	995.1	1159.0	1514.0	1937.9	2276.3	2737.6
5 Construction	143.3	484.9	1009.4	1856.6	2666.0	3149.8	3443.3	4221.5	5075.4	5683.0	6246.1	6769.0

Korea, Republic of

1.10 Gross Domestic Product by Kind of Activity, in Current Prices
(Continued)

Thousand Million Korean won

	1970	1975	1977	1978	1979	1980	1981	1982	1983	1984	1985	1986
6 Wholesale and retail trade, restaurants and hotels	442.2	1760.8	2605.3	3316.8	4117.8	4967.5	6166.9	6906.8	7743.7	8872.1	9721.6	11294.9
7 Transport, storage and communication	185.7	606.2	1169.2	1603.2	2175.0	2915.4	3893.7	4616.5	5277.4	5789.6	6210.9	6965.5
8 Finance, insurance, real estate and business services	236.6	692.6	1394.3	2008.3	2774.3	4171.7	4480.4	4462.3	5873.1	6701.6	8018.4	9207.6
9 Community, social and personal services	93.4	302.6	488.5	684.1	857.3	1192.5	1442.0	1760.5	2112.9	2406.6	2663.9	2975.0
Total, Industries	2480.3	9296.9	16085.3	21799.4	28303.9	34442.1	42311.8	46626.9	54063.9	61569.2	67678.5	77722.3
Producers of Government Services	210.3	649.7	1296.5	1648.6	2123.8	2823.6	3522.2	4226.5	4711.1	5060.2	5651.3	6270.5
Other Producers	53.1	202.6	360.0	454.9	551.6	705.3	920.1	1168.1	1391.1	1566.9	1823.6	2073.7
Subtotal	2743.7	10149.2	17741.8	23902.9	30979.3	37971.0	46754.1	52021.5	60166.1	68196.3	75153.4	86066.5
Less: Imputed bank service charge	42.4	159.5	321.2	498.5	760.4	1191.4	1177.3	662.6	1228.9	1509.8	1846.2	2300.6
Plus: Import duties	58.5	234.2	564.6	838.1	1005.2	1135.3	1446.9	1553.8	2065.7	2180.2	2203.5	2744.0
Plus: Value added tax	...	...	...	...	...	...	...	...	...	...	...	...
Equals: Gross Domestic Product	2759.8	10223.9	17985.2	24242.5	31224.1	37914.9	47023.7	52912.7	61002.9	68866.7	75510.7	86509.9

1.11 Gross Domestic Product by Kind of Activity, in Constant Prices

Thousand Million Korean won

	1970	1975	1977	1978	1979	1980	1981	1982	1983	1984	1985	1986
At constant prices of: 1980												
1 Agriculture, hunting, forestry and fishing	4989.6	6289.1	7132.4	6426.6	6899.1	5524.7	6759.7	6980.6	7436.0	7453.2	7809.2	8156.5
2 Mining and quarrying	362.0	511.1	573.4	604.4	563.2	520.0	616.1	626.4	685.0	742.4	792.9	824.2
3 Manufacturing	2613.4	5895.5	8455.5	10259.4	11340.0	11214.3	12058.9	12558.9	14095.6	16188.0	16805.0	19736.4
4 Electricity, gas and water	161.5	345.1	456.2	611.9	660.5	786.2	844.4	881.5	1131.1	1420.3	1697.6	2025.7
5 Construction	1184.4	1745.1	2471.5	3084.4	3225.3	3149.8	3035.3	3594.9	4275.6	4539.5	4749.2	5094.9
6 Wholesale and retail trade, restaurants and hotels	2237.6	3914.2	4606.2	5061.7	5226.8	4967.5	5353.7	5637.0	6141.9	6716.0	7107.4	8209.0
7 Transport, storage and communication	789.7	1456.6	2050.2	2428.4	2827.1	2915.4	3072.3	3288.1	3668.4	3974.2	4170.2	4613.8
8 Finance, insurance, real estate and business services	1428.8	2222.6	3031.4	3390.4	3676.9	4171.7	4128.0	4464.3	4945.8	5468.5	6313.0	7134.9
9 Community, social and personal services	543.8	794.0	934.8	1024.7	1116.9	1192.5	1210.4	1304.2	1452.8	1590.1	1700.4	1831.5
Total, Industries	14310.8	23173.3	29711.6	32891.9	35535.8	34442.1	37078.8	39335.9	43832.2	48092.2	51144.9	57626.9
Producers of Government Services	2152.8	2395.0	2523.4	2619.7	2713.8	2823.6	2934.1	3022.6	3090.8	3112.4	3167.0	3263.0
Other Producers	373.2	557.9	612.3	648.4	680.1	705.3	739.3	793.0	857.7	925.8	1010.5	1096.3
Subtotal	16836.8	26126.2	32847.3	36160.0	38929.7	37971.0	40752.2	43151.5	47780.7	52130.4	55322.4	61986.2
Less: Imputed bank service charge	248.2	558.9	848.5	950.7	1125.8	1191.4	1277.2	1444.3	1593.1	1853.6	2199.7	2680.5
Plus: Import duties	296.7	580.5	834.7	1201.7	1295.7	1135.3	1248.3	1328.5	1556.1	1595.7	1551.7	1860.7
Plus: Value added tax	...	...	...	...	...	...	...	...	...	...	...	...
Equals: Gross Domestic Product	16885.3	26147.8	32833.5	36411.0	39099.6	37914.9	40723.3	43035.7	47743.7	51872.5	54674.4	61166.4

1.12 Relations Among National Accounting Aggregates

Thousand Million Korean won

	1970	1975	1977	1978	1979	1980	1981	1982	1983	1984	1985	1986
Gross Domestic Product	2759.8	10223.9	17985.2	24242.5	31224.1	37914.9	47023.7	52912.7	61002.9	68866.7	75510.7	86509.9
Plus: Net factor income from the rest of the world	17.1	-159.3	-256.6	-305.7	-483.0	-1242.6	-1897.5	-2188.1	-2017.1	-2458.5	-2660.9	-2676.9
Factor income from the rest of the world	42.7	76.2	133.8	233.1	312.2	468.2	681.9	770.1	804.6	984.8	1139.9	1309.9
Less: Factor income to the rest of the world	25.6	235.5	390.4	538.8	795.2	1710.8	2579.4	2958.2	2821.7	3443.3	3800.8	3986.8
Equals: Gross National Product	2776.9	10064.6	17728.6	23936.8	30741.1	36672.3	45126.2	50724.6	58985.8	66408.2	72849.8	83833.0
Less: Consumption of fixed capital	175.1	759.2	1339.2	1710.4	2344.2	2896.2	3617.5	4390.2	5191.2	6070.2	6657.3	7758.7

Korea, Republic of

1.12 Relations Among National Accounting Aggregates
(Continued)

Thousand Million Korean won

	1970	1975	1977	1978	1979	1980	1981	1982	1983	1984	1985	1986
Equals: National Income	2601.8	9305.4	16389.4	22226.4	28396.9	33776.1	41508.7	46334.4	53794.6	60338.0	66192.5	76074.3
Plus: Net current transfers from the rest of the world	57.3	132.1	261.5	527.3	751.6	996.4	1356.2	1584.9	1535.6	1569.8	1498.6	1738.9
Current transfers from the rest of the world	67.9	186.7	381.9	626.6	880.3	1221.1	1603.9	1880.5	1838.4	1872.7	1848.3	2033.7
Less: Current transfers to the rest of the world	10.6	54.6	120.4	99.3	128.7	224.7	247.7	295.6	302.8	302.9	349.7	294.8
Equals: National Disposable Income	2659.1	9437.5	16650.9	22753.7	29148.5	34772.5	42864.9	47919.3	55330.2	61907.8	67691.1	77813.2
Less: Final consumption	2327.3	8369.0	13225.3	17403.2	22591.4	29054.1	35881.0	40111.6	44035.3	47857.4	52019.2	56358.5
Equals: Net Saving	331.8	1068.5	3425.6	5350.5	6557.1	5718.4	6983.9	7807.7	11294.9	14050.4	15671.9	21454.7
Less: Surplus of the nation on current transactions	-194.2	-900.0	42.1	-504.9	-1996.6	-3210.1	-3062.1	-1954.5	-1263.7	-1096.3	-758.2	4048.0
Statistical discrepancy	-18.6	39.4	181.2	58.2	176.4	-35.8	15.5	357.2	-129.0	-9.6	-442.6	115.7
Equals: Net Capital Formation	507.4	2007.9	3564.7	5913.6	8730.1	8892.7	10061.5	10119.4	12429.6	15137.1	15987.5	17522.4

2.1 Government Final Consumption Expenditure by Function, in Current Prices

Thousand Million Korean won

	1970	1975	1977	1978	1979	1980	1981	1982	1983	1984	1985	1986
1 General public services	...	146.4	286.9	379.5	477.7	645.2	831.4	1024.9	1133.2	1215.3	1293.0	1454.6
2 Defence	...	600.7	943.4	1243.5	1454.9	2124.0	2569.5	2780.9	2987.1	3004.9	3561.0	3876.6
3 Public order and safety	...	77.5	155.7	200.0	257.4	343.4	477.7	557.8	677.9	695.8	771.8	830.3
4 Education	...	209.2	397.8	489.6	603.6	810.8	994.7	1228.0	1392.2	1537.7	1768.6	1979.2
5 Health	...	14.1	30.9	37.9	54.8	71.1	94.6	87.2	100.8	105.4	102.5	121.6
6 Social security and welfare	...	10.8	17.7	24.8	37.2	45.9	64.3	97.5	104.7	120.9	121.6	160.1
7 Housing and community amenities	...	13.8	20.8	37.5	54.3	71.1	75.5	72.4	56.4	43.6	44.3	58.2
8 Recreational, cultural and religious affairs	...	9.9	13.5	18.4	25.5	32.2	43.9	44.3	49.2	52.7	49.6	70.3
9 Economic services	...	31.3	37.2	51.6	69.1	93.8	195.7	178.4	210.1	251.3	128.2	269.5
A Fuel and energy	...	0.8	2.2	3.9	5.0	6.5	29.9	48.0	67.3	33.3	0.5	57.4
B Agriculture, forestry, fishing and hunting	...	20.7	22.7	34.6	49.2	63.7	117.7	88.3	104.4	125.1	80.1	158.8
C Mining, manufacturing and construction, except fuel and energy	...	2.8	3.5	3.8	4.3	5.7	17.7	29.9	29.8	61.5	43.5	47.7
D Transportation and communication	...	7.0	8.8	9.3	10.6	17.9	30.4	12.2	8.6	31.4	4.1	5.6
E Other economic affairs	...	...	...	...	...	...	...	...	...	...	...	...
10 Other functions	...	7.5	15.2	18.4	24.9	30.5	36.1	38.9	41.8	51.5	52.8	64.2
Total Government Final Consumption Expenditure	263.4	1121.1	1919.2	2501.2	3059.4	4268.0	5383.4	6110.3	6753.4	7079.1	7893.4	8884.6

2.2 Government Final Consumption Expenditure by Function, in Constant Prices

Thousand Million Korean won

	1970	1975	1977	1978	1979	1980	1981	1982	1983	1984	1985	1986
				At constant prices of:1980								
1 General public services	...	479.6	547.5	603.3	613.2	645.2	695.6	705.4	749.0	738.7	734.5	804.6
2 Defence	...	1522.7	1676.4	1949.0	1926.8	2124.0	2170.9	2133.4	2258.1	2229.5	2576.6	2768.4
3 Public order and safety	...	260.8	313.1	332.7	340.5	343.4	408.1	435.6	468.9	457.7	462.5	474.0
4 Education	...	672.1	723.6	772.2	774.8	810.8	842.1	894.0	919.8	965.9	1091.5	1090.6
5 Health	...	50.1	70.9	70.0	70.6	71.1	77.4	74.0	83.4	84.5	79.7	88.8
6 Social security and welfare	...	37.0	37.6	39.9	43.8	45.9	48.8	62.7	59.8	61.2	60.2	76.4
7 Housing and community amenities	...	48.8	56.0	77.6	80.7	71.1	58.0	56.0	42.9	34.3	33.2	45.5
8 Recreational, cultural and religious affairs	...	25.4	28.2	33.0	35.2	32.2	34.6	33.2	34.7	36.3	33.2	47.3
9 Economic services	...	76.8	72.3	86.4	91.8	93.8	164.9	143.0	162.0	188.8	95.1	194.3
A Fuel and energy	...	2.7	5.1	6.0	7.1	6.5	22.0	38.4	46.1	20.9	0.3	34.0
B Agriculture, forestry, fishing and hunting	...	51.6	42.8	57.0	64.4	63.7	103.3	79.0	86.7	103.7	62.4	123.3
C Mining, manufacturing and construction, except fuel and energy	...	5.8	6.2	6.1	5.4	5.7	15.1	23.2	23.8	44.6	30.0	33.0
D Transportation and communication	...	16.7	18.2	16.4	14.9	17.9	24.2	8.4	5.4	19.6	2.4	3.4
E Other economic affairs	...	...	...	...	...	...	...	...	...	...	...	...
10 Other functions	...	21.2	28.7	29.6	31.6	30.5	31.5	31.8	32.3	38.1	38.7	45.1
Total Government Final Consumption Expenditure	2152.1	3194.5	3554.3	3993.7	4009.2	4268.0	4531.9	4569.1	4810.9	4835.0	5145.2	5625.0

Korea, Republic of

2.3 Total Government Outlays by Function and Type

Thousand Million Korean won

		Final Consumption Expenditures			Subsidies	Other Current Transfers & Property Income	Total Current Disbursements	Gross Capital Formation	Other Capital Outlays	Total Outlays
		Total	Compensation of Employees	Other						

1980

1	General public services	645.2	483.0	162.2	...	...	...	108.2	...	...
2	Defence	2124.0	800.1	1323.9	...	...	...	15.5	...	...
3	Public order and safety	343.4	252.2	91.2	...	...	...	70.0	...	...
4	Education	810.8	935.9	-125.1	...	...	...	252.8	...	...
5	Health	71.1	72.0	-0.9	1.0	...	...	25.2	...	...
6	Social security and welfare	45.9	36.1	9.8	...	...	...	25.5	...	...
7	Housing and community amenities	71.1	39.1	32.0	3.0	...	...	422.2	...	...
8	Recreation, culture and religion	32.2	12.7	19.5	...	...	...	50.0	...	...
9	Economic services	93.8	90.0	3.8	134.1	...	...	633.9	...	...
	A Fuel and energy	6.5	8.4	-1.9	71.4	...	...	25.4	...	...
	B Agriculture, forestry, fishing and hunting	63.7	50.0	13.7	9.3	...	...	100.7	...	...
	C Mining (except fuels), manufacturing and construction	5.7	12.3	-6.6	39.5	...	...	72.2	...	...
	D Transportation and communication	17.9	19.3	-1.4	13.9	...	...	435.6	...	...
	E Other economic affairs	...	...	...	...	...	...	...	...	...
10	Other functions	30.5	14.6	15.9	243.0	...	...	57.2	...	...
	Total	4268.0	2735.7	1532.3	381.1	805.6	5454.7	1660.5	-12.0	7103.2

1981

1	General public services	831.4	599.1	232.3	...	...	...	126.2	...	...
2	Defence	2569.5	968.6	1600.9	...	...	...	7.8	...	...
3	Public order and safety	477.7	319.1	158.6	...	...	...	74.8	...	...
4	Education	994.7	1179.3	-184.6	0.1	...	...	393.2	...	...
5	Health	94.6	92.6	2.0	1.1	...	...	36.8	...	...
6	Social security and welfare	64.3	49.6	14.7	0.1	...	...	25.1	...	...
7	Housing and community amenities	75.5	53.1	22.4	6.7	...	...	349.3	...	...
8	Recreation, culture and religion	43.9	18.8	25.1	...	...	...	50.6	...	...
9	Economic services	195.7	115.0	80.7	110.5	...	...	807.8	...	...
	A Fuel and energy	29.9	14.5	15.4	52.6	...	...	25.3	...	...
	B Agriculture, forestry, fishing and hunting	117.7	60.2	57.5	4.8	...	...	200.4	...	...
	C Mining (except fuels), manufacturing and construction	17.7	14.8	2.9	50.5	...	...	60.6	...	...
	D Transportation and communication	30.4	25.5	4.9	2.6	...	...	521.5	...	...
	E Other economic affairs	...	...	...	...	...	...	...	...	...
10	Other functions	36.1	17.8	18.3	297.9	...	...	50.0	...	...
	Total	5383.4	3413.0	1970.4	416.4	1040.1	6839.9	1921.6	25.2	8786.7

1982

1	General public services	1024.9	772.3	252.6	...	...	...	105.1	...	...
2	Defence	2780.9	1122.0	1658.9	...	...	...	10.6	...	...
3	Public order and safety	557.8	374.0	183.8	...	...	...	104.6	...	...
4	Education	1228.0	1469.2	-241.2	2.6	...	...	442.4	...	...
5	Health	87.2	92.2	-5.0	1.2	...	...	44.8	...	...
6	Social security and welfare	97.5	59.8	37.7	...	...	...	22.7	...	...
7	Housing and community amenities	72.4	46.2	26.2	3.8	...	...	495.8	...	...
8	Recreation, culture and religion	44.3	18.4	25.9	...	...	...	60.2	...	...
9	Economic services	178.4	121.2	57.2	126.5	...	...	991.2	...	...
	A Fuel and energy	48.0	17.7	30.3	54.4	...	...	22.3	...	...
	B Agriculture, forestry, fishing and hunting	88.3	54.1	34.2	5.9	...	...	133.1	...	...
	C Mining (except fuels), manufacturing and construction	29.9	16.8	13.1	29.0	...	...	202.7	...	...
	D Transportation and communication	12.2	32.6	-20.4	37.2	...	...	633.1	...	...
	E Other economic affairs	...	...	...	...	...	...	...	...	...
10	Other functions	38.9	18.6	20.3	288.7	...	...	52.2	...	...
	Total	6110.3	4093.9	2016.4	422.8	1351.2	7884.3	2329.6	-18.9	10195.0

Korea, Republic of

2.3 Total Government Outlays by Function and Type
(Continued)

Thousand Million Korean won

| | | Final Consumption Expenditures | | | Other Current | Total | Gross | Other | |
| | | | Compensation | | | Transfers & | Current | Capital | Capital | Total |
		Total	of Employees	Other	Subsidies	Property Income	Disbursements	Formation	Outlays	Outlays

1983

1	General public services	1133.2	857.9	275.3	0.5	...	...	172.1	...	...
2	Defence	2987.1	1159.4	1827.7	...	...	...	11.1	...	...
3	Public order and safety	677.9	455.6	222.3	...	...	...	78.4	...	...
4	Education	1392.2	1691.7	-299.5	0.1	...	...	438.8	...	...
5	Health	100.8	98.0	2.8	1.6	...	...	39.2	...	...
6	Social security and welfare	104.7	76.3	28.4	...	...	...	58.7	...	...
7	Housing and community amenities	56.4	52.8	3.6	2.5	...	...	574.8	...	...
8	Recreation, culture and religion	49.2	22.3	26.9	...	...	...	109.5	...	...
9	Economic services	210.1	138.4	71.7	72.7	...	...	1207.2	...	...
	A Fuel and energy	67.3	18.1	49.2	30.5	...	...	7.6	...	...
	B Agriculture, forestry, fishing and hunting	104.4	66.0	38.4	4.7	...	...	231.3	...	...
	C Mining (except fuels), manufacturing and construction	29.8	15.2	14.6	0.3	...	...	172.1	...	...
	D Transportation and communication	8.6	39.1	-30.5	37.2	...	...	796.2	...	...
	E Other economic affairs	...	...	...	...	...	...	...	...	...
10	Other functions	41.8	21.0	20.8	425.6	...	...	57.2	...	...
	Total	6753.4	4573.4	2180.0	503.0	1578.7	8835.1	2747.0	6.6	11588.7

1984

1	General public services	1215.3	956.9	258.4	1.9	...	...	163.5	...	...
2	Defence	3004.9	1193.2	1811.7	...	...	...	14.6	...	...
3	Public order and safety	695.8	481.3	214.5	...	...	...	108.4	...	...
4	Education	1537.7	1845.1	-307.4	1.9	...	...	527.1	...	...
5	Health	105.4	100.3	5.1	1.3	...	...	50.0	...	...
6	Social security and welfare	120.9	96.0	24.9	...	...	...	94.2	...	...
7	Housing and community amenities	43.6	49.1	-5.5	2.7	...	...	645.6	...	...
8	Recreation, culture and religion	52.7	22.9	29.8	...	...	...	114.9	...	...
9	Economic services	251.3	146.4	104.9	84.2	...	...	1357.7	...	...
	A Fuel and energy	33.3	19.6	13.7	17.0	...	...	32.9	...	...
	B Agriculture, forestry, fishing and hunting	125.1	62.5	62.6	9.5	...	...	181.8	...	...
	C Mining (except fuels), manufacturing and construction	61.5	23.4	38.1	0.3	...	...	273.3	...	...
	D Transportation and communication	31.4	40.9	-9.5	57.4	...	...	869.7	...	...
	E Other economic affairs	...	...	...	...	...	...	...	...	...
10	Other functions	51.5	23.2	28.3	518.3	...	...	103.8	...	...
	Total	7079.1	4914.4	2164.7	610.3	1836.3	9525.7	3179.8	-15.9	12689.6

1985

1	General public services	1200.0	1074.4	210.0	0.0	...	...	150.0	...	...
2	Defence	3561.0	1303.2	2257.8	...	...	...	12.2	...	...
3	Public order and safety	771.8	548.7	223.1	...	...	...	113.2	...	...
4	Education	1768.6	2089.8	-321.2	2.6	...	...	554.5	...	...
5	Health	102.5	106.1	-3.6	2.8	...	...	64.5	...	...
6	Social security and welfare	121.6	105.5	16.1	...	...	...	40.2	...	...
7	Housing and community amenities	44.3	55.4	-11.1	3.6	...	...	772.5	...	...
8	Recreation, culture and religion	49.6	26.0	23.6	...	...	...	167.9	...	...
9	Economic services	128.2	166.3	-38.1	42.1	...	...	1429.6	...	...
	A Fuel and energy	0.5	25.9	-25.4	17.9	...	...	50.7	...	...
	B Agriculture, forestry, fishing and hunting	80.1	69.0	11.1	4.9	...	...	193.9	...	...
	C Mining (except fuels), manufacturing and construction	43.5	26.5	17.0	4.1	...	...	327.1	...	...
	D Transportation and communication	4.1	44.9	-40.8	15.2	...	...	857.9	...	...
	E Other economic affairs	...	...	...	...	...	...	...	...	...
10	Other functions	52.8	23.6	29.2	470.2	...	...	112.3	...	...
	Total	7893.4	5499.0	2394.4	524.6	2046.8	10464.8	3426.5	-102.9	13788.4

Korea, Republic of

2.5 Private Final Consumption Expenditure by Type and Porpose, in Current Prices

Thousand Million Korean won

	1970	1975	1977	1978	1979	1980	1981	1982	1983	1984	1985	1986
Final Consumption Expenditure of Resident Households													
1 Food, beverages and tobacco	1123.4	3887.8	5949.2	7573.3	9655.2	11859.7	14922.5	15937.7	16845.8	17922.1	19365.0	20465.5
2 Clothing and footwear	208.1	723.9	1104.1	1471.2	1763.2	2130.4	2437.1	2478.9	2734.8	2971.8	2928.7	3102.4
3 Gross rent, fuel and power	189.7	599.3	985.6	1321.2	1853.4	2527.7	3121.1	3508.5	3963.3	4455.7	4867.4	5353.9
4 Furniture, furnishings and household equipment and operation	81.0	316.5	564.9	829.8	1131.1	1183.8	1252.3	1381.6	1595.6	1942.2	2043.6	2304.2
5 Medical care and health expenses	50.5	228.6	365.5	532.0	722.8	971.7	1171.1	1399.8	1636.0	1784.6	1914.5	2121.6
6 Transport and communication	123.2	472.4	736.3	1047.9	1479.9	2137.9	2532.1	3077.8	3447.7	3876.8	4212.3	4748.6
7 Recreational, entertainment, education and cultural services	117.2	450.4	771.9	974.8	1329.5	1812.0	2473.1	3034.5	3512.7	3913.0	4249.5	4860.4
8 Miscellaneous goods and services	155.5	568.5	884.8	1164.0	1482.5	2034.1	2429.3	2950.8	3305.8	3598.8	4224.2	4750.8
Total Final Consumption Expenditure in the Domestic Market by Households, of which	2048.6	7247.4	11362.3	14914.2	19417.6	24657.3	30338.6	33769.6	37041.7	40465.0	43805.2	47707.4
A Durable goods	40.3	178.5	328.8	520.4	729.9	714.3	929.6	1025.6	1313.0	1573.3	1543.9	1901.7
B Semi-durable goods	286.4	1046.1	1681.4	2260.3	2747.9	3323.3	3659.0	3788.0	4150.5	4526.1	4667.2	5119.4
C Non-durable goods	1289.1	4450.0	6759.6	8665.4	11138.3	13933.2	17522.3	18826.0	19943.0	21304.3	23049.1	24580.0
D Services	432.8	1572.8	2592.5	3468.1	4801.8	6686.5	8227.7	10130.0	11635.2	13061.3	14545.0	16106.3
Plus: Direct purchases abroad by resident households	2.2	6.7	11.1	26.4	57.1	84.0	160.9	248.8	219.7	264.1	322.6	250.2
Less: Direct purchases in the domestic market by non-resident households	6.8	67.7	171.4	181.8	129.2	198.8	274.8	318.3	368.1	430.2	559.1	1111.0
Equals: Final Consumption Expenditure of Resident Households	2044.0	7186.4	11202.0	14758.8	19345.5	24542.5	30224.7	33700.1	36893.3	40298.9	43568.7	46846.6
Final Consumption Expenditure of Private Non-profit Institutions Serving Households													
1 Research and science	...	0.6	1.0	1.4	1.8	2.3	2.9	3.4	4.2	4.5	5.2	5.3
2 Education	...	16.8	35.0	41.8	55.3	74.6	33.1	17.8	70.7	97.1	109.8	123.4
3 Medical and other health services	...	12.0	15.6	22.5	34.9	43.9	61.4	85.3	101.4	126.4	149.7	165.5
4 Welfare services	...	9.5	15.3	20.8	24.8	33.0	24.0	48.6	56.7	66.6	73.3	82.1
5 Recreational and related cultural services	...	...	...	...	...	...	...	...	...	...	...	...
6 Religious organisations	...	...	...	...	...	...	...	...	...	...	...	...
7 Professional and labour organisations serving households	...	...	...	...	...	...	...	...	...	...	...	...
8 Miscellaneous	...	22.6	37.2	56.7	69.7	89.8	151.5	146.1	155.6	184.8	219.1	251.0
Equals: Final Consumption Expenditure of Private Non-profit Organisations Serving Households	19.9	61.5	104.1	143.2	186.5	243.6	272.9	301.2	388.6	479.4	557.1	627.3
Private Final Consumption Expenditure	2063.9	7247.9	11306.1	14902.0	19532.0	24786.1	30497.6	34001.3	37281.9	40778.3	44125.8	47473.9

2.6 Private Final Consumption Expenditure by Type and Purpose, in Constant Prices

Thousand Million Korean won

	1970	1975	1977	1978	1979	1980	1981	1982	1983	1984	1985	1986
At constant prices of:1980													
Final Consumption Expenditure of Resident Households													
1 Food, beverages and tobacco	6942.1	9255.8	10428.6	10955.8	11990.7	11859.7	12116.7	12566.4	13261.9	13662.7	14173.1	15028.6
2 Clothing and footwear	1065.1	1676.5	1987.6	2309.6	2225.6	2130.4	2168.2	2071.4	2227.4	2296.4	2290.6	2378.1
3 Gross rent, fuel and power	1511.9	1917.5	2145.4	2313.2	2449.1	2527.7	2596.6	2700.5	2855.5	3070.7	3251.1	3512.2
4 Furniture, furnishings and household equipment and operation	333.2	698.2	937.6	1235.1	1383.3	1183.8	1136.4	1191.3	1343.0	1528.7	1591.6	1788.6
5 Medical care and health expenses	269.0	597.7	741.5	855.4	945.2	971.7	1028.4	1168.0	1335.9	1435.1	1535.1	1634.2
6 Transport and communication	656.5	1158.1	1598.3	1890.2	2158.9	2137.9	2216.0	2357.7	2632.0	2857.7	3039.1	3349.7
7 Recreational, entertainment, education and cultural services	886.4	1258.2	1442.2	1554.0	1730.7	1812.0	2127.8	2335.0	2584.7	2856.5	2985.1	3385.4
8 Miscellaneous goods and services	896.8	1438.8	1676.5	1799.4	1926.1	2034.1	2056.9	2231.8	2416.3	2643.8	3013.8	3233.4
Total Final Consumption Expenditure in the Domestic Market by Households, of which	12561.0	18000.8	20957.7	22912.7	24809.6	24657.3	25447.0	26622.1	28656.7	30351.6	31879.5	34310.2
A Durable goods	126.6	288.3	459.0	708.6	873.5	714.3	912.4	972.0	1227.8	1468.0	1476.2	1842.8
B Semi-durable goods	1377.6	2402.8	2945.8	3458.1	3423.6	3323.3	3285.8	3213.2	3435.5	3568.1	3675.0	3948.4

Korea, Republic of

2.6 Private Final Consumption Expenditure by Type and Purpose, in Constant Prices
(Continued)

Thousand Million Korean won

	1970	1975	1977	1978	1979	1980	1981	1982	1983	1984	1985	1986
					At constant prices of:1980							
C Non-durable goods	7862.5	10630.6	12079.5	12837.2	14053.6	13933.2	14238.6	14795.1	15689.6	16284.2	16982.2	18126.1
D Services	3194.3	4679.1	5473.4	5908.8	6458.9	6686.5	7010.2	7641.8	8303.8	9031.3	9746.1	10392.9
Plus: Direct purchases abroad by resident households	11.9	13.8	19.0	37.7	77.5	84.0	133.5	199.0	156.5	174.5	192.7	117.3
Less: Direct purchases in the domestic market by non-resident households	30.8	149.7	298.4	276.8	166.3	198.8	227.6	245.4	273.4	312.5	395.9	769.7
Equals: Final Consumption Expenditure of Resident Households	12542.1	17864.9	20678.3	22673.6	24720.8	24542.5	25352.9	26575.7	28539.8	30213.6	31676.3	33657.8
		Final Consumption Expenditure of Private Non-profit Institutions Serving Households										
1 Research and science	...	1.3	1.8	2.0	2.3	2.3	2.4	2.6	3.0	3.1	3.5	3.4
2 Education	...	50.2	61.8	63.5	69.8	74.6	26.5	11.9	43.1	56.7	60.1	64.8
3 Medical and other health services	...	26.1	28.6	35.4	43.2	43.9	52.3	66.4	76.6	93.9	109.0	117.3
4 Welfare services	...	22.8	28.5	32.8	32.2	33.0	19.7	35.9	39.5	45.1	48.7	53.4
5 Recreational and related cultural services	...	...	...	...	...	...	...	...	...	...	...	...
6 Religious organisations	...	...	...	...	...	...	...	...	...	...	...	...
7 Professional and labour organisations serving households	...	...	...	...	...	...	...	...	...	...	...	...
8 Miscellaneous	...	53.9	71.0	89.3	90.7	89.8	124.5	105.5	113.8	125.9	148.8	167.8
Equals: Final Consumption Expenditure of Private Non-profit Organisations Serving Households	107.7	154.3	191.7	223.0	238.2	243.6	225.4	222.3	276.0	324.7	370.1	406.7
Private Final Consumption Expenditure	12649.8	18019.2	20870.0	22806.6	24960.0	24786.1	25578.3	26798.0	28815.8	30538.3	32046.4	34064.5

2.11 Gross Fixed Capital Formation by Kind of Activity of Owner, ISIC Divisions, in Current Prices

Thousand Million Korean won

	1970	1975	1977	1978	1979	1980	1981	1982	1983	1984	1985	1986
					All Producers							
1 Agriculture, hunting, forestry and fishing	112.9	285.4	524.7	713.9	940.1	955.0	1001.9	1107.5	1404.8	1612.7	1492.9	...
2 Mining and quarrying	2.6	15.1	39.9	56.4	72.0	80.8	107.7	127.6	132.3	150.4	171.3	...
3 Manufacturing	105.4	640.1	1424.0	2179.5	2845.7	2650.7	2742.0	3221.2	3374.5	4536.9	5795.0	...
4 Electricity, gas and water	35.0	157.5	353.2	529.3	888.7	1115.0	1392.8	1561.3	1928.8	1730.5	1825.4	...
5 Construction	6.8	44.4	147.8	187.1	254.0	318.4	366.8	463.3	434.5	540.7	550.1	...
6 Wholesale and retail trade, restaurants and hotels	32.8	113.4	181.1	307.2	342.9	423.4	571.4	912.4	702.5	883.6	941.0	...
7 Transport, storage and communication	14.3	228.4	401.9	668.0	951.8	1447.9	1887.6	1891.5	2879.0	2773.7	3061.8	...
8 Finance, insurance, real estate and business services	214.8	653.6	1010.0	1755.1	2361.7	2937.2	2669.5	3464.2	4472.6	4853.0	4670.8	...
9 Community, social and personal services	20.8	74.0	134.1	170.0	211.4	246.8	269.7	407.9	403.6	533.7	501.5	...
Total Industries	545.4	2211.9	4216.7	6566.5	8868.3	10175.2	11009.4	13156.9	15732.6	17615.2	19009.8	...
Producers of Government Services	141.2	338.2	623.0	921.3	1323.0	1660.5	1921.6	2329.6	2747.0	3179.8	3426.5	...
Private Non-Profit Institutions Serving Households	...	...	...	...	...	...	...	...	...	...	...	...
Total	686.6	2550.1	4839.7	7487.8	10191.3	11835.7	12931.0	15486.5	18479.6	20795.0	22436.3	...

2.12 Gross Fixed Capital Formation by Kind of Activity of Owner, ISIC Divisions, in Constant Prices

Thousand Million Korean won

	1970	1975	1977	1978	1979	1980	1981	1982	1983	1984	1985	1986
					At constant prices of:1980							
					All Producers							
1 Agriculture, hunting, forestry and fishing	669.7	738.7	1031.5	1186.2	1202.1	955.0	863.6	863.2	1085.4	1197.6	1120.8	...
2 Mining and quarrying	10.0	33.2	72.8	89.5	93.2	80.8	93.8	105.8	107.8	121.1	132.6	...
3 Manufacturing	554.5	1408.6	2595.0	3460.4	3683.2	2650.7	2454.0	2694.3	2754.6	3675.5	4494.7	...
4 Electricity, gas and water	184.2	346.8	643.5	840.4	1150.3	1115.0	1248.1	1306.6	1582.7	1411.2	1423.2	...

Korea, Republic of

2.12 Gross Fixed Capital Formation by Kind of Activity of Owner, ISIC Divisions, in Constant Prices
(Continued)

Thousand Million Korean won

	1970	1975	1977	1978	1979	1980	1981	1982	1983	1984	1985	1986
					At constant prices of:1980							
5 Construction	35.7	97.8	269.4	297.0	328.8	318.4	325.7	383.7	352.8	433.7	432.2	...
6 Wholesale and retail trade, restaurants and hotels	172.6	249.7	330.0	487.8	443.8	423.4	503.3	754.9	574.8	722.8	731.3	...
7 Transport, storage and communication	75.3	503.0	732.3	1060.6	1231.9	1448.0	1611.7	1551.4	2304.0	2193.8	2318.1	...
8 Finance, insurance, real estate and business services	1181.1	1651.2	2051.0	2984.8	3095.5	2937.2	2350.6	2896.5	3685.3	3913.0	3664.8	...
9 Community, social and personal services	109.2	162.8	244.4	269.9	273.6	246.8	240.8	338.6	326.2	429.8	387.9	...
Total Industries	2995.9	5191.8	7969.9	10676.6	11502.4	10175.3	9691.6	10895.0	12773.6	14098.5	14705.6	...
Producers of Government Services	775.9	793.9	1177.7	1498.0	1715.9	1660.4	1667.9	1925.1	2243.3	2519.0	2650.1	...
Private Non-Profit Institutions Serving Households	...	...	...	...	...	...	...	...	...	...	...	...
Total	3771.8	5985.7	9147.6	12174.6	13218.3	11835.7	11359.5	12820.1	15016.9	16617.5	17355.7	...

2.17 Exports and Imports of Goods and Services, Detail

Thousand Million Korean won

	1970	1975	1977	1978	1979	1980	1981	1982	1983	1984	1985	1986
					Exports of Goods and Services							
1 Exports of merchandise, f.o.b.	272.3	2450.7	4792.0	6027.3	7055.9	10373.3	13881.1	14758.0	17980.0	21241.0	23044.9	29866.0
2 Transport and communication	33.0	232.7	437.1	567.2	863.4	1576.8	2213.2	2582.2	2775.8	2970.9	2768.4	2902.8
A In respect of merchandise imports	13.8	85.8	165.5	236.3	351.0	599.4	770.0	803.5	860.8	1019.9	967.6	895.1
B Other	19.2	146.9	271.6	330.9	512.4	977.4	1443.2	1778.7	1915.0	1951.0	1800.8	2007.7
3 Insurance service charges	3.4	17.3	41.7	48.8	65.1	80.9	70.2	73.2	74.7	92.6	75.1	98.8
A In respect of merchandise imports	1.9	7.8	11.5	15.6	21.2	30.3	39.7	40.7	44.6	52.8	48.1	51.6
B Other	1.5	9.5	30.2	33.2	43.9	50.6	30.5	32.5	30.1	39.8	27.0	47.2
4 Other commodities	15.8	60.3	347.5	455.0	392.9	479.3	690.5	997.4	968.9	1004.2	774.2	1201.5
5 Adjustments of merchandise exports to change-of-ownership basis	...	...	...	...	...	...	...	...	...	...	...	...
6 Direct purchases in the domestic market by non-residential households	6.8	67.7	171.4	181.8	129.2	198.8	274.8	318.3	368.1	430.2	559.1	1111.0
7 Direct purchases in the domestic market by extraterritorial bodies	57.7	26.1	58.5	55.6	57.0	56.3	61.7	73.2	78.2	90.7	105.2	160.5
Total Exports of Goods and Services	389.0	2854.8	5848.2	7335.7	8563.5	12765.4	17191.5	18802.3	22245.7	25829.6	27326.9	35340.6
					Imports of Goods and Services							
1 Imports of merchandise, c.i.f.	612.5	3461.6	5347.8	7364.7	9915.8	14203.7	17462.5	17880.0	20611.9	23559.2	24508.3	27711.0
A Imports of merchandise, f.o.b.	557.5	3208.8	5004.0	6874.6	9187.2	13021.4	16285.2	16705.5	19386.1	22065.8	23037.9	26174.2
B Transport of services on merchandise imports	52.9	243.5	330.5	471.8	703.7	1147.5	1131.1	1127.1	1173.7	1430.1	1408.2	1465.3
By residents	13.8	85.8	165.5	236.3	351.0	599.4	770.0	803.5	860.8	1019.9	967.6	895.1
By non-residents	39.1	157.7	165.0	235.5	352.7	548.1	361.1	323.6	312.9	410.2	440.6	570.2
C Insurance service charges on merchandise imports	2.1	9.3	13.3	18.3	24.9	34.8	46.2	47.4	52.1	63.3	62.2	71.5
By residents	1.9	7.8	11.5	15.6	21.2	30.3	39.7	40.8	44.6	52.8	48.1	51.6
By non-residents	0.2	1.5	1.8	2.7	3.7	4.5	6.5	6.6	7.5	10.5	14.1	19.9
2 Adjustments of merchandise imports to change-of-ownership basis	...	...	...	...	...	...	...	...	...	...	...	...
3 Other transport and communication	7.3	136.6	251.3	328.5	431.1	841.7	1114.5	1131.3	1123.2	1071.0	1177.2	1377.6
4 Other insurance service charges	1.6	23.9	35.0	48.0	43.6	16.8	71.6	91.1	59.1	60.7	84.5	78.5
5 Other commodities	25.2	67.9	141.5	264.1	340.1	509.9	800.1	720.3	930.9	1027.5	763.8	853.9
6 Direct purchases abroad by government	8.8	30.9	24.3	30.5	41.0	73.2	102.7	82.1	83.1	54.7	66.4	83.4
7 Direct purchases abroad by resident households	2.2	6.7	11.1	26.4	57.1	84.0	160.9	248.8	219.7	264.1	322.6	250.2
Total Imports of Goods and Services	657.6	3727.6	5811.0	8062.2	10828.7	15729.3	19712.3	20153.6	23027.9	26037.2	26922.8	30354.6
Balance of Goods and Services	-268.6	-872.8	37.2	-726.5	-2265.2	-2963.9	-2520.8	-1351.3	-782.2	-207.6	404.1	4986.0
Total Imports and Balance of Goods and Services	389.0	2854.8	5848.2	7335.7	8563.5	12765.4	17191.5	18802.3	22245.7	25829.6	27326.9	35340.6

Korea, Republic of

4.1 Derivation of Value Added by Kind of Activity, in Current Prices

Thousand Million Korean won

	1980 Gross Output	1980 Intermediate Consumption	1980 Value Added	1981 Gross Output	1981 Intermediate Consumption	1981 Value Added	1982 Gross Output	1982 Intermediate Consumption	1982 Value Added	1983 Gross Output	1983 Intermediate Consumption	1983 Value Added
						All Producers						
1 Agriculture, hunting, forestry and fishing	7604.1	2079.4	5524.7	10229.2	2786.9	7442.3	11096.9	3365.4	7731.5	12221.7	3929.1	8292.6
A Agriculture and hunting	...	...	4663.5	...	...	6352.4	...	...	6427.2	...	...	6746.4
B Forestry and logging	...	...	347.1	...	...	383.7	...	...	592.4	...	...	635.2
C Fishing	...	...	514.1	...	...	706.2	...	...	711.9	...	...	911.0
2 Mining and quarrying	746.4	226.4	520.0	1106.7	372.4	734.3	1134.6	362.0	772.6	1290.1	417.0	873.1
A Coal mining	...	...	238.7	...	...	365.9	...	...	415.4	...	...	414.7
B Crude petroleum and natural gas production	...	...	...	...	...	...	...	...	-	...	...	-
C Metal ore mining	...	...	36.7	...	...	47.3	...	...	31.1	...	...	32.1
D Other mining	...	...	244.6	...	...	321.1	...	...	326.1	...	...	426.3
3 Manufacturing	48083.2	36868.9	11214.3	59348.7	45634.9	13713.8	64439.2	49443.0	14996.2	71462.8	54161.1	17301.7
A Manufacture of food, beverages and tobacco	10419.7	8151.2	2268.5	12069.6	9258.2	2811.4	13685.9	10481.3	3204.6	14623.9	11034.2	3589.7
B Textile, wearing apparel and leather industries	8122.8	6142.9	1979.9	10379.9	7852.6	2527.3	10838.7	8203.1	2635.6	11958.7	8948.8	3009.9
C Manufacture of wood and wood products, including furniture	982.1	817.6	164.5	1084.5	901.6	182.9	977.0	795.8	181.2	1106.2	880.8	225.4
D Manufacture of paper and paper products, printing and publishing	1478.1	1060.0	418.1	1798.4	1298.0	500.4	1874.3	1381.9	492.4	2087.4	1533.7	553.7
E Manufacture of chemicals and chemical petroleum, coal, rubber and plastic products	11889.3	9297.9	2591.4	14566.9	11642.1	2924.8	15315.7	12132.6	3183.1	16720.8	13129.2	3591.6
F Manufacture of non-metallic mineral products, except products of petroleum and coal	1762.8	1205.8	557.0	2018.6	1392.4	626.2	2353.6	1646.1	707.5	2860.2	1963.2	897.0
G Basic metal industries	4977.4	4257.1	720.3	6785.6	5774.1	1011.5	7355.8	6199.8	1156.0	7972.7	6703.4	1269.3
H Manufacture of fabricated metal products, machinery and equipment	7808.4	5507.5	2300.9	9977.1	7071.8	2905.3	11307.5	8126.7	3180.8	13361.2	9477.7	3883.5
I Other manufacturing industries	642.6	428.9	213.7	668.1	444.1	224.0	730.7	475.7	255.0	771.7	490.1	281.6
4 Electricity, gas and water	1993.4	1207.2	786.2	2726.8	1731.7	995.1	3196.3	2037.3	1159.0	3549.8	2035.8	1514.0
A Electricity, gas and steam	...	...	745.7	...	...	930.3	...	...	1063.8	...	...	1387.4
B Water works and supply	...	...	40.5	...	...	64.8	...	...	95.2	...	...	126.6
5 Construction	7411.4	4261.6	3149.8	8010.1	4566.8	3443.3	10058.7	5837.2	4221.5	12014.7	6939.3	5075.4
6 Wholesale and retail trade, restaurants and hotels	7244.3	2276.8	4967.5	8904.0	2737.1	6166.9	9919.9	3013.1	6906.8	11155.0	3411.3	7743.7
A Wholesale and retail trade	...	...	4301.9	...	...	5363.9	...	...	5965.8	...	...	6663.5
B Restaurants and hotels	...	...	665.6	...	...	803.0	...	...	941.0	...	...	1080.2
Restaurants	...	...	466.0	...	...	551.2	...	...	638.8	...	...	736.9
Hotels and other lodging places	...	...	199.6	...	...	251.8	...	...	302.2	...	...	343.3
7 Transport, storage and communication	5597.3	2681.9	2915.4	7435.7	3542.0	3893.7	8705.1	4088.6	4616.5	9895.0	4617.6	5277.4
A Transport and storage	...	...	2364.0	...	...	3175.2	...	...	3559.5	...	...	4006.6
B Communication	...	...	551.4	...	...	718.5	...	...	1057.0	...	...	1270.8
8 Finance, insurance, real estate and business services	5316.1	1144.4	4171.7	5974.1	1493.7	4480.4	6252.3	1790.0	4462.3	7911.5	2038.4	5873.1
A Financial institutions	...	...	1712.4	...	...	1539.3	...	...	927.8	...	...	1445.4
B Insurance	...	...	211.0	...	...	272.1	...	...	300.1	...	...	443.8
C Real estate and business services	...	...	2248.3	...	...	2669.0	...	...	3148.4	...	...	3983.9
9 Community, social and personal services	1092.3	899.8	1192.5	2315.4	873.4	1442.0	2782.6	1022.1	1760.5	3277.1	1164.2	2112.9
Total, Industries	85888.5	51446.4	34442.1	106050.7	63738.9	42311.8	117585.6	70958.7	46626.9	132777.7	78713.8	54063.9
Producers of Government Services	4905.5	2081.9	2823.6	6183.4	2661.2	3522.2	7154.7	2928.2	4226.5	8020.6	3309.5	4711.1
Other Producers	1041.7	336.4	705.3	1358.5	438.4	920.1	1698.0	529.9	1168.1	1995.4	604.3	1391.1
Total	91835.7	53864.7	37971.0	113592.6	66838.5	46754.1	126438.3	74416.8	52021.5	142793.7	82627.6	60166.1
Less: Imputed bank service charge	...	-1191.4	1191.4	...	-1177.3	1177.3	...	-662.6	662.6	...	-1228.9	1228.9
Import duties	1135.3	...	1135.3	1446.9	...	1446.9	1553.8	...	1553.8	2065.7	...	2065.7
Value added tax	...	...	...	...	...	...	...	...	...	...	...	...
Total	92971.0	55056.1	37914.9	115039.5	68015.8	47023.7	127992.1	75079.4	52912.7	144859.4	83856.5	61002.9

Korea, Republic of

4.1 Derivation of Value Added by Kind of Activity, in Current Prices

Thousand Million Korean won

	1984			1985		
	Gross Output	Intermediate Consumption	Value Added	Gross Output	Intermediate Consumption	Value Added

All Producers

	Gross Output 1984	Interm. Cons. 1984	Value Added 1984	Gross Output 1985	Interm. Cons. 1985	Value Added 1985
1 Agriculture, hunting, forestry and fishing	13421.7	4240.5	9181.2	14625.7	4467.7	10158.0
A Agriculture and hunting	...	...	7620.5	...	...	8439.2
B Forestry and logging	...	...	667.4	...	...	625.4
C Fishing	...	...	893.3	...	...	1093.4
2 Mining and quarrying	1428.0	450.2	977.8	1631.0	532.8	1098.2
A Coal mining	...	...	453.2	...	...	505.6
B Crude petroleum and natural gas production	...	...	-	...	...	...
C Metal ore mining	...	...	32.1	...	...	30.0
D Other mining	...	...	492.5	...	...	562.6
3 Manufacturing	81810.1	61790.7	20019.4	86506.3	65221.2	21285.1
A Manufacture of food, beverages and tobacco	15604.4	11755.7	3848.7	16983.3	12884.8	4098.5
B Textile, wearing apparel and leather industries	13285.5	9868.6	3416.9	13594.7	10088.9	3505.8
C Manufacture of wood and wood products, including furniture	1202.2	962.2	240.0	1148.5	914.5	234.0
D Manufacture of paper and paper products, printing and publishing	2272.8	1685.4	587.4	2365.2	1746.7	618.6
E Manufacture of chemicals and chemical petroleum, coal, rubber and plastic products	18564.6	14487.8	4076.8	19664.4	15225.3	4439.1
F Manufacture of non-metallic mineral products, except products of petroleum and coal	3098.3	2098.0	1000.3	3132.0	2114.3	1017.7
G Basic metal industries	8855.0	7399.9	1455.1	9073.6	7572.6	1501.0
H Manufacture of fabricated metal products, machinery and equipment	17975.4	12912.8	5062.6	19533.9	14024.3	5509.6
I Other manufacturing industries	951.9	620.3	331.6	1010.6	649.9	360.7
4 Electricity, gas and water	3886.2	1948.3	1937.9	4213.8	1937.5	2276.3
A Electricity, gas and steam	...	...	1807.4	...	...	2143.3
B Water works and supply	...	...	130.5	...	...	133.0
5 Construction	13243.8	7560.8	5683.0	14242.6	7996.5	6246.1
6 Wholesale and retail trade, restaurants and hotels	12800.3	3928.2	8872.1	13958.1	4236.5	9721.6
A Wholesale and retail trade	...	...	7711.8	...	...	8452.0
B Restaurants and hotels	...	...	1160.3	...	...	1269.6
Restaurants	...	...	780.3	...	...	859.3
Hotels and other lodging places	...	...	380.0	...	...	410.3
7 Transport, storage and communication	10797.3	5007.7	5789.6	11412.6	5201.7	6210.9
A Transport and storage	...	...	4249.2	...	...	4505.2
B Communication	...	...	1540.4	...	...	1705.7
8 Finance, insurance, real estate and business services	9104.6	2403.0	6701.6	10654.4	2636.0	8018.4
A Financial institutions	...	...	1752.7	...	...	2272.9
B Insurance	...	...	498.8	...	...	723.0
C Real estate and business services	...	...	4450.1	...	...	5022.5
9 Community, social and personal services	3677.5	1270.9	2406.6	4049.4	1385.5	2663.9
Total, Industries	50169.5	88600.3	61569.2	61293.9	93615.4	67678.5
Producers of Government Services	8494.0	3433.8	5060.2	9648.0	3996.7	5651.3
Other Producers	2242.4	675.5	1566.9	2586.6	763.0	1823.6
Total	60905.9	92709.6	68196.3	73528.5	98375.1	75153.4
Less: Imputed bank service charge	...	-1509.8	1509.8	-	-1846.2	1846.2
Import duties	2180.2	...	2180.2	2203.5	-	2203.5
Value added tax	...	...	...	...	...	...
Total	63086.1	94219.4	68866.7	75732.0	00221.3	75510.7

Korea, Republic of

4.2 Derivation of Value Added by Kind of Activity, in Constant Prices

Thousand Million Korean won

At constant prices of: 1980

All Producers

		1980 Gross Output	1980 Intermediate Consumption	1980 Value Added	1981 Gross Output	1981 Intermediate Consumption	1981 Value Added	1982 Gross Output	1982 Intermediate Consumption	1982 Value Added	1983 Gross Output	1983 Intermediate Consumption	1983 Value Added
1	Agriculture, hunting, forestry and fishing	7604.1	2079.4	5524.7	9025.2	2265.5	6759.7	9348.1	2367.5	6980.6	10251.9	2815.9	7436.0
A	Agriculture and hunting	...	...	4663.5	...	...	5796.6	...	...	6051.6	...	...	6432.7
B	Forestry and logging	...	...	347.1	...	...	367.0	...	...	323.3	...	...	423.9
C	Fishing	...	...	514.1	...	...	596.1	...	...	605.7	...	...	579.4
2	Mining and quarrying	746.4	226.4	520.0	829.4	213.3	616.1	825.2	198.8	626.4	877.4	192.4	685.0
A	Coal mining	...	...	238.7	...	...	289.8	...	...	306.2	...	...	320.1
B	Crude petroleum and natural gas production	...	...	-	...	...	-	...	...	-	...	...	-
C	Metal ore mining	...	...	36.7	...	...	40.6	...	...	38.6	...	...	37.7
D	Other mining	...	...	244.6	...	...	285.7	...	...	281.6	...	...	327.2
3	Manufacturing	48083.2	36868.9	11214.3	50656.6	38597.7	12058.9	52972.2	40413.3	12558.9	58553.2	44457.6	14095.6
A	Manufacture of food, beverages and tobacco	...	...	2268.5	...	...	2339.0	...	...	2495.4	...	...	2727.8
B	Textile, wearing apparel and leather industries	...	...	1979.9	...	...	2212.2	...	...	2214.0	...	...	2364.6
C	Manufacture of wood and wood products, including furniture	...	...	164.5	...	...	171.8	...	...	162.8	...	...	186.4
D	Manufacture of paper and paper products, printing and publishing	...	...	418.1	...	...	446.2	...	...	450.2	...	...	497.2
E	Manufacture of chemicals and chemical petroleum, coal, rubber and plastic products	...	...	2591.4	...	...	2562.8	...	...	2573.2	...	...	2860.4
F	Manufacture of non-metallic mineral products, except products of petroleum and coal	...	...	557.0	...	...	550.4	...	...	601.5	...	...	724.8
G	Basic metal industries	...	...	720.3	...	...	863.0	...	...	950.2	...	...	1053.6
H	Manufacture of fabricated metal products, machinery and equipment	...	...	2300.9	...	...	2707.1	...	...	2894.5	...	...	3450.2
I	Other manufacturing industries	...	...	213.7	...	...	206.4	...	...	217.1	...	...	230.6
4	Electricity, gas and water	1993.4	1207.2	786.2	2157.6	1313.2	844.4	2302.5	1421.0	881.5	2635.5	1504.4	1131.1
A	Electricity, gas and steam	...	...	745.7	...	...	794.5	...	...	830.3	...	...	1061.1
B	Water works and supply	...	...	40.5	...	...	49.9	...	...	51.2	...	...	70.0
5	Construction	7411.4	4261.6	3149.8	6998.5	3963.2	3035.3	8416.7	4821.8	3594.9	9949.8	5674.2	4275.6
6	Wholesale and retail trade, restaurants and hotels	7244.3	2276.8	4967.5	7719.7	2366.0	5353.7	8082.5	2445.5	5637.0	8836.4	2694.5	6141.9
A	Wholesale and retail trade	...	...	4301.9	...	...	4690.2	...	...	4923.5	...	...	5347.7
B	Restaurants and hotels	...	...	665.6	...	...	663.5	...	...	713.5	...	...	794.2
	Restaurants	...	...	466.0	...	...	448.6	...	...	483.8	...	...	540.5
	Hotels and other lodging places	...	...	199.6	...	...	214.9	...	...	229.7	...	...	253.7
7	Transport, storage and communication	5597.3	2681.9	2915.4	5994.1	2921.8	3072.3	6566.7	3278.6	3288.1	7244.8	3576.4	3668.4
A	Transport and storage	...	...	2364.0	...	...	2473.1	...	...	2720.5	...	...	2989.5
B	Communication	...	...	551.4	...	...	599.2	...	...	567.6	...	...	678.9
8	Finance, insurance, real estate and business services	5316.1	1144.4	4171.7	5415.6	1287.6	4128.0	5865.2	1400.9	4464.3	6421.5	1475.7	4945.8
A	Financial institutions	...	...	1712.4	...	...	1573.1	...	...	1656.0	...	...	1777.5
B	Insurance	...	...	211.0	...	...	222.3	...	...	296.2	...	...	334.0
C	Real estate and business services	...	...	2240.0	...	...	2332.6	...	...	2512.1	...	...	2834.3
9	Community, social and personal services	1892.3	699.8	1192.5	1935.9	725.5	1210.4	2082.5	778.3	1304.2	2316.4	863.6	1452.8
	Total, Industries	85888.5	51446.4	34442.1	90732.6	53653.8	37078.8	96461.6	57125.7	39335.9	107086.9	63254.7	43832.2
	Producers of Government Services	4905.5	2081.9	2823.6	5205.3	2271.2	2934.1	5350.0	2327.4	3022.6	5713.6	2622.8	3090.8
	Other Producers	1041.7	336.4	705.3	1103.6	364.3	739.3	1191.9	398.9	793.0	1301.2	443.5	857.7
	Total	91835.7	53864.7	37971.0	97041.5	56289.3	40752.2	103003.5	59852.0	43151.5	114101.7	66321.0	47780.7
	Less: Imputed bank service charge	...	-1191.4	1191.4	...	-1277.2	1277.2	...	-1444.3	1444.3	...	-1593.1	1593.1
	Import duties	1135.3	...	1135.3	1248.3	...	1248.3	1328.5	...	1328.5	1556.1	...	1556.1
	Value added tax	...	...	...	...	...	...	...	...	...	...	...	...
	Total	92971.0	55056.1	37914.9	98289.8	57566.5	40723.3	104332.0	61296.3	43035.7	115657.8	67914.1	47743.7

Korea, Republic of

4.2 Derivation of Value Added by Kind of Activity, in Constant Prices

Thousand Million Korean won

At constant prices of: 1980

All Producers

		1984 Gross Output	1984 Intermediate Consumption	1984 Value Added	1985 Gross Output	1985 Intermediate Consumption	1985 Value Added
1	Agriculture, hunting, forestry and fishing	10397.1	2943.9	7453.2	10858.5	3049.3	7809.2
	A Agriculture and hunting	...	...	6369.0	...	...	6704.1
	B Forestry and logging	...	...	456.9	...	...	435.5
	C Fishing	...	...	627.3	...	...	669.6
2	Mining and quarrying	955.7	213.3	742.4	1019.3	226.4	792.9
	A Coal mining	...	...	345.3	...	...	364.3
	B Crude petroleum and natural gas production	...	...	-	...	...	...
	C Metal ore mining	...	...	39.3	...	...	38.0
	D Other mining	...	...	357.8	...	...	390.6
3	Manufacturing	65887.9	49699.9	16188.0	68488.8	51683.8	16805.0
	A Manufacture of food, beverages and tobacco	...	...	2979.4	...	...	3141.4
	B Textile, wearing apparel and leather industries	...	...	2476.6	...	...	2530.3
	C Manufacture of wood and wood products, including furniture	...	...	195.3	...	...	182.5
	D Manufacture of paper and paper products, printing and publishing	...	...	525.7	...	...	549.3
	E Manufacture of chemicals and chemical petroleum, coal, rubber and plastic products	...	...	3246.0	...	...	3408.6
	F Manufacture of non-metallic mineral products, except products of petroleum and coal	...	...	793.4	...	...	804.4
	G Basic metal industries	...	...	1152.4	...	...	1178.9
	H Manufacture of fabricated metal products, machinery and equipment	...	...	4542.1	...	...	4736.8
	I Other manufacturing industries	...	...	277.1	...	...	272.8
4	Electricity, gas and water	2895.2	1474.9	1420.3	3120.3	1422.7	1697.6
	A Electricity, gas and steam	...	...	1358.3	...	...	1632.9
	B Water works and supply	...	...	62.0	...	...	64.7
5	Construction	10637.2	6097.7	4539.5	11160.1	6410.9	4749.2
6	Wholesale and retail trade, restaurants and hotels	9683.7	2967.7	6716.0	10223.1	3115.7	7107.4
	A Wholesale and retail trade	...	...	5887.3	...	...	6228.8
	B Restaurants and hotels	...	...	828.7	...	...	878.6
	Restaurants	...	...	548.8	...	...	...
	Hotels and other lodging places	...	...	279.9	...	...	...
7	Transport, storage and communication	7755.1	3780.9	3974.2	8089.3	3919.1	4170.2
	A Transport and storage	...	...	3115.5	...	...	3227.1
	B Communication	...	...	858.7	...	...	943.1
8	Finance, insurance, real estate and business services	7193.6	1725.1	5468.5	8196.8	1883.8	6313.0
	A Financial institutions	...	...	2067.8	...	...	2556.8
	B Insurance	...	...	374.4	...	...	513.3
	C Real estate and business services	...	...	3026.3	...	...	3242.9
9	Community, social and personal services	2538.5	948.4	1590.1	2716.3	1015.9	1700.4
	Total, Industries	17944.0	69851.8	48092.2	23872.5	72727.6	51144.9
	Producers of Government Services	5801.4	2689.0	3112.4	6289.0	3122.0	3167.0
	Other Producers	1419.5	493.7	925.8	1567.6	557.1	1010.5
	Total	25164.9	73034.5	52130.4	31729.1	76406.7	55322.4
	Less: Imputed bank service charge	...	-1853.6	1853.6	...	-2199.7	2199.7
	Import duties	1595.7	...	1595.7	1551.7	...	1551.7
	Value added tax	...	...	...	...	...	...
	Total	26760.6	74888.1	51872.5	33280.8	78606.4	54674.4

Korea, Republic of

4.3 Cost Components of Value Added

Thousand Million Korean won

	1980						1981					
	Compensation of Employees	Capital Consumption	Net Operating Surplus	Indirect Taxes	Less: Subsidies Received	Value Added	Compensation of Employees	Capital Consumption	Net Operating Surplus	Indirect Taxes	Less: Subsidies Received	Value Added
	All Producers											
1 Agriculture, hunting, forestry and fishing	751.8	158.4	4590.2	24.3	...	5524.7	907.7	207.3	6296.6	30.7	...	7442.3
2 Mining and quarrying	369.7	58.1	157.1	-64.9	...	520.0	433.3	92.7	250.3	-42.0	...	734.3
3 Manufacturing	4334.9	1286.7	3226.8	2365.9	...	11214.3	5296.9	1585.5	3956.8	2874.6	...	13713.8
A Manufacture of food, beverages and tobacco	514.5	135.1	396.4	1222.5	...	2268.5	619.9	166.2	488.0	1537.3	...	2811.4
B Textile, wearing apparel and leather industries	1012.7	212.9	615.9	138.4	...	1979.9	1312.0	266.6	776.5	172.2	...	2527.3
C Manufacture of wood and wood products, including furniture	125.4	20.5	-8.4	27.0	...	164.5	123.3	20.2	6.4	33.0	...	182.9
D Manufacture of paper and paper products, printing and publishing	232.5	34.4	125.0	26.2	...	418.1	277.3	41.2	149.3	32.6	...	500.4
E Manufacture of chemicals and chemical petroleum, coal, rubber and plastic products	749.7	314.5	903.2	624.0	...	2591.4	829.1	362.1	1051.8	681.8	...	2924.8
F Manufacture of non-metallic mineral products, except products of petroleum and coal	241.5	93.9	184.5	37.1	...	557.0	272.6	104.0	203.9	45.7	...	626.2
G Basic metal industries	247.8	205.1	247.2	20.2	...	720.3	352.7	287.2	346.2	25.4	...	1011.5
H Manufacture of fabricated metal products, machinery and equipment	1107.9	259.0	680.1	253.9	...	2300.9	1403.4	326.2	848.9	326.8	...	2905.3
I Other manufacturing industries	102.9	11.3	82.9	16.6	...	213.7	106.6	11.8	85.8	19.8	...	224.0
4 Electricity, gas and water	145.0	155.2	444.3	41.7	...	786.2	158.9	189.1	594.4	52.7	...	995.1
5 Construction	1832.7	96.8	917.3	303.0	...	3149.8	1898.1	114.2	1053.4	377.6	...	3443.3
6 Wholesale and retail trade, restaurants and hotels	1363.2	193.9	3395.0	15.4	...	4967.5	1650.5	235.9	4250.4	30.1	...	6166.9
7 Transport, storage and communication	1348.4	488.8	894.7	183.5	...	2915.4	1719.3	614.1	1310.0	250.3	...	3893.7
8 Finance, insurance, real estate and business services	1125.1	290.0	2348.8	407.8	...	4171.7	1493.0	363.6	2144.2	479.6	...	4480.4
9 Community, social and personal services	600.5	38.6	431.1	122.3	...	1192.5	724.4	48.9	516.3	152.4	...	1442.0
Total, Industries	11871.3	2766.5	16405.3	3399.0	...	34442.1	14282.1	3451.3	20372.4	4206.0	...	42311.8
Producers of Government Services	2735.7	86.2	-	1.7	...	2823.6	3413.0	107.4	-	1.8	...	3522.2
Other Producers	659.2	43.5	-	2.6	...	705.3	858.3	58.8	-	3.0	...	920.1
Total	15266.2	2896.2	16405.3	3403.3	...	37971.0	18553.4	3617.5	20372.4	4210.8	...	46754.1
Less: Imputed bank service charge	...	...	1191.4	...		1191.4	...	...	1177.3	...		1177.3
Import duties	...	...	...	1135.3		1135.3	...	...	...	1446.9		1446.9
Value added tax	...	...	...	...		...	...	...	...	...		...
Total a	15266.2	2896.2	15213.9	4538.6		37914.9	18553.4	3617.5	19195.1	5657.7		47023.7

	1982						1983					
	Compensation of Employees	Capital Consumption	Net Operating Surplus	Indirect Taxes	Less: Subsidies Received	Value Added	Compensation of Employees	Capital Consumption	Net Operating Surplus	Indirect Taxes	Less: Subsidies Received	Value Added
	All Producers											
1 Agriculture, hunting, forestry and fishing	974.4	236.8	6483.7	36.6	...	7731.5	1188.2	385.5	6678.7	40.2	...	8292.6
2 Mining and quarrying	445.4	147.1	210.8	30.7	...	772.6	407.8	166.3	213.4	4.4	...	873.1
3 Manufacturing	5717.2	1754.4	4260.7	3263.9	...	14996.2	6641.6	1979.8	4883.2	3797.1	...	17301.7
A Manufacture of food, beverages and tobacco	713.4	205.4	464.1	1821.7	...	3204.6	794.1	202.4	525.6	2067.6	...	3589.7

Korea, Republic of

4.3 Cost Components of Value Added
(Continued)

Thousand Million Korean won

	1982						1983					
	Compensation of Employees	Capital Consumption	Net Operating Surplus	Indirect Taxes	Less: Subsidies Received	Value Added	Compensation of Employees	Capital Consumption	Net Operating Surplus	Indirect Taxes	Less: Subsidies Received	Value Added
B Textile, wearing apparel and leather industries	1354.4	276.9	806.8	197.5	...	2635.6	1550.5	310.0	909.0	240.4	...	3009.9
C Manufacture of wood and wood products, including furniture	107.1	17.4	19.4	37.3	...	181.2	135.3	21.4	23.0	45.7	...	225.4
D Manufacture of paper and paper products, printing and publishing	269.2	40.1	145.3	37.8	...	492.4	296.1	46.1	165.5	46.0	...	553.7
E Manufacture of chemicals and chemical petroleum, coal, rubber and plastic products	912.0	403.0	1188.5	679.6	...	3183.1	1060.5	453.3	1330.8	747.0	...	3591.6
F Manufacture of non-metallic mineral products, except products of petroleum and coal	304.8	117.7	231.5	53.5	...	707.5	386.7	150.0	294.8	65.5	...	897.0
G Basic metal industries	407.8	325.4	392.6	30.2	...	1156.0	454.3	352.9	426.2	35.9	...	1269.3
H Manufacture of fabricated metal products, machinery and equipment	1529.6	355.4	916.6	379.2	...	3180.8	1835.6	429.5	1104.8	513.6	...	3883.5
I Other manufacturing industries	118.9	13.1	95.9	27.1	...	255.0	128.5	14.2	103.5	35.4	...	281.6
4 Electricity, gas and water	177.8	305.9	612.6	62.7	...	1159.0	287.0	384.2	766.7	76.1	...	1514.0
5 Construction	2332.4	144.8	1299.1	445.2	...	4221.5	2835.0	166.7	1529.6	544.1	...	5075.4
6 Wholesale and retail trade, restaurants and hotels	1830.3	260.2	4707.9	108.4	...	6906.8	2077.5	295.0	5313.2	58.0	...	7743.7
7 Transport, storage and communication	1891.2	842.1	1583.1	300.1	...	4616.5	2463.6	953.2	1489.9	370.7	...	5277.4
8 Finance, insurance, real estate and business services	1823.1	435.4	1525.0	678.8	...	4462.3	2198.1	567.4	2160.5	947.1	...	5873.1
9 Community, social and personal services	897.3	59.9	608.6	194.7	...	1760.5	1090.9	72.5	715.3	234.2	...	2112.9
Total, Industries	16089.1	4186.6	21291.5	5059.7	...	46626.9	19279.7	4970.6	23750.5	6063.1	...	54063.9
Producers of Government Services	4093.9	130.8	-	1.8	...	4226.5	4573.4	135.5	-	2.2	...	4711.1
Other Producers	1091.6	72.8	-	3.7	...	1168.1	1301.1	85.1	-	4.9	...	1391.1
Total	21274.6	4390.2	21291.5	5065.2	...	52021.5	25154.2	5191.2	23750.5	6070.2	...	60166.1
Less: Imputed bank service charge	...	...	662.6	...	...	662.6	...	...	1228.9	...	...	1228.9
Import duties	...	...	...	1553.8	...	1553.8	...	...	...	2065.7	...	2065.7
Value added tax	...	...	...	...	...	...	...	...	...	...	...	...
Total a	21274.6	4390.2	20628.9	6619.0	...	52912.7	25154.2	5191.2	22521.6	8135.9	...	61002.9

	1984						1985					
	Compensation of Employees	Capital Consumption	Net Operating Surplus	Indirect Taxes	Less: Subsidies Received	Value Added	Compensation of Employees	Capital Consumption	Net Operating Surplus	Indirect Taxes	Less: Subsidies Received	Value Added
				All Producers								
1 Agriculture, hunting, forestry and fishing	1217.2	410.9	7507.4	45.7	...	9181.2	1325.5	452.4	8329.7	50.4	...	10158.0
2 Mining and quarrying	565.6	192.0	224.8	-4.6	...	977.8	645.4	222.5	234.5	-4.2	...	1098.2
3 Manufacturing	7788.3	2419.4	5672.4	4139.3	...	20019.4	8268.8	2571.9	6018.7	4425.7	...	21285.1
A Manufacture of food, beverages and tobacco	900.2	221.0	514.5	2213.0	...	3848.7	986.6	232.3	545.6	2333.9	...	4098.5
B Textile, wearing apparel and leather industries	1714.3	411.0	1036.5	255.1	...	3416.9	1756.5	418.5	1057.9	272.9	...	3505.8
C Manufacture of wood and wood products, including furniture	138.6	21.1	31.1	49.2	...	240.0	132.1	20.8	28.7	52.5	...	234.0
D Manufacture of paper and paper products, printing and publishing	294.0	51.0	193.4	49.0	...	587.4	310.8	53.8	200.8	53.2	...	618.6
E Manufacture of chemicals and chemical petroleum, coal, rubber and plastic products	1148.0	543.2	1544.1	841.5	...	4076.8	1237.9	588.8	1649.0	963.5	...	4439.1
F Manufacture of non-metallic mineral products, except products of petroleum and coal	436.4	148.6	345.2	70.1	...	1000.3	440.0	153.2	348.8	75.7	...	1017.7
G Basic metal industries	504.4	450.7	461.6	38.4	...	1455.1	521.4	467.5	470.8	41.3	...	1501.0
H Manufacture of fabricated metal products, machinery and equipment	2500.9	553.8	1422.4	585.5	...	5062.6	2722.6	616.2	1584.6	586.3	...	5509.6
I Other manufacturing industries	151.5	19.0	123.6	37.5	...	331.6	160.9	20.7	132.7	46.4	...	360.7
4 Electricity, gas and water	241.6	445.2	1169.9	81.2	...	1937.9	329.7	533.7	1325.2	87.7	...	2276.3

Korea, Republic of

4.3 Cost Components of Value Added
(Continued)

Thousand Million Korean won

	1984						1985					
	Compensation of Employees	Capital Consumption	Net Operating Surplus	Indirect Taxes	Less: Subsidies Received	Value Added	Compensation of Employees	Capital Consumption	Net Operating Surplus	Indirect Taxes	Less: Subsidies Received	Value Added
5 Construction	3270.0	182.1	1644.3	586.6	...	5683.0	3667.8	193.2	1755.2	629.9	...	6246.1
6 Wholesale and retail trade, restaurants and hotels	2387.0	341.9	6162.2	-19.0	...	8872.1	2583.3	369.5	6686.8	82.0	...	9721.6
7 Transport, storage and communication	2703.8	1118.1	1550.2	417.5	...	5789.6	2839.7	1231.1	1643.6	496.5	...	6210.9
8 Finance, insurance, real estate and business services	2344.3	637.8	2689.1	1030.4	...	6701.6	2736.1	731.8	3470.5	1080.0	...	8018.4
9 Community, social and personal services	1272.2	83.9	795.4	255.1	...	2406.6	1388.1	91.3	873.7	310.8	...	2663.9
Total, Industries	21790.0	5831.3	27415.7	6532.2	...	61569.2	23784.4	6397.4	30337.9	7158.8	...	67678.5
Producers of Government Services	4914.4	143.7	-	2.1	...	5060.2	5499.0	150.6	-	1.7	...	5651.3
Other Producers	1466.6	95.2	-	5.1	...	1566.9	1707.8	109.3	-	6.5	...	1823.6
Total	28171.0	6070.2	27415.7	6539.4	...	68196.3	30991.2	6657.3	30337.9	7167.0	...	75153.4
Less: Imputed bank service charge	...	...	1509.8	...	...	1509.8	...	...	1846.2	...	...	1846.2
Import duties	...	...	...	2180.2	...	2180.2	...	...	...	2203.5	...	2203.5
Value added tax	...	...	...	...	...	...	...	...	...	...	...	...
Total [a]	28171.0	6070.2	25905.9	8719.6	...	68866.7	30991.2	6657.3	28491.7	9370.5	...	75510.7

a) Column 4 refers to indirect taxes less subsidies received.

Kuwait

Source. Reply to the United Nations National Accounts Questionnaire from the Central Office of Statistics, Ministry of Planning, Kuwait City. Official estimates are published by the same Office in 'National Accounts Statistics' and 'National Accounts and Input-output Tables of Kuwait', 1976.

General note. The estimates shown in the following tables have been prepared in accordance with the United Nations System of National Accounts so far as the existing data would permit.

1.1 Expenditure on the Gross Domestic Product, in Current Prices

Million Kuwaiti dinars

	1970	1975	1977	1978	1979	1980	1981	1982	1983	1984	1985	1986
1 Government final consumption expenditure	139	386	586	616	764	865	993	1197	1298	1357	1457	1445
2 Private final consumption expenditure	396	756	1363	1478	1780	2388	2664	3317	2796	2879	2668	2585
3 Gross capital formation	124	444	945	863	934	1078	1162	1565	1507	1320	1259	990
A Increase in stocks	-2	26	129	69	144	105	89	129	-18	14	-37	-
B Gross fixed capital formation	126	418	815	794	790	973	1073	1436	1525	1306	1296	990
Residential buildings									...	...	...	...
Non-residential buildings	63	155	336	421	508	607	636	816	...	...	...	...
Other construction and land improvement etc.									...	...	...	...
Other	63	263	479	373	282	366	437	620	...	...	...	...
4 Exports of goods and services	614	2806	2918	3008	5333	6065	4855	3386	3596	3862	3463	2442
5 Less: Imports of goods and services	248	907	1760	1700	1971	2655	2688	3253	3063	3037	2929	2464
Statistical discrepancy	1	-1	...	-1	-1	...	...	...	...	...	...	...
Equals: Gross Domestic Product	1026	3485	4052	4264	6840	7741	6986	6212	6134	6381	5918	4998

1.2 Expenditure on the Gross Domestic Product, in Constant Prices

Million Kuwaiti dinars

	1970	1975	1977	1978	1979	1980	1981	1982	1983	1984	1985	1986
					At constant prices of:1984							
1 Government final consumption expenditure	461	750	974	1009	1041	1108	1100	1255	1316	1357	1401	1318
2 Private final consumption expenditure	970	1286	2049	2075	2333	2927	3044	3514	2830	2879	2632	2524
3 Gross capital formation	284	637	1302	1113	1098	1150	1160	1499	1461	1320	1259	917
A Increase in stocks	-5	38	165	88	172	114	91	130	-18	14	-37	-
B Gross fixed capital formation	289	599	1137	1025	926	1036	1069	1369	1479	1306	1296	917
4 Exports of goods and services	8898	6497	6339	6800	8200	5667	4172	2968	3515	3862	3520	3953
5 Less: Imports of goods and services	491	1204	2092	2059	2247	2883	2688	2910	2971	3037	2942	2245
Statistical discrepancy	-255	-140	-550	-326	-616	-182	-482	-722	-88	-	81	46
Equals: Gross Domestic Product	9867	7826	8022	8612	9809	7787	6306	5604	6063	6381	5951	6513

1.3 Cost Components of the Gross Domestic Product

Million Kuwaiti dinars

	1970	1975	1977	1978	1979	1980	1981	1982	1983	1984	1985	1986
1 Indirect taxes, net	...	...	37	25	33	41	56	22	-16	-14	-2	...
A Indirect taxes	...	...	56	49	58	72	92	99	86	74	68	...
B Less: Subsidies	...	...	19	24	25	31	36	77	102	88	70	...
2 Consumption of fixed capital	...	...	129	169	217	263	290	337	346	403	401	...
3 Compensation of employees paid by resident producers to:	...	...	688	792	973	1197	1387	1623	1779	1854	1852	...
4 Operating surplus	...	...	3197	3278	5617	6240	5253	4230	4025	4138	3667	...
Equals: Gross Domestic Product	...	...	4051	4264	6840	7741	6986	6212	6134	6381	5918	...

Kuwait

1.7 External Transactions on Current Account, Summary

Million Kuwaiti dinars

	1970	1975	1977	1978	1979	1980	1981	1982	1983	1984	1985	1986
Payments to the Rest of the World
1 Imports of goods and services	248	907	1760	1700	1971	2655	2688	3253	3063	3037	2929	2464
2 Factor income to the rest of the world	212	106	57	81	115	173	206	217	197	248	200	175
3 Current transfers to the rest of the world	54	310	358	339	356	427	463	438	452	408	473	368
4 Surplus of the nation on current transactions	203	1813	1306	1686	3879	4293	3841	1404	1542	1887	1448	1790
Payments to the Rest of the World and Surplus of the Nation on Current Transactions	717	3136	3481	3806	6321	7548	7198	5312	5254	5580	5050	4797
Receipts From The Rest of the World
1 Exports of goods and services	614	2806	2918	3008	5333	6065	4855	3386	3596	3862	3463	2442
2 Factor income from rest of the world	103	330	563	798	988	1483	2343	1926	1658	1718	1587	2355
3 Current transfers from rest of the world	...	...	...	...	...	...	...	...	...	...	...	...
Receipts from the Rest of the World on Current Transactions	717	3136	3481	3806	6321	7548	7198	5312	5254	5580	5050	4797

1.10 Gross Domestic Product by Kind of Activity, in Current Prices

Million Kuwaiti dinars

	1970	1975	1977	1978	1979	1980	1981	1982	1983	1984	1985	1986
1 Agriculture, hunting, forestry and fishing	2	6	8	10	12	14	24	29	28	35	39	52
2 Mining and quarrying	619	2459	2483	2526	4415	5089	4121	2765	3040	3403	2985	1843
3 Manufacturing	43	195	241	283	567	427	415	308	375	300	377	555
4 Electricity, gas and water [a]	7	13	21	24	26	-74	-167	-231	-221	-178	-151	-94
5 Construction	28	74	158	176	219	278	263	262	274	272	198	156
6 Wholesale and retail trade, restaurants and hotels	85	221	371	401	434	596	664	768	546	574	549	514
7 Transport, storage and communication	29	60	77	89	115	181	215	291	275	265	240	250
8 Finance, insurance, real estate and business services	78	150	248	283	429	509	578	1022	736	587	493	470
9 Community, social and personal services	18	34	43	47	51	80	92	98	101	104	104	101
Total, Industries	910	3212	3650	3839	6268	7100	6205	5312	5154	5362	4834	3847
Producers of Government Services	106	242	343	369	506	558	683	794	883	924	996	1063
Other Producers	3	7	11	14	17	22	20	23	24	31	28	29
Subtotal	1019	3461	4004	4222	6791	7680	6908	6129	6061	6317	5858	4939
Less: Imputed bank service charge	...	...	...	...	...	...	...	...	...	...	...	...
Plus: Import duties	7	24	48	42	49	61	78	83	73	64	60	59
Plus: Value added tax	...	...	...	...	...	...	...	...	...	...	...	...
Equals: Gross Domestic Product	1026	3485	4052	4264	6840	7741	6986	6212	6134	6381	5918	4998

a) Beginning 1980, the cost of fuel (natural gas, crude petroleum and gas-oil) consumed in the production of electricity and water has been taken into account as intermediate consumption in estimating the value added of item 'Electricity, gas and water'.

1.11 Gross Domestic Product by Kind of Activity, in Constant Prices

Million Kuwaiti dinars

	1970	1975	1977	1978	1979	1980	1981	1982	1983	1984	1985	1986
At constant prices of: 1984
1 Agriculture, hunting, forestry and fishing	12	12	11	13	12	13	21	24	28	35	41	54
2 Mining and quarrying	8735	6096	5758	6231	7300	4866	3298	2406	3117	3403	3103	3768
3 Manufacturing	132	255	281	300	298	294	285	310	308	300	314	318
4 Electricity, gas and water	-30	-61	-79	-92	-112	-117	-129	-150	-161	-178	-196	-215
5 Construction	69	125	238	247	287	341	301	278	277	272	195	152
6 Wholesale and retail trade, restaurants and hotels	207	364	534	550	561	714	745	811	555	574	546	507
7 Transport, storage and communication	68	97	112	124	151	225	251	310	277	265	236	233
8 Finance, insurance, real estate and business services	211	274	353	390	415	461	523	556	560	588	587	580
9 Community, social and personal services	55	75	89	85	82	116	120	111	103	103	104	100

Kuwait

1.11 Gross Domestic Product by Kind of Activity, in Constant Prices
(Continued)

Million Kuwaiti dinars

	1970	1975	1977	1978	1979	1980	1981	1982	1983	1984	1985	1986
				At constant prices of:1984								
Total, Industries	9459	7237	7277	7848	8995	6913	5415	4656	5064	5362	4930	5497
Producers of Government Services	385	542	664	687	732	776	784	847	903	924	934	937
Other Producers	8	16	24	25	27	32	29	26	24	31	27	26
Subtotal	9852	7795	7965	8560	9754	7721	6228	5529	5991	6317	5891	6459
Less: Imputed bank service charge	...	...	...	...	...	...	...	...	...	...	...	...
Plus: Import duties	15	32	57	52	56	66	78	75	71	64	60	54
Plus: Value added tax	...	...	...	...	...	...	...	...	...	...	...	...
Equals: Gross Domestic Product	9867	7827	8022	8612	9810	7787	6306	5604	6062	6381	5951	6513

1.12 Relations Among National Accounting Aggregates

Million Kuwaiti dinars

	1970	1975	1977	1978	1979	1980	1981	1982	1983	1984	1985	1986
Gross Domestic Product	1026	3485	4051	4264	6840	7741	6986	6212	6134	6381	5918	4998
Plus: Net factor income from the rest of the world	-110	224	506	717	873	1310	2137	1709	1461	1470	1387	2180
Factor income from the rest of the world	103	330	563	798	988	1483	2343	1926	1658	1718	...	...
Less: Factor income to the rest of the world	213	106	57	81	115	173	206	217	197	248	...	...
Equals: Gross National Product	916	3709	4557	4981	7713	9051	9123	7921	7595	7851	7305	7178
Less: Consumption of fixed capital	58	93	129	169	217	263	290	337	345	403	401	421
Equals: National Income	858	3616	4428	4812	7496	8788	8833	7584	7250	7448	6904	6757
Plus: Net current transfers from the rest of the world	-54	-310	-358	-339	-356	-427	-463	-438	-452	-408	-473	-368
Current transfers from the rest of the world	...	...	...	...	...	...	...	...	...	...	...	...
Less: Current transfers to the rest of the world	54	310	358	339	356	427	463	438	452	408	473	368
Equals: National Disposable Income	804	3306	4070	4473	7140	8361	8370	7146	6798	7040	6431	6389
Less: Final consumption	535	1142	1949	2093	2544	3253	3657	4514	4094	4235	4126	4030
Equals: Net Saving	269	2164	2121	2380	4596	5108	4713	2632	2703	2805	2305	2359
Less: Surplus of the nation on current transactions	203	1813	1306	1686	3879	4293	3841	1404	1541	1887	1448	1790
Equals: Net Capital Formation	66	351	815	694	717	815	872	1228	1162	918	857	569

2.1 Government Final Consumption Expenditure by Function, in Current Prices

Million Kuwaiti dinars

	1970	1975	1977	1978	1979	1980	1981	1982	1983	1984	1985	1986
1 General public services												
2 Defence	60	195	314	337	362	412	467	571	636	673	749	708
3 Public order and safety												
4 Education	33	90	127	130	190	197	225	269	283	295	316	332
5 Health	16	39	56	59	73	102	126	159	168	173	182	187
6 Social security and welfare	2	6	9	9	17	22	26	30	29	30	31	34
7 Housing and community amenities	7	18	23	27	35	43	51	60	70	75	65	69
8 Recreational, cultural and religious affairs	6	16	20	23	34	33	36	42	47	51	52	53
9 Economic services	15	22	37	35	53	56	62	66	65	60	62	62
10 Other functions	...	...	...	...	...	...	...	...	...	...	...	...
Total Government Final Consumption Expenditure	139	386	586	620	764	865	993	1197	1298	1356	1457	1445

Kuwait

2.2 Government Final Consumption Expenditure by Function, in Constant Prices

Million Kuwaiti dinars

	1970	1975	1977	1978	1979	1980	1981	1982	1983	1984	1985	1986
	\multicolumn{12}{c	}{At constant prices of:1984}
1 General public services												
2 Defence	208	382	498	510	501	517	469	569	638	673	707	623
3 Public order and safety												
4 Education	113	183	237	249	264	280	287	310	309	295	306	310
5 Health	49	72	88	97	98	128	146	164	165	173	173	169
6 Social security and welfare	7	13	16	16	23	25	29	31	27	30	31	34
7 Housing and community amenities	24	34	43	46	48	54	63	69	74	74	75	75
8 Recreational, cultural and religious affairs	21	30	36	37	47	43	46	49	49	51	51	51
9 Economic services	39	36	56	54	60	61	60	63	54	60	58	56
10 Other functions	...	...	...	...	...	...	...	...	...	...	...	...
Total Government Final Consumption Expenditure	461	750	974	1009	1041	1108	1100	1255	1316	1356	1401	1318

4.1 Derivation of Value Added by Kind of Activity, in Current Prices

Million Kuwaiti dinars

	1980 Gross Output	1980 Intermediate Consumption	1980 Value Added	1981 Gross Output	1981 Intermediate Consumption	1981 Value Added	1982 Gross Output	1982 Intermediate Consumption	1982 Value Added	1983 Gross Output	1983 Intermediate Consumption	1983 Value Added
	\multicolumn{12}{c	}{All Producers}
1 Agriculture, hunting, forestry and fishing	27	13	14	37	13	24	45	16	29	45	17	28
A Agriculture and hunting	24	13	11	29	12	17	38	15	23	39	16	23
B Forestry and logging	...	...	...	...	...	...	...	...	...	...	...	...
C Fishing	3	-	3	8	1	7	7	1	6	6	1	5
2 Mining and quarrying	5134	45	5089	4165	44	4121	2819	54	2765	3096	56	3040
A Coal mining	...	...	...	...	...	...	...	...	...	...	...	...
B Crude petroleum and natural gas production	5125	39	5086	4153	38	4115	2816	53	2763	3093	55	3038
C Metal ore mining	...	...	...	...	...	...	...	...	...	...	...	...
D Other mining	9	6	3	12	6	6	3	1	2	3	1	2
3 Manufacturing	1702	1275	427	1759	1344	415	2084	1776	308	2112	1737	375
A Manufacture of food, beverages and tobacco	78	49	29	79	50	29	90	58	32	96	58	38
B Textile, wearing apparel and leather industries	33	10	23	31	10	21	35	12	23	36	12	24
C Manufacture of wood and wood products, including furniture	43	24	19	45	25	20	35	20	15	32	17	15
D Manufacture of paper and paper products, printing and publishing	25	12	13	31	15	16	34	17	17	34	18	16
E Manufacture of chemicals and chemical petroleum, coal, rubber and plastic products	1333	1069	264	1334	1102	232	1627	1516	111	1674	1491	183
F Manufacture of non-metallic mineral products, except products of petroleum and coal	84	54	30	95	63	32	122	82	40	112	69	43
G Basic metal industries	9	3	6	6	4	2	7	3	4	8	4	4
H Manufacture of fabricated metal products, machinery and equipment	94	53	41	136	75	61	132	67	65	118	67	51
I Other manufacturing industries	3	1	2	2	-	2	2	1	1	2	1	1
4 Electricity, gas and water [a]	44	118	-74	51	217	-166	52	282	-230	58	279	-221
A Electricity, gas and steam	19	91	-72	24	172	-148	24	224	-200	29	221	-192
B Water works and supply	25	27	-2	27	45	-18	28	58	-30	29	58	-29
5 Construction	627	349	278	594	331	263	592	330	262	665	391	274
6 Wholesale and retail trade, restaurants and hotels	760	165	595	848	184	664	965	197	768	758	212	546
A Wholesale and retail trade	691	137	554	771	153	618	878	163	715	672	174	498
B Restaurants and hotels	69	28	41	77	31	46	87	34	53	86	38	48
7 Transport, storage and communication	323	142	181	376	161	215	457	166	291	435	160	275
A Transport and storage	289	139	150	326	157	169	402	162	240	375	156	219
B Communication	34	3	31	50	4	46	55	4	51	60	4	56
8 Finance, insurance, real estate and business services	580	71	509	659	81	578	1083	61	1022	797	61	736
A Financial institutions	192	25	167	248	32	216	390	23	367	312	21	291

Kuwait

4.1 Derivation of Value Added by Kind of Activity, in Current Prices
(Continued)

Million Kuwaiti dinars

	1980 Gross Output	1980 Intermediate Consumption	1980 Value Added	1981 Gross Output	1981 Intermediate Consumption	1981 Value Added	1982 Gross Output	1982 Intermediate Consumption	1982 Value Added	1983 Gross Output	1983 Intermediate Consumption	1983 Value Added
B Insurance	19	4	15	20	4	16	22	4	18	23	5	18
C Real estate and business services	370	43	327	391	45	346	671	34	637	462	35	427
9 Community, social and personal services	118	38	80	134	43	91	128	30	98	133	33	100
A Sanitary and similar services	5	1	4	7	1	6	11	1	10	12	3	9
B Social and related community services	25	8	17	28	8	18	30	8	22	35	10	25
Educational services	14	4	10	14	4	10	13	4	9	16	5	11
Medical, dental, other health and veterinary services	11	4	7	12	4	8	17	4	13	19	5	14
C Recreational and cultural services	3	1	2	4	2	2	5	4	1	4	2	2
D Personal and household services	85	28	57	97	32	65	82	17	65	82	18	64
Total, Industries	9317	2217	7100	8623	2418	6205	8225	2912	5313	8099	2946	5153
Producers of Government Services	876	319	557	1006	324	682	1214	420	794	1317	434	883
Other Producers	28	6	22	25	5	20	27	5	22	28	5	23
Total	10222	2542	7680	9654	2747	6907	9466	3337	6129	9444	3385	6059
Less: Imputed bank service charge	...	...	...	...	...	...	...	...	...	...	...	...
Import duties	61	-	61	78	-	78	83	-	83	74	-	74
Value added tax	...	...	...	...	...	...	...	...	...	...	...	...
Total	10282	2542	7740	9732	2747	6985	9549	3337	6212	9518	3385	6133

	1984 Gross Output	1984 Intermediate Consumption	1984 Value Added	1985 Gross Output	1985 Intermediate Consumption	1985 Value Added	1986 Gross Output	1986 Intermediate Consumption	1986 Value Added
				All Producers					
1 Agriculture, hunting, forestry and fishing	55	20	35	62	23	39	...	...	52
A Agriculture and hunting	49	19	30	56	22	34	...	...	48
B Forestry and logging	...	...	...	...	...	...	...	...	...
C Fishing	6	1	5	6	1	5	...	...	4
2 Mining and quarrying	3453	50	3403	3037	53	2984	...	...	1843
A Coal mining	...	...	...	...	...	...	...	...	...
B Crude petroleum and natural gas production	3444	44	3400	3033	50	2983	...	...	1842
C Metal ore mining	...	...	...	...	...	...	...	...	...
D Other mining	9	6	3	4	3	1	...	...	1
3 Manufacturing	2030	1730	300	2226	1849	377	...	...	555
A Manufacture of food, beverages and tobacco	93	56	37	103	63	40	...	...	45
B Textile, wearing apparel and leather industries	39	14	25	38	12	26	...	...	26
C Manufacture of wood and wood products, including furniture	34	18	16	32	18	14	...	...	12
D Manufacture of paper and paper products, printing and publishing	34	17	17	39	20	19	...	...	17
E Manufacture of chemicals and chemical petroleum, coal, rubber and plastic products	1631	1513	118	1810	1615	195	...	...	383
F Manufacture of non-metallic mineral products, except products of petroleum and coal	89	49	40	87	53	34	...	...	34
G Basic metal industries	3	1	2	8	4	4	...	...	2
H Manufacture of fabricated metal products, machinery and equipment	105	61	44	106	62	44	...	...	36
I Other manufacturing industries	2	1	1	3	2	1	...	...	1
4 Electricity, gas and water [a]	61	239	-178	62	213	-151	...	...	-94
A Electricity, gas and steam	32	189	-157	33	168	-135	...	...	-87
B Water works and supply	20	50	21	20	46	16	...	...	-7

Kuwait

4.1 Derivation of Value Added by Kind of Activity, in Current Prices
(Continued)

Million Kuwaiti dinars

		1984 Gross Output	1984 Intermediate Consumption	1984 Value Added	1985 Gross Output	1985 Intermediate Consumption	1985 Value Added	1986 Gross Output	1986 Intermediate Consumption	1986 Value Added
5	Construction	767	495	272	623	425	198	...	...	156
6	Wholesale and retail trade, restaurants and hotels	795	221	574	727	178	549	...	...	514
	A Wholesale and retail trade	710	181	529	637	137	500	...	...	470
	B Restaurants and hotels	85	40	45	90	41	49	...	...	44
7	Transport, storage and communication	446	181	265	379	139	240	...	...	250
	A Transport and storage	383	176	207	315	131	184	...	...	191
	B Communication	63	5	58	64	8	56	...	...	59
8	Finance, insurance, real estate and business services	650	63	587	554	61	493	...	...	469
	A Financial institutions	299	22	277	245	23	222	...	...	217
	B Insurance	28	5	23	24	5	19	...	...	16
	C Real estate and business services	323	36	287	285	33	252	...	...	236
9	Community, social and personal services	136	33	103	138	34	104	...	...	101
	A Sanitary and similar services	17	3	14	13	2	11	...	...	10
	B Social and related community services	35	9	26	39	11	28	...	...	26
	Educational services	17	5	12	21	7	14	...	...	15
	Medical, dental, other health and veterinary services	18	4	14	18	4	14	...	...	11
	C Recreational and cultural services	2	1	1	2	1	1	...	...	1
	D Personal and household services	82	20	62	84	20	64	...	...	64
	Total, Industries	8393	3032	5361	7808	2975	4833	...	...	3846
	Producers of Government Services	1375	451	924	1477	481	996	...	...	1063
	Other Producers	39	8	31	32	4	28	...	...	29
	Total	9807	3491	6316	9317	3460	5857	...	...	4938
	Less: Imputed bank service charge	...	...	...	...	...	...	...	...	...
	Import duties	64	-	64	60	-	60	...	...	59
	Value added tax	...	...	...	...	...	...	...	...	...
	Total	9871	3491	6380	9377	3460	5917	...	...	4997

a) Beginning 1980, the cost of fuel (natural gas, crude petroleum and gas-oil) consumed in the production of electricity and water has been taken into account as intermediate consumption in estimating the value added of item 'Electricity, gas and water'.

4.2 Derivation of Value Added by Kind of Activity, in Constant Prices

Million Kuwaiti dinars

		1980 Gross Output	1980 Intermediate Consumption	1980 Value Added	1981 Gross Output	1981 Intermediate Consumption	1981 Value Added	1982 Gross Output	1982 Intermediate Consumption	1982 Value Added	1983 Gross Output	1983 Intermediate Consumption	1983 Value Added
						At constant prices of:1984							
						All Producers							
1	Agriculture, hunting, forestry and fishing	...	...	13	...	...	21	...	...	24	...	...	28
	A Agriculture and hunting	...	...	10	...	...	15	...	...	14	...	...	23
	B Forestry and logging	...	...	...	...	...	...	...	...	...	...	...	...
	C Fishing	...	...	3	...	...	6	...	...	5	...	...	5
2	Mining and quarrying	...	...	4865	...	...	3298	...	...	2406	...	...	3117
	A Coal mining	...	...	...	...	...	...	...	...	...	...	...	...
	B Crude petroleum and natural gas production	...	...	4862	...	...	3293	...	...	2404	...	...	3116
	C Metal ore mining	...	...	...	...	...	...	...	...	...	...	...	...
	D Other mining	...	...	3	...	...	5	...	...	2	...	...	1

Kuwait

4.2 Derivation of Value Added by Kind of Activity, in Constant Prices
(Continued)

Million Kuwaiti dinars

At constant prices of: 1984

	1980 Gross Output	1980 Intermediate Consumption	1980 Value Added	1981 Gross Output	1981 Intermediate Consumption	1981 Value Added	1982 Gross Output	1982 Intermediate Consumption	1982 Value Added	1983 Gross Output	1983 Intermediate Consumption	1983 Value Added
3 Manufacturing	...	...	294	...	...	285	...	...	310	...	...	308
A Manufacture of food, beverages and tobacco	...	...	33	...	...	31	...	...	33	...	...	38
B Textile, wearing apparel and leather industries	...	...	25	...	...	21	...	...	24	...	...	24
C Manufacture of wood and wood products, including furniture	...	...	23	...	...	22	...	...	17	...	...	15
D Manufacture of paper and paper products, printing and publishing	...	...	16	...	...	19	...	...	19	...	...	18
E Manufacture of chemicals and chemical petroleum, coal, rubber and plastic products	...	...	111	...	...	98	...	...	111	...	...	115
F Manufacture of non-metallic mineral products, except products of petroleum and coal	...	...	31	...	...	33	...	...	41	...	...	43
G Basic metal industries	...	...	6	...	...	3	...	...	4	...	...	4
H Manufacture of fabricated metal products, machinery and equipment	...	...	47	...	...	57	...	...	60	...	...	50
I Other manufacturing industries	...	...	2	...	...	1	...	...	1	...	...	1
4 Electricity, gas and water	...	...	-117	...	...	-129	...	...	-150	...	...	-161
A Electricity, gas and steam	...	...	-102	...	...	-113	...	...	-132	...	...	-141
B Water works and supply	...	...	-14	...	...	-15	...	...	-18	...	...	-20
5 Construction	...	...	341	...	...	301	...	...	278	...	...	277
6 Wholesale and retail trade, restaurants and hotels	...	...	714	...	...	745	...	...	810	...	...	555
A Wholesale and retail trade	...	...	645	...	...	673	...	...	743	...	...	501
B Restaurants and hotels	...	...	69	...	...	72	...	...	67	...	...	54
7 Transport, storage and communication	...	...	225	...	...	250	...	...	310	...	...	277
A Transport and storage	...	...	194	...	...	204	...	...	259	...	...	221
B Communication	...	...	31	...	...	46	...	...	51	...	...	56
8 Finance, insurance, real estate and business services	...	...	461	...	...	523	...	...	556	...	...	560
A Financial institutions	...	...	197	...	...	251	...	...	267	...	...	268
B Insurance	...	...	17	...	...	15	...	...	18	...	...	18
C Real estate and business services	...	...	247	...	...	257	...	...	271	...	...	274
9 Community, social and personal services	...	...	116	...	...	120	...	...	111	...	...	103
A Sanitary and similar services	...	...	5	...	...	7	...	...	12	...	...	10
B Social and related community services	...	...	25	...	...	20	...	...	23	...	...	25
Educational services	...	...	14	...	...	12	...	...	10	...	...	11
Medical, dental, other health and veterinary services	...	...	11	...	...	8	...	...	13	...	...	14
C Recreational and cultural services	...	...	2	...	...	3	...	...	1	...	...	2
D Personal and household services	...	...	84	...	...	90	...	...	75	...	...	66
Total, Industries	...	...	6912	...	...	5414	...	...	4655	...	...	5064
Producers of Government Services	...	...	776	...	...	784	...	...	847	...	...	903
Other Producers	...	...	32	...	...	29	...	...	26	...	...	24
Total	...	...	7720	...	...	6227	...	...	5528	...	...	5991
Less: Imputed bank service charge	...	...	...	...	...	...	...	...	...	...	...	...
Import duties	...	...	67	...	...	78	...	...	75	...	...	71
Value added tax	...	...	...	...	...	...	...	...	...	...	...	...
Total	...	...	7787	...	...	6305	...	...	5603	...	...	6062

Kuwait

4.2 Derivation of Value Added by Kind of Activity, in Constant Prices

Million Kuwaiti dinars

		1984			1985			1986		
		Gross Output	Intermediate Consumption	Value Added	Gross Output	Intermediate Consumption	Value Added	Gross Output	Intermediate Consumption	Value Added
		At constant prices of: 1984								
		All Producers								
1	Agriculture, hunting, forestry and fishing	...	...	35	...	...	40	...	...	54
	A Agriculture and hunting	...	...	30	...	...	35	...	...	51
	B Forestry and logging	...	...	...	...	...	...	...	...	...
	C Fishing	...	...	5	...	...	5	...	...	3
2	Mining and quarrying	...	...	3403	...	...	3103	...	...	3768
	A Coal mining	...	...	...	...	...	...	...	...	...
	B Crude petroleum and natural gas production	...	...	3400	...	...	3103	...	...	3768
	C Metal ore mining	...	...	...	...	...	...	...	...	...
	D Other mining	...	...	3	...	...	1	...	...	1
3	Manufacturing	...	...	300	...	...	314	...	...	318
	A Manufacture of food, beverages and tobacco	...	...	37	...	...	40	...	...	44
	B Textile, wearing apparel and leather industries	...	...	25	...	...	26	...	...	23
	C Manufacture of wood and wood products, including furniture	...	...	16	...	...	15	...	...	13
	D Manufacture of paper and paper products, printing and publishing	...	...	17	...	...	20	...	...	17
	E Manufacture of chemicals and chemical petroleum, coal, rubber and plastic products	...	...	118	...	...	129	...	...	141
	F Manufacture of non-metallic mineral products, except products of petroleum and coal	...	...	40	...	...	33	...	...	33
	G Basic metal industries	...	...	2	...	...	3	...	...	2
	H Manufacture of fabricated metal products, machinery and equipment	...	...	44	...	...	47	...	...	44
	I Other manufacturing industries	...	...	1	...	...	1	...	...	1
4	Electricity, gas and water	...	...	-178	...	...	-196	...	...	-215
	A Electricity, gas and steam	...	...	-157	...	...	-174	...	...	-191
	B Water works and supply	...	...	-21	...	...	-22	...	...	-23
5	Construction	...	...	272	...	...	195	...	...	152
6	Wholesale and retail trade, restaurants and hotels	...	...	574	...	...	546	...	...	507
	A Wholesale and retail trade	...	...	528	...	...	498	...	...	463
	B Restaurants and hotels	...	...	46	...	...	48	...	...	44
7	Transport, storage and communication	...	...	265	...	...	236	...	...	232
	A Transport and storage	...	...	207	...	...	180	...	...	180
	B Communication	...	...	58	...	...	56	...	...	52
8	Finance, insurance, real estate and business services	...	...	587	...	...	587	...	...	580
	A Financial institutions	...	...	277	...	...	273	...	...	266
	B Insurance	...	...	23	...	...	18	...	...	17
	C Real estate and business services	...	...	287	...	...	296	...	...	297
9	Community, social and personal services	...	...	103	...	...	104	...	...	100
	A Sanitary and similar services	...	...	14	...	...	17	...	...	16
	B Social and related community services	...	...	26	...	...	27	...	...	26
	Educational services	...	...	12	...	...	15	...	...	15
	Medical, dental, other health and veterinary services	...	...	14	...	...	12	...	...	11
	C Recreational and cultural services	...	...	1	...	...	1	...	...	1
	D Personal and household services	...	...	62	...	...	59	...	...	57

Kuwait

4.2 Derivation of Value Added by Kind of Activity, in Constant Prices
(Continued)

Million Kuwaiti dinars

	1984 Gross Output	1984 Intermediate Consumption	1984 Value Added	1985 Gross Output	1985 Intermediate Consumption	1985 Value Added	1986 Gross Output	1986 Intermediate Consumption	1986 Value Added
				At constant prices of:1984					
Total, Industries	...	...	5361	...	...	4929	...	...	5496
Producers of Government Services	...	...	924	...	...	934	...	...	936
Other Producers	...	...	31	...	...	26	...	...	26
Total	...	...	6316	...	...	5889	...	...	6458
Less: Imputed bank service charge	...	...	...	...	...	...	...	...	...
Import duties	...	...	64	...	...	61	...	...	54
Value added tax	...	...	...	...	...	...	...	...	...
Total	...	...	6380	...	...	5950	...	...	6512

Lebanon

Source. Reply to the United Nations National Accounts Questionnaire from the Direction Centrale de la Statistique, Ministere du plan, Beyrouth. The official estimates are published annually by the Direction Centrale de la Statistique in 'Les Comptes Economiques'.

General note. The official estimates of Lebanon have been adjusted by the Direction Centrale de la Statistique to conform to the United Nations System of National Accounts so far as the existing data would permit.

1.1 Expenditure on the Gross Domestic Product, in Current Prices

Million Lebanese pounds

	1970	1975	1977	1978	1979	1980	1981	1982	1983	1984	1985	1986
1 Government final consumption expenditure	512	...	1702	2012	2559	3515	4219	4850	...	...	...	...
2 Private final consumption expenditure	4197	...	7530	7627	9661	12905	15488	15840	...	...	...	...
3 Gross capital formation	905	...	1710	1640	2010	2196	3459	1179	...	...	...	...
A Increase in stocks	-33	...	...	...	...	...	...	...	...	...	...	...
B Gross fixed capital formation	938	...	...	...	...	...	...	...	...	...	...	...
4 Exports of goods and services	1149	...	1561	2120	4168	5460	5724	5255	...	...	...	...
5 Less: Imports of goods and services	1897	...	4304	4600	7248	10076	12090	14525	...	...	...	...
Equals: Gross Domestic Product	4866	...	8199	8799	11150	14000	16800	12599	...	...	...	...

1.3 Cost Components of the Gross Domestic Product

Million Lebanese pounds

	1970	1975	1977	1978	1979	1980	1981	1982	1983	1984	1985	1986
1 Indirect taxes, net	344	...	482	509	682	683	436	306	...	...	...	...
A Indirect taxes	464	...	...	...	...	...	...	...	...	...	...	...
B Less: Subsidies	120	...	...	...	...	...	...	...	...	...	...	...
2 Consumption of fixed capital	275	...	...	...	...	...	...	...	...	...	...	...
3 Compensation of employees paid by resident producers to:	4247	...	...	...	...	...	...	...	...	...	...	...
4 Operating surplus		...	...	...	...	...	...	...	...	...	...	...
Equals: Gross Domestic Product	4866	...	8199	8799	11150	14000	16800	12599	...	...	...	...

1.7 External Transactions on Current Account, Summary

Million Lebanese pounds

	1970	1975	1977	1978	1979	1980	1981	1982	1983	1984	1985	1986
Payments to the Rest of the World												
1 Imports of goods and services	1897	...	...	...	...	...	...	...	...	...	...	...
2 Factor income to the rest of the world	299	...	...	...	...	...	...	...	...	...	...	...
3 Current transfers to the rest of the world	...	...	...	...	...	...	...	...	...	...	...	...
4 Surplus of the nation on current transactions	-38	...	...	...	...	...	...	...	...	...	...	...
Payments to the Rest of the World and Surplus of the Nation on Current Transactions	2158	...	...	...	...	...	...	...	...	...	...	...
Receipts From The Rest of the World												
1 Exports of goods and services	1149	...	...	...	...	...	...	...	...	...	...	...
2 Factor income from rest of the world	1009	...	...	...	...	...	...	...	...	...	...	...
3 Current transfers from rest of the world	...	...	...	...	...	...	...	...	...	...	...	...
Receipts from the Rest of the World on Current Transactions	2158	...	...	...	...	...	...	...	...	...	...	...

1.10 Gross Domestic Product by Kind of Activity, in Current Prices

Million Lebanese pounds

	1970	1975	1977	1978	1979	1980	1981	1982	1983	1984	1985	1986
1 Agriculture, hunting, forestry and fishing	445	...	700	751	952	1288	1435	1076	...	...	...	...
2 Mining and quarrying	661	...	...	...	...	...	...	...	...	...	...	...
3 Manufacturing		...	1070	1148	1455	1702	2192	1644	...	...	...	...
4 Electricity, gas and water	113	...	445	478	605	708	911	683	...	...	...	...
5 Construction	219	...	280	300	381	447	575	431	...	...	...	...
6 Wholesale and retail trade, restaurants and hotels	1527	...	2320	2490	3155	4008	4753	3565	...	...	...	...
7 Transport, storage and communication	401	...	630	676	857	530	628	471	...	...	...	...
8 Finance, insurance, real estate and business services	595	...	1036	1112	1408	2349	2785	2089	...	...	...	...
9 Community, social and personal services	482	...	883	948	1201	1526	1809	1357	...	...	...	...

Lebanon

1.10 Gross Domestic Product by Kind of Activity, in Current Prices
(Continued)

Million Lebanese pounds

	1970	1975	1977	1978	1979	1980	1981	1982	1983	1984	1985	1986
Total, Industries	4442	...	7363	7903	10014	12557	15087	11316	...	...	...	...
Producers of Government Services	424	...	836	897	1136	1443	1712	1284	...	...	...	...
Other Producers	...	...	...	...	...	...	...	...	...	...	...	...
Subtotal	4866	...	8199	8799	11150	14000	16800	12600	...	...	...	...
Less: Imputed bank service charge	...	...	...	...	...	...	...	...	...	...	...	...
Plus: Import duties	...	...	...	...	...	...	...	...	...	...	...	...
Plus: Value added tax	...	...	...	...	...	...	...	...	...	...	...	...
Equals: Gross Domestic Product	4866	...	8199	8799	11150	14000	16800	12600	...	...	...	...

1.12 Relations Among National Accounting Aggregates

Million Lebanese pounds

	1970	1975	1977	1978	1979	1980	1981	1982	1983	1984	1985	1986
Gross Domestic Product	4866	...	...	...	...	...	...	...	...	...	...	...
Plus: Net factor income from the rest of the world	165	...	...	...	...	...	...	...	...	...	...	...
Equals: Gross National Product	5031	...	...	...	...	...	...	...	...	...	...	...
Less: Consumption of fixed capital	275	...	...	...	...	...	...	...	...	...	...	...
Equals: National Income	4756	...	...	...	...	...	...	...	...	...	...	...
Plus: Net current transfers from the rest of the world	...	...	...	...	...	...	...	...	...	...	...	...
Equals: National Disposable Income	...	...	...	...	...	...	...	...	...	...	...	...
Less: Final consumption	4709	...	...	...	...	...	...	...	...	...	...	...
Equals: Net Saving	...	...	...	...	...	...	...	...	...	...	...	...
Less: Surplus of the nation on current transactions	...	...	...	...	...	...	...	...	...	...	...	...
Equals: Net Capital Formation	630	...	...	...	...	...	...	...	...	...	...	...

Lesotho

General note. The preparation of national accounts statistics in Lesotho is undertaken by the Bureau of Statistics, Maseru. The official estimates together with methodological notes on sources and methods are published in a series of reports entitled 'National Accounts'. The estimates are generally in accordance with the classifications and definitions recommended in the United Nations System of National Accounts (SNA). The following tables have been prepared from successive replies to the United Nations national accounts questionnaire. When the scope and coverage of the estimates differ for conceptual or statistical reasons from the definitions and classifications recommended in SNA, a footnote is indicated to the relevant tables.

Sources and methods:

(a) Gross domestic product. Gross domestic product if estimated mainly through the production approach.

(b) Expenditure on the gross domestic product. All items of GDP by expenditure type are estimated through the expenditure approach. Government final consumption expenditure, consisting of wages and salaries and purchases of goods and services, is obtained from government accounts. The government expenditure is classified by the type of service provided by the central authorities. The estimates of private final consumption expenditure are based on the rural household survey undertaken in 1967-1969 and on the urban household survey carried out in six district towns from May 1972 to May 1973. Recently, this item has been estimated as a residual. Increase in stocks is estimated mainly from questionnaires and surveys carried out for the agricultural sector. Gross fixed capital formation consists of the value of purchases and own-account construction of fixed assets by government, private and public enterprises, individuals and non-profit institutions. Various sources such as questionnaires are used to collect the information. For the agricultural sector only, increase in stocks is included in this item. Estimates of exports and imports of merchandise are obtained from foreign trade statistics with adjustments made for differences in coverage and valuation. Exports are recorded f.o.b. at the border of Lesotho and imports are also recorded f.o.b. at the point of dispatch. Gross domestic product by expenditure type is not estimated at constant prices.

(c) Cost-structure of the gross domestic product. Wages and salaries are derived from the government accounts and other returns. Estimates of operating surplus are derived as residuals from the production accounts of all sectors. Depreciation is obtained from returned questionnaires and no estimate is available for the government or subsistence sectors. Indirect taxes consist mainly of revenue received by Lesotho as a member of the customs agreement with Botswana, South Africa and Swaziland. Subsidy figures consist of government contributions to defray part of the operating expenses of government and other enterprises.

(d) Gross domestic product by kind of economic activity. The table of GDP by kind of economic activity is prepared in factor values. The production approach is used to estimate the value added of the different industries except for producers of government services in which case the income approach is used. The Agricultural Division of the Bureau of Statistics carries out regular annual surveys. The 1970 census of agriculture and the 1973 agricultural survey are used to derive estimates of cereal production, assuming a wastage of 6 per cent during the various stages of harvest. The 1967-69 rural household survey is used for fruit and vegetable production estimates. For livestock, balance sheets prepared by the Agricultural Division of the Bureau of Statistics provide changes in stock estimates, to which the average values for different types of livestock are applied. For meat production, average carcass weights are applied to the numbers of livestock slaughtered which are obtained from the Ministry of Health and annual production surveys. The value of diamonds sold to licenced dealers by diggers is regarded as the value of diamonds exported from Lesotho. The receipts from diamonds are regarded as a contribution by the mining sector to GDP. Data on quantities and values of diamonds are obtained monthly from the Department of Mines and Geology. For manufacturing, data are derived from questionnaires prepared specially for manufacturing enterprises while data for handicrafts are based on the 1967-1969 rural household consumption and expenditure survey. Data for electricity and water are obtained from the balance sheets of the electricity corporation and accounts of the concerned ministry. Special questionnaires filled in by building contractors are used for the construction sector. Estimates of own-account contribution are included. For the trade sector, questionnaires are used for large enterprises while the results of a survey conducted in 1970-1971 are used for small enterprises. Estimates of the public transport and communication sector are based on government accounts supplemented by inquiries while estimates of private transport are obtained from the concerned enterprises. For the financial sector, special inquiries directed at the banks and the headquarters of insurance companies are used. For ownership of dwellings, government accounts provide information for the public sector while questionnaires returned by businesses and institutions are used for the private sector. The 1972-73 urban household survey is used to estimate imputed rent. Information relating to general government services is obtained from the government accounts. Data on other services are obtained through questionnaires and special inquiries. GDP by kind of economic activity is not estimated at constant prices.

1.1 Expenditure on the Gross Domestic Product, in Current Prices

Million Lesotho maloti

		1970	1975	1977	1978	1979	1980	1981	1982	1983	1984	1985	1986
1	Government final consumption expenditure	6.2	23.1 / 21.3	29.2	40.9	52.4	98.9	108.6	99.0	111.2	124.9	168.3	194.6
2	Private final consumption expenditure	63.2	183.9 / 167.2	264.2	300.7	353.7	395.3	473.7	593.4	707.9	804.4	879.1	1002.3
3	Gross capital formation	6.0	27.3 / 20.7	42.0	60.1	84.6	100.7	116.3	140.5	100.5	160.7	183.0	215.1
	A Increase in stocks	0.8	3.8 / -	1.7	9.1	10.9	7.2	8.9	-2.5	0.3	10.1	-2.3	2.0
	B Gross fixed capital formation	5.1	23.5 / 20.7	40.3	51.0	73.7	93.5	107.4	143.0	100.2	150.6	185.3	213.1
	Residential buildings	...	3.2 / 11.2[a]										
	Non-residential buildings	...	5.8 / ...	23.2	30.3	40.3	52.3	55.2	83.2	59.7	72.5	84.0	96.0
	Other construction and land improvement etc.	...	3.2 / ...										
	Other	2.7	11.4 / 0.5	17.1	20.7	33.4	41.2	52.2	60.8	40.5	78.1	101.3	117.1
4	Exports of goods and services	5.7	16.2 / 14.6	18.0	36.4	50.0	61.9	63.4	63.9	59.8	69.7	83.3	95.4
5	Less: Imports of goods and services	28.6	139.5 / 113.2	185.3	206.3	296.4	359.5	433.6	527.6	584.3	689.0	743.2	860.2
	Equals: Gross Domestic Product [b]	52.5	111.0 / 110.6	168.1	231.8	244.3	297.3	328.4	369.2	395.1	470.7	570.5	647.2

a) Including item 'Residential buildings' through 'Other construction and land improvement etc.'
b) First series, estimates refer to year beginning 1 April.

Lesotho

1.3 Cost Components of the Gross Domestic Product

Million Lesotho maloti

	1970	1975	1977	1978	1979	1980	1981	1982	1983	1984	1985	1986
1 Indirect taxes, net	4.7	12.9 / 13.2	23.6	46.3	28.8	32.9	41.8	69.5	86.7	95.5	113.8	130.5
2 Consumption of fixed capital	...	3.0	...	...	...	...	...	...	...	...	...	...
3 Compensation of employees paid by resident producers to:	...	30.3 / 97.4[a]										
A Resident households	...	30.3 / ...	144.5	185.5	215.5	264.4	286.6	299.7	308.4	375.2	456.7	516.7
B Rest of the world	...	- / ...										
4 Operating surplus	42.5	64.8 / ...										
Equals: Gross Domestic Product [b]	52.5	111.0 / 110.6	168.1	231.9	244.3	297.3	328.4	369.2	395.1	470.7	570.5	647.2

a) Including item 'Compensation of employees paid by resident producers to:' through 'Operating surplus'.
b) First series, estimates refer to year beginning 1 April.

1.7 External Transactions on Current Account, Summary

Million Lesotho maloti

	1970	1975	1977	1978	1979	1980	1981	1982	1983	1984	1985	1986
Payments to the Rest of the World												
1 Imports of goods and services	...	139.5 / 113.2	185.3	206.3	296.4	359.5	433.6	527.6	584.3	689.0	743.2	860.2
A Imports of merchandise c.i.f.	...	137.8 / 106.7	179.1	195.9	275.2	331.5	405.5	497.7	539.4	629.1	654.9	744.3
B Other	...	1.7 / 6.5	6.2	10.4	21.2	28.8	28.1	29.9	44.9	59.9	88.3	115.9
2 Factor income to the rest of the world	...	3.2 / 4.8	4.2	4.4	5.0	5.7	7.7	16.4	13.9	16.3	20.0	23.7
A Compensation of employees	...	... / ...										
B Property and entrepreneurial income	...	... / 4.8	4.2	4.4	5.0	5.7	7.7	16.4	13.9	16.3	20.0	23.7
3 Current transfers to the rest of the world [a]	...	0.3 / ...	...	...	...	...	...	...	...	...	...	...
4 Surplus of the nation on current transactions	...	-11.5 / 1.5	-8.9	12.2	1.4	-8.7	-42.9	-41.6	-11.5	7.7	23.4	-30.9
Payments to the Rest of the World and Surplus of the Nation on Current Transactions [b]	...	131.6 / 119.5	180.6	222.9	302.8	356.5	398.4	502.4	586.7	713.0	786.6	853.0
Receipts From The Rest of the World												
1 Exports of goods and services	...	16.2 / 14.6	18.0	36.4	50.0	61.9	63.4	63.9	59.8	69.7	83.3	95.4
A Exports of merchandise f.o.b.	...	10.6 / 9.2	12.2	28.7	38.9	46.6	44.6	40.6	34.6	41.8	51.8	59.9
B Other	...	5.7 / 5.4	5.8	7.7	11.1	15.3	18.8	23.3	25.2	27.9	31.5	35.5
2 Factor income from rest of the world	...	104.2 / 93.9	144.1	157.7	183.2	210.7	262.5	389.3	437.0	503.5	534.3	607.1
A Compensation of employees	...	100.4 / 90.4	141.0	154.3	178.9	205.0	255.0	378.0	421.0	475.9	499.0	583.6
B Property and entrepreneurial income	...	3.8 / 3.5	3.1	3.4	4.3	5.7	7.5	11.3	16.0	27.6	35.3	23.5
3 Current transfers from rest of the world [a]	...	11.1 / 11.0	18.5	28.8	69.6	83.9	72.5	49.2	89.9	139.8	169.0	150.5
Receipts from the Rest of the World on Current Transactions [b]	...	131.6 / 119.5	180.6	222.9	302.8	356.5	398.4	502.4	586.7	713.0	786.6	853.0

a) Current transfers from the rest of the world is net of current transfers to the rest of the world.
b) First series, estimates refer to year beginning 1 April.

Lesotho

1.8 Capital Transactions of The Nation, Summary

Million Lesotho maloti

	1970	1975	1977	1978	1979	1980	1981	1982	1983	1984	1985	1986
Finance of Gross Capital Formation												
Gross saving	...	15.8 / 22.2	33.1	72.3	86.0	92.0	73.4	98.9	89.0	168.4	206.4	184.2
1 Consumption of fixed capital	...	3.0 / ...	...	...	...	...	...	...	...	...	...	...
2 Net saving	...	12.8 / ...	...	...	...	...	...	...	...	...	...	...
Less: Surplus of the nation on current transactions	...	-11.5 / 1.5	-8.9	12.2	1.4	-8.7	-42.9	-41.6	-11.5	7.7	23.4	-30.9
Finance of Gross Capital Formation a	...	27.3 / 20.7	42.0	60.1	84.6	100.7	116.3	140.5	100.5	160.7	183.0	215.1
Gross Capital Formation												
Increase in stocks	...	3.8 / -	1.7	9.1	10.9	7.2	8.9	-2.5	0.3	10.1	-2.3	2.0
Gross fixed capital formation	...	23.5 / 20.7	40.3	51.0	73.7	93.5	107.4	143.0	100.2	150.6	185.3	213.1
1 General government	...	12.6 / 10.8	33.8	40.6	44.4	44.4	61.0	64.3	59.2	69.0	73.7	84.8
2 Corporate and quasi-corporate enterprises	...	10.9 / 9.9	6.5	10.4	29.3	49.1	46.4	78.7	41.0	81.6	111.6	128.3
A Public	...	... / ...	...	...	...	...	...	...	...	...	...	...
B Private	...	10.9 / 9.9	6.5	10.4	29.3	49.1	46.4	78.7	41.0	81.6	111.6	128.3
3 Other	...	... / ...	...	...	...	...	...	...	...	...	...	...
Gross Capital Formation a	...	27.3 / 20.7	42.0	60.1	84.6	100.7	116.3	140.5	100.5	160.7	183.0	215.1

a) First series, estimates refer to year beginning 1 April.

1.10 Gross Domestic Product by Kind of Activity, in Current Prices

Million Lesotho maloti

	1970	1975	1977	1978	1979	1980	1981	1982	1983	1984	1985	1986
1 Agriculture, hunting, forestry and fishing	16.7	31.1 / 31.7	49.6	55.2	65.7	70.0	74.1	63.9	75.3	98.0	111.0	108.6
2 Mining and quarrying	0.7	0.5 / 0.5	1.2	15.4	18.6	20.7	16.0	13.5	0.8	0.6	1.6	1.9
3 Manufacturing a	2.1	5.6 / 5.6	7.2	10.1	11.9	13.9	16.8	22.2	29.1	40.5	45.7	59.2
4 Electricity, gas and water	0.2	0.8 / 0.8	1.6	1.8	2.0	2.2	2.0	2.5	2.1	3.4	4.7	5.0
5 Construction	1.4	6.0 / 6.0	12.4	16.2	21.5	28.0	29.5	44.5	31.9	38.8	50.0	57.5
6 Wholesale and retail trade, restaurants and hotels	11.2	21.5 / 21.6	26.6	27.8	28.7	33.2	36.8	44.7	52.6	63.7	77.7	92.5
7 Transport, storage and communication	0.6	2.6 / 2.6	4.4	4.9	3.6	3.7	4.3	4.7	6.8	9.3	11.4	13.5
8 Finance, insurance, real estate and business services	7.4	13.5 / 13.5	18.7	23.2	23.5	26.4	34.8	42.9	40.6	60.5	65.2	74.6
9 Community, social and personal services	0.5	0.8 / 6.9	9.1	11.5	16.7	27.2	31.0	28.2	29.6	31.6	41.0	47.4
Total, Industries	40.7	82.4 / 89.2	130.8	166.1	192.2	225.3	245.3	267.1	259.5	346.4	408.3	460.2
Producers of Government Services	4.3	7.8 / 7.2	11.7	17.2	22.2	38.7	47.3	44.5	45.9	49.3	67.0	78.6
Other Producers	2.8	7.9 / 1.0	2.0	2.2	3.2	3.2	3.6	4.1	3.4	3.9	4.7	5.4
Subtotal b	47.0	98.1 / 97.4	144.5	185.5	217.6	267.2	296.2	315.7	328.1	399.6	480.0	544.2
Less: Imputed bank service charge	...	... / ...	...	...	2.1	2.8	9.6	16.0	19.7	24.4	23.3	27.5
Plus: Import duties	...	... / ...	...	...	...	...	...	...	...	...	...	...
Plus: Value added tax	...	... / ...	...	...	...	...	...	...	...	...	...	...
Plus: Other adjustments c	4.7	12.9 / 13.2	23.6	46.3	28.8	32.9	41.8	69.5	86.7	95.5	113.8	130.5
Equals: Gross Domestic Product d	52.5	111.0 / 110.6	168.1	231.8	244.3	297.3	328.4	369.2	395.1	470.7	570.5	647.2

a) Item 'Manufacturing' includes handicrafts.
b) Gross domestic product in factor values.
c) Item 'Other adjustments' refers to indirect taxes net of subsidies.
d) First series, estimates refer to year beginning 1 April.

Lesotho

1.11 Gross Domestic Product by Kind of Activity, in Constant Prices

Million Lesotho maloti

	1970	1975	1977	1978	1979	1980	1981	1982	1983	1984	1985	1986
					At constant prices of:1980							
1 Agriculture, hunting, forestry and fishing	...	...	...	...	...	70.0	68.3	59.7	66.5	71.6	74.4	65.1
2 Mining and quarrying	...	...	...	...	...	20.7	11.6	15.7	1.4	1.4	2.6	2.1
3 Manufacturing [a]	...	...	...	...	...	13.9	15.0	17.3	19.8	24.5	24.2	27.7
4 Electricity, gas and water	...	...	...	...	...	2.2	2.5	2.7	2.6	2.7	2.9	3.1
5 Construction	...	...	...	...	...	28.0	25.7	32.5	19.8	21.4	24.4	33.2
6 Wholesale and retail trade, restaurants and hotels	...	...	...	...	...	33.2	32.9	35.0	37.1	41.5	43.1	46.6
7 Transport, storage and communication	...	...	...	...	...	3.7	3.8	4.0	5.2	5.8	6.3	6.9
8 Finance, insurance, real estate and business services	...	...	...	...	...	26.4	30.5	33.7	36.7	39.9	37.8	39.1
9 Community, social and personal services	...	...	...	...	...	27.2	28.8	26.3	27.6	29.5	28.2	32.7
Total, Industries	...	...	...	...	...	225.3	219.1	226.9	216.7	238.3	243.9	256.5
Producers of Government Services	...	...	...	...	...	38.7	44.0	41.5	42.8	45.9	44.7	52.4
Other Producers	...	...	...	...	...	3.2	3.2	3.2	2.4	2.5	2.6	2.8
Subtotal [b]	...	...	...	...	...	267.2	266.3	271.6	261.9	286.7	291.2	311.7
Less: Imputed bank service charge	...	...	...	...	...	2.8	8.4	12.4	14.0	15.9	13.0	14.0
Plus: Import duties	...	...	...	...	...	...	...	...	...	...	...	...
Plus: Value added tax	...	...	...	...	...	...	...	...	...	...	...	...
Plus: Other adjustments [c]	...	...	...	...	...	32.9	35.2	36.7	35.1	35.4	33.0	31.7
Equals: Gross Domestic Product [d]	...	...	...	...	...	297.3	293.1	295.9	283.0	306.2	311.2	329.4

a) Item 'Manufacturing' includes handicrafts.
b) Gross domestic product in factor values.
c) Item 'Other adjustments' refers to indirect taxes net of subsidies.
d) First series, estimates refer to year beginning 1 April.

1.12 Relations Among National Accounting Aggregates

Million Lesotho maloti

	1970	1975	1977	1978	1979	1980	1981	1982	1983	1984	1985	1986
Gross Domestic Product [a]	52.5	111.0 / 110.6	168.1	231.8	244.3	297.3	328.4	369.2	395.1	470.7	570.5	647.2
Plus: Net factor income from the rest of the world	22.3	101.0 / 89.1	139.9	153.3	178.2	205.0	254.8	372.9	423.1	487.2	514.3	583.4
Factor income from the rest of the world	...	104.2 / 93.9	144.1	157.7	183.2	210.7	262.5	389.3	437.0	503.5	534.3	607.1
Less: Factor income to the rest of the world	...	3.2 / 4.8	4.2	4.4	5.0	5.7	7.7	16.4	13.9	16.3	20.0	23.7
Equals: Gross National Product	74.8	212.0 / 199.7	308.0	385.1	422.5	502.3	583.2	742.1	818.2	957.9	1084.8	1230.6
Less: Consumption of fixed capital	...	3.0 / ...	...	...	...	...	...	...	...	...	...	...
Equals: National Income [ba]	...	209.0 / 199.7	308.0	385.1	422.5	502.3	583.2	742.1	818.2	957.9	1084.8	1230.6
Plus: Net current transfers from the rest of the world	...	10.8 / 11.0	18.5	28.8	69.6	83.9	72.5	49.2	89.9	139.8	169.0	150.5
Current transfers from the rest of the world	...	11.1 / ...	...	...	...	...	...	...	...	...	...	...
Less: Current transfers to the rest of the world	...	0.3 / ...	...	...	...	...	...	...	...	...	...	...
Equals: National Disposable Income [ca]	...	219.8 / 210.7	326.5	413.9	492.1	586.2	655.7	791.3	908.1	1097.7	1253.8	1381.1
Less: Final consumption	...	207.0 / 188.5	293.4	341.6	406.1	494.2	582.3	692.4	819.1	929.3	1047.4	1196.9
Equals: Net Saving [da]	...	12.8 / 22.2	33.1	72.3	86.0	92.0	73.4	98.9	89.0	168.4	206.4	184.2
Less: Surplus of the nation on current transactions	...	-11.5 / 1.5	-8.9	12.2	1.4	-8.7	-42.9	-41.6	-11.5	7.7	23.4	-30.9
Equals: Net Capital Formation [ea]	...	24.3 / 20.7	42.0	60.1	84.6	100.7	116.3	140.5	100.5	160.7	183.0	215.1

a) First series, estimates refer to year beginning 1 April.
b) Item 'National income' includes consumption of fixed capital.
c) Item 'National disposable income' includes consumption of fixed capital.
d) Item 'Net saving' includes consumption of fixed capital.
e) Item 'Net capital formation' includes consumption of fixed capital.

Lesotho

2.1 Government Final Consumption Expenditure by Function, in Current Prices

Million Lesotho maloti

	1970	1975	1977	1978	1979	1980	1981	1982	1983	1984	1985	1986
1 General public services	...	5.7 / 5.3	7.0	10.1	13.8	26.4	35.4	21.2	28.1	33.6	47.7	59.4
2 Defence	...	... / ...	...	...	...	...	...	...	...	...	...	...
3 Public order and safety	...	3.8 / 3.5	5.1	7.7	9.6	20.4	20.7	24.8	24.5	28.0	41.0	46.0
4 Education	...	6.4 / 5.8	7.9	10.1	12.8	25.6	24.8	24.3	27.1	29.9	36.5	42.4
5 Health	...	1.6 / 1.5[a]	2.3	2.9	4.2	7.3	7.1	8.3	10.5	10.8	14.0	15.9
6 Social security and welfare	...	... / ...										
7 Housing and community amenities	...	... / ...	...	...	...	...	...	...	...	...	...	...
8 Recreational, cultural and religious affairs	...	... / ...	...	...	...	...	...	...	...	...	...	...
9 Economic services	...	5.6 / 5.2	6.9	10.1	12.0	19.3	20.5	20.3	21.0	22.5	29.0	30.9
A Fuel and energy	...	... / ...	...	...	...	...	...	...	...			...
B Agriculture, forestry, fishing and hunting	...	2.0 / 2.0	3.7	4.8	5.8	10.4	9.6	9.0	9.4	10.5	13.0	14.1
C Mining, manufacturing and construction, except fuel and energy	...	... / 0.3	0.6	1.1	0.6	1.0	1.4	0.9	0.8	1.2	1.6	1.8
D Transportation and communication	...											
E Other economic affairs	...	3.5 / 2.9	2.6	4.2	5.6	7.8	9.6	10.3	10.7	10.8	14.4	15.0
10 Other functions	...	... / ...	...	...	...	...	...	...	...	...	...	...
Total Government Final Consumption Expenditure [b]	6.2	23.1 / 21.3	29.3	40.9	52.5	99.0	108.6	99.0	111.2	124.8	168.3	194.6

a) Including item 'Social security and welfare'.
b) First series, estimates refer to year beginning 1 April.

Liberia

General note. The preparation of national accounts statistics in Liberia is undertaken by the Ministry of Planning and Economic Affairs, Monrovia. The official estimates are published annually in 'Economic Survey of Liberia'. A description of the sources and methods used for the national accounts estimation is found in 'Sources and Methods of Estimation of National Product, 1970-1973' and 'The New Series and Methodology for Estimating Gross Domestic Product, 1973' published in 1975 and 1978 respectively. The estimates are generally in accordance with the classifications and definitions recommended in the United Nations System of National Accounts (SNA). The following tables have been prepared from successive replies to the United Nations national accounts questionnaire. When the scope and coverage of the estimates differ for conceptual or statistical reasons from the definitions and classifications recommended in SNA, a footnote is indicated to the relevant tables.

Sources and methods:

(a) Gross domestic product. Gross domestic product is estimated mainly through the income approach.

(b) Expenditure on the gross domestic product. The expenditure approach is used to estimate government final consumption expenditure, increase in stocks and exports and imports of goods and services. The commodity-flow approach is used to estimate private final consumption expenditure and gross fixed capital formation. The main sources used for estimating government final consumption expenditure are the monthly revenue and expenditure reports contained in 'Government Accounts of Liberia'. For private expenditure on imported goods, the c.i.f. value and import duties are obtained directly from the import statistics of consumer goods while the trade and transport margin is put at 35 per cent of the c.i.f. value. For local production, estimates are obtained from the production statistics of goods and services. Changes in stocks are estimated for iron-ore only. The sources used are the annual reports of the iron-ore companies and an analysis based on the difference between production and exports. The estimate is obtained by finding the difference between the quantities produced and the quantities exported and applying the average export prices. Gross fixed capital formation is estimated as value of local production plus imports minus exports plus transport costs, trade mark-ups, duties paid, etc. For machinery and equipment, the estimates are based on foreign trade statistics. For construction, the estimates are prepared by analysing import and local production of construction materials, the data of which are obtained from import statistics and the survey of establishments. The estimates of imports and exports of goods and services are based on the foreign trade statistics. Figures on exports and imports are supplemented by estimates for non-factor services. Constant price series of government expenditure is estimated by using employment data to extrapolate the base-year figures. The base-year value for stocks of iron-ore is extrapolated by using a volume indicator. For the remaining components of GDP by expenditure type, the current values are deflated by price indexes.

(c) Cost-structure of the gross domestic product. The estimates of compensation of employees, operating surplus and consumption of fixed capital are obtained from income tax files, replies to the national accounts questionnaires and from annual reports and financial accounts. The estimates of indirect taxes and subsidies are based on income tax returns for the main activities.

(d) Gross domestic product by kind of economic activity. The table of GDP by kind of economic activity is prepared in factor values. The income approach is used to estimate the value added of most industries. When data are available, the production and expenditure approaches are also used. For the agricultural sector, value added of rubber production is estimated from the financial accounts of the rubber concessions, the income tax statements of all rubber companies, and from information obtained from local rubber farmers. For other agricultural crops and fishing, value added is obtained from the income tax files. The value added of forestry is arrived at from an input-output study of the industry, based on the national accounts surveys. For the mining of iron-ore, value added is obtained directly from the financial accounts of the companies. Information of production components of manufacturing is obtained from income tax files, semi-annual questionnaires and other supplementary series. An extrapolation is made for non-reporting establishments. The value added of electricity, gas and water is obtained directly from the annual reports and accounts of concerned enterprises and their replies to the national accounts questionnaires. Estimates of the construction sector are derived mainly by using the commodity-flow approach. Domestic production of commodities used in construction is estimated and adjusted for exports, imports and changes in stocks and supplementary data on transport costs, dealers' margins, etc. is added. The value of imported construction materials and production statistics of locally produced construction are obtained. Information on substantial development of land undertaken is supplied by the companies. A combination of the production approach and the income approach is used for the trade sector. The output is equal to the gross margin. The income tax data and the technique of extrapolation are used to arrive at value added. The extrapolation process involves separating the large establishments from the others, extrapolating the value added by the change registered by comparable establishments and finally identifying new establishments and treating them as an additional contributor to value added. The estimates of the transport sector are derived from various sources such as national accounts questionnaire, income tax files and reports of the Motor Vehicle Division. The gross output of the financial sector is equal to the sum of actual service charges and imputed service charges. The data required for the value added are obtained through a questionnaire. The estimates of real estate and ownership of dwellings are obtained by extrapolating the 1967 estimate by means of the population growth rate and the rent component of the consumer price index. For producers of government services, the main source is the detailed analysis of the government accounts. The value added of other private services are extrapolated by the change in compensation of employees, interest, depreciation and operating surplus obtained from the income tax files. For the constant price estimates, price deflation is used for manufacturing, construction and trade sectors. For the remaining sectors, value added is extrapolated by using volume indexes.

1.1 Expenditure on the Gross Domestic Product, in Current Prices

Million Liberian dollars

	1970	1975	1977	1978	1979	1980	1981	1982	1983	1984	1985	1986
1 Government final consumption expenditure	45.1	73.2	120.0	139.0	156.6	182.0	200.1	222.4	169.1	160.2	137.3	135.8
2 Private final consumption expenditure	206.4	257.6	363.1	402.0	436.2	430.0	647.2	650.4	723.0	710.2	706.8	662.6
3 Gross capital formation	88.4	216.7	245.3	218.6	280.0	245.2	198.1	236.0	190.8	194.6	134.3	122.8
A Increase in stocks [a]	8.4	55.5	11.0	-41.5	-17.6	49.1	18.5	42.9	7.7	25.7	7.8	7.8
B Gross fixed capital formation	80.0	161.2	234.3	260.1	297.6	196.1	179.6	193.1	183.1	168.9	126.5	115.0
4 Exports of goods and services	240.1	403.7	459.0	500.0	553.6	613.5	540.7	510.6	463.5	489.0	470.2	459.4
5 Less: Imports of goods and services	172.2	371.9	521.9	548.6	587.4	614.0	560.9	478.5	479.2	411.5	322.8	370.2
Statistical discrepancy	...	30.3	40.7	62.7	52.3	59.9	29.1	-47.6	18.4	-69.6	-69.0	24.4
Equals: Gross Domestic Product	407.8	609.6	706.2	773.7	891.3	916.6	1054.3	1093.3	1085.6	1072.9	1056.8	1034.8

a) Item 'Increase in stocks' includes only increase in iron ore stocks. Beginning 1981, it includes increase in iron ore and rubber stocks.

Liberia

1.2 Expenditure on the Gross Domestic Product, in Constant Prices

Million Liberian dollars

	1970	1975	1977	1978	1979	1980	1981	1982	1983	1984	1985	1986
					At constant prices of: 1971				1981			
1 Government final consumption expenditure	49.6	48.8	57.3	60.2	64.0	61.0	58.5 / 200.1	218.9	169.0	156.8	136.9	134.3
2 Private final consumption expenditure	209.5	161.5	218.4	217.0	202.0	171.0	163.5 / 647.2	620.9	650.0	621.1	625.0	593.4
3 Gross capital formation	76.4	116.6	111.5	97.1	122.0	116.9	87.1 / 198.1	234.3	193.4	173.3	120.2	104.4
A Increase in stocks	-4.3[a]	26.6[a]	3.7[a]	-28.2[a]	-11.3[a]	21.7[a]	-4.5[a] / 18.5	40.5	5.4	20.6	6.5	6.5
B Gross fixed capital formation	80.7	90.0	107.8	125.3	133.3	95.2	91.6 / 179.6	193.8	188.0	152.7	113.7	97.9
4 Exports of goods and services	261.0	211.7	204.1	239.1	236.0	237.0	217.4 / 540.7	471.0	460.1	489.5	473.0	449.0
5 Less: Imports of goods and services	187.2	187.5	219.2	223.6	267.0	187.0	169.0 / 560.9	454.0	473.1	375.1	317.4	314.6
Statistical discrepancy	...	23.4	24.1	29.2	82.0	12.5	17.9 / 29.1	-18.3	36.5	-35.8	-28.7	25.8
Equals: Gross Domestic Product	409.3	374.5	396.2	419.0	439.0	411.4	395.4 / 1054.3	1072.8	1035.9	1029.8	1009.0	992.3

a) Item 'Increase in stocks' includes only increase in iron ore stocks. Beginning 1981, it includes increase in iron ore and rubber stocks.

1.3 Cost Components of the Gross Domestic Product

Million Liberian dollars

	1970	1975	1977	1978	1979	1980	1981	1982	1983	1984	1985	1986
1 Indirect taxes, net	28.5	50.5	84.7	103.7	114.2	115.8	116.5	118.2	106.8	103.0	96.0	86.6
2 Consumption of fixed capital	54.8	...	...	...	...	...	...	...	...	...	...	...
3 Compensation of employees paid by resident producers to:	324.5	...	...	...	...	...	...	...	...	...	...	...
4 Operating surplus		...	...	...	...	...	...	...	...	...	...	...
Equals: Gross Domestic Product	407.8	609.6	706.2	773.7	891.3	916.6	1054.3	1093.3	1085.6	1072.9	1056.8	1034.8

1.10 Gross Domestic Product by Kind of Activity, in Current Prices

Million Liberian dollars

	1970	1975	1977	1978	1979	1980	1981	1982	1983	1984	1985	1986
1 Agriculture, hunting, forestry and fishing	94.4	82.0	90.2	118.3	139.7	159.0	297.0	284.0	334.5	350.7	352.0	335.1
2 Mining and quarrying	115.6	231.8	153.8	130.2	134.8	153.0	127.4	150.3	123.2	107.4	128.2	129.6
3 Manufacturing	15.2	36.3	50.2	53.7	82.0	77.0	62.9	65.2	59.6	68.5	64.8	64.7
4 Electricity, gas and water	5.6	8.5	9.3	13.2	17.2	19.1	22.7	25.0	28.9	22.5	16.6	18.3
5 Construction	18.4	28.8	44.1	50.1	63.0	32.5	37.0	39.7	39.8	34.6	32.2	29.0
6 Wholesale and retail trade, restaurants and hotels	42.6	49.2	82.9	85.0	93.0	79.0	59.1	74.9	70.4	62.5	60.2	56.7
7 Transport, storage and communication	31.8	40.7	53.7	59.2	66.0	61.0	76.2	77.0	80.4	80.7	71.4	75.3
8 Finance, insurance, real estate and business services	23.7	40.2	49.3	55.6	68.2	76.6	85.8	90.2	100.9	110.3	109.0	115.2
9 Community, social and personal services	9.0	21.4	32.5	...	...	31.5	28.6	29.6	31.7	27.7	31.4	31.0
Total, Industries	356.3	520.5	566.0	...	...	688.7	796.7	836.7	869.4	872.9	866.7	854.9
Producers of Government Services	23.0	43.8	71.0	...	...	123.6	154.4	154.9	127.1	121.7	114.4	113.0

Liberia

1.10 Gross Domestic Product by Kind of Activity, in Current Prices
(Continued)

Million Liberian dollars

	1970	1975	1977	1978	1979	1980	1981	1982	1983	1984	1985	1986
Other Producers	3.4	...	...	...	...	...	...	...	...	...	...	...
Subtotal [a]	382.7	564.3	637.0	675.0	791.4	812.3	951.1	991.6	996.5	994.6	981.1	967.9
Less: Imputed bank service charge	3.4	4.7	3.8	5.0	14.1	11.5	13.3	16.5	17.7	24.7	20.3	19.7
Plus: Import duties	18.1	33.2	58.8	72.1	77.4	67.6	80.3	67.3	60.3	57.0	57.5	...
Plus: Value added tax	...	...	-11.7	...	...	...	...	...	...	...	...	...
Plus: Other adjustments [b]	10.4	16.8	25.9	31.6	36.8	48.2	36.2	50.9	46.5	46.0	37.8	...
Equals: Gross Domestic Product	407.8	609.6	706.2	773.7	891.3	916.6	1054.3	1093.3	1085.6	1072.9	1056.8	1034.8

a) Gross domestic product in factor values.
b) Item 'Other adjustments' refers to net indirect taxes other than import duties.

1.11 Gross Domestic Product by Kind of Activity, in Constant Prices

Million Liberian dollars

	1970	1975	1977	1978	1979	1980	1981	1982	1983	1984	1985	1986
		At constant prices of: 1971					1981					
1 Agriculture, hunting, forestry and fishing	89.3	50.1	54.9	59.9	62.8	63.0	49.4 / 297.0	297.9	305.0	323.2	339.2	342.3
2 Mining and quarrying	121.2	116.2	94.3	93.3	99.1	111.0	100.8 / 127.4	120.9	96.0	99.4	92.0	94.3
3 Manufacturing	15.7	23.1	29.2	30.7	33.0	26.0	23.6 / 62.9	66.0	65.4	68.3	67.2	65.1
4 Electricity, gas and water	4.9	6.6	7.7	7.9	8.0	7.8	7.9 / 22.7	26.9	23.4	23.6	24.0	24.0
5 Construction	17.4	14.1	19.2	22.0	25.0	15.0	18.0 / 37.0	33.3	38.2	29.8	30.5	26.7
6 Wholesale and retail trade, restaurants and hotels	40.4	27.6	29.5	30.2	31.0	25.0	23.0 / 59.1	68.9	67.1	56.9	57.4	52.4
7 Transport, storage and communication	32.7	35.5	41.0	43.0	44.0	35.0	33.4 / 76.2	88.8	86.4	84.7	72.7	71.1
8 Finance, insurance, real estate and business services	24.1	26.7	27.2	28.0	30.0	30.0	31.1 / 85.8	83.6	88.7	86.3	86.5	87.3
9 Community, social and personal services	9.1	18.7	23.8	...	...	17.0	16.0 / 28.6	30.5	31.4	27.1	30.0	28.0
Total, Industries	354.8	318.6	326.8	...	...	330.3	303.2 / 796.7	816.8	801.6	799.3	799.5	791.2
Producers of Government Services	25.2	29.2	31.3	...	...	39.6	50.4 / 154.4	154.9	152.5	146.0	137.3	135.6
Other Producers	3.4	...	...	...	...	...	...	...	...	...	...	...
Subtotal	383.4[a]	347.8[a]	358.1[a]	372.2[a]	393.5[a]	369.9[a]	353.6[a] / 951.1	971.7	954.1	945.3	936.8	926.8
Less: Imputed bank service charge	3.3	4.3	3.9	4.0	4.5	3.7	4.3 / 13.3	12.4	14.7	11.1	13.0	13.7
Plus: Import duties	...	...	...	...	...	...	...	...	...	...	...	...
Plus: Value added tax	...	...	...	...	...	...	...	...	...	...	...	...
Plus: Other adjustments	29.2[b]	31.0[b]	42.0[b]	50.8[b]	50.0[b]	45.2[b]	45.8[b] / 116.5	113.5	96.5	95.6	85.2	79.2
Equals: Gross Domestic Product	409.3	374.5	396.2	419.0	439.0	411.4	395.4 / 1054.3	1072.8	1035.9	1029.8	1009.0	992.3

a) Gross domestic product in factor values.
b) Item 'Other adjustments' refers to net indirect taxes other than import duties.

Liberia

1.12 Relations Among National Accounting Aggregates

Million Liberian dollars

	1970	1975	1977	1978	1979	1980	1981	1982	1983	1984	1985	1986
Gross Domestic Product	...	...	...	...	...	...	1054.3	1093.3	1085.6	1072.9	1056.8	1034.8
Plus: Net factor income from the rest of the world	...	...	...	...	...	...	-125.2	-175.5	-141.9	-170.1	-70.6	-110.9
Equals: Gross National Product	...	...	...	...	...	...	929.1	917.8	943.7	902.8	986.2	923.9
Less: Consumption of fixed capital	...	...	...	...	...	...	118.3	115.8	115.8	98.6	85.2	90.8
Equals: National Income	...	...	...	...	...	...	810.8	802.0	827.9	804.2	901.0	833.1
Plus: Net current transfers from the rest of the world	...	...	...	...	...	...	...	...	...	...	...	...
Equals: National Disposable Income	...	...	...	...	...	...	...	...	...	...	...	...
Less: Final consumption	...	...	...	...	...	...	...	...	...	...	...	...
Equals: Net Saving	...	...	...	...	...	...	...	...	...	...	...	...
Less: Surplus of the nation on current transactions	...	...	...	...	...	...	...	...	...	...	...	...
Equals: Net Capital Formation	...	...	...	...	...	...	...	...	...	...	...	...

Libyan Arab Jamahiriya

General note. The preparation of national accounts statistics in Libyan Arab Jamahiriya is undertaken by the Ministry of Planning, Tripoli. The official estimates are published in a series of publications entitled 'National Accounts of Libya'. A detailed description of the sources and methods used for the national accounts estimation is contained in a publication entitled 'National Accounts Statistics of the Libyan Arab Republic - Sources and Methods' published in 1972. The estimates are generally in accordance with the classifications and definitions recommended in the United Nations System of National Accounts (SNA). The following tables have been prepared from successive replies to the United Nations national accounts questionnaire. When the scope and coverage of the estimates differ for conceptual or statistical reasons from the definitions and classifications recommended in SNA, a footnote is indicated to the relevant tables.

Sources and methods:

(a) Gross domestic product. Gross domestic product is estimated mainly through the production approach.

(b) Expenditure on the gross domestic product. The expenditure approach is used to estimate government final consumption expenditure and imports and exports of goods and services. This approach is also used for gross fixed capital formation, although supported by the commodity-flow method for machinery and equipment. The commodity-flow method is used for the estimation of private expenditure on goods while other approaches are used for the estimation of expenditure on services. For government final consumption expenditure, the estimates are obtained from actual revenue and expenditure data supplied by the Ministry of Finance, by municipalities and by the National Social Insurance Institutions. The estimates are classified both by purpose and by kind of expenditure. The estimates of private expenditures on goods are obtained from the external trade statistics by commodity and from data on locally produced goods, import duties, trade margins and average retail prices. The estimates of capital formation for the petroleum sector are obtained from Annual Survey of Petroleum Mining Industry and for the general government, the most important source is the data on actual expenditure in the central government development budgets. For machinery and equipment, external trade data are used, adding duties paid and other costs and deducting value of re-export from c.i.f. value of imports. Exports and imports of goods and services are estimated from data supplied by the Bank of Libya. For the constant price estimates, price deflation is used for most of the expenditure items, the current values being deflated by various price indexes such as nation-wide cost of living index, price index of imported consumer goods and appropriate unit value indexes for different capital goods. Personal expenditures on items such as food and transport equipment are extrapolated by quantity indicators.

(c) Cost-structure of the gross domestic product. In estimating the cost-structure components of GDP, depreciation of the petroleum sector is obtained from the Annual Survey of Petroleum Mining Industry. For other sectors, depreciation is estimated as a certain percentage of gross domestic product according to international experience and judgement about the prevailing situation in the Libyan economy. Indirect taxes are estimated from the central government and local authorities' annual accounts, while subsidies are estimated on the basis of the ordinary and the development budgets. No information for compensation of employees and operating surplus is available about the methods of estimation.

(d) Gross domestic product by kind of economic activity. The table of gross domestic product by kind of economic activity is prepared at market prices, i.e. producers' values. The production approach is used to estimate value added of the majority of industries. The income approach is used for transport, storage and communication, public administration and defence and other services. The expenditure approach is used for the construction sector, whereas value added of the trade sectors is based upon the use of the commodity-flow method. All data required for the estimation of the agriculture sector are supplied by the Ministry of Agriculture. The agricultural statistics are based on reports made by the local authorities of the Ministry of Agriculture and data derived from the reporting system are verified by the agricultural census held in 1974. Petroleum mining, which accounts for more than two-thirds of GDP, is carried out by petroleum mining concession holding units and by non-concession holding units which are engaged in prospecting and drilling activities on a contract basis. Gross output of the concession holding units is made up of value of exports, value of domestic sales, value of changes in stocks, cost of surveys and exploration, value of work done for others and miscellaneous sources of income. The value of exports based on f.o.b. values, is reported by crude petroleum exporting companies, while the value of the other output is contained in the Annual Survey of Petroleum Mining Industry. The total value of inputs consists of the cost of materials consumed and the value of services purchased. For the activities of the non-concession holding units, a survey is undertaken on an annual basis since 1970. The basic source of information for manufacturing is the annual survey conducted since 1965 and published in 'Report of the Annual Survey of Large Manufacturing Establishments'. The data derived from the surveys are adjusted to exclude trade activity. Estimates for gross output and value added are then worked out for all establishments, including those engaging less than 20 persons which are not covered by the annual surveys. The main sources of information for the construction sector are the government budgets, statements by the municipalities and the annual surveys of the petroleum mining industry and of the large manufacturing establishments. The value added of construction is estimated as a percentage of the total expenditure on construction made by all sectors of the economy. There are no comprehensive statistics which could be used for a direct compilation of value added originating in trade. The estimation is instead based on an indirect method, according to which the income accruing to the trade sector is estimated as a percentage of the value of goods transacted during the year. The value added of road transport is based on the number of vehicles in operation and the estimated value added per vehicle. Transport data are supplied by Ministry of Communication Road Department and Libyan Arab Airline. Data for banking and insurance are supplied by Bank of Libya. The income accrued from ownership of dwellings is based on the estimation of the number of dwelling units existing each year and on the application of an average annual rent per unit. Estimates for the producers of government services are based on actual revenue and expenditure of the government sectors. Other services estimates are derived by applying an average gross income per person to the number of persons engaged in the different activities. For the constant price estimates, double deflation is used for the agricultural sector with the quantity of output and input valued at average 1963-1965 prices. Value added of crude oil production, electricity, gas and water, construction and transport is extrapolated by quantity indexes of output. For other activities in the petroleum sector, the current value is deflated by a price index roughly reflecting changes in the cost of its main goods and services. For manufacturing, trade, financial sector and other services, different kinds of price indexes are used, such as cost of living index and price index of domestic manufacturing goods.

1.1 Expenditure on the Gross Domestic Product, in Current Prices

Million Libyan dinars

	1970	1975	1977	1978	1979	1980	1981	1982	1983	1984	1985	1986
1 Government final consumption expenditure	220.7	1044.3	1400.3	1691.8	2006.6	2350.5	2720.5	2965.5	...	...	...	...
2 Private final consumption expenditure	395.5	1193.5	1482.2	1665.2	1894.7	2327.5	3127.3	3383.8	...	...	...	...
3 Gross capital formation	246.3	1154.7	1398.3	1552.0	1965.3	2518.8	2930.9	2311.8	...	...	...	...
A Increase in stocks	3.6	100.0	30.0	20.0	110.0	95.0	120.0	-50.0	...	...	...	...
B Gross fixed capital formation	242.7	1054.7	1368.3	1532.0	1855.3	2423.8	2810.9	2361.8	...	...	...	...
Residential buildings	...	235.5	245.6	256.5	214.8	250.6	325.2	...	...	...	...	...
Non-residential buildings	...	166.5	228.2	255.6	356.9	419.9	540.5	...	...	...	...	...
Other construction and land improvement etc.	...	285.7	459.0	535.6	659.7	914.2	999.3	...	...	...	...	...
Other	...	367.0	435.5	484.3	623.9	839.1	945.9	...	...	...	...	...
4 Exports of goods and services	870.0	2053.2	3430.8	2978.1	4801.4	6737.0	4868.4	4104.5	...	...	...	...
5 Less: Imports of goods and services	403.2	1665.7	1948.6	2199.5	2821.7	3398.7	4306.2	3920.0	...	...	...	...
Equals: Gross Domestic Product	1329.3	3780.0	5763.0	5687.6	7846.4	10535.1	9340.9	8845.6	8531.0	7574.0	7203.0	6473.0

Libyan Arab Jamahiriya

1.2 Expenditure on the Gross Domestic Product, in Constant Prices

Million Libyan dinars

	1970	1975	1977	1978	1979	1980	1981	1982	1983	1984	1985	1986
				At constant prices of:								
			1975						1980			
1 Government final consumption expenditure	...	1044.3	1362.7	1619.0	1884.1	2141.0 / 2350.5	2566.5	2696.0	...	...	...	...
2 Private final consumption expenditure	...	1193.5	1403.8	1518.6	1679.9	1995.3 / 2327.5	3053.9	3026.3	...	...	...	...
3 Gross capital formation	...	1154.7	1233.1	1307.1	1538.2	1781.5 / 2518.8	2746.2	2095.2	...	...	...	...
A Increase in stocks	...	100.0	25.0	15.0	100.0	90.0 / 95.0	112.0	-45.5	...	...	...	...
B Gross fixed capital formation	...	1054.7	1208.1	1292.1	1438.2	1691.5 / 2423.8	2634.2	2140.7	...	...	...	...
Residential buildings	...	235.5	217.4	243.2	265.6	180.1 / ...						
Non-residential buildings	...	166.5	201.9	225.9	246.5	332.8 / ...						
Other construction and land improvement etc.	...	285.7	409.2	437.3	475.9	635.4 / ...						
Other	...	367.0	379.6	385.7	450.2	543.2 / ...						
4 Exports of goods and services	...	2053.2	2869.5	2728.3	2958.1	2443.1 / 6737.0	4314.2	4549.1	...	...	...	...
5 Less: Imports of goods and services	...	1665.7	1813.0	1949.8	2369.2	2630.8 / 3398.7	4102.5	3685.0	...	...	...	...
Equals: Gross Domestic Product	...	3780.0	5056.1	5223.2	5691.1	5730.1 / 10535.1	8578.3	8681.6	...	...	...	...

1.3 Cost Components of the Gross Domestic Product

Million Libyan dinars

	1970	1975	1977	1978	1979	1980	1981	1982	1983	1984	1985	1986
1 Indirect taxes, net	41.0	105.7	150.3	191.5	243.4	297.9	385.9	315.6	...	...	...	...
A Indirect taxes	50.5	219.9	264.2	307.3	393.3	509.4	575.8	528.0	...	...	...	...
B Less: Subsidies	9.5	114.2	113.9	115.8	149.9	211.5	189.9	212.4	...	...	...	...
2 Consumption of fixed capital	109.0	166.1	207.5	237.4	263.2	338.3	392.4	475.9	...	...	...	...
3 Compensation of employees paid by resident producers to:	268.8	1048.2	1431.7	1635.4	1848.9	2162.7	2546.7	2635.2	...	...	...	...
A Resident households	217.5	976.5	1354.2	...	...	...	...	...	...	...	...	...
B Rest of the world	51.3	71.7	77.5	...	...	...	...	...	...	...	...	...
4 Operating surplus	910.5	2460.0	3973.5	3623.3	5490.9	7736.2	6015.9	5418.9	...	...	...	...
A Corporate and quasi-corporate enterprises	...	...										...
B Private unincorporated enterprises	...	...	...	...	...	...	...	...	...	...	...	...
C General government	...	3.3	...	...	...	...	...	...	...	...	...	...
Equals: Gross Domestic Product	1329.3	3780.0	5763.0	5687.6	7846.3	10535.1	9340.9	8845.6	...	...	...	...

1.4 General Government Current Receipts and Disbursements

Million Libyan dinars

	1970	1975	1977	1978	1979	1980	1981	1982	1983	1984	1985	1986
					Receipts							
1 Operating surplus	...	3.3	5.3	3.1	10.9	15.9	...	...	...	...	...	...
2 Property and entrepreneurial income	490.1	1408.4	2860.7	2405.0	3950.5	6497.9	...	...	...	...	...	...
3 Taxes, fees and contributions	80.5	363.4	508.0	595.4	740.3	919.8	...	...	...	...	...	...
A Indirect taxes	50.5	219.9	264.2	307.3	393.3	509.4	...	...	...	...	...	...

Libyan Arab Jamahiriya

1.4 General Government Current Receipts and Disbursements
(Continued)

Million Libyan dinars

	1970	1975	1977	1978	1979	1980	1981	1982	1983	1984	1985	1986
B Direct taxes	16.2	83.4	145.5	195.9	225.5	283.9	...	...	...	...	...	...
C Social security contributions	8.9	48.8	83.2	75.4	76.9	86.0	...	...	...	...	...	...
D Compulsory fees, fines and penalties	4.9	11.3	15.1	16.8	44.6	40.5	...	...	...	...	...	...
4 Other current transfers	7.2	9.5	2.0	3.7	2.5	1.7	...	...	...	...	...	...
Total Current Receipts of General Government	577.8	1784.7	3375.8	3007.2	4704.2	7435.4	...	...	...	...	...	...

Disbursements

	1970	1975	1977	1978	1979	1980	1981	1982	1983	1984	1985	1986
1 Government final consumption expenditure	220.7	1044.3	1400.3	1691.8	2006.6	2350.5	...	...	...	...	...	...
A Compensation of employees	...	413.9	...	...	...	...	...	...	...	...	...	...
B Consumption of fixed capital	...	20.5	...	...	...	...	...	...	...	...	...	...
C Purchases of goods and services, net	...	...	...	...	...	...	...	...	...	...	...	...
D Less: Own account fixed capital formation	...	...	...	...	...	...	...	...	...	...	...	...
E Indirect taxes paid, net	...	...	...	...	...	...	...	...	...	...	...	...
2 Property income	...	...	...	...	...	...	...	...	...	...	...	...
3 Subsidies	9.5	114.2	113.9	115.8	149.9	211.5	...	...	...	...	...	...
4 Other current transfers	68.4	90.3	116.1	160.7	216.4	337.6	...	...	...	...	...	...
A Social security benefits	...	30.6	35.4	43.9	52.3	49.9	...	...	...	...	...	...
B Social assistance grants	6.5	9.0	16.5	34.2	49.3	81.3	...	...	...	...	...	...
C Other	68.4	50.7	64.2	82.7	114.9	206.4	...	...	...	...	...	...
5 Net saving	279.2	536.0	1745.5	1038.9	2331.0	4535.7	...	...	...	...	...	...
Total Current Disbursements and Net Saving of General Government	577.8	1784.7	3375.8	3007.2	4704.2	7435.4	...	...	...	...	...	...

1.7 External Transactions on Current Account, Summary

Million Libyan dinars

	1970	1975	1977	1978	1979	1980	1981	1982	1983	1984	1985	1986

Payments to the Rest of the World

	1970	1975	1977	1978	1979	1980	1981	1982	1983	1984	1985	1986
1 Imports of goods and services	403.2	1665.7	1948.6	2199.5	2821.7	3398.7	4306.2	3920.0	...	...	...	...
A Imports of merchandise c.i.f.	372.2	1454.8	1663.8	1957.6	2469.0	3057.8	...	...	...	...	...	...
B Other	31.0	210.9	284.8	241.9	352.7	340.9	...	...	...	...	...	...
2 Factor income to the rest of the world	252.6	495.3	588.2	535.8	678.9	668.2	860.1	836.4	...	...	...	...
A Compensation of employees	51.3	71.7	77.5	161.5	301.9	311.5	453.2	466.2	...	...	...	...
B Property and entrepreneurial income	201.3	423.6	510.7	374.3	377.0	356.7	406.9	370.2	...	...	...	...
3 Current transfers to the rest of the world	43.4	50.1	45.4	37.7	70.1	30.1	41.7	39.1	...	...	...	...
4 Surplus of the nation on current transactions	208.1	-93.6	921.0	304.1	1362.0	3025.3	149.6	-424.6	...	...	...	...
Payments to the Rest of the World and Surplus of the Nation on Current Transactions	907.3	2117.5	3503.2	3077.1	4932.7	7122.3	5357.6	4370.9	...	...	...	...

# Libyan Arab Jamahiriya

1.7 External Transactions on Current Account, Summary
(Continued)

Million Libyan dinars

	1970	1975	1977	1978	1979	1980	1981	1982	1983	1984	1985	1986
Receipts From The Rest of the World												
1 Exports of goods and services	870.0	2053.2	3430.8	2978.1	4801.4	6737.0	4868.4	4104.5	...	...	...	...
A Exports of merchandise f.o.b.	857.6	2011.8	3387.8	2941.0	4766.4	6697.4	...	...	...	...	...	...
B Other	12.4	41.4	43.0	37.1	35.0	39.6	...	...	...	...	...	...
2 Factor income from rest of the world	36.6	63.5	71.5	93.9	125.8	379.5	481.6	256.9	...	...	...	...
A Compensation of employees	-	-	-	-	-	...	...	...	...	...	...	...
B Property and entrepreneurial income	36.6	63.5	71.5	93.9	125.8	...	...	...	...	...	...	...
3 Current transfers from rest of the world	0.7	0.8	0.9	5.1	5.8	5.8	7.6	9.5	...	...	...	...
Receipts from the Rest of the World on Current Transactions	907.3	2117.5	3503.2	3077.1	4932.7	7122.3	5357.6	4370.9	...	...	...	...

1.8 Capital Transactions of The Nation, Summary

Million Libyan dinars

	1970	1975	1977	1978	1979	1980	1981	1982	1983	1984	1985	1986
Finance of Gross Capital Formation												
Gross saving	454.3	1061.1	2319.3	1856.1	3327.3	5544.1	3080.5	1887.2	...	...	...	...
1 Consumption of fixed capital	109.0	166.1	207.5	237.4	263.2	338.3	392.4	475.9	...	...	...	...
A General government	...	18.4	30.0	37.6	50.3	63.7	...	...	...	...	...	...
B Corporate and quasi-corporate enterprises	...	...	...	...	...	...	...	...	...	...	...	...
C Other	...	...	...	...	...	...	...	...	...	...	...	...
2 Net saving	345.3	895.0	2111.8	1618.7	3064.1	5205.8	2688.1	1411.3	...	...	...	...
A General government	279.2	536.0	1745.5	1038.9	2331.0	4535.7	...	...	...	...	...	...
B Corporate and quasi-corporate enterprises	...	...	...	...	...	...	...	...	...	...	...	...
C Other	...	...	...	...	...	...	...	...	...	...	...	...
Less: Surplus of the nation on current transactions	208.1	-93.6	921.0	304.1	1362.0	3025.3	149.6	-424.6	...	...	...	...
Finance of Gross Capital Formation	246.3	1154.7	1398.3	1552.0	1965.3	2518.8	2930.6	2311.8	...	...	...	...
Gross Capital Formation												
Increase in stocks	3.6	100.0	30.0	20.0	110.0	95.0	120.0	-50.0	...	...	...	...
Gross fixed capital formation	242.7	1054.7	1368.3	1532.0	1855.3	2423.8	2810.9	2361.8	...	...	...	...
1 General government	3.3	834.1	1171.5	1284.4	1672.6	2223.3	...	...	...	...	...	...
2 Corporate and quasi-corporate enterprises	...	...	...	...	...	...	...	...	...	...	...	...
3 Other	...	...	...	...	...	...	...	...	...	...	...	...
Gross Capital Formation	246.3	1154.7	1398.3	1552.0	1965.3	2518.8	2930.9	2311.8	...	...	...	...

Libyan Arab Jamahiriya

1.10 Gross Domestic Product by Kind of Activity, in Current Prices

Million Libyan dinars

	1970	1975	1977	1978	1979	1980	1981	1982	1983	1984	1985	1986
1 Agriculture, hunting, forestry and fishing	33.1	82.9	90.0	122.1	140.4	164.9	204.3	217.2	...	...	...	...
2 Mining and quarrying [a]	814.3	1981.8	3304.4	2842.0	4586.8	6620.7	4709.4	4265.2	...	...	...	...
3 Manufacturing	22.5	65.5	124.7	148.7	185.8	213.9	240.8	304.9	...	...	...	...
4 Electricity, gas and water	6.2	17.6	26.1	31.0	40.0	49.7	55.7	69.2	...	...	...	...
5 Construction	87.8	434.7	602.0	682.8	726.7	935.7	1202.5	1053.9	...	...	...	...
6 Wholesale and retail trade, restaurants and hotels	47.0	224.6	292.0	338.9	383.2	481.7	556.5	522.7	...	...	...	...
7 Transport, storage and communication	43.2	175.8	220.1	250.9	291.2	335.3	385.5	387.3	...	...	...	...
8 Finance, insurance, real estate and business services	67.9	229.9	301.4	348.2	383.4	441.3	495.4	467.6	...	...	...	...
9 Community, social and personal services	68.2	201.9	288.1	318.8	351.0	381.0	421.1	469.9	...	...	...	...
Total, Industries	1190.2	3414.7	5248.8	5083.4	7088.5	9624.2	8271.2	7757.9	...	...	...	...
Producers of Government Services	98.1	258.3	362.2	410.8	512.5	611.1	683.8	772.1	...	...	...	...
Other Producers	...	1.3	1.7	1.9	2.0	2.0	-	-	...	...	...	...
Subtotal [b]	1288.3	3674.3	5612.7	5496.1	7603.0	10237.3	8955.0	8530.0	...	...	...	...
Less: Imputed bank service charge	...	...	...	...	...	...	...	...	...	...	...	...
Plus: Import duties	...	...	...	...	...	...	...	...	...	...	...	...
Plus: Value added tax	...	...	...	...	...	...	...	...	...	...	...	...
Plus: Other adjustments [c]	41.0	105.7	150.3	191.5	243.4	297.9	385.9	315.6	...	...	...	...
Equals: Gross Domestic Product	1329.3	3780.0	5763.0	5687.6	7846.4	10535.1	9340.9	8845.6	...	...	...	...

a) Item 'Mining and quarrying' includes oil and gas production.
b) Gross domestic product in factor values.
c) Item 'Other adjustments' refers to indirect taxes net of subsidies.

1.11 Gross Domestic Product by Kind of Activity, in Constant Prices

Million Libyan dinars

	1970	1975	1977	1978	1979	1980	1981	1982	1983	1984	1985	1986
	1964		**1975**			**1980**						
1 Agriculture, hunting, forestry and fishing	17.2	82.9	79.1	85.9	91.2	104.9 / 164.9	177.9	185.9	...	...	...	...
2 Mining and quarrying	660.4	1981.8[a]	2741.7[a]	2647.6[a]	2853.1[a]	2478.0[a] / 6620.7[a]	4200.3[a]	4414.8[a]	...	...	...	...
3 Manufacturing	20.5	65.5	121.1	141.0	136.0	157.0 / 213.9	220.8	280.5	...	...	...	...
4 Electricity, gas and water	4.7	17.6	26.1	31.0	40.0	49.7 / 49.7	54.1	64.2	...	...	...	...
5 Construction	41.8	434.7	528.0	559.7	567.7	660.9 / 935.7	1085.5	942.8	...	...	...	...
6 Wholesale and retail trade, restaurants and hotels	37.5	224.6	270.6	294.7	314.1	349.1 / 481.7	515.3	493.1	...	...	...	...
7 Transport, storage and communication	36.5	175.8	203.5	223.6	246.2	274.1 / 335.3	376.0	373.4	...	...	...	...
8 Finance, insurance, real estate and business services	50.3	229.9	288.0	320.0	339.6	376.8 / 441.3	476.2	452.4	...	...	...	...
9 Community, social and personal services	51.0	203.2	286.2	318.2	348.3	376.6 / 382.9	411.1	440.3	...	...	...	...

Libyan Arab Jamahiriya

1.11 Gross Domestic Product by Kind of Activity, in Constant Prices
(Continued)

Million Libyan dinars

	1970	1975	1977	1978	1979	1980	1981	1982	1983	1984	1985	1986
		1964			At constant prices of: 1975				1980			
Total, Industries	919.9	3416.0	4544.3	4621.7	4936.2	4827.1 9626.1	7517.2	7647.4	...	...	...	...
Producers of Government Services	73.4	258.3	361.5	410.0	511.5	605.1 611.1	670.2	718.6	...	...	...	...
Other Producers	...	...	...	...	...	...						
Subtotal	993.3	3674.3	4905.8	5031.7	5447.7	5432.2 10237.2	8187.4	8366.0	...	...	...	...
Less: Imputed bank service charge		...	...	...	...	...	...	...				
Plus: Import duties		...	...	...	...	...	...	...				
Plus: Value added tax		...	...	...	...	...	...	...				
Equals: Gross Domestic Product	993.3	3674.3[b]	4905.8[b]	5031.7[b]	5447.7[b]	5432.2[b] 10237.2[b]	8187.4[b]	8366.0[b]	...	...	...	...

a) Item 'Mining and quarrying' includes oil and gas production.
b) Gross domestic product in factor values.

1.12 Relations Among National Accounting Aggregates

Million Libyan dinars

	1970	1975	1977	1978	1979	1980	1981	1982	1983	1984	1985	1986
Gross Domestic Product	1329.3	3780.0	5763.0	5687.6	7846.3	10535.1	9340.9	8845.6	...	...	...	...
Plus: Net factor income from the rest of the world	-216.0	-431.8	-516.7	-441.9	-553.1	-288.7	-378.5	-579.5	...	...	...	...
Factor income from the rest of the world	36.6	63.5	71.5	93.9	125.8	379.5	481.6	256.9	...	...	...	...
Less: Factor income to the rest of the world	252.6	495.3	588.2	535.8	678.9	668.2	860.1	836.4	...	...	...	...
Equals: Gross National Product	1113.3	3348.2	5246.3	5245.7	7293.2	10246.4	8962.4	8266.1	...	...	...	...
Less: Consumption of fixed capital	109.0	166.1	207.5	237.4	263.2	338.3	392.4	475.9	...	...	...	...
Equals: National Income	1004.3	3182.1	5038.8	5008.3	7030.0	9908.1	8570.0	7790.2	...	...	...	...
Plus: Net current transfers from the rest of the world	-42.7	-49.3	-44.5	-32.6	-64.3	-24.3	-34.1	-29.6	...	...	...	...
Current transfers from the rest of the world	0.7	0.8	0.9	5.1	5.8	5.8	7.6	9.5	...	...	...	...
Less: Current transfers to the rest of the world	43.4	50.1	45.4	37.7	70.1	30.1	41.7	39.1	...	...	...	...
Equals: National Disposable Income	961.6	3132.8	4994.3	4975.7	6965.7	9883.8	8535.9	7760.6	...	...	...	...
Less: Final consumption	616.2	2237.8	2882.5	3357.0	3901.3	4678.0	5847.8	6349.3	...	...	...	...
Equals: Net Saving	345.3	895.0	2111.8	1618.7	3064.1	5205.8	2688.1	1411.3	...	...	...	...
Less: Surplus of the nation on current transactions	208.1	-93.6	921.0	304.1	1362.0	3025.3	149.6	-424.6	...	...	...	...
Equals: Net Capital Formation	137.3	988.6	1190.8	1314.6	1702.1	2180.5	2538.5	1835.9	...	...	...	...

Libyan Arab Jamahiriya

2.1 Government Final Consumption Expenditure by Function, in Current Prices

Million Libyan dinars

	1970	1975	1977	1978	1979	1980	1981	1982	1983	1984	1985	1986
1 General public services	47.7						...	...	...	...	...	...
2 Defence	91.2	763.9	966.4	1201.6	1381.2	1617.7	...	...	...	...	...	...
3 Public order and safety							...	...	...	...	...	...
4 Education	33.0	132.0	188.6	210.5	237.8	271.2	...	...	...	...	...	...
5 Health	16.2	65.1	102.2	121.8	144.5	174.4	...	...	...	...	...	...
6 Social security and welfare	1.4	17.7	36.9	34.9	55.0	54.4	...	...	...	...	...	...
7 Housing and community amenities	7.0	18.1	27.9	32.0	34.7	29.3	...	...	...	...	...	...
8 Recreational, cultural and religious affairs	6.0	12.2	22.2	24.3	20.4	21.3	...	...	...	...	...	...
9 Economic services	18.2	35.0	56.3	66.7	133.0	182.1	...	...	...	...	...	...
10 Other functions	...	...				...	...	...	...	...	...	...
Total Government Final Consumption Expenditure	220.7	1044.3	1400.3	1691.8	2006.6	2350.5	...	...	...	...	...	...

2.2 Government Final Consumption Expenditure by Function, in Constant Prices

Million Libyan dinars

	1970	1975	1977	1978	1979	1980	1981	1982	1983	1984	1985	1986
				At constant prices of:1975								
1 General public services	...						...	...	...	...	...	...
2 Defence	...	763.9	936.1	1142.3	1282.8	1454.1	...	...	...	...	...	...
3 Public order and safety	...						...	...	...	...	...	...
4 Education	...	132.4	186.6	206.4	231.4	258.4	...	...	...	...	...	...
5 Health	...	65.1	99.4	117.1	136.2	159.3	...	...	...	...	...	...
6 Social security and welfare	...	17.7	36.6	34.1	53.9	53.1	...	...	...	...	...	...
7 Housing and community amenities	...	18.1	27.0	30.5	32.8	27.3	...	...	...	...	...	...
8 Recreational, cultural and religious affairs	...	12.2	21.7	23.7	19.7	20.2	...	...	...	...	...	...
9 Economic services	...	34.9	55.3	64.9	127.3	168.6	...	...	...	...	...	...
10 Other functions	...	...	...	...	...	...	...	...	...	...	...	...
Total Government Final Consumption Expenditure	...	1044.3	1362.7	1619.0	1884.1	2141.0	...	...	...	...	...	...

2.5 Private Final Consumption Expenditure by Type and Porpose, in Current Prices

Million Libyan dinars

	1970	1975	1977	1978	1979	1980	1981	1982	1983	1984	1985	1986
				Final Consumption Expenditure of Resident Households								
1 Food, beverages and tobacco	152.0	...	...	...	...	...	...	...	...	...	...	...
A Food	136.5	...	...	...	...	...	...	...	...	...	...	...
B Non-alcoholic beverages	3.2	...	...	...	...	...	...	...	...	...	...	...
C Alcoholic beverages	1.1	...	...	...	...	...	...	...	...	...	...	...
D Tobacco	11.2	...	...	...	...	...	...	...	...	...	...	...
2 Clothing and footwear	39.6	...	...	...	...	...	...	...	...	...	...	...
3 Gross rent, fuel and power	71.6	...	...	...	...	...	...	...	...	...	...	...
4 Furniture, furnishings and household equipment and operation	17.6	...	...	...	...	...	...	...	...	...	...	...
A Household operation	5.3	...	...	...	...	...	...	...	...	...	...	...
B Other	12.3	...	...	...	...	...	...	...	...	...	...	...
5 Medical care and health expenses	11.8	...	...	...	...	...	...	...	...	...	...	...
6 Transport and communication	51.0	...	...	...	...	...	...	...	...	...	...	...
A Personal transport equipment	7.4	...	...	...	...	...	...	...	...	...	...	...
B Other	43.6	...	...	...	...	...	...	...	...	...	...	...
7 Recreational, entertainment, education and cultural services	14.6	...	...	...	...	...	...	...	...	...	...	...
8 Miscellaneous goods and services	24.5	...	...	...	...	...	...	...	...	...	...	...

Libyan Arab Jamahiriya

2.5 Private Final Consumption Expenditure by Type and Porpose, in Current Prices
(Continued)

Million Libyan dinars

	1970	1975	1977	1978	1979	1980	1981	1982	1983	1984	1985	1986
A Personal care	18.4	...	...	...	...	...	...	...	...	...	...	...
B Expenditures in restaurants, cafes and hotels	5.2	...	...	...	...	...	...	...	...	...	...	...
C Other	0.9	...	...	...	...	...	...	...	...	...	...	...
Total Final Consumption Expenditure in the Domestic Market by Households, of which	382.7	...	...	...	...	...	...	...	...	...	...	...
A Durable goods	38.0	...	...	...	...	...	...	...	...	...	...	...
B Semi-durable goods	54.9	...	...	...	...	...	...	...	...	...	...	...
C Non-durable goods	187.0	...	...	...	...	...	...	...	...	...	...	...
D Services	102.8	...	...	...	...	...	...	...	...	...	...	...
Plus: Direct purchases abroad by resident households	19.5	...	...	...	...	...	...	...	...	...	...	...
Less: Direct purchases in the domestic market by non-resident households	10.1	...	...	...	...	...	...	...	...	...	...	...
Equals: Final Consumption Expenditure of Resident Households	392.1	...	...	...	...	...	...	...	...	...	...	...

Final Consumption Expenditure of Private Non-profit Institutions Serving Households

	1970	1975	1977	1978	1979	1980	1981	1982	1983	1984	1985	1986
Equals: Final Consumption Expenditure of Private Non-profit Organisations Serving Households	...	...	...	...	...	...	...	...	...	...	...	...
Statistical discrepancy	3.4	...	...	...	...	...	...	...	...	...	...	...
Private Final Consumption Expenditure	395.5	...	...	...	...	...	...	...	...	...	...	...

2.6 Private Final Consumption Expenditure by Type and Purpose, in Constant Prices

Million Libyan dinars

	1970	1975	1977	1978	1979	1980	1981	1982	1983	1984	1985	1986

At constant prices of:1964

Final Consumption Expenditure of Resident Households

	1970	1975	1977	1978	1979	1980	1981	1982	1983	1984	1985	1986
1 Food, beverages and tobacco	118.6	...	...	...	...	...	...	...	...	...	...	...
A Food	107.1	...	...	...	...	...	...	...	...	...	...	...
B Non-alcoholic beverages	3.0	...	...	...	...	...	...	...	...	...	...	...
C Alcoholic beverages	0.7	...	...	...	...	...	...	...	...	...	...	...
D Tobacco	7.8	...	...	...	...	...	...	...	...	...	...	...
2 Clothing and footwear	36.9	...	...	...	...	...	...	...	...	...	...	...
3 Gross rent, fuel and power	56.0	...	...	...	...	...	...	...	...	...	...	...
4 Furniture, furnishings and household equipment and operation	16.9	...	...	...	...	...	...	...	...	...	...	...
A Household operation	4.2	...	...	...	...	...	...	...	...	...	...	...
B Other	12.7	...	...	...	...	...	...	...	...	...	...	...
5 Medical care and health expenses	7.9	...	...	...	...	...	...	...	...	...	...	...
6 Transport and communication	36.9	...	...	...	...	...	...	...	...	...	...	...
A Personal transport equipment	6.5	...	...	...	...	...	...	...	...	...	...	...
B Other	30.4	...	...	...	...	...	...	...	...	...	...	...
7 Recreational, entertainment, education and cultural services	14.1	...	...	...	...	...	...	...	...	...	...	...
8 Miscellaneous goods and services	16.2	...	...	...	...	...	...	...	...	...	...	...
A Personal care	11.9	...	...	...	...	...	...	...	...	...	...	...
B Expenditures in restaurants, cafes and hotels	3.6	...	...	...	...	...	...	...	...	...	...	...

Libyan Arab Jamahiriya

2.6 Private Final Consumption Expenditure by Type and Purpose, in Constant Prices
(Continued)

Million Libyan dinars

	1970	1975	1977	1978	1979	1980	1981	1982	1983	1984	1985	1986
				At constant prices of:1964								
C Other	0.7	...	...	...	...	...	...	...	...	...	...	...
Total Final Consumption Expenditure in the Domestic Market by Households, of which	303.5	...	...	...	...	...	...	...	...	...	...	...
Plus: Direct purchases abroad by resident households	15.5	...	...	...	...	...	...	...	...	...	...	...
Less: Direct purchases in the domestic market by non-resident households	7.6	...	...	...	...	...	...	...	...	...	...	...
Equals: Final Consumption Expenditure of Resident Households	311.4	...	...	...	...	...	...	...	...	...	...	...
			Final Consumption Expenditure of Private Non-profit Institutions Serving Households									
Equals: Final Consumption Expenditure of Private Non-profit Organisations Serving Households	...	...	...	...	...	...	...	...	...	...	...	...
Statistical discrepancy	4.5	...	...	...	...	...	...	...	...	...	...	...
Private Final Consumption Expenditure	315.9	...	...	...	...	...	...	...	...	...	...	...

2.7 Gross Capital Formation by Type of Good and Owner, in Current Prices

Million Libyan dinars

	1980			
	TOTAL	Total Private	Public Enterprises	General Government
Increase in stocks, total	95.0	...	...	...
Gross Fixed Capital Formation, Total	2423.8	200.5	...	2223.3
1 Residential buildings	250.6	53.3	...	197.4
2 Non-residential buildings	419.9	5.0	...	414.9
3 Other construction	726.0	40.2	...	685.8
4 Land improvement and plantation and orchard development	188.2	0.6	...	187.6
5 Producers' durable goods	653.3	77.1	...	576.1
A Transport equipment	81.2	38.6	...	42.6
B Machinery and equipment	572.1	38.5	...	533.5
6 Breeding stock, dairy cattle, etc.	9.4	3.9	...	5.5
Statistical discrepancy [a]	176.4	20.4	...	156.0
Total Gross Capital Formation	2518.8	...	...	...

a) Item 'Statistical discrepancy' refers to furnishing and supplies and other assets.

2.8 Gross Capital Formation by Type of Good and Owner, in Constant Prices

Million Libyan dinars

	1980				1981			
	TOTAL	Total Private	Public Enterprises	General Government	TOTAL	Total Private	Public Enterprises	General Government
	At constant prices of:1975							
Increase in stocks, total	90.0	...	...	...	...	...	...	...
Gross Fixed Capital Formation, Total	1691.5	...	...	...	1853.5	...	...	...
1 Residential buildings	180.1	...	...	...	342.0	...	...	...
2 Non-residential buildings	332.8	...	...	...	317.0	...	...	...
3 Other construction	499.1	...	...	...	461.0	...	...	...
4 Land improvement and plantation and orchard development	136.3	...	...	...	152.0	...	...	...
5 Producers' durable goods	421.8	...	...	...	444.5	...	...	...
A Transport equipment	54.8	...	...	...	46.5	...	...	...
B Machinery and equipment	367.0	...	...	...	398.0	...	...	...
6 Breeding stock, dairy cattle, etc.	7.6	...	...	...	5.0	...	...	...
Statistical discrepancy [a]	113.8	...	...	...	132.0	...	...	...
Total Gross Capital Formation	1781.5	...	...	...	...	...	...	...

a) Item 'Statistical discrepancy' refers to furnishing and supplies and other assets.

Libyan Arab Jamahiriya

2.11 Gross Fixed Capital Formation by Kind of Activity of Owner, ISIC Divisions, in Current Prices

Million Libyan dinars

	1970	1975	1977	1978	1979	1980	1981	1982	1983	1984	1985	1986
					All Producers							
1 Agriculture, hunting, forestry and fishing	...	149.9	188.4	217.5	234.2	334.2	375.9	247.7	...	...	...	...
2 Mining and quarrying	...	28.4	47.7	102.0	89.8	102.3	70.0	55.0	...	...	...	...
3 Manufacturing	...	121.5	164.6	163.2	269.8	431.8	442.9	342.7	...	...	...	...
4 Electricity, gas and water	...	135.1	195.2	205.5	284.3	370.8	261.3	252.0	...	...	...	...
5 Construction	...	28.4	31.2	16.2	20.0	22.8	25.0	30.0	...	...	...	...
6 Wholesale and retail trade, restaurants and hotels	...	5.9	14.5	23.4	59.9	83.2	107.0	90.0	...	...	...	...
7 Transport, storage and communication	...	157.7	228.5	268.1	320.8	439.4	703.8	690.4	...	...	...	...
8 Finance, insurance, real estate and business services	...	235.7	246.6	257.4	215.9	251.7	324.0	234.7	...	...	...	...
9 Community, social and personal services	...	100.7	117.4	125.9	177.2	197.5	305.3	265.1	...	...	...	...
Total Industries	...	963.3	1234.1	1379.2	1671.9	2233.7	2615.2	2207.6	...	...	...	...
Producers of Government Services	...	91.4	134.2	152.6	183.6	190.1	195.7	154.2	...	...	...	...
Private Non-Profit Institutions Serving Households	...	...	...	...	...	...	...	...	...	...	...	...
Total	...	1054.7	1368.3	1532.0	1855.3	2423.8	2810.9	2361.8	...	...	...	...

2.12 Gross Fixed Capital Formation by Kind of Activity of Owner, ISIC Divisions, in Constant Prices

Million Libyan dinars

	1970	1975	1977	1978	1979	1980	1981	1982	1983	1984	1985	1986
				At constant prices of:1975								
					All Producers							
1 Agriculture, hunting, forestry and fishing	...	149.9	169.9	185.5	185.4	244.4	...	...	...	...	...	...
2 Mining and quarrying	...	28.4	41.5	83.0	68.0	70.0	...	...	...	...	...	...
3 Manufacturing	...	121.5	143.5	134.3	200.9	277.5	...	...	...	...	...	...
4 Electricity, gas and water	...	135.1	168.3	168.7	213.0	255.4	...	...	...	...	...	...
5 Construction	...	28.4	28.4	13.7	15.5	16.4	...	...	...	...	...	...
6 Wholesale and retail trade, restaurants and hotels	...	5.9	12.8	19.8	47.7	59.9	...	...	...	...	...	...
7 Transport, storage and communication	...	157.7	203.5	227.2	252.0	311.8	...	...	...	...	...	...
8 Finance, insurance, real estate and business services	...	235.7	218.2	222.9	171.8	182.4	...	...	...	...	...	...
9 Community, social and personal services	...	100.7	103.9	107.8	139.7	139.3	...	...	...	...	...	...
A Sanitary and similar services	...	...	...	...	...	...	...	...	...	...	...	...
B Social and related community services	...	...	...	...	...	...	...	...	...	...	...	...
Educational services	...	73.1	68.6	63.7	77.9	83.5	...	...	...	...	...	...
Medical, dental, other health and veterinary services	...	26.2	33.5	43.2	60.7	47.7	...	...	...	...	...	...
C Recreational and cultural services	...	...	...	...	...	...	...	...	...	...	...	...
D Personal and household services	...	1.4	1.8	0.9	1.1	0.7	...	...	...	...	...	...
Total Industries	...	963.3	1090.1	1162.9	1294.0	1557.1	...	...	...	...	...	...
Producers of Government Services	...	91.4	118.1	129.2	144.2	134.4	...	...	...	...	...	...
Private Non Profit Institutions Serving Households	...	...	...	...	...	...	...	...	...	...	...	...
Total	...	1054.7	1208.1	1292.1	1438.2	1691.5	...	...	...	...	...	...

Libyan Arab Jamahiriya

2.17 Exports and Imports of Goods and Services, Detail

Million Libyan dinars

	1970	1975	1977	1978	1979	1980	1981	1982	1983	1984	1985	1986
Exports of Goods and Services												
1 Exports of merchandise, f.o.b.	857.6	2011.8	3387.8	2941.0	4766.4	6697.4	...	...	...	...	...	...
2 Transport and communication							...	...	...	...	...	...
3 Insurance service charges							...	...	...	...	...	...
4 Other commodities	12.4	41.4	43.0	37.1	35.0	39.6	...	...	...	...	...	...
5 Adjustments of merchandise exports to change-of-ownership basis							...	...	...	...	...	...
6 Direct purchases in the domestic market by non-residential households							...	...	...	...	...	...
7 Direct purchases in the domestic market by extraterritorial bodies							...	...	...	...	...	...
Total Exports of Goods and Services	870.0	2053.2	3430.8	2978.1	4801.4	6737.0	...	...	...	...	...	...
Imports of Goods and Services												
1 Imports of merchandise, c.i.f.	372.2	1454.8	1663.8	1957.6	2469.0	3057.8	...	...	...	...	...	...
2 Adjustments of merchandise imports to change-of-ownership basis	...	...				...						
3 Other transport and communication						340.9	...	...	...	...	...	...
4 Other insurance service charges							...	...	...	...	...	...
5 Other commodities	31.0	210.9	284.8	241.9	352.7		...	...	...	...	...	...
6 Direct purchases abroad by government							...	...	...	...	...	...
7 Direct purchases abroad by resident households							...	...	...	...	...	...
Total Imports of Goods and Services	403.2	1665.7	1948.6	2199.5	2821.7	3398.7	...	...	...	...	...	...
Balance of Goods and Services	466.8	387.5	1482.2	778.6	1979.7	3338.3	...	...	...	...	...	...
Total Imports and Balance of Goods and Services	870.0	2053.2	3430.8	2978.1	4801.4	6737.0	...	...	...	...	...	...

4.1 Derivation of Value Added by Kind of Activity, in Current Prices

Million Libyan dinars

	1980 Gross Output	Intermediate Consumption	Value Added
All Producers			
1 Agriculture, hunting, forestry and fishing	233.7	68.8	164.9
A Agriculture and hunting	227.7	67.2	160.5
B Forestry and logging	1.1	0.2	0.9
C Fishing	4.9	1.4	3.5
2 Mining and quarrying [a]	6862.2	241.5	6620.7
A Coal mining	-	-	-
B Crude petroleum and natural gas production	6801.2	229.3	6571.9
C Metal ore mining	-	-	-
D Other mining	61.0	12.2	48.8

Libyan Arab Jamahiriya

4.1 Derivation of Value Added by Kind of Activity, in Current Prices
(Continued)

Million Libyan dinars

	1980 Gross Output	1980 Intermediate Consumption	1980 Value Added
3 Manufacturing	623.0	409.1	213.9
A Manufacture of food, beverages and tobacco	110.7	74.5	36.2
B Textile, wearing apparel and leather industries	26.9	17.7	9.2
C Manufacture of wood and wood products, including furniture	21.3	14.4	6.9
D Manufacture of paper and paper products, printing and publishing	12.5	4.9	7.6
E Manufacture of chemicals and chemical petroleum, coal, rubber and plastic products [b]	363.8	252.1	111.7
F Manufacture of non-metallic mineral products, except products of petroleum and coal [b]	41.6	21.2	20.4
G Basic metal industries	34.3	17.5	16.8
H Manufacture of fabricated metal products, machinery and equipment			
I Other manufacturing industries	11.9	6.8	5.1
4 Electricity, gas and water	107.4	57.7	49.7
A Electricity, gas and steam	106.0	57.3	48.7
B Water works and supply	1.4	0.4	1.0
5 Construction	1701.5	765.8	935.7
6 Wholesale and retail trade, restaurants and hotels	598.6	116.9	481.7
A Wholesale and retail trade	558.3	102.7	455.6
B Restaurants and hotels	40.3	14.2	26.1
7 Transport, storage and communication	455.5	120.2	335.3
A Transport and storage	454.3	119.9	334.4
B Communication	1.2	0.3	0.9
8 Finance, insurance, real estate and business services	457.5	16.2	441.3
A Financial institutions	204.4	10.5	193.9
B Insurance	19.4	1.8	17.6
C Real estate and business services	233.7	3.9	229.8
Real estate, except dwellings	21.0	1.6	19.4
Dwellings	212.7	2.3	210.4
9 Community, social and personal services	496.7	115.8	380.9
A Sanitary and similar services	*	-	-
B Social and related community services	445.6	110.1	335.5
Educational services	271.2	50.4	220.8
Medical, dental, other health and veterinary services	174.4	59.7	114.7
C Recreational and cultural services	5.3	1.1	4.2
D Personal and household services	45.8	4.6	41.2
Total, Industries	11536.1	1912.0	9624.2
Producers of Government Services	1934.7	1323.6	611.1
Other Producers	2.8	0.8	2.0
Total [c]	13473.6	3236.4	10237.3
Less: Imputed bank service charge	...	...	...
Import duties	...	...	...
Value added tax	...	...	...
Total	...	...	...

a) Item 'Mining and quarrying' includes oil and gas production.
b) Petroleum products and liquified gas industries are included in item 'Manufacture of non-metallic mineral products'.
c) Gross domestic product in factor values.

Libyan Arab Jamahiriya

4.3 Cost Components of Value Added

Million Libyan dinars

	Compensation of Employees	Capital Consumption	Net Operating Surplus	Indirect Taxes	Less: Subsidies Received	Value Added
			1980			
			All Producers			
1 Agriculture, hunting, forestry and fishing	46.3	24.5	94.1	...	...	164.9
A Agriculture and hunting	44.0	23.9	92.6	...	...	160.5
B Forestry and logging	0.7	0.1	0.1	...	...	0.9
C Fishing	1.6	0.5	1.4	...	...	3.5
2 Mining and quarrying [a]	128.5	73.3	6418.9	...	...	6620.7
A Coal mining	...	...	...	...	...	...
B Crude petroleum and natural gas production	108.8	63.5	6399.6	...	...	6571.9
C Metal ore mining	...	...	...	...	...	...
D Other mining	19.7	9.8	19.3	...	...	48.8
3 Manufacturing	71.6	24.8	117.5	...	...	213.9
A Manufacture of food, beverages and tobacco	18.8	10.1	7.3	...	...	36.2
B Textile, wearing apparel and leather industries	8.5	1.2	-0.5	...	...	9.2
C Manufacture of wood and wood products, including furniture	6.5	1.4	-1.0	...	...	6.9
D Manufacture of paper and paper products, printing and publishing	4.9	0.8	1.9	...	...	7.6
E Manufacture of chemicals and chemical petroleum, coal, rubber and plastic products [b]	12.2	6.7	92.8	...	...	111.7
F Manufacture of non-metallic mineral products, except products of petroleum and coal [b]	10.9	3.0	6.5	...	...	20.4
G Basic metal industries	7.7	1.3	7.8	...	...	16.8
H Manufacture of fabricated metal products, machinery and equipment	...	...	...	...	...	...
I Other manufacturing industries	2.1	0.3	2.7	...	...	5.1
4 Electricity, gas and water	30.5	19.2	-	...	...	49.7
A Electricity, gas and steam	29.7	19.0	-	...	...	48.7
B Water works and supply	0.8	0.2	-	...	...	1.0
5 Construction	692.1	53.9	189.7	...	...	935.7
6 Wholesale and retail trade, restaurants and hotels	80.6	10.4	390.7	...	...	481.7
A Wholesale and retail trade	69.5	7.0	379.1	...	...	455.6
B Restaurants and hotels	11.1	3.4	11.6	...	...	26.1
7 Transport, storage and communication	152.2	53.8	129.3	...	...	335.3
A Transport and storage	152.0	53.7	128.7	...	...	334.4
B Communication	0.2	0.1	0.6	...	...	0.9
8 Finance, insurance, real estate and business services	22.7	36.4	382.2	...	...	441.3
A Financial institutions	15.6	1.7	176.6	...	...	193.9
B Insurance	2.5	0.4	14.7	...	...	17.6
C Real estate and business services	4.6	34.3	190.9	...	...	229.8
Real estate, except dwellings	3.5	1.9	14.0	...	...	19.4
Dwellings	1.1	32.4	176.9	...	...	210.4
9 Community, social and personal services	339.6	27.9	13.5	...	...	381.0
A Sanitary and similar services	-	-	-	...	...	-
B Social and related community services	308.7	26.8	-	...	...	335.5
Educational services	206.3	14.5	-	...	...	220.8
Medical, dental, other health and veterinary services	102.4	12.3	-	...	...	114.7
C Recreational and cultural services	1.1	0.5	2.6	...	...	4.2
D Personal and household services	29.8	0.5	10.9	...	...	41.2

Libyan Arab Jamahiriya

4.3 Cost Components of Value Added
(Continued)

Million Libyan dinars

	\multicolumn{6}{c}{1980}
	Compensation of Employees	Capital Consumption	Net Operating Surplus	Indirect Taxes	Less: Subsidies Received	Value Added
Total, Industries c	1564.1	324.2	7735.9	...	...	9624.2
Producers of Government Services	...	...	...	...	...	...
Other Producers	...	...	...	...	...	...
Total	...	...	...	...	...	...
Less: Imputed bank service charge	...	...	...	...	...	...
Import duties	...	...	...	...	...	...
Value added tax	...	...	...	...	...	...
Total	...	...	...	...	...	...

a) Item 'Mining and quarrying' includes oil and gas production.
b) Petroleum products and liquified gas industries are included in item 'Manufacture of non-metallic mineral products'.
c) Gross domestic product in factor values.

Luxembourg

Source. Reply to the United Nations National Accounts Questionnaire from the Service Central de la Statistique et des Etudes Economiques, Ministere de L'Economie Nationale, Luxembourg. The official estimates and descriptions are published by the Service in 'Cahiers Economiques, Serie B, Comptes Nationaux'.

General note. The official estimates have been adjusted by the Service to conform to the United Nations System of National Accounts so far as the existing data would permit.

1.1 Expenditure on the Gross Domestic Product, in Current Prices

Million Luxembourg francs

	1970	1975	1977	1978	1979	1980	1981	1982	1983	1984	1985	1986
1 Government final consumption expenditure	5781	12951	16286	17553	19517	22182	24668	26097	28227	30111	32053	35451
2 Private final consumption expenditure [a]	27802	50117	61092	65023	70649	78085	86252	95756	104180	112602	120523	125286
3 Gross capital formation	14392	20118	21260	28380	27234	34204	35228	39900	42349	50010	46853	43798
A Increase in stocks	1691	-3941	-4444	1392	-2542	-1713	-851	-71	4545	11482	8745	-2199
B Gross fixed capital formation	12701	24059	25704	26988	29776	35917	36079	39971	37804	38528	38108	45997
Residential buildings	2448	6962	6106	5903	6585	7256	7469	7537	...	...	...	...
Non-residential buildings	5087	10307	9802	11078	12873	15377	16050	18911	...	...	...	...
Other construction and land improvement etc.									...	...	...	...
Other	5166	6790	9796	10007	10244	13262	12434	14234	...	...	...	...
4 Exports of goods and services	48893	80245	89079	93998	111058	117308	122498	141101	157403	196361	223552	226356
5 Less: Imports of goods and services	41826	76689	85157	92739	106313	118850	126955	144068	157416	192573	212071	208344
Equals: Gross Domestic Product [b]	55042	86742	102560	112215	122145	132929	141691	158786	174743	196511	210910	222547

a) Item 'Private consumption expenditure' refers to expenditure in the domestic market only.
b) Data in this table have been revised, therefore they are not strictly comparable with the unrevised data in the other tables.

1.2 Expenditure on the Gross Domestic Product, in Constant Prices

Million Luxembourg francs

	1970	1975	1977	1978	1979	1980	1981	1982	1983	1984	1985	1986
	At constant prices of: 1975 / 1980											
1 Government final consumption expenditure	10222 / 16436	19544	20677	21048	21518	22182	22493	22825	23258	23646	23957	24400
2 Private final consumption expenditure	38842 / 52851[a]	67955[a]	71473[a]	73522[a]	75971[a]	78085[a]	79358[a]	79509[a]	79405[a]	81322[a]	82725[a]	85440[a]
3 Gross capital formation	21657 / 32818	30147	27932	32628	30473	34204	33274	33784	33921	37226	36532	32064
A Increase in stocks	1276 / 5168	-1973	-2630	1657	-1771	-1713	-393	-30	3798	7794	8192	-760
B Gross fixed capital formation	20381 / 27650	32120	30562	30971	32244	35917	33667	33814	30123	29432	28340	32824
Residential buildings	4340 / 5990	9608	7384	6886	7223	7256	6922	6445	...	...	...	...
Non-residential buildings	8640 / 11721	13779	11854	12920	14118	15377	14913	16436	...	...	...	...
Other construction and land improvement etc.									...	...	...	...
Other	7401 / 9616	8737	11427	11201	10896	13262	11644	11388	...	...	...	...
4 Exports of goods and services	67973 / 84263	99570	104679	108364	118685	117308	113107	114063	119856	141396	154358	160805
5 Less: Imports of goods and services	65212 / 84663	99076	101545	107555	115245	118850	115573	115477	117704	135850	144255	144989
Equals: Gross Domestic Product [b]	73482 / 101705	118140	123216	128007	131402	132929	132659	134704	138736	147740	153317	157720

a) Item 'Private consumption expenditure' refers to expenditure in the domestic market only.
b) Data in this table have been revised, therefore they are not strictly comparable with the unrevised data in the other tables.

1.3 Cost Components of the Gross Domestic Product

Million Luxembourg francs

	1970	1975	1977	1978	1979	1980	1981	1982	1983	1984	1985	1986
1 Indirect taxes, net	4716	8907	9587	11259	11572	14029	13862	16226	20563	23750	27007	24861
A Indirect taxes	5412	11377	13785	15688	16347	19024	20542	24118	30132	32638	36039	34285
B Less: Subsidies	696	2470	4198	4429	4775	4995	6680	7892	9569	8888	9032	9424
2 Consumption of fixed capital	7863	12365	12055	12808	14602	15921	16961	18144	20180	22610	23980	25100
3 Compensation of employees paid by resident producers to:	25594	54890	67517	71274	77057	85181	93545	100045	106740	115253	121840	131991

Luxembourg

1.3 Cost Components of the Gross Domestic Product
(Continued)

Million Luxembourg francs

	1970	1975	1977	1978	1979	1980	1981	1982	1983	1984	1985	1986
A Resident households	23817	49589	60927	64207	69504	76699	84289	89931	95497	102879	107964	115529
B Rest of the world	1777	5301	6590	7067	7553	8482	9256	10114	11243	12374	13876	16462
4 Operating surplus	16869	10580	13401	16874	18914	17798	17323	24371	27260	34898	38083	40595
A Corporate and quasi-corporate enterprises	...	...	...	...	...	...	...	...	...	...	...	...
B Private unincorporated enterprises	...	...	...	...	...	...	...	...	...	...	...	...
C General government	769	1433	2081	2249	2226	2679	2660	2705	...	...	...	...
Equals: Gross Domestic Product [a]	55042	86742	102560	112215	122145	132929	141691	158786	174743	196511	210910	222547

a) Data in this table have been revised, therefore they are not strictly comparable with the unrevised data in the other tables.

1.4 General Government Current Receipts and Disbursements

Million Luxembourg francs

	1970	1975	1977	1978	1979	1980	1981	1982	1983	1984	1985	1986
Receipts												
1 Operating surplus	769	1433	2081	2249	2226	2679	2699	3009	3115	3163	...	...
2 Property and entrepreneurial income	1249	2492	2927	3251	4098	5331	5923	6376	6280	6087	...	...
3 Taxes, fees and contributions	16881	36759	48506	54289	54810	59993	64274	72245	85315	91571	...	...
A Indirect taxes	5341	11086	13529	15394	16041	18094	19233	22552	27921	30045	32797	...
B Direct taxes	6674	14709	20531	23779	22775	24015	25699	28844	35060	36953	41485	...
C Social security contributions	4866	10964	14446	15116	15994	17884	19342	20849	22334	24573	...	...
D Compulsory fees, fines and penalties	...	...	...	...	...	...	...	...	...	...	...	...
4 Other current transfers	589	1436	1926	2089	2369	2712	3226	3423	3487	3873	...	...
Total Current Receipts of General Government	19488	42120	55440	61878	63503	70715	76122	85053	98197	104694	...	...
Disbursements												
1 Government final consumption expenditure	5781	12951	16286	17553	19517	22182	24668	26097	28227	30110	...	...
2 Property income	622	738	911	1062	1006	1127	1281	1650	1802	2108	...	...
A Interest	622	738	911	1062	1006	1127	1281	1650	1802	2108	...	...
B Net land rent and royalties	-	-	-	-	-	-	-	-	-	-	...	...
3 Subsidies	696	2189	3785	3424	4191	4484	6460	7370	9278	8639	...	...
4 Other current transfers	8671	19580	25593	28029	30326	33439	37562	40796	43257	46835	...	...
A Social security benefits	7504	16850	22597	24586	26881	30235	33855	37028	39586	42817	...	...
B Social assistance grants	...	...	...	...	...	...	...	...	...	...	...	...
C Other	1167	2730	2996	3443	3445	3204	3707	3768	3671	4018	...	...
5 Net saving	3718	6662	8865	11810	8463	9483	6151	9140	15633	17002	...	...
Total Current Disbursements and Net Saving of General Government	19488	42120	55440	61878	63503	70715	76122	85053	98197	104694	...	...

1.7 External Transactions on Current Account, Summary

Million Luxembourg francs

	1970	1975	1977	1978	1979	1980	1981	1982	1983	1984	1985	1986
Payments to the Rest of the World												
1 Imports of goods and services	41575	76028	84290	91849	105318	117509	124977	141250	...	...	...	...
A Imports of merchandise c.i.f.	38213	69234	76085	83350	95089	105622	111326	124638	...	...	...	...
B Other	3362	6794	8205	8499	10229	11887	13651	16612	...	...	...	...
2 Factor income to the rest of the world	11164	69676	84517	109088	190763	325073	537540	549461	...	...	...	...
A Compensation of employees	1775	5293	6576	7065	7554	8497	9293	9997	...	...	...	...
B Property and entrepreneurial income	9389	64383	77941	102023	183209	316576	528247	539464	...	...	...	...
3 Current transfers to the rest of the world	1235	3043	4404	4589	5162	5479	6439	7654	...	...	...	...
A Indirect taxes to supranational organizations	71	281	256	294	306	1051	1352	1781	...	...	...	...
B Other current transfers	1164	2762	4148	4295	4856	4428	5087	5873	...	...	...	...
4 Surplus of the nation on current transactions	8023	13323	20389	21010	26513	26565	29064	41997	...	...	...	...
Payments to the Rest of the World and Surplus of the Nation on Current Transactions	61997	162070	193600	226536	327756	474626	698020	740362	...	...	...	...

Luxembourg

1.7 External Transactions on Current Account, Summary
(Continued)

Million Luxembourg francs

	1970	1975	1977	1978	1979	1980	1981	1982	1983	1984	1985	1986
Receipts From The Rest of the World												
1 Exports of goods and services	48615	79063	86859	91933	108816	114689	119244	135625	...	...	...	...
A Exports of merchandise f.o.b.	42517	65309	68585	72333	85845	87929	88563	101898	...	...	...	...
B Other	6098	13754	18274	19600	22971	26760	30681	33727	...	...	...	...
2 Factor income from rest of the world	12801	80842	103817	130881	215482	356239	574967	600533	...	...	...	...
A Compensation of employees	1412	4179	5740	6489	7384	8030	9250	10754	...	...	...	...
B Property and entrepreneurial income	11389	76663	98077	124392	208098	348209	565717	589779	...	...	...	...
3 Current transfers from rest of the world	581	2165	2924	3722	3458	3698	3809	4204	...	...	...	...
A Subsidies from supranational organisations	-	281	413	1005	584	511	220	222	...	...	...	...
B Other current transfers	581	1884	2511	2717	2874	3187	3589	3982	...	...	...	...
Receipts from the Rest of the World on Current Transactions	61997	162070	193600	226536	327756	474626	698020	740362	...	...	...	...

1.8 Capital Transactions of The Nation, Summary

Million Luxembourg francs

	1970	1975	1977	1978	1979	1980	1981	1982	1983	1984	1985	1986
Finance of Gross Capital Formation												
Gross saving	22704	34458	43514	50829	54787	60631	67935	95792	111490	127607	138082	146404
1 Consumption of fixed capital	7863	12365	12055	12808	14602	15921	16961	18144	20180	22610	23980	25100
A General government	505	880	1092	1253	1351	1499	1734	1960	...	...	...	...
B Corporate and quasi-corporate enterprises	...	...	...	...	...	...	...	...	...	...	...	...
C Other	...	...	...	...	...	...	...	...	...	...	...	...
2 Net saving	14841	22093	31459	38021	40185	44710	50974	77648	91310	104997	114102	121304
A General government	3419	6447	8519	11268	8621	9077	6146	8299	...	...	...	...
B Corporate and quasi-corporate enterprises	...	...	...	...	...	...	...	...	...	...	...	...
C Other	...	...	...	...	...	...	...	...	...	...	...	...
Less: Surplus of the nation on current transactions	8312	14340	22254	22449	27553	26427	32707	55892	69141	77597	91229	102606
Finance of Gross Capital Formation	14392	20118	21260	28380	27234	34204	35228	39900	42349	50010	46853	43798
Gross Capital Formation												
Increase in stocks	1691	-3941	-4444	1392	-2542	-1713	-851	-71	4545	11482	8745	-2199
Gross fixed capital formation	12701	24059	25704	26988	29776	35917	36079	39971	37804	38528	38108	45997
1 General government	1788	5223	5711	5931	6950	8398	8639	10244	...	...	...	...
2 Corporate and quasi-corporate enterprises	...	...	...	...	...	...	...	...	...	...	...	...
3 Other	...	...	...	...	...	...	...	...	...	...	...	...
Gross Capital Formation	14392	20118	21260	28380	27234	34204	35228	39900	42349	50010	46853	43798

1.10 Gross Domestic Product by Kind of Activity, in Current Prices

Million Luxembourg francs

	1970	1975	1977	1978	1979	1980	1981	1982	1983	1984	1985	1986
1 Agriculture, hunting, forestry and fishing	2119	2947	3055	3481	3619	3460	3894	5413	4984	5293	...	...
2 Mining and quarrying	675	720	623	446	467	501	468	177	190	170	...	...
3 Manufacturing	23789	25363	29525	33536	36849	37809	38590	46692	50499	60522	...	...
4 Electricity, gas and water	1520	2429	2807	2907	3086	3088	3638	4122	4640	5229	...	...
5 Construction	3452	7488	7658	7926	8368	10026	10088	10039	11124	11414	...	...
6 Wholesale and retail trade, restaurants and hotels	6918	13609	16516	17468	19715	22051	24836	28260	31352	34147	...	...
7 Transport, storage and communication	2711	4281	5367	6083	6848	7102	7503	7559	9197	10997	...	...
8 Finance, insurance, real estate and business services [a]	2631	11443	16942	17574	14929	12699	12300	20699	31329	30135	...	...
9 Community, social and personal services [a]	6808	12434	15686	17135	18503	20376	22066	24034	26087	26969	...	...

Luxembourg

1.10 Gross Domestic Product by Kind of Activity, in Current Prices
(Continued)

Million Luxembourg francs

	1970	1975	1977	1978	1979	1980	1981	1982	1983	1984	1985	1986
Total, Industries	50623	80714	98179	106556	112384	117112	123383	146995	169402	184876	...	...
Producers of Government Services	4464	9918	12723	13700	15139	17121	19116	20252	21874	23868	...	...
Other Producers	156	344	451	506	545	600	687	746	824	893	...	...
Subtotal	55243	90976	111353	120762	128068	134833	143186	167993	192100	209637	...	...
Less: Imputed bank service charge	2300	11022	16395	17105	14867	12911	13203	21722	31373	29701	...	...
Plus: Import duties	929	2089	2306	2460	2600	4279	3811	4142	6375	6853	...	...
Plus: Value added tax	1166	4449	5061	5703	5886	6693	7749	9289	10525	12223	...	...
Equals: Gross Domestic Product [b]	55038	86492	102325	111820	121687	132894	141543	159702	177627	199012	...	...

a) Business services are included in item 'Community, social and personal services'.
b) The branch breakdown used in this table (GDP by kind of activity) is according to the classification NACE/CLIO.

1.11 Gross Domestic Product by Kind of Activity, in Constant Prices

Million Luxembourg francs

	1970	1975	1977	1978	1979	1980	1981	1982	1983	1984	1985	1986
					At constant prices of 1980							
1 Agriculture, hunting, forestry and fishing	3802	3645	3511	3771	3710	3460	3554	4337	3800	4105	...	...
2 Mining and quarrying	1234	844	671	493	493	501	427	162	164	140	...	...
3 Manufacturing	33045	33713	35324	36791	38207	37809	35917	36971	38950	43289	...	...
4 Electricity, gas and water	2385	3202	3177	3280	3228	3088	3089	2913	2959	3089	...	...
5 Construction	7626	9806	8969	9149	9257	10026	10010	9413	9932	9732	...	...
6 Wholesale and retail trade, restaurants and hotels	12689	18210	19277	19765	21411	22051	22857	23896	24592	25259	...	...
7 Transport, storage and communication	4315	5575	6083	6519	7084	7102	7190	7223	7464	8431	...	...
8 Finance, insurance, real estate and business services [a]	2666	7642	8683	9723	10908	12699	13133	13001	13610	13819	...	...
9 Community, social and personal services [a]	14429	16700	18018	18999	19538	20376	20608	20767	21010	20868	...	...
Total, Industries	82191	99337	103713	108490	113836	117112	116785	118683	122481	128732	...	...
Producers of Government Services	12686	15085	15960	16246	16608	17121	17361	17618	17951	18217	...	...
Other Producers	422	505	540	560	580	600	622	645	667	688	...	...
Subtotal	95299	114927	120213	125296	131024	134833	134768	136946	141099	147637	...	...
Less: Imputed bank service charge	1940	6820	8201	9279	10961	12911	13620	13772	13487	13389	...	...
Plus: Import duties	2929	3503	4532	4691	4559	4279	3338	3287	3369	3563	...	...
Plus: Value added tax	4282	6058	6004	6532	6386	6693	7142	7101	6896	7534	...	...
Equals: Gross Domestic Product [b]	100570	117668	122548	127240	131008	132894	131628	133562	137877	145345	...	...

a) Business services are included in item 'Community, social and personal services'.
b) The branch breakdown used in this table (GDP by kind of activity) is according to the classification NACE/CLIO.

1.12 Relations Among National Accounting Aggregates

Million Luxembourg francs

	1970	1975	1977	1978	1979	1980	1981	1982	1983	1984	1985	1986
Gross Domestic Product	55042	86742	102560	112215	122145	132929	141691	158786	174743	196511	210910	222547
Plus: Net factor income from the rest of the world	1000	11095	19816	22051	24507	29977	39662	61918	72958	78247	84067	89695
Factor income from the rest of the world	12844	81018	103578	130048	212203	348095	563264	595529	496774	568190	568655	525044
Less: Factor income to the rest of the world	10944	69323	83762	107997	187696	318118	523602	533611	423816	489943	484588	435349
Equals: Gross National Product	56942	98437	122376	134266	146652	162906	181353	220704	247701	274758	294977	312242
Less: Consumption of fixed capital	7863	12365	12055	12808	14602	15921	16961	18144	20180	22610	23980	25100
Equals: National Income	49079	86072	110321	121458	132050	146985	164392	202560	227521	252148	270997	287142
Plus: Net current transfers from the rest of the world	-655	-911	-1484	-861	-1699	-2008	-2498	-3059	-3804	-4438	-4319	-5101
Current transfers from the rest of the world	581	2165	2924	3722	3458	3698	3809	4204	...	...	...	...
Less: Current transfers to the rest of the world	1235	3043	4404	4589	5162	5479	6439	7654	...	...	...	...
Equals: National Disposable Income	48424	85161	108837	120597	130351	144977	161894	199501	223717	247710	266678	282041
Less: Final consumption	33583	63068	77378	82576	90166	100267	110920	121853	132407	142713	152576	160737
Equals: Net Saving	14841	22093	31459	38021	40185	44710	50974	77648	91310	104997	114102	121304
Less: Surplus of the nation on current transactions	8312	14340	22254	22449	27553	26427	32707	55892	69141	77597	91229	102606
Equals: Net Capital Formation	6529	7753	9205	15572	12632	18283	18267	21756	22169	27400	22873	18698

Luxembourg

2.5 Private Final Consumption Expenditure by Type and Porpose, in Current Prices

Million Luxembourg francs

	1970	1975	1977	1978	1979	1980	1981	1982	1983	1984	1985	1986
	\multicolumn{12}{c}{Final Consumption Expenditure of Resident Households}
1 Food, beverages and tobacco	7902	12911	16064	16446	17378	18480	20440	24159	26872	27782	29294	...
A Food	6598	10054	12064	12250	12592	13103	14202	15681	16832	18014	18697	...
B Non-alcoholic beverages	176	230	281	281	332	355	426	511	560	567	685	...
C Alcoholic beverages	528	906	1058	1075	1232	1423	1620	1750	1784	1787	1884	...
D Tobacco	600	1721	2661	2840	3222	3599	4192	6217	7696	7414	8028	...
2 Clothing and footwear	2623	4429	4880	5268	5572	5875	6400	6745	7373	7460	8270	...
3 Gross rent, fuel and power	4865	9069	11359	12537	13829	15200	17262	19406	22068	24364	26403	...
A Fuel and power	1486	2600	3554	3927	4798	5610	6538	7792	9108	9979	10803	...
B Other	3379	6469	7805	8610	9031	9590	10724	11614	12960	14385	15600	...
4 Furniture, furnishings and household equipment and operation	2624	5356	6212	6312	6620	7498	8191	8741	9412	10581	11565	...
5 Medical care and health expenses	1490	3220	4361	4883	5243	5863	6362	7043	7287	7941	8390	...
6 Transport and communication	3029	6534	8740	9800	11272	13359	15454	17818	18976	20028	21282	...
7 Recreational, entertainment, education and cultural services	1109	2010	2410	2530	2530	2707	2930	3457	3833	4193	4336	...
8 Miscellaneous goods and services	4186	7290	8522	8837	10099	11310	11740	12563	13793	15226	16293	...
Total Final Consumption Expenditure in the Domestic Market by Households, of which	27828	50819	62548	66613	72543	80292	88779	99932	109614	117575	125833	...
Plus: Direct purchases abroad by resident households	1356	2442	3020	3195	3435	3770	4324	5033	5540	5980	6458	...
Less: Direct purchases in the domestic market by non-resident households	1382	3144	4476	4785	5329	5977	6851	9209	10974	10953	11768	...
Equals: Final Consumption Expenditure of Resident Households [a]	27802	50117	61092	65023	70649	78085	86252	95756	104180	112602	120523	...
	\multicolumn{12}{c}{Final Consumption Expenditure of Private Non-profit Institutions Serving Households}
Equals: Final Consumption Expenditure of Private Non-profit Organisations Serving Households	...	...	...	...	...	...	...	...	...	...	...	...
Private Final Consumption Expenditure	27802	50117	61092	65023	70649	78085	86252	95756	104180	112602	120523	...

a) Item 'Final consumption expenditure of resident households' includes consumption expenditure of private non-profit institutions serving households.

2.6 Private Final Consumption Expenditure by Type and Purpose, in Constant Prices

Million Luxembourg francs

	1970	1975	1977	1978	1979	1980	1981	1982	1983	1984	1985	1986
	\multicolumn{12}{c}{At constant prices of:1980}
	\multicolumn{12}{c}{Final Consumption Expenditure of Resident Households}
1 Food, beverages and tobacco	14228	16729	17414	17406	17915	18480	18742	19803	20346	19648	20689	...
A Food	12059	12946	13013	13009	13066	13103	13138	13145	13125	13134	13186	...
B Non-alcoholic beverages	283	325	342	318	356	355	386	448	458	449	526	...
C Alcoholic beverages	841	1115	1143	1128	1259	1423	1460	1435	1353	1298	1328	...
D Tobacco	1045	2343	2916	2951	3234	3599	3758	4775	5410	4767	5649	...
2 Clothing and footwear	5064	6252	6155	6086	6036	5875	5960	5938	6073	5846	6181	...
3 Gross rent, fuel and power	10067	12836	13799	14857	15194	15200	15634	15712	16422	16983	17625	...
A Fuel and power	3585	4153	4875	5315	5600	5610	5724	5900	6328	6481	6726	...

Luxembourg

2.6 Private Final Consumption Expenditure by Type and Purpose, in Constant Prices
(Continued)

Million Luxembourg francs

	1970	1975	1977	1978	1979	1980	1981	1982	1983	1984	1985	1986
				At constant prices of:1980								
B Other	6482	8683	8924	9542	9594	9590	9910	9812	10094	10502	10899	...
4 Furniture, furnishings and household equipment and operation	4267	6601	7105	6967	7077	7498	7700	7474	7321	7739	8199	...
5 Medical care and health expenses	2996	4178	4931	5414	5538	5863	5932	6181	6021	6268	6188	...
6 Transport and communication	5939	9535	11178	11979	12818	13359	14037	14020	14005	13955	14349	...
7 Recreational, entertainment, education and cultural services	1927	2482	2632	2733	2664	2707	2805	3065	3097	3110	3107	...
8 Miscellaneous goods and services	8412	10294	9963	9877	10765	11310	10874	10784	10061	10443	10633	...
Total Final Consumption Expenditure in the Domestic Market by Households, of which	52900	68907	73177	75319	78007	80292	81684	82977	83346	83992	86971	...
Plus: Direct purchases abroad by resident households	2578	3311	3533	3613	3694	3770	3978	4179	4212	4272	4464	...
Less: Direct purchases in the domestic market by non-resident households	2627	4263	5237	5410	5730	5977	6304	7647	8344	7825	8134	...
Equals: Final Consumption Expenditure of Resident Households [a]	52851	67955	71474	73521	75970	78085	79358	79509	79214	80439	83301	...

Final Consumption Expenditure of Private Non-profit Institutions Serving Households

| Equals: Final Consumption Expenditure of Private Non-profit Organisations Serving Households | ... | ... | ... | ... | ... | ... | ... | ... | ... | ... | ... | ... |
| Private Final Consumption Expenditure | 52851 | 67955 | 71474 | 73521 | 75970 | 78085 | 79358 | 79509 | 79214 | 80439 | 83301 | ... |

a) Item 'Final consumption expenditure of resident households' includes consumption expenditure of private non-profit institutions serving households.

2.11 Gross Fixed Capital Formation by Kind of Activity of Owner, ISIC Divisions, in Current Prices

Million Luxembourg francs

	1970	1975	1977	1978	1979	1980	1981	1982	1983	1984	1985	1986
					All Producers							
1 Agriculture, hunting, forestry and fishing	664	1149	489	1046	1122	1166	1310	1693	1987	...	...	...
2 Mining and quarrying	152	47	45	21	59	54	7	12	15	...	...	...
A Coal mining	...	...	...	...	...	...	...	...	...	...	...	...
B Crude petroleum and natural gas production	...	...	...	...	...	...	...	...	...	...	...	...
C Metal ore mining	126	34	33	2	-	1	-	-	-	...	...	...
D Other mining	26	13	12	19	59	53	7	12	15	...	...	...
3 Manufacturing	4549	5275	6285	6167	7145	7846	8722	7570	7841	...	...	...
A Manufacturing of food, beverages and tobacco	411	638	363	389	462	524	714	535	602	...	...	...
B Textile, wearing apparel and leather industries	12	108	140	60	48	54	39	86	35	...	...	...
C Manufacture of wood, and wood products, including furniture [a]	...	...	...	...	...	...	...	...	...	...	...	...
D Manufacture of paper and paper products, printing and publishing	35	99	343	323	199	151	157	178	181	...	...	...
E Manufacture of chemicals and chemical petroleum, coal, rubber and plastic products	902	601	589	403	438	998	823	1499	1680	...	...	...
F Manufacture of non-metalic mineral products except products of petroleum and coal	140	530	1549	298	390	817	2227	590	837	...	...	...
G Basic metal industries	2526	2701	2849	4365	5115	4498	3429	3414	3715	...	...	...
H Manufacture of fabricated metal products, machinery and equipment	493	262	420	289	444	724	1283	1230	729	...	...	...
I Other manufacturing industries [a]	23	30	23	34	49	80	50	38	62	...	...	...
4 Electricity, gas and water	553	1016	996	891	872	1010	1116	1074	1225	...	...	...
5 Construction	315	348	466	550	581	837	687	764	786	...	...	...
6 Wholesale and retail trade, restaurants and hotels	889	1256	1649	1841	2085	2524	2766	3232	3542	...	...	...
A Wholesale and retail trade	641	924	1349	1561	1725	1984	2107	2235	2391	...	...	...
B Restaurants and hotels	248	332	300	280	360	540	659	997	1151	...	...	...
7 Transport, storage and communication	667	1421	1979	2656	2232	4083	2067	2823	2740	...	...	...

Luxembourg

2.11 Gross Fixed Capital Formation by Kind of Activity of Owner, ISIC Divisions, in Current Prices
(Continued)

Million Luxembourg francs

	1970	1975	1977	1978	1979	1980	1981	1982	1983	1984	1985	1986
A Transport and storage	476	974	1396	1727	1495	3267	1282	1821	2230	...	...	...
B Communication	191	447	583	929	737	816	785	1002	510	...	...	...
8 Finance, insurance, real estate and business services [b]	2691	7813	7026	6542	7729	8793	9172	9950	10168	...	...	...
A Financial institutions	215	834	913	621	969	1289	1546	2735	2463	...	...	...
B Insurance	28	17	7	18	101	226	206	165	105	...	...	...
C Real estate and business services	2448	6962	6106	5903	6659	7278	7420	7050	7600	...	...	...
Real estate except dwellings	...	...	...	...	...	...	...	...	...	...	...	...
Dwellings	2448	6962	6106	5903	6659	7278	7420	7050	7600	...	...	...
9 Community, social and personal services [b]	428	503	1023	1321	992	1202	1402	3240	1608	...	...	...
Total Industries	10908	18828	19958	21035	22817	27515	27249	30358	29912	...	...	...
Producers of Government Services	1788	5223	5711	5931	6950	8398	8909	9358	8909	...	...	...
Private Non-Profit Institutions Serving Households	5	8	35	22	9	4	16	34	48	...	...	...
Total	12701	24059	25704	26988	29776	35917	36174	39750	38869	...	...	...

a) Item 'Manufacture of wood and wood products, including furniture' is included in item 'Other manufacturing industries'.
b) Business services are included in item 'Community, social and personal services'.

2.12 Gross Fixed Capital Formation by Kind of Activity of Owner, ISIC Divisions, in Constant Prices

Million Luxembourg francs

	1970	1975	1977	1978	1979	1980	1981	1982	1983	1984	1985	1986
	\multicolumn{12}{c}{At constant prices of: 1980}											
	\multicolumn{12}{c}{All Producers}											
1 Agriculture, hunting, forestry and fishing	1645	1641	578	1201	1218	1166	1243	1481	1666	...	...	...
2 Mining and quarrying	286	61	54	24	64	54	7	10	12	...	...	...
A Coal mining	...	...	...	...	...	...	...	...	...	...	...	...
B Crude petroleum and natural gas production	...	...	...	...	...	...	...	...	...	...	...	...
C Metal ore mining	236	44	40	2	-	1	-	-	-	...	...	...
D Other mining	50	17	14	22	64	53	7	10	12	...	...	...
3 Manufacturing	9191	6869	7362	6947	7637	7846	8150	6173	5866	...	...	...
A Manufacturing of food, beverages and tobacco	823	846	425	439	495	524	668	437	455	...	...	...
B Textile, wearing apparel and leather industries	24	524	175	75	51	54	36	70	26	...	...	...
C Manufacture of wood, and wood products, including furniture [a]	...	...	...	...	...	...	...	...	...	...	...	...
D Manufacture of paper and paper products, printing and publishing	70	127	405	366	215	151	147	145	138	...	...	...
E Manufacture of chemicals and chemical petroleum, coal, rubber and plastic products	1870	773	692	454	469	998	769	1223	1267	...	...	...
F Manufacture of non-metalic mineral products except products of petroleum and coal	281	718	1815	339	419	817	2080	487	631	...	...	...
G Basic metal industries	5050	3500	3326	4906	5462	4498	3204	2767	2754	...	...	...
H Manufacture of fabricated metal products, machinery and equipment	1026	342	497	329	473	724	1199	1013	549	...	...	...
I Other manufacturing industries [a]	47	39	27	39	53	80	47	31	46	...	...	...
4 Electricity, gas and water	1232	1319	1197	1026	943	1010	1038	932	1026	...	...	...
5 Construction	626	451	554	630	625	837	641	623	591	...	...	...
6 Wholesale and retail trade, restaurants and hotels	1658	1610	1922	2083	2241	2524	2601	2702	2756	...	...	...
A Wholesale and retail trade	1144	1187	1571	1769	1855	1984	1980	1860	1842	...	...	...
B Restaurants and hotels	514	423	351	314	386	540	621	842	914	...	...	...
7 Transport, storage and communication	1415	1843	2367	3056	2416	4083	1930	2393	2206	...	...	...
A Transport and storage	995	1279	1682	2006	1622	3267	1195	1540	1787	...	...	...

Luxembourg

2.12 Gross Fixed Capital Formation by Kind of Activity of Owner, ISIC Divisions, in Constant Prices
(Continued)

Million Luxembourg francs

	1970	1975	1977	1978	1979	1980	1981	1982	1983	1984	1985	1986
				At constant prices of:1980								
B Communication	420	564	685	1050	794	816	735	853	419	...	...	...
8 Finance, insurance, real estate and business services [b]	6630	10736	8463	7611	8459	8793	8500	8455	8054	...	...	...
Real estate except dwellings	...	...	...	...	...	...	...	...	...	...	...	...
Dwellings	6101	9608	7385	6886	7305	7270	6854	6020	6060	...	...	...
9 Community, social and personal services [b]	786	653	1173	1504	1069	1202	1324	2707	1247	...	...	...
Total Industries	23469	25183	23670	24082	24672	27515	25434	25476	23424	...	...	...
Producers of Government Services	4173	6927	6851	6864	7562	8398	8288	8133	7398	...	...	...
Private Non-Profit Institutions Serving Households	8	10	41	25	10	4	15	29	38	...	...	...
Total	27650	32120	30562	30971	32244	35917	33737	33638	30860	...	...	...

a) Item 'Manufacture of wood and wood products, including furniture' is included in item 'Other manufacturing industries'.
b) Business services are included in item 'Community, social and personal services'.

2.17 Exports and Imports of Goods and Services, Detail

Million Luxembourg francs

	1970	1975	1977	1978	1979	1980	1981	1982	1983	1984	1985	1986
					Exports of Goods and Services							
1 Exports of merchandise, f.o.b.	42517	65309	68585	72333	85845	87929	88563	101898	...	...	...	...
2 Transport and communication	4744	11454	15454	16580	19711	23160	26656	29279	...	...	...	...
3 Insurance service charges	...	...	...	...	...	...	...	...	...	...	...	...
4 Other commodities	...	...	...	...	...	...	...	...	...	...	...	...
5 Adjustments of merchandise exports to change-of-ownership basis	...	...	...	...	...	...	...	...	...	...	...	...
6 Direct purchases in the domestic market by non-residential households	1354	2300	2820	3020	3260	3600	4025	4448	...	...	...	...
7 Direct purchases in the domestic market by extraterritorial bodies	...	...	...	...	...	...	...	...	...	...	...	...
Total Exports of Goods and Services	48615	79063	86859	91933	108816	114689	119244	135625	...	...	...	...
					Imports of Goods and Services							
1 Imports of merchandise, c.i.f.	38213	69234	76085	83350	95089	105622	111326	124638	...	...	...	...
2 Adjustments of merchandise imports to change-of-ownership basis	2006	4352	5185	5304	6794	8117	9327	11579	...	...	...	...
3 Other transport and communication	...	...	...	...	...	...	...	...	...	...	...	...
4 Other insurance service charges	...	...	...	...	...	...	...	...	...	...	...	...
5 Other commodities	...	...	...	...	...	...	...	...	...	...	...	...
6 Direct purchases abroad by government	...	...	...	...	...	...	...	...	...	...	...	...
7 Direct purchases abroad by resident households	1356	2442	3020	3195	3435	3770	4324	5033	...	...	...	...
Total Imports of Goods and Services	41575	76028	84290	91849	105318	117509	124977	141250	...	...	...	...
Balance of Goods and Services	7040	3035	2569	84	3498	-2820	-5733	-5625	...	...	...	...
Total Imports and Balance of Goods and Services	48615	79063	86859	91933	108816	114689	119244	135625	...	...	...	...

4.3 Cost Components of Value Added

Million Luxembourg francs

	1980						1981					
	Compensation of Employees	Capital Consumption	Net Operating Surplus	Indirect Taxes	Less: Subsidies Received	Value Added	Compensation of Employees	Capital Consumption	Net Operating Surplus	Indirect Taxes	Less: Subsidies Received	Value Added
					All Producers							
1 Agriculture, hunting, forestry and fishing	212	...	3494	...	...	3460	219	...	3752	...	...	3894
A Agriculture and hunting	...	...	...	...	...	3053	...	...	...	...	...	3481
B Forestry and logging	...	...	...	...	...	407	...	...	...	...	...	413
C Fishing	...	...	...	...	...	...	...	...	...	...	...	...
2 Mining and quarrying	...	...	...	...	...	501	...	...	...	...	...	468
A Coal mining	...	...	...	...	...	-	...	...	...	...	...	-
B Crude petroleum and natural gas production	...	...	...	...	...	-	...	...	...	...	...	-
C Metal ore mining	...	...	...	...	...	323	...	...	...	...	...	273

Luxembourg

4.3 Cost Components of Value Added
(Continued)

Million Luxembourg francs

	1980						1981					
	Compensation of Employees	Capital Consumption	Net Operating Surplus	Indirect Taxes	Less: Subsidies Received	Value Added	Compensation of Employees	Capital Consumption	Net Operating Surplus	Indirect Taxes	Less: Subsidies Received	Value Added
D Other mining	...	...	...	...	...	178	...	...	...	...	...	195
3 Manufacturing	27505	...	9891	...	...	37809	28599	...	9667	...	...	38590
A Manufacture of food, beverages and tobacco	1563	...	1246	...	...	3519	1691	...	1296	...	...	3098
B Textile, wearing apparel and leather industries	402	...	555	...	...	976	446	...	542	...	...	1037
C Manufacture of wood and wood products, including furniture	240	...	139	...	...	...	244	...	121	...	...	...
D Manufacture of paper and paper products, printing and publishing	853	...	346	...	...	1210	924	...	463	...	...	1388
E Manufacture of chemicals and chemical petroleum, coal, rubber and plastic products	3463	...	2018	...	...	5438	3674	...	2458	...	...	6212
F Manufacture of non-metallic mineral products, except products of petroleum and coal	1446	...	969	...	...	2300	1603	...	887	...	...	2388
G Basic metal industries	15252	...	2933	...	...	18048	15383	...	2195	...	...	17610
H Manufacture of fabricated metal products, machinery and equipment	4286	...	1685	...	...	5923	4634	...	1705	...	...	6469
I Other manufacturing industries	...	...	...	...	...	395	...	...	...	...	...	388
4 Electricity, gas and water	1149	...	1830	...	...	3088	1224	...	2264	...	...	3638
5 Construction	7274	...	2414	...	...	10026	7467	...	2413	...	...	10088
6 Wholesale and retail trade, restaurants and hotels	...	...	...	...	...	22051	...	...	...	...	...	24836
A Wholesale and retail trade	...	...	...	...	...	18957	...	...	...	...	...	21441
B Restaurants and hotels	...	...	...	...	...	3094	...	...	...	...	...	3395
7 Transport, storage and communication	7760	...	2500	...	...	7102	8539	...	2742	...	...	7503
A Transport and storage	6110	...	1702	...	...	4639	6715	...	1814	...	...	4739
B Communication	1650	...	798	...	...	2463	1824	...	928	...	...	2764
8 Finance, insurance, real estate and business services [a]	8742	...	3956	...	...	12699	10437	...	2416	...	...	12300
9 Community, social and personal services [a]	17214	...	23133	...	...	20376	20222	...	25034	...	...	22066
Total, Industries	69856	...	47218	...	...	117112	76707	...	48288	...	...	123383
Producers of Government Services	15558	...	1499	...	...	17121	17310	...	1734	...	...	19116
Other Producers	570	...	30	...	...	600	653	...	34	...	...	687
Total	85984	...	48747	...	...	134833	94670	...	50056	...	...	143186
Less: Imputed bank service charge	...	...	786	...	...	12911	...	...	776	...	...	13203
Import duties	...	...	...	...	...	4279	...	...	...	...	...	3811
Value added tax	...	...	...	...	...	6693	...	...	...	...	...	7749
Total [b]	85984	...	47961	...	...	132894	94670	...	49280	...	...	141543

	1982						1983					
	Compensation of Employees	Capital Consumption	Net Operating Surplus	Indirect Taxes	Less: Subsidies Received	Value Added	Compensation of Employees	Capital Consumption	Net Operating Surplus	Indirect Taxes	Less: Subsidies Received	Value Added
All Producers													
1 Agriculture, hunting, forestry and fishing	234	...	5314	...	...	5413	...	...	...	...	...	4984
A Agriculture and hunting	...	...	...	...	...	4967	...	...	...	...	...	4511
B Forestry and logging	...	...	...	...	...	446	...	...	...	...	...	473
C Fishing	...	...	...	...	...	...	...	...	...	...	...	...
2 Mining and quarrying	...	...	...	...	...	177	...	...	...	...	...	190
A Coal mining	...	...	...	...	...	-	...	...	...	...	...	-
B Crude petroleum and natural gas production	...	...	...	...	...	...	...	...	...	...	...	...
C Metal ore mining	...	...	...	...	...	-	...	...	...	...	...	-
D Other mining	...	...	...	...	...	177	...	...	...	...	...	190

Luxembourg

4.3 Cost Components of Value Added
(Continued)

Million Luxembourg francs

	1982						1983					
	Compensation of Employees	Capital Consumption	Net Operating Surplus	Indirect Taxes	Less: Subsidies Received	Value Added	Compensation of Employees	Capital Consumption	Net Operating Surplus	Indirect Taxes	Less: Subsidies Received	Value Added
3 Manufacturing	29753	...	13891	...	...	46692	...	...	...	...	...	50499
A Manufacture of food, beverages and tobacco	1764	...	1697	...	...	4593	...	...	...	...	...	5138
B Textile, wearing apparel and leather industries	459	...	700	...	...	1001	...	...	...	...	...	1221
C Manufacture of wood and wood products, including furniture	257	...	111	...	...	...	...	...	...	...	...	...
D Manufacture of paper and paper products, printing and publishing	986	...	563	...	...	1475	...	...	...	...	...	1617
E Manufacture of chemicals and chemical petroleum, coal, rubber and plastic products	3905	...	3354	...	...	7738	...	...	...	...	...	9251
F Manufacture of non-metallic mineral products, except products of petroleum and coal	1720	...	1726	...	...	3238	...	...	...	...	...	3690
G Basic metal industries	15769	...	4139	...	...	21511	...	...	...	...	...	21753
H Manufacture of fabricated metal products, machinery and equipment	4893	...	1601	...	...	6715	...	...	...	...	...	7384
I Other manufacturing industries	...	...	...	...	...	421	...	...	...	...	...	445
4 Electricity, gas and water	1281	...	2952	...	...	4122	...	...	...	...	...	4640
5 Construction	7820	...	2012	...	...	10039	...	...	...	...	...	11124
6 Wholesale and retail trade, restaurants and hotels	...	...	...	...	...	28260	...	...	...	...	...	31352
A Wholesale and retail trade	...	...	...	...	...	24674	...	...	...	...	...	27306
B Restaurants and hotels	...	...	...	...	...	3586	...	...	...	...	...	4046
7 Transport, storage and communication	8865	...	2828	...	...	7559	...	...	...	...	...	9197
A Transport and storage	6912	...	1913	...	...	4684	...	...	...	...	...	5771
B Communication	1953	...	915	...	...	2875	...	...	...	...	...	3426
8 Finance, insurance, real estate and business services [a]	12385	...	7495	...	...	20699	...	...	...	...	...	31329
9 Community, social and personal services [a]	21940	...	27872	...	...	24034	...	...	...	...	...	26087
Total, Industries	82278	...	62364	...	...	146995	...	...	...	...	...	169402
Producers of Government Services	18384	...	1960	...	...	20252	...	...	...	...	...	21874
Other Producers	709	...	37	...	...	746	...	...	...	...	...	824
Total	101371	...	64361	...	...	167993	...	...	...	...	...	192100
Less: Imputed bank service charge	...	...	1077	...	...	21722	...	...	...	...	...	31373
Import duties	...	...	...	...	...	4142	...	...	...	...	...	6375
Value added tax	...	...	...	...	...	9289	...	...	...	...	...	10525
Total [b]	101371	...	63284	...	...	159702	...	...	...	...	...	177627

	1984						
	Compensation of Employees	Capital Consumption	Net Operating Surplus	Indirect Taxes	Less: Subsidies Received	Value Added

All Producers

	Compensation of Employees	Capital Consumption	Net Operating Surplus	Indirect Taxes	Less: Subsidies Received	Value Added
1 Agriculture, hunting, forestry and fishing	...	...	...	...	...	5293
A Agriculture and hunting	...	...	...	...	...	4823
B Forestry and logging					...	470
C Fishing	...					...
2 Mining and quarrying	...	...	...	...	...	170
A Coal mining	...	...	...	...	...	*
B Crude petroleum and natural gas production	...	...	...	...	...	-
C Metal ore mining	...	...	...	...	...	-
D Other mining	...	...	...	...	...	170

Luxembourg

4.3 Cost Components of Value Added
(Continued)

Million Luxembourg francs

	Compensation of Employees	Capital Consumption	Net Operating Surplus	Indirect Taxes	Less: Subsidies Received	Value Added
	\multicolumn{6}{c}{1984}
3 Manufacturing	...	...	...	...	...	60522
A Manufacture of food, beverages and tobacco	...	...	...	...	...	5249
B Textile, wearing apparel and leather industries	...	...	...	...	...	1251
C Manufacture of wood and wood products, including furniture	...	...	...	...	...	...
D Manufacture of paper and paper products, printing and publishing	...	...	...	...	...	1757
E Manufacture of chemicals and chemical petroleum, coal, rubber and plastic products	...	...	...	...	...	10860
F Manufacture of non-metallic mineral products, except products of petroleum and coal	...	...	...	...	...	3837
G Basic metal industries	...	...	...	...	...	28008
H Manufacture of fabricated metal products, machinery and equipment	...	...	...	...	...	9101
I Other manufacturing industries	...	...	...	...	...	459
4 Electricity, gas and water	...	...	...	...	...	5229
5 Construction	...	...	...	...	...	11414
6 Wholesale and retail trade, restaurants and hotels	...	...	...	...	...	34147
A Wholesale and retail trade	...	...	...	...	...	29801
B Restaurants and hotels	...	...	...	...	...	4346
7 Transport, storage and communication	...	...	...	...	...	10997
A Transport and storage	...	...	...	...	...	7133
B Communication	...	...	...	...	...	3864
8 Finance, insurance, real estate and business services [a]	...	...	...	...	...	30135
9 Community, social and personal services [a]	...	...	...	...	...	26969
Total, Industries	...	...	...	...	...	184876
Producers of Government Services	...	...	...	...	...	23868
Other Producers	...	...	...	...	...	893
Total	...	...	...	...	...	209637
Less: Imputed bank service charge	...	...	...	...	...	29701
Import duties	...	...	...	...	...	6853
Value added tax	...	...	...	...	...	12223
Total [b]	...	...	...	...	...	199012

a) Business services are included in item 'Community, social and personal services'.
b) The branch breakdown used in this table (GDP by kind of activity) is according to the classification NACE/CLIO.

Madagascar

Source. Reply to the United Nations National Accounts Questionnaire from the Institut National de la Statistique et de la Recherche Economique, Ministere des Finances et du Commerce, Tananarive.

General note. The official estimates of Madagascar have been adjusted by the Institut National de la Statistique et de la Recherche Economique to conform to the United Nations System of National Accounts so far as the existing data would permit.

1.1 Expenditure on the Gross Domestic Product, in Current Prices

Million Malagasy francs

	1970	1975	1977	1978	1979	1980	1981	1982	1983	1984	1985	1986
1 Government final consumption expenditure	46100	60400	72800	81600	103000	117800	129100	149500	165300	185000	209700	...
2 Private final consumption expenditure [a]	167200	301100	343100	360600	444300	526100	604600	799000	973400	1058100	1208600	...
3 Gross capital formation	38900	50600	60200	70400	150800	162400	142500	133000	160700	185700	217700	...
A Increase in stocks	...	...	2200	...	...	4800	-5800	3600	...	...	...	...
B Gross fixed capital formation	...	...	58000	...	...	157600	148300	129400	...	...	...	...
4 Exports of goods and services	56800	74500	97600	96100	95300	96800	96400	125700	139700	214200	225000	...
5 Less: Imports of goods and services	59600	91400	105600	122100	198300	213300	183600	211100	218000	273900	307600	...
Equals: Gross Domestic Product	249400	395200	468100	486600	595100	689800	789000	996100	1221100	1369100	1553400	

a) Item 'Private final consumption expenditure' has been obtained as a residual.

1.2 Expenditure on the Gross Domestic Product, in Constant Prices

Million Malagasy francs

	1970	1975	1977	1978	1979	1980	1981	1982	1983	1984	1985	1986
	At constant prices of: 1970									1984		
1 Government final consumption expenditure	46100	44600	47100	49800	57100	59600	59500	57700	57900	185000	189600	...
2 Private final consumption expenditure [a]	167200	167200	167200	163600	175100	175800	157400	161700	162700	1058100	1070500	...
3 Gross capital formation	38900	37600	31100	28700	51900	49200	34300	28000	27800	185700	189300	...
A Increase in stocks	2500	...	1100	...	...	...	...	...	...	...	...	...
B Gross fixed capital formation	36400	...	30000	...	...	...	...	...	...	...	...	...
4 Exports of goods and services	56800	58400	50300	50700	51400	48700	37300	38100	33400	214200	223300	...
5 Less: Imports of goods and services	59600	50400	40300	44100	62400	58000	37000	38600	32900	273900	272500	...
Equals: Gross Domestic Product	249400	257400	255400	248700	273100	275300	251500	246900	248900	1369100	1400200	...

a) Item 'Private final consumption expenditure' has been obtained as a residual.

1.3 Cost Components of the Gross Domestic Product

Million Malagasy francs

	1970	1975	1977	1978	1979	1980	1981	1982	1983	1984	1985	1986
1 Indirect taxes, net	29700	33600	47200	56400	67400	...	...	...	...	...	...	...
A Indirect taxes	32400	36400	...	...	...	...	...	...	...	...	...	...
B Less: Subsidies	2700	2800	...	...	...	...	...	...	...	...	...	...
2 Consumption of fixed capital	...	...	5800	6200	7000	...	...	...	...	...	...	...
3 Compensation of employees paid by resident producers to:	...	...	405100	414200	507500	...	...	...	...	...	...	...
4 Operating surplus	...	...				...	...	...	...	...	...	...
Equals: Gross Domestic Product	249400	395200	468100	486600	595100	...	...	...	...	...	...	...

1.7 External Transactions on Current Account, Summary

Million Malagasy francs

	1970	1975	1977	1978	1979	1980	1981	1982	1983	1984	1985	1986
	Payments to the Rest of the World											
1 Imports of goods and services	51599	103744	100231	...	...	...	...	...	...	...	...	...
A Imports of merchandise c.i.f.	39534	88862	96119	...	...	...	...	...	...	...	...	...
B Other	12065	14882	4112	...	...	...	...	...	...	...	...	...
2 Factor income to the rest of the world	11002	8473	7938	...	...	...	...	...	...	...	...	...

Madagascar

1.7 External Transactions on Current Account, Summary
(Continued)

Million Malagasy francs

	1970	1975	1977	1978	1979	1980	1981	1982	1983	1984	1985	1986
A Compensation of employees	6904	6291	6178	...	...	...	...	...	...	...	...	...
B Property and entrepreneurial income	4098	2182	1760	...	...	...	...	...	...	...	...	...
By general government	353	701	...	...	...	...	...	...	...	...	...	...
By corporate and quasi-corporate enterprises	3745	1481	...	...	...	...	...	...	...	...	...	...
By other	...	...	...	...	...	...	...	...	...	...	...	...
3 Current transfers to the rest of the world	1267	2202	515	...	...	...	...	...	...	...	...	...
4 Surplus of the nation on current transactions	-1007	-22677	-4671	...	...	...	...	...	...	...	...	...
Payments to the Rest of the World and Surplus of the Nation on Current Transactions	62861	91742	104013	...	...	...	...	...	...	...	...	...

Receipts From The Rest of the World

	1970	1975	1977	1978	1979	1980	1981	1982	1983	1984	1985	1986
1 Exports of goods and services	45671	76124	88053	...	...	...	...	...	...	...	...	...
A Exports of merchandise f.o.b.	40222	68506	86153	...	...	...	...	...	...	...	...	...
B Other	5449	7618	1900	...	...	...	...	...	...	...	...	...
2 Factor income from rest of the world	...	8684	7246	...	...	...	...	...	...	...	...	...
A Compensation of employees	...	7619	6726	...	...	...	...	...	...	...	...	...
B Property and entrepreneurial income	516	1065	520	...	...	...	...	...	...	...	...	...
By general government	20	...	...	...	...	...	...	...	...	...	...	...
By corporate and quasi-corporate enterprises	-	...	...	...	...	...	...	...	...	...	...	...
By other	496	1065	520	...	...	...	...	...	...	...	...	...
3 Current transfers from rest of the world	18688	6934	8714	...	...	...	...	...	...	...	...	...
Receipts from the Rest of the World on Current Transactions	62861	91742	104013	...	...	...	...	...	...	...	...	...

1.10 Gross Domestic Product by Kind of Activity, in Current Prices

Million Malagasy francs

	1970	1975	1977	1978	1979	1980	1981	1982	1983	1984	1985	1986
1 Agriculture, hunting, forestry and fishing	73800	162400	185700	187600	212500	249100	313600	409700	525300	580600	653200	...
2 Mining and quarrying												...
3 Manufacturing	46000	70600	89900	93600	114500	124300	125300	149900	185400	213900	254100	...
4 Electricity, gas and water												...
5 Construction												...
6 Wholesale and retail trade, restaurants and hotels												...
7 Transport, storage and communication	82700	104900	116700	122100	163500	197700	230100	298700	361500	400600	451300	...
8 Finance, insurance, real estate and business services												...
9 Community, social and personal services												...
Total, Industries	202500	337900	392300	403300	490500	571100	669000	858300	1072200	1195100	1358600	...
Producers of Government Services	33700	42400	52500	59600	72600	83600	90400	107600	115200	128000	142000	...
Other Producers [a]	...	...	...	...	...	...	...	...	...	...	...	...
Subtotal	236200	380300	444800	462900	563100	654700	759400	965900	1187400	1323100	1500600	...
Less: Imputed bank service charge	...	...	...	...	...	...	...	...	...	...	...	...
Plus: Import duties	13200	14900	23300	23700	32000	35100	29600	30200	33700	46000	52800	...
Plus: Value added tax	...	...	...	...	...	...	...	...	...	...	...	...
Equals: Gross Domestic Product	249400	395200	468100	486600	595100	689800	789000	996100	1221100	1369100	1553400	...

a) Item 'Other producers' is included in item 'Community, social and personal services'.

Madagascar

1.11 Gross Domestic Product by Kind of Activity, in Constant Prices

Million Malagasy francs

	1970	1975	1977	1978	1979	1980	1981	1982	1983	1984	1985	1986
	\multicolumn{9}{c}{At constant prices of: 1970}		1984	
1 Agriculture, hunting, forestry and fishing	73800	80900	76300	71300	76400	78300	74800	77800	79700	580600	591700	...
2 Mining and quarrying										...	...	...
3 Manufacturing	46000	51400	48100	50100	56500	55000	42400	36400	36900	213900	223500	...
4 Electricity, gas and water												...
5 Construction												
6 Wholesale and retail trade, restaurants and hotels												...
7 Transport, storage and communication	82600	83900	85600	80700	90100	90700	84500	83600	82900	400600	409200	...
8 Finance, insurance, real estate and business services												...
9 Community, social and personal services												...
Total, Industries	202400	216200	210000	202100	223000	224000	201700	197800	199500	1195100	1224400	...
Producers of Government Services	33700	32200	35500	37300	40000	41700	43800	44200	44700	128000	129200	...
Other Producers a	...	...	...	...	...	...	...	...	...	...	...	...
Subtotal	236100	248400	245500	239400	263000	265700	245500	242000	244200	1323100	1353600	...
Less: Imputed bank service charge	...	...	...	...	...	...	...	...	...	...	...	...
Plus: Import duties	13200	9000	9900	9300	10100	9600	6000	4900	4700	46000	46600	...
Plus: Value added tax	...	...	...	...	...	...	...	...	...	...	...	...
Equals: Gross Domestic Product	249400	257400	255400	248700	273100	275300	251500	246900	248900	1369100	1400200	...

a) Item 'Other producers' is included in item 'Community, social and personal services'.

1.12 Relations Among National Accounting Aggregates

Million Malagasy francs

	1970	1975	1977	1978	1979	1980	1981	1982	1983	1984	1985	1986
Gross Domestic Product	249400	395200	468100	486600	595100	689800	...	...	...	...	...	...
Plus: Net factor income from the rest of the world	-6300	211	-692	-600	-900	-1000	...	...	...	...	...	...
Factor income from the rest of the world	...	8684	7246	...	...	...	...	...	...	...	...	...
Less: Factor income to the rest of the world	...	8973	7938	...	...	...	...	...	...	...	...	...
Equals: Gross National Product	243100	395411	467408	486000	594200	688800	...	...	...	...	...	...
Less: Consumption of fixed capital	...	...	5800	6200	7000	...	...	...	...	...	...	...
Equals: National Income	...	...	461608	479800	587200	...	...	...	...	...	...	...
Plus: Net current transfers from the rest of the world	17421	4732	8199	...	...	...	...	...	...	...	...	...
Current transfers from the rest of the world	18688	6934	8714	...	...	...	...	...	...	...	...	...
Less: Current transfers to the rest of the world	1267	2202	515	...	...	...	...	...	...	...	...	...
Equals: National Disposable Income	...	...	469807	...	...	...	...	...	...	...	...	...
Less: Final consumption	...	...	415900	...	...	...	...	...	...	...	...	...
Equals: Net Saving	...	...	53907	...	...	...	...	...	...	...	...	...
Less: Surplus of the nation on current transactions	...	...	...	...	...	...	...	...	...	...	...	...
Equals: Net Capital Formation	...	...	...	...	...	...	...	...	...	...	...	...

Madagascar

2.17 Exports and Imports of Goods and Services, Detail

Million Malagasy francs

	1970	1975	1977	1978	1979	1980	1981	1982	1983	1984	1985	1986
				Exports of Goods and Services								
1 Exports of merchandise, f.o.b.	40268	68480	...	...	...	...	...	...	...	...	...	...
2 Transport and communication	...	3020	...	...	...	...	...	...	...	...	...	...
3 Insurance service charges	...	...	...	...	...	...	...	...	...	...	...	...
4 Other commodities	...	...	...	...	...	...	...	...	...	...	...	...
5 Adjustments of merchandise exports to change-of-ownership basis	...	...	...	...	...	...	...	...	...	...	...	...
6 Direct purchases in the domestic market by non-residential households	...	...	...	...	...	...	...	...	...	...	...	...
7 Direct purchases in the domestic market by extraterritorial bodies	...	...	...	...	...	...	...	...	...	...	...	...
Total Exports of Goods and Services	45669	80600	...	...	...	...	...	...	...	...	...	...
				Imports of Goods and Services								
1 Imports of merchandise, c.i.f.	...	84730	...	...	...	...	...	...	...	...	...	...
A Imports of merchandise, f.o.b.	39434	71040	...	...	...	...	...	...	...	...	...	...
B Transport of services on merchandise imports	...	12190	...	...	...	...	...	...	...	...	...	...
C Insurance service charges on merchandise imports	...	1500	...	...	...	...	...	...	...	...	...	...
By residents	...	...	...	...	...	...	...	...	...	...	...	...
By non-residents	...	1500	...	...	...	...	...	...	...	...	...	...
2 Adjustments of merchandise imports to change-of-ownership basis	...	...	...	...	...	...	...	...	...	...	...	...
3 Other transport and communication	...	...	...	...	...	...	...	...	...	...	...	...
4 Other insurance service charges	...	...	...	...	...	...	...	...	...	...	...	...
5 Other commodities	...	...	...	...	...	...	...	...	...	...	...	...
6 Direct purchases abroad by government	...	...	...	...	...	...	...	...	...	...	...	...
7 Direct purchases abroad by resident households	...	...	...	...	...	...	...	...	...	...	...	...
Total Imports of Goods and Services	51599	91400	...	...	...	...	...	...	...	...	...	...
Balance of Goods and Services	-5930	-10800	...	...	...	...	...	...	...	...	...	...
Total Imports and Balance of Goods and Services	45669	80600	...	...	...	...	...	...	...	...	...	...

Malawi

General note. The preparation of national accounts statistics in Malawi is undertaken by the National Statistical Office, Zomba. The official estimates are published in a series of reports entitled 'National Accounts Report'. A detailed description of the sources and methods used for national accounts estimates is found in 'National Accounts Handbook, Sources and Methods' published in 1985. The estimates are generally in accordance with the classifications and definitions recommended in the United Nations System of National Accounts (SNA). The following tables have been prepared from successive replies to the United Nations national accounts questionnaire. When the scope and coverage of the estimates differ for conceptual or statistical reasons from the definitions and classifications recommended in SNA, a footnote is indicated to the relevant tables.

Sources and methods:

(a) Gross domestic product. Gross domestic product is estimated mainly through the production approach.

(b) Expenditure on the gross domestic product. The expenditure approach is used to estimate government final consumption expenditure, increase in stocks, investment in building and construction and exports and imports of goods and services. The commodity-flow approach is used to estimate the gross capital formation of transport equipment, plant and machinery whereas private final consumption expenditure is estimated as a residual. Government expenditure is estimated by netting out rent from the total of Malawi Government Revenue Expenditure on Revenue and Development Account Expenditure and final consumption as shown in 'Public Sector Financial Statistics'. Changes in recorded stocks of the monetary sector are obtained from the annual economic surveys and annual reports of the Agricultural Development and Marketing Corporation. Unrecorded stocks, i.e., imported goods, are estimated on the basis of information received from businessmen and the Ministry of Trade and Industry. Estimates of non-monetary stocks are estimated from annual economic surveys, reports of the Veterinary Department and from the Agricultural Development and Marketing Corporation. Estimates of investments in building and construction are obtained directly from large enterprises and government. For fixed operating and auxiliary equipment, installation costs are estimated at 25 per cent of the price of deliveries. Other equipment is valued at estimated delivered prices. 15 per cent of the private cars and bicyles are assumed to be imported by government and private industry and are treated as capital formation. Export and imports of goods and services are based on the balance of payments report. For the constant price estimates, price deflation is used to estimate all items of GDP by expenditure type.

(c) Cost-structure of the gross domestic product. Estimates of compensation of employees, operating surplus and consumption of fixed capital are based on data obtained from the annual survey of ecomomic activities. Data on indirect taxes and subsidies are taken from the financial statistics of the public sector.

(d) Gross domestic product by kind of economic activity. The table of GDP by kind of economic activity is prepared in factor values. The production approach is used to estimate the value added of most industries. The value added of large and medium-scale establishments, was generally taken from the Annual Economic Survey 1973-1979 and from the Medium Business Annual Review. Estimates of agricultural output are based mainly on the annual reports of the Agricultural Development and Marketing Corporation and on agricultural surveys undertaken by the National Statistical Office. Net income of farmers from sales of crops to the corporation is derived by deducting from total farm receipts the expenditure on cotton spraying and 50 per cent of the expenditure on fertilizers, seeds and tools. Income from sales of crops to other dealers is calculated as 50 per cent of the free-on-rail export value of the crops, whereas income from sales in local village and urban markets is calculated from estimates of the annual consumption of main food crops by the African population. For livestock production, estimates are based on live-weight purchases by butchers and the Cold Storage Commission which re published in the annual reports of the Veterinary Department. Increase in herds is estimated from the annual livestock censuses and the national sample survey of agriculture. For forestry, the National Statistical Office makes estimates of the retail value of firewood sales less the cost of axes and hatchets. An assumption on the quantities of firewood consumed per household is made for nonmarketed firewood. The Fisheries Department provides estimates for the fishing sector. Own-consumption of fish is estimated as 10 per cent of the landed value of the total fish catch. The estimates of large mining entreprises are based on the annual economic survey. For large manufacturing enterprises employing 20 persons or more, the annual economic survey is used to estimate gross output and intermediate consumption. The estimates of enterprises such as grain-milling, tailoring, fish-curing, handicrafts, etc. are based on agricultural sample surveys, information from the Ministry of Trade and Industry, data supplied by the Buildings Department, etc. The sources for the estimates of electricity, gas and water are the annual economic surveys and the public sector financial statistics. For government construction, the annual reports of the Ministry of Works and Supplies and the estimates prepared by the National Statisticial Office are used as sources. For private construction, the quarterly building inquiries and the annual economic surveys are used for the larger enterprises while data from agricultural surveys are used for other construction including own-account construction. It is assumed that the ratio of value added to total receipts for the large construction enterprises also applies to small operators. The annual economic survey is the source used to estimate activity of larger trade enterprises while the annual reviews of small businesses are used for other enterprises. The wage component of gross output is derived from data on average employment per store and minimum wage rates. For the transport sector, the annual economic survey is also used for the larger enterprises while the annual reports of the Road Traffic Commissioner are used for the small transport operators. It is assumed that average value added per vehicle for the larger operators applies equally to the small enterprises. Value added of financial institutions is estimated on the basis of the quarterly employment inquiries, documents of banks, information from the Ministry of Finance and the Accountant-General's annual reports. Rental value are obtained from various sources such as the public sector financial statistics, the Accountant-General's annual reports and reports of the Commissioner for Taxes.ng income survey, respectively. Value added of public administration and defence is obtained from the detailed analysis of government accounts. For private services, estimates are based on quarterly employment and earnings inquiries, agricultural surveys, annual inquiries of domestic servants, annual economic surveys and information supplied by the Ministry of Trade and Industry. GDP by kind of economic activity is not estimated at constant prices.

1.1 Expenditure on the Gross Domestic Product, in Current Prices

Million Malawi kwacha

		1970	1975	1977	1978	1979	1980	1981	1982	1983	1984	1985	1986
1	Government final consumption expenditure	41.0	74.7	98.6	134.2	164.2	193.9	198.0	218.3	235.9	268.0	344.0	412.8
2	Private final consumption expenditure [a]	192.3	365.2	483.4	502.2	577.0	728.6	806.5	923.1	1111.6	1183.0	1511.4	1678.6
3	Gross capital formation	69.6	178.6	179.7	307.8	261.4	...	...	...	...	...	...	...
A	Increase in stocks [a]	8.5	46.8	18.1	60.7	29.5	...	...	...	...	...	...	...
B	Gross fixed capital formation	61.1	131.8	161.6	247.1	231.9	222.1	167.8	181.7	187.0	222.7	259.5	252.2
	Residential buildings	26.0	...	...	...	...	...	...	...	...	...	...	...
	Non-residential buildings	...	...	...	...	...	...	...	...	...	...	...	...
	Other construction and land improvement etc.	...	...	...	...	...	...	...	...	...	...	...	...
	Other	35.1	...	...	...	...	...	...	...	...	...	...	...
4	Exports of goods and services	58.7	-88.8	-33.7	-143.5	-170.7	249.7	284.4	280.2	298.2	484.4	475.0	503.6
5	Less: Imports of goods and services	94.5					390.1	348.6	359.3	407.1	451.2	568.2	559.6
	Equals: Gross Domestic Product	267.1	529.7	728.0	800.7	831.9	1005.2	1108.1	1244.0	1435.9	1706.9	2021.7	2287.6

a) Beginning 1980, item 'Increase in stocks' is included in item 'Private final consumption expenditure'.

Malawi

1.2 Expenditure on the Gross Domestic Product, in Constant Prices

Million Malawi kwacha

	1970	1975	1977	1978	1979	1980	1981	1982	1983	1984	1985	1986
	\multicolumn{5}{c}{At constant prices of: 1964}				1978			
1 Government final consumption expenditure	38.6	...	...	...	...	157.2	150.6	153.9	153.5	165.9	183.6	191.6
2 Private final consumption expenditure	167.2	...	...	...	...	543.1[a]	541.3[a]	571.6[a]	603.0[a]	555.9[a]	633.2[a]	608.2[a]
3 Gross capital formation	52.3	...	...	...	...	...	...	...	...	...	...	...
A Increase in stocks	7.1	...	...	...	...	...	...	...	...	...	...	...
B Gross fixed capital formation	45.2	...	...	...	...	174.0	118.0	114.8	111.9	108.5	108.0	77.4
4 Exports of goods and services	-32.1	...	...	...	...	273.6	224.7	202.3	209.0	277.4	262.4	250.9
5 Less: Imports of goods and services		...	...	...	...	308.8	239.7	228.7	232.8	217.5	259.0	195.2
Equals: Gross Domestic Product	226.0	...	...	...	...	839.1	794.9	813.9	844.6	890.2	928.2	932.9

a) Beginning 1980, item 'Increase in stocks' is included in item 'Private final consumption expenditure'.

1.3 Cost Components of the Gross Domestic Product

Million Malawi kwacha

	1970	1975	1977	1978	1979	1980	1981	1982	1983	1984	1985	1986
1 Indirect taxes, net	17.8	35.0	44.1	58.2	74.1	103.5	107.8	116.1	139.6	178.1	216.0	214.5
A Indirect taxes	18.2	...	...	...	...	...	...	...	...	...	...	...
B Less: Subsidies	0.4	...	...	...	...	...	...	...	...	...	...	...
2 Consumption of fixed capital [a]	...	29.8	42.0	56.7	56.5	...	...	...	...	...	...	...
3 Compensation of employees paid by resident producers to:	69.4	130.3	165.0	207.2	223.1	...	...	...	...	...	...	...
A Resident households	64.6	...	...	...	...	...	...	...	...	...	...	...
B Rest of the world	4.9	...	...	...	...	...	...	...	...	...	...	...
4 Operating surplus [a]	179.8	334.6	476.9	478.6	478.2	...	...	...	...	...	...	...
Equals: Gross Domestic Product	267.1	529.7	728.0	800.7	831.9	1005.2	1108.1	1244.0	1435.9	1706.9	2021.7	2287.6

a) Item 'Operating surplus' includes consumption of fixed capital.

1.4 General Government Current Receipts and Disbursements

Million Malawi kwacha

	1970	1975	1977	1978	1979	1980	1981	1982	1983	1984	1985	1986
	\multicolumn{12}{c}{Receipts}
1 Operating surplus	...	...	...	...	...	...	...	...	...	...	...	...
2 Property and entrepreneurial income	...	...	...	...	...	...	...	...	...	...	...	...
3 Taxes, fees and contributions	...	75.0	92.8	123.1	140.7	175.1	184.4	208.8	...	...	...	...
A Indirect taxes	...	35.0	44.1	58.2	74.1	98.4	113.2	122.4	...	...	...	...
B Direct taxes	...	30.5	43.2	57.2	59.4	64.9	61.9	79.9	...	...	...	...
C Social security contributions	...	...	...	...	...	...	...	...	...	...	...	...
D Compulsory fees, fines and penalties	...	9.5	5.5	7.7	7.2	11.8	9.3	6.5	...	...	...	...
4 Other current transfers	...	7.3	18.0	32.8	38.1	40.6	41.4	34.5	...	...	...	...
Total Current Receipts of General Government	...	82.3	110.8	155.9	178.8	215.7	225.8	243.3	...	...	...	...
	\multicolumn{12}{c}{Disbursements}
1 Government final consumption expenditure	...	74.7	98.6	134.2	164.2	193.9	198.0	218.3	235.9	268.0	344.0	412.8

Malawi

1.4 General Government Current Receipts and Disbursements
(Continued)

Million Malawi kwacha

	1970	1975	1977	1978	1979	1980	1981	1982	1983	1984	1985	1986
A Compensation of employees	...	39.8	47.5	61.3	68.3	74.1	84.4	99.0	111.7	127.3	149.5	172.4
B Consumption of fixed capital	...	3.7	5.4	5.9	5.7	...	...	...	...	...	...	...
C Purchases of goods and services, net	...	31.2	45.7	67.0	90.2	119.8	113.6	119.3	124.2	140.7	194.5	240.4
D Less: Own account fixed capital formation	...	...	...	...	...	...	...	...	...	...	...	...
E Indirect taxes paid, net	...	...	...	...	...	...	...	...	...	...	...	...
2 Property income	...	...	...	...	...	...	...	...	...	...	...	...
3 Subsidies	...	...	...	...	...	...	...	...	...	...	...	...
4 Other current transfers	...	...	...	...	...	...	...	...	...	...	...	...
5 Net saving	...	7.6	12.2	21.7	14.6	17.6	4.1	14.5	...	...	...	...
Total Current Disbursements and Net Saving of General Government	...	82.3	110.8	155.9	178.8	215.7	225.8	243.3	...	...	...	...

1.7 External Transactions on Current Account, Summary

Million Malawi kwacha

	1970	1975	1977	1978	1979	1980	1981	1982	1983	1984	1985	1986
Payments to the Rest of the World												
1 Imports of goods and services	94.5	...	...	...	...	...	...	...	...	...	...	...
A Imports of merchandise c.i.f.	77.3	...	...	...	...	...	...	...	...	...	...	...
B Other	17.2	...	...	...	...	...	...	...	...	...	...	...
2 Factor income to the rest of the world	16.1	...	...	...	...	...	...	...	...	...	...	...
A Compensation of employees	4.9	...	...	...	...	...	...	...	...	...	...	...
B Property and entrepreneurial income	11.2	...	...	...	...	...	...	...	...	...	...	...
3 Current transfers to the rest of the world	0.3	...	...	...	...	...	...	...	...	...	...	...
4 Surplus of the nation on current transactions	-34.7	...	...	...	...	...	...	...	...	...	...	...
Payments to the Rest of the World and Surplus of the Nation on Current Transactions	76.2	...	...	...	...	...	...	...	...	...	...	...
Receipts From The Rest of the World												
1 Exports of goods and services	58.7	...	...	...	...	...	...	...	...	...	...	...
A Exports of merchandise f.o.b.	47.9	...	...	...	...	...	...	...	...	...	...	...
B Other	10.8	...	...	...	...	...	...	...	...	...	...	...
2 Factor income from rest of the world	10.0	...	...	...	...	...	...	...	...	...	...	...
A Compensation of employees	8.2	...	...	...	...	...	...	...	...	...	...	...
B Property and entrepreneurial income	1.9	...	...	...	...	...	...	...	...	...	...	...
3 Current transfers from rest of the world	7.5	...	...	...	...	...	...	...	...	...	...	...
Receipts from the Rest of the World on Current Transactions	76.2	...	...	...	...	...	...	...	...	...	...	...

1.10 Gross Domestic Product by Kind of Activity, in Current Prices

Million Malawi kwacha

	1970	1975	1977	1978	1979	1980	1981	1982	1983	1984	1985	1986
1 Agriculture, hunting, forestry and fishing [a]	139.8	194.9	299.3	296.5	319.7	...	...	...	...	...	...	...
2 Mining and quarrying	0.4	...	...	...	...	...	...	...	...	...	...	...
3 Manufacturing	24.8	69.1	82.9	99.1	110.1	...	...	...	...	...	...	...
4 Electricity, gas and water	2.9	7.9	10.5	12.5	15.7	...	...	...	...	...	...	...
5 Construction	8.5	23.8	31.4	46.3	29.9	...	...	...	...	...	...	...

Malawi

1.10 Gross Domestic Product by Kind of Activity, in Current Prices
(Continued)

Million Malawi kwacha

	1970	1975	1977	1978	1979	1980	1981	1982	1983	1984	1985	1986
6 Wholesale and retail trade, restaurants and hotels	24.6	74.6	113.9	104.9	97.7	...	...	...	...	...	...	...
7 Transport, storage and communication	9.5	35.9	36.5	45.0	40.4	...	...	...	...	...	...	...
8 Finance, insurance, real estate and business services	6.6	24.6	33.6	43.4	51.1	...	...	...	...	...	...	...
9 Community, social and personal services	14.5	20.8	21.1	26.9	30.8	...	...	...	...	...	...	...
Total, Industries	231.6	451.6	629.2	674.6	695.4	...	...	...	...	...	...	...
Producers of Government Services	17.9	43.5	52.9	67.2	74.0	...	...	...	...	...	...	...
Other Producers	2.5	19.6	26.1	29.3	33.7	...	...	...	...	...	...	...
Subtotal	252.0	514.7	708.2	771.1	803.1	...	...	...	...	...	...	...
Less: Imputed bank service charge	2.7	9.0	11.4	12.1	23.8	...	...	...	...	...	...	...
Plus: Import duties	...	22.0	27.3	38.1	49.0	...	...	...	...	...	...	...
Plus: Value added tax	...	2.9	3.9	3.6	3.6	...	...	...	...	...	...	...
Plus: Other adjustments	17.8	...	...	...	...	...	...	...	...	...	...	...
Equals: Gross Domestic Product	267.1	529.7	728.0	800.7	831.9	...	...	...	...	...	...	...

a) Item 'Agriculture, hunting, forestry and fishing' includes all non-monetary output.

1.11 Gross Domestic Product by Kind of Activity, in Constant Prices

Million Malawi kwacha

	1970	1975	1977	1978	1979	1980	1981	1982	1983	1984	1985	1986
				At constant prices of:1978								
1 Agriculture, hunting, forestry and fishing	...	230.3	286.5	294.9	304.1	284.1	260.7	278.7	290.6	309.8	307.4	312.3
2 Mining and quarrying	...	...	...	...	...	...	...	...	...	...	...	...
3 Manufacturing	...	81.1	80.5	84.8	88.5	89.0	92.0	91.8	98.3	100.8	101.1	101.0
4 Electricity, gas and water	...	10.8	11.8	12.5	13.2	14.1	14.3	14.6	15.8	16.3	16.4	17.3
5 Construction	...	33.9	36.1	46.2	42.7	43.4	35.8	36.0	33.0	33.8	39.3	49.5
6 Wholesale and retail trade, restaurants and hotels	...	91.9	89.0	104.8	105.1	108.5	96.1	93.8	97.7	101.8	113.9	107.7
7 Transport, storage and communication	...	43.9	40.1	44.7	51.5	51.8	48.2	46.8	47.3	46.7	49.5	52.2
8 Finance, insurance, real estate and business services	...	31.0	37.8	43.3	50.6	51.4	47.4	47.0	50.3	51.3	54.9	55.7
9 Community, social and personal services	...	26.1	26.0	26.9	28.1	29.1	30.5	31.0	33.2	34.3	35.6	36.3
Total, Industries	...	549.0	607.3	658.1	683.8	671.4	624.9	639.7	666.2	694.8	718.1	732.0
Producers of Government Services	...	58.2	64.0	67.2	72.3	79.0	85.1	89.8	93.9	96.1	106.5	108.7
Other Producers	...	22.6	27.0	29.3	31.5	32.3	31.7	32.6	33.9	35.2	36.2	37.1
Subtotal	...	629.8	698.3	754.6	787.6	782.7	741.7	762.1	794.0	826.1	860.8	877.8
Less: Imputed bank service charge	...	11.3	12.8	12.1	20.4	20.7	19.0	19.0	20.3	20.7	22.1	22.5
Plus: Import duties	...	...	...	...	...	...	...	...	...	...	...	...
Plus: Value added tax	...	...	...	...	...	...	...	...	...	...	...	...
Equals: Gross Domestic Product a	...	618.5	685.5	742.5	767.2	762.0	722.7	743.1	773.7	805.4	838.7	855.3

a) Gross domestic product in factor values.

1.12 Relations Among National Accounting Aggregates

Million Malawi kwacha

	1970	1975	1977	1978	1979	1980	1981	1982	1983	1984	1985	1986
Gross Domestic Product	267.1	529.7	728.0	800.7	831.9	1005.2	1108.1	1244.0	1435.9	1706.9	2021.7	2287.6
Plus: Net factor income from the rest of the world	-6.1	10.7	-23.0	-4.0	-34.8	-81.1	-74.3	-74.0	-75.4	-78.8	-90.9	-113.2
Factor income from the rest of the world	10.0	...	...	...	...	...	...	...	...	...	...	...
Less: Factor income to the rest of the world	16.1	...	...	...	...	...	...	...	...	...	...	...
Equals: Gross National Product	261.0	540.4	705.0	796.7	797.1	924.1	1033.8	1170.0	1360.5	1628.1	1930.8	2174.4

Malawi

1.12 Relations Among National Accounting Aggregates
(Continued)

Million Malawi kwacha

	1970	1975	1977	1978	1979	1980	1981	1982	1983	1984	1985	1986
Less: Consumption of fixed capital	...	29.8	42.0	56.7	56.5	...	...	...	...	...	...	...
Equals: National Income	...	510.6	663.0	740.0	740.6	...	...	...	...	...	...	...
Plus: Net current transfers from the rest of the world	7.3	12.2	23.0	37.8	37.8	40.6	41.4	38.3	34.7	34.5	42.1	51.0
Equals: National Disposable Income	...	522.8	686.0	777.8	778.4	...	...	...	...	...	...	...
Less: Final consumption	233.3	439.9	582.0	636.4	741.2	...	...	...	...	...	...	...
Equals: Net Saving	...	82.9	104.0	141.4	37.2	...	...	...	...	...	...	...
Less: Surplus of the nation on current transactions	-34.7	...	...	...	...	...	...	...	...	...	...	...
Equals: Net Capital Formation	...	...	...	...	...	...	...	...	...	...	...	...

2.17 Exports and Imports of Goods and Services, Detail

Million Malawi kwacha

		1970	1975	1977	1978	1979	1980	1981	1982	1983	1984	1985	1986
	Exports of Goods and Services												
1	Exports of merchandise, f.o.b.	47.9	...	...	...	...	...	...	...	...	...	...	...
2	Transport and communication	3.7	...	...	...	...	...	...	...	...	...	...	...
	A In respect of merchandise imports	0.8	...	...	...	...	...	...	...	...	...	...	...
	B Other	2.9	...	...	...	...	...	...	...	...	...	...	...
3	Insurance service charges	1.1	...	...	...	...	...	...	...	...	...	...	...
4	Other commodities	2.2	...	...	...	...	...	...	...	...	...	...	...
5	Adjustments of merchandise exports to change-of-ownership basis	...	...	...	...	...	...	...	...	...	...	...	...
6	Direct purchases in the domestic market by non-residential households	3.8	...	...	...	...	...	...	...	...	...	...	...
7	Direct purchases in the domestic market by extraterritorial bodies	...	...	...	...	...	...	...	...	...	...	...	...
	Total Exports of Goods and Services	58.7	...	...	...	...	...	...	...	...	...	...	...
	Imports of Goods and Services												
1	Imports of merchandise, c.i.f.	77.3	...	...	...	...	...	...	...	...	...	...	...
	A Imports of merchandise, f.o.b.	68.4	...	...	...	...	...	...	...	...	...	...	...
	B Transport of services on merchandise imports	9.0	...	...	...	...	...	...	...	...	...	...	...
	By residents	...	...	...	...	...	...	...	...	...	...	...	...
	By non-residents	9.0	...	...	...	...	...	...	...	...	...	...	...
	C Insurance service charges on merchandise imports	...	...	...	...	...	...	...	...	...	...	...	...
2	Adjustments of merchandise imports to change-of-ownership basis	...	...	...	...	...	...	...	...	...	...	...	...
3	Other transport and communication	4.9	...	...	...	...	...	...	...	...	...	...	...
4	Other insurance service charges	2.8	...	...	...	...	...	...	...	...	...	...	...
5	Other commodities	3.0	...	...	...	...	...	...	...	...	...	...	...
6	Direct purchases abroad by government	6.5	...	...	...	...	...	...	...	...	...	...	...
7	Direct purchases abroad by resident households	...	...	...	...	...	...	...	...	...	...	...	...
	Total Imports of Goods and Services	94.5	...	...	...	...	...	...	...	...	...	...	...
	Balance of Goods and Services	-35.9	...	...	...	...	...	...	...	...	...	...	...
	Total Imports and Balance of Goods and Services	58.7	...	...	...	...	...	...	...	...	...	...	...

Malaysia

General note. The preparation of national accounts statistics in Malaysia is undertaken by the Department of Statistics, Kuala Lumpur. The official estimates are published in a series of reports entitled 'Malaysia National Accounts Statistics'. The estimates are generally in accordance with the classifications and definitions recommended in the United Nations System of National Accounts (SNA, 1968). Since 1970, the publication of estimates of National Accounts have been on a Malaysia basis. The following tables have been prepared from successive replies to the United Nations National Accounts Questionnaire. When the scope and coverage of the estimates differ for conceptual or statistical reasons from the definitions and classifications recommended in SNA, a footnote is indicated to the relevant tables.

Sources and methods:

(a) Gross domestic product. Gross domestic product is estimated mainly through the production approach

(b) Expenditure on the gross domestic product. All components of GDP by expenditure type are estimated through the expenditure approach (by 'commodity flow'). Data on government final consumption expenditure are obtained from the annual accounts of the various levels of government. Estimates of private consumption expenditure have been made by allocating the available supply of consumer goods and services from import and local production to consumption accounts for the various component items. Estimates of changes in stocks are derived from annual censuses and government accounts. Gross fixed capital formation includes not only building, construction, machinery and equipment but also investment in plantation and small-holders' perennial crops. For building and construction, information is obtained from the annual surveys of construction industries for the private enterprises, institutions and households and from annual financial reports and analysis of accounts of the general government and public corporations. For machinery and equipment, mark-ups derived from the 1967 census of distributive trades, transport charges, indirect taxes etc. are added to the c.i.f. values to obtain the final value of capital formation. Data on domestic production are provided by the annual surveys of manufacturing industries. Information for the estimation of investment in perennial crops is derived from the annual censuses of the various crops. Export and import data are recorded at the time of crossing the customs boundaries. GDP by expenditure type is not estimated at constant prices.

(c) Cost-structure of the gross domestic product. Estimates for compensation of employees are derived from statistics covering output, input and government accounts for all sectors except for the agricultural sector which is obtained from the census of population and the labour force survey. Indirect taxes are obtained from government accounts. The allocation according to industries and households are based on information from the production statistics, tax regulations and assumed relationships to known items. Operating surplus including depreciation is obtained as a residual.

(d) Gross domestic product by kind of economic activity. The table of GDP by kind of economic activity is prepared at market prices, i.e., producers' values. The production approach is used to estimate the value added of all industries except government services and part of the private services which are estimated through the income approach. Information on the production volume of the various agricultural crops, except paddy, is based on the 1973 household budget survey and updated with acreage, yield and price data. Input are obtained from the relevant agricultural economic bulletins. For paddy, data on production from the Ministry of Agriculture are used while the prices are derived from the National Padi Board's approved buying prices, rice mills' purchase prices and retail prices prior to 1972. Since 1972, the Department compiles a producer price index for all goods. Information on intermediate consumption is based on input coefficients extracted from reports of the economic survey of paddy production in 1967/68. Data on the production of palmoil, coconut, copra and tea, are obtained from monthly and annual reports submitted by the estates. Statistics on livestock, forestry and fishing are obtained from the Veterinary Services, the Department of Forestry and the Department of Fishery, respectively. Salting, drying and other forms of fish preservation are treated as manufacturing and therefore are not included in the value of fishing. For the mining sector the value of production, inputs and other related information are obtained from the oil companies for crude oil, from annual censuses for mining and from an annual survey for stone-quarrying. The annual surveys of manufacturing industries are used for estimating the gross value of production and intermediate consumption of manufacturing. For industries not covered, censuses of manufacturing industries in 1968 and 1973 have been used as bench-marks. Data relating to electricity and water are obtained from the detailed accounts of the producers. For construction, the information is obtained from the annual survey of construction industries supplemented by the analysis of government accounts and public corporations. The value of services rendered by the trade sector is calculated as the gross mark-up. Mark-ups are added to the producers' values of commodities, the total of which is treated as deliveries from the 'distributive trades' industry to other industries. Mark-ups and intermediate consumption are calculated from sources such as the census of distributive trades, import prices, ex-factory prices and retail prices. For restaurants and hotels, estimates are based on the 1971 census of selected service trades in the urban areas. The estimates of the value of production for road transport are made on the basis of the number of vehicle registered and the 1971 census of selected industries. For the financial sector, information is obtained from concerned institutions. The household expenditure survey in 1973 is used as the basis for the calculation of rent paid on dwellings and imputed rent of owner-occupied dwellings. Business services rendered by professionals in the private sector are valued by means of data collected from the annual census of professions and institutions. Information on producers of government services is derived from the analysis of government financial statements. For private services, estimates are obtained from a variety of sources such as the census of professions and institutions, the 1971 census of selected industries and employment data. For the constant price estimates, value added of agriculture, mining and quarrying, manufacturing, electricity and water transport sectors is extrapolated by a quantity index for output. For education and health, trends in the number of persons engaged are used. For the remaining industries, construction, trade, ownership of dwellings and public services, estimates of current prices are retained.

1.1 Expenditure on the Gross Domestic Product, in Current Prices

Million Malaysian ringgit

	1970	1975	1977	1978	1979	1980	1981	1982	1983	1984	1985	1986
1 Government final consumption expenditure	1742	3924	5388	6090	6475	8811	10425	11469	12156	11741	11844	12127
2 Private final consumption expenditure	6349	13086	16798	19584	22406	26946	30594	33226	35998	39594	40360	36574
3 Gross capital formation	2016	5221	7586	10104	13423	16217	20157	23338	25109	26697	21315	17869
A Increase in stocks	315	-381	243	723	1173	-380	-602	593	575	1306	-1809	-996
B Gross fixed capital formation	1701	5602	7343	9381	12250	16597	20759	22745	24534	25391	23124	18865
Residential buildings	250	...	...	1058	...	...	...	...	...	...	...	...
Non-residential buildings	288	...	...	2270	...	...	...	...	...	...	...	...
Other construction and land improvement etc.	378	...	...	1682	...	...	...	...	...	...	...	...
Other	785	...	...	4371	...	...	...	...	...	...	...	...
4 Exports of goods and services	4332	10172	16279	18585	26004	30676	30154	31846	36298	43171	42537	40722
5 Less: Imports of goods and services	3851	10071	13711	16477	21884	29342	33717	37300	39996	41653	38509	36148
Equals: Gross Domestic Product	10588	22332	32340	37886	46424	53308	57613	62579	69565	79550	77547	71144

Malaysia

1.2 Expenditure on the Gross Domestic Product, in Constant Prices

Million Malaysian ringgit

	1970	1975	1977	1978	1979	1980	1981	1982	1983	1984	1985	1986
			At constant prices of:									
		1970						1978				
1 Government final consumption expenditure	1742	3117	3714	3931 / 6090	6195	7750	8784	9552	9989	9500	9417	9536
2 Private final consumption expenditure	6349	9631	11283	12398 / 19584	21698	24445	25686	26531	27376	29142	29299	26369
3 Gross capital formation	2016	3670	5011	5418 / 10104	11455	13612	15952	18245	19638	20713	16586	13684
A Increase in stocks	315	-266	275	299 / 723	285	-319	-498	478	445	952	-1302	-917
B Gross fixed capital formation	1701	3936	4736	5119 / 9381	11170	13931	16450	17767	19193	19761	17888	14601
4 Exports of goods and services	4332	7179	8746	9410 / 18585	21924	22619	22431	24826	27889	31733	31875	37486
5 Less: Imports of goods and services	3851	6232	7879	8893 / 16477	19844	23914	25251	28724	31310	33347	30027	29216
Equals: Gross Domestic Product	10588	17365	20875	22264 / 37886	41428	44512	47002	50430	53582	57741	57150	57859

1.3 Cost Components of the Gross Domestic Product

Million Malaysian ringgit

	1970	1975	1977	1978	1979	1980	1981	1982	1983	1984	1985	1986
1 Indirect taxes, net	1549	3366	5449	6099	7671	9066	8836	8758	10425	12066	11650	9943
A Indirect taxes	1551	...	...	6099	...	...	...	...	...	...	...	...
B Less: Subsidies	2	...	...	-	...	...	...	...	...	...	...	...
2 Consumption of fixed capital a	...	...	...	...	...	...	...	...	...	...	...	...
3 Compensation of employees paid by resident producers to:	3726	...	...	11966	...	...	...	...	...	...	...	...
4 Operating surplus a	5313	...	...	19821	...	...	...	...	...	...	...	...
Equals: Gross Domestic Product	10588	22332	32340	37886	46424	53308	57613	62579	69565	79550	77547	71144

a) Item 'Operating surplus' includes consumption of fixed capital.

1.4 General Government Current Receipts and Disbursements

Million Malaysian ringgit

	1970	1975	1977	1978	1979	1980	1981	1982	1983	1984	1985	1986
					Receipts							
1 Operating surplus	50	...	...	...	...	...	...	...	...	...	...	...
2 Property and entrepreneurial income	290	...	...	...	...	...	...	...	...	...	...	...
3 Taxes, fees and contributions	2355	...	...	...	...	...	...	...	...	...	...	...
A Indirect taxes	1551	...	...	...	...	...	...	...	...	...	...	...
B Direct taxes	588	...	...	...	...	...	...	...	...	...	...	...
C Social security contributions	206	...	...	...	...	...	...	...	...	...	...	...
D Compulsory fees, fines and penalties	10	...	...	...	...	...	...	...	...	...	...	...
4 Other current transfers	304	...	...	...	...	...	...	...	...	...	...	...
Total Current Receipts of General Government	2999	...	...	...	...	...	...	...	...	...	...	...
					Disbursements							
1 Government final consumption expenditure	1742	...	...	...	...	...	...	...	...	...	...	...
A Compensation of employees	1199	...	...	...	...	...	...	...	...	...	...	...
B Consumption of fixed capital	111	...	...	...	...	...	...	...	...	...	...	...
C Purchases of goods and services, net	576	...	...	...	...	...	...	...	...	...	...	...
D Less: Own account fixed capital formation	...	...	...	...	...	...	...	...	...	...	...	...
E Indirect taxes paid, net	-144	...	...	...	...	...	...	...	...	...	...	...
2 Property income	126	...	...	...	...	...	...	...	...	...	...	...

Malaysia

1.4 General Government Current Receipts and Disbursements
(Continued)

Million Malaysian ringgit

	1970	1975	1977	1978	1979	1980	1981	1982	1983	1984	1985	1986
3 Subsidies	2	...	...	...	...	...	...	...	...	...	...	...
4 Other current transfers	421	...	...	...	...	...	...	...	...	...	...	...
A Social security benefits	129	...	...	...	...	...	...	...	...	...	...	...
B Social assistance grants	...	...	...	...	...	...	...	...	...	...	...	...
C Other	292	...	...	...	...	...	...	...	...	...	...	...
5 Net saving	708	...	...	...	...	...	...	...	...	...	...	...
Total Current Disbursements and Net Saving of General Government	2999	...	...	...	...	...	...	...	...	...	...	...

1.7 External Transactions on Current Account, Summary

Million Malaysian ringgit

	1970	1975	1977	1978	1979	1980	1981	1982	1983	1984	1985	1986
Payments to the Rest of the World												
1 Imports of goods and services	3851	...	...	16477	...	...	...	...	...	...	...	...
A Imports of merchandise c.i.f.	3401	...	...	14690	...	...	...	...	...	...	...	...
B Other	450	...	...	1787	...	...	...	...	...	...	...	...
2 Factor income to the rest of the world	536	...	...	2581	...	...	...	...	...	...	...	...
3 Current transfers to the rest of the world	470	...	...	280	...	...	...	...	...	...	...	...
4 Surplus of the nation on current transactions	-30	...	...	304	...	...	...	...	...	...	...	...
Payments to the Rest of the World and Surplus of the Nation on Current Transactions	4827	...	...	19642	...	...	...	...	...	...	...	...
Receipts From The Rest of the World												
1 Exports of goods and services	4332	...	...	18585	...	...	...	...	...	...	...	...
A Exports of merchandise f.o.b.	4105	...	...	17067	...	...	...	...	...	...	...	...
B Other	227	...	...	1518	...	...	...	...	...	...	...	...
2 Factor income from rest of the world	219	...	...	881	...	...	...	...	...	...	...	...
3 Current transfers from rest of the world	276	...	...	176	...	...	...	...	...	...	...	...
Receipts from the Rest of the World on Current Transactions	4827	...	...	19642	...	...	...	...	...	...	...	...

1.10 Gross Domestic Product by Kind of Activity, in Current Prices

Million Malaysian ringgit

	1970	1975	1977	1978	1979	1980	1981	1982	1983	1984	1985	1986
1 Agriculture, hunting, forestry and fishing	3051	...	...	9513	...	...	...	...	...	...	...	...
2 Mining and quarrying	735	...	...	3912	...	...	...	...	...	...	...	...
3 Manufacturing	1554	...	...	7189	...	...	...	...	...	...	...	...
4 Electricity, gas and water	203	...	...	531	...	...	...	...	...	...	...	...
5 Construction	395	...	...	1571	...	...	...	...	...	...	...	...
6 Wholesale and retail trade, restaurants and hotels	1269	...	...	4156	...	...	...	...	...	...	...	...
7 Transport, storage and communication	549	...	...	1867	...	...	...	...	...	...	...	...
8 Finance, insurance, real estate and business services	912	...	...	3177	...	...	...	...	...	...	...	...
9 Community, social and personal services	221	...	...	798	...	...	...	...	...	...	...	...
Total, Industries	8889	...	...	32714	...	...	...	...	...	...	...	...
Producers of Government Services	1268	...	...	4105	...	...	...	...	...	...	...	...
Other Producers	67	...	...	102	...	...	...	...	...	...	...	...
Subtotal	10224	...	...	36921	...	...	...	...	...	...	...	...
Less: Imputed bank service charge	106	...	...	585	...	...	...	...	...	...	...	...
Plus: Import duties	470	...	...	1550	...	...	...	...	...	...	...	...
Plus: Value added tax	...	...	...	...	...	...	...	...	...	...	...	...
Equals: Gross Domestic Product	10588	22332	32340	37886	...	...	...	...	...	...	...	...

Malaysia

1.11 Gross Domestic Product by Kind of Activity, in Constant Prices

Million Malaysian ringgit

	1970	1975	1977	1978	1979	1980	1981	1982	1983	1984	1985	1986
		At constant prices of:										
		1970						1978				
1 Agriculture, hunting, forestry and fishing	3051	4804	5519	5610 / 9513	10060	10189	10684	11375	11302	11623	11914	12389
2 Mining and quarrying	735	792	967	1054 / 3912	4586	4487	4289	4617	5342	6073	5985	6433
3 Manufacturing	1554	2850	3735	4081 / 7189	8004	8742	9155	9668	10429	11711	11263	12111
4 Electricity, gas and water	203	365	442	499 / 530	584	640	689	721	798	890	948	1027
5 Construction	395	654	800	919 / 1572	1761	2066	2367	2598	2867	2988	2738	2355
6 Wholesale and retail trade, restaurants and hotels	1269	2219	2592	2824 / 4156	4669	5383	5694	6104	6583	7107	6911	6147
7 Transport, storage and communication	549	1071	1290	1415 / 1867	2107	2542	2847	2984	3138	3464	3630	3851
8 Finance, insurance, real estate and business services	912	1468	1675	1823 / 3177	3434	3687	3953	4231	4570	4892	5093	5073
9 Community, social and personal services	221	388	463	498 / 798	841	912	950	1024	1076	1130	1181	1231
Total, Industries	8889	14611	17483	18723 / 32714	36046	38648	40628	43322	46105	49878	49663	50617
Producers of Government Services	1268	2210	2719	2831 / 4106	4375	4563	5649	6027	6328	6817	6957	7253
Other Producers	67	90	95	97 / 101	107	109	115	117	117	119	119	121
Subtotal	10224	16911	20297	21651 / 36921	40528	43320	46392	49466	52550	56814	56739	57991
Less: Imputed bank service charge	106	211	244	302 / 585	733	854	877	1152	1397	1595	1834	1891
Plus: Import duties	470	665	822	915 / 1550	1633	2046	2087	2116	2429	2522	2245	1759
Plus: Value added tax	...	...	...	... / ...	...	...	...	...	...	...	...	...
Equals: Gross Domestic Product	10588	17365	20875	22264 / 37886	41428	44512	47602	50430	53582	57741	57150	57859

1.12 Relations Among National Accounting Aggregates

Million Malaysian ringgit

	1970	1975	1977	1978	1979	1980	1981	1982	1983	1984	1985	1986
Gross Domestic Product	10588	22332	32340	37886	46424	53308	57613	62579	69565	79550	77547	71144
Plus: Net factor income from the rest of the world	-317	-726	-1276	-1700	-2070	-1918	-2011	-2889	-4411	-5368	-5709	-5293
Factor income from the rest of the world	219	...	...	881	...	...	...	...	...	...	...	...
Less: Factor income to the rest of the world	536	...	...	2581	...	...	...	...	...	...	...	...
Equals: Gross National Product	10271	21606	31064	36186	44354	51390	55602	59690	65154	74182	71838	65851
Less: Consumption of fixed capital	...	...	...	...	...	...	...	...	...	...	...	...
Equals: National Income [a]	10271	...	...	36186	...	...	...	...	...	...	...	...
Plus: Net current transfers from the rest of the world	-194	...	...	-104	...	...	...	...	...	...	...	...
Current transfers from the rest of the world	276	...	...	176	...	...	...	...	...	...	...	...
Less: Current transfers to the rest of the world	470	...	...	280	...	...	...	...	...	...	...	...
Equals: National Disposable Income [b]	10077	...	...	36082	...	...	...	...	...	...	...	...
Less: Final consumption	8091	17010	22186	25674	...	...	...	...	...	...	...	...
Equals: Net Saving [c]	1986	...	...	10408	...	...	...	...	...	...	...	...
Less: Surplus of the nation on current transactions	-30	...	...	304	...	...	...	...	...	...	...	...
Equals: Net Capital Formation [d]	2016	...	...	10104	...	...	...	...	...	...	...	...

a) Item 'National income' includes consumption of fixed capital.
b) Item 'National disposable income' includes consumption of fixed capital.
c) Item 'Net saving' includes consumption of fixed capital.
d) Item 'Net capital formation' includes consumption of fixed capital.

Malaysia

2.1 Government Final Consumption Expenditure by Function, in Current Prices

Million Malaysian ringgit

	1970	1975	1977	1978	1979	1980	1981	1982	1983	1984	1985	1986
1 General public services	444	...	...	1261	...	...	...	...	...	...	...	...
2 Defence	442	...	...	1645	...	...	...	...	...	...	...	...
3 Public order and safety		...	...		...	...	...	...	...	...	...	...
4 Education	434	...	...	1636	...	...	...	...	...	...	...	...
5 Health	150	...	...	601	...	...	...	...	...	...	...	...
6 Social security and welfare		...	...		...	...	...	...	...	...	...	...
7 Housing and community amenities	79	...	...	933	...	...	...	...	...	...	...	...
8 Recreational, cultural and religious affairs		...	...		...	...	...	...	...	...	...	...
9 Economic services	193	...	...		...	...	...	...	...	...	...	...
10 Other functions	...	...	...	14	...	...	...	...	...	...	...	...
Total Government Final Consumption Expenditure	1742	3924	5388	6090	6475	8811	10425	11469	12156	11741	11844	12127

2.5 Private Final Consumption Expenditure by Type and Porpose, in Current Prices

Million Malaysian ringgit

	1970	1975	1977	1978	1979	1980	1981	1982	1983	1984	1985	1986
Final Consumption Expenditure of Resident Households											
1 Food, beverages and tobacco	2875	...	...	7908	...	...	...	...	...	...	...	...
A Food	2392	...	...	6623	...	...	...	...	...	...	...	...
B Non-alcoholic beverages	37	...	...	163	...	...	...	...	...	...	...	...
C Alcoholic beverages	129	...	...	382	...	...	...	...	...	...	...	...
D Tobacco	317	...	...	740	...	...	...	...	...	...	...	...
2 Clothing and footwear	348	...	...	1109	...	...	...	...	...	...	...	...
3 Gross rent, fuel and power	862	...	...	2051	...	...	...	...	...	...	...	...
4 Furniture, furnishings and household equipment and operation	392	...	...	1479	...	...	...	...	...	...	...	...
A Household operation	162	...	...	421	...	...	...	...	...	...	...	...
B Other	230	...	...	1058	...	...	...	...	...	...	...	...
5 Medical care and health expenses	133	...	...	420	...	...	...	...	...	...	...	...
6 Transport and communication	856	...	...	3481	...	...	...	...	...	...	...	...
A Personal transport equipment	180	...	...	1221	...	...	...	...	...	...	...	...
B Other	676	...	...	2260	...	...	...	...	...	...	...	...
7 Recreational, entertainment, education and cultural services	347	...	...	1252	...	...	...	...	...	...	...	...
A Education	50	...	...	101	...	...	...	...	...	...	...	...
B Other	297	...	...	1151	...	...	...	...	...	...	...	...
8 Miscellaneous goods and services	519	...	...	1623	...	...	...	...	...	...	...	...
A Personal care	217	...	...	622	...	...	...	...	...	...	...	...
B Expenditures in restaurants, cafes and hotels	248	...	...	798	...	...	...	...	...	...	...	...
C Other	54	...	...	203	...	...	...	...	...	...	...	...
Total Final Consumption Expenditure in the Domestic Market by Households, of which	6332	...	...	19323	...	...	...	...	...	...	...	...
A Durable goods	356	...	...	2391	...	...	...	...	...	...	...	...
B Semi-durable goods	831	...	...	2527	...	...	...	...	...	...	...	...
C Non-durable goods	3501	...	...	9883	...	...	...	...	...	...	...	...
D Services	1644	...	...	4522	...	...	...	...	...	...	...	...
Plus: Direct purchases abroad by resident households	184	...	...	883	...	...	...	...	...	...	...	...
Less: Direct purchases in the domestic market by non-resident households	167	...	...	622	...	...	...	...	...	...	...	...
Equals: Final Consumption Expenditure of Resident Households [a]	6349	...	...	19584	...	...	...	...	...	...	...	...
Final Consumption Expenditure of Private Non-profit Institutions Serving Households											
Equals: Final Consumption Expenditure of Private Non-profit Organisations Serving Households	...	...	...	...	...	...	...	...	...	...	...	...
Private Final Consumption Expenditure	6349	...	...	19584	...	...	...	...	...	...	...	...

a) Item 'Final consumption expenditure of resident households' includes consumption expenditure of private non-profit institutions serving households.

Malaysia

2.17 Exports and Imports of Goods and Services, Detail

Million Malaysian ringgit

	1970	1975	1977	1978	1979	1980	1981	1982	1983	1984	1985	1986
Exports of Goods and Services												
1 Exports of merchandise, f.o.b.	4105	...	...	17067	...	...	...	...	...	...	...	...
2 Transport and communication	5	...	...	696	...	...	...	...	...	...	...	...
3 Insurance service charges	...	...	...	16	...	...	...	...	...	...	...	...
4 Other commodities	5	...	...	184	...	...	...	...	...	...	...	...
5 Adjustments of merchandise exports to change-of-ownership basis	50	...	...	...	...	...	...	...	...	...	...	...
6 Direct purchases in the domestic market by non-residential households	167	...	...	622	...	...	...	...	...	...	...	...
7 Direct purchases in the domestic market by extraterritorial bodies	...	...	...	...	...	...	...	...	...	...	...	...
Total Exports of Goods and Services	4332	10172	16279	18585	...	...	...	...	...	...	...	...
Imports of Goods and Services												
1 Imports of merchandise, c.i.f.	3401	...	...	14690	...	...	...	...	...	...	...	...
2 Adjustments of merchandise imports to change-of-ownership basis	...	...	...	...	...	...	...	...	...	...	...	...
3 Other transport and communication	85	...	...	381	...	...	...	...	...	...	...	...
4 Other insurance service charges	11	...	...	39	...	...	...	...	...	...	...	...
5 Other commodities	170	...	...	484	...	...	...	...	...	...	...	...
6 Direct purchases abroad by government	...	...	...	883	...	...	...	...	...	...	...	...
7 Direct purchases abroad by resident households	184	...	...		...	...	...	...	...	...	...	...
Total Imports of Goods and Services	3851	10071	13711	16477	...	...	...	...	...	...	...	...
Balance of Goods and Services	481	101	2568	2108	...	...	...	...	...	...	...	...
Total Imports and Balance of Goods and Services	4332	10172	16279	18585	...	...	...	...	...	...	...	...

Maldives

Source. Reply to the United Nations National Accounts Questionnaire from the Department of information and broadcasting, Male. Official estimates are published by the ministry of planning and development in the Statistical Yearbook.

General note. The estimates shown in the following tables have been prepared in accordance with the United Nations System of National Accounts so far as the existing data would permit.

1.1 Expenditure on the Gross Domestic Product, in Current Prices

Million Maldivian Rufiyaa

	1970	1975	1977	1978	1979	1980	1981	1982	1983	1984	1985	1986
1 Government final consumption expenditure	...	...	...	...	...	56.8	49.0	65.0	76.0	94.8	...	...
2 Private final consumption expenditure	...	...	...	...	...	270.3	344.0	367.0	385.0	416.0	...	...
3 Gross capital formation	...	...	...	...	...	117.4	99.0	105.0	178.0	220.0	...	...
A Increase in stocks	...	...	...	...	...	...	...	1.6	12.0	8.0	...	...
B Gross fixed capital formation	...	...	...	...	...	...	...	103.0	166.0	212.0	...	...
4 Exports of goods and services	...	...	...	...	...	142.4	196.0	240.0	288.0	300.0	...	...
5 Less: Imports of goods and services	...	...	...	...	...	231.3	313.0	345.0	464.0	495.0	...	...
Equals: Gross Domestic Product [a]	...	...	...	...	...	355.6	376.0	432.0	466.0	537.0	596.0	...

a) Data for this table have not been revised, therefore, data for some years are not comparable with those of other tables.

1.2 Expenditure on the Gross Domestic Product, in Constant Prices

Million Maldivian Rufiyaa

	1970	1975	1977	1978	1979	1980	1981	1982	1983	1984	1985	1986
			At constant prices of:									
			1980					1982			1984	
1 Government final consumption expenditure	...	...	42.9	37.1	42.6	56.8 / 45.0	46.0	60.0	70.0 / 83.6	94.8	...	...
2 Private final consumption expenditure	...	...	132.9	182.4	237.7	270.3 / 321.0	354.0	363.0	374.0 / 380.8	416.0	...	...
3 Gross capital formation	...	...	24.7	41.6	48.6	117.4 / 87.0	105.0	105.0	109.0 / 178.0	220.0	...	...
A Increase in stocks	...	...				...	...	...	... / 12.0	8.0	...	...
B Gross fixed capital formation	...	...				...	...	...	... / 166.0	212.0	...	...
4 Exports of goods and services	...	...	106.6	108.7	133.1	142.4 / 175.0	225.0	239.0	261.0 / 288.0	300.0	...	...
5 Less: Imports of goods and services	...	...	70.7	98.8	162.1	231.3 / 254.0	312.0	322.0	352.0 / 464.0	495.0	...	...
Equals: Gross Domestic Product	...	...	236.3	271.0	299.9	355.6 / 374.0	418.0	445.0	462.0 / 475.4	537.0	...	...

1.10 Gross Domestic Product by Kind of Activity, in Current Prices

Million Maldivian Rufiyaa

	1970	1975	1977	1978	1979	1980	1981	1982	1983	1984	1985	1986
1 Agriculture, hunting, forestry and fishing	...	...	...	...	...	111.5	130.5	130.3	149.3	167.5	176.3	212.7
2 Mining and quarrying	...	...	...	...	...	5.8	10.3	10.7	11.1	11.4	11.7	12.0
3 Manufacturing	...	...	...	...	...	14.3	16.8	21.4	27.2	30.4	33.5	38.1
4 Electricity, gas and water	...	...	...	...	...							
5 Construction	...	...	...	...	...	30.2	27.7	32.8	34.2	40.7	48.9	52.9
6 Wholesale and retail trade, restaurants and hotels	...	...	...	...	...	40.0	36.6	49.5	69.4	87.7	97.2	103.5
7 Transport, storage and communication	...	...	...	...	...	17.2	84.2	41.6	58.7	101.3	135.7	159.3
8 Finance, insurance, real estate and business services	...	...	...	...	...	8.2	11.7	13.4	15.4	19.6	26.0	29.3
9 Community, social and personal services	...	...	...	...	...	54.5	7.7	9.6	16.5	41.5	38.0	34.1

Maldives

1.10 Gross Domestic Product by Kind of Activity, in Current Prices
(Continued)

Million Maldivian Rufiyaa

	1970	1975	1977	1978	1979	1980	1981	1982	1983	1984	1985	1986
Total, Industries	...	...	...	...	...	281.1	325.6	309.3	381.8	500.1	567.3	641.9
Producers of Government Services	...	...	...	...	...	39.5	18.5	22.2	37.6	42.7	45.8	55.5
Other Producers	...	...	...	...	...	...	...	...	...	...	...	...
Subtotal	...	...	...	...	...	320.6	344.1	331.5	381.8	542.8	613.1	697.4
Less: Imputed bank service charge	...	...	...	...	...	...	...	...	...	...	...	...
Plus: Import duties	...	...	...	...	...	...	...	...	...	...	...	...
Plus: Value added tax	...	...	...	...	...	...	...	...	...	...	...	...
Equals: Gross Domestic Product	...	...	...	...	...	320.6	344.1	331.5	381.8	542.8	613.1	697.4

1.11 Gross Domestic Product by Kind of Activity, in Constant Prices

Million Maldivian Rufiyaa

	1970	1975	1977	1978	1979	1980	1981	1982	1983	1984	1985	1986
			At constant prices of: 1980				1982			1985		
1 Agriculture, hunting, forestry and fishing	...	...	102.9	98.1	96.9	114.9 / 128.7	138.9 / 150.2	140.7	145.6	157.3	176.3	174.3
2 Mining and quarrying	...	...	0.8	3.2	4.8	5.6 / 5.6	5.4 / 9.0	9.6	10.4	11.0	11.7	12.4
3 Manufacturing	...	...	7.9	10.0	12.5	14.9 / 12.7[a]	16.0 / 19.3	25.9	29.8	32.1	33.5	36.0
4 Electricity, gas and water	...	...	1.2	1.7	0.7	0.9 / ...						
5 Construction	...	...	11.8	25.6	35.4	42.0 / 39.6	28.6 / 28.5	33.4	34.4	40.8	48.9	52.8
6 Wholesale and retail trade, restaurants and hotels	...	...	...	...	...	44.0	44.3 / 36.6	49.5	69.4	87.7	97.2	103.5
7 Transport, storage and communication	...	...	12.8	15.5	18.4	21.8 / 19.4	21.0 / 82.8	39.7	53.6	92.5	122.7	145.6
8 Finance, insurance, real estate and business services	...	...	43.6	62.5	74.4	88.2 / 12.5	14.7 / 15.3	16.2	17.5	20.9	26.0	28.3
9 Community, social and personal services	...	...	6.8	8.0	9.6	11.4 / 58.4	72.1 / 8.2	10.0	17.1	42.2	38.0	33.4
Total, Industries	...	...	187.7	224.4	252.7	299.6 / 320.9	340.9 / 349.9	325.0	377.8	484.5	554.3	586.3
Producers of Government Services	...	...	48.6	46.6	47.2	56.0 / 44.9	54.9 / 18.5	22.2	37.6	42.7	45.8	55.5
Other Producers	...	...	...	...	...	...	...	...	...	...	...	...
Subtotal	...	...	236.3	271.0	299.9	355.6 / 365.8	395.8 / 368.4	347.2	415.4	527.2	600.1	641.8
Less: Imputed bank service charge	...	...				...	...	...	...	...	...	...
Plus: Import duties	...	...				...	...	...	...	...	...	...
Plus: Value added tax	...	...				...	...	...	...	...	...	...
Equals: Gross Domestic Product	...	...	236.3	271.0	299.9	355.6 / 365.8	395.8 / 368.4	347.2	415.4	527.2	600.1	641.8

a) Including item 'Electricity, gas and water'.

2.1 Government Final Consumption Expenditure by Function, in Current Prices

Million Maldivian Rufiyaa

	1970	1975	1977	1978	1979	1980	1981	1982	1983	1984	1985	1986
1 General public services	...	...	...	...	...	...	...	19.6	27.5	31.3	36.2	44.9
2 Defence	...	...	...	...	...	...	...	11.4	14.1	16.1	18.1	22.6
3 Public order and safety	...	...	...	...	...	...	...					
4 Education	...	...	...	...	...	...	...	9.7	13.1	15.0	17.5	22.5
5 Health	...	...	...	...	...	...	...	7.4	7.1	8.1	9.5	11.5

Maldives

2.1 Government Final Consumption Expenditure by Function, in Current Prices
(Continued)

Million Maldivian Rufiyaa

	1970	1975	1977	1978	1979	1980	1981	1982	1983	1984	1985	1986
6 Social security and welfare	...	...	...	...	...	...	...	27.1	13.7	7.0	6.8	7.4
7 Housing and community amenities	...	...	...	...	...	...	...	4.4	5.2	6.0	9.7	10.8
8 Recreational, cultural and religious affairs	...	...	...	...	...	...	...					
9 Economic services	...	...	...	...	...	...	...	9.0	10.1	14.3	14.3	7.8
A Fuel and energy	...	...	...	...	...	...	...	...	...	...	...	...
B Agriculture, forestry, fishing and hunting	...	...	...	...	...	...	...	1.2	1.5	1.8	1.7	2.6
C Mining, manufacturing and construction, except fuel and energy	...	...	...	...	...	...	...	...	...	...	...	...
D Transportation and communication	...	...	...	...	...	...	...	6.8	6.9	10.2	10.4	2.3
E Other economic affairs	...	...	...	...	...	...	...	1.0	1.7	2.3	2.2	2.9
10 Other functions	...	...	...	...	...	...	...	4.2	4.4	5.1	8.8	11.3
Total Government Final Consumption Expenditure	...	...	...	...	...	...	...	92.8	95.2	102.9	120.9	138.8

Mali

Source. 'Comptes economiques de Mali, 1971'. Service de la statistique, Bamako, Koulouba. On 1 June 1984, Mali joined the French Community in Africa of which the legal tender is CFA francs. Two Mali francs is equivalent to one CFA franc.

General note. The estimates shown in the following tables have been prepared in accordance with the United Nations System of National Accounts so far as the existing data would permit.

1.1 Expenditure on the Gross Domestic Product, in Current Prices
Thousand Million CFA francs

	1970	1975	1977	1978	1979	1980	1981	1982	1983	1984	1985	1986
1 Government final consumption expenditure	...	...	8.3	9.4	11.3	12.6	36.6	39.6	44.9	49.6	...	...
2 Private final consumption expenditure	...	...	150.0	172.8	213.6	246.5	315.6	321.0	339.0	367.0	...	...
3 Gross capital formation	...	...	37.9	46.1	47.5	50.6	93.0	118.5	118.0	144.9	...	...
A Increase in stocks	...	...	3.6	4.0	3.8	3.0	...	...	...	...	...	...
B Gross fixed capital formation	...	...	34.4	42.1	43.8	47.6	...	...	...	...	...	...
4 Exports of goods and services	...	...	39.2	30.0	37.2	53.3	55.6	62.6	78.8	96.8	...	...
5 Less: Imports of goods and services	...	...	51.3	65.4	76.9	90.0	120.6	130.0	158.5	188.1	...	...
Equals: Gross Domestic Product	152.6	269.0	204.6	217.8	259.6	300.6	380.2	411.7	421.9	470.2	...	...

1.3 Cost Components of the Gross Domestic Product
Thousand Million CFA francs

	1970	1975	1977	1978	1979	1980	1981	1982	1983	1984	1985	1986
1 Indirect taxes, net	...	...	...	13.6	16.9	14.5	28.9	30.6	...	...	...	...
A Indirect taxes	...	...	...	17.6	17.7	17.3	30.9	33.0	...	...	...	...
B Less: Subsidies	...	...	...	4.0	0.8	2.8	2.0	2.5	...	...	...	...
2 Consumption of fixed capital	...	...	...	...	...	...	22.6	24.3	...	...	...	...
3 Compensation of employees paid by resident producers to:	...	...	...	49.5	59.2	68.5	81.0	90.7	...	...	...	...
4 Operating surplus [a]	...	...	...	154.0	180.2	208.6	197.6	221.0	...	...	...	...
Equals: Gross Domestic Product	...	...	...	217.8	259.6	300.6	330.0	366.5	...	...	...	...

a) Item 'Operating surplus' includes consumption of fixed capital.

1.4 General Government Current Receipts and Disbursements
Thousand Million CFA francs

	1970	1975	1977	1978	1979	1980	1981	1982	1983	1984	1985	1986
Receipts												
1 Operating surplus	...	...	...	...	...	...	-	-	...	...	...	...
2 Property and entrepreneurial income	...	...	...	...	...	...	-	0.3	...	...	...	...
3 Taxes, fees and contributions	...	...	...	...	...	...	45.8	48.5	...	...	...	...
A Indirect taxes	...	...	...	...	...	...	30.9	33.0	...	...	...	...
B Direct taxes	...	...	...	...	...	...	10.0	10.8	...	...	...	...
C Social security contributions	...	...	...	...	...	...	4.4	4.1	...	...	...	...
D Compulsory fees, fines and penalties	...	...	...	...	...	...	0.6	0.7	...	...	...	...
4 Other current transfers	...	...	...	...	...	...	30.8	31.8	...	...	...	...
Total Current Receipts of General Government	...	...	...	...	...	...	76.7	80.7	...	...	...	...
Disbursements												
1 Government final consumption expenditure	...	...	...	...	...	...	35.0	38.1	...	...	...	...
2 Property income	...	...	...	...	...	...	3.9	7.0	...	...	...	...
3 Subsidies	...	...	...	...	...	...	2.0	2.5	...	...	...	...
4 Other current transfers	...	...	...	...	...	...	12.8	11.2	...	...	...	...
A Social security benefits	...	...	...	...	...	...	1.7	1.9	...	...	...	...
B Social assistance grants	...	...	...	...	...	...	...	...	...	...	...	...
C Other	...	...	...	...	...	...	11.2	9.3	...	...	...	...
5 Net saving	...	...	...	...	...	...	22.9	21.9	...	...	...	...
Total Current Disbursements and Net Saving of General Government	...	...	...	...	...	...	76.7	80.7	...	...	...	...

Mali

1.7 External Transactions on Current Account, Summary

Thousand Million CFA francs

	1970	1975	1977	1978	1979	1980	1981	1982	1983	1984	1985	1986
Payments to the Rest of the World												
1 Imports of goods and services	...	...	...	...	...	...	120.6	130.0	...	...	...	...
A Imports of merchandise c.i.f.	...	...	...	...	...	...	104.6	109.2	...	...	...	...
B Other	...	...	...	...	...	...	16.0	20.7	...	...	...	...
2 Factor income to the rest of the world	...	...	...	...	...	...	8.0	12.7	...	...	...	...
A Compensation of employees	...	...	...	...	...	...	4.2	4.8	...	...	...	...
B Property and entrepreneurial income	...	...	...	...	...	...	3.9	8.0	...	...	...	...
3 Current transfers to the rest of the world	...	...	...	...	...	...	1.3	1.7	...	...	...	...
4 Surplus of the nation on current transactions	...	...	...	...	...	...	-31.0	-37.1	...	...	...	...
Payments to the Rest of the World and Surplus of the Nation on Current Transactions	...	...	...	...	...	...	98.9	107.2	...	...	...	...
Receipts From The Rest of the World												
1 Exports of goods and services	...	...	...	...	...	...	55.6	62.6	...	...	...	...
A Exports of merchandise f.o.b.	...	...	...	...	...	...	41.9	47.9	...	...	...	...
B Other	...	...	...	...	...	...	13.5	14.6	...	...	...	...
2 Factor income from rest of the world	...	...	...	...	...	...	12.5	12.8	...	...	...	...
A Compensation of employees	...	...	...	...	...	...	12.5	12.8	...	...	...	...
B Property and entrepreneurial income	...	...	...	...	...	...	...	...	...	...	...	...
3 Current transfers from rest of the world	...	...	...	...	...	...	30.8	31.8	...	...	...	...
Receipts from the Rest of the World on Current Transactions	...	...	...	...	...	...	98.9	107.3	...	...	...	...

1.10 Gross Domestic Product by Kind of Activity, in Current Prices

Thousand Million CFA francs

	1970	1975	1977	1978	1979	1980	1981	1982	1983	1984	1985	1986
1 Agriculture, hunting, forestry and fishing	...	...	...	...	...	...	174.7	194.4	...	...	...	...
2 Mining and quarrying	...	...	...	...	...	...	24.1	26.9	...	...	...	...
3 Manufacturing	...	...	...	...	...	...			...	...	...	...
4 Electricity, gas and water	...	...	...	...	...	...	1.9	2.4	...	...	...	...
5 Construction	...	...	...	...	...	...	20.8	21.0	...	...	...	...
6 Wholesale and retail trade, restaurants and hotels	...	...	...	...	...	...	53.4	60.5	...	...	...	...
7 Transport, storage and communication	...	...	...	...	...	...	10.5	12.6	...	...	...	...
8 Finance, insurance, real estate and business services	...	...	...	...	...	...	4.9	6.3	...	...	...	...
9 Community, social and personal services	...	...	...	...	...	...	9.2	11.5	...	...	...	...
Statistical discrepancy	...	...	...	...	...	...	4.4	2.0	...	...	...	...
Total, Industries	...	...	...	...	...	...	303.7	337.5	...	...	...	...
Producers of Government Services	...	...	...	...	...	...	26.3	29.1	...	...	...	...
Other Producers	...	...	...	...	...	...	...	...	...	...	...	...
Subtotal	...	...	...	...	...	...	330.0	366.5	...	...	...	...
Less: Imputed bank service charge	...	...	...	...	...	...	...	...	...	...	...	...
Plus: Import duties	...	...	...	...	...	...	...	...	...	...	...	...
Plus: Value added tax	...	...	...	...	...	...	...	...	...	...	...	...
Equals: Gross Domestic Product	...	...	...	...	...	...	330.0	366.5	...	...	...	...

Mali

1.12 Relations Among National Accounting Aggregates

Thousand Million CFA francs

	1970	1975	1977	1978	1979	1980	1981	1982	1983	1984	1985	1986
Gross Domestic Product	76.3	129.5	204.6	217.8	259.6	300.6	330.0	366.5	395.4	...	...	...
Plus: Net factor income from the rest of the world	0.9	4.2	5.6	-8.9	-7.4	-7.4	4.5	0.3	8.9	...	...	...
Factor income from the rest of the world	...	...	...	...	...	...	12.5	13.0	...	...	...	...
Less: Factor income to the rest of the world	...	...	...	...	...	...	8.0	12.7	...	...	...	...
Equals: Gross National Product	77.2	183.7	210.2	208.9	252.4	293.2	334.5	366.7	404.3	...	...	...
Less: Consumption of fixed capital	3.0	...	...	...	...	...	22.6	24.3	...	...	...	...
Equals: National Income	74.2	...	...	...	...	...	311.9	342.5	...	...	...	...
Plus: Net current transfers from the rest of the world	...	...	...	...	...	...	29.5	30.1	...	...	...	...
Current transfers from the rest of the world	...	...	...	...	...	...	30.8	31.8	...	...	...	...
Less: Current transfers to the rest of the world	...	...	...	...	...	...	1.3	1.7	...	...	...	...
Equals: National Disposable Income	...	...	...	...	...	...	341.4	372.6	...	...	...	...
Less: Final consumption	...	...	...	...	...	...	313.7	329.3	...	...	...	...
Equals: Net Saving	...	...	...	...	...	...	27.8	43.3	...	...	...	...
Less: Surplus of the nation on current transactions	...	...	...	...	...	...	-31.0	-37.1	...	...	...	...
Statistical discrepancy	...	...	...	...	...	...	-1.0	1.3	...	...	...	...
Equals: Net Capital Formation	...	...	...	...	...	...	57.8	81.7	...	...	...	...

Malta

General note. The preparation of national accounts statistics in Malta is undertaken by the Central Office of Statistics, Valetta. The offical estimates and methodological notes are published annually in 'National Accounts of the Maltese Islands'. The estimates are generally in accordance with the definitions and classifications recommended in the United Nations System of National Accounts (SNA). Input-output tables are published in the above-mentioned publication. The following tables have been prepared from successive replies to the United Nations national accounts questionaire. When the scope and coverage of the estimates differ for conceptual or statistical reasons from the definitions and classification recommended in SNA, a footnote is indicated to the relevant tables.

Sources and methods:

(a) Gross domestic product. Gross domestic product is estimated mainly through the income approach.

(b) Expenditure on the gross domestic product. The expenditure approach is used to estimate government final consumption expenditure and exports and imports of goods and services. This approach, in combination with the commodity-flow approach is used for gross fixed capital formation and private final consumption expenditure. Increase in stocks is obtained as a residual. The estimates of government consumption expenditure is based on returns from all government departments. Excluded are current expenditure on national insurance benefits, subsidies and grants to persons and expenditure on fixed capital assets and on addition to stocks. Private consumption expenditure represents expenditure on consumer goods and services by persons and non-profit making bodies at market prices. Gross fixed capital formation constitutes expenditure on fixed assets for the replacement of and addition to existing assets. The estimates are based on an analysis of government expenditure, import data and censuses of production. The estimates of exports and imports of goods and services are based on data available from trade returns, banking statistics and estimates of expenditure on services, supplemented by ad hoc inquiries. For the constant price estimates, government final consumption expenditure, gross fixed capital formation and exports and imports of goods and services are deflated by appropriate indexes. For private consumption expenditure, extensive use is made of the various subindexes that make up the retail price index.

(c) Cost-structure of the gross domestic product. Compensation of employees includes employers' contributions to national insurance. For the private sector, employees' incomes are taken from annual reports of labours inspectors except in the manufacturing, quarrying and construction sectors, for which data are taken from the censuses of production. Government wages and salaries are estimated on the basis of department returns, while the services submit actual figures of their wage and salary bill. Profits are estimated from income tax data for professionals, annual censuses of production for manufacturing and ad hoc inquiries for other activities. For trade, gross profits are arrived at by assessing wholesale and retail profits on the basis of calculated turnovers. Income from property is estimated on the basis of actual rents received by the government plus rents earned by the private sector which is based on data obtained in the census of population, housing and employment in 1967 and interest earned from local sources. Indirect taxes cover items such as customs and excise duties, business licenses, stamp duties, motor vehicle licenses, etc. While subsidies include grants to farmers, price-stabilization payment, loss incurred on water and milk supplies, etc.

(d) Gross domestic product by kind of economic activity. The table of GDP by kind of economic activity is prepared in factor values. The income approach is used to estimate the value added of most industries except agriculture and fishing, for which the production approach is used. For most sectors of GDP by economic activity, separate estimates are available for wages and salaries, income from self-employment and other trading income. The contribution of each industry also includes provision for depreciation. The sources of these estimates are described in the cost-structure of GDP above. GDP by kind of economic activity is not estimated at constant prices.

1.1 Expenditure on the Gross Domestic Product, in Current Prices

Thousand Maltese pounds

	1970	1975	1977	1978	1979	1980	1981	1982	1983	1984	1985	1986
1 Government final consumption expenditure	18350	30523	39734	46091	53678	63364	75407	85216	82257	80321	84309	89508
2 Private final consumption expenditure	73855	118660	172420	186371	206006	253485	279434	305724	306705	317475	333239	347895
3 Gross capital formation	31034	38957	62256	65104	82992	96457	118154	145625	137090	133233	133754	130506
A Increase in stocks a	3221	1475	2262	4789	4795	9383	12557	25504	5460	6780	7883	8179
B Gross fixed capital formation	27813	37482	59994	60315	78197	87074	105597	120121	131630	126453	125871	122327
Residential buildings	4946	5509	13776	17629	21065	20875	30155	38634				
Non-residential buildings	4750	2497							50960	48661	41197	44779
Other construction and land improvement etc.	2960	6397	11422	10896	9867	10658	11215	11317				
Other	15157	23079	34796	31790	47265	55541	64227	70170	80670	77792	84674	77548
4 Exports of goods and services	47098	137327	207366	229569	290769	356647	355918	319799	307647	323539	345155	365702
5 Less: Imports of goods and services	75516	159710	241996	249518	307666	377989	392462	394578	376143	393516	420475	421742
Equals: Gross Domestic Product	94821	165757	239780	277617	325779	391964	436451	461786	457556	461052	475982	511869

a) Item 'Increase in stocks' includes a statistical discrepancy.

1.2 Expenditure on the Gross Domestic Product, in Constant Prices

Thousand Maltese pounds

	1970	1975	1977	1978	1979	1980	1981	1982	1983	1984	1985	1986
					At constant prices of:							
		1954					1973					
1 Government final consumption expenditure	11300		26700	31400	34600	38200	38900	41800	44300	43800	42700	45100	47100
2 Private final consumption expenditure	60300		101900	130600	136300	140400	149100	154000	158500	160700	167100	175400	180300
3 Gross capital formation	20200		28900	38700	40000	44000	48900	58900	78500	67000	64000	62800	58300
A Increase in stocks a	3200		1500	2300	4800	4800	9400	12600	25400	5500	6800	7900	8200
B Gross fixed capital formation	17000		27400	36400	35200	39200	39500	46300	53100	61500	57200	54900	50100
4 Exports of goods and services	32200		105600	140200	146800	171500	192000	170100	146600	143900	149700	160800	169400
5 Less: Imports of goods and services	58800		110900	141100	135600	148700	166200	153400	150400	139500	145000	158400	158500
Equals: Gross Domestic Product	65200		152200	199800	222100	245400	262700	271400	277600	275900	278500	285700	297100

a) Item 'Increase in stocks' includes a statistical discrepancy.

Malta

1.3 Cost Components of the Gross Domestic Product

Thousand Maltese pounds

	1970	1975	1977	1978	1979	1980	1981	1982	1983	1984	1985	1986
1 Indirect taxes, net	12620	12813	19881	26357	32128	43352	45917	44041	40426	39675	45432	50103
A Indirect taxes	14828	20002	26882	30116	36159	45744	47897	46852	43794	43706	49452	54885
B Less: Subsidies	2208	7189	7001	3759	4031	2392	1980	2811	3368	4031	4020	4782
2 Consumption of fixed capital	2927	5432	8547	10040	11085	12896	14363	15738	19753	20990	21423	23200
3 Compensation of employees paid by resident producers to:	47147	82975	113054	131460	152669	180553	203805	228625	223584	217928	222942	231617
4 Operating surplus	32127	64537	98298	109760	129897	155163	172366	173382	173793	182459	186185	206949
Equals: Gross Domestic Product	94821	165757	239780	277617	325779	391964	436451	461786	457556	461052	475982	511869

1.4 General Government Current Receipts and Disbursements

Thousand Maltese pounds

	1970	1975	1977	1978	1979	1980	1981	1982	1983	1984	1985	1986
					Receipts							
1 Operating surplus	569	336	721	1212	1373	3142	8906	5297	5206	8688	4982	16712
2 Property and entrepreneurial income	3348	14321	19180	25918	34440	50064	55259	58238	43930	49996	46046	37403
3 Taxes, fees and contributions	19121	40124	55849	66280	88299	108972	121315	127977	124173	118905	127249	131722
A Indirect taxes	14828	20002	26882	30116	36159	45744	47897	46852	43794	43706	49452	54885
B Direct taxes [a]	4205	19869	28710	35906	51828	62890	73142	80766	79950	74731	77349	76453
C Social security contributions [a]	...	...	...	...	...	...	...	...	...	...	...	...
D Compulsory fees, fines and penalties	88	253	257	258	312	338	276	359	429	468	448	384
4 Other current transfers	2252	2607	3388	3338	3585	3663	4282	4244	4652	5229	5344	5311
Total Current Receipts of General Government [b]	25290	57388	79138	96748	127697	165841	189762	195756	177961	182818	183621	191148
					Disbursements							
1 Government final consumption expenditure	18350	30523	39734	46091	53878	63364	75407	85216	82257	80321	84309	89508
A Compensation of employees	13504	22289	30090	33346	39126	44444	51513	58152	57348	68618	78392	82730
B Consumption of fixed capital	654	1808	2732	2899	2731	3127	3746	4996	5624	5972	5917	6778
C Purchases of goods and services, net	...	...	...	...	...	...	...	...	...	...	...	...
D Less: Own account fixed capital formation	...	...	...	...	...	...	...	...	...	...	...	...
E Indirect taxes paid, net	...	...	...	...	...	...	...	...	...	...	...	...
2 Property income	1940	1711	1693	1672	1667	1666	1641	1630	1611	1700	1705	1716
3 Subsidies	2208	7189	7001	3759	4031	2392	1980	2811	3368	4031	4020	4782
4 Other current transfers	4350	16013	23669	28704	31695	40312	51410	59402	61484	65351	65021	66668
5 Net saving	-1558	1952	7041	16522	36626	58107	59324	46697	29241	31415	28566	28474
Total Current Disbursements and Net Saving of General Government [b]	25290	57388	79138	96748	127697	165841	189762	195756	177961	182818	183621	191148

a) Item 'Social security contributions' is included in item 'Direct taxes on Income'.
b) Public enterprises is included in general government.

1.5 Current Income and Outlay of Corporate and Quasi Corporate Enterprises, Summary

Thousand Maltese pounds

	1970	1975	1977	1978	1979	1980	1981	1982	1983	1984	1985	1986
					Receipts							
1 Operating surplus	9493	26770	41258	43838	46404	52235	59863	68790	69703	72729	76329	74824
2 Property and entrepreneurial income received	576	945	1257	1395	3107	4618	5474	5412	3826	3876	4209	4387
3 Current transfers	...			...	...			...	...	...	...	...
Total Current Receipts [a]	10069	27715	42515	45233	49511	56853	65337	74202	73529	76605	80538	79211
					Disbursements							
1 Property and entrepreneurial income	4015	10307	14859	18606	27908	29296	31397	33484	30107	35279	38000	35066
2 Direct taxes and other current payments to general government	1934	3064	4972	7142	10705	10260	11376	17065	16032	14728	15194	15354
3 Other current transfers	...	...	...	...	...	...	...	...	...	...	...	...
4 Net saving	4120	14344	22684	19485	10898	17297	22564	23653	25390	26598	27335	28791
Total Current Disbursements and Net Saving [a]	10069	27715	42515	45233	49511	56853	65337	74202	73529	76605	80538	79211

a) Public enterprises is included in general government.

Malta

1.6 Current Income and Outlay of Households and Non-Profit Institutions

Thousand Maltese pounds

	1970	1975	1977	1978	1979	1980	1981	1982	1983	1984	1985	1986
					Receipts							
1 Compensation of employees	47147	82975	113054	131460	152669	180553	203805	228625	223584	217928	222942	231617
2 Operating surplus of private unincorporated enterprises	19668	28968	43596	45572	47574	57940	66268	72020	73370	75774	79082	84042
3 Property and entrepreneurial income	11706	23472	27972	29036	39538	48676	50878	50767	49599	53845	54036	54419
4 Current transfers	13591	27549	40738	43177	45457	53668	64994	74126	77252	81334	79638	80236
A Social security benefits	4000	15759	23325	28468	31408	40035	51125	59130	61211	65100	64726	66412
B Social assistance grants												
C Other	9591	11790	17413	14709	14049	13633	13869	14996	16041	16234	14912	13824
Total Current Receipts	92112	162964	225360	249245	285238	340837	385945	425538	423805	428881	435698	450314
					Disbursements							
1 Private final consumption expenditure	73855	118660	172420	186371	206006	253485	279434	305724	306705	317475	333239	347895
2 Property income	...	...	...	...	...	...	...	...	...	...	...	...
3 Direct taxes and other current transfers n.e.c. to general government	2359	17058	23995	29022	41435	52968	62042	64060	64347	60471	62603	61483
A Social security contributions	795	5981	9153	12390	16758	23464	28450	30482	31304	29492	30766	31466
B Direct taxes	1476	10824	14585	16374	24365	29166	33316	33219	32614	30511	31389	29569
C Fees, fines and penalties	88	253	257	258	312	338	276	359	429	468	448	448
4 Other current transfers	2047	3222	3846	4850	5432	6095	7053	6308	6499	8095	7420	7530
5 Net saving	13851	24024	25099	29002	32365	28289	37416	49446	46254	42840	32436	33406
Total Current Disbursements and Net Saving	92112	162964	225360	249245	285238	340837	385945	425538	423805	428881	435698	450314

1.7 External Transactions on Current Account, Summary

Thousand Maltese pounds

	1970	1975	1977	1978	1979	1980	1981	1982	1983	1984	1985	1986
					Payments to the Rest of the World							
1 Imports of goods and services	75516	159710	241996	249518	307666	377989	392462	394578	376143	393516	420475	421742
2 Factor income to the rest of the world	3503	5623	8241	12233	22019	19929	19679	11801	9874	9199	10758	17195
A Compensation of employees	...	...	...	...	...	...	...	...	...	...	...	...
B Property and entrepreneurial income	3503	5623	8241	12233	22019	19929	19679	11801	9874	9199	10758	17195
3 Current transfers to the rest of the world	1309	1730	1665	2445	2654	2915	3156	2383	2173	3185	2465	2560
4 Surplus of the nation on current transactions	-11694	6795	1115	9945	7982	20132	15513	-10091	-16452	-11390	-23994	-16635
Payments to the Rest of the World and Surplus of the Nation on Current Transactions	68634	173858	253017	274141	340321	420965	430810	398671	371738	394510	409704	424862
					Receipts From The Rest of the World							
1 Exports of goods and services	47098	137327	207366	229569	290769	356647	355918	319799	307647	323539	345155	365702
2 Factor income from rest of the world	10781	23880	27375	29166	34983	50479	60923	63829	47997	54669	49543	45251
A Compensation of employees	...	...	...	...	...	...	...	...	...	...	...	...
B Property and entrepreneurial income	10781	23880	27375	29166	34983	50479	60923	63829	47997	54669	49543	45251
3 Current transfers from rest of the world	10755	12651	18276	15406	14569	13839	13969	15043	16094	16302	15006	13909
Receipts from the Rest of the World on Current Transactions	68634	173858	253017	274141	340321	420965	430810	398671	371738	394510	409704	424862

1.8 Capital Transactions of The Nation, Summary

Thousand Maltese pounds

	1970	1975	1977	1978	1979	1980	1981	1982	1983	1984	1985	1986
					Finance of Gross Capital Formation							
Gross saving	19340	45752	63371	75049	90974	116589	133667	135534	120638	121843	109760	113871
1 Consumption of fixed capital	2927	5432	8547	10040	11085	12896	14363	15738	19753	20990	21423	23200
A General government [a]	654	1808	2732	2899	2731	3127	3746	4996	5624	5972	5917	6778
B Corporate and quasi-corporate enterprises	715	1820	3677	4627	5501	6718	7087	7285	10097	11594	12269	12946
Public	...	...	...	...	...	...	...	...	...	...	...	...
Private	715	1820	3677	4627	5501	6718	7087	7285	10097	11594	12269	12946

Malta

1.8 Capital Transactions of The Nation, Summary
(Continued)

Thousand Maltese pounds

	1970	1975	1977	1978	1979	1980	1981	1982	1983	1984	1985	1986
C Other	1558	1804	2138	2514	2853	3051	3530	3457	4032	3424	3237	3476
2 Net saving	16413	40320	54824	65009	79889	103693	119304	119796	100885	100853	88337	90671
A General government	-1558	1952	7041	16522	36626	58107	59324	46697	29241	31415	28566	28474
B Corporate and quasi-corporate enterprises	4120	14344	22684	19485	10898	17297	22564	23653	25390	26598	27335	28791
Public	...	...	...	...	...	...	...	...	...	...	...	...
Private	4120	14344	22684	19485	10898	17297	22564	23653	25390	26598	27335	28791
C Other	13851	24024	25099	29002	32365	28289	37416	49446	46254	42840	32436	33406
Less: Surplus of the nation on current transactions	-11694	6795	1115	9945	7982	20132	15513	-10091	-16452	-11390	-23994	-16635
Finance of Gross Capital Formation	31034	38957	62256	65104	82992	96457	118154	145629	137090	133233	133754	130506

Gross Capital Formation

	1970	1975	1977	1978	1979	1980	1981	1982	1983	1984	1985	1986
Increase in stocks [b]	3221	1475	2262	4789	4795	9383	12557	25504	5460	6780	7883	8179
Gross fixed capital formation	27813	37482	59994	60315	78197	87074	105597	120121	131630	126453	125871	122327
1 General government [a]	10074	17982	22783	21868	21885	25543	30609	33375	23747	25124	25330	25795
2 Corporate and quasi-corporate enterprises	3470	7551	18503	17129	32186	38903	44043	43354	72964	60601	57982	53344
A Public	...	...	...	...	...	...	...	...	...	...	...	...
B Private	3470	7551	18503	17129	32186	38903	44043	43354	72964	60601	57982	53344
3 Other	14269	11949	18708	21318	24126	22628	30945	43392	34919	40728	42559	43188
Gross Capital Formation	31034	38957	62256	65104	82992	96457	118154	145625	137090	133233	133754	130506

a) Public enterprises is included in general government.
b) Item 'Increase in stocks' includes a statistical discrepancy.

1.10 Gross Domestic Product by Kind of Activity, in Current Prices

Thousand Maltese pounds

	1970	1975	1977	1978	1979	1980	1981	1982	1983	1984	1985	1986
1 Agriculture, hunting, forestry and fishing	5813	9210	12895	11357	11529	13289	15038	16767	18731	19346	19375	20419
2 Mining and quarrying [a]	6206	9209	10526	11662	13533	15655	17073	23546	23511	19660	20758	18869
3 Manufacturing	17865	46684	72597	84445	99976	115358	121384	125024	120036	124706	126929	134676
4 Electricity, gas and water [b]	4289	5859	8332	10340	11661	15635	23586	21958	21119	24985	22278	34704
5 Construction [a]	...	...	...	...	...	...	...	...	...	...	...	...
6 Wholesale and retail trade, restaurants and hotels [c]	13597	21732	33161	39139	45766	51001	57421	63184	64010	66077	66696	67647
7 Transport, storage and communication	2845	6686	10234	11863	14679	22230	22596	20396	24050	23391	23955	26240
8 Finance, insurance, real estate and business services [d]	7287	14511	18556	22934	29252	37269	45519	50303	51475	53517	57131	61255
9 Community, social and personal services [cd]	4268	9253	16408	21082	28129	33731	36404	38415	36850	33605	34894	35639
Total, Industries	62170	123144	182709	212822	254525	304168	339021	359593	359782	365287	372016	399449
Producers of Government Services	19221	28728	35684	37291	39126	44444	51513	58152	57348	56090	58534	62317
Other Producers	810	1072	1506	1147								
Subtotal [e]	82201	152044	219099	251260	293651	348612	390534	417745	417130	421377	430550	461766
Less: Imputed bank service charge	...	...	...	...	...	...	...	...	...	...	...	...
Plus: Import duties	...	...	...	...	...	...	...	...	...	...	...	...
Plus: Value added tax	...	...	...	...	...	...	...	...	...	...	...	...
Plus: Other adjustments [f]	12620	12813	19881	26357	32128	43352	45917	44041	40426	39675	45432	50103
Equals: Gross Domestic Product	94821	165757	239780	277617	325779	391964	436451	461786	457666	461052	475982	511869

a) Item 'Construction' is included in 'Mining and quarrying'.
b) Item 'Electricity, gas and water' refers mainly to government enterprises.
c) Restaurants and hotels are included in item 'Community, social and personal services'.
d) Business services are included in item 'Community, social and personal services'.
e) Gross domestic product in factor values.
f) Item 'Other adjustments' refers to indirect taxes net of subsidies.

1.12 Relations Among National Accounting Aggregates

Thousand Maltese pounds

	1970	1975	1977	1978	1979	1980	1981	1982	1983	1984	1985	1986
Gross Domestic Product	94821	165757	239780	277617	325779	391964	436451	461786	457556	461052	475982	511869
Plus: Net factor income from the rest of the world	7278	18257	19134	16933	12964	30550	41244	52028	38123	45470	38785	28056
Equals: Gross National Product	102099	184014	258914	294550	338743	422514	477695	513814	495679	506522	514767	539925
Less: Consumption of fixed capital	2927	5432	8547	10040	11085	12896	14363	15738	19753	20990	21423	23200
Equals: National Income	99172	178582	250367	284510	327658	409618	463332	498076	475926	485532	493344	516725

Malta

1.12 Relations Among National Accounting Aggregates
(Continued)

Thousand Maltese pounds

	1970	1975	1977	1978	1979	1980	1981	1982	1983	1984	1985	1986
Plus: Net current transfers from the rest of the world	9446	10921	16611	12961	11915	10924	10813	12660	13921	13117	12541	11349
Current transfers from the rest of the world	10755	12651	18276	15406	14569	13839	13969	15043	16094	16302	15006	13909
Less: Current transfers to the rest of the world	1309	1730	1665	2445	2654	2915	3156	2383	2173	3185	2465	2560
Equals: National Disposable Income	108618	189503	266978	297471	339573	420542	474145	510736	489847	498649	505885	528074
Less: Final consumption	92205	149183	212154	232462	259684	316849	354841	390940	388962	397796	417548	437403
Equals: Net Saving	16413	40320	54824	65009	79889	103693	119304	119796	100885	100853	88337	90671
Less: Surplus of the nation on current transactions	-11694	6795	1115	9945	7982	20132	15513	-10091	-16452	-11390	-23994	-16635
Equals: Net Capital Formation	28107	33525	53709	55064	71907	83561	103791	129887	117337	112243	112331	107306

2.1 Government Final Consumption Expenditure by Function, in Current Prices

Thousand Maltese pounds

		1970	1975	1977	1978	1979	1980	1981	1982	1983	1984	1985	1986
1	General public services	2968	7360	7992	7921	9284	9583	9819	10887	10718	9575	10804	11478
2	Defence	2743	4170	6123	6674	8150	9264	11419	14339	14169	13826	14636	15265
3	Public order and safety												
4	Education	5594	6842	10138	10930	13397	15500	18252	20266	19666	18528	19484	20197
5	Health	4135	6222	8209	10902	11923	15133	17587	20731	20723	20680	21108	22980
6	Social security and welfare	423	658	841	1014	1344	1449	1950	1792	1704	2160	2146	2385
7	Housing and community amenities	1750	4514	5201	7453	8292	10711	14265	14428	12606	12768	13314	14041
8	Recreational, cultural and religious affairs	...	...	...	...	...	...	...	...	...	...	...	...
9	Economic services	499	757	1230	1197	1288	1724	2115	2773	2671	2784	2817	3162
10	Other functions	238	-	-	-	-	-	-	-	-	-	-	-
	Total Government Final Consumption Expenditure	18350	30523	39734	46091	53678	63364	75407	85216	82257	80321	84309	89508

2.5 Private Final Consumption Expenditure by Type and Porpose, in Current Prices

Thousand Maltese pounds

		1970	1975	1977	1978	1979	1980	1981	1982	1983	1984	1985	1986
		\multicolumn{12}{c}{Final Consumption Expenditure of Resident Households}											
1	Food, beverages and tobacco	32801	53120	69950	81798	93447	114993	127180	133047	131847	131301	141513	140887
	A Food	23445	37618	48846	56270	60828	74501	83668	92140	93762	92954	101225	98285
	B Non-alcoholic beverages	2626	3222	3763	3415	3938	5248	6932	9938	9907	10811	12920	13599
	C Alcoholic beverages	3638	5462	9657	13426	18391	21626	22559	17354	15545	14810	14840	16224
	D Tobacco	3092	6818	7684	8687	10290	13618	14021	13615	12633	12726	12528	12779
2	Clothing and footwear	9333	13877	17762	19140	23914	29375	29725	25951	25184	27014	33039	36247
3	Gross rent, fuel and power	5845	9953	13136	14385	19655	25042	26296	21867	22225	22423	22828	24102
	A Fuel and power	...	...	4989	5100	5813	8232	8827	6730	7196	8102	8032	8525
	B Other	...	...	8147	9285	13842	16810	17469	15137	15029	14321	14796	15577
4	Furniture, furnishings and household equipment and operation	8696	16377	24155	25318	30804	37639	35917	35771	35141	35517	33534	35252
	A Household operation	1359	4469	6865	6981	7854	8966	9037	10310	9766	10925	10888	9544
	B Other	7337	11908	17290	18337	22950	28673	26880	25461	25375	24592	22646	25708
5	Medical care and health expenses [a]	2210	6820	8127	10498	10625	10675	10404	12198	12593	13404	12524	14620
6	Transport and communication	5988	18647	27789	30884	38198	50689	50870	51151	50726	51042	57969	60127
	A Personal transport equipment	4499	12705	19731	20700	24579	32420	31796	32819	31425	33893	37189	38974
	B Other	1489	5942	8058	10184	13619	18269	19074	18332	19301	17149	20780	21153
7	Recreational, entertainment, education and cultural services	5179	9667	13863	15187	16749	21953	23169	23114	21009	22527	21490	24949
	A Education	...	...	816	987	1096	1731	1342	1470	1406	1547	1547	1677
	B Other	...	...	13047	14200	15653	20222	21827	21644	19603	20980	19943	23272
8	Miscellaneous goods and services [a]	7637	13690	23147	28663	37004	56717	61696	55498	52976	54457	56749	63976
	A Personal care	3208	4266	7600	8278	11641	11421	12020	13109	10645	11048	10777	10903
	B Expenditures in restaurants, cafes and hotels	...	7177	13716	18006	22154	41083	46490	37455	38181	39240	41531	48744

Malta

2.5 Private Final Consumption Expenditure by Type and Porpose, in Current Prices
(Continued)

Thousand Maltese pounds

	1970	1975	1977	1978	1979	1980	1981	1982	1983	1984	1985	1986
C Other	...	2247	1831	2379	3209	4213	3186	4934	4150	4169	4441	4329
Total Final Consumption Expenditure in the Domestic Market by Households, of which	77689	142151	197929	225873	270396	347083	365257	358597	351701	357685	379646	400160
Plus: Direct purchases abroad by resident households	2051	4596	8890	10250	11837	18336	19591	23707	22804	22890	23443	27085
Less: Direct purchases in the domestic market by non-resident households	5885	28087	34399	49752	76227	111934	105414	76580	67800	63100	69850	79350
Equals: Final Consumption Expenditure of Resident Households [b]	73855	118660	172420	186371	206006	253485	279434	305724	306705	317475	333239	347895

Final Consumption Expenditure of Private Non-profit Institutions Serving Households

	1970	1975	1977	1978	1979	1980	1981	1982	1983	1984	1985	1986
Equals: Final Consumption Expenditure of Private Non-profit Organisations Serving Households	...	...	...	...	...	...	...	...	...	...	...	...
Private Final Consumption Expenditure	73855	118660	172420	186371	206006	253485	279434	305724	306705	317475	333239	347895

a) Item 'Medical care and health expenses' refers to chemists' goods only, other components are included in item 'Miscellaneous goods and services'.
b) Item 'Final consumption expenditure of resident households' includes consumption expenditure of private non-profit institutions serving households.

2.6 Private Final Consumption Expenditure by Type and Purpose, in Constant Prices

Thousand Maltese pounds

	1970	1975	1977	1978	1979	1980	1981	1982	1983	1984	1985	1986
		1954				**At constant prices of:**			**1973**			

Final Consumption Expenditure of Resident Households

	1970	1975	1977	1978	1979	1980	1981	1982	1983	1984	1985	1986
1 Food, beverages and tobacco	25362	48951	57444	65159	70787	71139	69605	67851	68081	68583	74885	72805
A Food	18075	36212	41265	45832	47718	49096	48375	48370	50067	50433	56105	53027
B Non-alcoholic beverages	2951	1591	1887	1712	1974	2581	2507	3490	3482	3799	4541	4779
C Alcoholic beverages	2777	4819	7662	10287	12938	10585	9954	7578	6816	6468	6481	7086
D Tobacco	1559	6329	6630	7328	8157	8877	8769	8413	7716	7883	7758	7913
2 Clothing and footwear	9156	12675	16322	17198	20691	24392	24026	19323	18730	20156	24540	25590
3 Gross rent, fuel and power	5517	8776	10625	11526	15568	18526	19043	16102	16329	16120	16501	17434
A Fuel and power	...	...	2976	3088	3098	3418	3515	2689	3013	3457	3426	3661
B Other	...	...	7649	8438	12470	15108	15528	13413	13316	12663	13075	13773
4 Furniture, furnishings and household equipment and operation	7046	14125	18651	19122	21115	24330	21869	20766	20976	20963	19723	20943
A Household operation	1070	3613	4901	5022	4634	4577	4000	4838	4752	5321	5303	4560
B Other	5976	10512	13750	14099	16481	19753	17503	15928	16224	15642	14420	16383
5 Medical care and health expenses [a]	1991	6014	6710	8426	8335	8036	8376	7488	7421	7904	7415	8577
6 Transport and communication	4386	12308	15797	16453	17552	18854	16823	15292	15326	15437	17698	18549
A Personal transport equipment	3121	6662	10191	10475	10330	11163	9692	9369	8786	9166	10603	11132
B Other	1265	5040	5606	6078	7222	7691	7131	5923	6540	6271	7095	7417
7 Recreational, entertainment, education and cultural services	4406	8399	11735	12518	13438	15012	14089	13874	12538	13482	12854	14489
A Education	...	...	596	721	801	1265	981	1075	1028	1131	1131	1226

Malta

2.6 Private Final Consumption Expenditure by Type and Purpose, in Constant Prices
(Continued)

Thousand Maltese pounds

	1970	1975	1977	1978	1979	1980	1981	1982	1983	1984	1985	1986
	At constant prices of:											
	1954						**1973**					
B Other	...	...	11139	11797	12639	13747	13108	12799	11510	12351	11723	13263
8 Miscellaneous goods and services [a]	5714	11711	17665	21060	25297	34978	32701	31538	31159	32016	33367	37615
Total Final Consumption Expenditure in the Domestic Market by Households, of which	63578	122959	154949	171462	192783	215267	207252	192234	190559	194661	206983	216002
Plus: Direct purchases abroad by resident households	1298	3304	4775	4999	5091	6739	6660	7141	6602	6489	6182	6725
Less: Direct purchases in the domestic market by non-resident households	4580	24377	29105	40197	57504	72940	59956	40862	36422	34027	37761	42401
Equals: Final Consumption Expenditure of Resident Households [b]	60296	101886	130619	136264	140370	149066	153956	158513	160739	167123	175404	180326
	Final Consumption Expenditure of Private Non-profit Institutions Serving Households											
Equals: Final Consumption Expenditure of Private Non-profit Organisations Serving Households	...	...	...	...	...	...	...	...	...	...	...	...
Private Final Consumption Expenditure	60296	101886	130619	136264	140370	149066	153956	158513	160739	167123	175404	180326

a) Item 'Medical care and health expenses' refers to chemists' goods only, other components are included in item 'Miscellaneous goods and services'.
b) Item 'Final consumption expenditure of resident households' includes consumption expenditure of private non-profit institutions serving households.

2.7 Gross Capital Formation by Type of Good and Owner, in Current Prices

Thousand Maltese pounds

	\multicolumn{4}{c}{1980}	\multicolumn{4}{c}{1981}	\multicolumn{4}{c}{1982}
	TOTAL	Total Private	Public Enterprises	General Government	TOTAL	Total Private	Public Enterprises	General Government	TOTAL	Total Private	Public Enterprises	General Government
Increase in stocks, total	9383	2036	6971	376	12557	7160	5856	-459	25504	19229	3096	3179
Gross Fixed Capital Formation, Total	87074	61531	5070	20473	105597	74988	13466	17143	120121	86746	19214	14161
1 Residential buildings	20875	...	...	...	30155	25760	...	4395				
2 Non-residential buildings		...	...	...			...		50020	33366	5635	11019
3 Other construction	10658	...	...	...	11215	...	...	...				
4 Land improvement and plantation and orchard development		...	...	...		...	...	...				
5 Producers' durable goods	55541	44782	3115	7644	64227	49228	10004	4995	70101	53380	13579	3142
A Transport equipment	13153	13040	...	...	13828	13595	...	...	14508	14273	...	...
B Machinery and equipment	42388	31742	...	...	50399	35633	...	...	55593	39107	...	...
6 Breeding stock, dairy cattle, etc.	...	...	...	...	...	...	...	...	...	...	...	...
Total Gross Capital Formation	96457	63567	12041	20849	118154	82148	19322	16684	145625	105975	22310	17340

	\multicolumn{4}{c}{1983}	\multicolumn{4}{c}{1984}	\multicolumn{4}{c}{1985}
	TOTAL	Total Private	Public Enterprises	General Government	TOTAL	Total Private	Public Enterprises	General Government	TOTAL	Total Private	Public Enterprises	General Government
Increase in stocks, total	5460	9479	-7588	3569	6780	-1372	5197	2955	7883	9446	-5000	3437
Gross Fixed Capital Formation, Total	131630	107883	11371	12376	126453	101329	14199	10925	125871	100541	16453	8877
1 Residential buildings												
2 Non-residential buildings	50960	37400	4035	9527	48661	37076	2964	8621	41197	30806	3382	7009
3 Other construction												
4 Land improvement and plantation and orchard development												
5 Producers' durable goods	80670	70483	7338	2849	77792	64253	11235	2304	84674	69735	13071	1868
A Transport equipment	33135	32972	...	...	14559	14449	...	...	15939	15755	...	...
B Machinery and equipment	47535	37511	...	...	63233	49804	...	...	68735	53980	...	...
6 Breeding stock, dairy cattle, etc.	...	...	...	...	...	...	...	...	...	...	...	...
Total Gross Capital Formation	137090	117362	3783	15945	133233	99957	19396	13880	133754	109987	11453	12314

Malta

2.7 Gross Capital Formation by Type of Good and Owner, in Current Prices

Thousand Maltese pounds

	1986 TOTAL	Total Private	Public Enterprises	General Government
Increase in stocks, total	8179	3500	324	4355
Gross Fixed Capital Formation, Total	122327	96532	16210	9585
1 Residential buildings				
2 Non-residential buildings	44779	32925	3607	8247
3 Other construction				
4 Land improvement and plantation and orchard development				
5 Producers' durable goods	77548	63607	12603	1338
A Transport equipment	16676	16491	...	...
B Machinery and equipment	60872	47116	...	...
6 Breeding stock, dairy cattle, etc.	...	...	...	...
Total Gross Capital Formation	130506	100032	16534	13940

2.11 Gross Fixed Capital Formation by Kind of Activity of Owner, ISIC Divisions, in Current Prices

Thousand Maltese pounds

	1970	1975	1977	1978	1979	1980	1981	1982	1983	1984	1985	1986
					All Producers							
1 Agriculture, hunting, forestry and fishing	292	468	1064	1000	1010	1180	1270	1447	1363	1603	1355	1697
2 Mining and quarrying [a]	1182	1472	0021	2222	3725	1432	2692	4976	4761	6340	5743	5598
3 Manufacturing	4918	7670	11928	10951	18936	22693	28095	24882	23301	26298	30578	21641
4 Electricity, gas and water	4153	617	1189	1611	...	...	...	...	...	...	...	...
5 Construction [a]	...	...	...	...	...	...	...	...	...	...	...	...
6 Wholesale and retail trade, restaurants and hotels	2053	1770	3703	3470	8230	12085	7912	6721	4143	4606	4829	10000
7 Transport, storage and communication	3617	5004	7895	9255	9416	11184	14415	15582	37345	31486	32016	27326
8 Finance, insurance, real estate and business services [b]	4578	3305	6746	10421	11928	9792	18179	29274	32985	26898	22821	26174
9 Community, social and personal services [b]	1099	1276	3754	3578	3067	2165	2425	3864	3985	4098	3199	4096
Total Industries	21892	21582	40200	42508	56312	61531	74988	86746	107883	101329	100541	96532
Producers of Government Services	5921	15900	19794	17807	21885	25543	30609	33375	23747	25124	25330	25795
Private Non-Profit Institutions Serving Households	...	...	...	...	...	...	...	...	...	...	...	...
Total	27813	37482	59994	60315	78197	87074	105597	120121	131630	126453	125871	122327

a) Item 'Construction' is included in item 'Mining and quarrying'.
b) Finance, insurance and business services are included in item 'Community, social and personal services'.

3.12 General Government Income and Outlay Account: Total and Subsectors

Thousand Maltese pounds

	1980 Total General Government	Central Government	State or Provincial Government	Local Government	Social Security Funds	1981 Total General Government	Central Government	State or Provincial Government	Local Government	Social Security Funds
					Receipts					
1 Operating surplus	3142	...	...	...	...	8906	...	...	...	...
2 Property and entrepreneurial income	50064	...	...	...	...	55259	...	...	...	...
A Withdrawals from public quasi-corporations	...	...	...	...	...	...	...	...	...	...
B Interest	48261	...	...	...	...	49195	...	...	...	...
C Dividends		...	...	...	...		...	...	...	...
D Net land rent and royalties	1803	...	...	...	...	6064	...	...	...	...
3 Taxes, fees and contributions	108972	...	...	...	...	121315	...	...	...	...
A Indirect taxes	45744	...	...	...	...	47897	...	...	...	...
B Direct taxes [a]	62890	...	...	...	...	73142	...	...	...	...
Income [a]	62890	...	...	...	...	73142	...	...	...	...
Other	-	...	...	...	...	-	...	...	...	...
C Social security contributions [a]	...	...	...	...	...	...	...	...	...	...
D Fees, fines and penalties	338	...	...	...	...	276	...	...	...	...

Malta

3.12 General Government Income and Outlay Account: Total and Subsectors
(Continued)

Thousand Maltese pounds

		1980					1981				
		Total General Government	Central Government	State or Provincial Government	Local Government	Social Security Funds	Total General Government	Central Government	State or Provincial Government	Local Government	Social Security Funds
4	Other current transfers	3663	...	...	...	...	4282	...	...	...	...
	A Casualty insurance claims	-	...	...	...	...		...	...	...	...
	B Transfers from other government subsectors	...	...	...	...	...	...	...	...	...	...
	C Transfers from the rest of the world	206	...	...	...	...	100	...	...	...	...
	D Other transfers, except imputed	3457	...	...	...	...	4182	...	...	...	...
	E Imputed unfunded employee pension and welfare contributions	-	...	...	...	...	-	...	...	...	...
Total Current Receipts [b]		165841	...	...	...	...	189762	...	...	...	...

Disbursements

		Total General Government	Central	State/Prov	Local	Social Security	Total General Government	Central	State/Prov	Local	Social Security
1	Government final consumption expenditure	63364	...	...	...	...	75407	...	...	...	...
2	Property income	1666	...	...	...	...	1641	...	...	...	...
	A Interest	1666	...	...	...	...	1641	...	...	...	...
	B Net land rent and royalties	...	...	...	...	...	...	...	...	...	...
3	Subsidies	2392	...	...	...	...	1980	...	...	...	...
4	Other current transfers	40312	...	...	...	...	51410	...	...	...	...
	A Casualty insurance premiums, net	-	...	...	...	...		...	...	...	...
	B Transfers to other government subsectors	...	...	...	...	...	...	...	...	...	...
	C Social security benefits	...	...	...	...	...	...	...	...	...	...
	D Social assistance grants	...	...	...	...	...	...	...	...	...	...
	E Unfunded employee pension and welfare benefits	...	...	...	...	...	...	...	...	...	...
	F Transfers to private non-profit institutions serving households	...	...	...	...	...	...	...	...	...	...
	G Other transfers n.e.c.	...	...	...	...	...	...	...	...	...	...
	H Transfers to the rest of the world	277	...	...	...	...	285	...	...	...	...
Net saving		58107	...	...	...	...	59324	...	...	...	...
Total Current Disbursements and Net Saving [b]		165841	...	...	...	...	189762	...	...	...	...

		1982					1983				
		Total General Government	Central Government	State or Provincial Government	Local Government	Social Security Funds	Total General Government	Central Government	State or Provincial Government	Local Government	Social Security Funds

Receipts

1	Operating surplus	5297	...	...	...	...	5206	...	...	...	...
2	Property and entrepreneurial income	58238	...	...	...	...	43930	...	...	...	...
	A Withdrawals from public quasi-corporations	...	...	...	...	...	...	...	...	...	...
	B Interest	51683	...	...	...	...	37825	...	...	...	...
	C Dividends										
	D Net land rent and royalties	6555	...	...	...	...	6105	...	...	...	...
3	Taxes, fees and contributions	127977	...	...	...	...	124173	...	...	...	...
	A Indirect taxes	46852	...	...	...	...	43794	...	...	...	...
	B Direct taxes [a]	80766	...	...	...	...	79950	...	...	...	...
	Income [a]	80766	...	...	...	...	79950	...	...	...	...
	Other	-	...	...	...	...	-	...	...	...	...
	C Social security contributions [a]	...	...	...	...	...	...	...	...	...	...
	D Fees, fines and penalties	359	...	...	...	...	429	...	...	...	...
4	Other current transfers	4244	...	...	...	...	4652	...	...	...	...
	A Casualty insurance claims	-	...	...	...	...	-	...	...	...	...
	B Transfers from other government subsectors	...	...	...	...	...	...	...	...	...	...
	C Transfers from the rest of the world	47	...	...	...	...	53	...	...	...	...
	D Other transfers, except imputed	4197	...	...	...	...	4599	...	...	...	...
	E Imputed unfunded employee pension and welfare contributions	-	...	...	...	...	-	...	...	...	...

Malta

3.12 General Government Income and Outlay Account: Total and Subsectors
(Continued)

Thousand Maltese pounds

	1982					1983				
	Total General Government	Central Government	State or Provincial Government	Local Government	Social Security Funds	Total General Government	Central Government	State or Provincial Government	Local Government	Social Security Funds
Total Current Receipts [b]	195756	...	...	...	...	177961	...	...	...	...

Disbursements

1 Government final consumption expenditure	85216	...	...	...	...	82257	...	...	...	...
2 Property income	1630	...	...	...	...	1611	...	...	...	...
A Interest	1630	...	...	...	...	1611	...	...	...	...
B Net land rent and royalties	...	...	...	...	...	...	...	...	...	...
3 Subsidies	2811	...	...	...	...	3368	...	...	...	...
4 Other current transfers	59402	...	...	...	...	61484	...	...	...	...
A Casualty insurance premiums, net	-	...	...	...	...	-	...	...	...	...
B Transfers to other government subsectors	...	...	...	...	...	...	...	...	...	...
C Social security benefits	...	...	...	...	...	...	...	...	...	...
D Social assistance grants	...	...	...	...	...	...	...	...	...	...
E Unfunded employee pension and welfare benefits	...	...	...	...	...	...	...	...	...	...
F Transfers to private non-profit institutions serving households	...	...	...	...	...	...	...	...	...	...
G Other transfers n.e.c.	...	...	...	...	...	...	...	...	...	...
H Transfers to the rest of the world	272	...	...	...	...	273	...	...	...	...
Net saving	46697	...	...	...	...	29241	...	...	...	...
Total Current Disbursements and Net Saving [b]	195756	...	...	...	...	177961	...	...	...	...

	1984					1985				
	Total General Government	Central Government	State or Provincial Government	Local Government	Social Security Funds	Total General Government	Central Government	State or Provincial Government	Local Government	Social Security Funds

Receipts

1 Operating surplus	8688	...	...	...	...	4982	...	...	...	...
2 Property and entrepreneurial income	49996	...	...	...	...	46046	...	...	...	...
A Withdrawals from public quasi-corporations	...	...	...	...	...	...	...	...	...	...
B Interest	44085	...	...	...	...	39948	...	...	...	...
C Dividends		...	...	...	...		...	...	...	...
D Net land rent and royalties	5911	...	...	...	...	6098	...	...	...	...
3 Taxes, fees and contributions	118905	...	...	...	...	127249	...	...	...	...
A Indirect taxes	43706	...	...	...	...	49452	...	...	...	...
B Direct taxes [a]	74731	...	...	...	...	77349	...	...	...	...
Income [a]	74731	...	...	...	...	77349	...	...	...	...
Other	-	...	...	...	...	-	...	...	...	...
C Social security contributions [a]	...	...	...	...	...	...	...	...	...	...
D Fees, fines and penalties	468	...	...	...	...	448	...	...	...	...
4 Other current transfers	5229	...	...	...	...	5344	...	...	...	...
A Casualty insurance claims	-	...	...	...	...	-	...	...	...	...
B Transfers from other government subsectors	...	...	...	...	...	...	...	...	...	...
C Transfers from the rest of the world	68	...	...	...	...	94	...	...	...	...
D Other transfers, except imputed	...	...	...	...	...	5250	...	...	...	...
E Imputed unfunded employee pension and welfare contributions	-	...	...	...	...	-	...	...	...	...
Total Current Receipts [b]	182818	...	...	...	...	183621	...	...	...	...

Disbursements

1 Government final consumption expenditure	80321	...	...	...	...	84309	...	...	...	...
2 Property income	1700	...	...	...	...	1705	...	...	...	...
A Interest	1700	...	...	...	...	1705	...	...	...	...
B Net land rent and royalties	...	...	...	...	...	...	...	...	...	...
3 Subsidies	4031	...	...	...	...	4020	...	...	...	...

Malta

3.12 General Government Income and Outlay Account: Total and Subsectors
(Continued)

Thousand Maltese pounds

	1984					1985				
	Total General Government	Central Government	State or Provincial Government	Local Government	Social Security Funds	Total General Government	Central Government	State or Provincial Government	Local Government	Social Security Funds
4 Other current transfers	65351	...	...	...	...	65021	...	...	...	...
A Casualty insurance premiums, net	-	...	...	...	...	-	...	...	...	...
B Transfers to other government subsectors	...	...	...	...	...	...	...	...	...	...
C Social security benefits	...	...	...	...	...	...	...	...	...	...
D Social assistance grants	...	...	...	...	...	...	...	...	...	...
E Unfunded employee pension and welfare benefits	...	...	...	...	...	...	...	...	...	...
F Transfers to private non-profit institutions serving households	...	...	...	...	...	...	...	...	...	...
G Other transfers n.e.c.	...	...	...	...	...	...	...	...	...	...
H Transfers to the rest of the world	251	...	...	...	...	295	...	...	...	...
Net saving	31415	...	...	...	...	28566	...	...	...	...
Total Current Disbursements and Net Saving [b]	182818	...	...	...	...	183621	...	...	...	...

	1986				
	Total General Government	Central Government	State or Provincial Government	Local Government	Social Security Funds
Receipts					
1 Operating surplus	16712	...	...	...	...
2 Property and entrepreneurial income	37403	...	...	...	...
A Withdrawals from public quasi-corporations	...	...	...	...	...
B Interest	31662	...	...	...	...
C Dividends		...	...	...	...
D Net land rent and royalties	5742	...	...	...	...
3 Taxes, fees and contributions	131722	...	...	...	...
A Indirect taxes	54885	...	...	...	...
B Direct taxes [a]	76453	...	...	...	...
Income [a]	76453	...	...	...	...
Other	...	...	...	...	...
C Social security contributions [a]	...	...	...	...	...
D Fees, fines and penalties	384	...	...	...	...
4 Other current transfers	5311	...	...	...	...
A Casualty insurance claims	...	...	...	...	...
B Transfers from other government subsectors	...	...	...	...	...
C Transfers from the rest of the world	85	...	...	...	...
D Other transfers, except imputed	5226	...	...	...	...
E Imputed unfunded employee pension and welfare contributions	-	...	...	...	...
Total Current Receipts [b]	191148	...	...	...	...
Disbursements					
1 Government final consumption expenditure	89508	...	...	...	...
2 Property income	1716	...	...	...	...
A Interest	1716	...	...	...	...
B Net land rent and royalties	...	...	...	...	...
3 Subsidies	4782	...	...	...	...

Malta

3.12 General Government Income and Outlay Account: Total and Subsectors
(Continued)

Thousand Maltese pounds

	1986 Total General Government	Central Government	State or Provincial Government	Local Government	Social Security Funds
4 Other current transfers	66668	...	...	...	...
A Casualty insurance premiums, net	-	...	...	...	...
B Transfers to other government subsectors	...	...	...	...	...
C Social security benefits	...	...	...	...	...
D Social assistance grants	...	...	...	...	...
E Unfunded employee pension and welfare benefits	...	...	...	...	...
F Transfers to private non-profit institutions serving households	...	...	...	...	...
G Other transfers n.e.c.	...	...	...	...	...
H Transfers to the rest of the world	256	...	...	...	...
Net saving	28474	...	...	...	...
Total Current Disbursements and Net Saving [b]	191148	...	...	...	...

a) Item 'Social security contributions' is included in item 'Direct taxes on income'.
b) Public enterprises is included in general government.

3.13 General Government Capital Accumulation Account: Total and Subsectors

Thousand Maltese pounds

	1980 Total General Government	Central Government	State or Provincial Government	Local Government	Social Security Funds	1981 Total General Government	Central Government	State or Provincial Government	Local Government	Social Security Funds
					Finance of Gross Accumulation					
1 Gross saving	61234	...	...	...	...	63070	...	...	...	...
A Consumption of fixed capital	3127	...	...	...	...	3746	...	...	...	...
B Net saving	58107	...	...	...	...	59324	...	...	...	...
2 Capital transfers	6351	...	...	...	...	19995	...	...	...	...
A From other government subsectors	...	...	...	...	...	...	...	...	...	...
B From other resident sectors	1753	...	...	...	...	1955	...	...	...	...
C From rest of the world	4598	...	...	...	...	18040	...	...	...	...
Finance of Gross Accumulation [a]	67585	...	...	...	...	83065	...	...	...	...
					Gross Accumulation					
1 Gross capital formation	32890	...	...	...	...	36006	...	...	...	...
A Increase in stocks	7347	...	...	...	...	5397	...	...	...	...
B Gross fixed capital formation	25543	...	...	...	...	30609	...	...	...	...
2 Purchases of land, net	-	...	...	...	...	-	...	...	...	...
3 Purchases of intangible assets, net	-	...	...	...	...	-	...	...	...	...
4 Capital transfers	759	...	...	...	...	1086	...	...	...	...
A To other government subsectors	...	...	...	...	...	1	...	...	...	...
B To other resident sectors	759	...	...	...	...	1085	...	...	...	...
C To rest of the world	...	...	...	...	...	...	...	...	...	...
Net lending	33936	...	...	...	...	45973	...	...	...	...
Gross Accumulation [a]	67585	...	...	...	...	83065	...	...	...	...

	1982 Total General Government	Central Government	State or Provincial Government	Local Government	Social Security Funds	1983 Total General Government	Central Government	State or Provincial Government	Local Government	Social Security Funds
					Finance of Gross Accumulation					
1 Gross saving	51693	...	...	...	...	34865	...	...	...	...
A Consumption of fixed capital	4996	...	...	...	...	5624	...	...	...	...
B Net saving	46697	...	...	...	...	29241	...	...	...	...
2 Capital transfers	10776	...	...	...	...	9393	...	...	...	...
A From other government subsectors	...	...	...	...	...	...	...	...	...	...
B From other resident sectors	1721	...	...	...	...	1824	...	...	...	...
C From rest of the world	9055	...	...	...	...	7569	...	...	...	...
Finance of Gross Accumulation [a]	62469	...	...	...	...	44258	...	...	...	...
					Gross Accumulation					
1 Gross capital formation	39650	...	...	...	...	19728	...	...	...	...

Malta

3.13 General Government Capital Accumulation Account: Total and Subsectors
(Continued)

Thousand Maltese pounds

	1982					1983				
	Total General Government	Central Government	State or Provincial Government	Local Government	Social Security Funds	Total General Government	Central Government	State or Provincial Government	Local Government	Social Security Funds
A Increase in stocks	6275	...	...	...	...	-4019	...	...	...	...
B Gross fixed capital formation	33375	...	...	...	...	23747	...	...	...	...
2 Purchases of land, net	-	...	...	...	...	-	...	...	...	...
3 Purchases of intangible assets, net	-	...	...	...	...	-	...	...	...	...
4 Capital transfers	591	...	...	...	...	435	...	...	...	...
A To other government subsectors	...	...	...	...	...	...	...	...	...	...
B To other resident sectors	591	...	...	...	...	435	...	...	...	...
C To rest of the world	...	...	...	...	...	...	...	...	...	...
Net lending	22228	...	...	...	...	24095	...	...	...	...
Gross Accumulation [a]	62469	...	...	...	...	44258	...	...	...	...

	1984					1985				
	Total General Government	Central Government	State or Provincial Government	Local Government	Social Security Funds	Total General Government	Central Government	State or Provincial Government	Local Government	Social Security Funds

Finance of Gross Accumulation

1 Gross saving	37387	...	...	...	...	34483	...	...	...	...
A Consumption of fixed capital	5972	...	...	...	...	5917	...	...	...	...
B Net saving	31415	...	...	...	...	28566	...	...	...	...
2 Capital transfers	9298	...	...	...	...	2040	...	...	...	...
A From other government subsectors	...	...	...	...	...	...	...	...	...	...
B From other resident sectors	2116	...	...	...	...	1596	...	...	...	...
C From rest of the world	7182	...	...	...	...	444	...	...	...	...
Finance of Gross Accumulation [a]	46685	...	...	...	...	36523	...	...	...	...

Gross Accumulation

1 Gross capital formation	33276	...	...	...	...	23767	...	...	...	...
A Increase in stocks	8152	...	...	...	...	-1563	...	...	...	...
B Gross fixed capital formation	25124	...	...	...	...	25330	...	...	...	...
2 Purchases of land, net	-	...	...	...	...	-	...	...	...	...
3 Purchases of intangible assets, net	-	...	...	...	...	-	...	...	...	...
4 Capital transfers	543	...	...	...	...	246	...	...	...	...
A To other government subsectors	...	...	...	...	...	...	...	...	...	...
B To other resident sectors	543	...	...	...	...	246	...	...	...	...
C To rest of the world	...	...	...	...	...	...	...	...	...	...
Net lending	12866	...	...	...	...	12510	...	...	...	...
Gross Accumulation [a]	46685	...	...	...	...	36523	...	...	...	...

	1986				
	Total General Government	Central Government	State or Provincial Government	Local Government	Social Security Funds

Finance of Gross Accumulation

1 Gross saving	35252	...	...	...	...
A Consumption of fixed capital	6778	...	...	...	...
B Net saving	28474	...	...	...	...
2 Capital transfers	2923	...	...	...	...
A From other government subsectors	...	...	...	...	...
B From other resident sectors	1584	...	...	...	...
C From rest of the world	1339	...	...	...	...
Finance of Gross Accumulation [a]	38175	...	...	...	...

Gross Accumulation

1 Gross capital formation	30474	...	...	...	...
A Increase in stocks	4679	...	...	...	...
B Gross fixed capital formation	25795	...	...	...	...

Malta

3.13 General Government Capital Accumulation Account: Total and Subsectors
(Continued)

Thousand Maltese pounds

	1986				
	Total General Government	Central Government	State or Provincial Government	Local Government	Social Security Funds
2 Purchases of land, net	-	...	...	...	...
3 Purchases of intangible assets, net	-	...	...	...	...
4 Capital transfers	206	...	...	...	...
A To other government subsectors	...	...	...	...	...
B To other resident sectors	206	...	...	...	...
C To rest of the world	...	...	...	...	...
Net lending	7495	...	...	...	...
Gross Accumulation [a]	38175	...	...	...	...

a) Public enterprises is included in general government.

3.22 Corporate and Quasi-Corporate Enterprise Income and Outlay Account: Total and Sectors

Thousand Maltese pounds

	1980			1981			1982			1983		
	TOTAL	Non-Financial	Financial	TOTAL	Non-Financial	Financial	TOTAL	Non-Financial	Financial	TOTAL	Non-Financial	Financial
					Receipts							
1 Operating surplus	52235	43201	9034	59863	53807	6056	68790	59316	9474	69703	62505	7198
2 Property and entrepreneurial income	4618	4618	-	5474	5474	-	5412	5412	-	3826	3826	-
A Withdrawals from quasi-corporate enterprises	4618	4618	-	5474	5474	-	5412	5412	-	3826	3826	-
B Interest	...	...	...	...	...	...	...	...	...	...	...	...
C Dividends	...	...	...	...	...	...	...	...	...	...	...	...
D Net land rent and royalties	...	...	...	...	...	...	...	...	...	...	...	...
3 Current transfers	...	...	...	...	...	...	...	...	...	...	...	...
Total Current Receipts	56853	47819	9034	65337	59281	6056	74202	64728	9474	73529	66331	7198
					Disbursements							
1 Property and entrepreneurial income	...	...	...	...	...	...	...	...	...	...	...	...
A Withdrawals from quasi-corporations	9970	9970	-	6129	6129	-	6268	6268	-	3547	3547	-
B Interest	...	...	...	...	...	...	...	...	...	...	...	...
C Dividends	...	...	...	...	...	...	...	...	...	...	...	...
D Net land rent and royalties	...	...	...	...	...	...	...	...	...	...	...	...
2 Direct taxes and other current transfers n.e.c. to general government	10260	7324	2936	11376	9408	1968	17065	13986	3079	16032	13693	2339
A Direct taxes	10260	7324	2936	11376	9408	1968	17065	13986	3079	16032	13693	2339
On income	10260	7324	2936	11376	9408	1968	17065	13986	3079	16032	13693	2339
Other	...	...	...	...	...	...	...	...	...	...	...	...
B Fines, fees, penalties and other current transfers n.e.c.				...	...	...	...	...	...	...	...	...
3 Other current transfers	...	...	...	...	...	...	...	...	...	...	...	...
Net saving	17297	14180	3117	32564	21021	1640	20050	21202	2371	25390	24141	1249
Total Current Disbursements and Net Saving	56853	47819	9034	65337	59281	6056	74202	64728	9474	73529	66331	7198

	1984			1985			1986		
	TOTAL	Non-Financial	Financial	TOTAL	Non-Financial	Financial	TOTAL	Non-Financial	Financial
					Receipts				
1 Operating surplus	72729	65309	7420	70329	67289	6040	74894	65799	9102
2 Property and entrepreneurial income	3876	3876	-	4209	4209	-	4387	4387	-
A Withdrawals from quasi-corporate enterprises	3876	3876	-	4209	4209	-	4387	4387	-
B Interest	...	...	...	...	...	...	...	...	...
C Dividends	...	...	...	...	...	...	...	...	...
D Net land rent and royalties	...	...	...	...	...	...	...	...	...
3 Current transfers	...	...	...	...	...	...	...	...	...
Total Current Receipts	76605	69185	7420	80538	71498	9040	79211	70109	9102
					Disbursements				
1 Property and entrepreneurial income	...	...	...	...	...	...	...	...	...

Malta

3.22 Corporate and Quasi-Corporate Enterprise Income and Outlay Account: Total and Sectors
(Continued)

Thousand Maltese pounds

	1984 TOTAL	1984 Non-Financial	1984 Financial	1985 TOTAL	1985 Non-Financial	1985 Financial	1986 TOTAL	1986 Non-Financial	1986 Financial
A Withdrawals from quasi-corporations	4820	4820	-	6842	6842	-	4743	4743	-
B Interest	...	...	...	31167	28397	2770	30323	27737	2586
C Dividends	...	...	...						
D Net land rent and royalties	...	...	...	...	...	...	...	...	...
2 Direct taxes and other current transfers n.e.c. to general government	14728	12317	2411	15194	12256	2938	15354	12396	2958
A Direct taxes	14728	12317	2411	15194	12256	2938	15354	12396	2958
On income	14728	12317	2411	15194	12256	2938	15354	12396	2958
Other	...	...	...	...	...	...	...	...	...
B Fines, fees, penalties and other current transfers n.e.c.	...	...	...	...	...	...	...	...	...
3 Other current transfers	...	...	...	...	...	...	...	...	...
Net saving	26598	26094	504	27335	24003	3332	28791	25233	3558
Total Current Disbursements and Net Saving	76605	69185	7420	80538	71498	9040	79211	70109	9102

3.23 Corporate and Quasi-Corporate Enterprise Capital Accumulation Account: Total and Sectors

Thousand Maltese pounds

	1980 TOTAL	1980 Non-Financial	1980 Financial	1981 TOTAL	1981 Non-Financial	1981 Financial	1982 TOTAL	1982 Non-Financial	1982 Financial	1983 TOTAL	1983 Non-Financial	1983 Financial
Finance of Gross Accumulation
1 Gross saving	24015	20415	3600	29651	27899	1752	30938	28325	2613	35487	33983	1504
A Consumption of fixed capital	6718	6575	143	7087	6878	209	7285	7043	242	10097	9842	255
B Net saving	17297	13840	3457	22564	21021	1543	23653	21282	2371	25390	24141	1249
2 Capital transfers	...	...	...	...	...	...	...	...	...	...	...	...
Finance of Gross Accumulation	24015	20415	3600	29651	27899	1752	30938	28325	2613	35487	33983	1504
Gross Accumulation
1 Gross capital formation	40914	40914	-	50782	50782	-	62394	62394	-	82193	82193	-
A Increase in stocks	2011	2011	-	6739	6739	-	19040	19040	-	9229	9229	-
B Gross fixed capital formation	38903	38903	-	44043	44043	-	43354	43354	-	72964	72964	-
2 Purchases of land, net	...	...	...	...	...	...	...	...	...	...	...	...
3 Purchases of intangible assets, net	...	...	...	...	...	...	...	...	...	...	...	...
4 Capital transfers	...	...	...	...	...	...	...	...	...	...	...	...
Net lending	-16899	-20499	3600	-21131	-22883	1752	-31456	-34069	2613	-46706	-48210	1504
Gross Accumulation	24015	20415	3600	29651	27899	1752	30938	28325	2613	35487	33983	1504

	1984 TOTAL	1984 Non-Financial	1984 Financial	1985 TOTAL	1985 Non-Financial	1985 Financial	1986 TOTAL	1986 Non-Financial	1986 Financial
Finance of Gross Accumulation
1 Gross saving	38192	37397	795	39604	35961	3643	41737	37836	3901
A Consumption of fixed capital	11594	11303	291	12269	11958	311	12946	12603	343
B Net saving	26598	26094	504	27335	24003	3332	28791	25233	3558
2 Capital transfers	...	...	...	...	...	...	...	...	...
Finance of Gross Accumulation	38192	37397	795	39604	35961	3643	41737	37836	3901
Gross Accumulation
1 Gross capital formation	59271	59271	-	67028	67028	-	56344	56344	-
A Increase in stocks	-1330	-1330	-	9046	9046	-	3000	3000	-
B Gross fixed capital formation	60601	60601	-	57982	57982	-	53344	53344	-
2 Purchases of land, net	...	...	...	...	...	...	...	...	...
3 Purchases of intangible assets, net	...	...	...	...	...	...	...	...	...
4 Capital transfers	...	...	...	...	...	...	...	...	...
Net lending	-21079	-21874	795	-27424	-31067	3643	-14607	-18508	3901
Gross Accumulation	38192	37397	795	39604	35961	3643	41737	37836	3901

Malta

3.32 Household and Private Unincorporated Enterprise Income and Outlay Account

Thousand Maltese pounds

	1970	1975	1977	1978	1979	1980	1981	1982	1983	1984	1985	1986
					Receipts							
1 Compensation of employees	47147	82975	113054	131460	152669	180553	203805	228625	223584	217928	222942	231617
A Wages and salaries	46259	79323	107652	125265	144290	168821	189580	213384	207932	203182	207559	215884
B Employers' contributions for social security	888	3652	5402	6195	8379	11732	14225	15241	15652	14746	15383	15733
C Employers' contributions for private pension & welfare plans	...	...	...	...	...	...	...	...	...	...	...	...
2 Operating surplus of private unincorporated enterprises	19668	28968	43596	45572	47574	57940	66268	72020	73370	75774	79082	84042
3 Property and entrepreneurial income	11706	23472	27972	29036	39538	48676	50878	50767	49599	53845	54036	54419
A Withdrawals from private quasi-corporations	...	...	...	...	...	...	...	...	...	...	...	...
B Interest												
C Dividends	11706	23472	27972	29036	39538	48676	50878	50767	49599	53845	54036	54419
D Net land rent and royalties												
3 Current transfers	13591	27549	40738	43177	45457	53668	64994	74126	77252	81334	79638	80236
A Casualty insurance claims	...	...	...	...	...	...	...	...	...	...	...	...
B Social security benefits	4000	15759	23325	28468	31408	40035	51125	59130	61211	65100	64726	66412
C Social assistance grants												
D Unfunded employee pension and welfare benefits	-	-	-	-	-	-	-	-	-	-	-	-
E Transfers from general government	...	...	...	...	...	...	...	...	...	...	...	...
F Transfers from the rest of the world	9591	11790	17413	14709	14049	13633	13869	14996	16041	16234	14912	13824
G Other transfers n.e.c.	...	...	...	...	...	...	...	...	...	...	...	...
Total Current Receipts	92112	162964	225360	249245	285238	340837	385945	425538	423805	428881	435698	450314
					Disbursements							
1 Final consumption expenditures	73855	118660	172420	186371	206006	253485	279434	305724	306705	317475	333239	347895
A Market purchases	...	...	...	...	...	...	...	...	...	...	...	...
B Gross rents of owner-occupied housing	1251	2135	2594	2657	2778	2965	3586	3758	3884	3932	4184	4307
C Consumption from own-account production	...	...	...	...	...	...	...	...	...	...	...	...
2 Property income	...	...	...	...	...	...	...	...	...	...	...	...
3 Direct taxes and other current transfers n.e.c. to government	2359	17058	23995	29022	41435	52968	62042	64060	64347	60471	62603	61483
A Social security contributions	795	5981	9153	12390	16758	23464	28450	30482	31304	29492	30766	31466
B Direct taxes	1476	10824	14585	16374	24365	29166	33316	33219	32614	30511	31389	29569
Income taxes	1476	10824	14585	16374	24365	29166	33316	33219	32614	30511	31389	29569
Other	...	...	...	...	...	...	...	...	...	...	...	...
C Fees, fines and penalties	88	253	257	258	312	338	276	359	429	468	448	448
4 Other current transfers	2047	3222	3846	4850	5432	6095	7053	6308	6499	8095	7420	7530
A Net casualty insurance premiums	...	...	...	...	...	...	...	...	...	...	...	...
B Transfers to private non-profit institutions serving households	...	...	...	...	...	...	...	...	...	...	...	...
C Transfers to the rest of the world	959	1476	1321	2209	2367	2638	2871	2111	1900	5161	5250	5226
D Other current transfers, except imputed	1088	1746	2525	2641	3065	3457	4182	4197	4599	2934	2170	2304
E Imputed employee pension and welfare contributions	-	-	-	-	-	-	-	-	-	-	-	-
Net saving	13851	24024	25099	29002	32365	28289	37416	49446	46254	42840	32436	33406
Total Current Disbursements and Net Saving	92112	162964	225360	249245	285238	340837	385945	425538	423805	428881	435698	450314

3.33 Household and Private Unincorporated Enterprise Capital Accumulation Account

Thousand Maltese pounds

	1970	1975	1977	1978	1979	1980	1981	1982	1983	1984	1985	1986
					Finance of Gross Accumulation							
1 Gross saving	15409	25828	27237	31516	35218	31340	40946	52903	50286	46264	35673	36882
A Consumption of fixed capital	1558	1804	2138	2514	2853	3051	3530	3457	4032	3424	3237	3476
B Net saving	13851	24024	25099	29002	32365	28289	37416	49446	46254	42840	32436	33406
2 Capital transfers [a]	-862	615	3492	2689	...	...	...	...	...	...	...	...

Malta

3.33 Household and Private Unincorporated Enterprise Capital Accumulation Account
(Continued)

Thousand Maltese pounds

	1970	1975	1977	1978	1979	1980	1981	1982	1983	1984	1985	1986
Total Finance of Gross Accumulation	14547	26443	30729	34205	...	...	...	...	...	...	...	...
					Gross Accumulation							
1 Gross Capital Formation	15804	10295	18764	21597	24406	22653	31366	43581	35169	40686	42959	43688
A Increase in stocks	1535	-1654	56	279	280	25	421	189	250	-42	400	500
B Gross fixed capital formation	14269	11949	18708	21318	24126	22628	30945	43392	34919	40728	42559	43188
2 Purchases of land, net	...	...	...	...	...	...	...	...	...	...	...	...
3 Purchases of intangibles, net	...	...	...	...	...	...	...	...	...	...	...	...
4 Capital transfers	...	...	...	...	...	...	...	...	...	...	...	...
Net lending	-1257	16148	11965	12608	...	...	...	...	...	...	...	...
Total Gross Accumulation	14547	26443	30729	34205	...	...	...	...	...	...	...	...

a) Capital transfers received are recorded net of capital transfers paid.

3.51 External Transactions: Current Account: Detail

Thousand Maltese pounds

	1970	1975	1977	1978	1979	1980	1981	1982	1983	1984	1985	1986
					Payments to the Rest of the World							
1 Imports of goods and services	75516	159710	241996	249518	307666	377989	392462	394578	376143	393516	420475	421742
2 Factor income to the rest of the world	3503	5623	8241	12233	22019	19929	19679	11801	9874	9199	10758	17195
A Compensation of employees	...	...	...	...	...	...	...	...	...	...	...	...
B Property and entrepreneurial income	3503	5623	8241	12233	22019	19929	19679	11801	9874	9199	10758	17195
3 Current transfers to the rest of the world	1309	1730	1665	2445	2654	2915	3156	2383	2173	3185	2465	2560
A Indirect taxes by general government to supranational organizations	...	...	...	...	...	...	...	...	...	...	...	...
B Other current transfers	1309	1730	1665	2445	2654	2915	3156	2383	2173	3185	2465	2560
By general government	350	254	344	236	287	277	285	272	273	251	295	256
By other resident sectors	959	1476	1321	2209	2367	2638	2871	2111	1900	2934	2170	2304
4 Surplus of the nation on current transactions	-11694	6795	1115	9945	7982	20132	15513	-10091	-16452	-11390	-23994	-16635
Payments to the Rest of the World, and Surplus of the Nation on Current Transfers	68634	173858	253017	274141	340321	420965	430810	398671	371738	394510	409704	424862
					Receipts From The Rest of the World							
1 Exports of goods and services	47098	137327	207366	229569	290769	356647	355918	319799	307647	323539	345155	365702
2 Factor income from the rest of the world	10781	23880	27375	29166	34983	50479	60923	63829	47997	54669	49543	45251
A Compensation of employees	...	...	...	...	...	...	...	...	...	...	...	...
B Property and entrepreneurial income	10781	23880	27375	29166	34983	50479	60923	63829	47997	54669	49543	45251
3 Current transfers from the rest of the world	10755	12651	18276	15406	14569	13839	13969	15043	16094	16302	15006	13909
A Subsidies to general government from supranational organizations	...	...	...	...	...	...	...	...	...	...	...	...
B Other current transfers	10755	12651	18276	15406	14569	13839	13969	15043	16094	16302	15006	13909
To general government	1164	861	863	697	520	206	100	47	53	68	94	85
To other resident sectors	9591	11790	17413	14709	14049	13633	13869	14996	16041	16234	14912	13824
Receipts from the Rest of the World on Current Transfers	68634	173858	253017	274141	340321	420965	430810	398671	371738	394510	409704	424862

Malta

3.52 External Transactions: Capital Accumulation Account

Thousand Maltese pounds

	1970	1975	1977	1978	1979	1980	1981	1982	1983	1984	1985	1986
Finance of Gross Accumulation												
1 Surplus of the nation on current transactions	-11694	6795	1115	9945	7982	20132	15513	-10091	-16452	-11390	-23994	-16635
2 Capital transfers from the rest of the world	9394	18257	18356	20669	10764	8981	24138	18145	14787	16557	13170	16751
A By general government	6500	17037	13834	16474	5042	4598	18040	9055	7569	7182	444	1339
B By other resident sectors	2894	1220	4522	4195	5722	4383	6098	9090	7218	9375	12726	15412
Total Finance of Gross Accumulation	-2300	25052	19471	30614	18746	29113	39651	8054	-1664	5167	-10824	116
Gross Accumulation												
1 Capital transfers to the rest of the world	...	...	...	...	...	...	...	...	...	...	...	...
2 Purchases of intangible assets, n.e.c., net, from the rest of the world	-	-	-	-	-	-	-	-	-	-	-	-
Net lending to the rest of the world	-2300	25052	19471	30614	18746	29113	39651	8054	-1665	5167	-10824	106
Total Gross Accumulation	-2300	25052	19471	30614	18746	29113	39651	8054	-1665	5167	-10824	106

4.1 Derivation of Value Added by Kind of Activity, in Current Prices

Thousand Maltese pounds

	1980			1981			1982			1983		
	Gross Output	Intermediate Consumption	Value Added	Gross Output	Intermediate Consumption	Value Added	Gross Output	Intermediate Consumption	Value Added	Gross Output	Intermediate Consumption	Value Added
All Producers												
1 Agriculture, hunting, forestry and fishing	...	...	13289	...	...	15038	...	...	16767	...	...	18731
2 Mining and quarrying [a]	...	...	15655	...	...	17073	...	...	23546	...	...	23511
3 Manufacturing	...	...	115358	...	...	121384	...	...	125024	...	...	120036
A Manufacture of food, beverages and tobacco	...	...	15543	...	...	18413	...	...	20814	...	...	19903
B Textile, wearing apparel and leather industries	...	...	36559	...	...	36531	...	...	36189	...	...	33665
C Manufacture of wood and wood products, including furniture	...	...	5306	...	...	5622	...	...	6223	...	...	5466
D Manufacture of paper and paper products, printing and publishing	...	...	8266	...	...	7790	...	...	6829	...	...	6979
E Manufacture of chemicals and chemical petroleum, coal, rubber and plastic products	...	...	7423	...	...	6879	...	...	6325	...	...	7005
F Manufacture of non-metallic mineral products, except products of petroleum and coal	...	...	2786	...	...	2957	...	...	3448	...	...	3965
G Basic metal industries	...	...	4319	...	...	-	...	...	-	...	...	-
H Manufacture of fabricated metal products, machinery and equipment	...	...	25558	...	...	34823	...	...	35710	...	...	32537
I Other manufacturing industries	...	...	9598	...	...	8369	...	...	9486	...	...	10616
4 Electricity, gas and water [b]	...	...	15635	...	...	23586	...	...	21958	...	...	21119
5 Construction [a]	...	...	...	...	...	...	...	...	...	...	...	...
6 Wholesale and retail trade, restaurants and hotels [c]	...	...	51001	...	...	57421	...	...	63184	...	...	64010
7 Transport, storage and communication	...	...	22230	...	...	22596	...	...	20396	...	...	24050
8 Finance, insurance, real estate and business services [d]	...	...	37269	...	...	46610	...	...	50303	...	...	51475
9 Community, social and personal services [cd]	...	...	33731	...	...	36404	...	...	38415	...	...	36850
Total, Industries	...	...	304168	...	...	339021	...	...	359593	...	...	359782
Producers of Government Services	...	...	44444	...	...	51513	...	...	58152	...	...	57348
Other Producers	...	...		...	...		...	...		...	...	
Total [e]	...	...	348612	...	...	390534	...	...	417745	...	...	417130
Less: Imputed bank service charge	...	...	...	...	...	...	...	...	...	...	...	...
Import duties	...	...	...	...	...	...	...	...	...	...	...	...
Value added tax	...	...	...	...	...	...	...	...	...	...	...	...
Other adjustments [f]	...	...	43352	...	...	45917	...	...	44041	...	...	40426
Total	...	...	391964	...	...	436451	...	...	461786	...	...	457556

Malta

4.1 Derivation of Value Added by Kind of Activity, in Current Prices

Thousand Maltese pounds

	1984 Gross Output	1984 Intermediate Consumption	1984 Value Added	1985 Gross Output	1985 Intermediate Consumption	1985 Value Added	1986 Gross Output	1986 Intermediate Consumption	1986 Value Added
				All Producers					
1 Agriculture, hunting, forestry and fishing	...	...	19346	...	...	19375	...	...	20419
2 Mining and quarrying [a]	...	...	19660	...	...	20758	...	...	18869
3 Manufacturing	...	...	124706	...	...	126929	...	...	134676
A Manufacture of food, beverages and tobacco	...	...	20431	...	...	22813	...	...	...
B Textile, wearing apparel and leather industries	...	...	35052	...	...	35091	...	...	...
C Manufacture of wood and wood products, including furniture	...	...	5065	...	...	4220	...	...	...
D Manufacture of paper and paper products, printing and publishing	...	...	8661	...	...	8383	...	...	...
E Manufacture of chemicals and chemical petroleum, coal, rubber and plastic products	...	...	7962	...	...	8352	...	...	...
F Manufacture of non-metallic mineral products, except products of petroleum and coal	...	...	4891	...	...	3626	...	...	...
G Basic metal industries	...	...	-	...	...	-	...	...	...
H Manufacture of fabricated metal products, machinery and equipment	...	...	31607	...	...	33431	...	...	...
I Other manufacturing industries	...	...	11037	...	...	11013	...	...	...
4 Electricity, gas and water [b]	...	...	24985	...	...	22278	...	...	34704
5 Construction [a]	...	...	...	...	...	...	...	...	...
6 Wholesale and retail trade, restaurants and hotels [c]	...	...	66077	...	...	66696	...	...	67647
7 Transport, storage and communication	...	...	23391	...	...	23955	...	...	26240
8 Finance, insurance, real estate and business services [d]	...	...	53517	...	...	57131	...	...	61255
9 Community, social and personal services [cd]	...	...	33605	...	...	34894	...	...	35639
Total, Industries	...	...	365287	...	...	372016	...	...	399449
Producers of Government Services	...	...	56090	...	...	58534	...	...	62317
Other Producers	...	...		...	...		...	...	
Total [e]	...	...	421377	...	...	430550	...	...	461766
Less: Imputed bank service charge	...	...	...	...	...	...	...	...	...
Import duties	...	...	...	...	...	...	...	...	...
Value added tax	...	...	...	...	...	...	...	...	...
Other adjustments [f]	...	...	39675	...	...	45432	...	...	50103
Total	...	...	461052	...	...	475982	...	...	511869

a) Item 'Construction' is included in item 'Mining and quarrying'.
b) Item 'Electricity, gas and water' refers mainly to government enterprises.
c) Restaurants and hotels are included in item 'Community, social and personal services'.
d) Business services are included in item 'Community, social and personal services'.
e) Gross domestic product in factor values.
f) Item 'Other adjustments' refers to indirect taxes net of subsidies.

4.3 Cost Components of Value Added

Thousand Maltese pounds

	1980 Compensation of Employees	1980 Capital Consumption	1980 Net Operating Surplus	1980 Indirect Taxes	1980 Less: Subsidies Received	1980 Value Added	1981 Compensation of Employees	1981 Capital Consumption	1981 Net Operating Surplus	1981 Indirect Taxes	1981 Less: Subsidies Received	1981 Value Added
						All Producers						
1 Agriculture, hunting, forestry and fishing	1366	...	11923	...	...	13289	1699	...	13339	...	...	15038
2 Mining and quarrying [a]	12337	...	3318	...	...	15655	12936	...	4137	...	...	17073
3 Manufacturing	67560	...	47798	...	...	115358	73420	...	47964	...	...	121384
4 Electricity, gas and water [b]	10213	...	5422	...	...	15635	12259	...	11327	...	...	23586
5 Construction [a]	...	...	...	...	...	...	...	...	...	...	...	...
6 Wholesale and retail trade, restaurants and hotels [c]	8253	...	42748	...	...	51001	10282	...	47139	...	...	57421
7 Transport, storage and communication	9757	...	12473	...	...	22230	11215	...	11381	...	...	22596
8 Finance, insurance, real estate and business services [d]	5137	...	32132	...	...	37269	5839	...	39680	...	...	45519
9 Community, social and personal services [cd]	21486	...	12245	...	...	33731	24642	...	11762	...	...	36404

Malta

4.3 Cost Components of Value Added
(Continued)

Thousand Maltese pounds

	1980						1981					
	Compensation of Employees	Capital Consumption	Net Operating Surplus	Indirect Taxes	Less: Subsidies Received	Value Added	Compensation of Employees	Capital Consumption	Net Operating Surplus	Indirect Taxes	Less: Subsidies Received	Value Added
Total, Industries	136109	...	168059	...	...	304168	152292	...	186729	...	...	339021
Producers of Government Services	44444	...	...	...	...	44444	51513	...	...	...	...	51513
Other Producers		...	...	...	...			...	...	...	...	
Total [ef]	180553	...	168059	...	...	348612	203805	...	186729	...	...	390534
Less: Imputed bank service charge	...	...	...	...	...	...	...	...	...	...	...	...
Import duties	...	...	...	...	...	...	...	...	...	...	...	...
Value added tax	...	...	...	...	...	...	...	...	...	...	...	...
Other adjustments [g]	...	...	...	45744	2392	43352	...	...	...	47897	1980	45917
Total	180553	...	168059	45744	2392	391964	203805	...	186729	47897	1980	436451

	1982						1983					
	Compensation of Employees	Capital Consumption	Net Operating Surplus	Indirect Taxes	Less: Subsidies Received	Value Added	Compensation of Employees	Capital Consumption	Net Operating Surplus	Indirect Taxes	Less: Subsidies Received	Value Added
	All Producers											
1 Agriculture, hunting, forestry and fishing	2072	...	14695	...	...	16767	1975	...	16756	...	...	18731
2 Mining and quarrying [a]	16804	...	6742	...	...	23546	16923	...	6588	...	...	23511
3 Manufacturing	78328	...	46696	...	...	125024	75103	...	44933	...	...	120036
4 Electricity, gas and water [b]	13396	...	8562	...	...	21958	12498	...	8621	...	...	21119
5 Construction [a]	...	...	...	...	...	...	...	...	...	...	...	...
6 Wholesale and retail trade, restaurants and hotels [c]	11668	...	51516	...	...	63184	11931	...	52079	...	...	64010
7 Transport, storage and communication	11674	...	8722	...	...	20396	11945	...	12105	...	...	24050
8 Finance, insurance, real estate and business services [d]	7942	...	42361	...	...	50303	7933	...	43542	...	...	51475
9 Community, social and personal services [cd]	28589	...	9826	...	...	38415	27928	...	8922	...	...	36850
Total, Industries	170473	...	189120	...	...	359593	166236	...	193546	...	...	359782
Producers of Government Services	58152	...	...	...	...	58152	57348	...	...	...	...	57348
Other Producers		...	...	...	...			...	...	...	...	
Total [ef]	228625	...	189120	...	...	417745	223584	...	193546	...	...	417130
Less: Imputed bank service charge	...	...	...	...	...	...	...	...	...	...	...	...
Import duties	...	...	...	...	...	...	...	...	...	...	...	...
Value added tax	...	...	...	...	...	...	...	...	...	...	...	...
Other adjustments [g]	...	...	...	46852	2811	44041	...	...	...	43794	3368	40426
Total	228625	...	189120	46852	2811	461786	223584	...	193546	43794	3368	457556

	1984						1985					
	Compensation of Employees	Capital Consumption	Net Operating Surplus	Indirect Taxes	Less: Subsidies Received	Value Added	Compensation of Employees	Capital Consumption	Net Operating Surplus	Indirect Taxes	Less: Subsidies Received	Value Added
	All Producers											
1 Agriculture, hunting, forestry and fishing	1830	...	17516	...	...	19346	1783	...	17592	...	...	19375
2 Mining and quarrying [a]	14224	...	5436	...	...	19660	14495	...	6263	...	...	20758
3 Manufacturing	75470	...	49236	...	...	124706	76029	...	50900	...	...	126929
4 Electricity, gas and water [b]	12763	...	12222	...	...	24985	13609	...	8669	...	...	22278
5 Construction [a]	...	...	...	...	...	...	...	...	...	...	...	...
6 Wholesale and retail trade, restaurants and hotels [c]	12294	...	53783	...	...	66077	12452	...	54244	...	...	66696
7 Transport, storage and communication	12491	...	10900	...	...	23391	12901	...	11054	...	...	23955
8 Finance, insurance, real estate and business services [d]	7988	...	45529	...	...	53517	8264	...	40077	...	...	57131
9 Community, social and personal services [cd]	24778	...	8827	...	...	33605	24885	...	10009	...	...	34894
Total, Industries	161838	...	203449	...	...	365287	164408	...	207608	...	...	372016
Producers of Government Services	56090	...	...	...	...	56090	58534	...	...	...	...	58534
Other Producers		...	...	...	...			...	...	...	...	
Total [ef]	217928	...	203449	...	...	421377	222942	...	207608	...	...	430550
Less: Imputed bank service charge	...	...	...	...	...	...	...	...	...	...	...	...
Import duties	...	...	...	...	...	...	...	...	...	...	...	...
Value added tax	...	...	...	...	...	...	...	...	...	...	...	...
Other adjustments [g]	...	...	...	43706	4031	39675	...	...	...	49452	4020	45432
Total	217928	...	203449	43706	4031	461052	222942	...	207608	49452	4020	475982

Malta

Thousand Maltese pounds

4.3 Cost Components of Value Added

	Compensation of Employees	Capital Consumption	Net Operating Surplus	Indirect Taxes	Less: Subsidies Received	Value Added
			1986			
			All Producers			
1 Agriculture, hunting, forestry and fishing	1774	...	18645	...	...	20419
2 Mining and quarrying a	13676	...	5193	...	...	18869
3 Manufacturing	80856	...	53820	...	...	134676
4 Electricity, gas and water b	13636	...	21068	...	...	34704
5 Construction a	...	...	...	...	...	...
6 Wholesale and retail trade, restaurants and hotels c	12834	...	54813	...	...	67647
7 Transport, storage and communication	12569	...	13671	...	...	26240
8 Finance, insurance, real estate and business services d	8983	...	52272	...	...	61255
9 Community, social and personal services cd	24972	...	10667	...	...	35639
Total, Industries	169300	...	230149	...	...	399449
Producers of Government Services	62317	...		...	...	62317
Other Producers		...	...	...	...	
Total ef	231617	...	230149	...	...	461766
Less: Imputed bank service charge	...	...	...	...	...	...
Import duties	...	...	...	...	...	...
Value added tax	...	...	...	...	...	...
Other adjustments g	...	...	...	54885	4782	50103
Total	231617	...	230149	54885	4782	511869

a) Item 'Construction' is included in item 'Mining and quarrying'.
b) Item 'Electricity, gas and water' refers mainly to government enterprises.
c) Restaurants and hotels are included in item 'Community, social and personal services'.
d) Business services are included in item 'Community, social and personal services'.
e) Gross domestic product in factor values.
f) Column 'Consumption of fixed capital' is included in column 'Net operating surplus'.
g) Item 'Other adjustments' refers to indirect taxes net of subsidies.

Martinique

Source. Reply to the United Nations National Accounts Questionnaire from the Institute national de la statistique et des studes economiques (INSEE), Paris.
General note. The estimates shown in the following tables have been adjusted by the INSEE to conform to the United Nations System of National Accounts so far as the existing data would permit.

1.1 Expenditure on the Gross Domestic Product, in Current Prices

Million French francs

	1970	1975	1977	1978	1979	1980	1981	1982	1983	1984	1985	1986
1 Government final consumption expenditure	489.6	1140.5	1481.8	1668.9	1919.6	2236.5	2567.9	3065.8	3534.9	3896.1	4212.8	...
2 Private final consumption expenditure	1395.3	2714.5	3637.1	4211.1	4892.0	5499.4	6549.5	8013.4	9038.9	9840.7	10948.8	...
3 Gross capital formation	366.5	567.7	720.2	795.3	1027.6	1461.5	1460.3	1698.6	2001.6	1978.1	2085.1	...
A Increase in stocks	-10.2	-44.4	44.6	38.5	15.8	187.4	92.3	13.6	-28.3	-61.6	-52.7	
B Gross fixed capital formation	376.7	612.1	675.6	756.8	1011.8	1274.1	1368.0	1685.0	2029.9	2039.7	2137.8	
4 Exports of goods and services	166.8	407.7	630.3	564.1	567.4	528.6	894.6	992.8	1261.8	1355.7	1458.9	...
5 Less: Imports of goods and services	817.7	1472.9	2072.9	2268.9	2868.6	3624.4	4227.3	4896.4	5722.9	6050.9	6128.7	...
Equals: Gross Domestic Product	1600.5	3357.5	4396.5	4970.7	5538.0	6101.6	7245.0	8874.2	10114.3	11019.7	12576.9	...

1.3 Cost Components of the Gross Domestic Product

Million French francs

	1970	1975	1977	1978	1979	1980	1981	1982	1983	1984	1985	1986
1 Indirect taxes, net	186.9	339.1	461.8	499.5	555.3	687.7	790.5	958.6	...	...	...	...
A Indirect taxes	208.4	372.7	501.6	565.9	631.8	775.3	939.2	1123.4	...	...	...	...
B Less: Subsidies	21.5	33.6	39.8	66.4	76.5	87.6	148.7	164.8	...	...	...	...
2 Consumption of fixed capital [a]	...	...	...	...	...	...	...	...	...	...	...	...
3 Compensation of employees paid by resident producers to:	1037.4	2194.1	2939.1	3334.7	3809.8	4432.1	5092.0	6159.5	...	...	...	...
4 Operating surplus [a]	376.2	824.3	995.0	1130.5	1172.9	981.8	1362.5	1756.1	...	...	...	...
Equals: Gross Domestic Product	1600.5	3357.5	4396.5	4970.7	5538.0	6101.6	7245.0	8874.2	10114.3	11019.7	12576.9	...

a) Item 'Operating surplus' includes consumption of fixed capital.

1.7 External Transactions on Current Account, Summary

Million French francs

	1970	1975	1977	1978	1979	1980	1981	1982	1983	1984	1985	1986
				Payments to the Rest of the World								
1 Imports of goods and services	817.7	1472.9	2072.9	2268.8	2868.6	3624.4	4227.3	4896.4				
2 Factor income to the rest of the world	31.2	88.8	106.6	158.4	182.9	213.4	275.3	322.3	...	...	...	...
A Compensation of employees	-	-	-	-	-	-	-	-				
B Property and entrepreneurial income	31.2	88.8	106.6	158.4	182.9	213.4	275.3	322.3				
3 Current transfers to the rest of the world	16.1	17.9	20.3	49.2	58.2	80.9	104.8	117.9				
4 Surplus of the nation on current transactions	-123.8	70.8	31.2	-54.3	-336.1	-639.3	-513.2	-590.6				
Payments to the Rest of the World and Surplus of the Nation on Current Transactions	741.2	1650.4	2231.0	2422.1	2773.6	3279.4	4094.2	4746.0	...	...	...	...
				Receipts From The Rest of the World								
1 Exports of goods and services	166.8	407.7	630.3	564.1	567.3	528.6	894.6	992.8				
2 Factor income from rest of the world	8.9	18.4	34.5	60.0	74.9	114.2	174.7	201.0				
A Compensation of employees	-	-	-	-	-	-	-	-				
B Property and entrepreneurial income	8.9	18.4	34.5	60.0	74.9	114.2	174.7	201.0				
3 Current transfers from rest of the world	565.5	1224.3	1566.2	1798.0	2131.4	2636.6	3024.0	3552.2				
Receipts from the Rest of the World on Current Transactions	741.2	1650.4	2231.0	2422.1	2773.6	3279.4	4094.2	4746.0	...	...	...	...

1.10 Gross Domestic Product by Kind of Activity, in Current Prices

Million French francs

	1970	1975	1977	1978	1979	1980	1981	1982	1983	1984	1985	1986
1 Agriculture, hunting, forestry and fishing	...	344.1	433.7	506.7	424.5	372.9	531.2	691.1	...	...	...	...
2 Mining and quarrying	...	207.1	230.8	267.1	306.1	303.5	419.7	527.9	...	...	...	...
3 Manufacturing	...								...	...	...	...
4 Electricity, gas and water	...	80.9	105.5	83.5	106.9	97.9	87.8	89.6				
5 Construction	...	170.6	154.0	170.1	167.5	225.8	258.5	310.4				

Martinique

1.10 Gross Domestic Product by Kind of Activity, in Current Prices
(Continued)

Million French francs

	1970	1975	1977	1978	1979	1980	1981	1982	1983	1984	1985	1986
6. Wholesale and retail trade, restaurants and hotels	...	599.3	815.7	841.2	990.8	1037.3	1196.3	1478.2	...	...	...	...
7. Transport, storage and communication	...	105.0	116.9	147.7	199.6	220.3	269.2	372.5	...	...	...	...
8. Finance, insurance, real estate and business services	...	282.1	365.2	491.5	556.0	427.8	627.6	762.6	...	...	...	...
9. Community, social and personal services	...	398.0	630.3	703.1	812.6	1118.4	1288.9	1512.9	...	...	...	...
Total, Industries	...	2187.1	2852.1	3210.9	3564.0	3803.9	4679.2	5745.2	...	...	...	...
Producers of Government Services	...	991.5	1299.2	1500.0	1682.7	1985.6	2254.4	2712.8	...	...	...	...
Other Producers	...	51.4	79.2	95.3	104.6	115.4	137.4	162.0	...	...	...	...
Subtotal	1505.2	3230.0	4230.5	4806.2	5351.3	5904.9	7071.0	8620.0	...	...	...	...
Less: Imputed bank service charge	45.0	116.0	152.2	196.4	231.7	308.6	418.0	479.8	...	...	...	...
Plus: Import duties	77.0	113.3	155.4	174.3	205.6	247.5	284.2	344.5	...	...	...	...
Plus: Value added tax	63.3	130.2	162.8	186.6	212.9	257.8	307.8	389.5	...	...	...	...
Equals: Gross Domestic Product	1600.5	3357.5	4396.5	4970.7	5538.1	6101.6	7245.0	8874.2	10114.3	11019.7	12576.9	...

1.12 Relations Among National Accounting Aggregates

Million French francs

	1970	1975	1977	1978	1979	1980	1981	1982	1983	1984	1985	1986
Gross Domestic Product	1600.5	3357.5	4396.5	4970.7	5538.0	6101.6	7245.0	8874.2	10114.3	11019.7	12576.9	...
Plus: Net factor income from the rest of the world	-22.3	-70.4	-72.1	-98.4	-108.0	-99.2	-100.6	-121.3	...	...	...	...
Factor income from the rest of the world	8.9	18.4	34.5	60.0	74.9	114.2	174.7	201.0	...	...	...	...
Less: Factor income to the rest of the world	31.2	88.8	106.6	158.4	182.9	213.4	275.3	322.3	...	...	...	...
Equals: Gross National Product	1578.2	3287.1	4324.4	4872.3	5430.0	6002.4	7144.4	8752.9	...	...	...	...
Less: Consumption of fixed capital	...	...	...	...	...	...	...	...	...	...	...	...
Equals: National Income	...	...	...	...	...	...	...	...	...	...	...	...
Plus: Net current transfers from the rest of the world	549.4	1206.4	1545.9	1748.8	2073.2	2555.7	2920.1	3434.4	...	...	...	...
Current transfers from the rest of the world	565.5	1224.3	1566.2	1798.0	2131.4	2636.6	3024.9	3552.3	...	...	...	...
Less: Current transfers to the rest of the world	16.1	17.9	20.3	49.2	58.2	80.9	104.8	117.9	...	...	...	...
Equals: National Disposable Income	...	...	...	...	...	...	...	...	...	...	...	...
Less: Final consumption	1884.9	3855.0	5118.9	5880.1	6811.7	7773.6	9117.4	11079.2	...	...	...	...
Equals: Net Saving	...	...	...	...	...	...	...	...	...	...	...	...
Less: Surplus of the nation on current transactions	-123.8	70.8	31.2	-54.3	-336.1	-639.3	-513.3	-590.5	...	...	...	...
Equals: Net Capital Formation	...	...	...	...	...	...	...	...	...	...	...	...

Mauritania

Source. Reply to the United Nations National Accounts Questionnaire from the Direction de la Statistique et des Etudes Economiques, Ministere de la Planification et du Developpement Industriel, Nouakchott. The official estimates are published annually in 'Comptes Economiques'.

General note. The estimates shown in the following tables have been prepared in accordance with the United Nations System of National Accounts so far as the existing data would permit.

1.1 Expenditure on the Gross Domestic Product, in Current Prices

Million Mauritanian ouguiyas

	1970	1975	1977	1978	1979	1980	1981	1982	1983	1984	1985	1986
1 Government final consumption expenditure	1853	5060	8784	9370	9523	9183	9224	9885	10127	10189	...	...
2 Private final consumption expenditure	5998	11652	14213	17407	22126	28504	32381	30733	32214	33180	...	...
3 Gross capital formation	2559	9144	10924	6713	8078	10200	15925	18708	19682	16280	...	...
A Increase in stocks	220	2128	1131	2673	2172	2400	6353	8108	8317	1580	...	...
B Gross fixed capital formation	2339	7016	9793	4040	5906	7800	9572	10600	11365	14700	...	...
4 Exports of goods and services	4760	7986	8150	7421	8821	11566	12128	15434	18820	18821	...	...
5 Less: Imports of goods and services	3840	13247	17073	16003	17648	21383	26419	32091	34922	33970	...	...
Equals: Gross Domestic Product [a]	11330	20595	24988	24908	30853	38070	43239	42669	45921	44500	...	...

a) Data in this table have been revised, therefore they are not strictly comparable with the unrevised data in the other tables.

1.7 External Transactions on Current Account, Summary

Million Mauritanian ouguiyas

	1970	1975	1977	1978	1979	1980	1981	1982	1983	1984	1985	1986
Payments to the Rest of the World												
1 Imports of goods and services	...	13247	17073	16003	17648	21383	26419	32091	32549	32644	...	...
A Imports of merchandise c.i.f.	...	8987	12760	12048	13117	14751	18653	22083	20732	19276	...	...
B Other	...	4260	4313	3955	4531	6632	7766	10008	11817	13368	...	...
2 Factor income to the rest of the world	...	262	711	922	1049	1023	2076	1874	2373	1325	...	...
A Compensation of employees	...	7	10	12	15	18	16	15	17	10	...	...
B Property and entrepreneurial income	...	255	701	910	1034	1005	2060	1859	2356	1315	...	...
3 Current transfers to the rest of the world	...	1344	1344	1523	1987	2202	1509	2155	1938	1904	...	...
4 Surplus of the nation on current transactions	...	-2781	-4785	-3295	-4485	-6171	-10747	-14348	-11690	-7534	...	...
Payments to the Rest of the World and Surplus of the Nation on Current Transactions	...	12072	14343	15153	16199	18437	19257	21772	25170	28339	...	...
Receipts From The Rest of the World												
1 Exports of goods and services	...	7986	8150	7421	8821	11566	12128	15434	20241	20567	...	...
A Exports of merchandise f.o.b.	...	7212	7172	5474	6754	9013	9411	12426	17286	18745	...	...
B Other	...	774	978	1947	2067	2553	2717	3008	2955	1822	...	...
2 Factor income from rest of the world	...	232	219	180	558	815	1018	1008	550	595	...	...
A Compensation of employees	...	17	24	35	40	46	46	50	50	55	...	...
B Property and entrepreneurial income	...	215	195	145	518	769	972	958	500	540	...	...
3 Current transfers from rest of the world	...	3854	5974	7552	6820	6056	6111	5330	4929	7177	...	...
Receipts from the Rest of the World on Current Transactions	...	12072	14343	15153	16199	18437	19257	21772	25170	28339	...	...

1.10 Gross Domestic Product by Kind of Activity, in Current Prices

Million Mauritanian ouguiyas

	1970	1975	1977	1978	1979	1980	1981	1982	1983	1984	1985	1986
1 Agriculture, hunting, forestry and fishing	3114	5137	5605	6131	8769	12262	15223	13028	11982	8564	...	...
2 Mining and quarrying	2810	4028	3708	2476	3079	4505	4831	5342	4369	4426	...	...
3 Manufacturing	525	918	1280	1444	1615	1997	2337	2408	3685	3808	...	...
4 Electricity, gas and water											...	...
5 Construction	700	1114	1700	1179	1929	2314	2726	2888	3175	3505	...	...
6 Wholesale and retail trade, restaurants and hotels	660	2239	2424	2533	2968	3424	3100	3834	4708	5688	...	...
7 Transport, storage and communication	605	966	1742	1940	2371	2584	2710	3007	3179	3188	...	...
8 Finance, insurance, real estate and business services	927	1416	1856	2078	2350	2632	2500	2500	2585	2685	...	...
9 Community, social and personal services											...	...

Mauritania

1.10 Gross Domestic Product by Kind of Activity, in Current Prices
(Continued)

Million Mauritanian ouguiyas

	1970	1975	1977	1978	1979	1980	1981	1982	1983	1984	1985	1986
Total, Industries	9341	15818	18315	17781	23081	29718	33427	33007	33683	31864	...	...
Producers of Government Services	1297	3059	4646	5165	5616	5943	6938	6166	7720	7800	...	...
Other Producers	...	...	...	...	...	...	...	...	...	...	...	...
Subtotal [a]	10638	18877	22961	22946	28697	35661	40365	39173	41403	39664	...	...
Less: Imputed bank service charge	...	...	...	...	...	...	...	...	...	...	...	...
Plus: Import duties	...	...	...	...	...	...	...	...	...	...	...	...
Plus: Value added tax	...	...	...	...	...	...	...	...	...	...	...	...
Plus: Other adjustments [b]	692	1718	2037	1962	2156	2409	2874	3496	4518	4836	...	...
Equals: Gross Domestic Product [c]	11330	20595	24998	24908	30853	38070	43239	42669	45921	44500	...	...

a) Gross domestic product in factor values.
b) Item 'Other adjustments' refers to indirect taxes net of subsidies.
c) Data in this table have been revised, therefore they are not strictly comparable with the unrevised data in the other tables.

1.11 Gross Domestic Product by Kind of Activity, in Constant Prices

Million Mauritanian ouguiyas

	1970	1975	1977	1978	1979	1980	1981	1982	1983	1984	1985	1986
	At constant prices of:1973											
1 Agriculture, hunting, forestry and fishing	4653	3743	3270	3287	3528	3317	4464	3884	3398	2743	...	...
2 Mining and quarrying	2930	2471	2377	1548	1866	2189	2336	2115	2127	2129	...	...
3 Manufacturing	720	712	862	902	1011	997	1297	1216	1412	1403	...	...
4 Electricity, gas and water											...	...
5 Construction	917	779	971	674	1037	1157	1250	1162	1280	1300	...	...
6 Wholesale and retail trade, restaurants and hotels	824	1722	1534	1490	1604	1712	1670	1706	1803	1812	...	...
7 Transport, storage and communication	755	732	995	965	1270	1119	1320	1310	1325	1358	...	...
8 Finance, insurance, real estate and business services	1157	1089	1175	1222	1270	1316	...	...	...	...	...	...
9 Community, social and personal services												
Total, Industries	11956	11248	11184	10088	10715	11807	...	...	...	...	...	...
Producers of Government Services	961	2683	3630	3689	3694	3552	3304	2680	3027	3037	...	...
Other Producers	...	...	...	...	...	...	...	...	...	...	...	...
Subtotal [a]	12917	13931	14814	13777	15280	15359	15641	14070	14372	13782	...	...
Less: Imputed bank service charge	...	...	...	...	...	...	...	...	...	...	...	...
Plus: Import duties	...	...	...	...	...	...	...	...	...	...	...	...
Plus: Value added tax	...	...	...	...	...	...	...	...	...	...	...	...
Plus: Other adjustments [b]	...	1507	1591	1401	1418	1456	1844	2076	2179	2110	...	...
Equals: Gross Domestic Product [c]	12917	15438	16405	15178	16698	16815	17485	16149	16551	15892	...	...

a) Gross domestic product in factor values.
b) Item 'Other adjustments' refers to indirect taxes net of subsidies.
c) Data in this table have been revised, therefore they are not strictly comparable with the unrevised data in the other tables.

1.12 Relations Among National Accounting Aggregates

Million Mauritanian ouguiyas

	1970	1975	1977	1978	1979	1980	1981	1982	1983	1984	1985	1986
Gross Domestic Product	11330	20595	24998	24908	30853	38070	43239	42669	45921	44500	...	...
Plus: Net factor income from the rest of the world	...	-30	-492	-742	-491	-208	-1058	-866	-1823	-730	...	...
Factor income from the rest of the world	...	232	219	180	25	815	1018	1008	550	595	...	...
Less: Factor income to the rest of the world	...	262	711	922	541	1023	2076	1874	2373	1325	...	...
Equals: Gross National Product	...	20565	24506	24166	30362	37862	42181	41803	44098	43770	...	...
Less: Consumption of fixed capital	...	...	...	...	...	...	...	...	...	...	...	...
Equals: National Income [a]	...	20565	24506	24166	30362	37862	42181	41803	44098	43770	...	...
Plus: Net current transfers from the rest of the world	...	2510	4630	6029	4833	3854	4602	3175	2991	5273	...	...
Current transfers from the rest of the world	...	...	...	...	...	6056	6111	5330	4929	7177	...	...
Less: Current transfers to the rest of the world	...	...	...	...	...	2202	1509	2155	1938	1904	...	...
Equals: National Disposable Income [b]	...	23075	29136	30195	35195	41716	46783	44978	47089	49043	...	...
Less: Final consumption	...	...	...	...	...	...	...	...	...	...	...	...
Equals: Net Saving	...	...	...	...	...	...	...	...	...	...	...	...
Less: Surplus of the nation on current transactions	...	...	...	...	...	...	...	...	...	...	...	...
Equals: Net Capital Formation	...	...	...	...	...	...	...	...	...	...	...	...

a) Item 'National income' includes consumption of fixed capital.
b) Item 'National disposable income' includes consumption of fixed capital.

Mauritania

2.1 Government Final Consumption Expenditure by Function, in Current Prices

Million Mauritanian ouguiyas

	1970	1975	1977	1978	1979	1980	1981	1982	1983	1984	1985	1986
1 General public services	...	1285.7	1723.9	...	...	...	...	...	...	...	...	...
2 Defence	...	439.9	1497.0	...	...	...	...	...	...	...	...	...
3 Public order and safety	...	...	...	...	...	...	...	...	...	...	...	...
4 Education	...	598.0	1161.9	...	...	...	...	...	...	...	...	...
5 Health	...	191.7	254.0	...	...	...	...	...	...	...	...	...
6 Social security and welfare	...	29.1	51.0	...	...	...	...	...	...	...	...	...
7 Housing and community amenities	...	-	-	...	...	...	...	...	...	...	...	...
8 Recreational, cultural and religious affairs	...	145.5	101.5	...	...	...	...	...	...	...	...	...
9 Economic services	...	320.7	346.5	...	...	...	...	...	...	...	...	...
10 Other functions	...	2187.4	3541.2	...	...	...	...	...	...	...	...	...
Total Government Final Consumption Expenditure	...	5198.0	8677.0	...	...	...	...	...	...	...	...	...

2.17 Exports and Imports of Goods and Services, Detail

Million Mauritanian ouguiyas

	1970	1975	1977	1978	1979	1980	1981	1982	1983	1984	1985	1986
Exports of Goods and Services												
1 Exports of merchandise, f.o.b.	...	7212	7172	5474	6754	9013	9411	12426	17286	18745	...	...
2 Transport and communication	...	207	437	578	736	725	1001	1046	566	559	...	...
A In respect of merchandise imports	...	66	27	2	6	1	-	-	-	-	...	...
B Other	...	141	410	576	730	724	1001	1046	566	559	...	...
3 Insurance service charges	...	...	...	...	...	...	...	...	...	...	...	...
4 Other commodities	...	136	47	247	48	99	435	693	922	593	...	...
5 Adjustments of merchandise exports to change-of-ownership basis	...	-	-	-	-	...	...	...	...	...	...	...
6 Direct purchases in the domestic market by non-residential households	...	207	281	845	1039	1420	960	840	519	670	...	...
7 Direct purchases in the domestic market by extraterritorial bodies	...	244	213	277	244	309	321	429	382	439	...	...
Total Exports of Goods and Services	4760	7986	8150	7421	8821	11566	12128	15434	20241	20567	...	...
Imports of Goods and Services												
1 Imports of merchandise, c.i.f.	...	8987	12760	12048	13117	14751	18653	22083	20732	19276	...	...
A Imports of merchandise, f.o.b.	...	8987	12760	12048	13117	14751	18653	22083	20732	19276	...	...
B Transport of services on merchandise imports	...	...	...	...	...	...	...	...	...	...	...	...
C Insurance service charges on merchandise imports	...	...	...	...	...	...	...	...	...	...	...	...
2 Adjustments of merchandise imports to change-of-ownership basis	...	...	...	...	...	...	...	...	...	...	...	...
3 Other transport and communication	...	1861	1762	1728	2184	3862	4693	4937	6137	6421	...	...
4 Other insurance service charges	...					...	...	...	...	...	...	...
5 Other commodities	...	1827	1739	1247	1395	1584	2145	3617	4366	5194	...	...
6 Direct purchases abroad by government	...	185	340	504	445	587	245	497	354	791	...	...
7 Direct purchases abroad by resident households	...	396	472	476	507	599	683	957	960	962	...	...
Total Imports of Goods and Services	3840	13247	17073	16003	17648	21383	26419	32091	32549	32644	...	...
Balance of Goods and Services	920	-5261	-8923	-8582	-8827	...	...	...	...	...	...	...
Total Imports and Balance of Goods and Services	4760	7986	8150	7421	8821	...	...	...	...	...	...	...

Mauritius

General note. The preparation of national accounts statistics in Mauritius is undertaken by the Central statistical Office, Rose Hill. The official estimates are published periodically in 'National Accounts of Mauritius'. The following presentation on sources and methods is mainly based on information received from the central Statistical Office. The estimates are generally in accordance with the Clasifications and definitions recommended in the United Nations System of National Accounts (SNA). The following tables have been prepared from successive replies to the United Nations national accounts questionnaire. When the scope and coverage of the estimates differ for conceptual or statistical reasons from the definitions and classifications recommended in SNA, a footnote is indicated to the relevant tables.

Sources and methods:

(a) Gross domestic product. Gross domestic product is estimated mainly through the production approach.

(b) Expenditure on the gross domestic product. The expenditure approach is used to estimate government final consumption expenditure and exports and imports of goods and services. This approach, in combination with the commodity-flow approach is used to estimate gross fixed capital formation. The commodity-flow approach is used for private final consumption expenditure supplemented by the expenditure approach for expenditure on services. Government consumption expenditure is estimated on the basis of the annual financial reports of the government and the municipal and town councils. The sources of data for private expenditure on goods include the 1972 census of population, the annual trade reports of the Customs Department, the annual financial reports of the government and special surveys of wholesale and retail margins, costs and profits. Figures of imported goods are extracted and reclassified from the foreign trade statistics and added to the figures for local production, both valued at market prices. Expenditure on services and private expenditure abroad are estimated on the basis of data from financial reports of the government, the censuses, records of income Tax Office and annual reports of the Ministry of Education. Information of investment on new buildings is obtained from records of building permits issued, records of the municipal and town councils and from returns of industrial and building companies. Investment on plantations is estimated from the returns of agricultural concerns and reports of the Chamber of Agriculture and the Tobacco Board. For machinery and equipment, figures on imports are derived from the annual trade reports and returns from industrial firms. Charges for transport, trade margins and installation costs are added to the c.i.f. values. Domestic production figures are obtained from the annual returns of manufacturing firms. Estimates of exports and imports of goods and services are based on sources such as the annual trade reports of the Customs Department, monthly returns from banks, records of Post Office and balance-of-payments. GDP by expenditure type at constant prices has not been estimated since 1966.

(c) Cost-structure of the gross domestic product. Information on compensation of employees for large establishments of all sectors, except the sugar industry is available from questionnaires sent out in connexion with the census of production and income tax returns. For the sugar sector, detailed figures of payments in cash and in kind are supplied by all sugar estates with factories while figures from employment records, statutory wage rates and the quantity of canes produced are used for the remaining sugar industry. Wages and salaries for the public sector are obtained from a bi-annual survey of all government departments and ministries. Operating surplus is estimated through the use of questionnaires and income-tax statistics for the private sector and production accounts for the government sector. For consumption of fixed capital, all sugar estates with factories provide data on a replacement cost basis while for other capital goods, the estimates are based on expected lifetime. Data on indirect taxes and subsidies are obtained from government and municipal council records.

(d) Gross domestic product by kind of economic activity. The table of GDP by kind of economic activity is prepared in factor values. The production approach is used to estimate value added of most industries. The income approach is used for some private services and for public administration and defence. For the agricultural sector, estimates are made on an item-by-item basis using annual statistical returns, annual surveys and reports supplemented by direct inquiries among producers and distributors. Sources used for sugar production are reports of the Chamber of Agriculture and financial statements of the Mauritius Sugar Syndicate. The estimates for mining and quarrying refer only to salt production and sand quarries and are provided directly by the concerned enterprises. The estimates for manufacturing are obtained through similar methods as those used for the agricultural sector. For sugar and related products, data are obtained from returns furnished by the factories and distilleries, reports and statistics of the Chamber of Agriculture and financial statements of the Mauritius Sugar Syndicate. The estimates of electricity and water are based on information provided by the concerned enterprises and the financial reports of the government. Information on private construction is obtained from records of building permits issued and from the municipal and town councils. Information furnished by the building contractors and financial reports of the government are used for public construction. For trade, information is obtained from the Income Tax Office and from imports and local production statistics. Special questionnaires on receipts and expenditure are sent to large hotel and restaurant enterprises as well as to large transport enterprises. Informatiom on public transport is available from the Accountant-General's records. For the financial sector, the most important sources are the Central Bank, income-tax returns of commercial banks and annual reports of the Registrar of insurance Companies. Special questionnaires are also sent to insurance companies. The estimates for ownership of dwellings are based on the 1972 census of population and records of building permits issued. For public administration and defence, detailed information is available from treasury records. For the private services, information is obtained from the population census and special questionnaires sent to large enterprises. For the constant price estimates, current values are generally deflated by appropriate price indexes. In cases where production is homogeneous, e.g. Sugar production value added is extrapolated by volume indexes.

1.1 Expenditure on the Gross Domestic Product, in Current Prices

Million Mauritius rupees

	1970	1975	1977	1978	1979	1980	1981	1982	1983	1984	1985	1986
1 Government final consumption expenditure	166	443	798	933	1009	1224	1422	1624	1706	1835	1915	2075
2 Private final consumption expenditure	734	1878	3593	4174	5144	6562	7269	8301	8874	9841	11118	11845
3 Gross capital formation	145	1138	1630	1923	2385	1803	2578	2130	2229	3165	3900	3915
A Increase in stocks	...	...	120	153	420	-225	338	30	-71	570	800	-
B Gross fixed capital formation	145	1138	1510	1770	1965	2028	2240	2100	2300	2595	3100	3915
Residential buildings	33	264	476	588	718	685	730	735	700	740	730	775
Non-residential buildings	23	201	281	264	235	223	248	245	277	350	635	660
Other construction and land improvement etc.	40	180	161	319	345	327	402	480	527	495	425	645
Other	49	493	592	599	667	793	860	640	796	1010	1310	1835
4 Exports of goods and services	22	2184	2656	2705	3260	4450	4566	5529	5953	6989	8895	11907
5 Less: Imports of goods and services		2227	3235	3477	4158	5342	5626	5859	5999	7470	9210	10498
Equals: Gross Domestic Product	1067	3416	5442	6258	7640	8697	10209	11725	12763	14360	16618	19240

Mauritius

1.2 Expenditure on the Gross Domestic Product, in Constant Prices

Million Mauritius rupees

	1970	1975	1977	1978	1979	1980	1981	1982	1983	1984	1985	1986
					At constant prices of: 1976				1982			
1 Government final consumption expenditure	...	...	668	695	682	688	713	727 / 1624	1665	1727	1727	1762
2 Private final consumption expenditure	...	...	3121	3210	3240	3059	2965	3071 / 8301	8463	8844	9295	9760
3 Gross capital formation	...	...	1480	1608	1685	988	1213	908 / 2130	2097	2520	2964	3954
A Increase in stocks	...	...	110	138	308	-132	173	14 / 30	-70	220	434	903
B Gross fixed capital formation	...	...	1370	1470	1377	1120	1040	894 / 2100	2167	2300	2530	3051
Residential buildings	...	...	445	500	517	418	382	348 / 735	667	662	631	651
Non-residential buildings	...	...	262	220	165	130	120	107 / 245	263	311	540	542
Other construction and land improvement etc.	...	...	146	265	238	185	180	204 / 480	502	445	364	531
Other	...	...	517	485	457	387	349	235 / 640	735	882	995	1327
4 Exports of goods and services	...	...	2710	2701	2790	2843	2701	2971 / 5529	5580	5810	6504	8494
5 Less: Imports of goods and services	...	...	2967	3010	3010	2733	2462	2265 / 5859	6035	6578	7305	9676
Equals: Gross Domestic Product	...	...	5012	5204	5387	4845	5130	5412 / 11725	11770	12323	13185	14294

1.3 Cost Components of the Gross Domestic Product

Million Mauritius rupees

	1970	1975	1977	1978	1979	1980	1981	1982	1983	1984	1985	1986
1 Indirect taxes, net	155	326	666	764	1100	1308	1444	1705	2150	2310	2738	3185
A Indirect taxes	155	359	734	825	1136	1326	1455	1717	2180	2355	2784	3285
B Less: Subsidies	-	33	68	61	36	18	11	12	30	45	46	100
2 Consumption of fixed capital [a]	...	...	...	...	...	...	...	...	...	...	...	...
3 Compensation of employees paid by resident producers to:	516	1568	2705	3046	3470	3953	4482	4972	5400	5915	6570	7700
4 Operating surplus [a]	396	1522	2071	2448	3070	3436	4283	5048	5213	6135	7310	8355
Equals: Gross Domestic Product	1067	3416	5442	6258	7640	8697	10209	11725	12763	14360	16618	19240

a) Item 'Operating surplus' includes consumption of fixed capital.

1.4 General Government Current Receipts and Disbursements

Million Mauritius rupees

	1970	1975	1977	1978	1979	1980	1981	1982	1983	1984	1985	1986
					Receipts							
1 Operating surplus	...	...	...	...	...	...	23	43	62	67	92	98
2 Property and entrepreneurial income	10	40	56	80	106	125	129	176	180	135	303	328
3 Taxes, fees and contributions	205	957	1086	1205	1615	1845	2193	2492	3042	3263	3754	4402
A Indirect taxes	155	359	734	826	1136	1326	1455	1717	2180	2355	2784	3285
B Direct taxes	50	598	329	354	367	379	464	457	509	529	545	650
C Social security contributions	...	...	9	9	90	115	248	287	322	344	387	423
D Compulsory fees, fines and penalties	...	...	14	16	22	25	26	31	31	35	38	44
4 Other current transfers	8	62	...	...	1	3	14	72	29	51	216	218
Total Current Receipts of General Government	226	1065	1142	1285	1722	1973	2359	2783	3313	3516	4365	5046

Mauritius

1.4 General Government Current Receipts and Disbursements
(Continued)

Million Mauritius rupees

	1970	1975	1977	1978	1979	1980	1981	1982	1983	1984	1985	1986
					Disbursements							
1 Government final consumption expenditure	166	443	798	933	1009	1224	1422	1624	1706	1835	1915	2075
A Compensation of employees	...	...	674	774	872	1043	1242	1421	1471	1522	1598	1725
B Consumption of fixed capital	...	...	...	...	...	...	...	...	...	...	...	...
C Purchases of goods and services, net	...	...	124	159	137	180	180	203	235	313	317	350
D Less: Own account fixed capital formation	...	...	...	...	...	...	...	...	...	...	...	...
E Indirect taxes paid, net	...	...	...	...	...	...	...	...	...	...	...	...
2 Property income	...	...	92	133	253	332	410	866	759	848	929	963
3 Subsidies	1	33	68	61	36	18	11	12	30	45	46	100
4 Other current transfers	37	345	293	388	481	478	659	825	860	774	880	854
A Social security benefits [a]	...	...	...	...	...	...	...	328	389	449	503	563	598
B Social assistance grants	...	...	...	...	...	...	...					
C Other	...	...	...	...	...	...	...	331	436	411	272	317	256
Statistical discrepancy	...	75	...	...	...	...	...	...	...	...	...	...
5 Net saving	22	169	-109	-230	-57	-79	-143	-544	-42	14	595	1054
Total Current Disbursements and Net Saving of General Government	226	1065	1142	1285	1722	1973	2359	2783	3313	3516	4365	5046

a) Item 'Social security benefits' includes unfounded employee welfare benefits.

1.5 Current Income and Outlay of Corporate and Quasi-Corporate Enterprises, Summary

Million Mauritius rupees

	1970	1975	1977	1978	1979	1980	1981	1982	1983	1984	1985	1986
					Receipts							
1 Operating surplus	...	...	...	...	...	...	...	2067	1925	2522	3125	...
2 Property and entrepreneurial income received	...	...	...	...	...	...	...	666	699	740	1156	...
3 Current transfers	...	...	...	...	...	...	...	346	396	472	454	...
Total Current Receipts	...	...	...	...	...	...	...	3079	3020	3734	4735	...
					Disbursements							
1 Property and entrepreneurial income	...	...	...	...	...	...	...	777	923	1049	1604	...
2 Direct taxes and other current payments to general government	...	...	...	...	...	...	...	181	204	188	233	...
3 Other current transfers	...	...	...	...	...	...	...	302	363	462	389	...
4 Net saving	...	...	...	...	...	...	...	1819	1530	2035	2509	...
Total Current Disbursements and Net Saving	...	...	...	...	...	...	...	3079	3020	3734	4735	...

1.6 Current Income and Outlay of Households and Non-Profit Institutions

Million Mauritius rupees

	1970	1975	1977	1978	1979	1980	1981	1982	1983	1984	1985	1986
					Receipts							
1 Compensation of employees	516	1568	...	...	...	...	...	4972	5400	5915	6570	...
2 Operating surplus of private unincorporated enterprises	...	...	...	...	...	...	...	2939	3227	3546	4093	...
3 Property and entrepreneurial income	256	832	...	...	...	...	...	419	473	576	629	...
4 Current transfers	46	271	...	...	...	...	...	1052	1156	1162	1315	...
A Social security benefits [a]	...	...	...	...	...	...	...	389	449	503	563	...
B Social assistance grants	...	...	...	...	...	...	...					
C Other	...	...	...	...	...	...	...	663	707	659	752	...
Statistical discrepancy	...	-9	...	...	...	...	...	...	...	...	...	...
Total Current Receipts	818	2662	...	...	...	...	...	9382	10256	11199	12607	...

Mauritius

1.6 Current Income and Outlay of Households and Non-Profit Institutions
(Continued)

Million Mauritius rupees

		1970	1975	1977	1978	1979	1980	1981	1982	1983	1984	1985	1986
						Disbursements							
1	Private final consumption expenditure	734	1832	...	...	...	...	...	8301	8874	9891	11118	...
2	Property income	...	...	...	...	...	...	...	110	161	180	255	...
3	Direct taxes and other current transfers n.e.c. to general government	30	135	...	...	...	...	...	595	658	720	737	...
	A Social security contributions	...	...	...	...	...	...	...	287	322	344	387	...
	B Direct taxes	...	...	...	...	...	...	...	283	311	348	320	...
	C Fees, fines and penalties	...	...	...	...	...	...	...	25	25	28	30	...
4	Other current transfers	6	8	...	...	...	...	...	122	147	146	176	...
5	Net saving	48	687	...	...	...	...	...	254	416	262	321	...
	Total Current Disbursements and Net Saving	818	2662	...	...	...	...	...	9382	10256	11199	12607	...

a) Item 'Social security benefits' includes unfounded employee welfare benefits.

1.7 External Transactions on Current Account, Summary

Million Mauritius rupees

		1970	1975	1977	1978	1979	1980	1981	1982	1983	1984	1985	1986
						Payments to the Rest of the World							
1	Imports of goods and services	515	2227	3235	3477	4158	5342	5626	5859	5999	7470	9210	10498
	A Imports of merchandise c.i.f.	414	1965	2885	3051	3602	4661	4922	5008	5164	6528	8083	9183
	B Other	101	262	350	426	550	681	704	851	835	942	1127	1315
2	Factor income to the rest of the world	12	45	51	83	130	216	470	541	514	666	730	805
	A Compensation of employees	-	-	-	-	-	-	-	-	-	-	-	-
	B Property and entrepreneurial income	12	45	51	83	130	216	470	541	514	666	730	805
3	Current transfers to the rest of the world	10	23	24	30	47	60	64	53	80	75	76	85
4	Surplus of the nation on current transactions	42	127	-512	-735	-927	-911	-1321	-457	-237	-716	-459	1348
	Payments to the Rest of the World and Surplus of the Nation on Current Transactions	579	2422	2798	2855	3408	4707	4839	5996	6356	7495	9557	12736
						Receipts From The Rest of the World							
1	Exports of goods and services	531	2268	2656	2705	3259	4450	4566	5529	5953	6989	8895	11907
	A Exports of merchandise f.o.b.	388	1848	2030	1969	2427	3332	2999	3985	4346	5201	6639	9045
	B Other	143	420	626	736	832	1118	1567	1544	1607	1788	2256	2862
2	Factor income from rest of the world	17	61	34	35	24	38	62	43	29	40	30	76
	A Compensation of employees	-	1	-	-	-	-	-	-	-	-	-	-
	B Property and entrepreneurial income	17	60	34	35	24	38	62	43	29	40	30	76
3	Current transfers from rest of the world	31	93	108	115	125	219	211	424	374	466	632	753
	Receipts from the Rest of the World on Current Transactions	579	2422	2798	2855	3408	4707	4839	5996	6356	7495	9557	12736

1.10 Gross Domestic Product by Kind of Activity, in Current Prices

Million Mauritius rupees

		1970	1975	1977	1978	1979	1980	1981	1982	1983	1984	1985	1986
1	Agriculture, hunting, forestry and fishing	222	1034	939	977	1224	914	1257	1530	1465	1736	2123	2395
2	Mining and quarrying	1	4	9	11	12	15	16	17	18	19	20	22
3	Manufacturing	146	564	699	801	972	1127	1377	1560	1678	2183	2864	3730
4	Electricity, gas and water	29	69	99	118	161	209	188	260	245	296	397	462
5	Construction	48	217	406	506	552	561	588	625	655	690	775	895

Mauritius

1.10 Gross Domestic Product by Kind of Activity, in Current Prices
(Continued)

Million Mauritius rupees

	1970	1975	1977	1978	1979	1980	1981	1982	1983	1984	1985	1986
6 Wholesale and retail trade, restaurants and hotels	91	279	575	630	779	1050	1219	1290	1455	1640	1834	2210
7 Transport, storage and communication	108	281	447	563	653	837	997	1112	1230	1372	1510	1700
8 Finance, insurance, real estate and business services	90	160	826	981	1139	1416	1635	1883	2044	2232	2446	2575
9 Community, social and personal services	126	342	211	251	303	361	442	525	569	593	624	672
Total, Industries	861	2950	4211	4838	5795	6490	7719	8802	9359	10761	12593	14661
Producers of Government Services	51	140	615	705	793	952	1104	1275	1327	1379	1447	1565
Other Producers	...	...	30	39	46	54	60	71	81	92	96	104
Subtotal [a]	912	3090	4856	5582	6634	7496	8883	10148	10767	12232	14136	16330
Less: Imputed bank service charge	...	...	80	88	94	107	118	128	154	182	256	275
Plus: Import duties	...	...	...	...	...	...	...	...	...	...	...	...
Plus: Value added tax	...	...	...	...	...	...	...	...	...	...	...	...
Plus: Other adjustments [b]	155	326	666	764	1100	1308	1444	1705	2150	2310	2738	3185
Equals: Gross Domestic Product	1067	3416	5442	6258	7640	8697	10209	11725	12763	14360	16618	19240

a) Gross domestic product in factor values.
b) Item 'Other adjustments' refers to indirect taxes net of subsidies.

1.11 Gross Domestic Product by Kind of Activity, in Constant Prices

Million Mauritius rupees

	1970	1975	1977	1978	1979	1980	1981	1982	1983	1984	1985	1986
			At constant prices of: 1976					1982				
1 Agriculture, hunting, forestry and fishing	...	...	938	939	977	643	784	936 / 1530	1331	1341	1492	1613
2 Mining and quarrying	...	...	7	7	7	7	7	7 / 17	17	17	17	18
3 Manufacturing	...	...	666	717	754	701	762	802 / 1560	1576	1768	2038	2380
4 Electricity, gas and water	...	...	81	89	97	97	97	117 / 250	243	267	315	343
5 Construction	...	...	381	400	370	307	292	280 / 625	633	646	698	780
6 Wholesale and retail trade, restaurants and hotels	...	...	533	538	582	558	568	542 / 1290	1373	1455	1527	1665
7 Transport, storage and communication	...	...	410	431	437	423	434	454 / 1112	1151	1209	1260	1348
8 Finance, insurance, real estate and business services	...	...	702	734	763	761	794	831 / 1765	1812	1872	1935	1990
9 Community, social and personal services	...	...	215	231	252	252	265	286 / 596	627	646	652	675
Total, Industries	...	...	3933	4086	4239	3749	4003	4255 / 8745	8763	9221	9934	10812
Producers of Government Services	...	...	522	547	563	569	591	604 / 1275	1300	1320	1330	1343
Other Producers	...	...	...	...	...	...	...	...	...	...	...	...
Subtotal [a]	...	...	4455	4633	4802	4318	4594	4859 / 10020	10063	10541	11264	12155
Less: Imputed bank service charge	...	...	...	...	...	...	...	...	...	...	...	...
Plus: Import duties	...	...	...	...	...	...	...	...	...	...	...	...
Plus: Value added tax	...	...	...	...	...	...	...	...	...	...	...	...
Plus: Other adjustments [b]	...	...	557	571	585	527	536	553 / 1705	1707	1782	1921	2139
Equals: Gross Domestic Product	...	...	5012	5204	5387	4845	5130	5412 / 11725	11770	12323	13185	14294

a) Gross domestic product in factor values.
b) Item 'Other adjustments' refers to indirect taxes net of subsidies.

Mauritius

1.12 Relations Among National Accounting Aggregates

Million Mauritius rupees

	1970	1975	1977	1978	1979	1980	1981	1982	1983	1984	1985	1986
Gross Domestic Product	1067	3416	5442	6258	7640	8697	10209	11725	12763	14360	16618	19240
Plus: Net factor income from the rest of the world	7	17	-17	-48	-106	-178	-408	-498	-485	-626	-700	-729
Factor income from the rest of the world	...	...	34	35	24	38	62	43	29	40	30	76
Less: Factor income to the rest of the world	...	...	51	83	130	216	470	541	514	666	730	805
Equals: Gross National Product	1074	3433	5425	6210	7534	8519	9801	11227	12278	13734	15918	18511
Less: Consumption of fixed capital	...	...	...	...	...	...	...	...	...	...	...	...
Equals: National Income [a]	1074	3433	5425	6210	7534	8519	9801	11227	12278	13734	15918	18511
Plus: Net current transfers from the rest of the world	11	35	84	85	78	159	147	371	294	391	556	668
Current transfers from the rest of the world	...	...	108	115	125	219	211	424	374	466	632	753
Less: Current transfers to the rest of the world	...	...	24	30	47	60	64	53	80	75	76	85
Equals: National Disposable Income [b]	1085	3467	5509	6295	7612	8678	9948	11598	12572	14125	16474	19179
Less: Final consumption	900	2321	4391	5107	6153	7786	8691	9925	10580	11676	13033	13920
Equals: Net Saving [c]	185	1146	1118	1188	1459	892	1257	1673	1992	2449	3441	5259
Less: Surplus of the nation on current transactions	...	...	...	...	...	...	...	...	...	...	...	...
Equals: Net Capital Formation	...	...	...	...	...	...	...	...	...	...	...	...

a) Item 'National income' includes consumption of fixed capital.
b) Item 'National disposable income' includes consumption of fixed capital.
c) Item 'Net saving' includes consumption of fixed capital.

2.1 Government Final Consumption Expenditure by Function, in Current Prices

Million Mauritius rupees

		1970	1975	1977	1978	1979	1980	1981	1982	1983	1984	1985	1986
1	General public services	...	...	128	152	142	147	173	208	215	254	298	329
2	Defence	...	...	-	-	-	22	27	34	34	42	38	42
3	Public order and safety	...	...	98	112	154	157	171	193	208	221	247	269
4	Education	...	...	181	211	232	299	349	384	435	419	440	480
5	Health	...	...	151	170	184	228	256	283	296	328	336	364
6	Social security and welfare	...	...	18	22	22	27	29	30	37	48	56	63
7	Housing and community amenities	...	...	65	77	80	84	90	105	116	105	72	81
8	Recreational, cultural and religious affairs	...	...	14	19	19	23	26	36	32	34	35	39
9	Economic services	...	...	143	170	176	237	301	351	333	384	393	408
	A Fuel and energy	...	...	1	4	1	1	1	1	1	1	1	1
	B Agriculture, forestry, fishing and hunting	...	...	49	52	53	82	88	135	123	145	169	180
	C Mining, manufacturing and construction, except fuel and energy	...	...	65	75	85	108	160	172	167	172	164	172
	D Transportation and communication	...	...	3	3	4	3	4	5	7	8	8	9
	E Other economic affairs	...	...	25	36	33	43	48	38	35	58	51	46
10	Other functions	...	...	-	-	-	-	-	-	-	-	-	-
	Total Government Final Consumption Expenditure	...	...	798	933	1009	1224	1422	1624	1706	1835	1915	2075

Mauritius

2.3 Total Government Outlays by Function and Type

Million Mauritius rupees

	Final Consumption Expenditures Total	Compensation of Employees	Other	Subsidies	Other Current Transfers & Property Income	Total Current Disbursements	Gross Capital Formation	Other Capital Outlays	Total Outlays
1982									
1 General public services	208	141	67	4	9	221	...	...	...
2 Defence	34	28	6	-	-	34	...	...	...
3 Public order and safety	193	181	12	-	-	193	...	...	...
4 Education	384	368	16	-	130	514	...	...	...
5 Health	283	231	52	-	2	285	...	...	...
6 Social security and welfare	30	32	-2	-	392	422	...	...	...
7 Housing and community amenities	105	93	13	-	2	107	...	...	...
8 Recreation, culture and religion	36	30	6	3	5	44	...	...	...
9 Economic services	351	318	33	5	285	641	...	...	...
A Fuel and energy	1	1	-	-	-	1	...	...	...
B Agriculture, forestry, fishing and hunting	135	132	3	-	2	137	...	...	...
C Mining (except fuels), manufacturing and construction	172	149	23	5	-	177	...	...	...
D Transportation and communication	5	5	-	-	-	5	...	...	...
E Other economic affairs	38	31	7	-	283	321	...	...	...
10 Other functions	-	-	-	-	866	866	...	...	...
Total	1624	1421	203	12	1691	3327	...	...	...
1983									
1 General public services	215	148	67	-	9	224	...	...	...
2 Defence	34	30	4	-	-	34	...	...	...
3 Public order and safety	208	187	21	-	-	208	...	...	...
4 Education	435	387	48	-	125	560	...	...	...
5 Health	296	238	58	-	1	297	...	...	...
6 Social security and welfare	37	37	-	-	452	489	...	...	...
7 Housing and community amenities	116	106	10	-	1	117	...	...	...
8 Recreation, culture and religion	32	25	7	3	6	41	...	...	...
9 Economic services	333	313	20	27	266	627	...	...	...
A Fuel and energy	1	1	-	-	1	2	...	...	...
B Agriculture, forestry, fishing and hunting	123	128	-5	15	7	146	...	...	...
C Mining (except fuels), manufacturing and construction	167	145	22	8	-	175	...	...	...
D Transportation and communication	7	7	-	4	-	11	...	...	...
E Other economic affairs	35	32	3	-	258	293	...	...	...
10 Other functions	-	-	-	-	759	759	...	...	...
Total	1706	1471	235	30	1619	3355	...	...	...
1984									
1 General public services	254	162	92	-	18	272	...	...	...
2 Defence	42	31	11	-	-	42	...	...	...
3 Public order and safety	221	196	25	-	-	221	...	...	...
4 Education	419	393	26	-	144	563	...	...	...
5 Health	328	242	86	-	2	330	...	...	...
6 Social security and welfare	48	40	8	-	507	555	...	...	...
7 Housing and community amenities	105	96	9	-	9	114	...	...	...
8 Recreation, culture and religion	34	27	7	3	7	44	...	...	...
9 Economic services	384	335	49	42	87	513	...	...	...
A Fuel and energy	1	1	-	-	1	2	...	...	...
B Agriculture, forestry, fishing and hunting	145	148	-3	26	8	179	...	...	...
C Mining (except fuels), manufacturing and construction	172	146	26	11	-	183	...	...	...
D Transportation and communication	8	7	1	5	1	14	...	...	...
E Other economic affairs	58	33	25	-	77	135	...	...	...
10 Other functions	-	-	-	-	848	848	...	...	...
Total	1835	1522	313	45	1622	3502	...	...	...

Mauritius

2.3 Total Government Outlays by Function and Type
(Continued)

Million Mauritius rupees

	Final Consumption Expenditures Total	Compensation of Employees	Other	Subsidies	Other Current Transfers & Property Income	Total Current Disbursements	Gross Capital Formation	Other Capital Outlays	Total Outlays
1985									
1 General public services	298	195	103	-	10	308	...	...	...
2 Defence	38	31	7	-	-	38	...	...	...
3 Public order and safety	247	214	33	-	-	247	...	...	...
4 Education	440	414	26	-	147	587	...	...	...
5 Health	336	248	88	-	4	340	...	...	...
6 Social security and welfare	56	48	8	-	563	619	...	...	...
7 Housing and community amenities	72	70	2	9	1	82	...	...	...
8 Recreation, culture and religion	35	26	9	2	7	44	...	...	...
9 Economic services	393	352	41	35	148	576	...	...	...
A Fuel and energy	1	1	-	-	1	2	...	...	...
B Agriculture, forestry, fishing and hunting	169	161	8	24	4	197	...	...	...
C Mining (except fuels), manufacturing and construction	164	149	15	5	-	169	...	...	...
D Transportation and communication	8	7	1	6	5	19	...	...	...
E Other economic affairs	51	34	17	-	138	189	...	...	...
10 Other functions	-	-	-	-	929	929	...	...	...
Total	1915	1598	317	46	1809	3770	...	...	...
1986									
1 General public services	329	207	122	-	17	346	...	...	...
2 Defence	42	32	10	-	-	42	...	...	...
3 Public order and safety	269	233	36	-	-	269	...	...	...
4 Education	480	449	31	-	149	629	...	...	...
5 Health	364	272	92	-	3	367	...	...	...
6 Social security and welfare	63	51	12	-	603	666	...	...	...
7 Housing and community amenities	81	77	4	10	-	91	...	...	...
8 Recreation, culture and religion	39	27	12	2	7	48	...	...	...
9 Economic services	408	377	31	87	75	570	...	...	...
A Fuel and energy	1	1	-	-	2	3	...	...	...
B Agriculture, forestry, fishing and hunting	180	176	4	77	1	257	...	...	...
C Mining (except fuels), manufacturing and construction	172	159	13	5	-	177	...	...	...
D Transportation and communication	9	8	1	6	1	16	...	...	...
E Other economic affairs	46	33	13	-	71	117	...	...	...
10 Other functions	-			-	903	903	...	...	...
Total	2075	1725	350	100	1817	3992	...	...	...

2.7 Gross Capital Formation by Type of Good and Owner, in Current Prices

Million Mauritius rupees

	1980 TOTAL	Total Private	Public Enterprises	General Government	1981 TOTAL	Total Private	Public Enterprises	General Government	1982 TOTAL	Total Private	Public Enterprises	General Government
Increase in stocks, total	-225	...	...	...	338	...	...	...	30	...	...	...
Gross Fixed Capital Formation, Total	2020	1298	...	730	2240	1375	...	865	2100	1345	...	755
1 Residential buildings	685	573	...	112	730	637	...	93	735	655	...	80
2 Non-residential buildings	223	120	...	103	248	143	...	105	245	164	...	81
3 Other construction	327	27	...	300	402	31	...	371	480	46	...	434

Mauritius

2.7 Gross Capital Formation by Type of Good and Owner, in Current Prices
(Continued)

Million Mauritius rupees

	1980				1981				1982			
	TOTAL	Total Private	Public Enterprises	General Government	TOTAL	Total Private	Public Enterprises	General Government	TOTAL	Total Private	Public Enterprises	General Government
4 Land improvement and plantation and orchard development	...	...	...	...	...	...	...	...	...	...	...	...
5 Producers' durable goods	793	578	...	215	860	564	...	296	640	480	...	160
A Transport equipment	246	208	...	38	242	136	...	106	120	86	...	34
Passenger cars	46	43	...	3	52	37	...	15	45	41	...	4
Other	200	165	...	35	190	99	...	91	75	45	...	30
B Machinery and equipment	547	370	...	177	618	428	...	190	520	394	...	126
6 Breeding stock, dairy cattle, etc.	...	...	...	...	...	...	...	...	...	...	...	...
Total Gross Capital Formation	1803	...	...	...	2578	...	...	...	2130	...	...	...

	1983				1984				1985			
	TOTAL	Total Private	Public Enterprises	General Government	TOTAL	Total Private	Public Enterprises	General Government	TOTAL	Total Private	Public Enterprises	General Government
Increase in stocks, total	-73	...	...	...	570	...	...	...	800	...	...	...
Gross Fixed Capital Formation, Total	2300	1485	...	815	2595	1770	...	825	3100	2100	...	1000
1 Residential buildings	700	634	...	66	740	685	...	55	730	678	...	52
2 Non-residential buildings	277	207	...	70	350	260	...	90	635	375	...	260
3 Other construction	527	50	...	477	495	74	...	421	425	60	...	365
4 Land improvement and plantation and orchard development	...	...	...	...	...	...	...	...	...	...	...	...
5 Producers' durable goods	796	594	...	202	1010	751	...	259	1310	987	...	323
A Transport equipment	151	89	...	62	201	159	...	42	270	197	...	73
Passenger cars	40	35	...	5	56	47	...	9	85	75	...	10
Other	111	54	...	57	145	112	...	33	185	122	...	63
B Machinery and equipment	645	505	...	140	809	592	...	217	1040	790	...	250
6 Breeding stock, dairy cattle, etc.	...	...	...	...	...	...	...	...	...	...	...	...
Total Gross Capital Formation	2229	...	...	...	3165	...	...	...	3900	...	...	...

	1986			
	TOTAL	Total Private	Public Enterprises	General Government
Increase in stocks, total	-	...	...	...
Gross Fixed Capital Formation, Total	3915	...	...	...
1 Residential buildings	775	...	...	...
2 Non-residential buildings	660	...	...	...
3 Other construction	645	...	...	...
4 Land improvement and plantation and orchard development	...	...	...	...
5 Producers' durable goods	1835	...	...	...
A Transport equipment	485	...	...	...
Passenger cars	155	...	...	...
Other	330	...	...	...
B Machinery and equipment	1350	...	...	...
6 Breeding stock, dairy cattle, etc.	...	...	...	...
Total Gross Capital Formation	3915	...	...	...

2.11 Gross Fixed Capital Formation by Kind of Activity of Owner, ISIC Divisions, in Current Prices

Million Mauritius rupees

	1970	1975	1977	1978	1979	1980	1981	1982	1983	1984	1985	1986
All Producers												
1 Agriculture, hunting, forestry and fishing	23	120	116	119	135	102	127	135	102	123	130	130
2 Mining and quarrying	-	-	-	-	-	-	-	-	-	-	-	-
3 Manufacturing	16	292	271	268	296	279	302	315	337	503	740	1070
4 Electricity, gas and water	12	71	83	144	100	170	243	350	467	316	285	230

Mauritius

2.11 Gross Fixed Capital Formation by Kind of Activity of Owner, ISIC Divisions, in Current Prices
(Continued)

Million Mauritius rupees

	1970	1975	1977	1978	1979	1980	1981	1982	1983	1984	1985	1986
5 Construction	5	22	38	45	48	62	74	45	36	29	80	135
6 Wholesale and retail trade, restaurants and hotels	5	37	70	80	85	101	111	90	131	184	330	300
7 Transport, storage and communication	32	184	254	308	405	380	374	235	330	453	435	955
8 Finance, insurance, real estate and business services	36	265	497	611	748	760	773	780	744	788	815	875
9 Community, social and personal services	16	103	38	28	33	40	50	70	63	95	135	75
Total Industries	145	1094	1367	1603	1850	1894	2054	2020	2210	2491	2950	3770
Producers of Government Services	-	44	143	167	115	134	186	80	90	104	150	145
Private Non-Profit Institutions Serving Households	...	...	...	...	...	...	...	...	...	...	...	...
Total	145	1138	1510	1770	1965	2028	2240	2100	2300	2595	3100	3915

2.12 Gross Fixed Capital Formation by Kind of Activity of Owner, ISIC Divisions, in Constant Prices

Million Mauritius rupees

	1970	1975	1977	1978	1979	1980	1981	1982	1983	1984	1985	1986
		1970	At constant prices of: 1976							1982		

All Producers

	1970	1975	1977	1978	1979	1980	1981	1982	1983	1984	1985	1986
1 Agriculture, hunting, forestry and fishing	23	56	105	100	95	58	60	53 / 135	107	122	120	115
2 Mining and quarrying	-	-	... / -					-	-	-	-	-
3 Manufacturing	16	119	240	220	205	141	127	117 / 315	314	442	580	805
4 Electricity, gas and water	12	29	73	116	68	88	104	136 / 350	438	280	231	180
5 Construction	5	10	33	36	33	30	30	18 / 45	33	25	60	97
6 Wholesale and retail trade, restaurants and hotels	5	14	64	66	59	56	50	40 / 90	123	162	269	236
7 Transport, storage and communication	32	72	225	248	274	192	158	92 / 235	300	388	341	721
8 Finance, insurance, real estate and business services	36	87	464	519	538	458	401	367 / 780	708	704	697	725
9 Community, social and personal services	...	...	35	24	24	22	26	34 / 70	60	86	110	59
Total Industries	129	387	1239	1329	1296	1045	956	857 / 2020	2083	2209	2408	2938
Producers of Government Services	16	...	101	141	81	75	84	37 / 80	84	91	122	113
Private Non-Profit Institutions Serving Households	...	58	...	...	...	...	...	... / ...	...	...	...	...
Total	145	445	1370	1470	1377	1120	1040	894 / 2100	2167	2300	2530	3051

Mauritius

2.17 Exports and Imports of Goods and Services, Detail

Million Mauritius rupees

	1970	1975	1977	1978	1979	1980	1981	1982	1983	1984	1985	1986
Exports of Goods and Services												
1 Exports of merchandise, f.o.b.	388	1848	2030	1969	2427	3332	2999	3985	4346	5201	6639	9045
2 Transport and communication	68	168	265	291	333	449	507	669	712	777	985	1143
A In respect of merchandise imports	14	14	1	5	...	20	35	33	34	26	30	38
B Other	54	154	264	286	333	429	472	636	678	751	955	1105
3 Insurance service charges	2	5	15	11	11	17	214	11	12	14	10	13
A In respect of merchandise imports	-	-	-	-	-	-	-	-	-	-	-	-
B Other	2	5	15	11	11	17	214	11	12	14	10	13
4 Other commodities	29	77	105	149	186	267	344	334	327	302	342	466
5 Adjustments of merchandise exports to change-of-ownership basis	-	-	-	-	-	-	-	-	-	-	-	-
6 Direct purchases in the domestic market by non-residential households	27	135	210	230	260	325	433	450	503	631	845	1190
7 Direct purchases in the domestic market by extraterritorial bodies	17	35	31	55	42	60	69	80	53	64	74	50
Total Exports of Goods and Services [a]	531	2268	2656	2705	3259	4450	4566	5529	5953	6989	8895	11907
Imports of Goods and Services												
1 Imports of merchandise, c.i.f.	414	1965	2885	3051	3602	4661	4922	5008	5164	6528	8083	9183
A Imports of merchandise, f.o.b.	360	1679	2430	2580	3055	3965	4260	4313	4516	5727	7056	8197
B Transport of services on merchandise imports	54	286	455	471	547	696	662	695	648	801	1027	986
C Insurance service charges on merchandise imports	...	...	...	...	...	...	...	...	...	...	...	...
2 Adjustments of merchandise imports to change-of-ownership basis	...	...	...	...	...	...	...	...	...	...	...	...
3 Other transport and communication	59	85	127	161	216	296	305	342	302	349	468	460
4 Other insurance service charges	4	38	26	43	53	68	57	98	83	95	128	129
5 Other commodities	11	36	75	87	92	95	119	143	173	183	198	306
6 Direct purchases abroad by government	27	103	122	135	195	222	223	268	277	315	333	420
7 Direct purchases abroad by resident households												
Total Imports of Goods and Services [a]	515	2227	3235	3477	4158	5342	5626	5859	5999	7470	9210	10498
Balance of Goods and Services	16	41	-579	-772	-899	-892	-1060	-330	-46	-481	-315	1409
Total Imports and Balance of Goods and Services [a]	531	2268	2656	2705	3259	4450	4566	5529	5953	6989	8895	11907

a) Data in this table have been revised, therefore they are not strictly comparable with the unrevised data in the other tables.

4.1 Derivation of Value Added by Kind of Activity, in Current Prices

Million Mauritius rupees

	1980			1981			1982			1983		
	Gross Output	Intermediate Consumption	Value Added	Gross Output	Intermediate Consumption	Value Added	Gross Output	Intermediate Consumption	Value Added	Gross Output	Intermediate Consumption	Value Added
All Producers												
1 Agriculture, hunting, forestry and fishing	1523	609	914	1984	727	1257	2345	815	1530	2316	861	1455
2 Mining and quarrying	34	19	15	35	19	16	38	21	17	40	22	18
3 Manufacturing	5008	3397	1611	6198	4210	1988	7038	4789	2249	7498	5104	2394
4 Electricity, gas and water	381	172	209	456	268	188	502	242	260	558	313	245
5 Construction	1558	997	561	1653	1065	588	1700	1075	625	1780	1124	656
6 Wholesale and retail trade, restaurants and hotels	1839	737	1102	2076	802	1274	2254	902	1352	2431	928	1503
7 Transport, storage and communication	1514	666	848	1760	748	1012	1962	839	1123	2201	960	1241
8 Finance, insurance, real estate and business services	1734	299	1436	1982	325	1657	2296	383	1913	2470	397	2073
9 Community, social and personal services	633	222	411	729	229	500	829	229	600	892	231	661

Mauritius

4.1 Derivation of Value Added by Kind of Activity, in Current Prices
(Continued)

Million Mauritius rupees

	1980 Gross Output	1980 Intermediate Consumption	1980 Value Added	1981 Gross Output	1981 Intermediate Consumption	1981 Value Added	1982 Gross Output	1982 Intermediate Consumption	1982 Value Added	1983 Gross Output	1983 Intermediate Consumption	1983 Value Added
Total, Industries	14225	7118	7107	16873	8393	8480	18964	9295	9669	20186	9940	10246
Producers of Government Services	1170	218	952	1328	224	1104	1520	245	1275	1608	281	1327
Other Producers	58	5	54	66	7	60	76	5	71	86	5	81
Total	15454	7341	8113	18267	8624	9644	20560	9545	11015	21880	10226	11654
Less: Imputed bank service charge	...	-107	107	...	-118	118	...	-128	128	...	-154	154
Import duties	691	...	691	684	...	684	839	...	839	1262	...	1262
Value added tax	...	...	...	...	...	...	...	...	...	...	...	...
Total	16145	7448	8697	18951	8742	10210	21399	9673	11726	23142	10380	12762

	1984 Gross Output	1984 Intermediate Consumption	1984 Value Added	1985 Gross Output	1985 Intermediate Consumption	1985 Value Added
			All Producers			
1 Agriculture, hunting, forestry and fishing	2607	886	1721	3098	990	2108
2 Mining and quarrying	42	23	19	44	24	20
3 Manufacturing	9160	6323	2837	11610	7999	3611
4 Electricity, gas and water	648	351	297	797	400	397
5 Construction	1910	1226	684	2148	1380	768
6 Wholesale and retail trade, restaurants and hotels	2537	842	1695	2849	941	1908
7 Transport, storage and communication	2512	1129	1383	2891	1372	1519
8 Finance, insurance, real estate and business services	2799	532	2267	3056	573	2483
9 Community, social and personal services	964	275	689	1036	310	726
Total, Industries	23179	11587	11592	27529	13989	13540
Producers of Government Services	1717	338	1379	1785	338	1447
Other Producers	97	5	92	100	4	96
Total	24993	11930	13063	29414	14331	15083
Less: Imputed bank service charge	...	-181	181	...	-256	256
Import duties	1478	...	1478	1791	...	1791
Value added tax	...	...	...	...	...	...
Total	26471	12111	14360	31205	14587	16618

4.3 Cost Components of Value Added

Million Mauritius rupees

	1980 Compensation of Employees	1980 Capital Consumption	1980 Net Operating Surplus	1980 Indirect Taxes	1980 Less: Subsidies Received	1980 Value Added	1981 Compensation of Employees	1981 Capital Consumption	1981 Net Operating Surplus	1981 Indirect Taxes	1981 Less: Subsidies Received	1981 Value Added
					All Producers							
1 Agriculture, hunting, forestry and fishing	737	...	177	-	...	914	840	...	417	-	...	1257
2 Mining and quarrying	8	...	7	-	...	15	8	...	8	-	...	16
3 Manufacturing	589	...	538	484	...	1611	684	...	694	610	...	1988
4 Electricity, gas and water	114	...	95	-	...	209	121	...	67	-	...	188
5 Construction	376	...	185	-	...	561	380	...	208	-	...	588
6 Wholesale and retail trade, restaurants and hotels	333	...	717	52	...	1102	377	...	842	55	...	1274
7 Transport, storage and communication	485	...	352	11	...	848	556	...	441	15	...	1012
8 Finance, insurance, real estate and business services	152	...	1264	20	...	1436	177	...	1458	22	...	1657
9 Community, social and personal services	153	...	208	50	...	411	175	...	267	58	...	500
Total, Industries [ab]	2947	...	3543	617	...	7107	3318	...	4402	760	...	8480
Producers of Government Services	952	...	...	...	...	952	1104	...	...	...	...	1104
Other Producers	54	...	...	...	...	54	60	...	...	...	...	60
Total [ab]	3953	...	3543	617	...	8113	4482	...	4402	760	...	9644
Less: Imputed bank service charge	...	...	107	...	...	107	...	...	118	...	...	118
Import duties	...	...	...	691	...	691	...	...	...	684	...	684
Value added tax	...	...	...	...	...	...	...	...	...	...	...	...
Total [ab]	3953	...	3436	1308	...	8697	4482	...	4284	1444	...	10210

Mauritius

4.3 Cost Components of Value Added

Million Mauritius rupees

	1982						1983					
	Compensation of Employees	Capital Consumption	Net Operating Surplus	Indirect Taxes	Less: Subsidies Received	Value Added	Compensation of Employees	Capital Consumption	Net Operating Surplus	Indirect Taxes	Less: Subsidies Received	Value Added
					All Producers							
1 Agriculture, hunting, forestry and fishing	900	...	630	-	...	1530	974	...	491	-10	...	1455
2 Mining and quarrying	9	...	8	...	...	17	9	...	9	-	...	18
3 Manufacturing	754	...	806	689	...	2249	841	...	836	717	...	2394
4 Electricity, gas and water	140	...	120	-	...	260	150	...	95	-	...	245
5 Construction	400	...	225	-	...	625	420	...	235	1	...	656
6 Wholesale and retail trade, restaurants and hotels	420	...	870	61	...	1351	469	...	986	234	...	1503
7 Transport, storage and communication	596	...	515	12	...	1123	660	...	570	11	...	1241
8 Finance, insurance, real estate and business services	205	...	1678	30	...	1913	248	...	1796	29	...	2073
9 Community, social and personal services	202	...	324	74	...	600	221	...	348	92	...	661
Total, Industries [a,b]	3626	...	5176	866	...	9668	3992	...	5366	1074	...	10246
Producers of Government Services	1275	...	...	...	...	1275	1327	...	...	...	...	1327
Other Producers	71	...	...	...	...	71	81	...	...	...	...	81
Total [a,b]	4972	...	5176	866	...	11014	5400	...	5366	1074	...	11654
Less: Imputed bank service charge	...	...	128	...	...	128	...	...	154	...	...	154
Import duties	...	...	...	839	...	839	...	...	...	1076	...	1262
Value added tax	...	...	...	...	...	...	...	...	...	...	...	...
Total [a,b]	4972	...	5048	1705	...	11725	5400	...	5212	2150	...	12762

	1984						1985					
	Compensation of Employees	Capital Consumption	Net Operating Surplus	Indirect Taxes	Less: Subsidies Received	Value Added	Compensation of Employees	Capital Consumption	Net Operating Surplus	Indirect Taxes	Less: Subsidies Received	Value Added
					All Producers							
1 Agriculture, hunting, forestry and fishing	994	...	742	-15	...	1721	1043	...	1080	-15	...	2108
2 Mining and quarrying	10	...	9	-	...	19	10	...	10	-	...	20
3 Manufacturing	1043	...	1139	655	...	2837	1320	...	1543	748	...	3611
4 Electricity, gas and water	156	...	141	-	...	297	155	...	242	-	...	397
5 Construction	450	...	240	-6	...	684	480	...	295	-7	...	768
6 Wholesale and retail trade, restaurants and hotels	523	...	1116	273	...	1695	650	...	1184	74	...	1908
7 Transport, storage and communication	753	...	619	11	...	1383	791	...	719	9	...	1519
8 Finance, insurance, real estate and business services	284	...	1947	36	...	2267	329	...	2117	37	...	2483
9 Community, social and personal services	231	...	363	95	...	689	249	...	376	101	...	726
Total, Industries [a,b]	4444	...	6316	1049	...	11592	5027	...	7566	947	...	13540
Producers of Government Services	1379	...	...	...	...	1379	1447	...	...	...	...	1447
Other Producers	92	...	...	...	...	92	96	...	...	...	...	96
Total [a,b]	5915	...	6316	1049	...	13063	6570	...	7566	947	...	15083
Less: Imputed bank service charge	...	...	181	...	...	181	...	...	256	...	...	256
Import duties	...	...	...	1261	...	1478	...	...	...	1791	...	1791
Value added tax	...	...	...	...	...	...	...	...	...	...	...	...
Total [a,b]	5915	...	6135	2310	...	14360	6570	...	7310	2738	...	16618

a) Column 4 refers to indirect taxes less subsidies received.
b) Column 'Consumption of fixed capital' is included in column 'Net operating surplus'.

Mexico

General note. The preparation of national accounts statistics in Mexico is undertaken by the Direccion General de Estadistica of the Instituto Nacional de Estadistica, Geografia e Informatica (Ministry of Programming and the Budget). The official estimates are published annually in 'Sistema de Cuentas Naconales de Mexico'. The estimates are generally in accordance with the classifications and definitions recommended in the United Nations System of National Accounts (SNA). Input-output tables for 1950, 1960, 1970 and 1975 have been published. The following tables have been prepared from successive replies to the United Nations national accounts questionnaire. A revision of the national accounts estimates is presently undertaken by the Direccion General de Estadistica. The new series will be published in the 1981 edition of this publication. When the scope and coverage of the estimates differ for conceptual or statistical reasons from the definitions and classifications recommended in SNA, a footnote is indicated to the relevant tables.

Sources and methods:

(a) Gross domestic product. The main approach used to estimate GDP is the production approach.

(b) Expenditure on the gross domestic product. The expenditure approach is used to estimate government final consumption expenditure, increase in stocks, and exports and imports of goods and services. The estimates of gross fixed capital formation is largely based on the commodity-flow approach, whereas private final consumption expenditure is calculated as a residual. The estimates of government consumption expenditure are based on government accounts. For gross fixed capital formation the values from the input-output table of 1960 are extrapolated by value indexes for each of the principal components. The indexes are constructed by using special quantity and price indexes. Exports and imports of goods are estimated from the table of external transactions, which is based on the balance of payments. For the calculation of constant prices, general government expenditure is deflated by a specially constructed price index covering wages and salaries as well as prices of goods and services. As in the case of current prices, private consumption expenditure in constant prices is calculated as a residual. Gross domestic investment is first estimated in constant prices and later converted into current prices. Exports and imports of goods and services are deflated by specially constructed price indexes.

(c) Cost-structure of the gross domestic product. The estimates of compensation of employees for general government, petroleum and electricity production, financial institutions and partly for the transport sector, are based on direct current information on wages, salaries, etc. In the case of manufacturing, mining and private services the estimates are based on ratios of wages and salaries to gross output taken from sample surveys. For construction, trade and agriculture, employment indexes are constructed on the basis of data on occupation from the population censuses of 1960 and 1970, projected by production indexes and indexes of average wages. The estimates of consumption of fixed capital, are based on an approximation to the perpetual inventory method. Each year depreciation of the capital stock, valued at replacement cost, is estimated, based on assumptions regarding the economic life of the fixed assets. The price indexes required are derived implicitly from the estimation of gross fixed capital at 1960 prices. Government accounts are used in the estimation of indirect taxes and subsidies. Operating surplus is estimated as a residual.

(d) Gross domestic product by kind of economic activity. The table of GDP by kind of economic activity is prepared at market prices, i.e. producers' values. The production approach is used to estimate value added of all industries with direct relation to the input-output table of 1960. The income approach or the expenditure approach are used for some sectors. The estimation of gross output, intermediate consumption and value added is based on the 1960 input-output table, from which extrapolations are made by means of value indexes. These value indexes are, in general, the products of price indexes and volume indexes. The volume index for agricultural production is based on statistics of gross output of more than 60 commodities. The index for livestock production is based on statistics of animals slaughtered for domestic consumption and export, live animals exported and inventory changes. The intermediate consumption of crop and livestock production in 1960 is extrapolated by value indexes for the principal components and commodities used. For petroleum and other mining, the volume indexes are based on data from the concerned authorities. The intermediate consumption of 1960 is extrapolated by value indexes for the principal components and commodities used, based on various surveys. The volume index for manufacturing, which covers 200 products, is based on data from several authorities and through direct inquiries to industry associations and manufacturers. Input is extrapolated by value indicators. The index for construction is compiled on the basis of the apparent consumption of a few construction materials. Fixed input-output coefficients of 1960 are used. The volume index for trade is based on estimates of trade margins on locally produced and imported goods. Gross margins are based on data from the commercial censuses and special surveys. Input is extrapolated by a weighed value index. The volume index for transport and communications is based on data from the concerned authorities and companies. Input is extrapolated by quantity indexes. Value added of financial institutions and insurance is estimated through the income approach. For real estate output is extrapolated by value index for housing construction and industrial rents. Fixed input-output coefficients are used at constant prices. Current prices are obtained through the use of a specially constructed price index of principal commodities. The population censuses and household budget surveys are used to impute the rents of owner-occupied dwellings. The volume index for public administration and defense is obtained by compiling an index of wages, salaries and other compensation paid to the government employees. For the computation of constant prices, double deflation is used for all sectors, except the community, social and personal services sector. Output is extrapolated by means of output or volume indexes in all sectors in which double deflation is used. The input of the base-year is extrapolated by quantity indexes in all sectors except for the electricity, construction, restaurants and hotels, financing and services sectors, in which cases either deflation by price indexes is done or constant input-output coefficients are assumed. In the community, social and personal services sector, various approaches are used to estimate output in constant prices, such as double deflation, extrapolation of value added and deflation by price indexes.

1.1 Expenditure on the Gross Domestic Product, in Current Prices

Thousand Million Mexican pesos

	1970	1975	1977	1978	1979	1980	1981	1982	1983	1984	1985	1986
1 Government final consumption expenditure	32	113	199	255	334	463 / 449	660	1026	1574	2722	4374	7235
2 Private final consumption expenditure	320	756	1226	1544	1976	2651 / 2909	3945	6036	10882	18590	30349	53692
3 Gross capital formation	101	261	422	552	796	1203 / 1214	1678	2244	3710	5853	10375	14655
A Increase in stocks	12	25	59	59	78	170 / 107	61	-4	573	566	1300	-745
B Gross fixed capital formation	89	236	363	492	718	1033 / 1107	1617	2249	3137	5287	9076	15400
Residential buildings	21	61	98	109	151	206 / 199	276	431	744	1201	2003	3633
Non-residential buildings	12	25	34	47	66	96 / 144	209	322	397	713	1123	1542
Other construction and land improvement etc.	18	50	82	133	188	286 / 278	422	600	737	1146	1839	3127
Other	38	100	150	204	314	445 / 486	710	896	1259	2197	4030	7098
4 Exports of goods and services	34	76	191	245	343	537 / 470	630	1302	3397	5122	7294	13734
5 Less: Imports of goods and services	43	106	189	258	382	578 / 580	793	1011	1684	2815	4990	9962
Equals: Gross Domestic Product	444	1100	1849	2337	3068	4276 / 4470	6128	9798	17879	29472	47403	79353

Mexico

1.2 Expenditure on the Gross Domestic Product, in Constant Prices

Thousand Million Mexican pesos

	1970	1975	1977	1978	1979	1980	1981	1982	1983	1984	1985	1986
	\multicolumn{5}{c}{At constant prices of: 1970}		\multicolumn{6}{c}{1980}	
1 Government final consumption expenditure	32	54	57	62	68	75 / 449	495	505	519	553	558	570
2 Private final consumption expenditure	320	425	454	491	534	575 / 2909	3123	3046	2883	2977	3073	2988
3 Gross capital formation	101	151	147	164	193	236 / 1214	1393	1055	770	817	915	728
A Increase in stocks	12	19	23	22	22	39 / 107	107	-16	2	-	31	-49
B Gross fixed capital formation	89	132	124	143	172	197 / 1107	1286	1070	768	817	884	777
Residential buildings	21	32	34	32	35	36 / 199	214	218	205	215	233	228
Non-residential buildings	12	13	11	13	15	17 / 144	164	159	103	116	119	90
Other construction and land improvement etc.	18	27	27	37	44	52 / 278	329	285	204	201	200	179
Other	38	61	51	61	79	93 / 486	580	409	255	284	332	280
4 Exports of goods and services	34	43	58	64	72	77 / 479	534	650	739	781	749	761
5 Less: Imports of goods and services	43	64	58	70	91	120 / 580	683	424	281	331	375	321
Equals: Gross Domestic Product	444	610	658	712	777	842 / 4470	4862	4832	4629	4796	4920	4725

1.3 Cost Components of the Gross Domestic Product

Thousand Million Mexican pesos

	1970	1975	1977	1978	1979	1980	1981	1982	1983	1984	1985	1986
1 Indirect taxes, net	22	63	107	138	207	355 / 343	458	858	1326	2375	4435	6631
A Indirect taxes	25	79	139	175	260	434 / 432	579	1135	1924	3164	5688	8537
B Less: Subsidies	3	16	32	37	53	80 / 89	122	277	598	789	1254	1907
2 Consumption of fixed capital	24	60	107	136	178	237 / 384	527	956	2176	3359	5317	10853
3 Compensation of employees paid by resident producers to:	158	419	719	886	1157	1542 / 1611	2295	3450	5251	8450	13586	22539
4 Operating surplus	240	559	917	1177	1525	2143 / 2133	2847	4533	9126	15287	24065	39331
Equals: Gross Domestic Product	444	1100	1849	2337	3068	4276 / 4470	6128	9798	17879	29472	47403	79353

1.7 External Transactions on Current Account, Summary

Thousand Million Mexican pesos

	1970	1975	1977	1978	1979	1980	1981	1982	1983	1984	1985	1986
	\multicolumn{12}{c}{Payments to the Rest of the World}
1 Imports of goods and services	43	106	189	258	382	578 / 580	793	1011	1684	2815	4990	9962
A Imports of merchandise c.i.f.	31	82	133	190	287	449 / 456	615	722	1141	2000	3602	7187
B Other	12	24	56	68	95	129 / 124	178	288	544	815	1388	2775
2 Factor income to the rest of the world	8	22	52	68	96	143 / 157	257	640	1269	2042	2699	5463
A Compensation of employees	-	-	-	-	-	- / ...	...	...	...	...	...	...
B Property and entrepreneurial income	8	22	52	68	96	143 / 157	257	640	1269	2042	2699	5463
3 Current transfers to the rest of the world	-	-	1	1	1	1 / 1	1	1	5	4	7	8
4 Surplus of the nation on current transactions	-13	-46	-37	-61	-111	-152 / -224	-365	-50	704	765	354	-291
Payments to the Rest of the World and Surplus of the Nation on Current Transactions	38	81	205	265	368	570 / 514	686	1602	3661	5627	8049	15141

Mexico

1.7 External Transactions on Current Account, Summary
(Continued)

Thousand Million Mexican pesos

	1970	1975	1977	1978	1979	1980	1981	1982	1983	1984	1985	1986
						Receipts From The Rest of the World						
1 Exports of goods and services	34	76	191	245	343	537 / 479	638	1502	3397	5122	7294	13734
A Exports of merchandise f.o.b.	34	76	191	245	343	537 / 347	476	1211	2655	3994	5575	9762
B Other	-	-	-	-	-	- / 131	162	292	743	1128	1720	3971
2 Factor income from rest of the world	2	4	9	15	19	26 / 29	40	82	214	424	603	1085
A Compensation of employees	2	2	6	6	5	4 / 4	5	10	23	44	89	205
B Property and entrepreneurial income	1	1	4	9	13	22 / 24	35	72	191	380	513	880
3 Current transfers from rest of the world	1	2	4	5	6	7 / 7	8	18	50	80	152	322
Receipts from the Rest of the World on Current Transactions	30	81	205	265	368	570 / 514	686	1602	3661	5627	8049	15141

1.10 Gross Domestic Product by Kind of Activity, in Current Prices

Thousand Million Mexican pesos

	1970	1975	1977	1978	1979	1980	1981	1982	1983	1984	1985	1986
1 Agriculture, hunting, forestry and fishing	54	123	195	240	281	357 / 368	503	720	1302	2530	4007	7400
2 Mining and quarrying [a]	11	31	60	77	129	288 / 141	144	298	1264	1647	2196	2871
3 Manufacturing [a]	105	258	443	553	717	988 / 991	1329	2037	3780	6633	11093	19589
4 Electricity, gas and water	5	10	22	24	31	42 / 44	56	88	167	282	449	987
5 Construction	24	66	104	139	194	276 / 287	427	635	804	1298	2065	3373
6 Wholesale and retail trade, restaurants and hotels	115	277	446	560	743	1000 / 1250	1695	2903	5073	8362	13332	21149
7 Transport, storage and communication	21	63	114	150	200	279 / 286	395	606	1172	2004	3152	5636
8 Finance, insurance, real estate and business services	51	107	168	215	269	349 / 396	554	843	1440	2310	3659	6477
9 Community, social and personal services	38	90	160	204	273	377 / 401	569	926	1700	2693	4410	7599
Total, Industries	425	1024	1711	2164	2838	3956 / 4165	5673	9055	16793	27762	44663	75147
Producers of Government Services	25	88	159	199	263	368 / ...	...	...	...	...	...	...
Other Producers	...	...	...	...	...	... / 353	521	830	1232	2065	3293	5232
Subtotal	450	1112	1870	2363	3101	4324 / 4518	6194	9884	18025	29827	47956	80380
Less: Imputed bank service charge	5	12	21	26	33	48 / 48	66	86	146	355	554	1026
Plus: Import duties	...	...	...	...	...	...	...	...	...	...	...	...
Plus: Value added tax	...	...	...	...	...	...	...	...	...	...	...	...
Equals: Gross Domestic Product	444	1100	1849	2337	3068	4276 / 4470	6128	9798	17879	29472	47403	79353

a) Basic petroleum manufacturing is included in item 'Mining and quarrying'.

Mexico

1.11 Gross Domestic Product by Kind of Activity, in Constant Prices

Thousand Million Mexican pesos

	1970	1975	1977	1978	1979	1980	1981	1982	1983	1984	1985	1986
			At constant prices of: 1970						1980			
1 Agriculture, hunting, forestry and fishing	54	63	68	72	71	76 / 368	391	383	391	401	416	405
2 Mining and quarrying [a]	11	15	16	19	22	27 / 141	162	177	175	179	179	172
3 Manufacturing [a]	105	148	162	177	196	210 / 991	1055	1026	946	993	1053	993
4 Electricity, gas and water	5	8	10	11	12	13 / 44	49	54	55	58	62	64
5 Construction	24	33	32	37	41	46 / 287	329	305	247	260	266	239
6 Wholesale and retail trade, restaurants and hotels	115	158	166	179	200	216 / 1250	1382	1370	1267	1298	1313	1223
7 Transport, storage and communication	21	38	42	48	55	63 / 286	314	291	283	298	306	296
8 Finance, insurance, real estate and business services	51	68	73	77	81	82 / 396	421	440	456	481	499	515
9 Community, social and personal services	38	48	53	57	61	66 / 401	428	433	435	431	430	411
Total, Industries	425	578	623	676	738	800 / 4165	4532	4480	4254	4400	4525	4318
Producers of Government Services	25	39	42	44	49	53	...	...	...	...	...	...
Other Producers	...	...	...	...	...	353	385	409	434	459	458	470
Subtotal	450	617	665	721	787	853 / 4518	4916	4889	4688	4858	4983	4789
Less: Imputed bank service charge	5	7	8	9	10	11 / 48	54	57	59	62	63	63
Plus: Import duties	...	...	...	...	...	...	...	...	...	...	...	...
Plus: Value added tax	...	...	...	...	...	...	...	...	...	...	...	...
Equals: Gross Domestic Product	444	610	658	712	777	842 / 4470	4862	4832	4629	4796	4920	4725

a) Basic petroleum manufacturing is included in item 'Mining and quarrying'.

1.12 Relations Among National Accounting Aggregates

Thousand Million Mexican pesos

	1970	1975	1977	1978	1979	1980	1981	1982	1983	1984	1985	1986
Gross Domestic Product	444	1100	1849	2337	3068	4276 / 4470	6128	9798	17879	29472	47403	79353
Plus: Net factor income from the rest of the world	-6	-18	-43	-53	-77	-117 / -129	-217	-558	-1055	-1618	-2096	-4377
Factor income from the rest of the world	2	4	9	15	19	26 / 29	40	82	214	424	603	1085
Less: Factor income to the rest of the world	8	22	52	68	96	143 / 157	257	640	1269	2042	2699	5463
Equals: Gross National Product	439	1082	1806	2285	2990	4159 / 4341	5911	9240	16824	27854	45307	74976
Less: Consumption of fixed capital	24	60	107	136	178	237 / 384	527	956	2176	3359	5317	10853

Mexico

1.12 Relations Among National Accounting Aggregates
(Continued)

Thousand Million Mexican pesos

	1970	1975	1977	1978	1979	1980	1981	1982	1983	1984	1985	1986
Equals: National Income	415	1022	1700	2149	2812	3923 / 3958	5383	8283	14648	24495	39990	64123
Plus: Net current transfers from the rest of the world	1	2	4	4	5	6 / 6	7	17	45	76	145	314
Current transfers from the rest of the world	1	2	4	5	6	7 / 7	8	18	50	80	152	322
Less: Current transfers to the rest of the world	-	-	1	1	1	1 / 1	1	1	5	4	7	8
Equals: National Disposable Income	416	1024	1703	2153	2817	3929 / 3964	5390	8300	14693	24571	40135	64437
Less: Final consumption	352	869	1425	1799	2310	3114 / 3358	4605	7062	12455	21312	34723	60927
Equals: Net Saving	64	155	278	354	507	815 / 607	785	1238	2238	3260	5412	3510
Less: Surplus of the nation on current transactions	-13	-46	-37	-61	-111	-152 / -224	-365	-50	704	765	354	-291
Equals: Net Capital Formation	77	201	316	415	618	966 / 830	1150	1288	1534	2494	5058	3802

2.5 Private Final Consumption Expenditure by Type and Porpose, in Current Prices

Thousand Million Mexican pesos

	1970	1975	1977	1978	1979	1980	1981	1982	1983	1984	1985	1986
Final Consumption Expenditure of Resident Households												
1 Food, beverages and tobacco	129	319	516	626	760	989	1304	2042	3742	6404	...	...
2 Clothing and footwear	37	82	131	169	223	304	402	654	1170	1843	...	...
3 Gross rent, fuel and power	40	78	119	148	182	236	314	502	869	1467	...	...
4 Furniture, furnishings and household equipment and operation	40	90	154	195	263	355	462	764	1338	2141	...	...
5 Medical care and health expenses	9	25	45	57	75	107	155	274	530	899	...	...
6 Transport and communication	25	66	110	148	197	273	375	642	1264	2227	...	...
7 Recreational, entertainment, education and cultural services	15	37	62	80	110	149	203	327	528	873	...	...
8 Miscellaneous goods and services	29	75	124	158	210	285	400	687	1223	2059	...	...
Total Final Consumption Expenditure in the Domestic Market by Households, of which	325	772	1260	1581	2021	2698	3616	5891	10672	17912	...	...
A Durable goods	29	68	110	153	212	290	383	602	897	1455	...	...
B Semi-durable goods	194	467	756	924	1158	1531	2017	3260	6017	10221	...	...
C Non-durable goods											...	...
D Services	102	237	394	503	651	877	1216	2030	3758	6237	...	...
Plus: Direct purchases abroad by resident households	9	17	43	49	68	94	153	231	288	408	...	...
Less: Direct purchases in the domestic market by non-resident households	15	33	77	86	112	140	184	346	604	852	...	...
Equals: Final Consumption Expenditure of Resident Households [a]	320	756	1226	1544	1976	2651	3584	5776	10356	17469	...	...
Final Consumption Expenditure of Private Non-profit Institutions Serving Households												
Equals: Final Consumption Expenditure of Private Non-profit Organisations Serving Households	...	...	...	...	...	...	...	...	...	...	...	...
Private Final Consumption Expenditure	320	756	1226	1544	1976	2651	3584	5776	10356	17469	...	...

a) Item 'Final consumption expenditure of resident households' includes consumption expenditure of private non-profit institutions serving households.

Mexico

2.6 Private Final Consumption Expenditure by Type and Purpose, in Constant Prices

Thousand Million Mexican pesos

	1970	1975	1977	1978	1979	1980	1981	1982	1983	1984	1985	1986
					At constant prices of: 1970							
				Final Consumption Expenditure of Resident Households								
1 Food, beverages and tobacco	129	169	180	190	201	215	226	234	232	...	...	...
2 Clothing and footwear	37	49	54	57	63	65	69	71	65	...	...	...
3 Gross rent, fuel and power	40	49	53	55	58	60	63	67	68	...	...	...
4 Furniture, furnishings and household equipment and operation	40	52	58	63	71	75	78	82	71	...	...	...
5 Medical care and health expenses	9	17	19	21	24	26	28	30	30	...	...	...
6 Transport and communication	25	38	41	47	53	59	65	64	56	...	...	...
7 Recreational, entertainment, education and cultural services	15	21	24	27	30	32	34	35	30	...	...	...
8 Miscellaneous goods and services	29	39	40	44	49	52	55	59	54	...	...	...
Total Final Consumption Expenditure in the Domestic Market by Households, of which	325	434	469	504	547	583	619	641	605	621	...	...
A Durable goods	29	43	45	53	61	67	72	69	50	51	...	...
B Semi-durable goods	194	257	277	293	317	337	358	376	358	369	...	...
C Non-durable goods											...	...
D Services	102	134	147	157	169	179	189	197	197	202	...	...
Plus: Direct purchases abroad by resident households	9	12	15	16	19	23	32	20	11	15	...	...
Less: Direct purchases in the domestic market by non-resident households	15	20	30	29	33	32	34	38	40	45	...	...
Equals: Final Consumption Expenditure of Resident Households a	320	425	454	491	534	575	617	623	577	591	...	...
			Final Consumption Expenditure of Private Non-profit Institutions Serving Households									
Equals: Final Consumption Expenditure of Private Non-profit Organisations Serving Households	...	...	...	...	...	...	...	...	...	...	...	...
Private Final Consumption Expenditure	320	425	454	491	534	575	617	623	577	591	...	...

a) Item 'Final consumption expenditure of resident households' includes consumption expenditure of private non-profit institutions serving households.

4.1 Derivation of Value Added by Kind of Activity, in Current Prices

Thousand Million Mexican pesos

	1980			1981			1982			1983		
	Gross Output	Intermediate Consumption	Value Added	Gross Output	Intermediate Consumption	Value Added	Gross Output	Intermediate Consumption	Value Added	Gross Output	Intermediate Consumption	Value Added
						All Producers						
1 Agriculture, hunting, forestry and fishing	...	...	368	...	...	503	...	...	720	...	...	1392
2 Mining and quarrying a	...	...	141	...	...	144	...	...	298	...	...	1264
A Coal mining	...	...	2	...	...	3	...	...	4	...	...	12
B Crude petroleum and natural gas production	...	...	82	...	...	83	...	...	196	...	...	1039
C Metal ore mining	...	...	34	...	...	26	...	...	48	...	...	126
D Other mining	...	...	23	...	...	31	...	...	49	...	...	87

Mexico

4.1 Derivation of Value Added by Kind of Activity, in Current Prices
(Continued)

Thousand Million Mexican pesos

	1980 Gross Output	1980 Intermediate Consumption	1980 Value Added	1981 Gross Output	1981 Intermediate Consumption	1981 Value Added	1982 Gross Output	1982 Intermediate Consumption	1982 Value Added	1983 Gross Output	1983 Intermediate Consumption	1983 Value Added
3 Manufacturing [a]	...	...	991	...	...	1329	...	...	2037	...	...	3780
A Manufacture of food, beverages and tobacco	...	...	243	...	...	322	...	...	522	...	...	979
B Textile, wearing apparel and leather industries	...	...	136	...	...	175	...	...	257	...	...	491
C Manufacture of wood and wood products, including furniture	...	...	42	...	...	54	...	...	80	...	...	141
D Manufacture of paper and paper products, printing and publishing	...	...	54	...	...	74	...	...	113	...	...	214
E Manufacture of chemicals and chemical petroleum, coal, rubber and plastic products	...	...	153	...	...	206	...	...	339	...	...	716
F Manufacture of non-metallic mineral products, except products of petroleum and coal	...	...	69	...	...	95	...	...	146	...	...	269
G Basic metal industries	...	...	61	...	...	80	...	...	113	...	...	214
H Manufacture of fabricated metal products, machinery and equipment	...	...	216	...	...	298	...	...	428	...	...	696
I Other manufacturing industries	...	...	17	...	...	25	...	...	38	...	...	59
4 Electricity, gas and water	...	...	44	...	...	56	...	...	88	...	...	167
5 Construction	...	...	287	...	...	427	...	...	635	...	...	804
6 Wholesale and retail trade, restaurants and hotels	...	...	1250	...	...	1695	...	...	2903	...	...	5073
7 Transport, storage and communication	...	...	286	...	...	395	...	...	606	...	...	1172
8 Finance, insurance, real estate and business services	...	...	396	...	...	554	...	...	843	...	...	1440
9 Community, social and personal services	...	...	401	...	...	569	...	...	926	...	...	1700
Total, Industries	...	...	4165	...	...	5673	...	...	9055	...	...	16793
Producers of Government Services	...	...	353	...	...	521	...	...	830	...	...	1232
Other Producers	...	...	...	...	...	...	...	...	...	...	...	...
Total	...	...	4518	...	...	6194	...	...	9884	...	...	18025
Less: Imputed bank service charge	...	...	48	...	...	66	...	...	86	...	...	146
Import duties	...	...	...	...	...	...	...	...	...	...	...	...
Value added tax	...	...	...	...	...	...	...	...	...	...	...	...
Total	...	...	4470	...	...	6128	...	...	9798	...	...	17879

	1984 Gross Output	1984 Intermediate Consumption	1984 Value Added	1985 Gross Output	1985 Intermediate Consumption	1985 Value Added	1986 Gross Output	1986 Intermediate Consumption	1986 Value Added
All Producers									
1 Agriculture, hunting, forestry and fishing	...	...	2533	...	...	4307	...	...	7466
2 Mining and quarrying [a]	...	...	1647	...	...	2196	...	...	2871
A Coal mining	...	...	26	...	...	45	...	...	57
B Crude petroleum and natural gas production	...	...	1312	...	...	1672	...	...	1814
C Metal ore mining	...	...	147	...	...	175	...	...	405
D Other mining	...	...	163	...	...	305	...	...	595

Mexico

4.1 Derivation of Value Added by Kind of Activity, in Current Prices
(Continued)

Thousand Million Mexican pesos

	1984 Gross Output	1984 Intermediate Consumption	1984 Value Added	1985 Gross Output	1985 Intermediate Consumption	1985 Value Added	1986 Gross Output	1986 Intermediate Consumption	1986 Value Added
3 Manufacturing [a]	...	...	6633	...	...	11093	...	...	19589
A Manufacture of food, beverages and tobacco	...	...	1719	...	...	2884	...	...	5573
B Textile, wearing apparel and leather industries	...	...	770	...	...	1237	...	...	2087
C Manufacture of wood and wood products, including furniture	...	...	245	...	...	429	...	...	724
D Manufacture of paper and paper products, printing and publishing	...	...	379	...	...	639	...	...	1153
E Manufacture of chemicals and chemical petroleum, coal, rubber and plastic products	...	...	1208	...	...	1991	...	...	3566
F Manufacture of non-metallic mineral products, except products of petroleum and coal	...	...	461	...	...	801	...	...	1406
G Basic metal industries	...	...	443	...	...	638	...	...	1085
H Manufacture of fabricated metal products, machinery and equipment	...	...	1295	...	...	2278	...	...	3676
I Other manufacturing industries	...	...	112	...	...	196	...	...	318
4 Electricity, gas and water	...	...	282	...	...	449	...	...	987
5 Construction	...	...	1298	...	...	2065	...	...	3373
6 Wholesale and retail trade, restaurants and hotels	...	...	8362	...	...	13332	...	...	21149
7 Transport, storage and communication	...	...	2004	...	...	3152	...	...	5636
8 Finance, insurance, real estate and business services	...	...	2310	...	...	3659	...	...	6477
9 Community, social and personal services	...	...	2693	...	...	4410	...	...	7599
Total, Industries	...	...	27762	...	...	44663	...	...	75147
Producers of Government Services	...	...	2065	...	...	3293	...	...	5232
Other Producers	...	...	...	...	...	...	...	...	...
Total	...	...	29827	...	...	47956	...	...	80380
Less: Imputed bank service charge	...	...	355	...	...	554	...	...	1026
Import duties	...	...	...	...	...	...	...	...	...
Value added tax	...	...	...	...	...	...	...	...	...
Total	...	...	29472	...	...	47403	...	...	79353

a) Basic petroleum manufacturing is included in item 'Mining and quarrying'.

4.2 Derivation of Value Added by Kind of Activity, in Constant Prices

Thousand Million Mexican pesos

	1980 Gross Output	1980 Intermediate Consumption	1980 Value Added	1981 Gross Output	1981 Intermediate Consumption	1981 Value Added	1982 Gross Output	1982 Intermediate Consumption	1982 Value Added	1983 Gross Output	1983 Intermediate Consumption	1983 Value Added
			At constant prices of: 1980									
			All Producers									
1 Agriculture, hunting, forestry and fishing	...	...	368	...	...	391	...	...	383	...	...	391
2 Mining and quarrying [a]	...	...	141	...	...	162	...	...	177	...	...	175
A Coal mining	...	...	2	...	...	3	...	...	3	...	...	3
B Crude petroleum and natural gas production	...	...	82	...	...	96	...	...	111	...	...	108
C Metal ore mining	...	...	34	...	...	39	...	...	39	...	...	43
D Other mining	...	...	23	...	...	25	...	...	24	...	...	22

Mexico

4.2 Derivation of Value Added by Kind of Activity, in Constant Prices
(Continued)

Thousand Million Mexican pesos

	1980 Gross Output	1980 Intermediate Consumption	1980 Value Added	1981 Gross Output	1981 Intermediate Consumption	1981 Value Added	1982 Gross Output	1982 Intermediate Consumption	1982 Value Added	1983 Gross Output	1983 Intermediate Consumption	1983 Value Added
					At constant prices of:1980							
3 Manufacturing a	...	...	991	...	...	1055	...	...	1026	...	...	946
A Manufacture of food, beverages and tobacco	...	...	243	...	...	254	...	...	265	...	...	262
B Textile, wearing apparel and leather industries	...	...	136	...	...	144	...	...	137	...	...	130
C Manufacture of wood and wood products, including furniture	...	...	42	...	...	42	...	...	41	...	...	38
D Manufacture of paper and paper products, printing and publishing	...	...	54	...	...	57	...	...	57	...	...	53
E Manufacture of chemicals and chemical petroleum, coal, rubber and plastic products	...	...	153	...	...	167	...	...	171	...	...	168
F Manufacture of non-metallic mineral products, except products of petroleum and coal	...	...	69	...	...	71	...	...	69	...	...	64
G Basic metal industries	...	...	61	...	...	64	...	...	58	...	...	54
H Manufacture of fabricated metal products, machinery and equipment	...	...	216	...	...	237	...	...	208	...	...	163
I Other manufacturing industries	...	...	17	...	...	20	...	...	19	...	...	15
4 Electricity, gas and water	...	...	44	...	...	49	...	...	54	...	...	55
5 Construction	...	...	287	...	...	329	...	...	305	...	...	247
6 Wholesale and retail trade, restaurants and hotels	...	...	1250	...	...	1382	...	...	1370	...	...	1267
7 Transport, storage and communication	...	...	286	...	...	314	...	...	291	...	...	283
8 Finance, insurance, real estate and business services	...	...	396	...	...	421	...	...	440	...	...	456
9 Community, social and personal services	...	...	401	...	...	428	...	...	433	...	...	435
Total, Industries	...	...	4165	...	...	4532	...	...	4480	...	...	4254
Producers of Government Services	...	...	353	...	...	385	...	...	409	...	...	434
Other Producers	...	...	...	...	...	...	...	...	...	...	...	...
Total	...	...	4518	...	...	4916	...	...	4889	...	...	4688
Less: Imputed bank service charge	...	...	48	...	...	54	...	...	57	...	...	59
Import duties	...	...	...	...	...	...	...	...	...	...	...	...
Value added tax	...	...	...	...	...	...	...	...	...	...	...	...
Total	...	...	4470	...	...	4862	...	...	4832	...	...	4629

	1984 Gross Output	1984 Intermediate Consumption	1984 Value Added	1985 Gross Output	1985 Intermediate Consumption	1985 Value Added	1986 Gross Output	1986 Intermediate Consumption	1986 Value Added
			At constant prices of:1980						
			All Producers						
1 Agriculture, hunting, forestry and fishing	...	...	401	...	...	416	...	...	405
2 Mining and quarrying a	...	...	179	...	...	179	...	...	172
A Coal mining	...	...	3	...	...	3	...	...	3
B Crude petroleum and natural gas production	...	...	109	...	...	107	...	...	99
C Metal ore mining	...	...	43	...	...	45	...	...	45
D Other mining	...	...	23	...	...	25	...	...	24

Mexico

4.2 Derivation of Value Added by Kind of Activity, in Constant Prices
(Continued)

Thousand Million Mexican pesos

	1984 Gross Output	1984 Intermediate Consumption	1984 Value Added	1985 Gross Output	1985 Intermediate Consumption	1985 Value Added	1986 Gross Output	1986 Intermediate Consumption	1986 Value Added
				At constant prices of:1980					
3 Manufacturing [a]	...	...	993	...	...	1053	...	...	993
A Manufacture of food, beverages and tobacco	...	...	265	...	...	275	...	...	274
B Textile, wearing apparel and leather industries	...	...	131	...	...	134	...	...	127
C Manufacture of wood and wood products, including furniture	...	...	40	...	...	40	...	...	39
D Manufacture of paper and paper products, printing and publishing	...	...	56	...	...	61	...	...	59
E Manufacture of chemicals and chemical petroleum, coal, rubber and plastic products	...	...	179	...	...	189	...	...	182
F Manufacture of non-metallic mineral products, except products of petroleum and coal	...	...	68	...	...	73	...	...	68
G Basic metal industries	...	...	61	...	...	61	...	...	57
H Manufacture of fabricated metal products, machinery and equipment	...	...	177	...	...	200	...	...	170
I Other manufacturing industries	...	...	17	...	...	19	...	...	17
4 Electricity, gas and water	...	...	58	...	...	62	...	...	64
5 Construction	...	...	260	...	...	266	...	...	239
6 Wholesale and retail trade, restaurants and hotels	...	...	1298	...	...	1313	...	...	1223
7 Transport, storage and communication	...	...	298	...	...	306	...	...	296
8 Finance, insurance, real estate and business services	...	...	481	...	...	499	...	...	515
9 Community, social and personal services	...	...	431	...	...	430	...	...	411
Total, Industries	...	...	4400	...	...	4525	...	...	4318
Producers of Government Services	...	...	459	...	...	458	...	...	470
Other Producers	...	...	...	...	...	...	...	...	...
Total	...	...	4858	...	...	4983	...	...	4789
Less: Imputed bank service charge	...	...	62	...	...	63	...	...	63
Import duties	...	...	...	...	...	...	...	...	...
Value added tax	...	...	...	...	...	...	...	...	...
Total	...	...	4796	...	...	4920	...	...	4725

a) Basic petroleum manufacturing is included in item 'Mining and quarrying'.

Mongolia

Source. The official data are published annually in 'National Economy of the Mongolian People's Republic'.

General note. The estimates shown in the following tables have been prepared in accordance with the System of Material Product Balances. Therefore, these estimates are not comparable in concept and coverage with those conforming to the United Nations System of National Accounts.

2a Net Material Product by Kind of Activity of the Material Sphere in Current Market Prices

Percentages

	1970	1975	1977	1978	1979	1980	1981	1982	1983	1984	1985	1986
1 Agriculture and forestry	25.3	22.4	17.1	19.5	18.0	15.0	16.4	17.9	18.0	17.0	16.2	21.0
2 Industrial activity	22.6	24.7	27.5	27.3	27.8	29.3	29.4	30.9	32.2	32.3	32.6	33.7
3 Construction	5.8	5.4	5.5	5.4	5.7	6.1	5.6	5.1	4.8	5.0	5.0	5.8
4 Wholesale and retail trade and restaurants and other eating and drinking places	36.5	36.2	37.0	35.4	35.9	36.3	35.9	33.8	32.8	33.0	33.0	25.7
5 Transport and communication	7.5	9.1	10.6	10.2	10.5	11.2	10.9	10.5	10.5	11.0	11.5	11.7
A Transport	6.9	8.2	9.7	9.3	9.5	10.1	9.7	9.3	9.2	9.6	10.1	10.2
B Communication	0.6	0.9	0.9	0.9	1.0	1.1	1.2	1.2	1.3	1.4	1.4	1.5
6 Other activities of the material sphere	2.3	2.2	2.3	2.2	2.1	2.0	1.8	1.8	1.7	1.7	1.7	2.1
Net material product	100.0	100.0	100.0	100.0	100.0	100.0	100.0	100.0	100.0	100.0	100.0	100.0

2b Net Material Product by Kind of Activity of the Material Sphere in Constant Market Prices

Index numbers 1970=100

	1970	1975	1977	1978	1979	1980	1981	1982	1983	1984	1985	1986
					At constant prices of:1970							
1 Agriculture and forestry	100	111	78	98	97	81	95	109	109	99	109	115
2 Industrial activity	100	181	224	240	273	295	321	355	390	424	447	457
3 Construction	100	135	144	152	172	188	188	190	193	202	210	232
4 Wholesale and retail trade and restaurants and other eating and drinking places a	100	122	135	142	153	160	171	179	187	194	200	211
5 Transport and communication	100	175	215	226	246	266	285	306	327	347	376	422
A Transport	100	172	215	225	243	262	277	295	312	330	359	404
B Communication	100	200	223	246	286	313	379	426	493	532	559	621
6 Other activities of the material sphere	100	139	149	153	155	157	157	171	176	175	175	198
Net material product	100	138	148	161	175	181	196	213	226	236	249	262

a) Item 'Other activities of the material sphere' is included in item 'Wholesale and retail trade and restaurants and other eating and drinking places'.

6b Capital Formation by Kind of Activity of the Material and Non-Material Spheres in Constant Market Prices

Million Mongolian tugriks

	1970	1975	1977	1978	1979	1980	1981	1982	1983	1984	1985	1986
					At constant prices of:1960							
					Gross Fixed Capital Formation							
1 Agriculture and forestry	293	...	...	...	...	...	...	...	...	...	...	...
2 Industrial activity	327	...	...	...	...	...	...	...	...	...	...	...
3 Construction	52	...	...	...	...	...	...	...	...	...	...	...
4 Wholesale and retail trade and restaurants and other eating and drinking places	28	...	...	...	...	...	...	...	...	...	...	...
5 Transport and communication	95	...	...	...	...	...	...	...	...	...	...	...
6 Other activities of the material sphere	...	...	...	...	...	...	...	...	...	...	...	...
Total Material Sphere	794	...	...	...	...	...	...	...	...	...	...	...
7 Housing except owner-occupied, communal and miscellaneous personal services	109	...	...	...	...	...	...	...	...	...	...	...
8 Education, culture and art	96	...	...	...	...	...	...	...	...	...	...	...
9 Health and social welfare services and sports	42	...	...	...	...	...	...	...	...	...	...	...
Total Non-Material Sphere Serving Individuals	247	...	...	...	...	...	...	...	...	...	...	...
10 Government	...	...	...	...	...	...	...	...	...	...	...	...
11 Finance, credit and insurance	...	...	...	...	...	...	...	...	...	...	...	...
12 Research, scientific and technological institutes	...	...	...	...	...	...	...	...	...	...	...	...
13 Other activities of the non-material sphere	...	...	...	...	...	...	...	...	...	...	...	...
Total Non-Material Sphere Serving the Community as a Whole	21	...	...	...	...	...	...	...	...	...	...	...
14 Owner-occupied dwellings	...	...	...	...	...	...	...	...	...	...	...	...
Total Gross Fixed Capital Formation	1062	...	...	...	...	...	...	...	...	...	...	...

Montserrat

Source. Government of Montserrat, Statistics Office, 'National Accounts Statistics 1975-82'.

General note. The estimates shown in the following tables have been prepared in accordance with the United Nations System of National Accounts so far as the existing data would permit.

1.1 Expenditure on the Gross Domestic Product, in Current Prices

Million East Caribbean dollars

	1970	1975	1977	1978	1979	1980	1981	1982	1983	1984	1985	1986
1 Government final consumption expenditure	...	6.3	6.7	7.8	9.9	12.2	14.1	16.9	17.9	19.3	20.3	21.3
2 Private final consumption expenditure	...	27.1	32.4	37.2	47.4	71.2	76.5	81.9	83.7	90.2	96.4	102.1
3 Gross capital formation	...	8.7	9.8	14.2	19.6	26.8	33.7	32.1	25.6	24.7	26.2	40.8
A Increase in stocks	...	0.3	0.6	2.3	1.4	5.2	4.3	1.5	2.0	2.5	1.5	3.2
B Gross fixed capital formation	...	8.4	9.2	11.9	18.2	21.6	29.4	30.6	23.6	22.2	24.7	37.6
Residential buildings	...											
Non-residential buildings		6.2	6.3	6.6	11.0	11.4	14.4	18.6	12.9	13.9	16.0	19.1
Other construction and land improvement etc.	...											
Other	...	2.2	2.9	5.3	7.2	10.2	15.0	12.0	10.7	8.3	8.7	18.5
4 Exports of goods and services	...	1.5	2.5	5.6	3.1	4.8	8.9	10.5	18.5	12.7	11.7	11.5
5 Less: Imports of goods and services	...	18.2	20.8	29.6	37.7	49.7	59.9	60.4	59.2	53.3	54.5	61.5
Equals: Gross Domestic Product	...	25.4	30.5	35.2	43.2	65.4	73.3	81.0	86.5	93.6	100.1	114.1

1.2 Expenditure on the Gross Domestic Product, in Constant Prices

Million East Caribbean dollars

	1970	1975	1977	1978	1979	1980	1981	1982	1983	1984	1985	1986
					At constant prices of: 1977							
1 Government final consumption expenditure	...	6.9	6.7	7.0	7.0	7.5	8.3	9.1	9.4	9.4	10.1	9.8
2 Private final consumption expenditure	...	32.9	32.4	31.0	37.4	40.4	38.8	40.0	38.2	38.9	42.4	41.4
3 Gross capital formation	...	12.4	9.9	12.6	15.0	18.0	20.6	18.6	13.2	12.3	13.5	20.2
A Increase in stocks	...	0.5	0.6	2.1	1.0	3.0	2.3	0.8	1.1	0.7	0.8	1.6
B Gross fixed capital formation	...	11.9	9.2	10.5	14.0	15.0	18.3	17.6	12.1	11.6	12.7	18.6
Residential buildings	...											
Non-residential buildings		8.5	6.3	5.9	8.7	8.2	8.9	10.6	6.9	7.4	8.5	10.2
Other construction and land improvement etc.	...											
Other	...	3.4	2.9	4.6	5.3	6.8	9.4	7.0	5.2	4.1	4.2	8.4
4 Exports of goods and services	...	2.0	2.5	5.6	2.5	3.3	5.8	6.0	9.2	6.3	5.8	5.6
5 Less: Imports of goods and services	...	22.7	20.8	23.8	25.7	29.3	32.4	30.7	28.4	24.6	27.5	30.4
Equals: Gross Domestic Product	...	31.3	30.5	32.4	36.2	39.9	41.1	42.8	41.6	42.3	44.3	46.6

1.4 General Government Current Receipts and Disbursements

Thousand East Caribbean dollars

	1970	1975	1977	1978	1979	1980	1981	1982	1983	1984	1985	1986
					Receipts							
1 Operating surplus	...	...	...	...	...	...	...	...	...	...	...	...
2 Property and entrepreneurial income	...	529	894	653	1073	1090	1994	...	...	...	...	...
3 Taxes, fees and contributions	...	4471	5407	6198	9021	12840	15453	...	...	...	...	...
A Indirect taxes	...	2551	3046	3438	5305	7948	9807	10020	9980	10554	11890	...
B Direct taxes	...	1000	1507	1705	2358	2853	3299	4040	5210	5686	5100	...
C Social security contributions	...	-	-	-	-	-	-	...	...	...	...	...
D Compulsory fees, fines and penalties	...	920	854	1055	1358	2039	2347	...	...	...	...	...
4 Other current transfers	...	66	669	706	432	763	570	785	865	1099	349	...
Total Current Receipts of General Government	...	5066	6970	7557	10526	14693	18017	19776	20920	21559	22119	...
					Disbursements							
1 Government final consumption expenditure	...	6280	6704	7786	9906	12242	14119	16877	17929	19279	20279	...

Montserrat

1.4 General Government Current Receipts and Disbursements
(Continued)

Thousand East Caribbean dollars

	1970	1975	1977	1978	1979	1980	1981	1982	1983	1984	1985	1986
A Compensation of employees	...	4709	4780	5439	7281	8700	8828	10792	12109	13400	14068	...
B Consumption of fixed capital	...	...	...	...	...	...	...	...	...	...	...	...
C Purchases of goods and services, net	...	1571	1924	2347	2625	3542	5291	6085	5820	5879	6211	...
D Less: Own account fixed capital formation	...	...	...	...	...	...	...	...	...	...	...	...
E Indirect taxes paid, net	...	...	...	...	...	...	...	...	...	...	...	...
2 Property income	...	80	75	54	45	57	303	370	326	268	257	...
A Interest	...	80	75	54	45	57	303	370	326	268	257	...
B Net land rent and royalties	...	-	-	-	-	-	-	-	-	-	-	...
3 Subsidies	...	116	104	93	80	120	135	-	130	139	155	...
4 Other current transfers	...	674	847	789	873	1096	1175	1378	1593	1668	1105	...
5 Net saving	...	-2084	-760	-1165	-378	1178	2285	1151	942	205	323	...
Total Current Disbursements and Net Saving of General Government	...	5066	6970	7557	10526	14693	18017	19776	20920	21559	22119	...

1.10 Gross Domestic Product by Kind of Activity, in Current Prices

Million East Caribbean dollars

	1970	1975	1977	1978	1979	1980	1981	1982	1983	1984	1985	1986
1 Agriculture, hunting, forestry and fishing	...	1.2	1.3	1.5	2.0	2.4	3.0	3.3	3.3	3.9	4.1	4.8
2 Mining and quarrying	...	0.2	0.2	0.4	0.4	0.4	0.5	1.1	0.7	1.1	1.2	1.3
3 Manufacturing	...	1.4	1.8	2.3	3.0	3.4	4.1	4.0	5.3	5.6	5.1	6.5
4 Electricity, gas and water	...	0.7	0.9	1.1	1.0	1.9	2.0	2.1	3.0	3.3	3.3	3.7
5 Construction	...	2.8	2.8	3.0	4.9	5.3	6.4	8.3	5.7	6.2	7.1	8.5
6 Wholesale and retail trade, restaurants and hotels	...	4.2	5.9	6.8	6.6	10.6	15.0	16.1	16.1	16.0	17.0	20.5
7 Transport, storage and communication	...	1.5	2.0	3.1	3.6	4.3	5.2	6.5	8.5	9.7	11.0	12.2
8 Finance, insurance, real estate and business services	...	6.7	7.4	7.9	8.9	17.7	15.7	16.7	19.8	20.7	21.5	24.2
9 Community, social and personal services	...	2.8	3.4	4.1	5.0	8.6	10.0	16.6	11.4	13.1	14.1	13.9
Total, Industries	...	21.5	25.7	30.2	35.4	54.6	61.9	68.9	73.8	79.6	84.4	95.6
Producers of Government Services	...	0.8	2.8	3.0	4.0	4.9	4.9	5.8	6.6	7.7	8.3	10.4
Other Producers	...	...	...	...	...	...	...	...	...	...	...	...
Subtotal a	...	22.3	28.5	33.2	39.4	59.5	66.8	74.7	80.4	87.3	92.7	106.0
Less: Imputed bank service charge	...	-0.8	1.1	1.2	1.3	1.9	2.8	3.7	3.6	4.0	4.1	4.8
Plus: Import duties	...	...	...	...	...	...	...	...	...	...	...	...
Plus: Value added tax	...	...	...	...	...	...	...	...	...	...	...	...
Plus: Other adjustments b	...	2.3	2.9	3.3	5.2	7.8	9.3	10.0	9.7	10.3	11.5	12.9
Equals: Gross Domestic Product	...	25.4	30.5	35.2	43.2	65.4	73.3	81.0	86.5	93.6	100.1	114.1

a) Gross domestic product in factor values.
b) Item 'Other adjustments' refers to indirect taxes net of subsidies.

1.11 Gross Domestic Product by Kind of Activity, in Constant Prices

Million East Caribbean dollars

	1970	1975	1977	1978	1979	1980	1981	1982	1983	1984	1985	1986
					At constant prices of:1977							
1 Agriculture, hunting, forestry and fishing	...	1.6	1.3	1.3	1.6	1.5	1.7	1.6	1.4	1.7	1.8	1.9
2 Mining and quarrying	...	0.3	0.2	0.3	0.3	0.3	0.3	0.7	0.3	0.5	0.5	0.5
3 Manufacturing	...	1.7	1.8	2.4	2.8	3.1	3.5	3.4	3.6	3.5	3.5	3.8
4 Electricity, gas and water	...	0.8	0.9	1.0	1.0	1.1	1.1	1.1	1.2	1.3	1.3	1.4
5 Construction	...	3.8	2.8	2.6	2.9	2.6	4.0	4.7	3.1	3.3	3.3	4.5
6 Wholesale and retail trade, restaurants and hotels	...	6.3	5.9	6.5	6.8	7.7	8.1	8.2	8.0	7.6	8.0	8.2
7 Transport, storage and communication	...	1.9	2.0	2.5	2.6	2.8	2.9	3.1	3.2	3.2	3.5	3.5
8 Finance, insurance, real estate and business services	...	7.5	7.4	7.8	8.2	8.5	8.7	8.8	8.9	9.2	9.4	9.8
9 Community, social and personal services	...	3.3	3.5	3.5	3.6	5.0	4.9	4.7	4.5	4.6	4.7	4.2
Total, Industries	...	27.2	25.9	28.0	30.8	33.7	35.2	36.3	34.2	34.9	36.5	37.8
Producers of Government Services	...	2.6	2.8	2.8	2.9	3.2	3.1	3.3	3.6	3.9	4.1	4.8

Montserrat

1.11 Gross Domestic Product by Kind of Activity, in Constant Prices
(Continued)

Million East Caribbean dollars

	1970	1975	1977	1978	1979	1980	1981	1982	1983	1984	1985	1986
				At constant prices of:1977								
Other Producers	...	...	...	...	...	...	...	...	...	...	...	...
Subtotal a	...	29.8	28.7	30.8	33.7	36.9	38.3	39.6	37.8	38.8	40.6	42.6
Less: Imputed bank service charge	...	1.4	1.1	1.1	1.3	1.6	1.6	1.6	1.6	1.7	1.7	1.8
Plus: Import duties	...	...	...	...	...	...	...	...	...	...	...	...
Plus: Value added tax	...	...	...	...	...	...	...	...	...	...	...	...
Plus: Other adjustments b	...	3.0	2.9	2.9	3.8	4.6	4.4	4.8	5.4	5.2	5.3	5.8
Equals: Gross Domestic Product	...	31.3	30.5	32.4	36.2	39.9	41.1	42.8	41.6	42.3	44.2	46.6

a) Gross domestic product in factor values.
b) Item 'Other adjustments' refers to indirect taxes net of subsidies.

2.1 Government Final Consumption Expenditure by Function, in Current Prices

Thousand East Caribbean dollars

	1970	1975	1977	1978	1979	1980	1981	1982	1983	1984	1985	1986
1 General public services	...	1066	995	1254	2066	2281	2378	3109	2715	3786	3802	...
2 Defence	...	20	25	24	34	71	43	56	63	59	59	...
3 Public order and safety	...	847	794	889	1205	1373	1486	1752	1961	2031	2301	...
4 Education	...	1371	1396	1427	1987	2222	2513	2772	3170	3727	4533	...
5 Health	...	1239	1141	1456	1853	2298	2502	2822	3121	3063	3093	...
6 Social security and welfare	...	552	683	856	711	1225	1174	1522	1652	1275	982	...
7 Housing and community amenities	...	54	39	53	89	75	148	141	135	-45	188	...
8 Recreational, cultural and religious affairs	...	29	37	40	55	64	75	175	249	120	341	...
9 Economic services	...	1114	1591	1703	1876	2500	3793	4475	4832	5250	4963	...
A Fuel and energy	...	-8	30	35	43	54	63	69	191	-	-	...
B Agriculture, forestry, fishing and hunting	...	285	409	349	454	732	661	732	914	1380	1569	...
C Mining, manufacturing and construction, except fuel and energy	...	224	320	351	341	457	956	1416	2436	3391	2433	...
D Transportation and communication	...	577	587	716	912	1173	1641	1959	868	420	927	...
E Other economic affairs	...	36	245	252	126	84	472	299	423	59	34	...
10 Other functions	...	-12	9	84	30	133	7	38	-	13	17	...
Total Government Final Consumption Expenditure	...	6280	6704	7786	9906	12242	14119	16862	17929	19279	20279	...

4.1 Derivation of Value Added by Kind of Activity, in Current Prices

Million East Caribbean dollars

	1980 Gross Output	1980 Intermediate Consumption	1980 Value Added	1981 Gross Output	1981 Intermediate Consumption	1981 Value Added
			All Producers			
1 Agriculture, hunting, forestry and fishing	...	...	2.4	...	...	3.0
A Agriculture and hunting	...	...	1.7	...	...	2.3
B Forestry and logging	...	...	0.4	...	...	0.4
C Fishing	...	...	0.3	...	...	0.3
2 Mining and quarrying	...	...	0.4	...	...	0.5
3 Manufacturing	...	...	3.5	...	...	4.1
4 Electricity, gas and water	...	...	1.9	...	...	2.0
5 Construction	...	...	5.3	...	...	6.4
6 Wholesale and retail trade, restaurants and hotels	...	...	10.7	...	...	15.0
A Wholesale and retail trade	...	...	8.9	...	...	12.6
B Restaurants and hotels	...	...	1.7	...	...	2.4
Restaurants	...	...	0.1	...	...	0.2
Hotels and other lodging places	...	...	1.6	...	...	2.2
7 Transport, storage and communication	...	...	4.3	...	...	5.2
A Transport and storage	...	...	3.5	...	...	4.3
B Communication	...	...	0.8	...	...	0.9
8 Finance, insurance, real estate and business services	...	...	17.7	...	...	15.7
A Financial institutions	...	...	2.3	...	...	2.7

Montserrat

4.1 Derivation of Value Added by Kind of Activity, in Current Prices
(Continued)

Million East Caribbean dollars

	1980 Gross Output	1980 Intermediate Consumption	1980 Value Added	1981 Gross Output	1981 Intermediate Consumption	1981 Value Added
B Insurance	...	...	0.4	...	...	0.8
C Real estate and business services	...	...	15.0	...	...	12.2
Real estate, except dwellings	...	...	1.2	...	...	1.5
Dwellings	...	...	13.8	...	...	10.7
9 Community, social and personal services	...	...	8.6	...	...	10.0
A Sanitary and similar services	...	...	-	...	...	-
B Social and related community services	...	...	5.8	...	...	7.2
C Recreational and cultural services	...	...	2.0	...	...	1.9
D Personal and household services	...	...	0.8	...	...	0.9
Total, Industries	...	...	54.6	...	...	61.9
Producers of Government Services	...	...	4.9	...	...	4.9
Other Producers	...	...	...	...	...	...
Total [a]	...	...	59.5	...	...	66.8
Less: Imputed bank service charge	...	...	1.9	...	...	2.8
Import duties	...	...	...	...	...	...
Value added tax	...	...	...	...	...	...
Other adjustments [b]	...	...	7.8	...	...	9.3
Total	...	...	65.4	...	...	73.3
Memorandum Item: Mineral fuels and power	...	...	1.4	...	...	...

a) Gross domestic product in factor values.
b) Item 'Other adjustments' refers to indirect taxes net of subsidies.

Morocco

Source. Reply to the United Nations National Accounts Questionnaire from the Division du Plan et des Etudes Economiques, Rabat. Official estimates are published by the Division in 'Comptes de la Nation'.

General note. The estimates have been adjusted by the Division du Plan et des Etudes Economiques to conform to the United Nations System of National Accounts so far as the existing data would permit. It should be noted that the domestic territory is defined to include all de facto residents, such as foreign diplomats and troops.

1.1 Expenditure on the Gross Domestic Product, in Current Prices

Thousand Million Moroccan Dirhams

	1970	1975	1977	1978	1979	1980	1981	1982	1983	1984	1985	1986
1 Government final consumption expenditure	2.40	5.86	10.33	11.47	13.23	14.28	16.77	19.24	18.71	19.25	20.79	23.32
2 Private final consumption expenditure	14.53	24.80	32.58	36.44	40.81	47.12	53.32	61.78	64.12	73.94	81.75	91.26
3 Gross capital formation	3.70	9.25	16.18	14.03	15.19	15.87	17.19	20.97	19.76	23.85	27.37	27.26
A Increase in stocks	0.71	0.21	0.28	0.30	0.32	1.06	0.36	-0.12	-0.78	1.39	2.41	1.00
B Gross fixed capital formation	2.99	9.04	15.90	13.73	14.87	14.81	16.83	21.09	20.54	22.46	24.96	26.26
4 Exports of goods and services	3.54	8.43	8.83	9.35	10.83	13.23	16.29	18.52	21.15	26.90	32.20	32.91
5 Less: Imports of goods and services	4.15	11.93	18.16	16.14	18.02	20.34	26.83	30.43	29.10	38.41	42.81	40.42
Equals: Gross Domestic Product	20.02	36.41	49.76	55.15	62.04	70.16	76.74	90.09	94.64	105.54	119.31	134.33

1.2 Expenditure on the Gross Domestic Product, in Constant Prices

Thousand Million Moroccan Dirhams

	1970	1975	1977	1978	1979	1980	1981	1982	1983	1984	1985	1986
				At constant prices of: 1960								
1 Government final consumption expenditure	2.36	4.17	6.21	...	...	...	...	...	...	...	...	...
2 Private final consumption expenditure	14.34	17.21	18.07	...	...	...	...	...	...	...	...	...
3 Gross capital formation	2.81	5.61	8.00	...	...	...	...	...	...	...	...	...
A Increase in stocks	0.07	0.13	-0.28	...	...	...	...	...	...	...	...	...
B Gross fixed capital formation	2.74	5.48	8.28	...	...	...	...	...	...	...	...	...
4 Exports of goods and services	3.54	3.96	4.96	...	...	...	...	...	...	...	...	...
5 Less: Imports of goods and services	4.15	6.47	8.22	...	...	...	...	...	...	...	...	...
Equals: Gross Domestic Product	18.89	24.49	29.03	...	...	...	...	...	...	...	...	...

1.3 Cost Components of the Gross Domestic Product

Thousand Million Moroccan Dirhams

	1970	1975	1977	1978	1979	1980	1981	1982	1983	1984	1985	1986
1 Indirect taxes, net	2.55	3.20	6.54	6.37	7.50	9.70	...	...	...	...	...	...
2 Consumption of fixed capital	...	...	...	...	...	...	...	...	...	...	...	...
3 Compensation of employees paid by resident producers to:	6.47	11.69	16.35	17.54	20.55	23.22	...	...	...	...	...	...
4 Operating surplus [a]	11.00	21.53	26.87	31.24	34.00	37.10	...	...	...	...	...	...
Equals: Gross Domestic Product	20.02	36.41	49.76	55.15	62.04	70.16	76.74	90.09	94.63	105.54	119.31	134.33

a) Item 'Operating surplus' includes consumption of fixed capital.

1.7 External Transactions on Current Account, Summary

Thousand Million Moroccan Dirhams

	1970	1975	1977	1978	1979	1980	1981	1982	1983	1984	1985	1986
				Payments to the Rest of the World								
1 Imports of goods and services	4.15	11.93	18.16	16.14	18.02	20.34	26.83	30.43	29.10	38.41	42.81	40.42
2 Factor income to the rest of the world	0.45	0.66	1.34	1.74	2.22	2.80	4.38	5.05	5.12	5.77	8.15	7.37
A Compensation of employees	0.03	0.03	0.03	0.04	0.04	0.04	0.04	0.06	0.04	0.05	-	0.02
B Property and entrepreneurial income	0.42	0.63	1.31	1.70	2.18	2.76	4.34	4.99	5.08	5.72	8.15	7.35
3 Current transfers to the rest of the world	0.25	0.38	0.49	0.49	0.55	0.64	0.76	0.57	0.31	0.43	0.69	0.79
4 Surplus of the nation on current transactions	-0.57	-2.05	-7.93	-5.40	-5.77	-5.57	-9.34	-11.43	-5.91	-8.91	-8.05	-1.53
Payments to the Rest of the World and Surplus of the Nation on Current Transactions	4.28	10.91	12.05	12.96	15.01	18.21	22.62	24.60	28.62	35.71	43.60	47.04

Morocco

1.7 External Transactions on Current Account, Summary
(Continued)

Thousand Million Moroccan Dirhams

	1970	1975	1977	1978	1979	1980	1981	1982	1983	1984	1985	1986
	\multicolumn{12}{c}{Receipts From The Rest of the World}
1 Exports of goods and services	3.54	8.43	8.83	9.35	10.83	13.23	16.29	18.52	21.15	26.90	32.20	32.91
2 Factor income from rest of the world	0.13	0.45	0.57	0.62	0.76	1.07	1.33	0.95	0.12	0.14	0.52	0.39
A Compensation of employees	0.04	0.23	0.29	0.35	0.42	0.43	0.54	0.54	0.04	0.05	0.08	0.09
B Property and entrepreneurial income	0.09	0.22	0.28	0.27	0.34	0.64	0.79	0.41	0.08	0.09	0.44	0.30
3 Current transfers from rest of the world	0.61	2.02	2.64	2.98	3.43	3.91	5.00	5.14	7.36	8.67	10.88	13.74
Receipts from the Rest of the World on Current Transactions	4.28	10.91	12.05	12.96	15.01	18.21	22.62	24.60	28.63	35.71	43.60	47.04

1.10 Gross Domestic Product by Kind of Activity, in Current Prices

Thousand Million Moroccan Dirhams

	1970	1975	1977	1978	1979	1980	1981	1982	1983	1984	1985	1986
1 Agriculture, hunting, forestry and fishing	3.99	6.52	8.15	10.44	11.12	12.71	11.42	16.26	16.13	17.55	21.00	20.59
2 Mining and quarrying	0.66	3.30	2.08	2.08	2.75	3.43	4.26	4.04	3.99	5.26	5.62	4.79
3 Manufacturing	3.25	6.23	8.24	9.37	10.44	12.01	13.42	14.57	15.95	17.36	20.22	23.50
4 Electricity, gas and water	0.64	0.90	1.21	1.34	2.14	2.37	2.73	3.25	3.44	3.94	4.72	4.67
5 Construction	0.85	2.38	4.67	4.51	4.94	4.84	5.36	6.60	6.70	6.90	7.81	7.41
6 Wholesale and retail trade, restaurants and hotels	3.92	6.25	8.04	8.57	9.16	10.18	10.85	12.34	12.95	14.68	16.02	17.98
7 Transport, storage and communication	0.84	1.55	2.16	2.47	2.64	3.12	3.43	3.98	4.48	5.68	5.87	6.69
8 Finance, insurance, real estate and business services	0.30	0.71	1.09	1.20	1.33	1.54	1.89	2.42	2.56	3.28	3.68	4.54
9 Community, social and personal services [a]	4.71	8.05	11.53	12.72	14.80	17.20	...	...	...	...	...	...
Total, Industries	...	...	...	...	...	...	...	...	...	...	...	...
Producers of Government Services [a]	...	...	...	...	...	...	...	...	...	...	...	...
Other Producers [a]	...	...	...	...	...	...	...	...	...	...	...	...
Subtotal	19.16	35.89	47.18	52.69	59.30	67.19	72.70	...	...	...	...	...
Less: Imputed bank service charge	0.28	0.69	1.02	1.11	1.20	1.41	1.64	2.19	2.27	2.98	3.67	4.41
Plus: Import duties	1.14	1.21	3.60	3.57	3.94	4.24	5.38	6.38	6.38	7.02	7.47	7.72
Plus: Value added tax	...	...	...	...	...	...	...	...	...	...	...	...
Equals: Gross Domestic Product	20.02	36.41	49.76	55.15	62.04	70.16	76.74	90.09	94.64	105.54	119.31	134.33

a) Items 'Other producers' and 'Producers of government services' are included in item 'Community, social and personal services'.

1.11 Gross Domestic Product by Kind of Activity, in Constant Prices

Thousand Million Moroccan Dirhams

	1970	1975	1977	1978	1979	1980	1981	1982	1983	1984	1985	1986
	\multicolumn{12}{c}{At constant prices of: 1969}
1 Agriculture, hunting, forestry and fishing	3.72	3.47	3.51	4.14	4.07	4.32	3.33	3.99	3.84	3.83	4.30	5.28
2 Mining and quarrying	0.65	0.72	0.87	0.92	0.98	0.93	0.92	0.87	0.93	0.99	0.97	0.93
3 Manufacturing	3.21	4.33	4.93	5.19	5.27	5.52	5.52	5.52	5.73	5.64	5.74	5.92
4 Electricity, gas and water	0.64	0.89	1.01	1.02	1.62	1.33	1.38	1.46	1.53	1.54	1.58	1.54
5 Construction	0.78	1.60	2.09	1.67	1.62	1.47	1.43	1.60	1.52	1.45	1.54	1.37
6 Wholesale and retail trade, restaurants and hotels	3.61	4.81	5.54	5.55	5.66	6.41	6.22	6.57	6.58	6.70	6.89	7.21
7 Transport, storage and communication	0.84	1.09	1.35	1.49	1.53	1.56	1.63	1.75	1.81	1.90	1.96	2.05
8 Finance, insurance, real estate and business services	0.30	0.50	0.62	0.63	0.63	0.67	0.73	0.85	0.85	0.96	1.06	1.14
9 Community, social and personal services [a]	4.91	6.06	7.50	7.93	8.53	9.23	...	...	...	...	...	...
Total, Industries	...	...	...	...	...	...	...	...	...	...	...	...
Producers of Government Services [a]	...	...	...	...	...	...	...	...	...	...	...	...
Other Producers [a]	...	...	...	...	...	...	...	...	...	...	...	...
Subtotal	18.64	23.47	27.81	28.53	29.92	31.25	30.50	...	...	...	...	...
Less: Imputed bank service charge	0.28	0.48	0.58	0.57	0.58	0.61	0.64	0.77	0.75	0.81	1.01	1.11
Plus: Import duties	0.99	1.63	2.10	1.62	1.66	1.76	1.84	1.91	1.87	2.04	2.07	2.08
Plus: Value added tax	...	...	...	...	...	...	...	...	...	...	...	...
Equals: Gross Domestic Product	19.35	24.62	28.93	29.58	31.00	32.13	31.71	33.87	34.65	35.41	36.95	39.10

a) Items 'Other producers' and 'Producers of government services' are included in item 'Community, social and personal services'.

Morocco

1.12 Relations Among National Accounting Aggregates

Thousand Million Moroccan Dirhams

	1970	1975	1977	1978	1979	1980	1981	1982	1983	1984	1985	1986
Gross Domestic Product	20.02	36.41	49.76	55.15	62.04	70.16	76.74	90.09	94.64	105.54	119.31	134.33
Plus: Net factor income from the rest of the world	-0.32	-0.19	-0.77	-1.11	-1.46	-1.73	-3.05	-4.10	-5.00	-5.63	-7.63	-6.98
Factor income from the rest of the world	0.13	0.45	0.57	0.62	0.76	1.07	1.33	0.95	0.12	0.14	0.52	0.39
Less: Factor income to the rest of the world	0.45	0.66	1.34	1.74	2.22	2.80	4.38	5.05	5.12	5.77	8.15	7.37
Equals: Gross National Product	19.70	36.22	48.99	54.04	60.58	68.43	73.69	85.99	89.63	99.91	112.68	127.35
Less: Consumption of fixed capital	...	...	...	...	...	...	...	...	...	...	...	...
Equals: National Income [a]	19.70	36.22	48.99	54.04	60.58	68.43	73.69	85.99	89.63	99.91	112.68	127.35
Plus: Net current transfers from the rest of the world	0.36	1.64	2.16	2.50	2.89	3.27	4.24	4.57	7.05	8.24	10.19	12.95
Current transfers from the rest of the world	0.61	2.02	2.64	2.98	3.43	3.91	5.00	5.14	7.36	8.67	10.88	13.74
Less: Current transfers to the rest of the world	0.25	0.38	0.49	0.48	0.54	0.64	0.76	0.57	0.31	0.43	0.69	0.79
Equals: National Disposable Income [b]	20.06	37.86	51.15	56.54	63.47	71.70	77.93	90.57	96.68	108.14	121.87	140.32
Less: Final consumption	16.93	30.66	42.91	47.91	54.04	61.40	70.09	81.02	82.83	93.20	102.54	114.59
Equals: Net Saving [c]	3.13	7.20	8.24	8.63	9.43	10.30	7.84	9.55	13.85	14.94	19.33	25.73
Less: Surplus of the nation on current transactions	-0.57	-2.05	-7.93	-5.40	-5.77	-5.57	-9.34	-11.43	-5.91	-8.91	-8.05	-1.53
Equals: Net Capital Formation [d]	3.70	9.25	16.18	14.03	15.19	15.87	17.19	20.97	19.76	23.85	27.38	27.26

a) Item 'National income' includes consumption of fixed capital.
b) Item 'National disposable income' includes consumption of fixed capital.
c) Item 'Net saving' includes consumption of fixed capital.
d) Item 'Net capital formation' includes consumption of fixed capital.

2.17 Exports and Imports of Goods and Services, Detail

Thousand Million Moroccan Dirhams

	1970	1975	1977	1978	1979	1980	1981	1982	1983	1984	1985	1986
Exports of Goods and Services												
1 Exports of merchandise, f.o.b.												
2 Transport and communication	2.46	6.94	5.93	6.26	7.62	9.64	12.00	12.47	14.76	19.12	21.75	22.25
3 Insurance service charges												
4 Other commodities	0.41	0.31	1.42	1.44	1.54	...	...	...	...	...	...	...
5 Adjustments of merchandise exports to change-of-ownership basis	...	...	...	...	...	...	...	...	...	...	...	...
6 Direct purchases in the domestic market by non-residential households [a]	0.67	1.18	1.48	1.65	1.67	...	...	...	...	...	...	...
7 Direct purchases in the domestic market by extraterritorial bodies	...	...	...	...	...	...	...	...	...	...	...	...
Total Exports of Goods and Services	3.54	8.43	8.83	9.35	10.83	13.23	16.29	18.52	21.15	26.90	32.20	32.91
Imports of Goods and Services												
1 Imports of merchandise, c.i.f.												
A Imports of merchandise, f.o.b.	3.47	11.05	17.10	15.10	16.96	18.48	24.67	27.63	26.50	35.29	39.57	36.61
B Transport of services on merchandise imports												
C Insurance service charges on merchandise imports												
2 Adjustments of merchandise imports to change-of-ownership basis	...	...	...	...	...	...	...	...	...	...	...	...
3 Other transport and communication	...	...	...	...	...	...	...	...	...	...	...	...
4 Other insurance service charges	...	...	...	...	...	...	...	...	...	...	...	...
5 Other commodities	0.68	0.88	1.06	1.04	1.05	...	...	...	...	...	...	...
6 Direct purchases abroad by government	...	...	...	...	...	...	...	...	...	...	...	...
7 Direct purchases abroad by resident households	...	...	...	...	...	...	...	...	...	...	...	...
Total Imports of Goods and Services	4.15	11.93	18.16	16.14	18.02	20.34	26.83	30.43	29.10	38.41	42.81	40.42
Balance of Goods and Services	-0.61	-3.50	-9.33	-6.79	-7.19	-7.11	-10.54	-11.91	-7.95	-11.51	-10.61	-7.51
Total Imports and Balance of Goods and Services	3.54	8.43	8.83	9.35	10.83	13.23	16.29	18.52	21.15	26.90	32.20	32.91

a) Item 'Direct purchases in the domestic market by non-resident households' refers to foreign tourists and agencies.

Mozambique

Source. The estimates are published by the Direccao Nacional de Estatistica in 'Infermacao Estadistica'.

General note. The estimates shown in the following tables have been prepared in accordance with the United Nations System of National Accounts so far as the existing data would permit.

1.1 Expenditure on the Gross Domestic Product, in Current Prices

Thousand Million Mozambique Meticais

	1970	1975	1977	1978	1979	1980	1981	1982	1983	1984	1985	1986
1 Government final consumption expenditure	...	...	...	...	...	14	17	19	21	22	24	...
2 Private final consumption expenditure	...	...	...	...	...	64	65	77	80	93	127	...
3 Gross capital formation	...	...	...	...	...	15	16	18	9	11	10	...
4 Exports of goods and services	...	...	...	...	...	-14	-16	-21	-19	-18	-15	...
5 Less: Imports of goods and services	...	...	...	...	...							...
Equals: Gross Domestic Product	...	...	...	...	...	78	82	92	91	109	147	...

1.3 Cost Components of the Gross Domestic Product

Thousand Million Mozambique Meticais

	1970	1975	1977	1978	1979	1980	1981	1982	1983	1984	1985	1986
1 Indirect taxes, net	...	...	...	...	...	8	8	8	8	9	6	...
A Indirect taxes	...	...	...	...	...	8	9	9	9	10	7	...
B Less: Subsidies	...	...	...	...	...	-	1	1	1	1	1	...
2 Consumption of fixed capital	...	...	...	...	...	5	5	5	4	4	4	...
3 Compensation of employees paid by resident producers to:	...	...	...	...	...	65	69	79	79	96	137	...
4 Operating surplus	...	...	...	...	...							...
Equals: Gross Domestic Product	...	...	...	...	...	78	82	92	91	100	147	...

1.12 Relations Among National Accounting Aggregates

Thousand Million Mozambique Meticais

	1970	1975	1977	1978	1979	1980	1981	1982	1983	1984	1985	1986
Gross Domestic Product	...	...	...	...	...	78	82	92	91	109	147	...
Plus: Net factor income from the rest of the world	...	...	...	...	...	1	-	-1	1	-	-	...
Equals: Gross National Product	...	...	...	...	...	79	81	91	92	109	147	...
Less: Consumption of fixed capital	...	...	...	...	...	5	5	5	4	4	4	...
Equals: National Income	...	...	...	...	...	74	76	86	88	105	143	...
Plus: Net current transfers from the rest of the world	...	...	...	...	...	...	...	...	...	...	...	...
Equals: National Disposable Income	...	...	...	...	...	...	...	...	...	...	...	...
Less: Final consumption	...	...	...	...	...	...	...	...	...	...	...	...
Equals: Net Saving	...	...	...	...	...	...	...	...	...	...	...	...
Less: Surplus of the nation on current transactions	...	...	...	...	...	...	...	...	...	...	...	...
Equals: Net Capital Formation	...	...	...	...	...	...	...	...	...	...	...	...

Nepal

Source. Reply to the United Nations National Accounts Questionnaire from the National Income Division, Central Bureau of Statistics, Kathmandu.
General note. The official estimates of Nepal have been prepared in accordance with the United Nations System of National Accounts so far as the existing data would permit.

1.1 Expenditure on the Gross Domestic Product, in Current Prices

Million Nepalese rupees — Fiscal year ending 15 July

	1970	1975	1977	1978	1979	1980	1981	1982	1983	1984	1985	1986
1 Government final consumption expenditure	...	1257	1260	1471	1889	1565	1922	2638	2563	3021	3647	...
2 Private final consumption expenditure	...	13652	13688	15721	17741	19195	22411	25488	28140	32432	34203	...
A Households	...	13494	13530	15567	17557	19040	22190	25333	27861	32103	33845	...
B Private non-profit institutions serving households	...	158	158	154	184	155	221	155	279	329	358	...
3 Gross capital formation	...	2402	2769	3507	3514	4270	4808	5098	6799	7402	8636	...
A Increase in stocks	...	179	188	213	251	589	509	-151	52	444	488	...
B Gross fixed capital formation	...	2223	2581	3294	3263	3681	4299	5249	6747	6958	8148	...
Residential buildings	...	...	671	803	875	1021	1203	...	...	...	...	...
Non-residential buildings	...	...	1163	1626	1713	1765	2140	...	...	...	...	...
Other construction and land improvement etc.	...	...						...	...	...	...	...
Other	...	...	747	865	675	895	956	...	...	...	...	...
4 Exports of goods and services	...	1475	2037	2086	2618	2695	3523	3592	3455	4196	5371	...
5 Less: Imports of goods and services	...	2215	2474	3053	3547	4374	5357	5828	7196	7661	9318	...
Equals: Gross Domestic Product	...	16571	17280	19732	22215	23351	27307	30988	33761	39390	42539	...

1.3 Cost Components of the Gross Domestic Product

Million Nepalese rupees — Fiscal year ending 15 July

	1970	1975	1977	1978	1979	1980	1981	1982	1983	1984	1985	1986
1 Indirect taxes, net	...	635	1025	1306	1436	1465	1841	1951	2117	2386	2890	...
2 Consumption of fixed capital	...	698	767	959	1088	1091	1283	1427	1583	1748	1960	...
3 Compensation of employees paid by resident producers to:	...	9944	10121	11433	12069	13251	16328	16665	18603	...	...	...
4 Operating surplus	...	5294	5367	6034	7622	7544	7855	10945	11458	...	...	...
Equals: Gross Domestic Product	...	16571	17280	19732	22215	23351	27307	30988	33761	39390	42539	...

1.4 General Government Current Receipts and Disbursements

Million Nepalese rupees — Fiscal year ending 15 July

	1970	1975	1977	1978	1979	1980	1981	1982	1983	1984	1985	1986
Receipts												
1 Operating surplus	...	...	...	...	...	...	...	...	...	...	...	...
2 Property and entrepreneurial income	...	...	...	...	...	93	...	...	...	...	...	...
3 Taxes, fees and contributions	...	...	...	...	...	2216	...	...	...	...	...	...
A Indirect taxes	...	...	...	...	...	1465	...	...	...	...	...	...
B Direct taxes	...	...	...	...	...	115	...	...	...	...	...	...
C Social security contributions	...	...	...	...	...	413	...	...	...	...	...	...
D Compulsory fees, fines and penalties	...	...	...	...	...	223	...	...	...	...	...	...
4 Other current transfers	...	...	...	...	...	319	...	...	...	...	...	...
Total Current Receipts of General Government	...	...	...	...	...	2628	...	...	...	...	...	...
Disbursements												
1 Government final consumption expenditure	...	...	...	...	...	1565	...	...	...	...	...	...
A Compensation of employees	...	...	...	...	...	867	...	...	...	...	...	...
B Consumption of fixed capital	...	...	...	...	...	...	...	...	...	...	...	...
C Purchases of goods and services, net	...	...	...	...	...	699	...	...	...	...	...	...
D Less: Own account fixed capital formation	...	...	...	...	...	...	...	...	...	...	...	...
E Indirect taxes paid, net	...	...	...	...	...	...	...	...	...	...	...	...
2 Property income	...	...	...	...	...	...	...	...	...	...	...	...
3 Subsidies	...	...	...	...	...	5	...	...	...	...	...	...
4 Other current transfers	...	...	...	...	...	67	...	...	...	...	...	...
5 Net saving	...	...	...	...	...	991	...	...	...	...	...	...
Total Current Disbursements and Net Saving of General Government	...	...	...	...	...	2628	...	...	...	...	...	...

Nepal

1.7 External Transactions on Current Account, Summary

Million Nepalese rupees — Fiscal year ending 15 July

	1970	1975	1977	1978	1979	1980	1981	1982	1983	1984	1985	1986
Payments to the Rest of the World												
1 Imports of goods and services	...	2215	2474	3053	3547	4374	5357	5828	7196	7661	9318	...
A Imports of merchandise c.i.f.	...	1815	2045	2516	2912	3569	4443	4948	6333	6534	7825	...
B Other	...	400	429	537	635	805	914	880	863	1127	1493	...
2 Factor income to the rest of the world	...	46	33	29	38	53	57	59	56	84	124	...
3 Current transfers to the rest of the world	...	-	-	-	-	-	-	-	-	-	-	...
4 Surplus of the nation on current transactions	...	-119	254	-291	40	-341	-296	-393	-1670	-1384	-1850	...
Payments to the Rest of the World and Surplus of the Nation on Current Transactions	...	2142	2761	2791	3625	4086	5118	5494	5582	6361	7592	...
Receipts From The Rest of the World												
1 Exports of goods and services	...	1475	2037	2086	2618	2695	3523	3592	3455	4196	5371	...
A Exports of merchandise f.o.b.	...	890	1189	1065	1304	1166	1613	1496	1136	1710	2765	...
B Other	...	585	848	1021	1314	1529	1910	2096	2319	2486	2608	...
2 Factor income from rest of the world	...	313	352	320	428	547	644	674	753	709	784	...
3 Current transfers from rest of the world	...	354	372	385	579	844	951	1228	1374	1456	1437	...
Receipts from the Rest of the World on Current Transactions	...	2142	2761	2791	3625	4086	5118	5494	5582	6361	7592	...

1.10 Gross Domestic Product by Kind of Activity, in Current Prices

Million Nepalese rupees — Fiscal year ending 15 July

	1970	1975	1977	1978	1979	1980	1981	1982	1983	1984	1985	1986
1 Agriculture, hunting, forestry and fishing	5922	9949 / 11435	10389	11616	13365	13520	15510	17715	19082	22570	24366	29603
2 Mining and quarrying	4	3 / 22	26	25	34	42	58	66	85	111	117	139
3 Manufacturing [a]	787	1458 / 664	736	794	848	936	1049	1243	1460	1816	1923	2271
4 Electricity, gas and water	18	34 / 34	39	42	48	60	67	82	127	158	167	197
5 Construction	192	172 / 583	1020	1338	1559	1570	1974	2342	2377	2576	2728	3223
6 Wholesale and retail trade, restaurants and hotels	363	738 / 540	636	707	724	889	953	1068	1199	1520	1609	1901
7 Transport, storage and communication	192	453 / 690	852	1093	1248	1541	1889	1992	2129	2468	2613	3087
8 Finance, insurance, real estate and business services	857	1119 / 1095	1412	1534	1613	1833	2077	2366	2594	2937	3110	3674
9 Community, social and personal services [b]	256	544 / 873	1145	1277	1340	1495	1889	2163	2591	2848	3016	3562
Total, Industries	8591	14470 / 15936	16255	18426	20779	21886	25466	29037	31644	37004	39649	47657
Producers of Government Services [b]	177	332 / ...	...	...	...	...	...	...	...	...	...	...
Other Producers [b]	...	... / ...	...	...	...	...	...	...	...	...	...	...
Subtotal [c]	8768	14802 / 15936	16255	18426	20779	21886	25466	29037	31644	37004	39649	47657
Less: Imputed bank service charge	...	... / ...	...	...	...	...	...	...	...	...	...	...
Plus: Import duties	...	... / ...	...	...	...	...	...	...	...	...	...	...
Plus: Value added tax	...	... / ...	...	...	...	...	...	...	...	...	...	...
Plus: Other adjustments [d]	...	... / 635	1025	1306	1436	1465	1841	1951	2117	2386	2890	3421
Equals: Gross Domestic Product	8768	14802 / 16571	17280	19732	22215	23351	27307	30988	33761	39390	42539	51078

a) Item 'Manufacturing' includes cottage industries.
b) Items 'Other producers' and 'Producers of government services' are included in item 'Community, social and personal services'.
c) Gross domestic product in factor values.
d) Item 'Other adjustments' refers to indirect taxes net of subsidies.

Nepal

1.11 Gross Domestic Product by Kind of Activity, in Constant Prices

Million Nepalese rupees — Fiscal year ending 15 July

	1970	1975	1977	1978	1979	1980	1981	1982	1983	1984	1985	1986
		1965			At constant prices of:		1975					
1 Agriculture, hunting, forestry and fishing	5922	4530 / 11550	11141	11141	11480	10933	12066	12616	12478	13668	13990	14608
2 Mining and quarrying	...	...	...	...	...	...	...	...	...	...	...	...
3 Manufacturing	...	...	...	...	...	...	...	...	...	...	...	...
4 Electricity, gas and water	...	...	...	...	...	...	...	...	...	...	...	...
5 Construction	...	...	...	...	...	...	...	...	...	...	...	...
6 Wholesale and retail trade, restaurants and hotels	...	...	...	...	...	...	...	...	...	...	...	...
7 Transport, storage and communication	...	...	...	...	...	...	...	...	...	...	...	...
8 Finance, insurance, real estate and business services	...	...	...	...	...	...	...	...	...	...	...	...
9 Community, social and personal services	...	...	...	...	...	...	...	...	...	...	...	...
Total, Industries	...	...	...	...	...	...	...	...	...	...	...	...
Producers of Government Services	...	...	...	...	...	...	...	...	...	...	...	...
Other Producers	...	...	...	...	...	...	...	...	...	...	...	...
Subtotal	...	...	...	...	...	...	...	...	...	...	...	...
Less: Imputed bank service charge	...	...	...	...	...	...	...	...	...	...	...	...
Plus: Import duties	...	...	...	...	...	...	...	...	...	...	...	...
Plus: Value added tax	...	...	...	...	...	...	...	...	...	...	...	...
Equals: Gross Domestic Product	6367	6965 / 16571	17822	18607	19048	18606	20158	20920	20297	22262	22920	23848

1.12 Relations Among National Accounting Aggregates

Million Nepalese rupees — Fiscal year ending 15 July

	1970	1975	1977	1978	1979	1980	1981	1982	1983	1984	1985	1986
Gross Domestic Product	...	16571	17280	19732	22215	23351	27307	30988	33761	39390	42539	...
Plus: Net factor income from the rest of the world	...	267	319	291	390	494	587	615	697	625	660	...
Factor income from the rest of the world	...	313	352	320	428	547	644	674	753	709	784	...
Less: Factor income to the rest of the world	...	46	33	29	38	53	57	59	56	84	124	...
Equals: Gross National Product	...	16838	17599	20023	22605	23845	27894	31603	34458	40015	43199	...
Less: Consumption of fixed capital	...	698	767	959	1088	1091	1283	1427	1583	1748	1960	...
Equals: National Income	...	16140	16832	19064	21517	22754	26611	30176	32875	38267	41239	...
Plus: Net current transfers from the rest of the world	...	354	372	385	579	844	951	1228	1374	1456	1437	...
Current transfers from the rest of the world	...	354	372	385	579	844	951	1228	1374	1456	1437	...
Less: Current transfers to the rest of the world	...	-	-	-	-	-	-	-	-	-	-	...
Equals: National Disposable Income	...	16494	17204	19449	22096	23598	27562	31404	34249	39723	42676	...
Less: Final consumption	...	14909	14948	17192	19630	20760	24333	28126	30703	35453	37850	...
Equals: Net Saving	...	1585	2256	2257	2466	2838	3229	3278	3546	4270	4826	...
Less: Surplus of the nation on current transactions	...	-119	254	-291	40	-341	-296	-393	-1670	-1384	-1850	...
Equals: Net Capital Formation	...	1704	2002	2548	2426	3179	3525	3671	5216	5654	6676	...

Netherlands

General note. The preparation of national accounts statistics in the Netherlands is undertaken by the Central Bureau of Statistics, Voorburg. The official estimates together with methodological notes are published annually in 'Nationale Rekeningen' (National Accounts). The estimates are generally in accordance with the classifications and definitions recommended in the United Nations System of National Accounts (SNA). The first annual publication on input-output tables, covering the years 1948-1957, was issued in 1960. The following tables have been prepared from successive replies to the United Nations national accounts questionnaire. When the scope and coverage of the estimates differ for conceptual or statistical reasons from the definitions and classifications recommended in SNA, a footnote is indicated to the relevant tables.

Sources and methods:

(a) Gross domestic product. The main approach used to estimate GDP is the production approach.

(b) Expenditure on the gross domestic product. The expenditure approach is used to estimate government final consumption expenditure, gross fixed capital formation and exports and imports of goods and services. A combination of the commodity-flow approach and the expenditure approach is used for the estimation of private final consumption expenditure, private gross fixed capital formation and increase in stocks. The main sources for estimating general government consumption expenditure are the final accounts of the various agencies. The data sources for exports and imports of goods and services are foreign trade statistics for merchandise and balance of payments data and survey data for services. Constant prices are obtained through deflation with price indexes for all expenditure components, except government consumption expenditure referring to wages and salaries, which is extrapolated by employment data.

(c) Cost-structure of the gross domestic product. The main source for the compilation of compensation of employees is data from the social security institutions in the case of employees in enterprises and accounts data in the case of general government employees. Operating surplus is obtained as a residual within the framework of the annual input-output tables. Estimates of the consumption of fixed capital are made by the Central Bureau of Statistics, based on the perpetual inventory method. Information on indirect taxes and subsidies is provided by government agencies.

(d) Gross domestic product by kind of economic activity. The table on GDP by kind of economic activity is prepared at market prices net of value added tax for which breakdown by kind of economic activity is not available. The production approach is used to estimate value added of most industries. This is done within the framework of detailed input-output tables using the commodity-flow approach. The income approach is used to estimate value added of producers of government services, business services and most community, social and personal services. For the agricultural sector, the main sources of information are the annual surveys of crop production and unpublished reports of statutory trade offices. Data on the structure of production costs are provided by annual farm management surveys. Statistics on sales of horticulture produce in special markets are also available. Net increase of livestock is evaluated on the basis of frequent samples, and on average annual prices per category. Regarding crude petroleum and natural gas production the information base consists of data supplied by all individual enterprises. The information base for manufacturing consists mainly of an annual survey of all enterprises with more than 10 employees. Recent bench-mark information is given by a census of establishments conducted for 1978. The census covers all establishments and collects information on kind of economic activity and employment. For the private construction sector, annual production surveys are available. For general government, data are available on the capital expenditure. The production of buildings is covered by quarterly progress reports from the municipalities. The production value is estimated on the basis of the production of work completed. Bench-mark data for wholesale and retail trade are available for certain years. For some parts of the trade sector annual production surveys are available. Surveys are planned to be held for other parts. Annual surveys are carried out for the transport sector. Information on railways and communications is derived directly from the few existing enterprises. Inter-urban public transportation by bus is covered by statements by government agencies. For the estimation of value added of credit institutions, the required data are collected on the basis of an annual survey. Data of insurance companies are obtained both from an annual survey and from the companies' accounts. The value of dwellings corresponds to total rents, including the imputed rents of owner-occupied houses. Cost accounts for houses are published by housing corporations. For producers of government services the main sources are the accounts of the agencies. Considerable gaps exist regarding some sub-sectors of private services. In these cases data are collected from various sources such as income tax data and social security information. For the constant price estimates, double deflation is used for agriculture and fishing. Current output quantities are valued at base-year prices where quantities are available, otherwise deflated by representative price indexes. Some input categories are valued at base year prices while others are deflated by price index. Value added of mining and quarrying, manufacturing, electricity, gas, water, transport and communication is calculated by double deflation. For trade, output at constant prices is extrapolated by quantity indicators for output, input categories are deflated by price indexes. Value added at constant prices of financing, insurance and business services is generally extrapolated by means of volume indexes of material output and factor input. For producers of government services, net value added at constant prices is extrapolated by means of a value added index based on quantity data of factor services. For private services value added is extrapolated by indexes of employment.

1.1 Expenditure on the Gross Domestic Product, in Current Prices

Million Netherlands guilders

	1970	1975	1977	1978	1979	1980	1981	1982	1983	1984	1985	1986
1 Government final consumption expenditure	18660	38250	47850	52610	57170	60260	62750	65120	66580	66390	67550	68240
2 Private final consumption expenditure	70820	128950	164310	179170	192430	205780	213230	221830	229860	236750	247230	255210
3 Gross capital formation	33810	45380	59430	65120	67990	72510	64490	66140	70020	76300	81300	88780
A Increase in stocks	2450	-940	1540	1820	1500	1720	-3090	-1020	560	1990	2350	4610
B Gross fixed capital formation	31360	46320	57890	63300	66490	70790	67580	67160	69460	74310	78950	84170
Residential buildings	7240	11690	16140	17730	18280	20840	20130	19540	19470	20400	19410	20100
Non-residential buildings	6520	8700	10940	12460	13740	15120	13710	12900	11960	12310	11970	13150
Other construction and land improvement etc.	4380	6470	6840	7240	7240	8030	8010	7630	7360	7960	7750	7370
Other	13220	19460	23970	25870	27230	26800	25730	27090	30670	33640	39820	43550
4 Exports of goods and services	54300	109720	130740	133340	155060	176810	204620	212600	210770	240500	266200	231990
5 Less: Imports of goods and services	56410	102340	127400	133230	156690	178620	192240	196830	205210	227750	245690	214650
Equals: Gross Domestic Product	121180	219960	274930	297010	316960	336740	352050	368800	381020	400250	416590	429570

1.2 Expenditure on the Gross Domestic Product, in Constant Prices

Million Netherlands guilders

	1970	1975	1977	1978	1979	1980	1981	1982	1983	1984	1985	1986
	\multicolumn{12}{c}{At constant prices of: 1980}
1 Government final consumption expenditure	46180	52100	56080	58260	59920	60260	61460	61860	62630	62260	63070	64200
2 Private final consumption expenditure	145980	173880	191520	199810	205760	205780	200610	198260	199990	201990	205770	212090
3 Gross capital formation	72960	65030	72920	75100	73410	72510	60920	60000	62430	66420	70030	75850
A Increase in stocks	3340	-1030	2000	2390	1950	1720	-2500	-840	330	970	1180	2050
B Gross fixed capital formation	69620	66060	70920	72710	71460	70790	63420	60840	62100	65450	68850	73800
Residential buildings	18890	17900	20640	20950	19910	20840	18840	17790	17720	18510	17850	18470
Non-residential buildings	16260	13370	14110	14750	14990	15120	12920	11910	11070	11340	11100	12170
Other construction and land improvement etc.	11220	9960	8830	8590	7910	8030	7540	6990	6670	7040	6700	6430
Other	23250	24830	27340	28420	28650	26800	24120	24150	26640	28560	33200	36730
4 Exports of goods and services	107320	145450	156990	162170	174180	176810	179540	179510	185820	199560	210410	211820
5 Less: Imports of goods and services	119670	140510	159200	169210	179410	178620	168160	169970	176580	185380	196400	202770
Equals: Gross Domestic Product	252770	295950	318310	326130	333860	336740	334370	329660	334290	344850	352880	361190

Netherlands

1.3 Cost Components of the Gross Domestic Product

Million Netherlands guilders

	1970	1975	1977	1978	1979	1980	1981	1982	1983	1984	1985	1986
1 Indirect taxes, net	11550	20210	26730	29300	29800	32020	32900	32700	33920	35380	36930	40190
A Indirect taxes	13600	24140	33600	37000	38580	41120	41720	42760	45140	47990	50690	53670
B Less: Subsidies	2050	3930	6870	7700	8780	9100	8820	10060	11220	12610	13760	13480
2 Consumption of fixed capital	10260	20010	24240	26670	29290	32490	35620	37860	39190	41190	42760	43720
3 Compensation of employees paid by resident producers to:	67170	131170	159540	172770	185920	197840	201530	207480	209640	210000	216120	223850
A Resident households	66780	130510	158850	172020	185120	196930	200520	206340	208520	208880	214900	222640
B Rest of the world	390	660	690	750	800	910	1010	1140	1120	1120	1220	1210
4 Operating surplus	32200	48570	64420	68270	70950	74390	82800	90820	98270	113680	120780	121810
A Corporate and quasi-corporate enterprises	32200	48570	64420	68270	70950	74390	82800	90820	98270	113680	120780	121810
B Private unincorporated enterprises												
C General government	...	...	...	...	...	...	...	...	...	...	...	...
Equals: Gross Domestic Product	121180	219960	274930	297010	315960	336740	352850	368860	381020	400250	416590	429570

1.4 General Government Current Receipts and Disbursements

Million Netherlands guilders

	1970	1975	1977	1978	1979	1980	1981	1982	1983	1984	1985	1986
Receipts												
1 Operating surplus	...	...	...	...	...	...	...	...	...	...	...	...
2 Property and entrepreneurial income	2960	8690	13840	14230	16710	20000	25290	26950	28170	32530	35780	30250
3 Taxes, fees and contributions	46580	96520	120940	132680	141130	153570	159040	167330	178160	179390	186820	191940
A Indirect taxes	13590	22550	31080	34570	35040	37450	37990	38710	41000	43400	45680	48040
B Direct taxes	15810	34530	41860	45500	48500	53500	53280	54290	51890	51030	52880	57620
C Social security contributions	16760	38530	46860	51420	56310	61220	66140	72490	83300	82860	85950	83940
D Compulsory fees, fines and penalties	420	910	1140	1190	1280	1400	1630	1840	1970	2100	2310	2340
4 Other current transfers	1360	3100	4000	4210	4660	4270	4300	4320	4220	4440	4470	4580
Total Current Receipts of General Government	50900	108310	138780	151120	162500	177840	188630	198600	210550	216360	227070	226770
Disbursements												
1 Government final consumption expenditure	18660	38250	47850	52610	57170	60260	62750	65120	66580	66390	67550	68240
A Compensation of employees	13510	28880	35970	39140	41980	44080	45020	46720	46950	46410	46810	47100
B Consumption of fixed capital	800	1600	1820	2080	2150	2400	2560	2420	2300	2620	2720	2730
C Purchases of goods and services, net	4520	8080	10350	11640	13300	14000	15390	16170	17490	17580	18200	18490
D Less: Own account fixed capital formation	210	460	530	550	560	580	580	570	560	640	630	540
E Indirect taxes paid, net	40	150	240	300	300	360	360	380	400	420	450	460
2 Property income	4160	8250	10620	11850	13260	15660	19340	23180	26500	29860	32150	32610
A Interest	4160	8250	10620	11850	13260	15660	19340	23180	26500	29860	32150	32610
B Net land rent and royalties	...	...	...	...	...	...	...	...	...	...	...	...
3 Subsidies	1570	2140	3690	4070	4240	4980	5520	6220	6710	7410	8110	7710
4 Other current transfers	21930	55580	71850	80680	87300	94260	102730	112860	118420	119370	121570	123420
A Social security benefits	16760	39960	51950	58730	64720	70920	75690	80610	81400	81570	83250	84590
B Social assistance grants	2410	7770	10170	10660	11590	12700	15600	20490	24730	24870	22510	22560
C Other	2760	7850	9730	11290	10990	10640	11440	11760	12290	12930	15810	16270
5 Net saving	4580	4090	4770	1910	530	2680	-1710	-8780	-7660	-6670	-2310	-5210
Total Current Disbursements and Net Saving of General Government	50900	108310	138780	151120	162500	177840	188630	198600	210550	216360	227070	226770

Netherlands

1.5 Current Income and Outlay of Corporate and Quasi-Corporate Enterprises, Summary

Million Netherlands guilders

	1970	1975	1977	1978	1979	1980	1981	1982	1983	1984	1985	1986
Receipts												
1 Operating surplus	32200	48570	64420	68270	70950	74390	82800	90820	98270	113680	120780	121810
2 Property and entrepreneurial income received [a]	11210	32540	39950	46530	58440	73520	89240	93600	91000	97200	102150	100020
3 Current transfers	3590	6810	9450	10290	11020	11540	12840	12710	13210	13600	14270	14590
Total Current Receipts	47000	87920	113820	125090	140410	159450	184880	197130	202480	224480	237200	236420
Disbursements												
1 Property and entrepreneurial income [a]	34270	69300	87560	98510	113120	132540	154080	165560	165370	179920	188290	185270
2 Direct taxes and other current payments to general government	3050	7410	8180	8300	8260	10170	11100	11340	10850	10300	13060	14370
3 Other current transfers	3590	6810	9450	10290	11020	11540	12840	12710	13210	13600	14270	14590
4 Net saving	6090	4400	8630	7990	8010	5200	6860	7520	13050	20660	21580	22190
Total Current Disbursements and Net Saving	47000	87920	113820	125090	140410	159450	184880	197130	202480	224480	237200	236420

a) For the period 1970-1976, property and entrepreneurial income paid by non-financial corporate and quasi-corporate enterprises is net of property income received.

1.6 Current Income and Outlay of Households and Non-Profit Institutions

Million Netherlands guilders

	1970	1975	1977	1978	1979	1980	1981	1982	1983	1984	1985	1986
Receipts												
1 Compensation of employees	67200	131260	159690	172850	186020	197960	201640	207690	209810	210150	216200	223830
A From resident producers	66780	130510	158850	172020	185120	196930	200520	206340	208520	208880	214900	222640
B From rest of the world	420	750	840	830	900	1030	1120	1350	1290	1270	1300	1190
2 Operating surplus of private unincorporated enterprises	...	...	...	...	...	...	...	...	...	...	...	...
3 Property and entrepreneurial income [a]	24790	36210	45760	50160	52070	55850	59890	69490	74830	81100	85600	89040
4 Current transfers	23400	57780	75190	83670	91890	98960	107570	117480	123270	123920	126240	127860
A Social security benefits	16660	39750	51630	58310	64230	70370	75100	79900	80730	80870	82520	83790
B Social assistance grants	2450	7870	10280	10770	11700	12820	15710	20600	24840	25010	22640	22680
C Other	4290	10160	13280	14590	15960	15770	16760	16980	17700	18040	21080	21390
Total Current Receipts	115390	225250	280640	306680	329980	352770	369100	394660	407910	415170	428040	440730
Disbursements												
1 Private final consumption expenditure	70820	128950	164310	179170	192430	205780	213230	221830	229860	236750	247230	255210
2 Property income [a]	...	...	1030	1320	1670	1910	2070	1890	1740	1700	1740	1790
3 Direct taxes and other current transfers n.e.c. to general government	29940	66560	81680	89810	97830	105950	109950	117280	126310	125690	128080	129530
A Social security contributions	16760	38530	46860	51420	56310	61220	66140	72490	83300	82860	85950	83940
B Direct taxes	12760	27120	33680	37200	40240	43330	42180	42950	41040	40730	39820	43250
C Fees, fines and penalties	420	910	1140	1190	1280	1400	1630	1840	1970	2100	2310	2340
4 Other current transfers	3450	7370	9690	10520	11760	11800	12070	12480	12700	13280	13770	13950
5 Net saving	11180	22370	23930	25850	26290	27240	31480	41180	37300	37750	37220	40250
Total Current Disbursements and Net Saving	115390	225250	280640	306680	329980	352770	369100	394660	407910	415170	428040	440730

a) For 1970-1976, property income received is net of property income paid.

1.7 External Transactions on Current Account, Summary

Million Netherlands guilders

	1970	1975	1977	1978	1979	1980	1981	1982	1983	1984	1985	1986
Payments to the Rest of the World												
1 Imports of goods and services	56410	102340	127400	133230	156690	178620	192240	196830	205210	227750	245690	214650
A Imports of merchandise c.i.f.	49140	90890	111700	115680	137550	156120	168420	171710	179580	200240	216520	184860
B Other	7270	11450	15700	17550	19140	22500	23820	25120	25630	27510	29170	29790
2 Factor income to the rest of the world	4180	8990	9750	11610	15730	22710	31090	32400	27810	31370	31060	28490
A Compensation of employees	390	660	690	750	800	910	1010	1140	1120	1120	1220	1210
B Property and entrepreneurial income	3790	8330	9060	10860	14930	21800	30080	31260	26690	30250	29840	27280
By general government	...	...	...	...	...	...	...	...	...	...	...	...
By corporate and quasi-corporate enterprises	3790	8330	9060	10860	14930	21800	30080	31260	26690	30250	29840	27280

Netherlands

1.7 External Transactions on Current Account, Summary
(Continued)

Million Netherlands guilders

	1970	1975	1977	1978	1979	1980	1981	1982	1983	1984	1985	1986
By other	...	...	...	...	...	...	...	...	...	...	...	...
3 Current transfers to the rest of the world	890	4320	5650	6640	7120	7690	8170	8770	8900	10100	10980	11830
A Indirect taxes to supranational organizations	10	1590	2520	2430	3540	3670	3730	4050	4140	4590	5010	5630
B Other current transfers	880	2730	3130	4210	3580	4020	4440	4720	4760	5510	5970	6200
4 Surplus of the nation on current transactions	-1700	5490	2140	-2700	-3870	-4900	7760	11640	11860	16630	17950	12170
Payments to the Rest of the World and Surplus of the Nation on Current Transactions	59780	121140	144940	148780	175670	204120	239260	249640	253780	285850	305680	267140

Receipts From The Rest of the World

	1970	1975	1977	1978	1979	1980	1981	1982	1983	1984	1985	1986
1 Exports of goods and services	54300	109720	130740	133340	155060	176810	204620	212600	219770	248560	266200	231990
A Exports of merchandise f.o.b.	43010	88960	106530	107460	128460	147080	171330	177620	185010	210630	226190	194190
B Other	11290	20760	24210	25880	26600	29730	33290	34980	34760	37930	40010	37800
2 Factor income from rest of the world	4740	8970	10240	10930	15000	22090	30130	32020	28370	30870	32490	28110
A Compensation of employees	420	750	840	830	900	1030	1120	1350	1290	1270	1300	1190
B Property and entrepreneurial income	4320	8220	9400	10100	14100	21060	29010	30670	27080	29600	31190	26920
By general government	...	50	60	60	40	40	110	100	80	70	130	60
By corporate and quasi-corporate enterprises	...	7710	8700	9310	13240	20100	27830	29140	25470	27940	29470	25290
By other	...	460	640	730	820	920	1070	1430	1530	1590	1590	1570
3 Current transfers from rest of the world	740	2450	3960	4510	5610	5220	4510	5020	5640	6420	6990	7040
A Subsidies from supranational organisations	480	1790	3180	3630	4540	4120	3300	3840	4510	5200	5650	5770
B Other current transfers	260	660	780	880	1070	1100	1210	1180	1130	1220	1340	1270
Receipts from the Rest of the World on Current Transactions	59780	121140	144940	148780	175670	204120	239260	249640	253780	285850	305680	267140

1.8 Capital Transactions of The Nation, Summary

Million Netherlands guilders

	1970	1975	1977	1978	1979	1980	1981	1982	1983	1984	1985	1986

Finance of Gross Capital Formation

	1970	1975	1977	1978	1979	1980	1981	1982	1983	1984	1985	1986
Gross saving	32110	50870	61570	62420	64120	67610	72250	77780	81880	92930	99250	100950
1 Consumption of fixed capital	10260	20010	24240	26670	29290	32490	35620	37860	39190	41190	42760	43720
A General government	800	1600	1820	2080	2150	2400	2560	2420	2300	2620	2720	2730
B Corporate and quasi-corporate enterprises [a]	9460	18410	22420	24590	27140	30090	33060	35440	36890	38570	40040	40990
C Other [a]	...	...	...	...	...	...	...	...	...	...	...	...
2 Net saving	21850	30860	37330	35750	34830	35120	36630	39920	42690	51740	56490	57230
A General government	4580	4090	4770	1910	530	2680	-1710	-8780	-7660	-6670	-2310	-5210
B Corporate and quasi-corporate enterprises	6090	4400	8630	7990	8010	5200	6860	7520	13050	20660	21580	22190
C Other	11180	22370	23930	25850	26290	27240	31480	41180	37300	37750	37220	40250
Less: Surplus of the nation on current transactions	-1700	5490	2140	-2700	-3870	-4900	7760	11640	11860	16630	17950	12170
Finance of Gross Capital Formation	33810	45380	59430	65120	67990	72510	64490	66140	70020	76300	81300	88780

Gross Capital Formation

	1970	1975	1977	1978	1979	1980	1981	1982	1983	1984	1985	1986
Increase in stocks	2450	-940	1540	1820	1500	1720	-3090	-1020	560	1990	2350	4610
Gross fixed capital formation	31360	46320	57890	63300	66490	70790	67580	67160	69460	74310	78950	84170
1 General government	5670	8640	9280	9640	9800	10970	11100	10620	10190	11190	10520	9550
2 Corporate and quasi-corporate enterprises [a]	25690	37680	48610	53660	56690	59820	56480	56540	59270	63120	68430	74620
3 Other [a]	...	...	...	...	...	...	...	...	...	...	...	...
Gross Capital Formation	33810	45380	59430	65120	67990	72510	64490	66140	70020	76300	81300	88780

a) Item 'Other' is included in item 'Corporate and quasi-corporate enterprises'.

Netherlands

1.9 Gross Domestic Product by Institutional Sectors of Origin

Million Netherlands guilders

	1970	1975	1977	1978	1979	1980	1981	1982	1983	1984	1985	1986
	\multicolumn{12}{c}{Domestic Factor Incomes Originating}
1 General government	13510	28880	35970	39140	41980	44080	45020	46720	46950	46410	46810	47100
2 Corporate and quasi-corporate enterprises [a]	85860	150860	187990	201900	214890	228150	239310	251580	260960	277270	290090	298560
A Non-financial	84770	149260	185500	198910	211610	224630	236070	248570	257900	273950	286740	295000
B Financial	1090	1600	2490	2990	3280	3520	3240	3010	3060	3320	3350	3560
3 Households and private unincorporated enterprises [a]	...	...	...	...	...	...	...	...	...	...	...	...
4 Non-profit institutions serving households [a]	...	...	...	...	...	...	...	...	...	...	...	...
Subtotal: Domestic Factor Incomes	99370	179740	223960	241040	256870	272230	284330	298300	307910	323680	336900	345660
Indirect taxes, net	11550	20210	26730	29300	29800	32020	32900	32700	33920	35380	36930	40190
A Indirect taxes	13600	24140	33600	37000	38580	41120	41720	42760	45140	47990	50690	53670
B Less: Subsidies	2050	3930	6870	7700	8780	9100	8820	10060	11220	12610	13760	13480
Consumption of fixed capital	10260	20010	24240	26670	29290	32490	35620	37860	39190	41190	42760	43720
Gross Domestic Product	121180	219960	274930	297010	315960	336740	352850	368860	381020	400250	416590	429570

a) The estimates of Households and private unincorporated enterprises and Non-profit institutions serving households are included in item 'Corporate and quasi corporate enterprises'.

1.10 Gross Domestic Product by Kind of Activity, in Current Prices

Million Netherlands guilders

	1970	1975	1977	1978	1979	1980	1981	1982	1983	1984	1985	1986
1 Agriculture, hunting, forestry and fishing	6696	9752	11416	11772	11330	11676	14557	15932	16124	17259	17170	18590
2 Mining and quarrying	1897	8883	13035	12555	14545	19151	25563	25972	27328	31091	35340	23840
3 Manufacturing [a]	31320	48234	55060	57952	60084	60365	59780	64670	67463	72569	74410	85080
4 Electricity, gas and water	2608	4908	6195	6509	6639	7172	7606	8159	8412	8367	8560	9330
5 Construction	9380	14936	18328	20690	21508	23760	23056	22444	21413	21357	20780	21640
6 Wholesale and retail trade, restaurants and hotels [b]	17238	29617	36584	39614	42106	43437	44575	47051	48461	51175	53330	55380
7 Transport, storage and communication	8768	14186	17719	18740	20271	21298	22265	22395	23152	24590	26710	27050
8 Finance, insurance, real estate and business services	11593	24881	34024	38962	43251	46893	50314	54273	60108	63012	65830	69340
9 Community, social and personal services [ab]	10247	22839	28809	31976	34656	37528	39452	41626	42776	43278	44060	46170
Statistical discrepancy	13	-6	...	-10	...	...	12	8	13	12	...	...
Total, Industries	99760	178230	221170	238760	254390	271280	287180	302530	315250	332710	346190	356420
Producers of Government Services	14350	30630	38030	41520	44430	46840	47940	49520	49650	49450	49980	50290
Other Producers	500	750	900	990	1020	1050	1060	1090	1070	1090	1110	1140
Subtotal	114610	209610	260100	281270	299840	319170	336180	353140	365970	383250	397280	407850
Less: Imputed bank service charge	2340	6360	8130	9310	10590	11460	12660	14080	16150	16420	16770	16880
Plus: Import duties	1820	2920	3690	3800	4300	4440	4220	4580	4770	5130	5670	6330
Plus: Value added tax	7090	13790	19270	21250	22410	24590	25110	25220	26430	28290	30410	32270
Equals: Gross Domestic Product	121180	219960	274930	297010	315960	336740	352850	368860	381020	400250	416590	429570

a) Item 'Manufacturing' includes manufacture of medical, surgical and dental equipment.
b) Repair services are included in item 'Community, social and personal services'.

1.11 Gross Domestic Product by Kind of Activity, in Constant Prices

Million Netherlands guilders

	1970	1975	1977	1978	1979	1980	1981	1982	1983	1984	1985	1986
	\multicolumn{12}{c}{At constant prices of: 1980}
1 Agriculture, hunting, forestry and fishing	7930	9670	10160	10910	11370	11680	13290	14270	14740	15650	15330	16900
2 Mining and quarrying												
3 Manufacturing [a]	62900	79900	85180	85410	87750	86680	85070	90090	83080	87140	90380	90490
4 Electricity, gas and water												
5 Construction	26560	25460	25060	24860	23460	23760	21860	20730	20110	20730	20720	20960
6 Wholesale and retail trade, restaurants and hotels [b]												
7 Transport, storage and communication	103320	123080	134950	140630	146470	149160	149610	150090	151720	157430	161480	166720
8 Finance, insurance, real estate and business services												
9 Community, social and personal services [ab]												

Netherlands

1.11 Gross Domestic Product by Kind of Activity, in Constant Prices
(Continued)

Million Netherlands guilders

	1970	1975	1977	1978	1979	1980	1981	1982	1983	1984	1985	1986
					At constant prices of:1980							
Total, Industries	200790	238110	255350	261810	269050	271280	260830	266070	270550	280950	287910	295070
Producers of Government Services	36500	41480	44210	45280	46050	46840	47680	47820	47690	47760	48220	48350
Other Producers	1230	1040	1070	1070	1060	1050	1030	1000	980	990	990	990
Subtotal	238520	280630	300630	308160	316160	319170	318540	314890	319220	329700	337120	344410
Less: Imputed bank service charge	5960	9200	9700	10460	11250	11460	11910	12380	12360	12330	12520	12850
Plus: Import duties	3360	3690	4120	4270	4490	4440	4250	4400	4550	4380	5010	5580
Plus: Value added tax	16850	20830	23260	24160	24460	24590	23490	22750	22880	23100	23270	24050
Equals: Gross Domestic Product	252770	295950	318310	326130	333860	336740	334370	329660	334290	344850	352880	361190

a) Item 'Manufacturing' includes manufacture of medical, surgical and dental equipment.
b) Repair services are included in item 'Community, social and personal services'.

1.12 Relations Among National Accounting Aggregates

Million Netherlands guilders

	1970	1975	1977	1978	1979	1980	1981	1982	1983	1984	1985	1986
Gross Domestic Product	121180	219960	274930	297010	315960	336740	352850	368860	381020	400250	416590	429570
Plus: Net factor income from the rest of the world	560	-20	490	-680	-730	-620	-960	-380	560	-500	1430	-380
Factor income from the rest of the world	4740	8970	10240	10930	15000	22090	30130	32020	28370	30870	32490	28110
Less: Factor income to the rest of the world	4180	8990	9750	11610	15730	22710	31090	32400	27810	31370	31060	28490
Equals: Gross National Product	121740	219940	275420	296330	315230	336120	351890	368480	381580	399750	418020	429190
Less: Consumption of fixed capital	10260	20010	24240	26670	29290	32490	35620	37860	39190	41190	42760	43720
Equals: National Income	111480	199930	251180	269660	285940	303630	316270	330620	342390	358560	375260	385470
Plus: Net current transfers from the rest of the world	-150	-1870	-1690	-2130	-1510	-2470	-3660	-3750	-3260	-3680	-3990	-4790
Current transfers from the rest of the world	740	2450	3960	4510	5610	5220	4510	5020	5640	6420	6990	7040
Less: Current transfers to the rest of the world	890	4320	5650	6640	7120	7690	8170	8770	8900	10100	10980	11830
Equals: National Disposable Income	111330	198060	249490	267530	284430	301160	312610	326870	339130	354880	371270	380680
Less: Final consumption	89480	167200	212160	231780	249600	266040	275980	286950	296440	303140	314780	323450
Equals: Net Saving	21850	30860	37330	35750	34830	35120	36630	39920	42690	51740	56490	57230
Less: Surplus of the nation on current transactions	-1700	5490	2140	-2700	-3870	-4900	7760	11640	11860	16630	17950	12170
Equals: Net Capital Formation	23550	25370	35190	38450	38700	40020	28870	28280	30830	35110	38540	45060

2.1 Government Final Consumption Expenditure by Function, in Current Prices

Million Netherlands guilders

	1970	1975	1977	1978	1979	1980	1981	1982	1983	1984	1985	1986
1 General public services [a]	...	...	...	...	...	...	...	...	...	...	...	...
2 Defence	3880	6460	7920	8770	9720	10170	10790	11430	12360	12230	11930	12100
3 Public order and safety	...	...	...	...	...	...	...	...	...	...	...	...
4 Education [b]	6410	14010	17220	18770	20140	21130	21650	21970	21480	21200	21570	21880
5 Health [a]	...	...	...	...	...	...	...	...	...	...	...	...
6 Social security and welfare [c]	630	1330	1730	1910	2140	2400	2650	2890	2990	3070	3140	3160
7 Housing and community amenities [a]												
8 Recreational, cultural and religious affairs	7740	16450	20980	23160	25170	26560	27660	28830	29750	29890	30910	31100
9 Economic services												
10 Other functions [a]												
Total Government Final Consumption Expenditure	18660	38250	47850	52610	57170	60260	62750	65120	66580	66390	67550	68240

a) Items 'General public service' and 'Health' are included in items 'Housing and community amenities' through 'Other functions'.
b) Item 'Education' refers to school only.
c) Item 'Social security and welfare' refers to social security only.

Netherlands

2.3 Total Government Outlays by Function and Type

Million Netherlands guilders

	Final Consumption Expenditures Total	Compensation of Employees	Other	Subsidies	Other Current Transfers & Property Income	Total Current Disbursements	Gross Capital Formation	Other Capital Outlays	Total Outlays
1980									
1 General public services [a]	...	...	...	...	...	...	...	...	...
2 Defence	10170	6460	3710	-	500	10670	-	10	10680
3 Public order and safety	...	...	...	...	...	...	...	...	...
4 Education [b]	21130	17160	3970	-	1400	22530	1630	10	24170
5 Health [a]	...	...	...	...	...	...	...	...	...
6 Social security and welfare [c]	2400	1510	890	-	70940	73340	-	90	73430
7 Housing and community amenities [a]									
8 Recreation, culture and religion	26560	18950	7610	4980	33860	65400	9340	8750	83490
9 Economic services									
10 Other functions [a]									
Total	60260	44080	16180	4980	106700	171940	10970	8860	191770
1981									
1 General public services [a]	...	...	...	...	...	...	...	...	...
2 Defence	10790	6640	4150	-	520	11310	-	200	11510
3 Public order and safety	...	...	...	...	...	...	...	...	...
4 Education [b]	21650	17470	4180	-	1450	23100	1510	-	24610
5 Health [a]	...	...	...	...	...	...	...	...	...
6 Social security and welfare [c]	2650	1640	1010	-	75790	78440	-	80	78520
7 Housing and community amenities [a]									
8 Recreation, culture and religion	27660	19270	8390	5520	40630	73810	9590	10150	93550
9 Economic services									
10 Other functions [a]									
Total	62750	45020	17730	5520	118390	186660	11100	10430	208190
1982									
1 General public services [a]	...	...	...	...	...	...	...	...	...
2 Defence	11430	6840	4590	-	540	11970	-	110	12080
3 Public order and safety	...	...	...	...	...	...	...	...	...
4 Education [b]	21970	17890	4080	-	1420	23390	1460	10	24860
5 Health [a]	...	...	...	...	...	...	...	...	...
6 Social security and welfare [c]	2890	1840	1050	-	80720	83610	-	70	83680
7 Housing and community amenities [a]									
8 Recreation, culture and religion	28830	20150	8680	6220	49220	84270	9160	10450	103880
9 Economic services									
10 Other functions [a]									
Total	65120	46720	18400	6220	131900	203240	10620	10640	224500
1983									
1 General public services [a]	...	...	...	...	...	...	...	...	...
2 Defence	12360	6840	5520	-	510	12870	-	10	12880
3 Public order and safety	...	...	...	...	...	...	...	...	...
4 Education [b]	21480	17600	3880	-	1440	22920	1210	-	24130
5 Health [a]	...	...	...	...	...	...	...	...	...
6 Social security and welfare [c]	2990	1900	1090	-	81500	84490	-	70	84560
7 Housing and community amenities [a]									
8 Recreation, culture and religion	29750	20610	9140	6710	56630	93090	8980	10290	112360
9 Economic services									
10 Other functions [a]									
Total	66580	46960	19600	6710	140080	213370	10190	10370	233930

Netherlands

2.3 Total Government Outlays by Function and Type
(Continued)

Million Netherlands guilders

	Final Consumption Expenditures - Total	Compensation of Employees	Other	Subsidies	Other Current Transfers & Property Income	Total Current Disbursements	Gross Capital Formation	Other Capital Outlays	Total Outlays
1984									
1 General public services a	...	...	...	...	...	...	...	...	...
2 Defence	12230	6930	5300	-	570	12800	-	10	12810
3 Public order and safety	...	...	...	...	...	...	...	...	...
4 Education b	21200	17170	4030	-	1480	22680	1300	- -	23980
5 Health a	...	...	...	...	...	...	...	...	...
6 Social security and welfare c	3070	1930	1140	-	81690	84760	-	80	84840
7 Housing and community amenities a									
8 Recreation, culture and religion	29890	20380	9510	7410	59490	96790	9890	11780	118460
9 Economic services									
10 Other functions a									
Total	66390	46410	19980	7410	143230	217030	11190	11870	240090
1985									
1 General public services a	...	...	...	...	...	...	...	...	...
2 Defence	11930	6800	5130	-	580	12510	-	20	12530
3 Public order and safety	...	...	...	...	...	...	...	...	...
4 Education b	21570	17340	4230	-	1590	23160	1250	-	24410
5 Health a	...	...	...	...	...	...	...	...	...
6 Social security and welfare c	3140	1990	1150	-	83380	86520	-	90	86610
7 Housing and community amenities a									
8 Recreation, culture and religion	30910	20680	10230	8110	62160	101180	9270	11750	122200
9 Economic services									
10 Other functions a									
Total	67550	46810	20740	8110	147710	223370	10520	11860	245750
1986									
1 General public services a	...	...	...	...	...	...	...	...	...
2 Defence	12100	6860	5240	-	630	12730	-	20	12750
3 Public order and safety	...	...	...	...	...	...	...	...	...
4 Education b	21880	17710	4170	-	1770	23650	1130	-	24780
5 Health a	...	...	...	...	...	...	...	...	...
6 Social security and welfare c	3160	2000	1160	-	84700	87860	-	100	87960
7 Housing and community amenities a									
8 Recreation, culture and religion	31100	20530	10570	7710	62230	101040	8420	14270	123730
9 Economic services									
10 Other functions a									
Total	68240	47100	21140	7710	149330	225280	9550	14390	249220

a) Items 'General public service' and 'Health' are included in items 'Housing and community amenities' through 'Other functions'.
b) Item 'Education' refers to school only.
c) Item 'Social security and welfare' refers to social security only.

2.5 Private Final Consumption Expenditure by Type and Porpose, in Current Prices

Million Netherlands guilders

	1970	1975	1977	1978	1979	1980	1981	1982	1983	1984	1985	1986
Final Consumption Expenditure of Resident Households												
1 Food, beverages and tobacco	18250	28350	34720	35990	37620	39610	41840	43860	44750	46510	47390	47630
A Food	14430	21860	27050	27790	28780	30630	32390	33910	34520	36020	36680	36860
B Non-alcoholic beverages	...	...	820	940	1050	1090	1140	1310	1360	1300	1380	1370
C Alcoholic beverages	...	...	3620	3730	4120	4060	4340	4620	4690	4790	4810	4910
D Tobacco	1830	2760	3230	3530	3670	3830	3970	4020	4180	4400	4520	4490
2 Clothing and footwear	7490	11770	13670	14480	15340	16170	15770	15690	15690	15770	16840	18270
3 Gross rent, fuel and power a	8810	17960	22880	25520	29170	32640	36410	39670	42540	44820	48090	48560
A Fuel and power	2550	5190	6530	7440	9200	10530	12150	12770	13200	14000	15850	14460
B Other	6260	12770	16350	18080	19970	22110	24260	26900	29340	30820	32240	34100
4 Furniture, furnishings and household equipment and operation	8160	12810	16450	17650	17720	18590	17570	17190	17400	17260	17870	18810
A Household operation	1770	2750	3320	3530	3690	3940	4070	4300	4310	4460	4670	4860

Netherlands

2.5 Private Final Consumption Expenditure by Type and Porpose, in Current Prices
(Continued)

Million Netherlands guilders

	1970	1975	1977	1978	1979	1980	1981	1982	1983	1984	1985	1986
B Other	6390	10060	13130	14120	14030	14650	13500	12890	13090	12800	13200	13950
5 Medical care and health expenses	5950	14480	18680	20890	22750	24830	26580	28410	29220	29750	30500	31600
6 Transport and communication	6600	13790	18160	19740	21620	21810	22500	23070	24330	24710	26200	27230
A Personal transport equipment	2380	4940	7520	8110	8420	6760	6630	6950	7990	7960	8910	10360
B Other	4220	8850	10640	11630	13200	15050	15870	16120	16340	16750	17290	16870
7 Recreational, entertainment, education and cultural services	5930	12470	15920	17890	18700	20050	20300	20380	21250	21960	22690	23700
A Education	...	...	500	550	600	660	700	710	730	740	760	800
B Other	...	...	15420	17340	18100	19390	19600	19670	20520	21220	21930	22900
8 Miscellaneous goods and services	9030	16370	21160	23130	25220	27310	28180	29150	30050	31820	32940	33980
A Personal care	1970	3120	4060	4420	4740	5100	5190	5150	5390	5650	5920	6300
B Expenditures in restaurants, cafes and hotels	3720	5900	7510	8170	8860	9660	10050	10560	10880	11770	12090	12290
C Other	3340	7350	9590	10540	11620	12550	12940	13440	13780	14400	14930	15390
Total Final Consumption Expenditure in the Domestic Market by Households, of which	70220	128000	161640	175290	188140	201010	209150	217420	225230	232600	242520	249780
A Durable goods	...	...	23160	24830	24670	23270	21830	21550	22740	22250	23550	25840
B Semi-durable goods	...	...	26530	28940	30890	33120	32640	32410	32870	33570	35580	38240
C Non-durable goods	...	...	51750	55020	59740	64790	69570	72680	74210	77550	80720	79060
D Services	...	...	60200	66500	72840	79830	84890	90780	95410	99230	102670	106640
Plus: Direct purchases abroad by resident households	2470	4470	6440	7670	8100	9450	9410	9630	9870	10200	10830	11280
Less: Direct purchases in the domestic market by non-resident households	1870	3520	3770	3790	3890	4680	5330	5220	5240	6050	6120	5850
Equals: Final Consumption Expenditure of Resident Households [b]	70820	128950	164310	179170	192430	205780	213230	221830	229860	236750	247230	255210

Final Consumption Expenditure of Private Non-profit Institutions Serving Households

	1970	1975	1977	1978	1979	1980	1981	1982	1983	1984	1985	1986
Equals: Final Consumption Expenditure of Private Non-profit Organisations Serving Households	...	...	...	...	...	...	...	...	...	...	...	...
Private Final Consumption Expenditure	70820	128950	164310	179170	192430	205780	213230	221830	229860	236750	247230	255210

a) Item 'Gross rent, fuel and power' includes maintenance expenditure.
b) Item 'Final consumption expenditure of resident households' includes consumption expenditure of private non-profit institutions serving households.

2.6 Private Final Consumption Expenditure by Type and Purpose, in Constant Prices

Million Netherlands guilders

	1970	1975	1977	1978	1979	1980	1981	1982	1983	1984	1985	1986

At constant prices of: 1980

Final Consumption Expenditure of Resident Households

	1970	1975	1977	1978	1979	1980	1981	1982	1983	1984	1985	1986
1 Food, beverages and tobacco	30830	35430	37630	38520	39700	39610	39780	39590	40110	40100	40330	40770
A Food	24810	27140	28500	29310	29900	30630	30800	30710	31140	31500	31860	32310
B Non-alcoholic beverages	...	...	890	1000	1120	1090	1140	1180	1270	1180	1190	1220
C Alcoholic beverages	...	...	4050	4160	4540	4060	4160	4120	4160	4130	4050	4070
D Tobacco	3170	4000	4190	4050	4140	3830	3680	3580	3540	3290	3230	3170
2 Clothing and footwear	16010	15750	16130	16180	16420	16170	15180	14500	14320	14130	14400	15150
3 Gross rent, fuel and power [a]	20400	26880	28960	30410	32300	32640	32610	32700	33390	34180	35520	36240
A Fuel and power	7670	9020	9410	9970	11140	10530	9880	9270	9250	9410	10060	9980
B Other	12730	17860	19550	20440	21160	22110	22730	23490	24140	24770	25460	26260
4 Furniture, furnishings and household equipment and operation	15080	16050	18530	19230	18760	18590	16670	15770	15760	15500	15700	16220
A Household operation	3610	3600	3830	3920	3950	3940	3900	3960	3920	4000	4090	4140
B Other	11470	12450	14700	15310	14810	14650	12770	11810	11840	11500	11610	12080
5 Medical care and health expenses	17730	21190	22590	23400	24000	24830	25150	25490	25720	26370	26790	27660
6 Transport and communication	13620	18250	21410	22690	23710	21810	21010	20670	21020	20910	21550	22860
A Personal transport equipment	4490	6450	8380	8770	8950	6760	6390	6260	6860	6710	7280	8070
B Other	9130	11800	13030	13920	14760	15050	14620	14410	14160	14200	14270	14790
7 Recreational, entertainment, education and cultural services	10910	15130	17600	19000	19450	20050	19510	18880	19190	19710	19880	20490
A Education	...	...	610	620	640	660	650	620	550	540	540	550

Netherlands

2.6 Private Final Consumption Expenditure by Type and Purpose, in Constant Prices
(Continued)

Million Netherlands guilders

	1970	1975	1977	1978	1979	1980	1981	1982	1983	1984	1985	1986
					At constant prices of:1980							
B Other	...	...	16990	18380	18810	19390	18860	18260	18640	19170	19340	19940
8 Miscellaneous goods and services	19260	22900	24560	25210	26450	27310	27060	26900	26710	27590	27960	28510
A Personal care	4110	4220	4670	4840	5040	5100	5060	4930	5080	5300	5430	5760
B Expenditures in restaurants, cafes and hotels	7490	8470	8690	8930	9290	9660	9450	9440	9300	9670	9680	9640
C Other	7660	10210	11200	11440	12120	12550	12550	12530	12330	12620	12850	13110
Total Final Consumption Expenditure in the Domestic Market by Households, of which	143840	171580	187410	194640	200790	201010	196970	194560	196220	198490	202130	207900
A Durable goods	...	...	25190	26440	25840	23270	21040	20030	20750	20240	21000	22570
B Semi-durable goods	...	...	30720	31810	32870	33120	31570	30150	30040	30260	30860	32330
C Non-durable goods	...	...	59650	62110	65150	64790	63910	63030	63300	63730	64560	65320
D Services	...	...	71850	74280	76930	79830	80450	81350	82130	84260	85710	87680
Plus: Direct purchases abroad by resident households	5790	7060	8420	9330	9080	9450	8630	8320	8310	8420	8510	8840
Less: Direct purchases in the domestic market by non-resident households	3650	4760	4310	4160	4110	4680	4990	4620	4540	4920	4870	4650
Equals: Final Consumption Expenditure of Resident Households [b]	145980	173880	191520	199810	205760	205780	200610	198260	199990	201990	205770	212090

Final Consumption Expenditure of Private Non-profit Institutions Serving Households

	1970	1975	1977	1978	1979	1980	1981	1982	1983	1984	1985	1986
Equals: Final Consumption Expenditure of Private Non-profit Organisations Serving Households	...	...	...	...	...	...	...	...	...	...	...	...
Private Final Consumption Expenditure	145980	173880	191520	199810	205760	205780	200610	198260	199990	201990	205770	212090

a) Item 'Gross rent, fuel and power' includes maintenance expenditure.
b) Item 'Final consumption expenditure of resident households' includes consumption expenditure of private non-profit institutions serving households.

2.7 Gross Capital Formation by Type of Good and Owner, in Current Prices

Million Netherlands guilders

	1980				1981				1982			
	TOTAL	Total Private	Public Enterprises	General Government	TOTAL	Total Private	Public Enterprises	General Government	TOTAL	Total Private	Public Enterprises	General Government
Increase in stocks, total [a]	1720	1720	...	...	-3090	-3090	...	...	-1020	-1020	...	...
Gross Fixed Capital Formation, Total [ba]	70790	59820	...	10970	67580	56480	...	11100	67160	56540	...	10620
1 Residential buildings	20840	20840	...	...	20130	20130	...	...	19540	19540	...	...
2 Non-residential buildings	15120	11960	...	3160	13710	10600	...	3110	12900	9820	...	3080
3 Other construction	8030	1700	...	6330	8010	1570	...	6440	7630	1480	...	6150
4 Land improvement and plantation and orchard development			...				...				...	
5 Producers' durable goods	24740	23260	...	1480	23900	22350	...	1550	25320	23930	...	1390
A Transport equipment	7080	6760	...	320	6160	5820	...	340	7310	6990	...	320
Passenger cars	2640	...	...	...	2520	...	...	...	2760	...	...	...
Other	4440	...	...	...	3640	...	...	...	4550	...	...	...
B Machinery and equipment	17660	16500	...	1160	17740	16530	...	1210	18010	16940	...	1070
6 Breeding stock, dairy cattle, etc.	60	60	...	...	150	150	...	...	140	140	...	...
Statistical discrepancy [c]	2000	2000	...	...	1680	1680	...	...	1630	1630	...	...
Total Gross Capital Formation [ba]	72510	61540	...	10970	64490	53390	...	11100	66140	55520	...	10620

	1983				1984				1985			
	TOTAL	Total Private	Public Enterprises	General Government	TOTAL	Total Private	Public Enterprises	General Government	TOTAL	Total Private	Public Enterprises	General Government
Increase in stocks, total [a]	560	560	...	...	1990	1990	...	...	2350	2350	...	...
Gross Fixed Capital Formation, Total [ba]	69460	59270	...	10190	74310	63120	...	11190	78950	68430	...	10520
1 Residential buildings	19470	19470	...	...	20400	20400	...	...	19410	19410	...	...
2 Non-residential buildings	11960	9080	...	2880	12310	9420	...	2890	11970	9580	...	2390
3 Other construction	7360	1320	...	6040	7960	1220	...	6740	7750	1250	...	6500
4 Land improvement and plantation and orchard development			...				...				...	

Netherlands

2.7 Gross Capital Formation by Type of Good and Owner, in Current Prices
(Continued)

Million Netherlands guilders

	1983 TOTAL	1983 Total Private	1983 Public Enterprises	1983 General Government	1984 TOTAL	1984 Total Private	1984 Public Enterprises	1984 General Government	1985 TOTAL	1985 Total Private	1985 Public Enterprises	1985 General Government
5 Producers' durable goods	28590	27320	...	1270	31960	30400	...	1560	38140	36510	...	1630
A Transport equipment	9410	9120	...	290	9100	8770	...	330	10720	10400	...	320
Passenger cars	3330	...	...	...	3600	...	...	...	4260	...	...	...
Other	6080	...	...	...	5500	...	...	...	6460	...	...	...
B Machinery and equipment	19180	18200	...	980	22860	21630	...	1230	27420	26110	...	1310
6 Breeding stock, dairy cattle, etc.	190	190	...	...	-150	-150	...	...	-270	-270	...	...
Statistical discrepancy [c]	1890	1890	...	...	1830	1830	...	...	1950	1950	...	...
Total Gross Capital Formation [ba]	70020	59830	...	10190	76300	65110	...	11190	81300	70780	...	10520

	1986 TOTAL	1986 Total Private	1986 Public Enterprises	1986 General Government
Increase in stocks, total [a]	4610	4610	...	...
Gross Fixed Capital Formation, Total [ba]	84170	74620	...	9550
1 Residential buildings	20100	20100	...	...
2 Non-residential buildings	13150	11120	...	2030
3 Other construction	7370	1470	...	5900
4 Land improvement and plantation and orchard development			...	
5 Producers' durable goods	41320	39700	...	1020
A Transport equipment	12180	11880	...	300
Passenger cars	5150	...	...	...
Other	7030	...	...	...
B Machinery and equipment	29140	27820	...	1320
6 Breeding stock, dairy cattle, etc.	-190	-190	...	...
Statistical discrepancy [c]	2420	2420	...	...
Total Gross Capital Formation [ba]	88780	79230	...	9550

a) Column 'Public enterprises' is included in column 'Total private'.
b) Gross capital formation are estimated by user rather than by owner base.
c) Item 'Statistical discrepancy' refers to transfers costs on existing fixed capital goods.

2.8 Gross Capital Formation by Type of Good and Owner, in Constant Prices

Million Netherlands guilders

	1980 TOTAL	1980 Total Private	1980 Public Enterprises	1980 General Government	1981 TOTAL	1981 Total Private	1981 Public Enterprises	1981 General Government	1982 TOTAL	1982 Total Private	1982 Public Enterprises	1982 General Government
					At constant prices of:1980							
Increase in stocks, total [a]	1720	1720	...	...	-2500	-2500	...	...	-840	-840	...	...
Gross Fixed Capital Formation, Total [ba]	70790	59820	...	10970	63420	52900	...	10460	60840	51120	...	9720
1 Residential buildings	20840	20840	...	...	18840	18840	...	...	17790	17790	...	...
2 Non-residential buildings	15120	11960	...	3160	12920	10000	...	2920	11910	9070	...	2840
3 Other construction	8030	1700	...	6330	7540	1470	...	6070	6990	1360	...	5630
4 Land improvement and plantation and orchard development			...				...				...	
5 Producers' durable goods	24740	23260	...	1480	22160	20690	...	1470	22150	20900	...	1250
A Transport equipment	7080	6760	...	320	5890	5560	...	330	6560	6270	...	290
Passenger cars	2640	...	...	...	2470	...	...	...	2540	...	...	...
Other	4440	...	...	...	3420	...	...	...	4020	...	...	...
B Machinery and equipment	17660	16500	...	1160	16270	15130	...	1140	15590	14630	...	960
6 Breeding stock, dairy cattle, etc.	60	60	...	...	130	130	...	...	100	100	...	...
Statistical discrepancy [c]	2000	2000	...	...	1830	1830	...	...	1900	1900	...	...
Total Gross Capital Formation [ba]	72510	61540	...	10970	60920	50460	...	10460	60000	50280	...	9720

Netherlands

2.8 Gross Capital Formation by Type of Good and Owner, in Constant Prices

Million Netherlands guilders

	1983 TOTAL	1983 Total Private	1983 Public Enterprises	1983 General Government	1984 TOTAL	1984 Total Private	1984 Public Enterprises	1984 General Government	1985 TOTAL	1985 Total Private	1985 Public Enterprises	1985 General Government
				At constant prices of:1980								
Increase in stocks, total a	330	330	...	...	970	970	...	...	1180	1180	...	...
Gross Fixed Capital Formation, Total ba	62100	52830	...	9270	65450	55480	...	9970	68850	59650	...	9200
1 Residential buildings	17720	17720	...	...	18510	18510	...	...	17850	17850	...	...
2 Non-residential buildings	11070	8400	...	2670	11340	8660	...	2680	11100	8870	...	2230
3 Other construction	6670	1190	...	5480	7040	1070	...	5970	6700	1090	...	5610
4 Land improvement and plantation and orchard development			...				...				...	
5 Producers' durable goods	24370	23250	...	1120	26680	25360	...	1320	31310	29950	...	1360
A Transport equipment	8050	7800	...	250	7550	7290	...	260	8610	8350	...	260
Passenger cars	2930	...	...	...	3000	...	...	...	3480	...	...	...
Other	5120	...	...	...	4550	...	...	...	5130	...	...	...
B Machinery and equipment	16320	15450	...	870	19130	18070	...	1060	22700	21600	...	1100
6 Breeding stock, dairy cattle, etc.	140	140	...	...	-140	-140	...	...	-230	-230	...	...
Statistical discrepancy c	2130	2130	...	...	2020	2020	...	...	2120	2120	...	...
Total Gross Capital Formation ba	62430	53160	...	9270	66420	56450	...	9970	70030	60830	...	9200

	1986 TOTAL	1986 Total Private	1986 Public Enterprises	1986 General Government
		At constant prices of:1980		
Increase in stocks, total a	2050	2050	...	...
Gross Fixed Capital Formation, Total ba	73800	65410	...	8390
1 Residential buildings	18470	18470	...	...
2 Non-residential buildings	12170	10280	...	1890
3 Other construction	6430	1280	...	5150
4 Land improvement and plantation and orchard development			...	
5 Producers' durable goods	34400	33050	...	1350
A Transport equipment	9710	9470	...	240
Passenger cars	4030	...	...	...
Other	5680	...	...	...
B Machinery and equipment	24690	23580	...	1110
6 Breeding stock, dairy cattle, etc.	-170	-170	...	...
Statistical discrepancy c	2500	2500	...	...
Total Gross Capital Formation ba	75850	67460	...	8390

a) Column 'Public enterprises' is included in column 'Total private'.
b) Gross capital formation are estimated by user rather than by owner base.
c) Item 'Statistical discrepancy' refers to transfers costs on existing fixed capital goods.

2.11 Gross Fixed Capital Formation by Kind of Activity of Owner, ISIC Divisions, in Current Prices

Million Netherlands guilders

	1970	1975	1977	1978	1979	1980	1981	1982	1983	1984	1985	1986
					All Producers							
1 Agriculture, hunting, forestry and fishing	1150	1870	3230	3880	4510	3870	3120	3390	3820	3760	4050	4700
A Agriculture and hunting	...	...	3230	3880	4490	3810	2970	3160	3470	...	...	...
B Forestry and logging	...	...	...	...	...	...	...	...	...	...	...	...
C Fishing	...	...	-	-	20	60	150	120	150	...	...	...
2 Mining and quarrying	400	1430	1210	1200	1070	1060	1370	1690	1470	1530	2230	...
A Coal mining	...	...	...	...	...	...	...	...	...	...	...	...
B Crude petroleum and natural gas production	...	...	1210	1200	1070	1060	1370	1690	...	...	...	...
C Metal ore mining	...	...	...	...	...	...	...	...	...	...	...	...
D Other mining	...	...	...	...	...	...	...	...	...	...	...	...

Netherlands

2.11 Gross Fixed Capital Formation by Kind of Activity of Owner, ISIC Divisions, in Current Prices
(Continued)

Million Netherlands guilders

	1970	1975	1977	1978	1979	1980	1981	1982	1983	1984	1985	1986
3 Manufacturing [a]	6970	7450	8850	10310	11330	11970	11230	11260	11730	13980	16870	...
A Manufacturing of food, beverages and tobacco	...	...	1830	2330	2820	3050	2660	2590				
B Textile, wearing apparel and leather industries	...	...	280	290	330	310	240	310				
C Manufacture of wood, and wood products, including furniture	...	...	260	290	300	280	200	200				
D Manufacture of paper and paper products, printing and publishing	...	...	660	900	1280	1120	1190	1140				
E Manufacture of chemicals and chemical petroleum, coal, rubber and plastic products	...	...	2990	2910	2710	2750	2900	3140				
F Manufacture of non-metalic mineral products except products of petroleum and coal	...	...	620	720	660	830	640	450				
G Basic metal industries	...	...	240	280	370	430	490	420				
H Manufacture of fabricated metal products, machinery and equipment	...	...	1880	2450	2670	3050	2740	2930				
I Other manufacturing industries	...	...	90	140	190	150	170	160				
4 Electricity, gas and water	1860	2950	2930	2710	2770	3070	3080	2540	2280	2440	2530	...
5 Construction	620	700	1180	1360	1200	1150	1040	890	1120	1250	1640	...
6 Wholesale and retail trade, restaurants and hotels [b]	2100	2710	3680	3840	4160	4240	3700	3600	3630	4120	4890	5710
7 Transport, storage and communication	2510	4750	5340	6020	6190	6020	5540	6530	8110	7590	8600	9420
A Transport and storage	...	...	4210	4650	4840	4560	4150	5130	6340	...	...	...
B Communication	...	...	1130	1370	1350	1460	1390	1380	1450	...	...	...
8 Finance, insurance, real estate and business services	7760	12750	17980	19750	20170	22470	21520	20890	21070	21990	21080	22180
A Financial institutions	170	170	190	200	200	210	230	250	270	300	320	360
B Insurance	80	80	90	90	90	100	110	120	130	140	150	160
C Real estate and business services [c]	7510	12500	17700	19460	19880	22160	21180	20520	20670	21550	20610	21660
Real estate except dwellings	...	...	...	...	...	...	...	...	...	...	...	...
Dwellings	7510	12500	17700	19460	19880	22160	21180	20520	20670	21200	20210	...
9 Community, social and personal services [bc]	2320	3070	4210	4590	5290	5970	5880	5750	6040	6460	6540	7080
Total Industries [d]	25690	37680	48610	53660	56690	59820	56480	56540	59270	63120	68430	74620
Producers of Government Services	5670	8640	9280	9640	9800	10970	11100	10620	10190	11190	10520	9550
Private Non-Profit Institutions Serving Households [d]	...	...	...	...	...	...	...	...	...	...	...	...
Total [e]	31360	46320	57890	63300	66490	70790	67580	67160	69460	74310	78950	84170

a) Repair services are included in item 'Manufacturing'.
b) Restaurants and hotels are included in item 'Community, social and personal services'.
c) Business services are included in item 'Community, social and personal services'.
d) Item 'Private non-profit institutions serving households' is included with various industries above.
e) Gross capital formation are estimated by user rather than by owner base.

2.12 Gross Fixed Capital Formation by Kind of Activity of Owner, ISIC Divisions, in Constant Prices

Million Netherlands guilders

	1970	1975	1977	1978	1979	1980	1981	1982	1983	1984	1985	1986
	At constant prices of:1980 — All Producers											
1 Agriculture, hunting, forestry and fishing	2520	2640	3930	4440	4860	3870	2930	3060	3390	3240	3450	4020
2 Mining and quarrying												
3 Manufacturing [a]	18090	16130	16380	17400	17430	17250	15510	14430	14350	16330	19590	21890
4 Electricity, gas and water												

Netherlands

2.12 Gross Fixed Capital Formation by Kind of Activity of Owner, ISIC Divisions, in Constant Prices
(Continued)

Million Netherlands guilders

	1970	1975	1977	1978	1979	1980	1981	1982	1983	1984	1985	1986
At constant prices of:1980												
5 Construction	...	...	...	...	...	...	...	...	...	...	...	...
6 Wholesale and retail trade, restaurants and hotels [b]	4140	3800	4410	4350	4480	4240	3510	3260	3210	3580	4190	4840
7 Transport, storage and communication	4560	6080	6100	6650	6550	6020	5150	5770	6920	6410	7090	7890
8 Finance, insurance, real estate and business services [bc]	25880	24350	28300	28550	27500	28440	25860	24600	24960	25920	25330	26770
9 Community, social and personal services [c]	...	...	...	...	...	...	...	...	...	...	...	...
Total Industries [d]	55190	53000	59120	61390	60820	59820	52960	51120	52830	55480	59650	65410
Producers of Government Services	14430	13060	11800	11320	10640	10970	10460	9720	9270	9970	9200	8390
Private Non-Profit Institutions Serving Households [d]	...	...	...	...	...	...	...	...	...	...	...	...
Total [e]	69620	66060	70920	72710	71460	70790	63420	60840	62100	65450	68850	73800

a) Repair services are included in item 'Manufacturing'.
b) Restaurants and hotels are included in item 'Finance, insurance, real estate and business services'.
c) Item 'Community, social and personal services' is included in item 'Finance, insurance, real estate and business services'.
d) Item 'Private non-profit institutions serving households' is included with various industries above.
e) Gross capital formation are estimated by user rather than by owner base.

2.17 Exports and Imports of Goods and Services, Detail

Million Netherlands guilders

	1970	1975	1977	1978	1979	1980	1981	1982	1983	1984	1985	1986
Exports of Goods and Services												
1 Exports of merchandise, f.o.b.	43010	88960	106530	107460	128460	147080	171330	177620	185010	210630	226190	194190
2 Transport and communication	6360	8930	10550	10680	11950	13760	15350	15180	15560	16930	18020	16370
A In respect of merchandise imports	370	360	270	280	340	380	430	430	400	500	550	430
B Other	5990	8570	10280	10400	11610	13380	14920	14750	15160	16430	17470	15940
3 Insurance service charges	270	450	800	850	800	830	1100	920	1030	860	910	950
4 Other commodities	2790	7860	9090	10560	9960	10460	11510	13660	12930	14090	14960	14630
5 Adjustments of merchandise exports to change-of-ownership basis	...	...	...	...	...	...	...	...	...	...	...	...
6 Direct purchases in the domestic market by non-residential households	1870	3520	3770	3790	3890	4680	5330	5220	5240	6050	6120	5850
7 Direct purchases in the domestic market by extraterritorial bodies												
Total Exports of Goods and Services	54300	109720	130740	133340	155060	176810	204620	212600	219770	248560	266200	231990
Imports of Goods and Services												
1 Imports of merchandise, c.i.f.	49140	90890	111700	115680	137550	156120	168420	171710	179580	200240	216520	184860
A Imports of merchandise, f.o.b.	45920	85540	105380	109080	129610	147200	158330	161810	170390	188700	203680	174820
B Transport of services on merchandise imports	3080	5080	5970	6240	7530	8480	9620	9460	8770	11030	12320	9620
By residents	370	360	270	280	340	380	430	430	400	500	550	430
By non-residents	2710	4720	5700	5960	7190	8100	9190	9030	8370	10530	11770	9190
C Insurance service charges on merchandise imports	140	270	350	360	410	440	470	440	420	510	520	420
By residents	...	...	...	...	...	...	...	...	...	...	...	...
By non-residents	140	270	350	360	410	440	470	440	420	510	520	420
2 Adjustments of merchandise imports to change-of-ownership basis	...	...	...	...	...	...	...	...	...	...	...	...
3 Other transport and communication	240	480	570	670	750	960	1040	1140	1120	1200	1260	1280
4 Other insurance service charges	330	590	610	700	820	930	1000	1040	1050	1090	1160	1210
5 Other commodities	4230	5910	8080	8510	9390	11160	12370	13310	13590	15020	15920	16020
6 Direct purchases abroad by government												
7 Direct purchases abroad by resident households	2470	4470	6440	7670	8180	9450	9410	9630	9870	10200	10830	11280
Total Imports of Goods and Services	56410	102340	127400	133230	156690	178620	192240	196830	205210	227750	245690	214650
Balance of Goods and Services	-2110	7380	3340	110	-1630	-1810	12380	15770	14560	20810	20510	17340
Total Imports and Balance of Goods and Services	54300	109720	130740	133340	155060	176810	204620	212600	219770	248560	266200	231990

Netherlands

3.11 General Government Production Account: Total and Subsectors

Million Netherlands guilders

	1980					1981				
	Total General Government	Central Government	State or Provincial Government	Local Government	Social Security Funds	Total General Government	Central Government	State or Provincial Government	Local Government	Social Security Funds
Gross Output										
1 Sales	3200	1750	...	1450	-	3290	1730	...	1560	-
2 Services produced for own use	60260	27010	...	30850	2400	62750	28200	...	31900	2650
3 Own account fixed capital formation	580	-	...	580	-	580	-	...	580	-
Gross Output [a]	64040	28760	...	32880	2400	66620	29930	...	34040	2650
Gross Input										
Intermediate Consumption	17200	9970	...	6340	890	18680	10780	...	6890	1010
Subtotal: Value Added	46840	18790	...	26540	1510	47940	19150	...	27150	1640
1 Indirect taxes, net	360	130	-	230	-	360	120	-	240	-
A Indirect taxes	360	130	...	230	-	360	120	...	240	-
B Less: Subsidies	...	...	...	...	...	...	...	...	...	...
2 Consumption of fixed capital	2400	660	...	1740	-	2560	710	...	1850	-
3 Compensation of employees	44080	18000	...	24570	1510	45020	18320	...	25060	1640
A To residents	44080	18000	...	24570	1510	45020	18320	...	25060	1640
B To the rest of the world	...	...	...	...	...	...	...	...	...	...
4 Net Operating surplus	...	...	...	...	...	...	...	...	...	...
Gross Input [a]	64040	28760	...	32880	2400	66620	29930	...	34040	2650

	1982					1983				
	Total General Government	Central Government	State or Provincial Government	Local Government	Social Security Funds	Total General Government	Central Government	State or Provincial Government	Local Government	Social Security Funds
Gross Output										
1 Sales	3700	1900	...	1800	-	4040	2110	...	1930	-
2 Services produced for own use	65120	29310	...	32920	2890	66580	30660	...	32930	2990
3 Own account fixed capital formation	570	-	...	570	-	560	-	...	560	-
Gross Output [a]	69390	31210	...	35290	2890	71180	32770	...	35420	2990
Gross Input										
Intermediate Consumption	19870	11520	...	7300	1050	21530	12920	...	7520	1090
Subtotal: Value Added	49520	19690	...	27990	1840	49650	19850	...	27900	1900
1 Indirect taxes, net	380	140	-	240	-	400	130	-	270	-
A Indirect taxes	380	140	...	240	-	400	130	...	270	-
B Less: Subsidies	...	...	...	...	...	...	...	...	...	...
2 Consumption of fixed capital	2420	630	...	1790	-	2300	670	...	1630	-
3 Compensation of employees	46720	18920	...	25960	1840	46950	19050	...	26000	1900
A To residents	46720	18920	...	25960	1840	46950	19050	...	26000	1900
B To the rest of the world	...	...	...	...	...	...	...	...	...	...
4 Net Operating surplus	...	...	...	...	...	...	...	...	...	...
Gross Input [a]	69390	31210	...	35290	2890	71180	32770	...	35420	2990

	1984					1985				
	Total General Government	Central Government	State or Provincial Government	Local Government	Social Security Funds	Total General Government	Central Government	State or Provincial Government	Local Government	Social Security Funds
Gross Output										
1 Sales	4360	2310	...	2050	-	4450	2280	...	2170	-
2 Services produced for own use	66390	30720	...	32600	3070	67550	31290	...	33120	3140
3 Own account fixed capital formation	640	-	...	640	-	630	-	...	630	-
Gross Output [a]	71390	33030	...	35290	3070	72630	33570	...	35920	3140
Gross Input										
Intermediate Consumption	21940	13040	...	7760	1140	22650	13410	...	8090	1150
Subtotal: Value Added	49450	19990	...	27530	1930	49980	20160	...	27830	1990
1 Indirect taxes, net	420	150	-	270	-	450	170	-	280	-
A Indirect taxes	420	150	...	270	-	450	170	...	280	-
B Less: Subsidies	...	...	...	...	...	...	...	...	...	...
2 Consumption of fixed capital	2620	800	...	1820	-	2720	840	...	1880	-
3 Compensation of employees	46410	19040	...	25440	1930	46810	19150	...	25670	1990
A To residents	46410	19040	...	25440	1930	46810	19150	...	25670	1990
B To the rest of the world	...	...	...	...	...	...	...	...	...	...
4 Net Operating surplus	...	...	...	...	...	...	...	...	...	...
Gross Input [a]	71390	33030	...	35290	3070	72630	33570	...	35920	3140

Netherlands

3.11 General Government Production Account: Total and Subsectors

Million Netherlands guilders

	1986				
	Total General Government	Central Government	State or Provincial Government	Local Government	Social Security Funds
Gross Output					
1 Sales	4890	2520	...	2370	-
2 Services produced for own use	68240	31660	...	33420	3160
3 Own account fixed capital formation	540	-	...	540	-
Gross Output a	73670	34180	...	36330	3160
Gross Input					
Intermediate Consumption	23380	14030	...	8190	1160
Subtotal: Value Added	50290	20150	...	28140	2000
1 Indirect taxes, net	460	170	-	290	-
A Indirect taxes	460	170	...	290	-
B Less: Subsidies	...	...	...	...	...
2 Consumption of fixed capital	2730	880	...	1850	-
3 Compensation of employees	47100	19100	...	26000	2000
A To residents	47100	19100	...	26000	2000
B To the rest of the world	...	...	...	...	...
4 Net Operating surplus	...	...	...	...	...
Gross Input a	73670	34180	...	36330	3160

a) Local Government includes provincial governmnet and other regional government entities.

3.12 General Government Income and Outlay Account: Total and Subsectors

Million Netherlands guilders

	1980					1981				
	Total General Government	Central Government	State or Provincial Government	Local Government	Social Security Funds	Total General Government	Central Government	State or Provincial Government	Local Government	Social Security Funds
Receipts										
1 Operating surplus	...	...	...	...	...	...	...	...	...	...
2 Property and entrepreneurial income	20000	14120	...	4890	990	25290	18830	...	5440	1020
A Withdrawals from public quasi-corporations	2600	550	...	2050	-	2900	630	...	2270	-
B Interest	6690	3170	...	2530	990	7560	3720	...	2820	1020
C Dividends	10710	10400		310	-	14830	14480	...	350	-
D Net land rent and royalties			...					...		
3 Taxes, fees and contributions	153570	88730	...	3620	61220	159040	88660	...	4240	66140
A Indirect taxes	37450	35250	...	2200	-	37990	35480	...	2510	-
B Direct taxes	53500	52760	...	740	-	53280	52350	...	930	-
Income	50680	50680	...	-	-	50410	50410	...	-	-
Other	2820	2080	...	740	-	2870	1940	...	930	-
C Social security contributions	61220	-	...	-	61220	66140	-	...	-	66140
D Fees, fines and penalties	1400	720	...	680	-	1630	830	...	800	-
4 Other current transfers	4270	1990	...	46050	11500	4300	1950	...	49830	9880
A Casualty insurance claims	80	20	...	60	-	100	-	...	100	-
B Transfers from other government subsectors	...	-	...	43790	11480	...	-	...	47510	9850
C Transfers from the rest of the world	140	140	...	-	-	140	140	...	-	-
D Other transfers, except imputed	330	90	...	240	-	340	90	...	250	-
E Imputed unfunded employee pension and welfare contributions	3720	1740	...	1960	20	3720	1720	...	1970	30
Total Current Receipts a	177840	104840	...	54560	73710	188630	109440	...	59510	77040
Disbursements										
1 Government final consumption expenditure	60260	27010	...	30850	2400	62750	28200	...	31900	2650
2 Property income b	15660	7090	...	8560	10	19340	9420	...	9840	80
A Interest	15660	7090	...	8560	10	19340	9420	...	9840	80
B Net land rent and royalties	...	...	...	...	...	...	...	...	...	...
3 Subsidies	4980	2940	...	2040	...	5520	3380	...	2140	...

Netherlands

3.12 General Government Income and Outlay Account: Total and Subsectors
(Continued)

Million Netherlands guilders

	1980					1981				
	Total General Government	Central Government	State or Provincial Government	Local Government	Social Security Funds	Total General Government	Central Government	State or Provincial Government	Local Government	Social Security Funds
4 Other current transfers	94260	65130	...	13460	70940	102730	68230	...	16140	75720
A Casualty insurance premiums, net	80	20	...	60	-	100	-	...	100	-
B Transfers to other government subsectors	...	55270	...	-	-	...	57360	...	-	-
C Social security benefits	70920	-	...	-	70920	75690	-	...	-	75690
D Social assistance grants	12700	2980	...	9720	-	15600	3380	...	12220	-
E Unfunded employee pension and welfare benefits	3720	1740	...	1960	20	3720	1720	...	1970	30
F Transfers to private non-profit institutions serving households	5140	3450	...	1690	-	5700	3900	...	1800	-
G Other transfers n.e.c.	220	190	...	30	-	260	210	...	50	-
H Transfers to the rest of the world	1480	1480	...	-	-	1660	1660	...	-	-
Net saving	2680	2670	...	-350	360	-1710	210	...	-510	-1410
Total Current Disbursements and Net Saving a	177840	104840	...	54560	73710	188630	100440	...	59510	77040

	1982					1983				
	Total General Government	Central Government	State or Provincial Government	Local Government	Social Security Funds	Total General Government	Central Government	State or Provincial Government	Local Government	Social Security Funds

Receipts

1 Operating surplus	...	...	...	...	...	...	...	...	...	...
2 Property and entrepreneurial income	26950	20330	...	5840	780	28170	21060	...	6430	680
A Withdrawals from public quasi-corporations	3300	850	...	2450	-	3400	700	...	2700	-
B Interest	7890	4250	...	2860	780	8810	4910	...	3220	680
C Dividends	15760	15230	...	530	-	15960	15450	...	510	-
D Net land rent and royalties			...					...		
3 Taxes, fees and contributions	167330	90080	...	4760	72490	178160	90000	...	4860	83300
A Indirect taxes	38710	35890	...	2820	-	41000	38230	...	2770	-
B Direct taxes	54290	53210	...	1080	-	51890	50760	...	1130	-
Income	51300	51300	...	-	-	48850	48850	...	-	-
Other	2990	1910	...	1080	-	3040	1910	...	1130	-
C Social security contributions	72490	-	...	-	72490	83300	-	...	-	83300
D Fees, fines and penalties	1840	980	...	860	-	1970	1010	...	960	-
4 Other current transfers	4320	2040	...	58170	7840	4220	1990	...	61680	3600
A Casualty insurance claims	80	-	...	80	-	70	-	...	70	-
B Transfers from other government subsectors	...	-	...	55920	7810	...	-	...	59480	3570
C Transfers from the rest of the world	190	190	...	-	-	160	160	...	-	-
D Other transfers, except imputed	320	100	...	220	-	320	100	...	220	-
E Imputed unfunded employee pension and welfare contributions	3730	1750	...	1950	30	3670	1730	...	1910	30
Total Current Receipts a	198600	112450	...	68770	81110	210550	113050	...	72970	87580

Disbursements

1 Government final consumption expenditure	65120	29310	...	32920	2890	66580	30660	...	32930	2990
2 Property income b	23180	12450	...	10620	110	26500	15230	...	11170	100
A Interest	23180	12450	...	10620	110	26500	15230	...	11170	100
B Net land rent and royalties	...	...	...	...	...	...	...	...	...	...
3 Subsidies	6220	3480	...	2740	...	6710	3800	...	2910	...

1015

Netherlands

3.12 General Government Income and Outlay Account: Total and Subsectors
(Continued)

Million Netherlands guilders

	1982					1983				
	Total General Government	Central Government	State or Provincial Government	Local Government	Social Security Funds	Total General Government	Central Government	State or Provincial Government	Local Government	Social Security Funds
4 Other current transfers	112860	75670	...	20280	80640	118420	76120	...	23920	81430
A Casualty insurance premiums, net	80	-	...	80	-	70	-	...	70	-
B Transfers to other government subsectors	...	63730	...	-	-	...	63050	...	-	-
C Social security benefits	80610	-	...	-	80610	81400	-	...	-	81400
D Social assistance grants	20490	4200	...	16290	-	24730	4860	...	19870	-
E Unfunded employee pension and welfare benefits	3730	1750	...	1950	30	3670	1730	...	1910	30
F Transfers to private non-profit institutions serving households	5870	3950	...	1920	-	6460	4460	...	2000	-
G Other transfers n.e.c.	250	210	...	40	-	270	200	...	70	-
H Transfers to the rest of the world	1830	1830	...	-	-	1820	1820	...	-	-
Net saving	-8780	-8460	...	2210	-2530	-7660	-12760	...	2040	3060
Total Current Disbursements and Net Saving [a]	198600	112450	...	68770	81110	210550	113050	...	72970	87580

	1984					1985				
	Total General Government	Central Government	State or Provincial Government	Local Government	Social Security Funds	Total General Government	Central Government	State or Provincial Government	Local Government	Social Security Funds

Receipts

1 Operating surplus	...	...	...	...	...	...	...	...	...	...
2 Property and entrepreneurial income	32530	24750	...	6960	820	35780	27480	...	7430	870
A Withdrawals from public quasi-corporations	3400	610	...	2790	-	3900	980	...	2920	-
B Interest	10500	6050	...	3630	820	10800	6160	...	3770	870
C Dividends	18630	18090	...	540	-	21080	20340	...	740	-
D Net land rent and royalties			...					...		
3 Taxes, fees and contributions	179390	91510	...	5020	82860	186820	95340	...	5530	85950
A Indirect taxes	43400	40540	...	2860	-	45680	42510	...	3170	-
B Direct taxes	51030	49860	...	1170	-	52880	51620	...	1260	-
Income	47790	47790	...	-	-	49480	49480	...	-	-
Other	3240	2070	...	1170	-	3400	2140	...	1260	-
C Social security contributions	82860	-	...	-	82860	85950	-	...	-	85950
D Fees, fines and penalties	2100	1110	...	990	-	2310	1210	...	1100	-
4 Other current transfers	4440	2200	...	60790	2940	4470	2190	...	62420	2750
A Casualty insurance claims	80	-	...	80	-	100	-	...	100	-
B Transfers from other government subsectors	...	-	...	58580	2910	...	-	...	60170	2720
C Transfers from the rest of the world	270	270	...	-	-	300	300	...	-	-
D Other transfers, except imputed	400	180	...	220	-	290	70	...	220	-
E Imputed unfunded employee pension and welfare contributions	3690	1750	...	1910	30	3780	1820	...	1930	30
Total Current Receipts [a]	216360	118460	...	72770	86620	227070	125010	...	75380	89570

Disbursements

1 Government final consumption expenditure	66390	30720	...	32600	3070	67550	31290	...	33120	3140
2 Property income [b]	29860	17920	...	11830	110	32150	20020	...	12030	100
A Interest	29860	17920	...	11830	110	32150	20020	...	12030	100
B Net land rent and royalties	...	...	...	...	...	...	...	...	...	...
3 Subsidies	7410	3920	...	3490	...	8110	3840	...	4270	...

1016

Netherlands

3.12 General Government Income and Outlay Account: Total and Subsectors
(Continued)

Million Netherlands guilders

	1984					1985				
	Total General Government	Central Government	State or Provincial Government	Local Government	Social Security Funds	Total General Government	Central Government	State or Provincial Government	Local Government	Social Security Funds
4 Other current transfers	119370	74800	...	24460	81600	121570	76550	...	24630	83280
A Casualty insurance premiums, net	80	-	...	80	-	100	-	...	100	-
B Transfers to other government subsectors	...	61490	...	-	-	...	62890	...	-	-
C Social security benefits	81570	-	...	-	81570	83250	-	...	-	83250
D Social assistance grants	24870	4450	...	20420	-	22510	4550	...	17960	-
E Unfunded employee pension and welfare benefits	3690	1750	...	1910	30	3780	1820	...	1930	30
F Transfers to private non-profit institutions serving households	6510	4510	...	2000	-	8980	4390	...	4590	-
G Other transfers n.e.c.	250	200	...	50	-	240	190	...	50	-
H Transfers to the rest of the world	2400	2400	...	-	-	2710	2710	...	-	-
Net saving	-6670	-8900	...	390	1840	-2310	-6690	...	1330	3050
Total Current Disbursements and Net Saving [a]	216360	118460	...	72770	86620	227070	125010	...	75380	89570

	1986				
	Total General Government	Central Government	State or Provincial Government	Local Government	Social Security Funds

Receipts

1 Operating surplus	...	...	...	...	...
2 Property and entrepreneurial income	30250	22310	...	7280	660
A Withdrawals from public quasi-corporations	3500	600	...	2000	-
B Interest	11100	6810	...	3630	660
C Dividends	15650	14900		750	-
D Net land rent and royalties			...		
3 Taxes, fees and contributions	191940	102490	...	5510	83940
A Indirect taxes	48040	44960	...	3080	-
B Direct taxes	57620	56360	...	1260	-
Income	54130	54130	...	-	-
Other	3490	2230	...	1260	-
C Social security contributions	83940	-	...	-	83940
D Fees, fines and penalties	2340	1170	...	1170	-
4 Other current transfers	4580	2160	...	62410	2150
A Casualty insurance claims	110	-	...	110	-
B Transfers from other government subsectors	...	-	...	60020	2120
C Transfers from the rest of the world	280	280	...	-	-
D Other transfers, except imputed	290	60	...	230	-
E Imputed unfunded employee pension and welfare contributions	3900	1820	...	2050	30
Total Current Receipts [a]	226770	126960	...	75200	86750

Disbursements

1 Government final consumption expenditure	68240	31660	...	33420	3160
2 Property income [b]	32610	20740	...	11790	80
A Interest	32610	20740	...	11790	80
B Net land rent and royalties	...	...	...	...	...
3 Subsidies	7710	3710	...	4000	...

Netherlands

3.12 General Government Income and Outlay Account: Total and Subsectors
(Continued)

Million Netherlands guilders

	\multicolumn{5}{c}{1986}
	Total General Government	Central Government	State or Provincial Government	Local Government	Social Security Funds
4 Other current transfers	123420	76680	...	24260	84620
A Casualty insurance premiums, net	110	-	...	110	-
B Transfers to other government subsectors	...	62140	...	-	-
C Social security benefits	84590	-	...	-	84590
D Social assistance grants	22560	5170	...	17390	-
E Unfunded employee pension and welfare benefits	3900	1820	...	2050	30
F Transfers to private non-profit institutions serving households	9130	4450	...	4680	-
G Other transfers n.e.c.	220	190	...	30	-
H Transfers to the rest of the world	2910	2910	...	-	-
Net saving	-5210	-5830	...	1730	-1110
Total Current Disbursements and Net Saving [a]	226770	126960	...	75200	86750

a) Local Government includes provincial governmnet and other regional government entities.
b) Item 'Property income' includes payments and receipts of property income from other subsectors of general government.

3.13 General Government Capital Accumulation Account: Total and Subsectors

Million Netherlands guilders

	\multicolumn{5}{c}{1980}	\multicolumn{5}{c}{1981}
	Total General Government	Central Government	State or Provincial Government	Local Government	Social Security Funds	Total General Government	Central Government	State or Provincial Government	Local Government	Social Security Funds
	\multicolumn{10}{c}{Finance of Gross Accumulation}
1 Gross saving	5080	3330	...	1390	360	850	920	...	1340	-1410
A Consumption of fixed capital	2400	660	...	1740	-	2560	710	...	1850	-
B Net saving	2680	2670	...	-350	360	-1710	210	...	-510	-1410
2 Capital transfers	1200	1070	...	2160	200	1360	1350	...	2750	200
A From other government subsectors	...	30	...	2000	200	...	150	...	2590	200
B From other resident sectors	1100	940	...	160	-	1260	1100	...	160	-
C From rest of the world	100	100	...	-	-	100	100	...	-	-
Finance of Gross Accumulation [a]	6280	4400	...	3550	560	2210	2270	...	4090	-1210
	\multicolumn{10}{c}{Gross Accumulation}
1 Gross capital formation	10970	3160	...	7810	-	11100	3300	...	7800	-
A Increase in stocks	...	...	...	...	...	...	...	...	...	...
B Gross fixed capital formation	10970	3160	...	7810	-	11100	3300	...	7800	-
Own account	580	-	...	580	-	580	-	...	580	-
Other	10390	3160	...	7230	-	10520	3300	...	7220	-
2 Purchases of land, net	...	...	...	...	...	...	...	...	...	...
3 Purchases of intangible assets, net	...	...	...	...	...	...	...	...	...	...
4 Capital transfers	8860	10190	...	810	90	10430	12120	...	1170	80
A To other government subsectors	...	2200	...	30	-	...	2790	...	150	-
B To other resident sectors	8250	7380	...	780	90	9670	8570	...	1020	80
C To rest of the world	610	610	...	-	-	760	760	...	-	-
Net lending [b]	-13550	-8950	...	-5070	470	-19320	-13150	...	-4880	-1290
Gross Accumulation [a]	6280	4400	...	3550	560	2210	2270	...	4090	-1210

	\multicolumn{5}{c}{1982}	\multicolumn{5}{c}{1983}
	Total General Government	Central Government	State or Provincial Government	Local Government	Social Security Funds	Total General Government	Central Government	State or Provincial Government	Local Government	Social Security Funds
	\multicolumn{10}{c}{Finance of Gross Accumulation}
1 Gross saving	-6360	-7830	...	4000	-2530	-5360	-12090	...	3670	3060
A Consumption of fixed capital	2420	630	...	1790	-	2300	670	...	1630	-
B Net saving	-8780	-8460	...	2210	-2530	-7660	-12760	...	2040	3060
2 Capital transfers	1510	1320	...	3170	200	1690	1510	...	3400	200

Netherlands

3.13 General Government Capital Accumulation Account: Total and Subsectors
(Continued)

Million Netherlands guilders

	1982					1983				
	Total General Government	Central Government	State or Provincial Government	Local Government	Social Security Funds	Total General Government	Central Government	State or Provincial Government	Local Government	Social Security Funds
A From other government subsectors	...	90	...	2890	200	...	90	...	3130	200
B From other resident sectors	1430	1150	...	280	-	1550	1280	...	270	-
C From rest of the world	80	80	...	-	-	140	140	...	-	-
Finance of Gross Accumulation [a]	-4850	-6510	...	7170	-2330	-3670	-10580	...	7070	3260

Gross Accumulation

1 Gross capital formation	10620	2870	...	7750	-	10190	2880	...	7310	-
A Increase in stocks	...	...	...	...	...	...	...	...	...	...
B Gross fixed capital formation	10620	2870	...	7750	-	10190	2880	...	7310	-
Own account	570	-	...	570	-	560	-	...	560	-
Other	10050	2870	...	7180	-	9630	2880	...	6750	-
2 Purchases of land, net	...	...	...	...	...	...	...	...	...	...
3 Purchases of intangible assets, net	...	...	...	...	...	...	...	...	...	...
4 Capital transfers	10640	12630	...	1120	70	10370	12310	...	1410	70
A To other government subsectors	...	3090	...	90	-	...	3330	...	90	-
B To other resident sectors	9830	8730	...	1030	70	9750	8360	...	1320	70
C To rest of the world	810	810	...	-	-	620	620	...	-	-
Net lending [b]	-26110	-22010	...	-1700	-2400	-24230	-25770	...	-1650	3190
Gross Accumulation [a]	-4850	-6510	...	7170	-2330	-3670	-10580	...	7070	3260

	1984					1985				
	Total General Government	Central Government	State or Provincial Government	Local Government	Social Security Funds	Total General Government	Central Government	State or Provincial Government	Local Government	Social Security Funds

Finance of Gross Accumulation

1 Gross saving	-4050	-8100	...	2210	1840	410	-5850	...	3210	3050
A Consumption of fixed capital	2620	800	...	1820	-	2720	840	...	1880	-
B Net saving	-6670	-8900	...	390	1840	-2310	-6690	...	1330	3050
2 Capital transfers	2080	1610	...	3910	200	2060	1820	...	4100	180
A From other government subsectors	...	10	...	3430	200	...	20	...	3840	180
B From other resident sectors	1960	1480	...	480	-	1880	1620	...	260	-
C From rest of the world	120	120	...	-	-	180	180	...	-	-
Finance of Gross Accumulation [a]	-1970	-6490	...	6120	2040	2470	-4030	...	7310	3230

Gross Accumulation

1 Gross capital formation	11190	3190	...	8000	-	10520	3160	...	7360	-
A Increase in stocks	...	...	...	...	...	...	...	...	...	...
B Gross fixed capital formation	11190	3190	...	8000	-	10520	3160	...	7360	-
Own account	640	-	...	640	-	630	-	...	630	-
Other	10550	3190	...	7360	-	9890	3160	...	6730	-
2 Purchases of land, net	...	...	...	...	...	...	...	...	...	...
3 Purchases of intangible assets, net	...	...	...	...	...	...	...	...	...	...
4 Capital transfers	11870	13790	...	1640	80	11860	14010	...	1800	90
A To other government subsectors	...	3630	...	10	-	...	4020	...	20	-
B To other resident sectors	11380	9670	...	1630	80	11350	9480	...	1780	90
C To rest of the world	490	490	...	-	-	510	510	...	-	-
Net lending [b]	-25030	-23470	...	-3520	1960	-19910	-21200	...	-1850	3140
Gross Accumulation [a]	1070	6400	...	6120	2040	2470	4030	...	7310	3230

	1986				
	Total General Government	Central Government	State or Provincial Government	Local Government	Social Security Funds

Finance of Gross Accumulation

1 Gross saving	-2480	-4950	...	3580	-1110
A Consumption of fixed capital	2730	880	...	1850	-
B Net saving	-5210	-5830	...	1730	-1110
2 Capital transfers	2220	1980	...	3830	180

1019

Netherlands

3.13 General Government Capital Accumulation Account: Total and Subsectors
(Continued)

Million Netherlands guilders

	1986				
	Total General Government	Central Government	State or Provincial Government	Local Government	Social Security Funds
A From other government subsectors	...	20	...	3570	180
B From other resident sectors	2100	1840	...	260	-
C From rest of the world	120	120	...	-	-
Finance of Gross Accumulation [a]	-260	-2970	...	7410	-930
	Gross Accumulation				
1 Gross capital formation	9550	2940	...	6610	-
A Increase in stocks	...	...	...	...	...
B Gross fixed capital formation	9550	2940	...	6610	-
Own account	540	-	...	540	-
Other	9010	2940	...	6070	-
2 Purchases of land, net	...	...	...	...	...
3 Purchases of intangible assets, net	...	...	...	...	...
4 Capital transfers	14390	16410	...	1650	100
A To other government subsectors	...	3750	...	20	-
B To other resident sectors	13770	12040	...	1630	100
C To rest of the world	620	620	...	-	-
Net lending [b]	-24200	-22320	...	-850	-1030
Gross Accumulation [a]	-260	-2970	...	7410	-930

a) Local Government includes provincial governmnet and other regional government entities.
b) Net lending of the capital accumulation account and the capital finance account have not been reconciled and are different due to different statistical sources.

3.14 General Government Capital Finance Account, Total and Subsectors

Million Netherlands guilders

	1980					1981				
	Total General Government	Central Government	State or Provincial Government	Local Government	Social Security Funds	Total General Government	Central Government	State or Provincial Government	Local Government	Social Security Funds
	Acquisition of Financial Assets									
1 Gold and SDRs	...	...	...	...	...	...	...	...	...	...
2 Currency and transferable deposits	1624	1581	...	39	4	-650	-548	...	-130	28
3 Other deposits	-1116	-	...	-909	-207	-974	-	...	329	-1303
4 Bills and bonds, short term [a]	26	-	...	4	22	18	-	...	-4	22
5 Bonds, long term	-56	-	...	-	-56	-73	-	...	-	-73
6 Corporate equity securities	-	-	...	-	-	-	-	...	-	-
7 Short-term loans, n.e.c. [a]	-270	-368	...	-65	163	-179	-	...	-39	-140
8 Long-term loans, n.e.c.	11834	5637	...	6010	187	13920	7420	...	6470	30
9 Other receivables	...	...	...	...	...	...	...	...	...	...
10 Other assets	...	...	...	...	...	...	...	...	...	...
Total Acquisition of Financial Assets [b]	12042	6850	...	5079	113	12062	6872	...	6626	-1436
	Incurrence of Liabilities									
1 Currency and transferable deposits	207	207	...	-	-	146	146	...	-	-
2 Other deposits	-89	-89	...	-	-	-1073	-1073	...	-	-
3 Bills and bonds, short term [a]	3319	3319	...	-	-	2215	2215	...	-	-
4 Bonds, long term	5355	5976	...	-621	-	8790	9381	...	-591	-
5 Short-term loans, n.e.c. [a]	3190	-53	...	3021	222	-223	-100	...	-710	587
6 Long-term loans, n.e.c.	14851	7450	...	7221	180	22039	9718	...	12225	96
7 Other payables	...	...	...	...	...	...	...	...	...	...
8 Other liabilities	...	...	...	...	...	...	...	...	...	...
Total Incurrence of Liabilities	26833	16810	...	9621	402	31894	20287	...	10924	683
Statistical discrepancy	-1241	-1010	...	528	-759	-512	-265	...	582	-829
Net Lending [c]	-13550	-8950	...	-5070	470	-19320	-13150	...	-4880	-1290
Incurrence of Liabilities and Net Worth [b]	12042	6850	...	5079	113	12062	6872	...	6626	-1436

Netherlands

3.14 General Government Capital Finance Account, Total and Subsectors
Million Netherlands guilders

	1982 Total General Government	1982 Central Government	1982 State or Provincial Government	1982 Local Government	1982 Social Security Funds	1983 Total General Government	1983 Central Government	1983 State or Provincial Government	1983 Local Government	1983 Social Security Funds
	Acquisition of Financial Assets									
1 Gold and SDRs	...	...	...	...	...	...	...	...	...	...
2 Currency and transferable deposits	378	320	...	64	-6	-1	-190	...	159	30
3 Other deposits	-402	-	...	-72	-330	1509	-	...	566	943
4 Bills and bonds, short term [a]	-142	-	...	3	-145	-44	-	...	6	-50
5 Bonds, long term	-8	-	...	-	-8	-	-	...	-	-
6 Corporate equity securities	-	-	...	-	-	-	-	...	-	-
7 Short-term loans, n.e.c. [a]	251	-	...	306	-55	-400	-	...	338	-738
8 Long-term loans, n.e.c.	11490	6200	...	5550	-260	10172	5247	...	4990	-65
9 Other receivables	...	...	...	...	...	...	...	...	...	...
10 Other assets	...	...	...	...	...	...	...	...	...	...
Total Acquisition of Financial Assets [b]	11567	6520	...	5851	-804	11236	5057	...	6059	120
	Incurrence of Liabilities									
1 Currency and transferable deposits	53	53	...	-	-	45	45	...	-	-
2 Other deposits	-9	-9	...	-	-	-379	-379	...	-	-
3 Bills and bonds, short term [a]	1239	1239	...	-	-	-255	-255	...	-	-
4 Bonds, long term	16177	16645	...	-468	-	20604	21264	...	-660	-
5 Short-term loans, n.e.c. [a]	-2506	310	...	-3375	559	-1932	-123	...	-401	-1408
6 Long-term loans, n.e.c.	19912	9436	...	10858	-382	17686	9672	...	7901	113
7 Other payables	...	...	...	...	...	...	...	...	...	...
8 Other liabilities	...	...	...	...	...	...	...	...	...	...
Total Incurrence of Liabilities	34866	27674	...	7015	177	35769	30224	...	6840	-1295
Statistical discrepancy	2811	856	...	536	1419	107	833	...	959	-1685
Net Lending [c]	-26110	-22010	...	-1700	-2400	-24640	-26000	...	-1740	3100
Incurrence of Liabilities and Net Worth [b]	11567	6520	...	5851	-804	11236	5057	...	6059	120

a) Bills are included in item 'Short-term loans, n.e.c.'.
b) Local Government includes provincial governmnet and other regional government entities.
c) Net lending of the capital accumulation account and the capital finance account have not been reconciled and are different due to different statistical sources.

3.21 Corporate and Quasi-Corporate Enterprise Production Account: Total and Sectors
Million Netherlands guilders

	1980 TOTAL	1980 Non-Financial	1980 Financial	1980 ADDENDUM: Total, including Unincorporated	1981 TOTAL	1981 Non-Financial	1981 Financial	1981 ADDENDUM: Total, including Unincorporated	1982 TOTAL	1982 Non-Financial	1982 Financial	1982 ADDENDUM: Total, including Unincorporated
	Gross Output											
1 Output for sale	573070	561520	11550	573070	610000	598300	11700	610000	629030	617200	11830	629030
2 Imputed bank service charge	11460	...	11460	11460	12660	...	12660	12660	14080	...	14080	14080
3 Own-account fixed capital formation	1720	1720	...	1720	1970	1970	...	1970	2020	2020	...	2020
Gross Output	586250	563240	23010	586250	624630	600270	24360	624630	645130	619220	25910	645130
	Gross Input											
Intermediate consumption	296350	277760	18590	296350	319720	299570	20150	319720	325790	303870	21920	325790
1 Imputed banking service charge	11460	...	11460	11460	12660	...	12660	12660	14080	...	14080	14080
2 Other intermediate consumption	284890	277760	7130	284890	307060	299570	7490	307060	311710	303870	7840	311710
Subtotal: Value Added	289900	285480	4420	289900	304910	300700	4210	304910	319340	315350	3990	319340
1 Indirect taxes, net	31660	31020	640	31660	32540	31860	680	32540	32320	31650	670	32320
A Indirect taxes	40760	40110	650	40760	41360	40680	680	41360	42380	41700	680	42380
B Less: Subsidies	9100	9090	10	9100	8820	8820	-	8820	10060	10050	10	10060
2 Consumption of fixed capital	30090	29830	260	30090	33060	32770	290	33060	35440	35130	310	35440
3 Compensation of employees	153760	145030	8730	153760	156510	147230	9280	156510	160760	150870	9890	160760
A To residents	152850	144120	8730	152850	155500	146220	9280	155500	159620	149730	9890	159620
B To the rest of the world	910	910	...	910	1010	1010	...	1010	1140	1140	...	1140
4 Net operating surplus	74390	79600	-5210	74390	82800	88840	-6040	82800	90820	97700	-6880	90820
Gross Input	586250	563240	23010	586250	624630	600270	24360	624630	645130	619220	25910	645130

Netherlands

3.21 Corporate and Quasi-Corporate Enterprise Production Account: Total and Sectors
Million Netherlands guilders

	1983 TOTAL	1983 Non-Financial	1983 Financial	1983 ADDENDUM: Total, including Unincorporated	1984 TOTAL	1984 Non-Financial	1984 Financial	1984 ADDENDUM: Total, including Unincorporated	1985 TOTAL	1985 Non-Financial	1985 Financial	1985 ADDENDUM: Total, including Unincorporated
Gross Output												
1 Output for sale	649480	637190	12290	649480	700680	687660	13020	700680	728320	714550	13770	728320
2 Imputed bank service charge	16150	...	16150	16150	16420	...	16420	16420	16770	...	16770	16770
3 Own-account fixed capital formation	2070	2070	...	2070	2370	2370	...	2370	2550	2550	...	2550
Gross Output	667700	639260	28440	667700	719470	690030	29440	719470	747640	717100	30540	747640
Gross Input												
Intermediate consumption	336330	312030	24300	336330	368670	343720	24950	368670	381030	355060	25970	381030
1 Imputed banking service charge	16150	...	16150	16150	16420	...	16420	16420	16770	...	16770	16770
2 Other intermediate consumption	320180	312030	8150	320180	352250	343720	8530	352250	364260	355060	9200	364260
Subtotal: Value Added	331370	327230	4140	331370	350800	346310	4490	350800	366610	362040	4570	366610
1 Indirect taxes, net	33520	32770	750	33520	34960	34140	820	34960	36480	35620	860	36480
A Indirect taxes	44740	43980	760	44740	47570	46740	830	47570	50240	49370	870	50240
B Less: Subsidies	11220	11210	10	11220	12610	12600	10	12610	13760	13750	10	13760
2 Consumption of fixed capital	36890	36560	330	36890	38570	38220	350	38570	40040	39680	360	40040
3 Compensation of employees	162690	152510	10180	162690	163590	153280	10310	163590	169310	158570	10740	169310
A To residents	161570	151390	10180	161570	162470	152160	10310	162470	168090	157350	10740	168090
B To the rest of the world	1120	1120	...	1120	1120	1120	...	1120	1220	1220	...	1220
4 Net operating surplus	98270	105390	-7120	98270	113680	120670	-6990	113680	120780	128170	-7390	120780
Gross Input	667700	639260	28440	667700	719470	690030	29440	719470	747640	717100	30540	747640

	1986 TOTAL	1986 Non-Financial	1986 Financial	1986 ADDENDUM: Total, including Unincorporated
Gross Output				
1 Output for sale	703690	689150	14540	703690
2 Imputed bank service charge	16880	...	16880	16880
3 Own-account fixed capital formation	2600	2600	...	2600
Gross Output	723170	691750	31420	723170
Gross Input				
Intermediate consumption	343890	317350	26540	343890
1 Imputed banking service charge	16880	...	16880	16880
2 Other intermediate consumption	327010	317350	9660	327010
Subtotal: Value Added	379280	374400	4880	379280
1 Indirect taxes, net	39730	38790	940	39730
A Indirect taxes	53210	52260	950	53210
B Less: Subsidies	13480	13470	10	13480
2 Consumption of fixed capital	40990	40610	380	40990
3 Compensation of employees	176750	165580	11170	176750
A To residents	175540	164370	11170	175540
B To the rest of the world	1210	1210	...	1210
4 Net operating surplus	121810	129420	-7610	121810
Gross Input	723170	691750	31420	723170

3.22 Corporate and Quasi-Corporate Enterprise Income and Outlay Account: Total and Sectors
Million Netherlands guilders

	1980 TOTAL	1980 Non-Financial	1980 Financial	1981 TOTAL	1981 Non-Financial	1981 Financial	1982 TOTAL	1982 Non-Financial	1982 Financial	1983 TOTAL	1983 Non-Financial	1983 Financial
Receipts												
1 Operating surplus	74390	79600	-5210	82800	88840	-6040	90820	97700	-6880	98270	105390	-7120
2 Property and entrepreneurial income [a]	73520	10370	63140	89240	11620	77620	93600	10860	82740	91000	10100	80900
A Withdrawals from quasi-corporate enterprises	1080	...	1080	1140	...	1140	1200	...	1200	1370	...	1370
B Interest	66530	5700	60830	81310	6200	75110	85260	5500	79760	81860	4600	77260
C Dividends	5910	4670	1230	6790	5420	1370	7140	5360	1780	7770	5500	2270
D Net land rent and royalties												

Netherlands

3.22 Corporate and Quasi-Corporate Enterprise Income and Outlay Account: Total and Sectors
(Continued)

Million Netherlands guilders

	1980 TOTAL	1980 Non-Financial	1980 Financial	1981 TOTAL	1981 Non-Financial	1981 Financial	1982 TOTAL	1982 Non-Financial	1982 Financial	1983 TOTAL	1983 Non-Financial	1983 Financial
3 Current transfers	11540	3250	8290	12840	3560	9280	12710	3480	9230	13210	3570	9640
A Casualty insurance claims	2550	2330	220	3150	2680	470	2910	2640	270	3110	2750	360
B Casualty insurance premiums, net, due to be received by insurance companies	7830	-	7830	8570	-	8570	8720	-	8720	9040	-	9040
C Current transfers from the rest of the world	-	-	-	-	-	-	-	-	-	-	-	-
D Other transfers except imputed	150	-	150	150	-	150	150	-	150	150	-	150
E Imputed unfunded employee pension and welfare contributions	1010	920	90	970	880	90	930	840	90	910	820	90
Total Current Receipts [b]	159450	93220	66220	184880	104020	80860	197130	112040	85090	202480	119060	83420

Disbursements

	1980 TOTAL	1980 Non-Fin	1980 Fin	1981 TOTAL	1981 Non-Fin	1981 Fin	1982 TOTAL	1982 Non-Fin	1982 Fin	1983 TOTAL	1983 Non-Fin	1983 Fin
1 Property and entrepreneurial income [a]	132540	80180	52360	154080	88520	65560	165560	96170	69390	165370	99570	65800
A Withdrawals from quasi-corporations	3680	3610	70	4040	4030	10	4500	4490	10	4770	4770	-
B Interest	67880	34500	33380	82380	38700	43680	83690	39600	44090	75690	38500	37190
C Dividends	60980	42070	18910	67660	45790	21870	77370	52080	25290	84910	56300	28610
D Net land rent and royalties												
2 Direct taxes and other current transfers n.e.c. to general government	10170	8760	1410	11100	9680	1420	11340	10100	1240	10850	9730	1120
A Direct taxes	10170	8760	1410	11100	9680	1420	11340	10100	1240	10850	9730	1120
On income	10170	8760	1410	11100	9680	1420	11340	10100	1240	10850	9730	1120
Other	...	...	...	...	...	...	...	...	...	...	...	...
B Fines, fees, penalties and other current transfers n.e.c.	...	...	...	...	...	...	...	...	...	...	...	...
3 Other current transfers	11540	3250	8290	12840	3560	9280	12710	3480	9230	13210	3570	9640
A Casualty insurance premiums, net	2550	2330	220	3150	2680	470	2910	2640	270	3110	2750	360
B Casualty insurance claims liability of insurance companies	7830	-	7830	8570	-	8570	8720	-	8720	9040	-	9040
C Transfers to private non-profit institutions	...	...	...	...	...	...	...	...	...	...	...	...
D Unfunded employee pension and welfare benefits	1010	920	90	970	880	90	930	840	90	910	820	90
E Social assistance grants	150	-	150	150	-	150	150	-	150	150	-	150
F Other transfers n.e.c.	...	...	...	...	...	...	...	...	...	...	...	...
G Transfers to the rest of the world	...	...	...	...	...	...	...	...	...	...	...	...
Net saving	5200	1030	4160	6860	2260	4600	7520	2290	5230	13050	6190	6860
Total Current Disbursements and Net Saving [b]	159450	93220	66220	184880	104020	80860	197130	112040	85090	202480	119060	83420

	1984 TOTAL	1984 Non-Financial	1984 Financial	1985 TOTAL	1985 Non-Financial	1985 Financial	1986 TOTAL	1986 Non-Financial	1986 Financial

Receipts

	1984 TOTAL	1984 Non-Fin	1984 Fin	1985 TOTAL	1985 Non-Fin	1985 Fin	1986 TOTAL	1986 Non-Fin	1986 Fin
1 Operating surplus	113680	120670	-6990	120780	128170	-7390	121810	129420	-7610
2 Property and entrepreneurial income [a]	97200	10370	86830	102150	12980	89170	100020	11650	88370
A Withdrawals from quasi-corporate enterprises	1470	...	1470	1580	...	1580	1660	...	1660
B Interest	87910	5300	82610	90720	6200	84520	89410	6200	83210
C Dividends	7820	5070	2750	9850	6780	3070	8950	5450	3500
D Net land rent and royalties									

Netherlands

3.22 Corporate and Quasi-Corporate Enterprise Income and Outlay Account: Total and Sectors
(Continued)

Million Netherlands guilders

	1984 TOTAL	1984 Non-Financial	1984 Financial	1985 TOTAL	1985 Non-Financial	1985 Financial	1986 TOTAL	1986 Non-Financial	1986 Financial
3 Current transfers	13600	3700	9900	14270	3780	10490	14590	3770	10820
A Casualty insurance claims	3060	2880	180	3190	2990	200	3290	3080	210
B Casualty insurance premiums, net, due to be received by insurance companies	9480	-	9480	10050	-	10050	10380	-	10380
C Current transfers from the rest of the world	-	-	-	-	-	-	-	-	-
D Other transfers except imputed	140	-	140	130	-	130	120	-	120
E Imputed unfunded employee pension and welfare contributions	920	820	100	900	790	110	800	690	110
Total Current Receipts [b]	224480	134740	89740	237200	144930	92270	236420	144840	91580

Disbursements

	1984 TOTAL	1984 Non-Financial	1984 Financial	1985 TOTAL	1985 Non-Financial	1985 Financial	1986 TOTAL	1986 Non-Financial	1986 Financial
1 Property and entrepreneurial income [a]	179920	108040	71880	188290	113730	74560	185270	111600	73670
A Withdrawals from quasi-corporations	4870	4700	170	5480	4930	550	5160	5150	10
B Interest	79960	39700	40260	79690	39900	39790	76700	39600	37100
C Dividends	95090	63640	31450	103120	68900	34220	103410	66850	36560
D Net land rent and royalties									
2 Direct taxes and other current transfers n.e.c. to general government	10300	8900	1400	13060	11820	1240	14370	13070	1300
A Direct taxes	10300	8900	1400	13060	11820	1240	14370	13070	1300
On income	10300	8900	1400	13060	11820	1240	14370	13070	1300
Other	...	...	...	...	...	...	...	...	...
B Fines, fees, penalties and other current transfers n.e.c.	...	...	...	...	...	...	...	...	...
3 Other current transfers	13600	3700	9900	14270	3780	10490	14590	3770	10820
A Casualty insurance premiums, net	3060	2880	180	3190	2990	200	3290	3080	210
B Casualty insurance claims liability of insurance companies	9480	-	9480	10050	-	10050	10380	-	10380
C Transfers to private non-profit institutions	...	...	...	...	...	...	...	...	...
D Unfunded employee pension and welfare benefits	920	820	100	900	790	110	800	690	110
E Social assistance grants	140	-	140	130	-	130	120	-	120
F Other transfers n.e.c.	...	...	...	...	...	...	...	...	...
G Transfers to the rest of the world	...	...	...	...	...	...	...	...	...
Net saving	20660	14100	6560	21580	15600	5980	22190	16400	5790
Total Current Disbursements and Net Saving [b]	224480	134740	89740	237200	144930	92270	236420	144840	91580

a) For the period 1970-1976, property and entrepreneurial income paid by non-financial corporate and quasi-corporate enterprises is net of property income received.
b) Column 'Non-Financial' includes unincorporated private enterprises.

3.23 Corporate and Quasi-Corporate Enterprise Capital Accumulation Account: Total and Sectors

Million Netherlands guilders

	1980 TOTAL	1980 Non-Financial	1980 Financial	1981 TOTAL	1981 Non-Financial	1981 Financial	1982 TOTAL	1982 Non-Financial	1982 Financial	1983 TOTAL	1983 Non-Financial	1983 Financial
	\multicolumn{12}{c	}{Finance of Gross Accumulation}
1 Gross saving	35290	30860	4430	39920	35030	4890	42960	37420	5540	49940	42750	7190
A Consumption of fixed capital	30090	29830	260	33060	32770	290	35440	35130	310	36890	36560	330
B Net saving	5200	1030	4170	6860	2260	4600	7520	2290	5230	13050	6190	6860
2 Capital transfers	7690	7300	390	9090	8710	380	9220	8710	510	9110	8570	540
A From resident sectors	7690	7300	390	9090	8710	380	9220	8710	510	9110	8570	540
B From the rest of the world	...	...	...	...	...	...	...	...	...	...	...	...
Finance of Gross Accumulation [a]	42980	38160	4820	49010	43740	5270	52180	46130	6050	59050	51320	7730
	\multicolumn{12}{c	}{Gross Accumulation}
1 Gross capital formation	61540	61230	310	53390	53050	340	55520	55150	370	59830	59430	400
A Increase in stocks	1720	1720	-	-3090	-3090	-	-1020	-1020	-	560	560	-
B Gross fixed capital formation	59820	59510	310	56480	56140	340	56540	56170	370	59270	58870	400

Netherlands

3.23 Corporate and Quasi-Corporate Enterprise Capital Accumulation Account: Total and Sectors
(Continued)

Million Netherlands guilders

	1980			1981			1982			1983		
	TOTAL	Non-Financial	Financial	TOTAL	Non-Financial	Financial	TOTAL	Non-Financial	Financial	TOTAL	Non-Financial	Financial
Own account	1720	1720	-	1970	1970	-	2020	2020	-	2070	2070	-
Other	58100	57790	310	54510	54170	340	54520	54150	370	57200	56800	400
2 Purchases of land, net	...	...	...	...	...	...	...	...	...	...	...	...
3 Purchases of intangible assets, net	...	...	...	...	...	...	...	...	...	...	...	...
4 Capital transfers b	640	360	280	740	480	260	1110	720	390	1290	870	420
A To resident sectors	640	360	280	740	480	260	1110	720	390	1290	870	420
B To the rest of the world	...	...	...	...	...	...	...	...	...	...	...	...
Net lending c	-19200	-23430	4230	-5120	-9790	4670	-4450	-9740	5290	-2070	-8980	6910
Gross Accumulation a	42980	38160	4820	49010	43740	5270	52180	46130	6050	59050	51320	7730

	1984			1985			1986		
	TOTAL	Non-Financial	Financial	TOTAL	Non-Financial	Financial	TOTAL	Non-Financial	Financial
Finance of Gross Accumulation										
1 Gross saving	59230	52320	6910	61620	55280	6340	63180	57010	6170
A Consumption of fixed capital	38570	38220	350	40040	39680	360	40990	40610	380
B Net saving	20660	14100	6560	21580	15600	5980	22190	16400	5790
2 Capital transfers	10690	9820	870	10600	9840	760	13010	12410	600
A From resident sectors	10690	9820	870	10600	9840	760	13010	12410	600
B From the rest of the world	...	...	...	...	...	...	...	...	...
Finance of Gross Accumulation a	69920	62140	7780	72220	65120	7100	76190	69420	6770
Gross Accumulation										
1 Gross capital formation	65110	64670	440	70780	70310	470	79230	78710	520
A Increase in stocks	1990	1990	-	2350	2350	-	4610	4610	-
B Gross fixed capital formation	63120	62680	440	68430	67960	470	74620	74100	520
Own account	2370	2370	-	2550	2550	-	2600	2600	-
Other	60750	60310	440	65880	65410	470	72020	71500	520
2 Purchases of land, net	...	...	...	...	...	...	...	...	...
3 Purchases of intangible assets, net	...	...	...	...	...	...	...	...	...
4 Capital transfers b	1890	1150	740	1680	1060	620	1550	1120	430
A To resident sectors	1890	1150	740	1680	1060	620	1550	1120	430
B To the rest of the world	...	...	...	...	...	...	...	...	...
Net lending c	2920	-3680	6600	-240	-6250	6010	-4590	-10410	5820
Gross Accumulation a	69920	62140	7780	72220	65120	7100	76190	69420	6770

a) Column 'Non-Financial' includes unincorporated private enterprises.
b) Capital transfers from financial enterprises to resident sectors on imputed transaction that is equal to the capital transfer received by pension funds from general government in order to supplement the net equity of households in life insurance and pension funds.
c) Net lending of the capital accumulation account and the capital finance account have not been reconciled and are different due to different statistical sources.

3.24 Corporate and Quasi-Corporate Enterprise Capital Finance Account: Total and Sectors

Million Netherlands guilders

	1980			1981			1982			1983		
	TOTAL	Non-Financial	Financial	TOTAL	Non-Financial	Financial	TOTAL	Non-Financial	Financial	TOTAL	Non-Financial	Financial
Acquisition of Financial Assets												
1 Gold and SDRs	96	-	96	422	-	422	532	-	532	-732	-	-732
2 Currency and transferable deposits	6329	3250	3079	-2293	-1236	-1057	11212	6974	4238	7875	7039	836
3 Other deposits	27387	10468	16919	37911	19466	18445	6458	11116	-4658	3456	2770	686
4 Bills and bonds, short term	3293	-166	3459	2197	-98	2295	1381	86	1295	-211	126	-337
5 Bonds, long term	6262	3540	2722	9408	3967	5441	17274	6530	10744	23181	8448	14733
6 Corporate equity securities	479	1073	-594	2407	2407	...	1200	-262	1462	2609	-494	3103
7 Short term loans, n.e.c.	14749	1529	13220	15356	5467	9889	1269	907	362	8905	1764	7141
8 Long term loans, n.e.c.	47479	4782	42697	43792	5897	37895	38953	3303	35650	37787	3965	33822
9 Trade credits and advances	...	...	...	...	...	...	...			...	...	...
10 Other receivables	...	...	...	...	...	...	...			...	...	...
11 Other assets	26396	26396	...	26718	26718	...	30042	30042	...	32670	32670	...
Total Acquisition of Financial Assets a	132470	50872	81598	135918	62588	73330	108321	58696	49625	115540	56288	59252
Incurrence of Liabilities												
1 Currency and transferable deposits	5240	-	5240	539	-	539	9153	-	9153	7606	-	7606

Netherlands

3.24 Corporate and Quasi-Corporate Enterprise Capital Finance Account: Total and Sectors
(Continued)

Million Netherlands guilders

	1980 TOTAL	1980 Non-Financial	1980 Financial	1981 TOTAL	1981 Non-Financial	1981 Financial	1982 TOTAL	1982 Non-Financial	1982 Financial	1983 TOTAL	1983 Non-Financial	1983 Financial
2 Other deposits	37736	14	37722	41485	-160	41645	8118	25	8093	10970	157	10813
3 Bills and bonds, short term [b]	...	...	...	...	...	...	...	...	...	...	...	...
4 Bonds, long term	4398	910	3488	1485	182	1303	490	-173	663	932	-394	1326
5 Corporate equity securities	953	1799	-846	901	1165	-264	2913	2695	218	2115	1248	867
6 Short-term loans, n.e.c. [b]	7476	4739	2737	6917	4424	2493	-2004	-2320	316	3879	818	3061
7 Long-term loans, n.e.c.	38761	34238	4523	28254	29920	-1666	23959	25815	-1856	25367	23392	1975
8 Net equity of households in life insurance and pension fund reserves [c]	26206	-	26206	26398	-	26398	29752	-	29752	32430	-	32430
9 Proprietors' net additions to the accumulation of quasi-corporations	...	...	...	...	...	...	...	...	...	...	...	...
10 Trade credit and advances	...	...	...	...	...	...	...	...	...	...	...	...
11 Other accounts payable	...	...	...	...	...	...	...	...	...	...	...	...
12 Other liabilities	249	-	249	276	-	276	-	-	-	...	...	...
Total Incurrence of Liabilities [a]	121019	41700	79319	106255	35531	70724	72381	26042	46339	83299	25221	58078
Statistical discrepancy	3901	5842	-1941	3723	5787	-2064	330	2334	-2004	-2869	3047	-5916
Net Lending [d]	7550	3330	4220	25940	21270	4670	35610	30320	5290	35110	28020	7090
Incurrence of Liabilities and Net Lending [a]	132470	50872	81598	135918	62588	73330	108321	58696	49625	115540	56288	59252

a) Column 'Non-Financial' includes unincorporated private enterprises.
b) Bills are included in item 'Short-term loans, n.e.c.'.
c) Item 'Net equity of households in life insurance and pension fund reserves' includes technical reserves of casualty insurance.
d) Net lending of the capital accumulation account and the capital finance account have not been reconciled and are different due to different statistical sources.

3.32 Household and Private Unincorporated Enterprise Income and Outlay Account

Million Netherlands guilders

	1970	1975	1977	1978	1979	1980	1981	1982	1983	1984	1985	1986
Receipts												
1 Compensation of employees	67200	131260	159690	172850	186020	197960	201640	207690	209810	210150	216200	223830
A Wages and salaries	53940	101360	123470	133850	143360	152080	155080	160320	159850	160550	165630	172520
B Employers' contributions for social security	8870	20090	24560	26500	29270	31350	32300	33250	35360	35410	36900	37510
C Employers' contributions for private pension & welfare plans	4390	9810	11660	12500	13390	14530	14260	14120	14600	14190	13670	13800
2 Operating surplus of private unincorporated enterprises	...	...	...	...	...	...	...	...	...	...	...	...
3 Property and entrepreneurial income [a]	24790	36210	45760	50160	52070	55850	59890	69490	74830	81100	85600	89040
A Withdrawals from private quasi-corporations	...	...	-	-	-	-	-	-	-	-	-	-
B Interest	...	...	7200	8600	9890	12530	14220	15910	14460	14610	14660	12590
C Dividends	...	...	38560	41560	42180	43320	45670	53580	60370	66490	70940	76450
D Net land rent and royalties	...	...	-	-	-	-	-	-	-	-	-	-
3 Current transfers	23400	57780	75190	83670	91890	98960	107570	117480	123270	123920	126240	127860
A Casualty insurance claims	1350	2760	3710	4130	4550	4870	5190	5360	5570	5860	6270	6470
B Social security benefits	16660	39750	51630	58310	64230	70370	75100	79900	80730	80870	82520	83790
C Social assistance grants	2450	7870	10280	10770	11700	12820	15710	20600	24840	25010	22640	22680
D Unfunded employee pension and welfare benefits	1450	3400	4450	4710	5270	4730	4690	4660	4580	4610	4680	4700
E Transfers from general government	1260	3490	4510	5030	5210	5210	5810	5970	6580	6620	9090	9230
F Transfers from the rest of the world	230	510	610	720	930	960	1070	990	970	950	1040	990
G Other transfers n.e.c.	-	-	-	-	-	-	-	-	-	-	-	-
Total Current Receipts [bc]	115390	225250	280640	306680	329980	352770	369100	394660	407910	415170	428040	440730
Disbursements												
1 Final consumption expenditures	70820	128950	164310	179170	192430	205780	213230	221830	229860	236750	247230	255210
2 Property income [a]	...	...	1030	1320	1670	1910	2070	1890	1740	1700	1740	1790
A Interest	...	...	1030	1320	1670	1910	2070	1890	1740	1700	1740	1790
B Net land rent and royalties	...	...	...	...	...	...	...	...	...	...	...	...
3 Direct taxes and other current transfers n.e.c. to government	29940	66560	81680	89810	97830	105950	109950	117280	126310	125690	128080	129530
A Social security contributions	16760	38530	46860	51420	56310	61220	66140	72490	83300	82860	85950	83940
B Direct taxes	12760	27120	33680	37200	40240	43330	42180	42950	41040	40730	39820	43250
Income taxes	12050	25790	31820	34970	37710	40510	39310	39960	38000	37490	36420	39760

Netherlands

3.32 Household and Private Unincorporated Enterprise Income and Outlay Account
(Continued)

Million Netherlands guilders

	1970	1975	1977	1978	1979	1980	1981	1982	1983	1984	1985	1986
Other	710	1330	1860	2230	2530	2820	2870	2990	3040	3240	3400	3490
C Fees, fines and penalties	420	910	1140	1190	1280	1400	1630	1840	1970	2100	2310	2340
4 Other current transfers	3450	7370	9690	10530	11760	11890	12370	12480	12700	13280	13770	13950
A Net casualty insurance premiums	1350	2760	3710	4130	4550	4870	5190	5360	5570	5860	6270	6470
B Transfers to private non-profit institutions serving households	...	...	...	...	...	...	...	...	...	...	...	...
C Transfers to the rest of the world	470	990	1270	1400	1650	1960	2150	2140	2230	2410	2530	2490
D Other current transfers, except imputed	180	220	260	290	290	330	340	320	320	400	290	290
E Imputed employee pension and welfare contributions	1450	3400	4450	4710	5270	4730	4690	4660	4580	4610	4680	4700
Net saving	11180	22370	23930	25850	26290	27240	31480	41180	37300	37750	37220	40250
Total Current Disbursements and Net Saving [bc]	115390	225250	280640	306680	329980	352770	369100	394660	407910	415170	428040	440730

a) For 1970-1976, property income received is net of property income paid.
b) Private non-profit institutions serving households is included in household and private unincorporated enterprise.
c) Private unincorporated enterprises are included in corporate and quasi-corporate enterprises.

3.33 Household and Private Unincorporated Enterprise Capital Accumulation Account

Million Netherlands guilders

	1970	1975	1977	1978	1979	1980	1981	1982	1983	1984	1985	1986
Finance of Gross Accumulation
1 Gross saving	11180	22370	23930	25850	26290	27240	31480	41180	37300	37750	37220	40250
A Consumption of fixed capital	...	...	...	...	...	...	...	...	...	...	...	...
B Net saving	11180	22370	23930	25850	26290	27240	31480	41180	37300	37750	37220	40250
2 Capital transfers	780	1580	1500	1360	1440	1150	1230	1540	1600	1930	1910	1760
A From resident sectors [a]	640	1360	1200	1100	1110	840	840	1000	1060	1430	1370	1190
B From the rest of the world	140	220	300	260	330	310	390	540	540	500	540	570
Total Finance of Gross Accumulation [bc]	11960	23950	25430	27210	27730	28390	32710	42720	38900	39680	39130	42010
Gross Accumulation
1 Gross Capital Formation	...	...	...	...	...	...	...	...	...	...	...	...
2 Purchases of land, net	...	...	...	...	...	...	...	...	...	...	...	...
3 Purchases of intangibles, net	...	...	...	...	...	...	...	...	...	...	...	...
4 Capital transfers	430	600	890	1020	1190	1330	1410	1470	1290	1430	1430	1650
A To resident sectors	270	360	520	590	710	740	780	710	680	810	820	980
B To the rest of the world	160	240	370	430	480	590	630	760	610	620	610	670
Net lending	11530	23350	24540	26190	26540	27060	31300	41250	37610	38250	37700	40360
Total Gross Accumulation [bc]	11960	23950	25430	27210	27730	28390	32710	42720	38900	39680	39130	42010

a) Capital transfers from financial enterprises to resident sectors on imputed transaction that is equal to the capital transfer received by pension funds from general government in order to supplement the net equity of households in life insurance and pension funds.
b) Private non-profit institutions serving households is included in household and private unincorporated enterprise.
c) Private unincorporated enterprises are included in corporate and quasi-corporate enterprises.

0.51 External Transactions: Current Account: Detail

Million Netherlands guilders

	1970	1975	1977	1978	1979	1980	1981	1982	1983	1984	1985	1986
Payments to the Rest of the World
1 Imports of goods and services	56410	102340	127400	133230	156690	178620	192240	196830	205210	227750	245690	214650
A Imports of merchandise c.i.f.	49140	90890	111700	115680	137550	156120	168420	171710	179580	200240	216520	184860
B Other	7270	11450	15700	17550	19140	22500	23820	25120	25630	27510	29170	29790
2 Factor income to the rest of the world	4100	8990	9750	11610	15730	22710	31090	32400	27810	31370	31060	28490
A Compensation of employees	390	660	690	750	800	910	1010	1140	1120	1120	1220	1210
B Property and entrepreneurial income	3790	8330	9060	10860	14930	21800	30080	31260	26690	30250	29840	27280
By general government	...	...	...	...	...	...	...	...	...	...	...	...
By corporate and quasi-cororate enterprises	3790	8330	9060	10860	14930	21800	30080	31260	26690	30250	29840	27280

Netherlands

3.51 External Transactions: Current Account: Detail
(Continued)

Million Netherlands guilders

	1970	1975	1977	1978	1979	1980	1981	1982	1983	1984	1985	1986
By other	...	...	...	...	...	...	...	...	...	...	...	...
3 Current transfers to the rest of the world	890	4320	5650	6640	7120	7690	8170	8770	8900	10100	10980	11830
A Indirect taxes by general government to supranational organizations	10	1590	2520	2430	3540	3670	3730	4050	4140	4590	5010	5630
B Other current transfers	880	2730	3130	4210	3580	4020	4440	4720	4760	5510	5970	6200
By general government	410	1740	1860	2810	1930	2060	2290	2580	2530	3100	3440	3710
By other resident sectors	470	990	1270	1400	1650	1960	2150	2140	2230	2410	2530	2490
4 Surplus of the nation on current transactions	-1700	5490	2140	-2700	-3870	-4900	7760	11640	11860	16630	17950	12170
Payments to the Rest of the World, and Surplus of the Nation on Current Transfers	59780	121140	144940	148780	175670	204120	239260	249640	253780	285850	305680	267140

Receipts From The Rest of the World

	1970	1975	1977	1978	1979	1980	1981	1982	1983	1984	1985	1986
1 Exports of goods and services	54300	109720	130740	133340	155060	176810	204620	212600	219770	248560	266200	231990
A Exports of merchandise f.o.b.	43010	88960	106530	107460	128460	147080	171330	177620	185010	210630	226190	194190
B Other	11290	20760	24210	25880	26600	29730	33290	34980	34760	37930	40010	37800
2 Factor income from the rest of the world	4740	8970	10240	10930	15000	22090	30130	32020	28370	30870	32490	28110
A Compensation of employees	420	750	840	830	900	1030	1120	1350	1290	1270	1300	1190
B Property and entrepreneurial income	4320	8220	9400	10100	14100	21060	29010	30670	27080	29600	31190	26920
By general government	...	50	60	60	40	40	110	100	80	70	130	60
By corporate and quasi-corporate enterprises	...	7710	8700	9310	13240	20100	27830	29140	25470	27940	29470	25290
By other	...	460	640	730	820	920	1070	1430	1530	1590	1590	1570
3 Current transfers from the rest of the world	740	2450	3960	4510	5610	5220	4510	5020	5640	6420	6990	7040
A Subsidies to general government from supranational organizations	480	1790	3180	3630	4540	4120	3300	3840	4510	5200	5650	5770
B Other current transfers	260	660	780	880	1070	1100	1210	1180	1130	1220	1340	1270
To general government	30	150	170	160	140	140	140	190	160	270	300	280
To other resident sectors	230	510	610	720	930	960	1070	990	970	950	1040	990
Receipts from the Rest of the World on Current Transfers	59780	121140	144940	148780	175670	204120	239260	249640	253780	285850	305680	267140

3.52 External Transactions: Capital Accumulation Account

Million Netherlands guilders

	1970	1975	1977	1978	1979	1980	1981	1982	1983	1984	1985	1986

Finance of Gross Accumulation

	1970	1975	1977	1978	1979	1980	1981	1982	1983	1984	1985	1986
1 Surplus of the nation on current transactions	-1700	5490	2140	-2700	-3870	-4900	7760	11640	11860	16630	17950	12170
2 Capital transfers from the rest of the world	260	310	370	390	450	410	490	620	680	620	720	690
A By general government	120	90	70	130	120	100	100	80	140	120	180	120
B By other resident sectors	140	220	300	260	330	310	390	540	540	500	540	570
Total Finance of Gross Accumulation	-1440	5800	2510	-2310	-3420	-4490	8250	12260	12540	17250	18670	12860

Gross Accumulation

	1970	1975	1977	1978	1979	1980	1981	1982	1983	1984	1985	1986
1 Capital transfers to the rest of the world	500	530	740	800	1030	1200	1390	1570	1230	1110	1120	1290
A By general government	340	290	370	370	550	610	760	810	620	490	510	620
B By other resident sectors	160	240	370	430	480	590	630	760	610	620	610	670
2 Purchases of intangible assets, n.e.c., net, from the rest of the world	...	...	...	...	...	...	...	...	...	...	...	...
Net lending to the rest of the world [a]	-1940	5270	1770	-3110	-4450	-5690	6860	10690	11310	16140	17550	11570
Total Gross Accumulation	-1440	5800	2510	-2310	-3420	-4490	8250	12260	12540	17250	18670	12860

a) Net lending of the capital accumulation account and the capital finance account have not been reconciled and are different due to different statistical sources.

Netherlands

3.53 External Transactions: Capital Finance Account

Million Netherlands guilders

	1970	1975	1977	1978	1979	1980	1981	1982	1983	1984	1985	1986
Acquisitions of Foreign Financial Assets											
1 Gold and SDR's	316	-	-	-	255	249	276	-	-	...	...	...
2 Currency and transferable deposits	534	320	1004	592	-296	226	2803	1578	628	...	...	...
3 Other deposits	5181	10657	11635	16705	18689	28782	21702	-811	5373	...	...	...
4 Bills and bonds, short term	...	...	...	...	...	...	...	...	...	...	...	...
5 Bonds, long term	2105	1044	3370	2409	2386	4240	1826	2119	1352	...	...	...
6 Corporate equity securities	913	936	1397	1206	1931	2496	1617	3769	1670	...	...	...
7 Short-term loans, n.e.c.	2464	-641	-2099	-124	1383	178	1325	-1032	-2310	...	...	...
8 Long-term loans	2428	2275	864	2142	4022	3466	5022	2355	6834	...	...	...
9 Proprietors' net additions to accumulation of quasi-corporate, non-resident enterprises	...	...	...	...	...	...	...	...	...	...	...	...
10 Trade credit and advances	...	...	...	...	...	...	...	...	...	...	...	...
11 Other [a]	6	10	-40	-80	-80	-190	-320	-290	-240	...	...	...
Total Acquisitions of Foreign Financial Assets	13947	14601	16131	22850	28290	39447	34251	7688	13307		...	...
Incurrence of Foreign Liabilities											
1 Currency and transferable deposits [b]	3948	3785	1224	109	1706	2732	-825	3962	851	...	...	...
2 Other deposits	2467	10120	7270	9525	10350	17406	18227	-2864	-253	...	...	...
3 Bills and bonds, short term	...	...	...	...	...	...	...	...	...	...	...	...
4 Bonds, long term	-12	219	430	804	45	693	886	2718	2997	...	...	...
5 Corporate equity securities	2110	3499	2018	2641	997	2022	3123	2056	2164	...	...	...
6 Short-term loans, n.e.c.	901	-110	612	1520	4228	3991	9808	4998	4248	...	...	...
7 Long-term loans	1527	3660	6622	6787	10297	9167	12441	8927	11740	...	...	...
8 Non-resident proprietors' net additions to accumulation of resident quasi-corporate enterprises	...	...	...	...	...	...	...	...	...	...	...	...
9 Trade credit and advances	...	...	...	...	...	...	...	...	...	...	...	...
10 Other [c]	762	102	132	-838	-2127	96	422	532	-732	...	...	...
Total Incurrence of Liabilities	11703	21275	18308	20548	25496	36107	44082	20329	21015	...	...	...
Statistical discrepancy	304	-1724	-487	-478	-1286	-2660	-3211	-3141	2762	...	...	...
Net Lending [d]	1940	-4950	-1690	2780	4080	6000	-6620	-9500	-10470	...	...	...
Total Incurrence of Liabilities and Net Lending	13947	14601	16131	22850	28290	39447	34251	7688	13307	...	...	...

a) Item 'Other' of 'Acquisitions of foreign financial assets' refers to insurance technical reserves.
b) For 1979, item 'Currency and transferable deposits' includes 3979 million guilders in European Currency Units.
c) Item 'Other' of 'Incurrence of liabilities' refers to SDRs and financial gold.
d) Net lending of the capital accumulation account and the capital finance account have not been reconciled and are different due to different statistical sources.

4.1 Derivation of Value Added by Kind of Activity, in Current Prices

Million Netherlands guilders

	1980			1981			1982			1983		
	Gross Output	Intermediate Consumption	Value Added	Gross Output	Intermediate Consumption	Value Added	Gross Output	Intermediate Consumption	Value Added	Gross Output	Intermediate Consumption	Value Added
All Producers											
1 Agriculture, hunting, forestry and fishing	27370	15694	11676	31442	16885	14557	33493	17561	15932	34724	18600	16124
A Agriculture and hunting	26746	15399	11347	30701	16528	14173	32690	17143	15547	33830	18149	15681
B Forestry and logging												
C Fishing	624	295	329	741	357	384	803	418	385	894	451	443
2 Mining and quarrying	21893	2742	19151	28764	3201	25563	30049	4077	25972	31501	4173	27328
A Coal mining	...	...	...	...	...	...	...	...	...	...	...	...
B Crude petroleum and natural gas production	20868	2217	18651	27760	2729	25031	28947	3530	25417	30229	3495	26734
C Metal ore mining	...	...	...	...	...	...	...	...	...	...	...	...
D Other mining	1025	525	500	1004	472	532	1102	547	555	1272	678	594

Netherlands

4.1 Derivation of Value Added by Kind of Activity, in Current Prices
(Continued)

Million Netherlands guilders

	1980 Gross Output	1980 Intermediate Consumption	1980 Value Added	1981 Gross Output	1981 Intermediate Consumption	1981 Value Added	1982 Gross Output	1982 Intermediate Consumption	1982 Value Added	1983 Gross Output	1983 Intermediate Consumption	1983 Value Added
3 Manufacturing	220709	160344	60365	235777	175997	59780	242374	177704	64670	251817	184354	67463
A Manufacture of food, beverages and tobacco	56578	45812	10766	63168	51873	11295	66969	54518	12451	69467	56917	12550
B Textile, wearing apparel and leather industries	8609	6060	2549	8158	5742	2416	8351	5825	2526	8286	5843	2443
C Manufacture of wood and wood products, including furniture	5157	3145	2012	4917	3090	1827	4695	2971	1724	4747	3075	1672
D Manufacture of paper and paper products, printing and publishing	16822	10267	6555	17357	10712	6645	17719	10749	6970	17942	10746	7196
E Manufacture of chemicals and chemical petroleum, coal, rubber and plastic products	63586	51823	11763	70240	59456	10784	70388	58146	12242	76839	62363	14476
F Manufacture of non-metallic mineral products, except products of petroleum and coal	5822	3282	2540	5665	3364	2301	5520	3323	2197	5488	3260	2228
G Basic metal industries	8755	6246	2509	9182	6817	2365	9282	6359	2923	9509	6667	2842
H Manufacture of fabricated metal products, machinery and equipment	52325	31830	20495	53950	33092	20858	56224	33930	22294	56069	33443	22626
I Other manufacturing industries	3055	1879	1176	3140	1851	1289	3226	1883	1343	3470	2040	1430
4 Electricity, gas and water	18511	11339	7172	22219	14613	7606	23145	14986	8159	23759	15347	8412
A Electricity, gas and steam	17112	11068	6044	20781	14332	6449	21583	14695	6888	22078	15051	7027
B Water works and supply	1399	271	1128	1438	281	1157	1562	291	1271	1681	296	1385
5 Construction	55239	31479	23760	52469	29413	23056	50324	27880	22444	48847	27434	21413
6 Wholesale and retail trade, restaurants and hotels	68101	24664	43437	69541	24966	44575	72704	25653	47051	74281	25820	48461
A Wholesale and retail trade	58292	20596	37696	59328	20721	38607	61954	21162	40792	63238	21276	41962
B Restaurants and hotels	9809	4068	5741	10213	4245	5968	10750	4491	6259	11043	4544	6499
7 Transport, storage and communication	34215	12917	21298	36791	14526	22265	37103	14708	22395	37651	14499	23152
A Transport and storage	26745	11858	14887	28885	13378	15507	28671	13501	15170	28811	13289	15522
B Communication	7470	1059	6411	7906	1148	6758	8432	1207	7225	8840	1210	7630
8 Finance, insurance, real estate and business services	59336	12443	46893	63406	13092	50314	68016	13743	54273	74128	14020	60108
A Financial institutions	13815	2863	10952	15141	3064	12077	16805	3288	13517	19300	3513	15787
B Insurance	9188	4266	4922	9221	4436	4785	9106	4547	4559	9140	4649	4491
C Real estate and business services	36333	5314	31019	39044	5592	33452	42105	5908	36197	45688	5858	39830
Real estate, except dwellings	...	...	...	...	...	...	...	...	...	...	...	...
Dwellings	19153	2797	16356	21276	2888	18388	23765	3006	20759	26142	2934	23208
9 Community, social and personal services [a]	49181	11653	37528	51997	12545	39452	54915	13289	41626	56488	13712	42776
A Sanitary and similar services	...	...	...	...	...	...	...	...	...	...	...	...
B Social and related community services	23778	4910	18868	25432	5459	19973	27215	5960	21255	28068	6180	21888
Educational services	...	...	...	...	...	...	...	...	...	...	...	...
Medical, dental, other health and veterinary services	23778	4910	18868	25432	5459	19973	27215	5960	21255	28068	6180	21888
C Recreational and cultural services	5647	2059	3588	5924	2113	3811	6300	2176	4124	6773	2320	4453
D Personal and household services [a]	19756	4684	15072	20641	4973	15668	21400	5153	16247	21647	5212	16435
Statistical discrepancy	1615	1615	...	1834	1822	12	2117	2109	8	2234	2221	13
Total, Industries	556170	284890	271280	594240	307060	287180	614240	311710	302530	635430	320180	315250
Producers of Government Services	64040	17200	46840	66620	18680	47940	69390	19870	49520	71180	21530	49650
Other Producers	1050	...	1050	1060	...	1060	1090	...	1090	1070	...	1070
Total	621260	302090	319170	661920	325740	336180	684720	331580	353140	707680	341710	365970
Less: Imputed bank service charge	...	-11460	11460	...	-12660	12660	...	-14080	14080	...	-16150	16150
Import duties	4440	...	4440	4220	...	4220	4580	...	4580	4770	...	4770
Value added tax [b]	24590	...	24590	25110	...	25110	25220	...	25220	26430	...	26430
Total	650290	313550	336740	691250	338400	352850	714520	345660	368860	738880	357860	381020

Netherlands

4.1 Derivation of Value Added by Kind of Activity, in Current Prices

Million Netherlands guilders

	1984 Gross Output	1984 Intermediate Consumption	1984 Value Added	1985 Gross Output	1985 Intermediate Consumption	1985 Value Added	1986 Gross Output	1986 Intermediate Consumption	1986 Value Added
All Producers									
1 Agriculture, hunting, forestry and fishing	36630	19371	17259	...	...	17170	...	...	18590
A Agriculture and hunting	35661	18876	16785	...	...	...	...	...	...
B Forestry and logging				...	...	...	...	...	...
C Fishing	969	495	474	...	...	...	...	...	...
2 Mining and quarrying	35291	4200	31091	...	...	35340	...	...	23840
A Coal mining	...	...	...	...	...	...	...	...	...
B Crude petroleum and natural gas production	33933	3526	30407	...	...	...	...	...	...
C Metal ore mining	...	...	...	...	...	...	...	...	...
D Other mining	1358	674	684	...	...	...	...	...	...
3 Manufacturing	279477	206908	72569	...	...	74410	...	...	85080
A Manufacture of food, beverages and tobacco	76054	62934	13120	...	...	...	...	...	...
B Textile, wearing apparel and leather industries	8864	6365	2400	...	...	...	...	...	...
C Manufacture of wood and wood products, including furniture	4743	3095	1648	...	...	...	...	...	...
D Manufacture of paper and paper products, printing and publishing	19592	12148	7444	...	...	...	...	...	...
E Manufacture of chemicals and chemical petroleum, coal, rubber and plastic products	86640	70020	16611	...	...	...	...	...	...
F Manufacture of non-metallic mineral products, except products of petroleum and coal	5876	3468	2408	...	...	...	...	...	...
G Basic metal industries	11764	8256	3508	...	...	...	...	...	...
H Manufacture of fabricated metal products, machinery and equipment	62139	38366	23773	...	...	...	...	...	...
I Other manufacturing industries	3805	2247	1558	...	...	...	...	...	...
4 Electricity, gas and water	25200	16833	8367	...	...	8560	...	...	9330
A Electricity, gas and steam	23483	16523	6960	...	...	...	...	...	...
B Water works and supply	1717	310	1407	...	...	...	...	...	...
5 Construction	51008	29651	21357	...	...	20780	...	...	21640
6 Wholesale and retail trade, restaurants and hotels	79350	28175	51175	...	...	53330	...	...	55380
A Wholesale and retail trade	67428	23200	44228	...	...	...	...	...	...
B Restaurants and hotels	11922	4975	6947	...	...	...	...	...	...
7 Transport, storage and communication	40110	15520	24590	...	...	26710	...	...	27050
A Transport and storage	30966	14238	16728	...	...	...	...	...	...
B Communication	9144	1282	7862	...	...	...	...	...	...
8 Finance, insurance, real estate and business services	77803	14791	63012	...	...	65830	...	...	69340
A Financial institutions	19776	3689	16087	...	...	...	...	...	...
B Insurance	9663	4849	4814	...	...	...	...	...	...
C Real estate and business services	48364	6253	42111	...	...	...	...	...	...
Real estate, except dwellings	...	...	...	...	...	...	...	...	...
Dwellings	27574	3063	24511	...	...	...	...	...	...
9 Community, social and personal services [a]	57513	14235	43278	...	...	44060	...	...	46170
A Sanitary and similar services	...	...	...	...	...	...	...	...	...
B Social and related community services	28467	6361	22106	...	...	...	...	...	...
Educational services	...	...	...	...	...	...	...	...	...
Medical, dental, other health and veterinary services	28467	6361	22106	...	...	...	...	...	...
C Recreational and cultural services	6959	2434	4525	...	...	...	...	...	...
D Personal and household services [a]	22087	5440	16647	...	...	...	...	...	...
Statistical discrepancy	2578	2566	12	...	...	...	...	...	...

Netherlands

4.1 Derivation of Value Added by Kind of Activity, in Current Prices
(Continued)

Million Netherlands guilders

	1984 Gross Output	1984 Intermediate Consumption	1984 Value Added	1985 Gross Output	1985 Intermediate Consumption	1985 Value Added	1986 Gross Output	1986 Intermediate Consumption	1986 Value Added
Total, Industries	684960	352250	332710	710450	364260	346190	683430	327010	356420
Producers of Government Services	71390	21940	49450	72630	22650	49980	73670	23380	50290
Other Producers	1090	...	1090	1110	...	1110	1140	...	1140
Total	757440	374190	383250	784190	386910	397280	758240	350390	407850
Less: Imputed bank service charge	...	-16420	16420	...	-16770	16770	...	-16880	16880
Import duties	5130	...	5130	5670	...	5670	6330	...	6330
Value added tax b	28290	...	28290	30410	...	30410	32270	...	32270
Total	790860	390610	400250	820270	403680	416590	796840	367270	429570

a) Repair services are included in item 'Community, social and personal services'.
b) Item 'Value added tax' includes selective investment levy.,

4.3 Cost Components of Value Added

Million Netherlands guilders

	1980 Compensation of Employees	1980 Capital Consumption	1980 Net Operating Surplus	1980 Indirect Taxes	1980 Less: Subsidies Received	1980 Value Added	1981 Compensation of Employees	1981 Capital Consumption	1981 Net Operating Surplus	1981 Indirect Taxes	1981 Less: Subsidies Received	1981 Value Added
					All Producers							
1 Agriculture, hunting, forestry and fishing	2492	1800	7127	435	178	11676	2577	1970	9583	500	73	14557
A Agriculture and hunting	2342	1730	7005	431	161	11347	2400	1890	9437	495	49	14173
B Forestry and logging												
C Fishing	150	70	122	4	17	329	177	80	146	5	24	384
2 Mining and quarrying	528	780	17803	40	-	19151	576	930	24014	43	-	25563
A Coal mining	...	...	...	...	-	...	...	...	...	...	...	...
B Crude petroleum and natural gas production	357	690	17584	20	...	18651	405	820	23784	22	...	25031
C Metal ore mining	...	...	...	...	...	...	...	...	...	...	...	...
D Other mining	171	90	219	20	...	500	171	110	230	21	...	532
3 Manufacturing	43678	8340	5971	5847	3471	60365	44482	9220	3340	6014	3276	59780
A Manufacture of food, beverages and tobacco	6913	1670	2338	2886	3041	10766	7197	1870	1818	2990	2580	11295
B Textile, wearing apparel and leather industries	2280	400	-115	24	40	2549	2066	420	-57	25	38	2416
C Manufacture of wood and wood products, including furniture	1627	200	186	7	8	2012	1549	210	67	7	6	1827
D Manufacture of paper and paper products, printing and publishing	4832	650	1040	37	4	6555	4918	710	985	38	6	6645
E Manufacture of chemicals and chemical petroleum, coal, rubber and plastic products	6589	2540	-89	2743	20	11763	6876	2850	-1743	2824	23	10784
F Manufacture of non-metallic mineral products, except products of petroleum and coal	1808	430	289	14	1	2540	1764	480	43	15	1	2301
G Basic metal industries	1836	590	59	24	-	2509	1883	650	-184	16	-	2365
H Manufacture of fabricated metal products, machinery and equipment	17005	1780	1954	110	354	20495	17431	1940	2000	96	609	20858
I Other manufacturing industries	788	80	309	2	3	1176	798	90	411	3	13	1289
4 Electricity, gas and water	2557	2410	2158	47	-	7172	2612	2720	2223	51	-	7606
A Electricity, gas and steam	2141	2050	1806	47	-	6044	2190	2320	1888	51	-	6449
B Water works and supply	416	360	352	-	-	1128	422	400	335	-	-	1157
5 Construction	17704	1090	4910	120	64	23760	16300	1190	5487	130	51	23056
6 Wholesale and retail trade, restaurants and hotels	26012	3280	13974	598	427	43437	26473	3470	14270	656	294	44575
A Wholesale and retail trade	23836	2940	10827	505	412	37696	24222	3110	11007	550	282	38607
B Restaurants and hotels	2176	340	3147	93	15	5741	2251	360	3263	106	12	5968
7 Transport, storage and communication	15418	4690	3221	320	2351	21298	15792	5090	3655	349	2621	22265
A Transport and storage	11308	3590	2033	307	2351	14887	11629	3900	2270	329	2621	15507
B Communication	4110	1100	1188	13	-	6411	4163	1190	1385	20	-	6758
8 Finance, insurance, real estate and business services	17784	5770	21750	3330	1741	46893	18899	6350	23458	3299	1692	50314
A Financial institutions	5486	130	5204	138	6	10952	5873	150	5897	161	4	12077

Netherlands

4.3 Cost Components of Value Added
(Continued)

Million Netherlands guilders

	\multicolumn{6}{c	}{1980}	\multicolumn{6}{c}{1981}
	Compensation of Employees	Capital Consumption	Net Operating Surplus	Indirect Taxes	Less: Subsidies Received	Value Added	Compensation of Employees	Capital Consumption	Net Operating Surplus	Indirect Taxes	Less: Subsidies Received	Value Added
B Insurance	3241	130	1042	510	1	4922	3407	140	719	520	1	4785
C Real estate and business services	9057	5510	15504	2682	1734	31019	9619	6060	16842	2618	1687	33452
Real estate, except dwellings	...	...	...	...	...	...	...	...	...	...	...	...
Dwellings	581	5100	11055	1343	1723	16356	620	5600	12285	1561	1678	18388
9 Community, social and personal services [a]	26536	1930	8936	196	70	37528	27734	2120	9432	214	48	39452
A Sanitary and similar services	...	...	...	...	...	...	...	...	...	...	...	...
B Social and related community services	11770	1450	5538	111	1	18868	12356	1600	5905	115	3	19973
Educational services	...	...	...	...	...	...	...	...	...	...	...	...
Medical, dental, other health and veterinary services	11770	1450	5538	111	1	18868	12356	1600	5905	115	3	19973
C Recreational and cultural services	2025	120	831	23	11	3588	2764	130	894	26	3	3811
D Personal and household services [a]	12141	360	2567	62	58	15072	12614	390	2633	73	42	15668
Statistical discrepancy	1	...	...	-3	-2	...	5	...	-2	14	5	12
Total, Industries	152710	30090	85850	10930	8300	271280	155450	33060	95460	11270	8060	287180
Producers of Government Services	44080	2400	-	360	-	46840	45020	2560	-	360	-	47940
Other Producers	1050	...	-	-	-	1050	1060	...	-	-	-	1060
Total	197840	32490	85850	11290	8300	319170	201530	35620	95460	11630	8060	336180
Less: Imputed bank service charge	...	...	11460	...	...	11460	...	...	12660	...	...	12660
Import duties	...	...	...	4440	...	4440	...	...	...	4220	...	4220
Value added tax [b]	...	...	...	24590	...	24590	...	...	...	25110	...	25110
Other adjustments	...	...	...	800	800	...	...	...	...	760	760	...
Total	197840	32490	74390	41120	9100	336740	201530	35620	82800	41720	8820	352850

	\multicolumn{6}{c	}{1982}	\multicolumn{6}{c}{1983}
	Compensation of Employees	Capital Consumption	Net Operating Surplus	Indirect Taxes	Less: Subsidies Received	Value Added	Compensation of Employees	Capital Consumption	Net Operating Surplus	Indirect Taxes	Less: Subsidies Received	Value Added
	\multicolumn{12}{c}{**All Producers**}
1 Agriculture, hunting, forestry and fishing	2727	2100	10683	556	134	15932	2926	2200	10656	565	223	16124
A Agriculture and hunting	2543	2000	10568	549	113	15547	2736	2090	10505	557	207	15681
B Forestry and logging												
C Fishing	184	100	115	7	21	385	190	110	151	8	16	443
2 Mining and quarrying	645	1070	24215	42	-	25972	691	1150	25442	45	-	27328
A Coal mining	...	...	...	...	-	...	...	...	...	...	-	...
B Crude petroleum and natural gas production	465	940	23990	22	...	25417	512	1010	26187	25	...	26734
C Metal ore mining	...	...	...	...	...	...	...	...	...	...	...	...
D Other mining	180	130	225	20	...	555	179	140	255	20	...	594

Netherlands

4.3 Cost Components of Value Added
(Continued)

Million Netherlands guilders

	1982						1983					
	Compensation of Employees	Capital Consumption	Net Operating Surplus	Indirect Taxes	Less: Subsidies Received	Value Added	Compensation of Employees	Capital Consumption	Net Operating Surplus	Indirect Taxes	Less: Subsidies Received	Value Added
3 Manufacturing	45658	9900	6528	6214	3630	64670	45626	10240	8779	6833	4015	67463
A Manufacture of food, beverages and tobacco	7515	2020	2652	3257	2993	12451	7652	2100	2553	3576	3331	12550
B Textile, wearing apparel and leather industries	1974	430	161	27	66	2526	1895	440	164	29	85	2443
C Manufacture of wood and wood products, including furniture	1478	220	30	7	11	1724	1403	220	54	9	14	1672
D Manufacture of paper and paper products, printing and publishing	5075	760	1100	40	5	6970	5122	800	1238	42	6	7196
E Manufacture of chemicals and chemical petroleum, coal, rubber and plastic products	7229	3070	-771	2736	22	12242	7544	3190	774	2993	25	14476
F Manufacture of non-metallic mineral products, except products of petroleum and coal	1746	510	-72	15	2	2197	1684	520	11	16	3	2228
G Basic metal industries	1941	700	267	15	-	2923	2000	720	106	16	-	2842
H Manufacture of fabricated metal products, machinery and equipment	17869	2090	2747	114	526	22294	17492	2150	3381	147	544	22626
I Other manufacturing industries	831	100	414	3	5	1343	834	100	498	5	7	1430
4 Electricity, gas and water	2664	2940	2504	51	-	8159	2695	3020	2642	55	-	8412
A Electricity, gas and steam	2268	2500	2069	51	-	6888	2308	2570	2095	54	-	7027
B Water works and supply	396	440	435	-	-	1271	387	450	547	1	-	1385
5 Construction	15591	1270	5539	132	88	22444	14830	1330	5234	131	112	21413
6 Wholesale and retail trade, restaurants and hotels	26769	3680	16196	724	318	47051	27464	3820	16792	839	454	48461
A Wholesale and retail trade	24424	3300	12757	608	297	40792	25030	3430	13210	719	427	41962
B Restaurants and hotels	2345	380	3439	116	21	6259	2434	390	3582	120	27	6499
7 Transport, storage and communication	16323	5480	3444	378	3230	22395	16700	5770	3605	393	3316	23152
A Transport and storage	12002	4160	1876	362	3230	15170	12299	4390	1772	377	3316	15522
B Communication	4321	1320	1568	16	-	7225	4401	1380	1833	16	-	7630
8 Finance, insurance, real estate and business services	20028	6710	25920	3393	1778	54273	20708	6950	31042	3637	2229	60108
A Financial institutions	6329	160	6859	176	7	13517	6558	170	8854	214	9	15787
B Insurance	3563	150	341	507	2	4559	3619	160	170	545	3	4491
C Real estate and business services	10136	6400	18720	2710	1769	36197	10531	6620	22018	2878	2217	39830
Real estate, except dwellings	...	...	...	...	...	...	...	...	...	...	...	...
Dwellings	669	5910	14225	1708	1753	20759	715	6110	16867	1712	2196	23208
9 Community, social and personal services [a]	29257	2290	9880	280	81	41626	29981	2410	10223	266	104	42776
A Sanitary and similar services	...	...	...	...	...	...	...	...	...	...	...	...
B Social and related community services	13177	1730	6174	179	5	21255	13573	1810	6367	144	6	21888
Educational services	...	...	...	...	...	...	...	...	...	...	...	...
Medical, dental, other health and veterinary services	13177	1730	6174	179	5	21255	13573	1810	6367	144	6	21888
C Recreational and cultural services	2927	140	1034	28	5	4124	2989	150	1291	30	7	4453
D Personal and household services	13153	420	2672	73	71	16247	13419	450	2565	92	91	16435
Statistical discrepancy	8	...	-9	10	1	8	-1	...	5	6	-3	13
Total, Industries	159670	35440	104900	11780	9260	302530	161620	36890	114420	12770	10450	315250
Producers of Government Services	46720	2420	-	380	-	49520	46950	2300	-	400	-	49650
Other Producers	1090	...	-	-	-	1090	1070	...	-	-	-	1070
Total	207480	37860	104900	12160	9260	353140	209640	39190	114420	13170	10450	365970
Less: Imputed bank service charge	...	...	14080	...	...	14080	...	...	16150	...	...	16150
Import duties	...	...	...	4580	...	4580	...	...	...	4770	...	4770
Value added tax [b]	...	...	...	25220	...	25220	...	...	...	26430	...	26430
Other adjustments	...	...	...	800	800	...	...	...	...	770	770	...
Total	207480	37860	90820	42760	10060	368860	209640	39190	98270	45140	11220	381020

Netherlands

4.3 Cost Components of Value Added

Million Netherlands guilders

		1984					1985					
		Compensation of Employees	Capital Consumption	Net Operating Surplus	Indirect Taxes	Less: Subsidies Received	Value Added	Compensation of Employees	Capital Consumption	Net Operating Surplus	Indirect Taxes	Less: Subsidies Received	Value Added
						All Producers							
1	Agriculture, hunting, forestry and fishing	2957	2340	11488	575	101	17259	...	...	...	...	...	17170
	A Agriculture and hunting	2755	2210	11348	567	95	16785	...	...	...	...	...	...
	B Forestry and logging							...	...	...	...	...	...
	C Fishing	202	130	140	8	6	474	...	...	...	...	...	...
2	Mining and quarrying	736	1250	29062	43	-	31091	...	...	...	...	...	35340
	A Coal mining	...	...	...	...	-	...	...	...	...	...	...	...
	B Crude petroleum and natural gas production	562	1100	28723	22	...	30407	...	...	...	...	...	...
	C Metal ore mining	...	...	...	...	...	...	...	...	...	...	...	...
	D Other mining	174	150	339	21	...	684	...	...	...	...	...	...
3	Manufacturing	45666	10630	13638	7407	4772	72569	...	...	...	...	...	74410
	A Manufacture of food, beverages and tobacco	7704	2180	3644	3681	4089	13120	...	...	...	...	...	...
	B Textile, wearing apparel and leather industries	1841	430	282	28	82	2499	...	...	...	...	...	...
	C Manufacture of wood and wood products, including furniture	1353	220	81	9	15	1648	...	...	...	...	...	...
	D Manufacture of paper and paper products, printing and publishing	5235	850	1323	43	7	7444	...	...	...	...	...	...
	E Manufacture of chemicals and chemical petroleum, coal, rubber and plastic products	7570	3320	2294	3449	22	16611	...	...	...	...	...	...
	F Manufacture of non-metallic mineral products, except products of petroleum and coal	1680	530	185	16	3	2408	...	...	...	...	...	...
	G Basic metal industries	2025	740	726	17	-	3508	...	...	...	...	...	...
	H Manufacture of fabricated metal products, machinery and equipment	17413	2250	4498	159	547	23773	...	...	...	...	...	...
	I Other manufacturing industries	845	110	605	5	7	1558	...	...	...	...	...	...
4	Electricity, gas and water	2640	3090	2579	58	-	8367	...	...	...	...	...	8560
	A Electricity, gas and steam	2255	2620	2028	57	-	6960	...	...	...	...	...	...
	B Water works and supply	385	470	551	1	-	1407	...	...	...	...	...	...
5	Construction	14828	1380	5129	135	115	21357	...	...	...	...	...	20780
6	Wholesale and retail trade, restaurants and hotels	27726	3960	19219	783	513	51175	...	...	...	...	...	53330
	A Wholesale and retail trade	25190	3550	15309	661	482	44228	...	...	...	...	...	...
	B Restaurants and hotels	2536	410	3910	122	31	6947	...	...	...	...	...	...
7	Transport, storage and communication	16810	6160	4665	412	3457	24590	...	...	...	...	...	26710
	A Transport and storage	12417	4710	2670	388	3457	16728	...	...	...	...	...	...
	B Communication	4393	1450	1995	24	-	7862	...	...	...	...	...	...
8	Finance, insurance, real estate and business services	21263	7220	33599	3717	2787	63012	...	...	...	...	...	65830
	A Financial institutions	6651	180	9039	227	10	16087	...	...	...	...	...	...
	B Insurance	3661	170	393	593	3	4814	...	...	...	...	...	...
	C Real estate and business services	10951	6870	24167	2897	2774	42111	...	...	...	...	...	...
	Real estate, except dwellings	...	...	...	...	...	...	...	...	...	...	...	...
	Dwellings	758	6220	19401	1772	2750	24611	...	...	...	...	...	...
9	Community, social and personal services [a]	29864	2540	10720	265	111	43278	...	...	...	...	...	44060
	A Sanitary and similar services	...	...	...	...	...	...	...	...	...	...	...	...
	B Social and related community services	13354	1910	6704	144	6	22106	...	...	...	...	...	...
	Educational services	...	...	...	...	...	...	...	...	...	...	...	...
	Medical, dental, other health and veterinary services	13354	1910	6704	144	6	22106	...	...	...	...	...	...
	C Recreational and cultural services	2965	160	1376	31	7	4525	...	...	...	...	...	...
	D Personal and household services [a]	13545	470	2640	90	98	16647	...	...	...	...	...	...
	Statistical discrepancy	10	...	1	5	4	12	...	...	...	...	...	...

Netherlands

4.3 Cost Components of Value Added
(Continued)

Million Netherlands guilders

	1984						1985					
	Compensation of Employees	Capital Consumption	Net Operating Surplus	Indirect Taxes	Less: Subsidies Received	Value Added	Compensation of Employees	Capital Consumption	Net Operating Surplus	Indirect Taxes	Less: Subsidies Received	Value Added
Total, Industries	162500	38570	130100	13400	11860	332710	168200	40040	137550	13270	12870	346190
Producers of Government Services	46410	2620	-	420	-	49450	46810	2720	-	450	-	49980
Other Producers	1090	...	-	-	-	1090	1110	...	-	-	-	1110
Total	210000	41190	130100	13820	11860	383250	216120	42760	137550	13720	12870	397280
Less: Imputed bank service charge	...	...	16420	...	...	16420	...	...	16770	...	...	16770
Import duties	...	...	...	5130	...	5130	...	...	...	5670	...	5670
Value added tax [b]	...	...	...	28290	...	28290	...	...	...	30410	...	30410
Other adjustments	...	...	...	750	750	...	...	...	...	890	890	...
Total	210000	41190	113680	47990	12610	400250	216120	42760	120780	50690	13760	416590

a) Repair services are included in item 'Community, social and personal services'.
b) Item 'Value added tax' includes selective investment levy. ,

Netherlands Antilles

Source. Reply to the United Nations National Accounts Questionnaire from the Bureau Voor de Statistiek, Curacao. Official estimates together with detailed information on concepts, definitions, sources and methods of estimation utilized are published in 'Nationale Rekeningen, 1975'.

General note. The official estimates have been adjusted by the Bureau to conform to the United Nations System of National Accounts so far as the existing data would permit. It should be noted that estimates for Windward Islands are not included.

1.1 Expenditure on the Gross Domestic Product, in Current Prices

Million Netherlands Antillian guilders

	1970	1975	1977	1978	1979	1980	1981	1982	1983	1984	1985	1986
1 Government final consumption expenditure	...	...	...	...	469.1	568.3	649.1	726.7	...	...	...	...
2 Private final consumption expenditure	...	...	...	...	1305.1	1467.8	1702.9	1891.3	...	...	...	...
3 Gross capital formation	...	...	...	...	351.0	433.3	479.5	463.4	...	...	...	...
A Increase in stocks	...	...	...	...	88.7	49.3	64.9	35.3	...	...	...	...
B Gross fixed capital formation	...	...	...	...	262.3	384.0	414.6	428.1	...	...	...	...
4 Exports of goods and services [a]	...	...	...	...	1478.8	1791.2	1886.5	1787.6	...	...	...	...
5 Less: Imports of goods and services [a]	...	...	...	...	1730.4	2186.6	2313.9	2311.1	...	...	...	...
Equals: Gross Domestic Product	...	...	...	...	1873.6	2074.0	2404.1	2557.9	...	...	...	...

a) Exports and imports of merchandise are recorded on the basis of the crossing of frontiers. No data are available on the basis of changes in the ownership of the goods. Imports and exports are recorded on a cash basis and the imports and exports of oil refineries are not included in the estimates.

1.3 Cost Components of the Gross Domestic Product

Million Netherlands Antillian guilders

	1970	1975	1977	1978	1979	1980	1981	1982	1983	1984	1985	1986
1 Indirect taxes, net	...	...	...	...	120.3	137.5	131.8	123.3	...	...	...	...
A Indirect taxes	...	...	...	...	168.3	188.2	183.2	200.7	...	...	...	...
B Less: Subsidies	...	...	...	...	48.0	50.7	51.4	77.4	...	...	...	...
2 Consumption of fixed capital	...	...	...	...	140.0	158.1	187.4	206.1	...	...	...	...
3 Compensation of employees paid by resident producers to: [a]	...	...	...	...	1223.0	1442.1	1681.5	1865.8	...	...	...	...
A Resident households	...	...	...	...	1209.4	1403.3	1645.0	1823.6	...	...	...	...
B Rest of the world	...	...	...	...	13.6	38.8	36.5	42.2	...	...	...	...
4 Operating surplus	...	...	...	...	390.3	336.3	403.4	362.7	...	...	...	...
Equals: Gross Domestic Product [a]	...	...	...	...	1873.6	2074.0	2404.1	2557.9	...	...	...	...

a) The oil refineries in the Netherlands Antilles are now considered non-resident producers. Consequently, their compensation of employees to resident households is treated as wages and salaries paid by the rest of the world. Other cost components of these oil refineries are not included in GDP.

1.4 General Government Current Receipts and Disbursements

Million Netherlands Antillian guilders

	1970	1975	1977	1978	1979	1980	1981	1982	1983	1984	1985	1986
Receipts												
1 Operating surplus	...	...	...	...	-	-	-	-	...	...	...	...
2 Property and entrepreneurial income	...	...	...	...	20.4	8.2	28.5	12.7	...	...	...	...
3 Taxes, fees and contributions	...	...	...	...	511.9	608.5	707.6	741.1	...	...	...	...
A Indirect taxes	...	...	...	...	168.3	188.2	100.2	200.7	...	...	...	...
B Direct taxes [a]	...	...	...	...	264.8	328.7	409.7	410.7	...	...	...	...
C Social security contributions	...	...	...	...	70.0	00.1	107.5	124.4	...	...	...	...
D Compulsory fees, fines and penalties	...	...	...	...	5.5	5.5	7.2	5.3	...	...	...	...
4 Other current transfers [a]	...	...	...	...	148.1	215.3	289.1	434.5	...	...	...	...
Total Current Receipts of General Government	...	...	...	...	680.4	832.0	1025.2	1188.3	...	...	...	...
Disbursements												
1 Government final consumption expenditure	...	...	...	...	469.1	568.3	649.1	726.7	...	...	...	...
A Compensation of employees	...	...	...	...	342.2	395.5	469.1	536.4	...	...	...	...
B Consumption of fixed capital	...	...	...	...	7.2	8.1	9.9	11.1	...	...	...	...
C Purchases of goods and services, net	...	...	...	...	127.6	173.3	179.9	191.0	...	...	...	...
D Less: Own account fixed capital formation	...	...	...	...	8.4	9.1	10.4	12.4	...	...	...	...
E Indirect taxes paid, net	...	...	...	...	0.5	0.5	0.6	0.6	...	...	...	...
2 Property income	...	...	...	...	31.0	31.0	33.4	39.4	...	...	...	...
A Interest	...	...	...	...	31.0	31.0	33.4	39.4	...	...	...	...
B Net land rent and royalties	...	...	...	...	-	-	-	-	...	...	...	...

Netherlands Antilles

1.4 General Government Current Receipts and Disbursements
(Continued)

Million Netherlands Antillian guilders

	1970	1975	1977	1978	1979	1980	1981	1982	1983	1984	1985	1986
3 Subsidies	...	...	...	...	48.0	50.7	51.4	77.4	...	...	...	...
4 Other current transfers	...	...	...	...	147.5	172.3	206.0	236.1	...	...	...	...
A Social security benefits	...	...	...	...	71.3	80.4	102.2	116.3	...	...	...	...
B Social assistance grants	...	...	...	...	22.0	25.2	30.2	35.6	...	...	...	...
C Other	...	...	...	...	54.2	66.7	73.6	84.2	...	...	...	...
5 Net saving	...	...	...	...	-15.2	9.7	85.3	108.7	...	...	...	...
Total Current Disbursements and Net Saving of General Government	...	...	...	...	680.4	832.0	1025.2	1188.3	...	...	...	...

a) The profit taxes paid by the petroleum refineries and the off-shore companies are now considered as current transfers from the rest of the world.

1.7 External Transactions on Current Account, Summary

Million Netherlands Antillian guilders

	1970	1975	1977	1978	1979	1980	1981	1982	1983	1984	1985	1986
Payments to the Rest of the World												
1 Imports of goods and services [a]	...	...	...	...	1730.4	2186.6	2313.9	2311.1	...	...	...	...
A Imports of merchandise c.i.f.	...	...	...	...	1318.6	1610.0	1531.2	1636.4	...	...	...	...
B Other	...	...	...	...	411.8	576.6	782.7	674.7	...	...	...	...
2 Factor income to the rest of the world	...	...	...	...	101.6	141.0	110.8	111.8	...	...	...	...
A Compensation of employees	...	...	...	...	13.6	38.8	36.5	42.2	...	...	...	...
B Property and entrepreneurial income	...	...	...	...	88.0	102.2	74.3	69.6	...	...	...	...
By general government	...	...	...	...	21.5	21.8	17.9	17.2	...	...	...	...
By corporate and quasi-corporate enterprises	...	...	...	...	66.5	80.4	56.4	52.4	...	...	...	...
By other	...	...	...	...	-	-	-	-	...	...	...	...
3 Current transfers to the rest of the world	...	...	...	...	51.8	57.4	69.4	90.9	...	...	...	...
A Indirect taxes to supranational organizations	...	...	...	...	-	-	-	-	...	...	...	...
B Other current transfers	...	...	...	...	51.8	57.4	69.4	90.9	...	...	...	...
4 Surplus of the nation on current transactions	...	...	...	...	0.3	-89.0	44.0	109.2	...	...	...	...
Payments to the Rest of the World and Surplus of the Nation on Current Transactions	...	...	...	...	1884.1	2296.0	2538.1	2623.0	...	...	...	...
Receipts From The Rest of the World												
1 Exports of goods and services [a]	...	...	...	...	1478.8	1791.2	1886.5	1787.6	...	...	...	...
A Exports of merchandise f.o.b.	...	...	...	...	204.7	243.8	191.7	179.0	...	...	...	...
B Other	...	...	...	...	1274.1	1547.4	1694.8	1608.6	...	...	...	...
2 Factor income from rest of the world	...	...	...	...	254.6	288.6	360.1	416.6	...	...	...	...
A Compensation of employees [b]	...	...	...	...	202.0	231.6	255.4	287.5	...	...	...	...
B Property and entrepreneurial income	...	...	...	...	52.6	57.0	104.7	129.1	...	...	...	...
By general government	...	...	...	...	-	-	-	-	...	...	...	...
By corporate and quasi-corporate enterprises	...	...	...	...	39.9	39.2	33.5	41.9	...	...	...	...
By other	...	...	...	...	12.7	17.8	71.2	87.2	...	...	...	...
3 Current transfers from rest of the world	...	...	...	...	150.7	216.2	291.5	418.8	...	...	...	...
A Subsidies from supranational organisations	...	...	...	...	-	-	-	-	...	...	...	...
B Other current transfers	...	...	...	...	150.7	216.2	291.5	418.8	...	...	...	...
Receipts from the Rest of the World on Current Transactions	...	...	...	...	1884.1	2296.0	2538.1	2623.0	...	...	...	...

a) Exports and imports of merchandise are recorded on the basis of the crossing of frontiers. No data are available on the basis of changes in the ownership of the goods. Imports and exports are recorded on a cash basis and the imports and exports of oil refineries are not included in the estimates.

b) The oil refineries in the Netherlands Antilles are now considered non-resident producers. Consequently, their compensation of employees to resident households is treated as wages and salaries paid by the rest of the world. Other cost components of these oil refineries are not included in GDP.

Netherlands Antilles

1.8 Capital Transactions of The Nation, Summary

Million Netherlands Antillian guilders

	1970	1975	1977	1978	1979	1980	1981	1982	1983	1984	1985	1986
Finance of Gross Capital Formation												
Gross saving	...	...	...	...	351.3	344.3	523.5	572.6	...	...	...	...
1 Consumption of fixed capital	...	...	...	...	140.0	158.1	187.4	206.1	...	...	...	...
A General government	...	...	...	...	7.2	8.1	9.9	11.1	...	...	...	...
B Corporate and quasi-corporate enterprises	...	...	...	...	132.8	150.0	177.5	195.0	...	...	...	...
C Other	...	...	...	...	...	...	...	...	...	...	...	...
2 Net saving	...	...	...	...	211.3	186.2	336.1	366.5	...	...	...	...
A General government	...	...	...	...	-15.2	9.7	85.3	108.8	...	...	...	...
B Corporate and quasi-corporate enterprises	...	...	...	...	89.5	176.5	250.8	257.7	...	...	...	...
C Other	...	...	...	...	137.0	...	...	...	...	...	...	...
Less: Surplus of the nation on current transactions	...	...	...	...	0.3	-89.0	44.0	109.2	...	...	...	...
Finance of Gross Capital Formation	...	...	...	...	351.0	433.3	479.5	463.4	...	...	...	...
Gross Capital Formation												
Increase in stocks	...	...	...	...	88.7	49.3	64.9	35.3	...	...	...	...
Gross fixed capital formation	...	...	...	...	262.3	384.0	414.6	428.1	...	...	...	...
1 General government	...	...	...	...	57.4	44.9	39.4	51.0	...	...	...	...
2 Corporate and quasi-corporate enterprises	...	...	...	...	204.9	339.1	375.2	377.1	...	...	...	...
3 Other	...	...	...	...	...	...	...	...	...	...	...	...
Gross Capital Formation	...	...	...	...	351.0	433.3	479.5	463.4	...	...	...	...

1.9 Gross Domestic Product by Institutional Sectors of Origin

Million Netherlands Antillian guilders

	1970	1975	1977	1978	1979	1980	1981	1982	1983	1984	1985	1986
Domestic Factor Incomes Originating												
1 General government	...	...	...	...	342.2	395.5	469.1	536.4	...	...	...	...
2 Corporate and quasi-corporate enterprises	...	...	...	...					...	...	...	...
3 Households and private unincorporated enterprises	...	...	...	...	1271.1	1382.9	1615.8	1692.1	...	...	...	...
4 Non-profit institutions serving households	...	...	...	...					...	...	...	...
Subtotal: Domestic Factor Incomes	...	...	...	...	1613.3	1778.4	2084.9	2228.5	...	...	...	...
Indirect taxes, net	...	...	...	...	120.3	137.5	131.8	123.3	...	...	...	...
A Indirect taxes	...	...	...	...	168.3	188.2	183.2	200.7	...	...	...	...
B Less: Subsidies	...	...	...	...	48.0	50.7	51.4	77.4	...	...	...	...
Consumption of fixed capital	...	...	...	...	140.0	158.1	187.4	206.1	...	...	...	...
Gross Domestic Product	...	...	...	...	1873.6	2074.0	2404.1	2557.9	...	...	...	...

1.10 Gross Domestic Product by Kind of Activity, in Current Prices

Million Netherlands Antillian guilders

	1970	1975	1977	1978	1979	1980	1981	1982	1983	1984	1985	1986
1 Agriculture, hunting, forestry and fishing	...	...	...	...	9.1	11.5	10.3	10.8	...	...	...	...
2 Mining and quarrying	...	...	...	...					...	...	...	...
3 Manufacturing	...	...	...	...	133.5	159.8	172.9	185.6	...	...	...	...
4 Electricity, gas and water	...	...	...	...	38.6	40.3	57.3	54.9	...	...	...	...
5 Construction	...	...	...	...	155.6	186.8	190.1	198.3	...	...	...	...
6 Wholesale and retail trade, restaurants and hotels	...	...	...	...	489.5	531.8	636.0	668.7	...	...	...	...
7 Transport, storage and communication	...	...	...	...	337.0	353.8	379.0	336.0	...	...	...	...
8 Finance, insurance, real estate and business services	...	...	...	...	274.4	293.4	351.2	387.3	...	...	...	...
9 Community, social and personal services	...	...	...	...	146.2	161.7	205.0	250.4	...	...	...	...

Netherlands Antilles

1.10 Gross Domestic Product by Kind of Activity, in Current Prices
(Continued)

Million Netherlands Antillian guilders

	1970	1975	1977	1978	1979	1980	1981	1982	1983	1984	1985	1986
Total, Industries	...	...	...	...	1583.9	1739.1	2001.8	2092.0	...	...	...	...
Producers of Government Services	...	...	...	...	349.9	404.1	479.6	548.1	...	...	...	...
Other Producers	...	...	...	...	...	...	...	...	...	...	...	...
Subtotal	...	...	...	...	1933.8	2143.2	2481.4	2640.1	...	...	...	...
Less: Imputed bank service charge	...	...	...	...	60.2	69.2	77.3	82.2	...	...	...	...
Plus: Import duties	...	...	...	...	...	...	...	...	...	...	...	...
Plus: Value added tax	...	...	...	...	...	...	...	...	...	...	...	...
Equals: Gross Domestic Product	...	...	...	...	1873.6	2074.0	2404.1	2557.9	...	...	...	...

1.12 Relations Among National Accounting Aggregates

Million Netherlands Antillian guilders

	1970	1975	1977	1978	1979	1980	1981	1982	1983	1984	1985	1986
Gross Domestic Product	...	...	...	...	1873.6	2074.0	2404.1	2557.9	...	...	...	...
Plus: Net factor income from the rest of the world	...	...	...	...	153.0	147.6	249.3	304.8	...	...	...	...
Factor income from the rest of the world	...	...	...	...	254.6	288.6	360.1	416.6	...	...	...	...
Less: Factor income to the rest of the world	...	...	...	...	101.6	141.0	110.8	111.8	...	...	...	...
Equals: Gross National Product	...	...	...	...	2026.6	2221.6	2653.4	2862.7	...	...	...	...
Less: Consumption of fixed capital	...	...	...	...	140.0	158.1	187.4	206.1	...	...	...	...
Equals: National Income	...	...	...	...	1886.6	2063.5	2466.0	2656.6	...	...	...	...
Plus: Net current transfers from the rest of the world	...	...	...	...	98.9	158.8	222.1	327.9	...	...	...	...
Current transfers from the rest of the world	...	...	...	...	150.7	216.2	291.5	418.8	...	...	...	...
Less: Current transfers to the rest of the world	...	...	...	...	51.8	57.4	69.4	90.9	...	...	...	...
Equals: National Disposable Income	...	...	...	...	1985.5	2222.3	2688.1	2984.5	...	...	...	...
Less: Final consumption	...	...	...	...	1774.2	2036.1	2352.0	2618.0	...	...	...	...
Equals: Net Saving	...	...	...	...	211.3	186.2	336.1	366.5	...	...	...	...
Less: Surplus of the nation on current transactions	...	...	...	...	0.3	-89.0	44.0	109.2	...	...	...	...
Equals: Net Capital Formation	...	...	...	...	211.0	275.2	292.1	257.3	...	...	...	...

2.1 Government Final Consumption Expenditure by Function, in Current Prices

Million Netherlands Antillian guilders

		1970	1975	1977	1978	1979	1980	1981	1982	1983	1984	1985	1986
1	General public services	...	...	...	...	72.7	82.1	106.6	130.3	...	...	...	...
2	Defence	...	...	...	...	-	20.5	10.9	1.7	...	...	...	...
3	Public order and safety	...	...	...	...	47.0	49.7	69.1	81.6	...	...	...	...
4	Education	...	...	...	...	120.3	150.9	179.7	198.4	...	...	...	...
5	Health [a]	...	...	...	...	36.6	42.0	48.2	51.6	...	...	...	...
6	Social security and welfare	...	...	...	...	82.7	101.2	114.7	130.1	...	...	...	...
7	Housing and community amenities [a]	...	...	...	...	...	...	...	...	...	...	...	...
8	Recreational, cultural and religious affairs	...	...	...	...	11.5	12.3	14.8	16.6	...	...	...	...
9	Economic services	...	...	...	...	60.4	66.0	66.2	69.5	...	...	...	...
	A Fuel and energy	...	...	...	...					...	...	...	...
	B Agriculture, forestry, fishing and hunting	...	...	...	...	31.0	37.5	45.2	44.2	...	...	...	...
	C Mining, manufacturing and construction, except fuel and energy	...	...	...	...					...	...	...	...
	D Transportation and communication	...	...	...	...	29.4	28.5	21.0	25.3	...	...	...	...
	E Other economic affairs	...	...	...	...	-	-	-	-	...	...	...	...
10	Other functions	...	...	...	...	37.9	43.6	38.9	46.9	...	...	...	...
	Total Government Final Consumption Expenditure [b]	...	...	...	...	469.1	568.3	649.1	726.7	...	...	...	...

a) Housing and community amenities are included in health.
b) The estimates of government final consumption expenditure include estimates of non-commodity sales and commodities produced for which there is no available breakdown.

Netherlands Antilles

2.3 Total Government Outlays by Function and Type

Million Netherlands Antillian guilders

		Final Consumption Expenditures			Subsidies	Other Current Transfers & Property Income	Total Current Disbursements	Gross Capital Formation	Other Capital Outlays	Total Outlays
		Total	Compensation of Employees	Other						
		1980									
1	General public services [a]	82.1	67.3	14.8	-	38.1	120.2	9.4	...	...
2	Defence	20.5	-	20.5	-	-	20.5	-	...	...
3	Public order and safety	49.7	43.4	6.3	-	-	49.7	5.2	...	...
4	Education	150.9	131.6	19.3	-	14.8	165.7	10.5	...	...
5	Health [b]	42.0	28.4	13.6	1.4	-	43.4	3.1	...	...
6	Social security and welfare	101.2	43.0	58.2	-	108.7	209.9	0.3	...	...
7	Housing and community amenities [b]	...	...	...	...	...	...	...	...	...
8	Recreation, culture and religion	12.3	6.9	5.4	-	2.1	14.4	2.0	...	...
9	Economic services	66.0	32.5	33.5	49.2	-	115.2	13.1	...	...
	A Fuel and energy								...	...
	B Agriculture, forestry, fishing and hunting	37.5	24.4	13.1	48.5	-	86.0	6.0	...	...
	C Mining (except fuels), manufacturing and construction								...	...
	D Transportation and communication	28.5	8.1	20.4	0.7	-	29.2	7.1	...	...
	E Other economic affairs	-	-	-	-	-	-	-	...	...
10	Other functions	43.6	35.7	7.9	0.1	39.6	83.3	1.3	...	...
	Total [c]	568.3	388.8	179.5	50.7	203.3	822.3	44.9	64.9	932.1
		1981									
1	General public services [a]	106.6	84.7	21.9	-	41.6	148.2	8.5	...	...
2	Defence	10.9	0.1	10.8	-	-	10.9	-	...	...
3	Public order and safety	69.1	60.0	9.1	-	-	69.1	2.0	...	...
4	Education	179.7	157.3	22.4	-	16.8	196.5	6.8	...	...
5	Health [b]	48.2	33.4	14.8	-	-	48.2	4.8	...	...
6	Social security and welfare	114.7	45.0	69.7	0.4	136.7	251.8	1.2	...	...
7	Housing and community amenities [b]	...	...	...	...	...	...	...	...	...
8	Recreation, culture and religion	14.8	8.0	6.8	0.2	2.0	17.0	3.6	...	...
9	Economic services	66.2	38.6	27.6	50.5	-	116.7	9.7	...	...
	A Fuel and energy								...	...
	B Agriculture, forestry, fishing and hunting	45.2	28.3	16.9	45.3	-	90.5	6.6	...	...
	C Mining (except fuels), manufacturing and construction								...	...
	D Transportation and communication	21.0	10.3	10.7	5.2	-	26.2	3.1	...	...
	E Other economic affairs	-	-	-	-	-	-	-	...	...
10	Other functions	38.9	34.1	4.8	0.3	42.3	81.5	2.0	...	...
	Total [c]	649.1	461.2	187.9	51.4	239.4	939.9	39.4	63.3	1042.6
		1982									
1	General public services [a]	130.2	103.1	27.1	-	50.2	180.4	7.3	...	...
2	Defence	1.7	0.1	1.6	-	-	1.7	-	...	...
3	Public order and safety	81.6	69.4	12.2	-	-	81.6	2.5	...	...
4	Education	190.4	172.9	25.5	-	15.8	214.2	6.0	...	...
5	Health [b]	51.7	38.5	13.2	5.5	-	57.2	10.2	...	...
6	Social security and welfare	130.1	52.1	78.0	-	156.8	286.9	0.4	...	...
7	Housing and community amenities [b]	...	...	...	...	...	...	...	...	...
8	Recreation, culture and religion	16.6	9.6	7.0	0.3	2.4	19.3	8.4	...	...
9	Economic services	69.5	43.7	25.8	70.7	-	140.2	13.3	...	...

Netherlands Antilles

2.3 Total Government Outlays by Function and Type
(Continued)

Million Netherlands Antillian guilders

	Final Consumption Expenditures Total	Compensation of Employees	Other	Subsidies	Other Current Transfers & Property Income	Total Current Disbursements	Gross Capital Formation	Other Capital Outlays	Total Outlays
A Fuel and energy								...	...
B Agriculture, forestry, fishing and hunting	44.2	31.0	13.2	63.9	-	108.1	9.6	...	...
C Mining (except fuels), manufacturing and construction								...	...
D Transportation and communication	25.3	12.7	12.6	6.8	-	32.1	3.7	...	...
E Other economic affairs	-	-	-	-	-	-	-	...	...
10 Other functions	46.9	38.5	8.4	0.9	50.3	98.1	2.9	...	...
Total [c]	726.7	527.9	198.8	77.4	275.5	1079.6	51.0	72.4	1203.0

a) General public services of column 5 includes the total amount of unfunded employee pension and welfare benefits for which there is no available breakdown.
b) Housing and community amenities are included in health.
c) The estimates of government final consumption expenditure include estimates of non-commodity sales and commodities produced for which there is no available breakdown.

2.17 Exports and Imports of Goods and Services, Detail

Million Netherlands Antillian guilders

	1970	1975	1977	1978	1979	1980	1981	1982	1983	1984	1985	1986
Exports of Goods and Services
1 Exports of merchandise, f.o.b.	...	...	...	...	204.7	243.8	191.7	179.0	...	...	...	...
2 Transport and communication	...	...	...	...	439.3	493.2	474.2	377.3	...	...	...	...
3 Insurance service charges	...	...	...	...					...	...	...	...
4 Other commodities	...	...	...	...	135.1	188.8	239.9	247.4	...	...	...	...
5 Adjustments of merchandise exports to change-of-ownership basis	...	...	...	...	...	...	...	...	...	...	...	...
6 Direct purchases in the domestic market by non-residential households	...	...	...	...	569.7	714.7	785.7	759.4	...	...	...	...
7 Direct purchases in the domestic market by extraterritorial bodies	...	...	...	...	130.0	150.7	195.0	224.5	...	...	...	...
Total Exports of Goods and Services [a]	...	...	...	...	1478.8	1791.2	1886.5	1787.6	...	...	...	...
Imports of Goods and Services
1 Imports of merchandise, c.i.f.	...	...	...	...	1318.6	1610.0	1531.2	1636.4	...	...	...	...
2 Adjustments of merchandise imports to change-of-ownership basis	...	...	...	...	...	...	...	...	...	...	...	...
3 Other transport and communication	...	...	...	...	98.7	113.3	165.6	153.9	...	...	...	...
4 Other insurance service charges	...	...	...	...	...	...	...	...	...	...	...	...
5 Other commodities	...	...	...	...	211.5	346.6	485.7	366.4	...	...	...	...
6 Direct purchases abroad by government	...	...	...	...	8.6	12.7	13.4	12.9	...	...	...	...
7 Direct purchases abroad by resident households	...	...	...	...	93.0	104.0	118.0	141.5	...	...	...	...
Total Imports of Goods and Services [a]	...	...	...	...	1730.4	2186.6	2313.9	2311.1	...	...	...	...
Balance of Goods and Services	...	...	...	...	-251.6	-395.4	-427.4	-523.5	...	...	...	...
Total Imports and Balance of Goods and Services	...	...	...	...	1478.8	1791.2	1886.5	1787.6	...	...	...	...

a) Exports and imports of merchandise are recorded on the basis of the crossing of frontiers. No data are available on the basis of changes in the ownership of the goods.

New Caledonia

Source. Reply to the United Nations National Accounts Questionnaire from the Institute national de la statistique et des etudes economiques (INSEE), Paris.
General note. The estimates shown in the following tables have been adjusted by the INSEE to conform to the United Nations System of National Accounts so far as the existing data would permit.

1.1 Expenditure on the Gross Domestic Product, in Current Prices

Million CFP francs

	1970	1975	1977	1978	1979	1980	1981	1982	1983	1984	1985	1986
1 Government final consumption expenditure [a,b]	2852	12514	17189	19313	21851	25334	29473	35631	39773	46037	...	...
2 Private final consumption expenditure [a]	19686	33256	38223	39483	44240	49575	57147	65935	68606	72488	...	...
3 Gross capital formation	18641	18553	16653	15245	13285	19772	16362	19637	19145	18405	...	...
A Increase in stocks	450	...	...	-1442	-5900	-619	-904	-1247	-817	-2933	...	...
B Gross fixed capital formation	18191	...	...	16687	19185	20391	17266	20884	19962	21338	...	...
Residential buildings	...	3084	...	...	...	...	...	...	...	...	...	...
Non-residential buildings	...	...	...	...	...	...	...	...	...	...	...	...
Other construction and land improvement etc.	...	...	...	...	...	...	...	...	...	...	...	...
Other	...	...	...	...	...	...	...	...	...	...	...	...
4 Exports of goods and services	19647	26650	29761	20051	30184	31908	33794	30295	30964	42951	...	...
5 Less: Imports of goods and services	24437	27966	27931	25759	29643	37050	40631	43719	44763	53211	...	...
Statistical discrepancy [b,c]	1815	636	936	1087	1089	1308	159	314	436	-181	...	...
Equals: Gross Domestic Product	38204	63643	74831	69420	81006	90847	96304	108093	114161	126489	...	...

a) Beginning 1972, education and health are included in item 'Government final consumption expenditure' rather than in item 'Private final consumption expenditure'.
b) Government final consumption expenditure estimates are under-estimated since the system of national accounts used treats the government sector separately. Therefore this under estimation is rectified as a statistical discrepancy.
c) The accounting reconciliation is done at the level of the gross domestic production instead of gross domestic product. Therefore the statistical descrepancy reflects mainly the domestic salaries not accounted for elsewhere.

1.3 Cost Components of the Gross Domestic Product

Million CFP francs

	1970	1975	1977	1978	1979	1980	1981	1982	1983	1984	1985	1986
1 Indirect taxes, net	4152	3266	3232	3142	4540	3159	3708	3611	3543	4400	...	...
A Indirect taxes	4742	4712	...	...	...	...	7312	8036	8372	9617	...	...
B Less: Subsidies	590	1446	...	...	...	...	3604	4425	4829	5217	...	...
2 Consumption of fixed capital	16699	11911	10159	9979	12161	13694	9881	11594	10083	11482	...	...
3 Compensation of employees paid by resident producers to:	15984	32833	39611	41956	46563	55190	51492	61318	66930	73810	...	...
4 Operating surplus	1369	15633	21829	14343	17742	18804	31223	31570	33605	36797	...	...
Equals: Gross Domestic Product	38204	63643	74831	69420	81006	90847	96304	108093	114161	126489	...	...

1.4 General Government Current Receipts and Disbursements

Million CFP francs

	1970	1975	1977	1978	1979	1980	1981	1982	1983	1984	1985	1986
Receipts												
1 Operating surplus	...	...	...	...	...	...	...	...	...	...	...	...
2 Property and entrepreneurial income	...	...	...	...	...	...	...	...	...	...	...	...
3 Taxes, fees and contributions	...	...	...	...	...	...	19268	21359	24217	20279	...	...
A Indirect taxes	...	...	...	...	...	...	7312	8036	8372	9617	...	...
B Direct taxes	...	...	...	...	...	...	4983	5082	6490	7417	...	...
C Social security contributions	...	...	...	...	...	...	6973	8241	9355	11245	...	...
D Compulsory fees, fines and penalties	...	...	...	...	...	...	...	...	...	...	...	...
4 Other current transfers	...	...	...	...	...	...	30013	35952	40370	42875	...	...
Total Current Receipts of General Government	...	...	...	...	...	...	49281	57311	64587	71154	...	...
Disbursements												
1 Government final consumption expenditure	...	...	...	...	...	...	29473	35631	39773	46037	...	...
A Compensation of employees	...	...	...	...	...	...	21703	26084	29337	33679	...	...
B Consumption of fixed capital	...	...	...	...	...	...	...	...	...	...	...	...
C Purchases of goods and services, net	...	...	...	...	...	...	6339	7840	8236	9185	...	...
D Less: Own account fixed capital formation	...	...	...	...	...	...	...	...	...	...	...	...
E Indirect taxes paid, net	...	...	...	...	...	...	1431	1707	2200	3173	...	...
2 Property income	...	...	...	...	...	...	...	...	...	...	...	...

New Caledonia

1.4 General Government Current Receipts and Disbursements
(Continued)

Million CFP francs

	1970	1975	1977	1978	1979	1980	1981	1982	1983	1984	1985	1986
3 Subsidies	...	...	...	...	...	...	3604	4425	4829	5217	...	...
4 Other current transfers	...	...	...	...	...	...	11663	14307	16938	18403	...	...
A Social security benefits	...	...	...	...	...	...	3921	4713	5936	7021	...	...
B Social assistance grants	...	...	...	...	...	...	5107	6116	6698	7588	...	...
C Other	...	...	...	...	...	...	2635	3478	4304	3794	...	...
5 Net saving	...	...	...	...	...	...	4541	2948	3047	1497	...	...
Total Current Disbursements and Net Saving of General Government	...	...	...	...	...	...	49281	57311	64587	71154	...	...

1.5 Current Income and Outlay of Corporate and Quasi-Corporate Enterprises, Summary

Million CFP francs

	1970	1975	1977	1978	1979	1980	1981	1982	1983	1984	1985	1986
Receipts												
1 Operating surplus	...	...	...	...	...	...	41104	43164	43688	48279	...	...
2 Property and entrepreneurial income received	...	...	...	...	...	...	717	784	1675	2193	...	...
3 Current transfers	...	...	...	...	...	...	...	...	...	...	...	...
Total Current Receipts	...	...	...	...	...	...	41821	43948	45363	50472	...	...
Disbursements												
1 Property and entrepreneurial income	...	...	...	...	...	...	18383	20995	22286	22616	...	...
2 Direct taxes and other current payments to general government	...	...	...	...	...	...	3979	3253	3746	3670	...	...
3 Other current transfers	...	...	...	...	...	...	3034	3903	3888	4231	...	...
4 Net saving	...	...	...	...	...	...	16425	15797	15443	19955	...	...
Total Current Disbursements and Net Saving	...	...	...	...	...	...	41821	43948	45363	50472	...	...

1.6 Current Income and Outlay of Households and Non-Profit Institutions

Million CFP francs

	1970	1975	1977	1978	1979	1980	1981	1982	1983	1984	1985	1986
Receipts												
1 Compensation of employees	...	...	...	...	...	...	43801	52226	56677	61563	...	...
2 Operating surplus of private unincorporated enterprises	...	...	...	...	...	...	18383	20995	22286	22616	...	...
3 Property and entrepreneurial income	...	...	...	...	...	...	...	...	...	...	...	...
4 Current transfers	...	...	...	...	...	...	13070	16281	19082	20948	...	...
A Social security benefits	...	...	...	...	...	...	3921	4713	5936	7021	...	...
B Social assistance grants	...	...	...	...	...	...	5107	6116	6698	7588	...	...
C Other	...	...	...	...	...	...	4042	5452	6448	6339	...	...
Total Current Receipts	...	...	...	...	...	...	75254	89502	98045	105127	...	...
Disbursements												
1 Private final consumption expenditure	...	...	...	...	...	...	57147	65935	68606	72488	...	...
2 Property income	...	...	...	...	...	...	...	...	...	...	...	...
3 Direct taxes and other current transfers n.e.c. to general government	...	...	...	...	...	...	1208	2070	3010	4074	...	...
A Social security contributions	...	...	...	...	...	...	204	241	266	327	...	...
B Direct taxes	...	...	...	...	...	...	1004	1829	2744	3747	...	...
C Fees, fines and penalties	...	...	...	...	...	...	...	...	...	...	...	...
4 Other current transfers	...	...	...	...	...	...	2193	2955	3932	4240	...	...
5 Net saving	...	...	...	...	...	...	14706	18542	22497	24325	...	...
Total Current Disbursements and Net Saving	...	...	...	...	...	...	75254	89502	98045	105127	...	...

1.7 External Transactions on Current Account, Summary

Million CFP francs

	1970	1975	1977	1978	1979	1980	1981	1982	1983	1984	1985	1986
Payments to the Rest of the World												
1 Imports of goods and services	24437	27966	27931	25759	29643	37050	40631	43719	44763	53211	...	...
A Imports of merchandise c.i.f.	23069	27049	...	...	...	...	...	...	...	...	...	...
B Other	1368	917	...	...	...	...	...	...	...	...	...	...
2 Factor income to the rest of the world	...	...	...	...	...	...	...	...	...	...	...	...

New Caledonia

1.7 External Transactions on Current Account, Summary
(Continued)

Million CFP francs

	1970	1975	1977	1978	1979	1980	1981	1982	1983	1984	1985	1986
3 Current transfers to the rest of the world	59	109	217	312	375	470	...	...	...	...	...	...
4 Surplus of the nation on current transactions	-1256	7857	13574	11159	20847	18952	20238	18612	21842	27372	...	...
Payments to the Rest of the World and Surplus of the Nation on Current Transactions	23240	35932	41722	37230	50865	56472	60869	62331	66605	80583	...	...

Receipts From The Rest of the World

	1970	1975	1977	1978	1979	1980	1981	1982	1983	1984	1985	1986
1 Exports of goods and services	19647	26650	29761	20051	30184	31908	33794	30295	30964	42951	...	...
A Exports of merchandise f.o.b.	19277	25809	...	...	...	...	...	...	...	...	...	...
B Other	370	841	...	...	...	...	...	...	...	...	...	...
2 Factor income from rest of the world	...	...	...	...	...	...	...	...	...	...	...	...
3 Current transfers from rest of the world	3593	9282	11961	17179	20681	24565	27075	32036	35641	37632	...	...
Receipts from the Rest of the World on Current Transactions	23240	35932	41722	37230	50865	56472	60869	62331	66605	80583	...	...

1.10 Gross Domestic Product by Kind of Activity, in Current Prices

Million CFP francs

	1970	1975	1977	1978	1979	1980	1981	1982	1983	1984	1985	1986
1 Agriculture, hunting, forestry and fishing	1643	1901	2451	2196	2340	2719	1429	1820	2155	2252	...	...
2 Mining and quarrying	10981	16368	18000	7106	12902	14472	15901	13476	10591	16379	...	...
3 Manufacturing	1373	4003	4892	4289	4872	5231	4030	4985	5892	6215	...	...
4 Electricity, gas and water	594	1658	1616	1588	1810	2319	2332	2091	2318	2491	...	...
5 Construction	1488	8588	8002	7760	8240	8279	5432	6782	5290	5301	...	...
6 Wholesale and retail trade, restaurants and hotels [a]	13158	12889	14541	15339	16952	19351	24287	28395	30483	31274	...	...
7 Transport, storage and communication	1178	2611	2850	2408	2769	3395	4288	4761	4917	4227	...	...
8 Finance, insurance, real estate and business services	3605	4192	7743	11972	12226	13377	14549	16900	19814	20169	...	...
9 Community, social and personal services [a]		629									...	...
Total, Industries	34020	52839	60095	52658	62111	69142	72248	79210	81460	88308	...	...
Producers of Government Services	3847	10068	13800	15775	17806	20447	23134	27791	31537	36852	...	...
Other Producers	337	736	936	987	1089	1258	922	1092	1164	1329	...	...
Subtotal	38204	63643	74831	69420	81006	90847	96304	108093	114161	126489	...	...
Less: Imputed bank service charge	...	...	...	...	...	...	...	...	...	...		
Plus: Import duties	...	...	...	...	...	...	...	...	...	...		
Plus: Value added tax	...	...	...	...	...	...	...	...	...	...		
Equals: Gross Domestic Product	38204	63643	74831	69420	81006	90847	96304	108093	114161	126489	...	...

a) Restaurants and hotels are included in item 'Community, social and personal services'.

2.17 Exports and Imports of Goods and Services, Detail

Million CFP francs

	1970	1975	1977	1978	1979	1980	1981	1982	1983	1984	1985	1986

Exports of Goods and Services

	1970	1975	1977	1978	1979	1980	1981	1982	1983	1984	1985	1986
1 Exports of merchandise, f.o.b.	19277	25809	...	...	...	...	...	...	...	...	...	...
2 Transport and communication	...	...	...	...	...	...	...	...	...	...	...	...
3 Insurance service charges	...	...	...	...	...	...	...	...	...	...	...	...
4 Other commodities	...	...	...	...	...	...	...	...	...	...	...	...
5 Adjustments of merchandise exports to change-of-ownership basis	...	...	...	...	...	...	...	...	...	...	...	...
6 Direct purchases in the domestic market by non-residential households	370	841	...	...	...	...	...	...	...	...	...	...
7 Direct purchases in the domestic market by extraterritorial bodies	...	...	...	...	...	...	...	...	...	...	...	...
Total Exports of Goods and Services	19647	26650	...	...	...	...	...	...	...	...	...	...

Imports of Goods and Services

	1970	1975	1977	1978	1979	1980	1981	1982	1983	1984	1985	1986
1 Imports of merchandise, c.i.f.	23069	27049	...	...	...	...	...	...	...	...	...	...

New Caledonia

2.17 Exports and Imports of Goods and Services, Detail
(Continued)

Million CFP francs

	1970	1975	1977	1978	1979	1980	1981	1982	1983	1984	1985	1986
2 Adjustments of merchandise imports to change-of-ownership basis	...	...	...	...	...	...	...	...	...	...	...	...
3 Other transport and communication	...	...	...	...	...	...	...	...	...	...	...	...
4 Other insurance service charges	...	...	...	...	...	...	...	...	...	...	...	...
5 Other commodities	...	...	...	...	...	...	...	...	...	...	...	...
6 Direct purchases abroad by government	1368	917	...	...	...	...	...	...	...	...	...	...
7 Direct purchases abroad by resident households			...	...	...	...	...	...	...	...	...	...
Total Imports of Goods and Services	24437	27966	...	...	...	...	...	...	...	...	...	...
Balance of Goods and Services	-4790	-1316	...	...	...	...	...	...	...	...	...	...
Total Imports and Balance of Goods and Services	19647	26650	...	...	...	...	...	...	...	...	...	...

New Zealand

Source. Reply to the United Nations National Accounts Questionnaire from the Department of Statistics, Wellington. The official estimates and descriptions are published by the Department in the 'Annual Series National Income and Expenditure' and as appendices to the 'Monthly Abstract of Statistics'.

General note. The official estimates of New Zealand have been adjusted by the Department of Statistics to conform to the United Nations System of National Accounts so far as the existing data would permit.

1.1 Expenditure on the Gross Domestic Product, in Current Prices

Million New Zealand dollars — Fiscal year beginning 1 April

	1970	1975	1977	1978	1979	1980	1981	1982	1983	1984	1985	1986
1 Government final consumption expenditure	770	1732	2363 / 2363	2882	3314	4134	4988	5554	5839	6208	7279	9033
2 Private final consumption expenditure	3742	7098	9181 / 9181	10353	12105	14255	16645	18592	20060	22577	26414	30708
A Households	...	7010	9045 / 9045	10197	11921	14034	16367	18298	19771	22259	26038	30249
B Private non-profit institutions serving households	...	88	136 / 136	156	184	221	278	293	288	318	376	459
3 Gross capital formation	1418	3705	4228 / 3682	3639	4544	4802	6898	8125	8990	11129	12180	12998
A Increase in stocks [a]	204	459	683 / 137	-241	477	48	301	316	515	1524	791	1221
B Gross fixed capital formation	1214	3246	3545 / 3545	3880	4067	4754	6597	7809	8475	9605	11389	11777
Residential buildings	...	769	676 / 676	716	731	881	1180	1333	1555	1784	2085	...
Non-residential buildings	...	612	695 / 695	762	747	821	1034	1176	1250	1473	1982	...
Other construction and land improvement etc.	...	512	672 / 672	657	679	808	1136	1325	1379	1363	1463	...
Other	...	1352	1501 / 1501	1744	1900	2244	3247	3974	4201	4984	5860	...
4 Exports of goods and services	1296	2666	4125 / 4125	4687	5996	7003	8249	9116	10699	13317	14037	15040
5 Less: Imports of goods and services	1456	3430	4378 / 4378	4647	6256	7272	9168	10318	11090	14859	15093	14941
Statistical discrepancy	62	-102	-86 / -89	-53	-7	71	219	90	-168	295	52	40
Equals: Gross Domestic Product	5832	11668	15432 / 14884	16861	19696	22993	27831	31159	34330	38667	44869	52878

a) From 1977 onward, stock valuation adjustment is made for the estimates of value of physical increase in stocks.

1.2 Expenditure on the Gross Domestic Product, in Constant Prices

Million New Zealand dollars — Fiscal year beginning 1 April

At constant prices of: 1982

	1970	1975	1977	1978	1979	1980	1981	1982	1983	1984	1985	1986
1 Government final consumption expenditure	...	...	...	...	...	...	...	5554	5706	5737	5860	...
2 Private final consumption expenditure	...	...	...	...	...	...	...	18592	19110	19837	19912	...
A Households	...	...	...	...	...	...	...	18298	18814	19529	19579	...
B Private non-profit institutions serving households	...	...	...	...	...	...	...	293	296	308	333	...
3 Gross capital formation	...	...	...	...	...	...	...	8125	8507	9554	8936	...
A Increase in stocks [a]	...	...	...	...	...	...	...	316	322	1103	145	...
B Gross fixed capital formation	...	...	...	...	...	...	...	7809	8185	8451	8791	...
Residential buildings	...	...	...	...	...	...	...	1333	1476	1559	1615	...
Non-residential buildings	...	...	...	...	...	...	...	1170	1207	1343	1017	...
Other construction and land improvement etc.	...	...	...	...	...	...	...	1325	1341	1235	1180	...
Other	...	...	...	...	...	...	...	3974	4161	4313	4378	...
4 Exports of goods and services	...	...	...	...	...	...	...	9116	9862	10539	10902	...
5 Less: Imports of goods and services	...	...	...	...	...	...	...	10319	10280	11580	11214	...
Statistical discrepancy	...	...	...	...	...	...	...	90	-829	-322	101	...
Equals: Gross Domestic Product	...	...	...	...	...	...	...	31160	32076	33765	34497	...

a) From 1977 onward, stock valuation adjustment is made for the estimates of value of physical increase in stocks.

New Zealand

1.3 Cost Components of the Gross Domestic Product

Million New Zealand dollars

	1970	1975	1977	1978	1979	1980	1981	1982	1983	1984	1985	1986
1 Indirect taxes, net	518	712	1192 / 1192	1297	1646	1995	2336	2685	3192	3945	4478	6276
A Indirect taxes	577	1103	1469 / 1469	1725	1998	2343	2914	3440	3847	4543	4839	6542
B Less: Subsidies	59	391	277 / 277	428	352	348	578	755	655	598	361	266
2 Consumption of fixed capital	523	940	1169 / 1169	1297	1464	1678	1923	2216	2615	3085	3757	4281
3 Compensation of employees paid by resident producers to:	2945	6269	8091 / 8091	9399	10953	13018	15672	17168	17459	18986	22120	26045
A Resident households	2945	6269	8091 / 8091	9399	10953	13018	15672	17168	17459	18986	22120	26045
B Rest of the world	-	-	-	-	-	-	-	-	-	-	-	-
4 Operating surplus	1846	3747	4981 / 4432	4867	5634	6303	7900	9091	11064	12651	14514	16277
Equals: Gross Domestic Product a	5832	11668	15432 / 14884	16860	19697	22994	27831	31160	34330	38667	44869	52879

a) From 1977 onward, stock valuation adjustment is made for the estimates of value of physical increase in stocks.

1.7 External Transactions on Current Account, Summary

Million New Zealand dollars

	1970	1975	1977	1978	1979	1980	1981	1982	1983	1984	1985	1986
Payments to the Rest of the World												
1 Imports of goods and services	...	3430	4378	4647	6256	7272	9168	10318	11090	14859	15093	14942
A Imports of merchandise c.i.f.	...	...	3456	3540	4906	5576	7086	7888	8589	11697	11945	11369
B Other	...	...	922	1107	1350	1696	2082	2430	2501	3162	3148	3573
2 Factor income to the rest of the world	...	240	423	492	539	604	803	1068	1530	2179	2365	2640
A Compensation of employees	...	-	-	-	-	-	-	-	-	-	-	-
B Property and entrepreneurial income	...	240	423	492	539	604	803	1068	1530	2179	2365	2640
3 Current transfers to the rest of the world a	...	119	158	199	212	262	311	295	370	442	525	607
A Indirect taxes to supranational organizations	...	...	...	...	...	...	...	...	...	...	...	...
B Other current transfers	...	119	158	199	212	262	311	295	370	442	525	607
4 Surplus of the nation on current transactions	...	-905	-584	-402	-709	-740	-1502	-1944	-1605	-3236	-2916	-1899
Payments to the Rest of the World and Surplus of the Nation on Current Transactions	...	2884	4375	4936	6298	7398	8780	9737	11385	14244	15067	16290
Receipts From The Rest of the World												
1 Exports of goods and services	...	2666	4125	4687	5996	7003	8249	9116	10699	13317	14037	15040
A Exports of merchandise f.o.b.	...	...	3346	3820	4919	5715	6624	7230	8381	10423	10805	11566
B Other	...	...	779	867	1077	1288	1625	1886	2318	2894	3232	3474
2 Factor income from rest of the world	...	75	87	83	79	93	188	208	232	275	321	402
A Compensation of employees	...	-	-	-	-	-	-	-	-	-	-	-
B Property and entrepreneurial income	...	75	87	83	79	93	188	208	232	275	321	402
3 Current transfers from rest of the world a	...	143	163	166	223	302	343	413	454	652	709	846
A Subsidies from supranational organisations	...	...	...	...	...	...	...	...	...	...	...	...
B Other current transfers	...	143	163	166	223	302	343	413	454	652	709	846
Receipts from the Rest of the World on Current Transactions	...	2884	4375	4936	6298	7398	8780	9737	11385	14244	15067	16288

a) Item 'Current transfers to/from the rest of the world' includes also capital transfers.

New Zealand

1.10 Gross Domestic Product by Kind of Activity, in Current Prices

Million New Zealand dollars — Fiscal year beginning 1 April

	1970	1975	1977	1978	1979	1980	1981	1982	1983	1984	1985	1986
1 Agriculture, hunting, forestry and fishing	...	1163	1495 / 1496	1607	2395	2518	2662	2563	2949	3713	4165	...
2 Mining and quarrying	...	45	184 / 183	165	155	195	237	385	304	421	513	...
3 Manufacturing	...	2597	3472 / 3281	3771	4442	5082	6517	7236	7850	9166	10059	...
4 Electricity, gas and water	...	201	388 / 380	439	654	715	828	962	1066	1101	1383	...
5 Construction	...	868	913 / 906	933	965	1142	1512	1696	1862	2083	2536	...
6 Wholesale and retail trade, restaurants and hotels	...	2522	3180 / 2850	3246	3465	4400	5334	6208	7074	7406	8539	...
7 Transport, storage and communication	...	840	1254 / 1242	1429	1635	1861	2178	2533	2947	3212	3463	...
8 Finance, insurance, real estate and business services	...	1669	2237 / 2238	2499	2773	3185	3958	4574	5147	5971	7666	...
9 Community, social and personal services	...	453	565 / 565	653	752	874	1041	1178	1255	1493	1723	...
Total, Industries	...	10359	13688 / 13139	14744	17238	19972	24268	27334	30457	34565	40048	...
Producers of Government Services	...	1302	1728 / 1728	2137	2481	3106	3715	4088	4202	4389	5113	...
Other Producers	...	104	151 / 151	178	211	251	289	293	277	302	342	...
Subtotal	...	11765	15567 / 15017	17059	19930	23329	28273	31715	34935	39257	45503	...
Less: Imputed bank service charge	...	241	308 / 308	389	473	603	834	968	1100	1275	1455	...
Plus: Import duties	...	124	150 / 150	166	212	231	337	362	432	604	717	...
Plus: Value added tax	...	...	...	...	...	...	...	...	...	...	...	...
Plus: Other adjustments [a]	...	19	23 / 23	24	28	37	55	51	62	81	103	...
Equals: Gross Domestic Product [b]	...	11668	15432 / 14883	16860	19697	22994	27830	31160	34330	38666	44868	...

a) Item 'Other adjustments' relates to other indirect taxes and import duties not allocated to industries.
b) From 1977 onward, stock valuation adjustment is made for the estimates of value of physical increase in stocks.

1.11 Gross Domestic Product by Kind of Activity, in Constant Prices

Million New Zealand dollars — Fiscal year beginning 1 April

At constant prices of: 1982

	1970	1975	1977	1978	1979	1980	1981	1982	1983	1984	1985	1986
1 Agriculture, hunting, forestry and fishing	...	...	2038	1939	2196	2468	2459	2563	2462	2448	3013	...
2 Mining and quarrying	...	...	388	341	247	223	253	386	303	399	576	...
3 Manufacturing	...	...	6423	6413	6713	6613	7183	7235	7435	8224	7866	...
4 Electricity, gas and water	...	...	775	830	908	933	956	962	1062	1076	1102	...
5 Construction	...	...	1882	1672	1533	1516	1655	1696	1846	1909	2070	...
6 Wholesale and retail trade, restaurants and hotels	...	...	6179	6203	6135	6041	6362	6208	6402	6631	6522	...
7 Transport, storage and communication	...	...	2330	2393	2453	2450	2515	2532	2774	2994	3027	...
8 Finance, insurance, real estate and business services	...	...	4077	4228	4328	4444	4567	4574	4872	5139	5424	...
9 Community, social and personal services	...	...	1294	1350	1363	1381	1441	1471	1538	1589	1674	...
Total, Industries	...	...	25122	25111	25768	26067	27389	27627	28694	30407	31284	...
Producers of Government Services	...	...	3798	3928	3954	3974	4058	4088	4126	4135	4134	...
Other Producers	...	...	...	...	...	...	...	...	...	...	...	...
Subtotal	...	...	28920	29039	29722	30041	31447	31715	32820	34542	35418	...
Less: Imputed bank service charge	...	...	840	911	933	923	945	968	1126	1251	1414	...
Plus: Import duties	...	...	...	...	...	...	...	...	...	...	...	...
Plus: Value added tax	...	...	...	...	...	...	...	...	...	...	...	...
Plus: Other adjustments [a]	...	...	287	297	362	346	449	413	382	474	493	...
Equals: Gross Domestic Product [b]	...	...	28367	28425	29151	29464	30951	31160	32076	33765	34497	...

a) Item 'Other adjustments' relates to other indirect taxes and import duties not allocated to industries.
b) From 1977 onward, stock valuation adjustment is made for the estimates of value of physical increase in stocks.

New Zealand

1.12 Relations Among National Accounting Aggregates

Million New Zealand dollars — Fiscal year beginning 1 April

	1970	1975	1977	1978	1979	1980	1981	1982	1983	1984	1985	1986
Gross Domestic Product	5832	11668	15432 / 14883	16860	19697	22994	27831	31160	34330	38667	44868	52879
Plus: Net factor income from the rest of the world	-41	-165	-336 / -336	-409	-460	-511	-615	-860	-1298	-1904	-2044	-2238
Factor income from the rest of the world	...	75	87 / 87	83	79	93	188	208	232	275	321	402
Less: Factor income to the rest of the world	...	240	423 / 423	492	539	604	803	1068	1530	2179	2365	2640
Equals: Gross National Product	5791	11503	15096 / 14547	16451	19237	22483	27216	30300	33032	36763	42824	50641
Less: Consumption of fixed capital	523	940	1169 / 1169	1297	1464	1678	1923	2216	2615	3085	3757	4281
Equals: National Income	5268	10563	13928 / 13379	15154	17773	20804	25293	28084	30417	33678	39068	46360
Plus: Net current transfers from the rest of the world [a]	-9	24	5 / 5	-33	11	40	32	118	84	210	184	239
Current transfers from the rest of the world	...	143	163 / 163	166	223	302	343	413	454	652	709	846
Less: Current transfers to the rest of the world	...	119	158 / 158	199	212	262	311	295	370	442	525	607
Equals: National Disposable Income	5259	10587	13933 / 13384	15121	17784	20844	25325	28202	30501	33888	39252	46599
Less: Final consumption	4512	8830	11544 / 11544	13235	15419	18389	21633	24146	25899	28785	33693	39741
Equals: Net Saving	747	1757	2389 / 1840	1886	2365	2455	3692	4056	4602	5103	5559	6858
Less: Surplus of the nation on current transactions	-209	-905	-584 / -584	-402	-709	-740	-1502	-1944	-1605	-3236	-2916	-1899
Statistical discrepancy	-62	102	86 / 89	53	7	-71	-219	-90	168	-295	-52	-40
Equals: Net Capital Formation [b]	895	2764	3059 / 2513	2341	3081	3124	4975	5910	6375	8044	8423	8717

a) Item 'Current transfers to/from the rest of the world' includes also capital transfers.
b) From 1977 onward, stock valuation adjustment is made for the estimates of value of physical increase in stocks.

2.5 Private Final Consumption Expenditure by Type and Porpose, in Current Prices

Million New Zealand dollars — Fiscal year beginning 1 April

	1970	1975	1977	1978	1979	1980	1981	1982	1983	1984	1985	1986
Final Consumption Expenditure of Resident Households												
1 Food, beverages and tobacco	...	...	...	...	...	...	...	3556	3882	4256	4758	...
A Food	...	...	...	...	...	...	...	2518	2726	2985	3368	...
B Non-alcoholic beverages	...	...	...	...	...	...	...	632	692	759	827	...
C Alcoholic beverages	...	...	...	...	...	...	...	...	...	...	...	...
D Tobacco	...	...	...	...	...	...	...	406	464	512	563	...
2 Clothing and footwear	...	...	...	...	...	...	...	1362	1390	1552	1751	...
3 Gross rent, fuel and power	...	...	...	...	...	...	...	2892	3087	3460	4524	...
A Fuel and power	...	...	...	...	...	...	...	439	463	482	572	...
B Other	...	...	...	...	...	...	...	2453	2624	2978	3952	...
4 Furniture, furnishings and household equipment and operation	...	...	...	...	...	...	...	1713	1839	2067	2329	...
5 Medical care and health expenses	...	...	...	...	...	...	...	858	928	1034	1282	...
6 Transport and communication	...	...	...	...	...	...	...	3445	3753	4357	5041	...
A Personal transport equipment	...	...	...	...	...	...	...	1134	1195	1429	1543	...
B Other [a]	...	...	...	...	...	...	...	2311	2558	2928	3498	...
7 Recreational, entertainment, education and cultural services	...	...	...	...	...	...	...	1670	1840	2041	2308	...
8 Miscellaneous goods and services	...	...	...	...	...	...	...	2934	3211	3688	4425	...
A Personal care	...	...	...	...	...	...	...	691	715	815	974	...
B Expenditures in restaurants, cafes and hotels [b]	...	...	...	...	...	...	...	1526	1698	1954	2327	...
C Other [a]	...	...	...	...	...	...	...	717	798	919	1124	...
Total Final Consumption Expenditure in the Domestic Market by Households, of which	...	...	...	...	...	...	...	18431	19930	22454	26418	...

New Zealand

2.5 Private Final Consumption Expenditure by Type and Porpose, in Current Prices
(Continued)

Million New Zealand dollars — Fiscal year beginning 1 April

	1970	1975	1977	1978	1979	1980	1981	1982	1983	1984	1985	1986
A Durable goods	...	...	...	...	...	...	...	5671	5998	6851	7698	...
B Semi-durable goods	...	...	...	...	...	...	...	...	...	...	...	...
C Non-durable goods	...	...	...	...	...	...	...	5590	6071	6675	7647	...
D Services [a]	...	...	...	...	...	...	...	7169	7860	8928	11073	...
Plus: Direct purchases abroad by resident households	...	...	...	...	...	...	...	326	354	447	474	...
Less: Direct purchases in the domestic market by non-resident households	...	...	...	...	...	...	...	459	513	642	854	...
Equals: Final Consumption Expenditure of Resident Households	...	...	...	...	...	...	...	18298	19771	22259	26038	...

Final Consumption Expenditure of Private Non-profit Institutions Serving Households

	1970	1975	1977	1978	1979	1980	1981	1982	1983	1984	1985	1986
Equals: Final Consumption Expenditure of Private Non-profit Organisations Serving Households	...	...	...	...	...	...	...	293	288	318	376	...
Private Final Consumption Expenditure	...	...	...	...	...	...	...	18591	20059	22577	26414	...

a) Item 'Other' includes fringe benefits received by households.
b) Item 'Expenditures in restaurants, cafes and hotels' includes expenditure on alcohol consumed in chartered clubs, taverns and hotels and restaurants.

2.7 Gross Capital Formation by Type of Good and Owner, in Current Prices

Million New Zealand dollars — Fiscal year beginning 1 April

	1980 TOTAL	1980 Total Private	1980 Public Enterprises	1980 General Government	1981 TOTAL	1981 Total Private	1981 Public Enterprises	1981 General Government	1982 TOTAL	1982 Total Private	1982 Public Enterprises	1982 General Government
Increase in stocks, total [a]	48	...	...	...	301	...	...	...	316	...	...	...
Gross Fixed Capital Formation, Total	4754	3287	...	1469	6597	4603	...	1994	7809	5152	...	2657
1 Residential buildings	881	828	...	53	1180	1142	...	38	1333	1267	...	66
2 Non-residential buildings	821	460	...	361	1034	634	...	400	1176	682	...	494
3 Other construction	592	113	...	479	862	243	...	619	1054	204	...	850
4 Land improvement and plantation and orchard development	216	166	...	51	274	211	...	63	271	196	...	75
5 Producers' durable goods	2244	1720	...	525	3247	2373	...	874	3974	2802	...	1172
A Transport equipment	812	674	...	139	1217	883	...	334	1246	994	...	252
B Machinery and equipment	1432	1046	...	386	2030	1490	...	540	2728	1808	...	920
6 Breeding stock, dairy cattle, etc.	...	...	...	...	...	...	...	...	...	...	...	...
Total Gross Capital Formation	4802	...	...	...	6898	...	...	...	8125	...	...	...

	1983 TOTAL	1983 Total Private	1983 Public Enterprises	1983 General Government	1984 TOTAL	1984 Total Private	1984 Public Enterprises	1984 General Government	1985 TOTAL	1985 Total Private	1985 Public Enterprises	1985 General Government
Increase in stocks, total [a]	515	...	...	...	1524	...	...	...	791	...	...	...
Gross Fixed Capital Formation, Total	8475	5491	...	2984	9605	6917	...	2690	11389	7636	...	3751
1 Residential buildings	1555	1482	...	74	1784	1712	...	72	2085	1948	...	136
2 Non-residential buildings	1250	713	...	537	1473	917	...	556	1982	1232	...	750
3 Other construction	1129	224	...	905	1107	261	...	847	1276	214	...	1062
4 Land improvement and plantation and orchard development	250	180	...	70	256	179	...	77	187	116	...	71
5 Producers' durable goods	4291	2893	...	1398	4984	3847	...	1138	5859	4125	...	1732
A Transport equipment	1194	1002	...	192	1698	1560	...	138	2116	1546	...	569
B Machinery and equipment	3097	1891	...	1206	3286	2287	...	999	3743	2579	...	1163
6 Breeding stock, dairy cattle, etc.	...	...	...	...	...	...	...	...	...	...	...	...
Total Gross Capital Formation	8990	...	...	...	11129	...	...	...	12180	...	...	...

a) From 1977 onward, stock valuation adjustment is made for the estimates of value of physical increase in stocks.

New Zealand

2.9 Gross Capital Formation by Kind of Activity of Owner, ISIC Major Divisions, in Current Prices

Million New Zealand dollars — Fiscal year beginning 1 April

	1980 TGCF	1980 IS	1980 GFCF	1981 TGCF	1981 IS	1981 GFCF	1982 TGCF	1982 IS	1982 GFCF	1983 TGCF	1983 IS	1983 GFCF
						All Producers						
1 Agriculture, hunting, fishing and forestry	967	329	638	1166	346	820	1027	224	803	1444	606	838
2 Mining and quarrying	65	-5	70	65	14	51	62	-4	66	123	7	116
3 Manufacturing	550	-183	733	1264	-41	1305	2170	-53	2223	2001	-199	2200
4 Electricity, gas and water	379	-27	406	493	-17	510	598	6	592	656	42	614
5 Construction	149	-1	150	210	-3	213	206	11	195	224	5	219
6 Wholesale and retail trade, restaurants and hotels	368	-96	464	621	-6	627	758	93	665	785	-3	788
7 Transport, storage and communication	422	-3	425	720	-4	724	757	33	724	786	44	742
8 Finance, insurance, real estate and business services	1149	-	1149	1545	-	1545	1692	-	1692	2026	-	2026
9 Community, social and personal services	81	9	72	98	9	89	91	5	86	113	8	105
Total Industries	4133	25	4108	6183	299	5884	7359	313	7046	8164	512	7652
Producers of Government Services	602	23	579	635	2	633	693	4	689	737	3	734
Private Non-Profit Institutions Serving Households	67	-	67	81	-	81	74	-	74	90	-	90
Total a	4802	48	4754	6899	301	6598	8126	317	7809	8991	515	8476

	1984 TGCF	1984 IS	1984 GFCF	1985 TGCF	1985 IS	1985 GFCF
			All Producers			
1 Agriculture, hunting, fishing and forestry	1708	778	930	1960	1344	616
2 Mining and quarrying	121	4	117	161	2	159
3 Manufacturing	2495	306	2189	2368	-5	2373
4 Electricity, gas and water	567	5	562	521	-26	547
5 Construction	303	7	296	352	-12	364
6 Wholesale and retail trade, restaurants and hotels	1351	327	1024	580	-656	1236
7 Transport, storage and communication	1052	81	971	1802	142	1660
8 Finance, insurance, real estate and business services	2477	-	2477	3159	-	3159
9 Community, social and personal services	162	14	148	187	1	186
Total Industries	10231	1519	8712	11091	791	10300
Producers of Government Services	803	5	798	986	-	986
Private Non-Profit Institutions Serving Households	96	-	96	103	-	103
Total a	11130	1524	9606	12180	791	11389

a) From 1977 onward, stock valuation adjustment is made for the estimates of value of physical increase in stocks.

2.11 Gross Fixed Capital Formation by Kind of Activity of Owner, ISIC Divisions, in Current Prices

Million New Zealand dollars — Fiscal year beginning 1 April

	1970	1975	1977	1978	1979	1980	1981	1982	1983	1984	1985	1986
						All Producers						
1 Agriculture, hunting, forestry and fishing	...	246	316	406	530	638	820	803	838	930	616	...
A Agriculture and hunting	...	225	277	371	483	593	770	755	783	869	544	...
B Forestry and logging	...	22	24	25	26	36	43	27	31	37	41	...
C Fishing	...	...	15	10	21	9	7	21	24	24	31	...
2 Mining and quarrying	...	142	207	120	81	70	51	66	116	117	159	...

New Zealand

2.11 Gross Fixed Capital Formation by Kind of Activity of Owner, ISIC Divisions, in Current Prices
(Continued)

Million New Zealand dollars — Fiscal year beginning 1 April

	1970	1975	1977	1978	1979	1980	1981	1982	1983	1984	1985	1986
3 Manufacturing	...	361	388	460	547	733	1305	2223	2200	2189	2373	...
A Manufacturing of food, beverages and tobacco	...	124	120	165	222	348	393	394	393	440	429	...
B Textile, wearing apparel and leather industries	...	27	34	40	39	31	35	68	65	86	102	...
C Manufacture of wood, and wood products, including furniture	...	32	42	22	27	32	27	42	41	107	149	...
D Manufacture of paper and paper products, printing and publishing	...	50	37	70	71	86	115	137	141	239	194	...
E Manufacture of chemicals and chemical petroleum, coal, rubber and plastic products	...	39	41	62	62	98	382	1067	1010	779	634	...
F Manufacture of non-metallic mineral products except products of petroleum and coal	...	20	12	16	17	20	53	63	39	42	41	...
G Basic metal industries	...	9	23	21	20	29	172	301	343	284	560	...
H Manufacture of fabricated metal products, machinery and equipment	...	50	76	61	86	86	125	148	100	202	252	...
I Other manufacturing industries	...	1	4	3	3	3	3	3	8	10	12	...
4 Electricity, gas and water	...	305	385	411	377	406	510	592	614	562	547	...
5 Construction	...	77	96	74	115	150	213	195	219	296	364	...
6 Wholesale and retail trade, restaurants and hotels	...	224	222	300	454	464	627	665	788	1024	1236	...
7 Transport, storage and communication	...	417	466	539	321	425	724	724	742	971	1660	...
A Transport and storage	...	339	399	455	258	327	605	529	465	673	1216	...
B Communication	...	78	67	84	63	98	119	195	277	298	444	...
8 Finance, insurance, real estate and business services	...	1024	931	976	1011	1149	1545	1692	2026	2477	3159	...
9 Community, social and personal services	...	...	57	51	63	72	89	86	105	148	186	...
Total Industries	...	2797	3068	3339	3500	4108	5884	7046	7652	8712	10300	...
Producers of Government Services	...	408	430	492	513	579	633	689	734	798	986	...
Private Non-Profit Institutions Serving Households	...	40	47	49	54	67	81	74	90	96	103	...
Total	...	3246	3545	3880	4067	4754	6598	7809	8476	9606	11389	...

4.1 Derivation of Value Added by Kind of Activity, in Current Prices

Million New Zealand dollars — Fiscal year beginning 1 April

	1980 Gross Output	1980 Intermediate Consumption	1980 Value Added	1981 Gross Output	1981 Intermediate Consumption	1981 Value Added	1982 Gross Output	1982 Intermediate Consumption	1982 Value Added	1983 Gross Output	1983 Intermediate Consumption	1983 Value Added
All Producers												
1 Agriculture, hunting, forestry and fishing	5231	2713	2518	5808	3146	2662	6061	3499	2563	7037	4088	2949
A Agriculture and hunting [a]	4549	2388	2161	4992	2749	2243	5092	2975	2117	5900	3486	2413
B Forestry and logging	502	206	296	593	252	341	699	343	356	787	357	431
C Fishing [a]	180	119	61	223	145	78	270	181	90	350	245	105
2 Mining and quarrying	417	222	195	539	302	237	744	359	385	863	559	304

New Zealand

4.1 Derivation of Value Added by Kind of Activity, in Current Prices
(Continued)

Million New Zealand dollars — Fiscal year beginning 1 April

	1980 Gross Output	1980 Intermediate Consumption	1980 Value Added	1981 Gross Output	1981 Intermediate Consumption	1981 Value Added	1982 Gross Output	1982 Intermediate Consumption	1982 Value Added	1983 Gross Output	1983 Intermediate Consumption	1983 Value Added
3 Manufacturing	15732	10652	5082	19932	13414	6517	22007	14771	7236	23470	15620	7850
A Manufacture of food, beverages and tobacco	4701	3307	1394	5767	4119	1647	6656	4670	1986	7200	4842	2358
B Textile, wearing apparel and leather industries	1605	1046	560	1931	1216	716	2132	1376	756	2140	1432	708
C Manufacture of wood and wood products, including furniture	1043	676	367	1377	905	472	1374	932	442	1453	936	517
D Manufacture of paper and paper products, printing and publishing	1710	1104	606	2049	1325	724	2175	1372	803	2380	1535	844
E Manufacture of chemicals and chemical petroleum, coal, rubber and plastic products	1748	1278	470	2168	1573	595	2320	1651	668	2534	1860	674
F Manufacture of non-metallic mineral products, except products of petroleum and coal	539	312	227	764	427	337	872	499	373	904	506	399
G Basic metal industries	606	433	173	773	556	217	873	575	298	998	664	335
H Manufacture of fabricated metal products, machinery and equipment	3645	2416	1229	4913	3186	1726	5404	3565	1839	5642	3707	1934
I Other manufacturing industries	135	80	56	190	107	83	201	131	71	219	138	81
4 Electricity, gas and water	1468	753	715	1710	882	828	2084	1123	962	2237	1171	1066
5 Construction	3865	2723	1142	4934	3422	1512	5725	4029	1696	6272	4410	1862
6 Wholesale and retail trade, restaurants and hotels	9973	5573	4400	11972	6638	5334	13655	7447	6208	14847	7772	7074
7 Transport, storage and communication	3497	1636	1861	4127	1949	2178	4796	2263	2533	5236	2289	2947
A Transport and storage	2757	1524	1233	3274	1825	1449	3736	2112	1624	4066	2144	1922
B Communication	740	112	628	853	124	729	1060	151	909	1170	145	1025
8 Finance, insurance, real estate and business services	4852	1667	3185	6009	2051	3958	7100	2527	4574	7928	2781	5147
9 Community, social and personal services	1750	876	874	2154	1113	1041	2485	1307	1178	2745	1490	1255
Total, Industries	46787	26815	19972	57185	32916	24268	64659	37325	27334	70635	40178	30457
Producers of Government Services	4482	1376	3106	5398	1682	3715	6026	1938	4088	6353	2152	4202
Other Producers	439	188	251	507	218	289	539	246	293	531	254	277
Total	51709	28380	23329	63089	34817	28273	71223	39509	31715	77519	42583	34935
Less: Imputed bank service charge	...	-603	603	...	-834	834	...	-968	968	...	-1100	1100
Import duties	231	...	231	337	...	337	362	...	362	432	...	432
Value added tax	...	...	...	...	...	...	...	...	...	...	...	...
Other adjustments [b]	37	...	37	55	...	55	51	...	51	62	...	62
Total [c]	51977	28983	22994	63481	35651	27830	71636	40477	31160	78013	43683	34330

	1984 Gross Output	1984 Intermediate Consumption	1984 Value Added	1985 Gross Output	1985 Intermediate Consumption	1985 Value Added
	\multicolumn{6}{c}{All Producers}
1 Agriculture, hunting, forestry and fishing	8636	4924	3713	8697	4532	4165
A Agriculture and hunting [a]	7225	4249	2977	6900	3784	3116
B Forestry and logging	1024	413	612	1348	474	874
C Fishing [a]	387	262	124	449	274	175
2 Mining and quarrying	1051	630	421	1314	801	513

New Zealand

4.1 Derivation of Value Added by Kind of Activity, in Current Prices
(Continued)

Million New Zealand dollars — Fiscal year beginning 1 April

		1984 Gross Output	1984 Intermediate Consumption	1984 Value Added	1985 Gross Output	1985 Intermediate Consumption	1985 Value Added
3	Manufacturing	28116	18951	9166	30816	20757	10059
	A Manufacture of food, beverages and tobacco	7903	5403	2499	8574	5992	2582
	B Textile, wearing apparel and leather industries	2633	1800	834	2894	1934	960
	C Manufacture of wood and wood products, including furniture	1768	1153	615	2037	1334	703
	D Manufacture of paper and paper products, printing and publishing	2986	1851	1135	3321	2138	1183
	E Manufacture of chemicals and chemical petroleum, coal, rubber and plastic products	3131	2308	823	3535	2503	1032
	F Manufacture of non-metallic mineral products, except products of petroleum and coal	1040	604	436	1221	719	501
	G Basic metal industries	1245	803	442	1154	703	451
	H Manufacture of fabricated metal products, machinery and equipment	7102	4834	2269	7729	5229	2501
	I Other manufacturing industries	308	195	113	351	205	146
4	Electricity, gas and water	2496	1395	1101	3116	1732	1383
5	Construction	7009	4927	2083	8785	6248	2536
6	Wholesale and retail trade, restaurants and hotels	16334	8928	7406	18364	9825	8539
7	Transport, storage and communication	6071	2859	3212	6850	3386	3463
	A Transport and storage	4771	2650	2121	5345	3054	2291
	B Communication	1300	209	1091	1505	332	1172
8	Finance, insurance, real estate and business services	9269	3299	5971	11414	3747	7666
9	Community, social and personal services	3161	1669	1493	3902	2179	1723
	Total, Industries	82146	47580	34565	93257	53209	40048
	Producers of Government Services	6790	2401	4389	7998	2885	5113
	Other Producers	575	273	302	674	332	342
	Total	89510	50254	39257	101929	56426	45503
	Less: Imputed bank service charge	...	-1275	1275	...	-1455	1455
	Import duties	604	...	604	718	...	717
	Value added tax	...	...	...	...	...	...
	Other adjustments b	81	...	81	103	...	103
	Total c	90195	51529	38666	102750	57881	44868

a) Hunting is included in item 'Fishing'.
b) Item 'Other adjustments' relates to other indirect taxes and import duties not allocated to industries.
c) From 1977 onward, stock valuation adjustment is made for the estimates of value of physical increase in stocks.

4.2 Derivation of Value Added by Kind of Activity, in Constant Prices

Million New Zealand dollars — Fiscal year beginning 1 April

		1980 Gross Output	1980 Intermediate Consumption	1980 Value Added	1981 Gross Output	1981 Intermediate Consumption	1981 Value Added	1982 Gross Output	1982 Intermediate Consumption	1982 Value Added	1983 Gross Output	1983 Intermediate Consumption	1983 Value Added
		At constant prices of: 1982 — All Producers											
1	Agriculture, hunting, forestry and fishing	...	...	2468	...	...	2459	...	...	2563	...	...	2462
	A Agriculture and hunting a	...	...	2038	...	...	2015	...	...	2117	...	...	2000
	B Forestry and logging	...	...	349	...	...	358	...	...	356	...	...	365
	C Fishing a	...	...	81	...	...	86	...	...	90	...	...	97
2	Mining and quarrying	...	...	223	...	...	253	...	...	386	...	...	303

New Zealand

4.2 Derivation of Value Added by Kind of Activity, in Constant Prices
(Continued)

Million New Zealand dollars — Fiscal year beginning 1 April

	1980 Gross Output	1980 Intermediate Consumption	1980 Value Added	1981 Gross Output	1981 Intermediate Consumption	1981 Value Added	1982 Gross Output	1982 Intermediate Consumption	1982 Value Added	1983 Gross Output	1983 Intermediate Consumption	1983 Value Added
					At constant prices of:1982							
3 Manufacturing	...	...	6613	...	...	7183	...	...	7235	...	...	7435
A Manufacture of food, beverages and tobacco	...	...	1824	...	...	1872	...	...	1986	...	...	1998
B Textile, wearing apparel and leather industries	...	...	701	...	...	745	...	...	756	...	...	736
C Manufacture of wood and wood products, including furniture	...	...	436	...	...	489	...	...	442	...	...	468
D Manufacture of paper and paper products, printing and publishing	...	...	815	...	...	832	...	...	803	...	...	871
E Manufacture of chemicals and chemical petroleum, coal, rubber and plastic products	...	...	642	...	...	689	...	...	668	...	...	716
F Manufacture of non-metallic mineral products, except products of petroleum and coal	...	...	298	...	...	360	...	...	373	...	...	377
G Basic metal industries	...	...	258	...	...	285	...	...	298	...	...	334
H Manufacture of fabricated metal products, machinery and equipment	...	...	1639	...	...	1911	...	...	1909	...	...	1935
I Other manufacturing industries	...	...	...	...	...	...	...	...	...	...	...	...
4 Electricity, gas and water	...	...	933	...	...	956	...	...	962	...	...	1062
5 Construction	...	...	1516	...	...	1655	...	...	1696	...	...	1846
6 Wholesale and retail trade, restaurants and hotels	...	...	6041	...	...	6362	...	...	6208	...	...	6402
7 Transport, storage and communication	...	...	2450	...	...	2515	...	...	2532	...	...	2774
A Transport and storage	...	...	1623	...	...	1641	...	...	1623	...	...	1811
B Communication	...	...	827	...	...	874	...	...	909	...	...	963
8 Finance, insurance, real estate and business services	...	...	4444	...	...	4567	...	...	4574	...	...	4872
9 Community, social and personal services	...	...	1381	...	...	1441	...	...	1471	...	...	1538
Total, Industries	...	...	26067	...	...	27389	...	...	27627	...	...	28694
Producers of Government Services	...	...	3974	...	...	4058	...	...	4088	...	...	4126
Other Producers	...	...	...	...	...	...	...	...	...	...	...	...
Total	...	...	30041	...	...	31447	...	...	31715	...	...	32820
Less: Imputed bank service charge	...	...	923	...	...	945	...	...	968	...	...	1126
Import duties	...	...	...	...	...	...	...	...	...	...	...	...
Value added tax	...	...	...	...	...	...	...	...	...	...	...	...
Other adjustments [b]	...	...	346	...	...	449	...	...	413	...	...	382
Total [c]	...	...	29464	...	...	30951	...	...	31160	...	...	32076

	1984 Gross Output	1984 Intermediate Consumption	1984 Value Added	1985 Gross Output	1985 Intermediate Consumption	1985 Value Added
	At constant prices of:1982					
	All Producers					
1 Agriculture, hunting, forestry and fishing	...	...	2448	...	...	3013
A Agriculture and hunting [a]	...	...	1975	...	...	2512
B Forestry and logging	...	...	378	...	...	406
C Fishing [a]	...	...	95	...	...	95
2 Mining and quarrying	...	...	399	...	...	576

New Zealand

4.2 Derivation of Value Added by Kind of Activity, in Constant Prices
(Continued)

Million New Zealand dollars — Fiscal year beginning 1 April

	1984 Gross Output	1984 Intermediate Consumption	1984 Value Added	1985 Gross Output	1985 Intermediate Consumption	1985 Value Added
			At constant prices of: 1982			
3 Manufacturing	...	...	8224	...	...	7866
A Manufacture of food, beverages and tobacco	...	...	2085	...	...	1926
B Textile, wearing apparel and leather industries	...	...	819	...	...	797
C Manufacture of wood and wood products, including furniture	...	...	521	...	...	505
D Manufacture of paper and paper products, printing and publishing	...	...	986	...	...	990
E Manufacture of chemicals and chemical petroleum, coal, rubber and plastic products	...	...	818	...	...	791
F Manufacture of non-metallic mineral products, except products of petroleum and coal	...	...	412	...	...	427
G Basic metal industries	...	...	371	...	...	315
H Manufacture of fabricated metal products, machinery and equipment	...	...	2212	...	...	2115
I Other manufacturing industries	...	...	...	...	...	...
4 Electricity, gas and water	...	...	1076	...	...	1102
5 Construction	...	...	1909	...	...	2079
6 Wholesale and retail trade, restaurants and hotels	...	...	6631	...	...	6522
7 Transport, storage and communication	...	...	2994	...	...	3027
A Transport and storage	...	...	1948	...	...	1893
B Communication	...	...	1046	...	...	1134
8 Finance, insurance, real estate and business services	...	...	5139	...	...	5424
9 Community, social and personal services	...	...	1589	...	...	1674
Total, Industries	...	...	30407	...	...	31284
Producers of Government Services	...	...	4135	...	...	4134
Other Producers	...	...	...	...	...	...
Total	...	...	34542	...	...	35418
Less: Imputed bank service charge	...	...	1251	...	...	1414
Import duties	...	...	...	...	...	...
Value added tax	...	...	...	...	...	...
Other adjustments [b]	...	...	474	...	...	493
Total [c]	...	...	33765	...	...	34497

a) Hunting is included in item 'Fishing'.
b) Item 'Other adjustments' relates to other indirect taxes and import duties not allocated to industries.
c) From 1977 onward, stock valuation adjustment is made for the estimates of value of physical increase in stocks.

4.3 Cost Components of Value Added

Million New Zealand dollars — Fiscal year beginning 1 April

	1980 Compensation of Employees	1980 Capital Consumption	1980 Net Operating Surplus	1980 Indirect Taxes	1980 Less: Subsidies Received	1980 Value Added	1981 Compensation of Employees	1981 Capital Consumption	1981 Net Operating Surplus	1981 Indirect Taxes	1981 Less: Subsidies Received	1981 Value Added
				All Producers								
1 Agriculture, hunting, forestry and fishing	509	312	1651	86	40	2518	610	345	1876	104	274	2662
A Agriculture and hunting [a]	373	290	1450	81	33	2161	446	322	1600	90	202	2243
B Forestry and logging	110	11	177	4	6	296	135	13	198	4	10	341
C Fishing [a]	26	11	24	1	1	61	29	10	39	2	2	78
2 Mining and quarrying	55	33	86	22	1	195	65	29	117	27	-	237

New Zealand

4.3 Cost Components of Value Added
(Continued)

Million New Zealand dollars — Fiscal year beginning 1 April

	1980 Compensation of Employees	Capital Consumption	Net Operating Surplus	Indirect Taxes	Less: Subsidies Received	Value Added	1981 Compensation of Employees	Capital Consumption	Net Operating Surplus	Indirect Taxes	Less: Subsidies Received	Value Added
3 Manufacturing	3422	393	948	416	101	5082	4184	446	1486	512	107	6517
A Manufacture of food, beverages and tobacco	916	119	145	256	42	1394	1091	140	156	301	40	1647
B Textile, wearing apparel and leather industries	407	30	123	6	7	560	494	32	194	7	11	716
C Manufacture of wood and wood products, including furniture	246	24	95	3	2	367	314	26	131	3	2	472
D Manufacture of paper and paper products, printing and publishing	387	63	140	19	4	606	470	72	162	23	3	724
E Manufacture of chemicals and chemical petroleum, coal, rubber and plastic products	326	52	97	36	40	470	385	54	153	44	41	595
F Manufacture of non-metallic mineral products, except products of petroleum and coal	121	18	85	3	1	227	151	21	163	4	2	337
G Basic metal industries	104	15	53	1	-	173	129	16	72	2	1	217
H Manufacture of fabricated metal products, machinery and equipment	880	69	198	87	5	1229	1105	81	427	121	7	1726
I Other manufacturing industries	35	3	12	5	-	56	45	4	28	7	-	83
4 Electricity, gas and water	213	85	419	4	6	715	263	97	469	5	6	828
5 Construction	747	55	339	14	13	1142	888	63	552	18	9	1512
6 Wholesale and retail trade, restaurants and hotels	2041	227	1192	983	44	4400	2435	269	1486	1173	28	5334
7 Transport, storage and communication	1341	212	362	81	135	1861	1575	249	395	101	143	2178
A Transport and storage	907	163	220	76	133	1233	1053	196	245	94	140	1449
B Communication	434	49	142	5	2	628	522	53	150	7	3	729
8 Finance, insurance, real estate and business services	931	293	1577	386	2	3185	1158	346	1969	488	3	3958
9 Community, social and personal services	445	42	330	64	8	874	541	52	385	73	9	1041
Total, Industries	9704	1654	6906	2056	348	19972	11718	1896	8734	2498	578	24268
Producers of Government Services	3094	-	-	12	-	3106	3700	-	-	15	-	3715
Other Producers	220	25	-	7	-	251	254	27	-	8	-	289
Total	13018	1678	6906	2075	348	23329	15672	1923	8734	2521	578	28273
Less: Imputed bank service charge	...	...	603	...	...	603	...	...	834	...	...	834
Import duties	...	...	...	231	...	231	...	...	...	337	...	337
Value added tax	...	...	...	...	...	...	...	...	...	...	...	...
Other adjustments [b]	...	...	...	37	...	37	...	...	...	55	...	55
Total [cd]	13018	1678	6303	2343	348	22994	15672	1923	7900	2913	578	27830

	1982 Compensation of Employees	Capital Consumption	Net Operating Surplus	Indirect Taxes	Less: Subsidies Received	Value Added	1983 Compensation of Employees	Capital Consumption	Net Operating Surplus	Indirect Taxes	Less: Subsidies Received	Value Added
					All Producers							
1 Agriculture, hunting, forestry and fishing	636	380	1873	121	447	2563	658	417	2111	128	365	2949
A Agriculture and hunting [a]	478	351	1611	114	437	2117	485	386	1769	120	347	2413
B Forestry and logging	124	16	220	5	9	356	129	14	299	5	17	431
C Fishing [a]	34	13	42	2	1	90	44	17	43	3	1	105
2 Mining and quarrying	78	39	226	43	-	385	87	59	111	47	-	304

New Zealand

4.3 Cost Components of Value Added
(Continued)

Million New Zealand dollars — Fiscal year beginning 1 April

1982

	Compensation of Employees	Capital Consumption	Net Operating Surplus	Indirect Taxes	Less: Subsidies Received	Value Added
3 Manufacturing	4561	519	1684	571	99	7236
A Manufacture of food, beverages and tobacco	1225	160	294	343	37	1986
B Textile, wearing apparel and leather industries	514	38	207	8	11	756
C Manufacture of wood and wood products, including furniture	325	29	86	4	2	442
D Manufacture of paper and paper products, printing and publishing	509	86	186	25	3	803
E Manufacture of chemicals and chemical petroleum, coal, rubber and plastic products	405	60	194	47	37	668
F Manufacture of non-metallic mineral products, except products of petroleum and coal	173	26	172	4	2	373
G Basic metal industries	146	25	126	2	1	298
H Manufacture of fabricated metal products, machinery and equipment	1220	91	403	131	6	1839
I Other manufacturing industries	44	4	16	7	-	71
4 Electricity, gas and water	278	109	575	5	5	962
5 Construction	996	79	607	21	7	1696
6 Wholesale and retail trade, restaurants and hotels	2682	322	1787	1445	28	6208
7 Transport, storage and communication	1687	293	592	121	159	2533
A Transport and storage	1135	229	303	113	156	1624
B Communication	552	64	289	8	3	909
8 Finance, insurance, real estate and business services	1326	387	2273	590	2	4574
9 Community, social and personal services	600	62	443	82	9	1178
Total, Industries	12843	2188	10059	2999	755	27334
Producers of Government Services	4069	-	-	18	-	4088
Other Producers	256	28	-	9	-	293
Total	17168	2216	10059	3027	755	31715
Less: Imputed bank service charge	...	...	968	...	...	968
Import duties	...	...	...	362	...	362
Value added tax	...	...	...	...	...	...
Other adjustments [b]	...	...	...	51	...	51
Total [cd]	17168	2216	9091	3440	755	31160

1983

	Compensation of Employees	Capital Consumption	Net Operating Surplus	Indirect Taxes	Less: Subsidies Received	Value Added
3 Manufacturing	4482	617	2194	635	76	7850
A Manufacture of food, beverages and tobacco	1192	186	606	397	23	2358
B Textile, wearing apparel and leather industries	494	47	168	8	8	708
C Manufacture of wood and wood products, including furniture	316	36	163	5	2	517
D Manufacture of paper and paper products, printing and publishing	540	98	180	29	3	844
E Manufacture of chemicals and chemical petroleum, coal, rubber and plastic products	404	80	189	34	32	674
F Manufacture of non-metallic mineral products, except products of petroleum and coal	159	31	204	7	2	399
G Basic metal industries	150	32	151	2	1	335
H Manufacture of fabricated metal products, machinery and equipment	1183	102	510	144	5	1934
I Other manufacturing industries	44	5	23	9	-	81
4 Electricity, gas and water	294	137	635	5	5	1066
5 Construction	1034	94	718	22	6	1862
6 Wholesale and retail trade, restaurants and hotels	2733	394	2372	1606	30	7074
7 Transport, storage and communication	1720	357	903	128	162	2947
A Transport and storage	1174	270	517	120	159	1922
B Communication	546	87	386	8	3	1025
8 Finance, insurance, real estate and business services	1409	445	2634	661	2	5147
9 Community, social and personal services	621	68	486	90	10	1255
Total, Industries	13038	2587	12164	3324	655	30457
Producers of Government Services	4182	-	-	20	-	4202
Other Producers	239	28	-	10	-	277
Total	17459	2615	12164	3353	655	34935
Less: Imputed bank service charge	...	...	1100	...	...	1100
Import duties	...	...	...	432	...	432
Value added tax	...	...	...	...	...	...
Other adjustments [b]	...	...	...	62	...	62
Total [cd]	17459	2615	11064	3847	655	34330

1984

	Compensation of Employees	Capital Consumption	Net Operating Surplus	Indirect Taxes	Less: Subsidies Received	Value Added
All Producers						
1 Agriculture, hunting, forestry and fishing	740	499	2653	142	322	3713
A Agriculture and hunting [a]	554	464	2067	130	239	2977
B Forestry and logging	138	14	536	6	82	612
C Fishing [a]	48	21	50	6	1	124
2 Mining and quarrying	95	79	190	57	-	421

1985

	Compensation of Employees	Capital Consumption	Net Operating Surplus	Indirect Taxes	Less: Subsidies Received	Value Added
1 Agriculture, hunting, forestry and fishing	775	701	2622	162	96	4165
A Agriculture and hunting [a]	572	653	1832	145	87	3116
B Forestry and logging	145	20	710	7	8	874
C Fishing [a]	58	28	80	10	1	175
2 Mining and quarrying	100	108	227	77	-	513

New Zealand

4.3 Cost Components of Value Added
(Continued)

Million New Zealand dollars — Fiscal year beginning 1 April

		1984					1985					
	Compensation of Employees	Capital Consumption	Net Operating Surplus	Indirect Taxes	Less: Subsidies Received	Value Added	Compensation of Employees	Capital Consumption	Net Operating Surplus	Indirect Taxes	Less: Subsidies Received	Value Added
3 Manufacturing	4939	736	2823	746	79	9166	5551	877	2899	783	49	10059
A Manufacture of food, beverages and tobacco	1296	230	555	448	29	2499	1305	248	582	462	14	2582
B Textile, wearing apparel and leather industries	544	54	230	10	5	834	620	61	272	11	4	960
C Manufacture of wood and wood products, including furniture	349	39	223	6	2	615	406	48	243	7	1	703
D Manufacture of paper and paper products, printing and publishing	596	116	391	36	4	1135	723	129	295	40	4	1183
E Manufacture of chemicals and chemical petroleum, coal, rubber and plastic products	444	104	264	41	31	823	527	158	328	37	18	1032
F Manufacture of non-metallic mineral products, except products of petroleum and coal	170	31	228	9	2	436	200	38	254	11	1	501
G Basic metal industries	168	34	239	2	1	442	191	35	224	3	2	451
H Manufacture of fabricated metal products, machinery and equipment	1321	122	650	181	5	2269	1517	152	640	197	5	2501
I Other manufacturing industries	51	6	43	13	-	113	62	8	61	15	-	146
4 Electricity, gas and water	305	163	630	7	3	1101	373	182	824	8	4	1383
5 Construction	1131	106	824	26	4	2083	1301	118	1093	29	4	2536
6 Wholesale and retail trade, restaurants and hotels	3057	456	2047	1875	29	7406	3631	542	2491	1891	16	8539
7 Transport, storage and communication	1819	403	955	183	148	3212	2044	459	916	220	176	3463
A Transport and storage	1238	303	551	175	146	2121	1410	325	522	209	175	2291
B Communication	581	100	404	8	2	1091	634	134	394	11	1	1172
8 Finance, insurance, real estate and business services	1590	530	3164	688	2	5971	1950	642	4288	788	2	7666
9 Community, social and personal services	685	81	639	98	11	1493	785	91	760	99	12	1723
Total, Industries	14362	3053	13926	3822	598	34565	16510	3722	16121	4055	361	40048
Producers of Government Services	4364	-	-	26	-	4389	5083	...	...	30	-	5113
Other Producers	260	32	-	10	-	302	296	34	...	12	-	342
Total	18986	3085	13926	3858	598	39257	21889	3756	16121	4097	361	45503
Less: Imputed bank service charge	...	...	1275	...	...	1275	...	...	1455	...	...	1455
Import duties	...	...	...	604	...	604	...	...	...	717	...	717
Value added tax	...	...	...	...	...	...	...	...	...	...	...	...
Other adjustments [b]	...	...	...	81	...	81	...	...	...	103	...	103
Total [cd]	18986	3085	12651	4543	598	38666	22120	3756	14514	4839	361	44868

a) Hunting is included in item 'Fishing'.
b) Item 'Other adjustments' relates to other indirect taxes and import duties not allocated to industries.
c) From 1977 onward, stock valuation adjustment is made for the estimates of value of physical increase in stocks.
d) For year 1986, fringe benefits and fringe benefits tax are not included.

Nicaragua

Source. Reply to the United Nations National Accounts Questionnaire from the Departamento de Estudios Economicos, Banco Central de Nicaragua, Managua. The official estimates are published by the Banco Central in the 'Informe Anual'.

General note. The estimates shown in the following tables have been prepared in accordance with the United Nations System of National Accounts so far as the existing data would permit.

1.1 Expenditure on the Gross Domestic Product, in Current Prices

Million Nicaraguan cordobas

		1970	1975	1977	1978	1979	1980	1981	1982	1983	1984	1985	1986
1	Government final consumption expenditure	521	1007	1396	1762	2591	4107	5371	6646	10351	15913	41235	154039
2	Private final consumption expenditure	4038	8732	11101	10901	10739	18381	18094	19237	18655	24965	55616	243194
3	Gross capital formation	1011	2385	4018	1850	-833	3364	5777	5323	7401	10010	26702	73609
	A Increase in stocks	120	-126	435	-282	-1800	482	539	624	1011	1273	2782	13293
	B Gross fixed capital formation	891	2510	3583	2132	967	2882	5238	4699	6390	8737	23920	60316
	Residential buildings	89	417	438	221	...	...	...	...	...	...	...	...
	Non-residential buildings	125	555	666	445	...	...	...	...	...	...	...	...
	Other construction and land improvement etc.	140	165	230	143	...	...	...	...	...	...	...	...
	Other	537	1373	2249	1324	...	...	...	...	...	...	...	...
4	Exports of goods and services	1453	3122	5032	5160	6100	5039	5470	4530	6387	7404	17041	55672
5	Less: Imports of goods and services	1587	4113	5868	4686	4083	8999	10229	7386	9874	13262	25188	91772
	Equals: Gross Domestic Product	5436	11133	15679	14988	14514	21892	24483	28350	32920	45030	115404	435742

1.2 Expenditure on the Gross Domestic Product, in Constant Prices

Million Nicaraguan cordobas

		1970	1975	1977	1978	1979	1980	1981	1982	1983	1984	1985	1986
		\multicolumn{12}{c}{At constant prices of:1958}											
1	Government final consumption expenditure	293.9	407.6	508.3	625.6	...	...	...	...	...	...	...	...
2	Private final consumption expenditure	3365.7	4329.0	4763.3	4475.1	...	...	...	...	...	...	...	...
3	Gross capital formation	928.1	1049.7	1900.3	772.5	...	...	...	...	...	...	...	...
	A Increase in stocks	102.6	-101.3	343.0	-95.9	...	...	...	...	...	...	...	...
	B Gross fixed capital formation	825.5	1151.0	1557.3	868.4	...	...	...	...	...	...	...	...
	Residential buildings	80.8	207.5	197.5	119.9	...	...	...	...	...	...	...	...
	Non-residential buildings	113.0	282.1	329.9	224.3	...	...	...	...	...	...	...	...
	Other construction and land improvement etc.	126.9	83.3	113.7	59.7	...	...	...	...	...	...	...	...
	Other	504.8	578.1	916.2	464.5	...	...	...	...	...	...	...	...
4	Exports of goods and services	1403.2	2058.0	2042.9	2205.0	...	...	...	...	...	...	...	...
5	Less: Imports of goods and services	1326.6	1731.6	2390.3	1741.9	...	...	...	...	...	...	...	...
	Equals: Gross Domestic Product	4664.3	6112.7	6824.5	6336.3	...	...	...	...	...	...	...	...

1.3 Cost Components of the Gross Domestic Product

Million Nicaraguan cordobas

		1970	1975	1977	1978	1979	1980	1981	1982	1983	1984	1985	1986
1	Indirect taxes, net	459.2	1032.8	1486.1	1329.8	...	...	...	...	...	...	...	...
2	Consumption of fixed capital	217.4	445.3	627.0	500.5	...	...	...	...	...	...	...	...
3	Compensation of employees paid by resident producers to:	2906.1	6044.3	8481.3	8366.9	...	...	...	...	...	...	...	...
4	Operating surplus	1853.4	3610.6	5084.3	4691.8	...	...	...	...	...	...	...	...
	A Corporate and quasi-corporate enterprises	1861.2	3624.1	5098.5	4745.6	...	...	...	...	...	...	...	...
	B Private unincorporated enterprises					...	...	...	...	...	...	...	...
	C General government	7.8	13.5	14.2	50.0	...	...	...	...	...	...	...	...
	Equals: Gross Domestic Product	5436.1	11133.0	15679.0	14988.0	...	...	...	...	...	...	...	...

1.4 General Government Current Receipts and Disbursements

Million Nicaraguan cordobas

		1970	1975	1977	1978	1979	1980	1981	1982	1983	1984	1985	1986
		\multicolumn{12}{c}{Receipts}											
1	Operating surplus	-7.8	-13.5	-14.2	-53.8	...	...	...	...	...	...	...	...
2	Property and entrepreneurial income	...	...	...	...	...	...	...	...	...	...	...	...
3	Taxes, fees and contributions	637.6	1483.5	2075.8	1894.1	...	...	...	...	...	...	...	...
	A Indirect taxes [a]	459.2	1032.8	1486.2	1329.8	...	...	...	...	...	...	...	...

Nicaragua

1.4 General Government Current Receipts and Disbursements
(Continued)

Million Nicaraguan cordobas

	1970	1975	1977	1978	1979	1980	1981	1982	1983	1984	1985	1986
B Direct taxes	178.4	450.7	589.6	564.3	...	...	...	...	...	...	...	...
C Social security contributions	...	...	...	...	...	...	...	...	...	...	...	...
D Compulsory fees, fines and penalties	...	...	...	...	...	...	...	...	...	...	...	...
4 Other current transfers	30.8	87.4	79.9	68.8	...	...	...	...	...	...	...	...
Total Current Receipts of General Government	660.6	1557.4	2141.5	1909.1	...	...	...	...	...	...	...	...

Disbursements

	1970	1975	1977	1978	1979	1980	1981	1982	1983	1984	1985	1986
1 Government final consumption expenditure	521.4	1007.3	1396.3	1762.4	...	...	...	...	...	...	...	...
2 Property income	...	...	...	...	...	...	...	...	...	...	...	...
3 Subsidies [a]	...	...	...	...	...	...	...	...	...	...	...	...
4 Other current transfers	60.8	114.9	160.0	176.2	...	...	...	...	...	...	...	...
A Social security benefits	...	...	...	...	...	...	...	...	...	...	...	...
B Social assistance grants	...	...	...	...	...	...	...	...	...	...	...	...
C Other	60.8	114.9	160.0	176.2	...	...	...	...	...	...	...	...
5 Net saving	78.4	435.2	585.2	-29.5	...	...	...	...	...	...	...	...
Total Current Disbursements and Net Saving of General Government	660.6	1557.4	2141.5	1909.1	...	...	...	...	...	...	...	...

a) Item 'Subsidies' is netted out of item 'Indirect taxes'.

1.7 External Transactions on Current Account, Summary

Million Nicaraguan cordobas

	1970	1975	1977	1978	1979	1980	1981	1982	1983	1984	1985	1986

Payments to the Rest of the World

	1970	1975	1977	1978	1979	1980	1981	1982	1983	1984	1985	1986
1 Imports of goods and services	1586.9	4112.5	5868.1	4685.8	...	...	...	...	...	...	...	...
A Imports of merchandise c.i.f.	1250.4	2626.2	4457.6	4521.8	...	...	...	...	...	...	...	...
B Other	336.5	1486.3	1410.5	164.0	...	...	...	...	...	...	...	...
2 Factor income to the rest of the world	255.5	543.2	675.5	627.9	...	...	...	...	...	...	...	...
3 Current transfers to the rest of the world	11.0	5.6	5.8	3.8	...	...	...	...	...	...	...	...
4 Surplus of the nation on current transactions	-266.4	-1282.3	-1269.4	72.9	...	...	...	...	...	...	...	...
Payments to the Rest of the World and Surplus of the Nation on Current Transactions	1587.0	3379.0	5280.0	5390.4	...	...	...	...	...	...	...	...

Receipts From The Rest of the World

	1970	1975	1977	1978	1979	1980	1981	1982	1983	1984	1985	1986
1 Exports of goods and services	1453.2	3122.0	5031.6	5159.7	...	...	...	...	...	...	...	...
A Exports of merchandise f.o.b.	1250.4	2626.2	4457.6	4521.8	...	...	...	...	...	...	...	...
B Other	202.8	495.8	574.0	637.9	...	...	...	...	...	...	...	...
2 Factor income from rest of the world	79.1	127.4	159.6	153.3	...	...	...	...	...	...	...	...
3 Current transfers from rest of the world	54.7	129.6	88.8	77.4	...	...	...	...	...	...	...	...
Receipts from the Rest of the World on Current Transactions	1587.0	3379.0	5280.0	5390.4	...	...	...	...	...	...	...	...

1.8 Capital Transactions of The Nation, Summary

Million Nicaraguan cordobas

	1970	1975	1977	1978	1979	1980	1981	1982	1983	1984	1985	1986

Finance of Gross Capital Formation

	1970	1975	1977	1978	1979	1980	1981	1982	1983	1984	1985	1986
Gross saving	743.9	1095.3	2743.8	1917.7	...	...	...	...	...	...	...	...
1 Consumption of fixed capital	217.4	445.3	627.2	599.5	...	...	...	...	...	...	...	...
A General government	...	...	...	...	...	...	...	...	...	...	...	...
B Corporate and quasi-corporate enterprises	217.4	445.3	627.2	599.5	...	...	...	...	...	...	...	...
C Other	...	...	...	...	...	...	...	...	...	...	...	...
2 Net saving	526.5	650.0	2116.6	1318.2	...	...	...	...	...	...	...	...
A General government	78.4	435.2	585.2	-29.5	...	...	...	...	...	...	...	...
B Corporate and quasi-corporate enterprises	342.7	695.1	976.7	940.2	...	...	...	...	...	...	...	...

Nicaragua

1.8 Capital Transactions of The Nation, Summary
(Continued)

Million Nicaraguan cordobas	1970	1975	1977	1978	1979	1980	1981	1982	1983	1984	1985	1986
C Other	105.4	-480.3	554.7	407.5	...	...	...	...	...	...	...	...
Less: Surplus of the nation on current transactions	-266.4	-1282.3	-1269.4	72.9	...	...	...	...	...	...	...	...
Finance of Gross Capital Formation	1010.8	2384.6	4017.8	1850.3	...	...	...	...	...	...	...	...
Gross Capital Formation												
Increase in stocks	119.6	-125.7	434.8	-281.6	...	...	...	...	...	...	...	...
Gross fixed capital formation	891.2	2510.3	3583.0	2131.9	...	...	...	...	...	...	...	...
Gross Capital Formation	1010.8	2384.6	4017.8	1850.3	...	...	...	...	...	...	...	...

1.10 Gross Domestic Product by Kind of Activity, in Current Prices

Million Nicaraguan cordobas	1970	1975	1977	1978	1979	1980	1981	1982	1983	1984	1985	1986
1 Agriculture, hunting, forestry and fishing	1353.2	2490.6	3589.0	3701.2	...	...	...	...	...	...	...	...
2 Mining and quarrying [a]	33.5	39.1	39.5	45.5	...	...	...	...	...	...	...	...
3 Manufacturing [b]	1110.8	2459.9	3016.2	3149.0	...	...	...	...	...	...	...	...
4 Electricity, gas and water	84.1	174.8	310.2	302.5	...	...	...	...	...	...	...	...
5 Construction	173.3	603.9	708.2	429.2	...	...	...	...	...	...	...	...
6 Wholesale and retail trade, restaurants and hotels [c]	1153.3	2397.2	3834.0	3540.3	...	...	...	...	...	...	...	...
7 Transport, storage and communication	293.1	606.0	938.4	795.8	...	...	...	...	...	...	...	...
8 Finance, insurance, real estate and business services [d]	494.8	923.2	1240.1	1176.5	...	...	...	...	...	...	...	...
9 Community, social and personal services [cde]	365.2	728.8	1056.8	766.1	...	...	...	...	...	...	...	...
Total, Industries	5061.3	10423.5	14732.5	13906.1	...	...	...	...	...	...	...	...
Producers of Government Services	374.8	709.5	946.5	1081.9	...	...	...	...	...	...	...	...
Other Producers [e]	...	...	...	...	...	...	...	...	...	...	...	...
Subtotal	5436.1	11133.0	15678.9	14988.0	...	...	...	...	...	...	...	...
Less: Imputed bank service charge	...	...	...	...	...	...	...	...	...	...	...	...
Plus: Import duties	...	...	...	...	...	...	...	...	...	...	...	...
Plus: Value added tax	...	...	...	...	...	...	...	...	...	...	...	...
Equals: Gross Domestic Product	5436.1	11133.0	15679.0	14988.0	...	...	...	...	...	...	...	...

a) Item 'Mining and quarrying' refers to metal ore mining only.
b) For 1972, item 'Manufacturing' excludes damages by earthquake amounting to 21.7 million cordobas at current prices, and 17.9 million cordobas at constant prices.
c) Restaurants and hotels are included in item 'Community, social and personal services'.
d) Business services are included in item 'Community, social and personal services'.
e) Domestic service of households is included in item 'Community, social and personal services'.

1.11 Gross Domestic Product by Kind of Activity, in Constant Prices

Million Nicaraguan cordobas	1970	1975	1977	1978	1979	1980	1981	1982	1983	1984	1985	1986
	At constant prices of:1958											
1 Agriculture, hunting, forestry and fishing	1073.1	1427.9	1497.2	1594.0	...	...	...	...	...	...	...	...
2 Mining and quarrying [a]	32.3	25.8	17.2	12.4	...	...	...	...	...	...	...	...
3 Manufacturing [b]	1071.0	1426.6	1599.5	1598.0	...	...	...	...	...	...	...	...
4 Electricity, gas and water	125.5	175.2	225.6	210.7	...	...	...	...	...	...	...	...
5 Construction	158.3	304.2	340.4	199.9	...	...	...	...	...	...	...	...
6 Wholesale and retail trade, restaurants and hotels [c]	1008.1	1316.4	1470.1	1260.8	...	...	...	...	...	...	...	...
7 Transport, storage and communication	256.2	334.6	378.7	301.4	...	...	...	...	...	...	...	...
8 Finance, insurance, real estate and business services [d]	443.0	472.0	554.4	507.2	...	...	...	...	...	...	...	...
9 Community, social and personal services [cde]	319.2	327.4	429.1	303.2	...	...	...	...	...	...	...	...
Total, Industries	4486.7	5880.2	6516.2	5987.6	...	...	...	...	...	...	...	...
Producers of Government Services	211.3	287.1	344.6	384.1	...	...	...	...	...	...	...	...
Other Producers [e]	...	...	...	...	...	...	...	...	...	...	...	...
Subtotal	4698.0	6167.3	6860.8	6371.7	...	...	...	...	...	...	...	...
Less: Imputed bank service charge	33.7	54.6	36.3	35.4	...	...	...	...	...	...	...	...
Plus: Import duties	...	...	...	...	...	...	...	...	...	...	...	...
Plus: Value added tax	...	...	...	...	...	...	...	...	...	...	...	...
Equals: Gross Domestic Product	4664.3	6112.7	6824.5	6336.3	...	...	...	...	...	...	...	...

a) Item 'Mining and quarrying' refers to metal ore mining only.
b) For 1972, item 'Manufacturing' excludes damages by earthquake amounting to 21.7 million cordobas at current prices, and 17.9 million cordobas at constant prices.
c) Restaurants and hotels are included in item 'Community, social and personal services'.
d) Business services are included in item 'Community, social and personal services'.
e) Domestic service of households is included in item 'Community, social and personal services'.

Nicaragua

1.12 Relations Among National Accounting Aggregates

Million Nicaraguan cordobas

	1970	1975	1977	1978	1979	1980	1981	1982	1983	1984	1985	1986
Gross Domestic Product	5436.1	11133.0	15679.0	14988.0	14514.0	21892.0	24483.0	28350.0	32920.0	...	...	...
Plus: Net factor income from the rest of the world	-176.4	-415.8	-515.8	-474.6	-801.0	-922.0	-1016.0	-1380.0	-671.0	...	...	...
Equals: Gross National Product	5259.7	10717.2	15163.2	14513.4	13713.0	20970.0	23467.0	26970.0	32249.0	...	...	...
Less: Consumption of fixed capital	217.4	445.3	627.3	599.5	1204.0	876.0	1038.0	1182.0	1473.0	...	...	...
Equals: National Income	5042.3	10271.9	14535.9	13913.9	12509.0	20094.0	22429.0	25788.0	30776.0	...	...	...
Plus: Net current transfers from the rest of the world	43.7	124.0	83.0	73.6	...	...	...	...	...	...	...	...
Current transfers from the rest of the world	54.7	129.6	88.8	77.4	...	...	...	...	...	...	...	...
Less: Current transfers to the rest of the world	11.0	5.6	5.8	3.8	...	...	...	...	...	...	...	...
Equals: National Disposable Income	5086.0	10395.9	14618.9	13987.5	...	...	...	...	...	...	...	...
Less: Final consumption	4559.0	9738.9	12497.7	12663.8	...	...	...	...	...	...	...	...
Statistical discrepancy	-0.5	-7.0	-4.6	-5.5	...	...	...	...	...	...	...	...
Equals: Net Saving	526.5	650.0	2116.6	1318.2	...	...	...	...	...	...	...	...
Less: Surplus of the nation on current transactions	-266.4	-1282.3	-1269.4	72.9	...	...	...	...	...	...	...	...
Statistical discrepancy	0.5	7.0	4.5	5.5	...	...	...	...	...	...	...	...
Equals: Net Capital Formation	793.4	1939.3	3390.5	1250.8	...	...	...	...	...	...	...	...

2.17 Exports and Imports of Goods and Services, Detail

Million Nicaraguan cordobas

	1970	1975	1977	1978	1979	1980	1981	1982	1983	1984	1985	1986
Exports of Goods and Services												
1 Exports of merchandise, f.o.b.	1250.4	2626.2	4457.6	4521.8	...	...	...	...	...	...	...	...
2 Transport and communication	202.8	495.8	574.0	637.9	...	...	...	...	...	...	...	...
3 Insurance service charges					...	...	...	...	...	...	...	...
4 Other commodities	...	...	...	...	...	...	...	...	...	...	...	...
5 Adjustments of merchandise exports to change-of-ownership basis	...	...	...	...	...	...	...	...	...	...	...	...
6 Direct purchases in the domestic market by non-residential households	...	...	...	...	...	...	...	...	...	...	...	...
7 Direct purchases in the domestic market by extraterritorial bodies	...	...	...	...	...	...	...	...	...	...	...	...
Total Exports of Goods and Services	1453.2	3122.0	5031.6	5159.7	...	...	...	...	...	...	...	...
Imports of Goods and Services												
1 Imports of merchandise, c.i.f.	1250.4	2626.2	4457.6	4521.8	...	...	...	...	...	...	...	...
2 Adjustments of merchandise imports to change-of-ownership basis	...	...	...	...	...	...	...	...	...	...	...	...
3 Other transport and communication					...	...	...	...	...	...	...	...
4 Other insurance service charges	336.5	1486.3	1410.5	164.0	...	...	...	...	...	...	...	...
5 Other commodities					...	...	...	...	...	...	...	...
6 Direct purchases abroad by government	...	...	...	...	...	...	...	...	...	...	...	...
7 Direct purchases abroad by resident households	...	...	...	...	...	...	...	...	...	...	...	...
Total Imports of Goods and Services	1586.9	4112.5	5868.1	4685.8	...	...	...	...	...	...	...	...
Balance of Goods and Services	-133.7	-990.5	-836.5	473.9	...	...	...	...	...	...	...	...
Total Imports and Balance of Goods and Services	1453.2	3122.0	5031.6	5159.7	...	...	...	...	...	...	...	...

Niger

Source. Reply to the United Nations National Accounts Questionnaire from the Service de la Statistique et de la Mecanographie, Niamey.
General note. The estimates shown in the following tables have been adjusted by the Service to conform to the United Nations System of National Accounts so far as the existing data would permit.

1.1 Expenditure on the Gross Domestic Product, in Current Prices

Million CFA francs

	1970	1975	1977	1978	1979	1980	1981	1982	1983	1984	1985	1986
1 Government final consumption expenditure	13500	21000	31100	36500	43800	55200	70200	81000	87500	...	...	...
2 Private final consumption expenditure	94900	133100	206600	277800	312200	371300	410600	483200	522800	...	...	...
3 Gross capital formation	10500	19100	83600	100500	143200	171000	168400	181200	107000	...	...	...
A Increase in stocks	3000	4100	17700	12500	20000	19000	4500	26000	-12400	...	...	...
B Gross fixed capital formation	7500	15000	65900	88000	123200	152000	163900	155200	119400	...	...	...
4 Exports of goods and services	16700	37300	53700	77300	112500	132700	141800	139800	143700	...	...	...
5 Less: Imports of goods and services	24700	52800	86100	130000	169100	201700	189500	222200	173900	...	...	...
Equals: Gross Domestic Product [a]	111000	157700	288800	362100	442600	528500	601500	663000	687100	626400	682300	...

a) Data in this table have been revised, therefore they are not strictly comparable with the unrevised data in the other tables.

1.3 Cost Components of the Gross Domestic Product

Million CFA francs

	1970	1975	1977	1978	1979	1980	1981	1982	1983	1984	1985	1986
1 Indirect taxes, net	...	11834	19758	26749	35130	50725	...	...	...	...	...	...
A Indirect taxes	...	12071	20202	27102	35802	51079	...	...	...	...	...	...
B Less: Subsidies	...	237	444	353	672	354	...	...	...	...	...	...
2 Consumption of fixed capital	...	10107	15005	20557	28449	35967	...	...	...	...	...	...
3 Compensation of employees paid by resident producers to:	...	37827	54267	55459	69051	86552	...	...	...	...	...	...
4 Operating surplus	...	120585	199800	256402	310609	362964	...	...	...	...	...	...
A Corporate and quasi-corporate enterprises	...	...	...	...	...	...	...	...	...	...	...	...
B Private unincorporated enterprises	...	...	...	...	...	...	...	...	...	...	...	...
C General government	...	-27	780	43	-4	-2	...	...	...	...	...	...
Equals: Gross Domestic Product	...	180353	288830	359158	443239	536208	...	...	...	...	...	...

1.4 General Government Current Receipts and Disbursements

Million CFA francs

	1970	1975	1977	1978	1979	1980	1981	1982	1983	1984	1985	1986
					Receipts							
1 Operating surplus	...	...	...	...	...	...	...	...	...	...	...	...
2 Property and entrepreneurial income	...	1505	3783	...	...	...	...	...	...	...	...	...
3 Taxes, fees and contributions	...	20265	34674	...	...	...	...	...	...	...	...	...
A Indirect taxes	...	12071	20202	...	...	...	...	...	...	...	...	...
B Direct taxes	...	6580	12393	...	...	...	...	...	...	...	...	...
C Social security contributions	...	1301	1643	...	...	...	...	...	...	...	...	...
D Compulsory fees, fines and penalties	...	313	436	...	...	...	...	...	...	...	...	...
4 Other current transfers	...	20312	15860	...	...	...	...	...	...	...	...	...
Statistical discrepancy	...	-27	780	...	...	...	...	...	...	...	...	...
Total Current Receipts of General Government	...	42055	55097	...	...	...	...	...	...	...	...	...
					Disbursements							
1 Government final consumption expenditure	...	23634	31061	...	...	...	...	...	...	...	...	...
A Compensation of employees	...	14384	17143	...	...	...	...	...	...	...	...	...
B Consumption of fixed capital	...	1664	2936	...	...	...	...	...	...	...	...	...
C Purchases of goods and services, net	...	7610	10164	...	...	...	...	...	...	...	...	...
D Less: Own account fixed capital formation	...	...	...	...	...	...	...	...	...	...	...	...
E Indirect taxes paid, net	...	-24	818	...	...	...	...	...	...	...	...	...
2 Property income	...	684	1013	...	...	...	...	...	...	...	...	...

Niger

1.4 General Government Current Receipts and Disbursements
(Continued)

Million CFA francs

	1970	1975	1977	1978	1979	1980	1981	1982	1983	1984	1985	1986
3 Subsidies	...	237	444	...	...	...	...	...	...	...	...	...
4 Other current transfers	...	11717	9774	...	...	...	...	...	...	...	...	...
A Social security benefits	...	3130	4724	...	...	...	...	...	...	...	...	...
B Social assistance grants	...			...	...	...	...	...	...	...	...	...
C Other	...	8587	5050	...	...	...	...	...	...	...	...	...
5 Net saving	...	5783	12805	...	...	...	...	...	...	...	...	...
Total Current Disbursements and Net Saving of General Government	...	42055	55097	...	...	...	...	...	...	...	...	...

1.7 External Transactions on Current Account, Summary

Million CFA francs

	1970	1975	1977	1978	1979	1980	1981	1982	1983	1984	1985	1986
Payments to the Rest of the World												
1 Imports of goods and services	...	59501	79400	141919	175145	221275	...	...	...	...	...	...
2 Factor income to the rest of the world	...	3314	7000	14394	17436	18133	...	...	...	...	...	...
A Compensation of employees	...	...	...	158	198	231	...	...	...	...	...	...
B Property and entrepreneurial income	...	3314	7000	14236	17238	17902	...	...	...	...	...	...
3 Current transfers to the rest of the world	...	6990	8051	10561	13350	14725	...	...	...	...	...	...
4 Surplus of the nation on current transactions	...	-12777	-23991	-68643	-75538	-91629	...	...	...	...	...	...
Payments to the Rest of the World and Surplus of the Nation on Current Transactions	...	57028	70460	98231	130393	162512	...	...	...	...	...	...
Receipts From The Rest of the World												
1 Exports of goods and services	...	34603	52400	75620	115127	137805	...	...	...	...	...	...
2 Factor income from rest of the world	...	2814	3000	2856	3500	6653	...	...	...	...	...	...
A Compensation of employees	...	1759	1800	1624	1689	2043	...	...	...	...	...	...
B Property and entrepreneurial income	...	1055	1200	1232	1811	4610	...	...	...	...	...	...
3 Current transfers from rest of the world	...	19611	15060	19755	11766	18054	...	...	...	...	...	...
Receipts from the Rest of the World on Current Transactions	...	57028	70460	98231	130393	162512	...	...	...	...	...	...

1.8 Capital Transactions of The Nation, Summary

Million CFA francs

	1970	1975	1977	1978	1979	1980	1981	1982	1983	1984	1985	1986
Finance of Gross Capital Formation												
Gross saving	...	30248	59599	...	...	...	...	...	...	...	...	...
1 Consumption of fixed capital	...	10107	15005	...	...	...	...	...	...	...	...	...
A General government	...	1664	2936	...	...	...	...	...	...	...	...	...
B Corporate and quasi-corporate enterprises	...	...	...	...	...	...	...	...	...	...	...	...
C Other	...	...	...	...	...	...	...	...	...	...	...	...
2 Net saving	...	20141	44594	...	...	...	...	...	...	...	...	...
A General government	...	5783	12805	...	...	...	...	...	...	...	...	...
B Corporate and quasi-corporate enterprises	...	...	...	...	...	...	...	...	...	...	...	...
C Other	...	...	...	...	...	...	...	...	...	...	...	...
Less: Surplus of the nation on current transactions	...	-12777	-23991	...	...	...	...	...	...	...	...	...
Finance of Gross Capital Formation	...	43025	83590	...	...	...	...	...	...	...	...	...
Gross Capital Formation												
Increase in stocks	...	6280	17737	...	...	...	...	...	...	...	...	...
Gross fixed capital formation	...	36745	65853	...	...	...	...	...	...	...	...	...
1 General government	...	15770	23715	...	...	...	...	...	...	...	...	...
2 Corporate and quasi-corporate enterprises	...	20967	42120	...	...	...	...	...	...	...	...	...
3 Other	...	8	18	...	...	...	...	...	...	...	...	...
Gross Capital Formation	...	43025	83590	...	...	...	...	...	...	...	...	...

Niger

1.9 Gross Domestic Product by Institutional Sectors of Origin

Million CFA francs

	1970	1975	1977	1978	1979	1980	1981	1982	1983	1984	1985	1986
			Domestic Factor Incomes Originating									
1 General government	...	14357	17923	...	...	...	...	...	...	...	...	...
2 Corporate and quasi-corporate enterprises	...	...	...	...	...	...	...	...	...	...	...	...
3 Households and private unincorporated enterprises	...	123551	191571	...	...	...	...	...	...	...	...	...
4 Non-profit institutions serving households	...	121	135	...	...	...	...	...	...	...	...	...
Subtotal: Domestic Factor Incomes	...	158412	254067	...	...	...	...	...	...	...	...	...
Indirect taxes, net	...	11834	19758	...	...	...	...	...	...	...	...	...
A Indirect taxes	...	12071	20202	...	...	...	...	...	...	...	...	...
B Less: Subsidies	...	237	444	...	...	...	...	...	...	...	...	...
Consumption of fixed capital	...	10107	15005	...	...	...	...	...	...	...	...	...
Gross Domestic Product	...	180353	288830	...	...	...	...	...	...	...	...	...

1.10 Gross Domestic Product by Kind of Activity, in Current Prices

Million CFA francs

	1970	1975	1977	1978	1979	1980	1981	1982	1983	1984	1985	1986
1 Agriculture, hunting, forestry and fishing	...	88585	145734	166059	188746	228097	...	...	...	...	...	...
2 Mining and quarrying	...	10643	25444	36956	63074	67397	...	...	...	...	...	...
3 Manufacturing	...	13844	14665	15174	18228	19819	...	...	...	...	...	...
4 Electricity, gas and water	...	872	1489	1240	1153	2361	...	...	...	...	...	...
5 Construction	...	5055	10227	17086	24638	32120	...	...	...	...	...	...
6 Wholesale and retail trade, restaurants and hotels	...	17594	29368	40279	51059	62101	...	...	...	...	...	...
7 Transport, storage and communication	...	7485	10278	14587	18031	22632	...	...	...	...	...	...
8 Finance, insurance, real estate and business services	...	13168	19783	22585	27193	33565	...	...	...	...	...	...
9 Community, social and personal services	...	1644	1974	8236	9490	10985	...	...	...	...	...	...
Total, Industries	...	158890	258962	322202	401612	479077	...	...	...	...	...	...
Producers of Government Services	...	16024	20897	22836	25137	33809	...	...	...	...	...	...
Other Producers	...	865	1057	1501	2153	2536	...	...	...	...	...	...
Subtotal	...	175779	280916	346539	428902	515422	...	...	...	...	...	...
Less: Imputed bank service charge	...	2336	3834	3004	4757	6302	...	...	...	...	...	...
Plus: Import duties	...	6910	11748	15623	19094	27088	...	...	...	...	...	...
Plus: Value added tax	...	...	...	...	...	...	...	...	...	...	...	...
Equals: Gross Domestic Product	...	180353	288830	359158	443239	536208	...	...	...	...	...	...

1.12 Relations Among National Accounting Aggregates

Million CFA francs

	1970	1975	1977	1978	1979	1980	1981	1982	1983	1984	1985	1986
Gross Domestic Product	...	180353	288830	359158	443239	536208	...	...	...	...	...	...
Plus: Net factor income from the rest of the world	...	-500	-4000	-11538	-13936	11480	...	...	...	...	...	...
Factor income from the rest of the world	...	2814	3000	2856	3500	6653	...	...	...	...	...	...
Less: Factor income to the rest of the world	...	3314	7000	14394	17436	18133	...	...	...	...	...	...
Equals: Gross National Product	...	179853	284830	347620	429303	524728	...	...	...	...	...	...
Less: Consumption of fixed capital	...	10107	15005	20557	28449	35967	...	...	...	...	...	...
Equals: National Income	...	169746	269825	327063	400854	488761	...	...	...	...	...	...
Plus: Net current transfers from the rest of the world	...	12621	7009	9194	-1784	3329	...	...	...	...	...	...
Current transfers from the rest of the world	...	19611	15060	19755	11766	18054	...	...	...	...	...	...
Less: Current transfers to the rest of the world	...	6990	8051	10561	13350	14725	...	...	...	...	...	...
Equals: National Disposable Income	...	182367	276834	336257	399070	492090	...	...	...	...	...	...
Less: Final consumption	...	162226	232240	311921	362249	450574	...	...	...	...	...	...
Equals: Net Saving	...	20141	44594	24336	36821	41516	...	...	...	...	...	...
Less: Surplus of the nation on current transactions	...	-12777	-23991	-68643	-75538	-91621	...	...	...	...	...	...
Equals: Net Capital Formation	...	32918	68585	92979	112359	133137	...	...	...	...	...	...

Niger

2.11 Gross Fixed Capital Formation by Kind of Activity of Owner, ISIC Divisions, in Current Prices

Million CFA francs

	1970	1975	1977	1978	1979	1980	1981	1982	1983	1984	1985	1986
					All Producers							
1 Agriculture, hunting, forestry and fishing	...	10601	13471	...	...	...	...	...	...	...	...	...
A Agriculture and hunting	...	6002	7130	...	...	...	...	...	...	...	...	...
B Forestry and logging	...	4599	6341	...	...	...	...	...	...	...	...	...
C Fishing	...	...	...	...	...	...	...	...	...	...	...	...
2 Mining and quarrying	...	3182	16638	...	...	...	...	...	...	...	...	...
3 Manufacturing	...	1580	400	...	...	...	...	...	...	...	...	...
A Manufacturing of food, beverages and tobacco	...	483	243	...	...	...	...	...	...	...	...	...
B Textile, wearing apparel and leather industries	...	422	39	...	...	...	...	...	...	...	...	...
C Manufacture of wood, and wood products, including furniture	...	4	3	...	...	...	...	...	...	...	...	...
D Manufacture of paper and paper products, printing and publishing	...	49	39	...	...	...	...	...	...	...	...	...
E Manufacture of chemicals and chemical petroleum, coal, rubber and plastic products	...	72	12	...	...	...	...	...	...	...	...	...
F Manufacture of non-metalic mineral products except products of petroleum and coal	...	391	64	...	...	...	...	...	...	...	...	...
G Basic metal industries	...	...	...	...	...	...	...	...	...	...	...	...
H Manufacture of fabricated metal products, machinery and equipment	...	159	40	...	...	...	...	...	...	...	...	...
I Other manufacturing industries	...	...	...	...	...	...	...	...	...	...	...	...
4 Electricity, gas and water	...	542	490	...	...	...	...	...	...	...	...	...
5 Construction	...	681	1931	...	...	...	...	...	...	...	...	...
6 Wholesale and retail trade, restaurants and hotels	...	1896	3056	...	...	...	...	...	...	...	...	...
A Wholesale and retail trade	...	1870	3018	...	...	...	...	...	...	...	...	...
B Restaurants and hotels	...	26	38	...	...	...	...	...	...	...	...	...
7 Transport, storage and communication	...	1932	4458	...	...	...	...	...	...	...	...	...
A Transport and storage	...	1185	4149	...	...	...	...	...	...	...	...	...
B Communication	...	747	309	...	...	...	...	...	...	...	...	...
8 Finance, insurance, real estate and business services	...	481	1648	...	...	...	...	...	...	...	...	...
A Financial institutions	...	316	365	...	...	...	...	...	...	...	...	...
B Insurance	...	...	...	...	...	...	...	...	...	...	...	...
C Real estate and business services	...	165	1283	...	...	...	...	...	...	...	...	...
9 Community, social and personal services	...	72	28	...	...	...	...	...	...	...	...	...
A Sanitary and similar services	...	...	...	...	...	...	...	...	...	...	...	...
B Social and related community services	...	39	55	...	...	...	...	...	...	...	...	...
Educational services	...	39	55	...	...	...	...	...	...	...	...	...
Medical, dental, other health and veterinary services	...	-	-	...	...	...	...	...	...	...	...	...
C Recreational and cultural services	...	10	-54	...	...	...	...	...	...	...	...	...
D Personal and household services	...	23	27	...	...	...	...	...	...	...	...	...
Total Industries	...	20967	42120	...	...	...	...	...	...	...	...	...
Producers of Government Services	...	15770	23715	...	...	...	...	...	...	...	...	...
Private Non-Profit Institutions Serving Households	...	8	18	...	...	...	...	...	...	...	...	...
Total	...	36745	65853	...	...	...	...	...	...	...	...	...

Nigeria

General note. The preparation of national accounts statistics in Nigeria is undertaken by the Federal Office of Statistics, Lagos. The official estimates together with methodological notes on sources and methods are published in 'Gross Domestic Product of Nigeria'. Another publication 'National Accounts of Nigeria' with estimates dating back to 1958/59, was published in 1978. The estimates are generally in accordance with the definitions and classifications recommended in the United Nations System of National Accounts (SNA). Input-output tables have been published for the year 1959/60 in 'An Input-Output Analysis of the Nigerian Economy'. The following tables have been prepared from successive replies to the United Nations national accounts questionnaire. Estimates relate to fiscal year beginning 1 April. When the scope and coverage of the estimates differ for conceptual or statistical reasons from the definitions and classifications recommended in SNA, a footnote is indicated to the relevant tables.

Sources and methods:

(a) Gross domestic product. Gross domestic product is estimated mainly through the production approach.

(b) Expenditure on the gross domestic product. The expenditure approach is used to estimate government final consumption expenditure, exports and imports of goods and services and buildings and other construction of gross fixed capital formation. This approach, in combination with the commodity-flow approach is used to estimate investment in machinery and equipment. Private final consumption expenditure, which includes increase in stocks, is estimated as a residual. Government consumption expenditure is estimated from the annual economic analysis of the accounts of the public authorities. Useful information on private consumption expenditure will become available when the urban consumer survey and the rural consumption inquiry for 1974/75 are completed. The estimates of gross fixed capital formation for machinery, transport and other equipment are based on foreign trade statistics supplemented by information on import duties. A mark-up for trade, transport and installation charges of 33.3 per cent and 10 per cent is added to the import values of machinery and transport equipment respectively. The values of small concrete buildings are based on the value of cement used and of mud-walled houses on the estimated population in need of such houses. For the oil sector, the estimates of gross capital formation are compiled from the returns obtained from the oil companies. Sources for other sectors include the accounts of the Nigerian Coal Corp., the reports of the Nigerian Steel Development Authority, the Nigerian Railway Corp.and the Nigerian Shipping Line Ltd., and the accounts of the government. The main sources of information for exports and imports of goods and services are the balance of payments accounts.

(c) Cost-structure of the gross domestic product. Compensation of employees, operating surplus, and consumption of fixed capital are obtained as a residual by deducting net indirect taxes from the GDP. For indirect taxes and subsidies, the annual government accounts are used.

(d) Gross domestic product by kind of economic activity. The table of GDP by kind of economic activity is prepared in factor values. The production approach is used to estimate the value added of most industries. The income approach is used for producers of government services. Production estimates for 13 harvested agricultural crops are obtained from the national agriculture sample census in 1974/75 and the annual rural economic surveys. Estimates of output for green vegetables, tomatoes, oranges, bananas, sugar cane, coconut, pawpaw and pineapple are based on the average expenditure per household contained in the reports on inquiries into the income and expenditure patterns of lower and middle income households supplemented by export data. The values are reduced by 50 per cent for trade and transport charges. Foreign trade statistics provide the information for all other crops, except cocoa and tobacco which is estimated from information supplied by the Nigerian Produce Marketing CO., and from manufacturing companies. For livestock and its products, estimates are based on such data as foreign trade statistics, number of animals slaughtered, number of cattle that are milked, Lagos retail prices, etc. Non-monetary activities are covered in the estimates. The output of timber is estimated from the data on logs exported or used locally. Data on the production of fish are obtained from the Federal Fisheries Department. The annual reports of the Petroleum Division in the Federal Ministry of Mines and Power furnish information on production and f.o.b. values of crude oil and the quantity of gas sold. The same Ministry also furnishes data on production of metalliferous ores. This output is valued at f.o.b. prices. Information on the values of manufacturing output and intermediate consumption are obtained from the annual surveys of large establishments. Adjustment is made of value added by 20 per cent to cover small establishments. The estimates of electricity are based on annual reports of the concerned companies The sources of information on water supply are the actual expenditure of the Government bodies and annual accounts of water boards of corporations. Data for estimating value added in construction are obtained from accounts of public authorities and corporations government enterprises and the survey of large establishments engaged in mining, manufacturing and distributive activities. For smaller construction activities, sources such as the value of cement used, questionaire and actual of approved expenditure of public authorities are used. Trade is assumed to be 12.5 per cent of GDP in the base year 1958/59. For other years, value added is extrapolated by indexes. The bench-mark value added of road transport is based on the number of commercial vehicles. Other years' estimates are made by projecting the 1958/59 figure by the estimated number of tractors and commercial vehicles and using the CPI of transport services for five urban centres. The value added of railways, harbours, water and air transports are estimated from annual reports of concerned enterprises. The sources of information for estimating the value added of government services are the Accountant-General's reports and budget of the public authorities. For education, estimates are based on information obtained from the Federal Ministry of Education and the National Universities Commission for private institutions and on the number of teachers and an assumed average salary per teacher for other institutions. For private health institutions, the expenditure on personal emoluments is regarded as value added and assumed to grow at the same rate as for government institutions. The value added of other services, which includes the financial sector, is assumed to grow at an average annual rate of 13.8 per cent. For the constant price estimates, price deflation is used for the manufacturing, construction, part of transport and services sectors. For agriculture, the production of corps is either revalued at 1962/63 prices or deflated by retail prices. Value added of mining, electricity, trade and transport relating to passenger-miles and ton-miles is extrapolated by appropriate indicators.

1.1 Expenditure on the Gross Domestic Product, in Current Prices

Million Nigerian naira — Fiscal year beginning 1 April

	1970	1975	1977	1978	1979	1980	1981	1982	1983	1984	1985	1986
1 Government final consumption expenditure	577.6	2236.9	3826.9	4999.3	4881.7	5051.4	5503.5	5504.0	5560.7	...	...	...
2 Private final consumption expenditure	4143.4	13688.5	18824.3	23271.9	23847.0	28436.6	33853.3	36834.8	33843.0	...	...	...
3 Gross capital formation	882.7	5514.1	9921.9	9886.3	9580.2	11565.8	13991.7	11320.4	9316.6	...	...	...
A Increase in stocks	...	494.3	501.3	500.0	500.0	589.9	673.5	450.0	391.5	...	...	...
B Gross fixed capital formation	882.7	5019.8	9420.6	9386.3	9080.2	10976.0	13318.2	10870.4	8925.1	...	...	...
Residential buildings	...	552.3	884.8	...	...	...	...	...	...	...	...	...
Non-residential buildings	...	1469.2	1769.6	6191.7	6383.7	7342.3	8003.2	7206.3	6536.6	...	...	...
Other construction and land improvement etc.	...	1311.3	3351.5							...	...	...
Other	...	1687.0	3411.7	3194.6	2696.5	3633.7	5315.0	3664.1	2388.5	...	...	...
4 Exports of goods and services	953.8	5317.7	8370.0	6881.6	11016.9	14908.8	11375.8	9650.2	7806.7	...	...	...
5 Less: Imports of goods and services	937.0	4978.4	8432.7	10024.2	8243.1	11705.4	16081.9	12119.3	7875.3	...	...	...
Equals: Gross Domestic Product	5620.5	21778.7	32510.4	35014.9	41082.7	48257.2	48642.5	51190.1	48651.7	...	...	...

Nigeria

1.2 Expenditure on the Gross Domestic Product, in Constant Prices

Million Nigerian naira — Fiscal year beginning 1 April

	1970	1975	1977	1978	1979	1980	1981	1982	1983	1984	1985	1986
				At constant prices of:1977								
1 Government final consumption expenditure	...	2667.8	3826.9	4125.1	3149.5	2591.6	2930.4	2826.3	2848.8	...	...	...
2 Private final consumption expenditure	...	16374.0	18824.3	19206.9	15387.7	14594.2	18031.0	18914.0	17340.9	...	...	...
3 Gross capital formation	...	6628.2	9921.9	9336.1	8012.3	9218.2	10511.4	7990.0	6368.5	...	...	...
A Increase in stocks	...	642.8	501.3	498.2	468.5	562.1	625.3	416.9	365.8	...	...	...
B Gross fixed capital formation	...	5985.4	9420.6	8837.9	7543.8	8656.1	9885.2	7573.1	6002.7	...	...	...
Residential buildings	...	799.9	884.8	...	...	...	...	...	...	...	...	...
Non-residential buildings	...	2127.8	1769.6	5786.6	5556.8	6112.0	6408.2	5349.1	4624.4	...	...	...
Other construction and land improvement etc.	...	1311.3	3354.4							...	...	...
Other	...	1746.4	3411.7	3051.3	1987.0	2544.1	3477.0	2224.0	1378.3	...	...	...
4 Exports of goods and services	...	6809.7	8370.0	6844.6	10206.5	13294.8	9605.5	7426.7	5662.4	...	...	...
5 Less: Imports of goods and services	...	5131.9	8432.7	9002.4	6718.6	8613.3	10711.3	7296.8	4319.3	...	...	...
Equals: Gross Domestic Product	...	27347.8	32510.4	30510.3	30037.3	31085.5	30366.2	29860.1	27861.3	...	...	...

1.3 Cost Components of the Gross Domestic Product

Million Nigerian naira — Fiscal year beginning 1 April

	1970	1975	1977	1978	1979	1980	1981	1982	1983	1984	1985	1986
1 Indirect taxes, net	415.4	821.1	1227.0	1543.5	1176.2	1216.4	1597.1	1819.7	1879.0	...	...	...
A Indirect taxes	423.5	833.5	1244.8	1611.2	1233.8	1423.8	1887.5	2048.3	2136.2	...	...	...
B Less: Subsidies	8.1	12.4	17.8	67.7	57.6	207.4	290.4	228.6	257.2	...	...	...
2 Consumption of fixed capital	5205.1	759.8	1129.2	1032.5	998.8	1207.4	1465.0	1195.7	981.8	...	...	...
3 Compensation of employees paid by resident producers to:		5726.1	8342.7	10058.9	10221.7	11915.0	14003.2	15064.2	14019.8	...	...	...
A Resident households	...	5673.6	8213.5	9727.7	9932.7	11480.8	13486.8	14508.7	13659.4	...	...	...
B Rest of the world	...	52.5	129.2	331.2	289.0	434.2	516.4	555.6	360.4	...	...	...
4 Operating surplus	...	14471.0	21811.4	22380.0	28686.1	33918.5	31577.2	33110.5	31771.0	...	...	...
Equals: Gross Domestic Product	5620.5	21778.7	32510.4	35014.9	41082.7	48257.2	48642.5	51190.1	48651.7	...	...	...

1.7 External Transactions on Current Account, Summary

Million Nigerian naira — Fiscal year beginning 1 April

	1970	1975	1977	1978	1979	1980	1981	1982	1983	1984	1985	1986
				Payments to the Rest of the World								
1 Imports of goods and services	937.0	4978.4	8432.7	10024.2	8243.1	11705.4	16081.9	12119.3	7875.3	...	...	...
2 Factor income to the rest of the world	118.8	534.5	701.5	660.1	781.2	1468.6	1348.8	1317.4	1040.1	...	...	...
A Compensation of employees	...	52.5	129.2	331.2	289.0	434.2	516.4	555.6	360.4	...	...	...
B Property and entrepreneurial income	...	482.0	572.3	328.9	492.2	1034.4	832.4	761.8	679.7	...	...	...
3 Current transfers to the rest of the world	31.8	92.8	145.0	178.0	247.6	332.6	366.7	308.5	198.4	...	...	...
4 Surplus of the nation on current transactions	-50.0	42.6	-656.5	-3787.2	1924.1	1798.0	-5962.5	-3920.8	-1242.3	...	...	...
Payments to the Rest of the World and Surplus of the Nation on Current Transactions	1037.6	5648.3	8622.7	7075.1	11196.0	15304.6	11834.9	9824.4	7871.5	...	...	...

Nigeria

1.7 External Transactions on Current Account, Summary
(Continued)

Million Nigerian naira — Fiscal year beginning 1 April

	1970	1975	1977	1978	1979	1980	1981	1982	1983	1984	1985	1986
Receipts From The Rest of the World												
1 Exports of goods and services	953.8	5317.7	8370.0	6881.6	11016.9	14908.8	11375.8	9650.2	7806.7	...	...	...
2 Factor income from rest of the world	7.0	314.6	226.4	186.1	165.0	378.4	438.9	155.1	54.5	...	...	...
A Compensation of employees	...	5.0	-	2.2	5.6	6.9	7.7	6.7	5.0	...	...	...
B Property and entrepreneurial income	...	309.6	226.4	183.9	159.4	371.5	431.2	148.4	49.5	...	...	...
3 Current transfers from rest of the world	76.8	16.0	26.3	7.4	14.1	17.4	20.2	19.1	10.3	...	...	...
Receipts from the Rest of the World on Current Transactions	1037.6	5648.3	8622.7	7075.1	11196.0	15304.6	11834.9	9824.4	7871.5	...	...	...

1.10 Gross Domestic Product by Kind of Activity, in Current Prices

Million Nigerian naira — Fiscal year beginning 1 April

	1970	1975	1977	1978	1979	1980	1981	1982	1983	1984	1985	1986
1 Agriculture, hunting, forestry and fishing	2495.2	5354.7	7305.3	8053.9	9101.4	10079.3	9863.1	12410.3	12165.7	...	...	...
2 Mining and quarrying	540.7	4668.4	7905.0	8415.5	11339.5	15066.5	12400.1	11555.4	9923.0	...	...	...
3 Manufacturing	378.4	1170.4	1555.0	1785.0	2037.1	2354.4	2647.5	2726.3	2372.5	...	...	...
4 Electricity, gas and water	38.0	63.4	98.7	127.9	199.7	244.6	309.7	386.0	460.3	...	...	...
5 Construction	304.5	1814.6	2990.8	3077.2	3192.3	3671.2	4001.6	3603.0	3268.3	...	...	...
6 Wholesale and retail trade, restaurants and hotels	673.5	4378.6	6838.5	7104.1	8821.4	9722.9	10564.8	10593.8	10490.3	...	...	...
7 Transport, storage and communication	146.9	673.6	1039.3	1211.1	1447.0	1762.6	2129.0	2396.5	2187.7	...	...	...
8 Finance, insurance, real estate and business services	220.8	609.9	792.8	796.0	806.1	815.0	1161.7	1398.1	1494.3	...	...	...
9 Community, social and personal services	...	871.3	1081.4	1135.5	1216.5	1309.6	1398.1	1492.0	1499.0	...	...	...
Total, Industries	4798.0	19604.7	29606.8	31706.2	38161.0	45026.0	44475.6	46561.3	43861.1	...	...	...
Producers of Government Services	407.1	1352.9	1676.6	1765.2	1745.6	2014.9	2570.0	2809.1	2911.5	...	...	...
Other Producers	...	...	...	...	...	...	...	...	...	...	...	...
Subtotal a	5205.1	20957.6	31283.4	33471.4	39906.6	47040.9	47045.4	49370.4	46772.6	...	...	...
Less: Imputed bank service charge		...	...	...	...	...	...	...	...	...	...	...
Plus: Import duties	...	...	...	...	...	...	...	...	...	...	...	...
Plus: Value added tax	...	...	...	...	...	...	...	...	...	...	...	...
Plus: Other adjustments b	415.4	821.1	1227.0	1543.5	1176.1	1216.3	1597.1	1819.7	1879.1	...	...	...
Equals: Gross Domestic Product	5620.5	21778.7	32510.4	35014.9	41082.7	48257.2	48642.5	51190.1	48651.7	...	...	...
Memorandum Item: Mineral fuels and power	...	-47.7	-181.1	-391.9	-283.4	...	...	...	...	...	...	...

a) Gross domestic product in factor values.
b) Item 'Other adjustments' refers to indirect taxes net of subsidies.

Nigeria

1.11 Gross Domestic Product by Kind of Activity, in Constant Prices

Million Nigerian naira — Fiscal year beginning 1 April

	1970	1975	1977	1978	1979	1980	1981	1982	1983	1984	1985	1986
	1962				At constant prices of:			**1977**				
1 Agriculture, hunting, forestry and fishing	1835.8	6947.2	7305.3	6673.7	5785.8	6071.0	5720.7	6495.6	6155.0	...	...	...
2 Mining and quarrying	508.9	6276.5	7905.0	7073.7	8240.1	7406.7	5302.1	4645.3	4461.5	...	...	...
3 Manufacturing	317.6	1186.5	1555.0	1778.4	1908.6	2244.8	2458.3	2526.5	2216.7	...	...	...
4 Electricity, gas and water	24.5	86.0	98.7	110.3	136.8	143.3	169.5	189.4	199.4	...	...	...
5 Construction	266.2	1932.5	2990.8	2875.9	2778.8	3056.0	3204.1	2674.5	2312.2	...	...	...
6 Wholesale and retail trade, restaurants and hotels	515.3	5457.1	6838.5	6112.9	5744.8	6533.2	6941.3	6359.2	6092.7	...	...	...
7 Transport, storage and communication	138.2	964.2	1039.3	1083.7	1162.3	1311.4	1458.0	1523.8	1299.6	...	...	...
8 Finance, insurance, real estate and business services	192.7	679.2	792.8	746.0	713.8	689.7	932.6	1066.4	1089.8	...	...	...
9 Community, social and personal services	...	1047.5	1081.4	1074.4	1077.2	1091.5	1105.9	1120.8	1070.8	...	...	...
Total, Industries	3799.2	24576.8	29606.8	27528.9	27548.3	28547.5	27292.3	26601.5	24897.7	...	...	...
Producers of Government Services	387.4	1581.0	1676.6	1650.9	1584.3	1687.5	2150.8	2280.4	2143.0	...	...	...
Other Producers	...	...										
Subtotal [a]	4186.6	26157.8	31283.4	29179.7	29132.6	30235.0	29443.1	28881.8	27040.7			
Less: Imputed bank service charge	...	...										
Plus: Import duties	...	...										
Plus: Value added tax	...	...										
Plus: Other adjustments	...	1190.0[b]	1227.0[b]	1330.6[b]	904.7[b]	850.5[b]	923.1[b]	978.3[b]	820.6[b]	...	...	...
Equals: Gross Domestic Product	4186.6[a]	27347.8	32510.4	30510.3	30037.3	31085.5	30366.2	29860.1	27861.3			

a) Gross domestic product in factor values.
b) Item 'Other adjustments' refers to indirect taxes net of subsidies.

1.12 Relations Among National Accounting Aggregates

Million Nigerian naira — Fiscal year beginning 1 April

	1970	1975	1977	1978	1979	1980	1981	1982	1983	1984	1985	1986
Gross Domestic Product	...	21778.7	32510.4	35014.9	41082.7	48257.2	48642.5	51190.1	48651.7	...	...	...
Plus: Net factor income from the rest of the world	...	-219.9	-475.1	-474.0	-616.2	-1090.2	-909.9	-1162.3	-985.6	...	...	...
Factor income from the rest of the world	...	314.6	226.4	186.1	165.0	378.4	438.9	155.1	54.5			
Less: Factor income to the rest of the world	...	534.5	701.5	660.1	781.2	1468.6	1348.8	1317.4	1040.1			
Equals: Gross National Product	...	21558.8	32035.3	34540.9	40466.5	47167.0	47732.6	50027.8	47666.1			
Less: Consumption of fixed capital	...	759.8	1129.2	1032.5	998.8	1207.4	1465.0	1195.7	981.8			
Equals: National Income	...	20799.0	30906.1	33508.4	39467.7	45959.6	46267.6	48832.1	46684.3			
Plus: Net current transfers from the rest of the world	...	-76.8	-118.7	-170.6	-233.5	-315.2	-346.5	-289.4	-188.1			
Current transfers from the rest of the world	...	16.0	26.3	7.4	14.1	17.4	20.2	19.1	10.3			
Less: Current transfers to the rest of the world	...	92.8	145.0	178.0	247.6	332.6	366.7	308.5	198.4			
Equals: National Disposable Income	...	20722.2	30787.4	33337.8	39234.2	45644.4	45921.1	48542.7	46496.2			
Less: Final consumption	...	15925.4	22651.2	28271.2	28728.7	33488.0	39356.8	42338.8	39403.7			
Equals: Net Saving	...	4796.9	8136.2	5065.6	10505.5	12156.4	6564.3	6203.9	7092.5	...	...	...
Less: Surplus of the nation on current transactions	...	42.6	-656.5	-3787.2	1924.1	1798.0	-5962.5	-3920.8	-1242.3	...	...	...
Equals: Net Capital Formation	...	4754.3	8792.7	8853.8	8581.4	10358.4	12526.8	10124.7	8334.8	...	...	...

Nigeria

4.1 Derivation of Value Added by Kind of Activity, in Current Prices

Million Nigerian naira — Fiscal year beginning 1 April

	1980 Gross Output	1980 Intermediate Consumption	1980 Value Added	1981 Gross Output	1981 Intermediate Consumption	1981 Value Added	1982 Gross Output	1982 Intermediate Consumption	1982 Value Added	1983 Gross Output	1983 Intermediate Consumption	1983 Value Added
			All Producers									
1 Agriculture, hunting, forestry and fishing	...	...	10079.3	...	...	9863.1	...	...	12410.3	...	...	12165.7
A Agriculture and hunting	...	...	8545.7	...	...	7952.4	...	...	10092.8	...	...	9369.5
B Forestry and logging	...	...	315.0	...	...	321.7	...	...	329.7	...	...	337.7
C Fishing	...	...	1218.6	...	...	1589.0	...	...	1987.8	...	...	2458.5
2 Mining and quarrying	...	...	15066.5	...	...	12400.1	...	...	11555.4	...	...	9923.0
A Coal mining	...	...	0.1	...	...	0.1	...	...	-	...	...	-
B Crude petroleum and natural gas production	...	...	14192.7	...	...	11512.7	...	...	10758.6	...	...	9201.4
C Metal ore mining	...	...	16.8	...	...	16.6	...	...	12.7	...	...	10.4
D Other mining	...	...	856.8	...	...	870.8	...	...	784.1	...	...	711.3
3 Manufacturing	...	...	2354.4	...	...	2647.5	...	...	2726.3	...	...	2372.5
4 Electricity, gas and water	...	...	244.6	...	...	309.7	...	...	386.0	...	...	460.8
A Electricity, gas and steam	...	...	227.3	...	...	285.7	...	...	352.2	...	...	417.3
B Water works and supply	...	...	17.3	...	...	24.0	...	...	33.8	...	...	43.5
5 Construction	...	...	3671.2	...	...	4001.6	...	...	3603.0	...	...	3268.3
6 Wholesale and retail trade, restaurants and hotels	...	...	9722.9	...	...	10564.8	...	...	10593.8	...	...	10489.9
A Wholesale and retail trade	...	...	9617.2	...	...	10449.7	...	...	10463.6	...	...	10344.6
B Restaurants and hotels	...	...	105.7	...	...	115.1	...	...	130.1	...	...	145.3
7 Transport, storage and communication	...	...	1762.6	...	...	2128.9	...	...	2396.6	...	...	2187.7
A Transport and storage	...	...	1692.6	...	...	2055.0	...	...	2321.9	...	...	2109.6
B Communication	...	...	70.0	...	...	73.9	...	...	74.7	...	...	78.1
8 Finance, insurance, real estate and business services	...	...	815.0	...	...	1161.7	...	...	1398.1	...	...	1494.3
A Financial institutions	...	...	558.7	...	...	869.7	...	...	1069.0	...	...	1117.5
B Insurance	...	...	141.2	...	...	172.4	...	...	205.0	...	...	248.1
C Real estate and business services	...	...	115.1	...	...	119.6	...	...	124.1	...	...	128.7
9 Community, social and personal services	...	...	1309.6	...	...	1398.1	...	...	1492.0	...	...	1498.9
Total, Industries	...	...	45026.0	...	...	44475.6	...	...	46561.3	...	...	43861.1
Producers of Government Services	...	...	2014.9	...	...	2569.9	...	...	2809.1	...	...	2911.5
Other Producers	...	...	...	...	...	...	...	...	...	...	...	...
Total [a]	...	...	47040.9	...	...	47045.4	...	...	49370.4	...	...	46772.6
Less: Imputed bank service charge	...	...	...	...	...	...	...	...	...	...	...	...
Import duties	...	...	...	...	...	...	...	...	...	...	...	...
Value added tax	...	...	...	...	...	...	...	...	...	...	...	...
Total												

a) Gross domestic product in factor values.

4.2 Derivation of Value Added by Kind of Activity, in Constant Prices

Million Nigerian naira — Fiscal year beginning 1 April

	1980 Gross Output	1980 Intermediate Consumption	1980 Value Added	1981 Gross Output	1981 Intermediate Consumption	1981 Value Added	1982 Gross Output	1982 Intermediate Consumption	1982 Value Added	1983 Gross Output	1983 Intermediate Consumption	1983 Value Added
			At constant prices of: 1977									
			All Producers									
1 Agriculture, hunting, forestry and fishing	...	...	6071.0	...	...	5720.7	...	...	6495.6	...	...	6155.0
A Agriculture and hunting	...	...	5069.2	...	...	4699.8	...	...	5449.9	...	...	4976.8
B Forestry and logging	...	...	270.6	...	...	264.5	...	...	259.4	...	...	255.4
C Fishing	...	...	731.1	...	...	756.5	...	...	786.3	...	...	922.8
2 Mining and quarrying	...	...	7406.7	...	...	5302.1	...	...	4645.3	...	...	4461.5
A Coal mining	...	...	0.1	...	...	0.1	...	...	-	...	...	-
B Crude petroleum and natural gas production	...	...	6748.2	...	...	4613.1	...	...	4071.7	...	...	3966.2
C Metal ore mining	...	...	16.6	...	...	16.1	...	...	11.9	...	...	9.7
D Other mining	...	...	641.8	...	...	672.9	...	...	561.6	...	...	485.6
3 Manufacturing	...	...	2244.8	...	...	2458.3	...	...	2526.5	...	...	2216.7
4 Electricity, gas and water	...	...	143.3	...	...	169.5	...	...	189.4	...	...	199.4
A Electricity, gas and steam	...	...	129.3	...	...	151.4	...	...	165.0	...	...	169.8
B Water works and supply	...	...	13.9	...	...	18.2	...	...	24.3	...	...	29.6

Nigeria

4.2 Derivation of Value Added by Kind of Activity, in Constant Prices
(Continued)

Million Nigerian naira — Fiscal year beginning 1 April

	1980 Gross Output	1980 Intermediate Consumption	1980 Value Added	1981 Gross Output	1981 Intermediate Consumption	1981 Value Added	1982 Gross Output	1982 Intermediate Consumption	1982 Value Added	1983 Gross Output	1983 Intermediate Consumption	1983 Value Added
				At constant prices of: 1977								
5 Construction	...	...	3056.0	...	...	3204.1	...	...	2674.5	...	...	2312.2
6 Wholesale and retail trade, restaurants and hotels	...	...	6533.2	...	...	6941.3	...	...	6359.2	...	...	6092.7
A Wholesale and retail trade	...	...	6432.1	...	...	6831.6	...	...	6236.5	...	...	5956.8
B Restaurants and hotels	...	...	101.1	...	...	109.7	...	...	122.7	...	...	135.9
7 Transport, storage and communication	...	...	1311.4	...	...	1458.0	...	...	1523.8	...	...	1299.6
A Transport and storage	...	...	1247.0	...	...	1390.9	...	...	1457.2	...	...	1230.9
B Communication	...	...	64.4	...	...	67.1	...	...	66.6	...	...	68.7
8 Finance, insurance, real estate and business services	...	...	689.7	...	...	932.6	...	...	1066.4	...	...	1089.8
A Financial institutions	...	...	462.6	...	...	682.3	...	...	769.0	...	...	792.7
B Insurance	...	...	161.6	...	...	136.0	...	...	153.4	...	...	176.8
C Real estate and business services	...	...	65.5	...	...	114.2	...	...	144.0	...	...	120.2
Real estate, except dwellings	...	...	6.0	...	...	5.8	...	...	5.0	...	...	4.7
Dwellings	...	...	...	...	...	...	...	...	...	...	...	...
9 Community, social and personal services	...	...	1091.5	...	...	1105.9	...	...	1120.8	...	...	1070.8
Total, Industries	...	...	28547.5	...	...	27292.3	...	...	26601.5	...	...	24897.7
Producers of Government Services	...	...	1687.5	...	...	2150.8	...	...	2280.4	...	...	2143.0
Other Producers	...	...	...	...	...	...	...	...	...	...	...	...
Total [a]	...	...	30235.0	...	...	29443.1	...	...	28881.8	...	...	27040.7
Less: Imputed bank service charge	...	...	...	...	...	...	...	...	...	...	...	...
Import duties	...	...	...	...	...	...	...	...	...	...	...	...
Value added tax	...	...	...	...	...	...	...	...	...	...	...	...
Total	...	...	...	...	...	...	...	...	...	...	...	...

a) Gross domestic product in factor values.

Norway

General note. The preparation of national accounts statistics in Norway is undertaken by the Central Bureau of Statistics, Oslo. The official estimates are published annually in 'Nasjonalregnskap (National Accounts)'. A detailed description of the sources and methods is found in 'National Accounts of Norway - System and Methods of Estimation', No. 45 in the series Samfunnsokononieske Studier (Norwegian text) and No. 81/1 in the series RAPPORTER (English text), published in 1981. The estimates are generally in accordance with the classifications and definitions recommended in the United Nations system of National Accounts (SNA). Estimates conforming to the present SNA were published for the first time in 'Okonomisk Utsyn (Economic Survey) 1972'. The corresponding changes of concepts and classifications were published in 'Revidert Nasjonalregnskap (Revised National Accounts)' in 1975. Input-output tables were published in 1968 in 'Input-output data 1954, 1959 and 1964'. The following tables have been prepared from successive replies to the United Nations national accounts questionnaire. When the scope and coverage of the estimates differ for conceptual or statistical reasons from the definitions and classifications recommended in SNA, a footnote is indicated to the relevant tables.

Sources and methods:

(a) Gross domestic product. The main approach used to estimate GDP is the production approach.

(b) Expenditure on the gross domestic product. The expenditure approach is used to estimate all components of GDP by expenditure type, within the framework of detailed input-output tables using the commodity-flow method. Change in stocks, however, is primarily calculated as the difference between supply and other uses for each commodity. Government final consumption expenditure is mainly based on government accounts. Estimates of private consumption expenditure relating to consumer goods are based on turnover statistics and extrapolated by value indexes. Gross fixed capital formation is recorded at purchasers' prices which includes investment levies, but excludes value added tax. Exports and imports of goods and services are mainly based on foreign exchange statistics from the Bank of Norway and external trade statistics of the Central Bureau of Statistics. For the constant price estimates, double deflation and the commodity-flow approach are used within the framework of detailed annual input-output tables for all expenditure components. Current values are deflated by appropriate price indexes.

(c) Cost-structure of the gross domestic product. The value of compensation of employees is obtained through adding up wages and salaries by branch of activity. Censuses provide bench-mark data, while data from government accounts, quarterly earnings statistics and annual industrial statistics are used as extrapolators for the inter-censal years. Operating surplus is arrived at as a residual. Consumption of fixed capital is estimated by using the perpetual inventory method. Time series of gross investment at constant prices provide the basis for calculating consumption of fixed capital. Commodity taxes and subsidies are calculated on accrual basis through the commodity-flow method.

(d) Gross domestic product by kind of economic activity. The table of GDP by kind of economic activity is prepared at market prices, i.e. producers' values. The production approach is used to estimate value added of almost all industries. This is done within the framework of detailed input-output tables using the commodity-flow method. The income approach is used for producers of government services and part of other private services. The expenditure approach is used in the case of the trade sector. Agricultural production is estimated from data prepared by the Agricultural Budgeting Board. Information on prices is obtained from the Agricultural Price Reporting Office and from the marketing cooperatives. For mining and quarrying estimates are extracted from the annual industrial statistics, which include crude oil and natural gas production in the North Sea. For manufacturing use is made of the annual industrial statistics which supply detailed information on gross output and intermediate consumption by industrial activity and by commodity for all establishments employing five or more persons. The annual statistics of building and construction work give information on the number of establishments, persons engaged, value of production, cost of materials and gross fixed capital formation. Gross output of the trade sector is measured as the total of trade and transport margins plus some minor items. The margins are estimated as the aggregate difference between purchasers' values and producers' values, except for bench-mark years when mark-ups are estimated from information from government agencies, business organizations, surveys of consumer expenditure or from price data. The estimation of intermediate consumption is to a large extent based on ratios from bench-mark years. The estimates for railway, tramway, subway and suburban railway transport as well as air transport are based on detailed accounting data. For other land transport the statistical sources are the annual scheduled road transport statistics, data from censuses of establishments, etc. Summary accounts for financial institutions exist in the annual credit market statistics. For insurance the annual insurance statistics and extracts of accounts are used. Operating surplus of dwellings in the bench-mark year has been fixed as a certain percentage of reduced replacement cost of the dwelling stock in the base-year. For subsequent years gross output is extrapolated by using information on investments, repairs and clearing of old dwellings. Bench-mark estimates for business services are made from the censuses of establishments held every ten years and extrapolated by value indices based on annual statistics on services. For government services data are obtained from the municipal accounts and central government accounts including social insurance administration. For private services bench-mark estimates are to a large extent based on the censuses of establishments, and extrapolated by use of employment estimates and components of consumer price index. For the estimation of constant prices, double deflation and the commodity-flow approach are used within the framework of detailed annual input-output tables. In most sectors output is deflated by appropriate price indexes. However, output of crop and livestock products is valued at base-year prices, and extrapolation by quantity indicators is undertaken for restaurants and hotels, transport of goods and financial institutions.

1.1 Expenditure on the Gross Domestic Product, in Current Prices

Million Norwegian kroner

		1970	1975	1977	1978	1979	1980	1981	1982	1983	1984	1985	1986
1	Government final consumption expenditure	13533	28702	38625	43543	46585	53478	62616	70408	78214	84099	92804	102092
2	Private final consumption expenditure	43047	77615	103915	110670	120104	135242	155205	175310	192979	210921	246327	279796
3	Gross capital formation	24326	52335	69498	60765	65727	78902	84032	96071	99116	116267	121609	151743
	A Increase in stocks	3131	1544	-1576	-6941	-459	8104	-7761	3809	-4332	-1300	12675	9589
	B Gross fixed capital formation	21195	50791	71074	67706	66186	70798	91793	92262	103448	117567	108934	142154
	Residential buildings [a]	3984	8138	10321	11765	12552	13535	15055	17465	18526	19171	20431	24381
	Non-residential buildings	4102	8982	11340	12798	12910	14482	16138	16289	17047	17918	21150	26504
	Other construction and land improvement etc. [b]	3842	13734	22315	19681	17116	17682	29112	24379	36175	46106	33462	51621
	Other	9268	19937	27098	23461	23607	25098	31488	34130	31699	34372	33892	39648
4	Exports of goods and services	33400	62180	76264	87221	105407	134706	156299	165022	183921	214077	235384	194046
5	Less: Imports of goods and services	34431	72139	96768	89119	99154	117371	130467	144543	152031	172852	194308	211654
	Equals: Gross Domestic Product	79878	148702	191534	213080	238669	285046	327674	362269	402199	452512	501816	516023

a) Item 'Residential buildings' includes also summer cottages, temporary dwellings, logging camps, fishermens' quarters etc..
b) The estimates of 'Other construction' include oil drilling rigs, oil production platforms etc., pipelines for gas, oil and gas exploration and drilling.

Norway

1.2 Expenditure on the Gross Domestic Product, in Constant Prices

Million Norwegian kroner

	1970	1975	1977	1978	1979	1980	1981	1982	1983	1984	1985	1986
		1970			At constant prices of: 1975				1980			
1 Government final consumption expenditure	13533	17510 / 28702	32339	34068	35277	37191 / 53478	56763	58985	61727	63238	65358	67398
2 Private final consumption expenditure	43047	52069 / 77615	88039	86606	89389	91488 / 135242	136784	139199	141303	145139	160171	169862
3 Gross capital formation	24326	33813 / 52335	56242	46053	48263	52525 / 78902	76461	77337	75509	87173	79041	94634
A Increase in stocks	3131	1548 / 1544	-1727	-5418	-649	4344 / 8104	-7024	3041	-3109	-51	10158	7182
B Gross fixed capital formation	21195	32265 / 50791	57969	51471	48912	48181 / 70798	83485	74296	78618	87224	68883	87452
Residential buildings a	3984	5311 / 8138	8581	9361	9594	9376 / 13535	13695	14533	14420	14255	14472	15962
Non-residential buildings	4102	5914 / 8982	9403	10212	10053	10345 / 14482	14975	14016	13897	14068	15679	18349
Other construction and land improvement etc. b	3842	8885 / 13734	18817	15621	12828	11952 / 17682	25289	17861	26366	31619	22068	32491
Other	9268	12156 / 19937	21167	16277	16438	16508 / 25098	29526	27887	23935	27282	16664	20651
4 Exports of goods and services	33403	43319 / 62189	71704	77718	79723	81393 / 134795	136651	136451	146786	158841	175758	176859
5 Less: Imports of goods and services	34431	46487 / 72139	83807	72459	71954	74298 / 117371	119113	123467	123449	135177	143898	157647
Equals: Gross Domestic Product	79878	100224 / 148702	164517	171986	180698	188299 / 285046	287546	288505	301876	319214	336430	351106

a) Item 'Residential buildings' includes also summer cottages, temporary dwellings, logging camps, fishermens' quarters etc.. b) The estimates of 'Other construction' include oil drilling rigs, oil production platforms etc., pipelines for gas, oil and gas exploration and drilling.

1.3 Cost Components of the Gross Domestic Product

Million Norwegian kroner

	1970	1975	1977	1978	1979	1980	1981	1982	1983	1984	1985	1986
1 Indirect taxes, net	10450	17197	22216	21500	24363	29064	33901	38085	45294	52491	65056	71398
A Indirect taxes	14568	26455	36327	37946	41106	49025	55695	61747	69733	78200	91992	101084
B Less: Subsidies	4118	9258	14111	16446	16743	19961	21794	23662	24439	25709	26936	29686
2 Consumption of fixed capital	11026	21089	31060	34598	36878	41358	48053	55007	59614	62513	67506	74337
3 Compensation of employees paid by resident producers to:	41879	86186	112981	123964	129392	145421	164165	183356	198235	216350	239904	272985
A Resident households	41801	86120	112926	123900	129308	145331	163917	183086	197974	216070	239624	272700
B Rest of the world	77	66	56	64	84	90	248	270	261	280	280	285
4 Operating surplus	16522	24229	25277	33017	48035	69201	81554	85823	99055	121159	129350	97301
A Corporate and quasi-corporate enterprises	...	8244	3160	7102	23295	40749	48566	47944	58090	75152	79161	43136
B Private unincorporated enterprises	...	15399	21210	24567	23381	26780	30977	34462	36985	40805	44022	46942
C General government	...	586	906	1348	1358	1674	2010	3417	3979	5202	6167	7223
Equals: Gross Domestic Product	79877	148701	191534	213079	238668	285044	327673	362271	402198	452513	501816	516021

1.4 General Government Current Receipts and Disbursements

Million Norwegian kroner

	1970	1975	1977	1978	1979	1980	1981	1982	1983	1984	1985	1986
					Receipts							
1 Operating surplus	-	586	906	1348	1358	1674	2010	3417	3979	5202	6167	7223
2 Property and entrepreneurial income	1846	3053	4002	5871	7156	8303	10902	13040	15626	21445	24735	32875
3 Taxes, fees and contributions	32909	70152	92703	103669	115319	144657	160250	176332	194120	216898	250269	247436
A Indirect taxes	14568	26455	36327	37946	41106	49024	55696	61747	69733	78200	91992	101084
B Direct taxes	10591	23790	31583	37900	44201	61260	65657	70604	76722	87637	100600	78450
C Social security contributions	7730	19863	24733	27757	29914	34224	38699	43494	47149	50511	57314	67426
D Compulsory fees, fines and penalties	20	44	60	66	98	149	198	487	516	550	363	476

Norway

1.4 General Government Current Receipts and Disbursements
(Continued)

Million Norwegian kroner

	1970	1975	1977	1978	1979	1980	1981	1982	1983	1984	1985	1986
4 Other current transfers	...	...	...	...	...	...	...	...	...	3000	3078	3078
Total Current Receipts of General Government a	34755	73791	97611	110888	123833	154634	173162	192789	213725	246545	284249	290612

Disbursements

	1970	1975	1977	1978	1979	1980	1981	1982	1983	1984	1985	1986
1 Government final consumption expenditure	13533	28701	38625	43543	46585	53478	62616	70408	78213	84099	92804	102092
A Compensation of employees	8833	19550	26904	30145	32087	36574	42504	48526	53655	58470	64173	71084
B Consumption of fixed capital	578	1154	1616	1868	2026	2327	2658	2980	3186	3339	3840	4210
C Purchases of goods and services, net	4122	7997	10106	11530	12472	14577	17454	18902	21372	22291	24791	26798
D Less: Own account fixed capital formation	...	...	...	...	...	...	...	...	...	...	...	...
E Indirect taxes paid, net	...	...	...	...	...	...	...	...	...	...	...	...
2 Property income	1430	3156	5467	7015	8931	11182	12647	13834	16607	18807	21898	27650
A Interest	1430	3156	5467	7015	8931	11182	12647	13834	16607	18807	21898	27650
B Net land rent and royalties	...	...	...	...	...	...	...	...	...	...	...	...
3 Subsidies	4118	9258	14111	16446	16743	19960	21795	23662	24439	25708	26936	29686
4 Other current transfers	10084	21036	28497	33674	38961	43172	50255	57789	66076	71787	78029	86428
A Social security benefits	9785	20154	27049	31916	37023	40975	47636	54516	62212	67917	73820	81490
B Social assistance grants	...	...	...	...	...	...	...	...	...	...	...	...
C Other b	299	882	1448	1758	1938	2197	2619	3273	3864	3870	4209	4938
5 Net saving a	5590	11640	10911	10210	12613	26842	25849	27096	28390	46142	64583	44756
Total Current Disbursements and Net Saving of General Government a	34755	73791	97611	110888	123833	154634	173162	192789	213725	246543	284250	290612

a) Including local government enterprises.
b) Item 'Other' of Other current transfers refers to transfers to the rest of the world.

1.5 Current Income and Outlay of Corporate and Quasi-Corporate Enterprises, Summary

Million Norwegian kroner

	1970	1975	1977	1978	1979	1980	1981	1982	1983	1984	1985	1986

Receipts

	1970	1975	1977	1978	1979	1980	1981	1982	1983	1984	1985	1986
1 Operating surplus	...	8244	3160	7102	23295	40749	48566	47944	58090	75152	79161	43136
2 Property and entrepreneurial income received	...	14566	21214	26504	31343	40601	51981	63766	72577	82566	103635	134728
3 Current transfers	...	5278	8528	9789	10568	11484	14408	16823	18968	20360	19971	21291
Total Current Receipts	...	28088	32902	43395	65206	92834	114955	128533	149635	178078	202767	199155

Disbursements

	1970	1975	1977	1978	1979	1980	1981	1982	1983	1984	1985	1986
1 Property and entrepreneurial income	...	15512	23125	30664	37210	45719	58516	71642	80003	94487	109732	137190
2 Direct taxes and other current payments to general government	...	3400	5188	7494	11577	23531	26004	27965	32642	39025	47217	19864
3 Other current transfers	...	5646	8977	10388	11194	12227	15150	17711	19944	24650	24392	26008
4 Net saving	...	3530	-4388	-5151	5225	11357	15285	11215	17046	19917	21427	16094
Total Current Disbursements and Net Saving	...	28088	32902	43395	65206	92834	114955	128533	149635	178079	202768	199156

1.6 Current Income and Outlay of Households and Non-Profit Institutions

Million Norwegian kroner

	1970	1975	1977	1978	1979	1980	1981	1982	1983	1984	1985	1986

Receipts

	1970	1975	1977	1978	1979	1980	1981	1982	1983	1984	1985	1986
1 Compensation of employees	...	86162	112980	123960	129376	145396	164003	183181	198070	216178	239720	272800
A From resident producers	...	86120	112926	123900	129310	145330	163919	183085	197974	216070	239624	272700
B From rest of the world	...	42	54	60	66	66	84	96	96	108	96	108
2 Operating surplus of private unincorporated enterprises	...	15399	21210	24567	23381	26780	30977	34462	36985	40805	44022	46942
3 Property and entrepreneurial income	...	3492	4739	6179	7739	9612	11792	13711	16886	20392	24529	29364
4 Current transfers	...	21519	28863	33980	39230	43575	50675	58014	65937	72097	78495	86677
A Social security benefits	...	20154	27049	31916	37023	40975	47636	54516	62212	67917	73820	81490
B Social assistance grants	...	...	...	...	...	...	...	...	...	...	...	...
C Other	...	1365	1814	2064	2207	2600	3039	3498	3725	4180	4675	5187
Total Current Receipts	...	126572	167792	188686	199726	225363	257447	289368	317878	349472	386766	435791

Disbursements

	1970	1975	1977	1978	1979	1980	1981	1982	1983	1984	1985	1986
1 Private final consumption expenditure	...	77615	103915	110670	120104	135241	155205	175310	192979	210921	246327	279796

Norway

1.6 Current Income and Outlay of Households and Non-Profit Institutions
(Continued)

Million Norwegian kroner

	1970	1975	1977	1978	1979	1980	1981	1982	1983	1984	1985	1986
2 Property income	...	4343	6179	8199	9525	11230	14024	17572	21316	24081	30565	41289
3 Direct taxes and other current transfers n.e.c. to general government	...	40244	51043	58017	62419	71890	78278	86160	91281	99198	110743	126097
A Social security contributions	...	19863	24733	27757	29914	34224	38699	43494	47149	50511	57314	67426
B Direct taxes	...	20381	26310	30260	32505	37666	39579	42666	44132	48687	53429	58671
C Fees, fines and penalties	...	-	-	-	-	-	-	-	-	-	-	-
4 Other current transfers	...	986	1542	1698	1946	2265	2656	3427	3593	3650	4204	4892
5 Net saving	...	3384	5113	10102	5732	4737	7284	6899	8709	11623	-5072	-16283
Total Current Disbursements and Net Saving	...	126572	167792	188686	199726	225363	257447	289368	317878	349473	386767	435791

1.7 External Transactions on Current Account, Summary

Million Norwegian kroner

	1970	1975	1977	1978	1979	1980	1981	1982	1983	1984	1985	1986
Payments to the Rest of the World												
1 Imports of goods and services	34431	72139	96768	89119	99154	117371	130469	144543	152031	172852	194308	211654
A Imports of merchandise c.i.f.	26651	54366	72002	61979	70433	84543	90516	100458	102520	116542	133751	152574
B Other	7780	17773	24766	27140	28721	32828	39953	44085	49510	56311	60556	59080
2 Factor income to the rest of the world	1676	3706	6603	9635	12663	14841	19319	23431	23394	26651	27683	29323
A Compensation of employees	77	66	56	64	84	90	248	270	261	280	280	285
B Property and entrepreneurial income	1599	3640	6547	9571	12579	14751	19071	23161	23133	26371	27403	29038
3 Current transfers to the rest of the world	487	1356	2108	2478	2799	3212	3796	4791	5522	5506	6201	7221
A Indirect taxes to supranational organizations	-	-	-	-	-	-	-	-	-	-	-	-
B Other current transfers	487	1356	2108	2478	2799	3212	3796	4791	5522	5506	6201	7221
4 Surplus of the nation on current transactions	-1728	-12692	-26802	-11005	-5278	5448	12460	4146	14645	23929	26834	-32837
Payments to the Rest of the World and Surplus of the Nation on Current Transactions	34866	64509	78677	90227	109338	140872	166044	176911	195592	228938	255026	215361
Receipts From The Rest of the World												
1 Exports of goods and services	33403	62189	76264	87221	105407	134795	156288	165022	183921	214078	235383	194047
A Exports of merchandise f.o.b.	17715	38140	48747	57863	70007	92863	106899	114798	133249	156822	173023	135860
B Other	15688	24049	27517	29358	35400	41932	49390	50224	50672	57256	62361	58187
2 Factor income from rest of the world	1056	1791	1870	2453	3337	5321	8740	10727	10392	13509	18203	19985
A Compensation of employees	24	42	54	60	66	66	84	96	96	108	96	108
B Property and entrepreneurial income	1031	1749	1816	2393	3271	5255	8656	10631	10296	13401	18107	19877
3 Current transfers from rest of the world	408	529	543	553	594	756	1016	1161	1276	1350	1439	1331
A Subsidies from supranational organisations	-	-	-	-	-	-	-	-	-	-	-	-
B Other current transfers	408	529	543	553	594	756	1016	1161	1278	1350	1439	1331
Receipts from the Rest of the World on Current Transactions	34867	64509	78677	90227	109338	140872	166044	176910	195591	228937	255025	215363

1.8 Capital Transactions of The Nation, Summary

Million Norwegian kroner

	1970	1975	1977	1978	1979	1980	1981	1982	1983	1984	1985	1986
Finance of Gross Capital Formation												
Gross saving	22597	39643	42696	49759	60448	84350	96492	100218	113760	140197	148443	118905
1 Consumption of fixed capital	11024	21089	31060	34598	36878	41358	48053	55007	59614	62513	67506	74337
A General government [a]	578	2282	3057	3496	3825	4357	4910	5558	6010	6380	7187	7901
B Corporate and quasi-corporate enterprises	10446	13288	20213	22214	23564	26522	30556	35520	38644	40862	43913	48086
Public	1476	2141	3108	3606	3975	4776	5703	6473	7670	8055	9991	11587
Private	8970	11147	17105	18608	19589	21746	24853	29047	30974	32807	33922	36499
C Other [b]	...	5520	7790	8888	9489	10479	12587	13928	14961	15271	16405	18350
2 Net saving	11573	18554	11636	15161	23570	42992	48439	45211	54146	77684	80937	44568

Norway

1.8 Capital Transactions of The Nation, Summary
(Continued)

Million Norwegian kroner

	1970	1975	1977	1978	1979	1980	1981	1982	1983	1984	1985	1986
A General government [a]	5590	11640	10911	10210	12613	26842	25849	27096	28390	46142	64583	44756
B Corporate and quasi-corporate enterprises	5983	3530	-4388	-5151	5225	11357	15285	11215	17046	19917	21427	16094
Public	...	-77	1947	203	-850	5010	6642	9440	10795	10251	5459	7084
Private	...	3607	-6335	-5354	6075	6347	8643	1775	6251	9666	15968	9010
C Other [b]	...	3384	5113	10102	5732	4793	7307	6899	8709	11623	-5072	-16283
Less: Surplus of the nation on current transactions	-1728	-12692	-26802	-11005	-5278	5448	12460	4146	14644	23929	26834	-32836
Finance of Gross Capital Formation	24325	52335	69498	60764	65726	78902	84032	96072	99116	116268	121609	151741
Gross Capital Formation												
Increase in stocks	3131	1544	-1576	-6941	-460	8104	-7761	3809	-4332	-1300	12675	9589
Gross fixed capital formation	21194	50791	71074	67705	66186	70798	91793	92262	103448	117567	108934	142154
1 General government [a]	3578	9822	13093	15213	15140	16640	17576	18395	19406	19326	19719	22606
2 Corporate and quasi-corporate enterprises	17617	28655	39942	33144	32882	34035	54622	50118	60358	72384	58245	81398
A Public	3166	5419	8076	8081	7831	9625	13788	11015	19654	17282	20795	30533
B Private	14451	23236	31866	25063	25051	24410	40834	39103	40704	55102	37450	50865
3 Other [b]		12314	18039	19348	18164	20123	19595	23747	23684	25856	30970	38150
Gross Capital Formation	24325	52335	69498	60764	65726	78902	84032	96071	99116	116267	121609	151743

a) Local government enterprises are included in general government.
b) Beginning 1972, item 'Other' includes households and private unincorporated enterprises and non-profit institutions serving households.

1.9 Gross Domestic Product by Institutional Sectors of Origin

Million Norwegian kroner

	1970	1975	1977	1978	1979	1980	1981	1982	1983	1984	1985	1986
Domestic Factor Incomes Originating												
1 General government	8833	19550	26904	30145	32087	36574	42504	48526	53654	58470	64173	71084
2 Corporate and quasi-corporate enterprises [a]	49568	90864	111355	126836	145340	178049	203216	220652	243635	279039	305081	299202
3 Households and private unincorporated enterprises	...	...	...	...	...	...	...	...	...	...	...	...
4 Non-profit institutions serving households	...	...	...	...	...	...	...	...	...	...	...	...
Subtotal: Domestic Factor Incomes	58401	110415	138258	156981	177427	214622	245719	269179	297290	337509	369254	370286
Indirect taxes, net	10450	17197	22216	21500	24363	29064	33901	38085	45294	52491	65056	71398
A Indirect taxes	14568	26455	36327	37946	41106	49025	55695	61747	69733	78200	91992	101084
B Less: Subsidies	4118	9258	14111	16446	16743	19961	21794	23662	24439	25709	26936	29686
Consumption of fixed capital	11026	21089	31060	34598	36878	41358	48053	55007	59614	62513	67506	74337
Gross Domestic Product	79877	148701	191534	213079	238668	285044	327673	362271	402198	452513	501816	516021

a) The estimates of Households and private unincorporated enterprises and Non-profit institutions serving households are included in item 'Corporate and quasi-corporate enterprises'.

1.10 Gross Domestic Product by Kind of Activity, in Current Prices

Million Norwegian kroner

	1970	1975	1977	1978	1979	1980	1981	1982	1983	1984	1985	1986
1 Agriculture, hunting, forestry and fishing	4460	7115	9467	9815	10137	10969	12957	13437	13135	15042	15359	16484
2 Mining and quarrying	501	4400	8207	10756	21700	42070	51105	56514	60201	84770	91550	51992
3 Manufacturing	17259	32270	35963	37528	43820	45635	48575	51383	56724	64524	70236	79099
4 Electricity, gas and water	2165	4303	5084	6491	7486	8237	10158	11981	14312	16571	18796	20355
5 Construction	5593	10320	13402	15289	15254	16952	19673	22711	23848	24353	26909	29073
6 Wholesale and retail trade, restaurants and hotels	9943	17010	23940	20501	27085	33204	38475	42705	45475	49445	55305	62311
7 Transport, storage and communication	11780	16458	18755	20929	23116	26890	30755	31289	33852	37077	38651	44180
8 Finance, insurance, real estate and business services	7286	14369	19261	21310	24730	28244	34155	40859	45633	49318	55708	69870
9 Community, social and personal services	3780	7239	9638	10637	11339	12478	14009	15722	17701	18750	20652	23537
Total, Industries	62856	114383	143795	162257	185354	224747	259941	286660	318912	359858	393166	396901
Producers of Government Services	9412	20705	28519	32013	34114	38901	45162	51505	56841	61808	68013	75294
Other Producers	...	...	...	...	...	...	...	...	...	...	...	...

Norway

1.10 Gross Domestic Product by Kind of Activity, in Current Prices
(Continued)

Million Norwegian kroner

	1970	1975	1977	1978	1979	1980	1981	1982	1983	1984	1985	1986
Subtotal	72268	135087	172314	194270	219468	263648	305103	338165	375753	421667	461179	472195
Less: Imputed bank service charge	1709	4061	5629	6158	7278	8724	11349	14318	15960	15443	15857	22008
Plus: Import duties [a]	1328	2380	3984	2974	3253	3692	4248	5203	5764	6006	9032	11999
Plus: Value added tax [b]	7734	14312	18828	20143	21612	24703	28024	31536	34623	37794	44433	50212
Plus: Other adjustments [c]	256	983	2037	1851	1613	1726	1649	1683	2017	2489	3030	3624
Equals: Gross Domestic Product	79877	148702	191534	213080	238668	285045	327675	362269	402197	452512	501817	516022
Memorandum Item: Mineral fuels and power	2387	8182	12738	19726	30873	49587	59777	67331	80842	99676	108789	72444

a) Item 'Import duties' includes collection of customs duties, value added tax on imports and special excises or taxes on imports.
b) Item 'Value added tax' excludes value added tax on imports which is included in item 'Import duties'.
c) Item 'Other adjustments' refers to collection of investment levy on fixed capital formation and subsidies on residential and social buildings.

1.11 Gross Domestic Product by Kind of Activity, in Constant Prices

Million Norwegian kroner

	1970	1975	1977	1978	1979	1980	1981	1982	1983	1984	1985	1986
					At constant prices of:							
	1970	1970			1975				1980			
1 Agriculture, hunting, forestry and fishing	4460	4943 / 7115	7402	7155	7368	7515 / 10969	11959	12446	12319	13356	12687	12399
2 Mining and quarrying	591	2964 / 4493	7286	11722	14083	17360 / 42078	40498	40719	47866	55141	58079	60366
3 Manufacturing	17259	20328 / 32270	31671	30891	31883	31535 / 45635	44691	44787	44155	47013	49039	49779
4 Electricity, gas and water	2165	2831 / 4303	4141	4590	5022	4791 / 8237	8954	9094	10287	10614	10296	9690
5 Construction	5593	6922 / 10320	11419	12543	12354	12487 / 16952	16735	17031	17563	17768	18682	19501
6 Wholesale and retail trade, restaurants and hotels	9943	12803 / 17816	19561	19858	20560	20757 / 33264	32521	31907	31823	33351	36258	38674
7 Transport, storage and communication	11780	14038 / 16458	19264	19615	20263	21037 / 26890	27545	26530	27149	28501	28847	31242
8 Finance, insurance, real estate and business services	7286	8493 / 14369	16168	16515	17399	18141 / 28244	29310	30209	30274	31494	33374	36420
9 Community, social and personal services	3780	4525 / 7239	7935	8207	8551	8524 / 12478	12542	12699	13031	12965	13375	14052
Total, Industries	62856	77845 / 114383	124847	131095	137482	142147 / 224747	224754	225421	234466	250202	260637	272125
Producers of Government Services	9412	12403 / 20705	23852	25120	26209	27686 / 38901	41141	43393	44993	46248	47688	48745
Other Producers	...	...	...	...	...	...	...	...	...	...	...	...
Subtotal	72268	90248 / 135087	148699	156215	163691	169833 / 263648	265896	268814	279458	296450	308325	320870
Less: Imputed bank service charge	1709	1947 / 4061	4363	4480	4610	4797 / 8724	8985	9205	9543	10157	10897	11544
Plus: Import duties [a]	1328	1907 / 2380	2972	1917	2218	2475 / 3692	3869	4253	4092	4189	6119	6619
Plus: Value added tax [b]	7734	9712 / 14312	16158	16046	16659	16942 / 24703	25000	25399	25951	27309	30207	32150
Plus: Other adjustments [c]	256	304 / 983	1051	2289	2741	3846 / 1726	1767	-755	1918	1424	2676	3011
Equals: Gross Domestic Product	79877	100224 / 148702	164517	171987	180699	188299 / 285045	287546	288506	301877	319215	336430	351106
Memorandum Item: Mineral fuels and power	2387	5159 / 8182	10757	15694	18418	21355 / 49587	48637	49355	57407	65189	67819	69541

a) Item 'Import duties' includes collection of customs duties, value added tax on imports and special excises or taxes on imports.
b) Item 'Value added tax' excludes value added tax on imports which is included in item 'Import duties'.
c) Item 'Other adjustments' refers to collection of investment levy on fixed capital formation and subsidies on residential and social buildings.

Norway

1.12 Relations Among National Accounting Aggregates

Million Norwegian kroner

	1970	1975	1977	1978	1979	1980	1981	1982	1983	1984	1985	1986
Gross Domestic Product	79877	148701	191534	213079	238668	285045	327674	362270	402198	452512	501816	516022
Plus: Net factor income from the rest of the world	-621	-1915	-4733	-7182	-9326	-9520	-10579	-12704	-13002	-13142	-9480	-9338
Factor income from the rest of the world	1056	1791	1870	2453	3337	5321	8740	10727	10392	13509	18203	19985
Less: Factor income to the rest of the world	1677	3706	6603	9635	12663	14841	19319	23431	23394	26651	27683	29323
Equals: Gross National Product	79255	146786	186801	205897	229342	275525	317095	349565	389195	439370	492336	506684
Less: Consumption of fixed capital	11024	21089	31060	34598	36878	41358	48053	55007	59614	62512	67506	74338
Equals: National Income	68232	125697	155741	171299	192464	234167	269042	294559	329581	376858	424830	432346
Plus: Net current transfers from the rest of the world	-79	-827	-1565	-1925	-2205	-2456	-2780	-3630	-4244	-4156	-4762	-5890
Current transfers from the rest of the world	408	529	543	553	594	756	1016	1161	1278	1350	1439	1331
Less: Current transfers to the rest of the world	487	1356	2108	2478	2799	3212	3796	4791	5522	5506	6201	7221
Equals: National Disposable Income	68153	124870	154176	169374	190259	231711	266262	290929	325337	372702	420068	426456
Less: Final consumption	56579	106316	142540	154213	166689	188719	217821	245718	271192	295018	339131	381888
Equals: Net Saving	11573	18554	11636	15161	23570	42992	48441	45211	54146	77684	80937	44568
Less: Surplus of the nation on current transactions	-1728	-12692	-26802	-11005	-5278	5448	12460	4146	14645	23929	26834	-32836
Equals: Net Capital Formation	13301	31246	38438	26166	28848	37544	35981	41064	39501	53755	54103	77404

2.1 Government Final Consumption Expenditure by Function, in Current Prices

Million Norwegian kroner

		1970	1975	1977	1978	1979	1980	1981	1982	1983	1984	1985	1986
1	General public services	1156	2436	3273	3627	3684	4196	4805	5379	6050	6658	7325	8291
2	Defence	2821	4750	5741	6360	6789	8026	10235	11151	12559	12998	14427	15315
3	Public order and safety	541	1220	1692	1864	1971	2225	2617	2925	3186	3447	3758	4203
4	Education	3881	7959	10690	12073	12884	14372	16306	18534	20217	21744	24066	26816
5	Health	1927	5331	7858	8953	9734	11543	13467	15400	17690	19451	21509	23640
6	Social security and welfare	690	2118	3031	3541	3912	4668	5578	6369	6803	7218	8199	9010
7	Housing and community amenities	135	106	14	-10	-14	-23	-215	-298	-379	-500	-571	-616
8	Recreational, cultural and religious affairs	367	827	1184	1361	1469	1707	2037	2357	2668	2881	3162	3515
9	Economic services	1944	3884	5047	5681	5882	6534	7447	8334	9185	9869	10558	11483
	A Fuel and energy	15	61	91	132	163	89	120	158	138	-6	-42	93
	B Agriculture, forestry, fishing and hunting	240	465	575	623	668	725	852	971	1050	1106	1192	1370
	C Mining, manufacturing and construction, except fuel and energy	18	42	25	38	22	67	96	122	130	121	132	141
	D Transportation and communication	1342	2435	3130	3570	3649	4069	4571	5064	5449	5823	6238	6616
	E Other economic affairs	330	881	1226	1319	1379	1584	1807	2019	2418	2824	3038	3263
10	Other functions	73	71	94	92	274	229	340	257	235	333	372	435
	Total Government Final Consumption Expenditure	13533	28702	38625	43543	46585	53478	62616	70408	78214	84099	92804	102002

2.2 Government Final Consumption Expenditure by Function, in Constant Prices

Million Norwegian kroner

		1970	1975	1977	1978	1979	1980	1981	1982	1983	1984	1985	1986
		At constant prices of:											
		1970	1975				1980						
1	General public services	1156	1474 / 2436	2740	2838	2800	2923 / 4196	4349	4509	4801	4993	5183	5486
2	Defence	2821	2952 / 4750	4769	4959	5137	5456 / 8026	9242	9297	9904	10017	10484	10662
3	Public order and safety	541	738 / 1220	1418	1458	1499	1551 / 2225	2365	2454	2526	2593	2650	2775
4	Education	3881	4812 / 7959	8888	9451	9000	10045 / 14372	14897	15697	16064	16442	17066	17765
5	Health	1927	3216 / 5331	6602	6965	7305	8069 / 11543	12131	12826	13802	14288	14663	14960

Norway

2.2 Government Final Consumption Expenditure by Function, in Constant Prices
(Continued)

Million Norwegian kroner

	1970	1975	1977	1978	1979	1980	1981	1982	1983	1984	1985	1986
				At constant prices of:								
		1970		1975					1980			
6 Social security and welfare	690	1273 2118	2543	2770	2971	3264 4668	5016	5285	5312	5319	5676	5793
7 Housing and community amenities	135	63 106	11	-8	-10	-11 -23	-195	-236	-268	-304	-354	-361
8 Recreational, cultural and religious affairs	367	510 827	992	1074	1114	1197 1707	1850	1962	2052	2107	2174	2255
9 Economic services	1944	2430 3884	4255	4490	4453	4540 6534	6798	6976	7349	7531	7552	7777
A Fuel and energy	15	37 61	76	103	124	62 89	110	133	110	-4	-29	62
B Agriculture, forestry, fishing and hunting	240	281 465	481	487	505	501 725	777	816	835	836	844	909
C Mining, manufacturing and construction, except fuel and energy	18	25 42	21	30	17	47 67	88	102	101	90	92	92
D Transportation and communication	1342	1557 2435	2653	2840	2765	2827 4069	4186	4241	4393	4504	4517	4580
E Other economic affairs	330	530 881	1023	1030	1043	1103 1584	1638	1684	1910	2105	2129	2134
10 Other functions	73	43 71	79	72	208	159 229	310	214	186	252	264	287
Total Government Final Consumption Expenditure	13533	17510 28702	32339	34068	35277	37191 53478	56763	58985	61727	63238	65358	67398

2.5 Private Final Consumption Expenditure by Type and Porpose, in Current Prices

Million Norwegian kroner

	1970	1975	1977	1978	1979	1980	1981	1982	1983	1984	1985	1986
Final Consumption Expenditure of Resident Households
1 Food, beverages and tobacco	13883	23175	28564	30478	32464	36201	41360	46420	50743	54932	61734	69816
A Food	10504	17304	21480	23115	24280	27285	31381	35744	38758	41858	46838	52869
B Non-alcoholic beverages	467	808	1045	1158	1246	1327	1377	1726	1824	2008	2309	2841
C Alcoholic beverages	1650	3146	3848	3782	4368	4826	5412	5393	6144	6629	7522	8200
D Tobacco	1261	1917	2191	2423	2570	2764	3190	3557	4017	4436	5064	5906
2 Clothing and footwear	4535	6940	9332	9751	10501	11934	12975	13950	14352	15802	19073	21969
3 Gross rent, fuel and power	6084	10844	14276	16544	18493	21271	24881	28769	32708	36611	41908	45900
A Fuel and power	1736	3022	4205	5165	6173	7406	8846	10285	11570	13114	15915	16856
B Other	4348	7823	10071	11379	12320	13864	16036	18484	21138	23497	25992	29045
4 Furniture, furnishings and household equipment and operation	3606	7155	9672	10069	10721	11878	13215	14099	15102	16507	19031	21866
A Household operation [a]	837	1840	2420	2633	2717	3069	3418	3672	4055	4398	4869	5444
B Other	2769	5315	7252	7437	8004	8810	9798	10428	11047	12110	14162	16421
5 Medical care and health expenses	1729	3504	4400	4906	5249	5676	6387	7407	8180	8586	9067	9846
6 Transport and communication	5036	10056	15635	15090	17353	20220	23086	26502	29188	31811	41435	47152
A Personal transport equipment	1715	3674	6559	5113	6419	7406	8089	9694	10393	11363	18293	21835
B Other	3321	6382	9076	9977	10934	12814	14997	16808	18795	20448	23143	25316
7 Recreational, entertainment, education and cultural services	3313	6575	9048	9612	10361	11626	13403	14488	15979	17572	20132	23411
A Education	233	415	522	528	557	647	618	695	775	850	942	1071
B Other	3080	6160	8525	9084	9803	10979	12785	13794	15204	16722	19190	22340
8 Miscellaneous goods and services	4257	7628	9984	10668	11478	12968	15174	17139	19511	21742	25048	28595
A Personal care	738	1422	1829	1939	2003	2335	2710	3112	3546	3987	4565	5392
B Expenditures in restaurants, cafes and hotels	1564	2992	3958	4240	4560	5150	6042	6960	8066	9147	10492	11738

Norway

2.5 Private Final Consumption Expenditure by Type and Porpose, in Current Prices
(Continued)

Million Norwegian kroner

	1970	1975	1977	1978	1979	1980	1981	1982	1983	1984	1985	1986
C Other	1955	3214	4198	4489	4915	5483	6421	7068	7899	8609	9991	11465
Total Final Consumption Expenditure in the Domestic Market by Households, of which	42442	75876	100910	107120	116620	131773	150481	168774	185762	203563	237427	268553
A Durable goods	4526	9444	14810	13422	15270	16932	18851	20809	22127	24495	33798	39912
B Semi-durable goods	6973	11795	16034	16670	18061	20766	23235	25163	26282	28800	34586	39738
C Non-durable goods	18537	31935	40533	44184	47917	54529	62683	70534	77533	84513	96113	107013
D Services	12406	22701	29534	32844	35373	39545	45713	52269	59820	65755	72930	81890
Plus: Direct purchases abroad by resident households	1849	3864	5780	6761	6986	7414	9411	11592	12535	13197	15894	19125
Less: Direct purchases in the domestic market by non-resident households	1245	2125	2775	3211	3501	3945	4687	5056	5319	5839	6994	7883
Equals: Final Consumption Expenditure of Resident Households [b]	43047	77615	103915	110670	120104	135242	155205	175310	192979	210921	246327	279796

Final Consumption Expenditure of Private Non-profit Institutions Serving Households

	1970	1975	1977	1978	1979	1980	1981	1982	1983	1984	1985	1986
Equals: Final Consumption Expenditure of Private Non-profit Organisations Serving Households	...	...	...	...	...	...	...	...	...	...	...	...
Private Final Consumption Expenditure	43047	77615	103915	110670	120104	135242	155205	175310	192979	210921	246327	279796

a) Item 'Household operations' also includes repair of furniture and household goods.
b) Item 'Final consumption expenditure of resident households' includes consumption expenditure of private non-profit institutions serving households.

2.6 Private Final Consumption Expenditure by Type and Purpose, in Constant Prices

Million Norwegian kroner

	1970	1975	1977	1978	1979	1980	1981	1982	1983	1984	1985	1986
At constant prices of:		1970		1975					1980			

Final Consumption Expenditure of Resident Households

	1970	1975	1977	1978	1979	1980	1981	1982	1983	1984	1985	1986
1 Food, beverages and tobacco	13883	15426 / 23175	24178	24030	24811	25746 / 36201	34998	34498	34741	35261	37399	38758
A Food	10504	11528 / 17304	18225	18441	18669	19291 / 27285	27057	27203	27313	27566	28968	29968
B Non-alcoholic beverages	467	530 / 808	888	938	993	987 / 1327	1195	1313	1320	1371	1487	1685
C Alcoholic beverages	1650	2105 / 3146	3172	2823	3219	3453 / 4826	4275	3752	3845	3961	4367	4384
D Tobacco	1261	1263 / 1917	1892	1829	1931	2016 / 2764	2472	2230	2263	2363	2577	2722
2 Clothing and footwear	4535	4713 / 6940	7837	7528	7688	7968 / 11934	11627	11585	11308	11776	13262	14061
3 Gross rent, fuel and power	6084	7375 / 10844	12144	12778	13353	13709 / 21271	21817	22420	23068	23855	25484	26711
A Fuel and power	1736	1894 / 3022	3411	3520	3761	3706 / 7406	7380	7354	7232	7434	8268	8566
B Other	4348	5482 / 7823	8733	9259	9593	10003 / 13864	14437	15066	15836	16422	17215	18146
4 Furniture, furnishings and household equipment and operation	3606	4615 / 7155	8255	8148	8242	8102 / 11878	11623	11246	11174	11649	12790	13663
A Household operation [a]	837	1020 / 1840	1996	2096	2036	2073 / 3069	3079	2972	3052	3122	3210	3329
B Other	2769	3595 / 5315	6260	6053	6206	6120 / 8810	8544	8274	8122	8527	9575	10334
5 Medical care and health expenses	1729	2204 / 3504	3742	3851	3983	3705 / 5676	5771	6126	6345	6271	6168	6228
6 Transport and communication	5036	6813 / 10056	13012	11533	12485	12997 / 20220	20662	21663	21857	22514	28312	30196
A Personal transport equipment	1715	2547 / 3674	5523	3845	4324	4765 / 7406	7708	8568	8290	8273	12418	12940

Norway

2.6 Private Final Consumption Expenditure by Type and Purpose, in Constant Prices
(Continued)

Million Norwegian kroner

	1970	1975	1977	1978	1979	1980	1981	1982	1983	1984	1985	1986
		1970			At constant prices of: 1975				1980			
B Other	3321	4266 / 6382	7490	7688	8162	8232 / 12814	12955	13095	13567	14241	15894	17256
7 Recreational, entertainment, education and cultural services	3313	4716 / 6575	7852	7954	8343	8705 / 11626	12428	12128	12505	13162	14416	15908
A Education	233	257 / 415	431	404	414	458 / 647	563	564	586	604	634	692
B Other	3080	4459 / 6160	7422	7550	7929	8247 / 10979	11865	11564	11919	12558	13782	15216
8 Miscellaneous goods and services	4257	4892 / 7628	8320	8123	8357	8505 / 12968	13154	13191	13568	14393	15503	16553
A Personal care	738	940 / 1422	1571	1569	1584	1675 / 2335	2372	2389	2468	2619	2825	3114
B Expenditures in restaurants, cafes and hotels	1564	1952 / 2992	3100	3021	3155	3331 / 5150	5005	4812	4979	5319	5785	5948
C Other	1955	2000 / 3214	3648	3533	3618	3498 / 5483	5777	5989	6121	6455	6893	7492
Total Final Consumption Expenditure in the Domestic Market by Households, of which	42442	50754 / 75876	85339	83946	87262	89527 / 131773	132081	132856	134566	138881	153335	162078
A Durable goods	4526	6772 / 9444	12855	10897	11547	11756 / 16932	17462	18019	17662	18438	23960	25532
B Semi-durable goods	6973	7936 / 11795	13466	13112	13452	14065 / 20766	20840	20813	20596	21499	24428	26163
C Non-durable goods	18537	21065 / 31935	34201	34261	35514	36500 / 54529	53342	52988	53402	54372	58279	61056
D Services	12406	14982 / 22701	24818	25676	26748	27206 / 39545	40437	41036	42906	44572	46668	49327
Plus: Direct purchases abroad by resident households	1849	2736 / 3864	5030	5155	4723	4596 / 7414	8829	10159	10385	10036	11130	12315
Less: Direct purchases in the domestic market by non-resident households	1245	1421 / 2125	2330	2495	2595	2635 / 3945	4126	3816	3648	3778	4294	4530
Equals: Final Consumption Expenditure of Resident Households b	43047	52069 / 77615	88039	86606	89389	91488 / 135242	136784	139199	141303	145139	160171	169862

Final Consumption Expenditure of Private Non-profit Institutions Serving Households

Equals: Final Consumption Expenditure of Private Non-profit Organisations Serving Households		... / ...	...	...	...	... / ...	...	...	...	...	...	...
Private Final Consumption Expenditure	43047	52069 / 77615	88039	86606	89389	91488 / 135242	136784	139199	141303	145139	160171	169862

a) Item 'Household operations' also includes repair of furniture and household goods.
b) Item 'Final consumption expenditure of resident households' includes consumption expenditure of private non-profit institutions serving households.

2.7 Gross Capital Formation by Type of Good and Owner, in Current Prices

Million Norwegian kroner

	1980				1981				1982			
	TOTAL	Total Private	Public Enterprises	General Government	TOTAL	Total Private	Public Enterprises	General Government	TOTAL	Total Private	Public Enterprises	General Government
Increase in stocks, total	8104	8104	...	...	-7761	-7761	...	...	3809	3809	...	...
1 Goods producing industries	6369	6369	...	...	-4282	-4282	...	...	4231	4231	...	...
A Materials and supplies	...	...	...	...	...	...	...	...	...	...	...	...
B Work in progress a	6284	6284	...	...	-4191	-4191	...	...	4278	4278	...	...
C Livestock, except breeding stocks, dairy cattle, etc. b	85	85	...	...	-91	-91	...	...	-47	-47	...	...

Norway

2.7 Gross Capital Formation by Type of Good and Owner, in Current Prices
(Continued)

Million Norwegian kroner

	1980				1981				1982			
	TOTAL	Total Private	Public Enterprises	General Government	TOTAL	Total Private	Public Enterprises	General Government	TOTAL	Total Private	Public Enterprises	General Government
D Finished goods	...	...	...	...	...	...	...	...	...	...	...	...
2 Wholesale and retail trade	...	...	...	...	...	...	...	...	...	...	...	...
3 Other, except government stocks	1735	1735	...	...	-3479	-3479	...	...	-422	-422	...	...
4 Government stocks	...	...	...	...	...	...	...	...	...	...	...	...
Gross Fixed Capital Formation, Total	70798	59344	...	11454	91793	80190	...	11602	92262	80737	...	11525
1 Residential buildings c	13535	13489	...	46	15055	14986	...	69	17465	17693	...	-228
2 Non-residential buildings	14482	9405	...	5078	16138	10985	...	5153	16289	10949	...	5340
3 Other construction d	17146	12482	...	4665	28536	23968	...	4568	23775	19308	...	4467
4 Land improvement and plantation and orchard development	536	536	...	...	576	576	...	...	605	605	...	...
5 Producers' durable goods	24978	23312	...	1666	31412	29600	...	1812	34176	32230	...	1946
A Transport equipment	7359	7179	...	179	12341	11876	...	465	15043	14838	...	205
Passenger cars e	1585	1547	...	38	2305	1987	...	318	2369	2325	...	44
Other	5774	5633	...	142	10036	9890	...	147	12673	12513	...	161
B Machinery and equipment	17620	16133	...	1487	19071	17724	...	1347	19133	17392	...	1741
6 Breeding stock, dairy cattle, etc.	120	120	...	...	76	76	...	...	-46	-46	...	...
Total Gross Capital Formation	78902	67448	...	11454	84032	72429	...	11602	96071	84546	...	11525

	1983				1984				1985			
	TOTAL	Total Private	Public Enterprises	General Government	TOTAL	Total Private	Public Enterprises	General Government	TOTAL	Total Private	Public Enterprises	General Government
Increase in stocks, total	-4332	-4332	...	...	-1300	-1300	...	...	12675	12675	...	...
1 Goods producing industries	2116	2116	...	...	-2613	-2613	...	...	11101	11101	...	...
A Materials and supplies	...	...	...	...	...	...	...	...	...	...	...	...
B Work in progress a	2112	2112	...	...	-2649	-2649	...	...	11076	11076	...	...
C Livestock, except breeding stocks, dairy cattle, etc. b	4	4	...	...	36	36	...	...	25	25	...	...
D Finished goods	...	...	...	...	...	...	...	...	...	...	...	...
2 Wholesale and retail trade	...	...	...	...	...	...	...	...	...	...	...	...
3 Other, except government stocks	-6448	-6448	...	...	1313	1313	...	...	1574	1574	...	...
4 Government stocks	...	...	...	...	...	...	...	...	...	...	...	...
Gross Fixed Capital Formation, Total	103448	91037	...	12410	117567	104709	...	12858	108934	95645	...	13290
1 Residential buildings c	18526	19035	...	-509	19171	19636	...	-465	20431	21212	...	-781
2 Non-residential buildings	17047	11158	...	5889	17918	12098	...	5820	21150	15418	...	5732
3 Other construction d	35608	30689	...	4919	45579	40410	...	5169	33005	27504	...	5501
4 Land improvement and plantation and orchard development	567	567	...	...	527	527	...	...	457	457	...	...
5 Producers' durable goods	31700	29589	...	2111	34406	32071	...	2335	33973	31135	...	2838
A Transport equipment	13150	12932	...	219	11725	11484	...	241	8187	7929	...	258
Passenger cars e	2535	2483	...	52	2521	2467	...	54	3720	3651	...	69
Other	10615	10449	...	166	9204	9017	...	187	4467	4278	...	190
B Machinery and equipment	18550	16657	...	1893	22681	20587	...	2094	25786	23207	...	2579
6 Breeding stock, dairy cattle, etc.	...	...	...	...	-34	-34	...	...	-81	-81	...	...
Total Gross Capital Formation	99116	86705	...	12410	116267	103409	...	12858	121609	108320	...	13290

	1986			
	TOTAL	Total Private	Public Enterprises	General Government
Increase in stocks, total	9589	9589	...	...
1 Goods producing industries	-3415	-3415	...	...
A Materials and supplies	...	...	...	...
B Work in progress a	-3470	-3470	...	...
C Livestock, except breeding stocks, dairy cattle, etc. b	55	55	...	...

Norway

2.7 Gross Capital Formation by Type of Good and Owner, in Current Prices
(Continued)

Million Norwegian kroner

	\multicolumn{4}{c}{1986}
	TOTAL	Total Private	Public Enterprises	General Government
D Finished goods	...	...	...	...
2 Wholesale and retail trade	...	...	...	...
3 Other, except government stocks	13004	13004	...	...
4 Government stocks	...	...	...	...
Gross Fixed Capital Formation, Total	142154	126076	...	16078
1 Residential buildings c	24381	25039	...	-658
2 Non-residential buildings	26504	19215	...	7289
3 Other construction d	51177	44922	...	6255
4 Land improvement and plantation and orchard development	444	444	...	...
5 Producers' durable goods	39809	36617	...	3192
A Transport equipment	10371	10063	...	309
Passenger cars e	5408	5327	...	81
Other	4964	4736	...	228
B Machinery and equipment	29438	26555	...	2883
6 Breeding stock, dairy cattle, etc.	-161	-161	...	...
Total Gross Capital Formation	151743	135665	...	16078

a) Item 'Work in progress' includes work in progress in mining and manufacturing, ships, oil drilling and oil production platforms.
b) Item 'Livestock except breeding stocks, dairy cattles etc.' includes increase in stocks of fodder, timber and firewood.
c) Item 'Residential buildings' includes also summer cottages, temporary dwellings, logging camps, fishermens' quarters etc..
d) The estimates of 'Other construction' include oil drilling rigs, oil production platforms etc., pipelines for gas, oil and gas exploration and drilling.
e) Item 'Passenger cars' includes station wagons.

2.8 Gross Capital Formation by Type of Good and Owner, in Constant Prices

Million Norwegian kroner

	\multicolumn{4}{c}{1980}	\multicolumn{4}{c}{1981}	\multicolumn{4}{c}{1982}
	TOTAL	Total Private	Public Enterprises	General Government	TOTAL	Total Private	Public Enterprises	General Government	TOTAL	Total Private	Public Enterprises	General Government
	\multicolumn{12}{c}{At constant prices of: 1980}
Increase in stocks, total	8104	8104	...	...	-7024	-7024	...	...	3041	3041	...	...
1 Goods producing industries	6369	6369	...	...	-3875	-3875	...	...	3431	3431	...	...
A Materials and supplies	...	...	...	...	...	...	...	...	...	...	...	...
B Work in progress a	6284	6284	...	...	-3796	-3796	...	...	3470	3470	...	...
C Livestock, except breeding stocks, dairy cattle, etc. b	85	85	...	...	-79	-79	...	...	-39	-39	...	...
D Finished goods	...	...	...	...	...	...	...	...	...	...	...	...
2 Wholesale and retail trade	...	...	...	...	...	...	...	...	...	...	...	...
3 Other, except government stocks	1735	1735	...	...	-3149	-3149	...	...	-390	-390	...	...
4 Government stocks	...	...	...	...	...	...	...	...	...	...	...	...
Gross Fixed Capital Formation, Total	70798	59344	...	11454	83485	72717	...	10769	74296	64384	...	9913
1 Residential buildings c	13535	13489	...	46	13695	13631	...	64	14533	14717	...	-184
2 Non-residential buildings	14482	9405	...	5078	14975	10227	...	4748	14016	9477	...	4538
3 Other construction d	17146	12482	...	4665	24761	20542	...	4218	17356	13605	...	3751
4 Land improvement and plantation and orchard development	536	536	...	...	529	529	...	...	505	505	...	...
5 Producers' durable goods	24978	23312	...	1666	29458	27720	...	1738	27926	26118	...	1808
A Transport equipment	7359	7179	...	179	11085	10653	...	432	10491	10309	...	182
Passenger cars e	1585	1547	...	38	2137	1843	...	295	1625	1593	...	32
Other	5774	5633	...	142	8948	8811	...	137	8866	8716	...	150
B Machinery and equipment	17620	16133	...	1487	18373	17066	...	1306	17435	15809	...	1626
6 Breeding stock, dairy cattle, etc.	120	120	...	...	68	68	...	...	-39	-39	...	...
Total Gross Capital Formation	78902	67448	...	11454	76461	65693	...	10769	77337	67425	...	9913

Norway

2.8 Gross Capital Formation by Type of Good and Owner, in Constant Prices

Million Norwegian kroner

	1983				1984				1985			
	TOTAL	Total Private	Public Enterprises	General Government	TOTAL	Total Private	Public Enterprises	General Government	TOTAL	Total Private	Public Enterprises	General Government
	At constant prices of:1980										
Increase in stocks, total	-3109	-3109	...	...	-51	-51	...	...	10158	10158	...	...
1 Goods producing industries	1806	1806	...	...	-1724	-1724	...	...	7336	7336	...	...
A Materials and supplies	...	...	...	...	...	...	...	...	...	...	...	...
B Work in progress [a]	1802	1802	...	...	-1755	-1755	...	...	7315	7315	...	...
C Livestock, except breeding stocks, dairy cattle, etc. [b]	4	4	...	...	31	31	...	...	21	21	...	...
D Finished goods	...	...	...	...	...	...	...	...	...	...	...	...
2 Wholesale and retail trade	...	...	...	...	...	...	...	...	...	...	...	...
3 Other, except government stocks	-4915	-4915	...	...	1673	1673	...	...	2822	2822	...	...
4 Government stocks	...	...	...	...	...	...	...	...	...	...	...	...
Gross Fixed Capital Formation, Total	78618	68194	...	10425	87224	76553	...	10671	68883	58606	...	10277
1 Residential buildings [c]	14420	14829	...	-410	14255	14621	...	-365	14472	15049	...	-577
2 Non-residential buildings	13897	9195	...	4702	14068	9597	...	4470	15679	11581	...	4097
3 Other construction [d]	25911	21885	...	4027	31211	27198	...	4014	21737	17744	...	3993
4 Land improvement and plantation and orchard development	455	455	...	...	408	408	...	...	331	331	...	...
5 Producers' durable goods	23928	21822	...	2105	27311	24759	...	2552	16732	13969	...	2763
A Transport equipment	6581	6406	...	176	4110	3929	...	182	-6694	-6865	...	171
Passenger cars [e]	1477	1444	...	33	1478	1445	...	34	1986	1948	...	38
Other	5104	4961	...	143	2632	2484	...	148	-8679	-8813	...	133
B Machinery and equipment	17347	15417	...	1930	23201	20830	...	2371	23425	20833	...	2592
6 Breeding stock, dairy cattle, etc.	8	8	...	...	-29	-29	...	...	-67	-67	...	...
Total Gross Capital Formation	75509	65085	...	10425	87173	76502	...	10671	79041	68764	...	10277

	1986			
	TOTAL	Total Private	Public Enterprises	General Government
	At constant prices of:1980			
Increase in stocks, total	7182	7182	...	...
1 Goods producing industries	-1872	-1872	...	...
A Materials and supplies	...	...	...	...
B Work in progress [a]	-1910	-1910	...	...
C Livestock, except breeding stocks, dairy cattle, etc. [b]	38	38	...	...
D Finished goods	...	...	...	...
2 Wholesale and retail trade	...	...	...	...
3 Other, except government stocks	9053	9053	...	...
4 Government stocks	...	...	...	...
Gross Fixed Capital Formation, Total	87452	75520	...	11933
1 Residential buildings [c]	15962	16417	...	-456
2 Non-residential buildings	18349	13423	...	4926
3 Other construction [d]	32188	27867	...	4320
4 Land improvement and plantation and orchard development	303	303	...	...
5 Producers' durable goods	20792	17650	...	3143
A Transport equipment	-5941	-6123	...	182
Passenger cars [e]	2177	2142	...	35
Other	-8118	-8265	...	147
B Machinery and equipment	26733	23772	...	2961
6 Breeding stock, dairy cattle, etc.	-141	-141	...	...
Total Gross Capital Formation	94634	82702	...	11933

a) Item 'Work in progress' includes work in progress in mining and manufacturing, ships, oil drilling and oil production platforms.
b) Item 'Livestock except breeding stocks, dairy cattles etc.' includes increase in stocks of fodder, timber and firewood.
c) Item 'Residential buildings' includes also summer cottages, temporary dwellings, logging camps, fishermens' quarters etc..
d) The estimates of 'Other construction' include oil drilling rigs, oil production platforms etc., pipelines for gas, oil and gas exploration and drilling.
e) Item 'Passenger cars' includes station wagons.

Norway

2.11 Gross Fixed Capital Formation by Kind of Activity of Owner, ISIC Divisions, in Current Prices

Million Norwegian kroner

	1970	1975	1977	1978	1979	1980	1981	1982	1983	1984	1985	1986
					All Producers							
1 Agriculture, hunting, forestry and fishing	1398	2943	4656	5216	4882	5795	6258	5897	5186	5359	6165	6686
A Agriculture and hunting	973	2121	3556	3689	3717	4812	5156	4776	3955	3867	4412	4345
B Forestry and logging	131	231	269	310	317	326	369	361	386	415	450	471
C Fishing	294	591	830	1218	848	657	733	760	845	1077	1303	1870
2 Mining and quarrying	518	4381	11053	8531	6964	6833	18343	11578	15401	28388	20111	36516
A Coal mining	7	30	74	56	29	41	111	19	22	34	45	66
B Crude petroleum and natural gas production	313	4069	10696	8184	6594	6360	17696	11145	15042	28039	19705	36018
C Metal ore mining	72	161	124	94	128	205	300	200	136	119	109	192
D Other mining	126	121	159	196	213	226	237	215	201	195	253	240
3 Manufacturing	3234	6650	8778	8343	7331	9031	10855	9105	8258	9311	11978	17057
A Manufacturing of food, beverages and tobacco	613	879	1282	1451	1580	1593	1946	1897	1880	1970	2055	2549
B Textile, wearing apparel and leather industries	99	110	212	239	237	282	222	217	126	142	190	242
C Manufacture of wood, and wood products, including furniture	246	465	657	590	594	584	782	676	724	761	710	854
D Manufacture of paper and paper products, printing and publishing	383	886	1029	1276	1270	2155	2039	970	980	1304	1550	2217
E Manufacture of chemicals and chemical petroleum, coal, rubber and plastic products	414	1591	2364	1688	745	962	1177	1235	1150	1208	1835	3791
F Manufacture of non-metalic mineral products except products of petroleum and coal	141	235	380	452	335	350	492	517	288	401	606	776
G Basic metal industries	594	824	890	773	768	1181	1939	1511	967	1287	2108	3076
H Manufacture of fabricated metal products, machinery and equipment	730	1636	1909	1820	1758	1870	2189	2056	2103	2207	2864	3480
I Other manufacturing industries	15	25	56	54	43	55	68	24	40	32	60	72
4 Electricity, gas and water	1726	3267	4944	6013	6321	7000	7721	7960	8073	8266	8079	7843
A Electricity, gas and steam	1567	2877	4442	5392	5694	6380	7130	7353	7469	7665	7541	7220
B Water works and supply	159	390	502	622	627	620	591	608	604	601	538	623
5 Construction [a]	431	1789	3112	2405	1628	1588	1549	3165	3312	2382	3044	4185
6 Wholesale and retail trade, restaurants and hotels [b]	967	1976	2903	3056	3090	3285	3770	4141	4467	4464	5790	7351
A Wholesale and retail trade	922	1895	2798	2938	2966	3152	3618	3972	4286	4283	5563	7083
B Restaurants and hotels	44	82	105	119	125	133	152	169	181	181	227	268
7 Transport, storage and communication [c]	4351	11954	12560	8065	9043	7696	11595	15090	20250	18191	8318	8030
A Transport and storage	3912	10531	10507	5630	6382	4910	8720	11841	16709	14413	4183	3855
B Communication	439	1423	2053	2436	2661	2785	2875	3249	3541	3778	4136	4176
8 Finance, insurance, real estate and business services [d]	4619	10029	12661	14341	15540	16952	18732	22293	24437	26611	30191	36243
A Financial institutions	250	490	600	760	1061	1299	1926	1341	2359	2840	3583	3458
B Insurance	...	...	...	...	...	...	...	...	...	...	...	...
C Real estate and business services	4369	9538	12061	13582	14479	15653	16806	20952	22077	23770	26608	32785
Real estate except dwellings	430	1418	1765	1847	1973	2169	1825	3264	3047	4139	5400	7751
Dwellings	3939	8120	10296	11735	12506	13484	14981	17688	19030	19631	21208	25034
9 Community, social and personal services [e]	374	682	1085	998	1043	1166	1369	1509	1654	1737	1968	2165
Total Industries	17617	43670	61752	56969	55843	59344	80190	80737	91037	104709	95645	126076
Producers of Government Services	3578	7121	9322	10737	10343	11454	11602	11525	12410	12858	13290	16078
Private Non-Profit Institutions Serving Households	...	...	...	...	...	...	...	...	...	...	...	...
Total	21195	50791	71074	67706	66186	70798	91792	92262	103447	117567	108935	142154

a) Item 'Construction' also includes oil and natural gas exploration and drilling.
b) Item 'Wholesale and retail trade, restaurants and hotels' includes producers' durable goods, otherwise included in real estate.
c) Item 'Transport, storage and communication' includes pipeline transport for crude oil and natural gas.
d) Business services are included in item 'Community, social and personal services'.
e) Item 'Community, social and personal services' includes other private and business services but excludes commercial buildings.

Norway

2.12 Gross Fixed Capital Formation by Kind of Activity of Owner, ISIC Divisions, in Constant Prices

Million Norwegian kroner

	1970	1975	1977	1978	1979	1980	1981	1982	1983	1984	1985	1986
At constant prices of:	1970		1975						1980			

All Producers

1 Agriculture, hunting, forestry and fishing	1398	1953 / 2943	3848	4080	3562	3791 / 5795	5781	5042	4176	4181	4380	4465
A Agriculture and hunting	973	1377 / 2121	2860	2736	2688	3133 / 4812	4774	4126	3183	2991	3178	2885
B Forestry and logging	131	154 / 231	223	239	236	222 / 326	340	309	312	320	326	320
C Fishing	294	423 / 591	765	1104	638	437 / 657	667	608	681	869	876	1261
2 Mining and quarrying	518	2881 / 4381	9286	6659	5113	4275 / 6833	15334	7334	10522	19408	12877	22725
A Coal mining	7	21 / 30	64	47	24	33 / 41	103	16	18	28	33	48
B Crude petroleum and natural gas production	313	2668 / 4069	8989	6383	4822	3935 / 6360	14719	6954	10217	19082	12550	22334
C Metal ore mining	72	109 / 161	103	77	102	146 / 205	286	175	115	114	89	160
D Other mining	126	84 / 121	131	152	164	161 / 226	227	189	172	184	205	183
3 Manufacturing	3234	4603 / 6650	7397	6635	5858	6573 / 9031	10330	7997	7087	8718	9895	13581
A Manufacturing of food, beverages and tobacco	613	607 / 879	1079	1159	1267	1169 / 1593	1843	1659	1598	1801	1689	2034
B Textile, wearing apparel and leather industries	99	77 / 110	179	189	189	206 / 282	212	191	109	134	153	189
C Manufacture of wood, and wood products, including furniture	246	320 / 465	553	475	474	430 / 584	743	592	624	700	581	684
D Manufacture of paper and paper products, printing and publishing	383	621 / 886	866	1000	1011	1538 / 2155	1950	856	848	1254	1299	1805
E Manufacture of chemicals and chemical petroleum, coal, rubber and plastic products	414	1092 / 1591	1993	1353	593	691 / 962	1124	1086	996	1132	1488	2872
F Manufacture of non-metalic mineral products except products of petroleum and coal	141	162 / 235	319	359	265	256 / 350	469	453	249	371	494	610
G Basic metal industries	594	573 / 824	750	606	607	868 / 1181	1842	1334	831	1202	1731	2502
H Manufacture of fabricated metal products, machinery and equipment	730	1134 / 1636	1613	1452	1418	1372 / 1870	2082	1806	1799	2092	2410	2827
I Other manufacturing industries	15	17 / 25	47	44	35	42 / 55	64	21	34	32	51	58
4 Electricity, gas and water	1726	2111 / 3267	4246	4846	4816	4909 / 7000	7264	6917	6724	6581	6104	5556
A Electricity, gas and steam	1567	1861 / 2877	3814	4337	4327	4466 / 6380	6718	6406	6231	6118	5708	5108
B Water works and supply	159	250 / 390	432	509	489	443 / 620	547	511	493	463	396	448

Norway

2.12 Gross Fixed Capital Formation by Kind of Activity of Owner, ISIC Divisions, in Constant Prices
(Continued)

Million Norwegian kroner

	1970	1975	1977	1978	1979	1980	1981	1982	1983	1984	1985	1986
					At constant prices of:							
		1970			1975				1980			
5 Construction [a]	431	1167				1024						
		1789	2473	1714	1042	1588	1460	2453	2179	1756	2125	2485
6 Wholesale and retail trade, restaurants and hotels [b]	967	1503				2323						
		1976	2545	2238	2188	3285	3612	3604	3836	4022	4504	5257
A Wholesale and retail trade	922	1439				2225						
		1895	2446	2152	2100	3152	3467	3464	3684	3853	4323	5057
B Restaurants and hotels	44	65				98						
		82	99	87	88	133	145	140	152	169	181	200
7 Transport, storage and communication [c]	4351	5942				4630						
		11954	8819	4625	5772	7696	10460	10894	12575	9410	-5382	-5440
A Transport and storage	3912	4866				2589						
		10531	7009	2649	3662	4910	7701	7931	9258	5733	-9072	-9164
B Communication	439	1076				2040						
		1423	1810	1976	2109	2785	2760	2963	3317	3676	3690	3724
8 Finance, insurance, real estate and business services [d]	4619	6580				11833						
		10029	10588	11447	11932	16952	17152	18755	19459	20580	22215	24802
A Financial institutions	250	362				941						
		490	523	611	831	1299	1805	1179	2068	2610	3055	2896
B Insurance	...	...	...	...	...	...	...	...	...	...	...	...
		...				...						
C Real estate and business services	4369	6219				10893						
		9538	10065	10836	11101	15653	15347	17576	17391	17971	19160	21906
Real estate except dwellings	430	920				1553						
		1418	1505	1500	1544	2169	1721	2863	2566	3354	4114	5492
Dwellings	3939	5299				9340						
		8120	8560	9336	9557	13484	13626	14713	14825	14617	15046	16414
9 Community, social and personal services [e]	374	581				873						
		682	978	785	813	1166	1324	1388	1635	1898	1889	2089
Total Industries	17617	27321				40231						
		43670	50179	43029	41096	59344	72717	64384	68194	76553	58606	75520
Producers of Government Services	3578	4944				7950						
		7121	7789	8443	7817	11454	10769	9913	10425	10671	10277	11933
Private Non-Profit Institutions Serving Households	...	...	...	...	...	...	...	...	...	...	...	...
		...				...						
Total	21195	32265				48181						
		50791	57968	51472	48913	70798	83486	74297	78619	87224	68883	87453

a) Item 'Construction' also includes oil and natural gas exploration and drilling.
b) Item 'Wholesale and retail trade, restaurants and hotels' includes producers' durable goods, otherwise included in real estate.
c) Item 'Transport, storage and communication' includes pipeline transport for crude oil and natural gas.
d) Business services are included in item 'Community, social and personal services'.
e) Item 'Community, social and personal services' includes other private and business services but excludes commercial buildings.

Norway

2.13 Stocks of Reproducible Fixed Assets, by Type of Good and Owner, in Current Prices

Million Norwegian kroner

	TOTAL Gross	TOTAL Net	Total Private Gross	Total Private Net	Public Enterprises Gross	Public Enterprises Net	General Government Gross	General Government Net
1980								
1 Residential buildings a	...	238433	...	238433	...	...	...	...
2 Non-residential buildings	...	223155	...	142440	...	...	...	80715
3 Other construction b	...	282185	...	173976	...	...	...	108210
4 Land improvement and plantation and orchard development	...	42776	...	42776	...	...	...	...
5 Producers' durable goods	...	220515	...	210060	...	...	...	10455
A Transport equipment	...	91841	...	91169	...	...	...	672
Passenger cars c	...	5450	...	5346	...	...	...	103
Other	...	86391	...	85822	...	...	...	569
B Machinery and equipment	...	128674	...	118891	...	...	...	9783
6 Breeding stock, dairy cattle, etc.	...	3933	...	3933	...	...	...	...
Total	...	1011000	...	811618	...	...	...	199380
1981								
1 Residential buildings a	...	269938	...	269938	...	...	...	...
2 Non-residential buildings	...	251193	...	159925	...	...	...	91269
3 Other construction b	...	329514	...	207611	...	...	...	121903
4 Land improvement and plantation and orchard development	...	53235	...	53235	...	...	...	...
5 Producers' durable goods	...	240516	...	228994	...	...	...	11523
A Transport equipment	...	99868	...	98930	...	...	...	933
Passenger cars c	...	5872	...	5536	...	...	...	336
Other	...	93996	...	93399	...	...	...	597
B Machinery and equipment	...	140648	...	130058	...	...	...	10590
6 Breeding stock, dairy cattle, etc.	...	4435	...	4435	...	...	...	...
Total	...	1148830	...	924138	...	...	...	224695
1982								
1 Residential buildings a	...	314114	...	314114	...	...	...	...
2 Non-residential buildings	...	281116	...	179022	...	...	...	102094
3 Other construction b	...	379268	...	240741	...	...	...	136527
4 Land improvement and plantation and orchard development	...	56426	...	56426	...	...	...	...
5 Producers' durable goods	...	263458	...	250716	...	...	...	12742
A Transport equipment	...	108076	...	107110	...	...	...	966
Passenger cars c	...	7129	...	6771	...	...	...	358
Other	...	100947	...	100339	...	...	...	608
B Machinery and equipment	...	155382	...	143606	...	...	...	11776
6 Breeding stock, dairy cattle, etc.	...	4432	...	4432	...	...	...	...
Total	...	1298810	...	1045450	...	...	...	253363
1983								
1 Residential buildings a	...	346259	...	346259	...	...	...	...
2 Non-residential buildings	...	306603	...	194132	...	...	...	112471
3 Other construction b	...	407193	...	260251	...	...	...	146942
4 Land improvement and plantation and orchard development	...	53205	...	53205	...	...	...	...
5 Producers' durable goods	...	274326	...	261640	...	...	...	12686
A Transport equipment	...	114360	...	113398	...	...	...	962
Passenger cars c	...	7582	...	7244	...	...	...	339
Other	...	106778	...	106154	...	...	...	624
B Machinery and equipment	...	159966	...	148242	...	...	...	11723
6 Breeding stock, dairy cattle, etc.	...	4315	...	4315	...	...	...	...
Total	...	1391900	...	1119800	...	...	...	272099

Norway

2.13 Stocks of Reproducible Fixed Assets, by Type of Good and Owner, in Current Prices
(Continued)

Million Norwegian kroner

	TOTAL Gross	TOTAL Net	Total Private Gross	Total Private Net	Public Enterprises Gross	Public Enterprises Net	General Government Gross	General Government Net
1984								
1 Residential buildings a	...	376232	...	376232	...	...	...	...
2 Non-residential buildings	...	328853	...	208523	...	...	...	120330
3 Other construction b	...	458266	...	298404	...	...	...	159862
4 Land improvement and plantation and orchard development	...	62893	...	62893	...	...	...	...
5 Producers' durable goods	...	257221	...	244587	...	...	...	12634
A Transport equipment	...	101040	...	100108	...	...	...	933
Passenger cars c	...	7313	...	7038	...	...	...	275
Other	...	93728	...	93070	...	...	...	657
B Machinery and equipment	...	156181	...	144479	...	...	...	11701
6 Breeding stock, dairy cattle, etc.	...	4663	...	4663	...	...	...	...
Total	...	1488130	...	1195300	...	...	...	292826
1985								
1 Residential buildings a	...	409896	...	409896	...	...	...	...
2 Non-residential buildings	...	361195	...	228793	...	...	...	132402
3 Other construction b	...	498728	...	322012	...	...	...	176716
4 Land improvement and plantation and orchard development	...	66511	...	66511	...	...	...	...
5 Producers' durable goods	...	262352	...	246826	...	...	...	15525
A Transport equipment	...	77190	...	76252	...	...	...	938
Passenger cars c	...	8659	...	8424	...	...	...	235
Other	...	68531	...	67828	...	...	...	703
B Machinery and equipment	...	185161	...	170574	...	...	...	14587
6 Breeding stock, dairy cattle, etc.	...	5195	...	5195	...	...	...	...
Total	...	1603880	...	1279230	...	...	...	324644
1986								
1 Residential buildings a	...	461533	...	461533	...	...	...	...
2 Non-residential buildings	...	401588	...	257787	...	...	...	143801
3 Other construction b	...	550994	...	358943	...	...	...	192051
4 Land improvement and plantation and orchard development	...	68120	...	68120	...	...	...	...
5 Producers' durable goods	...	260059	...	243233	...	...	...	16826
A Transport equipment	...	59370	...	58426	...	...	...	943
Passenger cars c	...	12135	...	11932	...	...	...	203
Other	...	47234	...	46494	...	...	...	740
B Machinery and equipment	...	200689	...	184806	...	...	...	15883
6 Breeding stock, dairy cattle, etc.	...	5343	...	5343	...	...	...	...
Total	...	1747640	...	1394960	...	...	...	352678

a) Item 'Residential buildings' includes also summer cottages, temporary dwellings, logging camps, fishermens' quarters etc..
b) The estimates of 'Other construction' include oil drilling rigs, oil production platforms etc., pipelines for gas, oil and gas exploration and drilling.
c) Item 'Passenger cars' includes station wagons.

Norway

2.14 Stocks of Reproducible Fixed Assets, by Type of Good and Owner, in Constant Prices

Million Norwegian kroner

		TOTAL Gross	TOTAL Net	Total Private Gross	Total Private Net	Public Enterprises Gross	Public Enterprises Net	General Government Gross	General Government Net
					At constant prices of:1980				
					1980				
1	Residential buildings a	...	238433	...	238433	...	...	...	...
2	Non-residential buildings	...	223155	...	142440	...	...	...	80715
3	Other construction b	...	282185	...	173976	...	...	...	108210
4	Land improvement and plantation and orchard development	...	42776	...	42776	...	...	...	...
5	Producers' durable goods	...	220515	...	210060	...	...	...	10455
	A Transport equipment	...	91841	...	91169	...	...	...	672
	Passenger cars c	...	5450	...	5346	...	...	...	103
	Other	...	86391	...	85822	...	...	...	569
	B Machinery and equipment	...	128674	...	118891	...	...	...	9783
6	Breeding stock, dairy cattle, etc.	...	3933	...	3933	...	...	...	...
	Total d	...	1011000	...	811618	...	...	...	199380
					1981				
1	Residential buildings a	...	248271	...	248271	...	...	...	...
2	Non-residential buildings	...	233001	...	148901	...	...	...	84100
3	Other construction b	...	298082	...	185521	...	...	...	112561
4	Land improvement and plantation and orchard development	...	43234	...	43234	...	...	...	...
5	Producers' durable goods	...	224500	...	213428	...	...	...	11132
	A Transport equipment	...	89187	...	88326	...	...	...	861
	Passenger cars c	...	5482	...	5170	...	...	...	311
	Other	...	83705	...	83155	...	...	...	550
	B Machinery and equipment	...	135374	...	125102	...	...	...	10271
6	Breeding stock, dairy cattle, etc.	...	3967	...	3967	...	...	...	...
	Total d	...	1051120	...	843322	...	...	...	207793
					1982				
1	Residential buildings a	...	259043	...	259043	...	...	...	...
2	Non-residential buildings	...	241452	...	154474	...	...	...	86978
3	Other construction b	...	305862	...	189550	...	...	...	116312
4	Land improvement and plantation and orchard development	...	43713	...	43713	...	...	...	...
5	Producers' durable goods	...	226779	...	214976	...	...	...	11803
	A Transport equipment	...	86181	...	85378	...	...	...	803
	Passenger cars c	...	5139	...	4879	...	...	...	260
	Other	...	81042	...	80499	...	...	...	543
	B Machinery and equipment	...	140599	...	120608	...	...	...	11000
6	Breeding stock, dairy cattle, etc.	...	3955	...	3955	...	...	...	...
	Total d	...	1080800	...	865711	...	...	...	215093
					1983				
1	Residential buildings a	...	269773	...	269773	...	...	...	...
2	Non-residential buildings	...	249250	...	159513	...	...	...	89737
3	Other construction b	...	321208	...	200870	...	...	...	120338
4	Land improvement and plantation and orchard development	...	44171	...	44171	...	...	...	...
5	Producers' durable goods	...	224982	...	212284	...	...	...	12698
	A Transport equipment	...	79745	...	79001	...	...	...	744
	Passenger cars c	...	4737	...	4524	...	...	...	214
	Other	...	75008	...	74477	...	...	...	531
	B Machinery and equipment	...	145237	...	133283	...	...	...	11954
6	Breeding stock, dairy cattle, etc.	...	4088	...	4088	...	...	...	...
	Total d	...	1113470	...	890699	...	...	...	222773

Norway

2.14 Stocks of Reproducible Fixed Assets, by Type of Good and Owner, in Constant Prices
(Continued)

Million Norwegian kroner

	TOTAL Gross	TOTAL Net	Total Private Gross	Total Private Net	Public Enterprises Gross	Public Enterprises Net	General Government Gross	General Government Net
At constant prices of: 1980								
1984								
1 Residential buildings a	...	280143	...	280143	...	...	...	...
2 Non-residential buildings	...	256740	...	164484	...	...	...	92256
3 Other construction b	...	341014	...	216662	...	...	...	124352
4 Land improvement and plantation and orchard development	...	44518	...	44518	...	...	...	...
5 Producers' durable goods	...	226274	...	212329	...	...	...	13945
A Transport equipment	...	71580	...	70885	...	...	...	695
Passenger cars c	...	4512	...	4341	...	...	...	170
Other	...	67068	...	66544	...	...	...	524
B Machinery and equipment	...	154694	...	141444	...	...	...	13250
6 Breeding stock, dairy cattle, etc.	...	4253	...	4253	...	...	...	...
Total d	...	1152940	...	922389	...	...	...	230553
1985								
1 Residential buildings a	...	290785	...	290785	...	...	...	...
2 Non-residential buildings	...	264981	...	170837	...	...	...	94144
3 Other construction b	...	351613	...	223268	...	...	...	128345
4 Land improvement and plantation and orchard development	...	44782	...	44782	...	...	...	...
5 Producers' durable goods	...	216837	...	201549	...	...	...	15288
A Transport equipment	...	53624	...	52994	...	...	...	630
Passenger cars c	...	4784	...	4654	...	...	...	130
Other	...	48839	...	48340	...	...	...	500
B Machinery and equipment	...	163214	...	148555	...	...	...	14659
6 Breeding stock, dairy cattle, etc.	...	4466	...	4466	...	...	...	...
Total d	...	1173460	...	935687	...	...	...	237777
1986								
1 Residential buildings a	...	302625	...	302625	...	...	...	...
2 Non-residential buildings	...	275962	...	179039	...	...	...	96923
3 Other construction b	...	369305	...	236640	...	...	...	132665
4 Land improvement and plantation and orchard development	...	45026	...	45026	...	...	...	...
5 Producers' durable goods	...	212073	...	195188	...	...	...	16885
A Transport equipment	...	37212	...	36639	...	...	...	574
Passenger cars c	...	5134	...	5047	...	...	...	87
Other	...	32078	...	31592	...	...	...	486
B Machinery and equipment	...	174861	...	158550	...	...	...	16311
6 Breeding stock, dairy cattle, etc.	...	4325	...	4325	...	...	...	...
Total d	...	1209320	...	962843	...	...	...	246473

a) Item 'Residential buildings' includes also summer cottages, temporary dwellings, logging camps, fishermens' quarters etc..
b) The estimates of 'Other construction' include oil drilling rigs, oil production platforms etc., pipelines for gas, oil and gas exploration and drilling.
c) Item 'Passenger cars' includes station wagons.
d) Column 8 (General government, net) refers to stocks of reproducible fixed assets outside general government.

2.15 Stocks of Reproducible Fixed Assets by Kind of Activity, in Current Prices

Million Norwegian kroner

	1980 Gross	1980 Net	1981 Gross	1981 Net	1982 Gross	1982 Net	1983 Gross	1983 Net	1984 Gross	1984 Net	1985 Gross	1985 Net
1 Residential buildings a	...	238433	...	269938	...	314114	...	346259	...	376232	...	409896
2 Non-residential buildings	...	223155	...	251193	...	281116	...	306603	...	328853	...	361195
A Industries	...	142440	...	159925	...	179022	...	194132	...	208523	...	228793
1 Agriculture	...	35945	...	40362	...	44333	...	47237	...	49932	...	53572
2 Mining and quarrying	...	1224	...	1425	...	1549	...	1650	...	1699	...	1791
3 Manufacturing	...	44272	...	49831	...	55411	...	59460	...	62760	...	66981
4 Electricity, gas and water	...	15427	...	17222	...	19379	...	21248	...	22499	...	24349

Norway

2.15 Stocks of Reproducible Fixed Assets by Kind of Activity, in Current Prices
(Continued)

Million Norwegian kroner

	1980 Gross	1980 Net	1981 Gross	1981 Net	1982 Gross	1982 Net	1983 Gross	1983 Net	1984 Gross	1984 Net	1985 Gross	1985 Net
5 Construction	...	2132	...	2513	...	3063	...	3659	...	4078	...	4744
6 Wholesale and retail trade	...	...	...	...	...	...	...	...	...	...	...	...
7 Transport and communication	...	2078	...	2355	...	2670	...	2910	...	3175	...	3481
8 Finance, etc.	...	41362	...	46217	...	52617	...	57968	...	64381	...	73874
9 Community, social and personal services	...	...	...	...	...	...	...	...	...	...	...	...
B Producers of government services	...	80715	...	91269	...	102094	...	112471	...	120330	...	132402
C Other producers	...	...	...	...	...	...	...	...	...	...	...	...
3 Other construction [b]	...	282185	...	329514	...	379268	...	407193	...	458266	...	498728
A Industries	...	173976	...	207611	...	240741	...	260251	...	298404	...	322012
1 Agriculture [c]	...	2414	...	2745	...	3150	...	3429	...	3804	...	4430
2 Mining and quarrying [d]	...	44908	...	66040	...	81808	...	84607	...	103119	...	110706
3 Manufacturing	...	6179	...	6737	...	7442	...	8035	...	8349	...	10296
4 Electricity, gas and water	...	67330	...	75290	...	84526	...	89967	...	98339	...	105834
5 Construction [e]	...	6728	...	6925	...	8670	...	8515	...	8259	...	8111
6 Wholesale and retail trade	...	...	...	...	...	...	...	...	...	...	...	...
7 Transport and communication [f]	...	46416	...	49874	...	55145	...	65698	...	76535	...	82636
8 Finance, etc.	...	...	...	...	...	...	...	...	...	...	...	...
9 Community, social and personal services	...	...	...	...	...	...	...	...	...	...	...	...
B Producers of government services	...	108210	...	121903	...	138527	...	146942	...	159862	...	176716
C Other producers	...	...	...	...	...	...	...	...	...	...	...	...
4 Land improvement and development and plantation and orchard development	...	42776	...	53235	...	56426	...	53205	...	62893	...	66511
5 Producers' durable goods	...	220515	...	240516	...	263458	...	274326	...	257221	...	262352
A Industries	...	210060	...	228994	...	250716	...	261640	...	244587	...	246826
1 Agriculture [c]	...	21832	...	23984	...	25869	...	27193	...	27571	...	29860
2 Mining and quarrying [d]	...	3062	...	3516	...	3787	...	3750	...	5150	...	6368
3 Manufacturing	...	55564	...	60289	...	66346	...	66870	...	59875	...	72184
4 Electricity, gas and water	...	14664	...	16196	...	18673	...	20718	...	22410	...	24803
5 Construction [e]	...	6979	...	7118	...	7373	...	7318	...	6247	...	7017
6 Wholesale and retail trade	...	14827	...	15526	...	16940	...	17364	...	17349	...	20716
7 Transport and communication	...	85280	...	93560	...	101647	...	107887	...	94802	...	71337
8 Finance, etc. [g]	...	1535	...	1870	...	2380	...	2788	...	3422	...	5090
9 Community, social and personal services [g]	...	6318	...	6938	...	7701	...	7753	...	7700	...	9452
B Producers of government services	...	10455	...	11523	...	12742	...	12686	...	12634	...	15525
C Other producers	...	...	...	...	...	...	...	...	...	...	...	...
6 Breeding stock, dairy cattle, etc.	...	3933	...	4435	...	4432	...	4315	...	4663	...	5195
Total	...	1011000	...	1148830	...	1298810	...	1391900	...	1488130	...	1603880
Memorandum Item: Mineral Fuels and Power	...	133292	...	164010	...	193130	...	204709	...	234913	...	254512

	1986 Gross	1986 Net
1 Residential buildings [a]	...	461533
2 Non-residential buildings	...	401588
A Industries	...	257787
1 Agriculture	...	57485
2 Mining and quarrying	...	1942
3 Manufacturing	...	75359
4 Electricity, gas and water	...	26707
5 Construction	...	5576
6 Wholesale and retail trade	...	...
7 Transport and communication	...	3820

Norway

2.15 Stocks of Reproducible Fixed Assets by Kind of Activity, in Current Prices
(Continued)

Million Norwegian kroner

	1986 Gross	1986 Net
8 Finance, etc.	...	86898
9 Community, social and personal services	...	...
B Producers of government services	...	143801
C Other producers	...	...
3 Other construction [b]	...	550994
A Industries	...	358943
1 Agriculture [c]	...	5112
2 Mining and quarrying [d]	...	134721
3 Manufacturing	...	11945
4 Electricity, gas and water	...	112485
5 Construction [e]	...	11958
6 Wholesale and retail trade	...	...
7 Transport and communication [f]	...	82722
8 Finance, etc.	...	...
9 Community, social and personal services	...	...
B Producers of government services	...	192051
C Other producers	...	...
4 Land improvement and development and plantation and orchard development	...	68120
5 Producers' durable goods	...	260059
A Industries	...	243233
1 Agriculture [c]	...	32647
2 Mining and quarrying [d]	...	6658
3 Manufacturing	...	78157
4 Electricity, gas and water	...	27500
5 Construction [e]	...	7132
6 Wholesale and retail trade	...	24367
7 Transport and communication	...	50350
8 Finance, etc. [g]	...	6213
9 Community, social and personal services [g]	...	10209
B Producers of government services	...	16826
C Other producers	...	...
6 Breeding stock, dairy cattle, etc.	...	5343
Total	...	1747640
Memorandum Item: Mineral Fuels and Power	...	291433

a) Item 'Residential buildings' includes also summer cottages, temporary dwellings, logging camps, fishermens' quarters etc..
b) The estimates of 'Other construction' include oil drilling rigs, oil production platforms etc., pipelines for gas, oil and gas exploration and drilling.
c) Item 'Agriculture' refers to agriculture, forestry and fishing.
d) Item 'Mining and quarrying' also includes crude petroleum and natural gas production.
e) Item 'Construction' also includes oil and natural gas exploration and drilling.
f) Item 'Transport, storage and communication' includes pipeline transport for crude oil and natural gas.
g) Business services are included in item 'Community, social and personal services'.

2.16 Stocks of Reproducible Fixed Assets by Kind of Activity, in Constant Prices

Million Norwegian kroner

	1980 Gross	1980 Net	1981 Gross	1981 Net	1982 Gross	1982 Net	1983 Gross	1983 Net	1984 Gross	1984 Net	1985 Gross	1985 Net
	\multicolumn{12}{c}{At constant prices of:1980}
1 Residential buildings [a]	...	238433	...	248271	...	259043	...	269773	...	280143	...	290785
2 Non-residential buildings	...	223155	...	233001	...	241452	...	249250	...	256740	...	264981
A Industries	...	142440	...	148901	...	154474	...	159513	...	164484	...	170837
1 Agriculture	...	35945	...	37173	...	38070	...	38505	...	38755	...	38976
2 Mining and quarrying	...	1224	...	1324	...	1329	...	1336	...	1332	...	1338
3 Manufacturing	...	44272	...	46238	...	47323	...	48038	...	48649	...	49760
4 Electricity, gas and water	...	15427	...	16194	...	16999	...	17787	...	18170	...	18577

Norway

2.16 Stocks of Reproducible Fixed Assets by Kind of Activity, in Constant Prices
(Continued)

Million Norwegian kroner

	1980 Gross	1980 Net	1981 Gross	1981 Net	1982 Gross	1982 Net	1983 Gross	1983 Net	1984 Gross	1984 Net	1985 Gross	1985 Net
	\multicolumn{12}{c}{At constant prices of:1980}											
5 Construction	...	2132	...	2363	...	2687	...	3038	...	3293	...	3622
6 Wholesale and retail trade	...	...	...	...	...	...	...	...	...	...	...	...
7 Transport and communication	...	2078	...	2198	...	2293	...	2399	...	2481	...	2594
8 Finance, etc.	...	41362	...	43412	...	45773	...	48410	...	51805	...	55971
9 Community, social and personal services	...	...	...	...	...	...	...	...	...	...	...	...
B Producers of government services	...	80715	...	84100	...	86978	...	89737	...	92256	...	94144
C Other producers	...	...	...	...	...	...	...	...	...	...	...	...
3 Other construction [b]	...	282185	...	298082	...	305862	...	321208	...	341014	...	351613
A Industries	...	173976	...	185521	...	189550	...	200870	...	216662	...	223268
1 Agriculture [c]	...	2414	...	2537	...	2652	...	2792	...	2945	...	3198
2 Mining and quarrying [d]	...	44908	...	53817	...	54786	...	58235	...	67416	...	70000
3 Manufacturing	...	6170	...	6240	...	6275	...	6601	...	7049	...	7531
4 Electricity, gas and water	...	67330	...	70323	...	72610	...	74774	...	77205	...	79568
5 Construction [e]	...	6728	...	5954	...	6025	...	5888	...	5436	...	5180
6 Wholesale and retail trade	...	...	...	...	...	...	...	...	...	...	...	...
7 Transport and communication [f]	...	46416	...	46642	...	47202	...	52580	...	56611	...	57124
8 Finance, etc.	...	...	...	...	...	...	...	...	...	...	...	...
9 Community, social and personal services	...	...	...	...	...	...	...	...	...	...	...	...
B Producers of government services	...	108210	...	112561	...	116312	...	120338	...	124352	...	128345
C Other producers	...	...	...	...	...	...	...	...	...	...	...	...
4 Land improvement and development and plantation and orchard development	...	42776	...	43234	...	43713	...	44171	...	44518	...	44782
5 Producers' durable goods	...	220515	...	224560	...	226779	...	224982	...	226274	...	216837
A Industries	...	210060	...	213428	...	214976	...	212284	...	212329	...	201549
1 Agriculture [c]	...	21832	...	22194	...	22264	...	21928	...	21868	...	22021
2 Mining and quarrying [d]	...	3062	...	3381	...	3364	...	3306	...	5095	...	5544
3 Manufacturing	...	55564	...	58076	...	59051	...	59116	...	60670	...	62675
4 Electricity, gas and water	...	14664	...	15489	...	16513	...	17367	...	18242	...	18869
5 Construction [e]	...	6979	...	6918	...	6793	...	6563	...	6296	...	6099
6 Wholesale and retail trade	...	14827	...	14998	...	15236	...	15760	...	16552	...	17697
7 Transport and communication	...	85280	...	83830	...	82401	...	77692	...	71258	...	54364
8 Finance, etc. [g]	...	1535	...	1809	...	2194	...	2772	...	3757	...	4971
9 Community, social and personal services [g]	...	6318	...	6732	...	7102	...	7701	...	8591	...	9309
B Producers of government services	...	10455	...	11132	...	11803	...	12698	...	13945	...	15288
C Other producers	...	...	...	...	...	...	...	...	...	...	...	...
6 Breeding stock, dairy cattle, etc.	...	3933	...	3967	...	3955	...	4088	...	4253	...	4466
Total	...	1011000	...	1051120	...	1080800	...	1113470	...	1152940	...	1173460
Memorandum Item: Mineral Fuels and Power	...	133292	...	146714	...	151578	...	158612	...	172979	...	180189

	1986 Gross	1986 Net
	\multicolumn{2}{c}{At constant prices of:1980}	
1 Residential buildings [a]	...	302625
2 Non-residential buildings	...	275962
A Industries	...	179039
1 Agriculture	...	38970
2 Mining and quarrying	...	1340
3 Manufacturing	...	51942
4 Electricity, gas and water	...	18922

Norway

2.16 Stocks of Reproducible Fixed Assets by Kind of Activity, in Constant Prices
(Continued)

Million Norwegian kroner

	1986 Gross	1986 Net
		At constant prices of: 1980
5 Construction	...	3952
6 Wholesale and retail trade	...	...
7 Transport and communication	...	2716
8 Finance, etc.	...	61197
9 Community, social and personal services	...	...
B Producers of government services	...	96923
C Other producers	...	...
3 Other construction b	...	369305
A Industries	...	236640
1 Agriculture c	...	3506
2 Mining and quarrying d	...	82338
3 Manufacturing	...	8096
4 Electricity, gas and water	...	80479
5 Construction e	...	5165
6 Wholesale and retail trade	...	...
7 Transport and communication f	...	57056
8 Finance, etc.	...	...
9 Community, social and personal services	...	...
B Producers of government services	...	132665
C Other producers	...	...
4 Land improvement and development and plantation and orchard development	...	45026
5 Producers' durable goods	...	212073
A Industries	...	195188
1 Agriculture c	...	22470
2 Mining and quarrying d	...	6032
3 Manufacturing	...	66906
4 Electricity, gas and water	...	19521
5 Construction e	...	5936
6 Wholesale and retail trade	...	19377
7 Transport and communication	...	38697
8 Finance, etc. g	...	6117
9 Community, social and personal services g	...	10131
B Producers of government services	...	16885
C Other producers	...	...
6 Breeding stock, dairy cattle, etc.	...	4325
Total	...	1209320
Memorandum Item: Mineral Fuels and Power	...	195235

a) Item 'Residential buildings' includes also summer cottages, temporary dwellings, logging camps, fishermens' quarters etc..
b) The estimates of 'Other construction' include oil drilling rigs, oil production platforms etc., pipelines for gas, oil and gas exploration and drilling.
c) Item 'Agriculture' refers to agriculture, forestry and fishing.
d) Item 'Mining and quarrying' also includes crude petroleum and natural gas production.
e) Item 'Construction' also includes oil and natural gas exploration and drilling.
f) Item 'Transport, storage and communication' includes pipeline transport for crude oil and natural gas.
g) Business services are included in item 'Community, social and personal services'.

2.17 Exports and Imports of Goods and Services, Detail

Million Norwegian kroner

	1970	1975	1977	1978	1979	1980	1981	1982	1983	1984	1985	1986
					Exports of Goods and Services							
1 Exports of merchandise, f.o.b.	17715	38140	48747	57863	70007	92863	106899	114798	133249	156822	173023	135860
2 Transport and communication	13164	18054	19218	19808	26276	31500	36075	34728	34371	40191	43368	39064
A In respect of merchandise imports	241	470	566	464	498	505	516	517	551	580	610	600
B Other	12923	17584	18652	19344	25778	30995	35559	34211	33820	39611	42758	38464

Norway

2.17 Exports and Imports of Goods and Services, Detail
(Continued)

Million Norwegian kroner

	1970	1975	1977	1978	1979	1980	1981	1982	1983	1984	1985	1986
3 Insurance service charges	47	88	122	120	139	168	179	206	204	234	282	305
A In respect of merchandise imports	47	88	122	120	139	168	179	200	197	226	265	300
B Other	-	-	-	-	-	-	-	6	7	8	17	5
4 Other commodities	1206	3711	5292	6205	5461	6287	8413	10246	10790	11004	11727	10947
5 Adjustments of merchandise exports to change-of-ownership basis	...	...	...	...	...	...	...	...	...	...	...	...
6 Direct purchases in the domestic market by non-residential households	1271	2196	2885	3225	3524	3977	4722	5044	5307	5827	6983	7871
7 Direct purchases in the domestic market by extraterritorial bodies												
Total Exports of Goods and Services	33403	62189	76264	87221	105407	134795	156288	165022	183921	214078	235383	194047
Imports of Goods and Services												
1 Imports of merchandise, c.i.f.	26651	54366	72002	61979	70433	84543	90516	100458	102520	116542	133751	152574
A Imports of merchandise, f.o.b.	25956	52861	70313	60484	68805	82787	88586	98463	99945	113709	130441	149248
B Transport of services on merchandise imports	554	1197	1324	1154	1212	1255	1392	1397	1985	2154	2515	2426
By residents	241	470	566	464	498	505	516	517	551	580	610	600
By non-residents	313	727	758	690	714	750	876	880	1434	1574	1905	1826
C Insurance service charges on merchandise imports	141	308	365	341	416	501	538	598	590	679	795	900
By residents	*	-				*	*	-	-	-	-	-
By non-residents	141	308	365	341	416	501	538	598	590	679	795	900
2 Adjustments of merchandise imports to change-of-ownership basis	...	...	...	...	...	...	...	...	...	...	...	...
3 Other transport and communication	5355	9275	11176	11704	15246	17936	21038	22499	25379	27764	28206	24798
4 Other insurance service charges	43	503	281	253	306	663	401	356	579	903	833	144
5 Other commodities	527	4012	7316	8264	6067	6709	8978	9662	11042	14470	15648	15037
6 Direct purchases abroad by government	1855	3983	5993	6919	7102	7520	9536	11568	12511	13173	15870	19101
7 Direct purchases abroad by resident households												
Total Imports of Goods and Services	34431	72139	96768	89119	99154	117371	130469	144543	152031	172852	194308	211654
Balance of Goods and Services	-1028	-9950	-20504	-1898	6253	17424	25819	20479	31890	41226	41075	-17607
Total Imports and Balance of Goods and Services	33403	62189	76264	87221	105407	134795	156288	165022	183921	214078	235383	194047

3.12 General Government Income and Outlay Account: Total and Subsectors

Million Norwegian kroner

	1980					1981				
	Total General Government	Central Government	State or Provincial Government	Local Government	Social Security Funds	Total General Government	Central Government	State or Provincial Government	Local Government	Social Security Funds
					Receipts					
1 Operating surplus	1674	...	...	1674	...	2010	...	...	2010	...
2 Property and entrepreneurial income [a]	8303	5935	...	918	1450	10902	8321	...	929	1652
A Withdrawals from public quasi-corporations [a]	-1214	-1214	...	...	...	-845	-845	...	...	...
B Interest	9384	7016	...	918	1450	11629	9048	...	929	1652
C Dividends	133	133	...	...	...	118	118	...	...	...
D Net land rent and royalties	...	...	...	...	...	...	...	...	...	...
3 Taxes, fees and contributions	144657	88665	...	25217	30775	160250	94388	...	29409	36453
A Indirect taxes	19024	18300	...	407	130	55090	54940	...	609	147
B Direct taxes	61260	36530	...	24730	...	65657	36857	...	28800	...
Income [b]	38379	14299	...	24080	...	40599	12484	...	28115	...
Other	22881	22231	...	650	...	25058	24373	...	685	...
C Social security contributions	34224	3587	...	...	30637	38699	2393	...	...	36306
D Fees, fines and penalties	149	149	...	...	...	198	198	...	...	...

1099

Norway

3.12 General Government Income and Outlay Account: Total and Subsectors
(Continued)

Million Norwegian kroner

	1980					1981				
	Total General Government	Central Government	State or Provincial Government	Local Government	Social Security Funds	Total General Government	Central Government	State or Provincial Government	Local Government	Social Security Funds
4 Other current transfers	...	3816	...	17762	10922	...	4450	...	20623	12944
A Casualty insurance claims	...	-	...	...	...	...	-	...	...	...
B Transfers from other government subsectors	...	3816	...	17762	10922	...	4450	...	20623	12944
C Transfers from the rest of the world	...	...	...	...	...	...	...	...	...	...
D Other transfers, except imputed	...	...	...	...	...	...	...	...	...	...
E Imputed unfunded employee pension and welfare contributions	...	...	...	...	...	...	...	...	...	...
Total Current Receipts [c]	154634	98416	...	45571	43147	173162	107159	...	52971	51049
	Disbursements										
1 Government final consumption expenditure	53478	20417	...	32225	836	62616	24929	...	36737	950
2 Property income	11182	7813	...	3369	...	12647	8435	...	4212	...
A Interest	11182	7813	...	3369	...	12647	8435	...	4212	...
B Net land rent and royalties	...	...	...	...	...	...	...	...	...	...
3 Subsidies	19960	18845	...	866	249	21795	19656	...	1831	308
4 Other current transfers	43172	30116	...	5239	40317	50255	35710	...	5734	46828
A Casualty insurance premiums, net	...	...	...	...	...	...	...	...	...	...
B Transfers to other government subsectors	...	24565	...	998	6937	...	29387	...	1186	7444
C Social security benefits	40975	3354	...	4241	33380	47636	3704	...	4548	39384
D Social assistance grants	...	...	...	...	...	...	...	...	...	...
E Unfunded employee pension and welfare benefits	...	...	...	...	...	...	...	...	...	...
F Transfers to private non-profit institutions serving households	...	...	...	...	...	...	...	...	...	...
G Other transfers n.e.c.	...	...	...	...	...	...	...	...	...	...
H Transfers to the rest of the world	2186	2186	...	...	...	2617	2617	...	...	...
Net saving	26842	21225	...	3872	1745	25849	18429	...	4457	2963
Total Current Disbursements and Net Saving [c]	154634	98416	...	45571	43147	173162	107159	...	52971	51049

	1982					1983				
	Total General Government	Central Government	State or Provincial Government	Local Government	Social Security Funds	Total General Government	Central Government	State or Provincial Government	Local Government	Social Security Funds
	Receipts										
1 Operating surplus	3417	...	...	3417	...	3979	...	...	3979	...
2 Property and entrepreneurial income [a]	13040	9757	...	1381	1903	15626	11816	...	1574	2236
A Withdrawals from public quasi-corporations [a]	-1167	-1167	...	...	...	-589	-589	...	...	...
B Interest	13710	10426	...	1381	1903	15701	11891	...	1574	2236
C Dividends	497	497	...	...	...	514	514	...	...	...
D Net land rent and royalties	...	...	...	...	...	...	...	...	...	...
3 Taxes, fees and contributions	176332	102995	...	32690	40647	194120	115060	...	34872	44188
A Indirect taxes	61747	60794	...	771	182	69733	68600	...	931	202
B Direct taxes	70604	38685	...	31919	...	76722	42781	...	33941	...
Income [b]	42892	11751	...	31141	...	44674	11593	...	33081	...
Other	27712	26934	...	778	...	32048	31188	...	860	...
C Social security contributions	43494	3029	...	...	40465	47149	3163	...	...	43986
D Fees, fines and penalties	487	487	...	...	...	516	516	...	...	...
4 Other current transfers	...	5477	...	24204	14995	...	5472	...	26445	18026
A Casualty insurance claims	...	-	...	...	...	...	-	...	...	...
B Transfers from other government subsectors	...	5477	...	24204	14995	...	5472	...	26445	18026
C Transfers from the rest of the world	...	...	...	...	...	...	...	...	...	...
D Other transfers, except imputed	...	...	...	...	...	...	...	...	...	...
E Imputed unfunded employee pension and welfare contributions	...	...	...	...	...	...	...	...	...	...

Norway

3.12 General Government Income and Outlay Account: Total and Subsectors
(Continued)

Million Norwegian kroner

	1982					1983				
	Total General Government	Central Government	State or Provincial Government	Local Government	Social Security Funds	Total General Government	Central Government	State or Provincial Government	Local Government	Social Security Funds
Total Current Receipts c	192789	118229	...	61692	57545	213725	132348	...	66870	64450

Disbursements

1 Government final consumption expenditure	70408	27472	...	41940	997	78213	30456	...	46635	1122
2 Property income	13834	8767	...	5067	...	16607	10237	...	6370	...
A Interest	13834	8767	...	5067	...	16607	10237	...	6370	...
B Net land rent and royalties	...	...	...	...	...	...	...	...	...	...
3 Subsidies	23662	21326	...	2021	315	24439	22225	...	2209	6
4 Other current transfers	57789	41949	...	6596	53921	66076	47402	...	7474	61144
A Casualty insurance premiums, net	...	...	...	...	...	...	...	...	...	...
B Transfers to other government subsectors	...	34547	...	1376	8753	...	38844	...	1529	9570
C Social security benefits	54516	4129	...	5219	45168	62212	4694	...	5945	51573
D Social assistance grants	...	...	...	...	...	...	...	...	...	...
E Unfunded employee pension and welfare benefits	...	...	...	...	...	...	...	...	...	...
F Transfers to private non-profit institutions serving households	...	...	...	...	...	...	...	...	...	...
G Other transfers n.e.c.	...	...	...	...	...	...	...	...	...	...
H Transfers to the rest of the world	3271	3271	...	...	...	3850	3850	...	...	...
Net saving	27096	18716	...	6060	2312	28390	22029	...	4182	2179
Total Current Disbursements and Net Saving c	192789	118229	...	61693	57545	213725	132349	...	66870	64451

	1984					1985				
	Total General Government	Central Government	State or Provincial Government	Local Government	Social Security Funds	Total General Government	Central Government	State or Provincial Government	Local Government	Social Security Funds

Receipts

1 Operating surplus	5202	...	...	5202	...	6167	...	...	6167	...
2 Property and entrepreneurial income a	21445	16934	...	1935	2576	24735	19468	...	2427	2841
A Withdrawals from public quasi-corporations a	-833	-833	...	...	...	-2081	-2081	...	...	...
B Interest	21307	16796	...	1935	2576	25766	20498	...	2427	2841
C Dividends	971	971	...	...	...	1050	1050	...	...	...
D Net land rent and royalties	...	...	...	...	...	...	...	...	...	...
3 Taxes, fees and contributions	216898	131825	...	37436	47637	250269	153984	...	42807	53478
A Indirect taxes	78200	76936	...	1062	202	91992	90500	...	1283	209
B Direct taxes	87637	51263	...	36374	...	100600	59076	...	41524	...
Income b	49647	14308	...	35339	...	55555	15268	...	40287	...
Other	37990	36954	...	1035	...	45045	43808	...	1237	...
C Social security contributions	50511	3076	...	...	47435	57314	4045	...	...	53269
D Fees, fines and penalties	550	550	...	...	...	363	363	...	...	...
4 Other current transfers	3000	8486	...	31050	21584	3078	10321	...	34492	21497
A Casualty insurance claims	...	-	...	...	...	...	-	...	...	...
B Transfers from other government subsectors	...	5486	...	31050	21584	...	7243	...	34492	21497
C Transfers from the rest of the world	...	...	...	...	...	...	...	...	...	...
D Other transfers, except imputed	3000	3000	...	...	...	3078	3078	...	...	...
E Imputed unfunded employee pension and welfare contributions	...	...	...	...	...	...	...	...	...	...
Total Current Receipts c	246545	157245	...	75623	71797	284249	183773	...	85893	77816

Disbursements

1 Government final consumption expenditure	84099	31999	...	50958	1142	92804	34607	...	56887	1310
2 Property income	18807	11219	...	7588	...	21898	13300	...	8598	...
A Interest	18807	11219	...	7588	...	21898	13300	...	8598	...
B Net land rent and royalties	...	...	...	...	...	...	...	...	...	...
3 Subsidies	25708	23340	...	2363	6	26936	24355	...	2574	7

Norway

3.12 General Government Income and Outlay Account: Total and Subsectors
(Continued)

Million Norwegian kroner

	1984					1985				
	Total General Government	Central Government	State or Provincial Government	Local Government	Social Security Funds	Total General Government	Central Government	State or Provincial Government	Local Government	Social Security Funds
4 Other current transfers	71787	53445	...	8447	68015	78029	58272	...	9471	73518
A Casualty insurance premiums, net	...	...	...	...	...	...	...	...	...	...
B Transfers to other government subsectors	...	44664	...	1559	11897	...	48806	...	1531	12895
C Social security benefits	67917	4911	...	6888	56118	73820	5257	...	7940	60623
D Social assistance grants	...	...	...	...	...	...	...	...	...	...
E Unfunded employee pension and welfare benefits	...	...	...	...	...	...	...	...	...	...
F Transfers to private non-profit institutions serving households	...	...	...	...	...	...	...	...	...	...
G Other transfers n.e.c.	...	...	...	...	...	...	...	...	...	...
H Transfers to the rest of the world	3870	3870	...	...	...	4209	4209	...	...	...
Net saving	46142	37241	...	6268	2633	64583	53240	...	8362	2981
Total Current Disbursements and Net Saving [c]	246543	157244	...	75624	71796	284250	183774	...	85892	77816

	1986				
	Total General Government	Central Government	State or Provincial Government	Local Government	Social Security Funds
Receipts					
1 Operating surplus	7223	...	...	7223	...
2 Property and entrepreneurial income [a]	32875	26272	...	3185	3418
A Withdrawals from public quasi-corporations [a]	-3077	-3077	...	...	...
B Interest	34340	27737	...	3185	3418
C Dividends	1612	1612	...	...	...
D Net land rent and royalties	...	...	...	...	...
3 Taxes, fees and contributions	247436	137159	...	48143	62134
A Indirect taxes	101084	99369	...	1491	224
B Direct taxes	78450	31798	...	46652	...
Income [b]	62787	17385	...	45402	...
Other	15663	14413	...	1250	...
C Social security contributions	67426	5516	...	...	61910
D Fees, fines and penalties	476	476	...	...	...
4 Other current transfers	3078	9985	...	37055	18718
A Casualty insurance claims	...	-	...	...	...
B Transfers from other government subsectors	...	6907	...	37055	18718
C Transfers from the rest of the world	...	...	...	...	...
D Other transfers, except imputed	3078	3078	...	...	...
E Imputed unfunded employee pension and welfare contributions	...	...	...	...	...
Total Current Receipts [c]	290612	173416	...	95606	84270
Disbursements					
1 Government final consumption expenditure	102092	37891	...	62815	1386
2 Property income	27650	17822	...	9828	...
A Interest	27650	17822	...	9828	...
B Net land rent and royalties	...	...	...	...	...
3 Subsidies	29686	26300	...	3379	7

Norway

3.12 General Government Income and Outlay Account: Total and Subsectors
(Continued)

Million Norwegian kroner

	1986				
	Total General Government	Central Government	State or Provincial Government	Local Government	Social Security Funds
4 Other current transfers	86428	59960	...	9723	79425
A Casualty insurance premiums, net	...	...	...	...	...
B Transfers to other government subsectors	...	49337	...	861	12482
C Social security benefits	81490	5685	...	8862	66943
D Social assistance grants	...	...	...	...	...
E Unfunded employee pension and welfare benefits	...	...	...	...	...
F Transfers to private non-profit institutions serving households	...	...	...	...	...
G Other transfers n.e.c.	...	...	...	...	...
H Transfers to the rest of the world	4938	4938	...	...	...
Net saving	44756	31442	...	9861	3452
Total Current Disbursements and Net Saving c	290612	173415	...	95606	84270

a) Beginning 1975, loss on capital investments are deducted from item 'Withdrawals from public quasi-corporations.
b) Beginning 1975, income includes ordinary taxes on income and property.
c) General government and local government include municipal enterprises. Central government includes also sector for tax collection, i.e. values shown on accrued basis.

3.13 General Government Capital Accumulation Account: Total and Subsectors

Million Norwegian kroner

	1980					1981				
	Total General Government	Central Government	State or Provincial Government	Local Government	Social Security Funds	Total General Government	Central Government	State or Provincial Government	Local Government	Social Security Funds
	Finance of Gross Accumulation									
1 Gross saving	31200	21835	...	7620	1745	30759	19115	...	8681	2963
A Consumption of fixed capital	4358	610	...	3748	...	4910	686	...	4224	...
B Net saving	26842	21225	...	3872	1745	25849	18429	...	4457	2963
2 Capital transfers	...	...	...	...	...	...	...	...	...	...
Finance of Gross Accumulation a	31200	21835	...	7620	1745	30759	19115	...	8681	2963
	Gross Accumulation									
1 Gross capital formation	16640	3627	...	12972	41	17576	3780	...	13760	36
A Increase in stocks	...	...	...	...	...	...	...	...	...	...
B Gross fixed capital formation	16640	3627	...	12972	41	17576	3780	...	13760	36
2 Purchases of land, net	...	...	...	...	...	...	...	...	...	...
3 Purchases of intangible assets, net	...	...	...	...	...	...	...	...	...	...
4 Capital transfers	...	...	...	...	...	...	...	...	...	...
Net lending	14560	18208	...	-5352	1704	13183	15335	...	-5079	2927
Gross Accumulation a	31200	21835	...	7620	1745	30759	19115	...	8681	2963
	1982					1983				
	Total General Government	Central Government	State or Provincial Government	Local Government	Social Security Funds	Total General Government	Central Government	State or Provincial Government	Local Government	Social Security Funds
	Finance of Gross Accumulation									
1 Gross saving	32654	19465	...	10877	2312	34400	22812	...	9409	2179
A Consumption of fixed capital	5558	750	...	4808	...	6010	783	...	5227	...
B Net saving	27096	18715	...	6069	2312	28390	22029	...	4182	2179
2 Capital transfers	...	...	...	...	...	...	...	...	...	...
Finance of Gross Accumulation a	32654	19465	...	10877	2312	34400	22812	...	9409	2179
	Gross Accumulation									
1 Gross capital formation	18395	3811	...	14564	20	19406	4254	...	15125	26
A Increase in stocks	...	...	...	...	...	...	...	...	...	...
B Gross fixed capital formation	18395	3811	...	14564	20	19406	4254	...	15125	26
2 Purchases of land, net	...	...	...	...	...	...	...	...	...	...
3 Purchases of intangible assets, net	...	...	...	...	...	...	...	...	...	...
4 Capital transfers	...	...	...	...	...	...	...	...	...	...
Net lending	14259	15654	...	-3687	2292	14994	18558	...	-5716	2153
Gross Accumulation a	32654	19465	...	10877	2312	34400	22812	...	9409	2179

Norway

3.13 General Government Capital Accumulation Account: Total and Subsectors

Million Norwegian kroner

	1984					1985				
	Total General Government	Central Government	State or Provincial Government	Local Government	Social Security Funds	Total General Government	Central Government	State or Provincial Government	Local Government	Social Security Funds
Finance of Gross Accumulation											
1 Gross saving	52522	38054	...	11835	2633	71770	54190	...	14599	2981
A Consumption of fixed capital	6380	813	...	5567	...	7187	950	...	6237	...
B Net saving	46142	37241	...	6268	2633	64583	53240	...	8362	2981
2 Capital transfers	...	...	...	...	...	...	...	...	...	...
Finance of Gross Accumulation [a]	52522	38054	...	11835	2633	71770	54190	...	14599	2981
Gross Accumulation											
1 Gross capital formation	19326	4691	...	14562	73	19719	5045	...	14535	139
A Increase in stocks	...	...	...	...	...	...	...	...	...	...
B Gross fixed capital formation	19326	4691	...	14562	73	19719	5045	...	14535	139
2 Purchases of land, net	...	...	...	...	...	...	...	...	...	...
3 Purchases of intangible assets, net	...	...	...	...	...	...	...	...	...	...
4 Capital transfers	...	...	...	...	...	...	...	...	...	...
Net lending	33196	33363	...	-2727	2560	52051	49145	...	64	2842
Gross Accumulation [a]	52522	38054	...	11835	2633	71770	54190	...	14599	2981

	1986				
	Total General Government	Central Government	State or Provincial Government	Local Government	Social Security Funds
Finance of Gross Accumulation					
1 Gross saving	52657	32470	...	16734	3452
A Consumption of fixed capital	7901	1028	...	6873	...
B Net saving	44756	31442	...	9861	3452
2 Capital transfers	...	...	...	...	...
Finance of Gross Accumulation [a]	52657	32470	...	16734	3452
Gross Accumulation					
1 Gross capital formation	22606	5628	...	16897	81
A Increase in stocks	...	...	...	...	...
B Gross fixed capital formation	22606	5628	...	16897	81
2 Purchases of land, net	...	...	...	...	...
3 Purchases of intangible assets, net	...	...	...	...	...
4 Capital transfers	...	...	...	...	...
Net lending	30051	26842	...	-163	3371
Gross Accumulation [a]	52657	32470	...	16734	3452

a) General government and local government include municipal enterprises. Central government includes also sector for tax collection, i.e. values shown on accrued basis.

3.22 Corporate and Quasi-Corporate Enterprise Income and Outlay Account: Total and Sectors

Million Norwegian kroner

	1980			1981			1982			1983		
	TOTAL	Non-Financial	Financial	TOTAL	Non-Financial	Financial	TOTAL	Non-Financial	Financial	TOTAL	Non-Financial	Financial
Receipts												
1 Operating surplus	40749	44401	-3652	48566	53005	-4439	47944	53723	-5779	58090	64965	-6875
2 Property and entrepreneurial income	40601	6725	33876	51981	8795	43186	63766	10521	53245	72577	12516	60061
A Withdrawals from quasi-corporate enterprises	1192	1192	-	861	861	-	1260	1260	-	1290	1290	-
B Interest	37738	4043	33695	49011	6027	42984	60811	7824	52987	68168	8498	59670
C Dividends	1462	1281	181	1858	1656	202	1510	1252	258	2777	2386	391
D Net land rent and royalties	209	209	-	251	251	-	185	185	-	342	342	-

Norway

3.22 Corporate and Quasi-Corporate Enterprise Income and Outlay Account: Total and Sectors
(Continued)

Million Norwegian kroner

	1980			1981			1982			1983		
	TOTAL	Non-Financial	Financial	TOTAL	Non-Financial	Financial	TOTAL	Non-Financial	Financial	TOTAL	Non-Financial	Financial
3 Current transfers	11484	5842	5642	14408	7550	6858	16823	8372	8451	18968	9715	9253
A Casualty insurance claims	4040	4040	-	5014	5014	-	6076	6076	-	6412	6412	-
B Casualty insurance premiums, net, due to be received by insurance companies	5130	-	5130	6293	-	6293	7623	-	7623	7969	-	7969
C Current transfers from the rest of the world	...	...	...	...	...	...	...	...	...	...	...	...
D Other transfers except imputed	2314	1802	512	3101	2536	565	3124	2296	828	4587	3303	1284
E Imputed unfunded employee pension and welfare contributions	...	...	...	...	...	...	...	...	...	...	...	...
Total Current Receipts	92834	56968	35866	114955	69350	45605	128533	72616	55917	149635	87196	62439

Disbursements

	TOTAL	Non-Financial	Financial	TOTAL	Non-Financial	Financial	TOTAL	Non-Financial	Financial	TOTAL	Non-Financial	Financial
1 Property and entrepreneurial income	45719	21872	23847	58516	28379	30137	71642	34868	36774	80003	38258	41745
A Withdrawals from quasi-corporations	-22	-22	-	16	16	-	94	94	-	701	701	-
Public	-22	-22	-	16	16	-	94	94	-	701	701	-
Private	...	...	...	...	...	...	...	...	...	...	...	...
B Interest	40635	17202	23433	52302	22635	29667	63626	27381	36245	70076	29030	41046
C Dividends	4756	4342	414	5759	5289	470	7438	6909	529	8588	7889	699
D Net land rent and royalties	350	350	-	439	439	-	484	484	-	638	638	-
2 Direct taxes and other current transfers n.e.c. to general government	23531	23265	266	26004	25705	299	27965	27634	331	32642	32053	589
3 Other current transfers	12227	5340	6887	15150	7154	7996	17711	8010	9701	19944	9741	10203
A Casualty insurance premiums, net	4040	4040	-	5014	5014	-	6076	6076	-	6412	6412	-
B Casualty insurance claims liability of insurance companies	5130	-	5130	6293	-	6293	7623	-	7623	7969	-	7969
C Transfers to private non-profit institutions	...	...	...	...	...	...	...	...	...	...	...	...
D Unfunded employee pension and welfare benefits	...	...	...	...	...	...	...	...	...	...	...	...
E Social assistance grants	...	...	...	...	...	...	...	...	...	...	...	...
F Other transfers n.e.c.	3057	1300	1757	3843	2140	1703	4012	1934	2078	5563	3329	2234
G Transfers to the rest of the world	...	...	...	...	...	...	...	...	...	...	...	...
Net saving	11357	6491	4866	15285	8112	7173	11215	2104	9111	17046	7144	9902
Total Current Disbursements and Net Saving	92834	56968	35866	114955	69350	45605	128533	72616	55917	149635	87196	62439

	1984			1985			1986		
	TOTAL	Non-Financial	Financial	TOTAL	Non-Financial	Financial	TOTAL	Non-Financial	Financial

Receipts

1 Operating surplus	75152	82988	-7836	79161	87709	-8548	43136	52171	-9035
2 Property and entrepreneurial income	82566	12445	70121	103635	19153	84482	134728	24317	110411
A Withdrawals from quasi-corporate enterprises	1385	1385	-	2115	2115	-	3082	3082	-
B Interest	77940	8289	69651	97823	13923	83900	128193	18522	109671
C Dividends	2982	2512	470	3410	2828	582	3141	2401	740
D Net land rent and royalties	259	259	-	287	287	-	312	312	-
3 Current transfers	20360	10415	9945	19971	10630	9341	21291	10843	10448
A Casualty insurance claims	6986	6986	-	6929	6929	-	7450	7450	-
B Casualty insurance premiums, net, due to be received by insurance companies	8777	-	8777	8853	-	8853	9738	-	9738
C Current transfers from the rest of the world	...	...	...	...	...	...	...	...	...
D Other transfers except imputed	4597	3429	1168	4189	3701	488	4103	3393	710
E Imputed unfunded employee pension and welfare contributions	...	...	...	...	...	...	...	...	...
Total Current Receipts	178078	105848	72230	202767	117492	85275	199155	87331	111824

Norway

3.22 Corporate and Quasi-Corporate Enterprise Income and Outlay Account: Total and Sectors
(Continued)

Million Norwegian kroner

	1984 TOTAL	1984 Non-Financial	1984 Financial	1985 TOTAL	1985 Non-Financial	1985 Financial	1986 TOTAL	1986 Non-Financial	1986 Financial
	Disbursements								
1 Property and entrepreneurial income	94487	42513	51974	109732	44163	65569	137190	52059	85131
A Withdrawals from quasi-corporations	552	552	-	35	35	-	5	5	-
Public	552	552	-	35	35	-	5	.5	-
Private	...	...	...	...	...	...	...	...	...
B Interest	83536	32329	51207	98032	33429	64603	125403	41337	84066
C Dividends	9736	8969	767	10964	9998	966	10965	9900	1065
D Net land rent and royalties	663	663	-	701	701	-	817	817	-
2 Direct taxes and other current transfers n.e.c. to general government	39025	38436	589	47217	46599	618	19864	19138	726
3 Other current transfers	24650	10368	14282	24392	8622	15770	26008	9095	16913
A Casualty insurance premiums, net	6986	6986	-	6929	6929	-	7450	7450	-
B Casualty insurance claims liability of insurance companies	8777	-	8777	8853	-	8853	9738	-	9738
C Transfers to private non-profit institutions	...	...	...	...	...	...	...	...	...
D Unfunded employee pension and welfare benefits	...	...	...	...	...	...	...	...	...
E Social assistance grants	...	...	...	...	...	...	...	...	...
F Other transfers n.e.c.	8887	3382	5505	8610	1693	6917	8820	1645	7175
G Transfers to the rest of the world	...	...	...	...	...	...	...	...	...
Net saving	19917	14531	5386	21427	18109	3318	16094	7040	9054
Total Current Disbursements and Net Saving	178079	105848	72231	202768	117493	85275	199156	87332	111824

3.32 Household and Private Unincorporated Enterprise Income and Outlay Account

Million Norwegian kroner

	1970	1975	1977	1978	1979	1980	1981	1982	1983	1984	1985	1986
	Receipts											
1 Compensation of employees	...	86162	112980	123960	129376	145396	164003	183181	198070	216178	239720	272808
A Wages and salaries	...	73330	96706	105922	110565	124105	139799	156163	169236	185034	205452	233714
B Employers' contributions for social security	...	12832	16274	18038	18811	21291	24204	27018	28834	31144	34268	39094
C Employers' contributions for private pension & welfare plans	...	...	...	...	...	...	...	...	...	...	...	...
2 Operating surplus of private unincorporated enterprises	...	15399	21210	24567	23381	26780	30977	34462	36985	40805	44022	46942
3 Property and entrepreneurial income	...	3492	4739	6179	7739	9612	11792	13711	16886	20392	24529	29364
A Withdrawals from private quasi-corporations	...	...	...	...	...	...	...	...	...	...	...	...
B Interest	...	3132	4360	5865	7143	8516	10376	12461	15296	18719	22645	27763
C Dividends	...	360	379	314	596	1096	1416	1250	1590	1673	1884	1601
D Net land rent and royalties	...	...	...	...	...	...	...	...	...	...	...	...
3 Current transfers	...	21519	28863	33980	39230	43575	50675	58015	65937	72097	78495	86677
A Casualty insurance claims	...	468	822	912	987	1090	1279	1547	1557	1791	1923	2288
B Social security benefits	...	20154	27049	31916	37023	40975	47636	54516	62212	67917	73820	81490
C Social assistance grants	...	...	...	...	...	...	...	...	...	...	...	...
D Unfunded employee pension and welfare benefits	...	...	...	...	...	...	...	...	...	...	...	...
E Transfers from general government	...	...	...	...	...	...	...	...	...	...	...	...
F Transfers from the rest of the world	...	529	543	553	594	756	1016	1061	1178	1291	1426	1292
G Other transfers n.e.c.	...	368	449	599	626	754	744	890	990	1098	1326	1607
Total Current Receipts [a]	...	126572	167792	188686	199726	225363	257447	289369	317878	349472	386766	435791
	Disbursements											
1 Final consumption expenditures	...	77615	103915	110670	120104	135241	155205	175310	192979	210921	246327	279796
2 Property income	...	4343	6179	8199	9525	11230	14024	17572	21316	24081	30565	41289

Norway

3.32 Household and Private Unincorporated Enterprise Income and Outlay Account
(Continued)

Million Norwegian kroner

	1970	1975	1977	1978	1979	1980	1981	1982	1983	1984	1985	1986
A Interest	...	4343	6179	8199	9525	11230	14024	17572	21316	24081	30565	41289
B Net land rent and royalties	...	...	...	...	...	...	...	...	...	...	...	...
3 Direct taxes and other current transfers n.e.c. to government	...	40244	51043	58017	62419	71890	78278	86160	91281	99198	110743	126097
A Social security contributions	...	19863	24733	27757	29914	34224	38699	43494	47149	50511	57314	67426
B Direct taxes	...	20381	26310	30260	32505	37666	39579	42666	44132	48687	53429	58671
Income taxes	...	...	...	...	...	...	...	...	...	...	...	...
Other	...	...	...	...	...	...	...	...	...	...	...	...
C Fees, fines and penalties	...	...	...	...	...	...	...	...	...	...	...	...
4 Other current transfers	...	986	1542	1698	1946	2265	2656	3427	3593	3650	4204	4892
A Net casualty insurance premiums	...	468	822	912	987	1090	1279	1547	1557	1791	1924	2288
B Transfers to private non-profit institutions serving households	...	...	...	...	...	...	...	...	...	...	...	...
C Transfers to the rest of the world	...	474	660	720	861	1026	1179	1393	1520	1500	1933	2161
D Other current transfers, except imputed	...	44	60	66	98	140	190	407	510	359	347	443
E Imputed employee pension and welfare contributions	...	...	...	...	...	...	...	...	...	...	...	...
Net saving	...	3384	5113	10102	5732	4737	7284	6899	8709	11623	-5072	-16283
Total Current Disbursements and Net Saving a	...	126572	167792	188686	199726	225363	257447	289368	317878	349473	386767	435791

a) Column 'Farm' is included in column 'Non-farm entrepreneurial'.

3.51 External Transactions: Current Account: Detail

Million Norwegian kroner

	1970	1975	1977	1978	1979	1980	1981	1982	1983	1984	1985	1986
Payments to the Rest of the World
1 Imports of goods and services	34431	72139	96768	89119	99154	117371	130469	144543	152031	172852	194308	211654
A Imports of merchandise c.i.f.	26651	54366	72002	61979	70433	84543	90516	100458	102520	116542	133751	152574
B Other	7780	17773	24766	27140	28721	32828	39953	44085	49510	56311	60556	59080
2 Factor income to the rest of the world	1676	3706	6603	9635	12663	14841	19319	23431	23394	26651	27683	29323
A Compensation of employees	77	66	56	64	84	90	248	270	261	280	280	285
B Property and entrepreneurial income	1599	3640	6547	9571	12579	14751	19071	23161	23133	26371	27403	29038
3 Current transfers to the rest of the world	487	1356	2108	2478	2799	3212	3796	4791	5522	5506	6201	7221
A Indirect taxes by general government to supranational organizations	-	-	-	-	-	-	-	-	-	-	-	-
B Other current transfers	487	1356	2108	2478	2799	3212	3796	4791	5522	5506	6201	7221
By general government	299	882	1448	1758	1938	2186	2617	3271	3850	3870	4209	4938
By other resident sectors	188	474	660	720	861	1026	1179	1520	1672	1636	1992	2283
4 Surplus of the nation on current transactions	-1728	-12692	-26802	-11005	-5278	5448	12460	4146	14645	23929	26834	-32837
Payments to the Rest of the World, and Surplus of the Nation on Current Transfers	34866	64509	78677	90227	109338	140872	166044	176911	195592	228938	255026	215361
Receipts From The Rest of the World
1 Exports of goods and services	33403	62189	76264	87221	105407	134795	156288	165022	183921	214078	235383	194047
A Exports of merchandise f.o.b.	17715	38140	48747	57863	70007	92863	106899	114798	133249	156822	173023	135860

Norway

3.51 External Transactions: Current Account: Detail
(Continued)

Million Norwegian kroner

	1970	1975	1977	1978	1979	1980	1981	1982	1983	1984	1985	1986
B Other	15688	24049	27517	29358	35400	41932	49390	50224	50672	57256	62361	58187
2 Factor income from the rest of the world	1056	1791	1870	2453	3337	5321	8740	10727	10392	13509	18203	19985
A Compensation of employees	24	42	54	60	66	66	84	96	96	108	96	108
B Property and entrepreneurial income	1031	1749	1816	2393	3271	5255	8656	10631	10296	13401	18107	19877
3 Current transfers from the rest of the world	408	529	543	553	594	756	1016	1161	1278	1350	1439	1331
A Subsidies to general government from supranational organizations	-	-	-	-	-	-	-	-	-	-	-	-
B Other current transfers	408	529	543	553	594	756	1016	1161	1278	1350	1439	1331
To general government	-	-	-	-	-	-	-	-	-	-	-	-
To other resident sectors	408	529	543	553	594	756	1016	1161	1278	1350	1439	1331
Receipts from the Rest of the World on Current Transfers	34867	64509	78677	90227	109338	140872	166044	176910	195591	228937	255025	215363

3.52 External Transactions: Capital Accumulation Account

Million Norwegian kroner

	1970	1975	1977	1978	1979	1980	1981	1982	1983	1984	1985	1986
					Finance of Gross Accumulation							
1 Surplus of the nation on current transactions	-1728	-12692	-26802	-11005	-5278	5448	12460	4146	14645	23929	26834	-32836
2 Capital transfers from the rest of the world	...	...	...	...	...	...	...	...	...	...	...	...
Statistical discrepancy a	180	-	-	-	201	199	206	-	-	-	-	-
Total Finance of Gross Accumulation	-1548	-12692	-26802	-11005	-5077	5647	12666	4146	14645	23929	26834	-32836
					Gross Accumulation							
1 Capital transfers to the rest of the world	...	...	...	...	...	...	...	...	...	...	...	...
2 Purchases of intangible assets, n.e.c., net, from the rest of the world	-	-	-	-	-	-	-	-	-	-	-	-
Net lending to the rest of the world	-1548	-12692	-26802	-11005	-5077	5347	12666	4146	14645	23929	26834	-32836
Total Gross Accumulation	-1548	-12692	-26802	-11005	-5077	5647	12666	4146	14645	23929	26834	-32836

a) Item 'Statistical discrepancy' refers to allocation of SDRs.

3.53 External Transactions: Capital Finance Account

Million Norwegian kroner

	1970	1975	1977	1978	1979	1980	1981	1982	1983	1984	1985	1986
				Acquisitions of Foreign Financial Assets								
1 Gold and SDR's	180	5	45	33	298	115	275	774	-212	27	-53	745
2 Currency and transferable deposits	643	202	-100	-181	-97	87	81	221	1328	474	-171	7
3 Other deposits	-34	1446	632	3979	7597	14701	7440	6978	-4253	14851	-4319	-9602
4 Bills and bonds, short term	5	-	18	18	152	512	77	119	3566	12992	30283	1682
5 Bonds, long term	-	-	-	-	-	-	-	-	-	-	-	-
6 Corporate equity securities	219	68	547	79	-41	178	911	511	1187	1162	3790	3287
7 Short-term loans, n.e.c.	59	148	-39	-97	-	-514	1328	4034	2351	3972	260	1553
8 Long-term loans	881	893	1584	926	653	2013	1591	3282	4539	4286	9041	8709
9 Proprietors' net additions to accumulation of quasi-corporate, non-resident enterprises	-	-	-	-	-	-	-	-	-	-	-	-
10 Trade credit and advances	391	826	1209	2419	5448	781	1567	2394	2291	-841	516	-2123
11 Other	-51	817	-840	1413	1038	1941	489	980	1234	-	1087	646
Total Acquisitions of Foreign Financial Assets	2293	4405	3056	8589	15048	19814	13759	19293	12031	36923	40434	4904
				Incurrence of Foreign Liabilities								
1 Currency and transferable deposits	416	-76	-	-	-	-	-	-	-	-	-	-
2 Other deposits	-2	-160	2798	-2213	2472	7293	4661	7287	2693	12175	12863	9191
3 Bills and bonds, short term	-	-	-	-	-	-	-	-	-	-	-	-
4 Bonds, long term	380	2815	10163	12515	8926	-149	-4109	-4425	-7256	3442	10559	29506
5 Corporate equity securities	274	655	672	486	251	687	235	1029	1585	3838	1284	4190
6 Short-term loans, n.e.c.	-262	956	-1376	2204	343	1396	86	-766	-3933	-1764	5431	6629

Norway

3.53 External Transactions: Capital Finance Account
(Continued)

Million Norwegian kroner

	1970	1975	1977	1978	1979	1980	1981	1982	1983	1984	1985	1986
7 Long-term loans	1333	11749	13642	5826	3524	-1503	1993	10542	139	-2235	-7917	1967
8 Non-resident proprietors' net additions to accumulation of resident quasi-corporate enterprises	-	-	-	-	-	-	-	-	-	-	-	-
9 Trade credit and advances	639	372	1712	825	1728	10	-880	1699	345	1620	1714	-185
10 Other	585	-97	197	-2906	-163	1908	-902	521	994	-941	687	-941
Total Incurrence of Liabilities	3363	16214	27808	16737	17081	9642	1084	15887	-5433	16135	24621	50357
Statistical discrepancy [a]	478	883	2050	2857	3044	4525	10	-740	2819	-3141	-11021	-12616
Net Lending	-1548	-12692	-26802	-11005	-5077	5647	12665	4146	14645	23929	26834	-32837
Total Incurrence of Liabilities and Net Lending	2293	4405	3056	8589	15048	19814	13759	19293	12031	36923	40434	4904

a) Item 'Statistical discrepancy' refers to other short-term capital transactions and a statistical discrepancy.

4.1 Derivation of Value Added by Kind of Activity, in Current Prices

Million Norwegian kroner

	1980 Gross Output	1980 Intermediate Consumption	1980 Value Added	1981 Gross Output	1981 Intermediate Consumption	1981 Value Added	1982 Gross Output	1982 Intermediate Consumption	1982 Value Added	1983 Gross Output	1983 Intermediate Consumption	1983 Value Added
					All Producers							
1 Agriculture, hunting, forestry and fishing	22439	11469	10969	25510	12553	12957	27013	13576	13437	27599	14464	13135
A Agriculture and hunting	16465	9496	6969	18186	10339	7847	19650	11054	8597	19638	11688	7950
B Forestry and logging	2048	311	1737	2610	366	2244	2536	365	2171	2405	359	2046
C Fishing	3926	1662	2264	4714	1848	2866	4827	2157	2670	5556	2417	3139
2 Mining and quarrying	45905	3827	42078	56253	5068	51185	65140	8627	56514	78160	9929	68231
A Coal mining	111	79	32	186	125	61	186	130	55	191	108	84
B Crude petroleum and natural gas production	43523	2532	40991	53544	3565	49979	62436	7090	55346	75137	8282	66855
C Metal ore mining	1100	678	422	1258	767	492	1148	743	405	1263	792	470
D Other mining	1171	538	633	1265	611	654	1370	664	707	1569	747	822
3 Manufacturing	159133	113498	45635	176296	127721	48575	184297	132914	51383	193424	136699	56724
A Manufacture of food, beverages and tobacco	32824	27931	4894	38236	31800	6436	41740	34041	7699	44958	35924	9034
B Textile, wearing apparel and leather industries	4872	3017	1856	4811	2954	1857	4594	2892	1702	4293	2684	1609
C Manufacture of wood and wood products, including furniture	11812	7745	4067	12908	8716	4192	13367	9065	4303	13259	8964	4296
D Manufacture of paper and paper products, printing and publishing	16899	11322	5577	19725	13258	6467	20197	13476	6722	21859	13951	7908
E Manufacture of chemicals and chemical petroleum, coal, rubber and plastic products	26405	21031	5374	28746	24056	4689	29650	24520	5130	32801	27092	5709
F Manufacture of non-metallic mineral products, except products of petroleum and coal	4685	2860	1824	5271	3253	2019	5576	3456	2120	5744	3432	2312
G Basic metal industries	16273	10594	5679	15915	11430	4484	14792	10821	3971	18305	12137	6168
H Manufacture of fabricated metal products, machinery and equipment	44565	28528	16037	49924	31807	18117	53568	34171	19397	51340	32043	19297
I Other manufacturing industries	798	470	328	760	447	314	813	474	339	864	474	391
4 Electricity, gas and water	16401	8164	8237	19216	9058	10158	24062	12081	11981	28123	13811	14312
A Electricity, gas and steam	15824	7907	7917	18682	8803	9878	23425	11782	11643	27380	13485	13895
B Water works and supply	576	257	320	534	255	280	637	298	338	743	326	417
5 Construction	47590	30638	16952	53953	34281	19673	59555	36844	22711	63157	39309	23848
6 Wholesale and retail trade, restaurants and hotels	51992	18729	33264	59825	21350	38475	67956	25191	42765	73974	28499	45475
A Wholesale and retail trade	45300	15185	30115	51975	17279	34697	58913	20541	38372	63530	23201	40328
B Restaurants and hotels	6692	3544	3149	7850	4071	3779	9043	4650	4393	10445	5298	5147
7 Transport, storage and communication	56952	30062	26890	65811	35057	30755	69031	37742	31289	72963	39110	33852
A Transport and storage	49903	27722	22181	57149	32594	24556	58088	34703	23385	60096	35637	24459
B Communication	7049	2340	4709	8662	2463	6199	10943	3039	7904	12867	3473	9394
8 Finance, insurance, real estate and business services	41507	13263	28244	49638	15483	34155	59462	18604	40859	67441	21807	45633
A Financial institutions	11206	3059	8147	14409	3482	10926	18136	4283	13853	20781	5220	15562

Norway

4.1 Derivation of Value Added by Kind of Activity, in Current Prices
(Continued)

Million Norwegian kroner

	1980			1981			1982			1983		
	Gross Output	Intermediate Consumption	Value Added	Gross Output	Intermediate Consumption	Value Added	Gross Output	Intermediate Consumption	Value Added	Gross Output	Intermediate Consumption	Value Added
B Insurance	2183	1339	845	2047	1225	822	2053	1504	549	2339	1970	370
C Real estate and business services	28118	8865	19253	33182	10776	22406	39273	12816	26457	44320	14618	29702
Real estate, except dwellings	5071	2427	2644	6090	3030	3061	6761	3221	3539	7488	3492	3997
Dwellings	13389	3321	10067	15464	3855	11609	17784	4381	13402	20315	5314	15001
9 Community, social and personal services	16925	4447	12478	19048	5040	14009	21491	5770	15722	24232	6531	17701
A Sanitary and similar services	488	39	449	556	45	511	661	54	608	719	57	663
B Social and related community services	6924	2109	4815	7851	2455	5396	8987	2828	6159	10101	3238	6863
Educational services	1019	772	247	1109	947	162	1357	1159	198	1525	1345	180
Medical, dental, other health and veterinary services	4456	949	3508	5058	1064	3994	5818	1202	4616	6374	1318	5057
C Recreational and cultural services	2510	778	1732	2881	884	1997	3102	971	2131	3834	1210	2624
D Personal and household services	7003	1521	5482	7760	1656	6104	8741	1916	6824	9578	2027	7551
Total, Industries	458843	234096	224747	525550	265609	259941	578006	291347	286660	629072	310160	318912
Producers of Government Services	57363	18462	38901	67626	22464	45162	76579	25073	51505	85354	28512	56841
Other Producers	...	...	...	...	...	...	...	...	...	...	...	...
Total	516206	252558	263648	593176	288073	305103	654585	316420	338165	714425	338672	375753
Less: Imputed bank service charge	...	-8724	8724	...	-11349	11349	...	-14318	14318	...	-15960	15960
Import duties a	3692	...	3692	4248	...	4248	5203	...	5203	5764	...	5764
Value added tax b	56355	31651	24703	62377	34354	28024	69533	37997	31536	74087	39464	34623
Other adjustments c	1726	...	1726	1649	...	1649	1683	...	1683	2017	...	2017
Total	577979	292933	285045	661450	333776	327675	731004	368735	362269	796293	394096	402197
Memorandum Item: Mineral fuels and power	70899	21312	49587	84428	24651	59777	98395	31064	67331	116008	35166	80842

of which General Government:

	Gross Output	Intermediate Consumption	Value Added	Gross Output	Intermediate Consumption	Value Added	Gross Output	Intermediate Consumption	Value Added	Gross Output	Intermediate Consumption	Value Added
1 Agriculture, hunting, forestry and fishing	16	6	10	17	7	10	18	7	11	23	10	13
2 Mining and quarrying	...	...	...	...	...	...	...	...	...	...	...	...
3 Manufacturing	...	...	...	...	...	...	...	...	...	...	...	...
4 Electricity, gas and water	...	...	...	...	...	...	...	...	...	...	...	...
5 Construction	...	...	...	...	...	...	...	...	...	...	...	...
6 Wholesale and retail trade, restaurants and hotels	...	...	...	...	...	...	...	...	...	...	...	...
7 Transport and communication	3695	2890	805	4178	3243	935	4653	3587	1066	5052	3929	1123
8 Finance, insurance, real estate and business services	298	141	157	368	169	199	343	107	236	395	121	273
9 Community, social and personal services	53353	15425	37928	63063	19045	44018	71565	21373	50192	79884	24452	55432
Total, Industries of General Government	57363	18462	38901	67626	22464	45162	76579	25073	51505	85354	28512	56841
Producers of Government Services	...	...	...	...	...	...	...	...	...	...	...	...
Total, General Government	...	...	...	...	...	...	...	...	...	...	...	...

	1984			1985			1986		
	Gross Output	Intermediate Consumption	Value Added	Gross Output	Intermediate Consumption	Value Added	Gross Output	Intermediate Consumption	Value Added

All Producers

1 Agriculture, hunting, forestry and fishing	30397	15354	15042	32244	16886	15359	34860	18376	16484
A Agriculture and hunting	21629	12249	9380	22692	13411	9282	24165	14617	9548
B Forestry and logging	2880	420	2459	2953	438	2516	3169	441	2728
C Fishing	5888	2685	3203	6599	3037	3561	7527	3318	4209
2 Mining and quarrying	96398	11621	84778	107624	16074	91550	72682	20690	51992
A Coal mining	188	100	88	239	117	122	220	114	106
B Crude petroleum and natural gas production	93089	9702	83387	104071	13900	90171	68815	18318	50497
C Metal ore mining	1390	941	449	1494	1088	406	1501	1141	360
D Other mining	1732	878	854	1821	970	851	2147	1118	1030

Norway

4.1 Derivation of Value Added by Kind of Activity, in Current Prices
(Continued)

Million Norwegian kroner

		1984			1985			1986		
		Gross Output	Intermediate Consumption	Value Added	Gross Output	Intermediate Consumption	Value Added	Gross Output	Intermediate Consumption	Value Added
3	Manufacturing	217590	153066	64524	246733	176497	70236	255193	176094	79099
	A Manufacture of food, beverages and tobacco	48990	38744	10246	53010	41467	11544	58081	44346	13735
	B Textile, wearing apparel and leather industries	4643	2934	1709	5029	3218	1811	5276	3353	1923
	C Manufacture of wood and wood products, including furniture	13843	9431	4412	15161	10299	4862	16550	11097	5453
	D Manufacture of paper and paper products, printing and publishing	25266	15997	9269	28163	18028	10134	30122	19016	11107
	E Manufacture of chemicals and chemical petroleum, coal, rubber and plastic products	37358	30059	7299	39575	32066	7509	34197	23969	10228
	F Manufacture of non-metallic mineral products, except products of petroleum and coal	5867	3594	2272	6675	4194	2481	7938	4810	3128
	G Basic metal industries	23843	15471	8372	24485	17075	7410	22525	15886	6638
	H Manufacture of fabricated metal products, machinery and equipment	56826	36307	20519	73530	49510	24020	79270	52915	26355
	I Other manufacturing industries	955	529	427	1106	641	465	1236	703	533
4	Electricity, gas and water	32772	16201	16571	38151	19355	18796	39077	18723	20355
	A Electricity, gas and steam	31953	15828	16124	37234	18942	18292	38064	18272	19791
	B Water works and supply	819	372	447	917	413	504	1014	450	563
5	Construction	66660	42307	24353	73194	46285	26909	82773	53700	29073
6	Wholesale and retail trade, restaurants and hotels	80850	31405	49445	90852	35547	55305	101717	39406	62311
	A Wholesale and retail trade	68973	25305	43668	77171	28523	48648	86477	31667	54810
	B Restaurants and hotels	11877	6100	5777	13681	7024	6657	15240	7739	7502
7	Transport, storage and communication	82146	45069	37077	88649	49999	38651	92239	48059	44180
	A Transport and storage	67960	41146	26814	73379	45077	28302	74386	42338	32048
	B Communication	14186	3923	10263	15270	4922	10349	17853	5722	12131
8	Finance, insurance, real estate and business services	75172	25853	49318	86981	31273	55708	106062	36192	69870
	A Financial institutions	21090	6076	15015	23253	7179	16074	30780	8362	22418
	B Insurance	2750	2659	91	3057	3233	-176	3555	3175	380
	C Real estate and business services	51332	17119	34213	60672	20861	39811	71727	24655	47072
	Real estate, except dwellings	8281	3978	4303	9417	4574	4843	10433	4645	5788
	Dwellings	22569	5913	16656	24975	6970	18005	27921	8408	19513
9	Community, social and personal services	25730	6980	18750	28581	7928	20652	32413	8876	23537
	A Sanitary and similar services	770	57	714	943	80	862	1057	82	975
	B Social and related community services	10697	3501	7197	11382	3739	7642	12416	4001	8415
	Educational services	1672	1473	199	1852	1591	261	2096	1709	388
	Medical, dental, other health and veterinary services	6668	1399	5269	6879	1422	5457	7434	1515	5919
	C Recreational and cultural services	4066	1283	2783	4461	1407	3054	5091	1648	3443
	D Personal and household services	10197	2140	8057	11795	2702	9093	13849	3144	10705
Total, Industries		707714	347856	359858	793009	399844	393166	817017	420116	396901
Producers of Government Services		92249	30441	61808	102017	34004	68013	112708	37414	75294
Other Producers		...	...	...	...	...	...	...	...	...
Total		799963	378296	421667	895026	433847	461179	929725	457530	472195
Less: Imputed bank service charge		...	-15443	15443	...	-15857	15857	...	-22008	22008
Import duties a		6006	...	6006	9032	...	9032	11999	...	11999
Value added tax b		81225	43431	37794	93928	49495	44433	102730	52518	50212
Other adjustments c		2489	...	2489	3030	...	3030	3624	...	3624
Total		889683	437170	452512	1001020	499199	501817	1048080	532056	516022
Memorandum Item: Mineral fuels and power		140211	40535	99676	157303	48514	108789	117044	44600	72444

Norway

4.1 Derivation of Value Added by Kind of Activity, in Current Prices
(Continued)

Million Norwegian kroner

	1984 Gross Output	1984 Intermediate Consumption	1984 Value Added	1985 Gross Output	1985 Intermediate Consumption	1985 Value Added	1986 Gross Output	1986 Intermediate Consumption	1986 Value Added
				of which General Government:					
1 Agriculture, hunting, forestry and fishing	28	14	15	25	11	14	25	11	15
2 Mining and quarrying	...	...	...	...	...	...	...	...	...
3 Manufacturing	...	...	...	...	...	...	...	...	...
4 Electricity, gas and water	...	...	...	...	...	...	...	...	...
5 Construction	...	...	...	...	...	...	...	...	...
6 Wholesale and retail trade, restaurants and hotels	...	...	...	...	...	...	...	...	...
7 Transport and communication	5423	4248	1175	5813	4528	1285	6182	4788	1395
8 Finance, insurance, real estate and business services	501	159	341	559	179	380	615	204	411
9 Community, social and personal services	86297	26020	60277	95621	29287	66334	105886	32412	73474
Total, Industries of General Government	92249	30441	61808	102017	34004	68013	112708	37414	75294
Producers of Government Services	...	...	...	...	...	...	...	...	...
Total, General Government	...	...	...	...	...	...	...	...	...

a) Item 'Import duties' includes collection of customs duties, value added tax on imports and special excises or taxes on imports.
b) Item 'Value added tax' excludes value added tax on imports which is included in item 'Import duties'.
c) Item 'Other adjustments' refers to collection of investment levy on fixed capital formation and subsidies on residential and social buildings.

4.2 Derivation of Value Added by Kind of Activity, in Constant Prices

Million Norwegian kroner

	1980 Gross Output	1980 Intermediate Consumption	1980 Value Added	1981 Gross Output	1981 Intermediate Consumption	1981 Value Added	1982 Gross Output	1982 Intermediate Consumption	1982 Value Added	1983 Gross Output	1983 Intermediate Consumption	1983 Value Added
				At constant prices of: 1980								
				All Producers								
1 Agriculture, hunting, forestry and fishing	22439	11469	10969	23446	11488	11959	23996	11550	12446	23950	11631	12319
A Agriculture and hunting	16465	9496	6969	16698	9560	7138	17235	9540	7695	16732	9541	7191
B Forestry and logging	2048	311	1737	2269	326	1943	2114	297	1817	2069	277	1792
C Fishing	3926	1662	2264	4480	1602	2877	4646	1713	2933	5149	1813	3336
2 Mining and quarrying	45905	3827	42078	44986	4489	40498	47426	6707	40719	55212	7346	47866
A Coal mining	111	79	32	148	111	38	152	111	41	161	93	69
B Crude petroleum and natural gas production	43523	2532	40991	42541	3149	39391	45133	5471	39662	52778	6116	46662
C Metal ore mining	1100	678	422	1210	686	524	1025	594	431	1067	587	480
D Other mining	1171	538	633	1087	543	544	1116	532	585	1206	551	655
3 Manufacturing	159133	113498	45635	159566	114874	44691	156403	111616	44787	154361	110206	44155
A Manufacture of food, beverages and tobacco	32824	27931	4894	32732	28290	4443	33308	28874	4433	33705	29498	4207
B Textile, wearing apparel and leather industries	4872	3017	1856	4494	2767	1726	4045	2526	1518	3590	2193	1397
C Manufacture of wood and wood products, including furniture	11812	7745	4067	11848	7936	3912	11463	7714	3749	10847	7376	3471
D Manufacture of paper and paper products, printing and publishing	16899	11322	5577	17844	12108	5736	17185	11623	5562	17285	11604	5681
E Manufacture of chemicals and chemical petroleum, coal, rubber and plastic products	26405	21031	5374	25843	20504	5339	25707	19889	5817	27179	21200	5980
F Manufacture of non-metallic mineral products, except products of petroleum and coal	4685	2860	1824	4618	2860	1758	4526	2802	1724	4294	2620	1674
G Basic metal industries	16273	10594	5679	15809	10197	5612	14350	9007	5343	15915	9457	6458
H Manufacture of fabricated metal products, machinery and equipment	44565	28528	16037	45617	29783	15834	45050	28752	16297	40819	25872	14947
I Other manufacturing industries	798	470	328	761	430	331	771	429	342	728	387	341
4 Electricity, gas and water	16401	8164	8237	16851	7898	8954	18000	8906	9094	19807	9520	10287
A Electricity, gas and steam	15824	7907	7917	16385	7670	8715	17518	8667	8851	19320	9275	10045
B Water works and supply	576	257	320	466	228	239	482	239	243	488	246	242

Norway

4.2 Derivation of Value Added by Kind of Activity, in Constant Prices
(Continued)

Million Norwegian kroner

	1980 Gross Output	1980 Intermediate Consumption	1980 Value Added	1981 Gross Output	1981 Intermediate Consumption	1981 Value Added	1982 Gross Output	1982 Intermediate Consumption	1982 Value Added	1983 Gross Output	1983 Intermediate Consumption	1983 Value Added
				At constant prices of:1980								
5 Construction	47590	30638	16952	48238	31504	16735	48471	31441	17031	49487	31924	17563
6 Wholesale and retail trade, restaurants and hotels	51992	18729	33264	51178	18657	32521	51310	19403	31907	52344	20521	31823
A Wholesale and retail trade	45300	15185	30115	44632	15111	29521	45015	15916	29100	45878	16847	29032
B Restaurants and hotels	6692	3544	3149	6545	3546	2999	6294	3487	2807	6466	3675	2791
7 Transport, storage and communication	56952	30062	26890	58319	30774	27545	56512	29982	26530	55620	28471	27149
A Transport and storage	49903	27722	22181	50702	28543	22158	48537	27519	21018	47052	25841	21211
B Communication	7049	2340	4709	7617	2230	5387	7976	2463	5513	8568	2631	5938
8 Finance, insurance, real estate and business services	41507	13263	28244	43331	14021	29310	45300	15091	30209	46739	16465	30274
A Financial institutions	11206	3059	8147	11452	3044	8408	11753	3308	8445	12210	3756	8454
B Insurance	2183	1339	845	2090	1170	920	2260	1388	872	2288	1686	603
C Real estate and business services	28118	8865	19253	29789	9807	19982	31287	10395	20892	32241	11024	21217
Real estate, except dwellings	5071	2427	2644	5482	2727	2755	5481	2608	2873	5580	2667	2913
Dwellings	13389	3321	10067	13019	3507	10352	14482	3726	10756	15194	4231	10963
9 Community, social and personal services	16925	4447	12478	17110	4568	12542	17482	4783	12699	18105	5073	13031
A Sanitary and similar services	488	39	449	490	40	451	520	43	477	515	44	471
B Social and related community services	6924	2109	4815	7064	2194	4869	7370	2301	5069	7594	2406	5188
Educational services	1019	772	247	1007	835	172	1091	908	183	1140	976	165
Medical, dental, other health and veterinary services	4456	949	3508	4564	962	3602	4849	997	3852	4981	1003	3977
C Recreational and cultural services	2510	778	1732	2673	805	1868	2582	796	1787	2926	918	2008
D Personal and household services	7003	1521	5482	6883	1529	5354	7009	1643	5367	7070	1706	5364
Total, Industries	458843	234096	224747	463026	238271	224754	464900	239479	225421	475625	241159	234466
Producers of Government Services	57363	18462	38901	61296	20155	41141	64075	20682	43393	67216	22223	44993
Other Producers	...	...	...	...	...	...	...	...	...	...	...	...
Total	516206	252558	263648	524322	258427	265896	528975	260161	268814	542841	263383	279458
Less: Imputed bank service charge	...	-8724	8724	...	-8985	8985	...	-9205	9205	...	-9543	9543
Import duties [a]	3692	...	3692	3869	...	3869	4253	...	4253	4092	...	4092
Value added tax [b]	56355	31651	24703	55806	30806	25000	56803	31404	25399	57258	31307	25951
Other adjustments [c]	1726	...	1726	1767	...	1767	-755	...	-755	1918	...	1918
Total	577979	292933	285045	585764	298218	287546	589276	300770	288506	606109	304233	301877
Memorandum Item: Mineral fuels and power	70899	21312	49587	69407	20770	48637	73086	23730	49355	83062	25655	57407
				of which General Government:								
1 Agriculture, hunting, forestry and fishing	16	6	10	15	6	9	14	5	9	17	6	10
2 Mining and quarrying	...	...	...	...	...	...	...	...	...	...	...	...
3 Manufacturing	...	...	...	...	...	...	...	...	...	...	...	...
4 Electricity, gas and water	...	...	...	...	...	...	...	...	...	...	...	...
5 Construction	...	...	...	...	...	...	...	...	...	...	...	...
6 Wholesale and retail trade, restaurants and hotels	...	...	...	...	...	...	...	...	...	...	...	...
7 Transport and communication	3695	2890	805	3830	2975	855	3891	2986	905	4068	3141	927
8 Finance, insurance, real estate and business services	298	141	157	327	147	180	277	80	197	299	78	220
9 Community, social and personal services	53353	15425	37928	57125	17027	40097	59893	17612	42281	62833	18998	43835
Total, Industries of General Government	57363	18462	38901	61296	20155	41141	64075	20682	43393	67216	22223	44993
Producers of Government Services	...	...	...	...	...	...	...	...	...	...	...	...
Total, General Government	...	...	...	...	...	...	...	...	...	...	...	...

Norway

4.2 Derivation of Value Added by Kind of Activity, in Constant Prices

Million Norwegian kroner

	1984 Gross Output	1984 Intermediate Consumption	1984 Value Added	1985 Gross Output	1985 Intermediate Consumption	1985 Value Added	1986 Gross Output	1986 Intermediate Consumption	1986 Value Added
At constant prices of:1980 — All Producers									
1 Agriculture, hunting, forestry and fishing	25184	11828	13356	24726	12039	12687	25033	12634	12399
A Agriculture and hunting	17554	9548	8006	17069	9718	7351	16686	10028	6658
B Forestry and logging	2241	316	1925	2177	311	1866	2221	312	1909
C Fishing	5390	1964	3426	5480	2011	3469	6126	2294	3832
2 Mining and quarrying	63495	8354	55141	68609	10530	58079	73420	13053	60366
A Coal mining	152	85	67	183	75	108	173	70	102
B Crude petroleum and natural gas production	60939	6982	53958	65967	9068	56899	70606	11504	59102
C Metal ore mining	1134	671	464	1170	741	428	1204	762	442
D Other mining	1270	617	653	1290	646	644	1437	717	720
3 Manufacturing	162716	115703	47013	175478	126439	49039	176861	127082	49779
A Manufacture of food, beverages and tobacco	34195	30029	4166	34589	30407	4183	34605	30397	4208
B Textile, wearing apparel and leather industries	3652	2234	1417	3782	2298	1484	3763	2277	1485
C Manufacture of wood and wood products, including furniture	10795	7304	3490	11149	7550	3599	11384	7682	3702
D Manufacture of paper and paper products, printing and publishing	18581	12373	6208	19570	13078	6492	19684	13134	6550
E Manufacture of chemicals and chemical petroleum, coal, rubber and plastic products	29100	22031	7068	29631	22846	6786	29441	22550	6891
F Manufacture of non-metallic mineral products, except products of petroleum and coal	4197	2620	1577	4504	2878	1625	4951	3173	1778
G Basic metal industries	17695	10832	6863	18171	11533	6638	18021	11454	6567
H Manufacture of fabricated metal products, machinery and equipment	43737	27876	15861	53234	35379	17855	54114	35919	18195
I Other manufacturing industries	766	404	362	848	470	378	899	497	402
4 Electricity, gas and water	20576	9962	10614	21846	11550	10296	20596	10905	9690
A Electricity, gas and steam	20094	9699	10396	21347	11274	10073	20086	10618	9469
B Water works and supply	481	263	218	499	276	223	509	288	221
5 Construction	50438	32670	17768	52545	33863	18682	56678	37177	19501
6 Wholesale and retail trade, restaurants and hotels	55167	21817	33351	59582	23323	36258	63027	24352	38674
A Wholesale and retail trade	48270	17731	30539	52090	18806	33284	55365	19728	35636
B Restaurants and hotels	6898	4086	2811	7491	4517	2974	7662	4624	3038
7 Transport, storage and communication	59543	31042	28501	61604	32757	28847	64494	33252	31242
A Transport and storage	50382	28081	22301	51529	29218	22310	52774	29221	23553
B Communication	9161	2961	6199	10076	3539	6537	11720	4031	7689
8 Finance, insurance, real estate and business services	50017	18523	31494	54625	21251	33374	59339	22919	36420
A Financial institutions	12938	4159	8779	13881	4815	9066	14932	5339	9593
B Insurance	2552	2283	268	2627	2587	40	2760	2088	672
C Real estate and business services	34528	12081	22447	38117	13849	24268	41646	15491	26155
Real estate, except dwellings	5755	2795	2960	6204	3019	3185	6484	3125	3359
Dwellings	15740	4497	11243	16511	4978	11533	17407	5599	11808
9 Community, social and personal services	18204	5239	12965	19002	5627	13375	20036	5984	14052
A Sanitary and similar services	517	45	472	591	60	532	620	64	556
B Social and related community services	7617	2489	5128	7556	2523	5032	7696	2609	5087
Educational services	1171	1000	172	1218	1035	184	1288	1094	194
Medical, dental, other health and veterinary services	4880	1023	3857	4693	983	3710	4717	992	3726
C Recreational and cultural services	2987	940	2048	3172	983	2189	3468	1072	2396
D Personal and household services	7084	1765	5319	7683	2061	5622	8253	2239	6014

Norway

4.2 Derivation of Value Added by Kind of Activity, in Constant Prices
(Continued)

Million Norwegian kroner

	1984 Gross Output	1984 Intermediate Consumption	1984 Value Added	1985 Gross Output	1985 Intermediate Consumption	1985 Value Added	1986 Gross Output	1986 Intermediate Consumption	1986 Value Added
			At constant prices of: 1980						
Total, Industries	505340	255138	250202	538017	277380	260637	559482	287357	272125
Producers of Government Services	69159	22911	46248	71673	23985	47688	74216	25471	48745
Other Producers	...	...	...	...	...	...	...	...	...
Total	574499	278049	296450	609690	301365	308325	633698	312828	320870
Less: Imputed bank service charge	...	-10157	10157	...	-10897	10897	...	-11544	11544
Import duties [a]	4189	...	4189	6119	...	6119	6619	...	6619
Value added tax [b]	60007	32699	27309	65402	35195	30207	68661	36511	32150
Other adjustments [c]	1424	...	1424	2676	...	2676	3011	...	3011
Total	640119	320905	319215	683887	347457	336430	711989	360883	351106
Memorandum Item: Mineral fuels and power	92591	27402	65189	99192	31372	67819	102442	32901	69541
			of which General Government:						
1 Agriculture, hunting, forestry and fishing	19	8	11	15	5	10	14	5	9
2 Mining and quarrying	...	...	...	...	...	...	...	...	...
3 Manufacturing	...	...	...	...	...	...	...	...	...
4 Electricity, gas and water	...	...	...	...	...	...	...	...	...
5 Construction	...	...	...	...	...	...	...	...	...
6 Wholesale and retail trade, restaurants and hotels	...	...	...	...	...	...	...	...	...
7 Transport and communication	4191	3248	943	4203	3245	958	4280	3306	974
8 Finance, insurance, real estate and business services	349	95	253	363	97	266	370	103	267
9 Community, social and personal services	64601	19560	45041	67092	20637	46455	69552	22056	47495
Total, Industries of General Government	69159	22911	46248	71673	23985	47688	74216	25471	48745
Producers of Government Services	...	...	...	...	...	...	...	...	...
Total, General Government	...	...	...	...	...	...	...	...	...

a) Item 'Import duties' includes collection of customs duties, value added tax on imports and special excises or taxes on imports.
b) Item 'Value added tax' excludes value added tax on imports which is included in item 'Import duties'.
c) Item 'Other adjustments' refers to collection of investment levy on fixed capital formation and subsidies on residential and social buildings.

4.3 Cost Components of Value Added

Million Norwegian kroner

	1980 Compensation of Employees	1980 Capital Consumption	1980 Net Operating Surplus	1980 Indirect Taxes	1980 Less: Subsidies Received	1980 Value Added	1981 Compensation of Employees	1981 Capital Consumption	1981 Net Operating Surplus	1981 Indirect Taxes	1981 Less: Subsidies Received	1981 Value Added
				All Producers								
1 Agriculture, hunting, forestry and fishing	1226	3564	9857	272	3950	10969	1401	3944	11748	409	4544	12957
A Agriculture and hunting	344	2358	7626	97	3457	6969	369	2628	8481	139	3771	7847
B Forestry and logging	634	202	1072	19	190	1737	736	223	1515	22	252	2244
C Fishing	248	1005	1159	156	303	2264	296	1093	1752	248	522	2866
2 Mining and quarrying	2225	5082	30619	4271	119	42078	2717	7490	35857	5494	372	51185
A Coal mining	80	20	27	1	95	33	104	22	57	1	123	61
B Crude petroleum and natural gas production	1413	4745	30594	4239	...	40991	1830	7120	35565	5464	...	49979
C Metal ore mining	421	176	-174	19	21	422	449	193	81	15	246	492
D Other mining	310	142	172	12	3	633	334	155	154	14	3	654

Norway

4.3 Cost Components of Value Added
(Continued)

Million Norwegian kroner

		1980						1981				
	Compensation of Employees	Capital Consumption	Net Operating Surplus	Indirect Taxes	Less: Subsidies Received	Value Added	Compensation of Employees	Capital Consumption	Net Operating Surplus	Indirect Taxes	Less: Subsidies Received	Value Added
3 Manufacturing	34161	5552	8817	2671	5566	45635	37559	6068	7287	2991	5328	48575
A Manufacture of food, beverages and tobacco	4687	1010	1221	1883	3908	4894	5162	1097	1175	2181	3179	6436
B Textile, wearing apparel and leather industries	1489	184	274	22	113	1856	1485	196	284	21	128	1857
C Manufacture of wood and wood products, including furniture	2758	352	1007	59	109	4067	2990	390	921	64	173	4192
D Manufacture of paper and paper products, printing and publishing	4553	785	356	88	206	5577	4973	873	760	91	230	6467
E Manufacture of chemicals and chemical petroleum, coal, rubber and plastic products	3090	1038	1055	254	62	5374	3417	1107	-19	248	65	4689
F Manufacture of non-metallic mineral products, except products of petroleum and coal	1185	274	336	50	20	1824	1268	299	423	49	20	2019
G Basic metal industries	2975	741	2077	91	205	5679	3293	825	453	98	184	4484
H Manufacture of fabricated metal products, machinery and equipment	13151	1140	2443	222	920	16037	14699	1250	3255	237	1324	18117
I Other manufacturing industries	273	27	48	3	22	328	271	31	35	3	26	314
4 Electricity, gas and water	1943	2560	2239	1625	131	8237	2204	2842	3647	1644	180	10158
A Electricity, gas and steam	1840	2412	2149	1622	107	7917	2125	2675	3588	1641	151	9878
B Water works and supply	103	148	90	3	24	320	79	167	60	3	29	280
5 Construction	13268	2085	1485	192	78	16952	13984	2259	3290	207	66	19673
6 Wholesale and retail trade, restaurants and hotels	21343	3481	4805	6878	3242	33264	23893	3635	7185	7828	4065	38475
A Wholesale and retail trade	18800	3353	4301	6854	3193	30115	20938	3505	6466	7802	4014	34697
B Restaurants and hotels	2543	127	504	24	50	3149	2955	130	719	26	52	3779
7 Transport, storage and communication	18120	11033	-1470	881	1674	26890	20591	12827	-2073	942	1533	30755
A Transport and storage	14133	10107	-1177	792	1674	22181	16115	11780	-2669	863	1533	24556
B Communication	3987	927	-293	89	...	4709	4476	1047	596	80	...	6199
8 Finance, insurance, real estate and business services	8472	4785	16092	723	1828	28244	10269	5411	19574	831	1931	34155
A Financial institutions	3499	227	5788	24	1391	8147	4211	277	7835	27	1423	10926
B Insurance	1370	117	-646	4	1	845	1518	142	-842	5	1	822
C Real estate and business services	3604	4441	10951	695	437	19253	4540	4992	12581	800	508	22406
Real estate, except dwellings	17	778	1782	146	79	2644	19	854	2078	170	61	3061
Dwellings	152	3635	6372	246	337	10067	179	4106	7433	297	406	11609
9 Community, social and personal services	8089	889	5482	556	2539	12478	9045	920	6388	610	2955	14009
A Sanitary and similar services	329	...	120	...	...	449	355	...	156	...	...	511
B Social and related community services	3534	580	2395	2	1696	4815	4021	597	2735	3	1960	5396
Educational services	745	70	654	2	1223	247	846	71	687	3	1444	162
Medical, dental, other health and veterinary services	1308	476	1741	...	18	3508	1472	492	2048	...	18	3994
C Recreational and cultural services	589	173	1284	529	843	1732	686	188	1536	582	994	1997
D Personal and household services	3637	136	1683	25	...	5482	3983	135	1962	26	1	6104
Total, Industries	108847	39031	77925	18069	19126	224747	121661	45395	92904	20955	20974	259941
Producers of Government Services	36574	2327	...	...	...	38901	42504	2658	...	...	...	45162
Other Producers	...	...	...	...	...	...	...	...	...	...	...	...
Total	145421	41358	77925	18069	19126	263648	164165	48053	92904	20955	20974	305103
Less: Imputed bank service charge [a]	...	...	8724	...	...	8724	...	...	11349	...	...	11349
Import duties [b]	...	...	...	3693	1	3692	...	...	...	4249	1	4248
Value added tax [c]	...	...	...	24703	...	24703	...	...	...	28024	...	28024
Other adjustments	...	...	...	2560	834	1726	...	...	...	2468	819	1649
Total	145421	41358	69201	49025	19961	285045	164165	48053	81555	55696	21794	327675
of which General Government:												
1 Agriculture, hunting, forestry and fishing	10	...	...	...	...	10	10	...	...	...	...	10

Norway

4.3 Cost Components of Value Added
(Continued)

Million Norwegian kroner

1980 / 1981

	Compensation of Employees	Capital Consumption	Net Operating Surplus	Indirect Taxes	Less: Subsidies Received	Value Added	Compensation of Employees	Capital Consumption	Net Operating Surplus	Indirect Taxes	Less: Subsidies Received	Value Added
2 Mining and quarrying	...	...	...	...	...	...	...	...	...	...	...	...
3 Manufacturing	...	...	...	...	...	...	...	...	...	...	...	...
4 Electricity, gas and water	...	...	...	...	...	...	...	...	...	...	...	...
5 Construction	...	...	...	...	...	...	...	...	...	...	...	...
6 Wholesale and retail trade, restaurants and hotels	...	...	...	...	...	...	...	...	...	...	...	...
7 Transport and communication	559	246	...	...	...	805	658	278	...	...	...	935
8 Finance, insurance, real estate & business services	153	5	...	...	...	157	194	5	...	...	...	199
9 Community, social and personal services	35852	2076	...	...	...	37928	41642	2375	...	...	...	44018
Total, Industries of General Government	36574	2327	...	...	...	38901	42504	2658	...	...	...	45162
Producers of Government Services	...	...	...	...	...	...	...	...	...	...	...	...
Total, General Government	...	...	...	...	...	...	...	...	...	...	...	...

1982 / 1983

	Compensation of Employees	Capital Consumption	Net Operating Surplus	Indirect Taxes	Less: Subsidies Received	Value Added	Compensation of Employees	Capital Consumption	Net Operating Surplus	Indirect Taxes	Less: Subsidies Received	Value Added
					All Producers							
1 Agriculture, hunting, forestry and fishing	1413	4296	12484	368	5125	13437	1540	4511	12201	408	5526	13135
A Agriculture and hunting	394	2900	9694	127	4519	8597	427	3176	8936	147	4735	7950
B Forestry and logging	690	238	1465	27	250	2171	722	258	1322	33	288	2046
C Fishing	330	1157	1325	214	357	2670	391	1078	1944	229	502	3139
2 Mining and quarrying	3504	9690	37522	6199	402	56514	3946	10432	45392	8880	419	68231
A Coal mining	126	23	64	1	157	55	137	23	136	1	213	84
B Crude petroleum and natural gas production	2591	9295	37288	6172	...	55346	3007	10038	44961	8849	...	66855
C Metal ore mining	444	204	-16	15	241	405	419	198	38	18	203	470
D Other mining	344	169	186	12	4	707	384	173	257	12	4	822
3 Manufacturing	39868	6714	7001	3422	5623	51383	41462	6956	10286	3758	5738	56724
A Manufacture of food, beverages and tobacco	5632	1216	1400	2691	3239	7699	6051	1266	1920	2984	3187	9034
B Textile, wearing apparel and leather industries	1452	211	143	19	122	1702	1353	212	206	18	180	1609
C Manufacture of wood and wood products, including furniture	3129	431	868	59	185	4303	3176	448	899	65	292	4296
D Manufacture of paper and paper products, printing and publishing	5152	962	790	73	254	6722	5866	996	1218	77	248	7908
E Manufacture of chemicals and chemical petroleum, coal, rubber and plastic products	3639	1217	106	232	65	5130	3836	1254	446	240	66	5709
F Manufacture of non-metallic mineral products, except products of petroleum and coal	1365	330	404	41	20	2120	1392	338	563	45	24	2312
G Basic metal industries	3269	929	50	73	349	3971	3334	955	2373	72	566	6168
H Manufacture of fabricated metal products, machinery and equipment	15954	1385	3188	233	1363	19397	16169	1454	2568	256	1149	19297
I Other manufacturing industries	278	33	53	3	27	339	286	34	94	3	26	391
4 Electricity, gas and water	2479	3224	4686	1750	157	11981	2675	3511	6394	1888	156	14312
A Electricity, gas and steam	2390	3034	4608	1747	136	11643	2573	3310	6250	1885	123	13895
B Water works and supply	89	189	78	3	20	338	102	201	144	3	33	417
5 Construction	15675	2600	4274	207	45	22711	17069	2733	3942	237	133	23848
6 Wholesale and retail trade, restaurants and hotels	26834	3897	8516	7990	4472	42765	28678	3999	8764	8449	4414	45475
A Wholesale and retail trade	23410	3748	7654	7963	4413	38372	24924	3847	7489	8419	4350	40328
B Restaurants and hotels	3414	149	862	27	59	4393	3754	152	1275	30	64	5147
7 Transport, storage and communication	22632	14347	-5056	1038	1671	31289	23958	16332	-5810	1228	1856	33852
A Transport and storage	17381	13162	-6447	959	1671	23385	18363	15091	-8270	1130	1856	24459
B Communication	5251	1185	1391	79	...	7904	5596	1241	2460	98	...	9394
8 Finance, insurance, real estate and business services	12225	6242	23480	941	2030	40859	13978	6933	25773	1164	2214	45633
A Financial institutions	4898	335	10046	30	1457	13853	5644	386	11066	41	1576	15562

Norway

4.3 Cost Components of Value Added
(Continued)

Million Norwegian kroner

1982 / 1983

	Compensation of Employees	Capital Consumption	Net Operating Surplus	Indirect Taxes	Less: Subsidies Received	Value Added	Compensation of Employees	Capital Consumption	Net Operating Surplus	Indirect Taxes	Less: Subsidies Received	Value Added
B Insurance	1779	175	-1409	5	1	549	1995	206	-1837	6	1	370
C Real estate and business services	5548	5732	14843	907	573	26457	6339	6341	16544	1117	638	29702
Real estate, except dwellings	22	973	2457	177	89	3539	33	1063	2799	197	95	3997
Dwellings	205	4724	8561	370	457	13402	218	5243	9593	446	499	15001
9 Community, social and personal services	10199	1019	7233	708	3438	15722	11275	1020	8073	846	3512	17701
A Sanitary and similar services	410	...	198	...	...	608	464	...	198	...	...	663
B Social and related community services	4603	661	3097	3	2205	6159	5139	662	3306	4	2248	6863
Educational services	945	79	691	3	1519	198	1054	79	617	4	1574	180
Medical, dental, other health and veterinary services	1673	544	2406	...	7	4616	1836	545	2689	...	13	5057
C Recreational and cultural services	739	210	1736	678	1232	2131	830	209	2038	811	1264	2624
D Personal and household services	4447	148	2203	27	1	6824	4842	149	2530	31	1	7551
Total, Industries	134829	52028	100141	22624	22962	286660	144580	56428	115014	26857	23967	318912
Producers of Government Services	48526	2979	...	...	...	51505	53655	3186	...	...	...	56841
Other Producers	...	...	...	...	...	...	...	...	...	...	...	...
Total	183356	55007	100141	22624	22962	338165	198235	59614	115014	26857	23967	375753
Less: Imputed bank service charge [a]	...	...	14318	...	...	14318	...	...	15960	...	...	15960
Import duties [b]	...	...	...	5204	1	5203	...	...	...	5765	1	5764
Value added tax [c]	...	...	...	31536	...	31536	...	...	...	34623	...	34623
Other adjustments	...	...	...	2383	700	1683	...	...	...	2489	472	2017
Total	183356	55007	85823	61747	23663	362269	198235	59614	99054	69734	24440	402197

of which General Government:

	Compensation of Employees	Capital Consumption	Net Operating Surplus	Indirect Taxes	Less: Subsidies Received	Value Added	Compensation of Employees	Capital Consumption	Net Operating Surplus	Indirect Taxes	Less: Subsidies Received	Value Added
1 Agriculture, hunting, forestry and fishing	11	...	...	...	...	11	13	...	...	...	...	13
2 Mining and quarrying	...	...	...	...	...	...	...	...	...	...	...	...
3 Manufacturing	...	...	...	...	...	...	...	...	...	...	...	...
4 Electricity, gas and water	...	...	...	...	...	...	...	...	...	...	...	...
5 Construction	...	...	...	...	...	...	...	...	...	...	...	...
6 Wholesale and retail trade, restaurants and hotels	...	...	...	...	...	...	...	...	...	...	...	...
7 Transport and communication	760	306	...	...	...	1066	811	311	...	...	...	1123
8 Finance, insurance, real estate & business services	231	6	...	...	...	236	268	6	...	...	...	273
9 Community, social and personal services	47524	2668	...	...	...	50192	52563	2869	...	...	...	55432
Total, Industries of General Government	48526	2979	...	...	...	51505	53655	3186	...	...	...	56841
Producers of Government Services	...	...	...	...	...	...	...	...	...	...	...	...
Total, General Government	...	...	...	...	...	...	...	...	...	...	...	...

1984 / 1985

	Compensation of Employees	Capital Consumption	Net Operating Surplus	Indirect Taxes	Less: Subsidies Received	Value Added	Compensation of Employees	Capital Consumption	Net Operating Surplus	Indirect Taxes	Less: Subsidies Received	Value Added

All Producers

	Compensation of Employees	Capital Consumption	Net Operating Surplus	Indirect Taxes	Less: Subsidies Received	Value Added	Compensation of Employees	Capital Consumption	Net Operating Surplus	Indirect Taxes	Less: Subsidies Received	Value Added
1 Agriculture, hunting, forestry and fishing	1711	4591	13877	419	5556	15042	1937	4968	13832	508	5886	15359
A Agriculture and hunting	449	3325	10156	184	4735	9380	485	3629	10013	250	5095	9282
B Forestry and logging	825	271	1621	38	296	2459	880	296	1612	46	318	2516
C Fishing	437	995	2100	197	525	3203	573	1043	2207	212	474	3561
2 Mining and quarrying	5139	12935	56112	11137	544	84778	6203	14377	60265	11190	485	91550
A Coal mining	124	21	197	1	254	88	136	23	43	1	82	122
B Crude petroleum and natural gas production	4117	12573	55604	11094	...	83387	5122	13967	59955	11127	...	90171
C Metal ore mining	488	180	40	27	286	449	494	200	72	39	399	406
D Other mining	410	161	272	16	5	854	451	186	196	23	4	851

Norway

4.3 Cost Components of Value Added
(Continued)

Million Norwegian kroner

		1984					1985				
	Compensation of Employees	Capital Consumption	Net Operating Surplus	Indirect Taxes	Less: Subsidies Received	Value Added	Compensation of Employees	Capital Consumption	Net Operating Surplus	Indirect Taxes	Less: Subsidies Received	Value Added
3 Manufacturing	44940	6542	14581	4293	5832	64524	49573	7658	13725	5058	5778	70236
A Manufacture of food, beverages and tobacco	6488	1191	2370	3301	3104	10246	7007	1370	2713	3703	3249	11544
B Textile, wearing apparel and leather industries	1401	192	278	21	183	1709	1519	219	202	31	160	1811
C Manufacture of wood and wood products, including furniture	3316	423	866	72	265	4412	3620	494	877	96	226	4862
D Manufacture of paper and paper products, printing and publishing	6450	935	2036	101	253	9269	7254	1098	1713	142	73	10134
E Manufacture of chemicals and chemical petroleum, coal, rubber and plastic products	4191	1165	1692	319	68	7299	4394	1357	1375	438	56	7509
F Manufacture of non-metallic mineral products, except products of petroleum and coal	1485	313	452	46	24	2272	1662	365	411	66	23	2481
G Basic metal industries	3761	908	4391	105	793	8372	3972	1088	2569	149	368	7410
H Manufacture of fabricated metal products, machinery and equipment	17543	1383	2379	325	1111	20519	19783	1630	3773	428	1594	24020
I Other manufacturing industries	306	30	118	3	30	427	362	37	92	5	31	465
4 Electricity, gas and water	2942	3804	7598	2387	159	16571	3265	4150	8687	2844	149	18796
A Electricity, gas and steam	2832	3584	7448	2383	121	16124	3143	3912	8524	2838	124	18292
B Water works and supply	111	220	150	4	38	447	122	238	163	6	25	504
5 Construction	18168	2695	3457	287	254	24353	19531	2991	4234	380	227	26909
6 Wholesale and retail trade, restaurants and hotels	31548	3800	9367	9473	4744	49445	35398	4371	9688	10820	4972	55305
A Wholesale and retail trade	27270	3660	7970	9435	4666	43668	30566	4210	7998	10769	4895	48648
B Restaurants and hotels	4278	140	1397	39	78	5777	4832	162	1690	51	77	6657
7 Transport, storage and communication	24968	16233	-3604	1434	1954	37077	26605	15486	-3303	1834	1971	38651
A Transport and storage	18990	14931	-6514	1312	1906	26814	19905	13931	-5231	1648	1952	28302
B Communication	5978	1303	2910	121	49	10263	6700	1555	1928	186	20	10349
8 Finance, insurance, real estate and business services	16380	7583	26630	1333	2607	49318	19731	8472	28849	1706	3050	55708
A Financial institutions	6301	449	10113	44	1892	15015	7238	593	10502	57	2317	16074
B Insurance	2223	238	-2377	7	1	91	2571	311	-3066	8	1	-176
C Real estate and business services	7856	6895	18894	1282	714	34213	9922	7568	21413	1640	732	39811
Real estate, except dwellings	35	1171	2963	248	116	4303	38	1334	3233	340	103	4843
Dwellings	227	5689	10767	522	549	16656	246	6192	11535	611	578	18005
9 Community, social and personal services	12083	992	8584	991	3900	18750	13488	1193	9229	1113	4372	20652
A Sanitary and similar services	463	...	250			714	540	...	322			862
B Social and related community services	5551	643	3528	4	2529	7197	6120	773	3688	4	2942	7642
Educational services	1134	76	722	4	1737	199	1270	91	891	4	1995	261
Medical, dental, other health and veterinary services	1954	529	2807	...	21	5269	2047	636	2797	...	24	5457
C Recreational and cultural services	836	207	2105	945	1369	2783	1021	252	2159	1051	1420	3054
D Personal and household services	5232	142	2641	42	1	8057	5807	169	3060	58	1	9093
Total, Industries	157880	59174	136602	31753	25551	359858	175731	63666	145200	35452	26890	393166
Producers of Government Services	58470	3338				61808	64173	3840				68013
Other Producers	...	...	...	...	...	...	...	...	...	...	...	...
Total	216350	62513	136602	31753	25551	421667	239904	67506	145208	35452	26890	461179
Less: Imputed bank service charge [a]	...	...	15443	...	...	15443	...	...	15857	...	...	15857
Import duties [b]	...	...	...	6006	...	6006	...	...	...	9032	...	9032
Value added tax [c]	...	...	...	37794	...	37794	...	...	...	44433	...	44433
Other adjustments	...	...	...	2647	159	2489	...	...	...	3076	46	3030
Total	216350	62513	121159	78200	25710	452512	239904	67506	129351	91993	26936	501817

of which General Government:

1 Agriculture, hunting, forestry and fishing	15					15	14					14

1119

Norway

4.3 Cost Components of Value Added
(Continued)

Million Norwegian kroner

	1984						1985					
	Compensation of Employees	Capital Consumption	Net Operating Surplus	Indirect Taxes	Less: Subsidies Received	Value Added	Compensation of Employees	Capital Consumption	Net Operating Surplus	Indirect Taxes	Less: Subsidies Received	Value Added
2 Mining and quarrying	...	...	...	...	...	...	...	...	...	...	...	...
3 Manufacturing	...	...	...	...	...	...	...	...	...	...	...	...
4 Electricity, gas and water	...	...	...	...	...	...	...	...	...	...	...	...
5 Construction	...	...	...	...	...	...	...	...	...	...	...	...
6 Wholesale and retail trade, restaurants and hotels	...	...	...	...	...	...	...	...	...	...	...	...
7 Transport and communication	860	316	...	...	...	1175	904	382	...	...	...	1285
8 Finance, insurance, real estate & business services	336	6	...	...	...	341	373	7	...	...	...	380
9 Community, social and personal services	57260	3017	...	...	...	60277	62883	3451	...	...	...	66334
Total, Industries of General Government	58470	3338	...	...	...	61808	64173	3840	...	...	...	68013
Producers of Government Services	...	...	...	...	...	...	...	...	...	...	...	...
Total, General Government	...	...	...	...	...	...	...	...	...	...	...	...

	1986					
	Compensation of Employees	Capital Consumption	Net Operating Surplus	Indirect Taxes	Less: Subsidies Received	Value Added

All Producers

	Compensation of Employees	Capital Consumption	Net Operating Surplus	Indirect Taxes	Less: Subsidies Received	Value Added
1 Agriculture, hunting, forestry and fishing	2249	5416	14547	600	6327	16484
A Agriculture and hunting	527	3964	10264	313	5520	9548
B Forestry and logging	989	319	1718	53	350	2728
C Fishing	734	1133	2565	234	457	4209
2 Mining and quarrying	7536	17134	20951	6905	533	51992
A Coal mining	131	27	79	1	133	106
B Crude petroleum and natural gas production	6378	16702	20590	6827	...	50497
C Metal ore mining	520	209	-23	48	394	360
D Other mining	506	196	305	29	6	1030
3 Manufacturing	55648	8313	16263	5853	6978	79099
A Manufacture of food, beverages and tobacco	7988	1473	3465	4174	3365	13735
B Textile, wearing apparel and leather industries	1662	224	178	39	180	1923
C Manufacture of wood and wood products, including furniture	4033	530	1072	120	302	5453
D Manufacture of paper and paper products, printing and publishing	8148	1181	1868	178	269	11107
E Manufacture of chemicals and chemical petroleum, coal, rubber and plastic products	4829	1480	3415	545	41	10228
F Manufacture of non-metallic mineral products, except products of petroleum and coal	1957	392	715	82	19	3128
G Basic metal industries	4292	1208	1677	187	726	6638
H Manufacture of fabricated metal products, machinery and equipment	22341	1784	3744	523	2037	26355
I Other manufacturing industries	398	41	128	6	40	533
4 Electricity, gas and water	3639	4550	9236	3106	175	20355
A Electricity, gas and steam	3505	4300	9037	3099	149	19791
B Water works and supply	134	250	198	7	27	563
5 Construction	23132	3531	2149	469	209	29073
6 Wholesale and retail trade, restaurants and hotels	41121	5219	7586	12689	4303	62311
A Wholesale and retail trade	35280	5028	6092	12627	4217	54810
B Restaurants and hotels	5841	191	1494	62	86	7502
7 Transport, storage and communication	29145	14993	116	2228	2303	44180
A Transport and storage	21590	13299	-2548	1995	2288	32048
B Communication	7556	1694	2664	233	15	12131
8 Finance, insurance, real estate and business services	23932	9667	37830	2110	3669	69870
A Financial institutions	8438	711	15921	73	2725	22418

Norway

4.3 Cost Components of Value Added
(Continued)

Million Norwegian kroner

	1986					
	Compensation of Employees	Capital Consumption	Net Operating Surplus	Indirect Taxes	Less: Subsidies Received	Value Added
B Insurance	2877	386	-2894	11	1	380
C Real estate and business services	12618	8570	24803	2026	944	47072
Real estate, except dwellings	52	1563	3884	414	126	5788
Dwellings	281	6961	12321	707	757	19513
9 Community, social and personal services	15499	1305	10633	1277	5176	23537
A Sanitary and similar services	600	...	375	...	...	975
B Social and related community services	6880	846	4197	6	3514	8415
Educational services	1452	100	1206	6	2376	388
Medical, dental, other health and veterinary services	2262	696	2991	...	30	5919
C Recreational and cultural services	1201	270	2434	1198	1660	3443
D Personal and household services	6818	188	3628	73	2	10705
Total, Industries	201901	70127	119309	35237	29673	396901
Producers of Government Services	71084	4210	...	...	...	75294
Other Producers	...	...	...	...	...	...
Total	272985	74337	119309	35237	29673	472195
Less: Imputed bank service charge [a]	...	...	22008	...	...	22008
Import duties [b]	...	...	...	11999	...	11999
Value added tax [c]	...	...	...	50212	...	50212
Other adjustments	...	...	...	3637	13	3624
Total	272985	74337	97301	101085	29686	516022
of which General Government:							
1 Agriculture, hunting, forestry and fishing	15	...	...	...	...	15
2 Mining and quarrying	...	...	...	...	...	...
3 Manufacturing	...	...	...	...	...	...
4 Electricity, gas and water	...	...	...	...	...	...
5 Construction	...	...	...	...	...	...
6 Wholesale and retail trade, restaurants and hotels	...	...	...	...	...	...
7 Transport and communication	977	418	...	...	...	1395
8 Finance, insurance, real estate & business services	403	8	...	...	...	411
9 Community, social and personal services	69690	3785	...	...	...	73474
Total, Industries of General Government	71084	4210	...	...	...	75294
Producers of Government Services	...	...	...	...	...	...
Total, General Government	...	...	...	...	...	...

a) Item 'Import duties' includes collection of customs duties, value added tax on imports and special excises or taxes on imports.
b) Item 'Value added tax' excludes value added tax on imports which is included in item 'Import duties'.
c) Item 'Other adjustments' refers to collection of investment levy on fixed capital formation and subsidies on residential and social buildings.

Oman

Source. Reply to the United Nations National Accounts Questionnaire from the Directorate General of National Statistics, Development Council, Technical Secretariat, Muscat. Official estimates are published in the 'Statistical Yearbook, Fourth Issue, 1397 A.H., 1977 A.D.'.

General note. The estimates shown in the following tables have been adjusted by the United Nations Statistical Office to conform to the United Nations System of National Accounts so far as the existing data would permit.

1.1 Expenditure on the Gross Domestic Product, in Current Prices

Million rials Omani

	1970	1975	1977	1978	1979	1980	1981	1982	1983	1984	1985	1986
1 Government final consumption expenditure	13.7	...	268.5	272.3	354.7	499.2	656.4	715.2	779.8	808.0	894.1	853.4
2 Private final consumption expenditure [a]	20.7	...	246.2	310.3	337.4	576.8	590.6	794.7	802.2	938.5	1171.7	1076.9
3 Gross capital formation	14.7	...	289.5	273.5	335.4	465.7	583.5	706.7	736.9	913.2	953.1	898.4
A Increase in stocks [a]	...	...	...	...	...	...	...	...	...	...	...	...
B Gross fixed capital formation	14.7	...	289.5	273.5	335.4	465.7	583.5	706.7	736.9	913.2	953.1	898.4
4 Exports of goods and services	78.7	...	559.4	552.0	787.4	1294.0	1625.0	1532.0	1475.0	1532.0	1722.0	1108.0
5 Less: Imports of goods and services	21.0	...	416.8	461.2	525.0	772.2	965.0	1135.0	1054.0	1145.0	1285.0	1139.0
Equals: Gross Domestic Product	106.8	724.2	946.8	946.9	1289.9	2063.5	2490.5	2613.6	2739.9	3046.7	3455.9	2797.7

a) Item 'Increase in stocks' is included in item 'Private final consumption expenditure'.

1.3 Cost Components of the Gross Domestic Product

Million rials Omani

	1970	1975	1977	1978	1979	1980	1981	1982	1983	1984	1985	1986
1 Indirect taxes, net	...	...	...	...	...	...	...	...	...	...	...	...
2 Consumption of fixed capital	...	...	...	...	...	...	...	...	...	...	...	...
3 Compensation of employees paid by resident producers to:	...	...	211.4	238.3	303.9	424.4	555.2	655.7	749.3	884.8	994.1	996.8
4 Operating surplus	...	...	...	...	...	...	...	...	...	...	...	...
Equals: Gross Domestic Product	...	...	946.8	946.9	1289.9	2063.5	2490.5	2613.6	2739.9	3046.7	3455.9	2797.7

1.4 General Government Current Receipts and Disbursements

Million rials Omani

	1970	1975	1977	1978	1979	1980	1981	1982	1983	1984	1985	1986
Receipts												
1 Operating surplus	...	...	...	...	...	...	...	...	...	...	...	...
2 Property and entrepreneurial income [a]	...	...	489.4	464.5	642.4	854.0	1165.1	1133.2	1198.9	1300.4	...	...
3 Taxes, fees and contributions [b]	...	...	18.6	19.8	24.6	28.4	39.6	43.9	63.2	82.3	...	...
4 Other current transfers [c]	...	...	12.5	15.2	21.0	27.4	39.4	39.5	51.7	78.6	...	...
Total Current Receipts of General Government	...	...	...	...	...	...	...	...	...	...	...	...
Disbursements												
1 Government final consumption expenditure	...	...	268.5	272.3	354.7	499.2	656.4	715.2	779.8	808.0	...	...
A Compensation of employees	...	...	90.5	109.2	137.9	194.6	260.5	305.0	360.0	423.9	...	...
B Consumption of fixed capital	...	...	...	...	...	...	...	...	...	...	...	...
C Purchases of goods and services, net	...	...	178.0	163.1	216.8	304.6	395.9	410.2	419.8	384.1	...	...
D Less: Own account fixed capital formation	...	...	...	...	...	...	...	...	...	...	...	...
E Indirect taxes paid, net	...	...	...	...	...	...	...	...	...	...	...	...
2 Property income	...	...	...	...	...	...	...	...	...	...	...	...
A Interest	...	...	10.3	16.2	19.7	21.1	15.5	17.5	19.2	39.2	...	...
B Net land rent and royalties	...	...	...	...	...	...	...	...	...	...	...	...
3 Subsidies	...	...	...	...	...	...	...	...	...	...	...	...
4 Other current transfers	...	...	...	...	...	...	...	...	...	...	...	...
5 Net saving	...	...	...	...	...	...	...	...	...	...	...	...
Total Current Disbursements and Net Saving of General Government	...	...	...	...	...	...	...	...	...	...	...	...

a) Item 'Property and entrepreneurial income' refers to oil and gas revenue and interest from investment and rent.
b) Item 'Taxes fees and contributions' includes indirect taxes and compulsory fees, fines and penalties only.
c) Item 'Other transfers' represents income accrued from sales and services.

Oman

1.7 External Transactions on Current Account, Summary

Million rials Omani

	1970	1975	1977	1978	1979	1980	1981	1982	1983	1984	1985	1986
Payments to the Rest of the World
1 Imports of goods and services	...	...	416.8	461.2	525.0	772.2	965.0	1135.0	1054.0	1145.0	1285.0	1139.0
A Imports of merchandise c.i.f.	...	...	392.7	438.3	493.2	661.2	833.0	991.0	906.0	1013.0	1162.0	968.0
B Other	...	...	24.1	22.9	31.8	111.0	132.0	144.0	148.0	132.0	123.0	171.0
2 Factor income to the rest of the world	...	...	130.2	123.0	148.6	257.0	310.0	363.0	418.0	484.0	539.0	581.0
A Compensation of employees	...	...	76.6	83.3	97.2	137.0	172.0	206.0	254.0	297.0	327.0	340.0
B Property and entrepreneurial income	...	...	53.6	39.7	51.4	120.0	138.0	157.0	164.0	187.0	212.0	241.0
3 Current transfers to the rest of the world	...	...	...	...	...	...	...	...	...	...	...	...
4 Surplus of the nation on current transactions	...	...	12.4	-20.6	125.1	309.8	425.0	159.0	124.0	37.0	38.0	-369.0
Payments to the Rest of the World and Surplus of the Nation on Current Transactions	...	...	559.4	563.6	798.7	1339.0	1700.0	1657.0	1596.0	1666.0	1862.0	1351.0
Receipts From The Rest of the World
1 Exports of goods and services	...	...	559.4	552.0	787.4	1294.0	1625.0	1532.0	1475.0	1532.0	1722.0	1108.0
2 Factor income from rest of the world	...	...	-	11.6	11.3	45.0	75.0	125.0	121.0	134.0	140.0	243.0
A Compensation of employees	...	...	...	10.0	11.3	12.0	14.0	15.0	15.0	15.0	15.0	15.0
B Property and entrepreneurial income	...	...	-	1.6	-	33.0	61.0	110.0	106.0	119.0	125.0	228.0
3 Current transfers from rest of the world	...	...	...	...	...	...	...	...	...	...	...	...
Receipts from the Rest of the World on Current Transactions	...	...	559.4	563.6	798.7	1339.0	1700.0	1657.0	1596.0	1666.0	1862.0	1351.0

1.10 Gross Domestic Product by Kind of Activity, in Current Prices

Million rials Omani

	1970	1975	1977	1978	1979	1980	1981	1982	1983	1984	1985	1986
1 Agriculture, hunting, forestry and fishing	16.6	20.2	24.1	30.7	40.3	52.6	62.1	66.1	80.6	89.0	95.8	89.3
2 Mining and quarrying	71.6	486.8	532.8	493.8	719.7	1280.5	1476.4	1424.7	1384.6	1449.5	1654.1	997.2
3 Manufacturing	0.2	2.1	6.7	8.5	11.5	15.6	27.0	39.6	67.1	91.2	112.1	178.3
4 Electricity, gas and water	0.1	1.8	9.2	10.5	11.1	16.0	18.7	21.3	24.0	32.7	36.8	40.3
5 Construction	10.6	70.8	78.0	71.4	86.1	117.8	144.9	169.8	187.4	226.9	242.2	220.8
6 Wholesale and retail trade, restaurants and hotels	1.6	38.5	94.2	104.0	137.1	188.3	251.3	299.5	315.7	369.0	428.0	383.2
7 Transport, storage and communication	0.7	20.5	17.6	20.7	25.5	38.3	53.8	64.9	72.9	84.5	99.6	102.2
8 Finance, insurance, real estate and business services	2.1	19.1	96.2	100.1	123.1	162.8	206.6	231.2	250.1	275.9	295.9	286.3
9 Community, social and personal services	1.0	8.4	5.8	7.6	9.6	13.0	16.9	20.7	25.4	31.6	36.0	38.5
Total, Industries	104.5	671.2	864.0	847.3	1164.0	1884.9	2257.7	2337.8	2407.8	2650.3	3000.5	2336.1
Producers of Government Services	2.3	53.0	90.5	109.2	137.9	194.6	260.5	305.0	360.0	423.9	477.9	495.8
Other Producers	...	...	...	...	...	...	...	...	...	...	...	...
Subtotal	106.8	724.2	955.1	956.5	1301.9	2079.5	2518.2	2642.8	2767.8	3074.2	3478.4	2831.9
Less: Imputed bank service charge	...	...	12.9	14.2	19.0	24.6	39.0	43.9	49.6	59.2	63.6	71.2
Plus: Import duties	...	...	4.6	4.6	7.0	8.6	11.3	14.7	21.7	31.7	41.1	37.0
Plus: Value added tax	...	...	...	...	...	...	...	...	...	...	...	...
Equals: Gross Domestic Product	106.8	724.2	946.8	946.9	1289.9	2063.5	2490.5	2613.6	2739.9	3046.7	3455.9	2797.7

Oman

1.11 Gross Domestic Product by Kind of Activity, in Constant Prices

Million rials Omani

	1970	1975	1977	1978	1979	1980	1981	1982	1983	1984	1985	1986
				At constant prices of:1978								
1 Agriculture, hunting, forestry and fishing	...	...	...	30.7	40.7	49.0	49.7	54.1	64.2	70.4	83.1	73.7
2 Mining and quarrying	...	...	...	493.8	461.0	438.4	501.6	505.3	599.8	645.5	775.6	880.9
3 Manufacturing	...	...	...	8.5	10.5	12.5	20.6	30.2	47.8	67.5	83.4	76.3
4 Electricity, gas and water	...	...	...	10.5	14.0	16.7	18.4	26.3	29.9	44.8	47.5	78.0
5 Construction	...	...	...	71.4	74.6	91.4	107.1	142.3	174.7	221.3	239.3	235.4
6 Wholesale and retail trade, restaurants and hotels	...	...	...	104.0	117.5	139.0	180.4	224.6	238.6	286.9	316.6	250.4
7 Transport, storage and communication	...	...	...	20.7	23.9	33.2	43.2	51.3	59.0	73.4	86.5	84.5
8 Finance, insurance, real estate and business services	...	...	...	100.1	111.0	125.5	143.5	162.4	179.1	215.6	239.6	251.6
9 Community, social and personal services	...	...	...	7.6	9.4	12.1	15.1	18.3	22.8	29.5	34.0	34.8
Total, Industries	...	...	...	847.3	862.5	917.8	1079.6	1214.8	1415.9	1654.9	1905.6	1965.6
Producers of Government Services	...	...	...	109.2	137.4	144.6	170.2	176.6	203.9	235.6	248.1	239.1
Other Producers	...	...	...	...	...	...	...	...	...	...	...	...
Subtotal	...	...	...	956.5	999.9	1062.4	1249.8	1391.4	1619.8	1890.5	2153.7	2204.7
Less: Imputed bank service charge	...	...	...	14.2	18.4	21.5	32.2	35.3	40.7	52.8	58.1	60.1
Plus: Import duties	...	...	...	4.6	6.0	6.3	8.1	11.0	16.3	24.5	27.1	23.9
Plus: Value added tax	...	...	...	...	...	...	...	...	...	...	...	...
Equals: Gross Domestic Product	...	...	...	946.9	987.5	1047.2	1225.7	1367.1	1595.4	1862.2	2122.7	2168.5

1.12 Relations Among National Accounting Aggregates

Million rials Omani

	1970	1975	1977	1978	1979	1980	1981	1982	1983	1984	1985	1986
Gross Domestic Product	106.8	...	946.8	946.9	1289.9	2063.5	2490.5	2613.6	2739.9	3046.7	3455.9	2797.7
Plus: Net factor income from the rest of the world	-25.0	...	-130.2	-111.4	-137.3	-212.0	-235.0	-238.0	-297.0	-350.0	-399.0	-338.0
Factor income from the rest of the world	...	...	-	11.6	11.3	45.0	75.0	125.0	121.0	134.0	140.0	243.0
Less: Factor income to the rest of the world	...	...	130.2	123.0	148.6	257.0	310.0	363.0	418.0	484.0	539.0	581.0
Equals: Gross National Product	81.8	...	816.6	835.5	1152.6	1851.5	2255.5	2375.6	2442.9	2696.7	3056.9	2459.7
Less: Consumption of fixed capital	...	...	...	...	...	...	...	...	...	...	...	...
Equals: National Income	...	...	...	...	...	...	...	...	...	...	...	...
Plus: Net current transfers from the rest of the world	...	...	...	...	...	...	...	...	...	...	...	...
Equals: National Disposable Income	...	...	...	...	...	...	...	...	...	...	...	...
Less: Final consumption	...	...	...	...	...	...	...	...	...	...	...	...
Equals: Net Saving	...	...	...	...	...	...	...	...	...	...	...	...
Less: Surplus of the nation on current transactions	...	...	...	...	...	...	...	...	...	...	...	...
Equals: Net Capital Formation	...	...	...	...	...	...	...	...	...	...	...	...

2.1 Government Final Consumption Expenditure by Function, in Current Prices

Million rials Omani

	1970	1975	1977	1978	1979	1980	1981	1982	1983	1984	1985	1986
1 General public services	...	...	...	...	...	...	...	...	...	...	...	...
2 Defence	...	...	...	224.5	307.1	431.7	567.6	604.6	657.4	666.1	734.0	677.8
3 Public order and safety	...	...	...									
4 Education	...	...	14.3	16.4	21.9	31.8	44.6	55.6	66.8	72.7	83.1	97.1
5 Health	...	...	10.9	11.9	13.5	18.5	24.6	29.6	32.5	40.5	47.4	48.6
6 Social security and welfare	...	...	...	...	...	...	...	...	...	...	...	...
7 Housing and community amenities	...	...	...	...	...	...	...	...	...	...	...	...
8 Recreational, cultural and religious affairs	...	...	...	...	...	...	...	...	...	...	...	...
9 Economic services	...	...	...	...	...	...	...	...	...	...	...	...

Oman

2.1 Government Final Consumption Expenditure by Function, in Current Prices
(Continued)

Million rials Omani

	1970	1975	1977	1978	1979	1980	1981	1982	1983	1984	1985	1986
A Fuel and energy	...	...	...	...	...	...	...	...	...	...	...	...
B Agriculture, forestry, fishing and hunting	...	...	...	...	4.8	6.8	7.7	12.1	9.1	11.2	11.6	11.1
C Mining, manufacturing and construction, except fuel and energy	...	...	...	...	...	...	...	...	...	...	...	...
D Transportation and communication	...	...	...	20.9	9.4	12.0	14.9	17.0	17.7	20.4	21.6	19.8
E Other economic affairs	...	...	...	...	...	...	...	...	...	...	...	...
10 Other functions	...	...	...	...	...	...	...	...	...	...	...	...
Total Government Final Consumption Expenditure	...	...	269.9	273.7	356.7	500.8	659.4	718.9	783.5	810.9	897.7	853.4

4.1 Derivation of Value Added by Kind of Activity, in Current Prices

Million rials Omani

	1980 Gross Output	1980 Intermediate Consumption	1980 Value Added	1981 Gross Output	1981 Intermediate Consumption	1981 Value Added	1982 Gross Output	1982 Intermediate Consumption	1982 Value Added	1983 Gross Output	1983 Intermediate Consumption	1983 Value Added
					All Producers							
1 Agriculture, hunting, forestry and fishing	73.0	20.3	52.6	86.7	24.6	62.1	91.8	25.7	66.1	112.4	31.8	80.6
A Agriculture and hunting	49.7	12.4	37.2	53.9	13.5	40.5	60.9	15.2	45.7	71.3	17.8	53.5
B Forestry and logging	...	...	...	...	...	...	...	...	...	...	...	...
C Fishing	23.3	7.9	15.4	32.8	11.2	21.7	30.9	10.5	20.4	41.1	14.0	27.1
2 Mining and quarrying	1329.1	48.7	1280.4	1544.3	67.9	1476.4	1506.1	81.4	1424.7	1466.5	81.9	1384.6
A Coal mining	...	...	...	...	...	...	...	...	...	...	...	...
B Crude petroleum and natural gas production	1327.1	47.7	1279.4	1539.1	65.3	1473.8	1498.6	77.7	1420.9	1453.9	74.8	1379.1
C Metal ore mining	...	...	...	...	...	...	...	...	...	...	...	...
D Other mining	2.0	1.0	1.0	5.2	2.6	2.6	7.5	3.7	3.8	12.6	7.1	5.5
3 Manufacturing	38.8	23.2	15.6	69.7	42.7	27.0	89.5	49.9	39.6	257.2	190.1	67.1
4 Electricity, gas and water	36.3	20.3	16.0	47.9	29.2	18.7	53.4	32.1	21.3	63.7	39.7	24.0
A Electricity, gas and steam	30.2	17.5	12.7	40.3	26.4	13.9	44.3	28.4	15.9	52.1	35.6	16.5
B Water works and supply	6.1	2.8	3.3	7.6	2.8	4.8	9.1	3.7	5.4	11.6	4.1	7.5
5 Construction	294.5	176.7	117.8	362.4	217.5	145.0	424.6	254.8	169.8	468.8	281.4	187.4
6 Wholesale and retail trade, restaurants and hotels	277.4	89.1	188.3	367.1	115.7	251.3	438.2	138.8	299.5	463.4	147.8	315.7
A Wholesale and retail trade	261.6	78.5	183.1	346.3	103.9	242.4	412.6	123.8	288.8	432.8	129.9	303.0
B Restaurants and hotels	15.8	10.6	5.2	20.7	11.8	8.9	25.7	15.0	10.7	30.6	17.9	12.7
7 Transport, storage and communication	70.9	32.6	38.3	91.2	37.4	53.8	108.5	43.6	64.9	121.1	48.2	72.9
A Transport and storage	57.0	24.9	32.1	74.7	32.3	42.0	87.6	38.0	49.6	94.4	41.1	53.3
B Communication	13.9	7.7	6.2	17.0	5.1	11.8	20.9	5.6	15.3	26.7	7.1	19.6
8 Finance, insurance, real estate and business services	187.4	24.5	162.9	234.4	27.8	206.6	261.7	30.5	231.2	285.3	35.2	250.1
A Financial institutions	39.3	8.2	31.1	53.7	9.0	44.7	62.2	10.4	51.8	69.3	12.9	66.4
B Insurance	5.4	2.1	3.3	5.7	1.3	4.4	11.3	1.3	10.0	8.8	1.6	7.2
C Real estate and business services	142.8	14.3	128.5	175.1	17.5	157.6	188.2	18.8	169.4	207.2	20.7	186.5
9 Community, social and personal services	17.4	4.3	13.0	22.4	5.5	16.8	27.5	6.8	20.7	33.7	8.3	25.4
A Sanitary and similar services	...	...	...	...	...	...	...	...	...	...	...	...
B Social and related community services	2.0	0.4	1.6	2.7	0.6	2.2	3.5	0.7	2.8	4.4	0.9	3.5
Educational services	1.5	0.3	1.2	1.9	0.4	1.5	2.4	0.5	1.9	3.0	0.6	2.4
Medical, dental, other health and veterinary services	0.5	0.1	0.4	0.8	0.2	0.7	1.1	0.2	0.9	1.4	0.3	1.1
C Recreational and cultural services	8.6	3.4	5.2	10.7	4.2	6.5	12.9	5.0	7.9	15.3	6.0	9.3
D Personal and household services	6.8	0.6	6.2	8.9	0.8	8.1	11.1	1.1	10.0	14.0	1.4	12.6
Total, Industries	2324.8	439.7	1884.9	2826.1	568.3	2257.7	3001.3	663.6	2337.8	3272.1	864.4	2407.8
Producers of Government Services	500.8	306.2	194.6	659.4	398.9	260.5	718.9	413.9	305.0	783.5	423.5	360.0
Other Producers	...	...	...	...	...	...	...	...	...	...	...	...
Total	2825.6	745.9	2079.5	3485.5	967.2	2518.2	3720.2	1077.5	2642.8	4055.6	1287.9	2767.8
Less: Imputed bank service charge	...	-24.6	24.6	...	-39.0	39.0	...	-43.9	43.9	...	-49.6	49.6
Import duties	8.6	...	8.6	11.3	...	11.3	14.7	...	14.7	21.7	...	21.7
Value added tax	...	...	...	...	...	...	...	...	...	...	...	...
Total	2834.2	770.5	2063.5	3496.8	1006.2	2490.5	3734.9	1121.4	2613.6	4077.3	1337.5	2739.9

Oman

4.1 Derivation of Value Added by Kind of Activity, in Current Prices

Million rials Omani

	1984 Gross Output	1984 Intermediate Consumption	1984 Value Added	1985 Gross Output	1985 Intermediate Consumption	1985 Value Added	1986 Gross Output	1986 Intermediate Consumption	1986 Value Added
				All Producers					
1 Agriculture, hunting, forestry and fishing	124.5	35.5	89.0	132.9	37.1	95.8	123.7	34.4	89.3
A Agriculture and hunting	76.2	19.0	57.1	90.0	22.5	67.5	85.0	21.2	63.8
B Forestry and logging	...	...	...	...	...	...	...	...	...
C Fishing	48.3	16.4	31.9	42.9	14.6	28.3	38.7	13.2	25.5
2 Mining and quarrying	1542.4	92.9	1449.5	1761.4	107.3	1654.1	1116.3	119.1	997.2
A Coal mining	...	...	...	...	...	...	...	...	...
B Crude petroleum and natural gas production	1525.3	83.1	1442.3	1740.9	95.6	1645.3	1097.6	109.7	987.9
C Metal ore mining	...	...	...	...	...	...	...	...	...
D Other mining	17.1	9.8	7.2	20.5	11.7	8.8	18.7	9.4	9.3
3 Manufacturing	319.0	227.8	91.2	372.1	260.0	112.1	392.2	213.9	178.3
4 Electricity, gas and water	77.7	45.0	32.7	92.5	55.7	36.8	97.2	56.8	40.4
A Electricity, gas and steam	65.1	39.9	25.2	76.2	49.1	27.1	80.6	50.8	29.8
B Water works and supply	12.6	5.1	7.5	16.3	6.6	9.7	16.6	6.0	10.6
5 Construction	567.2	340.3	226.9	605.5	363.3	242.2	551.9	331.1	220.8
6 Wholesale and retail trade, restaurants and hotels	541.9	172.8	369.1	626.8	198.9	427.9	563.9	180.7	383.2
A Wholesale and retail trade	506.2	151.8	354.3	588.8	176.6	412.2	523.4	157.0	366.4
B Restaurants and hotels	35.7	21.0	14.7	38.0	22.3	15.7	40.5	23.7	16.8
7 Transport, storage and communication	139.1	54.6	84.5	163.9	64.3	99.6	169.9	67.7	102.2
A Transport and storage	106.4	46.2	60.2	120.7	52.5	68.2	122.0	53.3	68.7
B Communication	32.7	8.4	24.3	43.2	11.8	31.4	47.9	14.4	33.5
8 Finance, insurance, real estate and business services	315.4	39.5	275.9	333.0	37.1	295.9	328.2	41.9	286.3
A Financial institutions	80.5	14.2	66.3	84.9	11.1	73.8	96.0	17.5	78.5
B Insurance	15.6	3.4	12.2	20.2	3.2	17.0	23.6	3.5	20.1
C Real estate and business services	219.3	21.9	197.4	227.9	22.8	205.1	208.6	20.9	187.7
9 Community, social and personal services	41.9	10.3	31.6	47.9	11.9	36.0	51.4	12.9	38.5
A Sanitary and similar services	...	...	...	...	...	...	...	...	...
B Social and related community services	5.9	1.2	4.8	8.0	1.5	6.5	8.9	1.8	7.1
Educational services	4.1	0.8	3.3	5.8	1.1	4.7	6.5	1.3	5.2
Medical, dental, other health and veterinary services	1.8	0.4	1.5	2.2	0.4	1.8	2.4	0.5	1.9
C Recreational and cultural services	17.4	6.8	10.6	19.9	7.8	12.1	21.4	8.4	13.0
D Personal and household services	18.5	2.3	16.3	19.9	2.5	17.4	21.1	2.7	18.4
Total, Industries	3669.1	1018.7	2650.4	4136.0	1135.5	3000.5	3394.7	1058.6	2336.1
Producers of Government Services	810.9	387.0	423.9	897.7	419.8	477.9	853.4	357.6	495.8
Other Producers	...	...	...	...	...	...	...	...	...
Total	4480.0	1405.7	3074.3	5033.7	1555.3	3478.4	4248.1	1416.2	2831.9
Less: Imputed bank service charge	...	-59.2	59.2	...	-63.6	63.6	...	-71.2	71.2
Import duties	31.7	...	31.7	41.1	...	41.1	37.0	...	37.0
Value added tax	...	...	...	...	...	...	...	...	...
Total	4511.7	1464.9	3046.7	5074.8	1618.9	3455.9	4285.1	1487.4	2797.7

Pakistan

General note. The preparation of national accounts statistics in Pakistan is undertaken by the Federal Bureau of Statistics, Statistics Division of the Ministry of Finance and Economic Affairs, Karachi. The official estimates and methodological notes on sources and methods are published in a series of reports entitled 'National Accounts'. The estimates are generally in accordance with the classifications and definitions recommended in the United Nations System of National Accounts (SNA). Input-output tables have been published in 'A Summary of Input-Output Studies of the Economy of Pakistan'. The following tables have been prepared from successive replies to the United Nations national accounts questionnaire. Estimates relate to fiscal year beginning 1 July. It should be noted that the estimates for 1960-1969, except Table 4, GDP by Kind of Economic Activity, include data for Bangladesh. When the scope and coverage of the estimates differ for conceptual or statistical reasons from the definitions and classifications recommended in SNA, a footnote is indicated to the relevant tables.

Sources and methods:

(a) Gross domestic product. Gross domestic product is estimated mainly through the production approach.

(b) Expenditure on the gross domestic product. The expenditure approach is used to estimate government final consumption expenditure and exports and imports of goods and services. This approach, in combination with the commodity-flow approach is used to estimate gross capital formation. Private final consumption expenditure is derived as a residual. Government consumption expenditure is estimated by analyzing the budgets of the government bodies with an element of estimation made for the local sector for which the budgets are difficult to obtain. The basic information used in estimating increase in stocks is received from the Planning Commission. The estimates of gross fixed capital formation are classified by economic sectors. For agriculture, investment in construction is based on the rural construction survey for the years 1959/60 to 1963/64, the estimates are projected by the straight-line method using the 1963/64 data as bench-marks. Non-monetized investment is estimated on the basis of special studies carried out by research workers using 1965/66 as bench-mark. Investment in the mining and quarrying sector is estimated on the basis of data obtained in 1969/70 through inquiries into establishments. For large-scale manufacturing, investment estimates are based on sample surveys while the Karachi small industries survey in 1966 projected on the basis of the population growth rate is used for the small-scale manufacturing. Investment in machinery and equipment of the agricultural and mining sectors is estimated by the commodity-flow method. For the service sector, estimates are prepared from trade and domestic production data, annual budgets and annual questionnaires. Estimates of private residential construction are based on the rural construction survey, census reports, population growth and number of persons per household. Capital expenditure for the government bodies are based on the classification of their budgets. The estimates of exports of goods and services are obtained from the Statistics Division and the balance-of-payments. For the constant price estimates, all items of GDP by expenditure type are deflated by appropriate price indexes except gross fixed capital formation which is extrapolated by quantity indicators. Private consumption expenditure is obtained as residual.

(c) Cost-structure of the gross domestic product. Domestic factor incomes consisting of compensation of employees and operating surplus, is obtained as a residual, i.e., after subtracting depreciation and net indirect taxes from GDP. For depreciation, a flat rate is applied for the different sectors, 5 per cent for agriculture, mining and quarrying, small-scale manufacturing, public administration and defence and other private services, 10 per cent for large-scale manufacturing and parts of road transport, 2.5 per cent for construction, 2 per cent for trade and 20 per cent for ownership of dwellings in the rural areas and 25 per cent in the urban areas. Data of indirect taxes and subsidies are derived from budgets of the government bodies.

(d) Gross domestic product by kind of economic activity. The table of GDP by kind of economic activity is prepared in factor values. The production approach is used to estimate value added in agriculture, mining and quarrying, manufacturing, construction and electricity. The income approach is used for most of the remaining sectors. Production data of major agricultural crops are obtained from the Ministry of Agriculture. Corresponding harvest prices are obtained from the Provincial Directorates of Land Records. For minor crops harvest prices are taken at 80 per cent of the wholesale prices. Data on livestock products and wholesale prices are obtained from the Department of Agricultural Marketing and Grading. The current price estimates are derived indirectly by applying the wholesale price index to the constant price estimates. Production and price data of forestry and fishing are obtained from the concerned departments. The Natural Resources Division and the Provincial Mineral Development Department provide production and price data for the mining sector. Gross output is obtained by multiplying the output of each mineral by pit-head or well-head prices in the bench-mark year while annual output and index of wholesale prices are used for the current estimates. Bench-mark estimates for large-scale manufacturing are mainly based on the 1959/60 census of manufacturing industries. Other years' estimates are obtained by applying the quantum index of manufacturing to the bench-mark value. For small-scale manufacturing, bench-mark 1959/60 was computed on the basis of the number of persons engaged and on imputed gross value added per person. For other years, a uniform growth rate of 3 per cent is used in combination with the wholesale price index for manufacturing. The estimates for electricity and gas are based on data furnished by concerned companies while the estimates of water are included in public administration and defence sector. For construction, assumptions are based on the availability of cement for local consumption and on data from household income and expenditures surveys. Value added at constant factor cost thus obtained are adjusted by wholesale price index for manufacturing to arrive at current estimates. The value added of the trade sector is measured by net trade margins earned by traders on various types of products entering into wholesale and retail trade. The trade margins are estimated through special studies undertaken for this purpose. For the transport sector, data on income and expenditure are supplied by the concerned enterprises. The income per person in each category of the transport sector is estimated on the basis of data obtained from the findings of the Minimum Wage Board in 1963 and the 1961 Manpower Survey, projected according to the rate of annual increases in wages of the workers employed. For the financial sector, value added is based on data provided by the State Bank of Pakistan and various financial institutions. Bench-mark data for occupied dwellings are obtained from the housing census in 1960. For other years, it is estimated by applying the geometric growth obtained during 1950-60. For government services, the budgets of the government bodies are used. For private services, the number of persons engaged in the different occupations is obtained from the 1961 population census and extrapolated by the intercensal growth rate in the working force of this sector. For the constant price estimates, double deflation is used for agriculture. Price deflation is used for forestry and fishing, electricity and gas, transport, financial and community services. For mining, the annual output of each mineral is multiplied by the base year pit-head and well-head prices. Value added of the trade sector is obtained from the distribution of agricultural produce, manufactured and imported goods. Value added of manufacturing construction and ownership of dwellings is extrapolated by quantum indexes.

1.1 Expenditure on the Gross Domestic Product, in Current Prices

Million Pakistan rupees — Fiscal year beginning 1 July

		1970	1975	1977	1978	1979	1980	1981	1982	1983	1984	1985	1986
1	Government final consumption expenditure	5270	15165	19116	20339	23535	28998	34337	42499	51549	58080	66038	76244
2	Private final consumption expenditure	39030	101115	141769	160894	192741	227912	265939	293846	340111	396345	423387	457269
3	Gross capital formation	7892	24057	31505	34876	43345	47473	57032	63443	70928	80397	90319	103855
	A Increase in stocks	847		1000	1750	2000	4500	7858	6701	7489	8600	9000	9500
	B Gross fixed capital formation	7045	24057	30505	33126	41345	42973	49174	56742	63439	71797	81319	94355
	Residential buildings	...	2658	2971	3252	4052	4697	5710	7112	7673	8478	9152	...
	Non-residential buildings	...	4749	6144	5481	6822	8851	9702	10125	13529	14469	14592	...
	Other construction and land improvement etc.	...	7967	8380	8570	10665	11951	15857	16219	15308	18017	20526	...
	Other	...	8683	13010	15823	19806	17474	17905	23285	26929	30833	37049	...
4	Exports of goods and services	3922	13881	16629	21529	29485	35707	33033	44395	47835	49889	63268	79310
5	Less: Imports of goods and services	5323	23854	32600	42529	54578	62129	68501	82018	92222	106729	103475	114490
	Equals: Gross Domestic Product	50791	130364	176419	195109	234528	277961	321840	362165	418201	477982	539537	602188

Pakistan

1.2 Expenditure on the Gross Domestic Product, in Constant Prices

Million Pakistan rupees — Fiscal year beginning 1 July

	1970	1975	1977	1978	1979	1980	1981	1982	1983	1984	1985	1986
					At constant prices of:1959							
1 Government final consumption expenditure	3838	5398	5902	6134	6408	7182	7696	8472	9084	9469	10016	11071
2 Private final consumption expenditure	27938	34694	39919	43611	47245	49063	51068	53384	56820	62322	67052	69301
3 Gross capital formation	5103	6512	7189	7169	7335	7583	9087	9891	10341	11082	11763	13162
A Increase in stocks	617	-	257	422	429	854	1389	1125	1142	1247	1248	1264
B Gross fixed capital formation	4486	6512	6932	6747	6906	6729	7698	8766	9199	9835	10515	11898
4 Exports of goods and services	3697	3325	3222	3351	4247	4858	4567	5689	5479	5460	5330	6988
5 Less: Imports of goods and services	4356	5398	6285	7890	8274	7745	7709	8565	9184	10004	9944	9800
Equals: Gross Domestic Product	36220	44531	49947	52375	56961	60941	64709	68871	72540	78329	84217	90722

1.3 Cost Components of the Gross Domestic Product

Million Pakistan rupees — Fiscal year beginning 1 July

	1970	1975	1977	1978	1979	1980	1981	1982	1983	1984	1985	1986
1 Indirect taxes, net	4785	10628	16494	17071	23926	30365	32006	35975	45453	47093	54327	64913
A Indirect taxes	4978	13642	19604	24058	30333	35562	37440	43487	53557	56396	65916	78657
B Less: Subsidies	193	3014	3110	6987	6407	5197	5434	7512	8104	9303	11589	13744
2 Consumption of fixed capital	3208	7329	9826	10859	13072	15241	17787	20257	23711	26904	30325	33622
3 Compensation of employees paid by resident producers to:	42798	112407	150099	167179	197530	232355	272047	305933	349037	403985	454885	503653
4 Operating surplus												
Equals: Gross Domestic Product	50791	130364	176419	195109	234528	277961	321840	362165	418201	477982	539537	602188

1.10 Gross Domestic Product by Kind of Activity, in Current Prices

Million Pakistan rupees — Fiscal year beginning 1 July

	1970	1975	1977	1978	1979	1980	1981	1982	1983	1984	1985	1986
1 Agriculture, hunting, forestry and fishing	16236	38338	50567	54147	62164	71699	83426	90715	92165	108873	118670	127473
2 Mining and quarrying	243	968	1317	1464	2239	3149	3578	4199	5086	7153	11448	12616
3 Manufacturing	7723	17812	24023	27484	33553	40969	48419	55201	67475	75030	83670	95079
4 Electricity, gas and water	782	1713	2448	3397	4789	5928	6436	7274	8610	8738	11136	12385
5 Construction	1979	6739	8674	9667	11906	11449	12247	14567	19325	26464	30421	35261
6 Wholesale and retail trade, restaurants and hotels [a]	6954	18865	24983	28381	33759	40592	49738	55031	61559	72173	81045	89420
7 Transport, storage and communication	3017	8349	11282	13181	15486	19370	22937	25704	30659	34793	39429	44125
8 Finance, insurance, real estate and business services	2634	7377	9904	11152	12493	13858	16817	19641	23521	25947	28478	30613
9 Community, social and personal services [ab]	3475	10085	13572	15306	17950	21325	24770	27391	31215	35004	38860	42622
Total, Industries	43043	110246	146770	164179	194339	228339	268368	299723	339615	394175	443157	489594
Producers of Government Services	2963	9490	13155	13859	16263	19257	21466	26467	33133	36714	42053	47681
Other Producers [b]	...	...	...	...	...	...	...	...	...	...	...	...
Subtotal [c]	46006	119736	159925	178038	210602	247596	289834	326190	372748	430889	485210	537275
Less: Imputed bank service charge	...	...	...	...	...	...	...	...	...	...	...	...
Plus: Import duties	...	...	...	...	...	...	...	...	...	...	...	...
Plus: Value added tax	...	...	...	...	...	...	...	...	...	...	...	...
Plus: Other adjustments [d]	4785	10628	16494	17071	23926	30365	32006	35975	45453	47093	54327	64913
Equals: Gross Domestic Product	50791	130364	176419	195109	234528	277961	321840	362165	418201	477982	539537	602188

a) Restaurants and hotels are included in item 'Community, social and personal services'.
b) Item 'Other producers' is included in item 'Community, social and personal services'.
c) Gross domestic product in factor values.
d) Item 'Other adjustments' refers to indirect taxes net of subsidies.

1.11 Gross Domestic Product by Kind of Activity, in Constant Prices

Million Pakistan rupees — Fiscal year beginning 1 July

	1970	1975	1977	1978	1979	1980	1981	1982	1983	1984	1985	1986
					At constant prices of:1959							
1 Agriculture, hunting, forestry and fishing	12188	13659	14399	14845	15826	16405	16992	17637	16571	18600	19806	20967
2 Mining and quarrying	156	175	212	221	250	283	306	319	326	401	497	533
3 Manufacturing	5521	6588	7411	8025	8870	9837	11212	12032	13013	14102	15207	16339
4 Electricity, gas and water	741	985	1244	1366	1531	1698	1777	1916	2249	2345	2709	2979
5 Construction	1390	2094	2248	2371	2644	2749	2036	3175	3727	3838	4217	4692

Pakistan

1.11 Gross Domestic Product by Kind of Activity, in Constant Prices
(Continued)

Million Pakistan rupees — Fiscal year beginning 1 July

	1970	1975	1977	1978	1979	1980	1981	1982	1983	1984	1985	1986
					At constant prices of:1959							
6 Wholesale and retail trade, restaurants and hotels [a]	4566	5894	6460	6880	7399	7913	8765	9326	9680	10696	11490	12261
7 Transport, storage and communication	1981	2608	3029	3275	3495	3776	4042	4356	4821	5156	5590	6022
8 Finance, insurance, real estate and business services	1784	2408	2725	2859	2889	2831	3129	3516	3922	4079	4276	4435
9 Community, social and personal services [ab]	2276	2964	3319	3510	3711	3924	4149	4387	4639	4905	5187	5485
Total, Industries	30603	37375	41047	43352	46615	49416	53208	56664	58948	64122	68979	73713
Producers of Government Services	2133	3854	4657	4906	5209	5761	5844	6169	6658	7377	7707	8372
Other Producers [b]	...	...	...	...	...	...	...	...	...	...	...	...
Subtotal [c]	32736	41229	45704	48258	51824	55177	59052	62833	65606	71499	76686	82085
Less: Imputed bank service charge	...	...	...	...	...	...	...	...	...	...	...	...
Plus: Import duties	...	...	...	...	...	...	...	...	...	...	...	...
Plus: Value added tax	...	...	...	...	...	...	...	...	...	...	...	...
Plus: Other adjustments [d]	3484	3302	4243	4117	5137	5764	5657	6038	6934	6830	7531	8637
Equals: Gross Domestic Product	36220	44531	49947	52375	56961	60941	64709	68871	72540	78329	84217	90722

a) Restaurants and hotels are included in item 'Community, social and personal services'.
b) Item 'Other producers' is included in item 'Community, social and personal services'.
c) Gross domestic product in factor values.
d) Item 'Other adjustments' refers to indirect taxes net of subsidies.

1.12 Relations Among National Accounting Aggregates

Million Pakistan rupees — Fiscal year beginning 1 July

	1970	1975	1977	1978	1979	1980	1981	1982	1983	1984	1985	1986
Gross Domestic Product	50791	130364	176419	195109	234528	277961	321840	362165	418201	477982	539537	602188
Plus: Net factor income from the rest of the world	-82	2992	12139	14533	18284	22692	25349	39395	39595	38311	41359	35871
Equals: Gross National Product	50709	133356	188558	209642	252812	300653	347189	401560	457796	516293	580896	638059
Less: Consumption of fixed capital	3208	7329	9826	10859	13072	15241	17787	20257	23711	26904	30325	33622
Equals: National Income	47501	126027	178732	198783	239740	285412	329402	381303	434085	489389	550571	604437
Plus: Net current transfers from the rest of the world	...	...	...	...	...	...	...	...	...	...	...	...
Equals: National Disposable Income	...	...	...	...	...	...	...	...	...	...	...	...
Less: Final consumption	...	...	...	...	...	...	...	...	...	...	...	...
Equals: Net Saving	...	...	...	...	...	...	...	...	...	...	...	...
Less: Surplus of the nation on current transactions	...	...	...	...	...	...	...	...	...	...	...	...
Equals: Net Capital Formation	...	...	...	...	...	...	...	...	...	...	...	...

2.1 Government Final Consumption Expenditure by Function, in Current Prices

Million Pakistan rupees — Fiscal year beginning 1 July

	1970	1975	1977	1978	1979	1980	1981	1982	1983	1984	1985	1986
1 General public services	3742	11202	13438	14115	16776	17322	21132	25753	31259	34786	38761	40913
2 Defence												
3 Public order and safety	...	...	...	...	...	2206	2279	2884	3826	4347	4731	5192
4 Education	457	1567	2204	2361	2812	3304	3830	4987	6275	5531	6575	10048
5 Health	390	810	1252	1420	1285	1087	1244	1619	2088	2560	2936	3910
6 Social security and welfare	...	...	...	...	...	928	1204	1571	1670	1723	2105	2273
7 Housing and community amenities	...	...	...	...	...	685	802	766	974	974	1121	1257
8 Recreational, cultural and religious affairs	53	127	96	106	129	125	133	160	204	233	339	416
9 Economic services	458	1203	1680	1885	1749	3180	3589	4197	4711	7365	8915	11746
A Fuel and energy	...	...	...			127	146	162	205	235	275	362
B Agriculture, forestry, fishing and hunting	...	...	...	...	...	1799	2029	2796	3283	5727	6762	7995
C Mining, manufacturing and construction, except fuel and energy			...	...	...	127	145	194	207	337	378	1226
D Transportation and communication						399	511	570	626	592	695	848
E Other economic affairs	...	...	...	...	...	728	758	475	390	474	805	1315
10 Other functions	170	256	356	452	784	101	124	562	542	561	555	489
Total Government Final Consumption Expenditure	5270	15165	19116	20339	23535	28998	34337	42499	51549	58080	66038	76244

Pakistan

2.3 Total Government Outlays by Function and Type

Million Pakistan rupees — Fiscal year beginning 1 July

		Final Consumption Expenditures Total	Compensation of Employees	Other	Subsidies	Other Current Transfers & Property Income	Total Current Disbursements	Gross Capital Formation	Other Capital Outlays	Total Outlays
					1980					
1	General public services	17322	9067	8255	23	468	17813	1824	5	19642
2	Defence									
3	Public order and safety	2206	1612	594	-	722	2928	154	-	3082
4	Education	3364	2755	609	-	90	3454	654	2	4110
5	Health	1087	535	552	10	47	1144	602	-	1746
6	Social security and welfare	928	811	117	-	487	1415	18	-	1433
7	Housing and community amenities	685	441	244	6	-	691	599	-	1290
8	Recreation, culture and religion	125	56	69	164	82	371	190	-	561
9	Economic services	3180	1361	1819	2901	5637	11718	4631	18024	34373
	A Fuel and energy	127	36	91	-	-	127	639	16	782
	B Agriculture, forestry, fishing and hunting	1799	740	1059	2844	2013	6656	1360	14026	22042
	C Mining (except fuels), manufacturing and construction	127	51	76	-	613	740	189	-	929
	D Transportation and communication	399	124	275	32	2893	3324	2376	2464	8164
	E Other economic affairs	728	410	318	25	118	871	67	1518	2456
10	Other functions	101	35	66	220	18923	19244	295	169366	188905
	Total	28998	16673	12325	3324	26456	58778	8967	187397	255142
					1981					
1	General public services	21132	10257	10875	37	1294	22463	3613	28	26104
2	Defence									
3	Public order and safety	2279	1563	716	-	15	2294	172	-	2466
4	Education	3830	3188	642	-	852	4682	908	1	5591
5	Health	1244	605	639	16	56	1316	868	-	2184
6	Social security and welfare	1204	803	401	-	36	1240	28	-	1268
7	Housing and community amenities	802	502	300	10	958	1770	789	1	2560
8	Recreation, culture and religion	133	66	67	-	58	191	247	-	438
9	Economic services	3589	1562	2027	5011	3909	12509	5408	13615	31532
	A Fuel and energy	146	42	104	-	-	146	843	4	993
	B Agriculture, forestry, fishing and hunting	2029	857	1172	5009	1384	8422	1424	10595	20441
	C Mining (except fuels), manufacturing and construction	145	65	80	-	448	593	88	-	681
	D Transportation and communication	511	145	366	-	1993	2504	43	1608	4155
	E Other economic affairs	758	453	305	2	84	844	3010	1408	5262
10	Other functions	124	39	85	360	4693	5177	279	313559	319015
	Total	34337	18585	15752	5434	11871	51642	12312	327204	391158
					1982					
1	General public services	25753	11919	13834	617	1751	28121	2372	44	30537
2	Defence									
3	Public order and safety	2884	2086	798	-	19	2903	260	2	3165
4	Education	4987	4023	964	-	1078	6065	844	-	6909
5	Health	1619	739	880	-	84	1703	672	29	2404
6	Social security and welfare	1571	1373	198	-	97	1668	21	-	1689
7	Housing and community amenities	766	456	310	10	566	1342	916	4	2262
8	Recreation, culture and religion	160	74	86	-	90	250	161	-	411
9	Economic services	4197	1893	2304	6635	2358	13190	6613	18054	37857
	A Fuel and energy	162	68	94	15	-	177	635	6	818
	B Agriculture, forestry, fishing and hunting	2796	1297	1499	3156	1111	7063	1818	15192	24073
	C Mining (except fuels), manufacturing and construction	194	99	95	1723	385	2302	46	162	2510
	D Transportation and communication	570	133	437	36	81	687	3969	156	4812
	E Other economic affairs	475	296	179	1705	781	2961	145	2538	5644
10	Other functions	562	353	209	250	9398	10210	866	208963	220039
	Total	42499	22916	19583	7512	15441	65452	12725	227096	305273

Pakistan

2.3 Total Government Outlays by Function and Type
(Continued)

Million Pakistan rupees — Fiscal year beginning 1 July

		Final Consumption Expenditures Total	Compensation of Employees	Other	Subsidies	Other Current Transfers & Property Income	Total Current Disbursements	Gross Capital Formation	Other Capital Outlays	Total Outlays
					1983					
1	General public services	31259	15142	16117	1595	1670	34524	2908	34	37466
2	Defence									
3	Public order and safety	3826	2866	960	-	8	3834	365	-	4199
4	Education	6275	5025	1250	1	1080	7356	1257	-	8613
5	Health	2088	1020	1068	-	172	2260	1014	-	3274
6	Social security and welfare	1670	1483	187	-	30	1700	19	-	1719
7	Housing and community amenities	974	486	488	-	515	1489	1073	-	2562
8	Recreation, culture and religion	204	90	114	-	123	327	210	-	537
9	Economic services	4711	2249	2462	6508	12725	23944	6794	12285	43023
	A Fuel and energy	205	89	116	15	1132	1352	710	30	2092
	B Agriculture, forestry, fishing and hunting	3283	1613	1670	4546	1954	9783	2140	12062	23075
	C Mining (except fuels), manufacturing and construction	207	85	122	-	1151	1358	66	157	1581
	D Transportation and communication	626	187	439	297	7213	8136	3762	-	11898
	E Other economic affairs	390	275	115	1650	1275	3315	116	46	3477
10	Other functions	542	325	217	-	10833	11375	542	287680	299597
	Total	51549	28686	22863	8103	27156	86809	14182	299999	400990
					1984					
1	General public services	34786	16328	18458	2258	1866	38910	3272	38	42220
2	Defence									
3	Public order and safety	4347	3163	1184	-	9	4356	464	-	4820
4	Education	5531	4279	1252	-	1207	6738	1547	-	8285
5	Health	2560	1347	1213	-	192	2752	1109	-	3861
6	Social security and welfare	1723	1509	214	-	34	1757	23	-	1780
7	Housing and community amenities	974	521	453	-	576	1550	1157	-	2707
8	Recreation, culture and religion	233	135	98	-	137	370	236	-	606
9	Economic services	7365	4204	3161	5848	14221	27434	7523	13788	48745
	A Fuel and energy	235	76	159	89	1265	1589	651	34	2274
	B Agriculture, forestry, fishing and hunting	5727	3520	2207	4354	2184	12265	2365	13526	28156
	C Mining (except fuels), manufacturing and construction	337	132	205	-	1286	1623	96	176	1895
	D Transportation and communication	592	184	408	268	8061	8921	4275	-	13196
	E Other economic affairs	474	292	182	1137	1425	3036	136	52	3224
10	Other functions	561	301	260	1197	12106	10004	500	322874	337324
	Total	58080	31787	26293	9303	30348	97731	15917	336700	450348
					1985					
1	General public services	38761	18371	20390	2813	2058	43632	4363	43	48038
2	Defence									
3	Public order and safety	4731	3399	1332	-	10	4741	480	-	5221
4	Education	6575	5161	1414	-	1331	7906	1749	-	9655
5	Health	2936	1589	1347	-	212	3148	1325	-	4473
6	Social security and welfare	2105	1859	246	-	38	2143	26	-	2169
7	Housing and community amenities	1121	610	511	-	635	1756	1491	-	3247
8	Recreation, culture and religion	339	154	185	-	151	490	295	-	785
9	Economic services	8915	5051	3864	7285	15686	31886	7717	15702	55305
	A Fuel and energy	275	91	184	111	1395	1781	634	39	2454
	B Agriculture, forestry, fishing and hunting	6762	4221	2541	5424	2409	14595	2595	15401	32591
	C Mining (except fuels), manufacturing and construction	378	181	197	-	1418	1796	77	200	2073
	D Transportation and communication	695	222	473	334	8892	9921	4263	-	14184
	E Other economic affairs	805	336	469	1416	1572	3793	148	62	4003
10	Other functions	555	214	341	1491	13354	15400	678	367640	383718
	Total	66038	36408	29630	11589	33475	111102	18124	383385	512611

Pakistan

2.3 Total Government Outlays by Function and Type
(Continued)

Million Pakistan rupees — Fiscal year beginning 1 July

	Final Consumption Expenditures Total	Compensation of Employees	Other	Subsidies	Other Current Transfers & Property Income	Total Current Disbursements	Gross Capital Formation	Other Capital Outlays	Total Outlays
1986									
1 General public services	40913	19793	21120	3336	2356	46605	5050	50	51705
2 Defence									
3 Public order and safety	5192	3600	1592	-	12	5204	423	-	5627
4 Education	10048	8108	1940	-	1523	11571	2510	- -	14081
5 Health	3910	1951	1959	-	240	4150	1385	-	5535
6 Social security and welfare	2273	1965	308	-	45	2318	33	-	2351
7 Housing and community amenities	1257	735	522	-	726	1983	2225	-	4208
8 Recreation, culture and religion	416	201	215	-	173	589	322	-	911
9 Economic services	11746	4612	7134	8640	17966	38352	8304	18313	64969
A Fuel and energy	362	131	231	132	1598	2092	1100	45	3237
B Agriculture, forestry, fishing and hunting	7995	3442	4553	6433	2759	17187	2645	17965	37797
C Mining (except fuels), manufacturing and construction	1226	234	992	-	1625	2851	875	234	3960
D Transportation and communication	848	273	575	396	10183	11427	3507	-	14934
E Other economic affairs	1315	532	783	1679	1801	4795	177	69	5041
10 Other functions	489	316	173	1768	15298	17555	889	428841	447285
Total	76244	41281	34963	13744	38339	128327	21141	447204	596672

2.7 Gross Capital Formation by Type of Good and Owner, in Current Prices

Million Pakistan rupees — Fiscal year beginning 1 July

	1980 TOTAL	Total Private	Public Enterprises	General Government	1981 TOTAL	Total Private	Public Enterprises	General Government	1982 TOTAL	Total Private	Public Enterprises	General Government
Increase in stocks, total	4500	...	...	...	7858	...	...	...	6701	...	...	...
Gross Fixed Capital Formation, Total	42973	16874	17132	8967	49174	17916	18946	12312	56742	21738	22278	12725
1 Residential buildings	4697	3850	405	442	5710	4540	575	595	7112	5901	628	583
2 Non-residential buildings	8851	2993	2763	3095	9702	3264	2121	4317	10125	3632	2325	4168
3 Other construction	9646	93	5087	4466	13509	98	7053	6358	14033	199	6907	6927
4 Land improvement and plantation and orchard development	2305	1809	210	286	2348	1954	357	37	2186	1390	767	29
5 Producers' durable goods	17104	8008	8418	678	17542	7945	8592	1005	22823	10522	11283	1018
A Transport equipment	4230	2089	1996	145	4295	1890	2272	133	3851	2078	1544	229
Passenger cars	1544	813	659	72	1468	712	690	66	1354	826	411	117
Other	2686	1276	1337	73	2827	1178	1582	67	2497	1252	1133	112
B Machinery and equipment	12874	5919	6422	533	13247	6055	6320	872	18972	8444	9739	789
6 Breeding stock, dairy cattle, etc.	...	...	...	...	...	...	...	...	...	...	...	...
Statistical discrepancy [a]	370	121	249	-	363	115	248	-	462	94	368	-
Total Gross Capital Formation	47473	...	...	...	57032	...	...	...	63443	...	...	...

	1983 TOTAL	Total Private	Public Enterprises	General Government	1984 TOTAL	Total Private	Public Enterprises	General Government	1985 TOTAL	Total Private	Public Enterprises	General Government
Increase in stocks, total	7489	...	...	...	8600	...	...	...	9000	...	...	...
Gross Fixed Capital Formation, Total	63439	25645	23612	14182	71797	29712	26168	15917	81319	33307	29888	18124
1 Residential buildings	7673	6445	460	768	8478	7011	534	933	9152	7645	445	1062
2 Non-residential buildings	13529	5282	2974	5273	14470	6083	2584	5803	14593	4901	2942	6750
3 Other construction	12527	93	5668	6766	14363	118	6707	7538	15577	173	6957	8447

Pakistan

2.7 Gross Capital Formation by Type of Good and Owner, in Current Prices
(Continued)

Million Pakistan rupees — Fiscal year beginning 1 July

	1983 TOTAL	1983 Total Private	1983 Public Enterprises	1983 General Government	1984 TOTAL	1984 Total Private	1984 Public Enterprises	1984 General Government	1985 TOTAL	1985 Total Private	1985 Public Enterprises	1985 General Government
4 Land improvement and plantation and orchard development	2783	1975	770	38	3652	1998	1628	26	4948	2430	2490	28
5 Producers' durable goods	26441	11724	13380	1337	30532	14351	14565	1616	36733	18082	16814	1837
A Transport equipment	5360	2621	2408	331	8032	3395	4292	345	8417	3966	4059	392
Passenger cars	2012	1241	576	195	2510	1867	436	207	3127	2340	560	227
Other	3348	1380	1832	136	5522	1528	3856	138	5290	1626	3499	165
B Machinery and equipment	21081	9103	10972	1006	22500	10956	10273	1271	28316	14116	12755	1445
6 Breeding stock, dairy cattle, etc.	...	...	...	...	...	...	...	...	...	...	...	...
Statistical discrepancy a	486	126	360	-	301	151	150	-	316	76	240	-
Total Gross Capital Formation	70928	...	...	...	80397	...	...	...	90319	...	...	...

a) Item 'Statistical discrepancy' refers to furniture and fixture.

2.11 Gross Fixed Capital Formation by Kind of Activity of Owner, ISIC Divisions, in Current Prices

Million Pakistan rupees — Fiscal year beginning 1 July

	1970	1975	1977	1978	1979	1980	1981	1982	1983	1984	1985	1986
					All Producers							
1 Agriculture, hunting, forestry and fishing a	1475	4772	4904	4666	5924	6065	6301	7793	8636	8856	8792	10521
2 Mining and quarrying	26	71	376	144	161	384	418	288	897	1032	2149	2777
3 Manufacturing	1494	5000	8264	9146	10104	9195	9157	10556	12828	12936	16253	15506
A Manufacturing of food, beverages and tobacco	...	...	913	738	1147	563	856	983	1269	1772	1614	1427
B Textile, wearing apparel and leather industries	...	...	1180	1127	1495	1477	1151	1395	1488	1908	2826	4021
C Manufacture of wood, and wood products, including furniture	...	...	81	98	158	153	180	152	95	132	180	159
D Manufacture of paper and paper products, printing and publishing	...	...	93	121	189	240	577	461	640	520	752	740
E Manufacture of chemicals and chemical petroleum, coal, rubber and plastic products	...	...	2091	2227	1606	3307	1605	2513	3620	3446	3153	3303
F Manufacture of non-metalic mineral products except products of petroleum and coal	...	...	415	738	1914	1047	1171	1243	1707	1646	1533	936
G Basic metal industries	...	...	2968	3485	2995	1720	2633	2769	2382	1418	2937	541
H Manufacture of fabricated metal products, machinery and equipment	...	...	404	394	436	562	646	758	1272	1675	2620	3628
I Other manufacturing industries	...	...	119	218	164	126	338	282	355	419	638	751
4 Electricity, gas and water b	683	3186	2780	3028	2333	3382	3910	6195	6136	7949	8356	14291
5 Construction	100	682	922	899	1229	1760	1010	3094	2445	3176	3588	4777
6 Wholesale and retail trade, restaurants and hotels	...	...	...	...	...	...	...	...	...	...	...	...
7 Transport, storage and communication c	1269	2823	3202	3910	8659	6338	7152	6412	7759	10719	11289	11240
8 Finance, insurance, real estate and business services d	613	1459	2250	2476	3281	4118	4925	6428	7048	7588	8450	8968
9 Community, social and personal services d	443	1157	2149	2277	2814	2774	3083	3250	3508	3024	4318	5034
Total Industries e	6103	19151	24846	26546	34506	34006	36862	44017	49257	55880	63195	73214
Producers of Government Services	942	4907	5658	6580	6840	8967	12312	12725	14182	15917	18124	21141
Private Non-Profit Institutions Serving Households	...	...	...	...	...	...	...	...	...	...	...	...
Total	7045	24057	30505	33126	41345	42973	49174	56742	63439	71797	81319	94355

a) Item 'Agriculture, hunting, fishing and forestry' includes investment in Indus Basin Project made by WAPDA.
b) Item 'Electricity, gas and water' refers to electricity and gas only.
c) Item 'Transport, storage and communication' excludes storage.
d) Business services are included in item 'Community, social and personal services'.
e) The estimates of gross capital formation by kind of activity of owner refer to private and semi-public sector only.

Panama

General note. The preparation of national accounts statistics in Panama is undertaken by the Direccion de Estadistica y Censos Panama. Official estimates are published annually, from 1960 in 'Estadistica Panamena, Serie C, Ingreso Nacional' and from 1976 in the bulletin 'Situacion Economica'. The most detailed description of the sources and methods used for the national accounts estimation is found in 'Situacion Economica, Cuentas Nacionales: Anos 1973 a 1975', published in 1976. The estimates are generally in accordance with the classifications and definitions recommended in the United Nations System of National Accounts (SNA). The following tables have been prepared from successive replies to the United Nations national accounts questionnaire. When the scope and coverage of the estimates differ for conceptual or statistical reasons from the definitions and classifications recommended in SNA, a footnote is indicated to the relevant tables.

Sources and methods:

(a) Gross domestic product. Gross domestic product is estimated mainly through the income approach.

(b) Expenditure on the gross domestic product. The expenditure approach is used to estimate government final consumption expenditure as well as imports and exports of goods and services. The commodity-flow approach is used to estimate private final consumption expenditure and, to a large extent, gross capital formation. Data on government consumption expenditure are obtained from official documents and directly from the concerned agencies. Estimates of private consumption expenditure are based on data on locally produced and imported consumer goods. The gross value of construction is obtained by adding the cost of inputs of building materials to the estimated value added of the industry. Factor and non-factor services rendered by residents of Panama to the Former Canal Zone and to the Colon Free Zone are treated uniformly as non-factor services to the rest of the world. These services are, therefore, included in exports of goods and services. Constant prices are estimated by a combined use of extrapolation and price indexes. For government consumption expenditure, compensation of employees is extrapolated by the number of persons employed, whereas purchases of goods and services are deflated by a combination of price indexes. For private consumption expenditure, base-year estimates are extrapolated by means of indexes which refer to consumption at both current and constant prices. The final estimates are adjusted for the discrepancy between total demand and total supply. Current values of gross fixed capital formation are deflated by a price index for inputs in the case of buildings and other construction. The current value of transport equipment and machinery and equipment are extrapolated by a volume index obtained by deflating current values by an index based on the unit export value of machinery in supplier countries. Various price indexes are used for price deflation of exports and imports of goods and services.

(c) Cost-structure of the gross domestic product. Estimates of compensation of employees are based on data on average wages, and the percentage distribution of employees obtained from household surveys. To this informaton is added yearly estimates of salaries earned in the public and private sectors, employers' contribution to social security schemes and an estimate of the incomes of self-employed workers. Operating surplus is compiled from various items, such as property income, saving and direct taxes. The estimates on consumption of fixed capital, which exclude depreciation of government fixed capital, are based on accounting data of the private enterprises, obtained through direct surveys, and financial information of all autonomous and semi-autonomous entities included in the public sector. Estimates of indirect taxes are based on data from public finance, and on revenue figures from central government, municipalities and the Panamanian Institute of Tourism.

(d) Gross domestic product by kind of economic activity. The table of GDP by kind of economic activity is prepared in factor values. For the agriculture, forestry and fishing sector, value added is obtained by deducting inputs from gross value of production. Sources used to estimate agricultural production include the census of agriculture, agricultural surveys and, in the case of export products, external trade statistics. Price data are obtained from the current statistics on prices received by the agricultural producers. Value added in forestry is derived from a bench-mark estimate of sawn wood produced, the number of persons occupied and the ratio of output to employment, which is obtained from periodical industrial inquiries. In the case of fishing, estimates are based on fish landings in the Gulf of Panama, as published in 'Estadistica Panamena' and on the number of persons engaged in fishing, which is obtained from the latest population census. Value added of manufacturing is estimated by extrapolating the bench-mark estimate by an indicator based on the gross value of production by type of industrial activity. A similar approach is used for the electricity, gas and water sector, as well as the construction and the trade sectors. For the trade sector the indicator used is based on the current prices of products which are marketed through wholesale and retail trade. For transport, value added is estimated on the basis of the payments to factor of production. Value added for ownership of dwellings is obtained by aggregating estimates for different geographical areas of the country. For business services value added is estimated by utilizing an indicator of patent registrations in force for operating business at the end of each year. Financial reports relating to factor payments from central government, other government authorities and municipalities, form the data basis for estimates of public administration. A similar approach is applied for other public services, whereas for other private services value added is first estimated at constant prices and then inflated by price indices to arrive at value added at current prices. For the estimation of constant prices in the agricultural sector, the current quantities are valued at base-year prices. Base year estimates, for the manufacturing sector, are extrapolated by various indexes such as indexes of input quantities and quantum indexes of output. For construction, value added is extrapolated by a quantity index of inputs. For electricity, trade and transport value added is extrapolated by quantity indicators of output. For restaurants and hotels the indicators are based on tourist expenditure in Panama and on food and beverage quantities. For banks, value added is extrapolated using the balance of loans and deposits at the end of each year. For ownership of dwellings in urban areas, the construction of new dwellings is used as indicator, and for the rural areas the base-year estimate is extrapolated by an index of rural population growth. The value added of government services is extrapolated by an index of number of government employees. For other private services as well value added is extrapolated using various quantity indicators.

1.1 Expenditure on the Gross Domestic Product, in Current Prices

Million Panamanian balboas

	1970	1975	1977	1978	1979	1980	1981	1982	1983	1984	1985	1986
1 Government final consumption expenditure	152.3	353.3	412.1	482.9	567.2	680.5	812.9	962.6	941.5	1001.3	1043.6	1123.7
2 Private final consumption expenditure	618.8	1054.1	1242.6	1431.7	1693.8	2009.5	2107.4	2311.5	2480.0	2878.0	3080.2	2933.8
3 Gross capital formation	284.3	567.4	490.9	651.7	785.7	986.9	1167.2	1184.6	934.1	761.0	753.0	891.0
A Increase in stocks	22.4	31.9	45.0	45.4	124.5	120.5	87.6	-0.8	16.3	-18.9	-20.1	-4.1
B Gross fixed capital formation	261.9	535.5	445.9	606.3	661.2	866.4	1079.6	1185.4	917.8	779.9	773.1	895.1
Residential buildings	54.4	69.7	84.8	86.2	96.4	93.3	117.4	121.7	119.7	128.9	182.3	207.0
Non-residential buildings	48.4	109.8	77.4	115.1	187.1	219.7	225.8	236.0	221.9	145.3	170.8	186.4
Other construction and land improvement etc.	45.6	148.8	102.8	176.2	136.1	251.4	339.0	493.6	272.4	225.7	125.2	147.8
Other	113.5	207.2	180.9	228.8	241.6	302.0	397.4	334.1	303.8	280.0	294.8	353.9
4 Exports of goods and services	388.2	865.4	921.1	986.4	1124.8	1567.1	1632.0	1689.6	1709.5	1622.1	1735.2	1738.6
5 Less: Imports of goods and services	422.4	999.4	996.9	1100.2	1371.3	1685.2	1841.5	1869.4	1691.4	1696.9	1710.9	1565.9
Equals: Gross Domestic Product	1021.2	1840.8	2069.8	2452.5	2800.2	3558.8	3878.0	4278.9	4373.7	4565.5	4901.1	5121.2

1.2 Expenditure on the Gross Domestic Product, in Constant Prices

Million Panamanian balboas

	1970	1975	1977	1978	1979	1980	1981	1982	1983	1984	1985	1986
					At constant prices of:1970							
1 Government final consumption expenditure	152.3	234.3	250.4	261.5	269.1	284.8	334.9	365.5	343.8	348.4	354.0	383.7
2 Private final consumption expenditure	618.8	733.0	787.1	877.0	931.6	952.4	945.7	997.6	1053.5	1176.0	1196.8	1143.3
3 Gross capital formation	284.3	379.7	261.5	326.6	352.1	411.6	463.4	430.6	340.9	303.3	323.9	364.4
A Increase in stocks	22.4	18.7	16.9	23.4	52.2	46.3	37.3	0.5	7.9	-6.9	-7.5	0.5
B Gross fixed capital formation	261.9	361.0	244.6	303.2	299.9	365.3	426.1	430.1	333.0	310.2	331.4	363.9

Panama

1.2 Expenditure on the Gross Domestic Product, in Constant Prices
(Continued)

Million Panamanian balboas

	1970	1975	1977	1978	1979	1980	1981	1982	1983	1984	1985	1986
	\multicolumn{12}{c}{At constant prices of:1970}											
Residential buildings	54.4	44.5	44.8	44.0	42.6	37.0	42.8	41.4	39.6	43.1	60.8	67.0
Non-residential buildings	48.4	70.0	40.9	58.7	82.7	87.2	82.3	80.2	73.4	48.6	57.0	60.4
Other construction and land improvement etc.	45.6	94.9	54.4	89.9	60.1	99.8	123.5	167.7	90.1	75.4	41.8	47.9
Other	113.5	151.6	104.5	110.6	114.5	141.3	177.5	140.8	129.9	143.1	171.8	188.6
4 Exports of goods and services	388.2	467.0	503.7	538.8	531.6	764.5	740.7	800.1	793.9	743.3	796.8	812.8
5 Less: Imports of goods and services	422.4	528.3	481.3	553.1	568.1	667.5	665.9	675.2	606.4	653.4	663.1	636.8
Equals: Gross Domestic Product	1021.2	1285.7	1321.4	1450.8	1516.3	1745.8	1818.8	1918.6	1925.7	1917.6	2008.4	2067.4

1.3 Cost Components of the Gross Domestic Product

Million Panamanian balboas

	1970	1975	1977	1978	1979	1980	1981	1982	1983	1984	1985	1986
1 Indirect taxes, net	78.8	139.6	181.9	216.0	251.7	268.2	281.6	307.9	331.4	353.7	384.7	427.6
A Indirect taxes	81.4	142.5	183.6	221.7	255.1	269.7	285.4	313.7	336.4	358.8	390.0	432.9
B Less: Subsidies	2.6	2.9	1.7	5.7	3.4	1.6	3.8	5.0	5.0	5.1	5.3	5.3
2 Consumption of fixed capital	53.0	91.8	111.6	134.9	157.3	252.1	279.7	320.9	335.5	374.6	398.8	419.0
3 Compensation of employees paid by resident producers to:	511.0	942.8	1052.3	1218.7	1392.8	1624.6	1800.2	2049.5	2193.2	2301.1	2455.1	2598.4
4 Operating surplus	378.4	666.6	724.0	882.9	998.4	1413.9	1516.5	1600.6	1513.6	1536.1	1662.5	1676.2
Equals: Gross Domestic Product	1021.2	1840.8	2069.8	2452.5	2800.2	3558.8	3878.0	4278.9	4373.7	4565.5	4901.1	5121.2

1.4 General Government Current Receipts and Disbursements

Million Panamanian balboas

	1970	1975	1977	1978	1979	1980	1981	1982	1983	1984	1985	1986
	\multicolumn{12}{c}{Receipts}											
1 Operating surplus	-0.5	-0.3	-	0.3	0.1	-0.7	-0.9	-1.5	0.2	-0.1	-0.2	-0.7
2 Property and entrepreneurial income	27.0	57.2	58.1	59.3	63.4	89.2	97.7	107.1	133.6	141.0	188.1	164.9
3 Taxes, fees and contributions	193.4	380.0	491.1	548.0	671.7	833.2	951.4	1054.1	1159.5	1149.0	1250.8	1321.2
A Indirect taxes	81.4	142.5	183.6	221.7	255.1	269.7	285.4	313.7	336.4	358.8	390.0	432.9
B Direct taxes	55.7	117.5	136.3	136.7	170.9	226.6	284.2	300.8	354.1	304.7	342.4	366.2
C Social security contributions	47.8	103.1	150.7	163.5	199.9	236.9	279.8	339.6	361.7	371.5	394.0	394.7
D Compulsory fees, fines and penalties	8.5	16.9	20.5	26.1	45.8	100.0	102.0	100.0	107.3	114.0	124.4	127.4
4 Other current transfers	42.6	61.2	67.5	78.0	100.8	137.0	173.2	173.9	194.0	184.0	223.0	216.5
Total Current Receipts of General Government	262.5	498.1	616.7	685.6	836.0	1058.7	1221.4	1333.6	1487.3	1473.9	1661.7	1701.9
	\multicolumn{12}{c}{Disbursements}											
1 Government final consumption expenditure	152.3	353.3	412.1	482.9	567.2	680.5	812.9	962.6	941.5	1001.3	1043.6	1123.7
2 Property income	11.2	42.3	64.2	78.5	129.1	187.4	230.3	316.5	292.2	310.3	319.2	359.8
A Interest	11.2	42.3	64.2	78.5	129.1	187.4	230.3	316.5	292.2	310.3	319.2	359.8
B Net land rent and royalties	-	-	-	-	-	-	...	...	...	...	...	...
3 Subsidies	2.6	2.9	1.7	5.7	3.4	1.5	3.8	5.8	5.0	5.1	5.3	5.3
4 Other current transfers	39.5	83.7	105.2	118.0	155.9	197.8	239.9	281.4	306.7	329.8	362.8	369.8
A Social security benefits	18.2	45.9	66.0	74.8	87.2	99.1	121.7	134.6	156.4	174.4	198.6	200.7
B Social assistance grants	1.9	5.2	4.4	5.2	6.3	14.1	12.4	20.9	18.2	18.0	16.6	17.5
C Other	19.4	32.6	34.8	38.0	62.4	84.6	105.8	125.9	132.1	137.4	147.6	151.6
5 Net saving	56.9	15.9	33.5	0.5	-19.6	-8.5	-65.5	-232.7	-58.1	-172.6	-69.2	-156.7
Total Current Disbursements and Net Saving of General Government	262.5	498.1	616.7	685.6	836.0	1058.7	1221.4	1333.6	1487.3	1473.9	1661.7	1701.9

1.7 External Transactions on Current Account, Summary

Million Panamanian balboas

	1970	1975	1977	1978	1979	1980	1981	1982	1983	1984	1985	1986
	\multicolumn{12}{c}{Payments to the Rest of the World}											
1 Imports of goods and services	422.4	999.4	996.9	1100.2	1371.3	1685.2	1841.5	1869.4	1691.4	1696.9	1710.9	1565.9
A Imports of merchandise c.i.f.	363.5	906.1	881.1	966.4	1218.5	1483.9	1620.0	1636.9	1474.4	1468.3	1451.0	1326.5
B Other	58.9	93.3	115.8	133.8	152.8	201.3	221.5	232.5	217.0	228.6	259.9	239.4
2 Factor income to the rest of the world	41.0	396.1	547.6	854.4	1552.6	2760.6	3510.5	3793.5	2827.8	2620.9	2134.0	1812.3

Panama

1.7 External Transactions on Current Account, Summary
(Continued)

Million Panamanian balboas

	1970	1975	1977	1978	1979	1980	1981	1982	1983	1984	1985	1986
3 Current transfers to the rest of the world	19.1	39.5	46.7	54.7	61.4	58.1	54.8	63.9	70.4	61.3	39.0	38.8
4 Surplus of the nation on current transactions	-62.5	-169.3	-153.1	-189.5	-353.7	-213.8	-256.9	-282.7	60.1	-108.8	86.6	316.5
Payments to the Rest of the World and Surplus of the Nation on Current Transactions	420.0	1265.7	1438.1	1819.8	2631.6	4290.1	5149.9	5444.1	4649.7	4270.3	3970.5	3733.5

Receipts From The Rest of the World

	1970	1975	1977	1978	1979	1980	1981	1982	1983	1984	1985	1986
1 Exports of goods and services	388.2	865.4	921.1	986.4	1124.8	1567.1	1632.0	1689.6	1709.5	1622.1	1735.2	1738.6
A Exports of merchandise f.o.b.	158.3	466.0	402.4	387.4	451.8	525.5	495.0	488.8	426.5	368.2	393.4	400.1
B Other	229.9	399.4	518.7	599.0	673.0	1041.6	1137.0	1200.8	1283.0	1253.9	1341.8	1338.5
2 Factor income from rest of the world	14.5	376.6	484.5	797.0	1449.8	2650.6	3431.9	3654.6	2830.0	2497.3	2087.6	1858.3
A Compensation of employees	-	-	-	-	-	62.8	58.6	72.1	75.4	73.3	78.2	82.1
B Property and entrepreneurial income	14.5	376.6	484.5	797.0	1449.8	2587.8	3373.3	3582.5	2754.6	2424.0	2009.4	1776.2
3 Current transfers from rest of the world	17.3	23.7	32.5	36.4	57.0	72.4	86.0	99.9	110.2	150.9	147.7	136.6
Receipts from the Rest of the World on Current Transactions	420.0	1265.7	1438.1	1819.8	2631.6	4290.1	5149.9	5444.1	4649.7	4270.3	3970.5	3733.5

1.10 Gross Domestic Product by Kind of Activity, in Current Prices

Million Panamanian balboas

	1970	1975	1977	1978	1979	1980	1981	1982	1983	1984	1985	1986
1 Agriculture, hunting, forestry and fishing	149.1	205.6	263.5	288.5	304.2	320.4	359.3	371.2	408.4	415.9	450.6	478.6
2 Mining and quarrying	1.9	3.2	3.8	4.1	4.4	6.8	8.7	9.3	7.9	6.0	5.7	6.0
3 Manufacturing	127.3	236.0	234.0	252.6	293.3	356.0	375.6	394.0	401.0	411.0	420.0	422.1
4 Electricity, gas and water	21.8	41.4	63.7	82.5	95.0	113.8	142.4	152.6	153.5	194.9	212.1	227.2
5 Construction	68.2	151.5	122.6	172.7	194.4	258.4	295.2	378.4	271.5	225.0	229.8	257.0
6 Wholesale and retail trade, restaurants and hotels	161.0	318.4	362.3	422.7	493.6	618.2	667.6	681.3	647.5	655.4	693.5	701.0
7 Transport, storage and communication	61.2	129.3	172.4	217.8	263.6	408.2	427.4	497.0	601.1	590.6	640.8	640.4
8 Finance, insurance, real estate and business services	122.1	242.7	306.9	346.5	430.1	503.2	587.4	663.7	725.0	791.3	886.7	958.1
9 Community, social and personal services	68.2	141.0	164.5	181.2	206.5	246.9	273.1	344.0	358.5	379.5	397.1	418.5
Statistical discrepancy [a,b]	75.0	104.7	119.6	140.7	158.9	312.4	330.5	353.3	321.1	337.7	342.6	360.5
Total, Industries	855.8	1573.8	1813.3	2109.3	2444.0	3144.3	3467.2	3844.8	3895.5	4007.3	4278.9	4469.4
Producers of Government Services	117.8	241.8	277.6	329.7	399.4	446.4	468.5	534.2	595.1	673.7	731.1	758.9
Other Producers	21.3	23.4	21.3	26.9	30.3	37.2	42.4	46.2	50.7	56.3	57.6	59.7
Subtotal	994.9	1839.0	2112.2	2465.9	2873.7	3627.9	3978.1	4425.2	4541.3	4737.3	5067.6	5288.0
Less: Imputed bank service charge	10.6	42.4	87.9	70.4	141.6	147.5	183.7	237.4	263.9	280.6	285.1	309.4
Plus: Import duties	36.9	44.2	45.5	57.0	68.1	78.4	83.6	91.1	96.3	108.8	118.6	142.6
Plus: Value added tax	...	...	...	...	...	...	...	...	...	...	...	...
Equals: Gross Domestic Product	1021.2	1840.8	2069.8	2452.5	2800.2	3558.8	3878.0	4278.9	4373.7	4565.5	4901.1	5121.2

a) For 1970-1979, item 'Statistical discrepancy' refers to the services rendered to the area of the Panama Canal. Beginning 1980, the Treaty Torrijos-Carter was inforced, therefore all the activities of the area of the Panama Canal have been incorporated to the corresponding type of economic activity.

b) Beginning 1980, item 'Statistical discrepancy' refers to transport services sold by a resident enterprise 'Commission del Canal de Panama'. Due to the special characteristics of this enterprise it has been separated from the rest to facilitate the analysis of the estimates.

1.11 Gross Domestic Product by Kind of Activity, in Constant Prices

Million Panamanian balboas

	1970	1975	1977	1978	1979	1980	1981	1982	1983	1984	1985	1986
	At constant prices of:1970												
1 Agriculture, hunting, forestry and fishing	149.1	158.6	175.5	189.1	181.0	173.7	188.1	185.2	191.0	194.2	203.9	199.4
2 Mining and quarrying	1.9	2.5	2.1	2.2	2.4	3.1	3.8	4.1	3.4	2.6	2.4	2.5
3 Manufacturing	127.3	147.0	152.5	154.9	172.0	182.1	176.1	179.9	176.7	175.8	179.3	184.0
4 Electricity, gas and water	21.8	38.3	44.0	46.7	52.4	53.5	56.2	59.2	64.9	64.2	69.2	73.3
5 Construction	68.2	96.9	73.8	102.5	102.4	124.3	128.3	154.7	106.4	87.9	87.9	94.4
6 Wholesale and retail trade, restaurants and hotels	161.0	191.0	202.3	219.6	240.9	256.4	252.9	251.0	239.4	240.4	251.4	255.4
7 Transport, storage and communication	61.2	116.0	121.6	145.1	155.4	207.6	216.5	251.1	321.1	305.1	335.5	330.5
8 Finance, insurance, real estate and business services	122.1	178.8	193.8	199.7	222.9	227.2	243.5	252.6	262.7	271.9	283.2	300.8
9 Community, social and personal services	68.2	102.0	109.9	118.3	127.8	142.6	150.1	163.3	168.8	176.2	182.4	195.2
Statistical discrepancy [a,b]	75.0	74.7	71.4	74.3	76.4	175.5	188.4	204.7	175.0	174.6	177.0	185.9

Panama

1.11 Gross Domestic Product by Kind of Activity, in Constant Prices
(Continued)

Million Panamanian balboas

	1970	1975	1977	1978	1979	1980	1981	1982	1983	1984	1985	1986
					At constant prices of:1970							
Total, Industries	855.8	1105.8	1146.9	1252.4	1333.6	1546.0	1603.9	1705.8	1709.4	1692.9	1772.2	1821.4
Producers of Government Services	117.8	169.9	181.7	187.6	196.5	201.2	222.9	232.1	240.6	248.3	258.7	265.2
Other Producers	21.3	19.2	16.3	17.6	16.3	17.7	18.5	19.3	19.4	21.5	21.9	22.6
Subtotal	994.9	1294.9	1344.9	1457.6	1546.4	1764.9	1845.3	1957.2	1969.4	1962.7	2052.8	2109.2
Less: Imputed bank service charge	10.6	30.1	43.6	33.3	56.4	47.2	54.2	68.2	76.4	78.5	80.5	84.2
Plus: Import duties	36.9	20.9	20.1	26.5	26.3	28.1	27.7	29.6	32.7	33.4	36.1	42.4
Plus: Value added tax	...	...	...	...	...	...	...	...	...	...	...	...
Equals: Gross Domestic Product	1021.2	1285.7	1321.4	1450.8	1516.3	1745.8	1818.8	1918.6	1925.7	1917.6	2008.4	2067.4

a) For 1970-1979, item 'Statistical discrepancy' refers to the services rendered to the area of the Panama Canal. Beginning 1980, the Treaty Torrijos-Carter was inforced, therefore all the activities of the area of the Panama Canal have been incorporated to the corresponding type of economic activity.

b) Beginning 1980, item 'Statistical discrepancy' refers to transport services sold by a resident enterprise 'Commission del Canal de Panama'. Due to the special characteristics of this enterprise it has been separated from the rest to facilitate the analysis of the estimates.

1.12 Relations Among National Accounting Aggregates

Million Panamanian balboas

	1970	1975	1977	1978	1979	1980	1981	1982	1983	1984	1985	1986
Gross Domestic Product	1021.2	1840.8	2069.8	2452.5	2800.2	3558.8	3878.0	4278.9	4373.7	4565.5	4901.1	5121.2
Plus: Net factor income from the rest of the world	-26.5	-19.5	-63.1	-57.4	-102.8	-110.0	-78.6	-138.9	2.2	-123.6	-46.4	46.0
Factor income from the rest of the world	14.5	376.6	484.5	797.0	1449.8	2650.6	3431.9	3654.6	2830.0	2497.3	2087.6	1858.3
Less: Factor income to the rest of the world	41.0	396.1	547.6	854.4	1552.6	2760.6	3510.5	3793.5	2827.8	2620.9	2134.0	1812.3
Equals: Gross National Product	994.7	1821.3	2006.7	2395.1	2697.4	3448.8	3799.4	4140.0	4375.9	4441.9	4854.7	5167.2
Less: Consumption of fixed capital	53.0	91.8	111.6	134.9	157.3	252.1	279.7	320.9	335.5	374.6	398.8	419.0
Equals: National Income	941.7	1729.5	1895.1	2260.2	2540.1	3196.7	3519.7	3819.1	4040.4	4067.3	4455.9	4748.2
Plus: Net current transfers from the rest of the world	-1.8	-15.8	-14.2	-18.3	-4.4	14.3	31.2	36.0	39.8	89.6	108.7	97.8
Current transfers from the rest of the world	17.3	23.7	32.5	36.4	57.0	72.4	86.0	99.9	110.2	150.9	147.7	136.6
Less: Current transfers to the rest of the world	19.1	39.5	46.7	54.7	61.4	58.1	54.8	63.9	70.4	61.3	39.0	38.8
Equals: National Disposable Income	939.9	1713.7	1880.9	2241.9	2535.7	3211.0	3550.9	3855.1	4080.2	4156.9	4564.6	4846.0
Less: Final consumption	771.1	1407.4	1654.7	1914.6	2261.0	2690.0	2920.3	3274.1	3421.5	3879.3	4123.8	4057.5
Equals: Net Saving	168.8	306.3	226.2	327.3	274.7	521.0	630.6	581.0	658.7	277.6	440.8	788.5
Less: Surplus of the nation on current transactions	-62.5	-169.3	-153.1	-189.5	-353.7	-213.8	-256.9	-282.7	60.1	-108.8	86.6	316.5
Equals: Net Capital Formation	231.3	475.6	379.3	516.8	628.4	734.8	887.5	863.7	598.6	386.4	354.2	472.0

2.1 Government Final Consumption Expenditure by Function, in Current Prices

Million Panamanian balboas

	1970	1975	1977	1978	1979	1980	1981	1982	1983	1984	1985	1986
1 General public services	45.2	122.6	146.9	184.3	217.2	275.3	372.8	445.7	348.0	351.5	323.5	396.1
2 Defence												
3 Public order and safety	...	...	...	...	...	...	...	...	...	...	...	...
4 Education	44.9	91.3	103.4	114.9	133.6	157.0	174.8	191.3	211.2	232.3	250.5	259.9
5 Health	16.7	27.1	36.5	40.0	49.6	54.9	57.5	74.0	72.9	77.6	78.8	94.1
6 Social security and welfare	21.1	52.3	66.4	78.4	81.6	101.8	116.2	133.9	173.6	211.3	217.0	225.6
7 Housing and community amenities	3.5	12.5	12.9	14.5	17.8	14.8	12.2	16.6	21.3	27.8	28.8	26.9
8 Recreational, cultural and religious affairs	5.0	6.2	5.9	6.3	7.7	13.2	19.1	25.4	22.4	25.9	22.9	25.9
9 Economic services	14.8	31.6	29.7	33.7	46.7	63.5	60.3	75.7	92.1	74.9	114.0	95.2
10 Other functions	1.1	9.7	10.4	10.8	13.0	-			-	-	0.1	
Total Government Final Consumption Expenditure	152.3	353.3	412.1	482.9	567.2	680.5	812.9	962.6	941.5	1001.3	1043.6	1123.7

Panama

2.2 Government Final Consumption Expenditure by Function, in Constant Prices

Million Panamanian balboas

	1970	1975	1977	1978	1979	1980	1981	1982	1983	1984	1985	1986
					At constant prices of:1970							
1 General public services	45.2	78.7	85.1	97.9	100.9	115.2	153.7	169.3	127.1	122.3	109.7	134.1
2 Defence												
3 Public order and safety	...	...	...	...	...	...	...	...	...	...	...	...
4 Education	44.9	63.1	66.7	64.4	65.1	65.7	72.0	72.6	77.1	80.8	87.7	87.9
5 Health	16.7	18.0	22.1	21.6	23.4	23.0	23.6	28.1	26.6	27.0	26.7	35.2
6 Social security and welfare	21.1	34.6	40.1	41.9	38.7	42.6	47.9	50.9	63.4	73.5	73.6	76.4
7 Housing and community amenities	3.5	8.5	8.0	7.9	8.6	6.2	5.0	6.3	7.8	9.7	9.8	9.1
8 Recreational, cultural and religious affairs	5.0	4.1	3.7	3.5	3.6	5.5	7.9	9.6	8.2	9.0	7.8	8.8
9 Economic services	14.8	20.6	17.9	18.2	22.4	26.6	24.8	28.7	33.6	26.1	38.7	32.2
10 Other functions	1.1	6.7	6.8	6.1	6.4	-	-	-	-	-	-	...
Total Government Final Consumption Expenditure	152.3	234.3	250.4	261.5	269.1	284.8	334.9	365.5	343.8	348.4	354.0	383.7

2.7 Gross Capital Formation by Type of Good and Owner, in Current Prices

Million Panamanian balboas

	1980 TOTAL	1980 Total Private	1980 Public Enterprises	1980 General Government	1981 TOTAL	1981 Total Private	1981 Public Enterprises	1981 General Government	1982 TOTAL	1982 Total Private	1982 Public Enterprises	1982 General Government
Increase in stocks, total	120.5	93.3	27.2	...	87.6	84.0	3.6	...	-0.8	-14.5	13.7	...
1 Goods producing industries	64.1	...	...	...	84.0	...	...	...	7.3	...	...	...
2 Wholesale and retail trade	53.6	...	...	...	-0.2	...	...	...	-5.6	...	...	...
3 Other, except government stocks	...	...	...	...	...	...	...	...	...	...	...	...
4 Government stocks	2.8	...	...	...	3.8	...	...	...	-2.5	...	...	...
Gross Fixed Capital Formation, Total	866.4	513.8	352.6	...	1079.6	733.3	346.3	...	1185.4	712.5	472.9	...
1 Residential buildings	93.3	78.1	15.2	...	117.4	99.8	17.6	...	121.7	103.2	18.5	...
2 Non-residential buildings	219.7	199.2	20.5	...	225.8	204.8	21.0	...	236.0	187.5	48.5	...
3 Other construction	251.4	33.6	217.8	...	339.0	126.3	212.7	...	493.6	237.5	256.1	...
4 Land improvement and plantation and orchard development	...	...	...	...	...	...	...	...	...	...	...	...
5 Producers' durable goods	302.0	202.9	99.1	...	397.4	302.4	95.0	...	334.1	184.3	149.8	...
A Transport equipment	113.3	88.2	25.1	...	133.7	99.9	33.8	...	129.3	92.0	37.3	...
B Machinery and equipment	188.7	114.7	74.0	...	263.7	202.5	61.2	...	204.8	92.3	112.5	...
6 Breeding stock, dairy cattle, etc.	...	...	...	...	...	...	...	...	...	...	...	...
Total Gross Capital Formation	986.9	607.1	379.8	...	1167.2	817.3	349.9	...	1184.6	698.0	486.6	...

	1983 TOTAL	1983 Total Private	1983 Public Enterprises	1983 General Government	1984 TOTAL	1984 Total Private	1984 Public Enterprises	1984 General Government	1985 TOTAL	1985 Total Private	1985 Public Enterprises	1985 General Government
Increase in stocks, total	16.3	-3.8	20.1	...	-18.9	0.7	-19.6	...	-20.1	-12.8	-7.3	...
1 Goods producing industries	-2.7	...	...	...	-24.7	...	...	...	-8.9	...	...	...
2 Wholesale and retail trade	0.5	...	...	...	0.4	...	...	...	-3.5	...	...	...
3 Other, except government stocks	...	...	...	...	...	...	...	...	...	...	...	...
4 Government stocks	18.5	...	...	...	5.4	...	...	...	-7.7	...	...	...
Gross Fixed Capital Formation, Total	917.8	604.8	313.0	...	779.9	497.5	282.4	...	773.1	586.1	187.0	...
1 Residential buildings	119.7	108.8	10.9	...	128.9	111.8	17.1	...	182.3	163.9	18.4	...
2 Non-residential buildings	221.9	202.3	19.6	...	145.3	118.8	26.5	...	170.8	146.8	24.0	...
3 Other construction	272.4	62.3	210.1	...	225.7	38.6	187.1	...	125.2	45.9	79.3	...
4 Land improvement and plantation and orchard development	...	...	...	...	...	...	...	...	...	...	...	...
5 Producers' durable goods	303.8	231.4	72.4	...	280.0	228.3	51.7	...	294.8	229.5	65.3	...
A Transport equipment	103.4	77.7	25.7	...	105.4	89.3	16.1	...	117.6	94.1	23.5	...
B Machinery and equipment	200.4	153.7	46.7	...	174.6	139.0	35.6	...	177.2	135.4	41.8	...
6 Breeding stock, dairy cattle, etc.	...	...	...	...	...	...	...	...	...	...	...	...
Total Gross Capital Formation	934.1	601.0	333.1	...	761.0	498.2	262.8	...	753.0	573.3	179.7	...

Panama

2.7 Gross Capital Formation by Type of Good and Owner, in Current Prices

Million Panamanian balboas

	\multicolumn{4}{c}{1986}
	TOTAL	Total Private	Public Enterprises	General Government
Increase in stocks, total	-4.1	-1.4	-2.7	...
1 Goods producing industries	-22.1	...	...	...
2 Wholesale and retail trade	19.7	...	...	...
3 Other, except government stocks	...	...	...	...
4 Government stocks	-1.7	...	...	...
Gross Fixed Capital Formation, Total	895.1	717.4	177.7	...
1 Residential buildings	207.0	191.8	15.2	...
2 Non-residential buildings	186.4	169.5	16.9	...
3 Other construction	147.8	53.6	94.2	...
4 Land improvement and plantation and orchard development	...	...	...	...
5 Producers' durable goods	353.9	302.5	51.4	...
A Transport equipment	140.1	120.1	14.0	...
B Machinery and equipment	213.8	176.4	37.4	...
6 Breeding stock, dairy cattle, etc.	...	...	...	...
Total Gross Capital Formation	891.0	716.0	175.0	...

2.8 Gross Capital Formation by Type of Good and Owner, in Constant Prices

Million Panamanian balboas

	\multicolumn{4}{c}{1980}	\multicolumn{4}{c}{1981}	\multicolumn{4}{c}{1982}
	TOTAL	Total Private	Public Enterprises	General Government	TOTAL	Total Private	Public Enterprises	General Government	TOTAL	Total Private	Public Enterprises	General Government
	\multicolumn{12}{c}{At constant prices of:1970}
Increase in stocks, total	46.3	34.0	12.3	...	37.3	37.6	-0.3	...	0.5	-2.0	2.5	...
1 Goods producing industries	22.9	...	...	...	36.2	...	...	...	3.4	...	...	...
2 Wholesale and retail trade	21.5	...	...	...	-0.5	...	...	...	-1.0	...	...	...
3 Other, except government stocks	...	...	...	...	...	...	...	...	...	...	...	...
4 Government stocks	1.9	...	...	...	1.6	...	...	...	-1.9	...	...	...
Gross Fixed Capital Formation, Total	365.3	215.3	150.0	...	426.1	292.1	134.0	...	430.1	258.5	171.6	...
1 Residential buildings	37.0	30.9	6.1	...	42.8	36.4	6.4	...	41.4	35.1	6.3	...
2 Non-residential buildings	87.2	79.1	8.1	...	82.3	74.6	7.7	...	80.2	63.7	16.5	...
3 Other construction	99.8	13.4	86.4	...	123.5	46.0	77.5	...	167.7	80.7	87.0	...
4 Land improvement and plantation and orchard development	...	...	...	...	...	...	...	...	...	...	...	...
5 Producers' durable goods	141.3	91.9	49.4	...	177.5	135.1	42.4	...	140.8	79.0	61.8	...
A Transport equipment	35.3	27.5	7.8	...	60.7	45.4	15.3	...	54.4	39.8	14.6	...
B Machinery and equipment	106.0	64.4	41.6	...	116.8	89.7	27.1	...	86.4	39.2	47.2	...
6 Breeding stock, dairy cattle, etc.	...	...	...	...	...	...	...	...	...	...	...	...
Total Gross Capital Formation	411.6	249.3	162.3	...	463.4	329.7	133.7	...	430.6	256.5	174.1	...

	\multicolumn{4}{c}{1983}	\multicolumn{4}{c}{1984}	\multicolumn{4}{c}{1985}
	TOTAL	Total Private	Public Enterprises	General Government	TOTAL	Total Private	Public Enterprises	General Government	TOTAL	Total Private	Public Enterprises	General Government
	\multicolumn{12}{c}{At constant prices of:1970}
Increase in stocks, total	7.9	-2.9	10.8	...	-6.9	0.4	-7.3	...	-7.5	-1.9	-5.6	...
1 Goods producing industries	-0.4	...	...	...	-5.6	...	...	...	-2.5	...	...	...
2 Wholesale and retail trade	-1.7	...	...	...	1.5	...	...	...	-1.0	...	...	...
3 Other, except government stocks	...	...	...	...	...	...	...	...	...	...	...	...
4 Government stocks	10.0	...	...	...	-2.8	...	...	...	-4.0	...	...	...
Gross Fixed Capital Formation, Total	333.0	222.5	110.5	...	310.2	214.7	95.5	...	331.4	252.9	78.5	...
1 Residential buildings	39.6	36.0	3.6	...	43.1	37.4	5.7	...	60.8	54.7	6.1	...
2 Non-residential buildings	73.4	66.9	6.5	...	48.6	39.7	8.9	...	57.0	49.0	8.0	...

Panama

2.8 Gross Capital Formation by Type of Good and Owner, in Constant Prices
(Continued)

Million Panamanian balboas

	1983 TOTAL	1983 Total Private	1983 Public Enterprises	1983 General Government	1984 TOTAL	1984 Total Private	1984 Public Enterprises	1984 General Government	1985 TOTAL	1985 Total Private	1985 Public Enterprises	1985 General Government
				At constant prices of:1970								
3 Other construction	90.1	20.6	69.5	...	75.4	13.0	62.4	...	41.8	15.3	26.5	...
4 Land improvement and plantation and orchard development	...	...	...	...	...	...	...	...	...	...	...	...
5 Producers' durable goods	129.9	99.0	30.9	...	143.1	124.6	18.5	...	171.8	133.9	37.9	...
A Transport equipment	43.2	32.5	10.7	...	49.0	43.2	5.8	...	73.4	58.7	14.7	...
B Machinery and equipment	86.7	66.5	20.2	...	94.1	81.4	12.7	...	98.4	75.2	23.2	...
6 Breeding stock, dairy cattle, etc.	...	...	...	...	...	...	...	...	...	...	...	...
Total Gross Capital Formation	340.9	219.6	121.3	...	303.3	215.1	88.2	...	323.9	251.0	72.9	...

	1986 TOTAL	1986 Total Private	1986 Public Enterprises	1986 General Government
		At constant prices of:1970		
Increase in stocks, total	0.5	1.4	-0.9	...
1 Goods producing industries	-6.2	...	...	...
2 Wholesale and retail trade	7.3	...	...	...
3 Other, except government stocks	...	...	...	...
4 Government stocks	-0.6	...	...	...
Gross Fixed Capital Formation, Total	363.9	295.8	68.1	...
1 Residential buildings	67.0	62.1	4.9	...
2 Non-residential buildings	60.4	54.9	5.5	...
3 Other construction	47.9	17.4	30.5	...
4 Land improvement and plantation and orchard development	...	...	...	...
5 Producers' durable goods	188.6	161.4	27.2	...
A Transport equipment	77.6	69.8	7.8	...
B Machinery and equipment	111.0	91.6	19.4	...
6 Breeding stock, dairy cattle, etc.	...	...	...	...
Total Gross Capital Formation	364.4	297.2	67.2	...

2.17 Exports and Imports of Goods and Services, Detail

Million Panamanian balboas

	1970	1975	1977	1978	1979	1980	1981	1982	1983	1984	1985	1986
					Exports of Goods and Services							
1 Exports of merchandise, f.o.b.	158.3	466.0	402.4	387.4	451.8	525.5	495.0	488.8	426.5	368.2	393.4	400.1
2 Transport and communication	3.0	15.9	18.7	20.6	26.5	408.0	440.3	532.9	640.8	602.0	645.6	623.7
3 Insurance service charges	0.3	0.6	1.3	1.7	2.1	2.1	2.3	2.1	1.4	1.6	2.7	3.3
4 Other commodities	59.2	125.7	187.3	217.4	246.6	366.6	413.9	380.1	351.4	341.9	343.8	368.3
5 Adjustments of merchandise exports to change-of-ownership basis	...	...	...	...	...	...	...	...	...	...	...	...
6 Direct purchases in the domestic market by non-residential households	84.0	142.4	182.7	209.1	222.7	219.8	232.8	235.8	240.8	249.6	284.2	283.6
7 Direct purchases in the domestic market by extraterritorial bodies [a]	8.3	9.9	8.7	8.7	15.6	45.1	47.7	49.9	48.6	58.8	65.5	59.6
Statistical discrepancy	75.1	104.9	120.0	141.5	159.5	-	-	-	-	-	-	...
Total Exports of Goods and Services	388.2	865.4	921.1	986.4	1124.8	1567.1	1632.0	1689.6	1709.5	1622.1	1735.2	1738.6
					Imports of Goods and Services							
1 Imports of merchandise, c.i.f.	363.5	906.1	881.1	966.4	1218.5	1483.9	1620.0	1636.9	1474.4	1468.3	1451.0	1326.5

Panama

2.17 Exports and Imports of Goods and Services, Detail
(Continued)

Million Panamanian balboas

	1970	1975	1977	1978	1979	1980	1981	1982	1983	1984	1985	1986
A Imports of merchandise, f.o.b.	331.4	827.2	795.6	866.6	1095.2	1327.0	1453.0	1477.3	1329.5	1314.6	1301.5	1153.8
B Transport of services on merchandise imports	30.4	75.7	79.8	92.4	114.1	149.3	161.2	154.4	139.7	147.5	146.7	168.0
C Insurance service charges on merchandise imports	1.7	3.2	5.7	7.4	9.2	7.6	5.8	5.2	5.2	6.2	2.8	4.7
2 Adjustments of merchandise imports to change-of-ownership basis	...	...	...	...	...	...	...	...	...	...	...	...
3 Other transport and communication	12.9	17.0	20.6	22.4	26.1	42.4	46.8	45.8	46.0	59.8	58.8	50.3
4 Other insurance service charges	5.4	7.9	7.0	11.4	12.5	13.0	17.1	20.8	19.7	19.4	30.3	24.3
5 Other commodities	8.5	25.1	30.8	33.9	40.9	66.7	64.0	48.1	38.1	41.8	56.1	41.0
6 Direct purchases abroad by government	5.9	7.3	10.1	15.4	12.1	15.3	16.4	20.9	23.4	20.9	24.9	24.5
7 Direct purchases abroad by resident households	26.2	36.0	47.3	50.7	61.2	63.9	77.2	96.9	89.8	86.7	89.8	99.3
Total Imports of Goods and Services	422.4	999.4	996.9	1100.2	1371.3	1685.2	1841.5	1869.4	1691.4	1696.9	1710.9	1565.9
Balance of Goods and Services	-34.2	-134.0	-75.8	-113.8	-246.5	-118.1	-209.5	-179.8	18.1	-74.8	24.3	172.7
Total Imports and Balance of Goods and Services	388.2	865.4	921.1	986.4	1124.8	1567.1	1632.0	1689.6	1709.5	1622.1	1735.2	1738.6

a) Item 'Direct purchases in the domestic market by extra-territorial bodies' relates to compensation of employees and property and entrepreneurial income received by residents of Panama for services rendered in the Former Canal Zone and Colon Free Zone.

4.1 Derivation of Value Added by Kind of Activity, in Current Prices

Million Panamanian balboas

	1980 Gross Output	1980 Intermediate Consumption	1980 Value Added	1981 Gross Output	1981 Intermediate Consumption	1981 Value Added	1982 Gross Output	1982 Intermediate Consumption	1982 Value Added	1983 Gross Output	1983 Intermediate Consumption	1983 Value Added
						All Producers						
1 Agriculture, hunting, forestry and fishing	...	...	320.4	...	...	359.3	...	...	371.2	...	...	408.4
A Agriculture and hunting	...	...	272.6	...	...	318.3	...	...	323.7	...	...	357.2
B Forestry and logging	...	...	8.7	...	...	8.9	...	...	9.9	...	...	11.8
C Fishing	...	...	39.1	...	...	32.1	...	...	37.6	...	...	39.4
2 Mining and quarrying	...	...	6.8	...	...	8.7	...	...	9.3	...	...	7.9
3 Manufacturing	...	...	356.0	...	...	375.6	...	...	394.0	...	...	401.0
A Manufacture of food, beverages and tobacco	...	...	143.2	...	...	155.6	...	...	160.3	...	...	169.0
B Textile, wearing apparel and leather industries	...	...	44.1	...	...	44.8	...	...	46.1	...	...	45.2
C Manufacture of wood and wood products, including furniture	...	...	14.8	...	...	16.2	...	...	17.8	...	...	18.2
D Manufacture of paper and paper products, printing and publishing	...	...	27.1	...	...	26.5	...	...	27.1	...	...	30.1
E Manufacture of chemicals and chemical petroleum, coal, rubber and plastic products	...	...	69.7	...	...	72.3	...	...	76.4	...	...	76.3
F Manufacture of non-metallic mineral products, except products of petroleum and coal	...	...	30.6	...	...	33.5	...	...	36.8	...	...	33.6
G Basic metal industries	...	...	6.1	...	...	6.3	...	...	6.0	...	...	4.1
H Manufacture of fabricated metal products, machinery and equipment	...	...	19.4	...	...	19.6	...	...	22.6	...	...	23.0
I Other manufacturing industries	...	...	1.0	...	...	0.8	...	...	0.9	...	...	1.5
4 Electricity, gas and water	...	...	113.8	...	...	142.4	...	...	152.6	...	...	153.5
A Electricity, gas and steam	...	...	101.6	...	...	131.0	...	...	134.1	...	...	133.8
B Water works and supply	...	...	12.2	...	...	11.4	...	...	18.5	...	...	19.7
5 Construction	...	...	258.4	...	...	295.2	...	...	378.4	...	...	271.5
6 Wholesale and retail trade, restaurants and hotels	...	...	618.2	...	...	667.6	...	...	681.3	...	...	647.5
A Wholesale and retail trade	...	...	544.4	...	...	592.1	...	...	602.2	...	...	574.3
B Restaurants and hotels	...	...	73.8	...	...	75.5	...	...	79.1	...	...	73.2
7 Transport, storage and communication	...	...	408.2	...	...	427.4	...	...	497.0	...	...	601.1
A Transport and storage	...	...	352.8	...	...	356.3	...	...	413.9	...	...	509.5

Panama

4.1 Derivation of Value Added by Kind of Activity, in Current Prices
(Continued)

Million Panamanian balboas

	1980			1981			1982			1983		
	Gross Output	Intermediate Consumption	Value Added	Gross Output	Intermediate Consumption	Value Added	Gross Output	Intermediate Consumption	Value Added	Gross Output	Intermediate Consumption	Value Added
B Communication	...	...	55.4	...	...	71.1	...	...	83.1	...	...	91.6
8 Finance, insurance, real estate and business services	...	...	503.2	...	...	587.4	...	...	663.7	...	...	725.0
A Financial institutions	...	...	166.3	...	...	203.5	...	...	226.8	...	...	242.3
B Insurance	...	...	24.5	...	...	30.1	...	...	34.5	...	...	37.5
C Real estate and business services	...	...	312.4	...	...	353.8	...	...	402.4	...	...	445.2
Real estate, except dwellings	...	...	13.3	...	...	16.3	...	...	18.0	...	...	20.1
Dwellings	...	...	247.9	...	...	278.4	...	...	319.1	...	...	359.1
9 Community, social and personal services	...	...	246.9	...	...	273.1	...	...	344.0	...	...	358.5
A Sanitary and similar services	...	...	17.5	...	...	16.5	...	...	20.8	...	...	20.5
B Social and related community services	...	...	64.6	...	...	74.5	...	...	94.9	...	...	101.9
Educational services	...	...	16.3	...	...	17.2	...	...	22.1	...	...	22.5
Medical, dental, other health and veterinary services	...	...	48.3	...	...	57.3	...	...	72.8	...	...	79.4
C Recreational and cultural services	...	...	102.7	...	...	111.0	...	...	133.7	...	...	135.5
D Personal and household services	...	...	62.1	...	...	71.1	...	...	94.6	...	...	100.6
Statistical discrepancy [ab]	...	...	312.4	...	...	330.5	...	...	353.3	...	...	321.1
Total, Industries	...	...	3144.3	...	...	3467.2	...	...	3844.8	...	...	3895.5
Producers of Government Services	...	...	446.4	...	...	468.5	...	...	534.2	...	...	595.1
Other Producers	...	...	37.2	...	...	42.4	...	...	46.2	...	...	50.7
Total	...	...	3627.9	...	...	3978.1	...	...	4425.2	...	...	4541.3
Less: Imputed bank service charge	...	...	147.5	...	...	183.7	...	...	237.4	...	...	263.9
Import duties	...	...	78.4	...	...	83.6	...	...	91.1	...	...	96.3
Value added tax	...	...	...	...	...	...	...	...	...	...	...	...
Total	...	...	3558.8	...	...	3878.0	...	...	4278.9	...	...	4373.7

	1984			1985			1986		
	Gross Output	Intermediate Consumption	Value Added	Gross Output	Intermediate Consumption	Value Added	Gross Output	Intermediate Consumption	Value Added
				All Producers					
1 Agriculture, hunting, forestry and fishing	...	...	415.9	...	...	450.6	...	...	478.6
A Agriculture and hunting	...	...	366.1	...	...	393.0	...	...	383.9
B Forestry and logging	...	...	12.2	...	...	12.3	...	...	12.3
C Fishing	...	...	37.6	...	...	45.3	...	...	82.4
2 Mining and quarrying	...	...	6.0	...	...	5.7	...	...	6.0
3 Manufacturing	...	...	411.0	...	...	420.0	...	...	422.1
A Manufacture of food, beverages and tobacco	...	...	175.5	...	...	188.6	...	...	198.8
B Textile, wearing apparel and leather industries	...	...	47.0	...	...	48.6	...	...	46.6
C Manufacture of wood and wood products, including furniture	...	...	21.4	...	...	21.7	...	...	21.2
D Manufacture of paper and paper products, printing and publishing	...	...	32.1	...	...	34.9	...	...	34.3
E Manufacture of chemicals and chemical petroleum, coal, rubber and plastic products	...	...	76.5	...	...	69.8	...	...	60.2
F Manufacture of non-metallic mineral products, except products of petroleum and coal	...	...	27.6	...	...	26.9	...	...	31.0
G Basic metal industries	...	...	3.9	...	...	4.3	...	...	4.7
H Manufacture of fabricated metal products, machinery and equipment	...	...	24.1	...	...	22.4	...	...	22.0
I Other manufacturing industries	...	...	2.9	...	...	2.8	...	...	3.3
4 Electricity, gas and water	...	...	194.9	...	...	212.1	...	...	227.2
A Electricity, gas and steam	...	...	176.0	...	...	194.5	...	...	206.6
B Water works and supply	...	...	18.9	...	...	17.6	...	...	20.6

Panama

4.1 Derivation of Value Added by Kind of Activity, in Current Prices
(Continued)

Million Panamanian balboas

	1984			1985			1986		
	Gross Output	Intermediate Consumption	Value Added	Gross Output	Intermediate Consumption	Value Added	Gross Output	Intermediate Consumption	Value Added
5 Construction	...	...	225.0	...	...	229.8	...	...	257.0
6 Wholesale and retail trade, restaurants and hotels	...	...	655.4	...	...	693.5	...	...	701.0
A Wholesale and retail trade	...	...	575.1	...	...	604.0	...	...	615.2
B Restaurants and hotels	...	...	80.3	...	...	89.5	...	...	85.8
7 Transport, storage and communication	...	...	590.6	...	...	640.8	...	...	640.4
A Transport and storage	...	...	489.9	...	...	533.7	...	...	519.4
B Communication	...	...	100.7	...	...	107.1	...	...	121.0
8 Finance, insurance, real estate and business services	...	...	791.3	...	...	886.7	...	...	958.1
A Financial institutions	...	...	255.7	...	...	278.3	...	...	308.2
B Insurance	...	...	40.2	...	...	41.0	...	...	42.9
C Real estate and business services	...	...	495.4	...	...	567.4	...	...	607.0
Real estate, except dwellings	...	...	21.2	...	...	22.9	...	...	26.3
Dwellings	...	...	402.3	...	...	466.7	...	...	490.0
9 Community, social and personal services	...	...	379.5	...	...	397.1	...	...	418.5
A Sanitary and similar services	...	...	18.5	...	...	17.4	...	...	16.7
B Social and related community services	...	...	111.6	...	...	113.9	...	...	114.3
Educational services	...	...	20.7	...	...	21.3	...	...	21.4
Medical, dental, other health and veterinary services	...	...	90.9	...	...	92.6	...	...	92.9
C Recreational and cultural services	...	...	136.7	...	...	141.0	...	...	148.8
D Personal and household services	...	...	112.7	...	...	124.8	...	...	138.7
Statistical discrepancy [a,b]	...	...	337.7	...	...	342.6	...	...	360.5
Total, Industries	...	...	4007.3	...	...	4278.9	...	...	4469.4
Producers of Government Services	...	...	673.7	...	...	731.1	...	...	758.9
Other Producers	...	...	56.3	...	...	57.6	...	...	59.7
Total	...	...	4737.3	...	...	5067.6	...	...	5288.0
Less: Imputed bank service charge	...	...	280.6	...	...	285.1	...	...	309.4
Import duties	...	...	108.8	...	...	118.6	...	...	142.6
Value added tax	...	...	...	...	...	...	...	...	...
Total	...	...	4565.5	...	...	4901.1	...	...	5121.2

a) For 1970-1979, item 'Statistical discrepancy' refers to the services rendered to the area of the Panama Canal. Beginning 1980, the Treaty Torrijos-Carter was inforced, therefore all the activities of the area of the Panama Canal have been incorporated to the corresponding type of economic activity.

b) Beginning 1980, item 'Statistical discrepancy' refers to transport services sold by a resident enterprise 'Commission del Canal de Panama'. Due to the special characteristics of this enterprise it has been separated from the rest to facilitate the analysis of the estimates.

4.2 Derivation of Value Added by Kind of Activity, in Constant Prices

Million Panamanian balboas

	1980			1981			1982			1983		
	Gross Output	Intermediate Consumption	Value Added	Gross Output	Intermediate Consumption	Value Added	Gross Output	Intermediate Consumption	Value Added	Gross Output	Intermediate Consumption	Value Added
	At constant prices of:1970											
	All Producers											
1 Agriculture, hunting, forestry and fishing	...	...	173.7	...	...	188.1	...	...	185.2	...	...	191.0
A Agriculture and hunting	...	...	161.4	...	...	176.4	...	...	173.3	...	...	178.6
B Forestry and logging	...	...	5.0	...	...	4.9	...	...	5.1	...	...	5.5
C Fishing	...	...	7.3	...	...	6.8	...	...	6.8	...	...	6.9
2 Mining and quarrying	...	...	3.1	...	...	3.8	...	...	4.1	...	...	3.4

Panama

4.2 Derivation of Value Added by Kind of Activity, in Constant Prices
(Continued)

Million Panamanian balboas

	1980 Gross Output	1980 Intermediate Consumption	1980 Value Added	1981 Gross Output	1981 Intermediate Consumption	1981 Value Added	1982 Gross Output	1982 Intermediate Consumption	1982 Value Added	1983 Gross Output	1983 Intermediate Consumption	1983 Value Added
				At constant prices of: 1970								
3 Manufacturing	...	...	182.1	...	...	176.1	...	...	179.9	...	...	176.7
A Manufacture of food, beverages and tobacco	...	...	91.1	...	...	88.9	...	...	91.2	...	...	91.1
B Textile, wearing apparel and leather industries	...	...	22.3	...	...	21.9	...	...	21.1	...	...	16.8
C Manufacture of wood and wood products, including furniture	...	...	6.3	...	...	6.0	...	...	6.0	...	...	5.6
D Manufacture of paper and paper products, printing and publishing	...	...	12.5	...	...	11.0	...	...	11.6	...	...	13.0
E Manufacture of chemicals and chemical petroleum, coal, rubber and plastic products	...	...	23.6	...	...	22.1	...	...	23.2	...	...	24.7
F Manufacture of non-metallic mineral products, except products of petroleum and coal	...	...	13.4	...	...	12.7	...	...	13.3	...	...	12.1
G Basic metal industries	...	...	1.3	...	...	1.2	...	...	1.2	...	...	1.0
H Manufacture of fabricated metal products, machinery and equipment	...	...	10.2	...	...	10.1	...	...	10.5	...	...	9.9
I Other manufacturing industries	...	...	1.4	...	...	2.2	...	...	1.8	...	...	2.5
4 Electricity, gas and water	...	...	53.5	...	...	56.2	...	...	59.2	...	...	64.9
A Electricity, gas and steam	...	...	45.0	...	...	47.5	...	...	50.1	...	...	56.0
B Water works and supply	...	...	8.5	...	...	8.7	...	...	9.1	...	...	8.9
5 Construction	...	...	124.3	...	...	128.3	...	...	154.7	...	...	106.4
6 Wholesale and retail trade, restaurants and hotels	...	...	256.4	...	...	252.9	...	...	251.0	...	...	239.4
A Wholesale and retail trade	...	...	218.9	...	...	217.4	...	...	218.0	...	...	207.6
B Restaurants and hotels	...	...	37.5	...	...	35.5	...	...	33.0	...	...	31.8
7 Transport, storage and communication	...	...	207.6	...	...	216.5	...	...	251.1	...	...	321.1
A Transport and storage	...	...	187.4	...	...	195.0	...	...	228.2	...	...	297.5
B Communication	...	...	20.2	...	...	21.5	...	...	22.9	...	...	23.6
8 Finance, insurance, real estate and business services	...	...	227.2	...	...	243.5	...	...	252.6	...	...	262.7
A Financial institutions	...	...	60.3	...	...	67.1	...	...	70.5	...	...	76.3
B Insurance	...	...	12.3	...	...	14.2	...	...	14.0	...	...	14.3
C Real estate and business services	...	...	154.6	...	...	162.2	...	...	168.1	...	...	172.1
Real estate, except dwellings	...	...	9.0	...	...	11.9	...	...	12.8	...	...	12.9
Dwellings	...	...	121.9	...	...	125.2	...	...	129.2	...	...	102.8
9 Community, social and personal services	...	...	142.6	...	...	150.1	...	...	163.3	...	...	168.8
A Sanitary and similar services	...	...	6.3	...	...	6.3	...	...	6.7	...	...	6.2
B Social and related community services	...	...	31.1	...	...	32.5	...	...	35.6	...	...	36.8
Educational services	...	...	8.3	...	...	7.9	...	...	8.7	...	...	8.6
Medical, dental, other health and veterinary services	...	...	22.8	...	...	24.6	...	...	26.9	...	...	28.2
C Recreational and cultural services	...	...	76.0	...	...	80.1	...	...	86.5	...	...	89.1
D Personal and household services	...	...	29.2	...	...	31.2	...	...	34.5	...	...	36.7
Statistical discrepancy [a,b]	...	...	175.5	...	...	188.4	...	...	204.7	...	...	175.0
Total, Industries	...	...	1546.0	...	...	1603.9	...	...	1705.8	...	...	1709.4
Producers of Government Services	...	...	201.2	...	...	222.9	...	...	232.1	...	...	240.6
Other Producers	...	...	17.7	...	...	18.5	...	...	19.3	...	...	19.4
Total	...	...	1764.9	...	...	1845.3	...	...	1957.2	...	...	1969.4
Less: Imputed bank service charge	...	...	47.2	...	...	54.2	...	...	68.2	...	...	76.4
Import duties	...	...	28.1	...	...	27.7	...	...	29.6	...	...	32.7
Value added tax	...	...	...	...	...	...	...	...	...	...	...	...
Total	...	...	1745.8	...	...	1818.8	...	...	1918.6	...	...	1925.7

Panama

4.2 Derivation of Value Added by Kind of Activity, in Constant Prices

Million Panamanian balboas

	1984 Gross Output	1984 Intermediate Consumption	1984 Value Added	1985 Gross Output	1985 Intermediate Consumption	1985 Value Added	1986 Gross Output	1986 Intermediate Consumption	1986 Value Added
	\multicolumn{9}{c}{At constant prices of: 1970}								
	\multicolumn{9}{c}{All Producers}								
1 Agriculture, hunting, forestry and fishing	...	...	194.2	...	...	203.9	...	...	199.4
A Agriculture and hunting	...	...	182.0	...	...	188.9	...	...	180.7
B Forestry and logging	...	...	5.6	...	...	5.6	...	...	5.5
C Fishing	...	...	6.6	...	...	9.4	...	...	13.2
2 Mining and quarrying	...	...	2.6	...	...	2.4	...	...	2.5
3 Manufacturing	...	...	175.8	...	...	179.3	...	...	184.0
A Manufacture of food, beverages and tobacco	...	...	90.4	...	...	93.7	...	...	96.2
B Textile, wearing apparel and leather industries	...	...	18.2	...	...	18.6	...	...	18.9
C Manufacture of wood and wood products, including furniture	...	...	6.0	...	...	6.2	...	...	6.4
D Manufacture of paper and paper products, printing and publishing	...	...	13.1	...	...	14.0	...	...	13.3
E Manufacture of chemicals and chemical petroleum, coal, rubber and plastic products	...	...	24.6	...	...	24.2	...	...	24.3
F Manufacture of non-metallic mineral products, except products of petroleum and coal	...	...	10.5	...	...	10.1	...	...	11.7
G Basic metal industries	...	...	0.9	...	...	1.1	...	...	1.3
H Manufacture of fabricated metal products, machinery and equipment	...	...	9.6	...	...	8.9	...	...	9.0
I Other manufacturing industries	...	...	2.5	...	...	2.5	...	...	2.9
4 Electricity, gas and water	...	...	64.2	...	...	69.2	...	...	73.3
A Electricity, gas and steam	...	...	55.1	...	...	59.7	...	...	63.4
B Water works and supply	...	...	9.1	...	...	9.5	...	...	9.9
5 Construction	...	...	87.9	...	...	87.9	...	...	94.4
6 Wholesale and retail trade, restaurants and hotels	...	...	240.4	...	...	251.4	...	...	255.4
A Wholesale and retail trade	...	...	206.7	...	...	215.9	...	...	219.6
B Restaurants and hotels	...	...	33.7	...	...	35.5	...	...	35.8
7 Transport, storage and communication	...	...	305.1	...	...	335.5	...	...	330.5
A Transport and storage	...	...	280.3	...	...	309.5	...	...	303.5
B Communication	...	...	24.8	...	...	26.0	...	...	27.0
8 Finance, insurance, real estate and business services	...	...	271.9	...	...	283.2	...	...	300.8
A Financial institutions	...	...	79.7	...	...	83.6	...	...	91.4
B Insurance	...	...	14.3	...	...	15.0	...	...	15.3
C Real estate and business services	...	...	177.9	...	...	184.6	...	...	194.1
Real estate, except dwellings	...	...	12.9	...	...	13.2	...	...	14.9
Dwellings	...	...	136.4	...	...	140.3	...	...	146.1
9 Community, social and personal services	...	...	176.2	...	...	182.4	...	...	195.2
A Sanitary and similar services	...	...	5.4	...	...	4.9	...	...	4.0
B Social and related community services	...	...	40.4	...	...	41.5	...	...	43.4
Educational services	...	...	8.6	...	...	8.6	...	...	8.6
Medical, dental, other health and veterinary services	...	...	31.8	...	...	32.9	...	...	34.8
C Recreational and cultural services	...	...	89.5	...	...	91.3	...	...	97.4
D Personal and household services	...	...	40.9	...	...	44.7	...	...	49.8
Statistical discrepancy [a,b]	...	...	174.6	...	...	177.0	...	...	185.9

Panama

4.2 Derivation of Value Added by Kind of Activity, in Constant Prices
(Continued)

Million Panamanian balboas

	1984			1985			1986		
	Gross Output	Intermediate Consumption	Value Added	Gross Output	Intermediate Consumption	Value Added	Gross Output	Intermediate Consumption	Value Added
	At constant prices of: 1970								
Total, Industries	...	...	1692.9	...	...	1772.2	...	...	1821.4
Producers of Government Services	...	...	248.3	...	...	258.7	...	...	265.2
Other Producers	...	...	21.5	...	...	21.9	...	...	22.6
Total	...	...	1962.7	...	...	2052.8	...	...	2109.2
Less: Imputed bank service charge	...	...	78.5	...	...	80.5	...	...	84.2
Import duties	...	...	33.4	...	...	36.1	...	...	42.4
Value added tax	...	...	...	...	...	...	...	...	...
Total	...	...	1917.6	...	...	2008.4	...	...	2067.4

a) For 1970-1979, item 'Statistical discrepancy' refers to the services rendered to the area of the Panama Canal. Beginning 1980, the Treaty Torrijos-Carter was inforced, therefore all the activities of the area of the Panama Canal have been incorporated to the corresponding type of economic activity.

b) Beginning 1980, item 'Statistical discrepancy' refers to transport services sold by a resident enterprise 'Commission del Canal de Panama'. Due to the special characteristics of this enterprise it has been separated from the rest to facilitate the analysis of the estimates.

Papua New Guinea

General note. The preparation of national accounts statistics in Papua New Guinea is undertaken by the National Statistical Office (formerly Bureau of Statistics), Port Moresby. The official estimates are published in 'National Accounts Statistics'. A detailed description of the sources and methods used for the national accounts estimation is found in 'National Accounts Statistics 1960/61 - 1973/74', published in 1974. The estimates are generally in accordance with the classifications and definitions recommended in the United Nations System of National Accounts (SNA). Input-output tables for the years 1969/70, 1972/73 and 1976/77 were published in 1973, 1974 and 1982 respectively. The following tables have been prepared from successive replies to the United Nations national accounts questionnaire. When the scope and coverage of the estimates differ for conceptual or statistical reasons from the definitions and classfications recommended in SNA, a footnote is indicated to the relevant tables.

Sources and methods:

(a) Gross domestic product. Gross domestic product is estimated mainly through the income approach.

(b) Expenditure on the gross domestic product. All components of GDP by expenditure type are estimated through the expenditure approach. However, the commodity-flow approach is used for checking purposes in the case of a few items included under private consumption expenditure. The estimates of government consumption expenditure are based on Budget Papers, Annual Reports of the Commissioner for Local Government, Financial Statements of Provincial Government and Australian Budget Papers. The market component of household consumption expenditure is estimated mainly from the results of the retail sales and selected services survey. Estimates for items not covered by this survey are obtained from sources such as Budget Papers, the population census, various surveys of urban markets and village industry and taxation data. For some selected items, the estimates are checked and supplemented by data from international trade statistics using the commodity-flow approach. The non-market component of household consumption consists of food and firewood for own consumption and services of owner-occupied dwellings. Estimates of food produced for own consumption are calculated by using data from the Rural Industrial Bulletin and the estimated consumption per head of population. The annual quantity of firewood used per family is multiplied by average price and the number of families gathering firewood for own use. Construction and maintenance of housing is estimated by multiplying population data by the time spent and the minimum wage rate. Estimates of increase in stocks are based mainly on the Taxation Statistics Bulletin. For gross fixed capital formation by private industries, the principal source of information is the capital expenditure survey and for the public industries, the annual reports of the public enterprises. Exports and imports of goods and services are estimated mainly from the international trade statistics. For the constant price estimates of parts of government expenditure, private expenditure, gross fixed capital formation, increase in stocks and exports of merchandise, the current quantities are revalued at base-year prices. Regarding the market component of private consumption expenditure, building and construction, government expenditure on goods and services and imports of merchandise, the current values are deflated by appropriate price indexes.

(c) Cost-structure of the gross domestic product. Estimates of compensation of employees are based on taxation statistics, statistics of religious organizations and the Labour Information Bulletin. Adjustments are made for wages and salaries not covered by the above sources. Imputed wages referring to work provided to government and mission authorities are shown separately. Estimates of operating surplus for the market component are based mainly on taxation returns with some adjustments made to cover imputed bank service charge and to include producers not required to submit returns. For owner-occupied dwellings, operating surplus is calculated from information contained in the Building Statistics Bulletin. Consumption of fixed capital is estimated based on taxation data supplemented by annual reports for producers not covered. The Papua New Guinea Budget papers and the annual reports of the Commissioner for Local Government provide all the information needed to estimate indirect taxes and subsidies.

(d) Gross domestic product by kind of economic activity. The table of gross domestic product by kind of economic activity is prepared at market prices, i.e., producers' values. The income approach is used to estimate value added of most industries. Value added is defined as the sum of compensation of employees, operating surplus, consumption of fixed capital and net indirect taxes. The principal source is the income tax statistics, supplemented by annual reports of public and private enterprises. The reporting unit in these statistics is the enterprise (legal entity) rather than the establishment. For the major activities such as mining and quarrying, electricity, gas and water, and communication, in which cases almost the whole production is concentrated in a few enterprise units, the establishment type data are used. In cases where surveys data are used, adjustments and supplementary data are taken into account to cover activities not included. For the non-marketed production and contributions of free and partially-paid labour, estimates are available separately as sub-divisions of the relevant items as the amounts involved are quite substantial. As mentioned above, estimates of GDP by kind of economic activity are arrived at by subdividing the cost-structure components of total GDP into the various kinds of activity. Compensation of employees is classified in accordance with the industry information on individuals' tax returns. If an individual has more than one source of income, he is allocated to the industry category corresponding to his major source of income and all of his income is classed to that category. Data on operating surplus of private enterprises are classified on the basis of information given in the company tax statistics and in the statistics of individuals' income other than wages and salaries, while the industry categories of the operating surplus of public enterprises are determined by the nature of their productive activities. For industry allocation of consumption of fixed capital, the taxation data supplemented by other information in respect of producers not covered by the taxation statistics provide the basis. In the case of indirect taxes and subsidies, the industry allocation is made on the basis of the nature of indirect taxes and subsidies. GDP by kind of economic activity at constant prices is not estimated.

1.1 Expenditure on the Gross Domestic Product, in Current Prices

Million Papua New Guinea kina
Fiscal year beginning 1 July

	1970	1975	1977	1978	1979	1980	1981	1982	1983	1984	1985	1986
1 Government final consumption expenditure	183.1	367.2	337.7	353.3	371.4	411.2	454.4	468.1	471.3	505.1	537.3	551.8
2 Private final consumption expenditure	387.1	591.3	693.1	788.6	890.5	1051.3	1104.2	1117.9	1245.0	1343.6	1479.1	1554.2
3 Gross capital formation	291.6	193.4	280.5	296.3	383.3	430.6	458.1	562.5	626.2	605.2	500.7	603.9
A Increase in stocks	15.5	29.9	41.2	27.8	57.1	36.4	7.4	-14.2	-6.2	71.5	33.8	31.4
B Gross fixed capital formation	276.1	163.5	239.3	268.5	326.2	394.2	450.7	576.7	632.4	533.7	466.9	572.5
4 Exports of goods and services	113.6	400.4	584.0	579.1	742.5	727.6	612.0	611.3	766.1	800.2	1004.2	1090.0
5 Less: Imports of goods and services	354.2	470.9	600.8	627.5	744.3	910.8	987.6	1058.2	1129.6	1207.6	1243.0	1335.2
Statistical discrepancy	0.5	-13.0	4.0	23.4	-10.9	-11.8	9.2	14.5	-5.4	-5.2	0.9	-2.1
Equals: Gross Domestic Product [a]	621.7	1068.5	1298.5	1413.3	1632.5	1708.1	1681.2	1749.1	1973.7	2134.4	2279.2	2471.5

a) Second series, estimates relate to calendar year.

Papua New Guinea

1.2 Expenditure on the Gross Domestic Product, in Constant Prices

Million Papua New Guinea kina — Fiscal year beginning 1 July

	1970	1975	1977	1978	1979	1980	1981	1982	1983	1984	1985	1986
		1968	1972		At constant prices of: 1977				1981			
1 Government final consumption expenditure	151.8	232.5	337.7	343.4	349.6	337.8	324.8 / 454.4	422.6	414.1	419.3	429.3	420.5
2 Private final consumption expenditure	356.6	445.9	693.1	728.6	764.5	794.1	768.8 / 1104.2	1075.3	1119.0	1144.2	1221.2	1223.8
3 Gross capital formation	265.5	122.4	280.5	288.2	353.5	368.5	353.1 / 458.1	518.8	541.9	487.7	373.8	427.1
A Increase in stocks	14.6	20.3	41.2	27.8	52.6	29.2	5.3 / 7.4	-12.8	-5.3	54.4	20.7	16.8
B Gross fixed capital formation	250.9	102.1	239.3	260.4	300.9	339.3	347.8 / 450.7	531.6	547.2	433.3	353.1	410.3
4 Exports of goods and services	110.7	330.6	584.0	639.1	637.4	635.3	669.6 / 642.9	640.5	653.1	683.4	756.1	792.2
5 Less: Imports of goods and services	328.0	311.7	600.8	613.3	660.6	723.5	724.7 / 987.6	976.0	969.7	956.2	924.9	942.3
Statistical discrepancy	0.5	-9.4	4.0	23.8	-9.1	-10.0	6.7 / 9.2	14.0	-4.8	-4.3	0.7	-1.6
Equals: Gross Domestic Product	557.2	810.2	1298.5[a]	1409.7[a]	1435.2[a]	1402.3[a]	1398.3[a] / 1681.2[a]	1695.2[a]	1753.5[a]	1774.2[a]	1856.2[a]	1919.7[a]

a) The estimates with base year 1977 and 1981 relate to calendar year.

1.3 Cost Components of the Gross Domestic Product

Million Papua New Guinea kina — Fiscal year beginning 1 July

	1970	1975	1977	1978	1979	1980	1981	1982	1983	1984	1985	1986
1 Indirect taxes, net	30.2	57.9	79.7	82.9	98.3	110.0	114.6	134.4	151.9	179.2	189.7	212.0
A Indirect taxes	32.0	60.4	83.2	87.6	102.2	114.6	119.2	138.5	153.7	182.2	191.6	213.7
B Less: Subsidies	1.8	2.5	3.5	4.7	3.9	4.6	4.6	4.1	1.8	3.0	1.9	1.7
2 Consumption of fixed capital [a]	28.7	77.7	84.6	103.6	107.3	124.9	137.6	150.0	162.6	204.8	211.4	223.9
3 Compensation of employees paid by resident producers to:	296.9	505.8	518.0	552.0	594.7	676.2	747.7	763.4	792.9	872.3	871.5	939.0
A Resident households	296.9	505.8	517.8	551.5	593.8	675.4	747.1	762.5	792.2	871.7	870.9	938.4
B Rest of the world	-	-	0.2	0.5	0.9	0.7	0.6	0.8	0.8	0.6	0.6	0.6
4 Operating surplus	265.8	427.0	616.1	674.6	832.2	797.1	681.4	701.2	866.4	878.1	1006.6	1096.6
Equals: Gross Domestic Product [b]	621.7	1068.5	1298.5 / 1413.3	1632.5	1708.1	1681.2	1749.1	1973.7	2134.4	2279.2	2471.5	

a) Item 'Consumption of fixed capital' excludes consumption of fixed capital of producers of government-owned houses and hostels.
b) Second series, estimates relate to calendar year.

1.4 General Government Current Receipts and Disbursements

Million Papua New Guinea kina — Fiscal year beginning 1 July

	1970	1975	1977	1978	1979	1980	1981	1982	1983	1984	1985	1986
					Receipts							
1 Operating surplus	...	...	...	...	...	...	...	...	...	...	...	...
2 Property and entrepreneurial income	1.9	...	...	...	...	...	...	...	...	...	...	...
3 Taxes, fees and contributions	97.5	...	...	...	...	...	...	...	...	...	...	...
A Indirect taxes	32.0	60.4	83.2	87.6	102.2	114.6	119.2	138.5	153.7	182.2	191.6	213.7

# Papua New Guinea

1.4 General Government Current Receipts and Disbursements
(Continued)

Fiscal year beginning 1 July

Million Papua New Guinea kina

	1970	1975	1977	1978	1979	1980	1981	1982	1983	1984	1985	1986
B Direct taxes	64.3	...	...	...	...	...	...	...	...	...	...	...
C Social security contributions	-	...	...	...	...	...	...	...	...	...	...	...
D Compulsory fees, fines and penalties	1.2	3.0	...	...	...	...	...	...	...	...	...	...
4 Other current transfers	100.3	...	...	...	...	...	...	...	...	...	...	...
Total Current Receipts of General Government [a]	199.8	...	...	...	...	...	...	...	...	...	1479.1	1554.2

Disbursements

	1970	1975	1977	1978	1979	1980	1981	1982	1983	1984	1985	1986
1 Government final consumption expenditure	183.1	367.2	337.7	353.3	371.4	411.2	454.4	468.1	471.3	505.1	537.3	551.8
A Compensation of employees	61.6	...	...	...	...	...	...	...	...	...	...	...
B Consumption of fixed capital	2.4	...	...	...	...	...	...	...	...	...	...	...
C Purchases of goods and services, net	...	...	...	...	...	...	...	...	...	...	...	...
D Less: Own account fixed capital formation	...	...	...	...	...	...	...	...	...	...	...	...
E Indirect taxes paid, net	...	...	...	...	...	...	...	...	...	...	...	...
2 Property income	3.8	...	...	...	...	...	...	...	...	...	...	...
3 Subsidies	1.8	2.5	3.5	4.7	3.9	4.6	4.6	4.1	1.8	3.0	1.9	1.7
4 Other current transfers	2.5	...	...	...	...	...	...	...	...	...	...	...
5 Net saving	8.5	...	...	...	...	...	...	...	...	...	...	...
Total Current Disbursements and Net Saving of General Government [a]	199.7	...	...	...	...	...	...	...	...	...	...	...

a) Second series, estimates relate to calendar year.

1.5 Current Income and Outlay of Corporate and Quasi-Corporate Enterprises, Summary

Fiscal year beginning 1 July

Million Papua New Guinea kina

	1970	1975	1977	1978	1979	1980	1981	1982	1983	1984	1985	1986

Receipts

	1970	1975	1977	1978	1979	1980	1981	1982	1983	1984	1985	1986
1 Operating surplus	57.5	...	...	...	...	...	...	...	...	...	...	...
2 Property and entrepreneurial income received	29.3	...	...	...	...	...	...	...	...	...	...	...
3 Current transfers	5.8	...	...	...	...	...	...	...	...	...	...	...
Total Current Receipts	92.6	...	...	...	...	...	...	...	...	...	...	...

Disbursements

	1970	1975	1977	1978	1979	1980	1981	1982	1983	1984	1985	1986
1 Property and entrepreneurial income	60.3	...	...	...	...	...	...	...	...	...	...	...
2 Direct taxes and other current payments to general government	11.0	...	...	...	...	...	...	...	...	...	...	...
3 Other current transfers	6.7	...	...	...	...	...	...	...	...	...	...	...
4 Net saving	14.6	...	...	...	...	...	...	...	...	...	...	...
Total Current Disbursements and Net Saving	92.6	...	...	...	...	...	...	...	...	...	...	...

1.6 Current Income and Outlay of Households and Non-Profit Institutions

Fiscal year beginning 1 July

Million Papua New Guinea kina

	1970	1975	1977	1978	1979	1980	1981	1982	1983	1984	1985	1986

Receipts

	1970	1975	1977	1978	1979	1980	1981	1982	1983	1984	1985	1986
1 Compensation of employees	296.9	507.1	519.1	552.7	595.4	677.2	753.1	768.8	798.8	878.4	878.1	945.9
A From resident producers	296.9	505.8	517.8	551.5	593.8	675.4	747.1	762.5	792.2	871.5	870.9	938.4
B From rest of the world	-	1.3	1.3	1.2	1.6	1.8	6.0	6.3	6.6	6.9	7.2	7.5
2 Operating surplus of private unincorporated enterprises	...	...	...	...	...	...	...	...	...	...	...	...

Papua New Guinea

1.6 Current Income and Outlay of Households and Non-Profit Institutions
(Continued)

Million Papua New Guinea kina — Fiscal year beginning 1 July

	1970	1975	1977	1978	1979	1980	1981	1982	1983	1984	1985	1986
3 Property and entrepreneurial income	215.4	...	...	...	...	...	...	...	...	...	...	...
4 Current transfers	5.7	...	...	...	...	...	...	...	...	...	...	...
A Social security benefits	...	...	...	...	...	...	...	...	...	...	...	...
B Social assistance grants	...	...	...	...	...	...	...	...	...	...	...	...
C Other	3.2	...	...	...	...	...	...	...	...	...	...	...
Total Current Receipts [a]	518.0	...	...	...	...	...	...	...	...	...	...	...

Disbursements

	1970	1975	1977	1978	1979	1980	1981	1982	1983	1984	1985	1986
1 Private final consumption expenditure	387.1	591.3	693.1	788.6	890.5	1051.3	1104.2	1117.9	1245.0	1343.6	...	...
2 Property income	0.7	...	...	...	...	...	...	...	...	...	...	...
3 Direct taxes and other current transfers n.e.c. to general government	54.5	...	...	...	...	...	...	...	...	...	...	...
A Social security contributions	...	...	...	...	...	...	...	...	...	...	...	...
B Direct taxes	53.3	...	...	...	...	...	...	...	...	...	...	...
C Fees, fines and penalties	1.2	...	...	...	...	...	...	...	...	...	...	...
4 Other current transfers	8.5	...	...	...	...	...	...	...	...	...	...	...
5 Net saving	76.9	...	...	...	...	...	...	...	...	...	...	...
Total Current Disbursements and Net Saving [a]	518.0	...	...	...	...	...	...	...	...	...	...	...

a) Second series, estimates relate to calendar year.

1.7 External Transactions on Current Account, Summary

Million Papua New Guinea kina — Fiscal year beginning 1 July

Payments to the Rest of the World

	1970	1975	1977	1978	1979	1980	1981	1982	1983	1984	1985	1986
1 Imports of goods and services	354.2	470.9	600.9	627.5	744.3	910.8	987.6	1058.2	1129.6	1207.6	1243.0	1335.2
A Imports of merchandise c.i.f.	311.5	400.1	529.3	551.4	665.3	808.7	872.3	897.5	961.2	1018.2	1058.3	1137.7
B Other	42.7	70.8	71.6	76.1	79.0	102.1	115.3	160.7	168.4	189.4	184.7	197.5
2 Factor income to the rest of the world	36.4	55.6	53.3	49.9	76.8	100.4	98.2	122.5	174.8	124.1	151.4	170.2
A Compensation of employees	-	-	0.2	0.5	0.9	0.7	0.6	0.8	0.8	0.6	0.6	0.6
B Property and entrepreneurial income	36.4	55.6	53.1	49.4	75.9	99.7	97.6	121.7	174.0	123.5	150.8	169.6
3 Current transfers to the rest of the world	2.4	23.7	29.7	32.5	48.3	45.1	30.9	36.9	36.7	38.4	39.3	38.6
4 Surplus of the nation on current transactions	-163.7	54.5	98.5	69.6	82.8	-101.2	-242.8	-306.3	-277.8	-164.3	-114.3	-80.3
Payments to the Rest of the World and Surplus of the Nation on Current Transactions [a]	229.4	604.8	782.4	779.6	952.2	955.1	873.9	911.4	1063.3	1205.8	1319.4	1463.8

Receipts From The Rest of the World

	1970	1975	1977	1978	1979	1980	1981	1982	1983	1984	1985	1986
1 Exports of goods and services	113.6	400.4	584.0	579.1	742.5	737.6	642.9	644.3	766.1	893.2	1004.2	1098.8

Papua New Guinea

1.7 External Transactions on Current Account, Summary
(Continued)

Million Papua New Guinea kina — Fiscal year beginning 1 July

	1970	1975	1977	1978	1979	1980	1981	1982	1983	1984	1985	1986
A Exports of merchandise f.o.b.	77.4	345.3	521.2	510.9	656.6	640.3	555.6	552.7	674.3	793.3	901.6	994.5
B Other	36.2	55.1	62.8	68.2	85.9	97.3	87.4	91.6	91.8	99.9	102.6	104.3
2 Factor income from rest of the world	9.8	16.7	26.5	30.5	37.3	41.7	37.8	50.1	55.4	51.7	62.9	98.1
A Compensation of employees	-	1.3	1.3	1.2	1.6	1.8	6.0	6.3	6.6	6.9	7.2	7.5
B Property and entrepreneurial income	9.8	15.4	25.2	29.3	35.7	39.9	31.8	43.8	48.8	44.8	55.7	90.6
3 Current transfers from rest of the world	106.0	187.7	171.8	169.9	172.5	175.8	193.2	217.0	241.7	261.0	252.4	266.8
Receipts from the Rest of the World on Current Transactions [a]	229.3	604.8	782.4	779.6	952.2	955.0	873.9	911.4	1063.3	1205.8	1319.4	1463.8

a) Second series, estimates relate to calendar year.

1.8 Capital Transactions of The Nation, Summary

Million Papua New Guinea kina — Fiscal year beginning 1 July

	1970	1975	1977	1978	1979	1980	1981	1982	1983	1984	1985	1986
Finance of Gross Capital Formation												
Gross saving	128.4	234.9	382.9	389.3	455.2	317.7	224.4	270.8	343.0	435.7	387.4	521.5
1 Consumption of fixed capital [a]	28.7	77.7	84.6	103.6	107.3	124.9	137.6	150.0	162.6	204.8	211.4	223.9
A General government	2.4	...	...	...	...	...	...	...	...	...	...	...
B Corporate and quasi-corporate enterprises	23.3	...	...	...	...	...	...	...	...	...	...	...
Public	2.3	...	...	...	...	...	...	...	...	...	...	...
Private	21.0	...	...	...	...	...	...	...	...	...	...	...
C Other	3.0	...	...	...	...	...	...	...	...	...	...	...
2 Net saving	99.7	157.2	298.3	285.7	347.9	192.8	86.8	120.8	180.5	230.9	176.0	297.6
A General government	8.5	...	...	...	...	...	...	...	...	...	...	...
B Corporate and quasi-corporate enterprises	14.7	...	...	...	...	...	...	...	...	...	...	...
Public	3.8	...	...	...	...	...	...	...	...	...	...	...
Private	10.8	...	...	...	...	...	...	...	...	...	...	...
C Other	70.5	...	...	...	...	...	...	...	...	...	...	...
Less: Surplus of the nation on current transactions	-163.7	54.5	98.5	69.6	82.8	-101.2	-242.8	-306.3	-277.8	-164.3	-114.3	-80.3
Statistical discrepancy	-0.5	13.0	-4.0	-23.4	10.9	11.8	-9.2	-14.5	5.4	5.2	-0.9	2.1
Finance of Gross Capital Formation [b]	291.6	193.4	280.5	296.3	383.3	430.7	458.0	562.6	626.2	605.2	500.7	603.9
Gross Capital Formation												
Increase in stocks	15.5	29.9	41.2	27.8	57.1	36.4	7.4	-14.2	-6.2	71.5	33.8	31.4
Gross fixed capital formation	276.1	163.5	239.3	268.5	326.2	394.2	450.7	576.7	632.4	533.7	466.9	572.5
1 General government	43.1	51.6	65.3	66.5	90.0	123.1	107.3	84.5	80.0	100.0	100.1	119.3
2 Corporate and quasi-corporate enterprises	...	...	...	...	...	...	...	...	...	...	...	...
3 Other	...	...	...	...	...	...	...	...	...	...	...	...
Gross Capital Formation [b]	291.6	193.4	280.5	296.3	383.3	430.7	458.0	562.6	626.2	605.2	500.7	603.9

a) Item 'Consumption of fixed capital' excludes consumption of fixed capital of producers of government-owned houses and hostels.
b) Second series, estimates relate to calendar year.

Papua New Guinea

1.10 Gross Domestic Product by Kind of Activity, in Current Prices

Million Papua New Guinea kina — Fiscal year beginning 1 July

	1970	1975	1977	1978	1979	1980	1981	1982	1983	1984	1985	1986
1 Agriculture, hunting, forestry and fishing	215.5	316.2	...	497.5	552.8	565.7	561.4	567.2	647.8	...	...	...
2 Mining and quarrying	1.4	119.9	...	147.6	247.2	225.7	133.7	140.4	210.8	...	...	...
3 Manufacturing	34.7	92.1	...	134.0	152.2	162.3	166.6	164.6	178.8	...	...	...
4 Electricity, gas and water	6.9	10.0	...	17.0	20.8	6.3	19.9	19.4	28.8	...	...	...
5 Construction	109.7	68.9	...	52.4	54.6	64.2	70.5	82.0	84.7	...	...	...
6 Wholesale and retail trade, restaurants and hotels [a]	45.7	75.9	...	130.9	145.5	135.2	140.3	142.4	156.6	...	...	...
7 Transport, storage and communication	39.9	57.7	...	79.0	83.5	78.1	97.6	72.9	68.3	...	...	...
8 Finance, insurance, real estate and business services	24.8	62.4	...	65.8	80.9	139.4	126.1	172.3	187.4	...	...	...
9 Community, social and personal services [a]	60.8	244.9	...	160.2	166.5	182.8	199.8	212.7	225.8	...	...	...
Total, Industries	539.4	1048.0	...	1284.4	1504.0	1559.7	1515.9	1573.9	1789.0	...	...	...
Producers of Government Services	64.2	...	...	106.5	106.5	125.7	143.0	144.5	147.1	...	...	...
Other Producers	...	...	...	...	...	...	...	...	...	...	...	...
Subtotal	603.6	1048.0	...	1390.9	1610.5	1685.4	1658.9	1718.4	1936.1	...	...	...
Less: Imputed bank service charge	4.7	11.2	...	25.4	34.4	41.3	45.7	49.1	53.5	...	...	...
Plus: Import duties	22.7	31.7	...	47.8	56.4	64.1	68.1	79.7	91.1	...	...	...
Plus: Value added tax	...	...	...	...	...	...	...	...	...	...	...	...
Equals: Gross Domestic Product [b]	621.7	1068.5	...	1413.3	1632.5	1708.1	1681.2	1749.1	1973.7	...	...	...

a) Restaurants and hotels are included in item 'Community, social and personal services'.
b) Second series, estimates relate to calendar year.

1.12 Relations Among National Accounting Aggregates

Million Papua New Guinea kina — Fiscal year beginning 1 July

	1970	1975	1977	1978	1979	1980	1981	1982	1983	1984	1985	1986
Gross Domestic Product [a]	621.7	1068.5	1298.5	1413.3	1632.5	1708.1	1681.2	1749.1	1973.7	2134.4	2279.2	2471.5
Plus: Net factor income from the rest of the world	-26.6	-38.9	-26.7	-19.4	-39.5	-58.7	-60.4	-72.4	-119.4	-72.4	-88.5	-72.1
Factor income from the rest of the world	9.8	16.7	26.5	30.5	37.3	41.7	37.8	50.1	55.4	51.7	62.9	98.1
Less: Factor income to the rest of the world	36.4	55.6	53.3	49.9	76.8	100.4	98.2	122.5	174.8	124.1	151.4	170.2
Equals: Gross National Product [a]	595.1	1029.6	1271.8	1393.9	1593.0	1649.4	1620.8	1676.7	1854.3	2062.0	2190.7	2399.4
Less: Consumption of fixed capital [b]	28.7	77.7	84.6	103.6	107.3	124.9	137.6	150.0	162.6	204.8	211.4	223.9

Papua New Guinea

1.12 Relations Among National Accounting Aggregates
(Continued)

Million Papua New Guinea kina — Fiscal year beginning 1 July

	1970	1975	1977	1978	1979	1980	1981	1982	1983	1984	1985	1986
Equals: National Income [a]	566.4	951.8	1187.1	1290.2	1485.6	1524.5	1483.2	1526.6	1691.7	1857.1	1979.3	2175.5
Plus: Net current transfers from the rest of the world	103.5	164.0	142.0	137.4	124.2	130.7	162.3	180.1	205.1	222.6	213.1	228.2
Current transfers from the rest of the world	106.0	187.7	171.8	169.9	172.5	175.8	193.2	217.0	241.7	261.0	252.4	266.8
Less: Current transfers to the rest of the world	2.4	23.7	29.7	32.5	48.3	45.1	30.9	36.9	36.7	38.4	39.3	38.6
Equals: National Disposable Income [a]	669.9	1115.8	1329.2	1427.6	1609.8	1655.2	1645.5	1706.7	1896.8	2079.7	2192.4	2403.7
Less: Final consumption	570.2	958.5	1030.8	1141.9	1261.9	1462.5	1558.6	1586.0	1716.3	1848.8	2016.4	2106.1
Equals: Net Saving [a]	99.7	157.2	298.3	285.7	347.9	192.8	86.9	120.8	180.5	230.9	176.0	297.6
Less: Surplus of the nation on current transactions [a]	-163.7	54.5	98.5	69.6	82.8	-101.2	-242.8	-306.3	-277.8	-164.3	-114.3	-80.3
Statistical discrepancy	-0.5	13.0	-4.0	-23.4	10.9	11.8	-9.3	-14.5	5.4	5.2	-0.9	2.1
Equals: Net Capital Formation [a]	262.9	115.7	195.8	192.7	276.0	305.8	320.4	412.6	463.6	400.4	289.4	380.0

a) Second series, estimates relate to calendar year.
b) Item 'Consumption of fixed capital' excludes consumption of fixed capital of producers of government-owned houses and hostels.

2.1 Government Final Consumption Expenditure by Function, in Current Prices

Million Papua New Guinea kina — Fiscal year beginning 1 July

	1970	1975	1977	1978	1979	1980	1981	1982	1983	1984	1985	1986
1 General public services	46.7	...	...	...	...	...	...	...	...	...	...	...
2 Defence	16.0	...	...	...	...	...	...	...	...	...	...	...
3 Public order and safety		...	...	...	...	...	...	...	...	...	...	...
4 Education	27.7	...	...	...	...	...	...	...	...	...	...	...
5 Health	16.2	...	...	...	...	...	...	...	...	...	...	...
6 Social security and welfare	-	...	...	...	...	...	...	...	...	...	...	...
7 Housing and community amenities	2.7	...	...	...	...	...	...	...	...	...	...	...
8 Recreational, cultural and religious affairs	1.6	...	...	...	...	...	...	...	...	...	...	...
9 Economic services	72.2	...	...	...	...	...	...	...	...	...	...	...
10 Other functions	-	...	...	...	...	...	...	...	...	...	...	...
Total Government Final Consumption Expenditure	183.1	...	...	...	...	...	...	...	...	...	...	...

2.5 Private Final Consumption Expenditure by Type and Porpose, in Current Prices

Million Papua New Guinea kina — Fiscal year beginning 1 July

	1970	1975	1977	1978	1979	1980	1981	1982	1983	1984	1985	1986
Final Consumption Expenditure of Resident Households												
1 Food, beverages and tobacco [a]	236.2	...	...	...	...	...	...	...	...	...	...	...
A Food	201.8	...	...	...	...	...	...	...	...	...	...	...
B Non-alcoholic beverages	...	...	...	...	...	...	...	...	...	...	...	...
C Alcoholic beverages	...	...	...	...	...	...	...	...	...	...	...	...
D Tobacco	12.2	...	...	...	...	...	...	...	...	...	...	...
2 Clothing and footwear	11.5	...	...	...	...	...	...	...	...	...	...	...
3 Gross rent, fuel and power	36.5	...	...	...	...	...	...	...	...	...	...	...
4 Furniture, furnishings and household equipment and operation	25.5	...	...	...	...	...	...	...	...	...	...	...
5 Medical care and health expenses	3.4	...	...	...	...	...	...	...	...	...	...	...
6 Transport and communication	30.7	...	...	...	...	...	...	...	...	...	...	...
A Personal transport equipment	6.1	...	...	...	...	...	...	...	...	...	...	...

Papua New Guinea

2.5 Private Final Consumption Expenditure by Type and Porpose, in Current Prices
(Continued)

Million Papua New Guinea kina — Fiscal year beginning 1 July

	1970	1975	1977	1978	1979	1980	1981	1982	1983	1984	1985	1986
B Other	24.6	...	...									
7 Recreational, entertainment, education and cultural services	16.5	...	...									
A Education	0.5	...	...									
B Other	16.0	...	...									
8 Miscellaneous goods and services	6.6	...	...									
A Personal care	4.5	...	...									
B Expenditures in restaurants, cafes and hotels [a]	...	...	...									
C Other	...	...	...									
Total Final Consumption Expenditure in the Domestic Market by Households, of which	366.9	580.0	685.5	782.5	885.6	1044.6	1096.0	1110.8	1238.6	1337.2	1471.1	1546.2
A Durable goods	50.9	...	...									
B Semi-durable goods	...	...	...									
C Non-durable goods	254.4	...	...									
D Services	61.7	...	...									
Plus: Direct purchases abroad by resident households	18.2	15.9	13.1	12.3	11.9	15.3	15.9	14.8	13.3	13.5	14.5	15.0
Less: Direct purchases in the domestic market by non-resident households	9.7	4.6	5.5	6.2	7.0	8.7	7.8	7.7	6.9	7.1	6.5	7.0
Equals: Final Consumption Expenditure of Resident Households [b]	375.4	591.3	693.1	788.6	890.5	1051.3	1104.2	1117.9	1245.0	1343.6	1479.1	1554.2

Final Consumption Expenditure of Private Non-profit Institutions Serving Households

	1970	1975	1977	1978	1979	1980	1981	1982	1983	1984	1985	1986
1 Research and science	...	...	...									
2 Education	1.2	...	...									
3 Medical and other health services	0.7	...	...									
4 Welfare services	...	...	...									
5 Recreational and related cultural services	9.6	...	...									
6 Religious organisations	...	...	...									
7 Professional and labour organisations serving households	...	...	...									
8 Miscellaneous	...	...	...									
Equals: Final Consumption Expenditure of Private Non-profit Organisations Serving Households	11.6	...	...									
Private Final Consumption Expenditure [b]	387.1	591.3	693.1	788.6	890.5	1051.3	1104.2	1117.9	1245.0	1343.6	1479.1	1554.2

a) Item 'Food, beverages and tobacco' includes expenditure in restaurants, cafes and hotels.
b) Second series, estimates relate to calendar year.

2.11 Gross Fixed Capital Formation by Kind of Activity of Owner, ISIC Divisions, in Current Prices

Million Papua New Guinea kina — Fiscal year beginning 1 July

	1970	1975	1977	1978	1979	1980	1981	1982	1983	1984	1985	1986
All Producers												
1 Agriculture, hunting, forestry and fishing	7.1	...	...	...	...	...	...	...	...	...	...	...
2 Mining and quarrying	152.2	...	...	...	...	...	...	...	...	...	...	...
3 Manufacturing	8.2	...	...	...	...	...	...	...	...	...	...	...
4 Electricity, gas and water [a]	5.8	...	...	...	...	...	...	...	...	...	...	...

Papua New Guinea

2.11 Gross Fixed Capital Formation by Kind of Activity of Owner, ISIC Divisions, in Current Prices
(Continued)

Million Papua New Guinea kina — Fiscal year beginning 1 July

	1970	1975	1977	1978	1979	1980	1981	1982	1983	1984	1985	1986
5 Construction	5.6	...	...	...	...	...	...	...	...	...	...	...
6 Wholesale and retail trade, restaurants and hotels	...	...	...	...	...	...	...	...	...	...	...	...
7 Transport, storage and communication	...	...	...	...	...	...	...	...	...	...	...	...
8 Finance, insurance, real estate and business services [b]	7.4	...	...	...	...	...	...	...	...	...	...	...
9 Community, social and personal services [b]	43.4	...	...	...	...	...	...	...	...	...	...	...
Total Industries	229.7	...	...	...	...	...	...	...	...	...	...	...
Producers of Government Services	43.1	...	...	...	...	...	...	...	...	...	...	...
Private Non-Profit Institutions Serving Households	3.4	...	...	...	...	...	...	...	...	...	...	...
Total	276.1	...	...	...	...	...	...	...	...	...	...	...

a) Item 'Electricity, gas and water' also includes sanitary and similar services.
b) Finance, insurance, real estate (except owner-occupied dwellings) and business services are included in item 'Community, social and personal services'.

2.17 Exports and Imports of Goods and Services, Detail

Million Papua New Guinea kina — Fiscal year beginning 1 July

	1970	1975	1977	1978	1979	1980	1981	1982	1983	1984	1985	1986
Exports of Goods and Services												
1 Exports of merchandise, f.o.b. [a]	77.4	345.3	521.2	510.9	656.6	640.3	555.6	552.7	674.3	793.3	901.6	994.5
2 Transport and communication	17.1	24.7	31.5	34.0	37.5	46.1	51.2	54.4	58.0	64.7	66.7	68.3
A In respect of merchandise imports	5.1	15.1	17.9	18.4	20.2	22.3	22.5	24.1	25.5	28.2	28.8	29.3
B Other	12.1	9.7	13.5	15.6	17.3	23.8	28.7	30.3	32.5	36.5	37.9	39.0
3 Insurance service charges	...	0.7	0.9	1.0	1.3	1.5	1.1	1.3	0.4	1.4	2.1	2.3
A In respect of merchandise imports	...	0.5	0.8	0.9	1.3	1.4	1.0	1.2	0.3	1.2	1.8	2.0
B Other	...	0.2	0.1	0.1	0.1	0.1	0.1	0.1	0.1	0.2	0.3	0.3
4 Other commodities	9.4	25.1	25.9	27.0	40.1	41.1	27.3	28.3	26.5	26.7	27.3	26.7
5 Adjustments of merchandise exports to change-of-ownership basis	...	...	...	...	...	...	...	...	...	...	...	...
6 Direct purchases in the domestic market by non-residential households	9.7	4.6	5.5	6.2	7.0	8.7	7.8	7.7	6.9	7.1	6.5	7.0
7 Direct purchases in the domestic market by extraterritorial bodies	...	...	...	...	...	...	...	...	...	...	...	...
Total Exports of Goods and Services [b]	113.6	400.4	584.0	579.1	742.5	737.6	642.9	644.3	766.1	893.2	1004.2	1098.8
Imports of Goods and Services												
1 Imports of merchandise, c.i.f. [a]	311.5	400.1	529.3	551.4	665.3	808.7	872.3	897.5	961.2	1018.2	1058.3	1137.7
A Imports of merchandise, f.o.b.	277.6	341.2	451.7	470.3	560.7	687.3	751.5	760.0	817.3	856.7	876.1	949.7
B Transport of services on merchandise imports	33.9	58.2	75.3	78.9	101.4	117.8	117.0	133.6	139.6	157.0	177.5	182.9
By residents	5.1	15.1	17.9	18.4	20.2	22.3	22.5	24.1	26.5	28.2	28.8	29.3
By non-residents	28.8	43.1	59.7	60.5	81.2	95.5	94.5	109.5	113.1	128.7	148.7	153.6
C Insurance service charges on merchandise imports	...	0.8	2.3	2.2	3.3	3.6	3.9	4.0	4.3	4.5	4.6	5.0
By residents	...	0.5	0.8	0.9	1.3	1.4	1.0	1.2	0.3	1.2	1.8	2.0

Papua New Guinea

2.17 Exports and Imports of Goods and Services, Detail
(Continued)

Million Papua New Guinea kina   Fiscal year beginning 1 July

	1970	1975	1977	1978	1979	1980	1981	1982	1983	1984	1985	1986
By non-residents	...	0.3	1.5	1.3	2.0	2.2	2.9	2.8	4.0	3.4	2.8	3.0
2 Adjustments of merchandise imports to change-of-ownership basis	...	...	...	...	...	...	...	...	...	...	...	...
3 Other transport and communication	13.5	31.6	37.1	32.8	34.6	41.3	40.2	49.7	40.8	46.4	47.8	51.1
4 Other insurance service charges		4.3	3.0	8.0	7.7	9.5	9.9	10.4	9.6	9.8	10.2	10.6
5 Other commodities	11.7	18.1	20.0	21.7	23.8	34.0	46.7	83.8	100.5	116.1	109.6	117.5
6 Direct purchases abroad by government	...	...	...	1.3	1.1	1.9	2.4	2.1	4.2	3.7	2.7	3.4
7 Direct purchases abroad by resident households	17.5	16.8	13.1	12.3	11.9	15.4	16.1	14.8	13.3	13.5	14.5	15.0
Total Imports of Goods and Services [b]	354.2	470.9	600.9	627.5	744.3	910.8	987.6	1058.2	1129.6	1207.6	1243.0	1335.2
Balance of Goods and Services	-240.6	-70.5	-16.9	-48.4	-1.8	-173.2	-344.7	-413.9	-363.5	-314.4	-238.8	-236.4
Total Imports and Balance of Goods and Services [b]	113.6	400.4	584.0	579.1	742.5	737.6	642.9	644.3	766.1	893.2	1004.2	1098.8

a) Exports and imports of merchandise are recorded on the basis of the crossing of frontiers. No data are available on the basis of changes in the ownership of the goods.
b) Second series, estimates relate to calendar year.

Paraguay

General note. The preparation of national accounts statistics in Paraguay is undertaken by the Departamento de Estudios Economicos of the Banco Central del Paraguay, Asuncion. The official estimates are published by the Department in 'Cuentas Nacionales'. The following presentation is based mainly on a comprehensive description of sources and methods used in national accounting received from the Banco Central. The estimates are generally in accordance with the classifications and definitions recommended in the United Nations System of National Accounts (SNA). The following tables have been prepared from successive replies to the United Nations national accounts questionnaire. When the scope and coverage of the estimates differ for conceptual or statistical reasons from the definitions and classifications recommded in SNA, a footnote is indicated to the relevant tables.

Sources and methods :
(a) **Gross domestic product.** Gross domestic product is estimated mainly through the production approach.
(b) **Expenditure on the gross domestic product.** The expenditure approach is used to estimate government final consumption expenditure and exports and imports of goods and services. The commodity-flow approach is used for the estimation of gross fixed capital formation. Private final consumption expenditure is arrived at as a residual. The information needed to estimate government consumption expenditure is obtained from the Ministerio de Hacienda, which controls the budget of the public sector institutions. Increase in stock is estimated for livestock only. It is assumed to be the annual increase of the cattle production minus the number of cattle slaughtered. Gross fixed capital formation is estimated on the basis of import statistics for machinery, equipment, transport and communication. Estimates of the domestic production of these items as well as the gross value of production in the construction sector are also included. Exports and imports of goods and services are estimated on the basis of information furnished by the Division de Balanza de Pagos of the Banco Central. For the constant price estimates, the only information available is that the wholesale price index is used as a deflator.
(c) **Cost-structure of the gross domestic product.** Compensation of employees is estimated by combining the information on the number of persons employed, by economic sectors and the average wages paid in each productive sector. Depreciation is estimated on the basis of the average lifetime of each type of capital good established in the respective depreciation tables. Information on indirect taxes and subsidies are supplied by the Ministerio de Hacienda. Operating surplus is obtained as a residual.
(d) **Gross domestic product by kind of economic activity.** The table of GDP by kind of economic activity is prepared at market prices, i.e., producers' values. The production approach is used to estimate the value added of most industries. The income approach is used to estimate the value added of public administration and defence, part of transport and communication, and part of other private services. The gross output of the trade sector is based on the commodity-flow appraoch, applying a fixed percentage for value added. The value of agricultural production is obtained by multiplying quantities by prices. Information on prices and on most quantities are obtained from Ministerio de Agricultura y Ganaderia. Remaining quantities are estimated through the use of indirect indicators such as the rate of population growth. The value of livestock production is estimated by type of livestock. Slaughtering is estimated on the basis of information provided by the Direccion De Impuestos and the meat-processing industries while stocks of cattle are based on the 1956 agricultural census. Inputs for the agricultural section is assumed to be a certain percentage of the gross value of production. The production of mining and quarrying is estimated on the basis of the industrial production coefficients of lime and cement. Information on the manufacturing sector is obtained from the surveys of the Banco Central, and the 1955 and 1963 industrial censuses. The value added of each industrial group is determined on the basis of coefficients from the 1963 industrial census applied to the gross production values. The value added of electricity and water is mainly based on information from the concerned enterprises. For constuction, the source used is the production index for construction materials. This index is compared with permits granted by the municipalities expressed in quantitative measures, multiplied by the base-year value and inflated by the implicit price index of construction materials. Value added of the trade sector is assumed to be 30 percent of the values of locally manufactured goods, imported goods and agricultural products net of farm consumption. For motor transport, the number of vehicles by category is multiplied by the number of days worked and the gross income earned in the base year. The resulting amounts are then multiplied by value added coefficients for each category of vehicle. Non-mechanical transport is calculated on the basis of the index of agricultural production transported in rural areas by carts. For ownership of dwellings, the estimates are prepared on the basis of the number of dwellings by type of construction materials used. Value added is estimated by multiplying the paid and imputed rents by the number of dwellings. The value added of public administration and defence is estimated as the total compensation paid to government employees based on information furnished by the Presupuesto General de la Nacion. The value of public education is determined directly from the Presupuesto General de Gastos de la Nacion while that of private education is estimated at constant prices by multiplying the number of students enrolled by the annual education costs plus registration fees minus 20 percent for intermediate consumption. For health, information is obtained directly from the public health services and social security services and from the Ministerio de Salud Publica y Bienestar Social for the private sector. Estimates for domestic services are obtained by multiplying actual annual wages by employment figures which are assumed to increase at a rate of 3.3 percent in the urban area and 2.6 percent in the rural area. For other services, bench-mark estimates, based on the 1963 economic census, are projected by a specially constructed growth rate. For the constant price estimates, double deflation is used for the agricultural sector. The current quantities of mining and manufacturing are revalued at base-year prices. Value added of construction, transport and financial sectors is extrapolated by using quantity indicators. For electricity, gas and water, trade and services sectors, value added is deflated by using appropriate price indexes.

1.1 Expenditure on the Gross Domestic Product, in Current Prices
Million Paraguayan guaranies

	1970	1975	1977	1978	1979	1980	1981	1982	1983	1984	1985	1986
1 Government final consumption expenditure	6748	11972	16353	21500	24710	34732	48625	52272	58024	69280	90214	121790
2 Private final consumption expenditure	58042	142970	190062	225241	306501	399296	504074	552019	642198	831946	1066038	1426782
3 Gross capital formation	11034	45893	65072	87717	122972	161204	204283	188916	175229	245478	306451	417682
A Increase in stocks [a]	151	6350	2150	6461	6830	8550	10064	12045	10720	14300	18500	27072
B Gross fixed capital formation	10883	39543	62922	81256	116142	152654	194219	176871	164509	231178	287951	390610
Residential buildings												
Non-residential buildings	5463	18850	27800	40710	61066	90308	123000	115632	128351	133746	165776	220274
Other construction and land improvement etc												
Other [b]	5420	20693	35122	40546	55076	62346	71219	61239	36158	97432	122175	170336
4 Exports of goods and services	11176	25155	51293	50113	60130	77500	78107	89401	70054	197661	491785	540890
5 Less: Imports of goods and services	12078	35551	59158	71329	92802	112372	127400	145628	127391	273921	560598	673344
Equals: Gross Domestic Product	74921	190439	263612	322542	430514	560459	708689	737040	818114	1070444	1393890	1833800

a) Item 'Increase in stocks' includes livestock only.
b) Item 'Other' of gross capital formation includes communications equipments.

1.2 Expenditure on the Gross Domestic Product, in Constant Prices
Million Paraguayan guaranies

	1970	1975	1977	1978	1979	1980	1981	1982	1983	1984	1985	1986
	At constant prices of:1982											
1 Government final consumption expenditure	25720	28956	34527	40245	37494	42803	51126	52272	53919	50755	52800	53950
2 Private final consumption expenditure	230899	317410	388198	409266	403714	472573	524562	552019	543425	571717	575939	583729
3 Gross capital formation	36546	78810	108377	138528	161013	194465	227503	188916	154587	156940	158640	164500
A Increase in stocks [a]	629	15338	4545	12354	10179	10766	10741	12045	9404	10500	11700	13000
B Gross fixed capital formation	35917	63472	103832	126174	150834	183699	216762	176871	145183	146440	146940	151500

Paraguay

1.2 Expenditure on the Gross Domestic Product, in Constant Prices
(Continued)

Million Paraguayan guaranies

	1970	1975	1977	1978	1979	1980	1981	1982	1983	1984	1985	1986
					At constant prices of:1982							
Residential buildings												
Non-residential buildings	18030	30257	45875	63215	79307	108673	137277	115632	113185	91208	90296	91200
Other construction and land improvement etc.												
Other [b]	17887	33215	57957	62959	71527	75026	79485	61239	31998	55232	56644	60300
4 Exports of goods and services	42015	52005	62011	74452	132693	110070	83358	89461	75734	110171	151662	146828
5 Less: Imports of goods and services	39861	60730	97620	110759	120522	135225	142188	145628	112736	152677	172883	182784
Equals: Gross Domestic Product	295319	416451	495493	551732	614392	684686	744361	737040	714929	736906	766158	766223

a) Item 'Increase in stocks' includes livestock only.
b) Item 'Other' of gross capital formation includes communications equipments.

1.3 Cost Components of the Gross Domestic Product

Million Paraguayan guaranies

	1970	1975	1977	1978	1979	1980	1981	1982	1983	1984	1985	1986
1 Indirect taxes, net	5486	7879	10270	16212	27565	34536	41894	48210	45120	50726	66240	89455
A Indirect taxes	5507	7940	10342	16297	27586	34578	41946	48297	45166	50778	66350	89570
B Less: Subsidies	21	61	72	85	21	42	52	87	46	52	110	115
2 Consumption of fixed capital	3962	9800	24621	32253	49190	58630	77688	74285	72184	107900	145270	196530
3 Compensation of employees paid by resident producers to:	25770	65260	91600	106100	150900	195300	242850	245900	258243	342205	432120	561756
4 Operating surplus	39704	107500	137121	167977	202859	271993	346257	368645	442567	569613	750260	986059
Equals: Gross Domestic Product	74921	190439	263612	322542	430514	560459	708689	737040	818114	1070444	1393890	1833800

1.4 General Government Current Receipts and Disbursements

Million Paraguayan guaranies

	1970	1975	1977	1978	1979	1980	1981	1982	1983	1984	1985	1986
					Receipts							
1 Operating surplus	...	...	...	...	...	...	...	...	...	...	...	...
2 Property and entrepreneurial income	956	1429	2946	4909	10530	7609	8315	6561	7412	7800	9924	16396
3 Taxes, fees and contributions	7586	12073	17474	27718	42347	53255	66563	74383	75301	79755	105622	137416
A Indirect taxes	5507	7940	10342	16297	27586	34578	41946	48297	45166	50778	66350	89570
B Direct taxes	857	1573	2549	5062	6680	9097	11496	11528	13042	10407	16211	20869
C Social security contributions	1222	2560	4583	6359	8081	9580	13121	14558	17093	18570	23061	26977
D Compulsory fees, fines and penalties	...	...	...	...	...	...	...	...	...	...	...	...
4 Other current transfers	744	1012	2323	1024	1191	1452	1952	2591	3348	7660	8504	7500
Total Current Receipts of General Government	9286	14513	22743	33651	54068	62316	76830	83535	86061	95215	124050	161312
					Disbursements							
1 Government final consumption expenditure	6748	11972	16353	21500	24710	34732	48625	52272	58024	69280	90214	121790
2 Property income [a]	102	115	54	53	75	126	107	87	91	988	1208	1600
3 Subsidies	21	61	72	85	21	42	52	87	46	52	110	115
4 Other current transfers	1570	1966	2414	3798	5043	7047	9955	18923	17593	23260	29100	36329
A Social security benefits	...	...	...	...	...	...	...	...	...	...	...	...
B Social assistance grants	...	...	...	...	...	...	...	...	...	...	...	...
C Other	1570	1966	2414	3798	5043	7047	9955	18923	17593	23260	29100	36329
5 Net saving	844	399	3850	8215	24219	20369	18091	12166	10307	1635	3418	1478
Total Current Disbursements and Net Saving of General Government	9286	14513	22743	33651	54068	62316	76830	83535	86061	95215	124050	161312

a) Item 'Property income' relates to interest on public debt.

1.6 Current Income and Outlay of Households and Non-Profit Institutions

Million Paraguayan guaranies

	1970	1975	1977	1978	1979	1980	1981	1982	1983	1984	1985	1986
					Receipts							
1 Compensation of employees	25770	65260	91600	106100	150900	195300	242850	245900	258243	342205	432120	561756
2 Operating surplus of private unincorporated enterprises	...	...	...	...	...	...	...	...	...	...	...	...
3 Property and entrepreneurial income [a]	35982	100479	128117	154727	179825	251674	323321	347430	414301	531465	685437	905160
4 Current transfers	1570	1966	2414	3798	5043	7047	9955	18923	17593	23260	29100	36329

Paraguay

1.6 Current Income and Outlay of Households and Non-Profit Institutions
(Continued)

Million Paraguayan guaranies

	1970	1975	1977	1978	1979	1980	1981	1982	1983	1984	1985	1986
A Social security benefits	...	...	...	...	...	...	...	...	...	...	...	...
B Social assistance grants	...	...	...	...	...	...	...	...	...	...	...	...
C Other	1570	1966	2414	3798	5043	7047	9955	18923	17593	23260	29100	36329
Total Current Receipts	63322	167706	222131	264625	335768	454021	576126	612253	690137	896930	1146657	1503245
Disbursements												
1 Private final consumption expenditure	58042	142970	190062	225241	306501	399296	504074	552019	642198	831946	1066038	1426782
2 Property income [a]	...	...	...	...	...	...	...	...	...	...	...	...
3 Direct taxes and other current transfers n.e.c. to general government	1278	2662	4691	6484	8268	9840	13430	14982	17593	18976	23557	27548
4 Other current transfers	744	1012	2323	1024	1191	1452	1952	2591	3348	7660	8504	7500
5 Net saving	3259	21062	25055	31876	19808	43433	56670	42661	26998	38348	48558	41415
Total Current Disbursements and Net Saving	63322	167706	222131	264625	335768	454021	576126	612253	690137	896930	1146657	1503245

a) Item 'Property and entrepreneurial income' received is net of item 'Property income' paid.

1.8 Capital Transactions of The Nation, Summary

Million Paraguayan guaranies

	1970	1975	1977	1978	1979	1980	1981	1982	1983	1984	1985	1986
Finance of Gross Capital Formation												
Gross saving	8316	33961	57556	77574	100597	131692	164749	141012	122882	166793	224692	275959
1 Consumption of fixed capital	3962	9800	24621	32253	49190	58630	77688	74285	72184	107900	145270	196530
2 Net saving	4354	24161	32935	45321	51407	73062	87061	66727	50698	58800	79422	79429
A General government	844	399	3850	8215	24219	20369	18091	12166	10307	1635	3418	1478
B Corporate and quasi-corporate enterprises	251	2700	4030	5230	7380	9260	12300	11900	13393	18910	27446	36536
C Other	3259	21062	25055	31876	19808	43433	56670	42661	26998	38348	48558	41415
Less: Surplus of the nation on current transactions	-2718	-11932	-7516	-10143	-22375	-29512	-39534	-47904	-52347	-78685	-81759	-141723
Finance of Gross Capital Formation	11034	45893	65072	87717	122972	161204	204283	188916	175229	245478	306451	417682
Gross Capital Formation												
Increase in stocks	151	6350	2150	6461	6830	8550	10064	12045	10720	14300	18500	27072
Gross fixed capital formation	10883	39543	62922	81256	116142	152654	194219	176871	164509	231178	287951	390610
Gross Capital Formation	11034	45893	65072	87717	122972	161204	204283	188916	175229	245478	306451	417682

1.10 Gross Domestic Product by Kind of Activity, in Current Prices

Million Paraguayan guaranies

	1970	1975	1977	1978	1979	1980	1981	1982	1983	1984	1985	1986
1 Agriculture, hunting, forestry and fishing	24024	70284	89925	103431	135162	165136	196784	190645	211615	307113	403261	498923
2 Mining and quarrying	83	365	685	.4	1446	2285	2933	3141	3487	4359	5672	8350
3 Manufacturing	12498	29759	44977	54419	69610	92338	118469	120066	104270	172003	228115	296008
4 Electricity, gas and water	840	2739	4607	5982	7889	12923	15272	18120	20638	26064	30896	44791
5 Construction	2076	7163	10560	15470	23205	34317	46740	40544	54994	66873	82888	110137
6 Wholesale and retail trade, restaurants and hotels [ab]	18291	43594	66026	83986	112656	144870	188378	196158	217210	272599	360391	489776
7 Transport, storage and communication	2950	7600	10264	12994	17359	23784	29059	31107	34529	44059	57974	80083
8 Finance, insurance, real estate and business services [bc]	2281	5018	6077	7493	11229	14993	20091	22501	24977	30971	39163	52553
9 Community, social and personal services [ac]	7936	17424	20211	25263	37362	50698	64286	72000	79920	101178	129209	174917
Total, Industries	70070	183945	253329	309832	415918	541344	682012	704183	751040	1025219	1335569	1755538
Producers of Government Services	3943	6494	10283	12710	14595	19115	26677	32858	36472	45225	58321	78262
Other Producers	...	...	...	...	...	...	...	...	...	...	...	...
Subtotal	74921	190439	263612	322542	430513	560459	708689	737041	818114	1070444	1393890	1833800
Less: Imputed bank service charge	...	...	...	...	...	...	...	...	...	...	...	...
Plus: Import duties	...	...	...	...	...	...	...	...	...	...	...	...
Plus: Value added tax	...	...	...	...	...	...	...	...	...	...	...	...
Equals: Gross Domestic Product	74921	190439	263612	322542	430513	560459	708689	737041	818114	1070444	1393890	1833800

a) Restaurants and hotels are included in item 'Community, social and personal services'.
b) Finance is included in item 'Wholesale and retail trade, restaurants and hotels'.
c) Business services are included in item 'Community, social and personal services'.

Paraguay

1.11 Gross Domestic Product by Kind of Activity, in Constant Prices

Million Paraguayan guaranies

	1970	1975	1977	1978	1979	1980	1981	1982	1983	1984	1985	1986
	\multicolumn{12}{c}{At constant prices of: 1982}
1 Agriculture, hunting, forestry and fishing	89846	128157	141962	149112	159001	172524	189876	190645	185991	196990	206042	193467
2 Mining and quarrying	219	731	1276	1487	2118	2669	3070	3142	2912	2942	3073	3440
3 Manufacturing	54267	70036	86626	96712	106289	120422	125613	120966	115861	121075	127129	125345
4 Electricity, gas and water	2794	6135	8470	9923	11797	14025	14746	18120	17779	18164	19248	21218
5 Construction	7141	13491	20889	27573	35845	45164	52707	49544	46720	45604	45148	45600
6 Wholesale and retail trade, restaurants and hotels [a][b]	78258	105602	130220	148841	167446	185028	200570	196158	190171	193634	202759	209437
7 Transport, storage and communication	11702	18699	21608	23985	26743	29551	30497	31107	30742	31853	33468	35142
8 Finance, insurance, real estate and business services [b][c]	10699	13661	15993	17833	19705	21479	22961	22501	21448	21448	21662	22096
9 Community, social and personal services [a][c]	23438	42011	48173	54387	61403	68096	72727	72000	71133	72243	73688	75858
Total, Industries	278364	398523	475217	529853	590347	658958	712768	704182	682757	703953	732217	731603
Producers of Government Services	16955	17928	20277	21879	24045	25728	31594	32858	32172	32953	33941	34620
Other Producers	...	...	...	...	...	...	...	...	...	...	...	...
Subtotal	295319	416451	495493	551732	614392	684686	744361	737041	714929	736906	766158	766223
Less: Imputed bank service charge	...	...	...	...	...	...	...	...	...	...	...	...
Plus: Import duties	...	...	...	...	...	...	...	...	...	...	...	...
Plus: Value added tax	...	...	...	...	...	...	...	...	...	...	...	...
Equals: Gross Domestic Product	295319	416451	495493	551732	614392	684686	744361	737041	714929	736906	766158	766223

a) Restaurants and hotels are included in item 'Community, social and personal services'.
b) Finance is included in item 'Wholesale and retail trade, restaurants and hotels'.
c) Business services are included in item 'Community, social and personal services'.

1.12 Relations Among National Accounting Aggregates

Million Paraguayan guaranies

	1970	1975	1977	1978	1979	1980	1981	1982	1983	1984	1985	1986
Gross Domestic Product	74921	190439	263612	322542	430514	560459	708689	737040	818114	1070444	1393890	1833800
Plus: Net factor income from the rest of the world	-1816	-1536	359	1773	1294	5261	8759	8263	4990	-2425	-12946	-9269
Factor income from the rest of the world	...	...	4184	7449	10893	17247	22282	22119	20860	22904	39147	45841
Less: Factor income to the rest of the world	...	...	3825	5676	9599	11986	13523	13856	15870	25329	52093	55110
Equals: Gross National Product	73105	188903	263971	324315	431808	565720	717448	745303	823104	1068019	1380944	1824531
Less: Consumption of fixed capital	3962	9800	24621	32253	49190	58630	77688	74285	72184	107900	145270	196530
Equals: National Income	69143	179103	239350	292062	382618	507090	639760	671018	750920	960119	1235674	1628001
Plus: Net current transfers from the rest of the world	-	-	-	-	-	-	-	-	-	-	-	-
Equals: National Disposable Income	69143	179103	239350	292062	382618	507090	639760	671018	750920	960119	1235674	1628001
Less: Final consumption	64790	154942	206415	246741	331211	434028	552699	604291	700222	901226	1156252	1548572
Equals: Net Saving	4354	24161	32935	45321	51407	73062	87061	66727	50698	58893	79422	79429
Less: Surplus of the nation on current transactions	-2718	-11932	-7516	-10143	-22375	-29512	-39534	-47904	-52347	-78685	-81759	-141723
Equals: Net Capital Formation	7072	36093	40451	55464	73782	102574	126595	114632	103045	137578	161181	221152

4.1 Derivation of Value Added by Kind of Activity, in Current Prices

Million Paraguayan guaranies

	1980			1981			1982			1983		
	Gross Output	Intermediate Consumption	Value Added	Gross Output	Intermediate Consumption	Value Added	Gross Output	Intermediate Consumption	Value Added	Gross Output	Intermediate Consumption	Value Added
	\multicolumn{12}{c}{All Producers}
1 Agriculture, hunting, forestry and fishing	...	...	165137	...	...	196784	...	...	190645	...	...	211615
A Agriculture and hunting	...	...	148397	...	...	176087	...	...	171838	...	...	190740
B Forestry and logging	...	...	16402	...	...	20300	...	...	18370	...	...	20390
C Fishing	...	...	338	...	...	397	...	...	437	...	...	485
2 Mining and quarrying	...	...	2285	...	...	2933	...	...	3142	...	...	3487

Paraguay

4.1 Derivation of Value Added by Kind of Activity, in Current Prices
(Continued)

Million Paraguayan guaranies

	1980 Gross Output	1980 Intermediate Consumption	1980 Value Added	1981 Gross Output	1981 Intermediate Consumption	1981 Value Added	1982 Gross Output	1982 Intermediate Consumption	1982 Value Added	1983 Gross Output	1983 Intermediate Consumption	1983 Value Added
3 Manufacturing	...	...	92338	...	...	118469	...	...	120966	...	...	134273
A Manufacture of food, beverages and tobacco	...	...	31780	...	...	40520	...	...	48023	...	...	56380
B Textile, wearing apparel and leather industries	...	...	10349	...	...	15194	...	...	12473	...	...	13036
C Manufacture of wood and wood products, including furniture	...	...	14832	...	...	16734	...	...	17678	...	...	19276
D Manufacture of paper and paper products, printing and publishing	...	...	3506	...	...	4515	...	...	6334	...	...	6409
E Manufacture of chemicals and chemical petroleum, coal, rubber and plastic products	...	...	16709	...	...	21433	...	...	13866	...	...	14242
F Manufacture of non-metallic mineral products, except products of petroleum and coal	...	...	3826	...	...	4956	...	...	4526	...	...	5774
G Basic metal industries	...	...	172	...	...	348	...	...	446	...	...	530
H Manufacture of fabricated metal products, machinery and equipment	...	...	2326	...	...	3326	...	...	3842	...	...	4122
I Other manufacturing industries	...	...	8838	...	...	11442	...	...	13778	...	...	14504
4 Electricity, gas and water	...	...	12923	...	...	15271	...	...	18120	...	...	20638
A Electricity, gas and steam	...	...	11238	...	...	13148	...	...	15778	...	...	17514
B Water works and supply	...	...	1685	...	...	2123	...	...	2342	...	...	3124
5 Construction	...	...	34317	...	...	46740	...	...	49544	...	...	54994
6 Wholesale and retail trade, restaurants and hotels ab	...	...	144870	...	...	188378	...	...	196158	...	...	217210
7 Transport, storage and communication	...	...	23784	...	...	29059	...	...	31107	...	...	34529
8 Finance, insurance, real estate and business services bc	...	...	14993	...	...	20091	...	...	22500	...	...	24976
9 Community, social and personal services ac	...	...	50697	...	...	64286	...	...	72000	...	...	79920
Total, Industries	...	...	541344	...	...	682012	...	...	704183	...	...	781643
Producers of Government Services	...	...	19115	...	...	26678	...	...	32858	...	...	36472
Other Producers	...	...	...	...	...	...	...	...	...	...	...	...
Total	...	...	560459	...	...	708689	...	...	737040	...	...	818114
Less: Imputed bank service charge	...	...	...	...	...	...	...	...	...	...	...	...
Import duties	...	...	...	...	...	...	...	...	...	...	...	...
Value added tax	...	...	...	...	...	...	...	...	...	...	...	...
Total	...	...	560459	...	...	708689	...	...	737040	...	...	818114

	1984 Gross Output	1984 Intermediate Consumption	1984 Value Added	1985 Gross Output	1985 Intermediate Consumption	1985 Value Added	1986 Gross Output	1986 Intermediate Consumption	1986 Value Added
				All Producers					
1 Agriculture, hunting, forestry and fishing	...	...	307113	...	...	403261	...	...	498923
A Agriculture and hunting	...	...	273860	...	...	359230	...	...	429779
B Forestry and logging	...	...	32642	...	...	43243	...	...	68108
C Fishing	...	...	611	...	...	788	...	...	1036
2 Mining and quarrying	...	...	4359	...	...	5672	...	...	8350

Paraguay

4.1 Derivation of Value Added by Kind of Activity, in Current Prices
(Continued)

Million Paraguayan guaranies

	1984 Gross Output	1984 Intermediate Consumption	1984 Value Added	1985 Gross Output	1985 Intermediate Consumption	1985 Value Added	1986 Gross Output	1986 Intermediate Consumption	1986 Value Added
3 Manufacturing	...	...	172003	...	...	226115	...	...	296008
A Manufacture of food, beverages and tobacco	...	...	76307	...	...	106369	...	...	152186
B Textile, wearing apparel and leather industries	...	...	22086	...	...	28903	...	...	32408
C Manufacture of wood and wood products, including furniture	...	...	22948	...	...	25539	...	...	34641
D Manufacture of paper and paper products, printing and publishing	...	...	6077	...	...	7215	...	...	10231
E Manufacture of chemicals and chemical petroleum, coal, rubber and plastic products	...	...	16049	...	...	20917	...	...	23125
F Manufacture of non-metallic mineral products, except products of petroleum and coal	...	...	5770	...	...	6425	...	...	12229
G Basic metal industries	...	...	663	...	...	745	...	...	996
H Manufacture of fabricated metal products, machinery and equipment	...	...	6559	...	...	7819	...	...	9887
I Other manufacturing industries	...	...	15544	...	...	22183	...	...	20305
4 Electricity, gas and water	...	...	26064	...	...	30896	...	...	44791
A Electricity, gas and steam	...	...	22127	...	...	25780	...	...	37681
B Water works and supply	...	...	3937	...	...	5116	...	...	7110
5 Construction	...	...	66873	...	...	82888	...	...	110137
6 Wholesale and retail trade, restaurants and hotels ab	...	...	272599	...	...	360391	...	...	489776
7 Transport, storage and communication	...	...	44059	...	...	57974	...	...	80083
8 Finance, insurance, real estate and business services bc	...	...	30971	...	...	39163	...	...	52553
9 Community, social and personal services ac	...	...	101178	...	...	129209	...	...	174917
Total, Industries	...	...	1025219	...	...	1335569	...	...	1755538
Producers of Government Services	...	...	45225	...	...	58321	...	...	78262
Other Producers	...	...	...	...	...	...	...	...	...
Total	...	...	1070444	...	...	1393890	...	...	1833800
Less: Imputed bank service charge	...	...	...	...	...	...	...	...	...
Import duties	...	...	...	...	...	...	...	...	...
Value added tax	...	...	...	...	...	...	...	...	...
Total	...	...	1070444	...	...	1393890	...	...	1833800

a) Restaurants and hotels are included in item 'Community, social and personal services'.
b) Finance is included in item 'Wholesale and retail trade, restaurants and hotels'.
c) Business services are included in item 'Community, social and personal services'.

4.2 Derivation of Value Added by Kind of Activity, in Constant Prices

Million Paraguayan guaranies

	1980 Gross Output	1980 Intermediate Consumption	1980 Value Added	1981 Gross Output	1981 Intermediate Consumption	1981 Value Added	1982 Gross Output	1982 Intermediate Consumption	1982 Value Added	1983 Gross Output	1983 Intermediate Consumption	1983 Value Added
					At constant prices of:1982							
					All Producers							
1 Agriculture, hunting, forestry and fishing	...	...	172524	...	...	189876	...	...	190645	...	...	185991
A Agriculture and hunting	...	...	153692	...	...	169981	...	...	171838	...	...	167534
B Forestry and logging	...	...	18424	...	...	19471	...	...	18370	...	...	18039
C Fishing	...	...	408	...	...	424	...	...	437	...	...	418
2 Mining and quarrying	...	...	2669	...	...	3070	...	...	3142	...	...	2912

Paraguay

4.2 Derivation of Value Added by Kind of Activity, in Constant Prices
(Continued)

Million Paraguayan guaranies

	1980 Gross Output	1980 Intermediate Consumption	1980 Value Added	1981 Gross Output	1981 Intermediate Consumption	1981 Value Added	1982 Gross Output	1982 Intermediate Consumption	1982 Value Added	1983 Gross Output	1983 Intermediate Consumption	1983 Value Added
					At constant prices of:1982							
3 Manufacturing	...	...	120422	...	...	125613	...	...	120966	...	...	115861
A Manufacture of food, beverages and tobacco	...	...	40025	...	...	45456	...	...	48023	...	...	49523
B Textile, wearing apparel and leather industries	...	...	11276	...	...	13540	...	...	12473	...	...	11624
C Manufacture of wood and wood products, including furniture	...	...	22979	...	...	17655	...	...	17678	...	...	16977
D Manufacture of paper and paper products, printing and publishing	...	...	5261	...	...	5885	...	...	6334	...	...	3873
E Manufacture of chemicals and chemical petroleum, coal, rubber and plastic products	...	...	20816	...	...	20606	...	...	13866	...	...	13541
F Manufacture of non-metallic mineral products, except products of petroleum and coal	...	...	4645	...	...	5040	...	...	4526	...	...	4874
G Basic metal industries	...	...	377	...	...	430	...	...	446	...	...	445
H Manufacture of fabricated metal products, machinery and equipment	...	...	3609	...	...	3863	...	...	3842	...	...	3780
I Other manufacturing industries	...	...	11434	...	...	13138	...	...	13778	...	...	11224
4 Electricity, gas and water	...	...	14025	...	...	14746	...	...	18120	...	...	17779
A Electricity, gas and steam	...	...	12137	...	...	12623	...	...	15778	...	...	15014
B Water works and supply	...	...	1888	...	...	2123	...	...	2342	...	...	2765
5 Construction	...	...	45164	...	...	52707	...	...	49544	...	...	46720
6 Wholesale and retail trade, restaurants and hotels [ab]	...	...	185028	...	...	200570	...	...	196158	...	...	190171
7 Transport, storage and communication	...	...	29551	...	...	30497	...	...	31107	...	...	30742
8 Finance, insurance, real estate and business services [bc]	...	...	21479	...	...	22961	...	...	22501	...	...	21448
9 Community, social and personal services [ac]	...	...	68096	...	...	72727	...	...	72000	...	...	71133
Total, Industries	...	...	658958	...	...	712767	...	...	704182	...	...	682757
Producers of Government Services	...	...	25728	...	...	31594	...	...	32858	...	...	32172
Other Producers	...	...	...	...	...	...	...	...	...	...	...	...
Total	...	...	684686	...	...	744361	...	...	737041	...	...	714929
Less: Imputed bank service charge	...	...	...	...	...	...	...	...	...	...	...	...
Import duties	...	...	...	...	...	...	...	...	...	...	...	...
Value added tax	...	...	...	...	...	...	...	...	...	...	...	...
Total	...	...	684686	...	...	744361	...	...	737041	...	...	714929

	1984 Gross Output	1984 Intermediate Consumption	1984 Value Added	1985 Gross Output	1985 Intermediate Consumption	1985 Value Added	1986 Gross Output	1986 Intermediate Consumption	1986 Value Added
		At constant prices of:1982							
		All Producers							
1 Agriculture, hunting, forestry and fishing	...	...	196990	...	...	206042	...	...	193467
A Agriculture and hunting	...	...	178074	...	...	186954	...	...	172178
B Forestry and logging	...	...	18490	...	...	18649	...	...	20837
C Fishing	...	...	426	...	...	439	...	...	452
2 Mining and quarrying	...	...	2942	...	...	3073	...	...	3440

Paraguay

4.2 Derivation of Value Added by Kind of Activity, in Constant Prices
(Continued)

Million Paraguayan guaranies

	1984 Gross Output	1984 Intermediate Consumption	1984 Value Added	1985 Gross Output	1985 Intermediate Consumption	1985 Value Added	1986 Gross Output	1986 Intermediate Consumption	1986 Value Added
				At constant prices of: 1982					
3 Manufacturing	...	...	121075	...	...	127129	...	...	125345
A Manufacture of food, beverages and tobacco	...	...	52664	...	...	53588	...	...	57195
B Textile, wearing apparel and leather industries	...	...	12523	...	...	15352	...	...	12781
C Manufacture of wood and wood products, including furniture	...	...	16724	...	...	15302	...	...	15661
D Manufacture of paper and paper products, printing and publishing	...	...	4407	...	...	4487	...	...	4136
E Manufacture of chemicals and chemical petroleum, coal, rubber and plastic products	...	...	12470	...	...	14006	...	...	12838
F Manufacture of non-metallic mineral products, except products of petroleum and coal	...	...	4555	...	...	4003	...	...	5261
G Basic metal industries	...	...	519	...	...	550	...	...	553
H Manufacture of fabricated metal products, machinery and equipment	...	...	4794	...	...	6253	...	...	5406
I Other manufacturing industries	...	...	12419	...	...	13588	...	...	11512
4 Electricity, gas and water	...	...	18164	...	...	19248	...	...	21218
A Electricity, gas and steam	...	...	15344	...	...	16255	...	...	18060
B Water works and supply	...	...	2820	...	...	2993	...	...	3158
5 Construction	...	...	45604	...	...	45148	...	...	45600
6 Wholesale and retail trade, restaurants and hotels [ab]	...	...	193634	...	...	202759	...	...	209437
7 Transport, storage and communication	...	...	31853	...	...	33468	...	...	35142
8 Finance, insurance, real estate and business services [bc]	...	...	21448	...	...	21662	...	...	22096
9 Community, social and personal services [ac]	...	...	72243	...	...	73688	...	...	75858
Total, Industries	...	...	703953	...	...	732217	...	...	731603
Producers of Government Services	...	...	32953	...	...	33941	...	...	34620
Other Producers	...	...	...	...	...	...	...	...	...
Total	...	...	736906	...	...	766158	...	...	766223
Less: Imputed bank service charge	...	...	...	...	...	...	...	...	...
Import duties	...	...	...	...	...	...	...	...	...
Value added tax	...	...	...	...	...	...	...	...	...
Total	...	...	736906	...	...	766158	...	...	766223

a) Restaurants and hotels are included in item 'Community, social and personal services'.
b) Finance is included in item 'Wholesale and retail trade, restaurants and hotels'.
c) Business services are included in item 'Community, social and personal services'.

Peru

Source. Reply to the United Nations National Accounts Questionnaire from the Instituto Nacional de Estadistica, Lima. The official estimates are published in 'Cuentas Nacionales del Peru'.

General note. The estimates shown in the following tables have been prepared in accordance with the United Nations System of National Accounts so far as the existing data would permit.

1.1 Expenditure on the Gross Domestic Product, in Current Prices

Million Peruvian intis

	1970	1975	1977	1978	1979	1980	1981	1982	1983	1984	1985	1986
1 Government final consumption expenditure	231	575	1045	1520	301	667	1215	2260	4077	8104	22457	42342
2 Private final consumption expenditure					2131	3659	6738	11070	21099	45532	123412	254589
3 Gross capital formation	43	164	229	368	757	1640	3347	5644	7733	16517	44668	92125
A Increase in stocks	2	17	-18	-9	33	239	575	664	172	-221	414	9480
B Gross fixed capital formation	41	147	247	377	724	1402	2772	4981	7561	16738	44254	82645
Residential buildings	19	40	84	132	247	469	982	1955	3161	7081	19216	...
Non-residential buildings												...
Other construction and land improvement etc.	5	30	53	70	165	284	561	1055	1613	3611	9382	...
Other	17	76	109	174	311	649	1228	1970	2788	6046	15656	...
4 Exports of goods and services	50	72	190	394	968	1332	1735	2806	5880	13486	39611	43708
5 Less: Imports of goods and services	45	146	271	381	666	1329	2378	3829	6224	10794	30304	51742
Equals: Gross Domestic Product	280	665	1193	1901	3490	5968	10658	17950	32565	72845	199845	381022

1.2 Expenditure on the Gross Domestic Product, in Constant Prices

Million Peruvian intis

	1970	1975	1977	1978	1979	1980	1981	1982	1983	1984	1985	1986
	\multicolumn{12}{c}{At constant prices of 1970}
1 Government final consumption expenditure	2008	2527	2635	2414	301	368	362	410	374	357	370	385
2 Private final consumption expenditure					2131	2236	2356	2376	2167	2209	2256	2557
3 Gross capital formation	441	922	685	643	757	1031	1242	1153	716	645	579	856
A Increase in stocks	5	6	-38	-16	33	149	218	150	4	-23	-19	114
B Gross fixed capital formation	436	916	723	659	724	882	1024	1003	712	668	598	742
Residential buildings	186	250	248	247	247	272	300	311	251	249	...	...
Non-residential buildings											...	...
Other construction and land improvement etc.	46	158	137	123	166	191	225	222	172	176	...	...
Other	205	508	339	290	311	419	499	470	289	244	...	...
4 Exports of goods and services	651	606	708	800	968	879	854	906	812	886	925	811
5 Less: Imports of goods and services	582	842	738	558	666	868	1006	1028	723	592	541	680
Equals: Gross Domestic Product	2519	3213	3289	3299	3490	3647	3808	3817	3346	3506	3589	3929

1.3 Cost Components of the Gross Domestic Product

Million Peruvian intis

	1970	1975	1977	1978	1979	1980	1981	1982	1983	1984	1985	1986
1 Indirect taxes, net	23	46	49	165	361	573	1025	1710	2747	6197	19838	28670
A Indirect taxes	24	58	113	220	422	726	1195	1974	3152	6815	21608	31736
B Less: Subsidies	1	12	64	55	61	153	170	264	405	618	1770	3066
2 Consumption of fixed capital	17	41	91	144	196	321	553	945	1886	4253	11005	18834
3 Compensation of employees paid by resident producers to:	100	248	448	610	981	1772	3286	5703	10700	21601	54100	115635
A Resident households	...	...	...	...	977	1767	3275	5675	10631	21564	53849	115336
B Rest of the world	...	...	...	...	4	5	11	28	70	118	251	300
4 Operating surplus	141	331	605	982	1951	3303	5795	9592	17231	40714	114901	217882
Equals: Gross Domestic Product	280	665	1193	1901	3490	5968	10658	17950	32565	72845	199845	381022

1.4 General Government Current Receipts and Disbursements

Million Peruvian intis

	1970	1975	1977	1978	1979	1980	1981	1982	1983	1984	1985	1986
	\multicolumn{12}{c}{Receipts}
1 Operating surplus	...	...	...	...	4	5	8	20	37	147	582	951
2 Property and entrepreneurial income	...	...	...	...	34	213	399	571	939	1938	6780	6594
3 Taxes, fees and contributions	...	...	...	...	793	1333	2097	3338	5440	11528	32916	58285
A Indirect taxes	...	...	...	...	422	726	1195	1974	3152	6815	21608	31736

Peru

1.4 General Government Current Receipts and Disbursements
(Continued)

Million Peruvian intis

	1970	1975	1977	1978	1979	1980	1981	1982	1983	1984	1985	1986
B Direct taxes	...	...	...	...	280	424	512	782	1060	2115	4514	12355
C Social security contributions	...	...	...	...	84	168	332	513	1033	2053	5581	12495
D Compulsory fees, fines and penalties	...	...	...	...	7	15	58	69	195	545	1213	1699
4 Other current transfers	...	...	...	...	45	136	207	82	373	707	1668	1016
Total Current Receipts of General Government	...	...	...	...	875	1687	2712	4011	6789	14321	41947	66845

Disbursements

1 Government final consumption expenditure	...	...	...	...	301	667	1215	2260	4077	8104	22457	42342
2 Property income	...	...	...	...	124	228	357	519	1411	1759	4934	8332
A Interest	...	...	...	...	124	228	357	519	1411	1759	4934	8332
B Net land rent and royalties	...	...	...	...	...	...	...	...	...	...	...	...
3 Subsidies	...	...	...	...	61	153	170	264	405	618	1770	3066
4 Other current transfers	...	...	...	...	219	527	897	1098	2195	4342	11293	16634
A Social security benefits	...	...	...	...	79	150	281	481	918	1926	4462	10091
B Social assistance grants	...	...	...	...	...	...	...	...	...	...	...	...
C Other	...	...	...	...	140	377	616	617	1277	2416	6831	6543
5 Net saving [a]	...	...	...	...	170	111	73	-130	-1299	-502	1493	-3527
Total Current Disbursements and Net Saving of General Government	...	...	...	...	875	1687	2712	4011	6789	14321	41947	66845

a) Item 'Net saving' includes consumption of fixed capital.

1.5 Current Income and Outlay of Corporate and Quasi-Corporate Enterprises, Summary

Million Peruvian intis

	1970	1975	1977	1978	1979	1980	1981	1982	1983	1984	1985	1986

Receipts

1 Operating surplus	...	...	...	...	605	914	1359	2114	4132	11593	32880	41245
2 Property and entrepreneurial income received	...	...	...	...	299	583	1357	2280	4623	10950	26582	33463
3 Current transfers	...	...	...	...	127	298	538	741	1355	2552	7402	7805
Total Current Receipts	...	...	...	...	1033	1794	3253	5136	10109	25094	66865	82516

Disbursements

1 Property and entrepreneurial income	...	...	...	...	456	914	2052	3368	6498	16356	41973	47584
2 Direct taxes and other current payments to general government	...	...	...	...	241	381	441	680	891	1830	3907	11386
3 Other current transfers	...	...	...	...	33	65	137	234	552	956	2228	3667
4 Net saving [a]	...	...	...	...	302	435	622	854	2166	5950	18755	19879
Total Current Disbursements and Net Saving	...	...	...	...	1033	1794	3253	5137	10109	25094	66865	82516

a) Item 'Net saving' includes consumption of fixed capital.

1.6 Current Income and Outlay of Households and Non-Profit Institutions

Million Peruvian intis

	1970	1975	1977	1978	1979	1980	1981	1982	1983	1984	1985	1986

Receipts

1 Compensation of employees	...	...	...	...	983	1776	3290	5706	10703	21729	54395	116039
A From resident producers	...	...	...	...	977	1767	3275	5675	10631	21564	53849	115336
B From rest of the world	...	...	...	...	6	9	15	31	72	165	546	703
2 Operating surplus of private unincorporated enterprises	...	...	...	...	1539	2704	4981	8402	14950	33227	92444	194522
3 Property and entrepreneurial income	...	...	...	...	103	191	493	864	1625	2858	7456	9505
4 Current transfers	...	...	...	...	148	308	551	900	1693	3011	6647	14821
A Social security benefits	...	...	...	...	85	162	307	526	1021	2112	4685	10504
B Social assistance grants	...	...	...	...	...	...	...	...	...	...	...	...
C Other	...	...	...	...	...	...	...	...	...	...	...	...
Total Current Receipts	...	...	...	...	2773	4980	9314	15872	28972	60825	160943	334886

Disbursements

1 Private final consumption expenditure	...	...	...	...	2131	3659	6738	11070	21099	45532	123412	254589

Peru

1.6 Current Income and Outlay of Households and Non-Profit Institutions
(Continued)

Million Peruvian intis

	1970	1975	1977	1978	1979	1980	1981	1982	1983	1984	1985	1986
2 Property income	...	...	...	...	69	126	258	507	1054	1658	4433	4672
3 Direct taxes and other current transfers n.e.c. to general government	...	...	...	...	136	236	486	728	1499	3069	7625	15575
A Social security contributions	...	...	...	...	90	179	358	557	1136	2240	5805	12908
B Direct taxes	...	...	...	...	41	48	108	134	231	540	1092	1393
C Fees, fines and penalties	...	...	...	...	5	9	20	37	132	289	728	1274
4 Other current transfers	...	...	...	...	5	20	24	60	122	247	979	1912
5 Net saving [a]	...	...	...	...	432	938	1807	3507	5197	10318	24493	58138
Total Current Disbursements and Net Saving	...	...	...	...	2773	4980	9314	15872	28972	60825	160943	334886

a) Item 'Net saving' includes consumption of fixed capital.

1.7 External Transactions on Current Account, Summary

Million Peruvian intis

	1970	1975	1977	1978	1979	1980	1981	1982	1983	1984	1985	1986
Payments to the Rest of the World												
1 Imports of goods and services	...	...	...	...	666	1329	2377	3829	6224	10794	30304	51742
2 Factor income to the rest of the world	...	...	...	...	232	354	516	795	2031	4687	12172	12565
A Compensation of employees	...	...	...	...	4	5	11	28	70	118	251	300
B Property and entrepreneurial income	...	...	...	...	228	349	505	767	1961	4569	11921	12265
3 Current transfers to the rest of the world	...	...	...	...	1	3	4	5	16	47	207	205
4 Surplus of the nation on current transactions	...	...	...	...	147	-155	-844	-1413	-1669	-751	74	-17636
Payments to the Rest of the World and Surplus of the Nation on Current Transactions	...	...	...	...	1046	1531	2053	3216	6602	14777	42757	46876
Receipts From The Rest of the World												
1 Exports of goods and services	...	...	...	...	968	1332	1735	2806	5880	13486	39611	43708
2 Factor income from rest of the world	...	...	...	...	21	76	101	117	257	709	1945	1942
A Compensation of employees	...	...	...	...	6	9	15	31	72	165	546	703
B Property and entrepreneurial income	...	...	...	...	15	67	86	86	185	544	1399	1239
3 Current transfers from rest of the world	...	...	...	...	57	123	216	294	464	582	1202	1226
Receipts from the Rest of the World on Current Transactions	...	...	...	...	1046	1531	2053	3216	6602	14777	42757	46876

1.10 Gross Domestic Product by Kind of Activity, in Current Prices

Million Peruvian intis

	1970	1975	1977	1978	1979	1980	1981	1982	1983	1984	1985	1986
1 Agriculture, hunting, forestry and fishing	...	...	...	...	408	610	1098	1709	3426	7982	18239	...
2 Mining and quarrying	...	...	...	...	459	905	1257	1873	3589	7702	19314	...
3 Manufacturing	...	...	...	...	820	1206	1956	3317	6066	14859	48164	...
4 Electricity, gas and water	...	...	...	...	34	51	111	191	270	824	2547	...
5 Construction	...	...	...	...	181	342	737	1589	2172	4745	13367	...
6 Wholesale and retail trade, restaurants and hotels	...	...	...	...	623	1060	1932	3131	6145	13240	36271	...
7 Transport, storage and communication	...	...	...	...	221	380	712	1068	1817	4266	12360	...
8 Finance, insurance, real estate and business services	...	...	...	...	370	591	1238	2248	3836	8118	20746	...
9 Community, social and personal services	...	...	...	...	122	242	523	905	1750	3920	11010	...
Total, Industries	...	...	...	...	3241	5403	9564	16052	29071	65656	182018	...
Producers of Government Services	...	...	...	...	215	461	917	1567	3020	6438	14961	...
Other Producers	...	...	...	...	32	62	150	316	536	975	2604	...
Subtotal	...	...	...	...	3488	5926	10631	17935	32627	73069	199583	...
Less: Imputed bank service charge	...	...	...	...	76	118	284	404	767	1624	5888	...
Plus: Import duties	...	...	...	...	78	160	312	419	705	1400	3994	...
Plus: Value added tax	...	...	...	...	...	...	...	...	...	...	...	...
Equals: Gross Domestic Product [a]	...	...	...	...	3490	5968	10659	17950	32565	72845	197689	...

a) Data for this table have not been revised, therefore, data for some years are not comparable with those of other tables.

Peru

1.11 Gross Domestic Product by Kind of Activity, in Constant Prices

Million Peruvian intis

	1970	1975	1977	1978	1979	1980	1981	1982	1983	1984	1985	1986
					At constant prices of:1979							
1 Agriculture, hunting, forestry and fishing	...	...	...	...	408	382	416	428	382	427	440	...
2 Mining and quarrying	...	...	...	...	459	469	454	460	415	435	455	...
3 Manufacturing	...	...	...	...	820	866	873	864	718	757	809	...
4 Electricity, gas and water	...	...	...	...	34	39	42	45	38	38	40	...
5 Construction	...	...	...	...	181	202	225	230	181	183	165	...
6 Wholesale and retail trade, restaurants and hotels	...	...	...	...	623	654	689	689	590	604	617	...
7 Transport, storage and communication	...	...	...	...	224	236	251	248	230	231	234	...
8 Finance, insurance, real estate and business services	...	...	...	...	370	386	411	410	391	392	441	...
9 Community, social and personal services	...	...	...	...	122	127	134	132	128	133	139	...
Total, Industries	...	...	...	...	3241	3361	3495	3506	3073	3200	3340	...
Producers of Government Services	...	...	...	...	215	233	240	242	258	278	277	...
Other Producers	...	...	...	...	32	33	34	35	37	39	39	...
Subtotal	...	...	...	...	3488	3627	3769	3783	3368	3517	3656	...
Less: Imputed bank service charge	...	...	...	...	76	82	89	90	98	88	121	...
Plus: Import duties	...	...	...	...	78	102	128	124	76	77	60	...
Plus: Value added tax	...	...	...	...	...	...	...	...	...	...	...	...
Equals: Gross Domestic Product [a]	...	...	...	...	3490	3647	3808	3817	3346	3506	3595	...

a) Data for this table have not been revised, therefore, data for some years are not comparable with those of other tables.

1.12 Relations Among National Accounting Aggregates

Million Peruvian intis

	1970	1975	1977	1978	1979	1980	1981	1982	1983	1984	1985	1986
Gross Domestic Product	280	665	1193	1901	3490	5968	10658	17950	32565	72845	199845	381022
Plus: Net factor income from the rest of the world	-5	-9	-35	-88	-211	-278	-415	-678	-1773	-3977	-10227	-10622
Factor income from the rest of the world	...	...	...	...	21	76	101	117	257	709	1945	1942
Less: Factor income to the rest of the world	...	...	...	...	232	354	516	795	2031	4687	12172	12565
Equals: Gross National Product	275	657	1158	1814	3279	5690	10244	17272	30792	68867	189618	370400
Less: Consumption of fixed capital	17	41	91	144	196	321	553	945	1886	4253	11005	18834
Equals: National Income	259	616	1067	1670	3082	5369	9691	16328	28906	64614	178612	351566
Plus: Net current transfers from the rest of the world	3	2	4	8	56	120	213	289	448	535	994	1020
Current transfers from the rest of the world	...	...	...	...	57	123	216	294	464	582	1202	1226
Less: Current transfers to the rest of the world	...	...	...	...	1	3	4	5	16	47	207	205
Equals: National Disposable Income	262	618	1071	1678	3138	5489	9904	16617	29354	65149	179606	352586
Less: Final consumption	231	575	1045	1520	2432	4326	7953	13330	25176	53636	145869	296931
Equals: Net Saving	31	43	26	158	706	1163	1951	3287	4178	11513	33737	55655
Less: Surplus of the nation on current transactions	...	...	...	...	147	-155	-844	-1413	-1669	-751	74	-17636
Equals: Net Capital Formation	...	...	...	...	559	1318	2795	4700	5847	12264	33663	73291

2.1 Government Final Consumption Expenditure by Function, in Current Prices

Million Peruvian intis

	1970	1975	1977	1978	1979	1980	1981	1982	1983	1984	1985	1986
1 General public services	...	...	...	...	155	359	642	1347	2334	4388	12895	23826
2 Defence	...	...	...	...								
3 Public order and safety	...	...	...	...	...	...	...	...	...	...	...	...
4 Education	...	...	...	...	81	167	325	530	1008	2206	5551	10818
5 Health	...	...	...	...	27	52	101	152	346	685	1866	3565
6 Social security and welfare	...	...	...	...	7	14	26	52	72	160	427	796
7 Housing and community amenities	...	...	...	...	1	1	2	5	8	10	47	72
8 Recreational, cultural and religious affairs	...	...	...	...	5	24	23	42	76	58	319	567
9 Economic services	...	...	...	...	25	50	96	133	233	596	1352	2697
10 Other functions	...	...	...	...	...	...	...	...	...	...	...	...
Total Government Final Consumption Expenditure	...	...	...	...	301	667	1215	2260	4077	8104	22457	42342

Peru

2.5 Private Final Consumption Expenditure by Type and Porpose, in Current Prices

Million Peruvian intis

	1970	1975	1977	1978	1979	1980	1981	1982	1983	1984	1985	1986
Final Consumption Expenditure of Resident Households												
1 Food, beverages and tobacco	...	...	...	...	852	1356	2502	4005	8646	18373	47126	97532
2 Clothing and footwear	...	...	...	...	263	501	830	1212	1565	3413	10403	23989
3 Gross rent, fuel and power	...	...	...	...	106	154	243	404	698	1232	2726	4264
4 Furniture, furnishings and household equipment and operation	...	...	...	...	270	484	866	1354	2230	4974	14614	28605
5 Medical care and health expenses	...	...	...	...	80	132	250	432	919	1844	4943	10496
6 Transport and communication	...	...	...	...	158	266	495	891	1693	3781	11497	19775
7 Recreational, entertainment, education and cultural services	...	...	...	...	55	91	168	307	569	1309	3894	7400
8 Miscellaneous goods and services	...	...	...	...	347	674	1384	2464	4779	10607	28210	62529
Total Final Consumption Expenditure in the Domestic Market by Households, of which	...	...	...	...	2131	3659	6738	11070	21099	45532	123412	254589
Plus: Direct purchases abroad by resident households	...	...	...	...	...	...	...	...	...	...	...	...
Less: Direct purchases in the domestic market by non-resident households	...	...	...	...	...	...	...	...	...	...	...	...
Equals: Final Consumption Expenditure of Resident Households	...	...	...	...	2131	3659	6738	11070	21099	45532	123412	254589
Final Consumption Expenditure of Private Non-profit Institutions Serving Households												
Equals: Final Consumption Expenditure of Private Non-profit Organisations Serving Households	...	...	...	...	...	...	...	...	...	...	...	...
Private Final Consumption Expenditure	...	...	...	...	2131	3659	6738	11070	21099	45532	123412	254589

2.6 Private Final Consumption Expenditure by Type and Purpose, in Constant Prices

Million Peruvian intis

	1970	1975	1977	1978	1979	1980	1981	1982	1983	1984	1985	1986
At constant prices of: 1979												
Final Consumption Expenditure of Resident Households												
1 Food, beverages and tobacco	...	...	...	...	852	862	914	941	910	931	930	1062
2 Clothing and footwear	...	...	...	...	263	279	277	281	224	221	234	273
3 Gross rent, fuel and power	...	...	...	...	106	112	115	117	119	121	126	130
4 Furniture, furnishings and household equipment and operation	...	...	...	...	270	291	307	283	214	220	227	269
5 Medical care and health expenses	...	...	...	...	80	83	87	89	76	73	76	81
6 Transport and communication	...	...	...	...	158	174	185	188	163	166	164	179
7 Recreational, entertainment, education and cultural services	...	...	...	...	55	57	58	61	62	63	65	71
8 Miscellaneous goods and services	...	...	...	...	347	379	413	417	399	414	435	492
Total Final Consumption Expenditure in the Domestic Market by Households, of which	...	...	...	...	2131	2236	2356	2376	2167	2209	2256	2557
Plus: Direct purchases abroad by resident households	...	...	...	...	...	...	...	...	...	...	...	...
Less: Direct purchases in the domestic market by non-resident households	...	...	...	...	...	...	...	...	...	...	...	...
Equals: Final Consumption Expenditure of Resident Households	...	...	...	...	2131	2236	2356	2376	2167	2209	2256	2557
Final Consumption Expenditure of Private Non-profit Institutions Serving Households												
Equals: Final Consumption Expenditure of Private Non-profit Organisations Serving Households	...	...	...	...	...	...	...	...	...	...	...	...
Private Final Consumption Expenditure	...	...	...	...	2131	2236	2356	2376	2167	2209	2256	2557

Peru

2.7 Gross Capital Formation by Type of Good and Owner, in Current Prices

Million Peruvian intis

	1980 TOTAL	Total Private	Public Enterprises	General Government	1981 TOTAL	Total Private	Public Enterprises	General Government	1982 TOTAL	Total Private	Public Enterprises	General Government
Increase in stocks, total	239	204	35	-	575	471	105	-	664	479	185	-
Gross Fixed Capital Formation, Total	1402	1059	164	179	2772	2133	291	348	4981	3627	739	615
1 Residential buildings	469	...	...	...	982	...	...	...	1955	...	...	...
2 Non-residential buildings		...	...	...		...	...	...		...	...	...
3 Other construction	239	...	...	...	470	...	...	...	907	...	...	...
4 Land improvement and plantation and orchard development	45	...	...	...	91	...	...	...	148	...	...	...
5 Producers' durable goods	649	519	94	36	1228	1063	120	45	1970	1407	472	90
A Transport equipment	173	...	...	...	417	...	...	...	671	...	...	...
B Machinery and equipment	476	...	...	...	811	...	...	...	1299	...	...	...
6 Breeding stock, dairy cattle, etc.	...	...	...	...	...	...	...	...	...	...	...	...
Total Gross Capital Formation	1640	1263	199	179	3347	2604	396	348	5644	4106	924	615

	1983 TOTAL	Total Private	Public Enterprises	General Government	1984 TOTAL	Total Private	Public Enterprises	General Government	1985 TOTAL	Total Private	Public Enterprises	General Government
Increase in stocks, total	172	123	48	-	-221	-1062	842	-	414	-2138	2552	-
Gross Fixed Capital Formation, Total	7561	5241	1375	945	16738	12203	2024	2510	44254	34057	5211	4987
1 Residential buildings	3161	...	...	...	7081	...	...	...	19216	...	...	...
2 Non-residential buildings		...	...	...		...	...	...		...	...	...
3 Other construction	1291	...	...	...	3000	...	...	...	8082	...	...	...
4 Land improvement and plantation and orchard development	322	...	...	...	611	...	...	...	1300	...	...	...
5 Producers' durable goods	2788	1768	914	106	6046	4836	910	300	15656	11563	3371	722
A Transport equipment	887	...	...	...	2077	...	...	...	...	...	...	...
B Machinery and equipment	1902	...	...	...	3969	...	...	...	...	...	...	...
6 Breeding stock, dairy cattle, etc.	...	...	...	...	...	...	...	...	...	...	...	...
Total Gross Capital Formation	7733	5364	1423	945	16517	11141	2866	2510	44668	31919	7763	4987

	1986 TOTAL	Total Private	Public Enterprises	General Government
Increase in stocks, total	9480	8139	1340	-
Gross Fixed Capital Formation, Total	82645	64189	6539	11917
1 Residential buildings	...	...	...	...
2 Non-residential buildings	...	...	...	...
3 Other construction	...	...	...	...
4 Land improvement and plantation and orchard development	...	...	...	...
5 Producers' durable goods	27442	20431	5366	1645
A Transport equipment	...	...	...	...
B Machinery and equipment	...	...	...	...
6 Breeding stock, dairy cattle, etc.	...	...	...	...
Total Gross Capital Formation	92125	72328	7879	11917

3.11 General Government Production Account: Total and Subsectors

Million Peruvian intis

	1980 Total General Government	Central Government	State or Provincial Government	Local Government	Social Security Funds	1981 Total General Government	Central Government	State or Provincial Government	Local Government	Social Security Funds
Gross Output										
1 Sales	5	4	...	2	...	11	7	...	4	...
2 Services produced for own use	667	517	...	139	11	1215	946	...	247	22
3 Own account fixed capital formation	137	55	...	29	53	263	116	...	46	101
Gross Output	809	575	...	170	64	1489	1069	...	297	124
Gross Input										
Intermediate Consumption	288	234	...	30	23	452	362	...	47	43

Peru

3.11 General Government Production Account: Total and Subsectors
(Continued)

Million Peruvian intis

	1980					1981				
	Total General Government	Central Government	State or Provincial Government	Local Government	Social Security Funds	Total General Government	Central Government	State or Provincial Government	Local Government	Social Security Funds
Subtotal: Value Added	521	341	...	139	41	1037	707	...	250	80
1 Indirect taxes, net	12	8	...	3	1	41	32	...	7	2
A Indirect taxes	12	8	...	3	1	41	32	...	7	2
B Less: Subsidies	...	...	...	...	...	...	...	...	...	...
2 Consumption of fixed capital	...	...	...	...	...	...	...	...	...	...
3 Compensation of employees	504	330	...	134	39	988	670	...	239	78
4 Net Operating surplus	5	3	...	2	-	8	4	...	3	1
Gross Input	809	575	...	170	64	1489	1069	...	297	124

	1982					1983				
	Total General Government	Central Government	State or Provincial Government	Local Government	Social Security Funds	Total General Government	Central Government	State or Provincial Government	Local Government	Social Security Funds
					Gross Output					
1 Sales	19	16	...	3	...	31	25	...	6	...
2 Services produced for own use	2260	2116	...	98	46	4077	3821	...	195	61
3 Own account fixed capital formation	445	201	...	90	154	944	416	...	265	264
Gross Output	2724	2333	...	191	200	5052	4262	...	465	325
					Gross Input					
Intermediate Consumption	956	820	...	67	69	1610	1317	...	191	102
Subtotal: Value Added	1769	1513	...	125	131	3442	2945	...	273	223
1 Indirect taxes, net	53	48	...	2	3	26	19	...	3	4
A Indirect taxes	53	48	...	2	3	26	19	...	3	4
B Less: Subsidies	...	...	...	...	...	...	...	...	...	...
2 Consumption of fixed capital	...	...	...	...	...	...	...	...	...	...
3 Compensation of employees	1696	1454	...	114	128	3379	2907	...	254	218
4 Net Operating surplus	20	10	...	9	1	37	19	...	16	1
Gross Input	2724	2333	...	191	200	5052	4262	...	465	325

	1984					1985				
	Total General Government	Central Government	State or Provincial Government	Local Government	Social Security Funds	Total General Government	Central Government	State or Provincial Government	Local Government	Social Security Funds
					Gross Output					
1 Sales	65	53	...	11	...	165	131	...	33	-
2 Services produced for own use	8104	7543	...	437	124	22457	21062	...	1089	307
3 Own account fixed capital formation	2126	946	...	709	471	4858	2309	...	1399	1150
Gross Output	10294	8542	...	1157	595	27481	23502	...	2521	1457
					Gross Input					
Intermediate Consumption	2886	2222	...	498	166	9357	7815	...	1043	499
Subtotal: Value Added	7408	6320	...	659	429	18124	15687	...	1478	958
1 Indirect taxes, net	58	46	...	7	5	72	50	...	15	7
A Indirect taxes	58	46	...	7	5	72	50	...	15	7
B Less: Subsidies	...	...	...	...	...	...	...	...	...	...
2 Consumption of fixed capital	...	...	...	...	...	...	...	...	...	...
3 Compensation of employees	7203	6182	...	610	411	17470	15225	...	1332	912
4 Net Operating surplus	147	92	...	43	12	582	412	...	131	39
Gross Input	10294	8542	...	1157	595	27481	23502	...	2521	1457

	1986				
	Total General Government	Central Government	State or Provincial Government	Local Government	Social Security Funds
			Gross Output		
1 Sales	302	218	...	84	...
2 Services produced for own use	42342	39540	...	2083	718
3 Own account fixed capital formation	11319	4758	...	3148	3412
Gross Output	53962	44517	...	5315	4130
			Gross Input		
Intermediate Consumption	15888	12033	...	2324	1531
Subtotal: Value Added	38074	32484	...	2991	2599

Peru

3.11 General Government Production Account: Total and Subsectors
(Continued)

Million Peruvian intis

	1986				
	Total General Government	Central Government	State or Provincial Government	Local Government	Social Security Funds
1 Indirect taxes, net	226	147	...	27	52
A Indirect taxes	226	147	...	27	52
B Less: Subsidies	...	...	...	...	...
2 Consumption of fixed capital	...	...	...	...	...
3 Compensation of employees	36897	31708	...	2744	2445
4 Net Operating surplus	951	629	...	221	101
Gross Input	53962	44517	...	5315	4130

3.12 General Government Income and Outlay Account: Total and Subsectors

Million Peruvian intis

	1980					1981				
	Total General Government	Central Government	State or Provincial Government	Local Government	Social Security Funds	Total General Government	Central Government	State or Provincial Government	Local Government	Social Security Funds
Receipts										
1 Operating surplus	5	2	...	2	-	8	4	...	3	1
2 Property and entrepreneurial income	213	202	...	1	11	399	368	...	3	28
A Withdrawals from public quasi-corporations	...	...	...	...	...	...	...	...	...	...
B Interest	14	3	...	1	11	39	8	...	3	28
C Dividends	19	19	...	-	-	5	5	...	-	-
D Net land rent and royalties	180	180	...	-	-	355	355	...	-	-
3 Taxes, fees and contributions	1333	1197	...	20	116	2097	1814	...	51	231
A Indirect taxes	726	721	...	5	...	1195	1181	...	14	...
B Direct taxes	424	421	...	4	-	512	501	...	10	-
C Social security contributions	168	46	...	6	116	332	90	...	12	230
D Fees, fines and penalties	15	9	...	5	-	58	42	...	15	1
4 Other current transfers	136	15	...	120	-	207	20	...	188	-
A Casualty insurance claims	-	-	...	-	-	1	1	...	-	-
B Transfers from other government subsectors	...	...	...	...	...	...	...	...	...	...
C Transfers from the rest of the world	...	...	...	...	...	...	...	...	...	...
D Other transfers, except imputed	136	15	...	120	-	206	19	...	188	-
E Imputed unfunded employee pension and welfare contributions	...	...	...	...	...	...	...	...	...	...
Total Current Receipts	1687	1417	...	143	127	2712	2207	...	246	260
Disbursements										
1 Government final consumption expenditure	667	517	...	139	11	1215	946	...	247	22
2 Property income	228	228	...	-	-	357	357	...	-	-
A Interest	228	228	...	-	-	357	357	...	-	-
B Net land rent and royalties	...	...	...	...	...	...	...	...	...	...
3 Subsidies	153	153	...	-	-	170	170	...	-	-
4 Other current transfers	527	423	...	6	98	897	697	...	17	183
A Casualty insurance premiums, net	3	3	...	-	-	5	5	...	-	-
B Transfers to other government subsectors	...	...	...	...	...	...	...	...	...	...
C Social security benefits	150	46	...	6	98	281	90	...	12	179
D Social assistance grants	...	...	...	...	...	...	...	...	...	...
E Unfunded employee pension and welfare benefits	...	...	...	...	...	...	...	...	...	...
F Transfers to private non-profit institutions serving households	...	...	...	...	...	...	...	...	...	...
G Other transfers n.e.c.	374	374	...	-	-	611	602	...	5	4
H Transfers to the rest of the world	...	...	...	...	...	...	...	...	...	...
Net saving [a]	111	96	...	-3	18	73	38	...	-19	54
Total Current Disbursements and Net Saving	1687	1417	...	143	127	2712	2207	...	246	260

Peru

3.12 General Government Income and Outlay Account: Total and Subsectors

Million Peruvian intis

	1982					1983				
	Total General Government	Central Government	State or Provincial Government	Local Government	Social Security Funds	Total General Government	Central Government	State or Provincial Government	Local Government	Social Security Funds
Receipts										
1 Operating surplus	20	10	...	9	1	37	19	...	16	1
2 Property and entrepreneurial income	571	510	...	6	55	939	852	...	13	74
A Withdrawals from public quasi-corporations	...	...	...	...	...	...	...	...	...	...
B Interest	69	8	...	6	55	91	4	...	13	74
C Dividends	15	15	...	-	-	6	6	...	-	-
D Net land rent and royalties	488	488	...	-	-	842	842	...	-	-
3 Taxes, fees and contributions	3338	2942	...	54	343	5440	4517	...	211	712
A Indirect taxes	1974	1953	...	20	...	3152	2999	...	154	...
B Direct taxes	782	770	...	13	-	1060	1038	...	22	-
C Social security contributions	513	182	...	3	328	1033	387	...	8	638
D Fees, fines and penalties	69	37	...	18	15	195	93	...	27	74
4 Other current transfers	82	36	...	46	-	373	291	...	82	-
A Casualty insurance claims	1	1	...	-	-	7	7	...	-	-
B Transfers from other government subsectors	...	...	...	...	...	...	...	...	...	...
C Transfers from the rest of the world	...	...	...	...	...	...	...	...	...	...
D Other transfers, except imputed	81	35	...	46	-	366	284	...	82	-
E Imputed unfunded employee pension and welfare contributions	...	...	...	...	...	...	...	...	...	...
Total Current Receipts	4011	3498	...	115	398	6789	5680	...	322	787
Disbursements										
1 Government final consumption expenditure	2260	2116	...	98	46	4077	3821	...	195	61
2 Property income	519	518	...	-	1	1411	1403	...	-	8
A Interest	519	518	...	-	1	1411	1403	...	-	8
B Net land rent and royalties	...	...	...	...	...	...	...	...	...	...
3 Subsidies	264	264	...	-	-	405	405	...	-	-
4 Other current transfers	1098	783	...	9	306	2195	1634	...	21	540
A Casualty insurance premiums, net	9	9	...	-	-	18	18	...	-	-
B Transfers to other government subsectors	...	...	...	...	...	...	...	...	...	...
C Social security benefits	481	182	...	3	296	918	387	...	8	523
D Social assistance grants	...	...	...	...	...	...	...	...	...	...
E Unfunded employee pension and welfare benefits	...	...	...	...	...	...	...	...	...	...
F Transfers to private non-profit institutions serving households	...	...	...	...	...	...	...	...	...	...
G Other transfers n.e.c.	609	592	...	6	10	1259	1229	...	13	17
H Transfers to the rest of the world	...	...	...	...	...	...	...	...	...	...
Net saving [a]	-130	-182	...	7	45	-1299	-1583	...	106	178
Total Current Disbursements and Net Saving	4011	3498	...	115	398	6789	5680	...	322	787

	1984					1985				
	Total General Government	Central Government	State or Provincial Government	Local Government	Social Security Funds	Total General Government	Central Government	State or Provincial Government	Local Government	Social Security Funds
Receipts										
1 Operating surplus	147	92	...	43	12	582	412	...	131	39
2 Property and entrepreneurial income	1938	1740	...	35	163	6780	6305	...	135	341
A Withdrawals from public quasi-corporations	...	...	...	...	...	...	...	...	...	...
B Interest	206	8	...	35	163	654	181	...	135	338
C Dividends	128	128	...	-	-	345	345	...	-	-
D Net land rent and royalties	1604	1604	...	-	-	5781	5778	...	-	3
3 Taxes, fees and contributions	11528	9752	...	459	1317	32916	27503	...	1590	3825
A Indirect taxes	6815	6516	...	299	...	21608	20484	...	1124	...

Peru

3.12 General Government Income and Outlay Account: Total and Subsectors
(Continued)

Million Peruvian intis

	1984					1985				
	Total General Government	Central Government	State or Provincial Government	Local Government	Social Security Funds	Total General Government	Central Government	State or Provincial Government	Local Government	Social Security Funds
B Direct taxes	2115	2034	...	81	-	4514	4294	...	221	-
C Social security contributions	2053	881	...	19	1154	5581	2065	...	38	3479
D Fees, fines and penalties	545	321	...	60	163	1213	660	...	207	346
4 Other current transfers	707	560	...	147	1	1668	1512	...	155	-
A Casualty insurance claims	1	1	...	-	-	13	12	...	-	-
B Transfers from other government subsectors	...	...	...	...	...	...	...	...	...	...
C Transfers from the rest of the world	...	...	...	...	...	...	...	...	...	...
D Other transfers, except imputed	706	559	...	147	1	1655	1500	...	155	-
E Imputed unfunded employee pension and welfare contributions	...	...	...	...	...	...	...	...	...	...
Total Current Receipts	14321	12143	...	684	1493	41947	35732	...	2011	4204

Disbursements

1 Government final consumption expenditure	8104	7543	...	437	124	22457	21062	...	1089	307
2 Property income	1759	1738	...	3	18	4934	4901	...	3	30
A Interest	1759	1738	...	3	18	4934	4901	...	3	30
B Net land rent and royalties	...	...	...	...	...	...	...	...	...	...
3 Subsidies	618	618	...	-	-	1770	1770	...	-	-
4 Other current transfers	4342	3241	...	51	1050	11293	8808	...	85	2399
A Casualty insurance premiums, net	51	50	...	-	-	116	115	...	-	-
B Transfers to other government subsectors	...	...	...	...	...	...	...	...	...	...
C Social security benefits	1926	881	...	19	1027	4462	2065	...	38	2359
D Social assistance grants	...	...	...	...	...	...	...	...	...	...
E Unfunded employee pension and welfare benefits	...	...	...	...	...	...	...	...	...	...
F Transfers to private non-profit institutions serving households	...	...	...	...	...	...	...	...	...	...
G Other transfers n.e.c.	2365	2310	...	32	23	6715	6628	...	47	40
H Transfers to the rest of the world	...	...	...	...	...	...	...	...	...	...
Net saving [a]	-502	-997	...	193	303	1493	-809	...	833	1468
Total Current Disbursements and Net Saving	14321	12143	...	684	1493	41947	35732	...	2011	4204

	1986				
	Total General Government	Central Government	State or Provincial Government	Local Government	Social Security Funds

Receipts

1 Operating surplus	951	..	...	..	...
2 Property and entrepreneurial income	6594	..	...	..	...
A Withdrawals from public quasi-corporations	...	...	...	...	...
B Interest	521	...	...	...	...
C Dividends	247	..	...	..	...
D Net land rent and royalties	5826	..	...	..	...
3 Taxes, fees and contributions	58285	...	...	...	...
A Indirect taxes	31736	..	...	..	...
B Direct taxes	12355	..	...	..	...
C Social security contributions	12495	..	...	..	...
D Fees, fines and penalties	1699	..	...	..	...

Peru

3.12 General Government Income and Outlay Account: Total and Subsectors
(Continued)

Million Peruvian intis

	1986				
	Total General Government	Central Government	State or Provincial Government	Local Government	Social Security Funds
4 Other current transfers	1016	...	...	...	...
A Casualty insurance claims	18	..	..	..	...
B Transfers from other government subsectors	...	...	...	...	...
C Transfers from the rest of the world	...	...	...	...	...
D Other transfers, except imputed	998	..	...	..	...
E Imputed unfunded employee pension and welfare contributions	...	...	...	...	...
Total Current Receipts	66845	..	...	..	...

Disbursements

1 Government final consumption expenditure	42342	..	...	..	...
2 Property income	8332	..	...	..	...
A Interest	8332	..	...	..	...
B Net land rent and royalties	...	...	...	...	...
3 Subsidies	3066	..	...	..	...
4 Other current transfers	16634	...	...	...	...
A Casualty insurance premiums, net	132	..	...	..	...
B Transfers to other government subsectors	...	...	...	...	...
C Social security benefits	10091	..	...	..	...
D Social assistance grants	...	...	...	...	...
E Unfunded employee pension and welfare benefits	...	...	...	...	...
F Transfers to private non-profit institutions serving households	...	...	...	...	...
G Other transfers n.e.c.	6411	..	...	..	...
H Transfers to the rest of the world	...	...	...	...	...
Net saving [a]	-3527	..	...	..	...
Total Current Disbursements and Net Saving	66845	..	...	..	...

a) Item 'Net saving' includes consumption of fixed capital.

3.13 General Government Capital Accumulation Account: Total and Subsectors

Million Peruvian intis

	1980					1981				
	Total General Government	Central Government	State or Provincial Government	Local Government	Social Security Funds	Total General Government	Central Government	State or Provincial Government	Local Government	Social Security Funds

Finance of Gross Accumulation

1 Gross saving	111	96	...	-3	18	73	38	...	-19	54
2 Capital transfers	61	6	...	55		102	13	...	88	-
Finance of Gross Accumulation	172	102	...	52	18	175	51	...	70	54

Gross Accumulation

1 Gross capital formation	179	101	...	67	12	348	213	...	110	25
A Increase in stocks	-	-	...	-	-	-	-	...	.	-
B Gross fixed capital formation	179	101	...	67	12	348	213	...	110	25
2 Purchases of land, net	6	7	...	-	-	-1	-	...	-1	-
3 Purchases of intangible assets, net	...	...	...	...	...	...	...	...	...	...
4 Capital transfers	89	89	...	-	-	164	162	...	2	-
Net lending	-103	-94	...	-15	6	-337	-325	...	-41	29
Gross Accumulation	172	102	...	52	18	175	51	...	70	54

Peru

3.13 General Government Capital Accumulation Account: Total and Subsectors

Million Peruvian intis

1982

	Total General Government	Central Government	State or Provincial Government	Local Government	Social Security Funds
Finance of Gross Accumulation					
1 Gross saving	-130	-182	...	7	45
2 Capital transfers	128	26	...	101	-
Finance of Gross Accumulation	-3	-156	...	108	45
Gross Accumulation					
1 Gross capital formation	615	455	...	127	34
A Increase in stocks	-	-	...	-	-
B Gross fixed capital formation	615	455	...	127	34
2 Purchases of land, net	-	-1	...	-2	-
3 Purchases of intangible assets, net	...	...	...	...	...
4 Capital transfers	191	189	...	2	-
Net lending	-808	-800	...	-19	11
Gross Accumulation	-3	-156	...	108	45

1983

	Total General Government	Central Government	State or Provincial Government	Local Government	Social Security Funds
Finance of Gross Accumulation					
1 Gross saving	-1299	-1583	...	106	178
2 Capital transfers	296	68	...	227	-
Finance of Gross Accumulation	-1003	-1515	...	334	178
Gross Accumulation					
1 Gross capital formation	945	540	...	381	24
A Increase in stocks	-	-	...	-	-
B Gross fixed capital formation	945	540	...	381	24
2 Purchases of land, net	-1	1	...	-1	-
3 Purchases of intangible assets, net	...	...	...	...	...
4 Capital transfers	358	354	...	4	-
Net lending	-2306	-2410	...	-50	154
Gross Accumulation	-1003	-1515	...	334	178

1984

	Total General Government	Central Government	State or Provincial Government	Local Government	Social Security Funds
Finance of Gross Accumulation					
1 Gross saving	-502	-997	...	193	303
2 Capital transfers	697	206	...	491	-
Finance of Gross Accumulation	196	-791	...	684	303
Gross Accumulation					
1 Gross capital formation	2510	1582	...	896	32
A Increase in stocks	-	-	...	-	-
B Gross fixed capital formation	2510	1582	...	896	32
2 Purchases of land, net	-4	6	...	-11	-
3 Purchases of intangible assets, net	...	...	...	...	...
4 Capital transfers	713	710	...	3	-
Net lending	-3023	-3090	...	-204	270
Gross Accumulation	196	-791	...	684	303

1985

	Total General Government	Central Government	State or Provincial Government	Local Government	Social Security Funds
Finance of Gross Accumulation					
1 Gross saving	1493	-809	...	833	1468
2 Capital transfers	1477	443	...	1033	-
Finance of Gross Accumulation	2970	-365	...	1867	1468
Gross Accumulation					
1 Gross capital formation	4987	3247	...	1691	49
A Increase in stocks	-	-	...	-	-
B Gross fixed capital formation	4987	3247	...	1691	49
2 Purchases of land, net	-19	-6	...	-13	-
3 Purchases of intangible assets, net	...	...	...	...	...
4 Capital transfers	1723	1668	...	55	-
Net lending	-3721	-5274	...	134	1420
Gross Accumulation	2970	-365	...	1867	1468

1986

	Total General Government	Central Government	State or Provincial Government	Local Government	Social Security Funds
Finance of Gross Accumulation					
1 Gross saving	-3527	..	..	..	..
2 Capital transfers	2852	..	..	..	..
Finance of Gross Accumulation	-675	..	..	..	..
Gross Accumulation					
1 Gross capital formation	11917	..	..	..	..
A Increase in stocks	-	..	..	..	..
B Gross fixed capital formation	11917	..	..	..	..
2 Purchases of land, net	-12	..	..	..	..
3 Purchases of intangible assets, net	...	..	..	..	..
4 Capital transfers	3071	..	..	..	..
Net lending	-15652	..	..	..	..
Gross Accumulation	-675	..	..	..	..

3.14 General Government Capital Finance Account, Total and Subsectors

Million Peruvian intis

1980

	Total General Government	Central Government	State or Provincial Government	Local Government	Social Security Funds
Acquisition of Financial Assets					
1 Gold and SDRs	...	...	...	...	...
2 Currency and transferable deposits	-25	-33	...	-4	11
3 Other deposits	16	13	...	2	2
4 Bills and bonds, short term	-	-	...	-	-

1981

	Total General Government	Central Government	State or Provincial Government	Local Government	Social Security Funds
1 Gold and SDRs	...	...	...	...	...
2 Currency and transferable deposits	74	46	...	20	7
3 Other deposits	162	147	...	4	11
4 Bills and bonds, short term	2	-	...	1	1

Peru

3.14 General Government Capital Finance Account, Total and Subsectors
(Continued)

Million Peruvian intis

1980 / 1981

		1980				1981			
	Total General Government	Central Government	State or Provincial Government	Local Government	Social Security Funds	Total General Government	Central Government	State or Provincial Government	Local Government	Social Security Funds
5 Bonds, long term	1	-	...	-	1	7	-	...	-	7
6 Corporate equity securities	...	...	...	...	...	...	...	...	...	...
7 Short-term loans, n.e.c.	1	-	...	-	-	3	-	...	2	1
8 Long-term loans, n.e.c.	1	-	...	-	1	19	1	...	-	17
9 Other receivables	117	92	...	8	18	-83	-99	...	1	14
10 Other assets	223	222	...	1	-	187	186	...	1	-
Total Acquisition of Financial Assets	334	294	...	7	33	370	282	...	30	58

Incurrence of Liabilities

1 Currency and transferable deposits	...	...	...	...	...	...	...	...	...	...
2 Other deposits	2	-1	...	2	1	29	29	...	-	-
3 Bills and bonds, short term	-	-	...	-	-	1	1	...	-	-
4 Bonds, long term	67	67	...	-	-	120	120	...	-	-
5 Short-term loans, n.e.c.	-22	-23	...	1	-	208	198	...	9	1
6 Long-term loans, n.e.c.	335	335	...	-	-	170	159	...	10	-
7 Other payables	42	3	...	13	26	131	97	...	9	25
8 Other liabilities	15	9	...	5	1	36	27	...	7	2
Total Incurrence of Liabilities	439	390	...	22	27	695	631	...	37	27
Net Lending	-104	-96	...	-15	6	-325	-349	...	-6	30
Incurrence of Liabilities and Net Worth	334	294	...	7	33	370	282	...	30	58

1982 / 1983

		1982				1983			
	Total General Government	Central Government	State or Provincial Government	Local Government	Social Security Funds	Total General Government	Central Government	State or Provincial Government	Local Government	Social Security Funds

Acquisition of Financial Assets

1 Gold and SDRs	...	...	...	...	...	...	...	...	...	...
2 Currency and transferable deposits	-7	-7	...	9	-9	312	296	...	14	2
3 Other deposits	64	14	...	24	26	323	242	...	80	1
4 Bills and bonds, short term	2	1	...	1	1	68	2	...	2	64
5 Bonds, long term	-8	-	...	-	-8	98	-	...	1	97
6 Corporate equity securities	...	...	...	...	...	...	...	...	...	...
7 Short-term loans, n.e.c.	1	2	...	-	-1	3	-	...	4	-1
8 Long-term loans, n.e.c.	-9	-	...	2	-11	41	37	...	3	-
9 Other receivables	11	-201	...	26	186	-262	-564	...	-78	380
10 Other assets	310	309	...	1	-	860	851	...	9	-
Total Acquisition of Financial Assets	364	118	...	62	184	1444	864	...	35	544

Incurrence of Liabilities

1 Currency and transferable deposits	...	...	...	...	...	...	...	...	...	...
2 Other deposits	78	76	...	2	-	-56	-56	...	-	-
3 Bills and bonds, short term	1	1	...	-	-	-1	-1	...	-	-
4 Bonds, long term	59	59	...	-	-	100	100	...	-	-
5 Short-term loans, n.e.c.	-88	-79	...	-9	20	681	636	...	25	20
6 Long-term loans, n.e.c.	1058	1070	...	-11	-	2625	2637	...	-8	-4
7 Other payables	-20	-262	...	95	148	190	-226	...	52	365
8 Other liabilities	70	62	...	4	5	228	204	...	15	8
Total Incurrence of Liabilities	1180	926	...	81	173	3767	3294	...	84	389
Net Lending	-816	-808	...	-19	11	-2324	-2429	...	-49	155
Incurrence of Liabilities and Net Worth	364	118	...	62	184	1444	864	...	35	544

1984 / 1985

		1984				1985			
	Total General Government	Central Government	State or Provincial Government	Local Government	Social Security Funds	Total General Government	Central Government	State or Provincial Government	Local Government	Social Security Funds

Acquisition of Financial Assets

1 Gold and SDRs	...	...	...	...	...	...	...	...	...	...
2 Currency and transferable deposits	368	312	...	12	44	1802	1316	...	213	273
3 Other deposits	264	149	...	126	-11	649	264	...	283	102
4 Bills and bonds, short term	54	9	...	6	39	815	440	...	55	320

1177

Peru

3.14 General Government Capital Finance Account, Total and Subsectors
(Continued)

Million Peruvian intis

	1984					1985				
	Total General Government	Central Government	State or Provincial Government	Local Government	Social Security Funds	Total General Government	Central Government	State or Provincial Government	Local Government	Social Security Funds
5 Bonds, long term	-11	1	...	1	-13	204	-2	...	5	202
6 Corporate equity securities	...	...	...	...	...	...	...	...	...	...
7 Short-term loans, n.e.c.	7	5	...	1	1	479	439	...	13	27
8 Long-term loans, n.e.c.	72	6	...	2	64	74	7	...	35	32
9 Other receivables	-3590	-4031	...	-278	718	-637	-2148	...	-403	1913
10 Other assets	1263	1245	...	19	-	850	778	...	72	-
Total Acquisition of Financial Assets	-1573	-2305	...	-111	842	4236	1094	...	273	2869
Incurrence of Liabilities											
1 Currency and transferable deposits	...	...	...	...	...	...	...	...	...	...
2 Other deposits	5	5	...	1	-1	55	48	...	8	-
3 Bills and bonds, short term	-	-	...	-	-	-	-	...	-	-
4 Bonds, long term	320	320	...	-	-	1151	1152	...	-	-
5 Short-term loans, n.e.c.	490	469	...	4	17	631	589	...	24	18
6 Long-term loans, n.e.c.	5348	5286	...	6	56	16889	16875	...	6	9
7 Other payables	-5287	-5776	...	18	471	-11665	-13065	...	35	1365
8 Other liabilities	563	471	...	64	28	958	835	...	65	57
Total Incurrence of Liabilities	1438	774	...	93	572	8020	6432	...	138	1450
Net Lending	-3012	-3078	...	-204	270	-3784	-5339	...	135	1419
Incurrence of Liabilities and Net Worth	-1573	-2305	...	-111	842	4236	1094	...	273	2869

3.21 Corporate and Quasi-Corporate Enterprise Production Account: Total and Sectors

Million Peruvian intis

	1980				1981				1982			
	TOTAL	Non-Financial	Financial	ADDENDUM: Total, including Unincorporated	TOTAL	Non-Financial	Financial	ADDENDUM: Total, including Unincorporated	TOTAL	Non-Financial	Financial	ADDENDUM: Total, including Unincorporated
Gross Output												
1 Output for sale	...	...	...	...	...	...	...	...	...	...	...	...
2 Imputed bank service charge	...	...	...	...	...	...	...	...	...	...	...	...
3 Own-account fixed capital formation	...	...	...	...	...	...	...	...	...	...	...	...
Gross Output	5019	4802	217	...	8549	8075	474	...	14114	13347	767	...
Gross Input												
Intermediate consumption	2957	2777	180	...	5117	4724	393	...	8240	7628	612	...
1 Imputed banking service charge	119	...	119	...	284	...	284	...	404	...	404	...
2 Other intermediate consumption	61	...	61	...	109	...	109	...	208	...	208	...
Subtotal: Value Added	2063	2026	37	...	3431	3350	81	...	5874	5719	155	...
1 Indirect taxes, net	356	349	7	...	587	567	20	...	1152	1116	36	...
A Indirect taxes	503	492	11	...	749	726	23	...	1391	1354	37	...
B Less: Subsidies	147	143	4	...	162	159	3	...	239	238	1	...
2 Consumption of fixed capital	...	...	...	...	...	...	...	...	...	...	...	...
3 Compensation of employees	793	710	83	...	1486	1315	171	...	2606	2302	304	...
4 Net operating surplus	914	968	-54	...	1359	1469	-110	...	2114	2300	-186	...
Gross Input	5019	4802	217	...	8549	8075	474	...	14114	13347	767	...

	1983				1984				1985			
	TOTAL	Non-Financial	Financial	ADDENDUM: Total, including Unincorporated	TOTAL	Non-Financial	Financial	ADDENDUM: Total, including Unincorporated	TOTAL	Non-Financial	Financial	ADDENDUM: Total, including Unincorporated
Gross Output												
1 Output for sale	...	...	...	...	...	...	...	...	...	...	...	...
2 Imputed bank service charge	...	...	...	...	...	...	...	...	...	...	...	...
3 Own-account fixed capital formation	...	...	...	...	...	...	...	...	...	...	...	...
Gross Output	26352	24911	1441	...	61379	58075	3304	...	176811	166986	9825	...
Gross Input												
Intermediate consumption	15552	14350	1202	...	35879	33320	2559	...	104896	95881	9015	...
1 Imputed banking service charge	767	...	767	...	1624	...	1624	...	5716	...	5716	...
2 Other intermediate consumption	435	...	435	...	935	...	935	...	3299	...	3299	...

Peru

3.21 Corporate and Quasi-Corporate Enterprise Production Account: Total and Sectors
(Continued)

Million Peruvian intis

	1983				1984				1985			
	\multicolumn{3}{c|}{Corporate and Quasi-Corporate Enterprises}	ADDENDUM: Total,	\multicolumn{3}{c|}{Corporate and Quasi-Corporate Enterprises}	ADDENDUM: Total,	\multicolumn{3}{c|}{Corporate and Quasi-Corporate Enterprises}	ADDENDUM: Total,
	TOTAL	Non-Financial	Financial	including Unincorporated	TOTAL	Non-Financial	Financial	including Unincorporated	TOTAL	Non-Financial	Financial	including Unincorporated
Subtotal: Value Added	10800	10561	239	...	25500	24755	745	...	71915	71105	810	...
1 Indirect taxes, net	1875	1813	62	...	4450	4333	117	...	14973	14671	302	...
A Indirect taxes	2256	2194	62	...	4993	4876	117	...	16526	16224	302	...
B Less: Subsidies	381	381	-	...	543	543	-	...	1553	1553	-	...
2 Consumption of fixed capital	...	...	...	...	...	...	...	...	...	...	...	...
3 Compensation of employees	4795	4232	563	...	9456	8074	1382	...	24060	20990	3070	...
4 Net operating surplus	4132	4517	-385	...	11593	12347	-754	...	32880	35443	-2563	...
Gross Input	26352	24911	1441	...	61379	58075	3304	...	176811	166986	9825	...

	1986			
	\multicolumn{3}{c|}{Corporate and Quasi-Corporate Enterprises}	ADDENDUM: Total,
	TOTAL	Non-Financial	Financial	including Unincorporated

Gross Output

1 Output for sale	...	...	...	...
2 Imputed bank service charge	...	...	...	...
3 Own-account fixed capital formation	...	...	...	...
Gross Output	281977	264129	17848	...

Gross Input

Intermediate consumption	170009	153417	16592	...
1 Imputed banking service charge	11013	...	11013	...
2 Other intermediate consumption	5579	...	5579	...
Subtotal: Value Added	111968	110713	1256	...
1 Indirect taxes, net	19929	19345	584	...
A Indirect taxes	22746	22162	584	...
B Less: Subsidies	2817	2817	-	...
2 Consumption of fixed capital	...	...	...	...
3 Compensation of employees	50795	44937	5858	...
4 Net operating surplus	41245	46431	-5186	...
Gross Input	281977	264129	17848	...

3.22 Corporate and Quasi-Corporate Enterprise Income and Outlay Account: Total and Sectors

Million Peruvian intis

	1980			1981			1982			1983		
	TOTAL	Non-Financial	Financial	TOTAL	Non-Financial	Financial	TOTAL	Non-Financial	Financial	TOTAL	Non-Financial	Financial

Receipts

1 Operating surplus	914	968	-54	1359	1469	-110	2114	2300	-186	4132	4517	-385
2 Property and entrepreneurial income	583	136	447	1357	219	1138	2280	413	1867	4623	1061	3562
A Withdrawals from quasi-corporate enterprises	...	...	...	...	...	...	...	...	...	...	...	...
B Interest	572	127	445	1335	203	1132	2237	383	1854	4517	967	3550
C Dividends	8	5	3	15	9	6	31	18	13	80	68	12
D Net land rent and royalties	4	4	-	6	6	-	12	12	-	26	26	-
3 Current transfers	298	271	27	538	481	57	741	642	99	1355	1116	239
A Casualty insurance claims	44	19	25	91	41	50	145	58	87	314	98	216
B Casualty insurance premiums, net, due to be received by insurance companies	...	...	...	...	...	...	...	...	...	...	...	...
C Current transfers from the rest of the world	...	...	...	...	...	...	...	...	...	...	...	...
D Other transfers except imputed	242	242	-	421	421	-	552	552	-	938	938	-
E Imputed unfunded employee pension and welfare contributions	12	10	2	26	19	7	44	32	12	103	80	23
Total Current Receipts	1794	1374	420	3253	2169	1084	5136	3357	1779	10109	6693	3416

Disbursements

1 Property and entrepreneurial income	914	570	344	2052	1198	854	3368	1900	1468	6498	3699	2799
A Withdrawals from quasi-corporations	...	...	...	...	...	...	...	...	...	...	...	...

Peru

3.22 Corporate and Quasi-Corporate Enterprise Income and Outlay Account: Total and Sectors
(Continued)

Million Peruvian intis

	1980 TOTAL	1980 Non-Financial	1980 Financial	1981 TOTAL	1981 Non-Financial	1981 Financial	1982 TOTAL	1982 Non-Financial	1982 Financial	1983 TOTAL	1983 Non-Financial	1983 Financial
B Interest	568	246	322	1483	643	840	2590	1150	1440	4721	1957	2764
C Dividends	156	133	23	195	181	14	256	227	29	863	828	35
D Net land rent and royalties	192	192	-	374	374	-	522	522	-	913	913	-
2 Direct taxes and other current transfers n.e.c. to general government	381	363	18	441	390	51	680	640	40	891	812	79
A Direct taxes	376	358	18	403	354	49	648	610	38	828	750	78
B Fines, fees, penalties and other current transfers n.e.c.	5	5	-	38	36	2	32	30	2	63	62	1
3 Other current transfers	65	36	29	137	78	59	234	127	107	552	293	259
A Casualty insurance premiums, net	43	17	26	88	38	50	139	56	83	298	110	188
B Casualty insurance claims liability of insurance companies	...	...	...	...	...	...	...	...	...	...	...	...
C Transfers to private non-profit institutions	...	...	...	...	...	...	...	...	...	...	...	...
D Unfunded employee pension and welfare benefits	12	10	2	26	19	7	44	32	12	103	80	23
E Social assistance grants	...	...	...	...	...	...	...	...	...	...	...	...
F Other transfers n.e.c.	10	9	1	23	21	2	51	39	12	151	103	48
G Transfers to the rest of the world	...	...	...	...	...	...	...	...	...	...	...	...
Net saving a	435	406	29	622	503	119	854	690	164	2166	1888	278
Total Current Disbursements and Net Saving	1794	1374	420	3253	2169	1084	5137	3357	1780	10109	6693	3416

	1984 TOTAL	1984 Non-Financial	1984 Financial	1985 TOTAL	1985 Non-Financial	1985 Financial	1986 TOTAL	1986 Non-Financial	1986 Financial
Receipts									
1 Operating surplus	11593	12347	-754	32880	35443	-2563	41245	46431	-5186
2 Property and entrepreneurial income	10950	2798	8152	26582	6493	20089	33463	6692	26771
A Withdrawals from quasi-corporate enterprises	...	...	...	...	...	...	...	...	...
B Interest	10139	2043	8096	23845	3833	20012	31306	4837	26469
C Dividends	768	711	57	2637	2560	77	1962	1660	302
D Net land rent and royalties	45	45	-	99	99	-	196	196	-
3 Current transfers	2552	2092	460	7402	6269	1133	7805	6421	1384
A Casualty insurance claims	627	221	406	1718	619	1099	2068	716	1352
B Casualty insurance premiums, net, due to be received by insurance companies	...	...	...	...	...	...	...	...	...
C Current transfers from the rest of the world	...	...	...	...	...	...	...	...	...
D Other transfers except imputed	1737	1737	-	5460	5460	-	5324	5324	-
E Imputed unfunded employee pension and welfare contributions	188	134	54	224	190	34	413	381	32
Total Current Receipts	25094	17236	7858	66865	48206	18659	82516	59544	22972
Disbursements									
1 Property and entrepreneurial income	16356	9791	6565	41973	27438	14535	47584	31765	15819
A Withdrawals from quasi-corporations	...	...	...	...	...	...	...	...	...
B Interest	12673	6247	6426	29490	15343	14147	33987	18836	15151
C Dividends	1933	1795	138	6959	6571	388	7139	6470	669
D Net land rent and royalties	1748	1748	-	5524	5524	-	6460	6460	-
2 Direct taxes and other current transfers n.e.c. to general government	1830	1597	233	3907	3036	871	11386	10348	1038
A Direct taxes	1575	1343	232	3422	2555	867	10963	9930	1033
B Fines, fees, penalties and other current transfers n.e.c.	255	254	1	485	481	4	423	418	5

Peru

3.22 Corporate and Quasi-Corporate Enterprise Income and Outlay Account: Total and Sectors
(Continued)

Million Peruvian intis

	1984 TOTAL	1984 Non-Financial	1984 Financial	1985 TOTAL	1985 Non-Financial	1985 Financial	1986 TOTAL	1986 Non-Financial	1986 Financial
3 Other current transfers	956	466	490	2228	998	1230	3667	2138	1529
A Casualty insurance premiums, net	588	202	386	1562	500	1062	2063	771	1292
B Casualty insurance claims liability of insurance companies	...	...	...	...	...	...	...	...	...
C Transfers to private non-profit institutions	...	...	...	...	...	...	...	...	...
D Unfunded employee pension and welfare benefits	184	130	54	224	190	34	413	381	32
E Social assistance grants	...	...	...	...	...	...	...	...	...
F Other transfers n.e.c.	184	134	50	442	308	134	1191	986	205
G Transfers to the rest of the world	...	...	...	...	...	...	...	...	...
Net saving a	5950	5380	570	18755	16732	2023	19879	15293	4586
Total Current Disbursements and Net Saving	25094	17236	7858	66865	48206	18659	82516	59544	22972

a) Item 'Net saving' includes consumption of fixed capital.

3.23 Corporate and Quasi-Corporate Enterprise Capital Accumulation Account: Total and Sectors

Million Peruvian intis

	1980 TOTAL	1980 Non-Financial	1980 Financial	1981 TOTAL	1981 Non-Financial	1981 Financial	1982 TOTAL	1982 Non-Financial	1982 Financial	1983 TOTAL	1983 Non-Financial	1983 Financial
Finance of Gross Accumulation											
1 Gross saving	435	406	29	622	503	119	855	690	165	2166	1888	278
2 Capital transfers	47	12	35	97	15	82	141	31	110	760	287	473
Finance of Gross Accumulation	483	418	65	720	518	202	996	721	275	2926	2175	751
Gross Accumulation											
1 Gross capital formation	895	864	31	1752	1714	38	2962	2886	76	3806	3874	-68
A Increase in stocks	172	157	15	400	405	-5	491	480	11	59	239	-180
B Gross fixed capital formation	725	709	16	1352	1309	43	2473	2408	65	3745	3633	112
2 Purchases of land, net	1	-	1	7	1	6	4	-2	6	8	2	6
3 Purchases of intangible assets, net	...	...	...	...	...	...	...	...	...	...	...	...
4 Capital transfers	8	-	8	11	2	9	32	14	18	285	25	260
Net lending	-421	-446	25	-1050	-1198	148	-2002	-2177	175	-1174	-1725	551
Gross Accumulation	483	418	65	720	518	202	996	721	275	2926	2175	751

	1984 TOTAL	1984 Non-Financial	1984 Financial	1985 TOTAL	1985 Non-Financial	1985 Financial	1986 TOTAL	1986 Non-Financial	1986 Financial
Finance of Gross Accumulation								
1 Gross saving	5950	5380	570	18756	16732	2024	19879	15293	4586
2 Capital transfers	519	106	413	969	125	844	1515	220	1295
Finance of Gross Accumulation	6468	5486	982	19725	16857	2868	21395	15513	5882
Gross Accumulation								
1 Gross capital formation	7998	7526	472	33286	32245	1041	70234	68525	1709
A Increase in stocks	206	108	98	1248	1087	161	-496	-658	162
B Gross fixed capital formation	7792	7418	374	32038	31158	880	70709	69182	1546
2 Purchases of land, net	16	-4	20	15	-1	16	34	10	24
3 Purchases of intangible assets, net	...	...	...	...	...	...	...	...	...
4 Capital transfers	122	122	-	195	107	88	696	509	187
Net lending	1666	2157	491	13771	16404	1720	-49509	-53531	3902
Gross Accumulation	6468	5486	982	19725	16857	2868	21395	15513	5882

Peru

3.24 Corporate and Quasi-Corporate Enterprise Capital Finance Account: Total and Sectors

Million Peruvian intis

	1980 TOTAL	1980 Non-Financial	1980 Financial	1981 TOTAL	1981 Non-Financial	1981 Financial	1982 TOTAL	1982 Non-Financial	1982 Financial	1983 TOTAL	1983 Non-Financial	1983 Financial
Acquisition of Financial Assets												
1 Gold and SDRs	-19	-	-19	119	-	119	7	-	7	4	8	-4
2 Currency and transferable deposits	100	-38	138	131	12	119	-14	15	-29	540	91	449
3 Other deposits	465	-1	466	-263	-30	-233	891	86	805	1975	118	1857
4 Bills and bonds, short term	8	3	5	5	8	-3	21	-4	25	60	44	16
A Corporate and quasi-corporate, resident	8	3	5	5	8	-3	...	...	...	...	...	...
B Government	...	...	...	...	...	...	...	...	...	...	...	...
C Rest of the world	...	...	...	...	...	...	...	...	...	...	...	...
5 Bonds, long term	-19	-4	-15	145	1	144	77	3	74	-16	5	-21
6 Corporate equity securities	...	...	...	...	...	...	...	...	...	...	...	...
7 Short term loans, n.e.c.	176	-	176	981	4	977	681	81	600	2169	17	2152
8 Long term loans, n.e.c.	352	-	352	671	-	671	823	-	823	3233	-	3233
9 Trade credits and advances	...	...	...	...	...	...	...	...	...	...	...	...
10 Other receivables	106	59	47	405	177	228	699	376	323	4099	837	3262
11 Other assets	65	23	42	9	70	-61	127	90	37	-29	18	-47
Total Acquisition of Financial Assets	1234	42	1192	2204	242	1962	3313	647	2666	12130	1137	10993
Incurrence of Liabilities												
1 Currency and transferable deposits	347	-	347	399	-	399	511	-	511	2514	-	2514
2 Other deposits	491	-	491	844	-9	853	1308	3	1305	4084	5	4079
3 Bills and bonds, short term	76	-	76	-83	-	-83	19	-	19	2	-	2
4 Bonds, long term	11	4	7	31	-2	33	43	3	40	39	3	36
5 Corporate equity securities	...	...	...	...	...	...	...	...	...	...	...	...
6 Short-term loans, n.e.c.	-75	-3	-72	211	57	154	406	295	111	1410	186	1224
7 Long-term loans, n.e.c.	77	29	48	317	110	207	425	214	211	1085	279	806
8 Net equity of households in life insurance and pension fund reserves	...	...	...	...	...	...	...	...	...	...	...	...
9 Proprietors' net additions to the accumulation of quasi-corporations	...	...	...	...	...	...	...	...	...	...	...	...
10 Trade credit and advances	...	...	...	...	...	...	...	...	...	...	...	...
11 Other accounts payable	157	-34	191	333	200	133	660	467	193	2131	587	1544
12 Other liabilities	252	169	83	284	160	124	463	361	102	1443	1215	228
Total Incurrence of Liabilities	1336	165	1171	2334	516	1818	3835	1343	2492	12708	2275	10433
Net Lending	-102	-123	21	-131	-274	143	-522	-696	174	-577	-1138	561
Incurrence of Liabilities and Net Lending	1234	42	1192	2204	242	1962	3313	647	2666	12130	1137	10993

	1984 TOTAL	1984 Non-Financial	1984 Financial	1985 TOTAL	1985 Non-Financial	1985 Financial
Acquisition of Financial Assets						
1 Gold and SDRs	...	23	...	...	-77	...
2 Currency and transferable deposits	...	221	...	...	1108	...
3 Other deposits	...	127	...	...	2239	...
4 Bills and bonds, short term	...	78	...	...	-15	...
A Corporate and quasi-corporate, resident	...	...	...	...	...	...
B Government	...	...	...	...	...	...
C Rest of the world	...	...	...	...	...	...
5 Bonds, long term	...	19	...	...	3	...
6 Corporate equity securities	...	...	...	...	...	...
7 Short term loans, n.e.c.	...	34	...	...	133	...
8 Long term loans, n.e.c.	...	-	...	...	-	...
9 Trade credits and advances	...	...	...	...	...	...
10 Other receivables	...	2117	...	...	6954	...
11 Other assets	...	1454	...	...	1395	...
Total Acquisition of Financial Assets	...	4074	...	...	11739	...
Incurrence of Liabilities						
1 Currency and transferable deposits	...	...	...	...	...	...

Peru

3.24 Corporate and Quasi-Corporate Enterprise Capital Finance Account: Total and Sectors
(Continued)

Million Peruvian intis

	1984			1985		
	TOTAL	Non-Financial	Financial	TOTAL	Non-Financial	Financial
2 Other deposits	...	4	...	...	42	...
3 Bills and bonds, short term	...	-	...	...	-	...
4 Bonds, long term	...	6	...	...	48	...
5 Corporate equity securities	...	...	...	...	...	...
6 Short-term loans, n.e.c.	...	191	...	...	512	...
7 Long-term loans, n.e.c.	...	1563	...	...	4434	...
8 Net equity of households in life insurance and pension fund reserves	...	...	...	...	...	...
9 Proprietors' net additions to the accumulation of quasi-corporations	...	...	...	...	...	...
10 Trade credit and advances	...	...	...	...	...	...
11 Other accounts payable	...	2070	...	...	5495	...
12 Other liabilities	...	1828	...	...	4413	...
Total Incurrence of Liabilities	...	5663	...	...	14944	...
Net Lending	...	-1589	...	...	-3205	...
Incurrence of Liabilities and Net Lending	...	4074	...	...	11739	...

3.31 Household and Private Unincorporated Enterprise Production Account

Million Peruvian intis

	1970	1975	1977	1978	1979	1980	1981	1982	1983	1984	1985	1986
					Gross Output							
1 Output for sale	...	...	...	...	3117	5348	9538	15869	29067	64964	178425	346736
2 Non-marketed output	...	...	...	...	35	76	158	332	575	1059	3075	7755
Gross Output	...	...	...	...	3152	5424	9696	16201	29641	66023	181500	354490
					Gross Input							
Intermediate consumption	...	...	...	...	1293	2199	3819	6312	12023	27485	75742	130714
Subtotal: Value Added	...	...	...	...	1859	3225	5877	9890	17618	38538	105758	223776
1 Indirect taxes net liability of unincorporated enterprises	...	...	...	...	23	45	85	86	141	289	744	1311
A Indirect taxes	...	...	...	...	30	51	94	111	166	364	962	1560
B Less: Subsidies	...	...	...	...	7	6	9	25	25	75	218	249
2 Consumption of fixed capital	...	...	...	...	...	...	...	...	...	...	...	...
3 Compensation of employees	...	...	...	...	298	476	812	1401	2527	5022	12570	27943
4 Net operating surplus	...	...	...	...	1539	2704	4981	8402	14950	33227	92444	194522
Gross Input	...	...	...	...	3152	5424	9696	16201	29641	66023	181500	354490

3.32 Household and Private Unincorporated Enterprise Income and Outlay Account

Million Peruvian intis

	1970	1975	1977	1978	1979	1980	1981	1982	1983	1984	1985	1986
					Receipts							
1 Compensation of employees	...	...	...	...	983	1776	3290	5706	10703	21729	54395	116039
A Wages and salaries	...	...	...	...	893	1597	2932	5149	9567	19489	48590	103131
B Employers' contributions for social security	...	...	...	...	58	116	230	328	638	1154	3479	7425
C Employers' contributions for private pension & welfare plans	...	...	...	...	32	64	128	229	498	1086	2326	5482
2 Operating surplus of private unincorporated enterprises	...	...	...	...	1539	2704	4981	8402	14950	33227	92444	194522
3 Property and entrepreneurial income	...	...	...	...	103	191	493	864	1625	2858	7456	9505
A Withdrawals from private quasi-corporations	...	...	...	...	...	...	...	...	...	...	...	...
B Interest	...	...	...	...	52	118	395	683	956	1818	3515	4236
C Dividends	...	...	...	...	45	63	81	153	612	920	3625	4707
D Net land rent and royalties	...	...	...	...	6	9	16	27	57	120	317	562

Peru

3.32 Household and Private Unincorporated Enterprise Income and Outlay Account
(Continued)

Million Peruvian intis

	1970	1975	1977	1978	1979	1980	1981	1982	1983	1984	1985	1986
3 Current transfers	...	...	...	...	148	308	551	900	1693	3011	6647	14821
A Casualty insurance claims	...	...	...	...	2	4	5	11	32	79	153	266
B Social security benefits	...	...	...	...	85	162	307	526	1021	2112	4685	10504
C Social assistance grants	...	...	...	...	...	...	...	...	...	...	...	...
D Unfunded employee pension and welfare benefits	...	...	...	...	...	...	...	...	...	...	...	...
E Transfers from general government	...	...	...	...	...	...	...	...	...	...	...	...
F Transfers from the rest of the world	...	...	...	...	...	...	...	...	...	...	...	...
G Other transfers n.e.c.	...	...	...	...	61	142	239	363	640	820	1809	4051
Total Current Receipts	...	...	...	...	2773	4980	9314	15872	28972	60825	160943	334886
					Disbursements							
1 Final consumption expenditures	...	...	...	...	2131	3659	6738	11070	21099	45532	123412	254589
2 Property income	...	...	...	...	69	126	258	507	1054	1658	4433	4672
A Interest	...	...	...	...	68	123	252	498	1035	1620	3750	4505
B Net land rent and royalties	...	...	...	...	2	3	6	9	18	38	684	167
3 Direct taxes and other current transfers n.e.c. to government	...	...	...	...	136	236	486	728	1499	3069	7625	15575
A Social security contributions	...	...	...	...	90	179	358	557	1136	2240	5805	12908
B Direct taxes	...	...	...	...	41	48	108	134	231	540	1092	1393
Income taxes	...	...	...	...	...	...	...	...	...	...	...	...
Other	...	...	...	...	...	...	...	...	...	...	...	...
C Fees, fines and penalties	...	...	...	...	5	9	20	37	132	289	728	1274
4 Other current transfers	...	...	...	...	5	20	24	60	122	247	979	1912
A Net casualty insurance premiums	...	...	...	...	2	4	4	11	38	71	294	224
B Transfers to private non-profit institutions serving households	...	...	...	...	...	...	...	...	...	...	...	...
C Transfers to the rest of the world	...	...	...	...	...	...	...	...	...	...	...	...
D Other current transfers, except imputed	...	...	...	...	3	16	20	49	84	176	685	1688
E Imputed employee pension and welfare contributions	...	...	...	...	...	...	...	...	...	...	...	...
Net saving [a]	...	...	...	...	432	938	1807	3507	5197	10318	24493	58138
Total Current Disbursements and Net Saving	...	...	...	...	2773	4980	9314	15872	28972	60825	160943	334886

a) Item 'Net saving' includes consumption of fixed capital.

3.33 Household and Private Unincorporated Enterprise Capital Accumulation Account

Million Peruvian intis

	1970	1975	1977	1978	1979	1980	1981	1982	1983	1984	1985	1986
					Finance of Gross Accumulation							
1 Gross saving	...	...	...	...	432	938	1807	3507	5197	10318	24493	58138
2 Capital transfers	...	...	...	...	9	8	11	16	78	89	596	-
Total Finance of Gross Accumulation	...	...	...	...	440	947	1819	3523	5276	10407	25089	58138
					Gross Accumulation							
1 Gross Capital Formation	...	...	...	...	250	566	1246	2067	2982	6010	6396	9975
A Increase in stocks	...	...	...	...	-5	67	176	174	112	-426	-833	9975
B Gross fixed capital formation	...	...	...	...	255	499	1071	1893	2870	6436	7229	-
2 Purchases of land, net	...	...	...	...	-1	-8	-6	-3	-7	-11	4	-22
3 Purchases of intangibles, net	...	...	...	...	...	...	...	...	...	...	...	...
4 Capital transfers	...	...	...	...	1	3	3	-	-	-	-	-
Net lending	...	...	...	...	190	386	575	1460	2300	4408	18689	48185
Total Gross Accumulation	...	...	...	...	440	947	1819	3523	5276	10407	25089	58138

Peru

3.51 External Transactions: Current Account: Detail

Million Peruvian intis

	1970	1975	1977	1978	1979	1980	1981	1982	1983	1984	1985	1986
Payments to the Rest of the World												
1 Imports of goods and services	...	...	...	...	666	1329	2378	3829	6224	10794	30304	51742
2 Factor income to the rest of the world	...	...	...	...	232	354	516	795	2031	4687	12172	12565
A Compensation of employees	...	...	...	...	4	5	11	28	69	118	251	300
B Property and entrepreneurial income	...	...	...	...	228	349	505	767	1961	4569	11921	12265
3 Current transfers to the rest of the world	...	...	...	...	1	3	4	5	16	47	207	205
4 Surplus of the nation on current transactions	...	...	...	...	147	-155	-844	-1413	-1669	-751	74	-17636
Payments to the Rest of the World, and Surplus of the Nation on Current Transfers	...	...	...	...	1046	1531	2053	3216	6602	14777	42757	46876
Receipts From The Rest of the World												
1 Exports of goods and services	...	...	...	...	968	1332	1735	2806	5880	13486	39611	43708
2 Factor income from the rest of the world	...	...	...	...	21	76	101	117	257	709	1945	1942
A Compensation of employees	...	...	...	...	6	9	15	31	72	165	546	703
B Property and entrepreneurial income	...	...	...	...	15	67	86	86	185	544	1399	1239
3 Current transfers from the rest of the world	...	...	...	...	57	123	216	294	464	582	1202	1226
Receipts from the Rest of the World on Current Transfers	...	...	...	...	1046	1531	2053	3216	6602	14777	42757	46876

3.52 External Transactions: Capital Accumulation Account

Million Peruvian intis

	1970	1975	1977	1978	1979	1980	1981	1982	1983	1984	1985	1986
Finance of Gross Accumulation												
1 Surplus of the nation on current transactions	...	...	...	...	147	-155	-844	-1413	-1669	-751	74	-17636
2 Capital transfers from the rest of the world	...	...	...	...	13	17	32	63	490	470	1123	601
Total Finance of Gross Accumulation	...	...	...	...	160	-138	-812	-1350	-1179	-281	1197	-17035
Gross Accumulation												
1 Capital transfers to the rest of the world	...	...	...	...	...	...	...	...	...	...	...	...
2 Purchases of intangible assets, n.e.c., net, from the rest of the world	...	...	...	...	...	...	...	...	...	...	...	...
Net lending to the rest of the world	...	...	...	...	...	...	...	...	...	...	...	...
Total Gross Accumulation	...	...	...	...	160	-138	-812	-1350	-1179	-281	1197	-17035

3.53 External Transactions: Capital Finance Account

Million Peruvian intis

	1970	1975	1977	1978	1979	1980	1981	1982	1983	1984	1985	1986
Acquisitions of Foreign Financial Assets												
1 Gold and SDR's	...	...	...	...	...	...	...	...	...	...	...	...
2 Currency and transferable deposits	...	...	...	...	81	62	-9	185	741	...	...	...
3 Other deposits	...	...	...	...	-44	-3	-2	-213	128	...	...	...
4 Bills and bonds, short term	...	...	...	...	-	-	11	-19	-	...	...	...
5 Bonds, long term	...	...	...	...	-	-	-	-	-	...	...	...
6 Corporate equity securities	...	...	...	...	72	68	123	88	174	...	...	...
7 Short-term loans, n.e.c.	...	...	...	...	-103	-31	-13	641	-541	...	...	...
8 Long-term loans	...	...	...	...	149	202	211	1243	1821	...	...	...
9 Prporietors' net additions to accumulation of quasi-corporate, non-resident enterprises	...	...	...	...	...	...	...	...	...	...	...	...
10 Trade credit and advances	...	...	...	...	...	...	...	...	...	...	...	...
11 Other	...	...	...	...	4	100	41	21	52	...	...	...
Total Acquisitions of Foreign Financial Assets	...	...	...	...	160	397	362	1947	2374	...	...	...
Incurrence of Foreign Liabilities												
1 Currency and transferable deposits	...	...	...	...	207	-19	119	7	3	...	...	...

Peru

3.53 External Transactions: Capital Finance Account
(Continued)

Million Peruvian intis

		1970	1975	1977	1978	1979	1980	1981	1982	1983	1984	1985	1986
2	Other deposits	...	...	...	...	111	339	-345	258	205	...	...	...
3	Bills and bonds, short term	...	...	...	...	-	-	-	-	-	...	...	...
4	Bonds, long term	...	...	...	...	1	1	-	-2	6	...	...	...
5	Corporate equity securities	...	...	...	...	8	7	5	31	72	...	...	...
6	Short-term loans, n.e.c.	...	...	...	...	-	-1	-1	-1	-10	...	...	...
7	Long-term loans	...	...	...	...	4	5	-13	13	-9	...	...	...
8	Non-resident proprietors' net additions to accumulation of resident quasi-corporate enterprises	...	...	...	...	...	...	...	...	...	...	...	...
9	Trade credit and advances	...	...	...	...	...	...	...	...	...	...	...	...
10	Other	...	...	...	...	35	42	46	118	552	...	...	...
	Total Incurrence of Liabilities	...	...	...	...	364	374	-188	425	820	...	...	...
	Net Lending	...	...	...	...	-204	23	550	1522	1554	...	...	...
	Total Incurrence of Liabilities and Net Lending	...	...	...	...	160	397	362	1947	2374	...	...	...

4.1 Derivation of Value Added by Kind of Activity, in Current Prices

Million Peruvian intis

		1980			1981			1982			1983		
		Gross Output	Intermediate Consumption	Value Added	Gross Output	Intermediate Consumption	Value Added	Gross Output	Intermediate Consumption	Value Added	Gross Output	Intermediate Consumption	Value Added

All Producers

1	Agriculture, hunting, forestry and fishing	817	207	610	1466	368	1098	2311	602	1709	4672	1246	3426
	A Agriculture and hunting	776	195	581	1388	346	1042	2178	556	1622	4448	1171	3277
	B Forestry and logging												
	C Fishing	41	12	29	78	22	56	133	46	87	224	75	149
2	Mining and quarrying	1096	191	905	1576	319	1257	2430	557	1873	4751	1162	3589
	A Coal mining [a]	...	...	...	...	...	...	...	...	...	...	...	...
	B Crude petroleum and natural gas production	660	54	606	1078	92	986	1694	156	1538	2876	318	2558
	C Metal ore mining [a]	436	137	299	498	227	271	736	401	335	1875	844	1031
	D Other mining												
3	Manufacturing	4162	2956	1206	6794	4838	1956	10756	7439	3317	19916	13850	6066
	A Manufacture of food, beverages and tobacco	1113	797	316	2060	1453	607	3198	2212	986	6356	4507	1849
	B Textile, wearing apparel and leather industries	730	448	282	1049	618	431	1468	899	569	2109	1392	717
	C Manufacture of wood and wood products, including furniture	163	90	73	259	137	122	454	250	204	813	446	367
	D Manufacture of paper and paper products, printing and publishing	215	129	86	361	214	147	497	278	219	850	528	322
	E Manufacture of chemicals and chemical petroleum, coal, rubber and plastic products	747	776	-29	1286	1357	-71	2233	2159	74	4663	3962	701
	F Manufacture of non-metallic mineral products, except products of petroleum and coal	129	66	63	254	121	133	438	208	230	916	405	511
	G Basic metal industries	549	327	222	650	404	246	977	625	352	2200	1455	745
	H Manufacture of fabricated metal products, machinery and equipment	425	267	158	722	455	267	1232	693	539	1596	973	623
	I Other manufacturing industries	91	56	35	153	79	74	259	115	144	413	182	231
4	Electricity, gas and water	74	20	51	152	41	111	287	96	191	484	214	270
5	Construction	777	435	342	1590	853	737	3130	1541	1589	4941	2769	2172
6	Wholesale and retail trade, restaurants and hotels	1656	596	1060	3030	1098	1932	4981	1850	3131	9545	3400	6145
	A Wholesale and retail trade	1234	415	819	2227	764	1463	3527	1301	2225	6538	2207	4331
	B Restaurants and hotels	422	181	241	803	334	469	1454	549	906	3007	1193	1814
7	Transport, storage and communication	752	356	396	1375	663	712	2300	1211	1089	4323	2506	1817
8	Finance, insurance, real estate and business services	820	229	591	1649	411	1238	2973	725	2248	5279	1443	3836
	A Financial institutions	175	39	136	402	72	330	655	143	512	1253	316	937
	B Insurance	42	23	19	72	37	35	111	65	46	188	119	69
	C Real estate and business services	603	167	436	1175	302	873	2207	517	1690	3838	1008	2830
	Real estate, except dwellings	472	157	315	974	284	690	1875	481	1394	3283	930	2353

Peru

4.1 Derivation of Value Added by Kind of Activity, in Current Prices
(Continued)

Million Peruvian intis

	1980 Gross Output	1980 Intermediate Consumption	1980 Value Added	1981 Gross Output	1981 Intermediate Consumption	1981 Value Added	1982 Gross Output	1982 Intermediate Consumption	1982 Value Added	1983 Gross Output	1983 Intermediate Consumption	1983 Value Added
Dwellings	131	10	121	201	18	183	332	36	296	555	78	477
9 Community, social and personal services	321	79	242	671	148	523	1184	279	905	2286	536	1750
A Sanitary and similar services	...	...	...	...	...	...	...	...	...	...	...	...
B Social and related community services	109	30	79	215	52	163	396	91	305	837	182	655
Educational services	28	7	21	55	12	43	110	23	87	226	46	180
Medical, dental, other health and veterinary services	81	23	58	160	40	120	286	68	218	611	136	475
C Recreational and cultural services	212	49	163	456	96	360	788	188	600	1449	354	1095
D Personal and household services												
Total, Industries	10475	5072	5403	18303	8739	9564	30352	14300	16052	56197	27126	29071
Producers of Government Services	701	240	461	1273	356	917	2355	788	1567	4273	1253	3020
Other Producers	76	14	62	158	8	150	332	16	316	575	39	536
Total	11252	5326	5926	19734	9103	10631	33039	15104	17935	61045	28418	32627
Less: Imputed bank service charge	...	-118	118	...	-284	284	...	-404	404	...	-767	767
Import duties	160	...	160	312	...	312	419	...	419	705	...	705
Value added tax	...	...	...	...	...	...	...	...	...	...	...	...
Total [b]	11412	5444	5968	20046	9387	10659	33458	15508	17950	61750	29185	32565

	1984 Gross Output	1984 Intermediate Consumption	1984 Value Added	1985 Gross Output	1985 Intermediate Consumption	1985 Value Added
	\multicolumn{6}{c}{All Producers}
1 Agriculture, hunting, forestry and fishing	10964	2982	7982	27515	9276	18239
A Agriculture and hunting	10344	2760	7584	25645	8404	17241
B Forestry and logging						
C Fishing	620	222	398	1870	872	998
2 Mining and quarrying	10439	2737	7702	27642	8328	19314
A Coal mining [a]	...	...	...	...	...	...
B Crude petroleum and natural gas production	6808	775	6033	17862	2472	15390
C Metal ore mining [a]	3631	1962	1669	9780	5856	3924
D Other mining						
3 Manufacturing	47586	32727	14859	141482	93318	48164
A Manufacture of food, beverages and tobacco	15124	10655	4469	40191	27464	12727
B Textile, wearing apparel and leather industries	5341	3602	1739	17289	11269	6020
C Manufacture of wood and wood products, including furniture	1911	1032	879	5625	3039	2686
D Manufacture of paper and paper products, printing and publishing	2005	1197	838	5406	3362	2044
E Manufacture of chemicals and chemical petroleum, coal, rubber and plastic products	10538	9357	1181	33720	25566	8154
F Manufacture of non-metallic mineral products, except products of petroleum and coal	2008	862	1146	5553	2528	3025
G Basic metal industries	4814	3125	1689	14266	9686	4580
H Manufacture of fabricated metal products, machinery and equipment	4641	2466	2175	15962	8953	7009
I Other manufacturing industries	1174	431	743	3470	1451	2019
4 Electricity, gas and water	1198	374	824	3702	1155	2547

Peru

4.1 Derivation of Value Added by Kind of Activity, in Current Prices
(Continued)

Million Peruvian intis

	1984 Gross Output	1984 Intermediate Consumption	1984 Value Added	1985 Gross Output	1985 Intermediate Consumption	1985 Value Added
5 Construction	11117	6372	4745	29730	16363	13367
6 Wholesale and retail trade, restaurants and hotels	20605	7365	13240	57048	20777	36271
A Wholesale and retail trade	14245	4820	9425	39891	13928	25963
B Restaurants and hotels	6360	2545	3815	17157	6849	10308
7 Transport, storage and communication	9735	5469	4266	29169	16809	12360
8 Finance, insurance, real estate and business services	11416	3298	8118	30549	9803	20746
A Financial institutions	2911	685	2226	8471	1561	6910
B Insurance	393	250	143	1344	873	471
C Real estate and business services	8112	2363	5749	20734	7369	13365
Real estate, except dwellings	7196	2235	4961	18907	7018	11889
Dwellings	916	128	788	1827	351	1476
9 Community, social and personal services	5084	1164	3920	14453	3443	11010
A Sanitary and similar services	...	...	...	...	...	...
B Social and related community services	1861	368	1493	5061	1117	3944
Educational services	584	113	471	1783	343	1440
Medical, dental, other health and veterinary services	1277	255	1022	3278	774	2504
C Recreational and cultural services	3223	796	2427	9392	2326	7066
D Personal and household services						
Total, Industries	128144	62488	65656	361290	179272	182018
Producers of Government Services	8493	2055	6438	20599	5638	14961
Other Producers	1059	84	975	3075	471	2604
Total	137696	64627	73069	384964	185381	199583
Less: Imputed bank service charge	...	-1624	1624	...	-5888	5888
Import duties	1400	...	1400	3994	...	3994
Value added tax	...	...	...	...	...	...
Total b	139096	66251	72845	388958	191269	197689

a) 'Coal mining' is included in 'Other mining'.
b) Data for this table have not been revised, therefore, data for some years are not comparable with those of other tables.

4.2 Derivation of Value Added by Kind of Activity, in Constant Prices

Million Peruvian intis

	1980 Gross Output	1980 Intermediate Consumption	1980 Value Added	1981 Gross Output	1981 Intermediate Consumption	1981 Value Added	1982 Gross Output	1982 Intermediate Consumption	1982 Value Added	1983 Gross Output	1983 Intermediate Consumption	1983 Value Added
At constant prices of: 1979 — All Producers
1 Agriculture, hunting, forestry and fishing	515	133	382	562	146	416	578	150	428	516	134	382
A Agriculture and hunting	488	125	363	532	137	395	544	140	404	492	127	365
B Forestry and logging												
C Fishing	27	8	19	30	9	21	34	10	24	24	7	17
2 Mining and quarrying	596	127	469	577	123	454	585	125	460	534	119	415
A Coal mining a	...	...	...	...	...	...	...	...	...	...	...	...
B Crude petroleum and natural gas production	327	35	292	317	34	283	319	34	285	270	29	241
C Metal ore mining a	269	92	177	260	89	171	266	91	175	264	90	174
D Other mining												

Peru

4.2 Derivation of Value Added by Kind of Activity, in Constant Prices
(Continued)

Million Peruvian intis

		1980			1981			1982			1983		
		Gross Output	Intermediate Consumption	Value Added	Gross Output	Intermediate Consumption	Value Added	Gross Output	Intermediate Consumption	Value Added	Gross Output	Intermediate Consumption	Value Added
					At constant prices of:1979								
3	Manufacturing	2706	1840	866	2751	1878	873	2706	1842	864	2295	1577	718
	A Manufacture of food, beverages and tobacco	778	551	227	813	581	232	823	586	237	758	549	209
	B Textile, wearing apparel and leather industries	430	290	140	404	273	131	387	261	126	316	208	108
	C Manufacture of wood and wood products, including furniture	100	60	40	101	61	40	107	65	42	88	53	35
	D Manufacture of paper and paper products, printing and publishing	134	83	51	135	82	53	111	65	46	103	60	43
	E Manufacture of chemicals and chemical petroleum, coal, rubber and plastic products	510	410	100	534	427	107	538	431	107	452	373	79
	F Manufacture of non-metallic mineral products, except products of petroleum and coal	79	43	36	84	46	38	82	44	38	72	30	00
	G Basic metal industries	358	196	162	337	184	153	343	184	159	303	162	141
	H Manufacture of fabricated metal products, machinery and equipment	267	174	93	293	191	102	269	176	93	169	111	58
	I Other manufacturing industries	50	33	17	50	33	17	46	30	16	34	22	12
4	Electricity, gas and water	54	15	39	58	16	42	62	17	45	52	14	38
5	Construction	478	276	202	542	317	225	556	326	230	440	259	181
6	Wholesale and retail trade, restaurants and hotels	1023	369	654	1102	413	689	1105	416	689	950	360	590
	A Wholesale and retail trade	782	253	529	855	293	562	853	294	559	695	237	458
	B Restaurants and hotels	241	116	125	247	120	127	252	122	130	255	123	132
7	Transport, storage and communication	467	231	236	496	245	251	493	245	248	457	227	230
8	Finance, insurance, real estate and business services	535	149	386	571	160	411	572	162	410	543	152	391
	A Financial institutions	123	25	98	136	28	108	146	32	114	151	34	117
	B Insurance	25	14	11	24	13	11	21	13	8	17	12	5
	C Real estate and business services	387	110	277	411	119	292	405	117	288	375	106	269
	Real estate, except dwellings	292	104	188	315	113	202	307	111	196	276	100	176
	Dwellings	95	6	89	96	6	90	98	6	92	99	6	93
9	Community, social and personal services	176	49	127	186	52	134	185	53	132	176	48	128
	A Sanitary and similar services	...	...	...	...	...	...	...	...	...	...	...	...
	B Social and related community services	63	20	43	66	21	45	67	22	45	66	20	46
	Educational services	17	4	13	17	4	13	17	4	13	18	5	13
	Medical, dental, other health and veterinary services	46	16	30	49	17	32	50	18	32	48	15	33
	C Recreational and cultural services	113	29	84	120	31	89	118	31	87	110	28	82
	D Personal and household services												
	Total, Industries	6550	3189	3361	6845	3350	3495	6842	3336	3506	5963	2890	3073
	Producers of Government Services	388	155	233	381	141	240	430	188	242	393	135	258
	Other Producers	42	9	33	38	4	34	39	4	35	41	4	37
	Total	6980	3353	3627	7264	3495	3769	7311	3528	3783	6397	3029	3368
	Less: Imputed bank service charge	...	-82	82	...	-89	89	...	-90	90	...	-98	98
	Import duties	102	...	102	128	...	128	124	...	124	76	...	76
	Value added tax	...	...	...	...	...	...	...	...	...	...	...	...
	Total b	7082	3435	3647	7392	3584	3808	7435	3618	3817	6473	3127	3346

Peru

4.2 Derivation of Value Added by Kind of Activity, in Constant Prices

Million Peruvian intis

	1984 Gross Output	1984 Intermediate Consumption	1984 Value Added	1985 Gross Output	1985 Intermediate Consumption	1985 Value Added
		At constant prices of:1979 — All Producers				
1 Agriculture, hunting, forestry and fishing	577	150	427	595	155	440
A Agriculture and hunting	542	140	402	555	143	412
B Forestry and logging						
C Fishing	35	10	25	40	12	28
2 Mining and quarrying	559	124	435	588	133	455
A Coal mining [a]	...	...	...	...	...	...
B Crude petroleum and natural gas production	286	31	255	292	32	260
C Metal ore mining [a]	273	93	180	296	101	195
D Other mining						
3 Manufacturing	2419	1662	757	2530	1721	809
A Manufacture of food, beverages and tobacco	781	565	216	792	567	225
B Textile, wearing apparel and leather industries	347	230	117	385	255	130
C Manufacture of wood and wood products, including furniture	91	55	36	92	56	36
D Manufacture of paper and paper products, printing and publishing	102	59	43	95	55	40
E Manufacture of chemicals and chemical petroleum, coal, rubber and plastic products	488	401	87	507	406	101
F Manufacture of non-metallic mineral products, except products of petroleum and coal	69	37	32	65	35	30
G Basic metal industries	331	177	154	351	187	164
H Manufacture of fabricated metal products, machinery and equipment	175	115	60	207	136	71
I Other manufacturing industries	35	23	12	36	24	12
4 Electricity, gas and water	52	14	38	55	15	40
5 Construction	443	260	183	399	234	165
6 Wholesale and retail trade, restaurants and hotels	955	351	604	960	343	617
A Wholesale and retail trade	691	223	468	689	213	476
B Restaurants and hotels	264	128	136	271	130	141
7 Transport, storage and communication	459	228	231	463	229	234
8 Finance, insurance, real estate and business services	543	151	392	593	152	441
A Financial institutions	148	33	115	175	27	148
B Insurance	17	11	6	21	14	7
C Real estate and business services	378	107	271	397	111	286
Real estate, except dwellings	277	101	176	294	105	189
Dwellings	101	6	95	103	6	97
9 Community, social and personal services	180	47	133	187	48	139
A Sanitary and similar services	...	...	...	...	...	...
B Social and related community services	67	18	49	69	18	51
Educational services	19	5	14	20	5	15
Medical, dental, other health and veterinary services	48	13	35	49	13	36
C Recreational and cultural services	113	29	84	118	30	88
D Personal and household services						

Peru

4.2 Derivation of Value Added by Kind of Activity, in Constant Prices
(Continued)

Million Peruvian intis

	1984 Gross Output	1984 Intermediate Consumption	1984 Value Added	1985 Gross Output	1985 Intermediate Consumption	1985 Value Added
			At constant prices of: 1979			
Total, Industries	6187	2987	3200	6370	3030	3340
Producers of Government Services	375	97	278	371	94	277
Other Producers	43	4	39	47	8	39
Total	6605	3088	3517	6788	3132	3656
Less: Imputed bank service charge	...	-88	88	...	-121	121
Import duties	77	...	77	60	...	60
Value added tax	...	...	...	...	...	...
Total [b]	6682	3176	3506	6848	3253	3595

a) 'Coal mining' is included in 'Other mining'.
b) Data for this table have not been revised, therefore, data for some years are not comparable with those of other tables.

4.3 Cost Components of Value Added

Million Peruvian intis

	1980 Compensation of Employees	1980 Capital Consumption	1980 Net Operating Surplus	1980 Indirect Taxes	1980 Less: Subsidies Received	1980 Value Added	1981 Compensation of Employees	1981 Capital Consumption	1981 Net Operating Surplus	1981 Indirect Taxes	1981 Less: Subsidies Received	1981 Value Added
					All Producers							
1 Agriculture, hunting, forestry and fishing	129	16	464	1	...	610	223	29	845	1	...	1098
A Agriculture and hunting	118	10	452	1		581	202	18	821	1		1042
B Forestry and logging												
C Fishing	11	6	12	...	...	29	21	11	24	...		56
2 Mining and quarrying	89	37	690	89	...	905	162	70	933	92	...	1257
A Coal mining [a]	...	...	...	...	...	...	...	...	...	...	...	...
B Crude petroleum and natural gas production	21	1	531	53	...	606	46	35	847	58	...	986
C Metal ore mining [a]	68	36	159	36		299	116	35	86	34		271
D Other mining												
3 Manufacturing	343	101	494	341	73	1206	553	148	794	507	46	1956
A Manufacture of food, beverages and tobacco	81	25	156	98	44	316	134	42	300	146	15	607
B Textile, wearing apparel and leather industries	53	18	189	37	15	282	79	22	300	46	16	431
C Manufacture of wood and wood products, including furniture	14	3	53	4	1	73	23	5	89	6	1	122
D Manufacture of paper and paper products, printing and publishing	22	5	55	4	-	86	36	11	92	8	...	147
E Manufacture of chemicals and chemical petroleum, coal, rubber and plastic products	56	15	-224	127	3	-29	92	21	-403	225	6	-71
F Manufacture of non-metallic mineral products, except products of petroleum and coal	16	5	37	8	3	63	25	7	93	10	2	133
G Basic metal industries	36	15	137	35	1	222	65	23	131	29	2	246
H Manufacture of fabricated metal products, machinery and equipment	59	14	62	26	3	158	90	15	133	33	4	267
I Other manufacturing industries	6	1	29	2	3	35	9	2	59	4	-	74
4 Electricity, gas and water	27	13	6	5	-	51	58	25	17	11	...	111
5 Construction	114	20	201	7	...	342	197	42	487	11	...	737
6 Wholesale and retail trade, restaurants and hotels	186	12	871	63	72	1060	348	23	1552	122	113	1932
A Wholesale and retail trade	163	7	661	60	72	819	310	14	1134	118	113	1463
B Restaurants and hotels	23	5	210	3	...	241	38	9	418	4		469
7 Transport, storage and communication	108	57	215	18	2	396	201	98	385	34	6	712
8 Finance, insurance, real estate and business services	144	46	382	23	4	591	284	84	828	45	3	1238
A Financial institutions	77	6	51	5	3	136	160	8	153	11	2	330
B Insurance	6	-	7	6	...	19	11	1	11	12	...	35
C Real estate and business services	61	40	324	12	1	436	113	75	664	22	1	873
Real estate, except dwellings	61	28	216	11	1	315	113	56	501	21	1	690

Peru

4.3 Cost Components of Value Added
(Continued)

Million Peruvian intis

	1980						1981					
	Compensation of Employees	Capital Consumption	Net Operating Surplus	Indirect Taxes	Less: Subsidies Received	Value Added	Compensation of Employees	Capital Consumption	Net Operating Surplus	Indirect Taxes	Less: Subsidies Received	Value Added
Dwellings	...	12	108	1	...	121	...	19	163	1	-	183
9 Community, social and personal services	126	12	98	8	2	242	245	22	238	20	2	523
A Sanitary and similar services	...	...	...	...	...	...	...	...	...	...	...	...
B Social and related community services	55	4	20	2	2	79	110	5	46	4	2	163
Educational services	21	1	...	1	2	21	42	1	1	1	2	43
Medical, dental, other health and veterinary services	34	3	20	1	...	58	68	4	45	3	...	120
C Recreational and cultural services	71	8	78	6	...	163	135	17	192	16	...	360
D Personal and household services					...						...	
Total, Industries	1266	314	3421	555	153	5403	2271	541	6079	843	170	9564
Producers of Government Services	446	4	...	11	-	461	872	5	-	40	...	917
Other Producers	60	2	...	...	...	62	143	6	...	1	...	150
Total	1772	320	3421	566	153	5926	3286	552	6079	884	170	10631
Less: Imputed bank service charge	...	...	118	...	...	118	...	...	284	...	...	284
Import duties	...	...	...	160	...	160	...	...	...	312	...	312
Value added tax	...	...	...	...	...	...	...	...	...	...	...	...
Total [b]	1772	320	3303	726	153	5968	3286	552	5795	1196	170	10659

	1982						1983					
	Compensation of Employees	Capital Consumption	Net Operating Surplus	Indirect Taxes	Less: Subsidies Received	Value Added	Compensation of Employees	Capital Consumption	Net Operating Surplus	Indirect Taxes	Less: Subsidies Received	Value Added

All Producers

1 Agriculture, hunting, forestry and fishing	348	46	1314	1	...	1709	724	84	2617	1	...	3426
A Agriculture and hunting	310	28	1283	1	...	1622	665	55	2556	1	...	3277
B Forestry and logging					...						...	
C Fishing	38	18	31	...	...	87	59	29	61	...	...	149
2 Mining and quarrying	271	115	1365	122	...	1873	505	304	2588	192	...	3589
A Coal mining [a]	...	...	...	...	...	...	...	...	...	...	...	...
B Crude petroleum and natural gas production	81	63	1294	100	...	1538	194	173	2020	171	...	2558
C Metal ore mining [a]	190	52	71	22	...	335	311	131	568	21	...	1031
D Other mining					...						...	
3 Manufacturing	941	239	1281	926	70	3317	1678	507	2425	1576	120	6066
A Manufacture of food, beverages and tobacco	222	70	474	234	14	986	372	143	990	373	29	1849
B Textile, wearing apparel and leather industries	134	34	380	43	22	569	243	81	375	58	40	717
C Manufacture of wood and wood products, including furniture	40	9	150	7	2	204	72	17	272	9	3	367
D Manufacture of paper and paper products, printing and publishing	61	16	122	20	...	219	99	24	172	27	...	322
E Manufacture of chemicals and chemical petroleum, coal, rubber and plastic products	162	33	-518	412	15	74	328	66	-516	852	29	701
F Manufacture of non-metallic mineral products, except products of petroleum and coal	47	13	144	29	3	230	75	41	366	30	1	511
G Basic metal industries	98	37	181	40	4	352	160	89	461	40	5	745
H Manufacture of fabricated metal products, machinery and equipment	162	24	251	112	10	539	303	39	153	141	13	623
I Other manufacturing industries	15	3	97	29	...	144	26	7	152	46	-	231
4 Electricity, gas and water	142	45	-9	13	...	191	239	81	-68	20	2	270

Peru

4.3 Cost Components of Value Added
(Continued)

Million Peruvian intis

	1982						1983					
	Compensation of Employees	Capital Consumption	Net Operating Surplus	Indirect Taxes	Less: Subsidies Received	Value Added	Compensation of Employees	Capital Consumption	Net Operating Surplus	Indirect Taxes	Less: Subsidies Received	Value Added
5 Construction	359	82	1137	11	...	1589	530	130	1494	18	...	2172
6 Wholesale and retail trade, restaurants and hotels	580	39	2480	213	181	3131	1014	75	5039	267	250	6145
A Wholesale and retail trade	518	22	1659	207	181	2225	895	41	3387	258	250	4331
B Restaurants and hotels	62	17	821	6	-	906	119	34	1652	9	...	1814
7 Transport, storage and communication	337	164	540	57	9	1089	775	304	641	123	26	1817
8 Finance, insurance, real estate and business services	491	157	1482	119	1	2248	917	293	2455	171	...	3836
A Financial institutions	285	16	192	20	1	512	526	33	347	31	...	937
B Insurance	18	2	9	17	...	46	37	5	-4	31	...	69
C Real estate and business services	188	139	1281	82	...	1690	354	255	2112	109	...	2830
Real estate, except dwellings	188	108	1016	82	...	1394	354	203	1687	109	...	2353
Dwellings	...	31	265			296	...	52	425	...	...	477
9 Community, social and personal services	422	36	408	42	3	905	821	73	808	55	7	1750
A Sanitary and similar services	...	...	...	...	...	...	...	...	...	...	...	...
B Social and related community services	201	10	91	6	3	305	412	23	217	10	7	655
Educational services	85	2	2	1	3	87	173	7	4	3	7	180
Medical, dental, other health and veterinary services	116	8	89	5	-	218	239	16	213	7	...	475
C Recreational and cultural services	221	26	317	36	...	600	409	50	591	45	...	1095
D Personal and household services					...						...	
Total, Industries	3891	923	9998	1504	264	16052	7203	1851	17999	2423	405	29071
Producers of Government Services	1508	9	-	50	...	1567	2982	16	...	22	...	3020
Other Producers	303	12	...	1	...	316	516	19	...	1	...	536
Total	5702	944	9998	1555	264	17935	10701	1886	17999	2446	405	32627
Less: Imputed bank service charge	...	...	404	...	...	404	...	...	767	...	...	767
Import duties	...	...	...	419	...	419	...	...	...	705	...	705
Value added tax	...	...	...	...	...	...	...	...	...	...	...	...
Total [b]	5702	944	9594	1974	264	17950	10701	1886	17232	3151	405	32565

	1984						1985					
	Compensation of Employees	Capital Consumption	Net Operating Surplus	Indirect Taxes	Less: Subsidies Received	Value Added	Compensation of Employees	Capital Consumption	Net Operating Surplus	Indirect Taxes	Less: Subsidies Received	Value Added
					All Producers							
1 Agriculture, hunting, forestry and fishing	1391	207	6380	4	...	7982	3287	487	14457	8	...	18239
A Agriculture and hunting	1276	127	6179	2	...	7584	2986	289	13962	4	...	17241
B Forestry and logging					...						...	
C Fishing	115	80	201	2	...	398	301	198	495	4	...	998
2 Mining and quarrying	1087	476	5829	310	...	7702	2933	1358	14049	974	...	19314
A Coal mining [a]	...	...	...	...	...	...	...	...	...	...	...	...
B Crude petroleum and natural gas production	424	264	5083	262	...	6033	1153	700	12778	750	...	15390
C Metal ore mining [a]	663	212	746	48	...	1669	1780	658	1271	215	...	3924
D Other mining					...						...	

Peru

4.3 Cost Components of Value Added
(Continued)

Million Peruvian intis

		1984						1985				
	Compensation of Employees	Capital Consumption	Net Operating Surplus	Indirect Taxes	Less: Subsidies Received	Value Added	Compensation of Employees	Capital Consumption	Net Operating Surplus	Indirect Taxes	Less: Subsidies Received	Value Added
3 Manufacturing	3133	1293	7087	3704	358	14859	8008	3115	25240	13009	1208	48164
A Manufacture of food, beverages and tobacco	646	374	2737	822	110	4469	1577	760	8758	1960	328	12727
B Textile, wearing apparel and leather industries	451	176	1124	113	125	1739	1162	497	4606	231	476	6020
C Manufacture of wood and wood products, including furniture	122	58	685	18	4	879	315	143	2108	36	16	2586
D Manufacture of paper and paper products, printing and publishing	205	76	507	53	3	838	523	227	1199	107	12	2044
E Manufacture of chemicals and chemical petroleum, coal, rubber and plastic products	725	172	-1710	2055	61	1181	1909	433	-3029	9004	163	8154
F Manufacture of non-metallic mineral products, except products of petroleum and coal	126	114	850	62	6	1146	245	300	2369	132	21	3025
G Basic metal industries	329	194	1122	55	11	1689	843	509	3030	268	70	4580
H Manufacture of fabricated metal products, machinery and equipment	480	101	1259	372	37	2175	1274	211	4764	878	118	7009
I Other manufacturing industries	49	28	513	154	1	743	160	35	1435	393	4	2019
4 Electricity, gas and water	443	220	114	47	...	824	1023	705	683	136	...	2547
5 Construction	1055	292	3358	40	...	4745	2541	429	10321	76	...	13367
6 Wholesale and retail trade, restaurants and hotels	1888	159	10893	513	213	13240	3739	435	31467	1063	433	36271
A Wholesale and retail trade	1668	87	7396	487	213	9425	3243	240	21913	1000	433	25963
B Restaurants and hotels	220	72	3497	26	...	3815	496	195	9554	63	...	10308
7 Transport, storage and communication	1562	685	1798	259	38	4266	3213	1780	6884	536	53	12360
8 Finance, insurance, real estate and business services	2117	624	5019	358	...	8118	4019	1455	14403	869	-	20746
A Financial institutions	1308	88	775	55	...	2226	2042	220	4516	132	-	6910
B Insurance	74	12	-4	61	...	143	198	25	35	213	...	471
C Real estate and business services	735	524	4248	242	...	5749	1779	1210	9852	524	...	13365
Real estate, except dwellings	735	438	3546	242	...	4961	1779	1049	8537	524	...	11889
Dwellings	...	86	702	...	...	788	...	161	1315	...	...	1476
9 Community, social and personal services	1767	176	1860	126	9	3920	4178	487	6108	249	12	11010
A Sanitary and similar services	...	...	...	...	...	...	...	...	...	...	...	...
B Social and related community services	921	65	497	19	9	1493	2321	163	1437	35	12	3944
Educational services	444	18	12	6	9	471	1331	55	55	11	12	1440
Medical, dental, other health and veterinary services	477	47	485	13	...	1022	990	108	1382	24	...	2504
C Recreational and cultural services	846	111	1363	107	...	2427	1857	324	4671	214	...	7066
D Personal and household services					...						...	
Total, Industries	14443	4132	42338	5361	618	65656	32941	10251	123612	16920	1706	182018
Producers of Government Services	6291	95	...	52	...	6438	14754	87	...	120	...	14961
Other Producers	947	26	...	2	...	975	2530	70	...	4	...	2604
Total	21681	4253	42338	5415	618	73069	50225	10408	123612	17044	1706	199583
Less: Imputed bank service charge	...	...	1624	...	...	1624	...	...	5888	...	...	5888
Import duties	...	...	...	1400	...	1400	...	...	...	3994	...	3994
Value added tax	...	...	...	...	...	...	...	...	...	...	...	...
Total [b]	21681	4253	40714	6815	618	72845	50225	10408	117724	21038	1706	197689

a) 'Coal mining' is included in 'Other mining'.
b) Data for this table have not been revised, therefore, data for some years are not comparable with those of other tables.

Philippines

General note. The preparation of national accounts statistics in the Philippines is undertaken by the National Economic and Development Authority (NEDA), Manila. The official estimates with methodological notes are published in the annual NEDA National Income Series entitled 'The National Income Accounts'. An over-all revision was completed in 1976 and a detailed description of the framework, sources and methods used in national income estimation is found in 'Manual on the Philippine System of National Accounts: Framework, Sources and Methods' published in 1978 by NEDA. The estimates are generally in accordance with the classifications and definitions recommended in the United Nations System of National Accounts (SNA). In 1961, the first input-output study was published by the Office of Statistical Coordination and Standards. The following tables have been prepared from successive replies to the United Nations national accounts questionnaire. When the scope and coverage of the estimates differ for conceptual or statistical reasons from the definitions and classifications recommended in SNA, a footnote is indicated to the relevant tables.

Sources and methods:

(a) Gross domestic product. Gross domestic product is estimated mainly through the production approach.

(b) Expenditure on the gross domestic product. The expenditure approach is used to estimate all components of GDP by expenditure type except capital formation in machinery and equipment for which the commodity-flow approach is used. The commodity-flow approach and income-elasticity approach are also used for private consumption expenditure. Estimates of government consumption expenditure are taken from the Commission on Audit reports for national and local government and for the social security system from the Budget Commission and the two offices administering it. For personal consumption of goods, for which the statistics are available in quantity terms, the value of final consumption is obtained by multiplying consumption quantities by the appropriate retail prices. Consumption expenditure on each broad expenditure group is estimated in turn by using the commodity-flow method. Since the required data lag by at least a year, preliminary estimates are computed by using the income-elasticity approach. Bench-mark information on the levels and patterns of household expenditure are available from the family income and expenditure surveys for 1961, 1965 and 1971. Current data on supply are derived from production figures available from various sources such as censuses, surveys and concerned companies. The sources of data for increase in stocks include the integrated agricultural surveys and establishment surveys and censuses. For gross fixed capital formation, the net supply of durable equipment for domestic use is divided between consumption and capital formation by means of allocation ratios for each type of equipment. The 1969 survey of importers of durable equipment provided bench-mark data on importer-dealer ratios as well as trade and transport mark-up ratios. The ratios are updated by using the results of the annual trade establishments surveys. The primary sources of data for exports and imports of goods and services are the foreign trade statistics and the balance of payments. For the constant price estimates, wages and salaries of the government sector are extrapolated by an index of employment of government services. All the other components of GDP by expenditure type are deflated by appropriate price indexes.

(c) Cost-structure of the gross domestic product. Estimates of compensation of employees, operating surplus and depreciation are available from the annual surveys of establishments and reports of financial institutions and public utilities for the non-agricultural sectors and from studies on production costs for the agricultural sector. For depreciation, a global estimate for all sectors is derived by estimating the cost of replacement of existing stock by the use of the perpetual inventory method. The global estimate is then allocated to each sector, using a sectoral structure based on the reported levels of depreciation. The estimates of indirect taxes and subsidies are made on the basis of reports of the Commission on Audit, the Bureau of Internal Revenue, the Bureau of Customs, the Central Bank and other government agencies.

(d) Gross domestic product by kind of economic activity. The table of GDP by kind of economic activity is prepared at market prices, i.e., producers' values. The production approach is used to estimate value added of most industries. The income approach is used for producers of government services and a large part of private services. The expenditure approach is also used for construction. The sources used for the estimation of the agricultural sector are the 1971 census of agriculture, the integrated agricultural surveys which are conducted five times a year, the family income and expenditure surveys and data collected through administrative agencies and producers' associations. The value of agricultural and livestock production is obtained by multiplying the volume of output by the average prices received by the farmers. The cost ratios are obtained from cost-of-production studies and from the 1969 input-output tables. For fishery, the sources are the monthly reports from the operators and sustenance estimates based on growth-rates in selected municipalities. Estimates for mining are based on the annual reports from the Bureau of Mines, the surveys of establishments, the 1972 economic census and the financial statements of mining firms. For the organized sector of manufacturing, the sources of data include the economic census and the survey of establishments. For 5 out of 20 major industry groups, the commodity-flow approach is used, taking the supply and disposition ratios from the 1969 input-output tables. Basic data for electricity, gas and water are collected from concerned companies, government agencies and the surveys of establishments. Gross output of private construction is estimated on the basis of building construction statistics and building permits issued. Data for public construction are obtained from the annual report of the Commission on Audit and from quarterly questionnaires. Bench-mark estimates for trade are taken from the 1972 economic census. These are extrapolated by using the results of the surveys of trade establishments. An undercoverage allowance is made for trade activities not covered using employment data from the labour force survey and an estimate of value added per worker. The main sources of data for the transport sector are the 1972 economic census, the surveys of establishments and the financial reports of the concerned companies. Data for the financial sector are derived from financial statements compiled by the Central Bank. Bench mark estimates for the real estate sector are based on the results of the economic census and are extrapolated by the growth rates of real estate sales and mortgages. For the producers of government services, data are obtained from the annual report of the Commission on Audit. Bench-mark estimates for the private services are based on the economic census and are extrapolated by using appropriate price indexes for other years. For the domestic services, the value added is taken as the product of the number of persons employed and an estimate of value added per worker. For the constant price estimates, the value added of the agricultural and mining sectors are obtained by applying the base-year unit values to the volume of production. For the manufacturing, transport, financial and services sectors, value added is deflated by appropriate price indexes. Double deflation is used for electricity, gas and water, construction and trade.

1.1 Expenditure on the Gross Domestic Product, in Current Prices

Million Philippine pesos

	1970	1975	1977	1978	1979	1980	1981	1982	1983	1984	1985	1986
1 Government final consumption expenditure	3514	11115	14348	16127	18259	21191	24792	29215	29481	35567	42469	48553
2 Private final consumption expenditure	29552	76165	102626	118846	146577	178119	206942	234486	268188	403431	469133	474991
3 Gross capital formation	8303	33840	44369	51348	67687	81153	93261	96521	102526	91951	85402	82199
A Increase in stocks	1288	6708	7929	9043	11381	13160	13976	10495	7272	-8144	-4572	1225
B Gross fixed capital formation	7015	27132	36440	42305	56306	67993	79285	86026	95254	100095	89974	80974
Residential buildings	1278	4033	5974	6748	8854	11389	14783	15838	16954	24108	15164	16188
Non-residential buildings	904	3313	4937	5355	7242	9653	11207	13551	17656	19692	22368	11863
Other construction and land improvement etc.	417	4368	9489	10632	14475	16326	20017	21993	19751	20107	18696	18148
Other	4416	15418	16040	19570	25735	30625	33278	34644	40893	36188	33746	34775
4 Exports of goods and services	8096	21272	28925	32420	41460	53590	57806	56150	75267	117701	126571	155104
5 Less: Imports of goods and services	8236	29057	34754	41321	53558	68704	74359	79321	101138	118382	108506	116188
Statistical discrepancy a	289	1362	-1288	249	-2883	-699	-3184	3546	9772	10198	-5610	-17942
Equals: Gross Domestic Product	41518	114697	154226	177669	217542	264650	305258	340597	384096	540466	609459	626717

a) Item 'Statistical discrepancy' of increases in stocks, relates to the difference between the estimate of GDP through industrial origin approach and that of expenditure approach.

1.2 Expenditure on the Gross Domestic Product, in Constant Prices

Million Philippine pesos

	1970	1975	1977	1978	1979	1980	1981	1982	1983	1984	1985	1986
				At constant prices of:1972								
1 Government final consumption expenditure	4250	7263	7485	7710	7995	8294	8598	9145	8788	8255	8205	8551
2 Private final consumption expenditure	37468	46515	55147	58009	60818	59270	61617	63535	65348	66032	65977	66597
3 Gross capital formation	9929	18323	21121	22928	25493	26609	27220	26267	25119	14215	11124	10205
A Increase in stocks	1638	3349	3568	3893	4223	3872	3678	2580	2017	-1379	-702	124
B Gross fixed capital formation	8291	14974	17553	19035	21270	22737	23542	23687	23102	15594	11826	10081

Philippines

1.2 Expenditure on the Gross Domestic Product, in Constant Prices
(Continued)

Million Philippine pesos

	1970	1975	1977	1978	1979	1980	1981	1982	1983	1984	1985	1986
	\multicolumn{12}{c}{At constant prices of:1972}
Residential buildings	1519	2118	2696	2804	3044	3390	3869	3860	3710	3556	1928	1930
Non-residential buildings	1074	1740	2228	2225	2490	2873	2933	3302	3363	2905	2844	1414
Other construction and land improvement etc.	496	2294	4281	4406	5012	4860	5243	5359	4465	2985	2342	2161
Other	5202	8822	8348	9600	10724	11614	11497	11166	11064	6148	4712	4576
4 Exports of goods and services	8510	10220	14120	14657	15650	17741	17947	17486	19262	20846	19351	23560
5 Less: Imports of goods and services	10033	13276	14274	16116	18765	19377	18854	19510	21746	18175	13995	17555
Statistical discrepancy a	630	-608	-5132	-4404	-3229	31	-321	2076	3150	2754	-859	-588
Equals: Gross Domestic Product	50754	68437	78467	82784	87962	92567	96207	98999	99921	93927	89803	90770

a) Item 'Statistical discrepancy' of increases in stocks, relates to the difference between the estimate of GDP through industrial origin approach and that of expenditure approach.

1.3 Cost Components of the Gross Domestic Product

Million Philippine pesos

	1970	1975	1977	1978	1979	1980	1981	1982	1983	1984	1985	1986
1 Indirect taxes, net	3126	11161	13603	16851	22379	25759	25928	28665	34689	43920	48949	52329
A Indirect taxes	3292	11822	14059	17424	22967	26519	26705	29512	35608	44697	50216	53955
B Less: Subsidies	166	661	456	573	588	760	777	847	919	777	1267	1626
2 Consumption of fixed capital	3714	11304	14598	16759	20538	24543	30658	34664	39180	53749	67222	71682
3 Compensation of employees paid by resident producers to:	34678	92232	126025	144059	174626	214348	248672	277268	310227	442797	493288	502706
4 Operating surplus												
Equals: Gross Domestic Product	41518	114697	154226	177669	217543	264650	305258	340597	384096	540466	609459	626717

1.4 General Government Current Receipts and Disbursements

Million Philippine pesos

	1970	1975	1977	1978	1979	1980	1981	1982	1983	1984	1985	1986
	\multicolumn{12}{c}{Receipts}
1 Operating surplus	...	...	...	...	...	...	...	...	...	...	...	...
2 Property and entrepreneurial income	210	608	1355	1528	1891	2525	3404	4737	5801	7033	9317	12820
3 Taxes, fees and contributions	5032	16319	20357	25112	32125	37123	38255	41823	48499	62455	72091	78049
A Indirect taxes	3292	11822	14059	17424	22967	26519	26705	29512	35608	44697	50216	53955
B Direct taxes	1309	3432	4643	5712	6824	7912	8600	9061	9439	14281	18198	20187
C Social security contributions	431	1065	1655	1976	2334	2692	2950	3250	3452	3477	3677	3907
D Compulsory fees, fines and penalties	...	...	...	...	...	...	...	...	...	...	...	...
4 Other current transfers	95	301	154	265	208	240	281	407	624	948	2025	1915
Total Current Receipts of General Government	5337	17228	21866	26905	34224	39888	41940	46967	54924	70436	83433	92784
	\multicolumn{12}{c}{Disbursements}
1 Government final consumption expenditure	3514	11115	14348	16127	18259	21191	24792	29215	29481	35567	42469	48553
2 Property income	...	...	...	...	...	...	...	...	...	...	...	...
3 Subsidies	166	661	456	573	588	760	777	847	919	777	1267	1626
4 Other current transfers	698	1914	2397	3254	4279	4758	4869	6171	7921	13603	19662	24057
A Social security benefits	156	416	670	994	1083	1173	1418	1697	1992	2295	2350	2770
B Social assistance grants	...	...	...	...	...	...	...	...	...	...	...	...
C Other	542	1498	1727	2260	3196	3585	3451	4474	5930	11308	17312	21287
5 Net saving	959	3538	4665	6951	11098	13179	11502	10734	16604	20489	20035	18548
Total Current Disbursements and Net Saving of General Government	5337	17228	21866	26905	34224	39888	41940	46967	54924	70436	83433	92784

1.6 Current Income and Outlay of Households and Non-Profit Institutions

Million Philippine pesos

	1970	1975	1977	1978	1979	1980	1981	1982	1983	1984	1985	1986
	\multicolumn{12}{c}{Receipts}
1 Compensation of employees [a]	31864	86122	117905	134168	158292	193779	223531	247970	278068	416147	463849	470866
A From resident producers	31726	85384	116335	132035	154264	189058	217482	238595	265822	399752	444481	449609
B From rest of the world	138	738	1570	2133	4028	4721	6049	9375	12246	16395	19368	21257
2 Operating surplus of private unincorporated enterprises	...	...	...	...	...	...	...	...	...	...	...	...
3 Property and entrepreneurial income [a]	...	...	...	...	...	...	...	...	...	...	...	...

Philippines

1.6 Current Income and Outlay of Households and Non-Profit Institutions
(Continued)

Million Philippine pesos

	1970	1975	1977	1978	1979	1980	1981	1982	1983	1984	1985	1986
4 Current transfers	1242	3606	3964	4924	5952	6693	7473	8775	11546	11983	20936	29087
A Social security benefits	156	416	620	994	1083	1173	1418	1697	1992	2295	2350	2770
B Social assistance grants	527	1364	1550	1843	2373	2486	2460	3244	3952	6710	13120	15057
C Other	559	1826	1794	2089	2496	3034	3595	3834	5603	2978	5466	11260
Total Current Receipts	33106	89727	121869	139094	164244	200472	231004	256745	289615	428130	484785	499953

Disbursements

	1970	1975	1977	1978	1979	1980	1981	1982	1983	1984	1985	1986
1 Private final consumption expenditure	29552	76165	102626	118846	146577	178119	206942	234486	268188	403431	469133	474991
2 Property income	...	...	...	...	...	...	...	...	...	...	...	...
3 Direct taxes and other current transfers n.e.c. to general government	975	2494	4229	5046	6355	7202	7446	7808	8094	9577	13525	15419
A Social security contributions	431	1065	1635	1976	2334	2692	2950	3250	3452	3477	3677	3907
B Direct taxes	544	1429	2594	3070	4021	4510	4496	4558	4643	6100	9848	11512
C Fees, fines and penalties	...	...	...	...	...	...	...	...	...	...	...	...
4 Other current transfers	11	21	27	20	35	36	40	17	24	20	170	61
Statistical discrepancy	289	1362	-1268	249	-2952	-699	-3184	3546	9772	10198	-5610	-17942
5 Net saving	2279	9685	16255	14933	14229	15814	19760	10888	3537	4904	7567	27424
Total Current Disbursements and Net Saving	33106	89727	121869	139094	164244	200472	231004	256745	289615	428130	484785	499953

a) Item 'Property and entrepreneurial income' is included in item 'Compensation of employees'.

1.7 External Transactions on Current Account, Summary

Million Philippine pesos

	1970	1975	1977	1978	1979	1980	1981	1982	1983	1984	1985	1986
Payments to the Rest of the World												
1 Imports of goods and services	8236	29057	34754	41321	53556	68704	74359	79321	101138	118382	108506	116188
A Imports of merchandise c.i.f.	7371	26757	31017	37042	48144	61081	65816	69697	87448	106134	98582	106662
B Other	865	2300	3737	4279	5412	7623	8543	9624	13690	12248	9924	9526
2 Factor income to the rest of the world	896	2220	3443	4108	5104	7178	11800	17672	20990	35045	40985	38464
A Compensation of employees	18	56	41	32	44	65	71	69	74	20	19	122
B Property and entrepreneurial income	878	2164	3402	4076	5060	7113	11729	17603	20916	35025	40966	38342
3 Current transfers to the rest of the world	26	155	254	436	858	1135	1031	1247	2002	4618	4362	6291
4 Surplus of the nation on current transactions	-209	-6073	-5106	-7630	-9761	-13093	-15338	-25339	-26996	-14484	6253	33374
Payments to the Rest of the World and Surplus of the Nation on Current Transactions	8949	25359	33345	38235	49757	63924	71852	72901	97134	143561	160106	194317
Receipts From The Rest of the World												
1 Exports of goods and services	8096	21272	28925	32420	41460	53590	57806	56150	75267	117701	126571	155104
A Exports of merchandise f.o.b.	6608	16343	22994	24954	33506	42709	44378	42136	54609	88818	84126	95391
B Other	1488	4929	5931	7466	7954	10881	13428	14014	20658	28883	42445	59713
2 Factor income from rest of the world	199	1961	2472	3461	5593	7060	10170	12510	15640	21934	26044	26038
A Compensation of employees	138	738	1570	2133	4028	4721	6049	9375	12246	16395	19368	21257
B Property and entrepreneurial income	61	1223	902	1328	1565	2339	4121	3135	3394	5539	6676	4781
3 Current transfers from rest of the world	654	2126	1948	2354	2704	3274	3876	4241	6227	3926	7491	13175
Receipts from the Rest of the World on Current Transactions	8949	25359	33345	38235	49757	63924	71852	72901	97134	143561	160106	194317

1.8 Capital Transactions of The Nation, Summary

Million Philippine pesos

	1970	1975	1977	1978	1979	1980	1981	1982	1983	1984	1985	1986
Finance of Gross Capital Formation												
Gross saving	8094	27767	39263	43718	57924	68060	77923	71182	75530	77467	91655	115573
1 Consumption of fixed capital	3714	11304	14598	16759	20538	24543	30658	34664	39180	53749	67222	71682
2 Net saving	4380	16463	24665	26959	37386	43517	47265	36518	36350	23718	24433	43891
A General government	959	3538	4665	6951	11098	13179	11502	10734	16604	20489	20035	18548
B Corporate and quasi-corporate enterprises	1142	3240	3745	5075	12059	14524	16003	14896	16209	-1675	-3169	-2081

Philippines

1.8 Capital Transactions of The Nation, Summary
(Continued)

Million Philippine pesos

	1970	1975	1977	1978	1979	1980	1981	1982	1983	1984	1985	1986
C Other [a]	2279	9685	16255	14933	14229	15814	19760	10888	3537	4904	7567	27424
Less: Surplus of the nation on current transactions	-209	-6073	-5106	-7630	-9763	-13093	-15338	-25339	-26996	-14484	6253	33374
Finance of Gross Capital Formation	8303	33840	44369	51348	67687	81153	93261	96521	102526	91951	85402	82199
Gross Capital Formation												
Increase in stocks	1288	6708	7929	9043	11381	13160	13976	10495	7272	-8144	-4572	1225
Gross fixed capital formation	7015	27132	36440	42305	56306	67993	79285	86026	95254	100095	89974	80974
Gross Capital Formation	8303	33840	44369	51348	67687	81153	93261	96521	102526	91951	85402	82199

a) Item 'Other' of Net saving includes change in stocks which is mostly private.

1.10 Gross Domestic Product by Kind of Activity, in Current Prices

Million Philippine pesos

	1970	1975	1977	1978	1979	1980	1981	1982	1983	1984	1985	1986
1 Agriculture, hunting, forestry and fishing [a]	11863	33209	41982	47360	55543	61761	69391	76721	84546	139505	162519	163801
2 Mining and quarrying	1181	2000	2488	3333	5810	8095	6849	6106	7021	9714	11529	10198
3 Manufacturing	9780	28248	37392	43688	52144	64555	75151	83133	95172	137251	150523	154719
4 Electricity, gas and water	328	1057	1426	1669	2125	2761	3329	4042	5256	7980	10986	15184
5 Construction	1515	6813	11794	12591	16855	21311	26268	29302	30730	31209	27506	22685
6 Wholesale and retail trade, restaurants and hotels	6189	17171	24220	28638	36164	45322	53650	60888	71086	106367	125869	129282
7 Transport, storage and communication	1900	5834	8415	9894	12377	16444	19618	21376	24378	33820	38263	39078
8 Finance, insurance, real estate and business services	4182	10106	12861	15018	18312	22670	25017	28792	33048	34912	35194	37731
9 Community, social and personal services	1460	3428	4592	5252	6317	7670	9023	10516	11642	14257	16751	18179
Total, Industries	38398	107866	145170	167443	205647	250589	288295	320876	362879	515015	579140	590857
Producers of Government Services	2544	5573	7418	8619	9795	11493	13930	16389	17539	21254	26007	31753
Other Producers	576	1258	1639	1607	2101	2568	3032	3332	3678	4197	4312	4107
Subtotal	41518	114697	154226	177669	217543	264650	305258	340597	384096	540466	609459	626717
Less: Imputed bank service charge	...	...	...	...	...	...	...	...	...	...	...	...
Plus: Import duties	...	...	...	...	...	...	...	...	...	...	...	...
Plus: Value added tax	...	...	...	...	...	...	...	...	...	...	...	...
Equals: Gross Domestic Product	41518	114697	154226	177669	217543	264650	305258	340597	384096	540466	609459	626717

a) Item 'Agriculture, hunting, forestry and fishing' excludes hunting.

1.11 Gross Domestic Product by Kind of Activity, in Constant Prices

Million Philippine pesos

	1970	1975	1977	1978	1979	1980	1981	1982	1983	1984	1985	1986
	At constant prices of:1972											
1 Agriculture, hunting, forestry and fishing [a]	14821	18327	20770	21631	22606	23662	24608	25378	24845	25409	26252	27233
2 Mining and quarrying	1093	1445	1742	1809	2134	2236	2175	2016	1966	1755	1768	1558
3 Manufacturing	12367	17313	19672	21108	22239	23175	23959	24535	25108	23319	21541	21717
4 Electricity, gas and water	394	607	711	750	843	921	999	1084	1193	1342	1433	1547
5 Construction	1738	3958	5782	5944	6759	7139	7830	8079	7689	5866	4258	3382
6 Wholesale and retail trade, restaurants and hotels	7795	9781	11150	11987	12885	13664	14231	14672	15466	15540	15452	15728
7 Transport, storage and communication	2360	3610	4235	4501	4613	4827	5040	5165	5266	5032	4953	5084
8 Finance, insurance, real estate and business services	4767	6106	6725	7051	7506	8138	8032	8349	8698	6081	4950	5010
9 Community, social and personal services	1655	2402	2617	2732	2859	2991	3106	3209	3208	3018	2956	2970
Total, Industries	46990	63549	73404	77513	82444	86753	89980	92487	93438	87362	83563	84229
Producers of Government Services	3051	3940	4074	4251	4457	4700	5081	5339	5294	5585	5453	5811
Other Producers	713	948	989	1020	1061	1114	1146	1173	1188	980	787	730
Subtotal	50754	68437	78467	82784	87962	92567	96207	98999	99921	93927	89803	90770
Less: Imputed bank service charge	...	...	...	...	...	...	...	...	...	...	...	...
Plus: Import duties	...	...	...	...	...	...	...	...	...	...	...	...
Plus: Value added tax	...	...	...	...	...	...	...	...	...	...	...	...
Equals: Gross Domestic Product	50754	68437	78467	82784	87962	92567	96207	98999	99921	93927	89803	90770

a) Item 'Agriculture, hunting, forestry and fishing' excludes hunting.

Philippines

1.12 Relations Among National Accounting Aggregates

Million Philippine pesos

	1970	1975	1977	1978	1979	1980	1981	1982	1983	1984	1985	1986
Gross Domestic Product	41518	114697	154226	177669	217542	264650	305258	340597	384096	540466	609459	626717
Plus: Net factor income from the rest of the world	-697	-259	-971	-647	489	-118	-1630	-5162	-5350	-13111	-14941	-12426
Factor income from the rest of the world	199	1961	2472	3461	5593	7060	10170	12510	15640	21934	26044	26038
Less: Factor income to the rest of the world	896	2220	3443	4108	5104	7178	11800	17672	20990	35045	40985	38464
Equals: Gross National Product	40821	114438	153255	177022	218031	264532	303628	335435	378746	527355	594518	614291
Less: Consumption of fixed capital	3714	11304	14598	16759	20538	24543	30658	34664	39180	53749	67222	71682
Equals: National Income	37107	103134	138657	160263	197494	239989	272970	300771	339566	473606	527296	542609
Plus: Net current transfers from the rest of the world	628	1971	1694	1918	1846	2139	2845	2994	4225	-692	3129	6884
Current transfers from the rest of the world	654	2126	1948	2354	2704	3274	3876	4241	6227	3926	7491	13175
Less: Current transfers to the rest of the world	26	155	254	436	858	1135	1031	1247	2002	4618	4362	6291
Equals: National Disposable Income	37735	105105	140351	162181	199340	242128	275815	303765	343791	472914	530425	549493
Less: Final consumption	33066	87280	116974	134973	164836	199310	231734	263701	297669	438998	511602	523544
Statistical discrepancy	-289	-1362	1288	-249	2882	699	3184	-3546	-9772	-10198	5610	17942
Equals: Net Saving	4380	16463	24665	26959	37386	43517	47265	36518	36350	23718	24433	43891
Less: Surplus of the nation on current transactions	-209	-6073	-5106	-7630	-9763	-13093	-15338	-25339	-26996	-14484	6253	33374
Equals: Net Capital Formation	4589	22536	29771	34589	47149	56610	62603	61857	63346	38202	18180	10517

2.5 Private Final Consumption Expenditure by Type and Porpose, in Current Prices

Million Philippine pesos

	1970	1975	1977	1978	1979	1980	1981	1982	1983	1984	1985	1986
Final Consumption Expenditure of Resident Households												
1 Food, beverages and tobacco	17393	48735	60381	67746	82152	98022	114456	128533	147578	225744	264620	266116
A Food	15338	43327	55784	62468	75421	89974	105013	117475	135166	207966	243717	244488
B Non-alcoholic beverages	...	...	2309	2749	3665	4466	5269	6035	6858	9801	11494	11962
C Alcoholic beverages	...	...										
D Tobacco	906	2285	2288	2529	3066	3582	4174	5023	5554	8454	9409	9666
2 Clothing and footwear	1795	5407	6201	7087	8745	11078	12895	14656	16491	25213	28348	29103
3 Gross rent, fuel and power	3095	6713	10732	12469	15717	19702	23682	...	...	...	...	...
A Fuel and power	...	...	...	...	...	...	...	10315	12209	17947	21461	20902
B Other	...	...	...	...	...	...	...	...	...	...	...	...
4 Furniture, furnishings and household equipment and operation	1775	3656	7460	8722	10756	13146	14841	33785	38191	56597	65514	67237
A Household operation	712	1600	2455	3067	3900	4774	5511	23647	26946	40580	46607	47881
B Other	1063	2056	5005	5655	6856	8372	9330	10138	11245	16017	18907	19356
5 Medical care and health expenses	852	1828	2907	3332	4105	5059	5812	...	...	...	...	...
6 Transport and communication	764	1676	2720	3257	4415	5839	6790	7862	8835	13345	14866	14816
7 Recreational, entertainment, education and cultural services	1412	3123	4376	4813	6189	7663	8653	...	...	...	...	...
A Education	933	2057	2676	2975	3827	4756	5441	...	...	...	...	...
B Other	479	1066	1700	1838	2362	2907	3212	...	...	...	...	...
8 Miscellaneous goods and services	2466	5027	7841	11420	14498	17610	19813	...	...	...	...	...
A Personal care	753	1523	1794	2024	2535	3125	3579	...	...	...	...	...
B Expenditures in restaurants, cafes and hotels	...	...	...	...	...	...	...	...	...	...	...	...

Philippines

2.5 Private Final Consumption Expenditure by Type and Porpose, in Current Prices
(Continued)

Million Philippine pesos

	1970	1975	1977	1978	1979	1980	1981	1982	1983	1984	1985	1986
C Other	1713	3504	6047	9396	11963	14485	16234	...	...	...	...	...
Total Final Consumption Expenditure in the Domestic Market by Households, of which	29552	76165	102626	118846	146577	178119	206942	234486	268188	403431	469133	474995
Plus: Direct purchases abroad by resident households	...	...	...	...	...	...	...	...	...	...	...	...
Less: Direct purchases in the domestic market by non-resident households	...	...	...	...	...	...	...	...	...	...	...	...
Equals: Final Consumption Expenditure of Resident Households [a]	29552	76165	102626	118846	146577	178119	206942	234486	268188	403431	469133	474991

Final Consumption Expenditure of Private Non-profit Institutions Serving Households

	1970	1975	1977	1978	1979	1980	1981	1982	1983	1984	1985	1986
Equals: Final Consumption Expenditure of Private Non-profit Organisations Serving Households	...	...	...	...	...	...	...	...	...	...	...	...
Private Final Consumption Expenditure	29552	76165	102626	118846	146577	178119	206942	234486	268188	403431	469133	474991

a) Item 'Final consumption expenditure of resident households' includes consumption expenditure of private non-profit institutions serving households.

2.6 Private Final Consumption Expenditure by Type and Purpose, in Constant Prices

Million Philippine pesos

At constant prices of: 1967 (1970, 1975); 1972 (1977–1986)

Final Consumption Expenditure of Resident Households

	1970	1975	1977	1978	1979	1980	1981	1982	1983	1984	1985	1986
1 Food, beverages and tobacco	143126	175200	31158	32608	34030	35661	37138	38299	39416	40200	40299	40859
A Food	126514	154480	28666	29932	31230	32733	34061	35163	36221	36957	37061	37622
B Non-alcoholic beverages	...	...	1161	1275	1335	1399	1499	1518	1557	1590	1577	1586
C Alcoholic beverages	...	...										
D Tobacco	7394	8880	1331	1401	1465	1529	1578	1618	1638	1653	1661	1651
2 Clothing and footwear	13846	17460	2876	3008	3144	3295	3406	3493	3568	3599	3561	3545
3 Gross rent, fuel and power	25129	31370	5252	5501	5763	5946	6195	...	...	...	...	...
A Fuel and power	...	...	1521	1590	1663	1748	1816	1940	2010	2030	2050	2079
B Other	...	...	3731	3911	4100	4198	4379	...	...	...	...	...
4 Furniture, furnishings and household equipment and operation	13403	17170	7016	7357	7708	7991	8311	8452	8637	8660	8619	8647
A Household operation	5783	7400	4934	5171	5418	5579	5807	5910	6038	6057	6056	6082
B Other	7620	9770	2082	2186	2290	2412	2504	2542	2599	2603	2563	2565
5 Medical care and health expenses	6787	8580	1465	1536	1606	1689	1707	...	...	...	...	...
6 Transport and communication	6254	7990	1164	1223	1284	1357	1411	1448	1469	1488	1491	1504
7 Recreational, entertainment, education and cultural services	11023	14500	2207	2321	2437	2578	2687	...	...	...	...	...
A Education	7194	9470	1468	1543	1623	1719	1795	...	...	...	...	...
B Other	3829	5030	739	778	814	859	892	...	...	...	...	...
8 Miscellaneous goods and services	19152	23670	4009	4455	4846	4951	5141	...	...	...	...	...
A Personal care	5605	7100	943	986	1035	1085	1122	...	...	...	...	...
B Expenditures in restaurants, cafes and hotels	...	...	...	...	...	...	...	...	...	...	...	...

Philippines

2.6 Private Final Consumption Expenditure by Type and Purpose, in Constant Prices
(Continued)

Million Philippine pesos

	1970	1975	1977	1978	1979	1980	1981	1982	1983	1984	1985	1986
		1967			At constant prices of:		1972					
C Other	13547	16570	3066	3469	3811	3866	4019	...	...	...	...	...
Total Final Consumption Expenditure in the Domestic Market by Households, of which	238720	295940	55147	58009	60818	63468	65996	63535	65348	66032	65977	66597
Plus: Direct purchases abroad by resident households	...	...	...	...	...	...	...	...	...	...	...	...
Less: Direct purchases in the domestic market by non-resident households	...	...	...	...	...	...	...	...	...	...	...	...
Equals: Final Consumption Expenditure of Resident Households [a]	238720	295940	55147	58009	60818	63468	65996	63535	65348	66032	65977	66597

Final Consumption Expenditure of Private Non-profit Institutions Serving Households

Equals: Final Consumption Expenditure of Private Non-profit Organisations Serving Households	...	...	...	...	...	...	...	...	...	...	...	...
Private Final Consumption Expenditure	238720	295940	55147	58009	60818	63468	65996	63535	65348	66032	65977	66597

a) Item 'Final consumption expenditure of resident households' includes consumption expenditure of private non-profit institutions serving households.

2.17 Exports and Imports of Goods and Services, Detail

Million Philippine pesos

		1970	1975	1977	1978	1979	1980	1981	1982	1983	1984	1985	1986
	Exports of Goods and Services												
1	Exports of merchandise, f.o.b.	6608	16343	22994	24954	33506	42709	44378	42136	54609	88818	84126	95391
2	Transport and communication	273	975	1658	1562	1791	2357	2813	2120	2376	3548	5152	4504
	A In respect of merchandise imports	52	324	429	552	614	831	878	1059	1078	1114	1300	1245
	B Other	221	651	1229	1010	1177	1526	1935	1061	1298	2434	3852	3259
3	Insurance service charges	28	103	48	41	110	91	36	39	186	99	74	203
	A In respect of merchandise imports	23	44	37	25	21	8	13	21	10	-	-	-
	B Other	5	59	11	16	89	83	23	18	176	99	74	203
4	Other commodities	233	1799	1774	2842	2906	4308	5852	5724	9715	14830	21552	26870
5	Adjustments of merchandise exports to change-of-ownership basis	...	...	...	...	...	...	...	...	...	...	...	...
6	Direct purchases in the domestic market by non-residential households	557	747	1056	1523	1728	2380	2600	3792	5103	5847	9495	13197
7	Direct purchases in the domestic market by extraterritorial bodies	396	1305	1395	1498	1420	1745	2037	2339	3278	4559	6172	14939
	Total Exports of Goods and Services	8096	21272	28925	32420	41461	53590	57806	56150	75267	117701	126571	155104
	Imports of Goods and Services												
1	Imports of merchandise, c.i.f.	7371	26757	31017	37042	48146	61082	65815	69697	87448	106134	98582	106662
	A Imports of merchandise, f.o.b.	6651	24592	28550	34258	44892	57056	61911	64835	82234	100213	92659	98615
	B Transport of services on merchandise imports	685	2083	2396	2715	3180	3944	3779	4628	5120	5706	5792	7947
	By residents	53	329	434	559	621	842	899	1093	1048	1149	1320	1243
	By non-residents	632	1754	1962	2156	2559	3102	2880	3535	4072	4646	4472	6704
	C Insurance service charges on merchandise imports	35	82	71	69	74	82	125	204	94	126	132	100
	By residents	23	44	37	25	21	8	16	23	10	5	-	-

Philippines

2.17 Exports and Imports of Goods and Services, Detail
(Continued)

Million Philippine pesos

	1970	1975	1977	1978	1979	1980	1981	1982	1983	1984	1985	1986
By non-residents	12	38	34	44	53	74	109	211	84	121	132	100
2 Adjustments of merchandise imports to change-of-ownership basis	...	...	...	...	...	...	...	...	...	...	...	...
3 Other transport and communication	108	222	547	678	1278	1452	1980	1188	2246	1711	715	1059
4 Other insurance service charges	34	83	153	104	79	150	159	189	229	332	488	265
5 Other commodities	473	1342	2466	2548	3130	4786	5063	6733	8482	8973	7611	6637
6 Direct purchases abroad by government	92	553	465	770	691	918	870	920	1455	814	433	426
7 Direct purchases abroad by resident households	158	100	106	179	234	316	472	594	1278	418	677	1139
Total Imports of Goods and Services	8236	29057	34754	41321	53558	68704	74359	79321	101138	118382	108506	116188
Balance of Goods and Services	-141	-7785	-5829	-8901	-12097	-15114	-16553	-23171	-25871	-681	18065	38916
Total Imports and Balance of Goods and Services	8095	21272	28925	32420	41461	53590	57806	56150	75267	117701	126571	155104

4.1 Derivation of Value Added by Kind of Activity, in Current Prices

Million Philippine pesos

	1980 Gross Output	1980 Intermediate Consumption	1980 Value Added	1981 Gross Output	1981 Intermediate Consumption	1981 Value Added	1982 Gross Output	1982 Intermediate Consumption	1982 Value Added	1983 Gross Output	1983 Intermediate Consumption	1983 Value Added
All Producers												
1 Agriculture, hunting, forestry and fishing	...	...	61761	...	...	69391	...	...	76721	...	...	84546
A Agriculture and hunting [a]	...	...	43820	...	...	49419	...	...	54593	...	...	60215
B Forestry and logging	...	...	6743	...	...	6151	...	...	7351	...	...	7541
C Fishing	...	...	11198	...	...	13821	...	...	14777	...	...	16790
2 Mining and quarrying	...	...	8095	...	...	6849	...	...	6106	...	...	7021
A Coal mining [b]	...	...	...	...	...	...	...	...	...	...	...	...
B Crude petroleum and natural gas production	...	...	...	...	...	...	...	...	...	...	...	...
C Metal ore mining	...	...	6659	...	...	5174	...	...	4431	...	...	...
D Other mining [b]	...	...	1436	...	...	1675	...	...	1675	...	...	...
3 Manufacturing	...	...	64555	...	...	75151	...	...	83133	...	...	95172
A Manufacture of food, beverages and tobacco	...	...	24204	...	...	29318	...	...	33245	...	...	38136
B Textile, wearing apparel and leather industries	...	...	8130	...	...	9919	...	...	10445	...	...	11854
C Manufacture of wood and wood products, including furniture	...	...	2679	...	...	3257	...	...	3446	...	...	3866
D Manufacture of paper and paper products, printing and publishing	...	...	1551	...	...	1714	...	...	1748	...	...	2051
E Manufacture of chemicals and chemical petroleum, coal, rubber and plastic products	...	...	16236	...	...	17534	...	...	18751	...	...	21352
F Manufacture of non-metallic mineral products, except products of petroleum and coal	...	...	1832	...	...	1978	...	...	2289	...	...	2506
G Basic metal industries	...	...	2237	...	...	2217	...	...	2614	...	...	3126
H Manufacture of fabricated metal products, machinery and equipment	...	...	6832	...	...	8156	...	...	9331	...	...	10820
I Other manufacturing industries	...	...	854	...	...	1058	...	...	1264	...	...	1461
4 Electricity, gas and water	...	...	2761	...	...	3329	...	...	4042	...	...	5257
A Electricity, gas and steam	...	...	2427	...	...	2868	...	...	3461	...	...	4561
B Water works and supply	...	...	335	...	...	461	...	...	581	...	...	695
5 Construction	...	...	21311	...	...	26268	...	...	29302	...	...	30730
6 Wholesale and retail trade, restaurants and hotels	...	...	45322	...	...	53650	...	...	60888	...	...	71085
A Wholesale and retail trade	...	...	42050	...	...	49765	...	...	56356	...	...	66094
B Restaurants and hotels	...	...	3272	...	...	3885	...	...	4532	...	...	4991
7 Transport, storage and communication	...	...	16444	...	...	19618	...	...	21376	...	...	24378
A Transport and storage	...	...	...	...	...	...	...	...	...	...	...	20818
B Communication	...	...	...	...	...	...	...	...	...	...	...	3560
8 Finance, insurance, real estate and business services	...	...	22670	...	...	25017	...	...	28792	...	...	33048
A Financial institutions	...	...	9585	...	...	9463	...	...	10599	...	...	12031

Philippines

4.1 Derivation of Value Added by Kind of Activity, in Current Prices
(Continued)

Million Philippine pesos

	1980 Gross Output	1980 Intermediate Consumption	1980 Value Added	1981 Gross Output	1981 Intermediate Consumption	1981 Value Added	1982 Gross Output	1982 Intermediate Consumption	1982 Value Added	1983 Gross Output	1983 Intermediate Consumption	1983 Value Added
B Insurance	...	...	2864	...	...	3396	...	...	3926	...	...	4222
C Real estate and business services	...	...	10221	...	...	12158	...	...	14267	...	...	16795
Real estate, except dwellings	...	...	2396	...	...	2956	...	...	3589	...	...	4315
Dwellings	...	...	5763	...	...	6797	...	...	8027	...	...	9434
9 Community, social and personal services	...	...	7670	...	...	9023	...	...	10516	...	...	11642
A Sanitary and similar services	...	...	...	...	...	...	...	...	...	...	...	...
B Social and related community services	...	...	4458	...	...	5254	...	...	6168	...	...	7075
Educational services	...	...	1574	...	...	1835	...	...	2199	...	...	2472
Medical, dental, other health and veterinary services	...	...	2884	...	...	3419	...	...	3969	...	...	4603
C Recreational and cultural services	...	...	1346	...	...	1568	...	...	1721	...	...	1802
D Personal and household services	...	...	1866	...	...	2201	...	...	2627	...	...	2765
Total, Industries	...	...	250589	...	...	288295	...	...	320876	...	...	362878
Producers of Government Services	...	...	11493	...	...	13930	...	...	16389	...	...	17539
Other Producers	...	...	2568	...	...	3032	...	...	3332	...	...	3678
Total	...	...	264650	...	...	305258	...	...	340597	...	...	384096
Less. Imputed bank service charge	...	...	...	...	...	...	...	...	...	...	...	...
Import duties	...	...	...	...	...	...	...	...	...	...	...	...
Value added tax	...	...	...	...	...	...	...	...	...	...	...	...
Total	...	...	...	...	...	...	...	...	...	...	...	...

	1984 Gross Output	1984 Intermediate Consumption	1984 Value Added	1985 Gross Output	1985 Intermediate Consumption	1985 Value Added	1986 Gross Output	1986 Intermediate Consumption	1986 Value Added
All Producers									
1 Agriculture, hunting, forestry and fishing	...	...	139505	...	...	162519	...	...	163801
A Agriculture and hunting [a]	...	...	104346	...	...	123670	...	...	121222
B Forestry and logging	...	...	12043	...	...	10865	...	...	9874
C Fishing	...	...	23116	...	...	27984	...	...	32705
2 Mining and quarrying	...	...	9714	...	...	11529	...	...	10198
A Coal mining [b]	...	...	...	...	...	...	...	...	...
B Crude petroleum and natural gas production	...	...	...	...	...	...	...	...	...
C Metal ore mining	...	...	...	...	...	...	...	...	...
D Other mining [b]	...	...	...	...	...	...	...	...	...
3 Manufacturing	...	...	137251	...	...	150523	...	...	154719
A Manufacture of food, beverages and tobacco	...	...	58683	...	...	67206	...	...	66898
B Textile, wearing apparel and leather industries	...	...	16594	...	...	18047	...	...	22484
C Manufacture of wood and wood products, including furniture	...	...	4522	...	...	4682	...	...	3831
D Manufacture of paper and paper products, printing and publishing	...	...	3370	...	...	3751	...	...	4341
E Manufacture of chemicals and chemical petroleum, coal, rubber and plastic products	...	...	31284	...	...	30473	...	...	28683
F Manufacture of non-metallic mineral products, except products of petroleum and coal	...	...	2956	...	...	2668	...	...	2805
G Basic metal industries	...	...	5068	...	...	6459	...	...	6327
H Manufacture of fabricated metal products, machinery and equipment	...	...	11551	...	...	12715	...	...	14453
I Other manufacturing industries	...	...	3223	...	...	4522	...	...	4897
4 Electricity, gas and water	...	...	7980	...	...	10986	...	...	15184
A Electricity, gas and steam	...	...	6178	...	...	9799	...	...	13519
B Water works and supply	...	...	887	...	...	1187	...	...	1665

Philippines

4.1 Derivation of Value Added by Kind of Activity, in Current Prices
(Continued)

Million Philippine pesos

	1984 Gross Output	1984 Intermediate Consumption	1984 Value Added	1985 Gross Output	1985 Intermediate Consumption	1985 Value Added	1986 Gross Output	1986 Intermediate Consumption	1986 Value Added
5 Construction	...	...	31209	...	...	27506	...	...	22685
6 Wholesale and retail trade, restaurants and hotels	...	...	106367	...	...	125869	...	...	129282
A Wholesale and retail trade	...	...	99711	...	...	118370	...	...	121243
B Restaurants and hotels	...	...	6656	...	...	7499	...	...	8039
7 Transport, storage and communication	...	...	33820	...	...	38263	...	...	39078
A Transport and storage	...	...	28245	...	...	32204	...	...	32330
B Communication	...	...	5575	...	...	6059	...	...	6748
8 Finance, insurance, real estate and business services	...	...	34912	...	...	35194	...	...	37731
A Financial institutions	...	...	8471	...	...	2252	...	...	2949
B Insurance	...	...	5369	...	...	6502	...	...	6783
C Real estate and business services	...	...	21072	...	...	26440	...	...	27999
Real estate, except dwellings	...	...	3773	...	...	3331	...	...	3897
Dwellings	...	...	13590	...	...	18003	...	...	18662
9 Community, social and personal services	...	...	14257	...	...	16749	...	...	18179
A Sanitary and similar services	...	...	...	...	...	...	...	...	...
B Social and related community services	...	...	8811	...	...	10940	...	...	11834
Educational services	...	...	3114	...	...	4021	...	...	4288
Medical, dental, other health and veterinary services	...	...	5698	...	...	6920	...	...	7546
C Recreational and cultural services	...	...	2200	...	...	2406	...	...	2663
D Personal and household services	...	...	3245	...	...	3404	...	...	3682
Total, Industries	...	...	515015	...	...	579140	...	...	590857
Producers of Government Services	...	...	21254	...	...	26007	...	...	31753
Other Producers	...	...	4197	...	...	4312	...	...	4107
Total	...	...	540466	...	...	609459	...	...	626717
Less: Imputed bank service charge	...	...	...	...	...	...	...	...	...
Import duties	...	...	...	...	...	...	...	...	...
Value added tax	...	...	...	...	...	...	...	...	...
Total	...	...	...	...	...	...	...	...	...

a) Item 'Agriculture, hunting, forestry and fishing' excludes hunting.
b) 'Coal mining' is included in 'Other mining'.

4.2 Derivation of Value Added by Kind of Activity, in Constant Prices

Million Philippine pesos

	1980 Gross Output	1980 Intermediate Consumption	1980 Value Added	1981 Gross Output	1981 Intermediate Consumption	1981 Value Added	1982 Gross Output	1982 Intermediate Consumption	1982 Value Added	1983 Gross Output	1983 Intermediate Consumption	1983 Value Added

At constant prices of: 1972

All Producers

1 Agriculture, hunting, forestry and fishing	...	...	23662	...	...	24608	...	...	25378	...	...	24845
A Agriculture and hunting a	...	...	18400	...	...	19301	...	...	20141	...	...	19619
B Forestry and logging	...	...	1386	...	...	1175	...	...	983	...	...	819
C Fishing	...	...	3876	...	...	4132	...	...	4254	...	...	4407
2 Mining and quarrying	...	...	2236	...	...	2175	...	...	2016	...	...	1966
A Coal mining b	...	...	...	...	...	...	...	...	...	...	...	...
B Crude petroleum and natural gas production	...	...	...	...	...	...	...	...	...	...	...	...
C Metal ore mining	...	...	1946	...	...	1777	...	...	1574	...	...	1501
D Other mining b	...	...	290	...	...	398	...	...	442	...	...	465

Philippines

4.2 Derivation of Value Added by Kind of Activity, in Constant Prices
(Continued)

Million Philippine pesos

	1980 Gross Output	1980 Intermediate Consumption	1980 Value Added	1981 Gross Output	1981 Intermediate Consumption	1981 Value Added	1982 Gross Output	1982 Intermediate Consumption	1982 Value Added	1983 Gross Output	1983 Intermediate Consumption	1983 Value Added
					At constant prices of:1972							
3 Manufacturing	...	...	23175	...	...	23959	...	...	24535	...	...	25108
A Manufacture of food, beverages and tobacco	...	...	10190	...	...	10633	...	...	10960	...	...	11126
B Textile, wearing apparel and leather industries	...	...	2136	...	...	2354	...	...	2348	...	...	2363
C Manufacture of wood and wood products, including furniture	...	...	797	...	...	846	...	...	844	...	...	858
D Manufacture of paper and paper products, printing and publishing	...	...	515	...	...	532	...	...	531	...	...	564
E Manufacture of chemicals and chemical petroleum, coal, rubber and plastic products	...	...	4040	...	...	3915	...	...	3910	...	...	3982
F Manufacture of non-metallic mineral products, except products of petroleum and coal	...	...	574	...	...	540	...	...	569	...	...	587
G Basic metal industries	...	...	853	...	...	791	...	...	856	...	...	947
H Manufacture of fabricated metal products, machinery and equipment	...	...	3805	...	...	4052	...	...	4197	...	...	4347
I Other manufacturing industries	...	...	265	...	...	296	...	...	320	...	...	334
4 Electricity, gas and water	...	...	921	...	...	999	...	...	1084	...	...	1192
A Electricity, gas and steam	...	...	813	...	...	872	...	...	941	...	...	1029
B Water works and supply	...	...	108	...	...	127	...	...	143	...	...	163
5 Construction	...	...	7139	...	...	7830	...	...	8079	...	...	7689
6 Wholesale and retail trade, restaurants and hotels	...	...	13664	...	...	14231	...	...	14672	...	...	15466
A Wholesale and retail trade	...	...	12224	...	...	12731	...	...	13103	...	...	13930
B Restaurants and hotels	...	...	1440	...	...	1500	...	...	1569	...	...	1536
7 Transport, storage and communication	...	...	4827	...	...	5040	...	...	5165	...	...	5266
A Transport and storage	...	...	...	...	...	...	...	...	...	...	...	...
B Communication	...	...	...	...	...	...	...	...	...	...	...	...
8 Finance, insurance, real estate and business services	...	...	8138	...	...	7032	...	...	8349	...	...	8698
A Financial institutions	...	...	3323	...	...	2695	...	...	2905	...	...	3021
B Insurance	...	...	983	...	...	1024	...	...	1094	...	...	1077
C Real estate and business services	...	...	3832	...	...	4113	...	...	4350	...	...	4600
Real estate, except dwellings	...	...	792	...	...	880	...	...	962	...	...	1055
Dwellings	...	...	2023	...	...	2165	...	...	2291	...	...	2425
9 Community, social and personal services	...	...	2991	...	...	3106	...	...	3209	...	...	3208
A Sanitary and similar services	...	...	...	...	...	...	...	...	...	...	...	...
B Social and related community services	...	...	1758	...	...	1833	...	...	1897	...	...	1941
Educational services	...	...	786	...	...	821	...	...	865	...	...	877
Medical, dental, other health and veterinary services	...	...	972	...	...	1012	...	...	1032	...	...	1064
C Recreational and cultural services	...	...	477	...	...	494	...	...	506	...	...	493
D Personal and household services	...	...	756	...	...	770	...	...	800	...	...	774
Total, Industries	...	...	86753	...	...	89980	...	...	92487	...	...	93438
Producers of Government Services	...	...	4700	...	...	5081	...	...	5339	...	...	5294
Other Producers	...	...	1114	...	...	1146	...	...	1173	...	...	1188
Total	...	...	92567	...	...	96207	...	...	98999	...	...	99920
Less: Imputed bank service charge	...	...	...	...	...	...	...	...	...	...	...	...
Import duties	...	...	...	...	...	...	...	...	...	...	...	...
Value added tax	...	...	...	...	...	...	...	...	...	...	...	...
Total	...	...	...	...	...	...	...	...	...	...	...	...

Philippines

4.2 Derivation of Value Added by Kind of Activity, in Constant Prices

Million Philippine pesos

	1984 Gross Output	1984 Intermediate Consumption	1984 Value Added	1985 Gross Output	1985 Intermediate Consumption	1985 Value Added	1986 Gross Output	1986 Intermediate Consumption	1986 Value Added
At constant prices of: 1972 — All Producers									
1 Agriculture, hunting, forestry and fishing	...	...	25409	...	...	26252	...	...	27233
A Agriculture and hunting a	...	...	20315	...	...	21124	...	...	22028
B Forestry and logging	...	...	765	...	...	706	...	...	654
C Fishing	...	...	4329	...	...	4422	...	...	4551
2 Mining and quarrying	...	...	1755	...	...	1768	...	...	1558
A Coal mining b	...	...	...	...	...	...	...	...	...
B Crude petroleum and natural gas production	...	...	...	...	...	...	...	...	...
C Metal ore mining	...	...	1349	...	...	...	...	...	...
D Other mining b	...	...	406	...	...	...	...	...	...
3 Manufacturing	...	...	23319	...	...	21541	...	...	21717
A Manufacture of food, beverages and tobacco	...	...	11039	...	...	10412	...	...	10207
B Textile, wearing apparel and leather industries	...	...	2311	...	...	2016	...	...	2330
C Manufacture of wood and wood products, including furniture	...	...	730	...	...	645	...	...	508
D Manufacture of paper and paper products, printing and publishing	...	...	552	...	...	547	...	...	602
E Manufacture of chemicals and chemical petroleum, coal, rubber and plastic products	...	...	3390	...	...	3138	...	...	3030
F Manufacture of non-metallic mineral products, except products of petroleum and coal	...	...	481	...	...	375	...	...	377
G Basic metal industries	...	...	1121	...	...	1070	...	...	1018
H Manufacture of fabricated metal products, machinery and equipment	...	...	3270	...	...	2891	...	...	3197
I Other manufacturing industries	...	...	425	...	...	447	...	...	448
4 Electricity, gas and water	...	...	1342	...	...	1433	...	...	1547
A Electricity, gas and steam	...	...	1159	...	...	...	...	...	...
B Water works and supply	...	...	183	...	...	...	...	...	...
5 Construction	...	...	5866	...	...	4258	...	...	3382
6 Wholesale and retail trade, restaurants and hotels	...	...	15540	...	...	15452	...	...	15728
A Wholesale and retail trade	...	...	14073	...	...	14066	...	...	14337
B Restaurants and hotels	...	...	1467	...	...	1386	...	...	1391
7 Transport, storage and communication	...	...	5032	...	...	4953	...	...	5084
A Transport and storage	...	...	...	...	...	3813	...	...	3852
B Communication	...	...	...	...	...	1140	...	...	1232
8 Finance, insurance, real estate and business services	...	...	6081	...	...	4950	...	...	5010
A Financial institutions	...	...	1373	...	...	297	...	...	385
B Insurance	...	...	870	...	...	855	...	...	886
C Real estate and business services	...	...	3838	...	...	3798	...	...	3739
Real estate, except dwellings	...	...	628	...	...	442	...	...	482
Dwellings	...	...	2263	...	...	2391	...	...	2309
9 Community, social and personal services	...	...	3018	...	...	2956	...	...	2970
A Sanitary and similar services	...	...	...	...	...	...	...	...	...
B Social and related community services	...	...	1871	...	...	1957	...	...	1951
Educational services	...	...	855	...	...	890	...	...	866
Medical, dental, other health and veterinary services	...	...	1016	...	...	1067	...	...	1085
C Recreational and cultural services	...	...	457	...	...	402	...	...	420
D Personal and household services	...	...	690	...	...	597	...	...	599

Philippines

4.2 Derivation of Value Added by Kind of Activity, in Constant Prices
(Continued)

Million Philippine pesos

	1984			1985			1986		
	Gross Output	Intermediate Consumption	Value Added	Gross Output	Intermediate Consumption	Value Added	Gross Output	Intermediate Consumption	Value Added
	At constant prices of:1972								
Total, Industries	...	...	87362	...	...	83563	...	...	84229
Producers of Government Services	...	...	5585	...	...	5453	...	...	5811
Other Producers	...	...	980	...	...	787	...	...	730
Total	...	...	93927	...	...	89803	...	...	90770
Less: Imputed bank service charge	...	...	...	...	...	...	...	...	...
Import duties	...	...	...	...	...	...	...	...	...
Value added tax	...	...	...	...	...	...	...	...	...
Total	...	...	...	...	...	...	...	...	...

a) Item 'Agriculture, hunting, forestry and fishing' excludes hunting.
b) 'Coal mining' is included in 'Other mining'.

Poland

Source. Reply to the United Nations Material Balances Questionnaire from the Central Statistical Office of Poland, Warsaw. The official estimates are published annually in 'Rocznik Statystyczny' (Statistical Yearbook). Concepts, definitions and methods of estimation are described in the above Yearbook and also in 'Concise Statistical Yearbook of Poland' and in 'Rocznik Dochodu Narodowego, 1960-1965' (Yearbook of National Income, 1960-1965). The above publications are issued by the Central Statistical Office.

General note. The estimates shown in the following tables have been prepared in accordance with the System of Material Product Balances. Therefore, these estimates are not comparable in concept and coverage with those conforming to the United Nations System of National Accounts. In Poland, investments and general repairs in the socialized economy are financed from the state budget, credits granted by banks, depreciation funds, development fund of enterprises or enterprises, profit, receipts from the liquidation of fixed assets, various state and social funds designed as a whole or partially for investment, and from the so-called special funds construction activities of the housing and building associations are financed from their own funds (contributions of their members) and credits granted by banks. The estimates on national income for the years 1976-1980 were calculated according to the method of kind of activity. Beginning 1981, the method of enterprises has been adopted i.e., all activities of an enterprise are classified to one branch of activity only. Estimates using both methods are shown for the year 1980.

1a Net Material Product by Use at Current Market Prices

Thousand Million Polish zlotych

	1970	1975	1977	1978	1979	1980	1981	1982	1983	1984	1985	1986
1 Personal consumption	465.0	799.7 / 805.2	1039.6	1130.7	1245.5	1404.0 / 1409.3	1721.2	2929.3	3749.6	4455.8	5189.9 / 5205.9	6403.2
2 Material consumption in the units of the non-material sphere serving individuals [a]	...	... / ...	...	...	...	... / ...	...	...	...	...	... / ...	...
Consumption of the Population	465.0	799.7 / 805.2	1039.6	1130.7	1245.5	1404.0 / 1409.3	1721.2	2929.3	3749.6	4455.8	5189.9 / 5205.9	6403.2
3 Material consumption in the units of the non-material sphere serving the community as a whole [a]	83.0	146.6 / 152.3	205.1	228.7	247.4	264.5 / 255.1	276.4	525.7	687.9	885.1	1120.2 / 1083.6	1321.3
4 Net fixed capital formation	139.5	410.7 / 393.9	485.2	517.7	446.8	349.8 / 347.6	225.4	800.2	1053.6	1274.7	1539.7 / 1533.6	1950.0
5 Increase in material circulating assets and in stocks	44.0	102.0 / 102.0	93.0	96.2	59.0	13.8 / 40.5	-5.8	433.2	339.4	476.1	677.5 / 677.5	904.6
6 Losses												
7 Exports of goods and material services	17.7	-102.0 / -103.7	-86.8	-70.7	-63.3	-95.9 / -60.8	-56.8	64.6	93.5	90.1	59.1 / 157.3	118.0
8 Less: Imports of goods and material services												
Net Material Product [b]	749.2	1357.0 / 1349.7	1736.1	1902.6	1935.4	1936.2 / 1991.7	2160.4	4753.0	5924.0	7181.8	8586.4 / 8657.9	10697.1

a) Item 'Material consumption in units of the non-material sphere serving individuals' is included in item 'Material consumption in the units of the non-material sphere serving the community as a whole'.

b) Beginning 1975 the estimates of net material product shown in table 1a (Net Material Product by Use) differ from those shown in table 4 (Primary Income from Net Material Product). This is because net material product in table 1a is computed by means of the kind of activity method for which there was no possibility to single out elements of primary distribution while in table 4 there is primary distribution of net material product computed by means of the enterprise method.

Poland

1b Net Material Product by Use at Constant Market Prices

Thousand Million Polish zlotych

	1970	1975	1977	1978	1979	1980	1981	1982	1983	1984	1985	1986
		1971		**At constant prices of:** **1977**				**1982**			**1984**	
1 Personal consumption	470.4	706.3 875.5	1014.0	1023.7	1056.9	1081.1 3651.2	3502.3	2989.4	3176.0	3295.1	3367.6 4624.1	4855.2
2 Material consumption in the units of the non-material sphere serving individuals	...	... ...	...	...	...	... ...	...	...	...	...	... ...	...
Consumption of the Population	470.4	706.3 875.5	1014.0	1023.7	1056.9	1081.1 3651.2	3502.3	2989.4	3176.0	3295.1	3367.6 4624.1	4855.2
3 Material consumption in the units of the non-material sphere serving the community as a whole	81.8[a]	130.4[a] 168.1[a]	199.0[a]	209.8[a]	214.9[a]	217.4[a] 525.0[a]	482.5[a]	538.1[a]	554.8[a]	600.9[a]	640.4[a] 950.6	989.6
4 Net fixed capital formation	167.0	427.1 470.3	478.6	459.6	388.7	290.0 1326.1	1005.4	805.1	881.4	989.6	1037.7 838.3	888.0
5 Increase in material circulating assets and in stocks	46.8	82.6 109.1	76.3	84.1	50.9	19.7 108.2	33.0	165.0	136.0	102.3	132.6 468.8	489.8
6 Losses												
7 Exports of goods and material services	25.3	-85.0 -116.3	-77.4	-36.0	-10.0	-8.9 -102.0	-175.4	83.1	107.4	140.3	122.6 147.8	153.4
8 Less: Imports of goods and material services												
Net Material Product	791.3	1261.4 1506.7[b]	1690.5[b]	1741.2[b]	1701.4[b]	1599.3[b] 5508.5	4847.8	4580.7	4855.6	5128.2	5300.9 7029.6	7376.0

a) Item 'Material consumption in units of the non-material sphere serving individuals' is included in item 'Material consumption in the units of the non-material sphere serving the community as a whole'. b) The estimates are at constant prices as of January 1, 1977.

2a Net Material Product by Kind of Activity of the Material Sphere in Current Market Prices

Thousand Million Polish zlotych

	1970	1975	1977	1978	1979	1980	1981	1982	1983	1984	1985	1986
1 Agriculture and forestry	129.5	199.8 199.8	272.1	304.4	304.8	296.9 314.7	638.4	925.0	1088.5	1256.4	1398.7 1398.7	1650.2
A Agriculture and livestock [a]	108.6	166.4 166.4	227.1	257.2	256.7	246.3 260.6	576.5	758.5	907.7	1049.9	1155.9 1166.0	1352.6
B Forestry	10.6	15.1 15.1	16.2	15.7	14.5	15.1 24.2	24.9	73.3	85.9	93.6	115.8 115.8	139.7
C Other	10.3	18.3 18.3	28.8	31.5	33.6	35.5 29.9	37.0	93.2	94.9	112.9	127.0 127.0	157.9
2 Industrial activity [a]	408.7	803.3 803.3	910.9	993.8	1023.6	1062.8 1038.5	909.8	2387.6	2967.9	3561.8	4181.9 4117.1	5060.9

Poland

2a Net Material Product by Kind of Activity of the Material Sphere in Current Market Prices
(Continued)

Thousand Million Polish zlotych

	1970	1975	1977	1978	1979	1980	1981	1982	1983	1984	1985	1986
3 Construction	73.7	151.3 151.3	202.6	233.0	215.0	178.2 201.8	158.3	510.0	644.3	832.9	1064.5 1063.7	1378.9
4 Wholesale and retail trade and restaurants and other eating and drinking places	73.9	74.2 74.2	183.0	196.0	203.9	201.9 254.1	269.7	655.5	802.2	982.3	1207.2 1343.9	1708.3
5 Transport and communication	50.5	92.1 92.1	128.0	131.0	134.7	143.4 143.2	141.3	206.5	318.3	420.3	579.0 563.1	667.0
A Transport	44.9	78.9 78.9	111.5	113.5	112.1	116.3 115.8	113.7	166.5	261.3	355.7	488.5 472.6	562.4
B Communication	5.6	13.2 13.2	16.5	17.5	22.6	27.1 27.4	27.6	40.0	57.0	64.6	90.5 90.5	104.6
6 Other activities of the material sphere	12.9	28.3 29.0	39.5	44.4	53.4	53.0 39.4	42.9	68.4	102.8	128.1	155.1 171.4	231.8
Net material product	749.2	1349.0 1349.7	1736.1	1902.6	1935.4	1936.2 1991.7	2160.4	4753.0	5924.0	7181.8	8586.4 8657.9	10697.1

a) Inland water fishing is included in item 'Agriculture and livestock'. Ocean and coastal fishing and factory-vessel fishing are included in item 'Industrial activity'.

2b Net Material Product by Kind of Activity of the Material Sphere in Constant Market Prices

Thousand Million Polish zlotych

	1970	1975	1977	1978	1979	1980	1981	1982	1983	1984	1985	1986
		1971		1977	At constant prices of:			1982			1984	
1 Agriculture and forestry	149.6	154.6 246.3	248.1	267.6	248.3	213.1 773.9	787.4	829.4	877.3	926.3	928.3 1106.5	1176.0
A Agriculture and livestock	125.5[a]	121.0[a] 205.1[a]	203.1[a]	220.1[a]	201.5[a]	165.8[a] 601.9[a]	625.6[a]	661.5[a]	717.4[a]	760.4[a]	763.0[a] 917.5	981.8
B Forestry	13.8	14.6 16.6	16.2	15.9	14.7	15.4 62.9	66.7	73.2	82.6	89.1	90.4 95.0	100.2
C Other	10.3	19.0 24.6	28.8	31.6	32.1	31.9 109.1	95.1	94.7	77.3	76.8	74.9 94.0	94.0
2 Industrial activity	394.3[a]	657.5[a] 759.0[a]	892.9[a]	914.7[a]	898.8[a]	862.4[a] 2763.3[a]	2360.9[a]	2253.8[a]	2384.0[a]	2511.5[a]	2611.0[a] 3418.9	3571.2

Poland

2b Net Material Product by Kind of Activity of the Material Sphere in Constant Market Prices
(Continued)

Thousand Million Polish zlotych

	1970	1975	1977	1978	1979	1980	1981	1982	1983	1984	1985	1986
	1971		1977					1982			1984	
3 Construction	89.8	152.5 195.4	202.5	201.8	189.2	148.2 731.8	548.3	502.4	541.1	584.7	609.8 844.2	880.4
4 Wholesale and retail trade and restaurants and other eating and drinking places	93.5	159.8 158.8	180.0	180.3	185.5	185.7 893.6	827.9	720.1	750.8	777.4	810.3 1162.9	1224.4
5 Transport and communication	51.3	91.0 115.0	128.2	135.8	130.8	140.5 262.1	238.5	206.6	227.3	248.9	259.2 363.4	381.6
A Transport	...	... ...	...	...	...	... 224.5	201.3	166.6	177.4	195.4	203.3 299.5	312.9
B Communication	...	... ...	...	...	...	... 37.6	37.2	40.0	49.9	53.5	55.9 63.9	68.7
6 Other activities of the material sphere	12.8	46.0 32.2	38.8	41.0	48.8	49.4 83.8	84.8	68.4	75.1	79.4	82.3 133.7	142.4
Net material product	791.3	1261.4 1506.7[b]	1690.5[b]	1741.2[b]	1701.4[b]	1599.3[b] 5508.5	4847.8	4580.7	4855.6	5128.2	5300.9 7029.6	7376.0

a) Inland water fishing is included in item 'Agriculture and livestock'. Ocean and coastal fishing and factory-vessel fishing are included in item 'Industrial activity'.
b) The estimates are at constant prices as of January 1, 1977.

3 Primary Incomes by Kind of Activity of the Material Sphere in Current Market Prices

Thousand Million Polish zlotych

	1980		1981	
	Primary Income of the Population	Primary Income of Enterprises	Primary Income of the Population	Primary Income of Enterprises
1 Agriculture and forestry	292.5	22.2	602.4	36.0
A Agriculture and livestock [a]	255.9	4.7	553.2	23.3
B Forestry	10.4	13.8	14.3	10.6
C Other	26.2	3.7	34.9	2.1
2 Industrial activity [a]	409.1	629.4	515.1	394.7
3 Construction	134.3	61.6	163.0	-11.9
4 Wholesale and retail trade and restaurants and other eating and drinking places	89.9	165.0	131.3	139.9
5 Transport and communication	90.6	52.6	114.1	27.2
6 Other activities of the material sphere	38.4	1.0	45.0	-0.0
Total [b]	1054.8	931.8	1571.8	582.9

a) Inland water fishing is included in item 'Agriculture and livestock'. Ocean and coastal fishing and factory-vessel fishing are included in item 'Industrial activity'. b) Column 'Primary income of the population', includes net income of the owner of private farms and other private enterprises (equivalent to unincorporated enterprises in SNA).

4 Primary Incomes From Net Material Product

Thousand Million Polish zlotych

	1970	1975	1977	1978	1979	1980	1981	1982	1983	1984	1985	1986
				a) Primary Incomes of the Population								
1 Socialist sector	262.6	455.3 459.0	580.4	622.2	679.9	759.0 754.8	971.5	...	...	...	...	...
A State sector	224.8	378.6 382.1	471.9	504.6	552.5	623.2 618.5	793.0	...	...	...	...	...
B Co-operative sector	36.3	75.3 75.3	107.3	115.8	124.7	132.3 132.9	175.2	...	...	...	...	...
C Personal plots of households	1.5	1.4 1.4	1.2	1.8	2.7	3.5 3.4	3.3	...	...	...	...	...
2 Private sector	124.7	186.5 186.5	256.0	287.8	301.2	298.1 300.0	600.3	...	...	...	...	...
Sub-total	387.3	641.8 645.3	836.4	910.0	981.1	1057.1 1054.8	1571.8	...	...	...	...	...

Poland

4 Primary Incomes From Net Material Product
(Continued)

Thousand Million Polish zlotych

	1970	1975	1977	1978	1979	1980	1981	1982	1983	1984	1985	1986
				b) Primary incomes of the enterprises								
1 Socialist sector	344.0	668.0 / 665.2	860.4	946.6	908.4	827.8 / 888.8	533.1	...	...	...	...	...
A State sector	311.5	629.2 / 626.3	805.8	884.1	835.3	769.1 / 823.9	528.3	...	...	...	...	...
B Co-operative sector	32.5	38.8 / 38.9	54.6	62.5	73.1	58.7 / 64.9	4.8	...	...	...	...	...
2 Private sector	17.9	26.1 / 26.1	32.0	39.0	40.2	42.8 / 43.0	49.8	...	...	...	...	...
Sub-total	361.9	694.1 / 691.3	892.4	985.6	948.6	870.6 / 931.8	582.9	...	...	...	...	...
Total net material product	749.2	1335.9 / 1336.6	1728.8	1895.6	1929.7	1927.7 / 1986.6	2154.7	...	...	...	...	...

5a Supply and Disposition of Goods and Material Services in Current Market Prices

Thousand Million Polish zlotych

	Supply					Disposition				
	Gross Output at Producers Prices	Trade Margins and Transport Charges	Gross Output at Market Prices	Imports	Total Supply and Disposition	Intermediate Material Consumption including Depreciation	Final Consumption	Net Capital Formation	Losses	Exports
1982										
1 Agriculture and forestry a	1965.0	85.0	2050.0	81.0	2131.0	1646.0	477.0	-15.0	-	23.0
2 Industrial activity a	7088.0	726.0	7814.0	824.0	8638.0	4453.0	2589.0	802.0	-65.0	859.0
3 Construction	1114.0	1.0	1115.0	2.0	1117.0	202.0	91.0	756.0	-	68.0
4 Transport and communication	664.0	-	664.0	53.0	717.0	455.0	130.0	1.0	5.0	126.0
5 Other activities of the material sphere	249.0	4.0	253.0	2.0	255.0	143.0	104.0	6.0	-	2.0
Total b	11080.0	816.0	11896.0	962.0	12858.0	6899.0	3391.0	1550.0	-60.0	1078.0
1983										
1 Agriculture and forestry a	2232.0	105.0	2337.0	63.0	2400.0	1843.0	512.0	15.0	-	30.0
2 Industrial activity a	8656.0	975.0	9631.0	938.0	10569.0	5514.0	3407.0	728.0	-55.0	975.0
3 Construction	1415.0	2.0	1417.0	3.0	1420.0	268.0	113.0	985.0	-	54.0
4 Transport and communication	890.0	-	890.0	63.0	953.0	604.0	209.0	1.0	8.0	131.0
5 Other activities of the material sphere	317.0	5.0	322.0	3.0	325.0	186.0	133.0	4.0	-	2.0
Total b	13510.0	1087.0	14597.0	1070.0	15667.0	8415.0	4374.0	1733.0	-47.0	1192.0
1984										
1 Agriculture and forestry a	2484.0	136.0	2620.0	75.0	2695.0	2016.0	572.0	61.0	-	46.0
2 Industrial activity a	10453.0	1110.0	11563.0	1173.0	12736.0	6621.0	4074.0	922.0	-91.0	1210.0
3 Construction	1789.0	9.0	1798.0	1.0	1799.0	332.0	132.0	1267.0	-	68.0
4 Transport and communication	1102.0	-	1102.0	92.0	1194.0	745.0	259.0	2.0	8.0	180.0
5 Other activities of the material sphere	401.0	8.0	409.0	5.0	414.0	223.0	174.0	5.0	-	12.0
Total b	16229.0	1263.0	17492.0	1346.0	18838.0	9937.0	5211.0	2257.0	-83.0	1516.0

a) Inland water fishing is included in item 'Agriculture and livestock'. Ocean and coastal fishing and factory-vessel fishing are included in item 'Industrial activity'.
b) Column 2 (Trade margins and transport charges) refers to trade margins only, column 6 (Intermediate consumption including depreciation) excludes depreciation and column 9 (Losses) includes scraps and statistical discrepancies.

Poland

6a Capital Formation by Kind of Activity of the Material and Non-Material Spheres in Current Market Prices

Thousand Million Polish zlotych

	1970	1975	1977	1978	1979	1980	1981	1982	1983	1984	1985	1986
					Net Fixed Capital Formation							
1 Agriculture and forestry	22.6	54.6 / 54.6	86.5	88.8	85.7	54.4 / 51.0	49.2	134.6	187.1	202.3	195.2 / 195.2	218.8
2 Industrial activity	37.3	157.9 / 157.9	173.8	165.2	115.7	79.1 / 75.9	16.5	144.4	199.1	248.8	331.8 / 327.2	432.0
3 Construction	3.3	14.7 / 14.7	18.2	17.8	10.3	4.6 / 5.7	-6.3	-1.0	6.4	11.3	17.8 / 16.7	25.7
4 Wholesale and retail trade, restaurants and other eating and drinking places	3.2	7.4 / 7.4	7.5	7.0	5.3	4.0 / 4.9	3.8	17.2	25.4	30.1	34.4 / 33.8	59.7
5 Transport and communication	14.3	42.6 / 42.6	26.8	33.5	25.3	17.7 / 13.8	-6.2	12.5	21.4	43.3	67.7 / 73.0	93.1
6 Other activities of the material sphere	5.4	11.4 / 11.1	17.6	24.4	21.7	14.3 / 19.0	16.5	57.5	74.7	95.8	120.8 / 115.9	157.4
Total Material Sphere	86.1	288.6 / 288.3	330.4	336.7	264.0	174.1 / 170.3	73.5	365.2	514.1	631.6	767.7 / 761.8	086.7
7 Housing except owner-occupied, communal and miscellaneous personal services	19.2	48.2 / 46.8	71.8	95.7	97.3	92.9 / 94.2	73.1	190.3	239.9	292.0	344.6 / 344.6	424.5
8 Education, culture and art	8.9	15.0 / 15.0	17.6	17.1	15.7	14.9 / 12.7	11.8	37.1	48.8	62.8	86.2 / 86.2	113.2
9 Health and social welfare services and sports	4.4	15.7 / 15.7	16.4	18.5	21.2	19.7 / 19.7	18.4	43.2	55.6	73.5	97.9 / 97.8	129.4
Total Non-Material Sphere Serving Individuals	32.5	78.9 / 77.5	105.8	131.3	134.2	127.5 / 126.6	103.3	270.6	344.3	428.3	528.7 / 528.6	667.1
10 Government	...	... / ...	...	...	...	... / ...	...	...	...	...	... / ...	...
11 Finance, credit and insurance	...	... / ...	...	...	...	... / ...	...	...	...	...	... / ...	...
12 Research, scientific and technological institutes		... / ...	...	...	...	... / ...	...	...	...	...	... / ...	...
13 Other activities of the non-material sphere	...	... / ...	...	...	...	... / ...	...	...	...	...	... / ...	...
Total Non-Material Sphere Serving the Community as a Whole	10.6	20.0 / 20.1	25.6	23.2	22.4	27.6 / 30.1	28.6	72.5	78.7	96.3	110.6 / 110.4	146.3
14 Owner-occupied dwellings	10.3	8.0 / 8.0	23.4	26.5	26.2	20.6 / 20.6	20.0	91.9	116.5	118.5	132.7 / 132.8	149.9
Total Net Fixed Capital Formation [a]	139.5	395.5 / 393.9	485.2	517.7	446.8	349.8 / 347.6	225.4	800.2	1053.6	1274.7	1539.7 / 1533.6	1950.0
					Gross Fixed Capital Formation							
1 Agriculture and forestry	36.8	78.3 / 78.3	113.1	119.8	120.7	93.7 / 93.2	94.3	192.3	251.1	301.0	331.8 / 331.8	397.0

Poland

6a Capital Formation by Kind of Activity of the Material and Non-Material Spheres in Current Market Prices
(Continued)

Thousand Million Polish zlotych

	1970	1975	1977	1978	1979	1980	1981	1982	1983	1984	1985	1986
2 Industrial activity	87.7	227.4 / 227.4	264.5	269.2	228.8	203.3 / 202.1	151.2	293.0	353.4	469.1	615.2 / 612.5	804.3
3 Construction	10.0	27.9 / 27.9	34.7	36.6	31.0	26.7 / 26.6	15.2	18.2	24.6	36.3	47.1 / 47.1	63.2
4 Wholesale and retail trade and restaurants and other eating and drinking places	5.5	12.1 / 12.1	14.0	14.0	12.6	11.4 / 11.3	10.7	24.3	33.7	41.3	49.1 / 51.8	81.7
5 Transport and communciation	32.4	68.7 / 68.7	55.8	65.9	62.1	60.5 / 54.6	34.8	53.0	66.8	105.3	145.5 / 145.5	189.8
6 Other activities of the material sphere	7.2	15.3 / 15.3	22.9	30.2	28.9	21.5 / 27.0	25.3	68.9	88.5	116.8	149.3 / 149.3	199.0
Total Material Sphere	179.6	429.7 / 429.7	505.0	535.7	484.1	417.1 / 414.8	331.5	649.7	818.1	1069.8	1338.0 / 1338.0	1735.0
7 Housing except owner-occupied, communal and miscellaneous personal services	25.0	54.1 / 54.1	80.6	105.3	107.5	104.0 / 102.6	82.0	200.0	250.6	312.4	375.8 / 375.8	467.7
8 Education, culture and art	9.2	17.1 / 17.1	20.4	20.0	18.7	17.9 / 17.8	17.1	42.6	54.0	69.6	94.3 / 94.3	122.9
9 Health and social welfare services and sports	4.9	16.1 / 16.1	17.1	19.4	22.1	20.7 / 20.6	19.3	44.0	56.9	75.6	100.6 / 100.7	132.8
Total Non-Material Sphere Serving Individuals	39.1	87.3 / 87.3	118.1	144.7	148.3	142.6 / 141.0	118.4	286.6	361.5	457.6	570.7 / 570.8	723.4
10 Government	...	... / ...	...	...	...	... / ...	...	...	...	...	... / ...	...
11 Finance, credit and insurance	...	... / ...	...	...	...	... / ...	...	...	...	...	... / ...	...
12 Research, scientific and technological institutes	...	... / ...	...	...	...	... / ...	...	...	...	...	... / ...	...
13 Other activities of the non-material sphere	...	... / ...	...	...	...	... / ...	...	...	...	...	... / ...	...
Total Non-Material Sphere Serving the Community as a Whole	12.9	20.3 / 20.3	26.2	23.6	22.8	28.2 / 30.6	29.2	73.2	79.7	97.1	111.8 / 111.8	148.0
14 Owner-occupied dwellings	12.3	19.3 / 19.3	35.6	39.4	39.8	34.8 / 34.8	34.8	107.9	135.2	156.4	190.2 / 190.2	229.1
Total Gross Fixed Capital Formation	243.9	556.6 / 556.6	684.9	743.4	695.0	622.7 / 621.2	513.9	1117.4	1394.5	1780.9	2210.7 / 2210.8	2835.5

a) Computing of amortization according to spheres and divisions in 1972 and 1973 is not possible, therefore the sum of spheres is not equal to the total net investment outlays for fixed capital formation.

Poland

6b Capital Formation by Kind of Activity of the Material and Non-Material Spheres in Constant Market Prices

Thousand Million Polish zlotych

	1970	1975	1977	1978	1979	1980	1981	1982	1983	1984	1985	1986
		1971			At constant prices of: **1977**			**1982**			**1984**	

Net Fixed Capital Formation

	1970	1975	1977	1978	1979	1980	1981	1982	1983	1984	1985	1986
1 Agriculture and forestry	...	... / 69.2	84.7	82.6	77.0	48.1 / 216.5	197.8	139.4	149.8	151.7	127.2 / 61.9	52.6
2 Industrial activity	...	... / 188.7	171.7	146.1	97.4	56.7 / 338.8	203.6	144.5	160.0	198.8	229.3 / 84.0	104.1
3 Construction	...	... / 18.3	18.0	15.2	7.7	1.7 / 40.3	13.6	-0.9	3.6	10.0	12.2 / -7.5	-3.7
4 Wholesale and retail trade, restaurants and other eating and drinking places	...	... / 9.8	7.5	6.2	4.3	2.9 / 20.4	18.9	17.2	21.5	24.0	23.8 / 22.6	28.4
5 Transport and communication	...	... / 39.1	26.1	27.0	20.4	18.8 / 84.5	38.5	12.5	15.6	39.9	52.6 / 11.8	17.4
6 Other activities of the material sphere	...	... / 14.8	17.6	18.7	16.1	13.4 / 63.8	57.1	57.5	64.2	75.1	82.3 / 84.5	91.8
Total Material Sphere	...	... / 339.9	325.6	295.8	222.9	141.6 / 764.3	529.5	370.2	414.7	499.8	527.4 / 257.3	290.6
7 Housing except owner-occupied, communal and miscellaneous personal services	...	... / 57.9	71.8	78.9	81.4	75.5 / 289.4	229.0	190.3	209.9	221.6	226.4 / 270.7	269.6
8 Education, culture and art	...	... / 17.2	17.6	15.8	14.7	13.8 / 41.9	39.7	37.1	42.4	47.5	55.4 / 69.4	73.7
9 Health and social welfare services and sports	...	... / 18.0	16.4	17.1	19.5	18.3 / 52.4	46.4	43.2	48.6	55.4	62.5 / 81.5	88.2
Total Non-Material Sphere Serving Individuals	...	... / 93.1	105.8	111.8	115.6	107.6 / 383.7	315.1	270.6	300.9	324.5	344.3 / 421.6	431.5
10 Government	...	...	...	...	...	...	...	...	...	...	...	...
11 Finance, credit and insurance	...	...	...	...	...	...	...	...	...	...	...	...
12 Research, scientific and technological institutes	...	...	...	...	...	...	...	...	...	...	...	...
13 Other activities of the non-material sphere	...	...	...	...	...	...	...	...	...	...	...	...
Total Non-Material Sphere Serving the Community as a Whole	...	... / 23.2	25.6	29.7	28.8	26.4 / 83.5	78.4	72.4	69.1	72.6	95.0 / 93.4	100.9
14 Owner-occupied dwellings	...	... / 14.1	21.6	22.3	21.4	14.4 / 94.6	82.4	91.9	96.7	92.7	71.0 / 66.0	65.0
Total Net Fixed Capital Formation	...	... / 470.3	478.6	459.6	388.7	290.0 / 1326.1	1005.4	805.1	881.4	989.6	1037.7 / 838.3	888.0

Gross Fixed Capital Formation

	1970	1975	1977	1978	1979	1980	1981	1982	1983	1984	1985	1986
1 Agriculture and forestry	40.0	77.0 / 92.9	111.3	113.6	111.9	87.5 / 263.5	247.3	197.1	213.7	218.2	195.8 / 283.7	281.9

Poland

6b Capital Formation by Kind of Activity of the Material and Non-Material Spheres in Constant Market Prices
(Continued)

Thousand Million Polish zlotych

	1970	1975	1977	1978	1979	1980	1981	1982	1983	1984	1985	1986
					At constant prices of:							
		1971		1977				1982			1984	
2 Industrial activity	97.1	246.3 / 258.2	262.4	250.0	210.6	180.8 / 465.0	338.3	293.1	314.2	357.4	393.0 / 507.1	541.1
3 Construction	10.6	30.8 / 31.5	34.6	34.0	28.4	23.8 / 61.2	35.1	18.2	21.8	28.5	31.1 / 39.5	43.8
4 Wholesale and retail trade and restaurants and other eating and drinking places	6.2	12.9 / 14.6	14.0	13.1	11.6	10.2 / 26.8	25.8	24.3	29.8	32.8	32.5 / 49.3	56.4
5 Transport and communciation	34.8	73.4 / 65.2	55.7	59.1	55.3	55.6 / 125.4	79.5	53.0	59.7	84.7	97.9 / 122.6	132.1
6 Other activities of the material sphere	8.3	19.9 / 18.9	22.8	24.7	23.3	20.8 / 73.3	67.6	68.9	78.1	90.0	98.0 / 127.5	136.9
Total Material Sphere	197.0	460.3 / 481.3	500.8	494.5	441.1	378.7 / 1015.2	793.6	654.6	717.3	811.6	848.3 / 1129.7	1192.2
7 Housing except owner-occupied, communal and miscellaneous personal services	28.9	53.1 / 65.2	80.6	88.5	91.6	86.6 / 297.8	237.9	200.0	220.7	233.2	238.7 / 321.4	322.2
8 Education, culture and art	10.4	17.0 / 19.2	20.4	18.7	17.7	16.8 / 47.0	45.0	42.6	47.5	52.7	60.8 / 80.4	85.9
9 Health and social welfare services and sports	5.6	13.6 / 18.4	17.0	17.9	20.4	19.3 / 53.3	47.3	44.0	50.0	56.9	64.0 / 85.3	92.4
Total Non-Material Sphere Serving Individuals	44.9	83.7 / 102.8	118.0	125.1	129.7	122.7 / 398.1	330.2	286.6	318.2	342.8	363.5 / 487.1	500.5
10 Government	...	... / ...	...	...	...	... / ...	...	...	...	...	... / ...	...
11 Finance, credit and insurance	...	... / ...	...	...	...	... / ...	...	...	...	...	... / ...	...
12 Research, scientific and technological institutes	...	... / ...	...	...	...	... / ...	...	...	...	...	... / ...	...
13 Other activities of the non-material sphere	...	... / ...	...	...	...	... / ...	...	...	...	...	... / ...	...
Total Non-Material Sphere Serving the Community as a Whole	14.8	24.9 / 23.6	26.1	30.1	29.4	26.9 / 84.1	79.0	73.2	70.0	73.6	72.1 / 95.2	102.9
14 Owner-occupied dwellings	13.2	17.2 / 25.3	33.8	35.3	35.0	28.7 / 108.8	97.2	107.9	115.4	112.8	115.4 / 160.2	161.0
Total Gross Fixed Capital Formation	269.9	586.1 / 633.0	678.7	685.0	635.2	557.0 / 1606.2	1300.0	1122.3	1220.9	1340.8	1399.3 / 1872.2	1956.6

Poland

7a Final Consumption at Current Market Prices

Thousand Million Polish zlotych

	1970	1975	1977	1978	1979	1980	1981	1982	1983	1984	1985	1986
1 Personal consumption	465.0	799.7 805.2	1039.6	1130.7	1245.5	1404.0 1409.3	1721.2	2929.3	3749.6	4455.8	5189.9 5205.9	6403.2

a) Material Consumption in the Units of the Non-Material Sphere Serving Individuals

2 Total non-material sphere serving individuals	...	... ...	...	...	...	... ...	...	...	...	...	... ...	...

b) Material Consumption in the Units of the Non-Material Sphere Serving the Community as a Whole

3 Total non-material sphere serving the community as a whole	83.0	146.6 152.3	205.1	228.7	247.4	264.5 255.1	276.4	525.7	687.9	885.1	1120.2 1083.6	1321.3
Final consumption	548.0	946.3 957.5	1244.7	1359.4	1492.9	1668.5 1664.4	1997.6	3455.0	4437.5	5340.9	6310.1 6289.5	7724.5

7b Final Consumption at Constant Market Prices

Thousand Million Polish zlotych

	1970	1975	1977	1978	1979	1980	1981	1982	1983	1984	1985	1986

At constant prices of:

		1971		1977				1982			1984	
1 Personal consumption	470.4	706.3 875.5	1014.0	1023.7	1056.9	1081.1 3651.2	3502.3	2989.4	3176.0	3295.1	3367.6 4624.1	4855.2

a) Material Consumption in the Units of the Non-Material Sphere Serving Individuals

2 Total non-material sphere serving individuals	...	... ...	...	...	...	... ...	...	...	...	...	... ...	...

b) Material Consumption in the Units of the Non-Material Sphere Serving the Community as a Whole

3 Total non-material sphere serving the community as a whole	81.8	130.4 168.1	199.0	209.8	214.9	217.4 525.0	482.5	538.1	554.8	600.9	640.4 950.6	989.6
Final consumption	552.2	836.7 1043.6	1213.0	1233.5	1271.8	1298.5 4176.2	3984.8	3527.5	3730.8	3896.0	4008.0 5574.7	5844.8

Poland

8 Personal Consumption According to Source of Supply of Goods and Material Services in Current Market Prices

Thousand Million Polish zlotych

	1970	1975	1977	1978	1979	1980	1981	1982	1983	1984	1985	1986
1 Purchases of goods in state and co-operative retail trade	342.2	640.7 643.6	828.0	896.3	992.6	1105.0 1101.4	1272.6	2215.6	2902.5	3441.3	4001.5 4008.6	4960.7
2 Purchases of goods in the free market and from private retail trade	30.1	31.5 31.4	40.8	47.0	50.6	68.9 68.8	132.7	211.1	232.3	279.6	311.9 330.9	385.7
3 Goods produced on own account and received in kind	45.8	52.7 50.2	67.9	71.4	74.7	85.3 85.3	135.9	218.5	236.0	257.0	286.1 286.1	333.7
4 Payments for transport and communication services	16.8	29.5 31.6	39.1	41.9	46.1	52.6 54.9	63.2	83.0	138.9	167.1	208.7 208.7	255.6
5 Purchases of electricity, gas and water	8.0	12.7 9.1	10.7	11.4	12.6	13.8 13.8	15.2	30.8	33.4	38.8	46.1 46.1	58.2
6 Purchases directly from handicrafts, repair shops and the like	14.6	23.3 28.0	40.9	49.8	55.3	64.2 70.9	86.8	154.2	187.8	234.1	278.2 268.0	330.1
7 Consumption of fixed assets in respect of all dwellings	7.5	9.3 11.3	12.2	12.9	13.6	14.2 14.2	14.8	16.1	18.7	37.9	57.4 57.5	79.2
8 Other	...	... ...	...	...	...	... ...	...	...	...	...	... ...	...
Personal consumption	465.0	799.7 805.2	1039.6	1130.7	1245.5	1404.0 1409.3	1721.2	2929.3	3749.6	4455.8	5189.9 5205.9	6403.2

9a Total Consumption of the Population in Current Market Prices

Thousand Million Polish zlotych

	1970	1975	1977	1978	1979	1980	1981	1982	1983	1984	1985	1986
					By Object							
1 Housing except owner-occupied, communal and miscellaneous personal services	6.9	8.2 12.6	14.9	16.5	18.0	19.5 20.1	21.8	30.4	38.5	57.0	76.8 76.8	101.7
2 Education, culture and art	7.6	11.0 9.7	12.4	13.3	14.3	15.2 14.5	15.9	23.3	30.5	37.3	44.1 44.2	57.7
3 Health and social welfare services and sport	7.3	10.3 10.2	14.0	15.3	16.6	18.0 20.0	21.3	30.8	47.9	66.1	84.0 84.0	99.7
Statistical discrepancy [a]	5.9	9.5 8.8	9.7	10.7	12.1	11.9 11.0	14.0	15.9	24.3	32.9	44.1 44.2	59.1
Total consumption of non-material services	27.7	39.0 41.3	51.0	55.8	61.0	64.6 65.6	73.0	100.4	141.2	193.3	249.0 249.2	318.2
4 Personal consumption of goods and material services excluding depreciation of dwellings	455.9	790.4 793.9	1027.4	1117.8	1231.9	1389.8 1395.1	1706.4	2913.2	3730.9	4417.9	5132.5 5148.4	6324.0
Statistical discrepancy [b]	67.7	116.9 115.5	151.8	166.4	188.1	211.3 207.7	250.2	452.8	612.2	786.9	972.6 972.6	1178.2
Total consumption of the population	551.3	946.3 950.7	1230.2	1340.0	1481.0	1665.7 1668.4	2029.6	3466.4	4484.3	5398.1	6354.1 6370.2	7820.4

Poland

9a Total Consumption of the Population in Current Market Prices
(Continued)

Thousand Million Polish zlotych

	1970	1975	1977	1978	1979	1980	1981	1982	1983	1984	1985	1986
By Commodity and Service												
1 Food c	204.9	290.7 / 288.4	353.9	383.6	419.3	479.9 / 478.6	629.0	1274.1	1427.2	1651.7	1920.1 / 1928.4	2338.2
2 Beverages, coffee and tea	55.5	121.4 / 121.3	166.4	188.9	213.5	233.6 / 233.4	235.1	462.5	644.5	777.0	882.9 / 883.4	1064.6
3 Tobacco	13.2	21.6 / 21.6	33.1	34.2	38.6	41.4 / 41.3	60.9	77.2	98.4	107.2	113.7 / 113.7	148.4
4 Clothing and footwear	72.1	126.3 / 129.2	149.7	154.7	166.2	184.1 / 187.0	222.0	260.1	374.5	470.8	556.3 / 557.0	745.6
5 Gross rent	12.9	15.6 / 20.5	33.8	38.7	43.0	45.3 / 44.1	49.1	99.2	126.1	164.7	204.3 / 204.3	260.2
6 Fuel, electricity, water and gas	13.9	19.1 / 14.7	15.4	15.6	17.2	19.2 / 22.2	21.8	76.9	74.4	79.2	88.0 / 88.0	123.2
7 Furniture and household equipment	37.6	91.1 / 93.7	129.6	141.5	145.3	158.7 / 160.0	190.0	285.0	398.4	517.4	629.1 / 633.0	757.3
8 Health	41.6	73.8 / 73.8	93.5	101.7	114.6	134.6 / 134.3	158.9	256.5	326.1	389.4	483.4 / 483.3	602.4
9 Transport and communication	27.8	61.2 / 62.9	92.8	106.0	120.6	139.7 / 139.7	175.7	252.9	387.4	429.3	486.1 / 487.4	629.1
10 Education, recreation, sport	63.5	112.3 / 111.3	144.4	151.2	172.7	194.0 / 196.0	229.5	369.7	541.3	709.0	867.6 / 868.9	1051.0
11 Other	8.3	13.2 / 13.3	17.6	23.9	30.0	35.2 / 31.8	57.6	52.3	86.0	102.4	122.6 / 122.8	100.4
Total consumption of the population	551.3	946.3 / 950.7	1230.2	1340.0	1481.0	1665.7 / 1668.4	2029.6	3466.4	4484.3	5398.1	6354.1 / 6370.2	7820.4
By Mode of Acquisition												
1 Purchased	437.9	776.7 / 785.0	1010.5	1102.2	1218.2	1369.1 / 1375.4	1643.4	2795.1	3636.1	4354.2	5095.4 / 5111.5	6308.5
2 Free of charge	67.6	116.9 / 115.5	151.8	166.4	188.1	211.3 / 207.7	250.2	452.8	612.2	786.9	972.6 / 972.6	1178.2
3 From own production	45.8	52.7 / 50.2	67.9	71.4	74.7	85.3 / 85.3	136.0	218.5	236.0	257.0	286.1 / 286.1	333.7
Total consumption of the population	551.0	946.0 / 950.7	1230.2	1340.0	1481.0	1665.7 / 1668.4	2029.6	3466.4	4484.3	5398.1	6354.1 / 6370.2	7820.4

a) Item 'Statistical discrepancy' refers to other non-material services.
b) Except for an amount of 0.1 for 1970 which refers to statistical discrepancy, item 'Statistical discrepancy' refers to consumption from social funds, (benefits in kind).
c) For series 1, including consumption of food in schools, health institutions, sports institutions etc.

Portugal

General note. The preparation of national accounts statistics in Portugal is undertaken by the Instituto Nacional de Estatistica, Lisbon. The official estimates are published annually in the 'Annuario Estatistico'. A detailed description of the sources and methods used for the national accounts estimation is found in 'As Contas Nacionais Portuguesas 1958-1971', published by the Institute in 1972. The estimates are generally in accordance with the classification and definitions recommended in the United Nations System of National Accounts (SNA). Input-output table for 1959 has been published in 'Algunas Aplicacoes de Analise Input-Output a Matriz Portuguesa de 1959'. The following tables have been prepared from successive replies to the United Nations national accounts questionnaire. When the scope and coverage of the estimates differ for conceptual or statistical reasons from the definitions and classifications recommended in SNA, a footnote is indicated to the relevant tables.

Sources and methods:

(a) Gross domestic product. Gross domestic product is estimated mainly through the production approach.

(b) Expenditure on the gross domestic product. All items of GDP by expenditure type are estimated through the expenditure approach. The commodity-flow approach is also used for part of private final consumption expenditure. The estimates of government consumption expenditure are obtained from the government accounts. For private consumption expenditure, only estimates for food, beverages, tobacco, gross rent, fuel and power are made. For other components an estimate is derived as a residual between GDP and other final uses. The estimates of food, beverages and tobacco are based on retail prices and quantities consumed. Quantities consumed of other consumer products are available either through direct information or from production and foreign trade statistics, taking into account changes in producers' and wholesalers' stocks. Expenditures on house rent are estimated on the basis of information published in Estatisticas das Contribucoes e Impostos, adding 12 per cent for repairs. The calculation of increase in stocks is based on information on stock values supplied by corporations. Fixed capital formation in the private sector is estimated on the basis of annual surveys of corporation, the results of which are used to calculate increasing coefficients to be applied to total fixed capital formation. The annual construction surveys are used for the estimations of expenditure on new dwellings. For the public sector, investment is estimated from the revenue and expenditure data of the central government and other state organizations. Data for estimating exports and imports of goods and services are obtained from the balance of payments. For the constant price estimates, current values of government consumption expenditure, gross capital formation and exports and imports of goods and services are deflated by appropriate price indexes. For private consumption expenditure, the current quantities of the items estimated are revalued at base-year prices.

(c) Cost-structure of the gross domestic product. Wages and salaries for private sector are calculated per capita and applied to the number of employees which are obtained from the employment surveys submitted by the enterprises. Remuneration data for the government sector are obtained from government accounts. The data on employers' contributions to social security schemes are taken from 'seguro social'. Mathematical formulae are used to calculate consumption of fixed capital. Indirect taxes and subsidies are obtained directly from the government accounts.

(d) Gross domestic product by kind of economic activity. The table of GDP by kind of economic activity is prepared in factor values. The production approach is used to estimate value added of goods-production sectors whereas the income approach is used for the service sectors. The principal sources used to estimate agricultural production are Estadisticas Agricolas and the monthly Estado das Culturas e Previsao das Colheitas which contain data on quantities and prices. Data on intermediate consumption are supplied by the entities that supply the products. For products of forestry and logging not covered by statistics on agriculture, estimates are based on per capita data on consumption. For fishery, quantity and price data are obtained from fishery statistics while intermediate consumtpion is calculated as a percentage of the gross value of production. For the industrial activity sectors estimates are obtained directly from Estatisticas Industriais and the Anuario Estatistico. Adjustments are made for activities in the manufacturing sector not covered in these two sources by using the industrial census of 1957. Value added of electricity, gas and water is obtained directly from annual surveys of corporatons, non-corporations and local government services. The construction estimates are based on annual surveys of enterprises. For dwellings taxation statistics are used and the figures relating to floor area of new buildings are multiplied by the average cost of construction by region. For the trade sector, the annual surveys of corporations are used for the corporations while data on the economically active population and the value added per capita for the retail trade is used for the individual enterprises. Taxation statistics and information provided by corporation are used for restaurants and hotels. The value added of the transport sector is obtained from the concerned companies and from annual surveys. The estimates for the financial institutions are based on direct information whereas data published in 'Estatisticas das Contribucoes e Impostoa' are used for ownership of dwellings. For government services, value added is obtained through government accounts. For private services, estimates are obtained through the use of data from 'Estatisticas de Educacao' for education, inquiries held in various cities for domestic servants, number of tickets sold for recreational services and taxation statistics for other personal services. For the constant price estimates, double deflation is used for the agricultural sector. Value added for construction, trade, restaurants, services incidental to transport, financial institutions, and community services is deflated by appropriate price indexes. For industrial activity sectors, hotels, transport and ownership of dwellings, value added is extrapolated by quantity indexes.

1.1 Expenditure on the Gross Domestic Product, in Current Prices

Million Portuguese escudos

		1970	1975	1977	1978	1979	1980	1981	1982	1983	1984	1985	1986
1	Government final consumption expenditure	25245	57983	90200 87847	109670	137576	182608	225892	266600	333500	405500	501800	...
2	Private final consumption expenditure	122370	303768	470223 450377	535360	670255	845522	1045450	1274900	1584000	1986600	2387700	...
	A Households	...	...	... 448535	533128	667269	840705	1040150	...	...	...	...	...
	B Private non-profit institutions serving households	...	...	... 1842	2232	2986	4817	5300	...	...	...	...	...
3	Gross capital formation	41806	61471	157936 181744	239997	293016	412011	518815	653900	628500	610900	710100	...
	A Increase in stocks	10551	-12521	32436 15937	20223	29060	53164	55803	71900	-43900	-59000	-56600	...
	B Gross fixed capital formation	31255	73992	125500 165807	219774	263956	358847	463012	582000	672400	669900	766700	...
	Residential buildings	4441	14316	... 50867	65227	68053	88914	95811	...	...	...	...	...
	Non-residential buildings	11698	32642	... 9407	17462	20000	35856	36871	...	...	...	...	...
	Other construction and land improvement etc.	723	956	... 35155	47396	60909	78536	109950	...	...	...	...	...
	Other	14393	26078	... 70378	89689	114994	155541	220380	...	...	...	...	...
4	Exports of goods and services	41742	74067	110984 115298	158369	268723	343950	389515	474900	706400	1051400	1357800	...
5	Less: Imports of goods and services	53825	121050	205109 209431	256136	376265	528040	678536	822300	973300	1248900	1432600	...
	Equals: Gross Domestic Product	177338	376239	624234 625835	787260	993305	1256050	1501130	1848000	2279100	2805500	3524800	...

Portugal

1.2 Expenditure on the Gross Domestic Product, in Constant Prices

Million Portuguese escudos

	1970	1975	1977	1978	1979	1980	1981	1982	1983	1984	1985	1986
			At constant prices of:									
		1963					1977					
1 Government final consumption expenditure	18003	28057	33563 / 87847	91710	97490	105190	108140	111170	114170	117020	119010	...
2 Private final consumption expenditure	95288	136096	141704 / 450377	441370	440490	457670	466370	476160	471400	457260	461830	...
3 Gross capital formation	33684	22615	39289 / 181744	189630	207100	231290	243080	251330	197570	160780	159970	...
A Increase in stocks	8475	-5791	7213 / 15937	12000	33380	42630	44800	47300	8840	6020	9850	...
B Gross fixed capital formation	25209	28406	32076 / 165807	177630	173720	188660	198280	204030	188730	154760	150120	...
Residential buildings	3640	5103	...	...	...	...	...	...	...	...	...	...
Non-residential buildings	9658	11634	...	...	...	...	...	...	...	...	...	...
Other construction and land improvement etc.	421	407	...	...	...	...	...	...	...	...	...	...
Other	11490	11262	...	...	...	...	...	...	...	...	...	...
4 Exports of goods and services	33881	32715	34645 / 115298	130400	165740	173200	168000	178080	207820	237330	263670	...
5 Less: Imports of goods and services	43198	48909	56641 / 209431	206080	224010	247530	256690	270550	247010	240340	248270	...
Equals: Gross Domestic Product	137658	170574	192560 / 625835	647030	686810	719820	728900	746190	743060	702050	750210	...

1.3 Cost Components of the Gross Domestic Product

Million Portuguese escudos

	1970	1975	1977	1978	1979	1980	1981	1982	1983	1984	1985	1986
1 Indirect taxes, net	18306	34101	58400 / 57798	60538	74745	111544	133645	157500	199200	213800	347200	...
A Indirect taxes	21036	41741	79300 / 81546	96622	119679	176915	215073	261900	358100	426600	497600	...
B Less: Subsidies [a]	2730	7640	20900 / 23748	36084	44934	65371	81428	104400	158900	212800	150400	...
2 Consumption of fixed capital	9373	18022	27000 / 26090	35740	43270	53960	62040	79600	98500	121500	151600	...
3 Compensation of employees paid by resident producers to:	79313	224241	335734 / 345711	411200	503638	642966	788599	967300	1157100	1321000	1583300	...
A Resident households	77821	221597	... / 344329	409547	501676	639987	786066	...	...	...	...	...
B Rest of the world	1492	2644	... / 1382	1653	1962	2979	2533	...	...	...	...	...
4 Operating surplus	70346	99875	203100 / 196236	279782	371652	447581	516847	643600	824300	1149200	1442700	...
Equals: Gross Domestic Product	177338	376239	624234 / 625835	787260	993305	1256050	1501130	1848000	2279100	2805500	3524800	...

a) The 1973, 1975 and 1976 estimates for item 'Subsidies' in table 1.3 differ from those of table 1.4. In the first case they are entered on an accrual payment basis, in the second case they are entered on a cash payment basis.

1.4 General Government Current Receipts and Disbursements

Million Portuguese escudos

	1970	1975	1977	1978	1979	1980	1981	1982	1983	1984	1985	1986
					Receipts							
1 Operating surplus	274	144	363	982	1219	1092	1710	...	...	...	...	...
2 Property and entrepreneurial income	1710	1601	5203	8101	16254	10173	14793	...	...	...	...	...
3 Taxes, fees and contributions	40092	88888	177370	214420	270025	368528	466207	...	...	...	...	...
A Indirect taxes	21036	41741	81546	96622	119679	176915	215073	...	...	...	...	...
B Direct taxes	10819	20065	37573	47993	65880	81993	113224	...	...	...	...	...
C Social security contributions	8237	27082	58251	69805	84466	109620	137910	...	...	...	...	...
D Compulsory fees, fines and penalties	...	...	...	...	...	...	...	...	...	...	...	...

Portugal

1.4 General Government Current Receipts and Disbursements
(Continued)

Million Portuguese escudos

	1970	1975	1977	1978	1979	1980	1981	1982	1983	1984	1985	1986
4 Other current transfers	1010	2533	8181	8402	10230	14300	16494	...	...	...	...	...
Total Current Receipts of General Government	43086	93166	191117	231905	297728	394093	499204	...	...	...	...	...
				Disbursements								
1 Government final consumption expenditure	25245	57983	87847	109670	137576	182608	225892	...	...	...	...	...
A Compensation of employees	...	...	69644	87656	108472	144647	176711	...	...	...	...	...
B Consumption of fixed capital	...	55	...	...	...	...	...	...	...	...	...	...
C Purchases of goods and services, net	...	...	18198	22010	29064	37925	49167	...	...	...	...	...
D Less: Own account fixed capital formation	...	...	...	...	...	...	...	...	...	...	...	...
E Indirect taxes paid, net	...	...	5	4	40	36	14	...	...	...	...	...
2 Property income	975	2753	10754	21111	28557	38755	80122	...	...	...	...	...
A Interest	...	...	10747	21107	28532	38749	80115	...	...	...	...	...
B Net land rent and royalties	...	...	7	4	25	6	7	...	...	...	...	...
3 Subsidies [a]	2730	7473	23748	36084	44934	65371	81428	...	...	...	...	...
4 Other current transfers	5666	34249	70439	83112	98976	137435	177082	...	...	...	...	...
A Social security benefits	4537	23285	44906	58127	69813	100557	133493	...	...	...	...	...
B Social assistance grants	971	8963	19873	17754	20206	25072	32026	...	...	...	...	...
C Other	158	2001	5660	7231	8957	11806	11563	...	...	...	...	...
5 Net saving [b]	8470	-9292	-1671	-18072	-12315	-30076	-65320	...	...	...	...	...
Total Current Disbursements and Net Saving of General Government	43086	93166	191117	231905	297728	394093	499204	...	...	...	...	...

a) The 1973, 1975 and 1976 estimates for item 'Subsidies' in table 1.3 differ from those of table 1.4. In the first case they are entered on an accrual payment basis, in the second case they are entered on a cash payment basis.   b) Item 'Net saving' includes consumption of fixed capital.

1.5 Current Income and Outlay of Corporate and Quasi-Corporate Enterprises, Summary

Million Portuguese escudos

	1970	1975	1977	1978	1979	1980	1981	1982	1983	1984	1985	1986
					Receipts							
1 Operating surplus	...	...	45651	84250	124250	151159	165501	...	...	...	...	...
2 Property and entrepreneurial income received	...	...	74978	136349	190970	242937	347826	...	...	...	...	...
3 Current transfers	...	...	13609	17324	26953	38057	44353	...	...	...	...	...
Total Current Receipts	...	...	134238	237923	342173	432153	557680	...	...	...	...	...
					Disbursements							
1 Property and entrepreneurial income	...	...	97819	173566	270630	334635	487953	...	...	...	...	...
2 Direct taxes and other current payments to general government	...	...	9122	11220	15109	22670	30852	...	...	...	...	...
3 Other current transfers	...	...	14015	17598	28159	40386	47217	...	...	...	...	...
Statistical discrepancy	...	...	703	897	1049	1492	1929	...	...	...	...	...
4 Net saving [a]	...	...	12579	34642	27226	32970	-10271	...	...	...	...	...
Total Current Disbursements and Net Saving	...	...	134238	237923	342173	432153	557680	...	...	...	...	...

a) Item 'Net saving' includes consumption of fixed capital.

Portugal

1.6 Current Income and Outlay of Households and Non-Profit Institutions

Million Portuguese escudos

	1970	1975	1977	1978	1979	1980	1981	1982	1983	1984	1985	1986
Receipts												
1 Compensation of employees	79313	224241	345257	410589	503251	642028	788893	...	...	...	...	...
A From resident producers	...	...	344329	409547	501676	639987	786066	...	...	...	...	...
B From rest of the world	...	...	928	1042	1575	2041	2827	...	...	...	...	...
2 Operating surplus of private unincorporated enterprises	...	...	176312	230290	289453	349290	411676	...	...	...	...	...
3 Property and entrepreneurial income	57249	106839	32739	55166	112960	141575	205120	...	...	...	...	...
4 Current transfers	21378	61192	125871	166929	230547	304977	377589	...	...	...	...	...
A Social security benefits	4537	23285	66985	78680	92958	132634	173239	...	...	...	...	...
B Social assistance grants	...	...	...	...	...	...	...	...	...	...	...	...
C Other	16841	37907	58886	88249	137589	172343	204350	...	...	...		
Statistical discrepancy	...	...	703	897	1049	1492	1929	...	...	...	...	...
Total Current Receipts	157940	392272	680882	863871	1137260	1439360	1785210	...	...	...	...	...
Disbursements												
1 Private final consumption expenditure	122370	303768	450377	535360	670255	845522	1045450	...	...	...	...	...
2 Property income	...	...	11795	20016	42946	52935	62148	...	...	...	...	...
3 Direct taxes and other current transfers n.e.c. to general government	14303	41298	89172	109628	138829	173932	226852	...	...	...	...	...
A Social security contributions	8237	27082	60721	72855	88058	114609	144480	...	...	...	...	...
B Direct taxes	6066	14216	28451	36773	50771	59323	82372	...	...	...	...	...
C Fees, fines and penalties	...	...	...	...	...	...	...	...	...	...	...	...
4 Other current transfers	1309	2958	17233	20491	24370	32553	38880	...	...	...	...	...
5 Net saving	19958	44248	112305	178376	260860	334420	411882	...	...	...	...	...
Total Current Disbursements and Net Saving	157940	392272	680882	863871	1137260	1439360	1785210	...	...	...	...	...

1.7 External Transactions on Current Account, Summary

Million Portuguese escudos

	1970	1975	1977	1978	1979	1980	1981	1982	1983	1984	1985	1986
Payments to the Rest of the World												
1 Imports of goods and services	53825	121050	209431	256136	376265	528040	678536	...	...	...	...	...
A Imports of merchandise c.i.f.	42764	99598	194620	236361	345510	488209	630478	...	...	...	...	...
B Other	11061	21452	14811	19775	30755	39831	48058	...	...	...	...	...
2 Factor income to the rest of the world	1492	2644	10690	19786	29313	41736	74865	...	...	...	...	...

Portugal

1.7 External Transactions on Current Account, Summary
(Continued)

Million Portuguese escudos

	1970	1975	1977	1978	1979	1980	1981	1982	1983	1984	1985	1986
A Compensation of employees	1492	2644	1382	1653	1962	2979	2533	...	...	...	...	...
B Property and entrepreneurial income	...	...	9308	18133	27351	38757	72332	...	...	...	...	...
3 Current transfers to the rest of the world	547	1550	5765	7511	7517	6864	5650	...	...	...	...	...
A Indirect taxes to supranational organizations	...	...	...	...	...	...	...	...	...	...	...	...
B Other current transfers	547	1550	5765	7511	7517	6864	5650	...	...	...	...	...
4 Surplus of the nation on current transactions	3373	-20866	-58531	-45051	-17245	-74697	-182524	...	...	...	...	...
Payments to the Rest of the World and Surplus of the Nation on Current Transactions	59237	104378	167355	238382	395850	501943	576527	...	...	...	...	...

Receipts From The Rest of the World

	1970	1975	1977	1978	1979	1980	1981	1982	1983	1984	1985	1986
1 Exports of goods and services	41742	74067	115298	158369	268723	343950	389515	...	...	...	...	...
A Exports of merchandise f.o.b.	26596	49456	84973	114514	193115	247564	275979	...	...	...	...	...
B Other	15146	24611	30325	43855	75608	96386	113536	...	...	...	...	...
2 Factor income from rest of the world	2381	2275	2788	4098	6977	9158	12675	...	...	...	...	...
A Compensation of employees	2381	2275	928	1042	1575	2041	2827	...	...	...	...	...
B Property and entrepreneurial income	...	...	1860	3056	5402	7117	9848	...	...	...	...	...
3 Current transfers from rest of the world	15114	28036	49269	75915	120150	148835	174337	...	...	...	...	...
A Subsidies from supranational organisations	...	...	1765	554	664	563	1095	...	...	...	...	...
B Other current transfers	15114	28036	47504	75361	119486	148272	173242	...	...	...	...	...
Receipts from the Rest of the World on Current Transactions	59237	104378	167355	238382	395850	501943	576527	...	...	...	...	...

1.8 Capital Transactions of The Nation, Summary

Million Portuguese escudos

	1970	1975	1977	1978	1979	1980	1981	1982	1983	1984	1985	1986

Finance of Gross Capital Formation

	1970	1975	1977	1978	1979	1980	1981	1982	1983	1984	1985	1986
Gross saving	45179	40605	100500 / 123213	194946	275771	337314	336291	418500	484000	556400	815300	...
1 Consumption of fixed capital	9373	18022	27000 / 26090	35740	43270	53960	62040	79600	98500	121500	151600	...
A General government	...	55	...	...	...	...	...	...	...	...	...	...
B Corporate and quasi-corporate enterprises	9373	17967	...	...	...	...	...	...	...	...	...	...
Public	775	1340	...	...	...	...	...	...	...	...	...	...
Private	8598	16627	...	...	...	...	...	...	...	...	...	...
C Other	...	...	...	...	...	...	...	...	...	...	...	...
2 Net saving	35806	22583	73500 / 97123	159206	232501	283354	274251	338900	385500	434900	663700	...
A General government	8470	-9292	-1671	-18072	-12315	-30076	-65320	...	...	...	...	...
B Corporate and quasi-corporate enterprises	7378	-13156	12579	34642	27226	32970	-10271	...	...	...	...	...
Public	1336	5902	...	...	...	...	...	...	...	...	...	...
Private	6042	-19058	...	...	...	...	...	...	...	...	...	...

Portugal

1.8 Capital Transactions of The Nation, Summary
(Continued)

Million Portuguese escudos

	1970	1975	1977	1978	1979	1980	1981	1982	1983	1984	1985	1986
C Other	19958	45031	... 112305	178376	260860	334420	411882	...	...	...	...	...
Less: Surplus of the nation on current transactions	3373	-20866	-57436 -58531	-45051	-17245	-74697	-182524	-235400	-144500	-54500	105200	...
Finance of Gross Capital Formation	41806	61471	157936 181744	239997	293016	412011	518815	653900	628500	610900	710100	...

Gross Capital Formation

	1970	1975	1977	1978	1979	1980	1981	1982	1983	1984	1985	1986
Increase in stocks	10551	-12521	32436 15937	20223	29060	53164	55803	71900	-43900	-59000	-56600	...
Gross fixed capital formation	31255	73992	125500 165807	219774	263956	358847	463012	582000	672400	669900	766700	...
1 General government	3865	9068	... 18807	25822	37482	51605	74617	...	...	...	...	...
2 Corporate and quasi-corporate enterprises	...	...	84151	116563	143836	190220	239765	...	...	...	...	...
3 Other	...	...	62849	77389	82638	117022	148630	...	...	...	...	...
Gross Capital Formation	41806	61471	157936 181744	239997	293016	412011	518815	653900	628500	610900	710100	...

1.10 Gross Domestic Product by Kind of Activity, in Current Prices

Million Portuguese escudos

	1970	1975	1977	1978	1979	1980	1981	1982	1983	1984	1985	1986
1 Agriculture, hunting, forestry and fishing	28180	53022	74561	94000	115043	129899	134560	...	...	...	...	...
2 Mining and quarrying	916	2010	...	...	...	...	...	...	...	...	...	...
3 Manufacturing	53098	114817	174707	224320	303730	388982	470161	...	...	...	...	...
4 Electricity, gas and water	4311	6976	12046	16513	19954	26502	16097	...	...	...	...	...
5 Construction	8104	22619	47949	60719	65393	88852	113022	...	...	...	...	...
6 Wholesale and retail trade, restaurants and hotels	22820	47526	133798	168877	218701	272419	326190	...	...	...	...	...
7 Transport, storage and communication	10474	23628	35037	43534	54987	69341	93804	...	...	...	...	...
8 Finance, insurance, real estate and business services [a]	10274	21747	67171	95387	102692	131409	166562	...	...	...	...	...
9 Community, social and personal services [ab]	4464	8853	14976	18978	23619	30209	41011	...	...	...	...	...
Total, Industries	142641	301198	560245	722328	904119	1137610	1361410	...	...	...	...	...
Producers of Government Services	14674	38343	69649	87660	108512	144600	170725	...	...	...	...	...
Other Producers	1717	2597	7079	8362	10090	13282	16379	...	...	...	...	...
Subtotal [c]	159032	342138	636973	818350	1022720	1295580	1554510	...	...	...	...	...
Less: Imputed bank service charge	...	...	25928	44896	41902	55553	77588	...	...	...	...	...
Plus: Import duties	4153	8340	14790	13806	12486	16026	24208	...	...	...	...	...
Plus: Value added tax	...	...	...	...	...	...	...	...	...	...	...	...
Plus: Other adjustments [d]	14150	25701	...	...	...	...	...	...	...	...	...	...
Equals: Gross Domestic Product	177338	376239	625835	787260	993305	1256050	1501130	...	...	...	...	...
Memorandum Item: Mineral fuels and power	...	...	13252	18484	23919	29654	20823	...	...	...	...	...

a) Business services and real estate except dwellings are included in item 'Community, social and personal services'.
b) Repair services are included in item 'Community, social and personal services'.
c) For the first series, gross domestic product in factor values.
d) Item 'Other adjustments' refers to net indirect taxes other than import duties.

Portugal

1.11 Gross Domestic Product by Kind of Activity, in Constant Prices

Million Portuguese escudos

	1970	1975	1977	1978	1979	1980	1981	1982	1983	1984	1985	1986
		1963		At constant prices of:			1977					
1 Agriculture, hunting, forestry and fishing	19117	18093	... 74561	79012	95280	97420	87140	...	...	...	...	...
2 Mining and quarrying	606	951	...	...	...	...	...	...	...	...	...	...
3 Manufacturing	46285	59534	... 174707	183986	196310	204120	209050	...	...	...	...	...
4 Electricity, gas and water	4023	5706	12046	12250	13160	11000	8990	...	...	...	...	...
5 Construction	6607	8074	... 47949	54032	53870	57670	60380	...	...	...	...	...
6 Wholesale and retail trade, restaurants and hotels	17069	19487	133798	132918	136580	143260	145860	...	...	...	...	...
7 Transport, storage and communication	8455	11410	35037	35264	37800	41820	42550	...	...	...	...	...
8 Finance, insurance, real estate and business services	7896	10275	67171	79688	71250	75550	79170	...	...	...	...	...
9 Community, social and personal services	3066	3123	14976	14780	14960	15640	16220	...	...	...	...	...
Statistical discrepancy	...	...	-	-	-	-	2020	...	...	...	...	...
Total, Industries	113124	136653	... 560245	591930	619210	646480	651380	...	...	...	...	...
Producers of Government Services	10742	21411	69649	73703	78800	86090	90530	...	...	...	...	...
Other Producers	1219	903	7079	7203	7350	7350	7580	...	...	...	...	...
Subtotal	125085	158967	... 636973	672836	705360	739920	749490	...	...	...	...	...
Less: Imputed bank service charge	...	...	25928	37413	27010	28400	31510	...	...	...	...	...
Plus: Import duties	12573	11607	14790	11610	8530	8560	11480	...	...	...	...	...
Plus: Value added tax	...	...	...	...	...	...	...	...	...	...	...	...
Plus: Other adjustments	...	...	-	-	-70	-260	-560	...	...	...	...	...
Equals: Gross Domestic Product	137658	170574	... 625835	647033	686810	719820	728900	...	...	...	...	...

1.12 Relations Among National Accounting Aggregates

Million Portuguese escudos

	1970	1975	1977	1978	1979	1980	1981	1982	1983	1984	1985	1986
Gross Domestic Product	177338	376239	624234 625835	787260	993305	1256050	1501130	1848000	2279100	2805500	3524800	...
Plus: Net factor income from the rest of the world	889	-369	-6872 -7902	-15688	-22336	-32578	-62190	-103000	-119600	-177300	-196500	...
Factor income from the rest of the world	2381	2275	... 2788	4098	6977	9158	12675	...	...	...	...	...
Less: Factor income to the rest of the world	1492	2644	... 10690	19786	29313	41736	74865	...	...	...	...	...
Equals: Gross National Product	178227	375870	617362 617933	771572	970969	1223470	1438940	1745000	2159500	2628200	3328300	...
Less: Consumption of fixed capital	9373	18022	27000 26090	35740	43270	53960	62040	79600	98500	121500	151600	...

Portugal

1.12 Relations Among National Accounting Aggregates
(Continued)

Million Portuguese escudos

	1970	1975	1977	1978	1979	1980	1981	1982	1983	1984	1985	1986
Equals: National Income	168854	357848	590362 591843	735832	927699	1169510	1376900	1665400	2061000	2506700	3176700	...
Plus: Net current transfers from the rest of the world	14567	26486	43561 43504	68404	112633	141971	168687	215000	242000	320300	376500	...
Current transfers from the rest of the world	15114	28036	... 49269	75915	120150	148835	174337	...	...	...	...	...
Less: Current transfers to the rest of the world	547	1550	... 5765	7511	7517	6864	5650	...	...	...	...	...
Equals: National Disposable Income	183421	384334	633923 635347	804236	1040330	1311480	1545590	1880400	2303000	2827000	3553200	...
Less: Final consumption	147615	361751	560423 538224	645030	807831	1028130	1271340	1541500	1917500	2392100	2889500	...
Equals: Net Saving	35806	22583	73500 97123	159206	232501	283354	274251	338900	385500	434900	663700	...
Less: Surplus of the nation on current transactions	3373	-20866	-57436 -58531	-45051	-17245	-74697	-182524	-235400	-144500	-54500	105200	...
Equals: Net Capital Formation	32433	43449	130936 155654	204257	249746	358051	456775	574300	530000	489400	558500	...

2.1 Government Final Consumption Expenditure by Function, in Current Prices

Million Portuguese escudos

	1970	1975	1977	1978	1979	1980	1981	1982	1983	1984	1985	1986
1 General public services	6306	14592	11947	15425	20492	24705	29539	...	...	...	...	...
2 Defence	12730	16741	18170	21712	28047	36057	43001	...	...	...	...	...
3 Public order and safety	...	...	7501	9706	12005	15834	19232	...	...	...	...	...
4 Education	2918	13288	20644	24352	29567	42997	55279	...	...	...	...	...
5 Health	2752	11181	15746	19939	24131	32467	42661	...	...	...	...	...
6 Social security and welfare	530	2181	4942	6158	7977	11099	12748	...	...	...	...	...
7 Housing and community amenities	...	...	1506	1988	2510	3304	4230	...	...	...	...	...
8 Recreational, cultural and religious affairs	...	...	943	1234	1251	1980	2507	...	...	...	...	...
9 Economic services	...	...	6448	9156	11536	14120	16693	...	...	...	...	...
A Fuel and energy	...	...	31	34	25	11	15	...	...	...	...	...
B Agriculture, forestry, fishing and hunting	...	...	2232	3188	4256	5374	6251	...	...	...	...	...
C Mining, manufacturing and construction, except fuel and energy	...	...	437	530	849	1046	1362	...	...	...	...	...
D Transportation and communication	...	...	1214	1864	2049	1698	2217	...	...	...	...	...
E Other economic affairs	...	...	2534	3540	4357	5991	6848	...	...	...	...	...
10 Other functions	...	...	-	-	60	45	2	...	...	...	...	...
Total Government Final Consumption Expenditure	25245	57983	87847	109670	137576	182608	225892	...	...	...	...	...

Portugal

2.2 Government Final Consumption Expenditure by Function, in Constant Prices

Million Portuguese escudos

		1970	1975	1977	1978	1979	1980	1981	1982	1983	1984	1985	1986
		\multicolumn{12}{c}{At constant prices of:1963}
1	General public services	4676	7743	...	...	...	...	...	...	...	...	...	...
2	Defence	8965	8172	...	...	...	...	...	...	...	...	...	...
3	Public order and safety	...	...	...	...	...	...	...	...	...	...	...	...
4	Education	2096	6541	...	...	...	...	...	...	...	...	...	...
5	Health	1875	4566	...	...	...	...	...	...	...	...	...	...
6	Social security and welfare	391	1035	...	...	...	...	...	...	...	...	...	...
7	Housing and community amenities	...	...	...	...	...	...	...	...	...	...	...	...
8	Recreational, cultural and religious affairs	...	...	...	...	...	...	...	...	...	...	...	...
9	Economic services	...	...	...	...	...	...	...	...	...	...	...	...
10	Other functions	...	...	...	...	...	...	...	...	...	...	...	...
	Total Government Final Consumption Expenditure	18003	28057	...	...	...	...	...	...	...	...	...	...

2.3 Total Government Outlays by Function and Type

Million Portuguese escudos

		Final Consumption Expenditures Total	Compensation of Employees	Other	Subsidies	Other Current Transfers & Property Income	Total Current Disbursements	Gross Capital Formation	Other Capital Outlays	Total Outlays
		\multicolumn{10}{c}{1980}
1	General public services	24705	21209	3496	-	999	25704	5394	115	31213
2	Defence	36057	23023	13034	-	156	36213	115	4	36332
3	Public order and safety	15834	14798	1036	-	301	16135	602	18	16755
4	Education	42997	40433	2564	2	3936	46935	8490	455	55880
5	Health	32467	22266	10201	2	16758	49227	4138	73	53438
6	Social security and welfare	11099	9300	1799	-	110986	122085	1316	1042	124443
7	Housing and community amenities	3304	2874	430	1687	10	5001	7892	5006	17899
8	Recreation, culture and religion	1980	1404	576	-	1359	3339	1039	221	4599
9	Economic services	14120	9313	4807	63680	2681	80481	22607	9650	112738
	A Fuel and energy	11	-	11	367	-	378	3259	503	4140
	B Agriculture, forestry, fishing and hunting	5374	4042	1332	1202	28	6604	3540	347	10491
	C Mining (except fuels), manufacturing and construction	1046	710	336	15975	9	17030	169	3547	20746
	D Transportation and communication	1698	630	1068	8112	2491	12301	14351	3523	30175
	E Other economic affairs	5991	3931	2060	38024	153	44168	1288	1730	47186
10	Other functions	45	27	18	-	39004	39049	12	4100	43161
	Total	182608	144647	37961	65371	176190	424169	51605	20684	496458
		\multicolumn{10}{c}{1981}
1	General public services	29539	25403	4136	-	2093	31632	5790	-1150	36272
2	Defence	43001	26662	16339	-	5544	48545	1372	14	49931
3	Public order and safety	19232	18208	1024	-	1731	20963	1559	135	22657
4	Education	55279	51050	4229	11	3124	58414	10461	394	69269
5	Health	42661	28925	13736	36	18435	61132	6851	163	68146
6	Social security and welfare	12748	10136	2612	-	136713	149461	1082	1459	152002
7	Housing and community amenities	4230	3494	736	2087	85	6402	9190	848	16440
8	Recreation, culture and religion	2507	1860	647	-	1997	4504	1588	246	6338
9	Economic services	16693	10973	5720	79294	6388	102375	36724	13658	152757
	A Fuel and energy	15	-	15	816	-	831	4989	1326	7146
	B Agriculture, forestry, fishing and hunting	6251	4685	1566	1465	243	7959	3192	408	11559
	C Mining (except fuels), manufacturing and construction	1362	946	416	22940	110	24412	561	9261	34234
	D Transportation and communication	2217	760	1457	7567	5415	15199	26357	1672	43228
	E Other economic affairs	6848	4582	2266	46506	620	53974	1625	991	56590
10	Other functions	2	-	2	-	81094	81096	-	6458	87554
	Total	225892	176711	49181	81428	257204	564524	74617	22225	661366

Portugal

2.5 Private Final Consumption Expenditure by Type and Porpose, in Current Prices

Million Portuguese escudos

	1970	1975	1977	1978	1979	1980	1981	1982	1983	1984	1985	1986
Final Consumption Expenditure of Resident Households
1 Food, beverages and tobacco	66312	154974	185384	216167	271870	320460	392837	...	...	...	...	...
A Food	50974	116640	164496	187536	233396	278473	342130	...	...	...	...	...
B Non-alcoholic beverages	1933	4587	1089	1368	1666	2073	3052	...	...	...	...	...
C Alcoholic beverages	11275	28821	12006	17409	23568	22839	26700	...	...	...	...	...
D Tobacco	2130	4926	7793	9854	13240	17075	20955	...	...	...	...	...
2 Clothing and footwear	...	...	40948	48980	66390	91220	108766	...	...	...	...	...
3 Gross rent, fuel and power	7789	13664	30601	39338	43794	51722	59424	...	...	...	...	...
A Fuel and power	...	...	9034	12577	15470	20073	25607	...	...	...	...	...
B Other	...	...	21567	26761	28324	31640	33817	...	...	...	...	...
4 Furniture, furnishings and household equipment and operation	...	...	45287	50125	62150	87077	103457	...	...	...	...	...
A Household operation	...	...	14645	16079	20407	28214	34103	...	...	...	...	...
B Other	...	...	30642	34046	41743	58863	69354	...	...	...	...	...
5 Medical care and health expenses	...	...	17782	23547	29206	37141	45972	...	...	...	...	...
6 Transport and communication	...	...	57003	71339	92131	122577	164613	...	...	...	...	...
A Personal transport equipment	...	...	37915	46911	61546	82705	110566	...	...	...	...	...
B Other	...	...	19088	24428	30585	39872	54047	...	...	...	...	...
7 Recreational, entertainment, education and cultural services	...	...	22611	25858	32849	43384	57666	...	...	...	...	...
A Education	...	...	4954	5082	6379	7943	10788	...	...	...	...	...
B Other	...	...	17657	20776	26470	35441	46878	...	...	...	...	...
8 Miscellaneous goods and services	...	...	52732	67787	90731	114825	139498	...	...	...	...	...
A Personal care	...	...	4593	6033	7279	9780	12481	...	...	...	...	...
B Expenditures in restaurants, cafes and hotels	...	...	37528	49030	66189	82052	98089	...	...	...	...	...
C Other	...	...	10611	12724	17263	22993	28928	...	...	...	...	...
Total Final Consumption Expenditure in the Domestic Market by Households, of which	...	...	452348	543141	689121	868406	1072230	...	...	...	...	...
A Durable goods	...	...	33325	38152	47858	68817	93413	...	...	...	...	...
B Semi-durable goods	...	...	81244	94858	126640	169565	205546	...	...	...	...	...
C Non-durable goods	...	...	224695	267057	336104	406152	496010	...	...	...	...	...
D Services	...	...	113084	143074	178519	223872	277264	...	...	...	...	...
Plus: Direct purchases abroad by resident households	...	...	6737	9524	14694	17785	18814	...	...	...	...	...
Less: Direct purchases in the domestic market by non-resident households	...	...	10550	19537	36546	45486	50902	...	...	...	...	...
Equals: Final Consumption Expenditure of Resident Households	122370	303768	448535	533128	667269	840705	1040150	...	...	...	...	...
Final Consumption Expenditure of Private Non-profit Institutions Serving Households
1 Research and science	...	...	...					...	...	...	...	...

Portugal

2.5 Private Final Consumption Expenditure by Type and Porpose, in Current Prices
(Continued)

Million Portuguese escudos

	1970	1975	1977	1978	1979	1980	1981	1982	1983	1984	1985	1986
2 Education	...	...	9	11	15	18	26	...	...	...	...	...
3 Medical and other health services	...	...	28	27	28	42	42	...	...	...	...	...
4 Welfare services	...	...	1805	2194	2943	4757	5232	...	...	...	...	...
5 Recreational and related cultural services	...	...	...	...								
6 Religious organisations	...	...	...	...								
7 Professional and labour organisations serving households	...	...	...	...								
8 Miscellaneous	...	...	...	...								
Equals: Final Consumption Expenditure of Private Non-profit Organisations Serving Households	...	...	1842	2232	2986	4817	5300	...	...	...	...	...
Private Final Consumption Expenditure	122370	303768	450377	535360	670255	845522	1045450	...	...	...	...	...

2.6 Private Final Consumption Expenditure by Type and Purpose, in Constant Prices

Million Portuguese escudos

	1970	1975	1977	1978	1979	1980	1981	1982	1983	1984	1985	1986
At constant prices of: 1963												
Final Consumption Expenditure of Resident Households												
1 Food, beverages and tobacco	49433	62073	...	...	...	...	...	...	...	...	...	...
A Food	38684	45527	...	...	...	...	...	...	...	...	...	...
B Non-alcoholic beverages	1409	2828	...	...	...	...	...	...	...	...	...	...
C Alcoholic beverages	7425	10983	...	...	...	...	...	...	...	...	...	...
D Tobacco	1915	2735	...	...	...	...	...	...	...	...	...	...
2 Clothing and footwear	...	...	...	...	...	...	...	...	...	...	...	...
3 Gross rent, fuel and power	7163	9500	...	...	...	...	...	...	...	...	...	...
4 Furniture, furnishings and household equipment and operation	...	...	...	...	...	...	...	...	...	...	...	...
5 Medical care and health expenses	...	...	...	...	...	...	...	...	...	...	...	...
6 Transport and communication	...	...	...	...	...	...	...	...	...	...	...	...
7 Recreational, entertainment, education and cultural services	...	...	...	...	...	...	...	...	...	...	...	...
8 Miscellaneous goods and services	...	...	...	...	...	...	...	...	...	...	...	...
Total Final Consumption Expenditure in the Domestic Market by Households, of which	...	...	...	...	...	...	...	...	...	...	...	...
Plus: Direct purchases abroad by resident households	...	...	...	...	...	...	...	...	...	...	...	...
Less: Direct purchases in the domestic market by non-resident households	...	...	...	...	...	...	...	...	...	...	...	...
Equals: Final Consumption Expenditure of Resident Households	95288	136096	...	...	...	...	...	...	...	...	...	...
Final Consumption Expenditure of Private Non-profit Institutions Serving Households												
Equals: Final Consumption Expenditure of Private Non-profit Organisations Serving Households	...	...	...	...	...	...	...	...	...	...	...	...
Private Final Consumption Expenditure	95288	136096	...	...	...	...	...	...	...	...	...	...

Portugal

2.11 Gross Fixed Capital Formation by Kind of Activity of Owner, ISIC Divisions, in Current Prices

Million Portuguese escudos

	1970	1975	1977	1978	1979	1980	1981	1982	1983	1984	1985	1986
					All Producers							
1 Agriculture, hunting, forestry and fishing	1614	3227	8178	9186	12875	17049	19704	...	...	...	...	...
A Agriculture and hunting	1258	2568	6459	7386	9768	13847	16801	...	...	...	...	...
B Forestry and logging	...	...	296	555	824	944	1184	...	...	...	...	...
C Fishing	356	659	1423	1245	2283	2258	1719	...	...	...	...	...
2 Mining and quarrying	232	502	...	...	...	...	...	...	...	...	...	...
3 Manufacturing	9737	23162	34744	47937	61187	82754	110069	...	...	...	...	...
A Manufacturing of food, beverages and tobacco	...	...	3962	5639	6687	8729	12019	...	...	...	...	...
B Textile, wearing apparel and leather industries	...	...	4554	6158	9884	13316	21565	...	...	...	...	...
C Manufacture of wood, and wood products, including furniture	...	...	1196	1855	2604	3878	4690	...	...	...	...	...
D Manufacture of paper and paper products, printing and publishing	...	...	2766	2766	4007	4550	9654	...	...	...	...	...
E Manufacture of chemicals and chemical petroleum, coal, rubber and plastic products	...	...	11964	18100	19582	26003	23330	...	...	...	...	...
F Manufacture of non-metalic mineral products except products of petroleum and coal	...	...	3437	4677	5708	7221	10199	...	...	...	...	...
G Basic metal industries	...	...	1350	1674	1813	2956	2993	...	...	...	...	...
H Manufacture of fabricated metal products, machinery and equipment	...	...	4896	6188	9849	14638	23735	...	...	...	...	...
I Other manufacturing industries	...	...	619	880	1053	1463	1884	...	...	...	...	...
4 Electricity, gas and water	2581	7097	9321	17107	21487	26982	23729	...	...	...	...	...
5 Construction	679	1064	12167	9788	14215	23421	23415	...	...	...	...	...
6 Wholesale and retail trade, restaurants and hotels	2856	4248	9673	12913	16377	25918	31091	...	...	...	...	...
A Wholesale and retail trade	...	...	8868	11745	14492	22903	27914	...	...	...	...	...
B Restaurants and hotels	...	...	805	1168	1885	3015	3177	...	...	...	...	...
7 Transport, storage and communication	4470	9730	19741	28299	26712	31427	46939	...	...	...	...	...
A Transport and storage	...	...	16036	22968	16895	23178	37512	...	...	...	...	...
B Communication	...	...	3705	5331	9817	8240	9427	...	...	...	...	...
8 Finance, insurance, real estate and business services	4886	15210	54965	70283	76692	109024	137752	...	...	...	...	...
A Financial institutions	...	...	1221	1399	5137	7715	10003	...	...	...	...	...
B Insurance	...	...	715	726	1110	2042	2813	...	...	...	...	...
C Real estate and business services	...	...	53029	68158	70445	99267	124936	...	...	...	...	...
Real estate except dwellings	...	...	4305	5944	4450	10299	11949	...	...	...	...	...

Portugal

2.11 Gross Fixed Capital Formation by Kind of Activity of Owner, ISIC Divisions, in Current Prices
(Continued)

Million Portuguese escudos

	1970	1975	1977	1978	1979	1980	1981	1982	1983	1984	1985	1986
Dwellings	...	...	48724	62214	65995	88968	112987	...	...	...	...	...
9 Community, social and personal services	329	678	956	1648	3040	3508	4200	...	...	...	...	...
A Sanitary and similar services	...	...	...					...	...	...	...	...
B Social and related community services	...	...	161	357	1044	1091	1802	...	...	...	...	...
Educational services	...	...	41	97	166	162	403	...	...	...	...	...
Medical, dental, other health and veterinary services	...	...	120	260	878	929	1399	...	...	...	...	...
C Recreational and cultural services	...	...	795	1291	1996	2417	2398	...	...	...	...	...
D Personal and household services	...	...	...	...	...	...	...	...	...	...	...	...
Total Industries	27390	64924	149745	197161	232585	320083	396899	...	...	...	...	...
Producers of Government Services	3865	9068	16062	22613	31371	38764	66113	...	...	...	...	...
Private Non-Profit Institutions Serving Households	...	...	...	...	...	...	...	...	...	...	...	...
Total	31255	73992	165807	219774	263956	358847	463012	...	...	...	...	...

2.12 Gross Fixed Capital Formation by Kind of Activity of Owner, ISIC Divisions, in Constant Prices

Million Portuguese escudos

	1970	1975	1977	1978	1979	1980	1981	1982	1983	1984	1985	1986
	At constant prices of:1963											
	All Producers											
1 Agriculture, hunting, forestry and fishing	1196	1400	...	...	...	...	...	...	...	...	...	...
A Agriculture and hunting	910	1117	...	...	...	...	...	...	...	...	...	...
B Forestry and logging	...	...	...	...	...	...	...	...	...	...	...	...
C Fishing	286	283	...	...	...	...	...	...	...	...	...	...
2 Mining and quarrying	187	186	...	...	...	...	...	...	...	...	...	...
3 Manufacturing	7825	9318	...	...	...	...	...	...	...	...	...	...
4 Electricity, gas and water	2101	2593	...	...	...	...	...	...	...	...	...	...
5 Construction	544	448	...	...	...	...	...	...	...	...	...	...
6 Wholesale and retail trade, restaurants and hotels	2306	1678	...	...	...	...	...	...	...	...	...	...
7 Transport, storage and communication	3618	3771	...	...	...	...	...	...	...	...	...	...
8 Finance, insurance, real estate and business services	4011	5438	...	...	...	...	...	...	...	...	...	...
9 Community, social and personal services	263	269	...	...	...	...	...	...	...	...	...	...
Total Industries	22051	25102	...	...	...	...	...	...	...	...	...	...
Producers of Government Services	3158	3304	...	...	...	...	...	...	...	...	...	...
Private Non-Profit Institutions Serving Households	...	...	...	...	...	...	...	...	...	...	...	...
Total	25209	28406	...	...	...	...	...	...	...	...	...	...

2.17 Exports and Imports of Goods and Services, Detail

Million Portuguese escudos

	1970	1975	1977	1978	1979	1980	1981	1982	1983	1984	1985	1986
	Exports of Goods and Services											
1 Exports of merchandise, f.o.b.	26596	49456	84973	114514	193115	247564	275979	...	...	...	...	...
2 Transport and communication	1917	4208	15268	17856	28934	38810	47617	...	...	...	...	...
A In respect of merchandise imports	...	...	...	...	9234	13262	...	...	...	...	...	...
B Other	...	...	...	...	19700	25548	...	...	...	...	...	...

Portugal

2.17 Exports and Imports of Goods and Services, Detail
(Continued)

Million Portuguese escudos

	1970	1975	1977	1978	1979	1980	1981	1982	1983	1984	1985	1986
3 Insurance service charges	13229	20403	577	520	938	999	874	...	...	...	...	...
4 Other commodities			3930	5942	9190	11091	14143	...	...	...	...	...
5 Adjustments of merchandise exports to change-of-ownership basis	...	...	...	...	...	...	...	...	...	...	...	...
6 Direct purchases in the domestic market by non-residential households	...	...	10550	19537	36546	45486	50902	...	...	...	...	...
7 Direct purchases in the domestic market by extraterritorial bodies	...	...	...	...	...	...	...	...	...	...	...	...
Total Exports of Goods and Services	41742	74067	115298	158369	268723	343950	389515	...	...	...	...	...

Imports of Goods and Services

	1970	1975	1977	1978	1979	1980	1981	1982	1983	1984	1985	1986
1 Imports of merchandise, c.i.f.	42764	99598	194620	236361	345510	488209	630478	...	...	...	...	...
A Imports of merchandise, f.o.b.	39568	92125	176758	214799	314476	432343	573372	...	...	...	...	...
B Transport of services on merchandise imports	3196	7473	16105	19442	27982	50721	51491	...	...	...	...	...
By residents	...	...	5315	6416	9234	10202	10994	...	...	...	...	...
By non-residents	3196	7473	10790	13026	18748	37459	34497	...	...	...	...	...
C Insurance service charges on merchandise imports	...	...	1757	2120	3052	5145	5615	...	...	...	...	...
By residents	...	...	527	635	916	1316	1685	...	...	...	...	...
By non-residents	...	...	1230	1485	2136	3829	3930	...	...	...	...	...
2 Adjustments of merchandise imports to change-of-ownership basis	...	...	...	...	...	...	...	...	...	...	...	...
3 Other transport and communication			4417	6146	10533	14554	18832	...	...	...	...	...
4 Other insurance service charges	11061	21452	172	176	127	257	560	...	...	...	...	...
5 Other commodities			3485	3929	5401	7235	9852	...	...	...	...	...
6 Direct purchases abroad by government	...	...	...	...	...	...	...	...	...	...	...	...
7 Direct purchases abroad by resident households	...	...	6737	9524	14694	17785	18814	...	...	...	...	...
Total Imports of Goods and Services	53825	121050	209431	256136	376265	528040	678536	...	...	...	...	...
Balance of Goods and Services	-12083	-46983	-94133	-97767	-107542	-184090	-289021	...	...	...	...	...
Total Imports and Balance of Goods and Services	41742	74067	115298	158369	268723	343950	389515	...	...	...	...	...

3.11 General Government Production Account: Total and Subsectors

Million Portuguese escudos

	1980					1981				
	Total General Government	Central Government	State or Provincial Government	Local Government	Social Security Funds	Total General Government	Central Government	State or Provincial Government	Local Government	Social Security Funds

Gross Output

1 Sales	15843	13258	...	2253	332	19280	15950	...	2894	436
2 Services produced for own use	183809	160323	...	14471	9015	227812	198709	...	18648	10455
3 Own account fixed capital formation	...	...	...	...	...	...	...	...	...	...
Gross Output	199652	173581	...	16724	9347	247092	214659	...	21542	10891

Gross Input

Intermediate Consumption	48752	42486	...	4771	1495	62164	54142	...	5946	2076
Subtotal: Value Added	150900	131095	...	11953	7852	184928	160517	...	15596	8815

Portugal

3.11 General Government Production Account: Total and Subsectors
(Continued)

Million Portuguese escudos

		1980					1981			
		Total General Government	Central Government	State or Provincial Government	Local Government	Social Security Funds	Total General Government	Central Government	State or Provincial Government	Local Government	Social Security Funds
1	Indirect taxes, net	4142	4135	-	5	2	5151	5166	-	-18	3
	A Indirect taxes	4188	4142	...	44	2	5197	5174	...	20	3
	B Less: Subsidies	46	7	...	39	-	46	8	...	38	-
2	Consumption of fixed capital	...	...	...	...	...	...	...	...	...	...
3	Compensation of employees	145666	126186	...	11859	7621	178067	154196	...	15308	8563
4	Net Operating surplus [a]	1092	774	...	89	229	1710	1155	...	306	249
	Gross Input	199652	173581	...	16724	9347	247092	214659	...	21542	10891

a) Item 'Operating surplus' includes consumption of fixed capital.

3.12 General Government Income and Outlay Account: Total and Subsectors

Million Portuguese escudos

		1980					1981			
		Total General Government	Central Government	State or Provincial Government	Local Government	Social Security Funds	Total General Government	Central Government	State or Provincial Government	Local Government	Social Security Funds

Receipts

1	Operating surplus [ab]	1092	774	...	89	229	1710	1155	...	306	249
2	Property and entrepreneurial income	10173	9384	...	462	385	14793	13863	...	774	771
	A Withdrawals from public quasi-corporations [b]	-	...	...	...	...	-	...	...	...	...
	B Interest	3110	2508	...	275	385	8560	7876	...	528	771
	C Dividends	6843	6831	...	12	-	5930	5930	...	-	-
	D Net land rent and royalties	220	45	...	175	-	303	57	...	246	-
3	Taxes, fees and contributions	368528	249896	...	8526	110115	466207	318134	...	9621	138475
	A Indirect taxes	176915	175225	...	1195	495	215073	212992	...	1516	565
	B Direct taxes	81993	74671	...	7331	-	113224	105142	...	8105	-
	Income	79587	73121	...	6475	-	...	...	...	...	...
	Other	2406	1550	...	856	-	...	...	...	...	...
	C Social security contributions	109620	...	...	...	109620	137910	...	...	...	137910
	D Fees, fines and penalties	...	...	...	...	...	...	...	...	...	...
4	Other current transfers	14300	15131	...	14181	8208	16494	16595	...	16817	7713
	A Casualty insurance claims	37	-	...	8	29	46	-	...	18	28
	B Transfers from other government subsectors	...	2291	...	12942	7987	...	1118	...	16160	7353
	C Transfers from the rest of the world	857	841	...	-	16	1095	1077	...	-	18
	D Other transfers, except imputed	6252	5628	...	563	61	6623	6406	...	67	150
	E Imputed unfunded employee pension and welfare contributions	7154	6371	...	668	115	8730	7994	...	572	164
	Total Current Receipts	394093	275185	...	23258	118937	499204	349747	...	27518	147208

Disbursements

1	Government final consumption expenditure	182608	159453	...	14285	8870	225892	197233	...	18361	10298
2	Property income	38755	38515	...	298	-	80122	79847	...	586	304
	A Interest	38749	38511	...	296	-	80115	79843	...	583	304
	B Net land rent and royalties	6	4	...	2	...	7	4	...	3	...
3	Subsidies	65371	65069	...	303		81428	80942		486	

Portugal

3.12 General Government Income and Outlay Account: Total and Subsectors
(Continued)

Million Portuguese escudos

	1980 Total General Government	1980 Central Government	1980 State or Provincial Government	1980 Local Government	1980 Social Security Funds	1981 Total General Government	1981 Central Government	1981 State or Provincial Government	1981 Local Government	1981 Social Security Funds
4 Other current transfers	137435	51145	...	3617	105902	177082	61372	...	2692	137672
A Casualty insurance premiums, net	70	20		44	6	82	24	...	53	5
B Transfers to other government subsectors	...	20915	...	1986	328	...	23397	...	761	496
C Social security benefits	100557	...	...	...	100557	133493	...	...	...	133493
D Social assistance grants [c]	25072	20837	...	918	3317	32026	27206	...	1306	3514
E Unfunded employee pension and welfare benefits	7154	6371	...	668	115	8730	7994	...	572	164
F Transfers to private non-profit institutions serving households	282	282	...	-	...	584	584	...	-	...
G Other transfers n.e.c.	-	-	...	...	...	-	-	...	...	...
H Transfers to the rest of the world	4300	2720	...	1	1579	2167	2167	...	-	-
Net saving [d]	-30076	-38996	...	4755	4165	-65320	-69647	...	5393	-1066
Total Current Disbursements and Net Saving	394093	275185	...	23258	118937	499204	349747	...	27518	147208

a) Item 'Operating surplus' includes consumption of fixed capital.
b) Item 'Withdrawal from public quasi-corporate enterprises' is included in item 'Operating surplus'.
c) Item 'Social assistance grants' includes also transfers to households n.e.c.
d) Item 'Net saving' includes consumption of fixed capital.

3.13 General Government Capital Accumulation Account: Total and Subsectors

Million Portuguese escudos

	1980 Total General Government	1980 Central Government	1980 State or Provincial Government	1980 Local Government	1980 Social Security Funds	1981 Total General Government	1981 Central Government	1981 State or Provincial Government	1981 Local Government	1981 Social Security Funds
Finance of Gross Accumulation										
1 Gross saving	-30076	-38996	...	4755	4165	-65320	-69647	...	5393	-1066
A Consumption of fixed capital	...	...	...	...	...	...	...	...	...	...
B Net saving [a]	-30076	-38996	...	4755	4165	-65320	-69647	...	5393	-1066
2 Capital transfers	171688	171265	...	21133	1666	2627	2202	...	25089	1694
A From other government subsectors	-	14	...	20696	1666	-	137	...	24527	1694
B From other resident sectors	171577	171232	...	345	-	2560	2057	...	503	-
C From rest of the world	111	19	...	92	-	67	8	...	59	-
Finance of Gross Accumulation [b]	141612	132269	...	25888	5831	-62693	-67445	...	30482	628
Gross Accumulation										
1 Gross capital formation	51605	26442	...	24359	804	74617	40822	...	33170	625
A Increase in stocks	...	...	...	...	...	...	...	...	...	...
B Gross fixed capital formation	51605	26442	...	24359	804	74617	40822	...	33170	625
2 Purchases of land, net	1296	864	...	417	15	837	708	...	134	-5
3 Purchases of intangible assets, net	1	...	...	1	...	-	...	...	-	...
4 Capital transfers	19387	40210	...	568	985	21399	11669	...	1490	1598
A To other government subsectors	...	22354	...	11	11	...	26206	...	7	145
B To other resident sectors	14980	13450	...	556	974	15812	12070	...	1483	1453
C To rest of the world	4407	4406	...	1	-	5576	5576	...	-	-
Net lending	69323	64753	...	543	4027	-159535	-153633	...	-4312	-1590
Gross Accumulation [b]	141612	132269	...	25888	5831	-62693	-67445	...	30482	628

a) Item 'Net saving' includes consumption of fixed capital.
b) Data in this table have been revised, therefore they are not strictly comparable with the unrevised data in the other tables.

3.21 Corporate and Quasi-Corporate Enterprise Production Account: Total and Sectors

Million Portuguese escudos

	1980 Corporate and Quasi-Corporate Enterprises TOTAL	1980 Non-Financial	1980 Financial	1980 ADDENDUM: Total, including Unincorporated	1981 Corporate and Quasi-Corporate Enterprises TOTAL	1981 Non-Financial	1981 Financial	1981 ADDENDUM: Total, including Unincorporated
Gross Output								
1 Output for sale	1724830	1697560	27275	2405680	2144390	2109620	34773	2953240
2 Imputed bank service charge	55553	-	55553	55553	77588	-	77588	77588
3 Own-account fixed capital formation	...	...	...	...	...	...	...	...
Gross Output	1780390	1697560	82828	2461230	2221980	2109620	112361	3030830

Portugal

3.21 Corporate and Quasi-Corporate Enterprise Production Account: Total and Sectors
(Continued)

Million Portuguese escudos

	1980				1981			
	\multicolumn{3}{c}{Corporate and Quasi-Corporate Enterprises}	ADDENDUM: Total,	\multicolumn{3}{c}{Corporate and Quasi-Corporate Enterprises}	ADDENDUM: Total,
	TOTAL	Non-Financial	Financial	including Unincorporated	TOTAL	Non-Financial	Financial	including Unincorporated

Gross Input

	1980 TOTAL	Non-Fin	Fin	Addendum	1981 TOTAL	Non-Fin	Fin	Addendum
Intermediate consumption	1144780	1076800	67977	1375570	1456850	1362580	94264	1743180
1 Imputed banking service charge	55553	-	55553	55553	77588	-	77588	77588
2 Other intermediate consumption	1089230	1076800	12424	1320020	1379260	1362580	16676	1665590
Subtotal: Value Added	635607	620756	14851	1085660	765131	747034	18097	1287650
1 Indirect taxes, net	83274	73650	9624	91347	93740	81267	12473	104232
A Indirect taxes	147706	138042	9664	156672	174450	161977	12473	185614
B Less: Subsidies	64432	64392	40	65325	80710	80710	-	81382
2 Consumption of fixed capital	...	...	...	...	...	...	...	...
3 Compensation of employees	401174	371952	29222	493858	505890	468975	36915	606214
4 Net operating surplus a	151159	175154	-23995	500458	165501	196792	-31291	577206
Gross Input	1780390	1697560	82828	2461230	2221980	2109620	112361	3030830

a) Item 'Operating surplus' includes consumption of fixed capital.

3.22 Corporate and Quasi-Corporate Enterprise Income and Outlay Account: Total and Sectors

Million Portuguese escudos

	1980			1981		
	TOTAL	Non-Financial	Financial	TOTAL	Non-Financial	Financial

Receipts

	1980 TOTAL	Non-Fin	Fin	1981 TOTAL	Non-Fin	Fin
1 Operating surplus a	151159	175154	-23995	165501	196792	-31291
2 Property and entrepreneurial income	242937	22861	220076	347826	33485	314341
A Withdrawals from quasi-corporate enterprises	423	423	-	466	466	-
B Interest	240841	21192	219649	344936	31423	313513
C Dividends	1381	954	427	2053	1226	827
D Net land rent and royalties	292	292	-	371	370	1
3 Current transfers	38057	17066	20991	44353	19427	24926
A Casualty insurance claims	5690	5641	49	6189	6133	56
B Casualty insurance premiums, net, due to be received by insurance companies	14286	-	14286	16019	-	16019
C Current transfers from the rest of the world	...	...	...	...	...	...
D Other transfers except imputed	11521	6279	5242	13995	6905	7090
E Imputed unfunded employee pension and welfare contributions	6560	5146	1414	8150	6389	1761
Total Current Receipts	432153	215061	217072	557680	249704	307976

Disbursements

	1980 TOTAL	Non-Fin	Fin	1981 TOTAL	Non-Fin	Fin
1 Property and entrepreneurial income	334635	166457	168178	487953	248762	239191
A Withdrawals from quasi-corporations	...	...	...	...	...	...
B Interest	315164	152620	162544	468701	234365	234336
C Dividends	15771	10137	5634	14862	10074	4788
D Net land rent and royalties	3700	3700	-	4390	4323	67
2 Direct taxes and other current transfers n.e.c. to general government	22670	21278	1392	30852	28943	1909
A Direct taxes	22670	21278	1392	30852	28943	1909
B Fines, fees, penalties and other current transfers n.e.c.	...	...	...	...	...	...

Portugal

3.22 Corporate and Quasi-Corporate Enterprise Income and Outlay Account: Total and Sectors
(Continued)

Million Portuguese escudos

	1980 TOTAL	1980 Non-Financial	1980 Financial	1981 TOTAL	1981 Non-Financial	1981 Financial
3 Other current transfers	40386	12904	27482	47217	14040	33177
A Casualty insurance premiums, net	5904	5790	114	6175	6120	55
B Casualty insurance claims liability of insurance companies	14286	-	14286	16019	-	16019
C Transfers to private non-profit institutions	365	365	-	551	551	-
D Unfunded employee pension and welfare benefits	...	...	...	...	...	...
E Social assistance grants	10057	5146	4911	12791	6389	6402
F Other transfers n.e.c.	9774	1603	8171	11681	980	10701
G Transfers to the rest of the world	...	...	...	...	...	...
Statistical discrepancy [b]	1492	-	1492	1929	-	1929
Net saving [c]	32970	14442	18528	-10271	-42041	31770
Total Current Disbursements and Net Saving	432153	215081	217072	557680	249704	307976

a) Item 'Operating surplus' includes consumption of fixed capital.
b) Item 'Statistical discrepancy' refers to increase in technical reserves of pension funds.
c) Item 'Net saving' includes consumption of fixed capital.

3.23 Corporate and Quasi-Corporate Enterprise Capital Accumulation Account: Total and Sectors

Million Portuguese escudos

	1980 TOTAL	1980 Non-Financial	1980 Financial	1981 TOTAL	1981 Non-Financial	1981 Financial
Finance of Gross Accumulation						
1 Gross saving	32970	14442	18528	-10271	-42041	31770
A Consumption of fixed capital	...	...	...	...	...	...
B Net saving [a]	32970	14442	18528	-10271	-42041	31770
2 Capital transfers	16260	16168	92	17129	17102	27
Finance of Gross Accumulation	49230	30610	18620	6858	-24939	31797
Gross Accumulation						
1 Gross capital formation	243698	233941	9757	292271	279455	12816
A Increase in stocks	53478	53478	-	52506	52506	-
B Gross fixed capital formation	190220	180463	9757	239765	226949	12816
2 Purchases of land, net	6392	5320	1072	5952	4670	1282
3 Purchases of intangible assets, net	...	...	...	...	...	...
4 Capital transfers	173936	2481	171455	6753	3174	3579
Net lending	-374796	-211132	-163664	-298118	-312238	14120
Gross Accumulation	49230	30610	18620	6858	-24939	31797

a) Item 'Net saving' includes consumption of fixed capital.

3.24 Corporate and Quasi-Corporate Enterprise Capital Finance Account: Total and Sectors

Million Portuguese escudos

	1980 TOTAL	1980 Non-Financial	1980 Financial	1981 TOTAL	1981 Non-Financial	1981 Financial
Acquisition of Financial Assets						
1 Gold and SDRs	14438	-	14438	3036	-	3036
2 Currency and transferable deposits	36722	33125	3597	7265	5108	2157
3 Other deposits	1339	10326	-8987	-10242	14204	-24446
4 Bills and bonds, short term	4959	-	4959	15024	-	15024
5 Bonds, long term	-59896	499	-60395	156290	1274	155016
6 Corporate equity securities	-5020	-	-5020	-119	-	-119
7 Short term loans, n.e.c.	95944	7708	88236	139733	8	139725
8 Long term loans, n.e.c.	145948	716	145232	145360	-1750	147110
9 Trade credits and advances	15024	6768	8256	41142	20974	20168
10 Other receivables	...	...	...	...	...	...
11 Other assets [a]	2224	2205	19	1888	1874	14
Total Acquisition of Financial Assets	251682	61347	190335	499377	41692	457685
Incurrence of Liabilities						
1 Currency and transferable deposits	62190	-	62190	43985	-	43985

Portugal

3.24 Corporate and Quasi-Corporate Enterprise Capital Finance Account: Total and Sectors
(Continued)

Million Portuguese escudos

	1980 TOTAL	1980 Non-Financial	1980 Financial	1981 TOTAL	1981 Non-Financial	1981 Financial
2 Other deposits	273384	-	273384	369059	-	369059
3 Bills and bonds, short term	-809	-755	-54	11854	10909	945
4 Bonds, long term	...	...	...	...	...	...
5 Corporate equity securities	37337	36538	799	33289	32562	727
6 Short-term loans, n.e.c.	103416	134270	-30854	116886	120845	-3959
7 Long-term loans, n.e.c.	130274	121809	8465	146466	124442	22024
8 Net equity of households in life insurance and pension fund reserves	8058	-	8058	8508	-	8508
9 Proprietors' net additions to the accumulation of quasi-corporations	...	...	...	...	...	...
10 Trade credit and advances	-11879	-21308	9429	91703	87431	4272
11 Other accounts payable	...	...	...	...	...	...
12 Other liabilities	-3930	...	-3930	-2126	...	-2126
Total Incurrence of Liabilities	598041	270554	327487	819624	376189	443435
Statistical discrepancy	28437	1925	26512	-22129	-22259	130
Net Lending	-374796	-211132	-163664	-298118	-312238	14120
Incurrence of Liabilities and Net Lending	251682	61347	190335	499377	41692	457685

a) Item 'Other assets' refers to insurance reserves.

3.31 Household and Private Unincorporated Enterprise Production Account

Million Portuguese escudos

	1970	1975	1977	1978	1979	1980	1981	1982	1983	1984	1985	1986
					Gross Output							
1 Output for sale	...	...	334143	423389	551289	680844	808856	...	...	...	...	...
2 Non-marketed output	...	...	5553	5972	...	...	...	...	...	...	...	...
Gross Output	...	...	339696	429361	551289	680844	808856	...	...	...	...	...
					Gross Input							
Intermediate consumption	...	...	106332	134811	181851	230788	286335	...	...	...	...	...
Subtotal: Value Added	...	...	233364	294550	369438	450056	522521	...	...	...	...	...
1 Indirect taxes net liability of unincorporated enterprises	...	...	3254	3172	5891	8073	10492	...	...	...	...	...
A Indirect taxes	...	...	3918	4493	6405	8966	11164	...	...	...	...	...
B Less: Subsidies	...	...	664	1321	514	893	672	...	...	...	...	...
2 Consumption of fixed capital	...	...	...	...	...	...	...	...	...	...	...	...
3 Compensation of employees	...	...	53800	61090	74094	92684	100324	...	...	...	...	...
4 Net operating surplus a	...	...	176310	230288	289453	349299	411705	...	...	...	...	...
Gross Input	...	...	339696	429361	551289	680844	808856	...	...	...	...	...

a) Item 'Operating surplus' includes consumption of fixed capital.

3.32 Household and Private Unincorporated Enterprise Income and Outlay Account

Million Portuguese escudos

	1970	1975	1977	1978	1979	1980	1981	1982	1983	1984	1985	1986
					Receipts							
1 Compensation of employees	...	...	345257	410589	503251	642028	788893	...	...	...	...	...
2 Operating surplus of private unincorporated enterprises	...	...	176310	230288	289453	349299	411705	...	...	...	...	...
3 Property and entrepreneurial income	...	...	31818	54064	111372	139532	202101	...	...	...	...	...
A Withdrawals from private quasi-corporations	...	...	-	-	-	-	-	...	...	...	...	...
B Interest	...	...	28882	48252	103129	128416	191779	...	...	...	...	...
C Dividends	...	...	1976	4169	6058	7312	6491	...	...	...	...	...
D Net land rent and royalties	...	...	960	1643	2185	3804	3831	...	...	...	...	...

Portugal

3.32 Household and Private Unincorporated Enterprise Income and Outlay Account
(Continued)

Million Portuguese escudos

	1970	1975	1977	1978	1979	1980	1981	1982	1983	1984	1985	1986
3 Current transfers	...	...	124340	164493	227605	301347	371743	...	...	...	...	...
A Casualty insurance claims	...	...	3316	4440	6008	9217	10665	...	...	...	...	...
B Social security benefits	...	...	66985	78680	92958	132634	173239	...	...	...	...	...
C Social assistance grants	...	...	...	...	...	...	...	...	...	...	...	...
D Unfunded employee pension and welfare benefits	...	...	540	148	174	180	175	...	...	...	...	...
E Transfers from general government	...	...	...	...	...	...	...	...	...	...	...	...
F Transfers from the rest of the world	...	...	...	...	...	...	...	...	...	...	...	...
G Other transfers n.e.c.	...	...	53499	81225	128465	159316	187664	...	...	...	...	...
Statistical discrepancy a	...	...	703	897	1049	1492	1929	...	...	...	...	...
Total Current Receipts	...	...	678428	860331	1132730	1433700	1776370	...	...	...	...	...

Disbursements

	1970	1975	1977	1978	1979	1980	1981	1982	1983	1984	1985	1986
1 Final consumption expenditures	...	...	448535	533128	667269	840705	1040150	...	...	...	...	...
2 Property income	...	...	11739	19939	42849	52933	62050	...	...	...	...	...
A Interest	...	...	10756	18792	41611	50863	59942	...	...	...	...	...
B Net land rent and royalties	...	...	983	1147	1238	2070	2108	...	...	...	...	...
3 Direct taxes and other current transfers n.e.c. to government	...	...	89172	109628	138829	173932	226846	...	...	...	...	...
A Social security contributions	...	...	60721	72855	88058	114609	144480	...	...	...	...	...
B Direct taxes	...	...	28451	36773	50771	59323	82366	...	...	...	...	...
Income taxes	...	...	...	...	...	...	...	...	...	...	...	...
Other	...	...	...	...	...	...	...	...	...	...	...	...
C Fees, fines and penalties	...	...	...	...	...	...	...	...	...	...	...	...
4 Other current transfers	...	...	16777	20009	23375	31309	37565	...	...	...	...	...
A Net casualty insurance premiums	...	...	3272	3960	5704	7972	8849	...	...	...	...	...
B Transfers to private non-profit institutions serving households	...	...	1115	2188	2496	2700	4317	...	...	...	...	...
C Transfers to the rest of the world	...	...	3280	3511	2636	1792	1653	...	...	...	...	...
D Other current transfers, except imputed	...	...	3099	3923	4025	4933	5665	...	...	...	...	...
E Imputed employee pension and welfare contributions	...	...	6011	6427	8514	13912	17081	...	...	...	...	...
Net saving b	...	...	112205	177627	260408	334819	409765	...	...	...	...	...
Total Current Disbursements and Net Saving	...	...	678428	860331	1132730	1433700	1776370	...	...	...	...	...

a) Item 'Statistical discrepancy' refers to increase in technical reserves of pension funds.
b) Item 'Net saving' includes consumption of fixed capital.

3.33 Household and Private Unincorporated Enterprise Capital Accumulation Account

Million Portuguese escudos

	1970	1975	1977	1978	1979	1980	1981	1982	1983	1984	1985	1986

Finance of Gross Accumulation

	1970	1975	1977	1978	1979	1980	1981	1982	1983	1984	1985	1986
1 Gross saving	...	...	112205	177627	260408	334819	409765	...	...	...	...	...
A Consumption of fixed capital	...	...	...	...	...	...	...	...	...	...	...	...
B Net saving a	...	...	112205	177627	260408	334819	409765	...	...	...	...	...
2 Capital transfers	...	...	1067	886	2686	2020	4623	...	...	...	...	...
Total Finance of Gross Accumulation	...	...	113272	178513	263094	336839	414388	...	...	...	...	...

Gross Accumulation

	1970	1975	1977	1978	1979	1980	1981	1982	1983	1984	1985	1986
1 Gross Capital Formation	...	...	63410	83188	93197	117427	150521	...	...	...	...	...
A Increase in stocks	...	...	717	6218	10936	-314	3297	...	...	...	...	...
B Gross fixed capital formation	...	...	62693	76970	82261	117741	147224	...	...	...	...	...
2 Purchases of land, net	...	...	-1534	-2418	-3652	-7786	-6952	...	...	...	...	...
3 Purchases of intangibles, net	...	...	...	...	...	...	...	...	...	...	...	...
4 Capital transfers	...	...	854	789	848	1045	1798	...	...	...	...	...
Net lending	...	...	50542	96954	172701	226153	269021	...	...	...	...	...
Total Gross Accumulation	...	...	113272	178513	263094	336839	414388	...	...	...	...	...

a) Item 'Net saving' includes consumption of fixed capital.

Portugal

3.34 Household and Private Unincorporated Enterprise Capital Finance Account

Million Portuguese escudos

	1970	1975	1977	1978	1979	1980	1981	1982	1983	1984	1985	1986
Acquisition of Financial Assets												
1 Gold	...	...	-	-	-	-801	-	...	...	...	...	...
2 Currency and transferable deposits	...	...	15839	19876	43473	49428	34477	...	...	...	...	...
3 Other deposits	...	...	72442	116048	156502	238169	326196	...	...	...	...	...
4 Bills and bonds, short term	...	...	-	-	-	3460	6519	...	...	...	...	...
5 Bonds, long term	...	...	-	-1372	-784	69928	12505	...	...	...	...	...
6 Corporate equity securities	...	...	-	-	-	-59163	-5996	...	...	...	...	...
7 Short term loans, n.e.c.	...	...	3	-	-	-	-	...	...	...	...	...
8 Long term loans, n.e.c.	...	...	-	31	-25	-	-	...	...	...	...	...
9 Trade credit and advances	...	...	359	711	-2160	5114	2960	...	...	...	...	...
10 Net equity of households in life insurance and pension fund reserves	...	...	2591	3084	3737	5805	6603	...	...	...	...	...
11 Proprietors' net additions to the accumulation of quasi-corporations	...	...	...	...	...	...	...	...	...	...	...	...
12 Other	...	...	...	...	...	...	...	...	...	...	...	...
Total Acquisition of Financial Assets	...	...	91234	138378	200743	311940	383264	...	...	...	...	...
Incurrence of Liabilities												
1 Short term loans, n.e.c.	...	...	19690	15816	22100	21908	12587	...	...	...	...	...
2 Long term loans, n.e.c.	...	...	19793	29053	38780	47017	56832	...	...	...	...	...
3 Trade credit and advances	...	...	1862	3556	6063	8977	4092	...	...	...	...	...
4 Other accounts payable	...	...	...	...	...	...	...	...	...	...	...	...
5 Other liabilities	...	...	...	...	...	...	...	...	...	...	...	...
Total Incurrence of Liabilities	...	...	41345	48425	66943	77902	73511	...	...	...	...	...
Statistical discrepancy	...	...	-653	-7001	-38901	7885	40732	...	...	...	...	...
Net Lending	...	...	50542	96954	172701	226153	269021	...	...	...	...	...
Incurrence of Liabilities and Net Lending	...	...	91234	138378	200743	311940	383264	...	...	...	...	...

3.41 Private Non-Profit Institutions Serving Households: Production Account

Million Portuguese escudos

	1970	1975	1977	1978	1979	1980	1981	1982	1983	1984	1985	1986
Gross Output												
1 Sales	...	...	262	325	377	552	1060	...	...	...	...	...
2 Non-marketed output	...	...	2399	3580	4475	5961	6858	...	...	...	...	...
A Services produced for own use	...	...	2399	3580	4475	5961	6858	...	...	...	...	...
B Own account fixed capital formation	...	...	...	...	...	...	...	...	...	...	...	...
Gross Output	...	...	2661	3905	4852	6513	7918	...	...	...	...	...
Gross Input												
Intermediate consumption	...	...	1093	1447	1858	3051	3575	...	...	...	...	...
Subtotal: Value Added	...	...	1568	2458	2994	3462	4343	...	...	...	...	...
1 Indirect taxes, net	...	...	18	17	27	29	54	...	...	...	...	...
2 Consumption of fixed capital	...	...	...	...	...	...	...	...	...	...	...	...
3 Compensation of employees	...	...	1548	2439	2967	3442	4318	...	...	...	...	...
4 Net operating surplus [a]	...	...	2	2	-	-9	-29	...	...	...	...	...
Gross Input	...	...	2661	3905	4852	6513	7918	...	...	...	...	...

a) Item 'Operating surplus' includes consumption of fixed capital.

3.42 Private Non-Profit Institutions Serving Households: Income and Outlay Account

Million Portuguese escudos

	1970	1975	1977	1978	1979	1980	1981	1982	1983	1984	1985	1986
Receipts												
1 Operating surplus [a]	...	...	2	2	-	-9	-29	...	...	...	...	...
2 Property and entrepreneurial income	...	...	921	1102	1588	2043	3019	...	...	...	...	...
A Withdrawals from quasi-corporations	...	...	...	...	...	...	...	...	...	...	...	...
B Interest	...	...	319	427	600	960	1407	...	...	...	...	...
C Dividends	...	...	602	675	988	1083	1611	...	...	...	...	...
D Net land rent and royalties	...	...	-	-	-	-	1	...	...	...	...	...

Portugal

3.42 Private Non-Profit Institutions Serving Households: Income and Outlay Account
(Continued)

Million Portuguese escudos

	1970	1975	1977	1978	1979	1980	1981	1982	1983	1984	1985	1986
3 Current transfers	...	...	1531	2436	2942	3630	5846	...	...	...	...	...
A Casualty insurance claims	...	...	...	...	...	...	...	...	...	...	...	...
B Current transfers from general government	...	...	1509	2412	2911	3612	5815	...	...	...	...	...
C Other transfers from resident sectors	...	...	...	...	...	...	...	...	...	...	...	...
D Current transfers received from the rest of the world	...	...	...	...	...	...	...	...	...	...	...	...
E Imputed unfunded employee pension and welfare contributions	...	...	14	24	31	18	26	...	...	...	...	...
Total Current Receipts	...	...	2454	3540	4530	5664	8836	...	...	...	...	...
Disbursements												
1 Final consumption expenditures	...	...	1842	2232	2986	4817	5300	...	...	...	...	...
A Compensation of employees	...	...	1508	2373	2896	3333	4145	...	...	...	...	...
B Consumption of fixed capital	...	...	...	...	...	...	...	...	...	...	...	...
C Purchases of goods and services, net	...	...	334	-141	90	1484	1155	...	...	...	...	...
Purchases	...	...	1085	1421	1761	2932	3402	...	...	...	...	...
Less: Sales	...	...	751	1562	1671	1448	2247	...	...	...	...	...
2 Property income	...	...	56	77	97	2	98	...	...	...	...	...
A Interest	...	...	56	77	97	2	98	...	...	...	...	...
B Net land rent and royalties	...	...	...	...	...	...	...	...	...	...	...	...
3 Direct taxes and other transfers to general government	...	...	-	-	-	-	6	...	...	...	...	...
A Direct taxes	...	...	-	-	-	-	6	...	...	...	...	...
B Fees, fines and penalties	...	...	...	...	...	...	...	...	...	...	...	...
4 Other current transfers	...	...	456	482	995	1244	1315	...	...	...	...	...
A Net casualty insurance premiums	...	...	10	5	6	18	8	...	...	...	...	...
B Social assistance grants	...	...	127	95	247	225	373	...	...	...	...	...
C Unfunded employee pension and welfare benefits	...	...	...	...	...	...	...	...	...	...	...	...
D Current transfers to the rest of the world	...	...	162	157	247	267	234	...	...	...	...	...
E Other current transfers n.e.c.	...	...	157	225	495	734	700	...	...	...	...	...
Net saving b	...	...	100	749	452	-399	2117	...	...	...	...	...
Total Current Disbursements	...	...	2454	3540	4530	5664	8836	...	...	...	...	...

a) Item 'Operating surplus' includes consumption of fixed capital.
b) Item 'Net saving' includes consumption of fixed capital.

3.43 Private Non-Profit Institutions Serving Households: Capital Accumulation Account

Million Portuguese escudos

	1970	1975	1977	1978	1979	1980	1981	1982	1983	1984	1985	1986
Finance of Gross Accumulation												
1 Gross saving	...	...	100	749	452	-399	2117	...	...	...	...	...
A Consumption of fixed capital	...	...	...	...	...	...	...	...	...	...	...	...
B Net saving a	...	...	100	749	452	-399	2117	...	...	...	...	...
2 Capital transfers	...	...	38	61	-	104	103	...	...	...	...	...
Finance of Gross Accumulation	...	...	138	810	452	205	2220	...	...	...	...	...
Gross Accumulation												
1 Gross capital formation	...	...	156	419	377	-719	1406	...	...	...	...	...
A Increase in stocks	...	...	*	*	*	*	*	...	...	...	...	...
B Gross fixed capital formation	...	...	156	419	377	-719	1406	...	...	...	...	...
2 Purchases of land, net	...	...	...	...	...	...	...	...	...	...	...	...
3 Purchases of intangible assets, net	...	...	1	-1	2	-2	2	...	...	...	...	...
4 Capital transfers	...	...	14	10	-	-	52	...	...	...	...	...
Net lending	...	...	-33	382	73	426	760	...	...	...	...	...
Gross Accumulation	...	...	138	810	452	-295	2220	...	...	...	...	...

a) Item 'Net saving' includes consumption of fixed capital.

Portugal

3.44 Private Non-Profit Institutions Serving Households: Capital Finance Account

Million Portuguese escudos

	1970	1975	1977	1978	1979	1980	1981	1982	1983	1984	1985	1986
Acquisition of Financial Assets												
1 Gold	...	...	...	...	...	165	73	...	...	...	...	...
2 Currency and transferable deposits	...	...	-99	477	-768	512	856	...	...	...	...	...
3 Other deposits	...	...	3	99	182	1013	678	...	...	...	...	...
4 Bills and bonds, short term	...	...	...	...	...	...	...	...	...	...	...	...
5 Bonds, long term	...	...	-	-90	-11	-130	698	...	...	...	...	...
6 Corporate equity securities	...	...	-	-20	87	231	-1139	...	...	...	...	...
7 Short-term loans, n.e.c.	...	...	-	31	291	266	68	...	...	...	...	...
8 Long-term loans, n.e.c.	...	...	-	-8	22	68	18	...	...	...	...	...
9 Other receivables	...	...	-	-	-	-	2	...	...	...	...	...
10 Proprietors' net additions to the accumulation of quasi-corporations	...	...	...	...	...	...	...	...	...	...	...	...
11 Other assets	...	...	1	-	1	1	1	...	...	...	...	...
Total Acquisition of Financial Assets	...	...	-95	489	-196	2126	1255	...	...	...	...	...
Incurrence of Liabilities												
1 Short-term loans	...	...	-5	14	97	1675	545	...	...	...	...	...
2 Long-term loans	...	...	13	54	-36	127	-95	...	...	...	...	...
3 Other liabilities	...	...	-	-	-	2	3	...	...	...	...	...
Total Incurrence of Liabilities	...	...	8	68	61	1804	453	...	...	...	...	...
Statistical discrepancy	...	...	-70	39	-330	-104	42	...	...	...	...	...
Net Lending	...	...	-33	382	73	426	760	...	...	...	...	...
Incurrence of Liabilities and Net Lending	...	...	-95	489	-196	2126	1255	...	...	...	...	...

3.51 External Transactions: Current Account: Detail

Million Portuguese escudos

	1970	1975	1977	1978	1979	1980	1981	1982	1983	1984	1985	1986
Payments to the Rest of the World												
1 Imports of goods and services	53825	121050	209431	256136	376265	528040	678536	...	...	...	...	...
A Imports of merchandise c.i.f.	42764	99598	194620	236361	345510	488209	630478	...	...	...	...	...
B Other	11061	21452	14811	19775	30755	39831	48058	...	...	...	...	...
2 Factor income to the rest of the world	1492	2644	10690	19786	29313	41736	74865	...	...	...	...	...
A Compensation of employees	1492	2644	1382	1653	1962	2979	2533	...	...	...	...	...
B Property and entrepreneurial income	...	...	9308	18133	27351	38757	72332	...	...	...	...	...
3 Current transfers to the rest of the world	547	1550	5765	7511	7517	6864	5650	...	...	...	...	...
A Indirect taxes by general government to supranational organizations	...	...	...	...	...	...	...	...	...	...	...	...
B Other current transfers	547	1550	5765	7511	7517	6864	5650	...	...	...	...	...
By general government	158	1051	...	...	...	...	...	...	...	...	...	...
By other resident sectors	389	499	...	...	...	...	...	...	...	...	...	...
4 Surplus of the nation on current transactions	3373	-20866	-58531	-45051	-17245	-74697	-182524	...	...	...	...	...
Payments to the Rest of the World, and Surplus of the Nation on Current Transfers	59237	104378	167355	238382	395850	501943	576527	...	...	...	...	...
Receipts From The Rest of the World												
1 Exports of goods and services	41742	74067	115298	158369	268723	343950	389515	...	...	...	...	...
A Exports of merchandise f.o.b.	26596	49456	84973	114514	193115	247564	275979	...	...	...	...	...

Portugal

3.51 External Transactions: Current Account: Detail
(Continued)

Million Portuguese escudos

	1970	1975	1977	1978	1979	1980	1981	1982	1983	1984	1985	1986
B Other	15146	24611	30325	43855	75608	96386	113536	...	...	...	...	...
2 Factor income from the rest of the world	2381	2275	2788	4098	6977	9158	12675	...	...	...	...	...
A Compensation of employees	2381	2275	928	1042	1575	2041	2827	...	...	...	...	...
B Property and entrepreneurial income	...	...	1860	3056	5402	7117	9848	...	...	...	...	...
3 Current transfers from the rest of the world	15114	28036	49269	75915	120150	148835	174337	...	...	...	...	...
A Subsidies to general government from supranational organizations	...	...	1765	554	664	563	1095	...	...	...	...	...
B Other current transfers	15114	28036	47504	75361	119486	148272	173242	...	...	...	...	...
To general government	90	74	...	...	...	...	...	...	...	...	...	...
To other resident sectors	15024	27962	...	...	...	...	...	...	...	...	...	...
Receipts from the Rest of the World on Current Transfers	59237	104378	167355	238382	395850	501943	576527	...	...	...	...	...

3.52 External Transactions: Capital Accumulation Account

Million Portuguese escudos

	1970	1975	1977	1978	1979	1980	1981	1982	1983	1984	1985	1986
			Finance of Gross Accumulation									
1 Surplus of the nation on current transactions	3373	-20866	-58531	-45051	-17245	-74697	-182524	...	...	...	...	...
2 Capital transfers from the rest of the world	...	...	5	11	6	111	67	...	...	...	...	...
Total Finance of Gross Accumulation	3373	-20866	-58526	-45040	-17239	-74586	-182457	...	...	...	...	...
			Gross Accumulation									
1 Capital transfers to the rest of the world	...	...	242	528	1005	4407	5576	...	...	...	...	...
2 Purchases of intangible assets, n.e.c., net, from the rest of the world	...	...	-56	-39	-62	-99	-161	...	...	...	...	...
Net lending to the rest of the world	3373	-20866	-58712	-45529	-18182	-78894	-187872	...	...	...	...	...
Total Gross Accumulation	3373	-20866	-58526	-45040	-17239	-74586	-182457	...	...	...	...	...

3.53 External Transactions: Capital Finance Account

Million Portuguese escudos

	1970	1975	1977	1978	1979	1980	1981	1982	1983	1984	1985	1986
			Acquisitions of Foreign Financial Assets									
1 Gold and SDR's [a]	...	...	3225	-2401	-955	-3930	-2126	...	...	...	...	...
2 Currency and transferable deposits	...	...	-	477	-56	731	-54	...	...	...	...	...
3 Other deposits	...	...	-765	3447	-1427	896	-409	...	...	...	...	...
4 Bills and bonds, short term	...	...	...	...	...	...	...	...	...	...	...	...
5 Bonds, long term	...	...	-8	-556	-326	1480	326	...	...	...	...	...
6 Corporate equity securities	...	...	1784	1977	2263	5010	7287	...	...	...	...	...
7 Short-term loans, n.e.c.	...	...	46456	9972	-24889	38082	-3959	...	...	...	...	...
8 Long-term loans	...	...	5644	32067	39884	52527	90219	...	...	...	...	...
9 Proprietors' net additions to accumulation of quasi-corporate, non-resident enterprises	...	...	...	...	...	...	...	...	...	...	...	...
10 Trade credit and advances	...	...	...	...	...	...	...	...	...	...	...	...
11 Other	...	...	2027	366	23799	-21717	72154	...	...	...	...	...
Total Acquisitions of Foreign Financial Assets	...	...	58363	46239	38293	73079	163438	...	...	...	...	...
			Incurrence of Foreign Liabilities									
1 Currency and transferable deposits	...	...	-7675	-4991	9003	8389	1010	...	...	...	...	...

Portugal

3.53 External Transactions: Capital Finance Account
(Continued)

Million Portuguese escudos

	1970	1975	1977	1978	1979	1980	1981	1982	1983	1984	1985	1986
2 Other deposits	...	...	4466	20092	11742	-8791	-24015	...	...	...	...	...
3 Bills and bonds, short term	...	...	...	...	...	...	...	...	...	...	...	...
4 Bonds, long term	...	...	-30	-68	-80	-27	1142	...	...	...	...	...
5 Corporate equity securities	...	...	34	236	-589	572	182	...	...	...	...	...
6 Short-term loans, n.e.c.	...	...	-21	-875	-1607	7821	1801	...	...	...	...	...
7 Long-term loans	...	...	3354	2571	2279	3327	1526	...	...	...	...	...
8 Non-resident proprietors' net additions to accumulation of resident quasi-corporate enterprises	...	...	...	...	...	...	...	...	...	...	...	...
9 Trade credit and advances	...	...	856	1273	11033	-2640	12884	...	...	...	...	...
10 Other	...	...	...	...	...	...	...	...	...	...	...	...
Total Incurrence of Liabilities	...	...	984	18238	31781	8651	-5470	...	...	...	...	...
Statistical discrepancy	...	...	-1333	-17528	-11670	-14466	-18964	...	...	...	...	...
Net Lending	...	...	58712	45529	18182	78894	187872	...	...	...	...	...
Total Incurrence of Liabilities and Net Lending	...	...	58363	46239	38293	73079	163438	...	...	...	...	...

a) Item 'Gold and SDRs' includes also foreign currency.

4.1 Derivation of Value Added by Kind of Activity, in Current Prices

Million Portuguese escudos

	1980 Gross Output	1980 Intermediate Consumption	1980 Value Added	1981 Gross Output	1981 Intermediate Consumption	1981 Value Added
All Producers						
1 Agriculture, hunting, forestry and fishing	207060	77161	129899	231975	97415	134560
A Agriculture and hunting	159831	68681	91150	184398	88322	96076
B Forestry and logging	28168	1602	26566	25512	1493	24019
C Fishing	19061	6878	12183	22065	7600	14465
2 Mining and quarrying	...	...	...	...	...	...
3 Manufacturing	1220980	831997	388982	1490830	1020670	470161
A Manufacture of food, beverages and tobacco	278005	206456	71549	342156	254654	87502
B Textile, wearing apparel and leather industries	238806	150905	87901	264679	164543	100136
C Manufacture of wood and wood products, including furniture	63260	38604	24656	66213	39730	26483
D Manufacture of paper and paper products, printing and publishing	55178	33780	21398	71701	43568	28133
E Manufacture of chemicals and chemical petroleum, coal, rubber and plastic products	223488	188349	35139	304681	261406	43275
F Manufacture of non-metallic mineral products, except products of petroleum and coal	62945	30448	32497	81362	40048	41314
G Basic metal industries	44549	33554	10995	46294	32838	13456
H Manufacture of fabricated metal products, machinery and equipment	195212	109728	85484	240359	135640	104719
I Other manufacturing industries	59536	40173	19363	73389	48246	25143
4 Electricity, gas and water	63786	37284	26502	89732	73635	16097
5 Construction	222967	134115	88852	287330	174308	113022
6 Wholesale and retail trade, restaurants and hotels	406779	134360	272419	491231	165041	326190
A Wholesale and retail trade	316344	81467	234877	382483	102327	280156
B Restaurants and hotels	90435	52893	37542	108748	62714	46034
7 Transport, storage and communication	133189	63848	69341	173399	79595	93804
A Transport and storage	109975	60666	49309	140876	75114	65762
B Communication	23214	3182	20032	32523	4481	28042
8 Finance, insurance, real estate and business services [a]	161666	30257	131409	207160	40598	166562
A Financial institutions	69580	7312	62268	96610	10334	86276
B Insurance	12784	5112	7672	15156	6342	8814
C Real estate and business services	79302	17833	61469	95394	23922	71472
Real estate, except dwellings	55119	12415	42704	70324	17051	53273

Portugal

4.1 Derivation of Value Added by Kind of Activity, in Current Prices
(Continued)

Million Portuguese escudos

	1980 Gross Output	1980 Intermediate Consumption	1980 Value Added	1981 Gross Output	1981 Intermediate Consumption	1981 Value Added
Dwellings	24183	5418	18765	25070	6871	18199
9 Community, social and personal services [a][b]	42172	11963	30209	56231	15220	41011
A Sanitary and similar services	...	...	...	...	...	...
B Social and related community services	24591	5743	18848	33563	7326	26237
Educational services	7605	2135	5470	10570	2701	7869
Medical, dental, other health and veterinary services	16986	3608	13378	22993	4625	18368
C Recreational and cultural services	17581	6220	11361	22668	7894	14774
D Personal and household services	...	...	...	...	...	...
Total, Industries	2458600	1320990	1137610	3027890	1666490	1361410
Producers of Government Services	192613	47930	144683	238223	61498	176725
Other Producers	16185	2903	13282	19727	3348	16379
Total	2667400	1371820	1295580	3285840	1731330	1554510
Less: Imputed bank service charge	...	-55553	55553	...	-77588	77588
Import duties	16026	...	16026	24208	...	24208
Value added tax	...	...	...	...	...	...
Total	2683420	1427370	1256050	3310050	1808920	1501130
Memorandum Item: Mineral fuels and power	169728	140074	29654	250540	229717	20823

of which General Government:

	1980 Gross Output	1980 Intermediate Consumption	1980 Value Added	1981 Gross Output	1981 Intermediate Consumption	1981 Value Added
1 Agriculture, hunting, forestry and fishing	-	-	...	-	-	...
2 Mining and quarrying	-	-	-	-	-	-
3 Manufacturing	-	-	-	-	-	-
4 Electricity, gas and water	1040	554	486	1291	373	918
5 Construction	46	28	18	190	44	146
6 Wholesale and retail trade, restaurants and hotels	67	4	63	52	5	47
7 Transport and communication	-	-	-	-	-	-
8 Finance, insurance, real estate and business services	5886	236	5650	7293	240	7053
9 Community, social and personal services	-	-	-	43	4	39
Statistical discrepancy	-	-	...	-	-	...
Total, Industries of General Government	7039	822	6217	8869	666	8203
Producers of Government Services	...	...	...	...	...	...
Total, General Government	...	...	...	...	...	...

a) Business services and real estate except dwellings are Included In Item 'Community, social and personal services'.
b) Repair services are included in item 'Community, social and personal services'.

4.2 Derivation of Value Added by Kind of Activity, in Constant Prices

Million Portuguese escudos

	1980 Gross Output	1980 Intermediate Consumption	1980 Value Added	1981 Gross Output	1981 Intermediate Consumption	1981 Value Added
	At constant prices of:1977					
	All Producers					
1 Agriculture, hunting, forestry and fishing	...	...	97420	...	...	87140
A Agriculture and hunting	...	...	78240	...	...	71410
B Forestry and logging	...	...	12780	...	...	10180
C Fishing	...	...	6330	...	...	6150
2 Mining and quarrying	...	...	...	...	...	...

Portugal

4.2 Derivation of Value Added by Kind of Activity, in Constant Prices
(Continued)

Million Portuguese escudos

	1980 Gross Output	1980 Intermediate Consumption	1980 Value Added	1981 Gross Output	1981 Intermediate Consumption	1981 Value Added
				At constant prices of: 1977		
3 Manufacturing	...	...	204120	...	...	209050
A Manufacture of food, beverages and tobacco	...	...	38030	...	...	39160
B Textile, wearing apparel and leather industries	...	...	43390	...	...	44510
C Manufacture of wood and wood products, including furniture	...	...	11700	...	...	10200
D Manufacture of paper and paper products, printing and publishing	...	...	11900	...	...	12080
E Manufacture of chemicals and chemical petroleum, coal, rubber and plastic products	...	...	19410	...	...	20960
F Manufacture of non-metallic mineral products, except products of petroleum and coal	...	...	18660	...	...	19960
G Basic metal industries	...	...	6300	...	...	6420
H Manufacture of fabricated metal products, machinery and equipment	...	...	43270	...	...	43980
I Other manufacturing industries	...	...	11240	...	...	11920
4 Electricity, gas and water	...	...	11000	...	...	8990
5 Construction	...	...	57670	...	...	60380
6 Wholesale and retail trade, restaurants and hotels	...	...	143260	...	...	145860
A Wholesale and retail trade	...	...	126030	...	...	128450
B Restaurants and hotels	...	...	17270	...	...	17460
7 Transport, storage and communication	...	...	41820	...	...	42550
A Transport and storage	...	...	30380	...	...	30500
B Communication	...	...	11520	...	...	12110
8 Finance, insurance, real estate and business services [a]	...	...	75550	...	...	79170
A Financial institutions	...	...	32250	...	...	35600
B Insurance	...	...	3480	...	...	3300
C Real estate and business services	...	...	39980	...	...	40130
Real estate, except dwellings	...	...	22780	...	...	22640
Dwellings	...	...	16930	...	...	17360
9 Community, social and personal services [ab]	...	...	15640	...	...	16220
A Sanitary and similar services	...	...	...	...	...	...
B Social and related community services	...	...	10380	...	...	10870
Educational services	...	...	3330	...	...	3450
Medical, dental, other health and veterinary services	...	...	7070	...	...	7440
C Recreational and cultural services	...	...	5320	...	...	5420
D Personal and household services	...	...	...	...	...	...
Statistical discrepancy	...	...	...	...	...	2020
Total, Industries	...	...	646480	...	...	651380
Producers of Government Services	...	...	86090	...	...	90530
Other Producers	...	...	7350	...	...	7580
Total	...	...	739920	...	...	749490
Less: Imputed bank service charge	...	...	28400	...	...	31510
Import duties	...	...	8560	...	...	11480
Value added tax	...	...	...	...	...	...
Other adjustments	...	...	-260	...	...	-560
Total	...	...	719820	...	...	728900

a) Business services and real estate except dwellings are included in item 'Community, social and personal services'.
b) Repair services are included in item 'Community, social and personal services'.

Portugal

4.3 Cost Components of Value Added

Million Portuguese escudos

	1980 Compensation of Employees	Capital Consumption	Net Operating Surplus	Indirect Taxes	Less: Subsidies Received	Value Added	1981 Compensation of Employees	Capital Consumption	Net Operating Surplus	Indirect Taxes	Less: Subsidies Received	Value Added
					All Producers							
1 Agriculture, hunting, forestry and fishing	26602	...	102532	1967	1202	129899	28767	...	104991	2267	1465	134560
A Agriculture and hunting	16464	...	74097	1418	829	91150	16902	...	78631	1664	1121	96076
B Forestry and logging	543	...	25797	226	-	26566	678	...	23116	227	2	24019
C Fishing	9595	...	2638	323	373	12183	11187	...	3244	376	342	14465
2 Mining and quarrying	...	...	...	...	...	...	...	...	...	...	...	...
3 Manufacturing	205666	...	147691	51761	16136	388982	249307	...	177908	62781	19835	470161
A Manufacture of food, beverages and tobacco	24094	...	33164	20154	5863	71549	29705	...	39003	25140	6346	87502
B Textile, wearing apparel and leather industries	59750	...	24787	3808	444	87901	69402	...	27194	4526	986	100136
C Manufacture of wood and wood products, including furniture	12560	...	10782	1392	78	24656	14379	...	10474	1734	104	26483
D Manufacture of paper and paper products, printing and publishing	10128	...	10280	1293	293	21308	12650	...	14180	1702	400	20133
E Manufacture of chemicals and chemical petroleum, coal, rubber and plastic products	18213	...	14578	9320	6972	35139	22814	...	18096	9850	7485	43275
F Manufacture of non-metallic mineral products, except products of petroleum and coal	16106	...	14745	1776	130	32497	19797	...	19479	2434	396	41314
G Basic metal industries	6938	...	3679	569	191	10995	8581	...	4465	688	278	13456
H Manufacture of fabricated metal products, machinery and equipment	48060	...	26767	12780	2123	85484	60245	...	32885	15292	3703	104719
I Other manufacturing industries	9817	...	8909	679	42	19363	11725	...	12132	1355	69	25143
4 Electricity, gas and water	10845	...	15283	741	367	26502	13668	...	2118	1127	816	16097
5 Construction	60010	...	26604	2716	478	88852	75583	...	37837	3242	3640	113022
6 Wholesale and retail trade, restaurants and hotels	78550	...	149210	81165	36506	272419	96742	...	181258	92700	44510	326190
A Wholesale and retail trade	67412	...	124177	79744	36456	234877	82656	...	150875	90861	44236	280156
B Restaurants and hotels	11138	...	25033	1421	50	37542	14086	...	30383	1839	274	46034
7 Transport, storage and communication	55680	...	17245	3914	7498	69341	70769	...	25935	4667	7567	93804
A Transport and storage	42264	...	11638	2802	7395	49309	53557	...	16751	2968	7514	65762
B Communication	13416	...	5607	1112	103	20032	17212	...	9184	1699	53	28042
8 Finance, insurance, real estate and business services [a]	37119	...	82083	14649	2442	131409	46973	...	103887	18525	2823	166562
A Financial institutions	22991	...	31955	7362	40	62268	29397	...	47504	9375	-	86276
B Insurance	6231	...	-861	2302	-	7672	7518	...	-1802	3098	-	8814
C Real estate and business services	7897	...	50989	4985	2402	61469	10058	...	58185	6052	2823	71472
Real estate, except dwellings	7816	...	30743	4839	694	42704	9971	...	38143	5895	736	53273
Dwellings	81	...	20246	146	1708	18765	87	...	20042	157	2087	18199
9 Community, social and personal services [ab]	10594	...	16446	3911	742	30209	13754	...	22541	5488	772	41011
A Sanitary and similar services	...	...	...	...	...	...	...	...	...	...	...	...
B Social and related community services	5479	...	13120	253	4	18848	7131	...	18782	371	47	26237
Educational services	2525	...	2853	94	2	5470	3206	...	4536	138	11	7869
Medical, dental, other health and veterinary services	2954	...	10267	159	2	13378	3925	...	14246	233	36	18368
C Recreational and cultural services	5115	...	3326	3658	738	11361	6623	...	3759	5117	725	14774
D Personal and household services	...	...	...	...	...	...	...	...	...	...	...	...
Total, Industries [c]	485066	...	557094	160824	65371	1137610	595563	...	656475	190797	81428	1361410
Producers of Government Services	144647	...	-	36	-	144683	176711	...	-	14	-	176725
Other Producers	13253	...	-	29	-	13282	16325	...	-	54	-	16379
Total [c]	642966	...	557094	160889	65371	1295580	788599	...	656475	190865	81428	1554510
Less: Imputed bank service charge	...	...	55553	...	...	55553	...	...	77588	...	...	77588
Import duties	...	...	...	16026	...	16026	...	...	...	24208	...	24208
Value added tax	...	...	...	...	...	...	...	...	...	...	...	...
Total	642966	...	501541	176915	65371	1256050	788599	...	578887	215073	81428	1501130

Portugal

4.3 Cost Components of Value Added
(Continued)

Million Portuguese escudos

		1980					1981				
		Compensation of Employees	Capital Consumption	Net Operating Surplus	Indirect Taxes	Less: Subsidies Received	Value Added	Compensation of Employees	Capital Consumption	Net Operating Surplus	Indirect Taxes	Less: Subsidies Received	Value Added
		of which General Government:										
1	Agriculture, hunting, forestry and fishing	...	...	...	...	...	...	...	...	...	...	...	...
2	Mining and quarrying	-	...	-	-	-	-	-	...	-	-	-	-
3	Manufacturing	-	...	-	-	-	-	-	...	-	-	-	-
4	Electricity, gas and water	417	...	78	8	17	486	616	...	337	6	30	918
5	Construction	17	...	1	-	-	18	-	...	-	-	-	146
6	Wholesale and retail trade, restaurants and hotels	21	...	42	-	-	63	21	...	26	-	-	47
7	Transport and communication	-	...	-	-	-	-	-	...	-	-	-	-
8	Finance, insurance, real estate & business services	564	...	971	4144	29	5650	699	...	1142	5177	16	7053
9	Community, social and personal services	-	...	-	-	-	-	20	...	205	-	-	39
	Total, Industries of General Government	1019	...	1092	4152	46	6217	1356	...	1710	5183	46	8203
	Producers of Government Services	...	...	...	...	...	...	...	...	...	...	...	...
	Total, General Government	...	...	...	...	...	...	...	...	...	...	...	...

a) Business services and real estate except dwellings are included in item 'Community, social and personal services'.
b) Repair services are included in item 'Community, social and personal services'.
c) Column 'Consumption of fixed capital' is included in column 'Net operating surplus'.

Puerto Rico

General note. The preparation of national accounts statistics in Puerto Rico is undertaken by the Puerto Rico Planning Board, San Juan. The official estimates are published periodically in 'Ingreso y Producto-Puerto Rico Income and Product'. The following presentation of sources and methods is mainly based on information received from the Puerto Rico Planning Board. The estimates are generally in accordance with the classifications and definitions recommended in the United Nations System of National Accounts (SNA). The following tables have been prepared from successive replies to the United Nations national accounts questionnaire. When the scope and coverage of the estimates differ for conceptual or statistical reasons from the definitions and classifications recommended in SNA, a footnote is indicated to the relevant tables.

Sources and methods:

(a) Gross domestic product. Gross domestic product is estimated mainly through the expnditure approach.

(b) Expenditure on the gross domestic product. All components of GDP by expenditure type are estimated through the expenditure approach except private final consumption expenditure of goods and private investment in machinery and equipment which are estimated through the commodity-flow approach. Estimates of government consumption expenditure are based on special tabulations prepared by the Accounting Division of the Department of the Treasury. For personal consumption expenditure on goods, import data in f.o.b. values are obtained from the trade statistics whereas transport costs by commodity are computed by the Division of Economic Accounts. Estimates of locally produced goods are prepared by using the Puerto Rican censuses of manufactures as bench-marks and extrapolating these data for other years. Estimates of local sales of agricultural products are furnished by the Division of Agricultural Statistics. Adjustments for changes in trade inventories and mark-ups are made on the basis of data obtained from income tax returns and from the firms concerned. For some goods, the estimated quantity consumed is multiplied by the average price believed to have been paid by the consumer. Estimates of services are based on the gross receipts of the firms or organizations providing the services. Estimates of changes in stocks for the manufacturing sector are obtained through the use of census data which are extrapolated for the non-census years. For sugar and tobacco, quantity data from official sources are multiplied by the average export prices. For trade, inventories are calculated as percentages of sales from a sample of income tax returns. These percentages are then applied to the estimated total sales. Farm inventories of livestock are computed from data supplied by the Department of Agriculture. Estimates of gross fixed domestic investment in construction are obtained directly through surveys among the contractors. For those not covered by the surveys, data from building permits are used. Private investment in machinery and equipment is estimated on the basis of import statistics. For the government sector, capital expenditure estimates are based on direct surveys within the agencies and on special tabulations prepared by the Accounting Division of the Department of the Treasury. Sales to the rest of the world, i.e., to the federal government and other non-residents of Puerto Rico, include wages and salaries paid to federal employees and all purchases of goods and services by the federal government. These data are obtained from the records of the agencies themselves. Data on imports are obtained from the trade statistics issued by the United States Department of Commerce. For the constant price estimates, private final consumption expenditure is obtained by multiplying quantities by base-year prices where quantity data are available. Otherwise, the current estimates are deflated by appropriate price indexes. For all other components of GDP by expenditure type, price defaltion is used.

(c) Cost-structure of the gross domestic product. Basic data on wages and salaries are derived from records of the Bureau of Unemployment Insurance, from censuses of business and manufacturers and from income tax returns and other financial reports of private businesses and public corporations. The method used for estimating operating surplus in manufacturing, construction and some services consists in calculating, from a sample of income tax returns, ratios of profits and other property income to wages and salaries. These ratios are then applied to total wages and salaries. For some industries, the method is based on ratios of profits to gross receipts as reported on the income tax returns. Rental income of prsons is estimated by deducting from the total rent paid the rent received by businesses, government and the rest of the world. Depreciation is estimated by applying to the total wages and salaries the ratio of depreciation charges to wages and salaries or to gross receipts, in the case of trade, derived from income tax returns. Data on indirect taxes and subsidies are obtained in detail from government reports.

(d) Gross domestic product by kind of economic activity. The table of gross domestic product by kind of economic activity is prepared at market prices, i.e., producers' values. The income approach by distributive shares is used to estimate the value added of each industrial sector. The net income by distributive shares is available by industrial sector. Business transfer payments, depreciation and subsidies are distributed using direct information. Indirect business taxes are obtained from government reports and are broken down by industrial sector, using economic indicators such as data on local production and imports. For the constant price estimates, price deflation is used for the different economic activities of GDP.

1.1 Expenditure on the Gross Domestic Product, in Current Prices

Million United States dollars — Fiscal year beginning 1 July

	1970	1975	1977	1978	1979	1980	1981	1982	1983	1984	1985	1986
1 Government final consumption expenditure	913.8	1612.9	1867.4	2055.3	2280.8	2501.1	2418.3	2555.3	2886.2	3063.7	3214.0	3411.8
2 Private final consumption expenditure	4272.1	7485.7	9139.8	9913.3	10976.0	12123.4	12414.0	12991.2	13833.8	14871.4	15600.7	16706.3
3 Gross capital formation	1707.5	1973.7	1870.6	2063.8	2458.3	2264.8	1245.6	1429.0	2392.5	2296.1	2011.6	2776.2
A Increase in stocks	113.8	137.9	124.7	176.1	406.6	125.5	-542.1	-229.7	416.7	37.5	-308.3	-103.1
B Gross fixed capital formation	1593.7	1835.8	1745.9	1887.7	2051.8	2139.3	1787.7	1658.7	1975.7	2258.7	2319.9	2879.4
Residential buildings	408.7	424.2	477.2	443.9	435.5	417.4	387.1	359.5	330.8	373.7	360.9	458.6
Non-residential buildings	121.0	185.4	119.8	135.4	140.7	191.6	193.0	171.8	259.7	277.4	285.4	416.6
Other construction and land improvement etc.	612.8	685.7	536.7	621.0	726.9	767.5	656.4	502.1	637.2	664.5	567.0	760.8
Other	451.2	540.5	612.2	687.4	748.7	762.8	551.2	625.2	748.0	943.1	1106.5	1243.4
4 Exports of goods and services	2333.5	4200.8	5813.1	7230.7	8334.4	9565.5	10405.6	10193.4	10913.5	11568.1	12296.1	13623.9
5 Less: Imports of goods and services	3568.3	6276.8	7518.4	8476.9	9569.4	10631.9	10069.0	10181.4	11403.9	12116.1	11852.3	12872.9
Equals: Gross Domestic Product	5658.6	8996.4	11172.5	12786.2	14480.0	15823.0	16414.5	16987.5	18622.0	19683.2	21270.1	23645.4

1.2 Expenditure on the Gross Domestic Product, in Constant Prices

Million United States dollars — Fiscal year beginning 1 July

	1970	1975	1977	1978	1979	1980	1981	1982	1983	1984	1985	1986
	At constant prices of: 1954											
1 Government final consumption expenditure	548.1	690.3	754.6	813.5	860.8	902.4	863.4	896.7	965.9	1022.1	1066.7	1127.6
2 Private final consumption expenditure	2904.2	3473.7	3924.2	4037.0	3962.3	3971.9	3818.8	3916.7	4123.1	4020.0	4474.0	4724.8
3 Gross capital formation	1012.9	776.7	683.0	659.3	727.7	633.6	297.0	371.2	577.5	556.2	504.9	658.0
A Increase in stocks	72.2	53.8	64.9	41.8	113.5	65.6	-145.1	-35.9	107.9	14.9	-57.2	-11.7
B Gross fixed capital formation	940.7	722.9	618.0	617.5	614.1	568.0	442.1	407.2	469.6	541.4	562.0	669.7
Residential buildings	233.0	155.4	154.1	132.3	120.6	101.8	87.4	78.5	71.0	79.8	77.1	97.1
Non-residential buildings	69.0	67.9	38.7	40.3	39.0	46.7	43.6	37.5	55.7	59.2	60.8	88.2
Other construction and land improvement etc.	349.4	251.4	173.4	185.1	201.2	187.3	148.2	109.6	136.7	141.9	121.2	161.0
Other	289.3	248.2	251.8	259.8	253.3	232.2	162.9	181.6	206.2	260.6	302.9	323.4
4 Exports of goods and services	1507.4	1560.9	1919.5	2152.6	2101.0	2071.7	2112.0	2047.2	2167.6	2213.0	2408.6	2644.0
5 Less: Imports of goods and services	2704.2	2671.8	2873.1	2985.3	2900.9	2800.3	2571.2	2605.2	2900.3	3071.3	3062.8	3375.8
Equals: Gross Domestic Product	3268.3	3829.9	4408.3	4677.2	4750.9	4779.4	4550.0	4626.6	4933.8	5040.4	5391.4	5778.6

Puerto Rico

1.3 Cost Components of the Gross Domestic Product

Million United States dollars — Fiscal year beginning 1 July

	1970	1975	1977	1978	1979	1980	1981	1982	1983	1984	1985	1986
1 Indirect taxes, net	440.8	788.2	869.3	867.8	901.3	1008.5	1030.9	1211.0	1338.7	1371.9	1288.4	1459.1
A Indirect taxes	500.0	980.9	1099.0	1144.6	1184.5	1282.0	1333.7	1448.6	1672.8	1649.0	1567.1	1744.1
B Less: Subsidies	59.2	192.7	229.7	276.8	283.2	273.5	302.8	237.6	334.1	277.1	278.7	285.0
2 Consumption of fixed capital	406.3	622.8	732.3	799.3	861.2	932.8	1020.8	992.8	1131.3	1209.0	1281.2	1377.4
3 Compensation of employees paid by resident producers to:	2988.2	4819.3	5615.5	6290.2	6982.1	7570.5	7676.9	7738.4	8510.6	8956.4	9509.0	10180.6
A Resident households	2986.2	4799.9	5587.6	6262.2	6952.0	7538.1	7639.5	7703.5	8453.3	8887.4	9442.3	10117.6
B Rest of the world	2.0	19.4	27.9	28.0	30.1	32.4	37.4	34.9	57.3	69.0	66.7	63.0
4 Operating surplus	1589.4	3015.0	4141.5	4764.9	5665.3	6039.0	6491.0	6988.8	7676.5	8113.3	8939.5	10401.8
Statistical discrepancy	233.9	-248.9	-186.1	44.0	70.1	272.2	194.9	56.5	-35.1	32.6	252.0	226.5
Equals: Gross Domestic Product	5658.6	8996.4	11172.5	12786.2	14480.0	15823.0	16414.5	16987.5	18622.0	19683.2	21270.1	23645.4

1.7 External Transactions on Current Account, Summary

Million United States dollars — Fiscal year beginning 1 July

	1970	1975	1977	1978	1979	1980	1981	1982	1983	1984	1985	1986
Payments to the Rest of the World												
1 Imports of goods and services	3568.3	6276.8	7518.4	8476.9	9569.4	10631.9	10069.0	10181.4	11403.9	12116.1	11852.3	12872.9
A Imports of merchandise c.i.f.	3065.6	5502.8	6628.8	7488.9	8531.5	9521.7	8895.8	8915.3	10015.0	10667.9	10396.0	11246.0
B Other	502.7	774.0	889.6	988.0	1037.9	1110.2	1173.2	1266.1	1388.9	1448.2	1456.3	1626.9
2 Factor income to the rest of the world	697.1	1975.4	2800.9	3422.9	4285.9	4728.3	5092.4	5379.6	5904.1	6489.3	7042.8	8239.4
A Compensation of employees	2.0	19.4	27.9	28.0	30.1	32.4	37.4	34.9	57.3	69.0	66.7	63.0
B Property and entrepreneurial income	695.1	1956.0	2773.0	3394.9	4255.8	4695.9	5055.0	5344.7	5846.8	6420.3	6976.1	8176.4
By general government	35.2	97.2	123.0	116.5	115.9	141.3	142.8	159.5	201.8	211.2	201.5	211.7
By corporate and quasi-corporate enterprises	...	...	...	...	...	...	...	...	...	...	...	...
By other	...	...	...	...	...	...	...	...	...	...	...	...
3 Current transfers to the rest of the world	297.9	749.2	824.6	857.9	898.3	958.5	1010.0	1061.1	1198.6	1274.6	1376.7	1452.3
4 Surplus of the nation on current transactions	-1192.5	-1754.5	-1735.4	-1580.7	-1811.2	-1787.0	-337.2	-783.8	-1991.0	-2263.7	-1573.1	-2355.9
Payments to the Rest of the World and Surplus of the Nation on Current Transactions	3370.8	7246.9	9408.5	11177.0	12942.4	14531.7	15834.2	15838.3	16515.6	17616.3	18698.7	20208.7
Receipts From The Rest of the World												
1 Exports of goods and services	2333.5	4200.8	5813.1	7230.7	8334.4	9565.5	10405.6	10193.4	10913.5	11568.1	12296.1	13623.9
A Exports of merchandise f.o.b.	1826.5	3413.1	4880.3	6179.7	7139.7	8289.5	9052.7	8760.4	9408.8	9920.4	10610.5	11628.6
B Other	507.0	787.7	932.8	1051.0	1194.7	1276.0	1352.9	1433.0	1504.7	1647.7	1685.6	1995.3
2 Factor income from rest of the world	261.3	441.0	508.3	586.9	773.0	960.9	1172.5	1176.5	1104.7	1412.9	1411.8	1459.4
A Compensation of employees	200.9	231.3	260.0	266.6	265.7	317.5	332.9	356.9	386.1	416.1	428.7	447.4
B Property and entrepreneurial income	60.4	209.7	248.3	320.3	507.3	643.4	839.6	819.6	718.6	996.8	983.1	1012.0
By general government	6.5	3.3	8.9	5.7	9.2	7.3	10.8	11.1	14.5	12.6	11.1	8.8
By corporate and quasi-corporate enterprises	...	...	...	...	...	...	...	...	...	...	...	...
By other	...	...	...	...	...	...	...	...	...	...	...	...
3 Current transfers from rest of the world	776.0	2605.1	3087.1	3359.4	3835.0	4005.3	4256.1	4468.3	4497.4	4635.3	4990.8	5125.4
Receipts from the Rest of the World on Current Transactions	3370.8	7246.9	9408.5	11177.0	12942.4	14531.7	15834.2	15838.3	16515.6	17616.3	18698.7	20208.7

1.10 Gross Domestic Product by Kind of Activity, in Current Prices

Million United States dollars — Fiscal year beginning 1 July

	1970	1975	1977	1978	1979	1980	1981	1982	1983	1984	1985	1986
1 Agriculture, hunting, forestry and fishing	176.5	285.5	337.9	354.6	393.9	377.1	394.8	395.9	343.3	345.5	337.6	372.1
2 Mining and quarrying	10.4	9.3	9.5	9.1	11.2	11.0	10.8	11.0	9.7	10.8	10.8	13.4
3 Manufacturing	1333.8	2974.0	3920.3	4470.5	5322.5	5786.1	6017.0	6482.5	7266.2	7757.9	8298.5	9388.5
4 Electricity, gas and water	183.5	331.3	337.0	391.3	447.8	453.9	641.4	602.4	590.9	577.3	641.8	696.9
5 Construction [a]	474.2	386.3	331.5	349.6	359.0	399.4	344.0	311.0	296.1	326.2	315.8	394.8

Puerto Rico

1.10 Gross Domestic Product by Kind of Activity, in Current Prices
(Continued)

Million United States dollars — Fiscal year beginning 1 July

	1970	1975	1977	1978	1979	1980	1981	1982	1983	1984	1985	1986
6 Wholesale and retail trade, restaurants and hotels	1062.3	1660.9	2025.5	2252.7	2422.2	2621.2	2623.4	2566.5	2933.5	3089.5	3268.2	3685.7
7 Transport, storage and communication	298.2	495.4	630.2	707.1	787.0	849.3	899.9	865.0	1069.3	1017.5	1124.4	1175.5
8 Finance, insurance, real estate and business services	755.8	1089.2	1450.9	1673.9	1858.9	1995.1	2261.2	2518.6	2720.2	2862.1	3131.0	3515.3
9 Community, social and personal services	349.4	547.2	655.9	727.2	799.7	883.4	944.1	1009.0	1104.4	1156.8	1269.8	1362.6
Total, Industries	4644.1	7779.1	9698.7	10936.0	12402.2	13376.5	14136.6	14761.9	16333.6	17143.6	18397.9	20604.8
Producers of Government Services	736.1	1390.1	1570.8	1707.7	1896.3	2051.0	1952.0	2028.9	2172.8	2344.9	2443.8	2629.4
Other Producers	44.4	76.0	88.9	98.6	111.5	123.4	130.8	140.3	150.8	162.0	176.4	184.8
Subtotal	5424.6	9245.2	11358.4	12742.3	14410.0	15550.9	16219.4	16931.1	18657.2	19650.5	21018.1	23419.0
Less: Imputed bank service charge	...	...	...	...	...	...	...	...	...	...	...	...
Plus: Import duties	...	...	...	...	...	...	...	...	...	...	...	...
Plus: Value added tax	...	...	...	...	...	...	...	...	...	...	...	...
Plus: Other adjustments	233.9	-248.9	-186.1	44.0	70.1	272.2	194.9	56.5	-35.1	32.6	252.0	226.5
Equals: Gross Domestic Product	5658.6	8996.4	11172.5	12786.2	14480.0	15823.0	16414.5	16987.5	18622.0	19683.2	21270.1	23645.4

a) Item 'Construction' refers to contract construction only.

1.11 Gross Domestic Product by Kind of Activity, in Constant Prices

Million United States dollars — Fiscal year beginning 1 July

At constant prices of: 1954

	1970	1975	1977	1978	1979	1980	1981	1982	1983	1984	1985	1986
1 Agriculture, hunting, forestry and fishing	141.8	154.9	171.2	176.6	172.5	169.9	174.8	169.5	146.8	150.0	152.2	166.7
2 Mining and quarrying	5.9	4.3	4.1	4.0	4.5	3.9	3.6	3.5	3.0	3.2	3.1	3.8
3 Manufacturing	1012.9	1485.7	1747.2	1880.6	2016.4	2019.2	1978.8	2127.8	2330.4	2457.3	2672.8	2805.0
4 Electricity, gas and water	198.5	166.1	148.5	167.5	152.6	123.9	147.4	140.6	138.1	134.4	172.1	198.2
5 Construction a	270.4	141.6	107.1	104.2	99.4	97.4	77.7	67.9	63.5	69.6	67.4	83.8
6 Wholesale and retail trade, restaurants and hotels	685.1	753.3	822.3	853.2	816.4	795.9	762.9	733.6	817.2	852.4	897.3	980.0
7 Transport, storage and communication	188.7	208.1	259.5	288.6	294.0	289.6	302.1	249.9	330.7	327.4	354.1	370.3
8 Finance, insurance, real estate and business services	521.6	586.8	696.9	730.0	714.8	721.0	739.2	786.2	830.7	833.5	922.4	1069.1
9 Community, social and personal services	203.6	231.1	253.2	260.4	264.5	268.2	271.6	280.6	304.5	311.7	329.6	349.5
Total, Industries	3228.5	3731.9	4210.0	4465.1	4535.1	4489.5	4458.0	4559.6	4964.9	5139.5	5571.0	6026.4
Producers of Government Services	428.2	587.5	628.1	672.9	722.9	756.0	719.5	738.9	755.2	815.1	848.0	909.2
Other Producers	24.4	26.2	28.3	29.7	30.3	31.0	31.4	32.9	34.9	37.2	40.4	43.4
Subtotal	3681.1	4345.6	4866.4	5167.7	5288.3	5276.5	5208.9	5331.4	5755.0	5991.8	6459.4	6979.0
Less: Imputed bank service charge	...	...	...	...	...	...	...	...	...	...	...	...
Plus: Import duties	...	...	...	...	...	...	...	...	...	...	...	...
Plus: Value added tax	...	...	...	...	...	...	...	...	...	...	...	...
Plus: Other adjustments	-412.7	-515.8	-458.0	-490.6	-537.4	-497.2	-658.6	-704.8	-821.3	-951.2	-1068.1	-1200.2
Equals: Gross Domestic Product	3268.3	3829.9	4408.3	4677.2	4750.9	4779.4	4550.0	4626.6	4933.8	5040.4	5391.4	5778.6

a) Item 'Construction' refers to contract construction only.

1.12 Relations Among National Accounting Aggregates

Million United States dollars — Fiscal year beginning 1 July

	1970	1975	1977	1978	1979	1980	1981	1982	1983	1984	1985	1986
Gross Domestic Product	5658.6	8996.4	11172.5	12786.2	14480.0	15823.0	16414.5	16987.5	18622.0	19683.2	21270.1	23645.4
Plus: Net factor income from the rest of the world	-435.8	-1534.4	-2292.6	-2836.0	-3512.9	-3767.4	-3919.9	-4203.1	-4799.4	-5076.4	-5631.0	-6780.0
Factor income from the rest of the world	261.3	441.0	508.3	586.9	773.0	960.9	1172.5	1176.5	1104.7	1412.9	1411.8	1459.4
Less: Factor income to the rest of the world	697.1	1975.4	2800.9	3422.9	4285.9	4728.3	5092.4	5379.6	5904.1	6489.3	7042.8	8239.4
Equals: Gross National Product	5222.8	7462.0	8879.9	9950.2	10967.1	12055.6	12494.6	12784.4	13822.6	14606.8	15639.1	16865.4
Less: Consumption of fixed capital	406.3	622.8	732.3	799.3	861.2	932.8	1020.8	992.8	1131.3	1209.0	1281.2	1377.4

Puerto Rico

1.12 Relations Among National Accounting Aggregates
(Continued)

Million United States dollars — Fiscal year beginning 1 July

	1970	1975	1977	1978	1979	1980	1981	1982	1983	1984	1985	1986
Equals: National Income	4816.5	6839.2	8147.6	9150.9	10105.9	11122.8	11473.8	11791.6	12691.3	13397.8	14357.9	15488.0
Plus: Net current transfers from the rest of the world	478.1	1855.9	2262.5	2501.5	2936.7	3046.8	3246.1	3407.2	3298.8	3360.7	3614.1	3673.1
Current transfers from the rest of the world	776.0	2605.1	3087.1	3359.4	3835.0	4005.3	4256.1	4468.3	4497.4	4635.3	4990.8	5125.4
Less: Current transfers to the rest of the world	297.9	749.2	824.6	857.9	898.3	958.5	1010.0	1061.1	1198.6	1274.6	1376.7	1452.3
Equals: National Disposable Income	5294.6	8695.1	10410.1	11652.4	13042.6	14169.6	14719.9	15198.8	15990.1	16758.5	17972.0	19161.1
Less: Final consumption	5185.9	9098.6	11007.2	11968.6	13256.8	14624.5	14832.3	15546.4	16719.9	17935.1	18814.7	20118.2
Equals: Net Saving	108.7	-403.6	-597.1	-316.2	-214.1	-455.0	-112.4	-347.6	-729.8	-1176.6	-842.7	-957.1
Less: Surplus of the nation on current transactions	-1192.5	-1754.5	-1735.4	-1580.7	-1811.2	-1787.0	-337.2	-783.8	-1991.0	-2263.7	-1573.1	-2355.9
Equals: Net Capital Formation	1301.2	1350.9	1138.3	1264.5	1597.1	1332.0	224.8	436.2	1261.2	1087.1	730.4	1398.8

2.5 Private Final Consumption Expenditure by Type and Porpose, in Current Prices

Million United States dollars — Fiscal year beginning 1 July

	1970	1975	1977	1978	1979	1980	1981	1982	1983	1984	1985	1986
Final Consumption Expenditure of Resident Households												
1 Food, beverages and tobacco	1323.2	2577.4	2887.0	2999.2	3428.9	3699.8	3663.9	3822.2	3887.3	4198.9	4375.2	4733.6
A Food	996.8	2106.0	2324.9	2420.2	2779.5	2980.7	2936.0	3026.4	3087.3	3364.0	3492.4	3806.8
B Non-alcoholic beverages	...	...	...	...	...	...	...	...	...	...	...	...
C Alcoholic beverages	236.8	347.0	403.5	402.5	453.5	507.5	492.0	545.8	560.0	557.2	598.3	625.3
D Tobacco	89.5	124.4	158.6	176.5	195.9	211.6	235.9	250.0	240.0	277.7	284.6	301.5
2 Clothing and footwear	470.6	698.5	889.4	990.4	1016.1	1102.4	1119.3	1163.7	1313.8	1295.2	1325.8	1391.3
3 Gross rent, fuel and power	532.7	958.5	1221.1	1318.4	1511.9	1801.9	1961.4	2075.0	2188.4	2321.6	2431.0	2551.2
4 Furniture, furnishings and household equipment and operation	401.2	669.8	711.4	730.9	817.7	855.4	819.9	824.1	850.9	909.2	977.0	1103.9
A Household operation	100.0	170.4	204.5	204.8	231.3	243.3	246.6	256.0	236.0	269.7	278.9	289.9
B Other	301.2	499.4	506.9	526.1	586.4	612.1	573.3	568.1	614.9	639.5	698.1	814.0
5 Medical care and health expenses	184.5	289.6	410.0	479.3	486.0	534.7	586.9	631.4	698.0	844.3	912.2	1064.7
6 Transport and communication	569.3	1006.6	1325.0	1559.3	1780.5	2073.2	2005.4	2014.1	2268.4	2428.6	2579.4	2647.3
A Personal transport equipment	221.5	296.4	430.9	540.6	447.7	520.1	397.1	491.5	748.3	871.2	959.5	1034.5
B Other	347.8	710.2	894.1	1018.7	1332.8	1553.1	1608.3	1522.6	1520.1	1557.4	1619.9	1612.8
7 Recreational, entertainment, education and cultural services	248.5	513.4	707.0	751.2	735.7	814.8	868.1	906.9	936.3	1014.0	1019.0	1069.2
A Education	19.9	113.8	163.7	183.3	205.9	229.5	260.3	281.6	303.5	325.6	354.4	379.6
B Other	228.6	399.6	543.3	567.9	529.8	585.3	607.8	625.3	632.8	688.4	664.6	689.6
8 Miscellaneous goods and services	463.2	719.6	915.3	1012.0	1139.2	1199.3	1308.8	1411.9	1476.5	1616.9	1710.8	1876.9
A Personal care	111.5	180.5	217.8	239.4	291.3	328.2	375.6	403.3	426.8	440.2	437.7	456.7
B Expenditures in restaurants, cafes and hotels	141.0	222.2	293.1	341.7	378.2	412.5	417.2	396.2	415.1	453.2	497.5	549.4
C Other	210.7	316.9	404.4	430.9	469.7	458.6	516.0	612.4	634.6	723.5	775.6	870.8
Total Final Consumption Expenditure in the Domestic Market by Households, of which	4193.2	7433.4	9066.2	9840.7	10916.0	12081.5	12333.7	12849.3	13619.6	14628.7	15330.4	16438.1
Plus: Direct purchases abroad by resident households	250.3	327.2	395.3	460.5	471.7	467.3	524.9	542.3	579.0	615.2	628.3	761.9
Less: Direct purchases in the domestic market by non-resident households	239.3	398.6	490.3	573.9	628.0	665.1	715.3	707.3	698.9	738.8	762.8	918.5
Equals: Final Consumption Expenditure of Resident Households	4204.2	7362.0	8971.2	9727.3	10759.7	11883.7	12143.3	12684.3	13499.7	14505.1	15195.9	16281.5
Final Consumption Expenditure of Private Non-profit Institutions Serving Households												
1 Research and science	...	...	...	...	...	...	...	...	...	...	...	...
2 Education	20.6	...	...	...	...	...	...	...	...	...	...	...
3 Medical and other health services	45.2	114.6	156.0	171.8	200.0	219.9	248.1	281.3	307.2	338.1	373.6	391.8

Puerto Rico

2.5 Private Final Consumption Expenditure by Type and Porpose, in Current Prices
(Continued)

Million United States dollars — Fiscal year beginning 1 July

	1970	1975	1977	1978	1979	1980	1981	1982	1983	1984	1985	1986
4 Welfare services	...	...	...	...	...	...	...	...	...	...	...	...
5 Recreational and related cultural services	...	...	...	...	...	...	...	...	...	...	...	...
6 Religious organisations	2.1	9.1	12.5	14.2	16.3	19.7	22.6	25.6	26.9	28.1	31.3	32.9
7 Professional and labour organisations serving households	...	...	...	...	...	...	...	...	...	...	...	...
8 Miscellaneous	...	...	...	...	...	...	...	...	...	...	...	...
Equals: Final Consumption Expenditure of Private Non-profit Organisations Serving Households	67.9	123.7	168.5	186.0	216.3	239.6	270.7	306.9	334.1	366.2	404.9	424.7
Private Final Consumption Expenditure	4272.1	7485.7	9139.8	9913.3	10976.0	12123.4	12414.0	12991.2	13833.8	14871.4	15600.7	16706.3

2.6 Private Final Consumption Expenditure by Type and Purpose, in Constant Prices

Million United States dollars — Fiscal year beginning 1 July

	1970	1975	1977	1978	1979	1980	1981	1982	1983	1984	1985	1986

At constant prices of: 1954

Final Consumption Expenditure of Resident Households

	1970	1975	1977	1978	1979	1980	1981	1982	1983	1984	1985	1986
1 Food, beverages and tobacco	816.4	927.6	976.9	953.2	992.8	963.3	906.2	924.3	919.9	973.8	1012.5	1067.1
A Food	616.6	751.9	784.0	768.0	792.8	756.5	723.1	730.7	727.2	775.6	806.5	855.1
B Non-alcoholic beverages	...	...	...	...	...	...	...	...	...	...	...	...
C Alcoholic beverages	143.2	125.4	134.7	130.9	141.5	148.8	126.9	136.7	139.0	137.7	145.8	149.6
D Tobacco	56.6	50.3	58.2	54.3	58.5	58.0	56.2	56.9	53.7	60.5	60.3	62.3
2 Clothing and footwear	333.8	397.4	463.8	495.2	469.3	476.9	472.3	479.3	546.2	529.3	538.4	571.8
3 Gross rent, fuel and power	432.4	541.9	617.9	631.6	647.4	683.4	685.1	690.7	700.0	712.8	728.2	741.6
4 Furniture, furnishings and household equipment and operation	309.6	378.3	366.9	360.0	371.4	367.1	333.4	328.8	332.9	350.0	370.9	421.5
A Household operation	69.2	81.3	86.7	78.7	77.7	75.1	70.3	70.1	67.9	70.4	52.0	53.9
B Other	240.4	297.0	280.2	281.3	293.7	292.0	263.1	258.7	265.0	279.6	318.9	367.6
5 Medical care and health expenses	99.5	114.8	143.1	156.4	143.3	145.0	148.0	149.7	159.6	185.8	190.8	212.2
6 Transport and communication	385.7	457.2	555.3	610.0	573.3	588.7	536.9	548.6	634.2	680.7	721.2	729.9
A Personal transport equipment	132.7	133.0	176.0	204.6	155.0	160.6	114.7	141.5	210.3	238.2	253.0	244.7
B Other	253.0	324.2	379.6	405.4	418.3	428.1	422.2	407.1	423.9	442.5	468.2	485.2
7 Recreational, entertainment, education and cultural services	178.7	288.8	381.2	384.7	344.3	367.3	380.1	384.4	389.7	417.3	410.4	427.6
A Education	12.7	47.7	64.0	68.1	70.0	72.6	78.7	81.3	84.0	85.8	90.2	91.7
B Other	166.0	241.1	317.2	316.6	274.3	294.7	301.4	303.1	305.7	331.5	320.2	335.9
8 Miscellaneous goods and services	260.7	292.2	338.8	352.0	356.9	350.9	350.0	366.4	379.2	406.4	438.3	494.7
A Personal care	132.7	83.8	95.7	101.6	116.1	125.5	132.4	137.5	144.0	145.9	142.5	146.3
B Expenditures in restaurants, cafes and hotels	66.1	71.1	85.7	92.6	95.4	90.2	80.6	71.6	73.3	78.1	85.6	93.2
C Other	61.9	137.3	157.4	157.8	145.4	135.2	137.0	157.3	161.9	182.4	210.2	255.2
Total Final Consumption Expenditure in the Domestic Market by Households, of which	2816.8	3398.2	3843.9	3943.1	3898.7	3942.6	3812.0	3872.2	4061.7	4256.1	4410.7	4666.4
Plus: Direct purchases abroad by resident households	181.5	174.2	193.8	225.2	191.8	149.3	151.9	153.0	162.2	167.0	168.9	201.7
Less: Direct purchases in the domestic market by non-resident households	131.1	142.9	164.4	183.1	183.1	177.1	176.7	172.9	168.3	175.4	181.7	216.9
Equals: Final Consumption Expenditure of Resident Households	2867.2	3429.5	3873.3	3985.2	3907.4	3914.8	3787.2	3852.3	4055.6	4247.7	4397.9	4651.2

Final Consumption Expenditure of Private Non-profit Institutions Serving Households

	1970	1975	1977	1978	1979	1980	1981	1982	1983	1984	1985	1986
1 Research and science	...	...	...	...	...	...	...	...	...	...	...	...
2 Education	13.1	...	...	...	...	...	...	...	...	...	...	...
3 Medical and other health services	22.6	40.3	46.0	46.6	49.4	50.9	55.1	57.3	59.8	64.4	67.3	64.7

Puerto Rico

2.6 Private Final Consumption Expenditure by Type and Purpose, in Constant Prices
(Continued)

Million United States dollars — Fiscal year beginning 1 July

	1970	1975	1977	1978	1979	1980	1981	1982	1983	1984	1985	1986
					At constant prices of: 1954							
4 Welfare services	...	...	...	...	...	...	...	...	...	...	...	...
5 Recreational and related cultural services	...	...	...	...	...	...	...	...	...	...	...	...
6 Religious organisations	1.3	3.8	4.9	5.3	5.5	6.1	6.5	7.3	7.5	8.1	8.7	9.0
7 Professional and labour organisations serving households	...	...	...	...	...	...	...	...	...	...	...	...
8 Miscellaneous	...	...	...	...	...	...	...	...	...	...	...	...
Equals: Final Consumption Expenditure of Private Non-profit Organisations Serving Households	37.0	44.1	50.9	51.9	54.9	57.0	61.5	64.6	67.3	72.5	76.0	73.7
Private Final Consumption Expenditure	2904.2	3473.7	3924.1	4037.0	3962.3	3971.9	3848.8	3916.9	4123.1	4320.3	4474.0	4724.8

2.17 Exports and Imports of Goods and Services, Detail

Million United States dollars — Fiscal year beginning 1 July

	1970	1975	1977	1978	1979	1980	1981	1982	1983	1984	1985	1986
					Exports of Goods and Services							
1 Exports of merchandise, f.o.b.	1826.5	3413.1	4880.3	6179.7	7139.7	8289.5	9052.7	8760.4	9408.8	9920.4	10610.5	11628.6
2 Transport and communication	103.4	205.2	247.5	277.4	330.2	333.2	358.0	388.5	409.0	390.9	392.5	407.7
A In respect of merchandise imports	0.3	34.9	29.7	39.2	43.4	59.3	66.3	72.6	83.4	76.0	87.5	91.0
B Other	103.1	170.3	217.8	238.2	286.8	273.9	291.7	315.9	325.6	314.9	305.0	316.7
3 Insurance service charges	1.9	2.4	2.6	3.2	3.4	2.5	3.0	5.0	4.9	4.5	5.3	5.8
A In respect of merchandise imports	1.9	2.4	2.6	3.2	3.4	2.5	3.0	5.0	4.9	4.5	5.3	5.8
B Other	-	-	-	-	-	-	-	-	-	-	-	-
4 Other commodities	162.4	181.4	192.3	196.6	233.0	275.1	276.6	332.3	392.1	513.5	524.9	663.4
5 Adjustments of merchandise exports to change-of-ownership basis	...	...	...	...	...	...	...	...	...	...	...	...
6 Direct purchases in the domestic market by non-residential households	239.3	398.7	490.3	574.0	628.0	665.1	715.3	707.3	698.9	738.8	762.8	918.5
7 Direct purchases in the domestic market by extraterritorial bodies	...	...	...	...	...	...	...	...	...	...	...	...
Total Exports of Goods and Services	2333.5	4200.8	5813.1	7230.7	8334.4	9565.5	10405.6	10193.4	10913.5	11568.1	12296.1	13623.9
					Imports of Goods and Services							
1 Imports of merchandise, c.i.f.	3065.6	5502.8	6628.8	7488.9	8531.5	9521.7	8895.8	8915.3	10015.0	10667.9	10396.0	11246.0
A Imports of merchandise, f.o.b.	2832.8	5222.9	6316.2	7172.5	8189.3	9123.8	8523.8	8526.6	9519.9	10108.1	9830.0	10616.3
B Transport of services on merchandise imports	223.1	261.5	290.4	291.4	313.0	366.2	343.4	359.9	462.7	525.5	531.8	593.7
By residents	...	...	...	...	...	...	...	...	...	...	...	...
By non-residents	223.1	261.5	290.4	291.4	313.0	366.2	343.4	359.9	462.7	525.5	531.8	593.7
C Insurance service charges on merchandise imports	9.7	18.4	22.2	25.0	29.2	31.7	28.6	28.8	32.3	34.3	34.2	35.9
By residents	...	...	...	...	...	...	...	...	...	...	...	...
By non-residents	9.7	18.4	22.2	25.0	29.2	31.7	28.6	28.8	32.3	34.3	34.2	35.9
2 Adjustments of merchandise imports to change-of-ownership basis	...	...	...	...	...	...	...	...	...	...	...	...
3 Other transport and communication	106.8	266.2	286.7	290.6	288.9	342.3	323.5	376.7	413.5	411.5	396.7	430.2
4 Other insurance service charges	...	...	...	...	...	...	...	...	...	...	...	...
5 Other commodities	130.4	156.1	220.2	252.4	271.9	279.5	279.3	302.3	362.3	390.1	396.9	420.7
6 Direct purchases abroad by government	7.4	26.9	12.7	18.7	27.1	25.6	29.6	22.1	32.9	38.9	36.3	40.3
7 Direct purchases abroad by resident households	258.1	324.9	369.9	426.3	450.2	462.8	540.8	564.9	580.2	607.8	626.3	735.7
Total Imports of Goods and Services	3568.3	6276.8	7518.4	8476.9	9569.4	10631.9	10069.0	10181.4	11403.9	12116.1	11852.3	12872.9
Balance of Goods and Services	-1234.8	-2076.0	-1705.3	-1246.2	-1235.0	-1066.4	336.6	12.0	-490.4	-548.0	443.8	751.0
Total Imports and Balance of Goods and Services	2333.5	4200.8	5813.1	7230.7	8334.4	9565.5	10405.6	10193.4	10913.5	11568.1	12296.1	13623.9

Qatar

Source. Reply to the United Nations National Accounts Questionnaire from the Central Statistical Organization, Doha.
General note. The estimates shown in the following tables have been prepared in accordance with the United Nations System of National Accounts so far as the existing data would permit.

1.1 Expenditure on the Gross Domestic Product, in Current Prices

Million Qatari riyals

	1970	1975	1977	1978	1979	1980	1981	1982	1983	1984	1985	1986
1 Government final consumption expenditure	...	...	6190	6075	7955	5622	8143	7236	8203	9021	7882	...
2 Private final consumption expenditure	...	...				4477	5383	5868	5706	5856	5544	...
3 Gross capital formation	...	...	4708	4975	4551	4883	5596	7606	5176	4147	3998	...
A Increase in stocks	...	...	...	...	...	117	284	215	-544	-155	30	...
B Gross fixed capital formation	...	...	...	...	...	4766	5312	7391	5720	4302	3968	...
4 Exports of goods and services	...	...	8274	9249	14655	21127	21468	16753	12753	...	...	...
5 Less: Imports of goods and services	...	...	4850	4590	5378	7478	9063	9811	8296	7537	6610	...
Equals: Gross Domestic Product	...	...	14322	15709	21783	28631	31527	27652	23542	...	...	...

1.10 Gross Domestic Product by Kind of Activity, in Current Prices

Million Qatari riyals

	1970	1975	1977	1978	1979	1980	1981	1982	1983	1984	1985	1986
1 Agriculture, hunting, forestry and fishing	...	71	97	111	122	150	172	190	195	206	213	...
2 Mining and quarrying	...	6734	7890	8660	13664	19245	20175	15001	10790	...	...	...
3 Manufacturing	...	255	498	597	856	943	1491	1391	1464	1829	1770	...
4 Electricity, gas and water	...	19	46	62	85	64	83	89	133	165	191	...
5 Construction	...	766	1531	1340	1357	1556	1632	1829	1395	1411	1313	...
6 Wholesale and retail trade, restaurants and hotels	...	372	1398	1485	1660	1293	1858	1775	1587	1506	1186	...
7 Transport, storage and communication	...	156	307	370	415	399	409	458	450	480	450	...
8 Finance, insurance, real estate and business services	...	743	1087	1290	1523	1705	2022	2308	2030	1919	1899	...
9 Community, social and personal services	...	58	90	105	126	128	176	242	227	222	201	...
Total, Industries	...	9174	12944	14020	19808	25483	28018	23283	18272	...	...	...
Producers of Government Services	...	622	1502	1831	2143	3367	3865	4727	5553	6189	5748	...
Other Producers	...	44	61	71	83	100	102	104	105	105	105	...
Subtotal	...	9840	14507	15922	22034	28950	31985	28114	23930	...	...	...
Less: Imputed bank service charge	...	153	240	313	321	406	561	569	492	543	484	...
Plus: Import duties	...	20	55	100	70	87	103	107	104	118	129	...
Plus: Value added tax	...	...	...	...	...	...	...	...	...	...	...	...
Equals: Gross Domestic Product	...	9707	14322	15709	21783	28631	31527	27652	23542	...	...	...

1.11 Gross Domestic Product by Kind of Activity, in Constant Prices

Million Qatari riyals

	1970	1975	1977	1978	1979	1980	1981	1982	1983	1984	1985	1986
				At constant prices of: 1981								
1 Agriculture, hunting, forestry and fishing	...	...	...	...	...	148	172	189	184	192	193	...
2 Mining and quarrying	...	...	...	...	...	23524	20175	16342	...	...	...	...
3 Manufacturing	...	...	...	...	...	1470	1491	1622	1792	2141	2219	...
4 Electricity, gas and water	...	...	...	...	...	61	83	105	143	173	201	...
5 Construction	...	...	...	...	...	1600	1632	1795	1369	1481	1406	...
6 Wholesale and retail trade, restaurants and hotels	...	...	...	...	...	1272	1858	1702	1428	1362	1017	...
7 Transport, storage and communication	...	...	...	...	...	409	409	428	436	446	408	...
8 Finance, insurance, real estate and business services	...	...	...	...	...	1839	2022	2197	2052	2122	2108	...
9 Community, social and personal services	...	...	...	...	...	139	176	228	209	202	180	...
Total, Industries	...	...	...	...	...	30462	28018	24608	...	...	...	...
Producers of Government Services	...	...	...	...	...	3436	3865	4089	4422	4434	4476	...
Other Producers	...	...	...	...	...	109	102	98	97	96	94	...
Subtotal	...	...	...	...	...	34007	31985	28795	...	...	...	...
Less: Imputed bank service charge	...	...	...	...	...	441	561	537	453	495	432	...
Plus: Import duties	...	...	...	...	...	89	103	103	81	81	65	...
Plus: Value added tax	...	...	...	...	...	...	...	...	...	...	...	...
Equals: Gross Domestic Product	...	...	...	...	...	33655	31527	28361	...	...	...	...

Reunion

Source. Reply to the United Nations National Accounts Questionnaire from the Institute national de la statistique et des etudes economiques (INSEE), Paris. Official estimates and descriptions are published by the same Institute in 'Comptes Economiques de la Reunion'.

General note. The estimates shown in the following tables have been adjusted by the INSEE to conform to the United Nations System of National Accounts so far as the existing data would permit.

1.1 Expenditure on the Gross Domestic Product, in Current Prices

Million French francs

	1970	1975	1977	1978	1979	1980	1981	1982	1983	1984	1985	1986
1 Government final consumption expenditure	657.7	1542.7	2017.9	2194.8	2480.9	2868.0	3330.2	4058.4	4515.6	4864.5	5258.5	...
2 Private final consumption expenditure	1436.6	3399.8	4681.6	5207.9	6168.9	7120.4	8291.2	10296.5	11769.7	12900.3	14205.8	...
A Households	...	3386.3	4665.1	5173.1	6133.3	7079.7	8208.8	10152.9	11425.5	12737.3	...	...
B Private non-profit institutions serving households	...	13.5	16.5	34.8	35.6	40.7	82.4	143.6	344.2	163.0	...	...
3 Gross capital formation	539.4	1109.7	1124.7	1363.9	1570.1	1875.4	2085.1	2570.7	3064.3	3117.8	3426.9	...
A Increase in stocks	-32.9	140.6	44.9	103.8	138.2	130.4	92.0	72.6	87.6	24.7	125.3	...
B Gross fixed capital formation	572.3	969.1	1079.8	1260.1	1431.9	1744.9	1993.1	2498.1	2976.7	3093.1	3301.6	...
4 Exports of goods and services	282.1	268.5	560.7	521.0	594.9	556.0	763.2	787.4	881.5	855.5	1067.1	...
5 Less: Imports of goods and services	902.8	1780.8	2497.3	2690.2	3342.6	3971.2	4341.6	5426.9	6556.4	7046.6	7621.6	...
Equals: Gross Domestic Product	2013.4	4539.9	5887.6	6597.4	7472.2	8448.6	10128.2	12286.2	13674.7	14691.6	16336.6	...

1.3 Cost Components of the Gross Domestic Product

Million French francs

	1970	1975	1977	1978	1979	1980	1981	1982	1983	1984	1985	1986
1 Indirect taxes, net	252.6	462.6	652.2	647.7	709.1	871.9	1022.0	1262.5	...	...	...	...
2 Consumption of fixed capital	...	...	...	...	...	...	...	...	...	...	...	...
3 Compensation of employees paid by resident producers to:	1429.5	2826.2	3707.6	4202.5	4735.4	5481.0	6477.6	7682.5	8924.1	9500.0	10200.0	...
4 Operating surplus [a]	331.3	1251.1	1527.8	1747.2	2027.7	2095.6	2628.6	3341.2	...	...	...	...
Equals: Gross Domestic Product	2013.4	4539.9	5887.6	6597.4	7472.2	8448.6	10128.2	12286.2	13674.7	14691.6	16336.6	...

a) Item 'Operating surplus' includes consumption of fixed capital.

1.7 External Transactions on Current Account, Summary

Million French francs

	1970	1975	1977	1978	1979	1980	1981	1982	1983	1984	1985	1986
Payments to the Rest of the World												
1 Imports of goods and services	902.8	1780.8	2497.3	2690.2	3342.6	3971.2	4341.6	5380.3	...	...	...	...
2 Factor income to the rest of the world	43.9	87.6	153.2	198.8	239.4	278.8	315.4	400.5	...	...	...	...
A Compensation of employees	-	-	-	-	-	-	-	-	...	...	...	...
B Property and entrepreneurial income	43.9	87.6	153.2	198.8	239.4	278.8	315.4	400.5	...	...	...	...
3 Current transfers to the rest of the world	44.6	24.0	80.2	88.3	100.4	131.3	156.2	186.8	...	...	...	...
4 Surplus of the nation on current transactions	76.7	210.8	235.2	331.9	193.1	-73.4	442.1	-19.8	...	...	...	...
Payments to the Rest of the World and Surplus of the Nation on Current Transactions	1068.0	2103.2	2965.9	3309.2	3875.5	4308.0	5255.3	5947.8	...	...	...	...
Receipts From The Rest of the World												
1 Exports of goods and services	282.0	268.5	560.7	521.0	594.8	556.0	763.3	787.4	...	...	...	...
2 Factor income from rest of the world	6.9	19.4	58.4	104.4	138.8	197.8	274.9	416.4	...	...	...	...
A Compensation of employees	-	-	-	-	-	-	-	-	...	...	...	...
B Property and entrepreneurial income	6.9	19.4	58.4	104.4	138.8	197.8	274.9	416.4	...	...	...	...
3 Current transfers from rest of the world	779.1	1815.3	2346.8	2683.8	3141.9	3554.2	4217.1	4744.0	...	...	...	...
Receipts from the Rest of the World on Current Transactions	1068.0	2103.2	2965.9	3309.2	3875.5	4308.0	5255.3	5947.8	...	...	...	...

Reunion

1.10 Gross Domestic Product by Kind of Activity, in Current Prices

Million French francs

	1970	1975	1977	1978	1979	1980	1981	1982	1983	1984	1985	1986
1 Agriculture, hunting, forestry and fishing	...	283.3	306.0	477.3	519.3	498.5	646.2	828.2	...	...	...	...
2 Mining and quarrying	...	360.0	570.6	592.4	718.2	802.0	984.7	1125.8	...	...	...	...
3 Manufacturing	...								...	...	...	...
4 Electricity, gas and water	...	59.0	49.1	46.9	43.7	130.0	184.6	225.1	...	...	...	...
5 Construction	...	277.4	219.1	306.8	373.7	401.0	486.7	638.5	...	...	...	...
6 Wholesale and retail trade, restaurants and hotels	...	870.6	1209.2	1244.4	1324.9	1360.1	1525.0	1751.2	...	...	...	...
7 Transport, storage and communication	...	147.6	192.7	281.3	330.0	346.8	460.3	561.0	...	...	...	...
8 Finance, insurance, real estate and business services	...	357.2	483.9	600.8	737.7	883.2	1321.0	1340.7	...	...	...	...
9 Community, social and personal services	...	596.2	748.2	711.7	805.6	997.1	1095.9	1558.6	...	...	...	...
Total, Industries	1311.9	2951.3	3778.8	4261.6	4853.1	5418.7	6704.4	8029.1	...	...	...	...
Producers of Government Services	579.5	1342.8	1766.7	1989.1	2205.5	2569.1	2943.4	3495.7	...	...	...	...
Other Producers	31.5	71.8	88.6	108.7	118.4	166.4	217.8	301.5	...	...	...	...
Subtotal	1922.9	4365.9	5634.1	6359.4	7177.0	8154.2	9865.6	11826.3	...	...	...	...
Less: Imputed bank service charge	73.8	113.5	194.0	234.0	270.9	383.1	520.0	538.7	...	...	...	...
Plus: Import duties	82.7	120.1	240.4	223.7	266.5	334.7	379.5	488.1	...	...	...	...
Plus: Value added tax	81.6	167.4	207.2	248.3	299.6	338.8	403.0	510.6	...	...	...	...
Equals: Gross Domestic Product	2013.4	4539.9	5887.6	6597.4	7472.2	8448.6	10128.2	12286.2	...	...	...	...

1.12 Relations Among National Accounting Aggregates

Million French francs

	1970	1975	1977	1978	1979	1980	1981	1982	1983	1984	1985	1986
Gross Domestic Product	2013.4	4539.9	5887.6	6597.4	7472.2	8448.6	10128.2	12286.2	...	...	...	...
Plus: Net factor income from the rest of the world	-37.0	-68.2	-94.8	-94.4	-100.6	-81.0	-40.6	15.9	...	...	...	...
Factor income from the rest of the world	6.9	19.4	58.4	104.4	138.8	197.8	274.9	416.4	...	...	...	...
Less: Factor income to the rest of the world	43.9	87.6	153.2	198.8	239.4	278.8	315.5	400.5	...	...	...	...
Equals: Gross National Product	1976.4	4471.7	5792.8	6503.0	7371.6	8367.6	10087.4	12301.9	...	...	...	...
Less: Consumption of fixed capital	...	...	...	...	...	...	...	...	...	...	...	...
Equals: National Income	...	...	...	...	...	...	...	...	...	...	...	...
Plus: Net current transfers from the rest of the world	734.5	1791.3	2266.6	2595.6	3041.5	3422.9	4060.9	4557.2	...	...	...	...
Current transfers from the rest of the world	779.1	1815.3	2346.8	2683.8	3141.9	3554.2	4217.1	4744.0	...	...	...	...
Less: Current transfers to the rest of the world	44.6	24.0	80.2	88.2	100.4	131.3	156.2	186.8	...	...	...	...
Equals: National Disposable Income	...	...	...	...	...	...	...	...	...	...	...	...
Less: Final consumption	2094.3	4942.5	6699.5	7402.7	8649.8	9988.4	11621.5	14360.9	...	...	...	...
Equals: Net Saving	...	...	...	...	...	...	...	...	...	...	...	...
Less: Surplus of the nation on current transactions	76.7	210.8	235.2	331.8	193.1	-73.4	442.1	-19.8	...	...	...	...
Equals: Net Capital Formation	...	...	...	...	...	...	...	...	...	...	...	...

Romania

Source. Communication from the Central Statistical Board of Romania, Bucharest. Official estimates and descriptions are published annually in 'Anuarul Statistics' (Statistical Yearbook).

General note. The estimates shown in the following tables have been prepared in accordance with the System of Material Product Balances. Therefore, these estimates are not comparable in concept and coverage with those conforming to the United Nations System of National Accounts.

2a Net Material Product by Kind of Activity of the Material Sphere in Current Market Prices

Percentages

	1970	1975	1977	1978	1979	1980	1981	1982	1983	1984	1985	1986
1 Agriculture and forestry [a]	19.5 / 18.5	16.0 / 16.2	16.0	15.3	14.8	14.1	15.8	19.7	15.5	15.3	15.0	15.9
2 Industrial activity	60.3 / 58.0	56.2 / 59.8	57.0	57.9	58.5	58.6	57.2	55.7	60.2	61.0	62.7	62.5
3 Construction	9.8 / 10.4	7.6 / 7.6	10.7	10.2	9.6	8.8	8.5	7.4	7.8	7.7	7.8	7.6
4 Wholesale and retail trade and restaurants and other eating and drinking places	3.6 / ...	... / ...	...	...	...	...	...	...	...	...	...	...
5 Transport and communication	4.0 / 6.0	5.8 / 5.8	5.7	5.9	5.8	7.0	6.9	6.4	6.2	6.0	6.0	6.2
6 Other activities of the material sphere	2.8 / ...	... / ...	...	...	...	...	...	...	...	...	...	...
Net material product	100.0 / 100.0	100.0 / 100.0	100.0	100.0	100.0	100.0	100.0	100.0	100.0	100.0	100.0	100.0

a) Item 'Agriculture and forestry' refers to agriculture and livestock only.

2b Net Material Product by Kind of Activity of the Material Sphere in Constant Market Prices

Index numbers 1970 = 100

	1970	1975	1977	1978	1979	1980	1981	1982	1983	1984	1985	1986
	At constant prices of: 1985												
1 Agriculture and forestry	100	130	159	166	169	144	141	152	146	164	166	188
2 Industrial activity	100	186	223	244	263	279	290	295	313	336	362	389
3 Construction	100	144	189	192	195	195	189	191	208	221	231	239
4 Wholesale and retail trade and restaurants and other eating and drinking places	...	...	...	...	...	...	...	...	...	...	...	...
5 Transport and communication	100	169	187	197	205	221	229	234	230	238	241	259
6 Other activities of the material sphere	...	...	...	...	...	...	...	...	...	...	...	...
Net material product	100	171	206	222	235	242	247	254	263	284	300	322

6a Capital Formation by Kind of Activity of the Material and Non-Material Spheres in Current Market Prices

Million Romanian lei

	1970	1975	1977	1978	1979	1980	1981	1982	1983	1984	1985	1986
	Gross Fixed Capital Formation												
1 Agriculture and forestry	...	...	...	...	...	...	32821	33687	37481	40963	44686	43271
2 Industrial activity	...	...	...	...	...	...	105490	101545	111684	124094	119121	124668
3 Construction	...	...	...	...	...	...	7218	8312	8142	9542	11347	11304
4 Wholesale and retail trade and restaurants and other eating and drinking places	...	...	...	...	...	...	4866	5701	5237	5059	5233	5648
5 Transport and communciation	...	...	...	...	...	...	20631	26983	29183	26321	26369	22600
6 Other activities of the material sphere	...	...	...	...	...	...	...	...	...	...	...	...
Total Material Sphere	...	...	...	...	...	...	...	...	...	...	...	...
7 Housing except owner-occupied, communal and miscellaneous personal services [a]	...	...	...	...	...	...	30822	33405	34311	33638	32083	33883
8 Education, culture and art	...	...	...	...	...	...	1977	2048	1082	771	917	...
9 Health and social welfare services and sports	...	...	...	...	...	...	1091	1286	1099	1052	1109	...
Total Non-Material Sphere Serving Individuals	...	...	...	...	...	...	...	...	...	...	...	...

Romania

6a Capital Formation by Kind of Activity of the Material and Non-Material Spheres in Current Market Prices
(Continued)

Million Romanian lei

	1970	1975	1977	1978	1979	1980	1981	1982	1983	1984	1985	1986
10 Government	...	...	...	...	...	...	1117	1440	900	1110	1475	...
11 Finance, credit and insurance	...	...	...	...	...	...						...
12 Research, scientific and technological institutes	...	...	...	...	...	...	1239	1135	1064	1380	1416	...
13 Other activities of the non-material sphere	...	...	...	...	...	...	...	...	...	...	...	...
Total Non-Material Sphere Serving the Community as a Whole	...	...	...	...	...	...	...	...	...	...	...	...
14 Owner-occupied dwellings	...	...	...	...	...	...	...	...	...	...	...	...
Total Gross Fixed Capital Formation	...	...	...	...	...	...	207954	216354	230743	244714	246365	249347

a) Item 'Owner-occupied dwellings' is included in item 'Housing except owner-occupied, communal, and miscellaneous personal services'.

6b Capital Formation by Kind of Activity of the Material and Non-Material Spheres in Constant Market Prices

Million Romanian lei

	1970	1975	1977	1978	1979	1980	1981	1982	1983	1984	1985	1986
	\multicolumn{2}{c}{1963}	\multicolumn{5}{c}{At constant prices of: 1977}		\multicolumn{4}{c}{1981}	

Gross Fixed Capital Formation

	1970	1975	1977	1978	1979	1980	1981	1982	1983	1984	1985	1986
1 Agriculture and forestry	13102	18540 / 19498	24505	27302	26833	28008 / 29848	32821	...	...	...	...	...
2 Industrial activity	37961	67829 / 66125	80673	97164	104321	107058 / 111948	105490	...	...	...	...	...
3 Construction	3595	7317 / 6343	10747	12738	12745	9652 / 9910	7218	...	...	...	...	...
4 Wholesale and retail trade and restaurants and other eating and drinking places	2828	4849 / 5233	5381	5421	4591	4567 / 4926	4866	...	...	...	...	...
5 Transport and communciation	8469	14726 / 14766	17525	19908	20377	25286 / 26472	20631	...	...	...	...	...
6 Other activities of the material sphere	...	...	...	...	...	...	...	...	...	...	...	...
Total Material Sphere	...	...	...	...	...	...	...	...	...	...	...	...
7 Housing except owner-occupied, communal and miscellaneous personal services [a]	10181	17642 / 20419	22903	26462	28470	28391 / 33025	30822	...	...	...	...	...
8 Education, culture and art	1591	2673 / 2963	2973	2881	2524	2761 / 2972	1977	...	...	...	...	...
9 Health and social welfare services and sports	1143	1373 / 1523	1450	1251	962	1050 / 1150	1091	...	...	...	...	...
Total Non-Material Sphere Serving Individuals	...	...	...	...	...	...	...	...	...	...	...	...

# Romania

6b Capital Formation by Kind of Activity of the Material and Non-Material Spheres in Constant Market Prices
(Continued)

Million Romanian lei

	1970	1975	1977	1978	1979	1980	1981	1982	1983	1984	1985	1986
					At constant prices of:							
		1963		1977					1981			
10 Government	500	886				1218						
		971	1650	1449	1403	1347	1117	...	...	...	...	...
11 Finance, credit and insurance								...	...	...	...	...
12 Research, scientific and technological institutes	438	903				1349						
		869	1162	1200	1122	1401	1239	...	...	...	...	...
13 Other activities of the non-material sphere	...	...				...						
		...	...	...	...	...	...	...	...	...	...	...
Total Non-Material Sphere Serving the Community as a Whole	...	...				...						
		...	...	...	...	...	...	...	...	...	...	...
14 Owner-occupied dwellings	...	...				...						
		...	...	...	...	...	...	...	...	...	...	...
Total Gross Fixed Capital Formation	79990	137731				210451						
		139674	169260	196294	204368	223877	207954	...	...	...	...	...

a) Item 'Owner-occupied dwellings' is included in item 'Housing except owner-occupied, communal, and miscellaneous personal services'.

Rwanda

Source. Reply to the United Nations National Accounts Questionnaire from the Ministry of Planning, Kigali. Some official estimates together with information on concepts, definitions and methods of estimation are published in 'Comptes Economiques du Rwanda, 1969 et 1970'.

General note. The estimates shown in the following tables have been prepared in accordance with the United Nations System of National Accounts so far as the existing data would permit.

1.1 Expenditure on the Gross Domestic Product, in Current Prices

Thousand Million Rwanda francs

	1970	1975	1977	1978	1979	1980	1981	1982	1983	1984	1985	1986
1 Government final consumption expenditure	2.97	8.78	12.41	12.80	12.62	13.49	24.56	25.73	25.43	24.72	29.79	33.05
2 Private final consumption expenditure	17.60	41.24	50.86	62.10	73.62	89.97	96.40	100.44	112.15	122.31	129.55	114.65
3 Gross capital formation	1.62	7.25	10.79	13.46	11.57	17.43	16.31	21.89	17.70	23.32	29.26	30.04
A Increase in stocks	-0.03	0.29	1.65	2.14	-2.70	4.24	0.33	4.50	-1.50	0.49	0.65	-
B Gross fixed capital formation	1.65	6.96	9.14	11.32	14.27	13.19	15.98	17.39	19.20	22.83	28.61	30.04
4 Exports of goods and services	2.67	4.84	10.22	11.98	20.24	15.59	12.05	11.89	12.95	15.81	14.73	19.93
5 Less: Imports of goods and services	3.29	9.34	12.65	19.29	21.88	28.49	26.68	27.52	25.68	27.23	30.06	35.72
Equals: Gross Domestic Product	21.56	52.77	71.63	81.05	96.17	107.99	122.64	132.43	142.55	158.93	173.27	161.94

1.2 Expenditure on the Gross Domestic Product, in Constant Prices

Thousand Million Rwanda francs

	1970	1975	1977	1978	1979	1980	1981	1982	1983	1984	1985	1986
		1972			At constant prices of:			1976				
1 Government final consumption expenditure	...	...	...	...	...	...	...	...	...	...	...	...
2 Private final consumption expenditure	...	...	...	...	...	...	...	...	...	...	...	...
3 Gross capital formation	...	...	...	...	...	...	...	...	...	...	...	...
4 Exports of goods and services	...	...	...	...	...	...	...	...	...	...	...	...
5 Less: Imports of goods and services	...	...	...	...	...	...	...	...	...	...	...	...
Equals: Gross Domestic Product	22.37	...	65.07	71.46	78.16	...	...	...	...	...	...	...

1.3 Cost Components of the Gross Domestic Product

Thousand Million Rwanda francs

	1970	1975	1977	1978	1979	1980	1981	1982	1983	1984	1985	1986
1 Indirect taxes, net	...	3.25	6.44	5.95	8.24	8.26	7.81	9.22	9.46	11.67	13.02	...
A Indirect taxes	...	3.35	6.88	6.80	9.61	...	9.40	9.63	10.20	12.05	13.52	...
B Less: Subsidies	...	0.10	0.44	0.85	1.37	...	1.59	0.39	0.74	0.38	0.49	...
2 Consumption of fixed capital	...	1.49	2.11	2.58	3.06	6.06	3.74	4.80	5.29	6.81	7.27	...
3 Compensation of employees paid by resident producers to.	...	9.02	11.89	12.55	14.46	17.82	26.86	28.25	30.42	30.59	33.28	...
4 Operating surplus	...	39.01	51.19	59.97	70.41	75.85	84.23	90.16	97.39	109.86	119.70	...
Equals: Gross Domestic Product	21.56	52.77	71.63	81.05	96.17	107.99	122.64	132.43	142.55	158.93	173.27	...

1.7 External Transactions on Current Account, Summary

Thousand Million Rwanda francs

	1970	1975	1977	1978	1979	1980	1981	1982	1983	1984	1985	1986
				Payments to the Rest of the World								
1 Imports of goods and services		9.34	12.65	19.29	21.88	28.40	26.68	27.54	25.09	27.22	30.06	
2 Factor income to the rest of the world	...	0.05	0.13	0.89	0.94	1.45	1.60	1.78	1.59	1.48	1.81	...
3 Current transfers to the rest of the world	...	1.60	2.66	1.82	8.02	5.59	6.09	6.20	5.95	6.20	5.39	...
4 Surplus of the nation on current transactions	...	0.14	1.31	0.95	6.13	-9.49	-11.45	-12.81	-9.71	-9.34	-11.48	...
Payments to the Rest of the World and Surplus of the Nation on Current Transactions	...	11.13	16.75	22.95	36.97	26.04	22.92	22.71	23.52	25.56	25.78	...

Rwanda

1.7 External Transactions on Current Account, Summary
(Continued)

Thousand Million Rwanda francs

	1970	1975	1977	1978	1979	1980	1981	1982	1983	1984	1985	1986
	\multicolumn{12}{c}{Receipts From The Rest of the World}											
1 Exports of goods and services	...	4.84	10.22	11.98	20.24	15.59	12.05	11.89	12.95	15.81	14.73	...
2 Factor income from rest of the world	...	0.04	0.32	0.41	0.97	1.57	2.37	1.50	0.82	0.82	0.93	...
A Compensation of employees	...	...	...	...	...	...	0.04	0.02	0.02	0.02	0.02	...
B Property and entrepreneurial income	...	...	...	...	...	...	2.33	1.48	0.80	0.80	0.91	...
3 Current transfers from rest of the world	...	6.25	6.21	10.56	15.76	8.87	8.50	9.32	9.75	8.94	10.12	...
Receipts from the Rest of the World on Current Transactions	...	11.13	16.75	22.95	36.97	26.04	22.92	22.71	23.52	25.56	25.78	...

1.10 Gross Domestic Product by Kind of Activity, in Current Prices

Thousand Million Rwanda francs

	1970	1975	1977	1978	1979	1980	1981	1982	1983	1984	1985	1986
1 Agriculture, hunting, forestry and fishing	11.22	25.97	33.28	34.38	47.16	49.51	49.96	54.28	56.57	68.69	77.72	64.24
2 Mining and quarrying	0.47	1.05	1.88	1.84	1.84	1.84	0.81	0.62	0.72	0.57	0.46	0.31
3 Manufacturing	2.71	6.48	10.20	12.64	12.30	16.48	19.30	20.80	25.99	26.05	27.18	26.50
4 Electricity, gas and water	0.06	0.16	0.18	0.18	0.17	0.13	0.08	0.45	0.78	0.91	0.91	1.02
5 Construction	0.58	2.32	2.93	3.27	3.71	4.82	5.39	5.66	6.49	7.88	8.39	9.65
6 Wholesale and retail trade, restaurants and hotels	2.23	7.48	10.64	14.18	15.44	15.88	19.65	21.31	20.27	21.73	23.59	22.32
7 Transport, storage and communication	0.23	0.55	0.79	1.04	1.66	2.30	3.24	4.01	4.69	4.43	4.58	4.72
8 Finance, insurance, real estate and business services [a]	0.08	2.30	3.19	4.59	3.71	4.11	5.34	4.74	5.43	6.23	6.97	8.72
9 Community, social and personal services	2.48	4.85	6.40	6.11	7.21	9.17	15.39	16.69	17.93	17.80	18.24	19.15
Total, Industries	20.06	51.16	69.49	78.23	93.20	104.24	119.16	128.55	138.87	154.29	168.03	156.61
Producers of Government Services	...	...	...	...	...	...	...	...	...	...	...	...
Other Producers	...	...	...	...	...	...	...	...	...	...	...	...
Subtotal	20.06	51.16	69.49	78.23	93.20	104.24	119.16	128.55	138.87	154.29	168.03	156.61
Less: Imputed bank service charge [a]	...	...	...	...	...	...	...	...	...	...	...	...
Plus: Import duties	1.51	1.61	2.14	2.82	2.97	3.75	3.48	3.87	3.68	4.64	5.24	5.33
Plus: Value added tax	...	...	...	...	...	...	...	...	...	...	...	...
Equals: Gross Domestic Product	21.57	52.77	71.63	81.05	96.17	107.99	122.64	132.42	142.55	158.93	173.27	161.94

a) Item 'Less: Imputed bank service charge' is netted out of item 'Finance, insurance, real estate and business services'.

1.11 Gross Domestic Product by Kind of Activity, in Constant Prices

Thousand Million Rwanda francs

	1970	1975	1977	1978	1979	1980	1981	1982	1983	1984	1985	1986
	\multicolumn{12}{c}{At constant prices of:1976}											
1 Agriculture, hunting, forestry and fishing	...	...	30.68	31.52	38.31	...	...	...	...	...	...	...
2 Mining and quarrying	...	...	1.29	1.29	1.20	...	...	...	...	...	...	...
3 Manufacturing	...	...	8.43	8.94	8.86	...	...	...	...	...	...	...
4 Electricity, gas and water	...	...	0.19	0.18	0.17	...	...	...	...	...	...	...
5 Construction	...	...	2.90	3.13	3.55	...	...	...	...	...	...	...
6 Wholesale and retail trade, restaurants and hotels	...	...	9.70	12.99	12.75	...	...	...	...	...	...	...
7 Transport, storage and communication	...	...			0.89	...	...	...	...	...	...	...
8 Finance, insurance, real estate and business services [a]	...	...	3.00	4.31	3.81	...	...	...	...	...	...	...
9 Community, social and personal services	...	...	6.15	5.61	6.27	...	...	...	...	...	...	...
Total, Industries	...	...	63.06	68.92	75.81	...	...	...	...	...	...	...
Producers of Government Services	...	...	...	...	...	...	...	...	...	...	...	...
Other Producers	...	...	...	...	...	...	...	...	...	...	...	...
Subtotal	...	...	63.06	68.92	75.81	...	...	...	...	...	...	...
Less: Imputed bank service charge [a]	...	...	...	...	...	...	...	...	...	...	...	...
Plus: Import duties	...	...	2.01	2.54	2.35	...	...	...	...	...	...	...
Plus: Value added tax	...	...	...	...	...	...	...	...	...	...	...	...
Equals: Gross Domestic Product	...	...	65.07	71.46	78.16	...	...	...	...	...	...	...

a) Item 'Less: Imputed bank service charge' is netted out of item 'Finance, insurance, real estate and business services'.

Rwanda

1.12 Relations Among National Accounting Aggregates

Thousand Million Rwanda francs

	1970	1975	1977	1978	1979	1980	1981	1982	1983	1984	1985	1986
Gross Domestic Product	...	52.77	71.63	81.05	96.17	107.99	122.64	132.44	142.55	158.93	173.27	161.94
Plus: Net factor income from the rest of the world	...	-0.01	0.19	-0.48	0.03	0.12	0.77	-0.30	-0.77	-0.66	-0.88	-0.74
Factor income from the rest of the world	...	0.04	0.32	0.41	0.97	1.57	2.37	1.50	0.82	0.82	0.93	...
Less: Factor income to the rest of the world	...	0.05	0.13	0.89	0.94	1.45	1.60	1.80	1.59	1.48	1.81	...
Equals: Gross National Product	...	52.76	71.82	80.57	96.20	108.11	123.41	132.14	141.78	158.27	172.39	161.20
Less: Consumption of fixed capital	...	1.49	2.11	2.58	3.06	6.06	3.74	4.79	5.28	6.81	7.27	...
Equals: National Income	...	51.27	69.71	77.99	93.14	102.05	119.67	127.35	136.50	151.46	165.12	...
Plus: Net current transfers from the rest of the world	...	4.65	3.55	8.74	7.74	3.28	2.40	3.12	3.80	2.74	4.73	...
Current transfers from the rest of the world	...	6.25	6.21	10.56	15.76	8.87	8.50	9.32	9.75	8.94	10.12	...
Less: Current transfers to the rest of the world	...	1.60	2.66	1.82	8.02	5.59	6.10	6.20	5.95	6.20	5.39	...
Equals: National Disposable Income	...	55.92	73.26	86.73	100.88	105.33	122.07	130.47	140.30	154.20	169.85	...
Less: Final consumption	...	50.02	63.27	74.90	86.24	103.46	120.96	126.16	137.60	147.03	159.34	...
Equals: Net Saving	...	5.90	9.99	11.83	14.64	1.87	1.11	4.31	2.70	7.17	10.51	...
Less: Surplus of the nation on current transactions	...	0.14	1.31	0.95	6.13	-9.49	-11.45	-12.81	-9.71	-9.34	-11.48	...
Equals: Net Capital Formation	...	5.76	8.68	10.88	8.51	11.36	12.56	17.12	12.41	16.51	21.99	...

4.1 Derivation of Value Added by Kind of Activity, in Current Prices

Thousand Million Rwanda francs

	1980 Gross Output	1980 Intermediate Consumption	1980 Value Added	1981 Gross Output	1981 Intermediate Consumption	1981 Value Added	1982 Gross Output	1982 Intermediate Consumption	1982 Value Added	1983 Gross Output	1983 Intermediate Consumption	1983 Value Added
						All Producers						
1 Agriculture, hunting, forestry and fishing	51.33	1.82	49.51	51.32	1.36	49.96	55.66	1.38	54.28	58.19	1.62	56.57
A Agriculture and hunting	...	...	...	...	...	...	54.66	1.38	53.28	57.14	1.62	55.52
B Forestry and logging	...	...	...	...	...	...	0.75	-	0.75	0.78	-	0.78
C Fishing	...	...	...	...	...	...	0.25	-	0.25	0.28	-	0.28
2 Mining and quarrying	2.98	1.14	1.84	2.08	1.27	0.81	1.59	0.97	0.62	1.80	1.08	0.72
A Coal mining	...	...	...	...	...	...	...	...	...	...	...	...
B Crude petroleum and natural gas production	...	...	...	...	...	...	-	0.05	-0.05	0.02	0.04	-0.02
C Metal ore mining	...	...	...	...	...	...	1.41	0.92	0.49	1.60	1.04	0.56
D Other mining	...	...	...	...	...	...	0.17	-	0.17	0.18	-	0.18
3 Manufacturing	46.86	30.38	16.48	53.96	34.66	19.30	55.02	34.21	20.81	60.59	34.60	25.99
A Manufacture of food, beverages and tobacco	...	...	...	...	...	...	44.69	28.89	15.80	49.54	28.74	20.80
B Textile, wearing apparel and leather industries	...	...	...	...	...	...	3.04	1.51	1.53	3.55	2.02	1.53
C Manufacture of wood and wood products, including furniture	...	...	...	...	...	...	0.87	0.24	0.63	0.89	0.22	0.67
D Manufacture of paper and paper products, printing and publishing	...	...	...	...	...	...	0.31	0.19	0.12	0.39	0.18	0.21
E Manufacture of chemicals and chemical petroleum, coal, rubber and plastic products	...	...	...	...	...	...	2.06	1.43	0.63	1.99	1.48	0.51
F Manufacture of non-metallic mineral products, except products of petroleum and coal	...	...	...	...	...	...	1.18	0.15	1.03	1.25	0.15	1.10
G Basic metal industries	...	...	...	...	...	...	-	-	-	-	-	-
H Manufacture of fabricated metal products, machinery and equipment	...	...	...	...	...	...	2.86	1.81	1.05	2.98	1.81	1.17
I Other manufacturing industries	...	...	...	...	...	...	...	...	...	...	...	...
4 Electricity, gas and water	0.50	0.37	0.13	0.51	0.44	0.08	1.24	0.79	0.45	1.28	0.51	0.77
A Electricity, gas and steam	...	...	...	...	...	...	0.97	0.40	0.57	0.98	0.29	0.69
B Water works and supply	...	...	...	...	...	...	0.26	0.39	-0.13	0.30	0.22	0.09

Rwanda

4.1 Derivation of Value Added by Kind of Activity, in Current Prices
(Continued)

Thousand Million Rwanda francs

	1980 Gross Output	1980 Intermediate Consumption	1980 Value Added	1981 Gross Output	1981 Intermediate Consumption	1981 Value Added	1982 Gross Output	1982 Intermediate Consumption	1982 Value Added	1983 Gross Output	1983 Intermediate Consumption	1983 Value Added
5 Construction	9.39	4.57	4.82	9.48	4.09	5.39	8.93	3.27	5.66	10.47	3.98	6.49
6 Wholesale and retail trade, restaurants and hotels	17.57	1.69	15.88	21.56	1.91	19.65	23.40	2.09	21.31	22.32	2.04	20.28
A Wholesale and retail trade	...	...	...	...	...	...	22.76	1.82	20.94	21.59	1.74	19.85
B Restaurants and hotels	...	...	...	...	...	...	0.65	0.27	0.38	0.73	0.30	0.43
7 Transport, storage and communication	7.37	5.07	2.30	5.53	2.28	3.25	6.95	2.94	4.01	7.64	2.95	4.69
A Transport and storage	...	...	...	...	...	...	6.43	2.88	3.55	7.13	2.62	4.51
B Communication	...	...	...	...	...	...	0.51	0.06	0.45	0.51	0.33	0.18
8 Finance, insurance, real estate and business services [a]	7.90	3.79	4.11	9.40	4.06	5.34	8.45	3.71	4.74	9.11	3.68	5.43
A Financial institutions	...	...	...	...	...	...	3.69	2.78	0.91	2.91	2.48	0.43
B Insurance	...	...	...	...	...	...	-	-0.08	0.08	0.31	0.08	0.23
C Real estate and business services	...	...	...	...	...	...	5.36	1.02	4.34	5.88	1.12	4.76
9 Community, social and personal services	15.68	6.51	9.17	24.57	9.18	15.39	26.32	9.63	16.69	26.22	8.29	17.93
A Sanitary and similar services	...	...	...	...	...	...	...	...	...	...	...	...
B Social and related community services	...	...	...	...	...	...	...	...	...	...	...	...
Educational services	...	...	...	...	...	...	...	...	...	5.68	1.28	4.40
Medical, dental, other health and veterinary services	...	...	...	...	...	...	...	...	...	...	...	...
C Recreational and cultural services	...	...	...	...	...	...	...	...	...	0.40	0.29	0.11
D Personal and household services	...	...	...	...	...	...	...	...	...	...	...	...
Total, Industries	159.58	55.34	104.24	178.41	59.25	119.16	187.54	59.00	128.55	197.62	58.75	138.87
Producers of Government Services	...	...	...	...	...	...	...	...	...	...	...	...
Other Producers	...	...	...	...	...	...	...	...	...	...	...	...
Total	159.58	55.34	104.24	178.41	59.25	119.16	187.54	59.00	128.55	197.62	58.75	138.87
Less: Imputed bank service charge [a]	...	...	...	...	...	...	...	...	...	...	...	...
Import duties	3.75	-	3.75	3.48	-	3.48	3.87	-	3.87	3.68	-	3.68
Value added tax	...	...	...	...	...	...	...	...	...	...	...	...
Total	163.33	55.34	107.99	181.89	59.25	122.64	191.41	59.00	132.42	201.30	58.75	142.55

	1984 Gross Output	1984 Intermediate Consumption	1984 Value Added	1985 Gross Output	1985 Intermediate Consumption	1985 Value Added
	All Producers					
1 Agriculture, hunting, forestry and fishing	70.75	2.06	68.69	79.79	2.07	77.72
A Agriculture and hunting	69.66	2.06	67.60	...	...	...
B Forestry and logging	0.81	-	0.81	...	...	...
C Fishing	0.28	-	0.28	...	...	...
2 Mining and quarrying	0.88	0.31	0.57	0.68	0.22	0.46
A Coal mining	...	...	...	...	...	...
B Crude petroleum and natural gas production	0.03	0.01	0.02	...	...	...
C Metal ore mining	0.66	0.30	0.36	...	...	...
D Other mining	0.19	-	0.19	...	...	...

Rwanda

4.1 Derivation of Value Added by Kind of Activity, in Current Prices
(Continued)

Thousand Million Rwanda francs

		1984			1985		
		Gross Output	Intermediate Consumption	Value Added	Gross Output	Intermediate Consumption	Value Added
3	Manufacturing	62.64	36.59	26.05	71.04	43.86	27.18
	A Manufacture of food, beverages and tobacco	49.45	30.11	19.34	55.45	35.72	19.73
	B Textile, wearing apparel and leather industries	3.54	1.86	1.68	3.77	1.89	1.88
	C Manufacture of wood and wood products, including furniture	1.08	0.37	0.71	1.18	0.42	0.76
	D Manufacture of paper and paper products, printing and publishing	0.35	0.19	0.16	0.41	0.18	0.23
	E Manufacture of chemicals and chemical petroleum, coal, rubber and plastic products	2.50	1.60	0.90	3.22	2.30	0.92
	F Manufacture of non-metallic mineral products, except products of petroleum and coal	1.49	0.24	1.25	2.40	0.81	1.59
	G Basic metal industries	1.12	0.36	0.76	1.04	0.32	0.72
	H Manufacture of fabricated metal products, machinery and equipment	3.11	1.86	1.25	3.56	2.21	1.35
	I Other manufacturing industries	...	...	...	...	...	...
4	Electricity, gas and water	1.49	0.58	0.91	1.80	0.89	0.91
	A Electricity, gas and steam	1.10	0.44	0.66	1.32	0.60	0.72
	B Water works and supply	0.38	0.13	0.25	0.49	0.30	0.19
5	Construction	12.84	4.95	7.89	14.44	6.05	8.39
6	Wholesale and retail trade, restaurants and hotels	24.19	2.46	21.73	26.28	2.69	23.59
	A Wholesale and retail trade	23.12	1.90	21.22	25.09	2.06	23.03
	B Restaurants and hotels	1.07	0.57	0.50	1.19	0.63	0.56
7	Transport, storage and communication	9.92	5.50	4.42	10.83	6.26	4.57
	A Transport and storage	9.33	5.34	3.99	10.05	6.00	4.05
	B Communication	0.59	0.16	0.43	0.78	0.26	0.52
8	Finance, insurance, real estate and business services [a]	10.36	4.13	6.23	10.95	3.98	6.97
	A Financial institutions	3.52	2.80	0.72	3.47	2.52	0.95
	B Insurance	0.30	0.09	0.21	0.20	0.08	0.12
	C Real estate and business services	6.54	1.24	5.30	7.28	1.38	5.90
9	Community, social and personal services	26.63	8.83	17.80	31.79	13.55	18.24
	A Sanitary and similar services	...	...	...	...	...	...
	B Social and related community services	...	...	...	...	...	...
	Educational services	6.22	1.23	4.99	6.71	1.42	5.29
	Medical, dental, other health and veterinary services	...	...	...	...	...	...
	C Recreational and cultural services	0.30	0.15	0.15	0.31	0.20	0.11
	D Personal and household services	...	...	...	...	...	...
	Total, Industries	219.70	65.41	154.29	247.62	79.58	168.04
	Producers of Government Services		...	...	...	...	...
	Other Producers	...	...	...	...	...	...
	Total	219.70	65.41	154.29	247.62	79.58	168.04
	Less: Imputed bank service charge [a]						
	Import duties	4.64	-	4.64	5.24	-	5.24
	Value added tax	...	...	...	...	...	...
	Total	224.34	65.41	158.93	252.86	79.58	173.27

a) Item 'Less: Imputed bank service charge' is netted out of item 'Finance, insurance, real estate and business services'.

Rwanda

4.3 Cost Components of Value Added

Thousand Million Rwanda francs

		1980					1981				
		Compensation of Employees	Capital Consumption	Net Operating Surplus	Indirect Taxes	Less: Subsidies Received	Value Added	Compensation of Employees	Capital Consumption	Net Operating Surplus	Indirect Taxes	Less: Subsidies Received	Value Added

All Producers

		Comp. Emp.	Cap. Cons.	NOS	Ind. Tax	Subs.	VA	Comp. Emp.	Cap. Cons.	NOS	Ind. Tax	Subs.	VA
1	Agriculture, hunting, forestry and fishing	0.50	0.03	47.62	1.36	...	49.51	0.26	0.07	49.41	1.38	1.16	49.96
	A Agriculture and hunting	...	...	...	...	...	...	...	...	...	...	...	...
	B Forestry and logging	...	...	...	...	...	...	...	...	...	...	...	...
	C Fishing	...	...	...	...	...	...	...	...	...	...	...	...
2	Mining and quarrying	0.95	0.33	0.47	0.09	-	1.84	1.07	0.30	-0.70	0.14	-	0.81
	A Coal mining	...	...	...	...	...	...	...	...	...	...	...	...
	B Crude petroleum and natural gas production	...	...	...	...	...	...	...	...	...	...	...	...
	C Metal ore mining	...	...	...	...	...	...	...	...	...	...	...	...
	D Other mining	...	...	...	...	...	...	...	...	...	...	...	...
3	Manufacturing	1.88	0.64	11.17	2.79	...	16.48	2.24	0.71	13.33	3.30	0.28	19.30
	A Manufacture of food, beverages and tobacco	...	...	...	...	...	...	...	...	...	...	...	...
	B Textile, wearing apparel and leather industries	...	...	...	...	...	...	...	...	...	...	...	...
	C Manufacture of wood and wood products, including furniture	...	...	...	...	...	...	...	...	...	...	...	...
	D Manufacture of paper and paper products, printing and publishing	...	...	...	...	...	...	...	...	...	...	...	...
	E Manufacture of chemicals and chemical petroleum, coal, rubber and plastic products	...	...	...	...	...	...	...	...	...	...	...	...
	F Manufacture of non-metallic mineral products, except products of petroleum and coal	...	...	...	...	...	...	...	...	...	...	...	...
	G Basic metal industries	...	...	...	...	...	...	...	...	...	...	...	...
	H Manufacture of fabricated metal products, machinery and equipment	...	...	...	...	...	...	...	...	...	...	...	...
	I Other manufacturing industries	...	...	...	...	...	...	...	...	...	...	...	...
4	Electricity, gas and water	0.06	0.26	-0.19	-	-	0.13	0.21	0.15	-0.28	-	-	0.08
	A Electricity, gas and steam	...	...	...	...	...	...	...	...	...	...	...	...
	B Water works and supply	...	...	...	...	...	...	...	...	...	...	...	...
5	Construction	3.85	0.97	-	-	...	4.82	4.71	0.23	0.44	0.01	-	5.39
6	Wholesale and retail trade, restaurants and hotels	1.27	0.67	13.88	0.06	...	15.88	1.71	0.39	16.82	0.73	-	19.65
	A Wholesale and retail trade	...	...	...	...	...	...	...	...	...	...	...	...
	B Restaurants and hotels	...	...	...	...	...	...	...	...	...	...	...	...
7	Transport, storage and communication	0.62	0.56	1.03	0.09	-	2.30	0.69	0.15	2.45	0.09	0.13	3.25
	A Transport and storage	...	...	...	...	...	...	...	...	...	...	...	...
	B Communication	...	...	...	...	...	...	...	...	...	...	...	...
8	Finance, insurance, real estate and business services	0.43	1.71	1.87	0.10	-	4.11	0.61	1.72	2.76	0.26	0.01	5.34
	A Financial institutions	...	...	...	...	...	...	...	...	...	...	...	...
	B Insurance	...	...	...	...	...	...	...	...	...	...	...	...
	C Real estate and business services	...	...	...	...	...	...	...	...	...	...	...	...
9	Community, social and personal services	8.26	0.91	...	...	...	9.17	15.37	0.02	...	...	...	15.39
	A Sanitary and similar services	...	...	...	...	...	...	...	...	...	...	...	...
	B Social and related community services	...	...	...	...	...	...	...	...	...	...	...	...
	Educational services	...	...	...	...	...	...	...	...	...	...	...	...
	Medical, dental, other health and veterinary services	...	...	...	...	...	...	...	...	...	...	...	...
	C Recreational and cultural services	...	...	...	...	...	...	...	...	...	...	...	...
	D Personal and household services	...	...	...	...	...	...	...	...	...	...	...	...

Rwanda

4.3 Cost Components of Value Added
(Continued)

Thousand Million Rwanda francs

	1980							1981					
	Compensation of Employees	Capital Consumption	Net Operating Surplus	Indirect Taxes	Less: Subsidies Received	Value Added	Compensation of Employees	Capital Consumption	Net Operating Surplus	Indirect Taxes	Less: Subsidies Received	Value Added
Total, Industries	17.82	6.08	75.85	4.49	...	104.24	26.86	3.74	84.23	5.91	1.58	119.16
Producers of Government Services	...	...	...	...	...	...	...	...	...	...	...	...
Other Producers	...	...	...	...	...	...	...	...	...	...	...	...
Total	17.82	6.08	75.85	4.49	...	104.24	26.86	3.74	84.23	5.91	1.58	119.16
Less: Imputed bank service charge	...	...	...	...	...	...	...	...	...	...	...	...
Import duties	...	...	...	3.75	...	3.75	...	...	...	3.48	...	3.48
Value added tax	...	...	...	...	...	...	...	...	...	...	...	...
Total	17.82	6.08	75.85	8.24	...	107.99	26.86	3.74	84.23	9.40	1.58	122.64

	1982							1983					
	Compensation of Employees	Capital Consumption	Net Operating Surplus	Indirect Taxes	Less: Subsidies Received	Value Added	Compensation of Employees	Capital Consumption	Net Operating Surplus	Indirect Taxes	Less: Subsidies Received	Value Added
						All Producers						
1 Agriculture, hunting, forestry and fishing	0.23	0.07	52.81	1.41	0.24	54.28	0.30	0.06	55.57	1.11	0.47	56.57
A Agriculture and hunting	...	...	...	...	...	...	0.30	0.06	54.51	1.11	0.47	55.51
B Forestry and logging	...	...	...	...	...	...	-	-	0.78	-	-	0.78
C Fishing	...	...	...	...	...	...	-	-	0.28	-	-	0.28
2 Mining and quarrying	1.09	0.29	-0.84	0.08	-	0.62	1.15	0.33	-0.85	0.09	-	0.72
A Coal mining	...	...	...	...	...	...	...	...	...	...	...	...
B Crude petroleum and natural gas production	...	...	...	...	...	...	0.01	0.01	-0.04	-	-	-0.02
C Metal ore mining	...	...	...	...	...	...	1.07	0.32	-0.92	0.09	-	0.56
D Other mining	...	...	...	...	...	...	0.07	-	0.11	-	-	0.18
3 Manufacturing	2.65	0.72	14.16	3.38	0.10	20.81	2.81	0.91	18.38	4.04	0.14	25.99
A Manufacture of food, beverages and tobacco	...	...	...	...	...	...	0.94	0.56	15.40	4.00	0.10	20.80
B Textile, wearing apparel and leather industries	...	...	...	...	...	...	0.37	0.03	1.12	0.01	-	1.53
C Manufacture of wood and wood products, including furniture	...	...	...	...	...	...	0.31	0.02	0.34	-	-	0.67
D Manufacture of paper and paper products, printing and publishing	...	...	...	...	...	...	0.09	0.03	0.09	-	-	0.21
E Manufacture of chemicals and chemical petroleum, coal, rubber and plastic products	...	...	...	...	...	...	0.27	0.15	0.08	-	-	0.51
F Manufacture of non-metallic mineral products, except products of petroleum and coal	...	...	...	...	...	...	0.33	-	0.77	-	-	1.10
G Basic metal industries	...	...	...	...	...	...	...	...	...	...	...	...
H Manufacture of fabricated metal products, machinery and equipment	...	...	...	...	...	...	0.50	0.11	0.57	0.02	0.04	1.17
I Other manufacturing industries	...	...	...	...	...	...	...	...	...	...	...	0.77
4 Electricity, gas and water	0.11	0.35	-0.01	-	-	0.45	0.21	0.35	0.21	-	-	0.77
A Electricity, gas and steam	...	...	...	...	...	...	0.10	0.28	0.30	-	-	0.68
B Water works and supply	...	...	...	...	...	...	0.11	0.07	-0.09	-	-	0.09
5 Construction	4.92	0.26	0.47	0.01	-	5.66	5.55	0.30	0.63	0.01	-	6.49
6 Wholesale and retail trade, restaurants and hotels	1.82	0.94	17.77	0.78	-	21.31	1.92	0.90	16.62	0.84	-	20.28
A Wholesale and retail trade	...	...	...	...	...	...	1.67	0.81	16.53	0.84	-	19.85
B Restaurants and hotels	...	...	...	...	...	...	0.24	0.09	0.09	-	-	0.43
7 Transport, storage and communication	0.65	0.17	3.10	0.09	-	4.01	0.60	0.21	3.52	0.43	0.07	4.69
A Transport and storage	...	...	...	...	...	...	0.36	0.21	3.52	0.43	0.01	4.51
B Communication	...	...	...	...	...	...	0.23	-	-	-	0.06	0.18
8 Finance, insurance, real estate and business services	0.10	1.99	2.69	0.01	0.05	4.74	0.80	2.17	2.52	-	0.06	5.43
A Financial institutions	...	...	...	...	...	...	0.71	0.30	-0.52	-	0.06	0.44

Rwanda

4.3 Cost Components of Value Added
(Continued)

Thousand Million Rwanda francs

	1982						1983					
	Compensation of Employees	Capital Consumption	Net Operating Surplus	Indirect Taxes	Less: Subsidies Received	Value Added	Compensation of Employees	Capital Consumption	Net Operating Surplus	Indirect Taxes	Less: Subsidies Received	Value Added
B Insurance	...	...	...	...	...	...	0.08	0.01	0.14	-	-	0.23
C Real estate and business services	...	...	...	...	...	...	-	1.87	2.90	-	-	4.77
9 Community, social and personal services	16.67	0.02	...	...	...	16.69	17.08	0.06	0.79	...	...	17.93
A Sanitary and similar services	...	...	...	...	...	...	...	...	...	...	...	...
B Social and related community services	...	...	...	...	...	...	...	...	...	...	...	...
Educational services	...	...	...	...	...	...	4.40	...	...	...	...	4.40
Medical, dental, other health and veterinary services	...	...	...	...	...	...	...	...	...	...	...	...
C Recreational and cultural services	...	...	...	...	...	...	0.11	...	...	...	...	0.11
D Personal and household services	...	...	...	...	...	...	...	...	0.79	...	...	0.79
Total, Industries	28.24	4.81	90.15	5.76	0.39	128.57	30.42	5.29	97.39	6.52	0.74	138.87
Producers of Government Services	...	...	...	...	...	...	...	...	...	...	...	...
Other Producers	...	...	...	...	...	...	...	...	...	...	...	...
Total	28.24	4.81	90.15	5.76	0.39	128.57	30.42	5.29	97.39	6.52	0.74	138.87
Less: Imputed bank service charge	...	...	...	...	...	...	...	...	...	...	...	...
Import duties	...	...	...	3.87	...	3.87	...	...	...	3.68	...	3.68
Value added tax	...	...	...	...	...	...	...	...	...	...	...	...
Total	28.24	4.81	90.15	9.63	0.39	132.44	30.42	5.29	97.39	10.20	0.74	142.55

	1984						1985					
	Compensation of Employees	Capital Consumption	Net Operating Surplus	Indirect Taxes	Less: Subsidies Received	Value Added	Compensation of Employees	Capital Consumption	Net Operating Surplus	Indirect Taxes	Less: Subsidies Received	Value Added

All Producers

1 Agriculture, hunting, forestry and fishing	0.31	0.06	66.75	1.75	0.17	68.69	0.48	0.18	75.27	2.02	0.23	77.74
A Agriculture and hunting	0.31	0.06	65.66	1.75	0.17	67.61	...	...	...	...	...	...
B Forestry and logging	-	-	0.81	-	-	0.81	...	...	...	...	...	...
C Fishing	-	-	0.28	-	-	0.28	...	...	...	...	...	...
2 Mining and quarrying	1.01	0.31	-0.89	0.14	-	0.57	0.76	0.31	-0.61	-	-	0.46
A Coal mining	...	...	...	...	...	...	...	...	...	...	...	...
B Crude petroleum and natural gas production	0.01	-	0.01	-	-	0.02	...	...	...	...	...	...
C Metal ore mining	0.92	0.31	-1.02	0.14	-	0.36	...	...	...	...	...	...
D Other mining	0.08	-	0.12	-	-	0.20	...	...	...	...	...	...
3 Manufacturing	2.92	1.09	17.75	4.43	0.14	26.05	3.43	1.23	17.78	4.96	0.22	27.18
A Manufacture of food, beverages and tobacco	0.94	0.69	13.52	4.28	0.09	19.34	...	...	...	...	...	...
B Textile, wearing apparel and leather industries	0.36	0.02	1.29	0.01	-	1.68	...	...	...	...	...	...
C Manufacture of wood and wood products, including furniture	0.33	0.02	0.36	-	-	0.71	...	...	...	...	...	...
D Manufacture of paper and paper products, printing and publishing	0.09	0.04	0.02	0.02	-	0.16	...	...	...	...	...	...
E Manufacture of chemicals and chemical petroleum, coal, rubber and plastic products	0.32	0.15	0.46	0.02	0.04	0.91	...	...	...	...	...	...
F Manufacture of non-metallic mineral products, except products of petroleum and coal	0.34	-	0.92	-	-	1.25	...	...	...	...	...	...
G Basic metal industries	-	0.04	0.72	-	-	0.76	...	...	...	...	...	...
H Manufacture of fabricated metal products, machinery and equipment	0.55	0.14	0.46	0.10	0.01	1.25	...	...	...	...	...	...
I Other manufacturing industries	...	...	...	...	...	...	...	...	...	...	...	...
4 Electricity, gas and water	0.24	0.53	0.15	-	-	0.91	0.34	0.56	0.01	-	-	0.91
A Electricity, gas and steam	0.16	0.46	0.04	-	-	0.66	...	...	...	...	...	...
B Water works and supply	0.08	0.07	0.11	-	-	0.25	...	...	...	...	...	...

Rwanda

4.3 Cost Components of Value Added
(Continued)

Thousand Million Rwanda francs

			1984						1985			
		Compensation of Employees	Capital Consumption	Net Operating Surplus	Indirect Taxes	Less: Subsidies Received	Value Added	Compensation of Employees	Capital Consumption	Net Operating Surplus	Indirect Taxes	Less: Subsidies Received	Value Added
5	Construction	5.97	0.99	0.86	0.06	-	7.89	6.31	0.52	1.48	0.08	-	8.39
6	Wholesale and retail trade, restaurants and hotels	2.07	0.96	17.79	0.90	-	21.72	2.23	1.04	19.31	1.00	-	23.59
	A Wholesale and retail trade	1.73	0.87	17.73	0.89	-	21.22	...	...	...	...	...	...
	B Restaurants and hotels	0.34	0.09	0.06	0.01	-	0.50	...	...	...	...	...	...
7	Transport, storage and communication	0.83	0.50	2.97	0.12	-	4.43	1.49	0.91	1.97	0.21	-	4.58
	A Transport and storage	0.59	0.50	2.78	0.12	-	3.99	...	...	...	...	...	...
	B Communication	0.24	-	0.19	-	-	0.43	...	...	...	...	...	...
8	Finance, insurance, real estate and business services	0.72	2.30	3.27	-	0.07	6.23	1.06	2.45	3.50	-	0.04	6.97
	A Financial institutions	0.63	0.22	-0.07	-	0.07	0.72	...	...	...	...	...	...
	B Insurance	0.10	0.01	0.10	-	-	0.21	...	...	...	...	...	...
	C Real estate and business services	-	2.07	3.23	-	-	5.30	...	...	...	...	...	...
9	Community, social and personal services	16.51	0.07	1.21	...	...	17.80	17.19	0.07	0.98	...	...	18.24
	A Sanitary and similar services	...	...	...	...	...	...	...	...	...	...	...	...
	B Social and related community services	...	...	...	...	...	...	...	...	...	...	...	...
	Educational services	4.99	...	...	...	...	4.99	...	...	...	...	...	...
	Medical, dental, other health and veterinary services	...	...	...	...	...	...	...	...	...	...	...	...
	C Recreational and cultural services	0.15	...	...	...	...	0.15	...	...	...	...	...	...
	D Personal and household services	...	...	0.89	...	...	0.89	...	...	...	...	...	...
Total, Industries		30.58	6.81	109.85	7.40	0.38	154.29	33.28	7.27	119.69	8.28	0.49	168.03
Producers of Government Services		...	...	...	...	...	...	...	...	...	...	...	...
Other Producers		...	...	...	...	...	...	...	...	...	...	...	...
Total		30.58	6.81	109.85	7.40	0.38	154.29	33.28	7.27	119.69	8.28	0.49	168.03
Less: Imputed bank service charge		...	...	...	...	...	...	...	...	...	...	...	...
Import duties		...	...	...	4.64	...	4.64	...	...	...	5.24	...	5.24
Value added tax		...	...	...	...	...	...	...	...	...	...	...	...
Total		30.58	6.81	109.85	12.04	0.38	158.93	33.28	7.27	119.69	13.52	0.49	173.27

Saint Christopher and Nevis

Source. Reply to the United Nations National Accounts Questionnaire from the Ministry of Finance, St. Kitts-Nevis.
General note. The estimates shown in the following tables have been prepared in accordance with the United Nations System of National Accounts so far as the existing data would permit.

1.1 Expenditure on the Gross Domestic Product, in Current Prices

Thousand E.C. dollars

	1970	1975	1977	1978	1979	1980	1981	1982	1983	1984	1985	1986
1 Government final consumption expenditure	...	12140	16050	20130	22170	26310	38780	35520	35520	37520	...	...
2 Private final consumption expenditure	...	57085	47170	57550	73870	92690	108950	117200	140150	129560	...	...
3 Gross capital formation	...	9441	30800	25140	37250	49440	46060	55120	49910	53270	...	...
A Increase in stocks	...	1714	...	-	-	-	-	-	-	-	...	...
B Gross fixed capital formation	...	7727	30800	25140	37250	49440	46060	55120	49910	53270	...	...
Residential buildings	...	930	...	...	...	...	...	...	...	...	...	...
Non-residential buildings	...	1009	...	...	...	...	...	...	...	...	...	...
Other construction and land improvement etc.	...	439	...	...	...	...	...	...	...	...	...	...
Other	...	5346	...	...	...	...	...	...	...	...	...	...
4 Exports of goods and services	...	46841	51510	58600	64300	86730	92240	80630	78840	92820	...	...
5 Less: Imports of goods and services	...	51361	64810	69100	90200	125930	136610	130370	150390	145980	...	...
Equals: Gross Domestic Product	...	74146	80720	92320	107390	129240	149420	158100	154030	167190	...	...

1.3 Cost Components of the Gross Domestic Product

Thousand E.C. dollars

	1970	1975	1977	1978	1979	1980	1981	1982	1983	1984	1985	1986
1 Indirect taxes, net	...	12403	11520	16030	19860	26130	28880	20340	21940	...	...	...
A Indirect taxes	...	12403	12730	17820	22840	32220	35020	27270	25220	26700	...	...
B Less: Subsidies	...	-	1210	1790	2980	6090	6140	6930	3280	...	...	...
2 Consumption of fixed capital	...	2646	...	...	...	...	...	...	...	...	...	...
3 Compensation of employees paid by resident producers to:	...	49331	...	...	...	...	...	...	...	...	...	...
4 Operating surplus	...	9766	...	...	...	...	...	...	...	...	...	...
Equals: Gross Domestic Product	...	74146	80720	92320	107390	129240	149420	158100	154030	167190	...	...

1.10 Gross Domestic Product by Kind of Activity, in Current Prices

Thousand E.C. dollars

	1970	1975	1977	1978	1979	1980	1981	1982	1983	1984	1985	1986
1 Agriculture, hunting, forestry and fishing	8700	7832	13100	12180	13640	16510	13830	20310	16190	19720	16980	17410
2 Mining and quarrying	800	-	200	160	240	320	330	410	450	380	450	500
3 Manufacturing		27503	12540	13240	12790	15740	17880	18660	17550	22620	21940	23660
4 Electricity, gas and water	400	10	610	710	810	880	1110	1430	1360	1440	1530	1630
5 Construction	4000	3274	6590	5490	8120	10580	10850	13600	14960	12820	14860	16670

Saint Christopher and Nevis

1.10 Gross Domestic Product by Kind of Activity, in Current Prices
(Continued)

Thousand E.C. dollars

	1970	1975	1977	1978	1979	1980	1981	1982	1983	1984	1985	1986
6 Wholesale and retail trade, restaurants and hotels	4500	11226	8430	11530	14590	17480	19480	20830	22620	25890	30020	34710
7 Transport, storage and communication	1100	3343	5860	7320	7840	10000	15420	17450	16420	19540	21140	23900
8 Finance, insurance, real estate and business services	2600	7316	9050	9320	11090	11920	13320	16380	16310	19540	20870	22370
9 Community, social and personal services	1500	4035	3550	3530	3970	5200	6570	7300	7830	8400	9010	9650
Total, Industries	23600	64539	59930	63480	73090	88630	98790	116370	113690	130350	136800	150500
Producers of Government Services	5800	9606	11750	15970	18250	19200	26640	28550	29930	36080	37330	41540
Other Producers	...	...	...	...	...	...	...	...	...	...	...	...
Subtotal a	29400	74145	71680	79450	91340	107830	125430	144920	143620	166430	174130	192040
Less: Imputed bank service charge	...	...	2480	2930	3480	4360	3990	6180	7130	8920	8020	8620
Plus: Import duties	...	...	...	...	...	...	...	...	...	...	...	...
Plus: Value added tax	...	...	...	...	...	...	...	...	...	...	...	...
Equals: Gross Domestic Product a	...	74146	69200	76520	87860	103460	121440	138740	136490	157510	166110	183420

a) Gross domestic product in factor values.

1.11 Gross Domestic Product by Kind of Activity, in Constant Prices

Thousand E.C. dollars

	1970	1975	1977	1978	1979	1980	1981	1982	1983	1984	1985	1986
					At constant prices of:1977							
1 Agriculture, hunting, forestry and fishing	...	...	13100	13700	14860	13440	14090	14090	11500	11990	11720	11530
2 Mining and quarrying	...	...	200	150	180	230	240	280	310	260	290	320
3 Manufacturing	...	...	12540	13150	13310	13530	12150	13170	11720	13150	12440	13050
4 Electricity, gas and water	...	...	610	710	740	880	940	1000	1010	1070	1160	1270
5 Construction	...	...	6590	4940	6090	7720	7990	9490	10440	8720	9810	10300
6 Wholesale and retail trade, restaurants and hotels	...	...	8430	9960	11100	11970	12110	12680	13430	15170	17100	18840
7 Transport, storage and communication	...	...	5860	6180	6290	6880	9290	9410	9640	10480	11030	11850
8 Finance, insurance, real estate and business services	...	...	9050	8940	9460	9780	9760	10580	10750	11360	11870	12400
9 Community, social and personal services	...	...	3550	3310	3370	3750	4290	4500	4720	4950	5200	5460
Total, Industries	...	...	59930	61040	65400	68180	70860	75200	73520	77150	80620	85020
Producers of Government Services	...	...	11750	13070	14950	15690	16580	17750	18500	22400	23520	23910
Other Producers	...	...	...	...	...	...	...	...	...	...	...	...
Subtotal a	...	...	71680	74110	80350	83870	87440	92950	92020	99550	104140	108930
Less: Imputed bank service charge	...	...	2480	2640	3100	3590	3060	3250	3300	3630	3810	4040
Plus: Import duties	...	...	...	...	...	...	...	...	...	...	...	...
Plus: Value added tax	...	...	...	...	...	...	...	...	...	...	...	...
Equals: Gross Domestic Product a	...	...	69200	71470	77250	80280	84380	89700	88720	95920	100330	104890

a) Gross domestic product in factor values.

Saint Christopher and Nevis

1.12 Relations Among National Accounting Aggregates

Thousand E.C. dollars

	1970	1975	1977	1978	1979	1980	1981	1982	1983	1984	1985	1986
Gross Domestic Product	...	...	...	...	...	...	...	158100	154030	167190	...	...
Plus: Net factor income from the rest of the world	...	...	...	...	...	...	...	-9100	-2200	-800	-2200	...
Equals: Gross National Product	...	...	...	...	...	...	...	149000	151830	166390	...	...
Less: Consumption of fixed capital	...	...	...	...	...	...	...	...	...	...	...	...
Equals: National Income	...	...	...	...	...	...	...	...	...	...	...	...
Plus: Net current transfers from the rest of the world	...	...	...	...	...	...	...	35100	30500	31600	...	...
Equals: National Disposable Income	...	...	...	...	...	...	...	...	...	...	...	...
Less: Final consumption	...	...	...	...	...	...	...	...	...	...	...	...
Equals: Net Saving	...	...	...	...	...	...	...	...	...	...	...	...
Less: Surplus of the nation on current transactions	...	...	...	...	...	...	...	...	...	...	...	...
Equals: Net Capital Formation	...	...	...	...	...	...	...	...	...	...	...	...

Saint Lucia

Source. 'Economic Survey and Projections', British Development Division in the Caribbean.

General note. The estimates shown in the following tables have been prepared in accordance with the United Nations System of National Accounts so far as the existing data would permit.

1.1 Expenditure on the Gross Domestic Product, in Current Prices

Million E.C. dollars

	1970	1975	1977	1978	1979	1980	1981	1982	1983	1984	1985	1986
1 Government final consumption expenditure	...	23.2	37.0 / 34.3	35.8	46.3	59.4	73.4	87.9	97.5	102.7	...	...
2 Private final consumption expenditure	...	96.5	110.5 / 146.7	175.3	205.5	225.3	280.1	274.6	243.7	266.7	...	...
3 Gross capital formation	...	56.8	87.7 / 62.5	101.2	128.6	159.1	164.8	145.3	113.8	126.0	...	...
A Increase in stocks	...	6.7	9.9 / 10.4	16.9	21.4	26.2	27.5	24.2	19.0	21.0	...	...
B Gross fixed capital formation	...	50.1	77.8 / 52.1	84.3	107.2	132.9	137.3	121.1	94.8	105.0	...	...
4 Exports of goods and services	...	51.5	107.1 / 109.1	147.2	176.3	213.0	191.7	200.1	241.4	261.4	...	...
5 Less: Imports of goods and services	...	104.8	166.2 / 168.2	237.9	284.6	351.5	369.1	344.3	316.4	348.6	...	...
Equals: Gross Domestic Product	...	123.2	176.1 / 184.4	221.6	272.1	305.3	340.9	363.6	380.0	408.2	...	...

1.10 Gross Domestic Product by Kind of Activity, in Current Prices

Million E.C. dollars

	1970	1975	1977	1978	1979	1980	1981	1982	1983	1984	1985	1986
1 Agriculture, hunting, forestry and fishing	...	16.1	22.7 / 24.2	33.2	34.8	31.0	28.9	36.1	42.3	46.2	58.3	70.7
2 Mining and quarrying	...	1.5	1.2 / 1.0	1.3	3.1	3.9	4.1	3.2	2.2	2.3	2.3	2.5
3 Manufacturing	...	7.4	13.8 / 13.8	15.2	18.9	24.7	25.3	26.8	30.2	31.1	33.0	34.0
4 Electricity, gas and water	...	2.8	4.5 / 4.6	4.7	5.0	5.5	7.3	8.6	11.2	13.6	15.0	16.5
5 Construction	...	11.2	11.2 / 10.8	17.2	25.2	31.5	37.9	33.1	19.6	23.2	27.0	31.9
6 Wholesale and retail trade, restaurants and hotels	...	18.3	35.6 / 40.4	48.6	58.3	67.2	72.9	72.8	75.8	83.0	88.4	94.1
7 Transport, storage and communication	...	8.5	19.1 / 18.0	21.6	25.9	30.9	34.5	35.3	37.6	38.7	40.4	42.2
8 Finance, insurance, real estate and business services	...	16.3	18.5 / 17.2	20.6	25.0	28.9	36.8	40.0	41.5	42.5	43.8	45.2
9 Community, social and personal services	...	7.0	6.1 / 6.6	8.0	9.2	11.4	13.5	14.9	16.2	17.9	19.0	20.5
Total, Industries	...	89.1	132.7 / 136.6	170.4	205.4	235.0	261.2	270.8	276.6	298.5	327.2	357.6
Producers of Government Services	...	19.0	27.3 / 27.3	29.7	34.5	41.2	56.1	62.3	67.8	76.3	84.0	92.0
Other Producers	...	...	...	...	...	...	...	...	...	...	...	...
Subtotal a	...	108.1	160.0 / 163.9	200.1	239.9	276.2	317.3	333.1	344.4	374.8	411.2	449.6
Less: Imputed bank service charge	...	...	7.2 / 7.2	9.1	10.8	12.0	17.9	20.6	21.0	21.8	22.4	23.0
Plus: Import duties	...	...	... / ...	...	...	...	...	...	...	...	...	...
Plus: Value added tax	...	...	... / ...	...	...	...	...	...	...	...	...	...
Equals: Gross Domestic Product a	...	108.1	152.8 / 156.7	191.0	229.1	264.2	299.4	312.5	323.4	353.0	388.8	426.6

a) Gross domestic product in factor values.

1.11 Gross Domestic Product by Kind of Activity, in Constant Prices

Million E.C. dollars

	1970	1975	1977	1978	1979	1980	1981	1982	1983	1984	1985	1986
			At constant prices of: 1977									
1 Agriculture, hunting, forestry and fishing	...	...	24.2	29.3	27.9	22.1	18.8	25.0	28.7	31.0	34.8	39.1
2 Mining and quarrying	...	...	1.0	1.2	2.8	3.0	2.8	1.5	0.9	0.9	0.9	1.0
3 Manufacturing	...	...	13.8	16.0	13.4	15.5	15.8	17.0	18.8	18.8	19.3	19.6
4 Electricity, gas and water	...	...	4.6	5.1	5.9	5.7	5.8	6.0	6.6	7.1	7.6	8.0
5 Construction	...	...	10.8	15.3	18.2	18.7	19.8	17.2	9.7	10.9	12.5	14.5

Saint Lucia

1.11 Gross Domestic Product by Kind of Activity, in Constant Prices
(Continued)

Million E.C. dollars

	1970	1975	1977	1978	1979	1980	1981	1982	1983	1984	1985	1986
					At constant prices of:1977							
6 Wholesale and retail trade, restaurants and hotels	...	...	40.4	44.2	46.2	46.0	44.3	43.5	45.3	48.0	49.6	51.9
7 Transport, storage and communication	...	...	18.0	19.7	20.3	19.0	18.7	19.1	22.0	23.0	24.9	27.0
8 Finance, insurance, real estate and business services	...	...	17.2	18.5	19.6	20.0	20.9	21.6	22.8	23.1	24.0	24.7
9 Community, social and personal services	...	...	6.6	7.2	7.6	7.9	8.2	8.6	9.3	10.0	10.4	10.6
Total, Industries	...	...	136.6	156.5	161.9	157.9	155.1	159.5	164.1	172.8	184.0	196.4
Producers of Government Services	...	...	27.3	28.2	30.2	32.8	38.7	39.9	43.4	44.8	46.4	47.1
Other Producers	...	...	...	...	...	...	...	...	...	...	...	...
Subtotal [a]	...	...	163.9	184.7	192.1	190.7	193.8	199.4	207.5	217.6	230.4	243.5
Less: Imputed bank service charge	...	...	7.2	7.7	8.6	8.6	9.2	9.5	9.9	10.1	10.5	10.8
Plus: Import duties	...	...	...	...	...	...	...	...	...	...	...	...
Plus: Value added tax	...	...	...	...	...	...	...	...	...	...	...	...
Equals: Gross Domestic Product [a]	...	...	156.7	177.0	183.5	182.1	184.3	189.9	197.6	207.5	219.9	232.7

a) Gross domestic product in factor values.

Saint Vincent and the Grenadines

Source. 'The preparation of national accounts statistics in St. Vincent and the Grenadines is undertaken by the Statistical Office, Ministry of Finance, Planning and Development, Kingstown. The official estimates together with a description of the sources and methods used for the national accounts estimation are published in 'National Accounts of St. Vincent and the Grenadines'.

General note. The estimates shown in the following tables have been prepared in accordance with the United Nations System of National Accounts so far as the existing data would permit.

1.1 Expenditure on the Gross Domestic Product, in Current Prices

Million E.C. dollars

		1970	1975	1977	1978	1979	1980	1981	1982	1983	1984	1985	1986
1	Government final consumption expenditure	...	...	21.9	27.6	34.0	37.4	46.8	54.0	58.3	78.2	...	...
2	Private final consumption expenditure	...	...	81.7	87.4	120.4	136.9	144.5	171.4	170.4	153.3	...	...
3	Gross capital formation	...	...	33.9	34.4	48.6	62.8	64.1	68.4	73.7	84.3	...	...
	A Increase in stocks	...	...	-	-	-	-	-	-	-	-	...	...
	B Gross fixed capital formation	...	...	33.9	34.4	48.6	62.8	64.1	68.4	73.7	84.3	...	...
	Residential buildings	...	...									...	...
	Non-residential buildings	...	...	22.6	24.2	32.1	41.1	47.2	49.7	52.9	51.8	...	...
	Other construction and land improvement etc.	...	...									...	...
	Other	...	...	11.3	10.2	16.5	21.7	16.9	18.7	20.8	32.4	...	...
4	Exports of goods and services	...	...	42.7	74.0	76.3	89.5	116.0	135.9	165.9	192.0	...	...
5	Less: Imports of goods and services	...	...	86.0	103.9	140.2	170.9	178.8	204.7	221.9	238.8	...	...
	Equals: Gross Domestic Product	...	...	94.3	119.5	139.2	155.7	192.7	225.0	246.5	269.0	...	...

1.10 Gross Domestic Product by Kind of Activity, in Current Prices

Million E.C. dollars

		1970	1975	1977	1978	1979	1980	1981	1982	1983	1984	1985	1986
1	Agriculture, hunting, forestry and fishing	...	...	14.7	20.7	19.8	19.8	27.5	31.0	35.5	30.3	44.1	...
2	Mining and quarrying	...	...	0.3	0.3	0.4	0.5	0.6	0.6	0.6	0.6	0.7	...
3	Manufacturing	...	...	5.9	10.3	13.1	14.2	18.4	20.7	21.3	22.1	19.6	...
4	Electricity, gas and water	...	...	2.4	2.6	3.0	3.3	4.4	5.2	6.8	6.3	7.1	...
5	Construction	...	...	10.1	10.8	14.4	18.4	20.6	21.8	23.2	22.7	25.2	...
6	Wholesale and retail trade, restaurants and hotels	...	...	13.0	14.8	16.1	20.3	22.1	26.7	28.9	30.7	33.5	...
7	Transport, storage and communication	...	...	11.2	14.6	18.7	20.5	25.6	30.8	33.2	35.9	37.6	...
8	Finance, insurance, real estate and business services	...	...	7.6	9.9	12.4	15.1	18.3	20.5	22.0	22.7	22.9	...
9	Community, social and personal services	...	...	2.6	3.1	3.3	4.6	5.3	5.7	6.1	6.4	6.5	...
	Total, Industries	...	...	67.9	87.1	101.1	116.7	142.8	164.0	177.5	186.5	197.0	...
	Producers of Government Services	...	...	14.9	19.0	21.6	22.2	30.3	35.0	38.2	43.3	42.3	...
	Other Producers	...	...	...	...	...	...	...	...	...	...	...	...
	Subtotal [a]	...	...	82.8	106.0	122.7	138.9	173.1	199.0	215.7	229.8	239.3	...
	Less: Imputed bank service charge	...	...	3.2	4.5	5.5	7.4	8.5	10.8	11.4	13.0	11.0	...
	Plus: Import duties	...	...	...	...	...	...	...	...	...	...	...	...
	Plus: Value added tax	...	...	...	...	...	...	...	...	...	...	...	...
	Plus: Other adjustments [b]	...	...	14.7	18.0	21.0	24.2	20.2	00.0	42.2	52.2	45.8	...
	Equals: Gross Domestic Product	...	...	94.3	119.5	139.2	155.7	192.8	225.0	246.5	269.0	274.1	...

a) Gross domestic product in factor values
b) Item 'Other adjustments' refers to indirect taxes net of subsidies.

1.11 Gross Domestic Product by Kind of Activity, in Constant Prices

Million E.C. dollars

		1970	1975	1977	1978	1979	1980	1981	1982	1983	1984	1985	1986
					At constant prices of: 1977								
1	Agriculture, hunting, forestry and fishing	...	...	14.7	17.2	14.6	12.5	17.7	18.7	19.6	20.9	22.7	...
2	Mining and quarrying	...	...	0.3	0.3	0.3	0.3	0.3	0.3	0.3	0.3	0.4	...
3	Manufacturing	...	...	5.9	8.9	10.6	11.1	11.3	12.0	12.3	12.4	12.2	...
4	Electricity, gas and water	...	...	2.4	2.8	3.1	3.2	3.3	3.6	3.7	3.8	4.1	...
5	Construction	...	...	10.1	8.8	10.6	11.2	11.4	11.5	12.2	12.1	12.4	...
6	Wholesale and retail trade, restaurants and hotels	...	...	13.0	14.3	14.0	15.7	14.3	16.1	16.6	17.2	18.3	...
7	Transport, storage and communication	...	...	11.2	13.0	14.3	16.5	18.8	20.7	23.2	24.3	25.1	...
8	Finance, insurance, real estate and business services	...	...	7.6	7.7	8.1	8.5	8.6	8.8	8.9	9.3	9.1	...
9	Community, social and personal services	...	...	2.6	2.9	2.9	3.1	3.2	3.4	3.4	3.5	3.5	...

Saint Vincent and the Grenadines

1.11 Gross Domestic Product by Kind of Activity, in Constant Prices
(Continued)

Million E.C. dollars

	1970	1975	1977	1978	1979	1980	1981	1982	1983	1984	1985	1986
				At constant prices of:1977								
Total, Industries	...	...	67.9	75.8	78.4	82.2	88.9	95.0	100.3	103.7	107.8	...
Producers of Government Services	...	...	14.9	15.6	16.5	17.1	17.5	17.5	17.8	18.3	17.0	...
Other Producers	...	...	...	...	...	...	...	...	...	...	...	...
Subtotal [a]	...	...	82.8	91.3	94.8	99.3	106.4	112.5	118.1	122.0	124.8	...
Less: Imputed bank service charge	...	...	3.2	3.2	3.5	3.8	3.8	3.9	3.9	4.3	3.5	...
Plus: Import duties	...	...	...	...	...	...	...	...	...	...	...	...
Plus: Value added tax	...	...	...	...	...	...	...	...	...	...	...	...
Plus: Other adjustments	...	...	14.7	15.6	17.1	17.6	17.6	21.2	23.6	26.8	24.4	...
Equals: Gross Domestic Product [a]	...	...	94.3	103.7	108.5	113.1	120.1	129.8	137.7	144.5	145.7	...

a) Gross domestic product in factor values.

1.12 Relations Among National Accounting Aggregates

Million E.C. dollars

	1970	1975	1977	1978	1979	1980	1981	1982	1983	1984	1985	1986
Gross Domestic Product	...	...	94.3	119.5	139.2	155.7	192.7	225.0	...	...	...	...
Plus: Net factor income from the rest of the world	...	...	-	-	-0.3	-0.3	-0.5	-0.5	...	...	...	...
Equals: Gross National Product	...	...	93.4	119.5	138.9	155.4	192.2	224.5	...	...	...	...
Less: Consumption of fixed capital	...	...	...	...	...	...	...	...	...	...	...	...
Equals: National Income	...	...	...	...	...	...	...	...	...	...	...	...
Plus: Net current transfers from the rest of the world	...	...	...	...	...	...	...	...	...	...	...	...
Equals: National Disposable Income	...	...	...	...	...	...	...	...	...	...	...	...
Less: Final consumption	...	...	...	...	...	...	...	...	...	...	...	...
Equals: Net Saving	...	...	...	...	...	...	...	...	...	...	...	...
Less: Surplus of the nation on current transactions	...	...	...	...	...	...	...	...	...	...	...	...
Equals: Net Capital Formation	...	...	...	...	...	...	...	...	...	...	...	...

2.1 Government Final Consumption Expenditure by Function, in Current Prices

Million E.C. dollars

Fiscal year beginning 1 July

	1970	1975	1977	1978	1979	1980	1981	1982	1983	1984	1985	1986
1 General public services	...	...	2.5	4.7	5.6	4.5	7.1	...	...	...	...	...
2 Defence	...	...	-	-	-	-	-	...	...	...	...	...
3 Public order and safety	...	...	1.9	3.1	3.4	3.5	6.0	...	...	...	...	...
4 Education	...	...	6.5	9.4	8.8	9.3	15.7	...	...	...	...	...
5 Health	...	...	4.0	5.6	5.4	6.0	9.8	...	...	...	...	...
6 Social security and welfare	...	...	1.4	2.2	2.0	2.2	2.7	...	...	...	...	...
7 Housing and community amenities	...	...	0.5	0.7	1.4	1.4	2.7	...	...	...	...	...
8 Recreational, cultural and religious affairs	...	...	-	-	-	-	-	...	...	...	...	...
9 Economic services	...	...	5.0	6.5	7.6	11.4	5.2	...	...	...	...	...
A Fuel and energy	...	...	...	...	...	...	...	...	...	...	...	...
B Agriculture, forestry, fishing and hunting	...	...	1.1	1.6	1.6	1.9	3.7	...	...	...	...	...
C Mining, manufacturing and construction, except fuel and energy	...	...	3.9	4.8	5.9	9.5	1.3	...	...	...	...	...
D Transportation and communication	...	...	-	-	-	-	-	...	...	...	...	...
E Other economic affairs	...	...	-	0.1	0.1	0.1	0.2	...	...	...	...	...
10 Other functions	...	...	...	...	...	...	...	...	...	...	...	...
Total Government Final Consumption Expenditure	...	...	21.7	32.2	34.1	38.3	49.5	...	...	...	...	...

Samoa

Source. Reply to the United Nations National Accounts Questionnaire from the Department of Statistics, Apia.
General note. The estimates shown in the following tables have been prepared in accordance with the United Nations System of National Accounts so far as the existing data would permit.

1.1 Expenditure on the Gross Domestic Product, in Current Prices

Thousand Samoan tala	1970	1975	1977	1978	1979	1980	1981	1982	1983	1984	1985	1986
1 Government final consumption expenditure	...	...	...	...	...	...	...	...	...	...	...	...
2 Private final consumption expenditure	...	...	...	...	...	...	...	...	...	...	...	...
3 Gross capital formation	...	...	...	...	...	...	...	...	...	...	...	...
4 Exports of goods and services	5204.6	9600.0	...	...	...	...	...	...	...	...	...	...
5 Less: Imports of goods and services	10847.2	25168.0	...	...	...	...	...	...	...	...	...	...
Equals: Gross Domestic Product	...	...	...	...	...	...	...	...	...	...	...	...

Saudi Arabia

General note. The preparation of national accounts statistics in Saudi Arabia is undertaken by the Central Department of Statistics, Ministry of Finance and National Economy, Riyadh. The official estimates are published in the National Income Series entitled 'National Accounts of Saudi Arabia'. The most detailed description of the sources and methods used for the national accounts estimation is found in 'National Accounts of Saudi Arabia 1386-87 through 1391-92, A.H.' published in 1973. The estimates are generally in accordance with the classifications and definitions recommended in the United Nations System of National Accounts (SNA). The following tables have been prepared from successive replies to the United Nations national accounts questionnaire. The national accounts estimates shown relate to Hejra fiscal years. A Hejra fiscal year covers the period from the beginning of the seventh month of one Hejra calendar year through the end of the sixth month of the following year. When the scope and coverage of the estimates differ for conceptual or statistical reasons from the definitions and classifications recommended in SNA, a footnote is indicated to the relevant tables.

Sources and methods:

(a) Gross domestic product. Gross domestic product is estimated mainly through the production approach.

(b) Expenditure on the gross domestic product. All components of GDP by expenditure type are estimated through the expenditure approach except private final consumption expenditure and gross fixed capital formation of private transport establishments which are estimated by using the commodity-flow approach. Government consumption expenditure is calculated as the sum of compensation of employees and net current purchases of goods and services. Data are obtained from the appropriations in the government budget rather than from actual expenditure data. The estimates are, however, adjusted for under-spending. Estimates of private consumption expenditure are based on imports in c.i.f. values and gross output of domestically produced goods and services. Import duties are based on the customs tariffs whereas transport and distribution margins are based on assumed margin rates. In order to estimate the gross fixed capital formation of transport establishments, a detailed classification of import statistics is used to estimate the capital formation in transport equipment. For general government, public enterprises and private industries the estimates are based on surveys of industrial production, which include information on fixed assets. Gross capital formation of the oil sector is based on data provided by the oil companies through their annual returns. Exports of crude petroleum and petroleum products constitute over 99 per cent of total exports of merchandise. The data are obtained from annual returns of the oil companies. Non-petroleum exports and imports of merchandise are obtained from foreign trade statistics and balance of payment estimates. GDP by expenditure type at constant prices is not estimated.

(c) Cost-structure of the gross domestic product. Compensation of employees for the crude petroleum and petroleum refining industries is obtained from the annual returns provided by the oil companies. For most of the other industries, the estimates are determined on the basis of an estimated ratio of wages to gross output. Estimates of indirect taxes are made from revenue figures of the central and local governments while subsidies are calculated from information supplied by the Ministry of Finance. Gross operating surplus, including depreciation, is estimated as a residual.

(d) Gross domestic product by kind of economic activity. The table of GDP by kind of economic activity is prepared at market prices, i.e. producers' values. The production approach is used to estimate value added of the majority of industries. The income approach is used for mining other than extraction of crude petroleum and natural gas, mechanized road transport, ownership of dwellings, domestic services and producers of government services. For the agricultural sector, bench-mark estimates for 1967-68 on gross output and intermediate consumption were prepared based on the results of agricultural surveys conducted in the period 1960-1965. Other years' estimates are calculated by multiplying the 1967-68 figures by index numbers of physical output and producers' prices. The extraction of crude petroleum and natural gas are undertaken by Aramco, Getty, and Arabian Oil Company. The annual returns from these companies and from the Saudi Arabian Oil refineries provide details on sales, costs and capital expenditures which enable the calculation of gross output, intermediate consumption and compensation of employees for mining, manufacturing of petroleum products and construction. Internal prices of the oil companies are used for the calculation of sales figures and not the 'posted' prices which are used for calculating the payment of income tax. For other manufacturing, electricity, non-residential building construction, trade, water transport, financial services other than commercial banks, real estate, business services and private services, the estimates on gross output, intermediate consumption and compensation of employees for 1970 are available from the sample survey of establishments in 1971. Other years' estimates are calculated by multiplying the bench-mark year figures by quantity indexes, price indexes or assumed growth rates. Estimates on construction for the government sector are based on details of government appropriations. For the private sector, the value of construction of dwellings is derived by multiplying the estimated number of dwellings constructed by the estimated cost of construction per dwelling. For mechanized road transport, the estimated number of vehicles is multiplied by an estimated value added per vehicle while for the airlines, railways and the Tapline annual returns from the companies concerned provide data on gross output, intermediate consumption and compensation of employees. Commercial banks' figures for 1970 are obtained from a survey of the operations of commercial banks. An estimated index of growth of banking services is applied for other years. Estimates of government services are derived from a classification of government appropriations shown in the budget volumes. For the constant price estimates, the value added of the agricultural sector, manufacturing, electricity, trade, transport and other services is extrapolated by quantity indexes. Value added of crude petroleum and petroleum refining is extrapolated by quantity indexes compiled from figures on barrels produced. Different kinds of price indexes such as index of wage rates and cost of living index are used to deflate the value added of construction and the financial sectors.

1.1 Expenditure on the Gross Domestic Product, in Current Prices

Million Saudi Arabia riyals — Fiscal year beginning 1 July

	1970	1975	1977	1978	1979	1980	1981	1982	1983	1984	1985	1986
1 Government final consumption expenditure	3798	28883	47034	71904	77563	81915	128526	126900	121800	115600	113500	...
2 Private final consumption expenditure	6412	23903	54607	68608	102385	114905	126514	137300	143500	146000	122100	...
3 Gross capital formation	2727	34320	74502	69270	79722	112803	102513	112900	113400	94000	77200	...
A Increase in stocks a	-205	780	7611	-7384	-17346	6427	-19802	-2600	3300	2800	2300	...
B Gross fixed capital formation b	2932	33540	66891	76654	97068	106376	122315	115500	110100	91200	74900	...
Residential buildings	697	4912	7053	...	...	...	...	...	...	...	...	...
Non-residential buildings	192	8539	...	...	...	...	...	...	...	...	...	...
Other construction and land improvement etc.	1307	13439	...	...	...	...	...	...	...	...	...	...
Other	736	6337	14169	12682	17596	...	...	...	...	...	...	...
4 Exports of goods and services	15189	120284	140762	147236	258488	368425	354919	219400	168400	134700	102600	...
5 Less: Imports of goods and services	5205	42863	91505	107479	132351	157459	187754	181300	175900	159400	128700	...
Equals: Gross Domestic Product	22921	164526	225400	249539	385807	520589	524718	415200	371200	330900	286700	...

a) Item 'Increase in stocks' includes a statistical discrepancy.
b) Beginning 1974, item 'gross capital formation' includes other not classified capital goods.

1.3 Cost Components of the Gross Domestic Product

Million Saudi Arabia riyals — Fiscal year beginning 1 July

	1970	1975	1977	1978	1979	1980	1981	1982	1983	1984	1985	1986
1 Indirect taxes, net	350	-900	-903	-455	-1390	-981	-900	-700	-800	-500	-500	...
A Indirect taxes	430	665	1622	...	...	...	...	...	...	...	...	...
B Less: Subsidies	80	1565	2525	...	...	...	...	...	...	...	...	...
2 Consumption of fixed capital a	...	...	...	...	...	...	...	...	...	...	...	...
3 Compensation of employees paid by resident producers to:	4833	25007	50676	61140	75299	90177	525600	415900	372000	331400	287200	...
A Resident households	4305	23690	...	...	...	...						...
B Rest of the world	528	1316	...	...	...	...						...
4 Operating surplus a	17739	140419	175626	188854	311898	431393						...
Equals: Gross Domestic Product	22921	164526	225400	249539	385807	520589	524700	415200	371200	330900	286700	...

a) Item 'Operating surplus' includes consumption of fixed capital.

Saudi Arabia

1.7 External Transactions on Current Account, Summary

Million Saudi Arabia riyals — Fiscal year beginning 1 July

	1970	1975	1977	1978	1979	1980	1981	1982	1983	1984	1985	1986
Payments to the Rest of the World												
1 Imports of goods and services	5205	42863	91505	107479	132351	157500	187700	181300	175900	159400	...	...
A Imports of merchandise c.i.f.	4160	29652	60028	...	...	...	...	...	...	...	...	...
B Other	1045	13211	31477	...	...	...	...	...	...	...	...	...
2 Factor income to the rest of the world	6028	7670	16700	18200	36500	46400	39600	32900	31300	30300	...	...
A Compensation of employees	528	1316	9700	11300	13500	13900	18300	18100	18600	18400	...	...
B Property and entrepreneurial income	5500	6354	7000	6900	23000	32500	21300	14800	12700	11900	...	...
3 Current transfers to the rest of the world	1531	10389	13300	11800	18300	19300	...	...	...	...	...	...
4 Surplus of the nation on current transactions	2790	66912	26400	22800	90300	182300	175800	60000	8300	-10300	...	...
Payments to the Rest of the World and Surplus of the Nation on Current Transactions	15553	127834	147900	160300	277500	405500	403100	274200	215500	179400	...	...
Receipts From The Rest of the World												
1 Exports of goods and services	15189	120284	140762	147236	258488	368400	354900	219400	168400	134700	...	...
A Exports of merchandise f.o.b.	14319	116597	133728	...	...	...	...	...	...	...	...	...
B Other	870	3687	7034	...	...	...	...	...	...	...	...	...
2 Factor income from rest of the world	348	7537	7100	13100	19000	37100	48200	54800	47100	44700	...	...
A Compensation of employees	-	*	*	*				*	*	-	...	...
B Property and entrepreneurial income	348	7537	7100	13100	19000	37100	48200	54800	47100	44700	...	...
3 Current transfers from rest of the world	16	13	...	...	...	...	...	...	...	...	...	...
Receipts from the Rest of the World on Current Transactions	15553	127834	147900	160300	277500	405500	403100	274200	215500	179400	...	...

1.10 Gross Domestic Product by Kind of Activity, in Current Prices

Million Saudi Arabia riyals — Fiscal year beginning 1 July

	1970	1975	1977	1978	1979	1980	1981	1982	1983	1984	1985	1986
1 Agriculture, hunting, forestry and fishing	1016	1586	3909	4196	4648	5572	6740	8725	9400	11100	12600	...
2 Mining and quarrying	12632	110095	127181	132218	238579	342693	325297	194659	144900	112700	82800	...
3 Manufacturing	1958	8173	9974	12615	19295	25748	22384	23972	26700	27100	26200	...
4 Electricity, gas and water	298	151	204	248	271	399	-429	-850	-1000	-700	-800	...
5 Construction	1007	15854	31959	34764	43108	50348	58181	54903	50200	41600	34600	...
6 Wholesale and retail trade, restaurants and hotels	1068	6180	11049	13912	17760	21984	25064	28088	28400	27500	24200	...
7 Transport, storage and communication	1479	4077	9960	12764	15749	17123	19871	21489	24200	23500	20500	...
8 Finance, insurance, real estate and business services	1104	8444	12704	16180	18815	22325	25862	30183	31200	28400	20300	...
9 Community, social and personal services	265	1989	3293	4155	5261	5504	6813	8408	8400	9000	8600	...
Total, Industries	20826	156549	210233	231052	363486	491696	489783	369577	324400	280200	232000	...
Producers of Government Services	1805	7890	15146	18912	23384	29905	36361	46585	47600	51400	55200	...
Other Producers	...	...	...	...	...	...	...	...	...	...	...	...
Subtotal	22631	164439	225379	240064	386870	521601	526144	416162	372000	331600	287200	...
Less: Imputed bank service charge	50	547	1561	2342	3279	3607	3968	4364	4400	4600	4300	...
Plus: Import duties	340	634	1583	1917	2217	2595	2542	3400	3600	3900	3800	...
Plus: Value added tax	...	...	...	...	...	...	...	...	...	...	...	...
Equals: Gross Domestic Product	22921	164526	225400	249539	385807	520589	524718	415200	371200	330900	286700	...

Saudi Arabia

1.11 Gross Domestic Product by Kind of Activity, in Constant Prices

Million Saudi Arabia riyals — Fiscal year beginning 1 July

	1970	1975	1977	1978	1979	1980	1981	1982	1983	1984	1985	1986
		At constant prices of:										
		1969					1979					
1 Agriculture, hunting, forestry and fishing	1018	1221	1483 / 4200	4400	4700	4900	5200	5700	6200	6300	...	...
2 Mining and quarrying	9971	17622	19797 / 216900	221700	238600	248000	223900	134000	116700	96700	...	...
3 Manufacturing	1839	2187	2694 / 16100	17700	19300	20700	22100	24200	27400	27000	...	...
4 Electricity, gas and water	298	345	546 / 200	200	300	300	-400	-500	600	600	...	...
5 Construction	957	3309	4582 / 38500	39500	43100	47500	52300	49100	45300	41200	...	...
6 Wholesale and retail trade, restaurants and hotels	1051	2331	3555 / 11800	14200	17800	21000	24200	27300	27800	27600	...	...
7 Transport, storage and communication	1468	1580	2367 / 12000	13800	15700	17100	18500	20100	22400	22200	...	...
8 Finance, insurance, real estate and business services	1053	2608	3462 / 15100	16900	18800	20500	22200	23700	24100	23300	...	...
9 Community, social and personal services	253	363	470 / 4400	5100	5300	5700	6300	6700	6700	6500	...	...
Total, Industries	17908	31565	38956 / 319200	333500	363500	385800	374300	290300	277200	251300	...	...
Producers of Government Services	1722	2755	2953 / 20700	22000	23400	25800	27600	29600	30400	32000	...	...
Other Producers	...	...	...	...	...	...	...	...	...	...	...	...
Subtotal	19630	34320	41909 / 339900	355500	387000	411500	401900	319900	307600	283400	...	...
Less: Imputed bank service charge	48	70	144 / 1900	2600	3300	4100	4300	4500	4500	4600	...	...
Plus: Import duties	325	211	263 / 1900	2200	2200	2200	1900	2200	2100	1900	...	...
Plus: Value added tax	...	...	...	...	...	...	...	...	...	...	...	...
Equals: Gross Domestic Product	19907	34461	42028 / 339900	355100	385800	409700	399500	317600	305100	280600	...	...

1.12 Relations Among National Accounting Aggregates

Million Saudi Arabia riyals — Fiscal year beginning 1 July

	1970	1975	1977	1978	1979	1980	1981	1982	1983	1984	1985	1986
Gross Domestic Product	22921	164526	225400	249539	385807	520500	524700	415200	371200	330900	...	...
Plus: Net factor income from the rest of the world	-5680	-133	-9600	-5100	-17500	-9300	8600	21900	15800	14400	...	...
Factor income from the rest of the world	348	7537	7100	13100	19000	37100	48200	54800	47100	44700	...	...
Less: Factor income to the rest of the world	6028	7670	16700	18200	36500	46400	39600	32900	31300	30300	...	...
Equals: Gross National Product	17241	164393	215800	244439	368307	511200	533300	437100	387000	345300	...	...
Less: Consumption of fixed capital	...	...	...	...	...	...	...	...	...	...	...	...
Equals: National Income [a]	17242	164393	215800	244439	368307	511200	533300	437100	387000	345300	...	...
Plus: Net current transfers from the rest of the world	-1515	-10376	-13300	-11800	-18300	-19300	...	...	...	...	...	...
Current transfers from the rest of the world	16	13	...	...	...	...	...	...	...	...	...	...
Less: Current transfers to the rest of the world	1531	10389	13300	11800	18300	19300	...	...	...	...	...	...
Equals: National Disposable Income [b]	15727	154017	202500	232639	350007	491900	533300	437100	387000	345300	...	...
Less: Final consumption	10210	52785	101641	140512	179948	196800	255000	264200	265300	261600	...	...
Equals: Net Saving [c]	5517	101232	100900	92100	170100	295100	278300	172900	121700	83700	...	...
Less: Surplus of the nation on current transactions	2790	66912	26400	22800	90300	182300	175800	60000	8300	-10300	...	...
Equals: Net Capital Formation [d]	2727	34320	74500	69300	79800	112800	102500	112900	113400	94000	...	...

a) Item 'National income' includes consumption of fixed capital.
b) Item 'National disposable income' includes consumption of fixed capital.
c) Item 'Net saving' includes consumption of fixed capital.
d) Item 'Net capital formation' includes consumption of fixed capital.

Saudi Arabia

2.1 Government Final Consumption Expenditure by Function, in Current Prices

Million Saudi Arabia riyals — Fiscal year beginning 1 July

	1970	1975	1977	1978	1979	1980	1981	1982	1983	1984	1985	1986
1 General public services	646	2991	6541	...	...	...	...	...	...	...	...	...
2 Defence	1804	17473	26999	...	...	...	...	...	...	...	...	...
3 Public order and safety	...	...	...	...	...	...	...	...	...	...	...	...
4 Education	469	3074	5655	...	...	...	...	...	...	...	...	...
5 Health	153	826	1378	...	...	...	...	...	...	...	...	...
6 Social security and welfare	24	81	188	...	...	...	...	...	...	...	...	...
7 Housing and community amenities	57	-	27	...	...	...	...	...	...	...	...	...
8 Recreational, cultural and religious affairs	146	339	653	...	...	...	...	...	...	...	...	...
9 Economic services	332	2484	5184	...	...	...	...	...	...	...	...	...
10 Other functions	166	1614	409	...	...	...	...	...	...	...	...	...
Total Government Final Consumption Expenditure	3798	28883	47034	...	...	...	...	...	...	...	...	...

2.17 Exports and Imports of Goods and Services, Detail

Million Saudi Arabia riyals — Fiscal year beginning 1 July

	1970	1975	1977	1978	1979	1980	1981	1982	1983	1984	1985	1986
Exports of Goods and Services												
1 Exports of merchandise, f.o.b.	14319	116597	133728	...	...	...	...	...	...	...	...	...
2 Transport and communication	122	1070	1984	...	...	...	...	...	...	...	...	...
3 Insurance service charges	...	...	...	...	...	...	...	...	...	...	...	...
4 Other commodities	32	78	175	...	...	...	...	...	...	...	...	...
5 Adjustments of merchandise exports to change-of-ownership basis	...	...	...	...	...	...	...	...	...	...	...	...
6 Direct purchases in the domestic market by non-residential households	717	2539	3656	...	...	...	...	...	...	...	...	...
7 Direct purchases in the domestic market by extraterritorial bodies	...	...	...	...	...	...	...	...	...	...	...	...
Total Exports of Goods and Services [a]	15189	120284	139544	...	...	...	...	...	...	...	...	...
Imports of Goods and Services												
1 Imports of merchandise, c.i.f.	4160	29652	60028	...	...	...	...	...	...	...	...	...
2 Adjustments of merchandise imports to change-of-ownership basis	...	...	...	...	...	...	...	...	...	...	...	...
3 Other transport and communication	...	...	...	...	...	...	...	...	...	...	...	...
4 Other insurance service charges	...	...	...	...	...	...	...	...	...	...	...	...
5 Other commodities	94	856	1036	...	...	...	...	...	...	...	...	...
6 Direct purchases abroad by government	951	12355	20792	...	...	...	...	...	...	...	...	...
7 Direct purchases abroad by resident households				...	...	...	...	...	...	...	...	...
Total Imports of Goods and Services [a]	5205	42863	81856	...	...	...	...	...	...	...	...	...
Balance of Goods and Services	9984	77421	57688	...	...	...	...	...	...	...	...	...
Total Imports and Balance of Goods and Services [a]	15189	120284	139544	...	...	...	...	...	...	...	...	...

a) Data for this table have not been revised, therefore, data for some years are not comparable with those of other tables.

Senegal

Source. Reply to the United Nations National Accounts Questionnaire from the Direction de la Statistique, Dakar.
General note. The estimates shown in the following tables have been adjusted by the United Nations Statistical Office to conform to the United Nations System of National Accounts so far as the existing data would permit.

1.1 Expenditure on the Gross Domestic Product, in Current Prices

Thousand Million CFA francs

	1970	1975	1977	1978	1979	1980	1981	1982	1983	1984	1985	1986
1 Government final consumption expenditure	35.7	61.8	77.9	91.1	111.0	140.3	150.7	169.1	177.8	206.8	213.0	224.7
2 Private final consumption expenditure	177.3	294.5	363.6	385.1	446.7	504.0	551.9	635.5	672.8	758.1	925.5	986.1
3 Gross capital formation	37.7	72.3	84.6	86.2	108.4	97.3	110.1	132.9	188.9	160.7	157.8	179.4
A Increase in stocks	7.7	15.7	22.4	19.0	25.8	-2.9	7.7	8.4	55.8	8.9	-3.5	-3.6
B Gross fixed capital formation	30.0	56.6	62.2	67.2	82.6	100.2	102.4	124.5	133.1	151.8	161.3	183.0
4 Exports of goods and services	65.3	147.9	209.3	149.9	200.7	164.3	178.3	319.5	334.7	396.4	351.8	349.3
5 Less: Imports of goods and services	75.9	170.1	251.8	217.6	284.9	278.4	321.2	412.9	449.3	506.5	496.1	432.5
Equals: Gross Domestic Product	240.1	406.4	483.6	494.7	581.9	627.5	669.8	844.3	924.9	1015.5	1152.0	1307.0

1.2 Expenditure on the Gross Domestic Product, in Constant Prices

Thousand Million CFA francs

	1970	1975	1977	1978	1979	1980	1981	1982	1983	1984	1985	1986
	\multicolumn{12}{c}{At constant prices of:1977}											
1 Government final consumption expenditure	59.6	66.9	77.9	84.8	90.9	92.8	94.9	99.0	102.3	104.1	106.8	110.0
2 Private final consumption expenditure	293.5	328.0	363.6	365.0	388.4	395.3	397.1	398.5	417.1	400.8	442.2	442.2
3 Gross capital formation	72.7	88.2	84.6	80.4	90.9	70.0	70.9	75.9	79.5	77.3	70.9	75.8
A Increase in stocks	17.9	17.7	22.4	17.9	22.1	-2.2	5.3	5.1	2.2	4.7	-1.7	-1.6
B Gross fixed capital formation	54.8	70.5	62.2	62.5	68.8	72.2	65.6	70.8	77.3	72.6	72.6	77.4
4 Exports of goods and services	158.6	168.5	209.2	140.1	182.0	129.7	142.4	202.1	188.3	197.6	166.3	185.9
5 Less: Imports of goods and services	178.3	195.3	251.7	216.9	255.1	207.1	228.3	226.0	223.6	242.2	228.3	230.3
Equals: Gross Domestic Product	405.9	456.3	483.6	453.4	497.1	480.7	477.0	549.5	563.6	537.5	557.9	583.6

1.3 Cost Components of the Gross Domestic Product

Thousand Million CFA francs

	1970	1975	1977	1978	1979	1980	1981	1982	1983	1984	1985	1986
1 Indirect taxes, net	...	41.8	50.4	75.4	89.9	95.2	113.7	...	...	...	...	...
A Indirect taxes	...	53.7	64.1	91.2	101.6	...	...	...	...	...	...	...
B Less: Subsidies	...	11.9	13.7	15.8	11.7	...	...	...	...	...	...	...
2 Consumption of fixed capital	...	22.0	28.6	34.2	39.9	41.9	46.8	...	...	...	...	...
3 Compensation of employees paid by resident producers to:	...	117.2	148.0	172.5	193.4	...	...	...	...	...	...	...
4 Operating surplus	...	225.4	256.6	212.6	258.7	...	...	...	...	...	...	...
Equals: Gross Domestic Product	240.1	406.4	483.6	494.7	581.9	627.5	669.8	...	...	...	...	...

1.7 External Transactions on Current Account, Summary

Thousand Million CFA francs

	1970	1975	1977	1978	1979	1980	1981	1982	1983	1984	1985	1986
	\multicolumn{12}{c}{Payments to the Rest of the World}											
1 Imports of goods and services	...	170.1	251.8	217.6	284.9	278.4	...	...	...	...	...	...
A Imports of merchandise c.i.f.	...	145.6	210.9	...	...	...	...	...	...	...	...	...
B Other	...	24.5	40.9	...	...	...	...	...	...	...	...	...
2 Factor income to the rest of the world	...	20.9	18.3	23.6	22.1	22.6	...	...	...	...	...	...
A Compensation of employees	...	6.8	6.0	9.6	6.1	7.4	...	...	...	...	...	...
B Property and entrepreneurial income	...	14.1	12.3	14.0	16.0	15.2	...	...	...	...	...	...
3 Current transfers to the rest of the world	...	4.0	6.7	10.3	7.8	11.9	...	...	...	...	...	...
4 Surplus of the nation on current transactions	...	-18.2	-26.2	-54.5	-59.3	-66.0	...	...	...	...	...	...
Payments to the Rest of the World and Surplus of the Nation on Current Transactions	...	176.8	250.6	197.0	255.5	246.9	...	...	...	...	...	...
	\multicolumn{12}{c}{Receipts From The Rest of the World}											
1 Exports of goods and services	...	147.9	209.3	149.9	200.7	164.3	...	...	...	...	...	...

Senegal

1.7 External Transactions on Current Account, Summary
(Continued)

Thousand Million CFA francs

	1970	1975	1977	1978	1979	1980	1981	1982	1983	1984	1985	1986
A Exports of merchandise f.o.b.	...	107.8	163.9	90.5	133.4	103.8	...	...	...	...	...	...
B Other	...	40.1	45.4	59.4	67.3	60.5	...	...	...	...	...	...
2 Factor income from rest of the world	...	9.2	17.1	17.5	15.9	23.9	...	...	...	...	...	...
A Compensation of employees	...	7.7	14.9	15.3	14.1	21.3	...	...	...	...	...	...
B Property and entrepreneurial income	...	1.5	2.2	2.2	1.8	2.6	...	...	...	...	...	...
3 Current transfers from rest of the world	...	19.7	24.2	29.6	38.9	58.7	...	...	...	...	...	...
Receipts from the Rest of the World on Current Transactions	...	176.8	250.6	197.0	255.5	246.9	...	...	...	...	...	...

1.10 Gross Domestic Product by Kind of Activity, in Current Prices

Thousand Million CFA francs

	1970	1975	1977	1978	1979	1980	1981	1982	1983	1984	1985	1986
1 Agriculture, hunting, forestry and fishing	57.8	122.8	132.5	104.6	139.6	120.0	121.1	211.4	212.8	174.1	218.8	292.8
2 Mining and quarrying												
3 Manufacturing	42.3	79.5	91.9	92.9	109.0	118.5	128.8	113.9	141.4	208.1	252.0	262.5
4 Electricity, gas and water												
5 Construction	9.4	18.0	21.2	27.5	32.1	37.7	42.8	36.9	44.2	72.3	78.1	85.1
6 Wholesale and retail trade, restaurants and hotels	65.4	84.7	116.6	128.6	135.2							
7 Transport, storage and communication	17.4	28.6	28.6	30.8	36.6	236.5	254.6	346.5	392.6	396.2	434.2	488.3
8 Finance, insurance, real estate and business services	19.0	25.8	31.8	40.6	45.7							
9 Community, social and personal services												
Total, Industries	211.3	359.2	422.6	425.0	498.2	512.7	547.3	708.7	791.0	850.7	983.1	1128.7
Producers of Government Services	26.6	43.9	55.6	63.9	77.7	106.1	113.0	124.4	122.5	153.5	155.0	163.5
Other Producers	2.2	3.3	5.4	5.8	6.0	8.7	9.5	11.2	11.4	11.4	13.9	14.8
Subtotal	240.1	406.4	483.6	494.7	581.9	627.5	669.8	844.1	924.9	1015.5	1152.0	1307.0
Less: Imputed bank service charge	...	...	...	...	...	...	...	...	...	...	...	...
Plus: Import duties	...	...	...	...	...	...	...	...	...	...	...	...
Plus: Value added tax	...	...	...	...	...	...	...	...	...	...	...	...
Equals: Gross Domestic Product	240.1	406.4	483.6	494.7	581.9	627.5	669.8	844.1	924.9	1015.5	1152.0	1307.0

1.11 Gross Domestic Product by Kind of Activity, in Constant Prices

Thousand Million CFA francs

	1970	1975	1977	1978	1979	1980	1981	1982	1983	1984	1985	1986
				At constant prices of:1977								
1 Agriculture, hunting, forestry and fishing	111.6	124.2	102.5	101.2	120.7	105.2	99.3	123.9	129.9	107.1	115.6	131.3
2 Mining and quarrying												
3 Manufacturing	82.8	87.1	110.1	102.9	114.3	110.9	117.2	134.7	137.8	135.3	138.0	141.9
4 Electricity, gas and water												
5 Construction												
6 Wholesale and retail trade, restaurants and hotels												
7 Transport, storage and communication	163.7	184.9	177.0	185.3	187.3	192.9	184.8	211.1	212.7	207.4	211.5	213.6
8 Finance, insurance, real estate and business services												
9 Community, social and personal services												
Total, Industries	358.1	406.2	422.6	389.4	430.3	409.0	401.3	469.7	480.4	449.8	465.1	486.8
Producers of Government Services	44.0	47.1	55.6	58.4	61.5	65.7	69.2	73.3	76.7	81.2	84.0	87.8
Other Producers	3.8	3.0	5.4	5.6	5.3	6.0	6.5	6.5	6.5	6.5	8.8	8.9
Subtotal	405.9	456.3	483.6	453.4	497.1	480.7	477.0	549.5	563.6	537.5	557.9	583.5
Less: Imputed bank service charge	...	...	...	...	...	...	...	...	...	...	...	...
Plus: Import duties	...	...	...	...	...	...	...	...	...	...	...	...
Plus: Value added tax	...	...	...	...	...	...	...	...	...	...	...	...
Equals: Gross Domestic Product	405.9	456.3	483.6	453.4	497.1	480.7	477.0	549.5	563.6	537.5	557.9	583.5

Senegal

1.12 Relations Among National Accounting Aggregates

Thousand Million CFA francs

	1970	1975	1977	1978	1979	1980	1981	1982	1983	1984	1985	1986
Gross Domestic Product	240.1	406.4	483.6	494.7	581.9	627.5	669.8	844.3	924.9	1015.5	1152.0	1307.0
Plus: Net factor income from the rest of the world	5.1	4.0	16.3	13.2	24.9	24.3	23.4	-11.4	-10.1	-24.6	-36.8	-55.3
Equals: Gross National Product	245.2	410.4	499.9	507.9	606.8	651.8	693.2	832.9	914.8	990.9	1115.2	1251.7
Less: Consumption of fixed capital	...	22.0	28.6	34.2	39.9	41.9	46.8	87.1	107.7	110.7	157.8	179.4
Equals: National Income	...	388.4	471.3	473.7	566.9	609.9	646.4	745.8	807.1	880.2	957.4	1072.3
Plus: Net current transfers from the rest of the world	...	...	...	...	...	...	...	...	...	...	...	...
Equals: National Disposable Income	...	...	...	...	...	...	...	...	...	...	...	...
Less: Final consumption	...	...	...	...	...	...	...	...	...	...	...	...
Equals: Net Saving	...	...	...	...	...	...	...	...	...	...	...	...
Less: Surplus of the nation on current transactions	...	...	...	...	...	...	...	...	...	...	...	...
Equals: Net Capital Formation	...	...	...	...	...	...	...	...	...	...	...	...

Seychelles

Source. Reply to the United Nations National Accounts Questionnaire from the Department of Economic Development Planning and Housing, Unity House.
General note. The estimates shown in the following tables have been prepared in accordance with the United Nations System of National Accounts so far as the existing data would permit.

1.1 Expenditure on the Gross Domestic Product, in Current Prices

Million Seychelles rupees

	1970	1975	1977	1978	1979	1980	1981	1982	1983	1984	1985	1986
1 Government final consumption expenditure	...	...	117.1	149.5	211.4	270.0	308.5 / 308.5	338.0	325.9	327.7	384.1	...
2 Private final consumption expenditure	...	...	198.5	195.3	377.6	416.3	493.7 / 499.2	579.4	650.7	627.0	711.1	...
3 Gross capital formation	...	...	197.3	257.5	265.5	360.9	317.1 / 317.1	313.2	210.4	231.5	273.5	...
A Increase in stocks	...	...	6.8	4.1	8.9	16.7	-12.5 / -12.5	10.3	-9.5	4.6	-	...
B Gross fixed capital formation	...	...	190.5	253.4	256.6	344.2	329.6 / 329.6	302.9	219.9	226.9	273.5	...
Residential buildings	...	...	106.0	147.4	149.9	196.3	205.4 / 205.4	160.0	97.0	132.9	-	...
Non-residential buildings	...	...										...
Other construction and land improvement etc.	...	...	0.3	0.1	0.2	1.0	3.9 / 3.9	4.8	4.6	5.4	...	...
Other	...	...	84.2	87.9	106.5	146.9	120.3 / 120.3	138.0	118.3	85.7	...	...
4 Exports of goods and services	...	...	386.3	488.4	582.5	640.1	554.1 / 467.0	397.4	405.0	507.9	561.8	...
5 Less: Imports of goods and services	...	...	406.2	495.8	630.8	745.4	705.6 / 636.2	686.0	635.3	667.2	767.8	...
Equals: Gross Domestic Product [a]	...	292.0	493.0	594.9	806.2	941.9	971.8 / 955.6	942.0	956.8	1026.9	1162.7	...

a) Beginning 1981, gross national product rather than gross domestic product.

1.2 Expenditure on the Gross Domestic Product, in Constant Prices

Million Seychelles rupees

	1970	1975	1977	1978	1979	1980	1981	1982	1983	1984	1985	1986
					At constant prices of:1976							
1 Government final consumption expenditure	...	...	97.9	120.4	140.7	142.0	145.8	153.3	139.8	134.5	154.5	...
2 Private final consumption expenditure	...	...	206.5	257.7	291.2	277.2	267.8	313.2	342.4	320.8	356.1	...
3 Gross capital formation	...	...	165.3	192.1	184.3	202.7	182.1	216.5	128.4	141.1	163.8	...
A Increase in stocks	...	...	5.6	3.7	5.2	9.3	5.2	6.7	2.9	-3.8	-	...
B Gross fixed capital formation	...	...	159.7	188.4	179.1	193.4	176.9	209.8	125.5	144.9	163.8	...
4 Exports of goods and services	...	...	290.4	310.3	351.7	317.8 / -a	-160.5	-262.8	-204.3	-150.4	-185.9	...
5 Less: Imports of goods and services	...	...	366.6	459.5	477.5	461.8						...
Equals: Gross Domestic Product [b]	...	...	393.5	421.0	490.4	477.9 / -	435.2	420.2	406.3	446.1	488.5	...

a) Including item 'Less: Imports of goods and services'.
b) Beginning 1981, gross national product rather than gross domestic product.

Seychelles

1.3 Cost Components of the Gross Domestic Product

Million Seychelles rupees

	1970	1975	1977	1978	1979	1980	1981	1982	1983	1984	1985	1986
1 Indirect taxes, net	...	...	56.8	79.0	115.5	152.9	167.5	183.1	186.4	190.6	204.6	...
A Indirect taxes	...	...	56.8	79.0	115.5	152.9	167.5	183.1	186.4	...	...	...
B Less: Subsidies	...	...	-	-	-	-	-	-	-	...	...	...
2 Consumption of fixed capital	...	...	26.4	36.5	35.3	45.0	54.2	57.6	59.3	64.3	75.2	...
3 Compensation of employees paid by resident producers to:	...	...	175.5	212.9	289.8	356.9	410.5	402.8	401.8	419.5	447.4	...
4 Operating surplus	...	...	234.3	266.6	365.7	387.1	339.6	324.6	341.9	393.7	477.7	...
Equals: Gross Domestic Product	...	...	493.0	595.0	806.3	941.9	971.8	968.2	989.4	1068.1	1204.9	...

1.7 External Transactions on Current Account, Summary

Million Seychelles rupees

	1970	1975	1977	1978	1979	1980	1981	1982	1983	1984	1985	1986
Payments to the Rest of the World												
1 Imports of goods and services	...	...	406.2	495.8	630.8	745.4	705.6 / 636.2	686.0	635.3	667.2	767.8	752.1
A Imports of merchandise c.i.f.	...	...	349.5	427.3	534.8	631.4	589.0 / 587.5	639.3	592.1	614.7	702.7	661.7
B Other	...	...	56.7	68.5	96.0	114.0	116.6 / 48.7	46.7	43.2	52.5	65.1	90.4
2 Factor income to the rest of the world	...	...	38.7	47.3	72.2	56.3	34.2 / 16.3	26.2	32.6	41.2	42.2	54.3
A Compensation of employees	...	...	...	...	...	...	...	...	...	...	...	...
B Property and entrepreneurial income	...	...	...	...	...	...	16.3	26.2	32.6	41.2	42.2	54.3
3 Current transfers to the rest of the world	...	...	11.3	16.2	20.1	20.9	31.5 / 16.8	21.0	18.8	16.6	5.7	3.2
4 Surplus of the nation on current transactions	...	...	20.0	18.1	-60.7	-58.0	-113.6 / -121.7	-271.8	-185.1	-110.4	-151.8	-215.9
Payments to the Rest of the World and Surplus of the Nation on Current Transactions	...	...	476.2	577.4	662.4	764.6	657.7 / 547.6	461.4	501.6	614.6	663.9	593.7
Receipts From The Rest of the World												
1 Exports of goods and services	...	...	386.3	488.4	582.5	640.1	554.1 / 467.0	397.4	405.0	507.9	561.8	492.1
A Exports of merchandise f.o.b.	...	...	40.6	49.1	43.6	38.3	30.9 / 29.5	25.3	33.9	35.3	33.1	27.9
B Other	...	...	345.7	439.3	538.9	601.8	523.2 / 437.5	372.1	371.1	472.6	528.7	464.2
2 Factor income from rest of the world	...	...	9.1	9.0	15.9	22.2	19.6 / ...	...	...	...	...	...
3 Current transfers from rest of the world	...	...	80.8	80.0	64.0	102.3	84.0 / 80.6	64.0	96.6	106.7	102.7	101.6
Receipts from the Rest of the World on Current Transactions	...	...	476.2	577.4	662.4	764.6	657.7 / 547.6	461.4	501.6	614.6	663.9	593.7

1.10 Gross Domestic Product by Kind of Activity, in Current Prices

Million Seychelles rupees

	1970	1975	1977	1978	1979	1980	1981	1982	1983	1984	1985	1986
1 Agriculture, hunting, forestry and fishing	...	...	45.2	50.0	58.8	64.4	76.5	62.0	76.9	69.0	69.3	...
2 Mining and quarrying	...	...	0.8	1.1	1.2	0.7	0.2	-	-	-	...	...
3 Manufacturing	...	...	26.9	36.4	48.6	69.5	83.2	82.6	95.6	100.3	116.4	...
4 Electricity, gas and water	...	...	4.3	4.9	4.0	2.1	11.3	12.6	14.9	23.4	31.7	...
5 Construction	...	...	36.2	39.7	67.9	75.0	71.8	55.0	42.8	52.8	73.1	...
6 Wholesale and retail trade, restaurants and hotels	...	...	123.7	155.0	218.4	239.1	230.4	221.9	225.6	257.5	298.1	...
7 Transport, storage and communication	...	...	69.4	88.8	104.4	131.5	109.8	108.5	120.3	154.5	169.5	...
8 Finance, insurance, real estate and business services	...	...	64.5	72.7	99.4	117.6	115.9	120.4	111.2	106.3	119.2	...
9 Community, social and personal services [a]	...	...	13.6	15.5	22.2	24.4	22.2	23.2	28.6	28.0	33.3	...

Seychelles

1.10 Gross Domestic Product by Kind of Activity, in Current Prices
(Continued)

Million Seychelles rupees

	1970	1975	1977	1978	1979	1980	1981	1982	1983	1984	1985	1986
Total, Industries	...	...	384.6	464.1	624.9	724.3	721.3	686.2	715.9	791.9	910.6	...
Producers of Government Services	...	...	71.3	82.7	114.6	142.3	171.0	183.4	170.7	173.6	191.8	...
Other Producers [a]	...	...	...	...	...	...	...	...	...	...	...	...
Subtotal	...	...	455.9	546.8	739.5	866.6	892.3	869.6	886.6	965.5	1102.4	...
Less: Imputed bank service charge	...	...	8.3	11.6	20.0	29.8	34.1	29.6	25.8	26.0	31.9	...
Plus: Import duties	...	...	45.4	59.8	86.8	105.1	113.7	128.2	128.6	128.6	134.5	...
Plus: Value added tax	...	...	...	...	...	...	...	...	...	...	...	...
Equals: Gross Domestic Product	...	...	493.0	595.0	806.3	941.9	971.9	968.2	989.4	1068.1	1204.9	...

a) Item 'Other producers' is included in item 'Community, social and personal services'.

1.11 Gross Domestic Product by Kind of Activity, in Constant Prices

Million Seychelles rupees

	1970	1975	1977	1978	1979	1980	1981	1982	1983	1984	1985	1986
At constant prices of: 1976												
1 Agriculture, hunting, forestry and fishing	...	...	32.6	30.2	35.1	35.1	44.9	35.0	37.9	32.4	32.3	...
2 Mining and quarrying	...	...	0.7	0.8	0.9	0.5	0.2	-	-	-	-	...
3 Manufacturing	...	...	24.1	28.3	31.1	39.6	30.9	32.0	36.5	36.9	39.0	...
4 Electricity, gas and water	...	...	2.3	0.6	1.6	-4.0	-5.9	-6.2	-9.5	9.0	12.3	...
5 Construction	...	...	31.5	32.9	48.7	40.7	38.4	27.4	21.3	25.8	31.7	...
6 Wholesale and retail trade, restaurants and hotels	...	...	98.4	109.2	126.8	124.1	112.0	108.5	113.0	119.6	131.1	...
7 Transport, storage and communication	...	...	49.2	53.8	58.1	58.6	49.2	49.0	54.7	64.4	63.0	...
8 Finance, insurance, real estate and business services	...	...	57.1	56.1	68.6	72.1	64.3	68.3	60.9	54.4	64.5	...
9 Community, social and personal services [a]	...	...	12.7	12.0	14.4	12.2	10.2	12.1	10.3	9.1	10.5	...
Total, Industries	...	...	308.6	323.9	385.3	378.9	344.2	326.1	325.1	351.6	384.4	...
Producers of Government Services	...	...	58.4	67.2	76.6	74.9	82.3	84.1	76.0	75.8	79.2	...
Other Producers [a]	...	...	...	...	...	...	...	...	...	...	...	...
Subtotal	...	...	367.0	391.1	461.9	453.8	426.5	410.2	401.1	427.4	463.6	...
Less: Imputed bank service charge	...	...	7.5	10.2	15.0	18.0	18.6	16.3	13.4	13.6	14.0	...
Plus: Import duties	...	...	33.9	40.1	43.5	42.1	37.7	43.1	41.8	46.4	56.0	...
Plus: Value added tax	...	...	...	...	...	...	...	...	...	...	...	...
Equals: Gross Domestic Product	...	...	393.4	421.0	490.4	477.9	445.6	437.0	429.5	460.3	505.6	...

a) Item 'Other producers' is included in item 'Community, social and personal services'.

1.12 Relations Among National Accounting Aggregates

Million Seychelles rupees

	1970	1975	1977	1978	1979	1980	1981	1982	1983	1984	1985	1986
Gross Domestic Product	...	...	493.0	595.0	806.3	941.9	971.8	968.2	989.4	1068.0	1204.9	...
Plus: Net factor income from the rest of the world	...	...	-29.6	-38.3	-56.3	-34.1	16.3	26.2	-32.6	-41.2	-42.2	...
Factor income from the rest of the world	...	...	9.1	9.0	15.9	22.2	...	...	...	...	...	...
Less: Factor income to the rest of the world	...	...	38.7	47.3	72.2	56.3	...	...	...	...	...	...
Equals: Gross National Product	...	...	463.4	556.7	750.0	907.8	955.5	942.0	956.8	1026.8	1162.7	...
Less: Consumption of fixed capital	...	...	26.4	36.5	35.3	45.0	54.2	57.6	59.2	64.3	75.2	...
Equals: National Income	...	...	437.0	520.2	714.7	862.8	901.3	884.4	897.6	962.5	1087.5	...
Plus: Net current transfers from the rest of the world	...	...	69.5	63.8	43.9	81.4	63.8	43.0	77.8	90.1	96.4	...
Current transfers from the rest of the world	...	...	80.8	80.0	64.0	102.3	...	...	...	...	...	...
Less: Current transfers to the rest of the world	...	...	11.3	16.2	20.1	20.9	...	...	...	...	...	...
Equals: National Disposable Income	...	...	506.5	584.0	758.6	944.2	965.1	927.4	975.4	1052.6	1183.9	...
Less: Final consumption	...	...	315.6	344.8	589.0	686.3	807.2	917.4	976.7	954.7	1095.2	...
Equals: Net Saving	...	...	190.9	239.2	169.6	257.9	157.9	10.0	-1.3	97.9	88.7	...
Less: Surplus of the nation on current transactions	...	...	20.0	18.1	-60.7	-58.0	-121.7	-271.8	-185.1	-110.4	-151.8	...
Equals: Net Capital Formation	...	...	170.9	221.1	230.3	315.9	279.6	281.8	183.8	208.3	240.5	...

Seychelles

4.1 Derivation of Value Added by Kind of Activity, in Current Prices

Million Seychelles rupees

	1981 Gross Output	1981 Intermediate Consumption	1981 Value Added	1982 Gross Output	1982 Intermediate Consumption	1982 Value Added	1983 Gross Output	1983 Intermediate Consumption	1983 Value Added	1984 Gross Output	1984 Intermediate Consumption	1984 Value Added
					All Producers							
1 Agriculture, hunting, forestry and fishing	107.9	31.5	76.5	96.2	34.2	62.0	114.6	37.7	76.9	105.7	36.7	69.0
A Agriculture and hunting	62.6	18.0	44.6	57.0	22.0	35.0	70.3	24.5	45.8	68.9	25.8	43.1
B Forestry and logging	1.7	0.5	1.3	1.2	0.3	1.0	2.1	0.6	1.5	2.0	0.6	1.4
C Fishing	43.6	13.0	30.6	38.0	11.9	26.1	42.3	12.7	29.6	34.8	10.4	24.4
2 Mining and quarrying	...	...	...	...	...	...	...	...	...	...	...	...
3 Manufacturing	160.3	76.8	83.5	158.9	76.3	82.6	171.6	76.0	95.6	177.2	76.9	100.3
4 Electricity, gas and water	67.7	56.5	11.3	68.1	55.4	12.6	74.2	59.3	14.9	80.0	56.5	23.4
A Electricity, gas and steam	58.3	50.6	7.7	58.7	49.4	9.3	60.9	49.6	11.3	62.9	46.2	16.7
B Water works and supply	9.4	5.9	3.6	9.4	6.0	3.3	13.3	9.7	3.5	17.1	10.3	6.7
5 Construction	209.3	137.5	71.8	160.0	104.9	55.0	98.0	55.2	42.8	103.5	50.7	52.8
6 Wholesale and retail trade, restaurants and hotels	386.6	156.2	230.4	339.5	117.5	221.9	373.2	147.6	225.6	411.6	154.1	257.5
7 Transport, storage and communication	218.1	108.2	109.9	209.5	101.1	108.4	304.0	183.7	120.3	346.6	192.1	154.5
A Transport and storage	158.9	73.7	85.2	154.6	80.4	74.2	162.3	81.6	80.8	191.3	83.6	107.7
B Communication	59.2	34.5	24.7	54.9	20.7	34.3	141.7	102.1	39.6	155.2	108.5	46.8
8 Finance, insurance, real estate and business services	144.4	28.7	115.7	147.7	27.3	120.4	135.7	24.5	111.2	130.2	24.0	106.3
A Financial institutions	44.9	17.1	27.9	49.5	15.7	33.8	44.6	16.4	28.2	46.7	15.2	31.4
B Insurance	8.8	3.7	5.1	12.0	4.2	7.8	5.7	1.1	4.6	3.2	1.3	1.9
C Real estate and business services	90.7	7.9	82.7	86.2	7.5	78.8	85.4	7.0	78.4	80.3	7.5	73.0
Real estate, except dwellings	16.3	1.6	14.7	12.2	4.1	8.1	15.8	1.6	14.3	14.0	1.4	12.6
Dwellings	61.1	1.9	59.2	58.5	1.8	56.7	58.7	1.7	57.1	55.5	1.7	53.8
9 Community, social and personal services	37.0	14.8	22.2	41.0	17.8	23.2	41.5	12.9	28.6	40.5	12.5	28.0
Total, Industries	1331.5	610.3	721.2	1220.8	534.6	686.2	1312.8	596.9	715.9	1395.3	603.5	791.9
Producers of Government Services	322.8	151.8	171.0	356.0	172.6	183.4	341.9	171.2	170.7	345.2	171.6	173.6
Other Producers	...	...	...	...	...	...	...	...	...	...	...	...
Total	1654.2	762.0	892.2	1576.8	707.2	869.6	1654.7	768.1	886.6	1740.5	775.1	965.5
Less: Imputed bank service charge	...	-34.1	34.1	...	-29.6	29.6	...	-25.8	25.8	...	-26.0	26.0
Import duties	113.7	...	113.7	128.2	...	128.2	128.6	...	128.6	128.6	...	128.6
Value added tax	...	...	...	...	...	...	...	...	...	...	...	...
Total	1768.0	796.1	971.8	1705.0	736.8	968.2	1783.3	793.9	989.4	1869.1	801.1	1068.1

	1985 Gross Output	1985 Intermediate Consumption	1985 Value Added
		All Producers	
1 Agriculture, hunting, forestry and fishing	103.1	33.8	69.3
A Agriculture and hunting	71.3	27.0	44.3
B Forestry and logging	2.1	0.6	1.5
C Fishing	29.7	6.2	23.5
2 Mining and quarrying	...	...	...
3 Manufacturing	203.8	87.4	116.4
4 Electricity, gas and water	89.7	58.0	31.7
A Electricity, gas and steam	73.3	49.5	23.9
B Water works and supply	16.3	8.5	7.8
5 Construction	137.8	64.7	73.1
6 Wholesale and retail trade, restaurants and hotels	505.1	207.0	298.1
7 Transport, storage and communication	382.2	212.7	169.5
A Transport and storage	...	...	...
B Communication	...	...	...
8 Finance, insurance, real estate and business services	148.8	29.6	119.2
A Financial institutions	59.8	16.2	43.6
B Insurance	7.4	2.3	5.1
C Real estate and business services	81.6	11.1	70.5
Real estate, except dwellings	5.8	4.0	1.8

Seychelles

4.1 Derivation of Value Added by Kind of Activity, in Current Prices
(Continued)

Million Seychelles rupees

	1985		
	Gross Output	Intermediate Consumption	Value Added
Dwellings	65.2	1.9	63.3
9 Community, social and personal services	46.4	13.1	33.3
Total, Industries	1616.9	706.3	910.6
Producers of Government Services	390.6	198.9	191.8
Other Producers	...	...	...
Total	2007.5	905.2	1102.4
Less: Imputed bank service charge	...	-31.9	31.9
Import duties	134.5	...	134.5
Value added tax	...	...	...
Total	2142.0	937.1	1205.0

4.2 Derivation of Value Added by Kind of Activity, in Constant Prices

Million Seychelles rupees

	1981			1982			1983			1984		
	Gross Output	Intermediate Consumption	Value Added	Gross Output	Intermediate Consumption	Value Added	Gross Output	Intermediate Consumption	Value Added	Gross Output	Intermediate Consumption	Value Added

At constant prices of:1976

All Producers

1 Agriculture, hunting, forestry and fishing	62.3	17.0	44.9	56.0	20.9	35.1	59.3	21.4	37.9	54.0	21.6	32.4
A Agriculture and hunting	43.4	13.5	29.9	41.2	16.8	24.4	45.4	17.3	28.1	42.1	18.2	23.9
B Forestry and logging	1.9	0.5	1.4	1.3	0.2	1.1	1.0	0.3	0.7	1.3	0.3	1.0
C Fishing	16.7	3.0	13.7	13.4	3.9	9.5	12.9	3.8	9.1	10.6	3.1	7.5
2 Mining and quarrying	0.3	0.1	0.2	-	-	-	-	-	-	-	-	-
3 Manufacturing	68.9	38.0	30.9	71.5	39.6	31.9	75.7	39.2	36.5	76.0	39.2	36.9
4 Electricity, gas and water	23.6	29.4	-6.0	23.5	29.7	-6.2	26.7	36.2	-9.5	31.4	22.4	9.0
A Electricity, gas and steam	17.8	25.8	-8.1	18.7	26.6	-7.9	18.7	30.3	-11.6	21.2	16.2	5.0
B Water works and supply	5.8	3.6	2.1	4.8	3.1	1.7	8.0	5.9	2.1	10.2	6.2	4.0
5 Construction	111.9	73.5	38.4	79.6	52.2	27.4	48.7	27.4	21.3	50.7	24.8	25.8
6 Wholesale and retail trade, restaurants and hotels	193.0	81.0	112.0	179.1	70.5	108.6	196.0	82.9	113.1	211.3	91.6	119.6
7 Transport, storage and communication	137.3	88.2	49.2	130.8	81.8	49.0	160.8	106.2	54.6	175.4	110.9	64.4
A Transport and storage	96.7	61.2	35.6	89.1	57.7	31.5	90.4	55.4	35.0	106.4	62.7	43.7
B Communication	40.6	27.0	13.6	41.7	24.1	17.5	70.4	50.8	19.6	69.0	48.2	20.8
8 Finance, insurance, real estate and business services	80.1	15.7	64.4	83.9	15.6	68.3	73.2	12.4	60.8	67.3	12.8	54.4
A Financial institutions	22.9	9.3	13.6	25.1	8.6	16.5	21.7	8.1	13.6	21.9	8.1	13.8
B Insurance	4.5	2.0	2.5	6.1	2.3	3.8	2.5	0.6	1.9	1.5	0.7	0.8
C Real estate and business services	52.7	4.4	48.3	52.7	4.7	48.0	49.0	3.7	45.3	43.9	4.0	39.8
Real estate, except dwellings	8.4	0.9	7.6	7.6	0.8	6.8	8.2	0.8	7.4	7.1	0.7	6.4
Dwellings	33.6	1.0	32.6	32.5	1.0	31.5	32.6	1.0	31.6	28.9	0.9	28.0
9 Community, social and personal services	8.2	4.5	3.7	6.3	2.0	4.3	7.5	4.1	3.4	16.9	7.8	9.1
Total, Industries	685.3	347.3	338.0	630.7	312.3	318.4	647.9	329.8	318.1	683.0	331.1	351.6
Producers of Government Services	152.0	69.7	82.3	155.5	71.4	84.1	146.8	70.8	76.0	146.3	70.6	75.0
Other Producers	10.0	3.7	6.3	10.7	3.0	7.7	10.8	3.8	7.0	...	...	...
Total	847.3	420.7	426.6	796.9	386.7	410.2	805.5	404.4	401.1	829.3	401.7	427.4
Less: Imputed bank service charge	...	-18.6	18.6	...	-16.3	16.3	...	-13.4	13.4	...	-13.6	13.6
Import duties	37.7	...	37.7	43.1	...	43.1	41.8	...	41.8	46.4	...	46.4
Value added tax	...	...	...	...	...	...	...	...	...	...	...	...
Total	885.0	439.3	445.7	840.0	403.0	437.0	847.3	417.8	429.5	875.7	415.0	460.2

	1985		
	Gross Output	Intermediate Consumption	Value Added

At constant prices of:1976

All Producers

1 Agriculture, hunting, forestry and fishing	53.7	21.4	32.3
A Agriculture and hunting	42.3	18.7	23.6
B Forestry and logging	1.2	0.3	0.9
C Fishing	10.2	2.4	7.9
2 Mining and quarrying	...	...	...

Seychelles

4.2 Derivation of Value Added by Kind of Activity, in Constant Prices
(Continued)

Million Seychelles rupees

		1985 Gross Output	1985 Intermediate Consumption	1985 Value Added
				At constant prices of:1976
3	Manufacturing	85.6	46.6	39.0
4	Electricity, gas and water	35.0	22.7	12.3
	A Electricity, gas and steam	26.3	18.0	8.3
	B Water works and supply	8.7	4.7	4.0
5	Construction	65.8	34.1	31.7
6	Wholesale and retail trade, restaurants and hotels	246.7	115.5	131.1
7	Transport, storage and communication	177.3	114.3	63.0
	A Transport and storage	...	...	...
	B Communication	...	...	...
8	Finance, insurance, real estate and business services	80.4	15.9	64.5
	A Financial institutions	26.2	7.3	18.8
	B Insurance	3.2	1.0	2.2
	C Real estate and business services	51.0	7.6	43.5
	Real estate, except dwellings	2.5	1.8	0.7
	Dwellings	33.5	1.1	32.4
9	Community, social and personal services	15.4	4.9	10.5
	Total, Industries	759.9	375.4	384.4
	Producers of Government Services	164.3	85.1	79.2
	Other Producers	...	...	...
	Total	924.1	460.5	463.6
	Less: Imputed bank service charge	...	-14.0	14.0
	Import duties	56.0	...	56.0
	Value added tax	...	...	...
	Total	980.1	474.5	505.6

4.3 Cost Components of Value Added

Million Seychelles rupees

		1981 Compensation of Employees	1981 Capital Consumption	1981 Net Operating Surplus	1981 Indirect Taxes	1981 Less: Subsidies Received	1981 Value Added	1982 Compensation of Employees	1982 Capital Consumption	1982 Net Operating Surplus	1982 Indirect Taxes	1982 Less: Subsidies Received	1982 Value Added
					All Producers								
1	Agriculture, hunting, forestry and fishing	-	-	74.9	1.5	...	76.5	-	-	60.8	1.2	...	62.0
	A Agriculture and hunting	-	-	43.4	1.2	...	44.6	-	-	34.4	0.6	...	35.0
	B Forestry and logging	-	-	1.3	-	...	1.3	-	-	1.0	-	...	1.0
	C Fishing	-	-	30.3	0.4	...	30.6	-	-	25.4	0.6	...	26.1
2	Mining and quarrying	...	...	...	...	...	...	...	...	...	...	...	...
3	Manufacturing	22.4	8.1	21.1	31.8	...	83.5	24.5	8.5	15.1	34.5	...	82.6
4	Electricity, gas and water	12.9	3.9	-5.5	-	...	11.3	12.2	6.5	-6.2	-	...	12.6
	A Electricity, gas and steam	8.5	3.5	-4.3	-	...	7.7	7.1	5.8	-3.6	-	...	9.3
	B Water works and supply	4.4	0.3	-1.2	-	...	3.6	5.1	0.8	-2.6	-	...	3.3
5	Construction	46.1	3.0	22.7	-	...	71.8	36.1	3.3	15.6	-	...	55.0
6	Wholesale and retail trade, restaurants and hotels	53.7	6.4	151.6	18.6	...	230.4	41.8	7.0	159.3	13.8	...	221.9
	A Wholesale and retail trade	...	...	...	...	...	...	...	...	...	...	...	...
	B Restaurants and hotels	...	...	...	...	...	...	...	...	...	...	...	...
7	Transport, storage and communication	74.3	15.8	17.4	2.4	...	109.9	67.4	14.7	22.6	3.7	...	108.4
	A Transport and storage	57.1	9.3	16.3	2.4	...	85.2	49.2	9.2	12.0	3.7	...	74.2
	B Communication	17.1	6.5	1.1	-	...	24.7	18.1	5.5	10.7	-	...	34.3
8	Finance, insurance, real estate and business services	19.2	16.9	79.0	0.6	...	115.7	20.6	17.4	80.9	1.4	...	120.4
	A Financial institutions	11.0	1.1	15.7	-	...	27.9	13.4	1.9	18.3	0.2	...	33.8
	B Insurance	3.4	0.3	1.4	-	...	5.1	3.5	0.3	4.0	-	...	7.8
	C Real estate and business services	4.9	15.5	61.8	0.5	...	82.7	3.7	15.2	58.6	1.2	...	78.8
	Real estate, except dwellings	-	-	14.7	-	...	14.7	3.7	0.6	2.6	1.2	...	8.1

Seychelles

4.3 Cost Components of Value Added
(Continued)

Million Seychelles rupees

	1981						1982					
	Compensation of Employees	Capital Consumption	Net Operating Surplus	Indirect Taxes	Less: Subsidies Received	Value Added	Compensation of Employees	Capital Consumption	Net Operating Surplus	Indirect Taxes	Less: Subsidies Received	Value Added
Dwellings	-	15.3	43.9	-	...	59.2	-	14.6	42.1	-	...	56.7
9 Community, social and personal services	10.9	-	11.0	0.2	...	22.2	16.9	-	6.1	0.2	...	23.2
Total, Industries	239.6	54.1	372.2	55.3	...	721.2	219.6	57.5	354.2	54.9	...	686.2
Producers of Government Services	170.9	0.1	...	...	...	171.0	183.3	0.1	...	...	...	183.4
Other Producers	...	...	...	...	...	...	...	...	...	...	...	...
Total	410.5	54.0	372.2	55.2	...	892.2	402.9	57.6	354.3	54.8	...	869.6
Less: Imputed bank service charge	...	...	34.1	...	...	34.1	...	...	29.6	...	...	29.6
Import duties	...	...	...	112.2	...	113.7	...	...	...	128.2	...	128.2
Value added tax	...	...	...	...	...	...	...	...	...	...	...	...
Total	410.5	54.2	338.1	167.5	...	971.8	402.9	57.6	324.7	183.1	...	968.2

	1983						1984					
	Compensation of Employees	Capital Consumption	Net Operating Surplus	Indirect Taxes	Less: Subsidies Received	Value Added	Compensation of Employees	Capital Consumption	Net Operating Surplus	Indirect Taxes	Less: Subsidies Received	Value Added
					All Producers							
1 Agriculture, hunting, forestry and fishing	-	-	76.9	0.1	...	76.9	-	-	69.0	-	...	69.0
A Agriculture and hunting	-	-	45.8	-	...	45.8	-	-	43.1	-	...	43.1
B Forestry and logging	-	-	1.5	-	...	1.5	-	-	1.4	-	...	1.4
C Fishing	-	-	29.6	-	...	29.6	-	-	24.4	-	...	24.4
2 Mining and quarrying	...	...	...	...	...	...	...	...	...	...	...	...
3 Manufacturing	27.3	9.6	21.0	37.7	...	95.6	27.2	9.8	21.5	41.8	...	100.3
4 Electricity, gas and water	18.1	6.4	-10.5	1.0	...	14.9	18.4	6.0	-3.5	2.6	...	23.4
A Electricity, gas and steam	9.4	5.9	-4.7	0.7	...	11.3	9.6	5.7	-0.9	2.3	...	16.7
B Water works and supply	8.7	0.4	-5.8	0.3	...	3.5	8.8	0.3	-2.6	0.3	...	6.7
5 Construction	27.1	2.2	13.5	-	...	42.8	30.9	4.7	17.1	-	...	52.8
6 Wholesale and retail trade, restaurants and hotels	50.3	7.4	154.5	13.4	...	225.6	53.1	6.2	186.4	11.8	...	257.5
A Wholesale and retail trade	-	7.4	154.4	2.6	...	164.4	-	6.2	160.8	2.7	...	169.7
B Restaurants and hotels	50.3	-	-0.1	10.8	...	61.0	53.1	-	25.5	9.1	...	87.7
7 Transport, storage and communication	65.8	14.5	36.8	3.3	...	120.3	69.9	17.8	63.0	3.8	...	154.5
A Transport and storage	44.7	8.2	26.9	0.9	...	80.8	52.1	8.1	45.7	1.8	...	107.7
B Communication	21.1	6.2	9.8	2.4	...	39.6	17.8	9.8	17.2	2.0	...	46.8
8 Finance, insurance, real estate and business services	21.3	18.2	69.8	1.9	...	111.2	23.4	18.1	63.1	1.8	...	106.3
A Financial institutions	15.2	1.6	11.4	-	...	28.2	16.7	2.0	12.7	-	...	31.4
B Insurance	1.4	0.1	1.2	1.8	...	4.6	1.9	0.2	-1.9	1.8	...	1.9
C Real estate and business services	4.7	16.4	57.2	0.1	...	78.4	4.7	15.9	52.3	0.1	...	73.0
Real estate, except dwellings	-	-	14.3	-	...	14.3	-	-	12.6	-	...	12.6
Dwellings	-	15.6	41.5	-	...	57.1	-	15.0	38.8	-	...	53.9
9 Community, social and personal services	21.5	0.8	5.8	0.5	...	28.6	23.1	1.5	3.1	0.3	...	28.0
Total, Industries	231.2	59.2	367.7	57.8	...	715.9	246.0	64.2	419.7	62.0	...	791.9
Producers of Government Services	170.6	0.1	...	...	...	170.7	173.5	0.1	...	...	...	173.6
Other Producers	...	...	...	...	...	...	...	...	...	...	...	...
Total	401.9	59.1	367.7	57.9	...	886.5	419.5	64.3	419.7	62.0	...	965.5
Less: Imputed bank service charge	...	...	25.8	...	...	25.8	...	...	26.0	...	...	26.0
Import duties	...	...	...	128.6	...	128.6	...	...	...	128.6	...	128.6
Value added tax	...	...	...	...	...	...	...	...	...	...	...	...
Total	401.8	59.3	341.9	186.4	...	989.4	419.5	64.3	393.7	190.6	...	1000.1

	1985					
	Compensation of Employees	Capital Consumption	Net Operating Surplus	Indirect Taxes	Less: Subsidies Received	Value Added
			All Producers			
1 Agriculture, hunting, forestry and fishing	0.8	-	68.5	-	...	69.3
A Agriculture and hunting	-	-	44.3	-	...	44.3
B Forestry and logging	-	-	1.5	-	...	1.5
C Fishing	0.8	-	22.6	-	...	23.5

Seychelles

4.3 Cost Components of Value Added
(Continued)

Million Seychelles rupees

		1985					
		Compensation of Employees	Capital Consumption	Net Operating Surplus	Indirect Taxes	Less: Subsidies Received	Value Added
2	Mining and quarrying	...	...	...	...	...	...
3	Manufacturing	29.4	9.8	28.3	48.9	...	116.4
4	Electricity, gas and water	16.4	6.4	6.3	2.6	...	31.7
	A Electricity, gas and steam	9.8	6.3	5.2	2.6	...	23.9
	B Water works and supply	6.6	0.1	1.2	-	...	7.8
5	Construction	26.5	10.2	36.4	-	...	73.1
6	Wholesale and retail trade, restaurants and hotels	66.3	6.5	212.7	12.6	-	298.1
	A Wholesale and retail trade	...	...	...	...	...	...
	B Restaurants and hotels	...	...	...	...	...	...
7	Transport, storage and communication	70.3	21.2	74.8	3.3	-	169.5
	A Transport and storage	...	...	...	...	...	...
	B Communication	...	...	...	...	...	...
8	Finance, insurance, real estate and business services	23.2	19.7	74.4	2.0	...	119.2
	A Financial institutions	16.1	2.2	25.3	-	...	43.6
	B Insurance	1.9	0.1	1.1	1.9	...	5.1
	C Real estate and business services	5.2	17.3	48.0	0.1	...	70.5
	Real estate, except dwellings	0.8	0.7	0.1	-	...	1.8
	Dwellings	-	16.3	47.0	-	...	63.3
9	Community, social and personal services	22.8	1.3	8.3	0.8	...	33.3
Total, Industries		255.7	75.1	509.6	70.2	...	910.6
Producers of Government Services		191.7	0.1	-	-	...	191.8
Other Producers		...	...	...	...	...	...
Total		447.4	75.2	509.6	70.2	...	1102.4
Less: Imputed bank service charge		...	...	31.9	...	...	31.9
Import duties		...	...	...	134.5	...	134.5
Value added tax		...	...	...	...	...	...
Total		447.4	75.2	477.7	204.6	...	1204.9

Sierra Leone

General note. The preparation of national accounts statistics in Sierra Leone is undertaken by the Central Statistics Office, Freetown. Official estimates together with methodological notes are published in a series of reports entitled 'National Accounts of Sierra Leone'. The most detailed description of the sources and methods used for the national accounts estimation is found in the sixteenth edition of this report published in December 1987. The estimates are generally in accordance with the classifications and definitions recommended in the United Nations System of National Accounts (SNA). New and revised estimates for the years 1970/71 to 1975/76 were published in 1977, incorporating results of the 1974 population census and the Njala University survey on small-scale manufacturing in 1974. The following tables have been prepared from successive replies to the United Nations national accounts questionnaire. Estimates prior to 1967 relate to fiscal year beginning 1 April while estimates from 1966 relate to fiscal year beginning 1 July. When the scope and coverage of the estimates differ for conceptual or statistical reasons from the definitions and classifications recommended in SNA, a footnote is indicated to the relevant tables.

Sources and methods:

(a) **Gross domestic product.** Gross domestic product is estimated mainly through the income approach.

(b) **Expenditure on the gross domestic product.** The expenditure approach is used for the estimation of government final consumption expenditure and exports and imports of goods and services. A combination of the commodity-flow method and the expenditure approach is used to estimate private final consumption expenditure. The commodity-flow method is used to obtain estimates of gross capital formation. The actual expenditures incurred by the government are obtained from the government budget documents. The expenditure is classified by purpose, distinguishing between military and civilian purposes. Private final consumption expenditure estimates are compiled mainly by tracing the consumption goods through the distributive system to the ultimate consumer. Estimates for a few items of food and services are, however, prepared from data collected through the household expenditure survey and the report of the survey of business and industry. The figures on changes in stocks relate principally to diamonds, iron ore, bauxite, rice, export crops, stocks of all public companies, and all major manufacturing and trading establishments for which the completed questionnaires are received by the Central Statistics Office. The estimates of gross fixed capital formation are obtained through an analysis of production and imports of all capital goods classified by type and then marked up for distributive costs. Exports and imports of goods and services are estimated mainly from external trade statistics. GDP by expenditure type at constant prices is not estimated.

(c) **Cost-structure of the gross domestic product.** Estimates of domestic factor income are compiled from returns directly obtained from the companies concerned and then marked up for non-responding establishments. Analysis of indirect taxes and subsidies by industry was undertaken for the first time in 1976 to arrive at GDP by economic activity in producers' values. Information on depreciation is available only for some larger establishments.

(d) **Gross domestic product by kind of economic activity.** The table of gross domestic product by kind of economic activity is prepared at market prices, i.e. producers' values. Value added of the majority of industries is estimated through the income approach. The production approach is used to estimate the agricultural and mining sectors. Fairly reliable information on production of major agricultural crops is available only for 1970-71 and 1984-85 based on objective samples surveys. For other years the Ministry of Agriculture and Natural Resources estimate the production of these crops on the basis of reports received from their regional office. For other crops the main source is the Production Yearbook of the Food and Agriculture Organisation. The data required to estimate the value added of mining are obtained from the companies concerned while the value of diamonds smuggled out of the country is based on informal discussions with knowledgeable persons in the industry. The estimates of total income, wages and salaries, operating profits, etc. of a large sample of manufacturing establishments employing six or more persons are compiled from returns directly obtained from them, and then marked up for non-responding establishments using employment data as mark-up factors. The census of manufacturing establishments 1986-87 provided valuable data to strengthen the estimates for 1984 and 1985. The Njala University survey in 1974/75 was used to confirm estimates made for small-scale manufacturing which are based on employment projections and statistics of earnings. The commodity-flow method is used to estimate gross output and intermediate consumption of construction. Data from the government public works department and a number of private contractors are used for analysis of total construction expenditure. The commodity-flow method is also used for the trade sector, preparing aggregate trade margin estimates of all commodities marketed. Receipts and expenditure data are collected directly for national accounting purposes from a sample of trading establishments. For smaller trade establishments, estimates are obtained as a product of the number of persons engaged which is based on the 1974 census, and average earnings per person obtained from a bench-mark year and adjusted yearly. Transportation surveys and other data sources are used for bench-mark estimates in the transport sector. For the services sector, the imputed banking service charge is treated as a negative operating surplus of a nominal finance industry and deducted as a lump sum separately. The number of persons engaged in domestic services, obtained from the 1974 population census has been assumed to continue to grow at the average rate as indicated by the two censuses in 1963 and 1974. Government budgetary documents and unpublished records are used to obtain estimates for central government and local authorities. For the constant price estimates, double deflation is used for the agricultural components with current quantities valued at base-year prices of 1963/64 and 1972/73. Index of building costs is used for price deflation in the construction sector. For other industries, value added is extrapolated by quantity indexes of output obtained by price deflation or employment data. No single typical approach is used for mining and quarrying.

1.1 Expenditure on the Gross Domestic Product, in Current Prices

Million Sierra Leone leones — Fiscal year beginning 1 July

		1970	1975	1977	1978	1979	1980	1981	1982	1983	1984	1985	1986
1	Government final consumption expenditure	31.5	59.0	76.8	95.5	97.3	90.1	137.6	166.6	189.2	245.4	297.6	...
2	Private final consumption expenditure	267.8	528.9	719.3	879.8	1048.3	1171.5	1415.5	1647.3	2242.1	3615.7	5445.8	...
3	Gross capital formation	53.3	74.5	96.1	138.1	187.3	246.7	214.7	267.9	346.8	488.0	702.8	...
	A Increase in stocks	5.9	-2.3	-3.6	10.1	15.7	10.5	9.6	32.6	15.0	52.6	109.3	...
	B Gross fixed capital formation	47.4	76.8	99.7	128.0	171.6	236.2	205.1	235.3	331.8	435.4	593.5	...
	Residential buildings	...	...	...	...	...	...	...	...	...	...	...	...
	Non-residential buildings	24.8	47.5	62.6	62.8	109.2	131.3	128.2	124.9	188.1	290.9	373.1	...
	Other construction and land improvement etc.												...
	Other	22.6	29.3	37.1	65.2	62.4	104.9	76.9	110.4	143.7	144.5	220.4	...
4	Exports of goods and services a	109.0	142.6	199.4	233.4	264.2	297.4	252.9	207.7	200.0	400.0	855.0	...
5	Less: Imports of goods and services	113.0	191.5	241.5	317.6	441.6	513.5	416.1	413.4	338.6	502.5	948.5	...
	Equals: Gross Domestic Product	348.6	613.5	850.1	1029.2	1155.5	1292.2	1604.5	1876.1	2729.5	4309.8	6352.7	...

a) The estimates of exports of goods and services shown in table 1.1 differ from those shown in the other tables. These estimates include an upward adjustments for the estimated value of diamond smuggled out of the country.

1.3 Cost Components of the Gross Domestic Product

Million Sierra Leone leones — Fiscal year beginning 1 July

		1970	1975	1977	1978	1979	1980	1981	1982	1983	1984	1985	1986
1	Indirect taxes, net	32.0	54.9	99.8	96.7	92.6	118.6	100.5	76.9	104.8	138.5	219.7	...
	A Indirect taxes	33.8	56.0	99.8	97.1	92.7	118.6	100.7	77.3	105.6	139.4	223.4	...
	B Less: Subsidies	1.8	1.1	-	0.4	0.1	-	0.2	0.4	0.8	0.9	3.7	...
2	Consumption of fixed capital	30.9	49.3	69.1	81.2	102.9	124.0	152.5	182.6	280.1	410.2	511.4	...
3	Compensation of employees paid by resident producers to:	89.2	156.8	215.0	253.5	294.9	345.4	409.5	489.0	710.5	975.9	1364.5	...
4	Operating surplus	196.4	352.5	466.2	597.7	665.1	704.2	942.0	1127.6	1634.1	2785.2	4257.1	...
	Equals: Gross Domestic Product	348.6	613.5	850.1	1029.2	1155.5	1292.2	1604.5	1876.1	2729.5	4309.8	6352.7	...

Sierra Leone

1.7 External Transactions on Current Account, Summary

Million Sierra Leone leones — Fiscal year beginning 1 July

	1970	1975	1977	1978	1979	1980	1981	1982	1983	1984	1985	1986
Payments to the Rest of the World												
1 Imports of goods and services	113.0	191.5	241.5	317.6	441.6	513.5	416.1	413.4	338.6	502.5	948.5	...
A Imports of merchandise c.i.f.	96.9	167.6	208.5	290.8	388.6	447.5	360.4	368.5	286.9	418.3	781.6	...
B Other	16.1	23.9	33.0	26.8	53.0	66.0	55.7	44.9	51.7	84.2	166.9	...
2 Factor income to the rest of the world	9.2	13.8	19.2	41.2	44.9	23.7	43.4	43.6	40.0	81.8	-59.2	...
A Compensation of employees	...	...	...	...	...	...	...	...	...	...	...	...
B Property and entrepreneurial income	9.2	13.8	19.2	41.2	44.9	23.7	43.4	43.6	40.0	81.8	-59.2	...
3 Current transfers to the rest of the world	1.5	2.0	2.3	2.5	2.9	4.3	1.2	4.9	4.7	3.8	7.2	...
4 Surplus of the nation on current transactions	-14.9	-57.3	-43.8	-112.2	-195.5	-191.4	-165.3	-198.7	-33.1	-57.1	38.1	...
Payments to the Rest of the World and Surplus of the Nation on Current Transactions	108.8	150.0	219.2	249.1	293.9	350.1	295.4	263.2	350.2	531.0	934.6	...
Receipts From The Rest of the World												
1 Exports of goods and services	100.4	134.6	191.4	225.4	256.2	289.4	242.8	195.7	276.0	443.2	825.0	...
A Exports of merchandise f.o.b.	84.3	116.6	163.5	193.8	208.4	224.1	176.9	136.6	201.8	333.0	671.7	...
B Other	16.1	18.0	27.9	31.6	47.8	65.3	65.9	59.1	74.2	110.2	153.3	...
2 Factor income from rest of the world	2.6	4.0	2.2	0.5	0.4	0.8	0.7	0.2	0.5	0.6	1.3	...
A Compensation of employees	...	...	...	...	...	...	...	...	...	...	...	...
B Property and entrepreneurial income	2.6	4.0	2.2	0.5	0.4	0.8	0.7	0.2	0.5	0.5	1.3	...
3 Current transfers from rest of the world	5.8	11.4	25.6	23.2	37.3	59.9	51.9	67.3	73.7	87.2	108.3	...
Receipts from the Rest of the World on Current Transactions	108.8	150.0	219.2	249.1	293.9	350.1	295.4	263.2	350.2	531.0	934.6	...

1.10 Gross Domestic Product by Kind of Activity, in Current Prices

Million Sierra Leone leones — Fiscal year beginning 1 July

	1970	1975	1977	1978	1979	1980	1981	1982	1983	1984	1985	1986
1 Agriculture, hunting, forestry and fishing	96.5	220.0	303.8	342.4	369.0	399.4	552.3	690.7	1062.1	1873.0	2777.4	...
2 Mining and quarrying	57.5	63.4	75.8	119.3	128.1	121.8	95.2	101.4	140.5	275.8	787.2	...
3 Manufacturing	29.8	46.3	64.3	80.7	83.8	93.7	142.7	144.8	181.9	255.2	312.0	...
4 Electricity, gas and water	2.4	4.6	5.1	4.7	4.2	7.3	8.0	10.9	14.4	16.7	20.1	...
5 Construction	13.2	17.5	24.4	28.6	46.4	56.0	54.8	47.5	71.0	87.0	112.0	...
6 Wholesale and retail trade, restaurants and hotels	43.1	69.4	117.3	145.3	153.3	162.7	173.0	233.0	295.0	540.5	803.7	...
7 Transport, storage and communication	33.9	65.0	84.6	107.9	160.0	197.3	286.9	324.0	468.9	547.1	601.3	...
8 Finance, insurance, real estate and business services	26.4	47.3	59.7	67.5	80.2	96.7	126.0	146.9	269.7	465.5	604.0	...
9 Community, social and personal services [a]	8.7	17.3	20.8	24.8	25.2	32.9	64.0	73.9	98.1	142.6	200.9	...
Total, Industries	311.5	550.8	755.8	921.2	1050.2	1167.8	1502.9	1773.1	2601.9	4203.4	6218.6	...
Producers of Government Services	19.8	39.8	51.3	62.2	67.0	79.5	90.8	102.9	121.9	129.6	172.6	...
Other Producers [a]	1.4	2.0	2.2	2.5	2.5	2.5	...	...	...	...	...	...
Subtotal	332.7	592.6	809.3	985.9	1119.7	1249.8	1593.7	1876.0	2723.5	4333.0	6391.2	...
Less: Imputed bank service charge	3.3	8.3	7.3	6.7	6.9	6.4	29.5	31.9	39.0	85.0	140.0	...
Plus: Import duties	19.2	29.2	48.0	50.0	42.7	48.8	40.3	32.0	45.0	61.8	101.5	...
Plus: Value added tax	...	...	...	...	...	...	...	...	...	...	...	...
Equals: Gross Domestic Product	348.6	613.5	850.0	1029.2	1155.5	1292.2	1604.5	1876.1	2729.5	4309.8	6352.7	...

a) Beginning 1981, item 'Other producers' is included in item 'Community, social and personal services'.

1.11 Gross Domestic Product by Kind of Activity, in Constant Prices

Million Sierra Leone leones — Fiscal year beginning 1 July

	1970	1975	1977	1978	1979	1980	1981	1982	1983	1984	1985	1986
At constant prices of: 1972												
1 Agriculture, hunting, forestry and fishing	109.7	120.9	129.8	141.8	137.6	138.7	146.0	140.0	142.9	154.6	152.9	...
2 Mining and quarrying	70.0	51.7	27.4	29.1	33.2	26.2	22.3	19.9	22.6	19.1	26.0	...
3 Manufacturing	28.5	39.2	38.5	41.3	39.0	41.9	50.4	41.5	44.5	44.5	37.8	...
4 Electricity, gas and water	1.3	1.6	1.7	1.8	1.8	1.9	2.5	2.5	2.5	2.8	3.1	...
5 Construction	13.3	12.6	14.0	14.5	18.4	21.9	17.3	13.4	16.1	12.6	9.5	...

Sierra Leone

1.11 Gross Domestic Product by Kind of Activity, in Constant Prices
(Continued)

Million Sierra Leone leones — Fiscal year beginning 1 July

	1970	1975	1977	1978	1979	1980	1981	1982	1983	1984	1985	1986
					At constant prices of:1972							
6 Wholesale and retail trade, restaurants and hotels	47.3	45.7	54.5	52.1	53.0	64.7	65.2	74.4	61.5	57.5	56.7	...
7 Transport, storage and communication	34.8	40.5	42.4	47.2	51.5	50.3	59.5	58.8	60.4	52.6	39.9	...
8 Finance, insurance, real estate and business services	27.1	33.2	35.3	35.6	39.4	41.2	46.0	47.1	49.0	49.1	50.2	...
9 Community, social and personal services [a]	8.8	13.0	12.5	12.8	13.4	16.7	24.2	26.1	29.6	30.9	32.6	...
Total, Industries	340.8	358.4	356.1	376.2	387.3	403.5	433.4	423.7	429.1	423.7	408.7	...
Producers of Government Services	20.8	33.1	42.8	47.1	48.6	50.3	57.5	65.1	63.2	65.0	68.0	...
Other Producers [a]	1.4	1.7	1.8	1.8	1.8	1.8	...	...	...	...	...	...
Subtotal	363.0	393.2	400.7	425.1	437.7	455.6	490.9	488.8	492.3	488.7	476.7	...
Less: Imputed bank service charge	3.5	5.4	3.8	3.1	2.7	2.2	14.0	15.0	18.0	24.0	30.0	...
Plus: Import duties	26.2	20.8	18.9	24.7	25.1	35.2	20.0	16.0	22.0	18.0	19.0	...
Plus: Value added tax	...	...	...	...	...	...	...	...	...	...	...	...
Equals: Gross Domestic Product	385.7	408.6	415.8	446.7	460.1	488.6	496.9	489.8	496.3	482.7	465.7	...

a) Beginning 1981, item 'Other producers' is included in item 'Community, social and personal services'.

1.12 Relations Among National Accounting Aggregates

Million Sierra Leone leones — Fiscal year beginning 1 July

	1970	1975	1977	1978	1979	1980	1981	1982	1983	1984	1985	1986
Gross Domestic Product	348.6	613.5	850.1	1029.2	1155.5	1292.2	1604.5	1876.1	2729.5	4309.8	6352.7	...
Plus: Net factor income from the rest of the world	-6.6	-9.8	-17.0	-40.7	-44.5	-22.9	-42.7	-43.4	-39.5	-81.2	60.5	...
Factor income from the rest of the world	2.6	4.0	2.2	0.5	0.4	0.8	0.7	0.2	0.5	0.6	1.3	...
Less: Factor income to the rest of the world	9.2	13.8	19.2	41.2	44.9	23.7	43.4	43.6	40.0	81.8	-59.2	...
Equals: Gross National Product	342.0	603.7	833.0	988.5	1111.0	1269.3	1561.8	1832.7	2690.0	4228.6	6413.2	...
Less: Consumption of fixed capital	30.9	49.3	69.1	81.2	102.9	124.0	152.5	182.6	280.1	410.2	511.4	...
Equals: National Income	311.1	554.4	763.9	907.3	1008.1	1145.3	1409.3	1650.1	2409.9	3818.4	5901.8	...
Plus: Net current transfers from the rest of the world	4.3	9.4	23.3	20.7	34.4	55.6	50.7	62.4	69.0	83.4	101.1	...
Current transfers from the rest of the world	5.8	11.4	25.6	23.2	37.3	59.9	51.9	67.3	73.7	87.2	108.3	...
Less: Current transfers to the rest of the world	1.5	2.0	2.3	2.5	2.9	4.3	1.2	4.9	4.7	3.8	7.2	...
Equals: National Disposable Income	318.5	563.8	787.3	928.0	1042.5	1200.9	1460.0	1712.5	2478.9	3901.8	6002.9	...
Less: Final consumption	299.2	587.9	796.1	975.4	1145.6	1261.6	1553.1	1813.9	2431.3	3861.1	5743.4	...
Equals: Net Saving	19.3	-24.1	-8.8	-47.4	-103.1	-60.7	-93.1	-101.4	47.6	40.7	259.5	...
Less: Surplus of the nation on current transactions	-14.9	-57.3	-43.8	-112.2	-195.5	-191.4	-165.3	-198.7	-33.1	-57.1	38.1	...
Statistical discrepancy	-11.8	-8.0	-8.0	7.9	8.0	8.0	-10.0	-12.0	-14.0	-20.0	-30.0	...
Equals: Net Capital Formation	22.4	25.2	27.0	56.9	84.4	122.7	62.2	85.3	66.7	77.8	191.4	...

2.1 Government Final Consumption Expenditure by Function, in Current Prices

Million Sierra Leone leones — Fiscal year beginning 1 July

	1970	1975	1977	1978	1979	1980	1981	1982	1983	1984	1985	1986
1 General public services	9.85	22.98	34.41	44.31	102.41	43.40	49.07	43.38	55.13	56.34	136.33	...
2 Defence	3.41	9.00	11.09	16.55	11.73	13.88	18.32	18.02	19.72	21.60	35.16	...
3 Public order and safety	...	...	...	...	...	...	...	...	...	...	...	...
4 Education	10.23	23.84	29.97	32.61	38.10	47.22	72.28	58.49	73.69	74.68	90.91	...
5 Health	4.07	8.49	13.56	15.99	18.51	26.38	27.72	22.08	33.78	28.43	38.72	...
6 Social security and welfare	0.15	3.10	1.60	2.89	2.15	1.98	2.26	2.00	4.57	2.61	3.34	...
7 Housing and community amenities	1.19	4.99	6.30	6.56	6.26	4.37	7.43	3.92	4.87	3.30	7.05	...
8 Recreational, cultural and religious affairs	-	-	-	-	-	-	-	-	-	4.27	5.00	...
9 Economic services	17.89	49.57	45.36	67.30	97.47	123.02	110.50	138.51	120.51	146.74	348.09	...
10 Other functions	7.47	24.72	39.49	55.53	68.40	144.53	94.56	57.29	58.12	151.26	235.05	...
Total Government Final Consumption Expenditure [a,b]	54.26	146.69	182.58	241.74	345.03	404.78	382.14	343.69	370.39	489.23	899.65	...

a) Item 'Total government final consumption expenditure' includes development expenditure.
b) Only central government data are included in the general government estimates.

Sierra Leone

2.5 Private Final Consumption Expenditure by Type and Porpose, in Current Prices

Million Sierra Leone leones — Fiscal year beginning 1 July

	1970	1975	1977	1978	1979	1980	1981	1982	1983	1984	1985	1986
Final Consumption Expenditure of Resident Households												
1 Food, beverages and tobacco	143.5	301.1	409.4	...	...	...	695.8	912.3	1242.2	2172.9	3504.6	...
2 Clothing and footwear	37.7	66.5	95.8	...	...	...	126.9	121.2	144.6	179.7	190.1	...
3 Gross rent, fuel and power	27.3	47.2	54.8	...	...	...	143.5	177.8	298.9	585.6	821.6	...
4 Furniture, furnishings and household equipment and operation	23.0	36.8	59.6	...	...	...	90.4	106.0	107.2	130.9	170.3	...
5 Medical care and health expenses	3.5	5.7	9.6	...	...	...	15.6	20.6	35.2	56.8	85.8	...
6 Transport and communication	21.1	49.9	68.0	...	...	...	208.5	236.5	340.0	387.3	420.2	...
7 Recreational, entertainment, education and cultural services	10.1	23.4	28.5	...	...	...	49.7	52.5	71.6	99.0	121.3	...
8 Miscellaneous goods and services	5.4	8.1	12.8	...	...	...	24.6	23.6	27.0	39.0	53.6	...
Statistical discrepancy	-3.4	-11.2	-23.2				...	...	...	...	...	
Total Final Consumption Expenditure in the Domestic Market by Households, of which	268.2	527.5	715.3				1355.0	1650.5	2266.7	3651.2	5367.5	
Plus: Direct purchases abroad by resident households	2.8	4.8	6.8				4.0	6.2	6.8	8.1	10.8	
Less: Direct purchases in the domestic market by non-resident households	3.3	3.4	2.8				6.0	6.5	9.9	11.0	21.1	
Equals: Final Consumption Expenditure of Resident Households [a]	267.7	528.9	719.3				1353.0	1650.2	2263.6	3648.3	5357.2	
Final Consumption Expenditure of Private Non-profit Institutions Serving Households												
Equals: Final Consumption Expenditure of Private Non-profit Organisations Serving Households	...	...	...	...	...	...	...	...	...	...	...	...
Statistical discrepancy	...	...	...	...	...	...	62.5	-2.9	-21.5	-32.6	88.6	...
Private Final Consumption Expenditure	267.7	528.9	719.3	...	...	...	1415.5	1647.3	2242.1	3615.7	5445.8	...

a) Item 'Final consumption expenditure of resident households' includes consumption expenditure of private non-profit institutions serving households.

2.6 Private Final Consumption Expenditure by Type and Purpose, in Constant Prices

Million Sierra Leone leones — Fiscal year beginning 1 July

	1970	1975	1977	1978	1979	1980	1981	1982	1983	1984	1985	1986
	At constant prices of: 1963							1972				
Final Consumption Expenditure of Resident Households												
1 Food, beverages and tobacco	107.6	...	...	...	...	...	214.3	213.4	203.6	197.4	185.8	...
A Food	98.3	...	...	...	...	...	...	...	...	...	...	...
B Non-alcoholic beverages	5.0	...	...	...	...	...	...	...	...	...	...	...
C Alcoholic beverages		...	...	...	...	...	...	...	...	...	...	...
D Tobacco	4.3	...	...	...	...	...	...	...	...	...	...	...
2 Clothing and footwear	35.3	...	...	...	...	...	43.6	40.8	40.2	39.8	38.0	...
3 Gross rent, fuel and power	23.1	...	...	...	...	...	53.5	55.7	54.8	56.4	52.6	...
4 Furniture, furnishings and household equipment and operation	23.8	...	...	...	...	...	29.6	30.4	29.2	18.6	19.0	...
A Household operation	8.1	...	...	...	...	...	...	...	...	...	...	...
B Other	15.7	...	...	...	...	...	...	...	...	...	...	...
5 Medical care and health expenses	2.9	...	...	...	...	...	4.8	4.5	4.4	8.0	9.0	...
6 Transport and communication	25.8	...	...	...	...	...	29.9	27.5	27.7	28.5	21.9	...
A Personal transport equipment	3.4	...	...	...	...	...	...	...	...	...	...	...

Sierra Leone

2.6 Private Final Consumption Expenditure by Type and Purpose, in Constant Prices
(Continued)

Million Sierra Leone leones — Fiscal year beginning 1 July

	1970	1975	1977	1978	1979	1980	1981	1982	1983	1984	1985	1986
				At constant prices of: 1963					1972			
B Other	22.4	...	...	...	...	...	...	...	...	...	...	...
7 Recreational, entertainment, education and cultural services	11.3	...	...	...	...	...	19.2	18.2	23.1	28.6	30.7	...
A Education	7.2	...	...	...	...	...	...	...	...	...	...	...
B Other	4.1	...	...	...	...	...	...	...	...	...	...	...
8 Miscellaneous goods and services	5.4	...	...	...	...	...	6.8	6.5	6.6	4.3	4.5	...
A Personal care	2.0	...	...	...	...	...	...	...	...	...	...	...
B Expenditures in restaurants, cafes and hotels	...	...	...	...	...	...	...	...	...	...	...	...
C Other	3.4	...	...	...	...	...	...	...	...	...	...	...
Total Final Consumption Expenditure in the Domestic Market by Households, of which	235.2	...	...	...	...	...	400.7	397.0	389.6	381.6	361.5	...
Plus: Direct purchases abroad by resident households	2.2	...	...	...	...	...	0.9	1.4	1.1	1.4	0.9	...
Less: Direct purchases in the domestic market by non-resident households	3.7	...	...	...	...	...	1.4	1.5	1.6	2.0	1.8	...
Equals: Final Consumption Expenditure of Resident Households [a]	233.7	...	...	...	...	...	400.2	396.9	389.1	381.0	360.6	...

Final Consumption Expenditure of Private Non-profit Institutions Serving Households

	1970	1975	1977	1978	1979	1980	1981	1982	1983	1984	1985	1986
Equals: Final Consumption Expenditure of Private Non-profit Organisations Serving Households	...	...	...	...	...	...	...	...	...	...	...	...
Statistical discrepancy	...	...	...	...	...	...	18.5	-0.8	-3.8	-3.5	6.4	...
Private Final Consumption Expenditure	233.7	...	...	...	...	...	418.7	396.1	385.3	377.5	367.0	...

a) Item 'Final consumption expenditure of resident households' includes consumption expenditure of private non-profit institutions serving households.

2.7 Gross Capital Formation by Type of Good and Owner, in Current Prices

Million Sierra Leone leones — Fiscal year beginning 1 July

	1980 TOTAL	1980 Total Private	1980 Public Enterprises	1980 General Government	1981 TOTAL	1981 Total Private	1981 Public Enterprises	1981 General Government	1982 TOTAL	1982 Total Private	1982 Public Enterprises	1982 General Government
Increase in stocks, total	10.5	2.5	8.0	...	9.6	19.6	-10.0	...	32.6	23.2	9.4	...
Gross Fixed Capital Formation, total	236.2	147.2	35.2	53.8	205.1	124.4	20.2	60.5	235.3	164.9	12.6	57.8
1 Residential buildings												
2 Non-residential buildings	120.5	75.8	10.0	34.7	114.1	61.5	13.4	39.2	110.0	67.7	4.8	37.5
3 Other construction												
4 Land improvement and plantation and orchard development	10.8	-	-	10.8	14.1	-	-	14.1	14.9	-	-	14.9
5 Producers' durable goods	104.9	71.4	25.2	8.3	76.9	62.0	6.0	7.2	110.4	97.2	7.8	5.4
A Transport equipment	48.7	39.9	1.8	7.0	41.6	33.7	2.7	5.2	48.1	40.3	3.9	3.9
Passenger cars	23.0	...	...	...	19.4	...	...	...	18.7	...	...	...
Other	25.7	...	...	...	22.2	...	...	...	29.4	...	...	...
B Machinery and equipment	56.2	31.5	23.4	1.3	35.3	29.2	4.1	2.0	62.3	56.9	3.9	1.5
6 Breeding stock, dairy cattle, etc.	...	...	...	...	...	...	...	...	...	...	...	...
Total Gross Capital Formation	246.7	149.7	43.2	53.8	214.7	144.0	10.2	60.5	267.9	188.1	22.0	57.8

Sierra Leone

2.7 Gross Capital Formation by Type of Good and Owner, in Current Prices

Million Sierra Leone leones — Fiscal year beginning 1 July

	1983 TOTAL	1983 Total Private	1983 Public Enterprises	1983 General Government	1984 TOTAL	1984 Total Private	1984 Public Enterprises	1984 General Government	1985 TOTAL	1985 Total Private	1985 Public Enterprises	1985 General Government
Increase in stocks, total	15.0	18.0	-3.0	...	52.6	15.6	37.0	...	109.3	72.3	37.0	...
Gross Fixed Capital Formation, Total	331.8	295.9	13.9	22.0	435.4	256.6	92.5	86.3	593.5	378.5	64.1	150.9
1 Residential buildings												
2 Non-residential buildings	183.9	165.4	3.3	15.2	275.5	196.6	11.4	67.5	349.0	209.7	16.2	123.1
3 Other construction												
4 Land improvement and plantation and orchard development	4.2	-	-	4.2	15.4	-	-	15.4	24.1	-	0.1	24.0
5 Producers' durable goods	143.7	130.5	10.6	2.6	144.5	60.0	80.9	3.6	220.4	168.8	47.8	3.8
A Transport equipment	54.0	46.9	5.1	2.0	56.5	37.1	16.8	2.6	115.0	72.4	39.8	2.8
Passenger cars	24.2	...	...	...	19.6	...	...	...	37.3	...	...	...
Other	29.8	...	...	...	36.9	...	...	...	77.7	...	...	...
B Machinery and equipment	89.7	83.6	5.5	0.6	88.0	22.9	64.1	1.0	105.4	95.0	9.4	1.0
6 Breeding stock, dairy cattle, etc.	...	...	...	...	...	...	...	...	...	...	...	...
Total Gross Capital Formation	346.8	313.9	10.9	22.0	488.0	272.2	129.5	86.3	702.8	450.8	101.1	150.9

2.17 Exports and Imports of Goods and Services, Detail

Million Sierra Leone leones — Fiscal year beginning 1 July

	1970	1975	1977	1978	1979	1980	1981	1982	1983	1984	1985	1986
Exports of Goods and Services												
1 Exports of merchandise, f.o.b.	84.3	116.6	163.5	193.8	208.4	224.1	176.9	136.6	201.8	333.0	671.7	...
2 Transport and communication	...	...	...	...	...	...	...	...	...	...	...	...
3 Insurance service charges	...	...	...	...	...	...	...	...	...	...	...	...
4 Other commodities	16.1	18.0	27.9	31.6	47.8	65.3	65.9	59.1	74.2	110.2	153.3	...
5 Adjustments of merchandise exports to change-of-ownership basis	...	...	...	...	...	...	...	...	...	...	...	...
6 Direct purchases in the domestic market by non-residential households	...	...	...	...	...	...	...	...	...	...	...	...
7 Direct purchases in the domestic market by extraterritorial bodies	...	...	...	...	...	...	...	...	...	...	...	...
Total Exports of Goods and Services	100.4	134.6	191.4	225.4	256.2	289.4	242.8	195.7	276.0	443.2	825.0	...
Imports of Goods and Services												
1 Imports of merchandise, c.i.f.	96.9	167.6	208.5	290.8	388.6	447.5	360.4	368.5	286.9	418.3	781.6	...
A Imports of merchandise, f.o.b.	85.8	148.1	185.1	259.1	355.5	405.1	326.9	322.4	250.7	375.8	719.5	...
B Transport of services on merchandise imports	...	...	...	...	...	...	...	...	...	...	...	...
C Insurance service charges on merchandise imports	...	...	...	...	...	...	...	...	...	...	...	...
2 Adjustments of merchandise imports to change-of-ownership basis	...	...	...	...	...	...	...	...	...	...	...	...
3 Other transport and communication	...	...	...	...	...	...	...	...	...	...	...	...
4 Other insurance service charges	...	...	...	...	...	...	...	...	...	...	...	...
5 Other commodities	16.1	23.9	33.0	26.8	53.0	66.0	55.7	44.9	51.7	84.2	166.9	...
6 Direct purchases abroad by government	...	...	...	...	...	...	...	...	...	...	...	...
7 Direct purchases abroad by resident households	...	...	...	...	...	...	...	...	...	...	...	...
Total Imports of Goods and Services	113.0	191.5	241.5	317.6	441.6	513.5	416.1	413.4	338.6	502.5	948.5	...
Balance of Goods and Services	-12.5	-56.9	-50.1	-92.2	-185.4	-224.1	-173.3	-217.7	-62.6	-59.3	-123.5	...
Total Imports and Balance of Goods and Services	100.4	134.6	191.4	225.4	256.2	289.4	242.8	195.7	276.0	443.2	825.0	...

Sierra Leone

4.3 Cost Components of Value Added

Million Sierra Leone leones — Fiscal year beginning 1 July

1981 | 1982

	Compensation of Employees	Capital Consumption	Net Operating Surplus	Indirect Taxes	Less: Subsidies Received	Value Added	Compensation of Employees	Capital Consumption	Net Operating Surplus	Indirect Taxes	Less: Subsidies Received	Value Added
						All Producers						
1 Agriculture, hunting, forestry and fishing	60.9	18.6	459.1	13.7	...	552.3	92.3	25.2	568.5	4.7	...	690.7
2 Mining and quarrying	33.9	8.5	50.5	2.3	...	95.2	32.6	8.8	57.6	2.4	...	101.4
3 Manufacturing	17.7	5.9	76.6	42.5	...	142.7	21.4	6.7	80.2	36.5	...	144.8
4 Electricity, gas and water	3.8	2.6	1.6	...	...	8.0	5.2	2.9	2.8	...	...	10.9
5 Construction	28.8	4.0	22.0	...	...	54.8	19.6	3.8	24.1	...	...	47.5
6 Wholesale and retail trade, restaurants and hotels	50.1	17.2	105.0	0.7	...	173.0	68.1	23.2	141.1	0.6	...	233.0
7 Transport, storage and communication	51.9	77.0	157.2	1.0	0.2	286.9	61.5	89.5	172.5	0.9	0.4	324.0
8 Finance, insurance, real estate and business services	20.9	18.2	86.9	...	...	126.0	25.8	22.0	99.1	...	...	146.9
9 Community, social and personal services	50.7	0.5	12.6	0.2	...	64.0	59.6	0.5	13.6	0.2	...	73.9
Total, Industries [a]	318.7	152.5	971.5	60.4	...	1502.9	386.1	182.6	1159.5	45.3	0.4	1773.1
Producers of Government Services	90.8	...	...	...	...	90.8	102.9	...	...	...	...	102.9
Other Producers	...	...	...	...	...	...	...	...	...	...	...	...
Total [a]	409.5	152.5	971.5	60.4	0.2	1593.7	489.0	182.6	1159.5	45.3	0.4	1876.0
Less: Imputed bank service charge	...	...	29.5	...	...	29.5	...	...	31.9	...	...	31.9
Import duties	...	...	...	40.3	...	40.3	...	...	...	32.0	...	32.0
Value added tax	...	...	...	...	...	...	...	...	...	...	...	...
Total [a]	409.5	152.5	942.0	100.7	0.2	1604.5	489.0	182.6	1127.6	77.3	0.4	1876.1

1983 | 1984

	Compensation of Employees	Capital Consumption	Net Operating Surplus	Indirect Taxes	Less: Subsidies Received	Value Added	Compensation of Employees	Capital Consumption	Net Operating Surplus	Indirect Taxes	Less: Subsidies Received	Value Added
						All Producers						
1 Agriculture, hunting, forestry and fishing	155.3	44.9	852.4	9.5	...	1062.1	296.0	85.4	1486.3	5.3	...	1873.0
2 Mining and quarrying	47.7	9.0	81.2	2.6	...	140.5	48.0	41.9	180.1	5.8	...	275.8
3 Manufacturing	29.9	8.4	96.7	46.9	...	181.9	40.9	11.7	139.8	62.8	...	255.2
4 Electricity, gas and water	7.1	3.0	4.3	...	...	14.4	8.8	3.0	4.9	...	...	16.7
5 Construction	32.0	6.6	32.4	...	...	71.0	38.8	10.4	37.8	...	...	87.0
6 Wholesale and retail trade, restaurants and hotels	88.6	29.8	176.0	0.6	...	295.0	149.8	54.0	336.2	0.5	...	540.5
7 Transport, storage and communication	94.1	134.8	239.8	1.0	0.8	468.9	95.5	135.9	314.5	2.1	0.9	547.1
8 Finance, insurance, real estate and business services	51.3	43.0	175.4	...	...	269.7	34.9	67.2	362.9	0.5	...	465.5
9 Community, social and personal services	82.6	0.6	14.9	...	...	98.1	133.6	0.7	7.7	0.6	...	142.6
Total, Industries [a]	588.6	280.1	1673.1	60.6	0.8	2601.6	846.3	410.2	2870.2	77.6	0.9	4203.4
Producers of Government Services	121.9	...	...	...	...	121.9	129.6	...	...	...	...	129.6
Other Producers	...	...	...	...	...	...	...	...	...	...	...	...
Total [a]	710.5	280.1	1673.1	60.6	0.8	2723.5	975.9	410.2	2870.2	77.6	0.9	4333.0
Less: Imputed bank service charge	...	...	39.0	...	...	39.0	...	...	85.0	...	...	85.0
Import duties	...	...	...	45.0	...	45.0	...	...	...	61.8	...	61.8
Value added tax	...	...	...	...	...	...	...	...	...	...	...	...
Total [a]	710.5	280.1	1634.1	105.6	0.8	2729.5	975.9	410.2	2785.2	139.4	0.9	4309.8

1985

	Compensation of Employees	Capital Consumption	Net Operating Surplus	Indirect Taxes	Less: Subsidies Received	Value Added
					All Producers	
1 Agriculture, hunting, forestry and fishing	467.0	144.5	2128.7	37.2	...	2777.4
2 Mining and quarrying	108.6	54.3	618.5	5.8	...	787.2
3 Manufacturing	65.2	14.4	164.1	68.3	...	312.0
4 Electricity, gas and water	10.0	3.2	6.9	...	...	20.1

Sierra Leone

4.3 Cost Components of Value Added
(Continued)

Million Sierra Leone leones

Fiscal year beginning 1 July

1985

	Compensation of Employees	Capital Consumption	Net Operating Surplus	Indirect Taxes	Less: Subsidies Received	Value Added
5 Construction	40.0	11.1	60.9	...	...	112.0
6 Wholesale and retail trade, restaurants and hotels	222.0	80.0	498.0	3.7	...	803.7
7 Transport, storage and communication	74.4	113.0	412.6	5.0	3.7	601.3
8 Finance, insurance, real estate and business services	48.1	90.1	464.8	1.0	...	604.0
9 Community, social and personal services	156.6	0.8	42.6	0.9	...	200.9
Total, Industries [a]	1191.9	511.4	4397.1	121.9	3.7	6218.6
Producers of Government Services	172.6	...	...	...	...	172.6
Other Producers	...	...	...	...	...	...
Total [a]	1364.5	511.4	4397.1	121.9	3.7	6391.2
Less: Imputed bank service charge	...	...	140.0	...	...	140.0
Import duties	...	...	...	101.5	...	101.5
Value added tax	...	...	...	...	...	...
Total [a]	1364.5	511.4	4257.1	223.4	3.7	6352.7

a) Column 4 refers to indirect taxes less subsidies received.

Singapore

General note. The preparation of national accounts statistics in Singapore is undertaken by the Department of Statistics, Singapore. The official estimates together with a comprehensive description of the sources and methods used for the national accounts estimation is found in 'Singapore National Accounts, 1987' published by the Department of Statistics in April 1988. The estimates are generally in accordance with the classifications and definitions recommended in the United Nations System of National Accounts (SNA). The following tables have been prepared from successive replies to the United Nations national accounts questionnaire. When the scope and coverage of the estimates differ for conceptual or statistical reasons from the definitions and classifications recommended in SNA, a footnote is indicated to the relevant tables.

Sources and methods:

(a) Gross domestic product. Gross domestic product is estimated mainly through the production approach.

(b) Expenditure on the gross domestic product. The expenditure approach is used to estimate all components of GDP by expenditure type except private final expenditure on goods and capital expenditure on plant, machinery and equipment, for which the commodity-flow approach is used. The basic sources for estimating government final consumption expenditure are the annual financial statements of the Accountant-General, detailed income and expenditure statements of statutory boards and data collected from educational institutions. The estimates of private expenditure on goods are based on external trade statistics, data from the annual census of industrial production and on agricultural prduction data supplied by the Primary Production Department. Transport cost and distributor's margin are added to imports and local production values to arrive at market values of the commodities. Adjustments are made for stocks changes and for commodities with mulitple uses. Private expenditure on services are derived mainly from the results of surveys which are used as bench-mark estimates. Data used for the estimates of increase in stocks are derived from the annual censuses of industrial production and annual surveys of stocks conducted by the Department of Statistics. Capital formation in construction is estimated from the survey of capital expenditure on buildings, other construction and works. The estimates for capital formation of transport equipment are based on trade and prduction data as well as registration figures. The estimates of exports and imports of goods and services are based on balance-of-payments statistics. For the constant price estimates, all components of GDP by expenditure type are deflated by appropriate price indexes.

(c) Cost-structure of the gross domestic product. Estimates of the cost-structure of GDP are not made.

(d) Gross domestic product by kind of economic activity. The table of gross domestic product by kind of economic activity is prepared at market prices, i.e. producers' values. The production approach is used to estimate the value added of most industries. The income approach is used in the case of community, social and personal services and the transport sectors. Production data for the agricultural activities are estimated by the Primary Production Department based on two surveys conducted annually - the sample survey on pigs and poultry and the sample survey on vegetables. Fish production is based on fish caught and landed by locally registered fishing vessels while the estimates of output of live plants, flowers and aquarium fish are based on external trade statistics. Value added is calculated separately for each component as a fixed percentage of the value of production derived from the information available from the Department of Primary Production.

Value added of the mining sector is derived from the annual census of industrial production with adjustments made to conform to the national income concept. For manufacturing, basic data for establishments employing 10 or more workers are obtained from the annual census of industrial production. For smaller establishments, estimates are based on the censuses of industrial production for establishments with five to nine workers supplemented by estimates made from employment data and per capita value added referring to establishments engaging less than five workers. The data used for the estimates of electricity, gas and water are taken from detailed accounts provided by the Public Utilities Board. The Department of Statistics conducts annual inquiries to collect expenditure data on new construction and major extensions and alteration works. Value added is estimated as a fixed ratio of the total cost of work done, the ratio calculated from detailed cost estimates of Housing and Development Board Construction and the margin earned by the contractors. The wholesale and retail trades are divided into entrepot trade and domestic trade activities. Value added of the entrepot trade is taken as the gross margin on re-export, which is the difference between re-exports in f.o.b. values and the corresponding imports in c.i.f. values, less an allowance for transport and other costs. The data are extracted from the external trade statistics. For the domestic trade activities, estimates for retained imports are compiled from the external trade statistics while estimates for local production are based on agricultural output and the sales of the manufacturing sector to wholesalers and retailers. Vaue added is taken as the gross mark-up margin on the value of retained imports or local production less the costs of transport and other intermediate expenses. Data gathered in the surveys of wholesale and retail trade, restaurants and hotels were also been used. Bench-mark value added of the transort sector is derived from the surveys of services and detailed accounts from airlines and Port of Singapore Authority, etc. The communication services are run by the government and their value added is analyzed from government income and expenditure accounts. Value added of banks is equal to the sum of actual and imputed bank charges minus purchases of goods and services for intermediate consumption. The data are based on detailed accounts submitted by the respective banks. Value added of finance companies is equal to the net interest income received less intermediate inputs. Other financial institutions are estimated on the basis of bench-mark value added data computed from the survey of services, employment data and other appropriate indicators. Value added estimates of insurance are based on income and expenditure data contained in the annual report of the Insurance Commissioner. For real estate and business services, the estimates for the private establishments are based on the surveys of services. The estimates of owner-occupied dwellings are based on the annual value of properties as assessed for property tax. Government output is vaued at the cost of producing its services and value added is analysed from government financial statements, income and expenditure accounts of statutory boards and data provided by educational institutions and the Ministry of Education. The value added of domestic services consists of wages only and is estimated on the basis of the numbers employed and average earnings. For the constant price estimates, price deflation is used for agriculture, mining and quarrying, construction, trade, communication and services sectors. For manufacturing, electricity, gas and water and private services, value added is extrapolated by various output indicators. For transport, value added is either extrapolated by various indicators or deflated by price indexes.

1.1 Expenditure on the Gross Domestic Product, in Current Prices

Million Singapore dollars

	1970	1975	1977	1978	1979	1980	1981	1982	1983	1984	1985	1986
1 Government final consumption expenditure	692.5	1423.0	1716.3	1964.7	2033.6	2447.4	2788.6	3570.4	3995.3	4333.0	5548.5	5198.1
2 Private final consumption expenditure	3919.6	8120.7	9268.6	10149.1	11245.2	12911.3	14329.3	15282.5	16202.1	17569.5	17552.9	18096.1
3 Gross capital formation	2244.5	5370.4	5799.1	6957.4	8899.9	11627.6	13587.0	15658.8	17595.8	19417.3	16551.2	14566.3
A Increase in stocks	356.0	537.7	341.4	592.3	1380.3	1424.5	802.3	153.1	131.6	295.1	126.4	187.3
B Gross fixed capital formation	1888.5	4832.7	5457.7	6365.1	7519.6	10203.1	12784.7	15505.7	17464.2	19122.2	16424.8	14379.0
Residential buildings	363.6	1051.4	1245.7	1045.2	1017.3	1438.4	2060.7	3395.5	5516.8	6591.2	5265.4	3567.8
Non-residential buildings	244.1	648.7	670.4	963.4	1405.3	2069.7	3149.4	3912.4	4336.7	4200.5	3284.8	2133.7
Other construction and land improvement etc.	170.2	420.5	489.8	487.3	520.6	801.4	897.0	972.2	1023.1	1162.9	1457.2	2171.8
Other	1110.6	2712.1	3051.8	3869.2	4576.4	5893.6	6677.6	7225.6	6587.6	7167.6	6417.4	6505.7
4 Exports of goods and services	-1179.1	-1416.4	-424.2	-897.6	-1445.1	-2215.8	-1633.5	-1440.6	-663.8	-1113.0	-945.7	200.1
5 Less: Imports of goods and services												
Statistical discrepancy	127.4	54.7	320.8	-043.2	-210.0	320.2	268.0	-401.2	-396.6	-158.9	216.6	94.5
Equals: Gross Domestic Product	5804.9	13443.0	16039.0	17830.4	20523.0	25090.7	29339.4	32669.9	36732.8	40047.9	38923.5	38155.1

1.2 Expenditure on the Gross Domestic Product, in Constant Prices

Million Singapore dollars

	1970	1975	1977	1978	1979	1980	1981	1982	1983	1984	1985	1986
	At constant prices of: 1985
1 Government final consumption expenditure	1617.1	2327.4	2669.2	2976.3	2961.9	3241.5	3411.6	3863.8	4235.9	4457.2	5548.5	5541.6
2 Private final consumption expenditure	7482.1	11109.0	12341.2	13168.1	13971.4	14809.7	15491.3	16086.4	16852.1	17711.6	17552.9	18360.3
3 Gross capital formation	5043.3	7679.2	7852.6	9130.9	10854.4	12642.7	13541.0	15549.7	17309.9	18950.4	16551.2	14995.3
A Increase in stocks	1010.7	949.3	665.3	931.0	1596.7	1516.1	730.7	144.0	242.2	273.0	126.4	380.8
B Gross fixed capital formation	4032.6	6729.9	7187.3	8199.9	9257.7	11126.6	12810.3	15405.7	17067.7	18677.4	16424.8	14614.5

Singapore

1.2 Expenditure on the Gross Domestic Product, in Constant Prices
(Continued)

Million Singapore dollars

	1970	1975	1977	1978	1979	1980	1981	1982	1983	1984	1985	1986
					At constant prices of: 1985							
Residential buildings	1026.0	1583.9	1866.1	1530.7	1416.6	1573.1	1960.8	3403.2	5551.4	6549.5	5265.4	3720.6
Non-residential buildings	651.3	923.6	915.8	1306.0	1785.9	2188.8	3000.8	3788.2	4123.8	4098.5	3284.8	2219.1
Other construction and land improvement etc.	444.8	587.5	655.1	617.9	625.3	839.2	853.7	915.0	972.2	1132.7	1457.2	2255.7
Other	2012.1	3681.7	3912.1	4745.3	5429.9	6525.5	6995.0	7299.3	6420.3	6896.7	6417.4	6419.1
4 Exports of goods and services	-2316.9	-1975.0	-655.5	-1119.3	-1318.5	-1495.2	-1088.6	-2044.9	-1669.6	-1431.4	-945.7	359.9
5 Less: Imports of goods and services												
Statistical discrepancy	346.8	30.8	-64.2	-110.0	-184.5	-366.2	247.8	317.3	-191.1	-115.3	216.6	348.0
Equals: Gross Domestic Product	12172.4	19171.4	22143.3	24046.0	26284.7	28832.5	31603.1	33772.3	36537.2	39572.5	38923.5	39605.1

1.10 Gross Domestic Product by Kind of Activity, in Current Prices

Million Singapore dollars

	1970	1975	1977	1978	1979	1980	1981	1982	1983	1984	1985	1986
1 Agriculture, hunting, forestry and fishing	132.0	249.7	279.0	269.1	287.3	310.8	342.8	332.6	312.7	320.0	272.7	226.5
2 Mining and quarrying	19.2	45.9	47.9	37.5	42.1	82.2	104.7	128.1	140.6	132.2	111.3	75.6
3 Manufacturing	1152.5	3207.6	3980.9	4574.4	5700.9	7310.8	8359.4	8151.0	8905.1	9860.1	9180.7	10182.2
4 Electricity, gas and water	148.8	249.9	291.6	351.1	422.1	555.0	477.5	600.9	702.7	773.0	796.0	1074.6
5 Construction	385.2	1060.1	1168.1	1094.2	1209.3	1583.2	2129.8	3102.7	4154.8	4892.4	4117.3	3098.5
6 Wholesale and retail trade, restaurants and hotels	1516.2	3337.1	3914.3	4283.3	4844.8	5435.1	5840.0	6387.5	6667.4	6885.5	6636.3	6518.9
7 Transport, storage and communication	610.4	1478.2	2069.9	2550.6	2847.6	3517.3	4057.2	4429.0	4885.3	5213.6	5223.7	5287.5
8 Finance, insurance, real estate and business services	1004.2	2549.6	2861.0	3147.5	3686.4	4880.0	6586.6	7673.1	8777.5	9851.7	10523.0	10600.3
9 Community, social and personal services	319.7	614.6	671.9	735.8	813.2	852.1	1016.7	1209.3	1406.5	1531.6	1571.7	1698.6
Total, Industries	5288.2	12792.7	15284.6	17043.5	19853.7	24526.5	28914.7	32014.2	35952.6	39460.1	38432.7	38762.7
Producers of Government Services	451.5	964.4	1083.0	1184.3	1338.8	1548.3	1775.4	2284.1	2576.0	2901.1	3219.2	3023.9
Other Producers	...	...	...	...	...	...	...	...	...	...	...	...
Subtotal	5739.7	13757.1	16367.6	18227.8	21192.5	26074.8	30690.1	34298.3	38528.6	42361.2	41651.9	41786.6
Less: Imputed bank service charge	110.2	542.2	632.7	737.6	1039.2	1410.9	1778.6	2109.9	2306.8	2827.4	3196.5	4025.1
Plus: Import duties	175.4	228.1	304.1	340.2	369.7	426.8	427.9	481.5	511.0	514.1	468.1	393.6
Plus: Value added tax	...	...	...	...	...	...	...	...	...	...	...	...
Equals: Gross Domestic Product	5804.9	13443.0	16039.0	17830.4	20523.0	25090.7	29339.4	32669.9	36732.8	40047.9	38923.5	38155.1

1.11 Gross Domestic Product by Kind of Activity, in Constant Prices

Million Singapore dollars

	1970	1975	1977	1978	1979	1980	1981	1982	1983	1984	1985	1986
					At constant prices of: 1985							
1 Agriculture, hunting, forestry and fishing	256.1	275.2	309.5	306.7	308.1	308.1	300.9	284.3	290.7	306.0	272.7	240.8
2 Mining and quarrying	28.1	56.6	60.6	52.5	60.0	65.0	83.5	104.0	122.0	120.2	111.3	94.3
3 Manufacturing	3088.3	5088.1	6122.4	6787.6	7724.7	8497.3	9287.7	8962.5	9213.2	9904.2	9180.7	9952.1
4 Electricity, gas and water	219.9	336.5	416.1	491.4	536.5	578.0	620.4	650.2	707.8	762.1	796.0	839.9
5 Construction	1112.5	1685.5	1814.7	1686.8	1807.7	2010.5	2371.7	3248.8	4213.5	4873.6	4117.3	3177.9
6 Wholesale and retail trade, restaurants and hotels	2645.3	4000.5	4456.3	4767.6	5095.6	5452.8	5755.0	6091.9	6374.2	6738.9	6636.3	6604.2
7 Transport, storage and communication	879.2	1732.9	2296.4	2655.7	3038.5	3441.2	3888.7	4343.7	4670.7	5122.2	5223.7	5669.0
8 Finance, insurance, real estate and business services	1949.7	3742.5	4145.8	4433.0	4936.3	5823.2	6781.5	7466.9	8294.5	9325.1	10523.0	11143.9
9 Community, social and personal services	637.8	913.0	1005.8	1091.3	1136.4	1172.1	1239.6	1358.0	1453.8	1523.6	1571.7	1602.1
Total, Industries	10678.1	17597.5	20489.1	22272.6	24643.8	27348.2	30329.0	32510.3	35340.4	38675.9	38432.7	39324.2
Producers of Government Services	1193.0	1781.9	1913.2	2060.2	2185.6	2329.1	2444.8	2658.9	2878.5	3051.7	3219.2	3351.4
Other Producers	...	...	...	...	...	...	...	...	...	...	...	...
Subtotal	11834.7	19352.0	22399.1	24332.8	26829.4	29677.3	32773.8	35169.2	38218.9	41727.6	41651.9	42675.6
Less: Imputed bank service charge	160.2	581.2	653.7	707.1	991.6	1340.8	1653.8	1925.4	2191.7	2666.6	3196.5	3464.1
Plus: Import duties	356.1	324.9	389.2	420.3	446.9	496.0	483.1	528.5	510.0	511.5	468.1	393.6
Plus: Value added tax	...	...	...	...	...	...	...	...	...	...	...	...
Equals: Gross Domestic Product	12172.4	19171.4	22143.3	24046.0	26284.7	28832.5	31603.1	33772.3	36537.2	39572.5	38923.5	39605.1

Singapore

1.12 Relations Among National Accounting Aggregates

Million Singapore dollars

	1970	1975	1977	1978	1979	1980	1981	1982	1983	1984	1985	1986
Gross Domestic Product	5804.9	13443.0	16039.0	17830.4	20523.0	25090.7	29339.4	32669.9	36732.8	40047.9	38923.5	38155.1
Plus: Net factor income from the rest of the world	56.2	123.5	-187.3	-43.0	-78.9	-902.2	-1148.2	-894.2	-171.7	767.2	1406.9	1395.8
Equals: Gross National Product	5861.1	13566.5	15851.7	17787.4	20444.1	24188.5	28191.2	31775.7	36561.1	40815.1	40330.4	39550.9
Less: Consumption of fixed capital	308.9	1139.5	1796.8	2119.2	2431.8	2789.4	3261.5	3861.6	4073.0	4284.4	4629.3	4973.8
Equals: National Income	5552.2	12427.0	14054.9	15668.2	18012.3	21399.1	24929.7	27914.1	32488.1	36530.7	35701.1	34577.1
Plus: Net current transfers from the rest of the world	...	...	...	...	...	...	...	...	...	...	...	...
Equals: National Disposable Income	...	...	...	...	...	...	...	...	...	...	...	...
Less: Final consumption	...	...	...	...	...	...	...	...	...	...	...	...
Equals: Net Saving	...	...	...	...	...	...	...	...	...	...	...	...
Less: Surplus of the nation on current transactions	...	...	...	...	...	...	...	...	...	...	...	...
Equals: Net Capital Formation	...	...	...	...	...	...	...	...	...	...	...	...

2.5 Private Final Consumption Expenditure by Type and Porpose, in Current Prices

Million Singapore dollars

	1970	1975	1977	1978	1979	1980	1981	1982	1983	1984	1985	1986
Final Consumption Expenditure of Resident Households												
1 Food, beverages and tobacco	1399.3	2648.8	2967.0	3163.4	3476.6	3997.5	4561.8	4800.1	4932.0	5185.9	5121.5	5101.3
A Food	1085.0	2103.0	2348.7	2480.4	2741.5	3107.7	3583.6	3736.6	3723.7	3894.8	3818.3	3811.4
B Non-alcoholic beverages	57.3	107.3	128.1	137.3	155.8	197.2	219.5	218.6	269.2	259.6	290.7	301.6
C Alcoholic beverages	116.2	198.5	215.2	252.4	281.3	343.5	364.9	417.4	453.4	498.6	465.2	442.3
D Tobacco	140.8	240.0	275.0	293.3	298.0	349.1	393.8	427.5	485.7	532.9	547.3	546.0
2 Clothing and footwear	431.0	748.2	877.2	979.9	1117.0	1240.7	1408.4	1555.2	1681.8	1665.1	1569.4	1758.3
3 Gross rent, fuel and power	445.8	920.5	1067.6	1129.9	1219.7	1390.4	1493.1	1623.4	1745.3	1976.6	2184.9	2263.6
4 Furniture, furnishings and household equipment and operation	355.8	813.8	926.3	1006.6	1114.5	1322.9	1525.8	1602.1	1719.3	1943.2	2015.3	2051.6
A Household operation	100.7	201.4	191.1	208.2	231.2	251.7	297.3	336.3	418.0	458.9	489.1	542.6
B Other	255.1	612.4	735.2	798.4	883.3	1071.2	1228.5	1265.8	1301.3	1484.3	1526.2	1509.0
5 Medical care and health expenses	121.2	249.1	298.3	326.4	350.9	411.7	445.3	502.8	567.4	643.1	702.2	806.7
6 Transport and communication	543.3	1005.9	1325.4	1526.0	1820.4	2198.3	2345.5	2560.2	2743.1	2816.7	2678.7	2569.6
A Personal transport equipment	100.9	61.7	215.4	281.4	363.5	487.4	424.1	500.4	521.6	395.8	235.3	208.0
B Other	442.4	944.2	1110.0	1244.6	1456.9	1710.9	1921.4	2059.8	2221.5	2420.9	2443.4	2361.6
7 Recreational, entertainment, education and cultural services	441.1	1013.7	1144.7	1379.4	1647.7	1802.7	2153.8	2229.1	2421.0	2543.0	2453.5	2741.4
A Education	44.6	65.5	74.2	83.0	86.1	95.1	102.3	147.3	167.5	183.5	192.5	174.1
B Other	396.5	948.2	1070.5	1296.4	1561.6	1707.6	2051.5	2081.8	2253.5	2359.5	2261.0	2567.3
8 Miscellaneous goods and services	736.9	1693.7	1942.9	2205.5	2565.0	3133.1	3638.4	3684.4	3829.6	3910.1	3562.4	3685.7
A Personal care	77.6	157.4	186.9	237.0	264.5	288.7	330.4	408.4	432.5	474.3	456.1	457.4
B Expenditures in restaurants, cafes and hotels	274.7	672.9	846.4	939.5	1092.8	1276.6	1449.9	1406.6	1432.6	1479.4	1423.3	1400.1
C Other	384.6	863.4	909.6	1029.0	1207.7	1567.8	1858.1	1869.4	1964.5	1956.4	1683.0	1828.2
Total Final Consumption Expenditure in the Domestic Market by Households, of which	4474.4	9093.7	10549.4	11717.1	13311.8	15497.3	17572.1	18557.3	19639.5	20683.7	20287.9	20978.2
Plus: Direct purchases abroad by resident households	54.7	332.4	397.5	440.1	475.2	585.7	651.2	843.3	973.4	1049.5	1103.5	1145.7
Less: Direct purchases in the domestic market by non-resident households	609.5	1305.4	1678.3	2008.1	2541.8	3171.7	3894.0	4118.1	4410.8	4163.7	3838.5	4027.8
Equals: Final Consumption Expenditure of Resident Households a)	3919.6	8120.7	9268.6	10149.1	11245.2	12911.3	14329.3	15282.5	16202.1	17569.5	17552.9	18096.1
Final Consumption Expenditure of Private Non-profit Institutions Serving Households												
Equals: Final Consumption Expenditure of Private Non-profit Organisations Serving Households	...	...	...	...	...	...	...	...	...	...	...	...
Private Final Consumption Expenditure	3919.6	8120.7	9268.6	10149.1	11245.2	12911.3	14329.3	15282.5	16202.1	17569.5	17552.9	18096.1

a) Item 'Final consumption expenditure of resident households' includes consumption expenditure of private non-profit institutions serving households.

Singapore

2.6 Private Final Consumption Expenditure by Type and Purpose, in Constant Prices

Million Singapore dollars

	1970	1975	1977	1978	1979	1980	1981	1982	1983	1984	1985	1986
At constant prices of:1985											
Final Consumption Expenditure of Resident Households											
1 Food, beverages and tobacco	2985.4	3545.8	3957.4	4111.7	4363.8	4638.0	4810.1	4876.0	4962.4	5111.3	5121.5	5228.0
A Food	2287.6	2696.0	3030.1	3118.6	3325.6	3487.5	3643.3	3679.0	3663.2	3830.0	3818.3	3932.4
B Non-alcoholic beverages	119.5	147.8	175.9	188.6	193.2	234.3	229.1	210.8	261.1	255.9	290.7	302.7
C Alcoholic beverages	234.1	282.9	296.2	344.7	378.0	428.1	428.5	475.7	501.8	495.1	465.2	446.9
D Tobacco	347.9	421.4	456.6	459.8	467.0	488.1	509.2	510.5	536.3	530.3	547.3	946.0
2 Clothing and footwear	686.2	851.3	981.9	1068.3	1171.2	1281.2	1457.0	1580.0	1642.4	1647.3	1569.4	1812.9
3 Gross rent, fuel and power	870.4	1273.4	1407.9	1476.9	1528.3	1576.4	1630.9	1694.2	1794.9	1984.8	2184.9	2325.9
4 Furniture, furnishings and household equipment and operation	685.3	1096.6	1167.9	1211.1	1291.6	1451.9	1609.4	1641.4	1747.1	1953.3	2015.3	2011.9
A Household operation	223.5	286.9	300.0	301.4	324.7	329.8	369.6	385.4	435.9	459.9	489.1	513.4
B Other	471.9	811.8	869.5	909.7	966.9	1122.1	1239.8	1256.0	1311.2	1493.4	1526.2	1498.5
5 Medical care and health expenses	268.1	412.3	481.6	506.2	524.6	550.9	570.0	620.1	633.1	654.6	702.2	781.7
6 Transport and communication	1111.3	1524.4	1912.1	2139.6	2404.4	2618.4	2752.8	2861.2	2995.0	2967.3	2678.7	2648.5
A Personal transport equipment	164.8	77.2	237.6	280.1	348.3	460.8	394.8	471.7	499.5	386.8	235.3	168.2
B Other	942.4	1475.7	1678.0	1859.5	2056.1	2157.6	2358.0	2389.5	2495.5	2580.5	2443.4	2480.3
7 Recreational, entertainment, education and cultural services	623.2	1132.5	1244.4	1424.8	1612.7	1735.3	2047.0	2168.9	2480.4	2534.9	2453.5	2736.5
A Education	72.0	105.8	119.8	125.8	125.1	124.6	127.9	177.8	180.2	192.6	192.5	170.7
B Other	553.0	1026.4	1125.5	1299.0	1487.6	1610.7	1919.1	1991.1	2300.2	2342.3	2261.0	2565.8
8 Miscellaneous goods and services	1378.3	2241.6	2499.7	2787.2	3089.3	3378.1	3523.8	3633.1	3779.3	3884.1	3562.4	3739.1
A Personal care	149.0	213.2	249.7	309.0	332.6	351.5	364.2	407.9	445.0	484.0	456.1	452.3
B Expenditures in restaurants, cafes and hotels	562.9	980.4	1171.3	1281.5	1401.6	1372.3	1390.9	1356.2	1386.5	1428.5	1423.3	1469.0
C Other	655.6	1035.7	1078.6	1196.7	1355.1	1654.3	1768.7	1869.0	1947.8	1971.6	1683.0	1817.8
Total Final Consumption Expenditure in the Domestic Market by Households, of which	8506.3	12051.8	13607.9	14725.8	15985.9	17230.2	18401.0	19074.9	20034.6	20737.6	20287.9	21284.5
Plus: Direct purchases abroad by resident households	106.5	487.6	567.6	612.4	638.6	699.0	729.6	896.0	992.2	1049.7	1103.5	1162.4
Less: Direct purchases in the domestic market by non-resident households	996.4	1487.4	1861.1	2170.1	2653.1	3119.5	3639.3	3884.5	4174.7	4075.7	3838.5	4086.6
Equals: Final Consumption Expenditure of Resident Households	7482.1	11109.0	12341.2	13168.1	13971.4	14809.7	15491.3	16086.4	16852.1	17711.6	17552.9	18360.3
Final Consumption Expenditure of Private Non-profit Institutions Serving Households											
Equals: Final Consumption Expenditure of Private Non-profit Organisations Serving Households	...	...	...	...	...	...	...	...	...	...	...	...
Private Final Consumption Expenditure	7482.1	11109.0	12341.2	13168.1	13971.4	14809.7	15491.3	16086.4	16852.1	17711.6	17552.9	18360.3

Solomon Islands

Source. Reply to the United Nations National Accounts Questionnaire from the Statistics Division, Ministry of Finance, Honiara.
General note. The estimates have been adjusted by the United Nations Statistical Office to conform to the United Nations System of National Accounts so far as the existing data would permit.

1.1 Expenditure on the Gross Domestic Product, in Current Prices

Million Solomon Islands dollars

	1970	1975	1977	1978	1979	1980	1981	1982	1983	1984	1985	1986
1 Government final consumption expenditure	...	...	...	...	...	...	...	...	...	...	...	...
2 Private final consumption expenditure	...	...	...	...	...	...	...	...	...	...	...	...
3 Gross capital formation	...	...	...	...	...	...	...	...	...	...	...	...
4 Exports of goods and services	7.1	11.8	29.6	30.6	60.2	60.8	...	...	...	...	...	...
5 Less: Imports of goods and services [a]	10.0	21.8	25.8	30.9	50.5	61.5	...	...	...	...	...	...
Equals: Gross Domestic Product	28.6	51.2	73.5	85.8	112.7	119.4	140.6	158.5	141.4	193.5	193.1	...

a) Imports of merchandise, f.o.b. rather than c.i.f.

1.2 Expenditure on the Gross Domestic Product, in Constant Prices

Million Solomon Islands dollars

	1970	1975	1977	1978	1979	1980	1981	1982	1983	1984	1985	1986
				At constant prices of:1977								
1 Government final consumption expenditure	...	...	...	...	...	...	...	...	...	...	...	...
2 Private final consumption expenditure	...	...	...	...	...	...	...	...	...	...	...	...
3 Gross capital formation	...	...	...	...	...	...	...	...	...	...	...	...
4 Exports of goods and services	...	...	...	...	...	...	...	...	...	...	...	...
5 Less: Imports of goods and services	...	...	...	...	...	...	...	...	...	...	...	...
Equals: Gross Domestic Product	...	57.9	73.5	80.6	98.1	91.9	93.0	92.8	95.9	...	...	...

1.3 Cost Components of the Gross Domestic Product

Million Solomon Islands dollars

	1970	1975	1977	1978	1979	1980	1981	1982	1983	1984	1985	1986
1 Indirect taxes, net	2.2	3.4	5.4	6.2	10.5	10.8	14.5	18.0	18.0	...	...	...
2 Consumption of fixed capital	2.8	4.7	6.2	7.5	10.9	14.2	18.1	22.0	24.0	...	...	...
3 Compensation of employees paid by resident producers to:	7.9	14.6	21.7	25.2	27.1	31.3	39.2	45.2	50.0	...	...	...
4 Operating surplus	15.7	28.5	40.3	46.9	64.2	63.0	68.9	73.3	83.0	...	...	...
Equals: Gross Domestic Product	28.6	51.2	73.5	85.8	112.7	119.4	140.6	158.5	175.0	...	...	...

Somalia

Source. National Accounts estimates are published in 'National Accounts Aggregates of Somali Democratic Republic' by the Ministero Della Pianificazione Nazionale, Mogadishu.

General note. The estimates shown in the following tables have been prepared in accordance with the United Nations System of National Accounts so far as the existing data would permit.

1.1 Expenditure on the Gross Domestic Product, in Current Prices

Million Somali shillings

	1970	1975	1977	1978	1979	1980	1981	1982	1983	1984	1985	1986
1 Government final consumption expenditure	233	909	1128	1668	1937	3011	3273	...	...	...	...	...
2 Private final consumption expenditure	1811	3120	3924	5365	7234	8415	11103	...	...	...	...	...
3 Gross capital formation	318	1008	1987	1972	667	593	3097	...	...	...	...	...
A Increase in stocks	113	324	747	951	-490	-561	1810	...	...	...	...	...
B Gross fixed capital formation	205	684	1240	1021	1157	1154	1287	...	...	...	...	...
4 Exports of goods and services [a]	260	702	635	916	905	1221	1668	...	...	...	...	...
5 Less: Imports of goods and services [b]	378	1349	1336	2012	2808	3256	3080	...	...	...	...	...
Equals: Gross Domestic Product	2244	4390	6338	7909	7935	9984	16061	...	...	...	...	...

a) Item 'Exports of goods and services' includes exports of goods only.
b) Item 'Imports of goods and services' refers to imports of goods and non-factor services.

1.2 Expenditure on the Gross Domestic Product, in Constant Prices

Million Somali shillings

	1970	1975	1977	1978	1979	1980	1981	1982	1983	1984	1985	1986
At constant prices of: 1977												
1 Government final consumption expenditure	426	1146	1128	1516	1422	1388	1046	...	...	...	...	...
2 Private final consumption expenditure	3669	4710	3924	4848	4402	4365	4633	...	...	...	...	...
3 Gross capital formation	849	1145	1987	1748	664	527	1662	...	...	...	...	...
A Increase in stocks	333	466	747	766	-300	-315	846	...	...	...	...	...
B Gross fixed capital formation	516	679	1240	982	964	842	816	...	...	...	...	...
4 Exports of goods and services	765	789	635	673	637	754	686	...	...	...	...	...
5 Less: Imports of goods and services	912	2108	1336	1985	1168	1206	1035	...	...	...	...	...
Equals: Gross Domestic Product	4797	5682	6338	6800	5957	5823	6992	...	...	...	...	...

1.7 External Transactions on Current Account, Summary

Million Somali shillings

	1970	1975	1977	1978	1979	1980	1981	1982	1983	1984	1985	1986
Payments to the Rest of the World												
1 Imports of goods and services	...	1349	1336	2012	2808	3256	3080	...	...	...	...	...
A Imports of merchandise c.i.f.	...	1021	1106	1732	2481	2905	2681	...	...	...	...	...
B Other	...	328	230	280	327	351	399	...	...	...	...	...
2 Factor income to the rest of the world	...	20	6	16	46	41	104	...	...	...	...	...
A Compensation of employees	...	1	1	1	2	4	17	...	...	...	...	...
B Property and entrepreneurial income	...	19	5	15	44	37	88	...	...	...	...	...
3 Current transfers to the rest of the world	...	12	7	2	6	-	-	...	...	...	...	...
4 Surplus of the nation on current transactions	...	-1	-6	-406	-1296	-1128	-634	...	...	...	...	...
Payments to the Rest of the World and Surplus of the Nation on Current Transactions	...	1380	1342	1624	1564	2169	2550	...	...	...	...	...
Receipts From The Rest of the World												
1 Exports of goods and services	...	702	635	916	905	1221	1668	...	...	...	...	...
A Exports of merchandise f.o.b.	...	558	479	689	667	839	1103	...	...	...	...	...
B Other	...	144	156	227	238	382	565	...	...	...	...	...
2 Factor income from rest of the world	...	23	21	40	62	51	82	...	...	...	...	...
A Compensation of employees	...	2	2	3	2	19	45	...	...	...	...	...
B Property and entrepreneurial income	...	21	19	37	60	31	37	...	...	...	...	...
3 Current transfers from rest of the world	...	655	686	668	597	897	800	...	...	...	...	...
Receipts from the Rest of the World on Current Transactions	...	1380	1342	1624	1564	2169	2550	...	...	...	...	...

Somalia

1.10 Gross Domestic Product by Kind of Activity, in Current Prices

Million Somali shillings

	1970	1975	1977	1978	1979	1980	1981	1982	1983	1984	1985	1986
1 Agriculture, hunting, forestry and fishing	1066	2095	3193	3742	3256	4067	6899	...	...	...	...	...
2 Mining and quarrying	23	35	40	28	36	43	68	...	...	...	...	...
3 Manufacturing	186	226	439	433	458	574	850	...	...	...	...	...
4 Electricity, gas and water	15	38	46	44	50	58	127	...	...	...	...	...
5 Construction	105	204	302	206	283	389	506	...	...	...	...	...
6 Wholesale and retail trade, restaurants and hotels	172	407	477	687	702	1028	1509	...	...	...	...	...
7 Transport, storage and communication	133	323	325	302	365	772	1122	...	...	...	...	...
8 Finance, insurance, real estate and business services	91	228	312	450	554	670	1022	...	...	...	...	...
9 Community, social and personal services	52	108	149	170	216	361	660	...	...	...	...	...
Total, Industries	1842	3664	5282	6062	5920	7963	12763	...	...	...	...	...
Producers of Government Services	148	280	407	693	728	874	1151	...	...	...	...	...
Other Producers	...	...	...	...	...	...	...	...	...	...	...	...
Subtotal a	1990	3944	5689	6755	6648	8837	13914	...	...	...	...	...
Less: Imputed bank service charge												
Plus: Import duties	...	...	...	...	...	...	...	...	...	...	...	...
Plus: Value added tax												
Plus: Other adjustments b	254	448	650	1155	1287	1147	2147	...	...	...	...	...
Equals: Gross Domestic Product	2244	4390	6338	7909	7935	9984	16061	...	...	...	...	...

a) Gross domestic product in factor values.
b) Item 'Other adjustments' refers to indirect taxes net of subsidies.

1.11 Gross Domestic Product by Kind of Activity, in Constant Prices

Million Somali shillings

	1970	1975	1977	1978	1979	1980	1981	1982	1983	1984	1985	1986
					At constant prices of:1977							
1 Agriculture, hunting, forestry and fishing	2640	2747	3193	3226	2362	2512	3521	...	...	...	...	...
2 Mining and quarrying	15	38	46	44	50	58	54	...	...	...	...	...
3 Manufacturing	42	44	40	25	27	20	22	...	...	...	...	...
4 Electricity, gas and water	340	285	439	394	420	429	425	...	...	...	...	...
5 Construction	192	257	302	187	208	212	221	...	...	...	...	...
6 Wholesale and retail trade, restaurants and hotels	314	513	477	624	516	474	482	...	...	...	...	...
7 Transport, storage and communication	233	401	325	273	268	356	358	...	...	...	...	...
8 Finance, insurance, real estate and business services	165	344	312	409	407	415	436	...	...	...	...	...
9 Community, social and personal services	94	136	149	154	159	166	211	...	...	...	...	...
Total, Industries	4036	4765	5282	5336	4415	4642	5730	...	...	...	...	...
Producers of Government Services	270	353	407	630	597	652	576	...	...	...	...	...
Other Producers	...	...	...	...	...	...	...	...	...	...	...	...
Subtotal a	4306	5118	5689	5966	5012	5294	6306	...	...	...	...	...
Less: Imputed bank service charge	...	...	...	...	...	...	...	...	...	...	...	...
Plus: Import duties	...	...	...	...	...	...	...	...	...	...	...	...
Plus: Value added tax												
Plus: Other adjustments b	464	565	650	834	945	528	686	...	...	...	...	...
Equals: Gross Domestic Product	4770	5682	6338	6800	5957	5823	6992	...	...	...	...	...

a) Gross domestic product in factor values.
b) Item 'Other adjustments' refers to indirect taxes net of subsidies.

2.17 Exports and Imports of Goods and Services, Detail

Million Somali shillings

	1970	1975	1977	1978	1979	1980	1981	1982	1983	1984	1985	1986
				Exports of Goods and Services								
1 Exports of merchandise, f.o.b.	...	558	479	689	667	839	1103	...	...	...	...	...
2 Transport and communication	...	21	24	18	34	73	198	...	...	...	...	...
A In respect of merchandise imports	...	2	2	12	18	49	154	...	...	...	...	...
B Other	...	19	22	6	16	29	44	...	...	...	...	...
3 Insurance service charges	...	-	-	-	-	-	-	...	...	...	...	...

Somalia

2.17 Exports and Imports of Goods and Services, Detail
(Continued)

Million Somali shillings

	1970	1975	1977	1978	1979	1980	1981	1982	1983	1984	1985	1986
4 Other commodities	...	34	7	39	56	...	...	...	...	...	...	...
5 Adjustments of merchandise exports to change-of-ownership basis	...	-	-	-	-	-	-	...	...	...	...	...
6 Direct purchases in the domestic market by non-residential households	...	8	25	78	25	154	168	...	...	...	...	...
7 Direct purchases in the domestic market by extraterritorial bodies	...	82	99	92	122	145	198	...	...	...	...	...
Total Exports of Goods and Services	...	702	635	916	905	1221	1668	...	...	...	...	...
Imports of Goods and Services												
1 Imports of merchandise, c.i.f.	...	1021	1106	1732	2481	2905	2681	...	...	...	...	...
By residents	...	...	...	...	...	1221	1668	...	...	...	...	...
By non-residents	...	...	...	...	...	...	...	...	...	...	...	...
2 Adjustments of merchandise imports to change-of-ownership basis	...	-	-	-	-	-	-	...	...	...	...	...
3 Other transport and communication	...	39	31	23	23	80	37	...	...	...	...	...
4 Other insurance service charges	...	-	-	-	-	-	-	...	...	...	...	...
5 Other commodities	...	155	61	111	100	...	...	...	...	...	...	...
6 Direct purchases abroad by government	...	94	98	88	93	170	175	...	...	...	...	...
7 Direct purchases abroad by resident households	...	40	41	58	111	101	187	...	...	...	...	...
Total Imports of Goods and Services	...	1349	1336	2012	2808	3256	3080	...	...	...	...	...
Balance of Goods and Services	...	-647	-701	-1096	-1903	-2035	-1412	...	...	...	...	...
Total Imports and Balance of Goods and Services	...	702	635	916	905	1221	1668	...	...	...	...	...

South Africa

General note. The preparation of national accounts statistics in South Africa is undertaken by the South African Reserve Bank, Pretoria. The official estimates are published in the Bank's Quarterly Bulletin. A detailed description of the sources and methods used for the national accounts estimation is contained in a suplement to the Bulletin published in September 1981 entitled 'A Statistical Presentaton of South Africa's Quarterly National Accounts for the period 1946 to 1980'. The estimates are generally in accordance with the classifications and definitions recommended in the United Nations System of National Accounts (SNA). Input-output tables have been published in 'The South African Journal of Economics'. The following tables have been prepared from successive replies to the United Nations national accounts questionnaire. When the scope and coverage of the estimates differ for conceptual or statistical reasons from the definitions and classifications recommended in SNA, a footnote is indicated to the relevant tables.

Sources and methods:

(a) Gross domestic product. Gross domestic product is estimated mainly through the income approach.

(b) Expenditure on the gross domestic product. All items of GDP by expenditure type are estimated through the expenditure approach. Government expenditure is estimated through the use of published annual accounts and monthly issues from the Exchequer Account for the central authorities quarterly returns submitted directly to the Reserve Bank for the provincial authorities, and annual and quarterly data collected by the Department of Statistics for the local authorities. Estimates of private consumption expenditure are based on a variety of sources such as quarterly data on the agricultural products marketed for food, monthly excise figures for beverages and tobacco, monthly retail sales data for clothing, medicine, entertainment, etc., number of motor vehicles and cycles sold for transport equipment, number of dwelling units and average rent and income of concerned enterprises. The estimates of increase in stocks are based on census results and quarterly surveys. Information on investment in the public sector is obtained from published accounts updated by quarterly returns submitted to the Reserve Bank by concerned authorities. For the private sector, data on investment by the different sectors are obtained from various sources -- censuses and quarterly surveys for agriculture, manufacturing and mining, the value of buildings completed in urban areas for the sectors of commerce, private transport, financial institutions, etc. All relevant information for exports and imports of goods and services is based on balance-of-payments data. Official statistics and sample surveys of financial and non-financial companies are also used for exports and imports of services. For the constant price estimates, price deflation is used for government expenditure on goods and services, increase in stocks except agricultural stocks, gross fixed capital formation and exports and imports of goods and services. The net value of gold exports at constant prices is obtained by extrapolating the value of the base year on the basis of the number of kilograms of fine gold produced. The base-year values of government wages, salaries and allowances and private consumption expenditure are extrapolated by appropriate volume indexes. For agricultural stocks, values at constant prices are obtained by multiplying the change in the number of livestock by the average flock value.

(c) Cost-structure of the gross domestic product. Estimates of compensation of employees of all sectors of the economy are based on census results and monthly and quarterly data of wages, salaries and benefits paid to employees. Operating surplus is obtained from different sources for the different sectors of the economy-- data obtained from the Department of Agricultural Economics and Marketing for the agricultural sector, census results and quarterly surveys of financial statistics for mining, manufacturing, construction and trade, information from concerned enterprises for electricity, gas and water, financial data for the financial institutions, annual and monthly statistics for trade and communication and data on the number of residential units and indexes of house and flat rents for real estate. The straight-line method based on the original cost of the original assets is used for estimating consumption of fixed capital. Depreciation is based on replacement cost. Indirect taxes and subsidies are estimated on the basis of an analysis of government accounts by the Reserve Bank.

(d) Gross domestic product by kind of economic activity. The table of GDP by kind of economic activity is prepared in factor values. The income approach is used to estimate the value added of all industries except agriculture for which the production approach is used. The estimates of agricultural production are obtained by valuing physical output at net producers' prices. Data pertaining to agricultural and livestock production are obtained from the censuses of agriculture and forestry and the Agricultural Control Boards. For forestry and fishing, estimates are obtained from the Department of Forestry and from the censuses of Fisheries, respectively. Estimates of income originating from gold, coal, diamond and other mines are obtained from triennial censuses. For non-census years, estimates are based on various sources such as reports of the Government Mining Engineer and quarterly sample surveys of financial statistics of mining. Estimates of manufacturing are based on biennial censuses covering establishments employing three or more full-time workers or using power equipment. For other years, estimates are based on quarterly sample surveys supplemented by financial reports for public corporations and Auditor-General's reports and anual surveys of local authorities for government enterprises. Intermediate consumption is estimated in census years only. For electricity, gas and water, estimates are based on annual financial statements for corporations and on results of annual censuses for local authorities and private enterprises. The estimates of construction are based on biennial censuses of construction. For non-census years, sample surveys of wages and salaries and analysis of financial statements of important companies are used. The basic information for trade is obtained from the five-yearly censuses of distribution. For other years, estimates are based on sample surveys of trading establishments. Estimates for the transport sector are obtained from published data of concerned establishments, annual surveys and for the private sector, on the results of the five-yearly censuses. For communication, estimates are obtained from the reports of the Auditor-General. Estimates for banking, insurance and real estate are based on quarterly data collected from the financial institutions. Estimates for ownership of dwellings are based on the results of inquiries into housing and rent as part of the decennial population censuses which are updated by monthly data. Data from the annual rent surveys and monthly data of dwellings completed are used for estimating owner-occupied dwelling rents. For government services, information is obtained from government accounts. For private services, estimates are based on annual surveys, inquiry conducted concurrently with the population censuses and on workmen's compensation statistics. Estimates of the contribution to the GDP at constant prices by each major industry division are made on a quarterly basis. The value added of most industries is extrapolated by quantity indicators. Double deflation is used for agriculture and forestry. For financial institutions, business services and part of private service, value added is deflated by appropriate indexes.

1.1 Expenditure on the Gross Domestic Product, in Current Prices

Million South African rand

	1970	1975	1977	1978	1979	1980	1981	1982	1983	1984	1985	1986
1 Government final consumption expenditure	1564	3782	5155	5673	6543	8449	10378	12990	14809	18787	21695	26008
2 Private final consumption expenditure	7760	15478	19297	21510	24917	30922	37799	44134	50703	58517	65454	77093
A Households	7656	15214	18957	21143	24491	30405	37180	43347	49756	57436	64224	75748
B Private non-profit institutions serving households	104	264	340	367	426	517	619	787	947	1081	1230	1345
3 Gross capital formation	3684	8893	9264	9939	12574	18840	24033	20746	23206	26188	25124	27164
A Increase in stocks	490	783	-307	-403	323	2462	3901	1946	1303	57	-3495	-1834
B Gross fixed capital formation	3194	8110	9571	10342	12251	16378	20132	22692	24509	26131	28619	28998
Residential buildings	487	982	1000	1036	1280	1796	2311	2766	3366	3887	3568	3560
Non-residential buildings	530	1132	1572	1400	1608	1957	2606	3212	3506	4074	4419	4569
Other construction and land improvement etc. [a]	810	2292	2585	2860	3510	4683	5008	4812	5304	5468	5734	6039
Other	1367	3704	4414	5046	5853	7942	10207	11902	12333	12702	14898	14830
4 Exports of goods and services	2757	7388	10474	12959	16724	22219	20584	21833	23163	28261	40395	46499
5 Less: Imports of goods and services	3165	8119	8470	9867	11878	16959	21627	21813	19440	25931	28299	31866
Statistical discrepancy	308	32	-1406	-917	-2182	-1464	-84	1786	-2566	-8	-4228	-5203
Equals: Gross Domestic Product [b]	12908	27454	34314	39297	46698	62007	71083	79676	89875	105814	120141	139695

a) Land development includes transfer costs.
b) Estimates are prepared by the South African Reserve Bank. These estimates include the Republic of South Africa and Namibia.

South Africa

1.2 Expenditure on the Gross Domestic Product, in Constant Prices

Million South African rand

	1970	1975	1977	1978	1979	1980	1981	1982	1983	1984	1985	1986
	\multicolumn{12}{c}{At constant prices of:1980}
1 Government final consumption expenditure	4824	6663	7283	7347	7577	8449	8738	9221	9372	10097	10186	10363
2 Private final consumption expenditure	21197	27154	27385	27758	28395	30922	32946	33640	34259	35484	34118	34218
3 Gross capital formation	12219	16005	13315	12775	14192	18840	21225	15742	15527	16045	13053	11621
A Increase in stocks	1729	856	-515	-665	247	2462	3468	-1496	-890	-57	-2089	-849
B Gross fixed capital formation	10490	15149	13830	13440	13945	16378	17757	17238	16417	16102	15142	12470
Residential buildings	1658	1869	1489	1386	1491	1796	2004	2045	2154	2262	1859	1599
Non-residential buildings	1772	2129	2315	1858	1868	1958	2254	2366	2249	2371	2301	2049
Other construction and land improvement etc. [a]	2886	4565	3960	3898	4098	4682	4342	3571	3428	3216	2998	2714
Other	4204	6622	6086	6298	6488	7942	9157	9256	8586	8253	7984	6108
4 Exports of goods and services	17943	18676	21245	22208	22389	22219	20928	20948	19805	21442	23320	22828
5 Less: Imports of goods and services	14619	18509	14272	14374	14179	16959	19188	16189	13422	16103	13786	13467
Statistical discrepancy	...	...	...	1137	323	-1464	316	1110	-2433	-648	-1596	83
Equals: Gross Domestic Product [bc]	44557	54446	55265	56851	58697	62007	64965	64472	63108	66317	65295	65646

a) Land development includes transfer costs.
b) Estimates are prepared by the South African Reserve Bank. These estimates include the Republic of South Africa and Namibia.
c) For the years prior to 1978, existing series expressed in 1975 prices have been linked to the new 1980 base year without re-weighting. As a result, for the periods before 1978, the converted sub-totals and totals are not equal to the sum of their components.

1.3 Cost Components of the Gross Domestic Product

Million South African rand

	1970	1975	1977	1978	1979	1980	1981	1982	1983	1984	1985	1986
1 Indirect taxes, net	885	1608	2331	2779	3477	4044	5081	6683	6606	8386	9987	11793
A Indirect taxes	1032	1896	2798	3361	4058	4839	5974	7833	8480	10574	12594	14951
B Less: Subsidies	147	288	467	582	581	795	893	1150	1874	2188	2607	3158
2 Consumption of fixed capital	1359	3372	4902	5801	6886	8194	9860	12218	14453	16344	19722	24864
3 Compensation of employees paid by resident producers to:	7033	14822	18607	20653	23822	29358	36480	43387	48638	57262	63401	72663
A Resident households	6870	14348	18083	20077	23175	28607	35608	42401	47487	55969	61898	70897
B Rest of the world	163	474	524	576	647	751	872	986	1151	1293	1503	1766
4 Operating surplus	3631	7652	8474	10064	12513	20411	19662	17388	20178	23822	27031	30375
Equals: Gross Domestic Product [a]	12908	27454	34314	39297	46698	62007	71083	79676	89875	105814	120141	139695

a) Estimates are prepared by the South African Reserve Bank. These estimates include the Republic of South Africa and Namibia.

1.4 General Government Current Receipts and Disbursements

Million South African rand

	1970	1975	1977	1978	1979	1980	1981	1982	1983	1984	1985	1986
	\multicolumn{12}{c}{Receipts}
1 Operating surplus	...	...	...	...	...	...	...	...	...	...	...	...
2 Property and entrepreneurial income	164	455	467	654	656	1304	1056	573	772	1190	1468	1968
3 Taxes, fees and contributions	2418	5417	7104	8119	9689	12528	14514	17652	20363	24056	29636	34588
A Indirect taxes	1032	1896	2798	3361	4058	4839	5974	7833	8480	10574	12594	14951
B Direct taxes	1313	3350	4107	4531	5372	7369	8181	9386	11395	12912	16397	18925
C Social security contributions	36	71	86	109	129	169	184	228	263	296	333	372
D Compulsory fees, fines and penalties	37	100	113	118	130	151	175	205	225	274	312	340
4 Other current transfers	39	99	102	117	160	279	345	276	277	269	373	426
Total Current Receipts of General Government [a]	2621	5971	7673	8890	10505	14111	15915	18501	21412	25515	31477	36982
	\multicolumn{12}{c}{Disbursements}
1 Government final consumption expenditure	1564	3782	5156	5673	6543	8449	10378	12990	14809	18787	21695	26008
2 Property income	177	395	602	786	1424	1492	1708	2328	3290	4132	5201	5554
A Interest	177	395	602	786	1424	1492	1708	2328	3290	4132	5201	5554
B Net land rent and royalties	...	...	...	...	...	...	...	...	...	...	...	...

South Africa

1.4 General Government Current Receipts and Disbursements
(Continued)

Million South African rand

		1970	1975	1977	1978	1979	1980	1981	1982	1983	1984	1985	1986
3	Subsidies	147	288	467	582	581	795	893	1150	1874	2188	2607	3158
4	Other current transfers	294	692	940	1033	1234	1349	1532	2073	2475	2939	3662	4098
	A Social security benefits	42	73	109	138	143	176	164	200	264	352	471	588
	B Social assistance grants	251	614	823	889	1084	1166	1360	1862	2198	2571	3172	3490
	C Other	1	5	8	6	7	7	8	11	13	16	19	20
5	Net saving	439	814	508	816	723	2026	1404	-40	-1036	-2531	-1688	-1836
	Total Current Disbursements and Net Saving of General Government [a]	2621	5971	7673	8890	10505	14111	15915	18501	21412	25515	31477	36982

a) Estimates are prepared by the South African Reserve Bank. These estimates include the Republic of South Africa and Namibia.

1.6 Current Income and Outlay of Households and Non-Profit Institutions

Million South African rand

		1970	1975	1977	1978	1979	1980	1981	1982	1983	1984	1985	1986
	Receipts												
1	Compensation of employees	6872	14352	18090	20085	23185	28619	35623	42419	47508	55990	61921	70923
	A From resident producers	6870	14348	18083	20077	23175	28607	35608	42401	47488	55969	61898	70897
	B From rest of the world	2	4	7	8	10	12	15	18	20	21	23	20
2	Operating surplus of private unincorporated enterprises	...	...	...	...	...	...	...	...	...	...	...	...
3	Property and entrepreneurial income	1936	3825	5173	4974	6502	7738	6161	5390	8514	9860	13600	14421
4	Current transfers	367	840	1061	1181	1414	1554	1768	2360	2791	3293	4050	4503
	Total Current Receipts [a]	9175	19017	24324	26240	31101	37911	43552	50169	58813	69143	79571	89847
	Disbursements												
1	Private final consumption expenditure	7760	15478	19297	21510	24917	30922	37799	44134	50703	58517	65454	77093
2	Property income	...	...	...	...	...	...	...	...	...	...	...	...
3	Direct taxes and other current transfers n.e.c. to general government	586	1555	2190	2410	2437	2579	3358	4582	5689	8002	9492	10803
	A Social security contributions	...	...	...	...	...	...	...	...	...	...	...	...
	B Direct taxes	586	1555	2190	2410	2437	2579	3358	4582	5689	8002	9492	10803
	C Fees, fines and penalties	...	...	...	...	...	...	...	...	...	...	...	...
4	Other current transfers	47	76	147	120	106	104	120	121	129	139	165	184
5	Net saving	782	1908	2690	2200	3641	4306	2275	1332	2292	2485	4460	1767
	Total Current Disbursements and Net Saving [a]	9175	19017	24324	26240	31101	37911	43552	50169	58813	69143	79571	89847

a) Estimates are prepared by the South African Reserve Bank. These estimates include the Republic of South Africa and Namibia.

1.7 External Transactions on Current Account, Summary

Million South African rand

		1970	1975	1977	1978	1979	1980	1981	1982	1983	1984	1985	1986
	Payments to the Rest of the World												
1	Imports of goods and services	3165	8119	8470	9867	11878	16959	21627	21813	19440	25931	28299	31866
	A Imports of merchandise c.i.f.	2861	7382	7488	8751	10667	15516	19997	19956	17462	23667	25907	28713
	B Other	304	737	982	1116	1211	1443	1630	1858	1978	2264	2392	3153
2	Factor income to the rest of the world	623	1425	1840	2162	2555	3184	3835	4146	4702	5659	7855	9312
	A Compensation of employees	163	474	525	577	647	751	872	986	1150	1293	1503	1766
	B Property and entrepreneurial income	460	951	1315	1585	1908	2433	2963	3160	3552	4366	6352	7546
3	Current transfers to the rest of the world [a]	61	103	177	158	159	164	177	191	188	261	364	397
4	Surplus of the nation on current transactions	-868	-1813	412	1330	2880	2818	-4089	-3345	-78	-2220	5925	7196
	Payments to the Rest of the World and Surplus of the Nation on Current Transactions [b]	2981	7834	10899	13517	17472	23125	21550	22805	24202	29631	42443	48771
	Receipts From The Rest of the World												
1	Exports of goods and services	2757	7388	10474	12959	16724	22219	20584	21833	23163	28261	40395	46499

South Africa

1.7 External Transactions on Current Account, Summary
(Continued)

Million South African rand

	1970	1975	1977	1978	1979	1980	1981	1982	1983	1984	1985	1986
A Exports of merchandise f.o.b.	2290	6193	9088	11313	14816	19907	17917	18767	20136	24591	35925	41767
B Other	467	1195	1386	1646	1908	2312	2667	3066	3027	3670	4470	4732
2 Factor income from rest of the world	114	205	209	303	426	449	419	442	538	771	1326	1490
A Compensation of employees	2	4	7	8	10	12	15	18	20	21	23	26
B Property and entrepreneurial income	112	201	202	295	416	437	404	424	518	750	1303	1464
3 Current transfers from rest of the world	110	241	216	255	322	457	547	530	561	589	722	782
Receipts from the Rest of the World on Current Transactions [b]	2981	7834	10899	13517	17472	23125	21550	22805	24262	29621	42443	48771

a) Item 'Current transfers to/from the rest of the world' includes also capital transfers.
b) Estimates are prepared by the South African Reserve Bank. These estimates include the Republic of South Africa and Namibia.

1.8 Capital Transactions of The Nation, Summary

Million South African rand

	1970	1975	1977	1978	1979	1980	1981	1982	1983	1984	1985	1986
Finance of Gross Capital Formation												
Gross saving	2816	7080	9676	11269	15454	21658	19944	17401	23128	23968	31049	34360
1 Consumption of fixed capital	1359	3372	4902	5801	6886	8194	9860	12218	14453	16344	19722	24864
A General government	52	132	181	212	253	309	372	455	543	616	711	854
B Corporate and quasi-corporate enterprises	1307	3240	4721	5589	6633	7885	9488	11763	13910	15728	19011	24010
Public	334	865	1292	1516	1823	2431	2981	3667	4348	4941	5896	7394
Private	973	2375	3429	4073	4810	5454	6507	8096	9562	10787	13115	16616
C Other	-	-	-	-	-	-	-	-	-	-	-	-
2 Net saving	1457	3708	4774	5468	8568	13464	10084	5183	8675	7624	11327	9496
A General government	439	814	508	816	723	2026	1404	-40	-1036	-2531	-1688	-1836
B Corporate and quasi-corporate enterprises	236	986	1576	2452	4204	7132	6405	3891	7419	7670	8555	9565
C Other	782	1908	2690	2200	3641	4306	2275	1332	2292	2485	4460	1767
Less: Surplus of the nation on current transactions	-868	-1813	412	1330	2880	2818	-4089	-3345	-78	-2220	5925	7196
Finance of Gross Capital Formation [a]	3684	8893	9263	9939	12574	18840	24033	20746	23206	26188	25124	27164
Gross Capital Formation												
Increase in stocks	490	783	-307	-403	323	2462	3901	-1946	-1303	57	-3495	-1834
Gross fixed capital formation	3193	8110	9571	10342	12251	16378	20132	22692	24509	26131	28619	28998
1 General government	563	1296	1433	1411	1671	1909	2253	2353	2590	2832	3168	3729
2 Corporate and quasi-corporate enterprises	2631	6814	8138	8931	10580	14469	17879	20339	21919	23299	25451	25269
A Public	816	2748	3490	3876	4706	6160	6698	7519	7827	8003	9685	8903
B Private	1815	4066	4648	5055	5874	8309	11181	12820	14092	15296	15766	16366
3 Other	...	...	...	...	...	...	...	...	...	...	...	...
Gross Capital Formation [a]	3684	8893	9264	9939	12574	18840	24033	20746	23206	26188	25124	27164

a) Estimates are prepared by the South African Reserve Bank. These estimates include the Republic of South Africa and Namibia.

1.10 Gross Domestic Product by Kind of Activity, in Current Prices

Million South African rand

	1970	1975	1977	1978	1979	1980	1981	1982	1983	1984	1985	1986
1 Agriculture, hunting, forestry and fishing	973	2129	2532	2722	2885	4035	4787	4581	4096	5265	5907	7277
2 Mining and quarrying	1207	3182	4155	5497	7756	12729	10447	10409	12194	13210	17760	20953
3 Manufacturing	2796	5991	6963	7886	9579	12606	15646	16939	19456	22704	24311	27840
4 Electricity, gas and water	307	610	1140	1570	1777	1924	2164	2594	3181	3781	4480	5427
5 Construction	507	1362	1435	1472	1586	2080	2533	2898	3334	3674	3917	4215
6 Wholesale and retail trade, restaurants and hotels	1819	3667	4303	4595	4922	6806	8645	9376	10869	11486	12477	14242
7 Transport, storage and communication	1154	2395	3320	3670	4093	5045	5972	6623	7439	9336	9405	11335
8 Finance, insurance, real estate and business services	1733	3268	4076	4570	5386	6352	7664	9385	11459	13677	16470	18786
9 Community, social and personal services	228	389	519	609	678	820	945	1147	1466	1708	1920	2202
Total, Industries	10724	22993	28443	32591	38662	52397	58803	63952	73494	84841	96647	112277
Producers of Government Services	1132	2497	3267	3723	4342	5384	6837	8292	9604	12311	13906	16821

South Africa

1.10 Gross Domestic Product by Kind of Activity, in Current Prices
(Continued)

Million South African rand

	1970	1975	1977	1978	1979	1980	1981	1982	1983	1984	1985	1986
Other Producers	375	742	909	970	1070	1244	1459	1763	2005	2296	2603	2936
Subtotal [a]	12231	26232	32619	37284	44074	59025	67099	74007	85103	99448	113156	132034
Less: Imputed bank service charge	208	386	636	766	853	1062	1097	1014	1834	2020	3002	4132
Plus: Import duties	...	...	...	...	...	...	...	...	...	...	...	...
Plus: Value added tax	...	...	...	...	...	...	...	...	...	...	...	...
Plus: Other adjustments [b]	885	1608	2331	2779	3477	4044	5081	6683	6606	8386	9987	11793
Equals: Gross Domestic Product [c]	12908	27454	34314	39297	46698	62007	71083	79676	89875	105814	120141	139695

a) Gross domestic product in factor values.
b) Item 'Other adjustments' refers to indirect taxes net of subsidies.
c) Estimates of GDP by economic activity are prepared by the Department of Statistics. These estimates include the Republic of South Africa and Namibia.

1.11 Gross Domestic Product by Kind of Activity, in Constant Prices

Million South African rand

	1970	1975	1977	1978	1979	1980	1981	1982	1983	1984	1985	1986
					At constant prices of:1980							
1 Agriculture, hunting, forestry and fishing	2750	3339	3620	3740	3651	4035	4264	3892	3016	3333	3620	4203
2 Mining and quarrying	14741	12049	12677	12768	13043	12729	12565	12504	12529	12912	12907	12470
3 Manufacturing	7500	10006	9913	10632	11510	12606	13459	13052	12185	12554	11827	11900
4 Electricity, gas and water	983	1431	1566	1655	1770	1924	2145	2270	2287	2405	2567	2639
5 Construction	1614	2267	2062	1893	1918	2080	2195	2109	1994	2018	1873	1806
6 Wholesale and retail trade, restaurants and hotels	4788	6787	6376	6326	6098	6806	7446	7458	7720	8475	8040	7782
7 Transport, storage and communication	2898	3970	4149	4331	4713	5045	5365	5198	4892	5279	5235	5170
8 Finance, insurance, real estate and business services	4447	5411	5558	5691	5983	6352	6684	6848	7072	7389	7493	7666
9 Community, social and personal services	567	676	729	756	791	820	882	937	1001	1071	1074	1080
Total, Industries	40288	45936	46650	47792	49477	52397	55005	54268	52676	55436	54636	54716
Producers of Government Services	3656	4509	4918	5070	5208	5384	5512	5730	6018	6251	6292	6479
Other Producers	928	1137	1173	1195	1215	1244	1274	1313	1358	1409	1415	1425
Subtotal [a]	44872	51582	52741	54057	55900	59025	61791	61311	60052	63096	62343	62620
Less: Imputed bank service charge	737	948	931	951	978	1062	1201	1229	1256	1346	1356	1286
Plus: Import duties	...	...	...	...	...	...	...	...	...	...	...	...
Plus: Value added tax	...	...	...	...	...	...	...	...	...	...	...	...
Plus: Other adjustments [b]	2948	3763	3592	3745	3775	4044	4375	4390	4312	4567	4308	4312
Equals: Gross Domestic Product [c,d]	44557	54446	55265	56851	58697	62007	64965	64472	63108	66317	65295	65646

a) Gross domestic product in factor values.
b) Item 'Other adjustments' refers to indirect taxes net of subsidies.
c) Estimates of GDP by economic activity are prepared by the Department of Statistics. These estimates include the Republic of South Africa and Namibia.
d) For the years prior to 1978, existing series expressed in 1975 prices have been linked to the new 1980 base year without re-weighting. As a result, for the periods before 1978, the converted sub-totals and totals are not equal to the sum of their components.

1.12 Relations Among National Accounting Aggregates

Million South African rand

	1970	1975	1977	1978	1979	1980	1981	1982	1983	1984	1985	1986
Gross Domestic Product [a]	12908	27454	34314	39297	46698	62007	71083	79676	89875	105814	120141	139695
Plus: Net factor income from the rest of the world	-509	-1220	-1631	-1859	-2129	-2735	-3416	-3704	-4164	-4888	-6529	-7822
Factor income from the rest of the world	114	205	209	303	426	449	419	442	538	771	1326	1490
Less: Factor income to the rest of the world	623	1425	1840	2162	2555	3184	3835	4146	4702	5659	7855	9312
Equals: Gross National Product	12399	26234	32683	37438	44569	59272	67667	75972	85711	100926	113612	131873
Less: Consumption of fixed capital	1359	3372	4902	5801	6886	8194	9860	12218	14453	16344	19722	24864
Equals: National Income	11040	22862	27781	31637	37683	51078	57807	63754	71258	84582	93890	107009
Plus: Net current transfers from the rest of the world	49	138	39	97	163	293	370	339	363	338	358	385
Current transfers from the rest of the world	110	241	216	255	322	457	547	530	561	589	722	782
Less: Current transfers to the rest of the world [b]	61	103	177	158	159	164	177	191	198	251	364	397
Equals: National Disposable Income [a]	11089	23000	27820	31734	37846	51371	58177	64093	71621	84920	94248	107394
Less: Final consumption	9324	19260	24453	27183	31460	39371	48177	57124	65512	77304	87149	103101
Statistical discrepancy	-308	-32	1407	917	2182	1464	84	-1786	2566	8	4228	5203
Equals: Net Saving	1457	3708	4774	5468	8568	13464	10084	5183	8675	7624	11327	9496
Less: Surplus of the nation on current transactions	-868	-1813	412	1330	2880	2818	-4089	-3345	-78	-2220	5925	7196
Equals: Net Capital Formation [a]	2325	5521	4362	4138	5688	10646	14173	8528	8753	9844	5402	2300

a) Estimates are prepared by the South African Reserve Bank. These estimates include the Republic of South Africa and Namibia.
b) Item 'Current transfers to/from the rest of the world' includes also capital transfers.

South Africa

2.5 Private Final Consumption Expenditure by Type and Porpose, in Current Prices

Million South African rand

	1970	1975	1977	1978	1979	1980	1981	1982	1983	1984	1985	1986
Final Consumption Expenditure of Resident Households											
1 Food, beverages and tobacco	2500	5009	6472	7383	8685	10377	12791	14955	16917	19872	22253	27252
A Food	1797	3613	4606	5303	6283	7742	9766	11170	12832	14910	16956	20897
B Non-alcoholic beverages	90	200	264	263	332	408	427	515	588	782	880	1157
C Alcoholic beverages	394	807	1109	1264	1455	1462	1732	2253	2425	2821	2878	3447
D Tobacco	219	389	493	553	615	765	866	1017	1072	1359	1539	1751
2 Clothing and footwear	780	1587	1876	2030	2219	2746	3361	3792	4099	4518	4734	5599
3 Gross rent, fuel and power	961	1582	2071	2302	2575	3004	3640	4282	5250	6549	8128	9625
4 Furniture, furnishings and household equipment and operation	1084	2093	2395	2577	2954	3728	4504	5176	5842	6363	6697	7825
A Household operation	208	392	514	596	712	890	1108	1314	1577	1862	1893	2235
B Other	876	1701	1881	1981	2242	2838	3396	3862	4265	4501	4804	5590
5 Medical care and health expenses	252	537	736	828	913	1124	1324	1691	1984	2342	2674	3142
6 Transport and communication [a]	1101	2388	3006	3474	4210	5615	6831	7744	8683	9778	10999	12108
A Personal transport equipment	410	750	749	958	1150	1732	2213	2326	2673	2942	2480	2698
B Other	691	1638	2257	2516	3060	3883	4618	5418	6010	6836	8519	9410
7 Recreational, entertainment, education and cultural services	371	913	1104	1230	1372	1760	2153	2585	3100	3577	4062	4668
A Education	8	15	19	20	23	26	31	40	45	84	152	247
B Other	363	898	1085	1210	1349	1734	2122	2545	3055	3493	3910	4421
8 Miscellaneous goods and services	690	1402	1613	1769	2068	2571	3176	3781	4616	5339	5921	6531
A Personal care	159	277	330	366	417	495	612	739	883	1020	1157	1334
B Expenditures in restaurants, cafes and hotels	241	461	491	531	624	793	959	1082	1351	1563	1618	1705
C Other [a]	290	664	792	872	1027	1283	1605	1960	2382	2756	3146	3492
Total Final Consumption Expenditure in the Domestic Market by Households, of which	7739	15511	19273	21593	24996	30925	37780	44006	50491	58338	65468	76750
A Durable goods	934	1911	1978	2273	2672	3765	4757	5297	6085	6597	6120	6854
B Semi-durable goods	1475	3002	3591	3885	4282	5359	6586	7490	8493	9573	10571	12342
C Non-durable goods	3195	6572	8686	9862	11719	14166	17415	20350	23099	26998	30792	36920
D Services	2134	4026	5018	5573	6323	7635	9022	10869	12814	15170	17985	20634
Plus: Direct purchases abroad by resident households	161	353	391	363	446	570	674	785	872	971	902	1327
Less: Direct purchases in the domestic market by non-resident households [b]	244	650	707	813	951	1090	1274	1444	1607	1873	2146	2329
Equals: Final Consumption Expenditure of Resident Households	7656	15214	18957	21143	24491	30405	37180	43347	49756	57436	64224	75748
Final Consumption Expenditure of Private Non-profit Institutions Serving Households											
1 Research and science	...	...	...	...	...	...	...	...	...	...	...	...
2 Education	76	189	239	246	288	356	438	546	671	764	854	945
3 Medical and other health services	17	52	71	83	92	108	118	168	195	225	272	282
4 Welfare services	...	...	...	...	...	...	...	...	...	...	...	...
5 Recreational and related cultural services	8	15	20	27	34	40	49	58	65	75	86	99
6 Religious organisations	...	...	...	...	...	...	...	...	...	...	...	...
7 Professional and labour organisations serving households	...	...	...	...	...	...	...	...	...	...	...	...
8 Miscellaneous	3	8	10	11	12	13	14	15	16	17	18	19
Equals: Final Consumption Expenditure of Private Non-profit Organisations Serving Households	104	264	340	367	426	517	619	787	947	1081	1230	1345
Private Final Consumption Expenditure [c]	7760	15478	19297	21510	24917	30922	37799	44134	50703	58517	65454	77093

a) Packaged tours is included in item 'Transport and communication'.
b) Item 'Direct purchases in the domestic market by non-resident households' includes a statistical discrepancy.
c) Estimates are prepared by the South African Reserve Bank. These estimates include the Republic of South Africa and Namibia.

South Africa

2.6 Private Final Consumption Expenditure by Type and Purpose, in Constant Prices

Million South African rand

	1970	1975	1977	1978	1979	1980	1981	1982	1983	1984	1985	1986
At constant prices of: 1980												
Final Consumption Expenditure of Resident Households												
1 Food, beverages and tobacco	7266	8798	9491	9703	10040	10377	10714	11088	11269	11903	11830	12137
A Food	5596	6565	7111	7295	7451	7743	7999	8226	8456	8857	8991	9206
B Non-alcoholic beverages	224	360	355	316	365	408	373	385	385	431	418	462
C Alcoholic beverages	818	1270	1417	1475	1576	1462	1549	1690	1668	1761	1588	1636
D Tobacco	486	593	606	617	648	764	793	787	760	854	833	833
2 Clothing and footwear	1793	2448	2425	2379	2405	2746	2984	2934	2895	2855	2660	2694
3 Gross rent, fuel and power	2240	2627	2803	2863	2909	3004	3160	3215	3190	3343	3459	3497
4 Furniture, furnishings and household equipment and operation	2442	3448	3188	3151	3291	3728	3981	3999	4061	4046	3783	3694
A Household operation	572	745	827	842	839	890	998	1014	1050	1115	932	827
B Other	1854	2670	2357	2309	2452	2838	2983	2985	3011	2931	2851	2867
5 Medical care and health expenses	673	1063	1126	1142	1197	1232	1305	1399	1378	1513	1506	1450
6 Transport and communication [a]	3890	4930	4549	4920	4845	5615	6209	6179	6260	6495	5935	5892
A Personal transport equipment	1173	1335	1005	1175	1280	1732	1914	1745	1645	1528	1036	834
B Other	2661	3560	3562	3745	3565	3883	4295	4434	4615	4967	4899	5058
7 Recreational, entertainment, education and cultural services	1265	1914	1919	1943	1952	2156	2334	2458	2646	2717	2536	2350
A Education	258	346	344	351	354	382	310	399	418	432	419	386
B Other	1006	1568	1575	1592	1598	1774	2024	2059	2228	2285	2117	1964
8 Miscellaneous goods and services	1871	2425	2284	2242	2333	2585	2769	2832	3003	3081	2968	2769
A Personal care	326	477	465	450	462	505	559	574	586	594	578	547
B Expenditures in restaurants, cafes and hotels	749	826	729	704	726	793	797	784	868	893	823	736
C Other [a]	796	1122	1090	1088	1145	1287	1413	1474	1549	1594	1567	1486
Total Final Consumption Expenditure in the Domestic Market by Households, of which [b]	21414	27675	27846	28343	28972	31443	33456	34104	34702	35953	34677	34483
A Durable goods	2120	3064	2594	2723	2942	3765	4100	3979	3978	3781	2965	2611
B Semi-durable goods	3634	4934	4782	4704	4719	5359	5847	5808	5962	6025	5786	5732
C Non-durable goods	9939	12370	13114	13424	13631	14166	14935	15447	15863	16924	16605	16841
D Services	5721	7307	7356	7492	7680	8153	8574	8870	8899	9223	9321	9299
Plus: Direct purchases abroad by resident households	458	619	540	460	505	570	597	627	640	660	557	754
Less: Direct purchases in the domestic market by non-resident households [c]	675	1140	1001	1045	1082	1091	1107	1091	1083	1129	1116	1019
Equals: Final Consumption Expenditure of Resident Households [d,b]	21197	27154	27385	27758	28395	30922	32946	33640	34259	35484	34118	34218
Final Consumption Expenditure of Private Non-profit Institutions Serving Households												
Equals: Final Consumption Expenditure of Private Non-profit Organisations Serving Households	...	...	...	...	...	...	...	...	...	...	...	...
Private Final Consumption Expenditure [e,b]	21197	27154	27385	27758	28395	30922	32946	33640	34259	35484	34118	34218

a) Packaged tours is included in item 'Transport and communication'.
b) For the years prior to 1978, existing series expressed in 1975 prices have been linked to the new 1980 base year without re-weighting. As a result, for the periods before 1978, the converted sub-totals and totals are not equal to the sum of their components.
c) Item 'Direct purchases in the domestic market by non-resident households' includes a statistical discrepancy.
d) Item 'Final consumption expenditure of resident households' includes consumption expenditure of private non-profit institutions serving households.
e) Estimates are prepared by the South African Reserve Bank. These estimates include the Republic of South Africa and Namibia.

2.7 Gross Capital Formation by Type of Good and Owner, in Current Prices

Million South African rand

	1980				1981				1982			
	TOTAL	Total Private	Public Enterprises	General Government	TOTAL	Total Private	Public Enterprises	General Government	TOTAL	Total Private	Public Enterprises	General Government
Increase in stocks, total [a,b,c]	2462	2026	436	*	3901	3034	867	-	-1946	-1927	-19	-
1 Goods producing industries	239	...	...	...	985	...	...	...	-1314	...	...	...
2 Wholesale and retail trade [c]	1351	...	...	...	1913	...	...	...	-778	...	...	...
3 Other, except government stocks [c]	852	...	...	...	929	...	...	...	93	...	...	...
4 Government stocks [c]	20	...	...	...	74	...	...	...	53	...	...	...
Gross Fixed Capital Formation, Total	16378	8309	6160	1909	20132	11181	6698	2253	22692	12820	7519	2353
1 Residential buildings	1796	1179	...	...	2311	1608	...	...	2766	2066	...	...
2 Non-residential buildings	1957	892	...	...	2606	1369	...	...	3212	1911	...	...

South Africa

2.7 Gross Capital Formation by Type of Good and Owner, in Current Prices
(Continued)

Million South African rand

	1980				1981				1982			
	TOTAL	Total Private	Public Enterprises	General Government	TOTAL	Total Private	Public Enterprises	General Government	TOTAL	Total Private	Public Enterprises	General Government
3 Other construction	4330	671	...	...	4624	810	...	...	4380	823	...	...
4 Land improvement and plantation and orchard development [d]	353	...	...	...	383	...	...	...	432	...	...	...
5 Producers' durable goods	7942	5214	...	...	10207	7010	...	...	11901	7588	...	...
A Transport equipment	1893	1430	...	...	2569	1889	...	...	2915	1967	...	...
B Machinery and equipment	6049	3784	...	...	7637	5121	...	...	8986	5621	...	...
6 Breeding stock, dairy cattle, etc. [a]	...	...	...	...	...	...	...	...	...	...	...	...
Total Gross Capital Formation [e]	18840	10335	6596	1909	24033	14215	7563	2253	20746	10893	7500	2353

	1983				1984				1985			
	TOTAL	Total Private	Public Enterprises	General Government	TOTAL	Total Private	Public Enterprises	General Government	TOTAL	Total Private	Public Enterprises	General Government
Increase in stocks, total [abc]	-1303	-1309	6	-	57	190	-133	...	-3495	-3039	-456	...
1 Goods producing industries	-861	...	...	...	-124	...	...	...	-1763	...	...	...
2 Wholesale and retail trade [c]	-464	...	...	...	433	...	...	...	-734	...	...	...
3 Other, except government stocks [c]	109	...	...	...	-242	...	...	...	-990	...	...	...
4 Government stocks [c]	-87	...	...	...	-10	...	...	...	-8	...	...	...
Gross Fixed Capital Formation, Total	24509	14092	7827	2590	26131	15296	8003	2832	28619	15766	9685	3168
1 Residential buildings	3366	2511	...	...	3887	2988	...	...	3568	2830	...	...
2 Non-residential buildings	3506	2117	...	...	4074	2146	...	...	4419	2462	...	...
3 Other construction	4624	1012	...	...	4783	1147	...	...	5100	1348	...	...
4 Land improvement and plantation and orchard development [d]	678	...	...	...	725	725	...	...	634	634	...	...
5 Producers' durable goods	12335	7774	...	...	12702	8000	...	...	14900	8479	...	...
A Transport equipment	3172	2135	...	...	2868	2282	...	...	2904	2246	...	...
B Machinery and equipment	9163	5639	...	...	9834	5718	...	...	11996	6233	...	...
6 Breeding stock, dairy cattle, etc. [a]	...	...	...	...	...	...	...	...	...	...	...	...
Total Gross Capital Formation [e]	23206	12783	7833	2590	26188	15486	7870	2832	25124	12727	9229	3168

	1986			
	TOTAL	Total Private	Public Enterprises	General Government
Increase in stocks, total [abc]	-1834	-1829	-5	...
1 Goods producing industries	-386	...	...	...
2 Wholesale and retail trade [c]	-1521	...	...	...
3 Other, except government stocks [c]	256	...	...	...
4 Government stocks [c]	-183	...	...	...
Gross Fixed Capital Formation, Total	28998	16366	8903	3729
1 Residential buildings	3560	2795	...	...
2 Non-residential buildings	4569	2420	...	...
3 Other construction	5375	1678	...	...
4 Land improvement and plantation and orchard development [d]	664	664	...	...
5 Producers' durable goods	14830	8809	...	...
A Transport equipment	2839	2383	...	...
B Machinery and equipment	11991	6426	...	...
6 Breeding stock, dairy cattle, etc. [a]	...	...	...	...
Total Gross Capital Formation [e]	27164	14537	8898	3729

a) Item 'Breeding stocks, dairy cattle, etc.' is included in item 'Increase in stocks'.
b) Item 'Increase in stocks' excludes enterprises of commercial farms in business services, education, health and large unincorporated units of government enterprises.
c) The estimates of 'Increase in stocks' and their components are after inventory valuation adjustment.
d) Land development includes transfer costs.
e) Estimates are prepared by the South African Reserve Bank. These estimates include the Republic of South Africa and Namibia.

South Africa

2.8 Gross Capital Formation by Type of Good and Owner, in Constant Prices

Million South African rand

	1980 TOTAL	1980 Total Private	1980 Public Enterprises	1980 General Government	1981 TOTAL	1981 Total Private	1981 Public Enterprises	1981 General Government	1982 TOTAL	1982 Total Private	1982 Public Enterprises	1982 General Government
At constant prices of: 1980												
Increase in stocks, total [abc]	2462	2026	...	...	3468	2677	...	...	-1496	-1483	...	...
1 Goods producing industries	281	...	...	...	889	...	...	...	-1007	...	...	...
2 Wholesale and retail trade [c]	1238	...	...	...	1650	...	...	...	-694	...	...	...
3 Other, except government stocks [c]	923	...	...	...	862	...	...	...	164	...	...	...
4 Government stocks [c]	20	...	...	...	67	...	...	...	41	...	...	...
Gross Fixed Capital Formation, Total [d]	16378	8309	...	...	17756	9891	...	...	17230	9758	...	...
1 Residential buildings	1796	1179	...	...	2004	1396	...	...	2045	1530	...	...
2 Non-residential buildings	1958	892	...	...	2253	1182	...	...	2361	1406	...	...
3 Other construction	4330	671	...	...	4009	701	...	...	3251	616	...	...
4 Land improvement and plantation and orchard development [e]	352	...	...	...	332	...	...	...	320	...	...	...
5 Producers' durable goods	7942	5214	...	...	9158	6280	...	...	9253	5886	...	...
A Transport equipment	1893	1430	...	...	2253	1657	...	...	2157	1455	...	...
B Machinery and equipment	6049	3784	...	...	6905	4623	...	...	7096	4431	...	...
6 Breeding stock, dairy cattle, etc. [a]	...	...	...	...	...	...	...	...	...	...	...	...
Total Gross Capital Formation [f]	18840	10335	...	...	21224	12568	...	...	15734	8275	...	...

	1983 TOTAL	1983 Total Private	1983 Public Enterprises	1983 General Government	1984 TOTAL	1984 Total Private	1984 Public Enterprises	1984 General Government	1985 TOTAL	1985 Total Private	1985 Public Enterprises	1985 General Government
At constant prices of: 1980												
Increase in stocks, total [abc]	-890	-895	...	...	-57	26	...	...	-2089	-1821	...	...
1 Goods producing industries	-625	...	...	...	-85	...	...	...	-1015	...	...	...
2 Wholesale and retail trade [c]	-369	...	...	...	225	...	...	...	-498	...	...	...
3 Other, except government stocks [c]	166	...	...	...	-192	...	...	...	-572	...	...	...
4 Government stocks [c]	-62	...	...	...	-5	...	...	...	-4	...	...	...
Gross Fixed Capital Formation, Total [d]	16417	9439	...	...	16102	9397	...	...	15142	8282	...	...
1 Residential buildings	2154	1609	...	...	2262	1733	...	...	1859	1413	...	...
2 Non-residential buildings	2249	1359	...	...	2371	1399	...	...	2301	1268	...	...
3 Other construction	2992	656	...	...	2788	699	...	...	2665	788	...	...
4 Land improvement and plantation and orchard development [e]	436	...	...	...	428	428	...	...	333	333	...	...
5 Producers' durable goods	8586	5379	...	...	8253	5138	...	...	7984	4480	...	...
A Transport equipment	2032	1363	...	...	1684	1341	...	...	1431	1105	...	...
B Machinery and equipment	6554	4016	...	...	6569	3797	...	...	6553	3375	...	...
6 Breeding stock, dairy cattle, etc. [a]	...	...	...	...	...	...	...	...	...	...	...	...
Total Gross Capital Formation [f]	15527	8544	...	...	16045	9423	...	...	13053	6461	...	...

	1986 TOTAL	1986 Total Private	1986 Public Enterprises	1986 General Government
At constant prices of: 1980				
Increase in stocks, total [abc]	-849	-834	...	...
1 Goods producing industries	-202	...	...	...
2 Wholesale and retail trade [c]	-670	...	...	...
3 Other, except government stocks [c]	-50	...	...	...
4 Government stocks [c]	73	...	...	...
Gross Fixed Capital Formation, Total [d]	12470	6960	...	...
1 Residential buildings	1599	1255	...	...
2 Non-residential buildings	2049	1086	...	...

South Africa

2.8 Gross Capital Formation by Type of Good and Owner, in Constant Prices
(Continued)

Million South African rand

	1986			
	TOTAL	Total Private	Public Enterprises	General Government
	At constant prices of:1980			
3 Other construction	2415	751	...	...
4 Land improvement and plantation and orchard development e	299	299	...	...
5 Producers' durable goods	6108	3569	...	...
A Transport equipment	1046	876	...	...
B Machinery and equipment	5062	2693	...	...
6 Breeding stock, dairy cattle, etc. a	...	...	...	...
Total Gross Capital Formation f	11621	6126	...	...

a) Item 'Breeding stocks, dairy cattle, etc.' is included in item 'Increase in stocks'.
b) Item 'Increase in stocks' excludes enterprises of commercial farms in business services, education, health and large unincorporated units of government enterprises.
c) The estimates of 'Increase in stocks' and their components are after inventory valuation adjustment.
d) For the years prior to 1978, existing series expressed in 1975 prices have been linked to the new 1980 base year without re-weighting. As a result, for the periods before 1978, the converted sub-totals and totals are not equal to the sum of their components.
e) Land development includes transfer costs.
f) Estimates are prepared by the South African Reserve Bank. These estimates include the Republic of South Africa and Namibia.

2.11 Gross Fixed Capital Formation by Kind of Activity of Owner, ISIC Divisions, in Current Prices

Million South African rand

	1970	1975	1977	1978	1979	1980	1981	1982	1983	1984	1985	1986
	All Producers											
1 Agriculture, hunting, forestry and fishing	218	527	527	583	628	897	1248	1083	1006	870	945	933
2 Mining and quarrying	196	746	854	924	1305	1962	2290	2271	2173	2560	3182	4434
3 Manufacturing	594	1471	1767	2192	2821	4334	4750	4951	5300	4940	4524	4268
4 Electricity, gas and water	256	619	1255	1490	1739	1973	2309	3037	3629	4348	4877	4122
5 Construction	41	160	171	187	214	264	338	357	397	438	446	436
6 Wholesale and retail trade, restaurants and hotels	241	503	635	563	609	715	992	1314	1383	1655	2165	1706
7 Transport, storage and communication	351	1332	1456	1313	1430	1670	2326	3152	2952	2674	3266	3042
8 Finance, insurance, real estate and business services	684	1310	1348	1576	1733	2533	3434	3956	4849	5542	5685	5895
9 Community, social and personal services a	50	146	125	103	101	121	189	205	230	272	361	433
Total Industries bc	2631	6814	8138	8931	10580	14469	17876	20326	21919	23299	25451	25269
Producers of Government Services	563	1296	1433	1411	1671	1909	2253	2353	2590	2832	3168	3729
Private Non-Profit Institutions Serving Households a	...	...	...	...	...	...	...	...	...	...	...	...
Total b	3194	8110	9571	10342	12251	16378	20129	22679	24509	26131	28619	28998

a) Item 'Private non-profit institutions serving households' is included in item 'Community, social and personal services'.
b) Estimates are prepared by the South African Reserve Bank. These estimates include the Republic of South Africa and Namibia.
c) For the years prior to 1978, existing series expressed in 1975 prices have been linked to the new 1980 base year without re-weighting. As a result, for the periods before 1978, the converted sub-totals and totals are not equal to the sum of their components.

2.12 Gross Fixed Capital Formation by Kind of Activity of Owner, ISIC Divisions, in Constant Prices

Million South African rand

	1970	1975	1977	1978	1979	1980	1981	1982	1983	1984	1985	1986
	At constant prices of:1980											
	All Producers											
1 Agriculture, hunting, forestry and fishing	732	1020	771	742	694	897	1114	810	650	509	455	366
2 Mining and quarrying	723	1555	1228	1196	1474	1962	2019	1734	1467	1581	1690	1925
3 Manufacturing	1927	2711	2548	2853	3211	4334	4217	3828	3656	3151	2443	1821
4 Electricity, gas and water	822	1118	1768	1889	1943	1973	2069	2364	2513	2801	2651	1770

South Africa

2.12 Gross Fixed Capital Formation by Kind of Activity of Owner, ISIC Divisions, in Constant Prices
(Continued)

Million South African rand

	1970	1975	1977	1978	1979	1980	1981	1982	1983	1984	1985	1986
					At constant prices of:1980							
5 Construction	126	283	238	236	238	264	302	278	273	273	238	181
6 Wholesale and retail trade, restaurants and hotels	760	911	907	729	692	715	878	1000	932	1018	1142	733
7 Transport, storage and communication	1085	2424	2081	1684	1631	1670	2041	2372	1964	1639	1721	1277
8 Finance, insurance, real estate and business services	2237	2423	1964	2066	1988	2533	3003	2950	3143	3298	2957	2528
9 Community, social and personal services [a,b]	2096	2764	2331	2045	2074	2030	2113	1894	1819	1823	1845	1869
Total Industries [c,d]	8894	12844	11726	13440	13945	16378	17756	17230	16417	16093	15142	12470
Producers of Government Services [a]	...	...	...	...	...	...	...	...	...	...	...	...
Private Non-Profit Institutions Serving Households [b]	...	...	...	...	...	...	...	...	...	...	...	...
Total [c,d]	10490	15149	13830	13440	13945	16378	17756	17230	16417	16102	15142	12470

a) Item 'Producers of government services' is included in item 'Community, social and personal services'.
b) Item 'Private non-profit institutions serving households' is included in item 'Community, social and personal services'.
c) Estimates are prepared by the South African Reserve Bank. These estimates include the Republic of South Africa and Namibia.
d) For the years prior to 1978, existing series expressed in 1975 prices have been linked to the new 1980 base year without re-weighting. As a result, for the periods before 1978, the converted sub-totals and totals are not equal to the sum of their components.

2.17 Exports and Imports of Goods and Services, Detail

Million South African rand

	1970	1975	1977	1978	1979	1980	1981	1982	1983	1984	1985	1986
					Exports of Goods and Services							
1 Exports of merchandise, f.o.b.	2200	6100	9000	11313	14816	19907	17919	18768	20136	24591	35925	41767
2 Transport and communication	134	340	426	512	611	826	863	1028	835	980	1351	1772
3 Insurance service charges												
4 Other commodities	89	205	255	323	347	396	527	593	585	817	973	631
5 Adjustments of merchandise exports to change-of-ownership basis	-	-	-	-	-	-	-	-	-	-	-	-
6 Direct purchases in the domestic market by non-residential households	244	650	705	811	950	1090	1275	1444	1607	1873	2146	2329
7 Direct purchases in the domestic market by extraterritorial bodies	...	...	...	...	...	...	...	...	...	...	...	...
Total Exports of Goods and Services [a]	2757	7388	10474	12959	16724	22219	20584	21833	23163	28261	40395	46499
					Imports of Goods and Services							
1 Imports of merchandise, c.i.f.	2861	7382	7488	8751	10667	15518	19997	19956	17462	23667	25907	28713
A Imports of merchandise, f.o.b.	2582	6742	6881	8019	9739	14159	18109	18005	15863	21471	23045	25514
B Transport of services on merchandise imports	279	640	607	733	928	1359	1888	1951	1599	2196	2862	3199
C Insurance service charges on merchandise imports												
2 Adjustments of merchandise imports to change-of-ownership basis	...	...	...	...	...	...	...	...	...	...	...	...
3 Other transport and communication	142	383	590	753	765	871	955	1073	1106	1293	1490	1826
4 Other insurance service charges	...	...	...	...	...	...	...	...	...	...	...	...
5 Other commodities	...	...	...	...	...	...	...	...	...	...	...	...
6 Direct purchases abroad by government	...	...	...	...	...	...	...	...	...	...	...	...
7 Direct purchases abroad by resident households	162	354	392	362	446	570	674	785	872	971	902	1327
Total Imports of Goods and Services [a]	3165	8119	8470	9867	11878	16959	21626	21814	19440	25931	28299	31866
Balance of Goods and Services	-408	-731	2004	3092	4846	5260	-1042	19	3723	2330	12096	14633
Total Imports and Balance of Goods and Services [a]	2757	7388	10474	12959	16724	22219	20584	21833	23163	28261	40395	46499

a) Estimates are prepared by the South African Reserve Bank. These estimates include the Republic of South Africa and Namibia.

Spain

General note. The preparation of national accounts statistics in Spain is undertaken by the Instituto Nacional de Estadistica, Madrid. The official estimates are published by the Instituto in 'La Contabilidad Nacional de Espana'. A detailed description of the sources and methods used for the national accounts estimation is found in 'La Contabilidad Nacional de Espana, Base, 1970' published in 1977. In this publication, the Instituto introduced a new system of national accounts, the ESA system, which corresponds closely to the present United Nations System of National Accounts (SNA). Input output tables have been published by the organizacion Sindical Espanola in 'Tabla Input-output de la Economia Espanola'. The following tables have been prepared from successive replies to the United Nations national accounts questionnaire. When the scope and coverage of the estimates differ for conceptual or statistical reasons from the definitions and classifications recommended in SNA, a footnotes is indicated to the relevant tables.

Sources and methods:

(a) Gross domestic product. Gross domestic product is estimated mainly through the production approach.

(b) Expenditure on the gross domestic product. The expenditure approach is used to estimate government final consumption expenditure, increase in stocks and exports and imports of goods and services. This approach, in combination with the commodity-flow approach is used to estimate private consumption expenditure and gross fixed capital formation. Estimates of government expenditure are derived from the government accounts and for the social security funds, from basic accounting documents. Data obtained from the family budget expenditure surveys are used together with the commodity-flow method to arrive at the final estimates of private expenditure. For the estimation of changes in stocks, information is available from the Comisaria de Abastecimiento y Transportes and the Servicio Nacional de Cereales for the agricultural sector and from stock surveys for the industrial sectors. The basic data used for the estimation of gross fixed capital formation are obtained from various concerned agencies such as Ministerio de Agricultura for agricultural investments, Servicio Sindical de Estadistica for investments in the industrial sector, Comisaria del Plan de Desarrollo for public investments, reports from other enterprises, etc. The source of information for the estimation of exports and imports of goods and services is the balance of payments which is based on custom's statistics and information on external monetary flows. Supplementary information is obtained from the accounts of insurance companies and government accounts. For the constant prices estimates, all items of GDP by expenditure type are deflated by appropriate price indexes.

(c) Cost-structure of the gross domestic product. Wage statistics and social security data provided by the Instituto and the Ministerio de Sanidad u Seguridad Social are used to estimate compensation of employees. Operating surplus is obtained as a residual except interests of financial sector, rents of ownership of dwellings and imputed rents of public buildings for which separate estimates are made. The rate of consumption of fixed capital is based on average life of the existing stocks. Estimates of indirect taxes and subsidies are derived from the information used to compile the government accounts.

(d) Gross domestic product by kind of economic activity. The table of GDP by kind of economic activity is prepared in factor values. The production approach is used to estimate the value added of most industries. The income approach is used for government services and some service industries. Both production and income approaches are used for the trade sector, restaurants and hotels. The estimates of the agricultural sector are prepared by the Ministerio de Agricultura. Separate information on the volume and value of production of each subsector is available while intermediate consumption is estimated on a comprehensive basis. Value added of the fishing sector is estimated by using a fixed percentage between costs and value added based on data provided by the Sindicato Nacional de la Pescas. Annual mining statistics are obtained from the Direccion General de Minas y Combustibles supplemented by information obtained from the Ministerio de Industria. The estimates for manufacturing are based on industrial statistics compiled by the Ministerio de Industria, Ministerio de Agricultura and Servicio Sindical de Estadistica. The data used for estimating electricity, gas, and water are provided by the Ministerio de Industria, Servicio Sindical de Estadistica and Sindicato Nacional de Agua, Gas y Electricidad, respectively. The estimates of construction are based mainly on sample surveys supplemented by information on employment and material consumption obtained from the Ministerio de Obras Publicas and the Ministerio de Vivienda. For the trade sector, only scattered information is available on employment, wages and salaries, external trade and gross margins. However, a survey of domestic trade conducted for 1964 provided a detailed knowledge of the structure of this sector. For restaurants and hotels, estimates are based on information obtained from concerned agencies. The estimates for the transport sector are based on data supplied by the RENFE (a national enterprise) and other public and private companies for railways, data from the national airlines for air transport, passenger transport surveys and national surveys of goods transported for road transport and data from concerned maritime companies for water transport. The value added of communication is estimated directly on the basis of data provided by the State monopolies. For the financial and insurance sectors, the data are provided by the concerned institutions. For ownership of dwellings, the estimates are based on the resultes of family budget expenditure surveys. The rents are imputed by ascertaining the total dwelling costs, from which the net rent is derived as income on the capital. Estimates for producers of government services are based on data obtained from the Ministerio de Hacienda. The information for health and sanitary services in the private and public sectors is obtained from government accounts supplemented by the family budget expenditure surveys and censuses of health establishments. For other services, estimates are based on the number of persons employed, derived from the population censuses and checked against the data of input-output tables. The value added of domestic services and business services is obtained from sample surveys of family budget and accounting documents, respectively. For the constant price estimates, current estimates of most industries are deflated by appropriate price indexes. For agriculture and construction, double deflation is used.

1.1 Expenditure on the Gross Domestic Product, in Current Prices

Thousand Million Spanish pesetas

	1970	1975	1977	1978	1979	1980	1981	1982	1983	1984	1985	1986
1 Government final consumption expenditure	239.1	606.5	1018.6	1292.2	1574.7	1929.3	2242.2	2619.5	3090.9	3448.3	3906.6	4443.3
2 Private final consumption expenditure	1705.0	3929.7	6067.3	7290.7	8602.8	10080.4	11457.9	13143.3	14808.1	16370.0	18116.5	20400.2
3 Gross capital formation	705.1	1717.6	2296.9	2578.0	2940.9	3548.1	3638.2	4156.6	4470.2	4712.8	5286.2	6398.6
A Increase in stocks	21.1	126.3	96.8	27.7	98.7	179.9	-58.7	-14.4	-104.4	4.2	12.6	406.4
B Gross fixed capital formation	684.0	1591.3	2200.1	2550.3	2842.2	3368.2	3696.9	4171.0	4574.6	4708.6	5273.6	5992.2
Residential buildings	...	...	...	...	...	934.9	1029.3	1126.1	1136.0	1144.3	1183.5	1267.5
Non-residential buildings	...	...	...	...	...	1355.5	1479.8	1665.6	1925.5	2028.8	2303.6	2676.7
Other construction and land improvement etc.	...	...	...	...	...							
Other	...	...	...	...	...	1077.8	1187.8	1379.4	1513.1	1535.5	1786.5	2048.0
4 Exports of goods and services	348.4	816.0	1334.5	1710.8	1975.2	2409.8	3079.1	3672.2	4725.6	5943.5	6518.7	6453.9
5 Less: Imports of goods and services	373.3	1046.7	1522.3	1621.2	1935.9	2758.5	3428.3	4024.3	4860.1	5363.3	5914.8	5715.5
Statistical discrepancy	-0.1	-	-	-	-	-	-0.1	-	-	-	-	-
Equals: Gross Domestic Product	2624.2	6023.1	9195.0	11250.5	13157.7	15209.1	16989.0	19567.3	22234.7	25111.3	27913.2	31980.5

1.2 Expenditure on the Gross Domestic Product, in Constant Prices

Thousand Million Spanish pesetas

	1970	1975	1977	1978	1979	1980	1981	1982	1983	1984	1985	1986
					At constant prices of:1980							
1 Government final consumption expenditure	1129.8	1517.1	1686.2	1777.7	1851.9	1929.3	1965.5	2061.0	2141.7	2203.3	2305.5	2423.2
2 Private final consumption expenditure	6980.6	9152.3	9805.9	9898.5	10023.1	10080.4	10020.1	10038.5	10072.8	10034.1	10257.9	10621.7
3 Gross capital formation	2986.2	3895.2	3743.9	3535.0	3461.7	3548.1	3215.5	3265.1	3132.6	3009.6	3127.6	3573.7
A Increase in stocks	104.5	234.5	146.6	35.9	115.8	179.9	-43.1	-9.9	-59.1	2.8	7.4	207.4
B Gross fixed capital formation	2881.7	3660.7	3597.3	3499.1	3345.9	3368.2	3258.6	3275.0	3191.7	3006.8	3120.2	3366.3

Spain

1.2 Expenditure on the Gross Domestic Product, in Constant Prices
(Continued)

Thousand Million Spanish pesetas

	1970	1975	1977	1978	1979	1980	1981	1982	1983	1984	1985	1986
					At constant prices of:1980							
Residential buildings	...	...	...	...	...	934.9	919.0	892.4	835.3	782.6	770.9	786.3
Non-residential buildings	...	...	...	...	...	1355.5	1295.7	1314.1	1335.7	1280.8	1329.6	1454.0
Other construction and land improvement etc.	...	...	...	...	...							
Other	...	...	...	...	...	1077.8	1043.9	1068.6	1020.8	943.4	1019.7	1126.0
4 Exports of goods and services	1219.8	1712.3	2015.2	2230.3	2356.2	2409.8	2612.0	2736.7	3014.4	3367.9	3458.1	3510.1
5 Less: Imports of goods and services	1494.0	2336.0	2422.0	2397.4	2669.8	2758.5	2641.7	2745.4	2728.5	2700.5	2867.8	3310.7
Statistical discrepancy	-0.1	-	-	-0.1	-	-	-0.1	-	0.2	0.1	-0.1	-
Equals: Gross Domestic Product	10822.3	13940.9	14829.2	15044.0	15023.1	15209.1	15171.3	15355.9	15633.2	15914.5	16281.2	16818.0

1.3 Cost Components of the Gross Domestic Product

Thousand Million Spanish pesetas

	1970	1975	1977	1978	1979	1980	1981	1982	1983	1984	1985	1986
1 Indirect taxes, net	181.6	320.9	483.0	479.8	601.5	694.4	908.6	1033.3	1324.3	1567.8	1948.2	2782.6
A Indirect taxes	204.6	389.5	613.2	693.4	824.0	1009.5	1243.0	1522.3	1900.1	2271.4	2686.9	3557.4
B Less: Subsidies	23.0	68.6	130.2	213.6	222.5	315.1	334.4	489.0	575.8	703.6	738.7	774.8
2 Consumption of fixed capital	265.8	599.2	910.4	1105.7	1351.0	1615.4	1930.6	2253.7	2637.9	3029.6	3364.8	3631.8
3 Compensation of employees paid by resident producers to:	1186.0	3077.0	4805.0	5892.0	6870.0	7784.0	8714.9	9853.2	11132.4	11876.2	12957.2	14552.8
A Resident households	1186.0	3076.9	4804.9	5891.9	6869.8	7783.3	8714.6	9852.8	11132.0	11875.6	12956.3	14551.3
B Rest of the world	-	0.1	0.1	0.1	0.2	0.6	0.3	0.4	0.4	0.5	0.9	1.4
4 Operating surplus	990.8	2026.0	2996.6	3773.0	4335.1	5115.4	5434.9	6427.1	7140.0	8637.7	9643.1	11013.4
Statistical discrepancy	-	-	-	-	0.1	-0.1	-	-	0.1	-	-0.1	-0.1
Equals: Gross Domestic Product	2624.2	6023.1	9195.0	11250.5	13157.7	15209.1	16989.0	19567.3	22234.7	25111.3	27913.2	31980.5

1.4 General Government Current Receipts and Disbursements

Thousand Million Spanish pesetas

	1970	1975	1977	1978	1979	1980	1981	1982	1983	1984	1985	1986
					Receipts							
1 Operating surplus	...	...	...	...	...	...	...	...	...	...	...	...
2 Property and entrepreneurial income	...	...	...	...	...	152.4	222.5	288.9	307.1	251.7	324.7	...
3 Taxes, fees and contributions	...	...	...	...	...	3879.6	4535.4	5236.3	6435.5	7368.0	8419.5	...
A Indirect taxes	...	...	...	...	...	1009.5	1243.0	1522.3	1900.1	2271.4	2686.9	...
B Direct taxes [a]	...	...	...	...	...	1059.0	1221.1	1332.6	1748.1	2085.6	2378.4	...
C Social security contributions	...	...	...	...	...	1811.1	2071.3	2381.4	2787.3	3011.0	3354.2	...
D Compulsory fees, fines and penalties [a]	...	...	...	...	...	...	...	...	...	...	...	...
4 Other current transfers	...	...	...	...	...	489.1	536.3	611.8	696.0	729.7	884.0	...
Total Current Receipts of General Government	...	...	...	...	...	4521.1	5294.2	6137.0	7438.6	8349.4	9628.2	...
					Disbursements							
1 Government final consumption expenditure	...	...	...	...	...	1929.3	2242.2	2619.5	3090.9	3448.3	3906.6	...
A Compensation of employees	...	...	...	...	...	1488.2	1747.2	2000.1	2364.9	2634.4	2975.1	...
B Consumption of fixed capital	...	...	...	...	...	77.1	89.7	105.6	126.6	148.1	168.8	...
C Purchases of goods and services, net	...	...	...	...	...	364.0	405.3	513.8	599.5	665.8	762.6	...
D Less: Own account fixed capital formation	...	...	...	...	...	...	...	...	...	...	...	...
E Indirect taxes paid, net	...	...	...	...	...	...	...	...	...	...	...	...
2 Property income	...	...	...	...	...	110.9	135.6	190.5	290.4	509.3	900.0	...
3 Subsidies	...	...	...	...	...	315.1	334.4	489.0	575.8	703.6	738.7	...
4 Other current transfers	...	...	...	...	...	2156.3	2661.2	3045.6	3596.9	4015.9	4644.0	...
A Social security benefits	...	...	...	...	...	1926.3	2401.6	2747.5	3232.1	3642.9	4168.1	...
B Social assistance grants	...	...	...	...	...	...	...	...	...	...	...	...
C Other	...	...	...	...	...	230.0	259.6	298.2	364.8	372.9	476.0	...
5 Net saving	...	...	...	...	...	9.6	-79.1	-207.5	-115.4	-327.7	-561.1	...
Total Current Disbursements and Net Saving of General Government	...	...	...	...	...	4521.2	5294.3	6137.1	7438.6	8349.4	9628.2	...

a) Item 'Compulsory fees, fines and penalties' is included in item 'Direct taxes'.

Spain

1.5 Current Income and Outlay of Corporate and Quasi-Corporate Enterprises, Summary

Thousand Million Spanish pesetas

	1970	1975	1977	1978	1979	1980	1981	1982	1983	1984	1985	1986
Receipts												
1 Operating surplus	...	...	...	...	...	1558.4	1484.4	1755.9	1812.2	2383.0	2628.9	...
2 Property and entrepreneurial income received	...	...	...	...	...	1925.2	2656.8	3485.9	3992.8	4939.9	5209.4	...
3 Current transfers	...	...	...	...	...	376.9	443.9	520.7	634.4	659.1	750.7	...
Total Current Receipts	...	...	...	...	...	3860.5	4585.1	5762.5	6439.4	7982.0	8589.0	...
Disbursements												
1 Property and entrepreneurial income	...	...	...	...	...	2485.7	3465.5	4393.8	4923.5	5710.0	5871.6	...
2 Direct taxes and other current payments to general government	...	...	...	...	...	259.4	295.2	351.1	434.1	481.5	576.7	...
3 Other current transfers	...	...	...	...	...	449.9	539.3	675.1	800.6	814.6	936.5	...
Statistical discrepancy	...	...	...	...	...	10.4	2.2	1.5	-	25.3	47.0	...
4 Net saving	...	...	...	...	...	655.1	282.9	341.0	281.2	950.5	1157.1	...
Total Current Disbursements and Net Saving	...	...	...	...	...	3860.5	4585.1	5762.5	6439.4	7981.9	8588.9	...

1.6 Current Income and Outlay of Households and Non-Profit Institutions

Thousand Million Spanish pesetas

	1970	1975	1977	1978	1979	1980	1981	1982	1983	1984	1985	1986
Receipts												
1 Compensation of employees	...	...	...	...	...	7797.5	8734.4	9877.4	11162.3	11907.5	12988.7	...
A From resident producers	...	...	...	...	...	7783.3	8714.6	9852.8	11132.0	11875.6	12956.2	...
B From rest of the world	...	...	...	...	...	14.2	19.8	24.6	30.3	31.8	32.4	...
2 Operating surplus of private unincorporated enterprises	...	...	...	...	...	3557.0	3950.5	4671.2	5327.8	6254.7	7014.1	...
3 Property and entrepreneurial income	...	...	...	...	...	782.4	1077.1	1192.9	1324.0	1614.8	1918.8	...
4 Current transfers	...	...	...	...	...	2592.5	3181.3	3667.6	4279.5	4726.9	5430.6	...
A Social security benefits	...	...	...	...	...	2126.0	2639.2	3012.2	3509.2	3937.0	4497.1	...
B Social assistance grants	...	...	...	...	...	...	...	...	...	...	...	...
C Other	...	...	...	...	...	466.5	542.1	655.4	770.3	790.0	933.3	...
Statistical discrepancy	...	...	...	...	...	10.4	2.2	1.5	-	25.3	47.0	...
Total Current Receipts	...	...	...	...	...	14739.8	16945.5	19410.6	22093.6	24529.2	27399.2	...
Disbursements												
1 Private final consumption expenditure	...	...	...	...	...	10080.4	11457.9	13143.3	14808.1	16370.0	18116.5	...
2 Property income	...	...	...	...	...	406.9	612.9	692.4	798.2	1015.2	1043.3	...
3 Direct taxes and other current transfers n.e.c. to general government	...	...	...	...	...	2683.3	3070.3	3439.1	4152.6	4661.5	5200.5	...
A Social security contributions	...	...	...	...	...	1883.7	2144.4	2457.6	2838.7	3057.4	3398.8	...
B Direct taxes	...	...	...	...	...	799.6	925.9	981.5	1313.9	1604.0	1801.7	...
C Fees, fines and penalties	...	...	...	...	...	...	...	...	...	...	...	...
4 Other current transfers	...	...	...	...	...	665.3	758.5	853.6	1006.3	1067.4	1259.0	...
5 Net saving	...	...	...	...	...	903.7	1045.9	1282.4	1328.5	1415.1	1780.0	...
Total Current Disbursements and Net Saving	...	...	...	...	...	14739.6	16945.5	19410.8	22093.7	24529.2	27399.3	...

1.7 External Transactions on Current Account, Summary

Thousand Million Spanish pesetas

	1970	1975	1977	1978	1979	1980	1981	1982	1983	1984	1985	1986
Payments to the Rest of the World												
1 Imports of goods and services	...	...	...	...	...	2758.5	3428.3	4024.3	4860.1	5363.3	5914.8	5715.5
A Imports of merchandise c.i.f.	...	...	...	...	...	2480.7	3045.6	3561.1	4300.4	4753.3	5205.2	4971.3
B Other	...	...	...	...	...	277.8	382.7	463.3	559.6	610.0	709.6	744.1
2 Factor income to the rest of the world	...	...	...	...	...	256.9	429.3	496.3	552.4	641.5	645.2	543.1

Spain

1.7 External Transactions on Current Account, Summary
(Continued)

Thousand Million Spanish pesetas

	1970	1975	1977	1978	1979	1980	1981	1982	1983	1984	1985	1986
A Compensation of employees	...	...	...	...	...	0.6	0.3	0.4	0.4	0.5	0.9	1.4
B Property and entrepreneurial income	...	...	...	...	...	256.3	428.9	495.9	552.1	641.0	644.3	541.6
3 Current transfers to the rest of the world	...	...	...	...	...	34.9	44.9	51.1	71.0	69.3	118.9	238.7
A Indirect taxes to supranational organizations	...	...	...	...	...	...	...	...	...	...	...	106.6
B Other current transfers	...	...	...	...	...	34.9	44.9	51.1	71.0	69.3	118.9	132.1
4 Surplus of the nation on current transactions	...	...	...	...	...	-364.3	-458.0	-487.1	-338.0	354.8	454.6	553.5
Payments to the Rest of the World and Surplus of the Nation on Current Transactions	...	...	...	...	...	2686.0	3444.5	4084.6	5145.5	6428.9	7133.5	7050.8
					Receipts From The Rest of the World							
1 Exports of goods and services	...	...	...	...	...	2409.8	3079.1	3672.2	4725.6	5943.5	6518.7	6453.9
A Exports of merchandise f.o.b.	...	...	...	...	...	1531.6	1976.2	2372.2	3066.0	3936.1	4296.2	3938.2
B Other	...	...	...	...	...	878.2	1102.8	1300.0	1658.7	2007.4	2222.5	2515.7
2 Factor income from rest of the world	...	...	...	...	...	127.0	191.1	211.6	194.3	244.7	314.7	244.9
A Compensation of employees	...	...	...	...	...	14.2	19.8	24.6	30.3	31.8	32.4	38.3
B Property and entrepreneurial income	...	...	...	...	...	112.8	171.3	187.0	163.9	212.9	282.3	206.6
3 Current transfers from rest of the world	...	...	...	...	...	149.3	174.2	200.6	225.7	240.7	300.1	352.0
A Subsidies from supranational organisations	...	...	...	...	...	...	...	...	...	...	...	37.9
B Other current transfers	...	...	...	...	...	149.3	174.2	200.6	225.7	240.7	300.1	314.1
Receipts from the Rest of the World on Current Transactions	...	...	...	...	...	2686.1	3444.4	4084.4	5145.6	6428.9	7133.5	7050.8

1.8 Capital Transactions of The Nation, Summary

Thousand Million Spanish pesetas

	1970	1975	1977	1978	1979	1980	1981	1982	1983	1984	1985	1986
				Finance of Gross Capital Formation								
Gross saving	710.1	1540.4	2136.5	2692.8	3002.9	3183.8	3180.2	3669.5	4132.2	5067.6	5740.8	6952.1
1 Consumption of fixed capital	265.8	599.2	910.4	1105.7	1351.0	1615.4	1930.6	2253.7	2637.9	3029.6	3364.8	3631.8
A General government	...	...	...	...	...	77.1	89.7	105.6	126.6	148.1	168.8	...
B Corporate and quasi-corporate enterprises	...	...	...	...	...	1188.0	1415.4	1642.5	1932.4	2231.3	2504.1	...
C Other	...	...	...	...	...	350.2	425.5	505.6	578.9	650.3	691.9	...
2 Net saving	444.3	941.2	1226.1	1587.1	1651.9	1568.4	1249.6	1415.8	1494.3	2038.0	2376.0	3320.3
A General government	...	...	...	...	...	9.6	-79.1	-207.5	-115.4	-327.7	-561.1	...
B Corporate and quasi-corporate enterprises	...	...	...	...	...	655.1	282.9	341.0	281.2	950.5	1157.1	...
C Other	...	...	...	...	...	903.7	1045.9	1282.4	1328.5	1415.1	1780.0	...
Less: Surplus of the nation on current transactions	5.0	-177.2	-160.4	114.8	62.0	-364.3	-458.0	-487.1	-338.0	354.8	454.6	553.5
Statistical discrepancy	-	-	-	-	-	-	-	-	-	-	-	-
Finance of Gross Capital Formation	705.1	1717.6	2296.9	2578.0	2940.9	3548.1	3638.2	4156.6	4470.2	4712.8	5286.2	6398.6
				Gross Capital Formation								
Increase in stocks	21.1	126.3	96.8	27.7	98.7	179.9	-58.7	-14.4	-104.4	4.2	12.6	406.4
Gross fixed capital formation	684.0	1591.3	2200.1	2550.3	2842.2	3368.2	3696.9	4171.0	4574.6	4708.6	5273.6	5992.2
Gross Capital Formation	705.1	1717.6	2296.9	2578.0	2940.9	3548.1	3638.2	4156.6	4470.2	4712.8	5286.2	6398.6

1.9 Gross Domestic Product by Institutional Sectors of Origin

Thousand Million Spanish pesetas

	1970	1975	1977	1978	1979	1980	1981	1982	1983	1984	1985	1986
				Domestic Factor Incomes Originating								
1 General government	...	...	...	...	...	1488.2	1747.2	2000.1	2364.9	2634.4	2975.1	...
2 Corporate and quasi-corporate enterprises	...	...	...	...	...	11411.1	12402.7	14280.2	15907.5	17879.7	19625.1	...
A Non-financial	...	...	...	...	...	11116.6	12204.5	14160.4	15935.4	17838.2	19606.4	...
B Financial	...	...	...	...	...	294.6	198.1	119.8	-27.9	41.5	18.8	...

Spain

1.9 Gross Domestic Product by Institutional Sectors of Origin
(Continued)

Thousand Million Spanish pesetas

	1970	1975	1977	1978	1979	1980	1981	1982	1983	1984	1985	1986
3 Households and private unincorporated enterprises	...	...	...	...	...	...	...	...	...	...	...	...
4 Non-profit institutions serving households	...	...	...	...	...	...	...	...	...	...	...	...
Subtotal: Domestic Factor Incomes	2176.8	5103.0	7801.6	9665.0	11205.1	12899.4	14149.8	16280.3	18272.4	20513.9	22600.3	25566.2
Indirect taxes, net	181.6	320.9	483.0	479.8	601.5	694.4	908.6	1033.3	1324.3	1567.8	1948.2	2782.6
A Indirect taxes	204.6	389.5	613.2	693.4	824.0	1009.5	1243.0	1522.3	1900.1	2271.4	2686.9	3557.4
B Less: Subsidies	23.0	68.6	130.2	213.6	222.5	315.1	334.4	489.0	575.8	703.6	738.7	774.8
Consumption of fixed capital	265.8	599.2	910.4	1105.7	1351.0	1615.4	1930.6	2253.7	2637.9	3029.6	3364.8	3631.8
Statistical discrepancy	-	-	-	-	0.1	-0.1	-	-	0.1	-	-0.1	-0.1
Gross Domestic Product	2624.2	6023.1	9195.0	11250.5	13157.7	15209.1	16989.0	19567.3	22234.7	25111.3	27913.2	31980.5

1.10 Gross Domestic Product by Kind of Activity, in Current Prices

Thousand Million Spanish pesetas

	1970	1975	1977	1978	1979	1980	1981	1982	1983	1984	1985	1986
1 Agriculture, hunting, forestry and fishing	...	...	...	...	...	1073.4	1038.0	1225.9	1370.2	1642.7	1728.9	1758.7
2 Mining and quarrying	...	...	...	...	...	4284.3	4762.1	5326.2	6149.5	6903.6	7621.6	...
3 Manufacturing	...	...	...	...	...							...
4 Electricity, gas and water	...	...	...	...	...	309.0	426.7	562.2	591.7	765.8	880.0	...
5 Construction	...	...	...	...	...	1283.7	1328.6	1527.9	1631.7	1635.6	1781.5	2129.1
6 Wholesale and retail trade, restaurants and hotels	...	...	...	...	...	2772.8	3192.0	3717.6	4329.8	5019.7	5716.7	...
7 Transport, storage and communication	...	...	...	...	...	876.7	1036.2	1167.6	1362.3	1528.8	1664.7	...
8 Finance, insurance, real estate and business services [a]	...	...	...	...	...	2010.6	2298.5	2547.8	2724.6	3376.5	3678.8	...
9 Community, social and personal services [ab]	...	...	...	...	...	1297.5	1528.1	1895.7	2173.9	2460.6	2722.6	...
Total, Industries	...	...	...	...	...	13908.0	15610.3	17970.8	20333.7	23333.3	25794.8	29883.1
Producers of Government Services	...	...	...	...	...	1565.3	1836.8	2105.6	2491.5	2782.5	3144.0	3502.7
Other Producers [b]	...	...	...	...	...	...	...	...	...	...	...	...
Subtotal	...	...	...	...	...	15473.4	17447.1	20076.4	22825.2	26115.8	28938.8	33385.8
Less: Imputed bank service charge	...	...	...	...	...	535.8	756.3	889.1	1043.0	1478.0	1581.9	1854.3
Plus: Import duties	...	...	...	...	...	271.5	298.2	379.9	452.5	473.5	556.4	449.0
Plus: Value added tax	...	...	...	...	...							...
Plus: Other adjustments	...	...	...	...	...	0.1	-	0.1	-	-	-0.1	-
Equals: Gross Domestic Product	...	...	...	...	...	15209.1	16989.0	19567.3	22234.7	25111.3	27913.2	31980.5

a) Business services and real estate except dwellings are included in item 'Community, social and personal services'.
b) Item 'Other producers' is included in item 'Community, social and personal services'.

1.11 Gross Domestic Product by Kind of Activity, in Constant Prices

Thousand Million Spanish pesetas

	1970	1975	1977	1978	1979	1980	1981	1982	1983	1984	1985	1986
				At constant prices of:1980								
1 Agriculture, hunting, forestry and fishing	...	...	...	...	...	1073.4	971.7	956.9	1016.6	1104.1	1130.6	1005.9
2 Mining and quarrying	...	...	...	...	...	4284.3	4278.8	4214.2	4287.3	4303.9	4379.1	...
3 Manufacturing	...	...	...	...	...							...
4 Electricity, gas and water	...	...	...	...	...	309.0	303.6	312.2	312.5	345.8	368.0	...
5 Construction	...	...	...	...	...	1283.7	1281.1	1315.3	1316.6	1235.5	1263.3	1338.2
6 Wholesale and retail trade, restaurants and hotels	...	...	...	...	...	2772.8	2766.5	2804.8	2854.1	2928.4	2986.3	...
7 Transport, storage and communication	...	...	...	...	...	876.7	900.3	906.5	930.1	956.0	992.9	...
8 Finance, insurance, real estate and business services [a]	...	...	...	...	...	2010.6	2034.8	2065.9	2077.6	2142.5	2185.1	...
9 Community, social and personal services [ab]	...	...	...	...	...	1297.5	1309.8	1378.8	1394.4	1413.7	1418.1	...
Total, Industries	...	...	...	...	...	13908.0	13846.7	13954.7	14189.3	14429.9	14723.2	15190.6
Producers of Government Services	...	...	...	...	...	1565.3	1615.5	1683.0	1744.4	1798.5	1874.0	1933.0

Spain

1.11 Gross Domestic Product by Kind of Activity, in Constant Prices
(Continued)

Thousand Million Spanish pesetas

	1970	1975	1977	1978	1979	1980	1981	1982	1983	1984	1985	1986
					At constant prices of:1980							
Other Producers [b]	...	...	...	...	...	...	...	...	...	...	...	...
Subtotal	...	...	...	...	...	15473.4	15462.1	15637.7	15933.7	16228.3	16597.3	17123.6
Less: Imputed bank service charge	...	...	...	...	...	535.8	540.6	553.1	564.1	574.8	587.5	606.9
Plus: Import duties	...	...	...	...	...	271.5	249.8	271.3	263.6	261.0	271.4	301.2
Plus: Value added tax	...	...	...	...	...	...	...	...	...	...	...	...
Plus: Other adjustments	...	...	...	...	...	0.1	-0.1	-	-	-0.1	0.1	0.1
Equals: Gross Domestic Product	...	...	...	...	...	15209.1	15171.3	15355.9	15633.2	15914.5	16281.2	16818.0

a) Business services and real estate except dwellings are included in item 'Community, social and personal services'.
b) Item 'Other producers' is included in item 'Community, social and personal services'.

1.12 Relations Among National Accounting Aggregates

Thousand Million Spanish pesetas

	1970	1975	1977	1978	1979	1980	1981	1982	1983	1984	1985	1986
Gross Domestic Product	2624.2	6023.1	9195.0	11250.5	13157.7	15209.1	16989.0	19567.3	22234.7	25111.3	27913.2	31980.5
Plus: Net factor income from the rest of the world	-17.1	-18.5	-62.1	-87.4	-78.2	-130.0	-238.1	-284.7	-358.2	-396.8	-330.5	-298.1
Factor income from the rest of the world	4.6	35.5	32.5	55.3	91.1	127.0	191.1	211.6	194.3	244.7	314.7	244.9
Less: Factor income to the rest of the world	21.7	54.0	94.6	142.7	169.3	256.9	429.3	496.3	552.4	641.5	645.2	543.1
Equals: Gross National Product	2607.1	6004.6	9132.9	11163.2	13079.5	15079.1	16750.9	19282.7	21876.5	24714.5	27582.7	31682.4
Less: Consumption of fixed capital	265.8	599.2	910.4	1105.7	1351.0	1615.4	1930.6	2253.7	2637.9	3029.6	3364.8	3631.8
Equals: National Income	2341.3	5405.4	8222.5	10057.5	11728.5	13463.8	14820.3	17029.0	19238.6	21684.9	24217.9	28050.6
Plus: Net current transfers from the rest of the world	47.1	72.1	89.5	112.6	100.9	114.4	129.4	149.6	154.7	171.4	181.2	113.2
Current transfers from the rest of the world	50.5	90.0	130.3	156.8	159.0	149.3	174.2	200.6	225.7	240.7	300.1	352.0
Less: Current transfers to the rest of the world	3.5	18.1	40.7	44.3	58.0	34.9	44.9	51.1	71.0	69.3	118.9	238.8
Equals: National Disposable Income	2388.4	5477.5	8312.0	10170.1	11829.4	13578.2	14949.7	17178.6	19393.3	21856.3	24399.1	28163.8
Less: Final consumption	1944.1	4536.2	7085.9	8582.9	10177.5	12009.8	13700.0	15762.7	17899.0	19818.3	22023.1	24843.5
Equals: Net Saving	444.3	941.2	1226.1	1587.1	1651.9	1568.4	1249.6	1415.8	1494.3	2038.0	2376.0	3320.3
Less: Surplus of the nation on current transactions	5.0	-177.2	-160.4	114.8	62.0	-364.3	-458.0	-487.1	-338.0	354.8	454.6	553.5
Equals: Net Capital Formation	439.3	1118.4	1386.5	1472.3	1589.9	1932.7	1707.6	1903.0	1832.2	1683.2	1921.5	2766.8

2.5 Private Final Consumption Expenditure by Type and Porpose, in Current Prices

Thousand Million Spanish pesetas

		1970	1975	1977	1978	1979	1980	1981	1982	1983	1984	1985	1986
		\multicolumn{12}{c}{Final Consumption Expenditure of Resident Households}
1	Food, beverages and tobacco	...	...	...	...	...	2918.7	3296.4	3804.2	4231.9	4795.1	5327.3	5950.6
	A Food	...	...	...	...	...	2620.6	2936.8	3404.9	3788.1	4299.9	...	...
	B Non-alcoholic beverages	...	...	...	...	...	44.6	50.1	56.2	62.8	64.8	...	...
	C Alcoholic beverages	...	...	...	...	...	131.2	144.0	159.4	174.0	198.8	...	...
	D Tobacco	...	...	...	...	...	122.3	165.6	183.6	206.9	231.6	...	...
2	Clothing and footwear	...	...	...	...	...	839.8	943.6	1040.7	1154.0	1239.0	1394.9	1580.4
3	Gross rent, fuel and power	...	...	...	...	...	1716.5	1993.2	2290.1	2553.8	2833.1	3065.0	3328.6
	A Fuel and power	...	...	...	...	...	246.6	344.0	400.1	459.7	552.5	...	...
	D Other	...	...	...	...	...	1469.9	1649.2	1890.0	2094.1	2280.5		
4	Furniture, furnishings and household equipment and operation	...	...	...	...	...	810.5	888.2	989.5	1123.8	1228.1	1349.6	1549.4
5	Medical care and health expenses	...	...	...	...	...	394.4	447.7	528.9	591.5	627.5	684.0	748.3
6	Transport and communication	...	...	...	...	...	1409.0	1611.7	1824.7	2158.2	2395.7	2660.0	3035.1
	A Personal transport equipment	...	...	...	...	...	326.9	309.9	371.8	430.6	449.1	...	...
	B Other	...	...	...	...	...	1082.1	1301.9	1452.9	1727.6	1946.6	...	...
7	Recreational, entertainment, education and cultural services	...	...	...	...	...	708.4	813.6	943.8	1076.1	1141.7	1265.0	1464.9
	A Education	...	...	...	...	...	199.4	222.5	255.0	289.2	321.6	...	...
	B Other	...	...	...	...	...	509.0	591.1	688.8	786.9	820.2	...	...
8	Miscellaneous goods and services	...	...	...	...	...	1697.0	1996.8	2395.5	2778.7	3220.0	3565.4	4192.9
	A Personal care	...	...	...	...	...	140.6	158.6	179.7	206.1	229.0	...	...
	B Expenditures in restaurants, cafes and hotels	...	...	...	...	...	1178.8	1422.9	1755.8	2052.5	2409.7	...	...

Spain

2.5 Private Final Consumption Expenditure by Type and Porpose, in Current Prices
(Continued)

Thousand Million Spanish pesetas

	1970	1975	1977	1978	1979	1980	1981	1982	1983	1984	1985	1986
C Other	...	...	...	...	...	377.6	415.4	460.0	520.1	581.3	183.3	205.5
Total Final Consumption Expenditure in the Domestic Market by Households, of which	...	...	...	...	...	10494.3	11991.3	13817.4	15668.1	17480.1	19311.3	21850.2
Plus: Direct purchases abroad by resident households	...	...	...	...	...	94.7	103.6	123.4	142.8	153.6	193.5	235.8
Less: Direct purchases in the domestic market by non-resident households	...	...	...	...	...	508.5	637.0	797.6	1002.8	1263.7	1388.3	1685.8
Equals: Final Consumption Expenditure of Resident Households [a]	...	...	...	...	...	10080.4	11457.9	13143.3	14808.1	16370.0	18116.5	20400.2

Final Consumption Expenditure of Private Non-profit Institutions Serving Households

	1970	1975	1977	1978	1979	1980	1981	1982	1983	1984	1985	1986
Equals: Final Consumption Expenditure of Private Non-profit Organisations Serving Households	...	...	...	...	...	...	...	...	...	...	...	...
Private Final Consumption Expenditure	...	...	...	...	...	10080.4	11457.9	13143.3	14808.1	16370.0	18116.5	20400.2

a) Item 'Final consumption expenditure of resident households' includes consumption expenditure of private non-profit institutions serving households.

2.6 Private Final Consumption Expenditure by Type and Purpose, in Constant Prices

Thousand Million Spanish pesetas

	1970	1975	1977	1978	1979	1980	1981	1982	1983	1984	1985	1986

At constant prices of: 1980

Final Consumption Expenditure of Resident Households

	1970	1975	1977	1978	1979	1980	1981	1982	1983	1984	1985	1986
1 Food, beverages and tobacco	...	...	...	...	...	2918.7	2901.3	2900.3	2915.7	2927.3	2981.7	3009.2
A Food	...	...	...	...	...	2620.6	2601.7	2599.8	2617.8	2619.9	...	...
B Non-alcoholic beverages	...	...	...	...	...	44.6	42.8	42.0	41.5	39.5	...	...
C Alcoholic beverages	...	...	...	...	...	131.2	136.9	136.9	134.2	139.5	...	...
D Tobacco	...	...	...	...	...	122.3	119.8	121.6	122.2	128.4	...	...
2 Clothing and footwear	...	...	...	...	...	839.8	834.6	815.9	808.2	780.1	796.4	818.4
3 Gross rent, fuel and power	...	...	...	...	...	1716.5	1732.6	1752.7	1786.2	1825.9	1858.5	1906.8
A Fuel and power	...	...	...	...	...	246.6	243.6	241.4	246.3	259.8	...	...
B Other	...	...	...	...	...	1469.9	1489.0	1511.2	1539.9	1566.1	...	...
4 Furniture, furnishings and household equipment and operation	...	...	...	...	...	810.5	793.6	776.6	782.6	777.1	784.5	819.4
5 Medical care and health expenses	...	...	...	...	...	394.4	388.3	389.5	381.7	359.6	359.2	365.3
6 Transport and communication	...	...	...	...	...	1409.0	1374.1	1398.8	1424.2	1438.8	1502.4	1635.4
A Personal transport equipment	...	...	...	...	...	326.9	287.6	304.9	314.0	296.8	...	...
B Other	...	...	...	...	...	1082.1	1086.4	1093.9	1110.2	1142.0	...	...
7 Recreational, entertainment, education and cultural services	...	...	...	...	...	708.4	718.1	732.1	748.2	724.5	735.3	786.2
A Education	...	...	...	...	...	199.4	198.2	199.0	198.2	198.2	...	...
B Other	...	...	...	...	...	509.0	520.0	533.1	550.0	526.3	...	...
8 Miscellaneous goods and services	...	...	...	...	...	1697.0	1742.8	1768.7	1779.9	1832.3	1859.3	1950.2
A Personal care	...	...	...	...	...	140.6	139.2	140.6	136.4	137.7	...	...
B Expenditures in restaurants, cafes and hotels	...	...	...	...	...	1178.8	1237.8	1277.2	1296.4	1348.3	...	...
C Other	...	...	...	...	...	377.6	365.9	350.9	347.1	346.3	102.9	106.0
Total Final Consumption Expenditure in the Domestic Market by Households, of which	...	...	...	...	...	10494.3	10485.6	10534.5	10626.7	10665.5	10877.2	11290.9
Plus: Direct purchases abroad by resident households	...	...	...	...	...	94.7	85.6	90.0	83.6	84.2	97.4	112.0
Less: Direct purchases in the domestic market by non-resident households	...	...	...	...	...	508.5	551.0	586.0	637.5	715.6	716.7	781.2
Equals: Final Consumption Expenditure of Resident Households [a]	...	...	...	...	...	10080.4	10020.1	10038.5	10072.8	10034.1	10257.9	10621.7

Final Consumption Expenditure of Private Non-profit Institutions Serving Households

	1970	1975	1977	1978	1979	1980	1981	1982	1983	1984	1985	1986
Equals: Final Consumption Expenditure of Private Non-profit Organisations Serving Households	...	...	...	...	...	...	...	...	...	...	...	...
Private Final Consumption Expenditure	...	...	...	...	...	10080.4	10020.1	10038.5	10072.8	10034.1	10257.9	10621.7

a) Item 'Final consumption expenditure of resident households' includes consumption expenditure of private non-profit institutions serving households.

Spain

2.17 Exports and Imports of Goods and Services, Detail

Thousand Million Spanish pesetas

		1970	1975	1977	1978	1979	1980	1981	1982	1983	1984	1985	1986
	Exports of Goods and Services												
1	Exports of merchandise, f.o.b.	...	...	...	...	...	1531.6	1976.2	2372.2	3066.8	3936.1	4296.2	3938.2
2	Transport and communication [a]	...	...	...	...	...	254.3	309.1	335.9	434.4	483.8	543.1	496.8
3	Insurance service charges	...	...	...	...	...	26.1	30.2	31.3	33.7	44.8	47.0	43.1
4	Other commodities [a]	...	...	...	...	...	89.2	126.5	135.3	187.9	215.2	244.1	290.0
5	Adjustments of merchandise exports to change-of-ownership basis	...	...	...	...	...	...	...	...	...	...	...	...
6	Direct purchases in the domestic market by non-residential households	...	...	...	...	...	508.5	637.0	797.6	1002.8	1263.7	1388.3	1685.8
7	Direct purchases in the domestic market by extraterritorial bodies	...	...	...	...	...	...	...	...	...	...	...	...
	Total Exports of Goods and Services	...	...	...	...	...	2409.8	3079.1	3672.2	4725.6	5943.5	6518.7	6453.9
	Imports of Goods and Services												
1	Imports of merchandise, c.i.f.	...	...	...	...	...	2480.7	3045.6	3561.1	4300.4	4753.3	5205.2	4971.3
2	Adjustments of merchandise imports to change-of-ownership basis	...	...	...	...	...	...	...	...	...	...	...	...
3	Other transport and communication	...	...	...	...	...	55.9	93.4	108.2	142.4	164.9	155.3	151.0
4	Other insurance service charges	...	...	...	...	...	9.3	19.8	3.1	1.0	27.4	33.1	36.8
5	Other commodities	...	...	...	...	...	117.8	165.9	228.5	273.4	264.1	327.7	320.5
6	Direct purchases abroad by government	...	...	...	...	...	...	...	...	...	...	...	...
7	Direct purchases abroad by resident households	...	...	...	...	...	94.7	103.6	123.4	142.8	153.6	193.5	235.8
	Total Imports of Goods and Services	...	...	...	...	...	2758.5	3428.3	4024.3	4860.1	5363.3	5914.8	5715.5
	Balance of Goods and Services	...	...	...	...	...	-348.7	-349.2	-352.1	-134.5	580.2	603.9	738.4
	Total Imports and Balance of Goods and Services	...	...	...	...	...	2409.8	3079.1	3672.2	4725.6	5943.5	6518.7	6453.9

a) The estimates refer to transport only. Communication is included in item 'Other Commodities'.

3.11 General Government Production Account: Total and Subsectors

Thousand Million Spanish pesetas

	1980					1981				
	Total General Government	Central Government	State or Provincial Government	Local Government	Social Security Funds	Total General Government	Central Government	State or Provincial Government	Local Government	Social Security Funds
	Gross Output										
1 Sales	116.7	25.0	...	81.7	10.0	152.9	29.1	...	102.4	21.4
2 Services produced for own use	1939.0	1216.8	...	327.6	394.6	2254.5	1348.3	...	444.1	462.1
3 Own account fixed capital formation	...	...	...	...	...	...	...	...	...	...
Gross Output [a]	2055.7	1241.8	...	409.3	404.6	2407.4	1377.4	...	546.5	483.5
	Gross Input										
Intermediate Consumption	490.3	262.9	...	153.1	74.4	570.6	272.7	...	206.5	91.3
Subtotal: Value Added	1565.3	979.0	...	256.2	330.1	1836.8	1104.6	...	340.1	392.1
1 Indirect taxes, net	...	...	...	...	...	...	...	...	...	...
2 Consumption of fixed capital	77.1	50.9	...	18.4	7.8	89.7	60.2	...	21.5	8.0
3 Compensation of employees	1488.2	928.2	...	237.7	322.3	1747.2	1044.4	...	318.6	384.2
4 Net Operating surplus	...	...	...	...	...	...	...	...	...	...
Gross Input [a]	2055.6	1242.0	...	409.2	404.5	2407.5	1377.3	...	546.6	483.5

	1982					1983				
	Total General Government	Central Government	State or Provincial Government	Local Government	Social Security Funds	Total General Government	Central Government	State or Provincial Government	Local Government	Social Security Funds
	Gross Output										
1 Sales	178.3	29.1	...	119.8	29.5	212.7	31.5	...	134.6	46.7
2 Services produced for own use	2634.5	1527.5	...	585.1	521.9	3110.6	1723.4	...	803.4	583.9
3 Own account fixed capital formation	...	...	...	...	...	...	...	...	...	...
Gross Output [a]	2812.8	1556.6	...	704.9	551.4	3323.3	1754.9	...	938.0	630.6

Spain

3.11 General Government Production Account: Total and Subsectors
(Continued)

Thousand Million Spanish pesetas

	1982					1983				
	Total General Government	Central Government	State or Provincial Government	Local Government	Social Security Funds	Total General Government	Central Government	State or Provincial Government	Local Government	Social Security Funds
Gross Input											
Intermediate Consumption	707.2	343.0	...	250.5	113.7	831.9	411.5	...	296.9	123.5
Subtotal: Value Added	2105.6	1213.6	...	454.3	437.7	2491.5	1343.3	...	641.1	507.0
1 Indirect taxes, net	...	...	...	...	...	...	...	...	...	...
2 Consumption of fixed capital	105.6	71.1	...	26.6	7.9	126.6	82.1	...	35.7	8.8
3 Compensation of employees	2000.1	1142.5	...	427.8	429.8	2364.9	1261.2	...	605.4	498.2
4 Net Operating surplus	...	...	...	...	...	...	...	...	...	...
Gross Input [a]	2812.9	1556.6	...	704.9	551.4	3323.4	1754.8	...	938.0	630.5

	1984					1985				
	Total General Government	Central Government	State or Provincial Government	Local Government	Social Security Funds	Total General Government	Central Government	State or Provincial Government	Local Government	Social Security Funds
Gross Output											
1 Sales	267.0	44.9	...	169.1	53.0	310.2	37.1	...	199.0	74.1
2 Services produced for own use	3475.2	1767.7	...	1059.6	647.9	3931.3	1897.1	...	1310.6	723.6
3 Own account fixed capital formation	...	...	...	...	...	...	...	...	...	...
Gross Output [a]	3742.2	1812.6	...	1228.7	700.9	4241.5	1934.2	...	1509.6	797.7
Gross Input											
Intermediate Consumption	959.7	470.4	...	355.8	133.4	1097.5	478.4	...	456.8	162.3
Subtotal: Value Added	2782.5	1342.1	...	872.9	567.5	3144.0	1455.8	...	1052.8	635.4
1 Indirect taxes, net	...	...	...	...	...	...	...	...	...	...
2 Consumption of fixed capital	148.1	94.6	...	43.3	10.2	168.8	102.8	...	54.3	11.7
3 Compensation of employees	2634.4	1247.5	...	829.6	557.3	2975.1	1353.0	...	998.4	623.7
4 Net Operating surplus	...	...	...	...	...	...	...	...	...	...
Gross Input [a]	3742.2	1812.5	...	1228.7	700.9	4241.4	1934.2	...	1509.5	797.7

a) Local Government includes provincial governmnet and other regional government entities.

3.12 General Government Income and Outlay Account: Total and Subsectors

Thousand Million Spanish pesetas

	1980					1981				
	Total General Government	Central Government	State or Provincial Government	Local Government	Social Security Funds	Total General Government	Central Government	State or Provincial Government	Local Government	Social Security Funds
Receipts											
1 Operating surplus	...	...	...	...	...	...	...	...	...	...
2 Property and entrepreneurial income	152.4	138.3	...	9.0	5.2	222.5	201.5	...	14.0	7.0
A Withdrawals from public quasi-corporations	...	...	...	...	...	...	...	...	...	...
B Interest	71.0	61.3	...	6.7	3.0	87.3	73.3	...	10.2	3.8
C Dividends	81.4	77.0	...	2.2	2.2	135.2	128.2	...	3.8	3.2
D Net land rent and royalties	...	...	...	...	...	...	...	...	...	...
3 Taxes, fees and contributions	3879.6	1715.2	...	358.3	1806.1	4535.4	1943.8	...	526.9	2064.7
A Indirect taxes	1009.5	762.4	...	239.0	8.1	1243.0	918.3	...	316.4	8.3
B Direct taxes [a]	1059.0	939.7	...	119.3	-	1221.1	1010.6	...	210.5	-
C Social security contributions	1811.1	13.1	...	-	1798.0	2071.3	14.9	...	-	2056.4
D Fees, fines and penalties [a]	...	...	...	...	...	...	...	...	...	...
4 Other current transfers	489.1	474.4	...	83.4	299.0	536.3	547.3	...	103.4	423.8
A Casualty insurance claims	...	...	...	...	...	...	...	...	...	...
B Transfers from other government subsectors	...	28.7	...	41.4	297.7	...	63.8	...	55.9	418.4
C Transfers from the rest of the world	-	-	...	...	...	0.1	0.1	...	...	...
D Other transfers, except imputed	308.3	283.7	...	24.4	0.1	334.3	309.1	...	25.2	0.1
E Imputed unfunded employee pension and welfare contributions	180.8	162.0	...	17.5	1.2	201.9	174.3	...	22.4	5.2
Total Current Receipts [b]	4521.1	2327.9	...	450.7	2110.3	5294.2	2692.6	...	644.3	2495.5
Disbursements											
1 Government final consumption expenditure	1929.3	1207.2	...	327.6	394.6	2242.2	1336.0	...	444.1	462.1
2 Property income	110.9	81.2	...	29.5	0.2	135.6	103.7	...	31.8	0.1

Spain

3.12 General Government Income and Outlay Account: Total and Subsectors
(Continued)

Thousand Million Spanish pesetas

	1980 Total General Government	1980 Central Government	1980 State or Provincial Government	1980 Local Government	1980 Social Security Funds	1981 Total General Government	1981 Central Government	1981 State or Provincial Government	1981 Local Government	1981 Social Security Funds
3 Subsidies	315.1	288.4	...	26.7	...	334.4	306.9	...	27.5	...
4 Other current transfers	2156.3	767.4	...	36.9	1719.8	2661.2	929.6	...	95.5	2174.2
A Casualty insurance premiums, net	...	...	...	...	...	...	...	...	...	...
B Transfers to other government subsectors	...	308.0	...	5.9	53.9	...	445.1	...	40.9	52.2
C Social security benefits	1926.3	241.8	...	19.6	1664.8	2401.6	258.4	...	22.4	2120.8
D Social assistance grants	...	...	...	...	...	...	...	...	...	...
E Unfunded employee pension and welfare benefits	226.6	214.2	...	11.4	1.1	255.9	222.5	...	32.2	1.2
F Transfers to private non-profit institutions serving households	...	...	...	...	...	...	...	...	...	...
G Other transfers n.e.c.	...	...	...	...	...	...	...	...	...	...
H Transfers to the rest of the world	3.4	3.4	...	-	-	3.7	3.7	...	-	-
Net saving	9.6	-16.3	...	30.0	1.1	70.1	16.4	...	45.4	-140.9
Total Current Disbursements and Net Saving [b]	4521.2	2327.9	...	450.7	2110.5	5294.3	2692.6	...	644.3	2495.5

	1982 Total General Government	1982 Central Government	1982 State or Provincial Government	1982 Local Government	1982 Social Security Funds	1983 Total General Government	1983 Central Government	1983 State or Provincial Government	1983 Local Government	1983 Social Security Funds
Receipts										
1 Operating surplus	...	...	...	...	...	...	...	...	...	...
2 Property and entrepreneurial income	288.9	252.7	...	26.9	9.3	307.1	265.2	...	29.0	12.9
A Withdrawals from public quasi-corporations	...	...	...	...	...	...	...	...	...	...
B Interest	126.9	100.8	...	20.3	5.8	149.4	115.6	...	25.1	8.6
C Dividends	162.0	151.9	...	6.5	3.6	157.7	149.6	...	3.9	4.2
D Net land rent and royalties	...	...	...	...	...	...	...	...	...	...
3 Taxes, fees and contributions	5236.3	2144.7	...	717.5	2374.2	6435.5	2736.3	...	918.4	2780.9
A Indirect taxes	1522.3	1116.0	...	396.9	9.4	1900.1	1394.1	...	493.1	13.0
B Direct taxes [a]	1332.6	1012.0	...	320.6	-	1748.1	1322.7	...	425.3	-
C Social security contributions	2381.4	16.6	...	-	2364.8	2787.3	19.4	...	-	2767.9
D Fees, fines and penalties [a]	...	...	...	...	...	...	...	...	...	...
4 Other current transfers	611.8	632.8	...	157.0	828.1	696.0	684.4	...	315.6	770.0
A Casualty insurance claims	...	...	...	...	...	...	...	...	...	...
B Transfers from other government subsectors	...	85.3	...	98.6	822.2	...	71.5	...	241.4	761.1
C Transfers from the rest of the world	0.2	0.2	...			0.4	0.4	...	...	...
D Other transfers, except imputed	381.9	350.2	...	31.6	0.1	428.3	381.1	...	44.3	2.9
F Imputed unfunded employee pension and welfare contributions	229.7	197.1	...	26.8	5.8	267.2	231.3	...	29.9	6.0
Total Current Receipts [b]	6137.0	3030.2	...	901.4	3211.6	7438.6	3685.9	...	1263.0	3563.8
Disbursements										
1 Government final consumption expenditure	2619.5	1512.5	...	585.1	521.9	3090.9	1703.7	...	803.4	583.9
2 Property income	190.5	141.0	...	49.3	0.1	290.4	203.2	...	85.5	1.7
3 Subsidies	489.0	421.5	...	67.5	...	575.8	484.8	...	91.0	...

Spain

3.12 General Government Income and Outlay Account: Total and Subsectors
(Continued)

Thousand Million Spanish pesetas

	1982					1983				
	Total General Government	Central Government	State or Provincial Government	Local Government	Social Security Funds	Total General Government	Central Government	State or Provincial Government	Local Government	Social Security Funds
4 Other current transfers	3045.6	1422.6	...	123.9	2505.3	3596.9	1582.8	...	158.7	2929.4
A Casualty insurance premiums, net	...	...	...	...	...	...	...	...	...	...
B Transfers to other government subsectors	...	887.5	...	56.3	62.2	...	963.3	...	46.2	64.5
C Social security benefits	2747.5	279.7	...	26.8	2441.0	3232.1	339.1	...	29.9	2863.1
D Social assistance grants	...	...	...	...	...	...	...	...	...	...
E Unfunded employee pension and welfare benefits	291.3	248.5	...	40.7	2.0	355.2	270.7	...	82.7	1.8
F Transfers to private non-profit institutions serving households	...	...	...	...	...	...	...	...	...	...
G Other transfers n.e.c.	...	...	...	...	...	...	...	...	...	...
H Transfers to the rest of the world	6.9	6.9	...	-	-	9.6	9.6	...	-	-
Net saving	-207.5	-467.3	...	75.5	184.3	-115.4	-288.6	...	124.5	48.7
Total Current Disbursements and Net Saving [b]	6137.1	3030.3	...	901.3	3211.6	7438.6	3685.9	...	1263.1	3563.7

	1984					1985				
	Total General Government	Central Government	State or Provincial Government	Local Government	Social Security Funds	Total General Government	Central Government	State or Provincial Government	Local Government	Social Security Funds
Receipts										
1 Operating surplus	...	...	...	...	...	...	...	...	...	...
2 Property and entrepreneurial income	251.7	200.4	...	36.4	14.9	324.7	266.0	...	45.4	13.2
A Withdrawals from public quasi-corporations	...	...	...	...	...	...	...	...	...	...
B Interest	171.8	131.6	...	30.2	10.0	201.7	153.8	...	38.4	9.5
C Dividends	79.9	68.7	...	6.2	5.0	123.0	112.2	...	7.0	3.7
D Net land rent and royalties	...	...	...	...	...	...	...	...	...	...
3 Taxes, fees and contributions	7368.0	3118.8	...	1241.9	3007.3	8419.5	3386.6	...	1688.6	3344.4
A Indirect taxes	2271.4	1535.6	...	716.5	19.3	2686.9	1706.8	...	959.4	20.7
B Direct taxes [a]	2085.6	1560.2	...	525.4	-	2378.4	1649.2	...	729.2	-
C Social security contributions	3011.0	23.0	...	-	2988.0	3354.2	30.5	...	-	3323.7
D Fees, fines and penalties [a]	...	...	...	...	...	...	...	...	...	...
4 Other current transfers	729.7	756.7	...	397.2	957.9	884.0	855.6	...	357.5	1118.4
A Casualty insurance claims	...	...	...	...	...	...	...	...	...	...
B Transfers from other government subsectors	...	125.4	...	306.4	950.2	...	108.7	...	228.4	1110.3
C Transfers from the rest of the world	0.1	0.1	...	...	...	0.1	0.1	...	...	...
D Other transfers, except imputed	458.4	400.4	...	57.6	0.4	564.0	477.9	...	86.1	-
E Imputed unfunded employee pension and welfare contributions	271.2	230.7	...	33.2	7.3	319.9	268.9	...	42.9	8.1
Total Current Receipts [b]	8349.4	4075.9	...	1675.5	3980.1	9628.2	4508.2	...	2091.5	4476.0
Disbursements										
1 Government final consumption expenditure	3448.3	1740.8	...	1059.6	647.9	3906.6	1872.4	...	1310.6	723.6
2 Property income	509.3	410.4	...	98.9	0.1	900.0	776.1	...	123.4	0.4
3 Subsidies	703.6	586.2	...	117.4	...	738.7	561.2	...	166.9	10.7

Spain

3.12 General Government Income and Outlay Account: Total and Subsectors
(Continued)

Thousand Million Spanish pesetas

	1984 Total General Government	1984 Central Government	1984 State or Provincial Government	1984 Local Government	1984 Social Security Funds	1985 Total General Government	1985 Central Government	1985 State or Provincial Government	1985 Local Government	1985 Social Security Funds
4 Other current transfers	4015.9	1837.3	...	251.9	3308.7	4644.0	2044.8	...	260.1	3786.6
A Casualty insurance premiums, net	...	...	...	...	...	...	...	...	...	...
B Transfers to other government subsectors	...	1221.6	...	102.6	57.9	...	1289.9	...	84.1	73.5
C Social security benefits	3642.9	324.4	...	69.9	3248.6	4168.1	370.3	...	88.0	3709.8
D Social assistance grants	...	...	...	...	...	...	...	...	...	...
E Unfunded employee pension and welfare benefits	364.1	282.4	...	79.4	2.3	461.9	370.6	...	88.1	3.2
F Transfers to private non-profit institutions serving households	...	...	...	...	...	...	...	...	...	...
G Other transfers n.e.c.	...	...	...	...	...	...	...	...	...	...
H Transfers to the rest of the world	8.8	8.8	...	-	-	14.1	14.1	...	-	-
Net saving	-327.7	-498.8	...	147.7	23.4	-561.1	-746.4	...	230.4	-45.2
Total Current Disbursements and Net Saving [b]	8349.4	4075.9	...	1675.5	3980.1	9626.2	4508.1	...	2091.4	4476.1

a) Item 'Compulsory fees, fines and penalties' is included in item 'Direct taxes'.
b) Local Government includes provincial governmnet and other regional government entities.

3.13 General Government Capital Accumulation Account: Total and Subsectors

Thousand Million Spanish pesetas

	1980 Total General Government	1980 Central Government	1980 State or Provincial Government	1980 Local Government	1980 Social Security Funds	1981 Total General Government	1981 Central Government	1981 State or Provincial Government	1981 Local Government	1981 Social Security Funds
				Finance of Gross Accumulation						
1 Gross saving	86.7	34.6	...	48.4	3.7	10.6	76.6	...	66.9	-132.9
A Consumption of fixed capital	77.1	50.9	...	18.4	7.8	89.7	60.2	...	21.5	8.0
B Net saving	9.6	-16.3	...	30.0	-4.1	-79.1	16.4	...	45.4	-140.9
2 Capital transfers	32.6	20.0	...	44.4	0.6	81.5	24.5	...	53.0	3.9
Finance of Gross Accumulation [a]	119.3	54.6	...	92.8	4.3	92.1	101.1	...	119.9	-129.0
				Gross Accumulation						
1 Gross capital formation	276.0	170.6	...	84.0	21.3	365.2	231.6	...	106.7	26.9
A Increase in stocks	...	...	...	...	...	...	...	...	...	...
B Gross fixed capital formation	276.0	170.6	...	84.0	21.3	365.2	231.6	...	106.7	26.9
2 Purchases of land, net	8.0	4.6	...	3.4	...	24.8	6.5	...	18.2	0.1
3 Purchases of intangible assets, net	...	...	...	...	...	...	...	...	...	...
4 Capital transfers	234.1	259.6	...	6.8	0.1	366.6	352.8	...	13.3	0.5
Net lending	-398.7	-380.2	...	-1.3	-17.1	-664.6	-489.8	...	-18.3	-156.6
Gross Accumulation [a]	119.4	54.6	...	92.9	4.3	92.0	101.1	...	119.9	-129.1

	1982 Total General Government	1982 Central Government	1982 State or Provincial Government	1982 Local Government	1982 Social Security Funds	1983 Total General Government	1983 Central Government	1983 State or Provincial Government	1983 Local Government	1983 Social Security Funds
				Finance of Gross Accumulation						
1 Gross saving	-101.9	-396.2	...	102.1	192.2	11.2	-206.5	...	160.2	57.5
A Consumption of fixed capital	105.6	71.1	...	26.6	7.9	126.6	82.1	...	35.7	8.8
B Net saving	-207.5	-467.3	...	75.5	184.3	-115.4	-288.6	...	124.5	48.7
2 Capital transfers	91.9	23.0	...	68.0	0.9	139.5	26.2	...	108.9	4.4
Finance of Gross Accumulation [a]	-10.0	-373.2	...	170.1	193.1	150.7	-180.3	...	269.1	61.9
				Gross Accumulation						
1 Gross capital formation	574.5	298.9	...	236.7	38.9	607.7	346.7	...	226.2	34.8
A Increase in stocks	...	...	...	...	...	...	...	...	...	...
B Gross fixed capital formation	574.5	298.9	...	236.7	38.9	607.7	346.7	...	226.2	34.8
2 Purchases of land, net	27.2	3.7	...	23.5	0.1	24.3	10.6	...	13.6	0.1
3 Purchases of intangible assets, net	...	...	...	...	...	...	...	...	...	...
4 Capital transfers	488.2	451.5	...	36.4	0.3	585.7	512.3	...	73.0	0.5
Net lending	-1099.9	-1127.3	...	-126.5	153.8	-1067.1	-1050.0	...	-43.7	26.6
Gross Accumulation [a]	-10.0	-373.2	...	170.1	193.1	150.6	-180.4	...	269.1	62.0

Spain

3.13 General Government Capital Accumulation Account: Total and Subsectors

Thousand Million Spanish pesetas

	1984					1985				
	Total General Government	Central Government	State or Provincial Government	Local Government	Social Security Funds	Total General Government	Central Government	State or Provincial Government	Local Government	Social Security Funds

Finance of Gross Accumulation

1 Gross saving	-179.6	-404.2	...	191.0	33.6	-392.3	-643.6	...	284.7	-33.5
A Consumption of fixed capital	148.1	94.6	...	43.3	10.2	168.8	102.8	...	54.3	11.7
B Net saving	-327.7	-498.8	...	147.7	23.4	-561.1	-746.4	...	230.4	-45.2
2 Capital transfers	300.8	18.3	...	277.7	4.9	337.3	31.0	...	300.3	6.0
Finance of Gross Accumulation a	121.2	-385.9	...	468.7	38.5	-55.0	-612.6	...	585.0	-27.5

Gross Accumulation

1 Gross capital formation	722.0	310.8	...	371.8	39.5	994.6	325.2	...	619.8	49.5
A Increase in stocks	...	...	...	...	...	...	...	...	...	...
B Gross fixed capital formation	722.0	310.8	...	371.8	39.5	994.6	325.2	...	619.8	49.5
2 Purchases of land, net	37.9	10.3	...	27.9	-0.2	50.4	17.0	...	33.4	-
3 Purchases of intangible assets, net	...	...	...	...	...	...	...	...	...	...
4 Capital transfers	739.4	655.0	...	84.0	0.4	860.0	745.9	...	113.3	0.8
Net lending	-1378.1	-1362.0	...	-14.9	-1.2	-1960.0	-1700.6	...	-181.4	-78.0
Gross Accumulation a	121.2	-385.9	...	468.8	38.5	-55.0	-612.5	...	585.1	-27.7

a) Local Government includes provincial governmnet and other regional government entities.

3.21 Corporate and Quasi-Corporate Enterprise Production Account: Total and Sectors

Thousand Million Spanish pesetas

	1980				1981				1982			
	Corporate and Quasi-Corporate Enterprises			ADDENDUM: Total, including Unincorporated	Corporate and Quasi-Corporate Enterprises			ADDENDUM: Total, including Unincorporated	Corporate and Quasi-Corporate Enterprises			ADDENDUM: Total, including Unincorporated
	TOTAL	Non-Financial	Financial		TOTAL	Non-Financial	Financial		TOTAL	Non-Financial	Financial	

Gross Output

1 Output for sale	26417.0	25800.9	616.1	...	30020.1	29425.2	594.9	...	34280.6	33730.4	550.2	...
2 Imputed bank service charge	535.8	...	535.8	...	756.3	...	756.3	...	889.1	...	889.1	...
3 Own-account fixed capital formation	...	...	...	...	...	...	...	...	...	...	...	...
Gross Output	26952.8	25800.9	1151.9	...	30776.4	29425.2	1351.2	...	35169.7	33730.4	1439.3	...

Gross Input

Intermediate consumption	13580.5	12791.4	789.1	...	15922.4	14856.8	1065.6	...	18087.9	16864.8	1223.1	...
1 Imputed banking service charge	535.8	...	535.8	...	756.3	...	756.3	...	889.1	...	889.1	...
2 Other intermediate consumption	13044.7	12791.4	253.3	...	15166.1	14856.8	309.4	...	17198.9	16864.8	334.1	...
Subtotal: Value Added	13372.3	13009.5	362.8	...	14854.0	14568.4	285.6	...	17081.7	16865.6	216.2	...
1 Indirect taxes, net	422.9	394.9	28.1	...	610.4	574.7	35.7	...	653.4	611.5	41.9	...
A Indirect taxes	738.0	709.1	28.9	...	944.8	907.8	37.0	...	1142.4	1094.7	47.7	...
B Less: Subsidies	315.1	314.2	0.8	...	334.4	333.1	1.3	...	489.0	483.2	5.8	...
2 Consumption of fixed capital	1538.2	1498.1	40.2	...	1840.9	1789.2	51.7	...	2148.1	2093.7	54.4	...
3 Compensation of employees	6295.8	5849.7	446.0	...	6967.7	6443.2	524.5	...	7853.1	7232.0	621.2	...
4 Net operating surplus	5115.4	5266.8	-151.5	...	5434.9	5761.3	-326.4	...	6427.1	6928.4	-501.3	...
Gross Input	26952.8	25800.9	1151.9	...	30776.3	29425.2	1351.1	...	35169.6	33730.4	1439.3	...

	1983				1984				1985			
	Corporate and Quasi-Corporate Enterprises			ADDENDUM: Total, including Unincorporated	Corporate and Quasi-Corporate Enterprises			ADDENDUM: Total, including Unincorporated	Corporate and Quasi-Corporate Enterprises			ADDENDUM: Total, including Unincorporated
	TOTAL	Non-Financial	Financial		TOTAL	Non-Financial	Financial		TOTAL	Non-Financial	Financial	

Gross Output

1 Output for sale	39053.6	38575.9	477.8	...	44076.0	43448.9	627.2	...	48617.1	47900.9	716.2	...
2 Imputed bank service charge	1043.0	...	1043.0	...	1478.0	...	1478.0	...	1581.9	...	1581.9	...
3 Own-account fixed capital formation	...	...	...	...	...	...	...	...	...	...	...	...
Gross Output	40096.6	38575.9	1520.8	...	45554.0	43448.9	2105.2	...	50199.0	47900.9	2298.1	...

Gross Input

Intermediate consumption	20805.9	19374.0	1431.9	...	23698.6	21770.2	1928.4	...	25986.1	23898.2	2087.9	...
1 Imputed banking service charge	1043.0	...	1043.0	...	1478.0	...	1478.0	...	1581.9	...	1581.9	...
2 Other intermediate consumption	19762.9	19374.0	388.9	...	22220.7	21770.2	450.5	...	24404.2	23898.2	506.0	...
Subtotal: Value Added	19290.7	19201.9	88.8	...	21855.4	21678.7	176.7	...	24212.9	24002.7	210.2	...

Spain

3.21 Corporate and Quasi-Corporate Enterprise Production Account: Total and Sectors
(Continued)

Thousand Million Spanish pesetas

	1983 TOTAL	1983 Non-Financial	1983 Financial	ADDENDUM: Total, including Unincorporated	1984 TOTAL	1984 Non-Financial	1984 Financial	ADDENDUM: Total, including Unincorporated	1985 TOTAL	1985 Non-Financial	1985 Financial	ADDENDUM: Total, including Unincorporated
1 Indirect taxes, net	871.9	815.8	56.1	...	1094.2	1033.5	60.6	...	1391.8	1287.0	104.8	...
A Indirect taxes	1447.7	1386.1	61.6	...	1797.8	1719.7	78.0	...	2130.5	2013.9	116.6	...
B Less: Subsidies	575.8	570.3	5.5	...	703.6	686.2	17.4	...	738.7	726.9	11.8	...
2 Consumption of fixed capital	2511.3	2450.7	60.7	...	2881.5	2807.0	74.5	...	3195.9	3109.3	86.6	...
3 Compensation of employees	8767.5	8066.8	700.7	...	9241.8	8461.6	780.2	...	9982.1	9113.1	868.9	...
4 Net operating surplus	7140.0	7868.6	-728.6	...	8637.9	9376.6	-738.7	...	9643.1	10493.2	-850.2	...
Gross Input	40096.6	38575.9	1520.8	...	45554.0	43448.9	2105.0	...	50199.0	47900.8	2298.0	...

3.22 Corporate and Quasi-Corporate Enterprise Income and Outlay Account: Total and Sectors

Thousand Million Spanish pesetas

	1980 TOTAL	1980 Non-Financial	1980 Financial	1981 TOTAL	1981 Non-Financial	1981 Financial	1982 TOTAL	1982 Non-Financial	1982 Financial	1983 TOTAL	1983 Non-Financial	1983 Financial
Receipts												
1 Operating surplus	1558.4	1709.9	-151.5	1484.4	1810.8	-326.4	1755.9	2257.2	-501.3	1812.2	2540.7	-728.6
2 Property and entrepreneurial income	1925.2	178.6	1746.6	2656.8	174.6	2482.2	3485.9	284.7	3201.2	3992.8	335.1	3657.7
A Withdrawals from quasi-corporate enterprises	0.4	0.4	...	0.7	0.7	...	2.0	2.0	...	5.7	5.7	...
B Interest	1876.9	161.3	1715.6	2595.5	151.0	2444.4	3412.3	255.8	3156.5	3903.9	298.5	3605.4
C Dividends	45.9	14.9	31.0	58.5	20.8	37.8	68.3	23.5	44.8	79.7	27.3	52.3
D Net land rent and royalties	1.9	1.9	...	2.1	2.1	...	3.3	3.3	...	3.6	3.6	...
3 Current transfers	376.9	145.3	231.6	443.9	180.1	263.8	520.7	204.7	316.0	634.4	241.5	392.9
A Casualty insurance claims	32.6	32.6	...	37.2	37.2	...	45.0	45.0	...	61.4	61.4	...
B Casualty insurance premiums, net, due to be received by insurance companies	123.8	...	123.8	142.6	...	142.6	172.9	...	172.9	234.1	...	234.1
C Current transfers from the rest of the world	...	...	...	...	...	...	...	...	...	...	...	...
D Other transfers except imputed	84.9	4.2	80.6	90.9	1.7	89.2	101.0	2.3	98.8	105.7	0.4	105.3
E Imputed unfunded employee pension and welfare contributions	135.6	108.5	27.1	173.2	141.2	32.0	201.8	157.5	44.3	233.1	179.7	53.5
Total Current Receipts	3860.5	2033.8	1826.7	4585.1	2165.5	2419.6	5762.5	2746.6	3015.9	6439.4	3117.3	3322.0
Disbursements												
1 Property and entrepreneurial income	2485.7	1194.2	1291.6	3465.5	1621.7	1843.8	4393.8	1924.4	2469.3	4923.5	2167.3	2756.2
A Withdrawals from quasi-corporations	5.7	5.7	...	7.0	7.0	...	6.8	6.8	...	29.0	29.0	...
B Interest	2208.8	1019.5	1189.4	3083.7	1406.5	1677.3	3912.8	1655.5	2257.3	4394.0	1846.2	2547.8
C Dividends	255.2	153.0	102.2	358.3	191.7	166.6	453.4	241.4	212.0	471.3	262.9	208.4
D Net land rent and royalties	16.0	16.0	...	16.5	16.5	...	20.9	20.9	...	20.2	20.2	...
2 Direct taxes and other current transfers n.e.c. to general government	259.4	233.3	26.1	295.2	254.7	40.5	351.1	303.7	47.4	434.1	381.7	52.5
A Direct taxes	259.4	233.3	26.1	295.2	254.7	40.5	351.1	303.7	47.4	434.1	381.7	52.5
B Fines, fees, penalties and other current transfers n.e.c.	...	...	...	...	...	...	...	...	...	...	...	...
3 Other current transfers	449.9	210.8	239.0	539.3	269.5	269.9	675.1	322.2	353.0	800.6	414.2	386.5
A Casualty insurance premiums, net	45.2	38.1	7.1	51.7	48.4	3.3	62.0	55.5	6.5	85.2	81.3	3.9
B Casualty insurance claims liability of insurance companies	123.8	...	123.8	142.6	...	142.6	172.9	...	172.9	234.1	...	234.1
C Transfers to private non-profit institutions	...	...	...	...	...	...	...	...	...	...	...	...
D Unfunded employee pension and welfare benefits	200.1	108.5	91.7	239.7	141.2	98.5	271.4	157.5	113.9	279.7	179.7	100.0
E Social assistance grants	...	...	...	...	...	...	...	...	...	...	...	...
F Other transfers n.e.c.	80.7	64.3	16.4	105.3	79.9	25.4	168.9	109.2	59.7	201.6	153.2	48.4
G Transfers to the rest of the world	...	...	...	...	...	...	...	...	...	...	...	...
Statistical discrepancy	10.4	...	10.4	2.2	...	2.2	1.5	...	1.5	-	...	-
Net saving	655.1	395.5	259.6	282.9	19.7	263.2	341.0	196.3	144.7	281.2	154.3	126.9
Total Current Disbursements and Net Saving	3860.5	2033.8	1826.7	4585.1	2165.6	2419.6	5762.5	2746.6	3015.9	6439.4	3117.5	3322.1

Spain

3.22 Corporate and Quasi-Corporate Enterprise Income and Outlay Account: Total and Sectors

Thousand Million Spanish pesetas

	1984 TOTAL	1984 Non-Financial	1984 Financial	1985 TOTAL	1985 Non-Financial	1985 Financial
Receipts						
1 Operating surplus	2383.0	3121.6	-738.7	2628.9	3479.1	-850.2
2 Property and entrepreneurial income	4939.9	455.6	4484.3	5209.4	459.5	4749.9
A Withdrawals from quasi-corporate enterprises	2.6	2.6	...	-	-	...
B Interest	4847.6	423.3	4424.3	5098.8	422.3	4676.4
C Dividends	85.6	25.6	60.0	105.7	32.3	73.5
D Net land rent and royalties	4.1	4.1	...	4.9	4.9	...
3 Current transfers	659.1	266.1	393.0	750.7	298.1	452.6
A Casualty insurance claims	61.9	61.9	...	68.2	68.2	...
B Casualty insurance premiums, net, due to be received by insurance companies	238.7	...	238.7	272.6	...	272.6
C Current transfers from the rest of the world	...	...	...	...	...	...
D Other transfers except imputed	83.6	1.2	82.4	79.6	-	79.6
E Imputed unfunded employee pension and welfare contributions	275.0	203.0	72.0	330.4	229.9	100.4
Total Current Receipts	7982.0	3843.3	4138.6	8589.0	4236.7	4352.3
Disbursements						
1 Property and entrepreneurial income	5710.0	2631.6	3078.4	5871.6	2588.6	3283.0
A Withdrawals from quasi-corporations	26.4	26.4	...	-	-	...
B Interest	5255.5	2299.6	2955.9	5289.7	2183.2	3106.5
C Dividends	391.9	269.4	122.5	532.6	356.2	176.5
D Net land rent and royalties	36.1	36.1	...	49.3	49.3	...
2 Direct taxes and other current transfers n.e.c. to general government	481.5	416.0	65.6	576.7	498.7	78.0
A Direct taxes	481.5	416.0	65.6	576.7	498.7	78.0
B Fines, fees, penalties and other current transfers n.e.c.	...	...	...	...	...	...
3 Other current transfers	814.6	431.5	383.2	936.5	505.2	431.4
A Casualty insurance premiums, net	85.8	81.4	4.4	97.3	92.8	4.6
B Casualty insurance claims liability of insurance companies	238.7	...	238.7	272.6	...	272.6
C Transfers to private non-profit institutions	...	...	...	...	...	...
D Unfunded employee pension and welfare benefits	295.7	203.0	92.7	328.6	229.9	98.6
E Social assistance grants	...	...	...	...	...	...
F Other transfers n.e.c.	194.4	147.1	47.4	238.1	182.5	55.6
G Transfers to the rest of the world	...	...	...	...	...	...
Statistical discrepancy	25.3	...	25.3	47.0	...	47.0
Net saving	950.5	364.3	586.2	1157.1	644.2	512.9
Total Current Disbursements and Net Saving	7981.9	3843.4	4138.7	8588.9	4236.7	4352.3

3.23 Corporate and Quasi-Corporate Enterprise Capital Accumulation Account: Total and Sectors

Thousand Million Spanish pesetas

	1980 TOTAL	1980 Non-Financial	1980 Financial	1981 TOTAL	1981 Non-Financial	1981 Financial	1982 TOTAL	1982 Non-Financial	1982 Financial	1983 TOTAL	1983 Non-Financial	1983 Financial
Finance of Gross Accumulation												
1 Gross saving	1843.1	1543.3	299.8	1698.3	1383.3	314.9	1983.5	1784.4	199.1	2213.6	2026.0	187.6
A Consumption of fixed capital	1188.0	1147.8	40.2	1415.4	1363.6	51.7	1642.5	1588.1	54.4	1932.4	1871.7	60.7
B Net saving	655.1	395.5	259.6	282.9	19.7	263.2	341.0	196.3	144.7	281.2	154.3	126.9
2 Capital transfers	224.5	224.5	-	311.9	311.9	-	403.8	403.8	-	450.4	450.4	-
Finance of Gross Accumulation	2067.6	1767.8	299.8	2010.2	1695.2	314.9	2387.3	2188.2	199.1	2664.0	2476.4	187.6

Spain

3.23 Corporate and Quasi-Corporate Enterprise Capital Accumulation Account: Total and Sectors
(Continued)

Thousand Million Spanish pesetas

	1980 TOTAL	1980 Non-Financial	1980 Financial	1981 TOTAL	1981 Non-Financial	1981 Financial	1982 TOTAL	1982 Non-Financial	1982 Financial	1983 TOTAL	1983 Non-Financial	1983 Financial
						Gross Accumulation						
1 Gross capital formation	2369.4	2221.5	147.9	2278.2	2152.7	125.5	2460.0	2327.9	132.1	2713.4	2585.8	127.6
A Increase in stocks	...	...	...	...	...	...	...	...	...	...	...	...
B Gross fixed capital formation	2369.4	2221.5	147.9	2278.2	2152.7	125.5	2460.0	2327.9	132.1	2713.4	2585.8	127.6
2 Purchases of land, net	...	...	...	...	...	...	...	...	...	...	...	...
3 Purchases of intangible assets, net	...	...	...	...	...	...	...	...	...	...	...	...
4 Capital transfers	7.9	3.9	4.1	11.0	3.6	7.5	5.1	3.4	1.7	5.1	2.8	2.3
Net lending	-309.8	-457.5	147.8	-279.1	-461.0	181.9	-77.8	-143.1	65.3	-54.5	-112.2	57.8
Gross Accumulation	2067.5	1767.9	299.8	2010.1	1695.3	314.9	2387.3	2188.2	199.1	2664.0	2476.4	187.7

	1984 TOTAL	1984 Non-Financial	1984 Financial	1985 TOTAL	1985 Non-Financial	1985 Financial
			Finance of Gross Accumulation			
1 Gross saving	3181.8	2521.1	660.7	3661.2	3061.6	599.5
A Consumption of fixed capital	2231.3	2156.8	74.5	2504.1	2417.4	86.6
B Net saving	950.5	364.3	586.2	1157.1	644.2	512.9
2 Capital transfers	451.5	451.5	-	591.0	591.0	-
Finance of Gross Accumulation	3633.3	2972.6	660.7	4252.2	3652.6	599.5
			Gross Accumulation			
1 Gross capital formation	2738.1	2610.9	127.2	2980.9	2843.6	137.3
A Increase in stocks	...	...	...	...	...	...
B Gross fixed capital formation	2738.1	2610.9	127.2	2980.9	2843.6	137.3
2 Purchases of land, net	...	...	...	...	...	...
3 Purchases of intangible assets, net	...	...	...	...	...	...
4 Capital transfers	13.1	9.8	3.3	59.0	52.8	6.2
Net lending	882.1	351.9	530.2	1212.3	756.2	456.1
Gross Accumulation	3633.3	2972.6	660.7	4252.2	3652.6	599.6

3.32 Household and Private Unincorporated Enterprise Income and Outlay Account

Thousand Million Spanish pesetas

	1970	1975	1977	1978	1979	1980	1981	1982	1983	1984	1985	1986
					Receipts							
1 Compensation of employees	...	...	...	...	...	7797.5	8734.4	9877.4	11162.3	11907.5	12988.7	...
A Wages and salaries	...	...	...	...	...	6029.0	6698.7	7554.1	8494.5	9102.2	9812.4	...
B Employers' contributions for social security	...	...	...	...	...	1768.5	2035.7	2323.4	2667.8	2805.3	3176.3	...
C Employers' contributions for private pension & welfare plans												...
2 Operating surplus of private unincorporated enterprises	...	...	...	...	...	3557.0	3950.5	4671.2	5327.8	6254.7	7014.1	...
3 Property and entrepreneurial income	...	...	...	...	...	782.4	1077.1	1192.9	1324.0	1614.8	1918.8	...
A Withdrawals from private quasi-corporations	...	...	...	...	...	...	...	...	...	...	...	...
B Interest	...	...	...	...	...	670.1	946.4	1030.4	1132.3	1434.1	1701.4	...
C Dividends	...	...	...	...	...	102.3	129.5	161.2	190.1	179.1	215.6	...
D Net land rent and royalties	...	...	...	...	...	0.9	1.2	1.3	1.5	1.7	1.8	...
3 Current transfers	...	...	...	...	...	2592.5	3181.3	3667.6	4279.5	4726.9	5430.6	...
A Casualty insurance claims	...	...	...	...	...	91.7	105.3	128.3	174.0	176.7	205.6	...
B Social security benefits	...	...	...	...	...	2126.0	2639.2	3012.2	3509.2	3937.0	4497.1	...
C Social assistance grants	...	...	...	...	...	...	...	...	...	...	...	...
D Unfunded employee pension and welfare benefits	...	...	...	...	...	...	...	...	...	...	...	...
E Transfers from general government	...	...	...	...	...	...	...	...	...	...	...	...
F Transfers from the rest of the world	...	...	...	...	...	116.7	133.4	143.9	156.2	157.0	168.5	...
G Other transfers n.e.c.	...	...	...	...	...	258.1	303.4	383.2	440.1	456.3	559.2	...
Statistical discrepancy						10.4	2.2	1.5	-	25.3	47.0	
Total Current Receipts [a]	...	...	...	...	...	14739.8	16945.5	19410.6	22093.6	24529.2	27399.2	...

Spain

3.32 Household and Private Unincorporated Enterprise Income and Outlay Account
(Continued)

Thousand Million Spanish pesetas

	1970	1975	1977	1978	1979	1980	1981	1982	1983	1984	1985	1986
						Disbursements						
1 Final consumption expenditures	...	...	...	...	...	10080.4	11457.9	13143.3	14808.1	16370.0	18116.5	...
2 Property income	...	...	...	...	...	406.9	612.9	692.4	798.2	1015.2	1043.3	...
A Interest	...	...	...	...	...	406.9	612.9	692.4	798.2	1015.2	1043.3	...
B Net land rent and royalties	...	...	...	...	...	...	...	...	...	...	...	...
3 Direct taxes and other current transfers n.e.c. to government	...	...	...	...	...	2683.3	3070.3	3439.1	4152.6	4661.5	5200.5	...
A Social security contributions	...	...	...	...	...	1883.7	2144.4	2457.6	2838.7	3057.4	3398.8	...
B Direct taxes	...	...	...	...	...	799.6	925.9	981.5	1313.9	1604.0	1801.7	...
Income taxes	...	...	...	...	...	...	...	...	...	...	...	...
Other	...	...	...	...	...	...	...	...	...	...	...	...
C Fees, fines and penalties	...	...	...	...	...	...	...	...	...	...	...	...
4 Other current transfers	...	...	...	...	...	665.3	758.5	853.6	1006.3	1067.4	1259.0	...
A Net casualty insurance premiums	...	...	...	...	...	75.5	86.6	104.5	141.5	143.9	164.5	...
B Transfers to private non-profit institutions serving households	...	...	...	...	...	1.3	3.3	3.6	3.0	4.4	3.7	...
C Transfers to the rest of the world	...	...	...	...	...	0.5	0.9	1.5	2.1	3.2	21.5	...
D Other current transfers, except imputed	...	...	...	...	...	271.6	292.6	312.6	359.4	369.9	419.1	...
E Imputed employee pension and welfare contributions	...	...	...	...	...	316.4	375.1	431.5	500.4	546.1	650.3	...
Net saving	...	...	...	...	...	903.7	1045.9	1282.4	1328.5	1415.1	1780.0	...
Total Current Disbursements and Net Saving [a]	...	...	...	...	...	14739.6	16945.5	19410.8	22093.7	24529.2	27399.3	...

a) Private non-profit institutions serving households is included in household and private unincorporated enterprise.

3.33 Household and Private Unincorporated Enterprise Capital Accumulation Account

Thousand Million Spanish pesetas

	1970	1975	1977	1978	1979	1980	1981	1982	1983	1984	1985	1986
						Finance of Gross Accumulation						
1 Gross saving	...	...	...	...	...	1253.9	1471.4	1788.0	1907.4	2065.4	2471.9	...
A Consumption of fixed capital	...	...	...	...	...	350.2	425.5	505.6	578.9	650.3	691.9	...
B Net saving	...	...	...	...	...	903.7	1045.9	1282.4	1328.5	1415.1	1780.0	...
2 Capital transfers	...	...	...	...	...	12.1	18.3	28.4	40.8	48.3	50.6	...
Total Finance of Gross Accumulation [a]	...	...	...	...	...	1266.0	1489.7	1816.4	1948.2	2113.7	2522.5	...
						Gross Accumulation						
1 Gross Capital Formation	...	...	...	...	...	902.7	994.8	1122.2	1149.1	1252.8	1310.7	...
A Increase in stocks	...	...	...	...	...	...	...	...	...	...	...	...
B Gross fixed capital formation	...	...	...	...	...	902.7	994.8	1122.2	1149.1	1252.8	1310.7	...
2 Purchases of land, net	...	...	...	...	...	-8.0	-24.8	-27.2	-24.3	-37.9	-50.4	...
3 Purchases of intangibles, net	...	...	...	...	...	...	...	...	...	...	...	...
4 Capital transfers	...	...	...	...	...	28.3	35.6	33.5	42.2	53.4	65.2	...
Net lending	...	...	...	...	...	343.0	484.1	688.0	781.4	845.5	1197.0	...
Total Gross Accumulation [a]	...	...	...	...	...	1266.0	1489.7	1816.5	1948.4	2113.8	2522.5	...

a) Private non-profit institutions serving households is included in household and private unincorporated enterprise.

3.51 External Transactions: Current Account: Detail

Thousand Million Spanish pesetas

	1970	1975	1977	1978	1979	1980	1981	1982	1983	1984	1985	1986
						Payments to the Rest of the World						
1 Imports of goods and services	...	...	...	...	...	2758.5	3428.3	4024.3	4860.1	5363.3	5914.8	5715.5
A Imports of merchandise c.i.f.	...	...	...	...	...	2480.7	3045.6	3561.1	4300.4	4753.3	5205.2	4971.3
B Other	...	...	...	...	...	277.8	382.7	463.3	559.6	610.0	709.6	744.1
2 Factor income to the rest of the world	...	...	...	...	...	256.9	429.3	496.3	552.4	641.5	645.2	543.1

Spain

3.51 External Transactions: Current Account: Detail
(Continued)

Thousand Million Spanish pesetas

	1970	1975	1977	1978	1979	1980	1981	1982	1983	1984	1985	1986
A Compensation of employees	...	...	...	...	...	0.6	0.3	0.4	0.4	0.5	0.9	1.4
B Property and entrepreneurial income	...	...	...	...	...	256.3	428.9	495.9	552.1	641.0	644.3	541.6
3 Current transfers to the rest of the world	...	...	...	...	...	34.9	44.9	51.1	71.0	69.3	118.9	238.7
A Indirect taxes by general government to supranational organizations	...	...	...	...	...	...	...	...	...	...	...	106.6
B Other current transfers	...	...	...	...	...	34.9	44.9	51.1	71.0	69.3	118.9	132.1
By general government	...	...	...	...	...	3.4	3.7	6.9	9.6	8.8	14.1	55.0
By other resident sectors	...	...	...	...	...	31.5	41.2	44.2	61.4	60.4	104.8	77.2
4 Surplus of the nation on current transactions	...	...	...	...	...	-364.3	-458.0	-487.1	-338.0	354.8	454.6	553.5
Payments to the Rest of the World, and Surplus of the Nation on Current Transfers	...	...	...	...	...	2686.0	3444.5	4084.6	5145.5	6428.9	7133.5	7050.8

Receipts From The Rest of the World

	1970	1975	1977	1978	1979	1980	1981	1982	1983	1984	1985	1986
1 Exports of goods and services	...	...	...	...	...	2409.8	3079.1	3672.2	4725.6	5943.5	6518.7	6453.9
A Exports of merchandise f.o.b.	...	...	...	...	...	1531.6	1976.2	2372.2	3066.8	3936.1	4296.2	3938.2
B Other	...	...	...	...	...	878.2	1102.8	1300.0	1658.7	2007.4	2222.5	2515.7
2 Factor income from the rest of the world	...	...	...	...	...	127.0	191.1	211.6	194.3	244.7	314.7	244.9
A Compensation of employees	...	...	...	...	...	14.2	19.8	24.6	30.3	31.8	32.4	38.3
B Property and entrepreneurial income	...	...	...	...	...	112.8	171.3	187.0	163.9	212.9	282.3	206.6
3 Current transfers from the rest of the world	...	...	...	...	...	149.3	174.2	200.6	225.7	240.7	300.1	352.0
A Subsidies to general government from supranational organizations	...	...	...	...	...	...	...	...	...	...	...	37.9
B Other current transfers	...	...	...	...	...	149.3	174.2	200.6	225.7	240.7	300.1	314.1
To general government	...	...	...	...	...	-	0.1	0.2	0.4	0.1	0.1	31.9
To other resident sectors	...	...	...	...	...	149.3	174.1	200.4	225.3	240.6	300.0	282.1
Receipts from the Rest of the World on Current Transfers	...	...	...	...	...	2686.1	3444.4	4084.4	5145.6	6428.9	7133.5	7050.8

3.52 External Transactions: Capital Accumulation Account

Thousand Million Spanish pesetas

	1970	1975	1977	1978	1979	1980	1981	1982	1983	1984	1985	1986

Finance of Gross Accumulation

	1970	1975	1977	1978	1979	1980	1981	1982	1983	1984	1985	1986
1 Surplus of the nation on current transactions	...	...	...	...	...	-364.3	-458.0	-487.1	-338.0	354.8	454.6	553.5
2 Capital transfers from the rest of the world	...	...	...	...	...	0.4	0.6	0.2	0.4	-	0.1	40.6
Total Finance of Gross Accumulation	...	...	...	...	...	-363.9	-457.4	-486.9	-337.6	354.8	454.7	594.1

Gross Accumulation

	1970	1975	1977	1978	1979	1980	1981	1982	1983	1984	1985	1986
1 Capital transfers to the rest of the world	...	...	...	...	...	1.6	2.2	2.9	2.6	5.3	5.4	-
2 Purchases of intangible assets, n.e.c., net, from the rest of the world	...	...	...	...	...	...	...	...	...	...	...	...
Net lending to the rest of the world	...	...	...	...	...	-365.5	-459.7	-489.8	-340.2	349.5	449.3	594.1
Total Gross Accumulation	...	...	...	...	...	-363.9	-457.5	-486.9	-337.6	354.8	454.7	594.1

4.1 Derivation of Value Added by Kind of Activity, in Current Prices

Thousand Million Spanish pesetas

	1980			1981			1982			1983		
	Gross Output	Intermediate Consumption	Value Added	Gross Output	Intermediate Consumption	Value Added	Gross Output	Intermediate Consumption	Value Added	Gross Output	Intermediate Consumption	Value Added

All Producers

	Gross Output	Intermediate Consumption	Value Added	Gross Output	Intermediate Consumption	Value Added	Gross Output	Intermediate Consumption	Value Added	Gross Output	Intermediate Consumption	Value Added
1 Agriculture, hunting, forestry and fishing	2045.1	971.6	1073.4	2175.7	1137.7	1038.0	2544.7	1318.8	1225.9	2872.5	1502.3	1370.2
2 Mining and quarrying	...	...	...	...	...	...	...	...	...	...	...	...
3 Manufacturing	11872.2	7588.0	4284.3	13310.6	8548.5	4762.1	14941.4	9615.2	5326.2	17287.6	11138.1	6149.5
A Manufacture of food, beverages and tobacco	2471.5	1770.3	701.2	2826.9	2014.0	812.9	3240.9	2302.3	938.6	3743.3	2659.2	1084.1

Spain

4.1 Derivation of Value Added by Kind of Activity, in Current Prices
(Continued)

Thousand Million Spanish pesetas

		1980 Gross Output	1980 Intermediate Consumption	1980 Value Added	1981 Gross Output	1981 Intermediate Consumption	1981 Value Added	1982 Gross Output	1982 Intermediate Consumption	1982 Value Added	1983 Gross Output	1983 Intermediate Consumption	1983 Value Added
	B Textile, wearing apparel and leather industries	1013.4	571.0	442.4	1028.0	574.0	454.0	1151.9	648.2	503.7	1296.0	738.4	557.6
	C Manufacture of wood and wood products, including furniture	410.5	226.1	184.4	413.2	222.1	191.1	445.4	241.2	204.2	484.2	263.2	221.1
	D Manufacture of paper and paper products, printing and publishing	503.1	309.8	193.3	577.1	354.8	222.2	655.2	402.2	253.0	735.0	445.4	289.6
	E Manufacture of chemicals and chemical petroleum, coal, rubber and plastic products	...	...	...	...	...	...	...	...	...	...	...	...
	F Manufacture of non-metallic mineral products, except products of petroleum and coal	...	...	...	...	...	...	...	...	...	...	...	...
	G Basic metal industries	...	...	...	...	...	...	...	...	...	...	...	...
	H Manufacture of fabricated metal products, machinery and equipment	...	...	...	...	...	...	...	...	...	...	...	...
	I Other manufacturing industries	7473.7	4710.8	2763.0	8465.5	5383.5	3081.9	9448.0	6021.2	3426.7	11029.1	7031.9	3997.2
4	Electricity, gas and water	669.2	360.2	309.0	968.4	541.7	426.7	1181.9	619.7	562.2	1305.4	713.6	591.7
5	Construction	2443.4	1159.7	1283.7	2724.4	1395.7	1328.6	3070.3	1542.4	1527.9	3346.7	1715.0	1631.7
6	Wholesale and retail trade, restaurants and hotels	4234.1	1461.3	2772.8	4914.8	1722.8	3192.0	5731.0	2013.4	3717.6	6605.2	2275.4	4329.8
	A Wholesale and retail trade	2839.9	685.6	2154.3	3209.1	774.8	2434.3	3642.4	879.4	2763.0	4163.6	1005.2	3158.4
	B Restaurants and hotels	1394.2	775.7	618.5	1705.7	948.0	757.6	2088.7	1134.0	954.6	2441.6	1270.2	1171.5
7	Transport, storage and communication	1469.5	592.7	876.7	1794.2	758.1	1036.2	2031.5	864.0	1167.6	2381.9	1019.6	1362.3
	A Transport and storage	1217.2	568.5	648.7	1488.5	728.9	759.6	1678.5	826.8	851.8	1960.1	975.4	984.8
	B Communication	252.2	24.2	228.0	305.7	29.2	276.6	353.0	37.2	315.8	421.8	44.2	377.5
8	Finance, insurance, real estate and business services [a]	2634.6	624.0	2010.6	3022.2	723.8	2298.5	3354.3	806.4	2547.8	3642.6	918.0	2724.6
	A Financial institutions	...	...	...	...	...	...	...	...	...	...	...	...
	B Insurance	...	...	...	...	...	...	...	...	...	...	...	...
	C Real estate and business services	1482.7	370.7	1112.1	1671.0	414.4	1256.6	1915.0	472.4	1442.6	2121.8	529.1	1592.7
9	Community, social and personal services [ab]	1584.7	287.2	1297.5	1866.0	337.9	1528.1	2314.5	418.9	1895.7	2654.7	480.8	2173.9
	Total, Industries	26952.8	13044.7	13908.0	30776.4	15166.1	15610.3	35169.7	17198.9	17970.8	40096.6	19762.9	20333.7
	Producers of Government Services	2055.7	490.3	1565.3	2407.4	570.6	1836.8	2812.9	707.2	2105.6	3323.4	831.9	2491.5
	Other Producers [b]	...	...	...	...	...	...	...	...	...	...	...	...
	Total	29008.4	13535.1	15473.4	33183.8	15736.7	17447.1	37982.5	17906.1	20076.4	43420.0	20594.8	22825.2
	Less: Imputed bank service charge	...	-535.8	535.8	...	-756.3	756.3	...	-889.1	889.1	...	-1043.0	1043.0
	Import duties	271.5	...	271.5	298.2	...	298.2	379.9	...	379.9	452.5	...	452.5
	Value added tax	...	...	...	...	...	...	...	...	...	...	...	...
	Other adjustments	...	...	0.1	...	...	...	...	...	0.1	...	...	...
	Total	29279.9	14070.9	15209.1	33482.0	16493.0	16989.0	38362.4	18795.2	19567.3	43872.5	21637.8	22234.7

		1984 Gross Output	1984 Intermediate Consumption	1984 Value Added	1985 Gross Output	1985 Intermediate Consumption	1985 Value Added
		\multicolumn{6}{c}{**All Producers**}
1	Agriculture, hunting, forestry and fishing	3363.6	1720.9	1642.7	...	...	1728.9
2	Mining and quarrying	...	...	...	...	...	...
3	Manufacturing	19568.9	12665.3	6903.6	...	...	7621.6
	A Manufacture of food, beverages and tobacco	4307.0	3053.7	1253.3	...	...	1390.3

Spain

4.1 Derivation of Value Added by Kind of Activity, in Current Prices
(Continued)

Thousand Million Spanish pesetas

	1984 Gross Output	1984 Intermediate Consumption	1984 Value Added	1985 Gross Output	1985 Intermediate Consumption	1985 Value Added
B Textile, wearing apparel and leather industries	1449.3	832.7	616.6	...	...	683.2
C Manufacture of wood and wood products, including furniture	508.4	278.2	230.2	...	...	234.0
D Manufacture of paper and paper products, printing and publishing	858.3	512.5	345.8	...	...	369.1
E Manufacture of chemicals and chemical petroleum, coal, rubber and plastic products	...	...	...	...	...	...
F Manufacture of non-metallic mineral products, except products of petroleum and coal	...	...	...	...	...	...
G Basic metal industries	...	...	...	...	...	...
H Manufacture of fabricated metal products, machinery and equipment	...	...	...	...	...	...
I Other manufacturing industries	12446.0	7988.2	4457.8	...	...	4945.1
4 Electricity, gas and water	1435.2	669.4	765.8	...	...	880.0
5 Construction	3458.2	1822.6	1635.6	...	...	1781.5
6 Wholesale and retail trade, restaurants and hotels	7648.0	2628.4	5019.7	...	...	5716.7
A Wholesale and retail trade	4769.3	1151.5	3617.8	...	...	4071.0
B Restaurants and hotels	2878.7	1476.9	1401.8	...	...	1645.7
7 Transport, storage and communication	2662.3	1133.5	1528.8	...	...	1664.7
A Transport and storage	2173.6	1082.2	1091.5	...	...	1179.5
B Communication	488.6	51.3	437.3	...	...	485.2
8 Finance, insurance, real estate and business services [a]	4413.4	1036.8	3376.5	...	...	3678.8
A Financial institutions	...	...	...	...	...	...
B Insurance	...	...	...	...	...	...
C Real estate and business services	2308.3	586.4	1721.9	...	...	1886.7
9 Community, social and personal services [ab]	3004.4	543.9	2460.6	...	...	2722.6
Total, Industries	45554.0	22220.7	23333.3	...	...	25794.8
Producers of Government Services	3742.1	959.7	2782.5	...	...	3144.0
Other Producers [b]	...	...	...	...	...	...
Total	49296.1	23180.3	26115.8	...	...	28938.8
Less: Imputed bank service charge	...	-1478.0	1478.0	...	...	1581.9
Import duties	473.5	...	473.5	...	...	556.4
Value added tax	...	...	...	...	...	...
Other adjustments	...	...	...	...	...	-0.1
Total	49769.6	24658.3	25111.3	...	...	27913.2

a) Business services and real estate except dwellings are included in item 'Community, social and personal services'.
b) Item 'Other producers' is included in item 'Community, social and personal services'.

4.3 Cost Components of Value Added

Thousand Million Spanish pesetas

	1980 Compensation of Employees	1980 Capital Consumption	1980 Net Operating Surplus	1980 Indirect Taxes	1980 Less: Subsidies Received	1980 Value Added	1981 Compensation of Employees	1981 Capital Consumption	1981 Net Operating Surplus	1981 Indirect Taxes	1981 Less: Subsidies Received	1981 Value Added
					All Producers							
1 Agriculture, hunting, forestry and fishing	302.7	...	799.1	-28.3	...	1073.4	315.3	...	757.8	-35.1	...	1038.0
2 Mining and quarrying	...	...	...	...	...	...	...	...	...	...	...	...
3 Manufacturing	2404.6	...	1594.3	285.3	...	4284.3	2627.8	...	1734.0	400.3	...	4762.1
A Manufacture of food, beverages and tobacco	301.7	...	313.5	85.9	...	701.2	337.8	...	359.4	115.7	...	812.9

Spain

4.3 Cost Components of Value Added
(Continued)

Thousand Million Spanish pesetas

	1980						1981					
	Compensation of Employees	Capital Consumption	Net Operating Surplus	Indirect Taxes	Less: Subsidies Received	Value Added	Compensation of Employees	Capital Consumption	Net Operating Surplus	Indirect Taxes	Less: Subsidies Received	Value Added
B Textile, wearing apparel and leather industries	277.7	...	166.5	-1.8	...	442.4	279.7	...	170.4	3.9	...	454.0
C Manufacture of wood and wood products, including furniture	121.5	...	57.8	5.1	...	184.4	120.2	...	63.6	7.2	...	191.1
D Manufacture of paper and paper products, printing and publishing	119.2	...	78.9	-4.9	...	193.3	129.9	...	94.5	-2.2	...	222.2
E Manufacture of chemicals and chemical petroleum, coal, rubber and plastic products	...	...	...	...	...	...	...	...	...	...	...	...
F Manufacture of non-metallic mineral products, except products of petroleum and coal	...	...	...	...	...	...	...	...	...	...	...	...
G Basic metal industries	...	...	...	...	...	...	...	...	...	...	...	...
H Manufacture of fabricated metal products, machinery and equipment	...	...	...	...	...	...	...	...	...	...	...	...
I Other manufacturing industries	1584.4	...	977.5	201.0	...	2763.0	1760.2	...	1046.1	275.7	...	3081.9
4 Electricity, gas and water	116.4	...	170.0	22.6	...	309.0	144.1	...	241.8	40.8	...	426.7
5 Construction	889.2	...	351.6	42.9	...	1283.7	921.2	...	359.6	47.9	...	1328.6
6 Wholesale and retail trade, restaurants and hotels	1008.8	...	1729.4	34.7	...	2772.8	1106.9	...	2034.5	50.6	...	3192.0
A Wholesale and retail trade	803.9	...	1332.0	18.4	...	2154.3	857.2	...	1546.5	30.7	...	2434.3
B Restaurants and hotels	204.8	...	397.4	16.3	...	618.5	249.7	...	488.0	19.9	...	757.6
7 Transport, storage and communication	501.6	...	473.8	-98.6	...	876.7	586.8	...	541.3	-91.9	...	1036.2
A Transport and storage	380.9	...	383.5	-115.7	...	648.7	446.6	...	431.5	-118.6	...	759.6
B Communication	120.7	...	90.3	17.1	...	228.0	140.1	...	109.8	26.6	...	276.6
8 Finance, insurance, real estate and business services [a]	458.0	...	1509.8	42.9	...	2010.6	538.5	...	1709.1	50.9	...	2298.5
A Financial institutions	406.3	...	...	...	...	...	477.8	...	...	...	...	...
B Insurance	39.7	...	...	...	...	...	46.8	...	...	...	...	...
C Real estate and business services	12.0	...	1085.3	14.9	...	1112.1	14.0	...	1227.5	15.2	...	1256.6
9 Community, social and personal services [ab]	614.5	...	561.5	121.4	...	1297.5	727.1	...	654.0	147.0	...	1528.1
Total, Industries [cd]	6295.8	...	7189.4	422.9	...	13908.0	6967.7	...	8032.1	610.4	...	15610.3
Producers of Government Services	1488.2	...	77.1	...	...	1565.3	1747.2	...	89.7	...	...	1836.8
Other Producers [b]	...	...	...	...	...	...	...	...	...	...	...	...
Total [cd]	7784.0	...	7266.5	422.9	...	15473.4	8714.9	...	8121.8	610.4	...	17447.1
Less: Imputed bank service charge	...	...	535.8	...	...	535.8	...	...	756.3	...	...	756.3
Import duties	...	...	...	271.5	...	271.5	...	...	...	298.2	...	298.2
Value added tax	...	...	...	...	...	...	...	...	...	...	...	...
Other adjustments	...	...	...	...	...	0.1	...	...	...	...	...	-
Total [cd]	7784.0	...	6730.7	694.4	...	15209.1	8714.9	...	7365.5	908.6	...	16989.0

	1982						1983					
	Compensation of Employees	Capital Consumption	Net Operating Surplus	Indirect Taxes	Less: Subsidies Received	Value Added	Compensation of Employees	Capital Consumption	Net Operating Surplus	Indirect Taxes	Less: Subsidies Received	Value Added
					All Producers							
1 Agriculture, hunting, forestry and fishing	345.4	...	914.9	-34.5	...	1225.9	393.9	...	1021.8	-45.5	...	1370.2
2 Mining and quarrying	...	...	...	...	...	...	...	...	...	...	...	...
3 Manufacturing	2875.5	...	1975.3	475.4	...	5326.2	3156.3	...	2376.9	616.3	...	6149.5
A Manufacture of food, beverages and tobacco	381.0	...	407.0	150.5	...	938.6	430.7	...	461.3	192.1	...	1084.1

Spain

4.3 Cost Components of Value Added
(Continued)

Thousand Million Spanish pesetas

	1982							1983					
	Compensation of Employees	Capital Consumption	Net Operating Surplus	Indirect Taxes	Less: Subsidies Received	Value Added	Compensation of Employees	Capital Consumption	Net Operating Surplus	Indirect Taxes	Less: Subsidies Received	Value Added
B Textile, wearing apparel and leather industries	300.5	...	196.9	6.3	...	503.7	328.9	...	225.5	3.3	...	557.6
C Manufacture of wood and wood products, including furniture	127.0	...	68.0	9.2	...	204.2	136.5	...	73.9	10.6	...	221.1
D Manufacture of paper and paper products, printing and publishing	147.8	...	104.6	0.6	...	253.0	161.2	...	126.4	2.0	...	289.6
E Manufacture of chemicals and chemical petroleum, coal, rubber and plastic products	...	...	...	...	...	...	...	...	...	...	...	...
F Manufacture of non-metallic mineral products, except products of petroleum and coal	...	...	...	...	...	...	...	...	...	...	...	...
G Basic metal industries	...	...	...	...	...	...	...	...	...	...	...	...
H Manufacture of fabricated metal products, machinery and equipment	...	...	...	...	...	...	...	...	...	...	...	...
I Other manufacturing industries	1919.2	...	1198.8	308.7	...	3426.7	2099.1	...	1489.7	408.4	...	3997.2
4 Electricity, gas and water	173.3	...	350.4	38.5	...	562.2	200.2	...	334.7	56.9	...	591.7
5 Construction	1028.9	...	431.8	67.2	...	1527.9	1091.7	...	455.0	84.9	...	1631.7
6 Wholesale and retail trade, restaurants and hotels	1230.7	...	2418.8	68.1	...	3717.6	1418.4	...	2819.6	91.8	...	4329.8
A Wholesale and retail trade	934.3	...	1786.4	42.3	...	2763.0	1093.3	...	2006.4	58.6	...	3158.4
B Restaurants and hotels	296.3	...	632.4	25.9	...	954.6	325.1	...	813.1	33.2	...	1171.5
7 Transport, storage and communication	673.6	...	647.4	-153.5	...	1167.6	766.0	...	791.5	-195.2	...	1362.3
A Transport and storage	511.1	...	536.7	-196.0	...	851.8	583.3	...	640.0	-238.5	...	984.8
B Communication	162.5	...	110.7	42.6	...	315.8	182.7	...	151.5	43.2	...	377.5
8 Finance, insurance, real estate and business services [a]	637.7	...	1849.3	60.9	...	2547.8	719.4	...	1926.8	78.4	...	2724.6
A Financial institutions	567.6	...	...	...	...	...	637.7	...	...	...	...	...
B Insurance	53.6	...	...	...	...	...	62.9	...	...	...	...	...
C Real estate and business services	16.5	...	1407.1	18.9	...	1442.6	18.7	...	1551.6	22.4	...	1592.7
9 Community, social and personal services [ab]	888.0	...	876.4	131.3	...	1895.7	1021.5	...	968.2	184.2	...	2173.9
Total, Industries [cd]	7853.1	...	9464.3	653.4	...	17970.8	8767.5	...	10694.4	871.9	...	20333.7
Producers of Government Services	2000.1	...	105.6	...	...	2105.6	2364.9	...	126.6	...	...	2491.5
Other Producers [b]	...	...	...	...	...	...	...	...	...	...	...	...
Total [cd]	9853.2	...	9569.8	653.4	...	20076.4	11132.4	...	10820.9	871.9	...	22825.2
Less: Imputed bank service charge	...	...	889.1	...	...	889.1	...	...	1043.0	...	...	1043.0
Import duties	...	...	...	379.9	...	379.9	...	...	...	452.5	...	452.5
Value added tax	...	...	...	...	...	...	...	...	...	...	...	...
Other adjustments	...	...	...	...	...	0.1	...	...	...	...	...	...
Total [cd]	9853.2	...	8680.7	1033.3	...	19567.3	11132.4	...	9777.9	1324.4	...	22234.7

	1984							1985					
	Compensation of Employees	Capital Consumption	Net Operating Surplus	Indirect Taxes	Less: Subsidies Received	Value Added	Compensation of Employees	Capital Consumption	Net Operating Surplus	Indirect Taxes	Less: Subsidies Received	Value Added
					All Producers							
1 Agriculture, hunting, forestry and fishing	424.7	...	1254.4	-36.4	...	1642.7	470.0	...	...	...	...	1728.9
2 Mining and quarrying	...	...	...	...	...	...	...	...	...	...	...	...
3 Manufacturing	3348.8	...	2815.6	739.2	...	6903.6	3644.2	...	...	...	...	7621.6
A Manufacture of food, beverages and tobacco	475.3	...	550.5	227.5	...	1253.3	532.7	...	...	...	...	1390.3

Spain

4.3 Cost Components of Value Added
(Continued)

Thousand Million Spanish pesetas

	1984						1985					
	Compensation of Employees	Capital Consumption	Net Operating Surplus	Indirect Taxes	Less: Subsidies Received	Value Added	Compensation of Employees	Capital Consumption	Net Operating Surplus	Indirect Taxes	Less: Subsidies Received	Value Added
B Textile, wearing apparel and leather industries	347.3	...	264.5	4.8	...	616.6	392.4	...	...	...	...	683.2
C Manufacture of wood and wood products, including furniture	137.7	...	79.4	13.1	...	230.2	143.6	...	...	...	...	234.0
D Manufacture of paper and paper products, printing and publishing	172.7	...	164.4	8.6	...	345.8	170.7	...	...	...	...	369.1
E Manufacture of chemicals and chemical petroleum, coal, rubber and plastic products	...	...	...	...	...	...	...	...	...	...	...	...
F Manufacture of non-metallic mineral products, except products of petroleum and coal	...	...	...	...	...	...	...	...	...	...	...	...
G Basic metal industries	...	...	...	...	...	...	...	...	...	...	...	...
H Manufacture of fabricated metal products, machinery and equipment	...	...	...	...	...	...	...	...	...	...	...	...
I Other manufacturing industries	2215.7	...	1756.8	485.2	...	4457.8	2404.7	...	...	...	...	4945.1
4 Electricity, gas and water	209.1	...	470.2	86.6	...	765.8	229.7	...	...	...	...	880.0
5 Construction	997.6	...	518.8	119.2	...	1635.6	984.7	...	...	...	...	1781.5
6 Wholesale and retail trade, restaurants and hotels	1491.6	...	3406.9	121.2	...	5019.7	1612.5	...	...	...	...	5716.7
A Wholesale and retail trade	1119.0	...	2425.7	73.1	...	3617.8	1204.7	...	...	...	...	4071.0
B Restaurants and hotels	372.6	...	981.2	48.0	...	1401.8	407.9	...	...	...	...	1645.7
7 Transport, storage and communication	820.6	...	936.3	-228.1	...	1528.8	890.9	...	...	...	...	1664.7
A Transport and storage	620.3	...	753.2	-282.0	...	1091.5	668.0	...	...	...	...	1179.5
B Communication	200.3	...	183.2	53.9	...	437.3	222.9	...	...	...	...	485.2
8 Finance, insurance, real estate and business services [a]	800.9	...	2482.8	92.9	...	3376.5	891.9	...	...	...	...	3678.8
A Financial institutions	713.1	...	...	...	...	...	...	...	...	...	...	...
B Insurance	70.1	...	...	...	...	...	...	...	...	...	...	...
C Real estate and business services	20.7	...	1669.0	32.2	...	1721.9	23.0	...	...	...	...	1886.7
9 Community, social and personal services [ab]	1148.5	...	1112.2	199.8	...	2460.6	1258.1	...	...	...	...	2722.6
Total, Industries [cd]	9241.8	...	12997.2	1094.4	...	23333.3	9982.1	...	...	...	...	25794.8
Producers of Government Services	2634.4	...	148.1	...	...	2782.5	2975.1	...	...	...	...	3144.0
Other Producers [b]	...	...	...	...	...	...	...	...	...	...	...	...
Total [cd]	11876.2	...	13145.3	1094.4	...	26115.8	12957.2	...	...	...	...	28938.8
Less: Imputed bank service charge	...	...	1478.0	...	...	1478.0	...	...	...	...	...	1581.9
Import duties	...	...	...	473.5	...	473.5	...	...	...	...	...	556.4
Value added tax	...	...	...	...	...	...	...	...	...	...	...	...
Other adjustments	...	...	...	...	...	...	...	...	...	...	...	-0.1
Total [cd]	11876.2	...	11667.3	1567.9	...	25111.3	12957.2	...	...	...	...	27913.2

a) Business services and real estate except dwellings are included in item 'Community, social and personal services'.
b) Item 'Other producers' is included in item 'Community, social and personal services'.
c) Column 4 refers to indirect taxes less subsidies received.
d) Column 'Operating surplus' includes capital consumption and net indirect taxes'.

Sri Lanka

General note. The preparation of national accounts statistics in Sri Lanka is undertaken by the Department of Census and Statistics, Colombo. The official estimates are published by the Department in 'National Accounts in Sri Lanka'. The following presentation on sources and methods is based mainly on a report by the U.N. Regional Adviser of National Accounts entitled 'Assessment of sources, methods and reliability of estimates of gross domestic product by kind of economic activity in Sri Lanka (1975)' and on a detailed and comprehensive information received from the Department of Census and Statistics in 1978. The estimates are generally in accordance with the classifications and definitions recommended in the United Nations System of National Accounts (SNA). The following tables have been prepared from successve replies to the United Nations national accounts questionnaire. When the scope and coverage of the estimates differ for conceptual or statistical reasons from the definitions and classifications recommended in SNA, a footnote is indicated to the relevant tables.

Sources and methods:

(a) Gross domestic product. Gross domestic product is estimated mainly through the production approach.

(b) Expenditure on the gross domestic product. The expenditure approach is used to estimate government final consumption expenditure, gross fixed capital formation in the public sector and exports and imports of goods and services. This approach, in combination with the commodity-flow approach is used to estimate private final consumption expenditure. The commodity-flow approach is used for gross fixed capital formation in the private sector. Changes in stocks are estimated as a residual. General government expenditure consists of actual expenditure made by central government and current expenditure by the local government on goods and services which are obtained from the Treasury Votes Ledgers and the Ministry of Local Government, respectively. Private consumption expenditure is estimated by using the commodity-flow method on the basis of imports as well as domestic goods available for consumption. Bench-mark estimates for selected consumer items are avilable in value terms through the use of household survey data. These estimates are extrapolated by using the increase in population and price levels. For gross fixed capital formation in the public sector, direct estimates are prepared on the basis of information available in the budegetary accounts. For building and other construction, the supply of locally produced building materials are first compiled, adding 45 per cent to the production values for trade and transport margins while data on imported materials are obtained from customs returns adding import duties and 45 per cent for trade and transport margins. It has been found that building materials constitute 45 per cent of the construction cost with wages and profits at 55 per cent. For machinery and equipment, import statistics are analyzed in detail. Estimates for exports and imports of goods and services are based on foreign trade statistics and balance of payments data. For the constant price estimates, all items of GDP by expenditure type are deflated by appropriate price indices or extrapolated by using quantum indices.

(c) Cost-structure of the gross domestic product. Data on wages and salaries in the government sector are obtained from Treasury records. In order to estimate compensation of employees in the private sector, the percentages of wage component for the key sectors, obtained from the socio-economic survey data for 1980/1981, are applied to the respective activity. Based on special inquiries made, depreciation is assumed to be 33.3 per cent of the value of fixed assets up to 1978 and 20 per cent for the years 1979, 1980 and 1981. Indirect taxes are obtained from government revenue records and subsidies from treasury records.

(d) Gross domestic product by kind of economic activity. The table of GDP by kind of economic activity is prepared in producers values. The production approach is used to estimate value added of most industries. For livestock and forestry, the expenditure approach is used and for some of the service sectors like banking and transport, the income approach is used. Estimates of value added for tea and rubber have been revised by using the production approach. The estimation of coconut production is based on domestic and industrial consumption and exports. The annual cost-of-production returns are used for estimating inputs. The volume of paddy prodcution is estimated on the basis of acreage statistics obtained from a multistage sample survey of crop-cutting. Own-account consumption is estimated as 10 per cent of production. Bench-mark estimates for fruits and vegetables are based on the 1973 consumer finance survey. These are extrapolated for current years by increase in population and price levels. For livestock products, the per capita consumption obtained from the 1973 consumer finance survey is multiplied by each year's mid-year population. Production data for the mining and quarrying sector are obtained from the Department of Geological Survey. The value of input is assumed to be 15 per cent of the value of gross putput. For large-scale manufacturing, quantities and values of gross output and values of inputs are submitted in annual returns furnished by the registered industrial establishments. Bench-mark estimates for small-scale industries are obtained from the 1971 survey on the unorganized sector conducted by the Industrial Development Board. Extrapolation is done by using the growth in the labour force and the wage index. Data on electricity, gas and water are obtained from the Ceylon Electricity Board and the Ministry of Industries. The value added of construction activity in the private sector is based on locally produced and imported building materials obtained from the annual returns of manufacturing establishments and the customs returns, respectively. For the government sector, value of materials used in building and other construction accounts for 45 per cent of the gross value. This estimate is deducted from the value of the total supply of materials to obtain the value of material used in the private sector. Value added for the distributive trade is measured by net trade margins earned by traders on various types of products. Gross trade margin estimates are made seperately for exports, local market production, government and private imports, etc. From these estimates 15 per cent is deducted for input. Bench-mark estimates for hotels and restaurants have been obtained from the 1969/70 socio-economic survey. These estimates are extrapolated by population growth and a specially constructed index for meals consumed outside homes. For trnasport in the government sector, the expenditure on personal employment is taken as value added. The gross value of goods, transport and trade is obtained by applying specified distribution margins to the c.i.f. value in the case of imports and to the producer value in the case of locally produced goods. Wherever retail and producer prices are available the difference between them is taken as the distribution margin. For the financial sector, value added is based on data obtained from the Central Bank and concerned institutions. Bench-mark data for gross rental values have been obtained from the 1980/81 socio-economic survey. These estimates are applied to the housing stock, with an allowance made for rental increases. The value added of government services is obtained from the Treasury Accounts. For the private sector, value added is based on expenditure data obtained from the 1980/81 consumer finance survey, extrapolated by the growth in the labour force adjusted for changes in wages. For the constant price estimates, price deflation is used for most of the industries. For some agricultural products, electricity, gas and water, transport and government services, value added is extrapolated by a quantity index.

1.1 Expenditure on the Gross Domestic Product, in Current Prices

Million Sri Lanka rupees

	1970	1975	1977	1978	1979	1980	1981	1982	1983	1984	1985	1986
1 Government final consumption expenditure	1680	2697	3429	4851	5447	6667	7456	10407	12727	15442	19170	22990
2 Private final consumption expenditure	10165	21679	27088	31891	40052	53457	64581	77310	93075	108312	118101	130728
3 Gross capital formation	2746	3981	4871	9515	14339	22410	24286	28174	31374	34412	37876	38631
A Increase in stocks [a]	363	441	224	33	281	167	331	248	-210	150	225	137
B Gross fixed capital formation	2383	3540	4647	9482	14058	22243	23955	27926	31584	34262	37651	38494
Residential buildings	424	579	763	1234	2151	3808	5048	6138	6950	7238	9525	10694
Non-residential buildings	514	690	923	969	1479	2839	2350	2356	2858	2399	3039	4167
Other construction and land improvement etc.	673	968	1136	1900	2102	5113	7211	7472	7836	11075	9294	8966
Other	772	1302	1825	5378	8326	10483	9348	11960	13939	13550	15793	14667
4 Exports of goods and services	3478	7306	12311	14835	17660	21434	25892	27148	32016	44285	42394	42568
5 Less: Imports of goods and services	3908	9291	10979	16872	23969	36456	39558	45905	50381	54469	62396	63407
Statistical discrepancy	-	670	191	342	1391	825	1869	394	391	-639	2619	932
Equals: Gross Domestic Product	14161	27041	36912	44562	54920	68338	84527	97520	119202	147344	157763	172440

a) The estimates of 'Increase in stocks' for the years prior to 1975 include a statistical discrepancy.

1.2 Expenditure on the Gross Domestic Product, in Constant Prices

Million Sri Lanka rupees

	1970	1975	1977	1978	1979	1980	1981	1982	1983	1984	1985	1986
					At constant prices of:1975							
1 Government final consumption expenditure	2747	2697	2850	3654	3688	3626	3593	4208	3919	3953	4876	5714
2 Private final consumption expenditure	18338	21679	24987	25960	28569	31610	35390	37720	39188	39598	41986	44192
3 Gross capital formation	3866	3981	4225	5259	5891	6986	7434	7516	7262	6722	6696	6501
A Increase in stocks	771	441	171	22	169	75	127	91	-61	42	61	39
B Gross fixed capital formation	3095	3540	4054	5237	5722	6911	7306	7425	7324	6680	6635	6462

Sri Lanka

1.2 Expenditure on the Gross Domestic Product, in Constant Prices
(Continued)

Million Sri Lanka rupees

	1970	1975	1977	1978	1979	1980	1981	1982	1983	1984	1985	1986
					At constant prices of:1975							
Residential buildings	611	579	706	784	989	1178	1312	1527	1593	1505	1839	2050
Non-residential buildings	730	690	840	691	834	1108	774	726	813	613	742	1017
Other construction and land improvement etc.	925	968	1028	1450	1430	1808	2523	2516	2236	2686	2081	1987
Other	829	1302	1481	2312	2469	2817	2698	2656	2682	1876	1973	1408
4 Exports of goods and services	7326	7306	6480	7091	7746	8131	8375	9213	8936	10312	10828	11550
5 Less: Imports of goods and services	11842	9291	9954	13629	12743	13573	14061	15509	15420	15559	15062	16839
Statistical discrepancy	2709	670	732	3156	254	-1473	-3464	-3949	-2824	-1891	-4024	-3882
Equals: Gross Domestic Product [a]	23143	27041	29320	31492	33406	35308	37266	39199	41062	43136	45300	47236

a) The estimates before 1975 for this table have been calculated on the basis of 1963 prices and linked to the estimates for the years beginning 1975.

1.3 Cost Components of the Gross Domestic Product

Million Sri Lanka rupees

	1970	1975	1977	1978	1979	1980	1981	1982	1983	1984	1985	1986
1 Indirect taxes, net	664	749	1004	2116	3185	9174	10688	11163	15210	23102	22481	24318
A Indirect taxes	...	...	...	...	...	10163	11884	12176	16937	25245	24402	26437
B Less: Subsidies	...	...	...	...	...	988	1197	1013	1727	2143	1921	2119
2 Consumption of fixed capital	794	1180	1549	3161	2812	4449	4791	5585	6317	6852	7530	7699
3 Compensation of employees paid by resident producers to:	5103	12143	15421	19000	23945	31031	37636	44561	53729	64265	70748	78741
4 Operating surplus [a]	7237	12527	18523	19910	23307	22692	29211	35577	43765	53614	54160	60613
Statistical discrepancy [b]	363	441	415	375	1672	992	2200	642	181	-489	2844	1069
Equals: Gross Domestic Product	14161	27041	36912	44562	54920	68338	84527	97528	119202	147344	157763	172440

a) Item 'Operating surplus' has been obtained as a residual.
b) Item "Statistical discrepancy' includes 'Increase in stocks'.

1.4 General Government Current Receipts and Disbursements

Million Sri Lanka rupees

	1970	1975	1977	1978	1979	1980	1981	1982	1983	1984	1985	1986
					Receipts							
1 Operating surplus	...	...	...	...	...	...	...	...	...	...	...	...
2 Property and entrepreneurial income	10	25	23	30	30	1073	1360	1578	2149	3545	5168	5071
3 Taxes, fees and contributions	2509	4240	5508	10410	11225	12775	14267	15476	20765	31296	31095	32004
A Indirect taxes	2042	3423	4504	9217	9745	10163	11884	12176	16937	25245	24402	26437
B Direct taxes	425	770	937	1103	1357	2515	2250	3180	3703	5887	6232	5292
C Social security contributions	18	24	37	50	52	51	60	71	71	84	89	106
D Compulsory fees, fines and penalties	24	23	30	41	.71	47	72	49	55	79	372	169
4 Other current transfers	449	706	1013	1034	1220	286	357	573	2077	2270	2368	2796
Total Current Receipts of General Government [a]	2968	4971	6544	11474	12475	14134	15984	17627	24991	37110	38631	39871
					Disbursements							
1 Government final consumption expenditure	1680	2697	3429	4851	5447	6667	7456	10407	12727	15442	19170	22990
A Compensation of employees	924	1788	2279	2466	2883	3573	4162	5379	7260	8237	9244	11124
B Consumption of fixed capital	...	...	...	...	...	...	...	...	...	...	...	...
C Purchases of goods and services, net	756	909	1151	2385	2564	3094	3294	5029	5467	7205	9926	11866
D Less: Own account fixed capital formation	...	...	...	...	...	...	...	...	...	...	...	...
E Indirect taxes paid, net	...	...	...	...	...	...	...	...	...	...	...	...
2 Property income	...	...	...	...	...	2213	3738	5104	7369	7446	8488	9448
A Interest	...	...	...	...	...	2213	3738	5104	7369	7446	8488	9448
B Net land rent and royalties	...	...	...	...	...	...	...	...	...	...	...	...

Sri Lanka

1.4 General Government Current Receipts and Disbursements
(Continued)

Million Sri Lanka rupees

		1970	1975	1977	1978	1979	1980	1981	1982	1983	1984	1985	1986
3	Subsidies	...	...	...	...	...	988	1197	1013	1867	1463	1646	1548
4	Other current transfers	1330	2569	3124	5671	6141	4042	3638	3632	1731	3175	6378	2775
	A Social security benefits	...	...	...	...	...	...	...	...	...	...	...	...
	B Social assistance grants	...	...	...	...	...	...	...	...	...	...	...	...
	C Other	1084	2125	2513	4557	4931	...	...	...	...	...	...	...
5	Net saving	-41	-294	-10	952	887	223	-45	-2530	1297	9584	2949	3110
	Total Current Disbursements and Net Saving of General Government [a]	2968	4971	6544	11474	12475	14134	15984	17627	24991	37110	38631	39871

a) Prior to 1980, estimates are based on data extracted from Central Bank of Ceylon and from the Department of Census and Statistics (DC & S). Beginning 1980, the estimates are prepared by DC & S and are therefore, not comparable with the data prior to 1980.

1.6 Current Income and Outlay of Households and Non-Profit Institutions

Million Sri Lanka rupees

		1970	1975	1977	1978	1979	1980	1981	1982	1983	1984	1985	1986
	Receipts												
1	Compensation of employees	...	...	...	...	...	31031	37636	44561	53729	64265	70748	78741
2	Operating surplus of private unincorporated enterprises	...	...	...	...	...	...	...	...	...	...	...	...
3	Property and entrepreneurial income	...	...	...	...	...	21817	26033	30647	37935	41640	44772	51281
4	Current transfers	...	...	...	...	...	6100	8985	11055	12232	13982	15177	16049
	Total Current Receipts	...	...	...	...	...	58948	72654	86263	103896	119887	130697	146071
	Disbursements												
1	Private final consumption expenditure	...	...	...	...	...	53457	64581	77310	93076	100012	118101	130728
2	Property income	...	...	...	...	...	136	165	204	253	412	409	479
3	Direct taxes and other current transfers n.e.c. to general government	...	...	...	...	...	1671	2080	2636	2884	3860	4837	5637
	A Social security contributions	...	...	...	...	...	498	601	722	795	1057	1264	1281
	B Direct taxes	...	...	...	...	...	1173	1479	1914	2089	2803	3573	4356
	C Fees, fines and penalties	...	...	...	...	...	...	...	...	...	...	...	...
4	Other current transfers	...	...	...	...	...	530	830	866	894	1140	1329	1566
	Statistical discrepancy	...	...	...	...	...	-602	-1273	-1205	-941	-4959	-7529	-7411
5	Net saving [a]	...	...	...	...	...	3756	6271	6452	7731	11122	13550	15072
	Total Current Disbursements and Net Saving [a]	...	...	...	...	...	58948	72654	86263	103896	119887	130697	146071

a) Item 'Net saving' includes consumption of fixed capital.

1.7 External Transactions on Current Account, Summary

Million Sri Lanka rupees

		1970	1975	1977	1978	1979	1980	1981	1982	1983	1984	1985	1986
	Payments to the Rest of the World												
1	Imports of goods and services [a]	3908	9291	10979	16872	23060	36450	39558	45905	50381	54469	62396	63407
	A Imports of merchandise c.i.f.	3615	8801	10379	15600	22570	33915	36121	41420	45201	49046	55528	54898
	B Other	293	490	601	1272	1399	2541	3438	4486	5180	5423	6868	8509
2	Factor income to the rest of the world	235	295	422	551	854	1206	2502	2871	4270	4881	5706	5768
	A Compensation of employees	...	...	...	...	...	...	...	...	...	...	...	...
	B Property and entrepreneurial income	235	295	422	551	854	1206	2502	2871	4270	4881	5706	5768
3	Current transfers to the rest of the world	36	67	111	268	182	258	512	530	475	622	708	891
4	Surplus of the nation on current transactions	-543	-2166	1282	-1932	-5795	-13193	-11616	-15223	-15138	-6554	-16235	-16450
	Payments to the Rest of the World and Surplus of the Nation on Current Transactions	3636	7487	12794	15759	19210	24726	30956	34084	39987	53418	52575	53617
	Receipts From The Rest of the World												
1	Exports of goods and services [a]	3478	7306	12311	14835	17660	21434	25892	27148	32016	44285	42394	42568

1345

Sri Lanka

1.7 External Transactions on Current Account, Summary
(Continued)

Million Sri Lanka rupees

		1970	1975	1977	1978	1979	1980	1981	1982	1983	1984	1985	1986
	A Exports of merchandise f.o.b.	3103	6436	10911	13207	15282	17603	20507	21098	25038	37198	35729	33881
	B Other	375	870	1400	1629	2378	3831	5385	6050	6978	7088	6665	8687
2	Factor income from rest of the world	15	82	170	314	615	774	634	912	1056	1480	2261	1907
	A Compensation of employees	...	...	...	...	...	...	...	...	...	...	...	...
	B Property and entrepreneurial income	15	82	170	314	615	774	634	912	1056	1480	2261	1907
3	Current transfers from rest of the world	143	99	313	610	935	2518	4430	6024	6916	7653	7920	9142
	Receipts from the Rest of the World on Current Transactions	3636	7487	12794	15759	19210	24726	30956	34084	39987	53418	52575	53617

a) Prior to 1978, estimates of imports and exports of goods and services are valued at the Foreign Exchange Entitlment Certificate Rate (FEECR) which is a proxy to the unitary rate.

1.8 Capital Transactions of The Nation, Summary

Million Sri Lanka rupees

	1970	1975	1977	1978	1979	1980	1981	1982	1983	1984	1985	1986
Finance of Gross Capital Formation												
Gross saving	2203	1815	6153	7583	8544	9216	12670	12951	16236	27858	21641	22181
1 Consumption of fixed capital a	794	1180	1549	3161	2812	4449	4791	5585	6317	6852	7530	7699
2 Net saving	1409	635	4604	4422	5733	4768	7879	7366	9919	21006	14111	14482
Less: Surplus of the nation on current transactions	-543	-2166	1282	-1932	-5795	-13193	-11616	-15223	-15138	-6554	-16235	-16450
Statistical discrepancy	-	-	-	-	-	-	-	-	-	-	-	-
Finance of Gross Capital Formation	2746	3981	4871	9515	14339	22410	24286	28174	31374	34412	37876	38631
Gross Capital Formation												
Increase in stocks	363	441	224	33	281	167	331	248	-210	150	225	137
Gross fixed capital formation	2383	3540	4647	9482	14058	22243	23955	27926	31584	34262	37651	38494
1 General government b	572	1043	1225	2567	3773	5177	4242	4246	5428	6142	7758	8937
2 Corporate and quasi-corporate enterprises	1811	2496	3422	6915	10284	17066	19713	23680	26156	28121	29893	29557
A Public	...	...	...	...	...	...	...	...	...	...	...	...
B Private	1811	2496	3422	6915	10284	17066	19713	23680	26156	28121	29893	29557
3 Other	...	...	...	...	...	...	...	...	...	...	...	...
Gross Capital Formation	2746	3981	4871	9515	14339	22410	24286	28174	31374	34412	37876	38631

a) Item 'Consumption of fixed capital' includes depreciation of all private corporations as well as depreciation of fixed assets in other private unincorporated units.
b) Public enterprises is included in general government.

1.10 Gross Domestic Product by Kind of Activity, in Current Prices

Million Sri Lanka rupees

		1970	1975	1977	1978	1979	1980	1981	1982	1983	1984	1985	1986
1	Agriculture, hunting, forestry and fishing a	5080	7581	10723	12098	15199	17900	22787	25258	30468	37293	38506	39529
2	Mining and quarrying	90	323	412	587	646	910	1078	1159	1420	1209	1227	1670
3	Manufacturing a	2046	6652	9415	10071	10890	12422	14028	14644	17933	24301	26180	26914
4	Electricity, gas and water	73	117	150	169	352	547	1003	1543	1611	2507	2999	3062
5	Construction	848	1262	1591	2476	3702	6503	8037	8651	9902	11306	11939	13197
6	Wholesale and retail trade, restaurants and hotels	2357	4883	6495	8949	9896	11331	16168	19732	23901	26951	29061	32716
7	Transport, storage and communication	1307	2362	3056	3371	4848	6962	7383	9748	11635	15621	17429	19661
8	Finance, insurance, real estate and business services	699	1003	1308	1644	2852	3620	4624	5884	7226	8623	9235	10628
9	Community, social and personal services	327	621	792	991	1200	1513	1873	2093	2762	3057	3246	3594
	Total, Industries	12827	24804	33942	40354	49584	61708	76981	88711	106857	130868	139822	150971
	Producers of Government Services	1192	1825	2376	2660	2969	3573	4162	5379	7260	8237	9244	11124
	Other Producers	143	77	82	93	105	133	158	215	249	294	300	331
	Subtotal	14161	26706	36400	43108	52658	65414	81302	94305	114366	139399	149366	162426
	Less: Imputed bank service charge	...	...	...	...	...	...	...	...	...	...	...	...
	Plus: Import duties	...	334	512	1454	2262	2924	3225	3222	4836	7945	8397	10014
	Plus: Value added tax	...	...	...	...	...	...	...	...	...	...	...	...
	Equals: Gross Domestic Product	14161	27041	36912	44562	54920	68338	84527	97528	119202	147344	157763	172440

a) The estimates on processing of tea and rubber are included in the agricultural sector prior to 1975. From 1975 onward, they are included in the manufacturing sector.

Sri Lanka

1.11 Gross Domestic Product by Kind of Activity, in Constant Prices

Million Sri Lanka rupees

	1970	1975	1977	1978	1979	1980	1981	1982	1983	1984	1985	1986
					At constant prices of:1975							
1 Agriculture, hunting, forestry and fishing [a]	7191	7581	8242	8812	9209	9357	10058	10372	10994	10200	11146	11224
2 Mining and quarrying	149	323	373	436	411	475	500	479	575	693	673	918
3 Manufacturing [a]	4556	6652	6758	6866	7043	7071	7327	7281	7064	8300	8812	9345
4 Electricity, gas and water	97	117	126	132	166	181	203	222	226	253	274	294
5 Construction	1295	1262	1359	1505	1650	1947	2208	2157	2172	2200	2248	2419
6 Wholesale and retail trade, restaurants and hotels	4080	4883	5558	5925	6795	7564	8059	9408	10162	10907	11422	11983
7 Transport, storage and communication	2007	2362	2492	2782	3000	3460	3564	3658	4043	4531	4607	4718
8 Finance, insurance, real estate and business services	855	1003	1048	1092	1199	1269	1357	1512	1566	1649	1719	1772
9 Community, social and personal services	651	621	773	934	926	980	1076	1117	1196	1296	1299	1338
Statistical discrepancy	657	...	...	...	...	...	...	...	...	...	...	...
Total, Industries	21538	24804	26730	28484	30398	32305	34352	36206	37997	40029	42200	44011
Producers of Government Services	1529	1825	2046	2208	2195	2206	2236	2256	2272	2290	2334	2380
Other Producers	77	77	80	88	83	83	84	102	104	105	106	108
Subtotal [b]	23143	26706	28855	30780	32676	34594	36672	38564	40373	42432	44640	46499
Less: Imputed bank service charge	...	...	...	...	...	...	...	...	...	...	...	...
Plus: Import duties	...	334	464	712	729	714	595	635	689	704	660	737
Plus: Value added tax	...	...	...	...	...	...	...	...	...	...	...	...
Equals: Gross Domestic Product [b]	23143	27041	29320	31492	33406	35308	37266	39199	41062	43136	45300	47236

a) The estimates on processing of tea and rubber are included in the agricultural sector prior to 1975. From 1975 onward, they are included in the manufacturing sector.
b) The estimates before 1975 for this table have been calculated on the basis of 1963 prices and linked to the estimates for the years beginning 1975.

1.12 Relations Among National Accounting Aggregates

Million Sri Lanka rupees

	1970	1975	1977	1978	1979	1980	1981	1982	1983	1984	1985	1986
Gross Domestic Product	14161	27041	36912	44562	54920	68338	84527	97528	119202	147344	157763	172440
Plus: Net factor income from the rest of the world	-220	-213	-252	-237	-240	-432	-1868	-1959	-3214	-3401	-3445	-3861
Factor income from the rest of the world	15	82	170	314	615	774	634	912	1056	1480	2261	1907
Less: Factor income to the rest of the world	235	295	422	551	854	1206	2502	2871	4270	4881	5706	5768
Equals: Gross National Product	13941	26828	36660	44325	54681	67906	82659	95568	115988	143943	154318	168579
Less: Consumption of fixed capital	794	1180	1549	3161	2812	4449	4791	5585	6317	6852	7530	7699
Equals: National Income	13147	25648	35111	41164	51869	63457	77868	89983	109671	137091	146788	160880
Plus: Net current transfers from the rest of the world	107	32	202	342	754	2260	3918	5494	6441	7031	7212	8251
Current transfers from the rest of the world	143	99	313	610	935	2518	4430	6024	6916	7653	7920	9142
Less: Current transfers to the rest of the world	36	67	111	268	182	258	512	530	475	622	708	891
Equals: National Disposable Income	13254	25680	35313	41506	52623	65717	81786	95477	116112	144122	154000	169131
Less: Final consumption	11845	24375	30518	36742	45499	60124	72038	87717	105802	123755	137271	153718
Statistical discrepancy	...	-670	-191	-342	-1391	-825	-1869	-394	-391	639	-2619	-932
Equals: Net Saving	1409	635	4604	4422	5733	4768	7879	7366	9919	21006	14111	14482
Less: Surplus of the nation on current transactions	-543	-2166	1282	-1932	-5795	-13193	-11616	-15223	-15138	-6554	-16235	-16450
Equals: Net Capital Formation [a]	1952	2801	3322	6354	11527	17961	19495	22589	25057	27560	30346	30932

a) Item 'Net capital formation' includes a statistical discrepancy.

Sri Lanka

2.1 Government Final Consumption Expenditure by Function, in Current Prices

Million Sri Lanka rupees

		1970	1975	1977	1978	1979	1980	1981	1982	1983	1984	1985	1986
1	General public services	318	666	698	1497	1748	1860	2644	4346	4701	5816	6126	5281
2	Defence	92	193	227	283	485	585	625	687	1229	1748	4654	7877
3	Public order and safety	...	...	...	...	...	...	...	...	...	...	...	...
4	Education	472	681	910	1008	1167	1171	1508	1872	2380	2662	3154	3457
5	Health	236	332	461	522	626	738	823	954	1259	1521	1660	1733
6	Social security and welfare	183	336	428	640	596	756	930	1203	1681	1950	2228	3053
7	Housing and community amenities	2	25	30	37	52	61	67	87	133	130	83	73
8	Recreational, cultural and religious affairs	23	13	18	25	36	39	37	48	64	74	82	93
9	Economic services	354	451	658	839	738	1457	824	1211	1279	1541	1183	1423
10	Other functions	...	...	...	...	...	...	...	...	...	...	...	...
	Total Government Final Consumption Expenditure	1680	2697	3429	4851	5447	6667	7456	10407	12727	15442	19170	22990

2.2 Government Final Consumption Expenditure by Function, in Constant Prices

Million Sri Lanka rupees

		1970	1975	1977	1978	1979	1980	1981	1982	1983	1984	1985	1986
		\multicolumn{12}{c}{At constant prices of:1975}
1	General public services	522	666	580	1128	1183	1012	1276	1757	1448	1490	1555	1314
2	Defence	151	193	188	213	328	319	302	278	379	447	1185	1960
3	Public order and safety	...	...	...	...	...	...	...	...	...	...	...	...
4	Education	772	681	756	759	790	638	726	757	733	680	804	857
5	Health	385	332	383	393	424	403	395	386	388	391	424	429
6	Social security and welfare	299	336	356	482	403	410	449	486	518	498	566	760
7	Housing and community amenities	3	25	25	28	35	33	32	35	41	32	20	17
8	Recreational, cultural and religious affairs	39	13	15	19	24	22	18	19	20	20	20	23
9	Economic services	577	451	547	632	500	791	395	490	394	395	302	354
10	Other functions	...	...	...	...	...	...	...	...	...	...	...	...
	Total Government Final Consumption Expenditure [a]	2747	2697	2850	3654	3688	3626	3593	4208	3919	3953	4876	5714

a) The estimates before 1975 for this table have been calculated on the basis of 1963 prices and linked to the estimates for the years beginning 1975.

2.5 Private Final Consumption Expenditure by Type and Porpose, in Current Prices

Million Sri Lanka rupees

		1970	1975	1977	1978	1979	1980	1981	1982	1983	1984	1985	1986
		\multicolumn{12}{c}{**Final Consumption Expenditure of Resident Households**}
1	Food, beverages and tobacco	6539	15476	18972	22041	26957	33101	37270	44674	55616	62411	64194	69240
	A Food	5506	13724	16912	19411	23111	27298	30626	36974	47137	51684	52457	57307
	B Non-alcoholic beverages	43	60	57	66	76	88	77	52	233	659	292	626
	C Alcoholic beverages	344	594	539	978	1525	1884	1847	2809	2993	3111	3832	3474
	D Tobacco	647	1099	1463	1587	2245	3831	4720	4839	5253	6957	7613	7833
2	Clothing and footwear	618	1615	2044	1974	2532	3208	3923	4558	5794	6548	8044	9172
3	Gross rent, fuel and power	727	1047	1160	1362	2448	3112	3635	4704	5177	6174	6710	7033
	A Fuel and power	237	347	441	520	802	1050	1215	2171	2611	3334	3517	3729
	B Other	490	700	719	842	1646	2062	2419	2534	2566	2840	3193	3304
4	Furniture, furnishings and household equipment and operation	461	692	1149	1203	1828	2606	3281	3428	3492	3759	5312	5711
	A Household operation	258	326	529	555	851	805	1265	1472	1474	1452	1853	2000
	B Other	203	366	620	648	977	1801	2016	1956	2018	2307	3459	3711
5	Medical care and health expenses	291	310	439	523	644	896	1088	1236	1224	1508	1829	2597
6	Transport and communication	643	1229	1794	2711	3450	6467	9253	10696	12684	17678	18715	19959
	A Personal transport equipment	3	5	57	294	454	988	1199	1093	1466	1546	1630	1459
	B Other	640	1224	1738	2418	2996	5478	8055	9603	11217	16132	17085	18500
7	Recreational, entertainment, education and cultural services	687	689	1072	1245	1342	2064	2201	3393	3642	4189	5494	5411
	A Education	227	213	381	351	373	385	219	587	689	677	1387	1120
	B Other	460	477	690	894	969	1680	1982	2806	2953	3512	4107	4291
8	Miscellaneous goods and services	261	812	936	1123	1371	2235	2259	2467	2455	2942	3476	5497
	A Personal care	81	263	389	462	536	1202	887	952	1173	1367	2212	3537
	B Expenditures in restaurants, cafes and hotels	120	366	384	532	725	724	967	1308	991	1422	1106	1731

Sri Lanka

2.5 Private Final Consumption Expenditure by Type and Porpose, in Current Prices
(Continued)

Million Sri Lanka rupees

	1970	1975	1977	1978	1979	1980	1981	1982	1983	1984	1985	1986
C Other	60	183	163	129	110	309	405	208	291	153	158	228
Total Final Consumption Expenditure in the Domestic Market by Households, of which	10226	21869	27564	32182	40572	53689	62910	75156	90083	105208	113774	124620
Plus: Direct purchases abroad by resident households [a,b]	221	60	91	597	684	1656	4300	5201	5945	6839	7468	9316
Less: Direct purchases in the domestic market by non-resident households [c]	282	250	567	888	1204	1888	2629	3048	2952	3734	3141	3208
Equals: Final Consumption Expenditure of Resident Households [d]	10165	21679	27088	31891	40052	53457	64581	77310	93075	108312	118101	130728

Final Consumption Expenditure of Private Non-profit Institutions Serving Households

	1970	1975	1977	1978	1979	1980	1981	1982	1983	1984	1985	1986
Equals: Final Consumption Expenditure of Private Non-profit Organisations Serving Households	...	...	...	...	...	...	...	...	...	...	...	...
Private Final Consumption Expenditure	10165	21679	27088	31891	40052	53457	64581	77310	93075	108312	118101	130728

a) Estimates up to 1972 for 'Direct purchases abroad by resident households' have been obtained from the Central Bank. For 1973 and 1974, no estimates have been made. From 1975 onward, figures have been estimated independently by the Department of Census and Statistics.

b) For 1981 and 1982, transfers made by residents abroad are not included in item 'Direct Purchases Abroad by Resident Households' shown in table 2.17 but are included in the estimates shown in table 2.5.

c) Estimates up to 1974 for 'Direct purchases in the domestic market by non-resident households' have been obtained from the Central Bank. From 1975 onward, figures have been estimated independently by the Department of Census and Statistics.

d) Item 'Final consumption expenditure of resident households' includes consumption expenditure of private non-profit institutions serving households.

2.6 Private Final Consumption Expenditure by Type and Purpose, in Constant Prices

Million Sri Lanka rupees

	1970	1975	1977	1978	1979	1980	1981	1982	1983	1984	1985	1986
At constant prices of:1975												

Final Consumption Expenditure of Resident Households

	1970	1975	1977	1978	1979	1980	1981	1982	1983	1984	1985	1986
1 Food, beverages and tobacco	13725	15476	17201	16878	18604	18799	19201	19303	19851	18306	18718	18612
A Food	12509	13724	15504	15188	16530	16055	16534	16609	17025	15134	16001	16138
B Non-alcoholic beverages	47	60	51	40	40	44	31	20	37	284	119	120
C Alcoholic beverages	537	594	483	591	807	946	741	1089	1141	967	1115	859
D Tobacco	631	1099	1162	1061	1228	1755	1896	1585	1648	1921	1483	1495
2 Clothing and footwear	1039	1615	1901	1734	2146	2691	3169	3426	4144	4433	4628	4692
3 Gross rent, fuel and power	839	1047	1116	1144	1189	1197	1217	1419	1473	1455	1525	1582
A Fuel and power	347	347	405	418	447	441	452	644	690	710	772	814
B Other	492	700	711	726	742	755	765	775	783	745	753	768
4 Furniture, furnishings and household equipment and operation	756	692	1092	1008	1338	1648	1912	1675	1527	1481	1878	1863
A Household operation	311	326	486	465	627	526	694	748	652	560	678	640
B Other	445	366	606	544	710	1122	1218	927	876	921	1200	1223
5 Medical care and health expenses	507	310	404	439	475	585	602	628	541	582	669	830
6 Transport and communication	969	1229	1803	2730	2990	3404	3982	4596	4182	4950	5223	5255
A Personal transport equipment	4	5	57	295	394	520	516	470	479	430	454	384
B Other	965	1224	1746	2435	2596	2883	3466	4127	3703	4520	4769	4871
7 Recreational, entertainment, education and cultural services	1014	689	1071	1233	1112	1347	1207	1335	1315	1264	1545	1312
A Education	311	213	381	348	309	251	120	231	172	231	507	354
B Other	703	477	690	885	803	1096	1087	1104	1142	1033	1038	958
8 Miscellaneous goods and services	284	812	861	941	1010	1459	1103	1253	1086	1135	1271	1758
A Personal care	92	263	357	387	395	785	433	483	432	528	591	1132
B Expenditures in restaurants, cafes and hotels	128	366	353	446	534	473	472	664	555	548	614	554
C Other	64	183	150	108	81	202	198	106	100	59	66	72

Sri Lanka

2.6 Private Final Consumption Expenditure by Type and Purpose, in Constant Prices
(Continued)

Million Sri Lanka rupees

	1970	1975	1977	1978	1979	1980	1981	1982	1983	1984	1985	1986
					At constant prices of:1975							
Statistical discrepancy	-632	-	...	...	...	...	...	...	...	...	...	...
Total Final Consumption Expenditure in the Domestic Market by Households, of which	18502	21869	25449	26108	28863	31130	32393	33635	34119	33609	35457	35903
Plus: Direct purchases abroad by resident households [a,b]	238	60	91	597	684	1656	4011	5201	5945	6839	7468	9316
Less: Direct purchases in the domestic market by non-resident households [c]	402	250	553	745	978	1177	1014	1116	876	850	939	1026
Equals: Final Consumption Expenditure of Resident Households [d,e]	18338	21679	24987	25960	28569	31610	35390	37720	39188	39598	41986	44192

Final Consumption Expenditure of Private Non-profit Institutions Serving Households

| Equals: Final Consumption Expenditure of Private Non-profit Organisations Serving Households | ... | ... | ... | ... | ... | ... | ... | ... | ... | ... | ... | ... |
| Private Final Consumption Expenditure [e] | 18338 | 21679 | 24987 | 25960 | 28569 | 31610 | 35390 | 37720 | 39188 | 39598 | 41986 | 44192 |

a) Estimates up to 1972 for 'Direct purchases abroad by resident households' have been obtained from the Central Bank. For 1973 and 1974, no estimates have been made. From 1975 onward, figures have been estimated independently by the Department of Census and Statistics.
b) For 1981 and 1982, transfers made by residents abroad are not included in item 'Direct Purchases Abroad by Resident Households' shown in table 2.17 but are included in the estimates shown in table 2.5.
c) Estimates up to 1974 for 'Direct purchases in the domestic market by non-resident households' have been obtained from the Central Bank. From 1975 onward, figures have been estimated independently by the Department of Census and Statistics.
d) Item 'Final consumption expenditure of resident households' includes consumption expenditure of private non-profit institutions serving households.
e) The estimates before 1975 for this table have been calculated on the basis of 1963 prices and linked to the estimates for the years beginning 1975.

2.7 Gross Capital Formation by Type of Good and Owner, in Current Prices

Million Sri Lanka rupees

	1980 TOTAL	1980 Total Private	1980 Public Enterprises	1980 General Government	1981 TOTAL	1981 Total Private	1981 Public Enterprises	1981 General Government	1982 TOTAL	1982 Total Private	1982 Public Enterprises	1982 General Government
Increase in stocks, total [a]	167	128	...	39	331	272	...	59	248	210	...	38
Gross Fixed Capital Formation, Total	22243	17066	...	5177	23955	19713	...	4242	27926	23680	...	4246
1 Residential buildings	3808	3645	...	162	5048	4996	...	51	6138	5981	...	157
2 Non-residential buildings	2839	1388	...	1451	2350	1199	...	1151	2356	1359	...	997
3 Other construction	1661	520	...	1141	3147	2125	...	1022	3074	1722	...	1353
4 Land improvement and plantation and orchard development	3453	2755	...	698	4063	3156	...	908	4398	3315	...	1083
5 Producers' durable goods	10483	8759	...	1725	9348	8236	...	1111	11960	11303	...	657
A Transport equipment	3653	3158	...	495	2850	2430	...	420	6627	6257	...	369
B Machinery and equipment	6831	5600	...	1230	6497	5806	...	691	5333	5046	...	287
6 Breeding stock, dairy cattle, etc.	...	...	...	...	...	...	...	...	...	...	...	...
Total Gross Capital Formation [b]	22410	17194	...	5216	24286	19985	...	4301	28174	23890	...	4284

	1983 TOTAL	1983 Total Private	1983 Public Enterprises	1983 General Government	1984 TOTAL	1984 Total Private	1984 Public Enterprises	1984 General Government	1985 TOTAL	1985 Total Private	1985 Public Enterprises	1985 General Government
Increase in stocks, total [a]	-210	-174	...	-36	150	123	...	27	225	178	...	47
Gross Fixed Capital Formation, Total	31584	26156	...	5428	34262	28121	...	6142	37651	29893	...	7758
1 Residential buildings	6950	6883	...	67	7238	7186	...	53	9525	9477	...	48
2 Non-residential buildings	2858	1564	...	1294	2399	1633	...	766	3039	2154	...	885
3 Other construction	3848	1981	...	1867	4633	2069	...	2565	6490	2728	...	3762
4 Land improvement and plantation and orchard development	3988	2798	...	1191	6442	4784	...	1658	2804	1096	...	1708
5 Producers' durable goods	13939	12930	...	1009	13550	12449	...	1101	15793	14437	...	1355
A Transport equipment	5753	5414	...	339	5621	5184	...	437	5328	4506	...	822
B Machinery and equipment	8186	7516	...	671	7929	7266	...	664	10465	9931	...	533
6 Breeding stock, dairy cattle, etc.	...	...	...	...	...	...	...	...	...	...	...	...
Total Gross Capital Formation [b]	31374	25982	...	5392	34412	28244	...	6168	37876	30071	...	7805

Sri Lanka

2.7 Gross Capital Formation by Type of Good and Owner, in Current Prices

Million Sri Lanka rupees

	\multicolumn{4}{c}{1986}
	TOTAL	Total Private	Public Enterprises	General Government
Increase in stocks, total a	137	105	...	32
Gross Fixed Capital Formation, Total	38494	29557	...	8937
1 Residential buildings	10694	10495	...	199
2 Non-residential buildings	4167	2385	...	1782
3 Other construction	6197	3021	...	3176
4 Land improvement and plantation and orchard development	2769	1008	...	1761
5 Producers' durable goods	14667	12648	...	2019
A Transport equipment	4883	3682	...	1201
B Machinery and equipment	9784	8966	...	818
6 Breeding stock, dairy cattle, etc.	...	...	...	...
Total Gross Capital Formation b	38631	29662	...	8969

a) The estimates of 'Increase in stocks' for the years prior to 1975 include a statistical discrepancy.
b) Column 'Public Enterprises' is included in column 'General Government'.

2.8 Gross Capital Formation by Type of Good and Owner, in Constant Prices

Million Sri Lanka rupees

	\multicolumn{4}{c}{1980}	\multicolumn{4}{c}{1981}	\multicolumn{4}{c}{1982}
	TOTAL	Total Private	Public Enterprises	General Government	TOTAL	Total Private	Public Enterprises	General Government	TOTAL	Total Private	Public Enterprises	General Government
	\multicolumn{12}{c}{At constant prices of:1975}
Increase in stocks, total	75	58	...	18	127	105	...	23	91	77	...	14
Gross Fixed Capital Formation, Total	6911	5103	...	1809	7306	5922	...	1384	7425	6169	...	1257
1 Residential buildings	1178	1128	...	50	1312	1299	...	13	1527	1488	...	39
2 Non-residential buildings	1108	542	...	566	774	395	...	379	726	419	...	307
3 Other construction	690	216	...	474	1161	784	...	377	1053	590	...	463
4 Land improvement and plantation and orchard development	1118	864	...	255	1361	1067	...	294	1463	1139	...	325
5 Producers' durable goods	2817	2354	...	464	2698	2377	...	321	2656	2533	...	123
A Transport equipment	982	849	...	133	823	701	...	121	1250	1182	...	68
B Machinery and equipment	1836	1505	...	331	1875	1676	...	199	1406	1352	...	54
6 Breeding stock, dairy cattle, etc.	...	...	...	...	...	...	...	...	...	...	...	...
Total Gross Capital Formation a	6986	5160	...	1826	7434	6027	...	1407	7516	6245	...	1270

	\multicolumn{4}{c}{1983}	\multicolumn{4}{c}{1984}	\multicolumn{4}{c}{1985}
	TOTAL	Total Private	Public Enterprises	General Government	TOTAL	Total Private	Public Enterprises	General Government	TOTAL	Total Private	Public Enterprises	General Government
	\multicolumn{12}{c}{At constant prices of:1975}
Increase in stocks, total	-61	-51	...	-11	42	35	...	8	61	48	...	13
Gross Fixed Capital Formation, Total	7324	5852	...	1472	6680	5240	...	1432	6635	5016	...	1619
1 Residential buildings	1593	1577	...	15	1505	1494	...	11	1839	1830	...	9
2 Non-residential buildings	813	445	...	368	610	410	...	198	742	526	...	216
3 Other construction	1214	625	...	589	1288	575	...	713	1464	616	...	848
4 Land improvement and plantation and orchard development	1022	717	...	305	1398	1038	...	360	617	241	...	376
5 Producers' durable goods	2682	2488	...	194	1876	1723	...	152	1973	1804	...	169
A Transport equipment	1107	1042	...	65	778	718	...	61	666	563	...	103
B Machinery and equipment	1575	1446	...	129	1098	1006	...	92	1307	1241	...	66
6 Breeding stock, dairy cattle, etc.	...	...	...	...	...	...	...	...	...	...	...	...
Total Gross Capital Formation a	7263	5801	...	1461	6722	5282	...	1440	6696	5064	...	1632

Sri Lanka

2.8 Gross Capital Formation by Type of Good and Owner, in Constant Prices

Million Sri Lanka rupees

	\multicolumn{4}{c}{1986}
	TOTAL	Total Private	Public Enterprises	General Government
	\multicolumn{4}{c}{At constant prices of: 1975}
Increase in stocks, total	39	30	...	9
Gross Fixed Capital Formation, Total	6462	4704	...	1758
1 Residential buildings	2050	2012	...	38
2 Non-residential buildings	1017	582	...	435
3 Other construction	1393	679	...	714
4 Land improvement and plantation and orchard development	594	216	...	378
5 Producers' durable goods	1408	1215	...	193
A Transport equipment	469	354	...	115
B Machinery and equipment	939	861	...	78
6 Breeding stock, dairy cattle, etc.	...	...	...	...
Total Gross Capital Formation [a]	6501	4734	...	1767

a) Column 'Public Enterprises' is included in column 'General Government'.

2.17 Exports and Imports of Goods and Services, Detail

Million Sri Lanka rupees

	1970	1975	1977	1978	1979	1980	1981	1982	1983	1984	1985	1986
	\multicolumn{12}{c}{Exports of Goods and Services}
1 Exports of merchandise, f.o.b. [a][b]	3103	6436	10911	13207	15282	17603	20507	21098	25038	37198	35729	33881
2 Transport and communication	...	...	...	...	...	...	...	...	...	...	...	...
3 Insurance service charges	...	...	...	...	...	...	...	...	...	...	...	...
4 Other commodities [c]	93	620	833	741	1175	1943	2756	3003	4026	3353	3524	5479
5 Adjustments of merchandise exports to change-of-ownership basis	...	...	...	...	...	...	...	...	...	...	...	...
6 Direct purchases in the domestic market by non-residential households [d]	282	250	567	888	1204	1888	2629	3048	2952	3734	3141	3208
7 Direct purchases in the domestic market by extraterritorial bodies	...	...	...	...	...	...	...	...	...	...	...	...
Total Exports of Goods and Services	3478	7306	12311	14835	17660	21434	25892	27148	32016	44285	42394	42568
	\multicolumn{12}{c}{Imports of Goods and Services}
1 Imports of merchandise, c.i.f. [b]	3615	8801	10379	15600	22570	33915	36121	41420	45201	49046	55528	54898
2 Adjustments of merchandise imports to change-of-ownership basis	...	...	...	...	...	...	...	...	...	...	...	...
3 Other transport and communication	22	61	80	268	348	483	659	884	1256	1409	2077	2770
4 Other insurance service charges	8	11	19	33	26	41	55	114	185	261	278	755
5 Other commodities	42	358	410	375	342	361	189	217	-	-	-	-
6 Direct purchases abroad by government	...	...	...	...	...	...	...	...	...	...	...	...
7 Direct purchases abroad by resident households [e][f]	221	60	91	597	684	1656	4300	5202	5945	6839	7468	9316
Statistical discrepancy	...	...	...	...	...	...	-1766	-1930	-2206	-3086	-2955	-4332
Total Imports of Goods and Services	3908	9291	10979	16872	23969	36456	39558	45905	50381	54469	62396	63407
Balance of Goods and Services	-430	-1985	1332	-2037	-6309	-15022	-13667	-18758	-18365	-10184	-20002	-20839
Total Imports and Balance of Goods and Services	3478	7306	12311	14835	17660	21434	25892	27148	32016	44285	42394	42568

a) Item 'Exports of merchandise, f.o.b.' excludes merchandise purchases in the domestic market by non-resident households.
b) Prior to 1978, estimates of imports and exports of goods and services are valued at the Foreign Exchange Entitlment Certificate Rate (FEECR) which is a proxy to the unitary rate.
c) Item 'Other commodities' has been obtained as a residual.
d) Estimates up to 1974 for 'Direct purchases in the domestic market by non-resident households' have been obtained from the Central Bank. From 1975 onward, figures have been estimated independently by the Department of Census and Statistics.
e) Estimates up to 1972 for 'Direct purchases abroad by resident households' have been obtained from the Central Bank. For 1973 and 1974, no estimates have been made. From 1975 onward, figures have been estimated independently by the Department of Census and Statistics.
f) For 1981 and 1982, transfers made by residents abroad are not included in item 'Direct Purchases Abroad by Resident Households' shown in table 2.17 but are included in the estimates shown in table 2.5.

Sri Lanka

4.1 Derivation of Value Added by Kind of Activity, in Current Prices

Million Sri Lanka rupees

	1980 Gross Output	1980 Intermediate Consumption	1980 Value Added	1981 Gross Output	1981 Intermediate Consumption	1981 Value Added	1982 Gross Output	1982 Intermediate Consumption	1982 Value Added	1983 Gross Output	1983 Intermediate Consumption	1983 Value Added
					All Producers							
1 Agriculture, hunting, forestry and fishing [a]	...	...	17900	27496	4709	22787	31091	5834	25258	38474	8006	30468
A Agriculture and hunting	...	...	15824	24476	3944	20532	27574	4978	22596	34177	6676	27501
B Forestry and logging	...	...	946	944	-	944	1091	14	1077	1254	20	1234
C Fishing	...	...	1130	2076	765	1311	2427	841	1586	3043	1311	1733
2 Mining and quarrying	...	...	910	1268	190	1078	1364	205	1159	1566	146	1420
A Coal mining	...	...	...	...	...	...	...	...	...	...	...	...
B Crude petroleum and natural gas production	...	...	...	...	...	...	...	...	...	...	...	...
C Metal ore mining	...	...	...	...	...	...	...	...	...	...	...	...
D Other mining	...	...	910	1268	190	1078	1364	205	1159	1566	146	1420
3 Manufacturing [a]	...	...	12422	24837	10810	14028	35915	21271	14644	40913	22980	17933
A Manufacture of food, beverages and tobacco	...	...	6065	12956	6206	6750	14945	7421	7524	19718	10268	9451
B Textile, wearing apparel and leather industries	...	...	1550	2473	830	1643	2960	972	1988	2784	924	1860
C Manufacture of wood and wood products, including furniture	...	...	154	267	90	177	456	143	313	544	168	376
D Manufacture of paper and paper products, printing and publishing	...	...	255	448	156	292	414	144	270	426	148	278
E Manufacture of chemicals and chemical petroleum, coal, rubber and plastic products	...	...	1950	3577	1278	2299	13310	10633	2676	11332	8132	3200
F Manufacture of non-metallic mineral products, except products of petroleum and coal	...	...	925	1631	528	1103	1486	504	982	1534	518	1016
G Basic metal industries	...	...	108	192	67	125	119	42	77	243	85	158
H Manufacture of fabricated metal products, machinery and equipment	...	...	793	1278	447	831	331	116	215	612	214	398
I Other manufacturing industries	...	...	622	2015	1208	807	1895	1297	598	3721	2524	1197
4 Electricity, gas and water	...	...	547	1579	576	1003	2621	1078	1543	4145	2534	1611
A Electricity, gas and steam	...	...	547	1579	576	1003	2621	1078	1543	4145	2534	1611
B Water works and supply	...	...	...	...	...	...	...	...	...	...	...	...
5 Construction	...	...	6503	14536	6499	8037	15696	7045	8651	17686	7784	9902
6 Wholesale and retail trade, restaurants and hotels	...	...	11331	19725	3557	16168	23384	3653	19732	28408	4508	23901
A Wholesale and retail trade	...	...	10895	18753	3168	15585	22058	3139	18919	27398	4110	23288
B Restaurants and hotels	...	...	436	972	389	583	1326	513	812	1010	398	612
Restaurants	...	...	...	...	...	...	527	207	321	568	224	344
Hotels and other lodging places	...	...	...	...	...	...	799	307	492	442	174	268
7 Transport, storage and communication	...	...	6962	15592	8209	7383	20240	10492	9748	23711	12075	11635
A Transport and storage	...	...	...	15362	8209	7153	19814	10492	9322	22803	12075	10727
B Communication	...	...	...	230	-	230	426	-	426	908	-	908
8 Finance, insurance, real estate and business services	...	...	3620	5246	623	4624	6509	625	5884	7925	699	7226
A Financial institutions	...	...	1877	2689	113	2576	3848	115	3732	5149	117	5032
B Insurance	...	...										
C Real estate and business services	...	...	1743	2557	510	2047	2662	510	2152	2776	582	2194
Real estate, except dwellings	...	...	84	100	-	100	114	-	114	131	-	131
Dwellings	...	...	1659	2457	510	1947	2548	510	2039	2645	582	2063
9 Community, social and personal services	...	...	1513	2524	651	1873	2731	638	2093	3477	715	2762
A Sanitary and similar services	...	...	...	...	...	...	...	...	...	...	...	...
B Social and related community services	...	...	217	312	73	239	742	222	519	1003	267	736
C Recreational and cultural services	...	...	800	1302	461	840	1143	325	818	1323	336	987
D Personal and household services	...	...	496	911	117	794	847	91	756	1151	111	1039

Sri Lanka

4.1 Derivation of Value Added by Kind of Activity, in Current Prices
(Continued)

Million Sri Lanka rupees

	1980			1981			1982			1983		
	Gross Output	Intermediate Consumption	Value Added	Gross Output	Intermediate Consumption	Value Added	Gross Output	Intermediate Consumption	Value Added	Gross Output	Intermediate Consumption	Value Added
Total, Industries	...	...	61708	112805	35824	76981	139551	50840	88711	166304	59447	106857
Producers of Government Services	...	...	3573	7456	3294	4162	10407	5029	5379	12733	5473	7260
Other Producers	...	...	133	158	-	158	215	-	215	249	-	249
Total	...	...	65414	120419	39118	81302	150174	55869	94305	179286	64920	114366
Less: Imputed bank service charge	...	...	...	...	...	...	...	...	...	...	...	...
Import duties	...	...	2924	3225	-	3225	3222	-	3222	4836	-	4836
Value added tax	...	...	...	...	...	...	...	...	...	...	...	...
Total	...	...	68338	123644	39118	84527	153396	55869	97528	184121	64920	119202

	1984			1985			1986		
	Gross Output	Intermediate Consumption	Value Added	Gross Output	Intermediate Consumption	Value Added	Gross Output	Intermediate Consumption	Value Added
				All Producers					
1 Agriculture, hunting, forestry and fishing [a]	45132	7839	37293	47008	8502	38506	48918	9389	39529
A Agriculture and hunting	40222	6950	33272	41663	7457	34206	42773	8112	34661
B Forestry and logging	1444	13	1431	1652	15	1637	1723	13	1710
C Fishing	3466	876	2590	3693	1030	2663	4422	1264	3158
2 Mining and quarrying	1344	135	1209	1372	145	1227	1869	199	1670
A Coal mining	...	...	...	...	...	...	...	...	...
B Crude petroleum and natural gas production	...	...	...	...	...	...	...	...	...
C Metal ore mining	...	...	...	...	...	...	...	...	...
D Other mining	1344	135	1209	1372	145	1227	1869	199	1670
3 Manufacturing [a]	57899	33598	24301	58938	32758	26180	59866	32952	26914
A Manufacture of food, beverages and tobacco	29679	14423	15256	25868	11841	14027	28762	13905	14857
B Textile, wearing apparel and leather industries	8416	5323	3093	9731	5634	4097	10527	6217	4310
C Manufacture of wood and wood products, including furniture	655	207	448	980	317	663	913	292	621
D Manufacture of paper and paper products, printing and publishing	34	11	23	680	236	444	354	122	232
E Manufacture of chemicals and chemical petroleum, coal, rubber and plastic products	13834	11184	2650	12625	10345	2280	10596	8495	2101
F Manufacture of non-metallic mineral products, except products of petroleum and coal	964	313	651	1865	627	1238	1748	587	1161
G Basic metal industries	84	30	54	147	51	96	180	63	117
H Manufacture of fabricated metal products, machinery and equipment	1335	467	868	2894	1013	1881	3108	1087	2021
I Other manufacturing industries	2898	1640	1258	4148	2694	1454	3678	2184	1494
4 Electricity, gas and water	3304	797	2507	3369	370	2999	3520	458	3062
A Electricity, gas and steam	3304	797	2507	3369	370	2999	3520	458	3062
B Water works and supply	...	...	...	...	...	...	...	...	...
5 Construction	20411	9105	11306	21550	9611	11939	23667	10470	13197
6 Wholesale and retail trade, restaurants and hotels	32114	5163	26951	36616	7555	29061	41323	8607	32716
A Wholesale and retail trade	30683	4602	26081	35410	7082	28328	39565	7913	31652
B Restaurants and hotels	1431	561	870	1206	473	733	1758	694	1064
Restaurants	1012	397	615	804	315	489	1288	508	780
Hotels and other lodging places	419	164	255	402	158	244	470	186	284
7 Transport, storage and communication	31730	16109	15621	34413	16984	17429	36972	17311	19661
A Transport and storage	30772	16109	14663	33365	16984	16381	35827	17311	18516
B Communication	958	-	958	1048	-	1048	1145	-	1145
8 Finance, insurance, real estate and business services	9370	747	8623	10059	824	9235	11499	871	10628
A Financial institutions	6357	118	6239	6693	118	6575	8006	141	7865
B Insurance									
C Real estate and business services	3013	629	2384	3366	706	2660	3493	730	2763
Real estate, except dwellings	155	-	155	158	-	158	175	-	175

Sri Lanka

4.1 Derivation of Value Added by Kind of Activity, in Current Prices
(Continued)

Million Sri Lanka rupees

	1984 Gross Output	1984 Intermediate Consumption	1984 Value Added	1985 Gross Output	1985 Intermediate Consumption	1985 Value Added	1986 Gross Output	1986 Intermediate Consumption	1986 Value Added
Dwellings	2858	629	2229	3208	706	2502	3318	730	2588
9 Community, social and personal services	3840	783	3057	4055	809	3246	4507	913	3594
A Sanitary and similar services	...	...	...	...	...	...	...	...	...
B Social and related community services	1053	290	763	1127	303	824	1237	329	908
C Recreational and cultural services	1469	364	1105	1456	374	1082	1576	388	1188
D Personal and household services	1318	129	1189	1472	132	1340	1694	196	1498
Total, Industries	205144	74276	130868	217380	77558	139822	232141	81170	150971
Producers of Government Services	15442	7205	8237	19170	9926	9244	22990	11866	11124
Other Producers	294	-	294	300	-	300	331	-	331
Total	220880	81481	139399	236850	87484	149366	255462	93036	162426
Less: Imputed bank service charge	...	...	...	...	...	...	...	...	...
Import duties	7945	-	7945	8397	-	8397	10014	-	10014
Value added tax	...	...	...	...	...	...	...	...	...
Total	228825	81481	147344	245247	87484	157763	265476	93036	172440

a) The estimates on processing of tea and rubber are included in the agricultural sector prior to 1975. From 1975 onward, they are included in the manufacturing sector.

4.2 Derivation of Value Added by Kind of Activity, in Constant Prices

Million Sri Lanka rupees

	1980 Gross Output	1980 Intermediate Consumption	1980 Value Added	1981 Gross Output	1981 Intermediate Consumption	1981 Value Added	1982 Gross Output	1982 Intermediate Consumption	1982 Value Added	1983 Gross Output	1983 Intermediate Consumption	1983 Value Added
					At constant prices of: 1975							
					All Producers							
1 Agriculture, hunting, forestry and fishing a	...	...	9357	...	...	10058	...	...	10372	...	...	10994
A Agriculture and hunting	...	...	8542	...	...	9177	...	...	9411	...	...	9962
B Forestry and logging	...	...	287	...	...	279	...	...	317	...	...	373
C Fishing	...	...	528	...	...	602	...	...	644	...	...	660
2 Mining and quarrying	...	...	475	...	...	500	...	...	479	...	...	575
A Coal mining	...	...	...	...	...	...	...	...	...	...	...	...
B Crude petroleum and natural gas production	...	...	...	...	...	...	...	...	...	...	...	...
C Metal ore mining	...	...	...	...	...	...	...	...	...	...	...	...
D Other mining	...	...	475	...	...	500	...	...	479	...	...	575
3 Manufacturing a	...	...	7071	...	...	7327	...	...	7281	...	...	7064
A Manufacture of food, beverages and tobacco	...	...	3452	...	...	3526	...	...	3741	...	...	3973
B Textile, wearing apparel and leather industries	...	...	882	...	...	858	...	...	989	...	...	651
C Manufacture of wood and wood products, including furniture	...	...	88	...	...	92	...	...	156	...	...	151
D Manufacture of paper and paper products, printing and publishing	...	...	145	...	...	153	...	...	134	...	...	94
E Manufacture of chemicals and chemical petroleum, coal, rubber and plastic products	...	...	1110	...	...	1201	...	...	1331	...	...	1148
F Manufacture of non-metallic mineral products, except products of petroleum and coal	...	...	527	...	...	576	...	...	488	...	...	285
G Basic metal industries	...	...	62	...	...	65	...	...	38	...	...	61
H Manufacture of fabricated metal products, machinery and equipment	...	...	451	...	...	434	...	...	107	...	...	236
I Other manufacturing industries	...	...	354	...	...	421	...	...	297	...	...	465
4 Electricity, gas and water	...	...	181	...	...	203	...	...	222	...	...	226
A Electricity, gas and steam	...	...	181	...	...	203	...	...	...	...	...	...
B Water works and supply	...	...	...	...	...	...	...	...	...	...	...	...

Sri Lanka

4.2 Derivation of Value Added by Kind of Activity, in Constant Prices
(Continued)

Million Sri Lanka rupees

	1980			1981			1982			1983		
	Gross Output	Intermediate Consumption	Value Added	Gross Output	Intermediate Consumption	Value Added	Gross Output	Intermediate Consumption	Value Added	Gross Output	Intermediate Consumption	Value Added
	At constant prices of:1975											
5 Construction	...	...	1947	...	...	2208	...	...	2157	...	...	2172
6 Wholesale and retail trade, restaurants and hotels	...	...	7564	...	...	8059	...	...	9408	...	...	10162
A Wholesale and retail trade	...	...	7267	...	...	7719	...	...	8999	...	...	9731
B Restaurants and hotels	...	...	297	...	...	340	...	...	409	...	...	430
7 Transport, storage and communication	...	...	3460	...	...	3564	...	...	3658	...	...	4043
8 Finance, insurance, real estate and business services	...	...	1269	...	...	1357	...	...	1512	...	...	1566
A Financial institutions	...	...	541	...	...	622	...	...	762	...	...	805
B Insurance	...	...		...	...		...	...		...	...	
C Real estate and business services	...	...	728	...	...	735	...	...	750	...	...	761
Real estate, except dwellings	...	...	52	...	...	53	...	...	54	...	...	55
Dwellings	...	...	675	...	...	682	...	...	696	...	...	706
9 Community, social and personal services	...	...	980	...	...	1076	...	...	1117	...	...	1196
A Sanitary and similar services	...	...	...	...	...	...	...	...	...	...	...	...
B Social and related community services	...	...	138	...	...	133	...	...	309	...	...	367
C Recreational and cultural services	...	...	530	...	...	504	...	...	461	...	...	488
D Personal and household services	...	...	312	...	...	439	...	...	347	...	...	340
Total, Industries [b]	...	...	32305	...	...	34352	...	...	36206	...	...	37997
Producers of Government Services	...	...	2206	...	...	2236	...	...	2256	...	...	2272
Other Producers	...	...	83	...	...	84	...	...	102	...	...	104
Total [b]	...	...	34594	...	...	36672	...	...	38564	...	...	40373
Less: Imputed bank service charge	...	...	...	...	...	...	...	...	...	...	...	...
Import duties	...	...	714	...	...	595	...	...	635	...	...	689
Value added tax	...	...	...	...	...	...	...	...	...	...	...	...
Total [b]	...	...	35308	...	...	37266	...	...	39199	...	...	41062

	1984			1985			1986		
	Gross Output	Intermediate Consumption	Value Added	Gross Output	Intermediate Consumption	Value Added	Gross Output	Intermediate Consumption	Value Added
	At constant prices of:1975								
	All Producers								
1 Agriculture, hunting, forestry and fishing [a]	...	...	10200	...	...	11146	...	...	11224
A Agriculture and hunting	...	...	9359	...	...	10249	...	...	10276
B Forestry and logging	...	...	351	...	...	399	...	...	415
C Fishing	...	...	490	...	...	498	...	...	533
2 Mining and quarrying	...	...	693	...	...	673	...	...	918
A Coal mining	...	...	...	...	...	...	...	...	...
B Crude petroleum and natural gas production	...	...	...	...	...	...	...	...	...
C Metal ore mining	...	...	...	...	...	...	...	...	...
D Other mining	...	...	693	...	...	673	...	...	918

Sri Lanka

4.2 Derivation of Value Added by Kind of Activity, in Constant Prices
(Continued)

Million Sri Lanka rupees

	1984 Gross Output	1984 Intermediate Consumption	1984 Value Added	1985 Gross Output	1985 Intermediate Consumption	1985 Value Added	1986 Gross Output	1986 Intermediate Consumption	1986 Value Added
				At constant prices of:1975					
3 Manufacturing a	...	...	8300	...	...	8812	...	...	9345
A Manufacture of food, beverages and tobacco	...	...	4737	...	...	4435	...	...	5248
B Textile, wearing apparel and leather industries	...	...	1381	...	...	1497	...	...	1303
C Manufacture of wood and wood products, including furniture	...	...	126	...	...	175	...	...	168
D Manufacture of paper and paper products, printing and publishing	...	...	7	...	...	117	...	...	63
E Manufacture of chemicals and chemical petroleum, coal, rubber and plastic products	...	...	1298	...	...	1216	...	...	1185
F Manufacture of non-metallic mineral products, except products of petroleum and coal	...	...	125	...	...	231	...	...	226
G Basic metal industries	...	...	17	...	...	29	...	...	36
H Manufacture of fabricated metal products, machinery and equipment	...	...	272	...	...	563	...	...	617
I Other manufacturing industries	...	...	337	...	...	549	...	...	499
4 Electricity, gas and water	...	...	253	...	...	274	...	...	294
A Electricity, gas and steam	...	...	...	...	...	...	...	...	...
B Water works and supply	...	...	...	...	...	...	...	...	...
5 Construction	...	...	2200	...	...	2248	...	...	2419
6 Wholesale and retail trade, restaurants and hotels	...	...	10907	...	...	11422	...	...	11983
A Wholesale and retail trade	...	...	10291	...	...	10926	...	...	11421
B Restaurants and hotels	...	...	616	...	...	496	...	...	562
7 Transport, storage and communication	...	...	4531	...	...	4607	...	...	4718
8 Finance, insurance, real estate and business services	...	...	1649	...	...	1719	...	...	1772
A Financial institutions	...	...	879	...	...	938	...	...	976
B Insurance	...	...		...	...		...	...	
C Real estate and business services	...	...	770	...	...	781	...	...	795
Real estate, except dwellings	...	...	55	...	...	56	...	...	57
Dwellings	...	...	715	...	...	726	...	...	738
9 Community, social and personal services	...	...	1296	...	...	1299	...	...	1338
A Sanitary and similar services	...	...	...	...	...	...	...	...	...
B Social and related community services	...	...	372	...	...	393	...	...	413
C Recreational and cultural services	...	...	532	...	...	488	...	...	517
D Personal and household services	...	...	392	...	...	418	...	...	408
Total, Industries b	...	...	40029	...	...	42200	...	...	44011
Producers of Government Services	...	...	2298	...	...	2334	...	...	2380
Other Producers	...	...	105	...	...	106	...	...	108
Total b	...	...	42432	...	...	44640	...	...	46499
Less: Imputed bank service charge	...	...	...	...	...	...	...	...	...
Import duties	...	...	704	...	...	660	...	...	737
Value added tax	...	...	...	...	...	...	...	...	...
Total b	...	...	40136	...	...	45300	...	...	47236

a) The estimates on processing of tea and rubber are included in the agricultural sector prior to 1975. From 1975 onward, they are included in the manufacturing sector.

b) The estimates before 1975 for this table have been calculated on the basis of 1963 prices and linked to the estimates for the years beginning 1975.

Sri Lanka

4.3 Cost Components of Value Added

Million Sri Lanka rupees

	\multicolumn{6}{c	}{1983}	\multicolumn{6}{c	}{1984}
	Compensation of Employees	Capital Consumption	Net Operating Surplus	Indirect Taxes	Less: Subsidies Received	Value Added	Compensation of Employees	Capital Consumption	Net Operating Surplus	Indirect Taxes	Less: Subsidies Received	Value Added
\multicolumn{13}{c	}{All Producers}
1 Agriculture, hunting, forestry and fishing [a]	11898	...	17263	1461	154	30468	15269	...	22156	65	197	37293
2 Mining and quarrying	451	...	954	16	-	1420	381	...	806	22	-	1209
3 Manufacturing [a]	8509	...	3276	6930	782	17933	11417	...	4396	9368	880	24301
4 Electricity, gas and water	329	...	1178	104	-	1611	541	...	1942	24	-	2507
5 Construction	6809	...	2918	189	14	9902	7835	...	3358	116	3	11306
6 Wholesale and retail trade, restaurants and hotels [b]	8334	...	13590	6812	-	28736	8057	...	13145	13694	-	34896
7 Transport, storage and communication	4409	...	7851	152	776	11635	5956	...	10588	140	1063	15621
8 Finance, insurance, real estate and business services [c]	3790	...	2923	246	...	6960	4617	...	3277	456	...	8350
9 Community, social and personal services [dc]	1941	...	308	1029	...	3277	1955	...	310	1359	...	3624
Total, Industries [e]	46469	...	50262	16937	1727	111942	56028	...	59978	25244	2143	139107
Producers of Government Services	7260	...	...	...	...	7260	8237	...	...	...	...	8237
Other Producers [d]	...	...	...	...	...	...	...	...	...	...	...	...
Total [e]	53729	...	50262	16937	1727	119202	64265	...	59978	25244	2143	147344
Less: Imputed bank service charge	...	...	...	...	...	...	...	...	...	...	...	...
Import duties [b]	...	...	...	...	...	...	...	...	...	...	...	...
Value added tax	...	...	...	...	...	...	...	...	...	...	...	...
Total [e]	53729	...	50262	16937	1727	119202	64265	...	59977	25245	2143	147344

	\multicolumn{6}{c	}{1985}	\multicolumn{6}{c	}{1986}
	Compensation of Employees	Capital Consumption	Net Operating Surplus	Indirect Taxes	Less: Subsidies Received	Value Added	Compensation of Employees	Capital Consumption	Net Operating Surplus	Indirect Taxes	Less: Subsidies Received	Value Added
\multicolumn{13}{c	}{All Producers}
1 Agriculture, hunting, forestry and fishing [a]	15805	...	22932	54	285	38506	16245	...	23571	57	344	39529
2 Mining and quarrying	386	...	816	24	-	1227	530	...	1121	19	-	1670
3 Manufacturing [a]	14841	...	5715	6446	822	26180	16556	...	6375	4830	847	26914
4 Electricity, gas and water	645	...	2313	41	-	2999	656	...	2354	52	-	3062
5 Construction	8273	...	3545	124	3	11939	9031	...	3870	299	3	13197
6 Wholesale and retail trade, restaurants and hotels [b]	8448	...	13783	15227	-	37458	9060	...	14781	18889	-	42730
7 Transport, storage and communication	6506	...	11565	149	791	17429	7322	...	13016	231	908	19661
8 Finance, insurance, real estate and business services [c]	4653	...	3558	747	...	8957	5893	...	3927	512	...	10332
9 Community, social and personal services [dc]	1929	...	307	1588	...	3824	2307	...	366	1548	...	4221
Total, Industries [e]	61486	...	64534	24402	1901	148519	67600	...	69381	26437	2102	161316
Producers of Government Services	9264	...	...	...	20	9244	11141	...	...	...	17	11124
Other Producers [d]	...	...	...	...	...	...	...	...	...	...	...	...
Total [e]	70750	...	64534	24402	1921	157763	78741	...	69381	26437	2119	172440
Less: Imputed bank service charge	...	...	...	...	...	...	...	...	...	...	...	...
Import duties [b]	...	...	...	...	...	...	...	...	...	...	...	...
Value added tax	...	...	...	...	...	...	...	...	...	...	...	...
Total [e]	70748	...	64534	24402	1921	157763	78741	...	69381	26437	2119	172440

a) The estimates on processing of tea and rubber are included in the agricultural sector prior to 1975. From 1975 onward, they are included in the manufacturing sector.
b) Item 'Import duties' is included in item 'Wholesale and retail trade'.
c) Finance is included in item 'Community, social and personal services'.
d) Item 'Other producers' is included in item 'Community, social and personal services'.
e) Column 'Consumption of fixed capital' is included in column 'Net operating surplus'.

Sudan

General note. The preparation of national accounts statistics in Sudan is undertaken by the Department of Statistics, Khartoum. The official estimates together with the sources and methods used for the national accounts estimates are published in a series of publications entitled 'National Accounts and Supporting Tables'. The estimates are generally in accordance with the classifications and definitions recommended in the United Nations System of National Accounts (SNA). Input-output tables were published in 1964 in 'National Income of Sudan in 1961/62 (with preliminary estimates for 1962/63)'. The following tables have been prepared from successive replies to the United Nations national accounts questionnaire. From 1969 estimates relate to fiscal year beginning 1 July. When the scope and coverage of the estimates differ for conceptual or statistical reasons from the definitions and classifications recommended in SNA, a footnote is indicated to the relevant tables.

Sources and methods :

(a) Gross domestic product. Gross domestic product is estimated mainly through the production approach.

(b) Expenditure on the gross domestic product. All components of GDP by expenditure type are estimated through the expenditure approach except the estimates of gross fixed capital formation which are based partly on the commodity-flow method and partly on the expenditure approach. The sources of data for government final consumption expenditure are the actual figures available at Ministry of Treasury, Ministry of Local Government, different government units and public entities. For the central government, current and capital expenditure budgets are available, while for the local government figures on receipts and expenditures are available only for the six northern provinces, for the three southern provinces, budget figures have to be used. The estimates of private final consumption expenditure are based on the Household Budget Sample Survey 1967/68 which provided for the six northern provinces, data on average income and expenditure of households in the urban, semi-urban and rural areas. The number of households in these areas is based on the result of the 1973 Population Census. For the three southern provinces, which were not included in the Household Budget Sample Survey 1967/68, certain assumptions have been made to estimate their average expenditure per household. The expenditure by object per household has been calculated for 1967/68 to 1970/71 by multiplying an estimated rate of consumption increase by the number of urban, semi-urban and rural households in the North and the South. Increase in stocks is estimated partly on the basis of replies to questionnaires sent to public enterprises, producing industries and wholesale and retail trade companies. Capital formation estimates for central government and public entities are extracted from government capital expenditure accounts and for local government from the accounts of local councils. Total private expenditure on construction is obtained as a residual after deducting public expenditure on construction from total output of the construction sector. The expenditure on machinery and equipment is obtained from the statistics of imports classified by end-use. The data on external transactions are provided by the Bank of Sudan. The estimates of direct purchases by non-residents are based on a survey of the non-residents in Sudan. GDP by expenditure type at constant prices is not estimated.

(c) Cost-structure of the gross domestic product. In estimating the cost-structure components of GDP, compensation of employees is taken as the wage bill reported by manufacturing establishments and companies in the various economic activities. For the agriculture and primary sectors, compensation of employees is imputed from the employment side. Operating surplus is in most cases taken as the residual of gross output over total costs. Depreciation estimates of public corporations and private manufacturing enterprises are based on actual information available. Indirect taxes consist mainly of import and excise duties and are obtained from government budgets and accounts.

(d) Gross domestic product by kind of economic activity. The table of GDP by kind of economic activity is prepared at market prices, i.e. producers' values. Value added of most industries is estimated through the production approach. The income approach is used for government services and for electricity, gas and water. The commodity-flow method is used for the construction and trade sectors, while the expenditure approach is used for private services. For the agricultural sector, information on crop production is based on rough estimates furnished by the Ministry of Agriculture. To obtain the value of most crops, production figures are multiplied by auction or wholesale prices reduced by 10 per cent for transport and distribution margins. The estimates of value added of cotton, wheat, durra and ground-nuts are based on the records of Sudan Gezira Board which provides data on production, value and cost of production. The value of animal production is obtained through multiplying the assumed production per species by average producer price per head, supplied by the Department of Animal Resources. In the calculation of input and value added of livestock, dairy and poultry products, certain percentages have been adopted. There is a considerable difficulty in estimating the non-marketed production and own consumption in agriculture, as such information is only available from supply and disposition surveys which unfortunately have not been recently conducted. For forestry, hunting and fishing, data are supplied by the respective departments. The intermediate consumption of hunting and fishing is assumed to be a certain percentage of gross output. The gross output and value added of manufacturing are based on the Industrial Survey 1970/71 and on computed indexes of the value of production. The value added of industrial corporations are obtained from the balance sheets and profit and loss accounts of the corporations. Gross output of construction is estimated indirectly by calculating the total supplies of cement and the imported building materials. Intermediate consumption constitute 60 per cent of gross output. The market value of imported building materials is calculated by adding estimated margins to the c.i.f. value. For the domestic production of cement, an assumed average price per ton is applied. The construction of traditional buildings is estimated based on the 1973 Population Census and certain assumptions. For the trade sector, the trade margin of imported goods is calculated on the basis of c.i.f. value plus 5 per cent covering assumed duties and transport margin. For local production, it is assumed that 20 per cent of agricultural production represents own consumption. For the remaining marketable agricultural and industrial production, the trade margin is assumed to be 21.2 per cent. A rough estimate of the intermediate consumption is obtained by applying certain percentages and ratios. For transport, detailed data on receipts and expenditure are obtained from the accounts of the large public enterprises and by means of questionnaires and special surveys for other enterprises. Information on banks and insurance companies are obtained from the enterprises concerned. Gross output of banks is equated to the sum of actual service charges received plus imputed service charges. Data on intermediate consumption and factor income of banks and insurance companies are obtained from their balance sheet and profit and loss statements. The estimates of producers of government services are obtained from the Ordinary Budget or the extra-budgetary funds. For health services, entertainment and personal care, information is obtained from the institutions concerned and from the Household Sample Survey 1967/68 and the Population Census 1973. GDP by kind of economic activity at constant prices is not estimated.

1.1 Expenditure on the Gross Domestic Product, in Current Prices

Million Sudanese pounds — Fiscal year beginning 1 July

	1970	1975	1977	1978	1979	1980	1981	1982	1983	1984	1985	1986
1 Government final consumption expenditure	159.0	236.0	330.7	407.0	500.9	648.2	719.9	853.5	1112.5	...	...	...
2 Private final consumption expenditure	528.1	1371.1	2379.5	2605.7	2978.7	4211.5	5431.0	7956.8	9464.7	...	...	...
A Households	...	...	2336.4	...	2950.2	4176.5	5386.3	7897.2	9385.0	...	...	...
B Private non-profit institutions serving households	...	...	40.1	...	28.5	35.0	44.7	59.6	79.7	...	...	...
3 Gross capital formation	89.6	427.5	413.7	431.4	998.1	1078.2	1648.1	1627.3	1630.9	...	...	...
A Increase in stocks	16.4	65.5	90.4	92.0	228.9	80.4	372.7	32.9	-234.4	...	...	...
B Gross fixed capital formation	73.2	362.0	323.3	339.4	769.2	997.8	1275.4	1594.4	1865.3	...	...	...
Residential buildings	16.3	28.9	38.2	44.9	101.4	156.0	198.7	387.3	396.2	...	...	...
Non-residential buildings	2.4	17.2	30.0	63.9	58.4	85.3	123.3	179.0	192.6	...	...	...
Other construction and land improvement etc.	9.9	66.3	58.4	31.4	200.1	276.1	336.5	481.0	545.1	...	...	...
Other	44.6	249.6	196.7	199.2	409.3	480.4	616.9	547.1	731.4	...	...	...
4 Exports of goods and services	123.2	206.6	218.2	256.9	382.9	504.9	630.9	1095.8	1306.7	...	...	...
5 Less: Imports of goods and services	138.8	393.2	459.4	447.2	957.3	1356.9	1709.4	2347.6	2185.4	...	...	...
Equals: Gross Domestic Product	761.1	1848.0	2882.7	3253.8	3903.3	5085.9	6720.5	9185.8	11329.4	...	...	...

Sudan

1.2 Expenditure on the Gross Domestic Product, in Constant Prices

Million Sudanese pounds — Fiscal year beginning 1 July

	1970	1975	1977	1978	1979	1980	1981	1982	1983	1984	1985	1986
					At constant prices of:1981							
1 Government final consumption expenditure	...	...	...	...	...	...	719.9	617.3	626.8	...	...	...
2 Private final consumption expenditure	...	...	...	...	...	...	5431.0	5869.1	5352.7	...	...	...
A Households	...	...	...	...	...	...	5386.3	5822.3	5303.8	...	...	...
B Private non-profit institutions serving households	...	...	...	...	...	...	44.7	46.8	48.9	...	...	...
3 Gross capital formation	...	...	...	...	...	...	1648.1	1109.4	872.6	...	...	...
A Increase in stocks	...	...	...	...	...	...	372.7	47.5	-116.0	...	...	...
B Gross fixed capital formation	...	...	...	...	...	...	1275.4	1061.9	988.6	...	...	...
4 Exports of goods and services	...	...	...	...	...	...	630.9	822.2	807.1	...	...	...
5 Less: Imports of goods and services	...	...	...	...	...	...	1709.4	1656.7	1153.8	...	...	...
Statistical discrepancy	...	...	...	...	...	...	-	4.1	-27.7	...	...	...
Equals: Gross Domestic Product	...	...	...	...	...	...	6720.5	6765.4	6477.7	...	...	...

1.3 Cost Components of the Gross Domestic Product

Million Sudanese pounds — Fiscal year beginning 1 July

	1970	1975	1977	1978	1979	1980	1981	1982	1983	1984	1985	1986
1 Indirect taxes, net	110.1	225.7	305.4	357.6	349.1	427.8	483.8	847.2	895.9	...	...	...
A Indirect taxes	...	...	...	...	356.1	437.0	500.9	852.4	895.9	...	...	...
B Less: Subsidies	...	...	...	...	7.0	9.2	17.1	5.2	-	...	...	...
2 Consumption of fixed capital	53.2	166.1	269.2	222.5	359.9	458.0	640.9	1012.3	1245.0	...	...	...
3 Compensation of employees paid by resident producers to:	334.1	832.4	1275.5	1276.5	1371.2	1757.1	2347.8	3084.0	3895.1	...	...	...
A Resident households	333.0	831.4	...	...	1371.2	1757.1	2347.8	3084.0	3895.1	...	...	...
B Rest of the world	1.1	1.0	...	...	-	-	-	-	-	...	...	...
4 Operating surplus	263.7	623.8	1032.6	1397.2	1823.1	2443.0	3248.0	4242.3	5293.4	...	...	...
Equals: Gross Domestic Product	761.1	1848.0	2882.7	3253.8	3903.3	5085.9	6720.5	9185.8	11329.4	...	...	...

1.4 General Government Current Receipts and Disbursements

Million Sudanese pounds — Fiscal year beginning 1 July

	1970	1975	1977	1978	1979	1980	1981	1982	1983	1984	1985	1986
					Receipts							
1 Operating surplus	...	...	...	...	...	...	...	...	...	...	...	...
2 Property and entrepreneurial income	43.2	...	...	...	37.8	55.6	9.7	61.5	33.9	...	...	...
3 Taxes, fees and contributions	143.3	319.3	421.8	468.2	510.4	704.1	795.3	1243.7	1337.6	...	...	...
A Indirect taxes	110.1	227.7	309.8	357.6	329.7	460.2	503.0	833.8	869.3	...	...	...
B Direct taxes	22.2	43.3	58.8	69.4	93.5	134.8	160.1	198.9	229.9	...	...	...
C Social security contributions	0.8	2.6	3.8	9.2	13.9	21.0	24.4	31.0	34.7	...	...	...
D Compulsory fees, fines and penalties	10.2	45.7	49.4	32.0	73.3	88.1	107.8	180.0	203.7	...	...	...
4 Other current transfers	19.2	...	...	...	-	-	-	-	-	...	...	...
Total Current Receipts of General Government	205.7	...	...	...	548.2	759.7	805.0	1305.2	1371.5	...	...	...
					Disbursements							
1 Government final consumption expenditure	159.0	...	...	...	500.9	648.2	719.9	853.5	1112.5	...	...	...
A Compensation of employees	78.1	157.8	233.3	246.9	317.7	417.0	464.7	593.9	767.8	...	...	...
B Consumption of fixed capital	46.9	15.7	25.2	35.6	74.0	77.0	80.3	155.7	214.7	...	...	...
C Purchases of goods and services, net	...	...	...	...	109.2	154.2	174.9	103.9	130.0	...	...	...
D Less: Own account fixed capital formation	...	...	...	...	...	...	...	...	...	...	...	...
E Indirect taxes paid, net	-	2.0	4.4	-	...	...	...	...	...	...	...	...
2 Property income	-	...	...	...	123.3	153.5	179.3	256.6	321.5	...	...	...
A Interest	...	...	...	...	123.3	153.5	179.3	256.6	321.5	...	...	...
B Net land rent and royalties	...	...	...	...	...	...	...	...	...	...	...	...

Sudan

1.4 General Government Current Receipts and Disbursements
(Continued)

Million Sudanese pounds — Fiscal year beginning 1 July

	1970	1975	1977	1978	1979	1980	1981	1982	1983	1984	1985	1986
3 Subsidies	4.2	...	...	...	7.0	9.2	17.1	5.2	-	...	...	...
4 Other current transfers	46.2	...	...	...	26.8	26.4	35.2	53.6	73.5	...	...	...
A Social security benefits	2.7	...	...	...	...	...	...	...	...	...	...	...
B Social assistance grants	32.1	...	...	...	...	...	...	...	...	...	...	...
C Other	11.4	...	...	...	...	...	...	...	...	...	...	...
5 Net saving	-3.8	...	...	...	-109.8	-77.6	-146.5	136.3	-136.0	...	...	...
Total Current Disbursements and Net Saving of General Government	205.6	...	...	...	548.2	759.7	805.0	1305.2	1371.5	...	...	...

1.7 External Transactions on Current Account, Summary

Million Sudanese pounds — Fiscal year beginning 1 July

	1970	1975	1977	1978	1979	1980	1981	1982	1983	1984	1985	1986
Payments to the Rest of the World												
1 Imports of goods and services	138.8	393.2	459.4	447.2	957.3	1356.9	1709.4	2347.6	2185.4	...	...	...
A Imports of merchandise c.i.f.	119.1	362.8	416.1	382.0	867.9	1235.1	1514.4	2118.2	1900.6	...	...	...
B Other	19.7	30.4	43.3	65.2	89.4	121.8	195.0	229.4	284.8	...	...	...
2 Factor income to the rest of the world	6.1	27.5	21.9	32.7	33.8	52.6	147.2	187.4	316.8	...	...	...
A Compensation of employees	1.1	1.0	1.0	1.6	-	-	-	-	-	...	...	...
B Property and entrepreneurial income	5.0	26.5	20.9	31.1	33.8	52.6	147.2	187.4	316.8	...	...	...
3 Current transfers to the rest of the world	9.8	5.3	15.8	16.5	14.8	33.4	34.0	40.0	51.6	...	...	...
4 Surplus of the nation on current transactions	-22.5	-196.4	-233.0	-137.8	-212.8	-518.0	-795.3	-1100.1	-675.0	...	...	...
Payments to the Rest of the World and Surplus of the Nation on Current Transactions	132.2	229.6	264.1	358.6	793.1	924.9	1095.3	1474.9	1878.8	...	...	...
Receipts From The Rest of the World												
1 Exports of goods and services	123.2	206.6	218.2	256.9	382.9	504.9	630.9	1095.8	1306.7	...	...	...
A Exports of merchandise f.o.b.	106.6	188.3	187.3	214.6	281.3	326.5	340.8	589.4	873.3	...	...	...
B Other	16.6	18.3	30.9	42.3	101.6	178.4	290.1	506.4	433.4	...	...	...
2 Factor income from rest of the world	2.9	7.4	7.5	8.9	10.4	16.6	36.1	48.1	12.4	...	...	...
A Compensation of employees	2.3	2.6	2.7	5.4	-	-	-	-	-	...	...	...
B Property and entrepreneurial income	0.6	4.8	4.8	3.5	10.4	16.6	36.1	48.1	12.4	...	...	...
3 Current transfers from rest of the world	6.1	15.6	38.4	92.8	399.8	403.4	428.3	331.0	559.7	...	...	...
Receipts from the Rest of the World on Current Transactions	132.2	229.6	264.1	358.6	793.1	924.9	1095.3	1474.9	1878.8	...	...	...

1.8 Capital Transactions of The Nation, Summary

Million Sudanese pounds — Fiscal year beginning 1 July

	1970	1975	1977	1978	1979	1980	1981	1982	1983	1984	1985	1986
Finance of Gross Capital Formation												
Gross saving	...	...	...	...	785.3	560.2	852.8	527.2	955.9	...	...	...
1 Consumption of fixed capital	...	...	...	...	059.0	450.0	040.9	1012.3	1245.0	...	...	...
A General government	...	...	...	...	74.0	77.0	80.3	155.7	214.7	...	...	...
B Corporate and quasi-corporate enterprises	...	...	...	...	...	...	...	...	...	...	...	...
C Other	...	...	...	...	...	...	...	...	...	...	...	...
2 Net saving	...	...	...	...	425.4	102.2	211.9	-485.1	-289.1	...	...	...
A General government	...	...	...	...	-109.8	-77.6	-146.5	136.3	-136.0	...	...	...
B Corporate and quasi-corporate enterprises	...	...	...	...	...	...	...	...	...	...	...	...
C Other	...	...	...	...	...	...	...	...	...	...	...	...
Less: Surplus of the nation on current transactions	...	...	...	...	-212.8	-518.0	-795.3	-1100.1	-675.0	...	...	...
Finance of Gross Capital Formation	...	...	...	...	998.1	1078.2	1648.1	1627.3	1630.9	...	...	...

Sudan

1.8 Capital Transactions of The Nation, Summary
(Continued)

Million Sudanese pounds — Fiscal year beginning 1 July

	1970	1975	1977	1978	1979	1980	1981	1982	1983	1984	1985	1986
Gross Capital Formation												
Increase in stocks	...	...	...	...	228.9	80.4	372.7	32.9	-234.4	...	...	...
Gross fixed capital formation	...	...	...	...	769.2	997.8	1275.4	1594.4	1865.3	...	...	...
1 General government	...	...	...	...	96.9	86.0	118.3	77.6	101.5	...	...	...
2 Corporate and quasi-corporate enterprises	...	...	...	...	...	...	...	...	...	...	...	...
3 Other	...	...	...	...	...	...	...	...	...	...	...	...
Gross Capital Formation	...	...	...	...	998.1	1078.2	1648.1	1627.3	1630.9	...	...	...

1.10 Gross Domestic Product by Kind of Activity, in Current Prices

Million Sudanese pounds — Fiscal year beginning 1 July

	1970	1975	1977	1978	1979	1980	1981	1982	1983	1984	1985	1986
1 Agriculture, hunting, forestry and fishing	294.4	628.2	1051.9	1111.0	1298.4	1665.3	2401.9	2788.2	3339.4	...	...	...
2 Mining and quarrying	1.8	5.5	1.7	3.6	3.8	4.1	3.7	5.1	5.5	...	...	...
3 Manufacturing	67.4	155.6	215.1	282.5	336.5	394.6	466.1	670.1	869.7	...	...	...
4 Electricity, gas and water	16.6	28.6	38.6	45.0	65.5	69.4	76.4	93.6	175.3	...	...	...
5 Construction	23.3	88.8	118.6	124.0	204.6	296.0	381.9	604.9	666.7	...	...	...
6 Wholesale and retail trade, restaurants and hotels	113.6	315.3	555.8	641.3	574.3	791.5	949.3	1418.4	1978.6	...	...	...
7 Transport, storage and communication	50.7	192.4	279.1	363.7	416.1	488.1	691.4	927.1	1071.9	...	...	...
8 Finance, insurance, real estate and business services	41.8	138.8	191.8	219.0	368.2	551.8	795.0	1159.3	1383.0	...	...	...
9 Community, social and personal services	23.1	33.7	56.8	72.8	58.0	72.0	101.5	140.0	180.0	...	...	...
Total, Industries	632.7	1586.9	2509.4	2862.9	3325.4	4332.8	5867.2	7806.7	9670.1	...	...	...
Producers of Government Services	87.4	171.4	261.2	282.4	391.7	494.0	545.0	749.6	982.5	...	...	...
Other Producers	...	...	...	...	44.7	58.7	79.2	108.7	150.8	...	...	...
Subtotal	720.1	1758.3	2770.6	3145.3	3761.8	4885.5	6491.4	8665.0	10803.4	...	...	...
Less: Imputed bank service charge	10.3	20.3	37.2	41.6	51.9	79.6	107.8	132.9	142.4	...	...	...
Plus: Import duties	51.3	110.0	149.3	150.1	193.4	280.0	336.9	653.7	668.4	...	...	...
Plus: Value added tax	...	...	...	...	...	...	...	...	...	...	...	...
Equals: Gross Domestic Product	761.1	1848.0	2882.7	3253.8	3903.3	5085.9	6720.5	9185.8	11329.4	...	...	...

1.11 Gross Domestic Product by Kind of Activity, in Constant Prices

Million Sudanese pounds — Fiscal year beginning 1 July

	1970	1975	1977	1978	1979	1980	1981	1982	1983	1984	1985	1986
At constant prices of: 1981												
1 Agriculture, hunting, forestry and fishing	...	...	...	...	...	...	2401.9	2220.1	2164.3	...	...	...
2 Mining and quarrying	...	...	...	...	...	...	3.7	5.0	5.0	...	...	...
3 Manufacturing	...	...	...	...	...	...	466.1	511.5	503.6	...	...	...
4 Electricity, gas and water	...	...	...	...	...	...	76.4	94.5	102.2	...	...	...
5 Construction	...	...	...	...	...	...	381.9	460.7	399.4	...	...	...
6 Wholesale and retail trade, restaurants and hotels	...	...	...	...	...	...	949.3	979.5	905.5	...	...	...
7 Transport, storage and communication	...	...	...	...	...	...	691.4	706.9	672.3	...	...	...
8 Finance, insurance, real estate and business services	...	...	...	...	...	...	795.0	800.8	837.9	...	...	...
9 Community, social and personal services	...	...	...	...	...	...	101.5	110.0	110.3	...	...	...
Total, Industries	...	...	...	...	...	...	5867.2	5889.0	5700.5	...	...	...
Producers of Government Services	...	...	...	...	...	...	545.0	546.2	558.3	...	...	...
Other Producers	...	...	...	...	...	...	79.2	82.9	86.6	...	...	...
Subtotal	...	...	...	...	...	...	6491.4	6518.1	6345.4	...	...	...
Less: Imputed bank service charge	...	...	...	...	...	...	107.8	93.3	101.8	...	...	...
Plus: Import duties	...	...	...	...	...	...	336.9	340.6	234.1	...	...	...
Plus: Value added tax	...	...	...	...	...	...	...	...	...	...	...	...
Equals: Gross Domestic Product	...	...	...	...	...	...	6720.5	6765.4	6477.7	...	...	...

Sudan

1.12 Relations Among National Accounting Aggregates

Million Sudanese pounds — Fiscal year beginning 1 July

	1970	1975	1977	1978	1979	1980	1981	1982	1983	1984	1985	1986
Gross Domestic Product	761.1	1848.0	2882.7	3253.8	3903.3	5085.9	6720.5	9185.8	11329.4	...	...	...
Plus: Net factor income from the rest of the world	-3.2	-20.1	-14.4	-23.8	-23.4	-36.0	-111.1	-139.3	-304.4	...	...	...
Factor income from the rest of the world	2.9	7.4	7.5	8.9	10.4	16.6	36.1	48.1	12.4	...	...	...
Less: Factor income to the rest of the world	6.1	27.5	21.9	32.7	33.8	52.6	147.2	187.4	316.8	...	...	...
Equals: Gross National Product	757.9	1827.9	2868.3	3230.0	3879.9	5049.9	6609.4	9046.5	11025.0	...	...	...
Less: Consumption of fixed capital	53.2	166.1	269.2	222.5	359.9	458.0	640.9	1012.3	1245.0	...	...	...
Equals: National Income	704.7	1661.8	2599.1	3007.5	3520.0	4591.9	5968.5	8034.2	9780.0	...	...	...
Plus: Net current transfers from the rest of the world	-3.7	10.3	22.6	76.3	385.0	370.0	394.3	291.0	508.1	...	...	...
Current transfers from the rest of the world	6.1	15.6	38.4	92.8	399.8	403.4	428.3	331.0	559.7	...	...	...
Less: Current transfers to the rest of the world	9.8	5.3	15.8	16.5	14.8	33.4	34.0	40.0	51.6	...	...	...
Equals: National Disposable Income	701.0	1672.1	2621.7	3083.8	3905.0	4961.9	6362.8	8325.2	10288.1	...	...	...
Less: Final consumption	687.1	1607.1	2710.2	3012.7	3479.6	4859.7	6150.9	8810.3	10577.2	...	...	...
Equals: Net Saving	13.9	65.0	-88.5	71.1	425.4	102.2	211.9	-485.1	-289.1	...	...	...
Less: Surplus of the nation on current transactions	-22.5	-196.4	-233.0	-137.8	-212.8	-518.0	-795.3	-1100.1	-675.0	...	...	...
Equals: Net Capital Formation	36.4	261.4	144.5	208.9	638.2	620.2	1007.2	615.0	385.9	...	...	...

2.1 Government Final Consumption Expenditure by Function, in Current Prices

Million Sudanese pounds — Fiscal year beginning 1 July

	1970	1975	1977	1978	1979	1980	1981	1982	1983	1984	1985	1986
1 General public services [a]	69.8	109.4	149.1	185.4	134.6	193.9	181.2	236.1	360.4	...	...	...
2 Defence	28.0				101.1	124.3	133.6	161.8	250.4	...	...	...
3 Public order and safety [a]	...	...	...	...	...	...	...	...	...	...	...	...
4 Education	26.2	56.5	87.2	112.1	142.4	178.9	222.4	236.8	263.8	...	...	...
5 Health	14.2	22.3	28.0	31.1	35.8	38.6	70.1	73.1	56.2	...	...	...
6 Social security and welfare	...	...	...	...	...	...	...	...	...	...	...	...
7 Housing and community amenities	0.1	2.9	0.8	0.7	0.3	0.6	0.7	0.4	-2.0	...	...	...
8 Recreational, cultural and religious affairs	1.7	4.5	11.9	12.0	11.3	16.4	22.7	22.3	24.0	...	...	...
9 Economic services [b]	19.0	40.3	53.7	65.7	75.4	95.5	89.2	123.0	159.7	...	...	...
10 Other functions [b]	...	...	...	...	...	...	...	...	...	...	...	...
Total Government Final Consumption Expenditure	159.0	235.9	330.7	407.0	500.9	648.2	719.9	853.5	1112.5	...	...	...

a) Item 'Public order and safety' is included in item 'General public services'.
b) Item 'Other functions' is included in item 'Economic services'.

2.2 Government Final Consumption Expenditure by Function, in Constant Prices

Million Sudanese pounds — Fiscal year beginning 1 July

At constant prices of: 1981

	1970	1975	1977	1978	1979	1980	1981	1982	1983	1984	1985	1986
1 General public services	...	...	...	...	...	...	181.2	170.2	204.3	...	...	...
2 Defence	...	...	...	...	...	...	133.6	122.0	143.5	...	...	...
3 Public order and safety	...	...	...	...	...	...	...	...	...	...	...	...
4 Education	...	...	...	...	...	...	222.4	178.5	151.7	...	...	...
5 Health	...	...	...	...	...	...	70.1	53.9	31.0	...	...	...
6 Social security and welfare	...	...	...	...	...	...	...	...	...	...	...	...
7 Housing and community amenities	...	...	...	...	...	...	0.7	0.4	-1.0	...	...	...
8 Recreational, cultural and religious affairs	...	...	...	...	...	...	22.7	15.6	13.2	...	...	...
9 Economic services	...	...	...	...	...	...	89.2	76.7	84.1	...	...	...
10 Other functions	...	...	...	...	...	...	...	...	...	...	...	...
Total Government Final Consumption Expenditure	...	...	...	...	...	...	719.9	617.3	626.8	...	...	...

Sudan

2.3 Total Government Outlays by Function and Type

Million Sudanese pounds

Fiscal year beginning 1 July

	Final Consumption Expenditures Total	Compensation of Employees	Other	Subsidies	Other Current Transfers & Property Income	Total Current Disbursements	Gross Capital Formation	Other Capital Outlays	Total Outlays
1980									
1 General public services [a]	193.9	129.5	64.4	...	11.7	...	73.1	...	...
2 Defence	124.3	92.6	31.7	...	...	...	-	...	...
3 Public order and safety [a]	...	...	...	...	...	...	...	...	...
4 Education	178.8	116.5	62.3	...	5.0	...	5.0	...	...
5 Health	38.6	20.3	18.3	...	0.3	...	4.4	...	...
6 Social security and welfare	...	...	...	...	...	...	...	...	...
7 Housing and community amenities	0.6	0.5	0.1	...	...	...	0.4	...	...
8 Recreation, culture and religion	16.4	3.7	12.7	...	1.8	...	0.3	...	...
9 Economic services [b]	95.5	53.9	41.6	9.2	0.2	...	29.0	...	...
A Fuel and energy	...	...	...	...	...	...	...	...	...
B Agriculture, forestry, fishing and hunting	18.8	16.5	2.3	...	...	...	15.8	...	...
C Mining (except fuels), manufacturing and construction	29.5	8.1	21.4	...	...	...	0.9	...	...
D Transportation and communication	-7.8	4.6	-12.4	...	...	...	4.4	...	...
E Other economic affairs	55.0	24.7	30.3	...	...	...	7.9	...	...
10 Other functions [b]	...	...	...	...	7.4	...	...	...	...
Total	648.1	417.0	231.1	9.2	26.4	...	112.2	...	...
1981									
1 General public services [a]	181.2	120.0	61.2	...	13.5	...	110.0	...	...
2 Defence	133.6	100.9	32.7	...	...	...	-	...	...
3 Public order and safety [a]	...	...	...	...	...	...	...	...	...
4 Education	222.4	141.8	80.6	...	12.5	...	5.8	...	...
5 Health	70.1	41.1	29.0	...	0.3	...	5.1	...	...
6 Social security and welfare	...	...	...	...	...	...	...	...	...
7 Housing and community amenities	0.7	0.5	0.2	...	...	...	0.4	...	...
8 Recreation, culture and religion	22.7	6.8	15.9	...	0.2	...	1.4	...	...
9 Economic services [b]	89.2	53.6	35.6	17.1	-	...	33.3	...	...
A Fuel and energy	...	...	...	...	...	...	...	...	...
B Agriculture, forestry, fishing and hunting	20.1	18.2	1.9	...	...	...	18.3	...	...
C Mining (except fuels), manufacturing and construction	28.1	8.9	19.2	...	...	...	1.3	...	...
D Transportation and communication	-8.6	0.3	-8.9	...	...	...	5.6	...	...
E Other economic affairs	49.6	26.2	23.4	...	...	...	8.1	...	...
10 Other functions [b]	...	...	...	...	8.7	...	...	...	...
Total	719.7	464.7	255.2	17.1	35.2	...	156.0	...	...
1982									
1 General public services [a]	236.1	157.0	79.1	...	34.2	...	57.7	...	...
2 Defence	161.8	122.6	39.2	...	...	...	-	...	...
3 Public order and safety [a]	...	...	...	...	...	...	...	...	...
4 Education	236.8	188.4	48.4	...	2.9	...	13.6	...	...
5 Health	73.1	50.4	22.7	...	-	...	10.9	...	...
6 Social security and welfare	...	...	...	...	...	...	...	...	...
7 Housing and community amenities	0.4	0.9	-0.5	...	...	...	0.4	...	...
8 Recreation, culture and religion	22.3	10.9	11.4	...	1.1	...	1.4	...	...
9 Economic services [b]	123.0	63.7	59.3	5.2	0.7	...	48.3	...	...
A Fuel and energy	...	...	...	...	...	...	...	...	...
B Agriculture, forestry, fishing and hunting	18.1	23.5	-5.4	...	...	...	24.1	...	...
C Mining (except fuels), manufacturing and construction	40.7	10.3	30.4	...	...	...	2.7	...	...
D Transportation and communication	-9.0	3.4	-12.4	...	...	...	9.9	...	...
E Other economic affairs	73.2	26.5	46.7	...	...	...	11.6	...	...
10 Other functions [b]	...	...	...	...	14.7	...	...	...	...
Total	853.5	593.9	259.6	5.2	53.6	...	132.3	...	...

Sudan

2.3 Total Government Outlays by Function and Type
(Continued)

Million Sudanese pounds — Fiscal year beginning 1 July

		Final Consumption Expenditures		Subsidies	Other Current Transfers & Property Income	Total Current Disbursements	Gross Capital Formation	Other Capital Outlays	Total Outlays
		Total	Compensation of Employees	Other						

1983

		Total	Comp. of Employees	Other	Subsidies	Other Curr. Transfers	Total Curr. Disb.	Gross Cap. Formation	Other Cap. Outlays	Total Outlays
1	General public services [a]	360.4	262.8	97.6	...	51.4	...	75.6	...	...
2	Defence	250.4	188.5	61.9	...	...	...	-	...	...
3	Public order and safety [a]	...	...	...	...	...	...	...	...	...
4	Education	263.8	211.0	52.8	...	0.3	...	15.7	...	...
5	Health	56.2	26.6	29.6	...	0.4	...	9.6	...	...
6	Social security and welfare	...	...	...	...	...	...	...	...	...
7	Housing and community amenities	-1.0	1.0	-3.0	...	...	...	0.3	...	...
8	Recreation, culture and religion	24.0	12.2	11.8	...	1.3	...	0.9	...	...
9	Economic services [b]	159.7	65.7	94.0	...	0.4	...	59.4	...	...
	A Fuel and energy	...	...	...	...	...	...	...	...	...
	B Agriculture, forestry, fishing and hunting	22.3	24.5	-2.2	...	...	...	26.9	...	...
	C Mining (except fuels), manufacturing and construction	49.0	10.2	38.8	...	...	...	3.3	...	...
	D Transportation and communication	-11.1	3.7	-14.8	...	...	...	14.6	...	...
	E Other economic affairs	99.5	27.3	72.2	...	...	...	14.6	...	...
10	Other functions [b]	...	...	...	...	19.7	...	...	...	...
	Total	1112.5	767.8	344.7	-	73.5	...	161.5	...	...

a) Item 'Public order and safety' is included in item 'General public services'.
b) Item 'Other functions' is included in item 'Economic services'.

2.5 Private Final Consumption Expenditure by Type and Porpose, in Current Prices

Million Sudanese pounds — Fiscal year beginning 1 July

		1970	1975	1977	1978	1979	1980	1981	1982	1983	1984	1985	1986

Final Consumption Expenditure of Resident Households

		1970	1975	1977	1978	1979	1980	1981	1982	1983	1984	1985	1986
1	Food, beverages and tobacco	...	...	1672.0	...	1862.7	2670.5	3384.8	4767.8	6073.4	...	...	...
	A Food	...	...	1563.0	...	1796.2	2575.8	3251.1	4600.7	5905.8	...	...	...
	B Non-alcoholic beverages	...	...	5.0	...	14.7	16.5	22.0	32.9	52.8	...	...	...
	C Alcoholic beverages	...	...	39.6	...	19.9	26.3	34.4	27.4	2.4	...	...	...
	D Tobacco	...	...	64.4	...	31.9	51.9	77.3	106.8	112.4	...	...	...
2	Clothing and footwear	...	...	196.3	...	162.5	229.0	300.7	595.8	500.4	...	...	...
3	Gross rent, fuel and power	...	...	193.7	...	451.4	650.8	850.0	1209.6	1429.2	...	...	...
	A Fuel and power	...	...	...	...	151.2	212.1	250.1	315.6	352.7	...	...	...
	B Other	...	...	...	...	300.2	438.7	599.9	894.0	1076.5	...	...	...
4	Furniture, furnishings and household equipment and operation	...	...	82.2	...	134.9	179.5	250.0	444.0	513.0	...	...	...
	A Household operation	...	...	27.2	...	99.6	130.3	198.8	351.4	437.8	...	...	...
	D Other	...	...	55.0	...	35.3	49.2	51.2	92.6	75.2	...	...	...
5	Medical care and health expenses	...	...	49.1	...	131.9	185.3	282.4	420.5	385.8	...	...	...
6	Transport and communication	...	...	58.4	...	74.9	91.2	127.6	199.7	143.4	...	...	...
7	Recreational, entertainment, education and cultural services	...	...	61.8	...	38.7	54.3	58.6	91.0	69.4	...	...	...
	A Education			16.0									

Sudan

2.5 Private Final Consumption Expenditure by Type and Porpose, in Current Prices
(Continued)

Million Sudanese pounds — Fiscal year beginning 1 July

	1970	1975	1977	1978	1979	1980	1981	1982	1983	1984	1985	1986
B Other	...	...	45.8	...	...	...	...	...	...	...	...	...
8 Miscellaneous goods and services	...	...	23.4	...	86.8	111.3	142.5	191.2	259.7	...	...	...
Total Final Consumption Expenditure in the Domestic Market by Households, of which	...	...	2336.9	...	2943.8	4171.9	5396.6	7919.6	9374.3	...	...	...
Plus: Direct purchases abroad by resident households	...	...	22.5	...	17.0	29.8	22.1	24.8	58.3	...	...	...
Less: Direct purchases in the domestic market by non-resident households	...	...	23.0	...	10.6	25.2	32.4	47.2	47.6	...	...	...
Equals: Final Consumption Expenditure of Resident Households	...	...	2336.4	...	2950.2	4176.5	5386.3	7897.2	9385.0	...	...	...

Final Consumption Expenditure of Private Non-profit Institutions Serving Households

Equals: Final Consumption Expenditure of Private Non-profit Organisations Serving Households	...	...	43.1	...	28.5	35.0	44.7	59.6	79.7	...	...	...
Private Final Consumption Expenditure	...	...	2379.5	...	2978.7	4211.5	5431.0	7956.8	9464.7	...	...	...

2.6 Private Final Consumption Expenditure by Type and Purpose, in Constant Prices

Million Sudanese pounds — Fiscal year beginning 1 July

	1970	1975	1977	1978	1979	1980	1981	1982	1983	1984	1985	1986

At constant prices of: 1981

Final Consumption Expenditure of Resident Households

	1970	1975	1977	1978	1979	1980	1981	1982	1983	1984	1985	1986
1 Food, beverages and tobacco	...	...	...	...	...	...	3384.8	3595.3	3486.2	...	...	...
A Food	...	...	...	...	...	...	3251.1	3473.8	3392.9	...	...	...
B Non-alcoholic beverages	...	...	...	...	...	...	22.0	23.0	22.9	...	...	...
C Alcoholic beverages	...	...	...	...	...	...	34.4	20.0	1.5	...	...	...
D Tobacco	...	...	...	...	...	...	77.3	78.5	68.9	...	...	...
2 Clothing and footwear	...	...	...	...	...	...	300.7	355.5	226.5	...	...	...
3 Gross rent, fuel and power	...	...	...	...	...	...	850.0	898.1	898.9	...	...	...
A Fuel and power	...	...	...	...	...	...	250.1	269.8	247.2	...	...	...
B Other	...	...	...	...	...	...	599.9	628.3	651.7	...	...	...
4 Furniture, furnishings and household equipment and operation	...	...	...	...	...	...	250.0	305.0	181.8	...	...	...
A Household operation	...	...	...	...	...	...	30.1	31.5	32.9	...	...	...
B Other	...	...	...	...	...	...	219.9	273.5	148.9	...	...	...
5 Medical care and health expenses	...	...	...	...	...	...	282.4	329.6	235.9	...	...	...
6 Transport and communication	...	...	...	...	...	...	127.6	137.9	77.0	...	...	...
7 Recreational, entertainment, education and cultural services	...	...	...	...	...	...	58.6	71.6	42.6	...	...	...
8 Miscellaneous goods and services	...	...	...	...	...	...	142.5	147.9	152.6	...	...	...
Total Final Consumption Expenditure in the Domestic Market by Households, of which	...	...	...	...	...	...	5396.6	5840.9	5301.5	...	...	...
Plus: Direct purchases abroad by resident households	...	...	...	...	...	...	22.1	16.2	29.2	...	...	...
Less: Direct purchases in the domestic market by non-resident households	...	...	...	...	...	...	32.4	34.8	26.9	...	...	...
Equals: Final Consumption Expenditure of Resident Households	...	...	...	...	...	...	5386.3	5822.3	5303.8	...	...	...

Final Consumption Expenditure of Private Non-profit Institutions Serving Households

Equals: Final Consumption Expenditure of Private Non-profit Organisations Serving Households	...	...	...	...	...	...	...	...	...	...	...	...
Private Final Consumption Expenditure	...	...	...	...	...	...	...	...	...	...	...	...

Sudan

2.7 Gross Capital Formation by Type of Good and Owner, in Current Prices

Million Sudanese pounds — Fiscal year beginning 1 July

	1980 TOTAL	1980 Total Private	1980 Public Enterprises	1980 General Government	1981 TOTAL	1981 Total Private	1981 Public Enterprises	1981 General Government	1982 TOTAL	1982 Total Private	1982 Public Enterprises	1982 General Government
Increase in stocks, total	80.4	...	...	...	372.7	...	...	...	32.9	...	...	...
1 Goods producing industries	105.2	...	...	...	506.0	...	...	...	222.0	...	...	...
A Materials and supplies	...	...	...	...	...	...	...	...	...	...	...	...
B Work in progress	35.9	...	...	...	416.9	...	...	...	129.4	...	...	...
C Livestock, except breeding stocks, dairy cattle, etc.	69.3	...	...	...	89.1	...	...	...	92.6	...	...	...
D Finished goods	...	...	...	...	...	...	...	...	...	...	...	...
2 Wholesale and retail trade	19.4	...	...	...	-122.3	...	...	...	-93.0	...	...	...
3 Other, except government stocks	-44.2	...	...	...	-11.0	...	...	...	-96.1	...	...	...
4 Government stocks	...	...	...	...	...	...	...	...	...	...	...	...
Gross Fixed Capital Formation, Total	997.8	754.2	131.4	112.2	1275.4	908.5	211.1	155.8	1594.4	1144.3	317.9	132.2
1 Residential buildings	156.0	149.5	3.2	3.3	198.7	188.3	2.5	7.9	387.3	374.1	9.2	4.0
2 Non-residential buildings	85.3	21.6	22.5	41.2	123.3	28.4	43.7	51.2	179.0	68.9	57.8	52.3
3 Other construction	251.4	140.8	58.5	43.1	316.7	204.3	47.5	64.9	428.8	313.4	88.4	27.0
4 Land improvement and plantation and orchard development	24.7	-	20.3	4.4	19.8	-	16.3	3.5	52.2	-	30.0	22.2
5 Producers' durable goods	480.4	433.3	26.9	20.2	616.9	487.5	101.1	28.3	547.1	387.9	132.5	26.7
A Transport equipment	188.0	181.2	4.6	2.2	333.2	279.4	51.5	2.3	124.4	78.7	40.8	4.9
B Machinery and equipment	292.4	252.1	22.3	18.0	283.7	208.1	49.6	26.0	422.7	309.2	91.7	21.8
6 Breeding stock, dairy cattle, etc.	-	-	-	...	-	-	-	...	-	-	-	...
Total Gross Capital Formation	1078.2	...	...	112.2	1648.1	...	...	155.8	1627.3	...	...	132.2

	1983 TOTAL	1983 Total Private	1983 Public Enterprises	1983 General Government
Increase in stocks, total	-234.4	...	...	...
1 Goods producing industries	-71.1	...	...	...
A Materials and supplies	...	...	...	...
B Work in progress	-86.7	...	...	...
C Livestock, except breeding stocks, dairy cattle, etc.	15.6	...	...	...
D Finished goods	...	...	...	...
2 Wholesale and retail trade	-157.6	...	...	...
3 Other, except government stocks	-5.7	...	...	...
4 Government stocks	...	...	...	...
Gross Fixed Capital Formation, Total	1865.3	1390.7	312.8	161.8
1 Residential buildings	396.2	388.7	3.2	4.3
2 Non-residential buildings	192.6	60.0	55.9	76.7
3 Other construction	484.9	369.6	82.0	33.3
4 Land improvement and plantation and orchard development	60.2	-	51.9	8.3
5 Producers' durable goods	731.4	572.4	119.8	39.2
A Transport equipment	237.0	196.3	28.8	11.9
B Machinery and equipment	494.4	376.1	91.0	27.3
6 Breeding stock, dairy cattle, etc.	-	-	-	...
Total Gross Capital Formation	1630.9	...	...	161.8

2.11 Gross Fixed Capital Formation by Kind of Activity of Owner, ISIC Divisions, in Current Prices

Million Sudanese pounds — Fiscal year beginning 1 July

	1970	1975	1977	1978	1979	1980	1981	1982	1983	1984	1985	1986
					All Producers							
1 Agriculture, hunting, forestry and fishing	...	...	...	...	...	...	...	154.4	130.4	...	...	...
2 Mining and quarrying	...	...	...	...	...	...	...	0.5	0.6	...	...	...
3 Manufacturing	...	...	...	...	...	...	...	227.1	280.3	...	...	...
4 Electricity, gas and water	...	...	...	...	...	...	...	77.6	77.9	...	...	...

Sudan

2.11 Gross Fixed Capital Formation by Kind of Activity of Owner, ISIC Divisions, in Current Prices
(Continued)

Million Sudanese pounds — Fiscal year beginning 1 July

	1970	1975	1977	1978	1979	1980	1981	1982	1983	1984	1985	1986
A Electricity, gas and steam	...	...	...	...	...	...	...	66.4	65.5	...	...	...
B Water works and supply	...	...	...	...	...	...	...	11.2	12.4	...	...	...
5 Construction	...	...	...	...	...	...	...	98.6	35.5	...	...	...
6 Wholesale and retail trade, restaurants and hotels	...	...	...	...	...	...	...	106.6	120.7	...	...	...
7 Transport, storage and communication	...	...	...	...	...	...	...	34.6	38.3	...	...	...
A Transport and storage	...	...	...	...	...	...	...	31.1	34.5	...	...	...
B Communication	...	...	...	...	...	...	...	3.5	3.8	...	...	...
8 Finance, insurance, real estate and business services	...	...	...	...	...	...	...	756.4	818.3	...	...	...
A Financial institutions	...	...	...	...	...	...	...	...	...	...	...	...
B Insurance	...	...	...	...	...	...	...	...	...	...	...	...
C Real estate and business services	...	...	...	...	...	...	...	756.4	818.3	...	...	...
9 Community, social and personal services	...	...	...	...	...	...	...	...	...	...	...	...
Total Industries	...	...	...	...	...	...	...	1455.8	1502.0	...	...	...
Producers of Government Services	...	...	...	...	...	...	...	132.2	161.8	...	...	...
Private Non-Profit Institutions Serving Households	...	...	...	...	...	...	...	6.4	201.5	...	...	...
Total	...	...	...	...	...	...	...	1594.4	1865.3	...	...	...

2.17 Exports and Imports of Goods and Services, Detail

Million Sudanese pounds — Fiscal year beginning 1 July

	1970	1975	1977	1978	1979	1980	1981	1982	1983	1984	1985	1986
Exports of Goods and Services												
1 Exports of merchandise, f.o.b.	106.6	188.3	187.3	214.6	281.3	326.5	340.8	589.4	873.3	...	...	...
2 Transport and communication	1.2	4.1	4.4	5.3	8.7	13.1	14.8	31.6	8.8	...	...	...
3 Insurance service charges	0.8	0.3	0.1	0.9	0.2	0.3	0.5	0.6	0.2	...	...	...
4 Other commodities	1.7	2.0	3.4	3.9	82.1	139.8	242.4	427.0	376.8	...	...	...
5 Adjustments of merchandise exports to change-of-ownership basis	...	...	...	...	...	...	...	...	...	...	...	...
6 Direct purchases in the domestic market by non-residential households	12.9	11.9	23.0	32.2	10.6	25.2	32.4	47.2	47.6	...	...	...
7 Direct purchases in the domestic market by extraterritorial bodies	...	...	...	...	...	...	...	...	...	...	...	...
Total Exports of Goods and Services	123.2	206.6	218.2	256.9	382.9	504.9	630.9	1095.8	1306.7	...	...	...
Imports of Goods and Services												
1 Imports of merchandise, c.i.f.	119.1	362.8	416.1	382.0	867.9	1235.1	1514.4	2118.2	1900.6	...	...	...
A Imports of merchandise, f.o.b.	...	...	...	...	855.5	1218.7	1488.3	2093.5	1880.7	...	...	...
B Transport of services on merchandise imports	...	...	...	...	12.1	16.1	25.5	23.7	19.1	...	...	...
C Insurance service charges on merchandise imports	...	...	...	...	0.3	0.3	0.6	1.0	0.8	...	...	...
2 Adjustments of merchandise imports to change-of-ownership basis	...	...	...	...	...	...	...	...	...	...	...	...
3 Other transport and communication	4.2	3.1	7.1	10.0	12.1	16.1	25.5	23.7	19.1	...	...	...
4 Other insurance service charges	0.9	1.2	0.6	2.2	0.3	0.3	0.6	1.0	0.8	...	...	...
5 Other commodities	3.7	11.0	13.1	21.9	60.0	75.6	146.8	179.9	206.6	...	...	...
6 Direct purchases abroad by government	...	...	...	...	...	...	...	...	...	...	...	...
7 Direct purchases abroad by resident households	10.9	15.1	22.5	31.1	17.0	29.8	22.1	24.8	58.3	...	...	...
Total Imports of Goods and Services	138.8	393.2	459.4	447.2	957.3	1356.9	1709.4	2347.6	2185.4	...	...	...
Balance of Goods and Services	-15.6	-186.6	-241.2	-190.3	-574.4	-852.0	-1078.5	-1251.8	-878.7	...	...	...
Total Imports and Balance of Goods and Services	123.2	206.6	218.2	256.9	382.9	504.9	630.9	1095.8	1306.7	...	...	...

Sudan

4.1 Derivation of Value Added by Kind of Activity, in Current Prices

Million Sudanese pounds
Fiscal year beginning 1 July

	1980 Gross Output	1980 Intermediate Consumption	1980 Value Added	1981 Gross Output	1981 Intermediate Consumption	1981 Value Added	1982 Gross Output	1982 Intermediate Consumption	1982 Value Added	1983 Gross Output	1983 Intermediate Consumption	1983 Value Added
						All Producers						
1 Agriculture, hunting, forestry and fishing	2070.7	405.4	1665.3	2955.1	553.2	2401.9	3610.3	822.1	2788.2	4499.6	1160.2	3339.4
A Agriculture and hunting	1953.8	395.4	1558.4	2804.4	540.0	2264.4	3431.1	806.8	2624.3	4276.2	1140.1	3136.1
B Forestry and logging	88.7	5.8	82.9	110.6	7.2	103.4	135.5	8.8	126.7	156.2	10.1	146.1
C Fishing	28.2	4.2	24.0	40.1	6.0	34.1	43.7	6.5	37.2	67.2	10.0	57.2
2 Mining and quarrying	5.8	1.7	4.1	5.3	1.6	3.7	7.2	2.1	5.1	7.7	2.2	5.5
A Coal mining	...	...	...	...	...	...	...	...	...	...	...	...
B Crude petroleum and natural gas production	...	...	...	...	...	...	...	...	...	...	...	...
C Metal ore mining	...	...	...	...	...	...	...	...	...	...	...	...
D Other mining	5.8	1.7	4.1	5.3	1.6	3.7	7.2	2.1	5.1	7.7	2.2	5.5
3 Manufacturing	1001.7	607.1	394.6	1523.7	1057.6	466.1	2266.1	1595.9	670.2	2891.7	2022.0	869.7
A Manufacture of food, beverages and tobacco	423.8	246.1	177.7	581.1	342.2	238.9	815.8	485.1	330.7	1174.6	706.3	468.3
B Textile, wearing apparel and leather industries	127.4	80.3	47.1	373.4	319.8	53.6	594.9	507.6	87.3	735.4	633.7	101.7
C Manufacture of wood and wood products, including furniture	29.4	11.5	17.9	17.3	6.8	10.5	22.3	8.9	13.4	28.5	10.4	18.1
D Manufacture of paper and paper products, printing and publishing	34.4	17.6	16.8	34.8	23.1	11.7	57.8	40.6	17.2	62.3	43.5	18.8
E Manufacture of chemicals and chemical petroleum, coal, rubber and plastic products	269.2	183.1	86.1	343.3	270.8	72.5	519.5	408.8	110.7	572.4	447.8	124.6
F Manufacture of non-metallic mineral products, except products of petroleum and coal	37.3	19.6	17.7	45.3	23.1	22.2	85.7	45.4	40.3	124.8	66.9	57.9
G Basic metal industries	17.8	12.4	5.4	19.4	13.2	6.2	34.0	23.6	10.4	49.0	33.1	15.9
H Manufacture of fabricated metal products, machinery and equipment	57.5	34.5	23.0	102.6	53.4	49.2	127.1	68.7	58.4	132.7	70.7	62.0
I Other manufacturing industries	4.9	2.0	2.9	6.5	5.2	1.3	9.0	7.2	1.8	12.0	9.6	2.4
4 Electricity, gas and water	96.6	27.2	69.4	116.4	40.0	76.4	146.7	53.1	93.6	248.4	73.1	175.3
A Electricity, gas and steam	38.7	17.6	21.1	44.6	30.8	13.8	53.3	41.1	12.2	118.7	59.2	59.5
B Water works and supply	57.9	9.6	48.3	71.8	9.2	62.6	93.4	12.0	81.4	129.7	13.9	115.8
5 Construction	587.6	291.6	296.0	753.3	371.4	381.9	1193.8	588.9	604.9	1306.3	639.6	666.7
6 Wholesale and retail trade, restaurants and hotels	1150.4	358.9	791.5	1421.9	472.6	949.3	2100.9	682.5	1418.4	2717.8	739.2	1978.6
A Wholesale and retail trade	1064.1	310.4	753.7	1325.0	418.1	906.9	1982.2	618.9	1363.3	2569.6	660.1	1909.5
B Restaurants and hotels	86.3	48.5	37.8	96.9	54.5	42.4	118.7	63.6	55.1	148.2	79.1	69.1
Restaurants	49.1	30.4	18.7	54.9	34.0	20.9	74.6	46.2	28.4	99.4	61.6	37.8
Hotels and other lodging places	37.2	18.1	19.1	42.0	20.5	21.5	44.1	17.4	26.7	48.8	17.5	31.3
7 Transport, storage and communication	761.5	273.4	488.1	1089.2	397.8	691.4	1536.6	609.5	927.1	1880.3	808.4	1071.9
A Transport and storage	740.9	268.6	472.3	1065.0	392.6	672.4	1511.5	604.3	907.2	1847.8	799.1	1048.7
B Communication	20.6	4.8	15.8	24.2	5.2	19.0	25.1	5.2	19.9	32.5	9.3	23.2
8 Finance, insurance, real estate and business services	719.4	167.6	551.8	1076.7	281.7	795.0	1609.1	449.8	1159.3	1869.2	486.2	1383.0
A Financial institutions	139.3	17.3	122.0	193.3	21.2	172.1	253.0	31.6	221.4	306.4	46.7	259.7
B Insurance	11.6	0.7	10.9	13.2	0.8	12.4	16.5	1.3	15.2	23.5	1.9	21.6
C Real estate and business services	568.5	149.6	418.9	870.2	259.7	610.5	1339.6	416.9	922.7	1539.3	437.6	1101.7
9 Community, social and personal services	107.3	35.3	72.0	154.6	53.1	101.5	208.1	68.1	140.0	269.2	89.2	180.0
Total, Industries	6501.0	2168.2	4332.8	9096.2	3229.0	5867.2	12678.8	4872.0	7806.8	15690.2	6020.1	9670.1
Producers of Government Services	727.2	233.2	494.0	819.9	274.9	545.0	1011.4	261.8	749.6	1294.0	311.5	982.5
Other Producers	88.6	29.9	58.7	117.0	37.8	79.2	156.5	47.8	108.7	211.3	60.5	150.8
Total	7316.8	2431.3	4885.5	10033.1	3541.7	6491.4	13846.7	5181.6	8665.1	17195.5	6392.1	10803.4
Less: Imputed bank service charge	...	-79.6	79.6	...	-107.8	107.8	...	-132.9	132.9	...	-142.4	142.4
Import duties	280.0	-	280.0	336.9	-	336.9	653.7	-	653.7	668.4	-	668.4
Value added tax	...	...	...	...	...	...	...	...	...	...	...	...
Total	7596.8	2510.9	5085.9	10370.0	3649.5	6720.5	14500.4	5314.5	9185.9	17863.9	6534.5	11329.4

Sudan

4.2 Derivation of Value Added by Kind of Activity, in Constant Prices

Million Sudanese pounds
Fiscal year beginning 1 July

At constant prices of: 1981

All Producers

	1981 Gross Output	1981 Intermediate Consumption	1981 Value Added	1982 Gross Output	1982 Intermediate Consumption	1982 Value Added	1983 Gross Output	1983 Intermediate Consumption	1983 Value Added
1 Agriculture, hunting, forestry and fishing	...	...	2401.9	...	...	2220.1	...	...	2164.3
A Agriculture and hunting	...	...	2264.4	...	...	2088.5	...	...	2021.3
B Forestry and logging	...	...	103.4	...	...	98.9	...	...	108.8
C Fishing	...	...	34.1	...	...	32.7	...	...	34.2
2 Mining and quarrying	...	...	3.7	...	...	5.0	...	...	5.0
A Coal mining	...	...	...	...	...	...	...	...	...
B Crude petroleum and natural gas production	...	...	...	...	...	...	...	...	...
C Metal ore mining	...	...	...	...	...	...	...	...	...
D Other mining	...	...	3.7	...	...	5.0	...	...	5.0
3 Manufacturing	...	...	466.1	...	...	511.5	...	...	503.6
A Manufacture of food, beverages and tobacco	...	...	238.9	...	...	266.5	...	...	280.9
B Textile, wearing apparel and leather industries	...	...	53.6	...	...	59.2	...	...	53.9
C Manufacture of wood and wood products, including furniture	...	...	10.5	...	...	10.8	...	...	10.8
D Manufacture of paper and paper products, printing and publishing	...	...	11.7	...	...	12.2	...	...	12.8
E Manufacture of chemicals and chemical petroleum, coal, rubber and plastic products	...	...	72.5	...	...	78.4	...	...	75.9
F Manufacture of non-metallic mineral products, except products of petroleum and coal	...	...	22.2	...	...	29.5	...	...	31.1
G Basic metal industries	...	...	6.2	...	...	4.6	...	...	5.3
H Manufacture of fabricated metal products, machinery and equipment	...	...	49.2	...	...	48.9	...	...	31.5
I Other manufacturing industries	...	...	1.3	...	...	1.4	...	...	1.4
4 Electricity, gas and water	...	...	76.4	...	...	94.5	...	...	102.2
A Electricity, gas and steam	...	...	13.8	...	...	25.9	...	...	29.2
B Water works and supply	...	...	62.6	...	...	68.6	...	...	73.0
5 Construction	...	...	381.9	...	...	460.7	...	...	399.4
6 Wholesale and retail trade, restaurants and hotels	...	...	949.3	...	...	979.5	...	...	905.5
A Wholesale and retail trade	...	...	906.9	...	...	940.9	...	...	868.3
B Restaurants and hotels	...	...	42.4	...	...	38.6	...	...	37.2
7 Transport, storage and communication	...	...	691.4	...	...	706.9	...	...	672.3
A Transport and storage	...	...	672.4	...	...	691.5	...	...	658.7
B Communication	...	...	19.0	...	...	15.4	...	...	13.6
8 Finance, insurance, real estate and business services	...	...	795.0	...	...	800.3	...	...	837.9
A Financial institutions	...	...	172.1	...	...	148.4	...	...	162.6
B Insurance	...	...	12.4	...	...	17.6	...	...	17.6
C Real estate and business services	...	...	610.5	...	...	634.3	...	...	657.7
9 Community, social and personal services	...	...	101.5	...	...	110.0	...	...	110.3
Total, Industries	...	...	5867.2	...	...	5889.0	...	...	5700.5
Producers of Government Services	...	...	545.0	...	...	546.2	...	...	558.3
Other Producers	...	...	79.2	...	...	82.9	...	...	86.6
Total	...	...	6491.4	...	...	6518.1	...	...	6345.4
Less: Imputed bank service charge	...	...	107.8	...	...	93.3	...	...	101.8
Import duties	...	...	336.9	...	...	340.6	...	...	234.1
Value added tax	...	...	...	...	...	...	...	...	...
Total	...	...	6720.5	...	...	6765.4	...	...	6477.7

Sudan

4.3 Cost Components of Value Added

Million Sudanese pounds — Fiscal year beginning 1 July

		1980					1981					
		Compensation of Employees	Capital Consumption	Net Operating Surplus	Indirect Taxes	Less: Subsidies Received	Value Added	Compensation of Employees	Capital Consumption	Net Operating Surplus	Indirect Taxes	Less: Subsidies Received	Value Added

All Producers

		CoE 80	CC 80	NOS 80	IT 80	Sub 80	VA 80	CoE 81	CC 81	NOS 81	IT 81	Sub 81	VA 81
1	Agriculture, hunting, forestry and fishing	434.3	52.0	1169.5	9.5	...	1665.3	669.5	69.9	1656.2	6.3	...	2401.9
	A Agriculture and hunting	382.2	48.1	1119.3	8.8	...	1558.4	601.6	64.6	1592.7	5.5	...	2264.4
	B Forestry and logging	35.4	2.2	44.8	0.5	...	82.9	44.2	2.8	55.8	0.6	...	103.4
	C Fishing	16.7	1.7	5.4	0.2	...	24.0	23.7	2.5	7.7	0.2	...	34.1
2	Mining and quarrying	2.7	0.4	0.9	0.1	...	4.1	2.4	0.4	0.8	0.1	...	3.7
	A Coal mining	...	...	...	...	...	...	...	...	...	...	...	...
	B Crude petroleum and natural gas production	...	...	...	...	...	...	...	...	...	...	...	...
	C Metal ore mining	...	...	...	...	...	...	...	...	...	...	...	...
	D Other mining	2.7	0.4	0.9	0.1	...	4.1	2.4	0.4	0.8	0.1	...	3.7
3	Manufacturing	108.8	35.1	156.1	94.6	...	394.6	133.0	75.6	156.2	101.3	...	466.1
	A Manufacture of food, beverages and tobacco	33.3	14.0	96.2	34.2	...	177.7	42.7	32.7	128.2	35.3	...	238.9
	B Textile, wearing apparel and leather industries	22.3	6.8	10.5	7.5	...	47.1	43.4	25.1	-22.2	7.3	...	53.6
	C Manufacture of wood and wood products, including furniture	6.1	0.9	10.3	0.6	...	17.9	4.1	0.8	5.0	0.6	...	10.5
	D Manufacture of paper and paper products, printing and publishing	6.5	2.0	6.0	2.3	...	16.8	6.4	1.5	1.1	2.7	...	11.7
	E Manufacture of chemicals and chemical petroleum, coal, rubber and plastic products	22.1	6.7	21.7	35.6	...	86.1	11.8	10.3	12.7	37.7	...	72.5
	F Manufacture of non-metallic mineral products, except products of petroleum and coal	8.5	1.5	4.9	2.8	...	17.7	5.8	1.7	11.3	3.4	...	22.2
	G Basic metal industries	1.4	0.6	1.1	2.3	...	5.4	1.9	0.3	2.0	2.0	...	6.2
	H Manufacture of fabricated metal products, machinery and equipment	8.1	2.3	3.5	9.1	...	23.0	16.3	3.1	17.8	12.0	...	49.2
	I Other manufacturing industries	0.5	0.3	1.9	0.2	...	2.9	0.6	0.1	0.3	0.3	...	1.3
4	Electricity, gas and water	51.9	5.1	12.4	-	...	69.4	66.7	7.0	2.7	-	...	76.4
	A Electricity, gas and steam	8.5	3.7	8.9	-	...	21.1	12.4	4.4	-3.0	-	...	13.8
	B Water works and supply	43.4	1.4	3.5	-	...	48.3	54.3	2.6	5.7	-	...	62.6
5	Construction	143.9	16.1	133.0	3.0	...	296.0	184.3	20.4	173.5	3.7	...	381.9
6	Wholesale and retail trade, restaurants and hotels	252.5	20.5	487.1	31.4	...	791.5	339.2	27.8	560.4	21.9	...	949.3
	A Wholesale and retail trade	242.9	16.4	466.7	27.7	...	753.7	327.7	23.2	538.3	17.7	...	906.9
	B Restaurants and hotels	9.6	4.1	20.4	3.7	...	37.8	11.5	4.6	22.1	4.2	...	42.4
	Restaurants	4.1	-	14.6	-	...	18.7	4.6	-	16.3	-	...	20.9
	Hotels and other lodging places	5.5	4.1	5.8	3.7	...	19.1	6.9	4.6	5.8	4.2	...	21.5
7	Transport, storage and communication	202.5	66.7	213.3	5.6	...	488.1	277.3	89.9	316.2	8.0	...	691.4
	A Transport and storage	188.0	66.6	212.2	5.5	...	472.3	259.6	89.8	315.0	8.0	...	672.4
	B Communication	14.5	0.1	1.1	0.1	...	15.8	17.7	0.1	1.2	-	...	19.0
8	Finance, insurance, real estate and business services	57.9	182.8	308.5	2.6	...	551.8	84.8	263.0	443.0	4.2	...	795.0
	A Financial institutions	33.2	2.5	86.3	-	...	122.0	39.9	4.1	128.1	-	...	172.1
	B Insurance	0.9	-	10.0	-	...	10.9	1.2	0.1	11.1	-	...	12.4
	C Real estate and business services	23.8	180.3	212.2	2.6	...	418.9	43.7	258.8	303.8	4.2	...	610.5
9	Community, social and personal services	27.6	1.6	41.8	1.0	...	72.0	47.0	5.7	40.0	1.4	...	101.5
	Total, Industries [a]	1282.1	380.3	2522.6	147.8	...	4332.8	1804.8	559.7	3355.8	146.9	...	5867.2
	Producers of Government Services	417.0	77.0	-	-	...	494.0	464.7	80.3	-	-	...	545.0
	Other Producers	58.0	0.7	-	-	...	58.7	78.3	0.0			...	79.2
	Total [a]	1757.1	458.0	2522.6	147.8	...	4885.5	2347.8	640.9	3355.8	146.9	...	6491.4
	Less: Imputed bank service charge	...	...	79.6	...	...	79.6	...	...	107.8	...	...	107.8
	Import duties	...	...	...	280.0	...	280.0	...	...	...	336.9	...	336.9
	Value added tax	...	...	...	...	...	...	...	...	...	...	...	...
	Total [a]	1757.1	458.0	2443.0	427.8	...	5085.9	2347.8	640.9	3248.0	483.8	...	6720.5

Sudan

4.3 Cost Components of Value Added

Million Sudanese pounds — Fiscal year beginning 1 July

	Compensation of Employees	Capital Consumption	Net Operating Surplus	Indirect Taxes	Less: Subsidies Received	Value Added	Compensation of Employees	Capital Consumption	Net Operating Surplus	Indirect Taxes	Less: Subsidies Received	Value Added
	1982						1983					

All Producers

1 Agriculture, hunting, forestry and fishing	788.2	110.8	1880.5	8.7	...	2788.2	1062.6	135.0	2130.5	11.3	...	3339.4
A Agriculture and hunting	708.2	104.7	1803.7	7.7	...	2624.3	960.4	126.9	2038.7	10.1	...	3136.1
B Forestry and logging	54.2	3.4	68.4	0.7	...	126.7	62.5	3.9	78.9	0.8	...	146.1
C Fishing	25.8	2.7	8.4	0.3	...	37.2	39.7	4.2	12.9	0.4	...	57.2
2 Mining and quarrying	3.3	0.5	1.2	0.1	...	5.1	3.6	0.5	1.3	0.1	...	5.5
A Coal mining	...	...	...	...	...	...	...	...	...	...	...	...
B Crude petroleum and natural gas production	...	...	...	...	...	...	...	...	...	...	...	...
C Metal ore mining	...	...	...	...	...	...	...	...	...	...	...	...
D Other mining	3.3	0.5	1.2	0.1	...	5.1	3.6	0.5	1.3	0.1	...	5.5
3 Manufacturing	199.6	114.2	232.2	124.2	...	670.2	261.4	157.9	310.1	140.3	...	869.7
A Manufacture of food, beverages and tobacco	60.4	46.3	181.3	42.7	...	330.7	87.8	67.6	262.6	50.3	...	468.3
B Textile, wearing apparel and leather industries	68.0	40.5	-24.2	3.0	...	87.3	82.4	56.3	-40.4	3.4	...	101.7
C Manufacture of wood and wood products, including furniture	5.4	0.8	6.8	0.4	...	13.4	6.7	1.2	8.9	1.3	...	18.1
D Manufacture of paper and paper products, printing and publishing	11.3	2.6	1.9	1.4	...	17.2	12.1	2.8	2.0	1.9	...	18.8
E Manufacture of chemicals and chemical petroleum, coal, rubber and plastic products	17.9	15.6	19.2	58.0	...	110.7	21.9	19.1	23.4	60.2	...	124.6
F Manufacture of non-metallic mineral products, except products of petroleum and coal	11.4	3.4	20.9	4.6	...	40.3	22.9	5.3	25.3	4.4	...	57.9
G Basic metal industries	3.4	0.6	3.5	2.9	...	10.4	4.8	0.9	4.8	5.4	...	15.9
H Manufacture of fabricated metal products, machinery and equipment	20.9	4.0	22.8	10.7	...	58.4	21.6	4.1	23.5	12.8	...	62.0
I Other manufacturing industries	0.9	0.4	-	0.5	...	1.8	1.2	0.6	-	0.6	...	2.4
4 Electricity, gas and water	86.1	18.5	-11.0	-	...	93.6	118.3	21.5	35.5	-	...	175.3
A Electricity, gas and steam	15.2	13.3	-16.3	-	...	12.2	20.0	15.0	24.5	-	...	59.5
B Water works and supply	70.9	5.2	5.3	-	...	81.4	98.3	6.5	11.0	-	...	115.8
5 Construction	287.7	33.2	278.0	6.0	...	604.9	325.9	31.7	303.2	5.9	...	666.7
6 Wholesale and retail trade, restaurants and hotels	489.5	33.7	856.2	39.0	...	1418.4	573.1	36.2	1317.1	51.2	...	1978.6
A Wholesale and retail trade	469.6	29.9	829.6	34.2	...	1363.3	547.5	31.9	1283.2	45.9	...	1909.5
B Restaurants and hotels	19.9	3.8	26.6	4.8	...	55.1	25.6	4.3	33.9	5.3	...	69.1
Restaurants	13.0	1.1	14.0	0.3	...	28.4	17.3	1.5	18.6	0.4	...	37.8
Hotels and other lodging places	6.9	2.7	12.6	4.5	...	26.7	8.3	2.8	15.3	4.9	...	31.3
7 Transport, storage and communication	351.1	129.0	439.4	7.6	...	927.1	405.4	153.6	505.5	7.4	...	1071.9
A Transport and storage	339.1	128.5	432.0	7.6	...	907.2	391.5	152.1	497.7	7.4	...	1048.7
B Communication	12.0	0.5	7.4	-	...	19.9	13.9	1.5	7.8	-	...	23.2
8 Finance, insurance, real estate and business services	120.3	408.4	624.6	6.0	...	1159.3	155.6	481.8	736.6	9.0	...	1383.0
A Financial institutions	44.6	5.9	170.8	0.1	...	221.4	64.0	9.0	186.2	0.5	...	259.7
B Insurance	2.2	0.2	12.8	-	...	15.2	2.9	0.3	18.4	-	...	21.6
C Real estate and business services	73.5	402.3	441.0	5.9	...	922.7	88.7	472.5	532.0	8.5	...	1101.7
9 Community, social and personal services	56.8	7.1	74.2	1.9	...	140.0	72.0	10.7	95.0	2.3	...	180.0
Total, Industries [a]	2382.6	855.4	4375.3	193.5		7806.8	2977.9	1028.9	5435.8	227.5		9670.1
Producers of Government Services	593.9	155.7	-	-		749.6	767.8	214.7	-	-		982.5
Other Producers	107.5	1.2	-	-		108.7	149.4	1.4	-	-		150.8
Total [a]	3084.0	1012.3	4375.3	193.5		8665.1	3895.1	1245.0	5435.8	227.5		10803.4
Less: Imputed bank service charge	...	...	132.9	...		132.9	...	...	142.4	...		142.4
Import duties	...	...	...	653.7		653.7	...	...	...	668.4		668.4
Value added tax	...	...	...	...		...	...	...	...	...		...
Total [a]	3084.0	1012.3	4242.4	847.2		9185.9	3895.1	1245.0	5293.4	895.9		11329.4

a) Column 4 refers to indirect taxes less subsidies received.

Suriname

Source. Reply to the United Nations National Accounts Questionnaire from the Algemeen Bureau Voor de Statistiek, Parmaribo. The official estimates based on the present SNA are published by the Bureau in 'Nationale Rekeningen van Suriname'.

General note. The estimates shown in the following table have been prepared in accordance with the United Nations System of National Accounts so far as the existing data would permit.

1.1 Expenditure on the Gross Domestic Product, in Current Prices

Million Suriname guilders

	1970	1975	1977	1978	1979	1980	1981	1982	1983	1984	1985	1986
1 Government final consumption expenditure	...	194.9	282.0	335.1	342.7	338.5	430.7	520.1	437.2	498.8	588.5	732.5
2 Private final consumption expenditure	...	491.6	609.3	692.5	870.3	928.3	1060.9	1102.3	1331.2	1111.8	1050.3	917.8
3 Gross capital formation	...	300.9	478.8	477.3	357.3	420.6	555.0	507.3	275.6	203.9	137.0	94.3
A Increase in stocks	...	49.0	101.6	87.2	16.2	78.3	73.6	-8.8	-81.9	-110.1	-157.8	...
B Gross fixed capital formation	...	252.0	377.2	390.1	341.1	342.2	481.4	516.1	357.6	314.0	294.7	...
Residential buildings	...											...
Non-residential buildings	...	111.5	187.1	192.6	175.4	211.7	229.2	254.0	187.4	181.2	182.0	...
Other construction and land improvement etc.	...											...
Other	...	140.4	190.1	197.5	165.7	130.5	252.2	262.2	170.1	132.8	112.7	...
4 Exports of goods and services	...	578.0	707.0	814.0	917.0	1094.2	1009.8	909.5	775.5	749.4	639.8	569.4
5 Less: Imports of goods and services	...	634.0	795.0	848.0	922.0	1179.2	1258.1	1190.8	1032.8	819.1	674.3	562.9
Equals: Gross Domestic Product	...	930.8	1282.7	1471.0	1565.3	1602.3	1798.3	1848.8	1786.8	1744.8	1741.3	1751.1

1.3 Cost Components of the Gross Domestic Product

Million Suriname guilders

	1970	1975	1977	1978	1979	1980	1981	1982	1983	1984	1985	1986
1 Indirect taxes, net	...	195.8	180.6	234.9	226.3	247.7	269.6	245.1	226.4	214.1	183.0	146.5
A Indirect taxes	...	224.0	216.6	264.9	251.2	273.8	298.7	277.9	259.2	245.2	204.0	178.0
B Less: Subsidies	...	28.2	36.0	30.0	24.9	26.1	29.1	32.8	32.8	31.1	21.0	31.5
2 Consumption of fixed capital	...	91.0	134.1	145.6	168.4	171.6	186.4	182.3	182.5	173.0	174.6	180.8
3 Compensation of employees paid by resident producers to:	...	400.9	580.3	673.5	718.8	796.6	900.6	1076.2	1119.3	1160.5	1199.3	1192.8
4 Operating surplus	...	243.1	387.7	416.9	451.9	386.6	441.7	345.2	258.6	197.2	184.4	231.0
Equals: Gross Domestic Product	...	930.8	1282.7	1471.0	1565.3	1602.3	1798.3	1848.8	1786.8	1744.8	1741.3	1751.1

1.7 External Transactions on Current Account, Summary

Million Suriname guilders

	1970	1975	1977	1978	1979	1980	1981	1982	1983	1984	1985	1986
Payments to the Rest of the World												
1 Imports of goods and services	...	634.4	794.5	847.5	921.6	1179.2	1258.1	1190.8	1032.8	819.1	674.3	562.9
A Imports of merchandise c.i.f.	...	471.6	642.7	681.3	733.5	900.3	1013.7	921.2	803.7	617.3	532.9	425.7
B Other	...	162.8	151.8	166.2	188.1	278.9	244.4	269.6	229.1	201.8	141.4	137.2
2 Factor income to the rest of the world	...	46.1	74.2	70.1	98.9	76.4	41.7	51.6	49.6	6.4	5.8	8.1
A Compensation of employees	...	7.0	6.3	6.7	8.2	7.5	6.6	5.4	2.8	2.2	1.7	1.4
B Property and entrepreneurial income	...	39.1	67.9	63.4	90.7	68.9	35.1	46.2	46.8	4.2	4.1	6.7
3 Current transfers to the rest of the world	...	14.8	15.4	15.9	15.8	22.6	20.2	25.3	31.8	24.8	15.7	12.6
4 Surplus of the nation on current transactions	...	-85.2	-144.8	-82.1	-66.1	-104.6	-218.7	-273.7	-291.7	-80.4	-44.5	-7.5
Payments to the Rest of the World and Surplus of the Nation on Current Transactions	...	610.1	739.3	851.4	970.2	1174.2	1101.3	994.0	822.5	769.9	651.3	576.1
Receipts From The Rest of the World												
1 Exports of goods and services	...	577.7	707.2	813.6	916.7	1094.2	1009.8	909.5	775.5	749.4	639.8	569.4
A Exports of merchandise f.o.b.	...	495.3	617.9	702.4	792.7	918.2	845.7	765.1	654.7	650.8	560.8	524.6
B Other	...	82.4	89.3	112.0	124.0	176.0	164.1	144.4	120.8	98.6	79.0	44.8
2 Factor income from rest of the world	...	20.8	12.9	14.9	25.2	45.7	64.7	63.9	29.5	8.9	4.9	2.9
A Compensation of employees	...	2.7	1.0	1.3	1.3	1.2	1.9	0.7	1.4	1.2	1.0	0.1
B Property and entrepreneurial income	...	18.1	11.9	13.6	23.9	44.5	62.8	63.2	28.1	7.7	3.9	2.8
3 Current transfers from rest of the world	...	11.6	19.2	22.9	28.3	34.3	26.8	20.6	17.5	11.6	6.6	3.8
Receipts from the Rest of the World on Current Transactions	...	610.1	739.3	851.4	970.2	1174.2	1101.3	994.0	822.5	769.9	651.3	576.1

Suriname

1.10 Gross Domestic Product by Kind of Activity, in Current Prices

Million Suriname guilders

	1970	1975	1977	1978	1979	1980	1981	1982	1983	1984	1985	1986
1 Agriculture, hunting, forestry and fishing	...	58.5	92.1	91.7	116.0	122.7	140.1	144.3	126.9	134.5	142.7	166.0
2 Mining and quarrying	...	90.6	103.2	113.3	125.0	96.8	123.6	132.0	95.7	92.7	94.6	78.0
3 Manufacturing	...	152.3	202.9	225.3	239.6	249.1	271.2	225.8	195.3	197.4	206.6	212.9
4 Electricity, gas and water	...	22.5	34.2	46.7	62.1	87.1	73.4	69.7	92.9	88.0	66.4	50.4
5 Construction	...	33.9	127.2	104.2	102.6	88.6	106.8	110.2	99.7	106.5	97.2	101.9
6 Wholesale and retail trade, restaurants and hotels	...	142.4	200.9	246.8	270.9	273.3	286.7	314.5	310.6	271.2	267.8	267.3
7 Transport, storage and communication	...	48.3	61.4	82.5	77.8	84.1	98.6	100.2	106.2	111.4	127.7	137.0
8 Finance, insurance, real estate and business services	...	82.0	111.8	138.5	160.4	176.5	219.7	222.9	202.5	204.4	239.7	258.0
9 Community, social and personal services [a]	...	13.1	14.6	17.4	19.1	21.9	26.4	29.5	32.1	25.2	21.0	24.9
Total, Industries	...	643.6	948.2	1066.4	1173.5	1200.1	1346.4	1349.9	1261.8	1231.3	1263.7	1297.2
Producers of Government Services	...	118.4	182.3	210.9	221.6	225.9	276.1	346.3	373.9	374.1	383.8	411.1
Other Producers [a]	...	...	...	...	...	...	...	...	...	...	...	...
Subtotal [b]	...	761.9	1130.5	1277.3	1395.0	1425.9	1622.5	1696.2	1635.7	1605.4	1647.5	1708.3
Less: Imputed bank service charge	...	27.0	28.4	41.2	56.0	71.3	93.9	92.5	75.3	74.7	89.3	103.6
Plus: Import duties	...	...	...	...	...	...	...	...	...	...	...	...
Plus: Value added tax	...	...	...	...	...	...	...	...	...	...	...	...
Plus: Other adjustments [c]	...	195.8	180.6	234.9	226.3	247.7	269.6	245.1	226.4	214.1	183.4	146.5
Equals: Gross Domestic Product	...	930.8	1282.7	1471.0	1565.3	1602.3	1798.3	1848.8	1786.8	1744.8	1741.6	1751.2

a) Item 'Other producers' is included in item 'Community, social and personal services'.
b) Gross domestic product in factor values.
c) Item 'Other adjustments' refers to indirect taxes net of subsidies.

1.11 Gross Domestic Product by Kind of Activity, in Constant Prices

Million Suriname guilders

	1970	1975	1977	1978	1979	1980	1981	1982	1983	1984	1985	1986
					At constant prices of:1980							
1 Agriculture, hunting, forestry and fishing	...	96.9	115.4	110.2	121.8	122.7	138.9	134.7	122.9	127.6	129.4	134.4
2 Mining and quarrying	...	161.7	145.3	151.1	134.4	96.8	102.6	80.6	60.4	77.3	87.3	96.6
3 Manufacturing	...	262.1	277.3	295.0	278.4	249.1	256.1	214.0	193.6	187.5	199.6	196.9
4 Electricity, gas and water	...	50.8	70.7	77.3	86.0	87.1	78.0	63.3	64.0	63.9	59.0	53.0
5 Construction	...	56.5	153.6	116.3	105.0	88.6	106.3	104.5	94.4	98.1	87.0	77.2
6 Wholesale and retail trade, restaurants and hotels	...	236.1	279.8	318.5	306.8	273.3	263.8	269.7	255.2	214.9	191.3	161.0
7 Transport, storage and communication	...	77.3	86.9	95.6	83.6	84.1	82.4	84.1	90.6	93.0	105.0	109.4
8 Finance, insurance, real estate and business services	...	138.6	145.5	166.5	168.2	176.5	216.2	197.2	175.1	170.2	194.5	193.5
9 Community, social and personal services [a]	...	21.9	20.3	22.3	21.7	21.9	24.3	25.4	26.3	20.0	15.0	15.0
Total, Industries	...	1101.9	1294.9	1352.7	1306.0	1200.1	1268.6	1173.5	1082.5	1052.5	1068.1	1037.0
Producers of Government Services	...	173.3	224.2	259.5	221.6	225.9	276.1	298.5	322.3	322.5	330.9	354.4
Other Producers [a]	...	...	...	...	...	...	...	...	...	...	...	...
Subtotal	...	1275.2	1519.1	1612.2	1527.5	1425.9	1544.7	1472.0	1404.8	1375.0	1399.0	1391.4
Less: Imputed bank service charge	...	45.6	40.0	52.5	59.7	71.3	90.1	75.6	56.2	52.6	62.4	62.4
Plus: Import duties	...	...	...	...	...	...	...	...	...	...	...	...
Plus: Value added tax	...	...	...	...	...	...	...	...	...	...	...	...
Equals: Gross Domestic Product [b]	...	1229.6	1479.0	1559.7	1467.9	1354.6	1454.6	1396.4	1348.6	1322.4	1336.6	1329.0

a) Item 'Other producers' is included in item 'Community, social and personal services'.
b) Gross domestic product in factor values.

1.12 Relations Among National Accounting Aggregates

Million Suriname guilders

	1970	1975	1977	1978	1979	1980	1981	1982	1983	1984	1985	1986
Gross Domestic Product	...	930.8	1282.7	1471.0	1565.3	1602.3	1798.3	1848.8	1786.8	1744.8	1741.3	1751.1
Plus: Net factor income from the rest of the world	...	-25.3	-61.3	-55.2	-73.7	-30.7	23.0	12.3	-20.1	2.5	-0.9	-5.2
Factor income from the rest of the world	...	20.8	12.9	14.9	25.2	45.7	64.7	63.9	29.5	8.9	4.9	2.9
Less: Factor income to the rest of the world	...	46.1	74.2	70.1	98.9	76.4	41.7	51.6	49.6	6.4	5.8	8.1
Equals: Gross National Product	...	905.5	1221.4	1415.8	1491.6	1571.6	1821.3	1861.1	1766.7	1747.3	1740.4	1745.9
Less: Consumption of fixed capital	...	91.0	134.1	145.6	168.4	171.6	186.4	182.3	182.5	173.0	174.6	180.8

Suriname

1.12 Relations Among National Accounting Aggregates
(Continued)

Million Suriname guilders

	1970	1975	1977	1978	1979	1980	1981	1982	1983	1984	1985	1986
Equals: National Income	...	814.5	1087.3	1270.2	1323.3	1400.1	1634.9	1678.8	1584.2	1574.3	1565.8	1565.1
Plus: Net current transfers from the rest of the world	...	-3.2	3.8	7.0	12.5	11.7	6.6	-4.7	-14.3	-13.2	-9.1	-8.8
Current transfers from the rest of the world	...	11.6	19.2	22.9	28.3	34.3	26.8	20.6	17.5	11.6	6.6	3.8
Less: Current transfers to the rest of the world	...	14.8	15.4	15.9	15.8	22.6	20.2	25.3	31.8	24.8	15.7	12.6
Equals: National Disposable Income	...	811.3	1091.1	1277.2	1335.8	1411.8	1641.5	1674.1	1569.9	1561.1	1556.7	1556.3
Less: Final consumption	...	686.5	891.3	1027.6	1213.0	1266.8	1491.6	1622.8	1768.4	1610.6	1638.8	1650.3
Equals: Net Saving	...	124.8	199.9	249.6	122.8	145.0	149.9	51.3	-198.5	-49.5	-82.1	-93.9
Less: Surplus of the nation on current transactions	...	-85.2	-144.8	-82.1	-66.1	-104.0	-218.7	-273.7	-291.7	-80.4	-44.5	-7.5
Equals: Net Capital Formation	...	210.0	344.7	331.7	188.9	249.0	368.6	325.0	93.2	30.9	-37.6	-86.4

Swaziland

Source. Reply to the United Nations National Accounts Questionnaire from the Central Statistical Office, Mbabane. Official estimates are published annually in 'National Accounts Report', issued by the same Office.

General note. The official estimates of Swaziland have been prepared by the Statistical Office to conform to the United Nations System of National Accounts so far as the existing data would permit.

1.1 Expenditure on the Gross Domestic Product, in Current Prices

Million Swaziland emalangeni — Fiscal year ending 30 June

	1970	1975	1977	1978	1979	1980	1981	1982	1983	1984	1985	1986
1 Government final consumption expenditure	10.8	36.8	54.2	70.2	74.9	103.9	133.8	141.0	142.3	179.4	...	...
2 Private final consumption expenditure [a]	38.9	102.8	146.9	153.3	249.2	286.9	360.2	394.9	547.4	536.1	...	...
3 Gross capital formation	19.5	39.6	71.1	141.9	148.1	171.6	155.5	176.2	107.3	152.4	...	...
A Increase in stocks	2.4	-2.0	3.0	-3.0	6.0	23.8	15.3	23.4	-5.7	16.0	...	...
B Gross fixed capital formation	17.1	41.6	68.1	144.9	142.1	147.8	140.2	152.8	113.1	136.4	...	...
4 Exports of goods and services [b]	56.0	155.4	172.8	186.4	218.2	325.7	388.0	416.8	400.6	450.3	...	...
5 Less: Imports of goods and services [bc]	48.4	121.3	181.5	256.7	344.2	465.9	536.6	582.2	610.0	663.0	...	...
Equals: Gross Domestic Product	76.8	213.3	263.5	295.2	346.2	422.1	500.9	546.7	587.7	655.5	...	...

a) Item 'Private final consumption expenditure' shows significant increases from 1975 due to the sharp increases in salary. Estimates also include errors and omissions.
b) The estimates for imports and exports of goods and services and for the External Transaction Account are on calendar year basis.
c) The data on imports are adjusted for timing differences and therefore do not agree with the data shown in the External Transactions on Current Account table.

1.2 Expenditure on the Gross Domestic Product, in Constant Prices

Million Swaziland emalangeni — Fiscal year ending 30 June

	1970	1975	1977	1978	1979	1980	1981	1982	1983	1984	1985	1986
	\multicolumn{12}{c}{At constant prices of:1970}											
1 Government final consumption expenditure	10.8	19.6	...	...	...	...	...	...	...	...	...	...
2 Private final consumption expenditure	38.9	73.6	...	...	...	...	...	...	...	...	...	...
3 Gross capital formation	19.5	44.4	...	...	...	...	...	...	...	...	...	...
A Increase in stocks	2.4	3.9	...	...	...	...	...	...	...	...	...	...
B Gross fixed capital formation	17.1	40.5	...	...	...	...	...	...	...	...	...	...
4 Exports of goods and services	56.0	90.2	...	...	...	...	...	...	...	...	...	...
5 Less: Imports of goods and services	48.4	69.5	...	...	...	...	...	...	...	...	...	...
Equals: Gross Domestic Product	76.8	158.4	...	...	...	...	...	...	...	...	...	...

1.3 Cost Components of the Gross Domestic Product

Million Swaziland emalangeni — Fiscal year ending 30 June

	1970	1975	1977	1978	1979	1980	1981	1982	1983	1984	1985	1986
1 Indirect taxes, net	7.3	...	...	...	...	59.6	63.1	...	62.9	...	...	...
2 Consumption of fixed capital	7.7	...	...	...	...	26.1	33.6	...	46.6	...	...	...
3 Compensation of employees paid by resident producers to:	33.0	...	...	...	...	192.9	243.0	...	299.3	...	...	...
4 Operating surplus	28.8	...	...	...	...	143.5	161.2	...	178.9	...	...	...
Equals: Gross Domestic Product	76.8	...	...	...	...	422.1	500.9	...	587.7	...	...	...

1.4 General Government Current Receipts and Disbursements

Million Swaziland emalangeni — Fiscal year ending 30 June

	1970	1975	1977	1978	1979	1980	1981	1982	1983	1984	1985	1986
					Receipts							
1 Operating surplus	...	...	...	...	...	...	...	...	...	...	...	...
2 Property and entrepreneurial income	1.0	...	...	...	...	4.4	6.3	...	...	...	...	...
3 Taxes, fees and contributions	13.1	...	...	...	...	143.7	124.2	...	...	...	...	...
A Indirect taxes	7.3	...	...	...	...	103.4	78.4	...	...	...	...	...
B Direct taxes	5.3	...	...	...	...	37.4	43.8	...	...	...	...	...
C Social security contributions	-	...	...	...	...	-	-	...	...	...	...	...
D Compulsory fees, fines and penalties	0.5	...	...	...	...	2.9	2.0	...	...	...	...	...
4 Other current transfers	0.6	...	...	...	...	20.2	13.6	...	...	...	...	...
Total Current Receipts of General Government	14.8	...	...	...	...	168.3	144.1	...	...	...	...	...
					Disbursements							
1 Government final consumption expenditure	10.9	...	...	...	...	103.9	133.8	...	...	...	...	...

Swaziland

1.4 General Government Current Receipts and Disbursements
(Continued)

Million Swaziland emalangeni — Fiscal year ending 30 June

	1970	1975	1977	1978	1979	1980	1981	1982	1983	1984	1985	1986
A Compensation of employees	7.4	...	...	...	...	65.1	80.9	...	...	...	...	...
B Consumption of fixed capital	...	...	...	...	...	-	-	...	...	...	...	...
C Purchases of goods and services, net	...	...	...	...	...	38.8	52.9	...	...	...	...	...
D Less: Own account fixed capital formation	...	...	...	...	...	...	...	...	...	...	...	...
E Indirect taxes paid, net	...	...	...	...	...	...	...	...	...	...	...	...
2 Property income	1.9	...	...	...	...	0.4	9.4	...	...	...	...	...
3 Subsidies	-	...	...	...	...	...	...	...	...	...	...	...
4 Other current transfers	1.8	...	...	...	...	6.9	6.2	...	...	...	...	...
A Social security benefits	...	...	...	...	...	...	...	...	...	...	...	...
B Social assistance grants	0.7	...	...	...	...	...	...	...	...	...	...	...
C Other	1.1	...	...	...	...	...	...	...	...	...	...	...
5 Net saving	0.1	...	...	...	...	57.1	-5.3	...	...	...	...	...
Total Current Disbursements and Net Saving of General Government	14.8	...	...	...	...	168.3	144.1	...	...	...	...	...

1.7 External Transactions on Current Account, Summary

Million Swaziland emalangeni — Fiscal year ending 30 June

	1970	1975	1977	1978	1979	1980	1981	1982	1983	1984	1985	1986
Payments to the Rest of the World												
1 Imports of goods and services	48.4	121.3	181.5	256.7	344.6	465.9	536.6	582.2	610.0	662.7	...	...
A Imports of merchandise c.i.f.	...	94.4	144.2	199.1	271.8	405.5	442.7	469.0	516.3	535.5	...	...
B Other	...	26.9	37.3	57.6	72.9	60.4	93.9	113.2	93.7	127.2	...	...
2 Factor income to the rest of the world	10.7	17.1	15.6	56.0	31.1	27.9	38.0	27.4	38.8	40.3	...	...
A Compensation of employees	0.8	...	-	-	0.2	0.6	1.5	1.5	2.1	0.3	...	...
B Property and entrepreneurial income	9.9	17.1	15.6	56.0	30.9	27.3	36.5	25.9	36.7	40.0	...	...
3 Current transfers to the rest of the world	0.4	0.6	3.9	4.3	4.6	5.2	5.4	7.2	7.9	8.0	...	...
4 Surplus of the nation on current transactions	6.2	42.3	8.2	-84.7	-111.8	-95.7	-100.8	-82.9	-113.7	-61.3	...	...
Payments to the Rest of the World and Surplus of the Nation on Current Transactions [a]	65.7	181.3	209.2	232.3	268.5	403.3	479.2	533.9	543.0	649.7	...	...
Receipts From The Rest of the World												
1 Exports of goods and services	56.0	155.4	172.8	186.4	221.2	325.7	388.0	416.8	400.6	450.3	...	...
A Exports of merchandise f.o.b.	...	145.7	159.9	170.0	201.9	286.8	340.3	368.5	338.9	376.8	...	...
B Other	...	9.7	12.9	16.4	19.3	38.9	47.7	48.3	61.7	73.5	...	...
2 Factor income from rest of the world	1.3	12.4	8.6	9.8	8.9	22.1	43.8	42.9	69.4	102.6	...	...
A Compensation of employees	0.1	...	-	-	-	13.5	18.8	24.0	54.3	75.2	...	...
B Property and entrepreneurial income	1.2	12.4	8.6	9.8	8.9	8.6	25.0	18.9	15.1	27.4	...	...
3 Current transfers from rest of the world	8.4	13.5	27.7	36.0	38.4	55.5	47.4	74.3	72.9	96.8	...	...
Receipts from the Rest of the World on Current Transactions [a]	65.7	181.3	209.2	232.3	268.5	403.3	479.2	533.9	543.0	649.7	...	...

a) The estimates for imports and exports of goods and services and for the External Transaction Account are on calendar year basis.

1.10 Gross Domestic Product by Kind of Activity, in Current Prices

Million Swaziland emalangeni — Fiscal year ending 30 June

	1970	1975	1977	1978	1979	1980	1981	1982	1983	1984	1985	1986
1 Agriculture, hunting, forestry and fishing	18.1	...	...	...	...	90.2	104.7	102.1	111.2	131.0	...	...
2 Mining and quarrying	8.3	...	...	...	...	14.1	15.1	14.4	15.7	14.3	...	...
3 Manufacturing	9.1	...	...	...	...	79.6	89.1	100.8	89.7	108.5	...	...
4 Electricity, gas and water	1.6	...	...	...	...	4.4	7.2	8.7	9.3	10.3	...	...
5 Construction	1.8	...	...	...	...	16.2	21.4	24.8	25.3	26.9	...	...

Swaziland

1.10 Gross Domestic Product by Kind of Activity, in Current Prices
(Continued)

Million Swaziland emalangeni — Fiscal year ending 30 June

	1970	1975	1977	1978	1979	1980	1981	1982	1983	1984	1985	1986
6 Wholesale and retail trade, restaurants and hotels	10.5	...	...	...	...	35.6	42.3	54.8	63.8	68.1	...	...
7 Transport, storage and communication	5.6	...	...	...	...	20.5	24.8	32.0	36.8	42.1	...	...
8 Finance, insurance, real estate and business services	5.5	...	...	...	...	39.2	57.1	66.8	80.1	82.1	...	...
9 Community, social and personal services	1.9	...	...	...	...	5.7	7.4	9.4	10.8	12.5	...	...
Total, Industries	62.3	...	...	...	...	305.5	369.1	413.8	442.7	495.8	...	...
Producers of Government Services	7.4	...	...	...	...	61.1	76.0	85.4	97.2	103.7	...	...
Other Producers	...	...	...	...	...	6.7	9.3	9.1	10.5	12.0	...	...
Subtotal [a]	69.7	...	...	...	...	373.3	454.4	508.3	550.4	611.5	...	...
Less: Imputed bank service charge	0.8	...	...	...	...	10.9	16.5	23.6	25.5	28.0	...	...
Plus: Import duties	...	...	...	...	...	...	...	...	...	...	...	...
Plus: Value added tax	...	...	...	...	...	...	...	...	...	...	...	...
Plus: Other adjustments [b]	8.1	...	...	...	...	59.6	63.1	61.9	62.9	71.9	...	...
Equals: Gross Domestic Product	76.8	...	...	...	...	422.1	500.9	546.7	587.7	655.5	...	...

a) Gross domestic product in factor values.
b) Item 'Other adjustments' refers to indirect taxes net of subsidies.

1.11 Gross Domestic Product by Kind of Activity, in Constant Prices

Million Swaziland emalangeni — Fiscal year ending 30 June

	1970	1975	1977	1978	1979	1980	1981	1982	1983	1984	1985	1986
			At constant prices of:1980									
1 Agriculture, hunting, forestry and fishing	...	...	74.8	86.9	83.4	90.2	101.6	96.5	95.2	103.9	...	...
2 Mining and quarrying	...	...	15.3	15.4	14.5	14.1	14.6	12.8	10.7	10.8	...	...
3 Manufacturing	...	...	65.3	69.8	71.6	79.6	88.4	93.0	94.0	93.5	...	...
4 Electricity, gas and water	...	...	3.0	3.3	3.6	4.4	4.9	4.2	3.8	5.1	...	...
5 Construction	...	...	13.5	27.9	25.1	16.2	18.7	18.9	16.9	16.4	...	...
6 Wholesale and retail trade, restaurants and hotels	...	...	37.5	32.8	34.4	35.6	35.4	41.9	45.5	46.0	...	...
7 Transport, storage and communication	...	...	21.8	24.4	24.8	20.5	21.4	21.4	22.2	23.2	...	...
8 Finance, insurance, real estate and business services	...	...	33.9	35.7	37.6	39.2	41.9	42.4	43.0	43.5	...	...
9 Community, social and personal services	...	...	5.0	5.2	5.5	5.7	6.2	6.6	6.9	6.7	...	...
Total, Industries	...	...	270.1	301.4	300.5	305.5	333.1	337.7	338.2	349.1	...	...
Producers of Government Services	...	...	52.0	56.2	57.9	61.1	66.1	71.5	69.8	78.7	...	...
Other Producers	...	...	6.3	6.4	6.6	6.7	6.9	7.2	7.4	7.7	...	...
Subtotal [a]	...	...	328.4	364.1	365.0	373.3	406.1	416.4	415.4	435.5	...	...
Less: Imputed bank service charge	...	...	9.6	10.6	10.6	10.9	12.4	12.1	12.4	12.3	...	...
Plus: Import duties	...	...	...	...	...	...	...	...	...	...	...	...
Plus: Value added tax	...	...	...	...	...	...	...	...	...	...	...	...
Plus: Other adjustments [b]	...	...	74.1	49.5	56.0	59.6	57.5	48.8	44.8	47.4	...	...
Equals: Gross Domestic Product	...	...	392.8	403.0	410.2	422.1	451.1	453.0	447.8	470.6	...	...

a) Gross domestic product in factor values.
b) Item 'Other adjustments' refers to indirect taxes net of subsidies.

1.12 Relations Among National Accounting Aggregates

Million Swaziland emalangeni — Fiscal year ending 30 June

	1970	1975	1977	1978	1979	1980	1981	1982	1983	1984	1985	1986
Gross Domestic Product	76.8	213.4	263.5	295.2	346.2	422.1	500.9	546.7	587.7	655.5	...	...
Plus: Net factor income from the rest of the world	-9.4	-1.7	-2.8	-46.2	-22.2	-5.7	5.7	15.5	30.6	62.3	...	...
Factor income from the rest of the world	1.3	15.5	13.9	9.8	8.9	22.1	43.8	42.9	69.4	102.6	...	...
Less: Factor income to the rest of the world	10.7	17.2	16.7	56.0	31.1	27.9	38.0	27.4	38.8	40.3	...	...
Equals: Gross National Product	67.4	211.7	260.7	249.0	324.1	416.4	506.7	562.2	618.3	717.8	...	...
Less: Consumption of fixed capital	...	...	...	...	...	...	...	...	...	...	...	...

Swaziland

1.12 Relations Among National Accounting Aggregates
(Continued)

Million Swaziland emalangeni — Fiscal year ending 30 June

	1970	1975	1977	1978	1979	1980	1981	1982	1983	1984	1985	1986
Equals: National Income	...	...	...	...	...	...	...	...	...	...	...	...
Plus: Net current transfers from the rest of the world	8.0	9.8	19.6	31.7	33.8	50.3	42.0	67.1	65.0	88.8	...	...
Current transfers from the rest of the world	8.4	10.5	22.4	36.0	38.4	55.5	47.4	74.3	72.9	96.8	...	...
Less: Current transfers to the rest of the world	0.4	0.6	2.8	4.3	4.6	5.2	5.4	7.2	7.9	8.0	...	...
Equals: National Disposable Income [a]	75.4	221.5	280.3	280.7	357.9	466.7	548.7	629.2	683.3	806.6	...	...
Less: Final consumption	49.7	139.6	201.0	223.5	324.1	390.8	494.0	535.9	689.7	715.5	...	...
Equals: Net Saving [b]	25.7	81.9	79.3	57.2	33.7	75.9	54.7	93.3	-6.4	91.0	...	...
Less: Surplus of the nation on current transactions	...	...	...	-84.7	-111.8	-95.7	-100.8	-82.9	-113.7	-61.3	...	...
Equals: Net Capital Formation [c]	...	...	...	141.9	145.6	171.6	155.5	176.2	107.3	152.4	...	...

a) Item 'National disposable income' includes consumption of fixed capital.
b) Item 'Net saving' includes consumption of fixed capital.
c) Item 'Net capital formation' includes consumption of fixed capital.

2.9 Gross Capital Formation by Kind of Activity of Owner, ISIC Major Divisions, in Current Prices

Million Swaziland emalangeni — Fiscal year ending 30 June

	1980 Total Gross Capital Formation	1980 Increase in Stocks	1980 Gross Fixed Capital Formation	1981 Total Gross Capital Formation	1981 Increase in Stocks	1981 Gross Fixed Capital Formation	1983 Total Gross Capital Formation	1983 Increase in Stocks	1983 Gross Fixed Capital Formation
All Producers									
1 Agriculture, hunting, fishing and forestry	10.7	0.3	10.4	15.5	1.3	14.2	10.0	0.6	9.4
2 Mining and quarrying	2.6	1.5	1.1	2.3	1.2	1.1	-2.2	-2.5	0.3
3 Manufacturing	99.3	18.6	80.7	36.1	8.7	27.4	4.8	-6.3	11.1
4 Electricity, gas and water	1.8	-0.1	1.9	11.5	0.1	11.4	36.0	-	36.0
5 Construction	1.7	-0.4	2.1	5.9	0.3	5.6	0.6	-0.6	0.6
6 Wholesale and retail trade, restaurants and hotels	6.7	4.3	2.4	6.1	3.4	2.7	5.2	2.3	3.0
7 Transport, storage and communication	5.2	-0.5	5.7	10.6	-0.6	11.2	7.0	-0.1	7.1
8 Finance, insurance, real estate and business services	12.9	-	12.9	24.3	-	24.3	10.0	-	10.0
9 Community, social and personal services	0.7	0.1	0.6	1.4	0.8	0.6	1.0	0.4	0.6
Total Industries	141.6	23.8	117.8	113.7	15.2	98.5	72.4	-5.7	78.1
Producers of Government Services	30.1	-	30.1	39.7	-	39.7	33.7	-	33.7
Private Non-Profit Institutions Serving Households	-0.1	-	-0.1	2.1	-	2.1	1.3	-	1.3
Total	171.6	23.8	147.8	155.5	15.2	140.2	107.3	-5.7	113.1

4.1 Derivation of Value Added by Kind of Activity, in Current Prices

Million Swaziland emalangeni — Fiscal year ending 30 June

	1980 Gross Output	1980 Intermediate Consumption	1980 Value Added	1981 Gross Output	1981 Intermediate Consumption	1981 Value Added	1983 Gross Output	1983 Intermediate Consumption	1983 Value Added
All Producers									
1 Agriculture, hunting, forestry and fishing	140.2	50.1	90.2	163.0	58.3	104.7	183.5	72.3	111.2
A Agriculture and hunting	125.4	40.6	84.9	145.2	47.6	98.3	166.7	61.5	105.2
B Forestry and logging	14.8	9.5	5.3	17.8	10.7	6.4	16.8	10.8	6.1
C Fishing	...	...	...	...	...	...			
2 Mining and quarrying	23.9	9.8	14.1	25.8	10.7	15.1	26.7	11.0	15.7

Swaziland

4.1 Derivation of Value Added by Kind of Activity, in Current Prices
(Continued)

Million Swaziland emalangeni — Fiscal year ending 30 June

	1980 Gross Output	1980 Intermediate Consumption	1980 Value Added	1981 Gross Output	1981 Intermediate Consumption	1981 Value Added	1983 Gross Output	1983 Intermediate Consumption	1983 Value Added
3 Manufacturing	296.2	216.5	79.6	373.0	284.0	89.1	403.2	313.5	89.7
A Manufacture of food, beverages and tobacco	148.4	115.1	33.3	174.1	131.5	42.6	...	...	...
B Textile, wearing apparel and leather industries	12.5	10.3	2.2	21.7	19.3	2.4	...	...	...
C Manufacture of wood and wood products, including furniture	16.0	9.9	6.1	20.0	13.9	6.1	...	...	...
D Manufacture of paper and paper products, printing and publishing	60.8	36.4	24.4	63.7	45.7	18.0	...	...	...
E Manufacture of chemicals and chemical petroleum, coal, rubber and plastic products	35.5	26.9	8.5	55.6	43.7	11.9	...	...	...
F Manufacture of non-metallic mineral products, except products of petroleum and coal	3.1	2.2	0.9	6.7	5.4	1.3	...	...	...
G Basic metal industries	...	...	...	...	...	...	...	...	...
H Manufacture of fabricated metal products, machinery and equipment	19.2	15.2	4.0	30.8	24.2	6.6	...	...	...
I Other manufacturing industries	0.7	0.5	0.2	0.5	0.3	0.2	...	...	...
4 Electricity, gas and water	11.3	6.9	4.4	14.9	7.7	7.2	22.9	13.6	9.3
5 Construction	54.8	38.6	16.2	75.0	53.7	21.4	71.9	46.6	25.3
6 Wholesale and retail trade, restaurants and hotels	84.0	48.3	35.6	115.4	73.2	42.3	121.0	57.2	63.8
A Wholesale and retail trade	65.6	38.6	27.1	90.4	58.8	31.6	96.7	45.7	51.0
B Restaurants and hotels	18.4	9.8	8.6	25.1	14.4	10.7	24.3	11.5	12.8
7 Transport, storage and communication	45.8	25.3	20.5	64.5	39.7	24.8	83.2	46.5	36.8
A Transport and storage	39.7	22.4	17.3	53.5	34.3	19.2	69.4	41.1	28.3
B Communication	6.1	2.9	3.2	10.9	5.4	5.6	13.8	5.4	8.5
8 Finance, insurance, real estate and business services	61.8	22.6	39.2	83.1	26.0	57.1	107.3	27.2	80.1
A Financial institutions	28.6	16.4	12.3	37.9	15.7	22.2	36.9	10.9	26.0
B Insurance	3.1	1.8	1.4	4.3	2.4	1.9	8.7	2.8	6.0
C Real estate and business services	30.0	4.5	25.6	40.9	7.9	33.0	61.7	13.5	48.2
Real estate, except dwellings	5.4	1.2	4.3	10.0	2.0	8.0	20.7	5.8	14.8
Dwellings [a]	16.4	0.8	15.6	18.5	0.9	17.6	25.3	1.3	24.0
9 Community, social and personal services	11.8	6.0	5.7	15.3	7.9	7.4	24.2	13.4	10.8
A Sanitary and similar services	...	...	...	...	...	...	...	...	...
B Social and related community services	1.3	0.6	0.8	3.2	1.7	1.5	...	...	...
C Recreational and cultural services	2.7	1.3	1.4	3.3	1.6	1.7	...	...	...
D Personal and household services	7.7	4.2	3.5	8.9	4.6	4.2	...	...	...
Total, Industries	729.8	424.2	305.5	930.2	561.2	369.1	1043.9	601.3	442.7
Producers of Government Services	97.6	36.4	61.1	126.4	50.4	76.0	152.2	55.1	97.2
Other Producers	9.9	3.2	6.7	13.9	4.6	9.3	18.0	7.6	10.5
Total [b]	837.3	463.8	373.3	1070.5	616.2	454.4	1214.1	664.0	550.4
Less: Imputed bank service charge	...	-10.9	10.9	...	-16.5	16.5	...	-25.5	25.5
Import duties	...	...	...	...	...	...	...	...	...
Value added tax	...	...	...	...	...	...	...	...	...
Other adjustments [c]	59.6	...	59.6	63.1	...	63.1	62.9	...	62.9
Total	896.9	474.8	422.1	1133.6	632.7	500.9	1277.0	689.5	587.7

of which General Government:

1 Agriculture, hunting, forestry and fishing	...	...	...	...	...	...	...	...	...
2 Mining and quarrying	...	...	...	...	...	...	...	...	...
3 Manufacturing	...	...	...	...	...	...	...	...	...
4 Electricity, gas and water	...	...	...	...	...	...	...	...	...

Swaziland

4.1 Derivation of Value Added by Kind of Activity, in Current Prices
(Continued)

Million Swaziland emalangeni — Fiscal year ending 30 June

		1980			1981			1983	
	Gross Output	Intermediate Consumption	Value Added	Gross Output	Intermediate Consumption	Value Added	Gross Output	Intermediate Consumption	Value Added
5 Construction	5.5	2.9	2.7	5.9	2.6	3.3	...	...	...
6 Wholesale and retail trade, restaurants and hotels	...	...	...	...	...	...	...	...	...
7 Transport and communication	7.1	5.9	1.2	8.6	7.1	1.5	...	...	...
8 Finance, insurance, real estate and business services	...	...	...	...	...	...	...	...	...
9 Community, social and personal services	...	...	...	...	...	...	...	...	...
Total, Industries of General Government	12.6	8.8	3.9	14.5	9.7	4.8	...	...	...
Producers of Government Services	97.6	36.4	61.1	126.5	50.4	76.1	...	...	...
Total, General Government	110.3	45.2	65.1	141.0	60.1	80.9	...	...	...

a) Rented and owner-occupied dwellings are included in the category 'Dwelling' of item 'Finance, insurance, real estate and business services'.
b) Gross domestic product in factor values.
c) Item 'Other adjustments' refers to indirect taxes net of subsidies.

4.3 Cost Components of Value Added

Million Swaziland emalangeni — Fiscal year ending 30 June

		1980					1981				
	Compensation of Employees	Capital Consumption	Net Operating Surplus	Indirect Taxes	Less: Subsidies Received	Value Added	Compensation of Employees	Capital Consumption	Net Operating Surplus	Indirect Taxes	Less: Subsidies Received	Value Added

All Producers

	Comp. Empl.	Cap. Cons.	Net Op. Surp.	Ind. Taxes	Less Subs.	Val. Added	Comp. Empl.	Cap. Cons.	Net Op. Surp.	Ind. Taxes	Less Subs.	Val. Added
1 Agriculture, hunting, forestry and fishing	27.9	7.3	58.4	...	...	90.2	29.2	9.5	72.7	...	...	104.7
A Agriculture and hunting	22.0	6.1	60.2	...	...	84.9	23.2	8.5	72.6	...	...	98.3
B Forestry and logging	5.9	1.2	-1.8	...	...	5.3	6.0	1.0	-	...	...	6.4
C Fishing	...	...	...	...	...	...	...	...	...	...	...	...
2 Mining and quarrying	7.9	0.6	5.6	...	...	14.1	10.0	0.4	4.8	...	...	15.1
3 Manufacturing	30.3	9.2	40.1	...	...	79.6	38.9	10.8	39.4	...	...	89.1
A Manufacture of food, beverages and tobacco	13.0	5.0	15.3	...	...	33.3	16.2	5.1	21.3	...	...	42.6
B Textile, wearing apparel and leather industries	1.1	0.1	1.0	...	...	2.2	2.0	0.3	0.1	...	...	2.4
C Manufacture of wood and wood products, including furniture	2.6	0.4	3.1	...	...	6.1	4.0	0.3	1.8	...	...	6.1
D Manufacture of paper and paper products, printing and publishing	8.2	1.7	14.5	...	...	24.4	8.8	2.2	6.9	...	...	18.0
E Manufacture of chemicals and chemical petroleum, coal, rubber and plastic products	1.5	1.0	6.0	...	...	8.5	3.3	1.2	7.3	...	...	11.9
F Manufacture of non-metallic mineral products, except products of petroleum and coal	0.4	0.1	0.4	...	...	0.9	0.8	0.2	0.3	...	...	1.3
G Basic metal industries	...	...	...	...	...	...	...	...	...	...	...	...
H Manufacture of fabricated metal products, machinery and equipment	3.1	0.9	-	...	...	4.0	3.5	1.3	1.7	...	...	6.6
I Other manufacturing industries	0.3	-	-0.1	...	...	0.2	0.2	-	-	...	...	0.2
4 Electricity, gas and water	1.3	1.8	1.3	...	...	4.4	3.6	1.7	1.9	...	...	7.2
5 Construction	14.4	0.3	1.5	...	...	16.2	20.0	0.4	0.9	...	...	21.4
6 Wholesale and retail trade, restaurants and hotels	10.4	1.4	15.9	...	...	35.6	22.9	2.4	17.0	...	...	42.3
A Wholesale and retail trade	12.9	0.8	13.3	...	...	27.0	15.8	1.7	14.1	...	...	31.6
B Restaurants and hotels	5.5	0.6	2.6	...	...	8.6	7.1	0.6	2.9	...	...	10.7
7 Transport, storage and communication	10.0	3.3	7.1	...	...	20.5	12.4	4.7	7.8	...	...	24.8
A Transport and storage	8.2	2.7	6.4	...	...	17.3	10.2	3.5	5.5	...	...	19.2
B Communication	1.8	0.6	0.7	...	...	3.2	2.2	1.2	2.2	...	...	5.6
8 Finance, insurance, real estate and business services	10.8	1.4	27.1	...	...	39.2	15.7	3.0	38.5	...	...	57.1
A Financial institutions	6.9	0.9	4.5	...	...	12.3	9.5	1.9	10.8	...	...	22.2
B Insurance	0.6	-	0.8	...	...	1.4	0.8	-	1.1	...	...	1.9
C Real estate and business services	3.3	0.5	21.8	...	...	25.6	5.5	1.0	26.6	...	...	33.0
Real estate, except dwellings	...	...	...	...	...	...	0.4	0.7	6.8	...	...	7.9

Swaziland

4.3 Cost Components of Value Added
(Continued)

Million Swaziland emalangeni — Fiscal year ending 30 June

	1980						1981					
	Compensation of Employees	Capital Consumption	Net Operating Surplus	Indirect Taxes	Less: Subsidies Received	Value Added	Compensation of Employees	Capital Consumption	Net Operating Surplus	Indirect Taxes	Less: Subsidies Received	Value Added
Dwellings a	...	...	15.6	...	...	15.6	-	-	17.6	...	...	17.6
9 Community, social and personal services	4.2	0.5	1.0	...	...	5.7	5.1	0.7	1.6	...	...	7.4
A Sanitary and similar services	...	...	...	...	...	...	...	...	...	...	...	...
B Social and related community services	0.6	...	0.2	...	...	0.8	...	...	...	...	...	...
C Recreational and cultural services	0.9	0.5	-	...	...	1.5	...	...	...	...	...	...
D Personal and household services	2.7	...	0.8	...	...	3.5	...	...	...	...	...	...
Total, Industries	125.2	25.9	157.8	...	...	305.5	157.8	33.4	184.5	...	...	369.1
Producers of Government Services	61.1	-	-	...	...	61.1	76.0	-	-	...	...	76.0
Other Producers	6.6	0.1	-	...	...	6.7	9.2	0.1	-	...	...	9.3
Total b	192.9	26.0	157.8	...	...	373.7	243.0	33.5	184.5	...	...	454.4
Less: Imputed bank service charge	...	...	10.9	...	...	10.9	-	-	16.5	...	...	16.5
Import duties	...	...	...	...	...	...	...	...	...	...	...	...
Value added tax	...	...	...	...	...	...	...	...	...	...	...	...
Other adjustments c	...	...	...	...	...	59.6	...	...	...	...	...	63.1
Total	192.9	26.0	146.9	59.6	...	422.1	243.0	33.5	168.0	109.4	...	500.9

of which General Government:

1 Agriculture, hunting, forestry and fishing	...	...	...	...	...	...	...	...	...	...	...	...
2 Mining and quarrying	...	...	...	...	...	...	...	...	...	...	...	...
3 Manufacturing	...	...	...	...	...	...	...	...	...	...	...	...
4 Electricity, gas and water	...	...	...	...	...	...	...	...	...	...	...	...
5 Construction	2.7	-	-	...	...	2.7	3.4	...	...	...	...	3.4
6 Wholesale and retail trade, restaurants and hotels	...	...	...	...	...	...	...	...	...	...	...	...
7 Transport and communication	1.2	-	-	...	...	1.2	1.5	...	...	...	...	1.5
8 Finance, insurance, real estate & business services	...	...	...	...	...	...	...	...	...	...	...	...
9 Community, social and personal services	...	...	...	...	...	...	...	...	...	...	...	...
Total, Industries of General Government	3.9	-	-	...	...	3.9	4.9	...	...	...	...	4.9
Producers of Government Services	61.1	...	...	...	...	61.1	76.0	...	...	...	...	76.0
Total, General Government	65.0	...	...	...	...	65.0	80.9	...	...	...	...	80.9

	1983					
	Compensation of Employees	Capital Consumption	Net Operating Surplus	Indirect Taxes	Less: Subsidies Received	Value Added

All Producers

1 Agriculture, hunting, forestry and fishing	30.1	9.9	71.2	...	...	111.2
A Agriculture and hunting	25.0	9.1	71.1	...	...	105.2
B Forestry and logging	5.1	0.8	0.1	...	...	6.1
C Fishing	...	...	...	...	...	...
2 Mining and quarrying	9.8	0.2	5.8	...	...	15.7

Swaziland

4.3 Cost Components of Value Added
(Continued)

Million Swaziland emalangeni
Fiscal year ending 30 June

	Compensation of Employees	Capital Consumption	Net Operating Surplus	Indirect Taxes	Less: Subsidies Received	Value Added
	1983					
3 Manufacturing	48.3	13.0	28.4	...	...	89.7
A Manufacture of food, beverages and tobacco	...	...	...	...	...	...
B Textile, wearing apparel and leather industries	...	...	...	...	...	...
C Manufacture of wood and wood products, including furniture	...	...	...	...	...	...
D Manufacture of paper and paper products, printing and publishing	...	...	...	...	...	...
E Manufacture of chemicals and chemical petroleum, coal, rubber and plastic products	...	...	...	...	...	...
F Manufacture of non-metallic mineral products, except products of petroleum and coal	...	...	...	...	...	...
G Basic metal industries	...	...	...	...	...	...
H Manufacture of fabricated metal products, machinery and equipment	...	...	...	...	...	...
I Other manufacturing industries	...	...	...	...	...	...
4 Electricity, gas and water	4.3	2.1	2.9	...	...	9.3
5 Construction	21.6	2.0	1.7	...	...	25.3
6 Wholesale and retail trade, restaurants and hotels	32.1	2.8	28.9	...	...	63.8
A Wholesale and retail trade	22.4	2.0	26.7	...	...	51.0
B Restaurants and hotels	9.8	0.8	2.2	...	...	12.8
7 Transport, storage and communication	17.3	9.2	10.2	...	...	36.8
A Transport and storage	14.5	7.2	6.6	...	...	28.3
B Communication	2.8	2.1	3.6	...	...	8.5
8 Finance, insurance, real estate and business services	21.4	6.4	52.3	...	...	80.1
A Financial institutions	13.1	4.1	8.8	...	...	26.0
B Insurance	1.1	0.1	4.8	...	...	6.0
C Real estate and business services	7.2	2.2	38.7	...	...	48.2
Real estate, except dwellings	0.9	1.8	12.2	...	...	14.8
Dwellings [a]	-	-	24.0	...	...	24.0
9 Community, social and personal services	6.8	0.7	3.2	...	...	10.8
A Sanitary and similar services	...	...	...	...	...	...
B Social and related community services	...	...	...	...	...	...
C Recreational and cultural services	...	...	...	...	...	...
D Personal and household services	...	...	...	...	...	...
Total, Industries	191.7	46.3	204.6	...	...	442.7
Producers of Government Services	97.2	-	-	...	...	97.2
Other Producers	10.2	0.2	-	...	...	10.5
Total [b]	299.3	46.6	204.6	...	...	550.4
Less: Imputed bank service charge	-	-	25.5			25.5
Import duties	...	...	...	...	...	...
Value added tax	...	...	...	...	...	...
Other adjustments [c]	...	...	...	...	...	62.9
Total	299.3	46.6	178.9	62.9	...	587.7

of which General Government:

1 Agriculture, hunting, forestry and fishing	...	...	...	...	...	
2 Mining and quarrying	...	...	...	...	...	
3 Manufacturing	...	...	...	...	...	
4 Electricity, gas and water	...	...	...	...	...	

Swaziland

4.3 Cost Components of Value Added
(Continued)

Million Swaziland emalangeni   Fiscal year ending 30 June

	Compensation of Employees	Capital Consumption	Net Operating Surplus	Indirect Taxes	Less: Subsidies Received	Value Added
	1983					
5 Construction	...	...	...	...	...	...
6 Wholesale and retail trade, restaurants and hotels	...	...	...	...	...	...
7 Transport and communication	...	...	...	...	...	...
8 Finance, insurance, real estate & business services	...	...	...	...	...	...
9 Community, social and personal services	...	...	...	...	...	...
Total, Industries of General Government	...	...	...	...	...	...
Producers of Government Services	...	...	...	...	...	...
Total, General Government	...	...	...	...	...	...

a) Rented and owner-occupied dwellings are included in the category 'Dwelling' of item 'Finance, insurance, real estate and business services'.
b) Gross domestic product in factor values.
c) Item 'Other adjustments' refers to indirect taxes net of subsidies.

Sweden

General note. The preparation of national accounts statistics in Sweden is undertaken by Statistics, Sweden. The annual estimates of certain standard tables are published in a series of Statistical Reports entitled 'Nationalrakenskaper - National Accounts'. Supplementary and supporting tables are published separately in a set of five appendixes. Each series of the Statistical Reports contains some methodological notes. However, the most detailed description of the sources and methods used for the national accounts estimation at current and constant prices is found in 'Reports on Statistical Coordination 1979:11. Swedish National Accounts System. Sources and Methods'. The Swedish National Accounts System corresponds closely to the United Nations System of National Accounts. Separate input-output tables have been published for the years 1964, 1968, 1969, 1975 and 1980 in 'Input-Output tabeller for Sverige'. The following tables have been prepared from successive replies to the United Nations national accounts questionnaire. When the scope and coverage of the estimates differ for conceptual or statistical reasons from the definitions and classifications recommended in SNA, a footnote is indicated to the relevant tables.

Sources and methods:

(a) Gross domestic product. Gross domestic product is estimated mainly through the expenditure approach.

(b) Expenditure on the gross domestic product. All components of GDP by expenditure type are estimated through the expenditure approach. Government final consumption expenditure is calculated from the cost side. The calculations for the central government are based on the semi-annual groupings made by the National Accounting and Audit Bureau and on reports of the central government revenue. For local government the calculations are based on finance statistics compiled by Statistics Sweden. Private consumption expenditure consists of approximately 130 items, for which a number of estimation methods are used. The Swedish National Agriculture Marketing Board is the source for the estimate of food consumption, and for most of the remaining goods, the estimates are based on a combination of the Family Expenditure Survey and turnover statistics of retail trade. Gross capital formation estimates are derived from investment inquiries from the different sectors of economic activity and from government accounts data. Exports and imports of goods and services are mainly estimated from foreign trade statistics, and balance of payment statistics of the Swedish Central Bank. For the constant price estimates, price deflation is used for most of the expenditure items, the current values being deflated by various price indexes such as weighted consumer price indexes, adjusted export and import price indexes, price indexes for different capital goods, etc. Components of government consumption expenditure are deflated by relevant price indexes, except wages and salaries which are extrapolated by employment indexes.

(c) Cost-structure of the gross domestic product. In estimating the cost-structure components of GDP, compensation of employees is based on adjusted tax assessments and income statistics, adding employers' contributions to insurance and pensions from compilations in the insurance sector. Consumption of fixed capital is calculated from capital stock values obtained by the perpetual inventory method. Data on indirect taxes and subsidies are based on local government finance statistics and information from the National Accounting and Audit Bureau. Operating surplus, however, is arrived at as a residual.

(d) Gross domestic product by kind of economic activity. The table of gross domestic product by kind of economic activity is calculated in basic values. The production approach is used to estimate value added of the majority of industries. The income approach is applied to most government services as well as to the trade sector, construction and other private services. Statistics of the Agricultural Marketing Board is the main source of information for the estimation of agricultural production. Estimates of output and intermediate consumption of mining and manufacturing and electricity, gas and water are based on annual censuses. Special calculations are made to include establishments not included in the census. The annual statistics of financial accounting of enterprises as well as employment data obtained from the census of population are used for the trade sector. For the transport sector, the estimates are mainly based on official statistics and on financial accounting statistics. The output value of letting of dwellings and use of owner-occupied dwellings correspond to the item housing in private consumption. Input estimates are based on cost data from surveys of real estate costs. The financial statistics of enterprises are the main source for compiling estimates of the business services sector. Input is estimated on the basis of a fixed input-output relationship at constant prices. For government services the source is the National Accounting and Audit Bureau's statistics of government income and expenditure. For the constant price estimates, the general approach for all industries is double deflation. For the mining and manufacturing sectors deflation has been used at the level of establishment with previous year as base-year. For agriculture, forestry and fishing, current output quantities are revalued at base-year prices, while base-year values are extrapolated by employment figures for financing, insurance and producers of government services. For other industries different kinds of price indexes have been used, such as wholesale indexes, implicit price indexes, consumer price indexes, etc.

1.1 Expenditure on the Gross Domestic Product, in Current Prices

Million Swedish kronor

		1970	1975	1977	1978	1979	1980	1981	1982	1983	1984	1985	1986
1	Government final consumption expenditure	36916	71530	101615	115068	130657	151374	167414	182711	200560	218041	235879	253855
2	Private final consumption expenditure	92237	156908	198929	220480	243755	271831	301024	336650	365820	401987	442427	484553
	A Households	91176	154811	195682	216379	239430	266953	295825	330696	359334	394984	435006	476364
	B Private non-profit institutions serving households	1061	2097	3247	4101	4325	4878	5199	5954	6486	7003	7421	8189
3	Gross capital formation	44036	72931	75648	72676	92523	111891	104303	112143	122578	139158	162921	163895
	A Increase in stocks	5269	10013	-2399	-7423	962	5905	-5587	-6093	-9591	-7426	-1354	-6079
	B Gross fixed capital formation	38767	62918	78047	80099	91561	105986	109890	118236	132169	146584	164275	169974
	Residential buildings	9602	12055	14748	19212	22418	24490	25776	26947	28856	33070	35211	35607
	Non-residential buildings	16558	24239	29053	30086	33181	38362	39563	41606	45288	48289	50739	55066
	Other construction and land improvement etc.												
	Other [a]	12607	26624	34246	30801	35962	43134	44551	49683	58025	65225	78325	79301
4	Exports of goods and services	41515	84079	101332	110399	140508	156523	172527	201331	249528	284664	303509	308790
5	Less: Imports of goods and services	42478	85263	107508	112173	145196	166520	172228	205157	233121	254267	283852	277407
	Equals: Gross Domestic Product	172226	300785	370016	412450	462307	525099	573040	627678	705365	789583	860884	933686

a) Item 'Other' of gross capital formation includes a statistical discrepancy.

1.2 Expenditure on the Gross Domestic Product, in Constant Prices

Million Swedish kronor

		1970	1975	1977	1978	1979	1980	1981	1982	1983	1984	1985	1986
		\multicolumn{12}{c}{At constant prices of:1980}
1	Government final consumption expenditure	110825	128384	136873	141387	148084	151374	154439	155641	156882	160611	162923	166048
2	Private final consumption expenditure	231661	261433	269471	267564	274028	271831	270432	274144	269269	273207	281267	293493
	A Households	227617	256842	265051	263008	269338	266953	265522	268914	263889	267742	275828	287864
	B Private non-profit institutions serving households	4044	4591	4420	4556	4690	4878	4910	5230	5380	5465	5439	5629
3	Gross capital formation	113590	121556	102078	88700	102804	111891	95012	94045	93417	102237	112162	108386

Sweden

1.2 Expenditure on the Gross Domestic Product, in Constant Prices
(Continued)

Million Swedish kronor

	1970	1975	1977	1978	1979	1980	1981	1982	1983	1984	1985	1986
					At constant prices of:1980							
A Increase in stocks	13405	15073	-3189	-9365	360	5905	-5312	-5181	-7369	-3684	-138	-2844
B Gross fixed capital formation	100185	106483	105267	98065	102444	105986	100324	99226	100786	105921	112300	111230
Residential buildings	28476	25138	22434	25593	26051	24490	23340	22942	22657	24333	24485	23699
Non-residential buildings	40713	40300	38661	37027	37214	38362	35934	35248	35320	35361	35142	36784
Other construction and land improvement etc.												
Other [a]	30996	41045	44172	35445	39179	43134	41050	41036	42809	46227	52673	50747
4 Exports of goods and services	107872	129951	137537	148266	157364	156523	158281	165260	182904	195230	199456	205807
5 Less: Imports of goods and services	131301	149778	157141	148537	165801	166520	154651	161357	161940	169302	182910	193070
Equals: Gross Domestic Product	432647	491546	488818	497380	516479	525099	523513	527733	540532	561883	573898	580564

a) Item 'Other' of gross capital formation includes a statistical discrepancy.

1.3 Cost Components of the Gross Domestic Product

Million Swedish kronor

	1970	1975	1977	1978	1979	1980	1981	1982	1983	1984	1985	1986
1 Indirect taxes, net	18907	32412	41181	40311	42282	48694	57100	60719	70794	87104	99138	118272
A Indirect taxes	21754	41622	56463	57622	62001	71337	83784	91795	107644	126261	141245	163298
B Less: Subsidies	2847	9210	15282	17311	19719	22643	26684	31076	36850	39157	42107	45026
2 Consumption of fixed capital	16351	30538	40516	45963	51723	59421	66479	74675	84339	91752	99464	105865
3 Compensation of employees paid by resident producers to:	103018	183743	245104	272908	299946	337085	368363	389526	421599	461433	502379	549376
A Resident households	103012	183734	245086	272886	299918	337055	368293	389363	421219	461076	501964	548978
B Rest of the world	6	9	18	22	28	30	70	163	380	357	415	398
4 Operating surplus	33950	54092	43215	53268	68356	79899	81098	102758	128633	149294	159903	160173
A Corporate and quasi-corporate enterprises	8639	18876	-287	1956	16488	21313	19061	28818	46806	59090	63881	61793
B Private unincorporated enterprises	23920	33052	40617	49197	50273	56586	59727	71198	77420	85861	91411	93274
C General government	1391	2164	2885	2115	1595	2000	2310	2742	4407	4343	4611	5106
Equals: Gross Domestic Product	172226	300785	370016	412450	462307	525099	573040	627678	705365	789583	860884	933686

1.4 General Government Current Receipts and Disbursements

Million Swedish kronor

	1970	1975	1977	1978	1979	1980	1981	1982	1983	1984	1985	1986
					Receipts							
1 Operating surplus	1391	2164	2885	2115	1595	2000	2310	2742	4407	4343	4611	5106
2 Property and entrepreneurial income	5153	12030	16232	19208	22210	27121	32782	38910	45650	50891	57194	61799
3 Taxes, fees and contributions	69963	131725	188869	208869	229445	260498	292155	315679	358999	400969	433991	495461
A Indirect taxes	21754	41622	56463	57622	62001	71337	83784	91795	107644	126261	141245	163298
B Direct taxes	35010	63995	84237	94322	104369	113925	121835	136230	154440	169294	182952	205803
C Social security contributions	13059	25761	47779	56439	62525	74643	85833	86630	95653	103781	108206	124523
D Compulsory fees, fines and penalties	140	347	390	486	550	593	703	1024	1262	1633	1588	1837
4 Other current transfers	3833	6033	6459	6950	7689	7628	6913	12200	13251	14335	16837	11460
Total Current Receipts of General Government	80340	151952	214445	237142	260939	297247	334160	369531	422307	470538	512633	573826
					Disbursements							
1 Government final consumption expenditure	36916	71530	101615	115068	130657	151374	167414	182711	200560	218041	235879	253855
A Compensation of employees	25027	49476	71407	82887	93883	108627	118747	129076	139801	151694	161691	174978
B Consumption of fixed capital	1463	2768	3659	4142	4678	5367	6118	6915	7797	8509	9189	9738
C Purchases of goods and services, net	10200	17757	23587	26217	30503	35338	40025	43998	47306	52254	58870	62136
D Less: Own account fixed capital formation	...	...	...	...	...	...	...	...	...	...	...	...
E Indirect taxes paid, net	226	1529	2962	1822	1593	2042	2524	2722	5656	5584	6129	7003
2 Property income	3305	6666	9549	11230	14323	21887	31144	43953	51457	60991	73318	71109
A Interest	3225	6507	9288	11013	14170	21591	30771	43496	51063	60464	72738	70205
B Net land rent and royalties	80	159	261	217	153	296	373	457	394	527	580	904

Sweden

1.4 General Government Current Receipts and Disbursements
(Continued)

Million Swedish kronor

		1970	1975	1977	1978	1979	1980	1981	1982	1983	1984	1985	1986
3	Subsidies	2847	9210	15282	17311	19719	22643	26684	31076	36850	39157	42107	45026
4	Other current transfers	20451	47143	68075	79280	89642	102495	116209	127516	143225	152914	172339	189528
	A Social security benefits	12718	31634	47310	55733	63011	73396	84729	92730	104640	112335	125016	139567
	B Social assistance grants	4837	8768	11792	13501	15218	16457	17188	19782	21711	22315	27372	27795
	C Other	2896	6741	8973	10046	11413	12642	14292	15004	16874	18264	19951	22166
5	Net saving	16821	17403	19924	14253	6598	-1152	-7291	-15725	-9785	-565	-11010	14308
	Total Current Disbursements and Net Saving of General Government	80340	151952	214445	237142	260939	297247	334160	369531	422307	470538	512633	573826

1.5 Current Income and Outlay of Corporate and Quasi-Corporate Enterprises, Summary

Million Swedish kronor

		1970	1975	1977	1978	1979	1980	1981	1982	1983	1984	1985	1986
	Receipts												
1	Operating surplus	8639	18876	-287	1956	16488	21313	19061	28818	46806	59090	63881	61793
2	Property and entrepreneurial income received	16665	32197	46220	52319	63032	86631	111850	129435	141035	164058	192668	205287
3	Current transfers	7217	13975	20304	23967	24052	26181	33029	39754	41153	46413	56176	64643
	Total Current Receipts	32521	65048	66237	78242	103572	134125	163940	198007	228994	269561	312725	331723
	Disbursements												
1	Property and entrepreneurial income	18705	37150	51257	58151	67105	90562	115864	131212	147445	169616	194505	208376
2	Direct taxes and other current payments to general government	2667	3397	5614	4519	5167	6552	6334	8744	13012	14626	14536	17199
3	Other current transfers	5685	9232	12787	14388	15203	17026	23330	30234	32895	38908	46005	53312
4	Net saving	5464	15269	-3421	1184	16097	19985	18412	27817	35642	46411	57679	52836
	Total Current Disbursements and Net Saving	32521	65048	66237	78242	103572	134125	163940	198007	228994	269561	312725	331723

1.6 Current Income and Outlay of Households and Non-Profit Institutions

Million Swedish kronor

		1970	1975	1977	1978	1979	1980	1981	1982	1983	1984	1985	1986
	Receipts												
1	Compensation of employees	103026	183786	245217	273100	300130	337338	368631	389646	421456	461259	502173	549544
	A From resident producers	103012	183734	245086	272886	299918	337055	368293	389363	421219	461076	501964	548978
	B From rest of the world	14	52	131	214	212	283	338	283	237	183	209	566
2	Operating surplus of private unincorporated enterprises	23920	33052	40617	49197	50273	56586	59727	71198	77420	85861	91411	93274
3	Property and entrepreneurial income	7235	11471	15918	16235	18422	27267	34145	35833	38490	44130	52810	57244
4	Current transfers	22119	49409	70855	82342	92826	105996	120721	132961	149337	160190	179818	198264
	A Social security benefits	12718	31634	47310	55733	63011	73396	84729	92730	104640	112335	125016	139567
	B Social assistance grants	4899	10159	13853	15580	17496	19369	21148	23296	25737	26663	31932	33070
	C Other	4502	7616	9692	11029	12319	13231	14844	16935	18960	21192	22870	25627
	Total Current Receipts	156300	277718	372607	420874	461651	527187	583224	629638	686703	751440	826212	898326
	Disbursements												
1	Private final consumption expenditure	92237	156908	198929	220480	243755	271831	301024	336650	365820	401987	442427	484553
2	Property income	7107	11118	18366	19949	23686	32846	41477	43002	43292	48573	57159	61160
3	Direct taxes and other current transfers n.e.c. to general government	46388	87566	127874	147391	163166	183729	203509	217329	240110	261798	279994	315905
	A Social security contributions	13059	25761	47779	56439	62525	74643	85833	86630	95653	103781	108206	124523
	B Direct taxes	32398	60680	78804	89975	99353	107614	116701	127770	141798	155060	168591	188770
	C Fees, fines and penalties	931	1125	1291	977	1288	1472	1975	2926	2659	2957	3197	2612
4	Other current transfers	6535	13874	18403	21945	23076	23967	24689	30042	32268	34440	40927	39137
5	Net saving	4033	8252	9035	11109	7968	14814	12525	2615	5213	4642	5705	-2429
	Total Current Disbursements and Net Saving	156300	277718	372607	420874	461651	527187	583224	629638	686703	751440	826212	898326

Sweden

1.7 External Transactions on Current Account, Summary

Million Swedish kronor

	1970	1975	1977	1978	1979	1980	1981	1982	1983	1984	1985	1986
Payments to the Rest of the World												
1 Imports of goods and services	42478	85263	107508	112173	145196	166520	172228	205157	233121	254267	283852	277407
A Imports of merchandise c.i.f.	36730	73519	91492	93883	124661	143839	148735	177208	202038	221134	246761	233574
B Other	5748	11744	16016	18290	20535	22681	23493	27949	31083	33133	37091	43833
2 Factor income to the rest of the world	912	2084	4712	7344	7986	11947	21523	27599	31593	36530	42195	36155
A Compensation of employees	6	9	18	22	28	30	70	163	380	357	415	398
B Property and entrepreneurial income	906	2075	4694	7322	7958	11917	21453	27436	31213	36173	41780	35757
By general government [a]	10	2	217	977	1165	2981	6526	8664	11125	13295	14832	11983
By corporate and quasi-corporate enterprises	...	...	...	...	...	...	...	...	...	...	...	...
By other	...	...	...	...	...	...	...	...	...	...	...	...
3 Current transfers to the rest of the world	1235	3383	4839	5470	6267	6903	11378	14179	15641	16412	19530	20941
A Indirect taxes to supranational organizations	...	...	...	...	...	...	...	...	...	...	...	...
B Other current transfers	1235	3383	4839	5470	6267	6903	11378	14179	15641	16412	19530	20941
4 Surplus of the nation on current transactions	-1367	-1469	-9594	-167	-10137	-18823	-14178	-22761	-7169	3082	-11083	6685
Payments to the Rest of the World and Surplus of the Nation on Current Transactions	43258	89261	107465	124820	149312	166547	190951	224174	273186	310291	334494	341188
Receipts From The Rest of the World												
1 Exports of goods and services	41515	84679	101332	116399	140568	156523	172527	201331	249528	284664	303509	308790
A Exports of merchandise f.o.b.	35045	71727	85199	97703	117509	130246	143909	167088	209168	241362	258681	262571
B Other	6470	12952	16133	18696	23059	26277	28618	34243	40360	43302	44828	46219
2 Factor income from rest of the world	856	2891	4023	5968	6720	7924	12083	13730	14431	16255	19679	20008
A Compensation of employees	14	52	131	214	212	283	338	283	237	183	209	566
B Property and entrepreneurial income	842	2839	3892	5754	6508	7641	11745	13447	14194	16072	19470	19442
By general government [a]	149	395	666	1209	1341	1626	2415	2717	2712	2999	3572	4387
By corporate and quasi-corporate enterprises	...	...	...	...	...	...	...	...	...	...	...	...
By other	...	...	...	...	...	...	...	...	...	...	...	...
3 Current transfers from rest of the world	887	1691	2110	2453	2024	2100	6341	9113	9227	9372	11306	12390
A Subsidies from supranational organisations	...	...	...	...	...	...	...	...	...	...	...	...
B Other current transfers	887	1691	2110	2453	2024	2100	6341	9113	9227	9372	11306	12390
Receipts from the Rest of the World on Current Transactions	43258	89261	107465	124820	149312	166547	190951	224174	273186	310291	334494	341188

a) Only central government data are included in the general government estimates.

1.8 Capital Transactions of The Nation, Summary

Million Swedish kronor

	1970	1975	1977	1978	1979	1980	1981	1982	1983	1984	1985	1986
Finance of Gross Capital Formation												
Gross saving	42669	71462	66054	72509	82386	93068	90125	89382	115409	142240	151838	170580
1 Consumption of fixed capital	16351	30538	40516	45963	51723	59421	66479	74675	84339	91752	99464	105865
A General government	1885	3508	4631	5196	5863	6733	7654	8657	9747	10637	11410	12264
B Corporate and quasi-corporate enterprises	10203	19835	26241	29626	33326	37890	42178	47778	54433	58826	64484	68689
C Other	4263	7195	9644	11141	12534	14798	16647	18240	20159	22289	23570	24912
2 Net saving	26318	40924	25538	26546	30663	33647	23646	14707	31070	50488	52374	64715
A General government	16821	17403	19924	14253	6598	-1152	-7291	-15725	-9785	-565	-11010	14308
B Corporate and quasi-corporate enterprises	5464	15269	-3421	1184	16097	19985	18412	27817	35642	46411	57679	52836
C Other	4033	8252	9035	11109	7968	14814	12525	2615	5213	4642	5705	-2429
Less: Surplus of the nation on current transactions	-1367	-1469	-9594	-167	-10137	-18823	-14178	-22761	-7169	3082	-11083	6685
Finance of Gross Capital Formation	44036	72931	75648	72676	92523	111891	104303	112143	122578	139158	162921	163895

Sweden

1.8 Capital Transactions of The Nation, Summary
(Continued)

Million Swedish kronor

	1970	1975	1977	1978	1979	1980	1981	1982	1983	1984	1985	1986
Gross Capital Formation													
Increase in stocks	5269	10013	-2399	-7423	962	5905	-5587	-6093	-9591	-7426	-1354	-6079
Gross fixed capital formation	38767	62918	78047	80099	91561	105986	109890	118236	132169	146584	164275	169974
1 General government	10753	12808	16462	17834	19139	21836	23251	23809	25888	26903	27411	27599
2 Corporate and quasi-corporate enterprises	21289	36417	44211	42643	50278	61977	66577	75301	86646	98771	117635	124006
3 Other	6725	13693	17374	19622	22144	22173	20062	19126	19635	20910	19229	18369
Gross Capital Formation	44036	72931	75648	72676	92523	111891	104303	112143	122578	139158	162921	163895

1.9 Gross Domestic Product by Institutional Sectors of Origin

Million Swedish kronor

	1970	1975	1977	1978	1979	1980	1981	1982	1983	1984	1985	1986
Domestic Factor Incomes Originating													
1 General government	27384	53120	76354	87577	99489	115232	126097	137237	150122	162576	...	...
2 Corporate and quasi-corporate enterprises	77847	142658	160694	178565	208500	235000	253132	...	...	...	...	...
A Non-financial	77334	141422	159421	176379	205616	231731	249635	...	...	...	...	...
B Financial	513	1236	1273	2186	2923	3275	3497	...	...	...	...	...
3 Households and private unincorporated enterprises	30433	39988	48383	56671	56789	62958	66216	76061	...	...	...	...
4 Non-profit institutions serving households	1304	2069	2888	3363	3485	3788	4016	...	...	...	...	...
Subtotal: Domestic Factor Incomes	136968	237835	288319	326176	368302	416984	449461	492284	550232	610727	662282	709549
Indirect taxes, net	18907	32412	41181	40311	42282	48694	57100	60719	70794	87104	99138	118272
A Indirect taxes	21754	41622	56463	57622	62001	71337	83784	91795	107644	126261	141245	163298
B Less: Subsidies	2847	9210	15282	17311	19719	22643	26684	31076	36850	39157	42107	45026
Consumption of fixed capital	16351	30538	40516	45963	51723	59421	66479	74675	84339	91752	99464	105865
Gross Domestic Product	172226	300785	370016	412450	462307	525099	573040	627678	705365	789583	860884	933686

1.10 Gross Domestic Product by Kind of Activity, in Current Prices

Million Swedish kronor

	1970	1975	1977	1978	1979	1980	1981	1982	1983	1984	1985	1986
1 Agriculture, hunting, forestry and fishing	7088	13021	14601	14709	14703	16829	18625	20550	22486	25561	25887	28282
2 Mining and quarrying	1592	2384	1671	1262	1987	2449	2235	2484	3214	3833	4414	4029
3 Manufacturing	43110	79242	83055	88044	100924	111018	115712	125671	147050	168050	183325	200311
4 Electricity, gas and water	3129	6088	7790	10293	11520	13093	15148	15950	18797	21789	25240	26825
5 Construction	14268	22831	30273	31525	34707	38675	42844	44731	47311	50823	53708	56143
6 Wholesale and retail trade, restaurants and hotels	18761	34994	41684	45560	52085	58297	60413	65176	74330	86088	95965	105836
7 Transport, storage and communication	10737	18085	22061	24244	27268	31727	34638	37379	40662	44278	48521	55642
8 Finance, insurance, real estate and business services [a]	18889	31945	39770	46732	52209	58920	65122	74543	83284	91729	98608	110032
9 Community, social and personal services	5823	9478	12782	14184	15701	17230	18181	19934	22197	23716	27143	29182
Total, Industries	123397	218068	253687	276553	311104	348238	372918	406418	459331	515867	562801	616282
Producers of Government Services	26716	53773	78028	88851	100154	116036	127389	138713	153254	165787	177009	191719
Other Producers	1315	2136	3009	3437	3546	3860	4101	4571	4934	5246	5534	6060
Subtotal [b]	151428	273977	334724	368841	414804	468134	504408	549702	617519	686900	745344	814061
Less: Imputed bank service charge [a]	...	...	...	...	...	...	...	...	...	...	...	...
Plus: Import duties	1517	1424	1477	1311	1562	1760	1927	2160	2192	2520	2736	2985
Plus: Value added tax [c]	16677	20200	30900	42421	47110	54019	64447	71563	78599	89138	101729	108980
Plus: Other adjustments	2604	-2882	-3165	-123	-1169	1186	2258	4253	7055	11025	11075	7660
Equals: Gross Domestic Product	172226	300785	370016	412450	462307	525099	573040	627678	705365	789583	860884	933686
Memorandum Item: Mineral fuels and power [d]	3259	6982	7853	10002	11225	12740	14303	15264	18616	22194	25458	27846

a) Item 'Less: Imputed bank service charge' is netted out of item 'Finance, insurance, real estate and business services'.
b) Gross domestic product in basic values.
c) Item 'Value added tax' relates to value added tax and other taxes and subsidies on sales and production of commodities.
d) Item 'Mineral fuels and power' refers to ISIC categories 353 (Petroleum refineries), 354 (Manufacture of miscellaneous products of petroleum and coal) and 41 (Electricity, gas and steam).

Sweden

1.11 Gross Domestic Product by Kind of Activity, in Constant Prices

Million Swedish kronor

	1970	1975	1977	1978	1979	1980	1981	1982	1983	1984	1985	1986
	\multicolumn{12}{c}{At constant prices of: 1980}											
1 Agriculture, hunting, forestry and fishing	17449	17181	16047	16327	16257	16829	17067	18165	18993	19707	18914	19121
2 Mining and quarrying	2752	2707	2245	1858	2416	2449	2142	1793	1832	2073	2180	2006
3 Manufacturing	98776	113255	106789	103902	110588	111018	107398	106852	112342	119121	123075	123074
4 Electricity, gas and water	7249	10592	11302	12496	12929	13093	14098	13582	14335	16393	19224	19054
5 Construction	35638	36332	37852	37651	38393	38675	37896	38578	38778	39770	39590	40385
6 Wholesale and retail trade, restaurants and hotels	48382	56061	56205	55290	57979	58297	57279	57474	58447	59476	60862	62519
7 Transport, storage and communication	20204	26347	27607	28180	29654	31727	31027	31149	31028	33026	33887	35808
8 Finance, insurance, real estate and business services [a]	46086	53812	56009	56697	57522	58920	59689	60650	62717	64757	65956	66899
9 Community, social and personal services	13021	16141	17069	16860	17125	17230	16960	17255	17554	17443	18151	17931
Total, Industries	289557	332428	331125	329261	342863	348238	343556	345498	356026	371766	381839	386797
Producers of Government Services	81535	98090	104330	108629	113213	116036	118849	120301	122611	125214	126373	127864
Other Producers	4299	4080	3811	3861	3831	3860	3823	4042	4157	4198	4165	4282
Subtotal [b]	375391	434598	439266	441751	459907	468134	466228	469841	482794	501178	512377	518943
Less: Imputed bank service charge [a]	...	...	...	...	...	...	...	...	...	...	...	...
Plus: Import duties	1283	1399	1509	1436	1762	1760	1645	1654	1695	1882	2060	2481
Plus: Value added tax [c]	48679	52719	54455	54374	55801	54019	52579	53506	53140	53584	56330	57685
Plus: Other adjustments	7294	2830	-6412	-181	-991	1186	3061	2732	2903	5239	3131	1455
Equals: Gross Domestic Product	432647	491546	488818	497380	516479	525099	523513	527733	540532	561883	573898	580564
Memorandum Item: Mineral fuels and power [d]	6787	10146	10912	12227	12510	12740	13713	13252	14167	16285	18874	18308

a) Item 'Less: Imputed bank service charge' is netted out of item 'Finance, insurance, real estate and business services'.
b) Gross domestic product in basic values.
c) Item 'Value added tax' relates to value added tax and other taxes and subsidies on sales and production of commodities.
d) Item 'Mineral fuels and power' refers to ISIC categories 353 (Petroleum refineries), 354 (Manufacture of miscellaneous products of petroleum and coal) and 41 (Electricity, gas and steam).

1.12 Relations Among National Accounting Aggregates

Million Swedish kronor

	1970	1975	1977	1978	1979	1980	1981	1982	1983	1984	1985	1986
Gross Domestic Product	172226	300785	370016	412450	462307	525099	573040	627678	705365	789583	860884	933686
Plus: Net factor income from the rest of the world	-56	807	-689	-1376	-1266	-4023	-9440	-13869	-17162	-20275	-22516	-16147
Factor income from the rest of the world	856	2891	4023	5968	6720	7924	12083	13730	14431	16255	19679	20008
Less: Factor income to the rest of the world	912	2084	4712	7344	7986	11947	21523	27599	31593	36530	42195	36155
Equals: Gross National Product	172170	301592	369327	411074	461041	521076	563600	613809	688203	769308	838368	917539
Less: Consumption of fixed capital	16351	30538	40516	45963	51723	59421	66479	74675	84339	91752	99464	105865
Equals: National Income	155819	271054	328811	365111	409318	461655	497121	539134	603864	677556	738904	811674
Plus: Net current transfers from the rest of the world	-348	-1692	-2729	-3017	-4243	-4803	-5037	-5066	-6414	-7040	-8224	-8551
Current transfers from the rest of the world	887	1691	2110	2453	2024	2100	6341	9113	9227	9372	11306	12390
Less: Current transfers to the rest of the world	1235	3383	4839	5470	6267	6903	11378	14179	15641	16412	19530	20941
Equals: National Disposable Income	155471	269362	326082	362094	405075	456852	492084	534068	597450	670516	730680	803123
Less: Final consumption	129153	228438	300544	335548	374412	423205	468438	519361	566380	620028	678306	738408
Equals: Net Saving	26318	40924	25538	26546	30663	33647	23646	14707	31070	50488	52374	64715
Less: Surplus of the nation on current transactions	-1367	-1469	-9594	-167	-10137	-18823	-14178	-22761	-7169	3082	-11083	6685
Equals: Net Capital Formation	27685	42393	35132	26713	40800	52470	37824	37468	38239	47406	63457	58030

Sweden

2.1 Government Final Consumption Expenditure by Function, in Current Prices

Million Swedish kronor

	1970	1975	1977	1978	1979	1980	1981	1982	1983	1984	1985	1986
1 General public services [a]	4998	10023	13868	14768	17410	20256	22716	23727	26807	29284	31475	...
2 Defence	5712	9729	11581	12514	13814	16031	17901	19089	19446	20738	22460	...
3 Public order and safety												...
4 Education [a]	9093	15478	21380	23755	27337	31179	34183	37718	40885	43252	46451	...
5 Health	8256	17572	25809	29028	32200	38541	42603	46811	51776	56885	61997	...
6 Social security and welfare	3966	9035	15229	19258	22136	25410	27707	31396	35885	39539	43054	...
7 Housing and community amenities	847	1460	2060	2468	2411	2988	3231	3109	3188	3371	3589	...
8 Recreational, cultural and religious affairs	1762	4015	5900	6189	7073	8159	9085	10017	10867	11917	13020	...
9 Economic services	1949	3674	4974	5810	6728	7470	8382	9309	10202	11287	11836	...
10 Other functions	333	544	814	1278	1548	1340	1606	1535	1504	1768	1997	...
Total Government Final Consumption Expenditure	36916	71530	101615	115068	130657	151374	167414	182711	200560	218041	235879	253855

a) For 1982, general central government research is excluded from general administration and is included in item 'Education'.

2.2 Government Final Consumption Expenditure by Function, in Constant Prices

Million Swedish kronor

	1970	1975	1977	1978	1979	1980	1981	1982	1983	1984	1985	1986
					At constant prices of:1980							
1 General public services [a]	14535	17828	18953	18265	19824	20256	20974	20709	21371	21488	21810	...
2 Defence	15878	16226	15417	15336	15520	16031	15959	15469	14586	14664	14994	...
3 Public order and safety												...
4 Education [a]	25138	27564	28627	28980	30222	31179	31815	32489	32604	33058	32827	...
5 Health	27171	31211	34205	36252	37319	38541	39822	40332	41085	42300	40900	...
6 Social security and welfare	13506	18412	21051	23593	25028	25410	25779	26917	27924	28580	29847	...
7 Housing and community amenities	2513	2485	2628	3011	2791	2988	2922	2551	2366	2353	2298	...
8 Recreational, cultural and religious affairs	4887	6862	7728	7427	7955	8159	8305	8331	8258	8585	8846	...
9 Economic services	6063	6706	6856	6992	7676	7470	7480	7579	7534	7821	7705	...
10 Other functions	1134	1090	1408	1531	1749	1340	1383	1264	1154	1563	1613	...
Total Government Final Consumption Expenditure	110825	128384	136873	141387	148084	151374	154439	155641	156882	160511	163923	165948

a) For 1982, general central government research is excluded from general administration and is included in item 'Education'.

2.3 Total Government Outlays by Function and Type

Million Swedish kronor

	Final Consumption Expenditures Total	Compensation of Employees	Other	Subsidies	Other Current Transfers & Property Income	Total Current Disbursements	Gross Capital Formation	Other Capital Outlays	Total Outlays
					1980				
1 General public services [a]	20256	15035	5221	...	...	...	2832	...	...
2 Defence	16031	5522	10509	...	...	...	1910	...	...
3 Public order and safety				...	...	...		...	...
4 Education [a]	31179	23724	7455	...	...	...	3112	...	...
5 Health	38541	30669	7872	...	...	...	3357	...	...
6 Social security and welfare	25410	21811	3599	...	...	...	1519	...	...
7 Housing and community amenities	2988	1579	1409	...	...	...	3179	...	...
8 Recreation, culture and religion	8159	5173	2986	...	...	...	1224	...	...
9 Economic services	7470	4382	3088	...	...	...	5718	...	...
10 Other functions	1340	732	608	...	...	...	-	...	...
Total	151374	108627	42747	22643	124382	298399	22851	4010	325260
					1981				
1 General public services [a]	22716	16290	6426	...	...	...	2897	...	...
2 Defence	17901	6178	11723	...	...	...	1576	...	...
3 Public order and safety				...	...	...		...	...
4 Education [a]	34183	25840	8343	...	...	...	3522	...	...
5 Health	42603	33400	9203	...	...	...	3862	...	...
6 Social security and welfare	27707	24053	3654	...	...	...	1425	...	...
7 Housing and community amenities	3231	1672	1559	...	...	...	3245	...	...
8 Recreation, culture and religion	9085	5701	3384	...	...	...	1443	...	...
9 Economic services	8382	4759	3623	...	...	...	5817	...	...
10 Other functions	1606	854	752	...	...	...	-	...	...
Total	167414	118747	48667	26684	147353	341451	23787	6404	371642

Sweden

2.3 Total Government Outlays by Function and Type
(Continued)

Million Swedish kronor

		Final Consumption Expenditures Total	Compensation of Employees	Other	Subsidies	Other Current Transfers & Property Income	Total Current Disbursements	Gross Capital Formation	Other Capital Outlays	Total Outlays
	1982									
1	General public services [a]	23727	16864	6863	...	...	...	3045	...	...
2	Defence	19089	6695	12394	...	...	...	1527	...	...
3	Public order and safety				...	...	...		...	...
4	Education [a]	37718	27918	9800	...	...	...	3487	...	...
5	Health	46811	36682	10129	...	...	...	4374	...	...
6	Social security and welfare	31396	27014	4382	...	...	...	1209	...	...
7	Housing and community amenities	3109	1732	1377	...	...	...	3108	...	...
8	Recreation, culture and religion	10017	6125	3892	...	...	...	1475	...	...
9	Economic services	9309	5167	4142	...	...	...	6138	...	...
10	Other functions	1535	879	656	...	...	...	-	...	...
	Total	182711	129076	53635	31076	171469	385256	24363	10236	419855
	1983									
1	General public services [a]	26807	18338	8469	...	...	...	3325	...	...
2	Defence	19446	6617	12829	...	...	...	872	...	...
3	Public order and safety				...	...	...		...	...
4	Education [a]	40885	29781	11104	...	...	...	3405	...	...
5	Health	51776	39884	11892	...	...	...	4901	...	...
6	Social security and welfare	35885	30415	5470	...	...	...	1146	...	...
7	Housing and community amenities	3188	1819	1369	...	...	...	3093	...	...
8	Recreation, culture and religion	10867	6548	4319	...	...	...	1732	...	...
9	Economic services	10202	5519	4683	...	...	...	7453	...	...
10	Other functions	1504	880	624	...	...	...	-	...	...
	Total	200560	139801	60759	36850	194682	432092	25927	11110	469129
	1984									
1	General public services [a]	29284	19858	9426	...	...	...	3675	...	...
2	Defence	20738	6826	13912	...	...	...	-20	...	...
3	Public order and safety				...	...	...		...	...
4	Education [a]	43252	31682	11570	...	...	...	3427	...	...
5	Health	56885	43913	12972	...	...	...	5435	...	...
6	Social security and welfare	39539	33439	6100	...	...	...	1064	...	...
7	Housing and community amenities	3371	1922	1449	...	...	...	2882	...	...
8	Recreation, culture and religion	11917	7214	4703	...	...	...	1773	...	...
9	Economic services	11287	5838	5449	...	...	...	7832	...	...
10	Other functions	1768	1002	766	...	...	...	-	...	...
	Total	218041	151694	66347	39157	213905	471101	26068	6627	503798
	1985									
1	General public services [a]	31475	20911	10564	...	...	...	3679	...	...
2	Defence	22460	7218	15242	...	...	...	205	...	...
3	Public order and safety				...	...	...		...	...
4	Education [a]	46451	33634	12817	...	...	...	3538	...	...
5	Health	61997	47405	14592	...	...	...	5318	...	...
6	Social security and welfare	43054	35643	7411	...	...	...	1328	...	...
7	Housing and community amenities	3589	2033	1556	...	...	...	3073	...	...
8	Recreation, culture and religion	13020	7667	5353	...	...	...	1962	...	...
9	Economic services	11836	6092	5744	...	...	...	7633	...	...
10	Other functions	1997	1088	909	...	...	...	-	...	...
	Total	235879	161691	74188	42107	245657	523643	26736	8271	558650

Sweden

2.3 Total Government Outlays by Function and Type
(Continued)

Million Swedish kronor

		Final Consumption Expenditures		Subsidies	Other Current Transfers & Property Income	Total Current Disbursements	Gross Capital Formation	Other Capital Outlays	Total Outlays
		Total	Compensation of Employees	Other						

1986

		Total	Comp.	Other	Subsidies	Other Curr.	Total Curr. Disb.	Gross Cap. Form.	Other Cap. Outlays	Total Outlays
1	General public services [a]	...	...	...	...	...	...	...	...	...
2	Defence	...	...	...	...	...	...	...	...	...
3	Public order and safety	...	...	...	...	...	...	...	...	...
4	Education [a]	...	...	...	...	...	...	...	...	...
5	Health	...	...	...	...	...	...	...	...	...
6	Social security and welfare	...	...	...	...	...	...	...	...	...
7	Housing and community amenities	...	...	...	...	...	...	...	...	...
8	Recreation, culture and religion	...	...	...	...	...	...	...	...	...
9	Economic services	...	...	...	...	...	...	...	...	...
10	Other functions	...	...	...	...	...	...	...	...	...
	Total	253855	174978	78877	45026	260637	559518	27469	7963	594950

a) For 1982, general central government research is excluded from general administration and is included in item 'Education'.

2.5 Private Final Consumption Expenditure by Type and Porpose, in Current Prices

Million Swedish kronor

	1970	1975	1977	1978	1979	1980	1981	1982	1983	1984	1985	1986
Final Consumption Expenditure of Resident Households												
1 Food, beverages and tobacco	26584	41131	51476	55603	59897	66438	72743	81169	88878	98182	105164	112452
A Food	18989	28836	37000	40160	43848	48752	54058	60719	66643	74112	79506	85329
B Non-alcoholic beverages	650	1048	1128	1254	1169	1283	1384	1530	1633	1752	2009	2081
C Alcoholic beverages	4282	7407	8856	9300	9717	10582	11161	12189	13182	14068	14982	16182
D Tobacco	2663	3840	4492	4889	5163	5821	6140	6731	7420	8250	8667	8860
2 Clothing and footwear	7259	12252	15498	16626	18264	20159	21760	23510	25681	28449	32107	35935
3 Gross rent, fuel and power	19498	33622	43974	51083	58004	66756	75569	86579	94661	103256	114791	122057
A Fuel and power	2740	5706	8180	9648	11833	15131	17228	19450	20147	21970	26309	25536
B Other	16758	27916	35794	41435	46171	51625	58341	67129	74514	81286	88482	96521
4 Furniture, furnishings and household equipment and operation	6739	12484	15381	16212	17488	19051	19857	21779	23521	26027	27761	31040
A Household operation	1543	2251	2776	2970	3023	3193	3435	3761	4143	4451	4794	4273
B Other	5196	10233	12605	13242	14465	15858	16422	18018	19378	21576	22967	26767
5 Medical care and health expenses	1980	3185	4115	4444	4935	5729	6741	7748	8861	10029	10870	11951
6 Transport and communication	12706	22530	28212	32181	35907	39325	44413	51616	55792	61039	68835	77154
A Personal transport equipment	3436	6822	7432	8161	9128	8423	9083	11616	11783	12827	14273	19758
B Other	9270	15708	20780	24020	26779	30902	35330	40000	44009	48212	54562	57396
7 Recreational, entertainment, education and cultural services	7796	16097	20049	21537	23958	26495	29660	32240	34919	38479	41758	47197
A Education	180	291	338	363	406	464	489	504	564	636	672	682
B Other	7616	15806	19711	21174	23552	26031	29171	31736	34355	37843	41086	46515
8 Miscellaneous goods and services	6611	10551	12957	14249	15786	17228	18351	20095	22258	24575	27543	29846
A Personal care	2397	3841	4810	5169	5613	6105	6796	7492	8220	8894	9757	10614
B Expenditures in restaurants, cafes and hotels	3328	5337	6251	6830	7387	8074	8402	9341	10489	11915	13600	14665
C Other	886	1373	1896	2250	2756	2959	3153	3262	3549	3766	4186	4567
Total Final Consumption Expenditure in the Domestic Market by Households, of which	89173	151852	191662	211935	234239	261181	289094	324736	354571	390036	428829	467632
A Durable goods	9175	18091	21129	22274	24681	25389	26771	31068	32320	35551	38548	47423
B Semi-durable goods	14021	25591	32546	35789	39408	43476	47353	51720	56658	62750	69298	76923
C Non-durable goods	37803	61198	78035	85052	93613	106951	118522	132354	143676	157310	173076	180877

Sweden

2.5 Private Final Consumption Expenditure by Type and Porpose, in Current Prices
(Continued)

Million Swedish kronor

	1970	1975	1977	1978	1979	1980	1981	1982	1983	1984	1985	1986
D Services	28174	46972	59952	68820	76537	85365	96448	109594	122017	134425	147909	162409
Plus: Direct purchases abroad by resident households	2816	5242	7172	8174	9339	10191	11980	12766	13601	14872	17435	20772
Less: Direct purchases in the domestic market by non-resident households	813	2283	3152	3730	4148	4419	5249	6806	8838	9924	11258	12040
Equals: Final Consumption Expenditure of Resident Households	91176	154811	195682	216379	239430	266953	295825	330696	359334	394984	435006	476364

Final Consumption Expenditure of Private Non-profit Institutions Serving Households

	1970	1975	1977	1978	1979	1980	1981	1982	1983	1984	1985	1986
Equals: Final Consumption Expenditure of Private Non-profit Organisations Serving Households	1061	2097	3247	4101	4325	4878	5199	5954	6486	7003	7421	8189
Private Final Consumption Expenditure	92237	156908	198929	220480	243755	271831	301024	336650	365820	401987	442427	484553

2.6 Private Final Consumption Expenditure by Type and Purpose, in Constant Prices

Million Swedish kronor

	1970	1975	1977	1978	1979	1980	1981	1982	1983	1984	1985	1986

At constant prices of: 1980

Final Consumption Expenditure of Resident Households

	1970	1975	1977	1978	1979	1980	1981	1982	1983	1984	1985	1986
1 Food, beverages and tobacco	60732	64477	64670	64609	67166	66438	64706	65078	63667	63359	63325	63868
A Food	43366	45218	46083	46527	48740	48752	48042	47825	47085	46924	46889	47018
B Non-alcoholic beverages	1368	1287	1185	1234	1249	1283	1237	1284	1295	1310	1469	1448
C Alcoholic beverages	10530	12162	11828	11103	11310	10582	9823	10047	9575	9397	9347	9780
D Tobacco	5468	5810	5574	5745	5867	5821	5604	5922	5712	5728	5620	5622
2 Clothing and footwear	16238	19812	21154	20478	20489	20159	20522	20973	20673	21244	22485	23848
3 Gross rent, fuel and power	53406	59390	63236	64730	66265	66756	67016	67468	67684	68615	70993	71818
A Fuel and power	13572	13478	14895	15234	15651	15131	14528	14289	13997	14290	16046	16229
B Other	39834	45912	48341	49496	50614	51625	52488	53179	53687	54325	54947	55589
4 Furniture, furnishings and household equipment and operation	17481	19561	19805	19099	19260	19051	18205	18715	18416	18946	19054	20254
A Household operation	4240	3643	3693	3571	3366	3193	3176	3348	3421	3407	3412	3548
B Other	13241	15918	16112	15528	15894	15858	15029	15367	14995	15539	15642	16706
5 Medical care and health expenses	3725	5187	5424	5360	5563	5729	6026	6410	6528	6808	6894	7332
6 Transport and communication	31899	37825	39790	39957	40741	39325	39287	41764	40945	42042	44219	48107
A Personal transport equipment	8029	10435	9483	9218	9716	8423	8582	10182	9060	9059	9449	11840
B Other	23870	27390	30307	30739	31025	30902	30705	31582	31885	32983	34770	36267
7 Recreational, entertainment, education and cultural services	17748	25551	26271	25316	26231	26495	27006	27490	26989	27585	28401	30897
A Education	326	402	429	433	440	464	462	451	437	442	445	429
B Other	17422	25149	25842	24883	25791	26031	26544	27039	26552	27143	27956	30468
8 Miscellaneous goods and services	20466	19595	18673	17940	17941	17228	16907	17337	17388	17545	18323	18604
A Personal care	7399	6620	6962	6692	6662	6195	6454	6779	6644	6500	6759	7077
B Expenditures in restaurants, cafes and hotels	10300	10183	8568	8315	8261	8074	7451	7410	7407	7458	7662	7524
C Other	2767	2792	3143	2933	3018	2959	3002	3148	3337	3587	3902	4003
Total Final Consumption Expenditure in the Domestic Market by Households, of which	221695	251398	259023	257489	263656	261181	259675	265235	262290	266144	273694	284728
A Durable goods	21534	26983	26955	25749	26872	25389	25436	27946	26025	26806	27818	32539
B Semi-durable goods	33088	41525	43670	43128	43690	43476	43459	44231	43339	44492	46402	48748
C Non-durable goods	98761	104039	106688	106071	108932	106951	103989	104663	103212	103590	105548	107426
D Services	68312	78851	81710	82541	84162	85365	86791	88395	89714	91256	93926	96015
Plus: Direct purchases abroad by resident households	7884	9202	10253	10063	10398	10191	10529	9256	8251	8518	9448	10648
Less: Direct purchases in the domestic market by non-resident households	1962	3758	4225	4544	4716	4419	4682	5577	6652	6920	7314	7512
Equals: Final Consumption Expenditure of Resident Households	227617	256842	265051	263008	269338	266953	265522	268914	263889	267742	275828	287864

Final Consumption Expenditure of Private Non-profit Institutions Serving Households

	1970	1975	1977	1978	1979	1980	1981	1982	1983	1984	1985	1986
Equals: Final Consumption Expenditure of Private Non-profit Organisations Serving Households	4044	4591	4420	4556	4690	4878	4910	5230	5380	5465	5439	5629
Private Final Consumption Expenditure	231661	261433	269471	267564	274028	271831	270432	274144	269269	273207	281267	293493

Sweden

2.7 Gross Capital Formation by Type of Good and Owner, in Current Prices

Million Swedish kronor

	1980 TOTAL	1980 Total Private	1980 Public Enterprises	1980 General Government	1981 TOTAL	1981 Total Private	1981 Public Enterprises	1981 General Government	1982 TOTAL	1982 Total Private	1982 Public Enterprises	1982 General Government
Increase in stocks, total	5905	...	...	1015	-5587	...	...	536	-6093	...	...	554
1 Goods producing industries	3467	...	...	...	-2449	...	...	...	-6093	...	...	...
A Materials and supplies	915	...	...	...	-1052	...	...	...	-173	...	...	...
B Work in progress	-226	...	...	...	-3189	...	...	...	-3560	...	...	...
C Livestock, except breeding stocks, dairy cattle, etc.	10	...	...	...	-2	...	...	...	-51	...	...	...
D Finished goods	2768	...	...	...	1794	...	...	...	-2309	...	...	...
2 Wholesale and retail trade	1423	...	...	...	-3674	...	...	...	-554	...	...	...
3 Other, except government stocks	...	...	...	...	...	...	...	...	...	...	...	...
4 Government stocks	1015	...	...	1015	536	...	...	536	554	...	...	554
Gross Fixed Capital Formation, Total	105986	62992	25356	17638	109890	64456	26795	18639	118236	68487	30688	19061
1 Residential buildings	24490	18971	5519	-	25776	19189	6587	-	26947	19478	7469	-
2 Non-residential buildings	37109	11662	11657	13790	38262	11581	11860	14821	40188	11452	13755	14981
3 Other construction												
4 Land improvement and plantation and orchard development	1253	511	112	630	1301	538	126	637	1418	667	168	583
5 Producers' durable goods	38045	26759	8068	3218	38660	27257	8222	3181	43494	30701	9296	3497
A Transport equipment	7063	...	...	...	6204	...	...	...	7270	...	...	...
Passenger cars	1558	...	...	...	1450	...	...	...	1696	...	...	...
Other	5505	...	...	...	4754	...	...	...	5574	...	...	...
B Machinery and equipment	30982	...	...	...	32456	...	...	...	36224	...	...	...
6 Breeding stock, dairy cattle, etc.	378	378	...	...	393	393	...	...	390	390	...	...
Statistical discrepancy	4711	4711	...	...	5498	5498	...	...	5799	5799	...	...
Total Gross Capital Formation	111891	...	...	18653	104303	...	...	19175	112143	...	...	19615

	1983 TOTAL	1983 Total Private	1983 Public Enterprises	1983 General Government	1984 TOTAL	1984 Total Private	1984 Public Enterprises	1984 General Government	1985 TOTAL	1985 Total Private	1985 Public Enterprises	1985 General Government
Increase in stocks, total	-9591	...	...	39	-7426	...	...	-835	-1354	...	...	-675
1 Goods producing industries	-7082	...	...	...	-4767	...	...	...	332	...	...	...
A Materials and supplies	-927	...	...	...	-3363	...	...	...	-1072	...	...	...
B Work in progress	-2616	...	...	...	1362	...	...	...	566	...	...	...
C Livestock, except breeding stocks, dairy cattle, etc.	-61	...	...	...	-1	...	...	...	-57	...	...	...
D Finished goods	-3478	...	...	...	-2765	...	...	...	895	...	...	...
2 Wholesale and retail trade	-2548	...	...	...	-1824	...	...	...	-1011	...	...	...
3 Other, except government stocks	...	...	...	...	...	...	...	...	...	...	...	...
4 Government stocks	39	...	...	39	-835	...	...	-835	-675	...	...	-675
Gross Fixed Capital Formation, Total	132169	78636	32932	20601	146584	91294	33793	21497	164275	103404	39009	21862
1 Residential buildings	28856	21410	7446	-	33070	25208	7862	-	35211	25818	9393	-
2 Non-residential buildings	43763	12534	15155	16074	46695	14867	15331	16497	49010	16719	16110	16181
3 Other construction												
4 Land improvement and plantation and orchard development	1525	787	198	540	1594	915	214	465	1729	1009	232	488
5 Producers' durable goods	51097	36977	10133	3987	57605	42684	10386	4535	69830	51363	13274	5193
A Transport equipment	8119				11101				12904			
Passenger cars	3068	...	...	...	3967	...	...	...	5748	...	...	...
Other	5051	...	...	...	7134	...	...	...	7156	...	...	...
B Machinery and equipment	42978	...	...	...	46504	...	...	...	56926	...	...	...
6 Breeding stock, dairy cattle, etc.	462	462	...	...	440	440	...	...	452	452	...	...
Statistical discrepancy	6466	6466	...	...	7180	7180	...	...	8043	8043	...	...
Total Gross Capital Formation	122578	...	...	20640	139158	...	...	20662	162921	...	...	21187

Sweden

2.7 Gross Capital Formation by Type of Good and Owner, in Current Prices

Million Swedish kronor

	1986 TOTAL	Total Private	Public Enterprises	General Government
Increase in stocks, total	-6079	...	...	-130
1 Goods producing industries	-2733	...	...	...
A Materials and supplies	-389	...	...	...
B Work in progress	-1876	...	...	...
C Livestock, except breeding stocks, dairy cattle, etc.	-136	...	...	...
D Finished goods	-332	...	...	...
2 Wholesale and retail trade	-3216	...	...	...
3 Other, except government stocks	...	...	...	...
4 Government stocks	-130	...	...	-130
Gross Fixed Capital Formation, Total	169974	107425	40048	22501
1 Residential buildings	35607	26056	9551	-
2 Non-residential buildings	53130	20300	16697	16133
3 Other construction				
4 Land improvement and plantation and orchard development	1936	1153	268	515
5 Producers' durable goods	70491	51106	13532	5853
A Transport equipment	14131	...	...	...
Passenger cars	4529	...	...	...
Other	9602	...	...	...
B Machinery and equipment	56360	...	...	...
6 Breeding stock, dairy cattle, etc.	414	414	...	...
Statistical discrepancy	8396	8396	...	...
Total Gross Capital Formation	163895	...	...	22371

2.8 Gross Capital Formation by Type of Good and Owner, in Constant Prices

Million Swedish kronor

	1980 TOTAL	Total Private	Public Enterprises	General Government	1981 TOTAL	Total Private	Public Enterprises	General Government	1982 TOTAL	Total Private	Public Enterprises	General Government
				At constant prices of:1980								
Increase in stocks, total	5905	...	...	1015	-5312	...	...	450	-5181	...	...	391
1 Goods producing industries	3467	...	...	...	-2335	...	...	...	-5043	...	...	...
A Materials and supplies	915	...	...	...	-1090	...	...	...	-67	...	...	...
B Work in progress	-226	...	...	...	-2912	...	...	...	-2929	...	...	...
C Livestock, except breeding stocks, dairy cattle, etc.	10	...	...	...	-2	...	...	...	-47	...	...	...
D Finished goods	2768	...	...	...	1669	...	...	...	-2000	...	...	...
2 Wholesale and retail trade	1423	...	...	...	-3427	...	...	...	-529	...	...	...
3 Other, except government stocks	...	...	...	...	...	...	...	...	...	...	...	...
4 Government stocks	1015	...	...	1015	450	...	...	450	391	...	...	391
Gross Fixed Capital Formation, Total	105986	62992	25356	17638	100324	59140	24243	16941	99226	57549	25514	16163
1 Residential buildings	24490	18971	5519	...	23340	17537	5803	...	22942	16717	6225	...
2 Non-residential buildings	37109	11662	11657	13790	34723	10505	10759	13459	34009	9651	11592	12766
3 Other construction												
4 Land improvement and plantation and orchard development	1253	511	112	630	1211	505	118	588	1239	582	148	509
5 Producers' durable goods	38045	26759	8068	3218	35722	25265	7563	2894	35802	25365	7549	2888
A Transport equipment	7063	...	...	...	6004	...	...	...	6520	...	...	...
Passenger cars	1558	...	...	...	1376	...	...	...	1489	...	...	...
Other	5505	...	...	...	4628	...	...	...	5031	...	...	...
B Machinery and equipment	30982	...	...	...	29718	...	...	...	29282	...	...	...
6 Breeding stock, dairy cattle, etc.	378	378	...	...	351	351	...	...	322	322	...	...
Statistical discrepancy	4711	4711	...	...	4977	4977	...	...	4912	4912	...	...
Total Gross Capital Formation	111891	...	...	18653	95012	...	...	17391	94045	...	...	16554

Sweden

2.8 Gross Capital Formation by Type of Good and Owner, in Constant Prices

Million Swedish kronor

	1983 TOTAL	1983 Total Private	1983 Public Enterprises	1983 General Government	1984 TOTAL	1984 Total Private	1984 Public Enterprises	1984 General Government	1985 TOTAL	1985 Total Private	1985 Public Enterprises	1985 General Government
					At constant prices of:1980							
Increase in stocks, total	-7369	...	...	60	-3684	...	...	-454	-138	...	...	-416
1 Goods producing industries	-5683	...	...	...	-2345	...	...	...	776	...	...	...
A Materials and supplies	-1033	...	...	...	-1443	...	...	...	-191	...	...	...
B Work in progress	-2017	...	...	...	1011	...	...	...	434	...	...	...
C Livestock, except breeding stocks, dairy cattle, etc.	-55	...	...	...	-1	...	...	...	-42	...	...	...
D Finished goods	-2578	...	...	...	-1912	...	...	...	575	...	...	...
2 Wholesale and retail trade	-1746	...	...	...	-885	...	...	...	-498	...	...	...
3 Other, except government stocks	...	...	...	...	...	...	...	...	...	...	...	...
4 Government stocks	60	...	...	60	-454	...	...	-454	-416	...	...	-416
Gross Fixed Capital Formation, Total	100786	59948	24363	16475	105921	66050	24119	15752	112300	70835	26305	15160
1 Residential buildings	22657	16924	5733	...	24333	18595	5738	...	24485	18060	6425	...
2 Non-residential buildings	34120	9762	11277	13081	34205	10882	11108	12215	34001	11661	10987	11353
3 Other construction												
4 Land improvement and plantation and orchard development	1200	607	153	440	1156	648	151	357	1141	647	148	346
5 Producers' durable goods	37343	27189	7200	2954	40535	30233	7122	3180	46672	34466	8745	3461
A Transport equipment	6399	...	...	...	8454	...	...	...	8916	...	...	...
Passenger cars	2356	...	...	...	2805	...	...	...	3814	...	...	...
Other	4043	...	...	...	5640	...	...	...	5102	...	...	...
B Machinery and equipment	30944	...	...	...	32081	...	...	...	37756	...	...	...
6 Breeding stock, dairy cattle, etc.	353	353	...	...	318	318	...	...	305	305	...	...
Statistical discrepancy	5113	5113	...	...	5374	5374	...	...	5696	5696	...	...
Total Gross Capital Formation	93417	...	...	16535	102237	...	...	15298	112162	...	...	14744

	1986 TOTAL	1986 Total Private	1986 Public Enterprises	1986 General Government
	At constant prices of:1980			
Increase in stocks, total	-2844	...	...	-482
1 Goods producing industries	-1390	...	...	...
A Materials and supplies	154	...	...	...
B Work in progress	-1231	...	...	...
C Livestock, except breeding stocks, dairy cattle, etc.	-103	...	...	...
D Finished goods	-210	...	...	...
2 Wholesale and retail trade	-972	...	...	...
3 Other, except government stocks	...	...	...	...
4 Government stocks	-482	...	...	-482
Gross Fixed Capital Formation, Total	111230	70247	25941	15042
1 Residential buildings	23699	17547	6152	...
2 Non-residential buildings	35578	13580	11118	10880
3 Other construction				
4 Land improvement and plantation and orchard development	1206	696	161	349
5 Producers' durable goods	44030	32513	8510	3013
A Transport equipment	8914	...	...	...
Passenger cars	2712	...	...	...
Other	6202	...	...	...
B Machinery and equipment	35922	...	...	...
6 Breeding stock, dairy cattle, etc.	272	272	...	...
Statistical discrepancy	5639	5639	...	...
Total Gross Capital Formation	108386	...	...	14560

Sweden

2.9 Gross Capital Formation by Kind of Activity of Owner, ISIC Major Divisions, in Current Prices

Million Swedish kronor

	1980 Total Gross Capital Formation	1980 Increase in Stocks	1980 Gross Fixed Capital Formation	1981 Total Gross Capital Formation	1981 Increase in Stocks	1981 Gross Fixed Capital Formation	1982 Total Gross Capital Formation	1982 Increase in Stocks	1982 Gross Fixed Capital Formation	1983 Total Gross Capital Formation	1983 Increase in Stocks	1983 Gross Fixed Capital Formation
					All Producers							
1 Agriculture, hunting, fishing and forestry	4218	-156	4374	4642	116	4526	5651	364	5287	6036	66	5970
2 Mining and quarrying	1055	169	886	1000	304	696	675	8	667	55	-418	473
3 Manufacturing	20685	3407	17278	14618	-2793	17411	10258	-5976	16234	12676	-6112	18788
4 Electricity, gas and water	8447	47	8400	9936	-76	10012	11643	-489	12132	13257	-618	13875
5 Construction	1820	...	1820	1891	...	1891	1883	...	1883	2063	...	2063
6 Wholesale and retail trade, restaurants and hotels	6479	1423	5056	1427	-3674	5101	5215	-554	5769	4152	-2548	6700
7 Transport, storage and communication	9917	...	9917	9751	...	9751	11892	...	11892	12142	...	12142
8 Finance, insurance, real estate and business services	34860	...	34860	35229	...	35229	38282	...	38282	43729	...	43729
9 Community, social and personal services	1046	...	1046	1136	...	1136	1230	...	1230	1361	...	1361
Statistical discrepancy	4711	...	4711	5498	...	5498	5799	...	5799	6466	...	6466
Total Industries	93238	4890	88348	85128	-6123	91251	92528	-6647	99175	101938	-9630	111568
Producers of Government Services	18653	1015	17638	19175	536	18639	19615	554	19061	20640	39	20601
Private Non-Profit Institutions Serving Households	...	...	...	...	...	...	...	...	...	...	...	...
Total	111891	5905	105986	104303	-5587	109890	112143	-6093	118236	93417	-9591	132169
Memorandum Item: Mineral Fuels and Power [a]	...	...	6617	...	...	8354	...	...	10897	...	...	12885

	1984 Total Gross Capital Formation	1984 Increase in Stocks	1984 Gross Fixed Capital Formation	1985 Total Gross Capital Formation	1985 Increase in Stocks	1985 Gross Fixed Capital Formation	1986 Total Gross Capital Formation	1986 Increase in Stocks	1986 Gross Fixed Capital Formation
				All Producers					
1 Agriculture, hunting, fishing and forestry	6146	-314	6460	5678	-467	6145	5270	-150	5420
2 Mining and quarrying	281	-249	530	456	-105	561	454	-87	541
3 Manufacturing	19780	-2923	22703	30676	2331	28345	25799	-3222	29021
4 Electricity, gas and water	12142	-1281	13423	12333	-1427	13760	12461	726	11735
5 Construction	2310	...	2310	2389	...	2389	2504	...	2504
6 Wholesale and retail trade, restaurants and hotels	6293	-1824	8117	9022	-1011	10033	7661	-3216	10877
7 Transport, storage and communication	14778	...	14778	15535	...	15535	18224	...	18224
8 Finance, insurance, real estate and business services	48300	...	48300	56047	...	56047	58980	...	58980
9 Community, social and personal services	1286	...	1286	1555	...	1555	1775	...	1775
Statistical discrepancy	7180	...	7180	8043	...	8043	8396	...	8396
Total Industries	118496	-6591	125087	141734	-679	142413	141524	-5949	147473
Producers of Government Services	20662	-835	21497	21187	-675	21862	22371	-130	22501
Private Non-Profit Institutions Serving Households	...	...	...	...	...	...	...	...	...
Total	139158	-7426	146584	162921	-1354	164275	163895	-6079	169974
Memorandum Item: Mineral Fuels and Power [a]	...	...	11919	...	...	12267	...	...	10159

a) Item 'Mineral fuels and power' refers to ISIC categories 353 (Petroleum refineries), 354 (Manufacture of miscellaneous products of petroleum and coal) and 41 (Electricity, gas and steam).

2.10 Gross Capital Formation by Kind of Activity of Owner, ISIC Major Divisions, in Constant Prices

Million Swedish kronor

	1980 Total Gross Capital Formation	1980 Increase in Stocks	1980 Gross Fixed Capital Formation	1981 Total Gross Capital Formation	1981 Increase in Stocks	1981 Gross Fixed Capital Formation	1982 Total Gross Capital Formation	1982 Increase in Stocks	1982 Gross Fixed Capital Formation	1983 Total Gross Capital Formation	1983 Increase in Stocks	1983 Gross Fixed Capital Formation
				At constant prices of: 1980								
					All Producers							
1 Agriculture, hunting, fishing and forestry	4218	-156	4374	4258	92	4166	4698	284	4414	4463	34	4429
2 Mining and quarrying	1055	169	886	950	308	642	568	18	550	60	-288	348
3 Manufacturing	20685	3407	17278	13376	-2593	15969	8152	-5041	13193	8542	-5100	13642
4 Electricity, gas and water	8447	47	8400	8992	-142	9134	9735	-304	10039	10036	-329	10365

Sweden

2.10 Gross Capital Formation by Kind of Activity of Owner, ISIC Major Divisions, in Constant Prices
(Continued)

Million Swedish kronor

	1980 TGCF	1980 IS	1980 GFCF	1981 TGCF	1981 IS	1981 GFCF	1982 TGCF	1982 IS	1982 GFCF	1983 TGCF	1983 IS	1983 GFCF
	\multicolumn{12}{c}{At constant prices of: 1980}
5 Construction	1820	...	1820	1729	...	1729	1589	...	1589	1591	...	1591
6 Wholesale and retail trade, restaurants and hotels	6479	1423	5056	1291	-3427	4718	4311	-529	4840	3357	-1746	5103
7 Transport, storage and communication	9917	...	9917	9087	...	9087	10162	...	10162	9289	...	9289
8 Finance, insurance, real estate and business services	34860	...	34860	31922	...	31922	32329	...	32329	33831	...	33831
9 Community, social and personal services	1046	...	1046	1039	...	1039	1035	...	1035	1040	...	1040
Statistical discrepancy	4711	...	4711	4977	...	4977	4912	...	4912	5113	...	5113
Total Industries	93238	4890	88348	77621	-5762	83383	77491	-5572	83063	77322	-7429	84751
Producers of Government Services	18653	1015	17638	17391	450	16941	16554	391	16163	16095	60	16035
Private Non-Profit Institutions Serving Households	...	...	...	...	...	...	...	...	...	...	...	...
Total	111891	5905	105986	95012	-5312	100324	94045	-5181	99226	93417	-7369	100786
Memorandum Item: Mineral Fuels and Power a	...	...	6617	...	...	7634	...	...	8987	...	...	9563

	1984 TGCF	1984 IS	1984 GFCF	1985 TGCF	1985 IS	1985 GFCF	1986 TGCF	1986 IS	1986 GFCF
	\multicolumn{9}{c}{At constant prices of: 1980 — All Producers}
1 Agriculture, hunting, fishing and forestry	4229	-210	4447	3721	-292	4013	3214	-120	3340
2 Mining and quarrying	214	-156	370	312	-65	377	296	-52	348
3 Manufacturing	14513	-1435	15948	20732	1651	19081	16691	-1853	18544
4 Electricity, gas and water	8924	-536	9460	8647	-518	9165	8312	641	7671
5 Construction	1679	...	1679	1660	...	1660	1632	...	1632
6 Wholesale and retail trade, restaurants and hotels	4925	-885	5810	6285	-498	6783	6131	-972	7103
7 Transport, storage and communication	10997	...	10997	10662	...	10662	11751	...	11751
8 Finance, insurance, real estate and business services	35167	...	35167	38666	...	38666	39027	...	39027
9 Community, social and personal services	917	...	917	1038	...	1038	1133	...	1133
Statistical discrepancy	5374	...	5374	5696	...	5696	5639	...	5639
Total Industries	86939	-3230	90169	97418	278	97140	93826	-2362	96188
Producers of Government Services	15298	-454	15752	14744	-416	15160	14560	-482	15042
Private Non-Profit Institutions Serving Households	...	...	...	...	...	...	...	...	...
Total	102237	-3684	105921	112162	-138	112300	108386	-2844	111230
Memorandum Item: Mineral Fuels and Power a	...	...	8386	...	...	8164	...	...	6621

a) Item 'Mineral fuels and power' refers to ISIC categories 353 (Petroleum refineries), 354 (Manufacture of miscellaneous products of petroleum and coal) and 41 (Electricity, gas and steam).

2.11 Gross Fixed Capital Formation by Kind of Activity of Owner, ISIC Divisions, in Current Prices

Million Swedish kronor

	1970	1975	1977	1978	1979	1980	1981	1982	1983	1984	1985	1986
	\multicolumn{12}{c}{All Producers}
1 Agriculture, hunting, forestry and fishing	1201	3298	4175	4083	4372	4374	4526	5287	5970	6460	6145	5420
A Agriculture and hunting	748	2361	3157	3034	3194	3156	3182	3736	4224	4504	3997	3152
B Forestry and logging	425	903	964	953	1119	1163	1298	1490	1680	1850	2018	2177
C Fishing	28	34	54	96	59	55	46	61	66	106	130	91
2 Mining and quarrying	265	566	875	474	518	886	696	667	473	530	561	541
A Coal mining	...	...	...	...	...	...	...	...	...	...	...	...
B Crude petroleum and natural gas production	...	...	...	...	...	...	...	...	...	...	...	...
C Metal ore mining	220	474	551	380	404	742	628	565	332	353	356	355
D Other mining	45	92	324	94	114	144	68	102	141	177	205	186

Sweden

2.11 Gross Fixed Capital Formation by Kind of Activity of Owner, ISIC Divisions, in Current Prices
(Continued)

Million Swedish kronor

	1970	1975	1977	1978	1979	1980	1981	1982	1983	1984	1985	1986
3 Manufacturing	6556	13476	13361	11911	13296	17278	17411	16234	18788	22703	28345	29021
A Manufacturing of food, beverages and tobacco	727	963	1337	1446	1645	1933	1753	1589	1939	2053	2453	2428
B Textile, wearing apparel and leather industries	196	344	244	277	354	444	382	343	307	378	377	462
C Manufacture of wood, and wood products, including furniture	385	1171	1076	861	940	1387	1137	978	1337	1699	1518	1561
D Manufacture of paper and paper products, printing and publishing	1411	2637	3319	2538	2513	3261	4096	3783	4054	4859	7070	5968
E Manufacture of chemicals and chemical petroleum, coal, rubber and plastic products	742	1306	1516	1492	1924	2034	1852	2339	3278	2957	3768	3928
F Manufacture of non-metallic mineral products except products of petroleum and coal	269	585	488	854	672	609	502	430	410	484	596	703
G Basic metal industries	835	1592	1163	752	1057	2017	1671	1019	927	1336	1642	1514
H Manufacture of fabricated metal products, machinery and equipment	1964	4831	4171	3644	4150	5548	5976	5709	6476	8861	10728	12366
I Other manufacturing industries	27	47	47	47	41	45	42	44	60	76	193	91
4 Electricity, gas and water	3361	5654	7241	7025	6430	8400	10012	12132	13875	13423	13760	11735
A Electricity, gas and steam	2000	4096	5443	5151	4675	6463	8083	10322	11921	11699	12003	9906
B Water works and supply	1361	1558	1798	1874	1755	1937	1929	1810	1954	1724	1757	1829
5 Construction	672	1093	1170	1147	1417	1820	1891	1883	2063	2310	2389	2504
6 Wholesale and retail trade, restaurants and hotels	1949	3537	4285	4100	4687	5056	5101	5769	6700	8117	10033	10877
A Wholesale and retail trade	1775	3286	3987	3777	4327	4553	4686	5136	5822	7158	8854	9716
B Restaurants and hotels	174	251	298	323	360	503	415	633	878	959	1179	1161
7 Transport, storage and communication	3160	5828	7533	6749	8680	9917	9751	11892	12142	14778	15535	18224
A Transport and storage	1926	4262	5891	4368	5967	6392	5646	6871	7017	9488	8970	11062
B Communication	1234	1566	1642	2381	2713	3525	4105	5021	5125	5290	6565	7162
8 Finance, insurance, real estate and business services	12361	17055	20722	26177	31764	34860	35229	38282	43729	48300	56047	58980
A Financial institutions	257	522	554	524	686	680	603	592	555	1016	1219	1997
B Insurance	63	148	118	125	235	144	181	199	181	252	585	432
C Real estate and business services	12041	16385	20050	25528	30843	34036	34445	37491	42993	47032	54243	56551
Real estate except dwellings	1173	1617	1749	1995	2888	3020	2671	3247	3925	4270	5123	6409
Dwellings [a]	10488	13802	16714	21424	25099	26903	27787	28757	30488	34705	37012	37593
9 Community, social and personal services	413	535	798	756	907	1046	1136	1230	1361	1286	1555	1775
A Sanitary and similar services	99	97	164	153	173	215	219	210	192	233	186	342
B Social and related community services	12	29	35	12	21	22	19	17	24	34	72	46
Educational services [b]	12	29	35	12	21	22	19	17	24	34	72	46
Medical, dental, other health and veterinary services	-	-	-	-	-	-	-	-	-	-	-	-
C Recreational and cultural services	144	186	280	324	409	458	518	573	650	668	786	811
D Personal and household services	158	223	319	267	304	351	380	430	495	351	511	576
Statistical discrepancy	530	1977	5084	3434	3947	4711	5498	5799	6466	7180	8043	8396
Total Industries	30468	53019	65244	65856	76018	88348	91251	99175	111568	125087	142413	147473
Producers of Government Services	8299	9899	12803	14243	15543	17638	18639	19061	20601	21497	21862	22501
Private Non-Profit Institutions Serving Households	...	...	...	...	...	...	...	...	...	...	...	...
Total	38767	62918	78047	80099	91561	105986	109890	118236	132169	146584	164275	169974

a) Dwellings includes country lodges.
b) Item 'Educational services' includes research and scientific institutes (ISIC category 932).

Sweden

2.12 Gross Fixed Capital Formation by Kind of Activity of Owner, ISIC Divisions, in Constant Prices

Million Swedish kronor

		1970	1975	1977	1978	1979	1980	1981	1982	1983	1984	1985	1986
		\multicolumn{12}{c}{At constant prices of: 1980}
		\multicolumn{12}{c}{All Producers}
1	Agriculture, hunting, forestry and fishing	2877	5212	5459	4894	4883	4374	4166	4414	4429	4447	4013	3340
	A Agriculture and hunting	1798	3714	4137	3643	3560	3156	2930	3107	3117	3086	2621	1951
	B Forestry and logging	1035	1452	1257	1141	1259	1163	1195	1258	1264	1293	1310	1332
	C Fishing	44	46	65	110	64	55	41	49	48	68	82	57
2	Mining and quarrying	686	914	1144	562	570	886	642	550	348	370	377	348
	A Coal mining	...	...	...	...	...	...	...	...	...	...	...	...
	B Crude petroleum and natural gas production	...	...	...	...	...	...	...	...	...	...	...	...
	C Metal ore mining	570	769	723	452	445	742	578	466	244	247	240	229
	D Other mining	116	145	421	110	125	144	64	84	104	123	137	119
3	Manufacturing	16832	21643	17534	14107	14581	17278	15969	13193	13642	15948	19081	18544
	A Manufacturing of food, beverages and tobacco	1862	1541	1747	1715	1799	1933	1608	1297	1419	1455	1660	1548
	B Textile, wearing apparel and leather industries	502	553	319	329	389	444	350	278	223	265	254	295
	C Manufacture of wood, and wood products, including furniture	991	1887	1411	1022	1032	1387	1043	799	981	1197	1026	1004
	D Manufacture of paper and paper products, printing and publishing	3622	4207	4362	2999	2757	3261	3755	3064	2919	3395	4734	3795
	E Manufacture of chemicals and chemical petroleum, coal, rubber and plastic products	1906	2091	1992	1770	2113	2034	1701	1886	2364	2070	2532	2506
	F Manufacture of non metallic mineral products except products of petroleum and coal	690	934	640	1006	737	609	461	350	299	338	399	447
	G Basic metal industries	2142	2556	1528	888	1159	2017	1532	824	665	931	1096	956
	H Manufacture of fabricated metal products, machinery and equipment	5048	7797	5473	4322	4550	5548	5480	4660	4728	6243	7248	7934
	I Other manufacturing industries	69	77	62	56	45	45	39	35	44	54	132	59
4	Electricity, gas and water	7981	8922	9433	8421	7184	8400	9134	10039	10365	9460	9165	7671
	A Electricity, gas and steam	4785	6456	7093	6145	5208	6463	7385	8526	8876	8233	7989	6462
	B Water works and supply	3196	2466	2340	2276	1976	1937	1749	1513	1489	1227	1176	1209
5	Construction	1654	1752	1519	1373	1561	1820	1729	1589	1591	1679	1660	1632
6	Wholesale and retail trade, restaurants and hotels	4638	5490	5531	4919	5196	5056	4718	4840	5103	5810	6783	7103
	A Wholesale and retail trade	4308	5139	5171	4556	4809	4553	4336	4310	4432	5109	5957	6295
	B Restaurants and hotels	330	351	360	363	387	503	382	530	671	701	826	808
7	Transport, storage and communication	8245	8572	9038	7063	9163	9917	9087	10162	9289	10997	10662	11751
	A Transport and storage	5096	6140	6914	4252	6195	6392	5330	5957	5424	7176	6166	7076
	B Communication	3149	2432	2124	2811	2968	3525	3757	4205	3865	3821	4496	4675
8	Finance, insurance, real estate and business services	34911	33391	30379	34073	36450	34860	31922	32329	33831	35167	38666	39027
	A Financial institutions	518	756	678	608	741	680	546	490	419	725	843	1379
	B Insurance	141	225	148	146	251	144	165	165	138	181	403	296
	C Real estate and business services	34252	32410	29553	33319	35458	34036	31211	31674	33274	34261	37420	37352
	Real estate except dwellings	2785	2743	2367	2462	3225	3020	2426	2690	2984	3059	3514	4215
	Dwellings [a]	30779	28346	25272	28475	29174	26903	25102	24461	23935	25495	25692	24973
9	Community, social and personal services	1012	839	1038	900	1004	1046	1039	1035	1040	917	1038	1133
	A Sanitary and similar services	257	151	214	182	189	215	204	184	152	168	128	224
	B Social and related community services	29	45	43	12	21	22	19	16	19	26	50	29

Sweden

2.12 Gross Fixed Capital Formation by Kind of Activity of Owner, ISIC Divisions, in Constant Prices
(Continued)

Million Swedish kronor

	1970	1975	1977	1978	1979	1980	1981	1982	1983	1984	1985	1986
				At constant prices of:1980								
Educational services [b]	29	45	43	12	21	22	19	16	19	26	50	29
Medical, dental, other health and veterinary services	...	...	...	...	...	...	...	...	...	...	...	...
C Recreational and cultural services	341	286	368	389	463	458	464	472	491	470	514	512
D Personal and household services	385	357	413	317	331	351	352	363	378	253	346	368
Statistical discrepancy	1391	3569	7242	4386	4475	4711	4977	4912	5113	5374	5696	5639
Total Industries	80227	90304	88317	80698	85067	88348	83383	83063	84751	90169	97140	96188
Producers of Government Services	19958	16179	16950	17367	17377	17638	16941	16163	16035	15752	15160	15042
Private Non-Profit Institutions Serving Households	...	...	...	...	...	...	...	...	...	...	...	...
Total	100185	106483	105267	98065	102444	105986	100324	99226	100786	105921	112300	111230

a) Dwellings includes country lodges.
b) Item 'Educational services' includes research and scientific institutes (ISIC category 932).

2.14 Stocks of Reproducible Fixed Assets, by Type of Good and Owner, in Constant Prices

Million Swedish kronor

	TOTAL Gross	TOTAL Net	Total Private Gross	Total Private Net	Public Enterprises Gross	Public Enterprises Net	General Government Gross	General Government Net
				At constant prices of:1980				
				1980				
1 Residential buildings	991025	...	...	...	991025	...	-	...
2 Non-residential buildings	1039360	...	...	...	709610	...	329753	...
3 Other construction								
4 Land improvement and plantation and orchard development	...	...	...	...	...	...	...	...
5 Producers' durable goods	526203	...	...	...	491602	...	34601	...
A Transport equipment	56529	...	...	...	55136	...	1393	...
Passenger cars	27891	...	...	...	27455	...	436	...
Other	28638	...	...	...	27681	...	957	...
B Machinery and equipment	469674	...	...	...	436466	...	33208	...
6 Breeding stock, dairy cattle, etc.	...	...	...	...	...	...	...	...
Total [ab]	2556590	...	...	...	2192240	...	364354	...
				1981				
1 Residential buildings	1007600	...	...	...	1007600	...	-	...
2 Non-residential buildings	1070100	...	...	...	728838	...	341259	...
3 Other construction								
4 Land improvement and plantation and orchard development	...	...	...	...	...	...	...	...
5 Producers' durable goods	543193	...	...	...	506638	...	36555	...
A Transport equipment	56661	...	...	...	55186	...	1475	...
Passenger cars	27880	...	...	...	27432	...	448	...
Other	28781	...	...	...	27754	...	1027	...
B Machinery and equipment	486532	...	...	...	451452	...	35080	...
6 Breeding stock, dairy cattle, etc.	...	...	...	...	...	...	...	...
Total [ab]	2620890	...	...	...	2243080	...	377814	...
				1982				
1 Residential buildings	1023760	...	...	...	1023760	...	-	...
2 Non-residential buildings	1098570	...	...	...	746233	...	352337	...
3 Other construction								
4 Land improvement and plantation and orchard development	...	...	...	...	...	...	...	...
5 Producers' durable goods	558335	...	...	...	520198	...	38137	...
A Transport equipment	57822	...	...	...	56243	...	1579	...
Passenger cars	28391	...	...	...	27940	...	451	...
Other	29431	...	...	...	28303	...	1128	...
B Machinery and equipment	500513	...	...	...	463955	...	36558	...
6 Breeding stock, dairy cattle, etc.	...	...	...	...	...	...	...	...
Total [ab]	2680660	...	...	...	2290190	...	390474	...

Sweden

2.14 Stocks of Reproducible Fixed Assets, by Type of Good and Owner, in Constant Prices
(Continued)

Million Swedish kronor

		TOTAL Gross	TOTAL Net	Total Private Gross	Total Private Net	Public Enterprises Gross	Public Enterprises Net	General Government Gross	General Government Net
		\multicolumn{9}{c}{At constant prices of:1980}								
		\multicolumn{9}{c}{1983}								
1	Residential buildings	1037050	...	...	...	1037050	...	-	...
2	Non-residential buildings	1126600	...	...	...	764133	...	362468	...
3	Other construction		...	...	...		...		...
4	Land improvement and plantation and orchard development	...	...	...	...	...	...	...	...
5	Producers' durable goods	572724	...	...	...	533069	...	39655	...
	A Transport equipment	59160	...	...	...	57518	...	1642	...
	Passenger cars	28448	...	...	...	28021	...	427	...
	Other	30712	...	...	...	29497	...	1215	...
	B Machinery and equipment	513564	...	...	...	475551	...	38013	...
6	Breeding stock, dairy cattle, etc.	...	...	...	...	...	...	...	...
Total ab		2736380	...			2334250	...	402123	...

a) Column 'Total Private' is included in column 'Public Enterprise'.
b) Estimates of this table (Stocks of reproducible fixed assets) are stocks at January 1st each year.

2.16 Stocks of Reproducible Fixed Assets by Kind of Activity, in Constant Prices

Million Swedish kronor

		1980 Gross	1980 Net	1981 Gross	1981 Net	1982 Gross	1982 Net	1983 Gross	1983 Net
		\multicolumn{8}{c}{At constant prices of:1980}							
1	Residential buildings	991025	...	1007600	...	1023760	...	1037050	...
2	Non-residential buildings a	1039360	...	1070100	...	1098570	...	1126600	...
	A Industries	1700640	...	1736440	...	1769990	...	1801180	...
	1 Agriculture	68264	...	69075	...	69790	...	70631	...
	2 Mining and quarrying	9475	...	9807	...	10035	...	10257	...
	3 Manufacturing	165176	...	168274	...	170497	...	172477	...
	4 Electricity, gas and water	146015	...	151716	...	157719	...	164160	...
	5 Construction	8748	...	9184	...	9559	...	10010	...
	6 Wholesale and retail trade	51471	...	53222	...	54852	...	56508	...
	7 Transport and communication	104920	...	106974	...	109037	...	111397	...
	8 Finance, etc.	1130160	...	1151510	...	1171550	...	1188540	...
	9 Community, social and personal services	16403	...	16675	...	16949	...	17200	...
	B Producers of government services	329753	...	341259	...	352337	...	362468	...
	C Other producers	...	...	...	...	...	...	...	...
3	Other construction a	...	...	...	...	...	...	...	...
4	Land improvement and development and plantation and orchard development	...	...	...	...	...	...	...	...
5	Producers' durable goods	526203	...	543193	...	558335	...	572724	...
	A Industries	491602	...	506638	...	520198	...	533069	...
	1 Agriculture	39766	...	40400	...	41057	...	41606	...
	2 Mining and quarrying	10066	...	10437	...	10658	...	10779	...
	3 Manufacturing	229882	...	236483	...	242487	...	246381	...
	4 Electricity, gas and water	45492	...	47020	...	48912	...	51193	...
	5 Construction	17306	...	17212	...	17347	...	16956	...
	6 Wholesale and retail trade	40019	...	40736	...	41291	...	41616	...
	7 Transport and communication	82432	...	83735	...	84522	...	86327	...
	8 Finance, etc.	20931	...	25123	...	28567	...	32931	...
	9 Community, social and personal services	5708	...	5492	...	5357	...	5280	...
	B Producers of government services	34601	...	36555	...	38137	...	39655	...
	C Other producers	...	...	...	...	...	...	...	...
6	Breeding stock, dairy cattle, etc.	...	...	...	...	...	...	...	...
Total		2556590	...	2620890	...	2680660	...	2736380	...

a) Item 'Other construction' is included in item 'Non-residential buildings'.

Sweden

2.17 Exports and Imports of Goods and Services, Detail

Million Swedish kronor

	1970	1975	1977	1978	1979	1980	1981	1982	1983	1984	1985	1986
Exports of Goods and Services												
1 Exports of merchandise, f.o.b.	35045	71727	85199	97703	117509	130246	143909	167088	209168	241362	258681	262571
2 Transport and communication	4492	6888	7530	8696	10107	11386	15758	16541	18823	19400	20904	20490
A In respect of merchandise imports [a]	2984	3648	4453	5022	6139	6826	8357	8926	9554	9875	10586	9374
B Other	1508	3240	3077	3674	3968	4560	7401	7615	9269	9525	10318	11116
3 Insurance service charges [b]	...	...	...	...	...	...	...	...	...	...	...	...
4 Other commodities	1165	3781	5451	6270	8804	10472	7611	10896	12699	13978	12666	13689
5 Adjustments of merchandise exports to change-of-ownership basis	-	-	-	-	-	-	-	-	-	-	-	-
6 Direct purchases in the domestic market by non-residential households [c]	813	2283	3152	3730	4148	4419	5249	6806	8838	9924	11258	12040
7 Direct purchases in the domestic market by extraterritorial bodies	...	...	...	...	...	...	...	...	...	...	...	...
Total Exports of Goods and Services	41515	84679	101332	116399	140568	156523	172527	201331	249528	284664	303509	308790
Imports of Goods and Services												
1 Imports of merchandise, c.i.f.	36730	73519	91492	93883	124661	143839	148735	177208	202038	221134	246761	233574
A Imports of merchandise, f.o.b.	35070	71165	88564	90743	120709	140033	144791	172518	197313	216180	241980	227641
B Transport of services on merchandise imports	1533	2101	2612	2815	3521	3310	3433	4081	4023	4189	3900	5096
By residents	411	611	714	773	950	968	1097	1262	1183	1282	1631	1664
By non-residents	1122	1490	1898	2042	2571	2342	2336	2819	2840	2907	2269	3432
C Insurance service charges on merchandise imports	127	253	316	325	431	496	511	609	702	765	881	837
By residents	34	74	86	89	116	145	164	189	206	234	368	274
By non-residents	93	179	230	236	315	351	347	420	496	531	513	563
2 Adjustments of merchandise imports to change-of-ownership basis	...	...	...	...	...	...	...	...	...	...	...	...
3 Other transport and communication	1440	2767	3529	4303	4873	5696	6002	7495	7653	8556	8740	9948
4 Other insurance service charges [b]	...	...	...	...	...	...	...	...	...	...	...	...
5 Other commodities	1492	3735	5315	5813	6323	6794	5511	7688	9829	9705	10916	13113
6 Direct purchases abroad by government	...	...	...	...	...	...	...	...	...	...	...	...
7 Direct purchases abroad by resident households [c]	2816	5242	7172	8174	9339	10191	11980	12766	13601	14872	17435	20772
Total Imports of Goods and Services	42478	85263	107508	112173	145196	166520	172228	205157	233121	254267	283852	277407
Balance of Goods and Services	-963	-584	-6176	4226	-4628	-9997	299	-3826	16407	30397	19657	31383
Total Imports and Balance of Goods and Services	41515	84679	101332	116399	140568	156523	172527	201331	249528	284664	303509	308790

a) Transport and communication in respect of merchandise imports includes all freight services provided by Swedish transporters abroad.
b) Insurance service charges paid and received are calculated net.
c) Beginning 1975, items 'Direct purchases in the domestic market by non-residential households' and 'Direct purchase abroad by resident households' include gross amounts of Swedish bank-notes used for direct purchases abroad by residents and direct purchases in the domestic market.

3.11 General Government Production Account: Total and Subsectors

Million Swedish kronor

	1980					1981				
	Total General Government	Central Government	State or Provincial Government	Local Government	Social Security Funds	Total General Government	Central Government	State or Provincial Government	Local Government	Social Security Funds
Gross Output										
1 Sales	...	...	...	...	...	...	...	...	...	...
2 Services produced for own use	...	...	...	...	...	...	...	...	...	...
3 Own account fixed capital formation	...	...	...	...	...	...	...	...	...	...
Gross Output	...	...	...	...	...	...	...	...	...	...
Gross Input										
Intermediate Consumption	...	...	...	...	...	...	...	...	...	...
Subtotal: Value Added	...	...	...	...	...	...	...	...	...	...
1 Indirect taxes, net	...	...	...	...	...	...	...	...	...	...
2 Consumption of fixed capital	6733	1460	...	5255	18	7654	1643	...	5990	21
3 Compensation of employees	113232	...	...	...	...	123787	...	...	...	...
4 Net Operating surplus	2000	141	...	1859	-	2310	135	...	2175	-
Gross Input	...	...	...	...	...	...	...	...	...	...

Sweden

3.11 General Government Production Account: Total and Subsectors

Million Swedish kronor

	1982 Total General Government	Central Government	State or Provincial Government	Local Government	Social Security Funds	1983 Total General Government	Central Government	State or Provincial Government	Local Government	Social Security Funds
Gross Output										
1 Sales	...	...	...	...	...	...	...	...	...	...
2 Services produced for own use	...	...	...	...	...	...	...	...	...	...
3 Own account fixed capital formation	...	...	...	...	...	...	...	...	...	...
Gross Output	...	...	...	...	...	...	...	...	...	...
Gross Input										
Intermediate Consumption	...	...	...	...	...	...	...	...	...	...
Subtotal: Value Added	...	...	...	...	...	...	...	...	...	...
1 Indirect taxes, net	...	...	...	...	...	...	...	...	...	...
2 Consumption of fixed capital	8657	1860	...	6773	24	9747	2066	...	7651	30
3 Compensation of employees	134495	...	...	...	...	145715	...	...	...	...
4 Net Operating surplus	2742	145	...	2597	-	4407	145	...	4262	-
Gross Input	...	...	...	...	...	...	...	...	...	...

	1984 Total General Government	Central Government	State or Provincial Government	Local Government	Social Security Funds	1985 Total General Government	Central Government	State or Provincial Government	Local Government	Social Security Funds
Gross Output										
1 Sales	...	...	...	...	...	...	...	...	...	...
2 Services produced for own use	...	...	...	...	...	...	...	...	...	...
3 Own account fixed capital formation	...	...	...	...	...	...	...	...	...	...
Gross Output	...	...	...	...	...	...	...	...	...	...
Gross Input										
Intermediate Consumption	...	...	...	...	...	...	...	...	...	...
Subtotal: Value Added	...	...	...	...	...	...	...	...	...	...
1 Indirect taxes, net	...	...	...	...	...	...	...	...	...	...
2 Consumption of fixed capital	10637	2251	...	8358	28	11410	2339	...	9040	31
3 Compensation of employees	158233	...	...	...	...	...	...	...	...	...
4 Net Operating surplus	4343	208	...	4135	-	4611	160	...	4451	-
Gross Input	...	...	...	...	...	...	...	...	...	...

	1986 Total General Government	Central Government	State or Provincial Government	Local Government	Social Security Funds
Gross Output					
1 Sales	...	...	...	...	...
2 Services produced for own use	...	...	...	...	...
3 Own account fixed capital formation	...	...	...	...	...
Gross Output	...	...	...	...	...
Gross Input					
Intermediate Consumption	...	...	...	...	...
Subtotal: Value Added	...	...	...	...	...
1 Indirect taxes, net	...	...	...	...	...
2 Consumption of fixed capital	12264	2621	...	9613	30
3 Compensation of employees	...	...	...	...	...
4 Net Operating surplus	5106	205	...	4901	-
Gross Input	...	...	...	...	...

3.12 General Government Income and Outlay Account: Total and Subsectors

Million Swedish kronor

	1980 Total General Government	Central Government	State or Provincial Government	Local Government	Social Security Funds	1981 Total General Government	Central Government	State or Provincial Government	Local Government	Social Security Funds
Receipts										
1 Operating surplus	2000	141	...	1859	-	2310	135	...	2175	-
2 Property and entrepreneurial income	27121	8288	...	4815	14018	32782	10473	...	5504	16805
A Withdrawals from public quasi-corporations	2246	2246	...	-	-	2736	2736	...	-	-
B Interest	23860	5927	...	3972	13961	28924	7621	...	4564	16739

Sweden

3.12 General Government Income and Outlay Account: Total and Subsectors
(Continued)

Million Swedish kronor

	1980					1981				
	Total General Government	Central Government	State or Provincial Government	Local Government	Social Security Funds	Total General Government	Central Government	State or Provincial Government	Local Government	Social Security Funds
C Dividends	196	92	...	47	57	197	95	...	36	66
D Net land rent and royalties	819	23	...	796	-	925	21	...	904	-
3 Taxes, fees and contributions	260498	133390	...	77668	49440	292155	148615	...	86946	56594
A Indirect taxes	71337	69587	...	1750	-	83784	81521	...	2263	-
B Direct taxes	113925	38007	...	75918	-	121835	37152	...	84683	-
C Social security contributions	74643	25203	...	-	49440	85833	29239	...	-	56594
D Fees, fines and penalties	593	593	...	-	-	703	703	...	-	-
4 Other current transfers	7628	3700	...	51574	2944	6913	2530	...	56694	1655
A Casualty insurance claims	...	...	...	...	...	...	...	...	...	...
B Transfers from other government subsectors	...	3620	...	44026	2944	...	3451	...	48860	1655
C Transfers from the rest of the world	...	...	...	...	...	...	...	...	...	...
D Other transfers, except imputed	1479	289	...	1190	-	1672	243	...	1429	-
E Imputed unfunded employee pension and welfare contributions	6149	-209	...	6358	-	5241	-1164	...	6405	-
Total Current Receipts	297247	145519	...	135916	66402	334160	161753	...	151319	75054

Disbursements

	1980					1981				
1 Government final consumption expenditure	151374	45269	...	103748	2357	167414	48972	...	115918	2524
2 Property income	21887	17057	...	4814	16	31144	25512	...	5604	28
A Interest	21591	17057	...	4518	16	30771	25512	...	5231	28
B Net land rent and royalties	296	-	...	296	-	373	-	...	373	-
3 Subsidies	22643	14588	...	3885	4170	26684	17617	...	4770	4297
4 Other current transfers	102495	95142	...	14982	42961	116209	104813	...	15747	49615
A Casualty insurance premiums, net	199	199	...	-	-	422	422	...	-	-
B Transfers to other government subsectors	...	39682	...	5386	5522	...	42381	...	5548	6037
C Social security benefits	73396	36238	...	-	37158	84729	41470	...	-	43259
D Social assistance grants	16457	11054	...	5122	281	17188	11716	...	5153	319
E Unfunded employee pension and welfare benefits	3440	1650	...	1790	-	3580	1691	...	1889	-
F Transfers to private non-profit institutions serving households	4882	2198	...	2684	-	6068	2911	...	3157	-
G Other transfers n.e.c.	...	...	...	...	...	...	...	...	...	...
H Transfers to the rest of the world	4121	4121	...	-	-	4222	4222	...	-	-
Net saving	-1152	-26537	...	8487	16898	-7291	-35161	...	9280	18590
Total Current Disbursements and Net Saving	297247	145519	...	135916	66402	334160	161753	...	151319	75054

	1982					1983				
	Total General Government	Central Government	State or Provincial Government	Local Government	Social Security Funds	Total General Government	Central Government	State or Provincial Government	Local Government	Social Security Funds

Receipts

1 Operating surplus	2742	145	...	2597	-	4407	145	...	4262	-
2 Property and entrepreneurial income	38910	13778	...	5717	19415	45650	17698	...	5784	22168
A Withdrawals from public quasi-corporations	4146	4146	...	-	-	6631	6631	...	-	-
B Interest	33504	9489	...	4683	19332	37702	10935	...	4693	22074
C Dividends	246	121	...	42	83	254	123	...	37	94
D Net land rent and royalties	1014	22	...	992	-	1063	9	...	1054	-
3 Taxes, fees and contributions	315679	160802	...	97393	57484	358999	191154	...	107363	60482
A Indirect taxes	91795	89416	...	2379	-	107644	105183	...	2461	-
B Direct taxes	136230	41216	...	95014	-	154440	49140	...	104902	398
C Social security contributions	86630	29146	...	-	57484	95653	35569	...	-	60084
D Fees, fines and penalties	1024	1024	...	-	-	1262	1262	...	-	-

Sweden

3.12 General Government Income and Outlay Account: Total and Subsectors
(Continued)

Million Swedish kronor

	1982 Total General Government	1982 Central Government	1982 State or Provincial Government	1982 Local Government	1982 Social Security Funds	1983 Total General Government	1983 Central Government	1983 State or Provincial Government	1983 Local Government	1983 Social Security Funds
4 Other current transfers	12200	4870	...	61210	5494	13251	4640	...	67456	8936
A Casualty insurance claims	...	...	...	...	...	...	...	...	...	...
B Transfers from other government subsectors	...	3150	...	50730	5494	...	3239	...	55606	8936
C Transfers from the rest of the world	...	...	...	...	...	...	...	...	...	...
D Other transfers, except imputed	2699	341	...	2358	-	3437	460	...	2977	-
E Imputed unfunded employee pension and welfare contributions	9501	1379	...	8122	-	9814	941	...	8873	-
Total Current Receipts	369531	179595	...	166917	82393	422307	213637	...	184865	91586

Disbursements

	1982 Total	1982 Central	1982 State/Prov	1982 Local	1982 SSF	1983 Total	1983 Central	1983 State/Prov	1983 Local	1983 SSF
1 Government final consumption expenditure	182711	52153	...	127872	2686	200560	54554	...	143183	2823
2 Property income	43953	37653	...	6256	44	51457	44997	...	6424	36
A Interest	43496	37653	...	5799	44	51063	44997	...	6030	36
B Net land rent and royalties	457	-	...	457	-	394	-	...	394	-
3 Subsidies	31076	20841	...	5326	4909	36850	26023	...	5368	5459
4 Other current transfers	127516	113182	...	17626	56082	143225	126940	...	19858	64208
A Casualty insurance premiums, net	338	338	...	-	-	450	450	...	-	-
B Transfers to other government subsectors	...	47393	...	5155	6826	...	54831	...	5647	7303
C Social security benefits	92730	43834	...	-	48896	104640	48148	...	-	56492
D Social assistance grants	19782	12610	...	6812	360	21711	13486	...	7812	413
E Unfunded employee pension and welfare benefits	3944	1899	...	2045	-	4362	2090	...	2272	-
F Transfers to private non-profit institutions serving households	6343	2729	...	3614	-	7196	3069	...	4127	-
G Other transfers n.e.c.	...	...	...	...	...	...	...	...	...	...
H Transfers to the rest of the world	4379	4379	...	-	-	4866	4866	...	-	-
Net saving	-15725	-44234	...	9837	18672	-9785	-38877	...	10032	19060
Total Current Disbursements and Net Saving	369531	179595	...	166917	82393	422307	213637	...	184865	91586

	1984 Total General Government	1984 Central Government	1984 State or Provincial Government	1984 Local Government	1984 Social Security Funds	1985 Total General Government	1985 Central Government	1985 State or Provincial Government	1985 Local Government	1985 Social Security Funds

Receipts

1 Operating surplus	4343	208	...	4135	-	4611	160	...	4451	-
2 Property and entrepreneurial income	50891	19242	...	6409	25240	57194	22033	...	6761	28400
A Withdrawals from public quasi-corporations	7921	7921	...	-	-	9743	9743	...	*	*
B Interest	41377	11079	...	5179	25119	45522	11898	...	5377	28247
C Dividends	382	217	...	44	121	571	361	...	57	153
D Net land rent and royalties	1211	25	...	1186	-	1358	31	...	1327	-
3 Taxes, fees and contributions	400969	218867	...	115534	66568	433991	241611	...	123084	69296
A Indirect taxes	126261	123076	...	2564	621	141245	138788	...	1780	677
B Direct taxes	169294	55699	...	112970	625	182952	61111	...	121304	537
C Social security contributions	103781	38459	...	-	65322	108206	40124	...	-	68082
D Fees, fines and penalties	1600	1600	...	-	-	1588	1588	...	-	-
4 Other current transfers	14335	4364	...	74119	10449	16837	6336	...	80046	19740
A Casualty insurance claims	...	...	...	...	...	...	...	...	...	...
B Transfers from other government subsectors	...	3470	...	60678	10449	...	3606	...	65939	19740
C Transfers from the rest of the world	...	...	...	...	...	...	...	...	...	...
D Other transfers, except imputed	4131	496	...	3635	-	4299	314	...	3985	-
E Imputed unfunded employee pension and welfare contributions	10204	398	...	9806	-	12538	2416	...	10122	-
Total Current Receipts	470538	242681	...	200197	102257	512633	270140	...	214342	117436

Sweden

3.12 General Government Income and Outlay Account: Total and Subsectors
(Continued)

Million Swedish kronor

	1984					1985				
	Total General Government	Central Government	State or Provincial Government	Local Government	Social Security Funds	Total General Government	Central Government	State or Provincial Government	Local Government	Social Security Funds

Disbursements

1 Government final consumption expenditure	218041	58199	...	156936	2906	235879	61710	...	170996	3173
2 Property income	60991	54034	...	6849	108	73318	65815	...	7326	177
A Interest	60464	54034	...	6322	108	72738	65815	...	6746	177
B Net land rent and royalties	527	-	...	527	-	580	-	...	580	-
3 Subsidies	39157	27794	...	5543	5820	42107	29508	...	6307	6292
4 Other current transfers	152914	134871	...	21746	70894	172339	151151	...	24306	86167
A Casualty insurance premiums, net	718	718	...	-	-	401	401	...	-	-
B Transfers to other government subsectors	...	60688	...	6230	7679	...	69725	...	6498	13062
C Social security benefits	112335	49579	...	-	62756	125016	52481	...	-	72535
D Social assistance grants	22315	13309	...	8547	459	27372	16338	...	10464	570
E Unfunded employee pension and welfare benefits	4706	2265	...	2441	-	4939	2263	...	2676	-
F Transfers to private non-profit institutions serving households	7773	3245	...	4528	-	8788	4120	...	4668	-
G Other transfers n.e.c.	...	...	...	...	...	...	...	...	...	...
H Transfers to the rest of the world	5067	5067	...	-	-	5823	5823	...	-	-
Net saving	-565	-32217	...	9123	22529	-11010	-38044	...	5407	21627
Total Current Disbursements and Net Saving	470538	242681	...	200197	102257	512633	270140	...	214342	117436

	1986				
	Total General Government	Central Government	State or Provincial Government	Local Government	Social Security Funds

Receipts

1 Operating surplus	5106	205	...	4901	-
2 Property and entrepreneurial income	61799	25055	...	6072	30672
A Withdrawals from public quasi-corporations	11050	11050	...	-	-
B Interest	48495	13574	...	4528	30393
C Dividends	759	396	...	84	279
D Net land rent and royalties	1495	35	...	1460	-
3 Taxes, fees and contributions	495461	276914	...	138063	80484
A Indirect taxes	163298	160659	...	1832	807
B Direct taxes	205803	67669	...	136231	1903
C Social security contributions	124523	46749	...	-	77774
D Fees, fines and penalties	1837	1837	...	-	-
4 Other current transfers	11460	4701	...	77654	18314
A Casualty insurance claims	...	...	...	...	...
B Transfers from other government subsectors	...	3829	...	67066	18314
C Transfers from the rest of the world	...	...	...	...	...
D Other transfers, except imputed	2399	370	...	2029	-
E Imputed unfunded employee pension and welfare contributions	9061	502	...	8559	-
Total Current Receipts	573826	306875	...	226690	129470

Disbursements

1 Government final consumption expenditure	253855	67180	...	183312	3363
2 Property income	71109	63054	...	7960	95
A Interest	70205	63054	...	7056	95
B Net land rent and royalties	904	-	...	904	-
3 Subsidies	45026	31418	...	6629	6979

Sweden

3.12 General Government Income and Outlay Account: Total and Subsectors
(Continued)

Million Swedish kronor

		1986			
		Total General Government	Central Government	State or Provincial Government	Local Government	Social Security Funds
4	Other current transfers	189528	157669	...	25789	95279
	A Casualty insurance premiums, net	541	541	...	-	-
	B Transfers to other government subsectors	...	70218	...	6808	12183
	C Social security benefits	139567	56637	...	-	82930
	D Social assistance grants	27795	16846	...	10783	166
	E Unfunded employee pension and welfare benefits	5599	2469	...	3130	-
	F Transfers to private non-profit institutions serving households	9937	4869	...	5068	-
	G Other transfers n.e.c.	...	...	...	...	...
	H Transfers to the rest of the world	6089	6089	...	-	-
Net saving		14308	-12446	...	3000	23754
Total Current Disbursements and Net Saving		573826	306875	...	226600	120470

3.13 General Government Capital Accumulation Account: Total and Subsectors

Million Swedish kronor

		1980					1981				
		Total General Government	Central Government	State or Provincial Government	Local Government	Social Security Funds	Total General Government	Central Government	State or Provincial Government	Local Government	Social Security Funds
				Finance of Gross Accumulation							
1	Gross saving	5581	-25077	...	13742	16916	363	-33518	...	15270	18611
	A Consumption of fixed capital	6733	1460	...	5255	18	7654	1643	...	5990	21
	B Net saving	-1152	-26537	...	8487	16898	-7291	-35161	...	9280	18590
2	Capital transfers	1617	580	...	2893	-	1696	631	...	3323	-
	A From other government subsectors	...	-	...	1856	-	...	-	...	2258	-
	B From other resident sectors	1617	580	...	1037	-	1696	631	...	1065	-
	C From rest of the world	...	...	...	...	...	...	...	...	...	...
Finance of Gross Accumulation		7198	-24497	...	16635	16916	2059	-32887	...	18593	18611
				Gross Accumulation							
1	Gross capital formation	22851	5815	...	16996	40	23787	5077	...	18656	54
	A Increase in stocks	1015	1015	...	-	-	536	536	...	-	-
	B Gross fixed capital formation	21836	4800	...	16996	40	23251	4541	...	18656	54
2	Purchases of land, net	-526	151	...	-677	-	-78	118	...	-196	-
3	Purchases of intangible assets, net	...	...	...	...	...	...	...	...	...	...
4	Capital transfers	4536	6286	...	106	-	6482	8579	...	161	-
	A To other government subsectors	...	1822	...	34	...	...	2177	...	81	...
	B To other resident sectors	4536	4464	...	72	-	6482	6402	...	80	-
	C To rest of the world	...	...	...	...	...	...	...	...	...	...
Net lending [a]		-19663	-36749	...	210	16876	-28132	-46661	...	-28	18557
Gross Accumulation		7198	-24497	...	16635	16916	2059	-32887	...	18593	18611
		1982					1983				
		Total General Government	Central Government	State or Provincial Government	Local Government	Social Security Funds	Total General Government	Central Government	State or Provincial Government	Local Government	Social Security Funds
				Finance of Gross Accumulation							
1	Gross saving	-7000	-42374	...	16610	18696	-38	-36811	...	17683	19090
	A Consumption of fixed capital	8657	1860	...	6773	24	9747	2066	...	7651	30
	B Net saving	-15725	-44234	...	9837	18672	-9785	-38877	...	10032	19060
2	Capital transfers	1823	710	...	3244	-	1951	835	...	3319	-
	A From other government subsectors	...	-	...	2131	-	...	-	...	2203	-
	B From other resident sectors	1823	710	...	1113	-	1951	835	...	1116	-
	C From rest of the world	...	...	...	...	...	...	...	...	...	...
Finance of Gross Accumulation		-5245	-41664	...	19854	18696	1913	-35976	...	21002	19090
				Gross Accumulation							
1	Gross capital formation	24363	5451	...	18832	80	25927	5684	...	20198	45

Sweden

3.13 General Government Capital Accumulation Account: Total and Subsectors
(Continued)

Million Swedish kronor

	1982					1983				
	Total General Government	Central Government	State or Provincial Government	Local Government	Social Security Funds	Total General Government	Central Government	State or Provincial Government	Local Government	Social Security Funds
A Increase in stocks	554	554	...	-	-	39	39	...	-	-
B Gross fixed capital formation	23809	4897	...	18832	80	25888	5645	...	20198	45
2 Purchases of land, net	-6	116	...	-122	-	81	115	...	-34	-
3 Purchases of intangible assets, net	...	...	...	...	...	...	...	...	...	...
4 Capital transfers	10242	12189	...	184	-	11029	13030	...	202	-
A To other government subsectors	...	2027	...	104	-	...	2090	...	113	-
B To other resident sectors	10242	10162	...	80	-	11029	10940	...	89	-
C To rest of the world	...	...	...	...	...	...	...	...	...	...
Net lending [a]	-39844	-59420	...	960	18616	-35124	-54805	...	636	19045
Gross Accumulation	-5245	-41664	...	19854	18696	1913	-35976	...	21002	19090

	1984					1985				
	Total General Government	Central Government	State or Provincial Government	Local Government	Social Security Funds	Total General Government	Central Government	State or Provincial Government	Local Government	Social Security Funds

Finance of Gross Accumulation

1 Gross saving	10072	-29966	...	17481	22557	400	-35705	...	14447	21658
A Consumption of fixed capital	10637	2251	...	8358	28	11410	2339	...	9040	31
B Net saving	-565	-32217	...	9123	22529	-11010	-38044	...	5407	21627
2 Capital transfers	2108	1059	...	3688	-	2279	1193	...	2959	-
A From other government subsectors	...	-	...	2639	-	...	-	...	1873	-
B From other resident sectors	2108	1059	...	1049	-	2279	1193	...	1086	-
C From rest of the world	...	...	...	...	...	...	...	...	...	...
Finance of Gross Accumulation	12180	-28907	...	21169	22557	2679	-34512	...	17406	21658

Gross Accumulation

1 Gross capital formation	26068	5370	...	20652	46	26736	5292	...	21392	52
A Increase in stocks	-835	-835	...	-	-	-675	-675	...	-	-
B Gross fixed capital formation	26903	6205	...	20652	46	27411	5967	...	21392	52
2 Purchases of land, net	238	109	...	129	-	43	121	...	-78	-
3 Purchases of intangible assets, net	...	...	...	...	...	...	...	...	...	...
4 Capital transfers	6389	8867	...	161	-	8228	10003	...	98	-
A To other government subsectors	...	2574	...	65	-	...	1873	...	-	-
B To other resident sectors	6389	6293	...	96	-	8228	8130	...	98	-
C To rest of the world	...	...	...	...	...	...	...	...	...	...
Net lending [a]	-20515	-43253	...	227	22511	-32328	-49928	...	-4006	21606
Gross Accumulation	12180	-28907	...	21169	22557	2679	-34512	...	17406	21658

	1986				
	Total General Government	Central Government	State or Provincial Government	Local Government	Social Security Funds

Finance of Gross Accumulation

1 Gross saving	26572	-9825	...	12613	23784
A Consumption of fixed capital	12264	2621	...	9613	30
B Net saving	14308	-12446	...	3000	23754
2 Capital transfers	2139	1252	...	2734	-
A From other government subsectors	...	-	...	1847	-
B From other resident sectors	2139	1252	...	887	-
C From rest of the world	...	...	...	...	...
Finance of Gross Accumulation	28711	-8573	...	15347	23784

Gross Accumulation

1 Gross capital formation	27469	5596	...	21820	53
A Increase in stocks	-130	-130	...	-	-
B Gross fixed capital formation	27599	5726	...	21820	53

Sweden

3.13 General Government Capital Accumulation Account: Total and Subsectors
(Continued)

Million Swedish kronor

1986

	Total General Government	Central Government	State or Provincial Government	Local Government	Social Security Funds
2 Purchases of land, net	-1150	127	...	-1277	-
3 Purchases of intangible assets, net	...	...	...	...	...
4 Capital transfers	9113	10773	...	187	-
A To other government subsectors	...	1760	...	87	-
B To other resident sectors	9113	9013	...	100	-
C To rest of the world	...	...	...	...	...
Net lending a	-6721	-25069	...	-5383	23731
Gross Accumulation	28711	-8573	...	15347	23784

a) Net lending of the capital accumulation account and the capital finance account have not been reconciled and are different due to different statistical sources.

3.14 General Government Capital Finance Account, Total and Subsectors

Million Swedish kronor

	1980 Total General Government	Central Government	State or Provincial Government	Local Government	Social Security Funds	1981 Total General Government	Central Government	State or Provincial Government	Local Government	Social Security Funds
			Acquisition of Financial Assets							
1 Gold and SDRs	...	...	...	...	...	...	...	...	...	...
2 Currency and transferable deposits	1933	812	...	1003	118	2841	551	...	2382	-92
3 Other deposits a	868	-	...	868	-	86	-	...	86	-
4 Bills and bonds, short term b	100	-	...	100	-	-100	-	...	-100	-
5 Bonds, long term c	11200	-39	...	52	11187	14263	-12	...	228	14047
6 Corporate equity securities	1564	1238	...	232	94	2375	2054	...	167	154
7 Short-term loans, n.e.c.	14656	11622	...	1746	1288	13516	10365	...	2094	1057
8 Long-term loans, n.e.c.	...	...	...	...	...	...	...	...	...	...
9 Other receivables	...	...	...	...	...	...	...	...	...	...
10 Other assets	9917	4091	...	1643	4183	2051	-1019	...	-275	3345
Total Acquisition of Financial Assets	40238	17724	...	5644	16870	35032	11939	...	4582	18511
			Incurrence of Liabilities							
1 Currency and transferable deposits	...	...	...	...	...	...	...	...	...	...
2 Other deposits a	-	-	...	-	-	-	-	...	-	-
3 Bills and bonds, short term b	7444	7444	...	-	-	-743	-743	...	-	-
4 Bonds, long term c	35805	35821	...	-16	-	59731	58734	...	997	-
5 Short-term loans, n.e.c.	14766	12110	...	2656	-	7419	3437	...	3973	9
6 Long-term loans, n.e.c.	...	...	...	...	...	...	...	...	...	...
7 Other payables	...	...	...	...	...	...	...	...	...	...
8 Other liabilities	1337	-200	...	1538	-1	-979	15	...	-1053	59
Total Incurrence of Liabilities	59352	55175	...	4178	-1	65428	61443	...	3917	68
Net Lending d	-19114	-37451	...	1466	16871	-30396	-49504	...	665	18443
Incurrence of Liabilities and Net Worth	40238	17724	...	5644	16870	35032	11939	...	4582	18511

	1982 Total General Government	Central Government	State or Provincial Government	Local Government	Social Security Funds	1983 Total General Government	Central Government	State or Provincial Government	Local Government	Social Security Funds
			Acquisition of Financial Assets							
1 Gold and SDRs	...	...	...	...	...	...	...	...	...	...
2 Currency and transferable deposits	617	1310	...	-487	-206	-1493	-79	...	-1055	-359
3 Other deposits a	562	-	...	562	...	389	2	...	387	...
4 Bills and bonds, short term b	2159	-	...	2012	147	1291	164	...	774	353
5 Bonds, long term c	15285	58	...	-161	15388	17952	-281	...	1333	16900
6 Corporate equity securities	2037	1582	...	333	122	5473	5360	...	250	-137
7 Short-term loans, n.e.c.	12740	10185	...	914	1641	11239	9700	...	1077	462
8 Long-term loans, n.e.c.	...	...	...	...	...	...	...	...	...	...
9 Other receivables	...	...	...	...	...	...	...	...	...	...
10 Other assets	8699	3810	...	2768	2121	6948	3849	...	1631	1468
Total Acquisition of Financial Assets	42099	16945	...	5941	19213	41799	18715	...	4397	18687
			Incurrence of Liabilities							
1 Currency and transferable deposits	...	...	...	...	...	...	...	...	...	...

Sweden

3.14 General Government Capital Finance Account, Total and Subsectors
(Continued)

Million Swedish kronor

	1982					1983				
	Total General Government	Central Government	State or Provincial Government	Local Government	Social Security Funds	Total General Government	Central Government	State or Provincial Government	Local Government	Social Security Funds
2 Other deposits a	-	-	...	-	-	205	-	...	205	-
3 Bills and bonds, short term b	33741	33741	...	-	-	-5784	-5784	...	-	-
4 Bonds, long term c	26996	27105	...	-109	-	81395	81033	...	362	-
5 Short-term loans, n.e.c.	13932	11440	...	2489	3	4626	4031	...	591	4
6 Long-term loans, n.e.c.	...	...	...	...	...	...	...	...	...	...
7 Other payables	...	...	...	...	...	...	...	...	...	...
8 Other liabilities	5526	3165	...	2048	313	-911	-3180	...	2224	45
Total Incurrence of Liabilities	80195	75451	...	4428	316	79531	76100	...	3382	49
Net Lending d	-38096	-58506	...	1513	18897	-37732	-57385	...	1015	18638
Incurrence of Liabilities and Net Worth	42099	16945	...	5941	19213	41799	18715	...	4397	18687

	1984					1985				
	Total General Government	Central Government	State or Provincial Government	Local Government	Social Security Funds	Total General Government	Central Government	State or Provincial Government	Local Government	Social Security Funds

Acquisition of Financial Assets

1 Gold and SDRs	...	...	...	...	...	...	...	...	...	...
2 Currency and transferable deposits	1184	1781	...	-840	243	-1927	2364	...	-4482	191
3 Other deposits a	63	-2	...	-192	257	1627	779	...	440	408
4 Bills and bonds, short term b	768	264	...	-1042	1546	123	-148	...	643	-372
5 Bonds, long term c	16218	166	...	150	15902	14264	556	...	-311	14019
6 Corporate equity securities	2750	440	...	770	1540	2955	1258	...	543	1154
7 Short-term loans, n.e.c.	11838	9470	...	2357	11	7767	8529	...	-635	-127
8 Long-term loans, n.e.c.	...	...	...	...	...	...	...	...	...	...
9 Other receivables	...	...	...	...	...	...	...	...	...	...
10 Other assets	11947	8155	...	1455	2337	-801	-10961	...	4271	5889
Total Acquisition of Financial Assets	44768	20274	...	2658	21836	24008	2377	...	469	21162

Incurrence of Liabilities

1 Currency and transferable deposits	...	...	...	...	...	...	...	...	...	...
2 Other deposits a	6556	6517	...	39	-	11008	10678	...	330	-
3 Bills and bonds, short term b	38900	38900	...	-	-	21625	21625	...	-	-
4 Bonds, long term c	49724	49544	...	180	-	27092	26909	...	183	-
5 Short-term loans, n.e.c.	-31177	-32962	...	1782	3	1943	-3371	...	5312	2
6 Long-term loans, n.e.c.	...	...	...	...	...	...	...	...	...	...
7 Other payables	...	...	...	...	...	...	...	...	...	...
8 Other liabilities	-2	-	...	-17	15	-1256	-	...	-870	-386
Total Incurrence of Liabilities	64001	61999	...	1984	18	60412	55841	...	4955	-384
Net Lending d	-19233	-41725	...	674	21818	-36404	-53464	...	-4486	21546
Incurrence of Liabilities and Net Worth	44768	20274	...	2658	21836	24008	2377	...	469	21162

	1986				
	Total General Government	Central Government	State or Provincial Government	Local Government	Social Security Funds

Acquisition of Financial Assets

1 Gold and SDRs	...	...	...	...	...
2 Currency and transferable deposits	541	1961	...	-1615	195
3 Other deposits a	957	-499	...	-845	2301
4 Bills and bonds, short term b	-2422	-50	...	-1764	-608
5 Bonds, long term c	18542	1422	...	521	16599
6 Corporate equity securities	4733	1833	...	401	2499
7 Short-term loans, n.e.c.	-3654	-3775	...	-1560	1681
8 Long-term loans, n.e.c.	...	...	...	...	...
9 Other receivables	...	...	...	...	...
10 Other assets	15921	7727	...	5837	2357
Total Acquisition of Financial Assets	34618	8619	...	975	25024

Incurrence of Liabilities

1 Currency and transferable deposits	...	...	...	...	...
2 Other deposits a	17639	15813	...	1826	-
3 Bills and bonds, short term b	-6625	-6625	...	-	-

Sweden

3.14 General Government Capital Finance Account, Total and Subsectors
(Continued)

Million Swedish kronor

	1986				
	Total General Government	Central Government	State or Provincial Government	Local Government	Social Security Funds
4 Bonds, long term c	22297	20960	...	1337	-
5 Short-term loans, n.e.c.	4571	2570	...	2002	-1
6 Long-term loans, n.e.c.	...	...	...	...	...
7 Other payables	...	...	...	...	...
8 Other liabilities	2270	-	...	685	1585
Total Incurrence of Liabilities	40152	32718	...	5850	1584
Net Lending d	-5534	-24099	...	-4875	23440
Incurrence of Liabilities and Net Worth	34618	8619	...	975	25024

a) Item 'Other deposits' refers to certificate of deposit.
b) 'Bills and bonds' refer to Swedish treasury bills and special treasury bills.
c) Item 'Bonds, long-term' includes both short-term and long-term bonds.
d) Net lending of the capital accumulation account and the capital finance account have not been reconciled and are different due to different statistical sources.

3.21 Corporate and Quasi-Corporate Enterprise Production Account: Total and Sectors

Million Swedish kronor

	1980				1981				1982			
	\multicolumn{3}{c}{Corporate and Quasi-Corporate Enterprises}	ADDENDUM: Total, including Unincorporated	\multicolumn{3}{c}{Corporate and Quasi-Corporate Enterprises}	ADDENDUM: Total, including Unincorporated	\multicolumn{3}{c}{Corporate and Quasi-Corporate Enterprises}	ADDENDUM: Total, including Unincorporated
	TOTAL	Non-Financial	Financial		TOTAL	Non-Financial	Financial		TOTAL	Non-Financial	Financial	
Gross Output												
1 Output for sale	...	...	...	...	...	...	...	...	...	...	...	...
2 Imputed bank service charge	...	...	...	...	...	...	...	...	...	...	...	...
3 Own-account fixed capital formation	...	...	...	...	...	...	...	...	...	...	...	...
Gross Output	...	...	...	...	...	...	...	...	...	...	...	...
Gross Input												
Intermediate consumption	...	...	...	...	...	...	...	...	...	...	...	...
Subtotal: Value Added	...	...	...	...	...	...	...	...	...	...	...	...
1 Indirect taxes, net	...	...	...	...	...	...	...	...	...	...	...	...
2 Consumption of fixed capital	37890	37358	532	52688	42178	41574	604	58825	47778	47093	685	66018
3 Compensation of employees	213693	206230	7463	220065	234071	225880	8191	240560	...	...	...	...
4 Net operating surplus	21313	25501	-4188	77899	19061	23755	-4694	78788	28818	33945	-5127	100016
Gross Input	...	...	...	...	...	...	...	...	...	...	...	...

	1983				1984				1985			
	\multicolumn{3}{c}{Corporate and Quasi-Corporate Enterprises}	ADDENDUM: Total, including Unincorporated	\multicolumn{3}{c}{Corporate and Quasi-Corporate Enterprises}	ADDENDUM: Total, including Unincorporated	\multicolumn{3}{c}{Corporate and Quasi-Corporate Enterprises}	ADDENDUM: Total, including Unincorporated
	TOTAL	Non-Financial	Financial		TOTAL	Non-Financial	Financial		TOTAL	Non-Financial	Financial	
Gross Output												
1 Output for sale	...	...	...	...	...	...	...	...	...	...	...	...
2 Imputed bank service charge	...	...	...	...	...	...	...	...	...	...	...	...
3 Own-account fixed capital formation	...	...	...	...	...	...	...	...	...	...	...	...
Gross Output	...	...	...	...	...	...	...	...	...	...	...	...
Gross Input												
Intermediate consumption	...	...	...	...	...	...	...	...	...	...	...	...
Subtotal: Value Added	...	...	...	...	...	...	...	...	...	...	...	...
1 Indirect taxes, net	...	...	...	...	...	...	...	...	...	...	...	...
2 Consumption of fixed capital	54433	53662	771	74592	58826	57975	851	81115	64484	63538	946	88054
3 Compensation of employees	...	...	...	...	...	...	...	...	...	...	...	...
4 Net operating surplus	46806	53145	-6339	124225	59090	68228	-9138	144951	63881	74921	-11040	155292
Gross Input	...	...	...	...	...	...	...	...	...	...	...	...

	1986			
	\multicolumn{3}{c}{Corporate and Quasi-Corporate Enterprises}	ADDENDUM: Total, including Unincorporated
	TOTAL	Non-Financial	Financial	
Gross Output				
1 Output for sale	...	...	...	...
2 Imputed bank service charge	...	...	...	...
3 Own-account fixed capital formation	...	...	...	...
Gross Output	...	...	...	...

Sweden

3.21 Corporate and Quasi-Corporate Enterprise Production Account: Total and Sectors
(Continued)

Million Swedish kronor

	1986 Corporate and Quasi-Corporate Enterprises TOTAL	Non-Financial	Financial	ADDENDUM: Total, including Unincorporated
				Gross Input
Intermediate consumption	...	...	...	...
Subtotal: Value Added	...	...	...	...
1 Indirect taxes, net	...	...	...	...
2 Consumption of fixed capital	68689	67631	1058	93601
3 Compensation of employees	...	...	...	...
4 Net operating surplus	61793	74841	-13048	155067
Gross Input	...	...	...	...

3.22 Corporate and Quasi-Corporate Enterprise Income and Outlay Account: Total and Sectors

Million Swedish kronor

	1980 TOTAL	Non-Financial	Financial	1981 TOTAL	Non-Financial	Financial	1982 TOTAL	Non-Financial	Financial	1983 TOTAL	Non-Financial	Financial
						Receipts						
1 Operating surplus	21313	25501	-4188	19061	23755	-4694	28818	33945	-5127	46806	53145	-6339
2 Property and entrepreneurial income	86631	3911	82720	111850	4385	107465	129435	6240	123195	141035	6299	134736
A Withdrawals from quasi-corporate enterprises	...	...	...	...	...	...	...	...	...	...	...	...
B Interest	81630	-	81630	106227	-	106227	121406	-	121406	132848	-	132848
C Dividends	4813	3723	1090	4804	3566	1238	7117	5328	1789	7111	5223	1888
D Net land rent and royalties	188	188	-	819	819	-	912	912	-	1076	1076	-
3 Current transfers	26181	12459	13722	33029	12823	20206	39754	15394	24360	41153	15777	25376
A Casualty insurance claims	4077	4077	-	4517	4517	-	5177	5177	-	5584	5584	-
B Casualty insurance premiums, net, due to be received by insurance companies	5807	-	5807	11475	-	11475	15052	-	15052	15444	-	15444
C Current transfers from the rest of the world	884	884	-	73	73	-	-	-	-	-	-	-
D Other transfers except imputed	1750	1401	349	1887	1676	211	3942	3597	345	3742	3315	427
E Imputed unfunded employee pension and welfare contributions	13663	6097	7566	15077	6557	8520	15583	6620	8963	16383	6878	9505
Total Current Receipts	134125	41871	92254	163940	40963	122977	198007	55579	142428	228994	75221	153773
						Disbursements						
1 Property and entrepreneurial income	90562	30268	60294	115864	37601	78263	131212	41371	89841	147445	48905	98540
A Withdrawals from quasi-corporations	3683	2933	750	4251	3401	850	6089	4089	2000	9499	5499	4000
Public	2246	1496	750	2736	1886	850	4146	2146	2000	6631	2631	4000
Private	1437	1437	-	1515	1515	-	1943	1943	-	2868	2868	-
B Interest	79070	20519	58551	104019	27728	76291	115337	28891	86446	125539	32773	92766
C Dividends	6733	5740	993	6331	5209	1122	8412	7017	1395	10296	8522	1774
D Net land rent and royalties	1076	1076	-	1263	1263	-	1374	1374	-	2111	2111	-
2 Direct taxes and other current transfers n.e.c. to general government	6552	5376	1176	6334	4748	1586	8744	6922	1822	13012	10099	2913
A Direct taxes	6263	5248	1015	6091	4585	1506	8403	6727	1676	12552	9863	2689
B Fines, fees, penalties and other current transfers n.e.c.	289	128	161	243	163	80	341	195	146	460	236	224

Sweden

3.22 Corporate and Quasi-Corporate Enterprise Income and Outlay Account: Total and Sectors
(Continued)

Million Swedish kronor

	1980			1981			1982			1983		
	TOTAL	Non-Financial	Financial	TOTAL	Non-Financial	Financial	TOTAL	Non-Financial	Financial	TOTAL	Non-Financial	Financial
3 Other current transfers	17026	7340	9686	23330	6956	16374	30234	8099	22135	32895	10457	22438
A Casualty insurance premiums, net	4073	4073	-	3662	3662	-	4042	4042	-	4882	4882	-
B Casualty insurance claims liability of insurance companies	5896	-	5896	11768	-	11768	15408	-	15408	15677	-	15677
C Transfers to private non-profit institutions	...	...	...	...	...	...	...	...	...	...	...	...
D Unfunded employee pension and welfare benefits	5937	2607	3330	6803	2916	3887	7902	3256	4646	8779	3568	5211
E Social assistance grants	...	...	...	...	...	...	...	...	...	...	...	...
F Other transfers n.e.c.	1120	660	460	1097	378	719	2882	801	2081	3557	2007	1550
G Transfers to the rest of the world	...	...	...	...	...	...	...	...	...	...	...	...
Net saving	19985	-1113	21098	18412	-8342	26754	27817	-813	28630	35642	5760	29882
Total Current Disbursements and Net Saving	134125	41871	92254	163940	40963	122977	198007	55579	142428	228994	75221	153773

	1984			1985			1986		
	TOTAL	Non-Financial	Financial	TOTAL	Non-Financial	Financial	TOTAL	Non-Financial	Financial

Receipts

1 Operating surplus	59090	68228	-9138	63881	74921	-11040	61793	74841	-13048
2 Property and entrepreneurial income	164058	8126	155932	192668	11027	181641	205287	14828	190459
A Withdrawals from quasi-corporate enterprises	...	...	...	...	...	...	...	...	...
B Interest	153150	-	153150	178968	-	178968	187174	-	187174
C Dividends	9436	6654	2782	11247	8574	2673	16307	13022	3285
D Net land rent and royalties	1472	1472	-	2453	2453	-	1806	1806	-
3 Current transfers	46413	18138	28275	56176	20946	35230	64643	23295	41348
A Casualty insurance claims	7061	7061	-	7341	7341	-	8192	8192	-
B Casualty insurance premiums, net, due to be received by insurance companies	17037	-	17037	20600	-	20600	24333	-	24333
C Current transfers from the rest of the world	-	-	-	-	-	-	-	-	-
D Other transfers except imputed	4820	4230	590	7709	5933	1776	11022	7371	3651
E Imputed unfunded employee pension and welfare contributions	17495	6847	10648	20526	7672	12854	21096	7732	13364
Total Current Receipts	269561	94492	175069	312725	106894	205831	331723	112964	218759

Disbursements

1 Property and entrepreneurial income	169616	56453	113163	194505	60281	134224	208376	71243	137133
A Withdrawals from quasi-corporations	12550	8550	4000	14643	7982	6661	16195	8572	7623
Public	7921	3921	4000	9743	3082	6661	11050	3427	7623
Private	4629	4629	-	4900	4900	-	5145	5145	-
B Interest	143031	36433	106598	162362	38461	123901	168872	46793	122079
C Dividends	11990	9425	2565	15009	11347	3662	21141	13710	7431
D Net land rent and royalties	2045	2045	-	2491	2491	-	2168	2168	-
2 Direct taxes and other current transfers n.e.c. to general government	14626	12336	2290	14536	12687	1849	17199	11443	5756
A Direct taxes	14130	11999	2131	14222	12381	1841	16829	11082	5747
B Fines, fees, penalties and other current transfers n.e.c.	496	337	159	314	306	8	370	361	9

Sweden

3.22 Corporate and Quasi-Corporate Enterprise Income and Outlay Account: Total and Sectors
(Continued)

Million Swedish kronor

	1984 TOTAL	1984 Non-Financial	1984 Financial	1985 TOTAL	1985 Non-Financial	1985 Financial	1986 TOTAL	1986 Non-Financial	1986 Financial
3 Other current transfers	38908	12463	26445	46005	14773	31232	53312	17354	35958
A Casualty insurance premiums, net	5812	5812	-	6749	6749	-	8367	8367	-
B Casualty insurance claims liability of insurance companies	18017	-	18017	21341	-	21341	23835	-	23835
C Transfers to private non-profit institutions	...	...	...	...	...	...	...	...	...
D Unfunded employee pension and welfare benefits	9796	3750	6046	10568	3872	6696	11488	4082	7406
E Social assistance grants	...	...	...	...	...	...	...	...	...
F Other transfers n.e.c.	5283	2901	2382	7347	4152	3195	9622	4905	4717
G Transfers to the rest of the world	...	...	...	...	...	...	...	...	...
Net saving	46411	13240	33171	57679	19153	38526	52836	12924	39912
Total Current Disbursements and Net Saving	269561	94492	175069	312725	106894	205831	331723	112964	218759

3.23 Corporate and Quasi-Corporate Enterprise Capital Accumulation Account: Total and Sectors

Million Swedish kronor

	1980 TOTAL	1980 Non-Financial	1980 Financial	1981 TOTAL	1981 Non-Financial	1981 Financial	1982 TOTAL	1982 Non-Financial	1982 Financial	1983 TOTAL	1983 Non-Financial	1983 Financial
Finance of Gross Accumulation											
1 Gross saving	57875	36245	21630	60590	33232	27358	75595	46280	29315	90075	59422	30653
A Consumption of fixed capital	37890	37358	532	42178	41574	604	47778	47093	685	54433	53662	771
B Net saving	19985	-1113	21098	18412	-8342	26754	27817	-813	28630	35642	5760	29882
2 Capital transfers	3869	3869	-	5889	5889	-	9599	9599	-	10193	10193	-
A From resident sectors	3869	3869	...	5889	5889	...	9599	9599	...	10193	10193	...
B From the rest of the world	...	...	...	...	...	...	...	...	...	...	...	...
Finance of Gross Accumulation	61744	40114	21630	66479	39121	27358	85194	55879	29315	100268	69615	30653
Gross Accumulation											
1 Gross capital formation	66811	65775	1036	60566	59510	1056	68564	67472	1092	77016	75989	1027
A Increase in stocks	4834	4834	-	-6011	-6011	-	-6737	-6737	-	-9630	-9630	-
B Gross fixed capital formation	61977	60941	1036	66577	65521	1056	75301	74209	1092	86646	85619	1027
2 Purchases of land, net	-2352	-2451	99	-2560	-2739	179	-2051	-4002	1951	-1971	-4003	2032
3 Purchases of intangible assets, net	...	...	-	...	...	-	...	...	-	...	...	-
4 Capital transfers	259	259	-	266	266	-	278	278	-	279	279	-
A To resident sectors	259	259	...	266	266	...	278	278	...	279	279	...
B To the rest of the world	...	...	...	...	...	...	...	...	...	...	...	...
Net lending ab	-2974	-23469	20495	8207	-17916	26123	18403	-7869	26272	24944	-2650	27594
Gross Accumulation	61744	40114	21630	66479	39121	27358	85194	55879	29315	100268	69615	30653

	1984 TOTAL	1984 Non-Financial	1984 Financial	1985 TOTAL	1985 Non-Financial	1985 Financial	1986 TOTAL	1986 Non-Financial	1986 Financial
Finance of Gross Accumulation								
1 Gross saving	105237	71215	34022	122163	82691	39472	121525	80555	40970
A Consumption of fixed capital	58826	57975	851	64484	63538	946	68689	67631	1058
B Net saving	46411	13240	33171	57679	19153	38526	52836	12924	39912
2 Capital transfers	5503	5503	-	7189	7189	-	7968	7968	-
A From resident sectors	5503	5503	...	7189	7189	...	7968	7968	...
B From the rest of the world	...	...	...	...	...	...	...	...	...
Finance of Gross Accumulation	110740	76718	34022	129352	89880	39472	129493	88523	40970
Gross Accumulation								
1 Gross capital formation	92180	90473	1707	116956	114662	2294	118057	115018	3039
A Increase in stocks	-6591	-6591	-	-679	-679	-	-5949	-5949	-
B Gross fixed capital formation	98771	97064	1707	117635	115341	2294	124006	120967	3039

Sweden

3.23 Corporate and Quasi-Corporate Enterprise Capital Accumulation Account: Total and Sectors
(Continued)

Million Swedish kronor

		1984			1985			1986		
		TOTAL	Non-Financial	Financial	TOTAL	Non-Financial	Financial	TOTAL	Non-Financial	Financial
2	Purchases of land, net	-1932	-3988	2056	-1631	-3428	1797	-353	-2176	1823
3	Purchases of intangible assets, net	...	...	-	...	...	-	...	...	-
4	Capital transfers	262	262	-	272	272	-	222	222	-
	A To resident sectors	262	262	...	272	272	...	222	222	...
	B To the rest of the world	...	...	...	...	...	...	...	...	...
	Net lending ab	20230	-10029	30259	13755	-21626	35381	11567	-24541	36108
	Gross Accumulation	110740	76718	34022	129352	89880	39472	129493	88523	40970

a) Net lending of the capital accumulation account and the capital finance account have not been reconciled and are different due to different statistical sources.
b) Net lending excludes net acquisition of SDR.

3.24 Corporate and Quasi-Corporate Enterprise Capital Finance Account: Total and Sectors

Million Swedish kronor

		1980			1981			1982			1983		
		TOTAL	Non-Financial	Financial	TOTAL	Non-Financial	Financial	TOTAL	Non-Financial	Financial	TOTAL	Non-Financial	Financial

Acquisition of Financial Assets

1	Gold and SDRs	-253	-	-253	8	-	8	53	-	53	-920	-	-920
2	Currency and transferable deposits	10918	145	10773	20985	14121	6864	13031	5258	7773	12162	7612	4550
3	Other deposits a	12903	5413	7490	156	306	-150	23893	19093	4800	4840	7189	-2349
4	Bills and bonds, short term b	6312	-	6312	-3057	-	-3057	10252	-	10252	-2733	1484	-4217
5	Bonds, long term c	23805	32	23773	61620	3066	58554	20937	1005	19932	64502	14944	49558
6	Corporate equity securities	7017	5467	1550	13687	11430	2257	13327	9075	4252	14410	9605	4805
7	Short term loans, n.e.c.	66108	10615	55493	66889	9052	57837	87955	20483	67472	110744	36455	74289
8	Long term loans, n.e.c.	...	...	...	...	...	...	...	...	...	...	...	...
9	Trade credits and advances	9444	9444	-	9842	9842	-	12328	12328	-	18041	18041	-
10	Other receivables	...	...	...	...	...	...	...	...	...	...	...	...
11	Other assets	7634	7291	343	28230	1468	26762	19973	872	19101	25991	383	25608
	Total Acquisition of Financial Assets d	143888	38407	105481	198360	49285	149075	201749	68114	133635	247037	95713	151324

Incurrence of Liabilities

1	Currency and transferable deposits	27432	-	27432	43415	-	43415	27729	-	27729	26418	-	26418
2	Other deposits a	14661	-	14661	298	-	298	4281	-	4281	4948	378	4570
3	Bills and bonds, short term	...	...	...	...	...	...	...	...	...	...	...	...
4	Bonds, long term c	15378	-481	15859	24372	957	23415	26941	2863	24078	31901	3501	28400
5	Corporate equity securities	4120	3826	294	9194	7285	1909	11465	7211	4254	18296	11632	6664
6	Short-term loans, n.e.c.	64585	43027	21558	60458	35989	24469	65892	37615	28277	77306	54953	22353
7	Long-term loans, n.e.c.	...	...	...	...	...	...	...	...	...	...	...	...
8	Net equity of households in life insurance and pension fund reserves	3182	-	3182	4140	-	4140	4914	-	4914	9071	-	9071
9	Proprietors' net additions to the accumulation of quasi-corporations	1208	1208	-	1308	1308	-	1525	1525	-	1010	1010	-
10	Trade credit and advances e	7274	7274	-	8170	8170	-	10079	10079	-	13994	13994	-
11	Other accounts payable	...	...	...	...	...	...	...	...	...	...	...	...
12	Other liabilities	10048	7296	2752	35843	11299	24544	29276	14167	15109	39995	15213	24782
	Total Incurrence of Liabilities	147888	62150	85738	187198	65008	122190	182102	73460	108642	223839	101581	122258
	Net Lending f	-4000	-23743	19743	11162	-15723	26885	19647	-5346	24993	23198	-5868	29066
	Incurrence of Liabilities and Net Lending	143888	38407	105481	198360	49285	149075	201749	68114	133635	247037	95713	151324

		1984			1985			1986		
		TOTAL	Non-Financial	Financial	TOTAL	Non-Financial	Financial	TOTAL	Non-Financial	Financial

Acquisition of Financial Assets

1	Gold and SDRs	486	-	486	313	-	313	330	-	330
2	Currency and transferable deposits	17995	16401	1594	163	-7785	7948	24828	14566	10262
3	Other deposits a	-2376	-7666	5290	-3815	-315	-3500	8916	-657	9573
4	Bills and bonds, short term b	33576	-2912	36488	31100	17923	13177	-2460	-30587	28127
5	Bonds, long term c	25920	1649	24271	37380	2729	34651	88518	63267	25251
6	Corporate equity securities	25162	20094	5068	27791	23174	4617	38573	28068	10505
7	Short term loans, n.e.c.	121168	41003	80165	116996	38610	78386	227361	42010	185351
8	Long term loans, n.e.c.	...	...	...	...	...	...	...	...	...
9	Trade credits and advances	17225	17225	-	10554	10554	-	238	238	-

Sweden

3.24 Corporate and Quasi-Corporate Enterprise Capital Finance Account: Total and Sectors
(Continued)

Million Swedish kronor

	1984 TOTAL	1984 Non-Financial	1984 Financial	1985 TOTAL	1985 Non-Financial	1985 Financial	1986 TOTAL	1986 Non-Financial	1986 Financial
10 Other receivables	...	...	...	...	...	...	...	...	...
11 Other assets	44953	15514	29439	46397	13986	32411	67771	9812	57959
Total Acquisition of Financial Assets d	284109	101308	182801	266879	98876	168003	454075	126717	327358

Incurrence of Liabilities

	1984 TOTAL	1984 Non-Financial	1984 Financial	1985 TOTAL	1985 Non-Financial	1985 Financial	1986 TOTAL	1986 Non-Financial	1986 Financial
1 Currency and transferable deposits	38119	-	38119	11748	-	11748	60457	-	60457
2 Other deposits a	-1793	4464	-6257	-1968	4218	-6186	7681	3432	4249
3 Bills and bonds, short term	...	...	...	...	...	...	...	...	...
4 Bonds, long term c	36590	4287	32303	52322	5481	46841	98621	14128	84493
5 Corporate equity securities	23837	16025	7812	20703	13228	7475	37058	16178	20880
6 Short-term loans, n.e.c.	99072	63325	35747	89537	73955	15582	150579	106125	44454
7 Long-term loans, n.e.c.	...	...	...	...	...	...	...	...	...
8 Net equity of households in life insurance and pension fund reserves	9433	-	9433	10741	-	10741	15975	-	15975
9 Proprietors' net additions to the accumulation of quasi-corporations	332	332	-	1948	1948	-	2454	2454	-
10 Trade credit and advances e	16609	16609	-	13725	13725	-	2046	2046	-
11 Other accounts payable	...	...	...	...	...	...	...	...	...
12 Other liabilities	52507	16089	36418	51459	5272	46187	82803	23738	59065
Total Incurrence of Liabilities	274706	121131	153575	250215	117827	132388	457674	168101	289573
Net Lending f	9403	-19823	29226	16664	-18951	35615	-3599	-41384	37785
Incurrence of Liabilities and Net Lending	284109	101308	182801	266879	98876	168003	454075	126717	327358

a) Item 'Other deposits' refers to certificate of deposit.
b) 'Bills and bonds' refer to Swedish treasury bills and special treasury bills.
c) Item 'Bonds, long-term' includes both short-term and long-term bonds.
d) Item 'Total acquisition of financial assets' excludes net acquisition of SDRS except for 1982.
e) Item 'Trade credit advances' includes trade bills.
f) Net lending of the capital accumulation account and the capital finance account have not been reconciled and are different due to different statistical sources.

3.31 Household and Private Unincorporated Enterprise Production Account

Million Swedish kronor

	1970	1975	1977	1978	1979	1980	1981	1982	1983	1984	1985	1986

Gross Output

	1970	1975	1977	1978	1979	1980	1981	1982	1983	1984	1985	1986
1 Output for sale	...	...	...	...	...	...	...	...	...	...	...	...
2 Non-marketed output	...	...	...	...	...	...	...	...	...	...	...	...
Gross Output	...	...	...	...	...	...	...	...	...	...	...	...

Gross Input

	1970	1975	1977	1978	1979	1980	1981	1982	1983	1984	1985	1986
Intermediate consumption	...	...	...	...	...	...	...	...	...	...	...	...
Subtotal: Value Added	...	...	...	...	...	...	...	...	...	...	...	...
1 Indirect taxes net liability of unincorporated enterprises	...	...	...	...	...	...	...	...	...	...	...	...
2 Consumption of fixed capital	4263	7195	9644	11141	12534	14798	16647	18240	20159	22289	23570	24912
3 Compensation of employees	6513	6936	7766	7474	6516	6372	6489	4863	...	...	...	...
4 Net operating surplus	23920	33052	40617	49197	50273	56586	59727	71198	77420	85861	91411	93274
Gross Input	...	...	...	...	...	...	...	...	...	...	...	...

3.32 Household and Private Unincorporated Enterprise Income and Outlay Account

Million Swedish kronor

	1970	1975	1977	1978	1979	1980	1981	1982	1983	1984	1985	1986

Receipts

	1970	1975	1977	1978	1979	1980	1981	1982	1983	1984	1985	1986
1 Compensation of employees	103026	183786	245217	273100	300130	337338	368631	389646	421456	461259	502173	549544
A Wages and salaries	89529	147597	184775	201024	221110	245924	265729	281388	303641	334296	365807	400133
B Employers' contributions for social security	8133	24189	45427	53924	59713	71602	82584	83174	91618	99264	103302	119254
C Employers' contributions for private pension & welfare plans	5364	12000	15015	18152	19307	19812	20318	25084	26197	27699	33064	30157
2 Operating surplus of private unincorporated enterprises	23920	33052	40617	49197	50273	56586	59727	71198	77420	85861	91411	93274
3 Property and entrepreneurial income	7235	11471	15918	16235	18422	27267	34145	35833	38490	44130	52810	57244
A Withdrawals from private quasi-corporations	517	827	1058	1139	1287	1437	1515	1943	2868	4629	4900	5145
B Interest	5714	8911	12691	13079	14966	22723	29604	30129	30441	35375	42478	44663
C Dividends	885	1488	1745	1642	1833	2623	2398	3072	4238	3568	4833	6443
D Net land rent and royalties	119	245	424	375	336	484	628	689	943	558	599	993

Sweden

3.32 Household and Private Unincorporated Enterprise Income and Outlay Account
(Continued)

Million Swedish kronor

	1970	1975	1977	1978	1979	1980	1981	1982	1983	1984	1985	1986
3 Current transfers	22119	49409	70855	82342	92826	105996	120721	132961	149337	160190	179818	198264
A Casualty insurance claims	1046	1353	1984	2140	2231	2469	2818	3241	3517	4319	5241	5924
B Social security benefits	12718	31634	47310	55733	63011	73396	84729	92730	104640	112335	125016	139567
C Social assistance grants	4899	10159	13853	15580	17496	19369	21148	23296	25737	26663	31932	33070
D Unfunded employee pension and welfare benefits	3139	5666	6890	7886	8610	9377	10383	11846	13141	14502	15507	17087
E Transfers from general government	234	489	650	783	880	1029	1161	1313	1405	1577	1490	2008
F Transfers from the rest of the world	83	108	168	220	598	356	482	535	897	794	632	608
G Other transfers n.e.c.	...	...	...	...	...	...	...	...	...	...	...	...
Total Current Receipts [a]	156300	277718	372607	420874	461651	527187	583224	629638	686703	751440	826212	898326

Disbursements

	1970	1975	1977	1978	1979	1980	1981	1982	1983	1984	1985	1986
1 Final consumption expenditures	92237	156908	198929	220480	243755	271831	301024	336650	365820	401987	442427	484553
A Market purchases	81704	139119	175736	193461	213410	237649	262412	291994	315994	347613	383384	420381
B Gross rents of owner-occupied housing	10300	17500	22898	26716	30020	33871	38612	44656	49826	54374	59043	64172
C Consumption from own-account production	134	209	295	303	325	311	...	...	...	...	...	...
2 Property income	7107	11118	18366	19949	23686	32846	41477	43002	43292	48573	57159	61160
A Interest	6909	10787	18011	19493	23200	32230	40777	42234	42476	47655	56132	60030
Consumer debt	...	...	...	...	...	...	...	...	...	...	...	...
Mortgage	3540	6917	10765	11900	13105	17516	23269	25107	...	...	...	...
Other	...	...	...	...	...	...	...	...	...	...	...	...
B Net land rent and royalties	198	331	355	456	486	616	700	768	816	918	1027	1130
3 Direct taxes and other current transfers n.e.c. to government	46388	87566	127874	147391	163166	183729	203509	217329	240110	261798	279994	315905
A Social security contributions	13059	25761	47779	56439	62525	74643	85833	86630	95653	103781	108206	124523
B Direct taxes	32398	60680	78804	89975	99353	107614	115701	127773	141798	155060	168591	188770
Income taxes	...	...	...	...	...	...	...	...	...	...	...	...
Other	...	...	...	...	...	...	...	...	...	...	...	...
C Fees, fines and penalties	931	1125	1291	977	1288	1472	1975	2926	2659	2957	3197	2612
4 Other current transfers	6535	13874	18403	21945	23076	23967	24689	30042	32268	34440	40927	39137
A Net casualty insurance premiums	921	1157	2288	2638	2517	2527	2803	2992	3259	3861	4626	5776
B Transfers to private non-profit institutions serving households	...	...	...	...	...	...	...	...	...	...	...	...
C Transfers to the rest of the world	250	717	1100	1155	1252	1628	1568	1966	2812	2880	3237	3204
D Other current transfers, except imputed	...	...	...	...	...	...	...	...	...	...	...	...
E Imputed employee pension and welfare contributions	5364	12000	15015	18152	19307	19812	20318	25084	26197	27699	33064	30157
Net saving	4033	8252	9035	11109	7968	14814	12525	2615	5213	4642	5705	-2429
Total Current Disbursements and Net Saving [a]	156300	277718	372607	420874	461651	527187	583224	629638	686703	751440	826212	898326

a) Private non-profit institutions serving households is included in household and private unincorporated enterprise.

3.33 Household and Private Unincorporated Enterprise Capital Accumulation Account

Million Swedish kronor

	1970	1975	1977	1978	1979	1980	1981	1982	1983	1984	1985	1986

Finance of Gross Accumulation

	1970	1975	1977	1978	1979	1980	1981	1982	1983	1984	1985	1986
1 Gross saving	8296	15447	18679	22250	20502	29612	29172	20855	25372	26931	29275	22483
A Consumption of fixed capital	4263	7195	9644	11141	12534	14798	16647	18240	20159	22289	23570	24912
Owner-occupied housing	2312	3812	5388	6325	7494	9075	10169	11156	12147	13519	14553	15602
Other unincorporated enterprises	1951	3383	4256	4816	5040	5723	6478	7084	8012	8770	9017	9320
B Net saving	4033	8252	9035	11109	7968	14814	12525	2615	5213	4642	5705	-2429
2 Capital transfers	213	364	441	445	585	667	593	643	836	886	1039	1145
A From resident sectors	213	364	441	445	585	667	593	643	836	886	1039	1145
B From the rest of the world	...	...	...	...	...	...	...	...	...	...	...	...
Total Finance of Gross Accumulation [a]	8509	15811	19120	22695	21087	30279	29765	21498	26208	27817	30314	23628

Gross Accumulation

	1970	1975	1977	1978	1979	1980	1981	1982	1983	1984	1985	1986
1 Gross Capital Formation	6670	13614	17384	19497	22312	22229	19950	19216	19635	20910	19229	18369

Sweden

3.33 Household and Private Unincorporated Enterprise Capital Accumulation Account
(Continued)

Million Swedish kronor

	1970	1975	1977	1978	1979	1980	1981	1982	1983	1984	1985	1986
A Increase in stocks	-55	-79	10	-125	168	56	-112	90	...	...	...	...
B Gross fixed capital formation	6725	13693	17374	19622	22144	22173	20062	19126	19635	20910	19229	18369
Owner-occupied housing [bc]	5106	9884	12403	14748	16590	16545	14371	12404	11278	12437	10720	10626
Other gross fixed capital formation	1619	3809	4971	4874	5554	5628	5691	6722	8357	8473	8509	7743
2 Purchases of land, net [d]	943	1897	2212	2556	2888	2878	2638	2057	1890	1694	1588	1503
3 Purchases of intangibles, net	...	...	...	...	...	...	...	...	...	...	...	...
4 Capital transfers	557	852	1081	1173	1222	1358	1430	1545	1672	1846	2007	1917
A To resident sectors	557	852	1081	1173	1222	1358	1430	1545	1672	1846	2007	1917
B To the rest of the world	...	...	...	...	...	...	...	...	...	...	...	...
Net lending [e]	339	-552	-1557	-531	-5335	3814	5747	-1320	3011	3367	7490	1839
Total Gross Accumulation [a]	8509	15811	19120	22695	21087	30279	29765	21498	26208	27817	30314	23628

a) Private non-profit institutions serving households is included in household and private unincorporated enterprise.
b) Dwellings includes country lodges.
c) Item 'Owner occupied housing' excludes estate agents' commission.
d) Item 'Purchases of land, rent' includes estate agents' commission.
e) Net lending of the capital accumulation account and the capital finance account have not been reconciled and are different due to different statistical sources.

3.34 Household and Private Unincorporated Enterprise Capital Finance Account

Million Swedish kronor

	1970	1975	1977	1978	1979	1980	1981	1982	1983	1984	1985	1986
Acquisition of Financial Assets
1 Gold	...	...	...	...	...	...	...	...	...	...	...	...
2 Currency and transferable deposits	5093	14778	13607	16998	19190	22848	25530	19383	16029	16837	14059	31996
3 Other deposits [a]	...	...	...	...	...	...	...	...	...	6517	10678	15813
4 Bills and bonds, short term	-	-	1	-3	-	38	-9	-14	-17	4500	2100	-600
A Corporate and quasi-corporate	...	...	...	...	...	...	...	...	...	...	...	...
B Government	-	-	1	-3	-	38	-9	-14	-17	4500	2100	-600
C Rest of the world	...	...	...	...	...	...	...	...	...	...	...	...
5 Bonds, long term [b]	576	3479	3730	4842	5368	9512	2272	4620	8406	8334	9645	16177
6 Corporate equity securities	-831	-1032	-568	-1015	-2040	-1708	-2494	-267	-128	-730	-8448	5519
7 Short term loans, n.e.c.	536	959	321	430	750	3389	1758	3874	412	4078	64	5276
8 Long term loans, n.e.c.	...	...	...	...	...	...	...	...	...	...	...	...
9 Trade credit and advances [c]	493	-1119	-	24	50	52	101	107	114	121	129	-
10 Net equity of households in life insurance and pension fund reserves	1116	2269	1978	2275	2644	3182	4140	4914	9071	9433	10741	15975
11 Proprietors' net additions to the accumulation of quasi-corporations	...	...	...	...	...	...	...	...	...	...	...	...
12 Other [c]	2	-404	788	3357	849	-2966	4583	6130	6145	-4395	4607	1381
Total Acquisition of Financial Assets	6985	18930	19857	26908	26811	34347	35881	38747	40032	44695	43575	91537
Incurrence of Liabilities
1 Short term loans, n.e.c.	6678	18926	21384	27414	32023	31252	30096	39861	36781	40955	35801	89737
2 Long term loans, n.e.c.	...	...	...	...	...	...	...	...	...	...	...	...
3 Trade credit and advances	-	-	-	20	88	90	219	232	245	259	274	-
4 Other accounts payable	...	...	...	...	...	...	...	...	...	...	...	...
5 Other liabilities	...	...	...	...	...	...	...	...	...	...	...	...
Total Incurrence of Liabilities	6678	18926	21384	27434	32111	31342	30315	40093	37026	41214	36075	89737
Net Lending [d]	307	4	-1527	-526	-5300	3005	5566	-1346	3006	3481	7500	1800
Incurrence of Liabilities and Net Lending	6985	18930	19857	26908	26811	34347	35881	38747	40032	44695	43575	91537

a) Item 'Other deposits' refers to certificate of deposit.
b) Item 'Bonds, long-term' includes both short-term and long-term bonds.
c) Acquisition are reported net of incurrence of liabilities.
d) Net lending of the capital accumulation account and the capital finance account have not been reconciled and are different due to different statistical sources.

Sweden

3.41 Private Non-Profit Institutions Serving Households: Production Account

Million Swedish kronor

	1970	1975	1977	1978	1979	1980	1981	1982	1983	1984	1985	1986
					Gross Output							
1 Sales	...	...	...	...	...	...	...	...	...	...	...	...
2 Non-marketed output	...	...	...	...	...	...	...	...	...	...	...	...
Gross Output	1061	2097	3247	4101	4325	4878	5199	5954	6486	7003	7421	8189
					Gross Input							
Intermediate consumption	211	409	724	1175	1221	1419	1486	1788	1996	2217	2370	2601
Subtotal: Value Added	850	1688	2523	2926	3104	3459	3713	4166	4490	4786	5051	5588
1 Indirect taxes, net	7	52	100	62	53	64	77	87	176	171	186	214
2 Consumption of fixed capital	...	...	...	...	...	...	...	...	...	...	...	...
3 Compensation of employees	843	1636	2423	2864	3051	3395	3636	4079	4314	4615	4865	5374
4 Net operating surplus	...	...	...	...	...	...	...	...	...	...	...	...
Gross Input	1061	2097	3247	4101	4325	4878	5199	5954	6486	7003	7421	8189

3.44 Private Non-Profit Institutions Serving Households: Capital Finance Account

Million Swedish kronor

	1970	1975	1977	1978	1979	1980	1981	1982	1983	1984	1985	1986
				Acquisition of Financial Assets								
1 Gold	...	...	...	...	...	...	...	...	...	...	...	...
2 Currency and transferable deposits	...	...	...	296	...	...	...	...	...	...	...	...
3 Other deposits	...	...	...	...	...	...	...	...	...	...	...	...
4 Bills and bonds, short term	...	...	...	...	...	...	...	...	...	...	...	...
5 Bonds, long term	...	...	...	236	...	...	...	...	...	...	...	...
6 Corporate equity securities	...	...	...	93	...	...	...	...	...	...	...	...
7 Short-term loans, n.e.c.	...	...	...	...	...	...	...	...	...	...	...	...
8 Long-term loans, n.e.c.	...	...	...	...	...	...	...	...	...	...	...	...
9 Other receivables	...	...	...	...	...	...	...	...	...	...	...	...
10 Proprietors' net additions to the accumulation of quasi-corporations	...	...	...	...	...	...	...	...	...	...	...	...
11 Other assets	...	...	...	530	...	...	...	...	...	...	...	...
Total Acquisition of Financial Assets	...	...	...	1155	...	...	...	...	...	...	...	...
				Incurrence of Liabilities								
1 Short-term loans	...	...	...	...	...	...	...	...	...	...	...	...
2 Long-term loans	...	...	...	...	...	...	...	...	...	...	...	...
3 Other liabilities	...	...	...	131	...	...	...	...	...	...	...	...
Total Incurrence of Liabilities	...	...	...	131	...	...	...	...	...	...	...	...
Net Lending	...	...	...	1024	...	...	...	...	...	...	...	...
Incurrence of Liabilities and Net Lending	...	...	...	1155	...	...	...	...	...	...	...	...

3.51 External Transactions: Current Account: Detail

Million Swedish kronor

	1970	1975	1977	1978	1979	1980	1981	1982	1983	1984	1985	1986
				Payments to the Rest of the World								
1 Imports of goods and services	42478	85263	107508	112173	145196	166520	172228	205157	233121	254267	283852	277407
A Imports of merchandise o.i.f.	30730	73519	91492	93883	124661	143839	148735	177208	202038	221134	246761	233574
B Other	5748	11744	16016	18290	20535	22681	23493	27949	31083	33133	37091	43833
2 Factor income to the rest of the world	912	2084	4712	7344	7986	11947	21523	27599	31593	36530	42195	36155
A Compensation of employees	6	9	18	22	28	30	70	163	380	357	415	398
B Property and entrepreneurial income	906	2075	4694	7322	7958	11917	21453	27436	31213	36173	41780	35757
By general government [a]	10	2	217	677	1105	2901	6528	8664	11125	13295	14832	11983
By corporate and quasi-cororate enterprises	...	...	...	...	...	...	...	...	...	...	...	...

Sweden

3.51 External Transactions: Current Account: Detail
(Continued)

Million Swedish kronor

	1970	1975	1977	1978	1979	1980	1981	1982	1983	1984	1985	1986
By other	...	...	...	...	...	...	...	...	...	...	...	...
3 Current transfers to the rest of the world	1235	3383	4839	5470	6267	6903	11378	14179	15641	16412	19530	20941
A Indirect taxes by general government to supranational organizations	...	...	...	...	...	...	...	...	...	...	...	...
B Other current transfers	1235	3383	4839	5470	6267	6903	11378	14179	15641	16412	19530	20941
By general government	597	2067	2960	3388	4052	4121	4222	4379	4866	5067	5857	6112
By other resident sectors	638	1316	1879	2082	2215	2782	7156	9800	10775	11345	13673	14829
4 Surplus of the nation on current transactions	-1367	-1469	-9594	-167	-10137	-18823	-14178	-22761	-7169	3082	-11083	6685
Payments to the Rest of the World, and Surplus of the Nation on Current Transfers	43258	89261	107465	124820	149312	166547	190951	224174	273186	310291	334494	341188
Receipts From The Rest of the World												
1 Exports of goods and services	41515	84679	101332	116399	140568	156523	172527	201331	249528	284664	303509	308790
A Exports of merchandise f.o.b.	35045	71727	85199	97703	117509	130246	143909	167088	209168	241362	258681	262571
B Other	6470	12952	16133	18696	23059	26277	28618	34243	40360	43302	44828	46219
2 Factor income from the rest of the world	856	2891	4023	5968	6720	7924	12083	13730	14431	16255	19679	20008
A Compensation of employees	14	52	131	214	212	283	338	283	237	183	209	566
B Property and entrepreneurial income	842	2839	3892	5754	6508	7641	11745	13447	14194	16072	19470	19442
By general government [a]	149	395	666	1209	1341	1626	2415	2717	2712	2999	3572	4387
By corporate and quasi-corporate enterprises	...	...	...	...	...	...	...	...	...	...	...	...
By other	...	...	...	...	...	...	...	...	...	...	...	...
3 Current transfers from the rest of the world	887	1691	2110	2453	2024	2100	6341	9113	9227	9372	11306	12390
A Subsidies to general government from supranational organizations	...	...	...	...	...	...	...	...	...	...	...	...
B Other current transfers	887	1691	2110	2453	2024	2100	6341	9113	9227	9372	11306	12390
To general government	16	31	46	35	39	48	43	54	90	104	139	204
To other resident sectors	871	1660	2064	2418	1985	2052	6298	9059	9137	9268	11167	12184
Receipts from the Rest of the World on Current Transfers	43258	89261	107465	124820	149312	166547	190951	224174	273186	310291	334494	341188

a) Only central government data are included in the general government estimates.

3.52 External Transactions: Capital Accumulation Account

Million Swedish kronor

	1970	1975	1977	1978	1979	1980	1981	1982	1983	1984	1985	1986
Finance of Gross Accumulation												
1 Surplus of the nation on current transactions	-1367	-1469	-9594	-167	-10137	-18823	-14178	-22761	-7169	3082	-11083	6685
2 Capital transfers from the rest of the world	...	...	...	...	...	...	...	...	...	...	...	...
Total Finance of Gross Accumulation	-1367	-1469	-9594	-167	-10137	-18823	-14178	-22761	-7169	3082	-11083	6685
Gross Accumulation												
1 Capital transfers to the rest of the world	...	...	...	...	...	...	...	...	...	...	...	...
2 Purchases of intangible assets, n.e.c., net, from the rest of the world	...	...	...	...	...	...	...	...	...	...	...	...
Net lending to the rest of the world	-1367	-1469	-9594	-167	-10137	-18823	-14178	-22761	-7169	3082	-11083	6685
Total Gross Accumulation	-1367	-1469	-9594	-167	-10137	-18823	-14178	-22761	-7169	3082	-11083	6685

3.53 External Transactions: Capital Finance Account

Million Swedish kronor

	1970	1975	1977	1978	1979	1980	1981	1982	1983	1984	1985	1986
Acquisitions of Foreign Financial Assets												
1 Gold and SDR's	-134	-	27	41	89	-253	8	53	-920	486	313	330
2 Currency and transferable deposits	478	3230	5195	108	4185	9252	8289	5363	5056	-56	6023	4036
3 Other deposits [a]	...	...	...	...	...	...	...	...	...	...	...	...
4 Bills and bonds, short term [b]	208	5710	4014	2559	-3038	-992	-2410	-1060	4325	-56	11698	1143

Sweden

3.53 External Transactions: Capital Finance Account
(Continued)

Million Swedish kronor

	1970	1975	1977	1978	1979	1980	1981	1982	1983	1984	1985	1986
5 Bonds, long term c	21	83	-56	-110	131	378	457	679	1069	531	671	3307
6 Corporate equity securities	657	1051	544	808	1215	1836	3467	3455	5470	5201	4880	11661
7 Short-term loans, n.e.c.	1034	2170	2218	2445	3766	3024	5813	12004	12222	7162	3169	8263
8 Long-term loans	...	...	...	...	...	...	...	...	...	...	...	...
9 Prporietors' net additions to accumulation of quasi-corporate, non-resident enterprises	...	...	...	...	...	...	...	...	...	...	...	...
10 Trade credit and advances	1411	1135	2939	1911	1373	373	3513	2474	3129	1607	401	-100
11 Other	...	...	...	...	...	...	...	...	...	...	...	...
Total Acquisitions of Foreign Financial Assets d	3675	13379	14881	7762	7721	13618	19137	22968	30351	14875	27155	28640

Incurrence of Foreign Liabilities

	1970	1975	1977	1978	1979	1980	1981	1982	1983	1984	1985	1986
1 Currency and transferable deposits	21	24	127	150	335	985	2348	61	4776	2047	5476	7128
2 Other deposits a	-	-	-	-	-	892	69	110	-76	559	550	-366
3 Bills and bonds, short term b	-34	-	-	-	-	-	-	-	-	-	-	-
4 Bonds, long term c	342	3128	6874	2922	4650	7044	6405	13774	23505	36373	18796	988
5 Corporate equity securities	75	140	1	116	26	291	401	1348	5921	2188	5233	2348
6 Short-term loans, n.e.c.	1954	11246	15682	1621	13736	29474	21623	27120	8540	-21072	5623	24167
7 Long-term loans	...	...	...	...	...	...	...	...	...	...	...	...
8 Non-resident proprietors' net additions to accumulation of resident quasi-corporate enterprises	...	...	...	...	...	...	...	...	...	...	...	...
9 Trade credit and advances	1072	1818	-1120	759	1019	-1759	1959	350	787	1120	0717	1708
10 Other	...	...	...	...	...	...	...	...	...	...	...	...
Total Incurrence of Liabilities d	3430	16354	21564	5568	19766	36927	32805	42763	41879	21224	39395	35973
Statistical discrepancy	1612	-1506	2911	2361	-1908	-4486	510	2966	-4359	-9431	-1157	-14018
Net Lending d	-1367	-1469	-9594	-167	-10137	-18823	-14178	-22761	-7169	3082	-11083	6685
Total Incurrence of Liabilities and Net Lending d	3675	13379	14881	7762	7721	13618	19137	22968	30351	14875	27155	28640

a) Item 'Other deposits' refers to certificate of deposit.
b) 'Bills and bonds' refer to Swedish treasury bills and special treasury bills.
c) Item 'Bonds, long-term' includes both short-term and long-term bonds.
d) Beginning 1970 estimates of acquisition and incurrence of foreign liabilities are reported according to the financial accounts calculated by the Central Bureau of Statistics. Prior to 1970 estimates are based on the capital accounts of the balance of payment calculated by the Central Bank.

4.1 Derivation of Value Added by Kind of Activity, in Current Prices

Million Swedish kronor

	1980			1981			1982			1983		
	Gross Output	Intermediate Consumption	Value Added	Gross Output	Intermediate Consumption	Value Added	Gross Output	Intermediate Consumption	Value Added	Gross Output	Intermediate Consumption	Value Added

All Producers

1 Agriculture, hunting, forestry and fishing	28583	11754	16829	31878	13253	18625	35739	15189	20550	39059	16573	22486
A Agriculture and hunting	19345	9932	9413	21689	11225	10464	24909	12705	12204	26304	13938	12366
B Forestry and logging	8659	1613	7046	9580	1769	7811	10145	2187	7958	11933	2304	9629
C Fishing	579	209	370	609	259	350	685	297	388	822	331	491
2 Mining and quarrying	4597	2148	2449	4296	2061	2235	4530	2046	2484	5430	2216	3214
A Coal mining	...	...	...	...	...	...	...	...	...	...	...	...
B Crude petroleum and natural gas production	...	...	...	...	...	...	...	...	...	...	...	...
C Metal ore mining	3324	1614	1710	2997	1567	1430	3246	1540	1706	4112	1694	2418
D Other mining	1273	534	739	1299	494	805	1284	506	778	1318	522	796

Sweden

4.1 Derivation of Value Added by Kind of Activity, in Current Prices
(Continued)

Million Swedish kronor

	1980 Gross Output	1980 Intermediate Consumption	1980 Value Added	1981 Gross Output	1981 Intermediate Consumption	1981 Value Added	1982 Gross Output	1982 Intermediate Consumption	1982 Value Added	1983 Gross Output	1983 Intermediate Consumption	1983 Value Added
3 Manufacturing	327225	216207	111018	345893	230181	115712	382540	256869	125671	445495	298445	147050
A Manufacture of food, beverages and tobacco	43290	31640	11650	48017	35512	12505	55293	41749	13544	60345	44977	15368
B Textile, wearing apparel and leather industries	9311	5496	3815	9070	5351	3719	9299	5643	3656	10244	6163	4081
C Manufacture of wood and wood products, including furniture	26692	16846	9846	25258	16094	9164	26786	17579	9207	31499	20566	10933
D Manufacture of paper and paper products, printing and publishing	48078	32667	15411	52084	35745	16339	55684	36956	18728	66123	43972	22151
E Manufacture of chemicals and chemical petroleum, coal, rubber and plastic products	47184	36131	11053	50168	39775	10393	56210	43745	12465	67476	52522	14954
F Manufacture of non-metallic mineral products, except products of petroleum and coal	8521	4646	3875	8620	4730	3890	9578	5166	4412	10358	5609	4749
G Basic metal industries	26437	19975	6462	25374	19012	6362	28786	21195	7591	33850	25286	8564
H Manufacture of fabricated metal products, machinery and equipment	115145	66992	48153	124640	72119	52521	137956	82785	55171	162441	96992	65449
I Other manufacturing industries	2567	1814	753	2662	1843	819	2948	2051	897	3159	2358	801
4 Electricity, gas and water	20428	7335	13093	23763	8615	15148	26380	10430	15950	29395	10598	18797
A Electricity, gas and steam	18999	6829	12170	22094	8065	14029	24481	9799	14682	27426	9932	17494
B Water works and supply	1429	506	923	1669	550	1119	1899	631	1268	1969	666	1303
5 Construction	77215	38540	38675	83174	40330	42844	88992	44261	44731	95212	47901	47311
6 Wholesale and retail trade, restaurants and hotels	89617	31320	58297	95135	34722	60413	104837	39661	65176	118072	43742	74330
A Wholesale and retail trade	80548	26320	54228	85043	29116	55927	93433	33256	60177	105225	36672	68553
B Restaurants and hotels	9069	5000	4069	10092	5606	4486	11404	6405	4999	12847	7070	5777
7 Transport, storage and communication	60231	28504	31727	67709	33071	34638	75125	37746	37379	82868	42206	40662
A Transport and storage	46015	24071	21944	51542	28121	23421	56922	31458	25464	62297	34622	27675
B Communication	14216	4433	9783	16167	4950	11217	18203	6288	11915	20571	7584	12987
8 Finance, insurance, real estate and business services [a]	107811	48891	58920	124292	59170	65122	141598	67055	74543	160754	77470	83284
A Financial institutions	17511	18715	-1204	22537	23486	-949	25368	26553	-1185	30634	32457	-1823
B Insurance	5696	1350	4346	5918	1631	4287	5681	1863	3818	5717	2017	3700
C Real estate and business services	84604	28826	55778	95837	34053	61784	110549	38639	71910	124403	42996	81407
Real estate, except dwellings	6086	3257	2829	7578	3984	3594	9319	4731	4588	10663	5130	5533
Dwellings	55298	16319	38979	62743	19135	43608	72311	21819	50492	80600	24165	56435
9 Community, social and personal services	31218	13988	17230	34294	16113	18181	38309	18375	19934	41774	19577	22197
A Sanitary and similar services	6002	2075	3927	6323	2223	4100	7236	2516	4720	8043	2821	5222
B Social and related community services	5797	1721	4076	5920	1856	4064	6763	2092	4671	7565	2263	5302
Educational services	...	...	...	...	...	...	...	...	...	...	...	...
Medical, dental, other health and veterinary services	2102	838	1264	2191	965	1226	2693	1105	1588	3033	1169	1864
C Recreational and cultural services	7432	3805	3627	8772	4854	3918	9500	5643	3857	10450	5894	4556
D Personal and household services	11987	6387	5600	13279	7180	6099	14810	8124	6686	15716	8599	7117
Total, Industries	746925	398687	348238	810434	437516	372918	898050	491632	406418	1018060	558728	459331
Producers of Government Services	159207	43171	116036	176038	48649	127389	192891	54178	138713	211907	58653	153254
Other Producers	5279	1419	3860	5587	1486	4101	6359	1788	4571	6930	1996	4934
Total [b]	911411	443277	468134	992059	487651	504408	1097300	547598	549702	1236900	619377	617519
Less: Imputed bank service charge [a]	...	...	...	...	...	...	...	...	...	...	...	...
Import duties	1760	...	1760	1927	...	1927	2160	...	2160	2192	...	2192
Value added tax [c]	54019	...	54019	64447	...	64447	71563	...	71563	78599	...	78599
Other adjustments	1186	...	1186	2258	...	2258	4253	...	4253	7055	...	7055
Total	968376	443277	525099	1060690	487651	573040	1175280	547598	627678	1324740	619377	705365
Memorandum Item: Mineral fuels and power [d]	39259	26519	12740	43943	29640	14303	48935	33671	15264	56513	37897	18616

Sweden

4.1 Derivation of Value Added by Kind of Activity, in Current Prices

Million Swedish kronor

	1984 Gross Output	1984 Intermediate Consumption	1984 Value Added	1985 Gross Output	1985 Intermediate Consumption	1985 Value Added	1986 Gross Output	1986 Intermediate Consumption	1986 Value Added
			All Producers						
1 Agriculture, hunting, forestry and fishing	43778	18217	25561	44843	18956	25887	46546	18264	28282
A Agriculture and hunting	28864	15397	13467	28866	15973	12893	29718	15367	14351
B Forestry and logging	14031	2460	11571	15070	2593	12477	15924	2543	13381
C Fishing	883	360	523	907	390	517	904	354	550
2 Mining and quarrying	6418	2585	3833	7125	2711	4414	6557	2528	4029
A Coal mining	...	...	...	...	...	...	...	...	...
B Crude petroleum and natural gas production	...	...	...	...	...	...	...	...	...
C Metal ore mining	4967	1980	2987	5695	2162	3533	5068	1999	3069
D Other mining	1451	605	846	1430	549	881	1489	529	960
3 Manufacturing	508380	340330	168050	547128	363803	183325	562554	362243	200311
A Manufacture of food, beverages and tobacco	67880	51659	16221	72812	54486	18326	76376	55762	20614
B Textile, wearing apparel and leather industries	11445	6988	4457	12291	7314	4977	12601	7320	5281
C Manufacture of wood and wood products, including furniture	35756	23483	12273	35590	24198	11392	37764	26035	11729
D Manufacture of paper and paper products, printing and publishing	78048	51302	26746	83792	56154	27638	88630	59050	29580
E Manufacture of chemicals and chemical petroleum, coal, rubber and plastic products	74747	56450	18297	77889	57740	20149	67135	43860	23275
F Manufacture of non-metallic mineral products, except products of petroleum and coal	11119	6133	4986	11832	6510	5322	12412	6709	5703
G Basic metal industries	38509	29113	9396	40420	30296	10124	39010	27906	11104
H Manufacture of fabricated metal products, machinery and equipment	187365	112506	74859	208606	124312	84294	224544	132752	91792
I Other manufacturing industries	3511	2696	815	3896	2793	1103	4082	2849	1233
4 Electricity, gas and water	32936	11147	21789	38245	13005	25240	39048	12223	26825
A Electricity, gas and steam	30871	10410	20461	36030	12129	23901	36756	11358	25398
B Water works and supply	2065	737	1328	2215	876	1339	2292	865	1427
5 Construction	105008	54185	50823	109913	56205	53708	115672	59529	56143
6 Wholesale and retail trade, restaurants and hotels	133902	47814	86088	149453	53488	95965	163489	57653	105836
A Wholesale and retail trade	119152	39859	79293	132556	44509	88047	145110	48452	96658
B Restaurants and hotels	14750	7955	6795	16897	8979	7918	18379	9201	9178
7 Transport, storage and communication	91319	47041	44278	100542	52021	48521	110169	54527	55642
A Transport and storage	67804	37352	30452	74076	40523	33553	80745	42180	38565
B Communication	23515	9689	13826	26466	11498	14968	29424	12347	17077
8 Finance, insurance, real estate and business services [a]	180960	89231	91729	199019	100421	98598	223684	113652	110032
A Financial institutions	36465	38040	-1575	40169	42263	-2094	50737	52053	-1316
B Insurance	5371	2258	3113	5617	2524	3093	6217	2619	3598
C Real estate and business services	139124	48933	90191	153233	55634	97599	166730	58980	107750
Real estate, except dwellings	12393	6130	6263	13834	7783	6051	15889	7922	7967
Dwellings	87688	26680	61008	95671	29707	65964	104402	31954	72448
9 Community, social and personal services	45414	21698	23716	50388	23245	27143	54075	24893	29182
A Sanitary and similar services	8273	3089	5184	9341	3394	5947	9954	3358	6596
B Social and related community services	8263	2452	5811	9007	2685	6322	9411	2844	6567
Educational services	...	...	...	...	...	...	...	...	...
Medical, dental, other health and veterinary services	3175	1233	1942	3587	1374	2213	3827	1481	2346
C Recreational and cultural services	11558	6681	4877	12982	6865	6117	14339	7710	6629
D Personal and household services	17320	9476	7844	19058	10301	8757	20371	10981	9390
Total, Industries	1148120	632248	515867	1246660	683855	562801	1321790	705512	616282
Producers of Government Services	230810	65023	165787	249309	72300	177009	269073	77354	191719

Sweden

4.1 Derivation of Value Added by Kind of Activity, in Current Prices
(Continued)

Million Swedish kronor

	1984 Gross Output	1984 Intermediate Consumption	1984 Value Added	1985 Gross Output	1985 Intermediate Consumption	1985 Value Added	1986 Gross Output	1986 Intermediate Consumption	1986 Value Added
Other Producers	7463	2217	5246	7904	2370	5534	8661	2601	6060
Total [b]	1386390	699488	686900	1503870	758525	745344	1599530	785467	814061
Less: Imputed bank service charge [a]	...	...	...	...	...	...	...	...	...
Import duties	2520	...	2520	2736	...	2736	2985	...	2985
Value added tax [c]	89138	...	89138	101729	...	101729	108980	...	108980
Other adjustments	11025	...	11025	11075	...	11075	7660	...	7660
Total	1489070	699488	789583	1619410	758525	860884	1719150	785467	933686
Memorandum Item: Mineral fuels and power [d]	62095	39901	22194	67297	41839	25458	55687	27841	27846

a) Item 'Less: Imputed bank service charge' is netted out of item 'Finance, insurance, real estate and business services'.
b) Gross domestic product in basic values.
c) Item 'Value added tax' relates to value added tax and other taxes and subsidies on sales and production of commodities.
d) Item 'Mineral fuels and power' refers to ISIC categories 353 (Petroleum refineries), 354 (Manufacture of miscellaneous products of petroleum and coal) and 41 (Electricity, gas and steam).

4.2 Derivation of Value Added by Kind of Activity, in Constant Prices

Million Swedish kronor

	1980 Gross Output	1980 Intermediate Consumption	1980 Value Added	1981 Gross Output	1981 Intermediate Consumption	1981 Value Added	1982 Gross Output	1982 Intermediate Consumption	1982 Value Added	1983 Gross Output	1983 Intermediate Consumption	1983 Value Added
At constant prices of: 1980												
All Producers												
1 Agriculture, hunting, forestry and fishing	28583	11754	16829	28776	11709	17067	29970	11805	18165	30705	11712	18993
A Agriculture and hunting	19345	9932	9413	19442	9929	9513	20265	9894	10371	20128	9785	10343
B Forestry and logging	8659	1613	7046	8704	1549	7155	9079	1678	7401	9928	1687	8241
C Fishing	579	209	370	630	231	399	626	233	393	649	240	409
2 Mining and quarrying	4597	2148	2449	3929	1787	2142	3478	1685	1793	3481	1649	1832
A Coal mining	...	...	...	...	...	...	...	...	...	...	...	...
B Crude petroleum and natural gas production	...	...	...	...	...	...	...	...	...	...	...	...
C Metal ore mining	3324	1614	1710	2739	1340	1399	2385	1254	1131	2456	1241	1215
D Other mining	1273	534	739	1190	447	743	1093	431	662	1025	408	617
3 Manufacturing	327225	216207	111018	315712	208314	107398	315477	208625	106852	332940	220598	112342
A Manufacture of food, beverages and tobacco	43290	31640	11650	43031	31437	11594	43635	31879	11756	43262	31599	11663
B Textile, wearing apparel and leather industries	9311	5496	3815	8395	4943	3452	7809	4638	3171	7647	4545	3102
C Manufacture of wood and wood products, including furniture	26692	16846	9846	23793	15032	8761	24390	15516	8874	25720	16419	9301
D Manufacture of paper and paper products, printing and publishing	48078	32667	15411	46667	31802	14865	44742	30159	14583	48655	32948	15707
E Manufacture of chemicals and chemical petroleum, coal, rubber and plastic products	47184	36131	11053	43461	32712	10749	43391	32409	10982	48360	36538	11822
F Manufacture of non-metallic mineral products, except products of petroleum and coal	8521	4646	3875	7565	4166	3399	7682	4236	3446	7737	4243	3494
G Basic metal industries	26437	19975	6462	24930	18999	5931	25542	19242	6300	26690	20112	6578
H Manufacture of fabricated metal products, machinery and equipment	115145	66992	48153	115324	67417	47907	115615	68659	46956	122307	72258	50049
I Other manufacturing industries	2567	1814	753	2546	1806	740	2671	1887	784	2562	1936	626
4 Electricity, gas and water	20428	7335	13093	21597	7499	14098	21846	8264	13582	23103	8768	14335
A Electricity, gas and steam	18999	6829	12170	20176	7000	13176	20419	7735	12684	21721	8258	13463
B Water works and supply	1429	506	923	1421	499	922	1427	529	898	1382	510	872
5 Construction	77215	38540	38675	75009	37113	37896	75394	36816	38578	74677	35899	38778
6 Wholesale and retail trade, restaurants and hotels	89617	31320	58297	88173	30894	57279	88853	31379	57474	90230	31783	58447
A Wholesale and retail trade	80548	26320	54228	79170	25925	53245	79812	26390	53422	81094	26746	54348
B Restaurants and hotels	9069	5000	4069	9003	4969	4034	9041	4989	4052	9136	5037	4099
7 Transport, storage and communication	60231	28504	31727	60766	29739	31027	61463	30314	31149	61564	30536	31028
A Transport and storage	46015	24071	21944	46766	25308	21458	45918	25078	20840	44879	24705	20174
B Communication	14216	4433	9783	14000	4431	9569	15545	5236	10309	16685	5831	10854
8 Finance, insurance, real estate and business services [a]	107811	48891	58920	110661	50972	59689	114495	53845	60650	119178	56461	62717
A Financial institutions	17511	18715	-1204	18311	19584	-1273	19264	20480	-1216	21172	22317	-1145

Sweden

4.2 Derivation of Value Added by Kind of Activity, in Constant Prices
(Continued)

Million Swedish kronor

	1980 Gross Output	1980 Intermediate Consumption	1980 Value Added	1981 Gross Output	1981 Intermediate Consumption	1981 Value Added	1982 Gross Output	1982 Intermediate Consumption	1982 Value Added	1983 Gross Output	1983 Intermediate Consumption	1983 Value Added
					At constant prices of:1980							
B Insurance	5696	1350	4346	5776	1299	4477	6108	1552	4556	6350	1517	4833
C Real estate and business services	84604	28826	55778	86574	30089	56485	89123	31813	57310	91656	32627	59029
Real estate, except dwellings	6086	3257	2829	6368	3414	2954	6792	3646	3146	6969	3733	3236
Dwellings	55298	16319	38979	56247	17132	39115	57009	18072	38937	57744	18445	39299
9 Community, social and personal services	31218	13988	17230	31474	14514	16960	31796	14541	17255	31772	14218	17554
A Sanitary and similar services	6002	2075	3927	5955	2014	3941	6089	2025	4064	6284	2122	4162
B Social and related community services	5797	1721	4076	5617	1692	3925	5541	1680	3861	5589	1687	3902
Educational services	...	...	...	...	...	...	...	...	...	...	...	...
Medical, dental, other health and veterinary services	2102	838	1264	2108	853	1255	2120	859	1261	2100	850	1250
C Recreational and cultural services	7432	3805	3627	7781	4271	3510	7897	4308	3589	7913	4146	3767
D Personal and household services	11987	6387	5600	12121	6537	5584	12269	6528	5741	11986	6263	5723
Total, Industries	746925	398687	348238	736097	392541	343556	742772	397274	345498	767650	411624	356026
Producers of Government Services	159207	43171	116036	162214	43365	118849	164074	43773	120301	165511	42900	122611
Other Producers	5279	1419	3860	5261	1438	3823	5573	1531	4042	5729	1572	4157
Total [b]	911411	443277	468134	903572	437344	466228	912419	442578	469841	938890	456096	482794
Less: Imputed bank service charge [a]	...	...	...	...	...	...	...	...	...	...	...	...
Import duties	1760	...	1760	1645	...	1645	1654	...	1654	1695	...	1695
Value added tax [c]	54019	...	54019	52579	...	52579	53506	...	53506	53140	...	53140
Other adjustments	1186	...	1186	3061	...	3061	2732	...	2732	2903	...	2903
Total	968376	443277	525099	960857	437344	523513	970311	442578	527733	996628	456096	540532
Memorandum Item: Mineral fuels and power [d]	39259	26519	12740	37392	23679	13713	36957	23705	13252	40644	26477	14167

	1984 Gross Output	1984 Intermediate Consumption	1984 Value Added	1985 Gross Output	1985 Intermediate Consumption	1985 Value Added	1986 Gross Output	1986 Intermediate Consumption	1986 Value Added
				At constant prices of:1980					
				All Producers					
1 Agriculture, hunting, forestry and fishing	31598	11891	19707	30657	11743	18914	30404	11283	19121
A Agriculture and hunting	20853	9896	10957	20194	9716	10478	19831	9371	10460
B Forestry and logging	10068	1743	8325	9824	1778	8046	9996	1662	8334
C Fishing	677	252	425	639	249	390	577	250	327
2 Mining and quarrying	3890	1817	2073	4032	1852	2180	3763	1757	2006
A Coal mining	...	...	...	...	...	...	...	...	...
B Crude petroleum and natural gas production	...	...	...	...	...	...	...	...	...
C Metal ore mining	2843	1301	1462	3080	1463	1617	2863	1384	1479
D Other mining	1047	426	621	952	389	563	900	373	527

Sweden

4.2 Derivation of Value Added by Kind of Activity, in Constant Prices
(Continued)

Million Swedish kronor

	1984 Gross Output	1984 Intermediate Consumption	1984 Value Added	1985 Gross Output	1985 Intermediate Consumption	1985 Value Added	1986 Gross Output	1986 Intermediate Consumption	1986 Value Added
				At constant prices of:1980					
3 Manufacturing	351796	232675	119121	359185	236110	123075	363438	240364	123074
A Manufacture of food, beverages and tobacco	44083	32254	11829	44215	32335	11880	42493	31046	11447
B Textile, wearing apparel and leather industries	7889	4664	3225	7861	4668	3193	7692	4573	3119
C Manufacture of wood and wood products, including furniture	26693	17117	9576	25526	16482	9044	25750	16678	9072
D Manufacture of paper and paper products, printing and publishing	51645	35102	16543	53175	36038	17137	53972	36685	17287
E Manufacture of chemicals and chemical petroleum, coal, rubber and plastic products	49877	37719	12158	49976	37604	12372	51208	39381	11827
F Manufacture of non-metallic mineral products, except products of petroleum and coal	7852	4368	3484	7843	4359	3484	8064	4486	3578
G Basic metal industries	28040	20932	7108	28125	20924	7201	28603	21343	7260
H Manufacture of fabricated metal products, machinery and equipment	133069	78500	54569	139672	81685	57987	143049	84250	58799
I Other manufacturing industries	2648	2019	629	2790	2015	777	2607	1922	685
4 Electricity, gas and water	24722	8329	16393	28277	9053	19224	28347	9293	19054
A Electricity, gas and steam	23358	7793	15565	26856	8452	18404	26934	8697	18237
B Water works and supply	1364	536	828	1421	601	820	1413	596	817
5 Construction	77093	37323	39770	75754	36164	39590	77041	36656	40385
6 Wholesale and retail trade, restaurants and hotels	91536	32060	59476	94190	33328	60862	97086	34567	62519
A Wholesale and retail trade	82231	26928	55303	84605	28040	56565	87589	29329	58260
B Restaurants and hotels	9305	5132	4173	9585	5288	4297	9497	5238	4259
7 Transport, storage and communication	64687	31661	33026	66985	33098	33887	71853	36045	35808
A Transport and storage	46412	24800	21612	46864	25447	21417	50895	28164	22731
B Communication	18275	6861	11414	20121	7651	12470	20958	7881	13077
8 Finance, insurance, real estate and business services [a]	124628	59871	64757	127711	61755	65956	131516	64617	66899
A Financial institutions	22816	23910	-1094	23490	24656	-1166	25831	27054	-1223
B Insurance	6566	1698	4868	6803	1650	5153	7075	1617	5458
C Real estate and business services	95246	34263	60983	97418	35449	61969	98610	35946	62664
Real estate, except dwellings	7426	3978	3448	7735	4147	3591	8115	4350	7984
Dwellings	58237	18826	39411	59062	19320	39742	59761	19569	40192
9 Community, social and personal services	32149	14706	17443	32813	14662	18151	32806	14875	17931
A Sanitary and similar services	6451	2241	4210	6581	2285	4296	6249	2171	4078
B Social and related community services	5616	1690	3926	5727	1735	3992	5707	1745	3962
Educational services	...	...	...	...	...	...	...	...	...
Medical, dental, other health and veterinary services	2076	841	1235	2185	885	1300	2277	922	1355
C Recreational and cultural services	7891	4306	3585	8137	4081	4056	8422	4297	4125
D Personal and household services	12191	6469	5722	12368	6561	5807	12428	6662	5766
Total, Industries	802099	430333	371766	819604	437765	381839	836254	449457	386797
Producers of Government Services	169469	44255	125214	172684	46311	126373	175544	47680	127864
Other Producers	5794	1596	4198	5754	1589	4165	5925	1643	4282

Sweden

4.2 Derivation of Value Added by Kind of Activity, in Constant Prices
(Continued)

Million Swedish kronor

	1984			1985			1986		
	Gross Output	Intermediate Consumption	Value Added	Gross Output	Intermediate Consumption	Value Added	Gross Output	Intermediate Consumption	Value Added
				At constant prices of:1980					
Total [b]	977362	476184	501178	998042	485665	512377	1017720	498780	518943
Less: Imputed bank service charge [a]	...	...	...	...	...	...	...	...	...
Import duties	1882	...	1882	2060	...	2060	2481	...	2481
Value added tax [c]	53584	...	53584	56330	...	56330	57685	...	57685
Other adjustments	5239	...	5239	3131	...	3131	1455	...	1455
Total	1038070	476184	561883	1059560	485665	573898	1079340	498780	580564
Memorandum Item: Mineral fuels and power [d]	42442	26157	16285	46002	27128	18874	47237	28929	18308

a) Item 'Less: Imputed bank service charge' is netted out of item 'Finance, insurance, real estate and business services'.
b) Gross domestic product in basic values.
c) Item 'Value added tax' relates to value added tax and other taxes and subsidies on sales and production of commodities.
d) Item 'Mineral fuels and power' refers to ISIC categories 353 (Petroleum refineries), 354 (Manufacture of miscellaneous products of petroleum and coal) and 41 (Electricity, gas and steam).

4.3 Cost Components of Value Added

Million Swedish kronor

		1980						1981					
		Compensation of Employees	Capital Consumption	Net Operating Surplus	Indirect Taxes	Less: Subsidies Received	Value Added	Compensation of Employees	Capital Consumption	Net Operating Surplus	Indirect Taxes	Less: Subsidies Received	Value Added
						All Producers							
1	Agriculture, hunting, forestry and fishing	4767	3498	8434	379	249	16829	5173	3851	9502	450	351	18625
	A Agriculture and hunting	1904	2734	4768	256	249	9413	2117	3010	5396	292	351	10464
	B Forestry and logging	2835	679	3413	119	-	7046	3030	748	3879	154	-	7811
	C Fishing	28	85	253	4	-	370	26	93	227	4	-	350
2	Mining and quarrying	1593	522	297	37	-	2449	1628	576	-11	42	-	2235
	A Coal mining	...	...	...	...	...	...	...	...	...	...	...	...
	B Crude petroleum and natural gas production	...	...	...	...	...	...	...	...	...	...	...	...
	C Metal ore mining	1232	404	50	24	-	1710	1267	454	-319	28	-	1430
	D Other mining	361	118	247	13	-	739	361	122	308	14	-	805
3	Manufacturing	86936	13230	11854	1983	2985	111018	92634	14599	9494	2265	3280	115712
	A Manufacture of food, beverages and tobacco	6805	1340	3313	192	-	11650	7312	1472	3496	225	-	12505
	B Textile, wearing apparel and leather industries	3264	476	22	79	26	3815	3323	506	-185	88	13	3719
	C Manufacture of wood and wood products, including furniture	6504	1035	2148	159	-	9846	6549	1127	1310	178	-	9164
	D Manufacture of paper and paper products, printing and publishing	12352	2770	404	266	381	15411	12847	3090	451	300	349	16339
	E Manufacture of chemicals and chemical petroleum, coal, rubber and plastic products	7207	1606	2047	193	-	11053	7785	1769	655	184	-	10393
	F Manufacture of non-metallic mineral products, except products of petroleum and coal	2733	563	512	67	-	3875	2778	612	426	74	-	3890
	G Basic metal industries	6357	1414	-1435	126	-	6462	6765	1561	-2114	150	-	6362
	H Manufacture of fabricated metal products, machinery and equipment	39553	3966	4127	854	347	48153	43078	4398	4613	1014	582	52521
	I Other manufacturing industries	2161	60	716	47	2231	753	2197	64	842	52	2336	819
4	Electricity, gas and water	2958	4297	5920	115	197	13093	3301	4830	7151	138	272	15148
	A Electricity, gas and steam	2787	3423	5972	112	124	12170	3126	3897	7055	134	183	14029
	B Water works and supply	171	874	-52	3	73	923	175	933	96	4	89	1119
5	Construction	26277	1694	9895	809	-	38675	28392	1929	11593	930	-	42844
6	Wholesale and retail trade, restaurants and hotels	40911	3637	12522	1227	-	58297	44545	3951	10519	1398	-	60413
	A Wholesale and retail trade	37850	3392	11832	1154	-	54228	41134	3677	9808	1308	-	55927
	B Restaurants and hotels	3061	245	690	73	-	4069	3411	274	711	90	-	4486
7	Transport, storage and communication	22049	7647	4057	1346	3372	31727	23922	8358	4965	1516	4123	34638
	A Transport and storage	16402	4974	2738	1202	3372	21944	17673	5393	3083	1365	4093	23421
	B Communication	5647	2673	1319	144	-	9783	6249	2965	1882	151	30	11217
8	Finance, insurance, real estate and business services [ab]	20517	18898	22428	1732	4655	58920	22442	21604	25319	2317	6560	65122
	A Financial institutions	4910	352	-6577	111	-	-1204	5422	402	-6907	137	3	-949

Sweden

4.3 Cost Components of Value Added
(Continued)

Million Swedish kronor

	1980						1981					
	Compensation of Employees	Capital Consumption	Net Operating Surplus	Indirect Taxes	Less: Subsidies Received	Value Added	Compensation of Employees	Capital Consumption	Net Operating Surplus	Indirect Taxes	Less: Subsidies Received	Value Added
B Insurance	2553	180	1558	55	-	4346	2769	202	1249	67	-	4287
C Real estate and business services	13054	18366	27447	1566	4655	55778	14251	21000	30977	2113	6557	61784
Real estate, except dwellings	-	521	2210	120	22	2829	-	596	2893	132	27	3594
Dwellings	2360	16114	23699	1230	4424	38979	2566	18256	27369	1717	6300	43608
9 Community, social and personal services	14661	631	3975	354	2391	17230	15670	663	3995	409	2556	18181
A Sanitary and similar services	2205	44	1707	50	79	3927	2501	49	1587	61	98	4100
B Social and related community services	5185	26	703	111	1949	4076	5374	23	565	127	2025	4064
Educational services	...	...	...	...	...	...	...	...	...	...	...	...
Medical, dental, other health and veterinary services	2541	...	516	51	1844	1264	2644	...	417	59	1894	1226
C Recreational and cultural services	3020	...	898	72	363	3627	3306	...	961	84	433	3918
D Personal and household services	4251	48	1180	121	-	5600	4489	50	1423	137	-	6099
Total, Industries	220669	54054	79382	7982	13849	348238	237707	60361	82527	9465	17142	372918
Producers of Government Services	108627	5367	-	2042	-	116036	118747	6118	-	2524	-	127389
Other Producers	3788	-	-	72	-	3860	4016	-	-	85	-	4101
Total c	333084	59421	79382	10096	13849	468134	360470	66479	82527	12074	17142	504408
Less: Imputed bank service charge a	...	...	...	...	...	...	...	...	...	...	...	...
Import duties	...	...	...	1760	...	1760	...	...	...	1927	...	1927
Value added tax d	...	...	...	61372	7353	54019	...	...	...	72279	7832	64447
Other adjustments	4001	...	517	-1891	1441	1186	7893	...	-1429	-2496	1710	2258
Total	337085	59421	79899	71337	22643	525099	368363	66479	81098	83784	26684	573040

	1982						1983					
	Compensation of Employees	Capital Consumption	Net Operating Surplus	Indirect Taxes	Less: Subsidies Received	Value Added	Compensation of Employees	Capital Consumption	Net Operating Surplus	Indirect Taxes	Less: Subsidies Received	Value Added
	All Producers												
1 Agriculture, hunting, forestry and fishing	5330	4313	10757	502	352	20550	5712	4909	11241	984	360	22486
A Agriculture and hunting	2167	3371	6717	301	352	12204	2272	3836	6110	508	360	12366
B Forestry and logging	3132	834	3795	197	-	7958	3407	946	4809	467	-	9629
C Fishing	31	108	245	4	-	388	33	127	322	9	-	491
2 Mining and quarrying	1634	658	500	42	350	2484	1691	740	1097	76	390	3214
A Coal mining	...	...	...	...	...	...	...	...	...	...	...	...
B Crude petroleum and natural gas production	...	...	...	...	...	...	...	...	...	...	...	...
C Metal ore mining	1258	518	252	28	350	1706	1278	581	896	53	390	2418
D Other mining	376	140	248	14	-	778	413	159	201	23	-	796
3 Manufacturing	96003	16588	13391	2411	2722	125671	100329	18837	26351	4448	2915	147050
A Manufacture of food, beverages and tobacco	7700	1662	3949	233	-	13544	8071	1886	4998	413	-	15368
B Textile, wearing apparel and leather industries	3238	551	-201	85	17	3656	3278	598	74	156	25	4081
C Manufacture of wood and wood products, including furniture	6549	1257	1225	176	-	9207	6884	1433	2292	324	-	10933
D Manufacture of paper and paper products, printing and publishing	13249	3545	2001	307	374	18728	14176	4025	3800	612	462	22151
E Manufacture of chemicals and chemical petroleum, coal, rubber and plastic products	8105	2037	2050	273	-	12465	8658	2345	3576	375	-	14954
F Manufacture of non-metallic mineral products, except products of petroleum and coal	2787	683	868	74	-	4412	2736	759	1127	127	-	4749
G Basic metal industries	6789	1763	-1111	150	-	7591	6767	1971	-461	287	-	8564
H Manufacture of fabricated metal products, machinery and equipment	45173	5019	4150	1056	227	55171	47018	5742	10699	2035	45	65449
I Other manufacturing industries	2413	71	460	57	2104	897	2741	78	246	119	2383	801
4 Electricity, gas and water	3592	5585	6909	157	293	15950	3964	6461	8528	250	406	18797
A Electricity, gas and steam	3415	4547	6737	153	170	14682	3777	5299	8433	242	257	17494
B Water works and supply	177	1038	172	4	123	1268	187	1162	95	8	149	1303

Sweden

4.3 Cost Components of Value Added
(Continued)

Million Swedish kronor

	1982						1983					
	Compensation of Employees	Capital Consumption	Net Operating Surplus	Indirect Taxes	Less: Subsidies Received	Value Added	Compensation of Employees	Capital Consumption	Net Operating Surplus	Indirect Taxes	Less: Subsidies Received	Value Added
5 Construction	29357	2090	12449	835	-	44731	29952	2254	13611	1494	-	47311
6 Wholesale and retail trade, restaurants and hotels	46719	4452	12529	1476	-	65176	50359	5092	16194	2685	-	74330
A Wholesale and retail trade	42989	4129	11681	1378	-	60177	46236	4720	15110	2487	-	68553
B Restaurants and hotels	3730	323	848	98	-	4999	4123	372	1084	198	-	5777
7 Transport, storage and communication	26024	9350	5496	1600	5091	37379	27938	10629	5830	2286	6021	40662
A Transport and storage	18973	5979	4109	1437	5034	25464	20439	6837	4408	1961	5970	27675
B Communication	7051	3371	1387	163	57	11915	7499	3792	1422	325	51	12987
8 Finance, insurance, real estate and business services [a,b]	24551	23986	33293	2435	9722	74543	27936	26802	37006	3117	11577	83284
A Financial institutions	5955	460	-6663	150	1087	-1185	6559	521	-7459	285	1729	-1823
B Insurance	3040	225	480	73	-	3818	3458	250	-156	148	-	3700
C Real estate and business services	15556	23301	39476	2212	8635	71910	17919	26031	44621	2684	9848	81407
Real estate, except dwellings	-	677	3798	144	31	4588	-	771	4652	147	37	5533
Dwellings	2817	19825	34438	1781	8369	50492	3299	21499	39295	1912	9570	56435
9 Community, social and personal services	16410	738	4978	432	2624	19934	17418	818	5932	835	2806	22197
A Sanitary and similar services	2638	55	2071	65	109	4720	2781	61	2386	125	131	5222
B Social and related community services	5616	22	951	133	2051	4671	6060	23	1100	264	2145	5302
Educational services	...	...	...	...	...	...	...	...	...	...	...	...
Medical, dental, other health and veterinary services	2795	...	720	63	1990	1588	3018	...	813	130	2097	1864
C Recreational and cultural services	3516	...	714	91	464	3857	3726	...	1186	174	530	4556
D Personal and household services	4640	56	1847	143	-	6686	4851	69	1925	272	-	7117
Total, Industries	249620	67760	100302	9890	21154	406418	265299	76542	125790	16175	24475	459331
Producers of Government Services	129076	6915	-	2722	-	138713	139801	7797	-	5656	-	153254
Other Producers	4475	-	-	96	-	4571	4740	-	-	194	-	4934
Total [c]	383171	74675	100302	12708	21154	549702	409840	84339	125790	22025	24475	617519
Less: Imputed bank service charge [a]	...	...	...	...	...	...	...	...	...	...	...	...
Import duties	...	...	...	2160	...	2160	...	...	...	2192	...	2192
Value added tax [d]	...	...	...	79394	7831	71563	...	...	...	88155	9556	78599
Other adjustments	6355	...	2456	-2467	2091	4253	11759	...	2843	-4728	2819	7055
Total	389526	74675	102758	91795	31076	627678	421599	84339	128633	107644	36850	705365

	1984						1985					
	Compensation of Employees	Capital Consumption	Net Operating Surplus	Indirect Taxes	Less: Subsidies Received	Value Added	Compensation of Employees	Capital Consumption	Net Operating Surplus	Indirect Taxes	Less: Subsidies Received	Value Added
					All Producers								
1 Agriculture, hunting, forestry and fishing	6220	5210	13657	1044	570	25561	6332	5502	13605	996	548	25887
A Agriculture and hunting	2550	4193	6807	487	570	13467	2566	4454	5927	494	548	12893
B Forestry and logging	3625	877	6521	548	-	11571	3706	909	7370	492	-	12477
C Fishing	45	140	329	9	-	523	60	139	308	10	-	517
2 Mining and quarrying	1814	779	1164	76	-	3833	1976	818	1534	86	-	4414
A Coal mining	...	...	...	...	...	...	...	...	...	...	...	...
B Crude petroleum and natural gas production	...	...	...	...	...	...	...	...	...	...	...	...
C Metal ore mining	1343	611	982	51	-	2987	1429	643	1405	56	-	3533
D Other mining	471	168	182	25	-	846	547	175	129	30	-	881

Sweden

4.3 Cost Components of Value Added
(Continued)

Million Swedish kronor

			1984						1985			
	Compensation of Employees	Capital Consumption	Net Operating Surplus	Indirect Taxes	Less: Subsidies Received	Value Added	Compensation of Employees	Capital Consumption	Net Operating Surplus	Indirect Taxes	Less: Subsidies Received	Value Added
3 Manufacturing	111910	19981	34797	4512	3150	168050	124544	21313	35572	5219	3323	183325
A Manufacture of food, beverages and tobacco	8946	1983	4888	404	-	16221	9790	2102	5960	474	-	18326
B Textile, wearing apparel and leather industries	3604	611	127	158	43	4457	3889	625	344	175	56	4977
C Manufacture of wood and wood products, including furniture	7533	1510	2906	324	-	12273	8007	1571	1459	355	-	11392
D Manufacture of paper and paper products, printing and publishing	15990	4254	6341	628	467	26746	17617	4550	5223	712	464	27638
E Manufacture of chemicals and chemical petroleum, coal, rubber and plastic products	9885	2504	5518	390	-	18297	11097	2691	5864	497	-	20149
F Manufacture of non-metallic mineral products, except products of petroleum and coal	2974	789	1098	125	-	4986	3315	826	1037	144	-	5322
G Basic metal industries	6858	2057	216	265	-	9396	7609	2152	61	302	-	10124
H Manufacture of fabricated metal products, machinery and equipment	53178	6192	13393	2101	5	74859	59935	6709	15251	2426	27	84294
I Other manufacturing industries	2942	81	310	117	2635	815	3285	87	373	134	2776	1103
4 Electricity, gas and water	4245	7090	10635	248	429	21789	4557	7723	13246	268	554	25240
A Electricity, gas and steam	4080	5822	10585	242	268	20461	4383	6351	13269	261	363	23901
B Water works and supply	165	1268	50	6	161	1328	174	1372	-23	7	191	1339
5 Construction	32686	2374	14266	1497	-	50823	35519	2474	14039	1676	-	53708
6 Wholesale and retail trade, restaurants and hotels	56768	5558	20954	2808	-	86088	62735	6144	23859	3227	-	95965
A Wholesale and retail trade	51931	5139	19626	2597	-	79293	57153	5676	22236	2982	-	88047
B Restaurants and hotels	4837	419	1328	211	-	6795	5582	468	1623	245	-	7918
7 Transport, storage and communication	30807	11538	6393	2240	6700	44278	34232	12560	5852	2514	6637	48521
A Transport and storage	22724	7503	4965	1915	6655	30452	25089	8199	4734	2129	6598	33553
B Communication	8083	4035	1428	325	45	13826	9143	4361	1118	385	39	14968
8 Finance, insurance, real estate and business services [a,b]	32066	29839	37913	4068	12157	91729	34927	32793	37583	7418	14123	98598
A Financial institutions	7578	578	-9506	1132	1357	-1575	8314	641	-11370	1514	1193	-2094
B Insurance	3851	273	-1163	152	-	3113	4218	305	-1599	169	-	3093
C Real estate and business services	20637	28988	48582	2784	10800	90191	22395	31847	50552	5735	12930	97599
Real estate, except dwellings	-	862	5283	157	39	6263	-	968	5101	26	44	6051
Dwellings	3468	23601	42506	1965	10532	61008	...	...	...	...	...	...
9 Community, social and personal services	18807	874	6210	848	3023	23716	20597	948	7808	945	3155	27143
A Sanitary and similar services	3123	68	2003	128	138	5184	3427	75	2458	145	158	5947
B Social and related community services	6451	26	1407	257	2330	5811	6948	35	1529	282	2472	6322
Educational services	...	...	...	...	...	...	...	...	...	...	...	...
Medical, dental, other health and veterinary services	3144	...	1004	124	2330	1942	3416	...	1122	137	2462	2213
C Recreational and cultural services	4060	...	1180	192	555	4877	4452	...	1977	213	525	6117
D Personal and household services	5173	81	2319	271	-	7844	5770	97	2585	305	-	8757
Total, Industries	295323	83243	145989	17341	26029	515867	325419	90275	153098	22349	28340	562801
Producers of Government Services	151694	8509	-	5584	-	165787	161691	9189	-	6129	-	177009
Other Producers	5058	-	-	188	-	5246	5330	-	-	204	-	5534
Total [c]	452075	91752	145989	23113	26029	686900	492440	99464	153098	28682	28340	745344
Less: Imputed bank service charge [a]	...	...	...	...	...	...	...	...	...	...	...	...
Import duties	...	...	...	2520	...	2520	...	...	...	2736	...	2736
Value added tax [d]	...	...	...	98680	9542	89138	...	...	...	112446	10717	101729
Other adjustments	9358	...	3305	1948	3586	11025	9939	...	6805	-2619	3050	11075
Total	461433	91752	149294	126261	39157	789583	502379	99464	159903	141245	42107	860884

Sweden

4.3 Cost Components of Value Added

Million Swedish kronor

		Compensation of Employees	Capital Consumption	Net Operating Surplus	Indirect Taxes	Less: Subsidies Received	Value Added
		\multicolumn{6}{c}{1986}

All Producers

		Comp. of Employees	Capital Consumption	Net Operating Surplus	Indirect Taxes	Less: Subsidies Received	Value Added
1	Agriculture, hunting, forestry and fishing	6813	...	21277	1184	992	28282
	A Agriculture and hunting	2776	...	12011	546	982	14351
	B Forestry and logging	3958	...	8806	627	10	13381
	C Fishing	79	...	460	11	-	550
2	Mining and quarrying	2023	...	1914	92	-	4029
	A Coal mining	...	...	...	...	...	...
	B Crude petroleum and natural gas production	...	...	...	...	...	...
	C Metal ore mining	1439	...	1572	58	-	3069
	D Other mining	584	...	342	34	-	960
3	Manufacturing	133234	...	64825	5855	3603	200311
	A Manufacture of food, beverages and tobacco	11036	...	9018	560	-	20614
	B Textile, wearing apparel and leather industries	3973	...	1193	190	75	5281
	C Manufacture of wood and wood products, including furniture	8488	...	2842	399	-	11729
	D Manufacture of paper and paper products, printing and publishing	19035	...	10327	803	585	29580
	E Manufacture of chemicals and chemical petroleum, coal, rubber and plastic products	12116	...	10598	561	-	23275
	F Manufacture of non-metallic mineral products, except products of petroleum and coal	3497	...	2045	161	-	5703
	G Basic metal industries	7682	...	3102	320	-	11104
	H Manufacture of fabricated metal products, machinery and equipment	64005	...	25070	2717	-	91792
	I Other manufacturing industries	3402	...	630	144	2943	1233
4	Electricity, gas and water	4996	...	22097	341	609	26825
	A Electricity, gas and steam	4822	...	20635	334	393	25398
	B Water works and supply	174	...	1462	7	216	1427
5	Construction	38696	...	15533	1914	-	56143
6	Wholesale and retail trade, restaurants and hotels	68495	...	33839	3502	-	105836
	A Wholesale and retail trade	62527	...	30903	3228	-	96658
	B Restaurants and hotels	5968	...	2936	274	-	9178
7	Transport, storage and communication	38442	...	21103	2963	6866	55642
	A Transport and storage	27475	...	15429	2494	6833	38565
	B Communication	10967	...	5674	469	33	17077
8	Finance, insurance, real estate and business services [ab]	39549	1058	73611	10319	14505	110032
	A Financial institutions	9365	1058	10026	3053	866	-1310
	B Insurance	4624	...	-1221	195	-	3598
	C Real estate and business services	25560	...	88758	7071	13639	107750
	Real estate, except dwellings	*	...	7984	26	43	7967
	Dwellings	4447	...	75178	6168	13345	72448
9	Community, social and personal services	22021	...	9517	1068	3424	29182
	A Sanitary and similar services	3823	...	2759	168	154	6596
	B Social and related community services	7236	...	1798	313	2780	6567
	Educational services	...	...	...	...	...	...
	Medical, dental, other health and veterinary services	3742	...	1226	158	2780	2346
	C Recreational and cultural services	4776	...	2100	243	490	6629
	D Personal and household services	6186	...	2860	344	-	9390

Sweden

4.3 Cost Components of Value Added
(Continued)

Million Swedish kronor

	Compensation of Employees	Capital Consumption	Net Operating Surplus	Indirect Taxes	Less: Subsidies Received	Value Added
	\multicolumn{6}{c	}{1986}
Total, Industries	354269	96127	168647	27238	29999	616282
Producers of Government Services	174978	9738	-	7003	-	191719
Other Producers	5826	-	-	234	-	6060
Total [c]	535073	105865	168647	34475	29999	814061
Less: Imputed bank service charge [a]	...	...	...	...	...	...
Import duties	...	...	...	2985	...	2985
Value added tax [d]	...	...	...	120373	11393	108980
Other adjustments	14303	...	-8474	5465	3634	7660
Total	549376	105865	160173	163298	45026	933686

a) Item 'Less: Imputed bank service charge' is netted out of item 'Finance, insurance, real estate and business services'.
b) Column 'Operating Surplus' is reduced for imputed bank service charges.
c) Gross domestic product in basic values.
d) Item 'Value added tax' relates to value added tax and other taxes and subsidies on sales and production of commodities.

Switzerland

Source. Reply to the United Nations National Accounts Questionnaire from the Federal Bureau of Statistics, Bern. The official estimates are published annually by the Bureau in the September issue of 'La Vie Economique', and in 'Series revisees de la compatabilite nationale suisse, 1948-1976'.

General note. The estimates shown in the following tables have been adjusted to conform to the United Nations System of National Accounts so far as the existing data would permit.

1.1 Expenditure on the Gross Domestic Product, in Current Prices

Million Swiss francs

	1970	1975	1977	1978	1979	1980	1981	1982	1983	1984	1985	1986
1 Government final consumption expenditure	9505	17685	18895	19510	20520	21685	23545	25555	27355	28500	30420	31425
2 Private final consumption expenditure	53455	86270	92900	95540	101000	108335	116020	122440	127755	134035	141015	145460
3 Gross capital formation	29245	32200	30235	32925	37840	46320	47010	47095	48845	51300	55565	63495
A Increase in stocks	4290	-1455	-	435	3255	5820	2450	1795	1345	1500	1365	4500
B Gross fixed capital formation	24955	33655	30235	32490	34585	40500	44560	45300	47500	49800	54200	58995
Residential buildings												
Non-residential buildings	15455	22445	20170	21380	23410	27500	30800	31800	32750	34200	35900	38590
Other construction and land improvement etc.												
Other	9500	11210	10065	11110	11175	13000	13760	13500	14750	15600	18300	20405
4 Exports of goods and services	29710	44030	53445	53225	56015	62580	69100	69550	71760	80550	89015	89050
5 Less: Imports of goods and services	31250	40030	49685	49525	56830	68590	70920	68660	71850	81155	88065	86185
Equals: Gross Domestic Product	90665	140155	145790	151675	158545	170330	184755	195980	203865	213230	227950	242945

1.2 Expenditure on the Gross Domestic Product, in Constant Prices

Million Swiss francs

	1970	1975	1977	1978	1979	1980	1981	1982	1983	1984	1985	1986
					At constant prices of:1970							
1 Government final consumption expenditure	9505	10850	11105	11420	11540	11650	11935	12040	12495	12645	13060	13410
2 Private final consumption expenditure	53455	58615	61035	62390	63185	64845	65140	65140	66180	67195	68180	70260
3 Gross capital formation	29245	23295	22285	23895	27325	31260	29460	28285	29175	30445	32025	36580
A Increase in stocks	4290	-1210	-	250	2475	3945	1490	1060	790	875	780	2625
B Gross fixed capital formation	24955	24505	22285	23645	24850	27315	27970	27225	28385	29570	31245	33955
Residential buildings												
Non-residential buildings	15455	15905	14565	14910	15650	17070	17770	17490	18015	18750	19300	20120
Other construction and land improvement etc.												
Other	9500	8600	7720	8735	9200	10245	10200	9735	10370	10820	11945	13835
4 Exports of goods and services	29710	33425	40085	41575	42600	44760	46840	45445	45880	48805	52875	53005
5 Less: Imports of goods and services	31250	31790	39265	43555	46540	49890	49260	47970	50095	53640	56375	60570
Equals: Gross Domestic Product	90665	94395	95335	95725	98110	102625	104115	102940	103635	105450	109765	112685

1.3 Cost Components of the Gross Domestic Product

Million Swiss francs

	1970	1975	1977	1978	1979	1980	1981	1982	1983	1984	1985	1986
1 Indirect taxes, net	5615	7435	8020	8590	8890	9660	10510	10720	11320	11850	12630	13985
A Indirect taxes	6375	9115	9990	10775	11105	11910	12670	13315	14145	14895	15875	17345
B Less: Subsidies	760	1680	1970	2185	2215	2250	2160	2595	2825	3045	3245	3360
2 Consumption of fixed capital	10770	15245	15990	16430	16700	17960	19550	20400	20900	21700	23400	24395
3 Compensation of employees paid by resident producers to:	49605	85150	87690	92185	97095	104650	114120	122700	128155	133425	141525	150405
A Resident households	48535	82545	85510	89775	94500	101740	110670	118910	124330	129490	137300	145730
B Rest of the world	1070	2605	2180	2410	2595	2910	3450	3790	3825	3935	4225	4675
4 Operating surplus	24675	32325	34090	34470	35860	38060	40575	42160	43490	46255	50395	54160
Equals: Gross Domestic Product	90665	140155	145790	151675	158545	170330	184755	195980	203865	213230	227950	242945

1.4 General Government Current Receipts and Disbursements

Million Swiss francs

	1970	1975	1977	1978	1979	1980	1981	1982	1983	1984	1985	1986
					Receipts							
1 Operating surplus	-	-	-	-	-	-	-	-	-	-	-	-
2 Property and entrepreneurial income	1420	2235	2360	2245	2145	2505	2940	3020	2975	2995	3210	3430
3 Taxes, fees and contributions	22035	41780	45680	47745	48980	51925	56070	60330	63995	68640	72520	78665
A Indirect taxes	6375	9115	9990	10775	11105	11910	12670	13315	14145	14895	15875	17345

Switzerland

1.4 General Government Current Receipts and Disbursements
(Continued)

Million Swiss francs

	1970	1975	1977	1978	1979	1980	1981	1982	1983	1984	1985	1986
B Direct taxes	10130	20215	21505	21865	21965	23340	25480	27720	29085	31070	32500	35705
C Social security contributions	5065	11655	13260	14125	14845	15550	16710	18035	19390	21165	22495	23840
D Compulsory fees, fines and penalties	465	795	925	980	1065	1125	1210	1260	1375	1510	1650	1775
4 Other current transfers	565	960	1120	1285	1345	1480	1655	1905	2155	2430	2765	3020
Total Current Receipts of General Government	24020	44975	49160	51275	52470	55910	60665	65255	69125	74065	78495	85115

Disbursements

	1970	1975	1977	1978	1979	1980	1981	1982	1983	1984	1985	1986
1 Government final consumption expenditure	9505	17685	18895	19510	20520	21685	23545	25555	27355	28500	30420	31425
2 Property income	1330	2735	3170	3120	3025	3130	3375	3535	3630	3590	3695	3725
3 Subsidies	760	1680	1970	2185	2215	2250	2160	2595	2825	3045	3245	3360
4 Other current transfers	7700	18190	20260	21035	21655	22795	24245	27365	29085	31790	33320	35400
A Social security benefits	5670	14205	15905	16350	16840	17575	18600	21050	22425	24595	25555	27130
B Social assistance grants	1755	3295	3480	3685	3725	4000	4355	4835	5050	5395	5780	6125
C Other	275	690	875	1000	1090	1220	1290	1480	1610	1800	1985	2145
5 Net saving	4725	4685	4865	5425	5055	6050	7340	6205	6230	7140	7815	11205
Total Current Disbursements and Net Saving of General Government	24020	44975	49160	51275	52470	55910	60665	65255	69125	74065	78495	85115

1.6 Current Income and Outlay of Households and Non-Profit Institutions

Million Swiss francs

	1970	1975	1977	1978	1979	1980	1981	1982	1983	1984	1985	1986

Receipts

	1970	1975	1977	1978	1979	1980	1981	1982	1983	1984	1985	1986
1 Compensation of employees	48965	83370	86485	90735	95485	102760	111540	119810	125310	130490	138335	146740
A From resident producers	48535	82545	85510	89775	94500	101740	110670	118910	124330	129490	137300	145730
B From rest of the world	430	825	975	960	985	1020	870	900	980	1000	1035	1010
2 Operating surplus of private unincorporated enterprises [a]	...	...	...	...	...	...	...	...	...	...	...	...
3 Property and entrepreneurial income [ba]	20640	29715	30860	31055	32200	34115	37785	39395	40685	43750	45500	46200
4 Current transfers	7665	17775	19660	20310	20840	21915	23295	26225	27830	30345	31710	33640
A Social security benefits	5670	14205	15905	16350	16840	17575	18600	21050	22425	24595	25555	27130
B Social assistance grants	...	...	...	...	...	...	...	4835	5050	5395	5780	6125
C Other	1995	3570	3755	3960	4000	4340	4695	340	355	355	375	385
Total Current Receipts	77270	130860	137005	142100	148525	158790	172620	185430	193825	204585	215545	226580

Disbursements

	1970	1975	1977	1978	1979	1980	1981	1982	1983	1984	1985	1986
1 Private final consumption expenditure	53455	86270	92900	95540	101000	108335	116020	122440	127755	134035	141015	145460
2 Property income [b]	...	...	...	...	...	...	...	...	...	...	...	...
3 Direct taxes and other current transfers n.e.c. to general government	13855	29000	32245	33605	34790	36710	39730	42940	45475	49220	51755	55535
A Social security contributions	5065	11655	13260	14125	14845	15550	16710	18035	19390	21165	22495	23840
B Direct taxes	8790	17345	18985	19480	19945	21160	23020	24905	26085	28055	29260	31695
C Fees, fines and penalties	...	...	...	...	...	...	...	...	...	...	...	...
4 Other current transfers	1555	1810	1465	1420	1470	1835	2120	2260	2295	2345	2490	2605
5 Net saving	8405	13780	10395	11535	11265	11910	14750	17790	18300	18985	20285	22980
Total Current Disbursements and Net Saving	77270	130860	137005	142100	148525	158790	172620	185430	193825	204585	215545	226580

a) Item 'Operating surplus of private unincorporated enterprises' is included in item 'Property and entrepreneurial income'.
b) Item 'Property and entrepreneurial income' received is net of item 'Property income' paid.

1.7 External Transactions on Current Account, Summary

Million Swiss francs

	1970	1975	1977	1978	1979	1980	1981	1982	1983	1984	1985	1986

Payments to the Rest of the World

	1970	1975	1977	1978	1979	1980	1981	1982	1983	1984	1985	1986
1 Imports of goods and services	31250	40030	49685	49525	56830	68590	70920	68660	71850	81155	88065	86485
2 Factor income to the rest of the world	1610	3590	3295	3755	3835	4235	5290	5950	6650	6965	7845	9030
A Compensation of employees	1070	2605	2180	2410	2595	2910	3450	3790	3825	3935	4225	4675
B Property and entrepreneurial income	540	985	1115	1345	1240	1325	1840	2160	2825	3030	3620	4355

Switzerland

1.7 External Transactions on Current Account, Summary
(Continued)

Million Swiss francs

	1970	1975	1977	1978	1979	1980	1981	1982	1983	1984	1985	1986
3 Current transfers to the rest of the world	1830	2500	2340	2420	2560	3055	3410	3740	3905	4145	4475	4750
A Indirect taxes to supranational organizations	...	...	...	...	...	...	...	...	...	...	...	...
B Other current transfers	1830	2500	2340	2420	2560	3055	3410	3740	3905	4145	4475	4750
4 Surplus of the nation on current transactions	330	6820	8425	8040	4285	-795	5430	8010	8075	10260	12375	12135
Payments to the Rest of the World and Surplus of the Nation on Current Transactions	35020	52940	63745	63740	67510	75085	85050	86360	90480	102525	112760	112400

Receipts From The Rest of the World

	1970	1975	1977	1978	1979	1980	1981	1982	1983	1984	1985	1986
1 Exports of goods and services	29710	44030	53445	53225	56015	62580	69100	69550	71760	80550	89015	89050
2 Factor income from rest of the world	4875	8060	9405	9575	10480	11250	14510	15140	16735	19795	21250	20595
A Compensation of employees	430	825	975	960	985	1020	870	900	980	1000	1035	1010
B Property and entrepreneurial income	4445	7235	8430	8615	9495	10230	13640	14240	15755	18795	20215	19585
3 Current transfers from rest of the world	435	850	895	940	1015	1255	1440	1670	1985	2180	2495	2755
A Subsidies from supranational organisations	...	...	...	...	...	...	...	...	...	...	...	...
B Other current transfers	435	850	895	940	1015	1255	1440	1670	1985	2180	2495	2755
Receipts from the Rest of the World on Current Transactions	35020	52940	63745	63740	67510	75085	85050	86360	90480	102525	112760	112400

1.8 Capital Transactions of The Nation, Summary

Million Swiss francs

	1970	1975	1977	1978	1979	1980	1981	1982	1983	1984	1985	1986

Finance of Gross Capital Formation

	1970	1975	1977	1978	1979	1980	1981	1982	1983	1984	1985	1986
Gross saving	29575	39020	38660	40965	42125	45525	52440	55105	56920	61560	67940	75630
1 Consumption of fixed capital	10770	15245	15990	16430	16700	17960	19550	20400	20900	21700	23400	24395
2 Net saving	18805	23775	22670	24535	25425	27565	32890	34705	36020	39860	44540	51235
A General government	4725	4685	4865	5425	5055	6050	7340	6205	6230	7140	7815	10415
B Corporate and quasi-corporate enterprises	5675	5310	7410	7575	9105	9605	10800	10710	11490	13735	16440	17050
C Other	8405	13780	10395	11535	11265	11910	14750	17790	18300	18985	20285	23770
Less: Surplus of the nation on current transactions	330	6820	8425	8040	4285	-795	5430	8010	8075	10260	12375	12135
Finance of Gross Capital Formation	29245	32200	30235	32925	37840	46320	47010	47095	48845	51300	55565	63495

Gross Capital Formation

	1970	1975	1977	1978	1979	1980	1981	1982	1983	1984	1985	1986
Increase in stocks	4290	-1455	-	435	3255	5820	2450	1795	1345	1500	1365	4500
Gross fixed capital formation	24955	33655	30235	32490	34585	40500	44560	45300	47500	49800	54200	58995
Gross Capital Formation	29245	32200	30235	32925	37840	46320	47010	47095	48845	51300	55565	63495

1.12 Relations Among National Accounting Aggregates

Million Swiss francs

	1970	1975	1977	1978	1979	1980	1981	1982	1983	1984	1985	1986
Gross Domestic Product	90665	140155	145790	151675	158545	170330	184755	195980	203865	213230	227950	242945
Plus: Net factor income from the rest of the world	3265	4470	6110	5820	6645	7015	9220	9190	10085	12830	13405	11565
Factor income from the rest of the world	4875	8060	9405	9575	10480	11250	14510	15140	16735	19795	21250	20595
Less: Factor income to the rest of the world	1610	3590	3295	3755	3835	4235	5290	5950	6650	6965	7845	9030
Equals: Gross National Product	93930	144625	151900	157495	165190	177345	193975	205170	213950	226060	241355	254510
Less: Consumption of fixed capital	10770	15245	15990	16430	16700	17960	19550	20400	20900	21700	23400	24395

Switzerland

1.12 Relations Among National Accounting Aggregates
(Continued)

Million Swiss francs

	1970	1975	1977	1978	1979	1980	1981	1982	1983	1984	1985	1986
Equals: National Income	83160	129380	135910	141065	148490	159385	174425	184770	193050	204360	217955	230115
Plus: Net current transfers from the rest of the world	-1395	-1650	-1445	-1480	-1545	-1800	-1970	-2070	-1920	-1965	-1980	-1995
Current transfers from the rest of the world	435	850	895	940	1015	1255	1440	1670	1985	2180	2495	2755
Less: Current transfers to the rest of the world	1830	2500	2340	2420	2560	3055	3410	3740	3905	4145	4475	4750
Equals: National Disposable Income	81765	127730	134465	139585	146945	157585	172455	182700	191130	202395	215975	228120
Less: Final consumption	62960	103955	111795	115050	121520	130020	139565	147995	155110	162535	171435	176885
Equals: Net Saving	18805	23775	22670	24535	25425	27565	32890	34705	36020	39860	44540	51235
Less: Surplus of the nation on current transactions	330	6820	8425	8040	4285	-795	5430	8010	8075	10260	12375	12135
Equals: Net Capital Formation	18475	16955	14245	16495	21140	28360	27460	26695	27945	29600	32165	39100

2.5 Private Final Consumption Expenditure by Type and Porpose, in Current Prices

Million Swiss francs

	1970	1975	1977	1978	1979	1980	1981	1982	1983	1984	1985	1986
	\multicolumn{12}{c}{**Final Consumption Expenditure of Resident Households**}											
1 Food, beverages and tobacco	16805	25515	26330	26985	27955	29900	32085	33940	35330	36960	38655	40185
A Food	11665	18070	18880	19445	20140	21750	23290	24470	25530	26985	28250	29400
B Non-alcoholic beverages	5140	7445	7450	7540	7815	8150	8795	9470	9800	9975	10405	10785
C Alcoholic beverages	...	...	...	...	...	...	...	...	...	...	...	...
D Tobacco	...	...	...	...	...	...	...	...	...	...	...	...
2 Clothing and footwear	3550	4670	4665	4795	4855	5220	5555	5640	5855	6045	6340	6735
3 Gross rent, fuel and power	9185	16220	18185	18265	20060	20990	22270	23855	25120	26470	27805	27065
A Fuel and power	2515	4840	5680	5510	7090	7630	8095	8105	8235	8890	9380	7625
B Other	6670	11380	12505	12755	12970	13360	14175	15750	16885	17580	18425	19440
4 Furniture, furnishings and household equipment and operation	4115	5580	5655	5730	5910	6315	6550	6625	6735	6925	7125	7430
A Household operation	1125	1695	1715	1740	1715	1790	1845	1905	1960	2005	2050	2095
B Other	2990	3885	3940	3990	4195	4525	4705	4720	4775	4920	5075	5335
5 Medical care and health expenses	3320	6520	7265	7595	8030	8585	9280	10070	10815	11400	12130	12875
6 Transport and communication	5850	9125	10540	11120	11835	12775	13925	14240	14400	14770	15310	15710
A Personal transport equipment	1870	2390	3245	3715	3700	3825	4135	4215	4090	4100	4195	4885
B Other	3980	6735	7295	7405	8135	8950	9790	10025	10310	10670	11115	10825
7 Recreational, entertainment, education and cultural services [a]	4795	7840	8395	8575	9075	9925	10700	11315	11870	12620	13325	14020
8 Miscellaneous goods and services	4095	8010	8630	8850	9235	9820	10530	11230	11850	12435	13240	14165
A Personal care	1140	1810	1875	1900	1960	2075	2195	2340	2440	2560	2710	2845
B Expenditures in restaurants, cafes and hotels [a]	...	...	...	...	...	...	...	...	...	...	...	...
C Other	2955	6200	6755	6950	7275	7745	8335	8890	9410	9875	10530	11320
Total Final Consumption Expenditure in the Domestic Market by Households, of which	51715	83480	89665	91915	96955	103530	110895	116915	121975	127625	133930	138185
Plus: Direct purchases abroad by resident households	1740	2790	3235	3625	4045	4805	5125	5525	5780	6410	7085	7275
Less: Direct purchases in the domestic market by non-resident households [b]	...	...	...	...	...	...	...	...	...	...	...	...
Equals: Final Consumption Expenditure of Resident Households [c]	53455	86270	92900	95540	101000	108335	116020	122440	127755	134035	141015	145460
	\multicolumn{12}{c}{**Final Consumption Expenditure of Private Non-profit Institutions Serving Households**}											
Equals: Final Consumption Expenditure of Private Non-profit Organisations Serving Households	...	...	...	...	...	...	...	...	...	...	...	...
Private Final Consumption Expenditure	53455	86270	92900	95540	101000	108335	116020	122440	127755	134035	141015	145460

a) Item 'Expenditure in restaurants, cafes and hotels' is included in item 'Recreational, entertainment, education and cultural services'.
b) Item 'Direct purchases in the domestic market by non-resident households' is netted out from the appropriate items above.
c) Item 'Final consumption expenditure of resident households' includes consumption expenditure of private non-profit institutions serving households.

Switzerland

2.6 Private Final Consumption Expenditure by Type and Purpose, in Constant Prices

Million Swiss francs

	1970	1975	1977	1978	1979	1980	1981	1982	1983	1984	1985	1986
	\multicolumn{12}{c}{At constant prices of: 1970}

Final Consumption Expenditure of Resident Households

	1970	1975	1977	1978	1979	1980	1981	1982	1983	1984	1985	1986
1 Food, beverages and tobacco	16805	17715	18300	18125	18140	18340	18080	17980	18255	18530	18775	19170
A Food	11665	12785	13390	13240	13235	13360	13065	12920	13200	13445	13670	14010
B Non-alcoholic beverages	5140	4930	4910	4885	4905	4980	5015	5060	5055	5085	5105	5160
C Alcoholic beverages	...	...	...	...	...	...	...	...	...	...	...	...
D Tobacco	...	...	...	...	...	...	...	...	...	...	...	...
2 Clothing and footwear	3550	3180	3120	3165	3180	3300	3365	3285	3300	3310	3340	3425
3 Gross rent, fuel and power	9185	10755	11410	11655	11650	11910	12020	12080	12415	12700	12880	13135
A Fuel and power	2515	3070	3420	3610	3455	3560	3530	3455	3650	3795	3835	3945
B Other	6670	7685	7990	8045	8195	8350	8490	8625	8765	8905	9045	9190
4 Furniture, furnishings and household equipment and operation	4115	4050	4000	4010	4115	4255	4230	4090	4055	4110	4135	4230
A Household operation	1125	1195	1135	1145	1110	1120	1115	1095	1095	1095	1090	1090
B Other	2990	2855	2865	2865	3005	3135	3115	2995	2960	3015	3045	3140
5 Medical care and health expenses	3320	3740	3815	3885	3965	4105	4190	4230	4330	4395	4485	4585
6 Transport and communication	5850	6230	6790	7225	7330	7535	7755	7765	7750	7740	7715	8185
A Personal transport equipment	1870	1630	2090	2415	2295	2255	2300	2300	2200	2150	2115	2535
B Other	3980	4600	4700	4810	5035	5280	5455	5465	5550	5590	5600	5650
7 Recreational, entertainment, education and cultural services [a]	4795	5610	5770	5815	6100	6395	6555	6600	6740	6865	7030	7185
8 Miscellaneous goods and services	4095	5025	5185	5250	5345	5480	5545	5585	5705	5815	5960	6175
A Personal care	1140	1240	1235	1240	1285	1330	1355	1385	1400	1445	1495	1535
B Expenditures in restaurants, cafes and hotels [a]	...	...	...	...	...	...	...	...	...	...	...	...
C Other	2955	3785	3950	4010	4060	4150	4190	4200	4305	4370	4465	4640
Total Final Consumption Expenditure in the Domestic Market by Households, of which	51715	56305	58390	59130	59825	61320	61740	61615	62550	63465	64320	66090
Plus: Direct purchases abroad by resident households	1740	2310	2645	3260	3360	3525	3400	3525	3630	3730	3860	4170
Less: Direct purchases in the domestic market by non-resident households [b]	...	...	...	...	...	...	...	...	...	...	...	...
Equals: Final Consumption Expenditure of Resident Households [c]	53455	58615	61035	62390	63185	64845	65140	65140	66180	67195	68180	70260

Final Consumption Expenditure of Private Non-profit Institutions Serving Households

	1970	1975	1977	1978	1979	1980	1981	1982	1983	1984	1985	1986
Equals: Final Consumption Expenditure of Private Non-profit Organisations Serving Households	...	...	...	...	...	...	...	...	...	...	...	...
Private Final Consumption Expenditure	53455	58615	61035	62390	63185	64845	65140	65140	66180	67195	68180	70260

a) Item 'Expenditure in restaurants, cafes and hotels' is included in item 'Recreational, entertainment, education and cultural services'.
b) Item 'Direct purchases in the domestic market by non-resident households' is netted out from the appropriate items above.
c) Item 'Final consumption expenditure of resident households' includes consumption expenditure of private non-profit institutions serving households.

Syrian Arab Republic

General note. The preparation of national accounts statistics in Syrian Arab Republic is undertaken by the Directorate of National Accounts, Central Bureau of Statistics, Damascus. The official estimates are published annually in the 'Statistical Abstract', issued by the Central Bureau of Statistics. The following presentation of sources and methods is based on a report entitled: 'National Accounts of the Syrian Arab Republic and Syria's First Effort at Implementing Stages of the New United Nations System of National Accounts (SNA)'. The estimates are generally in accordance with the classifications and definitions recommended in the United Nations System of National Accounts. The following tables have been prepared from successive replies to the United Nations national accounts questionnaire. When the scope and coverage of the estimates differ for conceptual or statisitcal reasons from the definitions and classifications recommended in SNA, a footnote is indicated to the relevant tables.

Sources and methods:

(a) Gross domestic product. Gross domestic product is estimated mainly through the production approach.

(b) Expenditure on the gross domestic product. The expenditure approach is used to estimate government final consumption expenditure, exports and imports of goods and services, and part of changes in stocks. This approach, in combination with the commodity-flow approach, is used to estimate gross fixed capital formation. Private final consumption expenditure is obtained as a residual. The basic data for government final consumption expenditure estimates are available from the budgets of the State, the municipalities and religious endowment administrations. Stock fluctuations are not estimated. For gross fixed capital formation, detailed classification of import statistics are utilized for machinery and equipment. Added to the c.i.f. values are import duties, other indirect taxes and estimated trade margins. For construction in the private sector, estimates are obtained by multiplying the area of floor space indicated in the annual census by the average price per square metre and by adding thereto the value of repairs carried out. The estimates of exports and imports of goods and services are based on foreign trade statistics and balance-of-payments data. For the constant price estimates, price deflation is used for government final consumption expenditure and gross fixed capital formation. Price deflation and extrapolation by volume index are used for exports and imports of merchandise. Private consumption expenditure is obtained as a residual and no estimates for increase in stocks are made.

(c) Cost-structure of the gross domestic product. The cost-structure table of the GDP is not being estimated.

(d) Gross domestic product by kind of economic activity. The table of gross domestic product by kind of economic activity is prepared at market prices, i.e., producers' values. The production approach is used to estimate the value added of most industries. The income aproach is used for some private services and for producers of government services. The commodity-flow approach is used to estimate the gross output of the trade sector. The data on field and animal agricultural production are collected by the Ministry of Agriculture. Gross output and intermediate input are compiled per individual commodity group, estimated from figures gathered separately on quantities and prices. The agricultural prices were obtained through a census for the year 1971. For other years, only wholesale prices are known while producers' prices are derived on the basis of varying assumptions. Own-account consumption of agricultural production is mainly based on the sample survey conducted in 1970 and the 1968 family budget survey. Data for extractive industries, such as crude oil and phosphates, owned by the State are obtained from reports that include the size and value of production and intermediate consumption. Extractive industries in the private sector are based on industrial surveys. Data concerning industrial public enterprises are available from the Union of Industries. For the private sector, the Central Bureau of Statistics has undertaken a general economic survey for 1971, which covers all establishments employing more than nine persons and includes a sample of the smaller establishments. The frame for the survey was based on the 1970 population census. Other data sources has been used to cover establishments created after 1970. In the manufacture of food, the value of flour is multiplied by the ratio between the value of bread and the value of flour derived from the economic survey. Similar ratios between gross output and intermediate consumption and compensation of employees are used for the estimation of intermediate consumption and compensation of employees. The sources of data on the electricity and water industries are the accounts of the concerned enterprises. For construction, estimates of production values and intermediate consumption in the private sector are made by determining the value of construction projects completed during the year and adding to it the value of the completed portions of unfinished buildings and construction projects. The progress reports issued by the State Planning Commission are the prime source of data for construction in the public sector. For trade, gross margins are estimated as percentage mark-ups on commodity-flow values. The value of intermediate consumption is estimated as 8 percent of the production value. Information on railway and air transport and communication activities is supplied entirely by public enterprises. Gross output of road transport are based on the registration of licenses issued, and on gross revenue and cost data by type of unit, based on ad hoc transport sample surveys. Estimates of pipeline and sea transport are obtained from concerned enterprises. For banks, the production value is calculated by adding to actual expenditure imputed service charges. Estimates of insurance and real estate activities are derived from the concerned companies. The production value of the housing sector is estimated as rents paid to others for house leases plus the estimated rental value of owner-occupied houses. For community services, the basic data are available from the accounting records of public enterprises and the budgets of public authorities. The results of the 1971 general economic survey are used for some private services while proxy output indicators derived from the results of the 1970 population census and administrative records are used for other services. For the constant price estimates, double deflation is used for agriculture. Value added of all other economic activity sectors of GDP, except trade, is extrapolated by a quantity index. To obtain wholesale and retail trade margin at constant prices, the same percentages as those used for current prices are applied to the production values of the agricultural, mining and quarrying and manufacturing sectors.

1.1 Expenditure on the Gross Domestic Product, in Current Prices

Million Syrian pounds

		1970	1975	1977	1978	1979	1980	1981	1982	1983	1984	1985	1986
1	Government final consumption expenditure	1187	4338	5300	6499	8487	11870	13656	15103	16154	17079	19785	22940
2	Private final consumption expenditure	4966	13044	18769	21627	27399	34107	48256	44992	49686	49121	54155	63521
3	Gross capital formation	937	5916	9272	9876	10113	14116	15262	16270	17286	17865	19784	21937
	A Increase in stocks	40	760	-325	989	-81	...	...	...	...	...	...	...
	B Gross fixed capital formation	897	5156	9597	8887	10194	14116	15262	16270	17286	17865	19784	21937
	Residential buildings	215	849	1418	1627	1538	4036	4685	4650	3859	4471	5126	7394
	Non-residential buildings	59	337	725	642	968	1163	1047	1668	1825	2259	2335	2549
	Other construction and land improvement etc.	259	1329	2126	2462	3947	4269	4456	5580	6317	6705	7503	7653
	Other	364	2641	5328	4156	3741	4648	5074	4372	5285	4430	4820	...
4	Exports of goods and services	1190	4409	4908	4808	7253	9345	10290	9572	9714	9360	10245	10134
5	Less: Imports of goods and services	1432	6996	10984	10114	13950	18168	21687	17149	19549	18083	20744	20158
	Equals: Gross Domestic Product	6848	20711	27265	32696	39302	51270	65777	68788	73291	75342	83225	98374

1.2 Expenditure on the Gross Domestic Product, in Constant Prices

Million Syrian pounds

		1970	1975	1977	1978	1979	1980	1981	1982	1983	1984	1985	1986
		\multicolumn{12}{c}{At constant prices of:1980}												
1	Government final consumption expenditure	3701	8332	8585	9377	11862	11870	12445	13154	13855	15035	13913	15494
2	Private final consumption expenditure	8581	26036	25673	30177	31410	34107	42838	39227	40871	36883	41158	47841
3	Gross capital formation	3192	8636	13313	11567	11740	14116	14421	14896	15457	15742	16769	17337
	A Increase in stocks	...	...	...	...	...	...	...	...	...	...	...	...
	B Gross fixed capital formation	3192	8636	13313	11567	11740	14116	14421	14896	15457	15742	16769	17337

Syrian Arab Republic

1.2 Expenditure on the Gross Domestic Product, in Constant Prices
(Continued)

Million Syrian pounds

	1970	1975	1977	1978	1979	1980	1981	1982	1983	1984	1985	1986
					At constant prices of:1980							
Residential buildings	886	1422	2350	2625	2240	4036	4156	4266	3415	3888	4381	6060
Non-residential buildings	194	565	1012	827	1410	1163	930	1530	1615	1964	1996	2090
Other construction and land improvement etc.	848	2226	2827	2772	3459	4269	3934	5215	5692	5934	6525	6431
Other	1264	4423	7124	5343	4631	4648	5401	3885	4735	3956	3867	2756
4 Exports of goods and services	10042	10991	11026	10671	10219	9345	9758	10231	10636	10080	11578	15189
5 Less: Imports of goods and services	4938	13992	15919	15560	17438	18168	23319	19711	21965	21027	24993	30542
Equals: Gross Domestic Product	20578	40003	42678	46232	47793	51270	56143	57797	58855	56713	58425	65319

1.3 Cost Components of the Gross Domestic Product

Million Syrian pounds

	1970	1975	1977	1978	1979	1980	1981	1982	1983	1984	1985	1986
1 Indirect taxes, net	434	501	556	1848	428	1308	1316	2567	2504	2898	2798	3326
A Indirect taxes	540	1557	2005	2284	2543	3218	3326	3932	3924	3943	4198	4726
B Less: Subsidies	106	1056	1449	436	2115	1910	2010	1365	1420	1045	1400	1400
2 Consumption of fixed capital	305	582	882	1030	1149	1443	1967	2115	2243	2334	2731	3218
3 Compensation of employees paid by resident producers to:	...	...	...	...	...	...	...	...	...	...	...	...
4 Operating surplus	...	...	...	...	...	...	...	...	...	...	...	...
Equals: Gross Domestic Product	6848	20711	27265	32696	39302	51270	65777	68788	73291	75342	83225	98374

1.10 Gross Domestic Product by Kind of Activity, in Current Prices

Million Syrian pounds

	1970	1975	1977	1978	1979	1980	1981	1982	1983	1984	1985	1986
1 Agriculture, hunting, forestry and fishing	1382	3705	5000	6851	6857	10369	12759	13854	15627	14805	17463	23621
2 Mining and quarrying	157	2416	2695	2815	4524	6154	7004	6480	6024	6043	5948	3006
3 Manufacturing	1312	1535	2327	3585	3327	1825	5500	5176	5788	6047	6382	11057
4 Electricity, gas and water	91	222	288	338	395	394	526	-47	201	-55	191	102
5 Construction	201	960	1607	1781	2715	3574	3759	4327	4460	5006	5692	6704
6 Wholesale and retail trade, restaurants and hotels	1395	4603	7273	7893	9476	12693	16274	16846	17813	17701	18509	20114
7 Transport, storage and communication	733	2407	1735	1932	2786	3555	4810	5513	5968	6254	8196	9802
8 Finance, insurance, real estate and business services	731	1481	1966	2205	2591	3266	4113	4328	4202	4402	4181	4348
9 Community, social and personal services	116	281	590	710	810	926	1154	1407	1468	1818	2195	2519
Total, Industries	6118	17610	23481	28111	33481	42756	55899	57884	61551	62022	68757	81273
Producers of Government Services	712	3082	3760	4557	5790	8480	9840	10861	11693	13268	14408	17035
Other Producers	18	19	23	27	31	34	38	43	47	52	60	66
Subtotal	6848	20711	27265	32696	39302	51270	65777	68788	73291	75342	83225	98374
Less: Imputed bank service charge	...	...	...	...	...	...	...	...	...	...		
Plus: Import duties	...	...	...	...	...	...	...	...	...	...		
Plus: Value added tax	...	...	...	...	...	...	...	...	...	...		
Equals: Gross Domestic Product	6848	20711	27265	32696	39302	51270	65777	68788	73291	75342	83225	98374

1.11 Gross Domestic Product by Kind of Activity, in Constant Prices

Million Syrian pounds

	1970	1975	1977	1978	1979	1980	1981	1982	1983	1984	1985	1986
					At constant prices of:1980							
1 Agriculture, hunting, forestry and fishing	3842	6778	7033	8090	7423	10369	10765	10513	10458	9563	10169	11062
2 Mining and quarrying	2978	6955	6552	6489	6433	6154	7056	6937	7222	7287	7157	8316
3 Manufacturing	2037	3083	2430	2946	1959	1825	602	1025	1367	-327	211	1882
4 Electricity, gas and water	112	277	346	395	453	394	457	476	608	662	746	569
5 Construction	910	1749	2785	2804	3706	3574	3743	4140	4068	4528	5061	5853
6 Wholesale and retail trade, restaurants and hotels	4796	9197	10630	11134	11617	12693	15445	15512	15205	14259	14874	15743
7 Transport, storage and communication	1742	2934	2943	3056	3379	3555	4202	4225	4468	4698	5009	5184
8 Finance, insurance, real estate and business services	1435	2276	2620	2792	3142	3266	3574	3652	3370	3029	2897	3035
9 Community, social and personal services	344	463	785	906	987	926	986	1188	1238	1160	1199	1313

Syrian Arab Republic

1.11 Gross Domestic Product by Kind of Activity, in Constant Prices
(Continued)

Million Syrian pounds

	1970	1975	1977	1978	1979	1980	1981	1982	1983	1984	1985	1986
	\multicolumn{12}{c}{At constant prices of:1980}
Total, Industries	18196	33712	36124	39310	39189	42756	46830	47668	48004	44859	47323	52957
Producers of Government Services	2350	6269	6528	6894	8574	8480	9276	10089	10807	11806	11050	12307
Other Producers	32	22	26	28	30	34	37	40	44	48	52	55
Subtotal	20578	40003	42678	46232	47793	51270	56143	57797	58855	56713	58425	65319
Less: Imputed bank service charge	...	...	...	...	...	...	...	...	...	...	...	...
Plus: Import duties	...	...	...	...	...	...	...	...	...	...	...	...
Plus: Value added tax	...	...	...	...	...	...	...	...	...	...	...	...
Equals: Gross Domestic Product	20578	40003	42678	46232	47793	51270	56143	57797	58855	56713	58425	65319

2.11 Gross Fixed Capital Formation by Kind of Activity of Owner, ISIC Divisions, in Current Prices

Million Syrian pounds

	1970	1975	1977	1978	1979	1980	1981	1982	1983	1984	1985	1986
	\multicolumn{12}{c}{All Producers}
1 Agriculture, hunting, forestry and fishing	141	353	473	585	808	525	959	940	1471	2064	2606	2878
2 Mining and quarrying												
3 Manufacturing	230	2349	4799	3950	4391	4048	5117	5306	5033	4306	4328	4252
4 Electricity, gas and water												
5 Construction	...	...	...	...	...	...	...	...	...	...	...	...
6 Wholesale and retail trade, restaurants and hotels	...	...	...	...	...	...	...	...	...	...	...	...
7 Transport, storage and communication	187	960	1635	1213	1335	1629	2080	2395	2785	2212	2311	1853
8 Finance, insurance, real estate and business services	339	1494	2690	3139	3660	7914	7106	7629	7997	9283	10539	12954
9 Community, social and personal services												
Total Industries	897	5156	9597	8887	10194	14116	15262	16270	17286	17865	19784	21937
Producers of Government Services	...	...	...	...	...	...	...	...	...	...	...	...
Private Non-Profit Institutions Serving Households	...	...	...	...	...	...	...	...	...	...	...	...
Total	897	5156	9597	8887	10194	14116	15262	16270	17286	17865	19784	21937

2.12 Gross Fixed Capital Formation by Kind of Activity of Owner, ISIC Divisions, in Constant Prices

Million Syrian pounds

	1970	1975	1977	1978	1979	1980	1981	1982	1983	1984	1985	1986
	\multicolumn{12}{c}{At constant prices of:1980}
	\multicolumn{12}{c}{All Producers}
1 Agriculture, hunting, forestry and fishing	479	591	635	699	800	525	924	868	1328	1831	2261	2333
2 Mining and quarrying												
3 Manufacturing	847	3936	6435	4969	5169	4048	4866	4776	4575	3790	3712	3210
4 Electricity, gas and water												
5 Construction	...	...	...	...	...	...	...	...	...	...	...	...
6 Wholesale and retail trade, restaurants and hotels	...	...	...	...	...	...	...	...	...	...	...	...
7 Transport, storage and communication	556	1608	2178	1472	1350	1629	1940	2243	2457	1941	1836	1320
8 Finance, insurance, real estate and business services	1310	2501	4065	4427	4421	7914	6691	7009	7097	8180	8960	10474
9 Community, social and personal services												
Total Industries	3192	8636	13313	11567	11740	14116	14421	14896	15457	15742	16769	17337
Producers of Government Services	...	...	...	...	...	...	...	...	...	...	...	...
Private Non-Profit Institutions Serving Households	...	...	...	...	...	...	...	...	...	...	...	...
Total	3192	8636	13313	11567	11740	14116	14421	14896	15457	15742	16769	17337

Syrian Arab Republic

4.1 Derivation of Value Added by Kind of Activity, in Current Prices

Million Syrian pounds

	1980 Gross Output	1980 Intermediate Consumption	1980 Value Added	1981 Gross Output	1981 Intermediate Consumption	1981 Value Added	1982 Gross Output	1982 Intermediate Consumption	1982 Value Added	1983 Gross Output	1983 Intermediate Consumption	1983 Value Added
					All Producers							
1 Agriculture, hunting, forestry and fishing	12804	2435	10369	16270	3511	12759	17870	4016	13854	19492	3866	15626
2 Mining and quarrying	...	...	6154	...	...	7004	...	...	6480	...	...	6023
3 Manufacturing	...	...	1825	...	...	5500	...	...	5176	...	...	5788
A Manufacture of food, beverages and tobacco	...	...	716	...	...	382	...	...	-443	...	...	-275
B Textile, wearing apparel and leather industries	...	...	1837	...	...	1997	...	...	1225	...	...	1249
C Manufacture of wood and wood products, including furniture	...	...	530	...	...	452	...	...	421	...	...	453
D Manufacture of paper and paper products, printing and publishing	...	...	43	...	...	54	...	...	125	...	...	90
E Manufacture of chemicals and chemical petroleum, coal, rubber and plastic products	...	...	-2098	...	...	1626	...	...	1462	...	...	1181
F Manufacture of non-metallic mineral products, except products of petroleum and coal	...	...	213	...	...	289	...	...	707	...	...	965
G Basic metal industries	...	...	69	...	...	141	...	...	46	...	...	66
H Manufacture of fabricated metal products, machinery and equipment	...	...	474	...	...	516	...	...	1476	...	...	1670
I Other manufacturing industries	...	...	41	...	...	43	...	...	157	...	...	380
4 Electricity, gas and water	...	...	394	...	...	526	...	...	-47	...	...	201
5 Construction	9717	6143	3574	10413	6654	3759	12141	7814	4327	12223	7763	4460
6 Wholesale and retail trade, restaurants and hotels	14340	1647	12693	18341	2067	16274	18992	2146	16846	20094	2281	17813
7 Transport, storage and communication	5642	2087	3555	7718	2908	4810	8733	3220	5513	9538	3570	5968
8 Finance, insurance, real estate and business services	3478	212	3266	4368	255	4113	4558	230	4328	4506	304	4202
9 Community, social and personal services	1219	293	926	1584	430	1154	1890	483	1407	2019	551	1468
Total, Industries	70912	28156	42756	92401	36502	55899	100400	42516	57884	106514	44963	61551
Producers of Government Services	11989	3509	8480	13803	3963	9840	15214	4353	10861	16269	4576	11693
Other Producers	46	12	34	51	13	38	57	14	43	63	16	47
Total	82947	31677	51270	106255	40478	65777	115671	46883	68788	122846	49555	73291
Less: Imputed bank service charge	...	...	...	...	...	...	...	...	...	...	...	...
Import duties	...	...	...	...	...	...	...	...	...	...	...	...
Value added tax	...	...	...	...	...	...	...	...	...	...	...	...
Total	...	...	...	...	...	...	...	...	...	...	...	...

	1984 Gross Output	1984 Intermediate Consumption	1984 Value Added	1985 Gross Output	1985 Intermediate Consumption	1985 Value Added	1986 Gross Output	1986 Intermediate Consumption	1986 Value Added
				All Producers					
1 Agriculture, hunting, forestry and fishing	19338	4533	14805	22517	5054	17463	30976	7355	23621
2 Mining and quarrying	...	...	6043	6593	645	5948	3995	989	3006
3 Manufacturing	...	...	6047	...	...	6382	...	...	11057
A Manufacture of food, beverages and tobacco	...	...	517	...	...	215	...	...	647

Syrian Arab Republic

4.1 Derivation of Value Added by Kind of Activity, in Current Prices
(Continued)

Million Syrian pounds

	1984 Gross Output	1984 Intermediate Consumption	1984 Value Added	1985 Gross Output	1985 Intermediate Consumption	1985 Value Added	1986 Gross Output	1986 Intermediate Consumption	1986 Value Added
B Textile, wearing apparel and leather industries	...	...	976	...	...	1249	...	...	1604
C Manufacture of wood and wood products, including furniture	...	...	595	...	...	540	...	...	682
D Manufacture of paper and paper products, printing and publishing	...	...	84	...	...	138	...	...	106
E Manufacture of chemicals and chemical petroleum, coal, rubber and plastic products	...	...	1836	...	...	1690	...	...	5547
F Manufacture of non-metallic mineral products, except products of petroleum and coal	...	...	1129	...	...	1066	...	...	1421
G Basic metal industries	...	...	81	...	...	157	...	...	124
H Manufacture of fabricated metal products, machinery and equipment	...	...	723	...	...	1198	...	...	800
I Other manufacturing industries	...	...	106	...	...	129	...	...	126
4 Electricity, gas and water	...	...	-55	1977	1786	191	2042	1940	102
5 Construction	13653	8647	5006	15195	9503	5692	17864	11160	6704
6 Wholesale and retail trade, restaurants and hotels	19751	2049	17702	20604	2095	18509	22367	2253	20114
7 Transport, storage and communication	10095	3841	6254	12612	4416	8196	15134	5332	9802
8 Finance, insurance, real estate and business services	4708	306	4402	4508	327	4181	4685	337	4348
9 Community, social and personal services	2604	786	1818	3301	1106	2195	3778	1259	2519
Total, Industries	109953	47931	62022	118530	49773	68757	135675	54402	81273
Producers of Government Services	18569	5301	13268	19915	5507	14408	23093	6058	17035
Other Producers	70	18	52	80	20	60	88	22	66
Total	128592	53250	75342	138525	55300	83225	158856	60482	98374
Less: Imputed bank service charge	...	...	...	...	...	...	...	...	...
Import duties	...	...	...	...	...	...	...	...	...
Value added tax	...	...	...	...	...	...	...	...	...
Total	...	...	...	...	...	...	...	...	...

4.2 Derivation of Value Added by Kind of Activity, in Constant Prices

Million Syrian pounds

	1980 Gross Output	1980 Intermediate Consumption	1980 Value Added	1981 Gross Output	1981 Intermediate Consumption	1981 Value Added	1982 Gross Output	1982 Intermediate Consumption	1982 Value Added	1983 Gross Output	1983 Intermediate Consumption	1983 Value Added
	At constant prices of: 1980											
	All Producers											
1 Agriculture, hunting, forestry and fishing	12804	2435	10369	13731	2911	10765	13433	2920	10513	13437	2979	10458
2 Mining and quarrying	...	...	6154	...	...	7056	7374	437	6937	7725	503	7222
3 Manufacturing	...	...	1825	...	...	602	20160	19135	1025	21957	20590	1367
A Manufacture of food, beverages and tobacco	...	...	716	...	...	437	4010	3961	49	4488	4177	311
B Textile, wearing apparel and leather industries	...	...	1837	...	...	1863	3299	1927	1372	3998	2627	1371
C Manufacture of wood and wood products, including furniture	...	...	530	...	...	448	859	469	390	878	499	379
D Manufacture of paper and paper products, printing and publishing	...	...	43	...	...	44	205	109	96	278	180	98
E Manufacture of chemicals and chemical petroleum, coal, rubber and plastic products	...	...	-2098	...	...	-3138	6780	9689	-2909	6829	10101	-3272
F Manufacture of non-metallic mineral products, except products of petroleum and coal	...	...	213	...	...	244	1226	830	396	1419	869	550
G Basic metal industries	...	...	69	...	...	104	284	216	68	335	256	79
H Manufacture of fabricated metal products, machinery and equipment	...	...	474	...	...	559	2794	1371	1423	3015	1472	1543
I Other manufacturing industries	...	...	41	...	...	41	703	563	140	717	409	308
4 Electricity, gas and water	...	...	394	...	...	457	770	294	476	987	379	608

Syrian Arab Republic

4.2 Derivation of Value Added by Kind of Activity, in Constant Prices
(Continued)

Million Syrian pounds

	1980 Gross Output	1980 Intermediate Consumption	1980 Value Added	1981 Gross Output	1981 Intermediate Consumption	1981 Value Added	1982 Gross Output	1982 Intermediate Consumption	1982 Value Added	1983 Gross Output	1983 Intermediate Consumption	1983 Value Added
	\multicolumn{12}{c}{At constant prices of:1980}
5 Construction	9717	6143	3574	10111	6368	3743	11327	7187	4140	11005	6937	4068
6 Wholesale and retail trade, restaurants and hotels	14340	1647	12693	17317	1872	15445	17298	1786	15512	17077	1872	15205
7 Transport, storage and communication	5642	2087	3555	6688	2486	4202	6704	2479	4225	7049	2581	4468
8 Finance, insurance, real estate and business services	3478	212	3266	3793	219	3574	3892	240	3652	3615	245	3370
9 Community, social and personal services	1219	293	926	1325	339	986	1588	400	1188	1694	456	1238
Total, Industries	70912	28156	42756	79947	33117	46830	82546	34878	47668	84546	36542	48004
Producers of Government Services	11989	3509	8480	12579	3303	9276	13251	3162	10089	13955	3148	10807
Other Producers	46	12	34	49	12	37	54	14	40	60	16	44
Total	82947	31677	51270	92575	36432	56143	95851	38054	57797	98561	39706	58855
Less: Imputed bank service charge	...	...	...	...	...	...	...	...	...	...	...	...
Import duties	...	...	...	...	...	...	...	...	...	...	...	...
Value added tax	...	...	...	...	...	...	...	...	...	...	...	...
Total	...	...	...	...	...	...	...	...	...	...	...	...

	1984 Gross Output	1984 Intermediate Consumption	1984 Value Added	1985 Gross Output	1985 Intermediate Consumption	1985 Value Added	1986 Gross Output	1986 Intermediate Consumption	1986 Value Added
	\multicolumn{9}{c}{At constant prices of:1980}
	\multicolumn{9}{c}{All Producers}
1 Agriculture, hunting, forestry and fishing	12385	2822	9563	12986	2817	10169	14063	3001	11062
2 Mining and quarrying	7828	541	7287	7697	540	7157	9504	1188	8316
3 Manufacturing	21529	21856	-327	21106	20895	211	22616	20734	1882
A Manufacture of food, beverages and tobacco	4399	4346	53	3622	3836	-214	4178	4230	-52
B Textile, wearing apparel and leather industries	4185	3008	1177	4120	2593	1527	4244	2714	1530
C Manufacture of wood and wood products, including furniture	1056	509	547	1164	816	348	1046	475	571
D Manufacture of paper and paper products, printing and publishing	277	201	76	399	349	50	280	208	72
E Manufacture of chemicals and chemical petroleum, coal, rubber and plastic products	7344	11043	-3699	7848	10940	-3092	8038	10142	-2104
F Manufacture of non-metallic mineral products, except products of petroleum and coal	1621	911	710	1433	780	653	2358	1293	1065
G Basic metal industries	327	269	58	465	301	164	363	233	130
H Manufacture of fabricated metal products, machinery and equipment	2001	1300	871	1740	1068	678	1811	1231	580
I Other manufacturing industries	289	209	80	309	212	97	298	208	90
4 Electricity, gas and water	1209	547	662	1339	593	746	1133	564	569
5 Construction	12082	7554	4528	13239	8178	5061	15088	9235	5853
6 Wholesale and retail trade, restaurants and hotels	15861	1602	14259	16513	1639	14874	17446	1703	15743
7 Transport, storage and communication	7503	2805	4698	7683	2674	5009	7884	2700	5184
8 Finance, insurance, real estate and business services	3234	205	3029	3109	212	2897	3239	204	3035
9 Community, social and personal services	1653	493	1160	1792	593	1199	1949	636	1313
Total, Industries	83284	38425	44859	85464	38141	47323	92922	39965	52957
Producers of Government Services	15136	3330	11806	14004	2954	11050	15597	3290	12307
Other Producers	66	18	48	69	17	52	73	18	55
Total	98486	41773	56713	99537	41112	58425	108592	43273	65319
Less: Imputed bank service charge	...	...	...	...	...	...	...	...	...
Import duties	...	...	...	...	...	...	...	...	...
Value added tax	...	...	...	...	...	...	...	...	...
Total	...	...	...	...	...	...	...	...	...

Thailand

General note. The preparation of national accounts statistics in Thailand is undertaken by the Office of the National Economic Development Board, Bangkok. The official estimates together with methodological notes are published annually by the same office in 'National Income of Thailand'. The estimates are generally in accordance with the classifications and definitions recommended in the United Nations System of National Accounts (SNA). The following tables have been prepared from successive replies to the United Nations national accounts questionnaire. When the scope and coverage of the estimates differ from conceptual of statistical reasons from the definitions and classifications recommended in SNA, a footnote is indicated to the relevant tables.

Sources and methods:

(a) Gross domestic product. Gross domestic product is estimated mainly through the production approach.

(b) Expenditure on the gross domestic product. The expenditure approach is used to estimate government final consumption expenditure, increase in stocks and exports and imports of goods and services. The commodity-flow approach, supplemented by the expenditure approach, is used for the estimation of private final consumption expenditure and gross fixed capital formation. Estimates of government consumption expenditure are compiled from government accounts. Expenditure financed by foreign aids is added. For the main items of private consumption expenditure, the commodity-flow method is used. The per capita consumption of other items such as flour and chicken is based on family expenditure inquiries extrapolated by population and price changes. Stock changes in the private sector are estimated on the basis of commodity balance accounts. The estimate of private building activity is based on building permits issued for the urban areas and on municipal building construction costs. Additions are made for the imput profit of builders based on sample surveys, for permanent fixtures and fittings and for construction for own use. For the public sector questionnaires are sent to various government departments and enterprises. Estimates of other capital formation are based on foreign trade statistics. To the import values are added import duties, mark-ups and installation costs. Exports and imports of goods and services are derived directly from the balance-of-payments. For the constant prices estimates, current values of most of the expenditure items are deflated by appropriate price indexes. For private consumption expenditure, direct revaluation at base-year prices is used when information is available on quantities of commodities consumed.

(c) Cost-structure of the gross domestic product. Estimates of compensation of employees are derived from the cost of production estimated through surveys for the agricultural sector, from data on the average wage per worker multiplied by the construction sector, and for the public and financial sectors, the estimates are obtained from their records. Depreciation is estimated as 6.67 per cent and 10 per cent of GDP for building construction and equipment, respectively. Indirect taxes net of subsidies are estimated by the Comptroller-General's Department. Operating surplus is obtained as a residual.

(d) Gross domestic product by kind of economic activity. The table of GDP by kind of economic activity is prepared at market prices, i.e., producers' values. The production approach is used to estimate value added of most industries. However, the expenditure approach is used to estimate part of the agricultural sector, the income approach for public administration and defence and part of the private services and the commodity-flow approach for gross output of the trade sector. For the agricultural sector, annual production figures of paddy and 19 other principal crops are reported by the Department of Agriculture while vegetables and fruit production is based on consumption estimates. The production figure of each crop is multiplied by the average ex-farm prices. Annual livestock production estimates are based on inventory changes and the number of animals that are exported or slaughtered while cost estimates are based on information from the Department of Livestock Development. Own-account consumption of rice and fish, vegetables and fruits is based on the quantity consumed multiplied by local prices and on the 1962 household expenditure survey, respectively. The value of forestry production is estimated by multiplying the average price per unit by the total quantity produced. For mining and quarrying, the total production quantity of each mineral is multiplied by its average price to obtain the production value. Data on the gross value of production, intermediate consumption and value added in manufacturing by both private and public enterprises and registered partnership are obtained from reports submitted to the Comptroller-General's Department, the Ministry of Industry, the Department of Revenue and the Budget Bureau. For other manufacturing, value added is estimated by applying approximate value-added ratios to the gross value of production derived from financial statements and tax returns. The estimates of electricity, gas and water are computed directly from the financial statements of the various agencies. Construction expenditure in the public sector is reported directly to the National Statistical Office. Adjustments are made for non-reported construction. For the private sector, it is based on reported data such as building permits of municipalities or on average price of new houses. Intermediate cost for each type of construction is derived from questionnaires sent to contractors and information received from architects and engineers. The income originating in the trade sector is estimated by the commodity-flow method which traces the flows of consumer and producer goods of both domestic and foreign origin through the distribution channel. Gross margins are derived from the differences between retail prices and producers' prices. For the public transport and communications sectors, information is obtained directly from the financial statements of the agencies concerned. In the private sector, information is obtained from various sources such as the operating accounts of enterprises, registration and licence data and information on the earnings of companies that supply data. Value added of travel agencies is calculated from a tourist expenditure survey. For the financial sector, estimates are based on profit and loss statements for banking and insurance and on income tax returns for real-estate brokers and warehouse operators. Value added of ownership of dwelling represents the estimated rental value after expenses. Net rent is estimated by multiplying the estimated average net rent per dwelling by the estimated number of dwellings. For business services, value added of legal services for the base year is estimated from the number of lawyers practicing while average income is based on the labour survey and extrapolated by the growth rate of total criminal and civil cases. Other services such as auditing and engineering are estimated from auditing fees paid and the value of dwellings construction in the municipal area, respectively. Value added of public administration and defence are supplied by the Comptroller-General's Department. For other private services, including restaurants and hotels, data from the Department of Revenue licensing statistics and other data collected by the National Statistical Office are used. Both public and private education estimates are based on wages and salaries data of teachers. For the constant price estimates, price deflation is used to estimate the value added for most industries. For agriculture, when quantity figures of agricultural products are available, the base-year of mining and quarrying are extrapolated by quantity indicators. For public administration and defence, the number of employees by civil classification is used as an indicator of value added in real terms.

1.1 Expenditure on the Gross Domestic Product, in Current Prices

Million Thai baht

	1970	1975	1977	1978	1979	1980	1981	1982	1983	1984	1985	1986
1 Government final consumption expenditure	15620	30963	41676	53597	66937	82026	95731	110876	120665	130577	142782	147996
2 Private final consumption expenditure	92429	198514	260506	300470	353309	437960	511537	554732	618636	649633	685389	710619
3 Gross capital formation	35606	75747	102240	126950	160287	186258	194479	177772	212271	236645	244411	235705
A Increase in stocks	2880	9619	3608	10300	15931	9159	5412	-2126	6279	7846	12332	2571
B Gross fixed capital formation	32726	66128	98632	116650	144356	177099	189067	179898	205992	228799	232079	233134
Residential buildings	4057	7718	11329	15876	17484	19269	26524	29685	37549	39754	39052	41399
Non-residential buildings	5883	13176	17532	29025	29899	37478	38352	29051	27728	30575	32111	31647
Other construction and land improvement etc.	6561	7579	17834	11892	18970	32408	29036	39025	45265	53039	55711	56280
Other	16225	37655	51937	59857	78003	87944	95155	82137	95450	105431	105205	103808
4 Exports of goods and services	22715	57014	82198	101008	131820	167725	195751	210818	206964	241950	270849	310010
5 Less: Imports of goods and services	29316	70795	103377	119867	165846	204591	233765	211784	254073	262557	276993	274075
Statistical discrepancy	-994	7373	9787	7794	9733	15552	22433	3712	20450	-7385	-25084	-31893
Equals: Gross Domestic Product	136060	298816	393030	469952	556240	684930	786166	846126	924913	988863	1041354	1098362

1.2 Expenditure on the Gross Domestic Product, in Constant Prices

Million Thai baht

	1970	1975	1977	1978	1979	1980	1981	1982	1983	1984	1985	1986
	\multicolumn{12}{c}{At constant prices of:1972}
1 Government final consumption expenditure	16426	21908	27274	31816	36864	37352	40595	41850	42767	44830	46963	47688
2 Private final consumption expenditure	97978	134447	158455	166856	177204	185641	191573	196354	212645	223241	229757	235619
3 Gross capital formation	43121	50142	63860	69978	76009	74290	74426	64467	73923	79825	77790	72257
A Increase in stocks	3170	7731	4028	5794	6784	2858	1870	-265	2274	2888	3800	642
B Gross fixed capital formation	39951	42411	59832	64184	69225	71432	72556	64732	71649	76937	73990	71615

Thailand

1.2 Expenditure on the Gross Domestic Product, in Constant Prices
(Continued)

Million Thai baht

	1970	1975	1977	1978	1979	1980	1981	1982	1983	1984	1985	1986
At constant prices of: 1972												
Residential buildings	4334	4514	5704	7570	6572	6498	8958	9170	11198	11994	11407	11930
Non-residential buildings	6225	7730	9278	14516	13218	13639	13089	9386	8668	9498	9698	9308
Other construction and land improvement etc.	6965	4631	9533	5977	8077	11618	9840	12409	13816	16235	16576	16426
Other	22427	25536	35317	36121	41358	39677	40669	33767	37967	39210	36309	33951
4 Exports of goods and services	22855	30087	42722	49672	54478	59580	69864	82188	78492	88949	95958	103799
5 Less: Imports of goods and services	32313	38201	49208	53149	62710	64215	63748	56196	70821	71959	69097	75764
Statistical discrepancy	2025	5131	-5930	-4076	-4938	204	-1440	-4631	6163	-2708	-7502	3196
Equals: Gross Domestic Product	150092	203514	237173	261097	276907	292852	311270	324033	343169	362178	373869	386795

1.3 Cost Components of the Gross Domestic Product

Million Thai baht

	1970	1975	1977	1978	1979	1980	1981	1982	1983	1984	1985	1986
1 Indirect taxes, net	15765	31119	43717	51733	60903	71473	79879	83904	100947	111397	112575	121248
A Indirect taxes	15765	31411	44767	52725	64262	77122	84844	87290	104538	112808	117498	123483
B Less: Subsidies	-	292	1050	992	3359	5649	4965	3386	3591	1411	4923	2235
2 Consumption of fixed capital	10284	21014	28609	34428	41887	50640	59259	65649	73386	81773	89845	96290
3 Compensation of employees paid by resident producers to:	26851	61518	85439	109014	134314	169134	196110	231639	262739	282995	298171	314196
4 Operating surplus	83160	185165	235265	274777	319136	393683	450918	464934	487841	512698	540763	566628
Equals: Gross Domestic Product	136060	298816	393030	469952	556240	684930	786166	846126	924913	988863	1041354	1098362

1.4 General Government Current Receipts and Disbursements

Million Thai baht

	1970	1975	1977	1978	1979	1980	1981	1982	1983	1984	1985	1986
Receipts												
1 Operating surplus	...	...	...	...	...	...	...	...	...	...	...	...
2 Property and entrepreneurial income	946	2502	2411	2748	2830	4275	6595	7490	12680	7251	11087	14417
3 Taxes, fees and contributions	18084	37992	53575	64837	78707	94376	107814	112593	132994	145186	153329	159718
A Indirect taxes [a]	15765	31412	44767	52725	64262	77122	84844	87290	104538	112808	117498	123483
B Direct taxes	2319	6581	8808	12112	14445	17254	22970	25303	28456	32378	35831	36235
C Social security contributions	...	...	...	...	...	...	...	...	...	...	...	...
D Compulsory fees, fines and penalties	...	...	...	...	...	...	...	...	...	...	...	...
4 Other current transfers	1219	1334	1816	2412	3087	4874	5721	5952	5414	6665	8025	8541
Total Current Receipts of General Government	20249	41828	57802	69997	84624	103525	120130	126035	151088	159102	172441	182676
Disbursements												
1 Government final consumption expenditure	15620	30963	41676	53597	66937	82026	95731	110876	120665	130577	142782	147996
2 Property income	1442	3452	4836	6013	7792	10919	14051	18564	21158	25771	30291	35768
A Interest	1442	3452	4836	6013	7792	10919	14051	18564	21158	25771	30291	35768
B Net land rent and royalties	...	...	...	...	...	...	...	...	...	...	...	...
3 Subsidies [a]	...	292	1050	992	3359	5649	4965	3386	3591	1411	4923	2235
4 Other current transfers	303	244	357	333	366	507	360	271	867	1154	1029	1012
A Social security benefits	...	...	...	...	...	...	...	...	...	...	...	...
B Social assistance grants	...	...	...	...	...	...	...	...	...	...	...	...
C Other	303	244	357	333	366	507	360	271	867	1154	1029	1012
5 Net saving	2884	6877	9883	9062	6170	4424	5023	-7062	4807	189	-6584	-4335
Total Current Disbursements and Net Saving of General Government	20249	41828	57802	69997	84624	103525	120130	126035	151088	159102	172441	182676

a) For years before 1974, item 'Subsidies' is netted out of item 'Indirect taxes'.

1.6 Current Income and Outlay of Households and Non-Profit Institutions

Million Thai baht

	1970	1975	1977	1978	1979	1980	1981	1982	1983	1984	1985	1986
Receipts												
1 Compensation of employees	26851	61518	85439	109014	134314	169134	196110	231639	262739	282995	298171	314196
A From resident producers	26933	61389	84734	107214	130879	162142	186522	218579	244332	263292	276234	294014
B From rest of the world	-82	129	702	1800	3435	6992	9588	13060	18407	19703	21937	20182
2 Operating surplus of private unincorporated enterprises	71786	158631	200629	231001	264573	327273	362319	367850	374571	388267	401894	423687

Thailand

1.6 Current Income and Outlay of Households and Non-Profit Institutions
(Continued)

Million Thai baht

	1970	1975	1977	1978	1979	1980	1981	1982	1983	1984	1985	1986
3 Property and entrepreneurial income	8971	18790	25349	29068	34832	47757	58116	68029	77993	90714	101428	104942
4 Current transfers	489	1533	996	703	1076	2426	1760	2319	4821	3017	2960	3013
Total Current Receipts	108097	240472	312413	369786	434795	546590	618305	669837	720124	764993	804453	845838

Disbursements

	1970	1975	1977	1978	1979	1980	1981	1982	1983	1984	1985	1986
1 Private final consumption expenditure	92429	198514	260506	300470	353309	437960	511537	554732	618636	649633	685389	710619
2 Property income	458	1563	2616	3607	4332	5307	6762	7663	9730	11840	13619	13714
3 Direct taxes and other current transfers n.e.c. to general government	1416	2952	4112	5652	6597	7643	9503	12524	15257	17760	20442	20604
A Social security contributions	...	...	...	...	...	...	...	...	...	...	...	...
B Direct taxes	1416	2952	4112	5652	6597	7643	9503	12524	15257	17760	20442	20604
C Fees, fines and penalties	...	...	...	...	...	...	...	...	...	...	...	...
4 Other current transfers	393	876	1347	1458	1692	2024	2220	2591	2611	3316	3717	3854
5 Net saving	13401	36567	43832	58599	68865	93656	88283	92327	73890	82444	81286	97047
Total Current Disbursements and Net Saving	108097	240472	312413	369786	434795	546590	618305	669837	720124	764993	804453	845838

1.7 External Transactions on Current Account, Summary

Million Thai baht

	1970	1975	1977	1978	1979	1980	1981	1982	1983	1984	1985	1986

Payments to the Rest of the World

	1970	1975	1977	1978	1979	1980	1981	1982	1983	1984	1985	1986
1 Imports of goods and services	29316	70795	103377	119867	165846	204591	233765	211784	254073	262557	276993	274075
2 Factor income to the rest of the world	1257	4122	5051	8768	14014	17818	27581	32030	30619	36988	47648	49800
3 Current transfers to the rest of the world	164	223	268	244	254	395	316	355	444	458	693	730
4 Surplus of the nation on current transactions	-5210	-12253	-22085	-22937	-41712	-44587	-54900	-21933	-65722	-47171	-40824	23
Payments to the Rest of the World and Surplus of the Nation on Current Transactions	25527	62887	86611	105942	138402	178217	206762	222236	219414	252832	284510	324628

Receipts From The Rest of the World

	1970	1975	1977	1978	1979	1980	1981	1982	1983	1984	1985	1986
1 Exports of goods and services	22715	57014	82198	101008	131820	167725	195751	210818	206964	241950	270849	310010
2 Factor income from rest of the world	1636	3903	3037	3366	4223	5328	5794	5654	5249	5212	6729	7200
3 Current transfers from rest of the world	1176	1970	1376	1568	2359	5164	5217	5764	7201	5670	6932	7418
Receipts from the Rest of the World on Current Transactions	25527	62887	86611	105942	138402	178217	206762	222236	219414	252832	284510	324628

1.8 Capital Transactions of The Nation, Summary

Million Thai baht

	1970	1975	1977	1978	1979	1980	1981	1982	1983	1984	1985	1986

Finance of Gross Capital Formation

	1970	1975	1977	1978	1979	1980	1981	1982	1983	1984	1985	1986
Gross saving	29402	70867	89942	111807	128308	157223	162012	159551	166999	182089	178503	203835
1 Consumption of fixed capital	10284	21014	28609	34428	41887	50640	59259	65649	73386	81773	89845	96290
2 Net saving	19118	49853	61333	77379	86421	106583	102753	93902	93613	100316	88658	107545
A General government	2884	6877	9883	9062	6170	4424	5023	-7062	4807	189	-6584	-4335
B Corporate and quasi-corporate enterprises	2431	5161	7388	10930	11386	8503	9447	8637	14916	17683	13956	14833
C Other	13803	37815	44062	57387	68865	93656	88283	92327	73890	82444	81286	97047
Less: Surplus of the nation on current transactions	-5210	-12253	-22085	-22937	-41712	-44587	-54900	-21933	-65722	-47171	-40824	23
Statistical discrepancy	994	-7373	-9787	-7794	-9733	-15552	-22433	-3712	-20450	7385	25084	31893
Finance of Gross Capital Formation	35606	75747	102240	126950	160287	186258	194479	177772	212271	236645	244411	235705

Gross Capital Formation

	1970	1975	1977	1978	1979	1980	1981	1982	1983	1984	1985	1986
Increase in stocks	2880	9619	3608	10300	15931	9159	5412	-2126	6279	7846	12332	2571

Thailand

1.8 Capital Transactions of The Nation, Summary
(Continued)

Million Thai baht

	1970	1975	1977	1978	1979	1980	1981	1982	1983	1984	1985	1986
Gross fixed capital formation	32726	66128	98632	116650	144356	177099	189067	179898	205992	228799	232079	233134
1 General government	10478	15445	29670	36722	43089	67393	68600	66483	72924	81535	90888	88832
2 Corporate and quasi-corporate enterprises	22248	50683	68962	79928	101267	109706	120467	113415	133068	147264	141191	144302
A Public	...	...	...	...	...	...	...	...	...	...	...	...
B Private	22248	50683	68962	79928	101267	109706	120467	113415	133068	147264	141191	144302
3 Other	...	...	...	...	...	...	...	...	...	...	...	...
Gross Capital Formation	35606	75747	102240	126950	160287	186258	194479	177772	212271	236645	244411	235705

1.10 Gross Domestic Product by Kind of Activity, in Current Prices

Million Thai baht

	1970	1975	1977	1978	1979	1980	1981	1982	1983	1984	1985	1986
1 Agriculture, hunting, forestry and fishing	38493	94063	110929	129094	147076	173806	187886	188742	204443	191278	178533	183037
2 Mining and quarrying	2759	4062	8139	10610	12614	14493	13373	14807	16480	21291	29240	23347
3 Manufacturing	21814	53910	74676	89089	100740	134515	158272	164649	170200	190257	209014	226571
4 Electricity, gas and water	1625	3290	4384	5168	6075	6284	10743	14454	16319	18884	24070	28182
5 Construction	8261	12873	20251	24844	29240	39865	42008	43040	47129	52772	54373	55682
6 Wholesale and retail trade, restaurants and hotels	31079	62964	87867	105614	122199	152567	178383	192137	200173	219336	230901	248484
7 Transport, storage and communication	8588	18764	24706	29606	37844	45261	57281	63133	73708	83588	95160	101827
8 Finance, insurance, real estate and business services	8560	18974	24809	30450	37693	49269	60436	70933	83591	92914	98530	102157
9 Community, social and personal services	8735	17595	22459	27534	32136	40607	47139	56882	64319	69361	74397	79936
Total, Industries	129914	286495	378220	452009	534617	656667	755521	808777	882362	945681	994218	1049223
Producers of Government Services	6146	12321	14810	17943	21623	28263	30645	37349	42551	43182	47136	49139
Other Producers	...	...	...	...	...	...	...	...	...	...	...	...
Subtotal	136060	298816	393030	469952	556240	684930	786166	846126	924913	988863	1041354	1098362
Less: Imputed bank service charge	...	...	...	...	...	...	...	...	...	...	...	...
Plus: Import duties	...	...	...	...	...	...	...	...	...	...	...	...
Plus: Value added tax	...	...	...	...	...	...	...	...	...	...	...	...
Equals: Gross Domestic Product	136060	298816	393030	469952	556240	684930	786166	846126	924913	988863	1041354	1098362

1.11 Gross Domestic Product by Kind of Activity, in Constant Prices

Million Thai baht

	1970	1975	1977	1978	1979	1980	1981	1982	1983	1984	1985	1986
	At constant prices of: 1972										
1 Agriculture, hunting, forestry and fishing	48332	62081	65537	72513	71408	72784	77701	78502	81449	84144	86839	86215
2 Mining and quarrying	2555	2485	3526	4104	4531	4780	4623	4431	4414	5415	6001	6086
3 Manufacturing	23320	36787	48071	52521	57841	60597	64490	67318	72252	76811	77425	82612
4 Electricity, gas and water	1638	3181	4144	4500	5178	5560	6330	6755	7348	8088	8910	9527
5 Construction	8705	8514	11996	13583	14547	16576	15500	15097	15927	17680	17786	17911
6 Wholesale and retail trade, restaurants and hotels	31926	41969	48302	51809	54397	58087	61681	64255	66991	70186	72876	76117
7 Transport, storage and communication	9195	13445	14474	16205	17663	18811	20209	21715	23290	24605	25829	27180
8 Finance, insurance, real estate and business services	8806	13184	15397	17495	19871	21921	23920	26332	29639	32363	33377	33877
9 Community, social and personal services	9139	13509	16171	18201	19877	21313	23624	25795	27361	28780	29929	32020
Total, Industries	143616	195155	227618	250931	265313	280429	298078	310200	328671	348072	358972	371545
Producers of Government Services	6476	8359	9555	10166	11594	12423	13192	13833	14498	14106	14897	15250
Other Producers	...	...	...	...	...	...	...	...	...	...	...	...
Subtotal	150092	203514	237173	261097	276907	292852	311270	324033	343169	362178	373869	386795
Less: Imputed bank service charge	...	...	...	...	...	...	...	...	...	...	...	...
Plus: Import duties	...	...	...	...	...	...	...	...	...	...	...	...
Plus: Value added tax	...	...	...	...	...	...	...	...	...	...	...	...
Equals: Gross Domestic Product	150092	203514	237173	261097	276907	292852	311270	324033	343169	362178	373869	386795

Thailand

1.12 Relations Among National Accounting Aggregates

Million Thai baht

	1970	1975	1977	1978	1979	1980	1981	1982	1983	1984	1985	1986
Gross Domestic Product	136060	298816	393030	469952	556240	684930	786166	846126	924913	988863	1041354	1098362
Plus: Net factor income from the rest of the world	379	-219	-2014	-5402	-9791	-12490	-21787	-26376	-25370	-31776	-40919	-42600
Factor income from the rest of the world	1636	3903	3037	3366	4223	5328	5794	5654	5249	5212	6729	7200
Less: Factor income to the rest of the world	1257	4122	5051	8768	14014	17818	27581	32030	30619	36988	47648	49800
Equals: Gross National Product	136439	298597	391016	464550	546449	672440	764379	819750	899543	957087	1000435	1055762
Less: Consumption of fixed capital	10284	21014	28609	34428	41887	50640	59259	65649	73386	81773	89845	96290
Equals: National Income	126155	277583	362407	430122	504562	621800	705120	754101	826157	875314	910590	959472
Plus: Net current transfers from the rest of the world	1012	1747	1108	1324	2105	4769	4901	5409	6757	5212	6239	6688
Current transfers from the rest of the world	1176	1970	1376	1568	2359	5164	5217	5764	7201	5670	6932	7418
Less: Current transfers to the rest of the world	164	223	268	244	254	395	316	355	444	458	693	730
Equals: National Disposable Income	127167	279330	363515	431446	506667	626569	710021	759510	832914	880526	916829	966160
Less: Final consumption	108049	229477	302182	354067	420246	519986	607268	665608	739301	780210	828171	858615
Equals: Net Saving	19118	49853	61333	77379	86421	106583	102753	93902	93613	100316	88658	107545
Less: Surplus of the nation on current transactions	-5210	-12253	-22085	-22937	-41712	-44587	-54900	-21933	-65722	-47171	-40824	23
Statistical discrepancy	994	-7373	-9787	-7794	-9733	-15552	-22433	-3712	-20450	7385	25084	31893
Equals: Net Capital Formation	25322	54733	73631	92522	118400	135618	135220	112123	138885	154872	154566	139415

2.1 Government Final Consumption Expenditure by Function, in Current Prices

Million Thai baht

		1970	1975	1977	1978	1979	1980	1981	1982	1983	1984	1985	1986
1	General public services [a]	4722	8403	10710	12720	15862	21629	24623	29263	33321	34665	37269	38704
2	Defence [a]	6450	11000	17857	23420	29426	32450	39974	42395	45316	49894	56930	58946
3	Public order and safety												
4	Education	2989	7820	9532	12912	16284	21144	22590	29312	31818	34229	36172	37520
5	Health	568	1263	1827	2455	3065	4155	5366	6065	6621	7881	8720	8968
6	Social security and welfare	98	168	203	278	318	371	448	593	565	680	699	721
7	Housing and community amenities	...	...	...	...	...	...	...	...	...	...	...	...
8	Recreational, cultural and religious affairs	...	...	...	...	...	...	...	...	...	...	...	...
9	Economic services	744	2180	1347	1578	1707	1916	2294	2429	2442	2292	2239	2327
	A Fuel and energy	...	...	...	...	...	...	...	...	...	...	...	...
	B Agriculture, forestry, fishing and hunting	...	...	...	...	...	...	...	...	...	...	...	...
	C Mining, manufacturing and construction, except fuel and energy	...	...	...	...	...	...	...	...	...	...	...	...
	D Transportation and communication	744	2180	1347	1578	1707	1916	2294	2429	2442	2292	2239	2327
	E Other economic affairs	...	...	...	...	...	...	...	...	...	...	...	...
10	Other functions [b]	49	129	200	234	275	361	436	819	582	936	753	810
	Total Government Final Consumption Expenditure	15620	30963	41676	53597	66937	82026	95731	110876	120665	130577	142782	147996

a) Justice and police are included in item 'Defence'.
b) Item 'Other functions' includes items 'Housing and community amenities' and 'Recreational, cultural and religious affairs'.

2.2 Government Final Consumption Expenditure by Function, in Constant Prices

Million Thai baht

		1970	1975	1977	1978	1979	1980	1981	1982	1983	1984	1985	1986
		\multicolumn{12}{c}{At constant prices of:1972}
1	General public services [a]	4967	5920	6991	7484	8666	9748	10471	10995	12393	11774	12142	12360
2	Defence [a]	6777	7917	11766	14210	16422	15128	16823	16190	16443	17617	19149	19418
3	Public order and safety												
4	Education	3148	5380	6171	7421	8826	9390	9684	10921	10304	11365	11581	11773
5	Health	597	899	1196	1454	1682	1883	2273	2288	2346	2720	2875	2893
6	Social security and welfare	103	122	133	165	175	168	190	224	199	235	231	233
7	Housing and community amenities	...	...	...	...	...	...	...	...	...	...	...	...
8	Recreational, cultural and religious affairs	...	...	...	...	...	...	...	...	...	...	...	...
9	Economic services	782	1578	886	942	941	868	971	918	870	784	731	744

Thailand

2.2 Government Final Consumption Expenditure by Function, in Constant Prices
(Continued)

Million Thai baht

	1970	1975	1977	1978	1979	1980	1981	1982	1983	1984	1985	1986
					At constant prices of:1972							
A Fuel and energy	...	...	...	...	...	...	...	...	...	...	...	...
B Agriculture, forestry, fishing and hunting	...	...	...	...	...	...	...	...	...	...	...	...
C Mining, manufacturing and construction, except fuel and energy	...	...	...	...	...	...	...	...	...	...	...	...
D Transportation and communication	782	1578	886	942	941	868	971	918	870	784	731	744
E Other economic affairs	...	...	...	...	...	...	...	...	...	...	...	...
10 Other functions [b]	52	92	131	140	152	167	183	314	212	335	254	267
Total Government Final Consumption Expenditure	16426	21908	27274	31816	36864	37352	40595	41850	42767	44830	46963	47688

a) Justice and police are included in item 'Defence'.
b) Item 'Other functions' includes items 'Housing and community amenities' and 'Recreational, cultural and religious affairs'.

2.5 Private Final Consumption Expenditure by Type and Porpose, in Current Prices

Million Thai baht

	1970	1975	1977	1978	1979	1980	1981	1982	1983	1984	1985	1986
					Final Consumption Expenditure of Resident Households							
1 Food, beverages and tobacco	51474	111920	143638	164281	188079	226483	260576	276575	307513	310445	311174	319076
A Food	42866	93091	117837	135629	151928	183080	213176	223773	251171	249274	246973	253838
B Non-alcoholic beverages	2727	4805	6164	6583	8026	9682	10921	12304	13496	14716	15757	17133
C Alcoholic beverages	2467	7684	11510	13452	18109	21918	22736	25674	26206	28972	30894	29666
D Tobacco	3414	6340	8127	8617	10016	11803	13743	14824	16640	17483	17550	18439
2 Clothing and footwear	7621	17237	23485	29274	36642	47247	53953	58631	66173	73188	81157	87805
3 Gross rent, fuel and power	7775	13372	15942	17639	20626	26692	32362	35888	39869	43638	47295	50498
A Fuel and power	3552	6395	7637	8358	10358	14337	18028	19222	20472	21885	22905	23696
B Other	4223	6977	8305	9281	10268	12355	14334	16666	19397	21753	24390	26802
4 Furniture, furnishings and household equipment and operation	5323	10431	14444	17311	21955	27558	32285	33851	38339	41929	44906	46984
A Household operation	1966	4134	5327	5910	7168	8968	10917	12291	13703	14750	16178	17036
B Other	3357	6297	9117	11401	14787	18590	21368	21560	24636	27179	28728	29948
5 Medical care and health expenses	5255	11423	10469	12120	13512	18987	22459	26935	30921	33992	37498	40019
6 Transport and communication	6814	16150	22714	28042	34550	45296	59777	66833	73279	80047	93615	96994
A Personal transport equipment	1153	2388	4465	3445	3111	4127	4721	5070	6048	5963	4687	4560
B Other	5661	13762	18249	24597	31439	41169	55056	61763	67231	74084	88928	92434
7 Recreational, entertainment, education and cultural services	7666	17428	11302	12863	15418	18934	21596	24674	26722	28361	29995	30547
A Education	...	...	1352	1631	1961	2240	2627	3204	3893	3983	4185	4386
B Other	...	...	9950	11232	13457	16694	18969	21470	22829	24378	25810	26161
8 Miscellaneous goods and services	1404	2302	19935	24256	29111	37023	43958	49073	52974	58059	63895	67805
A Personal care	...	...	4401	5244	5966	7144	8545	9424	10281	11436	12681	12941
B Expenditures in restaurants, cafes and hotels	...	...	13663	16583	20169	26183	30996	34492	36646	40304	44396	47872
C Other	...	...	1871	2429	2976	3696	4417	5157	6047	6319	6818	6992
Total Final Consumption Expenditure in the Domestic Market by Households, of which	93332	200261	261929	305786	359893	448220	526966	572460	635790	669659	709535	739728
A Durable goods	...	9818	15336	16860	20390	25029	30016	30125	32759	30093	35948	36683
B Semi-durable goods	...	152656	198539	233133	272759	339978	397662	431137	479386	496598	518494	539731
C Non-durable goods	...											

Thailand

2.5 Private Final Consumption Expenditure by Type and Porpose, in Current Prices
(Continued)

Million Thai baht

	1970	1975	1977	1978	1979	1980	1981	1982	1983	1984	1985	1986
D Services	...	37787	48054	55793	66744	83213	99288	111198	123645	136368	155093	163314
Plus: Direct purchases abroad by resident households	1267	2735	3184	3579	4648	4989	6027	6151	7896	7291	7622	7424
Less: Direct purchases in the domestic market by non-resident households	2170	4482	4607	8895	11232	15249	21456	23879	25050	27317	31768	36533
Equals: Final Consumption Expenditure of Resident Households [a]	92429	198514	260506	300470	353309	437960	511537	554732	618636	649633	685389	710619

Final Consumption Expenditure of Private Non-profit Institutions Serving Households

	1970	1975	1977	1978	1979	1980	1981	1982	1983	1984	1985	1986
Equals: Final Consumption Expenditure of Private Non-profit Organisations Serving Households	...	...	...	...	...	...	...	...	...	...	...	...
Private Final Consumption Expenditure	92429	198514	260506	300470	353309	437960	511537	554732	618636	649633	685389	710619

a) Item 'Final consumption expenditure of resident households' includes consumption expenditure of private non-profit institutions serving households.

2.6 Private Final Consumption Expenditure by Type and Purpose, in Constant Prices

Million Thai baht

	1970	1975	1977	1978	1979	1980	1981	1982	1983	1984	1985	1986
At constant prices of: 1972											
Final Consumption Expenditure of Resident Households											
1 Food, beverages and tobacco	53885	71243	82372	85375	90775	92911	96021	96388	103316	107379	108892	111404
A Food	44822	56090	63515	64608	65961	67210	70477	71975	76588	79057	81816	84090
B Non-alcoholic beverages	2933	3877	4675	4858	5734	5177	5049	4950	5300	5757	6131	6582
C Alcoholic beverages	2715	5964	8255	9581	11707	12363	12055	12124	13155	13853	12638	12192
D Tobacco	3415	5312	5927	6328	7373	8161	8440	7339	8273	8712	8307	8540
2 Clothing and footwear	8847	12992	14989	16477	17177	17935	18631	19068	20007	20899	21912	22919
3 Gross rent, fuel and power	8068	9823	10780	11446	12099	12805	13504	14200	15238	16150	16891	17502
A Fuel and power	3711	4548	5095	5414	5710	6028	6339	6630	7069	7519	7809	8028
B Other	4357	5275	5685	6032	6389	6777	7165	7570	8169	8631	9082	9474
4 Furniture, furnishings and household equipment and operation	5696	7194	8938	10193	11427	12139	12932	12972	14496	16266	16828	17739
A Household operation	2206	2806	3299	3496	3863	4041	4314	4548	4817	5157	5423	5680
B Other	3490	4388	5639	6697	7564	8098	8618	8424	9679	11109	11405	12059
5 Medical care and health expenses	5691	9436	8666	9338	9756	10844	11820	13347	14774	15825	16952	17897
6 Transport and communication	7202	10255	12817	14518	14592	15710	16862	17832	19519	20917	22316	23382
A Personal transport equipment	1205	1521	2633	1857	1339	1393	1439	1504	1699	1577	1210	1103
B Other	5997	8734	10184	12661	13253	14317	15423	16328	17820	19340	21106	22279
7 Recreational, entertainment, education and cultural services	8134	12742	8539	9302	10147	11173	11546	12286	12947	13795	14105	14274
A Education	...	...	894	936	960	1025	1146	1272	1388	1356	1385	1425
B Other	...	...	7645	8366	9187	10148	10400	11014	11559	12439	12720	12849
8 Miscellaneous goods and services	1425	1749	11738	13270	14562	16304	17359	18273	19207	20601	22050	23147
A Personal care	...	...	2914	3132	3353	3503	3738	3856	4102	4383	4658	4720
B Expenditures in restaurants, cafes and hotels	...	...	7564	8607	9468	10966	11655	12281	12727	13789	14849	15879
C Other	...	...	1260	1531	1741	1835	1966	2136	2378	2429	2543	2548
Total Final Consumption Expenditure in the Domestic Market by Households, of which	98948	135434	158839	169919	180535	189821	198675	204366	219504	231832	239946	248264
A Durable goods	...	...	9361	9644	9997	10268	10990	10742	12395	12960	12824	13259
B Semi-durable goods	...	...	118904	127780	135925	141674	149653	154012	163260	172515	179183	186328
C Non-durable goods	...	...										

Thailand

2.6 Private Final Consumption Expenditure by Type and Purpose, in Constant Prices
(Continued)

Million Thai baht

	1970	1975	1977	1978	1979	1980	1981	1982	1983	1984	1985	1986
					At constant prices of:1972							
D Services	...	...	30574	32495	34613	37879	38032	39612	43849	46357	47939	48677
Plus: Direct purchases abroad by resident households	1267	2808	3269	3686	4767	5095	5784	5602	7191	6458	5881	5883
Less: Direct purchases in the domestic market by non-resident households	2237	3795	3653	6749	8098	9275	12886	13614	14050	15049	16070	18528
Equals: Final Consumption Expenditure of Resident Households [a]	97978	134447	158455	166856	177204	185641	191573	196354	212645	223241	229757	235619
	Final Consumption Expenditure of Private Non-profit Institutions Serving Households										
Equals: Final Consumption Expenditure of Private Non-profit Organisations Serving Households	...	...	...	...	...	...	...	...	...	...	...	...
Private Final Consumption Expenditure	97978	134447	158455	166856	177204	185641	191573	196354	212645	223241	229757	235619

a) Item 'Final consumption expenditure of resident households' includes consumption expenditure of private non-profit institutions serving households.

2.11 Gross Fixed Capital Formation by Kind of Activity of Owner, ISIC Divisions, in Current Prices

Million Thai baht

		1970	1975	1977	1978	1979	1980	1981	1982	1983	1984	1985	1986
						All Producers							
1	Agriculture, hunting, forestry and fishing	3495	6571	10773	12030	...	...	...	...	...	...	...	...
2	Mining and quarrying	724	1515	2181	2490	...	...	...	...	...	...	...	...
3	Manufacturing	5463	12913	17909	21093	...	...	...	...	...	...	...	...
4	Electricity, gas and water	1446	2758	6369	8546	...	...	...	...	...	...	...	...
5	Construction	1699	2911	4149	4772	...	...	...	...	...	...	...	...
6	Wholesale and retail trade, restaurants and hotels	3871	7182	9480	11547	...	...	...	...	...	...	...	...
7	Transport, storage and communication	5979	12134	18094	21716	...	...	...	...	...	...	...	...
8	Finance, insurance, real estate and business services	5704	11228	16494	21478	...	...	...	...	...	...	...	...
9	Community, social and personal services	3315	7218	10501	11293	...	...	...	...	...	...	...	...
	Total Industries	31696	64430	95950	114965	...	...	...	...	...	...	...	...
	Producers of Government Services	8226	12129	21647	25846	...	...	...	...	...	...	...	...
	Private Non-Profit Institutions Serving Households	...	...	...	...	...	...	...	...	...	...	...	...
	Statistical discrepancy	-7196	-10431	-18965	-24161	...	...	...	...	...	...	...	...
	Total	32726	66128	98632	116650	144356	177099	189067	179898	205992	228799	232079	...

4.1 Derivation of Value Added by Kind of Activity, in Current Prices

Million Thai baht

		1980			1981			1982			1983		
		Gross Output	Intermediate Consumption	Value Added	Gross Output	Intermediate Consumption	Value Added	Gross Output	Intermediate Consumption	Value Added	Gross Output	Intermediate Consumption	Value Added
						All Producers							
1	Agriculture, hunting, forestry and fishing	...	...	173806	...	...	187886	...	...	188742	...	...	204443
	A Agriculture and hunting	...	...	152089	...	...	163613	...	...	163460	...	...	178813
	B Forestry and logging	...	...	9733	...	...	11090	...	...	11132	...	...	11164
	C Fishing	...	...	11984	...	...	13183	...	...	14150	...	...	14466
2	Mining and quarrying	...	...	14493	...	...	13373	...	...	14807	...	...	16480
	A Coal mining	...	...	70	...	...	133	...	...	150	...	...	238
	B Crude petroleum and natural gas production	...	...	...	...	...	...	...	...	...	...	...	...
	C Metal ore mining	...	...	8415	...	...	6214	...	...	4855	...	...	3792
	D Other mining	...	...	6008	...	...	7026	...	...	9802	...	...	12450

Thailand

4.1 Derivation of Value Added by Kind of Activity, in Current Prices
(Continued)

Million Thai baht

	1980 Gross Output	1980 Intermediate Consumption	1980 Value Added	1981 Gross Output	1981 Intermediate Consumption	1981 Value Added	1982 Gross Output	1982 Intermediate Consumption	1982 Value Added	1983 Gross Output	1983 Intermediate Consumption	1983 Value Added
3 Manufacturing	...	...	134515	...	...	158272	...	...	164649	...	...	176200
A Manufacture of food, beverages and tobacco	...	...	38445	...	...	45240	...	...	47608	...	...	47619
B Textile, wearing apparel and leather industries	...	...	26472	...	...	30959	...	...	33162	...	...	35480
C Manufacture of wood and wood products, including furniture	...	...	4439	...	...	4972	...	...	4449	...	...	4841
D Manufacture of paper and paper products, printing and publishing	...	...	4646	...	...	5693	...	...	5962	...	...	5734
E Manufacture of chemicals and chemical petroleum, coal, rubber and plastic products	...	...	26766	...	...	31645	...	...	30896	...	...	32469
F Manufacture of non-metallic mineral products, except products of petroleum and coal	...	...	8561	...	...	9980	...	...	11273	...	...	12154
G Basic metal industries	...	...	2943	...	...	2610	...	...	2259	...	...	2241
H Manufacture of fabricated metal products, machinery and equipment	...	...	18812	...	...	22496	...	...	23041	...	...	28470
I Other manufacturing industries	...	...	3431	...	...	4677	...	...	5999	...	...	7192
4 Electricity, gas and water	...	...	6284	...	...	10743	...	...	14454	...	...	16319
A Electricity, gas and steam	...	...	5581	...	...	9855	...	...	13081	...	...	14433
B Water works and supply	...	...	703	...	...	888	...	...	1373	...	...	1886
5 Construction	...	...	39865	...	...	42008	...	...	43040	...	...	47129
6 Wholesale and retail trade, restaurants and hotels	...	...	152567	...	...	178383	...	...	192137	...	...	200173
A Wholesale and retail trade	...	...	128731	...	...	150293	...	...	159849	...	...	165812
B Restaurants and hotels	...	...	23836	...	...	28090	...	...	32288	...	...	34361
Restaurants	...	...	20787	...	...	24573	...	...	28404	...	...	30562
Hotels and other lodging places	...	...	3049	...	...	3517	...	...	3884	...	...	3799
7 Transport, storage and communication	...	...	45261	...	...	57281	...	...	63133	...	...	73708
A Transport and storage	...	...	41618	...	...	52935	...	...	57306	...	...	68280
B Communication	...	...	3643	...	...	4345	...	...	5827	...	...	5428
8 Finance, insurance, real estate and business services	...	...	49269	...	...	60436	...	...	70933	...	...	83591
A Financial institutions	...	...	37698	...	...	46929	...	...	54927	...	...	65330
B Insurance	...	...	3141	...	...	3834	...	...	4579	...	...	5575
C Real estate and business services	...	...	8431	...	...	9673	...	...	11427	...	...	12686
Real estate, except dwellings	...	...	1053	...	...	1262	...	...	1515	...	...	1476
Dwellings	...	...	7378	...	...	8411	...	...	9912	...	...	11210
9 Community, social and personal services	...	...	40607	...	...	47138	...	...	56882	...	...	64319
A Sanitary and similar services	...	...	...	...	...	...	...	...	...	...	...	...
B Social and related community services	...	...	27181	...	...	31631	...	...	39599	...	...	44724
Educational services	...	...	19148	...	...	22051	...	...	27874	...	...	31206
Medical, dental, other health and veterinary services	...	...	8033	...	...	9580	...	...	11725	...	...	13518
C Recreational and cultural services	...	...	3133	...	...	3522	...	...	3653	...	...	3954
D Personal and household services	...	...	10293	...	...	11985	...	...	13630	...	...	15641
Total, Industries	...	...	656667	...	...	755521	...	...	808777	...	...	882362
Producers of Government Services	...	...	28263	...	...	30645	...	...	37349	...	...	42551
Other Producers	...	...	...	...	...	...	...	...	...	...	...	...
Total	...	...	684930	...	...	786166	...	...	846126	...	...	924913
Less: Imputed bank service charge	...	...	...	...	...	...	...	...	...	...	...	...
Import duties	...	...	...	...	...	...	...	...	...	...	...	...
Value added tax	...	...	...	...	...	...	...	...	...	...	...	...
Total	...	...	684930	...	...	786166	...	...	846126	...	...	924913

Thailand

4.1 Derivation of Value Added by Kind of Activity, in Current Prices

Million Thai baht

		1984 Gross Output	1984 Intermediate Consumption	1984 Value Added	1985 Gross Output	1985 Intermediate Consumption	1985 Value Added	1986 Gross Output	1986 Intermediate Consumption	1986 Value Added
					All Producers					
1	Agriculture, hunting, forestry and fishing	...	...	191278	...	...	178533	...	...	183037
	A Agriculture and hunting	...	...	165875	...	...	151422	...	...	151574
	B Forestry and logging	...	...	12274	...	...	12304	...	...	13899
	C Fishing	...	...	13129	...	...	14807	...	...	17564
2	Mining and quarrying	...	...	21291	...	...	29240	...	...	23347
	A Coal mining	...	...	476	...	...	2142	...	...	2121
	B Crude petroleum and natural gas production	...	...	8370	...	...	14389	...	...	10364
	C Metal ore mining	...	...	4020	...	...	3505	...	...	1053
	D Other mining	...	...	8425	...	...	9204	...	...	9809
3	Manufacturing	...	...	196257	...	...	209014	...	...	226571
	A Manufacture of food, beverages and tobacco	...	...	55517	...	...	59615	...	...	57435
	B Textile, wearing apparel and leather industries	...	...	40483	...	...	45474	...	...	49801
	C Manufacture of wood and wood products, including furniture	...	...	5207	...	...	5265	...	...	5211
	D Manufacture of paper and paper products, printing and publishing	...	...	5991	...	...	6256	...	...	6571
	E Manufacture of chemicals and chemical petroleum, coal, rubber and plastic products	...	...	34617	...	...	38185	...	...	51228
	F Manufacture of non-metallic mineral products, except products of petroleum and coal	...	...	13443	...	...	14345	...	...	15022
	G Basic metal industries	...	...	2228	...	...	2876	...	...	2424
	H Manufacture of fabricated metal products, machinery and equipment	...	...	31600	...	...	29100	...	...	29182
	I Other manufacturing industries	...	...	7171	...	...	7898	...	...	9697
4	Electricity, gas and water	...	...	18884	...	...	24070	...	...	28182
	A Electricity, gas and steam	...	...	16990	...	...	20837	...	...	24362
	B Water works and supply	...	...	1894	...	...	3233	...	...	3820
5	Construction	...	...	52772	...	...	54373	...	...	55682
6	Wholesale and retail trade, restaurants and hotels	...	...	219336	...	...	230901	...	...	248484
	A Wholesale and retail trade	...	...	181993	...	...	189736	...	...	204095
	B Restaurants and hotels	...	...	37343	...	...	41165	...	...	44389
	Restaurants	...	...	33427	...	...	36870	...	...	39672
	Hotels and other lodging places	...	...	3916	...	...	4295	...	...	4717
7	Transport, storage and communication	...	...	83588	...	...	95160	...	...	101827
	A Transport and storage	...	...	77833	...	...	88389	...	...	94563
	B Communication	...	...	5755	...	...	6771	...	...	7264
8	Finance, insurance, real estate and business services	...	...	92914	...	...	98530	...	...	102157
	A Financial institutions	...	...	72357	...	...	75944	...	...	77623
	B Insurance	...	...	6251	...	...	6975	...	...	7527
	C Real estate and business services	...	...	14306	...	...	15611	...	...	17007
	Real estate, except dwellings	...	...	1969	...	...	2003	...	...	2098
	Dwellings	...	...	12337	...	...	13608	...	...	14909
9	Community, social and personal services	...	...	69361	...	...	74397	...	...	79936
	A Sanitary and similar services	...	...	...	...	...	...	...	...	...
	B Social and related community services	...	...	47762	...	...	51059	...	...	54015
	Educational services	...	...	32857	...	...	34445	...	...	36254
	Medical, dental, other health and veterinary services	...	...	14905	...	...	16614	...	...	17761
	C Recreational and cultural services	...	...	4344	...	...	4292	...	...	5054
	D Personal and household services	...	...	17255	...	...	19046	...	...	20867

Thailand

4.1 Derivation of Value Added by Kind of Activity, in Current Prices
(Continued)

Million Thai baht

	1984 Gross Output	1984 Intermediate Consumption	1984 Value Added	1985 Gross Output	1985 Intermediate Consumption	1985 Value Added	1986 Gross Output	1986 Intermediate Consumption	1986 Value Added
Total, Industries	...	...	945681	...	...	994218	...	...	1049223
Producers of Government Services	...	...	43182	...	...	47136	...	...	49139
Other Producers	...	...	...	...	...	...	...	...	...
Total	...	...	988863	...	...	1041354	...	...	1098362
Less: Imputed bank service charge	...	...	...	...	...	...	...	...	...
Import duties	...	...	...	...	...	...	...	...	...
Value added tax	...	...	...	...	...	...	...	...	...
Total	...	...	988863	...	...	1041354	...	...	1098362

4.2 Derivation of Value Added by Kind of Activity, in Constant Prices

Million Thai baht

	1980 Gross Output	1980 Intermediate Consumption	1980 Value Added	1981 Gross Output	1981 Intermediate Consumption	1981 Value Added	1982 Gross Output	1982 Intermediate Consumption	1982 Value Added	1983 Gross Output	1983 Intermediate Consumption	1983 Value Added
\multicolumn{13}{c}{At constant prices of: 1972}
\multicolumn{13}{c}{All Producers}
1 Agriculture, hunting, forestry and fishing	...	...	72784	...	...	77701	...	...	78502	...	...	81449
A Agriculture and hunting	...	...	63190	...	...	68028	...	...	69801	...	...	72251
B Forestry and logging	...	...	3318	...	...	2896	...	...	2682	...	...	2630
C Fishing	...	...	6276	...	...	6777	...	...	6019	...	...	6568
2 Mining and quarrying	...	...	4780	...	...	4623	...	...	4431	...	...	4414
A Coal mining	...	...	86	...	...	101	...	...	118	...	...	112
B Crude petroleum and natural gas production	...	...	...	...	...	...	...	...	...	...	...	...
C Metal ore mining	...	...	1898	...	...	1756	...	...	1460	...	...	1140
D Other mining	...	...	2796	...	...	2766	...	...	2853	...	...	3162
3 Manufacturing	...	...	60597	...	...	64490	...	...	67318	...	...	72252
A Manufacture of food, beverages and tobacco	...	...	19089	...	...	19555	...	...	20501	...	...	21046
B Textile, wearing apparel and leather industries	...	...	14720	...	...	15984	...	...	17349	...	...	18575
C Manufacture of wood and wood products, including furniture	...	...	1182	...	...	1260	...	...	1220	...	...	1347
D Manufacture of paper and paper products, printing and publishing	...	...	2624	...	...	2867	...	...	2864	...	...	2821
E Manufacture of chemicals and chemical petroleum, coal, rubber and plastic products	...	...	9754	...	...	10154	...	...	10388	...	...	11103
F Manufacture of non-metallic mineral products, except products of petroleum and coal	...	...	3387	...	...	3671	...	...	3779	...	...	4116
G Basic metal industries	...	...	710	...	...	593	...	...	533	...	...	539
H Manufacture of fabricated metal products, machinery and equipment	...	...	7783	...	...	8706	...	...	8674	...	...	10366
I Other manufacturing industries	...	...	1348	...	...	1700	...	...	2010	...	...	2339
4 Electricity, gas and water	...	...	5560	...	...	6330	...	...	6755	...	...	7348
A Electricity, gas and steam	...	...	5019	...	...	5801	...	...	6173	...	...	6728
B Water works and supply	...	...	541	...	...	529	...	...	582	...	...	620
5 Construction	...	...	16576	...	...	15500	...	...	15097	...	...	15927
6 Wholesale and retail trade, restaurants and hotels	...	...	58087	...	...	61681	...	...	64255	...	...	66991
A Wholesale and retail trade	...	...	48227	...	...	51103	...	...	52789	...	...	55076
B Restaurants and hotels	...	...	9860	...	...	10578	...	...	11466	...	...	11915
Restaurants	...	...	7820	...	...	8375	...	...	9075	...	...	9506
Hotels and other lodging places	...	...	2040	...	...	2202	...	...	2391	...	...	2409
7 Transport, storage and communication	...	...	18811	...	...	20209	...	...	21715	...	...	23290
A Transport and storage	...	...	15968	...	...	17370	...	...	19863	...	...	21733
B Communication	...	...	2843	...	...	2839	...	...	1852	...	...	1557
8 Finance, insurance, real estate and business services	...	...	21921	...	...	23920	...	...	26332	...	...	29639
A Financial institutions	...	...	15675	...	...	17317	...	...	19259	...	...	22078

Thailand

4.2 Derivation of Value Added by Kind of Activity, in Constant Prices
(Continued)

Million Thai baht

	1980 Gross Output	1980 Intermediate Consumption	1980 Value Added	1981 Gross Output	1981 Intermediate Consumption	1981 Value Added	1982 Gross Output	1982 Intermediate Consumption	1982 Value Added	1983 Gross Output	1983 Intermediate Consumption	1983 Value Added
					At constant prices of:1972							
B Insurance	...	...	1304	...	...	1415	...	...	1606	...	...	1884
C Real estate and business services	...	...	4942	...	...	5188	...	...	5467	...	...	5677
Real estate, except dwellings	...	...	440	...	...	465	...	...	531	...	...	499
Dwellings	...	...	4502	...	...	4723	...	...	4936	...	...	5178
9 Community, social and personal services	...	...	21313	...	...	23624	...	...	25795	...	...	27361
A Sanitary and similar services	...	...	...	...	...	...	...	...	...	...	...	...
B Social and related community services	...	...	12678	...	...	14302	...	...	15796	...	...	16588
Educational services	...	...	8381	...	...	9540	...	...	10438	...	...	10696
Medical, dental, other health and veterinary services	...	...	4297	...	...	4762	...	...	5358	...	...	5892
C Recreational and cultural services	...	...	2604	...	...	2881	...	...	3027	...	...	3268
D Personal and household services	...	...	6031	...	...	6441	...	...	6972	...	...	7505
Total, Industries	...	...	280429	...	...	298078	...	...	310200	...	...	328671
Producers of Government Services	...	...	12423	...	...	13192	...	...	13833	...	...	14498
Other Producers	...	...	...	...	...	...	...	...	...	...	...	...
Total	...	...	292852	...	...	311270	...	...	324033	...	...	343169
Less: Imputed bank service charge	...	...	...	...	...	...	...	...	...	...	...	...
Import duties	...	...	...	...	...	...	...	...	...	...	...	...
Value added tax	...	...	...	...	...	...	...	...	...	...	...	...
Total	...	...	292852	...	...	311270	...	...	324033	...	...	343169

	1984 Gross Output	1984 Intermediate Consumption	1984 Value Added	1985 Gross Output	1985 Intermediate Consumption	1985 Value Added	1986 Gross Output	1986 Intermediate Consumption	1986 Value Added
			At constant prices of:1972						
			All Producers						
1 Agriculture, hunting, forestry and fishing	...	...	84144	...	...	86839	...	...	86215
A Agriculture and hunting	...	...	75105	...	...	77623	...	...	76565
B Forestry and logging	...	...	2741	...	...	2658	...	...	2670
C Fishing	...	...	6298	...	...	6558	...	...	6980
2 Mining and quarrying	...	...	5415	...	...	6001	...	...	6086
A Coal mining	...	...	140	...	...	309	...	...	299
B Crude petroleum and natural gas production	...	...	574	...	...	925	...	...	873
C Metal ore mining	...	...	1244	...	...	991	...	...	1000
D Other mining	...	...	3457	...	...	3776	...	...	3914
3 Manufacturing	...	...	76811	...	...	77425	...	...	82612
A Manufacture of food, beverages and tobacco	...	...	22996	...	...	22431	...	...	23669
B Textile, wearing apparel and leather industries	...	...	19774	...	...	20935	...	...	22926
C Manufacture of wood and wood products, including furniture	...	...	1501	...	...	1449	...	...	1487
D Manufacture of paper and paper products, printing and publishing	...	...	2939	...	...	2967	...	...	3213
E Manufacture of chemicals and chemical petroleum, coal, rubber and plastic products	...	...	11298	...	...	11903	...	...	12846
F Manufacture of non-metallic mineral products, except products of petroleum and coal	...	...	4592	...	...	4624	...	...	4882
G Basic metal industries	...	...	586	...	...	778	...	...	777
H Manufacture of fabricated metal products, machinery and equipment	...	...	10947	...	...	9921	...	...	9823
I Other manufacturing industries	...	...	2278	...	...	2417	...	...	2989
4 Electricity, gas and water	...	...	8088	...	...	8910	...	...	9527
A Electricity, gas and steam	...	...	7397	...	...	8295	...	...	8892
B Water works and supply	...	...	691	...	...	615	...	...	635

Thailand

4.2 Derivation of Value Added by Kind of Activity, in Constant Prices
(Continued)

Million Thai baht

	1984 Gross Output	1984 Intermediate Consumption	1984 Value Added	1985 Gross Output	1985 Intermediate Consumption	1985 Value Added	1986 Gross Output	1986 Intermediate Consumption	1986 Value Added
				At constant prices of:1972					
5 Construction	...	...	17680	...	...	17786	...	...	17911
6 Wholesale and retail trade, restaurants and hotels	...	...	70186	...	...	72876	...	...	76117
A Wholesale and retail trade	...	...	57430	...	...	59120	...	...	61406
B Restaurants and hotels	...	...	12756	...	...	13756	...	...	14711
Restaurants	...	...	10210	...	...	11006	...	...	11668
Hotels and other lodging places	...	...	2546	...	...	2750	...	...	3043
7 Transport, storage and communication	...	...	24605	...	...	25829	...	...	27180
A Transport and storage	...	...	22863	...	...	23826	...	...	25208
B Communication	...	...	1742	...	...	2003	...	...	1972
8 Finance, insurance, real estate and business services	...	...	32363	...	...	33377	...	...	33877
A Financial institutions	...	...	24240	...	...	24843	...	...	24967
B Insurance	...	...	2094	...	...	2282	...	...	2421
C Real estate and business services	...	...	6029	...	...	6252	...	...	6489
Real estate, except dwellings	...	...	660	...	...	655	...	...	675
Dwellings	...	...	5369	...	...	5597	...	...	5814
9 Community, social and personal services	...	...	28780	...	...	29929	...	...	32020
A Sanitary and similar services	...	...	...	...	...	...	...	...	...
B Social and related community services	...	...	17114	...	...	17769	...	...	18529
Educational services	...	...	10782	...	...	10935	...	...	11301
Medical, dental, other health and veterinary services	...	...	6332	...	...	6834	...	...	7228
C Recreational and cultural services	...	...	3602	...	...	3636	...	...	4466
D Personal and household services	...	...	8064	...	...	8524	...	...	9025
Total, Industries	...	...	348072	...	...	358972	...	...	371545
Producers of Government Services	...	...	14106	...	...	14897	...	...	15250
Other Producers	...	...	...	...	...	...	...	...	...
Total	...	...	362178	...	...	373869	...	...	386795
Less: Imputed bank service charge	...	...	...	...	...	...	...	...	...
Import duties	...	...	...	...	...	...	...	...	...
Value added tax	...	...	...	...	...	...	...	...	...
Total	...	...	362178	...	...	373869	...	...	386795

4.3 Cost Components of Value Added

Million Thai baht

	1980 Compensation of Employees	1980 Capital Consumption	1980 Net Operating Surplus	1980 Indirect Taxes	1980 Less: Subsidies Received	1980 Value Added	1981 Compensation of Employees	1981 Capital Consumption	1981 Net Operating Surplus	1981 Indirect Taxes	1981 Less: Subsidies Received	1981 Value Added
					All Producers							
1 Agriculture, hunting, forestry and fishing	17894	...	155912	...	...	173806	22348	...	165538	...	...	187886
A Agriculture and hunting	...	...	...	...	...	...	...	...	...	...	...	...
B Forestry and logging	...	...	...	...	...	...	...	...	...	...	...	...
C Fishing	...	...	...	...	...	...	...	...	...	...	...	...
2 Mining and quarrying	2938	...	11555	...	...	14493	3356	...	10017	...	...	13373
A Coal mining	...	...	...	...	...	...	...	...	...	...	...	...
B Crude petroleum and natural gas production	...	...	...	...	...	...	...	...	...	...	...	...
C Metal ore mining	...	...	...	...	...	...	...	...	...	...	...	...
D Other mining	...	...	...	...	...	...	...	...	...	...	...	...

Thailand

4.3 Cost Components of Value Added
(Continued)

Million Thai baht

	1980 Compensation of Employees	1980 Capital Consumption	1980 Net Operating Surplus	1980 Indirect Taxes	1980 Less: Subsidies Received	1980 Value Added	1981 Compensation of Employees	1981 Capital Consumption	1981 Net Operating Surplus	1981 Indirect Taxes	1981 Less: Subsidies Received	1981 Value Added
3 Manufacturing	33263	...	101252	...	...	134515	39657	...	118615	...	...	158272
A Manufacture of food, beverages and tobacco	...	...	...	...	...	...	...	...	...	...	...	...
B Textile, wearing apparel and leather industries	...	...	...	...	...	...	...	...	...	...	...	...
C Manufacture of wood and wood products, including furniture	...	...	...	...	...	...	...	...	...	...	...	...
D Manufacture of paper and paper products, printing and publishing	...	...	...	...	...	...	...	...	...	...	...	...
E Manufacture of chemicals and chemical petroleum, coal, rubber and plastic products	...	...	...	...	...	...	...	...	...	...	...	...
F Manufacture of non-metallic mineral products, except products of petroleum and coal	...	...	...	...	...	...	...	...	...	...	...	...
G Basic metal industries	...	...	...	...	...	...	...	...	...	...	...	...
H Manufacture of fabricated metal products, machinery and equipment	...	...	...	...	...	...	...	...	...	...	...	...
I Other manufacturing industries	...	...	...	...	...	...	...	...	...	...	...	...
4 Electricity, gas and water	2937	...	3347	...	...	6284	3718	...	7025	...	...	10743
A Electricity, gas and steam	...	...	...	...	...	...	...	...	...	...	...	...
B Water works and supply	...	...	...	...	...	...	...	...	...	...	...	...
5 Construction	13680	...	26185	...	...	39865	15159	...	26849	...	...	42008
6 Wholesale and retail trade, restaurants and hotels	14759	...	137808	...	...	152567	17596	...	160787	...	...	178383
A Wholesale and retail trade	...	...	...	...	...	...	...	...	...	...	...	...
B Restaurants and hotels	...	...	...	...	...	...	...	...	...	...	...	...
Restaurants	...	...	...	...	...	...	...	...	...	...	...	...
Hotels and other lodging places	...	...	...	...	...	...	...	...	...	...	...	...
7 Transport, storage and communication	12665	...	32596	...	...	45261	14877	...	42404	...	...	57281
A Transport and storage	...	...	...	...	...	...	...	...	...	...	...	...
B Communication	...	...	...	...	...	...	...	...	...	...	...	...
8 Finance, insurance, real estate and business services	7023	...	42246	...	...	49269	8799	...	51637	...	...	60436
A Financial institutions	...	...	...	...	...	...	...	...	...	...	...	...
B Insurance	...	...	...	...	...	...	...	...	...	...	...	...
C Real estate and business services	...	...	...	...	...	...	...	...	...	...	...	...
Real estate, except dwellings	...	...	...	...	...	...	...	...	...	...	...	...
Dwellings	...	...	...	...	...	...	...	...	...	...	...	...
9 Community, social and personal services	28720	...	11887	...	...	40607	30366	...	16773	...	...	47139
A Sanitary and similar services	...	...	...	...	...	...	...	...	...	...	...	...
B Social and related community services	...	...	...	...	...	...	...	...	...	...	...	...
Educational services	...	...	...	...	...	...	...	...	...	...	...	...
Medical, dental, other health and veterinary services	...	...	...	...	...	...	...	...	...	...	...	...
C Recreational and cultural services	...	...	...	...	...	...	...	...	...	...	...	...
D Personal and household services	...	...	...	...	...	...	...	...	...	...	...	...
Total, Industries [a]	133879	...	522788	...	...	656667	155876	...	599645	...	...	755521
Producers of Government Services	28263	...	...	...	...	28263	30646	...	...	...	...	30040
Other Producers	...	...	...	...	...	...	...	...	...	...	...	...
Total [a]	162142	...	522788	...	...	684930	186522	...	599644	...	...	786167
Less: Imputed bank service charge	...	...	...	...	...	...	...	...	...	...	...	...
Import duties	...	...	...	...	...	...	...	...	...	...	...	...
Value added tax	...	...	...	...	...	...	...	...	...	...	...	...
Total [a]	162142	...	522788	...	...	684930	186522	...	599644	...	...	786166

Thailand

4.3 Cost Components of Value Added

Million Thai baht

		1982					1983				
		Compensation of Employees	Capital Consumption	Net Operating Surplus	Indirect Taxes	Less: Subsidies Received	Value Added	Compensation of Employees	Capital Consumption	Net Operating Surplus	Indirect Taxes	Less: Subsidies Received	Value Added

All Producers

		Comp.	Cap.	Net Op.	Ind. Tax	Subs.	VA	Comp.	Cap.	Net Op.	Ind. Tax	Subs.	VA
1	Agriculture, hunting, forestry and fishing	25376	...	163366	...	...	188742	27930	...	176513	...	...	204443
	A Agriculture and hunting	...	...	...	...	...	...	...	...	...	...	...	...
	B Forestry and logging	...	...	...	...	...	...	...	...	...	...	...	...
	C Fishing	...	...	...	...	...	...	...	...	...	...	...	...
2	Mining and quarrying	3425	...	11382	...	...	14807	2991	...	13489	...	...	16480
	A Coal mining	...	...	...	...	...	...	...	...	...	...	...	...
	B Crude petroleum and natural gas production	...	...	...	...	...	...	...	...	...	...	...	...
	C Metal ore mining	...	...	...	...	...	...	...	...	...	...	...	...
	D Other mining	...	...	...	...	...	...	...	...	...	...	...	...
3	Manufacturing	47287	...	117362	...	...	164649	52663	...	123537	...	...	176200
	A Manufacture of food, beverages and tobacco	...	...	...	...	...	...	...	...	...	...	...	...
	B Textile, wearing apparel and leather industries	...	...	...	...	...	...	...	...	...	...	...	...
	C Manufacture of wood and wood products, including furniture	...	...	...	...	...	...	...	...	...	...	...	...
	D Manufacture of paper and paper products, printing and publishing	...	...	...	...	...	...	...	...	...	...	...	...
	E Manufacture of chemicals and chemical petroleum, coal, rubber and plastic products	...	...	...	...	...	...	...	...	...	...	...	...
	F Manufacture of non-metallic mineral products, except products of petroleum and coal	...	...	...	...	...	...	...	...	...	...	...	...
	G Basic metal industries	...	...	...	...	...	...	...	...	...	...	...	...
	H Manufacture of fabricated metal products, machinery and equipment	...	...	...	...	...	...	...	...	...	...	...	...
	I Other manufacturing industries	...	...	...	...	...	...	...	...	...	...	...	...
4	Electricity, gas and water	4351	...	10103	...	...	14454	5349	...	10970	...	...	16319
	A Electricity, gas and steam	...	...	...	...	...	...	...	...	...	...	...	...
	B Water works and supply	...	...	...	...	...	...	...	...	...	...	...	...
5	Construction	15736	...	27304	...	...	43040	18923	...	28206	...	...	47129
6	Wholesale and retail trade, restaurants and hotels	19486	...	172651	...	...	192137	21805	...	178368	...	...	200173
	A Wholesale and retail trade	...	...	...	...	...	...	...	...	...	...	...	...
	B Restaurants and hotels	...	...	...	...	...	...	...	...	...	...	...	...
	Restaurants	...	...	...	...	...	...	...	...	...	...	...	...
	Hotels and other lodging places	...	...	...	...	...	...	...	...	...	...	...	...
7	Transport, storage and communication	17308	...	45825	...	...	63133	20128	...	53580	...	...	73708
	A Transport and storage	...	...	...	...	...	...	...	...	...	...	...	...
	B Communication	...	...	...	...	...	...	...	...	...	...	...	...
8	Finance, insurance, real estate and business services	10560	...	60373	...	...	70933	11801	...	71790	...	...	83591
	A Financial institutions	...	...	...	...	...	...	...	...	...	...	...	...
	B Insurance	...	...	...	...	...	...	...	...	...	...	...	...
	C Real estate and business services	...	...	...	...	...	...	...	...	...	...	...	...
	Real estate, except dwellings	...	...	...	...	...	...	...	...	...	...	...	...
	Dwellings	...	...	...	...	...	...	...	...	...	...	...	...
9	Community, social and personal services	37701	...	19181	...	...	56882	40191	...	24128	...	...	64319
	A Sanitary and similar services	...	...	...	...	...	...	...	...	...	...	...	...
	B Social and related community services	...	...	...	...	...	...	...	...	...	...	...	...

Thailand

4.3 Cost Components of Value Added
(Continued)

Million Thai baht

	1982						1983					
	Compensation of Employees	Capital Consumption	Net Operating Surplus	Indirect Taxes	Less: Subsidies Received	Value Added	Compensation of Employees	Capital Consumption	Net Operating Surplus	Indirect Taxes	Less: Subsidies Received	Value Added
Educational services	...	...	...	...	...	...	...	...	...	...	...	...
Medical, dental, other health and veterinary services	...	...	...	...	...	...	...	...	...	...	...	...
C Recreational and cultural services	...	...	...	...	...	...	...	...	...	...	...	...
D Personal and household services	...	...	...	...	...	...	...	...	...	...	...	...
Total, Industries a	181230	...	627547	...	...	808777	201781	...	680581	...	...	882362
Producers of Government Services	37349	...	...	...	...	37349	42551	...	...	...	...	42551
Other Producers	...	...	...	...	...	...	...	...	...	...	...	...
Total a	218579	...	627547	...	...	846126	244332	...	680581	...	...	924913
Less: Imputed bank service charge	...	...	...	...	...	...	...	...	...	...	...	...
Import duties	...	...	...	...	...	...	...	...	...	...	...	...
Value added tax	...	...	...	...	...	...	...	...	...	...	...	...
Total a	218579	...	627547	...	...	846126	244332	...	680581	...	...	924913

	1984						1985					
	Compensation of Employees	Capital Consumption	Net Operating Surplus	Indirect Taxes	Less: Subsidies Received	Value Added	Compensation of Employees	Capital Consumption	Net Operating Surplus	Indirect Taxes	Less: Subsidies Received	Value Added

All Producers

1 Agriculture, hunting, forestry and fishing	25194	...	168244	...	...	191278	23260	...	155273	...	...	178533
A Agriculture and hunting	...	...	...	...	...	165875	...	...	...	...	...	151422
B Forestry and logging	...	...	...	...	...	12274	...	...	...	...	...	12304
C Fishing	...	...	...	...	...	13129	...	...	...	...	...	14807
2 Mining and quarrying	3155	...	18136	...	...	21291	2701	...	26539	...	...	29240
A Coal mining	...	...	...	...	...	476	...	...	...	...	...	2142
B Crude petroleum and natural gas production	...	...	...	...	...	8370	...	...	...	...	...	14389
C Metal ore mining	...	...	...	...	...	4020	...	...	...	...	...	3505
D Other mining	...	...	...	...	...	8425	...	...	...	...	...	9204
3 Manufacturing	61387	...	135406	...	...	196257	64264	...	144750	...	...	209014
A Manufacture of food, beverages and tobacco	...	...	...	...	...	55517	...	...	...	...	...	59615
B Textile, wearing apparel and leather industries	...	...	...	...	...	40483	...	...	...	...	...	45474
C Manufacture of wood and wood products, including furniture	...	...	...	...	...	5207	...	...	...	...	...	5265
D Manufacture of paper and paper products, printing and publishing	...	...	...	...	...	5991	...	...	...	...	...	6256
E Manufacture of chemicals and chemical petroleum, coal, rubber and plastic products	...	...	...	...	...	34617	...	...	...	...	...	38185
F Manufacture of non-metallic mineral products, except products of petroleum and coal	...	...	...	...	...	13443	...	...	...	...	...	14245
G Basic metal industries	...	...	...	...	...	2228	...	...	...	...	...	2876
H Manufacture of fabricated metal products, machinery and equipment	...	...	...	...	...	31600	...	...	...	...	...	29100
I Other manufacturing industries	...	...	...	...	...	7171	...	...	...	...	...	7898
4 Electricity, gas and water	5996	...	12888	...	...	18884	6155	...	17915	...	...	24070
A Electricity, gas and steam	...	...	...	...	...	16990	...	...	...	...	...	20837
B Water works and supply	...	...	...	...	...	1894	...	...	...	...	...	3233
5 Construction	22473	...	30299	...	...	52772	23775	...	30598	...	...	54373
6 Wholesale and retail trade, restaurants and hotels	24024	...	195312	...	...	219336	25339	...	205562	...	...	230901
A Wholesale and retail trade	...	...	...	...	...	181993	...	...	...	...	...	189736
B Restaurants and hotels	...	...	...	...	...	37343	...	...	...	...	...	41165
Restaurants	...	...	...	...	...	...	...	...	...	...	...	36870
Hotels and other lodging places	...	...	...	...	...	...	...	...	...	...	...	4295
7 Transport, storage and communication	22472	...	61116	...	...	83588	24723	...	70437	...	...	95160
A Transport and storage	...	...	...	...	...	77833	...	...	...	...	...	88389

Thailand

4.3 Cost Components of Value Added
(Continued)

Million Thai baht

	1984						1985					
	Compensation of Employees	Capital Consumption	Net Operating Surplus	Indirect Taxes	Less: Subsidies Received	Value Added	Compensation of Employees	Capital Consumption	Net Operating Surplus	Indirect Taxes	Less: Subsidies Received	Value Added
B Communication	...	...	...	...	...	5755	...	...	...	...	...	6771
8 Finance, insurance, real estate and business services	12990	...	79924	...	...	92914	13616	...	84914	...	...	98530
A Financial institutions	...	...	...	...	...	72357	...	...	...	...	...	75944
B Insurance	...	...	...	...	...	6251	...	...	...	...	...	6975
C Real estate and business services	...	...	...	...	...	14306	...	...	...	...	...	15611
Real estate, except dwellings	...	...	...	...	...	...	...	...	...	...	...	2003
Dwellings	...	...	...	...	...	12337	...	...	...	...	...	13608
9 Community, social and personal services	42419	...	26942	...	...	69361	45265	...	29132	...	...	74397
A Sanitary and similar services	...	...	...	...	...	...	...	...	...	...	...	...
B Social and related community services	...	...	...	...	...	47762	...	...	...	...	...	...
Educational services	...	...	...	...	...	32857	...	...	...	...	...	...
Medical, dental, other health and veterinary services	...	...	...	...	...	14905	...	...	...	...	...	...
C Recreational and cultural services	...	...	...	...	...	4344	...	...	...	...	...	...
D Personal and household services	...	...	...	...	...	17255	...	...	...	...	...	...
Total, Industries [a]	220110	...	725571	...	...	945681	229098	...	765120	...	...	994218
Producers of Government Services	43182	...	...	...	...	43182	47136	...	...	...	...	47136
Other Producers	...	...	...	...	...	...	...	...	...	...	...	...
Total [a]	263292	...	725571	...	...	988863	276234	...	765120	...	...	...
Less: Imputed bank service charge	...	...	...	...	...	...	...	...	...	...	...	...
Import duties	...	...	...	...	...	...	...	...	...	...	...	...
Value added tax	...	...	...	...	...	...	...	...	...	...	...	...
Total [a]	263292	...	725571	...	...	988863	276234	...	765120	...	...	1041354

	1986					
	Compensation of Employees	Capital Consumption	Net Operating Surplus	Indirect Taxes	Less: Subsidies Received	Value Added

All Producers

1 Agriculture, hunting, forestry and fishing	24604	...	158433	...	...	183037
A Agriculture and hunting	...	...	...	...	...	151574
B Forestry and logging	...	...	...	...	...	13899
C Fishing	...	...	...	...	...	17564
2 Mining and quarrying	2506	...	20841	...	...	23347
A Coal mining	...	...	...	...	...	2121
B Crude petroleum and natural gas production	...	...	...	...	...	10364
C Metal ore mining	...	...	...	...	...	1053
D Other mining	...	...	...	...	...	9809

Thailand

4.3 Cost Components of Value Added
(Continued)

Million Thai baht

	Compensation of Employees	Capital Consumption	Net Operating Surplus	Indirect Taxes	Less: Subsidies Received	Value Added
			1986			
3 Manufacturing	70961	...	155610	...	...	226571
A Manufacture of food, beverages and tobacco	...	...	...	...	...	57435
B Textile, wearing apparel and leather industries	...	...	...	...	...	49801
C Manufacture of wood and wood products, including furniture	...	...	...	...	...	5211
D Manufacture of paper and paper products, printing and publishing	...	...	...	...	...	6571
E Manufacture of chemicals and chemical petroleum, coal, rubber and plastic products	...	...	...	...	...	51228
F Manufacture of non-metallic mineral products, except products of petroleum and coal	...	...	...	...	...	15022
G Basic metal industries	...	...	...	...	...	2424
H Manufacture of fabricated metal products, machinery and equipment	...	...	...	...	...	29182
I Other manufacturing industries	...	...	...	...	...	9697
4 Electricity, gas and water	6947	...	21235	...	...	28182
A Electricity, gas and steam	...	...	...	...	...	24362
B Water works and supply	...	...	...	...	...	3820
5 Construction	24646	...	31036	...	...	55682
6 Wholesale and retail trade, restaurants and hotels	26767	...	221717	...	...	248484
A Wholesale and retail trade	...	...	...	...	...	204095
B Restaurants and hotels	...	...	...	...	...	44389
Restaurants	...	...	...	...	...	39672
Hotels and other lodging places	...	...	...	...	...	4717
7 Transport, storage and communication	26222	...	75605	...	...	101827
A Transport and storage	...	...	...	...	...	94563
B Communication	...	...	...	...	...	7264
8 Finance, insurance, real estate and business services	14385	...	87772	...	...	102157
A Financial institutions	...	...	...	...	...	77623
B Insurance	...	...	...	...	...	7527
C Real estate and business services	...	...	...	...	...	17007
Real estate, except dwellings	...	...	...	...	...	2098
Dwellings	...	...	...	...	...	14909
9 Community, social and personal services	47837	...	32099	...	...	79936
A Sanitary and similar services	...	...	...	...	...	...
B Social and related community services	...	...	...	...	...	54015
Educational services	...	...	...	...	...	36254
Medical, dental, other health and veterinary services	...	...	...	...	...	17761
C Recreational and cultural services	...	...	...	...	...	5054
D Personal and household services	...	...	...	...	...	20867
Total, Industries [a]	244875	...	804348	...	...	1049223
Producers of Government Services	49139	...	...	...	...	49139
Other Producers	...	...	...	...	...	...
Total [a]	294014	...	804348	...	...	1098362
Less: Imputed bank service charge	...	...	...	...	...	...
Import duties	...	...	...	...	...	...
Value added tax	...	...	...	...	...	...
Total [a]	294014	...	804348	...	...	1098362

a) Column 'Operating surplus' includes capital consumption and net indirect taxes'.

Togo

Source. Reply to the United Nations National Accounts Questionnaire from the Haut Commissariat du Plan, Lome. The official estimates and descriptions are published by the Commissariat in 'Comptes Nationaux'.

General note. The estimates shown in the following tables have been prepared in accordance with the United Nations System of National Accounts so far as the existing data would permit.

1.1 Expenditure on the Gross Domestic Product, in Current Prices

Million CFA francs

	1970	1975	1977	1978	1979	1980	1981	1982	1983	1984	1985	1986
1 Government final consumption expenditure	7371	19210	28640	29254	32323	34655	38700	41800	40600	...	...	...
2 Private final consumption expenditure	56038	95638	106127	117239	134645	157193	180600	194900	201500	...	...	...
3 Gross capital formation	10604	36586	65598	93037	109406	86729	79100	70900	63300	...	...	...
A Increase in stocks	1366	7359	6916	4567	8000	16600	11400	7300	7000	...	...	...
B Gross fixed capital formation	9237	29227	58682	88470	101406	70129	67700	63600	56300	...	...	...
Residential buildings	2676	...	...	...	...	...	...	...	...	...	...	...
Non-residential buildings		...	...	...	...	...	...	...	...	...	...	...
Other construction and land improvement etc.	1928	...	...	...	...	...	...	...	...	...	...	...
Other	4633	...	...	...	...	...	...	...	...	...	...	...
4 Exports of goods and services	21642	35602	45021	60578	69959	90562	103400	110700	104600	...	...	...
5 Less: Imports of goods and services	22483	58734	76586	108024	130102	130267	143800	148600	128700	...	...	...
Equals: Gross Domestic Product [a]	73171	128302	168800	192084	216231	238872	258000	269700	281300	292100	...	...

a) Data in this table have been revised, therefore they are not strictly comparable with the unrevised data in the other tables.

1.2 Expenditure on the Gross Domestic Product, in Constant Prices

Million CFA francs

	1970	1975	1977	1978	1979	1980	1981	1982	1983	1984	1985	1986
				At constant prices of: 1970								
1 Government final consumption expenditure	7371	13170	16866	16890	18220	18211	18152	...	...	...	...	...
2 Private final consumption expenditure	56038	56159	59824	64276	62626	60297	60772	...	...	...	...	...
3 Gross capital formation	10603	23279	31072	39035	42685	34627	24263	...	...	...	...	...
A Increase in stocks	1366	4390	3586	1978	3135	6217	5372	...	...	...	...	...
B Gross fixed capital formation	9237	18889	27486	37057	39550	28410	18891	...	...	...	...	...
4 Exports of goods and services	21642	14061	15487	20417	27984	33541	35847	...	...	...	...	...
5 Less: Imports of goods and services	22483	26100	38602	47441	52750	52394	50589	...	...	...	...	...
Equals: Gross Domestic Product [a]	73171	80569	84647	93177	98757	94282	88445	...	...	...	...	...

a) Data in this table have been revised, therefore they are not strictly comparable with the unrevised data in the other tables.

1.3 Cost Components of the Gross Domestic Product

Million CFA francs

	1970	1975	1977	1978	1979	1980	1981	1982	1983	1984	1985	1986
1 Indirect taxes, net	6757	18142	18061	25206	26528	33065	35325	...	...	...	...	...
2 Consumption of fixed capital	4183	6188	8456	11463	14814	17900	19124	...	...	...	...	...
3 Compensation of employees paid by resident producers to:	23025	39509	54068	59417	64668	67112	71699	...	...	...	...	...
4 Operating surplus	39206	64463	88215	95998	110221	120795	129052	...	...	...	...	...
Equals: Gross Domestic Product [a]	73171	128302	168800	192084	216231	238872	255200	...	...	...	...	...

a) Data in this table have been revised, therefore they are not strictly comparable with the unrevised data in the other tables.

1.4 General Government Current Receipts and Disbursements

Million CFA francs

	1970	1975	1977	1978	1979	1980	1981	1982	1983	1984	1985	1986
					Receipts							
1 Operating surplus	...	...	...	...	...	...	...	...	...	...	...	...
2 Property and entrepreneurial income	358.8	...	...	...	...	...	...	...	...	...	...	...
3 Taxes, fees and contributions	9413.9	...	...	...	...	...	...	...	...	...	...	...
A Indirect taxes	7979.2	...	...	...	...	...	...	...	...	...	...	...
B Direct taxes	1414.0	...	...	...	...	...	...	...	...	...	...	...
C Social security contributions	-	...	...	...	...	...	...	...	...	...	...	...
D Compulsory fees, fines and penalties	20.7	...	...	...	...	...	...	...	...	...	...	...
4 Other current transfers	2472.6	...	...	...	...	...	...	...	...	...	...	...
Total Current Receipts of General Government	12245.3	...	...	...	...	...	...	...	...	...	...	...

Togo

1.4 General Government Current Receipts and Disbursements
(Continued)

Million CFA francs	1970	1975	1977	1978	1979	1980	1981	1982	1983	1984	1985	1986
Disbursements												
1 Government final consumption expenditure	5241.2	...	...	...	...	...	...	...	...	...	...	...
A Compensation of employees	4365.3	...	...	...	...	...	...	...	...	...	...	...
B Consumption of fixed capital	...	...	...	...	...	...	...	...	...	...	...	...
C Purchases of goods and services, net	1299.9	...	...	...	...	...	...	...	...	...	...	...
D Less: Own account fixed capital formation	...	...	...	...	...	...	...	...	...	...	...	...
E Indirect taxes paid, net	...	...	...	...	...	...	...	...	...	...	...	...
2 Property income	688.5	...	...	...	...	...	...	...	...	...	...	...
3 Subsidies	341.5	...	...	...	...	...	...	...	...	...	...	...
4 Other current transfers	4392.1	...	...	...	...	...	...	...	...	...	...	...
A Social security benefits	3575.2	...	...	...	...	...	...	...	...	...	...	...
B Social assistance grants		...	...	...	...	...	...	...	...	...	...	...
C Other	816.9	...	...	...	...	...	...	...	...	...	...	...
5 Net saving	1582.0	...	...	...	...	...	...	...	...	...	...	...
Total Current Disbursements and Net Saving of General Government	12245.3	...	...	...	...	...	...	...	...	...	...	...

1.6 Current Income and Outlay of Households and Non-Profit Institutions

Million CFA francs	1970	1975	1977	1978	1979	1980	1981	1982	1983	1984	1985	1986
Receipts												
1 Compensation of employees	36417	...	...	...	...	...	...	...	...	...	...	...
A From resident producers	36090	...	...	...	...	...	...	...	...	...	...	...
B From rest of the world	327	...	...	...	...	...	...	...	...	...	...	...
2 Operating surplus of private unincorporated enterprises	...	...	...	...	...	...	...	...	...	...	...	...
3 Property and entrepreneurial income	...	...	...	...	...	...	...	...	...	...	...	...
4 Current transfers	...	...	...	...	...	...	...	...	...	...	...	...
Total Current Receipts	...	...	...	...	...	...	...	...	...	...	...	...
Disbursements												
1 Private final consumption expenditure	59601	...	...	...	...	...	...	...	...	...	...	...
2 Property income	...	...	...	...	...	...	...	...	...	...	...	...
3 Direct taxes and other current transfers n.e.c. to general government	308	...	...	...	...	...	...	...	...	...	...	...
A Social security contributions	174	...	...	...	...	...	...	...	...	...	...	...
B Direct taxes	...	...	...	...	...	...	...	...	...	...	...	...
C Fees, fines and penalties	...	...	...	...	...	...	...	...	...	...	...	...
4 Other current transfers											...	...
5 Net saving	-364	...	...	...	...	...	...	...	...	...	...	...
Total Current Disbursements and Net Saving	...	...	...	...	...	...	...	...	...	...	...	...

1.7 External Transactions on Current Account, Summary

Million CFA francs	1970	1975	1977	1978	1979	1980	1981	1982	1983	1984	1985	1986
Payments to the Rest of the World												
1 Imports of goods and services	23508	58734	84405	122489	128759	138862	...	...	...	...	...	...
A Imports of merchandise c.i.f.	19551	...	...	...	...	...	...	...	...	...	...	...
B Other	3958	...	...	...	...	...	...	...	...	...	...	...
2 Factor income to the rest of the world	2114	2447	5062	6974	6485	6600	...	...	...	...	...	...

Togo

1.7 External Transactions on Current Account, Summary
(Continued)

Million CFA francs

	1970	1975	1977	1978	1979	1980	1981	1982	1983	1984	1985	1986
A Compensation of employees	340	55	104	98	95	100	...	...	...	...	...	...
B Property and entrepreneurial income	1775	2392	4958	6876	6390	6500	...	...	...	...	...	...
3 Current transfers to the rest of the world	609	3407	2906	3263	1200	3500	...	...	...	...	...	...
4 Surplus of the nation on current transactions	-1235	-16290	-21437	-49200	-45800	-37700	...	...	...	...	...	...
Payments to the Rest of the World and Surplus of the Nation on Current Transactions	24996	48298	70936	83526	90644	111262	...	...	...	...	...	...

Receipts From The Rest of the World

	1970	1975	1977	1978	1979	1980	1981	1982	1983	1984	1985	1986
1 Exports of goods and services	21498	35602	55450	66916	69959	90562	...	...	...	...	...	...
A Exports of merchandise f.o.b.	15910	...	...	...	...	...	...	...	...	...	...	...
B Other	5588	...	...	...	...	...	...	...	...	...	...	...
2 Factor income from rest of the world	848	2000	2254	1660	2185	2200	...	...	...	...	...	...
A Compensation of employees	327	615	543	460	495	500	...	...	...	...	...	...
B Property and entrepreneurial income	520	1385	1711	1200	1690	1700	...	...	...	...	...	...
3 Current transfers from rest of the world	2650	10696	13232	14950	18500	18500	...	...	...	...	...	...
Receipts from the Rest of the World on Current Transactions	24996	48298	70936	83526	90644	111262	...	...	...	...	...	...

1.10 Gross Domestic Product by Kind of Activity, in Current Prices

Million CFA francs

	1970	1975	1977	1978	1979	1980	1981	1982	1983	1984	1985	1986
1 Agriculture, hunting, forestry and fishing	27111	31646	45913	46889	58880	63640	69300	...	...	...	...	...
2 Mining and quarrying	3685	14924	11707	18932	17741	21876	22600	...	...	...	...	...
3 Manufacturing	6697	9004	11873	12307	11312	16633	16300	...	...	...	...	...
4 Electricity, gas and water	2001	3040	2893	3159	3482	4057	4100	...	...	...	...	...
5 Construction	2048	7083	9412	17539	16796	13948	11000	...	...	...	...	...
6 Wholesale and retail trade, restaurants and hotels	17716	21973	28155	30855	42215	45977	52900	...	...	...	...	...
7 Transport, storage and communication	5351	9268	11795	14234	13109	15331	17200	...	...	...	...	...
8 Finance, insurance, real estate and business services	2608	6720	8145	11443	12027	12656	15111	...	...	...	...	...
9 Community, social and personal services	2387	3785	4335	3981	4168	...	...	...	...	...	...	...
Total, Industries	69604	107443	134228	159339	179730	...	...	...	...	...	...	...
Producers of Government Services	5889	13112	19014	20812	22974	...	...	...	...	...	...	...
Other Producers	...	...	...	...	...	...	...	...	...	...	...	...
Subtotal	75493	120555	153242	180151	202704	223479	239511	...	...	...	...	...
Less: Imputed bank service charge	657	1747	1855	1900	2386	1756	1711	...	...	...	...	...
Plus: Import duties	...	8034	13582	13833	15913	17149	17400	...	...	...	...	...
Plus: Value added tax	...	...	...	...	...	...	...	...	...	...	...	...
Plus: Other adjustments	-1665	1460	3831	...	...	...	...	...	...	...	...	...
Equals: Gross Domestic Product [a]	73171	128302	168800	192084	216231	238872	255200	...	...	...	...	...

a) Data in this table have been revised, therefore they are not strictly comparable with the unrevised data in the other tables.

1.12 Relations Among National Accounting Aggregates

Million CFA francs

	1970	1975	1977	1978	1979	1980	1981	1982	1983	1984	1985	1986
Gross Domestic Product [a]	73171	128302	168800	192084	216231	238872	...	...	...	...	...	...
Plus: Net factor income from the rest of the world	-1100	-447	-2808	-4259	-4300	-4400	...	...	...	...	...	...
Factor income from the rest of the world	...	2000	2254	...	...	2200	...	...	...	...	...	...
Less: Factor income to the rest of the world	...	2447	5062	...	...	6600	...	...	...	...	...	...
Equals: Gross National Product	72071	127855	165992	187825	211931	234472	...	...	...	...	...	...
Less: Consumption of fixed capital	4183	6188	8456	11463	14814	17900	...	...	...	...	...	...

Togo

1.12 Relations Among National Accounting Aggregates
(Continued)

Million CFA francs

	1970	1975	1977	1978	1979	1980	1981	1982	1983	1984	1985	1986
Equals: National Income [a]	67888	121667	157536	176362	197117	216572	...	...	...	...	...	...
Plus: Net current transfers from the rest of the world	2928	7289	10326	11687	17300	15000	...	...	...	...	...	...
Current transfers from the rest of the world	...	10696	13232	14950	18500	18500	...	...	...	...	...	...
Less: Current transfers to the rest of the world	...	3407	2906	3263	1200	3500	...	...	...	...	...	...
Equals: National Disposable Income [a]	70816	128956	167862	188049	214417	231572	...	...	...	...	...	...
Less: Final consumption	63409	114848	134767	146493	166968	191848	...	...	...	...	...	...
Equals: Net Saving	7407	14108	33095	41556	47449	39724	...	...	...	...	...	...
Less: Surplus of the nation on current transactions	986	-16290	-24047	-40018	-47143	-29105	...	...	...	...	...	...
Equals: Net Capital Formation	6421	30398	57142	81574	94592	68829	...	...	...	...	...	...

a) Data in this table have been revised, therefore they are not strictly comparable with the unrevised data in the other tables.

2.1 Government Final Consumption Expenditure by Function, in Current Prices

Million CFA francs

		1970	1975	1977	1978	1979	1980	1981	1982	1983	1984	1985	1986
1	General public services	1689.0	...	...	...	...	...	...	...	...	...	...	...
2	Defence	797.3	...	...	...	...	...	...	...	...	...	...	...
3	Public order and safety		...	...	...	...	...	...	...	...	...	...	...
4	Education	1039.6	...	...	...	...	...	...	...	...	...	...	...
5	Health	641.8	...	...	...	...	...	...	...	...	...	...	...
6	Social security and welfare	53.8	...	...	...	...	...	...	...	...	...	...	...
7	Housing and community amenities	44.3	...	...	...	...	...	...	...	...	...	...	...
8	Recreational, cultural and religious affairs	42.6	...	...	...	...	...	...	...	...	...	...	...
9	Economic services	932.8	...	...	...	...	...	...	...	...	...	...	...
10	Other functions	-	...	...	...	...	...	...	...	...	...	...	...
	Total Government Final Consumption Expenditure	5241.2	...	...	...	...	...	...	...	...	...	...	...

2.5 Private Final Consumption Expenditure by Type and Porpuse, in Current Prices

Million CFA francs

		1970	1975	1977	1978	1979	1980	1981	1982	1983	1984	1985	1986

Final Consumption Expenditure of Resident Households

		1970	1975	1977	1978	1979	1980	1981	1982	1983	1984	1985	1986
1	Food, beverages and tobacco	38451.2	...	...	...	...	...	...	...	...	...	...	...
	A Food	35064.6	...	...	...	...	...	...	...	...	...	...	...
	B Non-alcoholic beverages	1787.7	...	...	...	...	...	...	...	...	...	...	...
	C Alcoholic beverages	...	...	...	...	...	...	...	...	...	...	...	...
	D Tobacco	1598.9	...	...	...	...	...	...	...	...	...	...	...
2	Clothing and footwear	5213.7	...	...	...	...	...	...	...	...	...	...	...
3	Gross rent, fuel and power	5974.7	...	...	...	...	...	...	...	...	...	...	...
4	Furniture, furnishings and household equipment and operation	2337.5	...	...	...	...	...	...	...	...	...	...	...
	A Household operation	736.3	...	...	...	...	...	...	...	...	...	...	...
	B Other	1601.2	...	...	...	...	...	...	...	...	...	...	...
5	Medical care and health expenses	952.0	...	...	...	...	...	...	...	...	...	...	...
6	Transport and communication	4964.7	...	...	...	...	...	...	...	...	...	...	...
	A Personal transport equipment	1236.6	...	...	...	...	...	...	...	...	...	...	...
	B Other	3728.1	...	...	...	...	...	...	...	...	...	...	...
7	Recreational, entertainment, education and cultural services	573.8	...	...	...	...	...	...	...	...	...	...	...
	A Education	334.4	...	...	...	...	...	...	...	...	...	...	...
	B Other	239.4	...	...	...	...	...	...	...	...	...	...	...
8	Miscellaneous goods and services	2057.4	...	...	...	...	...	...	...	...	...	...	...
	A Personal care	956.1	...	...	...	...	...	...	...	...	...	...	...
	B Expenditures in restaurants, cafes and hotels	324.8	...	...	...	...	...	...	...	...	...	...	...

Togo

2.5 Private Final Consumption Expenditure by Type and Porpose, in Current Prices
(Continued)

Million CFA francs

	1970	1975	1977	1978	1979	1980	1981	1982	1983	1984	1985	1986
C Other	776.5	...	...	...	...	...	...	...	...	...	...	...
Total Final Consumption Expenditure in the Domestic Market by Households, of which	60525.0	...	...	...	...	...	...	...	...	...	...	...
Plus: Direct purchases abroad by resident households	433.7	...	...	...	...	...	...	...	...	...	...	...
Less: Direct purchases in the domestic market by non-resident households	1213.4	...	...	...	...	...	...	...	...	...	...	...
Equals: Final Consumption Expenditure of Resident Households	59745.3	...	...	...	...	...	...	...	...	...	...	...

Final Consumption Expenditure of Private Non-profit Institutions Serving Households

	1970	1975	1977	1978	1979	1980	1981	1982	1983	1984	1985	1986
Equals: Final Consumption Expenditure of Private Non-profit Organisations Serving Households	...	...	...	...	...	...	...	...	...	...	...	...
Private Final Consumption Expenditure	59745.3	...	...	...	...	...	...	...	...	...	...	...

2.17 Exports and Imports of Goods and Services, Detail

Million CFA francs

	1970	1975	1977	1978	1979	1980	1981	1982	1983	1984	1985	1986
Exports of Goods and Services												
1 Exports of merchandise, f.o.b.	15910.2	...	...	...	...	...	...	...	...	...	...	...
2 Transport and communication	478.1	...	...	...	...	...	...	...	...	...	...	...
3 Insurance service charges	142.2	...	...	...	...	...	...	...	...	...	...	...
4 Other commodities	611.8	...	...	...	...	...	...	...	...	...	...	...
5 Adjustments of merchandise exports to change-of-ownership basis	3142.6	...	...	...	...	...	...	...	...	...	...	...
6 Direct purchases in the domestic market by non-residential households	1213.4	...	...	...	...	...	...	...	...	...	...	...
7 Direct purchases in the domestic market by extraterritorial bodies	...	...	...	...	...	...	...	...	...	...	...	...
Total Exports of Goods and Services	21498.3	...	...	...	...	...	...	...	...	...	...	...
Imports of Goods and Services												
1 Imports of merchandise, c.i.f.	19550.8	...	...	...	...	...	...	...	...	...	...	...
2 Adjustments of merchandise imports to change-of-ownership basis	1125.6	...	...	...	...	...	...	...	...	...	...	...
3 Other transport and communication	342.6	...	...	...	...	...	...	...	...	...	...	...
4 Other insurance service charges	296.3	...	...	...	...	...	...	...	...	...	...	...
5 Other commodities	433.7	...	...	...	...	...	...	...	...	...	...	...
6 Direct purchases abroad by government	1759.4	...	...	...	...	...	...	...	...	...	...	...
7 Direct purchases abroad by resident households		...	...	...	...	...	...	...	...	...	...	...
Total Imports of Goods and Services	23508.4	...	...	...	...	...	...	...	...	...	...	...
Balance of Goods and Services	-2010.1	...	...	...	...	...	...	...	...	...	...	...
Total Imports and Balance of Goods and Services	21498.3	...	...	...	...	...	...	...	...	...	...	...

Tonga

Source. Reply to the United Nations National Accounts Questionnaire from the Statistics Department, Nuku'alofa.
General note. The estimates shown in the following tables have been prepared in accordance with the United Nations System of National Accounts so far as the existing data would permit.

1.1 Expenditure on the Gross Domestic Product, in Current Prices

Million Tongan pa'anga — Fiscal year ending 30 June

	1970	1975	1977	1978	1979	1980	1981	1982	1983	1984	1985	1986
1 Government final consumption expenditure	2.3	3.2	4.7	5.8	6.0	6.9	7.7	10.8	10.3	...	...	...
2 Private final consumption expenditure	10.4	22.1	27.0	34.0	39.0	49.8	66.8	77.7	91.5	...	...	...
3 Gross capital formation	2.8	6.8	6.2	10.8	12.4	13.8	14.2	15.7	21.1	...	...	...
A Increase in stocks	-0.2	1.2	0.3	1.8	1.2	1.2	1.2	0.9	0.7	...	...	...
B Gross fixed capital formation	3.0	5.7	5.9	9.0	11.2	12.6	13.0	14.8	20.4	...	...	...
Residential buildings	...	...	...	...	...	3.9	2.1	3.2	6.6	...	...	...
Non-residential buildings	...	...	...	...	...	5.3	6.5	6.4	9.0	...	...	...
Other construction and land improvement etc.	...	...	...	...	...	0.1	0.1	0.1	0.2	...	...	...
Other	...	...	...	...	...	...	...	...	...	...	...	...
4 Exports of goods and services	3.3	10.3	10.4	10.5	10.4	14.1	14.3	16.5	14.3	...	...	...
5 Less: Imports of goods and services	5.4	17.6	17.6	24.6	27.9	31.7	36.6	41.0	50.9	...	...	...
Equals: Gross Domestic Product	13.3	28.3 / 24.8	30.8	36.3	39.9	52.9	54.4	64.2	72.7	...	...	...

1.3 Cost Components of the Gross Domestic Product

Million Tongan pa'anga — Fiscal year ending 30 June

	1970	1975	1977	1978	1979	1980	1981	1982	1983	1984	1985	1986
1 Indirect taxes, net	1.2	3.8	4.1	5.3	5.2	6.1	7.1	8.4	9.3	...	...	...
A Indirect taxes	...	...	...	...	...	...	7.3	8.7	9.7	...	...	...
B Less: Subsidies	...	...	...	...	...	...	0.2	0.3	0.4	...	...	...
2 Consumption of fixed capital	0.5	1.0	1.2	1.5	1.8	2.2	2.5	2.9	2.9	...	...	...
3 Compensation of employees paid by resident producers to:	6.5	9.5	11.5	12.8	17.2	18.6	24.1	28.5	32.2	...	...	...
A Resident households	6.5	...	...	...	...	...	...	...	...	...	...	...
B Rest of the world	-	...	...	...	...	...	...	...	...	...	...	...
4 Operating surplus	5.2	10.5	14.0	16.7	27.3	25.9	32.5	39.5	41.5	...	...	...
Equals: Gross Domestic Product	13.3	28.3 / 24.8	30.8	36.3	39.9	52.8	54.4	64.2	72.7	...	...	...

1.4 General Government Current Receipts and Disbursements

Million Tongan pa'anga — Fiscal year ending 30 June

	1970	1975	1977	1978	1979	1980	1981	1982	1983	1984	1985	1986
Receipts												
1 Operating surplus	...	0.1	0.1	0.2	0.2	0.2	0.4	0.9	...	...	...	...
2 Property and entrepreneurial income	...	0.2	-	-	-	0.3	0.7	0.6	...	...	...	...
3 Taxes, fees and contributions	...	4.3	4.9	6.5	6.5	7.8	9.1	10.7	...	...	...	...
A Indirect taxes	...	3.8	4.1	5.3	5.2	6.2	7.3	8.7	...	...	...	...
B Direct taxes	...	0.4	0.7	1.1	1.2	1.5	1.7	1.9	...	...	...	...
C Social security contributions	...	-	-	-	-	-	-	-	...	...	...	...
D Compulsory fees, fines and penalties	...	0.1	0.1	0.1	0.1	0.1	0.1	0.1	...	...	...	...
4 Other current transfers	...	-	0.1	0.1	0.1	0.2	0.2	0.3	...	...	...	...
Total Current Receipts of General Government [a]	...	4.6	5.0	6.8	6.8	8.5	10.4	12.5	...	...	...	...
Disbursements												
1 Government final consumption expenditure	...	3.3	4.7	5.4	5.9	6.3	6.9	9.2	...	...	...	...

Tonga

1.4 General Government Current Receipts and Disbursements
(Continued)

Million Tongan pa'anga — Fiscal year ending 30 June

	1970	1975	1977	1978	1979	1980	1981	1982	1983	1984	1985	1986
A Compensation of employees	...	2.2	3.4	3.7	3.9	4.3	4.3	5.8	...	...	...	...
B Consumption of fixed capital	...	...	...	...	...	...	...	...	...	...	...	...
C Purchases of goods and services, net	...	1.1	1.3	1.7	2.0	2.0	2.6	3.4	...	...	...	...
D Less: Own account fixed capital formation	...	...	...	...	...	...	...	...	...	...	...	...
E Indirect taxes paid, net	...	...	...	...	...	...	...	...	...	...	...	...
2 Property income	...	-	0.1	0.1	0.1	0.2	0.2	0.4	...	...	...	...
3 Subsidies	...	0.1	0.1	0.1	0.2	0.2	0.2	0.3	...	...	...	...
4 Other current transfers	...	0.2	0.3	0.4	0.5	0.5	0.6	0.6	...	...	...	...
5 Net saving [b]	...	1.0	-0.2	0.8	0.1	1.3	2.5	2.0	...	...	...	...
Total Current Disbursements and Net Saving of General Government [a]	...	4.6	5.0	6.8	6.8	8.5	10.4	12.5	...	...	...	...

a) Data for this table have not been revised, therefore, data for some years are not comparable with those of other tables.
b) Item 'Net saving' includes consumption of fixed capital.

1.7 External Transactions on Current Account, Summary

Million Tongan pa'anga — Fiscal year ending 30 June

	1970	1975	1977	1978	1979	1980	1981	1982	1983	1984	1985	1986
Payments to the Rest of the World												
1 Imports of goods and services	5.4	17.6	17.6	24.6	27.9	31.7	36.7	41.0	50.9	...	...	...
A Imports of merchandise c.i.f.	...	14.8	14.3	20.3	24.5	27.2	32.2	36.2	43.8	...	...	...
B Other	...	2.8	3.3	4.3	3.4	4.5	4.5	4.8	7.1	...	...	...
2 Factor income to the rest of the world	-	0.1	0.3	0.2	0.3	0.4	0.5	0.9	0.1	...	...	...
A Compensation of employees	-	...	...	-	0.3	0.3	0.5	0.8	0.1	...	...	...
B Property and entrepreneurial income	-	...	...	0.2	0.1	0.2	-	0.1	-	...	...	...
3 Current transfers to the rest of the world	0.3	0.5	1.4	0.8	0.8	1.0	2.0	2.9	6.2	...	...	...
4 Surplus of the nation on current transactions	-0.5	-0.6	-0.8	-6.0	-6.8	-4.7	-6.1	2.9	-13.7	...	...	...
Payments to the Rest of the World and Surplus of the Nation on Current Transactions	5.2	17.6	18.5	19.6	22.2	28.5	33.0	47.7	43.6	...	...	...
Receipts From The Rest of the World												
1 Exports of goods and services	3.3	10.3	10.4	10.5	10.4	14.1	14.3	16.4	14.3	...	...	...
A Exports of merchandise f.o.b.	...	5.6	5.6	5.3	5.0	7.7	7.1	6.7	3.8	...	...	...
B Other	...	4.7	4.8	5.2	5.5	6.4	7.2	9.7	10.6	...	...	...
2 Factor income from rest of the world	0.2	0.6	0.6	0.9	1.7	2.7	3.9	5.3	3.3	...	...	...
A Compensation of employees	-	...	...	0.1	0.3	0.8	2.7	2.8	3.3	...	...	...
B Property and entrepreneurial income	0.2	...	...	0.8	1.4	1.9	1.2	2.5	-	...	...	...
3 Current transfers from rest of the world	1.7	6.7	7.5	8.3	10.1	11.7	14.9	25.9	25.9	...	...	...
Receipts from the Rest of the World on Current Transactions	5.2	17.6	18.5	19.6	22.2	28.5	33.0	47.7	43.6	...	...	...

Tonga

1.8 Capital Transactions of The Nation, Summary

Million Tongan pa'anga — Fiscal year ending 30 June

	1970	1975	1977	1978	1979	1980	1981	1982	1983	1984	1985	1986
Finance of Gross Capital Formation												
Gross saving	2.2	6.2	5.5	4.7	5.7	10.9	10.2	18.9	...	...	...	...
1 Consumption of fixed capital	0.5	1.0	1.2	1.5	1.8	2.2	2.5	2.8	...	...	...	...
2 Net saving	1.7	5.2	4.3	3.2	3.9	8.7	7.8	16.1	...	...	...	...
Less: Surplus of the nation on current transactions	-0.5	-0.6	-0.8	-6.0	-6.8	-4.6	-6.6	2.5	...	...	...	...
Finance of Gross Capital Formation [a]	2.8	6.9	6.2	10.7	12.5	15.5	16.8	16.3	...	...	...	...
Gross Capital Formation												
Increase in stocks	-0.2	1.2	0.3	1.8	1.2	2.0	2.0	1.3	...	...	...	...
Gross fixed capital formation	3.0	5.7	5.9	9.0	11.2	13.6	14.8	15.0	...	...	...	...
1 General government	...	1.0	1.9	3.5	5.1	6.0	4.2	6.4	...	...	...	...
2 Corporate and quasi-corporate enterprises	...	4.7	4.0	5.5	6.1	7.5	10.6	8.6	...	...	...	...
A Public	...	0.4	0.7	0.7	0.8	1.3	2.1	0.9	...	...	...	...
B Private	...	4.3	3.3	4.8	5.3	6.2	8.5	7.7	...	...	...	...
3 Other	...	...	...	...	...	...	...	...	...	...	...	...
Gross Capital Formation [a]	2.8	6.9	6.2	10.7	12.5	15.5	16.8	16.3	...	...	...	...

a) Data for this table have not been revised, therefore, data for some years are not comparable with those of other tables.

1.9 Gross Domestic Product by Institutional Sectors of Origin

Million Tongan pa'anga — Fiscal year ending 30 June

	1970	1975	1977	1978	1979	1980	1981	1982	1983	1984	1985	1986
Domestic Factor Incomes Originating												
1 General government	...	...	...	...	3.8	4.5	4.5	6.2	...	...	...	...
2 Corporate and quasi-corporate enterprises	...	...	...	...	9.1	11.3	13.1	14.7	...	...	...	...
A Non-financial [a]	...	...	...	...	9.1	11.3	13.1	14.7	...	...	...	...
Public	...	...	...	...	4.5	5.4	5.5	6.1	...	...	...	...
Private	...	...	...	...	4.6	5.9	7.6	8.6	...	...	...	...
B Financial [a]	...	...	...	...	...	...	...	...	...	...	...	...
3 Households and private unincorporated enterprises	...	...	...	...	19.9	22.7	26.4	27.9	...	...	...	...
4 Non-profit institutions serving households	...	...	...	...	1.9	2.1	2.3	2.5	...	...	...	...
Subtotal: Domestic Factor Incomes [b]	...	...	...	...	34.7	40.0	40.3	51.2	...	...	...	...
Indirect taxes, net	...	...	...	...	5.2	6.1	7.3	8.7	...	...	...	...
Consumption of fixed capital	...	...	...	...	...	...	...	...	...	...	...	...
Gross Domestic Product [b]	...	...	...	...	40.0	46.8	53.5	59.9	...	...	...	...

a) Item 'Non-financial' includes also financial corporate and quasi-corporate enterprises.
b) Data for this table have not been revised, therefore, data for some years are not comparable with those of other tables.

1.10 Gross Domestic Product by Kind of Activity, in Current Prices

Million Tongan pa'anga — Fiscal year ending 30 June

	1970	1975	1977	1978	1979	1980	1981	1982	1983	1984	1985	1986
1 Agriculture, hunting, forestry and fishing	6.3	10.5	11.7	13.0	14.5	21.3	17.8	21.1	24.3	...	...	...
2 Mining and quarrying	0.1	0.1	0.1	0.2	0.2	0.3	0.4	0.4	0.4	...	...	...
3 Manufacturing	0.3	1.1	1.8	2.3	2.7	2.8	4.5	5.2	5.0	...	...	...
4 Electricity, gas and water	0.1	0.2	0.2	0.3	0.4	0.3	0.3	8.4	0.4	...	...	...
5 Construction	0.6	0.8	0.9	1.5	2.0	1.8	2.0	1.9	2.5	...	...	...

Tonga

1.10 Gross Domestic Product by Kind of Activity, in Current Prices
(Continued)

Million Tongan pa'anga — Fiscal year ending 30 June

	1970	1975	1977	1978	1979	1980	1981	1982	1983	1984	1985	1986
6 Wholesale and retail trade, restaurants and hotels	1.2	2.8	3.7	4.4	4.8	6.8	7.4	10.6	12.4	...	...	...
7 Transport, storage and communication	0.7	0.8	1.6	1.8	2.0	3.1	4.5	4.7	4.9	...	...	...
8 Finance, insurance, real estate and business services	0.7	1.5	1.9	2.3	2.5	3.8	2.9	3.2	4.0	...	...	...
9 Community, social and personal services [a]	0.9	3.2	4.8	5.2	5.7	6.5	7.5	8.3	9.5	...	...	...
Statistical discrepancy	...	...	...	...	...	...	-6.3	0.2	-9.1	...	...	...
Total, Industries	11.0	...	...	...	...	...	...	...	...	...	...	...
Producers of Government Services [a]	1.2	...	...	...	...	...	-0.2	-2.7	4.6	...	...	...
Other Producers [a]	...	...	...	...	...	...	...	...	...	...	...	...
Subtotal [b]	12.1	21.0	26.7	31.0	34.7	46.7	47.3	55.8	63.4	...	...	...
Less: Imputed bank service charge	...	...	...	...	0.2	0.3	0.4	0.5	0.7	...	...	...
Plus: Import duties	...	...	...	...	...	...	...	...	...	...	...	...
Plus: Value added tax	...	...	...	...	...	...	...	...	...	...	...	...
Plus: Other adjustments [c]	1.2	3.8	4.1	5.3	5.2	6.1	7.1	8.4	9.3	...	...	...
Equals: Gross Domestic Product	13.3	28.3 24.8	30.8	36.3	40.0	52.9	64.4	64.2	72.7	...	...	...

a) Items 'Other producers' and 'Producers of government services' are included in item 'Community, social and personal services'.
b) Gross domestic product in factor values.
c) Item 'Other adjustments' refers to indirect taxes net of subsidies.

1.11 Gross Domestic Product by Kind of Activity, in Constant Prices

Million Tongan pa'anga — Fiscal year ending 30 June

	1970	1975	1977	1978	1979	1980	1981	1982	1983	1984	1985	1986
					At constant prices of: 1975							
1 Agriculture, hunting, forestry and fishing	...	10.5	11.3	10.4	10.4	13.5	17.2	18.6	20.2	...	...	...
2 Mining and quarrying	...	0.1	0.1	0.2	0.2	0.2	0.3	0.2	0.3	...	...	...
3 Manufacturing	...	1.1	1.3	1.4	1.4	1.7	2.1	2.2	1.5	...	...	...
4 Electricity, gas and water	...	0.2	0.2	0.3	0.3	0.3	0.3	0.4	0.4	...	...	...
5 Construction	...	0.8	0.8	1.1	1.3	0.9	0.8	0.8	0.8	...	...	...
6 Wholesale and retail trade, restaurants and hotels	...	2.8	2.8	3.0	3.1	3.3	3.3	4.3	4.6	...	...	...
7 Transport, storage and communication	...	0.8	1.3	1.5	1.5	2.0	2.1	2.5	2.8	...	...	...
8 Finance, insurance, real estate and business services	...	1.5	1.7	1.8	2.2	2.5	2.5	3.3	3.6	...	...	...
9 Community, social and personal services [a]	...	3.2	3.4	3.6	3.7	3.9	3.8	5.0	5.3	...	...	...
Total, Industries	...	...	...	...	...	...	...	...	...	...	...	...
Producers of Government Services [a]	...	...	...	...	...	...	...	...	...	...	...	...
Other Producers [a]	...	...	...	...	...	...	...	...	...	...	...	...
Subtotal [b]	...	21.0	23.0	23.2	24.2	28.3	32.5	37.3	39.5	...	...	...
Less: Imputed bank service charge	...	...	...	...	...	...	...	...	...	...	...	...
Plus: Import duties	...	...	...	...	...	...	...	...	...	...	...	...
Plus: Value added tax	...	...	...	...	...	...	...	...	...	...	...	...
Plus: Other adjustments [c]	...	3.8	3.2	3.5	3.0	3.2	3.4	3.9	4.2	...	...	...
Equals: Gross Domestic Product	...	24.8	26.2	26.7	27.2	31.5	35.9	41.2	43.6	...	...	...

a) Items 'Other producers' and 'Producers of government services' are included in item 'Community, social and personal services'.
b) Gross domestic product in factor values.
c) Item 'Other adjustments' refers to indirect taxes net of subsidies.

Tonga

1.12 Relations Among National Accounting Aggregates

Million Tongan pa'anga — Fiscal year ending 30 June

	1970	1975	1977	1978	1979	1980	1981	1982	1983	1984	1985	1986
Gross Domestic Product	13.3	28.3 / 24.8	30.8	36.3	40.0	52.9	54.4	64.2	72.7	...	...	...
Plus: Net factor income from the rest of the world	0.2	0.5	0.3	0.7	1.3	2.3	3.4	4.4	3.2	...	...	...
Factor income from the rest of the world	0.2	0.6	0.6	0.9	1.7	2.7	3.9	5.3	3.3	...	...	...
Less: Factor income to the rest of the world	-	0.1	0.3	0.2	0.3	0.4	0.5	0.9	0.1	...	...	...
Equals: Gross National Product	13.5	25.3	31.1	37.0	41.2	55.2	57.8	68.6	75.9	...	...	...
Less: Consumption of fixed capital	0.5	1.0	1.2	1.5	1.8	2.2	2.5	2.9	2.9	...	...	...
Equals: National Income	13.0	27.7 / 24.4	29.9	35.5	39.5	53.0	55.3	65.7	73.0	...	...	...
Plus: Net current transfers from the rest of the world	1.4	6.1	6.1	7.5	9.3	10.7	12.9	23.0	19.7	...	...	...
Current transfers from the rest of the world	1.7	6.7	7.6	8.3	10.1	11.7	14.9	25.9	25.9	...	...	...
Less: Current transfers to the rest of the world	0.3	0.5	1.4	0.8	0.8	1.0	2.0	2.9	6.2	...	...	...
Equals: National Disposable Income	14.5	30.5	36.0	43.0	48.8	63.7	68.2	88.7	92.0	...	...	...
Less: Final consumption	12.7	25.3	31.7	39.8	45.0	56.7	74.5	88.5	101.8	...	...	...
Equals: Net Saving	1.7	5.2	4.3	3.2	3.9	7.0	5.7	15.7	4.5	...	...	...
Less: Surplus of the nation on current transactions	-0.5	-0.6	-0.8	-6.0	-6.8	-4.7	-6.1	2.9	-13.7	...	...	...
Equals: Net Capital Formation	2.3	5.9	5.0	9.2	10.7	11.7	11.8	12.8	18.2	...	...	...

2.1 Government Final Consumption Expenditure by Function, in Current Prices

Million Tongan pa'anga — Fiscal year ending 30 June

	1970	1975	1977	1978	1979	1980	1981	1982	1983	1984	1985	1986
1 General public services	...	...							...	...	...	...
2 Defence	...	...	1.9	1.9	2.1	2.8	3.2	4.3	...	...	...	...
3 Public order and safety	...	...							...	...	...	...
4 Education	...	0.5	0.9	1.0	1.1	1.2	1.2	1.6	...	...	...	...
5 Health	...	0.6	0.9	1.0	1.1	1.4	1.6	2.1	...	...	...	...
6 Social security and welfare	...	...	...	...	...	...	...	...	...	...	...	...
7 Housing and community amenities	...	0.1	0.2	0.2	0.3	0.3	0.3	0.2	...	...	...	...
8 Recreational, cultural and religious affairs	...	...	...	...	...	...	...	...	...	...	...	...
9 Economic services	...	0.6	0.8	1.3	1.4	1.3	1.3	2.9	...	...	...	...
A Fuel and energy	...	...	...	...	...	...	...	...	...	...	...	...
B Agriculture, forestry, fishing and hunting	...	0.2	0.3	0.4	0.5	0.5	0.5	0.7	...	...	...	...
C Mining, manufacturing and construction, except fuel and energy	...	0.3	0.4	0.7	0.7	0.7	0.7	1.8	...	...	...	...
D Transportation and communication	...	...	...	...	...	...	...	...	...	...	...	...
E Other economic affairs	...	0.1	0.1	0.2	0.2	0.2	0.2	0.4	...	...	...	...
10 Other functions	...	...	...	...	...	...	...	...	...	...	...	...
Total Government Final Consumption Expenditure	...	3.2	4.7	5.3	6.0	6.9	7.8	11.0	...	...	...	...

2.11 Gross Fixed Capital Formation by Kind of Activity of Owner, ISIC Divisions, in Current Prices

Million Tongan pa'anga — Fiscal year ending 30 June

All Producers

	1970	1975	1977	1978	1979	1980	1981	1982	1983	1984	1985	1986
1 Agriculture, hunting, forestry and fishing	0.2	0.5	0.9	1.7	2.3	1.4	1.6	4.0	...	...	...	...
A Agriculture and hunting	...	0.5	0.9	1.7	...	1.4	1.6	4.0	...	...	...	...
B Forestry and logging	...	...	...	...	...	...	...	...	...	...	...	...
C Fishing	...	...	...	...	...	...	...	...	...	...	...	...

Tonga

2.11 Gross Fixed Capital Formation by Kind of Activity of Owner, ISIC Divisions, in Current Prices
(Continued)

Million Tongan pa'anga — Fiscal year ending 30 June

	1970	1975	1977	1978	1979	1980	1981	1982	1983	1984	1985	1986
2 Mining and quarrying	0.1	... / -	-	-	0.1	0.1	-	-	...	...	...	...
A Coal mining	...	... / ...	...	...	...	...	...	...	...	...	...	...
B Crude petroleum and natural gas production	...	... / ...	...	...	...	...	...	...	...	...	...	...
C Metal ore mining	...	... / ...	...	...	...	...	...	...	...	...	...	...
D Other mining	0.1	... / -	-	-	0.1	0.1	-	-	...	...	...	...
3 Manufacturing	0.1	0.2	0.1	0.4	0.7	1.1	0.9	1.5	...	...	...	...
4 Electricity, gas and water	-	0.2	0.2	0.5	0.6	0.8	2.1	0.6	...	...	...	...
5 Construction	0.5	0.3	0.2	0.4	0.9	1.5	1.2	0.5	...	...	...	...
6 Wholesale and retail trade, restaurants and hotels	0.1	0.3	0.8	0.6	1.1	0.9	1.1	1.0	...	...	...	...
7 Transport, storage and communication	0.5	0.9	0.9	1.5	1.4	2.5	4.0	3.1	...	...	...	...
8 Finance, insurance, real estate and business services	-	2.6	2.0	2.4	2.6	2.3	2.8	3.1	...	...	...	...
9 Community, social and personal services	1.1	0.7	0.8	1.4	2.3	2.9	1.1	1.3	...	...	...	...
Total Industries	2.7	5.7	5.9	8.9	11.2	13.6	14.8	15.0	...	...	...	...
Producers of Government Services	0.3	...	...	...	...	...	...	...	...	...	...	...
Private Non-Profit Institutions Serving Households	...	...	...	...	...	...	...	...	...	...	...	...
Total	3.0	5.7	5.9	8.9	11.2	13.6	14.8	15.0	...	...	...	...

Trinidad and Tobago

Source. Reply to the United Nations National Accounts Questionnaire from the Central Statistical Office, Port-of-Spain. The official estimates are published by the Office in the 'National Income of Trinidad and Tobago' and in the 'Annual Statistical Digest'.

General note. The official estimates of Trinidad and Tobago have been adjusted by the Central Statistical Office to conform to the United Nations System of National Accounts so far as the existing data would permit. It should be noted that interest on the public debt is treated as a factor payment and is therefore included in National Income.

1.1 Expenditure on the Gross Domestic Product, in Current Prices

Million Trinidad and Tobago dollars

	1970	1975	1977	1978	1979	1980	1981	1982	1983	1984	1985	1986
1 Government final consumption expenditure	215	652	967	1148	1536	1805	2110	4032	3774	4091	4175	...
2 Private final consumption expenditure	986	2257	3605	4443	5663	6865	8197	11103	11574	11018	9333	...
3 Gross capital formation	425	1449	2008	2584	3213	4580	4541	5417	4969	4119	3889	...
A Increase in stocks	81	364	272	261	261	376	199	228	199	165	156	...
B Gross fixed capital formation	344	1085	1735	2323	2952	4204	4342	5189	4770	3954	3733	...
Residential buildings	91	250	465	565	1051	1257	1415	1725	1842	1647	1433	...
Non-residential buildings												...
Other construction and land improvement etc.	38	70	226	360	534	735	917	1360	1228	1098	955	...
Other	217	766	1044	1398	1367	2212	2011	2105	1700	1209	1344	...
4 Exports of goods and services	703	2808	3733	3766	4979	7550	7542	6694	5751	5976	5965	...
5 Less: Imports of goods and services	685	1866	2779	3391	4345	5834	5952	8070	7606	6285	5222	...
Equals: Gross Domestic Product	1644	5300	7533	8550	11046	14966	16438	19176	18461	18918	18140	...

1.2 Expenditure on the Gross Domestic Product, in Constant Prices

Million Trinidad and Tobago dollars

	1970	1975	1977	1978	1979	1980	1981	1982	1983	1984	1985	1986
	\multicolumn{12}{c}{At constant prices of:1970}
1 Government final consumption expenditure	215	347	355	398	499	529	607	737	568	604	608	...
2 Private final consumption expenditure	986	1217	1576	1762	1958	2021	2110	2565	2426	2051	1635	...
3 Gross capital formation	425	927	1095	1402	1447	1774	1479	1558	1389	1026	1077	...
4 Exports of goods and services	703	689	718	723	777	839	826	749	744	820	885	...
5 Less: Imports of goods and services	685	1168	1480	1665	2221	2380	2175	2815	2694	2311	2235	...
Statistical discrepancy	-	-130	-80	-218	29	-33	28	197	283	236	319	...
Equals: Gross Domestic Product	1644	1881	2184	2403	2490	2748	2874	2990	2715	2426	2290	...

1.3 Cost Components of the Gross Domestic Product

Million Trinidad and Tobago dollars

	1970	1975	1977	1978	1979	1980	1981	1982	1983	1984	1985	1986
1 Indirect taxes, net	94	90	112	49	-231	-588	-537	-856	-664	-141	-17	...
A Indirect taxes	109	212	413	418	492	637	681	819	969	1047	1155	...
B Less: Subsidies	16	122	302	370	723	1225	1218	1675	1633	1188	1173	...
2 Consumption of fixed capital	147	324	654	624	698	848	930	1142	1293	1399	1407	...
3 Compensation of employees paid by resident producers to:	846	1962	3067	3866	4951	6110	7652	10612	10660	10933	10978	...
4 Operating surplus	558	2924	3700	4012	5627	8597	8394	8278	7172	6727	5772	...
Equals: Gross Domestic Product	1644	5300	7533	8550	11046	14966	16438	19176	18461	18918	18140	...

1.4 General Government Current Receipts and Disbursements

Million Trinidad and Tobago dollars

	1970	1975	1977	1978	1979	1980	1981	1982	1983	1984	1985	1986
	\multicolumn{12}{c}{Receipts}
1 Operating surplus	...	...	...	...	...	...	...	...	...	...	...	...
2 Property and entrepreneurial income	42	266	421	438	576	781	908	851	897	829	883	...
3 Taxes, fees and contributions	248	1444	2386	2394	3206	5258	6037	6132	5510	5540	5344	...
A Indirect taxes	109	212	413	418	492	637	681	819	969	1047	1155	...
B Direct taxes	127	1205	1929	1934	2673	4537	5225	5183	4395	4337	3910	...
C Social security contributions	...	...	...	...	...	...	...	...	...	...	...	...
D Compulsory fees, fines and penalties	12	27	44	42	41	84	131	131	147	155	279	...
4 Other current transfers	-	11	17	19	23	37	39	49	62	79	89	...
Statistical discrepancy	3	4	5	7	6	5	4	8	8	22	11	...
Total Current Receipts of General Government	293	1725	2829	2859	3811	6082	6989	7039	6477	6469	6328	...

Trinidad and Tobago

1.4 General Government Current Receipts and Disbursements
(Continued)

Million Trinidad and Tobago dollars

	1970	1975	1977	1978	1979	1980	1981	1982	1983	1984	1985	1986
Disbursements												
1 Government final consumption expenditure	215	652	967	1148	1536	1805	2110	4032	3774	4091	4175	...
A Compensation of employees	178	561	829	992	1325	1522	1807	3577	3273	3522	3655	...
B Consumption of fixed capital	-	-	-	1	1	1	2	2	2	2	2	...
C Purchases of goods and services, net	37	91	138	156	210	282	302	452	499	566	518	...
D Less: Own account fixed capital formation	...	...	...	...	...	...	...	...	...	...	...	...
E Indirect taxes paid, net	...	...	...	...	...	...	...	...	...	...	...	...
2 Property income	22	47	43	80	126	125	179	161	197	313	466	...
A Interest												...
B Net land rent and royalties	...	...	...	...	...	...	...	...	...	...	...	
3 Subsidies	16	122	302	370	723	1225	1218	1675	1633	1188	1173	...
4 Other current transfers	22	94	127	154	263	294	346	456	590	682	806	...
A Social security benefits	7	25	37	66	85	93	101	139	162	172	173	...
B Social assistance grants												...
C Other	16	69	90	87	178	201	245	317	428	510	633	...
5 Net saving	19	811	1391	1107	1164	2633	3135	716	283	196	-292	...
Total Current Disbursements and Net Saving of General Government	293	1725	2829	2858	3811	6082	6989	7039	6477	6469	6328	...

1.7 External Transactions on Current Account, Summary

Million Trinidad and Tobago dollars

	1970	1975	1977	1978	1979	1980	1981	1982	1983	1984	1985	1986
Payments to the Rest of the World												
1 Imports of goods and services	685	1866	2779	3391	4345	5834	5952	8070	7606	6285	5222	...
2 Factor income to the rest of the world	141	275	649	487	995	1314	1309	1011	847	1020	1150	...
3 Current transfers to the rest of the world	10	52	79	95	114	162	222	340	290	303	260	...
4 Surplus of the nation on current transactions	-116	716	415	97	-87	803	891	-1865	-2435	-1290	-184	...
Payments to the Rest of the World and Surplus of the Nation on Current Transactions	720	2908	3921	4070	5367	8112	8374	7556	6309	6319	6448	...
Receipts From The Rest of the World												
1 Exports of goods and services	703	2808	3733	3766	4979	7550	7542	6694	5751	5976	5965	...
2 Factor income from rest of the world	11	94	185	300	384	558	827	857	553	338	478	...
3 Current transfers from rest of the world	6	6	4	4	4	4	5	5	5	5	5	...
Receipts from the Rest of the World on Current Transactions	720	2908	3921	4070	5367	8112	8374	7556	6309	6319	6448	...

1.10 Gross Domestic Product by Kind of Activity, in Current Prices

Million Trinidad and Tobago dollars

	1970	1975	1977	1978	1979	1980	1981	1982	1983	1984	1985	1986
1 Agriculture, hunting, forestry and fishing	80	174	261	302	322	337	386	433	472	527	595	...
2 Mining and quarrying	133	1865	2500	2349	3245	5928	5801	4760	3923	4019	3740	...
3 Manufacturing	397	792	1027	1074	1567	1338	1118	1349	1891	2020	1676	...
4 Electricity, gas and water	33	36	45	50	51	26	31	-4	-10	151	157	...
5 Construction	112	438	764	1224	1449	1885	2639	3152	2839	2542	2261	...
6 Wholesale and retail trade, restaurants and hotels	313	718	887	1166	1294	1431	1793	2313	2469	2757	2597	...
7 Transport, storage and communication	236	367	717	756	960	1444	1624	2005	1805	1529	1406	...
8 Finance, insurance, real estate and business services	122	364	597	774	1076	1434	1841	2167	2237	2205	2307	...
9 Community, social and personal services	111	257	393	465	593	728	809	1301	1385	1489	1553	...

Trinidad and Tobago

1.10 Gross Domestic Product by Kind of Activity, in Current Prices
(Continued)

Million Trinidad and Tobago dollars

	1970	1975	1977	1978	1979	1980	1981	1982	1983	1984	1985	1986
Total, Industries	1537	5011	7191	8161	10557	14551	16042	17476	17011	17239	16292	...
Producers of Government Services	139	453	636	763	1064	1174	1475	2868	2617	2799	2911	...
Other Producers	...	...	...	...	...	...	...	...	...	...	...	...
Subtotal	1676	5464	7827	8924	11621	15725	17517	20344	19628	20038	19203	...
Less: Imputed bank service charge	32	164	293	375	577	758	1079	1168	1167	1120	1060	...
Plus: Import duties	...	...	...	...	...	...	...	...	...	...	...	...
Plus: Value added tax	...	...	...	...	...	...	...	...	...	...	...	...
Equals: Gross Domestic Product	1644	5300	7533	8550	11046	14966	16438	19176	18461	18918	18140	...

1.11 Gross Domestic Product by Kind of Activity, in Constant Prices

Million Trinidad and Tobago dollars

	1970	1975	1977	1978	1979	1980	1981	1982	1983	1984	1985	1986
	\multicolumn{12}{c}{At constant prices of:1970}
1 Agriculture, hunting, forestry and fishing	80	80	78	75	72	67	66	68	66	67	74	...
2 Mining and quarrying	133	202	214	217	207	207	185	174	157	164	168	...
3 Manufacturing	397	369	425	448	460	471	440	450	445	428	412	...
4 Electricity, gas and water	33	40	50	53	59	66	75	89	96	100	99	...
5 Construction	112	201	248	350	374	410	474	486	399	323	260	...
6 Wholesale and retail trade, restaurants and hotels	313	381	384	458	428	489	533	560	483	447	402	...
7 Transport, storage and communication	236	201	318	293	326	440	468	515	438	300	268	...
8 Finance, insurance, real estate and business services	122	197	265	312	378	420	481	500	449	390	385	...
9 Community, social and personal services	111	135	146	152	177	176	184	175	179	175	176	...
Total, Industries	1537	1806	2128	2358	2481	2755	2906	3025	2712	2400	2244	...
Producers of Government Services	139	165	186	198	213	223	249	238	238	227	224	...
Other Producers	...	...	...	...	...	...	...	...	...	...	...	...
Subtotal	1676	1971	2314	2556	2694	2978	3155	3263	2950	2627	2468	...
Less: Imputed bank service charge	32	88	130	151	203	227	282	274	234	201	177	...
Plus: Import duties	...	...	...	...	...	...	...	...	...	...	...	...
Plus: Value added tax	...	...	...	...	...	...	...	...	...	...	...	...
Equals: Gross Domestic Product	1644	1881	2184	2403	2490	2748	2874	2990	2715	2426	2290	...

1.12 Relations Among National Accounting Aggregates

Million Trinidad and Tobago dollars

	1970	1975	1977	1978	1979	1980	1981	1982	1983	1984	1985	1986
Gross Domestic Product	1644	5300	7533	8550	11046	14966	16438	19176	18461	18918	18140	...
Plus: Net factor income from the rest of the world	-130	-181	-464	-187	-611	-756	-481	-154	-295	-682	-672	...
Factor income from the rest of the world	11	94	185	300	384	558	827	857	553	338	478	...
Less: Factor income to the rest of the world	141	275	649	487	995	1314	1309	1011	847	1020	1150	...
Equals: Gross National Product	1514	5119	7069	8363	10435	14210	15957	19022	18167	18236	17468	...
Less: Consumption of fixed capital	147	324	654	624	698	848	930	1142	1293	1399	1407	...
Equals: National Income	1367	4795	6414	7739	9737	13362	15027	17880	16874	16838	16061	...
Plus: Net current transfers from the rest of the world	-4	-46	-75	-91	-110	-157	-218	-336	-285	-299	-255	...
Current transfers from the rest of the world	6	6	4	4	4	4	5	5	5	5	5	...
Less: Current transfers to the rest of the world	10	52	79	95	114	162	222	340	290	303	260	...
Equals: National Disposable Income	1362	4749	6340	7648	9627	13205	14809	17544	16589	16539	15806	...
Less: Final consumption	1201	2908	4572	5591	7199	8670	10307	15134	15348	15109	13508	...
Equals: Net Saving	162	1841	1768	2057	2428	4536	4502	2410	1241	1431	2298	...
Less: Surplus of the nation on current transactions	-116	716	415	97	-87	803	891	-1865	-2435	-1290	-184	...
Equals: Net Capital Formation	278	1125	1353	1960	2515	3733	3610	4275	3676	2720	2482	...

Trinidad and Tobago

2.1 Government Final Consumption Expenditure by Function, in Current Prices

Million Trinidad and Tobago dollars

	1970	1975	1977	1978	1979	1980	1981	1982	1983	1984	1985	1986
1 General public services	...	...	...	...	...	...	306	787	494	592	671	...
2 Defence	...	...	...	...	...	...	...	...	...	...	...	...
3 Public order and safety	...	...	...	...	...	...	284	562	539	588	595	...
4 Education	...	...	...	...	...	...	374	792	751	828	847	...
5 Health	...	...	...	...	...	...	354	620	657	723	743	...
6 Social security and welfare	...	...	...	...	...	...	12	17	17	17	18	...
7 Housing and community amenities	...	...	...	...	...	...	139	218	236	262	265	...
8 Recreational, cultural and religious affairs	...	...	...	...	...	...	...	...	...	...	...	...
9 Economic services	...	...	...	...	...	...	628	1032	1081	1082	1039	...
A Fuel and energy	...	...	...	...	...	...	149	248	207	205	231	...
B Agriculture, forestry, fishing and hunting	...	...	...	...	...	...	101	162	200	183	175	...
C Mining, manufacturing and construction, except fuel and energy	...	...	...	...	...	...	40	52	66	62	56	...
D Transportation and communication	...	...	...	...	...	...	277	460	480	460	434	...
E Other economic affairs	...	...	...	...	...	...	61	110	128	172	143	...
10 Other functions	...	...	...	...	...	...	15	5	-2	-1	-2	...
Total Government Final Consumption Expenditure	...	...	...	...	...	...	2110	4032	3774	4091	4175	...

2.7 Gross Capital Formation by Type of Good and Owner, in Current Prices

Million Trinidad and Tobago dollars

	1980 TOTAL	Total Private	Public Enterprises	General Government	1981 TOTAL	Total Private	Public Enterprises	General Government	1982 TOTAL	Total Private	Public Enterprises	General Government
Increase in stocks, total	376	...	...	...	199	...	...	...	228	...	...	...
1 Goods producing industries	376	...	...	...	199	...	...	...	228	...	...	...
A Materials and supplies	122	...	...	...	160	...	...	...	114	...	...	...
B Work in progress	...	...	...	...	...	...	...	...	...	...	...	...
C Livestock, except breeding stocks, dairy cattle, etc.	...	...	...	...	...	...	...	...	...	...	...	...
D Finished goods	254	...	...	...	39	...	...	...	114	...	...	...
2 Wholesale and retail trade	...	...	...	...	...	...	...	...	...	...	...	...
3 Other, except government stocks	...	...	...	...	...	...	...	...	...	...	...	...
4 Government stocks	...	...	...	...	...	...	...	...	...	...	...	...
Gross Fixed Capital Formation, Total	4204	...	...	...	4342	...	...	...	5189	...	...	...
1 Residential buildings	1257	...	...	...	1415	...	...	...	1725	...	...	...
2 Non-residential buildings		...	...	...		...	...	...		...	...	...
3 Other construction	735	...	...	...	917	...	...	...	1360	...	...	...
4 Land improvement and plantation and orchard development	...	...	...	...	...	...	...	...	...	...	...	...
5 Producers' durable goods	1859	...	...	...	1646	...	...	...	1678	...	...	...
A Transport equipment	293	...	...	...	361	...	...	...	319	...	...	...
B Machinery and equipment	1567	...	...	...	1285	...	...	...	1359	...	...	...
6 Breeding stock, dairy cattle, etc.	...	...	...	...	...	...	...	...	...	...	...	...
Statistical discrepancy	353	...	...	...	365	...	...	...	427	...	...	...
Total Gross Capital Formation	4580	...	...	...	4541	...	...	...	5417	...	...	...

	1983 TOTAL	Total Private	Public Enterprises	General Government	1984 TOTAL	Total Private	Public Enterprises	General Government	1985 TOTAL	Total Private	Public Enterprises	General Government
Increase in stocks, total	199	...	...	...	165	...	...	...	156	...	...	...
1 Goods producing industries	199	...	...	...	165	...	...	...	156	...	...	...
A Materials and supplies	107	...	...	...	89	...	...	...	84	...	...	...
B Work in progress	...	...	...	...	...	...	...	...	...	...	...	...
C Livestock, except breeding stocks, dairy cattle, etc.	...	...	...	...	...	...	...	...	...	...	...	...
D Finished goods	91	...	...	...	76	...	...	...	72	...	...	...
2 Wholesale and retail trade	...	...	...	...	...	...	...	...	...	...	...	...
3 Other, except government stocks	...	...	...	...	...	...	...	...	...	...	...	...

Trinidad and Tobago

2.7 Gross Capital Formation by Type of Good and Owner, in Current Prices
(Continued)

Million Trinidad and Tobago dollars

	1983 TOTAL	1983 Total Private	1983 Public Enterprises	1983 General Government	1984 TOTAL	1984 Total Private	1984 Public Enterprises	1984 General Government	1985 TOTAL	1985 Total Private	1985 Public Enterprises	1985 General Government
4 Government stocks	...	...	...	...	...	...	...	...	...	...	...	...
Gross Fixed Capital Formation, Total	4770	...	...	...	3954	...	...	...	3733	...	...	...
1 Residential buildings	1842	...	...	...	1647	...	...	...	1433	...	...	...
2 Non-residential buildings		...	...	...		...	...	...		...	...	...
3 Other construction	1228	...	...	...	1098	...	...	...	955	...	...	...
4 Land improvement and plantation and orchard development	...	...	...	...	...	...	...	...	...	...	...	...
5 Producers' durable goods	1338	...	...	...	812	...	...	...	784	...	...	...
A Transport equipment	253	...	...	...	154	...	...	...	148	...	...	...
B Machinery and equipment	1085	...	...	...	659	...	...	...	636	...	...	...
6 Breeding stock, dairy cattle, etc.	...	...	...	...	...	...	...	...	...	...	...	...
Statistical discrepancy	362	...	...	...	397	...	...	...	560	...	...	...
Total Gross Capital Formation	4969	...	...	...	4119	...	...	...	3889	...	...	...

2.11 Gross Fixed Capital Formation by Kind of Activity of Owner, ISIC Divisions, in Current Prices

Million Trinidad and Tobago dollars

	1970	1975	1977	1978	1979	1980	1981	1982	1983	1984	1985	1986
					All Producers							
1 Agriculture, hunting, forestry and fishing	7	39	36	46	56	68	62	60				
2 Mining and quarrying	85	413	351	376	386	513	544	816	...	...	...	...
3 Manufacturing	122	327	393	736	433	1012	740	625				
A Manufacturing of food, beverages and tobacco	22	71	103	161	202	122	120	143				
B Textile, wearing apparel and leather industries	8	13	14	18	16	24	11	3				
C Manufacture of wood, and wood products, including furniture	1	11	16	41	20	21	9	16	...	...	...	...
D Manufacture of paper and paper products, printing and publishing	3	15	16	24	28	41	20	38				
E Manufacture of chemicals and chemical petroleum, coal, rubber and plastic products	73	175	178	423	95	709	483	265	...	...	...	...
F Manufacture of non-metalic mineral products except products of petroleum and coal									...	...	...	...
G Basic metal industries	14	37	59	63	63	81	83	145				
H Manufacture of fabricated metal products, machinery and equipment									...	...	...	...
I Other manufacturing industries	1	5	7	7	8	15	15	16	...	...	...	...
4 Electricity, gas and water	11	40	122	226	308	225	220	241	...	...	...	...
5 Construction	18	57	117	111	87	132	98	58	...	...	...	...
6 Wholesale and retail trade, restaurants and hotels	34	156	224	165	392	378	286	812				
A Wholesale and retail trade	23	146	208	157	370	355	268	792	...	...	...	...
B Restaurants and hotels	11	11	16	8	21	23	18	20	...	...	...	...
7 Transport, storage and communication	35	124	165	201	198	530	504	392	...	...	...	...
8 Finance, insurance, real estate and business services	57	185	338	347	810	850	840	902	...	...	...	...
9 Community, social and personal services	11	34	95	128	132	152	181	195	...	...	...	...
Total Industries [a]	380	1375	1841	2336	2800	3858	3474	4101	...	...	...	...
Producers of Government Services	45	74	167	248	413	722	1067	1316	...	...	...	...
Private Non-Profit Institutions Serving Households	...	...	...	...	...	...	...	...				
Total [a]	425	1449	2008	2584	3213	4580	4541	5417	...	...	...	...

a) The estimates of this table (Gross Fixed Capital Formation by kind of activity of owner) include increase in stocks.

Trinidad and Tobago

4.3 Cost Components of Value Added

Million Trinidad and Tobago dollars

	1980						1981					
	Compensation of Employees	Capital Consumption	Net Operating Surplus	Indirect Taxes	Less: Subsidies Received	Value Added	Compensation of Employees	Capital Consumption	Net Operating Surplus	Indirect Taxes	Less: Subsidies Received	Value Added
	All Producers											
1 Agriculture, hunting, forestry and fishing	181	10	165	...	18	337	210	11	188	...	23	386
2 Mining and quarrying	213	245	5460	10	...	5928	260	249	5284	8	...	5801
3 Manufacturing	779	130	634	63	268	1338	950	156	256	69	312	1118
A Manufacture of food, beverages and tobacco	217	36	204	50	210	296	258	50	192	49	258	291
B Textile, wearing apparel and leather industries	56	3	11	3	...	73	71	4	18	-	...	93
C Manufacture of wood and wood products, including furniture	37	9	15	...	...	61	42	8	-	...	...	49
D Manufacture of paper and paper products, printing and publishing	46	4	-4	...	...	46	61	6	8	...	...	75
E Manufacture of chemicals and chemical petroleum, coal, rubber and plastic products	293	64	310	7	59	614	336	68	-49	7	53	309
F Manufacture of non-metallic mineral products, except products of petroleum and coal												
G Basic metal industries	119	11	89	3	...	222	166	18	72	11	...	267
H Manufacture of fabricated metal products, machinery and equipment												
I Other manufacturing industries	12	3	10	1	...	25	15	4	15	1	...	35
4 Electricity, gas and water	175	21	11	1	183	26	210	17	13	1	209	31
5 Construction	1115	68	680	22	...	1885	1479	62	1065	33	...	2639
6 Wholesale and retail trade, restaurants and hotels	660	71	510	497	306	1431	768	83	765	522	345	1793
A Wholesale and retail trade	583	60	461	495	306	1293	679	69	706	520	345	1628
B Restaurants and hotels	77	11	49	2	...	138	90	13	59	3	...	164
7 Transport, storage and communication	978	204	685	27	450	1444	1329	231	363	30	329	1624
8 Finance, insurance, real estate and business services	319	97	1016	2	...	1434	412	117	1309	3	...	1841
9 Community, social and personal services	518	2	194	14	...	728	560	4	230	15	...	809
Total, Industries	4938	848	9355	636	1225	14551	6178	930	9473	681	1218	16042
Producers of Government Services	1172	1	...	...	...	1174	1474	2	...	...	...	1475
Other Producers	...	...	...	...	...	...	...	...	...	...	...	...
Total	6110	849	9355	636	1225	15725	7652	932	9473	681	1218	17517
Less: Imputed bank service charge	...	...	758	...	...	758	...	...	1079	...	...	1079
Import duties	...	...	...	...	...	...	...	...	...	...	...	...
Value added tax	...	...	...	...	...	...	...	...	...	...	...	...
Total	6110	848	8597	637	1225	14966	7652	930	8394	681	1218	16438

	1982						1983					
	Compensation of Employees	Capital Consumption	Net Operating Surplus	Indirect Taxes	Less: Subsidies Received	Value Added	Compensation of Employees	Capital Consumption	Net Operating Surplus	Indirect Taxes	Less: Subsidies Received	Value Added
	All Producers											
1 Agriculture, hunting, forestry and fishing	241	13	207	...	28	433	266	14	237	...	45	472
2 Mining and quarrying	338	327	4084	11	...	4760	385	316	3203	20	...	3923
3 Manufacturing	1097	201	352	79	379	1349	1234	249	721	112	426	1891
A Manufacture of food, beverages and tobacco	298	56	261	56	290	381	350	62	511	74	422	575

Trinidad and Tobago

4.3 Cost Components of Value Added
(Continued)

Million Trinidad and Tobago dollars

1982 / 1983

	Compensation of Employees	Capital Consumption	Net Operating Surplus	Indirect Taxes	Less: Subsidies Received	Value Added	Compensation of Employees	Capital Consumption	Net Operating Surplus	Indirect Taxes	Less: Subsidies Received	Value Added
B Textile, wearing apparel and leather industries	72	4	7	1	...	83	73	4	10	1	...	88
C Manufacture of wood and wood products, including furniture	47	9	3	...	...	59	49	14	8	...	...	72
D Manufacture of paper and paper products, printing and publishing	69	7	14	...	...	90	70	7	25	...	...	103
E Manufacture of chemicals and chemical petroleum, coal, rubber and plastic products	403	101	-26	6	90	394	453	115	70	17	4	650
F Manufacture of non-metallic mineral products, except products of petroleum and coal												
G Basic metal industries	194	21	82	15	...	311	225	44	85	18	...	372
H Manufacture of fabricated metal products, machinery and equipment					...						...	
I Other manufacturing industries	15	3	13	1	...	32	15	3	13	1	...	32
4 Electricity, gas and water	305	23	52	1	384	-4	356	25	-8	2	384	-10
5 Construction	1745	50	1318	39	...	3152	1684	66	1055	35	...	2839
6 Wholesale and retail trade, restaurants and hotels	1001	110	947	622	367	2313	1053	107	747	721	100	2469
A Wholesale and retail trade	899	94	881	618	367	2125	925	89	704	719	160	2277
B Restaurants and hotels	103	16	66	4	...	188	129	18	43	2	...	192
7 Transport, storage and communication	1524	287	666	45	516	2005	1260	363	754	46	618	1805
8 Finance, insurance, real estate and business services	524	127	1513	4	...	2167	786	149	1294	9	...	2237
9 Community, social and personal services	972	3	307	19	...	1301	1022	3	336	24	...	1385
Total, Industries	7747	1141	9446	820	1674	17476	8046	1292	8339	969	1633	17011
Producers of Government Services	2866	2	...	...	...	2868	2615	2	...	...	...	2617
Other Producers	...	...	...	...	...	...	...	...	...	...	...	...
Total	10612	1143	9446	820	1674	20344	10661	1294	8339	964	1633	19628
Less: Imputed bank service charge	...	...	1168	...	...	1168	...	...	1167	...	...	1167
Import duties	...	...	...	...	...	...	...	...	...	...	...	...
Value added tax	...	...	...	...	...	...	...	...	...	...	...	...
Total	10612	1142	8278	819	1675	19176	10660	1293	7172	969	1633	18461

1984 / 1985

	Compensation of Employees	Capital Consumption	Net Operating Surplus	Indirect Taxes	Less: Subsidies Received	Value Added	Compensation of Employees	Capital Consumption	Net Operating Surplus	Indirect Taxes	Less: Subsidies Received	Value Added
					All Producers							
1 Agriculture, hunting, forestry and fishing	290	15	254	...	31	527	324	18	282	...	29	595
2 Mining and quarrying	373	324	3302	21	...	4019	367	301	3051	20	...	3740
3 Manufacturing	1204	307	762	121	375	2020	1160	300	474	135	394	1676
A Manufacture of food, beverages and tobacco	384	66	451	84	375	610	416	72	360	102	284	666

Trinidad and Tobago

4.3 Cost Components of Value Added
(Continued)

Million Trinidad and Tobago dollars

	1984						1985					
	Compensation of Employees	Capital Consumption	Net Operating Surplus	Indirect Taxes	Less: Subsidies Received	Value Added	Compensation of Employees	Capital Consumption	Net Operating Surplus	Indirect Taxes	Less: Subsidies Received	Value Added
B Textile, wearing apparel and leather industries	67	5	8	1	...	81	69	5	-15	2	...	61
C Manufacture of wood and wood products, including furniture	54	15	9	...	...	78	42	12	7	...	...	61
D Manufacture of paper and paper products, printing and publishing	65	10	24	...	...	99	64	11	33	...	...	109
E Manufacture of chemicals and chemical petroleum, coal, rubber and plastic products	412	168	179	18	-	777	378	162	11	17	110	458
F Manufacture of non-metallic mineral products, except products of petroleum and coal												
G Basic metal industries	209	41	79	16	...	345	176	35	67	14	...	292
H Manufacture of fabricated metal products, machinery and equipment					...						...	
I Other manufacturing industries	14	3	12	1	...	30	15	3	12	1	...	31
4 Electricity, gas and water	398	40	-9	2	281	151	379	42	-2	3	265	157
5 Construction	1529	65	917	32	...	2542	1356	64	812	28	...	2261
6 Wholesale and retail trade, restaurants and hotels	1221	137	621	794	16	2757	1306	174	240	885	8	2597
A Wholesale and retail trade	1090	118	588	792	16	2573	1171	154	220	883	8	2420
B Restaurants and hotels	130	18	33	2	...	184	135	20	20	2	...	177
7 Transport, storage and communication	1195	327	447	45	485	1529	1170	292	381	41	478	1406
8 Finance, insurance, real estate and business services	818	180	1198	9	...	2205	853	212	1233	9	...	2307
9 Community, social and personal services	1108	3	354	24	...	1489	1153	3	362	35	...	1553
Total, Industries	8136	1398	7847	1048	1188	17239	8068	1406	6833	1156	1174	16292
Producers of Government Services	2797	2	...	...	...	2799	2909	2	...	...	...	2911
Other Producers	...	...	...	...	...	...	...	...	...	...	...	...
Total	10933	1400	7847	1048	1188	20038	10977	1408	6832	1156	1174	19203
Less: Imputed bank service charge	...	...	1120	...	...	1120	...	...	1060	...	...	1060
Import duties	...	...	...	...	...	...	...	...	...	...	...	...
Value added tax	...	...	...	...	...	...	...	...	...	...	...	...
Total	10933	1399	6727	1047	1188	18918	10978	1407	5772	1155	1173	18140

Tunisia

Source. Reply to the United Nations National Accounts Questionnaire from the Direction de la Planification, Ministere du Plan, Tunis. The official estimates are published annually by the same Office in 'l'Economie de la Tunisie en Chiffres'.

General note. The estimates shown in the following tables have been prepared in accordance with the United Nations System of National Accounts so far as the existing data would permit.

1.1 Expenditure on the Gross Domestic Product, in Current Prices

Million Tunisian dinars

	1970	1975	1977	1978	1979	1980	1981	1982	1983	1984	1985	1986
1 Government final consumption expenditure	127.4	254.5	354.7	406.1	444.4	512.2	615.7	792.8	925.6	1038.0	1137.0	...
2 Private final consumption expenditure	502.4	1082.6	1392.4	1553.2	1763.8	2178.7	2553.7	2996.0	3434.0	3932.0	4378.0	...
3 Gross capital formation	159.8	487.9	669.5	764.0	859.6	1039.5	1345.5	1505.1	1599.0	1999.8	1776.2	...
A Increase in stocks	4.8	39.9	-2.5	-7.0	-32.4	37.5	55.5	-69.9	-86.0	119.8	46.2	...
B Gross fixed capital formation	155.0	448.0	672.0	771.0	892.0	1002.0	1290.0	1575.0	1685.0	1880.0	1730.0	...
Residential buildings	22.3	75.0	106.0	122.0	143.0	188.0	198.0	266.0	327.0	365.0	378.0	...
Non-residential buildings	...	...	...	...	...	...	...	...	...	...	...	...
Other construction and land improvement etc.	...	...	...	...	...	...	...	...	...	...	...	...
Other	...	...	...	...	...	...	...	...	...	...	...	...
4 Exports of goods and services	166.2	545.6	648.5	769.0	1139.0	1424.6	1721.9	1773.3	1947.8	2113.7	2253.1	...
5 Less: Imports of goods and services	200.2	624.2	873.1	1008.4	1285.1	1614.5	2074.3	2279.2	2421.4	2842.5	2685.3	...
Equals: Gross Domestic Product	755.6	1741.4	2191.9	2483.9	2922.0	3540.5	4162.0	4788.0	5485.0	6241.0	6859.0	...

1.2 Expenditure on the Gross Domestic Product, in Constant Prices

Million Tunisian dinars

	1970	1975	1977	1978	1979	1980	1981	1982	1983	1984	1985	1986
		At constant prices of: 1972				1980						
1 Government final consumption expenditure	140.9	205.0	442.6	460.6	465.9	512.2	555.0	594.0	634.0	664.0	685.0	...
2 Private final consumption expenditure	555.1	860.0	1736.3	1833.8	1921.4	2178.7	2336.0	2403.0	2514.0	2657.0	2748.0	...
3 Gross capital formation	163.7	245.8	874.8	969.5	1030.1	1039.1	1196.0	1195.0	1172.0	1279.0	1072.0	...
A Increase in stocks	2.4	-67.0	16.9	69.5	66.0	37.1	51.0	-14.0	10.0	49.0	17.0	...
B Gross fixed capital formation	161.3	312.8	857.9	900.0	964.1	1002.0	1144.0	1209.0	1162.0	1230.0	1055.0	...
4 Exports of goods and services	185.3	275.5	1090.6	1172.1	1423.9	1424.6	1474.0	1372.0	1385.0	1422.0	1469.0	...
5 Less: Imports of goods and services	220.7	285.4	1238.4	1342.7	1545.0	1614.5	1824.0	1841.0	1800.0	1902.0	1654.0	...
Equals: Gross Domestic Product	824.3	1227.9	2905.9	3093.3	3296.3	3540.5	3736.0	3723.0	3905.0	4120.0	4320.0	...

1.3 Cost Components of the Gross Domestic Product

Million Tunisian dinars

	1970	1975	1977	1978	1979	1980	1981	1982	1983	1984	1985	1986
1 Indirect taxes, net	102.4	205.4	322.5	357.9	415.0	476.4	521.3	573.0	738.0	828.0	887.0	...
A Indirect taxes	106.3	240.0	361.3	413.0	483.9	553.6	651.0	...	...	...	...	...
B Less: Subsidies	3.9	34.6	38.8	55.1	68.9	77.2	129.7	...	...	...	...	...
2 Consumption of fixed capital	48.0	98.3	177.0	215.0	260.0	325.0	380.0	464.0	562.0	646.0	...	...
3 Compensation of employees paid by resident producers to:	605.2	1437.7	1692.4	1911.0	2247.0	2739.1	3260.7	3751.0	4185.0	4767.0	...	...
4 Operating surplus											...	...
Equals: Gross Domestic Product	755.6	1741.4	2191.9	2483.9	2922.0	3540.5	4162.0	4788.0	5485.0	6241.0	6859.0	...

1.4 General Government Current Receipts and Disbursements

Million Tunisian dinars

	1970	1975	1977	1978	1979	1980	1981	1982	1983	1984	1985	1986
					Receipts							
1 Operating surplus	...	...	...	...	...	...						
2 Property and entrepreneurial income	10.7	20.1	32.2	56.5	80.3	80.8 / 75.5	76.3	90.8	134.8	158.1	...	...
3 Taxes, fees and contributions	183.5	471.4	613.7	742.7	895.6	1109.8 / 1062.7	1321.4	1628.0	1825.5	2105.3	...	...
A Indirect taxes	106.4	231.6	356.6	425.6	477.3	567.4 / 553.6	651.0	798.6	983.2	1126.8	...	...

Tunisia

1.4 General Government Current Receipts and Disbursements
(Continued)

Million Tunisian dinars

	1970	1975	1977	1978	1979	1980	1981	1982	1983	1984	1985	1986
B Direct taxes	55.1	185.7	178.3	229.4	294.4	401.9 / 386.5	503.1	645.6	615.1	742.3	...	...
C Social security contributions	22.0	54.1	78.8	87.7	123.9	140.5 / 122.6	167.3	183.8	227.2	236.2	...	...
D Compulsory fees, fines and penalties	...	...	...	...	...	...	...	...	...	...	...	...
4 Other current transfers	1.8	6.9	17.3	21.1	38.6	56.9 / 44.8	28.2	21.8	28.7	28.9	...	...
Total Current Receipts of General Government [a]	196.0	498.4	663.2	820.3	1014.5	1247.5 / 1183.0	1425.9	1740.6	1989.0	2292.3	...	...

Disbursements

	1970	1975	1977	1978	1979	1980	1981	1982	1983	1984	1985	1986
1 Government final consumption expenditure	130.8	250.2	354.6	405.0	448.0	510.0 / 533.9	634.7	815.1	950.9	1067.7	...	...
2 Property income	9.9	17.2	21.5	30.3	44.9	57.4 / 57.6	63.3	87.9	105.8	130.9	...	...
3 Subsidies	4.7	16.9	43.0	56.7	71.1	85.6 / 77.2	129.7	190.8	183.2	280.6	...	...
4 Other current transfers	24.1	89.6	76.7	105.6	127.6	277.4 / 119.3	200.5	196.1	220.6	267.8	...	...
A Social security benefits	13.7	29.2	29.8	54.0	63.2	75.7 / 78.7	108.5	128.0	155.7	187.4	...	...
B Social assistance grants	7.8	58.3	40.2	37.6	40.8	47.1 / 29.8	77.7	59.0	58.2	73.1	...	...
C Other	2.6	2.1	6.7	14.0	23.6	154.6 / 10.8	14.3	9.1	6.7	7.3	...	...
5 Net saving	26.5	124.5	167.4	222.7	322.9	317.1 / 395.0	397.7	450.7	528.5	545.3	...	...
Total Current Disbursements and Net Saving of General Government [a]	196.0	498.4	663.2	820.3	1014.5	1247.5 / 1183.0	1425.9	1740.6	1989.0	2292.3	...	...

a) Data for this table have not been revised, therefore, data for some years are not comparable with those of other tables.

1.7 External Transactions on Current Account, Summary

Million Tunisian dinars

	1970	1975	1977	1978	1979	1980	1981	1982	1983	1984	1985	1986
Payments to the Rest of the World												
1 Imports of goods and services	200.2	624.2	873.1	1008.4	1285.1	1614.5	2074.3	2279.2	2421.4	2842.5	2685.3	...
A Imports of merchandise c.i.f.	167.7	572.8	782.4	899.7	1156.8	1467.1	1866.0	2002.0	2116.0	2481.9	2237.0	...
B Other	32.5	51.4	90.9	101.5	128.3	147.4	208.3	277.2	315.0	360.6	448.3	...
2 Factor income to the rest of the world	39.4	75.0	97.3	104.8	135.0	166.2	213.0	250.6	259.8	291.2	...	...
A Compensation of employees	14.9	11.3	13.6	8.8	8.1	8.1	5.7	6.9	6.3	5.0	...	...
B Property and entrepreneurial income	24.5	68.9	83.7	96.0	126.9	158.1	207.3	243.7	253.5	286.2	...	...
3 Current transfers to the rest of the world	2.2	5.7	7.2	8.6	5.8	...	...	...	...	...	...	...
4 Surplus of the nation on current transactions	-49.2	-85.1	-243.6	-242.6	-140.5	-167.7	-320.5	-453.3	-409.5	-680.0	-490.0	...
Payments to the Rest of the World and Surplus of the Nation on Current Transactions	192.7	619.8	734.2	878.9	1285.4	1613.0	1966.8	2076.5	2271.7	2453.7	...	...
Receipts From The Rest of the World												
1 Exports of goods and services	166.2	545.6	648.5	769.0	1139.0	1424.6	1721.9	1773.3	1947.8	2113.7	2253.1	...
A Exports of merchandise f.o.b.	98.8	345.6	398.3	468.4	726.7	970.0	1212.4	1169.4	1262.6	1399.1	1443.0	...
B Other	67.4	200.0	250.2	300.6	412.3	454.6	509.5	603.9	679.9	714.6	810.1	...
2 Factor income from rest of the world	19.0	74.6	78.9	100.9	136.4	188.4	244.9	303.2	323.9	340.0	...	...
A Compensation of employees	15.2	58.7	72.2	91.8	115.5	122.8	178.3	219.6	243.8	245.9	...	...
B Property and entrepreneurial income	3.8	16.8	6.7	9.1	20.9	65.6	66.6	83.6	80.1	94.1	...	...
3 Current transfers from rest of the world	7.4	4.7	6.8	9.0	10.0	...	...	...	...	...	...	...
Receipts from the Rest of the World on Current Transactions	192.7	619.8	734.2	878.9	1285.4	1613.0	1966.8	2076.5	2271.7	2453.7	...	...

Tunisia

1.10 Gross Domestic Product by Kind of Activity, in Current Prices

Million Tunisian dinars

	1970	1975	1977	1978	1979	1980	1981	1982	1983	1984	1985	1986
1 Agriculture, hunting, forestry and fishing	128.7	321.8	346.7	374.8	395.7	500.3	569.0	632.0	677.0	823.0	1040.0	...
2 Mining and quarrying	40.7	166.9	155.2	169.8	267.2	422.9	514.2	561.0	610.0	669.0	697.0	...
3 Manufacturing	63.5	158.1	231.3	274.8	338.1	417.3	494.0	536.0	614.0	731.0	827.0	...
4 Electricity, gas and water [a]	13.1	25.9	33.2	38.7	47.7	53.5	62.0	66.0	82.0	89.0	103.0	...
5 Construction	38.2	100.6	144.7	171.7	190.6	207.8	262.0	310.0	350.0	385.0	392.0	...
6 Wholesale and retail trade, restaurants and hotels [b]	148.1	355.7	405.6	449.8	517.3	621.7	743.0	901.0	1007.0	1142.0	1263.0	...
7 Transport, storage and communication	46.4	82.6	123.9	147.1	163.8	170.2	194.0	227.0	280.0	336.0	365.0	...
8 Finance, insurance, real estate and business services [cd]	53.8	75.0	100.5	118.6	139.0	163.0	194.0	221.0	240.0	249.0	272.0	...
9 Community, social and personal services [d]	17.0	61.7	73.2	89.9	118.3	138.9	161.0	185.0	213.0	197.0	222.0	...
Total, Industries	549.5	1348.3	1614.3	1835.2	2177.7	2695.6	3193.0	3639.0	4073.0	4621.0	5181.0	...
Producers of Government Services	103.7	187.7	255.1	290.8	328.6	368.5	448.0	571.0	671.0	792.0	850.0	...
Other Producers	...	...	...	...	...	...	...	...	...	...	...	...
Subtotal [e]	653.2	1536.0	1869.4	2126.0	2506.3	3064.1	3641.0	4210.0	4744.0	5413.0	6031.0	...
Less: Imputed bank service charge	...	...	...	...	...	...	...	...	...	...	...	...
Plus: Import duties	...	...	...	...	...	...	...	...	...	...	...	...
Plus: Value added tax	...	...	...	...	...	...	...	...	...	...	...	...
Plus: Other adjustments [f]	102.4	205.4	322.5	357.9	415.0	476.4	521.3	573.0	738.0	828.0	828.0	...
Equals: Gross Domestic Product	755.6	1741.4	2191.9	2483.9	2922.0	3540.5	4162.0	4788.0	5485.0	6241.0	6859.0	...

a) Item 'Electricity, gas and water' excludes gas.
b) Restaurants and hotels are included in item 'Community, social and personal services'.
c) Real estate refers to owner-occupied dwellings and rent only.
d) Finance, insurance and business services are included in item 'Community, social and personal services'.
e) Gross domestic product in factor values.
f) Item 'Other adjustments' refers to indirect taxes net of subsidies.

1.11 Gross Domestic Product by Kind of Activity, in Constant Prices

Million Tunisian dinars

	1970	1975	1977	1978	1979	1980	1981	1982	1983	1984	1985	1986
	At constant prices of: 1972					1980						
1 Agriculture, hunting, forestry and fishing	146.0	245.8	451.5	478.2	455.4	500.3	533.0	478.0	490.0	555.0	636.0	...
2 Mining and quarrying	51.1	62.9	325.6	367.8	403.8	422.9	413.0	395.0	431.0	422.0	409.0	...
3 Manufacturing	63.4	114.9	305.3	326.6	362.4	417.3	469.0	482.0	521.0	556.0	587.0	...
4 Electricity, gas and water [a]	13.1	19.9	38.7	42.5	48.8	53.5	58.5	61.0	67.0	72.0	76.0	...
5 Construction	50.6	63.4	168.2	174.6	195.6	207.8	237.0	245.0	250.0	258.0	256.0	...
6 Wholesale and retail trade, restaurants and hotels [b]	109.7	254.6	497.1	534.6	573.2	621.7	660.3	685.0	718.0	760.0	780.0	...
7 Transport, storage and communication	50.0	66.1	136.7	146.0	162.0	170.2	179.0	178.0	185.0	205.0	208.0	...
8 Finance, insurance, real estate and business services [cd]	53.8	69.8	137.7	145.4	153.9	163.0	170.0	176.0	183.0	190.0	197.0	...
9 Community, social and personal services [d]	66.2	45.9	94.6	102.1	129.6	138.9	143.8	130.0	121.0	121.0	148.0	...
Total, Industries	603.9	943.3	2154.8	2317.8	2485.2	2695.6	2863.6	2830.0	2966.0	3139.0	3297.0	...
Producers of Government Services	112.0	141.1	320.5	323.5	337.7	368.5	405.6	427.0	451.0	467.0	481.0	...
Other Producers	...	...	...	...	...	...	...	...	...	...	...	...
Subtotal [e]	715.9	1084.4	2475.3	2641.3	2822.9	3064.1	3269.2	3257.0	3417.0	3606.0	3778.0	...
Less: Imputed bank service charge	...	...	...	...	...	...	...	...	...	...	...	...
Plus: Import duties	...	...	...	...	...	...	...	...	...	...	...	...
Plus: Value added tax	...	...	...	...	...	...	...	...	...	...	...	...
Plus: Other adjustments [f]	108.4	143.5	430.6	452.0	473.4	476.4	467.4	466.0	488.0	516.0	541.0	...
Equals: Gross Domestic Product	824.3	1227.9	2905.9	3093.3	3296.3	3540.5	3736.6	3723.0	3905.0	4120.0	4320.0	...

a) Item 'Electricity, gas and water' excludes gas.
b) Restaurants and hotels are included in item 'Community, social and personal services'.
c) Real estate refers to owner-occupied dwellings and rent only.
d) Finance, insurance and business services are included in item 'Community, social and personal services'.
e) Gross domestic product in factor values.
f) Item 'Other adjustments' refers to indirect taxes net of subsidies.

Tunisia

1.12 Relations Among National Accounting Aggregates

Million Tunisian dinars

	1970	1975	1977	1978	1979	1980	1981	1982	1983	1984	1985	1986
Gross Domestic Product	755.6	1741.4	2191.9	2483.9	2922.0	3540.5	4162.0	4788.0	5485.0	6241.0	...	...
Plus: Net factor income from the rest of the world	-20.4	-0.4	-18.4	-3.9	1.4	22.2	31.9	52.6	64.1	48.8	...	...
Factor income from the rest of the world	19.0	74.6	78.9	100.9	136.4	188.4	244.9	303.2	323.9	340.0	...	...
Less: Factor income to the rest of the world	39.4	75.0	97.3	104.8	135.0	166.2	213.0	250.6	259.8	291.2	...	...
Equals: Gross National Product	735.2	1741.0	2173.5	2480.0	2923.4	3562.7	4193.9	4840.6	5549.1	6289.8	...	...
Less: Consumption of fixed capital	48.0	98.3	177.0	215.0	260.0	325.0	380.0	464.0	562.0	646.0	...	...
Equals: National Income	687.2	1642.7	1996.5	2265.0	2663.4	3237.7	3813.9	4376.6	4987.1	5643.8	...	...
Plus: Net current transfers from the rest of the world	5.3	-1.0	-0.4	0.4	4.2	...	...	...	...	...	...	...
Current transfers from the rest of the world	7.4	4.7	6.8	9.0	10.0	...	...	...	...	...	...	...
Less: Current transfers to the rest of the world	2.2	5.7	7.2	8.6	5.8	...	...	...	...	...	...	...
Equals: National Disposable Income	692.5	1641.7	1996.1	2265.4	2667.6	3237.7	3813.9	4376.6	4987.1	5643.8	...	...
Less: Final consumption	629.8	1337.1	1747.1	1959.3	2208.2	2690.9	3169.4	3788.8	4359.6	4970.0	...	...
Equals: Net Saving	62.7	304.6	249.0	306.1	459.4	546.8	644.5	587.8	627.5	673.8	...	...
Less: Surplus of the nation on current transactions	-49.2	-85.1	-243.6	-242.9	-140.5	-167.7	-320.5	-453.3	-409.5	-680.0	...	...
Equals: Net Capital Formation	111.9	389.7	492.6	549.0	599.9	714.5	965.0	1041.1	1037.0	1353.8	...	...

2.11 Gross Fixed Capital Formation by Kind of Activity of Owner, ISIC Divisions, in Current Prices

Million Tunisian dinars

	1970	1975	1977	1978	1979	1980	1981	1982	1983	1984	1985	1986
					All Producers							
1 Agriculture, hunting, forestry and fishing	13.8	40.7	46.5	59.6	108.5 / 110.5	149.5	178.1	205.0	259.0	274.0	...	...
2 Mining and quarrying	14.3	75.5	91.7	112.9	123.9 / 123.9	120.1	226.6	300.0	198.0	192.0	...	...
3 Manufacturing	17.8	83.3	125.1	166.5	162.1 / 165.8	133.9	216.0	289.5	361.5	360.0	...	...
4 Electricity, gas and water	10.0	35.0	55.8	48.8	104.4 / 104.4	71.9	89.4	113.0	151.0	216.0	...	...
5 Construction	...	6.0	3.0	2.0	1.0 / 9.8	10.2	12.0	13.0	15.0	20.0	...	...
6 Wholesale and retail trade, restaurants and hotels	13.6	10.6	12.1	16.8	16.3 / 5.4	6.5	3.5	7.0	10.0	18.0	...	...
7 Transport, storage and communication	12.8	51.2	82.1	71.9	138.0 / 125.5	211.0	235.4	269.0	203.0	222.0	...	...
8 Finance, insurance, real estate and business services	26.5	82.5	91.5	101.0	... / 143.0	188.0	198.0	230.0	283.0	325.0	...	...
9 Community, social and personal services	-	4.5	16.5	20.0	3.4 / 16.3	25.5	33.0	43.0	73.0	90.0	...	...
Total Industries	108.8	389.3	524.3	599.5	657.7 / 804.6	916.6	1192.0	1469.5	1553.5	1717.0	...	...
Producers of Government Services	...	...	...	...	...	...	...	...	...	...	...	...
Private Non-Profit Institutions Serving Households	42.7	77.7	110.7	125.5	236.3 / 87.4	85.4	98.0	105.5	131.5	163.0	...	...
Total [a]	151.5	461.0	665.0	764.0	894.0 / 892.0	1002.0	1290.0	1575.0	1685.0	1880.0	...	...

a) Data for this table have not been revised, therefore, data for some years are not comparable with those of other tables.

2.17 Exports and Imports of Goods and Services, Detail

Million Tunisian dinars

	1970	1975	1977	1978	1979	1980	1981	1982	1983	1984	1985	1986
					Exports of Goods and Services							
1 Exports of merchandise, f.o.b.	98.8	345.6	398.3	468.4	726.7	970.0 / 970.0	1212.4	1169.4	1262.6	1399.1	...	...
2 Transport and communication	13.6	44.2	50.6	62.6	...	104.0	122.3	150.1	153.1	157.6	...	...
3 Insurance service charges					...						...	...
4 Other commodities	31.6	119.0	135.0	166.7	...	276.5	312.3	367.2	416.0	390.0	...	...

Tunisia

2.17 Exports and Imports of Goods and Services, Detail
(Continued)

Million Tunisian dinars

	1970	1975	1977	1978	1979	1980	1981	1982	1983	1984	1985	1986
5 Adjustments of merchandise exports to change-of-ownership basis	...	...	...	...	...	... ...	...	...	...	...	...	...
6 Direct purchases in the domestic market by non-residential households [a]	22.0	36.8	64.6	71.3	...	... 29.5	44.2	42.5	57.2	102.0	...	...
7 Direct purchases in the domestic market by extraterritorial bodies	...	...	...	...	...	... 44.6	30.7	44.1	53.6	65.0	...	...
Total Exports of Goods and Services	166.2	545.6	648.5	769.0	1139.0	1424.6 1424.6	1721.9	1773.3	1942.5	2113.7	...	...
Imports of Goods and Services												
1 Imports of merchandise, c.i.f.	167.7	572.8	782.4	906.9	1156.8	1467.1 1467.1	1866.0	2002.0	2116.0	2481.9	...	...
A Imports of merchandise, f.o.b.	154.5	521.8	742.6	860.0	1098.0	1398.6 1398.6	1771.2	1900.8	1996.2	2353.9	...	...
B Transport of services on merchandise imports	13.2	51.0	39.8	46.9	58.8	68.5[b] 68.5	94.8	101.2	119.8	128.0	...	...
C Insurance service charges on merchandise imports						... ...						
2 Adjustments of merchandise imports to change-of-ownership basis	...	...	...	...	...	... ...	...	...	...	...	...	...
3 Other transport and communication	12.3	9.5	40.2	40.2	...	... 132.8	173.0	200.7	217.9	230.1	...	...
4 Other insurance service charges	...	...	...	...	...	... 39.9	76.1	90.5	124.9	148.6	...	...
5 Other commodities [c]	12.1	22.8	26.9	36.3	37.4	43.2 43.2	54.0	87.2	92.0	109.9	...	...
6 Direct purchases abroad by government	8.1	24.6	23.8	25.0	...	... ...	...	...	...	...	...	...
7 Direct purchases abroad by resident households					...	... ...	...	...	...	...	...	...
Total Imports of Goods and Services	200.2	629.7	873.3	1008.4	1285.0	1614.5 1614.5	2074.3	2279.2	2431.0	2842.5	...	...
Balance of Goods and Services	-34.0	-84.1	-224.8	-239.4	-146.0	-189.9 -189.9	-352.4	-505.9	-488.5	-728.8	...	...
Total Imports and Balance of Goods and Services [d]	166.2	545.6	648.5	769.0	1139.0	1424.6 1424.6	1721.9	1773.3	1942.5	2113.7	...	...

a) Item 'Direct purchases in the domestic market by non-residential households' refers to governmental and other services.
b) Including item 'Transport of services on merchandise imports' through 'Insurance service charges on merchandise imports'.
c) Item 'Other commodities' refers to tourism and travel.
d) Data for this table have not been revised, therefore, data for some years are not comparable with those of other tables.

Turkey

Source. Reply to the United Nations National Accounts Questionnaire from the State Institute of Statistics, Ankara. Methods of estimation, explanatory notes and primary sources are described annually in 'National Income of Turkey'.

General note. The official estimates have been prepared by the Institute to conform to the United Nations System of National Accounts so far as the existing data would permit.

1.1 Expenditure on the Gross Domestic Product, in Current Prices

Thousand Million Turkish liras

	1970	1975	1977	1978	1979	1980	1981	1982	1983	1984	1985	1986
1 Government final consumption expenditure	19	64	116	173	294	544	700	939	1176	1621	2332	3444
2 Private final consumption expenditure	102	366	573	846	1445	2992	4514	6160	8527	13646	20181	27052
3 Gross capital formation	29	132	244	306	507	1143	1570	1770	2259	3621	5802	9704
A Increase in stocks [a]	2	22	33	26	58	280	329	123	129	263	240	458
B Gross fixed capital formation [a]	27	111	211	280	449	864	1241	1647	2130	3358	5561	9246
Residential buildings	5	...	...	...	...	...	...	...	...	...	...	...
Non-residential buildings	6	...	...	...	...	...	...	...	...	...	...	...
Other construction and land improvement etc.	7	...	...	...	...	...	...	...	...	...	...	...
Other	9	...	...	...	...	...	...	...	...	...	...	...
4 Exports of goods and services	9	31	46	75	126	317	715	1275	1780	3559	5927	...
5 Less: Imports of goods and services	12	74	116	125	216	668	1085	1523	2210	4235	6690	...
Equals: Gross Domestic Product [b]	145	519	863	1275	2156	4328	6414	8620	11532	18212	27552	39155

a) Item 'Breeding stocks, dairy cattle, etc.' is included in item 'Increase in stocks'.
b) Data in this table have been revised, therefore they are not strictly comparable with the unrevised data in the other tables.

1.2 Expenditure on the Gross Domestic Product, in Constant Prices

Million Turkish liras

	1970	1975	1977	1978	1979	1980	1981	1982	1983	1984	1985	1986
	1968	\multicolumn{5}{c}{At constant prices of:}		1982					
1 Government final consumption expenditure	15541	656	751	825	839	913	921	939	955	984	1016	1105
2 Private final consumption expenditure	86238	5667	6656	6397	6199	5876	5911	6160	6468	6798	7002	7681
3 Gross capital formation	25045	1643	1883	1567	1558	1703	1795	1770	1863	2006	2201	2547
A Increase in stocks	1562	5	-121	-237	-182	138	204	123	167	217	187	255
B Gross fixed capital formation	23483	1638	2004	1804	1739	1565	1592	1647	1696	1789	2015	2292
Residential buildings	4723	...	...	...	...	...	...	...	...	...	...	...
Non-residential buildings	5020	...	...	...	...	...	...	...	...	...	...	...
Other construction and land improvement etc.	5939	...	...	...	...	...	...	...	...	...	...	...
Other	7801	...	...	...	...	...	...	...	...	...	...	...
4 Exports of goods and services	7298	501	539	609	534	574	931	1275	1460	1771	2041	...
5 Less: Imports of goods and services	10174	1610	2053	1400	1202	1198	1348	1523	1807	2106	2322	...
Equals: Gross Domestic Product	123948	6857	7776	7997	7927	7868	8211	8620	8940	9453	9937	10755

1.3 Cost Components of the Gross Domestic Product

Thousand Million Turkish liras

	1970	1975	1977	1978	1979	1980	1981	1982	1983	1984	1985	1986
1 Indirect taxes, net [a]	14	51	67	85	141	230	390	540	714	863	2026	3660
A Indirect taxes [a]	16	53	79	102	165	306	498	648	911	1206	2479	4003
B Less: Subsidies [a]	2	3	13	18	25	76	108	108	197	343	453	343
2 Consumption of fixed capital	9	30	48	71	121	242	358	477	630	1001	1515	2134
3 Compensation of employees paid by resident producers to:	42	141	236	349	...	...	...	...	...	...	...	...
A Resident households	42	140	232	347	...	...	...	...	...	...	...	...
B Rest of the world	-	1	5	2	...	...	...	...	...	...	...	...
4 Operating surplus	80	297	511	770	...	...	...	...	...	...	...	...
Equals: Gross Domestic Product	145	519	863	1275	2156	4328	6414	8620	11532	18212	27552	39155

a) The estimates of indirect taxes and subsidies are entered on accrual payment basis.

Turkey

1.4 General Government Current Receipts and Disbursements

Thousand Million Turkish liras

	1970	1975	1977	1978	1979	1980	1981	1982	1983	1984	1985	1986
Receipts												
1 Operating surplus	...	...	...	...	...	...	...	...	...	...	...	...
2 Property and entrepreneurial income	2	...	...	...	...	...	...	...	...	...	...	...
3 Taxes, fees and contributions	30	...	...	...	...	...	...	...	...	...	...	...
A Indirect taxes [a]	16	...	...	...	...	...	...	...	...	...	...	...
B Direct taxes	9	...	...	...	...	...	...	...	...	...	...	...
C Social security contributions	5	...	...	...	...	...	...	...	...	...	...	...
D Compulsory fees, fines and penalties	...	...	...	...	...	...	...	...	...	...	...	...
4 Other current transfers	3	...	...	...	...	...	...	...	...	...	...	...
Total Current Receipts of General Government	34	...	...	...	...	...	...	...	...	...	...	...
Disbursements												
1 Government final consumption expenditure	19	...	...	...	...	...	...	...	...	...	...	...
A Compensation of employees	14	...	...	...	...	...	...	...	...	...	...	...
B Consumption of fixed capital	-	...	...	...	...	...	...	...	...	...	...	...
C Purchases of goods and services, net	5	...	...	...	...	...	...	...	...	...	...	...
D Less: Own account fixed capital formation	...	...	...	...	...	...	...	...	...	...	...	...
E Indirect taxes paid, net	-	...	...	...	...	...	...	...	...	...	...	...
2 Property income	1	...	...	...	...	...	...	...	...	...	...	...
3 Subsidies [a]	2	...	...	...	...	...	...	...	...	...	...	...
4 Other current transfers	3	...	...	...	...	...	...	...	...	...	...	...
A Social security benefits	2	...	...	...	...	...	...	...	...	...	...	...
B Social assistance grants	...	...	...	...	...	...	...	...	...	...	...	...
C Other	1	...	...	...	...	...	...	...	...	...	...	...
5 Net saving	11	...	...	...	...	...	...	...	...	...	...	...
Total Current Disbursements and Net Saving of General Government	34	...	...	...	...	...	...	...	...	...	...	...

a) The estimates of indirect taxes and subsidies are entered on cash payment basis.

1.7 External Transactions on Current Account, Summary

Thousand Million Turkish liras

	1970	1975	1977	1978	1979	1980	1981	1982	1983	1984	1985	1986
Payments to the Rest of the World												
1 Imports of goods and services	12	76	113	122	197	...	...	...	...	...	...	...
A Imports of merchandise c.i.f.	11	69	105	113	179	...	...	...	...	...	...	...
B Other	2	7	8	8	19	...	...	...	...	...	...	...
2 Factor income to the rest of the world	1	3	14	13	21	...	...	...	...	...	...	...
A Compensation of employees	-	1	5	2	-	...	...	...	...	...	...	...
B Property and entrepreneurial income	1	2	9	11	21	...	...	...	...	...	...	...
3 Current transfers to the rest of the world				-	*	...	...	...	...	...	...	...
A Indirect taxes to supranational organizations	...	...	...	...	...	...	...	...	...	...	...	...
B Other current transfers	-	-	-	-	-	...	...	...	...	...	...	...
4 Surplus of the nation on current transactions	-1	-27	-61	-34	-45	...	...	...	...	...	...	...
Payments to the Rest of the World and Surplus of the Nation on Current Transactions	13	51	66	101	173	...	...	...	...	...	...	...
Receipts From The Rest of the World												
1 Exports of goods and services	9	34	42	72	108	...	...	...	...	...	...	...
A Exports of merchandise f.o.b.	7	20	31	55	76	...	...	...	...	...	...	...

Turkey

1.7 External Transactions on Current Account, Summary
(Continued)

Thousand Million Turkish liras

	1970	1975	1977	1978	1979	1980	1981	1982	1983	1984	1985	1986
B Other	2	13	10	16	32	...	...	...	...	...	...	...
2 Factor income from rest of the world	4	16	22	26	60	...	...	...	...	...	...	...
A Compensation of employees	4	16	21	25	59	...	...	...	...	...	...	...
B Property and entrepreneurial income	-	-	-	2	1	...	...	...	...	...	...	...
3 Current transfers from rest of the world	1	2	2	4	5	...	...	...	...	...	...	...
A Subsidies from supranational organisations	...	...	...	...	...	...	...	...	...	...	...	...
B Other current transfers	1	2	2	4	5	...	...	...	...	...	...	...
Receipts from the Rest of the World on Current Transactions	13	51	66	101	173	...	...	...	...	...	...	...

1.10 Gross Domestic Product by Kind of Activity, in Current Prices

Thousand Million Turkish liras

	1970	1975	1977	1978	1979	1980	1981	1982	1983	1984	1985	1986
1 Agriculture, hunting, forestry and fishing	39	139	224	306	473	940	1351	1710	2162	3465	4891	6621
2 Mining and quarrying	2	6	10	13	23	65	128	168	242	371	646	792
3 Manufacturing	27	98	154	264	470	971	1510	2080	2911	4642	6953	10236
4 Electricity, gas and water	2	8	15	22	33	86	131	211	265	520	1155	1761
5 Construction	10	25	43	66	106	218	293	366	459	717	1045	1573
6 Wholesale and retail trade, restaurants and hotels [a]	17	70	113	173	311	667	1029	1403	1933	3176	4763	6706
7 Transport, storage and communication	11	44	73	112	205	419	640	859	1155	1797	2741	3824
8 Finance, insurance, real estate and business services [b]	12	39	68	97	150	324	484	624	826	1344	1984	2832
9 Community, social and personal services [ab]	8	27	44	67	112	233	351	469	629	1012	1526	2168
Total, Industries	128	457	745	1121	1883	3924	5917	7889	10583	17044	25704	36513
Producers of Government Services	14	51	101	133	235	378	481	687	861	1056	1441	2073
Other Producers	...	...	...	...	...	...	...	...	...	...	...	...
Subtotal	142	507	847	1254	2119	4301	6398	8576	11444	18100	27145	38586
Less: Imputed bank service charge	2	9	15	19	28	59	98	121	160	275	416	589
Plus: Import duties	6	21	31	40	66	86	113	166	248	387	823	1158
Plus: Value added tax	...	...	...	...	...	...	...	...	...	...	...	...
Equals: Gross Domestic Product [c]	145	519	863	1275	2156	4328	6414	8620	11532	18212	27552	39155

a) Restaurants and hotels are included in item 'Community, social and personal services'.
b) Business services are included in item 'Community, social and personal services'.
c) Data in this table have been revised, therefore they are not strictly comparable with the unrevised data in the other tables.

1.11 Gross Domestic Product by Kind of Activity, in Constant Prices

Million Turkish liras

	1970	1975	1977	1978	1979	1980	1981	1982	1983	1984	1985	1986
					At constant prices of:1968							
1 Agriculture, hunting, forestry and fishing	32870	40889	43506	44745	45989	46766	46829	49722	49690	51426	52841	56701
2 Mining and quarrying	2165	2979	3386	3553	3713	3782	4067	4081	3995	4138	4618	5283
3 Manufacturing	24252	38478	44709	46131	43317	41619	45549	48473	52089	56908	60151	66467
4 Electricity, gas and water	1615	2811	3671	3862	4020	4148	4428	4918	5043	5447	6078	6984
5 Construction	8304	10532	12045	12545	13069	13173	13232	13298	13378	13645	14041	15187
6 Wholesale and retail trade, restaurants and hotels [a]	14270	24313	27779	28694	27909	27100	28942	30389	32274	34759	37018	40638
7 Transport, storage and communication	10095	16557	19399	19820	19239	18450	19122	19485	20030	21378	22512	24043
8 Finance, insurance, real estate and business services [b]	10066	13838	16343	17052	17652	18218	18648	19074	19442	20116	20707	21441
9 Community, social and personal services [ab]	6403	9202	10267	10596	10501	10396	10853	11377	11774	12491	13105	14246
Total, Industries	110040	159599	181105	186998	185409	183652	191670	200817	207716	220307	231071	250990
Producers of Government Services	11518	15471	17546	18629	19415	20546	21367	22521	23467	24070	24864	25774
Other Producers	...	...	...	...	...	...	...	...	...	...	...	...
Subtotal	121558	175070	198651	205627	204824	204198	213037	223338	231183	244377	255935	276764
Less: Imputed bank service charge	1964	2960	3508	3677	3787	3855	3928	3991	4011	4192	4338	4498
Plus: Import duties	4355	5651	6434	5364	4450	3613	3732	4121	4570	4853	5949	6495
Plus: Value added tax	...	...	...	...	...	...	...	...	...	...	...	...
Equals: Gross Domestic Product	123949	177761	201577	207314	205487	203956	212841	223468	231742	245038	257546	278761

a) Restaurants and hotels are included in item 'Community, social and personal services'.
b) Business services are included in item 'Community, social and personal services'.

Turkey

1.12 Relations Among National Accounting Aggregates

Thousand Million Turkish liras

	1970	1975	1977	1978	1979	1980	1981	1982	1983	1984	1985	1986
Gross Domestic Product	145	519	863	1275	2156	4328	6414	8620	11532	18212	27552	39155
Plus: Net factor income from the rest of the world	2	17	10	16	44	107	140	115	20	163	238	22
Factor income from the rest of the world	4	19	18	26	64	158	275	...	...	...	...	...
Less: Factor income to the rest of the world	1	2	8	11	22	55	138	...	...	...	...	...
Equals: Gross National Product	148	536	873	1291	2200	4435	6554	8735	11552	18375	27789	39177
Less: Consumption of fixed capital	9	30	48	71	121	242	358	477	630	1001	1515	2134
Equals: National Income	139	506	825	1220	2079	4193	6196	8258	10922	17374	26275	37043
Plus: Net current transfers from the rest of the world	1	2	...	...	...	-	-	-	-	-	-	-
Current transfers from the rest of the world	1	2	2	4	5	...	...	...	...	...	...	...
Less: Current transfers to the rest of the world	-	-	-	-	...	...	...	...	...	...	...	...
Equals: National Disposable Income	139	506	825	1220	2079	4193	6196	8258	10922	17374	26275	37043
Less: Final consumption	121	430	690	1019	1739	3536	5214	7099	9703	15268	22513	30496
Equals: Net Saving	19	76	135	201	340	657	982	1159	1220	2106	3762	6547
Less: Surplus of the nation on current transactions	-1	-27	-60	-34	-47	-244	-231	-134	-410	-513	-525	-1023
Equals: Net Capital Formation [a]	20	102	196	235	387	901	1213	1294	1629	2619	4287	7570

a) Data in this table have been revised, therefore they are not strictly comparable with the unrevised data in the other tables.

2.1 Government Final Consumption Expenditure by Function, in Current Prices

Thousand Million Turkish liras

	1970	1975	1977	1978	1979	1980	1981	1982	1983	1984	1985	1986
1 General public services [a]	5	...	...	...	...	...	...	...	...	...	...	...
2 Defence	5	...	...	...	...	...	...	...	...	...	...	...
3 Public order and safety [a]	...	...	...	...	...	...	...	...	...	...	...	...
4 Education	3	...	...	...	...	...	...	...	...	...	...	...
5 Health	2	...	...	...	...	...	...	...	...	...	...	...
6 Social security and welfare	-	...	...	...	...	...	...	...	...	...	...	...
7 Housing and community amenities	...	...	...	...	...	...	...	...	...	...	...	...
8 Recreational, cultural and religious affairs [b]	2	...	...	...	...	...	...	...	...	...	...	...
9 Economic services	2	...	...	...	...	...	...	...	...	...	...	...
10 Other functions	-	...	...	...	...	...	...	...	...	...	...	...
Total Government Final Consumption Expenditure	19	...	...	...	...	...	...	...	...	...	...	...

a) Item 'Public order and safety' is included in item 'General public services'.
b) Item 'Recreational, cultural and religious affairs' refers to Social and other community services.

2.7 Gross Capital Formation by Type of Good and Owner, in Current Prices

Thousand Million Turkish liras

	1980				1981				1982			
	TOTAL	Total Private	Public Enterprises	General Government	TOTAL	Total Private	Public Enterprises	General Government	TOTAL	Total Private	Public Enterprises	General Government
Increase in stocks, total	61	16	...	45	198	66	...	131	45	-7	...	51
1 Goods producing industries [ab]	43	16	...	27	167	66	...	101	3	-7	...	10
A Materials and supplies	15	-3	...	18	68	23	...	45	36	12	...	24
B Work in progress	3	6	...	-3	-8	-12	...	4	53	56	...	-3
C Livestock, except breeding stocks, dairy cattle, etc. [b]	-	-	...	-	-	...	...	-	-	-	...	-
D Finished goods	25	12	...	12	108	56	...	52	-86	-75	...	-11
2 Wholesale and retail trade [c]	18	-	...	18	24	-	...	24	32	-	...	32
3 Other, except government stocks	-	-	...	-	7	-	...	7	9	-	...	9
4 Government stocks	...	...	...	...	...	...	...	...	...	...	...	...
Gross Fixed Capital Formation, Total	690	211	...	479	1218	474	...	744	1636	659	...	977

1491

Turkey

2.7 Gross Capital Formation by Type of Good and Owner, in Current Prices
(Continued)

Thousand Million Turkish liras

	1980 TOTAL	1980 Total Private	1980 Public Enterprises	1980 General Government	1981 TOTAL	1981 Total Private	1981 Public Enterprises	1981 General Government	1982 TOTAL	1982 Total Private	1982 Public Enterprises	1982 General Government
1 Residential buildings	174	169	...	5	236	221	...	14	221	194	...	27
2 Non-residential buildings	119	27	...	92	243	35	...	208	403	42	...	360
3 Other construction	171	1	...	170	252	1	...	251	229	4	...	225
4 Land improvement and plantation and orchard development	...	...	...	...	...	...	...	...	...	...	...	...
5 Producers' durable goods	226	15	...	211	487	217	...	270	784	419	...	365
6 Breeding stock, dairy cattle, etc. [b]	...	...	...	...	...	...	...	...	...	...	...	...
Total Gross Capital Formation	751	227	...	524	1416	541	...	875	1680	652	...	1028

	1983 TOTAL	1983 Total Private	1983 Public Enterprises	1983 General Government	1984 TOTAL	1984 Total Private	1984 Public Enterprises	1984 General Government
Increase in stocks, total	...	...	...	...	...	...	...	...
1 Goods producing industries [a,b]	...	...	...	...	...	...	...	...
A Materials and supplies	...	...	...	...	...	...	...	...
B Work in progress	...	...	...	...	...	...	...	...
C Livestock, except breeding stocks, dairy cattle, etc. [b]	...	...	...	...	...	...	...	...
D Finished goods	...	...	...	...	...	...	...	...
2 Wholesale and retail trade [c]	...	...	...	...	...	...	...	...
3 Other, except government stocks	...	...	...	...	...	...	...	...
4 Government stocks	...	...	...	...	...	...	...	...
Gross Fixed Capital Formation, Total	2148	726	...	1422	3377	1488	...	1889
1 Residential buildings	319	298	...	20	500	472	...	28
2 Non-residential buildings	346	76	...	270	580	91	...	489
3 Other construction	542	4	...	537	725	3	...	721
4 Land improvement and plantation and orchard development	...	...	...	...	...	...	...	...
5 Producers' durable goods	942	348	...	594	1572	922	...	650
6 Breeding stock, dairy cattle, etc. [b]	...	...	...	...	...	...	...	...
Total Gross Capital Formation	...	...	...	...	...	...	...	...

a) Item 'Goods producing industries' excludes the stock changes of private agriculture.
b) Item 'Breeding stocks, dairy cattle, etc.' is included in item 'Increase in stocks'.
c) Item 'Wholesale and retail trade' excludes changes in stocks of private trade.

2.8 Gross Capital Formation by Type of Good and Owner, in Constant Prices

Million Turkish liras

	1980 TOTAL	1980 Total Private	1980 Public Enterprises	1980 General Government	1981 TOTAL	1981 Total Private	1981 Public Enterprises	1981 General Government	1982 TOTAL	1982 Total Private	1982 Public Enterprises	1982 General Government
	At constant prices of: 1973											
Increase in stocks, total	2654	832	...	1822	5856	1821	...	4035	1881	47	...	1834
1 Goods producing industries [a]	2091	832	...	1259	4834	1821	...	3013	438	47	...	391
A Materials and supplies	840	13	...	827	1777	455	...	1322	1190	541	...	649
B Work in progress	172	258	...	-86	-188	-284	...	96	1190	1249	...	-59
C Livestock, except breeding stocks, dairy cattle, etc. [b]	-2	-	...	-2	-	-	...	-	-13	-	...	-13
D Finished goods	1081	561	...	520	3245	1650	...	1595	-1929	-1743	...	-186
2 Wholesale and retail trade [c]	545	-	...	545	834	-	...	834	1206	-	...	1206
3 Other, except government stocks	18	-	...	18	188	-	...	188	237	-	...	237
4 Government stocks	...	...	...	...	...	...	...	...	...	...	...	...
Gross Fixed Capital Formation, Total	...	...	...	...	...	...	...	...	...	...	...	...
Total Gross Capital Formation	...	...	...	...	...	...	...	...	...	...	...	...

a) Item 'Goods producing industries' excludes the stock changes of private agriculture.
b) Item 'Breeding stocks, dairy cattle, etc.' is included in item 'Increase in stocks'.
c) Item 'Wholesale and retail trade' excludes changes in stocks of private trade.

Turkey

2.17 Exports and Imports of Goods and Services, Detail

Thousand Million Turkish liras

	1970	1975	1977	1978	1979	1980	1981	1982	1983	1984	1985	1986
Exports of Goods and Services												
1 Exports of merchandise, f.o.b.	7	20	31	55	76	...	...	...	...	...	...	...
2 Transport and communication	-	5	5	4	8	...	...	...	...	...	...	...
A In respect of merchandise imports	-	2	1	1	1	...	...	...	...	...	...	...
B Other	-	2	4	4	7	...	...	...	...	...	...	...
3 Insurance service charges	-	1	-	-	-	...	...	...	...	...	...	...
A In respect of merchandise imports	-	1	-	-	-	...	...	...	...	...	...	...
B Other	-	-	-	-	-	...	...	...	...	...	...	...
4 Other commodities	1	5	2	6	15	...	...	...	...	...	...	...
5 Adjustments of merchandise exports to change-of-ownership basis	-	-	-	-	-	...	...	...	...	...	...	...
6 Direct purchases in the domestic market by non-residential households	1	3	4	6	10	...	...	...	...	...	...	...
7 Direct purchases in the domestic market by extraterritorial bodies	...	...	...	...	...	...	...	...	...	...	...	...
Total Exports of Goods and Services	9	34	42	72	108	...	...	...	...	...	...	...
Imports of Goods and Services												
1 Imports of merchandise, c.i.f.	11	69	105	113	179	...	...	...	...	...	...	...
A Imports of merchandise, f.o.b.	10	63	93	101	159	...	...	...	...	...	...	...
B Transport of services on merchandise imports	1	5	10	11	17	...	...	...	...	...	...	...
By residents	...	...	...	...	...	...	...	...	...	...	...	...
By non-residents	1	5	10	11	17	...	...	...	...	...	...	...
C Insurance service charges on merchandise imports	-	1	1	2	2	...	...	...	...	...	...	...
By residents	...	...	...	...	...	...	...	...	...	...	...	...
By non-residents	-	1	1	2	2	...	...	...	...	...	...	...
2 Adjustments of merchandise imports to change-of-ownership basis	1	2	5	2	4	...	...	...	...	...	...	...
3 Other transport and communication	-	1	2	1	2	...	...	...	...	...	...	...
4 Other insurance service charges	-	-	-	-	-	...	...	...	...	...	...	...
5 Other commodities	1	3	1	5	13	...	...	...	...	...	...	...
6 Direct purchases abroad by government	...	...	...	...	...	...	...	...	...	...	...	...
7 Direct purchases abroad by resident households	...	...	...	...	...	...	...	...	...	...	...	...
Total Imports of Goods and Services	12	76	113	122	197	...	...	...	...	...	...	...
Balance of Goods and Services	-4	-42	-71	-50	-89	...	...	...	...	...	...	...
Total Imports and Balance of Goods and Services	9	34	42	72	108	...	...	...	...	...	...	...

3.51 External Transactions: Current Account: Detail

Thousand Million Turkish liras

	1970	1975	1977	1978	1979	1980	1981	1982	1983	1984	1985	1986
Payments to the Rest of the World												
1 Imports of goods and services	12	76	113	122	197	...	...	...	...	...	...	...
A Imports of merchandise c.i.f.	11	69	105	113	179	...	...	...	...	...	...	...
B Other	2	7	8	8	19	...	...	...	...	...	...	...
2 Factor income to the rest of the world	1	3	14	13	21	...	...	...	...	...	...	...

Turkey

3.51 External Transactions: Current Account: Detail
(Continued)

Thousand Million Turkish liras

	1970	1975	1977	1978	1979	1980	1981	1982	1983	1984	1985	1986
A Compensation of employees	-	1	5	2	-	...	...	...	...	...	...	...
B Property and entrepreneurial income	1	2	9	11	21	...	...	...	...	...	...	...
3 Current transfers to the rest of the world	-	-	-	-	-	...	...	...	...	...	...	...
A Indirect taxes by general government to supranational organizations	-	-	-	-	-	...	...	...	...	...	...	...
B Other current transfers	-	-	-	-	-	...	...	...	...	...	...	...
By general government	-	-	-	-	-	...	...	...	...	...	...	...
By other resident sectors	-	-	-	-	-	...	...	...	...	...	...	...
4 Surplus of the nation on current transactions	-1	-27	-61	-34	-45	...	...	...	...	...	...	...
Payments to the Rest of the World, and Surplus of the Nation on Current Transfers	13	51	66	101	173	...	...	...	...	...	...	...

Receipts From The Rest of the World

	1970	1975	1977	1978	1979	1980	1981	1982	1983	1984	1985	1986
1 Exports of goods and services	9	34	42	72	108	...	...	...	...	...	...	...
A Exports of merchandise f.o.b.	7	20	31	55	76	...	...	...	...	...	...	...
B Other	2	13	10	16	32	...	...	...	...	...	...	...
2 Factor income from the rest of the world	4	16	22	26	60	...	...	...	...	...	...	...
A Compensation of employees	4	16	21	25	59	...	...	...	...	...	...	...
B Property and entrepreneurial income	-	-	-	2	1	...	...	...	...	...	...	...
3 Current transfers from the rest of the world	1	2	2	4	5	...	...	...	...	...	...	...
A Subsidies to general government from supranational organizations	-	-	-	-	-	...	...	...	...	...	...	...
B Other current transfers	1	2	2	4	5	...	...	...	...	...	...	...
To general government	-	-	-	-	-	...	...	...	...	...	...	...
To other resident sectors	-	2	2	3	5	...	...	...	...	...	...	...
Receipts from the Rest of the World on Current Transfers	13	51	66	101	173	...	...	...	...	...	...	...

3.52 External Transactions: Capital Accumulation Account

Thousand Million Turkish liras

	1970	1975	1977	1978	1979	1980	1981	1982	1983	1984	1985	1986

Finance of Gross Accumulation

	1970	1975	1977	1978	1979	1980	1981	1982	1983	1984	1985	1986
1 Surplus of the nation on current transactions	-1	-27	-61	-34	-45	...	...	...	...	...	...	...
2 Capital transfers from the rest of the world	...	...	...	...	...	...	...	...	...	...	...	...
Total Finance of Gross Accumulation	-1	-27	-61	-34	-45	...	...	...	...	...	...	...

Gross Accumulation

	1970	1975	1977	1978	1979	1980	1981	1982	1983	1984	1985	1986
1 Capital transfers to the rest of the world	...	...	...	...	...	...	...	...	...	...	...	...
2 Purchases of intangible assets, n.e.c., net, from the rest of the world	...	...	...	...	...	...	...	...	...	...	...	...
Net lending to the rest of the world	-1	-27	-61	-34	-45	...	...	...	...	...	...	...
Total Gross Accumulation	-1	-27	-61	-34	-45	...	...	...	...	...	...	...

3.53 External Transactions: Capital Finance Account

Thousand Million Turkish liras

	1970	1975	1977	1978	1979	1980	1981	1982	1983	1984	1985	1986

Acquisitions of Foreign Financial Assets

	1970	1975	1977	1978	1979	1980	1981	1982	1983	1984	1985	1986
1 Gold and SDR's	-	-4	-	-	-	...	...	...	...	...	...	...
2 Currency and transferable deposits	2	6	-6	4	-11	...	...	...	...	...	...	...
3 Other deposits	-	-8	-4	-1	7	...	...	...	...	...	...	...
4 Bills and bonds, short term	...	...	...	...	...	...	...	...	...	...	...	...
5 Bonds, long term	...	...	...	...	...	...	...	...	...	...	...	...
6 Corporate equity securities	...	...	...	...	...	...	...	...	...	...	...	...
7 Short-term loans, n.e.c.	...	...	...	...	...	...	...	...	...	...	...	...

Turkey

3.53 External Transactions: Capital Finance Account
(Continued)

Thousand Million Turkish liras

	1970	1975	1977	1978	1979	1980	1981	1982	1983	1984	1985	1986
8 Long-term loans	...	...	...	...	...	...	...	...	...	...	...	...
9 Proprietors' net additions to accumulation of quasi-corporate, non-resident enterprises	...	...	...	...	...	...	...	...	...	...	...	...
10 Trade credit and advances	-	-2	-	-	-	...	...	...	...	...	...	...
11 Other	1	1	-	3	7	...	...	...	...	...	...	...
Total Acquisitions of Foreign Financial Assets	4	-7	-10	7	4	...	...	...	...	...	...	...

Incurrence of Foreign Liabilities

	1970	1975	1977	1978	1979	1980	1981	1982	1983	1984	1985	1986
1 Currency and transferable deposits	...	...	...	...	...	...	...	...	...	...	...	...
2 Other deposits	-	14	9	10	8	...	...	...	...	...	...	...
3 Bills and bonds, short term	...	...	...	...	...	...	...	...	...	...	...	...
4 Bonds, long term	...	...	...	...	...	...	...	...	...	...	...	...
5 Corporate equity securities	1	2	1	1	3	...	...	...	...	...	...	...
6 Short-term loans, n.e.c.	...	...	...	...	...	...	...	...	...	...	...	...
7 Long-term loans	2	4	5	17	-1	...	...	...	...	...	...	...
8 Non resident proprietors' net additions to accumulation of resident quasi-corporate enterprises	...	...	...	...	...	...	...	...	...	...	...	...
9 Trade credit and advances	-	-1	33	7	9	...	...	...	...	...	...	...
10 Other	3	-	-	-	-	...	...	...	...	...	...	...
Total Incurrence of Liabilities	5	20	49	36	20	...	...	...	...	...	...	...
Net Lending	-2	-27	-59	-30	-16	...	...	...	...	...	...	...
Total Incurrence of Liabilities and Net Lending	4	-7	-10	7	4	...	...	...	...	...	...	...

Uganda

General note. The preparation of national accounts statistics in Uganda is undertaken by the Statistics Division, Ministry of Planning and Economic Development, Entebbe. The official estimates are published in the 'Statistical Abstract'. The following presentation of sources and methods is mainly based on information received by the United Nations from the Statistical Division of Uganda. The estimates are generally in accordance with the classifications and definitions recommended in the United Nations System of National Accounts (SNA). The following tables have been prepared from successive replies to the United Nations national accounts questionnaire. When the scope and coverage of the estimates differ for conceptual or statistical reasons from the difinitions and classifications recommended in SNA, a footnote is indicated to the relevant tables.

Sources and methods:

(a) Gross domestic product. Gross domestic product is estimated mainly through the production approach.

(b) Expenditure on the gross domestic product. The expenditure approach is used to estimate government final consumption expenditure and exports and imports of goods and services. The commodity-flow approach is used to estimate gross capital formation. Private final consumption expenditure is obtained as a residual. Government final consumption expenditure is obtained from accounts of the government bodies. The estimates are recorded on a cash basis and are classified by purpose. Estimates of changes in stocks are prepared for coffee and livestock only, for which average prices are used. The value of capital expenditure on plant, machinery and transport equipment is estimated on the basis of import values, adding import duties, mark-ups for trade, transport and other miscellaneous charges. The estimates of construction are prepared on the basis of the estimated value of building materials as well as on wages and salaries paid. Own-account rural residential construction is estimated on the assumption that it keeps pace with the population growth. Estimates of government gross fixed capital formation are derived from the government fiscal and operating accounts. For exports and imports of goods and services, the Annual Trade Reports issued by the East African Customs Department and the balance-of-payments statistics are used. GDP by expenditure type at constant prices is not estimated.

(c) Cost-structure of the gross domestic product. For the government sector, wages and salaries are derived from the government accounts, for large-scale manufacturing they are obtained from the surveys of industrial production, for trade they are based on the 1966 census of distribution, with a constant ratio to total value added for other years and for services, they are taken from accounts of the services establishments or from the enumeration of employees. The estimates of consumption of fixed capital are built up by branch from various sources such as the annual surveys of industrial production and the accounts of enterprises in mining, electricity and water supply. Estimates of indirect taxes and subsidies are obtained from government accounts. Operating surplus is in most cases derived as a residual.

(d) Gross domestic product by kind of economic activity. The table of GDP by kind of economic activity is prepared in factor values. The production approach is used to estimate the value added of the goods-commodity-producing sectors. The income approach is used for the service-producing sectors except the trade sector, for which the commodity-flow approach is used. For the five major commercial agricultural crops: coffee, cotton, tea, tobacco and sugar cane, statistics of production and value are available annually from sources such as the Coffee Marketing Board, the annual surveys of industrial production and the Produce Marketing Board. For other crops, bench-mark estimates are based on the results of the census of agriculture in 1964/65. Production figures for other years are obtained by using population growth as an indicator. Estimates of subsistence production are based on ad hoc statistical inquiries conducted during the 1960s. Crop prices are collected monthly by the Ministry of Agriculture from selected markets. For intermediate consumption, input ratios are used. Livestock slaughtered for own consumption is evaluated at annual average auction prices while the marketed meat is evaluated at annual average retail prices adjusted for trade and transport margins. For forestry, the gross value of output of the public forests is taken to be equal to the gross revenue earned by the government from this activity. The main sources for estimating the mining industry are the annual surveys of industrial production. For manufacturing, the Statistics Division conducts annual surveys of industrial production covering all establishments employing 10 or more workers. The 1965 survey also covered small establishments employing 5 to 9 workers. The price data applicable for the large-scale sector are also used for the small-scale sector. The input ratios are mainly based on the 1965 survey results and assumed to remain constant. Estimates of electricity and water are obtained from the annual reports and accounts of the agencies involved. For construction, a bench-mark survey of building and construction activities was carried out in 1964 covering both small and large construction units and own-account construction in the organized sector. For trade, annual gross sales are determined by applying mark-ups based on the 1966 census of distribution and assuming stocks to remain constant. The value of gross sales is then related to inputs, wages and operating surplus on the basis of global norms derived from the 1966 census results. These norms are assumed to remain constant over the years. For restaurants and hotels, bench-mark information has been collected for 1967 from the profit and loss accounts of 50 hotels and resturants. The information collected are projected by means of either sales-tax data or data on wages and salaries. The estimates of railways, air transport and communications are obtained from the relevant corporations which are managed by the East African Community. For financial institutions, bench-mark information in terms of profit and loss accounts and balance-sheets of individual banks and other financial institutions has been analysed and estimates have been complied for 1969. For other years, these relationships have been applied to the number of employees in these institutions. Bench-mark information on insurance companies is available for 1967 and extrapolated by using management expenses. For real estate and ownership of dwellings, the estimates of rental values in urban areas are based on the records of the Land and Survey Department and the annual reports of the town councils. Bench-mark estimates for business services were collected in 1967 and are projected using as indicator the number of persons engaged in these services. For producers of government services, sources of data are the annual reports of government agencies and accounts of non-profit institutions. For other services, 1967 bench-mark estimates are extrapolated by the results of the annual enumeration of employees. For the constant price estimates, double deflation is used for agriculture, mining and quarrying, electricity, gas and water and trade sectors. For manufacturing and transport, value added is extrapolated by a quantity index for output. Price deflation is used for construction, restaurants and hotels and for financial and services sectors.

1.1 Expenditure on the Gross Domestic Product, in Current Prices

Million Uganda shillings

		1970	1975	1977	1978	1979	1980	1981	1982	1983	1984	1985	1986
1	Government final consumption expenditure	7897	21271	45551	62797	...	...	146188	301131	435250	580423	...	...
2	Private final consumption expenditure					...	...					...	...
3	Gross capital formation	1261	1712	2347	2481	...	...	4793	18313	41050	84101	...	...
	A Increase in stocks	100	171	540	600	...	...	2758	11256	31884	65322	...	...
	B Gross fixed capital formation	1161	1541	1807	1881	...	...	2035	7057	9166	18779	...	...
	Residential buildings	660	883	...	...	...	...	...	...	...	...	...	...
	Non-residential buildings	...	...	...	...	...	...	...	...	...	...	...	...
	Other construction and land improvement etc.	...	...	...	...	...	...	...	...	...	...	...	...
	Other	501	658	...	...	...	...	...	...	...	...	...	...
4	Exports of goods and services	2101	1837	4569	2550	...	...	6250	21853	48782	110400	...	...
5	Less: Imports of goods and services	1810	2318	3893	3524	...	...	16619	41356	49897	126734	...	...
	Equals: Gross Domestic Product	9449	22502	48574	64304	...	...	140612	299941	475185	648190	...	...

1.3 Cost Components of the Gross Domestic Product

Million Uganda shillings

		1970	1975	1977	1978	1979	1980	1981	1982	1983	1984	1985	1986
1	Indirect taxes, net	921	...	...	...	...	...	...	...	...	...	...	...
	A Indirect taxes	937	...	...	...	...	...	...	...	...	...	...	...
	B Less: Subsidies	16	...	...	...	...	...	...	...	...	...	...	...
2	Consumption of fixed capital [a]	...	...	...	...	...	...	...	...	...	...	...	...
3	Compensation of employees paid by resident producers to:	2136	...	...	...	...	...	...	...	...	...	...	...
4	Operating surplus [a]	6392	...	...	...	...	...	...	...	...	...	...	...
	Equals: Gross Domestic Product	9449	...	...	...	...	...	...	...	...	...	...	...

a) Item 'Operating surplus' includes consumption of fixed capital.

Uganda

1.10 Gross Domestic Product by Kind of Activity, in Current Prices

Million Uganda shillings

	1970	1975	1977	1978	1979	1980	1981	1982	1983	1984	1985	1986
1 Agriculture, hunting, forestry and fishing	4591	14996	...	...	...	...	...	...	...	...	...	...
2 Mining and quarrying	144	59	...	...	...	...	...	...	...	...	...	...
3 Manufacturing	782	1317	...	...	...	...	...	...	...	...	...	...
4 Electricity, gas and water	105	103	...	...	...	...	...	...	...	...	...	...
5 Construction	154	230	...	...	...	...	...	...	...	...	...	...
6 Wholesale and retail trade, restaurants and hotels	961	1342	...	...	...	...	...	...	...	...	...	...
7 Transport, storage and communication	263	430	...	...	...	...	...	...	...	...	...	...
8 Finance, insurance, real estate and business services [a]	633	1199	...	...	...	...	...	...	...	...	...	...
9 Community, social and personal services	66	42	...	...	...	...	...	...	...	...	...	...
Total, Industries	7699	19718	...	...	...	...	...	...	...	...	...	...
Producers of Government Services	731	1010	...	...	...	...	...	...	...	...	...	...
Other Producers	107	48	...	...	...	...	...	...	...	...	...	...
Subtotal [b]	8537	20776	...	...	...	...	...	...	...	...	...	...
Less: Imputed bank service charge [a]	...	...	...	...	...	...	...	...	...	...	...	...
Plus: Import duties	264	...	...	...	...	...	...	...	...	...	...	...
Plus: Value added tax	...	...	...	...	...	...	...	...	...	...	...	...
Plus: Other adjustments [c]	648	...	...	...	...	...	...	...	...	...	...	...
Equals: Gross Domestic Product	9449	...	...	...	...	...	...	...	...	...	...	...

a) Item 'Less: Imputed bank service charge' is netted out of item 'Finance, insurance, real estate and business services'.
b) Gross domestic product in factor values.
c) Item 'Other adjustments' refers to indirect taxes net of subsidies and a statistical discrepancy.

1.11 Gross Domestic Product by Kind of Activity, in Constant Prices

Million Uganda shillings

	1970	1975	1977	1978	1979	1980	1981	1982	1983	1984	1985	1986
	\multicolumn{12}{c}{At constant prices of: 1966}											
1 Agriculture, hunting, forestry and fishing	3774	3965	4097	4067	3497	3277	3500	3854	4239	...	...	...
2 Mining and quarrying	119	59	21	15	8	6	6	7	7	...	...	...
3 Manufacturing	631	504	479	372	246	261	247	282	290	...	...	...
4 Electricity, gas and water	109	104	102	103	77	91	109	105	97	...	...	...
5 Construction	122	92	84	79	72	37	38	43	47	...	...	...
6 Wholesale and retail trade, restaurants and hotels	825	592	623	587	537	465	448	498	541	...	...	...
7 Transport, storage and communication	276	322	266	167	134	168	182	200	208	...	...	...
8 Finance, insurance, real estate and business services [a]	542	602	681	720	661	663	664	680	704	...	...	...
9 Community, social and personal services	56	60	57	46	36	39	30	37	38	...	...	...
Total, Industries	6455	6301	6410	6156	5268	5007	5224	5706	6171	...	...	...
Producers of Government Services	731	1012	1067	997	1032	1078	1094	1130	1163	...	...	...
Other Producers	96	44	50	28	30	30	33	37	41	...	...	...
Subtotal [b]	7281	7356	7527	7181	6330	6115	6351	6870	7375	...	...	...
Less: Imputed bank service charge [a]	...	...	...	...	...	...	...	...	...	...	...	...
Plus: Import duties	...	...	...	...	...	...	...	...	...	...	...	...
Plus: Value added tax	...	...	...	...	...	...	...	...	...	...	...	...
Equals: Gross Domestic Product [b]	7282	7357	7527	7181	6330	6115	6351	6873	7375	...	...	...

a) Item 'Less: Imputed bank service charge' is netted out of item 'Finance, insurance, real estate and business services'.
b) Gross domestic product in factor values.

1.12 Relations Among National Accounting Aggregates

Million Uganda shillings

	1970	1975	1977	1978	1979	1980	1981	1982	1983	1984	1985	1986
Gross Domestic Product	9449	...	...	...	...	...	...	...	...	...	...	...
Plus: Net factor income from the rest of the world	-107	...	...	...	...	...	...	...	...	...	...	...
Equals: Gross National Product	9342	...	...	...	...	...	...	...	...	...	...	...
Less: Consumption of fixed capital	...	...	...	...	...	...	...	...	...	...	...	...
Equals: National Income [a]	9342	...	...	...	...	...	...	...	...	...	...	...

Uganda

1.12 Relations Among National Accounting Aggregates
(Continued)

Million Uganda shillings

	1970	1975	1977	1978	1979	1980	1981	1982	1983	1984	1985	1986
Plus: Net current transfers from the rest of the world	-39	...	...	...	...	...	...	...	...	...	...	...
Equals: National Disposable Income [b]	9303	...	...	...	...	...	...	...	...	...	...	...
Less: Final consumption	...	...	...	...	...	...	...	...	...	...	...	...
Equals: Net Saving	...	...	...	...	...	...	...	...	...	...	...	...
Less: Surplus of the nation on current transactions	...	...	...	...	...	...	...	...	...	...	...	...
Equals: Net Capital Formation	...	...	...	...	...	...	...	...	...	...	...	...

a) Item 'National income' includes consumption of fixed capital.
b) Item 'National disposable income' includes consumption of fixed capital.

Ukrainian SSR

Source. Communication from the Central Statistical Board of the Council of Ministers of the Ukrainian SSR, Kiev. The official estimates are published annually in 'Narodue Gospodarstvo Ukrainskoi SSR' (National Economy of the Ukrainian SSR).

General note. The estimates shown in the following tables have been prepared in accordance with the System of Material Product Balances. Therefore, these estimates are not comparable in concept and coverage with those conforming to the United Nations System of National Accounts.

2a Net Material Product by Kind of Activity of the Material Sphere in Current Market Prices

Thousand Million USSR Roubles

	1970	1975	1977	1978	1979	1980	1981	1982	1983	1984	1985	1986
1 Agriculture and forestry	13.9	14.3	16.9	17.3	...	...	...	...	...	...	...	...
2 Industrial activity	27.4	33.1	35.1	36.6	...	...	...	...	...	...	...	...
3 Construction	5.0	6.5	6.9	7.1	...	...	...	...	...	...	...	...
4 Wholesale and retail trade and restaurants and other eating and drinking places [a]	5.9	8.2	9.9	10.6	...	...	...	...	...	...	...	...
5 Transport and communication [b]	2.6	3.7	4.1	4.1	...	...	...	...	...	...	...	...
6 Other activities of the material sphere [a]	...	...	...	...	...	...	...	...	...	...	...	...
Net material product	54.8	65.8	72.9	75.9	76.4	77.5	82.6	87.5	92.3	96.2	96.6	97.4

a) Item 'Other activities of the material sphere' is included in item 'Wholesale and retail trade and restaurants and other eating and drinking places'.
b) Only goods transport and communication serving branches of material production are included in item 'Transport and Communication'.

2a Net Material Product by Kind of Activity of the Material Sphere in Current Market Prices

Percentages

	1970	1975	1977	1978	1979	1980	1981	1982	1983	1984	1985	1986
1 Agriculture and forestry	25.3	21.7	23.2	22.8	...	...	...	...	...	...	...	...
2 Industrial activity	50.0	50.3	48.1	48.2	...	...	...	...	...	...	...	...
3 Construction	9.2	9.9	9.5	9.4	...	...	...	...	...	...	...	...
4 Wholesale and retail trade and restaurants and other eating and drinking places [a]	10.7	12.5	13.6	14.0	...	...	...	...	...	...	...	...
5 Transport and communication [b]	4.8	5.6	5.6	5.4	...	...	...	...	...	...	...	...
6 Other activities of the material sphere [a]	...	...	...	...	...	...	...	...	...	...	...	...
Net material product	100.0	100.0	100.0	100.0	...	...	...	...	...	...	...	...

a) Item 'Other activities of the material sphere' is included in item 'Wholesale and retail trade and restaurants and other eating and drinking places'.
b) Only goods transport and communication serving branches of material production are included in item 'Transport and Communication'.

2b Net Material Product by Kind of Activity of the Material Sphere in Constant Market Prices

Index numbers 1960=100

	1970	1975	1977	1978	1979	1980	1981	1982	1983	1984	1985	1986
	At constant prices of: 1975											
1 Agriculture and forestry	116	...	...	...	...	...	...	...	...	...	...	...
2 Industrial activity	258	356	395	419	433	444	452	461	...	...	...	...
3 Construction	151	186	188	197	193	193	196	200	...	...	...	...
4 Wholesale and retail trade and restaurants and other eating and drinking places	197	258	276	284	291	410	444	475	...	...	...	...
5 Transport and communication	199	282	312	322	325	324	336	340	...	...	...	...
6 Other activities of the material sphere	...	...	...	...	...	...	...	...	...	...	...	...
Net material product	195	244	270	282	283	287	296	311	327	338	344	353

6b Capital Formation by Kind of Activity of the Material and Non-Material Spheres in Constant Market Prices

Million USSR Roubles

	1970	1975	1977	1978	1979	1980	1981	1982	1983	1984	1985	1986
	At constant prices of: 1984											
	Gross Fixed Capital Formation by Socio-economic Sector and Industrial Use											
1 State and co-operative (excluding collective farms)	14781	19848	20769	22023	21482	21325	21335	21966	24110	24438	25114	27620
A Industry	5462	7335	8040	8229	8012	8285	8301	8658	9190	9492	9660	10522
B Construction	438	535	560	574	636	643	601	602	572	554	622	560
C Agriculture and forestry [a]	2840	4340	4419	4632	4511	4489	4438	4539	4722	4648	4686	5116
D Transport and communication	1544	2090	2082	2881	2540	2201	2056	2121	3036	2705	2693	2948
E Residential building	2167	2746	2834	2881	2893	2823	2985	3092	3383	3670	3883	4478
F Trade and other	2330	2802	2834	2826	2890	2884	2954	2954	3207	3369	3570	3996
2 Collective farms	...	...	...	...	...	...	...	...	...	...	...	...
3 Other	...	...	...	...	...	...	...	...	...	...	...	...
Gross Fixed Capital Formation [b]	14781	19848	20769	22023	21482	21325	21335	21966	24110	24438	25114	27620

a) Item 'Agriculture and forestry' excludes forestry and procurement.
b) The estimates for this table are at constant prices of 1 January 1984.

United Arab Emirates

Source. Reply to the United Nations National Accounts Questionnaire from the Ministry of Foreign Affairs, Abu Dhabi.

General note. The estimates shown in the following tables have been prepared in accordance with the United Nations System of National Accounts so far as the existing data would permit.

1.1 Expenditure on the Gross Domestic Product, in Current Prices

Million U.A.E Dirhams

	1970	1975	1977	1978	1979	1980	1981	1982	1983	1984	1985	1986
1 Government final consumption expenditure	...	3261	7413	8163	9600	11992	21475	22000	19030	17696	19484	18314
2 Private final consumption expenditure	...	6215	11557	12501	15245	18968	24946	26846	27467	26744	27173	29877
3 Gross capital formation	...	12059	24966	23679	27643	31155	31801	32163	32203	29496	24933	22607
A Increase in stocks	...	-	2280	-2100	-799	1000	1158	480	535	380	475	510
B Gross fixed capital formation	...	12059	22686	25779	28442	30155	30643	31683	31668	29116	24458	22097
4 Exports of goods and services	...	29522	41779	40200	57201	85592	83662	71576	60874	60008	58266	39396
5 Less: Imports of goods and services	...	11597	22296	23874	29717	37874	40784	40152	36665	32101	30440	31850
Equals: Gross Domestic Product	...	39460	63419	60669	79972	109833	121100	112433	102909	101843	99416	78344

1.2 Expenditure on the Gross Domestic Product, in Constant Prices

Million U.A.E Dirhams

	1970	1975	1977	1978	1979	1980	1981	1982	1983	1984	1985	1986
					At constant prices of:1980							
1 Government final consumption expenditure	...	4667	8280	8570	10204	11992	20300	20042	18020	18381	19700	18402
2 Private final consumption expenditure	...	9344	15621	16785	17550	18968	23262	25669	26066	27364	28334	30038
3 Gross capital formation	...	16029	29378	27779	30009	31155	30114	29615	30527	30123	25596	21952
A Increase in stocks	...	-	3300	-3000	-1000	1000	1064	455	515	395	490	505
B Gross fixed capital formation	...	16029	26078	30779	31009	30155	29050	29160	30012	29728	25106	21447
4 Exports of goods and services	...	42145	53212	49544	66670	85592	77835	66714	58377	60583	58907	39855
5 Less: Imports of goods and services	...	19458	35255	33112	37554	37874	38557	38405	34565	33775	32314	32147
Equals: Gross Domestic Product	...	52727	71237	69566	86879	109833	112954	103635	98425	102676	100223	78100

1.3 Cost Components of the Gross Domestic Product

Million U.A.E Dirhams

	1970	1975	1977	1978	1979	1980	1981	1982	1983	1984	1985	1986
1 Indirect taxes, net	...	-175	-476	-601	-825	-1637	-2954	-3221	-2595	-2661	-2538	-2318
2 Consumption of fixed capital	...	2729	4885	5840	7129	9035	10384	13622	16582	17649	17027	15152
3 Compensation of employees paid by resident producers to:	...	5633	11442	12617	14166	16011	21123	23300	24297	24573	24997	24637
A Resident households	...	3923	8050	8952	10124	11639	14673	16300	16997	17761	18097	17487
B Rest of the world	...	1710	3392	3665	4042	4372	6450	7000	7300	6812	6900	7150
4 Operating surplus	...	31273	47568	42813	59502	86424	92547	78732	64625	62282	59930	40873
Equals: Gross Domestic Product	...	39460	63419	60669	79972	109833	121100	112433	102909	101843	99416	78344

1.7 External Transactions on Current Account, Summary

Million U.A.E Dirhams

	1970	1975	1977	1978	1979	1980	1981	1982	1983	1984	1985	1986
					Payments to the Rest of the World							
1 Imports of goods and services	...	11597	22296	23874	29717	37874	40784	40152	36665	32101	30440	31850
A Imports of merchandise c.i.f.	...	10912	20218	21473	26642	34116	35594	34795	30970	25530	24140	25100
B Other	...	685	2078	2401	3075	3758	5190	5357	5695	6571	6300	6750
2 Factor income to the rest of the world	...	4234	7613	7671	9496	10306	12770	12076	11600	10157	9800	8900
A Compensation of employees	...	1710	3392	3665	4042	4372	6450	7000	7300	6812	6900	7150
B Property and entrepreneurial income	...	2524	4221	4006	5454	5934	6320	5076	4300	3345	2900	1750
3 Current transfers to the rest of the world	...	2421	3514	3248	4774	6757	4016	2510	800	1064	1013	887
4 Surplus of the nation on current transactions	...	12697	11095	8989	18589	38909	34842	26138	21709	27286	27213	7159
Payments to the Rest of the World and Surplus of the Nation on Current Transactions	...	30949	44518	43782	62576	93846	92412	80876	70774	70608	68466	48796
					Receipts From The Rest of the World							
1 Exports of goods and services	...	29522	41779	40200	57201	85592	83662	71576	60874	60008	58266	39396

United Arab Emirates

1.7 External Transactions on Current Account, Summary
(Continued)

Million U.A.E Dirhams

	1970	1975	1977	1978	1979	1980	1981	1982	1983	1984	1985	1986
A Exports of merchandise f.o.b.	...	29112	41049	39444	56250	84512	82142	69980	59254	58440	56766	37776
B Other	...	410	730	756	951	1080	1520	1596	1620	1568	1500	1620
2 Factor income from rest of the world	...	1427	2739	3582	5375	8254	8750	9300	9900	10600	10200	9400
A Compensation of employees	...	...	...	...	...	...	...	...	...	...	...	...
B Property and entrepreneurial income	...	1427	2739	3582	5375	8254	8750	9300	9900	10600	10200	9400
3 Current transfers from rest of the world	...	...	...	...	...	...	...	...	...	...	...	...
Receipts from the Rest of the World on Current Transactions	...	30949	44518	43782	62576	93846	92412	80876	70774	70608	68466	48796

1.10 Gross Domestic Product by Kind of Activity, in Current Prices

Million U.A.E Dirhams

	1970	1975	1977	1978	1979	1980	1981	1982	1983	1984	1985	1986
1 Agriculture, hunting, forestry and fishing	...	329	491	604	680	827	1036	1144	1198	1349	1440	1540
2 Mining and quarrying	...	26462	35762	32825	48104	70767	70071	66280	46464	46042	45010	20453
3 Manufacturing	...	369	1853	2197	2534	4191	8077	9436	9584	9761	9255	8405
4 Electricity, gas and water	...	209	467	689	985	1297	1547	1851	1746	2076	2143	2308
5 Construction	...	4308	8474	8271	9338	9834	10475	10168	10520	9860	8882	8500
6 Wholesale and retail trade, restaurants and hotels	...	3248	6242	5589	6850	9094	10849	10913	9701	9154	8715	8820
7 Transport, storage and communication	...	1255	2662	2866	3420	3731	4950	5465	4780	4420	4188	4138
8 Finance, insurance, real estate and business services [a]	...	2219	5458	4429	4422	6129	9132	11375	12107	10617	10330	8707
9 Community, social and personal services [b]	...	382	610	675	740	814	1174	1380	1556	1602	1645	1758
Total, Industries	...	38781	62019	58145	77073	106684	117311	108012	97646	95781	91614	70629
Producers of Government Services	...	1364	3195	3981	4700	5989	8910	9632	9847	10356	11001	10957
Other Producers [b]	...	40	82	114	148	200	234	253	298	335	364	368
Subtotal [c]	...	40185	65296	62240	81921	112873	126455	117897	107791	106472	102979	81954
Less: Imputed bank service charge [a]	...	550	1401	970	1124	1403	2401	2243	2287	1968	1025	1292
Plus: Import duties	...	...	...	...	...	...	...	...	...	...	...	...
Plus: Value added tax	...	...	...	...	...	...	...	...	...	...	...	...
Plus: Other adjustments [d]	...	-175	-476	-601	-825	-1637	-2954	-3221	-2595	-2661	-2538	-2318
Equals: Gross Domestic Product	...	39460	63419	60669	79972	109833	121100	112433	102909	101843	99416	78344

a) For 1972-1974, imputed bank service charges are netted out of item 'Finance, insurance, real estate and business services.'
b) For 1972-1974, item 'Other producers' is included in item 'Community, social and personal services'.
c) Gross domestic product in factor values.
d) Item 'Other adjustments' refers to indirect taxes net of subsidies.

1.11 Gross Domestic Product by Kind of Activity, in Constant Prices

Million U.A.E Dirhams

	1970	1975	1977	1978	1979	1980	1981	1982	1983	1984	1985	1986
					At constant prices of: 1980							
1 Agriculture, hunting, forestry and fishing	...	367	563	649	732	827	1020	1079	1236	1400	1525	1617
2 Mining and quarrying	...	35938	41862	37824	52724	70767	65504	53487	45255	47327	45606	25621
3 Manufacturing	...	472	1923	2274	2542	4191	7990	9251	9116	9655	9443	8695
4 Electricity, gas and water	...	287	547	792	1122	1297	1509	1710	1742	2025	2225	2270
5 Construction	...	4770	7381	9749	9753	9834	9615	9692	10250	11650	9022	8652
6 Wholesale and retail trade, restaurants and hotels	...	4940	9054	8046	8316	9094	10384	10295	9574	9251	9025	9084
7 Transport, storage and communication	...	1608	2915	3188	3552	3731	3909	3880	3647	3890	3950	4075
8 Finance, insurance, real estate and business services [a]	...	2151	3992	4073	4824	6129	8484	8966	10907	10505	10290	8733
9 Community, social and personal services [b]	...	516	666	703	736	814	1126	1234	1472	1475	1580	1715
Total, Industries	...	51049	68903	67298	84301	106684	109541	99594	93199	97178	92666	70462
Producers of Government Services	...	2551	4189	4496	5125	5989	8104	8830	9491	9865	10792	10837

United Arab Emirates

1.11 Gross Domestic Product by Kind of Activity, in Constant Prices
(Continued)

Million U.A.E Dirhams

	1970	1975	1977	1978	1979	1980	1981	1982	1983	1984	1985	1986
					At constant prices of:1980							
Other Producers [b]	...	54	91	119	147	200	223	233	307	359	410	408
Subtotal [c]	...	53654	73183	71913	89573	112873	117868	108657	102997	107402	103868	81707
Less: Imputed bank service charge [a]	...	600	1227	1407	1514	1403	2180	2050	2130	1996	1064	1312
Plus: Import duties	...	...	...	...	...	...	...	...	...	...	...	...
Plus: Value added tax	...	...	...	...	...	...	...	...	...	...	...	...
Plus: Other adjustments [d]	...	-327	-720	-940	-1180	-1637	-2734	-2972	-2442	-2730	-2581	-2295
Equals: Gross Domestic Product	...	52727	71237	69566	86879	109833	112954	103635	98425	102676	100223	78100

a) For 1972-1974, imputed bank service charges are netted out of item 'Finance, insurance, real estate and business services.'
b) For 1972-1974, item 'Other producers' is included in item 'Community, social and personal services'.
c) Gross domestic product in factor values.
d) Item 'Other adjustments' refers to indirect taxes net of subsidies.

1.12 Relations Among National Accounting Aggregates

Million U.A.E Dirhams

	1970	1975	1977	1978	1979	1980	1981	1982	1983	1984	1985	1986
Gross Domestic Product	...	39460	63419	60669	79972	109833	121100	112433	102909	101843	99416	78344
Plus: Net factor income from the rest of the world	...	-2807	-4874	-4089	-4121	-2052	-4020	-2776	-1700	443	400	500
Factor income from the rest of the world	...	1427	2739	3582	5375	8254	8750	9300	9900	10600	10200	9400
Less: Factor income to the rest of the world	...	4234	7613	7671	9496	10306	12770	12076	11600	10157	9800	8900
Equals: Gross National Product	...	36653	58545	56580	75851	107781	117080	109657	101209	102286	99816	78844
Less: Consumption of fixed capital	...	2729	4885	5840	7129	9035	10384	13622	16582	17649	17027	15152
Equals: National Income	...	33924	53660	50740	68722	98746	106696	96035	84627	84637	82789	63692
Plus: Net current transfers from the rest of the world	...	-2421	-3514	-3248	-4774	-6757	-4016	-2510	-800	-1064	-1013	-887
Current transfers from the rest of the world	...	-	-	-	-	-	-	-	-	-	-	-
Less: Current transfers to the rest of the world	...	2421	3514	3248	4774	6757	4016	2510	800	1064	1013	887
Equals: National Disposable Income	...	31503	50146	47492	63948	91989	102680	93525	83827	83573	81776	62805
Less: Final consumption	...	9476	18970	20664	24845	30960	46421	48846	46497	44440	46657	48191
Equals: Net Saving	...	22027	31176	26828	39103	61029	56259	44679	37330	39133	35119	14614
Less: Surplus of the nation on current transactions	...	12697	11095	8989	18590	38909	34842	26138	21709	27286	27213	7159
Equals: Net Capital Formation	...	9330	20081	17839	20513	22120	21417	18541	15621	11847	7906	7455

2.11 Gross Fixed Capital Formation by Kind of Activity of Owner, ISIC Divisions, in Current Prices

Million U.A.E Dirhams

	1970	1975	1977	1978	1979	1980	1981	1982	1983	1984	1985	1986
					All Producers							
1 Agriculture, hunting, forestry and fishing	...	161	189	297	269	560	472	482	430	392	319	200
2 Mining and quarrying	...	2211	2977	3593	4334	5463	3949	3839	7724	8201	6955	6420
3 Manufacturing	...	2356	3034	5809	10712	9983	11855	12800	7633	6970	5700	4785
4 Electricity, gas and water	...	779	2534	3058	2193	2663	1900	2033	3565	3253	2599	2416
5 Construction	...	407	605	698	582	715	1016	1006	1080	736	592	600
6 Wholesale and retail trade, restaurants and hotels	...	311	1352	1476	1006	749	611	733	685	732	480	702
7 Transport, storage and communication	...	2111	5696	5467	4624	4139	4779	4612	4928	4547	3948	4000
8 Finance, insurance, real estate and business services	...	2638	4458	2902	1951	2483	2101	2070	2239	1328	1061	781
9 Community, social and personal services	...	7	8	10	12	15	30	40	45	41	80	100
Total Industries	...	10981	20853	23310	25683	26770	26713	27615	28329	26200	21734	20004
Producers of Government Services	...	1078	1833	2469	2759	3385	3930	4068	3339	2916	2724	2093
Private Non-Profit Institutions Serving Households	...	...	...	...	...	...	...	...	...	...	...	...
Total	...	12059	22686	25779	28442	30155	30643	31683	31668	29116	24458	22097

United Arab Emirates

2.12 Gross Fixed Capital Formation by Kind of Activity of Owner, ISIC Divisions, in Constant Prices

Million U.A.E Dirhams

	1970	1975	1977	1978	1979	1980	1981	1982	1983	1984	1985	1986
At constant prices of:1980												
All Producers												
1 Agriculture, hunting, forestry and fishing	...	244	247	368	301	560	313	...	...	...	...	...
2 Mining and quarrying	...	2521	3005	4010	4525	5463	...	...	...	...	...	...
3 Manufacturing	...	3348	3835	7105	11864	9983	...	...	...	...	...	...
4 Electricity, gas and water	...	1159	3308	3785	2458	2663	...	...	...	...	...	...
5 Construction	...	660	854	896	666	715	...	...	...	...	...	...
6 Wholesale and retail trade, restaurants and hotels	...	410	1507	1700	1063	749	...	...	...	...	...	...
7 Transport, storage and communication	...	3491	7080	6884	5173	4139	...	...	...	...	...	...
8 Finance, insurance, real estate and business services	...	2934	4394	3217	2032	2483	...	...	...	...	...	...
9 Community, social and personal services	...	11	11	13	14	15	...	...	...	...	...	...
Total Industries	...	14778	24241	27978	28096	26770	...	...	...	...	...	...
Producers of Government Services	...	1251	1837	2800	2908	3385	...	...	...	...	...	...
Private Non-Profit Institutions Serving Households	...	...	...	...	...	...	...	...	...	...	...	...
Total	...	16029	26078	30779	31004	30155	29050	29160	30012	29728	25106	21447

2.17 Exports and Imports of Goods and Services, Detail

Million U.A.E Dirhams

	1970	1975	1977	1978	1979	1980	1981	1982	1983	1984	1985	1986
Exports of Goods and Services												
1 Exports of merchandise, f.o.b.	...	29112	41049	39444	56250	84512	82142	69980	59254	58440	56766	37776
2 Transport and communication	...	301	467	482	601	659	900	950	850	900	800	850
3 Insurance service charges	...	...	...	...	...	...	...	...	...	...	...	...
4 Other commodities [a]	...	46	154	136	177	219	320	331	390	318	350	370
5 Adjustments of merchandise exports to change-of-ownership basis	...	...	...	...	...	...	...	...	...	...	...	...
6 Direct purchases in the domestic market by non-residential households	...	63	109	138	173	202	300	315	380	350	350	400
7 Direct purchases in the domestic market by extraterritorial bodies	...	...	...	...	...	...	...	...	...	...	...	...
Total Exports of Goods and Services	...	29522	41779	40200	57201	85592	83662	71576	60874	60008	58266	39396
Imports of Goods and Services												
1 Imports of merchandise, c.i.f.	...	10912	20218	21473	26642	34116	35594	34795	30970	25530	24140	25100
2 Adjustments of merchandise imports to change-of-ownership basis	...	...	...	...	...	...	...	...	...	...	...	...
3 Other transport and communication	...	191	591	654	849	976	1250	1438	1015	1463	1400	1500
4 Other insurance service charges	...	...	...	...	...	...	...	...	...	...	...	...
5 Other commodities [a]	...	436	1354	1517	2002	2507	3570	3519	4280	4708	4500	4800
6 Direct purchases abroad by government	...	58	133	230	224	275	370	400	400	400	400	450
7 Direct purchases abroad by resident households	...	...	...	...	...	...	...	...	...	...	...	...
Total Imports of Goods and Services	...	11597	22296	23874	29717	37874	40784	40152	36665	32101	30440	31850
Balance of Goods and Services	...	17925	19483	16326	27485	47718	42878	31424	24209	27907	27826	7546
Total Imports and Balance of Goods and Services	...	29522	41779	40200	57201	85592	83662	71576	60874	60008	58266	39396

a) Item 'Other commodities' refers to tourism and travel.

United Kingdom

General note. The preparation of national accounts statistics in United Kingdom is undertaken by the Central Statistical Office, London. Official estimates are published annually in 'National Income and Expenditure'. A comprehensive descripton of the sources and methods used in the preparation of the estimates is given in 'National Accounts Statistics, Sources and Methods', H.M.S.O., London, 1968. A new source of reference is 'The National Accounts - A Short Guide', H.M.S.O. London, 1981. Input-output tables for selected years are produced and published by the Central Statistical Office. The following tables have been prepared from successive replies to the United Nations national accounts questionnaire. When the scope and coverage of the estimates differ for conceptual or statistical reasons from the definitions and classifications recommended in SNA, a footnote is indicated to the relevant tables.

Sources and methods:

(a) **Gross domestic product.** The main approach used to estimate GDP is the expenditure approach.

(b) **Expenditure on the gross domestic product.** The expenditure approach is used to estimate all types of expenditure. Government final consumption expenditure is based on accounting data and departmental returns. Estimates for the central government are derived from the various exchequer and departmental accounts. Both the central government and the local government data are extensively rearranged to fit the concepts used in the national accounts. The estimates of private final consumption expenditure are built up commodity by commodity from a variety of independent sources. The sources available are statistics of supplies, sample surveys of consumers' expenditure, and statistics of sales by retail shops and other outlets. The major sources for estimating gross fixed capital formation in private industries are the annual censuses of production and annual inquiries into the distributive and service trades. Base-year estimates of dwellings are, however, based on the number of houses under construction and average prices. Changes are estimated from building output data obtained from contractors. The estimates of capital formation for the public sector are based on accounts. The statistics of exports and imports of goods and services are taken from the balance of payments accounts. Government final consumption expenditures referring to wages and salaries are estimated at constant prices partly by deflating by indexes of changes in rates of pay, but mostly by the use of volume indicators based on numbers employed. Goods and services are mainly deflated by composite base-weighted price indexes. No single-approach is used for all components of private final consumption expenditure. Most food, beverages and tobacco are revalued item by item at average base-year prices. Deflators constructed from components of the General Index of Retail Prices are used for other items. Price deflation is used for gross fixed capital formation. For buildings and other construction out-turn price indexes of successful tenders are used. For exports and imports of goods and services base-year figures on a balance of payments basis are extrapolated by means of volume changes for many goods. For other goods and services, however, mainly price deflation is used.

(c) **Cost-structure of the gross domestic product.** Information about wages and salaries paid in cash is obtained from the PAYE (Pay-As-You-Earn) system. The estimates of employers' contributions to national insurance and health are taken from the central government accounts. Estimates of operating surplus are provided through tax assessment data for profit incomes. Since they, however, are not available for the latest periods, the quarterly sample inquiry on company trading profits undertaken by the Inland Revenue is also used. Statistics of the trading surplus of public corporations, central government and local authority trading enterprises are taken from their accounts. The method used for estimating capital consumption is mainly the perpetual inventory method. Estimates of total taxes on expenditure and subsidies are available from government accounts.

(d) **Gross domestic product by kind of economic activity.** The income approach is used to estimate value added of most of the various economic activities. The production approach is applied in connexion with the estimates of agricultural income. The production figures of agriculture are based on estimates prepared by the departments concerned. Agricultural earnings, including payments in kind, are estimated by these departments from regular sample surveys. The estimate of income from farming is built up from very detailed estimates of output and expenditure. Information about crop areas and livestock numbers is collected from farmers by means of questionnaires, and estimates on the quantity harvested are based on the production acreage and the yield per acre. The estimates of mining and quarrying, manufacturing, electricity, gas and water and construction are built up from tax assessment data and production censuses. The censuses of production which are conducted annually, provide information on sales, employment, wages and salaries, purchases, expenditure, etc. For electricity, gas and water annual accounts data are also used, while for construction government accounts are among the sources. The estimates for the distributive trade are calculated from tax assessment data, number in employment and changes in average earnings. In the transport, storage and communication group, income data for the nationalized industries and public corporations are obtained from their annual reports, whereas for the remainder tax assessment data, annual censuses of employment and earnings inquiries are used. Tax assessment data and PAYE (Pay-As-You-Earn) statistics are mainly used as sources for financial institutions. Rents are based on the estimated rent income from various groups of property. Business services are mainly estimated from Inland Revenue data. The figures of central government wages and salaries are obtained from departments, while for local authorities they are derived from official publications. Tax assessment data are utilized to estimate the wage and salary bill for most services. Estimates at constant prices for the agricultural sector are obtained through double deflation. Output is valued at base-year prices, while input is valued at pre-subsidy base-year prices. Value added of all other sectors is obtained through extrapolation by indexes of production, volume or output.

1.1 Expenditure on the Gross Domestic Product, in Current Prices

Million Pounds Sterling

		1970	1975	1977	1978	1979	1980	1981	1982	1983	1984	1985	1986
1	Government final consumption expenditure	9037	23125	29487	33423	38908	49046	55470	60549	66006	69915	74070	79455
2	Private final consumption expenditure	31740	64992	86215	99419	117744	136725	152166	166553	181857	194595	212209	232569
	A Households	31143	63668	84453	97464	115520	133949	148916	162866	177701	189933	206942	226479
	B Private non-profit institutions serving households	597	1324	1762	1956	2225	2776	3250	3685	4157	4663	5265	6090
3	Gross capital formation	10118	19681	28860	32864	39087	38975	38574	43519	49324	55224	60905	64778
	A Increase in stocks [a]	382	-1354	1824	1804	2162	-2586	-2735	-1244	730	116	428	551
	B Gross fixed capital formation [a]	9736	21035	27036	31060	36925	41561	41309	44763	48594	55108	60477	64227
	Residential buildings	1870	4682	5699	6325	7649	8674	8132	8914	10447	11788	12069	14082
	Non-residential buildings	2946	7020	7647	8182	9637	11802	12471	13291	13260	14692	15083	15999
	Other construction and land improvement etc.	274	625	832	1103	1416	1561	1782	1937	2397	2676	2984	3476
	Other	4646	8708	12858	15450	18223	19524	18924	20621	22490	25952	30341	30670
4	Exports of goods and services	11934	27576	43944	48050	55685	63691	68407	73608	81004	92611	102706	98439
5	Less: Imports of goods and services	11482	29421	42968	45888	55096	58346	61148	68598	78134	93215	99178	101535
	Equals: Gross Domestic Product	51347	105953	145538	167868	196328	230091	253469	275631	300057	319130	350712	373706

a) Beginning 1973, 'Gross fixed capital formation' excludes the value of completed but unsold dwellings which is included in 'Increase in stocks'.

1.2 Expenditure on the Gross Domestic Product, in Constant Prices

Million Pounds Sterling

		1970	1975	1977	1978	1979	1980	1981	1982	1983	1984	1985	1986
		\multicolumn{12}{c}{At constant prices of:1980}
1	Government final consumption expenditure	38533	46397	46193	47258	48278	49046	49162	49665	50598	50995	50955	51405
2	Private final consumption expenditure	110482	124561	124335	131238	136786	136725	136644	137672	143147	146201	151603	160354
	A Households	108192	121990	121733	128565	134086	133949	133760	134612	139855	142677	147820	156161
	B Private non-profit institutions serving households	2324	2590	2621	2675	2700	2776	2885	3056	3292	3523	3784	4192
3	Gross capital formation	41482	38896	44043	44934	46457	38975	35170	38496	42303	45294	47010	47206

United Kingdom

1.2 Expenditure on the Gross Domestic Product, in Constant Prices
(Continued)

Million Pounds Sterling

	1970	1975	1977	1978	1979	1980	1981	1982	1983	1984	1985	1986
					At constant prices of:1980							
A Increase in stocks [a]	1412	-2644	2602	2208	2544	-2586	-2404	-1043	698	280	611	660
B Gross fixed capital formation [ab]	40070	41540	41441	42726	43913	41561	37574	39539	41605	45014	46399	46546
Residential buildings	8615	9140	8976	9048	9363	8674	7175	7632	8585	8793	8290	9118
Non-residential buildings	14396	14176	13101	12761	12436	11802	11292	12372	12478	13753	13594	13728
Other construction and land improvement etc.	1403	1552	1641	1802	1657	1561	1651	1814	1995	2152	2150	2219
Other	15879	16719	17737	19115	20457	19524	17456	17721	18547	20316	22365	21481
4 Exports of goods and services	42035	52352	60397	61408	63875	63691	63199	63652	64969	69440	73286	75636
5 Less: Imports of goods and services	41544	50162	52727	54670	60378	58346	56775	59593	63065	69124	71014	75446
Statistical discrepancy [c]	-693	-162	-20	-	-	-	-	-	-	-	-	-
Equals: Gross Domestic Product	190295	211882	222221	230168	235018	230091	227400	229892	237952	242806	251840	259155

a) Beginning 1973, 'Gross fixed capital formation' excludes the value of completed but unsold dwellings which is included in 'Increase in stocks'.
b) For years prior to 1978, components do not add up to total due to the method used to rebase to 1980 prices.
c) Price indexes based on 1963 were used to deflate the period 1960-1962, indexes based on 1970 were used to deflate the period 1963-1972, and indexes based on 1975 were used for the period 1973-1977. For subsequent years, price indices based on 1980 have been used for deflation purposes. The series were then linked at the component and total levels producing a residual difference shown as a statistical discrepancy.

1.3 Cost Components of the Gross Domestic Product

Million Pounds Sterling

	1970	1975	1977	1978	1979	1980	1981	1982	1983	1984	1985	1986
1 Indirect taxes, net	7231	9960	16091	18550	24655	30218	35536	39809	41930	43694	47953	54240
A Indirect taxes	8115	13646	19307	22179	29145	35829	41891	45674	48281	51338	55334	60792
B Less: Subsidies	884	3686	3216	3629	4490	5611	6355	5865	6351	7644	7381	6552
2 Consumption of fixed capital	4612	11632	16511	19382	22834	27963	31647	33676	36168	38892	42315	46004
3 Compensation of employees paid by resident producers to:	30623	68646	86790	99052	116065	137872	149731	158812	169826	180352	194759	209822
A Resident households	30544	68460	86512	98766	115778	137588	149453	158492	169485	179982	194353	209365
B Rest of the world	79	186	278	286	287	284	278	320	341	370	406	457
4 Operating surplus	9372	14361	25896	29891	33442	34095	37782	46592	54676	60741	69612	70600
A Corporate and quasi-corporate enterprises	3918	2971	10555	12353	13423	11574	12601	18247	24071	26539	32102	29327
B Private unincorporated enterprises	4827	10377	13948	15996	18276	20597	23141	26446	29169	33049	36036	39995
C General government	627	1013	1393	1542	1743	1924	2040	1899	1436	1153	1474	1278
Statistical discrepancy	-491	1354	250	993	-668	-57	-1227	-3258	-2543	-4549	-3927	-6960
Equals: Gross Domestic Product	51347	105953	145538	167868	196328	230091	253469	275631	300057	319130	350712	373706

1.4 General Government Current Receipts and Disbursements

Million Pounds Sterling

	1970	1975	1977	1978	1979	1980	1981	1982	1983	1984	1985	1986
					Receipts							
1 Operating surplus	605	1013	1393	1542	1743	1924	2040	1899	1436	1153	1474	1278
2 Property and entrepreneurial income	903	2021	2747	2977	3723	4979	5733	6817	6935	7568	8601	8857
3 Taxes, fees and contributions	18757	38212	50391	56099	67227	82228	95768	106272	114950	122995	134161	142777
A Indirect taxes	8149	13646	19307	22179	29145	35829	41891	45674	48281	51338	55334	60792
B Direct taxes	7915	17638	21428	23648	26399	32272	37769	42285	45628	49087	54373	55630
C Social security contributions	2655	6848	9508	10107	11531	13944	15923	18105	20800	22316	24216	26082
D Compulsory fees, fines and penalties	38	80	148	165	152	183	185	208	241	254	238	273
4 Other current transfers	488	1397	2016	2282	2588	3211	3898	4305	4720	5115	5432	5837
Total Current Receipts of General Government	20753	42643	56547	62900	75281	92342	107439	119293	128041	136821	149090	158749
					Disbursements							
1 Government final consumption expenditure	9015	23125	29487	33423	38908	49046	55470	60549	66006	69915	74070	79455
A Compensation of employees	5555	15188	18774	20878	23800	30092	34276	36530	39839	42064	44621	48370
B Consumption of fixed capital	301	778	1051	1184	1408	1746	1944	1973	2070	2172	2353	2541
C Purchases of goods and services, net	2598	6547	8709	10179	12108	15204	16724	19229	21744	23395	24830	26027
D Less: Own account fixed capital formation	150	192	274	304	336	456	427	495	557	564	567	676
E Indirect taxes paid, net	711	804	1227	1486	1928	2460	2953	3312	2910	2848	2833	3193
2 Property income	2025	4127	6288	7093	8671	10873	12700	13945	14159	15740	17469	17022

United Kingdom

1.4 General Government Current Receipts and Disbursements
(Continued)

Million Pounds Sterling

	1970	1975	1977	1978	1979	1980	1981	1982	1983	1984	1985	1986
A Interest	2025	4127	6288	7093	8671	10873	12700	13945	14159	15740	17469	17022
B Net land rent and royalties	...	...	...	...	...	...	...	...	...	...	...	...
3 Subsidies	884	3686	3216	3629	4490	5611	6355	5865	6351	7644	7381	6552
4 Other current transfers	4911	11532	17624	21331	24923	29727	36015	41969	45656	49384	54642	57647
A Social security benefits	2731	6519	9410	10738	12171	14804	17860	19348	20746	21977	23368	25509
B Social assistance grants	1289	3032	4707	6213	7683	9314	11848	15497	16983	18855	20948	22345
C Other	891	1981	3507	4380	5069	5609	6307	7124	7927	8552	10326	9793
Statistical discrepancy	84	479	515	498	601	792	739	720	759	827	793	983
5 Net saving	3834	-306	-583	-3074	-2312	-3707	-3840	-3755	-4890	-6689	-4657	-4910
Total Current Disbursements and Net Saving of General Government	20753	42643	56547	62900	75281	92342	107439	119293	128041	136821	149698	156749

1.5 Current Income and Outlay of Corporate and Quasi-Corporate Enterprises, Summary

Million Pounds Sterling

	1970	1975	1977	1978	1979	1980	1981	1982	1983	1984	1985	1986
Receipts												
1 Operating surplus	3918	2971	10555	12353	13423	11574	12601	18247	24071	26539	32102	29327
2 Property and entrepreneurial income received	5716	14947	18772	21512	33468	43902	47341	53329	54336	63750	78299	81427
3 Current transfers	...	...	...	...	...	...	...	...	...	...	...	...
Total Current Receipts	9634	17918	29327	33865	46891	55476	59942	71576	78407	90289	110401	110754
Disbursements												
1 Property and entrepreneurial income	7136	16239	19167	21831	33806	45832	48278	55349	55645	64033	77884	79099
2 Direct taxes and other current payments to general government	1736	2487	3334	4191	5194	6838	8836	10825	12412	14464	17081	15087
3 Other current transfers	36	42	43	45	51	52	62	69	86	102	114	134
4 Net saving	726	-850	6783	7798	7840	2754	2766	5333	10264	11690	15322	16434
Total Current Disbursements and Net Saving	9634	17918	29327	33865	46891	55476	59942	71576	78407	90289	110401	110754

1.6 Current Income and Outlay of Households and Non-Profit Institutions

Million Pounds Sterling

	1970	1975	1977	1978	1979	1980	1981	1982	1983	1984	1985	1986
Receipts												
1 Compensation of employees	30553	68494	86568	98826	115842	137657	149525	158568	169558	180053	194434	209445
A From resident producers	30544	68460	86512	98766	115778	137588	149453	158492	169485	179982	194353	209365
B From rest of the world	9	34	56	60	64	69	72	76	73	71	81	80
2 Operating surplus of private unincorporated enterprises	4827	10377	13948	15996	18276	20597	23141	26446	29169	33049	36036	39995
3 Property and entrepreneurial income	4031	6771	8440	9756	14141	18274	19802	22605	23569	27049	32983	34685
4 Current transfers	4596	10712	15692	18696	21807	26499	32400	37925	41275	44701	48325	52382
A Social security benefits	2751	6469	9333	10646	12072	14689	17675	19151	20495	21671	23017	25131
B Social assistance grants	1243	3019	4686	6185	7657	9278	11832	15504	17158	19006	21106	22562
C Other	602	1224	1673	1865	2078	2532	2893	3270	3622	4024	4202	4689
Total Current Receipts	44007	96354	124648	143274	170066	203027	224868	245544	263571	284852	311778	336507
Disbursements												
1 Private final consumption expenditure	31740	64992	86215	99420	117745	136725	152166	166551	181858	194596	212207	232569
2 Property income	1058	3095	4330	4729	6908	10073	11401	12940	13569	16908	22803	24353
3 Direct taxes and other current transfers n.e.c. to general government	8897	22079	27745	29723	32883	39556	45034	49763	54244	57178	61730	66883
A Social security contributions	2655	6848	9503	10101	11526	13939	15916	18095	20787	22301	24200	26067
B Direct taxes	6201	15151	18094	19457	21205	25434	28933	31460	33216	34623	37292	40543
C Fees, fines and penalties	41	80	148	165	152	183	185	208	241	254	238	273
4 Other current transfers	243	531	659	901	1044	1139	1175	1291	1250	1357	1500	1663
5 Net saving	2069	5657	5699	8501	11486	15534	15092	14999	12650	14813	13538	11039
Total Current Disbursements and Net Saving	44007	96354	124648	143274	170066	203027	224868	245544	263571	284852	311778	336507

United Kingdom

1.7 External Transactions on Current Account, Summary

Million Pounds Sterling

	1970	1975	1977	1978	1979	1980	1981	1982	1983	1984	1985	1986
Payments to the Rest of the World												
1 Imports of goods and services	11482	29421	42968	45889	55096	58346	61148	68598	78134	93215	99178	101535
A Imports of merchandise c.i.f.	9004	24150	35884	38599	46566	48587	50282	56202	64835	78376	84093	85024
B Other	2478	5271	7084	7290	8530	9759	10866	12396	13299	14839	15085	16511
2 Factor income to the rest of the world	821	5592	7601	9631	14241	21804	34878	41960	38700	45260	46035	40972
A Compensation of employees	79	186	278	286	287	284	278	320	341	370	406	457
B Property and entrepreneurial income	742	5406	7323	9345	13954	21520	34600	41640	38359	44890	45629	40515
By general government	319	491	565	650	681	895	940	1092	1189	1326	1475	1668
By corporate and quasi-corporate enterprises	423	4915	6758	8695	13273	20625	33660	40548	37170	43564	44154	38847
By other	...	...	...	...	...	...	...	...	...	...	...	...
3 Current transfers to the rest of the world	412	1234	2043	3019	3618	3899	4515	5298	5490	5938	6787	6118
A Indirect taxes to supranational organizations	-	349	752	985	1983	1897	2241	2936	3063	3296	3879	2890
B Other current transfers	412	885	1291	2034	1635	2002	2274	2362	2427	2642	2908	3228
4 Surplus of the nation on current transactions	630	-2194	-200	737	94	3512	5864	3474	2326	-1066	1684	-3171
Payments to the Rest of the World and Surplus of the Nation on Current Transactions	13345	34053	52412	59276	73049	87561	106405	119330	124650	143347	153684	145454
Receipts From The Rest of the World												
1 Exports of goods and services	11935	27577	43945	48051	55685	63691	68407	73609	81004	92611	102706	98439
A Exports of merchandise f.o.b.	8150	19330	31728	35063	40687	47422	50977	55565	60776	70367	78111	72843
B Other	3785	8247	12217	12988	14998	16269	17430	18044	20228	22244	24595	25596
2 Factor income from rest of the world	1181	5718	7553	9997	15965	21966	35169	42233	39899	46637	47467	43090
A Compensation of employees	9	34	56	60	64	69	72	76	73	71	81	80
B Property and entrepreneurial income	1172	5684	7497	9937	15901	21897	35097	42157	39826	46566	47386	43010
By general government	54	266	384	693	816	946	970	980	767	820	738	760
By corporate and quasi-corporate enterprises	1118	5418	7113	9244	15085	20951	34127	41177	39059	45746	46648	42250
By other	...	...	...	...	...	...	...	...	...	...	...	...
3 Current transfers from rest of the world	230	759	915	1228	1399	1904	2829	3489	3747	4099	3511	3925
A Subsidies from supranational organisations	-	342	184	344	380	573	742	855	1158	1442	1284	1470
B Other current transfers	230	417	731	884	1019	1331	2087	2634	2589	2657	2227	2455
Receipts from the Rest of the World on Current Transactions	13346	34054	52413	59276	73049	87561	106405	119331	124650	143347	153684	145454

1.8 Capital Transactions of The Nation, Summary

Million Pounds Sterling

	1970	1975	1977	1978	1979	1980	1981	1982	1983	1984	1985	1986
Finance of Gross Capital Formation												
Gross saving	11239	16133	28410	32608	39849	42544	45665	50251	54193	58707	66516	68567
1 Consumption of fixed capital	4612	11632	16511	19382	22834	27963	31647	33676	36168	38892	42315	46004
A General government	557	1411	1863	2089	2487	3097	3493	3547	3646	3854	4133	4445
B Corporate and quasi-corporate enterprises	3081	7689	11172	13145	15354	18802	21270	22764	24375	26055	28307	30566
Public	1129	2755	3836	4328	4977	6002	6674	6946	7212	7468	6212	6447
Private	1952	4934	7336	8817	10377	12800	14596	15818	17163	18587	22095	24119
C Other	974	2532	3476	4148	4993	6064	6884	7365	8147	8983	9875	10993
2 Net saving	6627	4501	11899	13226	17015	14581	14018	16575	18025	19815	24201	22563
A General government	3832	-306	-583	-3074	-2312	-3707	-3840	-3755	-4890	-6689	-4657	-4910
B Corporate and quasi-corporate enterprises	726	-850	6783	7798	7840	2754	2766	5333	10264	11690	15322	16434
Public	-412	-1514	-947	-937	-1936	-2152	-1519	-768	16	-1859	-1244	-378
Private	1138	664	7730	8735	9776	4906	4285	6101	10248	13549	16566	16812
C Other	2069	5657	5699	8501	11486	15534	15092	14999	12650	14813	13538	11039
Less: Surplus of the nation on current transactions	630	-2194	-200	737	94	3512	5864	3474	2326	-1066	1684	-3171

United Kingdom

1.8 Capital Transactions of The Nation, Summary
(Continued)

Million Pounds Sterling

	1970	1975	1977	1978	1979	1980	1981	1982	1983	1984	1985	1986
Statistical discrepancy	-491	1354	250	993	-668	-57	-1227	-3258	-2543	-4549	-3927	-6960
Finance of Gross Capital Formation	10118	19681	28860	32864	39087	38975	38574	43519	49324	55224	60905	64778
Gross Capital Formation												
Increase in stocks	382	-1354	1824	1804	2162	-2586	-2735	-1244	730	116	428	551
Gross fixed capital formation	9736	21035	27036	31060	36925	41561	41309	44763	48594	55108	60477	64227
1 General government	2443	4995	4817	4653	5145	5499	4568	4254	5680	6541	6581	7296
2 Corporate and quasi-corporate enterprises	5690	12224	16714	20198	23622	26778	27010	28553	28587	33661	38160	38808
A Public	1676	3920	4779	4944	5641	6653	6780	7114	7884	7405	5717	5555
B Private	4014	8304	11935	15254	17981	20125	20230	21439	20703	26256	32443	33253
3 Other	1603	3816	5505	6209	8158	9284	9731	11956	14327	14906	15736	18123
Gross Capital Formation	10118	19681	28860	32864	39087	38975	38574	43519	49324	55224	60905	64778

1.9 Gross Domestic Product by Institutional Sectors of Origin

Million Pounds Sterling

	1970	1975	1977	1978	1979	1980	1981	1982	1983	1984	1985	1986
Domestic Factor Incomes Originating												
1 General government	6552	16832	20881	23200	26544	33110	37560	39893	42889	45013	47921	51712
2 Corporate and quasi-corporate enterprises	25842	50523	71024	81846	95454	107201	114511	125738	137966	147386	163290	169825
A Non-financial	25260	49484	69607	80313	93016	105324	112782	122758	134152	144409	160195	166058
Public	3361	7787	10682	12136	13095	15599	17689	19851	20649	18017	16711	18527
Private	21899	41697	58925	68177	79921	89725	95093	102907	113503	126392	143484	147531
B Financial	582	1039	1417	1533	2438	1877	1729	2980	3814	2977	3095	3767
Public	-4	19	12	13	-4	-21	8	1	-4	12	7	4
Private	586	1020	1405	1520	2442	1898	1721	2979	3818	2965	3088	3763
3 Households and private unincorporated enterprises	7601	15652	20781	23897	27509	31656	35442	39773	43647	48694	53160	58885
A Owner-occupied housing	1296	3456	4669	5403	6522	7830	9114	10160	11013	11759	12838	13610
B Subsistence production	-	-	-	-	-	-	-	-	-	-	-	-
C Other	6305	12196	16112	18494	20987	23826	26328	29613	32634	36935	40322	45275
4 Non-profit institutions serving households	...	...	...	...	...	...	...	...	...	...	...	...
Subtotal: Domestic Factor Incomes	39995	83007	112686	128943	149507	171967	187513	205404	224502	241093	264371	280422
Indirect taxes, net	7231	9960	16091	18550	24655	30218	35536	39809	41930	43694	47953	54240
A Indirect taxes	8115	13646	19307	22179	29145	35829	41891	45674	48281	51338	55334	60792
B Less: Subsidies	884	3686	3216	3629	4490	5611	6355	5865	6351	7644	7381	6552
Consumption of fixed capital	4612	11632	16511	19382	22834	27963	31647	33676	36168	38892	42315	46004
Statistical discrepancy	-491	1354	250	993	-668	-57	-1227	-3258	-2543	-4549	-3927	-6960
Gross Domestic Product	51347	105953	145538	167868	196328	230091	253469	275631	300057	319130	350712	373706

1.10 Gross Domestic Product by Kind of Activity, in Current Prices

Million Pounds Sterling

	1970	1975	1977	1978	1979	1980	1981	1982	1983	1984	1985	1986
1 Agriculture, hunting, forestry and fishing	1242	2466	3353	3590	3922	4303	4837	5530	5365	6222	5627	5902
2 Mining and quarrying	616	1861	4288	5291	8510	12444	16031	18332	20777	22244	22897	12815
3 Manufacturing [a]	14947	27866	38875	44598	50259	54515	55152	59399	62774	67145	74782	81328
4 Electricity, gas and water [b]	1359	2764	4090	4500	4743	6389	7215	7764	8613	7260	8373	9413
5 Construction	2899	6266	7845	9139	10566	12022	12775	13874	15518	17064	18536	20061
6 Wholesale and retail trade, restaurants and hotels [a]	5949	11925	16527	19389	22120	24924	27112	29083	31993	35846	40521	45770
7 Transport, storage and communication	3691	7767	10224	11765	13206	14335	15830	17119	18228	19757	21426	23727
8 Finance, insurance, real estate and business services	6589	15428	22357	25461	31312	36851	41761	47495	51435	56312	63184	70386
9 Community, social and personal services [a]	2212	4409	6207	7094	8131	9231	10150	10630	12118	13693	15710	17906
Total, Industries	39504	80752	113766	130827	152769	175014	190863	209226	226821	245543	271056	287308
Producers of Government Services	5642	15641	19212	21418	24449	31184	35296	37601	41165	43484	46125	50576
Other Producers	705	1469	1850	2081	2446	3085	3610	3981	4320	4751	5239	5946

United Kingdom

1.10 Gross Domestic Product by Kind of Activity, in Current Prices
(Continued)

Million Pounds Sterling

	1970	1975	1977	1978	1979	1980	1981	1982	1983	1984	1985	1986
Subtotal [c]	45851	97862	134828	154326	179664	209283	229769	250808	272306	293778	322420	343830
Less: Imputed bank service charge	1244	3223	5631	6001	7323	9353	10609	11728	11636	13793	15734	17404
Plus: Import duties [d]	7231	6445	11686	13311	15859	18287	22490	25490	25896	25466	27162	31516
Plus: Value added tax	-	3515	4405	5239	8796	11931	13046	14319	16034	18228	20791	22724
Plus: Other adjustments [e]	-491	1354	250	993	-668	-57	-1227	-3258	-2543	-4549	-3927	-6960
Equals: Gross Domestic Product	51347	105953	145538	167868	196328	230091	253469	275631	300057	319130	350712	373706
Memorandum Item: Mineral fuels and power [f]	2065	5036	9218	10743	14627	20200	24201	26914	30697	30605	33131	24445

a) Repairs to consumer durables other than clothing are included in item 'Wholesale and retail trade, restaurants and hotels'.
b) Item 'Electricity, gas and water' includes nuclear fuel production.
c) Gross domestic product in factor values.
d) Item 'Import duties' refers to indirect taxes net of subsidies.
e) Item 'Other adjustments' refers to statistical discrepancy.
f) Item 'Mineral fuels and Power' includes water supply.

1.11 Gross Domestic Product by Kind of Activity, in Constant Prices

Index numbers 1980=100

	1970	1975	1977	1978	1979	1980	1981	1982	1983	1984	1985	1986
					At constant prices of:1980							
1 Agriculture, hunting, forestry and fishing	...	81.9	85.1	91.5	90.1	100.0	102.6	111.2	105.2	124.5	118.8	118.8
2 Mining and quarrying	...	73.9	77.4	77.1	98.8	100.0	106.6	117.3	124.9	118.5	128.8	133.7
3 Manufacturing [a]	...	105.0	109.0	109.7	109.5	100.0	94.0	94.2	96.9	100.8	103.8	104.7
4 Electricity, gas and water [b]	...	97.1	96.4	96.8	102.3	100.0	99.1	98.2	100.2	95.2	104.5	109.6
5 Construction	...	100.1	98.4	105.1	105.8	100.0	89.9	91.6	95.3	98.5	99.8	102.1
6 Wholesale and retail trade, restaurants and hotels [a]	...	97.5	97.8	103.5	106.5	100.0	98.4	100.3	104.6	109.5	114.8	120.4
7 Transport, storage and communication	...	92.5	94.6	96.9	101.3	100.0	100.2	99.2	102.1	106.4	112.1	116.7
8 Finance, insurance, real estate and business services	...	83.0	89.0	93.0	97.0	100.0	103.0	108.0	114.0	122.0	129.0	138.0
9 Community, social and personal services [a]	...	81.0	89.0	92.0	95.0	100.0	100.0	101.0	105.0	111.0	117.0	123.0
Total, Industries	...	...	...	...	...	...	...	...	...	...	...	...
Producers of Government Services	...	95.1	96.8	97.7	99.0	100.0	100.4	99.5	100.1	100.7	100.3	100.8
Other Producers	...	...	...	...	...	...	...	...	...	...	...	...
Subtotal	...	...	...	...	...	...	...	...	...	...	...	...
Less: Imputed bank service charge	...	78.0	82.0	87.0	94.0	100.0	105.0	111.0	120.0	131.0	140.0	157.0
Plus: Import duties	...	...	...	...	...	...	...	...	...	...	...	...
Plus: Value added tax	...	...	...	...	...	...	...	...	...	...	...	...
Equals: Gross Domestic Product [c]	...	92.0	96.6	99.9	102.9	100.0	98.4	100.1	103.3	106.7	110.7	114.0
Memorandum Item: Mineral fuels and power	...	51.9	73.6	84.3	100.4	100.0	104.1	110.4	116.5	110.5	120.8	126.1

a) Repairs to consumer durables other than clothing are included in item 'Wholesale and retail trade, restaurants and hotels'.
b) Item 'Electricity, gas and water' includes nuclear fuel production.
c) Gross domestic product in factor values.

1.12 Relations Among National Accounting Aggregates

Million Pounds Sterling

	1970	1975	1977	1978	1979	1980	1981	1982	1983	1984	1985	1986
Gross Domestic Product	51347	105953	145538	167868	196328	230091	253469	275631	300057	319130	350712	373706
Plus: Net factor income from the rest of the world	360	126	-48	366	1724	162	291	273	1199	1377	1432	2118
Factor income from the rest of the world	1181	5718	7553	9997	15965	21966	35169	42233	39899	46637	47467	43090
Less: Factor income to the rest of the world	821	5592	7601	9631	14241	21804	34878	41960	38700	45260	46035	40972
Equals: Gross National Product	51707	106079	145490	168234	198052	230253	253760	275904	301256	320507	352144	375824
Less: Consumption of fixed capital	4612	11632	16511	19382	22834	27963	31647	33676	36168	38892	42315	46004

United Kingdom

1.12 Relations Among National Accounting Aggregates
(Continued)

Million Pounds Sterling

	1970	1975	1977	1978	1979	1980	1981	1982	1983	1984	1985	1986
Equals: National Income	47095	94447	128979	148852	175218	202290	222113	242228	265088	281615	309829	329820
Plus: Net current transfers from the rest of the world	-182	-475	-1128	-1791	-2219	-1995	-1686	-1809	-1743	-1839	-3276	-2193
Current transfers from the rest of the world	230	759	915	1228	1399	1904	2829	3489	3747	4099	3511	3925
Less: Current transfers to the rest of the world	412	1234	2043	3019	3618	3899	4515	5298	5490	5938	6787	6118
Equals: National Disposable Income	46913	93972	127851	147061	172999	200295	220427	240419	263345	279776	306553	327627
Less: Final consumption	40777	88117	115702	132842	156652	185771	207636	227102	247863	264510	286279	312024
Statistical discrepancy	491	-1354	-250	-993	668	57	1227	3258	2543	4549	3927	6960
Equals: Net Saving	6627	4501	11899	13226	17015	14581	14018	16575	18025	19815	24201	22563
Less: Surplus of the nation on current transactions [a]	630	-2194	-200	737	94	3512	5864	3474	2326	-1066	1684	-3171
Statistical discrepancy	-491	1354	250	993	-668	-57	-1227	-3258	-2543	-4549	-3927	-6960
Equals: Net Capital Formation	5506	8049	12349	13482	16253	11012	6927	9843	13156	16332	18590	18774

a) Item 'Surplus of the nation on current transactions' includes net transfers abroad: 59 million in 1973 and 75 million in 1974.

2.1 Government Final Consumption Expenditure by Function, in Current Prices

Million Pounds Sterling

	1970	1975	1977	1978	1979	1980	1981	1982	1983	1984	1985	1986
1 General public services	...	...	1803	1949	2337	2840	3055	3338	3485	3455	3668	3965
2 Defence	...	...	6762	7507	8892	11370	12562	14333	15631	16953	17940	18176
3 Public order and safety	...	...	1929	2217	2680	3408	4050	4517	4957	5513	5766	6231
4 Education	...	...	6301	7057	8011	9852	11120	12025	12839	13404	13718	15583
5 Health	...	...	6375	7343	8488	10967	12628	13196	14990	15716	16752	18238
6 Social security and welfare	...	...	1851	2107	2482	3142	3658	4115	4435	4746	5332	5603
7 Housing and community amenities	...	...	906	1057	1274	1589	1734	1927	2115	2215	2463	2661
8 Recreational, cultural and religious affairs	...	...	615	710	849	1058	1159	1265	1449	1512	1519	1642
9 Economic services	...	...	1894	2292	2487	3074	3560	3860	4035	4229	4559	4815
A Fuel and energy	...	...	98	99	110	163	163	153	206	243	264	304
B Agriculture, forestry, fishing and hunting	...	...	262	306	327	430	456	479	495	443	433	497
C Mining, manufacturing and construction, except fuel and energy	...	...	166	224	188	193	374	385	365	404	464	433
D Transportation and communication	...	...	835	938	1094	1335	1523	1711	1752	1715	1844	1923
E Other economic affairs	...	...	533	725	768	953	1044	1132	1217	1424	1554	1658
10 Other functions	...	...	1051	1184	1408	1746	1944	1973	2070	2172	2353	2541
Total Government Final Consumption Expenditure	...	...	29487	33423	38908	49046	55470	60549	66006	69915	74070	79455

2.3 Total Government Outlays by Function and Type

Million Pounds Sterling

	Final Consumption Expenditures Total	Compensation of Employees	Other	Subsidies	Other Current Transfers & Property Income	Total Current Disbursements	Gross Capital Formation	Other Capital Outlays	Total Outlays
					1980				
1 General public services	2840	...	...	-	940	3780	390	40	4210
2 Defence	11370	...	...	-	38	11408	70	11	11489
3 Public order and safety	3408	...	...	-	98	3506	183	-	3689
4 Education	9852	...	...	-	2147	11999	575	184	12758
5 Health	10967	...	...	-	46	11013	616	-	11629
6 Social security and welfare	3142	...	...	-	25187	28329	92	1	28422
7 Housing and community amenities	1589	...	...	2558	264	4411	1895	846	7152
8 Recreation, culture and religion	1058	...	...	-	128	1186	227	14	1427
9 Economic services	3074	...	...	3053	3125	9252	1503	1357	12112

United Kingdom

2.3 Total Government Outlays by Function and Type
(Continued)

Million Pounds Sterling

	Final Consumption Expenditures Total	Compensation of Employees	Other	Subsidies	Other Current Transfers & Property Income	Total Current Disbursements	Gross Capital Formation	Other Capital Outlays	Total Outlays
A Fuel and energy	163	...	...	294	17	474	28	3	505
B Agriculture, forestry, fishing and hunting	430	...	...	722	43	1195	223	229	1647
C Mining (except fuels), manufacturing and construction	193	...	...	214	56	463	60	643	1166
D Transportation and communication	1335	...	...	1136	-	2471	1059	428	3958
E Other economic affairs	953	...	...	687	3009	4649	133	54	4836
10 Other functions	1746	...	...	-	8627	10373	-1	-	10372
Total	49046	...	...	5611	40600	95257	5550	2453	103260

1981

1 General public services	3055	...	...	-	1146	4201	346	33	4580
2 Defence	12562	...	...	-	54	12616	46	10	12672
3 Public order and safety	4050	...	...	-	92	4142	195	-	4337
4 Education	11120	...	...	-	2434	13554	563	201	14318
5 Health	12628	...	...	-	43	12671	700	-	13371
6 Social security and welfare	3658	...	...	-	31110	34768	96	1	34865
7 Housing and community amenities	1734	...	...	2163	383	4280	956	759	5995
8 Recreation, culture and religion	1159	...	...	-	156	1315	241	13	1569
9 Economic services	3560	...	...	4192	3305	11057	1364	4864	17285
A Fuel and energy	163	...	...	559	38	760	-5	10	765
B Agriculture, forestry, fishing and hunting	456	...	...	895	44	1395	134	218	1747
C Mining (except fuels), manufacturing and construction	374	...	...	267	117	758	52	4406	5216
D Transportation and communication	1523	...	...	1360	-	2883	1071	162	4116
E Other economic affairs	1044	...	...	1111	3106	5261	112	68	5441
10 Other functions	1944	...	...	-	9992	11936	-	-	11936
Total	55470	...	...	6355	48715	110540	4507	5881	120928

1982

1 General public services	3338	...	...	-	1111	4449	503	37	4989
2 Defence	14333	...	...	-	60	14393	72	35	14500
3 Public order and safety	4517	...	...	-	99	4616	245	-	4861
4 Education	12025	...	...	-	2564	14589	505	187	15281
5 Health	13196	...	...	-	61	13257	817	4	14078
6 Social security and welfare	4115	...	...	-	36266	40381	102	-	40483
7 Housing and community amenities	1927	...	...	1554	497	3978	-11	1140	5107
8 Recreation, culture and religion	1265	...	...	-	162	1427	265	4	1696
9 Economic services	3860	...	...	4311	3666	11837	1861	2473	16171
A Fuel and energy	153	...	...	581	72	806	-33	11	784
B Agriculture, forestry, fishing and hunting	479	...	...	910	50	1439	378	245	2062
C Mining (except fuels), manufacturing and construction	385	...	...	324	147	856	32	1792	2680
D Transportation and communication	1711	...	...	1616	71	3398	1362	350	5110
E Other economic affairs	1132	...	...	880	3326	5338	122	75	5535
10 Other functions	1973	...	...	-	11428	13401	-	-	13401
Total	60549	...	...	5865	55914	122328	4359	3880	130567

1983

1 General public services	3485	...	...	-	1221	4706	422	43	5171
2 Defence	15631	...	...	-	47	15678	171	23	15872
3 Public order and safety	4957	...	...	-	99	5056	256	-	5312
4 Education	12839	...	...	-	2772	15611	555	179	16345
5 Health	14990	...	...	-	76	15066	854	4	15924
6 Social security and welfare	4435	...	...	-	39317	43752	100	-	43852
7 Housing and community amenities	2115	...	...	1389	462	3966	1133	1933	7032
8 Recreation, culture and religion	1449	...	...	-	182	1631	323	3	1957
9 Economic services	4035	...	...	4962	3380	12377	2220	1409	16006

United Kingdom

2.3 Total Government Outlays by Function and Type
(Continued)

Million Pounds Sterling

		Final Consumption Expenditures Total	Compensation of Employees	Other	Subsidies	Other Current Transfers & Property Income	Total Current Disbursements	Gross Capital Formation	Other Capital Outlays	Total Outlays
	A Fuel and energy	206	...	...	953	152	1311	38	-	1349
	B Agriculture, forestry, fishing and hunting	495	...	...	1259	54	1808	464	270	2542
	C Mining (except fuels), manufacturing and construction	365	...	...	324	101	790	81	787	1658
	D Transportation and communication	1752	...	...	1642	84	3478	1482	308	5268
	E Other economic affairs	1217	...	...	784	2989	4990	155	44	5189
10	Other functions	2070	...	...	-	12259	14329	-	-	14329
	Total	66006	...	...	6351	59815	132172	6034	3594	141800
					1984					
1	General public services	3455	...	...	-	1338	4793	497	49	5339
2	Defence	16953	...	...	-	61	17014	203	17	17234
3	Public order and safety	5513	...	...	-	108	5621	292	-	5913
4	Education	13404	...	...	-	2865	16269	606	187	17062
5	Health	15716	...	...	-	91	15807	945	4	16756
6	Social security and welfare	4746	...	...	-	42610	47356	123	1	47480
7	Housing and community amenities	2215	...	...	1403	528	4146	1512	2271	7929
8	Recreation, culture and religion	1512	...	...	-	193	1705	400	1	2106
9	Economic services	4229	...	...	6241	3196	13666	1871	1266	16803
	A Fuel and energy	243	...	...	1982	206	2431	34	5	2470
	B Agriculture, forestry, fishing and hunting	443	...	...	1491	49	1983	27	277	2287
	C Mining (except fuels), manufacturing and construction	404	...	...	297	101	802	50	670	1522
	D Transportation and communication	1715	...	...	1595	92	3402	1581	257	5240
	E Other economic affairs	1424	...	...	876	2748	5048	179	57	5284
10	Other functions	2172	...	...	-	14134	16306	-	-	16306
	Total	69915	...	...	7644	65124	142683	6449	3796	152928
					1985					
1	General public services	3668	...	...	-	1377	5045	602	54	5701
2	Defence	17940	...	...	-	54	17994	268	21	18283
3	Public order and safety	5766	...	...	-	98	5864	327	-	6191
4	Education	13718	...	...	-	2905	16623	592	208	17423
5	Health	16752	...	...	-	117	16869	1005	4	17878
6	Social security and welfare	5332	...	...	-	46369	51701	152	-	51853
7	Housing and community amenities	2463	...	...	1402	572	4437	1272	1683	7392
8	Recreation, culture and religion	1519	...	...	-	298	1817	376	3	2196
9	Economic services	4559	...	...	5979	3474	14012	2618	1331	17961
	A Fuel and energy	264	...	...	1557	421	2242	49	-	2291
	B Agriculture, forestry, fishing and hunting	433	...	...	1385	49	1867	722	220	2809
	C Mining (except fuels), manufacturing and construction	464	...	...	253	86	803	77	797	1677
	D Transportation and communication	1844	...	...	1682	78	3604	1677	270	5551
	E Other economic affairs	1554	...	...	1102	2840	5496	93	44	5633
10	Other functions	2353	...	...	-	16847	19200	-	-	19200
	Total	74070	...	...	7381	72111	153562	7212	3304	164078
					1986					
1	General public services	3965	...	...	-	1449	5414	569	67	6050
2	Defence	18176	...	...	-	82	18258	358	12	18628
3	Public order and safety	6231	...	...	-	107	6338	354	-	6692
4	Education	15583	...	...	-	3047	18630	660	235	19525
5	Health	18238	...	...	-	125	18363	1078	5	19446
6	Social security and welfare	5603	...	...	-	50164	55767	189	-	55956
7	Housing and community amenities	2661	...	...	1452	800	4913	1626	1605	8144
8	Recreation, culture and religion	1642	...	...	-	290	1932	316	1	2249
9	Economic services	4815	...	...	5100	2826	12741	2254	1351	16346

United Kingdom

2.3 Total Government Outlays by Function and Type
(Continued)

Million Pounds Sterling

	Final Consumption Expenditures Total	Compensation of Employees	Other	Subsidies	Other Current Transfers & Property Income	Total Current Disbursements	Gross Capital Formation	Other Capital Outlays	Total Outlays
A Fuel and energy	304	...	...	766	593	1663	4	-	1667
B Agriculture, forestry, fishing and hunting	497	...	...	1608	21	2126	181	170	2477
C Mining (except fuels), manufacturing and construction	433	...	...	234	94	761	52	845	1658
D Transportation and communication	1923	...	...	1556	83	3562	1851	301	5714
E Other economic affairs	1658	...	...	936	2035	4629	166	35	4830
10 Other functions	2541	...	...	-	15779	18320	-4	-	18316
Total	79455	...	...	6552	74669	160676	7400	3276	171352

2.5 Private Final Consumption Expenditure by Type and Porpose, in Current Prices

Million Pounds Sterling

	1970	1975	1977	1978	1979	1980	1981	1982	1983	1984	1985	1986
Final Consumption Expenditure of Resident Households												
1 Food, beverages and tobacco	8236	15430	20811	23142	26227	29455	31683	33666	36098	38004	40136	42975
A Food	6194	11531	15523	17324	19606	22020	23364	24793	26379	27591	28871	30956
B Non-alcoholic beverages	155	430	524	603	758	856	843	856	1006	1051	1193	1386
C Alcoholic beverages	425	1144	1680	1913	2264	2481	2788	3018	3435	3733	4117	4283
D Tobacco	1462	2325	3084	3302	3599	4098	4688	4999	5278	5629	5955	6350
2 Clothing and footwear	2753	5206	6630	7830	9170	9875	10157	10925	12191	13326	14879	16388
3 Gross rent, fuel and power	5368	11622	15815	17772	20866	25180	30307	34618	36949	38947	42786	46099
A Fuel and power	1480	2887	4219	4613	5292	6355	7727	8696	9399	9575	10657	11148
B Other	3888	8735	11596	13159	15574	18825	22580	25922	27550	29372	32129	34951
4 Furniture, furnishings and household equipment and operation	2450	5006	6340	7533	8986	9925	10581	11189	12210	13033	14128	15432
A Household operation [a]	635	1150	1372	1547	1773	2171	2436	2608	2830	3100	3381	3627
B Other	1815	3856	4968	5986	7213	7754	8145	8581	9380	9933	10747	11805
5 Medical care and health expenses	290	547	743	845	1007	1267	1503	1769	2085	2332	2668	2997
6 Transport and communication	3961	9006	12172	14810	18704	21866	24404	26596	29706	31163	34175	36959
A Personal transport equipment	1081	2326	3199	4795	6450	6422	6548	7260	8754	8891	10143	11672
B Other	2880	6680	8973	10015	12254	15444	17856	19336	20952	22272	24032	25287
7 Recreational, entertainment, education and cultural services	2706	5987	8073	9394	11013	12853	14136	15476	16667	18000	19736	21927
A Education	171	374	650	783	883	1135	1336	1441	1432	1507	1625	1757
B Other	2535	5613	7423	8611	10130	11718	12800	14035	15235	16493	18111	20170
8 Miscellaneous goods and services	5477	11297	15362	17437	20675	24316	26525	28930	32589	36179	40263	44378
A Personal care	564	1067	1381	1563	1857	2134	2348	2596	2878	3255	3688	4056
B Expenditures in restaurants, cafes and hotels	3774	7613	10364	11601	13669	16159	17608	18712	20839	22813	24953	26515
C Other	1139	2617	3617	4273	5149	6023	6569	7622	8872	10111	11622	13807
Total Final Consumption Expenditure in the Domestic Market by Households, of which [b]	31241	64101	85946	98763	116648	134737	149296	163169	178495	190984	208771	227155
A Durable goods	2607	5872	7754	10152	13059	13449	13992	15377	17974	18751	20870	23582
B Semi-durable goods	5338	10733	14114	16882	19840	22054	22003	24540	26995	29312	32407	36052
C Non-durable goods	11448	22292	29986	32814	37856	43832	49087	53108	57156	60221	64460	67549
D Services	11848	25204	34092	38913	45892	55401	63335	70143	76369	82699	91033	99970
Plus: Direct purchases abroad by resident households	420	1009	1219	1592	2079	2648	3132	3483	3855	4275	4440	5641
Less: Direct purchases in the domestic market by non-resident households	518	1442	2712	2891	3207	3436	3512	3786	4649	5326	6269	6317
Equals: Final Consumption Expenditure of Resident Households	31143	63668	84453	97464	115520	133949	148916	162866	177701	189933	206942	226479
Final Consumption Expenditure of Private Non-profit Institutions Serving Households												
Equals: Final Consumption Expenditure of Private Non-profit Organisations Serving Households	597	1324	1762	1956	2225	2776	3250	3685	4157	4663	5265	6090
Private Final Consumption Expenditure [b,c]	31740	64992	86215	99420	117745	136725	152166	166551	181858	194596	212207	232569

a) Item 'Household operation' includes repairs to clothing and footwear, household equipment and miscellaneous goods, n.e.c.
b) The estimates of this table (Private final consumption expenditure by type and purpose) exclude the products of private gardens.
c) For years prior to 1978, components do not add up to total due to the method used to rebase to 1980 prices.

United Kingdom

2.6 Private Final Consumption Expenditure by Type and Purpose, in Constant Prices

Million Pounds Sterling

At constant prices of: 1980
Final Consumption Expenditure of Resident Households

	1970	1975	1977	1978	1979	1980	1981	1982	1983	1984	1985	1986
1 Food, beverages and tobacco [a]	27204	28184	28021	29191	29712	29455	28944	28571	29190	29008	29455	30331
A Food	21736	21307	21150	21725	22019	22020	21898	21799	22135	21889	22191	22918
B Non-alcoholic beverages	463	701	735	776	874	856	815	843	974	1002	1084	1256
C Alcoholic beverages	1110	1965	2236	2455	2603	2481	2431	2420	2611	2765	2919	2986
D Tobacco	4194	4246	3912	4235	4216	4098	3800	3509	3470	3352	3261	3171
2 Clothing and footwear	7439	8354	8529	9326	9990	9875	9787	10146	10913	11562	12365	13279
3 Gross rent, fuel and power [a]	21574	23294	23827	24291	25075	25180	25388	25565	26012	26400	27240	27864
A Fuel and power	5828	6107	6202	6314	6624	6355	6333	6210	6218	6149	6565	6730
B Other	15752	17191	17626	17977	18451	18825	19055	19355	19794	20251	20675	21134
4 Furniture, furnishings and household equipment and operation [a]	8296	9512	9117	9766	10293	9925	9939	10069	10580	10854	11273	11949
A Household operation [b]	2664	2372	2088	2087	2081	2171	2212	2192	2230	2313	2378	2443
B Other	5796	7172	7042	7679	8212	7754	7727	7877	8350	8541	8895	9506
5 Medical care and health expenses	1005	1093	1107	1155	1198	1267	1319	1408	1539	1627	1772	1920
6 Transport and communication [a]	15696	18549	18872	20526	21912	21866	22145	22408	24047	24287	25399	27218
A Personal transport equipment	4339	5315	4874	5998	6792	6422	6521	6707	7960	7652	8119	8728
B Other	11423	13220	13913	14528	15120	15444	15624	15701	16087	16635	17280	18490
7 Recreational, entertainment, education and cultural services	8035	10768	11383	12018	12559	12853	12909	13128	13689	14369	15186	16604
A Education	741	736	964	1072	1073	1135	1201	1110	1022	1011	1035	1045
B Other [a]	7330	10006	10408	10946	11486	11718	11708	12018	12667	13358	14151	15559
8 Miscellaneous goods and services [a]	19861	23837	23818	24539	25023	24316	23630	23592	24590	25539	26400	27589
A Personal care	1935	2203	2096	2153	2220	2134	2156	2187	2295	2445	2554	2662
B Expenditures in restaurants, cafes and hotels	14099	15954	15830	16132	16457	16159	15382	14868	15408	15715	16078	16150
C Other	3859	5665	5886	6254	6346	6023	6092	6537	6887	7379	7768	8777
Statistical discrepancy	-137	-111	-87	-	-	-	-	-	-	-	-	-
Total Final Consumption Expenditure in the Domestic Market by Households, of which [ac]	108973	123480	124587	130812	135762	134737	134061	134887	140560	143646	149090	156754
A Durable goods	8297	11232	10962	12475	14084	13449	13706	14396	16551	16717	17887	19739
B Semi-durable goods	16540	19873	20211	21967	22754	22054	21828	22467	23526	24592	25896	27851
C Non-durable goods	39956	41772	41869	43226	44176	43832	43435	43048	43769	43811	44819	46258
D Services	44559	50628	51594	53142	54749	55401	55089	54977	56712	58526	60486	62906
Plus: Direct purchases abroad by resident households	1345	1564	1355	1680	2115	2648	2808	2800	2849	2854	2925	3374
Less: Direct purchases in the domestic market by non-resident households	2028	2994	4185	3927	3791	3436	3109	3075	3554	3823	4195	3967
Equals: Final Consumption Expenditure of Resident Households [a]	108192	121990	121733	128565	134086	133949	133760	134612	139855	142677	147820	156161

Final Consumption Expenditure of Private Non-profit Institutions Serving Households

	1970	1975	1977	1978	1979	1980	1981	1982	1983	1984	1985	1986
Equals: Final Consumption Expenditure of Private Non-profit Organisations Serving Households	2324	2590	2621	2675	2700	2776	2885	3056	3292	3523	3784	4192
Statistical discrepancy	-34	-19	-19	-	-	-	-	-	-	-	-	-
Private Final Consumption Expenditure [ac]	110482	124561	124335	131240	136786	136725	136645	137668	143147	146200	151604	160353

a) For years prior to 1978, components do not add up to total due to the method used to rebase to 1980 prices.
b) Item 'Household operation' includes repairs to clothing and footwear, household equipment and miscellaneous goods, n.e.c.
c) The estimates of this table (Private final consumption expenditure by type and purpose) exclude the products of private gardens.

2.7 Gross Capital Formation by Type of Good and Owner, in Current Prices

Million Pounds Sterling

	1980				1981				1982			
	TOTAL	Total Private	Public Enterprises	General Government	TOTAL	Total Private	Public Enterprises	General Government	TOTAL	Total Private	Public Enterprises	General Government
Increase in stocks, total [a]	-2586	-2856	219	51	-2735	-2734	60	-61	-1244	-1610	261	105
1 Goods producing industries	-2358	-2577	219	-	-2154	-2249	95	-	-1165	-1468	303	-
A Materials and supplies	-1292	-1394	102	-	-1307	-1386	79	-	-360	-743	383	-
B Work in progress	-1031	-964	-67	-	-124	-159	35	-	-526	-495	-31	-
C Livestock, except breeding stocks, dairy cattle, etc.	-42	-42	-	-	-15	-15	-	-	46	46	-	-

United Kingdom

2.7 Gross Capital Formation by Type of Good and Owner, in Current Prices
(Continued)

Million Pounds Sterling

	1980 TOTAL	1980 Total Private	1980 Public Enterprises	1980 General Government	1981 TOTAL	1981 Total Private	1981 Public Enterprises	1981 General Government	1982 TOTAL	1982 Total Private	1982 Public Enterprises	1982 General Government
D Finished goods	7	-177	184	-	-708	-689	-19	-	-325	-276	-49	-
2 Wholesale and retail trade	-883	-885	2	-	-643	-651	8	-	10	7	3	-
3 Other, except government stocks	604	606	-2	-	123	166	-43	-	-194	-149	-45	-
4 Government stocks	51	-	-	51	-61	-	-	-61	105	-	-	105
Statistical discrepancy	-	-	-	-	-	-	-	-	-	-	-	-
Gross Fixed Capital Formation, Total a	41561	29409	6653	5499	41309	29961	6780	4568	44763	33395	7114	4254
1 Residential buildings	8674	6115	335	2224	8132	6174	309	1649	8914	6843	301	1770
2 Non-residential buildings	11802	6020	2637	3145	12471	6460	2700	3311	13291	6415	3034	3842
3 Other construction	...	...	...	...	...	...	...	...	...	...	...	...
4 Land improvement and plantation and orchard development	1561	2418	-173	-684	1782	2997	-42	-1173	1937	4261	-91	-2233
5 Producers' durable goods	19559	14891	3854	814	18921	14327	3813	781	20593	15848	3870	875
A Transport equipment	4566	3713	681	172	3849	3302	392	155	4292	3823	300	169
B Machinery and equipment	14993	11178	3173	642	15072	11025	3421	626	16301	12025	3570	706
6 Breeding stock, dairy cattle, etc.	-35	-35	-	-	3	3	-	-	28	28	-	-
Total Gross Capital Formation	38975	26553	6872	5550	38574	27227	6840	4507	43519	31785	7375	4359

	1983 TOTAL	1983 Total Private	1983 Public Enterprises	1983 General Government	1984 TOTAL	1984 Total Private	1984 Public Enterprises	1984 General Government	1985 TOTAL	1985 Total Private	1985 Public Enterprises	1985 General Government
Increase in stocks, total a	730	325	51	354	116	967	-759	-92	428	-82	-121	631
1 Goods producing industries	8	-57	65	-	-273	519	-792	-	-473	-359	-114	-
A Materials and supplies	-246	-352	106	-	-795	32	-827	-	320	158	162	-
B Work in progress	412	447	-35	-	211	165	46	-	-365	-420	55	-
C Livestock, except breeding stocks, dairy cattle, etc.	-15	-15	-	-	-17	-17	-	-	-73	-73	-	-
D Finished goods	-143	-137	-6	-	328	339	-11	-	-355	-24	-331	-
2 Wholesale and retail trade	194	192	2	-	476	476	-	-	210	210	-	-
3 Other, except government stocks	174	190	-16	-	5	-28	33	-	60	67	-7	-
4 Government stocks	354	-	-	354	-92	-	-	-92	631	-	-	631
Statistical discrepancy	-	-	-	-	-	-	-	-	-	-	-	-
Gross Fixed Capital Formation, Total a	48594	35030	7884	5680	55108	41162	7405	6541	60477	48179	5717	6581
1 Residential buildings	10447	7755	326	2366	11788	9042	318	2428	12069	9532	281	2256
2 Non-residential buildings	13260	6269	3082	3909	14692	7261	2868	4563	15083	7702	2675	4706
3 Other construction	...	...	...	...	...	...	...	...	...	...	...	...
4 Land improvement and plantation and orchard development	2397	4300	-156	-1747	2676	4611	-313	-1622	2984	5172	-407	-1781
5 Producers' durable goods	22497	16713	4632	1152	26080	20276	4502	1172	30329	25761	3168	1400
A Transport equipment	4540	3863	456	221	5604	4849	575	180	6436	5662	589	185
B Machinery and equipment	17957	12850	4176	931	20376	15427	3957	992	23893	20099	2579	1215
6 Breeding stock, dairy cattle, etc.	7	-7	-	-	-28	-28	-	-	12	12	-	*
Total Gross Capital Formation	49324	35355	7935	6034	55224	42129	6646	6449	60905	48097	5596	7212

	1986 TOTAL	1986 Total Private	1986 Public Enterprises	1986 General Government
Increase in stocks, total a	551	611	-164	104
1 Goods producing industries	-503	-344	-159	-
A Materials and supplies	-150	-122	-28	-
B Work in progress	22	117	-95	-
C Livestock, except breeding stocks, dairy cattle, etc.	-34	-34	-	-
D Finished goods	-341	-305	-36	-
2 Wholesale and retail trade	1002	1002	-	-
3 Other, except government stocks	-52	-47	-5	-
4 Government stocks	104	-	-	104

United Kingdom

2.7 Gross Capital Formation by Type of Good and Owner, in Current Prices
(Continued)

Million Pounds Sterling

	1986 TOTAL	Total Private	Public Enterprises	General Government
Statistical discrepancy	-	-	-	-
Gross Fixed Capital Formation, Total [a]	64227	51376	5555	7296
1 Residential buildings	14082	11360	258	2464
2 Non-residential buildings	15999	8182	2792	5025
3 Other construction	...	...	...	...
4 Land improvement and plantation and orchard development	3476	5625	-408	-1741
5 Producers' durable goods	30665	26204	2913	1548
A Transport equipment	6065	5413	453	199
B Machinery and equipment	24600	20791	2460	1349
6 Breeding stock, dairy cattle, etc.	5	5	-	-
Total Gross Capital Formation	64778	51987	5391	7400

a) Beginning 1973, 'Gross fixed capital formation' excludes the value of completed but unsold dwellings which is included in 'Increase in stocks'.

2.8 Gross Capital Formation by Type of Good and Owner, in Constant Prices

Million Pounds Sterling

	1980 TOTAL	Total Private	Public Enterprises	General Government	1981 TOTAL	Total Private	Public Enterprises	General Government	1982 TOTAL	Total Private	Public Enterprises	General Government
	At constant prices of:1980											
Increase in stocks, total [ab]	-2586	-2856	219	51	-2404	-2382	36	-58	-1043	-1322	194	85
1 Goods producing industries [b]	-2358	-2577	219	-	-2001	-2071	70	-	-938	-1169	231	-
A Materials and supplies	-1292	-1394	102	-	-1201	-1256	55	-	-300	-616	316	-
B Work in progress	-1031	-964	-67	-	-116	-149	33	-	-418	-392	-26	-
C Livestock, except breeding stocks, dairy cattle, etc.	-42	-42	-	-	-14	-14	-	-	40	40	-	-
D Finished goods	7	-177	184	-	-670	-652	-18	-	-260	-201	-59	-
2 Wholesale and retail trade	-883	-885	2	-	-569	-577	8	-	79	77	2	-
3 Other, except government stocks	604	606	-2	-	224	266	-42	-	-269	-230	-39	-
4 Government stocks	51	-	-	51	-58	-	-	-58	85	-	-	85
Statistical discrepancy	-	-	-	-	-	-	-	-	-	-	-	-
Gross Fixed Capital Formation, Total [ab]	41561	29409	6653	5499	37574	27448	6092	4034	39539	29635	6195	3709
1 Residential buildings	8674	6115	335	2224	7175	5455	271	1449	7632	5805	266	1561
2 Non-residential buildings	11802	6020	2637	3145	11292	5955	2388	2949	12372	6144	2737	3491
3 Other construction	...	...	...	...	...	...	...	...	...	...	...	...
4 Land improvement and plantation and orchard development	1561	2418	-173	-684	1651	2778	-38	-1089	1814	3997	-85	-2098
5 Producers' durable goods [b]	19559	14891	3854	814	17453	13257	3471	725	17697	13665	3277	755
A Transport equipment	4566	3713	681	172	3554	3055	355	144	3649	3246	258	145
B Machinery and equipment	14993	11178	3173	642	13899	10202	3116	581	14048	10419	3019	610
6 Breeding stock, dairy cattle, etc.	-35	-35	-	-	3	3	-	-	24	24	-	-
Statistical discrepancy	-	-	-	-	-	-	-	-	-	-	-	-
Statistical discrepancy	...	-	-	...	...	-	-	...	...	-	-	...
Total Gross Capital Formation	38975	26553	6872	5550	35170	25066	6128	3976	38496	28313	6389	3794

	1983 TOTAL	Total Private	Public Enterprises	General Government	1984 TOTAL	Total Private	Public Enterprises	General Government	1985 TOTAL	Total Private	Public Enterprises	General Government
				At constant prices of:1980								
Increase in stocks, total [ab]	698	311	99	288	280	924	-568	-76	611	53	14	544
1 Goods producing industries [b]	103	-9	112	-	-106	494	-600	-	-242	-251	9	-
A Materials and supplies	-172	-313	141	-	-602	26	-628	-	317	120	197	-
B Work in progress	356	384	-28	-	206	166	40	-	-269	-312	43	-
C Livestock, except breeding stocks, dairy cattle, etc.	-9	-9	-	-	-13	-13	-	-	-53	-53	-	-

1516

United Kingdom

2.8 Gross Capital Formation by Type of Good and Owner, in Constant Prices
(Continued)

Million Pounds Sterling

	1983				1984				1985			
	TOTAL	Total Private	Public Enterprises	General Government	TOTAL	Total Private	Public Enterprises	General Government	TOTAL	Total Private	Public Enterprises	General Government
				At constant prices of:1980								
D Finished goods	-72	-71	-1	-	303	315	-12	-	-237	-6	-231	-
2 Wholesale and retail trade	168	166	2	-	440	440	-	-	202	202	-	-
3 Other, except government stocks	139	154	-15	-	22	-10	32	-	107	102	5	-
4 Government stocks	288	-	-	288	-76	-	-	-76	544	-	-	544
Statistical discrepancy	-	-	-	-	-	-	-	-	-	-	-	-
Gross Fixed Capital Formation, Total ab	41605	29817	6653	5135	45014	33186	6045	5783	46399	36211	4533	5655
1 Residential buildings	8585	6243	283	2059	8793	6541	260	1992	8290	6287	222	1781
2 Non-residential buildings	12478	6089	2798	3591	13753	6977	2600	4176	13594	7127	2330	4137
3 Other construction	...	...	...	...	...	...	...	...	...	...	...	...
4 Land improvement and plantation and orchard development	1995	3586	-127	-1464	2152	3709	-251	-1306	2150	3740	-291	-1299
5 Producers' durable goods b	18553	13905	3699	949	20340	15983	3436	921	22356	19048	2272	1036
A Transport equipment	3763	3218	365	180	4299	3735	425	139	4574	4029	412	133
B Machinery and equipment	14790	10687	3334	769	16041	12248	3011	782	17782	15019	1860	903
6 Breeding stock, dairy cattle, etc.	-6	-6	-	-	-24	-24	-	-	9	9	-	-
Statistical discrepancy	-	-	-	-	-	-	-	-	-	-	-	-
Statistical discrepancy	...	-	...	...	...	-	...	...	...	-	...	...
Total Gross Capital Formation	42303	30128	6752	5423	45294	34110	5477	5707	47010	36264	4547	6199

	1986			
	TOTAL	Total Private	Public Enterprises	General Government
		At constant prices of:1980		
Increase in stocks, total ab	660	482	85	93
1 Goods producing industries b	-76	-157	81	-
A Materials and supplies	220	42	178	-
B Work in progress	-35	37	-72	-
C Livestock, except breeding stocks, dairy cattle, etc.	-24	-24	-	-
D Finished goods	-237	-212	-25	-
2 Wholesale and retail trade	823	823	-	-
3 Other, except government stocks	-180	-184	4	-
4 Government stocks	93	-	-	93
Statistical discrepancy	-	-	-	-
Gross Fixed Capital Formation, Total ab	46546	36159	4275	6112
1 Residential buildings	9118	7028	198	1892
2 Non-residential buildings	13728	7137	2340	4251
3 Other construction	...			
4 Land improvement and plantation and orchard development	2219	3596	-261	-1116
5 Producers' durable goods b	21479	18396	1998	1085
A Transport equipment	3999	3562	303	134
B Machinery and equipment	17480	14834	1695	951
6 Breeding stock, dairy cattle, etc.	2	2	-	-
Statistical discrepancy	-	-	-	-
Statistical discrepancy	...	-	...	...
Total Gross Capital Formation	47206	36641	4360	6205

a) Beginning 1973, 'Gross fixed capital formation' excludes the value of completed but unsold dwellings which is included in 'Increase in stocks'.
b) For years prior to 1978, components do not add up to total due to the method used to rebase to 1980 prices.

United Kingdom

2.9 Gross Capital Formation by Kind of Activity of Owner, ISIC Major Divisions, in Current Prices

Million Pounds Sterling

	1980			1981			1982			1983		
	Total Gross Capital Formation	Increase in Stocks	Gross Fixed Capital Formation	Total Gross Capital Formation	Increase in Stocks	Gross Fixed Capital Formation	Total Gross Capital Formation	Increase in Stocks	Gross Fixed Capital Formation	Total Gross Capital Formation	Increase in Stocks	Gross Fixed Capital Formation
	All Producers												
1 Agriculture, hunting, fishing and forestry	972	-51	1023	915	-33	948	1184	39	1145	1332	59	1273
2 Mining and quarrying	3647	84	3563	3556	-522	4078	3672	-439	4111	3616	-316	3932
3 Manufacturing	4157	-2321	6478	3753	-1565	5318	4189	-1291	5480	5650	-204	5854
4 Electricity, gas and water	2254	128	2126	2578	76	2502	3137	424	2713	3303	202	3101
5 Construction	270	-198	468	330	-110	440	645	102	543	864	267	597
6 Wholesale and retail trade, restaurants and hotels	2356	-883	3239	2580	-643	3223	3589	10	3579	3970	194	3776
7 Transport, storage and communication	3879	-3	3882	3316	-43	3359	3169	-44	3213	3769	-15	3784
8 Finance, insurance, real estate and business services	14821	607	14214	14629	166	14463	15901	-150	16051	17774	189	17585
9 Community, social and personal services	3229	49	3180	3251	-101	3352	3614	37	3577	4168	346	3822
Statistical discrepancy [a]	1620	-	1620	1924	-	1924	2098	-	2098	2500	-	2500
Total Industries	37205	-2588	39793	36832	-2775	39607	41198	-1312	42510	46946	722	46224
Producers of Government Services	1770	2	1768	1742	40	1702	2321	68	2253	2378	8	2370
Private Non-Profit Institutions Serving Households [b]	...	...	...	...	...	...	...	...	...	...	...	...
Total [c]	38975	-2586	41561	38574	-2735	41309	43519	-1244	44763	49324	730	48594
Memorandum Item: Mineral Fuels and Power	5587	212	5375	5799	-448	6247	6443	-15	6458	6518	-116	6634

	1984			1985			1986		
	Total Gross Capital Formation	Increase in Stocks	Gross Fixed Capital Formation	Total Gross Capital Formation	Increase in Stocks	Gross Fixed Capital Formation	Total Gross Capital Formation	Increase in Stocks	Gross Fixed Capital Formation
	All Producers								
1 Agriculture, hunting, fishing and forestry	1327	121	1206	766	-242	1008	876	-86	962
2 Mining and quarrying	3419	-269	3688	3252	-364	3616	3269	-242	3511
3 Manufacturing	7976	634	7342	8165	-570	8735	8554	-521	9075
4 Electricity, gas and water	2292	-775	3067	3303	272	3031	3219	-19	3238
5 Construction	536	16	520	963	431	532	899	365	534
6 Wholesale and retail trade, restaurants and hotels	4990	476	4514	5390	210	5180	6567	1002	5565
7 Transport, storage and communication	4653	33	4620	5057	1	5056	5159	35	5124
8 Finance, insurance, real estate and business services	20427	-28	20455	22748	59	22689	24450	-87	24537
9 Community, social and personal services	4135	-95	4230	5080	624	4456	4763	104	4659
Statistical discrepancy [a]	2931	-	2931	3386	-	3386	3926	-	3926
Total Industries	52686	113	52573	58110	421	57689	61682	551	61131
Producers of Government Services	2538	3	2535	2795	7	2788	3096	-	3096
Private Non-Profit Institutions Serving Households [b]	...	...	...	...	...	...	...	...	...
Total [c]	55224	116	55108	60905	428	60477	64778	551	64227
Memorandum Item: Mineral Fuels and Power	5295	-1044	6339	6173	-82	6255	6044	-268	6312

a) Column 'Gross fixed capital formation' is purchases less sales of land and existing buildings (excluding general government non-trading land) and column 'Increase in stocks' is an adjustment to reflect the deficiency on both coverage and quality of recorded data.
b) Item 'Private non-profit institutions serving households' is included with various industries above.
c) Beginning 1973, 'Gross fixed capital formation' excludes the value of completed but unsold dwellings which is included in 'Increase in stocks'.

2.10 Gross Capital Formation by Kind of Activity of Owner, ISIC Major Divisions, in Constant Prices

Million Pounds Sterling

	1980			1981			1982			1983		
	Total Gross Capital Formation	Increase in Stocks	Gross Fixed Capital Formation	Total Gross Capital Formation	Increase in Stocks	Gross Fixed Capital Formation	Total Gross Capital Formation	Increase in Stocks	Gross Fixed Capital Formation	Total Gross Capital Formation	Increase in Stocks	Gross Fixed Capital Formation
	At constant prices of: 1980												
	All Producers												
1 Agriculture, hunting, fishing and forestry	972	-51	1023	861	-26	887	1082	32	1050	1156	16	1140
2 Mining and quarrying	3647	84	3563	3324	-423	3747	3385	-310	3695	3212	-220	3432
3 Manufacturing	4157	-2321	6478	3349	-1516	4865	3591	-1113	4704	4648	-132	4780
4 Electricity, gas and water	2254	128	2126	2314	68	2246	2706	357	2349	2813	222	2591

United Kingdom

2.10 Gross Capital Formation by Kind of Activity of Owner, ISIC Major Divisions, in Constant Prices
(Continued)

Million Pounds Sterling

	1980 Total Gross Capital Formation	1980 Increase in Stocks	1980 Gross Fixed Capital Formation	1981 Total Gross Capital Formation	1981 Increase in Stocks	1981 Gross Fixed Capital Formation	1982 Total Gross Capital Formation	1982 Increase in Stocks	1982 Gross Fixed Capital Formation	1983 Total Gross Capital Formation	1983 Increase in Stocks	1983 Gross Fixed Capital Formation
						At constant prices of: 1980						
5 Construction	270	-198	468	307	-104	411	559	96	463	720	217	503
6 Wholesale and retail trade, restaurants and hotels	2356	-883	3239	2404	-569	2973	3257	79	3178	3451	168	3283
7 Transport, storage and communication	3879	-3	3882	3002	-42	3044	2740	-39	2779	3192	-10	3202
8 Finance, insurance, real estate and business services	14821	607	14214	13337	266	13071	13907	-230	14137	15219	149	15070
9 Community, social and personal services	3229	49	3180	2957	-95	3052	3236	25	3211	3697	282	3415
Statistical discrepancy [a]	1620	-	1620	1781	-	1781	1964	-	1964	2077	-	2077
Total Industries [b]	37205	-2588	39793	33636	-2441	36077	36427	-1103	37530	40185	692	39493
Producers of Government Services	1770	2	1768	1534	37	1497	2069	60	2009	2118	6	2112
Private Non-Profit Institutions Serving Households [c]	...	...	...	...	...	...	...	...	...	...	...	...
Statistical discrepancy	...	...	-	...	...	-	...	...	-	...	...	...
Total [db]	38975	-2586	41561	35170	-2404	37574	38496	-1043	39539	42303	698	41605
Memorandum Item: Mineral Fuels and Power	5587	212	5375	5346	-355	5701	5769	46	5723	5671	-	5671

	1984 Total Gross Capital Formation	1984 Increase in Stocks	1984 Gross Fixed Capital Formation	1985 Total Gross Capital Formation	1985 Increase in Stocks	1985 Gross Fixed Capital Formation	1986 Total Gross Capital Formation	1986 Increase in Stocks	1986 Gross Fixed Capital Formation
				At constant prices of: 1980					
				All Producers					
1 Agriculture, hunting, fishing and forestry	1155	78	1077	666	-186	852	762	9	753
2 Mining and quarrying	3069	-173	3242	2739	-228	2967	2590	-117	2707
3 Manufacturing	6286	536	5750	6019	-406	6425	5923	-406	6329
4 Electricity, gas and water	1900	-581	2481	2630	269	2361	2614	182	2432
5 Construction	450	34	416	711	309	402	632	256	376
6 Wholesale and retail trade, restaurants and hotels	4221	440	3781	4317	202	4115	5015	823	4192
7 Transport, storage and communication	3682	24	3658	3808	1	3807	3723	24	3699
8 Finance, insurance, real estate and business services	16294	-2	16296	17030	106	16924	17054	-204	17258
9 Community, social and personal services	3621	-78	3699	4243	539	3704	3763	93	3670
Statistical discrepancy [a]	2357	-	2357	2446	-	2446	2509	-	2509
Total Industries [b]	43035	278	42757	44609	606	44003	44585	660	43925
Producers of Government Services	2259	2	2257	2401	5	2396	2621	-	2621
Private Non-Profit Institutions Serving Households [c]	...	...	...	...	...	...	...	...	...
Statistical discrepancy	...	...	-	...	...	-	...	...	-
Total [db]	45294	280	45014	47010	611	46399	47206	660	46546
Memorandum Item: Mineral Fuels and Power	4610	-751	5361	5045	47	4998	4842	60	4782

a) Column 'Gross fixed capital formation' is purchases less sales of land and existing buildings (excluding general government non-trading land) and column 'Increase in stocks' is an adjustment to reflect the deficiency on both coverage and quality of recorded data.
b) For years prior to 1978, components do not add up to total due to the method used to rebase to 1980 prices.
c) Item 'Private non-profit institutions serving households' is included with various industries above.
d) Beginning 1973, 'Gross fixed capital formation' excludes the value of completed but unsold dwellings which is included in 'Increase in stocks'.

2.11 Gross Fixed Capital Formation by Kind of Activity of Owner, ISIC Divisions, in Current Prices

Million Pounds Sterling

	1970	1975	1977	1978	1979	1980	1981	1982	1983	1984	1985	1986
						All Producers						
1 Agriculture, hunting, forestry and fishing	288	586	786	953	959	1023	948	1145	1273	1206	1008	962
A Agriculture and hunting	258	518	720	873	887	949	870	1065	1183	1092	865	804
B Forestry and logging	23	38	37	48	51	66	77	75	86	103	123	143
C Fishing	7	30	29	32	21	8	1	5	4	11	20	15
2 Mining and quarrying	193	1642	2507	2781	2906	3563	4078	4111	3932	3688	3616	3511
A Coal mining	65	166	307	452	553	784	766	820	783	346	565	683
B Crude petroleum and natural gas production	128	1476	2200	2329	2353	2779	3312	3291	3149	3342	3051	2828
C Metal ore mining	...	...	...	...	...	...	...	...	...	...	...	...
D Other mining	...	...	...	...	...	...	...	...	...	...	...	...

United Kingdom

2.11 Gross Fixed Capital Formation by Kind of Activity of Owner, ISIC Divisions, in Current Prices
(Continued)

Million Pounds Sterling

	1970	1975	1977	1978	1979	1980	1981	1982	1983	1984	1985	1986
3 Manufacturing	2089	3458	4730	5624	6515	6478	5318	5480	5854	7342	8735	9075
A Manufacturing of food, beverages and tobacco	252	479	711	820	903	961	900	1002	996	1229	1393	1417
B Textile, wearing apparel and leather industries	124	182	204	266	299	235	181	238	249	336	384	449
C Manufacture of wood, and wood products, including furniture	33	74	108	126	169	171	105	113	136	157	192	236
D Manufacture of paper and paper products, printing and publishing	134	211	278	366	504	542	446	432	497	673	828	1001
E Manufacture of chemicals and chemical petroleum, coal, rubber and plastic products	81	104	193	214	248	256	196	205	233	324	391	346
F Manufacture of non-metalic mineral products except products of petroleum and coal	128	204	295	353	417	443	333	361	373	492	542	522
G Basic metal industries	214	549	654	504	438	389	297	263	251	381	360	353
H Manufacture of fabricated metal products, machinery and equipment	1106	1611	2238	2916	3471	3414	2808	2793	3057	3695	4592	4694
I Other manufacturing industries	17	44	49	59	66	67	52	73	62	55	53	57
4 Electricity, gas and water	782	1288	1392	1489	1696	2126	2502	2713	3101	3067	3031	3238
A Electricity, gas and steam	679	1140	1193	1232	1409	1812	2169	2347	2702	2651	2639	2801
B Water works and supply	103	148	199	257	287	314	333	366	399	416	392	437
5 Construction	159	349	407	484	586	468	440	543	597	520	532	534
6 Wholesale and retail trade, restaurants and hotels	640	1244	1907	2329	3040	3239	3223	3579	3776	4514	5180	5565
A Wholesale and retail trade	496	1030	1579	1910	2442	2573	2559	2886	3051	3743	4234	4475
B Restaurants and hotels	144	214	328	419	598	666	664	693	725	771	946	1090
7 Transport, storage and communication	1179	2179	2763	3153	3525	3882	3359	3213	3784	4620	5056	5124
A Transport and storage	745	1405	1888	2188	2383	2426	1894	1722	2099	2763	2756	2576
B Communication	434	774	875	965	1142	1456	1465	1491	1685	1857	2300	2548
8 Finance, insurance, real estate and business services	2533	6410	8251	9647	12131	14214	14463	16051	17585	20455	22689	24537
A Financial institutions	344	691	1132	1693	2387	2977	3161	3778	3655	5065	6370	5913
B Insurance	79	289	274	306	425	604	660	695	794	711	706	811
C Real estate and business services	2110	5430	6845	7648	9319	10633	10642	11578	13136	14679	15613	17813
Real estate except dwellings	240	748	1146	1323	1670	1959	2510	2664	2689	2891	3544	3731
Dwellings	1870	4682	5699	6325	7649	8674	8132	8914	10447	11788	12069	14082
9 Community, social and personal services	907	1811	2167	2229	2607	3180	3352	3577	3822	4230	4456	4659
A Sanitary and similar services	148	388	414	439	475	605	553	610	633	660	638	734
B Social and related community services	582	1096	1176	1174	1295	1556	1690	1802	1911	2114	2274	2447
Educational services	421	703	709	656	712	845	874	839	894	974	1041	1124
Medical, dental, other health and veterinary services	161	393	467	518	583	711	816	963	1017	1140	1233	1323
C Recreational and cultural services	177	327	577	616	837	1019	1109	1165	1278	1456	1544	1478
D Personal and household services	...	...	...	...	...	...	...	...	...	...	...	...
Statistical discrepancy	144	413	751	1082	1406	1620	1924	2098	2500	2931	3386	3926
Total Industries	8914	19380	25661	29771	35371	39793	39607	42510	46224	52573	57689	61131
Producers of Government Services	822	1655	1375	1289	1554	1768	1702	2253	2370	2535	2788	3096
Private Non-Profit Institutions Serving Households [a]	...	...	...	...	...	...	...	...	...	...	...	...
Total	9736	21035	27036	31060	36925	41561	41309	44763	48594	55108	60477	64227

a) Item 'Private non-profit institutions serving households' is included with various industries above.

United Kingdom

2.12 Gross Fixed Capital Formation by Kind of Activity of Owner, ISIC Divisions, in Constant Prices

Million Pounds Sterling

	1970	1975	1977	1978	1979	1980	1981	1982	1983	1984	1985	1986
	\multicolumn{12}{c}{At constant prices of:1980}											
	\multicolumn{12}{c}{All Producers}											
1 Agriculture, hunting, forestry and fishing	1305	1244	1214	1305	1145	1023	887	1050	1140	1077	852	753
A Agriculture and hunting	1198	1104	1113	1205	1068	949	814	979	1064	982	738	636
B Forestry and logging	90	75	56	66	57	66	71	67	73	85	98	106
C Fishing	27	65	46	34	20	8	2	4	3	10	16	11
2 Mining and quarrying	840	3219	3909	3927	3522	3563	3747	3695	3432	3242	2967	2707
A Coal mining	239	327	455	611	651	784	681	706	639	262	427	509
B Crude petroleum and natural gas production	582	2891	3453	3316	2871	2779	3066	2989	2793	2980	2540	2198
C Metal ore mining	...	...	...	...	...	...	...	...	...	...	...	...
D Other mining	...	...	...	...	...	...	...	...	...	...	...	...
3 Manufacturing	7966	6781	6774	7221	7496	6478	4865	4704	4780	5750	6425	6329
A Manufacturing of food, beverages and tobacco	1003	938	1041	1075	1047	961	817	852	803	959	1025	987
B Textile, wearing apparel and leather industries	492	389	295	344	346	235	165	205	209	267	292	326
C Manufacture of wood, and wood products, including furniture	149	155	159	166	197	171	95	97	111	121	139	168
D Manufacture of paper and paper products, printing and publishing	509	405	389	455	569	542	405	367	398	517	600	685
E Manufacture of chemicals and chemical petroleum, coal, rubber and plastic products	306	207	271	270	283	256	179	175	190	256	288	242
F Manufacture of non-metalic mineral products except products of petroleum and coal	488	399	410	454	478	443	305	309	304	386	403	370
G Basic metal industries	880	1093	941	653	503	389	272	227	207	297	267	248
H Manufacture of fabricated metal products, machinery and equipment	4081	3111	3198	3732	4000	3414	2579	2409	2507	2904	3372	3263
I Other manufacturing industries	58	84	70	72	73	67	48	63	51	43	39	40
4 Electricity, gas and water	3201	2528	2123	2066	2058	2126	2246	2349	2591	2481	2361	2432
A Electricity, gas and steam	2687	2229	1795	1677	1692	1812	1954	2028	2239	2119	2031	2075
B Water works and supply	494	294	326	389	366	314	292	321	352	362	330	357
5 Construction	630	710	590	614	670	468	411	463	503	416	402	376
6 Wholesale and retail trade, restaurants and hotels	2617	2511	2917	3158	3599	3239	2973	3178	3283	3781	4115	4192
A Wholesale and retail trade	1958	2083	2396	2571	2876	2573	2360	2548	2641	3113	3333	3345
B Restaurants and hotels	655	429	520	587	723	666	613	630	642	668	782	847
7 Transport, storage and communication	4489	4356	4085	4174	4116	3882	3044	2779	3202	3658	3807	3699
A Transport and storage	2806	2804	2786	2887	2787	2426	1714	1512	1777	2190	2085	1858
B Communication	1604	1554	1299	1287	1329	1456	1330	1267	1425	1468	1722	1841
8 Finance, insurance, real estate and business services	10913	12227	12593	13389	14525	14214	13071	14137	15070	16296	16024	17050
A Financial institutions	977	1233	1591	2166	2715	2977	2927	3363	3194	4235	4998	4472
B Insurance	385	578	460	461	532	604	614	663	762	657	622	671
C Real estate and business services	9678	10435	10554	10762	11278	10633	9530	10111	11114	11404	11304	12115
Real estate except dwellings	1115	1332	1589	1714	1915	1959	2355	2479	2529	2611	3014	2997
Dwellings	8615	9140	8976	9048	9363	8674	7175	7632	8585	8793	8290	9118
9 Community, social and personal services	3941	3518	3409	3198	3186	3180	3052	3211	3415	3699	3704	3670
A Sanitary and similar services	711	777	691	667	605	605	486	535	553	569	531	597
B Social and related community services	2507	2105	1836	1675	1583	1556	1545	1636	1739	1886	1920	1948

United Kingdom

2.12 Gross Fixed Capital Formation by Kind of Activity of Owner, ISIC Divisions, in Constant Prices
(Continued)

Million Pounds Sterling

	1970	1975	1977	1978	1979	1980	1981	1982	1983	1984	1985	1986
				At constant prices of:1980								
Educational services	1781	1342	1099	930	855	845	800	763	810	865	873	892
Medical, dental, other health and veterinary services	717	761	736	745	728	711	745	873	929	1021	1047	1056
C Recreational and cultural services	707	636	882	856	998	1019	1021	1040	1123	1244	1253	1125
D Personal and household services	...	...	...	...	...	...	...	...	...	...	...	...
Statistical discrepancy	742	1029	1482	1765	1638	1620	1781	1964	2077	2357	2446	2509
Total Industries	36604	38303	39172	40817	41955	39793	36077	37530	39493	42757	44003	43925
Producers of Government Services	3444	3220	2264	1909	1958	1768	1497	2009	2112	2257	2396	2621
Private Non-Profit Institutions Serving Households [a]	...	...	...	...	...	...	...	...	...	...	...	...
Statistical discrepancy	22	17	5	-	-	-	-	-	-	-	-	-
Total	40070	41540	41441	42726	43913	41561	37574	39539	41605	45014	46399	46546

a) Item 'Private non-profit institutions serving households' is included with various industries above.

2.13 Stocks of Reproducible Fixed Assets, by Type of Good and Owner, in Current Prices

Thousand Million Pounds Sterling

	TOTAL Gross	TOTAL Net	Total Private Gross	Total Private Net	Public Enterprises Gross	Public Enterprises Net	General Government Gross	General Government Net
				1980				
1 Residential buildings	359.8	248.6	242.2	157.6	10.1	8.7	107.6	82.3
2 Non-residential buildings								
3 Other construction	449.2	306.2	198.4	131.8	107.8	63.3	142.8	111.7
4 Land improvement and plantation and orchard development								
5 Producers' durable goods	348.8	197.5	224.1	130.3	112.2	59.7	12.4	7.5
A Transport equipment	56.1	29.5	40.9	23.3	13.5	5.4	1.6	0.8
B Machinery and equipment	292.7	168.0	183.2	107.0	98.7	54.3	10.8	6.7
6 Breeding stock, dairy cattle, etc.	...	...	...	...	...	...	...	...
Total [a]	1157.8	752.3	664.7	419.7	230.1	131.7	262.8	201.5
				1981				
1 Residential buildings	389.6	268.1	264.8	172.6	11.0	9.4	113.6	86.0
2 Non-residential buildings								
3 Other construction	474.4	322.5	208.1	137.2	114.1	67.1	152.0	118.8
4 Land improvement and plantation and orchard development								
5 Producers' durable goods	383.6	214.3	249.3	142.9	120.6	63.2	13.7	8.2
A Transport equipment	58.4	30.1	43.1	24.0	13.5	5.2	1.7	0.8
B Machinery and equipment	325.2	184.2	206.2	118.9	107.1	58.0	12.0	7.4
6 Breeding stock, dairy cattle, etc.	...	...	...	...	...	...	...	...
Total [a]	1247.6	804.9	722.2	452.7	245.7	139.7	279.3	213.0
				1982				
1 Residential buildings	406.9	278.7	283.4	185.0	11.4	9.7	112.0	83.9
2 Non-residential buildings								
3 Other construction	474.9	322.2	208.6	136.9	113.5	66.8	152.6	119.1
4 Land improvement and plantation and orchard development								
5 Producers' durable goods	415.4	229.0	272.7	154.5	127.9	65.7	14.9	8.9
A Transport equipment	60.1	30.4	44.8	24.5	13.5	5.0	1.8	0.9
B Machinery and equipment	355.3	198.6	227.9	130.0	114.4	60.7	13.1	8.0
6 Breeding stock, dairy cattle, etc.	...	...	...	...	...	...	...	...
Total [a]	1297.2	829.9	764.7	476.4	252.8	142.2	279.5	211.9

United Kingdom

2.13 Stocks of Reproducible Fixed Assets, by Type of Good and Owner, in Current Prices
(Continued)

Thousand Million Pounds Sterling

		TOTAL Gross	TOTAL Net	Total Private Gross	Total Private Net	Public Enterprises Gross	Public Enterprises Net	General Government Gross	General Government Net
	1983								
1	Residential buildings	440.7	300.6	312.8	204.4	12.1	10.2	115.7	85.9
2	Non-residential buildings								
3	Other construction	482.2	326.5	212.8	138.9	113.8	67.1	155.4	121.3
4	Land improvement and plantation and orchard development								
5	Producers' durable goods	445.8	242.8	293.9	164.3	135.9	69.0	16.1	9.6
	A Transport equipment	62.6	31.0	46.8	24.9	13.9	5.2	1.9	0.9
	B Machinery and equipment	383.2	211.8	247.1	139.4	122.0	63.8	14.2	8.7
6	Breeding stock, dairy cattle, etc.	...	...	...	...	...	...	...	...
	Total [a]	1368.7	869.9	819.5	507.6	261.8	146.3	287.2	216.8
	1984								
1	Residential buildings	479.9	326.2	345.5	226.0	13.1	11.0	121.3	89.2
2	Non-residential buildings								
3	Other construction	504.1	341.1	228.0	148.6	112.7	66.1	163.2	127.2
4	Land improvement and plantation and orchard development								
5	Producers' durable goods	481.7	260.2	353.4	194.3	110.9	55.5	17.6	10.5
	A Transport equipment	66.8	32.5	51.0	26.4	13.9	5.1	2.0	1.0
	B Machinery and equipment	415.0	227.7	302.4	167.9	97.1	50.4	15.6	9.5
6	Breeding stock, dairy cattle, etc.	...	...	...	...	...	...	...	...
	Total [a]	1465.7	927.5	926.9	568.9	236.7	132.6	302.1	226.9
	1985								
1	Residential buildings	519.0	350.9	380.1	248.3	13.8	11.5	125.0	90.9
2	Non-residential buildings								
3	Other construction	540.4	364.9	246.7	160.2	117.9	69.0	175.7	136.4
4	Land improvement and plantation and orchard development								
5	Producers' durable goods	521.2	280.5	386.0	211.8	116.0	57.3	19.4	11.6
	A Transport equipment	71.8	34.6	55.6	28.3	14.1	5.2	2.1	1.1
	B Machinery and equipment	449.4	245.9	330.4	183.5	101.9	52.1	17.3	10.5
6	Breeding stock, dairy cattle, etc.	...	...	...	...	...	...	...	...
	Total [a]	1580.6	996.3	1012.8	620.3	247.7	137.8	320.1	238.9
	1986								
1	Residential buildings	569.3	382.8	425.2	277.4	14.5	12.0	129.6	93.4
2	Non-residential buildings								
3	Other construction	570.7	384.0	280.2	180.7	106.2	61.9	184.3	141.4
4	Land improvement and plantation and orchard development								
5	Producers' durable goods	550.7	295.5	416.0	228.0	114.1	55.2	20.6	12.3
	A Transport equipment	74.4	35.7	58.2	29.5	14.2	5.2	2.0	1.0
	B Machinery and equipment	476.4	259.9	357.8	198.5	99.9	50.1	18.5	11.3
6	Breeding stock, dairy cattle, etc.	...	...	...	...	...	...	...	...
	Total [a]	1690.7	1062.3	1121.4	686.1	234.8	129.1	334.5	247.1

a) This table (Stocks of reproducible fixed assets) excludes breeding and producers livestock.

United Kingdom

2.14 Stocks of Reproducible Fixed Assets, by Type of Good and Owner, in Constant Prices

Thousand Million Pounds Sterling

	TOTAL Gross	TOTAL Net	Total Private Gross	Total Private Net	Public Enterprises Gross	Public Enterprises Net	General Government Gross	General Government Net
	\multicolumn{8}{c	}{At constant prices of: 1980}
	\multicolumn{8}{c	}{**1980**}
1 Residential buildings	338.2	233.6	228.3	148.5	9.4	8.1	100.6	76.9
2 Non-residential buildings								
3 Other construction	426.5	290.5	190.9	126.8	100.9	59.3	133.9	104.3
4 Land improvement and plantation and orchard development								
5 Producers' durable goods	334.1	189.2	214.8	124.8	107.3	57.0	12.0	7.3
A Transport equipment	53.7	28.2	39.1	22.2	13.0	5.2	1.6	0.8
B Machinery and equipment	280.4	161.0	175.7	102.6	94.3	51.9	10.4	6.5
6 Breeding stock, dairy cattle, etc.	...	...	...	...	...	...	...	...
Total [a]	1098.8	713.3	634.0	400.1	217.6	124.4	246.5	188.5
	\multicolumn{8}{c	}{**1981**}
1 Residential buildings	344.5	236.7	234.7	152.6	9.7	8.3	100.1	75.8
2 Non-residential buildings								
3 Other construction	434.5	295.0	196.3	129.5	101.1	59.6	136.3	106.0
4 Land improvement and plantation and orchard development								
5 Producers' durable goods	340.4	190.3	221.3	127.1	106.8	55.9	12.3	7.3
A Transport equipment	52.5	27.0	38.4	21.4	12.5	4.8	1.6	0.7
B Machinery and equipment	287.9	163.3	182.9	105.7	94.3	51.0	10.7	6.6
6 Breeding stock, dairy cattle, etc.	...	...	...	...	...	...	...	...
Total [a]	1119.4	722.0	652.3	409.2	217.6	123.8	248.7	189.1
	\multicolumn{8}{c	}{**1982**}
1 Residential buildings	351.1	240.1	242.9	158.0	9.9	8.5	98.3	73.6
2 Non-residential buildings								
3 Other construction	443.3	300.4	201.6	132.3	101.7	59.9	139.3	108.1
4 Land improvement and plantation and orchard development								
5 Producers' durable goods	346.5	191.3	227.5	129.2	106.5	54.6	12.5	7.4
A Transport equipment	51.3	25.9	37.9	20.7	11.9	4.4	1.5	0.7
B Machinery and equipment	295.2	165.4	189.6	108.5	94.6	50.2	11.0	6.7
6 Breeding stock, dairy cattle, etc.	...	...	...	...	...	...	...	...
Total [a]	1140.9	731.8	672.0	419.5	218.1	123.0	250.1	189.1
	\multicolumn{8}{c	}{**1983**}
1 Residential buildings	358.6	244.4	250.8	163.3	10.2	8.6	97.6	72.5
2 Non-residential buildings								
3 Other construction	452.1	305.7	207.1	135.1	101.9	60.3	142.4	110.3
4 Land improvement and plantation and orchard development								
5 Producers' durable goods	352.9	192.7	233.0	130.9	106.9	54.1	12.9	7.7
A Transport equipment	50.2	24.8	37.3	19.9	11.3	4.2	1.5	0.7
B Machinery and equipment	302.7	167.9	195.7	111.0	95.5	49.9	11.4	7.0
6 Breeding stock, dairy cattle, etc.	...	...	...	...	...	...	...	...
Total [a]	1163.6	742.8	690.9	429.3	219.0	123.0	252.9	190.5
	\multicolumn{8}{c	}{**1984**}
1 Residential buildings	366.4	248.8	258.5	168.3	10.5	8.8	97.4	71.7
2 Non-residential buildings								
3 Other construction	462.2	312.3	216.4	141.1	99.1	58.2	146.0	113.1
4 Land improvement and plantation and orchard development								
5 Producers' durable goods	360.6	195.5	264.9	146.4	82.4	41.2	13.4	7.9
A Transport equipment	49.9	24.2	37.8	19.6	10.7	3.9	1.5	0.7
B Machinery and equipment	310.7	171.3	227.1	126.8	71.7	37.2	11.9	7.2
6 Breeding stock, dairy cattle, etc.	...	...	...	...	...	...	...	...
Total [a]	1189.2	756.6	739.8	455.8	192.0	108.2	256.8	192.7

United Kingdom

2.14 Stocks of Reproducible Fixed Assets, by Type of Good and Owner, in Constant Prices
(Continued)

Thousand Million Pounds Sterling

	TOTAL Gross	TOTAL Net	Total Private Gross	Total Private Net	Public Enterprises Gross	Public Enterprises Net	General Government Gross	General Government Net
	\multicolumn{8}{c}{At constant prices of:1980}
	\multicolumn{8}{c}{**1985**}
1 Residential buildings	373.7	252.6	265.7	172.9	10.7	8.9	97.3	70.8
2 Non-residential buildings								
3 Other construction	472.0	318.5	221.8	144.2	99.9	58.5	149.6	115.8
4 Land improvement and plantation and orchard development								
5 Producers' durable goods	369.6	199.9	273.9	151.2	81.9	40.4	13.8	8.2
A Transport equipment	49.8	23.8	38.1	19.4	10.2	3.7	1.4	0.7
B Machinery and equipment	319.9	176.0	235.8	131.8	71.7	36.7	12.4	7.5
6 Breeding stock, dairy cattle, etc.	...	...	...	...	...	...	...	...
Total a	1215.3	771.0	761.4	468.3	192.5	107.8	260.7	194.8
	\multicolumn{8}{c}{**1986**}
1 Residential buildings	381.8	257.2	273.8	178.2	10.9	9.0	97.1	70.0
2 Non-residential buildings								
3 Other construction	481.9	324.6	240.1	155.0	88.3	51.5	152.7	118.1
4 Land improvement and plantation and orchard development								
5 Producers' durable goods	376.2	203.0	284.2	156.9	77.7	37.6	14.3	8.5
A Transport equipment	47.9	22.9	37.0	18.8	9.6	3.4	1.3	0.6
B Machinery and equipment	328.3	180.1	247.2	138.1	68.1	34.1	13.0	7.9
6 Breeding stock, dairy cattle, etc.	...	...	...	...	...	...	...	...
Total a	1239.9	784.8	798.1	490.1	176.9	98.1	264.1	196.6

a) This table (Stocks of reproducible fixed assets) excludes breeding and producers livestock.

2.15 Stocks of Reproducible Fixed Assets by Kind of Activity, in Current Prices

Thousand Million Pounds Sterling

	1980 Gross	1980 Net	1981 Gross	1981 Net	1982 Gross	1982 Net	1983 Gross	1983 Net	1984 Gross	1984 Net	1985 Gross	1985 Net
1 Residential buildings	359.8	248.6	389.6	268.1	406.9	278.7	440.7	300.6	479.9	326.2	519.0	350.9
2 Non-residential buildings a	...	...	...	...	...	...	...	...	...	...	...	...
3 Other construction ba	449.2	306.2	474.4	322.5	474.9	322.2	482.2	326.5	504.1	341.1	540.4	364.9
A Industries	385.4	246.2	405.7	258.0	405.3	257.0	410.4	259.4	428.5	270.7	459.3	289.5
1 Agriculture	13.6	8.1	14.2	8.3	14.3	8.3	14.6	8.4	15.5	8.9	16.7	9.4
2 Mining and quarrying c	21.3	13.5	23.6	14.8	24.6	15.3	25.7	15.9	27.6	17.0	30.0	18.1
3 Manufacturing d	75.2	43.0	76.7	43.4	74.9	41.9	74.4	41.0	76.6	41.8	81.2	44.0
4 Electricity, gas and water e	43.6	26.4	46.8	28.1	47.0	28.1	47.7	28.5	49.1	29.1	51.4	30.4
5 Construction	3.2	2.3	3.3	2.3	3.3	2.3	3.3	2.3	3.4	2.3	3.7	2.5
6 Wholesale and retail trade f	34.7	25.8	36.4	27.0	36.6	27.1	37.3	27.6	39.6	29.2	43.4	32.0
7 Transport and communication	45.1	23.2	47.5	24.5	46.9	24.3	46.8	24.4	47.9	25.1	50.0	26.4
8 Finance, etc. g	48.3	36.5	51.2	38.7	52.1	39.4	53.7	40.6	57.2	43.2	62.7	47.3
9 Community, social and personal services	100.4	68.2	106.0	71.7	105.7	71.3	106.8	71.8	111.6	74.9	120.2	80.4
B Producers of government services h	63.8	60.0	68.7	64.5	69.7	65.2	71.7	67.1	75.5	70.4	81.1	75.4
C Other producers	...	...	...	...	...	...	...	...	...	...	...	...
4 Land improvement and development and plantation and orchard development b	...	...	...	...	...	...	...	...	...	...	...	...
5 Producers' durable goods	348.8	197.5	383.6	214.3	415.4	229.0	445.8	242.8	481.7	260.2	521.2	280.5
A Industries	344.7	195.1	379.0	211.7	410.5	226.3	440.4	239.8	475.9	256.9	514.6	276.8
1 Agriculture	11.6	7.0	12.2	7.2	12.8	7.6	13.3	7.9	13.4	7.9	13.6	8.0
2 Mining and quarrying c	11.9	7.5	14.0	8.6	16.4	9.8	18.4	10.8	19.7	11.1	21.1	11.5
3 Manufacturing d	136.6	73.7	149.4	78.9	161.0	83.3	170.8	86.7	182.3	91.4	194.9	97.1
4 Electricity, gas and water e	54.4	30.3	59.4	32.7	64.1	34.9	68.2	36.8	72.4	38.7	76.5	40.5

United Kingdom

2.15 Stocks of Reproducible Fixed Assets by Kind of Activity, in Current Prices
(Continued)

Thousand Million Pounds Sterling

	1980 Gross	1980 Net	1981 Gross	1981 Net	1982 Gross	1982 Net	1983 Gross	1983 Net	1984 Gross	1984 Net	1985 Gross	1985 Net
5 Construction	9.7	5.3	10.5	5.6	11.2	5.8	11.7	6.0	12.2	6.2	12.8	6.3
6 Wholesale and retail trade [f]	28.0	17.0	31.4	18.9	34.6	20.7	37.7	22.4	41.8	24.9	46.5	27.7
7 Transport and communication	55.5	29.3	58.1	30.2	59.3	30.1	61.8	30.8	65.5	32.1	68.7	33.1
8 Finance, etc. [g]	23.2	16.7	28.4	20.3	33.8	23.9	39.4	27.4	47.1	32.3	57.0	39.0
9 Community, social and personal services	13.9	8.3	15.6	9.2	17.3	10.2	19.1	11.1	21.3	12.3	23.6	13.6
B Producers of government services [h]	4.1	2.4	4.5	2.6	4.9	2.8	5.3	3.0	5.9	3.3	6.6	3.7
C Other producers	...	...	...	...	...	...	...	...	...	...	...	...
6 Breeding stock, dairy cattle, etc.	...	...	...	...	...	...	...	...	...	...	...	...
Total	1157.8	752.3	1247.6	804.9	1297.2	829.9	1368.7	869.9	1465.7	927.5	1580.6	996.3

	1986 Gross	1986 Net
1 Residential buildings	569.3	382.8
2 Non-residential buildings [a]	...	...
3 Other construction [ba]	570.7	384.0
A Industries	486.3	306.0
1 Agriculture	17.7	9.8
2 Mining and quarrying [c]	31.9	18.8
3 Manufacturing [d]	85.4	45.8
4 Electricity, gas and water [e]	52.9	31.1
5 Construction	3.9	2.6
6 Wholesale and retail trade [f]	47.3	35.0
7 Transport and communication	51.2	27.3
8 Finance, etc. [g]	68.3	51.5
9 Community, social and personal services	127.6	85.0
B Producers of government services [h]	84.3	78.0
C Other producers	...	...
4 Land improvement and development and plantation and orchard development [b]	...	...
5 Producers' durable goods	550.7	295.5
A Industries	543.4	291.3
1 Agriculture	13.8	8.1
2 Mining and quarrying [c]	22.1	11.7
3 Manufacturing [d]	203.6	100.8
4 Electricity, gas and water [e]	79.4	41.5
5 Construction	13.2	6.4
6 Wholesale and retail trade [f]	50.4	30.1
7 Transport and communication	69.6	33.7
8 Finance, etc. [g]	65.8	44.3
9 Community, social and personal services	25.5	14.6
B Producers of government services [h]	7.3	4.2
C Other producers	...	...
6 Breeding stock, dairy cattle, etc.	...	...
Total	1690.7	1062.3

a) Item 'Non-residential buildings' is included in item 'Other construction'.
b) Item 'Land improvement and plantation and orchard development' is included in item 'Other construction'.
c) Item 'Mining and quarrying' refers to coal extraction and manufacture of solid fuels, coke ovens, extraction of mineral oil and natural gas. It excludes mineral mining.
d) Item 'Manufacturing' includes mineral mining, but excludes manufacture of solid fuels and coke ovens.
e) Item 'Electricity, gas and water' includes nuclear fuel production.
f) Item 'Wholesale and retail trade' includes hotels, catering and repairs.
g) Item 'Finance etc.' includes banking, finance, insurance, business services and leasing.
h) Item 'Producers of government services' includes public administration, national defence and compulsory social security. It also includes expenditure on roads.

United Kingdom

2.16 Stocks of Reproducible Fixed Assets by Kind of Activity, in Constant Prices

Thousand Million Pounds Sterling

	1980 Gross	1980 Net	1981 Gross	1981 Net	1982 Gross	1982 Net	1983 Gross	1983 Net	1984 Gross	1984 Net	1985 Gross	1985 Net
					At constant prices of: 1980							
1 Residential buildings	338.2	233.6	344.5	236.7	351.1	240.1	358.6	244.4	366.4	248.8	373.7	252.6
2 Non-residential buildings [a]	...	...	...	...	...	...	...	...	...	...	...	...
3 Other construction [b,a]	426.5	290.5	434.5	295.0	443.3	300.4	452.1	305.7	462.2	312.3	472.0	318.5
A Industries	367.0	234.7	373.7	238.1	380.7	241.9	387.7	245.7	395.7	250.4	403.3	254.7
1 Agriculture	13.1	7.8	13.4	7.9	13.8	8.0	14.2	8.2	14.7	8.4	15.0	8.4
2 Mining and quarrying [c]	20.3	12.9	21.8	13.7	23.1	14.4	24.2	15.0	25.4	15.7	26.4	16.0
3 Manufacturing [d]	72.4	41.4	72.5	41.0	72.5	40.5	72.4	39.9	72.6	39.6	72.9	39.4
4 Electricity, gas and water [e]	40.6	24.6	41.1	24.7	41.7	24.9	42.3	25.2	42.8	25.4	43.3	25.6
5 Construction	3.1	2.2	3.1	2.2	3.2	2.2	3.2	2.2	3.2	2.2	3.3	2.2
6 Wholesale and retail trade [f]	33.4	24.9	34.4	25.5	35.4	26.2	36.5	27.0	37.8	27.9	39.3	29.0
7 Transport and communication	42.2	21.8	42.2	21.9	42.1	21.9	42.1	22.0	42.3	22.2	42.4	22.4
8 Finance, etc. [g]	46.5	35.1	48.3	36.5	50.4	38.1	52.6	39.7	54.7	41.3	56.8	42.9
9 Community, social and personal services	95.4	64.8	96.9	65.5	98.5	66.4	100.2	67.3	102.1	68.4	104.0	69.5
B Producers of government services [h]	59.4	55.8	60.8	56.9	62.6	58.5	64.4	60.0	66.5	61.9	68.7	63.8
C Other producers	...	...	...	...	...	...	...	...	...	...	...	...
4 Land improvement and development and plantation and orchard development [b]	...	...	...	...	...	...	...	...	...	...	...	...
5 Producers' durable goods	334.1	189.2	340.4	190.3	346.5	191.3	352.9	192.7	360.6	195.5	369.6	199.9
A Industries	330.2	186.9	336.4	188.1	342.4	189.0	348.5	190.2	356.2	193.0	364.9	197.2
1 Agriculture	11.3	6.9	11.0	6.6	10.8	6.4	10.6	6.3	10.2	6.1	9.9	5.9
2 Mining and quarrying [c]	11.3	7.1	12.3	7.6	13.2	7.9	14.0	8.2	14.3	8.1	14.7	8.0
3 Manufacturing [d]	130.8	70.5	131.8	69.6	132.5	68.5	133.0	67.5	133.9	67.1	135.0	67.2
4 Electricity, gas and water [e]	52.0	29.0	52.3	28.8	52.6	28.7	53.1	28.7	53.5	28.6	53.7	28.5
5 Construction	9.3	5.1	9.3	4.9	9.3	4.9	9.4	4.8	9.3	4.7	9.2	4.6
6 Wholesale and retail trade [f]	26.8	16.3	27.8	16.7	28.9	17.3	30.0	17.8	31.3	18.6	32.7	19.5
7 Transport and communication	52.9	27.8	51.8	26.8	50.5	25.5	49.5	24.6	49.2	24.0	48.9	23.5
8 Finance, etc. [g]	22.4	16.2	26.0	18.6	29.8	21.1	33.5	23.4	38.1	26.4	43.8	30.3
9 Community, social and personal services	13.4	8.0	14.0	8.3	14.7	8.6	15.5	9.0	16.3	9.4	17.1	9.8
B Producers of government services [h]	3.9	2.3	4.0	2.3	4.2	2.3	4.3	2.4	4.5	2.5	4.7	2.7
C Other producers	...	...	...	...	...	...	...	...	...	...	...	...
6 Breeding stock, dairy cattle, etc.	...	...	...	...	...	...	...	...	...	...	...	...
Total	1098.8	713.3	1119.4	722.0	1140.9	731.8	1163.6	742.8	1189.2	756.6	1215.3	771.0

	1986 Gross	1986 Net
	At constant prices of: 1980	
1 Residential buildings	381.8	257.2
2 Non-residential buildings [a]	...	...
3 Other construction [b,a]	481.9	324.6
A Industries	410.8	258.7
1 Agriculture	15.2	8.4
2 Mining and quarrying [c]	27.0	16.0
3 Manufacturing [d]	73.1	39.2
4 Electricity, gas and water [e]	43.9	25.8
5 Construction	3.3	2.2
6 Wholesale and retail trade [f]	40.9	30.2
7 Transport and communication	42.5	22.6
8 Finance, etc. [g]	59.1	44.6
9 Community, social and personal services	105.9	70.6
B Producers of government services [h]	71.1	65.8

United Kingdom

2.16 Stocks of Reproducible Fixed Assets by Kind of Activity, in Constant Prices
(Continued)

Thousand Million Pounds Sterling

	1986 Gross	1986 Net
At constant prices of: 1980		
C Other producers	...	...
4 Land improvement and development and plantation and orchard development [b]	...	...
5 Producers' durable goods	376.2	203.0
A Industries	371.1	200.1
1 Agriculture	9.5	5.7
2 Mining and quarrying [c]	14.9	7.9
3 Manufacturing [d]	135.9	67.2
4 Electricity, gas and water [e]	54.0	28.3
5 Construction	9.1	4.4
6 Wholesale and retail trade [f]	34.0	20.4
7 Transport and communication	47.5	22.9
8 Finance, etc. [g]	48.5	33.1
9 Community, social and personal services	17.7	10.1
B Producers of government services [h]	5.0	2.9
C Other producers	...	...
6 Breeding stock, dairy cattle, etc.	...	...
Total	1239.9	784.8

a) Item 'Non-residential buildings' is included in item 'Other construction'.
b) Item 'Land improvement and plantation and orchard development' is included in item 'Other construction'.
c) Item 'Mining and quarrying' refers to coal extraction and manufacture of solid fuels, coke ovens, extraction of mineral oil and natural gas. It excludes mineral mining.
d) Item 'Manufacturing' includes mineral mining, but excludes manufacture of solid fuels and coke ovens.
e) Item 'Electricity, gas and water' includes nuclear fuel production.
f) Item 'Wholesale and retail trade' includes hotels, catering and repairs.
g) Item 'Finance etc.' includes banking, finance, insurance, business services and leasing.
h) Item 'Producers of government services' includes public administration, national defence and compulsory social security. It also includes expenditure on roads.

2.17 Exports and Imports of Goods and Services, Detail

Million Pounds Sterling

	1970	1975	1977	1978	1979	1980	1981	1982	1983	1984	1985	1986
Exports of Goods and Services												
1 Exports of merchandise, f.o.b.	8150	19330	31728	35063	40687	47422	50977	55565	60776	70367	78111	72843
2 Transport and communication	2132	4139	5495	5472	6500	7111	7160	6848	6984	7619	7753	7720
A In respect of merchandise imports	415	594	634	593	702	679	642	664	751	698	642	649
B Other [a]	1717	3545	4861	4879	5798	6432	6518	6184	6233	6921	7111	7071
3 Insurance service charges	210	322	599	643	635	537	739	782	919	1028	1759	2485
A In respect of merchandise imports	...	10	14	15	13	12	18	18	4	17	35	35
B Other	...	312	585	628	622	525	721	764	915	1011	1724	2450
4 Other commodities	925	2344	3411	3982	4656	5185	6019	6628	7676	8271	8814	9074
5 Adjustments of merchandise exports to change-of-ownership basis	...	...	...	...	...	...	...	...	...	...	...	...
6 Direct purchases in the domestic market by non-residential households	518	1442	2712	2891	3207	3436	3512	3786	4649	5326	6269	6317
7 Direct purchases in the domestic market by extraterritorial bodies	...	...	...	...	...	...	...	...	...	...	...	...
Total Exports of Goods and Services	11935	27577	43945	48051	55685	63691	68407	73609	81004	92611	102706	98439
Imports of Goods and Services												
1 Imports of merchandise, c.i.f.	9004	24150	35884	38599	46566	48587	50282	56202	64835	78376	84093	85024
A Imports of merchandise, f.o.b.	8184	22663	34012	36605	44136	46061	47617	53234	61611	74751	80289	81306
B Transport of services on merchandise imports	795	1426	1775	1882	2295	2385	2526	2786	3014	3373	3535	3429
By residents	415	594	634	593	702	679	642	664	751	698	642	649
By non-residents	380	832	1141	1289	1593	1706	1884	2122	2263	2675	2893	2780
C Insurance service charges on merchandise imports	26	62	98	112	135	141	139	183	210	252	269	289
By residents	...	10	14	15	13	12	18	18	4	17	35	35

United Kingdom

2.17 Exports and Imports of Goods and Services, Detail
(Continued)

Million Pounds Sterling

	1970	1975	1977	1978	1979	1980	1981	1982	1983	1984	1985	1986
By non-residents [b]	...	52	84	97	122	129	121	165	206	235	234	254
2 Adjustments of merchandise imports to change-of-ownership basis	...	...	...	...	...	...	...	...	...	...	...	...
3 Other transport and communication [a]	1371	2536	3417	3319	3854	4189	4441	4640	5038	5492	5616	5962
4 Other insurance service charges	...	...	...	...	...	...	...	...	...	...	...	...
5 Other commodities	687	1726	2448	2379	2597	2922	3293	4273	4406	5072	5029	4908
6 Direct purchases abroad by government	...	...	...	...	...	...	...	...	...	...	...	...
7 Direct purchases abroad by resident households	420	1009	1219	1592	2079	2648	3132	3483	3855	4275	4440	5641
Total Imports of Goods and Services	11482	29421	42968	45889	55096	58346	61148	68598	78134	93215	99178	101535
Balance of Goods and Services	453	-1844	977	2162	589	5345	7259	5011	2870	-604	3528	-3096
Total Imports and Balance of Goods and Services	11935	27577	43945	48051	55685	63691	68407	73609	81004	92611	102706	98439

a) Other transport and communication includes telecommunications and postal services.
b) Insurance service charges on merchandise imports by non-residents comprises both claims and insurance service charges on imports paid to overseas residents.

3.11 General Government Production Account: Total and Subsectors

Million Pounds Sterling

	1980					1981				
	Total General Government	Central Government	State or Provincial Government	Local Government	Social Security Funds	Total General Government	Central Government	State or Provincial Government	Local Government	Social Security Funds

Gross Output

1 Sales	...	...	...	...	...	...	...	...	...	...
2 Services produced for own use	56023	31453	...	23961	609	63698	35729	...	27235	734
3 Own account fixed capital formation	456	149	...	307	...	427	160	...	267	...
Gross Output	56479	31602	...	24268	609	64125	35889	...	27502	734

Gross Input

Intermediate Consumption	20632	15082	...	5236	314	22589	17204	...	5007	378
Subtotal: Value Added	35847	16520	...	19032	295	41536	18685	...	22495	356
1 Indirect taxes, net	-334	513	-	-853	6	503	614	-	-119	8
A Indirect taxes	2466	556	...	1904	6	2961	666	...	2287	8
B Less: Subsidies	2800	43	...	2757	...	2458	52	...	2406	...
2 Consumption of fixed capital	3097	713	...	2384	...	3493	805	...	2688	...
3 Compensation of employees	31160	15322	...	15549	289	35500	17245	...	17907	348
A To residents	30902	15064	...	15549	289	35242	16987	...	17907	348
B To the rest of the world	258	258	...	...	...	258	258	...	...	...
4 Net Operating surplus	1924	-28	...	1952	...	2040	21	...	2019	...
Gross Input	56479	31602	...	24268	609	64125	35889	...	27502	734

	1982					1983				
	Total General Government	Central Government	State or Provincial Government	Local Government	Social Security Funds	Total General Government	Central Government	State or Provincial Government	Local Government	Social Security Funds

Gross Output

1 Sales	...	...	...	...	...	...	...	...	...	...
2 Services produced for own use	70158	39384	...	30010	764	76092	43176	...	32154	762
3 Own account fixed capital formation	495	201	...	294	...	557	213	...	344	...
Gross Output	70653	39585	...	30304	764	76649	43389	...	32498	762

Gross Input

Intermediate Consumption	25995	19836	...	5769	390	29172	22127	...	6664	381
Subtotal: Value Added	44658	19749	...	24535	374	47477	21262	...	25834	381
1 Indirect taxes, net	1240	605	-	628	7	961	467	-	489	5
A Indirect taxes	3319	659	...	2653	7	2915	522	...	2388	5
B Less: Subsidies	2079	54	...	2025	...	1954	55	...	1899	...
2 Consumption of fixed capital	3547	850	...	2697	...	3646	893	...	2753	...
3 Compensation of employees	37972	18381	...	19224	367	41434	20155	...	20903	376
A To residents	37674	18083	...	19224	367	41112	19833	...	20903	376
B To the rest of the world	298	298	...	...	...	322	322	...	...	...
4 Net Operating surplus	1899	-87	...	1986	...	1436	-253	...	1689	...
Gross Input	70653	39585	...	30304	764	76649	43389	...	32498	762

United Kingdom

3.11 General Government Production Account: Total and Subsectors

Million Pounds Sterling

	1984					1985				
	Total General Government	Central Government	State or Provincial Government	Local Government	Social Security Funds	Total General Government	Central Government	State or Provincial Government	Local Government	Social Security Funds
Gross Output											
1 Sales	...	...	...	...	...	...	...	...	...	...
2 Services produced for own use	80198	45483	...	33934	781	84287	47660	...	35697	930
3 Own account fixed capital formation	564	196	...	368	...	567	208	...	359	...
Gross Output	80762	45679	...	34302	781	84854	47868	...	36056	930
Gross Input											
Intermediate Consumption	31009	23867	...	6753	389	31743	24298	...	6964	481
Subtotal: Value Added	49753	21812	...	27549	392	53111	23570	...	29092	449
1 Indirect taxes, net	906	361	-	542	3	1078	311	-	767	...
A Indirect taxes	2851	427	...	2421	3	2833	376	...	2457	-
B Less: Subsidies	1945	66	...	1879	...	1755	65	...	1690	...
2 Consumption of fixed capital	3854	943	...	2911	...	4133	1039	...	3094	...
3 Compensation of employees	43840	20957	...	22494	389	46426	22330	...	23647	449
A To residents	43490	20607	...	22494	389	46041	21945	...	23647	449
B To the rest of the world	350	350	...	...	...	385	385	...	...	...
4 Net Operating surplus	1153	-449	...	1602	...	1474	-110	...	1584	...
Gross Input	80762	45679	...	34302	781	84854	47868	...	36056	930

	1986				
	Total General Government	Central Government	State or Provincial Government	Local Government	Social Security Funds
Gross Output					
1 Sales	...	...	...	...	...
2 Services produced for own use	89682	50159	...	38646	877
3 Own account fixed capital formation	676	291	...	385	...
Gross Output	90358	50450	...	39031	877
Gross Input					
Intermediate Consumption	32741	25386	...	6912	443
Subtotal: Value Added	57617	25064	...	32119	434
1 Indirect taxes, net	1487	353	-	1134	...
A Indirect taxes	3193	421	...	2772	-
B Less: Subsidies	1706	68	...	1638	...
2 Consumption of fixed capital	4445	1152	...	3293	...
3 Compensation of employees	50407	23786	...	26187	434
A To residents	49977	23356	...	26187	434
B To the rest of the world	430	430	...	...	...
4 Net Operating surplus	1278	-227	...	1505	...
Gross Input	90358	50450	...	39031	877

3.12 General Government Income and Outlay Account: Total and Subsectors

Million Pounds Sterling

	1980					1981				
	Total General Government	Central Government	State or Provincial Government	Local Government	Social Security Funds	Total General Government	Central Government	State or Provincial Government	Local Government	Social Security Funds
Receipts											
1 Operating surplus	1924	-28	...	1952	...	2040	21	...	2019	...
2 Property and entrepreneurial income	4979	5896	...	707	626	5733	6812	...	738	617
A Withdrawals from public quasi-corporations	...	-	...	...	...	...	-	...	...	...
B Interest [a]	3657	4574	...	707	626	4194	5273	...	738	617
C Dividends	166	166	...	...	...	177	177	...	...	...
D Net land rent and royalties	1156	1156	...	...	...	1362	1362	...	...	...
3 Taxes, fees and contributions	82228	60000	...	8284	13944	95768	69434	...	10411	15923
A Indirect taxes	35829	27545	...	8284	...	41891	31480	...	10411	...
B Direct taxes	32272	32272	...	-	-	37769	37769	...	-	-
Income	31546	31546	...	-	...	36929	36929	...	-	...
Other	726	726	...	-	...	840	840	...	-	...
C Social security contributions	13944	-	...	-	13944	15923	-	...	-	15923
D Fees, fines and penalties	183	183	...	-	-	185	185	...	-	-

# United Kingdom

3.12 General Government Income and Outlay Account: Total and Subsectors
(Continued)

Million Pounds Sterling

	1980					1981				
	Total General Government	Central Government	State or Provincial Government	Local Government	Social Security Funds	Total General Government	Central Government	State or Provincial Government	Local Government	Social Security Funds
4 Other current transfers	3211	3055	...	14388	2803	3898	3807	...	16579	2989
A Casualty insurance claims	...	...	...	...	...	...	...	...	...	...
B Transfers from other government subsectors	...	1034	...	13233	2768	...	1333	...	15201	2943
C Transfers from the rest of the world	...	...	...	...	...	...	...	...	...	...
D Other transfers, except imputed	...	...	...	...	...	...	...	...	...	...
E Imputed unfunded employee pension and welfare contributions	3211	2021	...	1155	35	3898	2474	...	1378	46
Total Current Receipts [a]	92342	68923	...	25331	17373	107439	80074	...	29747	19529

Disbursements

	Total General Government	Central Government	State or Provincial Government	Local Government	Social Security Funds	Total General Government	Central Government	State or Provincial Government	Local Government	Social Security Funds
1 Government final consumption expenditure	49046	29403	...	19034	609	55470	33155	...	21581	734
2 Property income	10873	8890	...	4233	-	12700	10736	...	4397	1
A Interest	10873	8890	...	4233	-	12700	10736	...	4397	1
B Net land rent and royalties	...	...	...	...	...	...	...	...	...	...
3 Subsidies	5611	4569	...	1042	...	6355	5207	...	1148	...
4 Other current transfers	29727	29002	...	1887	15873	36015	34029	...	2224	19239
A Casualty insurance premiums, net	...	...	...	...	...	...	...	...	...	...
B Transfers to other government subsectors	...	16001	...	-	1034	...	18144	...	-	1333
C Social security benefits	14804	-	...	-	14804	17860	-	...	-	17860
D Social assistance grants	9314	8214	...	1100	...	11848	10717	...	1131	...
E Unfunded employee pension and welfare benefits	2419	1602	...	782	35	3159	2031	...	1082	46
F Transfers to private non-profit institutions serving households	1545	1540	...	5	...	1751	1740	...	11	...
G Other transfers n.e.c.	...	...	...	...	...	...	...	...	...	...
H Transfers to the rest of the world	1645	1645	...	-	...	1397	1397	...	-	...
Statistical discrepancy	792	419	...	373	...	739	443	...	296	...
Net saving	-3707	-3360	...	-1238	891	-3840	-3496	...	101	-445
Total Current Disbursements and Net Saving	92342	68923	...	25331	17373	107439	80074	...	29747	19529

	1982					1983				
	Total General Government	Central Government	State or Provincial Government	Local Government	Social Security Funds	Total General Government	Central Government	State or Provincial Government	Local Government	Social Security Funds

Receipts

1 Operating surplus	1899	-87	...	1986	...	1436	-253	...	1689	...
2 Property and entrepreneurial income	6817	7793	...	817	511	6935	8231	...	746	462
A Withdrawals from public quasi-corporations	...	-	...	...	...	...	-	...	...	...
B Interest [a]	4974	5950	...	817	511	4783	6079	...	746	462
C Dividends	243	243	...	...	...	265	265	...	...	...
D Net land rent and royalties	1600	1600	...	...	...	1887	1887	...	...	...
3 Taxes, fees and contributions	106272	76281	...	11886	18105	114950	81861	...	12289	20800
A Indirect taxes	45674	33788	...	11886	...	48281	35992	...	12289	...
B Direct taxes	42285	42285	...	-	-	45628	45628	...	-	-
Income	41263	41263	...	...	...	44444	44444	...	...	...
Other	1022	1022	...	...	...	1184	1184	...	...	...
C Social security contributions	18105	-	...	-	18105	20800	-	...	-	20800
D Fees, fines and penalties	208	208	...	-	-	241	241	...	-	-

United Kingdom

3.12 General Government Income and Outlay Account: Total and Subsectors
(Continued)

Million Pounds Sterling

	1982					1983				
	Total General Government	Central Government	State or Provincial Government	Local Government	Social Security Funds	Total General Government	Central Government	State or Provincial Government	Local Government	Social Security Funds
4 Other current transfers	4305	4309	...	17718	2309	4720	4748	...	20363	2841
A Casualty insurance claims	...	...	...	...	...	...	...	...	...	...
B Transfers from other government subsectors	...	1582	...	16190	2259	...	1741	...	18702	2789
C Transfers from the rest of the world	...	...	...	...	...	...	...	...	...	...
D Other transfers, except imputed	...	...	...	...	...	...	...	...	...	...
E Imputed unfunded employee pension and welfare contributions	4305	2727	...	1528	50	4720	3007	...	1661	52
Total Current Receipts [a]	119293	88296	...	32407	20925	128041	94587	...	35087	24103
Disbursements									
1 Government final consumption expenditure	60549	36372	...	23413	764	66006	39969	...	25275	762
2 Property income	13945	11901	...	4321	27	14159	12696	...	3939	28
A Interest	13945	11901	...	4321	27	14159	12696	...	3939	28
B Net land rent and royalties	...	...	...	...	...	...	...	...	...	...
3 Subsidies	5865	4484	...	1381	...	6351	4884	...	1467	...
4 Other current transfers	41969	38510	...	2510	20980	45656	41853	...	4496	22539
A Casualty insurance premiums, net	...	...	...	...	...	...	...	...	...	...
B Transfers to other government subsectors	...	18449	...	-	1582	...	21491	...	-	1741
C Social security benefits	19348	-	...	-	19348	20746	-	...	-	20746
D Social assistance grants	15497	14211	...	1286	...	16983	13812	...	3171	...
E Unfunded employee pension and welfare benefits	3585	2321	...	1214	50	3961	2594	...	1315	52
F Transfers to private non-profit institutions serving households	1974	1964	...	10	...	2303	2293	...	10	...
G Other transfers n.e.c.	...	...	...	...	...	...	...	...	...	...
H Transfers to the rest of the world	1565	1565	...	-	...	1663	1663	...	-	...
Statistical discrepancy	720	406	...	314	...	759	413	...	346	...
Net saving	-3755	-3377	...	468	-846	-4890	-5228	...	-436	774
Total Current Disbursements and Net Saving	119293	88296	...	32407	20925	128041	94587	...	35087	24103

	1984					1985				
	Total General Government	Central Government	State or Provincial Government	Local Government	Social Security Funds	Total General Government	Central Government	State or Provincial Government	Local Government	Social Security Funds
Receipts									
1 Operating surplus	1153	-449	...	1602	...	1474	-110	...	1584	...
2 Property and entrepreneurial income	7558	9254	...	696	482	8631	10568	...	765	538
A Withdrawals from public quasi-corporations	...	-	...	...	...	...	-	...	...	...
B Interest [a]	4826	6522	...	696	482	5954	7891	...	765	538
C Dividends	273	273	...	...	...	311	311	...	...	...
D Net land rent and royalties	2459	2459	...	...	...	2366	2366	...	...	...
3 Taxes, fees and contributions	122995	87904	...	12775	22316	134161	96365	...	13580	24216
A Indirect taxes	51338	38563	...	12775	...	55334	41754	...	13580	...
B Direct taxes	49087	49087	...	-	-	54373	54373	...	-	-
Income	47798	47798	...	-	...	52891	52891	...	-	...
Other	1289	1289	...	-	...	1482	1482	...	-	...
C Social security contributions	22316	-	...	-	22316	24216	-	...	-	24216
D Fees, fines and penalties	254	254	...	-	-	238	238	...	-	-

United Kingdom

3.12 General Government Income and Outlay Account: Total and Subsectors
(Continued)

Million Pounds Sterling

		1984					1985			
		Total General Government	Central Government	State or Provincial Government	Local Government	Social Security Funds	Total General Government	Central Government	State or Provincial Government	Local Government	Social Security Funds
4	Other current transfers	5115	5043	...	22093	2774	5432	5423	...	22524	2507
	A Casualty insurance claims	...	...	...	...	...	...	...	...	...	...
	B Transfers from other government subsectors	...	1844	...	20231	2720	...	2019	...	20559	2444
	C Transfers from the rest of the world	...	...	...	...	...	...	...	...	...	...
	D Other transfers, except imputed	...	...	...	...	...	...	...	...	...	...
	E Imputed unfunded employee pension and welfare contributions	5115	3199	...	1862	54	5432	3404	...	1965	63
	Total Current Receipts [a]	136821	101752	...	37166	25572	149698	112246	...	38453	27261
				Disbursements							
1	Government final consumption expenditure	69915	42467	...	26667	781	74070	45082	...	28058	930
2	Property income	15740	14583	...	4013	18	17469	16285	...	4420	4
	A Interest	15740	14583	...	4013	18	17469	16285	...	4420	4
	B Net land rent and royalties	...	...	...	...	...	...	...	...	...	...
3	Subsidies	7644	6198	...	1446	...	7381	6198	...	1183	...
4	Other current transfers	49384	44956	...	5348	23875	54642	48469	...	5745	25450
	A Casualty insurance premiums, net	...	...	...	...	...	...	...	...	...	...
	B Transfers to other government subsectors	...	22951	...	-	1844	...	23003	...	-	2019
	C Social security benefits	21077		...		21077	23368		...		23368
	D Social assistance grants	18855	15129	...	3726	...	20948	16898	...	4050	...
	E Unfunded employee pension and welfare benefits	4288	2622	...	1612	54	4639	2891	...	1685	63
	F Transfers to private non-profit institutions serving households	2476	2466	...	10	...	2700	2690	...	10	...
	G Other transfers n.e.c.	...	...	...	...	...	...	...	...	...	...
	H Transfers to the rest of the world	1788	1788	...	-	...	2987	2987	...	-	...
	Statistical discrepancy	827	577	...	250	...	793	513	...	280	...
	Net saving	-6689	-7029	...	-558	898	-4657	-4301	...	-1233	877
	Total Current Disbursements and Net Saving	136821	101752	...	37166	25572	149698	112246	...	38453	27261

		1986				
		Total General Government	Central Government	State or Provincial Government	Local Government	Social Security Funds
				Receipts		
1	Operating surplus	1278	-227	...	1505	...
2	Property and entrepreneurial income	6857	9208	...	878	577
	A Withdrawals from public quasi-corporations	...	-	...	...	...
	B Interest [a]	5592	7943	...	878	577
	C Dividends	324	324	...	...	...
	D Net land rent and royalties	941	941	...	...	...
3	Taxes, fees and contributions	142777	101588	...	15107	26082
	A Indirect taxes	60702	45685	...	15107	...
	B Direct taxes	55630	55630	...	-	-
	Income	54064	54064	...	-	-
	Other	1566	1566	...	-	...
	C Social security contributions	26082	-	...	-	26082
	D Fees, fines and penalties	273	273	...	-	-

United Kingdom

3.12 General Government Income and Outlay Account: Total and Subsectors
(Continued)

Million Pounds Sterling

	1986					
	Total General Government	Central Government	State or Provincial Government	Local Government	Social Security Funds
4 Other current transfers	5837	5921	...	23898	2350
A Casualty insurance claims	...	...	...	...	...
B Transfers from other government subsectors	...	2240	...	21804	2288
C Transfers from the rest of the world	...	...	...	...	...
D Other transfers, except imputed	...	...	...	...	...
E Imputed unfunded employee pension and welfare contributions	5837	3681	...	2094	62
Total Current Receipts a	156749	116490	...	41388	29009

Disbursements

1 Government final consumption expenditure	79455	47879	...	30699	877
2 Property income	17022	16587	...	4241	-
A Interest	17022	16587	...	4241	-
B Net land rent and royalties	...	...	...	...	...
3 Subsidies	6552	5474	...	1078	...
4 Other current transfers	57647	50097	...	6071	27811
A Casualty insurance premiums, net	...	...	...	...	...
B Transfers to other government subsectors	...	24092	...	-	2240
C Social security benefits	25509	-	...	-	25509
D Social assistance grants	22345	18126	...	4219	...
E Unfunded employee pension and welfare benefits	4854	2950	...	1842	62
F Transfers to private non-profit institutions serving households	3093	3083	...	10	...
G Other transfers n.e.c.	...	...	...	...	...
H Transfers to the rest of the world	1846	1846	...	-	...
Statistical discrepancy	983	731	...	252	...
Net saving	-4910	-4278	...	-953	321
Total Current Disbursements and Net Saving	156749	116490	...	41388	29009

a) Part of the receipts/payments of interests refers to receipts from/payments to subsectors of government. These are not included in the total for general government.

3.13 General Government Capital Accumulation Account: Total and Subsectors

Million Pounds Sterling

	1980					1981				
	Total General Government	Central Government	State or Provincial Government	Local Government	Social Security Funds	Total General Government	Central Government	State or Provincial Government	Local Government	Social Security Funds

Finance of Gross Accumulation

1 Gross saving	-610	-2647	...	1146	891	-347	-2691	...	2789	-445
A Consumption of fixed capital	3097	713	...	2384	-	3493	805	...	2688	-
B Net saving	-3707	-3360	...	-1238	891	-3840	-3496	...	101	-445
2 Capital transfers	494	451	...	338	...	780	745	...	352	...
A From other government subsectors	...	...	...	295	...	...	...	...	317	...
B From other resident sectors a	494	451	...	43	...	780	745	...	35	...
C From rest of the world	...	...	...	...	...	...	...	...	...	...
Finance of Gross Accumulation	-116	-2196	...	1484	891	433	-1946	...	3141	-445

Gross Accumulation

1 Gross capital formation	5550	1808	...	3742	...	4507	1792	...	2715	...
A Increase in stocks	51	51	...	...	...	-61	-61	...	...	...
B Gross fixed capital formation	5499	1757	...	3742	...	4568	1853	...	2715	...

United Kingdom

3.13 General Government Capital Accumulation Account: Total and Subsectors
(Continued)

Million Pounds Sterling

	1980					1981				
	Total General Government	Central Government	State or Provincial Government	Local Government	Social Security Funds	Total General Government	Central Government	State or Provincial Government	Local Government	Social Security Funds
2 Purchases of land, net	...	...	...	...	...	...	...	...	...	...
3 Purchases of intangible assets, net	...	...	...	...	...	...	...	...	...	...
4 Capital transfers	2453	2490	...	258	...	5881	5888	...	310	...
A To other government subsectors	...	295	...	...	...	...	317	...	...	...
B To other resident sectors	2453	2195	...	258	...	5881	5571	...	310	...
C To rest of the world	...	-	...	...	...	...	-	...	...	...
Net lending	-8119	-6494	...	-2516	891	-9955	-9626	...	116	-445
Gross Accumulation	-116	-2196	...	1484	891	433	-1946	...	3141	-445

	1982					1983				
	Total General Government	Central Government	State or Provincial Government	Local Government	Social Security Funds	Total General Government	Central Government	State or Provincial Government	Local Government	Social Security Funds

Finance of Gross Accumulation

1 Gross saving	-208	-2527	...	3165	-846	-1244	-4335	...	2317	774
A Consumption of fixed capital	3547	850	...	2697	-	3646	893	...	2753	-
B Net saving	-3755	-3377	...	468	-846	-4890	-5228	...	-436	774
2 Capital transfers	664	623	...	369	...	616	574	...	358	...
A From other government subsectors	...	...	...	328	...	...	...	...	316	...
B From other resident sectors [a]	664	623	...	41	...	616	574	...	42	...
C From rest of the world	...	...	...	...	...	...	...	...	...	...
Finance of Gross Accumulation	456	-1904	...	3534	-846	-628	-3761	...	2675	774

Gross Accumulation

1 Gross capital formation	4359	2268	...	2091	...	6034	2817	...	3217	...
A Increase in stocks	105	105	...	...	...	354	354	...	...	...
B Gross fixed capital formation	4254	2163	...	2091	...	5680	2463	...	3217	...
2 Purchases of land, net	...	...	...	...	...	...	...	...	...	...
3 Purchases of intangible assets, net	...	...	...	...	...	...	...	...	...	...
4 Capital transfers	3880	3666	...	542	...	3594	2773	...	1137	...
A To other government subsectors	...	328	...	...	...	...	316	...	...	...
B To other resident sectors	3880	3338	...	542	...	3594	2457	...	1137	...
C To rest of the world	...	-	...	...	...	...	-	...	...	...
Net lending	-7783	-7838	...	901	-846	-10256	-9351	...	-1679	774
Gross Accumulation	456	-1904	...	3534	-846	-628	-3761	...	2675	774

	1984					1985				
	Total General Government	Central Government	State or Provincial Government	Local Government	Social Security Funds	Total General Government	Central Government	State or Provincial Government	Local Government	Social Security Funds

Finance of Gross Accumulation

1 Gross saving	-2835	-6086	...	2353	898	-524	-3262	...	1861	877
A Consumption of fixed capital	3854	943	...	2911	-	4133	1039	...	3094	-
B Net saving	-6689	-7029	...	-558	898	-4657	-4301	...	-1233	877
2 Capital transfers	707	662	...	385	...	929	877	...	626	...
A From other government subsectors	...	...	...	340	...	...	...	...	574	...
B From other resident sectors [a]	707	662	...	45	...	929	877	...	52	...
C From rest of the world	...	...	...	...	...	...	...	...	...	...
Finance of Gross Accumulation	-2128	-5424	...	2738	898	405	-2385	...	2487	877

Gross Accumulation

1 Gross capital formation	6449	2674	...	3775	...	7212	3759	...	3453	...
A Increase in stocks	-92	-92	...	...	...	631	631	...	...	...
B Gross fixed capital formation	6541	2766	...	3775	...	6581	3128	...	3453	...

United Kingdom

3.13 General Government Capital Accumulation Account: Total and Subsectors
(Continued)

Million Pounds Sterling

	1984					1985				
	Total General Government	Central Government	State or Provincial Government	Local Government	Social Security Funds	Total General Government	Central Government	State or Provincial Government	Local Government	Social Security Funds
2 Purchases of land, net	...	...	...	...	...	...	...	...	...	...
3 Purchases of intangible assets, net	...	...	...	...	...	...	...	...	...	...
4 Capital transfers	3796	2802	...	1334	...	3304	3122	...	756	...
A To other government subsectors	...	340	...	...	...	...	574	...	...	...
B To other resident sectors	3796	2462	...	1334	...	3304	2548	...	756	...
C To rest of the world	...	-	...	...	...	...	-	...	...	...
Net lending	-12373	-10900	...	-2371	898	-10111	-9266	...	-1722	877
Gross Accumulation	-2128	-5424	...	2738	898	405	-2385	...	2487	877

	1986				
	Total General Government	Central Government	State or Provincial Government	Local Government	Social Security Funds
Finance of Gross Accumulation					
1 Gross saving	-465	-3126	...	2340	321
A Consumption of fixed capital	4445	1152	...	3293	-
B Net saving	-4910	-4278	...	-953	321
2 Capital transfers	1019	963	...	733	...
A From other government subsectors	...	...	...	677	...
B From other resident sectors [a]	1019	963	...	56	...
C From rest of the world	...	...	...	...	...
Finance of Gross Accumulation	554	-2163	...	3073	321
Gross Accumulation					
1 Gross capital formation	7400	3407	...	3993	...
A Increase in stocks	104	104	...	...	...
B Gross fixed capital formation	7296	3303	...	3993	...
2 Purchases of land, net	...	...	...	...	...
3 Purchases of intangible assets, net	...	...	...	...	...
4 Capital transfers	4708	4790	...	595	...
A To other government subsectors	...	677	...	...	...
B To other resident sectors	4708	4113	...	595	...
C To rest of the world	...	-	...	...	...
Net lending	-11554	-10360	...	-1515	321
Gross Accumulation	554	-2163	...	3073	321

a) Capital transfers from other resident sectors includes capital taxes and other capital receipts.

3.14 General Government Capital Finance Account, Total and Subsectors

Million Pounds Sterling

	1980					1981				
	Total General Government	Central Government	State or Provincial Government	Local Government	Social Security Funds	Total General Government	Central Government	State or Provincial Government	Local Government	Social Security Funds
Acquisition of Financial Assets											
1 Gold and SDRs	...	...	...	...	...	...	...	...	...	...
2 Currency and transferable deposits	489	474	...	15	...	-2500	-2550	...	50	...
3 Other deposits	-110	-142	...	32	...	-124	-189	...	65	...
4 Bills and bonds, short term	403	403	...	-	...	2559	2559	...	-	...
A Corporate and quasi-corporate enterprises, resident	403	403	...	-	...	2559	2559	...	-	...
B Other government subsectors	...	...	...	...	...	...	...	...	...	...
C Rest of the world	...	...	...	...	...	...	...	...	...	...
5 Bonds, long term	12	8	...	4	...	8	-6	...	14	...
A Corporations	...	...	...	...	...	...	...	...	...	...
B Other government subsectors	12	8	...	4	...	8	-6	...	14	...
C Rest of the world	...	...	...	...	...	...	...	...	...	...
6 Corporate equity securities	148	148	...	...	...	1649	1649	...	...	...
7 Short-term loans, n.e.c.	-147	-562	...	33	382	-2007	-482	...	9	-1534
8 Long-term loans, n.e.c.	4853	4430	...	423	...	-2550	-2785	...	235	...
A Mortgages	456	...	...	456	...	271	...	...	271	...

United Kingdom

3.14 General Government Capital Finance Account, Total and Subsectors
(Continued)

Million Pounds Sterling

	1980 Total General Government	1980 Central Government	1980 State or Provincial Government	1980 Local Government	1980 Social Security Funds	1981 Total General Government	1981 Central Government	1981 State or Provincial Government	1981 Local Government	1981 Social Security Funds
B Other	4397	4430	...	-33	...	-2821	-2785	...	-36	...
9 Other receivables	1248	995	...	-256	509	3680	2700	...	-109	1089
10 Other assets	9	9	...	...	...	-7	-7	...	...	...
Total Acquisition of Financial Assets	6905	5763	...	251	891	708	889	...	264	-445

Incurrence of Liabilities

	Total General Government	Central Government	State or Provincial Government	Local Government	Social Security Funds	Total General Government	Central Government	State or Provincial Government	Local Government	Social Security Funds
1 Currency and transferable deposits	266	266	...	...	...	527	527	...	...	...
2 Other deposits	1635	1738	...	-103	...	4138	4375	...	-237	...
3 Bills and bonds, short term	546	276	...	270	...	-986	-1160	...	174	...
4 Bonds, long term	10541	10678	...	-137	...	7958	8135	...	-177	...
5 Short-term loans, n.e.c.	285	-441	...	726	...	-203	-1787	...	1584	...
6 Long-term loans, n.e.c.	1268	-991	...	2259	...	-2179	-1229	...	-950	...
7 Other payables	29	-90	...	119	...	452	225	...	227	...
8 Other liabilities	665	665	...	...	...	1388	1388	...	...	...
Total Incurrence of Liabilities	15235	12101	...	3134	...	11095	10474	...	621	...
Statistical discrepancy [a]	-211	156	...	-367	...	-432	41	...	-473	...
Net Lending	-8119	-6494	...	-2516	891	-9955	-9626	...	116	-445
Incurrence of Liabilities and Net Worth	6905	5763	...	251	891	708	889	...	264	-445

	1982 Total General Government	1982 Central Government	1982 State or Provincial Government	1982 Local Government	1982 Social Security Funds	1983 Total General Government	1983 Central Government	1983 State or Provincial Government	1983 Local Government	1983 Social Security Funds

Acquisition of Financial Assets

	Total General Government	Central Government	State or Provincial Government	Local Government	Social Security Funds	Total General Government	Central Government	State or Provincial Government	Local Government	Social Security Funds
1 Gold and SDRs	...	...	...	...	...	...	...	...	...	...
2 Currency and transferable deposits	-1416	-1497	...	81	...	-533	-577	...	44	...
3 Other deposits	714	300	...	414	...	-45	-52	...	7	...
4 Bills and bonds, short term	4714	4714	...	-	...	-725	-725	...	-	...
A Corporate and quasi-corporate enterprises, resident	4714	4714	...	-	...	-725	-725	...	-	...
B Other government subsectors	...	...	...	...	...	...	...	...	...	...
C Rest of the world	...	...	...	...	...	...	...	...	...	...
5 Bonds, long term	-240	-242	...	2	...	134	116	...	18	...
A Corporations	...	...	...	...	...	...	...	...	...	...
B Other government subsectors	-240	-242	...	2	...	134	116	...	18	...
C Rest of the world	...	...	...	...	...	...	...	...	...	...
6 Corporate equity securities	-60	-60	...	...	...	-505	-505	...	...	...
7 Short-term loans, n.e.c.	-61	-484	...	-13	436	-277	-250	...	-1	-26
8 Long-term loans, n.e.c.	3481	3001	...	480	...	5193	5514	...	-321	...
A Mortgages	555	...	...	555	...	-306	...	...	-306	...
B Other	2926	3001	...	-75	...	5499	5514	...	-15	...
9 Other receivables	-1558	148	...	-424	-1282	1661	837	...	24	800
10 Other assets	10	-10	...	...	...	-8	-8	...	...	...
Total Acquisition of Financial Assets	5564	5870	...	540	-846	4895	4350	...	-229	774

Incurrence of Liabilities

	Total General Government	Central Government	State or Provincial Government	Local Government	Social Security Funds	Total General Government	Central Government	State or Provincial Government	Local Government	Social Security Funds
1 Currency and transferable deposits	300	300	...	...	...	786	786	...	...	...
2 Other deposits	3993	4995	...	-1002	...	3251	3262	...	-11	...
3 Bills and bonds, short term	-758	-323	...	-435	...	241	142	...	99	...
4 Bonds, long term	6290	6457	...	-167	...	9254	9490	...	-236	...
5 Short-term loans, n.e.c.	1016	522	...	494	...	-1036	-116	...	-920	...
6 Long-term loans, n.e.c.	822	29	...	793	...	1520	-844	...	2364	...
7 Other payables	38	183	...	-145	...	885	709	...	176	...
8 Other liabilities	1159	1159	...	...	...	579	579	...	...	...
Total Incurrence of Liabilities	12860	13322	...	-462	...	15480	14008	...	1472	...
Statistical discrepancy [a]	487	386	...	101	...	-329	-307	...	-22	...
Net Lending	-7783	-7838	...	901	-846	-10256	-9351	...	-1679	774
Incurrence of Liabilities and Net Worth	5564	5870	...	540	-846	4895	4350	...	-229	774

United Kingdom

3.14 General Government Capital Finance Account, Total and Subsectors

Million Pounds Sterling

	1984					1985				
	Total General Government	Central Government	State or Provincial Government	Local Government	Social Security Funds	Total General Government	Central Government	State or Provincial Government	Local Government	Social Security Funds

Acquisition of Financial Assets

1 Gold and SDRs	...	...	...	...	...	...	...	...	...	...
2 Currency and transferable deposits	-823	-757	...	-66	...	1743	1592	...	151	...
3 Other deposits	32	-92	...	124	...	368	-155	...	523	...
4 Bills and bonds, short term	3062	3062	...	-	...	1144	1129	...	15	...
A Corporate and quasi-corporate enterprises, resident	3062	3062	...	-	...	1144	1129	...	15	...
B Other government subsectors	...	...	...	...	...	...	...	...	...	...
C Rest of the world	...	...	...	...	...	...	...	...	...	...
5 Bonds, long term	-9	-22	...	13	...	-27	-28	...	1	...
A Corporations	...	...	...	...	...	...	...	...	...	...
B Other government subsectors	-9	-22	...	13	...	-27	-28	...	1	...
C Rest of the world	...	...	...	...	...	...	...	...	...	...
6 Corporate equity securities	-2431	-2431	...	...	...	-2344	-2344	...	...	...
7 Short-term loans, n.e.c.	787	-3	...	148	642	728	62	...	121	545
8 Long-term loans, n.e.c.	3538	3727	...	-189	...	5480	5972	...	-492	...
A Mortgages	-195	...	...	-195	...	-502	...	...	-502	...
B Other	3733	3727	...	6	...	5982	5972	...	10	...
9 Other receivables	1286	1161	...	-131	256	1068	733	...	3	332
10 Other assets	-9	-9	...	...	...	1	1	...	...	...
Total Acquisition of Financial Assets	5433	4636	...	-101	898	8161	6962	...	322	877

Incurrence of Liabilities

1 Currency and transferable deposits	617	617	...	...	...	429	429	...	...	...
2 Other deposits	4386	3723	...	663	...	2805	3173	...	-368	...
3 Bills and bonds, short term	94	-12	...	106	...	227	96	...	131	...
4 Bonds, long term	8220	8558	...	-338	...	8926	9555	...	-629	...
5 Short-term loans, n.e.c.	270	483	...	-213	...	-727	653	...	-1380	...
6 Long-term loans, n.e.c.	1902	-399	...	2301	...	5659	1034	...	4625	...
7 Other payables	1383	1293	...	90	...	738	640	...	98	...
8 Other liabilities	785	785	...	...	...	751	751	...	...	...
Total Incurrence of Liabilities	17657	15048	...	2609	...	18808	16331	...	2477	...
Statistical discrepancy [a]	149	488	...	-339	...	-536	-103	...	-433	...
Net Lending	-12373	-10900	...	-2371	898	-10111	-9266	...	-1722	877
Incurrence of Liabilities and Net Worth	5433	4636	...	-101	898	8161	6962	...	322	877

	1986				
	Total General Government	Central Government	State or Provincial Government	Local Government	Social Security Funds

Acquisition of Financial Assets

1 Gold and SDRs	...	...	...	...	...
2 Currency and transferable deposits	3370	3184	...	186	...
3 Other deposits	846	-149	...	995	...
4 Bills and bonds, short term	508	522	...	-14	...
A Corporate and quasi-corporate enterprises, resident	508	522	...	-14	...
B Other government subsectors	...	...	...	...	...
C Rest of the world	...	...	...	...	...
5 Bonds, long term	82	75	...	7	...
A Corporations	...	...	...	...	...
B Other government subsectors	82	75	...	7	...
C Rest of the world	...	...	...	...	...
6 Corporate equity securities	-3809	-3809	...	...	...
7 Short-term loans, n.e.c.	911	-75	...	619	367
8 Long-term loans, n.e.c.	4235	4730	...	-495	...
A Mortgages	-506	...	...	-506	...
B Other	4741	4730	...	11	...
9 Other receivables	-2298	-1573	...	-679	-46

United Kingdom

3.14 General Government Capital Finance Account, Total and Subsectors
(Continued)

Million Pounds Sterling

	\multicolumn{5}{c}{1986}
	Total General Government	Central Government	State or Provincial Government	Local Government	Social Security Funds
10 Other assets	119	119	...	...	...
Total Acquisition of Financial Assets	3964	3024	...	619	321

Incurrence of Liabilities

1 Currency and transferable deposits	674	674	...	...	...
2 Other deposits	1181	2196	...	-1015	...
3 Bills and bonds, short term	-126	3	...	-129	...
4 Bonds, long term	6668	6870	...	-202	...
5 Short-term loans, n.e.c.	-852	284	...	-1136	...
6 Long-term loans, n.e.c.	7359	2418	...	4941	...
7 Other payables	337	367	...	-30	...
8 Other liabilities	594	594	...	...	...
Total Incurrence of Liabilities	15835	13406	...	2429	...
Statistical discrepancy a	-317	-22	...	-295	...
Net Lending	-11554	-10360	...	-1515	321
Incurrence of Liabilities and Net Worth	3964	3024	...	619	321

a) Statistical discrepancy refers to adjustment made in order to reconcile the net lending of the Capital Accumulation Account and the Capital Finance Account.

3.22 Corporate and Quasi-Corporate Enterprise Income and Outlay Account: Total and Sectors

Million Pounds Sterling

	\multicolumn{3}{c}{1980}	\multicolumn{3}{c}{1981}	\multicolumn{3}{c}{1982}	\multicolumn{3}{c}{1983}
	TOTAL	Non-Financial	Financial	TOTAL	Non-Financial	Financial	TOTAL	Non-Financial	Financial	TOTAL	Non-Financial	Financial

Receipts

1 Operating surplus	11574	15933	-4359	12601	18059	-5458	18247	23522	-5275	24071	29718	-5647
2 Property and entrepreneurial income	43902	6685	37217	47341	7258	40083	53329	7467	45862	54336	8694	45642
A Withdrawals from quasi-corporate enterprises	43902	6685	37217	47341	7258	40083	53329	7467	45862	54336	8694	45642
B Interest	...	...	...	...	...	...	...	...	...	...	...	...
C Dividends	...	...	...	...	...	...	...	...	...	...	...	...
D Net land rent and royalties	...	...	...	...	...	...	...	...	...	...	...	...
3 Current transfers	...	...	...	...	...	...	...	...	...	...	...	...
Total Current Receipts	55476	22618	32858	59942	25317	34625	71576	30989	40587	78407	38412	39995

Disbursements

1 Property and entrepreneurial income	45832	17390	28442	48278	18231	30047	55349	20306	35043	55645	21450	34195
2 Direct taxes and other current transfers n.e.c. to general government	6838	5780	1058	8836	7836	1000	10825	9688	1137	12412	11114	1298
A Direct taxes	6838	5780	1058	8836	7836	1000	10825	9688	1137	12412	11114	1298
B Fines, fees, penalties and other current transfers n.e.c.	...	...	...	...	...	...	...	...	...	...	...	...
3 Other current transfers	52	43	9	62	51	11	69	57	12	86	71	15
A Casualty insurance premiums, net	...	...	...	...	...	...	...	...	...	...	...	...
B Casualty insurance claims liability of insurance companies	...	...	...	...	...	...	...	...	...	...	...	...
C Transfers to private non-profit institutions	52	43	9	62	51	11	69	57	12	86	71	15
D Unfunded employee pension and welfare benefits	...	...	...	...	...	...	...	...	...	...	...	...
E Social assistance grants	...	...	...	...	...	...	...	...	...	...	...	...
F Other transfers n.e.c.	...	...	...	...	...	...	...	...	...	...	...	...
G Transfers to the rest of the world	...	...	...	...	...	...	...	...	...	...	...	...
Net saving	2754	-595	3349	2766	-801	3567	5333	938	4395	10264	5777	4487
Total Current Disbursements and Net Saving	55476	22618	32858	59942	25317	34625	71576	30989	40587	78407	38412	39995

United Kingdom

3.22 Corporate and Quasi-Corporate Enterprise Income and Outlay Account: Total and Sectors
Million Pounds Sterling

	1984 TOTAL	1984 Non-Financial	1984 Financial	1985 TOTAL	1985 Non-Financial	1985 Financial	1986 TOTAL	1986 Non-Financial	1986 Financial
Receipts									
1 Operating surplus	26539	34261	-7722	32102	41023	-8921	29327	39132	-9805
2 Property and entrepreneurial income	63750	8606	55144	78299	10480	67819	81427	10852	70575
A Withdrawals from quasi-corporate enterprises	63750	8606	55144	78299	10480	67819	81427	10852	70575
B Interest	...	...	...	...	...	...	...	...	...
C Dividends	...	...	...	...	...	...	...	...	...
D Net land rent and royalties	...	...	...	...	...	...	...	...	...
3 Current transfers	...	...	...	...	...	...	...	...	...
Total Current Receipts	90289	42867	47422	110401	51503	58898	110754	49984	60770
Disbursements									
1 Property and entrepreneurial income	64033	22994	41039	77884	26915	50969	79099	27405	51694
2 Direct taxes and other current transfers n.e.c. to general government	14464	13171	1293	17081	15338	1743	15087	12876	2211
A Direct taxes	14464	13171	1293	17081	15338	1743	15087	12876	2211
B Fines, fees, penalties and other current transfers n.e.c.	...	...	...	...	...	...	...	...	...
3 Other current transfers	102	83	19	114	93	21	134	110	24
A Casualty insurance premiums, net	...	...	...	...	...	...	...	...	...
B Casualty insurance claims liability of insurance companies	...	...	...	...	...	...	...	...	...
C Transfers to private non-profit institutions	102	83	19	114	93	21	134	110	24
D Unfunded employee pension and welfare benefits	...	...	...	...	...	...	...	...	...
E Social assistance grants	...	...	...	...	...	...	...	...	...
F Other transfers n.e.c.	...	...	...	...	...	...	...	...	...
G Transfers to the rest of the world	...	...	...	...	...	...	...	...	...
Net saving	11690	6619	5071	15322	9157	6165	16434	9593	6841
Total Current Disbursements and Net Saving	90289	42867	47422	110401	51503	58898	110754	49984	60770

3.23 Corporate and Quasi-Corporate Enterprise Capital Accumulation Account: Total and Sectors
Million Pounds Sterling

	1980 TOTAL	1980 Non-Financial	1980 Financial	1981 TOTAL	1981 Non-Financial	1981 Financial	1982 TOTAL	1982 Non-Financial	1982 Financial	1983 TOTAL	1983 Non-Financial	1983 Financial
Finance of Gross Accumulation												
1 Gross saving	21556	17050	4506	24036	19030	5006	28097	22016	6081	34639	28179	6460
A Consumption of fixed capital	18802	17645	1157	21270	19831	1439	22764	21078	1686	24375	22402	1973
B Net saving	2754	-595	3349	2766	-801	3567	5333	938	4395	10264	5777	4487
2 Capital transfers	1340	1340	-	4872	4872	-	2336	2336	-	1423	1423	-
Finance of Gross Accumulation	22896	18390	4506	28908	23902	5006	30433	24352	6081	36062	29602	6460
Gross Accumulation												
1 Gross capital formation	24381	19135	5246	24547	19015	5532	27146	20982	6164	28807	23529	5278
A Increase in stocks	-2397	-2403	6	-2463	-2472	9	-1407	-1411	4	220	182	38
B Gross fixed capital formation	26778	21538	5240	27010	21487	5523	28553	22393	6160	28587	23347	5240
2 Purchases of land, net	...	...	...	...	...	...	...	...	...	...	...	...
3 Purchases of intangible assets, net	...	...	...	...	...	...	...	...	...	...	...	...
4 Capital transfers	150	150	-	411	144	267	184	96	88	222	222	-
A To resident sectors	150	150	-	411	144	267	184	96	88	222	222	-
B To the rest of the world	...	...	...	...	...	...	...	...	...	...	...	...
Net lending	-1635	-895	-740	3950	4743	-793	3103	3274	-171	7033	5851	1182
Gross Accumulation	22896	18390	4506	28908	23902	5006	30433	24352	6081	36062	29602	6460

United Kingdom

3.23 Corporate and Quasi-Corporate Enterprise Capital Accumulation Account: Total and Sectors
Million Pounds Sterling

		1984 TOTAL	1984 Non-Financial	1984 Financial	1985 TOTAL	1985 Non-Financial	1985 Financial	1986 TOTAL	1986 Non-Financial	1986 Financial
		\multicolumn{9}{c}{Finance of Gross Accumulation}								
1	Gross saving	37745	30369	7376	43629	34674	8955	47000	36856	10144
	A Consumption of fixed capital	26055	23750	2305	28307	25517	2790	30566	27263	3303
	B Net saving	11690	6619	5071	15322	9157	6165	16434	9593	6841
2	Capital transfers	1237	1237	-	1327	1327	-	2942	2942	-
	Finance of Gross Accumulation	38982	31606	7376	44956	36001	8955	49942	39798	10144
		\multicolumn{9}{c}{Gross Accumulation}								
1	Gross capital formation	33653	26699	6954	38013	30084	7929	39049	31763	7286
	A Increase in stocks	-8	-32	24	-147	-147	-	241	241	-
	B Gross fixed capital formation	33661	26731	6930	38160	30231	7929	38808	31522	7286
2	Purchases of land, net	...	...	...	...	...	...	...	...	...
3	Purchases of intangible assets, net	...	...	...	...	...	...	...	...	...
4	Capital transfers	245	245	-	258	258	-	231	231	-
	A To resident sectors	245	245	-	258	258	-	231	231	-
	B To the rest of the world	...	...	...	...	...	...	...	...	...
	Net lending	5084	4662	422	6685	5659	1026	10662	7804	2858
	Gross Accumulation	38982	31606	7376	44956	36001	8955	49942	39798	10144

3.24 Corporate and Quasi-Corporate Enterprise Capital Finance Account: Total and Sectors
Million Pounds Sterling

		1980 TOTAL	1980 Non-Financial	1980 Financial	1981 TOTAL	1981 Non-Financial	1981 Financial	1982 TOTAL	1982 Non-Financial	1982 Financial	1983 TOTAL	1983 Non-Financial	1983 Financial
		\multicolumn{12}{c}{Acquisition of Financial Assets}											
1	Gold and SDRs	...	...	...	...	...	...	...	...	...	...	...	...
2	Currency and transferable deposits	-479	-261	-218	2490	1546	944	1181	325	856	2565	2037	528
3	Other deposits	26844	3298	23546	29417	3972	25445	12818	2506	10312	20035	3477	16558
4	Bills and bonds, short term	2131	388	1743	-113	69	-182	-1865	50	-1915	2136	334	1802
	A Corporate and quasi-corporate, resident	1411	383	1028	845	80	765	-939	-20	-919	1913	236	1677
	B Government	720	5	715	-958	-11	-947	-926	70	-996	223	98	125
	C Rest of the world	...	...	...	...	...	...	...	...	...	...	...	...
5	Bonds, long term	9133	573	8560	8010	-55	8065	7907	-338	8245	10033	-1482	11515
	A Corporate, resident	...	...	...	...	...	...	...	...	...	...	...	...
	B Government	214	214	...	-339	-339	...	373	373	...	384	384	...
	C Rest of the world	...	...	...	...	...	...	...	...	...	...	...	...
6	Corporate equity securities	7376	2062	5314	7604	1392	6212	8531	2492	6039	9020	2469	6551
7	Short term loans, n.e.c.	19597	69	19528	24206	98	24108	20611	-3	20614	10995	44	10951
8	Long term loans, n.e.c.	9846	1413	8433	13101	2712	10389	17946	3303	14643	19682	3348	16334
	A Mortgages	6616	37	6579	8896	29	8867	13201	-30	13231	14753	-57	14810
	B Other	3230	1376	1854	4205	2683	1522	4745	3333	1412	4929	3405	1524
9	Trade credits and advances	490	490	...	3682	3682	...	514	514	...	1704	1704	...
	A Consumer credit	-126	-126	...	378	378	...	32	32	...	109	109	...
	B Other	616	616	...	3304	3304	...	482	482	...	1595	1595	...
10	Other receivables												
11	Other assets	-118	-123	5	72	69	3	-61	-54	-7	437	435	2
	Total Acquisition of Financial Assets	74820	7909	66911	88469	13485	74984	67582	8795	58787	76607	12366	64241
		\multicolumn{12}{c}{Incurrence of Liabilities}											
1	Currency and transferable deposits	2737	...	2737	6961	...	6961	6599	...	6599	7441	...	7441
2	Other deposits	47970	-145	48115	37364	-31	37395	29747	-3	29750	31972	18	31954
3	Bills and bonds, short term	2813	658	2155	15681	1499	14182	9926	2478	7448	4429	-559	4988
4	Bonds, long term	367	156	211	948	737	211	740	245	495	1255	605	650
5	Corporate equity securities	1708	1229	479	2870	1632	1238	2145	1008	1137	3800	1814	1986
6	Short-term loans, n.e.c.	7285	5665	1620	6986	4934	2052	6561	4181	2380	4819	2017	2802

United Kingdom

3.24 Corporate and Quasi-Corporate Enterprise Capital Finance Account: Total and Sectors
(Continued)

Million Pounds Sterling

	1980 TOTAL	1980 Non-Financial	1980 Financial	1981 TOTAL	1981 Non-Financial	1981 Financial	1982 TOTAL	1982 Non-Financial	1982 Financial	1983 TOTAL	1983 Non-Financial	1983 Financial
7 Long-term loans, n.e.c.	3852	3764	88	-2015	-2070	55	2844	2305	539	4529	3310	1219
8 Net equity of households in life insurance and pension fund reserves	12144	...	12144	14217	...	14217	14915	...	14915	15900	...	15900
9 Proprietors' net additions to the accumulation of quasi-corporations	...	...	...	...	...	...	...	...	...	...	...	...
10 Trade credit and advances	569	521	48	2259	2311	-52	117	89	28	1699	1679	20
11 Other accounts payable	...	...	...	...	...	...	...	...	...	...	...	...
12 Other liabilities	1360	615	745	3243	2885	358	-1118	-1295	177	1471	1358	113
Total Incurrence of Liabilities	80805	12463	68342	88514	11897	76617	72476	9008	63468	77315	10242	67073
Statistical discrepancy [a]	-4350	-3659	-691	-3995	-3155	-840	-7997	-3487	-4510	-7741	-3727	-4014
Net Lending	-1635	-895	-740	3950	4743	-793	3103	3274	-171	7033	5851	1182
Incurrence of Liabilities and Net Lending	74820	7909	66911	88469	13485	74984	67582	8795	58787	76607	12366	64241

	1984 TOTAL	1984 Non-Financial	1984 Financial	1985 TOTAL	1985 Non-Financial	1985 Financial	1986 TOTAL	1986 Non-Financial	1986 Financial
Acquisition of Financial Assets									
1 Gold and SDRs	...	...	...	...	...	...	...	...	...
2 Currency and transferable deposits	4703	1876	2827	3542	1721	1821	6701	3893	2808
3 Other deposits	18879	866	18013	33295	3735	29560	68109	7245	60864
4 Bills and bonds, short term	266	-212	478	1578	433	1145	4359	1038	3321
A Corporate and quasi-corporate, resident	296	-85	381	1381	466	915	4428	991	3437
B Government	-30	-127	97	197	-33	230	-69	47	-116
C Rest of the world	...	...	...	...	...	...	...	...	...
5 Bonds, long term	16689	285	16404	18529	-3285	21814	17820	-2073	19893
A Corporate, resident	...	...	...	...	...	...	...	...	...
B Government	-120	-120	...	-409	-409	...	-78	-78	...
C Rest of the world	...	...	...	...	...	...	...	...	...
6 Corporate equity securities	9695	4289	5406	18777	7562	11215	24472	6340	18132
7 Short term loans, n.e.c.	15845	65	15780	12255	17	12238	26813	276	26537
8 Long term loans, n.e.c.	20432	1523	18909	23260	717	22543	26658	-988	27646
A Mortgages	17252	-62	17314	19466	-93	19559	26170	-120	26290
B Other	3180	1585	1595	3794	810	2984	488	-868	1356
9 Trade credits and advances	540	540	...	624	624	...	447	447	...
A Consumer credit	200	200	...	118	118	...	-103	-103	...
B Other	340	340	...	506	506	...	550	550	...
10 Other receivables	...	...	...	...	...	...	...	...	...
11 Other assets	908	892	16	-123	-148	25	56	46	10
Total Acquisition of Financial Assets	87957	10124	77833	111737	11376	100361	175435	16224	159211
Incurrence of Liabilities									
1 Currency and transferable deposits	11362	...	11362	19238	...	19238	4688	...	4688
2 Other deposits	40170	-	40170	48891	-	48891	90546	91	90455
3 Bills and bonds, short term	1460	1508	-48	-5239	614	-5853	16938	1145	15793
4 Bonds, long term	1362	230	1132	8199	842	7357	5684	769	4915
5 Corporate equity securities	3462	1457	2005	6982	4194	2788	14563	6783	7780
6 Short-term loans, n.e.c.	13278	6331	6947	10879	5921	4958	23344	4291	19053
7 Long-term loans, n.e.c.	-2785	-1882	-903	2608	326	2282	-287	233	-520
8 Net equity of households in life insurance and pension fund reserves	17753	...	17753	18563	...	18563	19202	...	19202
9 Proprietors' net additions to the accumulation of quasi-corporations	...	...	...	...	...	...	...	...	...
10 Trade credit and advances	306	286	20	475	455	20	983	963	20
11 Other accounts payable	...	...	...	...	...	...	...	...	...
12 Other liabilities	1481	716	765	1215	54	1161	-1792	-313	-1479
Total Incurrence of Liabilities	87849	8646	79203	111811	12406	99405	173869	13962	159907
Statistical discrepancy [a]	-4976	-3184	-1792	-6759	-6689	-70	-9096	-5542	-3554
Net Lending	5084	4662	422	6685	5659	1026	10662	7804	2858
Incurrence of Liabilities and Net Lending	87957	10124	77833	111737	11376	100361	175435	16224	159211

a) Statistical discrepancy refers to adjustment made in order to reconcile the net lending of the Capital Accumulation Account and the Capital Finance Account.

United Kingdom

3.32 Household and Private Unincorporated Enterprise Income and Outlay Account

Million Pounds Sterling

	1970	1975	1977	1978	1979	1980	1981	1982	1983	1984	1985	1986
Receipts												
1 Compensation of employees	30553	68494	86568	98826	115842	137657	149525	158568	169558	180053	194434	209445
A Wages and salaries	27760	60333	74913	85629	100421	119027	127805	136188	145433	155052	168348	182579
B Employers' contributions for social security	1354	4068	5694	6069	6889	8210	8814	9344	10540	11263	12208	13257
C Employers' contributions for private pension & welfare plans	1439	4093	5961	7128	8532	10420	12906	13036	13585	13738	13878	13609
2 Operating surplus of private unincorporated enterprises	4827	10377	13948	15996	18276	20597	23141	26446	29169	33049	36036	39995
3 Property and entrepreneurial income	4031	6771	8440	9756	14141	18274	19802	22605	23569	27049	32983	34685
A Withdrawals from private quasi-corporations	...	...	...	...	...	...	...	...	...	...	...	...
B Interest	4031	6771	8440	9756	14141	18274	19802	22605	23569	27049	32983	34685
C Dividends	...	...	...	...	...	...	...	...	...	...	...	...
D Net land rent and royalties	...	...	...	...	...	...	...	...	...	...	...	...
3 Current transfers	4596	10712	15692	18696	21807	26499	32400	37925	41275	44701	48325	52382
A Casualty insurance claims	-	-	-	-	-	-	-	-	-	-	-	-
B Social security benefits	2751	6469	9333	10646	12072	14689	17675	19151	20495	21671	23017	25131
C Social assistance grants	1243	3019	4686	6185	7657	9278	11832	15504	17158	19006	21106	22562
D Unfunded employee pension and welfare benefits	-	-	-	-	-	-	-	-	-	-	-	-
E Transfers from general government	336	789	1016	1046	1187	1557	1736	1930	2100	2304	2528	2850
F Transfers from the rest of the world	230	393	614	774	840	923	1095	1271	1436	1618	1560	1705
G Other transfers n.e.c.	36	42	43	45	51	52	62	69	86	102	114	134
Total Current Receipts	44007	96354	124648	143274	170066	203027	224868	245544	263571	284852	311778	336507
Disbursements												
1 Final consumption expenditures	31740	64992	86215	99420	117745	136725	152166	166551	181858	194596	212207	232569
2 Property income	1058	3095	4330	4729	6908	10073	11401	12940	13569	16908	22803	24353
A Interest	1058	3095	4330	4729	6908	10073	11401	12940	13569	16908	22803	24353
Consumer debt	...	...	...	...	...	...	...	...	...	...	...	...
Mortgage	754	2115	2974	3007	4256	6160	6852	7581	7524	9434	12852	13622
Other	...	...	...	...	...	...	...	...	...	...	...	...
B Net land rent and royalties	...	...	...	...	...	...	...	...	...	...	...	...
3 Direct taxes and other current transfers n.e.c. to government	8897	22079	27745	29723	32883	39556	45034	49763	54244	57178	61730	66883
A Social security contributions	2655	6848	9503	10101	11526	13939	15916	18095	20787	22301	24200	26067
B Direct taxes	6201	15151	18094	19457	21205	25434	28933	31460	33216	34623	37292	40543
Income taxes	5964	14761	17564	18867	20604	24708	28093	30438	32032	33334	35810	38977
Other	237	390	530	590	601	726	840	1022	1184	1289	1482	1566
C Fees, fines and penalties	41	80	148	165	152	183	185	208	241	254	238	273
4 Other current transfers	243	531	659	901	1044	1139	1175	1291	1250	1357	1500	1663
A Net casualty insurance premiums	-	-	-	-	-	-	-	-	-	-	-	-
B Transfers to private non-profit institutions serving households	...	...	...	...	...	...	...	...	...	...	...	...
C Transfers to the rest of the world	243	531	659	901	1044	1139	1175	1291	1250	1357	1500	1663
D Other current transfers, except imputed	...	...	...	...	...	...	...	...	...	...	...	...
E Imputed employee pension and welfare contributions	-	-	-	-	-	-	-	-	-	-	-	-
Net saving	2069	5657	5699	8501	11486	15534	15092	14999	12650	14813	13538	11039
Total Current Disbursements and Net Saving	44007	96354	124648	143274	170066	203027	224868	245544	263571	284852	311778	336507

United Kingdom

3.33 Household and Private Unincorporated Enterprise Capital Accumulation Account

Million Pounds Sterling

	1970	1975	1977	1978	1979	1980	1981	1982	1983	1984	1985	1986
Finance of Gross Accumulation
1 Gross saving	3043	8189	9175	12649	16479	21598	21976	22364	20797	23796	23413	22032
A Consumption of fixed capital	974	2532	3476	4148	4993	6064	6884	7365	8147	8983	9875	10993
B Net saving	2069	5657	5699	8501	11486	15534	15092	14999	12650	14813	13538	11039
2 Capital transfers	207	426	841	1054	1095	1281	1179	1646	2419	2833	2238	2010
A From resident sectors	207	426	841	1054	1095	1281	1179	1646	2419	2833	2238	2010
B From the rest of the world	...	...	...	...	...	...	...	...	...	...	...	...
Total Finance of Gross Accumulation	3250	8615	10016	13703	17574	22879	23155	24010	23216	26629	25651	24042
Gross Accumulation
1 Gross Capital Formation	1623	3571	5860	6522	8546	9044	9520	12014	14483	15122	15680	18329
A Increase in stocks	20	-245	355	313	388	-240	-211	58	156	216	-56	206
B Gross fixed capital formation a	1603	3816	5505	6209	8158	9284	9731	11956	14327	14906	15736	18123
2 Purchases of land, net	...	...	...	...	...	...	...	...	...	...	...	...
3 Purchases of intangibles, net	...	...	...	...	...	...	...	...	...	...	...	...
4 Capital transfers	385	326	419	410	468	512	539	582	642	736	932	1032
A To resident sectors	385	326	419	410	468	512	539	582	642	736	932	1032
B To the rest of the world	...	...	...	...	...	...	...	...	...	...	...	...
Net lending	1242	4718	3737	6771	8560	13323	13096	11414	8091	10771	9039	4681
Total Gross Accumulation	3250	8615	10016	13703	17574	22879	23155	24010	23216	26629	25651	24042

a) Item 'Gross fixed capital formation' of household and private unincorporated enterprises includes net transactions in land and existing buildings.

3.34 Household and Private Unincorporated Enterprise Capital Finance Account

Million Pounds Sterling

	1970	1975	1977	1978	1979	1980	1981	1982	1983	1984	1985	1986
Acquisition of Financial Assets
1 Gold	...	...	...	...	...	...	...	...	...	...	...	...
2 Currency and transferable deposits	...	1704	2591	2632	1861	1382	1621	3020	2574	3432	7046	7204
3 Other deposits	...	4487	6200	8535	13356	15283	14316	14940	14413	16715	14527	15769
4 Bills and bonds, short term	...	...	...	...	...	...	...	...	...	...	...	...
5 Bonds, long term	...	880	325	-402	1407	403	1973	2983	3786	2397	7185	6319
A Corporate	...	80	11	-29	155	-59	275	866	2185	229	4053	1100
B Government	...	946	569	7	1539	1350	1970	2154	1342	2009	1492	3296
C Rest of the world	...	-146	-255	-380	-287	-888	-272	-32	259	159	1640	1923
6 Corporate equity securities	...	-1228	-2046	-1739	-3070	-2051	-2330	-3054	-2192	-3385	-4494	1404
7 Short term loans, n.e.c.	...	38	45	38	69	98	126	75	247	425	341	407
8 Long term loans, n.e.c.	...	-145	261	-14	-16	211	175	-619	-320	-192	-497	-767
A Mortgages	...	...	...	...	...	...	...	...	...	...	...	...
B Other	...	-145	261	-14	-16	211	175	-619	-320	-192	-497	-767
9 Trade credit and advances	...	...	...	...	...	...	...	...	...	...	...	...
10 Net equity of households in life insurance and pension fund reserves	...	4475	6923	8283	10770	12843	14863	15536	16591	18513	19282	20110
11 Proprietors' net additions to the accumulation of quasi-corporations	...	...	...	...	...	...	...	...	...	...	...	...
12 Other	...	33	48	104	233	272	195	337	374	625	970	586
Total Acquisition of Financial Assets	...	10244	14347	17437	24610	28441	30939	33223	35473	38530	44360	51032
Incurrence of Liabilities
1 Short term loans, n.e.c.	...	-493	1126	1509	2706	2966	3975	5015	4892	4191	6826	6007
2 Long term loans, n.e.c.	...	3613	4718	6232	7512	7972	10088	14516	15335	17693	20543	26393
A Mortgages	...	3613	4262	5441	6517	7369	9483	14127	14501	17034	19033	25732
B Other	...	-	456	791	995	603	605	389	834	659	1510	661
3 Trade credit and advances	...	140	150	214	674	-126	378	32	109	200	118	-103
A Consumer credit	...	140	150	214	674	-126	378	32	109	200	118	-103

United Kingdom

3.34 Household and Private Unincorporated Enterprise Capital Finance Account
(Continued)

Million Pounds Sterling

	1970	1975	1977	1978	1979	1980	1981	1982	1983	1984	1985	1986
B Other	...	...	...	...	...	...	...	...	...	...	...	...
4 Other accounts payable	...	35	12	29	213	13	252	-202	116	-45	-38	-201
5 Other liabilities	...	-8	-	-6	6	-1	16	-29	-2	-1	4	75
Total Incurrence of Liabilities	...	3287	6006	7978	11111	10824	14709	19332	20450	22038	27453	32171
Statistical discrepancy a	...	2239	4604	2687	4938	4294	3135	2479	6932	5721	7869	14180
Net Lending	...	4718	3737	6772	8561	13323	13095	11412	8091	10771	9038	4681
Incurrence of Liabilities and Net Lending	...	10244	14347	17437	24610	28441	30939	33223	35473	38530	44360	51032

a) Statistical discrepancy refers to adjustment made in order to reconcile the net lending of the Capital Accumulation Account and the Capital Finance Account.

3.51 External Transactions: Current Account: Detail

Million Pounds Sterling

	1970	1975	1977	1978	1979	1980	1981	1982	1983	1984	1985	1986
Payments to the Rest of the World
1 Imports of goods and services	11482	29421	42968	45889	55096	58346	61148	68598	78134	93215	99178	101535
A Imports of merchandise c.i.f.	9004	24150	35884	38599	46566	48587	50282	56202	64835	78376	84093	85024
B Other	2478	5271	7084	7290	8530	9759	10866	12396	13299	14839	15085	16511
2 Factor income to the rest of the world	821	5592	7601	9631	14241	21804	34878	41960	38700	45260	46035	40972
A Compensation of employees	79	186	278	286	287	284	278	320	341	370	406	457
B Property and entrepreneurial income	742	5406	7323	9345	13954	21520	34600	41640	38359	44890	45629	40515
By general government	319	491	565	650	681	895	940	1092	1189	1326	1475	1668
By corporate and quasi-cororate enterprises	423	4915	6758	8695	13273	20625	33660	40548	37170	43564	44154	38847
By other	...	...	...	...	...	...	...	...	...	...	...	...
3 Current transfers to the rest of the world	412	1234	2043	3019	3618	3899	4515	5298	5490	5938	6787	6118
A Indirect taxes by general government to supranational organizations	-	349	752	985	1983	1897	2241	2936	3063	3296	3879	2890
B Other current transfers	412	885	1291	2034	1635	2002	2274	2362	2427	2642	2908	3228
By general government	169	354	632	1133	591	863	1099	1071	1177	1285	1408	1565
By other resident sectors	243	531	659	901	1044	1139	1175	1291	1250	1357	1500	1663
4 Surplus of the nation on current transactions	630	-2194	-200	737	94	3512	5864	3474	2326	-1066	1684	-3171
Payments to the Rest of the World, and Surplus of the Nation on Current Transfers	13345	34053	52412	59276	73049	87561	106405	119330	124650	143347	153684	145454
Receipts From The Rest of the World
1 Exports of goods and services	11935	27577	43945	48051	55685	63691	68407	73609	81004	92611	102706	98439
A Exports of merchandise f.o.b.	8150	19330	31728	35063	40687	47422	50977	55565	60776	70367	78111	72843
B Other	3785	8247	12217	12988	14998	16269	17430	18044	20228	22244	24595	25596
2 Factor income from the rest of the world	1181	5718	7553	9997	15965	21966	35169	42233	39899	46637	47467	43090
A Compensation of employees	9	34	56	60	64	69	72	76	73	71	81	80
B Property and entrepreneurial income	1172	5684	7497	9937	15901	21897	35097	42157	39826	46566	47386	43010
By general government	54	266	384	693	816	946	970	980	767	820	738	760
By corporate and quasi-corporate enterprises	1118	5418	7113	9244	15085	20951	34127	41177	39059	45746	46648	42250
By other	...	...	...	...	...	...	...	...	...	...	...	...
3 Current transfers from the rest of the world	230	759	915	1228	1399	1904	2829	3489	3747	4099	3511	3925
A Subsidies to general government from supranational organizations	-	342	184	344	380	573	742	855	1158	1442	1284	1470
B Other current transfers	230	417	731	884	1019	1331	2087	2634	2589	2657	2227	2455
To general government	-	24	117	110	179	408	992	1363	1153	1039	667	750
To other resident sectors	230	393	614	774	840	923	1095	1271	1436	1618	1560	1705
Receipts from the Rest of the World on Current Transfers	13346	34054	52413	59276	73049	87561	106405	119331	124650	143347	153684	145454

United Kingdom

3.52 External Transactions: Capital Accumulation Account

Million Pounds Sterling

	1970	1975	1977	1978	1979	1980	1981	1982	1983	1984	1985	1986
Finance of Gross Accumulation												
1 Surplus of the nation on current transactions	630	-2194	-200	737	94	3512	5864	3474	2326	-1066	1684	-3171
2 Capital transfers from the rest of the world	...	...	...	...	...	...	...	...	...	...	...	...
Total Finance of Gross Accumulation	630	-2194	-200	737	94	3512	5864	3474	2326	-1066	1684	-3171
Gross Accumulation												
1 Capital transfers to the rest of the world	-	-	-	-	-	-	-	-	-	-	-	-
2 Purchases of intangible assets, n.e.c., net, from the rest of the world	...	...	...	...	...	...	...	...	...	...	...	...
Net lending to the rest of the world	630	-2194	-200	737	94	3512	5864	3474	2326	-1066	1684	-3171
Total Gross Accumulation	630	-2194	-200	737	94	3512	5864	3474	2326	-1066	1684	-3171

3.53 External Transactions: Capital Finance Account

Million Pounds Sterling

	1970	1975	1977	1978	1979	1980	1981	1982	1983	1984	1985	1986
Acquisitions of Foreign Financial Assets												
1 Gold and SDR's	-111	...	...	...	...	...	...	...	...	...	...	...
2 Currency and transferable deposits	103	-655	9588	-2329	1059	291	-2419	-1421	-607	-908	1758	2891
3 Other deposits	62	-	6199	14638	23872	22435	24805	9125	13642	13433	24478	53380
4 Bills and bonds, short term	24	-270	39	89	-225	287	1412	1056	548	652	105	1239
5 Bonds, long term	7	103	92	281	90	237	1540	4057	4397	10424	14002	16688
6 Corporate equity securities	274	257	369	1785	2159	4785	5163	3568	4002	1758	6986	11327
7 Short-term loans, n.e.c.	2955	7341	3811	5169	5641	9010	11566	7918	2287	-1025	-3654	-367
8 Long-term loans	291	496	1799	1939	3515	2877	4844	4188	5539	3080	1093	-1141
9 Proprietors' net additions to accumulation of quasi-corporate, non-resident enterprises	...	...	...	...	...	...	...	...	...	...	...	...
10 Trade credit and advances	157	107	318	343	710	59	530	-290	-	-	-	-
11 Other	...	...	...	...	...	...	...	...	...	...	...	...
Total Acquisitions of Foreign Financial Assets	3762	7379	22215	21915	36821	39981	47441	28201	29808	27414	44768	84017
Incurrence of Foreign Liabilities												
1 Currency and transferable deposits	-136	18	2636	-1136	3468	1902	3458	2693	3014	3759	9094	-9022
2 Other deposits	3526	7375	7769	16478	23029	30023	22698	14393	14462	22363	27984	60383
3 Bills and bonds, short term	-44	117	3898	2476	6718	1111	13677	7346	3805	-1123	-7625	13259
4 Bonds, long term	89	54	1262	42	1256	1597	455	432	953	929	5440	4819
5 Corporate equity securities	143	195	414	113	401	1020	1110	296	1479	1341	2029	3823
6 Short-term loans, n.e.c.	-960	1	395	14	-13	-2	-1	-115	-3	-343	-	1
7 Long-term loans	351	1765	2524	913	759	1059	12	1562	2368	-3888	1660	2198
8 Non-resident proprietors' net additions to accumulation of resident quasi-corporate enterprises	...	...	...	...	...	...	...	...	...	...	...	...
9 Trade credit and advances	193	65	130	163	364	-211	76	-107	-	-	-	-
10 Other	-	-	-	-	195	180	158	-	-	-	-	-
Total Incurrence of Liabilities	3162	9590	19028	19063	36177	36679	41643	26500	26078	23038	38582	75461
Statistical discrepancy [a]	-57	1337	3637	3108	-118	-267	-1292	-5031	-1138	894	574	4767
Net Lending	657	-3548	-450	-256	762	3569	7090	6732	4868	3482	5612	3789
Total Incurrence of Liabilities and Net Lending	3762	7379	22215	21915	36821	39981	47441	28201	29808	27414	44768	84017

a) Statistical discrepancy refers to adjustment made in order to reconcile the net lending of the Capital Accumulation Account and the Capital Finance Account.

4.3 Cost Components of Value Added

Million Pounds Sterling

	1980						1981					
	Compensation of Employees	Capital Consumption	Net Operating Surplus	Indirect Taxes	Less: Subsidies Received	Value Added	Compensation of Employees	Capital Consumption	Net Operating Surplus	Indirect Taxes	Less: Subsidies Received	Value Added
All Producers												
1 Agriculture, hunting, forestry and fishing	1274	1109	1920	...	...	4303	1354	1182	2301	...	...	4837
2 Mining and quarrying	3227	1980	7237	...	...	12444	3522	2344	10165	...	...	16031
3 Manufacturing [a]	43403	6497	4615	...	...	54515	44726	7146	3280	...	...	55152
4 Electricity, gas and water	3159	2257	973	...	...	6389	3589	2520	1106	...	...	7215

United Kingdom

4.3 Cost Components of Value Added
(Continued)

Million Pounds Sterling

1980 / 1981

	Compensation of Employees	Capital Consumption	Net Operating Surplus	Indirect Taxes	Less: Subsidies Received	Value Added	Compensation of Employees	Capital Consumption	Net Operating Surplus	Indirect Taxes	Less: Subsidies Received	Value Added
5 Construction	7582	547	3893	...	...	12022	7830	586	4359	...	...	12775
6 Wholesale and retail trade, restaurants and hotels [a]	18236	1827	4861	...	...	24924	20171	2037	4904	...	...	27112
7 Transport, storage and communication	10631	3913	-209	...	...	14335	11476	4415	-61	...	...	15830
8 Finance, insurance, real estate and business services	12623	5838	18390	...	...	36851	14476	6901	20384	...	...	41761
9 Community, social and personal services [a]	5582	382	3267	...	...	9231	6028	459	3663	...	...	10150
Total, Industries	105717	25849	43448	...	...	175014	113172	29300	48391	...	...	190863
Producers of Government Services	29438	1746	-	...	...	31184	33352	1944	-	...	...	35296
Other Producers	2717	368	-	...	...	3085	3207	403	-	...	...	3610
Total [b]	137872	27963	43448	...	...	209283	149731	31647	48391	...	...	229769
Less: Imputed bank service charge	...	...	9353	...	...	9353	...	...	10609	...	...	10609
Import duties [c]	...	...	...	...	...	19207	...	...	...	...	...	22400
Value added tax	...	...	...	11931	...	11931	...	...	...	13046	...	13046
Other adjustments [d]	...	...	...	23898	5611	-57	...	...	...	28845	6355	-1227
Total	137872	27963	34095	35829	5611	230091	149731	31647	37782	41891	6355	253469

1982 / 1983

	Compensation of Employees	Capital Consumption	Net Operating Surplus	Indirect Taxes	Less: Subsidies Received	Value Added	Compensation of Employees	Capital Consumption	Net Operating Surplus	Indirect Taxes	Less: Subsidies Received	Value Added
					All Producers							
1 Agriculture, hunting, forestry and fishing	1451	1210	2869	...	...	5530	1566	1246	2553	...	...	5365
2 Mining and quarrying	3768	2562	12002	...	...	18332	3672	2776	14329	...	...	20777
3 Manufacturing [a]	46266	7618	5515	...	...	59399	47336	7999	7439	...	...	62774
4 Electricity, gas and water	3761	2658	1345	...	...	7764	3796	2786	2031	...	...	8613
5 Construction	8103	633	5138	...	...	13874	8674	645	6199	...	...	15518
6 Wholesale and retail trade, restaurants and hotels [a]	21444	2211	5428	...	...	29083	23090	2325	6578	...	...	31993
7 Transport, storage and communication	11959	4525	635	...	...	17119	12733	4839	656	...	...	18228
8 Finance, insurance, real estate and business services	16643	7462	23390	...	...	47495	19090	8198	24147	...	...	51435
9 Community, social and personal services [a]	6217	556	3857	...	...	10630	6871	565	4682	...	...	12118
Total, Industries	119612	31294	58320	...	...	209226	126828	33681	66312	...	...	226821
Producers of Government Services	35628	1973	-	...	...	37601	39095	2070	-	...	...	41165
Other Producers	3572	409	-	...	...	3981	3903	417	-	...	...	4320
Total [b]	158812	33676	58320	...	...	250808	169826	36168	66312	...	...	272306
Less: Imputed bank service charge	...	...	11728	...	...	11728	...	...	11636	...	...	11636
Import duties [c]	...	...	...	...	...	25490	...	...	...	...	...	25896
Value added tax	...	...	...	14319	...	14319	...	...	...	16034	...	16034
Other adjustments [d]	...	...	...	31355	5865	-3250	...	...	...	32247	6351	-2543
Total	158812	33676	46592	45674	5865	275631	169826	36168	54676	48281	6351	300057

1984 / 1985

	Compensation of Employees	Capital Consumption	Net Operating Surplus	Indirect Taxes	Less: Subsidies Received	Value Added	Compensation of Employees	Capital Consumption	Net Operating Surplus	Indirect Taxes	Less: Subsidies Received	Value Added
					All Producers							
1 Agriculture, hunting, forestry and fishing	1616	1258	3348	...	...	6222	1741	1285	2601	...	...	5627
2 Mining and quarrying	1916	2944	17384	...	...	22244	3341	3144	16412	...	...	22897
3 Manufacturing [a]	50135	8368	8642	...	...	67145	53434	8975	12373	...	...	74782
4 Electricity, gas and water	3953	2913	394	...	...	7260	4081	3083	1209	...	...	8373
5 Construction	9115	672	7277	...	...	17064	9468	705	8363	...	...	18536
6 Wholesale and retail trade, restaurants and hotels [a]	24905	2502	8439	...	...	35846	26615	2754	11152	...	...	40521
7 Transport, storage and communication	13674	5176	907	...	...	19757	14458	5502	1466	...	...	21426
8 Finance, insurance, real estate and business services	21598	9256	25458	...	...	56312	24268	10467	28449	...	...	63184
9 Community, social and personal services [a]	7809	630	5254	...	...	13693	8800	723	6187	...	...	15710
Total, Industries	134721	36288	74534	...	...	245543	146206	39504	85346	...	...	271056
Producers of Government Services	41312	2172	-	...	...	43484	43772	2353	-	...	...	46125

United Kingdom

4.3 Cost Components of Value Added
(Continued)

Million Pounds Sterling

	1984							1985						
	Compensation of Employees	Capital Consumption	Net Operating Surplus	Indirect Taxes	Less: Subsidies Received	Value Added	Compensation of Employees	Capital Consumption	Net Operating Surplus	Indirect Taxes	Less: Subsidies Received	Value Added
Other Producers	4319	432	-	...	...	4751	4781	458	-	...	...	5239
Total [b]	180352	38892	74534	...	...	293778	194759	42315	85346	...	...	322420
Less: Imputed bank service charge	...	...	13793	...	...	13793	...	...	15734	...	...	15734
Import duties [c]	...	...	...	...	...	25466	...	...	...	...	...	27162
Value added tax	...	...	...	18228	...	18228	...	...	...	20791	...	20791
Other adjustments [d]	...	...	...	33110	7644	-4549	...	...	...	34543	7381	-3927
Total	180352	38892	60741	51338	7644	319130	194759	42315	69612	55334	7381	350712

	1986						
	Compensation of Employees	Capital Consumption	Net Operating Surplus	Indirect Taxes	Less: Subsidies Received	Value Added
	All Producers					
1 Agriculture, hunting, forestry and fishing	1735	1334	2833	...	...	5902
2 Mining and quarrying	3384	3350	6081	...	...	12815
3 Manufacturing [a]	56092	9506	15730	...	...	81328
4 Electricity, gas and water	4216	3248	1949	...	...	9413
5 Construction	10088	734	9239	...	...	20061
6 Wholesale and retail trade, restaurants and hotels [a]	28568	3006	14196	...	...	45770
7 Transport, storage and communication	15350	5822	2555	...	...	23727
8 Finance, insurance, real estate and business services	27426	11782	31178	...	...	70386
9 Community, social and personal services [a]	9467	859	7580	...	...	17906
Total, Industries	156326	42978	88004	...	...	287308
Producers of Government Services	48035	2541	-	...	...	50576
Other Producers	5461	485	-	...	...	5946
Total [b]	209822	46004	88004	...	...	343830
Less: Imputed bank service charge	...	...	17404	...	...	17404
Import duties [c]	...	...	...	...	...	31516
Value added tax	...	...	...	22724	...	22724
Other adjustments [d]	...	...	...	38068	6552	-6960
Total	209822	46004	70600	60792	6552	373706

a) Repairs to consumer durables other than clothing are included in item 'Wholesale and retail trade, restaurants and hotels'.
b) Gross domestic product in factor values.
c) Item 'Import duties' refers to indirect taxes net of subsidies.
d) Item 'Other adjustments' refers to statistical discrepancy.

United Rep. of Tanzania

General note. The preparation of national accounts statistics in the United Republic of Tanzania is undertaken by the Bureau of Statistics, Ministry of Finance, Economic Affairs and Planning, Dar es Salaam. Official estimates are published in the annual reports entitled 'Economic Surveys'. Detailed description of the sources and methods used for the national accounts estimation is found in the report 'National Accounts of Tanzania, 1976 to 1984: Sources and Methods' published in 1985. The estimates follow closely the classifications and definitions recommended in the United Nations System of National Accounts (SNA). Input-output tables have been compiled for 1969, 1970 and 1976. The following tables have been prepared from successive replies to the United Nations national accounts questionnaire. The estimates presented relate to Tanzania (mainland) only, i.e., the former territory of Tanganyika and excluding Zanzibar. When the scope and coverage of the estimates differ for conceptual or statistical reasons from the definitions and classifications recommended in SNA, a footnote is indicated to the relevant tables.

Sources and methods:

(a) Gross domestic product. Gross domestic product is estimated mainly through the income approach.

(b) Expenditure on the gross domestic product. Government final consumption expenditure and exports and imports of goods and services are estimated through the expenditure approach, while private final consumption expenditure and gross capital formation are compiled by using a combination of the commodity-flow and expenditure approaches. For government expenditure, actual central government revenue and expenditure, classified by purpose, are available from government documents. Revenue and expenditure details of local authorities are obtained from the Prime Minister's Office and from the local authorities themselves. For private consumption expenditure, estimates of domestic production of all commodities are compiled and allowances made for various intermediate uses and government and business purposes. The estimates are then marked up for distribution costs and adjusted for imports and exports. Data from the 1976/77 Household Budget Survey are used with regard to most expenditures on services. The estimate of change in stocks only covers the parastatal enterprises, export crops, livestock and those factories which were included in the survey of manufacturing industries. Estimates of gross fixed capital formation for the public sector are derived from detailed analysis of the accounts of the agencies concerned and from detailed statistics on imports of capital equipment. Own account rural residential construction has been estimated on the basis of building costs data, rental values and data on population growth. Exports and imports of goods and services are obtained from the balance of payment statements of the Bank of Tanzania. GDP by expenditure at constant prices is not estimated.

(c) Cost-structure of the gross domestic product. In estimating the cost structure components of GDP, estimates of compensation of employees are obtained from each industry group separately. In addition, information obtained from Employment and Earnings survey is used for the non-primary and mining industries groups. For agriculture, animal husbandry, forestry and fishing, the wage component of value added is fixed at 4.3 per cent of its value added based on the results of various farm surveys. Operating surplus estimates for each industrial sector is obtained from the companies concerned. Estimates of depreciation for fixed assets of the parastatal enterprises are provided by the establishments themselves and for other sectors, estimates are based on percentages obtained from previous surveys. Data on indirect taxes and subsidies are obtained by analyzing government recurrent revenue and expenditure.

(d) Gross domestic product by kind of economic activity. The table of gross domestic product by kind of economic activity is prepared at factor costs. The value added of agriculture, mining and manufacturing is estimated through the production approach while for the remaining industries, the income approach is used. For agriculture, the data on production, prices and cost of production of each export crop, available with the respective commodity boards, are utilized to derive estimates of their value added. For the non-export crops, similar data available from the Ministry of Agriculture and Livestock Development, Marketing Development Bureau, Bureau of Statistics and data collected through Economic and Household Budget Surveys and the 1976 Input-Output Table have been used. The 1969 and 1976-77 Household Budget Surveys provided information on the quantities of crops harvested and the value and quantity of crops sold for a number of food crops. Based on some assumptions regarding conversion factors for differing physical units and the adjustment from retail to producer prices, approximate values of the crop harvested at producers' prices have been worked out in a number of cases. For livestock, forestry and fishing, data are obtained from the concerned departments or sections of the Ministry of Agriculture and from the household budget surveys. The production costs incurred by producers of livestocks are based on scattered data available, from farm studies and informal discussions. For some minor crops and by-products, a very rough mark-up is established to cover their production. Data on mining are available in the annual Economic Surveys, obtained directly from Mines Division, Dodoma. The data obtained from Employment and Earnings Survey, census reports and monthly surveys are utilized for manufacturing. Bench-mark estimates of value added of manufacturing establishments were obtained from the Census of Industrial Production 1978 while current estimates are prepared mainly on the basis of annual surveys of manufacturing industries. The Annual Accounts and Supporting Schedules of Tanzania's electric company gives full details of its activities. Total volume of construction activity is estimated from a variety of sources and the estimates of factor incomes are specially collected from a large sample of contractors and building firms. Data collected through the 1969 and 1976/77 Household Budget Survey were used to re-examine estimates made for rural own account construction. For trade, transport and service industries, the data provided by the Employment and Earnings Surveys and the data on income and expenditure, specially collected from a large sample of such enterprises, together with the estimated gross trade margins, number of trade licenses, vehicle licenses, etc. provide the basis for estimation. Rental value of houses in the urban and rural areas are compiled on the basis of information on rented houses collected through the 1967 Population Census and the 1969 Household Budget Survey. For government services, data are collected from the agencies concerned and detailed analysis of their revenue and expenditure are undertaken. Information on the activities of East African Community are obtained from the East African Statistical Department. For the constant price estimates, double deflation is used for the agricultural, mining and quarrying, and construction sectors with current year quantities revalued at base-year prices. For the manufacturing, electricity, trade and transport sectors, value added is extrapolated by various quantity indicators and indexes. For the financial and service sectors, value added is deflated by different indexes such as employment index.

1.1 Expenditure on the Gross Domestic Product, in Current Prices

Million Tanzanian shillings

	1970	1975	1977	1978	1979	1980	1981	1982	1983	1984	1985	1986
1 Government final consumption expenditure	1208	3259	4308	5585	5956	5494	6105	8046	9443	10779	11437	12447
2 Private final consumption expenditure	6396	14171	17979	23363	25497	32486	37035	42261	52974	69683	92601	133588
3 Gross capital formation	2067	4004	7524	8094	9458	9685	10130	12235	9588	11975	17820	25878
A Increase in stocks	189	464	861	764	866	1055	1498	1410	1836	1645	2091	2487
B Gross fixed capital formation	1878	3540	6663	7330	8592	8630	8632	10825	7752	10330	15729	23391
Residential buildings	253	408	475	546	622	709	1001	1043	949	1291	1740	1960
Non-residential buildings	229	359	846	749	943	1126	1446	1373	898	1219	1275	2213
Other construction and land improvement etc.	528	926	1923	1755	2001	2524	2230	2985	1687	2203	2591	2162
Other	868	1847	3419	4280	5026	4271	3955	5424	4218	5617	10123	17056
4 Exports of goods and services	2200	3462	5627	4692	5131	5540	5994	4546	5111	6321	7453	14580
5 Less: Imports of goods and services	2607	5885	6570	9565	9759	11087	10162	8862	8761	13543	17480	37026
Statistical discrepancy	-91	-	...	...	...	...	...	...	...	...	...	...
Equals: Gross Domestic Product	9173	19011	28868	32169	36283	42118	49102	58226	68355	85215	111831	149467

United Rep. of Tanzania

1.2 Expenditure on the Gross Domestic Product, in Constant Prices

Million Tanzanian shillings

	1970	1975	1977	1978	1979	1980	1981	1982	1983	1984	1985	1986
		1966			At constant prices of:			1976				
1 Government final consumption expenditure	...	...	...	...	...	...	...	...	...	...	...	...
2 Private final consumption expenditure	...	...	...	...	...	...	...	...	...	...	...	...
3 Gross capital formation	1821	1894	6454	6223	6825	6103	6368	6563	4632	5405	6432	7672
A Increase in stocks	165	256	734	513	425	488	562	511	590	442	511	589
B Gross fixed capital formation	1656	1638	5720	5710	6400	5615	5806	6052	4042	4963	5921	7083
Residential buildings	218	232	414	425	443	439	551	516	412	478	527	515
Non-residential buildings	183	188	688	550	675	700	799	683	394	467	364	557
Other construction and land improvement etc.	421	485	1563	1289	1431	1569	1232	1485	740	844	740	544
Other	834	733	3055	3446	3851	2907	3224	3369	2496	3174	4290	5467
4 Exports of goods and services	...	...	...	...	...	...	...	...	...	...	...	...
5 Less: Imports of goods and services	...	...	...	...	...	...	...	...	...	...	...	...
Equals: Gross Domestic Product a	7680	9553	21853	22142	22943	23888	23666	24104	23472	23930	24561	25486

a) Gross domestic product in factor values.

1.3 Cost Components of the Gross Domestic Product

Million Tanzanian shillings

	1970	1975	1977	1978	1979	1980	1981	1982	1983	1984	1985	1986
1 Indirect taxes, net	958	2023	3170	3587	3966	4664	5196	5680	7347	8951	12501	18121
A Indirect taxes	994	2447	3392	3915	4222	4963	5730	6594	8391	9691	13031	18608
B Less: Subsidies	36	424	222	328	256	299	534	914	1044	740	530	487
2 Consumption of fixed capital	512	907	1014	1139	1270	1540	1542	1568	1619	1791	2216	2748
3 Compensation of employees paid by resident producers to:	2852	6082	5328	6110	6858	7940	9047	10168	11306	12570	13967	15816
4 Operating surplus	4851	9999	19356	21333	24192	27974	33317	40810	48083	61903	83145	112782
Equals: Gross Domestic Product	9173	19011	28868	32169	36283	42118	49102	58226	68355	85215	111831	149467

1.7 External Transactions on Current Account, Summary

Million Tanzanian shillings

	1970	1975	1977	1978	1979	1980	1981	1982	1983	1984	1985	1986
				Payments to the Rest of the World								
1 Imports of goods and services	2607	5885	6570	9565	9759	11087	10162	8862	8761	13543	17480	37026
A Imports of merchandise c.i.f.	...	...	6161	8798	8986	10003	9120	8392	8192	12960	16470	34329
B Other	...	...	409	767	773	1084	1042	470	569	583	1010	2697
2 Factor income to the rest of the world	101	90	180	192	166	226	266	257	232	190	734	3697
3 Current transfers to the rest of the world	184	359	249	239	210	209	192	168	270	303	286	917
4 Surplus of the nation on current transactions	-340	-1787	-69	-3645	-3252	-4604	-2456	-3440	-2715	-5968	-7660	-10225
Payments to the Rest of the World and Surplus of the Nation on Current Transactions	2552	4547	6930	6351	6883	6918	8164	5847	6548	8068	10840	31415

United Rep. of Tanzania

1.7 External Transactions on Current Account, Summary
(Continued)

Million Tanzanian shillings

	1970	1975	1977	1978	1979	1980	1981	1982	1983	1984	1985	1986
			Receipts From The Rest of the World									
1 Exports of goods and services	2200	3462	5627	4692	5131	5540	5994	4546	5111	6321	7453	14580
A Exports of merchandise f.o.b.	...	...	4464	3671	3980	4187	4373	3484	4001	5125	5718	11391
B Other	...	...	1163	1021	1151	1353	1621	1062	1110	1196	1735	3189
2 Factor income from rest of the world	77	37	92	147	95	114	90	26	21	17	30	416
3 Current transfers from rest of the world	275	1048	1211	1512	1657	1264	2080	1275	1416	1730	3357	16419
Receipts from the Rest of the World on Current Transactions	2552	4547	6930	6351	6883	6918	8164	5847	6548	8068	10840	31415

1.10 Gross Domestic Product by Kind of Activity, in Current Prices

Million Tanzanian shillings

	1970	1975	1977	1978	1979	1980	1981	1982	1983	1984	1985	1986
1 Agriculture, hunting, forestry and fishing	3381	7007	11131	12506	14728	16636	20338	26449	32737	41295	56235	77395
2 Mining and quarrying	105	101	243	228	284	329	299	266	249	337	251	474
3 Manufacturing [a]	828	1774	3287	3859	3868	4097	4501	4361	4869	5869	6861	8164
4 Electricity, gas and water	84	146	254	261	275	424	423	421	514	551	1071	2060
5 Construction	404	735	1111	1052	1229	1498	1614	1863	1252	1661	1977	2241
6 Wholesale and retail trade, restaurants and hotels	1046	2172	3407	3889	4344	4713	5479	6814	8148	10476	13599	18141
7 Transport, storage and communication	713	1453	1793	1917	2113	3019	3133	3395	3507	4826	7061	8550
8 Finance, insurance, real estate and business services	844	1650	2419	2686	2978	3744	4507	4891	5252	6140	6790	8192
9 Community, social and personal services [b]	920	2204	2596	2873	3342	3959	4732	5446	5772	6620	7284	8277
Total, Industries	8325	17242	26241	29271	33161	38419	45026	53906	62300	77775	101129	133494
Producers of Government Services [b]	...	...	...	...	...	...	...	...	...	...	...	...
Other Producers [b]	...	...	...	...	...	...	...	...	...	...	...	...
Subtotal [c]	8325	17242	26241	29271	33161	38419	45026	53906	62300	77775	101129	133494
Less: Imputed bank service charge	110	254	543	689	844	966	1120	1360	1202	1511	1799	2148
Plus: Import duties	...	...	...	...	...	...	...	...	...	...	...	...
Plus: Value added tax	...	...	...	...	...	...	...	...	...	...	...	...
Plus: Other adjustments [d]	958	2023	3170	3587	3966	4664	5196	5680	7347	8951	12501	18121
Equals: Gross Domestic Product	9173	19011	28868	32169	36285	42118	49102	58226	68355	85215	111831	149467

a) Item 'Manufacturing' includes handicrafts.
b) Items 'Other producers' and 'Producers of government services' are included in item 'Community, social and personal services'.
c) Gross domestic product in factor values.
d) Item 'Other adjustments' refers to indirect taxes net of subsidies.

United Rep. of Tanzania

1.11 Gross Domestic Product by Kind of Activity, in Constant Prices

Million Tanzanian shillings

	1970	1975	1977	1978	1979	1980	1981	1982	1983	1984	1985	1986
		1966			At constant prices of:			1976				
1 Agriculture, hunting, forestry and fishing	3205	3596	9150	8998	9066	9418	9511	9639	9597	9463	9788	10045
2 Mining and quarrying	97	73	231	189	200	189	193	193	174	176	163	160
3 Manufacturing [a]	716	903	2641	2730	2821	2683	2382	2304	2103	2159	2075	1935
4 Electricity, gas and water	92	139	244	286	318	400	417	420	413	439	461	523
5 Construction	327	392	915	783	879	932	890	930	549	629	577	572
6 Wholesale and retail trade, restaurants and hotels	984	1074	2782	2797	2839	2839	2725	2668	2612	2640	2662	2669
7 Transport, storage and communication	729	997	1652	1699	1634	1818	1652	1694	1473	1703	1848	1887
8 Finance, insurance, real estate and business services	763	941	2089	2208	2338	2483	2529	2702	2817	2920	2993	3073
9 Community, social and personal services [b]	866	1581	2611	2937	3349	3657	3916	4221	4450	4555	4761	5394
Total, Industries	7779	9696	22315	22627	23444	24419	24215	24771	24188	24684	25328	26258
Producers of Government Services [b]	...	...	...	...	...	...	...	...	...	...	...	...
Other Producers [b]	...	...	...	...	...	...	...	...	...	...	...	...
Subtotal [c]	7779	9696	22315	22627	23444	24419	24215	24771	24188	24684	25328	26258
Less: Imputed bank service charge	99	143	462	485	501	531	549	667	716	754	767	772
Plus: Import duties	...	...	...	...	...	...	...	...	...	...	...	...
Plus: Value added tax	...	...	...	...	...	...	...	...	...	...	...	...
Equals: Gross Domestic Product [c]	7680	9553	21853	22142	22943	23888	23666	24104	23472	23930	24561	25486

a) Item 'Manufacturing' includes handicrafts.
b) Items 'Other producers' and 'Producers of government services' are included in item 'Community, social and personal services'.
c) Gross domestic product in factor values.

1.12 Relations Among National Accounting Aggregates

Million Tanzanian shillings

	1970	1975	1977	1978	1979	1980	1981	1982	1983	1984	1985	1986
Gross Domestic Product	9173	19011	28868	32169	36285	42118	49102	58226	68355	85215	111831	149467
Plus: Net factor income from the rest of the world	-24	-53	-88	-45	-71	-112	-176	-231	-211	-173	-704	-3281
Factor income from the rest of the world	77	37	92	147	95	114	90	26	21	17	30	416
Less: Factor income to the rest of the world	101	90	180	192	166	226	266	257	232	190	734	3697
Equals: Gross National Product	9149	18958	28780	32124	36214	42006	48926	57995	68144	85042	111127	146186
Less: Consumption of fixed capital	512	907	1014	1139	1270	1540	1542	1568	1619	1791	2216	2748

United Rep. of Tanzania

1.12 Relations Among National Accounting Aggregates
(Continued)

Million Tanzanian shillings

	1970	1975	1977	1978	1979	1980	1981	1982	1983	1984	1985	1986
Equals: National Income	8637	18051	27766	30985	34944	40466	47384	56427	66525	83251	108911	143438
Plus: Net current transfers from the rest of the world	91	689	962	1273	1447	1055	1888	1107	1146	1427	3071	15502
Current transfers from the rest of the world	275	1048	1211	1512	1657	1264	2080	1275	1416	1730	3357	16419
Less: Current transfers to the rest of the world	184	359	249	239	210	209	192	168	270	303	286	917
Equals: National Disposable Income	8728	18740	28728	32258	36391	41521	49272	57534	67671	84678	111982	158940
Less: Final consumption	7604	17430	22287	28948	31453	37980	43140	50307	62417	80462	104038	146035
Statistical discrepancy	91	-	...	-	-	...	...	...	...	...	...	...
Equals: Net Saving	1215	1310	6441	3310	4936	3541	6132	7227	5254	4216	7944	12905
Less: Surplus of the nation on current transactions	-340	-1787	-69	-3645	-3252	-4604	-2456	-3440	-2715	-5968	-7660	-10225
Equals: Net Capital Formation	1555	3097	6510	6955	8188	8145	8588	10667	7969	10184	15604	23130

2.1 Government Final Consumption Expenditure by Function, in Current Prices

Million Tanzanian shillings   Fiscal year beginning 1 July

	1970	1975	1977	1978	1979	1980	1981	1982	1983	1984	1985	1986
1 General public services	296	648	937	1176	1592	1584	1712	2380	2257	3366	6558	7124
2 Defence	127	729	910	1349	3194	1110	1862	2308	2557	2744	3659	3176
3 Public order and safety	151	345	353	420	488	558	719	927	1040	1362	1326	1720
4 Education	289	757	1007	1324	1472	1653	1782	2298	2543	2503	1919	2245
5 Health	118	426	523	669	688	739	813	992	983	1171	1312	1313
6 Social security and welfare	9	21	18	24	37	52	44	51	61	62	125	66
7 Housing and community amenities	44	101	86	89	108	147	187	189	209	212	258	180
8 Recreational, cultural and religious affairs	56	130	169	174	240	277	322	381	385	440	589	138
9 Economic services	742	2630	2819	3404	4566	5222	5354	5495	5213	5573	6367	6988
A Fuel and energy [a]	102	603	401	460	773	647	545	677	647	712	987	1160
B Agriculture, forestry, fishing and hunting	218	945	859	882	934	1328	1272	1282	1233	1580	1639	2358
C Mining, manufacturing and construction, except fuel and energy	43	253	547	827	871	1406	1340	1555	1399	1492	1452	1293
D Transportation and communication	379	294	487	705	984	1109	1379	1482	1439	1295	1672	1742
E Other economic affairs		535	525	530	1004	732	819	500	494	494	623	435
10 Other functions	305	399	583	810	1378	1195	1802	3406	4042	4029	4232	7664
Total Government Final Consumption Expenditure [b]	2137	6186	7405	9439	13703	12537	14597	10427	19200	21461	26045	30614

a) Item 'Fuel and energy' includes water supply.
b) Only central government data are included in the general government estimates.

2.5 Private Final Consumption Expenditure by Type and Porpose, in Current Prices

Million Tanzanian shillings

	1970	1975	1977	1978	1979	1980	1981	1982	1983	1984	1985	1986
Final Consumption Expenditure of Resident Households
1 Food, beverages and tobacco	3575	9237	...	...	...	...	...	...	...	...	...	...
A Food	3266	8201	...	...	...	...	...	...	...	...	...	...
B Non-alcoholic beverages	24	43	...	...	...	...	...	...	...	...	...	...
C Alcoholic beverages	224	628	...	...	...	...	...	...	...	...	...	...
D Tobacco	61	365	...	...	...	...	...	...	...	...	...	...

United Rep. of Tanzania

2.5 Private Final Consumption Expenditure by Type and Porpose, in Current Prices
(Continued)

Million Tanzanian shillings

	1970	1975	1977	1978	1979	1980	1981	1982	1983	1984	1985	1986
2 Clothing and footwear	442	805	...	...	...	...	...	...	...	...	...	...
3 Gross rent, fuel and power	1019	1746	...	...	...	...	...	...	...	...	...	...
4 Furniture, furnishings and household equipment and operation	449	874	...	...	...	...	...	...	...	...	...	...
5 Medical care and health expenses	133	321	...	...	...	...	...	...	...	...	...	...
6 Transport and communication	392	577	...	...	...	...	...	...	...	...	...	...
7 Recreational, entertainment, education and cultural services	130	231	...	...	...	...	...	...	...	...	...	...
8 Miscellaneous goods and services	233	313	...	...	...	...	...	...	...	...	...	...
Total Final Consumption Expenditure in the Domestic Market by Households, of which	6373	14104	...	...	...	...	...	...	...	...	...	...
Plus: Direct purchases abroad by resident households	120	...	...	...	...	...	...	...	...	...	...	...
Less: Direct purchases in the domestic market by non-resident households	97	...	...	...	...	...	...	...	...	...	...	...
Equals: Final Consumption Expenditure of Resident Households [a]	6396	14171	...	...	...	...	...	...	...	...	...	...
Final Consumption Expenditure of Private Non-profit Institutions Serving Households												
Equals: Final Consumption Expenditure of Private Non-profit Organisations Serving Households	...	...	...	...	...	...	...	...	...	...	...	...
Private Final Consumption Expenditure	6396	14171	...	...	...	...	...	...	...	...	...	...

a) Item 'Final consumption expenditure of resident households' includes consumption expenditure of private non-profit institutions serving households.

2.11 Gross Fixed Capital Formation by Kind of Activity of Owner, ISIC Divisions, in Current Prices

Million Tanzanian shillings

	1970	1975	1977	1978	1979	1980	1981	1982	1983	1984	1985	1986
			All Producers									
1 Agriculture, hunting, forestry and fishing	117	234	448	676	686	698	677	846	972	1176	1608	2120
2 Mining and quarrying	31	48	24	16	8	46	41	41	104	72	105	155
3 Manufacturing	319	636	2232	1672	1865	1955	2561	3022	1724	1731	3072	5228
4 Electricity, gas and water	119	498	371	493	534	779	652	403	776	1197	1782	2587
5 Construction	77	82	222	326	420	500	730	1051	645	1136	1693	2458
6 Wholesale and retail trade, restaurants and hotels	54	72	437	410	200	151	105	504	131	287	426	622
7 Transport, storage and communication	756	1184	1726	2258	2524	1913	2077	2162	1887	2994	4456	6469
8 Finance, insurance, real estate and business services	322	642	438	485	562	687	771	884	305	300	446	647
9 Community, social and personal services [ab]	83	144	765	994	1793	1901	2018	1912	1208	1437	2138	3105
Total Industries	1878	3540	6663	7330	8592	8630	9632	10825	7752	10330	15729	23391
Producers of Government Services [a]	...	...	...	...	...	...	...	...	...	...	...	...
Private Non-Profit Institutions Serving Households [b]	...	...	...	...	...	...	...	...	...	...	...	...
Total	1878	3540	6663	7330	8592	8630	9632	10825	7752	10330	15729	23391

a) Item 'Producers of government services' is included in item 'Community, social and personal services'. b) Item 'Private non-profit institutions serving households' is included in item 'Community, social and personal services'.

United States

General note. The Bureau of Economic Analysis, is responsible for the preparation of national income accounts statistics in the United States. The official estimates are published in the 'Survey of Current Business, (Survey)'. A selected set of tables appears monthly and the full set appears in the July issue. The capital finance accounts and balance sheets are published by the Board of Governors of the Federal Reserve System. The official estimates are not totally consistent with the classifications and definitions used in the United Nations System of National Accounts (SNA). A summary explanation of the accounting framework appears in 'Introduction to National Economic Accounting' in the March 1985 'Survey'. Information on the sources and methods used to estimate the national accounts appears in 'GNP: An Overview of Source Data and Estimating Methods,' in the July 1987 'Survey'. Information on U.S. capital finance accounts and balance sheets is found in 'Introduction to the Flow of Funds', 1980, a publication of the Federal Reserve System. The most recent benchmark input-output accounts were published in 1984 in 'The Detailed Input-Output Structure of the U.S. Economy, 1977, Volumes 1 and 2'. Annual update tables also are prepared; see the january 1987 'Survey' for the 1981 accounts. The following tables have been prepared from successive national accounts questionnaires provided to the United Nations. The United States converts its official estimates as closely as possible to SNA definitions. When differences in scope and coverage from the SNA recommendations remain, footnotes are attached to the appropriate tables.

Sources and methods:

(a) Gross domestic product. Both the expenditure and income approach are used.

(b) Expenditure on the gross domestic product. The estimates of central government final consumption expenditures are based largely on budget statistics. The State and local government estimates are based largely on Census Bureau annual surveys of these governments. For private final consumption expenditures, benchmark estimates are taken from the detailed input-output tables, prepared every 5 years to coincide with comprehensive economic censuses. In addition major statistical sources include the Census Bureau merchandise trade series and the Decennial Census of Housing. Estimates for nonbenchmark years are extrapolations and interpolations of the benchmark data using Census Bureau surveys of retail store sales, service receipts, rental payments, and other public and private data sources. Annual estimates of gross fixed capital formation are largely based on surveys conducted by the Census Bureau and other government agencies, and private data for oil well drilling. Reports of government agencies are used for construction by the Federal government, federally-aided projects and public utility construction. Benchmark estimates of producers' durable equipment are largely based on Census of Manufactures shipments and merchandise trade using the commodity-flow method. Estimates for nonbenchmark years are extrapolations and interpolations of the benchmark data using Census Bureau annual and monthly survey data, merchandise trade statistics and an abbreviated commodity-flow method. Estimates of exports and imports of merchandise are based on customs documents tabulated by the Census Bureau. Service transactions are taken from the U.S. balance of payments accounts based on Bureau of Economic Analysis surveys and other government sources. Constant-dollar government final consumption expenditures are calculated in two parts. Employee compensation is obtained by extrapolating base-year figures with full-time equivalent employment measures, with detail by level of pay or experience. Purchases from business are obtained by deflation. The price indexes used are BEA indexes for national defense purchases, CPI, PPI, indexes of prices paid by farmers and a variety of others. Deflation is used for gross fixed capital formation, exports and imports of goods and services, and private final consumption expenditures, primarily using CPI and PPI, and other indexes.

(c) Cost-structure of the gross domestic product. The annual estimates of wages and salaries are taken mainly from administrative records of government agencies. The operating surplus is estimated in four separate parts: income of unincorporated enterprises, rental income of person, corporate profits, and net interest. Tabulations of tax returns are the primary source for nonfarm income, proprietors' income, corporate profits and net interest. Farm income is based on data compiled by the Department of Agriculture. Rental income of persons is based primarily on the decennial Census and a biennial survey of housing. Imputed rental receipts of owner-occupants of nonfarm dwellings are estimated using the rental-equivalency method. Rental receipts for both tenant-occupied and owner-occupied housing are adjusted to exclude expenses. Capital consumption allowances consist of depreciation, primarily based on tabulations of tax returns, and accidental damage to fixed capital, estimated by BEA. The estimates of depreciation that are based on capital consumption allowances with capital consumption adjustment are derived from perpetual inventory calculations from BEA's capital stock estimates. Indirect taxes include for the Federal government excise taxes and customs duties and for State and local government sales taxes and property taxes. Subsidies paid by the Federal government include payments to farmers and housing subsidies. Both components are estimated using the same sources as used for government final consumption.

(d) Gross domestic product by kind of economic activity. The table of GDP by kind of economic activity is prepared at market prices. The income approach is used to estimate value added of the various kinds of economic activities. The source data for the income components are described in (c) above. In many cases, the distribution by economic activity is provided by these source data. For six income components, it is based on the economic activity of the company. For corporate profits and corporate capital consumption allowances the distributions are converted by BEA to an establishment basis using Census Bureau and Department of Energy data. For nonfarm proprietors' income, noncorporate net interest, and noncorporate capital consumption allowances, they are assumed to be equivalent to an establishment distribution. For the other component, corporate net interest, no data are available for conversion to an establishment basis and the company basis is used. For income components where the source data provide no economic activity distributions, BEA estimates establishment distributions using various data and estimating methods. In the preparation of constant-dollar estimates, double deflation is used for farms; construction; manufacturing (except petroleum and coal products); railroad transportation; and electric, gas and sanitary services. Extrapolation of base year product by an indicator series is used for agricultural services, forestry, and fisheries; mining; manufacturing of petroleum and coal products; local and interurban transit; water and air transportation; pipelines (except natural gas); retail trade; finance, insurance and real estate; hotels and lodging places; private households; government and the following service sectors: transportation, business, personal, repairs, health, legal and education. Direct deflation is used for trucking and warehousing; communication; auto repair, services, and garages; motion pictures; amusement and recreation services; social services and membership organizations; and miscellaneous professional services. Data sources for double deflation includes Census Bureau shipments and cost of materials data; Department of Agriculture receipts, expenses, and prices; BEA input-output composition of intermediate consumption and Bureau of Labor Statistics price data. Data sources for extrapolation include Federal Reserve Board Index of Industrial Production; BEA estimates of persons engaged in production and hours worked; Department of Energy production; and BEA constant-dollar consumption measures. Bureau of Labor Statistics prices and average earnings are used for direct deflation.

1.1 Expenditure on the Gross Domestic Product, in Current Prices

Million United States dollars

		1970	1975	1977	1978	1979	1980	1981	1982	1983	1984	1985	1986
1	Government final consumption expenditure	189586	294219	345469	377292	418924	473722	525613	574090	617003	670110	728307	778586
2	Private final consumption expenditure	635842	1005820	1250010	1392720	1554720	1721220	1909680	2046300	2223660	2422200	2611730	2778410
3	Gross capital formation	179863	268163	395340	475075	515731	508253	591713	525237	568601	736220	738519	767658
	A Increase in stocks	1369	-4181	25240	30042	13102	-6014	32390	-12341	-9007	66204	22928	20858
	B Gross fixed capital formation	178494	272344	370100	445033	502629	514267	559323	537578	577608	670016	715591	746800
	Residential buildings	40488	61229	107266	127988	137567	121618	121311	104030	150990	179228	186748	216246
	Non-residential buildings	33794	45534	46251	56768	69566	77645	85326	88152	84531	99652	116223	114449
	Other construction and land improvement etc.	31514	50245	58112	69164	78657	91005	105826	104800	88919	94332	96596	90593
	Other	72698	115336	158471	191113	216839	223999	246860	240596	253168	296804	316024	325512
4	Exports of goods and services	59104	136346	155724	182013	223575	273347	292988	270904	264005	283250	281000	290182
5	Less: Imports of goods and services	55177	120625	179049	208188	248147	288074	310521	295137	319797	389441	399949	429341
	Equals: Gross Domestic Product	1009220	1583920	1967490	2218910	2464810	2688470	3009470	3121400	3353470	3722340	3959610	4185490

1.2 Expenditure on the Gross Domestic Product, in Constant Prices

Million United States dollars

		1970	1975	1977	1978	1979	1980	1981	1982	1983	1984	1985	1986
		\multicolumn{12}{c}{At constant prices of: 1980}
1	Government final consumption expenditure	432237	436443	448925	459057	467765	473722	478863	490247	507583	530591	558219	578922
2	Private final consumption expenditure	1271920	1472470	1622750	1688980	1725730	1721220	1747910	1766650	1855740	1945400	2034500	2120790
3	Gross capital formation	404932	405478	523997	573053	563914	508252	545308	460586	500322	645655	648220	666400
	A Increase in stocks	1268	-8263	31356	33840	11831	-6014	31744	-8271	-9716	54611	17220	17335
	B Gross fixed capital formation	403664	413741	492641	539213	552083	514266	513564	468857	510038	591044	631000	649065

United States

1.2 Expenditure on the Gross Domestic Product, in Constant Prices
(Continued)

Million United States dollars

	1970	1975	1977	1978	1979	1980	1981	1982	1983	1984	1985	1986
					At constant prices of:1980							
Residential buildings	99206	101769	149511	158494	151611	121618	112286	93118	132604	151490	154338	173854
Non-residential buildings	78414	68464	62337	69875	76827	77645	78120	76460	70649	79608	89836	85943
Other construction and land improvement etc.	84083	79615	83101	88269	88102	91005	95610	89709	81954	88247	87108	81202
Other	141961	163893	197691	222575	235544	223998	227548	209569	224831	271699	299718	308065
4 Exports of goods and services	134298	196195	206916	226912	246688	273347	272298	249641	243619	259544	265778	282210
5 Less: Imports of goods and services	191577	218856	292616	309750	313686	288074	295044	288541	323621	398202	420434	468243
Equals: Gross Domestic Product	2051810	2291730	2509970	2638250	2690410	2688470	2749340	2678580	2783640	2982980	3086280	3180070

1.3 Cost Components of the Gross Domestic Product

Million United States dollars

	1970	1975	1977	1978	1979	1980	1981	1982	1983	1984	1985	1986
1 Indirect taxes, net	89075	134910	157966	168539	179810	202558	239294	243352	260385	291184	310239	321413
A Indirect taxes	94026	139996	165661	178066	189352	213281	251476	258835	282560	313914	333151	347720
B Less: Subsidies	4951	5086	7695	9527	9542	10723	12182	15483	22175	22730	22912	26307
2 Consumption of fixed capital	105843	192851	236409	269346	311362	355816	403461	440644	455627	476888	503459	525193
3 Compensation of employees paid by resident producers to:	619072	952085	1181130	1334580	1497630	1646340	1817190	1918000	2032310	2224420	2382910	2517350
A Resident households	618875	951714	1180690	1334100	1497160	1645810	1816640	1917380	2031690	2223840	2382270	2516750
B Rest of the world	197	371	442	478	473	536	544	618	614	580	633	602
4 Operating surplus	196361	301570	392007	448356	476964	478832	545407	519455	599985	724487	768651	826443
A Corporate and quasi-corporate enterprises	87469	141733	203471	232504	246621	243149	273785	242589	301886	360190	369764	373163
B Private unincorporated enterprises	108892	159837	188536	215852	230343	235683	271622	276866	298099	364297	398887	453280
C General government	...	...	...	...	...	...	...	...	...	...	...	...
Statistical discrepancy	-1133	2502	-27	-1908	-965	4920	4124	-56	5170	5359	-5644	-4914
Equals: Gross Domestic Product	1009220	1583920	1967490	2218910	2464810	2688470	3009470	3121400	3353470	3722340	3959610	4185490

1.4 General Government Current Receipts and Disbursements

Million United States dollars

	1970	1975	1977	1978	1979	1980	1981	1982	1983	1984	1985	1986
					Receipts							
1 Operating surplus	...	...	...	...	...	...	...	...	...	...	...	...
2 Property and entrepreneurial income	5368	10900	12603	16705	23806	30344	38231	43721	46553	53180	59379	64101
3 Taxes, fees and contributions	279717	430963	553654	627297	704537	769959	881303	893825	948250	1054460	1142590	1206640
A Indirect taxes	94026	139996	165661	178066	189352	213281	251476	258835	282560	313914	333151	347720
B Direct taxes	137414	198624	270890	313446	357266	384793	427409	418758	431457	473774	517277	546340
C Social security contributions	46745	89637	113465	131716	153311	166617	196129	209139	226259	257654	281648	300394
D Compulsory fees, fines and penalties	1532	2706	3638	4069	4608	5268	6289	7093	7974	9120	10514	12187
4 Other current transfers	6658	14216	17821	19952	22446	26422	30134	32947	34863	34698	37709	38682
Total Current Receipts of General Government	291743	456079	584078	663954	750789	826725	949668	970493	1029670	1142340	1239680	1309420
					Disbursements							
1 Government final consumption expenditure	189586	294219	345469	377292	418924	473722	525613	574090	617003	670111	728307	778586
A Compensation of employees	120050	190050	223698	244345	264870	294059	323789	351777	374733	397767	427419	452809
B Consumption of fixed capital	13611	24335	27018	30439	35102	39919	42470	43597	44589	46215	49614	51442
C Purchases of goods and services, net	56797	80908	95716	103612	120187	141140	160653	179925	198893	227436	252796	275920
D Less: Own account fixed capital formation	872	1074	963	1104	1235	1396	1299	1209	1212	1307	1522	1585
E Indirect taxes paid, net	...	...	...	...	...	...	...	...	...	...	...	...
2 Property income	22686	38345	48731	57526	69522	84750	110997	130684	147964	176821	198524	210435
A Interest	22686	38345	48731	57526	69522	84750	110997	130684	147964	176821	198524	210435
B Net land rent and royalties	...	...	...	...	...	...	...	...	...	...	...	...

United States

1.4 General Government Current Receipts and Disbursements
(Continued)

Million United States dollars

		1970	1975	1977	1978	1979	1980	1981	1982	1983	1984	1985	1986
3	Subsidies	4951	5086	7695	9527	9542	10723	12182	15483	22175	22730	22912	26307
4	Other current transfers	81943	181330	208400	224397	251702	300631	340667	379862	408663	418561	448739	474412
	A Social security benefits	46470	105876	125616	133784	150502	180285	208948	242014	261039	265268	283754	300989
	B Social assistance grants	25098	57060	62876	68353	75403	89310	97367	99653	106850	111299	117008	124010
	C Other	10375	18394	19908	22260	25797	31036	34352	38195	40774	41994	47977	49413
5	Net saving	-7423	-62901	-26217	-4788	1099	-43101	-39791	-129626	-166139	-145883	-158804	-180316
	Total Current Disbursements and Net Saving of General Government	291743	456079	584078	663954	750789	826725	949668	970493	1029670	1142340	1239680	1309420

1.5 Current Income and Outlay of Corporate and Quasi-Corporate Enterprises, Summary

Million United States dollars

		1970	1975	1977	1978	1979	1980	1981	1982	1983	1984	1985	1986
						Receipts							
1	Operating surplus	87469	141733	203471	232504	246621	243149	273785	242589	301886	360190	369764	373163
2	Property and entrepreneurial income received	104532	206133	256026	309784	401589	501347	650062	715410	706394	798799	841818	866378
3	Current transfers	1416	2995	3670	4022	4671	5340	6117	6690	7118	7425	8198	8392
	Total Current Receipts	193417	350861	463167	546310	652881	749836	929964	964689	1015400	1166410	1219780	1247930
						Disbursements							
1	Property and entrepreneurial income	137841	258601	321199	386380	495238	620425	798236	871305	860024	958749	997257	1022790
2	Direct taxes and other current payments to general government	34356	50906	73044	83506	87996	84785	81143	63081	77241	93899	96712	105045
3	Other current transfers	3957	7757	9424	10313	11628	13649	14678	16765	18616	20776	23980	24680
4	Net saving	17263	33507	59500	66111	58019	30977	35907	13538	59517	92990	101831	95421
	Total Current Disbursements and Net Saving	193417	350861	463167	546310	652881	749836	929964	964689	1015400	1166410	1219780	1247930

1.6 Current Income and Outlay of Households and Non-Profit Institutions

Million United States dollars

		1970	1975	1977	1978	1979	1980	1981	1982	1983	1984	1985	1986
						Receipts							
1	Compensation of employees	619097	952048	1181080	1334490	1497580	1646250	1817140	1917900	2032250	2224440	2382900	2517440
	A From resident producers	618875	951714	1180690	1334100	1497160	1645810	1816640	1917380	2031690	2223840	2382270	2516750
	B From rest of the world	222	334	388	388	419	449	497	520	560	600	632	692
2	Operating surplus of private unincorporated enterprises	80171	125373	152915	176206	191871	180673	186772	175535	190882	234502	257251	289818
3	Property and entrepreneurial income	102238	151840	187372	215709	254103	310957	393037	432713	456218	513523	537412	567186
4	Current transfers	81220	183643	214379	230966	259007	308513	349572	389561	420011	429716	460633	486511
	A Social security benefits	46470	105876	125616	133784	150502	180285	208948	242014	261039	265268	283754	300989
	B Social assistance grants	25098	57060	62876	68353	75403	89310	97367	99653	106850	111299	117008	124010
	C Other	9652	20707	25887	28829	33102	38918	43257	47894	52122	53149	59871	61512
	Total Current Receipts	882726	1412900	1735750	1957370	2202560	2446400	2746520	2915710	3099360	3402180	3638200	3860960
						Disbursements							
1	Private final consumption expenditure	635812	1005820	1250010	1392720	1554720	1721220	1909680	2046300	2223660	2422200	2611730	2778410
2	Property income	16686	24428	30514	36687	43533	47376	51970	55548	61858	72508	82734	89933
3	Direct taxes and other current transfers n.e.c. to general government	151335	240061	314949	365725	427189	471893	548684	571909	588449	646649	712727	753876
	A Social security contributions	46745	89637	113465	131716	153311	166617	196129	209139	226259	257654	281648	300394
	B Direct taxes	103058	147718	197846	229940	269270	300008	346266	355677	354216	379875	420565	441295
	C Fees, fines and penalties	1532	2706	3638	4069	4608	5268	6289	7093	7974	9120	10514	12187
4	Other current transfers	9611	18890	23313	26062	29454	34439	38698	42169	44445	44907	49240	50323
5	Net saving	69252	123710	116965	136176	147663	171470	197489	199784	180950	215917	181766	188421
	Total Current Disbursements and Net Saving	882726	1412900	1735750	1957370	2202560	2446400	2746520	2915710	3099360	3402180	3638200	3860960

United States

1.7 External Transactions on Current Account, Summary

Million United States dollars

	1970	1975	1977	1978	1979	1980	1981	1982	1983	1984	1985	1986
Payments to the Rest of the World												
1 Imports of goods and services	55177	120625	179049	208188	248147	288074	310521	295137	319797	389441	399949	429341
A Imports of merchandise c.i.f. [a]	40855	99000	151851	176477	211930	247460	266462	249474	271341	334250	341016	367507
B Other	14322	21625	27198	31711	36217	40614	44059	45663	48456	55191	58933	61834
2 Factor income to the rest of the world	6316	14204	16218	23871	35425	43368	55259	58748	56682	72772	70529	74941
A Compensation of employees	197	371	442	478	473	536	544	618	614	580	633	602
B Property and entrepreneurial income	6119	13833	15776	23393	34952	42832	54715	58130	56068	72192	69896	74339
By general government	1024	4542	5542	8674	11122	12592	16878	18285	17825	19769	21306	22607
By corporate and quasi-corporate enterprises	5095	9291	10234	14719	23830	30240	37837	39845	38243	52423	48590	51732
By other	...	...	...	...	...	...	...	...	...	...	...	...
3 Current transfers to the rest of the world	6599	7858	6227	7044	8050	10023	9701	11103	11221	13747	16876	17548
A Indirect taxes to supranational organizations	...	...	...	...	...	...	...	...	...	...	...	...
B Other current transfers	6599	7858	6227	7044	8050	10023	9701	11103	11221	13747	16876	17548
4 Surplus of the nation on current transactions	3939	21596	-8710	-10138	1448	11830	9478	-953	-33485	-90948	-115911	-143853
Payments to the Rest of the World and Surplus of the Nation on Current Transactions	72031	164283	192784	228965	293070	353295	384959	364035	354215	385012	371443	377977
Receipts From The Rest of the World												
1 Exports of goods and services	59104	136346	155724	182013	223575	273347	292988	270904	264005	283250	281000	290182
A Exports of merchandise f.o.b. [a]	44280	109359	122820	144454	182986	224672	237894	213572	205637	223699	220205	224328
B Other	14824	26987	32904	37559	40589	48675	55094	57332	58368	59551	60795	65854
2 Factor income from rest of the world	12545	27202	36100	45740	68104	78368	90489	91626	88721	100420	88986	86077
A Compensation of employees	222	334	388	388	419	449	497	520	560	600	632	692
B Property and entrepreneurial income	12323	26868	35712	45352	67685	77919	89992	91106	88161	99820	88354	85385
By general government	907	1112	1625	1843	2295	2562	3680	4118	4832	5229	5503	6321
By corporate and quasi-corporate enterprises	11416	25756	34087	43509	65390	75357	86312	86988	83329	94591	82851	79064
By other	...	...	...	...	...	...	...	...	...	...	...	...
3 Current transfers from rest of the world	382	735	960	1212	1391	1580	1482	1505	1489	1342	1457	1718
A Subsidies from supranational organisations	...	...	...	...	...	...	...	...	...	...	...	...
B Other current transfers	382	735	960	1212	1391	1580	1482	1505	1489	1342	1457	1718
Receipts from the Rest of the World on Current Transactions	72031	164283	192784	228965	293070	353295	384959	364035	354215	385012	371443	377977

a) Valuation basis is essentially Free Along Side (F.A.S.).

1.8 Capital Transactions of The Nation, Summary

Million United States dollars

	1970	1975	1977	1978	1979	1980	1981	1982	1983	1984	1985	1986
Finance of Gross Capital Formation												
Gross saving	184935	287257	386657	466845	518143	515162	597066	524340	529955	639913	628252	628719
1 Consumption of fixed capital	105843	192851	236409	269346	311362	355816	403461	440644	455627	476888	503459	525193
A General government	13611	24335	27018	30439	35102	39919	42470	43597	44589	46215	49614	51442
B Corporate and quasi-corporate enterprises	55361	103091	128329	146174	168827	193465	223865	248861	257154	269726	285380	299925
Public	3411	6711	7879	9007	10510	12049	13150	13884	14436	15212	16240	17089
Private	51950	96380	120450	137167	158317	181416	210715	234977	242718	254514	269140	282836
C Other	36871	65425	81062	92733	107433	122432	137126	148186	153884	160947	168465	173826
2 Net saving	79092	94406	150248	197499	206781	159346	193605	83696	74328	163025	124793	103526
A General government	-7423	-62901	-26217	-4788	1099	-43101	-39791	-129626	-166139	-145882	-158804	-180316
B Corporate and quasi-corporate enterprises	17263	33597	59500	66111	58019	30977	35907	13538	59517	92990	101831	95421
Public	-444	-2803	-1943	-1320	-2640	-5256	-5377	-4243	-3415	1282	2262	1904
Private	17707	36400	61443	67431	60659	36233	41284	17781	62932	91708	99569	93517

United States

1.8 Capital Transactions of The Nation, Summary
(Continued)

Million United States dollars

	1970	1975	1977	1978	1979	1980	1981	1982	1983	1984	1985	1986
C Other	69252	123710	116965	136176	147663	171470	197489	199784	180950	215917	181766	188421
Less: Surplus of the nation on current transactions	3939	21596	-8710	-10138	1447	11829	9477	-953	-33485	-90948	-115911	-143853
Statistical discrepancy	-1133	2502	-27	-1908	-965	4920	4124	-56	5161	5359	-5644	-4914
Finance of Gross Capital Formation	179863	268163	395340	475075	515731	508253	591713	525237	568601	736220	738519	767658

Gross Capital Formation

	1970	1975	1977	1978	1979	1980	1981	1982	1983	1984	1985	1986
Increase in stocks	1369	-4181	25240	30042	13102	-6014	32390	-12341	-9007	66204	22928	20858
Gross fixed capital formation	178494	272344	370100	445033	502629	514267	559323	537578	577608	670016	715591	746800
1 General government	25077	33500	32262	37398	41087	47261	45749	46935	49367	51240	60239	64345
2 Corporate and quasi-corporate enterprises	88304	142896	185349	226503	256999	274429	310358	303373	305946	360465	391586	390516
A Public	7740	13661	15057	19431	19668	21708	22071	18830	18874	21633	23751	27226
B Private	80564	129235	170292	207072	237331	252721	288287	284543	287072	338832	367835	363290
3 Other	65113	95948	152489	181132	204543	192577	203216	187270	222295	258311	263766	291939
Gross Capital Formation	179863	268163	395340	475075	515731	508253	591713	525237	568601	736220	738519	767658

1.9 Gross Domestic Product by Institutional Sectors of Origin

Million United States dollars

	1970	1975	1977	1978	1979	1980	1981	1982	1983	1984	1985	1986

Domestic Factor Incomes Originating

	1970	1975	1977	1978	1979	1980	1981	1982	1983	1984	1985	1986
1 General government	120050	190050	223698	244345	264870	294059	323789	351777	374733	397767	427419	452809
2 Corporate and quasi-corporate enterprises	662975	1011580	1287010	1468360	1631100	1741830	1937830	1972940	2134690	2418410	2581980	2738800
3 Households and private unincorporated enterprises	4501	4634	5931	6247	6462	6586	7043	7596	8160	8928	9032	9349
A Owner-occupied housing	...	...	...	...	...	...	...	...	...	...	...	...
B Subsistence production	...	...	...	...	...	...	...	...	...	...	...	...
C Other	4501	4634	5931	6247	6462	6586	7043	7596	8160	8928	9032	9349
4 Non-profit institutions serving households	27907	47393	56503	63981	72167	82700	93930	105147	114710	123804	133127	142836
Subtotal: Domestic Factor Incomes	815433	1253660	1573140	1782930	1974600	2125170	2362600	2437460	2632290	2948910	3151560	3343800
Indirect taxes, net	89075	134910	157966	168539	179810	202558	239294	243352	260385	291184	310239	321413
A Indirect taxes	94026	139996	165661	178066	189352	213281	251476	258835	282560	313914	333151	347720
B Less: Subsidies	4951	5086	7695	9527	9542	10723	12182	15483	22175	22730	22912	26307
Consumption of fixed capital	105843	192851	236409	269346	311362	355816	403461	440644	455627	476888	503459	525193
Statistical discrepancy	-1133	2502	-27	-1908	-965	4920	4124	-56	5170	5359	-5644	-4914
Gross Domestic Product	1009220	1583920	1967490	2218910	2464810	2688470	3009470	3121400	3353470	3722340	3959610	4185490

1.10 Gross Domestic Product by Kind of Activity, in Current Prices

Million United States dollars

	1970	1975	1977	1978	1979	1980	1981	1982	1983	1984	1985	1986
1 Agriculture, hunting, forestry and fishing	27856	53037	54287	65114	77193	70320	83722	81370	66394	85305	84045	87069
2 Mining and quarrying	18791	41524	50469	56816	73139	107854	144398	132893	119060	120347	119264	96387
3 Manufacturing	254115	360183	468560	522763	566612	586438	649631	641021	689493	778413	806461	831844
4 Electricity, gas and water [a]	24055	42718	53342	58131	58663	68682	80847	92490	104001	119496	127365	132935
5 Construction	51053	77000	98743	116686	132712	139366	140321	142956	151321	173526	186618	200203
6 Wholesale and retail trade, restaurants and hotels	174064	280491	342643	384900	429917	455226	500354	525500	563712	635022	687516	727485
7 Transport, storage and communication	64905	99740	126281	143749	158544	173314	190158	197763	217833	237226	251475	261228
8 Finance, insurance, real estate and business services	186844	291899	371936	432204	490311	548516	622402	663127	740450	817524	800685	1000500
9 Community, social and personal services	78633	128259	159821	180214	199065	224472	250312	276551	302886	331136	359428	385160
Statistical discrepancy [b]	14497	22471	26031	29734	32001	33840	37976	40023	44085	51940	58551	62774
Total, Industries	895613	1397660	1753010	1990210	2218160	2408030	2700180	2793690	3005240	3349940	3580410	3785590
Producers of Government Services	133661	214385	250716	274784	299972	333978	366259	395374	419322	443982	477033	504251
Other Producers	...	...	...	...	...	...	...	...	...	...	...	...
Subtotal	1029270	1612050	2003730	2265000	2518130	2742010	3066440	3189070	3424560	3793920	4057440	4289840
Less: Imputed bank service charge	21407	36492	41616	51280	59814	65620	69681	76225	85345	88844	104345	113087
Plus: Import duties	2484	5864	5403	7100	7454	7160	8589	8609	9091	11904	12158	13654
Plus: Value added tax	...	...	...	...	...	...	...	...	...	...	...	...
Plus: Other adjustments [c]	-1133	2502	-27	-1908	-965	4920	4124	-56	5170	5359	-5644	-4914
Equals: Gross Domestic Product	1009220	1583920	1967490	2218910	2464800	2688470	3009470	3121400	3353470	3722340	3959610	4185490

a) Item 'Electricity, gas and water' also includes sanitary and similar services.
b) Item 'Statistical discrepancy' refers to government enterprises.
c) Item 'Other adjustments' refers to statistical discrepancy.

United States

1.11 Gross Domestic Product by Kind of Activity, in Constant Prices

Million United States dollars

	1970	1975	1977	1978	1979	1980	1981	1982	1983	1984	1985	1986
	At constant prices of: 1980											
1 Agriculture, hunting, forestry and fishing	65236	69958	66925	67729	71843	70320	81329	82539	67065	76496	87899	95094
2 Mining and quarrying	106499	99637	100255	102272	103566	107854	111078	104573	99450	105884	104127	94671
3 Manufacturing	444747	480455	565481	599805	613150	586438	597779	560720	594971	667550	697020	716679
4 Electricity, gas and water [a]	48473	64847	64559	66058	66947	68682	73749	73992	76401	83563	85194	83672
5 Construction	144375	128696	141870	151883	149366	139366	127320	121798	127020	137274	141584	145045
6 Wholesale and retail trade, restaurants and hotels	334209	391048	433994	454099	464232	455226	460673	459839	479268	521574	551307	578440
7 Transport, storage and communication	119441	137954	156379	168446	174879	173314	170659	164326	172136	181135	183401	187757
8 Finance, insurance, real estate and business services	366964	442017	479398	510680	536556	548516	565760	565002	584203	611029	635684	670421
9 Community, social and personal services	158717	188510	206036	215066	219657	224472	233150	237537	245786	256926	268204	277424
Statistical discrepancy [b]	26093	28879	30091	31572	32344	33840	33721	32658	33587	34497	35698	37235
Total, Industries	1814750	2032000	2244990	2367610	2432540	2408030	2455220	2402980	2479890	2675930	2790120	2886440
Producers of Government Services	294298	310846	317774	324443	328513	333978	337400	338089	340550	342795	348741	353243
Other Producers	...	...	...	...	...	...	...	...	...	...	...	...
Subtotal	2109050	2342850	2562760	2692050	2761050	2742010	2792620	2741070	2820440	3018720	3138860	3239680
Less: Imputed bank service charge	45559	55508	59237	62355	64032	65620	64762	67357	71386	72023	74305	76347
Plus: Import duties	5023	8412	7162	8747	8194	7160	7958	7817	8093	10294	10544	11887
Plus: Value added tax	...	...	...	...	...	...	...	...	...	...	...	...
Plus: Other adjustments [c]	-16703	-4026	-717	-191	-14799	4920	13525	-2951	26499	25991	11186	4853
Equals: Gross Domestic Product	2051810	2291730	2509970	2638250	2690420	2688470	2749340	2678580	2783640	2982980	3086280	3180070

a) Item 'Electricity, gas and water' also includes sanitary and similar services.
b) Item 'Statistical discrepancy' refers to government enterprises.
c) Item 'Other adjustments' refers to statistical discrepancy.

1.12 Relations Among National Accounting Aggregates

Million United States dollars

	1970	1975	1977	1978	1979	1980	1981	1982	1983	1984	1985	1986
Gross Domestic Product	1009220	1583920	1967490	2218910	2464810	2688470	3009470	3121400	3353470	3722340	3959610	4185490
Plus: Net factor income from the rest of the world	7253	17540	25424	30543	43801	47592	52108	51163	49864	47417	39763	33743
Factor income from the rest of the world	12545	27202	36100	45740	68104	78368	90489	91626	88721	100420	88986	86077
Less: Factor income to the rest of the world [a]	5292	9662	10676	15197	24303	30776	38381	40463	38857	53003	49223	52334
Equals: Gross National Product	1016470	1601460	1992910	2249450	2508610	2736060	3061580	3172560	3403340	3769750	3999370	4219230
Less: Consumption of fixed capital	105843	192851	236409	269346	311362	355816	403461	440644	455627	476888	503459	525193
Equals: National Income	910628	1408610	1756500	1980110	2197240	2380240	2658120	2731920	2947710	3292870	3495910	3694040
Plus: Net current transfers from the rest of the world	-6217	-7123	-5267	-5832	-6659	-8443	-8219	-9598	-9732	-12405	-15419	-15830
Current transfers from the rest of the world	382	735	960	1212	1391	1580	1482	1505	1489	1342	1457	1718
Less: Current transfers to the rest of the world	6599	7858	6227	7044	8050	10023	9701	11103	11221	13747	16876	17548
Equals: National Disposable Income	904411	1401480	1751240	1974270	2190590	2371800	2649900	2722320	2937980	3280460	3480500	3678210
Less: Final consumption	825428	1300030	1595470	1770010	1973650	2194940	2435290	2620390	2840660	3092310	3340040	3556990
Statistical discrepancy [b]	1133	-2502	27	1908	965	-4920	-4124	56	-5161	-5359	5644	4914
Equals: Net Saving [c]	79092	94406	150248	197499	206782	159347	193606	83696	74328	163025	124793	103526
Less: Surplus of the nation on current transactions	3939	21596	-8710	-10138	1448	11830	9478	-953	-33485	-90948	-115911	-143853
Statistical discrepancy [b]	-1133	2502	-27	-1908	-965	4920	4124	-56	5161	5359	-5644	-4914
Equals: Net Capital Formation	74020	75312	158931	205729	204369	152437	188252	84593	112974	259332	235060	242465

a) Item 'Factor income to the rest of the world' excludes factor income paid to the rest of the world by General Government.
b) Statistical Discrepancy is defined as the difference between GNP less charges against GNP other than Statistical Discrepancy. It arises because GNP and charges against GNP are independently derived by different methodologies. This Statistical Discrepancy after item 'Final consumption' is treated as a negative item and after item 'Surplus of the nations on current transactions', it is treated as a positive item.
c) Factor income paid to the rest of the world by general government is deducted from item 'Net saving'.

2.1 Government Final Consumption Expenditure by Function, in Current Prices

Million United States dollars

	1970	1975	1977	1978	1979	1980	1981	1982	1983	1984	1985	1986
1 General public services	10623	16798	21709	22994	26664	30441	33271	36951	39389	42996	45658	48041
2 Defence	74119	87738	100809	108743	121491	142013	166814	193341	213984	232750	259267	277733
3 Public order and safety	8421	16564	20310	22138	24427	26918	30365	34445	37763	41212	45301	49379
4 Education	44702	79445	93872	100361	111393	122828	133962	144928	153555	164744	176946	189782
5 Health	8651	16727	19700	21379	22583	25897	28358	29359	30839	33391	34641	37270

United States

2.1 Government Final Consumption Expenditure by Function, in Current Prices
(Continued)

Million United States dollars

	1970	1975	1977	1978	1979	1980	1981	1982	1983	1984	1985	1986
6 Social security and welfare	4326	9824	12855	14069	15495	17282	18799	19969	21021	23170	24531	25125
7 Housing and community amenities	4744	8847	10002	12527	13370	14528	13698	13527	13222	14834	15887	17300
8 Recreational, cultural and religious affairs	1864	3805	4513	5000	5390	5991	6226	6395	6462	6783	7395	8167
9 Economic services	27651	43194	47663	54592	61463	68661	73557	74492	78985	85800	93034	98516
A Fuel and energy	2137	5240	6909	8861	9042	8862	9993	8433	7499	8224	9463	10429
B Agriculture, forestry, fishing and hunting	2266	2863	2958	3510	3949	4474	4896	5570	6724	7781	8015	8022
C Mining, manufacturing and construction, except fuel and energy	2360	4106	4741	5189	6360	7124	8250	8264	8843	8554	9307	9191
D Transportation and communication	17788	25882	26861	30180	34523	39027	40800	42809	45874	50501	54920	58574
E Other economic affairs	3100	5103	6194	6852	7589	9174	9618	9416	10045	10740	11329	12300
10 Other functions	4485	11277	14036	15485	16648	19163	20563	20683	21783	24429	25647	27273
Total Government Final Consumption Expenditure	189586	294219	345469	377288	418924	473722	525613	574090	617003	670109	728307	778586

2.3 Total Government Outlays by Function and Type

Million United States dollars

	Final Consumption Expenditures Total	Compensation of Employees	Other	Subsidies	Other Current Transfers & Property Income	Total Current Disbursements	Gross Capital Formation	Other Capital Outlays	Total Outlays
1980									
1 General public services	30441	...	...	...	...	...	...	...	...
2 Defence	142013	...	...	...	...	...	...	...	...
3 Public order and safety	26918	...	...	...	...	...	...	...	...
4 Education	122828	...	...	...	...	...	...	...	...
5 Health	25897	...	...	...	...	...	...	...	...
6 Social security and welfare	17282	...	...	...	...	...	...	...	...
7 Housing and community amenities	14528	...	...	...	...	...	...	...	...
8 Recreation, culture and religion	5991	...	...	...	...	...	...	...	...
9 Economic services	68661	...	...	...	...	...	...	...	...
A Fuel and energy	8862	...	...	...	...	...	...	...	...
B Agriculture, forestry, fishing and hunting	4474	...	...	...	...	...	...	...	...
C Mining (except fuels), manufacturing and construction	7124	...	...	...	...	...	...	...	...
D Transportation and communication	39027	...	...	...	...	...	...	...	...
E Other economic affairs	9174	...	...	...	...	...	...	...	...
10 Other functions	19163	...	...	...	...	...	...	...	...
Total	473722	294059	179663	10723	385381	869826	48551	-2422	915955
1981									
1 General public services	33271	...	...	...	...	...	...	...	...
2 Defence	166814	...	...	...	...	...	...	...	...
3 Public order and safety	30365	...	...	...	...	...	...	...	...
4 Education	133962	...	...	...	...	...	...	...	...
5 Health	28358	...	...	...	...	...	...	...	...
6 Social security and welfare	18799	...	...	...	...	...	...	...	...
7 Housing and community amenities	13698	...	...	...	...	...	...	...	...
8 Recreation, culture and religion	6226	...	...	...	...	...	...	...	...
9 Economic services	73557	...	...	...	...	...	...	...	...
A Fuel and energy	9993	...	...	...	...	...	...	...	...
B Agriculture, forestry, fishing and hunting	4896	...	...	...	...	...	...	...	...
C Mining (except fuels), manufacturing and construction	8250	...	...	...	...	...	...	...	...
D Transportation and communication	40800	...	...	...	...	...	...	...	...
E Other economic affairs	9618	...	...	...	...	...	...	...	...
10 Other functions	20563	...	...	...	...	...	...	...	...
Total	525613	323789	201824	12182	451664	989459	50890	-3643	1036710

United States

2.3 Total Government Outlays by Function and Type
(Continued)

Million United States dollars

		Final Consumption Expenditures			Subsidies	Other Current Transfers & Property Income	Total Current Disbursements	Gross Capital Formation	Other Capital Outlays	Total Outlays
		Total	Compensation of Employees	Other						

1982

		Total								
1	General public services	36951	...	...	...	...	...	...	...	...
2	Defence	193341	...	...	...	...	...	...	...	...
3	Public order and safety	34445	...	...	...	...	...	...	...	...
4	Education	144928	...	...	...	...	...	...	...	...
5	Health	29359	...	...	...	...	...	...	...	...
6	Social security and welfare	19969	...	...	...	...	...	...	...	...
7	Housing and community amenities	13527	...	...	...	...	...	...	...	...
8	Recreation, culture and religion	6395	...	...	...	...	...	...	...	...
9	Economic services	74492	...	...	...	...	...	...	...	...
	A Fuel and energy	8433	...	...	...	...	...	...	...	...
	B Agriculture, forestry, fishing and hunting	5570	...	...	...	...	...	...	...	...
	C Mining (except fuels), manufacturing and construction	8264	...	...	...	...	...	...	...	...
	D Transportation and communication	42809	...	...	...	...	...	...	...	...
	E Other economic affairs	9416	...	...	...	...	...	...	...	...
10	Other functions	20683	...	...	...	...	...	...	...	...
	Total	574090	351777	222313	15483	510546	1100120	49711	-1636	1148190

1983

1	General public services	39389	...	...	...	...	...	...	...	...
2	Defence	213984	...	...	...	...	...	...	...	...
3	Public order and safety	37763	...	...	...	...	...	...	...	...
4	Education	153555	...	...	...	...	...	...	...	...
5	Health	30839	...	...	...	...	...	...	...	...
6	Social security and welfare	21021	...	...	...	...	...	...	...	...
7	Housing and community amenities	13222	...	...	...	...	...	...	...	...
8	Recreation, culture and religion	6462	...	...	...	...	...	...	...	...
9	Economic services	78985	...	...	...	...	...	...	...	...
	A Fuel and energy	7499	...	...	...	...	...	...	...	...
	B Agriculture, forestry, fishing and hunting	6724	...	...	...	...	...	...	...	...
	C Mining (except fuels), manufacturing and construction	8843	...	...	...	...	...	...	...	...
	D Transportation and communication	45874	...	...	...	...	...	...	...	...
	E Other economic affairs	10045	...	...	...	...	...	...	...	...
10	Other functions	21783	...	...	...	...	...	...	...	...
	Total	617003	374733	242270	22175	556627	1195810	52835	-2854	1245790

1984

1	General public services	42996	...	...	...	...	...	...	...	...
2	Defence	232750	...	...	...	...	...	...	...	...
3	Public order and safety	41212	...	...	...	...	...	...	...	...
4	Education	164744	...	...	...	...	...	...	...	...
5	Health	33391	...	...	...	...	...	...	...	...
6	Social security and welfare	23170	...	...	...	...	...	...	...	...
7	Housing and community amenities	14834	...	...	...	...	...	...	...	...
8	Recreation, culture and religion	6783	...	...	...	...	...	...	...	...
9	Economic services	85800	...	...	...	...	...	...	...	...
	A Fuel and energy	8224	...	...	...	...	...	...	...	...
	B Agriculture, forestry, fishing and hunting	7781	...	...	...	...	...	...	...	...
	C Mining (except fuels), manufacturing and construction	8554	...	...	...	...	...	...	...	...
	D Transportation and communication	50501	...	...	...	...	...	...	...	...
	E Other economic affairs	10740	...	...	...	...	...	...	...	...
10	Other functions	24429	...	...	...	...	...	...	...	...
	Total	670109	397767	272344	22730	595382	1288220	53383	-1515	1340090

United States

2.3 Total Government Outlays by Function and Type
(Continued)

Million United States dollars

	Final Consumption Expenditures Total	Compensation of Employees	Other	Subsidies	Other Current Transfers & Property Income	Total Current Disbursements	Gross Capital Formation	Other Capital Outlays	Total Outlays
1985									
1 General public services	45658	...	...	...	...	...	...	...	...
2 Defence	259267	...	...	...	...	...	...	...	...
3 Public order and safety	45301	...	...	...	...	...	...	...	...
4 Education	176946	...	...	...	...	...	...	...	...
5 Health	34641	...	...	...	...	...	...	...	...
6 Social security and welfare	24531	...	...	...	...	...	...	...	...
7 Housing and community amenities	15887	...	...	...	...	...	...	...	...
8 Recreation, culture and religion	7395	...	...	...	...	...	...	...	...
9 Economic services	93034	...	...	...	...	...	...	...	...
A Fuel and energy	9463	...	...	...	...	...	...	...	...
B Agriculture, forestry, fishing and hunting	8015	...	...	...	...	...	...	...	...
C Mining (except fuels), manufacturing and construction	9307	...	...	...	...	...	...	...	...
D Transportation and communication	54920	...	...	...	...	...	...	...	...
E Other economic affairs	11329	...	...	...	...	...	...	...	...
10 Other functions	25647	...	...	...	...	...	...	...	...
Total	728307	427419	300888	22912	647263	1398480	61956	1496	1461930
1986									
1 General public services	48041	...	...	...	...	...	...	...	...
2 Defence	277733	...	...	...	...	...	...	...	...
3 Public order and safety	49379	...	...	...	...	...	...	...	...
4 Education	189782	...	...	...	...	...	...	...	...
5 Health	37270	...	...	...	...	...	...	...	...
6 Social security and welfare	25125	...	...	...	...	...	...	...	...
7 Housing and community amenities	17300	...	...	...	...	...	...	...	...
8 Recreation, culture and religion	8167	...	...	...	...	...	...	...	...
9 Economic services	98516	...	...	...	...	...	...	...	...
A Fuel and energy	10429	...	...	...	...	...	...	...	...
B Agriculture, forestry, fishing and hunting	8022	...	...	...	...	...	...	...	...
C Mining (except fuels), manufacturing and construction	9191	...	...	...	...	...	...	...	...
D Transportation and communication	58574	...	...	...	...	...	...	...	...
E Other economic affairs	12300	...	...	...	...	...	...	...	...
10 Other functions	27273	...	...	...	...	...	...	...	...
Total	778586	452809	325777	20307	604847	1489740	64402	-366	1553780

2.4 Composition of General Government Social Security Benefits and Social Assistance Grants to Households

Million United States dollars

	1980 Social Security Benefits	1980 Social Assistance Grants	1981 Social Security Benefits	1981 Social Assistance Grants	1982 Social Security Benefits	1982 Social Assistance Grants	1983 Social Security Benefits	1983 Social Assistance Grants	1984 Social Security Benefits	1984 Social Assistance Grants	1985 Social Security Benefits	1985 Social Assistance Grants
1 Education benefits	...	9318	...	10332	...	9716	...	10489	...	10480	...	10813
2 Health benefits	...	26671	...	31041	...	33982	...	37264	...	40553	...	44291
3 Social security and welfare benefits	180285	50279	208948	53343	242014	53744	261039	56806	265268	58140	283754	59813
4 Housing and community amenities	...	167	...	163	...	96	...	16	...	16	...	83
5 Recreation and cultural benefits	...	312	...	408	...	264	...	425	...	520	...	326
6 Other	...	2563	...	2080	...	1851	...	1832	...	1581	...	1682
Total	180285	89310	208948	97367	242014	99653	261039	106832	265268	111299	283754	117008

United States

2.4 Composition of General Government Social Security Benefits and Social Assistance Grants to Households
Million United States dollars

	1986 Social Security Benefits	1986 Social Assistance Grants
1 Education benefits	...	10611
2 Health benefits	...	48411
3 Social security and welfare benefits	300989	62285
4 Housing and community amenities	...	318
5 Recreation and cultural benefits	...	464
6 Other	...	1921
Total	300989	124010

2.5 Private Final Consumption Expenditure by Type and Porpose, in Current Prices
Million United States dollars

	1970	1975	1977	1978	1979	1980	1981	1982	1983	1984	1985	1986
Final Consumption Expenditure of Resident Households												
1 Food, beverages and tobacco	118018	177961	204360	221360	246179	269655	292539	310611	326598	344907	361570	376826
A Food	89915	135675	156330	170384	189675	207663	225806	240171	250415	265885	278286	289820
B Non-alcoholic beverages	5054	8099	9140	9955	11076	12130	13188	14036	14630	15526	16252	16922
C Alcoholic beverages	12257	19119	21910	23359	26134	29112	30809	31749	33306	32950	35017	35896
D Tobacco	10792	15068	16980	17662	19294	20750	22736	24655	28247	30546	32015	34188
2 Clothing and footwear	52283	75766	89817	101293	109315	116945	128589	133619	146029	158508	170402	181827
3 Gross rent, fuel and power	114628	187514	233231	261375	295465	338021	381325	416048	445858	479053	514748	547252
A Fuel and power	19584	36984	48702	54119	62586	74345	82919	91391	97473	102595	106425	103601
B Other	95044	150530	184529	207256	232879	263676	298406	324657	348385	376458	408323	443651
4 Furniture, furnishings and household equipment and operation	46397	67259	83817	92517	102263	108191	115915	118458	129008	141128	149181	159329
A Household operation	13589	18630	23070	25365	27726	29864	32283	34022	35805	38191	39803	42409
B Other	32808	48629	60747	67152	74537	78327	83632	84436	93203	102937	109378	116920
5 Medical care and health expenses	59930	107576	139828	157137	178170	205113	240347	270020	295381	326602	356781	389582
6 Transport and communication	95099	155230	210795	232532	257831	277136	304717	315806	346689	384489	415223	424386
A Personal transport equipment	30826	47851	75113	84341	84916	77104	85258	92611	112666	138992	157799	175365
B Other	64273	107379	135682	148191	172915	200032	219459	223195	234023	245497	257424	249021
7 Recreational, entertainment, education and cultural services	54550	89143	107968	120774	134446	147175	165244	178166	196146	216359	236693	255998
A Education	12530	20580	24153	26970	30273	34314	38861	41939	46184	50465	55480	60266
B Other	42020	68563	83815	93804	104173	112861	126383	136227	149962	165894	181213	195732
8 Miscellaneous goods and services	90423	140921	175878	201246	226479	254850	277992	298450	329472	359885	393941	431272
A Personal care	20280	30579	38362	42908	46606	51321	55417	56897	62596	67849	71973	77562
B Expenditures in restaurants, cafes and hotels	37340	59778	73951	84953	98252	108806	116017	122758	134418	145934	156213	168315
C Other	32803	50564	63565	73385	81621	94723	106558	118795	132458	146102	165755	185395
Total Final Consumption Expenditure in the Domestic Market by Households, of which	631328	1001370	1245690	1388230	1550150	1717090	1906670	2041180	2215180	2410930	2598540	2766470
A Durable goods	67119	106331	148142	165466	174880	171918	187634	197917	228590	269708	299783	330500
B Semi-durable goods	93060	138574	166740	185819	202304	216974	237810	247421	269778	293002	312481	330886
C Non-durable goods	185929	294526	347218	379495	433467	492329	538543	566020	595236	624902	652981	653489
D Services	285220	461939	583594	657454	739497	835865	942681	1029820	1121580	1223320	1333290	1451600
Plus: Direct purchases abroad by resident households [a]	7177	9817	11293	12577	13976	15691	17026	18777	21308	24640	27022	27112
Less: Direct purchases in the domestic market by non-resident households	2663	5372	6982	8095	9402	11558	14013	13651	12828	13373	13828	15178
Equals: Final Consumption Expenditure of Resident Households [b]	635842	1005820	1250010	1392720	1554720	1721220	1909680	2046300	2223660	2422200	2611730	2778410
Final Consumption Expenditure of Private Non-profit Institutions Serving Households												
Equals: Final Consumption Expenditure of Private Non-profit Organisations Serving Households	...	...	...	...	...	...	...	...	...	...	...	...
Private Final Consumption Expenditure	635842	1005820	1250010	1392720	1554720	1721220	1909680	2046300	2223660	2422200	2611730	2778410

a) Item 'Direct purchases abroad by resident households' includes direct purchases abroad by resident households less value of gifts in kind, sent abroad, net.
b) Item 'Final consumption expenditure of resident households' includes consumption expenditure of private non-profit institutions serving households.

United States

2.6 Private Final Consumption Expenditure by Type and Purpose, in Constant Prices

Million United States dollars

		1970	1975	1977	1978	1979	1980	1981	1982	1983	1984	1985	1986
		\multicolumn{12}{c}{At constant prices of: 1980}
		\multicolumn{12}{c}{Final Consumption Expenditure of Resident Households}
1	Food, beverages and tobacco	241780	244225	264994	261233	264428	269655	270472	275644	283556	287571	296931	300133
	A Food	198817	188207	205585	202052	203464	207663	208411	214126	222062	226386	234504	237918
	B Non-alcoholic beverages	4834	11159	11967	11768	11880	12130	12149	12469	12939	13185	13658	13852
	C Alcoholic beverages	20290	25021	26988	27230	28275	29112	28859	28534	28864	28019	29000	28613
	D Tobacco	17839	19838	20454	20183	20808	20750	21053	20515	19691	19980	19770	19751
2	Clothing and footwear	77756	91406	100363	109815	114326	116945	123833	125705	134408	143649	149303	159610
3	Gross rent, fuel and power	246265	293232	309313	322866	332350	338021	340915	343258	348144	355868	364899	374456
	A Fuel and power	63864	68729	74166	76811	76667	74345	71504	71655	72796	73684	75618	77319
	B Other	182400	224504	235147	246055	255683	263676	269411	271603	275348	282184	289281	297136
4	Furniture, furnishings and household equipment and operation	87295	92790	102910	107359	110980	108191	107386	103795	109757	118080	122674	128491
	A Household operation	31943	28523	29346	30016	30380	29864	29420	29353	30065	31498	31796	32635
	B Other	55352	64267	73564	77342	80600	78327	77967	74442	79692	86581	90878	95856
5	Medical care and health expenses	121869	164446	181509	189058	197584	205113	216332	222380	227284	234112	240967	250915
6	Transport and communication	210224	250468	294130	307066	302162	277136	276684	278164	300284	323631	342391	359783
	A Personal transport equipment	55104	67296	92961	97157	91007	77104	78237	80154	94636	111207	123203	134119
	B Other	155120	183171	201169	209909	211154	200032	198447	198010	205648	212424	219189	225664
7	Recreational, entertainment, education and cultural services	86116	119529	131644	139636	145614	147176	154303	159095	170954	185585	201182	217082
	A Education	28603	31428	32249	33351	33884	34314	35211	35889	37890	39567	42120	44170
	B Other	57513	88102	99395	106285	111730	112862	119093	123206	133065	146018	159062	172912
8	Miscellaneous goods and services	188524	210845	232510	246372	253204	254850	254762	251673	270550	282581	298361	315180
	A Personal care	39681	44821	50089	52741	53108	51321	51636	50965	53920	57043	59335	62743
	B Expenditures in restaurants, cafes and hotels	78559	89398	97604	103405	107801	108806	106398	106386	111445	115674	118658	122647
	C Other	70285	76626	84817	90226	92295	94723	96727	94323	105185	109864	120368	129790
	Total Final Consumption Expenditure in the Domestic Market by Households, of which	1259830	1466940	1617370	1683400	1720650	1717090	1744690	1759720	1844940	1931080	2017010	2105650
	A Durable goods	101396	142285	181058	191037	189209	171919	175701	177998	201354	231920	256618	283369
	B Semi-durable goods	148430	176677	195014	208919	216212	216974	225281	226108	241275	259015	269675	283721
	C Non-durable goods	435662	457273	490591	495868	497544	492329	488799	493695	507434	515494	528449	537751
	D Services	574340	690706	750711	787581	817682	835865	854906	861914	894875	924646	962266	1000810
	Plus: Direct purchases abroad by resident households [a]	17521	13777	14716	15531	15641	15691	15904	18403	21123	24552	27605	25856
	Less: Direct purchases in the domestic market by non-resident households	5426	8254	9342	9954	10556	11558	12676	11469	10322	10231	10112	10723
	Equals: Final Consumption Expenditure of Resident Households [b]	1271920	1472470	1622750	1688980	1725730	1721220	1747910	1766650	1855740	1945400	2034500	2120790
	\multicolumn{12}{c}{Final Consumption Expenditure of Private Non-profit Institutions Serving Households}
	Equals: Final Consumption Expenditure of Private Non-profit Organisations Serving Households	...	...	...	...	...	...	...	...	...	...	...	...
	Private Final Consumption Expenditure	1271920	1472470	1622750	1688980	1725730	1721220	1747910	1766650	1855740	1945400	2034500	2120790

a) Item 'Direct purchases abroad by resident households' includes direct purchases abroad by resident households less value of gifts in kind, sent abroad, net.
b) Item 'Final consumption expenditure of resident households' includes consumption expenditure of private non-profit institutions serving households.

2.7 Gross Capital Formation by Type of Good and Owner, in Current Prices

Million United States dollars

	\multicolumn{4}{c	}{1980}	\multicolumn{4}{c	}{1981}	\multicolumn{4}{c}{1982}
	TOTAL	Total Private	Public Enterprises	General Government	TOTAL	Total Private	Public Enterprises	General Government	TOTAL	Total Private	Public Enterprises	General Government
Increase in stocks, total	-6014	-8329	1025	1290	32390	24007	3242	5141	-12341	-24532	9415	2776
1 Goods producing industries [a]	-4524	-4524	...	...	9034	9034	...	...	-16528	-16528	...	...
A Materials and supplies	-709	-709	...	...	-4701	-4701	...	...	-6997	-6997	...	...
B Work in progress	1917	1917	...	...	-35	-35	...	...	-5188	-5188	...	...
C Livestock, except breeding stocks, dairy cattle, etc. [b]	1339	1339	...	...	286	286	...	...	-690	-690	...	...

United States

2.7 Gross Capital Formation by Type of Good and Owner, in Current Prices
(Continued)

Million United States dollars

	1980				1981				1982			
	TOTAL	Total Private	Public Enterprises	General Government	TOTAL	Total Private	Public Enterprises	General Government	TOTAL	Total Private	Public Enterprises	General Government
D Finished goods	-7071	-7071	...	...	13484	13484	...	...	-3653	-3653	...	...
2 Wholesale and retail trade	-682	-682	...	...	8383	8383	...	...	-6082	-6082	...	...
3 Other, except government stocks	-2098	-3123	1025	...	9832	6590	3242	...	7493	-1922	9415	...
4 Government stocks	1290	...	...	1290	5141	...	...	5141	2776	...	...	2776
Gross Fixed Capital Formation, Total	514267	445298	21708	47261	559323	491503	22071	45749	537578	471813	18830	46935
1 Residential buildings [c]	121618	119453	1321	844	121311	118999	1400	912	104030	101847	1151	1032
2 Non-residential buildings	77645	61016	336	16293	85326	69505	463	15358	88152	73095	386	14671
3 Other construction	91005	52887	18156	19962	105826	68993	17603	19230	104800	70200	14589	20011
4 Land improvement and plantation and orchard development	...	...	...	...	...	...	...	...	...	...	...	...
5 Producers' durable goods	223999	211942	1895	10162	246860	234006	2605	10249	240596	226671	2704	11221
A Transport equipment	49336	44917	...	4419	51292	46248	...	5044	47377	42516	...	4861
Passenger cars	12522	11359	...	1163	14337	13129	...	1208	13543	12347	...	1196
Other	36814	33558	...	3256	36955	33119	...	3836	33834	30169	...	3665
B Machinery and equipment [d]	174663	167025	1895	5743	195568	187758	2605	5205	193219	184155	2704	6360
6 Breeding stock, dairy cattle, etc.	...	...	...	...	...	...	...	...	...	...	...	...
Total Gross Capital Formation	508253	436969	22733	48551	591713	515510	25313	50890	525237	447281	28245	49711

	1983				1984				1985			
	TOTAL	Total Private	Public Enterprises	General Government	TOTAL	Total Private	Public Enterprises	General Government	TOTAL	Total Private	Public Enterprises	General Government
Increase in stocks, total	-9007	-7081	-5394	3468	66204	67688	-3627	2143	22928	9976	11235	1717
1 Goods producing industries [a]	-13265	-13265	...	...	28751	28751	...	...	-11408	-11408	...	...
A Materials and supplies	-508	-508	...	...	5232	5232	...	...	-3396	-3396	...	...
B Work in progress	-601	-601	...	...	9994	9994	...	...	-1798	-1798	...	...
C Livestock, except breeding stocks, dairy cattle, etc. [b]	-467	-467	...	...	-1697	-1697	...	...	-1915	-1915	...	...
D Finished goods	-11689	-11689	...	...	15222	15222	...	...	-4299	-4299	...	...
2 Wholesale and retail trade	6319	6319	...	...	30057	30057	...	...	13983	13983	...	...
3 Other, except government stocks	-5529	-135	-5394	...	5253	8880	-3627	...	18636	7401	11235	...
4 Government stocks	3468	...	...	3468	2143	...	...	2143	1717	...	...	1717
Gross Fixed Capital Formation, Total	577608	509367	18874	49367	670016	597143	21633	51240	715591	631601	23751	60239
1 Residential buildings [c]	150990	148375	1271	1344	179228	176485	1465	1278	186748	183962	1178	1608
2 Non-residential buildings	84531	68970	478	15083	99652	84265	417	14970	116223	97572	598	18053
3 Other construction	88919	55079	13907	19933	94332	56850	15994	21488	96596	54943	17406	24247
4 Land improvement and plantation and orchard development	...	...	...	...	...	...	...	...	...	...	...	...
5 Producers' durable goods	253168	236943	3218	13007	296804	279543	3757	13504	316024	295124	4569	16331
A Transport equipment	54427	49456	...	4971	65875	59781	...	6094	71066	63809	...	7257
Passenger cars	18639	17347	...	1292	19629	18276	...	1353	19248	17871	...	1377
Other	35788	32109	...	3679	46246	41505	...	4741	51818	45938	...	5880
B Machinery and equipment [d]	198741	187487	3218	8036	230929	219762	3757	7410	244958	231315	4569	9074
6 Breeding stock, dairy cattle, etc. [b]	...	...	...	...	...	...	...	...	...	...	...	...
Total Gross Capital Formation	568601	502286	13480	52835	736220	664831	18006	53383	738519	641577	34986	61956

	1986			
	TOTAL	Total Private	Public Enterprises	General Government
Increase in stocks, total	20858	15735	5066	57
1 Goods producing industries [a]	-5713	-5713	...	...
A Materials and supplies	-2244	-2244	...	...
B Work in progress	-1465	-1465	...	...
C Livestock, except breeding stocks, dairy cattle, etc. [b]	-1470	-1470	...	...

United States

2.7 Gross Capital Formation by Type of Good and Owner, in Current Prices
(Continued)

Million United States dollars

	\multicolumn{4}{c	}{1986}
	TOTAL	Total Private	Public Enterprises	General Government
D Finished goods	-534	-534	...	...
2 Wholesale and retail trade	10958	10958	...	...
3 Other, except government stocks	15556	10490	5066	...
4 Government stocks	57	...	...	57
Gross Fixed Capital Formation, Total	746800	655229	27226	64345
1 Residential buildings c	216246	212921	1641	1684
2 Non-residential buildings	114449	93064	390	20995
3 Other construction	90593	44330	20164	26099
4 Land improvement and plantation and orchard development	...	...	...	...
5 Producers' durable goods	325512	304914	5031	15567
A Transport equipment	75238	68173	...	7065
Passenger cars	22105	20709	...	1396
Other	53133	47464	...	5669
B Machinery and equipment d	250274	236741	5031	8502
6 Breeding stock, dairy cattle, etc. b	...	...	...	...
Total Gross Capital Formation	767658	670964	32292	64402

a) Item 'Goods producing industries' includes only manufacturing and farming.
b) Item 'Breeding stocks, dairy cattle, etc.' is included in item 'Increase in stocks'.
c) The estimates of residential buildings of government enterprises and general government are included in the respective columns of item 'Residential buildings' in tables 2.7 and 2.8. These estimates are included in item 'Real estate' in tables 2.9-2.12 and are therefore excluded from the estimates of government enterprises and general government of these tables. This latter classification is followed in tables 2.13-2.16.
d) Item 'Machinery and equipment' includes all producers durable goods of public enterprises.

2.8 Gross Capital Formation by Type of Good and Owner, in Constant Prices

Million United States dollars

	\multicolumn{4}{c	}{1980}	\multicolumn{4}{c	}{1981}	\multicolumn{4}{c	}{1982}
	TOTAL	Total Private	Public Enterprises	General Government	TOTAL	Total Private	Public Enterprises	General Government	TOTAL	Total Private	Public Enterprises	General Government
	\multicolumn{12}{c	}{At constant prices of:1980}
Increase in stocks, total	-6014	-8329	1025	1290	31744	21702	3884	6158	-8271	-22971	11353	3347
1 Goods producing industries a	-4524	-4524	...	...	8020	8020	...	...	-15837	-15837	...	...
A Materials and supplies	-709	-709	...	...	17942	17942	...	...	-7471	-7471	...	...
B Work in progress	1917	1917	...	...	-861	-861	...	...	-5384	-5384	...	...
C Livestock, except breeding stocks, dairy cattle, etc. b	1339	1339	...	...	278	278	...	...	-723	-723	...	...
D Finished goods	-7071	-7071	...	...	-9339	-9339	...	...	-2259	-2259	...	...
2 Wholesale and retail trade	-682	-682	...	...	7867	7867	...	...	-5573	-5573	...	...
3 Other, except government stocks	-2098	-3123	1025	...	9699	5815	3884	...	9792	-1561	11353	...
4 Government stocks	1290	...	...	1290	6158	...	...	6158	3347	...	...	3347
Gross Fixed Capital Formation, Total	514266	445207	21700	47201	513564	449005	21295	43204	466057	407350	18147	43353
1 Residential buildings c	121618	119453	1321	844	112286	110124	1309	853	93118	91114	1057	947
2 Non-residential buildings	77645	67010	338	10293	78120	63582	425	14113	76460	63379	335	12746
3 Other construction	91005	52887	18156	19962	95610	59723	17151	18736	89709	55644	14364	19701
4 Land improvement and plantation and orchard development	...	...	...	...	...	...	...	...	...	...	...	...
5 Producers' durable goods	223998	211941	1895	10162	227548	215636	2410	9502	209569	197219	2391	9959
A Transport equipment	49336	44917	...	4419	48153	43582	...	4571	43264	39071	...	4193
Passenger cars	12522	11359	...	1163	15007	13841	...	1166	14907	13777	...	1130
Other	36814	33558	...	3256	33146	29741	...	3405	28356	25293	...	3063
B Machinery and equipment d	174662	167024	1895	5743	179395	172054	2410	4931	166306	158148	2391	5766
6 Breeding stock, dairy cattle, etc. b	...	...	...	...	...	...	...	...	...	...	...	...
Total Gross Capital Formation	508252	436968	22733	48551	545308	470767	25179	49362	460586	384385	29500	46700

United States

2.8 Gross Capital Formation by Type of Good and Owner, in Constant Prices

Million United States dollars

	1983				1984				1985			
	TOTAL	Total Private	Public Enterprises	General Government	TOTAL	Total Private	Public Enterprises	General Government	TOTAL	Total Private	Public Enterprises	General Government
	At constant prices of:1980											
Increase in stocks, total	-9716	-7617	-5876	3777	54611	56258	-4026	2379	17220	5703	9991	1526
1 Goods producing industries a	-12381	-12381	...	...	23051	23051	...	...	-12078	-12078	...	...
A Materials and supplies	-828	-828	...	...	5717	5717	...	...	-3959	-3959	...	...
B Work in progress	-1399	-1399	...	...	9434	9434	...	...	-1860	-1860	...	...
C Livestock, except breeding stocks, dairy cattle, etc. b	-823	-823	...	...	-2664	-2664	...	...	-2923	-2923	...	...
D Finished goods	-9331	-9331	...	...	10564	10564	...	...	-3336	-3336	...	...
2 Wholesale and retail trade	4729	4729	...	...	25826	25826	...	...	11525	11525	...	...
3 Other, except government stocks	-5841	35	-5876	...	3355	7381	-4026	...	16247	6256	9991	...
4 Government stocks	3777	...	...	3777	2379	...	...	2379	1526	...	...	1526
Gross Fixed Capital Formation, Total	510038	446623	18218	45197	591044	525111	20298	45635	631000	558588	21028	51384
1 Residential buildings c	132604	130240	1149	1215	151490	149100	1277	1113	154338	151975	999	1364
2 Non-residential buildings	70649	57617	400	12632	79608	67288	334	11986	89836	75439	462	13935
3 Other construction	81954	48259	13847	19848	88247	52149	15403	20695	87108	49687	15637	21784
4 Land improvement and plantation and orchard development	...	...	...	...	...	...	...	...	...	...	...	...
5 Producers' durable goods	224831	210507	2822	11502	271699	256574	3284	11841	299718	281487	3930	14301
A Transport equipment	48983	44810	...	4173	59762	54778	...	4984	62773	57046	...	5727
Passenger cars	19950	18749	...	1201	23588	22288	...	1300	23072	21790	...	1282
Other	29033	26061	...	2972	36173	32490	...	3683	39700	35256	...	4444
B Machinery and equipment d	175848	165697	2822	7329	211938	201796	3284	6857	236946	224441	3930	8574
6 Breeding stock, dairy cattle, etc. b	...	...	...	...	...	...	...	...	...	...	...	...
Total Gross Capital Formation	500322	439006	12342	48974	645655	581369	16272	48014	648220	564291	31019	52910

	1986			
	TOTAL	Total Private	Public Enterprises	General Government
	At constant prices of:1980			
Increase in stocks, total	17335	11920	5355	60
1 Goods producing industries a	-6351	-6351	...	...
A Materials and supplies	-2747	-2747	...	...
B Work in progress	-1453	-1453	...	...
C Livestock, except breeding stocks, dairy cattle, etc. b	-2212	-2212	...	...
D Finished goods	61	61	...	...
2 Wholesale and retail trade	9149	9149	...	...
3 Other, except government stocks	14477	9122	5355	...
4 Government stocks	60	...	...	60
Gross Fixed Capital Formation, Total	649065	571834	23770	53460
1 Residential buildings c	173854	171119	1350	1385
2 Non-residential buildings	85943	69920	292	15731
3 Other construction	81202	40290	17832	23080
4 Land improvement and plantation and orchard development	...	...	...	...
5 Producers' durable goods	308065	290505	4296	13264
A Transport equipment	61904	56568	...	5336
Passenger cars	22533	21291	...	1242
Other	39371	35277	...	4094
B Machinery and equipment d	246161	233937	4296	7928
6 Breeding stock, dairy cattle, etc. b	...	...	...	...
Total Gross Capital Formation	666400	583754	29125	53520

a) Item 'Goods producing industries' includes only manufacturing and farming.
b) Item 'Breeding stocks, dairy cattle, etc.' is included in item 'Increase in stocks'.
c) The estimates of residential buildings of government enterprises and general government are included in the respective columns of item 'Residential buildings' in tables 2.7 and 2.8. These estimates are included in item 'Real estate' in tables 2.9-2.12 and are therefore excluded from the estimates of government enterprises and general government of these tables. This latter classification is followed in tables 2.13-2.16.
d) Item 'Machinery and equipment' includes all producers durable goods of public enterprises.

United States

2.9 Gross Capital Formation by Kind of Activity of Owner, ISIC Major Divisions, in Current Prices

Million United States dollars

	1980 TGCF	1980 IS	1980 GFCF	1981 TGCF	1981 IS	1981 GFCF	1982 TGCF	1982 IS	1982 GFCF	1983 TGCF	1983 IS	1983 GFCF
					All Producers							
1 Agriculture, hunting, fishing and forestry	14075	-5928	20003	24715	5751	18964	13865	-1429	15294	7416	-7482	14898
2 Mining and quarrying	34830	-154	34984	53707	2197	51510	53150	600	52550	33447	-1860	35307
3 Manufacturing	76745	1404	75341	85204	3283	81921	63224	-15099	78323	58642	-5783	64425
4 Electricity, gas and water	24634	-723	25357	28027	773	27254	25478	-1908	27386	24687	-1365	26052
5 Construction	6449	-1984	8433	10347	627	9720	4035	-82	4117	5234	954	4280
6 Wholesale and retail trade, restaurants and hotels	33496	-682	34178	50244	8383	41861	38252	-6082	44334	61269	6319	54950
7 Transport, storage and communication	51646	266	51380	54468	-156	54624	51454	-503	51957	55239	180	55059
8 Finance, insurance, real estate and business services a	169547	-395	169942	175406	809	174597	164090	-62	164152	207515	238	207277
9 Community, social and personal services	14995	-133	15128	20278	2340	17938	18987	33	18954	23888	1718	22170
Statistical discrepancy ba	21412	1025	20387	23913	3242	20671	27094	9415	17679	12209	-5394	17603
Total Industries	447829	-7304	455133	526309	27249	499060	459629	-15117	474746	489546	-12475	502021
Producers of Government Services a	47707	1290	46417	49978	5141	44837	48679	2776	45903	51491	3468	48023
Private Non-Profit Institutions Serving Households	12718	-	12718	15426	-	15426	16928	-	16928	27564	-	27564
Statistical discrepancy	-1	-	-1	-	-	-	1	-	1	-	-	-
Total	508253	-6014	514267	591713	32390	559323	525237	-12341	537578	568601	-9007	577608

	1984 TGCF	1984 IS	1984 GFCF	1985 TGCF	1985 IS	1985 GFCF	1986 TGCF	1986 IS	1986 GFCF
				All Producers					
1 Agriculture, hunting, fishing and forestry	21905	7146	14759	8593	-3612	12205	10918	-1073	11991
2 Mining and quarrying	36507	-28	36535	32753	193	32560	21334	1042	20292
3 Manufacturing	97955	21605	76350	76521	-7796	84317	75535	-4640	80175
4 Electricity, gas and water	32752	2345	30407	41942	-245	42187	40415	127	40288
5 Construction	8864	3538	5326	10514	3909	6605	11885	4563	7322
6 Wholesale and retail trade, restaurants and hotels	97795	30057	67738	86040	13983	72057	84655	10958	73697
7 Transport, storage and communication	58508	1449	57059	60224	1841	58383	63898	2503	61395
8 Finance, insurance, real estate and business services a	267436	846	266590	283470	329	283141	312995	316	312679
9 Community, social and personal services	28746	730	28016	28371	1374	26997	30848	1939	28909
Statistical discrepancy ba	16541	-3627	20168	33808	11235	22573	30651	5066	25585
Total Industries	667009	64061	602948	662236	21211	641025	683134	20801	662333
Producers of Government Services a	52105	2143	49962	60348	1717	58631	62718	57	62661
Private Non-Profit Institutions Serving Households	17106	-	17106	15935	-	15935	21806	-	21806
Statistical discrepancy									
Total	736220	66204	670016	738519	22928	715591	767658	20858	746800

a) The estimates of residential buildings of government enterprises and general government are included in the respective columns of item 'Residential buildings' in tables 2.7 and 2.8. These estimates are included in item 'Real estate' in tables 2.9-2.12 and are therefore excluded from the estimates of government enterprises and general government of these tables. This latter classification is followed in tables 2.13-2.16. b) Item 'Statistical discrepancy' refers to government enterprises.

2.10 Gross Capital Formation by Kind of Activity of Owner, ISIC Major Divisions, in Constant Prices

Million United States dollars

	1980 TGCF	1980 IS	1980 GFCF	1981 TGCF	1981 IS	1981 GFCF	1982 TGCF	1982 IS	1982 GFCF	1983 TGCF	1983 IS	1983 GFCF
				At constant prices of:1980								
				All Producers								
1 Agriculture, hunting, fishing and forestry	14075	-5928	20003	22108	5008	17100	11378	-1481	12859	5462	-6502	11964
2 Mining and quarrying	34830	-154	34984	44773	1874	42899	39434	498	38936	29387	-1580	30967
3 Manufacturing	76745	1404	75341	77797	3012	74785	53158	-14356	67514	49507	-5878	55385
4 Electricity, gas and water	24634	-723	25357	25205	533	24672	21312	-1558	22870	20102	-1086	21188

United States

2.10 Gross Capital Formation by Kind of Activity of Owner, ISIC Major Divisions, in Constant Prices
(Continued)

Million United States dollars

	1980 Total Gross Capital Formation	1980 Increase in Stocks	1980 Gross Fixed Capital Formation	1981 Total Gross Capital Formation	1981 Increase in Stocks	1981 Gross Fixed Capital Formation	1982 Total Gross Capital Formation	1982 Increase in Stocks	1982 Gross Fixed Capital Formation	1983 Total Gross Capital Formation	1983 Increase in Stocks	1983 Gross Fixed Capital Formation
					At constant prices of:1980							
5 Construction	6449	-1984	8433	9496	682	8814	3416	-12	3428	4415	922	3493
6 Wholesale and retail trade, restaurants and hotels	33496	-682	34178	46340	7867	38473	33275	-5573	38848	52936	4729	48207
7 Transport, storage and communication	51645	265	51380	48949	-142	49091	42825	-462	43287	44313	181	44132
8 Finance, insurance, real estate and business services [a]	169547	-395	169942	161879	839	161040	145447	-32	145479	182463	266	182197
9 Community, social and personal services	14995	-133	15128	18364	2028	16336	16293	2	16291	20356	1331	19025
Statistical discrepancy [ba]	21412	1025	20387	23302	3884	19418	27491	11353	16138	9909	-5876	15785
Total Industries	447827	-7305	455132	478213	25585	452628	394029	-11621	405650	418849	-13493	432342
Producers of Government Services [a]	47707	1290	46417	48679	6158	42521	46107	3347	42760	48084	3777	44307
Private Non-Profit Institutions Serving Households	12718	...	12718	18415	...	18415	20447	...	20447	33389	...	33389
Statistical discrepancy [c]	-	1	-1	1	1	-	3	3	-	-	-	-
Total	508252	-6014	514266	545308	31744	513564	460586	-8271	468857	500322	-9716	510038

	1984 Total Gross Capital Formation	1984 Increase in Stocks	1984 Gross Fixed Capital Formation	1985 Total Gross Capital Formation	1985 Increase in Stocks	1985 Gross Fixed Capital Formation	1986 Total Gross Capital Formation	1986 Increase in Stocks	1986 Gross Fixed Capital Formation
			At constant prices of:1980						
			All Producers						
1 Agriculture, hunting, fishing and forestry	16081	4615	11466	4529	-4827	9356	7432	-1658	9090
2 Mining and quarrying	34485	-21	34506	31494	166	31328	21284	1034	20250
3 Manufacturing	83621	18436	65185	65601	-7251	72852	63750	-4693	68443
4 Electricity, gas and water	25895	1758	24137	32730	-172	32902	31071	108	30963
5 Construction	7343	3092	4251	8568	3350	5218	9640	3922	5718
6 Wholesale and retail trade, restaurants and hotels	84687	25826	58861	73538	11525	62013	72733	9149	63584
7 Transport, storage and communication	45551	1233	44318	46156	1570	44586	48358	2334	46024
8 Finance, insurance, real estate and business services [a]	230691	753	229938	245723	298	245425	268903	286	268617
9 Community, social and personal services	24063	568	23495	23557	1044	22513	25330	1439	23891
Statistical discrepancy [ba]	13645	-4026	17671	28943	9991	18952	26638	5355	21283
Total Industries	566062	52234	513828	560840	15694	545146	575139	17276	557863
Producers of Government Services [a]	47441	2379	45062	51318	1526	49792	52234	60	52174
Private Non-Profit Institutions Serving Households	32154	...	32154	36062	...	36062	39028	...	39028
Statistical discrepancy [c]	-2	-2	-	-	-	-	-1	-1	-
Total	645655	54611	591044	648220	17220	631000	666400	17335	649065

a) The estimates of residential buildings of government enterprises and general government are included in the respective columns of item 'Residential buildings' in tables 2.7 and 2.8. These estimates are included in item 'Real estate' in tables 2.9-2.12 and are therefore excluded from the estimates of government enterprises and general government of these tables. This latter classification is followed in tables 2.13-2.16.
b) Item 'Statistical discrepancy' refers to government enterprises.
c) Item 'Statistical discrepancy' refers to residual (deflation) error to adjust total Gross Fixed Capital Formation by Kind of Activity of Owner (Table 2.12) to Gross Fixed Capital Formation by Type of Good and Owner (Table 2.8).

2.11 Gross Fixed Capital Formation by Kind of Activity of Owner, ISIC Divisions, in Current Prices

Million United States dollars

	1970	1975	1977	1978	1979	1980	1981	1982	1983	1984	1985	1986
					All Producers							
1 Agriculture, hunting, forestry and fishing	7258	12860	17307	18432	21773	20003	18964	15294	14898	14759	12205	11991
2 Mining and quarrying	5093	12234	18511	22995	28367	34984	51510	52550	35307	36535	32560	20292
A Coal mining	476	1385	2943	3074	3410	3615	4744	3871	2729	2526	2521	2182
B Crude petroleum and natural gas production	3868	9023	13406	17434	21860	28341	43506	45151	30027	31113	27414	16196
C Metal ore mining	431	1071	1284	1477	1780	1685	1663	1790	1654	1933	1717	1316
D Other mining	318	756	879	1009	1317	1342	1597	1737	897	963	907	598

United States

2.11 Gross Fixed Capital Formation by Kind of Activity of Owner, ISIC Divisions, in Current Prices
(Continued)

Million United States dollars

	1970	1975	1977	1978	1979	1980	1981	1982	1983	1984	1985	1986
3 Manufacturing	23812	38487	47989	58172	67280	75341	81921	78323	64425	76350	84317	80175
A Manufacturing of food, beverages and tobacco	2211	3645	4535	5209	5644	6454	6918	7610	6554	7105	7692	7651
B Textile, wearing apparel and leather industries	1195	1458	2014	2150	2224	2509	2500	2203	2241	2790	2516	2436
C Manufacture of wood, and wood products, including furniture	815	1501	2164	2422	2697	2637	2298	1895	1779	2465	2582	3094
D Manufacture of paper and paper products, printing and publishing	2248	3782	4880	5899	7048	7982	7488	8247	7849	8790	10454	10781
E Manufacture of chemicals and chemical petroleum, coal, rubber and plastic products	5478	10306	11945	12883	14649	15332	17643	19373	14346	14598	15408	14083
F Manufacture of non-metalic mineral products except products of petroleum and coal	948	1629	1784	2679	2803	3259	2650	2297	1697	2240	2637	2313
G Basic metal industries	2670	4328	4559	5089	5745	6082	6844	5320	4304	4118	4580	4092
H Manufacture of fabricated metal products, machinery and equipment	7992	11518	15549	21256	25790	30304	34934	30766	25130	33613	37834	34966
I Other manufacturing industries	255	320	559	587	680	782	647	612	524	630	613	760
4 Electricity, gas and water	10424	15206	19446	19999	20754	25357	27254	27386	26052	30407	42187	40288
5 Construction	3176	5154	6251	8805	9257	8433	9720	4117	4280	5326	6605	7322
6 Wholesale and retail trade, restaurants and hotels	11510	18190	22115	29847	35206	34178	41861	44334	54950	67738	72057	73697
A Wholesale and retail trade	10187	16881	20617	27848	32374	30875	37751	39781	49044	59752	63414	64877
B Restaurants and hotels	1323	1310	1499	1998	2832	3303	4109	4553	5906	7986	8642	8821
Restaurants	...	...	...	...	...	...	...	...	...	...	...	...
Hotels and other lodging places	1323	1310	1499	1998	2832	3303	4109	4553	5906	7986	8642	8821
7 Transport, storage and communication	16591	25636	34396	43895	51611	51380	54624	51957	55059	57059	58383	61395
A Transport and storage	7329	12301	15825	20946	23578	23990	23844	20183	21367	21006	19645	19351
B Communication	9262	13335	18571	22949	28032	27390	30780	31774	33693	36053	38738	42044
8 Finance, insurance, real estate and business services	53500	74677	126976	151961	182747	169942	174597	164152	207277	266590	283141	312679
A Financial institutions	2998	6533	8420	10400	12273	13312	15203	16518	18561	27329	31130	33106
B Insurance	644	920	1027	1313	1488	1799	1881	1862	2048	5331	8297	10030
C Real estate and business services	49858	67224	117529	140248	168986	154830	157513	145771	186668	233930	243715	269542
Real estate except dwellings	9038	8713	16001	19893	28109	29512	34227	37519	42337	48531	50884	49486
Dwellings	40820	58511	101528	120355	140877	125318	123286	108252	144331	185399	192831	220056
9 Community, social and personal services	5554	8559	11971	13110	14448	15128	17938	18954	22170	28016	26997	28909
A Sanitary and similar services	...	...	...	...	...	...	...	...	...	...	...	...
B Social and related community services	2055	3112	4020	4092	4287	5106	6390	7263	8321	9038	9086	9605
Educational services	94	118	153	132	142	198	187	231	244	245	289	311
Medical, dental, other health and veterinary services	1283	1847	2405	2431	2901	3814	5414	6354	7133	7781	7658	8004
C Recreational and cultural services	1078	1654	1971	2264	2865	2879	2988	2931	3031	4081	4593	4396
D Personal and household services	2421	3794	5980	6753	7297	7143	8560	8759	10818	14897	13319	14908
Statistical discrepancy [a]	6811	13530	14584	18580	18783	20387	20671	17679	17603	20168	22573	25585
Total Industries	143729	224534	319546	385795	450226	455133	499060	474746	502021	602948	641025	662333
Producers of Government Services	24847	32816	31692	36798	40494	46417	44837	45903	48023	49962	58631	62661
Private Non-Profit Institutions Serving Households	9918	14994	18862	22440	11909	12718	15426	16928	27564	17106	15935	21806
Statistical discrepancy	1	-	-	-	-	-1	-	1	-	-	-	-
Total	178495	272344	370100	445033	502629	514267	559323	537578	577608	670016	715591	746800

a) Item 'Statistical discrepancy' refers to government enterprises.

United States

2.12 Gross Fixed Capital Formation by Kind of Activity of Owner, ISIC Divisions, in Constant Prices

Million United States dollars

		1970	1975	1977	1978	1979	1980	1981	1982	1983	1984	1985	1986
						At constant prices of:1980							
						All Producers							
1	Agriculture, hunting, forestry and fishing	16717	19826	23067	22659	24407	20003	17100	12859	11964	11466	9356	9090
2	Mining and quarrying	15265	21944	27024	29250	31526	34984	42899	38936	30967	34506	31328	20250
	A Coal mining	1187	2244	4004	3799	3784	3615	4182	3133	2168	1969	1939	1687
	B Crude petroleum and natural gas production	12276	16761	20083	22380	24309	28341	35819	32904	26750	30269	27379	17101
	C Metal ore mining	1025	1713	1754	1836	1979	1685	1481	1476	1334	1525	1325	1013
	D Other mining	776	1226	1183	1235	1454	1342	1416	1423	715	744	685	448
3	Manufacturing	51886	56405	61893	69528	73843	75341	74785	67514	55385	65185	72852	68443
	A Manufacturing of food, beverages and tobacco	4831	5363	5931	6297	6224	6454	6292	6555	5565	5893	6328	6142
	B Textile, wearing apparel and leather industries	2664	2184	2682	2630	2451	2509	2256	1868	1874	2265	2007	1901
	C Manufacture of wood, and wood products, including furniture	1835	2299	2885	2962	2989	2637	2070	1610	1494	2006	2078	2426
	D Manufacture of paper and paper products, printing and publishing	5017	5577	6297	7073	7732	7982	6780	7029	6656	7347	8784	8913
	E Manufacture of chemicals and chemical petroleum, coal, rubber and plastic products	12105	14889	15238	15332	16129	15332	16114	16679	12175	12174	12797	11481
	F Manufacture of non-metalic mineral products except products of petroleum and coal	2182	2451	2279	3172	3053	3259	2433	2014	1521	2031	2477	2188
	G Basic metal industries	5798	6383	5881	6082	6322	6082	6202	4496	3597	3382	3737	3276
	H Manufacture of fabricated metal products, machinery and equipment	16913	16782	19964	25270	28191	30304	32050	26738	22056	29556	34129	31485
	I Other manufacturing industries	541	476	735	711	751	782	588	525	446	531	513	630
4	Electricity, gas and water	24349	23571	24590	23582	22908	25357	24672	22870	21188	24137	32902	30963
5	Construction	7476	8001	8367	10830	10310	8433	8814	3428	3493	4251	5218	5718
6	Wholesale and retail trade, restaurants and hotels	24328	26458	28428	35555	38548	34178	38473	38848	48207	58861	62013	63584
	A Wholesale and retail trade	21394	24526	26463	33145	35435	30875	34720	34902	43217	52354	55114	56680
	B Restaurants and hotels	2934	1932	1966	2411	3113	3303	3753	3945	4990	6507	6900	6904
	Restaurants	...	...	...	...	...	...	...	...	...	...	...	...
	Hotels and other lodging places	2934	1932	1966	2411	3113	3303	3753	3945	4990	6507	6900	6904
7	Transport, storage and communication	32338	34583	40817	49547	54757	51380	49091	43287	44132	44318	44586	46024
	A Transport and storage	16077	17913	20060	24448	25483	23990	20997	16753	17435	16614	15270	14819
	B Communication	16262	16670	20757	25099	29274	27390	28094	26534	26696	27704	29316	31205
8	Finance, insurance, real estate and business services	123216	118661	171725	184527	199450	169942	161040	145479	182197	229938	245425	268617
	A Financial institutions	5862	9113	10327	11655	12852	13312	14049	14722	17709	27031	33259	37465
	B Insurance	1125	1081	1152	1363	1478	1799	1854	1824	2237	6628	11004	14929
	C Real estate and business services	116229	108467	160246	171509	185119	154830	145137	128933	162251	196280	201161	216223
	Real estate except dwellings	17536	12253	19925	23212	30298	29512	31034	32156	36008	40431	41917	40374
	Dwellings	98693	96214	140321	148297	154821	125318	114103	96777	126244	155849	159244	175849
9	Community, social and personal services	11286	12420	15517	15707	15852	15128	16336	16291	19025	23495	22513	23891
	A Sanitary and similar services	...	...	...	...	...	...	...	...	...	...	...	...
	B Social and related community services	4290	4512	5232	4881	4638	5106	5844	6268	7241	7694	7742	8258

United States

2.12 Gross Fixed Capital Formation by Kind of Activity of Owner, ISIC Divisions, in Constant Prices
(Continued)

Million United States dollars

	1970	1975	1977	1978	1979	1980	1981	1982	1983	1984	1985	1986
					At constant prices of:1980							
Educational services	137	129	164	134	138	198	183	224	267	290	386	468
Medical, dental, other health and veterinary services	2655	2641	3081	2863	3137	3814	4955	5465	6105	6467	6249	6492
C Recreational and cultural services	2018	2326	2434	2645	3107	2879	2738	2536	2591	3445	3897	3717
D Personal and household services	4978	5582	7852	8181	8106	7143	7754	7488	9193	12355	10874	11916
Statistical discrepancy [a]	17131	20396	19883	23044	20700	20387	19418	16138	15785	17671	18952	21283
Total Industries	323993	342265	421311	464229	492300	455132	452628	405650	432342	513828	545146	557863
Producers of Government Services	60577	50688	45033	47101	45452	46417	42521	42760	44307	45062	49792	52174
Private Non-Profit Institutions Serving Households	19093	20789	26297	27883	14331	12718	18415	20447	33389	32154	36062	39028
Statistical discrepancy	-	-1	-	-	-	-1	-	-	-	-	-	-
Total	403663	413741	492641	539213	552083	514266	513564	468857	510038	591044	631000	649065

a) Item 'Statistical discrepancy' refers to government enterprises.

2.13 Stocks of Reproducible Fixed Assets, by Type of Good and Owner, in Current Prices

Thousand Million United States dollars

	TOTAL Gross	TOTAL Net	Total Private Gross	Total Private Net	Public Enterprises Gross	Public Enterprises Net	General Government Gross	General Government Net
				1980				
1 Residential buildings [a]	4155	2718	4070	2661	54	38	31	20
2 Non-residential buildings	2111	1296	1455	886	41	28	614	382
3 Other construction	2578	1564	1036	585	511	333	1032	646
4 Land improvement and plantation and orchard development	...	...	...	...	...	...	...	...
5 Producers' durable goods	2562	1445	2382	1353	24	14	157	79
A Transport equipment	...	...	549	312	...	...	...	...
Passenger cars	...	...	92	63	...	...	...	...
Other	...	...	458	249	...	...	...	...
B Machinery and equipment	...	...	1832	1041	...	...	...	...
6 Breeding stock, dairy cattle, etc.	...	...	...	...	...	...	...	...
Total	11407	7023	8943	5484	630	413	1834	1127
				1981				
1 Residential buildings [a]	4565	2974	4471	2911	60	41	34	21
2 Non-residential buildings	2361	1438	1638	991	45	30	678	417
3 Other construction	2746	1656	1186	672	548	356	1012	628
4 Land improvement and plantation and orchard development	...	...	...	...	...	...	...	...
5 Producers' durable goods	2911	1631	2712	1530	28	16	171	85
A Transport equipment	...	...	605	338	...	...	...	...
Passenger cars	...	...	100	68	...	...	...	...
Other	...	...	505	270	...	...	...	...
B Machinery and equipment	...	...	2107	1192	...	...	...	...
6 Breeding stock, dairy cattle, etc.	...	...	...	...	...	...	...	...
Total	12583	7700	10007	6104	680	444	1895	1152
				1982				
1 Residential buildings [a]	4543	2937	4450	2876	59	40	34	21
2 Non-residential buildings	2450	1480	1709	1027	47	31	694	422
3 Other construction	2811	1685	1256	710	563	364	992	611
4 Land improvement and plantation and orchard development	...	...	...	...	...	...	...	...
5 Producers' durable goods	3138	1736	2928	1629	31	18	179	89
A Transport equipment	...	...	627	344	...	...	...	...
Passenger cars	...	...	105	70	...	...	...	...
Other	...	...	523	274	...	...	...	...
B Machinery and equipment	...	...	2301	1285	...	...	...	...
6 Breeding stock, dairy cattle, etc.	...	...	...	...	...	...	...	...
Total	12941	7838	10343	6242	699	453	1899	1143

United States

2.13 Stocks of Reproducible Fixed Assets, by Type of Good and Owner, in Current Prices
(Continued)

Thousand Million United States dollars

		TOTAL Gross	TOTAL Net	Total Private Gross	Total Private Net	Public Enterprises Gross	Public Enterprises Net	General Government Gross	General Government Net
				1983					
1	Residential buildings [a]	4899	3160	4798	3094	64	43	37	23
2	Non-residential buildings	2651	1585	1862	1109	48	32	740	444
3	Other construction	2822	1682	1225	689	583	373	1015	620
4	Land improvement and plantation and orchard development	...	...	...	...	...	...	...	...
5	Producers' durable goods	3261	1783	3044	1671	34	20	183	92
	A Transport equipment	...	...	650	354	...	...	...	...
	Passenger cars	...	...	117	79	...	...	...	...
	Other	...	...	532	274	...	...	...	...
	B Machinery and equipment	...	...	2394	1317	...	...	...	...
6	Breeding stock, dairy cattle, etc.	...	...	...	...	...	...	...	...
	Total	13632	8209	10929	6563	729	467	1975	1179
				1984					
1	Residential buildings [a]	5203	3358	5096	3289	67	45	39	25
2	Non-residential buildings	2812	1668	2008	1189	51	34	753	445
3	Other construction	2989	1772	1272	713	615	391	1102	669
4	Land improvement and plantation and orchard development	...	...	...	...	...	...	...	...
5	Producers' durable goods	3415	1866	3190	1748	37	22	188	96
	A Transport equipment	...	...	678	372	...	...	...	...
	Passenger cars	...	...	127	88	...	...	...	...
	Other	...	...	550	284	...	...	...	...
	B Machinery and equipment	...	...	2512	1376	...	...	...	...
6	Breeding stock, dairy cattle, etc.	...	...	...	...	...	...	...	...
	Total	14419	8663	11566	6939	770	490	2083	1234
				1985					
1	Residential buildings [a]	5479	3538	5367	3466	70	46	42	26
2	Non-residential buildings	2987	1763	2126	1256	54	35	808	473
3	Other construction	3137	1848	1290	717	648	408	1200	723
4	Land improvement and plantation and orchard development	...	...	...	...	...	...	...	...
5	Producers' durable goods	3558	1942	3321	1815	41	24	196	103
	A Transport equipment	...	...	706	391	...	...	...	...
	Passenger cars	...	...	137	96	...	...	...	...
	Other	...	...	569	295	...	...	...	...
	B Machinery and equipment	...	...	2614	1424	...	...	...	...
6	Breeding stock, dairy cattle, etc.	...	...	...	...	...	...	...	...
	Total	15161	9092	12103	7254	813	513	2245	1325
				1986					
1	Residential buildings [a]	5874	3802	5754	3726	75	48	45	28
2	Non-residential buildings	3152	1850	2264	1330	55	36	832	484
3	Other construction	3167	1852	1301	715	668	419	1198	718
4	Land improvement and plantation and orchard development	...	...	...	...	...	...	...	...
5	Producers' durable goods	3730	2036	3479	1899	45	27	205	110
	A Transport equipment	...	...	739	411	...	...	...	...
	Passenger cars	...	...	150	105	...	...	...	...
	Other	...	...	589	306	...	...	...	...
	B Machinery and equipment	...	...	2740	1488	...	...	...	...
6	Breeding stock, dairy cattle, etc.	...	...	...	...	...	...	...	...
	Total	15922	9539	12798	7670	844	530	2280	1340

a) The estimates of residential buildings of government enterprises and general government are included in the respective columns of item 'Residential buildings' in tables 2.7 and 2.8. These estimates are included in item 'Real estate' in tables 2.9-2.12 and are therefore excluded from the estimates of government enterprises and general government of these tables. This latter classification is followed in tables 2.13-2.16.

United States

2.14 Stocks of Reproducible Fixed Assets, by Type of Good and Owner, in Constant Prices

Thousand Million United States dollars

		TOTAL Gross	TOTAL Net	Total Private Gross	Total Private Net	Public Enterprises Gross	Public Enterprises Net	General Government Gross	General Government Net
		\multicolumn{8}{c}{At constant prices of: 1980}
		\multicolumn{8}{c}{**1980**}
1	Residential buildings [a]	3982	2603	3900	2548	52	36	30	19
2	Non-residential buildings	2018	1239	1391	847	40	27	586	365
3	Other construction	2382	1446	900	504	496	324	986	618
4	Land improvement and plantation and orchard development	...	...	...	...	...	...	...	...
5	Producers' durable goods	2474	1396	2302	1307	23	13	149	75
	A Transport equipment	...	...	512	291	...	...	...	...
	Passenger cars	...	...	89	61	...	...	...	...
	Other	...	...	422	229	...	...	...	...
	B Machinery and equipment	...	...	1791	1016	...	...	...	...
6	Breeding stock, dairy cattle, etc.	...	...	...	...	...	...	...	...
	Total	10856	6684	8494	5206	611	401	1751	1077
		\multicolumn{8}{c}{**1981**}
1	Residential buildings [a]	4061	2644	3977	2588	53	37	30	19
2	Non-residential buildings	2072	1262	1437	869	41	28	593	365
3	Other construction	2441	1478	934	526	508	330	999	621
4	Land improvement and plantation and orchard development	...	...	...	...	...	...	...	...
5	Producers' durable goods	2572	1441	2006	1352	25	14	151	75
	A Transport equipment	...	...	518	290	...	...	...	...
	Passenger cars	...	...	92	62	...	...	...	...
	Other	...	...	426	228	...	...	...	...
	B Machinery and equipment	...	...	1879	1062	...	...	...	...
6	Breeding stock, dairy cattle, etc.	...	...	...	...	...	...	...	...
	Total	11145	6825	8745	5336	628	409	1773	1080
		\multicolumn{8}{c}{**1982**}
1	Residential buildings [a]	4122	2666	4037	2610	54	37	31	19
2	Non-residential buildings	2122	1282	1480	890	42	28	599	364
3	Other construction	2491	1499	962	541	517	334	1012	625
4	Land improvement and plantation and orchard development	...	...	...	...	...	...	...	...
5	Producers' durable goods	2639	1460	2462	1369	26	15	151	76
	A Transport equipment	...	...	518	285	...	...	...	...
	Passenger cars	...	...	94	63	...	...	...	...
	Other	...	...	424	222	...	...	...	...
	B Machinery and equipment	...	...	1944	1085	...	...	...	...
6	Breeding stock, dairy cattle, etc.	...	...	...	...	...	...	...	...
	Total	11374	6907	8940	5410	640	414	1794	1084
		\multicolumn{8}{c}{**1983**}
1	Residential buildings [a]	4210	2716	4123	2659	55	37	32	20
2	Non-residential buildings	2166	1295	1517	904	43	28	605	363
3	Other construction	2533	1511	981	547	526	336	1026	628
4	Land improvement and plantation and orchard development	...	...	...	...	...	...	...	...
5	Producers' durable goods	2711	1485	2530	1392	28	16	153	77
	A Transport equipment	...	...	524	286	...	...	...	...
	Passenger cars	...	...	102	69	...	...	...	...
	Other	...	...	422	218	...	...	...	...
	B Machinery and equipment	...	...	2006	1105	...	...	...	...
6	Breeding stock, dairy cattle, etc.	...	...	...	...	...	...	...	...
	Total	11620	7007	9151	5501	652	417	1817	1088

United States

2.14 Stocks of Reproducible Fixed Assets, by Type of Good and Owner, in Constant Prices
(Continued)

Thousand Million United States dollars

	TOTAL Gross	TOTAL Net	Total Private Gross	Total Private Net	Public Enterprises Gross	Public Enterprises Net	General Government Gross	General Government Net
	\multicolumn{8}{c}{At constant prices of:1980}							
	\multicolumn{8}{c}{**1984**}							
1 Residential buildings [a]	4327	2793	4238	2735	56	37	33	21
2 Non-residential buildings	2218	1315	1563	925	44	29	611	361
3 Other construction	2580	1529	1004	557	535	340	1040	632
4 Land improvement and plantation and orchard development	...	...	...	...	...	...	...	...
5 Producers' durable goods	2812	1541	2627	1444	30	17	155	79
A Transport equipment	...	...	534	294	...	...	...	...
Passenger cars	...	...	107	74	...	...	...	...
Other	...	...	426	220	...	...	...	...
B Machinery and equipment	...	...	2093	1150	...	...	...	...
6 Breeding stock, dairy cattle, etc.	...	...	...	...	...	...	...	...
Total	11936	7177	9432	5662	665	423	1839	1093
	\multicolumn{8}{c}{**1985**}							
1 Residential buildings [a]	4443	2869	4352	2811	57	37	34	21
2 Non-residential buildings	2278	1345	1615	954	45	29	618	361
3 Other construction	2626	1545	1026	565	546	344	1055	636
4 Land improvement and plantation and orchard development	...	...	...	...	...	...	...	...
5 Producers' durable goods	2925	1606	2735	1505	32	19	158	83
A Transport equipment	...	...	545	302	...	...	...	...
Passenger cars	...	...	112	78	...	...	...	...
Other	...	...	432	224	...	...	...	...
B Machinery and equipment	...	...	2190	1202	...	...	...	...
6 Breeding stock, dairy cattle, etc.	...	...	...	...	...	...	...	...
Total	12272	7365	9727	5834	680	429	1864	1102
	\multicolumn{8}{c}{**1986**}							
1 Residential buildings [a]	4576	2961	4483	2901	58	38	35	22
2 Non-residential buildings	2331	1368	1661	975	46	30	625	363
3 Other construction	2662	1551	1033	560	558	350	1071	642
4 Land improvement and plantation and orchard development	...	...	...	...	...	...	...	...
5 Producers' durable goods	3039	1670	2844	1564	35	21	160	86
A Transport equipment	...	...	555	309	...	...	...	...
Passenger cars	...	...	117	82	...	...	...	...
Other	...	...	438	227	...	...	...	...
B Machinery and equipment	...	...	2289	1255	...	...	...	...
6 Breeding stock, dairy cattle, etc.	...	...	...	...	...	...	...	...
Total	12609	7551	10021	6001	697	438	1891	1112

a) The estimates of residential buildings of government enterprises and general government are included in the respective columns of item 'Residential buildings' in tables 2.7 and 2.8. These estimates are included in item 'Real estate' in tables 2.9-2.12 and are therefore excluded from the estimates of government enterprises and general government of these tables. This latter classification is followed in tables 2.13-2.16.

2.15 Stocks of Reproducible Fixed Assets by Kind of Activity, in Current Prices

Thousand Million United States dollars

	1980 Gross	1980 Net	1981 Gross	1981 Net	1982 Gross	1982 Net	1983 Gross	1983 Net	1984 Gross	1984 Net	1985 Gross	1985 Net
1 Residential buildings [a]	4155	2718	4565	2974	4543	2937	4899	3160	5203	3358	5479	3538
2 Non-residential buildings	2111	1296	2361	1438	2450	1480	2651	1585	2812	1668	2987	1763
3 Other construction	2578	1564	2746	1656	2811	1685	2822	1682	2989	1772	3137	1848
A Industries	2757	1653	3100	1854	3249	1935	3365	1991	3571	2103	3727	2186
1 Agriculture	136	83	151	91	155	92	166	97	174	100	179	101
2 Mining and quarrying	272	146	360	199	397	221	331	183	339	186	345	187
3 Manufacturing	367	209	409	232	423	238	454	251	482	263	500	270
4 Electricity, gas and water	436	262	477	285	498	295	519	304	538	312	553	318

United States

2.15 Stocks of Reproducible Fixed Assets by Kind of Activity, in Current Prices
(Continued)

Thousand Million United States dollars

	1980 Gross	1980 Net	1981 Gross	1981 Net	1982 Gross	1982 Net	1983 Gross	1983 Net	1984 Gross	1984 Net	1985 Gross	1985 Net
5 Construction	23	17	25	18	26	19	29	20	31	21	32	21
6 Wholesale and retail trade	217	142	248	162	262	170	289	186	317	203	345	222
7 Transport and communication	376	199	405	216	420	223	438	234	462	248	459	244
8 Finance, etc.	237	148	272	171	292	184	327	205	364	231	404	259
9 Community, social and personal services	142	85	159	95	166	98	182	107	197	115	209	121
Statistical discrepancy ba	552	361	593	386	610	395	631	405	666	424	701	443
B Producers of government services a	1646	1028	1691	1046	1686	1032	1755	1063	1855	1114	2007	1196
C Other producers c	286	178	316	195	326	198	353	212	375	223	390	229
4 Land improvement and development and plantation and orchard development	...	...	...	...	...	...	...	...	...	...	...	...
5 Producers' durable goods	2562	1445	2911	1631	3138	1736	3261	1783	3415	1866	3558	1942
A Industries	2376	1351	2706	1528	2923	1627	3038	1669	3185	1747	3317	1814
1 Agriculture	183	98	202	106	211	106	215	104	212	100	206	93
2 Mining and quarrying	86	50	103	59	112	61	109	56	106	52	103	48
3 Manufacturing	742	425	844	482	910	513	929	513	962	526	998	542
4 Electricity, gas and water	181	103	206	115	221	122	227	123	235	128	251	140
5 Construction	70	41	07	46	07	43	83	39	70	36	77	35
6 Wholesale and retail trade	194	107	218	120	235	129	255	143	281	162	302	175
7 Transport and communication	472	269	540	307	588	331	621	346	652	360	677	369
8 Finance, etc.	281	169	325	193	361	211	386	225	423	249	451	266
9 Community, social and personal services	137	76	155	86	168	92	180	100	197	112	212	122
Statistical discrepancy b	24	14	28	16	31	18	34	20	37	22	41	24
B Producers of government services	157	79	171	85	179	89	183	92	188	96	196	103
C Other producers c	29	15	33	18	37	20	39	21	42	23	45	25
6 Breeding stock, dairy cattle, etc.	...	...	...	...	...	...	...	...	...	...	...	...
Total	11407	7023	12583	7700	12941	7838	13632	8209	14419	8663	15161	9092

	1986 Gross	1986 Net
1 Residential buildings a	5874	3802
2 Non-residential buildings	3152	1850
3 Other construction	3167	1852
A Industries	3879	2262
1 Agriculture	184	102
2 Mining and quarrying	331	173
3 Manufacturing	522	278
4 Electricity, gas and water	569	324
5 Construction	34	22
6 Wholesale and retail trade	376	241
7 Transport and communication	470	250
8 Finance, etc.	446	289
9 Community, social and personal services	223	129
Statistical discrepancy ba	724	455
B Producers of government services a	2030	1202
C Other producers c	410	238
4 Land improvement and development and plantation and orchard development	...	...
5 Producers' durable goods	3730	2036
A Industries	3476	1898
1 Agriculture	197	87
2 Mining and quarrying	97	43
3 Manufacturing	1035	558
4 Electricity, gas and water	269	152

United States

2.15 Stocks of Reproducible Fixed Assets by Kind of Activity, in Current Prices
(Continued)

Thousand Million United States dollars

	1986 Gross	1986 Net
5 Construction	76	35
6 Wholesale and retail trade	329	192
7 Transport and communication	705	380
8 Finance, etc.	493	291
9 Community, social and personal services	230	134
Statistical discrepancy [b]	45	27
B Producers of government services	205	110
C Other producers [c]	49	28
6 Breeding stock, dairy cattle, etc.	...	...
Total	15922	9539

a) The estimates of residential buildings of government enterprises and general government are included in the respective columns of item 'Residential buildings' in tables 2.7 and 2.8. These estimates are included in item 'Real estate' in tables 2.9-2.12 and are therefore excluded from the estimates of government enterprises and general government of these tables. This latter classification is followed in tables 2.13-2.16. b) Item 'Statistical discrepancy' refers to government enterprises. c) Item 'Other producers' consists of non-profit institutions serving individuals.

2.16 Stocks of Reproducible Fixed Assets by Kind of Activity, in Constant Prices

Thousand Million United States dollars

	1980 Gross	1980 Net	1981 Gross	1981 Net	1982 Gross	1982 Net	1983 Gross	1983 Net	1984 Gross	1984 Net	1985 Gross	1985 Net
					At constant prices of:1980							
1 Residential buildings [a]	3982	2603	4061	2644	4122	2666	4210	2716	4327	2793	4443	2869
2 Non-residential buildings	2018	1239	2072	1262	2122	1282	2166	1295	2218	1315	2278	1345
3 Other construction	2382	1446	2441	1478	2491	1499	2533	1511	2580	1529	2626	1545
A Industries	2603	1562	2691	1613	2767	1651	2829	1673	2904	1708	2986	1750
1 Agriculture	130	80	133	80	134	80	136	79	136	78	136	77
2 Mining and quarrying	248	133	269	149	288	160	301	165	316	173	327	177
3 Manufacturing	350	200	359	203	367	206	370	205	375	204	380	205
4 Electricity, gas and water	385	232	395	236	403	239	409	239	416	241	424	244
5 Construction	22	16	22	16	23	16	24	16	24	16	25	16
6 Wholesale and retail trade	207	136	218	142	227	147	235	152	247	158	262	169
7 Transport and communication	362	192	365	194	367	195	368	196	370	197	373	199
8 Finance, etc.	227	142	240	151	255	160	268	169	286	182	309	199
9 Community, social and personal services	136	82	140	83	144	85	148	87	154	89	159	92
Statistical discrepancy [ba]	536	351	550	358	559	362	569	365	579	369	591	373
B Producers of government services [a]	1572	983	1592	986	1612	988	1632	991	1651	993	1673	997
C Other producers [c]	273	171	278	171	282	172	287	173	292	174	296	174
4 Land improvement and development and plantation and orchard development	...	...	...	...	...	...	...	...	...	...	...	...
5 Producers' durable goods	2474	1396	2572	1441	2639	1460	2711	1485	2812	1541	2925	1606
A Industries	2291	1303	2386	1348	2452	1366	2523	1390	2623	1444	2733	1507
1 Agriculture	174	93	175	91	172	86	168	81	163	77	156	71
2 Mining and quarrying	81	47	85	48	87	48	85	44	83	41	80	37
3 Manufacturing	722	414	753	430	775	437	786	435	805	441	828	452
4 Electricity, gas and water	172	98	175	98	178	98	181	98	185	100	197	109
5 Construction	74	39	76	40	71	35	67	31	63	29	61	28
6 Wholesale and retail trade	194	107	202	111	210	116	227	128	250	145	270	158
7 Transport and communication	441	251	460	262	473	266	487	271	499	275	510	277
8 Finance, etc.	276	165	296	176	315	184	340	199	378	224	421	253
9 Community, social and personal services	135	75	140	78	146	80	154	85	167	95	178	103
Statistical discrepancy [b]	23	13	25	14	26	15	28	16	30	17	32	19
B Producers of government services	149	75	151	75	151	76	153	77	155	79	158	83
C Other producers [c]	28	15	29	15	30	16	32	17	34	19	36	20
6 Breeding stock, dairy cattle, etc.	...	...	...	...	...	...	...	...	...	...	...	...
Total	10856	6684	11145	6825	11374	6907	11620	7007	11936	7177	12272	7365

United States

2.16 Stocks of Reproducible Fixed Assets by Kind of Activity, in Constant Prices

Thousand Million United States dollars

		1986 Gross	1986 Net
		At constant prices of:1980	
1	Residential buildings a	4576	2961
2	Non-residential buildings	2331	1368
3	Other construction	2662	1551
	A Industries	3050	1775
	1 Agriculture	136	75
	2 Mining and quarrying	326	170
	3 Manufacturing	383	204
	4 Electricity, gas and water	432	246
	5 Construction	25	16
	6 Wholesale and retail trade	275	176
	7 Transport and communication	375	200
	8 Finance, etc.	331	214
	9 Community, social and personal services	164	94
	Statistical discrepancy ba	604	379
	B Producers of government services a	1696	1005
	C Other producers c	301	175
4	Land improvement and development and plantation and orchard development	...	...
5	Producers' durable goods	3039	1670
	A Industries	2846	1569
	1 Agriculture	149	66
	2 Mining and quarrying	76	33
	3 Manufacturing	847	458
	4 Electricity, gas and water	206	116
	5 Construction	59	27
	6 Wholesale and retail trade	293	173
	7 Transport and communication	521	281
	8 Finance, etc.	469	283
	9 Community, social and personal services	191	111
	Statistical discrepancy b	35	21
	B Producers of government services	160	86
	C Other producers c	39	22
6	Breeding stock, dairy cattle, etc.	...	...
	Total	12609	7551

a) The estimates of residential buildings of government enterprises and general government are included in the respective columns of item 'Residential buildings' in tables 2.7 and 2.8. These estimates are included in item 'Real estate' in tables 2.9-2.12 and are therefore excluded from the estimates of government enterprises and general government of these tables. This latter classification is followed in tables 2.13-2.16.
b) Item 'Statistical discrepancy' refers to government enterprises.
c) Item 'Other producers' consists of non-profit institutions serving individuals.

2.17 Exports and Imports of Goods and Services, Detail

Million United States dollars

	1970	1975	1977	1978	1979	1980	1981	1982	1983	1984	1985	1986
Exports of Goods and Services												
1 Exports of merchandise, f.o.b. a	44280	109359	122820	144454	182986	224672	237894	213572	205637	223699	220205	224328
2 Transport and communication	3669	6879	8456	9739	12127	14209	15671	15491	15627	16837	17106	18752
3 Insurance service charges	...	...	...	...	...	...	...	...	...	...	...	...
4 Other commodities	8492	14736	17466	19725	19060	22908	25410	28190	29913	29341	29861	31924
5 Adjustments of merchandise exports to change-of-ownership basis	...	...	...	...	...	...	...	...	...	...	...	...
6 Direct purchases in the domestic market by non-residential households	2663	5372	6982	8095	9402	11558	14013	13651	12828	13373	13828	15178
7 Direct purchases in the domestic market by extraterritorial bodies	...	...	...	...	...	...	...	...	...	...	...	...
Total Exports of Goods and Services	59104	136346	155724	182013	223575	273347	292988	270904	264005	283250	281000	290182

United States

2.17 Exports and Imports of Goods and Services, Detail
(Continued)

Million United States dollars

	1970	1975	1977	1978	1979	1980	1981	1982	1983	1984	1985	1986
					Imports of Goods and Services							
1 Imports of merchandise, c.i.f. [a]	40855	99000	151851	176477	211930	247460	266462	249474	271341	334250	341016	367507
A Imports of merchandise, f.o.b. [a]	40855	99000	151851	176477	211930	247460	266462	249474	271341	334250	341016	367507
B Transport of services on merchandise imports	...	...	...	...	...	...	...	...	...	...	...	...
C Insurance service charges on merchandise imports	...	...	...	...	...	...	...	...	...	...	...	...
2 Adjustments of merchandise imports to change-of-ownership basis	...	...	...	...	...	...	...	...	...	...	...	...
3 Other transport and communication	2843	5708	7972	9124	10906	11790	12474	11710	12222	14843	15852	17099
4 Other insurance service charges	...	...	...	...	...	...	...	...	...	...	...	...
5 Other commodities	4036	5830	7694	9784	11035	12755	14139	14766	14479	15309	15470	17078
6 Direct purchases abroad by government	...	...	...	...	...	...	...	...	...	...	...	...
7 Direct purchases abroad by resident households	7443	10087	11532	12803	14276	16069	17446	19187	21755	25039	27611	27657
Total Imports of Goods and Services	55177	120625	179049	208188	248147	288074	310521	295137	319797	389441	399949	429341
Balance of Goods and Services	3927	15721	-23325	-26175	-24572	-14727	-17533	-24233	-55792	-106191	-118949	-139159
Total Imports and Balance of Goods and Services	59104	136346	155724	182013	223575	273347	292988	270904	264005	283250	281000	290182

a) Valuation basis is essentially Free Along Side (F.A.S.).

3.12 General Government Income and Outlay Account: Total and Subsectors

Million United States dollars

	1980					1981				
	Total General Government	Central Government	State or Provincial Government	Local Government	Social Security Funds	Total General Government	Central Government	State or Provincial Government	Local Government	Social Security Funds
					Receipts					
1 Operating surplus	...	...	...	...	...	...	...	...	...	...
2 Property and entrepreneurial income	30344	10188	...	19307	849	38231	13466	...	23777	988
A Withdrawals from public quasi-corporations	...	...	...	...	...	...	...	...	...	...
B Interest	30247	10188	...	19210	849	38105	13466	...	23651	988
C Dividends	97	...	...	97	...	126	...	...	126	...
D Net land rent and royalties	...	...	...	...	...	...	...	...	...	...
3 Taxes, fees and contributions	769959	360490	...	242852	166617	881303	413794	...	271380	196129
A Indirect taxes	213281	38822	...	174459	...	251476	56183	...	195293	...
B Direct taxes	384793	321436	...	63357	...	427409	357352	...	70057	...
Income	378496	321436	...	57060	...	420706	357352	...	63354	...
Other	6297	...	...	6297	...	6703	...	...	6703	...
C Social security contributions	166617	...	...	...	166617	196129	...	...	...	196129
D Fees, fines and penalties	5268	232	...	5036	...	6289	259	...	6030	...
4 Other current transfers	26422	31690	...	88990	5626	30134	35875	...	88257	6408
A Casualty insurance claims	...	...	...	...	...	...	...	...	...	...
B Transfers from other government subsectors	...	5268	...	88990	5626	...	5741	...	88257	6408
C Transfers from the rest of the world	21	21	...	-	...	34	34	...	-	...
D Other transfers, except imputed	2731	2731	...	...	...	2910	2910	...	...	...
E Imputed unfunded employee pension and welfare contributions	23670	23670	...	...	...	27190	27190	...	...	...
Total Current Receipts [ab]	826725	402368	...	351149	173092	949668	463135	...	383414	203525
					Disbursements					
1 Government final consumption expenditure	473722	207081	...	266641	5580	525613	236000	...	289613	6106
2 Property income	84750	65392	...	19358	...	110997	88153	...	22844	...
A Interest	84750	65392	...	19358	...	110997	88153	...	22844	...
B Net land rent and royalties	...	...	...	...	...	...	...	...	...	...
3 Subsidies	10723	10369	...	354	...	12182	11780	...	402	...

United States

3.12 General Government Income and Outlay Account: Total and Subsectors
(Continued)

Million United States dollars

		1980				1981			
	Total General Government	Central Government	State or Provincial Government	Local Government	Social Security Funds	Total General Government	Central Government	State or Provincial Government	Local Government	Social Security Funds
4 Other current transfers	300631	166801	...	47849	180285	340667	172771	...	53248	208948
A Casualty insurance premiums, net	...	...	...	...	...	...	...	...	...	...
B Transfers to other government subsectors	...	94304	...	...	...	...	94300	...	...	...
C Social security benefits	180285	...	...	...	180285	208948	...	...	...	208948
D Social assistance grants	89310	41501	...	47809	...	97367	44119	...	53248	...
E Unfunded employee pension and welfare benefits [c]	23710	23670	...	40	...	27131	27131	...	-	...
F Transfers to private non-profit institutions serving households	...	...	...	...	...	...	...	...	...	...
G Other transfers n.e.c.	...	...	...	...	...	...	...	...	...	...
H Transfers to the rest of the world	7326	7326	...	...	...	7221	7221	...	...	...
Net saving	-43101	-47275	...	16947	-12773	-39791	-45569	...	17307	-11529
Total Current Disbursements and Net Saving [ab]	826725	402368	...	351149	173092	949668	463135	...	383414	203525

		1982				1983			
	Total General Government	Central Government	State or Provincial Government	Local Government	Social Security Funds	Total General Government	Central Government	State or Provincial Government	Local Government	Social Security Funds

Receipts

1 Operating surplus	...	...	...	...	...	...	...	...	...	...
2 Property and entrepreneurial income	43721	16157	...	26309	1255	46553	18079	...	26976	1498
A Withdrawals from public quasi-corporations	...	...	...	...	...	...	...	...	...	...
B Interest	43567	16157	...	26155	1255	46377	18079	...	26800	1498
C Dividends	154	...	...	154	...	176	...	...	176	...
D Net land rent and royalties	...	...	...	...	...	...	...	...	...	...
3 Taxes, fees and contributions	893825	393973	...	290713	209139	948250	401515	...	320476	226259
A Indirect taxes	258835	48085	...	210750	...	282560	51599	...	230961	...
B Direct taxes	418758	345577	...	73181	...	431457	349435	...	82022	...
Income	411498	345577	...	65921	...	423616	349435	...	74181	...
Other	7260	...	...	7260	...	7841	...	...	7841	...
C Social security contributions	209139	...	...	...	209139	226259	...	...	...	226259
D Fees, fines and penalties	7093	311	...	6782	...	7974	481	...	7493	...
4 Other current transfers	32947	38917	...	84271	6322	34863	41370	...	86683	5963
A Casualty insurance claims	...	...	...	...	...	...	...	...	...	...
B Transfers from other government subsectors	...	5970	...	84271	6322	...	6507	...	86683	5963
C Transfers from the rest of the world	117	117	...	-	...	35	35	...	-	...
D Other transfers, except imputed	3093	3093	...	...	...	3221	3221	...	...	...
E Imputed unfunded employee pension and welfare contributions	29737	29737	...	...	...	31607	31607	...	...	...
Total Current Receipts [ab]	970493	449047	...	401293	216716	1029670	460964	...	434135	233720

Disbursements

1 Government final consumption expenditure	574090	264347	...	309743	6385	617003	289218	...	327785	6971
2 Property income	130684	103559	...	27125	...	147964	115617	...	32347	...
A Interest	130684	103559	...	27125	...	147964	115617	...	32347	...
B Net land rent and royalties	...	...	...	...	...	...	...	...	...	...
3 Subsidies	15483	15029	...	454	...	22175	21666	...	509	...

United States

3.12 General Government Income and Outlay Account: Total and Subsectors
(Continued)

Million United States dollars

		1982					1983			
		Total General Government	Central Government	State or Provincial Government	Local Government	Social Security Funds	Total General Government	Central Government	State or Provincial Government	Local Government	Social Security Funds
4	Other current transfers	379862	171115	...	56911	242014	408663	178524	...	61282	261039
	A Casualty insurance premiums, net	...	...	...	...	...	...	...	...	...	...
	B Transfers to other government subsectors	...	90178	...	...	...	...	92182	...	...	...
	C Social security benefits	242014	...	...	...	242014	261039	...	...	...	261039
	D Social assistance grants	99653	42742	...	56911	...	106850	45568	...	61282	...
	E Unfunded employee pension and welfare benefits [c]	29741	29741	...	-	...	32052	32052	...	-	...
	F Transfers to private non-profit institutions serving households	...	...	...	...	...	...	...	...	...	...
	G Other transfers n.e.c.	...	...	...	...	...	...	...	...	...	...
	H Transfers to the rest of the world	8454	8454	...	...	...	8722	8722	...	...	...
Net saving		-129626	-105003	...	7060	-31683	-166139	-144061	...	12212	-34290
Total Current Disbursements and Net Saving [ab]		970493	449047	...	401293	216716	1029670	460964	...	434135	233720

		1984					1985			
		Total General Government	Central Government	State or Provincial Government	Local Government	Social Security Funds	Total General Government	Central Government	State or Provincial Government	Local Government	Social Security Funds

Receipts

1	Operating surplus	...	...	...	...	...	...	...	...	...	...
2	Property and entrepreneurial income	53180	20274	...	31088	1818	59379	21292	...	36052	2035
	A Withdrawals from public quasi-corporations	...	...	...	...	...	...	...	...	...	...
	B Interest	53016	20274	...	30924	1818	59164	21292	...	35837	2035
	C Dividends	164	...	...	164	...	215	...	...	215	...
	D Net land rent and royalties	...	...	...	...	...	...	...	...	...	...
3	Taxes, fees and contributions	1054460	435170	...	361638	257654	1142590	471501	...	389441	281648
	A Indirect taxes	313914	55718	...	258196	...	333151	55226	...	277925	...
	B Direct taxes	473774	378962	...	94812	...	517277	415613	...	101664	...
	Income	465222	378962	...	86260	...	508092	415613	...	92479	...
	Other	8552	...	...	8552	...	9185	...	...	9185	...
	C Social security contributions	257654	...	...	...	257654	281648	...	...	...	281648
	D Fees, fines and penalties	9120	490	...	8630	...	10514	662	...	9852	...
4	Other current transfers	34698	41373	...	94028	9550	37709	44913	...	100173	12037
	A Casualty insurance claims	...	...	...	...	...	...	...	...	...	...
	B Transfers from other government subsectors	...	6675	...	94028	9550	...	7204	...	100173	12037
	C Transfers from the rest of the world	38	38	...	-	...	52	52	...	-	...
	D Other transfers, except imputed	3371	3371	...	...	...	3401	3401	...	...	...
	E Imputed unfunded employee pension and welfare contributions	31289	31289	...	...	...	34256	34256	...	...	...
Total Current Receipts [ab]		1142340	496817	...	486754	269022	1239680	537706	...	525666	295720

Disbursements

1	Government final consumption expenditure	670111	315613	...	354498	7148	728307	343820	...	384487	7699
2	Property income	176821	139775	...	37046	...	198524	156076	...	42448	...
	A Interest	176821	139775	...	37046	...	198524	156076	...	42448	...
	B Net land rent and royalties	...	...	...	...	...	...	...	...	...	...
3	Subsidies	22730	22120	...	610	...	22912	22222	...	690	...

United States

3.12 General Government Income and Outlay Account: Total and Subsectors
(Continued)

Million United States dollars

		1984				1985			
	Total General Government	Central Government	State or Provincial Government	Local Government	Social Security Funds	Total General Government	Central Government	State or Provincial Government	Local Government	Social Security Funds
4 Other current transfers	418561	191046	...	65352	265268	448739	206412	...	70288	283754
A Casualty insurance premiums, net	...	...	...	...	...	...	...	...	...	...
B Transfers to other government subsectors	...	103105	...	...	...	...	111715	...	...	...
C Social security benefits	265268	...	...	...	265268	283754	...	...	...	283754
D Social assistance grants	111299	45947	...	65352	...	117008	46720	...	70288	...
E Unfunded employee pension and welfare benefits [c]	31069	31069	...	-	...	34486	34486	...	-	...
F Transfers to private non-profit institutions serving households	...	...	...	...	...	...	...	...	...	...
G Other transfers n.e.c.	...	...	...	...	...	...	...	...	...	...
H Transfers to the rest of the world	10925	10925	...	...	...	13491	13491	...	...	...
Net saving	-145883	-171737	...	29248	-3394	-158804	-190824	...	27753	4267
Total Current Disbursements and Net Saving [ab]	1142340	496817	...	486754	269022	1239680	537706	...	525666	295720

		1986			
	Total General Government	Central Government	State or Provincial Government	Local Government	Social Security Funds
			Receipts		
1 Operating surplus	...	...	...	...	...
2 Property and entrepreneurial income	64101	21593	...	40274	2234
A Withdrawals from public quasi-corporations	...	...	...	...	...
B Interest	63851	21593	...	40024	2234
C Dividends	250	...	...	250	...
D Net land rent and royalties	...	...	...	...	...
3 Taxes, fees and contributions	1206640	490500	...	415747	300394
A Indirect taxes	347720	50881	...	296839	...
B Direct taxes	546340	438914	...	107426	...
Income	536526	438914	...	97612	...
Other	9814	...	...	9814	...
C Social security contributions	300394	...	...	...	300394
D Fees, fines and penalties	12187	705	...	11482	...
4 Other current transfers	38682	45878	...	107374	14852
A Casualty insurance claims	...	...	...	...	...
B Transfers from other government subsectors	...	7196	...	107374	14852
C Transfers from the rest of the world	97	97	...	-	...
D Other transfers, except imputed	3374	3374	...	...	...
E Imputed unfunded employee pension and welfare contributions	35211	35211	...	...	...
Total Current Receipts [ab]	1309420	557971	...	563395	317480
			Disbursements		
1 Government final consumption expenditure	778586	365124	...	413462	7720
2 Property income	210435	162435	...	48000	...
A Interest	210435	162435	...	48000	...
B Net land rent and royalties	...	...	...	...	...
3 Subsidies	26307	25500	...	807	...

1583

United States

3.12 General Government Income and Outlay Account: Total and Subsectors
(Continued)

Million United States dollars

1986

	Total General Government	Central Government	State or Provincial Government	Local Government	Social Security Funds
4 Other current transfers	474412	219103	...	76022	300989
A Casualty insurance premiums, net	...	...	...	...	...
B Transfers to other government subsectors	...	121702	...	...	...
C Social security benefits	300989	...	...	...	300989
D Social assistance grants	124010	47988	...	76022	...
E Unfunded employee pension and welfare benefits c	35211	35211	...	-	...
F Transfers to private non-profit institutions serving households	...	...	...	...	...
G Other transfers n.e.c.	...	...	...	...	...
H Transfers to the rest of the world	14202	14202	...	...	...
Net saving	-180316	-214191	...	25104	8771
Total Current Disbursements and Net Saving ab	1309420	557971	...	563395	317480

a) State or provincial government is included in local government.
b) Intergovernmental transfers (not shown separately) are included in column 1. Therefore, column 1 is not equal to the sum of columns 2, 3, 4 and 5.
c) Item 'Unfunded employee pension and welfare benefits' also includes wage accruals less disbursements.

3.13 General Government Capital Accumulation Account: Total and Subsectors

Million United States dollars

	1980					1981				
	Total General Government	Central Government	State or Provincial Government	Local Government	Social Security Funds	Total General Government	Central Government	State or Provincial Government	Local Government	Social Security Funds

Finance of Gross Accumulation

1 Gross saving	-3182	-39291	...	48882	-12773	2679	-36833	...	51041	-11529
A Consumption of fixed capital	39919	7984	...	31935	...	42470	8736	...	33734	...
B Net saving	-43101	-47275	...	16947	-12773	-39791	-45569	...	17307	-11529
2 Capital transfers	9988	7724	...	2264	...	10446	8075	...	2371	...
A From other government subsectors	...	...	...	...	...	...	...	...	...	...
B From other resident sectors	8836	6572	...	2264	...	9353	6982	...	2371	...
C From rest of the world	1152	1152	...	...	...	1093	1093	...	...	...
Finance of Gross Accumulation a	6806	-31567	...	51146	-12773	13125	-28758	...	53412	-11529

Gross Accumulation

1 Gross capital formation	48551	10195	...	38356	...	50890	14269	...	36621	...
A Increase in stocks	1290	1059	...	231	...	5141	4993	...	148	...
B Gross fixed capital formation	47261	9136	...	38125	...	45749	9276	...	36473	...
Own account	1396	107	...	1289	...	1299	98	...	1201	...
Other	45865	9029	...	36836	...	44450	9178	...	35272	...
2 Purchases of land, net	2377	342	...	2035	...	2384	165	...	2219	...
3 Purchases of intangible assets, net	-4799	-4376	...	-423	...	-6027	-5706	...	-321	...
4 Capital transfers	-	-	...	...	...	-	-	...	...	...
A To other government subsectors	...	...	...	...	...	...	...	...	...	...
B To other resident sectors	...	...	...	...	...	...	...	...	...	...
C To rest of the world	-	-	...	...	...	-	-	...	...	...
Net lending b	-39323	-37728	...	11178	-12773	-34122	-37486	...	14893	-11529
Gross Accumulation a	6806	-31567	...	51146	-12773	13125	-28758	...	53412	-11529

	1982					1983				
	Total General Government	Central Government	State or Provincial Government	Local Government	Social Security Funds	Total General Government	Central Government	State or Provincial Government	Local Government	Social Security Funds

Finance of Gross Accumulation

1 Gross saving	-86029	-95783	...	41437	-31683	-121550	-134659	...	47399	-34290
A Consumption of fixed capital	43597	9220	...	34377	...	44589	9402	...	35187	...
B Net saving	-129626	-105003	...	7060	-31683	-166139	-144061	...	12212	-34290
2 Capital transfers	10207	7619	...	2588	...	8455	5889	...	2566	...

United States

3.13 General Government Capital Accumulation Account: Total and Subsectors
(Continued)

Million United States dollars

	1982					1983				
	Total General Government	Central Government	State or Provincial Government	Local Government	Social Security Funds	Total General Government	Central Government	State or Provincial Government	Local Government	Social Security Funds
A From other government subsectors	...	...	...	...	...	...	...	...	...	...
B From other resident sectors	10207	7619	...	2588	...	8455	5889	...	2566	...
C From rest of the world	-	-	...	...	...	-	-	...	...	...
Finance of Gross Accumulation a	-75822	-88164	...	44025	-31683	-113095	-128770	...	49965	-34290
Gross Accumulation										
1 Gross capital formation	49711	13629	...	36082	...	52835	14654	...	38181	...
A Increase in stocks	2776	2739	...	37	...	3468	3099	...	369	...
B Gross fixed capital formation	46935	10890	...	36045	...	49367	11555	...	37812	...
Own account	1209	90	...	1119	...	1212	89	...	1123	...
Other	45726	10800	...	34926	...	48155	11466	...	36689	...
2 Purchases of land, net	2354	146	...	2208	...	2327	68	...	2259	...
3 Purchases of intangible assets, net	-3990	-3813	...	-177	...	-5181	-5051	...	-130	...
4 Capital transfers	-	-	...	...	...	-	-	...	...	...
A To other government subsectors	...	...	...	...	...	...	...	...	...	...
B To other resident sectors	...	...	...	...	...	...	...	...	...	...
C To rest of the world	-	-	...	...	...	-	-	...	...	...
Net lending b	-123897	-98126	...	5912	-31683	-163076	-138441	...	9655	-34290
Gross Accumulation a	-75822	-88164	...	44025	-31683	-113095	-128770	...	49965	-34290

	1984					1985				
	Total General Government	Central Government	State or Provincial Government	Local Government	Social Security Funds	Total General Government	Central Government	State or Provincial Government	Local Government	Social Security Funds
Finance of Gross Accumulation										
1 Gross saving	-99668	-162135	...	65861	-3394	-109190	-180906	...	67449	4267
A Consumption of fixed capital	46215	9602	...	36613	...	49614	9918	...	39696	...
B Net saving	-145883	-171737	...	29248	-3394	-158804	-190824	...	27753	4267
2 Capital transfers	8487	6096	...	2391	...	9049	6487	...	2562	...
A From other government subsectors	...	...	...	...	...	...	...	...	...	...
B From other resident sectors	8487	6096	...	2391	...	9049	6487	...	2562	...
C From rest of the world	-	-	...	...	...	-	-	...	...	...
Finance of Gross Accumulation a	-91181	-156039	...	68252	-3394	-100141	-174419	...	70011	4267
Gross Accumulation										
1 Gross capital formation	53383	12275	...	41108	...	61956	14424	...	47532	...
A Increase in stocks	2143	2011	...	132	...	1717	1499	...	218	...
B Gross fixed capital formation	51240	10264	...	40976	...	60239	12925	...	47314	...
Own account	1307	84	...	1223	...	1522	85	...	1437	...
Other	40033	10180	...	39753	...	58717	12840	...	45877	...
2 Purchases of land, net	2744	150	...	2594	...	3006	216	...	2790	...
3 Purchases of intangible assets, net	-4259	-4083	...	-176	...	-1510	-1370	...	-140	...
4 Capital transfers	-	-	...	...	...	-	-	...	...	...
A To other government subsectors	...	...	...	...	...	...	...	...	...	...
B To other resident sectors	...	...	...	...	...	...	...	...	...	...
C To rest of the world	-	-	...	...	...	-	-	...	...	...
Net lending b	-143049	-164381	...	24726	-3394	-163593	-187689	...	19829	4267
Gross Accumulation a	-91181	-156039	...	68252	-3394	-100141	-174419	...	70011	4267

	1986				
	Total General Government	Central Government	State or Provincial Government	Local Government	Social Security Funds
Finance of Gross Accumulation					
1 Gross saving	-128874	-204106	...	66461	8771
A Consumption of fixed capital	51442	10085	...	41357	...
B Net saving	-180316	-214191	...	25104	8771
2 Capital transfers	9888	7089	...	2799	...

United States

3.13 General Government Capital Accumulation Account: Total and Subsectors
(Continued)

Million United States dollars

	1986				
	Total General Government	Central Government	State or Provincial Government	Local Government	Social Security Funds
A From other government subsectors	...	...	...	...	...
B From other resident sectors	9888	7089	...	2799	...
C From rest of the world	-	-	...	...	...
Finance of Gross Accumulation a	-118986	-197017	...	69260	8771
	Gross Accumulation				
1 Gross capital formation	64402	11118	...	53284	...
A Increase in stocks	57	520	...	-463	...
B Gross fixed capital formation	64345	10598	...	53747	...
Own account	1585	81	...	1504	...
Other	62760	10517	...	52243	...
2 Purchases of land, net	2927	192	...	2735	...
3 Purchases of intangible assets, net	-3293	-3173	...	-120	...
4 Capital transfers	-	-	...	...	...
A To other government subsectors	...	...	...	...	...
B To other resident sectors	...	...	...	...	...
C To rest of the world	-	-	...	...	...
Net lending b	-183022	-205154	...	13361	8771
Gross Accumulation a	-118986	-197017	...	69260	8771

a) State or provincial government is included in local government.
b) Net lending of the capital accumulation account and the capital finance account have not been reconciled and are different due to different statistical sources.

3.14 General Government Capital Finance Account, Total and Subsectors

Million United States dollars

	1980					1981				
	Total General Government	Central Government	State or Provincial Government	Local Government	Social Security Funds	Total General Government	Central Government	State or Provincial Government	Local Government	Social Security Funds
	Acquisition of Financial Assets									
1 Gold and SDRs	4961	4961	...	...	...	4736	4736	...	...	...
2 Currency and transferable deposits	-3143	-2536	...	-607	...	-1099	375	...	-1474	...
3 Other deposits	-1926	-210	...	-1716	...	7307	-142	...	7449	...
4 Bills and bonds, short term	2132	-	...	2132	...	-6984	-	...	-6984	...
5 Bonds, long term	...	...	...	...	...	...	...	...	...	...
6 Corporate equity securities	...	...	...	...	...	...	...	...	...	...
7 Short-term loans, n.e.c.	16180	16180	...	...	...	19107	19107	...	...	...
8 Long-term loans, n.e.c.	17288	7506	...	9782	...	12621	4939	...	7682	...
9 Other receivables	3778	3778	...	...	...	2542	2542	...	...	...
10 Other assets	-3286	-4340	...	1054	...	-8154	-9130	...	976	...
Total Acquisition of Financial Assets	35984	25339	...	10645	...	30076	22427	...	7649	...
	Incurrence of Liabilities									
1 Currency and transferable deposits	...	...	...	...	...	...	...	...	...	...
2 Other deposits	...	...	...	...	...	...	...	...	...	...
3 Bills and bonds, short term	38398	36661	...	1737	...	24208	23070	...	1138	...
4 Bonds, long term	57201	42639	...	14562	...	68821	64412	...	4409	...
5 Short-term loans, n.e.c.	924	-	...	924	...	1238	-	...	1238	...
6 Long-term loans, n.e.c.	-104	-104	...	...	...	-109	-109	...	...	...
7 Other payables	3253	1272	...	1981	...	1585	478	...	1107	...
8 Other liabilities	8187	8187	...	...	...	12334	12334	...	...	...
Total Incurrence of Liabilities	107859	88655	...	19204	...	108077	100185	...	7892	...
Net Lending a	-71875	-63316	...	-8559	...	-78001	-77758	...	-243	...
Incurrence of Liabilities and Net Worth	35984	25339	...	10645	...	30076	22427	...	7649	...

United States

3.14 General Government Capital Finance Account, Total and Subsectors

Million United States dollars

	1982					1983				
	Total General Government	Central Government	State or Provincial Government	Local Government	Social Security Funds	Total General Government	Central Government	State or Provincial Government	Local Government	Social Security Funds

Acquisition of Financial Assets

1 Gold and SDRs	4438	4438	...	...	...	2892	2892	...	...	...
2 Currency and transferable deposits	4874	6429	...	-1555	...	-8943	-8263	...	-680	...
3 Other deposits	11644	472	...	11172	...	531	-451	...	982	...
4 Bills and bonds, short term	6755	-	...	6755	...	27488	-	...	27488	...
5 Bonds, long term	...	...	...	...	...	...	...	...	...	...
6 Corporate equity securities	...	...	...	...	...	...	...	...	...	...
7 Short-term loans, n.e.c.	13572	13572	...	...	...	8435	8435	...	...	...
8 Long-term loans, n.e.c.	7603	2364	...	5239	...	9106	1220	...	7886	...
9 Other receivables	4792	4792	...	...	...	3766	3766	...	...	...
10 Other assets	-9964	-8556	...	-1408	...	7929	6003	...	1926	...
Total Acquisition of Financial Assets	43714	23511	...	20203	...	51204	13602	...	37602	...

Incurrence of Liabilities

1 Currency and transferable deposits	...	...	...	...	...	...	...	...	...	...
2 Other deposits	...	...	...	...	...	...	...	...	...	...
3 Bills and bonds, short term	71679	64948	...	6731	...	43539	45020	...	-1481	...
4 Bonds, long term	110284	96434	...	13850	...	176012	141618	...	34394	...
5 Short-term loans, n.e.c.	967	-	...	967	...	1109	-	...	1109	...
6 Long-term loans, n.e.c.	-119	-119	...	...	...	-81	-81	...	...	...
7 Other payables	2620	1682	...	938	...	3650	2858	...	792	...
8 Other liabilities	13734	13734	...	...	...	16720	16720	...	...	...
Total Incurrence of Liabilities	199165	176679	...	22486	...	240949	206135	...	34814	...
Net Lending [a]	-155451	-153168	...	-2283	...	-189745	-192533	...	2788	...
Incurrence of Liabilities and Net Worth	43714	23511	...	20203	...	51204	13602	...	37602	...

	1984					1985				
	Total General Government	Central Government	State or Provincial Government	Local Government	Social Security Funds	Total General Government	Central Government	State or Provincial Government	Local Government	Social Security Funds

Acquisition of Financial Assets

1 Gold and SDRs	2596	2596	...	...	...	1907	1907	...	...	...
2 Currency and transferable deposits	10294	5263	...	5031	...	14062	12991	...	1071	...
3 Other deposits	10270	532	...	9738	...	19693	40	...	19653	...
4 Bills and bonds, short term	17633	-	...	17633	...	80485	-	...	80485	...
5 Bonds, long term	...	...	...	...	...	...	...	...	...	...
6 Corporate equity securities	...	...	...	...	...	...	...	...	...	...
7 Short-term loans, n.e.c.	16597	16597	...	...	...	14928	14928	...	...	...
8 Long-term loans, n.e.c.	10704	469	...	10235	...	11649	1841	...	9808	...
9 Other receivables	5082	5082	...	...	...	3679	3679	...	...	...
10 Other assets	5900	2047	...	3853	...	-1480	-2735	...	1255	...
Total Acquisition of Financial Assets	79076	32586	...	46490	...	144923	32651	...	112272	...

Incurrence of Liabilities

1 Currency and transferable deposits	...	...	...	...	...	...	...	...	...	...
2 Other deposits	...	...	...	...	...	...	...	...	...	...
3 Bills and bonds, short term	26412	30068	...	-3656	...	69014	67712	...	1302	...
4 Bonds, long term	192176	168834	...	23342	...	238283	155978	...	82305	...
5 Short-term loans, n.e.c.	7741	...	...	7741	...	8179	...	...	8179	...
6 Long-term loans, n.e.c.	-100	-100	...	...	...	-69	-69	...	...	...
7 Other payables	4015	3033	...	982	...	5475	4392	...	1083	...
8 Other liabilities	23615	23615	...	...	...	24174	24174	...	...	...
Total Incurrence of Liabilities	253859	225450	...	28409	...	345056	252187	...	92869	...
Net Lending [a]	-174783	-192864	...	18081	...	-200133	-219536	...	19403	...
Incurrence of Liabilities and Net Worth	79076	32586	...	46490	...	144923	32651	...	112272	...

United States

3.14 General Government Capital Finance Account, Total and Subsectors

Million United States dollars

	1986				
	Total General Government	Central Government	State or Provincial Government	Local Government	Social Security Funds
Acquisition of Financial Assets					
1 Gold and SDRs	-741	-741	...	...	...
2 Currency and transferable deposits	3915	408	...	3507	...
3 Other deposits	4197	185	...	4012	...
4 Bills and bonds, short term	36574	-	...	36574	...
5 Bonds, long term	...	...	...	...	...
6 Corporate equity securities	...	...	...	...	...
7 Short-term loans, n.e.c.	8996	8996	...	...	...
8 Long-term loans, n.e.c.	12315	517	...	11798	...
9 Other receivables	121	121	...	...	...
10 Other assets	1893	73	...	1820	...
Total Acquisition of Financial Assets	67270	9559	...	57711	...
Incurrence of Liabilities					
1 Currency and transferable deposits	...	...	...	...	...
2 Other deposits	...	...	...	...	...
3 Bills and bonds, short term	50659	46509	...	4150	...
4 Bonds, long term	207278	168543	...	38735	...
5 Short-term loans, n.e.c.	1437	...	...	1437	...
6 Long-term loans, n.e.c.	-36	-36	...	...	...
7 Other payables	1731	555	...	1176	...
8 Other liabilities	22025	22025	...	...	...
Total Incurrence of Liabilities	283094	237596	...	45498	...
Net Lending [a]	-215824	-228037	...	12213	...
Incurrence of Liabilities and Net Worth	67270	9559	...	57711	...

a) Net lending of the capital accumulation account and the capital finance account have not been reconciled and are different due to different statistical sources.

3.22 Corporate and Quasi-Corporate Enterprise Income and Outlay Account: Total and Sectors

Million United States dollars

	1980			1981			1982			1983		
	TOTAL	Non-Financial	Financial	TOTAL	Non-Financial	Financial	TOTAL	Non-Financial	Financial	TOTAL	Non-Financial	Financial
Receipts												
1 Operating surplus	243149	224025	19124	273785	260962	12823	242589	237847	4742	301886	284910	16976
2 Property and entrepreneurial income	501347	113475	387872	650062	140242	509820	715410	147570	567840	706394	145838	560556
A Withdrawals from quasi-corporate enterprises	...	...	...	...	...	...	...	...	...	...	...	...
B Interest	448345	80331	368014	597094	108047	489047	660144	114039	546105	647973	111886	536087
C Dividends	53002	33144	19858	52968	32195	20773	55266	33531	21735	58421	33952	24469
D Net land rent and royalties	...	...	...	...	...	...	...	...	...	...	...	...
3 Current transfers	5340	5340	...	6117	6117	...	6690	6690	...	7118	7118	...
A Casualty insurance claims	...	...	...	...	...	...	...	...	...	...	...	...
B Casualty insurance premiums, net, due to be received by insurance companies												
C Current transfers from the rest of the world	...	...	...	...	...	...	...	...	...	...	...	...
D Other transfers except imputed	1048	1048	...	1107	1107	...	1185	1185	...	1238	1238	...
E Imputed unfunded employee pension and welfare contributions	4292	4292	...	5010	5010	...	5505	5505	...	5880	5880	...
Total Current Receipts	749836	342840	406996	929964	407321	522643	964689	392107	572582	1015400	437866	577532
Disbursements												
1 Property and entrepreneurial income	620425	241968	378457	798236	297435	500801	871305	317229	554076	860024	310788	549236
A Withdrawals from quasi-corporations	...	...	...	...	...	...	...	...	...	...	...	...
B Interest	514555	147654	366901	683980	197300	486680	752109	211455	540654	732872	198583	534289

United States

3.22 Corporate and Quasi-Corporate Enterprise Income and Outlay Account: Total and Sectors
(Continued)

Million United States dollars

	1980 TOTAL	1980 Non-Financial	1980 Financial	1981 TOTAL	1981 Non-Financial	1981 Financial	1982 TOTAL	1982 Non-Financial	1982 Financial	1983 TOTAL	1983 Non-Financial	1983 Financial
C Dividends	105870	94314	11556	114256	100135	14121	119196	105774	13422	127152	112205	14947
D Net land rent and royalties	...	...	...	...	...	...	...	...	...	...	...	...
2 Direct taxes and other current transfers n.e.c. to general government	84785	67006	17779	81143	63887	17256	63081	46258	16823	77241	59437	17804
A Direct taxes	84785	67006	17779	81143	63887	17256	63081	46258	16823	77241	59437	17804
On income	84785	67006	17779	81143	63887	17256	63081	46258	16823	77241	59437	17804
Other	...	...	...	...	...	...	...	...	...	...	...	...
B Fines, fees, penalties and other current transfers n.e.c.	...	...	...	...	...	...	...	...	...	...	...	...
3 Other current transfers	13649	12165	1484	14678	13287	1391	16765	14890	1875	18616	16544	2072
A Casualty insurance premiums, net	...	...	...	...	...	...	...	...	...	...	...	...
B Casualty insurance claims liability of insurance companies	-	...	-	-	...	-	-	...	-	-	...	-
C Transfers to private non-profit institutions	2359	2109	250	2514	2298	216	2906	2688	218	3627	3321	306
D Unfunded employee pension and welfare benefits	4292	4292	...	5010	5010	...	5505	5505	...	5880	5880	...
E Social assistance grants	2847	1674	1173	2438	1332	1106	3247	1665	1582	3545	1860	1685
F Other transfers n.e.c.	4151	4090	61	4716	4647	69	5107	5032	75	5564	5483	81
G Transfers to the rest of the world	...	...	...	...	...	...	...	...	...	...	...	...
Net saving	30977	21701	9276	35007	32712	3195	13538	13730	-192	59517	51097	8420
Total Current Disbursements and Net Saving	749836	342840	406996	929964	407321	522643	964689	392107	572582	1015400	437866	577532

	1984 TOTAL	1984 Non-Financial	1984 Financial	1985 TOTAL	1985 Non-Financial	1985 Financial	1986 TOTAL	1986 Non-Financial	1986 Financial
Receipts									
1 Operating surplus	360190	354359	5831	369764	366880	2884	373163	365494	7669
2 Property and entrepreneurial income	798799	166506	632293	841818	164933	676885	866378	167125	699253
A Withdrawals from quasi-corporate enterprises	...	...	...	...	...	...	...	...	...
B Interest	738684	130572	608112	775572	126670	648902	795311	125435	669876
C Dividends	60115	35934	24181	66246	38263	27983	71067	41690	29377
D Net land rent and royalties	...	...	...	...	...	...	...	...	...
3 Current transfers	7425	7425	...	8198	8198	...	8392	8392	...
A Casualty insurance claims									
B Casualty insurance premiums, net, due to be received by insurance companies	...	...	...				...	...	...
C Current transfers from the rest of the world	...	...	...				...	...	...
D Other transfers except imputed	1294	1294	...	1387	1387	...	1368	1368	...
E Imputed unfunded employee pension and welfare contributions	6131	6131	...	6811	6811	...	7024	7024	...
Total Current Receipts	1166410	528290	638124	1219780	540011	679769	1247930	541011	706922
Disbursements									
1 Property and entrepreneurial income	950740	341162	617587	997257	344893	652364	1022790	353308	669479
A Withdrawals from quasi-corporations	...	...	...	...	...	...	...	...	...
B Interest	823103	223980	599123	854705	223408	631297	870506	222157	648349
C Dividends	135646	117182	18464	142552	121485	21067	152281	131151	21130
D Net land rent and royalties	...	...	...	...	...	...	...	...	...
2 Direct taxes and other current transfers n.e.c. to general government	93899	73523	20376	96712	69930	26782	105045	78272	26773
A Direct taxes	93899	73523	20376	96712	69930	26782	105045	78272	26773
On income	93899	73523	20376	96712	69930	26782	105045	78272	26773
Other	...	...	...	...	...	...	...	...	...
B Fines, fees, penalties and other current transfers n.e.c.	...	...	...	...	...	...	...	...	...

United States

3.22 Corporate and Quasi-Corporate Enterprise Income and Outlay Account: Total and Sectors
(Continued)

Million United States dollars

		1984			1985			1986		
		TOTAL	Non-Financial	Financial	TOTAL	Non-Financial	Financial	TOTAL	Non-Financial	Financial
3	Other current transfers	20776	18300	2476	23980	21259	2721	24680	21771	2909
A	Casualty insurance premiums, net	...	...	...	...	...	...	...	...	...
B	Casualty insurance claims liability of insurance companies	80	...	80	103	...	103	164	...	164
C	Transfers to private non-profit institutions	4059	3717	342	5227	4786	441	5096	4666	430
D	Unfunded employee pension and welfare benefits	6131	6131	...	6811	6811	...	7024	7024	...
E	Social assistance grants	3735	1780	1955	4357	2289	2068	4747	2543	2204
F	Other transfers n.e.c.	6771	6672	99	7482	7373	109	7649	7538	111
G	Transfers to the rest of the world	...	...	...	...	...	...	...	...	...
	Net saving	92990	95305	-2315	101831	103929	-2098	95421	87660	7761
	Total Current Disbursements and Net Saving	1166410	528290	638124	1219780	540011	679769	1247930	541011	706922

3.23 Corporate and Quasi-Corporate Enterprise Capital Accumulation Account: Total and Sectors

Million United States dollars

		1980			1981			1982			1983		
		TOTAL	Non-Financial	Financial	TOTAL	Non-Financial	Financial	TOTAL	Non-Financial	Financial	TOTAL	Non-Financial	Financial

Finance of Gross Accumulation

1	Gross saving	224442	206295	18147	259772	246092	13680	262399	250573	11826	316671	295319	21352
A	Consumption of fixed capital	193465	184594	8871	223865	213380	10485	248861	236843	12018	257154	244222	12932
B	Net saving	30977	21701	9276	35907	32712	3195	13538	13730	-192	59517	51097	8420
2	Capital transfers	...	...	...	...	...	...	...	...	...	...	...	...
	Finance of Gross Accumulation	224442	206295	18147	259772	246092	13680	262399	250573	11826	316671	295319	21352

Gross Accumulation

1	Gross capital formation	274147	259048	15099	329967	310436	19531	290296	263787	26509	299498	285221	14277
A	Increase in stocks	-282	-1131	849	19609	16202	3407	-13077	-22249	9172	-6448	-788	-5660
B	Gross fixed capital formation	274429	260179	14250	310358	294234	16124	303373	286036	17337	305946	286009	19937
2	Purchases of land, net	-2377	-2377	...	-2384	-2384	...	-2354	-2354	...	-2327	-2327	...
3	Purchases of intangible assets, net	4799	4799	...	6027	6027	...	3990	3990	...	5181	5181	...
4	Capital transfers	...	...	...	...	...	...	...	...	...	...	...	...
	Net lending [a]	-52127	-55175	3048	-73838	-67987	-5851	-29533	-14850	-14683	14319	7244	7075
	Gross Accumulation	224442	206295	18147	259772	246092	13680	262399	250573	11826	316671	295319	21352

		1984			1985			1986		
		TOTAL	Non-Financial	Financial	TOTAL	Non-Financial	Financial	TOTAL	Non-Financial	Financial

Finance of Gross Accumulation

1	Gross saving	362716	350572	12144	387211	372929	14282	395346	369112	26234
A	Consumption of fixed capital	269726	255267	14459	285380	269000	16380	299925	281452	18473
B	Net saving	92990	95305	-2315	101831	103929	-2098	95421	87660	7761
2	Capital transfers	...	...	...	...	...	...	...	...	...
	Finance of Gross Accumulation	362716	350572	12144	387211	372929	14282	395346	369112	26234

Gross Accumulation

1	Gross capital formation	414426	388413	26013	414408	366620	47788	410521	364978	45543
A	Increase in stocks	53961	57550	-3589	22822	11599	11223	20005	14695	5310
B	Gross fixed capital formation	360465	330863	29602	391586	355021	36565	390516	350283	40233
2	Purchases of land, net	-2744	-2744	...	-3006	-3006	...	-2927	-2927	...
3	Purchases of intangible assets, net	4259	4259	...	1510	1510	...	3293	3293	...
4	Capital transfers	...	...	...	...	...	...	...	...	...
	Net lending [a]	-53225	-39356	-13869	-25701	7805	-33506	-15541	3768	-19309
	Gross Accumulation	362716	350572	12144	387211	372929	14282	395346	369112	26234

a) Net lending of the capital accumulation account and the capital finance account have not been reconciled and are different due to different statistical sources.

United States

3.24 Corporate and Quasi-Corporate Enterprise Capital Finance Account: Total and Sectors

Million United States dollars

	1980 TOTAL	1980 Non-Financial	1980 Financial	1981 TOTAL	1981 Non-Financial	1981 Financial	1982 TOTAL	1982 Non-Financial	1982 Financial	1983 TOTAL	1983 Non-Financial	1983 Financial
Acquisition of Financial Assets												
1 Gold and SDRs	-12	...	-12	-9	...	-9	-3	...	-3	-27	...	-27
2 Currency and transferable deposits	10985	4762	6223	4409	302	4107	15447	8379	7068	7387	6691	696
3 Other deposits	27492	9295	18197	54850	15747	39103	40853	11359	29494	29027	19743	9284
4 Bills and bonds, short term	169288	3060	166228	201975	13962	188013	230796	18264	212532	241717	24333	217384
5 Bonds, long term	...	...	...	...	...	...	...	...	...	...	...	...
6 Corporate equity securities	44252	19222	25030	37603	9624	27979	23534	-2370	25904	51473	373	51100
7 Short term loans, n.e.c.	71766	224	71542	109096	1866	107230	70613	542	70071	88884	3344	85540
8 Long term loans, n.e.c.	96322	...	96322	78635	...	78635	66911	...	66911	173552	...	173552
9 Trade credits and advances	48231	48231	...	23181	23181	...	-15650	-15650	...	62223	62223	...
10 Other receivables	...	...	...	...	...	...	...	...	...	...	...	...
11 Other assets	66107	23618	42489	69330	17340	51990	107508	26471	81037	45022	8372	36650
Total Acquisition of Financial Assets	534431	108412	426019	579070	82022	497048	540009	46995	493014	699258	125079	574179
Incurrence of Liabilities												
1 Currency and transferable deposits	16142	...	16142	28105	...	28105	37389	...	37389	40212	...	40212
2 Other deposits	166127	...	166127	126707	...	126707	171542	...	171542	232360	...	232360
3 Bills and bonds, short term	10380	5585	4795	37829	16882	20947	-7647	-6516	-1131	18671	2648	16023
4 Bonds, long term	83721	38519	45202	86132	36192	49940	111002	33809	77193	110613	25457	85156
5 Corporate equity securities	32738	28190	4548	19575	13846	5729	38202	25196	13006	69655	39830	29825
6 Short-term loans, n.e.c.	41282	33959	7323	74168	54865	19303	46036	42961	3075	21518	28682	-7164
7 Long-term loans, n.e.c.	1694	1734	-40	-1930	-1950	20	-1107	-1220	113	3530	3505	25
8 Net equity of households in life insurance and pension fund reserves	109710	...	109710	107871	...	107871	127073	...	127073	139352	...	139352
9 Proprietors' net additions to the accumulation of quasi-corporations	...	...	...	...	...	...	...	...	...	...	...	...
10 Trade credit and advances	39583	39583	...	30813	30813	...	4966	4966	...	40753	40753	...
11 Other accounts payable	...	...	...	...	...	...	...	...	...	...	...	...
12 Other liabilities	57591	-1734	59325	136518	-6795	143313	63499	-14062	77561	44548	5758	38790
Total Incurrence of Liabilities	558968	145836	413132	645788	143853	501935	590955	85134	505821	721212	146633	574579
Net Lending [a]	-24537	-37424	12887	-66718	-61831	-4887	-50946	-38139	-12807	-21954	-21554	-400
Incurrence of Liabilities and Net Lending	534431	108412	426019	579070	82022	497048	540009	46995	493014	699258	125079	574179

	1984 TOTAL	1984 Non-Financial	1984 Financial	1985 TOTAL	1985 Non-Financial	1985 Financial	1986 TOTAL	1986 Non-Financial	1986 Financial
Acquisition of Financial Assets									
1 Gold and SDRs	-25	...	-25	-6	...	-6	-26	...	-26
2 Currency and transferable deposits	10320	6682	3638	25402	9754	15648	21891	11462	10429
3 Other deposits	28603	8140	20463	27055	7335	20620	47733	15665	32068
4 Bills and bonds, short term	274121	21450	252671	329806	9198	320608	493968	19109	474859
5 Bonds, long term	...	...	...	...	...	...	...	...	...
6 Corporate equity securities	22540	2821	19719	60070	17268	42802	78158	28047	50111
7 Short term loans, n.e.c.	192703	3753	188950	162396	3156	159240	173211	962	172249
8 Long term loans, n.e.c.	200845	...	200845	222792	...	222792	285492	...	285492
9 Trade credits and advances	16358	16358	...	35240	35240	...	10865	10865	...
10 Other receivables	...	...	...	...	...	...	...	...	...
11 Other assets	116135	27884	88251	140510	17706	122804	125084	13013	112071
Total Acquisition of Financial Assets	891600	117088	774512	1004170	99657	904508	1236380	99123	1137250
Incurrence of Liabilities									
1 Currency and transferable deposits	47274	...	47274	83337	...	83337	125300	...	125300
2 Other deposits	258565	...	258565	192607	...	192607	155806	...	155806
3 Bills and bonds, short term	43476	23110	20366	54892	13543	41349	20654	-9439	30093
4 Bonds, long term	177720	66671	111049	245417	96353	149064	357050	111375	245675
5 Corporate equity securities	-11785	-48907	37122	36666	-61009	97675	117178	-54393	171571
6 Short-term loans, n.e.c.	122250	105918	16332	74257	56399	17858	109031	85574	23457

United States

3.24 Corporate and Quasi-Corporate Enterprise Capital Finance Account: Total and Sectors
(Continued)

Million United States dollars

	1984 TOTAL	1984 Non-Financial	1984 Financial	1985 TOTAL	1985 Non-Financial	1985 Financial	1986 TOTAL	1986 Non-Financial	1986 Financial
7 Long-term loans, n.e.c.	744	333	411	488	433	55	2792	2713	79
8 Net equity of households in life insurance and pension fund reserves	134213	...	134213	174977	...	174977	180213	...	180213
9 Proprietors' net additions to the accumulation of quasi-corporations	...	...	...	...	...	...	...	...	...
10 Trade credit and advances	34423	34423	...	32985	32985	...	2992	2992	...
11 Other accounts payable	...	...	...	...	...	...	...	...	...
12 Other liabilities	179571	665	178906	154783	-1761	156544	223670	1046	222624
Total Incurrence of Liabilities	986451	182213	804238	1050410	136943	913466	1294690	139868	1154820
Net Lending a	-94851	-65125	-29726	-46244	-37286	-8958	-58310	-40745	-17565
Incurrence of Liabilities and Net Lending	891600	117088	774512	1004170	99657	904508	1236380	99123	1137250

a) Net lending of the capital accumulation account and the capital finance account have not been reconciled and are different due to different statistical sources.

3.32 Household and Private Unincorporated Enterprise Income and Outlay Account

Million United States dollars

	1970	1975	1977	1978	1979	1980	1981	1982	1983	1984	1985	1986
					Receipts							
1 Compensation of employees	619097	952048	1181080	1334490	1497580	1646250	1817140	1917900	2032250	2224440	2382900	2517440
A Wages and salaries	552044	815624	995183	1120980	1253590	1373840	1512350	1588340	1678840	1841730	1977900	2092650
B Employers' contributions for social security	23839	46691	61075	71466	82513	88861	103522	109676	119773	138976	147401	155727
C Employers' contributions for private pension & welfare plans	43214	89733	124822	142042	161474	183553	201266	219888	233641	243733	257599	269067
2 Operating surplus of private unincorporated enterprises	80171	125373	152915	176206	191871	180673	186772	175535	190882	234502	257251	289818
3 Property and entrepreneurial income	102238	151840	187372	215709	254103	310957	393037	432713	456218	513523	537412	567186
A Withdrawals from private quasi-corporations	...	...	...	...	...	...	...	...	...	...	...	...
B Interest	61840	109586	140999	163407	200362	251489	318489	355166	374304	429458	452139	469224
C Dividends	22215	28720	38180	43007	48103	52868	61288	63930	68731	75531	76306	81214
D Net land rent and royalties	18183	13534	8193	9295	5638	6600	13260	13617	13183	8534	8967	16748
3 Current transfers	81220	183643	214379	230966	259007	308513	349572	389561	420011	429716	460633	486511
A Casualty insurance claims	...	...	...	...	...	...	...	...	...	...	...	...
B Social security benefits	46470	105876	125616	133784	150502	180285	208948	242014	261039	265268	283754	300989
C Social assistance grants	25098	57060	62876	68353	75403	89310	97367	99653	106850	111299	117008	124010
D Unfunded employee pension and welfare benefits a	6186	14448	18332	20428	23781	28002	32141	35246	37932	37200	41297	42235
E Transfers from general government	...	...	...	...	...	...	...	...	...	...	...	...
F Transfers from the rest of the world	381	730	941	1206	1371	1559	1448	1388	1454	1304	1405	1621
G Other transfers n.e.c.	3085	5529	6614	7195	7950	9357	9668	11260	12736	14645	17169	17656
Total Current Receipts	882726	1412900	1735750	1957370	2202560	2446400	2746520	2915710	3099360	3402180	3638200	3860960
					Disbursements							
1 Final consumption expenditures	635842	1005820	1250010	1392720	1554720	1721220	1909680	2046300	2223660	2422200	2611730	2778410
A Market purchases	570853	901084	1120960	1246210	1388270	1531800	1696430	1815340	1977610	2157660	2328070	2472460
B Gross rents of owner-occupied housing	64213	103602	127885	145383	165208	188283	212130	229913	244974	263477	282732	305055
C Consumption from own-account production	725	1212	1092	1112	1183	1058	1044	965	1073	1063	930	889
2 Property income	16686	24428	30514	36687	43533	47376	51970	55548	61858	72508	82734	89933
A Interest	16686	24428	30514	36687	43533	47376	51970	55548	61858	72508	82734	89933
Consumer debt	16686	24428	30514	36687	43533	47376	51970	55548	61858	72508	82734	89933
Mortgage	...	...	...	...	...	...	...	...	...	...	...	...
Other	...	...	...	...	...	...	...	...	...	...	...	...
B Net land rent and royalties	...	...	...	...	...	...	...	...	...	...	...	...
3 Direct taxes and other current transfers n.e.c. to government	151335	240061	314949	365725	427189	471893	548684	571909	588449	646649	712727	753876
A Social security contributions	46745	89637	113465	131716	153311	166617	196129	209139	226259	257654	281648	300394
B Direct taxes	103058	147718	197846	229940	269270	300008	346266	355677	354216	379875	420565	441295
Income taxes	99744	143294	192865	224471	263452	293711	339563	348417	346375	371323	411380	431481

United States

3.32 Household and Private Unincorporated Enterprise Income and Outlay Account
(Continued)

Million United States dollars

	1970	1975	1977	1978	1979	1980	1981	1982	1983	1984	1985	1986
Other	3314	4424	4981	5469	5818	6297	6703	7260	7841	8552	9185	9814
C Fees, fines and penalties	1532	2706	3638	4069	4608	5268	6289	7093	7974	9120	10514	12187
4 Other current transfers	9611	18890	23313	26062	29454	34439	38698	42169	44445	44907	49240	50323
A Net casualty insurance premiums	...	...	...	...	...	...	...	...	...	...	...	...
B Transfers to private non-profit institutions serving households	...	...	...	...	...	...	...	...	...	...	...	...
C Transfers to the rest of the world	1538	1684	1841	2094	2357	2698	2481	2649	2499	2822	3385	3346
D Other current transfers, except imputed	1887	2658	3040	3269	3497	3779	4017	4278	4459	4665	4788	4742
E Imputed employee pension and welfare contributions	6186	14548	18432	20699	23600	27962	32200	35242	37487	37420	41067	42235
Net saving	69252	123710	116965	136176	147663	171470	197489	199784	180950	215917	181766	188421
Total Current Disbursements and Net Saving	882726	1412900	1735750	1957370	2202560	2446400	2746520	2915710	3099360	3402180	3638200	3860960

a) Item 'Unfunded employee pension and welfare benefits' also includes wage accruals less disbursements.

3.33 Household and Private Unincorporated Enterprise Capital Accumulation Account

Million United States dollars

	1970	1975	1977	1978	1979	1980	1981	1982	1983	1984	1985	1986
Finance of Gross Accumulation												
1 Gross saving	106123	189135	198027	228909	255096	293902	334615	347970	334834	376864	350231	362247
A Consumption of fixed capital	36871	65425	81062	92733	107433	122432	137126	148186	153884	160947	168465	173826
Owner-occupied housing	14329	25718	32718	37897	43917	49164	53844	56770	59585	62612	67059	69811
Other unincorporated enterprises	22542	39707	48344	54836	63516	73268	83282	91416	94299	98335	101406	104015
B Net saving	69252	123710	116965	136176	147663	171470	197489	199784	180950	215917	181766	188421
2 Capital transfers	...	...	...	...	...	...	...	...	...	...	...	...
Total Finance of Gross Accumulation	106123	189135	198027	228909	255096	293902	334615	347970	334834	376864	350231	362247
Gross Accumulation												
1 Gross Capital Formation	65539	98072	155445	185238	208520	185555	210856	185230	216268	268411	262155	292735
A Increase in stocks	426	2124	2956	4106	3977	-7022	7640	-2040	-6027	10100	-1611	796
B Gross fixed capital formation	65113	95948	152489	181132	204543	192577	203216	187270	222295	258311	263766	291939
Owner-occupied housing	27123	48815	87405	101600	92670	79471	82081	70941	124164	132615	141341	173842
Other gross fixed capital formation	37990	47133	65084	79532	111873	113106	121135	116329	98131	125696	122425	118097
2 Purchases of land, net	...	...	...	...	...	...	...	...	...	...	...	...
3 Purchases of intangibles, net	...	...	...	...	...	...	...	...	...	...	...	...
4 Capital transfers	4764	6448	9276	7242	7593	8836	9353	10207	8455	8487	9049	9888
A To resident sectors	4764	6448	9276	7242	7593	8836	9353	10207	8455	8487	9049	9888
B To the rest of the world	...	...	...	...	...	...	...	...	...	...	...	...
Net lending a	35820	84615	33306	36429	38983	99511	114406	152533	110111	99966	79027	59624
Total Gross Accumulation	106123	189135	198027	228909	255096	293902	334615	347970	334834	376864	350231	362247

a) Net lending of the capital accumulation account and the capital finance account have not been reconciled and are different due to different statistical sources.

3.34 Household and Private Unincorporated Enterprise Capital Finance Account

Million United States dollars

	1970	1975	1977	1978	1979	1980	1981	1982	1983	1984	1985	1986
Acquisition of Financial Assets												
1 Gold	...	...	...	...	...	...	...	...	...	...	...	...
2 Currency and transferable deposits	8002	6103	10738	22336	26718	10283	25176	17736	36786	16667	39162	99286
3 Other deposits	43553	79010	106852	106121	106627	154603	174187	150752	156457	275770	140113	154108
4 Bills and bonds, short term	660	14086	19624	37851	60562	22193	44303	62600	85112	126406	153657	531
5 Bonds, long term	...	...	...	...	...	...	...	...	...	...	...	...
6 Corporate equity securities	-609	-3933	-7051	-12489	-23661	-10871	-39504	-5159	4113	-55994	-32428	21742
7 Short term loans, n.e.c.	960	1244	-744	2005	2233	673	3422	1604	4811	8327	8351	4036
8 Long term loans, n.e.c.	2408	3335	7860	11946	16678	17450	17991	10844	926	5834	3264	1055
9 Trade credit and advances	...	...	...	...	...	...	...	...	...	...	...	...
10 Net equity of households in life insurance and pension fund reserves	24189	71921	78560	95022	101834	118503	117911	139000	153591	152399	194081	201284
11 Proprietors' net additions to the accumulation of quasi-corporations	...	...	...	...	...	...	...	...	...	...	...	...

United States

3.34 Household and Private Unincorporated Enterprise Capital Finance Account
(Continued)

Million United States dollars

	1970	1975	1977	1978	1979	1980	1981	1982	1983	1984	1985	1986
12 Other	3209	10552	14546	17050	9318	1664	-15512	14514	26691	14679	43282	50752
Total Acquisition of Financial Assets	83302	182318	239385	279842	299309	314498	327974	391891	468487	544088	549482	532794
Incurrence of Liabilities												
1 Short term loans, n.e.c.	11451	14668	52600	67329	68790	32878	60061	41923	77777	104697	105173	86418
2 Long term loans, n.e.c.	29964	56590	124404	146595	163393	129470	111286	86584	180135	216739	237286	296106
3 Trade credit and advances	1316	2631	3225	6221	2949	2448	2453	395	1719	3956	4246	3270
4 Other accounts payable	...	...	...	...	...	...	...	...	...	...	...	...
5 Other liabilities	-1350	2784	5602	4869	5277	10834	4482	13056	20402	6076	46971	5061
Total Incurrence of Liabilities	41381	76673	185831	225014	240409	175630	178282	141958	280033	331468	393676	390855
Net Lending [a]	41921	105645	53554	54828	58900	138868	149692	249933	188454	212620	155806	141939
Incurrence of Liabilities and Net Lending	83302	182318	239385	279842	299309	314498	327974	391891	468487	544088	549482	532794

a) Net lending of the capital accumulation account and the capital finance account have not been reconciled and are different due to different statistical sources.

3.51 External Transactions: Current Account: Detail

Million United States dollars

	1970	1975	1977	1978	1979	1980	1981	1982	1983	1984	1985	1986
Payments to the Rest of the World												
1 Imports of goods and services	55177	120625	179049	208188	248147	288074	310521	295137	319797	389441	399949	429341
A Imports of merchandise c.i.f. [a]	40855	99000	151851	176477	211930	247460	266462	249474	271341	334250	341016	367507
B Other	14322	21625	27198	31711	36217	40614	44059	45663	48456	55191	58933	61834
2 Factor income to the rest of the world	6316	14204	16218	23871	35425	43368	55259	58748	56682	72772	70529	74941
A Compensation of employees	197	371	442	478	473	536	544	618	614	580	633	602
B Property and entrepreneurial income	6119	13833	15776	23393	34952	42832	54715	58130	56068	72192	69896	74339
By general government	1024	4542	5542	8674	11122	12592	16878	18285	17825	19769	21306	22607
By corporate and quasi-corporate enterprises	5095	9291	10234	14719	23830	30240	37837	39845	38243	52423	48590	51732
By other	...	...	...	...	...	...	...	...	...	...	...	...
3 Current transfers to the rest of the world	6599	7858	6227	7044	8050	10023	9701	11103	11221	13747	16876	17548
A Indirect taxes by general government to supranational organizations	...	...	...	...	...	...	...	...	...	...	...	...
B Other current transfers	6599	7858	6227	7044	8050	10023	9701	11103	11221	13747	16876	17548
By general government	5061	6174	4386	4950	5693	7325	7220	8454	8722	10925	13491	14202
By other resident sectors	1538	1684	1841	2094	2357	2698	2481	2649	2499	2822	3385	3346
4 Surplus of the nation on current transactions	3939	21596	-8710	-10138	1448	11830	9478	-953	-33485	-90948	-115911	-143853
Payments to the Rest of the World, and Surplus of the Nation on Current Transfers	72031	164283	192784	228965	293070	353295	384959	364035	354215	385012	371443	377977
Receipts From The Rest of the World												
1 Exports of goods and services	59104	136346	155724	182013	223575	273347	292988	270904	264005	283250	281000	290182
A Exports of merchandise f.o.b. [a]	44280	109359	122820	144454	182986	224672	237894	213572	205637	223699	220205	224328
B Other	14824	26987	32904	37559	40589	48675	55094	57332	58368	59551	60795	65854
2 Factor income from the rest of the world	12545	27202	36100	45740	68104	78368	90489	91626	88721	100420	88986	86077
A Compensation of employees	222	334	388	388	419	449	497	520	560	600	632	692
B Property and entrepreneurial income	12323	26868	35712	45352	67685	77919	89992	91106	88161	99820	88354	85385
By general government	907	1112	1625	1843	2295	2562	3680	4118	4832	5229	5503	6321
By corporate and quasi-corporate enterprises	11416	25756	34087	43509	65390	75357	86312	86988	83329	94591	82851	79064

United States

3.51 External Transactions: Current Account: Detail
(Continued)

Million United States dollars

	1970	1975	1977	1978	1979	1980	1981	1982	1983	1984	1985	1986
By other	...	...	...	...	...	...	...	...	...	...	...	...
3 Current transfers from the rest of the world	382	735	960	1212	1391	1580	1482	1505	1489	1342	1457	1718
A Subsidies to general government from supranational organizations	...	...	...	...	...	...	...	...	...	...	...	...
B Other current transfers	382	735	960	1212	1391	1580	1482	1505	1489	1342	1457	1718
To general government	1	5	19	6	20	21	34	117	35	38	52	97
To other resident sectors	381	730	941	1206	1371	1559	1448	1388	1454	1304	1405	1621
Receipts from the Rest of the World on Current Transfers	72031	164283	192784	228965	293070	353295	384959	364035	354215	385012	371443	377977

a) Valuation basis is essentially Free Along Side (F.A.S.).

3.52 External Transactions: Capital Accumulation Account

Million United States dollars

	1970	1975	1977	1978	1979	1980	1981	1982	1983	1984	1985	1986
Finance of Gross Accumulation												
1 Surplus of the nation on current transactions	3939	21596	-8710	-10138	1448	11830	9478	-953	-33485	-90948	-115911	-143853
2 Capital transfers from the rest of the world	867	-	-	-	1139	1152	1093	-	-	-	-	-
A By general government	867	-	-	-	1139	1152	1093	-	-	-	-	-
B By other resident sectors	...	...	...	...	...	...	...	...	...	...	...	...
Total Finance of Gross Accumulation	4806	21596	-8710	-10138	2587	12982	10571	-953	-33485	-90948	-115911	-143853
Gross Accumulation												
1 Capital transfers to the rest of the world	-	-	-	-	-	-	-	-	-	-	-	-
A By general government	-	-	-	-	-	-	-	-	-	-	-	-
B By other resident sectors	...	...	...	...	...	...	...	...	...	...	...	...
2 Purchases of intangible assets, n.e.c., net, from the rest of the world	...	...	...	...	...	...	...	...	...	...	...	...
Net lending to the rest of the world a	4806	21596	-8710	-10138	2586	12981	10570	-953	-33485	-90948	-115911	-143853
Total Gross Accumulation	4806	21596	-8710	-10138	2586	12981	10570	-953	-33485	-90948	-115911	-143853

a) Net lending of the capital accumulation account and the capital finance account have not been reconciled and are different due to different statistical sources.

3.53 External Transactions: Capital Finance Account

Million United States dollars

	1970	1975	1977	1978	1979	1980	1981	1982	1983	1984	1985	1986
Acquisitions of Foreign Financial Assets												
1 Gold and SDR's	64	66	239	-1184	1201	16	1823	1372	65	979	897	246
2 Currency and transferable deposits	-2545	783	136	452	-68	8138	3353	3592	1130	2151	2960	-559
3 Other deposits	-375	826	1315	2449	6107	2800	12567	2382	2973	-4747	-2190	...
4 Bills and bonds, short term	700	-90	1854	-3170	3593	4091	6922	8517	-122	969	-7351	-5376
5 Bonds, long term	874	7168	5051	4181	3701	1202	5487	6614	3000	8812	3703	2561
6 Corporate equity securities	8666	13323	12298	15706	26248	21588	9837	-1000	4056	3765	20957	28788
A Subsidiaries abroad	7590	14244	11890	16057	25223	19222	9624	-2370	373	2821	17268	28047
B Other	1076	-921	408	-351	1025	2366	213	1370	3683	944	3689	741
7 Short-term loans, n.e.c.	1133	6650	6032	22171	5996	16463	7240	-1011	7892	-2616	-1446	327
8 Long-term loans	...	...	...	...	...	...	...	...	...	...	...	...
9 Proprietors' net additions to accumulation of quasi-corporate, non-resident enterprises	...	...	...	...	...	...	...	...	...	...	...	...
10 Trade credit and advances	963	665	499	-274	1512	1745	203	-2726	242	-494	-615	-423
11 Other	-1683	-501	-3106	16689	5673	-2386	29113	8858	9109	13839	3985	542
Total Acquisitions of Foreign Financial Assets	7896	28890	24318	57020	53963	53657	76545	26598	28425	17658	20990	26106
Incurrence of Foreign Liabilities												
1 Currency and transferable deposits	521	-316	2400	-248	4244	17	-3785	-3660	1605	1940	1565	2679
2 Other deposits	-1664	1456	-400	1145	1173	1214	2270	6813	514	4560	3708	-2659
3 Bills and bonds, short term	10257	5651	11033	21165	-21521	9755	-4490	-4365	12719	18567	-6960	25474
4 Bonds, long term	717	2587	26638	8244	9168	14223	21126	25539	8257	26253	67749	66062
5 Corporate equity securities	2161	7270	6403	10274	13472	20672	31057	17714	16929	22587	25460	44114
A Subsidiaries of non-resident incorporated units	1464	2603	3728	7852	11813	15315	25296	13810	11519	25568	20491	26357

United States

3.53 External Transactions: Capital Finance Account
(Continued)

Million United States dollars

	1970	1975	1977	1978	1979	1980	1981	1982	1983	1984	1985	1986
B Other	697	4667	2675	2422	1659	5357	5761	3904	5410	-2981	4969	17757
6 Short-term loans, n.e.c.	...	...	...	...	...	...	...	...	...	...	...	...
7 Long-term loans	...	...	...	...	...	...	...	...	...	...	...	...
8 Non-resident proprietors' net additions to accumulation of resident quasi-corporate enterprises	...	...	...	...	...	...	...	...	...	...	...	...
9 Trade credit and advances	1558	1837	1873	4116	214	3494	-207	26	-1340	1353	457	362
10 Other	-8634	-13629	-7097	14587	24990	-25272	1031	-44184	16397	13063	32304	26703
Total Incurrence of Liabilities	4916	4856	40850	59283	31740	24103	47002	-2117	55081	88323	124283	162735
Net Lending a	2980	24034	-16532	-2467	25898	31233	27395	30834	-28350	-71703	-105374	-127540
Total Incurrence of Liabilities and Net Lending	7896	28890	24318	56816	57638	55336	74397	28717	26731	16620	18909	35195

a) Net lending of the capital accumulation account and the capital finance account have not been reconciled and are different due to different statistical sources.

4.1 Derivation of Value Added by Kind of Activity, in Current Prices

Million United States dollars

	1980 Gross Output	1980 Intermediate Consumption	1980 Value Added	1981 Gross Output	1981 Intermediate Consumption	1981 Value Added	1982 Gross Output	1982 Intermediate Consumption	1982 Value Added	1983 Gross Output	1983 Intermediate Consumption	1983 Value Added
						All Producers						
1 Agriculture, hunting, forestry and fishing a	...	...	70320	...	...	83722	...	...	81370	...	...	66394
2 Mining and quarrying	...	...	107854	...	...	144398	...	...	132893	...	...	119060
A Coal mining	...	...	12994	...	...	13900	...	...	15222	...	...	14405
B Crude petroleum and natural gas production	...	...	85345	...	...	121341	...	...	110794	...	...	96928
C Metal ore mining	...	...	3876	...	...	3893	...	...	2344	...	...	2554
D Other mining	...	...	5639	...	...	5264	...	...	4533	...	...	5173
3 Manufacturing	...	...	586438	...	...	649631	...	...	641021	...	...	689493
A Manufacture of food, beverages and tobacco	...	...	60009	...	...	66791	...	...	70960	...	...	77143
B Textile, wearing apparel and leather industries	...	...	36269	...	...	39133	...	...	38212	...	...	41406
C Manufacture of wood and wood products, including furniture	...	...	27505	...	...	26572	...	...	25832	...	...	31406
D Manufacture of paper and paper products, printing and publishing	...	...	55098	...	...	60724	...	...	65616	...	...	70636
E Manufacture of chemicals and chemical petroleum, coal, rubber and plastic products	...	...	80446	...	...	93591	...	...	99882	...	...	110809
F Manufacture of non-metallic mineral products, except products of petroleum and coal	...	...	19155	...	...	19181	...	...	18320	...	...	20336
G Basic metal industries	...	...	44527	...	...	50183	...	...	35606	...	...	30618
H Manufacture of fabricated metal products, machinery and equipment	...	...	253728	...	...	281546	...	...	275320	...	...	296680
I Other manufacturing industries	...	...	9701	...	...	11910	...	...	11273	...	...	10459
4 Electricity, gas and water b	...	...	68682	...	...	80847	...	...	92490	...	...	104001
5 Construction	...	...	139366	...	...	140321	...	...	142956	...	...	151321
6 Wholesale and retail trade, restaurants and hotels	...	...	455226	...	...	500354	...	...	525500	...	...	563712
A Wholesale and retail trade c	...	...	436120	...	...	479816	...	...	503628	...	...	539199
B Restaurants and hotels c	...	...	19106	...	...	20538	...	...	21872	...	...	24513
Restaurants	...	...	...	...	...	...	...	...	...	...	...	...
Hotels and other lodging places	...	...	19106	...	...	20538	...	...	21872	...	...	24513
7 Transport, storage and communication	...	...	173314	...	...	190158	...	...	197763	...	...	217833
A Transport and storage	...	...	106575	...	...	113560	...	...	111878	...	...	121532
B Communication	...	...	66739	...	...	76598	...	...	85885	...	...	96301
8 Finance, insurance, real estate and business services	...	...	548516	...	...	622462	...	...	663127	...	...	746450
A Financial institutions	...	...	71758	...	...	85350	...	...	91003	...	...	113134
B Insurance	...	...	52441	...	...	51522	...	...	48423	...	...	55857
C Real estate and business services	...	...	424317	...	...	485590	...	...	523701	...	...	577459
Real estate, except dwellings	...	...	220307	...	...	252338	...	...	269660	...	...	303845

United States

4.1 Derivation of Value Added by Kind of Activity, in Current Prices
(Continued)

Million United States dollars

	1980 Gross Output	1980 Intermediate Consumption	1980 Value Added	1981 Gross Output	1981 Intermediate Consumption	1981 Value Added	1982 Gross Output	1982 Intermediate Consumption	1982 Value Added	1983 Gross Output	1983 Intermediate Consumption	1983 Value Added
Dwellings	...	...	204010	...	...	233252	...	...	254041	...	...	273614
9 Community, social and personal services	...	...	224472	...	...	250312	...	...	276551	...	...	302886
A Sanitary and similar services [b]	...	...		...	...		...	...		...	...	
B Social and related community services	...	...	150851	...	...	171208	...	...	192446	...	...	210699
Educational services	...	...	16020	...	...	17560	...	...	19162	...	...	21026
Medical, dental, other health and veterinary services	...	...	108533	...	...	125242	...	...	142712	...	...	156831
C Recreational and cultural services	...	...	17631	...	...	19803	...	...	21653	...	...	23605
D Personal and household services	...	...	55990	...	...	59301	...	...	62452	...	...	68582
Statistical discrepancy [d]	...	...	33840	...	...	37976	...	...	40023	...	...	44085
Total, Industries	...	...	2408030	...	...	2700180	...	...	2793690	...	...	3005240
Producers of Government Services	...	...	333978	...	...	366259	...	...	395374	...	...	419322
Other Producers	...	...	...	...	...	...	...	...	...	...	...	...
Total	...	...	2742010	...	...	3066440	...	...	3189070	...	...	3424560
Less: Imputed bank service charge	...	...	65620	...	...	69681	...	...	76225	...	...	85345
Import duties	...	...	7160	...	...	8589	...	...	8609	...	...	9091
Value added tax	...	...		...	...		...	...		...	...	
Other adjustments [e]	...	...	4920	...	...	4124	...	...	-56	...	...	5170
Total	...	...	2688470	...	...	3009470	...	...	3121400	...	...	3353470

of which General Government:

	1980 Gross Output	1980 Intermediate Consumption	1980 Value Added	1981 Gross Output	1981 Intermediate Consumption	1981 Value Added	1982 Gross Output	1982 Intermediate Consumption	1982 Value Added	1983 Gross Output	1983 Intermediate Consumption	1983 Value Added
1 Agriculture, hunting, forestry and fishing	...	...	...	...	...	...	...	...	...	...	...	...
2 Mining and quarrying	...	...	...	...	...	...	...	...	...	...	...	...
3 Manufacturing	...	...	...	...	...	...	...	...	...	...	...	...
4 Electricity, gas and water	...	...	...	...	...	...	...	...	...	...	...	...
5 Construction	...	...	...	...	...	...	...	...	...	...	...	...
6 Wholesale and retail trade, restaurants and hotels	...	...	...	...	...	...	...	...	...	...	...	...
7 Transport and communication	...	...	...	...	...	...	...	...	...	...	...	...
8 Finance, insurance, real estate and business services	...	...	...	...	...	...	...	...	...	...	...	...
9 Community, social and personal services	...	...	...	...	...	...	...	...	...	...	...	...
Total, Industries of General Government	...	...	33840	...	...	37976	...	...	40023	...	...	44085
Producers of Government Services	...	...	...	...	...	...	...	...	...	...	...	...
Total, General Government	...	...	...	...	...	...	...	...	...	...	...	...

	1984 Gross Output	1984 Intermediate Consumption	1984 Value Added	1985 Gross Output	1985 Intermediate Consumption	1985 Value Added	1986 Gross Output	1986 Intermediate Consumption	1986 Value Added
			All Producers						
1 Agriculture, hunting, forestry and fishing [a]	...	...	85305	...	...	84045	...	...	87069
2 Mining and quarrying	...	...	120347	...	...	119264	...	...	96387
A Coal mining	...	...	14680	...	...	14447	...	...	13731
B Crude petroleum and natural gas production	...	...	97175	...	...	96139	...	...	74011
C Metal ore mining	...	...	2255	...	...	2366	...	...	2674
D Other mining	...	...	6237	...	...	6312	...	...	5971

United States

4.1 Derivation of Value Added by Kind of Activity, in Current Prices
(Continued)

Million United States dollars

	1984 Gross Output	1984 Intermediate Consumption	1984 Value Added	1985 Gross Output	1985 Intermediate Consumption	1985 Value Added	1986 Gross Output	1986 Intermediate Consumption	1986 Value Added
3 Manufacturing	...	...	778413	...	...	806461	...	...	831844
A Manufacture of food, beverages and tobacco	...	...	79953	...	...	82896	...	...	84479
B Textile, wearing apparel and leather industries	...	...	42072	...	...	40852	...	...	42550
C Manufacture of wood and wood products, including furniture	...	...	35475	...	...	35913	...	...	38424
D Manufacture of paper and paper products, printing and publishing	...	...	80031	...	...	85700	...	...	90021
E Manufacture of chemicals and chemical petroleum, coal, rubber and plastic products	...	...	121300	...	...	122725	...	...	131746
F Manufacture of non-metallic mineral products, except products of petroleum and coal	...	...	23114	...	...	24382	...	...	25503
G Basic metal industries	...	...	36545	...	...	35053	...	...	35123
H Manufacture of fabricated metal products, machinery and equipment	...	...	345955	...	...	364738	...	...	369738
I Other manufacturing industries	...	...	13968	...	...	14202	...	...	14260
4 Electricity, gas and water [b]	...	...	119496	...	...	127365	...	...	132935
5 Construction	...	...	173526	...	...	186618	...	...	200203
6 Wholesale and retail trade, restaurants and hotels	...	...	635022	...	...	687516	...	...	727485
A Wholesale and retail trade [c]	...	...	607693	...	...	657652	...	...	695298
B Restaurants and hotels [c]	...	...	27329	...	...	29864	...	...	32187
Restaurants	...	...	...	...	...	...	...	...	...
Hotels and other lodging places	...	...	27329	...	...	29864	...	...	32187
7 Transport, storage and communication	...	...	237226	...	...	251475	...	...	261228
A Transport and storage	...	...	134622	...	...	141723	...	...	145409
B Communication	...	...	102604	...	...	109752	...	...	115819
8 Finance, insurance, real estate and business services	...	...	817524	...	...	899685	...	...	1000500
A Financial institutions	...	...	114306	...	...	125792	...	...	138549
B Insurance	...	...	56347	...	...	62623	...	...	80749
C Real estate and business services	...	...	646871	...	...	711270	...	...	781202
Real estate, except dwellings	...	...	351277	...	...	387514	...	...	425808
Dwellings	...	...	295594	...	...	323756	...	...	355394
9 Community, social and personal services	...	...	331136	...	...	359428	...	...	385160
A Sanitary and similar services [b]	...	...	...	...	...	...	...	...	...
B Social and related community services	...	...	229156	...	...	247695	...	...	266880
Educational services	...	...	23557	...	...	25246	...	...	26768
Medical, dental, other health and veterinary services	...	...	169823	...	...	184459	...	...	199529
C Recreational and cultural services	...	...	25486	...	...	28819	...	...	30337
D Personal and household services	...	...	76494	...	...	82914	...	...	87943
Statistical discrepancy [d]	...	...	51940	...	...	58551	...	...	62774
Total, Industries	...	...	3349940	...	...	3580410	...	...	3785590
Producers of Government Services	...	...	443982	...	...	477033	...	...	504251
Other Producers	...	...	...	...	...	...	...	...	...
Total	...	...	3793920	...	...	4057440	...	...	4289840
Less: Imputed bank service charge	...	...	88844	...	...	104345	...	...	113087
Import duties	...	...	11904	...	...	12158	...	...	13654
Value added tax	...	...	...	...	...	...	...	...	...
Other adjustments [e]	...	...	5359	...	...	-5644	...	...	-4914
Total	...	...	3722340	...	...	3959610	...	...	4185490

of which General Government:

1 Agriculture, hunting, forestry and fishing	...	...	...	...	...	...	...	...	...

United States

4.1 Derivation of Value Added by Kind of Activity, in Current Prices
(Continued)

Million United States dollars

		1984			1985			1986		
		Gross Output	Intermediate Consumption	Value Added	Gross Output	Intermediate Consumption	Value Added	Gross Output	Intermediate Consumption	Value Added
2	Mining and quarrying	...	...	...	...	...	...	...	...	...
3	Manufacturing	...	...	...	...	...	...	...	...	...
4	Electricity, gas and water	...	...	...	...	...	...	...	...	...
5	Construction	...	...	...	...	...	...	...	...	...
6	Wholesale and retail trade, restaurants and hotels	...	...	...	...	...	...	...	...	...
7	Transport and communication	...	...	...	...	...	...	...	...	...
8	Finance, insurance, real estate and business services	...	...	...	...	...	...	...	...	...
9	Community, social and personal services	...	...	...	...	...	...	...	...	...
	Total, Industries of General Government	...	...	51940	...	...	58551	...	...	62774
	Producers of Government Services	...	...	...	...	...	...	...	...	...
	Total, General Government	...	...	...	...	...	...	...	...	...

a) Item 'Agriculture, hunting, forestry and fishing' excludes hunting.
b) Item 'Electricity, gas and water' also includes sanitary and similar services.
c) Restaurants is included in Retail Trade.
d) Item 'Statistical discrepancy' refers to government enterprises.
e) Item 'Other adjustments' refers to statistical discrepancy.

4.2 Derivation of Value Added by Kind of Activity, in Constant Prices

Million United States dollars

		1980			1981			1982			1983		
		Gross Output	Intermediate Consumption	Value Added	Gross Output	Intermediate Consumption	Value Added	Gross Output	Intermediate Consumption	Value Added	Gross Output	Intermediate Consumption	Value Added

At constant prices of: 1980

All Producers

1	Agriculture, hunting, forestry and fishing a	...	...	70320	...	...	81329	...	...	82539	...	...	67065
2	Mining and quarrying	...	...	107854	...	...	111078	...	...	104573	...	...	99450
	A Coal mining	...	...	12994	...	...	12931	...	...	13151	...	...	12437
	B Crude petroleum and natural gas production	...	...	85345	...	...	88250	...	...	84287	...	...	79584
	C Metal ore mining	...	...	3876	...	...	4138	...	...	2537	...	...	2368
	D Other mining	...	...	5639	...	...	5760	...	...	4597	...	...	5060
3	Manufacturing	...	...	586438	...	...	597779	...	...	560720	...	...	594971
	A Manufacture of food, beverages and tobacco	...	...	60009	...	...	62039	...	...	63962	...	...	64405
	B Textile, wearing apparel and leather industries	...	...	36269	...	...	36239	...	...	33981	...	...	36118
	C Manufacture of wood and wood products, including furniture	...	...	27505	...	...	25947	...	...	22911	...	...	25472
	D Manufacture of paper and paper products, printing and publishing	...	...	55098	...	...	56250	...	...	58358	...	...	61495
	E Manufacture of chemicals and chemical petroleum, coal, rubber and plastic products	...	...	80446	...	...	84170	...	...	83404	...	...	89292
	F Manufacture of non-metallic mineral products, except products of petroleum and coal	...	...	19155	...	...	17966	...	...	16524	...	...	17896
	G Basic metal industries	...	...	44527	...	...	46348	...	...	34004	...	...	28922
	H Manufacture of fabricated metal products, machinery and equipment	...	...	253728	...	...	267144	...	...	236867	...	...	261764
	I Other manufacturing industries	...	...	9701	...	...	11676	...	...	10709	...	...	9609
4	Electricity, gas and water b	...	...	68682	...	...	73749	...	...	73992	...	...	76401
5	Construction	...	...	139366	...	...	127320	...	...	121798	...	...	127020
6	Wholesale and retail trade, restaurants and hotels	...	...	455226	...	...	460673	...	...	459839	...	...	479268
	A Wholesale and retail trade c	...	...	436120	...	...	441889	...	...	441545	...	...	460272
	B Restaurants and hotels c	...	...	19106	...	...	18784	...	...	18293	...	...	18996
	Restaurants	...	...	...	...	...	...	...	...	...	...	...	...
	Hotels and other lodging places	...	...	19106	...	...	18784	...	...	18293	...	...	18996
7	Transport, storage and communication	...	...	173314	...	...	170659	...	...	164326	...	...	172136
	A Transport and storage	...	...	106575	...	...	100185	...	...	91443	...	...	93799

United States

4.2 Derivation of Value Added by Kind of Activity, in Constant Prices
(Continued)

Million United States dollars

	1980 Gross Output	1980 Intermediate Consumption	1980 Value Added	1981 Gross Output	1981 Intermediate Consumption	1981 Value Added	1982 Gross Output	1982 Intermediate Consumption	1982 Value Added	1983 Gross Output	1983 Intermediate Consumption	1983 Value Added
				At constant prices of:1980								
B Communication	...	...	66739	...	...	70474	...	...	72882	...	...	78338
8 Finance, insurance, real estate and business services	...	...	548516	...	...	565760	...	...	565002	...	...	584203
A Financial institutions	...	...	71758	...	...	74073	...	...	77364	...	...	78569
B Insurance	...	...	52441	...	...	52950	...	...	54553	...	...	55246
C Real estate and business services	...	...	424317	...	...	438738	...	...	433084	...	...	450389
Real estate, except dwellings	...	...	220307	...	...	228085	...	...	220246	...	...	233666
Dwellings	...	...	204010	...	...	210653	...	...	212838	...	...	216724
9 Community, social and personal services	...	...	224472	...	...	233150	...	...	237537	...	...	245786
A Sanitary and similar services [b]	...	...	...	...	...	...	...	...	...	...	...	...
B Social and related community services	...	...	150851	...	...	158599	...	...	162728	...	...	167719
Educational services	...	...	16020	...	...	16478	...	...	16916	...	...	17547
Medical, dental, other health and veterinary services	...	...	108533	...	...	115634	...	...	119245	...	...	123120
C Recreational and cultural services	...	...	17631	...	...	18605	...	...	19360	...	...	20198
D Personal and household services	...	...	55990	...	...	55947	...	...	55449	...	...	57869
Statistical discrepancy [d]	...	...	33840	...	...	33721	...	...	32658	...	...	33587
Total, Industries	...	...	2408030	...	...	2455220	...	...	2402980	...	...	2479890
Producers of Government Services	...	...	333978	...	...	337400	...	...	338089	...	...	340550
Other Producers	...	...	...	...	...	...	...	...	...	...	...	...
Total	...	...	2742010	...	...	2792620	...	...	2741070	...	...	2820440
Less: Imputed bank service charge	...	...	65620	...	...	64762	...	...	67357	...	...	71386
Import duties	...	...	7160	...	...	7958	...	...	7817	...	...	8093
Value added tax	...	...	...	...	...	...	...	...	...	...	...	...
Other adjustments [e]	...	...	4920	...	...	13525	...	...	-2951	...	...	26499
Total	...	...	2688470	...	...	2749340	...	...	2678580	...	...	2783640

of which General Government:

	1980 GO	1980 IC	1980 VA	1981 GO	1981 IC	1981 VA	1982 GO	1982 IC	1982 VA	1983 GO	1983 IC	1983 VA
1 Agriculture, hunting, forestry and fishing	...	...	...	...	...	...	...	...	...	...	...	...
2 Mining and quarrying	...	...	...	...	...	...	...	...	...	...	...	...
3 Manufacturing	...	...	...	...	...	...	...	...	...	...	...	...
4 Electricity, gas and water	...	...	...	...	...	...	...	...	...	...	...	...
5 Construction	...	...	...	...	...	...	...	...	...	...	...	...
6 Wholesale and retail trade, restaurants and hotels	...	...	...	...	...	...	...	...	...	...	...	...
7 Transport and communication	...	...	...	...	...	...	...	...	...	...	...	...
8 Finance, insurance, real estate and business services	...	...	...	...	...	...	...	...	...	...	...	...
9 Community, social and personal services	...	...	...	...	...	...	...	...	...	...	...	...
Total, Industries of General Government	...	...	33840	...	...	33721	...	...	32658	...	...	33587
Producers of Government Services	...	...	...	...	...	...	...	...	...	...	...	...
Total, General Government	...	...	...	...	...	...	...	...	...	...	...	...

	1984 Gross Output	1984 Intermediate Consumption	1984 Value Added	1985 Gross Output	1985 Intermediate Consumption	1985 Value Added	1986 Gross Output	1986 Intermediate Consumption	1986 Value Added
			At constant prices of:1980						
			All Producers						
1 Agriculture, hunting, forestry and fishing [a]	...	...	76496	...	...	87899	...	...	95094
2 Mining and quarrying	...	...	105884	...	...	104127	...	...	94671
A Coal mining	...	...	13980	...	...	13989	...	...	13617
B Crude petroleum and natural gas production	...	...	83529	...	...	81733	...	...	72905
C Metal ore mining	...	...	2784	...	...	2653	...	...	2675
D Other mining	...	...	5590	...	...	5751	...	...	5474

United States

4.2 Derivation of Value Added by Kind of Activity, in Constant Prices
(Continued)

Million United States dollars

	1984 Gross Output	1984 Intermediate Consumption	1984 Value Added	1985 Gross Output	1985 Intermediate Consumption	1985 Value Added	1986 Gross Output	1986 Intermediate Consumption	1986 Value Added
				At constant prices of:1980					
3 Manufacturing	...	...	667550	...	...	697020	...	...	716679
A Manufacture of food, beverages and tobacco	...	...	63091	...	...	63968	...	...	63463
B Textile, wearing apparel and leather industries	...	...	36647	...	...	35051	...	...	35435
C Manufacture of wood and wood products, including furniture	...	...	28756	...	...	28647	...	...	29520
D Manufacture of paper and paper products, printing and publishing	...	...	64081	...	...	65591	...	...	65978
E Manufacture of chemicals and chemical petroleum, coal, rubber and plastic products	...	...	92579	...	...	90108	...	...	94594
F Manufacture of non-metallic mineral products, except products of petroleum and coal	...	...	19631	...	...	20158	...	...	20160
G Basic metal industries	...	...	33365	...	...	32819	...	...	33745
H Manufacture of fabricated metal products, machinery and equipment	...	...	315372	...	...	346388	...	...	359875
I Other manufacturing industries	...	...	14026	...	...	14291	...	...	13908
4 Electricity, gas and water [b]	...	...	83563	...	...	85194	...	...	83672
5 Construction	...	...	137274	...	...	141584	...	...	145045
6 Wholesale and retail trade, restaurants and hotels			521574			551307			578440
A Wholesale and retail trade [c]	...	...	502218	...	...	531661	...	...	559061
B Restaurants and hotels [c]	...	...	19355	...	...	19646	...	...	19379
Restaurants	...	...	...	...	...	...	...	...	...
Hotels and other lodging places	...	...	19355	...	...	19646	...	...	19379
7 Transport, storage and communication	...	...	181135	...	...	183401	...	...	187757
A Transport and storage	...	...	101965	...	...	103044	...	...	106560
B Communication	...	...	79171	...	...	80356	...	...	81197
8 Finance, insurance, real estate and business services	...	...	611029	...	...	635684	...	...	670421
A Financial institutions	...	...	81730	...	...	83366	...	...	86861
B Insurance	...	...	56884	...	...	61015	...	...	67880
C Real estate and business services	...	...	472414	...	...	491303	...	...	515680
Real estate, except dwellings	...	...	250241	...	...	261336	...	...	277119
Dwellings	...	...	222174	...	...	229967	...	...	238560
9 Community, social and personal services	...	...	256926	...	...	268204	...	...	277424
A Sanitary and similar services [b]	...	...	...	...	...	...	...	...	...
B Social and related community services	...	...	174852	...	...	180757	...	...	187995
Educational services	...	...	18261	...	...	18754	...	...	18905
Medical, dental, other health and veterinary services	...	...	128531	...	...	133420	...	...	139354
C Recreational and cultural services	...	...	20644	...	...	22441	...	...	22810
D Personal and household services	...	...	61431	...	...	65007	...	...	66620
Statistical discrepancy [d]	...	...	34497	...	...	35698	...	...	37235
Total, Industries			2675930			2790120			2886440
Producers of Government Services	...	...	342795	...	...	348741	...	...	353243
Other Producers	...	...	...	...	...	...	...	...	...
Total	...	...	3018720	...	...	3138860	...	...	3239680
Less: Imputed bank service charge	...	...	72023	...	...	74305	...	...	76347
Import duties	...	...	10294	...	...	10544	...	...	11887
Value added tax	...	...	...	...	...	...	...	...	...
Other adjustments [e]	...	...	25991	...	...	11186	...	...	4853
Total	...	...	2982980	...	...	3086280	...	...	3180070

United States

4.2 Derivation of Value Added by Kind of Activity, in Constant Prices
(Continued)

Million United States dollars

	1984			1985			1986		
	Gross Output	Intermediate Consumption	Value Added	Gross Output	Intermediate Consumption	Value Added	Gross Output	Intermediate Consumption	Value Added

At constant prices of: 1980

of which General Government:

1 Agriculture, hunting, forestry and fishing	...	...	...	...	...	...	...	...	...
2 Mining and quarrying	...	...	...	...	...	...	...	...	...
3 Manufacturing	...	...	...	...	...	...	...	...	...
4 Electricity, gas and water	...	...	...	...	...	...	...	...	...
5 Construction	...	...	...	...	...	...	...	...	...
6 Wholesale and retail trade, restaurants and hotels	...	...	...	...	...	...	...	...	...
7 Transport and communication	...	...	...	...	...	...	...	...	...
8 Finance, insurance, real estate and business services	...	...	...	...	...	...	...	...	...
9 Community, social and personal services	...	...	...	...	...	...	...	...	...
Total, Industries of General Government	...	...	34497	...	...	35698	...	...	37235
Producers of Government Services	...	...	...	...	...	...	...	...	...
Total, General Government	...	...	...	...	...	...	...	...	...

a) Item 'Agriculture, hunting, forestry and fishing' excludes hunting.
b) Item 'Electricity, gas and water' also includes sanitary and similar services.
c) Restaurants is included in Retail Trade.
d) Item 'Statistical discrepancy' refers to government enterprises.
e) Item 'Other adjustments' refers to statistical discrepancy and residual.

4.3 Cost Components of Value Added

Million United States dollars

	1980						1981					
	Compensation of Employees	Capital Consumption	Net Operating Surplus	Indirect Taxes	Less: Subsidies Received	Value Added	Compensation of Employees	Capital Consumption	Net Operating Surplus	Indirect Taxes	Less: Subsidies Received	Value Added

All Producers

1 Agriculture, hunting, forestry and fishing a	15049	12275	40874	3195	1073	70320	15507	13168	53111	3488	1552	83722
2 Mining and quarrying	28773	17917	44225	16939	-	107854	35830	23333	50499	34739	3	144398
A Coal mining	7785	1842	2018	1349	-	12994	8183	1953	2333	1434	3	13900
B Crude petroleum and natural gas production	15290	14598	40525	14932	...	85345	21322	20154	47254	32611	...	121341
C Metal ore mining	2948	368	167	393	...	3876	3450	229	-188	402	...	3893
D Other mining	2750	1109	1515	265	...	5639	2875	997	1100	292	...	5264
3 Manufacturing	436141	56943	67817	25813	276	586438	475363	68461	78730	27279	202	649631
A Manufacture of food, beverages and tobacco	34917	5649	10639	8804	...	60009	37661	6615	13420	9095	...	66791
B Textile, wearing apparel and leather industries	29185	1768	4900	416	...	36269	31231	1961	5487	454	...	39133
C Manufacture of wood and wood products, including furniture	18901	3228	4874	502	...	27505	19850	3348	2919	455	...	26572
D Manufacture of paper and paper products, printing and publishing	39381	4896	9650	1171	...	55098	43223	5978	10201	1322	...	60724
E Manufacture of chemicals and chemical petroleum, coal, rubber and plastic products	51255	11157	10173	7861	...	80446	56838	13391	15135	8227	...	93591
F Manufacture of non-metallic mineral products, except products of petroleum and coal	14333	2319	2001	502	...	19155	15118	2484	1037	542	...	19181
G Basic metal industries	33139	6199	4061	1128	...	44527	36019	7238	5682	1244	...	50183
H Manufacture of fabricated metal products, machinery and equipment	208249	20821	19742	5192	276	253728	228187	26232	21676	5653	202	281546
I Other manufacturing industries	6781	906	1777	237	...	9701	7236	1214	3173	287	...	11910
4 Electricity, gas and water b	21996	14014	21797	10875	-	68682	24912	15801	27623	12511	-	80847
5 Construction	92672	7460	36646	2588	-	139366	97859	8107	31637	2718	-	140321
6 Wholesale and retail trade, restaurants and hotels	276074	27828	86374	64950	-	455226	301568	33023	95546	70217	-	500354
A Wholesale and retail trade c	264708	25521	82279	63612	-	436120	288538	30004	92560	68714	-	479816
B Restaurants and hotels	11366	2307	4095	1338	...	19106	13030	3019	2986	1503	...	20538
Restaurants c	...	...	...	...	...	...	...	...	...	...	...	...
Hotels and other lodging places	11366	2307	4095	1338	...	19106	13030	3019	2986	1503	...	20538
7 Transport, storage and communication	106133	28165	29796	10887	1667	173314	115924	33661	30998	11288	1713	190158

United States

4.3 Cost Components of Value Added
(Continued)

Million United States dollars

		1980						1981					
		Compensation of Employees	Capital Consumption	Net Operating Surplus	Indirect Taxes	Less: Subsidies Received	Value Added	Compensation of Employees	Capital Consumption	Net Operating Surplus	Indirect Taxes	Less: Subsidies Received	Value Added
	A Transport and storage	70933	14610	17913	4786	1667	106575	75731	17623	17372	4547	1713	113560
	B Communication	35200	13555	11883	6101	...	66739	40193	16038	13626	6741	...	76598
8	Finance, insurance, real estate and business services	174411	63305	247940	65851	2991	548516	199053	74941	276850	75199	3581	622462
	A Financial institutions	47105	6738	14728	3187	...	71758	53744	9110	18826	3670	...	85350
	B Insurance	33154	2084	11938	5377	112	52441	36492	2522	6840	5668	-	51522
	C Real estate and business services	94152	54483	221274	57287	2879	424317	108817	63309	251184	65861	3581	485590
	Real estate, except dwellings	92000	24768	88201	16299	961	220307	106459	31106	95924	20003	1154	252338
	Dwellings	2152	29715	133073	40988	1918	204010	2358	32203	155260	45858	2427	233252
9	Community, social and personal services	165270	10875	43304	5023	-	224472	187077	12208	45579	5448	-	250312
	A Sanitary and similar services [b]	...	...	...	...	...	...	...	...	...	...	...	...
	B Social and related community services	123875	2795	23201	980	...	150851	141761	3595	24799	1053	...	171208
	Educational services	14815	178	924	103	...	16020	16529	220	722	89	...	17560
	Medical, dental, other health and veterinary services	83299	2264	22231	739	...	108533	97442	2930	24056	814	...	125242
	C Recreational and cultural services	11982	2203	1703	1743	...	17631	13286	2769	1915	1833	...	19803
	D Personal and household services	29413	5877	18400	2300	...	55990	32030	5844	18865	2562	...	59301
Statistical discrepancy [d]		35763	5023	-2230	...	4716	33840	40306	5507	-2706	...	5131	37976
Total, Industries		1352280	243805	616543	206121	10723	2408030	1493400	288210	687867	242887	12182	2700180
Producers of Government Services		294059	39919	...	...	...	333978	323789	42470	...	...	...	366259
Other Producers		...	...	...	...	...	...	...	...	...	...	...	...
Total		1646340	283724	616543	206121	10723	2742010	1817190	330680	687867	242887	12182	3066440
Less: Imputed bank service charge		...	...	65620	...	...	65620	...	...	69681	...	...	69681
Import duties		...	...	...	7160	...	7160	...	...	...	8589	...	8589
Value added tax		...	...	...	...	...	...	...	...	...	...	...	...
Other adjustments [e]		...	...	...	4920	...	4920	...	...	...	4124	...	4124
Total [f]		1646340	283724	550923	218201	10723	2688470	1817190	330680	618186	255600	12182	3009470

of which General Government:

1	Agriculture, hunting, forestry and fishing	...	...	...	...	...	...	...	...	...	...	...	...
2	Mining and quarrying	...	...	...	...	...	...	...	...	...	...	...	...
3	Manufacturing	...	...	...	...	...	...	...	...	...	...	...	...
4	Electricity, gas and water	...	...	...	...	...	...	...	...	...	...	...	...
5	Construction	...	...	...	...	...	...	...	...	...	...	...	...
6	Wholesale and retail trade, restaurants and hotels	...	...	...	...	...	...	...	...	...	...	...	...
7	Transport and communication	...	...	...	...	...	...	...	...	...	...	...	...
8	Finance, insurance, real estate & business services	...	...	...	...	...	...	...	...	...	...	...	...
9	Community, social and personal services	...	...	...	...	...	...	...	...	...	...	...	...
Total, Industries of General Government		35763	5023	-2230	...	4716	33840	40306	5507	-2706	...	5131	37976
Producers of Government Services		...	...	...	...	...	...	...	...	...	...	...	...
Total, General Government		...	...	...	...	...	...	...	...	...	...	...	...

		1982						1983					
		Compensation of Employees	Capital Consumption	Net Operating Surplus	Indirect Taxes	Less: Subsidies Received	Value Added	Compensation of Employees	Capital Consumption	Net Operating Surplus	Indirect Taxes	Less: Subsidies Received	Value Added

All Producers

1	Agriculture, hunting, forestry and fishing [a]	16993	14338	48854	3575	2390	81370	17183	14877	38703	3550	7919	66394
2	Mining and quarrying	37454	29627	38334	27485	7	132893	33107	36728	28034	21193	2	119060
	A Coal mining	8883	2169	2055	2122	7	15222	7473	2623	2321	1990	2	14405
	B Crude petroleum and natural gas production	23123	26489	36522	24660	...	110794	20618	32578	25202	18530	...	96928
	C Metal ore mining	2628	199	-893	410	...	2344	2140	329	-304	389	...	2554
	D Other mining	2820	770	650	293	...	4533	2876	1198	815	284	...	5173

United States

4.3 Cost Components of Value Added
(Continued)

Million United States dollars

	\multicolumn{6}{c	}{1982}	\multicolumn{6}{c}{1983}
	Compensation of Employees	Capital Consumption	Net Operating Surplus	Indirect Taxes	Less: Subsidies Received	Value Added	Compensation of Employees	Capital Consumption	Net Operating Surplus	Indirect Taxes	Less: Subsidies Received	Value Added
3 Manufacturing	473056	78761	61154	28249	199	641021	490606	88306	74630	35989	38	689493
A Manufacture of food, beverages and tobacco	39582	8504	13918	8956	...	70960	40706	9917	14422	12098	...	77143
B Textile, wearing apparel and leather industries	30105	2143	5476	488	...	38212	32152	2200	6541	513	...	41406
C Manufacture of wood and wood products, including furniture	18977	3399	2911	545	...	25832	21709	3836	5309	552	...	31406
D Manufacture of paper and paper products, printing and publishing	45862	7174	11123	1457	...	65616	49255	7890	11893	1598	...	70636
E Manufacture of chemicals and chemical petroleum, coal, rubber and plastic products	59725	16059	15575	8523	...	99882	62470	17881	17835	12623	...	110809
F Manufacture of non-metallic mineral products, except products of petroleum and coal	14458	2704	584	574	...	18320	15162	2742	1822	610	...	20336
G Basic metal industries	30198	7115	-3078	1371	...	35606	28173	6217	-5201	1429	...	30618
H Manufacture of fabricated metal products, machinery and equipment	226706	30317	12450	6046	199	275320	233324	35928	21210	6256	38	296680
I Other manufacturing industries	7443	1346	2195	289	...	11273	7655	1695	799	310	...	10459
4 Electricity, gas and water [b]	28368	18373	31606	14143	-	92490	30589	21487	36362	15563	-	104001
5 Construction	97703	9004	33498	2751	-	142956	100485	9622	38073	3141	-	151321
6 Wholesale and retail trade, restaurants and hotels	318080	38210	95727	73483	-	525500	338495	40921	102397	81899	-	563712
A Wholesale and retail trade [c]	303953	34714	93154	71807	-	503628	322933	36908	99385	79973	-	539199
B Restaurants and hotels	14127	3496	2573	1676	...	21872	15562	4013	3012	1926	...	24513
Restaurants [c]	...	...	...	...	...	...	...	...	...	...	...	...
Hotels and other lodging places	14127	3496	2573	1676	...	21872	15562	4013	3012	1926	...	24513
7 Transport, storage and communication	121324	35621	30519	11929	1630	197763	124765	43160	36631	15250	1973	217833
A Transport and storage	76055	16865	15783	4805	1630	111878	78203	19096	20153	6053	1973	121532
B Communication	45269	18756	14736	7124	...	85885	46562	24064	16478	9197	...	96301
8 Finance, insurance, real estate and business services	222278	82246	280720	82723	4840	663127	249470	96061	316187	90381	5649	746450
A Financial institutions	61477	10988	14754	3784	...	91003	70865	12802	25352	4115	...	113134
B Insurance	39848	2888	-361	6048	-	48423	42838	4150	2048	6821	-	55857
C Real estate and business services	120953	68370	266327	72891	4840	523701	135767	79109	288787	79445	5649	577459
Real estate, except dwellings	118368	33713	97469	22209	2099	269660	133121	41897	106370	24991	2534	303845
Dwellings	2585	34657	168858	50682	2741	254041	2646	37212	182417	54454	3115	273614
9 Community, social and personal services	208325	14670	47668	5888	-	276551	227095	17239	52049	6503	-	302886
A Sanitary and similar services [b]	...	...	...	...	...	...	...	...	...	...	...	...
B Social and related community services	159811	4495	26957	1183	...	192446	174728	5544	29080	1347	...	210699
Educational services	18005	267	791	99	...	19162	19825	337	763	101	...	21026
Medical, dental, other health and veterinary services	111951	3760	26081	920	...	142712	122838	4759	28150	1084	...	156831
C Recreational and cultural services	14401	3438	1900	1914	...	21653	15732	4060	1771	2042	...	23605
D Personal and household services	34113	6737	18811	2791	...	62452	36635	7635	21198	3114	...	68582
Statistical discrepancy [d]	42644	5979	-2183	...	6417	40023	45778	6438	-1537	...	6594	44085
Total, Industries	1566230	326829	665897	250226	15483	2793690	1657570	374839	721529	273469	22175	3005240
Producers of Government Services	351777	43597	...	...	...	395374	374733	44589	...	...	...	419322
Other Producers	...	...	...	...	...	...	...	...	...	...	...	...
Total	1918000	370426	665897	250226	15483	3189070	2032310	419428	721529	273469	22175	3424560
Less: Imputed bank service charge	...	...	76225	...	...	76225	...	...	85345	...	...	85345
Import duties	...	...	...	8609	...	8609	...	...	...	9091	...	9091
Value added tax	...	...	...	...	...	...	...	...	...	...	...	...
Other adjustments [e]	...	...	...	-56	...	-56	...	...	...	5170	...	5170
Total [f]	1918000	370426	589672	258779	15483	3121400	2032310	419428	636184	287730	22175	3353470

United States

4.3 Cost Components of Value Added
(Continued)

Million United States dollars

	1982						1983					
	Compensation of Employees	Capital Consumption	Net Operating Surplus	Indirect Taxes	Less: Subsidies Received	Value Added	Compensation of Employees	Capital Consumption	Net Operating Surplus	Indirect Taxes	Less: Subsidies Received	Value Added
				of which General Government:								
1 Agriculture, hunting, forestry and fishing	...	...	...	...	...	...	...	...	...	...	...	...
2 Mining and quarrying	...	...	...	...	...	...	...	...	...	...	...	...
3 Manufacturing	...	...	...	...	...	...	...	...	...	...	...	...
4 Electricity, gas and water	...	...	...	...	...	...	...	...	...	...	...	...
5 Construction	...	...	...	...	...	...	...	...	...	...	...	...
6 Wholesale and retail trade, restaurants and hotels	...	...	...	...	...	...	...	...	...	...	...	...
7 Transport and communication	...	...	...	...	...	...	...	...	...	...	...	...
8 Finance, insurance, real estate & business services	...	...	...	...	...	...	...	...	...	...	...	...
9 Community, social and personal services	...	...	...	...	...	...	...	...	...	...	...	...
Total, Industries of General Government	42644	5979	-2183	...	6417	40023	45778	6438	-1537	...	6594	44085
Producers of Government Services	...	...	...	...	...	...	...	...	...	...	...	...
Total, General Government	...	...	...	...	...	...	...	...	...	...	...	...

	1984						1985					
	Compensation of Employees	Capital Consumption	Net Operating Surplus	Indirect Taxes	Less: Subsidies Received	Value Added	Compensation of Employees	Capital Consumption	Net Operating Surplus	Indirect Taxes	Less: Subsidies Received	Value Added
				All Producers								
1 Agriculture, hunting, forestry and fishing [a]	17840	15422	55729	3357	7043	85305	18890	14959	53015	3477	6296	84045
2 Mining and quarrying	35251	40589	24359	20149	1	120347	34931	45231	21620	17484	2	119264
A Coal mining	8219	2613	1745	2104	1	14680	8000	2987	1263	2199	2	14447
B Crude petroleum and natural gas production	21768	36148	21978	17281	...	97175	21787	40182	19693	14477	...	96139
C Metal ore mining	2115	286	-570	424	...	2255	1837	341	-259	447	...	2366
D Other mining	3149	1542	1206	340	...	6237	3307	1721	923	361	...	6312
3 Manufacturing	540658	96170	102160	39433	8	778413	564765	105407	96266	40027	4	806461
A Manufacture of food, beverages and tobacco	42027	10997	14948	11981	...	79953	43487	11820	16060	11529	...	82896
B Textile, wearing apparel and leather industries	33758	2738	5006	570	...	42072	32786	3135	4303	628	...	40852
C Manufacture of wood and wood products, including furniture	24362	3703	6520	890	...	35475	25251	3753	6234	675	...	35913
D Manufacture of paper and paper products, printing and publishing	54359	9707	14165	1800	...	80031	58002	10539	15203	1956	...	85700
E Manufacture of chemicals and chemical petroleum, coal, rubber and plastic products	66468	19417	21355	14060	...	121300	69136	19770	19665	14154	...	122725
F Manufacture of non-metallic mineral products, except products of petroleum and coal	16616	3039	2777	682	...	23114	17016	2792	3829	745	...	24382
G Basic metal industries	30358	3642	960	1585	...	36545	29324	5570	-1554	1713	...	35053
H Manufacture of fabricated metal products, machinery and equipment	264525	40454	33472	7512	8	345955	281541	45121	29857	8223	4	364738
I Other manufacturing industries	8185	2473	2957	353	...	13968	8222	2907	2669	404	...	14202
4 Electricity, gas and water [b]	32776	25335	44453	16932	-	119496	35194	26664	45843	19664	-	127365
5 Construction	113890	10826	45245	3565	-	173526	124899	11107	46713	3899	-	186618
6 Wholesale and retail trade, restaurants and hotels	376248	46184	119019	93571	-	635022	404523	56539	124177	102277	-	687516
A Wholesale and retail trade [c]	358578	41440	116274	91401	-	607693	385182	51655	120941	99874	-	657652
B Restaurants and hotels	17670	4744	2745	2170	...	27329	19341	4884	3236	2403	...	29864
Restaurants [c]	...	...	...	...	...	...	...	...	...	...	...	...
Hotels and other lodging places	17670	4744	2745	2170	...	27329	19341	4884	3236	2403	...	29864
7 Transport, storage and communication	132382	46170	43685	16858	1869	237226	137914	54146	43000	18188	1773	251475
A Transport and storage	85159	20345	24112	6875	1869	134622	89009	23892	23343	7252	1773	141723
B Communication	47223	25825	19573	9983	...	102604	48905	30254	19657	10936	...	109752
8 Finance, insurance, real estate and business services	282348	110656	330298	100969	6747	817524	317037	127816	353508	108227	6903	899685
A Financial institutions	77490	14563	17436	4817	...	114306	86526	19569	14312	5385	...	125792

United States

4.3 Cost Components of Value Added
(Continued)

Million United States dollars

	1984						1985					
	Compensation of Employees	Capital Consumption	Net Operating Surplus	Indirect Taxes	Less: Subsidies Received	Value Added	Compensation of Employees	Capital Consumption	Net Operating Surplus	Indirect Taxes	Less: Subsidies Received	Value Added
B Insurance	46240	4800	-1940	7247	-	56347	50961	5886	-2503	8279	-	62623
C Real estate and business services	158618	91293	314802	88905	6747	646871	179550	102361	341699	94563	6903	711270
Real estate, except dwellings	155711	50978	118156	29840	3408	351277	176334	57879	125072	31109	2880	387514
Dwellings	2907	40315	196646	59065	3339	295594	3216	44482	216627	63454	4023	323756
9 Community, social and personal services	245895	20023	58042	7176	-	331136	264013	21062	66603	7750	-	359428
A Sanitary and similar services b	...	...	...	...	...	...	...	...	...	...	...	...
B Social and related community services	187711	6967	32975	1503	...	229156	201772	7320	36932	1671	...	247695
Educational services	21930	402	1075	150	...	23557	23592	456	1026	172	...	25246
Medical, dental, other health and veterinary services	131282	5726	31654	1161	...	169823	141081	6533	35571	1274	...	184459
C Recreational and cultural services	17001	4691	1612	2182	...	25486	18151	4653	3748	2267	...	28819
D Personal and household services	41183	8365	23455	3491	...	76494	44090	9089	25923	3812	...	82914
Statistical discrepancy d	49363	6942	2697	...	7062	51940	53320	7522	5643	...	7934	58551
Total, Industries	1826650	418317	825687	302010	22730	3349940	1955490	470453	856388	320993	22912	3580410
Producers of Government Services	397767	46215	...	...	...	443982	427419	49614	...	...	...	477033
Other Producers	...	...	...	...	...	...	...	...	...	...	...	...
Total	2224420	464532	825687	302010	22730	3793920	2382910	520067	856388	320993	22912	4057440
Less: Imputed bank service charge	...	...	88844	...	...	88844	...	...	104345	...	...	104345
Import duties	...	...	...	11904	...	11904	...	...	...	12158	...	12158
Value added tax	...	...	...	...	...	...	...	...	...	...	...	...
Other adjustments e	...	...	...	5359	...	5359	...	...	...	-5644	...	-5644
Total f	2224420	464532	736843	319273	22730	3722340	2382910	520067	752043	327507	22912	3959610

of which General Government:

1 Agriculture, hunting, forestry and fishing	...	...	...	...	...	...	...	...	...	...	...	...
2 Mining and quarrying	...	...	...	...	...	...	...	...	...	...	...	...
3 Manufacturing	...	...	...	...	...	...	...	...	...	...	...	...
4 Electricity, gas and water	...	...	...	...	...	...	...	...	...	...	...	...
5 Construction	...	...	...	...	...	...	...	...	...	...	...	...
6 Wholesale and retail trade, restaurants and hotels	...	...	...	...	...	...	...	...	...	...	...	...
7 Transport and communication	...	...	...	...	...	...	...	...	...	...	...	...
8 Finance, insurance, real estate & business services	...	...	...	...	...	...	...	...	...	...	...	...
9 Community, social and personal services	...	...	...	...	...	...	...	...	...	...	...	...
Total, Industries of General Government	49363	6942	2697	...	7062	51940	53320	7522	5643	...	7934	58551
Producers of Government Services	...	...	...	...	...	...	...	...	...	...	...	...
Total, General Government	...	...	...	...	...	...	...	...	...	...	...	...

	1986					
	Compensation of Employees	Capital Consumption	Net Operating Surplus	Indirect Taxes	Less: Subsidies Received	Value Added

All Producers

1 Agriculture, hunting, forestry and fishing a	19812	14309	59066	3432	9550	87069
2 Mining and quarrying	30688	42834	11576	11290	1	96387
A Coal mining	7700	2629	1319	2084	1	13731
B Crude petroleum and natural gas production	17920	38388	9240	8463	...	74011
C Metal ore mining	1686	278	317	393	...	2674
D Other mining	3382	1539	700	350	...	5971

United States

4.3 Cost Components of Value Added
(Continued)

Million United States dollars

	Compensation of Employees	Capital Consumption	Net Operating Surplus	Indirect Taxes	Less: Subsidies Received	Value Added
	\multicolumn{6}{c}{1986}
3 Manufacturing	576924	104633	106339	43948	-	831844
A Manufacture of food, beverages and tobacco	45208	11880	15559	11832	...	84479
B Textile, wearing apparel and leather industries	33752	3045	5073	680	...	42550
C Manufacture of wood and wood products, including furniture	26506	3407	7783	728	...	38424
D Manufacture of paper and paper products, printing and publishing	61214	10496	16203	2108	...	90021
E Manufacture of chemicals and chemical petroleum, coal, rubber and plastic products	70585	18617	25787	16757	...	131746
F Manufacture of non-metallic mineral products, except products of petroleum and coal	17601	2522	4579	801	...	25503
G Basic metal industries	28264	5509	-503	1853	...	35123
H Manufacture of fabricated metal products, machinery and equipment	285337	46147	29512	8742	-	369738
I Other manufacturing industries	8457	3010	2346	447	...	14260
4 Electricity, gas and water [b]	37285	27425	49297	18928	-	132935
5 Construction	133177	10086	52771	4169	-	200203
6 Wholesale and retail trade, restaurants and hotels	428604	60356	128920	109605		727405
A Wholesale and retail trade [c]	407767	55238	125286	107007	-	695298
B Restaurants and hotels	20837	5118	3634	2598	...	32187
Restaurants [c]	...	...	...	...		...
Hotels and other lodging places	20837	5118	3634	2598	...	32187
7 Transport, storage and communication	141893	54778	47139	19243	1825	261228
A Transport and storage	92070	22357	24932	7875	1825	145409
B Communication	49823	32421	22207	11368	...	115819
8 Finance, insurance, real estate and business services	357408	141457	394199	115191	7755	1000500
A Financial institutions	100556	22283	9888	5822	...	138549
B Insurance	56368	6721	7755	9905	-	80749
C Real estate and business services	200484	112453	376556	99464	7755	781202
Real estate, except dwellings	196992	64317	136646	31560	3707	425808
Dwellings	3492	48136	239910	67904	4048	355394
9 Community, social and personal services	282920	21830	72150	8260	-	385160
A Sanitary and similar services [b]	...	...	...	...	...	...
B Social and related community services	216759	7815	40488	1818	...	266880
Educational services	25000	456	1122	190	...	26768
Medical, dental, other health and veterinary services	152184	7031	38926	1388	...	199529
C Recreational and cultural services	19473	4459	4072	2333	...	30337
D Personal and household services	46688	9556	27590	4109	...	87943
Statistical discrepancy [d]	55834	8179	5937	...	7176	62774
Total, Industries	2064550	485887	927394	334066	26307	3785590
Producers of Government Services	452809	51442	...	...	...	504251
Other Producers	...	...	...	...	...	...
Total	2517350	537329	927394	334066	26307	4289840
Less: Imputed bank service charge	...	...	113087	...	...	113087
Import duties	...	...	...	13654	...	13654
Value added tax	...	...	...	...	...	...
Other adjustments [e]	...	...	...	-4914	...	-4914
Total [f]	2517350	537329	814307	342806	26307	4185490

United States

4.3 Cost Components of Value Added
(Continued)

Million United States dollars

	1986					
	Compensation of Employees	Capital Consumption	Net Operating Surplus	Indirect Taxes	Less: Subsidies Received	Value Added
	of which General Government:					
1 Agriculture, hunting, forestry and fishing	...	...	...	...	...	...
2 Mining and quarrying	...	...	...	...	...	...
3 Manufacturing	...	...	...	...	...	...
4 Electricity, gas and water	...	...	...	...	...	...
5 Construction	...	...	...	...	...	...
6 Wholesale and retail trade, restaurants and hotels	...	...	...	...	...	...
7 Transport and communication	...	...	...	...	...	...
8 Finance, insurance, real estate & business services	...	...	...	...	...	...
9 Community, social and personal services	...	...	...	...	...	...
Total, Industries of General Government	55834	8179	5937	...	7176	62774
Producers of Government Services	...	...	...	...	...	...
Total, General Government	...	...	...	...	...	...

a) Item 'Agriculture, hunting, forestry and fishing' excludes hunting.
b) Item 'Electricity, gas and water' also includes sanitary and similar services.
c) Restaurants is included in Retail Trade.
d) Item 'Statistical discrepancy' refers to government enterprises.
e) Item 'Other adjustments' refers to statistical discrepancy.

f) Totals shown in columns 2 and 3, capital consumption and net operating surplus, differ from the estimates shown in table 1.3 by the amount of total capital consumption adjustment (including that of government enterprises) which is included in table 1.3 and not in this table. Industry detail in this table is not available for capital consumption adjustment.

Uruguay

General note. The preparation of national accounts statistics in Uruguay is undertaken by the Banco Central del Uruguay, Montevideo. The official estimates together with some methological notes are published annually by the Banco Central in 'Producto e Ingreso Nacionales'. The following presentation of sources and methods is mainly based on a report entitled 'Metodologia del Calculo de las cuentas de actividades, a precios corrientes'. The estimates are generally in accordance with the classifications and definitions recommended in the United Nations System of National Accounts (SNA). The following tables have been prepared from successive replies to the United Nations national accounts questionnaire. When the scope and coverage of the estimates differ for conceptual or statistical reasons from the definitions and classifications recommended in SNA, a footnote is indicated to the relevant tables.

Sources and methods:

(a) Gross domestic product. Gross domestic product is estimated mainly through the production approach.

(b) Expenditure on the gross domestic product. All components of GDP by expenditure type are estimated through the expenditure approach except private final consumption expenditure and gross investment in machinery and equipments which are estimated by the commodity-flow approach. The estimates of government final consumption expenditure are based on the budgetary programmes of the different institutional subsectors. The items are analyzed in accordance with the government disbursements which are classified into ten different items. The commodity-flow approach is used to estimate private final consumption expenditure by separating the current products according to their origin and source. These estimates are periodically checked by surveys of homes and of family budgets. The estimates of increase in stocks refer to stock variations for meat and wool only. The estimates of imported machinery and equipment are based on c.i.f. import values classified by industry of origin, principal groups of goods and sectors of destination. Customs duties, indirect taxes, trade margins, etc. are then added. Domestically produced capital goods are estimated in the same manner. The estimates of exports and imports of goods and services are based on the foreign trade statistics which are adjusted for unregistered transactions. The balance-of-payments data are also used. For the constant price estimates, price deflation is used for government purchases of goods and services, public construction and exports and imports of services. For government compensation of employees, increase in stocks, private construction, investment in machinery and equipment and exports and imports of goods, the base-year estimates are extrapolated by quantity index. Private consumption expenditure is obtained as a residual.

(c) Cost-structure of the gross domestic product. The estimates of wages and salaries in the agricultural sector are estimated by using employment data and average wages obtained from censuses and extrapolated and interpolated by using indices of physical volumes. For private construction, the ratio of wages and salaries to the value of building is determined for the different types of construction work. For the trade sector, wages and salaries are measured from employment data obtained from the 1963 population census and extrapolated by volume index of commercialized merchandise. For the public sectors, compensation of employees is obtained directly from the government enterprises. In general, consumption of fixed capital is valued at original cost. Information of indirect taxes and subsidies is available directly for registered tax classifications by economic branch. Profits of government monopoly enterprises are treated as indirect taxes while deficits are treated as subsidies. Operating surplus is obtained as a residual.

(d) Gross domestic product by kind of economic activity. The table of GDP by kind of economic activity is prepared in factor values. The production approach is used to estimate the value added of most industries. However, the income approach is used for producers of government services, part of the construction sector and part of the services sector. The Ministerio de Ganaderia y Agricultura conducts censuses and surveys every four years, covering agricultural establishments of over one hectare. The censuses include various type of information such as ownership, locations, land tenure conditions, production, stocks, etc. The Ministerio also conducts annual sample surveys on principal crops, wool production, etc. The gross value of livestock production is based on the number of livestock, adjusted for imports and exports and changes in stocks. Data on mining production and prices are provided by the Instituto Geologico del Uruguay and the Camara de la Construccion, respectively. The estimates of intermediate consumption are based on the 1968 national economic census. For manufacturing, quarterly and annual surveys are conducted. They provide data on labour force, salaries and wages, raw materials, manufactured products, costs, etc. The value of electricity and water production is obtained directly from the concerned enterprises which are government monopolies. The data of gas production are furnished by the concerned companies. Basic information used to estimate the gross value of production in the building sector is obtained from the administrative records of the public sector. For private building, the municipal records provide data on approved licences, quantity, size and type of construction. This information is adjusted on the basis of surveys on time extension of buildings and areas. The accounting records of the central government and public enterprises supply the information used to estimate the gross production value of public buildings. The estimates of the trade sector are based on the gross value of commercialized production while intermediate consumption is obtained from an analysis of the accounts of certain enterprises. The Banco Central del Uruguay conducts surveys of trade channels and trade margins. For restaurants and hotels, the estimates are based on studies carried out in 1962 extrapolated by price and volume indexes. The production values of railways, air transport and ports are estimated from the data supplied by the respective government enterprises. For other transport, data are obtained directly from concerned enterprises and from licence permits issued. Bench-mark estimates of cargo transport were prepared for 1961. These estimates are projected by the use of an index of receipts. Information on water transport, storage and communication is obtained directly from a special maritime commission, from the Mercado de Frutos, and from the accounts of government enterprises, respectively. The estimates of banking services are obtained from administrative records. For real estate, the value of production is determined as the amount of gross rents paid or imputed for housing services. Owner-occupied dwellings are imputed in accordance with the average rents for rented houses. The estimates of business services are based on the number of persons employed and average wages. For producers of government services, the estimates are based on budgetary programmes of the institutional subsectors. For domestic service, data from the 1963 population census are extrapolated on the basis of information from employment agencies. For other private services, bench-mark studies referring to 1961 are extrapolated by the most suitable indicators. For the constant price estimates, value added of most industries is extrapolated by a quantity index. Double deflation is used for all components of the agricultural sector and price deflation is used for public construction.

1.1 Expenditure on the Gross Domestic Product, in Current Prices

Million Uruguayan pesos

	1970	1975	1977	1978	1979	1980	1981	1982	1983	1984	1985	1986
1 Government final consumption expenditure	92	1116	2451	3821	6789	11482	17336	20100	25653	36851	69084	129582
2 Private final consumption expenditure	448	6244	15018	22919	43441	69890	91147	94076	137826	216282	392451	691858
3 Gross capital formation	69	1102	3028	4951	9975	15994	18802	18555	18427	29115	39771	72164
A Increase in stocks [a]	-	12	-2	8	663	572	-403	-827	-1902	1784	1467	2885
B Gross fixed capital formation	69	1090	3030	4943	9312	15422	19205	19382	20329	27331	38304	69279
Residential buildings	37	734	1687	3122	5935	10324	13880	14931	14568	20663	27124	45000
Non residential buildings												
Other construction and land improvement etc.	4	36	57	93	208	227	157	178	289	455	605	1150
Other	28	320	1286	1728	3169	4871	5168	4273	5472	6213	10575	23129
4 Exports of goods and services	73	1017	3774	5530	9400	13861	17987	18072	44700	72065	122080	227097
5 Less: Imports of goods and services	81	1613	4356	6291	11980	19023	22819	22107	41600	59954	103228	175664
Equals: Gross Domestic Product	601	8166	19915	30930	57625	92204	122453	128696	185006	294359	520158	945037

a) Item 'Increase in stocks' refers to increase in stocks of wool and livestock in the private sector, and to stocks held by the public sector.

1.2 Expenditure on the Gross Domestic Product, in Constant Prices

Million Uruguayan pesos

	1970	1975	1977	1978	1979	1980	1981	1982	1983	1984	1985	1986
	\multicolumn{12}{c}{At constant prices of:1978}
1 Government final consumption expenditure	3047	3334	3465	3821	4302	4244	4562	4452	4322	4347	4479	4820
2 Private final consumption expenditure	21972	22758	22158	22919	24163	26232	26854	24257	21926	20497	20920	22141
3 Gross capital formation	2740	3057	4335	4951	6132	6461	5888	4815	3052	3111	2399	2545
A Increase in stocks [a]	-111	-84	14	8	250	206	-179	-350	-419	102	104	62
B Gross fixed capital formation	2851	3141	4321	4943	5882	6255	6067	5165	3471	3009	2295	2483

Uruguay

1.2 Expenditure on the Gross Domestic Product, in Constant Prices
(Continued)

Million Uruguayan pesos

	1970	1975	1977	1978	1979	1980	1981	1982	1983	1984	1985	1986
	At constant prices of:1978											
Residential buildings	1619	2049	2371	3122	3537	3757	3840	3638	2412	2239	1557	1507
Non-residential buildings												
Other construction and land improvement etc.	64	56	58	93	122	91	54	54	46	41	37	43
Other	1168	1036	1892	1728	2223	2407	2173	1473	1013	729	701	933
4 Exports of goods and services	3053	4086	5300	5530	5893	6106	6483	5801	6697	6744	6892	8164
5 Less: Imports of goods and services	4955	5305	5874	6291	7652	8235	8318	7187	5740	4883	4879	5981
Equals: Gross Domestic Product	25857	27930	29384	30930	32838	34808	35469	32138	30257	29816	29811	31689

a) Item 'Increase in stocks' refers to increase in stocks of wool and livestock in the private sector, and to stocks held by the public sector.

1.3 Cost Components of the Gross Domestic Product

Million Uruguayan pesos

	1970	1975	1977	1978	1979	1980	1981	1982	1983	1984	1985	1986
1 Indirect taxes, net	81	1058	2770	4638	7867	12665	16550	16735	22874	38224	71704	135879
A Indirect taxes	92	1224	3258	5357	8864	14552	19239	20181	27787	44405	79960	...
B Less: Subsidies	11	166	488	719	996	1887	2689	3446	4913	6181	8256	...
2 Consumption of fixed capital	22	343	954	1557	2933	4858	6050	6105	6404	8609	12066	21823
3 Compensation of employees paid by resident producers to:	269	3206	6894	10255	17030	28367	39890	45956	55671	81446	166138	...
4 Operating surplus a	229	3559	9297	14480	29795	46314	59963	59900	100057	166080	270250	...
Equals: Gross Domestic Product	601	8166	19915	30930	57625	92204	122453	128696	185006	294359	520158	945037

a) Item 'Operating surplus' has been obtained as a residual.

1.4 General Government Current Receipts and Disbursements

Million Uruguayan pesos

	1970	1975	1977	1978	1979	1980	1981	1982	1983	1984	1985	1986
	Receipts											
1 Operating surplus	...	...	...	...	...	...	...	...	...	...	...	...
2 Property and entrepreneurial income	2	5	17	54	203	185	169	447	193	294	444	...
3 Taxes, fees and contributions	167	2063	5458	8778	14380	24119	30563	33390	46553	69942	131052	...
A Indirect taxes	92	1224	3258	5357	8864	14552	19239	20181	27787	44405	79960	...
B Direct taxes	16	221	739	956	1528	3680	3885	4320	6980	9210	18573	...
C Social security contributions	59	618	1461	2465	3988	5887	7439	8889	11786	16327	32519	...
D Compulsory fees, fines and penalties	...	...	...	...	...	...	...	...	...	...	...	...
4 Other current transfers	...	...	...	...	...	...	...	...	...	...	...	...
Total Current Receipts of General Government	169	2068	5475	8832	14583	24304	30732	33837	46746	70236	131496	...
	Disbursements											
1 Government final consumption expenditure	92	1116	2451	3821	6789	11482	17336	20100	25653	36851	69084	...
2 Property income a	2	28	28	86	97	290	412	1769	3556	4823	6424	...
3 Subsidies	11	166	488	719	996	1887	2689	3446	4913	6181	8256	...
4 Other current transfers	57	670	1528	2447	3790	6722	12419	15662	18637	25176	42923	...
A Social security benefits	60	692	1550	2482	3834	6783	12501	15776	18935	25612	43783	...
B Social assistance grants	...	...	...	...	...	...	...	...	...	...	...	...
C Other	-3	-22	-22	-35	-44	-61	-82	-114	-298	-436	-860	...
5 Net saving	7	88	980	1759	2911	3923	-2124	-7140	-6013	-2795	4809	...
Total Current Disbursements and Net Saving of General Government	169	2068	5475	8832	14583	24304	30732	33837	46746	70236	131496	...

a) Item 'Property income' relates to interest on public debt.

1.10 Gross Domestic Product by Kind of Activity, in Current Prices

Million Uruguayan pesos

	1970	1975	1977	1978	1979	1980	1981	1982	1983	1984	1985	1986
1 Agriculture, hunting, forestry and fishing	67	851	2192	2946	6020	8860	9987	9942	16686	30415	48937	93270
2 Mining and quarrying	6	43	185	255	565	1191	1613	1465	2425	3080	4737	8811
3 Manufacturing	114	1756	4132	6363	13603	20603	24152	21724	38336	67279	121879	222154
4 Electricity, gas and water a	8	145	249	366	562	1185	1774	2587	4209	6589	12698	24076
5 Construction	20	336	725	1326	2544	4182	5965	6494	5621	6989	9596	17202

Uruguay

1.10 Gross Domestic Product by Kind of Activity, in Current Prices
(Continued)

Million Uruguayan pesos

	1970	1975	1977	1978	1979	1980	1981	1982	1983	1984	1985	1986
6 Wholesale and retail trade, restaurants and hotels	86	1349	3524	5248	10063	14910	19150	16401	24839	41746	...	...
7 Transport, storage and communication	45	542	1195	1709	2993	5083	6982	7898	11617	17304	31514	59454
8 Finance, insurance, real estate and business services	50	698	1815	3350	5709	10241	16315	21480	28585	41887	...	...
9 Community, social and personal services	24	279	709	1079	1844	3053	4493	5430	7269	9996	...	...
Total, Industries	420	5999	14726	22643	43903	69308	90431	93421	139587	225285	...	...
Producers of Government Services	77	881	1872	2914	4856	8490	12958	15406	18956	25765	48090	87174
Other Producers	23	228	547	735	999	1741	2514	3134	3589	5085	...	...
Subtotal b	520	7108	17145	26292	49758	79539	105903	111961	162132	256135	448454	809158
Less: Imputed bank service charge	...	...	...	...	...	...	...	...	...	...	...	...
Plus: Import duties	...	...	...	...	...	...	...	...	...	...	...	...
Plus: Value added tax	...	...	...	...	...	...	...	...	...	...	...	...
Plus: Other adjustments c	81	1058	2770	4638	7867	12665	16550	16735	22874	38224	71704	135879
Equals: Gross Domestic Product	601	8166	19915	30930	57625	92204	122453	128696	185006	294359	520158	945037

a) Item 'Electricity, gas and water' includes sewage services.
b) Gross domestic product in factor values.
c) Item 'Other adjustments' refers to indirect taxes net of subsidies.

1.11 Gross Domestic Product by Kind of Activity, in Constant Prices

Million Uruguayan pesos

	1970	1975	1977	1978	1979	1980	1981	1982	1983	1984	1985	1986
					At constant prices of:1978							
1 Agriculture, hunting, forestry and fishing	3197	3001	3150	2946	2933	3408	3596	3332	3402	3171	3315	3420
2 Mining and quarrying	151	207	238	255	317	374	367	290	248	205	166	191
3 Manufacturing	5058	5565	6017	6364	6818	6980	6662	5536	5148	5292	5207	5837
4 Electricity, gas and water a	281	314	338	366	379	408	430	435	444	441	454	487
5 Construction	686	876	1015	1326	1490	1546	1593	1545	1026	913	656	646
6 Wholesale and retail trade, restaurants and hotels	4451	4602	4948	5248	5726	6214	6341	5063	4591	4518	...	...
7 Transport, storage and communication	1485	1563	1712	1709	1885	2041	2025	1802	1717	1711	1695	1861
8 Finance, insurance, real estate and business services	2607	3269	3097	3350	3461	3645	3909	4070	4047	...	...	...
9 Community, social and personal services	1122	1066	1061	1079	1103	1104	1139	1118	1039	...	...	...
Total, Industries	19038	20463	21582	22643	24112	25720	26062	23191	21662	...	...	...
Producers of Government Services	2333	2524	2629	2914	3143	3147	3365	3373	3427	3446	3549	...
Other Producers	597	759	763	735	659	733	746	755	631	...	...	...
Subtotal b	21968	23746	24974	26292	27914	29600	30173	27319	25720	25345	25341	26937
Less: Imputed bank service charge	...	...	...	...	...	...	...	...	...	...	...	...
Plus: Import duties	...	...	...	...	...	...	...	...	...	...	...	...
Plus: Value added tax	...	...	...	...	...	...	...	...	...	...	...	...
Plus: Other adjustments c	3889	4184	4410	4638	4924	5208	5296	4819	4537	4471	4470	4752
Equals: Gross Domestic Product	25857	27930	29384	30930	32838	34808	35469	32138	30257	29816	29811	31689

a) Item 'Electricity, gas and water' includes sewage services.
b) Gross domestic product in factor values.
c) Item 'Other adjustments' refers to indirect taxes net of subsidies.

1.12 Relations Among National Accounting Aggregates

Million Uruguayan pesos

	1970	1975	1977	1978	1979	1980	1981	1982	1983	1984	1985	1986
Gross Domestic Product	601	8166	19915	30930	57625	92204	122453	128696	185006	294359	520158	945037
Plus: Net factor income from the rest of the world	-6	-168	-317	-465	-454	-912	-797	-2729	-9895	-20210	-35592	-41616
Equals: Gross National Product	595	7998	19598	30465	57171	91292	121656	125967	175111	274149	484566	903421
Less: Consumption of fixed capital	22	343	954	1557	2933	4858	6050	6105	6404	8609	12066	21823
Equals: National Income	573	7655	18644	28908	54238	86434	115606	119862	168707	265540	472500	881598
Plus: Net current transfers from the rest of the world	3	35	31	44	56	79	105	145	380	559	1093	3832
Equals: National Disposable Income	576	7690	18675	28952	54294	86513	115711	120007	169087	266099	473593	885430
Less: Final consumption	540	7360	17469	26740	50230	81372	108483	114176	163479	253133	461535	821440
Equals: Net Saving	36	330	1206	2212	4064	5141	7228	5831	5608	12966	12058	63990
Less: Surplus of the nation on current transactions	-11	-429	-868	-1182	-2978	-5995	-5524	-6619	-6415	-7540	-15647	13649
Equals: Net Capital Formation	47	759	2074	3394	7042	11136	12752	12450	12023	20506	27705	50341

Uruguay

2.7 Gross Capital Formation by Type of Good and Owner, in Current Prices

Million Uruguayan pesos

	\multicolumn{4}{c	}{1980}	\multicolumn{4}{c	}{1981}	\multicolumn{4}{c}{1982}
	TOTAL	Total Private	Public Enterprises	General Government	TOTAL	Total Private	Public Enterprises	General Government	TOTAL	Total Private	Public Enterprises	General Government
Increase in stocks, total [a]	572	572	-	...	-403	-403	-	...	-827	-827	-	...
Gross Fixed Capital Formation, Total	15422	10520	4902	...	19205	13046	6159	...	19382	10147	9235	...
1 Residential buildings	10324	6557	3767	...	13880	8365	5515	...	14931	7942	6989	...
2 Non-residential buildings	...	...	...	...	...	...	...	...	...	...	...	...
3 Other construction	...	...	...	...	...	...	...	...	...	...	...	...
4 Land improvement and plantation and orchard development	227	227	-	...	157	157	-	...	178	178	-	...
5 Producers' durable goods	4871	3736	1135	...	5168	4524	644	...	4273	2027	2246	...
6 Breeding stock, dairy cattle, etc.	...	...	...	...	...	...	...	...	...	...	...	...
Total Gross Capital Formation	15994	11092	4902	...	18802	12643	6159	...	18555	9320	9235	...

	\multicolumn{4}{c	}{1983}	\multicolumn{4}{c	}{1984}	\multicolumn{4}{c}{1985}
	TOTAL	Total Private	Public Enterprises	General Government	TOTAL	Total Private	Public Enterprises	General Government	TOTAL	Total Private	Public Enterprises	General Government
Increase in stocks, total [a]	-1902	-1902	-	...	1784	1784	-	-	1467	1467	-	...
Gross Fixed Capital Formation, Total	20329	12808	7521	...	27331	15345	11986	-	38304	24060	14244	...
1 Residential buildings	14568	8776	5792	...	20663	9401	11262	-	27124	14113	13011	...
2 Non-residential buildings	...	...	...	...	...	...	...	...	...	...	...	...
3 Other construction	...	...	...	...	...	...	...	...	...	...	...	...
4 Land improvement and plantation and orchard development	289	289	-	...	455	455	-	-	605	605	-	...
5 Producers' durable goods	5472	3743	1729	...	6213	5489	724	-	10575	9342	1233	...
6 Breeding stock, dairy cattle, etc.	...	...	...	...	...	...	...	...	...	...	...	...
Total Gross Capital Formation	18427	10906	7521	...	29115	17129	11986	...	39771	25527	14244	...

	\multicolumn{4}{c}{1986}
	TOTAL	Total Private	Public Enterprises	General Government
Increase in stocks, total [a]	2885	2885	-	...
Gross Fixed Capital Formation, Total	69279	41888	27391	...
1 Residential buildings	45000	21905	23095	...
2 Non-residential buildings	...	...	...	...
3 Other construction	...	...	...	...
4 Land improvement and plantation and orchard development	1150	1150	-	...
5 Producers' durable goods	23129	18833	4296	...
6 Breeding stock, dairy cattle, etc.	...	...	...	...
Total Gross Capital Formation	72164	44773	27391	...

a) Item 'Increase in stocks' refers to increase in stocks of wool and livestock in the private sector, and to stocks held by the public sector.

2.8 Gross Capital Formation by Type of Good and Owner, in Constant Prices

Million Uruguayan pesos

	\multicolumn{4}{c	}{1980}	\multicolumn{4}{c	}{1981}	\multicolumn{4}{c}{1982}
	TOTAL	Total Private	Public Enterprises	General Government	TOTAL	Total Private	Public Enterprises	General Government	TOTAL	Total Private	Public Enterprises	General Government
\multicolumn{13}{c}{At constant prices of:1978}
Increase in stocks, total [a]	206	206	-	...	-179	-179	-	...	-350	-350	-	...
Gross Fixed Capital Formation, Total	6255	4312	1943	...	6067	4287	1780	...	5165	2680	2485	...
1 Residential buildings	3757	2396	1361	...	3840	2326	1514	...	3638	1945	1693	...
2 Non-residential buildings	...	...	...	...	...	...	...	...	...	...	...	...
3 Other construction	...	...	...	...	...	...	...	...	...	...	...	...
4 Land improvement and plantation and orchard development	91	91	-	...	54	54	-	...	54	54	-	...
5 Producers' durable goods	2407	1825	582	...	2173	1907	266	...	1473	681	792	...
6 Breeding stock, dairy cattle, etc.	...	...	...	...	...	...	...	...	...	...	...	...
Total Gross Capital Formation	6461	4518	1943	...	5888	4108	1780	...	4815	2330	2485	...

Uruguay

2.8 Gross Capital Formation by Type of Good and Owner, in Constant Prices

Million Uruguayan pesos

	1983 TOTAL	1983 Total Private	1983 Public Enterprises	1983 General Government	1984 TOTAL	1984 Total Private	1984 Public Enterprises	1984 General Government	1985 TOTAL	1985 Total Private	1985 Public Enterprises	1985 General Government
At constant prices of: 1978												
Increase in stocks, total [a]	-419	-419	-	...	102	102	-	...	104	104	-	...
Gross Fixed Capital Formation, Total	3471	2205	1266	...	3009	1699	1310	...	2295	1459	836	...
1 Residential buildings	2412	1453	959	...	2239	1013	1226	...	1557	806	751	...
2 Non-residential buildings	...	...	...	...	...	...	...	...	...	...	...	...
3 Other construction	...	...	...	...	...	...	...	...	...	...	...	...
4 Land improvement and plantation and orchard development	46	46	-	...	41	41	-	...	37	37	-	...
5 Producers' durable goods	1013	706	307	...	729	645	84	...	701	616	85	...
6 Breeding stock, dairy cattle, etc.	...	...	...	...	...	...	...	...	...	...	...	...
Total Gross Capital Formation	3052	1786	1266	...	3111	1801	1310	...	2399	1563	836	...

	1986 TOTAL	1986 Total Private	1986 Public Enterprises	1986 General Government
At constant prices of: 1978				
Increase in stocks, total [a]	62	62	-	...
Gross Fixed Capital Formation, Total	2483	1526	957	...
1 Residential buildings	1507	730	777	...
2 Non-residential buildings	...	...	...	...
3 Other construction	...	...	...	...
4 Land improvement and plantation and orchard development	43	43	-	...
5 Producers' durable goods	933	753	180	...
6 Breeding stock, dairy cattle, etc.	...	...	...	...
Total Gross Capital Formation	2545	1588	957	...

a) Item 'Increase in stocks' refers to increase in stocks of wool and livestock in the private sector, and to stocks held by the public sector.

USSR

Source. Communication from the Central Statistical Office of the USSR, Moscow. The official estimates and descriptions are published annually in 'Narodnoe Khozyaistvo SSSR' (National Economy of the USSR).

General note. The estimates shown in the following tables have been prepared in accordance with the System of Material Product Balances. Therefore, these estimates are not comparable in concept and coverage with those conforming to the United Nations System of National Accounts. It should be noted that the estimates for the USSR include those for the Byelorussian SSR and the Ukrainian SSR. Separate country chapters for those two Republics of the USSR are shown in this Yearbook.

1a Net Material Product by Use at Current Market Prices

Thousand Million USSR roubles

	1970	1975	1977	1978	1979	1980	1981	1982	1983	1984	1985	1986
1 Personal consumption	...	...	...	...	...	...	...	...	...	...	...	...
2 Material consumption in the units of the non-material sphere serving individuals	...	...	...	...	...	...	...	...	...	...	...	...
Consumption of the Population	201.3	266.4	292.5	307.9	323.6	345.5	364.9	378.5	393.0	407.2	418.4	427.6
3 Material consumption in the units of the non-material sphere serving the community as a whole												
4 Net fixed capital formation [a,b]	84.2	96.6	106.9	112.7	109.3	108.6	113.0	134.4	143.4	151.8	150.3	148.4
5 Increase in material circulating assets and in stocks [a,b,c]												
6 Losses	...	...	...	...	...	...	...	...	...	...	...	...
7 Exports of goods and material services	...	...	...	...	...	...	...	...	...	...	...	...
8 Less: Imports of goods and material services	...	...	...	...	...	...	...	...	...	...	...	...
Net Material Product	285.5	363.0	399.4	420.6	432.9	454.1	477.9	512.9	536.4	559.0	568.7	576.0

a) Changes in work-in-progress on construction are included in item 'Increase in material circulating assets and in stocks'.
b) Increase in productive livestock and draught animals is included in item 'Net fixed capital formation'.
c) Item 'Increase in material circulating assets and in stocks' includes increase in value of young animals.

2a Net Material Product by Kind of Activity of the Material Sphere in Current Market Prices

Thousand Million USSR roubles

	1970	1975	1977	1978	1979	1980	1981	1982	1983	1984	1985	1986
1 Agriculture and forestry	63.1	61.5	71.6	74.4	73.2	68.9	73.1	80.9	111.1	115.7	112.8	121.2
2 Industrial activity [a]	148.3	191.2	207.0	220.4	226.5	238.1	248.0	266.6	253.8	262.1	263.1	258.0
3 Construction	30.0	41.3	44.6	46.2	46.7	47.6	49.0	51.9	53.2	59.4	62.3	70.3
4 Wholesale and retail trade and restaurants and other eating and drinking places	32.2	46.3	57.3	60.1	68.6	80.6	88.5	92.9	97.0	99.6	105.3	101.4
5 Transport and communication	16.3	23.0	25.1	25.2	25.6	27.0	28.1	31.6	33.2	33.7	35.0	36.5
6 Other activities of the material sphere	...	...	...	...	...	...	...	...	...	...	...	...
Net material product	289.9	363.3	405.6	426.3	440.6	462.2	486.7	523.9	548.3	570.5	578.5	587.4

a) Item 'Industrial activity' includes turnover taxes realized in prices on industrial goods.

2b Net Material Product by Kind of Activity of the Material Sphere in Constant Market Prices

Index numbers 1960 = 100

	1970	1975	1977	1978	1979	1980	1981	1982	1983	1984	1985	1986
				At constant prices of: 1983								
1 Agriculture and forestry	...	...	...	...	...	...	...	104	111	107	105	113
							98					
2 Industrial activity	246	365	113	118	123	128	132	107	111	115	120	125
							104					
3 Construction	176	235	106	112	113	117	120	105	110	113	117	131
							103					
4 Wholesale and retail trade and restaurants and other eating and drinking places	189	256	109	114	117	121	125	104	107	111	114	117
							104					
5 Transport and communication	216	306	109	114	115	120	125	107	112	113	116	120
							104					
6 Other activities of the material sphere	...	...	...	...	...	...	...	...	...	...	...	...
Net material product	199	262	111	116	119	124	128	107	112	115	119	124
							103					

USSR

6b Capital Formation by Kind of Activity of the Material and Non-Material Spheres in Constant Market Prices

Thousand Million USSR roubles

		1970	1975	1977	1978	1979	1980	1981	1982	1983	1984	1985	1986
		\multicolumn{12}{c}{At constant prices of:1980}
		\multicolumn{12}{c}{Gross Fixed Capital Formation}
1	Agriculture and forestry	16.0	26.1	27.8	29.0	29.5	29.8	30.6	31.0	32.0	31.1	31.5	33.5
2	Industrial activity	32.5	44.9	48.9	51.1	51.2	53.3	55.3	56.8	60.4	62.7	65.5	71.0
3	Construction	3.3	4.8	5.1	5.7	5.8	6.0	5.9	6.4	6.2	5.8	6.1	6.8
4	Wholesale and retail trade and restaurants and other eating and drinking places [a]	...	...	...	...	...	...	...	...	...	...	...	...
5	Transport and communciation	9.0	14.4	15.6	18.2	18.1	18.1	18.8	19.8	21.5	22.3	21.9	22.8
6	Other activities of the material sphere	...	...	...	...	...	...	...	...	...	...	...	...
	Total Material Sphere	...	...	...	...	...	...	...	...	...	...	...	...
7	Housing except owner-occupied, communal and miscellaneous personal services	15.8	19.2	20.1	20.7	20.5	21.1	22.5	24.0	25.8	27.3	28.1	30.9
8	Education, culture and art [a]	15.6	19.1	21.2	21.9	22.5	22.6	23.4	23.9	25.1	25.1	26.4	29.4
9	Health and social welfare services and sports [a]												
	Total Non-Material Sphere Serving Individuals	...	...	...	...	...	...	...	...	...	...	...	...
10	Government	...	...	...	...	...	...	...	...	...	...	...	...
11	Finance, credit and insurance	...	...	...	...	...	...	...	...	...	...	...	...
12	Research, scientific and technological institutes	...	...	...	...	...	...	...	...	...	...	...	...
13	Other activities of the non-material sphere	...	...	...	...					...	...	...	...
	Total Non-Material Sphere Serving the Community as a Whole	...	...	...	...	...	...	...	...	...	...	...	...
14	Owner-occupied dwellings	...	...	...	...	...	...	...	...	...	...	...	...
	Total Gross Fixed Capital Formation	92.2	128.5	138.7	146.6	147.6	150.9	156.5	161.9	171.0	174.3	179.5	194.4

a) Item 'Wholesale and retail trade, restaurants etc.' is included in item 'Education, culture, and art' through 'Health and social welfare services and sports'.

Venezuela

General note. The preparation of national accounts statistics in Venezuela is undertaken by the Banco Central de Venezuela. The official estimates are published annually by the Banco in 'Memorias o Informes Economicas'. A detailed description of the sources and methods used for the national accounts estimation is found in 'Metodologia de las Cuentas Nacionales de Venezuela' and in 'Practicas en materia de cuentas' published by the Banco. The estimates are generally in accordance with the classifications and defininitions recommended in the United Nations System of National Accounts (SNA). The following tables have been prepared from successive replies to the United Nations national accounts questionnaire. When the scope and coverage of the estimates differ for conceptual or statistical reasons from the definitions and classifications recommended in SNA, a footnote is indicated to the relevant tables.

Sources and methods :

(a) Gross domestic product. Gross domestic product is estimated mainly through the production approach.

(b) Expenditure on the gross domestic product. The expenditure approach is used to estimate government final consumption expenditure and exports and imports of goods and services. The commodity-flow approach is used for private consumption expenditure and gross fixed capital formation. Increase in stocks is obtained as a residual. The estimates of government final consumption expenditures are based on information obtained from government budgets and financial statements of the government entities. For private consumption expenditure on imported goods, estimates are based on the value of imports f.o.b. Values of locally produced goods are based on the production account of agriculture, manufacturing and the services. Trade margins based on surveys are used to estimate purchasers' values. The information used to estimate gross fixed capital formation include data on construction, manufacturing production, sales of vechiles and livestock and imported capital goods. The data on petroleum and iron-ore exports are obtained from the Ministerio de Energia y Minas while exports of other merchandise are obtained from the Oficina Central de Estadisticas e Informatica. The Corporacion de turismo, the embassies as well as companies engaged in transports, communication and insurance also provide export data. Import data are mainly provided by the Oficina Central de Estadisticas e Informatica. For the constant price estimates, only information for gross fixed capital formation is available. The item is deflated by price indexes constructed separately for construction, machinery and equipment and transport equipment. For other aggregates of this item, the estimates are obtained directly at constant prices.

(c) Cost-structure of the gross domestic product. In estimating the cost structure components of GDP, estimates of compensation of employees, operating surplus and depreciation are obtained for each industry group separately. For agriculture, forestry and fishing, they are estimated as a percentage of the gross value of production based on factore and coefficients from a 1968 study. For the mining sector, information from the Ministerio de Energia e Minas are used for petroleum activity and iron-ore mining. For manufacturing, estimates are based on cost structure data by the Ministerio de Hacienda supplemented by information from public enterprises and petroleum refineries. A survey conducted by the Banco in 1968-70 provides coefficients for the trade sector. Financial statements are used for public enterprises railway transport, communication, financial institutions and insurance. Input coefficients obtained from surveys are used for road transport and private services. Data on indirect taxes and subsidies are obtained from government sources.

(d) Gross domestic product by kind of economic activity. The table of GDP by kind of economic activity at market prices, i.e., producers' values. The production approach is used to estimate the value added of most industries. The income approach is used to estimate producers of government services. domestic services and part of other private services. The information on gross output in the agricultural sector is furnished annually by the Ministerio de Agricultura y Cria on the basis of field survey conducted during the summer (January-April) and the winter(May-December). These surveys give information on cultivated areas and physical production of the principal crops. The value of production is first calculated in constant prices by multiplying the physical production of each item by the respective producers' prices in 1968 and then converting it to current values by using the producers' price index estimated by the Banco. Value added is obtained by applying the cost structure estimated for 1968. For crude petroleum and refinery products, a production account covering all enterprises in the petroleum sector is constructed on the basis of information provided by the Ministerio de Energia y Minas. Crude petroleum is separated from refinery production on the basis of annual survey data. During the period 1968-1975, exports were calculated at official fiscal prices for export as declared by foreign concessionaires while from 1976 onwards, the prices reported by the nationalized enterprises have been used. Value added for the manufacturing industries is estimated by applying to the gross value of production by kind of economic activity the cost structure information on companies. Bench-mark estimates on gross value of manufacturing production have been prepared based on the third industrial survey conducted in 1971. These estimates are extrapolated by the annual changes in the index of industrial production through annual surveys. The Instituto Nacional de Obras Sanitarias provides information on production and cost structure of water supply. For public construction, information is obtained from censuses conducted by the Banco. For private construction requiring permits, estimates are based on construction coefficients per capita which are available for 14 urben centres through a Survey. The estimates for the federal district are calculated independently through a survey and through using information on construction permits. Non-permit construction estimates are agriculture. Bench-mark estimates for each of the activities in the trade sector have been prepared for 1968-1970 by using the results of a national survey conducted by the Banco. Since 1970, over-all estimates are made by extrapolating the total value of production by an index of market sales. Adjustments are made to account for the public enterprises by using their respective financial statements. Value added in the private transport sector is estimated by applying the sample coefficient, obtained through surveys, to the receipts for each type of services. For the public sector, information is obtained directly from concerned enterprises. The value added of the financial institutions is obtained as the difference between the value of production and intermediate consumption. For ownership of dwellings, the value of production is estimated from the total number of occupied dwellings and the annual average rent, adjusted by the rent item in the cost-of-living index. For real estate and business services, the production value is estimated by projecting the annual changes of incomes obtained from surveys. The value added of government services constitutes the renumeration of employees of the various government agencies and the consumption of fixed capital of the administrative organizations. For private services, coefficients of value added obtained from surveys are used. For the constant price estimates, value added of agriculture and mining is extrapolated by quantum indexes. For other industries, current values are deflated by various price indexes.

1.1 Expenditure on the Gross Domestic Product, in Current Prices

Million Venezuelan bolivares

	1970	1975	1977	1978	1979	1980	1981	1982	1983	1984	1985	1986
1 Government final consumption expenditure	6635	15943	22959	24056	27758	35123	42643	42594	41339	43565	48737	53770
2 Private final consumption expenditure	27267	56286	80110	94762	110329	135375	160533	182239	183435	209834	232180	271883
3 Gross capital formation	15743	36444	64668	72413	65651	62791	65409	75330	34149	51345	54580	82044
A Increase in stocks	4206	5846	4184	576	98	-1354	-4374	5167	-21197	1751	-2890	4496
B Gross fixed capital formation	11537	30598	60484	71837	65553	64145	69783	70163	55346	49594	57470	77548
Residential buildings	2503	7045	11164	14406	16238	17228	16272	12354	10209	8095	7055	9538
Non-residential buildings	3820	8959	19821	23423	22763	20548	23452	27412	24319	18227	19915	27604
Other construction and land improvement etc.	355	586	740	710	400	451	707	748	786	437	379	1120
Other	4859	14008	28759	33298	26152	25918	29352	29649	20032	22835	30121	39286
4 Exports of goods and services	12226	39278	43506	41957	64024	85463	89614	75197	74067	105159	101597	97745
5 Less: Imports of goods and services	9846	29853	55537	64128	60025	64551	72991	84092	42498	62373	65063	101582
Equals: Gross Domestic Product	52025	118098	155706	169060	207737	254201	285208	291268	290492	347530	372031	403860

1.2 Expenditure on the Gross Domestic Product, in Constant Prices

Million Venezuelan bolivares

	1970	1975	1977	1978	1979	1980	1981	1982	1983	1984	1985	1986
					At constant prices of:1968							
1 Government final consumption expenditure	...	...	...	...	...	...	...	...	...	...	...	...
2 Private final consumption expenditure	...	...	...	...	...	...	...	...	...	...	...	...
3 Gross capital formation	...	...	...	...	...	...	...	...	...	...	...	...
A Increase in stocks	...	...	...	...	...	...	...	...	...	...	...	...
B Gross fixed capital formation	10949	18929	31361	32610	26074	22290	22959	22102	16280	13209	14167	15145

Venezuela

1.2 Expenditure on the Gross Domestic Product, in Constant Prices
(Continued)

Million Venezuelan bolivares

	1970	1975	1977	1978	1979	1980	1981	1982	1983	1984	1985	1986
	\multicolumn{12}{c}{At constant prices of:1968}
Residential buildings	2450	4127	5271	6053	5980	5403	4669	3290	2552	1830	1430	1592
Non-residential buildings	3682	5305	9561	10063	8566	6583	6814	7228	6075	4149	4128	4636
Other construction and land improvement etc.	344	346	355	304	150	143	205	198	197	100	79	188
Other	4473	9151	16174	16190	11378	10161	11271	11386	7456	7130	8530	8729
4 Exports of goods and services	...	...	...	...	...	...	...	...	...	...	...	...
5 Less: Imports of goods and services	...	...	...	...	...	...	...	...	...	...	...	...
Equals: Gross Domestic Product	50634	64417	74777	76376	77396	75857	75628	76144	71867	70894	71089	74756

1.3 Cost Components of the Gross Domestic Product

Million Venezuelan bolivares

	1970	1975	1977	1978	1979	1980	1981	1982	1983	1984	1985	1986
1 Indirect taxes, net	2836	4572	5212	4544	6649	7996	8416	9776	20387	20395	27277	10048
A Indirect taxes	2947	5599	6832	6648	8997	11378	12013	12910	22693	22568	28983	12903
B Less: Subsidies	111	1027	1620	2104	2348	3382	3597	3134	2306	2173	1706	2855
2 Consumption of fixed capital	4824	7523	10520	12485	14912	17104	19869	21666	24031	26628	29982	35158
3 Compensation of employees paid by resident producers to:	21098	45807	63727	75831	86602	105143	119642	124529	123625	128398	144170	169314
A Resident households	21001	45731	63727	75831	86602	105143	119642	124529	123578	128334	144170	169314
B Rest of the world	97	76	-	-	-	-	-	-	47	64	-	-
4 Operating surplus	23267	60196	76247	76200	99574	123958	137281	135297	122449	172109	170602	189340
Equals: Gross Domestic Product	52025	118098	155706	169060	207737	254201	285208	291268	290492	347630	372031	400860

1.4 General Government Current Receipts and Disbursements

Million Venezuelan bolivares

	1970	1975	1977	1978	1979	1980	1981	1982	1983	1984	1985	1986
	\multicolumn{12}{c}{Receipts}
1 Operating surplus	-63	-143	94	46	94	88	91	106	94	112	109	...
2 Property and entrepreneurial income	3019	9573	...	12382	11941	14342	18290	21482	26983	29871	28491	...
3 Taxes, fees and contributions	9036	36512	...	33661	51120	72296	80393	68287	66978	110993	98104	...
A Indirect taxes	2948	5599	6832	6648	8997	11378	12013	12910	20863	19588	28721	...
B Direct taxes	5121	28972	...	23440	37378	54910	61996	48491	41014	84667	62594	...
C Social security contributions	845	1694	...	2718	3062	4258	4397	4734	4735	4879	5314	...
D Compulsory fees, fines and penalties	122	247	...	855	1683	1750	1987	2152	366	1859	1475	...
4 Other current transfers	243	365	...	11691	14039	13758	17804	17785	16569	18003	22073	...
Total Current Receipts of General Government	12235	46307	...	57780	77194	100484	116578	107660	110624	158979	148777	...
	\multicolumn{12}{c}{Disbursements}
1 Government final consumption expenditure	6635	15943	22959	24056	27758	35123	42643	42594	41339	43565	48737	...
A Compensation of employees	5745	12894	18198	20054	23579	30030	34851	35171	34421	35788	40083	...
B Consumption of fixed capital	26	20	25	43	42	48	52	51	82	97	132	...
C Purchases of goods and services, net	1263	3086	4799	4023	4137	5045	7740	7372	6836	7680	8522	...
D Less: Own account fixed capital formation	399	57	63	64	...	...	...	...	...	...	...	...
E Indirect taxes paid, net	...	...	...	...	...	...	...	...	...	...	...	...
2 Property income	205	323	...	2515	2915	5585	5992	6399	7231	11619	12814	...
A Interest	...	...	...	2515	2915	5585	5992	6399	7231	11619	12814	...
B Net land rent and royalties	...	...	...	...	...	...	...	...	...	...	...	...
3 Subsidies	111	1027	1620	2104	2348	3382	3597	3134	2306	2173	1706	...
4 Other current transfers	510	1678	...	12019	13999	17046	20720	23760	27446	37232	43773	...
A Social security benefits	158	516	...	780	905	1298	1584	1783	1759	1864	2055	...
B Social assistance grants	184	734	...	870	710	1081	955	906	2805	3261	3945	...
C Other	168	428	...	10369	12384	14667	18181	21071	22882	32107	37773	...
5 Net saving	4774	27336	...	17086	30174	39348	43626	31773	32302	64390	41747	...
Total Current Disbursements and Net Saving of General Government	12235	46307	...	57780	77194	100484	116578	107660	110624	158979	148777	...

Venezuela

1.7 External Transactions on Current Account, Summary

Million Venezuelan bolivares

		1970	1975	1977	1978	1979	1980	1981	1982	1983	1984	1985	1986
		\multicolumn{12}{c}{Payments to the Rest of the World}
1	Imports of goods and services	9846	29853	55537	64128	60025	64551	72991	84092	42498	62373	65063	101582
	A Imports of merchandise c.i.f.	8363	25860	48026	53574	47661	50783	56218	62977	33082	49365	54749	87875
	B Other	1483	3993	7511	10554	12364	13768	16773	21115	9416	13008	10314	13707
2	Factor income to the rest of the world	2768	2764	3711	5136	6519	8487	13080	17539	16957	22279	27622	32995
	A Compensation of employees	97	76	-	-	-	-	-	-	47	64	-	-
	B Property and entrepreneurial income	2671	2688	3711	5136	6519	8487	13080	17539	16910	22215	27622	32995
3	Current transfers to the rest of the world	317	659	1215	1746	1746	1879	1750	2738	988	863	867	954
	A Indirect taxes to supranational organizations	...	...	...	...	...	...	...	...	...	...	...	...
	B Other current transfers	...	...	...	...	...	...	...	...	988	863	867	954
4	Surplus of the nation on current transactions	-458	9118	-13606	-24546	1498	20236	17120	-18186	20720	33389	20898	-20632
	Payments to the Rest of the World and Surplus of the Nation on Current Transactions	12473	42394	46857	46464	69788	95153	104941	86183	81163	118904	114450	114899
		\multicolumn{12}{c}{Receipts From The Rest of the World}
1	Exports of goods and services	12226	39278	43506	41957	64024	85463	89614	75197	74067	105159	101597	97745
	A Exports of merchandise f.o.b.	11616	37724	41349	39265	61461	82497	86374	70738	69078	99871	96010	88737
	B Other	610	1554	2157	2692	2563	2966	3240	4459	4989	5288	5587	9008
2	Factor income from rest of the world	238	3108	3347	4503	5760	9690	15327	10986	7096	13745	12853	17154
	A Compensation of employees	-	-	-	-	-	-	-	-	75	50	54	-
	B Property and entrepreneurial income	238	3108	3347	4503	5760	9690	15327	10986	7021	13695	12799	17154
3	Current transfers from rest of the world	9	8	4	4	4	-	-	-	-	-	-	-
	Receipts from the Rest of the World on Current Transactions	12473	42394	46857	46464	69788	95153	104941	86183	81163	118904	114450	114899

1.10 Gross Domestic Product by Kind of Activity, in Current Prices

Million Venezuelan bolivares

		1970	1975	1977	1978	1979	1980	1981	1982	1983	1984	1985	1986
1	Agriculture, hunting, forestry and fishing	3714	6974	9270	10137	11940	14436	16413	17676	19536	23886	29192	36122
2	Mining and quarrying	9293	30486	32862	30430	45507	62188	66944	54389	46922	69662	58623	36227
3	Manufacturing	8319	18851	24794	26544	34743	41197	43089	46784	49293	67675	79170	92722
4	Electricity, gas and water [a]	845	1407	1829	2124	2499	2579	3977	4900	5398	5773	6985	7652
5	Construction	2084	6201	11488	14316	14753	14479	15683	15657	14317	10335	11146	14805
6	Wholesale and retail trade, restaurants and hotels	5625	11205	15780	17461	19192	20834	23245	25704	33339	38292	41795	48583
7	Transport, storage and communication	5458	11063	17130	21923	23452	25184	30769	35631	33266	37725	43377	53941
8	Finance, insurance, real estate and business services	7536	15014	20704	23331	27386	37883	46277	49953	51820	57999	61593	68396
9	Community, social and personal services	2209	4781	6678	7480	8160	9579	10981	11166	11421	13197	14714	16779
	Total, Industries	45083	105982	140535	153746	187632	228359	257378	261860	265312	324544	346595	375227
	Producers of Government Services	5771	12914	18223	20097	23621	30078	34903	35222	34503	35885	40215	43717
	Other Producers	645	1238	1537	1725	2108	2499	2966	3187	3777	3994	4414	5026
	Subtotal	51499	120134	160295	175568	213361	260936	295247	300269	303592	364423	391224	423970
	Less: Imputed bank service charge	1065	5098	8458	9857	10693	13104	16378	15879	16101	19916	22685	24998
	Plus: Import duties	1591	3062	3869	3349	5069	6369	6339	6878	3001	3023	3492	4888
	Plus: Value added tax	...	...	...	...	...	...	...	...	...	...	...	...
	Equals: Gross Domestic Product	52025	118098	155706	169060	207737	254201	285208	291268	290492	347530	372031	403860

a) Item 'Electricity, gas and water' excludes gas.

Venezuela

1.11 Gross Domestic Product by Kind of Activity, in Constant Prices

Million Venezuelan bolivares

	1970	1975	1977	1978	1979	1980	1981	1982	1983	1984	1985	1986
	\multicolumn{12}{c}{At constant prices of:1968}
1 Agriculture, hunting, forestry and fishing	3544	4236	4403	4545	4677	4765	4676	4843	4863	4901	5180	5489
2 Mining and quarrying	9780	6594	6077	6004	6526	6103	5948	5340	5002	5098	4868	5221
3 Manufacturing	8264	10634	12331	12899	13324	13660	13322	13863	13626	14247	14561	15300
4 Electricity, gas and water [a]	859	1483	1689	1674	1933	1950	2256	2533	2635	2634	2703	2924
5 Construction	2015	3661	5510	6115	5519	4609	4511	4131	3583	2350	2253	2608
6 Wholesale and retail trade, restaurants and hotels	5416	7364	8655	8655	8211	6907	6724	6897	7012	6643	6453	6635
7 Transport, storage and communication	5223	7664	9603	10368	9851	9805	10155	10508	9080	8806	9218	9649
8 Finance, insurance, real estate and business services [b]	7226	11739	14279	14245	14504	14023	15133	14645	14600	15660	15864	16561
9 Community, social and personal services	2134	3756	4695	4778	4757	4872	4848	4492	4226	4330	4252	4363
Total, Industries	44461	57131	67242	69283	69302	66694	67573	67252	64627	64669	65352	68750
Producers of Government Services	5082	7850	9281	9431	10073	10498	10586	10593	10399	10357	10160	10434
Other Producers	619	822	821	806	826	835	847	863	861	843	898	935
Subtotal	50162	65803	77344	79520	80201	78027	79006	78708	75887	75869	76410	80119
Less: Imputed bank service charge	1040	3287	4675	4848	5203	4777	5697	4910	4904	5637	5989	6055
Plus: Import duties	1512	1901	2108	1704	2398	2607	2319	2346	884	662	668	692
Plus: Value added tax	...	...	...	...	...	...	...	...	...	...	...	...
Equals: Gross Domestic Product	50634	64417	74777	76376	77396	75857	75628	76144	71867	70894	71089	74756

a) Item 'Electricity, gas and water' excludes gas.
b) Item 'Finance, insurance, real estate and business services' includes the imputation applied to the financial intermediaries.

1.12 Relations Among National Accounting Aggregates

Million Venezuelan bolivares

	1970	1975	1977	1978	1979	1980	1981	1982	1983	1984	1985	1986
Gross Domestic Product	52025	118098	155706	169060	207737	254201	285208	291268	290492	347530	372031	403860
Plus: Net factor income from the rest of the world	-2530	344	-364	-633	-759	1203	2247	-6553	-9861	-8534	-14769	-15841
Factor income from the rest of the world	238	3108	3347	4503	5760	9690	15327	10986	7096	13745	12853	17154
Less: Factor income to the rest of the world	2768	2764	3711	5136	6519	8487	13080	17539	16957	22279	27622	32995
Equals: Gross National Product	49495	118442	155342	168427	206978	255404	287455	284715	280631	338996	357262	388019
Less: Consumption of fixed capital	4824	7523	10520	12485	14912	17104	19869	21666	24031	26628	29982	35158
Equals: National Income	44671	110919	144822	155942	192066	238300	267586	263049	256600	312368	327280	352861
Plus: Net current transfers from the rest of the world	-308	-651	-1211	-1742	-1742	-1879	-1750	-2738	-988	-863	-867	-954
Current transfers from the rest of the world	9	8	4	4	4	-	-	-	-	-	-	-
Less: Current transfers to the rest of the world	317	659	1215	1746	1746	1879	1750	2738	988	863	867	954
Equals: National Disposable Income	44363	110268	143611	154200	190324	236421	265836	260311	255612	311505	326413	351907
Less: Final consumption	33902	72229	103069	118818	138087	170498	203176	224833	224774	253399	280917	325653
Equals: Net Saving	10461	38039	40542	35382	52237	65923	62660	35478	30838	58106	45496	26254
Less: Surplus of the nation on current transactions	-458	9118	-13606	-24546	1498	20236	17120	-18186	20720	33389	20898	-20632
Equals: Net Capital Formation	10919	28921	54148	59928	50739	45687	45540	53664	10118	24717	24598	46886

2.1 Government Final Consumption Expenditure by Function, in Current Prices

Million Venezuelan bolivares

	1970	1975	1977	1978	1979	1980	1981	1982	1983	1984	1985	1986
1 General public services	1271	3312	4956	5971	6871	9469	9524	8316	8373	7277	8742	...
2 Defence	938	2259	3755	2583	3023	3240	3905	4903	4220	6033	5817	...
3 Public order and safety	...	...	...	...	...	...	...	...	...	...	...	...
4 Education	1879	4777	6900	7494	8563	11449	13239	14068	13482	15381	17117	...
5 Health	1300	2154	2886	3306	3370	3925	5397	5484	7244	7416	8572	...
6 Social security and welfare	426	1215	1655	1772	2029	2605	4371	4322	2466	3190	3548	...
7 Housing and community amenities	195	372	265	320	399	737	1078	1162	1116	1267	1684	...
8 Recreational, cultural and religious affairs	62	189	323	386	343	662	791	988	964	705	885	...
9 Economic services	564	1665	2219	2224	3160	3036	4163	3351	3474	2296	2372	...
10 Other functions	...	...	...	...	...	175	-	-	-	-	-	...
Total Government Final Consumption Expenditure	6635	15943	22959	24056	27758	35123	42643	42594	41339	43565	48737	...

Venezuela

2.5 Private Final Consumption Expenditure by Type and Porpose, in Current Prices

Million Venezuelan bolivares

	1970	1975	1977	1978	1979	1980	1981	1982	1983	1984	1985	1986
Final Consumption Expenditure of Resident Households												
1 Food, beverages and tobacco	10744	22713	32655	37281	45983	59004	74727	85767	97157	111230	121761	142926
A Food	...	...	...	...	...	...	...	60004	69953	82572	96739	...
B Non-alcoholic beverages	...	...	...	...	...	...	...	5342	3533	4036	4387	...
C Alcoholic beverages	...	...	...	...	...	...	...	17777	20660	21999	17327	...
D Tobacco	...	...	...	...	...	...	...	2644	3011	2623	3308	...
2 Clothing and footwear	1898	4444	4954	6301	7198	7467	7758	8379	7596	8275	10673	11552
3 Gross rent, fuel and power	2985	4690	5285	5894	7194	11178	14107	15996	17665	18569	19527	22836
4 Furniture, furnishings and household equipment and operation	2173	5252	7031	7877	8729	9660	9318	10090	8302	10293	14454	16120
5 Medical care and health expenses	1260	2377	3059	3447	3861	4917	5326	5864	7595	8880	11206	11552
6 Transport and communication	3863	7206	11293	12403	13804	14413	17197	21255	20138	21595	24791	31970
7 Recreational, entertainment, education and cultural services	2315	4994	7296	9057	9724	12763	12955	13170	10246	11908	15469	16926
8 Miscellaneous goods and services	1456	3366	4570	6176	6811	8072	9138	9661	7949	9403	10854	14776
Total Final Consumption Expenditure in the Domestic Market by Households, of which	26694	55042	76143	88436	103304	127474	150526	170182	176648	200153	228735	268658
A Durable goods	2152	4938	7732	9572	9911	10970	11122	11322	6437	6831	8885	...
B Semi-durable goods	3073	7077	8648	11816	13172	14948	15738	17288	15055	17284	21583	...
C Non-durable goods	13144	27723	38249	43317	52954	67990	84226	97951	109663	126327	142197	...
D Services	8325	15304	21514	23731	27267	33566	39440	43621	45493	49711	56070	...
Plus: Direct purchases abroad by resident households	616	1609	4190	6613	7092	8046	9651	12052	8592	13001	7651	10099
Less: Direct purchases in the domestic market by non-resident households	246	819	800	963	873	1168	920	1482	3302	4697	5745	8711
Equals: Final Consumption Expenditure of Resident Households	27064	55832	79533	94086	109523	134352	159257	180752	181938	208457	230641	270046
Final Consumption Expenditure of Private Non-profit Institutions Serving Households												
Equals: Final Consumption Expenditure of Private Non-profit Organisations Serving Households	203	454	577	676	806	1023	1276	1487	1497	1377	1539	1837
Private Final Consumption Expenditure	27267	56286	80110	94762	110329	135375	160533	182239	183435	209834	232180	271883

2.11 Gross Fixed Capital Formation by Kind of Activity of Owner, ISIC Divisions, in Current Prices

Million Venezuelan bolivares

	1970	1975	1977	1978	1979	1980	1981	1982	1983	1984	1985	1986
All Producers												
1 Agriculture, hunting, forestry and fishing	767	1862	2014	1958	1863	2091	2651	2131	1270	1794	3357	...
2 Mining and quarrying	1478	1296	2396	4099	6194	9116	12338	15645	12344	9589	10044	...
3 Manufacturing [a]	1588	4052	5991	5624	3148	4262	2843	2642	903	913	1869	...
4 Electricity, gas and water	387	2196	6499	7575	7789	6301	10495	14355	12434	7876	8764	...
5 Construction [b]	...	...	...	...	...	...	...	...	...	...	...	...
6 Wholesale and retail trade, restaurants and hotels [a]	628	1311	105	125	65	120	65	14	30	56	-14	...
7 Transport, storage and communication	447	1523	3494	4690	6897	5455	5747	6352	6124	4450	6606	...
8 Finance, insurance, real estate and business services [c]	323	726	1350	2285	2889	2633	4023	4410	4242	3413	4865	...
9 Community, social and personal services [bc]	4292	12666	32037	36706	30692	26616	20874	14609	5970	14754	12417	...
Total Industries	9910	25632	53886	63062	59537	56594	59036	60158	43317	42845	47908	...
Producers of Government Services	1448	4618	6179	8263	5434	6806	9816	8911	10935	5562	8237	...
Private Non-Profit Institutions Serving Households	179	348	419	512	582	745	931	1094	1094	1187	1325	...
Total	11537	30598	60484	71837	65553	64145	69783	70163	55346	49594	57470	...

a) Beginning 1977, items 'Manufacturing', 'Wholesale and retail trade', 'Restaurant and hotels', refer only to gross fixed public investment.
b) Item 'Construction' is included in item 'Community, social and personal services'.
c) Business services and real estate except dwellings are included in item 'Community, social and personal services'.

Venezuela

2.12 Gross Fixed Capital Formation by Kind of Activity of Owner, ISIC Divisions, in Constant Prices

Million Venezuelan bolivares

	1970	1975	1977	1978	1979	1980	1981	1982	1983	1984	1985	1986
	\multicolumn{12}{c}{At constant prices of:1968}											
	\multicolumn{12}{c}{All Producers}											
1 Agriculture, hunting, forestry and fishing	728	1152	1044	889	741	727	872	671	365	478	827	...
2 Mining and quarrying	1402	802	1242	1860	2464	3168	4059	4928	3542	2553	2475	...
3 Manufacturing [a]	1507	2507	3106	2553	1252	1481	935	832	259	243	461	...
4 Electricity, gas and water	368	1359	3370	3439	3099	2189	3453	4522	3569	2098	2160	...
5 Construction [b]	...	...	...	...	...	...	...	...	...	...	...	...
6 Wholesale and retail trade, restaurants and hotels [a]	596	811	55	57	26	42	21	4	9	15	-3	...
7 Transport, storage and communication	424	942	1812	2129	2743	1895	1891	2001	1757	1185	1628	...
8 Finance, insurance, real estate and business services [c]	307	449	700	1038	1148	915	1324	1389	1217	909	1199	...
9 Community, social and personal services [bc]	4073	7835	16611	16662	12208	9249	6868	4602	2110	3931	3062	...
Total Industries	9405	15857	27940	28627	23681	19666	19423	18949	12828	11412	11809	...
Producers of Government Services	1374	2857	3204	3751	2161	2365	3230	2808	3138	1481	2030	...
Private Non-Profit Institutions Serving Households	170	215	217	232	232	259	300	345	314	310	327	...
Total	10949	18929	31361	32610	26074	22290	22959	22102	16280	13209	14166	...

a) Beginning 1977, items 'Manufacturing', 'Wholesale and retail trade', 'Restaurant and hotels', refer only to gross fixed public investment.
b) Item 'Construction' is included in item 'Community, social and personal services'.
c) Business services and real estate except dwellings are included in item 'Community, social and personal services'.

2.17 Exports and Imports of Goods and Services, Detail

Million Venezuelan bolivares

	1970	1975	1977	1978	1979	1980	1981	1982	1983	1984	1985	1986
	\multicolumn{12}{c}{Exports of Goods and Services}											
1 Exports of merchandise, f.o.b.	11616	37724	41349	39265	61461	82497	86374	70738	69078	99871	96010	88737
2 Transport and communication	251	528	870	1232	1140	1181	1571	1885	2246	2748	1902	2791
A In respect of merchandise imports	97	301	326	295	271	137	180	364	439	914	541	1652
B Other	154	227	544	937	869	1044	1391	1521	1807	1834	1361	1139
3 Insurance service charges	88	90	226	206	332	463	364	869	280	57	102	216
A In respect of merchandise imports	9	27	29	26	24	56	43	167	23	13	7	62
B Other	79	63	197	180	308	407	321	702	257	44	95	154
4 Other commodities	25	117	261	291	218	154	385	223	1012	227	514	1446
5 Adjustments of merchandise exports to change-of-ownership basis	-	-	-	-	-	-	-	-	-	-	-	-
6 Direct purchases in the domestic market by non-residential households	246	819	800	963	873	1040	800	1323	1451	2256	3069	4555
7 Direct purchases in the domestic market by extraterritorial bodies	-	-	-	-	-	128	120	159	-	-	-	-
Total Exports of Goods and Services	12226	39278	43506	41957	64024	85463	89614	75197	74067	105159	101597	97745
	\multicolumn{12}{c}{Imports of Goods and Services}											
1 Imports of merchandise, c.i.f.	8363	25860	48026	53574	47661	50783	56218	62977	33082	49365	54749	87875
A Imports of merchandise, f.o.b.	7537	22941	43630	48082	42817	46554	51887	58180	29997	45767	50030	80385
B Transport of services on merchandise imports	761	2682	4039	5046	4452	4163	4295	4664	3047	3573	4692	7490
By residents	...	...	...	...	...	...	...	...	...	...	...	...
By non-residents	761	2682	4039	5046	4452	4163	4295	4664	3047	3573	4692	7490
C Insurance service charges on merchandise imports	65	237	357	446	392	66	36	133	38	25	27	-
By residents	...	...	...	...	...	...	...	...	...	...	...	...

Venezuela

2.17 Exports and Imports of Goods and Services, Detail
(Continued)

Million Venezuelan bolivares

	1970	1975	1977	1978	1979	1980	1981	1982	1983	1984	1985	1986
By non-residents	65	237	357	446	392	66	36	133	38	25	27	-
2 Adjustments of merchandise imports to change-of-ownership basis	-	-	-	-	-	-	-	-	-	-	-	-
3 Other transport and communication	220	340	1057	1164	1378	1968	2375	1730	1268	3674	2497	1939
4 Other insurance service charges	119	92	227	217	325	449	501	1041	191	164	149	339
5 Other commodities	436	1704	1494	1948	2927	2582	3570	5247	2724	2275	3212	5325
6 Direct purchases abroad by government	92	248	543	612	642	723	676	1045	805	624	718	841
7 Direct purchases abroad by resident households	616	1609	4190	6613	7092	8046	9651	12052	4428	6271	3738	5263
Total Imports of Goods and Services	9846	29853	55537	64128	60025	64551	72991	84092	42498	62373	65063	101582
Balance of Goods and Services	2380	9425	-12031	-22171	3999	20912	16623	-8895	31569	42786	36534	-3837
Total Imports and Balance of Goods and Services	12226	39278	43506	41957	64024	85463	89614	75197	74067	105159	101597	97745

4.1 Derivation of Value Added by Kind of Activity, in Current Prices

Million Venezuelan bolivares

	1980 Gross Output	1980 Intermediate Consumption	1980 Value Added	1981 Gross Output	1981 Intermediate Consumption	1981 Value Added	1982 Gross Output	1982 Intermediate Consumption	1982 Value Added	1983 Gross Output	1983 Intermediate Consumption	1983 Value Added
						All Producers						
1 Agriculture, hunting, forestry and fishing	18141	3705	14436	20630	4217	16413	22092	4416	17676	24433	4897	19536
A Agriculture and hunting	17394	3600	13794	20074	4138	15936	21119	4282	16837	23163	4719	18444
B Forestry and logging	149	22	127	179	27	152	202	26	176	226	34	192
C Fishing	598	83	515	377	52	325	771	108	663	1044	144	900
2 Mining and quarrying	68588	6400	62188	74332	7388	66944	65047	10658	54389	53344	6422	46922
A Coal mining [a]	...	...	...	...	...	...	...	...	...	...	...	...
B Crude petroleum and natural gas production	66631	5633	60998	72310	6679	65631	63337	10069	53268	51835	5981	45854
C Metal ore mining [a]	...	...	...	...	...	...	...	...	...	...	...	...
D Other mining [a]	1957	767	1190	2022	709	1313	1710	589	1121	1509	441	1068
3 Manufacturing	123884	82687	41197	132006	88917	43089	142722	95938	46784	142958	93665	49293
A Manufacture of food, beverages and tobacco	36754	26141	10613	41577	29041	12536	46877	32658	14219	49374	34570	14804
B Textile, wearing apparel and leather industries	8022	5476	2546	8459	5750	2709	8530	5826	2704	8831	6030	2801
C Manufacture of wood and wood products, including furniture	2319	1641	678	2095	1491	604	2116	1502	614	2114	1501	613
D Manufacture of paper and paper products, printing and publishing	5776	3718	2058	6673	4301	2372	7405	4771	2634	7797	5031	2766
E Manufacture of chemicals and chemical petroleum, coal, rubber and plastic products	39932	23518	16414	40390	24641	15749	42284	26466	15818	40704	23787	16917
F Manufacture of non-metallic mineral products, except products of petroleum and coal	4689	2729	1960	5199	3020	2179	5717	3330	2387	4989	2895	2094
G Basic metal industries	8190	5608	2582	7519	5202	2317	8897	5364	3533	10538	5683	4855
H Manufacture of fabricated metal products, machinery and equipment	17293	13216	4077	19290	14905	4385	20028	15410	4618	17685	13516	4169
I Other manufacturing industries	909	640	269	804	566	238	868	611	257	926	652	274
4 Electricity, gas and water	4834	2255	2579	6682	2705	3977	7771	2871	4900	8097	2699	5398
A Electricity, gas and steam [b]	4041	1603	2438	5633	2015	3618	6371	2154	4217	6918	2295	4623
B Water works and supply	793	652	141	1049	690	359	1400	717	683	1179	404	775
5 Construction	34382	19903	14479	37242	21559	15683	37181	21524	15657	34003	19686	14317
6 Wholesale and retail trade, restaurants and hotels	33348	12514	20834	37092	13847	23245	40435	14731	25704	48960	15621	33339
A Wholesale and retail trade	30048	11123	18925	33705	12422	21283	36810	13220	23590	45356	14122	31234
B Restaurants and hotels	3300	1391	1909	3387	1425	1962	3625	1511	2114	3604	1499	2105
7 Transport, storage and communication	38575	13391	25184	46268	15499	30769	52243	16612	35631	50639	17373	33266
A Transport and storage	36369	12701	23668	42977	14473	28504	48017	15621	32396	46027	16628	29399
B Communication	2206	690	1516	3291	1026	2265	4226	991	3235	4612	745	3867
8 Finance, insurance, real estate and business services	49502	11619	37883	60365	14088	46277	65781	15828	49953	67201	15381	51820
A Financial institutions	16121	3306	12815	20407	4104	16303	20094	4457	15637	20607	4148	16459

Venezuela

4.1 Derivation of Value Added by Kind of Activity, in Current Prices
(Continued)

Million Venezuelan bolivares

	1980 Gross Output	1980 Intermediate Consumption	1980 Value Added	1981 Gross Output	1981 Intermediate Consumption	1981 Value Added	1982 Gross Output	1982 Intermediate Consumption	1982 Value Added	1983 Gross Output	1983 Intermediate Consumption	1983 Value Added
B Insurance	2905	1594	1311	2933	1862	1071	3327	2090	1237	3633	2302	1331
C Real estate and business services	30476	6719	23757	37025	8122	28903	42360	9281	33079	42961	8931	34030
9 Community, social and personal services	13749	4170	9579	15808	4827	10981	16282	5116	11166	16559	5138	11421
A Sanitary and similar services	120	209	-89	121	267	-146	140	412	-272	141	508	-367
B Social and related community services [c]	7643	1486	6157	8973	1746	7227	9585	1883	7702	10162	2018	8144
Educational services	2896	564	2332	3513	685	2828	3917	764	3153	4340	847	3493
Medical, dental, other health and veterinary services	320	187	133	369	216	153	424	248	176	489	286	203
C Recreational and cultural services	2559	399	2160	2966	545	2421	2732	507	2225	2440	306	2134
D Personal and household services	3427	2076	1351	3748	2269	1479	3825	2314	1511	3816	2306	1510
Total, Industries	385003	156644	228359	430425	173047	257378	449554	187694	261860	446194	180882	265312
Producers of Government Services	35775	5697	30078	43098	8195	34903	43250	8028	35222	42165	7662	34503
Other Producers	3130	631	2499	3753	787	2966	4104	917	3187	4699	922	3777
Total	423908	162972	260936	477276	182029	295247	496908	196639	300269	493058	189466	303592
Less: Imputed bank service charge	...	-13104	13104	...	-16378	16378	...	-15879	15879	...	-16101	16101
Import duties	6369	...	6369	6339	...	6339	6878	...	6878	3001	...	3001
Value added tax	...	...	...	...	...	...	...	...	...	...	...	...
Total	430277	176076	254201	483615	198407	285208	503786	212518	291268	496059	205567	290492

	1984 Gross Output	1984 Intermediate Consumption	1984 Value Added	1985 Gross Output	1985 Intermediate Consumption	1985 Value Added	1986 Gross Output	1986 Intermediate Consumption	1986 Value Added
				All Producers					
1 Agriculture, hunting, forestry and fishing	29894	6008	23886	36751	7559	29192	45232	9110	36122
A Agriculture and hunting	27961	5739	22222	34740	7284	27456	41870	8642	33228
B Forestry and logging	247	37	210	216	33	183	276	42	234
C Fishing	1686	232	1454	1795	242	1553	3086	426	2660
2 Mining and quarrying	77271	7609	69662	68096	9473	58623	48732	12505	36227
A Coal mining [a]	...	...	...	...	...	...	...	...	...
B Crude petroleum and natural gas production	75362	7074	68288	65855	8658	57197	45758	11510	34248
C Metal ore mining [a]	...	...	...	1048	393	655	1351	504	847
D Other mining [a]	1909	535	1374	1193	422	771	1623	491	1132
3 Manufacturing	188100	120425	67675	222187	143017	79170	259724	167002	92722
A Manufacture of food, beverages and tobacco	58624	41902	16722	70291	50590	19701	82113	59228	22885
B Textile, wearing apparel and leather industries	12346	8382	3964	13218	8961	4257	15587	10574	5013
C Manufacture of wood and wood products, including furniture	2372	1683	689	2660	1886	774	3327	2359	968
D Manufacture of paper and paper products, printing and publishing	10579	6829	3750	11834	7616	4218	13834	8910	4924
E Manufacture of chemicals and chemical petroleum, coal, rubber and plastic products	58607	31987	26620	73995	40469	33526	78877	42508	36369
F Manufacture of non-metallic mineral products, except products of petroleum and coal	5728	3310	2418	6872	3961	2911	9015	5243	3772
G Basic metal industries	17976	9730	8246	19033	11106	7927	25056	13822	11234
H Manufacture of fabricated metal products, machinery and equipment	20791	15844	4947	23284	17724	5560	30695	23500	7195
I Other manufacturing industries	1077	758	319	1000	704	296	1220	858	362
4 Electricity, gas and water	9784	4011	5773	11445	4460	6985	12681	5029	7652
A Electricity, gas and steam [b]	8535	3529	5006	10165	4049	6116	11510	4618	6892
B Water works and supply	1249	482	767	1280	411	869	1171	411	760

Venezuela

4.1 Derivation of Value Added by Kind of Activity, in Current Prices
(Continued)

Million Venezuelan bolivares

	1984 Gross Output	1984 Intermediate Consumption	1984 Value Added	1985 Gross Output	1985 Intermediate Consumption	1985 Value Added	1986 Gross Output	1986 Intermediate Consumption	1986 Value Added
5 Construction	24544	14209	10335	26469	15323	11146	35156	20351	14805
6 Wholesale and retail trade, restaurants and hotels	55269	16977	38292	61283	19488	41795	72463	23880	48583
A Wholesale and retail trade	51326	15345	35981	57354	17865	39489	67595	21858	45737
B Restaurants and hotels	3943	1632	2311	3929	1623	2306	4868	2022	2846
7 Transport, storage and communication	59641	21916	37725	70341	26964	43377	87738	33797	53941
A Transport and storage	54649	21474	33175	63967	25986	37981	80103	32773	47330
B Communication	4992	442	4550	6374	978	5396	7635	1024	6611
8 Finance, insurance, real estate and business services	73934	15935	57999	79828	18235	61593	89320	20924	68396
A Financial institutions	25582	4303	21279	28622	5383	23239	33862	6742	27120
B Insurance	3838	2404	1434	4344	3041	1303	5265	3686	1579
C Real estate and business services	44514	9228	35286	46862	9811	37051	50193	10496	39697
9 Community, social and personal services	18713	5516	13197	21287	6573	14714	24623	7844	16779
A Sanitary and similar services	344	350	-6	389	646	-257	461	779	-318
B Social and related community services c	11419	2277	9142	13230	2651	10579	15047	3093	11954
Educational services	4835	943	3892	5720	1115	4605	6183	1237	4946
Medical, dental, other health and veterinary services	574	336	238	677	396	281	830	490	340
C Recreational and cultural services	2768	360	2408	2948	415	2533	3355	466	2889
D Personal and household services	4182	2529	1653	4720	2861	1859	5760	3506	2254
Total, Industries	537150	212606	324544	597687	251092	346595	675669	300442	375227
Producers of Government Services	44701	8816	35885	50143	9928	40215	55623	11906	43717
Other Producers	4842	848	3994	5363	949	4414	6153	1127	5026
Total	586693	222270	364423	653193	261969	391224	737445	313475	423970
Less: Imputed bank service charge	...	-19916	19916	...	-22685	22685	...	-24998	24998
Import duties	3023	...	3023	3492	...	3492	4888	-	4888
Value added tax	...	...	...	...	...	...	...	...	...
Total	589716	242186	347530	656685	284654	372031	742333	338473	403860

a) Items 'Coal mining' and 'Metal ore mining' are included in item 'Other mining'.
b) Item 'Electricity, gas and water' excludes gas.
c) Social and related community services includes in addition to Educational and health services (item 33 and 34) also the services of commercial and professional associations.

4.2 Derivation of Value Added by Kind of Activity, in Constant Prices

Million Venezuelan bolivares

	1980 Gross Output	1980 Intermediate Consumption	1980 Value Added	1981 Gross Output	1981 Intermediate Consumption	1981 Value Added	1982 Gross Output	1982 Intermediate Consumption	1982 Value Added	1983 Gross Output	1983 Intermediate Consumption	1983 Value Added
	\multicolumn{12}{c}{At constant prices of:1968}
	\multicolumn{12}{c}{All Producers}
1 Agriculture, hunting, forestry and fishing	6218	1453	4765	6131	1455	4676	6334	1491	4843	6319	1456	4863
A Agriculture and hunting	6050	1430	4620	5979	1433	4546	6174	1469	4705	6162	1434	4728
B Forestry and logging	39	6	33	39	6	33	39	5	34	38	6	32
C Fishing	129	17	112	113	16	97	121	17	104	119	16	103
2 Mining and quarrying	6751	648	6103	6900	952	5948	6387	1047	5340	6010	1008	5002
A Coal mining	...	...	...	...	...	...	...	...	...	...	...	...
B Crude petroleum and natural gas production	5881	415	5466	6041	721	5320	5658	842	4816	5414	849	4565
C Metal ore mining	499	121	378	485	118	367	368	91	277	289	60	229
D Other mining	371	112	259	374	113	261	361	114	247	307	99	208

Venezuela

4.2 Derivation of Value Added by Kind of Activity, in Constant Prices
(Continued)

Million Venezuelan bolivares

	1980 Gross Output	1980 Intermediate Consumption	1980 Value Added	1981 Gross Output	1981 Intermediate Consumption	1981 Value Added	1982 Gross Output	1982 Intermediate Consumption	1982 Value Added	1983 Gross Output	1983 Intermediate Consumption	1983 Value Added
				At constant prices of:1968								
3 Manufacturing	43081	29421	13660	42429	29107	13322	43662	29799	13863	42014	28388	13626
A Manufacture of food, beverages and tobacco	15611	10848	4763	15684	10723	4961	16209	11079	5130	16519	11375	5144
B Textile, wearing apparel and leather industries	2909	1985	924	2822	1920	902	2803	1915	888	2827	1934	893
C Manufacture of wood and wood products, including furniture	623	436	187	501	353	148	489	343	146	459	321	138
D Manufacture of paper and paper products, printing and publishing	1836	1183	653	1993	1285	708	2090	1348	742	2157	1393	764
E Manufacture of chemicals and chemical petroleum, coal, rubber and plastic products	9510	6009	3501	8995	5793	3202	9481	6195	3286	9013	5801	3212
F Manufacture of non-metallic mineral products, except products of petroleum and coal	1458	851	607	1446	844	602	1511	884	627	1315	768	547
G Basic metal industries	3228	2068	1160	3142	2156	986	3277	2066	1211	3084	1767	1317
H Manufacture of fabricated metal products, machinery and equipment	7763	5940	1823	7720	5944	1776	7647	5860	1787	6479	4916	1563
I Other manufacturing industries	143	101	42	126	89	37	155	109	46	161	113	48
4 Electricity, gas and water	3620	1670	1950	3745	1489	2256	3968	1435	2533	3951	1316	2635
A Electricity, gas and steam [a]	3071	1219	1852	3253	1165	2088	3432	1160	2272	3510	1165	2345
B Water works and supply	549	451	98	492	324	168	536	275	261	441	151	290
5 Construction	10950	6341	4609	10852	6341	4511	9866	5735	4131	8511	4928	3583
6 Wholesale and retail trade, restaurants and hotels	11053	4146	6907	10724	4000	6724	10845	3948	6897	10297	3285	7012
A Wholesale and retail trade	9986	3696	6290	9795	3609	6186	9919	3562	6357	9447	2941	6506
B Restaurants and hotels	1067	450	617	929	391	538	926	386	540	850	344	506
7 Transport, storage and communication	15795	5990	9805	15681	5526	10155	15967	5459	10508	14268	5188	9080
A Transport and storage	14456	5571	8885	14270	5086	9184	14575	5133	9442	12920	4970	7950
B Communication	1339	419	920	1411	440	971	1392	326	1066	1348	218	1130
8 Finance, insurance, real estate and business services	18461	4438	14023	19924	4791	15133	19478	4833	14645	19100	4500	14600
A Financial institutions	5877	1205	4672	7098	1428	5670	6213	1378	4835	5985	1205	4780
B Insurance	1396	766	630	1320	838	482	1339	841	498	1335	846	489
C Real estate and business services	11188	2467	8721	11506	2525	8981	11926	2614	9312	11780	2449	9331
9 Community, social and personal services	6784	1912	4872	6754	1906	4848	6340	1848	4492	6126	1900	4226
A Sanitary and similar services	53	92	-39	45	99	-54	48	139	-91	44	159	-115
B Social and related community services [b]	3470	606	2783	3405	703	2792	3456	705	2751	3042	920	2722
Educational services	1357	264	1093	1420	277	1143	1489	290	1199	1532	299	1233
Medical, dental, other health and veterinary services	190	111	79	195	114	81	210	123	87	224	131	93
C Recreational and cultural services	1880	293	1587	1994	366	1628	1697	315	1382	1364	171	1193
D Personal and household services	1372	831	541	1220	738	482	1139	689	450	1076	650	426
Total, Industries	122713	56019	66694	123140	55567	67573	122847	55595	67252	116596	51969	64627
Producers of Government Services	12487	1989	10498	13072	2486	10586	13008	2415	10593	12708	2309	10399
Other Producers	1046	211	835	1072	225	847	1111	248	863	1071	210	861
Total	136246	58219	78027	137284	58278	79006	136966	58258	78708	130375	54488	75887
Less: Imputed bank service charge	...	-4777	4777	...	-5697	5697	...	-4910	4910	...	-4904	4904
Import duties	2607	...	2607	2319	...	2319	2346	...	2346	884	...	884
Value added tax	...	...	...	...	...	...	...	...	...	...	...	...
Total	138853	62996	75857	139603	63975	75628	139312	63168	76144	131259	59392	71867

Venezuela

4.2 Derivation of Value Added by Kind of Activity, in Constant Prices

Million Venezuelan bolivares

	1984 Gross Output	1984 Intermediate Consumption	1984 Value Added	1985 Gross Output	1985 Intermediate Consumption	1985 Value Added	1986 Gross Output	1986 Intermediate Consumption	1986 Value Added
	At constant prices of: 1968								
	All Producers								
1 Agriculture, hunting, forestry and fishing	6399	1498	4901	6790	1610	5180	7164	1675	5489
A Agriculture and hunting	6230	1475	4755	6624	1587	5037	6977	1649	5328
B Forestry and logging	34	5	29	25	4	21	28	4	24
C Fishing	135	18	117	141	19	122	159	22	137
2 Mining and quarrying	6131	1033	5098	5847	979	4868	7101	1880	5221
A Coal mining	...	...	...	...	...	...	...	...	...
B Crude petroleum and natural gas production	5437	844	4593	4957	652	4305	6129	1542	4587
C Metal ore mining	411	97	314	565	212	353	625	233	392
D Other mining	283	92	191	325	115	210	347	105	242
3 Manufacturing	44838	30591	14247	43260	28699	14561	45652	30352	15300
A Manufacture of food, beverages and tobacco	16589	11565	5024	16633	11624	5009	17684	12595	5089
B Textile, wearing apparel and leather industries	3286	2242	1044	3221	2198	1023	3449	2355	1094
C Manufacture of wood and wood products, including furniture	451	316	135	468	327	141	543	380	163
D Manufacture of paper and paper products, printing and publishing	2504	1619	885	2414	1557	857	2588	1671	917
E Manufacture of chemicals and chemical petroleum, coal, rubber and plastic products	9502	6082	3420	8226	4666	3560	7644	4028	3616
F Manufacture of non-metallic mineral products, except products of petroleum and coal	1412	821	591	1494	868	626	1700	994	706
G Basic metal industries	3420	1909	1511	3846	2222	1624	3908	2169	1739
H Manufacture of fabricated metal products, machinery and equipment	7529	5935	1594	6829	5193	1636	7990	6057	1933
I Other manufacturing industries	145	102	43	129	44	85	146	103	43
4 Electricity, gas and water	4469	1835	2634	4443	1740	2703	4847	1923	2924
A Electricity, gas and steam [a]	4016	1660	2356	4062	1618	2444	4422	1774	2648
B Water works and supply	453	175	278	381	122	259	425	149	276
5 Construction	5581	3231	2350	5350	3097	2253	6193	3585	2608
6 Wholesale and retail trade, restaurants and hotels	9589	2946	6643	9462	3009	6453	9910	3275	6635
A Wholesale and retail trade	8786	2627	6159	8752	2716	6036	9144	2957	6187
B Restaurants and hotels	803	319	484	710	293	417	766	318	448
7 Transport, storage and communication	14795	5989	8806	14842	5624	9218	15551	5902	9649
A Transport and storage	12645	5063	7582	13238	5378	7860	13876	5677	8199
B Communication	2150	926	1224	1604	246	1358	1675	225	1450
8 Finance, insurance, real estate and business services	20100	4440	15660	20691	4827	15864	21796	5235	16561
A Financial institutions	6912	1163	5749	7254	1364	5890	7806	1554	6252
B Insurance	1295	811	484	1324	927	397	1540	1078	462
C Real estate and business services	11893	2466	9427	12113	2536	9577	12450	2603	9847
9 Community, social and personal services	6140	1810	4330	5990	1738	4252	6203	1840	4363
A Sanitary and similar services	115	117	-2	97	161	-64	109	184	-75
B Social and related community services [b]	3617	877	2740	3568	741	2827	3677	756	2921
Educational services	1543	301	1242	1612	314	1298	1643	329	1314
Medical, dental, other health and veterinary services	234	137	97	241	141	100	261	154	107
C Recreational and cultural services	1348	175	1173	1231	173	1058	1216	169	1047
D Personal and household services	1060	641	419	1094	663	431	1201	731	470

Venezuela

4.2 Derivation of Value Added by Kind of Activity, in Constant Prices
(Continued)

Million Venezuelan bolivares

	1984 Gross Output	1984 Intermediate Consumption	1984 Value Added	1985 Gross Output	1985 Intermediate Consumption	1985 Value Added	1986 Gross Output	1986 Intermediate Consumption	1986 Value Added
			At constant prices of:1968						
Total, Industries	118042	53373	64669	116675	51323	65352	124417	55667	68750
Producers of Government Services	12901	2544	10357	12668	2508	10160	13275	2841	10434
Other Producers	1022	179	843	1091	193	898	1145	210	935
Total	131965	56096	75869	130434	54024	76410	138837	58718	80119
Less: Imputed bank service charge	...	-5637	5637	...	-5989	5989	...	-6055	6055
Import duties	662	...	662	668	...	668	692	...	692
Value added tax	...	...	...	...	...	...	...	...	...
Total	132627	61733	70894	131102	60013	71089	139529	64773	74756

a) Item 'Electricity, gas and water' excludes gas.
b) Social and related community services includes in addition to Educational and health services (item 33 and 34) also the services of commercial and professional associations.

4.3 Cost Components of Value Added

Million Venezuelan bolivares

		1980 Compensation of Employees	1980 Capital Consumption	1980 Net Operating Surplus	1980 Indirect Taxes	1980 Less: Subsidies Received	1980 Value Added	1981 Compensation of Employees	1981 Capital Consumption	1981 Net Operating Surplus	1981 Indirect Taxes	1981 Less: Subsidies Received	1981 Value Added
						All Producers							
1	Agriculture, hunting, forestry and fishing	5460	1072	8370	-	466	14436	6178	1150	9287	-	202	16413
	A Agriculture and hunting	5135	1009	8116	...	466	13794	5951	1108	9079	...	202	15936
	B Forestry and logging	37	0	87	...	...	127	45	4	103		...	152
	C Fishing	288	60	167	...	...	515	182	38	105	...	...	325
2	Mining and quarrying	3873	1649	56105	561	...	62188	4448	1981	60134	381	...	66944
	A Coal mining a	...	...	...	...	...	...	...	...	...	...	...	...
	B Crude petroleum and natural gas production	3243	1523	55679	553	...	60998	3737	1841	59679	374	...	65631
	C Metal ore mining a	...	...	...	...	...	...	...	...	...	...	...	...
	D Other mining a	630	126	426	8	...	1190	711	140	455	7	...	1313
3	Manufacturing	15411	3288	20374	3073	949	41197	16732	3986	19848	3685	1162	43089
	A Manufacture of food, beverages and tobacco	3914	850	4511	2287	949	10613	4563	1001	5609	2525	1162	12536
	B Textile, wearing apparel and leather industries	1586	176	756	28	...	2546	1676	192	814	27	...	2709
	C Manufacture of wood and wood products, including furniture	439	55	172	12	...	678	387	51	155	11	...	604
	D Manufacture of paper and paper products, printing and publishing	1024	266	738	30	...	2058	1171	311	854	36	...	2372
	E Manufacture of chemicals and chemical petroleum, coal, rubber and plastic products	3343	604	11822	645	...	16414	3579	739	10418	1013	...	15749
	F Manufacture of non-metallic mineral products, except products of petroleum and coal	918	349	675	18	...	1960	1018	383	759	19	...	2179
	G Basic metal industries	1947	631	-3	7	...	2582	1943	945	-578	7	...	2317
	H Manufacture of fabricated metal products, machinery and equipment	2089	334	1611	43	...	4077	2261	343	1737	44	...	4385
	I Other manufacturing industries	151	23	92	3	...	269	134	21	80	3	...	238
4	Electricity, gas and water	1994	568	-96	113	...	2579	1975	629	1203	170	...	3977
	A Electricity, gas and steam b	1189	543	593	113	...	2438	1395	603	1450	170	...	3618
	B Water works and supply	805	25	-689	-	...	141	580	26	-247	-	...	359
5	Construction	10315	571	3483	110	...	14479	11173	618	3774	118	...	15683
6	Wholesale and retail trade, restaurants and hotels	12692	1839	7451	531	1679	20834	14132	2040	8319	580	1826	23245
	A Wholesale and retail trade	11530	1591	7030	453	1679	18925	12941	1786	7881	501	1826	21283
	B Restaurants and hotels	1162	248	421	78	...	1909	1191	254	438	79	...	1962
7	Transport, storage and communication	11699	3199	10348	127	189	25184	13580	3550	13732	150	243	30769
	A Transport and storage	10481	2928	10322	126	189	23668	12174	3245	13178	150	243	28504
	B Communication	1218	271	26	1	...	1516	1406	305	554	-	...	2265
8	Finance, insurance, real estate and business services	7623	4301	25643	316	...	37883	9459	5210	31210	398	...	46277
	A Financial institutions	4822	327	7564	102	...	12815	6055	403	9708	137	...	16303

Venezuela

4.3 Cost Components of Value Added
(Continued)

Million Venezuelan bolivares

1980

	Compensation of Employees	Capital Consumption	Net Operating Surplus	Indirect Taxes	Less: Subsidies Received	Value Added
B Insurance	586	36	621	68	...	1311
C Real estate and business services	2215	3938	17458	146	...	23757
9 Community, social and personal services	3579	537	5384	178	99	9579
A Sanitary and similar services	365	-	-454	-	...	-89
B Social and related community services c	1955	318	3888	95	99	6157
Educational services	1682	151	592	6	99	2332
Medical, dental, other health and veterinary services	78	16	31	8	...	133
C Recreational and cultural services	491	73	1562	34	...	2160
D Personal and household services	768	146	388	49	...	1351
Total, Industries	72646	17024	137062	5009	3382	228359
Producers of Government Services	30030	48	...	...	...	30078
Other Producers	2467	32	...	...	...	2499
Total	105143	17104	137062	5009	3382	260936
Less: Imputed bank service charge	...	...	13104	...	...	13104
Import duties	...	...	...	6369	...	6369
Value added tax	...	...	...	...	...	...
Total	105143	17104	123958	11378	3382	254201

1981

	Compensation of Employees	Capital Consumption	Net Operating Surplus	Indirect Taxes	Less: Subsidies Received	Value Added
B Insurance	735	24	227	85	...	1071
C Real estate and business services	2669	4783	21275	176	...	28903
9 Community, social and personal services	4188	613	6152	192	164	10981
A Sanitary and similar services	513	-	-659	-	...	-146
B Social and related community services c	2351	374	4559	107	164	7227
Educational services	2037	183	766	6	164	2828
Medical, dental, other health and veterinary services	90	18	36	9	...	153
C Recreational and cultural services	485	79	1822	35	...	2421
D Personal and household services	839	160	430	50	...	1479
Total, Industries	81865	19777	153659	5674	3597	257378
Producers of Government Services	34851	52	...	...	...	34903
Other Producers	2926	40	...	...	...	2966
Total	119642	19869	153659	5674	3597	295247
Less: Imputed bank service charge	...	...	16378	...	...	16378
Import duties	...	...	...	6339	...	6339
Value added tax	...	...	...	...	...	...
Total	119642	19869	137281	12013	3597	285208

1982

All Producers

	Compensation of Employees	Capital Consumption	Net Operating Surplus	Indirect Taxes	Less: Subsidies Received	Value Added
1 Agriculture, hunting, forestry and fishing	6527	1264	10225	-	340	17676
A Agriculture and hunting	6099	1188	9890	...	340	16837
B Forestry and logging	52	-	124	...	...	176
C Fishing	376	76	211	...	...	663
2 Mining and quarrying	4729	2254	46124	1282	...	54389
A Coal mining a	...	...	...	...	...	...
B Crude petroleum and natural gas production	4175	2090	45727	1276	...	53268
C Metal ore mining a	...	...	...	...	...	...
D Other mining a	554	164	397	6	...	1121
3 Manufacturing	18359	4436	21908	3293	1212	46784
A Manufacture of food, beverages and tobacco	5255	1137	7068	1971	1212	14219
B Textile, wearing apparel and leather industries	1686	192	806	20	...	2704
C Manufacture of wood and wood products, including furniture	395	50	161	8	...	614
D Manufacture of paper and paper products, printing and publishing	1304	343	959	28	...	2634
E Manufacture of chemicals and chemical petroleum, coal, rubber and plastic products	3898	1015	9697	1208	...	15818
F Manufacture of non-metallic mineral products, except products of petroleum and coal	1118	426	829	14	...	2387
G Basic metal industries	2193	887	445	8	...	3533
H Manufacture of fabricated metal products, machinery and equipment	2366	364	1854	34	...	4618
I Other manufacturing industries	144	22	89	2	...	257
4 Electricity, gas and water	2503	866	1331	200	...	4900
A Electricity, gas and steam b	1395	832	1790	200	...	4217
B Water works and supply	1108	34	-459	-	...	683

1983

	Compensation of Employees	Capital Consumption	Net Operating Surplus	Indirect Taxes	Less: Subsidies Received	Value Added
1 Agriculture, hunting, forestry and fishing	7270	1436	11208	-	378	19536
A Agriculture and hunting	6710	1327	10785	...	378	18444
B Forestry and logging	57	5	130	...	...	192
C Fishing	503	104	293	...	...	900
2 Mining and quarrying	5763	2877	37192	1090	...	46922
A Coal mining a	...	...	...	...	...	...
B Crude petroleum and natural gas production	5223	2689	36857	1085	...	45854
C Metal ore mining a	...	...	...	...	...	...
D Other mining a	540	188	335	5	...	1068
3 Manufacturing	18425	4778	18903	8256	1069	49293
A Manufacture of food, beverages and tobacco	5424	1186	3321	5942	1069	14804
B Textile, wearing apparel and leather industries	1745	196	796	64	...	2801
C Manufacture of wood and wood products, including furniture	395	50	142	26	...	613
D Manufacture of paper and paper products, printing and publishing	1359	365	952	90	...	2766
E Manufacture of chemicals and chemical petroleum, coal, rubber and plastic products	3971	1211	9920	1815	...	16917
F Manufacture of non-metallic mineral products, except products of petroleum and coal	976	363	717	38	...	2094
G Basic metal industries	2255	1047	1368	185	...	4855
H Manufacture of fabricated metal products, machinery and equipment	2146	336	1597	90	...	4169
I Other manufacturing industries	154	24	90	6	...	274
4 Electricity, gas and water	2492	1033	1651	222	...	5398
A Electricity, gas and steam b	1626	959	1816	222	...	4623
B Water works and supply	866	74	-165	-	...	775

Venezuela

4.3 Cost Components of Value Added
(Continued)

Million Venezuelan bolivares

1982 / 1983

	Compensation of Employees	Capital Consumption	Net Operating Surplus	Indirect Taxes	Less: Subsidies Received	Value Added	Compensation of Employees	Capital Consumption	Net Operating Surplus	Indirect Taxes	Less: Subsidies Received	Value Added
5 Construction	11154	617	3800	86	...	15657	10201	563	3421	132	...	14317
6 Wholesale and retail trade, restaurants and hotels	15008	2225	9290	483	1302	25704	14989	2364	7618	8876	508	33339
A Wholesale and retail trade	13747	1937	8783	425	1302	23590	13731	2078	7160	8773	508	31234
B Restaurants and hotels	1261	288	507	58	...	2114	1258	286	458	103	...	2105
7 Transport, storage and communication	13226	3363	19000	128	86	35631	11780	3963	17352	285	114	33266
A Transport and storage	11647	2981	17727	127	86	32396	9716	3424	16088	285	114	29399
B Communication	1579	382	1273	1	...	3235	2064	539	1264	-	...	3867
8 Finance, insurance, real estate and business services	10231	5906	33394	422	...	49953	9967	6207	35062	584	...	51820
A Financial institutions	6108	422	8926	181	...	15637	5870	542	9783	264	...	16459
B Insurance	881	45	215	96	...	1237	959	49	251	72	...	1331
C Real estate and business services	3242	5439	24253	145	...	33079	3138	5616	25028	248	...	34030
9 Community, social and personal services	4481	637	6104	138	194	11166	4587	681	6143	247	237	11421
A Sanitary and similar services	541	-	-813	-	...	-272	385	16	-768	-	...	-367
B Social and related community services c	2607	403	4807	79	194	7702	2872	430	4938	141	237	8144
Educational services	2272	204	867	4	194	3153	2517	225	981	7	237	3493
Medical, dental, other health and veterinary services	104	21	44	7	...	176	120	24	46	13	...	203
C Recreational and cultural services	478	70	1655	22	...	2225	476	70	1549	39	...	2134
D Personal and household services	855	164	455	37	...	1511	854	165	424	67	...	1510
Total, Industries	86218	21568	151176	6032	3134	261860	85474	23902	138550	19692	2306	265312
Producers of Government Services	35171	51	...	...	...	35222	34421	82	...	...	...	34503
Other Producers	3140	47	...	...	...	3187	3730	47	...	...	...	3777
Total	124529	21666	151176	6032	3134	300269	123625	24031	138550	19692	2306	303592
Less: Imputed bank service charge	...	...	15879	...	...	15879	...	...	16101	...	...	16101
Import duties	...	...	...	6878	...	6878	...	...	...	3001	...	3001
Value added tax	...	...	...	...	...	...	...	...	...	...	...	...
Total	124529	21666	135297	12910	3134	291268	123625	24031	122449	22693	2306	290492

1984 / 1985

	Compensation of Employees	Capital Consumption	Net Operating Surplus	Indirect Taxes	Less: Subsidies Received	Value Added	Compensation of Employees	Capital Consumption	Net Operating Surplus	Indirect Taxes	Less: Subsidies Received	Value Added
					All Producers							
1 Agriculture, hunting, forestry and fishing	8961	1755	13590	-	420	23886	9578	2095	17519	-	-	29192
A Agriculture and hunting	8086	1581	12975	...	420	22222	8660	1908	16888	...	...	27456
B Forestry and logging	62	5	143	...	...	210	52	9	122	...	...	183
C Fishing	813	169	472	...	...	1454	866	178	509	...	...	1553
2 Mining and quarrying	5370	3243	59145	1904	...	69662	7050	3457	47527	589	...	58623
A Coal mining a	...	...	...	...	...	...	...	...	...	...	...	...
B Crude petroleum and natural gas production	4779	3084	58525	1900	...	68288	6407	3309	46902	579	...	57197
C Metal ore mining a	...	...	...	...	...	...	321	46	279	9	...	655
D Other mining a	591	159	620	4	...	1374	322	102	346	1	...	771

Venezuela

4.3 Cost Components of Value Added
(Continued)

Million Venezuelan bolivares

	1984						1985					
	Compensation of Employees	Capital Consumption	Net Operating Surplus	Indirect Taxes	Less: Subsidies Received	Value Added	Compensation of Employees	Capital Consumption	Net Operating Surplus	Indirect Taxes	Less: Subsidies Received	Value Added
3 Manufacturing	21879	5990	33465	7209	868	67675	25520	6448	34464	13135	397	79170
A Manufacture of food, beverages and tobacco	6221	1357	5237	4775	868	16722	7380	1614	909	10195	397	19701
B Textile, wearing apparel and leather industries	2447	278	1167	72	...	3964	2614	304	1193	146	...	4257
C Manufacture of wood and wood products, including furniture	445	57	164	23	...	689	499	63	167	45	...	774
D Manufacture of paper and paper products, printing and publishing	1836	498	1320	96	...	3750	2098	544	1374	202	...	4218
E Manufacture of chemicals and chemical petroleum, coal, rubber and plastic products	4569	1425	18658	1968	...	26620	5590	1541	24233	2162	...	33526
F Manufacture of non-metallic mineral products, except products of petroleum and coal	1118	407	861	32	...	2418	1345	485	1014	67	...	2911
G Basic metal industries	2515	1539	4039	153	...	8246	2977	1417	3417	116	...	7927
H Manufacture of fabricated metal products, machinery and equipment	2549	401	1911	86	...	4947	2851	454	2075	180	...	5560
I Other manufacturing industries	179	28	108	4	...	319	166	26	82	22	...	296
4 Electricity, gas and water	2424	1208	1854	287	...	5773	2750	1407	2492	336	...	6985
A Electricity, gas and steam [b]	1680	1134	1905	287	...	5006	1966	1362	2452	336	...	6116
B Water works and supply	744	74	-51	-	...	767	784	45	40	-	...	869
5 Construction	7363	407	2477	88	...	10335	7940	440	2671	95	...	11146
6 Wholesale and retail trade, restaurants and hotels	16319	2576	11237	8844	684	38292	18863	2972	12604	8288	932	41795
A Wholesale and retail trade	14951	2268	10701	8745	684	35981	17501	2663	12082	8175	932	39489
B Restaurants and hotels	1368	308	536	99	...	2311	1362	309	522	113	...	2306
7 Transport, storage and communication	11425	4009	21857	434	-	37725	13366	5283	24519	209	-	43377
A Transport and storage	9397	3483	19865	430	-	33175	11623	4740	21412	206	-	37981
B Communication	2028	526	1992	4	...	4550	1743	543	3107	3	...	5396
8 Finance, insurance, real estate and business services	9928	6543	41001	527	...	57999	8900	6878	43269	2546	...	61593
A Financial institutions	5597	632	14843	207	...	21279	6487	693	15903	156	...	23239
B Insurance	1024	58	266	86	...	1434	1137	65	66	35	...	1303
C Real estate and business services	3307	5853	25892	234	...	35286	1276	6120	27300	2355	...	37051
9 Community, social and personal services	4990	757	7399	252	201	13197	5754	822	8222	293	377	14714
A Sanitary and similar services	141	1	-148	-	...	-6	169	2	-428	-	...	-257
B Social and related community services [c]	3209	483	5507	144	201	9142	3785	536	6463	172	377	10579
Educational services	2804	251	1031	7	201	3892	3317	297	1358	10	377	4605
Medical, dental, other health and veterinary services	141	28	56	13	...	238	166	33	64	18	...	281
C Recreational and cultural services	706	93	1569	40	...	2408	743	85	1661	44	...	2533
D Personal and household services	934	180	471	68	...	1653	1057	199	526	77	...	1859
Total, Industries	88659	26488	192025	19545	2173	324544	99721	29802	193287	25491	1706	346595
Producers of Government Services	35788	97	...	...	...	35885	40083	132	...	...	...	40215
Other Producers	3951	43	...	...	...	3994	4366	48	...	...	...	4414
Total	128398	26628	192025	19545	2173	364423	144170	29982	193287	25491	1706	391224
Less: Imputed bank service charge	...	...	19916	...	...	19916	...	...	22685	...	...	22685
Import duties	...	...	...	3023	...	3023	...	...	...	3492	...	3492
Value added tax	...	...	...	...	...	...	...	...	...	...	...	...
Total	128398	26628	172109	22568	2173	347530	144170	29982	170602	28983	1706	372031

Venezuela

4.3 Cost Components of Value Added

Million Venezuelan bolivares

		Compensation of Employees	Capital Consumption	Net Operating Surplus	Indirect Taxes	Less: Subsidies Received	Value Added
		\multicolumn{6}{c}{1986}
		\multicolumn{6}{c}{All Producers}
1	Agriculture, hunting, forestry and fishing	13298	2671	20153	-	-	36122
	A Agriculture and hunting	11742	2357	19129	...	-	33228
	B Forestry and logging	69	5	160	...	...	234
	C Fishing	1487	309	864	...	...	2660
2	Mining and quarrying	6504	3899	25275	549	...	36227
	A Coal mining [a]	...	...	...	...	...	...
	B Crude petroleum and natural gas production	5700	3710	24311	527	...	34248
	C Metal ore mining [a]	360	61	405	21	...	847
	D Other mining [a]	444	128	559	1	...	1132
3	Manufacturing	30205	7647	56542	-472	1200	92722
	A Manufacture of food, beverages and tobacco	8609	1873	18173	-4570	1200	22885
	B Textile, wearing apparel and leather industries	3073	364	1641	-65	...	5013
	C Manufacture of wood and wood products, including furniture	623	79	286	-20	...	968
	D Manufacture of paper and paper products, printing and publishing	2399	635	1984	-94	...	4924
	E Manufacture of chemicals and chemical petroleum, coal, rubber and plastic products	6283	1749	23777	4560	...	36369
	F Manufacture of non-metallic mineral products, except products of petroleum and coal	1764	645	1400	-37	...	3772
	G Basic metal industries	3569	1692	6125	-152	...	11234
	H Manufacture of fabricated metal products, machinery and equipment	3682	578	3024	-89	...	7195
	I Other manufacturing industries	203	32	132	-5	...	362
4	Electricity, gas and water	2532	1584	3173	363	...	7652
	A Electricity, gas and steam [b]	1966	1559	3005	362	...	6892
	B Water works and supply	566	25	168	1	...	760
5	Construction	10547	583	3506	169	...	14805
6	Wholesale and retail trade, restaurants and hotels	23194	3652	17018	5963	1244	48583
	A Wholesale and retail trade	21517	3272	16390	5802	1244	45737
	B Restaurants and hotels	1677	380	628	161	...	2846
7	Transport, storage and communication	15504	6322	31823	292	-	53941
	A Transport and storage	13735	5862	27445	288	-	47330
	B Communication	1769	460	4378	4	...	6611
8	Finance, insurance, real estate and business services	12667	7540	47482	707	...	68396
	A Financial institutions	7413	926	18487	294	...	27120
	B Insurance	1379	79	79	42	...	1579
	C Real estate and business services	3875	6535	28916	371	...	39697
9	Community, social and personal services	6361	1019	9366	444	411	16779
	A Sanitary and similar services	225	-	-543	-	...	-318
	B Social and related community services [c]	4114	592	7422	237	411	11954
	Educational services	3586	309	1448	14	411	4946
	Medical, dental, other health and veterinary services	207	42	61	30	...	340
	C Recreational and cultural services	740	102	1972	75	...	2889
	D Personal and household services	1282	325	515	132	...	2254

Venezuela

4.3 Cost Components of Value Added
(Continued)

Million Venezuelan bolivares

	Compensation of Employees	Capital Consumption	Net Operating Surplus	Indirect Taxes	Less: Subsidies Received	Value Added
	\multicolumn{6}{c}{1986}					
Total, Industries	120812	34917	214338	8015	2855	375227
Producers of Government Services	43533	184	...	...	...	43717
Other Producers	4969	57	...	...	...	5026
Total	169314	35158	214338	8015	2855	423970
Less: Imputed bank service charge	...	...	24998	...	...	24998
Import duties	...	...	...	4888	...	4888
Value added tax	...	...	...	...	...	...
Total	169314	35158	189340	12903	2855	403860

a) Items 'Coal mining' and 'Metal ore mining' are included in item 'Other mining'.
b) Item 'Electricity, gas and water' excludes gas.

c) Social and related community services includes in addition to Educational and health services (item 33 and 34) also the services of commercial and professional associations.

Viet Nam

Source. 'Statistical Data of the Socialist Republic of Viet Nam, 1978' published by the General Statistical Office, Hanoi.
General note. The estimates shown in the following tables have been prepared in accordance with the United Nations System of National Accounts so far as the existing data would permit.

1.1 Expenditure on the Gross Domestic Product, in Current Prices

Million Dongs

	1970	1975	1977	1978	1979	1980	1981	1982	1983	1984	1985	1986
1 Government final consumption expenditure	...	...	...	...	...	...	...	...	...	...	...	...
2 Private final consumption expenditure	...	...	...	...	...	...	...	...	...	...	...	...
3 Gross capital formation	...	...	...	...	...	...	...	...	...	...	...	...
4 Exports of goods and services	...	...	...	...	...	...	...	...	...	...	...	...
5 Less: Imports of goods and services	...	...	...	...	...	...	...	...	...	...	...	...
Equals: Gross Domestic Product	...	18258	20305	20742	...	...	...	...	...	...	...	...

Yemen

Source. Reply to the United Nations National Accounts Questionnaire from the Central Planning Organization, Sanaa. The official estimates and descriptions are published in the 'National Accounts of Yemen Arab Republic', issued by the same Organization.

General note. The official estimates of Yemen have been prepared in accordance with the United Nations System of National Accounts so far as the existing data would permit.

1.1 Expenditure on the Gross Domestic Product, in Current Prices

Million Yemeni rials — Fiscal year beginning 1 July

	1970	1975	1977	1978	1979	1980	1981	1982	1983	1984	1985	1986
1 Government final consumption expenditure	161	701	1279	1839	2255	3007	3891	6416	7449	7135	5543	6898
2 Private final consumption expenditure	1477	4939	7971	10648	12342	12910	12467	13530	14189	14837	29404	33999
3 Gross capital formation	251	900	3210	3994	4761	5005	5530	5362	3981	3755	4472	4988
A Increase in stocks	31	155	407	30	355	107	219	240	-148	-90	-75	50
B Gross fixed capital formation	220	745	2803	3964	4406	4898	5311	5122	4129	3845	4547	4938
4 Exports of goods and services	29	214	242	474	803	805	1130	958	1126	1178	1164	1155
5 Less: Imports of goods and services	391	1866	4483	6774	8465	9046	9636	10397	9575	8955	9644	9568
Equals: Gross Domestic Product [a]	1527	4888	8219	10181	11696	12681	13382	15869	17170	17950	30939	37472

a) Beginning 1981, estimates relate to calendar year.

1.2 Expenditure on the Gross Domestic Product, in Constant Prices

Million Yemeni rials — Fiscal year beginning 1 July

	1970	1975	1977	1978	1979	1980	1981	1982	1983	1984	1985	1986
	At constant prices of 1975						At constant prices of 1981					
1 Government final consumption expenditure	435	1516	1884	2221	2463	3103	3891	5263	5762	5493	3791	4290
2 Private final consumption expenditure	2739	10288	10864	12249	12238	12120	12467	13308	13541	13696	17206	16984
3 Gross capital formation	542	2163	5395	5978	6425	6433	5530	5155	3673	3370	3344	3108
A Increase in stocks	73	301	542	35	377	110	219	235	-140	-81	-42	23
B Gross fixed capital formation	469	1862	4853	5943	6048	6323	5311	4920	3813	3451	3386	3085
4 Exports of goods and services	50	417	324	548	847	824	1130	939	1023	1038	711	560
5 Less: Imports of goods and services	674	5261	7556	9374	9760	9529	9636	9949	8769	8001	5913	4688
Equals: Gross Domestic Product [a]	3092	9123	10911	11622	12213	12951	13382	14716	15230	15596	19139	20254

a) Beginning 1981, estimates relate to calendar year.

1.3 Cost Components of the Gross Domestic Product

Million Yemeni rials — Fiscal year beginning 1 July

	1970	1975	1977	1978	1979	1980	1981	1982	1983	1984	1985	1986
1 Indirect taxes, net	70	431	1361	1453	1811	1868	1792	1943	2327	2397	2974	2863
2 Consumption of fixed capital	33	98	186	235	279	309	313	360	393	421	839	1038
3 Compensation of employees paid by resident producers to:	294	4359	6672	8493	9606	10504	11277	13566	14450	15132	27126	33571
4 Operating surplus	1130	...	...	...	...	...	...	...	...	...	...	...
Equals: Gross Domestic Product [a]	1527	4888	8219	10181	11696	12681	13382	15869	17170	17950	30939	37472

a) Beginning 1981, estimates relate to calendar year.

Yemen

1.7 External Transactions on Current Account, Summary

Million Yemeni rials — Fiscal year beginning 1 July

	1970	1975	1977	1978	1979	1980	1981	1982	1983	1984	1985	1986
Payments to the Rest of the World												
1 Imports of goods and services	391	1866	4483	6774	8465	9046	9636	10397	9575	8955	9644	9568
2 Factor income to the rest of the world	...	...	...	...	...	...	...	...	...	...	...	...
By general government	...	...	3210	...	...	...	...	...	...	...	...	...
By corporate and quasi-corporate enterprises	...	...	...	...	...	...	...	...	...	...	...	...
By other	...	...	...	...	...	...	...	...	...	...	...	...
3 Current transfers to the rest of the world	...	...	...	...	...	...	...	...	...	...	...	...
4 Surplus of the nation on current transactions	-82	1100	1473	-621	-1480	-2980	-2990	-2665	-2451	-1663	-2210	-1158
Payments to the Rest of the World and Surplus of the Nation on Current Transactions [a]	309	2966	5956	6153	6985	6066	6646	7732	7124	7292	7434	8410
Receipts From The Rest of the World												
1 Exports of goods and services	29	214	242	474	803	805	1130	958	1126	1178	1164	1155
2 Factor income from rest of the world [b]	129	763	1332	1743	2160	1899	1938	6774	5998	6114	6270	7255
A Compensation of employees	119	581	975	1217	1423	1356	1484	...	...	...	...	...
B Property and entrepreneurial income	10	182	357	526	737	543	454	...	...	...	...	...
3 Current transfers from rest of the world [b]	151	1989	4382	3936	4022	3362	3579	...	...	...	...	...
Receipts from the Rest of the World on Current Transactions [a]	309	2966	5956	6153	6985	6066	6646	7732	7124	7292	7434	8410

a) Beginning 1981, estimates relate to calendar year.
b) Net factor income and net current transfers are shown in items 2 and 3, respectively, of the receipt from the rest of the world.

1.10 Gross Domestic Product by Kind of Activity, in Current Prices

Million Yemeni rials — Fiscal year beginning 1 July

	1970	1975	1977	1978	1979	1980	1981	1982	1983	1984	1985	1986
1 Agriculture, hunting, forestry and fishing	785	2011	2409	3049	3458	3579	3685	3799	3596	3712	8033	10680
2 Mining and quarrying [a]	15	32	100	133	149	149	156	168	190	210	241	506
3 Manufacturing	67	257	381	504	655	730	820	1043	1254	1453	3365	4620
4 Electricity, gas and water	4	17	23	38	66	90	117	138	170	220	257	320
5 Construction	79	236	796	1060	1033	1110	1098	1215	1255	1365	1541	1285
6 Wholesale and retail trade, restaurants and hotels	251	1012	1531	1790	1935	2131	2185	2369	2476	2614	4169	4896
7 Transport, storage and communication	47	150	308	370	431	461	497	610	665	710	3489	4106
8 Finance, insurance, real estate and business services	100	258	508	635	788	946	1117	1274	1503	1635	3598	4166
9 Community, social and personal services	12	42	78	101	121	130	131	155	162	182	242	286

Yemen

1.10 Gross Domestic Product by Kind of Activity, in Current Prices
(Continued)

Million Yemeni rials — Fiscal year beginning 1 July

	1970	1975	1977	1978	1979	1980	1981	1982	1983	1984	1985	1986
Total, Industries	1360	4015	6133	7680	8636	9316	9806	10771	11274	12107	... 24935	30865
Producers of Government Services	127	509	858	1202	1505	1906	2129	3477	3912	3857	... 3643	4410
Other Producers	7	14	19	21	23	24	24	27	31	34	... 38	50
Subtotal	1494	4538	7010	8903	10164	11246	11959	14275	15217	15998	... 28616	35325
Less: Imputed bank service charge	20	44	95	108	138	274	211	246	260	288	... 651	716
Plus: Import duties	53	394	1304	1386	1670	1709	1634	1840	2213	2240	... 2974	2863
Plus: Value added tax	...	...	...	...	...	...	...	...	...	...	...	...
Equals: Gross Domestic Product [b]	1527	4888	8219	10181	11696	12681	13382	15869	17170	17950	... 30939	37472

a) For 1986, item 'Mining and Quarrying' includes crude petroleum production.
b) Beginning 1981, estimates relate to calendar year.

1.11 Gross Domestic Product by Kind of Activity, in Constant Prices

Million Yemeni rials — Fiscal year beginning 1 July

At constant prices of: 1975 (1970); 1981 (1981 onwards)

	1970	1975	1977	1978	1979	1980	1981	1982	1983	1984	1985	1986
1 Agriculture, hunting, forestry and fishing	1547	3409	2802	3265	3404	3578	3685	3854	3418	3414	... 3704	4126
2 Mining and quarrying	27	67[a]	134[a]	154[a]	163[a]	154[a]	156[a]	163[a]	178[a]	187[a]	... 172[a]	397[a]
3 Manufacturing	142	425	511	597	688	741	820	987	1216	1345	... 2404	2662
4 Electricity, gas and water	8	35	46	59	78	91	117	138	173	216	... 239	286
5 Construction	151	591	1276	1473	1238	1196	1098	1167	1159	1225	... 1101	857
6 Wholesale and retail trade, restaurants and hotels	465	1764	1847	1812	1996	2131	2185	2303	2259	2317	... 2553	2728
7 Transport, storage and communication	92	323	429	446	452	465	497	596	593	620	... 2406	2549
8 Finance, insurance, real estate and business services	197	556	702	685	738	969	1117	1274	1477	1556	... 2436	2597
9 Community, social and personal services	27	85	105	117	123	127	131	154	154	160	... 138	159
Total, Industries	2656	7255	7852	8608	8880	9452	9806	10636	10627	11040	... 15153	16361
Producers of Government Services	314	1100	1265	1453	1643	1963	2129	2472	2763	2724	... 2291	2314
Other Producers	9	14	19	21	23	24	24	27	31	32	... 36	40
Subtotal	2979	8369	9136	10082	10546	11439	11959	13135	13421	13796	... 17480	18715
Less: Imputed bank service charge	51	98	142	133	155	295	211	251	248	260	... 465	482
Plus: Import duties	164	852	1917	1673	1822	1807	1634	1832	2057	2060	... 2124	2021
Plus: Value added tax	...	...	...	...	...	...	...	...	...	...	...	...
Equals: Gross Domestic Product	3092[b]	9123[a]	10911[a]	11622[a]	12213[a]	12951[a]	13382[a]	14716[a]	15230[a]	15596[a]	19139[a]	20254[a]

a) For 1986, item 'Mining and Quarrying' includes crude petroleum production.
b) Beginning 1981, estimates relate to calendar year.

Yemen

1.12 Relations Among National Accounting Aggregates

Million Yemeni rials — Fiscal year beginning 1 July

	1970	1975	1977	1978	1979	1980	1981	1982	1983	1984	1985	1986
Gross Domestic Product	1527	4888	8219	10181	11696	12681	13382	15869	17170	17950	30939	37472
Plus: Net factor income from the rest of the world [a]	129	763	1332	1743	2160	1899	1938	6774	5998	6114	6270	7255
Equals: Gross National Product	1656	5651	9551	11924	13856	14580	15320	...	...	...	...	...
Less: Consumption of fixed capital	33	98	186	235	279	309	313	360	393	421	839	1038
Equals: National Income	1623	5553	9365	11689	13577	14271	15007	...	...	...	...	...
Plus: Net current transfers from the rest of the world [a]	151	1989	4382	3936	4022	3362	3579	...	...	...	...	...
Equals: National Disposable Income	1774	7542	13747	15625	17599	17633	18586	22283	22775	23643	36370	43689
Less: Final consumption	1638	5640	9250	12487	14597	15917	16358	19946	21638	21972	34947	40897
Equals: Net Saving	136	1902	4497	3138	3002	1716	2227	2337	1137	1671	1423	2792
Less: Surplus of the nation on current transactions	-82	1100	1473	-621	-1480	-2980	-2990	-2665	-2451	-1663	-2210	-1158
Equals: Net Capital Formation [b]	218	802	3024	3759	4482	4696	5217	5002	3588	3334	3633	3950

a) Beginning 1982, item 'Net factor income from abroad' includes item 'Net current transfers from the rest of the world'.
b) Beginning 1981, estimates relate to calendar year.

2.11 Gross Fixed Capital Formation by Kind of Activity of Owner, ISIC Divisions, in Current Prices

Million Yemeni rials — Fiscal year beginning 1 July

	1970	1975	1977	1978	1979	1980	1981	1982	1983	1984	1985	1986
					All Producers							
1 Agriculture, hunting, forestry and fishing	...	57	231	317	311	383	269	341	402	416	619	526
2 Mining and quarrying	...	...	60	29	30	44	60	66	67	70	35	52
3 Manufacturing	...	52	228	418	355	372	364	237	187	168	578	451
4 Electricity, gas and water	...	...	127	192	324	609	768	661	552	505	839	801
5 Construction	...	10	165	210	270	303	80	52	54	56	104	116
6 Wholesale and retail trade, restaurants and hotels	...	...	...	...	...	...	430	229	227	219	269	257
7 Transport, storage and communication	...	220	831	1016	1504	1506	941	1053	531	445	322	571
8 Finance, insurance, real estate and business services	...	311	700	841	909	965	817	700	840	792	864	1001
A Financial institutions	...	...	...	...	...	...	27	22	68	59	44	78
B Insurance	...	...	...	...	...	...	...	...	...	...	...	...
C Real estate and business services	...	311	700	841	909	965	790	678	772	733	820	923
9 Community, social and personal services	...	95	461	941	703	716	1583	1783	1271	1174	917	1163
Total Industries [a]	...	745	2803	3964	4406	4898	5311	5122	4129	3845	4547	4930
Producers of Government Services	...	...	...	...	...	...	...	...	...	...	...	...
Private Non-Profit Institutions Serving Households	...	...	...	...	...	...	...	...	...	...	...	...
Total	...	...	...	...	...	...	...	...	...	...	...	...

a) Beginning 1981, estimates relate to calendar year.

Yemen

2.12 Gross Fixed Capital Formation by Kind of Activity of Owner, ISIC Divisions, in Constant Prices

Million Yemeni rials — Fiscal year beginning 1 July

	1970	1975	1977	1978	1979	1980	1981	1982	1983	1984	1985	1986
					At constant prices of: 1981							
					All Producers							
1 Agriculture, hunting, forestry and fishing	...	141	412	561	449	526	269	328	373	371	461	329
2 Mining and quarrying	...	...	107	46	46	66	59	64	60	65	26	32
3 Manufacturing	...	129	458	705	563	573	364	227	172	147	430	282
4 Electricity, gas and water	...	...	253	320	494	897	768	635	509	464	625	500
5 Construction	...	25	333	355	441	476	80	50	50	49	77	72
6 Wholesale and retail trade, restaurants and hotels	...	...	...	...	...	...	430	220	209	191	200	161
7 Transport, storage and communication	...	550	1390	1788	2055	1905	941	1012	490	394	240	357
8 Finance, insurance, real estate and business services	...	778	1068	1110	1005	930	817	672	775	690	644	626
A Financial institutions	...	...	...	...	...	...	27	21	62	54	32	49
B Insurance	...	...	...	...	...	...	...	...	...	...	...	...
C Real estate and business services	...	778	1068	1110	1005	930	790	651	713	636	612	577
9 Community, social and personal services	...	239	832	1058	995	950	1583	1712	1175	1080	683	726
Total Industries [a]	...	1862	4853	5943	6048	6323	5311	4920	3813	3451	3386	3085
Producers of Government Services	...	...	...	...	...	...	...	...	...	...	...	...
Private Non-Profit Institutions Serving Households	...	...	...	...	...	...	...	...	...	...	...	...
Total	...	...	...	...	...	...	...	...	...	...	...	...

a) Beginning 1981, estimates relate to calendar year.

4.1 Derivation of Value Added by Kind of Activity, in Current Prices

Million Yemeni rials — Fiscal year beginning 1 July

	1985 Gross Output	1985 Intermediate Consumption	1985 Value Added	1986 Gross Output	1986 Intermediate Consumption	1986 Value Added
			All Producers			
1 Agriculture, hunting, forestry and fishing	11476	3443	8033	16430	5750	10680
2 Mining and quarrying	330	89	241	662	156	506
A Coal mining	...	...	...	...	...	...
B Crude petroleum and natural gas production	...	...	...	325	65	260
C Metal ore mining	...	...	...	...	...	...
D Other mining	...	...	...	337	91	246
3 Manufacturing	7692	4327	3365	10675	6055	4620
4 Electricity, gas and water	492	235	257	685	365	320
5 Construction	3436	1895	1541	3022	1737	1285
6 Wholesale and retail trade, restaurants and hotels	5072	903	4169	5968	1072	4896
7 Transport, storage and communication	4743	1254	3489	5583	1477	4106
8 Finance, insurance, real estate and business services	3957	359	3598	4570	404	4166
9 Community, social and personal services	303	61	242	359	73	286
Total, Industries [a]	37501	12566	24935	47954	17089	30865
Producers of Government Services	5609	1966	3643	7010	2600	4410
Other Producers	45	7	38	65	15	50
Total	43155	14539	28616	55029	19704	35325
Less: Imputed bank service charge	...	-651	651	...	-716	716
Import duties	2974	...	2974	2863	...	2863
Value added tax	...	...	...	...	...	...
Total [a]	46129	15190	30939	57892	20420	37472

a) Beginning 1981, estimates relate to calendar year.

Yemen

4.2 Derivation of Value Added by Kind of Activity, in Constant Prices

Million Yemeni rials
Fiscal year beginning 1 July

		1985			1986	
	Gross Output	Intermediate Consumption	Value Added	Gross Output	Intermediate Consumption	Value Added

At constant prices of: 1981

All Producers

1	Agriculture, hunting, forestry and fishing	5292	1588	3704	6347	2221	4126
2	Mining and quarrying	235	63	172	512	115	397
	A Coal mining	...	...	...	...	...	...
	B Crude petroleum and natural gas production	...	...	...	325	65	260
	C Metal ore mining	...	...	...	...	...	...
	D Other mining	...	...	...	187	50	137
3	Manufacturing	5495	3091	2404	6201	3539	2662
4	Electricity, gas and water	457	218	239	612	326	286
5	Construction	2455	1354	1101	2015	1158	857
6	Wholesale and retail trade, restaurants and hotels	3115	562	2553	3326	598	2728
7	Transport, storage and communication	3271	865	2406	3466	917	2549
8	Finance, insurance, real estate and business services	2686	250	2436	2858	261	2597
9	Community, social and personal services	173	35	138	200	41	159
	Total, Industries [a]	23179	8026	15153	25537	9176	16361
	Producers of Government Services	3837	1546	2291	4359	2045	2314
	Other Producers	43	7	36	52	12	40
	Total	27059	9579	17480	29948	11233	18715
	Less: Imputed bank service charge	...	-465	465	...	-482	482
	Import duties	2124	...	2124	2021	...	2021
	Value added tax	...	...	...	...	...	...
	Total [a]	29183	10044	19139	31969	11715	20254

a) Beginning 1981, estimates relate to calendar year.

4.3 Cost Components of Value Added

Million Yemeni rials
Fiscal year beginning 1 July

		1980					1981				
		Compensation of Employees	Capital Consumption	Net Operating Surplus	Indirect Taxes	Less: Subsidies Received	Value Added	Compensation of Employees	Capital Consumption	Net Operating Surplus	Indirect Taxes	Less: Subsidies Received	Value Added

All Producers

1	Agriculture, hunting, forestry and fishing	421	...	3016	...	...	3579	428	...	3069	...	...	3648
2	Mining and quarrying	36	...	106	...	...	149	38	...	112	...	...	156
3	Manufacturing	133	...	398	...	...	730	275	...	411	...	...	854
4	Electricity, gas and water	19	...	58	...	...	80	26	...	81	...	...	111
5	Construction	617	...	420	...	...	1088	603	...	410	...	...	1080
6	Wholesale and retail trade, restaurants and hotels	224	...	1930	...	...	2260	231	...	1878	...	...	2188
7	Transport, storage and communication	78	...	234	...	...	461	84	...	229	...	...	470
8	Finance, insurance, real estate and business services	133	...	1346	...	...	1536	134	...	1370	...	...	1565
9	Community, social and personal services	8	...	111	...	...	130	9	...	103	...	...	131
	Total, Industries [ab]	1670	...	7619	...	...	10013	1828	...	7662	...	...	10203
	Producers of Government Services	1741	...	...	...	...	1748	1958	...	...	...	...	1965
	Other Producers	24	...	...	...	...	24	24	...	...	...	...	24
	Total	3435	...	7619	...	...	11785	3810	...	7662	...	...	12192
	Less: Imputed bank service charge	...	...	864	...	...	864	...	...	705	...	...	705
	Import duties	...	...	...	...	...	1709	...	...	...	...	...	1633
	Value added tax	...	...	...	...	...	...	...	...	...	...	...	...
	Total [ab]	3435	...	6755	...	...	12630	3810	...	6957	...	...	13120

Yemen

4.3 Cost Components of Value Added

Million Yemeni rials — Fiscal year beginning 1 July

	Compensation of Employees	Capital Consumption	Net Operating Surplus	Indirect Taxes	Less: Subsidies Received	Value Added
			1982			
			All Producers			
1 Agriculture, hunting, forestry and fishing	447	...	3209	...	...	3813
2 Mining and quarrying	41	...	120	...	...	167
3 Manufacturing	320	...	478	...	...	991
4 Electricity, gas and water	36	...	114	...	...	155
5 Construction	649	...	441	...	...	1161
6 Wholesale and retail trade, restaurants and hotels	258	...	2094	...	...	2445
7 Transport, storage and communication	96	...	261	...	...	525
8 Finance, insurance, real estate and business services	128	...	1379	...	...	1569
9 Community, social and personal services	10	...	116	...	...	146
Total, Industries ab	1985	...	8212	...	...	10972
Producers of Government Services	2454	...	...	...	...	2463
Other Producers	26	...	...	...	...	26
Total	4465	...	8212	...	...	13461
Less: Imputed bank service charge	...	...	670	...	...	670
Import duties	...	...	...	...	...	1846
Value added tax	...	...	...	...	...	...
Total ab	4465	...	7542	...	...	14637

a) Beginning 1981, estimates relate to calendar year.
b) Data for this table have not been revised, therefore, data for some years are not comparable with those of other tables.

Yemen

4.2 Derivation of Value Added by Kind of Activity, in Constant Prices

Million Yemeni rials — Fiscal year beginning 1 July

At constant prices of: 1981 — All Producers

	1985 Gross Output	1985 Intermediate Consumption	1985 Value Added	1986 Gross Output	1986 Intermediate Consumption	1986 Value Added
1 Agriculture, hunting, forestry and fishing	5292	1588	3704	6347	2221	4126
2 Mining and quarrying	235	63	172	512	115	397
A Coal mining	...	...	...	...	...	...
B Crude petroleum and natural gas production	...	...	...	325	65	260
C Metal ore mining	...	...	...	...	...	...
D Other mining	...	...	...	187	50	137
3 Manufacturing	5495	3091	2404	6201	3539	2662
4 Electricity, gas and water	457	218	239	612	326	286
5 Construction	2455	1354	1101	2015	1158	857
6 Wholesale and retail trade, restaurants and hotels	3115	562	2553	3326	598	2728
7 Transport, storage and communication	3271	865	2406	3466	917	2549
8 Finance, insurance, real estate and business services	2686	250	2436	2858	261	2597
9 Community, social and personal services	173	35	138	200	41	159
Total, Industries a	23179	8026	15153	25537	9176	16361
Producers of Government Services	3837	1546	2291	4359	2045	2314
Other Producers	43	7	36	52	12	40
Total	27059	9579	17480	29948	11233	18715
Less: Imputed bank service charge	...	-465	465	...	-482	482
Import duties	2124	...	2124	2021	...	2021
Value added tax	...	...	...	...	...	...
Total a	29183	10044	19139	31969	11715	20254

a) Beginning 1981, estimates relate to calendar year.

4.3 Cost Components of Value Added

Million Yemeni rials — Fiscal year beginning 1 July

All Producers

	1980 Compensation of Employees	1980 Capital Consumption	1980 Net Operating Surplus	1980 Indirect Taxes	1980 Less: Subsidies Received	1980 Value Added	1981 Compensation of Employees	1981 Capital Consumption	1981 Net Operating Surplus	1981 Indirect Taxes	1981 Less: Subsidies Received	1981 Value Added
1 Agriculture, hunting, forestry and fishing	421	...	3016	...	...	3579	428	...	3069	...	...	3648
2 Mining and quarrying	36	...	106	...	...	149	38	...	112	...	...	156
3 Manufacturing	133	...	398	...	...	730	275	...	411	...	...	854
4 Electricity, gas and water	19	...	58	...	...	80	26	...	81	...	...	111
5 Construction	617	...	420	...	...	1088	603	...	410	...	...	1080
6 Wholesale and retail trade, restaurants and hotels	224	...	1930	...	...	2260	231	...	1878	...	...	2199
7 Transport, storage and communication	78	...	234	...	...	461	84	...	229	...	...	470
8 Finance, insurance, real estate and business services	133	...	1346	...	...	1536	134	...	1370	...	...	1565
9 Community, social and personal services	8	...	111	...	...	130	9	...	103	...	...	131
Total, Industries ab	1670	...	7619	...	...	10013	1828	...	7662	...	...	10203
Producers of Government Services	1741					1748	1958		...	...	...	1965
Other Producers	24	...	...	...	...	24	24	...	...	...	...	24
Total	3435	...	7619	...	...	11785	3810	...	7662	...	...	12192
Less: Imputed bank service charge	...	...	864	...	...	864	...	...	705	...	...	705
Import duties	...	...	...	...	...	1709	...	...	...	...	...	1633
Value added tax	...	...	...	...	...	...	...	...	...	...	...	...
Total ab	3435	...	6755	...	...	12630	3810	...	6957	...	...	13120

Yemen

4.3 Cost Components of Value Added

Million Yemeni rials
Fiscal year beginning 1 July

	Compensation of Employees	Capital Consumption	Net Operating Surplus	Indirect Taxes	Less: Subsidies Received	Value Added
			1982			
			All Producers			
1 Agriculture, hunting, forestry and fishing	447	...	3209	...	...	3813
2 Mining and quarrying	41	...	120	...	...	167
3 Manufacturing	320	...	478	...	...	991
4 Electricity, gas and water	36	...	114	...	...	155
5 Construction	649	...	441	...	...	1161
6 Wholesale and retail trade, restaurants and hotels	258	...	2094	...	...	2445
7 Transport, storage and communication	96	...	261	...	...	525
8 Finance, insurance, real estate and business services	128	...	1379	...	...	1569
9 Community, social and personal services	10	...	116	...	...	146
Total, Industries [ab]	1985	...	8212	...	...	10972
Producers of Government Services	2454	...	...	...	...	2463
Other Producers	26	...	...	...	...	26
Total	4465	...	8212	...	...	13461
Less: Imputed bank service charge	...	...	670	...	...	670
Import duties	...	...	...	...	...	1846
Value added tax	...	...	...	...	...	...
Total [ab]	4465	...	7542	...	...	14637

a) Beginning 1981, estimates relate to calendar year.
b) Data for this table have not been revised, therefore, data for some years are not comparable with those of other tables.

Yugoslavia

Source. Reply to the United Nations National Accounts Questionnaire from the Federal Institute for Statistics, Belgrade. The official estimates and descriptions are published annually in 'Statisticki Godisnjak' (Statistical Yearbook), issued by the same Office.

General note. The estimates shown in the following tables have been prepared in accordance with the United Nations System of National Accounts so far as the existing data would permit.

1.1 Expenditure on the Gross Domestic Product, in Current Prices

Thousand Million Yugoslav dinars

	1970	1975	1977	1978	1979	1980	1981	1982	1983	1984	1985	1986
1 Government final consumption expenditure	30	98	148	177	228	291	381	500	643	932	1666	3348
2 Private final consumption expenditure	96	295	429	528	672	881	1226	1624	2243	3389	5951	11782
3 Gross capital formation	65	218	326	411	539	731	983	1227	1660	2691	4702	8996
A Increase in stocks	14	54	58	54	91	186	298	373	631	1233	2093	3949
B Gross fixed capital formation	52	163	268	357	448	546	685	855	1030	1458	2609	5047
4 Exports of goods and services	32	102	128	147	201	322	446	600	851	1704	2638	3763
5 Less: Imports of goods and services	40	149	190	223	329	476	570	744	950	1864	2774	3930
Statistical discrepancy	-1	13	-5	-28	-16	-26	-56	-48	-165	-199	-232	-559
Equals: Gross Domestic Product	182	577	835	1013	1294	1724	2410	3159	4283	6653	11951	23400

1.2 Expenditure on the Gross Domestic Product, in Constant Prices

Thousand Million Yugoslav dinars

	1970	1975	1977	1978	1979	1980	1981	1982	1983	1984	1985	1986
				At constant prices of:1980								
1 Government final consumption expenditure	187	229	254	265	278	281	268	268	263	265	269	281
2 Private final consumption expenditure	538	718	760	979	879	878	799	790	726	655	658	686
3 Gross capital formation	362	493	615	521	738	718	793	782	824	903	897	731
A Increase in stocks	48	76	122	-24	158	172	301	317	404	523	533	431
B Gross fixed capital formation	314	417	493	545	580	546	492	465	420	380	364	300
4 Exports of goods and services	213	270	292	306	314	336	321	302	284	304	319	310
5 Less: Imports of goods and services	282	372	394	404	453	413	358	309	283	280	279	296
Equals: Gross Domestic Product	1015	1337	1527	1665	1746	1781	1791	1790	1765	1791	1809	1884

1.3 Cost Components of the Gross Domestic Product

Thousand Million Yugoslav dinars

	1970	1975	1977	1978	1979	1980	1981	1982	1983	1984	1985	1986
1 Indirect taxes, net	15	47	79	97	129	152	218	261	399	599	876	1747
A Indirect taxes	16	62	105	123	163	195	269	340	508	771	1193	2364
B Less: Subsidies	1	15	26	26	34	43	51	79	109	172	317	617
2 Consumption of fixed capital	17	61	84	103	129	175	236	375	529	779	1325	2492
3 Compensation of employees paid by resident producers to:	...	...	...	...	...	...	...	...	...	...	...	...
4 Operating surplus	...	...	...	...	...	...	...	...	...	...	...	...
Statistical discrepancy	151	469	673	813	1037	1397	1956	2524	3354	5275	9749	19161
Equals: Gross Domestic Product	182	577	835	1013	1294	1724	2410	3159	4283	6653	11950	23400

1.10 Gross Domestic Product by Kind of Activity, in Current Prices

Thousand Million Yugoslav dinars

	1970	1975	1977	1978	1979	1980	1981	1982	1983	1984	1985	1986
1 Agriculture, hunting, forestry and fishing	30	84	112	113	147	201	304	435	620	896	1376	2899
2 Mining and quarrying	4	13	17	20	24	39	57	77	104	200	336	514
3 Manufacturing	49	160	221	272	344	481	699	918	1264	2065	4125	7621
4 Electricity, gas and water	4	14	21	25	32	45	60	79	91	145	264	565
5 Construction	19	54	79	100	128	168	226	272	322	447	820	1589
6 Wholesale and retail trade, restaurants and hotels	17	63	88	111	145	195	264	359	503	774	1305	2610
7 Transport, storage and communication	12	44	59	74	97	127	177	228	310	469	890	1735
8 Finance, insurance, real estate and business services	4	17	27	37	44	60	80	108	134	220	420	890
9 Community, social and personal services	19	81	131	166	204	255	324	423	534	838	1539	3230
Statistical discrepancy	-	1	1	-	-	-	-	-	-	-	-	-
Total, Industries	159	530	756	916	1165	1571	2192	2898	3884	6054	11075	21653
Producers of Government Services	8	...	...	...	...	...	...	...	...	...	...	...

Yugoslavia

1.10 Gross Domestic Product by Kind of Activity, in Current Prices
(Continued)

Thousand Million Yugoslav dinars

	1970	1975	1977	1978	1979	1980	1981	1982	1983	1984	1985	1986
Other Producers	...	...	...	...	...	...	...	...	...	...	...	...
Subtotal	167	530	756	916	1165	1571	2192	2898	3884	6054	11075	21653
Less: Imputed bank service charge	...	...	...	...	...	...	...	...	...	...	...	...
Plus: Import duties [a]	15	47	79	97	129	152	218	261	399	599	877	1747
Plus: Value added tax	...	...	...	...	...	...	...	...	...	...	...	...
Plus: Other adjustments	-	-	-	-	-	-	-	-	-	-	-	-
Equals: Gross Domestic Product	182	577	835	1013	1294	1724	2410	3159	4283	6653	11952	23400

a) Item 'Import duties' refers to indirect taxes net of subsidies.

1.11 Gross Domestic Product by Kind of Activity, in Constant Prices

Million Yugoslav dinars

	1970	1975	1977	1978	1979	1980	1981	1982	1983	1984	1985	1986
					At constant prices of: 1972							
1 Agriculture, hunting, forestry and fishing	41900	48800	54100	51200	54000	55200	56600	60700	60300	61415	57510	61415
2 Mining and quarrying	...	...	...	...	...	...	...	...	...	...	...	...
3 Manufacturing	73242	107154	121595	132101	142900	148820	155270	155084	157335	165365	169830	176453
4 Electricity, gas and water	4782	6907	8515	8983	9549	10425	10506	10669	11300	10545	10870	11215
5 Construction	24800	30000	34300	38200	41800	42000	40000	37000	32200	30836	30325	29905
6 Wholesale and retail trade, restaurants and hotels	47600	63000	66000	72500	76800	77600	76500	76900	75700	73835	73490	75336
7 Transport, storage and communication	17600	24000	26900	29700	30900	32100	32500	31600	32000	33294	34426	36007
8 Finance, insurance, real estate and business services	3804	9504	11931	14047	13921	14611	14015	14178	12690	12810	13715	13960
9 Community, social and personal services	...	...	...	...	...	...	...	...	...	...	...	...
Total, Industries	...	...	...	...	...	...	...	...	...	...	...	...
Producers of Government Services	...	...	...	...	...	...	...	...	...	...	...	...
Other Producers	...	...	...	...	...	...	...	...	...	...	...	...
Subtotal	...	...	...	...	...	...	...	...	...	...	...	...
Less: Imputed bank service charge	...	...	...	...	...	...	...	...	...	...	...	...
Plus: Import duties	...	...	...	...	...	...	...	...	...	...	...	...
Plus: Value added tax	...	...	...	...	...	...	...	...	...	...	...	...
Equals: Gross Domestic Product	...	...	...	...	...	...	...	...	...	...	...	...

1.12 Relations Among National Accounting Aggregates

Thousand Million Yugoslav dinars

	1970	1975	1977	1978	1979	1980	1981	1982	1983	1984	1985	1986
Gross Domestic Product	182	577	835	1013	1294	1724	2410	3159	4283	6653	11951	23400
Plus: Net factor income from the rest of the world	4	29	36	53	59	91	103	124	116	223	291	420
Factor income from the rest of the world	...	35	43	62	75	127	162	212	229	462	654	918
Less: Factor income to the rest of the world	...	6	7	9	16	36	59	88	112	239	363	498
Equals: Gross National Product	186	606	872	1066	1353	1814	2513	3283	4399	6876	12242	23820
Less: Consumption of fixed capital	17	61	84	103	129	175	236	375	529	779	1325	2492
Equals: National Income	169	545	788	963	1224	1640	2277	2908	3870	6097	10917	21328
Plus: Net current transfers from the rest of the world	...	...	...	...	...	...	...	...	...	...	...	...
Equals: National Disposable Income	...	...	...	...	...	...	...	...	...	...	...	...
Less: Final consumption	...	...	...	...	...	...	...	...	...	...	...	...
Equals: Net Saving	...	...	...	...	...	...	...	...	...	...	...	...
Less: Surplus of the nation on current transactions	...	...	...	...	...	...	...	...	...	...	...	...
Equals: Net Capital Formation	...	...	...	...	...	...	...	...	...	...	...	...

Zaire

General note. The preparation of national accounts statistics in Zaire is undertaken by Institut de Recherche Scientifique, Kinshasa. Official estimates are published by the Banque du Zaire in 'Rapport Annuel'. The estimates are generally in accordance with the classifications and definitions recommended in the United Nations System of National Accounts (SNA). The following tables have been prepared from succesive replies to the United Nations national accounts questionnaire. When the scope and coverage of the estimates differ from conceptual or statistical reasons from the definitions and classifications recommend in SNA, a footnote is indicated to the relevant tables.

Sources and methods:

(a) Gross domestic product. Gross domestic product is estimated mainly through the production approach.

(b) Expenditure on the gross domestic product. The expenditure approach is used to estimate government final consumption expenditure and exports and imports of goods and services. This approach, together with the commodity flow approach, is used to estimate private final consumption expenditure and gross capital formation. The estimates of government consumption expenditure are derived from the government accounts. Information on private consumption expenditure is obtained from household sample surveys on expenditure conducted by the Institut National de la Statistique in the principal urban centres. The results of these surveys are extrapolated to cover the whole country. Some items are calculated as residuals by using the commodity-flow approach. For increase in stocks, information on the value of stocks at the beginning and end of the accounting year are obtained from the annual surveys of enterprises. For gross fixed capital formation, the estimates, using the commodity-flow approach, are based on information on acquisition of capital goods obtained from the surveys of enterprises. The estimates of capital formation by the general government, public enterprises and public corporations are derived from accounts while information from external trade statistics are used for machinery and equipment. The estimates of exports and imports of goods and services are derived from the balance of payments. The estimates of GDP by expenditure type at constant prices are obtained by applying to the value added at current prices the corresponding implicit price indexes.

(c) Cost-structure of the gross domestic product. The total of wages and salaries is estimated by extrapolating the bench-mark average wages and salaries from a special inquiry by indexes of yearly changes and multiplying the result by the number of employees. The estimates are adjusted to include the value of free lodging. Salaries paid by the government are obtained from budgetary accounts while those paid by enterprises are based on the annual reports of the Caisse des pensions. Estimates of income for unincorporated enterprises are derived from the estimates made of gross product from the production side. Estimates for the foreign population are based on the number of persons engaged in the various professions and their estimated average income. Income from property relates only to net rents and distributed profits received by the foreign population. The accounts of large enterprises are analysed to derive dividends and novelties received as well as direct taxes on corporations and corporate saving. General government income from property and entrepreneurship is derived from the budgets and accounts. The estimates of consumption of fixed capital are based on the results of the annual surveys of enterprises. Small enterprises are not included in the estimates. The annual surveys of enterprises also provide data on indirect taxes and subsidies.

(d) Gross domestic product by kind of economic activity. The table of GDP by kind of economic activity is prepared at market prices, i.e., producers' values. The production approach by commodity-flows is used to estimate the value of most industries. The income approach is used to estimate the value of public administration, defence and some private services. The Department de l'agriculture publishes annual statistical reports on agricultural production, livestock, forestry and fishing. Bench-mark estimates on gross output and value added have been prepared for 1970 based on a census of agriculture and livestock in the modern sector. In addition to this, the annual surveys of enterprises provide the values and the costs of production for the agricultural enterprises. For the modern agricultural sector, total production is valued on the basis of farm-gate prices while for the traditional sector, prices paid at the first sales point are used. The gross value of production in the mining and quarrying sector is estimated on the basis of data supplied by the Mining Service or is obtained from the annual surveys of enterprises. For large industrial enterprises, the annual surveys of industrial enterprises provide estimates of production and value added. For medium-sized and small enterprises, 1973 bench-mark data are obtained from a survey conducted at Kinshasa. These estimates are extrapolated for the country as a whole with a 90 per cent weighting for the city of Kinshasa. The data on electricity, gas and water are obtained from the public enterprises by means of a questionnaire. The estimates of construction in the private sector are based on the surveys of enterprises while the government budget and accounts are used for the public sector. Information on building permits issued in urban areas is used adjusted by means of average cost data per square meter of construction to give an estimate of construction for the whole country. For small construction, the 1973 data obtained from the survey conducted at Kinshasa are extrapolated by assuming that Kinshasa represent 77 per cent of the whole country. The annual surveys of enterprises which furnish information on purchases, services and value added are used to estimate the gross output in large organized trade enterprises. The gross output of the transportation sector is assumed to be equivalent to the gross receipts of transport enterprises. For the financial institutions, data are obtained from the surveys of enterprises as well as from the concerned enterprises directly. The estimates of services such as education, medical services, recreation, etc. are derived from profit-and-loss accounts, budgets of agencies and other offical statitics. For other services, the annual surveys of enterprises and household surveys of domestic servants provide the necessary data. The estimates of government services are derived from government accounts. The estimates of GDP by kind of economic activity at constant prices are obtained by applying to the value at current prices the corresponding implicit price indexes.

1.1 Expenditure on the Gross Domestic Product, in Current Prices

Million Zaires

	1970	1975	1977	1978	1979	1980	1981	1982	1983	1984	1985	1986
1 Government final consumption expenditure	266.0	451.9	772.2	893.0	1857.0	2756.0	4190.0	5948.0	8676.0	14999.0	17134.0	...
2 Private final consumption expenditure	413.0	1220.0	2849.0	3812.0	6686.0	10426.0	15275.0	17094.0	36794.0	34363.0	70360.0	...
3 Gross capital formation	245.0	612.8	1524.0	1007.0	2179.0	4277.0	5967.0	7493.0	11492.0	29322.0	43364.0	...
A Increase in stocks	42.0	65.3	152.0	57.0	653.0	842.0	1292.0	1225.0	2010.0	8523.0	11378.0	...
B Gross fixed capital formation	203.0	547.5	1372.0	950.0	1526.0	3435.0	4675.0	6268.0	9482.0	20799.0	31980.0	...
4 Exports of goods and services	415.0	520.0	1117.0	1216.0	2742.0	6102.0	8349.0	10013.0	23387.0	76783.0	106269.0	...
5 Less: Imports of goods and services	400.6	885.0	2305.0	1448.0	2359.0	6379.0	10001.0	9437.0	21214.0	55883.0	89911.0	...
Equals: Gross Domestic Product a)	938.0	1919.0	3956.0	5481.0	11105.0	17183.0	23781.0	31110.0	59134.0	99723.0	147263.0	203416.0

a) Data in this table have been revised, therefore they are not strictly comparable with the unrevised data in the other tables.

1.2 Expenditure on the Gross Domestic Product, in Constant Prices

Million Zaires

	1970	1975	1977	1978	1979	1980	1981	1982	1983	1984	1985	1986
				At constant prices of:1970								
1 Government final consumption expenditure	260.9	224.4	214.3	...	...	...	...	...	...	...	...	...
2 Private final consumption expenditure	432.7	464.5	424.4	...	...	...	...	...	...	...	...	...
3 Gross capital formation	244.1	349.2	497.5	...	...	...	...	...	...	...	...	...
A Increase in stocks	42.0	28.3	27.5	...	...	...	...	...	...	...	...	...
B Gross fixed capital formation	202.1	320.9	470.0	...	...	...	...	...	...	...	...	...
4 Exports of goods and services	415.0	554.0	891.4	...	...	...	...	...	...	...	...	...
5 Less: Imports of goods and services	400.6	526.6	1040.5	...	...	...	...	...	...	...	...	...
Equals: Gross Domestic Product	952.1	1065.5	987.1	...	...	...	...	...	...	...	...	...

Zaire

1.3 Cost Components of the Gross Domestic Product

Million Zaires

	1970	1975	1977	1978	1979	1980	1981	1982	1983	1984	1985	1986
1 Indirect taxes, net	217.1	250.4	335.0	...	...	...	...	...	...	...	...	...
A Indirect taxes	217.4	262.4	354.4	...	...	...	...	...	...	...	...	...
B Less: Subsidies	0.3	12.0	19.4	...	...	...	...	...	...	...	...	...
2 Consumption of fixed capital	69.2	193.8	270.4	...	...	...	...	...	...	...	...	...
3 Compensation of employees paid by resident producers to:	665.8	1448.2	3268.6	...	...	...	...	...	...	...	...	...
4 Operating surplus				...	...	...	...	...	...	...	...	...
Equals: Gross Domestic Product	952.1	1892.4	3874.0	...	...	...	...	...	...	...	...	...

1.10 Gross Domestic Product by Kind of Activity, in Current Prices

Million Zaires

	1970	1975	1977	1978	1979	1980	1981	1982	1983	1984	1985	1986
1 Agriculture, hunting, forestry and fishing	158.8	373.6	1013.3	...	...	...	...	...	...	...	...	...
2 Mining and quarrying	211.2	200.2	341.4	...	...	...	...	...	...	...	...	...
3 Manufacturing	77.5	191.6	280.2	...	...	...	...	...	...	...	...	...
4 Electricity, gas and water	8.7	10.2	11.2	...	...	...	...	...	...	...	...	...
5 Construction	45.0	111.7	144.6	...	...	...	...	...	...	...	...	...
6 Wholesale and retail trade, restaurants and hotels [a]	106.4	326.5	853.7	...	...	...	...	...	...	...	...	...
7 Transport, storage and communication	75.9	82.3	84.2	...	...	...	...	...	...	...	...	...
8 Finance, insurance, real estate and business services [b]	19.4	44.3	116.5	...	...	...	...	...	...	...	...	...
9 Community, social and personal services [ab]	84.0	236.1	521.5	...	...	...	...	...	...	...	...	...
Total, Industries	786.9	1576.5	3366.6	...	...	...	...	...	...	...	...	...
Producers of Government Services	119.3	248.8	461.3	...	...	...	...	...	...	...	...	...
Other Producers	...	...	...	...	...	...	...	...	...	...	...	...
Subtotal	906.2	1825.3	3827.9	...	...	...	...	...	...	...	...	...
Less: Imputed bank service charge	4.8	18.4	45.0	...	...	...	...	...	...	...	...	...
Plus: Import duties	50.7	85.5	91.1	...	...	...	...	...	...	...	...	...
Plus: Value added tax	...	...	...	...	...	...	...	...	...	...	...	...
Equals: Gross Domestic Product	952.1	1892.4	3874.0	...	...	...	...	...	...	...	...	...

a) Restaurants and hotels are included in item 'Community, social and personal services'.
b) Insurance, real estate and business services are included in item 'Community, social and personal services'.

1.11 Gross Domestic Product by Kind of Activity, in Constant Prices

Million Zaires

	1970	1975	1977	1978	1979	1980	1981	1982	1983	1984	1985	1986
				At constant prices of:1970								
1 Agriculture, hunting, forestry and fishing	158.8	172.6	177.2	...	...	...	...	...	...	...	...	...
2 Mining and quarrying	211.2	242.1	228.0	...	...	...	...	...	...	...	...	...
3 Manufacturing	77.5	92.1	83.0	...	...	...	...	...	...	...	...	...
4 Electricity, gas and water	8.7	10.2	11.2	...	...	...	...	...	...	...	...	...
5 Construction	45.0	58.1	40.6	...	...	...	...	...	...	...	...	...
6 Wholesale and retail trade, restaurants and hotels [a]	106.4	131.1	133.1	...	...	...	...	...	...	...	...	...
7 Transport, storage and communication	75.9	82.3	66.8	...	...	...	...	...	...	...	...	...
8 Finance, insurance, real estate and business services [b]	19.4	17.8	18.2	...	...	...	...	...	...	...	...	...
9 Community, social and personal services [ab]	84.0	94.8	81.3	...	...	...	...	...	...	...	...	...
Total, Industries	786.9	901.1	839.4	...	...	...	...	...	...	...	...	...
Producers of Government Services	119.3	135.2	165.8	...	...	...	...	...	...	...	...	...
Other Producers	...	...	...	...	...	...	...	...	...	...	...	...
Subtotal	906.2	1036.3	1005.2	...	...	...	...	...	...	...	...	...
Less: Imputed bank service charge	4.8	18.4	45.0	...	...	...	...	...	...	...	...	...
Plus: Import duties	50.7	47.6	26.9	...	...	...	...	...	...	...	...	...
Plus: Value added tax	...	...	...	...	...	...	...	...	...	...	...	...
Equals: Gross Domestic Product	952.1	1065.5	987.1	...	...	...	...	...	...	...	...	...

a) Restaurants and hotels are included in item 'Community, social and personal services'.
b) Insurance, real estate and business services are included in item 'Community, social and personal services'.

Zaire

1.12 Relations Among National Accounting Aggregates

Million Zaires

	1970	1975	1977	1978	1979	1980	1981	1982	1983	1984	1985	1986
Gross Domestic Product [a]	938.0	1919.0	3956.0	5481.0	11105.0	17183.0	23781.0	31110.0	59134.0	99723.0	147263.0	...
Plus: Net factor income from the rest of the world	-55.9	-94.0	-150.6	-180.0	-384.0	-742.0	-935.0	-1647.0	-2562.0	-11452.0	-4084.0	...
Equals: Gross National Product	882.1	1825.0	3805.4	5301.0	10721.0	16441.0	22846.0	29463.0	56572.0	88271.0	143179.0	...
Less: Consumption of fixed capital	69.2	195.0	272.4	382.0	439.0	548.0	837.0	1220.0	1725.0	2501.0	4331.0	...
Equals: National Income	813.0	1630.0	3533.0	4919.0	10282.0	15893.0	22009.0	28243.0	54847.0	85770.0	138848.0	...
Plus: Net current transfers from the rest of the world	28.4	57.3	131.5	...	...	...	...	...	...	...	...	...
Equals: National Disposable Income	841.3	1687.3	3664.5	...	...	...	...	...	...	...	...	...
Less: Final consumption	...	...	...	...	...	...	...	...	...	...	...	...
Equals: Net Saving	...	...	...	...	...	...	...	...	...	...	...	...
Less: Surplus of the nation on current transactions	...	...	...	...	...	...	...	...	...	...	...	...
Equals: Net Capital Formation	...	...	...	...	...	...	...	...	...	...	...	...

a) Data in this table have been revised, therefore they are not strictly comparable with the unrevised data in the other tables.

Zambia

General note. The preparation of national accounts statistics in Zambia is undertaken by the Central Statistical Office (CSO), Lusaka. The official estimates are published in November-December issue of the Monthly Digest of Statistics. A description of the sources and methods used for the National Accounts estimation is found in 'National Accounts and Input-Output Tables, 1971' and 'National Accounts, 1972' published in August 1975 and June 1978, respectively. The estimates are generally in accordance with the classifications and definitions recommended in the United Nations System of National Accounts (SNA). The following tables have been prepared from successive replies to the United Nations national accounts questionnaire. When the scope and coverage of the estimates differ for conceptual or statistical reasons from the definitions and classifications recommended in SNA, a footnote is indicated to the relevant tables.

Sources and methods:

(a) Gross domestic product. Gross domestic product is estimated mainly through the production approach.

(b) Expenditure on the gross domestic product. All components of GDP by expenditure type are estimated through the expenditure approach except for the total estimate of private consumption expenditure which is obtained as a residual. However, a detailed breakdown is obtained through the use of the expenditure approach. Data used to estimate government expenditure are contained in 'Financial Statistics of the Government Sector' supplemented by detailed tabulations prepared by the CSO. The 'Urban Household Budget Survey in Low-cost Housing Areas, 1966-1968' and the household budget surveys 1974/75 for the urban and rural areas provide a detailed breakdown for the private consumption expenditure. Data on changes in stocks are collected through the annual national income inquiries and the balance sheets supplied by the enterprises. These two sources as well as government accounts are also used to estimate gross fixed capital formation. For transport equipment and machinery, furniture etc., the estimates are based closely on end-use groupings of imports and domestic products. Transactions with the rest of the world are estimated from the balance of payments statistics. Data on exports and imports are obtained from the annual statements of external trade prepared by the CSO. The CSO also undertakes a special inquiry on international transactionsof all major private and public sector enterprises. For the constant price estimates, the current values of the expenditure items are deflated by various price indexes such as weighted index of wages and prices, consumer price index, implicit price index, etc.

(c) Cost-structure of the gross domestic product. The estimates of compensation of employees are based on information obtained through the annual income inquiries, the annual censuses of production and construction and other sources. Grossing-up factors to account for non-responding units are worked out on the basis of employment data collected through the quarterly employment surveys. Compensation of employees includes an estimated figure for domestic servant based on the 1969 population census data projected by an assumed 5 per cent annual growth rate. Consumption of fixed capital figures are obtained from the balance sheets of enterprises. Depreciation is imputed for some government enterprises and government administration and for owner-occupied buildings in urban and rural areas. Indirect taxes estimates are derived from the annual national income inquiries, the annual censuses of industrial production and construction data. Operating surplus is obtained as a residual.

(d) Gross domestic product by kind of economic activity. The table of GDP by kind of economic activity is prepared at market prices, i.e., producers' values. The production approach is used to estimate the value added of nearly all industries. The income approach is used for the value added of producers of government services. The accounts of the agricultural sector have been divided into a commercial sector and a subsistence sector. The commercial sector includes all surplus production of the rural areas, the output of agricultural extension services, own-account capital formation and retentions by commercial farmers. The estimates for the subsistence sector are restricted to own consumption by traditional producers. The Quarterly Agricultural Statistical Bulletin gives information on intakes of agricultural products, official producer prices and input prices. Intake data are used for estimating surplus productions of commercial and non-commercial farmers. The output of agricultural extension services relates to tenant schemes of the Tobacco Board of Zambia and the extension services of the government. The estimates of own-account capital formation of livestocks are based on the annual surveys of agricultural and pastoral production and on annual censuses of livestock. The estimates of retentions by commercial farmers are also based on the annual surveysof agricultural and pastoral production. The 1971/72 survey included, for the first time, information on intermediate inputs of commercial farmers. This information is used for non-commercial farmers as well. The average input-output ratio for 1972 has been applied to agricultural output for earlier years. For later years, a constant real input-output ratio is assumed. Estimates of the subsistence sector's own-consumed production are derived from total production estimates by subtracting surplus production, covered by the commercial sector estimates. This is done for crops on the basis of the first sample census of non-commercial farms held during the crop year 1970/71. The annual censuses of industrial production provide the data for the estimates of mining and quarrying, manufacturing and electricity and water. For mining, the financial statements of the mining companies are also used. For manufacturing, extensive data on output and input of goods and services are available from the censuses. Provisions for non-responding establishments are made on the basis of employment data. The annual censuses of construction by contractors provide data for the construction sector. For own-account construction by households, the Ministry of Local Government and Housing provides information on the number, type and cost of houses. The principal source for the services sectors-trade, transport, communication, financial and community services - is the annual national income inquiry. Questionnaires are sent out annually to all large and medium-sized establishments and on a sample basis for small establishments using a short form. Information by kind of economic activity, is requested on employment, earnings, operating and non-operating incomes and expenditure, appropriation of surplus, capital investment and input and output of materials. For owner-occupied dwellings, rents are estimated on the basis of cost of houses and their life and on data from the household budget surveys. For producers of government services, estimates are based on financial statistics of the government sector. For constant price estimates, double deflation is used for the agricultural and mining sectors. For the remaining sectors, the current values are deflated by various price indexes.

1.1 Expenditure on the Gross Domestic Product, in Current Prices

Million Zambian kwacha

	1970	1975	1977	1978	1979	1980	1981	1982	1983	1984	1985	1986
1 Government final consumption expenditure	206.0	435.7	525.0	537.8	633.0	781.6	986.0	995.9	1008.8	1240.1	1686.7	3002.3
2 Private final consumption expenditure a	490.0	814.5	1022.8	1251.5	1412.6	1691.9	2262.2	2312.1	2645.5	2848.5	4146.8	7496.6
3 Gross capital formation	367.0	642.0	490.0	537.0	376.0	713.3	673.3	602.9	575.0	724.0	1053.0	1791.0
A Increase in stocks	-12.0	40.0	7.0	100.0	-74.0	155.0	63.3	-15.1	-40.0	101.4	328.5	730.3
B Gross fixed capital formation	379.0	602.0	483.0	437.0	450.0	558.3	610.0	618.0	615.0	622.6	724.5	1060.7
Residential buildings	47.0	...	...	...	...	...	...	...	...	...	...	...
Non-residential buildings	43.0	...	...	...	...	...	...	...	...	...	...	...
Other construction and land improvement etc.	137.0	...	...	...	...	...	...	...	...	...	...	...
Other	151.0	...	...	...	...	...	...	...	...	...	...	...
4 Exports of goods and services	685.0	575.0	781.5	755.3	1208.3	1268.0	998.0	993.1	1280.7	1755.1	2627.8	5602.4
5 Less: Imports of goods and services	471.0	883.8	832.9	830.9	969.5	1391.2	1434.1	1311.5	1328.8	1636.7	2465.7	5794.4
Equals: Gross Domestic Product	1278.0	1583.4	1986.4	2250.7	2660.4	3063.6	3485.4	3595.3	4181.2	4931.0	7048.6	12097.9

a) Item 'Private final consumption expenditure' has been obtained as a residual.

1.2 Expenditure on the Gross Domestic Product, in Constant Prices

Million Zambian kwacha

	1970	1975	1977	1978	1979	1980	1981	1982	1983	1984	1985	1986
			At constant prices of:									
			1970					1977				
1 Government final consumption expenditure	206.0	287.2	277.0 / 525.0	473.0	473.4	531.3	611.3	541.5	454.6	483.8	460.1	488.9
2 Private final consumption expenditure	490.0	565.2	488.5 / 1022.8	1034.5	1143.6	1104.0	1176.4	1089.0	1102.1	1113.5	1281.9	1080.7
3 Gross capital formation	367.0	427.3	205.8 / 490.0	474.8	266.7	439.1	390.5	298.9	226.5	242.0	261.2	308.5
A Increase in stocks	-12.0	33.8	-0.2 / 7.0	90.3	-45.0	94.0	38.1	-10.6	-21.1	30.1	62.4	127.2
B Gross fixed capital formation	379.0	393.5	206.0 / 483.0	384.5	311.7	345.1	352.4	309.5	247.6	211.9	198.8	181.3

1646

Zambia

1.2 Expenditure on the Gross Domestic Product, in Constant Prices
(Continued)

Million Zambian kwacha

	1970	1975	1977	1978	1979	1980	1981	1982	1983	1984	1985	1986
		At constant prices of:										
		1970					1977					
Residential buildings	47.0	...	...	...	...	...	...	...	...	...	...	...
Non-residential buildings	43.0	...	...	...	...	...	...	...	...	...	...	...
Other construction and land improvement etc.	137.0	...	...	...	...	...	...	...	...	...	...	...
Other	151.0	...	...	...	...	...	...	...	...	...	...	...
4 Exports of goods and services	685.0	683.2	807.3 / 781.5	731.2	652.8	632.7	552.0	640.4	567.3	536.9	506.1	545.8
5 Less: Imports of goods and services	471.0	454.9	335.3 / 832.9	689.6	629.5	710.4	596.4	465.4	392.7	383.0	424.4	465.4
Statistical discrepancy	-	-69.9	-15.1 / ...	-26.1	30.0	-0.9	-14.9	-45.1	61.0	18.3	-47.8	93.7
Equals: Gross Domestic Product	1278.0	1438.1	1428.2 / 1986.4	1997.8	1937.0	1995.8	2118.9	2059.3	2010.0	2011.5	2041.4	2052.2

1.3 Cost Components of the Gross Domestic Product

Million Zambian kwacha

	1970	1975	1977	1978	1979	1980	1981	1982	1983	1984	1985	1986
1 Indirect taxes, net [a]	68.0	117.7	189.8	240.4	237.0	221.0	357.0	345.2	632.1	666.0	740.2	2031.5
A Indirect taxes [a]	87.0	207.7	274.8	288.5	342.3	417.8	467.5	502.1	714.3	758.5	928.6	2365.3
B Less: Subsidies [a]	19.0	90.0	85.0	42.1	105.3	196.8	110.2	156.9	82.2	91.6	188.4	333.8
2 Consumption of fixed capital	136.0	243.0	290.9	299.6	307.5	339.1	383.4	405.8	426.4	630.3	948.5	1711.6
3 Compensation of employees paid by resident producers to:	481.0	802.0	973.2	1110.4	1234.1	1436.8	1722.7	1920.1	1974.2	2162.9	2859.3	4278.9
A Resident households	481.0	802.0	973.2	1110.4	1234.1	1436.8	1722.7	1920.1	1974.2	2162.9	2859.3	4278.9
B Rest of the world	-	-	-	-	-	-	-	-	-	-	-	-
4 Operating surplus	592.0	420.7	532.5	594.3	881.8	1066.7	1022.0	924.2	1148.5	1470.9	2500.6	4075.9
Equals: Gross Domestic Product	1278.0	1583.4	1986.4	2250.9	2660.4	3063.6	3485.4	3595.3	4181.2	4931.0	7048.6	12097.9

a) The estimates of indirect taxes and subsidies are entered on accrual payment basis.

1.7 External Transactions on Current Account, Summary

Million Zambian kwacha

	1970	1975	1977	1978	1979	1980	1981	1982	1983	1984	1985	1986
	Payments to the Rest of the World											
1 Imports of goods and services	470.5	883.8	832.9	830.9	969.5	1391.2	1434.1	1311.5	1328.8	1636.7	2465.7	5794.4
A Imports of merchandise c.i.f.	408.0	760.9	663.9	648.4	745.2	1085.8	1097.3	1083.9	1067.2	1345.1	2103.6	5224.6
B Other	62.5	122.9	169.0	182.5	224.3	305.4	336.8	227.6	261.6	291.6	362.1	569.8
2 Factor income to the rest of the world	62.2	82.5	96.1	112.9	128.4	233.8	115.3	230.9	250.0	380.0	599.5	1249.9
A Compensation of employees	-	-	-	-	-	-	-	-	-	-	-	...
B Property and entrepreneurial income	62.2	82.5	96.1	112.9	128.4	233.8	115.3	230.9	250.0	380.0	599.5	1249.9
3 Current transfers to the rest of the world	110.5	87.2	82.2	70.6	113.2	166.1	140.4	67.1	59.5	89.5	109.8	318.5
4 Surplus of the nation on current transactions	77.0	-465.2	-208.1	-230.9	35.8	-490.3	-648.5	-570.9	-298.5	-317.0	-429.2	-1070.2
Payments to the Rest of the World and Surplus of the Nation on Current Transactions	720.1	588.3	803.1	783.6	1246.9	1300.8	1041.3	1038.6	1340.0	1789.2	2745.8	5692.6
	Receipts From The Rest of the World											
1 Exports of goods and services	685.4	575.0	781.5	755.3	1208.3	1268.0	998.0	993.1	1280.7	1755.1	2627.8	5602.4
A Exports of merchandise f.o.b.	727.2	530.9	710.0	707.0	1107.6	1140.2	866.3	877.6	1150.4	1618.4	2447.5	5247.0

Zambia

1.7 External Transactions on Current Account, Summary
(Continued)

Million Zambian kwacha

	1970	1975	1977	1978	1979	1980	1981	1982	1983	1984	1985	1986
B Other	-41.8	44.1	64.9	47.4	100.7	118.8	131.7	115.5	130.1	136.7	180.3	355.4
2 Factor income from rest of the world	28.8	7.9	8.0	6.8	8.8	5.2	17.4	11.7	3.6	8.6	5.0	10.0
A Compensation of employees	-	-	-	-	-	-	-	-	-	-	-	-
B Property and entrepreneurial income	28.8	7.9	8.0	6.8	8.8	5.2	17.4	11.7	3.6	8.6	5.0	10.0
By general government	...	...	...	...	...	0.5	0.2	0.9	0.9	1.3	1.0	...
By corporate and quasi-corporate enterprises	...	...	...	...	...	-	0.2	-	-	-	-	...
By other	...	...	...	...	...	4.7	17.0	10.8	3.0	7.3	4.0	...
3 Current transfers from rest of the world	5.9	5.4	13.6	21.5	29.8	27.6	25.9	31.0	55.7	25.5	113.0	80.2
Receipts from the Rest of the World on Current Transactions	720.1	588.3	803.1	783.6	1246.9	1300.8	1041.3	1038.6	1340.0	1789.2	2745.8	5692.6

1.10 Gross Domestic Product by Kind of Activity, in Current Prices

Million Zambian kwacha

	1970	1975	1977	1978	1979	1980	1981	1982	1983	1984	1985	1986
1 Agriculture, hunting, forestry and fishing	126.3	206.4	325.6	363.0	397.2	435.3	553.8	492.2	593.7	717.2	925.2	1304.6
2 Mining and quarrying	458.0	215.2	233.7	286.8	469.3	501.7	488.4	396.6	641.6	673.8	1101.9	2978.6
3 Manufacturing	129.1	250.3	353.0	430.1	486.7	566.1	684.1	740.4	829.8	1010.6	1610.0	2431.5
4 Electricity, gas and water	17.7	43.0	47.6	57.7	59.9	61.0	66.3	72.2	70.4	69.7	71.1	72.3
5 Construction	90.3	151.2	113.7	111.5	101.2	136.5	111.7	127.0	133.1	153.3	182.9	304.0
6 Wholesale and retail trade, restaurants and hotels	133.6	157.5	223.7	260.0	287.9	361.2	410.9	452.9	524.9	646.8	944.1	1293.0
7 Transport, storage and communication	45.6	88.5	131.4	125.5	148.6	161.5	171.1	193.2	227.4	251.3	325.5	598.3
8 Finance, insurance, real estate and business services	87.6	159.8	201.8	222.3	258.4	290.9	325.0	363.3	403.6	517.2	683.7	1027.7
9 Community, social and personal services	11.3	10.9	16.5	18.1	20.1	23.4	29.3	33.3	35.4	40.1	46.8	58.1
Total, Industries	1099.5	1282.8	1646.9	1875.0	2229.3	2537.6	2840.6	2871.1	3459.9	4080.0	5891.2	10068.1
Producers of Government Services	134.7	217.4	312.9	344.1	381.8	444.6	557.5	631.9	673.5	760.2	887.5	1101.6
Other Producers	21.4	40.2	...	...	...	...	...	...	...	...	...	...
Subtotal	1255.6	1540.4	1959.9	2219.1	2611.1	2982.2	3398.1	3503.0	4133.4	4840.2	6778.7	11169.7
Less: Imputed bank service charge	9.7	19.0	22.5	23.5	29.0	31.1	33.7	38.8	44.9	49.6	64.2	111.1
Plus: Import duties	32.1	62.0	49.0	55.1	78.3	112.5	121.0	131.1	92.7	140.4	334.1	1039.5
Plus: Value added tax	...	...	...	...	...	...	...	...	...	...	...	...
Equals: Gross Domestic Product	1278.0	1583.4	1986.4	2250.7	2660.4	3063.6	3485.4	3595.3	4181.2	4931.0	7048.6	12097.9

1.11 Gross Domestic Product by Kind of Activity, in Constant Prices

Million Zambian kwacha

	1970	1975	1977	1978	1979	1980	1981	1982	1983	1984	1985	1986
			At constant prices of:									
		1970					1977					
1 Agriculture, hunting, forestry and fishing	126.3	157.0	168.2 / 325.6	327.5	309.7	303.9	328.7	290.3	314.6	332.2	343.8	363.8
2 Mining and quarrying	458.0	427.9	469.7 / 233.7	245.2	195.1	205.2	214.8	215.2	221.7	200.0	185.4	173.9
3 Manufacturing	129.1	157.6	141.4 / 353.0	370.5	392.9	383.5	430.2	415.1	384.5	389.3	419.5	421.2
4 Electricity, gas and water	17.7	48.9	57.8 / 47.6	60.6	63.4	65.8	71.0	75.8	72.2	70.9	72.7	74.1
5 Construction	90.3	138.5	90.4 / 113.7	104.1	89.0	102.8	78.9	84.0	88.6	88.6	77.1	81.1
6 Wholesale and retail trade, restaurants and hotels	133.6	123.8	114.5 / 223.7	224.7	210.9	236.3	248.6	231.8	227.6	216.9	226.0	218.2
7 Transport, storage and communication	45.6	57.6	61.5 / 131.4	119.4	123.9	117.5	118.3	118.8	119.4	116.2	108.7	107.1
8 Finance, insurance, real estate and business services	87.6	132.9	125.5 / 201.8	194.5	207.0	211.3	218.3	226.5	234.5	242.0	239.6	246.1
9 Community, social and personal services	11.3	7.0	7.0 / 16.4	16.6	16.4	17.3	19.6	19.7	17.8	17.8	18.3	18.1

Zambia

1.11 Gross Domestic Product by Kind of Activity, in Constant Prices
(Continued)

Million Zambian kwacha

	1970	1975	1977	1978	1979	1980	1981	1982	1983	1984	1985	1986
		1970			At constant prices of:			1977				
Total, Industries	1099.5	1251.2	1236.0 / 1646.9	1663.1	1608.3	1643.6	1728.4	1677.2	1680.9	1673.9	1691.1	1703.6
Producers of Government Services	134.7	140.9	142.5 / 313.0	312.9	312.2	328.7	372.3	374.2	337.9	337.1	347.3	343.4
Other Producers	21.4	32.7	40.8 / ...	...	...	...	...	...	...	...	...	...
Subtotal	1255.6	1424.8	1419.4 / 1959.9	1976.0	1920.5	1972.3	2100.7	2051.4	2018.8	2011.0	2038.4	2047.0
Less: Imputed bank service charge	9.7	13.6	11.0 / 22.5	18.8	20.6	18.8	18.2	19.8	18.5	17.5	16.9	16.8
Plus: Import duties	32.1	26.9	19.8 / 49.0	40.6	37.1	42.3	36.4	27.7	18.5	18.0	19.9	22.0
Plus: Value added tax	...	...	...	...	...	...	...	...	...	...	...	...
Equals: Gross Domestic Product	1278.0	1438.1	1428.2 / 1986.4	1997.8	1937.0	1995.8	2118.9	2059.3	2018.8	2011.5	2041.4	2052.2

1.12 Relations Among National Accounting Aggregates

Million Zambian kwacha

	1970	1975	1977	1978	1979	1980	1981	1982	1983	1984	1985	1986
Gross Domestic Product	1278.0	1583.4	1986.4	2250.7	2660.4	3063.6	3485.4	3595.3	4181.2	4931.0	7048.6	12097.9
Plus: Net factor income from the rest of the world	-33.4	-74.6	-88.1	-106.1	-119.6	-228.6	-97.9	219.2	246.1	371.4	-504.5	-1209.9
Factor income from the rest of the world	28.8	7.9	8.0	6.8	8.8	5.2	17.4	11.7	3.6	8.6	5.0	10.0
Less: Factor income to the rest of the world	62.2	82.5	96.1	112.9	128.4	233.8	115.3	230.9	250.0	380.0	599.5	1249.9
Equals: Gross National Product	1244.6	1508.8	1898.3	2144.6	2540.8	2835.0	3387.5	3376.1	3934.8	4559.6	6454.1	10858.0
Less: Consumption of fixed capital	136.0	243.0	290.0	299.6	307.5	339.1	383.4	405.8	426.4	630.3	948.5	1711.6
Equals: National Income	1108.0	1265.8	1608.3	1845.0	2233.3	2495.9	3004.1	2970.3	3508.4	3929.3	5505.6	9146.4
Plus: Net current transfers from the rest of the world	-105.0	-81.8	-68.6	-49.1	-83.4	-138.5	-114.5	-36.1	-3.8	-64.0	3.2	-238.3
Current transfers from the rest of the world	5.9	5.4	13.6	21.5	29.8	27.6	25.9	31.0	55.7	25.5	113.0	80.2
Less: Current transfers to the rest of the world	110.5	87.2	82.2	70.6	113.2	166.1	140.4	67.1	59.5	89.5	109.8	318.5
Equals: National Disposable Income	1003.0	1184.0	1539.7	1795.9	2149.9	2357.4	2889.6	2934.2	3504.6	3865.3	5508.8	8908.1
Less: Final consumption	696.0	1250.2	1547.8	1789.3	2045.6	2473.3	3248.2	3308.0	3654.3	4088.6	5833.5	10498.9
Equals: Net Saving	307.9	-66.2	-8.1	6.6	104.3	-115.9	-358.6	-373.8	-149.7	-223.3	-324.7	-1590.8
Less: Surplus of the nation on current transactions	77.0	-465.2	-208.1	-230.8	35.8	-490.3	-648.5	-570.9	-298.7	-317.0	-429.2	-1670.2
Equals: Net Capital Formation	231.0	399.0	200.0	237.4	68.5	374.2	289.9	197.1	148.8	93.7	104.5	79.4

2.17 Exports and Imports of Goods and Services, Detail

Million Zambian kwacha

		1970	1975	1977	1978	1979	1980	1981	1982	1983	1984	1985	1986
					Exports of Goods and Services								
1	Exports of merchandise, f.o.b.	727.2	530.9	716.6	707.9	1107.6	1038.5	950.9	969.7	1061.8	1192.0	1494.7	5247.0
2	Transport and communication	-	44.8	62.2	66.5	66.8	72.7	69.4	64.9	80.0	87.6	118.3	234.4
	A In respect of merchandise imports	-	35.8	48.0	49.3	37.9	48.5	35.8	27.3	37.0	41.1	52.3	157.4
	B Other	-	9.0	14.2	17.2	28.9	24.2	33.6	37.6	43.0	46.5	66.0	77.0
3	Insurance service charges	2.4	-	-	-	-	...	...	...	...	...	...	...
	A In respect of merchandise imports		-	-	-	-	...	...	...	...	...	...	...
	B Other	2.4	-	-	-	-	...	...	...	...	...	...	...
4	Other commodities	4.8	8.0	10.2	13.7	12.9	9.5	14.1	2.0	2.0	2.5	4.0	5.0
5	Adjustments of merchandise exports to change-of-ownership basis	-54.0	-14.7	-15.8	-42.8	9.0	110.7	-84.6	-89.5	100.4	426.4	952.8	-
6	Direct purchases in the domestic market by non-residential households	5.0	6.0	8.3	10.0	12.0	16.6	27.0	23.0	23.3	23.0	24.0	48.0
7	Direct purchases in the domestic market by extraterritorial bodies	...	...	...	...	...	20.0	21.2	23.0	25.0	23.6	34.0	68.0
	Total Exports of Goods and Services	685.4	575.0	781.5	755.3	1208.3	1268.0	998.0	993.1	1292.5	1755.1	2627.8	5602.4
					Imports of Goods and Services								
1	Imports of merchandise, c.i.f.	408.0	760.9	663.9	648.4	745.2	1085.8	1097.3	1083.9	1067.2	1345.1	2103.6	5224.6

Zambia

2.17 Exports and Imports of Goods and Services, Detail
(Continued)

Million Zambian kwacha

	1970	1975	1977	1978	1979	1980	1981	1982	1983	1984	1985	1986
A Imports of merchandise, f.o.b.	347.7	609.6	532.0	494.8	599.8	878.7	926.4	932.0	895.2	1109.9	1790.0	4294.1
B Transport of services on merchandise imports	54.5	139.0	122.4	...	...	207.1	170.9	151.9	172.0	235.2	313.6	930.5
By residents	-	35.8	48.0	48.0	41.1	...	...	...	...	...	...	...
By non-residents	54.5	103.2	74.4	...	...	207.1	170.9	151.9	172.0	235.2	313.6	930.5
C Insurance service charges on merchandise imports	5.8	12.3	9.5	...	...	...	...	...	...	...	...	...
By residents	-	-	-	...	...	...	...	...	...	...	...	...
By non-residents	5.8	12.3	9.5	...	...	...	...	...	...	...	...	...
2 Adjustments of merchandise imports to change-of-ownership basis	...	...	...	...	...	...	...	...	...	...	...	...
3 Other transport and communication	14.0	32.0	47.4	53.0	89.2	88.4	77.6	79.4	100.0	110.3	157.0	183.3
4 Other insurance service charges	1.4	-	-	-	-	...	...	...	...	...	...	...
5 Other commodities	27.2	61.6	96.2	80.5	88.2	164.5	180.0	50.6	118.7	120.0	126.4	109.0
6 Direct purchases abroad by government	1.5	5.7	11.0	17.7	21.1	10.0	19.3	17.8	16.6	17.6	27.0	130.0
7 Direct purchases abroad by resident households	18.4	23.6	14.4	31.3	25.8	42.5	59.9	79.7	26.3	43.5	51.7	146.6
Total Imports of Goods and Services	470.5	883.8	832.9	830.9	969.5	1391.2	1434.1	1311.4	1328.4	1636.5	2465.7	5793.5
Balance of Goods and Services	214.9	-308.8	-51.4	-75.6	238.8	-123.2	-436.1	-318.3	-36.3	118.6	162.1	-191.1
Total Imports and Balance of Goods and Services	685.4	575.0	781.5	755.3	1208.3	1268.0	998.0	993.1	1292.1	1755.1	2627.8	5602.4

4.1 Derivation of Value Added by Kind of Activity, in Current Prices

Million Zambian kwacha

	1980 Gross Output	1980 Intermediate Consumption	1980 Value Added	1981 Gross Output	1981 Intermediate Consumption	1981 Value Added	1982 Gross Output	1982 Intermediate Consumption	1982 Value Added	1983 Gross Output	1983 Intermediate Consumption	1983 Value Added
						All Producers						
1 Agriculture, hunting, forestry and fishing	...	...	435.3	...	...	553.8	...	...	492.2	...	...	593.7
A Agriculture and hunting	...	...	386.8	...	...	504.2	...	...	426.5	...	...	521.5
B Forestry and logging	...	...	27.8	...	...	29.4	...	...	32.4	...	...	34.2
C Fishing	...	...	20.7	...	...	20.2	...	...	33.3	...	...	38.0
2 Mining and quarrying	...	...	501.7	...	...	488.4	...	...	396.6	...	...	641.6
A Coal mining	...	...	...	...	...	...	...	...	...	...	...	...
B Crude petroleum and natural gas production	...	...	...	...	...	...	...	...	...	...	...	...
C Metal ore mining	...	...	490.1	...	...	472.7	...	...	381.6	...	...	619.1
D Other mining	...	...	11.6	...	...	15.7	...	...	15.0	...	...	22.5
3 Manufacturing	...	...	566.1	...	...	684.1	...	...	740.4	...	...	829.8
A Manufacture of food, beverages and tobacco	...	...	266.0	...	...	317.5	...	...	351.3	...	...	393.9
B Textile, wearing apparel and leather industries	...	...	72.1	...	...	89.3	...	...	100.3	...	...	104.0
C Manufacture of wood and wood products, including furniture	...	...	19.1	...	...	33.3	...	...	32.3	...	...	16.2
D Manufacture of paper and paper products, printing and publishing	...	...	20.4	...	...	20.6	...	...	19.6	...	...	23.2
E Manufacture of chemicals and chemical petroleum, coal, rubber and plastic products	...	...	69.5	...	...	87.1	...	...	74.9	...	...	83.4
F Manufacture of non-metallic mineral products, except products of petroleum and coal	...	...	27.0	...	...	48.5	...	...	58.9	...	...	81.2
G Basic metal industries	...	...	8.1	...	...	8.2	...	...	6.0	...	...	11.8
H Manufacture of fabricated metal products, machinery and equipment	...	...	78.3	...	...	73.0	...	...	89.6	...	...	107.5
I Other manufacturing industries	...	...	5.6	...	...	6.6	...	...	7.5	...	...	8.6
4 Electricity, gas and water	...	...	61.0	...	...	66.3	...	...	72.2	...	...	70.4

Zambia

4.1 Derivation of Value Added by Kind of Activity, in Current Prices
(Continued)

Million Zambian kwacha

	1980			1981			1982			1983		
	Gross Output	Intermediate Consumption	Value Added	Gross Output	Intermediate Consumption	Value Added	Gross Output	Intermediate Consumption	Value Added	Gross Output	Intermediate Consumption	Value Added
5 Construction	...	...	136.5	...	...	111.7	...	...	127.0	...	...	133.1
6 Wholesale and retail trade, restaurants and hotels	...	...	361.2	...	...	410.9	...	...	452.9	...	...	524.9
A Wholesale and retail trade	...	...	301.5	...	...	328.0	...	...	355.5	...	...	401.6
B Restaurants and hotels	...	...	59.7	...	...	82.9	...	...	97.4	...	...	123.3
7 Transport, storage and communication	...	...	161.5	...	...	171.1	...	...	193.2	...	...	227.4
A Transport and storage	...	...	135.1	...	...	142.8	...	...	161.1	...	...	189.2
B Communication	...	...	26.4	...	...	28.3	...	...	32.1	...	...	38.2
8 Finance, insurance, real estate and business services	...	...	290.9	...	...	325.0	...	...	363.3	...	...	403.6
A Financial institutions	...	...	110.0	...	...	119.2	...	...	137.3	...	...	156.6
B Insurance	...	...		...	...		...	...		...	...	
C Real estate and business services	...	...	180.9	...	...	205.8	...	...	226.0	...	...	247.0
9 Community, social and personal services a	...	...	468.0	...	...	586.8	...	...	665.2	...	...	708.9
A Sanitary and similar services	...	...	202.8	...	...	262.0	...	...	290.0	...	...	281.0
B Social and related community services	...	...	196.4	...	...	244.4	...	...	287.7	...	...	324.7
Educational services	...	...	148.2	...	...	180.2	...	...	211.2	...	...	237.0
Medical, dental, other health and veterinary services	...	...	48.2	...	...	64.2	...	...	76.5	...	...	87.7
C Recreational and cultural services	...	...	18.8	...	...	24.9	...	...	25.6	...	...	30.0
D Personal and household services	...	...	50.0	...	...	55.5	...	...	61.9	...	...	73.0
Total, Industries	...	...	...	...	...	...	...	...	...	...	...	...
Producers of Government Services a	...	...	...	...	...	...	...	...	...	...	...	...
Other Producers a	...	...	...	...	...	...	...	...	...	...	...	...
Total	...	...	2982.2	...	...	3398.1	...	...	3503.0	...	...	4133.4
Less: Imputed bank service charge	...	...	31.1	...	...	33.7	...	...	38.8	...	...	44.9
Import duties	...	...	112.5	...	...	121.0	...	...	131.1	...	...	92.7
Value added tax	...	...	...	...	...	...	...	...	...	...	...	...
Total	...	...	3063.6	...	...	3485.4	...	...	3595.3	...	...	4181.2

	1984			1985			1986		
	Gross Output	Intermediate Consumption	Value Added	Gross Output	Intermediate Consumption	Value Added	Gross Output	Intermediate Consumption	Value Added

All Producers

	Gross Output	Intermediate Consumption	Value Added	Gross Output	Intermediate Consumption	Value Added	Gross Output	Intermediate Consumption	Value Added
1 Agriculture, hunting, forestry and fishing	...	...	717.2	...	...	925.2	...	...	1304.6
A Agriculture and hunting	...	...	624.1	...	...	775.3	...	...	1049.6
B Forestry and logging	...	...	44.5	...	...	72.2	...	...	162.8
C Fishing	...	...	48.6	...	...	77.7	...	...	92.2
2 Mining and quarrying	...	...	673.8	...	...	1101.9	...	...	2978.1
A Coal mining	...	...	...	...	...	...	...	...	...
B Crude petroleum and natural gas production	...	...	...	...	...	...	...	...	...
C Metal ore mining	...	...	644.8	...	...	1056.8	...	...	2886.2
D Other mining	...	...	29.0	...	...	45.1	...	...	91.9

Zambia

4.1 Derivation of Value Added by Kind of Activity, in Current Prices
(Continued)

Million Zambian kwacha

	1984 Gross Output	1984 Intermediate Consumption	1984 Value Added	1985 Gross Output	1985 Intermediate Consumption	1985 Value Added	1986 Gross Output	1986 Intermediate Consumption	1986 Value Added
3 Manufacturing	...	...	1010.6	...	...	1610.0	...	...	2431.5
A Manufacture of food, beverages and tobacco	...	...	442.2	...	...	593.1	...	...	803.2
B Textile, wearing apparel and leather industries	...	...	130.5	...	...	212.6	...	...	274.9
C Manufacture of wood and wood products, including furniture	...	...	22.8	...	...	43.8	...	...	99.6
D Manufacture of paper and paper products, printing and publishing	...	...	34.9	...	...	95.4	...	...	156.7
E Manufacture of chemicals and chemical petroleum, coal, rubber and plastic products	...	...	108.6	...	...	194.8	...	...	339.0
F Manufacture of non-metallic mineral products, except products of petroleum and coal	...	...	69.8	...	...	129.7	...	...	113.5
G Basic metal industries	...	...	13.0	...	...	13.2	...	...	17.5
H Manufacture of fabricated metal products, machinery and equipment	...	...	177.6	...	...	309.6	...	...	599.5
I Other manufacturing industries	...	...	11.2	...	...	17.8	...	...	27.6
4 Electricity, gas and water	...	...	69.7	...	...	71.1	...	...	72.3
5 Construction	...	...	153.3	...	...	183.2	...	...	304.0
6 Wholesale and retail trade, restaurants and hotels	...	...	646.8	...	...	944.1	...	...	1293.3
A Wholesale and retail trade	...	...	520.8	...	...	763.0	...	...	1049.4
B Restaurants and hotels	...	...	126.0	...	...	181.1	...	...	243.9
7 Transport, storage and communication	...	...	251.3	...	...	325.5	...	...	598.3
A Transport and storage	...	...	205.5	...	...	260.0	...	...	477.8
B Communication	...	...	45.8	...	...	65.5	...	...	120.5
8 Finance, insurance, real estate and business services	...	...	517.2	...	...	683.7	...	...	1027.7
A Financial institutions	...	...	172.9	...	...	69.0	...	...	97.6
B Insurance	...	...		...	...	159.9	...	...	298.7
C Real estate and business services	...	...	344.3	...	...	454.8	...	...	631.4
9 Community, social and personal services [a]	...	...	800.3	...	...	934.3	...	...	1159.7
A Sanitary and similar services	...	...	318.5	...	...	391.7	...	...	480.2
B Social and related community services	...	...	360.2	...	...	404.7	...	...	507.5
Educational services	...	...	259.0	...	...	292.1	...	...	384.1
Medical, dental, other health and veterinary services	...	...	101.2	...	...	112.6	...	...	123.4
C Recreational and cultural services	...	...	34.0	...	...	41.8	...	...	51.2
D Personal and household services	...	...	87.6	...	...	96.1	...	...	120.8
Total, Industries	...	...	...	...	...	...	...	...	...
Producers of Government Services [a]	...	...	...	...	...	...	...	...	...
Other Producers [a]	...	...	...	...	...	...	...	...	...
Total	...	...	4840.2	...	...	6779.0	...	...	11169.5
Less: Imputed bank service charge	...	...	49.6	...	...	64.2	...	...	111.1
Import duties	...	...	140.4	...	...	334.1	...	...	1039.5
Value added tax	...	...	...	...	...	...	...	...	...
Total	...	...	4931.0	...	...	7048.9	...	...	12097.9

a) Items 'Other producers' and 'Producers of government services' are included in item 'Community, social and personal services'.

Zambia

4.2 Derivation of Value Added by Kind of Activity, in Constant Prices

Million Zambian kwacha

	1980 Gross Output	1980 Intermediate Consumption	1980 Value Added	1981 Gross Output	1981 Intermediate Consumption	1981 Value Added	1982 Gross Output	1982 Intermediate Consumption	1982 Value Added	1983 Gross Output	1983 Intermediate Consumption	1983 Value Added
	\multicolumn{12}{c}{At constant prices of:1977}											
	\multicolumn{12}{c}{All Producers}											
1 Agriculture, hunting, forestry and fishing	...	...	303.9	...	...	328.7	...	...	290.3	...	...	314.6
A Agriculture and hunting	...	...	273.8	...	...	299.3	...	...	257.7	...	...	279.8
B Forestry and logging	...	...	14.5	...	...	14.9	...	...	15.3	...	...	15.8
C Fishing	...	...	15.6	...	...	14.5	...	...	17.3	...	...	19.0
2 Mining and quarrying	...	...	205.2	...	...	214.8	...	...	215.2	...	...	221.7
A Coal mining	...	...	...	...	...	...	...	...	...	...	...	...
B Crude petroleum and natural gas production	...	...	...	...	...	...	...	...	...	...	...	...
C Metal ore mining	...	...	198.2	...	...	206.3	...	...	206.1	...	...	215.0
D Other mining	...	...	7.0	...	...	8.5	...	...	9.1	...	...	6.7
3 Manufacturing	...	...	383.5	...	...	430.2	...	...	415.1	...	...	384.5
A Manufacture of food, beverages and tobacco	...	...	180.7	...	...	203.4	...	...	196.0	...	...	182.8
B Textile, wearing apparel and leather industries	...	...	62.2	...	...	69.4	...	...	73.3	...	...	63.1
C Manufacture of wood and wood products, including furniture	...	...	11.8	...	...	16.0	...	...	13.8	...	...	6.7
D Manufacture of paper and paper products, printing and publishing	...	...	11.7	...	...	11.1	...	...	12.0	...	...	11.3
E Manufacture of chemicals and chemical petroleum, coal, rubber and plastic products	...	...	45.7	...	...	58.8	...	...	47.5	...	...	44.5
F Manufacture of non-metallic mineral products, except products of petroleum and coal	...	...	14.9	...	...	17.6	...	...	16.5	...	...	19.6
G Basic metal industries	...	...	4.5	...	...	3.9	...	...	3.3	...	...	3.6
H Manufacture of fabricated metal products, machinery and equipment	...	...	48.4	...	...	45.8	...	...	48.7	...	...	49.3
I Other manufacturing industries	...	...	3.6	...	...	4.2	...	...	4.0	...	...	3.8
4 Electricity, gas and water	...	...	65.8	...	...	71.0	...	...	75.8	...	...	72.2
5 Construction	...	...	102.8	...	...	78.9	...	...	84.0	...	...	88.6
6 Wholesale and retail trade, restaurants and hotels	...	...	236.3	...	...	248.6	...	...	231.8	...	...	227.6
A Wholesale and retail trade	...	...	196.2	...	...	195.2	...	...	178.5	...	...	171.8
B Restaurants and hotels	...	...	40.1	...	...	53.4	...	...	53.3	...	...	55.8
7 Transport, storage and communication	...	...	117.5	...	...	118.3	...	...	118.8	...	...	119.4
A Transport and storage	...	...	96.1	...	...	97.3	...	...	97.1	...	...	95.6
B Communication	...	...	21.4	...	...	21.0	...	...	21.7	...	...	23.8
8 Finance, insurance, real estate and business services	...	...	211.3	...	...	218.3	...	...	226.5	...	...	234.5
A Financial institutions	...	...	66.8	...	...	65.0	...	...	70.8	...	...	66.2
B Insurance	...	...		...	...		...	...		...	...	
C Real estate and business services	...	...	144.5	...	...	153.3	...	...	155.7	...	...	168.3
9 Community, social and personal services [a]	...	...	346.0	...	...	391.9	...	...	393.9	...	...	355.7
A Sanitary and similar services	...	...	147.8	...	...	172.2	...	...	168.6	...	...	138.5
B Social and related community services	...	...	143.1	...	...	160.7	...	...	167.3	...	...	159.9
Educational services	...	...	108.0	...	...	118.5	...	...	122.8	...	...	116.7
Medical, dental, other health and veterinary services	...	...	35.1	...	...	42.2	...	...	44.5	...	...	43.2
C Recreational and cultural services	...	...	13.7	...	...	16.4	...	...	14.9	...	...	14.8
D Personal and household services	...	...	41.4	...	...	42.6	...	...	43.1	...	...	42.5

Zambia

4.2 Derivation of Value Added by Kind of Activity, in Constant Prices
(Continued)

Million Zambian kwacha

	1980			1981			1982			1983		
	Gross Output	Intermediate Consumption	Value Added	Gross Output	Intermediate Consumption	Value Added	Gross Output	Intermediate Consumption	Value Added	Gross Output	Intermediate Consumption	Value Added
	At constant prices of:1977											
Total, Industries	...	...	...	...	...	...	...	...	...	...	...	...
Producers of Government Services a	...	...	...	...	...	...	...	...	...	...	...	...
Other Producers a	...	...	...	...	...	...	...	...	...	...	...	...
Total	...	...	1972.3	...	...	2100.7	...	...	2051.4	...	...	2018.8
Less: Imputed bank service charge	...	...	18.8	...	...	18.2	...	...	19.8	...	...	18.5
Import duties	...	...	42.3	...	...	36.4	...	...	27.1	...	...	18.5
Value added tax	...	...	...	...	...	...	...	...	...	...	...	...
Total	...	...	1995.8	...	...	2118.9	...	...	2059.3	...	...	2018.8

	1984			1985			1986		
	Gross Output	Intermediate Consumption	Value Added	Gross Output	Intermediate Consumption	Value Added	Gross Output	Intermediate Consumption	Value Added
	At constant prices of:1977								
	All Producers								
1 Agriculture, hunting, forestry and fishing	...	...	332.2	...	...	343.8	...	...	363.8
A Agriculture and hunting	...	...	294.2	...	...	300.0	...	...	316.1
B Forestry and logging	...	...	15.3	...	...	19.3	...	...	23.2
C Fishing	...	...	22.7	...	...	24.5	...	...	24.5
2 Mining and quarrying	...	...	200.0	...	...	185.4	...	...	173.9
A Coal mining	...	...	...	...	...	...	...	...	...
B Crude petroleum and natural gas production	...	...	...	...	...	...	...	...	...
C Metal ore mining	...	...	193.5	...	...	179.0	...	...	167.6
D Other mining	...	...	6.5	...	...	6.4	...	...	6.3
3 Manufacturing	...	...	389.3	...	...	419.5	...	...	421.2
A Manufacture of food, beverages and tobacco	...	...	180.2	...	...	174.8	...	...	184.9
B Textile, wearing apparel and leather industries	...	...	60.5	...	...	74.3	...	...	64.3
C Manufacture of wood and wood products, including furniture	...	...	8.0	...	...	9.3	...	...	10.3
D Manufacture of paper and paper products, printing and publishing	...	...	11.5	...	...	15.3	...	...	18.9
E Manufacture of chemicals and chemical petroleum, coal, rubber and plastic products	...	...	46.1	...	...	42.9	...	...	43.0
F Manufacture of non-metallic mineral products, except products of petroleum and coal	...	...	15.1	...	...	26.1	...	...	15.5
G Basic metal industries	...	...	3.8	...	...	3.6	...	...	3.4
H Manufacture of fabricated metal products, machinery and equipment	...	...	60.2	...	...	68.9	...	...	76.7
I Other manufacturing industries	...	...	3.9	...	...	4.3	...	...	4.2
4 Electricity, gas and water	...	...	70.9	...	...	72.7	...	...	74.1
5 Construction	...	...	88.6	...	...	77.1	...	...	81.1
6 Wholesale and retail trade, restaurants and hotels	...	...	216.9	...	...	226.0	...	...	218.2
A Wholesale and retail trade	...	...	167.9	...	...	174.7	...	...	169.0
B Restaurants and hotels	...	...	49.0	...	...	51.3	...	...	49.2
7 Transport, storage and communication	...	...	116.2	...	...	108.7	...	...	107.1
A Transport and storage	...	...	91.2	...	...	82.9	...	...	81.7
B Communication	...	...	25.0	...	...	25.8	...	...	25.4
8 Finance, insurance, real estate and business services	...	...	242.0	...	...	239.6	...	...	246.1
A Financial institutions	...	...	62.5	...	...	22.4	...	...	20.1
B Insurance	...	...		...	...	38.2	...	...	40.1
C Real estate and business services	...	...	179.5	...	...	179.0	...	...	185.9
9 Community, social and personal services a	...	...	354.9	...	...	365.6	...	...	361.5
A Sanitary and similar services	...	...	137.4	...	...	141.3	...	...	137.3
B Social and related community services	...	...	158.7	...	...	163.1	...	...	158.5

Zambia

4.2 Derivation of Value Added by Kind of Activity, in Constant Prices
(Continued)

Million Zambian kwacha

	1984 Gross Output	1984 Intermediate Consumption	1984 Value Added	1985 Gross Output	1985 Intermediate Consumption	1985 Value Added	1986 Gross Output	1986 Intermediate Consumption	1986 Value Added
				At constant prices of:1977					
Educational services	...	...	115.8	...	...	119.0	...	...	115.7
Medical, dental, other health and veterinary services	...	...	42.9	...	...	44.1	...	...	42.8
C Recreational and cultural services	...	...	14.7	...	...	15.1	...	...	14.7
D Personal and household services	...	...	44.1	...	...	46.1	...	...	50.8
Total, Industries	...	...	...	...	...	...	...	...	...
Producers of Government Services [a]	...	...	...	...	...	...	...	...	...
Other Producers [a]	...	...	...	...	...	...	...	...	...
Total	...	...	2011.0	...	...	2038.4	...	...	2047.0
Less: Imputed bank service charge	...	...	17.5	...	...	16.9	...	...	16.8
Import duties	...	...	18.0	...	...	19.9	...	...	22.0
Value added tax	...	...	...	...	...	...	...	...	...
Total	...	...	2011.5	...	...	2041.4	...	...	2052.2

a) Items 'Other producers' and 'Producers of government services' are included in item 'Community, social and personal services'.

Zimbabwe

General note. The prepration of national accounts statistics in Zimbabwe is undertaken by the Central Statistical Office, Hararel. The official estimates together with methodological notes are published annually in 'National Accounts of Zimbabwe Rhodesia'. The estimates are generally in accordance with the classifications and definitions recommended in the United Nations System of National AccoUnts (SNA). The following tables have been prepared from successive replies to the United Nations national accounts questionnaire. When the scope and coverage of the estimates differ for conceptual or statistical reasons from the definitions and classifications recommended in SNA, a footnote is indicated to the relevant tables.

Sources and methods:

(a) Gross domestic product. Gross domestic product is estimated mainly through the production approach.

(b) Expenditure on the gross domestic product. All items of GDP by expenditure type are estimated through the use of the expenditure approach combined with the commodity-flow approach except private consumption expenditure which is derived as a residual. In general, the commodity-flow approach determines to which consuming sector or group the commodities would be allocated. For government expenditure, detailed accounts are available from each department of the central government while the local authorities and certain controlled organizations and funds provide copies of their annual financial statement. Total private consumption expenditure is to a large extent derived as a residual. However, supplementary information is obtained from returns of major suppliers of consumer products and from family budget surveys. The estimates are checked by turnover statistics of retailers. Data on changes in stocks are available from the annual censuses of production, agriculture and livestock and from the 1975 census of road transport and for the trade sector, from turnover indexes. Expenditure on capital goods are available in the anual censuses of agriculture and production, the annual analysis of public sector accounts and the annual surveys of financial institutions. The data from these sources are classified by industry, sector and type of asset. The value of new buildings construction is estimated from monthly surveys of private contractors and public sector producers. The estimates include own-account construction of dwellings and service charges of capital nature. Tabulations of exports and imports classified by industry of origin and commodity are used to determine the proportion of each group's output sold abroad and the value of imports at the border. Valuation adjustments are made to bring all trade to a uniform f.o.b. or free-on-rail valuation at the border of the exporting country. For the constant price estimates of all expenditure items deflation is done with the use of appropriate price indexes.

(c) Cost-structure of the gross domestic product. Wages and salaries paid in industrial activity sectors are obtained from the annual censuses of industrial production. The estimates are adjusted from fiscal to calendar year and projected using ratios derived from the quarterly employment inquiries. This latter soUrce also provides wage data for the financial, trade and service sectors. Wages and salaries paid in the agricultural sector are taken from the results of qUarterly censuses of farmers. Estimates of indirect taxes and subsidies are obtained from government accounts. Gross operating surplus, including depreciation, is estimated as a residual.

(d) Gross domestic product by kind of economic activity. The table of GDP by kind of economic activity is prepared in factor values. The production approach is used to estimate value added of most industries. For the service sector, the income approach is used while for the trade sector, the estimates are made by projecting the results of the latest census of distribution. Information on the gross output of agriculture is available either from regular annual censuses or from records of sales to official marketing authorities. ValUe of own-accout consumption for some items is estimated on the basis of forecasts of total production less recorded sales and for other items, on the basis of assumed average consumption rates. The gross output of forestry and logging is estimated to include the cost of plantation development, sales and increase in stocks of cut timber, etc. For agricultural services, estimates are based on a survey held in 1974 of the main estalishments. For the industrial activity sector and construction, complete output and input accounts are available from the annual censuses of production. The results are converted from fiscal to calendar-year basis and extrapolated by indcators such as turnover, mineral output, construction work done and prices. The gross output of establishments classified to manufacturing which also engage in distribution activity includes the sales margin only on goods purchased for resale without further processing. Estimates of output and input of the trade sector are made by extrapolating the results of the 1969 census of distribution, using turnover indicators. For transport, the production account is based on the results of the 1975 census of road transport supplemented by the accounts of concerned companies. Estimates of financial institutions are based on the results of annual surveys taken together with statutory statistical returns rendered by registered institutions. The 1969 census of population provided information on the number of dwellings by type of dwelling, as well as the average gross rents paid for rented dwellings and these are updated using the consumer price rent index. The ratio between rented and owner-occupied dwellings are assumed to have remained constant since 1969. Cost of inputs into dwellings are estimated on a unit basis from annual surveys. Value added of private domestic services is estimated as wages in cash and in kind paid. Value added of education, health and other services are based on income tax statistics and wage data collected through the quarterly employment inquiries. GDP by kind of economic activity is estimated at constant prices mainly by the use of volume indices at commodity group levels for goods producing industries, trade (volume of goods handled), transport (volume of traffic by types) and services like education (combined index of students and teachers). In the case of the rest of the services, the total employment in each year is used as the indicator for constant price estimates.

1.1 Expenditure on the Gross Domestic Product, in Current Prices

Million Zimbabwean dollars

	1970	1975	1977	1978	1979	1980	1981	1982	1983	1984	1985	1986
1 Government final consumption expenditure	126	256	382	451	537	677	763	973	1145	1341	1511	...
2 Private final consumption expenditure	740	1225	1344	1550	1937	2219	2975	3394	3765	4245	4737	...
A Households	717	1196	1312	1516	1903	2184	2940	3357	3726	4199	4682	...
B Private non-profit institutions serving households	23	29	32	34	34	35	35	37	39	46	52	...
3 Gross capital formation	202	540	420	281	358	648	1026	1102	1418	1074	1869	...
A Increase in stocks	27	72	41	-60	-37	120	196	63	195	-36	522	...
B Gross fixed capital formation	175	468	379	341	395	528	830	1039	1223	1110	1347	...
Residential buildings	29	57	48	36	30	34	53	57	52	47	43	...
Non-residential buildings	18	91	98	56	73	107	183	203	247	243	223	...
Other construction and land improvement etc.	59	142	92	67	108	109	193	398	381	63	49	...
Other	69	178	141	182	184	278	401	381	543	757	1032	...
4 Exports of goods and services	11	590	610	675	798	1043	1117	1141	1345	1708	2124	...
5 Less: Imports of goods and services		613	558	593	803	1146	1442	1450	1542	1673	2139	...
Equals: Gross Domestic Product	1079	1998	2198	2363	2826	3441	4439	5160	6132	6696	8099	...

1.2 Expenditure on the Gross Domestic Product, in Constant Prices

Million Zimbabwean dollars

	1970	1975	1977	1978	1979	1980	1981	1982	1983	1984	1985	1986
					At constant prices of:1980							
1 Government final consumption expenditure	226	348	425	599	615	677	791	845	931	1020	1081	...
2 Private final consumption expenditure	1646	2033	1844	1995	2242	2219	2605	2620	2606	2520	2176	...
A Households	1601	1996	1811	1952	2207	2184	2574	2593	2578	2491	2145	...
B Private non-profit institutions serving households	45	37	33	43	35	35	31	27	28	29	31	...
3 Gross capital formation	563	986	540	358	392	646	950	815	860	562	814	...

Zimbabwe

1.2 Expenditure on the Gross Domestic Product, in Constant Prices
(Continued)

Million Zimbabwean dollars

	1970	1975	1977	1978	1979	1980	1981	1982	1983	1984	1985	1986
	\multicolumn{12}{l}{At constant prices of:1980}
A Increase in stocks	55	86	-19	-84	-51	118	228	27	120	-14	312	...
B Gross fixed capital formation	508	899	559	442	443	528	722	788	740	576	502	...
Residential buildings	93	109	74	50	36	34	43	40	31	24	20	...
Non-residential buildings	64	174	151	78	87	107	147	141	145	127	104	...
Other construction and land improvement etc.	164	252	134	91	124	109	160	279	227	33	24	...
Other	189	364	200	223	196	278	372	328	337	392	354	...
4 Exports of goods and services	30	1229	988	1027	855	1042	1123	1151	1155	1078	1138	...
5 Less: Imports of goods and services		1277	903	902	860	1146	1450	1463	1325	1056	1146	...
Statistical discrepancy [a]	155	-25	170	-79	-138	2	-114	67	-139	-127	356	...
Equals: Gross Domestic Product	2620	3294	3064	2998	3105	3441	3905	4035	4088	3997	4419	...

a) Item 'Statistical discrepancy' refers to the difference between gross domestic product obtained by the product approach and that obtained by the expenditure approach.

1.3 Cost Components of the Gross Domestic Product

Million Zimbabwean dollars

	1970	1975	1977	1978	1979	1980	1981	1982	1983	1984	1985	1986
1 Indirect taxes, net	68	96	129	104	172	217	384	540	896	744	...	...
A Indirect taxes	87	137	223	238	262	317	504	709	956	1040	...	...
B Less: Subsidies	19	41	94	134	90	100	120	169	60	296		
2 Consumption of fixed capital [a]	...	...	...	...	...	...	...	...	...	...	...	...
3 Compensation of employees paid by resident producers to:	559	1049	1249	1380	1562	1900	2329	2797	3130	3525		
4 Operating surplus [a]	454	852	822	878	1092	1322	1727	1822	2107	2426		
Equals: Gross Domestic Product	1079	1998	2198	2363	2826	3441	4439	5160	6132	6696	...	...

a) Item 'Operating surplus' includes consumption of fixed capital.

1.4 General Government Current Receipts and Disbursements

Million Zimbabwean dollars

	1970	1975	1977	1978	1979	1980	1981	1982	1983	1984	1985	1986
	\multicolumn{12}{l}{Receipts}
1 Operating surplus	...	...	...	...	...	...	...	...	...	...	...	...
2 Property and entrepreneurial income [a]	50	43	51	52	57	56	56	79	107	124	142	...
3 Taxes, fees and contributions	172	393	514	509	548	705	1052	1424	1753	1913	2110	...
A Indirect taxes	87	137	224	238	262	316	507	709	956	1051	1148	...
B Direct taxes	82	250	284	265	281	383	539	707	783	856	955	...
C Social security contributions	1	4	5	5	5	5	5	7	13	6	7	...
D Compulsory fees, fines and penalties	2	2	1	1	1	1	1	1	1	-	-	...
4 Other current transfers	11	22	27	31	32	54	72	62	68	93	103	...
Total Current Receipts of General Government [b]	233	458	593	593	637	815	1180	1565	1928	2130	2355	...
	\multicolumn{12}{l}{Disbursements}
1 Government final consumption expenditure	126	237	372	439	516	663	750	1007	1138	1334	1526	...
2 Property income	23	34	46	55	72	93	125	193	242	310	380	...
3 Subsidies	20	35	100	134	90	100	120	169	82	296	281	...
4 Other current transfers	40	57	77	94	113	158	184	269	370	364	454	...
A Social security benefits	1	2	3	2	3	3	4	4	6	5	6	...
B Social assistance grants [c]	18	20	33	48	60	74	71	77	75	79	85	...
C Other	20	36	41	43	49	81	109	188	289	280	363	...
Statistical discrepancy [d]	...	...	...	...	...	33	46	46	18	28	40	...
5 Net saving [e]	24	94	-2	-129	-154	-232	-45	-119	78	-202	-326	...
Total Current Disbursements and Net Saving of General Government [b]	233	458	593	593	637	815	1180	1565	1928	2130	2355	...

a) Item 'Property and entrepreneural income' includes consumption of fixed capital.
b) Estimates of general government cover central & local government.
c) Item 'Social assistance grants' refers to pensions.
d) Item 'Statistical discrepancy' represents unclassified estimates.
e) Item 'Net saving' includes consumption of fixed capital.

Zimbabwe

1.5 Current Income and Outlay of Corporate and Quasi-Corporate Enterprises, Summary

Million Zimbabwean dollars

	1970	1975	1977	1978	1979	1980	1981	1982	1983	1984	1985	1986
Receipts												
1 Operating surplus [a]	269	584	535	617	791	993	...	...	...	...	...	...
2 Property and entrepreneurial income received	81	162	197	210	241	292	...	...	...	...	...	...
3 Current transfers	34	72	103	117	120	150	...	...	...	...	...	...
Total Current Receipts	384	818	835	944	1152	1436	...	...	...	...	...	...
Disbursements												
1 Property and entrepreneurial income	145	286	349	351	419	496	...	...	...	...	...	...
2 Direct taxes and other current payments to general government	46	148	162	133	131	177	...	...	...	...	...	...
3 Other current transfers	59	129	172	194	199	250	...	...	...	...	...	...
4 Net saving [b]	134	256	152	266	403	513	...	...	...	...	...	...
Total Current Disbursements and Net Saving [c]	384	818	835	944	1152	1436	...	...	...	...	...	...

a) Item 'Operating surplus' includes consumption of fixed capital.
b) Item 'Net saving' includes consumption of fixed capital.
c) Corporate and quasi-corporate enterprises includes companies, financial institutions & public corporations.

1.7 External Transactions on Current Account, Summary

Million Zimbabwean dollars

	1970	1975	1977	1978	1979	1980	1981	1982	1983	1984	1985	1986
Payments to the Rest of the World												
1 Imports of goods and services	...	613	558	593	803	1146	1442	1450	1542	1673	2139	...
A Imports of merchandise c.i.f.	275	494	422	443	595	861	1059	1114	1087	1237	1555	...
B Other	...	119	136	150	208	285	383	336	455	436	584	...
2 Factor income to the rest of the world	...	67	73	67	97	115	187	272	339	287	316	...
A Compensation of employees	...	11	12	13	23	23	31	36	44	51	55	...
B Property and entrepreneurial income	...	56	61	54	73	92	156	236	295	236	261	...
By general government	...	1	3	1	3	5	20	63	94	128	152	...
By corporate and quasi-corporate enterprises	...	43	40	34	47	57	98	125	150	74	89	...
By other	...	12	18	19	23	31	38	48	52	34	21	...
3 Current transfers to the rest of the world	...	30	31	33	40	71	86	97	116	127	129	...
4 Surplus of the nation on current transactions	-13	-88	-9	25	-74	-157	-439	-533	-454	-102	-146	...
Payments to the Rest of the World and Surplus of the Nation on Current Transactions	...	622	653	718	866	1175	1276	1286	1543	1984	2438	...
Receipts From The Rest of the World												
1 Exports of goods and services	...	590	610	675	798	1043	1118	1141	1345	1708	2124	...
A Exports of merchandise f.o.b.	265	542	566	625	734	929	1001	998	1174	1484	...	...
B Other	...	48	43	50	64	114	117	143	164	226	...	...
2 Factor income from rest of the world	...	21	25	26	43	68	72	78	91	92	94	...
A Compensation of employees	...	1	1	1	1	2	4	14	16	19	17	...
B Property and entrepreneurial income	...	20	25	25	43	66	68	64	75	73	77	...
By general government	...	-	-	-	-	-	8	14	12	12	12	...
By corporate and quasi-corporate enterprises	...	16	20	18	34	50	44	37	43	42	54	...
By other	...	4	5	7	8	15	17	13	20	19	11	...
3 Current transfers from rest of the world	...	11	18	18	25	64	86	67	107	184	220	...
Receipts from the Rest of the World on Current Transactions	...	622	653	718	866	1175	1276	1286	1543	1984	2438	...

Zimbabwe

1.9 Gross Domestic Product by Institutional Sectors of Origin

Million Zimbabwean dollars

	1970	1975	1977	1978	1979	1980	1981	1982	1983	1984	1985	1986
					Domestic Factor Incomes Originating							
1 General government	138	261	359	418	479	563	698	869	1130	1282	...	...
2 Corporate and quasi-corporate enterprises	617	1226	1257	1432	1699	2020	2551	2966	3314	3343	...	...
A Non-financial	602	1191	1220	1396	1658	1969	2487	2884	3211	3228	...	...
Public	90	155	184	200	212	198	234	261	343	524	...	...
Private	512	1036	1036	1196	1446	1771	2253	2623	2868	2704	...	...
B Financial	15	35	37	36	41	51	64	82	103	115	...	...
Public	-1	14	14	21	30	45	41	41	53	37	...	...
Private	16	21	13	15	11	6	23	41	50	78	...	...
3 Households and private unincorporated enterprises	232	386	420	365	428	551	743	699	697	1226	...	...
A Owner-occupied housing	15	21	24	22	20	18	24	25	26	25	...	...
B Subsistence production	...	...	...	...	...	...	...	...	...	...	...	...
C Other	217	365	396	343	408	533	719	674	671	1200	...	...
4 Non-profit institutions serving households	24	31	35	43	47	88	63	85	97	101	...	...
Subtotal: Domestic Factor Incomes [a]	1011	1902	2069	2259	2654	3224	4055	4620	5236	5952	...	...
Indirect taxes, net	68	96	129	104	172	217	384	540	896	744	...	...
A Indirect taxes	87	137	223	238	262	317	504	709	956	1040	...	...
B Less: Subsidies	19	41	94	134	90	100	120	169	60	296	...	...
Consumption of fixed capital	...	...	...	...	...	...	...	...	...	...	...	...
Gross Domestic Product	1079	1998	2198	2363	2826	3441	4439	5160	6132	6696	...	...

a) Item 'Domestic factor incomes' includes consumption of fixed capital.

1.10 Gross Domestic Product by Kind of Activity, in Current Prices

Million Zimbabwean dollars

	1970	1975	1977	1978	1979	1980	1981	1982	1983	1984	1985	1986
1 Agriculture, hunting, forestry and fishing	153	323	334	292	325	451	646	658	506	673	951	935
2 Mining and quarrying	71	131	149	156	226	285	252	217	393	457	526	571
3 Manufacturing	209	447	460	515	625	802	1016	1121	1360	1533	2118	2489
4 Electricity, gas and water [a]	32	50	56	62	71	70	78	73	195	239	277	463
5 Construction	55	94	84	68	92	91	138	190	258	270	229	239
6 Wholesale and retail trade, restaurants and hotels	152	258	242	356	425	451	603	718	744	768	957	1071
7 Transport, storage and communication	88	145	166	178	188	211	306	362	364	436	470	467
8 Finance, insurance, real estate and business services [b]	69	130	149	150	167	202	240	283	334	342	403	455
9 Community, social and personal services [b]	140	246	290	312	347	478	588	777	857	964	1085	1224
Total, Industries	969	1824	1930	2089	2466	3041	3867	4399	5011	5682	7016	7914
Producers of Government Services	63	130	204	239	270	291	309	367	398	438	468	508
Other Producers	...	...	...	...	...	...	...	...	...	...	...	...
Subtotal [c]	1032	1954	2134	2328	2736	3332	4176	4766	5409	6120	7484	8422
Less: Imputed bank service charge	21	52	65	69	82	108	121	146	173	168	181	190
Plus: Import duties	...	...	...	...	...	...	...	...	...	...	...	...
Plus: Value added tax	...	...	...	...	...	...	...	...	...	...	...	...
Plus: Other adjustments [d]	68	96	129	104	172	217	384	540	896	744	796	1005
Equals: Gross Domestic Product	1079	1998	2198	2363	2826	3441	4439	5160	6132	6696	8099	9237

a) Item 'Electricity, gas and water' excludes gas.
b) Business services are included in item 'Community, social and personal services'.
c) Gross domestic product in factor values.
d) Item 'Other adjustments' refers to indirect taxes net of subsidies.

1.11 Gross Domestic Product by Kind of Activity, in Constant Prices

Million Zimbabwean dollars

	1970	1975	1977	1978	1979	1980	1981	1982	1983	1984	1985	1986
					At constant prices of 1980							
1 Agriculture, hunting, forestry and fishing	357	460	403	444	444	451	515	478	403	496	614	540
2 Mining and quarrying	251	299	309	292	292	285	278	284	280	291	288	285
3 Manufacturing	513	729	653	629	697	802	881	877	852	809	902	915
4 Electricity, gas and water [a]	97	94	58	70	64	70	70	63	68	70	79	108
5 Construction	113	156	109	91	89	91	105	101	93	86	64	60

Zimbabwe

1.11 Gross Domestic Product by Kind of Activity, in Constant Prices
(Continued)

Million Zimbabwean dollars

	1970	1975	1977	1978	1979	1980	1981	1982	1983	1984	1985	1986
At constant prices of:1980												
6 Wholesale and retail trade, restaurants and hotels	287	378	337	329	339	451	456	451	392	366	410	415
7 Transport, storage and communication	193	196	165	167	173	211	221	226	224	226	246	244
8 Finance, insurance, real estate and business services [b]	160	271	258	225	195	202	249	282	255	244	260	241
9 Community, social and personal services [b]	363	439	440	427	425	478	561	637	674	703	750	785
Total, Industries	2334	3022	2732	2674	2718	3041	3336	3399	3241	3291	3613	3593
Producers of Government Services	158	198	245	277	277	291	339	333	338	364	370	391
Other Producers	...	...	...	...	...	...	...	...	...	...	...	...
Subtotal [c]	2492	3220	2977	2951	2995	3332	3675	3732	3579	3655	3983	3984
Less: Imputed bank service charge	54	86	91	87	90	108	106	114	114	100	96	90
Plus: Import duties	...	...	...	...	...	...	...	...	...	...	...	...
Plus: Value added tax	...	...	...	...	...	...	...	...	...	...	...	...
Plus: Other adjustments [d]	182	160	178	134	200	217	336	417	623	442	532	529
Equals: Gross Domestic Product	2620	3294	3064	2998	3105	3441	3905	4035	4088	3997	4419	4423

a) Item 'Electricity, gas and water' excludes gas.
b) Business services are included in item 'Community, social and personal services'.
c) Gross domestic product in factor values.
d) Item 'Other adjustments' refers to indirect taxes net of subsidies.

1.12 Relations Among National Accounting Aggregates

Million Zimbabwean dollars

	1970	1975	1977	1978	1979	1980	1981	1982	1983	1984	1985	1986
Gross Domestic Product	1079	1998	2198	2363	2826	3441	4439	5160	6136	6696	8099	...
Plus: Net factor income from the rest of the world	-21	-46	-48	-42	-53	-47	-115	-194	-248	-195	-223	...
Factor income from the rest of the world	...	21	25	26	43	68	72	78	91	92	94	...
Less: Factor income to the rest of the world	...	67	73	67	97	115	187	272	339	287	316	...
Equals: Gross National Product	1059	1952	2150	2321	2773	3394	4324	4966	5884	6501	7874	...
Less: Consumption of fixed capital	...	...	...	...	...	...	...	...	...	...	...	...
Equals: National Income [a]	1059	1952	2150	2321	2773	3394	4324	4966	5884	6501	7874	...
Plus: Net current transfers from the rest of the world	-3	-19	-13	-15	-15	-6	1	-30	-9	56	91	...
Current transfers from the rest of the world	...	11	18	18	25	64	87	67	107	183	220	...
Less: Current transfers to the rest of the world	...	30	31	33	40	70	86	97	116	127	129	...
Equals: National Disposable Income [b]	1055	1933	2137	2306	2758	3388	4325	4936	5875	6557	7965	...
Less: Final consumption	866	1481	1726	2001	2474	2896	3738	4367	4910	5586	6245	...
Equals: Net Saving [c]	189	452	411	305	284	492	587	569	965	971	1720	...
Less: Surplus of the nation on current transactions	-13	-88	-9	25	-74	-157	-439	-533	-454	-102	-146	...
Equals: Net Capital Formation [d]	202	540	420	281	358	648	1026	1102	1418	1074	1869	...

a) Item 'National income' includes consumption of fixed capital.
b) Item 'National disposable income' includes consumption of fixed capital.
c) Item 'Net saving' includes consumption of fixed capital.
d) Item 'Net capital formation' includes consumption of fixed capital.

2.1 Government Final Consumption Expenditure by Function, in Current Prices

Million Zimbabwean dollars

	1970	1975	1977	1978	1979	1980	1981	1982	1983	1984	1985	1986
1 General public services												...
2 Defence	60	135	262	314	375	487	439	510	541	653	747	
3 Public order and safety												...
4 Education	17	44	54	61	66	99	144	260	300	363	415	...
5 Health	13	24	29	37	40	54	70	95	106	128	146	...
6 Social security and welfare	...	...	...	...	...	...	...	...	...	...	...	...
7 Housing and community amenities	10	18	19	18	21	26	35	34	53	46	53	...
8 Recreational, cultural and religious affairs	3	8	9	10	10	13	18	32	38	37	43	...
9 Economic services	6	28	33	31	26	53	75	101	93	92	105	...
10 Other functions	-3	-20	-34	-32	-22	-69	-31	-25	7	15	17	...
Total Government Final Consumption Expenditure [a]	106	237	372	439	516	663	750	1007	1138	1334	1526	...

a) Estimates of general government cover central & local government.

Zimbabwe

2.3 Total Government Outlays by Function and Type

Million Zimbabwean dollars

	Final Consumption Expenditures — Total	Compensation of Employees	Other	Subsidies	Other Current Transfers & Property Income	Total Current Disbursements	Gross Capital Formation	Other Capital Outlays	Total Outlays
1980									
1 General public services		...	...	...					
2 Defence	487	...	...	...	7	494	24	2	520
3 Public order and safety		...	...	...					
4 Education	99	...	...	...	103	202	6	...	208
5 Health	54	...	...	...	9	63	7	...	70
6 Social security and welfare	...	...	...	...	...	...	...	...	...
7 Housing and community amenities	26	...	...	...	-	26	35	...	61
8 Recreation, culture and religion	13	...	...	...	89	102	1	-	103
9 Economic services	53	...	...	100	13	166	37	...	203
10 Other functions	-69	...	...	...	7	-62	10	2	-50
Total ab	663	518	145	100	284	1047	120	4	1171
1981									
1 General public services		...	...	...					
2 Defence	439	...	...	...	4	443	30	5	478
3 Public order and safety		...	...	...					
4 Education	144	...	...	...	156	300	10	...	310
5 Health	70	...	...	...	23	93	7	...	100
6 Social security and welfare	...	...	...	...	...	...	...	...	...
7 Housing and community amenities	35	...	...	...	-	35	39	...	74
8 Recreation, culture and religion	18	...	...	...	92	110	1	-	111
9 Economic services	75	...	...	120	17	212	56	...	268
10 Other functions	-31	...	...	...	5	-26	12	2	-12
Total ab	750	626	124	120	355	1225	155	7	1387
1982									
1 General public services		...	...	...					
2 Defence	510	...	...	...	2	512	37	14	563
3 Public order and safety		...	...	...					
4 Education	260	...	...	...	263	523	22	-	545
5 Health	95	...	...	...	32	127	6	1	134
6 Social security and welfare	...	...	...	...	...	...	...	...	...
7 Housing and community amenities	34	...	...	...	-	34	45	-	79
8 Recreation, culture and religion	32	...	...	...	136	168	10	-	178
9 Economic services	101	...	...	169	26	296	140	...	436
10 Other functions	-25	...	...	...	10	-15	10	5	-
Total ab	1007	829	178	169	508	1684	270	20	1974
1983									
1 General public services		...	...	...					
2 Defence	541	...	...	...	3	544	51	5	600
3 Public order and safety		...	...	...					
4 Education	300	...	...	...	279	579	33	-	612
5 Health	106	...	...	...	29	135	8	5	148
6 Social security and welfare	...			...	...	...	...	...	...
7 Housing and community amenities	53	...	...	...	2	55	42	-	97
8 Recreation, culture and religion	48			...	110	158	7		361
9 Economic services	93	...	...	82	40	215	153	...	369
10 Other functions	7	...	...	...	9	16	7	6	29
Total ab	1138	925	213	82	630	1850	301	17	2168

Zimbabwe

2.3 Total Government Outlays by Function and Type
(Continued)

Million Zimbabwean dollars

	Final Consumption Expenditures Total	Compensation of Employees	Other	Subsidies	Other Current Transfers & Property Income	Total Current Disbursements	Gross Capital Formation	Other Capital Outlays	Total Outlays
				1984					
1 General public services		...	...	...					
2 Defence	653	...	...	...	12	665	61	12	738
3 Public order and safety		...	...	...					
4 Education	363	...	...	...	324	687	33	...	720
5 Health	128	...	...	...	39	167	12	3	182
6 Social security and welfare	...	...	...	...	...	...	...	...	...
7 Housing and community amenities	46	...	...	...	-	46	43	...	89
8 Recreation, culture and religion	37	...	...	...	166	203	8	-	211
9 Economic services	92	...	...	296	51	439	168	...	607
10 Other functions	15	...	...	...	8	23	2	4	29
Total [ab]	1334	1064	270	296	702	2332	327	19	2678
				1985					
1 General public services		...	...	...					
2 Defence	747	...	...	...	20	767	67	13	847
3 Public order and safety		...	...	...					
4 Education	415	...	...	...	405	820	37	-	857
5 Health	146	...	...	...	62	208	13	3	224
6 Social security and welfare	...	...	...	...	...	...	...	...	...
7 Housing and community amenities	53	...	...	...	-	53	47	-	100
8 Recreation, culture and religion	43	...	...	...	100	143	9	-	152
9 Economic services	105	...	...	281	145	531	185	-	716
10 Other functions	17	...	...	...	9	26	2	5	33
Total [ab]	1526	1217	309	281	874	2681	360	21	3062

a) Estimates of general government cover central & local government.
b) Property income and net of inter-governmental transfers in column 5 are included in the total and not in the breakdowns. Also included in the same total are some unclassified estimates.

2.5 Private Final Consumption Expenditure by Type and Porpose, in Current Prices

Million Zimbabwean dollars

	1970	1975	1977	1978	1979	1980	1981	1982	1983	1984	1985	1986
				Final Consumption Expenditure of Resident Households								
1 Food, beverages and tobacco	266	436	503	575	748	800	954	1096	1175	1220	1661	...
A Food	185	304	337	377	489	461	509	532	477	512	735	...
B Non-alcoholic beverages	10	24	31	34	44	106	133	207	300	303	449	...
C Alcoholic beverages	71	108	135	164	215	233	312	357	398	405	477	...
D Tobacco												...
2 Clothing and footwear	96	151	154	204	268	290	415	475	444	462	573	...
3 Gross rent, fuel and power	99	175	181	223	277	308	423	488	651	866	847	...
A Fuel and power	30	65	71	92	113	127	190	255	400	532	503	...
B Other	69	110	110	131	164	181	233	233	251	334	344	...
4 Furniture, furnishings and household equipment and operation	77	123	127	139	152	275	376	364	360	427	346	...
A Household operation	47	79	75	86	101	215	299	284	272	340	258	...
B Other	30	44	52	53	51	60	77	80	88	87	88	...
5 Medical care and health expenses	30	57	64	95	111	94	119	133	153	156	167	...
6 Transport and communication [a]	20	32	24	28	38	55	96	115	114	87	97	...
7 Recreational, entertainment, education and cultural services	35	51	58	59	68	92	127	156	218	229	216	...
A Education	17	21	23	27	29	53	79	104	157	159	150	...
B Other	18	30	35	32	39	39	48	52	61	70	66	...
8 Miscellaneous goods and services [a]	120	191	241	237	303	331	508	563	624	749	799	...
A Personal care	...	...	...	...	...	...	...	...	...	...	...	...
B Expenditures in restaurants, cafes and hotels	48	76	99	115	143	149	263	302	342	415	444	...
C Other	72	115	142	122	160	182	245	261	282	334	355	...

Zimbabwe

2.5 Private Final Consumption Expenditure by Type and Porpose, in Current Prices
(Continued)

Million Zimbabwean dollars

	1970	1975	1977	1978	1979	1980	1981	1982	1983	1984	1985	1986
Statistical discrepancy	-1	...	...	...	...	...	...	...	...	...	...	...
Total Final Consumption Expenditure in the Domestic Market by Households, of which	740	1215	1352	1560	1964	2242	3015	3388	3738	4196	4707	...
A Durable goods	66	111	99	114	139	271	394	400	386	426	355	...
B Semi-durable goods	...	...	...	...	...	...	...	...	...	...	...	...
C Non-durable goods	462	764	852	1012	1302	1367	1740	2026	2226	2450	3012	...
D Services	212	340	401	434	523	605	881	963	1126	1320	1340	...
Plus: Direct purchases abroad by resident households	...	...	...	...	...	...	...	...	...	...	...	...
Less: Direct purchases in the domestic market by non-resident households	23	19	40	44	61	58	75	31	12	-3	25	...
Equals: Final Consumption Expenditure of Resident Households	717	1196	1312	1516	1903	2184	2940	3357	3726	4199	4682	...
	\multicolumn{12}{c}{Final Consumption Expenditure of Private Non-profit Institutions Serving Households}
1 Research and science	...	...	...	...	...	...	...	...	...	...	...	...
2 Education	13	16	18	19	18	17	17	17	16	...	...	...
3 Medical and other health services	3	4	5	5	5	6	6	3	3	...	...	...
4 Welfare services	...	...	...	...	...	...	...	...	...	...	...	...
5 Recreational and related cultural services	...	...	...	...	...	...	...	...	...	...	...	...
6 Religious organisations	...	...	...	...	...	...	...	...	...	...	...	...
7 Professional and labour organisations serving households	...	...	...	...	...	...	...	...	...	...	...	...
8 Miscellaneous	7	9	9	10	11	12	12	17	20	...	...	...
Equals: Final Consumption Expenditure of Private Non-profit Organisations Serving Households	23	29	32	34	34	35	35	37	39	46	52	...
Private Final Consumption Expenditure	740	1225	1344	1550	1937	2219	2975	3394	3768	4245	4737	...

a) Item 'Transport and communication' includes personal transport equipment only. Communication is included in item 'Miscellaneous good and services'.

2.6 Private Final Consumption Expenditure by Type and Purpose, in Constant Prices

Million Zimbabwean dollars

	1970	1975	1977	1978	1979	1980	1981	1982	1983	1984	1985	1986
	\multicolumn{12}{c}{At constant prices of:1980}
	\multicolumn{12}{c}{Final Consumption Expenditure of Resident Households}
1 Food, beverages and tobacco	625	829	725	774	915	800	817	838	757	686	605	...
A Food	406	515	435	457	545	461	432	406	298	282	272	...
B Non-alcoholic beverages	22	40	49	42	45	106	105	143	174	149	149	...
C Alcoholic beverages	197	274	241	275	325	233	280	289	285	255	184	...
D Tobacco												...
2 Clothing and footwear	193	227	192	242	293	290	363	369	306	278	231	...
3 Gross rent, fuel and power	187	249	240	281	293	308	367	365	467	452	379	...
A Fuel and power	86	122	124	144	125	127	155	197	254	263	183	...
B Other	101	127	116	137	168	181	212	168	213	189	196	...
4 Furniture, furnishings and household equipment and operation	163	204	164	169	172	275	326	275	244	264	188	...
A Household operation	89	119	88	97	108	215	267	235	206	228	164	...
B Other	74	85	76	72	64	60	59	40	38	36	24	...
5 Medical care and health expenses	72	98	90	121	125	94	109	105	113	106	99	...
6 Transport and communication a	43	60	32	33	41	55	93	107	78	47	44	...
7 Recreational, entertainment, education and cultural services	110	101	86	82	82	92	133	141	187	175	155	...
A Education	63	48	44	45	40	53	87	96	143	129	117	...
B Other	47	53	42	37	42	39	46	45	44	46	38	...
8 Miscellaneous goods and services a	264	303	341	311	356	331	430	417	433	484	454	...
A Personal care	...	...	...	...	...	...	...	...	...	...	...	...
B Expenditures in restaurants, cafes and hotels	117	126	141	154	169	149	215	214	220	250	233	...
C Other	147	177	200	157	187	182	215	203	213	234	221	...
Total Final Consumption Expenditure in the Domestic Market by Households, of which	1657	2068	1871	2012	2275	2242	2638	2615	2585	2490	2157	...

Zimbabwe

2.6 Private Final Consumption Expenditure by Type and Purpose, in Constant Prices
(Continued)

Million Zimbabwean dollars

	1970	1975	1977	1978	1979	1980	1981	1982	1983	1984	1985	1986
					At constant prices of:1980							
A Durable goods	132	179	120	130	150	271	360	341	284	276	207	...
B Semi-durable goods	...	...	...	...	...	...	...	...	...	...	...	...
C Non-durable goods	1051	1354	1205	1331	1520	1367	1502	1566	1475	1394	1185	...
D Services	474	535	545	551	605	605	776	708	826	820	765	...
Plus: Direct purchases abroad by resident households	...	...	...	...	...	...	...	...	...	...	...	...
Less: Direct purchases in the domestic market by non-resident households	56	72	60	60	67	58	63	22	7	-1	12	...
Equals: Final Consumption Expenditure of Resident Households	1601	1996	1811	1952	2207	2184	2574	2593	2578	2491	2145	...
Final Consumption Expenditure of Private Non-profit Institutions Serving Households												
Equals: Final Consumption Expenditure of Private Non-profit Organisations Serving Households	45	37	33	43	35	35	31	27	28	29	31	...
Private Final Consumption Expenditure	1646	2033	1844	1995	2242	2219	2605	2620	2606	2520	2176	...

a) Item 'Transport and communication' includes personal transport equipment only. Communication is included in item 'Miscellaneous good and services'.

2.7 Gross Capital Formation by Type of Good and Owner, in Current Prices

Million Zimbabwean dollars

	1980				1981				1982			
	TOTAL	Total Private	Public Enterprises	General Government	TOTAL	Total Private	Public Enterprises	General Government	TOTAL	Total Private	Public Enterprises	General Government
Increase in stocks, total	120	...	...	...	196	...	...	...	63	...	...	...
1 Goods producing industries	164	...	...	...	377	...	...	...	378	...	...	...
A Materials and supplies	63	...	...	...	96	...	...	...	48	...	...	...
B Work in progress	...	...	...	...	...	...	...	...	...	...	...	...
C Livestock, except breeding stocks, dairy cattle, etc.	67	...	...	...	199	...	...	...	256	...	...	...
D Finished goods	34	...	...	...	82	...	...	...	74	...	...	...
2 Wholesale and retail trade	104	...	...	...	262	...	...	...	69	...	...	...
3 Other, except government stocks	9	...	...	...	15	...	...	...	43	...	...	...
4 Government stocks		...	...	...		...	...	...		...	...	...
Statistical discrepancy a	-157	...	...	...	-458	...	...	...	-427	...	...	...
Gross Fixed Capital Formation, Total	528	366	45	117	830	593	82	155	1039	523	277	239
1 Residential buildings	34	6	2	26	53	17	2	34	57	11	-	46
2 Non-residential buildings	107	90	1	16	183	158	2	23	203	139	14	50
3 Other construction	109	37	19	53	193	92	38	63	398	59	244	96
4 Land improvement and plantation and orchard development	...	...	...	...	...	...	...	...	...	...	...	...
5 Producers' durable goods	278	233	23	22	401	326	40	35	381	314	19	47
A Transport equipment	84	75	2	7	106	90	4	12	136	113	6	17
B Machinery and equipment	194	158	21	15	295	236	36	23	245	201	13	30
6 Breeding stock, dairy cattle, etc.	...	...	...	...	...	...	...	...	...	...	...	...
Total Gross Capital Formation	648	...	...	...	1026	...	...	...	1102	...	...	...

	1983				1984				1985			
	TOTAL	Total Private	Public Enterprises	General Government	TOTAL	Total Private	Public Enterprises	General Government	TOTAL	Total Private	Public Enterprises	General Government
Increase in stocks, total	195	...	...	...	-36	...	...	...	522	...	...	...
1 Goods producing industries	1119	...	...	...	-77	...	...	...	442	...	...	...
A Materials and supplies	76	...	...	...	21	...	...	...	45	...	...	...
B Work in progress	...	...	...	...	...	...	...	...	...	...	...	...
C Livestock, except breeding stocks, dairy cattle, etc.	455	...	...	...	-123	...	...	...	145	...	...	...
D Finished goods	588	...	...	...	25	...	...	...	252	...	...	...
2 Wholesale and retail trade	-84	...	...	...	222	...	...	...	311	...	...	...
3 Other, except government stocks	33	...	...	...	47	...	...	...	33	...	...	...
4 Government stocks		...	...	...		...	...	...		...	...	...

Zimbabwe

2.7 Gross Capital Formation by Type of Good and Owner, in Current Prices
(Continued)

Million Zimbabwean dollars

	1983 TOTAL	Total Private	Public Enterprises	General Government	1984 TOTAL	Total Private	Public Enterprises	General Government	1985 TOTAL	Total Private	Public Enterprises	General Government
Statistical discrepancy [a]	-873	...	...	...	-228	...	...	...	-264	...	...	...
Gross Fixed Capital Formation, Total	1223	506	413	305	1110	608	221	281	1347	...	...	...
1 Residential buildings	52	9	3	40	47	8	3	35	43	...	...	...
2 Non-residential buildings	247	130	36	80	243	161	36	46	223	...	...	...
3 Other construction	381	49	207	126	63	56	-147	155	49	...	...	...
4 Land improvement and plantation and orchard development	...	...	...	...	...	...	...	...	...	...	...	...
5 Producers' durable goods	545	318	167	58	757	383	329	45	1032	...	...	...
A Transport equipment	132	102	13	17	158	141	10	7	175	...	...	...
B Machinery and equipment	411	216	154	41	599	242	319	38	857	...	...	...
6 Breeding stock, dairy cattle, etc.	...	...	...	...	...	...	...	...	...	...	...	...
Total Gross Capital Formation	1418	...	...	...	1074	...	...	...	1869	...	...	...

a) Item 'Statistical discrepancy' refers to revaluation adjustment.

2.8 Gross Capital Formation by Type of Good and Owner, in Constant Prices

Million Zimbabwean dollars

	1980 TOTAL	Total Private	Public Enterprises	General Government	1981 TOTAL	Total Private	Public Enterprises	General Government	1982 TOTAL	Total Private	Public Enterprises	General Government
	At constant prices of: 1980											
Increase in stocks, total	118	...	...	...	228	...	...	...	27	...	...	...
1 Goods producing industries	45	...	...	...	76	...	...	...	34	...	...	...
A Materials and supplies	40	...	...	...	38	...	...	...	-3	...	...	...
B Work in progress	...	...	...	...	...	...	...	...	...	...	...	...
C Livestock, except breeding stocks, dairy cattle, etc.	-7	...	...	...	8	...	...	...	16	...	...	...
D Finished goods	11	...	...	...	30	...	...	...	21	...	...	...
2 Wholesale and retail trade	72	...	...	...	149	...	...	...	-32	...	...	...
3 Other, except government stocks	3	...	...	...	3	...	...	...	25	...	...	...
4 Government stocks		...	...	...		...	...	...		...	...	...
Gross Fixed Capital Formation, Total	528	...	...	...	722	...	...	...	788	...	...	...
1 Residential buildings	34	...	...	...	43	...	...	...	40	...	...	...
2 Non-residential buildings	107	...	...	...	147	...	...	...	141	...	...	...
3 Other construction	109	...	...	...	160	...	...	...	279	...	...	...
4 Land improvement and plantation and orchard development	...	...	...	...	...	...	...	...	...	...	...	...
5 Producers' durable goods	278	...	...	...	372	...	...	...	328	...	...	...
A Transport equipment	84	...	...	...	105	...	...	...	126	...	...	...
B Machinery and equipment	194	...	...	...	267	...	...	...	202	...	...	...
6 Breeding stock, dairy cattle, etc.	...	...	...	...	...	...	...	...	...	...	...	...
Total Gross Capital Formation	646	...	...	...	950	...	...	...	815	...	...	...

	1983 TOTAL	Total Private	Public Enterprises	General Government	1984 TOTAL	Total Private	Public Enterprises	General Government	1985 TOTAL	Total Private	Public Enterprises	General Government
	At constant prices of: 1980											
Increase in stocks, total	120	...	...	...	-14	...	...	...	312	...	...	...
1 Goods producing industries	313	...	...	...	-103	...	...	...	149	...	...	...
A Materials and supplies	-5	...	...	...	-28	...	...	...	13	...	...	...
B Work in progress	...	...	...	...	...	...	...	...	...	...	...	...
C Livestock, except breeding stocks, dairy cattle, etc.	-19	...	...	...	-15	...	...	...	15	...	...	...
D Finished goods	337	...	...	...	-60	...	...	...	121	...	...	...
2 Wholesale and retail trade	-201	...	...	...	73	...	...	...	149	...	...	...
3 Other, except government stocks	8	...	...	...	16	...	...	...	14	...	...	...
4 Government stocks		...	...	...		...	...	...		...	...	...
Gross Fixed Capital Formation, Total	740	...	...	...	576	...	...	...	502	...	...	...

Zimbabwe

2.8 Gross Capital Formation by Type of Good and Owner, in Constant Prices
(Continued)

Million Zimbabwean dollars

	1983				1984				1985			
	TOTAL	Total Private	Public Enterprises	General Government	TOTAL	Total Private	Public Enterprises	General Government	TOTAL	Total Private	Public Enterprises	General Government
	At constant prices of: 1980												
1 Residential buildings	31	...	...	...	24	...	...	...	20	...	...	...
2 Non-residential buildings	145	...	...	...	127	...	...	...	104	...	...	...
3 Other construction	227	...	...	...	33	...	...	...	24	...	...	...
4 Land improvement and plantation and orchard development	...	...	...	...	...	...	...	...	...	...	...	...
5 Producers' durable goods	337	...	...	...	392	...	...	...	354	...	...	...
A Transport equipment	90	...	...	...	93	...	...	...	80	...	...	...
B Machinery and equipment	247	...	...	...	299	...	...	...	274	...	...	...
6 Breeding stock, dairy cattle, etc.	...	...	...	...	...	...	...	...	...	...	...	...
Total Gross Capital Formation	860	...	...	...	562	...	...	...	814	...	...	...

2.11 Gross Fixed Capital Formation by Kind of Activity of Owner, ISIC Divisions, in Current Prices

Million Zimbabwean dollars

	1970	1975	1977	1978	1979	1980	1981	1982	1983	1984	1985	1986
	All Producers											
1 Agriculture, hunting, forestry and fishing	23	38	45	42	44	53	91	116	81	92	...	...
2 Mining and quarrying	25	40	66	59	83	83	133	94	89	89	...	...
3 Manufacturing	31	115	49	44	50	123	201	168	196	234	...	...
4 Electricity, gas and water [a]	9	36	19	18	14	26	47	133	288	171	...	...
5 Construction	3	9	4	3	6	12	26	35	33	17	...	...
6 Wholesale and retail trade, restaurants and hotels	10	17	17	19	24	43	50	47	28	100	...	...
7 Transport, storage and communication	15	60	36	33	37	48	60	160	137	83	...	...
8 Finance, insurance, real estate and business services [b]	31	62	57	45	62	49	87	95	106	106	...	...
9 Community, social and personal services [b]	10	26	29	26	25	29	62	78	84	87	...	...
A Sanitary and similar services	...	...	...	...	...	...	...	...	...	...	...	...
B Social and related community services	...	18	20	19	18	15	25	38	42	37	...	...
Educational services	...	12	13	11	10	8	18	30	31	24	...	...
Medical, dental, other health and veterinary services	...	6	7	8	8	7	7	8	11	13	...	...
C Recreational and cultural services	...	8	9	7	7	14	37	40	42	50	...	...
D Personal and household services	...	...	...	...	...	...	...	...	...	...	...	...
Total Industries	157	403	322	289	345	466	757	926	1042	979	...	...
Producers of Government Services	18	65	57	52	50	62	73	113	181	131	...	...
Private Non-Profit Institutions Serving Households	...	...	...	...	...	...	...	...	...	...	...	...
Total	175	468	379	341	395	528	830	1039	1223	1110	1347	...

a) Item 'Electricity, gas and water' excludes gas.
b) Business services are included in item 'Community, social and personal services'.

2.12 Gross Fixed Capital Formation by Kind of Activity of Owner, ISIC Divisions, in Constant Prices

Million Zimbabwean dollars

	1970	1975	1977	1978	1979	1980	1981	1982	1983	1984	1985	1986
	At constant prices of: 1980											
	All Producers											
1 Agriculture, hunting, forestry and fishing	64	73	65	55	49	53	83	93	51	50	...	...
2 Mining and quarrying	67	77	97	76	92	83	114	72	54	46	...	...
3 Manufacturing	85	226	71	56	54	123	179	135	121	121	...	...
4 Electricity, gas and water [a]	25	69	27	22	15	26	41	94	174	83	...	...

Zimbabwe

2.7 Gross Capital Formation by Type of Good and Owner, in Current Prices
(Continued)

Million Zimbabwean dollars

	1983 TOTAL	1983 Total Private	1983 Public Enterprises	1983 General Government	1984 TOTAL	1984 Total Private	1984 Public Enterprises	1984 General Government	1985 TOTAL	1985 Total Private	1985 Public Enterprises	1985 General Government
Statistical discrepancy [a]	-873	...	...	...	-228	...	...	...	-264	...	...	...
Gross Fixed Capital Formation, Total	1223	506	413	305	1110	608	221	281	1347	...	...	...
1 Residential buildings	52	9	3	40	47	8	3	35	43	...	...	...
2 Non-residential buildings	247	130	36	80	243	161	36	46	223	...	...	...
3 Other construction	381	49	207	126	63	56	-147	155	49	...	...	...
4 Land improvement and plantation and orchard development	...	...	...	...	...	...	...	...	...	...	...	...
5 Producers' durable goods	545	318	167	58	757	383	329	45	1032	...	...	...
A Transport equipment	132	102	13	17	158	141	10	7	175	...	...	...
B Machinery and equipment	411	216	154	41	599	242	319	38	857	...	...	...
6 Breeding stock, dairy cattle, etc.	...	...	...	...	...	...	...	...	...	...	...	...
Total Gross Capital Formation	1418	...	...	...	1074	...	...	...	1869	...	...	...

a) Item 'Statistical discrepancy' refers to revaluation adjustment.

2.8 Gross Capital Formation by Type of Good and Owner, in Constant Prices

Million Zimbabwean dollars

	1980 TOTAL	1980 Total Private	1980 Public Enterprises	1980 General Government	1981 TOTAL	1981 Total Private	1981 Public Enterprises	1981 General Government	1982 TOTAL	1982 Total Private	1982 Public Enterprises	1982 General Government
					At constant prices of:1980							
Increase in stocks, total	118	...	...	...	228	...	...	...	27	...	...	...
1 Goods producing industries	45	...	...	...	76	...	...	...	34	...	...	...
A Materials and supplies	40	...	...	...	38	...	...	...	-3	...	...	...
B Work in progress	...	...	...	...	...	...	...	...	...	...	...	...
C Livestock, except breeding stocks, dairy cattle, etc.	-7	...	...	...	8	...	...	...	16	...	...	...
D Finished goods	11	...	...	...	30	...	...	...	21	...	...	...
2 Wholesale and retail trade	72	...	...	...	149	...	...	...	-32	...	...	...
3 Other, except government stocks	3	...	...	...	3	...	...	...	25	...	...	...
4 Government stocks												
Gross Fixed Capital Formation, Total	528	...	...	...	722	...	...	...	788	...	...	...
1 Residential buildings	34	...	...	...	43	...	...	...	40	...	...	...
2 Non-residential buildings	107	...	...	...	147	...	...	...	141	...	...	...
3 Other construction	109	...	...	...	160	...	...	...	279	...	...	...
4 Land improvement and plantation and orchard development	...	...	...	...	...	...	...	...	...	...	...	...
5 Producers' durable goods	278	...	...	...	372	...	...	...	328	...	...	...
A Transport equipment	84	...	...	...	105	...	...	...	126	...	...	...
B Machinery and equipment	194	...	...	...	267	...	...	...	202	...	...	...
6 Breeding stock, dairy cattle, etc.	...	...	...	...	...	...	...	...	...	...	...	...
Total Gross Capital Formation	646	...	...	...	950	...	...	...	815	...	...	...

	1983 TOTAL	1983 Total Private	1983 Public Enterprises	1983 General Government	1984 TOTAL	1984 Total Private	1984 Public Enterprises	1984 General Government	1985 TOTAL	1985 Total Private	1985 Public Enterprises	1985 General Government
					At constant prices of:1980							
Increase in stocks, total	120	...	...	...	-14	...	...	...	919	...	...	...
1 Goods producing industries	313	...	...	...	-103	...	...	...	149	...	...	...
A Materials and supplies	-5	...	...	...	-28	...	...	...	13	...	...	...
B Work in progress	...	...	...	...	...	...	...	...	...	...	...	...
C Livestock, except breeding stocks, dairy cattle, etc.	-19	...	...	...	-15	...	...	...	15	...	...	...
D Finished goods	337	...	...	...	-60	...	...	...	121	...	...	...
2 Wholesale and retail trade	-201	...	...	...	73	...	...	...	149	...	...	...
3 Other, except government stocks	8	...	...	...	16	...	...	...	14	...	...	...
4 Government stocks												
Gross Fixed Capital Formation, Total	740	...	...	...	576	...	...	...	502	...	...	...

Zimbabwe

2.8 Gross Capital Formation by Type of Good and Owner, in Constant Prices
(Continued)

Million Zimbabwean dollars

	1983 TOTAL	1983 Total Private	1983 Public Enterprises	1983 General Government	1984 TOTAL	1984 Total Private	1984 Public Enterprises	1984 General Government	1985 TOTAL	1985 Total Private	1985 Public Enterprises	1985 General Government
				At constant prices of:1980								
1 Residential buildings	31	...	...	...	24	...	...	...	20	...	...	...
2 Non-residential buildings	145	...	...	...	127	...	...	...	104	...	...	...
3 Other construction	227	...	...	...	33	...	...	...	24	...	...	...
4 Land improvement and plantation and orchard development	...	...	...	...	...	...	...	...	...	...	...	...
5 Producers' durable goods	337	...	...	...	392	...	...	...	354	...	...	...
A Transport equipment	90	...	...	...	93	...	...	...	80	...	...	...
B Machinery and equipment	247	...	...	...	299	...	...	...	274	...	...	...
6 Breeding stock, dairy cattle, etc.	...	...	...	...	...	...	...	...	...	...	...	...
Total Gross Capital Formation	860	...	...	...	562	...	...	...	814	...	...	...

2.11 Gross Fixed Capital Formation by Kind of Activity of Owner, ISIC Divisions, in Current Prices

Million Zimbabwean dollars

	1970	1975	1977	1978	1979	1980	1981	1982	1983	1984	1985	1986
					All Producers							
1 Agriculture, hunting, forestry and fishing	23	38	45	42	44	53	91	116	81	92	...	...
2 Mining and quarrying	25	40	66	59	83	83	133	94	89	89	...	...
3 Manufacturing	31	115	49	44	50	123	201	168	196	234	...	...
4 Electricity, gas and water [a]	9	36	19	18	14	26	47	133	288	171	...	...
5 Construction	3	9	4	3	6	12	26	35	33	17	...	...
6 Wholesale and retail trade, restaurants and hotels	10	17	17	19	24	43	50	47	28	100	...	...
7 Transport, storage and communication	15	60	36	33	37	48	60	160	137	83	...	...
8 Finance, insurance, real estate and business services [b]	31	62	57	45	62	49	87	95	106	106	...	...
9 Community, social and personal services [b]	10	26	29	26	25	29	62	78	84	87	...	...
A Sanitary and similar services	...	...	...	...	...	...	...	...	...	...	...	...
B Social and related community services	...	18	20	19	18	15	25	38	42	37	...	...
Educational services	...	12	13	11	10	8	18	30	31	24	...	...
Medical, dental, other health and veterinary services	...	6	7	8	8	7	7	8	11	13	...	...
C Recreational and cultural services	...	8	9	7	7	14	37	40	42	50	...	...
D Personal and household services	...	...	...	...	...	...	...	...	...	...	...	...
Total Industries	157	403	322	289	345	466	757	926	1042	979	...	...
Producers of Government Services	18	65	57	52	50	62	73	113	181	131	...	...
Private Non-Profit Institutions Serving Households	...	...	...	...	...	...	...	...	...	...	...	...
Total	175	468	379	341	395	528	830	1039	1223	1110	1347	...

a) Item 'Electricity, gas and water' excludes gas.
b) Business services are included in item 'Community, social and personal services'.

2.12 Gross Fixed Capital Formation by Kind of Activity of Owner, ISIC Divisions, in Constant Prices

Million Zimbabwean dollars

	1970	1975	1977	1978	1979	1980	1981	1982	1983	1984	1985	1986
					At constant prices of:1980							
					All Producers							
1 Agriculture, hunting, forestry and fishing	64	73	65	55	49	53	83	93	51	50	...	...
2 Mining and quarrying	67	77	97	76	92	83	114	72	54	46	...	...
3 Manufacturing	85	226	71	56	54	123	179	135	121	121	...	...
4 Electricity, gas and water [a]	25	69	27	22	15	26	41	94	174	83	...	...

Zimbabwe

2.12 Gross Fixed Capital Formation by Kind of Activity of Owner, ISIC Divisions, in Constant Prices
(Continued)

Million Zimbabwean dollars

	1970	1975	1977	1978	1979	1980	1981	1982	1983	1984	1985	1986
	\multicolumn{12}{c}{At constant prices of:1980}
5 Construction	7	19	6	3	6	12	24	29	21	9	...	...
6 Wholesale and retail trade, restaurants and hotels	31	35	25	24	28	44	45	37	18	53	...	...
7 Transport, storage and communication	45	114	54	40	40	48	54	122	86	45	...	...
8 Finance, insurance, real estate and business services [b]	100	118	87	62	74	49	71	67	63	55	...	...
9 Community, social and personal services [b]	32	51	44	35	28	29	52	57	50	45	...	...
A Sanitary and similar services	...	...	...	...	...	...	...	...	...	...	...	...
B Social and related community services	19	35	26	22	17	16	31	28	25	19	...	...
Educational services	11	23	15	11	8	8	15	22	19	12	...	...
Medical, dental, other health and veterinary services	8	12	11	11	9	8	6	6	6	7	...	...
C Recreational and cultural services	13	16	13	9	8	14	31	29	25	26	...	...
D Personal and household services	...	...	...	...	...	...	...	...	...	...	...	...
Total Industries	456	782	476	373	386	466	661	707	638	508	...	...
Producers of Government Services	54	117	83	69	57	62	61	81	102	68	...	...
Private Non-Profit Institutions Serving Households	...	...	...	...	...	...	...	...	...	...	...	...
Total	510	899	559	442	443	528	722	788	740	576	502	465

a) Item 'Electricity, gas and water' excludes gas.
b) Business services are included in item 'Community, social and personal services'.

4.1 Derivation of Value Added by Kind of Activity, in Current Prices

Million Zimbabwean dollars

	1980 Gross Output	1980 Intermediate Consumption	1980 Value Added	1981 Gross Output	1981 Intermediate Consumption	1981 Value Added	1982 Gross Output	1982 Intermediate Consumption	1982 Value Added	1983 Gross Output	1983 Intermediate Consumption	1983 Value Added
	\multicolumn{12}{c}{All Producers}
1 Agriculture, hunting, forestry and fishing	778	327	451	1120	474	646	1194	537	658	1099	593	506
2 Mining and quarrying	468	183	285	485	233	252	440	223	217	629	235	393
3 Manufacturing	2204	1402	802	2837	1821	1016	3219	2098	1121	3349	1989	1360
A Manufacture of food, beverages and tobacco	638	461	177	785	573	211	1053	778	275	1149	758	391
B Textile, wearing apparel and leather industries	400	262	138	546	350	197	550	355	195	511	306	205
C Manufacture of wood and wood products, including furniture	74	42	32	111	63	48	110	64	46	98	51	47
D Manufacture of paper and paper products, printing and publishing	115	67	48	157	88	68	179	101	78	207	100	106
E Manufacture of chemicals and chemical petroleum, coal, rubber and plastic products	284	181	103	380	236	144	412	265	147	499	317	182
F Manufacture of non-metallic mineral products, except products of petroleum and coal	63	30	33	88	55	33	118	55	63	114	49	66
G Basic metal industries	289	169	120	263	168	95	230	155	75	289	182	107
H Manufacture of fabricated metal products, machinery and equipment	311	173	138	465	262	202	522	299	223	453	212	241
I Other manufacturing industries	30	18	13	42	25	17	45	26	19	30	14	16
4 Electricity, gas and water [a]	163	93	70	186	108	78	181	108	73	331	136	195
A Electricity, gas and steam	146	87	59	169	101	68	156	98	58	319	126	193
B Water works and supply	17	6	10	17	7	10	25	10	15	12	10	2

Zimbabwe

4.1 Derivation of Value Added by Kind of Activity, in Current Prices
(Continued)

Million Zimbabwean dollars

		1980			1981			1982			1983		
		Gross Output	Intermediate Consumption	Value Added	Gross Output	Intermediate Consumption	Value Added	Gross Output	Intermediate Consumption	Value Added	Gross Output	Intermediate Consumption	Value Added
5	Construction	255	168	91	341	203	138	463	273	190	536	278	258
6	Wholesale and retail trade, restaurants and hotels	893	438	451	1176	573	603	1231	512	718	1208	464	744
	A Wholesale and retail trade	837	404	433	1112	537	575	1155	475	680	1110	412	697
	B Restaurants and hotels	52	34	18	64	36	28	75	37	38	98	51	46
7	Transport, storage and communication	410	199	211	548	243	306	656	294	362	740	376	364
8	Finance, insurance, real estate and business services [b]	269	67	202	311	71	240	382	99	283	439	104	334
	A Financial institutions	184	25	159	211	26	185	267	39	228	315	39	276
	B Insurance												
	C Real estate and business services	85	42	43	100	45	55	115	60	55	124	65	59
9	Community, social and personal services [b]	619	141	478	756	166	588	996	219	777	1146	289	857
	A Sanitary and similar services	...	...	...	...	...	...	...	...	...	...	...	...
	B Social and related community services	309	69	240	366	68	297	502	87	415	583	131	452
	Educational services	213	44	169	249	33	215	351	42	309	417	74	343
	Medical, dental, other health and veterinary services	96	25	71	117	35	82	151	45	106	166	57	109
	C Recreational and cultural services	245	72	173	318	98	219	409	132	277	475	158	317
	D Personal and household services	65	-	65	72	-	72	85	-	85	88	-	88
	Total, Industries	6059	3018	3041	7760	3892	3867	8762	4363	4399	9477	4464	5011
	Producers of Government Services	586	295	291	603	294	309	730	363	367	820	422	398
	Other Producers	...	...	...	...	...	...	...	...	...	...	...	...
	Total [c]	6645	3313	3332	8363	4186	4176	9492	4726	4766	10297	4886	5409
	Less: Imputed bank service charge	...	-108	108	...	-121	121	...	-146	146	...	-173	173
	Import duties	...	...	...	...	...	...	...	...	...	...	...	...
	Value added tax	...	...	...	...	...	...	...	...	...	...	...	...
	Other adjustments [d]	217	...	217	384	...	384	540	...	540	900	...	900
	Total	6862	3420	3443	8747	4308	4439	10032	4872	5160	11197	5059	6132

		1984		
		Gross Output	Intermediate Consumption	Value Added

All Producers

1	Agriculture, hunting, forestry and fishing	1317	644	673
2	Mining and quarrying	729	272	457
3	Manufacturing	3405	1872	1533
	A Manufacture of food, beverages and tobacco	...	...	...
	B Textile, wearing apparel and leather industries	...	...	...
	C Manufacture of wood and wood products, including furniture	...	...	...
	D Manufacture of paper and paper products, printing and publishing	...	...	...
	E Manufacture of chemicals and chemical petroleum, coal, rubber and plastic products	...	...	...
	F Manufacture of non-metallic mineral products, except products of petroleum and coal	...	...	...
	G Basic metal industries	...	...	...
	H Manufacture of fabricated metal products, machinery and equipment	...	...	...
	I Other manufacturing industries	...	...	...
4	Electricity, gas and water [a]	405	166	239
	A Electricity, gas and steam	...	...	...
	B Water works and supply	...	...	...

Zimbabwe

4.1 Derivation of Value Added by Kind of Activity, in Current Prices
(Continued)

Million Zimbabwean dollars

		1984	
	Gross Output	Intermediate Consumption	Value Added
5 Construction	555	285	270
6 Wholesale and retail trade, restaurants and hotels	1452	684	768
A Wholesale and retail trade	1331	616	715
B Restaurants and hotels	121	69	52
7 Transport, storage and communication	857	422	436
8 Finance, insurance, real estate and business services [b]	483	141	342
A Financial institutions	341	59	282
B Insurance			
C Real estate and business services	142	82	60
9 Community, social and personal services [b]	1296	332	964
A Sanitary and similar services	...	...	...
B Social and related community services	665	134	531
Educational services	508	93	415
Medical, dental, other health and veterinary services	157	41	116
C Recreational and cultural services	544	198	346
D Personal and household services	87	-	87
Total, Industries	10499	4818	5682
Producers of Government Services	816	377	438
Other Producers	...	...	...
Total [c]	11315	5195	6120
Less: Imputed bank service charge	...	-168	168
Import duties	...	...	...
Value added tax	...	...	...
Other adjustments [d]	744	...	744
Total	12059	5363	6696

a) Item 'Electricity, gas and water' excludes gas.
b) Business services are included in item 'Community, social and personal services'.
c) Gross domestic product in factor values.
d) Item 'Other adjustments' refers to indirect taxes net of subsidies.

4.3 Cost Components of Value Added

Million Zimbabwean dollars

	1980						1981					
	Compensation of Employees	Capital Consumption	Net Operating Surplus	Indirect Taxes	Less: Subsidies Received	Value Added	Compensation of Employees	Capital Consumption	Net Operating Surplus	Indirect Taxes	Less: Subsidies Received	Value Added
					All Producers							
1 Agriculture, hunting, forestry and fishing	146	...	305	...	...	451	216	...	430	...	...	646
2 Mining and quarrying	116	...	169	...	...	285	158	...	94	...	...	252
3 Manufacturing	402	...	400	...	...	802	541	...	475	...	...	1016
A Manufacture of food, beverages and tobacco	90	...	86	...	...	176	115	...	96	...	...	211

Zimbabwe

4.3 Cost Components of Value Added
(Continued)

Million Zimbabwean dollars

		1980						1981				
	Compensation of Employees	Capital Consumption	Net Operating Surplus	Indirect Taxes	Less: Subsidies Received	Value Added	Compensation of Employees	Capital Consumption	Net Operating Surplus	Indirect Taxes	Less: Subsidies Received	Value Added
B Textile, wearing apparel and leather industries	62	...	76	...	...	138	89	...	108	...	...	197
C Manufacture of wood and wood products, including furniture	18	...	14	...	...	32	26	...	22	...	...	48
D Manufacture of paper and paper products, printing and publishing	31	...	16	...	...	47	41	...	27	...	...	68
E Manufacture of chemicals and chemical petroleum, coal, rubber and plastic products	45	...	59	...	...	104	59	...	85	...	...	144
F Manufacture of non-metallic mineral products, except products of petroleum and coal	15	...	18	...	...	33	22	...	11	...	...	33
G Basic metal industries	51	...	69	...	...	120	69	...	26	...	...	95
H Manufacture of fabricated metal products, machinery and equipment	83	...	56	...	...	139	113	...	89	...	...	202
I Other manufacturing industries	7	...	6	...	...	13	7	...	10	...	...	17
4 Electricity, gas and water [a]	27	...	43	...	...	70	30	...	48	...	...	78
A Electricity, gas and steam	25	...	34	...	...	59	28	...	40	...	...	68
B Water works and supply	2	...	9	...	...	11	2	...	8	...	...	10
5 Construction	81	...	9	...	...	91	110	...	28	...	...	138
6 Wholesale and retail trade, restaurants and hotels	203	...	248	...	...	451	197	...	406	...	...	603
A Wholesale and retail trade	185	...	249	...	...	434	176	...	399	...	...	575
B Restaurants and hotels	19	...	-1	...	...	18	21	...	7	...	...	28
7 Transport, storage and communication	194	...	17	...	...	211	218	...	88	...	...	306
8 Finance, insurance, real estate and business services [b]	78	...	124	...	...	202	100	...	140	...	...	240
A Financial institutions	74	...	85	...	...	159	95	...	90	...	...	185
B Insurance		...		...	...			...		...	...	
C Real estate and business services	4	...	39	...	...	43	5	...	50	...	...	55
9 Community, social and personal services [b]	392	...	86	...	...	478	479	...	109	...	...	586
A Sanitary and similar services	...	...	...	...	...	...	...	...	...	...	...	...
B Social and related community services	218	...	22	...	...	240	272	...	29	...	...	301
Educational services	169	...	-	...	...	169	216	...	1	...	...	215
Medical, dental, other health and veterinary services	49	...	22	...	...	71	56	...	26	...	...	82
C Recreational and cultural services	110	...	63	...	...	173	135	...	84	...	...	219
D Personal and household services	65	...	-	...	...	65	72	...	-	...	...	72
Total, Industries	1639	...	1405	...	...	3041	2048	...	1817	...	...	3867
Producers of Government Services	263	...	27	...	...	291	281	...	28	...	...	309
Other Producers	...	...	...	...	...	...	...	...	...	...	...	...
Total [c]	1902	...	1432	...	...	3332	2329	...	1843	...	...	4176
Less: Imputed bank service charge	...	...	108	...	...	108	...	...	121	...	...	121
Import duties	...	...	...	...	...	...	...	...	...	...	...	...
Value added tax	...	...	...	...	...	...	...	...	...	...	...	...
Other adjustments [d]	...	...	...	217	...	217	...	...	...	384	...	384
Total [c]	1900	...	1322	217	...	3441	2329	...	1727	384	...	4439

of which General Government:

1 Agriculture, hunting, forestry and fishing	5	...	-1	...	...	4	10	...	...	...	...	10
2 Mining and quarrying	...	...	...	...	...	...	...	...	...	...	...	...
3 Manufacturing	4	...	5	...	...	9	5	...	4	...	...	9
4 Electricity, gas and water	17	...	28	...	...	45	19	...	34	...	...	53

Zimbabwe

4.3 Cost Components of Value Added
(Continued)

Million Zimbabwean dollars

	1980							1981					
	Compensation of Employees	Capital Consumption	Net Operating Surplus	Indirect Taxes	Less: Subsidies Received	Value Added	Compensation of Employees	Capital Consumption	Net Operating Surplus	Indirect Taxes	Less: Subsidies Received	Value Added
5 Construction	35	...	-2	...	...	33	40	...	3	...	...	43
6 Wholesale and retail trade, restaurants and hotels	3	...	4	...	...	7	4	...	4	...	...	8
7 Transport and communication	8	...	...	...	...	8	8	...	...	...	...	8
8 Finance, insurance, real estate & business services	...	...	28	...	...	28	...	...	28	...	...	28
9 Community, social and personal services	170	...	...	...	...	170	258	...	...	...	...	258
Total, Industries of General Government	242	...	62	...	...	304	344	...	73	...	...	417
Producers of Government Services	263	...	...	...	...	263	281	...	...	...	...	281
Total, General Government	505	...	62	...	...	567	625	...	73	...	...	698

	1982							1983					
	Compensation of Employees	Capital Consumption	Net Operating Surplus	Indirect Taxes	Less: Subsidies Received	Value Added	Compensation of Employees	Capital Consumption	Net Operating Surplus	Indirect Taxes	Less: Subsidies Received	Value Added
					All Producers							
1 Agriculture, hunting, forestry and fishing	248	...	410	...	...	658	275	...	231	...	...	506
2 Mining and quarrying	179	...	38	...	...	217	161	...	232	...	...	393
3 Manufacturing	640	...	472	...	...	1121	702	...	660	...	...	1360
A Manufacture of food, beverages and tobacco	...	...	...	...	...	275	160	...	230	...	...	390
B Textile, wearing apparel and leather industries	...	...	...	...	...	195	128	...	77	...	...	205
C Manufacture of wood and wood products, including furniture	...	...	...	...	...	46	33	...	15	...	...	48
D Manufacture of paper and paper products, printing and publishing	50	...	28	...	...	78	53	...	53	...	...	100
E Manufacture of chemicals and chemical petroleum, coal, rubber and plastic products	71	...	77	...	...	148	84	...	97	...	...	181
F Manufacture of non-metallic mineral products, except products of petroleum and coal	27	...	36	...	...	63	27	...	38	...	...	65
G Basic metal industries	67	...	7	...	...	74	79	...	27	...	...	107
H Manufacture of fabricated metal products, machinery and equipment	134	...	89	...	...	223	129	...	113	...	...	242
I Other manufacturing industries	11	...	8	...	...	19	9	...	7	...	...	14
4 Electricity, gas and water [a]	34	...	39	...	...	73	35	...	160	...	...	195
A Electricity, gas and steam	32	...	26	...	...	58	34	...	159	...	...	193
B Water works and supply	2	...	13	...	...	15	2	...	1	...	...	3
5 Construction	142	...	48	...	...	190	134	...	125	...	...	258
6 Wholesale and retail trade, restaurants and hotels	189	...	529	...	...	718	336	...	407	...	...	744
A Wholesale and retail trade	168	...	512	...	...	680	308	...	390	...	...	698
B Restaurants and hotels	22	...	17	...	...	39	29	...	18	...	...	47
7 Transport, storage and communication	263	...	99	...	...	362	295	...	69	...	...	364
8 Finance, insurance, real estate and business services [b]	122	...	161	...	...	283	144	...	190	...	...	334
A Financial institutions	117	...	111	...	...	228	138	...	138	...	...	276
B Insurance												
C Real estate and business services	5	...	50	...	...	55	6	...	53	...	...	59
9 Community, social and personal services [b]	642	...	136	...	...	778	700	...	157	...	...	857
A Sanitary and similar services	...	...	...	...	...	...	...	...	...	...	...	...
B Social and related community services	386	...	30	...	...	416	420	...	32	...	...	452

Zimbabwe

4.3 Cost Components of Value Added
(Continued)

Million Zimbabwean dollars

	1982						1983					
	Compensation of Employees	Capital Consumption	Net Operating Surplus	Indirect Taxes	Less: Subsidies Received	Value Added	Compensation of Employees	Capital Consumption	Net Operating Surplus	Indirect Taxes	Less: Subsidies Received	Value Added
Educational services	310	...	-1	...	...	309	344	...	-1	...	...	343
Medical, dental, other health and veterinary services	76	...	30	...	...	106	76	...	32	...	...	109
C Recreational and cultural services	171	...	106	...	...	277	192	...	125	...	...	317
D Personal and household services	85	...	-	...	...	85	88	...	-	...	...	88
Total, Industries	2468	...	1931	...	...	4399	2782	...	2230	...	...	5011
Producers of Government Services	330	...	37	...	...	367	348	...	50	...	...	398
Other Producers	...	...	...	...	...	...	...	...	...	...	...	...
Total c	2798	...	1968	...	...	4766	3130	...	2280	...	...	5409
Less: Imputed bank service charge	...	...	146	...	...	146	...	...	173	...	...	173
Import duties	...	...	...	...	...	...	...	...	...	...	...	...
Value added tax	...	...	...	...	...	...	...	...	...	...	...	...
Other adjustments d	...	...	...	540	...	540	...	...	...	896	...	896
Total c	2797	...	1822	540	...	5160	3130	...	2107	896	...	6132

of which General Government:

	Compensation of Employees	Capital Consumption	Net Operating Surplus	Indirect Taxes	Less: Subsidies Received	Value Added	Compensation of Employees	Capital Consumption	Net Operating Surplus	Indirect Taxes	Less: Subsidies Received	Value Added
1 Agriculture, hunting, forestry and fishing	20	...	-2	...	...	18	13	...	1	...	...	14
2 Mining and quarrying	...	...	...	...	...	...	...	...	...	...	...	...
3 Manufacturing	7	...	5	...	...	12	44	...	8	...	...	52
4 Electricity, gas and water	22	...	19	...	...	41	26	...	141	...	...	167
5 Construction	52	...	-4	...	...	48	44	...	36	...	...	80
6 Wholesale and retail trade, restaurants and hotels	5	...	5	...	...	10	5	...	12	...	...	17
7 Transport and communication	9	...	...	...	...	9	10	...	...	...	...	10
8 Finance, insurance, real estate & business services	...	...	37	...	...	37	...	...	50	...	...	50
9 Community, social and personal services	363	...	...	...	...	363	390	...	...	...	...	390
Total, Industries of General Government	478	...	60	...	...	538	531	...	248	...	...	779
Producers of Government Services	330	...	...	...	...	330	348	...	...	...	...	348
Total, General Government	808	...	60	...	...	868	879	...	248	...	...	1127

	1984						
	Compensation of Employees	Capital Consumption	Net Operating Surplus	Indirect Taxes	Less: Subsidies Received	Value Added

All Producers

	Compensation of Employees	Capital Consumption	Net Operating Surplus	Indirect Taxes	Less: Subsidies Received	Value Added
1 Agriculture, hunting, forestry and fishing	313	...	360	...	...	673
2 Mining and quarrying	193	...	264	...	...	457
3 Manufacturing	763	...	770	...	...	1533
A Manufacture of food, beverages and tobacco	...	...	...	...	...	...
B Textile, wearing apparel and leather industries	...	...	...	...	...	...
C Manufacture of wood and wood products, including furniture	...	...	...	...	...	...
D Manufacture of paper and paper products, printing and publishing	...	...	...	...	...	...
E Manufacture of chemicals and chemical petroleum, coal, rubber and plastic products	...	...	...	...	...	...
F Manufacture of non-metallic mineral products, except products of petroleum and coal	...	...	...	...	...	...
G Basic metal industries	...	...	...	...	...	...
H Manufacture of fabricated metal products, machinery and equipment	...	...	...	...	...	...
I Other manufacturing industries	...	...	...	...	...	...
4 Electricity, gas and water a	46	...	193	...	...	239
A Electricity, gas and steam	...	...	...	...	...	...
B Water works and supply	...	...	...	...	...	...

Zimbabwe

4.3 Cost Components of Value Added
(Continued)

Million Zimbabwean dollars

1984

	Compensation of Employees	Capital Consumption	Net Operating Surplus	Indirect Taxes	Less: Subsidies Received	Value Added
5 Construction	167	...	103	...	...	270
6 Wholesale and retail trade, restaurants and hotels	356	...	411	...	...	768
A Wholesale and retail trade	327	...	390	...	...	715
B Restaurants and hotels	29	...	23	...	...	52
7 Transport, storage and communication	332	...	104	...	...	436
8 Finance, insurance, real estate and business services [b]	158	...	184	...	...	342
A Financial institutions	151	...	131	...	...	282
B Insurance		...		...	...	
C Real estate and business services	7	...	53	...	...	60
9 Community, social and personal services [b]	805	...	158	...	...	964
A Sanitary and similar services	...	...	...	...	...	...
B Social and related community services	507	...	23	...	...	531
Educational services	416	...	-1	...	...	415
Medical, dental, other health and veterinary services	91	...	24	...	...	116
C Recreational and cultural services	211	...	135	...	...	346
D Personal and household services	87	...	-	...	...	87
Total, Industries	3134	...	2547	...	...	5682
Producers of Government Services	391	...	47	...	...	438
Other Producers	...	...	...	...	...	...
Total [c]	3525	...	2594		...	6120
Less: Imputed bank service charge	...	...	168	...	...	168
Import duties	...	...	...	...	...	...
Value added tax	...	...	...	...	...	...
Other adjustments [d]	...	...	...	744	...	744
Total [c]	3525	...	2426	744	...	6696

of which General Government:

1 Agriculture, hunting, forestry and fishing	11	...	3	...		14
2 Mining and quarrying	...	...	...	...	...	...
3 Manufacturing	8	...	9	...	...	17
4 Electricity, gas and water	14	...	170	...	...	184
5 Construction	82	...	30	...	...	112
6 Wholesale and retail trade, restaurants and hotels	6	...	15	...	...	21
7 Transport and communication	12	...			...	12
8 Finance, insurance, real estate & business services	...	...	47	...	...	47
9 Community, social and personal services	484	...	...	...	...	484
Total, Industries of General Government	617	...	274	...	...	801
Producers of Government Services	391	...	...	...	...	391
Total General Government	1008		274		...	1282

a) Item 'Electricity, gas and water' excludes gas.
b) Business services are included in item 'Community, social and personal services'.
c) Column 'Consumption of fixed capital' is included in column 'Net operating surplus'.
d) Item 'Other adjustments' refers to indirect taxes net of subsidies.

كيفية الحصول على منشورات الأمم المتحدة

يمكن الحصول على منشورات الأمم المتحدة من المكتبات ودور التوزيع في جميع أنحاء العالم . استعلم عنها من المكتبة التي تتعامل معها أو اكتب إلى : الأمم المتحدة ، قسم البيع في نيويورك أو في جنيف .

如何购取联合国出版物

联合国出版物在全世界各地的书店和经售处均有发售。请向书店询问或写信到纽约或日内瓦的联合国销售组。

HOW TO OBTAIN UNITED NATIONS PUBLICATIONS

United Nations publications may be obtained from bookstores and distributors throughout the world. Consult your bookstore or write to: United Nations, Sales Section, New York or Geneva.

COMMENT SE PROCURER LES PUBLICATIONS DES NATIONS UNIES

Les publications des Nations Unies sont en vente dans les librairies et les agences dépositaires du monde entier. Informez-vous auprès de votre libraire ou adressez-vous à : Nations Unies, Section des ventes, New York ou Genève.

КАК ПОЛУЧИТЬ ИЗДАНИЯ ОРГАНИЗАЦИИ ОБЪЕДИНЕННЫХ НАЦИЙ

Издания Организации Объединенных Наций можно купить в книжных магазинах и агентствах во всех районах мира. Наводите справки об изданиях в вашем книжном магазине или пишите по адресу: Организация Объединенных Наций, Секция по продаже изданий, Нью-Йорк или Женева.

COMO CONSEGUIR PUBLICACIONES DE LAS NACIONES UNIDAS

Las publicaciones de las Naciones Unidas están en venta en librerías y casas distribuidoras en todas partes del mundo. Consulte a su librero o diríjase a: Naciones Unidas, Sección de Ventas, Nueva York o Ginebra.

Litho in United Nations, New York
88-41067—February 1989—4,175
ISBN 92-1-161305-1

10000
(not to be sold separately)

United Nations publication
Sales No. E.89.XVII.7, Part II
ST/ESA/STAT/SER.X/11

DOES NOT CIRCULATE

WITHDRAWN

WILLIAM F. MAAG LIBRARY
YOUNGSTOWN STATE UNIVERSITY